PENTATEUCH AND HAFTORAHS

ספר

חמשה חומשי תורה

עם ההפטרות

נדפס על פי המסורה ומתורגם אַנגלית

עם פירוש קצר

מלאכת סיעת הוגי תורה ובראשם

יוסף צבי הערץ

רב הכולל דמלכות בריטאניה ומדינותיה

כרך ראשון

בראשית, שמות, ויקרא

THE
PENTATEUCH
AND
HAFTORAHS

HEBREW TEXT, ENGLISH TRANSLATION
AND COMMENTARY

EDITED BY

DR. J. H. HERTZ
CHIEF RABBI OF THE BRITISH EMPIRE

VOLUME I

GENESIS, EXODUS, LEVITICUS

Printed in U. S. A.

PREFACE TO THE AMERICAN EDITION

The nature and purpose of this commentary to the Pentateuch and Haftorahs are fully set out in the prefaces following. I cannot, however, refrain from adding that the reception given to this *Chumesh* fully justified the many years of labour entailed in its production. The original edition in five volumes was soon followed by a one-volume edition. It has, furthermore, been translated into other languages, something quite unusual in the case of a commentary. In addition to German and Hungarian translations, a Hebrew rendering of it is appearing in the Holy Land. And now, a special reprint of the work is published for the use of my brethren in America. This gives me particular joy as I shall thus, in a small measure, repay the great debt I owe to the most powerful and conscious of Jewries, where, a half-century ago, I received the training for my sacred calling.

That this work, in the original and in translation, continue, under Divine blessing, to be of help in the spread of Jewish religious knowledge and the consequent strengthening of Jewish religious loyalty is the prayer of

J. H. HERTZ,
Chief Rabbi

Rosh Chodesh Nisan 5701
March 29, 1941

FROM THE PREFACE TO THE FIRST EDITION[1]

This work, which gives the text in Hebrew and English, accompanied by a brief exposition of both the Pentateuch and the Haftorahs for use in Synagogue, School, and Home, supplies a long-felt want among English-speaking Jews. The glosses on the Pentateuch (without the Haftorahs) by David Levi and Isaac Delgado were published 140 years ago, and are, besides, unobtainable today. In 1844, De Sola, Lindenthal, and Raphall began a commentary on the Sacred Scriptures, of which *Genesis* alone appeared. The English translation, however, was fantastic, the notes voluminous, and the Haftorahs were not included. Kalisch's volumes on *Genesis, Exodus,* and *Leviticus* were not written for the Synagogue or for the Jewish Home. All other Jewish Scriptural publications in England and America, either omitted the Hebrew text or were without a Commentary for general use.

Text. I am deeply grateful to the Committee of the British and Foreign Bible Society for their courtesy in generously granting me the use of the plates of their standard and beautiful edition of the Hebrew Text.

Commentary. In the preparation of the Commentary I have had the valuable assistance of Dr. J. Abelson (Gen. I-XI and Numbers); Dr. A. Cohen (Gen. XII-XXXVI, Exodus XXI-XL, Levitious, and Deut economy (I-XVI); the late

[1] Published in 5 vols., Oxford University Press, 1929-1936.

Rev. G. Friedlaender (Gen. XXXVII-L, and Exod. I-XX); and the Rev. S. Frampton (the Haftorahs, Genesis to Numbers). In placing their respective manuscripts at my disposal, they allowed me the widest editorial discretion. I have condensed or enlarged, re-cast or re-written at will, myself supplying the Additional Notes as well as nearly all the introductory and concluding comments on the various sections. To my collaborators, as well as to Prof. I. Epstein and the Rev. M. Rosenbaum for much helpful criticism, I would herewith express my heart-felt thanks.

AUTHORITIES. Jewish and non-Jewish commentators — ancient, medieval, and modern — have been freely drawn upon. "Accept the true from whatever source it comes," is sound Rabbinic doctrine — even if it be from the pages of a devout Christian expositor or of an iconoclastic Bible scholar, Jewish or non-Jewish. This does not affect the Jewish Traditional character of work. My conviction that the criticism of the Pentateuch associated with the name of Wellhausen is a perversion of history and a desecration of religion, is unshaken; likewise, my refusal to eliminate the Divine either from history or from human life. . . .

In concluding this labour of love, I recall the sacred memory of one, cut off in the midst of her years, whose wise counsel and religious enthusiasm induced me to undertake, amid the distractions and duties of my office, the vital task of a People's Commentary on the Pentateuch. And I offer praise to Almighty God for having given me life, strength, and opportunity to see the completion of that task.

J. H. HERTZ.

London, Lag be-Omer, 5696
10 *May,* 1936

FROM THE PREFACE TO THE ONE-VOLUME EDITION

The Translation in this new edition is the Version of the Holy Scriptures issued by the Jewish Publication Society of America in 1917. I wish to record my deep gratitude to the President, Mr. J. Solis-Cohen, junr., and the Executive of the Society for their courtesy in granting me the privilege of reprinting it.

A further word must be said as to the nature of the Commentary. Its aim is two-fold; the exposition, firstly, of the "plain sense" of the Sacred Text; and, secondly, of its religious message as affecting everyday problems of human existence, and guiding the life of Israel and Humanity. In this way alone is a commentary in true line with the tradition of Rashi and the ancient Jewish expositors of the Bible.

J. H. H.

London, 10 *Marchesvan,* 5698
15 *October,* 1937

TABLE OF CONTENTS

ERRATA

VOLUME I

PAGE 373. 3. *kindle no fire.* This command has been understood by certain Jewish sects to prohibit even the *enjoyment* of light or fire on the Sabbath; the Rabbis, however, apply it only to the act of *producing* fire. Food prepared by fire on the Sabbath is, however, prohibited.

ספר בראשית

THE BOOK OF GENESIS

ספר בראשית

THE BOOK OF GENESIS

The Hebrew name for the First Book of Moses was originally *Sefer Maaseh Bereshith*, 'Book of Creation.' This was rendered into Greek by *Genesis*, 'origin,' because it gives an account of the creation of the world and the beginnings of life and society. Its current Jewish name is בראשית *Bereshith* ('In the beginning') which is the first Hebrew word in its opening sentence. *Bereshith* is also the name of Chap. I–VI, 8, the first of the fifty-four weekly Torah Readings (Sedrahs) on Sabbath mornings.

If the Pentateuch (which is a Greek word meaning the *five books* of Moses) were merely a code of civil and religious laws, it would have opened with the twelfth chapter of Exodus, which contains the earliest specific commandment given to Israel (Rashi). But it is far more than a code of law: it is the Torah, *i.e.* the Divine Teaching given to Israel, and the Message of Israel to mankind. Therefore, it describes the origins of the Jewish people; traces its kinship to the other portions of the human family—all being of one blood and offspring of one common stock; and goes back to the creation of the world, which it declares to be the work of One Almighty and Beneficent God. All this is told in the first eleven chapters of Genesis. The remaining thirty-nine chapters give the story of the Fathers of the Jewish people—Abraham, Isaac, Jacob and his children.

For the place of the tales of Genesis in human education, see p. 141.

1 CHAPTER I

1. In the beginning God created the heaven and the earth. 2. Now the earth was unformed and void, and darkness was upon the face of the deep; and the spirit of God hovered over the face of the waters. 3. And God said: 'Let there be light.' And there was light. 4. And God saw the light, that it was good; and God divided the light from the darkness. 5. And God called the light Day, and the darkness He called Night. And there was evening and there was morning, one day.

CAP. I. א א

א 2 בְּרֵאשִׁית בָּרָא אֱלֹהִים אֵת הַשָּׁמַיִם וְאֵת הָאָרֶץ׃ וְהָאָרֶץ
הָיְתָה תֹהוּ וָבֹהוּ וְחֹשֶׁךְ עַל־פְּנֵי תְהוֹם וְרוּחַ אֱלֹהִים
3 מְרַחֶפֶת עַל־פְּנֵי הַמָּיִם׃ וַיֹּאמֶר אֱלֹהִים יְהִי אוֹר וַיְהִי־
4 אוֹר׃ וַיַּרְא אֱלֹהִים אֶת־הָאוֹר כִּי־טוֹב וַיַּבְדֵּל אֱלֹהִים בֵּין
ה הָאוֹר וּבֵין הַחֹשֶׁךְ׃ וַיִּקְרָא אֱלֹהִים ׀ לָאוֹר יוֹם וְלַחֹשֶׁךְ
קָרָא לָיְלָה וַיְהִי־עֶרֶב וַיְהִי־בֹקֶר יוֹם אֶחָד׃ פ

v. 1. ב רבתי

I. BERESHITH

(CHAPTERS I–VI, 8)

ORIGIN OF THE UNIVERSE AND THE BEGINNINGS OF THE HUMAN RACE

CREATION OF THE WORLD. CHAPTER I–II, 3

1. *In the beginning.* Verse 1 is a majestic summary of the story of Creation: God is the beginning, nay, the Cause of all things. The remainder of the chapter gives details of the successive acts of creation. Ages untold may have elapsed between the calling of matter into being and the reduction of chaos to ordered arrangement.

God. Heb. *Elohim.* The existence of the Deity is throughout Scripture assumed: it is not a matter for argument or doubt. *Elohim* is the general designation of the Divine Being in the Bible, as the fountain and source of all things. *Elohim* is a plural form, which is often used in Hebrew to denote plenitude of might. Here it indicates that God comprehends and unifies all the forces of eternity and infinity.

created. The Heb. word is in the singular, thus precluding any idea that its subject, *Elohim*, is to be understood in a plural sense. The term **ברא** is used exclusively of Divine activity. Man is spoken of as 'making' or 'forming', but never as 'creating', *i.e.* producing something out of nothing.

the heaven and the earth. The visible world; that which is above (heaven), and that which is below (earth).

2. *the earth.* The material out of which the universe is formed.

the deep. Heb. *tehom*, the abyss.

spirit of God. The mysterious, unseen, and irresistible presence of the Divine Being.

hovered. The Heb. word occurs again only in Deut. XXXII, 11, where it is descriptive of the eagle hovering over the young to care for them and protect them. Matter in itself is lifeless. The Spirit of God quickens it and transforms it into material for a living world. The Jerusalem Targum translates this verse: 'And the earth was vacancy and desolation, solitary of the sons of men and void of every animal, and darkness was upon the face of the abyss; and the Spirit of Mercies from before the LORD breathed upon the face of the waters.'

3–5. FIRST DAY. CREATION OF LIGHT.

3. *And God said.* 'By the word of the LORD were the heavens made,' Psalm XXXIII, 6. One of the names for God in later Jewish literature is 'He who spake and the world came into existence' (Authorised Prayer Book, p. 16). 'The phrase *God said* must be taken as a figurative equivalent of "God willed"' (Saadyah).

let there be light. A sublimely simple phrase to express a sublime fact. This light, which is distinct from that radiated later on from the sun, disperses the darkness that enshrouded the Deep (*v.* 2). The old question, Whence did the light issue before the sun was made, is answered by the nebular theory! The great astronomer Halley, wrote: 'These nebulæ reply fully to the difficulty which has been raised against the Mosaic description of creation, in asserting that light could not be generated without the sun.'

4. *that it was good.* *i.e.* fulfils the will of the Creator. Repeated *v.* 10, 12, 18, 21, 25, 31. For the significance of this refrain, see Additional Note A, p. 193.

5. *called.* In calling the light Day, God defines the significance of light in human life. In the Bible account of Creation, everything centres round man and is viewed from his angle.

And there was evening. The day, according to the Scriptural reckoning of time, begins with the preceding evening. Thus, the observance of the Day of Atonement is to be 'from even unto even' (Lev. XXIII, 32); and similarly of the Sabbath and Festivals.

¶ 6. And God said: 'Let there be a firmament in the midst of the waters, and let it divide the waters from the waters.' 7. And God made the firmament, and divided the waters which were under the firmament from the waters which were above the firmament; and it was so. 8. And God called the firmament Heaven. And there was evening and there was morning, a second day. ¶ 9. And God said: 'Let the waters under the heaven be gathered together unto one place, and let the dry land appear.' And it was so. 10. And God called the dry land Earth, and the gathering together of the waters called He Seas; and God saw that it was good. 11. And God said: 'Let the earth put forth grass, herb yielding seed, and fruit-tree bearing fruit after its kind, wherein is the seed thereof, upon the earth.' And it was so. 12. And the earth brought forth grass, herb yielding seed after its kind, and tree bearing fruit, wherein is the seed thereof, after its kind; and God saw that it was good. 13. And there was evening and there was morning, a third day.* ii a. ¶ 14. And God said: 'Let there be lights in the firmament of the heaven to divide the day from the night; and let them be for signs, and for seasons, and for days and

6 וַיֹּאמֶר אֱלֹהִים יְהִי רָקִיעַ בְּתוֹךְ הַמָּיִם וִיהִי מַבְדִּיל בֵּין
7 מַיִם לָמָיִם׃ וַיַּעַשׂ אֱלֹהִים אֶת־הָרָקִיעַ וַיַּבְדֵּל בֵּין הַמַּיִם
אֲשֶׁר מִתַּחַת לָרָקִיעַ וּבֵין הַמַּיִם אֲשֶׁר מֵעַל לָרָקִיעַ וַיְהִי־
8 כֵן׃ וַיִּקְרָא אֱלֹהִים לָרָקִיעַ שָׁמָיִם וַיְהִי־עֶרֶב וַיְהִי־בֹקֶר
יוֹם שֵׁנִי׃ פ
9 וַיֹּאמֶר אֱלֹהִים יִקָּווּ הַמַּיִם מִתַּחַת הַשָּׁמַיִם אֶל־מָקוֹם אֶחָד
י וְתֵרָאֶה הַיַּבָּשָׁה וַיְהִי־כֵן׃ וַיִּקְרָא אֱלֹהִים ׀ לַיַּבָּשָׁה אֶרֶץ
11 וּלְמִקְוֵה הַמַּיִם קָרָא יַמִּים וַיַּרְא אֱלֹהִים כִּי־טוֹב׃ וַיֹּאמֶר
אֱלֹהִים תַּדְשֵׁא הָאָרֶץ דֶּשֶׁא עֵשֶׂב מַזְרִיעַ זֶרַע עֵץ פְּרִי
עֹשֶׂה פְּרִי לְמִינוֹ אֲשֶׁר זַרְעוֹ־בוֹ עַל־הָאָרֶץ וַיְהִי־כֵן׃
12 וַתּוֹצֵא הָאָרֶץ דֶּשֶׁא עֵשֶׂב מַזְרִיעַ זֶרַע לְמִינֵהוּ וְעֵץ עֹשֶׂה־
13 פְּרִי אֲשֶׁר זַרְעוֹ־בוֹ לְמִינֵהוּ וַיַּרְא אֱלֹהִים כִּי־טוֹב׃ וַיְהִי־
שני עֶרֶב וַיְהִי־בֹקֶר יוֹם שְׁלִישִׁי׃* פ
14 וַיֹּאמֶר אֱלֹהִים יְהִי מְאֹרֹת בִּרְקִיעַ הַשָּׁמַיִם לְהַבְדִּיל בֵּין
הַיּוֹם וּבֵין הַלָּיְלָה וְהָיוּ לְאֹתֹת וּלְמוֹעֲדִים וּלְיָמִים וְשָׁנִים׃

v. 11. הד' בזק' ובספרי ספרד ברביע

one day. Not an ordinary day but a Day of God (יומו של הקב״ה), an age. With Him a thousand years, nay a thousand thousand ages, are but as a day that is past; Psalm xc, 4. 'Earthly and human measurement of time, by a clock of human manufacture, cannot apply to the first three days, as the sun was not then in existence. The beginning of each period of creation is called morning; its close, evening' (Delitzsch); in the same way, we speak of the morning and evening of life.

6–8. SECOND DAY. THE FIRMAMENT

6. *firmament.* Sky, arch of heaven.

waters from the waters. i.e. the waters above the firmament (the mists and clouds that come down to earth in the shape of rain), from the waters on earth (rivers and seas).

7. *and it was so.* Fulfilment follows immediately upon the Divine fiat. 'For He spake, and it was done; He commanded, and it stood fast' (Psalm xxxiii, 9).

8. *Heaven.* In the Bible, Heaven (*shamayim*) is represented as the habitation of God, in the figurative sense in which the Temple is similarly described: 'Behold heaven and the heaven of heavens cannot contain Thee; how much less this house which I have builded!' (I Kings viii, 27).

and there was evening. On the second day, the usual formula, 'And God saw that it was good,' is omitted. The work begun on that day did not terminate until the middle of the third day. Hence, an uncompleted piece of work could not properly be pronounced 'good' (Rashi).

a second day. Or, 'the second day'; similarly, *v.* 13, 19, and 23.

9–13. THIRD DAY. SEA, LAND, AND VEGETATION

9. *be gathered together.* As long as the face of the earth was covered by the 'deep' (*v.* 2), life was impossible for man or beast. God therefore decreed boundaries for the waters; cf. Psalm civ, 6–8.

10. *Earth.* Here it signifies that part of the terrestrial surface which was to be the abode of man and the scene of his activity.

that it was good. i.e. a fitting stage for the drama of human history.

11. *put forth.* In creating the earth, God implanted in it the forces that at His command produced the vegetation.

12. *that it was good.* As food for man and beast (cf. *v.* 29 f).

14–19. FOURTH DAY. CREATION OF HEAVENLY BODIES

14. *lights.* The Heb. word signifies sources of light; hence, 'luminaries' would be a better translation.

Other ancient peoples ascribed to the sun, moon and stars a beneficent or malevolent potency over the lives of men and nations. Here,

טו וְהָיוּ לִמְאוֹרֹת בִּרְקִיעַ הַשָּׁמַיִם לְהָאִיר עַל־הָאָרֶץ וַיְהִי־
16 כֵן׃ וַיַּעַשׂ אֱלֹהִים אֶת־שְׁנֵי הַמְּאֹרֹת הַגְּדֹלִים אֶת־הַמָּאוֹר
הַגָּדֹל לְמֶמְשֶׁלֶת הַיּוֹם וְאֶת־הַמָּאוֹר הַקָּטֹן לְמֶמְשֶׁלֶת
17 הַלַּיְלָה וְאֵת הַכּוֹכָבִים׃ וַיִּתֵּן אֹתָם אֱלֹהִים בִּרְקִיעַ
18 הַשָּׁמָיִם לְהָאִיר עַל־הָאָרֶץ׃ וְלִמְשֹׁל בַּיּוֹם וּבַלַּיְלָה
וּלֲהַבְדִּיל בֵּין הָאוֹר וּבֵין הַחֹשֶׁךְ וַיַּרְא אֱלֹהִים כִּי־טוֹב׃
19 וַיְהִי־עֶרֶב וַיְהִי־בֹקֶר יוֹם רְבִיעִי׃ פ
כ וַיֹּאמֶר אֱלֹהִים יִשְׁרְצוּ הַמַּיִם שֶׁרֶץ נֶפֶשׁ חַיָּה וְעוֹף יְעוֹפֵף
21 עַל־הָאָרֶץ עַל־פְּנֵי רְקִיעַ הַשָּׁמָיִם׃ וַיִּבְרָא אֱלֹהִים אֶת־
הַתַּנִּנִם הַגְּדֹלִים וְאֵת כָּל־נֶפֶשׁ הַחַיָּה ׀ הָרֹמֶשֶׂת אֲשֶׁר
שָׁרְצוּ הַמַּיִם לְמִינֵהֶם וְאֵת כָּל־עוֹף כָּנָף לְמִינֵהוּ וַיַּרְא
22 אֱלֹהִים כִּי־טוֹב׃ וַיְבָרֶךְ אֹתָם אֱלֹהִים לֵאמֹר פְּרוּ וּרְבוּ
23 וּמִלְאוּ אֶת־הַמַּיִם בַּיַּמִּים וְהָעוֹף יִרֶב בָּאָרֶץ׃ וַיְהִי־עֶרֶב
וַיְהִי־בֹקֶר יוֹם חֲמִישִׁי׃* פ שלישי
24 וַיֹּאמֶר אֱלֹהִים תּוֹצֵא הָאָרֶץ נֶפֶשׁ חַיָּה לְמִינָהּ בְּהֵמָה
כה וָרֶמֶשׂ וְחַיְתוֹ־אֶרֶץ לְמִינָהּ וַיְהִי־כֵן׃ וַיַּעַשׂ אֱלֹהִים אֶת־
חַיַּת הָאָרֶץ לְמִינָהּ וְאֶת־הַבְּהֵמָה לְמִינָהּ וְאֵת כָּל־רֶמֶשׂ
26 הָאֲדָמָה לְמִינֵהוּ וַיַּרְא אֱלֹהִים כִּי־טוֹב׃ וַיֹּאמֶר אֱלֹהִים
נַעֲשֶׂה אָדָם בְּצַלְמֵנוּ כִּדְמוּתֵנוּ וְיִרְדּוּ בִדְגַת הַיָּם וּבְעוֹף

v. 18. נ"א ולהבדיל v. 21. חסר י' בתראה

years; 15. and let them be for lights in the firmament of the heaven to give light upon the earth.' And it was so. 16. And God made the two great lights: the greater light to rule the day, and the lesser light to rule the night; and the stars. 17. And God set them in the firmament of the heaven to give light upon the earth, 18. and to rule over the day and over the night, and to divide the light from the darkness; and God saw that it was good. 19. And there was evening and there was morning, a fourth day. ¶ 20. And God said: 'Let the waters swarm with swarms of living creatures, and let fowl fly above the earth in the open firmament of heaven.' 21. And God created the great sea-monsters, and every living creature that creepeth, wherewith the waters swarmed, after its kind, and every winged fowl after its kind; and God saw that it was good. 22. And God blessed them, saying: 'Be fruitful, and multiply, and fill the waters in the seas, and let fowl multiply in the earth.' 23. And there was evening and there was morning, a fifth day.* iii a. ¶ 24. And God said: 'Let the earth bring forth the living creature after its kind, cattle, and creeping thing, and beast of the earth after its kind.' And it was so. 25. And God made the beast of the earth after its kind, and the cattle after their kind, and every thing that creepeth upon the ground after its kind; and God saw that it was good. 26. And God said: 'Let us make man in our image, after our likeness; and let them have dominion over the fish of the sea, and over the fowl of the air, and over the

however, all idolatry and superstition are swept away. These lights are works of one Almighty God, and are created for His appointed purposes; see Jer. x, 2.

for signs. To help man locate his position when moving over the surface of the earth: they were primitive man's compass.

for seasons. To regulate the calendar. The 'seasons' are spring, summer, autumn, and winter; also seed-time and harvest. The Heb. word for 'seasons' later acquired the meaning of 'festivals', since these were fixed by the year's seasons.

15. *light upon the earth.* Without which life and growth are impossible.

16. *and the stars.* They are mentioned last and without explanation, because they play a subordinate part in the life of man, as compared with the sun and moon.

20–23. Fifth Day. Fishes and Birds

20. *swarm.* Or, 'teem.' Heb. *sharatz.* Movement as well as fecundity is implied. It is used in connection with fishes and aquatic animals, rodents and insects.

fowl. Collective noun, meaning winged things.

in the open firmament. In mid-air; in the face of, or over against, the firmament.

21. *creature.* lit. 'soul.' In Hebrew, *soul* is used more widely than in English, often denoting, as here, merely a living being.

22. *God blessed them.* No blessing was bestowed upon the vegetation, as its growth is dependent upon sun and rain, and not upon its own volition.

24–31. Sixth Day. Land Animals and Man

24. *earth bring forth.* The seeds and possibility of life implanted within her on the first day of Creation (Rashi).

cattle. All domestic animals.

creeping thing. Reptiles.

beast of the earth. Wild animals.

26. *let us make man.* Mankind is described as in a special sense created by God Himself.

cattle, and over all the earth, and over every creeping thing that creepeth upon the earth.' 27. And God created man in His own image, in the image of God created He him; male and female created He them. 28. And God blessed them; and God said unto them: 'Be fruitful, and multiply, and replenish the earth, and subdue it; and have dominion over the fish of the sea, and over the fowl of the air, and over every living thing that creepeth upon the earth.' 29. And God said: 'Behold, I have given you every herb yielding seed, which is upon the face of all the earth, and every tree, in which is the fruit of a tree yielding seed—to you it shall be for food; 30. and to every beast of the earth, and to every fowl of the air, and to every thing that creepeth upon the earth, wherein there is a living soul, [I have given] every green herb for food.' And it was so. 31. And God saw every thing that He had made, and, behold, it was very good. And there was evening and there was morning, the sixth day.

הַשָּׁמַיִם וּבַבְּהֵמָה וּבְכָל־הָאָרֶץ וּבְכָל־הָרֶמֶשׂ הָרֹמֵשׂ עַל־
27 הָאָרֶץ׃ וַיִּבְרָא אֱלֹהִים ׀ אֶת־הָאָדָם בְּצַלְמוֹ בְּצֶלֶם אֱלֹהִים
28 בָּרָא אֹתוֹ זָכָר וּנְקֵבָה בָּרָא אֹתָם׃ וַיְבָרֶךְ אֹתָם אֱלֹהִים
וַיֹּאמֶר לָהֶם אֱלֹהִים פְּרוּ וּרְבוּ וּמִלְאוּ אֶת־הָאָרֶץ וְכִבְשֻׁהָ
וּרְדוּ בִּדְגַת הַיָּם וּבְעוֹף הַשָּׁמַיִם וּבְכָל־חַיָּה הָרֹמֶשֶׂת עַל־
29 הָאָרֶץ׃ וַיֹּאמֶר אֱלֹהִים הִנֵּה נָתַתִּי לָכֶם אֶת־כָּל־עֵשֶׂב ׀
זֹרֵעַ זֶרַע אֲשֶׁר עַל־פְּנֵי כָל־הָאָרֶץ וְאֶת־כָּל־הָעֵץ אֲשֶׁר־
ל בּוֹ פְרִי־עֵץ זֹרֵעַ זָרַע לָכֶם יִהְיֶה לְאָכְלָה׃ וּלְכָל־חַיַּת
הָאָרֶץ וּלְכָל־עוֹף הַשָּׁמַיִם וּלְכֹל ׀ רוֹמֵשׂ עַל־הָאָרֶץ אֲשֶׁר־
31 בּוֹ נֶפֶשׁ חַיָּה אֶת־כָּל־יֶרֶק עֵשֶׂב לְאָכְלָה וַיְהִי־כֵן׃ וַיַּרְא
אֱלֹהִים אֶת־כָּל־אֲשֶׁר עָשָׂה וְהִנֵּה־טוֹב מְאֹד וַיְהִי־עֶרֶב
וַיְהִי־בֹקֶר יוֹם הַשִּׁשִּׁי׃ פ

To enhance the dignity of this last work and to mark the fact that man differs in kind from the animals, Scripture represents God as deliberating over the making of the human species (Abarbanel). It is not 'let man be created' or 'let man be made', but 'let us make man'. The use of the plural, 'let *us* make man,' is the Heb. idiomatic way of expressing deliberation, as in XI, 7; or, it is the plural of Majesty, royal commands being conveyed in the first person plural, as in Ezra IV, 18.

man. Heb. '*Adam.*' The word is used here, as frequently in the Bible, in the sense of 'human being'. It is derived from *adamah* 'earth', to signify that man is earth-born; see II, 7.

in our image, after our likeness. Man is made in the 'image' and 'likeness' of God: his character is potentially Divine. 'God created man to be immortal, and made him to be an image of His own eternity' (Wisdom of Solomon II, 23). Man alone among living creatures is gifted, like his Creator, with moral freedom and will. He is capable of knowing and loving God, and of holding spiritual communion with Him; and man alone can guide his actions in accordance with Reason. 'On this account he is said to have been made in the form and likeness of the Almighty' (Maimonides). Because man is endowed with Reason, he can subdue his impulses in the service of moral and religious ideals, and is born to bear rule over Nature. Psalm VIII says of man, 'O LORD . . . Thou hast made him but little lower than the angels, and crownest him with glory and honour. Thou hast made him to have dominion over the works of Thy hands.'

27. *male and female.* A general statement; man and woman, both alike, are in their spiritual nature akin to God.

28. *and God blessed them.* Cf. *v.* 22. Here the words, 'And God said unto them,' are added, indicating a more intimate relationship between Him and human beings.

be fruitful and multiply. This is the first precept (*mitzvah*) given to man. The duty of building a home and rearing a family figures in the rabbinic Codes as the first of the 613 *Mitzvoth* (commandments) of the Torah.

and subdue it. 'The secret of all modern science is in the first chapter of Genesis. Belief in the dominion of spirit over matter, of mind over nature, of man over the physical and the animal creation, was essential to the possession of that dominion' (Lyman Abbott). 'What we call the will or volition of Man . . . has become a power in nature, an imperium in imperio, which has profoundly modified not only Man's own history, but that of the whole living world, and the face of the planet on which he lives' (Ray Lankester).

29. In the primitive ideal age (as also in the Messianic future, see Isaiah XI, 7), the animals were not to prey on one another.

31. *very good.* Each created thing is 'good' in itself; but when combined and united, the totality is proclaimed 'very good'. Everything in the universe was as the Creator willed it—nothing superfluous, nothing lacking—a harmony. 'This harmony bears witness to the unity of God who planned this unity of Nature' (Luzzatto).

2 CHAPTER II

1. And the heaven and the earth were finished, and all the host of them. 2. And on the seventh day God finished His work which He had made; and He rested on the seventh day from all His work which He had made. 3. And God blessed the seventh day, and hallowed it; because that in it He rested from all His work which God in creating had made.* iv a; ii s.
¶ 4. These are the generations of the heaven and of the earth when they were created, in the day that the LORD God made earth

CAP. II. ב ב

א 2 וַיְכֻלּוּ הַשָּׁמַיִם וְהָאָרֶץ וְכָל־צְבָאָם׃ וַיְכַל אֱלֹהִים בַּיּוֹם
הַשְּׁבִיעִי מְלַאכְתּוֹ אֲשֶׁר עָשָׂה וַיִּשְׁבֹּת בַּיּוֹם הַשְּׁבִיעִי
3 מִכָּל־מְלַאכְתּוֹ אֲשֶׁר עָשָׂה׃ וַיְבָרֶךְ אֱלֹהִים אֶת־יוֹם
הַשְּׁבִיעִי וַיְקַדֵּשׁ אֹתוֹ כִּי בוֹ שָׁבַת מִכָּל־מְלַאכְתּוֹ אֲשֶׁר־
בָּרָא אֱלֹהִים לַעֲשׂוֹת׃* רביעי פ (שני לספ')
4 אֵלֶּה תוֹלְדוֹת הַשָּׁמַיִם וְהָאָרֶץ בְּהִבָּרְאָם בְּיוֹם עֲשׂוֹת יְהוָה

ה' זעירא v. 4.

CHAPTER II, 1–3. THE SABBATH

The Torah was not originally divided into chapters. Such division originated in the Middle Ages; and, because of its convenience, found its way into the *printed* Hebrew text. Sometimes, as here, the division is misleading. Thus, the next three verses belong to the preceding chapter, and form its worthy and incomparable conclusion.

1. *were finished.* The Heb. verb implies not only completion but perfection.

host. lit. 'army'; the totality of the universe conceived as an organized whole, a cosmos.

2. *seventh day.* 'What did the world lack after the six days' toil? Rest. So God finished His labours on the seventh day by the creation of a day of rest, the Sabbath' (Midrash).

finished. Better, '*had finished*' (Mendelssohn, M. Friedlander).

rested. Heb. 'desisted', from creating. In the fourth commandment (Exod. xx, 11) God is said to have 'rested' (*vayanach*) on the seventh day. This ascribing of human actions to God is called *anthropomorphism*, and is employed in the Bible to make intelligible to the finite, human mind that which relates to the Infinite. The Talmudic saying, דברה תורה כלשון בני אדם 'The Torah speaks the ordinary language of men,' became a leading principle in later Jewish interpretation of Scripture.

3. *God blessed.* The Creator endowed the Sabbath with a blessing which would be experienced by all who observed it. On the Sabbath, the Talmud says, the Jew receives an 'additional soul', נשמה יתרה; *i.e.* his spiritual nature is heightened through the influence of the holy day.

hallowed. lit. 'set apart' from profane usage. The Sabbath demands more than stoppage of work. It is specifically marked off as a day consecrated to God and the life of the spirit.

in creating had made. lit. 'which God created to make', *i.e.* to continue acting (Ibn Ezra, Abarbanel) throughout time by the unceasing operation of Divine laws. This thought is contained in the Prayer Book (p. 39): 'In His goodness He reneweth the creation every day continually.' Or, as the Rabbis say, the work of creation continues, and the world is still in the process of creation, as long as the conflict between good and evil remains undecided. Ethically the world is thus still 'unfinished', and it is man's glorious privilege to help finish it. He can by his life hasten the triumph of the forces of good in the universe.

See Additional Note A ('The Creation Chapter'), p. 193.

THE BEGINNINGS OF THE HUMAN RACE

(*a*) THE GARDEN OF EDEN

CHAPTERS II, 4–III

Chapter II is *not* another account of Creation. No mention is made in it of the formation of the dry land, the sea, the sun, moon or stars. It is nothing else but the sequel of the preceding chapter. In Chap. I man is considered as part of the general scheme of created things. Chap. II *supplements* the brief mention of the creation of man in *v.* 27 of the last chapter, by describing the formation of man and woman and their first dwelling place, as preliminary to the Temptation, and the consequent expulsion from the Garden of Eden in Chap. III. Only such details as are indispensable for the understanding of that event are given.

4. *These are the generations of the heaven and of the earth.* Some consider these words as a summary of the preceding chapter (Rashi). Elsewhere, however, in ten different sections of the Book of Genesis, such opening words ('these are the generations') always refer to the things that *follow: e.g.* 'These are the generations of Adam' (VI, 9), means, these are the descendants of Adam. In the same way, 'the generations of the heavens and the earth' here begins the account of man, the offspring of heaven and earth; or, the history of Adam and his family.

in the day that. Heb. idiom for 'at the time when'.

LORD God. Heb. *Adonay Elohim.* The two most important Names of the Deity are here used. 'LORD' is the usual English translation of *Adonay*. *Adonay* is the prescribed traditional reading of the Divine Name expressed in the four Hebrew letters Y H W H—which is never

ה אֱלֹהִים אֶרֶץ וְשָׁמָיִם׃ וְכֹל ׀ שִׂיחַ הַשָּׂדֶה טֶרֶם יִהְיֶה
בָאָרֶץ וְכָל־עֵשֶׂב הַשָּׂדֶה טֶרֶם יִצְמָח כִּי לֹא הִמְטִיר יְהוָה
6 אֱלֹהִים עַל־הָאָרֶץ וְאָדָם אַיִן לַעֲבֹד אֶת־הָאֲדָמָה׃ וְאֵד
7 יַעֲלֶה מִן־הָאָרֶץ וְהִשְׁקָה אֶת־כָּל־פְּנֵי־הָאֲדָמָה׃ וַיִּיצֶר
יְהוָה אֱלֹהִים אֶת־הָאָדָם עָפָר מִן־הָאֲדָמָה וַיִּפַּח בְּאַפָּיו
8 נִשְׁמַת חַיִּים וַיְהִי הָאָדָם לְנֶפֶשׁ חַיָּה׃ וַיִּטַּע יְהוָה אֱלֹהִים

and heaven. ¶ 5. No shrub of the field was yet in the earth, and no herb of the field had yet sprung up; for the LORD God had not caused it to rain upon the earth, and there was not a man to till the ground; 6. but there went up a mist from the earth, and watered the whole face of the ground. 7. Then the LORD God formed man of the dust of the ground, and breathed into his nostrils the breath of life; and man became a living soul. 8. And the LORD God planted a garden eastward, in Eden; and there He

pronounced as written. This Divine Name is spoken of as the *Tetragrammaton*, which is a Greek word meaning 'the Name of four letters'. The High Priest of old pronounced it *as written*, on the Day of Atonement during the Temple Service; whereupon all the people fell on their faces and exclaimed, 'Blessed be His Name whose glorious Kingdom is for ever and ever.' The Heb. root of that Divine Name means 'to be'; *Adonay* thus expresses the eternal self-existence of Him who is the Author of all existence. A possible rendering, therefore, for *Adonay* is 'The Eternal', and this has been adopted in some Jewish versions of Scripture.

The other and more general Divine Name is *Elohim*. Whereas *Adonay* is used whenever the Divine is spoken of in close relationship with men or nations, *Elohim* denotes God as the Creator and Moral Governor of the Universe. The Rabbis find a clear distinction in the use of these two terms: *Adonay* (LORD) describes the Deity stressing His lovingkindness, His acts of mercy and condescension and revelation to mankind (**מדת הרחמים**); while *Elohim* (God) emphasizes His justice and rulership (**מדת הדין**). The Midrash says, 'Thus spake the Holy One, blessed be He: If I create the world by Mercy alone, sin will abound; if by Justice alone, how can the world endure? I will create it by both.' In the first chapter of Genesis, which treats of the Universe as a whole, *Elohim* ('God') is used; but in the second chapter which begins the story of man, that Divine Name is no longer used alone, but together with *Adonay* ('LORD God'). There was soon need for the exercise of the Divine mercy. See Additional Note, p. 199.

earth and heaven. Since the centre of interest now turns to man, earth is mentioned before heaven.

5. *no shrub*. Vegetation remained in the same state as on the day of its creation (see I, 11), through lack of rain.

not a man. The edible fruits of the earth require not only God's gift of rain, but also man's cultivation. Man must be a co-worker with God in making this earth a garden.

6. *there went up*. 'There used to go up.' The Heb. verb expresses repeated action.

a mist. In Assyrian, the word means the 'overflow of a river', and it may here have the same significance.

watered. The vegetation did not therefore decay, though there was insufficient moisture for growth.

7. *formed*. The Heb. **וייצר**, is from the same root, *yatzar*, as is used of the potter moulding clay into a vessel, possibly to remind us that man is 'as clay in the hands of the potter'. The Rabbis point to the fact that in this verse the word for 'formed' (*vayyitzer*) is written with two *yods*, whereas in *v*. 19 when relating the creation of animals, it has only one *yod* (**ויצר**). Man alone, they declare, is endowed with both a *Yetzer tob* (a good inclination) and a *Yetzer ra* (an evil inclination); whereas animals have no moral discrimination or moral conflict. Another explanation is, man alone is a citizen of two worlds; he is both of earth and of heaven.

dust of the ground. 'From which part of the earth's great surface did He gather the dust?' ask the Rabbis. Rabbi Meir answered, 'From every part of the habitable earth was the dust taken for the formation of Adam.' In a word, men of all lands and climes are brothers. Other Rabbis held that the dust was taken from the site on which the Holy Temple, with the altar of Atonement, was in later ages to be built. That means, though man comes from the dust, sin is not a permanent part of his nature. Man can overcome sin, and through repentance attain to at-one-ment with his Maker.

a living soul. The term may mean nothing more than 'living entity'. The Targum, however, renders it by 'a speaking spirit'; *viz*. a personality endowed with the faculty of thinking and expressing his thoughts in speech.

8–17. THE GARDEN

8. *garden*. The ancient Versions translate it by the Persian word 'Paradise', lit. enclosure or park.

eastward. Either, 'in the East,' the home of the earliest civilization; or, situated east of Eden. The Targum translates it, 'aforetime.'

Eden. The Heb. word means 'delight'; but it is probably the name of a country, *Edinu* (signifying 'plain, steppe'); and may denote the extensive plain watered by the rivers Tigris and Euphrates.

put the man whom He had formed. 9. And out of the ground made the LORD God to grow every tree that is pleasant to the sight, and good for food; the tree of life also in the midst of the garden, and the tree of the knowledge of good and evil. 10. And a river went out of Eden to water the garden; and from thence it was parted, and became four heads. 11. The name of the first is Pishon; that is it which compasseth the whole land of Havilah, where there is gold; 12. and the gold of that land is good; there is bdellium and the onyx stone. 13. And the name of the second river is Gihon; the same is it that compasseth the whole land of Cush. 14. And the name of the third river is [1]Tigris; that is it which goeth toward the east of Asshur. And the fourth river is the Euphrates. 15. And the LORD God took the man, and put him into the garden of Eden to dress it and to keep it. 16. And the LORD God commanded the man, saying: 'Of every tree of the garden thou mayest freely eat; 17. but of the tree of the knowledge of good and evil, thou shalt not eat of it:

9 גַּן־בְּעֵדֶן מִקֶּדֶם וַיָּשֶׂם שָׁם אֶת־הָאָדָם אֲשֶׁר יָצָר׃ וַיַּצְמַח
יְהוָה אֱלֹהִים מִן־הָאֲדָמָה כָּל־עֵץ נֶחְמָד לְמַרְאֶה וְטוֹב
לְמַאֲכָל וְעֵץ הַחַיִּים בְּתוֹךְ הַגָּן וְעֵץ הַדַּעַת טוֹב וָרָע׃
י וְנָהָר יֹצֵא מֵעֵדֶן לְהַשְׁקוֹת אֶת־הַגָּן וּמִשָּׁם יִפָּרֵד וְהָיָה
11 לְאַרְבָּעָה רָאשִׁים׃ שֵׁם הָאֶחָד פִּישׁוֹן הוּא הַסֹּבֵב אֵת
12 כָּל־אֶרֶץ הַחֲוִילָה אֲשֶׁר־שָׁם הַזָּהָב׃ וּזֲהַב הָאָרֶץ הַהִוא
13 טוֹב שָׁם הַבְּדֹלַח וְאֶבֶן הַשֹּׁהַם׃ וְשֵׁם־הַנָּהָר הַשֵּׁנִי גִּיחוֹן
14 הוּא הַסּוֹבֵב אֵת כָּל־אֶרֶץ כּוּשׁ׃ וְשֵׁם־הַנָּהָר הַשְּׁלִישִׁי
חִדֶּקֶל הוּא הַהֹלֵךְ קִדְמַת אַשּׁוּר וְהַנָּהָר הָרְבִיעִי הוּא
טו פְרָת׃ וַיִּקַּח יְהוָה אֱלֹהִים אֶת־הָאָדָם וַיַּנִּחֵהוּ בְגַן־עֵדֶן
16 לְעָבְדָהּ וּלְשָׁמְרָהּ׃ וַיְצַו יְהוָה אֱלֹהִים עַל־הָאָדָם לֵאמֹר
17 מִכֹּל עֵץ־הַגָּן אָכֹל תֹּאכֵל׃ וּמֵעֵץ הַדַּעַת טוֹב וָרָע לֹא

[1] Heb. *Hiddekel.*

The phrase 'Garden of Eden' became in course of time descriptive of any place possessing beauty and fertility. In later Jewish literature, it signifies the Heavenly Paradise where the souls of the righteous repose in felicity.

9. *tree of life.* The fruit of which prolongs life, or renders immortal. The phrase also occurs in a purely figurative sense, *e.g.* Prov. III, 18.

the knowledge of good and evil. The Targum paraphrase is, 'the tree, the eaters of whose fruits know to distinguish between good and evil.' The expression 'good and evil' denotes the knowledge which infancy lacks and experience acquires ('Your children which this day have no knowledge of good or evil', Deut. I, 39). 'Knowledge of good and evil' may also mean, knowledge of all things, *i.e.* omniscience; see III, 5.

10. *it was parted.* After passing through the Garden, it divided into four separate streams.

11. *Pishon.* Nowhere else mentioned in the Bible.

Havilah. Cf. X, 29. N.E. of Arabia, on the Persian Gulf. Arabia was famed in antiquity for its gold.

12. *bdellium.* Possibly the pearl.

13. *Gihon.* Like the Pishon, the identity of this river is a matter of conjecture.

Cush. Usually rendered Ethiopia; but it may also denote some territory in Asia.

14. *Asshur.* Assyria; which lies some distance East of the Tigris and possibly includes Babylonia.

Euphrates. No further description is given, because it was universally known as 'the great River' (Deut. I, 7) and '*the* River' (Exod. XXIII, 31, Isa. VII, 20).

15–16. *to dress it and to keep it. i.e.* to till it and guard it from running wild. Not indolence but congenial work is man's Divinely allotted portion. 'See what a great thing is work! The first man was not to taste of anything until he had done some work. Only after God told him to cultivate and keep the garden, did He give him permission to eat of its fruits' (Aboth di Rabbi Nathan).

17. *thou shalt not eat.* Man's most sacred privilege is freedom of will, the ability to obey or to disobey his Maker. This sharp limitation of self-gratification, this 'dietary law', was to test the use he would make of his freedom; and it thus begins the moral discipline of man. Unlike the beast, man has also a spiritual life, which demands the subordination of man's desires to the law of God. The will of God revealed in His Law is the one eternal and unfailing guide as to what constitutes good and evil—and not man's instincts, or even his Reason, which in the hour of temptation often call light darkness and darkness light.

thou shalt surely die. i.e. thou must inevitably become mortal (Symmachus). While this explanation removes the difficulty that Adam and Eve lived a long time after they had eaten of the forbidden fruit, it assumes that man was created to be a deathless being. A simpler explanation is that in view of all the circumstances of the temptation, the All-merciful God mercifully modified the penalty, and they did not die on the day of their sin.

for in the day that thou eatest thereof thou shalt surely die.' ¶ 18. And the LORD God said: 'It is not good that the man should be alone; I will make him a help meet for him.' 19. And out of the ground the LORD God formed every beast of the field, and every fowl of the air; and brought them unto the man to see what he would call them; and whatsoever the man would call every living creature, that was to be the name thereof.* iii s. 20. And the man gave names to all cattle, and to the fowl of the air, and to every beast of the field; but for Adam there was not found a help meet for him. 21. And the LORD God caused a deep sleep to fall upon the man, and he slept; and He took one of his ribs, and closed up the place with flesh instead thereof. 22. And the rib, which the LORD God had taken from the man, made He a woman, and brought her unto the man. 23. And the man said: 'This is now bone of my bones, and flesh of my flesh; she shall be called [1]Woman, because she was taken out of [2]Man.' 24. Therefore shall a man leave his father and

18 תֹאכַל מִמֶּנּוּ כִּי בְּיוֹם אֲכָלְךָ מִמֶּנּוּ מוֹת תָּמוּת׃ וַיֹּאמֶר
יְהוָה אֱלֹהִים לֹא־טוֹב הֱיוֹת הָאָדָם לְבַדּוֹ אֶעֱשֶׂה־לּוֹ עֵזֶר
19 כְּנֶגְדּוֹ׃ וַיִּצֶר יְהוָה אֱלֹהִים מִן־הָאֲדָמָה כָּל־חַיַּת הַשָּׂדֶה
וְאֵת כָּל־עוֹף הַשָּׁמַיִם וַיָּבֵא אֶל־הָאָדָם לִרְאוֹת מַה־יִּקְרָא־
לוֹ וְכֹל אֲשֶׁר יִקְרָא־לוֹ הָאָדָם נֶפֶשׁ חַיָּה הוּא שְׁמוֹ׃*
כ וַיִּקְרָא הָאָדָם שֵׁמוֹת לְכָל־הַבְּהֵמָה וּלְעוֹף הַשָּׁמַיִם וּלְכֹל
21 חַיַּת הַשָּׂדֶה וּלְאָדָם לֹא־מָצָא עֵזֶר כְּנֶגְדּוֹ׃ וַיַּפֵּל יְהוָה
אֱלֹהִים ׀ תַּרְדֵּמָה עַל־הָאָדָם וַיִּישָׁן וַיִּקַּח אַחַת מִצַּלְעֹתָיו
22 וַיִּסְגֹּר בָּשָׂר תַּחְתֶּנָּה׃ וַיִּבֶן יְהוָה אֱלֹהִים ׀ אֶת־הַצֵּלָע אֲשֶׁר־
23 לָקַח מִן־הָאָדָם לְאִשָּׁה וַיְבִאֶהָ אֶל־הָאָדָם׃ וַיֹּאמֶר הָאָדָם
זֹאת הַפַּעַם עֶצֶם מֵעֲצָמַי וּבָשָׂר מִבְּשָׂרִי לְזֹאת יִקָּרֵא אִשָּׁה
24 כִּי מֵאִישׁ לֻקְחָה־זֹּאת׃ עַל־כֵּן יַעֲזָב־אִישׁ אֶת־אָבִיו וְאֶת־

[1] Heb. *Ishshah*. [2] Heb. *Ish*.

*(שלישי לספ׳) v. 22. קמץ ומלרע

18–25. CREATION OF WOMAN

18. *it is not good.* From this verse the Rabbis deduce that marriage is a Divine institution, a holy estate in which alone man lives his true and complete life. Celibacy is contrary to nature.

a help. A wife is not a man's shadow or subordinate, but his other self, his 'helper', in a sense which no other creature on earth can be.

meet for him. To match him. The Heb. term *k'negdo*, may mean either 'at his side', *i.e.* fit to associate with; or, 'as over against him', *i.e.* corresponding to him.

19. Better, *The LORD God, having formed out of the ground every beast of the field, and every fowl of heaven, brought them unto the man* (S. R. Hirsch, Delitzsch, and W. H. Green). See I, 21, 25. The fishes are not alluded to because they are precluded from becoming man's companions.

call them. Man alone has language, and can give birth to languages. In giving names to earth's creatures, he would establish his dominion over them (I, 26, 28). The name would also reflect the impression produced on his mind by each creature, and indicate whether he regarded it as a fit companion for himself.

20. *but for Adam.* The dignity of human nature could not, in few words, be more beautifully expressed (Dillmann).

21. *a deep sleep.* As in XV, 12, the word implies that something mysterious and awe-inspiring was about to take place.

one of his ribs. Woman was not formed from the dust of the earth, but from man's own body. 'We have here a wonderfully conceived allegory designed to set forth the moral and social relation of the sexes to each other, the dependence of woman upon man, her close relationship to him, and the foundation existing in nature for the attachment springing up between them. The woman is formed out of the man's side; hence it is the wife's natural duty to be at hand, ready at all times to be a "help" to her husband; it is the husband's natural duty ever to cherish and defend his wife, as part of his own self' (Driver).

22. *made.* lit. 'builded'; the Rabbis connected this striking use of ויבן with the noun בינה, 'understanding,' intuition, and remarked, 'This teaches that God has endowed woman with greater intuition than He has man.'

23. *bone of my bones.* The phrase passed into popular speech (XXIX, 14).

woman. The Heb. word *Ishshah;* that for man is *Ish.* The similarity in sound emphasizes the spiritual identity of man and woman.

24. *shall a man leave.* Or, 'therefore doth a man leave his father and his mother, and doth cleave . . . and they become one flesh.' Rashi says: 'These words are by the Holy Spirit (רוח הקודש)'; *i.e.* this verse is not spoken by Adam, but is the inspired comment of Moses in order to inculcate the Jewish ideal of marriage as a unique tie which binds a man to his wife even closer than to his parents.

The Biblical ideal is the monogamic marriage; a man shall cleave 'to his *wife*', not to his wives. The sacredness of marriage relations, according to Scripture, thus goes back to the very birth of human society; nay, it is part of the scheme of his mother, and shall cleave unto his wife, and they shall be one flesh. 25. And they were both naked, the man and his wife, and were not ashamed.

3

CHAPTER III

1. Now the serpent was more subtle than any beast of the field which the LORD God had made. And he said unto the woman: 'Yea, hath God said: Ye shall not eat of any tree of the garden?' 2. And the woman said unto the serpent: 'Of the fruit of the trees of the garden we may eat; 3. but of the fruit of the tree which is in the midst of the garden, God hath said: Ye shall not eat of it, neither shall ye touch it, lest ye die.' 4. And the serpent said unto the woman: 'Ye shall not surely die; 5. for God doth know that in the day ye eat thereof, then your eyes shall be opened, and ye shall be as God, knowing good and evil.' 6. And when the woman saw that

כה אִמּוֹ וְדָבַק בְּאִשְׁתּוֹ וְהָיוּ לְבָשָׂר אֶחָד׃ וַיִּהְיוּ שְׁנֵיהֶם
עֲרוּמִּים הָאָדָם וְאִשְׁתּוֹ וְלֹא יִתְבֹּשָׁשׁוּ׃

ג

CAP. III. ג

א וְהַנָּחָשׁ הָיָה עָרוּם מִכֹּל חַיַּת הַשָּׂדֶה אֲשֶׁר עָשָׂה יְהוָה
אֱלֹהִים וַיֹּאמֶר אֶל־הָאִשָּׁה אַף כִּי־אָמַר אֱלֹהִים לֹא תֹאכְלוּ
2 מִכֹּל עֵץ הַגָּן׃ וַתֹּאמֶר הָאִשָּׁה אֶל־הַנָּחָשׁ מִפְּרִי עֵץ־הַגָּן
3 נֹאכֵל׃ וּמִפְּרִי הָעֵץ אֲשֶׁר בְּתוֹךְ־הַגָּן אָמַר אֱלֹהִים לֹא
4 תֹאכְלוּ מִמֶּנּוּ וְלֹא תִגְּעוּ בּוֹ פֶּן־תְּמֻתוּן׃ וַיֹּאמֶר הַנָּחָשׁ
ה אֶל־הָאִשָּׁה לֹא־מוֹת תְּמֻתוּן׃ כִּי יֹדֵעַ אֱלֹהִים כִּי בְּיוֹם
אֲכָלְכֶם מִמֶּנּוּ וְנִפְקְחוּ עֵינֵיכֶם וִהְיִיתֶם כֵּאלֹהִים יֹדְעֵי טוֹב

ב׳ v. 25. דגש אחר שורק

Creation. The Rabbinic term for marriage is קידושין, lit. 'the sanctities,' sanctification; the purpose of marriage being to preserve and sanctify that which had been made in the image of God; see *Marriage, Divorce, and the Position of Woman, in Judaism* (Additional Notes, Deut.).

one flesh. One entity, sharing the joys and burdens of life.

25. *not ashamed.* Before eating of the forbidden fruit (see on *v.* 9 above), they were like children in the Orient, who in the innocence and ignorance of childhood run about unclothed.

CHAPTER III, 1–8. THE TRIAL OF MAN'S FREEDOM

1. *the serpent.* According to the Rabbinic legend, the serpent in its original state had the power of speech, and its intellectual powers exceeded those of all other animals, and it was envy of man that made it plot his downfall.

subtle. The same Heb. root signifies both 'naked' and 'subtle, clever, mischievous'. Seeming simplicity is often the most dangerous weapon of cunning. The gliding stealthy movement of the serpent is a fitting symbol of the insidious progress of temptation.

yea, hath God said. lit. 'Is it really so, that God (*Elohim*) hath said'—a statement expressing surprise and incredulity with the object of creating doubt in the reasonableness of the Divine prohibition.

2. *the woman.* Guileless and unsuspecting, she falls into the trap—even enlarges on God's command.

3. *neither shall ye touch it.* There was no word concerning 'touching' in the original prohibition. This exaggeration on the part of the woman, says the Midrash, was the cause of her fall.

4. *ye shall not surely die.* The serpent boldly denies the validity of God's threat.

5. God assigned no reason for the command; the serpent suggests one; *viz.* when God gave His order, it was not for man's benefit, but because God was envious of what man would become, if he ate the forbidden fruit.

opened. To new sources of knowledge, hidden from ordinary sight—a strong appeal to the curiosity of the woman.

as God. i.e. you will become endowed with a power which is at present reserved exclusively to Himself, *viz.* omniscience (Sforno); and, having acquired omniscience, you will be in a position to repudiate His authority.

good and evil. A Heb. idiom for 'all things' (Cheyne, Ehrlich); cf. II Sam. XIV, 17. The same Heb. idiom occurs in a negative form in XXIV, 50 and XXXI, 24, 29, where it means 'nothing at all'. The ordinary explanation of the phrase 'good and evil' in the literal sense, assumes that God would for any reason withhold from man the ability to discern between what is morally right and wrong—a view which contradicts the spirit of Scripture. Moreover, Adam would not have been made 'in the image of God' if he did not from the first possess the faculty of distinguishing between good and evil. And if he lacked such faculty, his obedience or disobedience to any command whatsoever, could have no moral significance. None of these objections holds good in regard to the temporary withholding of ordinary knowledge from Adam, pending his decision to work with or against God.

6. *the woman saw.* Though the tempter did not tell the woman to eat the fruit, he had woven the spell. The woman looked upon the tree with a new longing—it was good to eat, a delight to the eyes, and it would give wisdom. She turns her the tree was good for food, and that it was a delight to the eyes, and that the tree was to be desired to make one wise, she took of the fruit thereof, and did eat; and she gave also unto her husband with her, and he did eat. 7. And the eyes of them both were opened, and they knew that they were naked; and they sewed fig-leaves together, and made themselves girdles. 8. And they heard the voice of the LORD God walking in the garden toward the cool of the day; and the man and his wife hid themselves from the presence of the LORD God amongst the trees of the garden. 9. And the LORD God called unto the man, and said unto him: 'Where art thou?' 10. And he said: 'I heard Thy voice in the garden, and I was afraid, because I was naked; and I hid myself.' 11. And He said: 'Who told thee that thou wast naked? Hast thou eaten of the tree, whereof I commanded thee that thou shouldest not eat?' 12. And the man said: 'The woman whom Thou gavest to be with me, she gave me of the tree, and I did eat.' 13. And the LORD God said unto the woman: 'What is this thou hast done?' And the woman said: 'The serpent beguiled me, and I did eat.' 14. And the LORD God said unto the serpent: 'Because thou hast done

6 וָרָע׃ וַתֵּרֶא הָאִשָּׁה כִּי טוֹב הָעֵץ לְמַאֲכָל וְכִי תַאֲוָה־הוּא
לָעֵינַיִם וְנֶחְמָד הָעֵץ לְהַשְׂכִּיל וַתִּקַּח מִפִּרְיוֹ וַתֹּאכַל וַתִּתֵּן
7 גַּם־לְאִישָׁהּ עִמָּהּ וַיֹּאכַל׃ וַתִּפָּקַחְנָה עֵינֵי שְׁנֵיהֶם וַיֵּדְעוּ כִּי
עֵירֻמִּם הֵם וַיִּתְפְּרוּ עֲלֵה תְאֵנָה וַיַּעֲשׂוּ לָהֶם חֲגֹרֹת׃
8 וַיִּשְׁמְעוּ אֶת־קוֹל יְהוָה אֱלֹהִים מִתְהַלֵּךְ בַּגָּן לְרוּחַ הַיּוֹם
וַיִּתְחַבֵּא הָאָדָם וְאִשְׁתּוֹ מִפְּנֵי יְהוָה אֱלֹהִים בְּתוֹךְ עֵץ הַגָּן׃
9 וַיִּקְרָא יְהוָה אֱלֹהִים אֶל־הָאָדָם וַיֹּאמֶר לוֹ אַיֶּכָּה׃ וַיֹּאמֶר
אֶת־קֹלְךָ שָׁמַעְתִּי בַּגָּן וָאִירָא כִּי־עֵירֹם אָנֹכִי וָאֵחָבֵא׃
11 וַיֹּאמֶר מִי הִגִּיד לְךָ כִּי עֵירֹם אָתָּה הֲמִן־הָעֵץ אֲשֶׁר צִוִּיתִיךָ
12 לְבִלְתִּי אֲכָל־מִמֶּנּוּ אָכָלְתָּ׃ וַיֹּאמֶר הָאָדָם הָאִשָּׁה אֲשֶׁר
13 נָתַתָּה עִמָּדִי הִוא נָתְנָה־לִּי מִן־הָעֵץ וָאֹכֵל׃ וַיֹּאמֶר יְהוָה
אֱלֹהִים לָאִשָּׁה מַה־זֹּאת עָשִׂית וַתֹּאמֶר הָאִשָּׁה הַנָּחָשׁ
14 הִשִּׁיאַנִי וָאֹכֵל׃ וַיֹּאמֶר יְהוָה אֱלֹהִים ׀ אֶל־הַנָּחָשׁ כִּי עָשִׂיתָ

v. 6. פתח באס״ף

back upon the impulses of gratitude, love, and duty to God. The story mirrors human experience.

with her. Either, 'who was with her,' or, 'to eat with her.' The desire for companionship in guilt is characteristic of sin.

7. *were opened.* The knowledge attained is neither of happiness, wisdom, or power, but of consciousness of sin and its conflict with the will of God (Ryle). Next come shame, fear, and the attempt to hide.

naked. They forfeited their innocence. Rashi gives a metaphorical interpretation to the words: 'They knew that they were naked'—naked of all sense of gratitude and obedience to the Divine will: one precept alone had they been asked to obey, and even this proved too much for them!

fig-leaves. Because they were the largest and best suited for a loin-covering.

8. *the voice.* Or, 'sound.'

toward the cool of the day. *i.e.* towards evening when, in the Orient, a cooling breeze arises (Song of Songs II, 17). It was this evening wind that carried to Adam and Eve the sound which heralded the approach of God.

hid themselves. Conscience makes cowards of them.

9–21. THE SENTENCE

9. *where art thou?* The Midrash explains that this question was asked out of consideration for Adam to afford him time to recover his self-possession. '*Where art thou?* is the call which, after every sin, resounds in the ears of the man who seeks to deceive himself and others concerning his sin' (Dillmann).

10. *because I was naked.* The Rabbis maintain that 'one sin leads to another sin'. Adam commits a further offence by attempting to conceal the truth by means of this excuse.

11. *hast thou eaten?* An opportunity is given Adam for full confession and expression of contrition. A sin unconfessed and unrepented is a sin constantly committed.

12. Finding his excuse useless, Adam throws the blame upon everybody but himself. First of all it is 'the woman'; then he insolently fixes a share of the responsibility upon God—'whom Thou gavest to be with me.'

13. Instead of a question, the words may be taken as an exclamation, 'What is this thou hast done!'

14. *the serpent.* As the tempter and instigator of the offence, sentence is passed upon it first; and as the tempter, the serpent is cursed, and not its dupes and victims.

shalt thou go . . . shalt thou eat. Better, *upon thy belly thou goest and dust thou eatest.* 'Till the eighteenth century it was the general belief that the serpent had been walking upright and was now reduced to crawling. This is quite un-Biblical.

this, cursed art thou from among all cattle, and from among all beasts of the field; upon thy belly shalt thou go, and dust shalt thou eat all the days of thy life. 15. And I will put enmity between thee and the woman, and between thy seed and her seed; they shall bruise thy head, and thou shalt bruise their heel.' ¶ 16. Unto the woman He said: 'I will greatly multiply thy pain and thy travail; in pain thou shalt bring forth children; and thy desire shall be to thy husband, and he shall rule over thee.' ¶ 17. And unto Adam He said: 'Because thou hast hearkened unto the voice of thy wife, and hast eaten of the tree, of which I commanded thee, saying: Thou shalt not eat of it; cursed is the ground for thy sake; in toil shalt thou eat of it all the days of thy life. 18. Thorns also and thistles shall it bring forth to thee; and thou shalt eat the herb of the field. 19. In the sweat of thy face shalt thou eat bread, till thou return unto the ground; for out of it wast thou taken; for dust thou art, and unto dust shalt thou return.' 20. And the man called his wife's name [1]Eve; because she was the mother of all living. 21. And the LORD God made for

זֹאת אָרוּר אַתָּה מִכָּל־הַבְּהֵמָה וּמִכֹּל חַיַּת הַשָּׂדֶה עַל־
טו גְּחֹנְךָ תֵלֵךְ וְעָפָר תֹּאכַל כָּל־יְמֵי חַיֶּיךָ׃ וְאֵיבָה ׀ אָשִׁית
בֵּינְךָ וּבֵין הָאִשָּׁה וּבֵין זַרְעֲךָ וּבֵין זַרְעָהּ הוּא יְשׁוּפְךָ רֹאשׁ
16 וְאַתָּה תְּשׁוּפֶנּוּ עָקֵב׃ ס אֶל־הָאִשָּׁה אָמַר הַרְבָּה אַרְבֶּה
עִצְּבוֹנֵךְ וְהֵרֹנֵךְ בְּעֶצֶב תֵּלְדִי בָנִים וְאֶל־אִישֵׁךְ תְּשׁוּקָתֵךְ
17 וְהוּא יִמְשָׁל־בָּךְ׃ ס וּלְאָדָם אָמַר כִּי שָׁמַעְתָּ לְקוֹל
אִשְׁתֶּךָ וַתֹּאכַל מִן־הָעֵץ אֲשֶׁר צִוִּיתִיךָ לֵאמֹר לֹא תֹאכַל
מִמֶּנּוּ אֲרוּרָה הָאֲדָמָה בַּעֲבוּרֶךָ בְּעִצָּבוֹן תֹּאכֲלֶנָּה כֹּל יְמֵי
18 חַיֶּיךָ׃ וְקוֹץ וְדַרְדַּר תַּצְמִיחַ לָךְ וְאָכַלְתָּ אֶת־עֵשֶׂב הַשָּׂדֶה׃
19 בְּזֵעַת אַפֶּיךָ תֹּאכַל לֶחֶם עַד שׁוּבְךָ אֶל־הָאֲדָמָה
כִּי מִמֶּנָּה לֻקָּחְתָּ כִּי־עָפָר אַתָּה וְאֶל־עָפָר תָּשׁוּב׃
כ וַיִּקְרָא הָאָדָם שֵׁם אִשְׁתּוֹ חַוָּה כִּי הִוא הָיְתָה אֵם כָּל־

[1] Heb. *Havvah*, that is, *Life*.

The meaning is, Continue to crawl on thy belly and eat dust. Henceforth it will be regarded as a curse, recalling to men thy attempt to drag them to the dust' (B. Jacob).

All the days of thy life. As long as thy species lasts.

15. *enmity*. The sight of the serpent will create loathing in man, and fear of its deadly sting will call forth an instinctive desire to destroy it.

bruise. Because of its position on the ground, the serpent strikes at the heel of man; while the man deals the fatal blow by crushing its head. Therefore the victory will rest with man.

16. *greatly multiply . . . over thee*. Better, *Much, much will I make thy pain and thy travail; in pain wilt thou bring forth children, and thy desire is unto thy husband and he ruleth over thee* (B. Jacob). This is no sentence upon the woman. It does not contain the term 'cursed'. Moreover, God himself pronounced the fruitfulness of man a blessing (I, 28), and therewith woman's pain and travail are inextricably bound up, being part of woman's physical being. The words addressed to the woman are therefore parenthetical, and signify in effect: 'Thee I need not punish. A sufficiency of woe and suffering is thine because of thy physical being' (B. Jacob).

thy desire. In spite of the pangs of travail, the longing for motherhood remains the most powerful instinct in woman.

17. *cursed is the ground*. It was Adam's duty from the beginning to till the ground (II, 15): but the work would now become much more laborious. The soil would henceforth yield its produce only as the result of hard and unceasing toil.

for thy sake. Only as long as Adam lived was the earth under a curse; see on V, 29 and VIII, 21.

18. *thou shalt eat the herb*. Render, '*whereas thou eatest the herb of the field*.' The spontaneous growth of the soil will be weeds, which are unsuitable for human consumption. Man's food is the herb, which he can only acquire by toil.

19. *in the sweat*. 'The necessity of labour has proved man's greatest blessing, and has been the cause of all progress and improvement' (Ryle).

20. *the mother of all living*. This translation is incorrect. Render, *the mother of all humankind*. Otherwise, some word must be supplied after 'living', so as to exclude animal life (Onkelos, Saadyah). W. Robertson Smith has shown that the word חי in the text, which is here wrongly translated, 'living,' is the primitive Semitic word for 'clan'; Eve was the mother of every human clan, the mother of mankind. חי in this sense occurs also in I Sam. XVIII, 18 ('Who am I, and who are my kinsfolk, ומי חיי, or my father's family, etc.' RV Margin).

21. *The LORD God made*. Despite their sin, God had not withdrawn His care from them. Divine punishment is at once followed by Divine pity.

Adam and for his wife garments of skins, and clothed them.* v a; iv s. ¶ 22. And the LORD God said: 'Behold, the man is become as one of us, to know good and evil; and now, lest he put forth his hand, and take also of the tree of life, and eat, and live for ever.' 23. Therefore the LORD God sent him forth from the garden of Eden, to till the ground from whence he was taken. 24. So He drove out the man; and He placed at the east of the garden of Eden the cherubim, and the flaming sword which turned every way, to keep the way to the tree of life.

4 CHAPTER IV

1. And the man knew Eve his wife; and she conceived and bore Cain, and said: 'I have [1]gotten a man with the help of the

[1] Heb. *kanah*, to get.

21 חַי׃ וַיַּעַשׂ יְהוָה אֱלֹהִים לְאָדָם וּלְאִשְׁתּוֹ כָּתְנוֹת עוֹר
וַיַּלְבִּשֵׁם׃* חמישי פ (רביעי לספ')
22 וַיֹּאמֶר ׀ יְהוָה אֱלֹהִים הֵן הָאָדָם הָיָה כְּאַחַד מִמֶּנּוּ לָדַעַת
טוֹב וָרָע וְעַתָּה ׀ פֶּן־יִשְׁלַח יָדוֹ וְלָקַח גַּם מֵעֵץ הַחַיִּים
23 וְאָכַל וָחַי לְעֹלָם׃ וַיְשַׁלְּחֵהוּ יְהוָה אֱלֹהִים מִגַּן־עֵדֶן לַעֲבֹד
24 אֶת־הָאֲדָמָה אֲשֶׁר לֻקַּח מִשָּׁם׃ וַיְגָרֶשׁ אֶת־הָאָדָם וַיַּשְׁכֵּן
מִקֶּדֶם לְגַן־עֵדֶן אֶת־הַכְּרֻבִים וְאֵת לַהַט הַחֶרֶב הַמִּתְהַפֶּכֶת
לִשְׁמֹר אֶת־דֶּרֶךְ עֵץ הַחַיִּים׃ ס

ד CAP. IV. ד

א וְהָאָדָם יָדַע אֶת־חַוָּה אִשְׁתּוֹ וַתַּהַר וַתֵּלֶד אֶת־קַיִן וַתֹּאמֶר

garments of skin. Better suited for the rough life in front of them than the apron of leaves they were wearing.

and clothed them. This is one of the passages on which the Rabbis base the Jewish ideal of *Imitatio Dei*, the duty of imitating God's ways of lovingkindness and pity. 'The beginning and the end of the Torah is the bestowal of loving-kindnesses,' they say; 'at the beginning of the Torah, God clothes Adam; and at its end, He buries Moses.'

22–24. THE EXPULSION FROM EDEN

22. *man is become as one of us.* As one of the angels; or, 'us' is a plural of Majesty (cf. I, 26), meaning, man is become as God—omniscient. Man, having through disobedience secured the faculty of unlimited knowledge, there was real danger that his knowledge would outstrip his sense of obedience to Divine Law. In our own day, we see that deep insight into Nature's secrets, if unrestrained by considerations of humanity, may threaten the very existence of mankind; *e.g.* through chemical warfare.

live for ever. Through further disobedience he could secure deathlessness. Immortality, however, that had been secured through disobedience and lived in sin, an immortal life of Intellect without Conscience, would defeat the purpose of man's creation (Sforno). Therefore, not only for his punishment, but for his salvation, to bring him back from the sinister course on which he had entered, God sent man forth from the Garden. Man, having sunk into sin, must rise again through the spiritual purification of suffering and death (Strack).

24. *drove out.* Sin drives man from God's presence; and when man banishes God from his world, he dwells in a wilderness instead of a Garden of Eden.

at the east. Either because man dwelt to the east of the Garden, or because the entrance was on that side.

cherubim. What these really were is a matter of uncertainty. According to Rashi, they were 'angels of destruction'. The first man was forbidden to enter the Garden again, and the slightest attempt on his part to do so would bring down upon him instant destruction. In the Bible generally, the cherubim are symbols of God's presence (Exod. XXV, 18).

to keep the way. Though the entrance to Eden was guarded by the angels with the flaming sword, the gentler angel of mercy did not forsake them in their exile. Adam and Eve discovered Repentance—the Rabbis tell us—and thereby they came nearer to God outside of Eden than when in Eden.

(*b*) CAIN, SETH, AND THEIR DESCENDANTS. CHAPTERS IV AND V

IV, 1–16. CAIN AND ABEL

This narrative describes the spread of sin, issuing in violence and death!

1. *gotten.* The derivation is based on the resemblance of sound between Cain and the Heb. root *kanah*—to acquire.

with the help of the LORD. The four Heb. words spoken by Eve are very obscure. The traditional interpretation makes 'a man' refer to Cain; and the words, an expression of thanksgiving for her child. Others refer 'man' to husband (cf. XXIX, 32). The sequel to the act of disobedience in the Garden would have caused estrangement between husband and wife; and Eve rejoices in the birth of a child, because through Cain, she wins back her husband.

Lord.' 2. And again she bore his brother Abel. And Abel was a keeper of sheep, but Cain was a tiller of the ground. 3. And in process of time it came to pass, that Cain brought of the fruit of the ground an offering unto the Lord. 4. And Abel, he also brought of the firstlings of his flock and of the fat thereof. And the Lord had respect unto Abel and to his offering; 5. but unto Cain and to his offering He had not respect. And Cain was very wroth, and his countenance fell. 6. And the Lord said unto Cain: 'Why art thou wroth? and why is thy countenance fallen? 7. If thou doest well, shall it not be lifted up? and if thou doest not well, sin coucheth at the door; and unto thee is its desire, but thou mayest rule over it.' 8. And Cain spoke unto Abel his brother. And it came to pass, when they were in the field, that Cain rose up against Abel his brother, and slew him. ¶ 9. And the Lord said unto Cain: 'Where is Abel thy brother?' And he said: 'I know not; am I my brother's keeper?' 10. And He said: 'What hast thou done? the voice of thy

2 קָנִיתִי אִישׁ אֶת־יְהוָה׃ וַתֹּסֶף לָלֶדֶת אֶת־אָחִיו אֶת־הָבֶל
3 וַיְהִי־הֶבֶל רֹעֵה צֹאן וְקַיִן הָיָה עֹבֵד אֲדָמָה׃ וַיְהִי מִקֵּץ
4 יָמִים וַיָּבֵא קַיִן מִפְּרִי הָאֲדָמָה מִנְחָה לַיהוָה׃ וְהֶבֶל הֵבִיא
גַם־הוּא מִבְּכֹרוֹת צֹאנוֹ וּמֵחֶלְבֵהֶן וַיִּשַׁע יְהוָה אֶל־הֶבֶל
ה וְאֶל־מִנְחָתוֹ׃ וְאֶל־קַיִן וְאֶל־מִנְחָתוֹ לֹא שָׁעָה וַיִּחַר לְקַיִן
6 מְאֹד וַיִּפְּלוּ פָּנָיו׃ וַיֹּאמֶר יְהוָה אֶל־קָיִן לָמָּה חָרָה לָךְ
7 וְלָמָּה נָפְלוּ פָנֶיךָ׃ הֲלוֹא אִם־תֵּיטִיב שְׂאֵת וְאִם לֹא
תֵיטִיב לַפֶּתַח חַטָּאת רֹבֵץ וְאֵלֶיךָ תְּשׁוּקָתוֹ וְאַתָּה תִּמְשָׁל־
8 בּוֹ׃ וַיֹּאמֶר קַיִן אֶל־הֶבֶל אָחִיו* וַיְהִי בִּהְיוֹתָם בַּשָּׂדֶה וַיָּקָם
9 קַיִן אֶל־הֶבֶל אָחִיו וַיַּהַרְגֵהוּ׃ וַיֹּאמֶר יְהוָה אֶל־קַיִן אֵי
י הֶבֶל אָחִיךָ וַיֹּאמֶר לֹא יָדַעְתִּי הֲשֹׁמֵר אָחִי אָנֹכִי׃ וַיֹּאמֶר

v. 3. מלרע v. 4. ב׳ רפה v. 8. בלא פסקא

2. *Abel.* In Assyrian, *ablu* means 'son'. The Heb. word signifies 'a breath', like his life, so tragically brief. As the younger brother, Abel is given the lighter task of caring for the flocks; while Cain assists his father in the cultivation of the soil.

3. *an offering.* This is the first mention of worship in Scripture. The religious instinct is part of man's nature, and sacrifice is the earliest outward expression of that worship. Its purpose was to express acknowledgment of His bounty to the Giver of all.

4. *firstlings.* The most highly-prized among the flocks.

the fat. The richest part of the animal.

had respect unto. *i.e.* accepted.

5. *but unto Cain.* Unlike Abel's, his sacrifice is rejected because of the difference of spirit in which it was offered. The Lord looks to the heart.

his countenance fell. In disappointment and dejection.

7. *shall it not be lifted up?* Alluding to the 'countenance' that had fallen. God mercifully intervenes to arrest the progress of evil thoughts. Another interpretation is, 'Shall there not be acceptance?'

sin coucheth. Sin is compared to a ravenous beast lying in wait for its prey. It crouches at the entrance of the house, to spring upon its victim as soon as the door is opened. By harbouring feelings of vexation, Cain opened the door of his heart to the evil passions of envy, anger, violence, which eventually ended in murder.

and unto thee. Passion and evil imagination are ever assaulting the heart of man; yet he can conquer them, if only he resist them with determination.

8. *and Cain spoke unto Abel.* What is said is not mentioned. The ancient Versions supply some such words as, 'let us go into the field.' This is unnecessary, as Scripture often omits words (see II Chron. I, 2) which are obvious, and can be gathered from the context (Ehrlich).

in the field. Far away from their parents' home, where Cain had his brother at his mercy; cf. Deut. XXII, 25.

9. *where is . . . brother?* As in III, 9, the object of the question is not information, but to elicit a confession of guilt (Rashi).

am I my brother's keeper? Cain's answer is both false and insolent. Only a murderer altogether renounces the obligations of brotherhood.

10. *what hast thou done?* The note of interrogation should be replaced by a note of exclamation. The meaning is: What a deed of horror hast thou wrought! This is further indicated by the fact that the word 'brother' is used no less than six times in verses 8–11.

blood. The Heb. word is in the plural. In slaying Abel, Cain slew also Abel's unborn descendants. 'He who destroys a single human life is as if he destroyed a whole world' (Talmud).

crieth unto Me. For vengeance. See Job XVI, 18, 'Oh, earth, cover not thou my blood, and let my cry have no resting-place.'

brother's blood crieth unto Me from the
ground. 11. And now cursed art thou
from the ground, which hath opened her
mouth to receive thy brother's blood from
thy hand. 12. When thou tillest the ground,
it shall not henceforth yield unto thee her
strength; a fugitive and a wanderer shalt
thou be in the earth.' 13. And Cain said
unto the LORD: 'My punishment is greater
than I can bear. 14. Behold, Thou hast
driven me out this day from the face of
the land; and from Thy face shall I be
hid; and I shall be a fugitive and a wanderer
in the earth; and it will come to pass, that
whosoever findeth me will slay me.' 15.
And the LORD said unto him: 'Therefore
whosoever slayeth Cain, vengeance shall
be taken on him sevenfold.' And the LORD
set a sign for Cain, lest any finding him
should smite him. ¶ 16. And Cain went out
from the presence of the LORD, and dwelt
in the land of [1]Nod, on the east of Eden.
17. And Cain knew his wife; and she
conceived, and bore Enoch; and he builded
a city, and called the name of the city after
the name of his son Enoch. 18. And unto
Enoch was born Irad; and Irad begot
Mehujael; and [2]Mehujael begot Methushael;
and Methushael begot Lamech.*v s. 19.
And Lamech took unto him two wives;

[1] That is, *Wandering*. [2] Heb. *Mehijael*.

11 מָה עָשִׂיתָ קוֹל דְּמֵי אָחִיךָ צֹעֲקִים אֵלַי מִן־הָאֲדָמָה׃ וְעַתָּה
אָרוּר אָתָּה מִן־הָאֲדָמָה אֲשֶׁר פָּצְתָה אֶת־פִּיהָ לָקַחַת אֶת־
12 דְּמֵי אָחִיךָ מִיָּדֶךָ׃ כִּי תַעֲבֹד אֶת־הָאֲדָמָה לֹא־תֹסֵף תֵּת־כֹּחָהּ
13 לָךְ נָע וָנָד תִּהְיֶה בָאָרֶץ׃ וַיֹּאמֶר קַיִן אֶל־יְהוָה גָּדוֹל עֲוֺנִי
14 מִנְּשֹׂא׃ הֵן גֵּרַשְׁתָּ אֹתִי הַיּוֹם מֵעַל פְּנֵי הָאֲדָמָה וּמִפָּנֶיךָ אֶסָּתֵר
טו וְהָיִיתִי נָע וָנָד בָּאָרֶץ וְהָיָה כָל־מֹצְאִי יַהַרְגֵנִי׃ וַיֹּאמֶר לוֹ יְהוָה
לָכֵן כָּל־הֹרֵג קַיִן שִׁבְעָתַיִם יֻקָּם וַיָּשֶׂם יְהוָה לְקַיִן אוֹת לְבִלְתִּי
16 הַכּוֹת־אֹתוֹ כָּל־מֹצְאוֹ׃ וַיֵּצֵא קַיִן מִלִּפְנֵי יְהוָה וַיֵּשֶׁב בְּאֶרֶץ
17 נוֹד קִדְמַת־עֵדֶן׃ וַיֵּדַע קַיִן אֶת־אִשְׁתּוֹ וַתַּהַר וַתֵּלֶד אֶת־
חֲנוֹךְ וַיְהִי בֹּנֶה עִיר וַיִּקְרָא שֵׁם הָעִיר כְּשֵׁם בְּנוֹ חֲנוֹךְ׃
18 וַיִּוָּלֵד לַחֲנוֹךְ אֶת־עִירָד וְעִירָד יָלַד אֶת־מְחוּיָאֵל וּמְחִיָּיאֵל
19 יָלַד אֶת־מְתוּשָׁאֵל וּמְתוּשָׁאֵל יָלַד אֶת־לָמֶךְ׃ *וַיִּקַּח־לוֹ לָמֶךְ

* (חמישי לספ׳)

11. *from the ground.* Or, 'more than the ground,' upon which a curse had been pronounced (III, 17).

12. *when thou tillest.* Wherever he lives, the curse will follow him and the soil will be barren for him. The remainder of his existence will consequently be an unceasing vagabondage.

13. *my punishment.* The Heb. word עון means both the consequences of a sin, *i.e.* punishment, and the sin itself. The Targum renders 'mine iniquity is too great to be pardoned'. The Heb. word translated 'than I can bear' can also be rendered 'to be forgiven'. Rashi understands the phrase as a question, 'Is my iniquity too great to be forgiven?'

14. *land.* He complains that he is banished into the desert, to share the fate of an outlaw.

and from Thy face. To be 'hidden from the face of God' (Deut. XXXI, 18) is to forfeit Divine protection. 'This anguished cry of Cain reveals him as a man not wholly bad, one to whom banishment from the Divine presence is a distinct ingredient in his cup of misery' (Skinner).

whosoever findeth me. Cain feared death at the hands of some future 'avenger of blood'; cf. Num. XXXV, 10 f.

15. *sevenfold.* The number 'seven' is occasionally used in the Bible to express an indefinite large number; cf. Lev. XXVI, 27: Prov. XXIV, 16. Cain's murderer shall be visited with a punishment far greater than that exacted of Abel's, as God had now made manifest His abhorrence of bloodshed to all.

set a sign for Cain. According to the Rabbis, Cain was a repentant sinner. God, therefore, reassured him that he would not be regarded as a common, intentional murderer. God's mercy to the guilty who repents of his sin is infinitely greater than that of man. The popular expression, *the brand of Cain*, in the sense of the sign of the murderer, arises from a complete misunderstanding of the passage.

16. *from the presence of the LORD.* Having forfeited God's favour, Cain withdraws from the neighbourhood of Eden, which was the special abode of the Divine Presence.

17–24. DESCENDANTS OF CAIN

17. *his wife.* The marriage of brother and sister was quite common in primitive times, but the Hebrew people looked upon it with such abhorrence (cf. Lev. XVIII, 9) that Scripture makes no reference to the identity of the wife in this passage.

he builded a city. lit. 'he was building a city'; did not necessarily complete it. Cain said in his heart, 'If it is decreed upon me to be a wanderer on the earth, the decree shall not apply to my offspring' (Nachmanides).

19. *two wives.* This is especially mentioned, as it was a departure from the ideal expounded in II, 14.

the name of the one was Adah, and the name of the other Zillah. 20. And Adah bore Jabal; he was the father of such as dwell in tents and have cattle. 21. And his brother's name was Jubal; he was the father of all such as handle the harp and pipe. 22. And Zillah, she also bore Tubal-cain, the forger of every cutting instrument of brass and iron; and the sister of Tubal-cain was Naamah. 23. And Lamech said unto his wives:

> Adah and Zillah, hear my voice;
> Ye wives of Lamech, hearken unto my speech;
> For I have slain a man for wounding me,
> And a young man for bruising me;
> 24. If Cain shall be avenged sevenfold,
> Truly Lamech seventy and sevenfold.

25. And Adam knew his wife again; and she bore a son, and called his name [1]Seth: 'for God [2]hath appointed me another seed instead of Abel; for Cain slew him.' 26. And to Seth, to him also there was born a son; and he called his name Enosh; then began men to call upon the name of the LORD.*vi.

5

Chapter V

1. This is the book of the generations of Adam. In the day that God created man, in the likeness of God made He him; 2. male and female created He them, and

כ שְׁתֵּי נָשִׁים שֵׁם הָאַחַת עָדָה וְשֵׁם הַשֵּׁנִית צִלָּה׃ וַתֵּלֶד עָדָה
21 אֶת־יָבָל הוּא הָיָה אֲבִי יֹשֵׁב אֹהֶל וּמִקְנֶה׃ וְשֵׁם אָחִיו יוּבָל הוּא
22 הָיָה אֲבִי כָּל־תֹּפֵשׂ כִּנּוֹר וְעוּגָב׃ וְצִלָּה גַם־הִוא יָלְדָה אֶת־
תּוּבַל קַיִן לֹטֵשׁ כָּל־חֹרֵשׁ נְחֹשֶׁת וּבַרְזֶל וַאֲחוֹת תּוּבַל־קַיִן
23 נַעֲמָה׃ וַיֹּאמֶר לֶמֶךְ לְנָשָׁיו עָדָה וְצִלָּה שְׁמַעַן קוֹלִי נְשֵׁי
לֶמֶךְ הַאְזֵנָּה אִמְרָתִי כִּי אִישׁ הָרַגְתִּי לְפִצְעִי וְיֶלֶד
24 לְחַבֻּרָתִי׃ כִּי שִׁבְעָתַיִם יֻקַּם־קָיִן וְלֶמֶךְ שִׁבְעִים וְשִׁבְעָה׃
כה וַיֵּדַע אָדָם עוֹד אֶת־אִשְׁתּוֹ וַתֵּלֶד בֵּן וַתִּקְרָא אֶת־שְׁמוֹ
שֵׁת כִּי שָׁת־לִי אֱלֹהִים זֶרַע אַחֵר תַּחַת הֶבֶל כִּי הֲרָגוֹ
26 קָיִן׃ וּלְשֵׁת גַּם־הוּא יֻלַּד־בֵּן וַיִּקְרָא אֶת־שְׁמוֹ אֱנוֹשׁ אָז
הוּחַל לִקְרֹא בְּשֵׁם יְהוָה׃* ס ששי

ה

Cap. V. ה

א זֶה סֵפֶר תּוֹלְדֹת אָדָם בְּיוֹם בְּרֹא אֱלֹהִים אָדָם בִּדְמוּת
2 אֱלֹהִים עָשָׂה אֹתוֹ׃ זָכָר וּנְקֵבָה בְּרָאָם וַיְבָרֶךְ אֹתָם
3 וַיִּקְרָא אֶת־שְׁמָם אָדָם בְּיוֹם הִבָּרְאָם׃ וַיְחִי אָדָם שְׁלֹשִׁים
וּמְאַת שָׁנָה וַיּוֹלֶד בִּדְמוּתוֹ כְּצַלְמוֹ וַיִּקְרָא אֶת־שְׁמוֹ שֵׁת׃

[1] Heb. *Sheth*. [2] Heb. *shath*.

ד' v. 23. א' נחה

20. *father. i.e.* the first, the originator of pastoral life. Abel had been the keeper of sheep (v. 2); but Jabal widened the class of animals which could be domesticated.

21. *harp and pipe.* Music, according to Hebrew tradition, is thus the most ancient art, dating from the beginnings of the human race.

22. *brass.* The Heb. is more accurately translated 'copper', since it was a metal dug from the earth (Deut. VIII, 9). Brass is an alloy. The discovery of the use of metals forms an important step in the progress of civilization.

Naamah. The word means, 'pleasant, gracious.' Jewish legend states she became the wife of Noah.

23, 24. A triumphal song on the invention of the weapons mentioned in the preceding verse. Lamech possibly committed an act of involuntary homicide on some young person. He turns to his wives and says boastfully, 'See! I have taken a man's life, though he only inflicted a bruise on me. Should the necessity arise, I feel able to lay low any assailant that crosses my path. If Cain, though unarmed, was promised a sevenfold vengeance on a foe, I, equipped with the weapons invented by Tubal-Cain, will be able to exact a vengeance very much greater!' This heathen song marks the growth of the spirit of Cain.

26. *Enosh.* In Heb. poetry, *enosh* means 'man'.

to call upon. Then men began to pray to God (Ibn Ezra); or, once more call upon God under the name *Adonay*, Lord, which seems to have been forgotten among the descendants of Cain (Hoffmann).

Chaps. II–IV record the sin of Adam and Eve, their expulsion from Eden, the murder of Abel, Cain's descendants reaching in Lamech the climax of boastful and unrestrained violence. Piety, however, does not perish with Abel, and it reaches a new development in the days of Enosh (W. H. Green).

Chapter V. Descendants of Seth

1. *this is the book.* Heb. *sefer* does not always mean a volume; it may be used of any written document. Rabbinic tradition states the Torah is not one continuous work, written at one definite moment. 'The Torah was given to Moses in separate scrolls' (תורה מגילה מגילה נתנה). The formula, 'These are the generations,' which

4 וַיִּהְיוּ יְמֵי־אָדָם אַחֲרֵי הוֹלִידוֹ אֶת־שֵׁת שְׁמֹנֶה מֵאֹת שָׁנָה
ה וַיּוֹלֶד בָּנִים וּבָנוֹת׃ וַיִּהְיוּ כָּל־יְמֵי אָדָם אֲשֶׁר־חַי תְּשַׁע
6 מֵאוֹת שָׁנָה וּשְׁלֹשִׁים שָׁנָה וַיָּמֹת׃ ס וַיְחִי־שֵׁת חָמֵשׁ
7 שָׁנִים וּמְאַת שָׁנָה וַיּוֹלֶד אֶת־אֱנוֹשׁ׃ וַיְחִי־שֵׁת אַחֲרֵי הוֹלִידוֹ
אֶת־אֱנוֹשׁ שֶׁבַע שָׁנִים וּשְׁמֹנֶה מֵאוֹת שָׁנָה וַיּוֹלֶד בָּנִים
8 וּבָנוֹת׃ וַיִּהְיוּ כָּל־יְמֵי־שֵׁת שְׁתֵּים עֶשְׂרֵה שָׁנָה וּתְשַׁע מֵאוֹת
9 שָׁנָה וַיָּמֹת׃ ס וַיְחִי אֱנוֹשׁ תִּשְׁעִים שָׁנָה וַיּוֹלֶד אֶת־קֵינָן׃
י וַיְחִי אֱנוֹשׁ אַחֲרֵי הוֹלִידוֹ אֶת־קֵינָן חֲמֵשׁ עֶשְׂרֵה שָׁנָה
11 וּשְׁמֹנֶה מֵאוֹת שָׁנָה וַיּוֹלֶד בָּנִים וּבָנוֹת׃ וַיִּהְיוּ כָּל־יְמֵי
12 אֱנוֹשׁ חָמֵשׁ שָׁנִים וּתְשַׁע מֵאוֹת שָׁנָה וַיָּמֹת׃ ס וַיְחִי קֵינָן
13 שִׁבְעִים שָׁנָה וַיּוֹלֶד אֶת־מַהֲלַלְאֵל׃ וַיְחִי קֵינָן אַחֲרֵי הוֹלִידוֹ
אֶת־מַהֲלַלְאֵל אַרְבָּעִים שָׁנָה וּשְׁמֹנֶה מֵאוֹת שָׁנָה וַיּוֹלֶד
14 בָּנִים וּבָנוֹת׃ וַיִּהְיוּ כָּל־יְמֵי קֵינָן עֶשֶׂר שָׁנִים וּתְשַׁע מֵאוֹת
טו שָׁנָה וַיָּמֹת׃ ס וַיְחִי מַהֲלַלְאֵל חָמֵשׁ שָׁנִים וְשִׁשִּׁים שָׁנָה
16 וַיּוֹלֶד אֶת־יָרֶד׃ וַיְחִי מַהֲלַלְאֵל אַחֲרֵי הוֹלִידוֹ אֶת־יֶרֶד
שְׁלֹשִׁים שָׁנָה וּשְׁמֹנֶה מֵאוֹת שָׁנָה וַיּוֹלֶד בָּנִים וּבָנוֹת׃
17 וַיִּהְיוּ כָּל־יְמֵי מַהֲלַלְאֵל חָמֵשׁ וְתִשְׁעִים שָׁנָה וּשְׁמֹנֶה מֵאוֹת
18 שָׁנָה וַיָּמֹת׃ ס וַיְחִי־יֶרֶד שְׁתַּיִם וְשִׁשִּׁים שָׁנָה וּמְאַת
19 שָׁנָה וַיּוֹלֶד אֶת־חֲנוֹךְ׃ וַיְחִי־יֶרֶד אַחֲרֵי הוֹלִידוֹ אֶת־חֲנוֹךְ
כ שְׁמֹנֶה מֵאוֹת שָׁנָה וַיּוֹלֶד בָּנִים וּבָנוֹת׃ וַיִּהְיוּ כָּל־יְמֵי־יֶרֶד
21 שְׁתַּיִם וְשִׁשִּׁים שָׁנָה וּתְשַׁע מֵאוֹת שָׁנָה וַיָּמֹת׃ ס וַיְחִי
22 חֲנוֹךְ חָמֵשׁ וְשִׁשִּׁים שָׁנָה וַיּוֹלֶד אֶת־מְתוּשָׁלַח׃ וַיִּתְהַלֵּךְ

blessed them, and called their name Adam, in the day when they were created. 3. And Adam lived a hundred and thirty years, and begot a son in his own likeness, after his image; and called his name Seth. 4. And the days of Adam after he begot Seth were eight hundred years; and he begot sons and daughters. 5. And all the days that Adam lived were nine hundred and thirty years; and he died. ¶ 6. And Seth lived a hundred and five years, and begot Enosh. 7. And Seth lived after he begot Enosh eight hundred and seven years, and begot sons and daughters. 8. And all the days of Seth were nine hundred and twelve years; and he died. ¶ 9. And Enosh lived ninety years, and begot Kenan. 10. And Enosh lived after he begot Kenan eight hundred and fifteen years, and begot sons and daughters. 11. And all the days of Enosh were nine hundred and five years; and he died. ¶ 12. And Kenan lived seventy years, and begot Mahalalel. 13. And Kenan lived after he begot Mahalalel eight hundred and forty years, and begot sons and daughters. 14. And all the days of Kenan were nine hundred and ten years; and he died. ¶ 15. And Mahalalel lived sixty and five years, and begot Jared. 16. And Mahalalel lived after he begot Jared eight hundred and thirty years, and begot sons and daughters. 17. And all the days of Mahalalel were eight hundred ninety and five years; and he died. ¶ 18. And Jared lived a hundred sixty and two years, and begot Enoch. 19. And Jared lived after he begot Enoch eight hundred years, and begot sons and daughters. 20. And all the days of Jared were nine hundred sixty and two years; and he died. ¶ 21. And Enoch lived sixty and five years, and begot Methuselah. 22. And Enoch walked with

occurs ten times in Genesis, each time beginning a new section, would mark the beginning of such scroll or 'book'. This explains why some sections, as this Chapter, have introductory verses *which recall or summarize facts mentioned in earlier sections*.

The book of the generations of Adam. Heb. זה ספר תולדת אדם. One of the early Rabbis, Ben Azzai, translated these words, 'This is the book of the generations of *Man*,' and declared them to be 'a great, fundamental teaching of the Torah'. As all human beings are traced back to one parent, he taught, they must necessarily be brothers. These words, therefore, proclaim the vital truth of the Unity of the Human Race, and the consequent doctrine of the Brotherhood of Man. 'This is the book of the generations of Man'—not black, not white, not great, not small, but *Man*. In these Scriptural words we have a concept quite unknown in the ancient world—Humanity. And only the belief in One God could lead to such a clear affirmation of the unity of mankind.

in the likeness. A reminder of the dignity of man's nature.

5. Various theories have been propounded to explain the abnormally long lives of these antediluvians. Maimonides holds that only the distinguished individuals named in this chapter lived these long years, but others lived a more or less normal span. The idea that men in primeval times lived extraordinarily long lives is common to the traditions of most ancient peoples.

Two names in this series of descendants of Seth, Enoch and Lamech are identical with those among the children of Cain. In both cases, however, the connection makes it evident that they represent different characters.

God after he begot Methuselah three hundred years, and begot sons and daughters. 23. And all the days of Enoch were three hundred sixty and five years. 24. And Enoch walked with God, and he was not; for God took him.*vii. ¶ 25. And Methuselah lived a hundred eighty and seven years, and begot Lamech. 26. And Methuselah lived after he begot Lamech seven hundred eighty and two years, and begot sons and daughters. 27. And all the days of Methuselah were nine hundred sixty and nine years; and he died. ¶ 28. And Lamech lived a hundred eighty and two years, and begot a son. 29. And he called his name Noah, saying: 'This same shall [1]comfort us in our work and in the toil of our hands, which cometh from the ground which the LORD hath cursed.' 30. And Lamech lived after he begot Noah five hundred ninety and five years, and begot sons and daughters. 31. And all the days of Lamech were seven hundred seventy and seven years; and he died. ¶ 32. And Noah was five hundred years old; and Noah begot Shem, Ham, and Japheth.

חֲנוֹךְ אֶת־הָאֱלֹהִים אַחֲרֵי הוֹלִידוֹ אֶת־מְתוּשֶׁלַח שְׁלֹשׁ
23 מֵאוֹת שָׁנָה וַיּוֹלֶד בָּנִים וּבָנוֹת׃ וַיְהִי כָּל־יְמֵי חֲנוֹךְ חָמֵשׁ
24 וְשִׁשִּׁים שָׁנָה וּשְׁלֹשׁ מֵאוֹת שָׁנָה׃ וַיִּתְהַלֵּךְ חֲנוֹךְ אֶת־
שביעי כה הָאֱלֹהִים וְאֵינֶנּוּ כִּי־לָקַח אֹתוֹ אֱלֹהִים׃ * ס וַיְחִי מְתוּשֶׁלַח
26 שֶׁבַע וּשְׁמֹנִים שָׁנָה וּמְאַת שָׁנָה וַיּוֹלֶד אֶת־לָמֶךְ׃ וַיְחִי
מְתוּשֶׁלַח אַחֲרֵי הוֹלִידוֹ אֶת־לֶמֶךְ שְׁתַּיִם וּשְׁמוֹנִים שָׁנָה
27 וּשְׁבַע מֵאוֹת שָׁנָה וַיּוֹלֶד בָּנִים וּבָנוֹת׃ וַיִּהְיוּ כָּל־יְמֵי
מְתוּשֶׁלַח תֵּשַׁע וְשִׁשִּׁים שָׁנָה וּתְשַׁע מֵאוֹת שָׁנָה וַיָּמֹת׃ ס
28 וַיְחִי־לֶמֶךְ שְׁתַּיִם וּשְׁמֹנִים שָׁנָה וּמְאַת שָׁנָה וַיּוֹלֶד בֵּן׃
29 וַיִּקְרָא אֶת־שְׁמוֹ נֹחַ לֵאמֹר זֶה יְנַחֲמֵנוּ מִמַּעֲשֵׂנוּ וּמֵעִצְּבוֹן
ל יָדֵינוּ מִן־הָאֲדָמָה אֲשֶׁר אֵרְרָהּ יְהוָה׃ וַיְחִי־לֶמֶךְ אַחֲרֵי
הוֹלִידוֹ אֶת־נֹחַ חָמֵשׁ וְתִשְׁעִים שָׁנָה וַחֲמֵשׁ מֵאֹת
31 שָׁנָה וַיּוֹלֶד בָּנִים וּבָנוֹת׃ וַיְהִי כָּל־יְמֵי־לֶמֶךְ שֶׁבַע
32 וְשִׁבְעִים שָׁנָה וּשְׁבַע מֵאוֹת שָׁנָה וַיָּמֹת׃ ס וַיְהִי־
נֹחַ בֶּן־חֲמֵשׁ מֵאוֹת שָׁנָה וַיּוֹלֶד נֹחַ אֶת־שֵׁם אֶת־חָם
וְאֶת־יָפֶת׃

6

CHAPTER VI

1. And it came to pass, when men began to multiply on the face of the earth, and daughters were born unto them, 2. that the sons of God saw the daughters of men that they were fair; and they took them

CAP. VI. ו

ו
א וַיְהִי כִּי־הֵחֵל הָאָדָם לָרֹב עַל־פְּנֵי הָאֲדָמָה וּבָנוֹת יֻלְּדוּ
2 לָהֶם׃ וַיִּרְאוּ בְנֵי־הָאֱלֹהִים אֶת־בְּנוֹת הָאָדָם כִּי טֹבֹת הֵנָּה

[1] Heb. *nahem*, to comfort.

ה׳ v. 29. הקורא יטעים הגרש קודם התלשא

22. *walked with God.* To avoid the anthropomorphism, Onkelos renders, 'Enoch walked in the fear of God,' and the Jerusalem Targum, 'served in truth before the Lord.' Whereas the other men enumerated merely existed and preserved the race physically, Enoch led a life of intimate companionship with God in that morally deteriorating age. The Heb. idiom 'to walk with God' is employed to express a righteous course of life, as though the man who is thus described, walked with and was accompanied by his Maker. A similar phrase is used concerning Noah (vi, 9).

24. *and he was not.* These words may mean either that, as a reward for his piety, Enoch did not meet with the ordinary fate of mortals, but like Elijah he was taken to Heaven without the agony of death; or, that Enoch died prematurely. Rashi explains that although Enoch was pious, he was weak and liable to go astray. To avert such a calamity, he was removed from earth.

for God took him. This description of death is profoundly significant. We come from God, and to Him do we return. To die is to be taken by God, in whose Presence there is life eternal.

Rabbinical legend was very busy with the story of Enoch. He was the repository of the mysteries of the universe; and even higher honours were later accorded to him in the circles of the Jewish mystics.

29. *comfort.* See on III, 17. Only as long as Adam lived was the earth under a curse; and as, according to the chronology of this chapter, Noah was the first man born after the death of Adam, his birth becomes the presage of a new age to mankind (B. Jacob). Instead of 'comfort us', Rashi translates 'shall give us rest'—referring to the invention of the plough, that was attributed to Noah, by which human labour was much lightened.

CHAPTER VI, 1–8. THE GROWING CORRUPTION OF MANKIND

2. *sons of God.* Is the literal translation of the Heb. phrase *beney Elohim.*

Among several ancient peoples there was a belief that there once existed a race of men of gigantic strength and stature who were the offspring of human mothers and celestial fathers, and we are supposed to have an echo of that legend in this Biblical passage. Philo, Josephus

wives, whomsoever they chose. 3. And
the LORD said: 'My spirit shall not abide
in man for ever, for that he also is flesh;
therefore shall his days be a hundred and
twenty years.' 4. The Nephilim were in
the earth in those days, and also after
that, when the sons of God came in unto
the daughters of men, and they bore
children to them; the same were the mighty
men that were of old, the men of renown.*m.
¶ 5. And the LORD saw that the wicked-
ness of man was great in the earth, and
that every imagination of the thoughts of
his heart was only evil continually. 6.
And it repented the LORD that He had

3 וַיִּקְחוּ לָהֶם נָשִׁים מִכֹּל אֲשֶׁר בָּחָרוּ׃ וַיֹּאמֶר יְהוָה לֹא
יָדוֹן רוּחִי בָאָדָם לְעֹלָם בְּשַׁגַּם הוּא בָשָׂר וְהָיוּ יָמָיו מֵאָה
4 וְעֶשְׂרִים שָׁנָה׃ הַנְּפִלִים הָיוּ בָאָרֶץ בַּיָּמִים הָהֵם וְגַם אַחֲרֵי־
כֵן אֲשֶׁר יָבֹאוּ בְּנֵי הָאֱלֹהִים אֶל־בְּנוֹת הָאָדָם וְיָלְדוּ לָהֶם
הֵמָּה הַגִּבֹּרִים אֲשֶׁר מֵעוֹלָם אַנְשֵׁי הַשֵּׁם׃* פ מפטיר
ה וַיַּרְא יְהוָה כִּי רַבָּה רָעַת הָאָדָם בָּאָרֶץ וְכָל־יֵצֶר
6 מַחְשְׁבֹת לִבּוֹ רַק רַע כָּל־הַיּוֹם׃ וַיִּנָּחֶם יְהוָה כִּי־עָשָׂה

and the author of the Book of Jubilees were misled into this interpretation by the analogy of these heathen fables. There is, however, no trace in Genesis of 'fallen angels' or rebellious angels; and the idea of inter-marriage of angels and human beings is altogether foreign to Hebrew thought. The mythological explanation of this passage was in all ages repelled by a large body of Jewish and non-Jewish commentators, though it has been revived by many moderns.

Others render *beney Elohim* by 'sons of the great' (in poetic Hebrew, *elohim* often means 'mighty', cf. Ps. XXIX, 1). This verse would thus state that the sons of the nobles took them wives of the daughters of the people, who were powerless to resist. These marriages were the result of mere unbridled passion, and are an indication of the licence and oppression in that time.

'Sons of God' may, however, also mean those who serve God and obey Him, those nourished and brought up in the love of Him as their Father and Benefactor (Exod. IV, 22; Deut. XIV, 1; XXXII, 5; Isa. I, 2; Hos. II, 1). It is quite in accord with Biblical usage that those who adhered to the true worship of God—the children of Seth—are called 'sons of God'; and that, in contrast to these, the daughters of the line of Cain should be spoken of as 'daughters of men' (Ibn Ezra, Mendelssohn, S. R. Hirsch, W. H. Green).

Verses 1–4 would then point out the calamitous consequences to mankind when the pious sons of Seth merged with those who had developed a Godless civilization and who, with all their progress in arts and inventions, had ended in depravity and despair. Through intermarriage, the sons of Seth sink to the level of the ungodly race; and likewise deserved the doom that, with the exception of one family, was to overtake mankind. These verses are thus the first warning in the Torah against intermarriage with idolaters.

3. *abide in.* The above interpretation is borne out by this verse. For, if 'fallen angels' were in question, and if it was wrong for them to marry human women, the angels surely were the chief offenders; and yet the sentence falls exclusively upon *man*. 'In God's judgments there is no unrighteousness, partiality, or even the appearance of partiality' (Keil).

for that he also is flesh. Another translation is, 'by reason of their going astray they are flesh.' Despite the fact that man is created in the Divine image, he has proved by his proneness to err that he is 'flesh'; *i.e.* the earthly side of his nature too readily overpowers the spiritual.

a hundred and twenty years. i.e. his days are numbered: but I will not at once destroy him. There shall yet be an interval of 120 years, before I bring the Deluge upon mankind (Targum); a respite to the human race to give them time for repentance (Ibn Ezra).

4. *Nephilim.* Or, 'giants.' They existed before the intermarriages took place. The mention of Nephilim in Num. XIII, 33, is no reason to assume that they survived the Flood. The excited imagination of the Spies expresses its terror at the men of great stature whom they saw at Hebron, by saying that they must be the old antediluvian giants (W. H. Green).

men of renown. By reason of their abnormal physical strength, they gained for themselves a reputation as heroes. But enduring fame does not rest upon such qualifications as these Nephilim possessed. Their fate was to disappear from the earth, and humanity was to continue through Noah, 'a righteous man, and blameless in his generation.'

5. *wickedness.* This verse and the two that follow form the climax to the previous four verses in which the moral depravity of the age is depicted. Retribution is swiftly coming.

imagination. The desires; the whole bent of his thoughts.

heart. In Heb. the heart is the seat of mind, intellect, purpose.

6. *repented.* See note to Chap. II, 2. Here the feelings of a human being are ascribed to God. 'He who destroys his own work seems to repent of having made it' (Ibn Ezra).

grieved Him. A touching indication of the Divine love for His creation. God is grieved at made man on the earth, and it grieved Him at His heart. 7. And the LORD said: 'I will blot out man whom I have created from the face of the earth; both man, and beast, and creeping thing, and fowl of the air; for it repenteth Me that I have made them.' 8. But Noah found grace in the eyes of the LORD.

7 אֶת־הָֽאָדָם בָּאָרֶץ וַיִּתְעַצֵּב אֶל־לִבּֽוֹ׃ וַיֹּאמֶר יְהוָה אֶמְחֶה
אֶת־הָאָדָם אֲשֶׁר־בָּרָאתִי מֵעַל פְּנֵי הָאֲדָמָה מֵאָדָם עַד־
בְּהֵמָה עַד־רֶמֶשׂ וְעַד־עוֹף הַשָּׁמָיִם כִּי נִחַמְתִּי כִּי עֲשִׂיתִֽם׃
8 וְנֹחַ מָצָא חֵן בְּעֵינֵי יְהוָֽה׃

the frustration of His purposes for the human race—the possibility of such frustration being the price of man's freedom of will. According to Biblical thought, God glories in the beauty of His handiwork; how great then must His grief be, when His handiwork is soiled through human wickedness!

7. *I will blot out man.* 'In the Divine economy of the universe, men or nations, or generations, that thwart God's purpose, have no permanent title to life' (Kent).

and beast. Rashi remarks: 'Beast and creeping thing and fowl were all created for man's sake. When, therefore, man disappears, what necessity is there for preserving the animals alive!' But a comparison with Jonah IV, 11, where the innocence of the animals as well as of the little children, is invoked by the Prophet in his plea for Nineveh, suggests that in the Biblical view all life, whether human or animal, forms one organic whole; see *v.* 12 of this chapter.

8. *grace.* Favour. 'Righteousness delivereth from death.' On what grounds Noah won the Divine approval, is told in the next verse.

For Additional Notes on THE CREATION CHAPTER and THE GARDEN OF EDEN, see pp. 193–196.

THE HAFTORAH

The Haftorah (the Heb. term is *haphtarah*, 'conclusion') is the Lesson from the Prophets recited immediately after the Reading of the Law. Long before the destruction of the Second Temple, the custom had grown up of *concluding* the Reading of the Torah on Sabbaths, Fasts and Festivals with a selection from the 'Earlier Prophets' (Joshua, Judges, Samuel and Kings) or from the 'Later Prophets' (Isaiah, Jeremiah, Ezekiel and the Book of the Twelve Prophets). We possess no historical data concerning the institution of these Lessons. A medieval author on the Liturgy states that a little more than two thousand years ago (168 B.C.E.), Antiochos Epiphanes, king of Syria and Palestine, forbade the reading of the Torah under penalty of death. The Scribes, thereupon, substituted a chapter of the Prophets cognate to the portion of the Law that ought to have been read. But whatever be the exact origin of the Haftorah, there is always some similarity between the Sedrah and the Prophetic selection. Even when the latter does not contain an explicit reference to the events of the Sedrah, it reinforces the teaching of the weekly Reading upon the mind of the worshipper by a Prophetic message of consolation and hope.

HAFTORAH BERESHITH הפטרת בראשית

ISAIAH XLII, 5–XLIII, 10

Chapter XLII

5. Thus saith God the Lord,
He that created the heavens, and stretched them forth,
He that spread forth the earth and that which cometh out of it,
He that giveth breath unto the people upon it,
And spirit to them that walk therein:

6. I the Lord have called thee in righteousness,
And have taken hold of thy hand,
And kept thee, and set thee for a covenant of the people,
For a light of the nations;

7. To open the blind eyes,
To bring out the prisoners from the dungeon,
And them that sit in darkness out of the prison-house.

8. I am the Lord, that is My name;
And My glory will I not give to another,
Neither My praise to graven images.

Cap. XLII. מב

כֹּה־אָמַר ה
הָאֵל ׀ יְהוָה בּוֹרֵא הַשָּׁמַיִם וְנוֹטֵיהֶם רֹקַע הָאָרֶץ וְצֶאֱצָאֶיהָ
6 נֹתֵן נְשָׁמָה לָעָם עָלֶיהָ וְרוּחַ לַהֹלְכִים בָּהּ׃ אֲנִי יְהוָה
קְרָאתִיךָ בְצֶדֶק וְאַחְזֵק בְּיָדֶךָ וְאֶצׇּרְךָ וְאֶתֶּנְךָ לִבְרִית עָם
7 לְאוֹר גּוֹיִם׃ לִפְקֹחַ עֵינַיִם עִוְרוֹת לְהוֹצִיא מִמַּסְגֵּר אַסִּיר
8 מִבֵּית כֶּלֶא יֹשְׁבֵי חֹשֶׁךְ׃ אֲנִי יְהוָה הוּא שְׁמִי וּכְבוֹדִי
9 לְאַחֵר לֹא־אֶתֵּן וּתְהִלָּתִי לַפְּסִילִים׃ הָרִאשֹׁנוֹת הִנֵּה־בָאוּ
וַחֲדָשׁוֹת אֲנִי מַגִּיד בְּטֶרֶם תִּצְמַחְנָה אַשְׁמִיעַ אֶתְכֶם׃

9. Behold, the former things are come to pass,
And new things do I declare;
Before they spring forth I tell you of them.

Isaiah XLII, 5–XLIII, 10. Israel's Destiny

The connection between the Sedrah and the Prophetical Lesson is found in the opening words of the Haftorah (*v.* 5) which speak of God as the Creator of Heaven and Earth. The first chapters of Genesis, after describing the Creation, recount the growth of sin and violence among the children of men. The Prophet, likewise, proclaims the omnipotence and sovereignty of the Creator of the Universe, and proceeds to declare unto Israel his mission to rescue the world from moral degeneracy.

These chapters are taken from the second portion of the Book of Isaiah. This part of the Book of Isaiah is sometimes called 'The Prophecy of Restoration'. It is addressed to the Jews in Babylon who had been deported from Judea, after the first destruction of Jerusalem in the year 586 b.c.e., and who were longing for the day when they would be free to return to the Holy Land and Holy City. During the years of weary waiting, the Prophet consoles his suffering brethren by setting before them the sublime mission of Israel: God had called Israel to be His witness before all peoples, to be ' a light unto the nations', and to point the way of righteousness and salvation to all the children of men.

5–9. God promises Israel, the 'Servant of the Lord', Divine aid in the achievement of his sacred task.

6. *in righteousness.* *i.e.* for My righteous purpose; I will strengthen thee ('hold thy hand') to accomplish thy destiny ('to be a light unto the nations').

a covenant of the people. Or, 'a covenant to mankind.' The knowledge of God and practice of righteousness which it is Israel's mission to spread will, when consummated, bind all peoples together in a covenant of peace (Kimchi). All the Prophets preach the moral unity of mankind.

a light of the nations. Better, '*unto the nations*.'

7. *to open the blind eyes.* To enlighten those who are blind to the truth, to free those who are in spiritual bondage.

8. *My name.* The name *Adonay* conveys the unique reality, and the power to confer reality, of the Divine Being. This 'glory' would be forfeited if His predictions should fail (Cheyne).

9. *former things are come to pass.* Former events, like the victories of Cyrus, have taken place in accordance with the utterances of the Prophets. Now, as surely, these new prophecies of the exaltation of the Servant of the Lord, through these victories, shall likewise come to pass.

10. Sing unto the LORD a new song,
And His praise from the end of the earth;
Ye that go down to the sea, and all that is therein,
The isles, and the inhabitants thereof.

11. Let the wilderness and the cities thereof lift up their voice,
The villages that Kedar doth inhabit;
Let the inhabitants of Sela exult,
Let them shout from the top of the mountains.

12. Let them give glory unto the LORD,
And declare His praise in the islands.

13. The LORD will go forth as a mighty man,
He will stir up jealousy like a man of war;
He will cry, yea, He will shout aloud,
He will prove Himself mighty against His enemies.

14. I have long time held My peace,
I have been still, and refrained Myself;
Now will I cry like a travailing woman,
Gasping and panting at once.

15. I will make waste mountains and hills,
And dry up all their herbs;
And I will make the rivers islands,
And will dry up the pools.

י שִׁירוּ לַיהוָה שִׁיר חָדָשׁ תְּהִלָּתוֹ מִקְצֵה הָאָרֶץ יוֹרְדֵי הַיָּם
11 וּמְלֹאוֹ אִיִּים וְיֹשְׁבֵיהֶם׃ יִשְׂאוּ מִדְבָּר וְעָרָיו חֲצֵרִים תֵּשֵׁב
12 קֵדָר יָרֹנּוּ יֹשְׁבֵי סֶלַע מֵרֹאשׁ הָרִים יִצְוָחוּ׃ יָשִׂימוּ לַיהוָה
13 כָּבוֹד וּתְהִלָּתוֹ בָּאִיִּים יַגִּידוּ׃ יְהוָה כַּגִּבּוֹר יֵצֵא כְּאִישׁ
מִלְחָמוֹת יָעִיר קִנְאָה יָרִיעַ אַף־יַצְרִיחַ עַל־אֹיְבָיו יִתְגַּבָּר׃
14 הֶחֱשֵׁיתִי מֵעוֹלָם אַחֲרִישׁ אֶתְאַפָּק כַּיּוֹלֵדָה אֶפְעֶה אֶשֹּׁם
טו וְאֶשְׁאַף יָחַד׃ אַחֲרִיב הָרִים וּגְבָעוֹת וְכָל־עֶשְׂבָּם אוֹבִישׁ
16 וְשַׂמְתִּי נְהָרוֹת לָאִיִּים וַאֲגַמִּים אוֹבִישׁ׃ וְהוֹלַכְתִּי עִוְרִים
בְּדֶרֶךְ לֹא יָדָעוּ בִּנְתִיבוֹת לֹא־יָדְעוּ אַדְרִיכֵם אָשִׂים מַחְשָׁךְ
לִפְנֵיהֶם לָאוֹר וּמַעֲקַשִּׁים לְמִישׁוֹר אֵלֶּה הַדְּבָרִים עֲשִׂיתִם

16. And I will bring the blind by a way that they knew not,
In paths that they knew not will I lead them;
I will make darkness light before them,
And rugged places plain.
These things will I do,
And I will not leave them undone.

v. 16. קמץ בז״ק

Cyrus, the creator of the Persian Empire, is one of the great men in history. Whether as king, general or statesman, he has no superior among the rulers of the Orient. To the Greeks he appeared the ideal king; and in Israel the Prophets hailed him as God's Anointed, as the chosen Agent for the ending of idolatry and tyranny among the nations. In the year 549, before the Common Era, he became king of the Medes, and when in 538 he conquered Babylon, he was master of Western Asia. Cyrus perceived the value of Jewish gratitude and loyalty, and one of his first acts was a proclamation to the Jewish exiles in Babylon, granting them the right to return to Jerusalem and rebuild the Temple. This 'Cyrus Declaration' is preserved in the last verse of the last book of the Hebrew Bible, II Chronicles xxxvi, 23.

10–13. Hymn of Praise to God, because of the restoration of Israel, which the Prophet foretells (Ibn Ezra); also because of the glad tidings that a Servant-People has been Divinely chosen to carry God's message to mankind. Therefore, all peoples will unite in this song—even all Nature is here figuratively represented as sharing in the rejoicing at the glorious news (Kimchi).

10. *new song.* 'A song of a kind which has not before been heard, concerning new events of a kind never before displayed' (R. Levy).

13. There are obstacles to the consummation of the great events foretold, but God will manifest His power to remove them.

jealousy. i.e. ardour of battle, against heathen gods after whom His people had gone astray.

cry. Shout aloud, according to the manner of warriors in battle (Kimchi).

14–17. Are a continuation of the verses 1–9. They are full of bold anthropomorphisms.

14. *I have long time held My peace.* Perhaps at Israel's sufferings, and the desolation of the Holy Land. Now shall God's power be manifest. The scales will fall from the eyes of those who are spiritually blind.

cry. Burst the bonds of restraint.

17. They shall be turned back, greatly ashamed,
That trust in graven images,
That say unto molten images:
'Ye are our gods.'

18. Hear, ye deaf,
And look, ye blind, that ye may see.

19. Who is blind, but My servant?
Or deaf, as My messenger that I send?
Who is blind as he that is whole-hearted,
And blind as the LORD's servant?

20. Seeing many things, thou observest not;
Opening the ears, he heareth not.

21. The LORD was pleased, for His righteousness' sake,
To make the teaching great and glorious.*

22. But this is a people robbed and spoiled,
They are all of them snared in holes,
And they are hid in prison-houses;
They are for a prey, and none delivereth,
For a spoil, and none saith: 'Restore.'

23. Who among you will give ear to this?
Who will hearken and hear for the time to come?

24. Who gave Jacob for a spoil, and Israel to the robbers?
Did not the LORD?
He against whom we have sinned,
And in whose ways they would not walk,
Neither were they obedient unto His law.

25. Therefore He poured upon him the fury of His anger,
And the strength of battle;
And it set him on fire round about, yet he knew not,
And it burned him, yet he laid it not to heart.

17 וְלֹא עֲזַבְתִּים׃ נָסֹגוּ אָחוֹר יֵבֹשׁוּ בֹשֶׁת הַבֹּטְחִים בַּפָּסֶל
18 הָאֹמְרִים לְמַסֵּכָה אַתֶּם אֱלֹהֵינוּ׃ הַחֵרְשִׁים שְׁמָעוּ
19 וְהַעִוְרִים הַבִּיטוּ לִרְאוֹת׃ מִי עִוֵּר כִּי אִם־עַבְדִּי וְחֵרֵשׁ
כְּמַלְאָכִי אֶשְׁלָח מִי עִוֵּר כִּמְשֻׁלָּם וְעִוֵּר כְּעֶבֶד יְהוָה׃
כ 21 רָאִית* רַבּוֹת וְלֹא תִשְׁמֹר פָּקוֹחַ אָזְנַיִם וְלֹא יִשְׁמָע׃ יְהוָה
22 חָפֵץ לְמַעַן צִדְקוֹ יַגְדִּיל תּוֹרָה וְיַאְדִּיר׃* וְהוּא עַם־בָּזוּז
וְשָׁסוּי הָפֵחַ בַּחוּרִים כֻּלָּם וּבְבָתֵּי כְלָאִים הָחְבָּאוּ הָיוּ לָבַז
23 וְאֵין מַצִּיל מְשִׁסָּה וְאֵין־אֹמֵר הָשַׁב׃ מִי בָכֶם יַאֲזִין זֹאת
24 יַקְשִׁב וְיִשְׁמַע לְאָחוֹר׃ מִי־נָתַן לִמְשׁוֹסָּה יַעֲקֹב וְיִשְׂרָאֵל
לְבֹזְזִים הֲלוֹא יְהוָה זוּ חָטָאנוּ לוֹ וְלֹא־אָבוּ בִדְרָכָיו הָלוֹךְ
כה וְלֹא שָׁמְעוּ בְּתוֹרָתוֹ׃ וַיִּשְׁפֹּךְ עָלָיו חֵמָה אַפּוֹ וֶעֱזוּז
מִלְחָמָה וַתְּלַהֲטֵהוּ מִסָּבִיב וְלֹא יָדָע וַתִּבְעַר־בּוֹ וְלֹא־
יָשִׂים עַל־לֵב׃

CAP. XLIII. מג

א וְעַתָּה כֹּה־אָמַר יְהוָה בֹּרַאֲךָ יַעֲקֹב וְיֹצֶרְךָ יִשְׂרָאֵל אַל־

CHAPTER XLIII

1. But now thus saith the LORD that created thee, O Jacob,
And He that formed thee, O Israel:

* Sephardim conclude here.

מב׳ v. 20. ראות קרי* כאן מסיימין הספרדים v. 24. למשיסה קרי.. v. 25. קמץ בז״ק

17. *ashamed.* Put to shame.

18–21. The Restoration would offer Israel the opportunity of beginning his Divinely appointed work. But how great is the contrast between the ideal Israel and the real! Israel's mission should begin with Israel.

19. *Whole-hearted.* The meaning of the verse is, 'Who is blind but he who should be My servant . . . who is deaf but he who should be whole-hearted with Me.'

20. So many wondrous happenings in Israel's history should have opened the eyes of the soul.

21. *the LORD was pleased.* God sent His messengers to proclaim His Teaching, and to render His Torah great and glorious, by making it effective amongst all nations.

22–25. How is the pitiable plight of Israel, the homelessness and bondage of the Exile, to be reconciled with the assertion of God's power? Israel's sufferings are due to disobedience and rebellion. He rebukes Israel's insensibility to God's message, and urges a better understanding of the significance of God's dealings with Israel. Israel's disasters are a moral discipline leading to the purification and deliverance of His chastened People.

CHAPTER XLIII, 1–10. ISRAEL, GOD'S WITNESS

1. *I have redeemed.* The perfect tense of the verbs is used to express the certainty of this future event. This is called the 'Prophetic perfect': the Prophet is so confident that the Divine

2 תִּירָא כִּי גְאַלְתִּיךָ קָרָאתִי בְשִׁמְךָ לִי־אָתָּה׃ כִּי־תַעֲבֹר
בַּמַּיִם אִתְּךָ אָנִי וּבַנְּהָרוֹת לֹא יִשְׁטְפוּךָ כִּי־תֵלֵךְ בְּמוֹ־אֵשׁ
3 לֹא תִכָּוֶה וְלֶהָבָה לֹא תִבְעַר־בָּךְ׃ כִּי אֲנִי יְהוָה אֱלֹהֶיךָ
קְדוֹשׁ יִשְׂרָאֵל מוֹשִׁיעֶךָ נָתַתִּי כָפְרְךָ מִצְרַיִם כּוּשׁ וּסְבָא
4 תַּחְתֶּיךָ׃ מֵאֲשֶׁר יָקַרְתָּ בְעֵינַי נִכְבַּדְתָּ וַאֲנִי אֲהַבְתִּיךָ וְאֶתֵּן
ה אָדָם תַּחְתֶּיךָ וּלְאֻמִּים תַּחַת נַפְשֶׁךָ׃ אַל־תִּירָא כִּי־אִתְּךָ
6 אָנִי מִמִּזְרָח אָבִיא זַרְעֶךָ וּמִמַּעֲרָב אֲקַבְּצֶךָּ׃ אֹמַר לַצָּפוֹן
תֵּנִי וּלְתֵימָן אַל־תִּכְלָאִי הָבִיאִי בָנַי מֵרָחוֹק וּבְנוֹתַי מִקְצֵה
7 הָאָרֶץ׃ כֹּל הַנִּקְרָא בִשְׁמִי וְלִכְבוֹדִי בְּרָאתִיו יְצַרְתִּיו אַף־
8 עֲשִׂיתִיו׃ הוֹצִיא עַם־עִוֵּר וְעֵינַיִם יֵשׁ וְחֵרְשִׁים וְאָזְנַיִם לָמוֹ׃
9 כָּל־הַגּוֹיִם נִקְבְּצוּ יַחְדָּו וְיֵאָסְפוּ לְאֻמִּים מִי בָהֶם יַגִּיד זֹאת
וְרִאשֹׁנוֹת יַשְׁמִיעֻנוּ יִתְּנוּ עֵדֵיהֶם וְיִצְדָּקוּ וְיִשְׁמְעוּ וְיֹאמְרוּ

Fear not, for I have redeemed thee,
I have called thee by thy name, thou art Mine.

2. When thou passest through the waters, I will be with thee,
And through the rivers, they shall not overflow thee;
When thou walkest through the fire, thou shalt not be burned,
Neither shall the flame kindle upon thee.

3. For I am the LORD thy God,
The Holy One of Israel, thy Saviour;
I have given Egypt as thy ransom,
Ethiopia and Seba for thee.

4. Since thou art precious in My sight, and honourable,
And I have loved thee;
Therefore will I give men for thee,
And peoples for thy life.

5. Fear not, for I am with thee;
I will bring thy seed from the east,
And gather thee from the west;

6. I will say to the north: 'Give up,'
And to the south: 'Keep not back,
Bring My sons from far,
And My daughters from the end of the earth;

7. Every one that is called by My name,
And whom I have created for My glory,
I have formed him, yea, I have made him.'

8. The blind people that have eyes shall be brought forth,
And the deaf that have ears.

9. All the nations are gathered together,
And the peoples are assembled;
Who among them can declare this,
And announce to us former things?
Let them bring their witnesses, that they may be justified;
And let them hear, and say: 'It is truth.'

v. 9. קמץ בז״ק

promise will be fulfilled, that he describes the future event as if it had already been seen or heard by him. Thus, the Prophet does not say, 'Babylon will fall,' but, 'Fallen is Babylon'—he sees it as a heap of ruins.

2. What a marvellous summary of Jewish history since the Exile!

3. *thy ransom.* The Prophet foresees the impending downfall of the Egyptian lands (*Seba* is identified by some as a place on the African side of the Red Sea) before the Persian arms (Cambyses, son of Cyrus, was the actual conqueror). Accordingly, the acquisition of these new territories is described as the equivalent (the 'ransom') to Persia for the emancipation of the exiled Jews (Ibn Ezra).

4. *men.* Israel's ransom is paid not in gold, but in whole nations.

5–7. The Jewish Dispersion is now known to have been more widespread than was formerly believed. Israel's scattered sons shall, however, not be lost, but shall be ingathered from all parts of the earth.

8–10. The nations and the Servant are summoned to God's judgment throne.

8. *brought forth.* Even if many are unaware of the full significance of their history, Israel is nevertheless a competent witness to the bare external facts; it has *heard* the predictions and *seen* them fulfilled (Skinner).

9. *former things. i.e.* past events in Israel's history which had been announced by Prophets before they occurred. If foreign nations can make such claims, let them bring forth their witnesses to support ('justify') them. They cannot; but Israel can testify to God's rule in history, and His sovereignty over the world. Therefore once again,

10. Ye are My witnesses, saith the Lord,
And My servant whom I have chosen;
That ye may know and believe Me, and understand
That I am He;
Before Me there was no God formed,
Neither shall any be after Me.

י אֱמֶת׃ אַתֶּם עֵדַי נְאֻם־יְהוָה וְעַבְדִּי אֲשֶׁר בָּחָרְתִּי לְמַעַן
תֵּדְעוּ וְתַאֲמִינוּ לִי וְתָבִינוּ כִּי־אֲנִי הוּא לְפָנַי לֹא־נוֹצַר אֵל
וְאַחֲרַי לֹא־יִהְיֶה׃

10. *ye are My witnesses.* Israel's high vocation as God's witnesses, to the end that every succeeding generation shall 'know, understand and believe' in Him as the One Creator of the Universe and only Saviour of men and nations.

'Israel's "Heroic History", as Manasseh ben Israel called it, is in truth never-ending. Each Jew and each Jewess is making his or her mark, or his or her stain, upon the wonderful unfinished history of the Jews, the history which Herder called the greatest poem of all time. *Ye are my witnesses, saith the LORD.* Loyal and steadfast witnesses is it, or self-seeking and suborned ones? A witness of some sort every Jew born is bound to be. He must fulfil his mission, and through good report and through evil report, he must add his item of evidence to the record' (Katie Magnus).

ו פ פ פ ב 2

6 ¶9. These are the generations of Noah. Noah was in his generations a man righteous and whole-hearted; Noah walked with God. 10. And Noah begot three sons, Shem, Ham, and Japheth. 11. And the earth was corrupt before God, and the earth was filled with violence. 12. And God saw the earth, and, behold, it was corrupt; for all flesh had corrupted their way upon the earth. ¶ 13. And God said unto Noah: 'The end of all flesh is come before Me; for the earth is filled with violence through them; and, behold, I will destroy them with the earth. 14. Make thee an ark of gopher wood; with rooms shalt thou make the ark, and shalt pitch it within and without with pitch. 15. And this is how thou shalt make it: the length of the ark three hundred cubits, the breadth of it fifty cubits, and the height of it thirty cubits. 16. A light shalt thou make to the ark, and to a cubit

9 אֵלֶּה תּוֹלְדֹת נֹחַ נֹחַ אִישׁ צַדִּיק תָּמִים הָיָה בְּדֹרֹתָיו
י אֶת־הָאֱלֹהִים הִתְהַלֶּךְ־נֹחַ׃ וַיּוֹלֶד נֹחַ שְׁלֹשָׁה בָנִים אֶת־
11 שֵׁם אֶת־חָם וְאֶת־יָפֶת׃ וַתִּשָּׁחֵת הָאָרֶץ לִפְנֵי הָאֱלֹהִים
12 וַתִּמָּלֵא הָאָרֶץ חָמָס׃ וַיַּרְא אֱלֹהִים אֶת־הָאָרֶץ וְהִנֵּה
נִשְׁחָתָה כִּי־הִשְׁחִית כָּל־בָּשָׂר אֶת־דַּרְכּוֹ עַל־הָאָרֶץ׃ ס
13 וַיֹּאמֶר אֱלֹהִים לְנֹחַ קֵץ כָּל־בָּשָׂר בָּא לְפָנַי כִּי־מָלְאָה
14 הָאָרֶץ חָמָס מִפְּנֵיהֶם וְהִנְנִי מַשְׁחִיתָם אֶת־הָאָרֶץ׃ עֲשֵׂה
לְךָ תֵּבַת עֲצֵי־גֹפֶר קִנִּים תַּעֲשֶׂה אֶת־הַתֵּבָה וְכָפַרְתָּ אֹתָהּ
טו מִבַּיִת וּמִחוּץ בַּכֹּפֶר׃ וְזֶה אֲשֶׁר תַּעֲשֶׂה אֹתָהּ שְׁלֹשׁ מֵאוֹת
אַמָּה אֹרֶךְ הַתֵּבָה חֲמִשִּׁים אַמָּה רָחְבָּהּ וּשְׁלֹשִׁים אַמָּה

II. NOACH

(CHAPTERS VI, 9–XI, 32)

THE FLOOD. CHAPTERS VI, 9–IX

On the Flood and its parallels in Babylonian literature, see Additional Notes C and E, pp. 196–198.

CHAPTER VI, 9–22. THE BUILDING OF THE ARK

9. *these are the generations. i.e.* this is the story of Noah. This phrase, as in II, 4, introduces a new section of the history.

righteous. In his actions, in his relationship with his fellows.

whole-hearted. 'Blameless' (RV); faultless.

in his generations. The Rabbis point out that these words may be understood as stating that, despite the depravity which raged around him, he remained unspotted and untainted by corruption. It may, however, also mean that in *his* generations, *i.e.* judged by the low standard of his age, Noah was righteous; but had he lived in the period of Abraham, he would not have been conspicuous for goodness.

Noah walked with God. But Abraham, Scripture later tells us, walked *before* God. A father takes his young child by the hand so that the latter walks *with* him, but he allows an older, maturer child to walk *before* him. In moral strength, Abraham was the superior of Noah (Midrash).

10. A new section begins with *v.* 9. Hence the sons who had been enumerated in V, 32 are again referred to, because they figure in the story which forms the theme of this section.

11. *the earth. i.e.* the inhabitants of the earth. So again in XLI, 57.

corrupt. The Rabbis understand this as an allusion to gross immorality.

before God. Either in open and flagrant defiance of God, or what they did was an offence in the sight of God.

violence. Ruthless outrage of the rights of the weak by the strong.

12. *all flesh.* Including the animals. Their corruption manifested itself in the development of ferocity.

way. Manner of life, conduct.

13. *the end.* The destruction.

is come before Me. i.e. has come before God's mind, has been determined by Him.

with the earth. With the things that are upon the surface of the earth.

14. *make thee an ark. i.e.* a ship. The Rabbis say that the construction of the Ark occupied Noah for 120 years, in order to give his contemporaries an opportunity to repent. Their curiosity would naturally be aroused by what Noah was doing; and he would answer their enquiry by warning them of the judgment which God was bringing on mankind. They, however, scoffed at him and gave no heed to his words.

gopher wood. A resinous wood, which would not admit the water; probably the cypress.

rooms. lit. 'nests'; separate stalls for the different species of animals.

15. *this is how.* These are the measurements and directions.

a cubit. Roughly eighteen inches.

16. *a light.* The unusual word here used for light means in the plural (dual) 'noon'. Legend shalt thou finish it upward; and the door of the ark shalt thou set in the side thereof; with lower, second, and third stories shalt thou make it. 17. And I, behold, I do bring the flood of waters upon the earth, to destroy all flesh, wherein is the breath of life, from under heaven; every thing that is in the earth shall perish. 18. But I will establish My covenant with thee; and thou shalt come into the ark, thou, and thy sons, and thy wife, and thy sons' wives with thee. 19. And of every living thing of all flesh, two of every sort shalt thou bring into the ark, to keep them alive with thee; they shall be male and female. 20. Of the fowl after their kind, and of the cattle after their kind, of every creeping thing of the ground after its kind, two of every sort shall come unto thee, to keep them alive. 21. And take thou unto thee of all food that is eaten, and gather it to thee; and it shall be for food for thee, and for them.' 22. Thus did Noah; according to all that God commanded him, so did he.* ii.

7

Chapter VII

1. And the Lord said unto Noah: 'Come thou and all thy house into the ark; for thee have I seen righteous before Me in this generation. 2. Of every clean beast thou shalt take to thee seven and seven, each with his mate; and of the beasts that are not clean two [and two], each with

16 קוֹמָתָהּ׃ צֹהַר ׀ תַּעֲשֶׂה לַתֵּבָה וְאֶל־אַמָּה תְּכַלֶּנָּה מִלְמַעְלָה
וּפֶתַח הַתֵּבָה בְּצִדָּהּ תָּשִׂים תַּחְתִּיִּם שְׁנִיִּם וּשְׁלִשִׁים
17 תַּעֲשֶׂהָ׃ וַאֲנִי הִנְנִי מֵבִיא אֶת־הַמַּבּוּל מַיִם עַל־הָאָרֶץ
לְשַׁחֵת כָּל־בָּשָׂר אֲשֶׁר־בּוֹ רוּחַ חַיִּים מִתַּחַת הַשָּׁמָיִם כֹּל
18 אֲשֶׁר־בָּאָרֶץ יִגְוָע׃ וַהֲקִמֹתִי אֶת־בְּרִיתִי אִתָּךְ וּבָאתָ אֶל־
19 הַתֵּבָה אַתָּה וּבָנֶיךָ וְאִשְׁתְּךָ וּנְשֵׁי־בָנֶיךָ אִתָּךְ׃ וּמִכָּל־הָחַי
מִכָּל־בָּשָׂר שְׁנַיִם מִכֹּל תָּבִיא אֶל־הַתֵּבָה לְהַחֲיֹת אִתָּךְ
כ זָכָר וּנְקֵבָה יִהְיוּ׃ מֵהָעוֹף לְמִינֵהוּ וּמִן־הַבְּהֵמָה לְמִינָהּ
מִכֹּל רֶמֶשׂ הָאֲדָמָה לְמִינֵהוּ שְׁנַיִם מִכֹּל יָבֹאוּ אֵלֶיךָ
21 לְהַחֲיוֹת׃ וְאַתָּה קַח־לְךָ מִכָּל־מַאֲכָל אֲשֶׁר יֵאָכֵל וְאָסַפְתָּ
22 אֵלֶיךָ וְהָיָה לְךָ וְלָהֶם לְאָכְלָה׃ וַיַּעַשׂ נֹחַ כְּכֹל אֲשֶׁר צִוָּה
שני אֹתוֹ אֱלֹהִים כֵּן עָשָׂה׃*

ז Cap. VII ז

א וַיֹּאמֶר יְהוָה לְנֹחַ בֹּא־אַתָּה וְכָל־בֵּיתְךָ אֶל־הַתֵּבָה כִּי־
2 אֹתְךָ רָאִיתִי צַדִּיק לְפָנַי בַּדּוֹר הַזֶּה׃ מִכֹּל ׀ הַבְּהֵמָה
הַטְּהוֹרָה תִּקַּח־לְךָ שִׁבְעָה שִׁבְעָה אִישׁ וְאִשְׁתּוֹ וּמִן־
3 הַבְּהֵמָה אֲשֶׁר לֹא טְהֹרָה הִוא שְׁנַיִם אִישׁ וְאִשְׁתּוֹ׃ גַּם־

ו׳ v. 19. הה״א בקמץ

relates that it was a precious stone, which illuminated the whole interior of the Ark.

to a cubit. The precise meaning of these words is doubtful. The 'light' (which must be thought of as a kind of casement near to the roof) was to measure a cubit in height; or there was to be a space of a cubit between the roof and the top of the casement.

17. *and I, behold, I.* These emphatic words bring out the thought of the terrible necessity of the Flood.

18. *covenant*. A covenant means an agreement or compact between two parties, for the observance of which pledges are given. Here it is used in the simple sense of a promise. God will fulfil His promise to spare Noah and his family.

22. *thus did Noah. i.e.* he made the ark and collected provisions. The act of bringing the animals into the ark is described in the next chapter.

Chapter VII, 1–9. Entering the Ark

1. *righteous*. In vi, 9, Noah was described as 'righteous and blameless'. Since the present verse was addressed *to* Noah, whereas vi, 9 was spoken *of* him in his absence, the Rabbis deduced the rule: 'Utter only a part of a man's praise in his presence, but thou mayest speak the whole of a man's praise in his absence.' Most people unfortunately give utterance to the whole of a man's *blame* in his absence, graciously contenting themselves with only a portion of such blame in his presence.

2. *clean beast*. According to Rashi, this means 'of every beast which at a later period would be considered clean by the people of Israel' (Lev. xi and Deut. xiv). But more probably, the distinction between clean and unclean in this passage is based on the fitness of the animal to be used as a sacrifice to God; cf. viii, 20, where it is narrated that Noah offered upon the altar 'of every clean beast, and of every clean fowl'.

seven and seven. i.e. seven pairs; seven males and seven females. The *general* direction in vi, 19 to take a pair of each kind of animal into the ark in order to preserve alive the various species, is here supplemented by the more *specific* injunction, when the time arrived for entering the ark, that *of the clean beasts* there shall be seven of each species. As Rashi points out, he required additional clean animals for sacrifice

מֵעוֹף הַשָּׁמַיִם שִׁבְעָה שִׁבְעָה זָכָר וּנְקֵבָה לְחַיּוֹת זֶרַע עַל־
4 פְּנֵי כָל־הָאָרֶץ׃ כִּי לְיָמִים עוֹד שִׁבְעָה אָנֹכִי מַמְטִיר עַל־
הָאָרֶץ אַרְבָּעִים יוֹם וְאַרְבָּעִים לָיְלָה וּמָחִיתִי אֶת־כָּל־
ה הַיְקוּם אֲשֶׁר עָשִׂיתִי מֵעַל פְּנֵי הָאֲדָמָה׃ וַיַּעַשׂ נֹחַ כְּכֹל
6 אֲשֶׁר־צִוָּהוּ יְהוָה׃ וְנֹחַ בֶּן־שֵׁשׁ מֵאוֹת שָׁנָה וְהַמַּבּוּל הָיָה
7 מַיִם עַל־הָאָרֶץ׃ וַיָּבֹא נֹחַ וּבָנָיו וְאִשְׁתּוֹ וּנְשֵׁי־בָנָיו אִתּוֹ אֶל־
8 הַתֵּבָה מִפְּנֵי מֵי הַמַּבּוּל׃ מִן־הַבְּהֵמָה הַטְּהוֹרָה וּמִן
הַבְּהֵמָה אֲשֶׁר אֵינֶנָּה טְהֹרָה וּמִן־הָעוֹף וְכֹל אֲשֶׁר־רֹמֵשׂ
9 עַל־הָאֲדָמָה׃ שְׁנַיִם שְׁנַיִם בָּאוּ אֶל־נֹחַ אֶל־הַתֵּבָה זָכָר
י וּנְקֵבָה כַּאֲשֶׁר צִוָּה אֱלֹהִים אֶת־נֹחַ׃ וַיְהִי לְשִׁבְעַת הַיָּמִים
11 וּמֵי הַמַּבּוּל הָיוּ עַל־הָאָרֶץ׃ בִּשְׁנַת שֵׁשׁ־מֵאוֹת שָׁנָה לְחַיֵּי־
נֹחַ בַּחֹדֶשׁ הַשֵּׁנִי בְּשִׁבְעָה־עָשָׂר יוֹם לַחֹדֶשׁ בַּיּוֹם הַזֶּה
נִבְקְעוּ כָּל־מַעְיְנוֹת תְּהוֹם רַבָּה וַאֲרֻבֹּת הַשָּׁמַיִם נִפְתָּחוּ׃
12 וַיְהִי הַגֶּשֶׁם עַל־הָאָרֶץ אַרְבָּעִים יוֹם וְאַרְבָּעִים לָיְלָה׃
13 בְּעֶצֶם הַיּוֹם הַזֶּה בָּא נֹחַ וְשֵׁם־וְחָם וָיֶפֶת בְּנֵי־נֹחַ וְאֵשֶׁת
14 נֹחַ וּשְׁלֹשֶׁת נְשֵׁי־בָנָיו אִתָּם אֶל־הַתֵּבָה׃ הֵמָּה וְכָל־הַחַיָּה
לְמִינָהּ וְכָל־הַבְּהֵמָה לְמִינָהּ וְכָל־הָרֶמֶשׂ הָרֹמֵשׂ עַל־

his mate; 3. of the fowl also of the air, seven and seven, male and female; to keep seed alive upon the face of all the earth. 4. For yet seven days, and I will cause it to rain upon the earth forty days and forty nights; and every living substance that I have made will I blot out from off the face of the earth.' 5. And Noah did according unto all that the LORD commanded him. ¶ 6. And Noah was six hundred years old when the flood of waters was upon the earth. 7. And Noah went in, and his sons, and his wife, and his sons' wives with him, into the ark, because of the waters of the flood. 8. Of clean beasts, and of beasts that are not clean, and of fowls, and of every thing that creepeth upon the ground, 9. there went in two and two unto Noah into the ark, male and female, as God commanded Noah. 10. And it came to pass after the seven days, that the waters of the flood were upon the earth. 11. In the six hundredth year of Noah's life, in the second month, on the seventeenth day of the month, on the same day were all the fountains of the great deep broken up, and the windows of heaven were opened. 12. And the rain was upon the earth forty days and forty nights. ¶ 13. In the selfsame day entered Noah, and Shem, and Ham, and Japheth, the sons of Noah, and Noah's wife, and the three wives of his sons with them, into the ark; 14. they, and every beast after its kind, and all the cattle after their kind, and every creeping thing that creepeth upon

on leaving the ark. From the phrasing of the verse, Malbim shows that the command is concerning Noah's *domestic* animals. (Hence the phrase איש ואשתו instead of זכר ונקבה in VI, 19.)

beasts that are not clean. Of Noah's domestic animals—such as hares, asses, camels—he was to take two each. The phrase 'that are not clean' is itself noteworthy. It is a circumlocution which might have been avoided by the use of the simple word 'unclean'. The Talmud bases on this verse its admonition to avoid impure and unrefined language in conversation.

4. *for yet seven days.* To give Noah time to carry out the instructions which had been given him.

5. *according unto all.* Cf. VI, 22. There it refers to the construction of the ark; here it implies the strict fulfilment of the directions enumerated in the preceding verses.

9. *two and two.* In couples.

10–24. 'THE WINDOWS OF HEAVEN WERE OPENED'

11. *in the second month.* The Rabbis differ as to whether the year is here reckoned as beginning in Nisan or Tishri. On the view that the year commenced with Tishri, the Flood began about November, which is the time of the rainy season. More probably, the Flood began in May, which is the time of the inundation of the Babylonian plain.

the great deep. The *tehom* of I, 2. There was a seismic upheaval; the earth was swept by a gigantic tidal wave, and simultaneously there was a torrential downpour of rain.

windows of heaven. For the expression, cf. II Kings VII, 2, 19; Mal. III, 10; as if the vast reservoirs of water thought of as stored above the sky (I, 7) were coming down through special openings, constantly and in resistless strength.

12. *rain.* lit. 'heavy rain.' There was a continuous downpour for the period of time specified.

13. After a summary of the Flood-story (*v.* 6–12) we have a more detailed description of the event.

selfsame day. i.e. the day determined by God.

14. *every bird of every sort.* lit. 'every bird of every wing'; *i.e.* every species of winged creature.

the earth after its kind, and every fowl after its kind, every bird of every sort. 15. And they went in unto Noah into the ark, two and two of all flesh wherein is the breath of life. 16. And they that went in, went in male and female of all flesh, as God commanded him; and the LORD shut him in.* iii. 17. And the flood was forty days upon the earth; and the waters increased, and bore up the ark, and it was lifted up above the earth. 18. And the waters prevailed, and increased greatly upon the earth; and the ark went upon the face of the waters. 19. And the waters prevailed exceedingly upon the earth; and all the high mountains that were under the whole heaven were covered. 20. Fifteen cubits upward did the waters prevail; and the mountains were covered. 21. And all flesh perished that moved upon the earth, both fowl, and cattle, and beast, and every swarming thing that swarmeth upon the earth, and every man; 22. all in whose nostrils was the breath of the spirit of life, whatsoever was in the dry land, died. 23. And He blotted out every living substance which was upon the face of the ground, both man, and cattle, and creeping thing, and fowl of the heaven; and they were blotted out from the earth; and Noah only was left, and they that were with him in the ark. 24. And the waters prevailed upon the earth a hundred and fifty days.

הָאָרֶץ לְמִינֵהוּ וְכָל־הָעוֹף לְמִינֵהוּ כֹּל צִפּוֹר כָּל־כָּנָף׃
טו וַיָּבֹאוּ אֶל־נֹחַ אֶל־הַתֵּבָה שְׁנַיִם שְׁנַיִם מִכָּל־הַבָּשָׂר אֲשֶׁר־
16 בּוֹ רוּחַ חַיִּים׃ וְהַבָּאִים זָכָר וּנְקֵבָה מִכָּל־בָּשָׂר בָּאוּ
שלישי 17 כַּאֲשֶׁר צִוָּה אֹתוֹ אֱלֹהִים וַיִּסְגֹּר יְהוָה בַּעֲדוֹ׃ * וַיְהִי הַמַּבּוּל
אַרְבָּעִים יוֹם עַל־הָאָרֶץ וַיִּרְבּוּ הַמַּיִם וַיִּשְׂאוּ אֶת־הַתֵּבָה
18 וַתָּרָם מֵעַל הָאָרֶץ׃ וַיִּגְבְּרוּ הַמַּיִם וַיִּרְבּוּ מְאֹד עַל־הָאָרֶץ
19 וַתֵּלֶךְ הַתֵּבָה עַל־פְּנֵי הַמָּיִם׃ וְהַמַּיִם גָּבְרוּ מְאֹד מְאֹד
עַל־הָאָרֶץ וַיְכֻסּוּ כָּל־הֶהָרִים הַגְּבֹהִים אֲשֶׁר־תַּחַת כָּל־
כ הַשָּׁמָיִם׃ חֲמֵשׁ עֶשְׂרֵה אַמָּה מִלְמַעְלָה גָּבְרוּ הַמָּיִם וַיְכֻסּוּ
21 הֶהָרִים׃ וַיִּגְוַע כָּל־בָּשָׂר ׀ הָרֹמֵשׂ עַל־הָאָרֶץ בָּעוֹף וּבַבְּהֵמָה
22 וּבַחַיָּה וּבְכָל־הַשֶּׁרֶץ הַשֹּׁרֵץ עַל־הָאָרֶץ וְכֹל הָאָדָם׃ כֹּל
אֲשֶׁר נִשְׁמַת־רוּחַ חַיִּים בְּאַפָּיו מִכֹּל אֲשֶׁר בֶּחָרָבָה מֵתוּ׃
23 וַיִּמַח* אֶת־כָּל־הַיְקוּם ׀ אֲשֶׁר ׀ עַל־פְּנֵי הָאֲדָמָה מֵאָדָם
עַד־בְּהֵמָה עַד־רֶמֶשׂ וְעַד־עוֹף הַשָּׁמַיִם וַיִּמָּחוּ מִן־הָאָרֶץ
24 וַיִּשָּׁאֶר אַךְ־נֹחַ וַאֲשֶׁר אִתּוֹ בַּתֵּבָה׃ וַיִּגְבְּרוּ הַמַּיִם עַל־
הָאָרֶץ חֲמִשִּׁים וּמְאַת יוֹם׃

8

CHAPTER VIII

1. And God remembered Noah, and every living thing, and all the cattle that were with him in the ark; and God made a wind to pass over the earth, and the waters

ח

CAP. VIII. ח

א וַיִּזְכֹּר אֱלֹהִים אֶת־נֹחַ וְאֵת כָּל־הַחַיָּה וְאֶת־כָּל־הַבְּהֵמָה
אֲשֶׁר אִתּוֹ בַּתֵּבָה וַיַּעֲבֵר אֱלֹהִים רוּחַ עַל־הָאָרֶץ וַיָּשֹׁכּוּ

ז׳ v. 23. המ׳ רפה

16. *The LORD shut him in.* This means either literally that God fastened the door so that it withstood the violence of the storm; or it is a beautifully naïve figure of speech to denote the Divine protection which encompassed Noah. Hence the employment of the term Lord, *Adonay*, for this act of Divine mercy (cf. note on II, 4).

17. *the waters increased.* After it had rained for forty days, the waters were sufficiently deep to bear the ark which, as Rashi remarks, had previously been like a heavily-laden ship stuck in shallow water and unable to move.

18. *the waters prevailed.* They covered the earth. It will be noted that there were three stages in the increase of the waters. The first was marked by the lifting of the ark (*v.* 17); the second by the floating of the ark (*v.* 18); the third by the total submergence of the mountains (*v.* 19).

20. *fifteen cubits upward.* This means that the waters rose twenty-two and a half feet above the top of the highest mountain.

21. What had been foretold in VI, 17 was literally fulfilled.

every man. i.e. the entire human race outside the ark.

24. *prevailed.* Dominated the earth. After forty days' downpour, the waters reached their highest point, and remained so for a period of one hundred and ten days. After 150 days had passed from the commencement of the Flood, the waters began to diminish.

CHAPTER VIII, 1–5. THE DIMINUTION OF WATERS

1. *God remembered.* His covenanted promise to Noah that He would preserve him, and all that were with him in the ark (Ibn Ezra). The animals are expressly included in the kindly

2 הַמָּיִם׃ וַיִּסָּכְרוּ מַעְיְנֹת תְּהוֹם וַאֲרֻבֹּת הַשָּׁמָיִם וַיִּכָּלֵא
3 הַגֶּשֶׁם מִן־הַשָּׁמָיִם׃ וַיָּשֻׁבוּ הַמַּיִם מֵעַל הָאָרֶץ הָלוֹךְ וָשׁוֹב
4 וַיַּחְסְרוּ הַמַּיִם מִקְצֵה חֲמִשִּׁים וּמְאַת יוֹם׃ וַתָּנַח הַתֵּבָה
בַּחֹדֶשׁ הַשְּׁבִיעִי בְּשִׁבְעָה־עָשָׂר יוֹם לַחֹדֶשׁ עַל הָרֵי אֲרָרָט׃
ה וְהַמַּיִם הָיוּ הָלוֹךְ וְחָסוֹר עַד הַחֹדֶשׁ הָעֲשִׂירִי בָּעֲשִׂירִי
6 בְּאֶחָד לַחֹדֶשׁ נִרְאוּ רָאשֵׁי הֶהָרִים׃ וַיְהִי מִקֵּץ אַרְבָּעִים
7 יוֹם וַיִּפְתַּח נֹחַ אֶת־חַלּוֹן הַתֵּבָה אֲשֶׁר עָשָׂה׃ וַיְשַׁלַּח אֶת־
הָעֹרֵב וַיֵּצֵא יָצוֹא וָשׁוֹב עַד־יְבֹשֶׁת הַמַּיִם מֵעַל הָאָרֶץ׃
8 וַיְשַׁלַּח אֶת־הַיּוֹנָה מֵאִתּוֹ לִרְאוֹת הֲקַלּוּ הַמַּיִם מֵעַל פְּנֵי
9 הָאֲדָמָה׃ וְלֹא־מָצְאָה הַיּוֹנָה מָנוֹחַ לְכַף־רַגְלָהּ וַתָּשָׁב
אֵלָיו אֶל־הַתֵּבָה כִּי מַיִם עַל־פְּנֵי כָל־הָאָרֶץ וַיִּשְׁלַח יָדוֹ
י וַיִּקָּחֶהָ וַיָּבֵא אֹתָהּ אֵלָיו אֶל־הַתֵּבָה׃ וַיָּחֶל עוֹד שִׁבְעַת
11 יָמִים אֲחֵרִים וַיֹּסֶף שַׁלַּח אֶת־הַיּוֹנָה מִן־הַתֵּבָה׃ וַתָּבֹא
אֵלָיו הַיּוֹנָה לְעֵת עֶרֶב וְהִנֵּה עֲלֵה־זַיִת טָרָף בְּפִיהָ וַיֵּדַע

assuaged; 2. the fountains also of the deep and the windows of heaven were stopped, and the rain from heaven was restrained. 3. And the waters returned from off the earth continually; and after the end of a hundred and fifty days the waters decreased. 4. And the ark rested in the seventh month, on the seventeenth day of the month, upon the mountains of Ararat. 5. And the waters decreased continually until the tenth month; in the tenth month, on the first day of the month, were the tops of the mountains seen. ¶ 6. And it came to pass at the end of forty days, that Noah opened the window of the ark which he had made. 7. And he sent forth a raven, and it went forth to and fro, until the waters were dried up from off the earth. 8. And he sent forth a dove from him, to see if the waters were abated from off the face of the ground. 9. But the dove found no rest for the sole of her foot, and she returned unto him to the ark, for the waters were on the face of the whole earth; and he put forth his hand, and took her, and brought her in unto him into the ark. 10. And he stayed yet other seven days; and again he sent forth the dove out of the ark. 11. And the dove came in to him at eventide; and lo in her mouth an olive-leaf freshly plucked; so Noah knew

thought of God. As there is no forgetfulness with God, so we cannot really apply the term remembrance to him (Kimchi). This phrase which is in continual use in devotion is only a human way of speaking of the Divine.

assuaged. The Heb. verb is used of anger being calmed down (Esther II, 1). The waters grew calm after the fury of the storm.

3. *returned .... continually. i.e.* kept gradually diminishing.

an hundred and fifty days. Cf. VII, 24. The Flood commenced on the 17th day of the second month (VII, 11); and 150 days later, on the 17th of the seventh month, the waters had decreased to such an extent that the ark grounded on the mountains of Ararat.

4. *the mountains of Ararat.* Ararat is the name of a country; see Isa. XXXVII, 38, where the Septuagint translates Ararat by Armenia. Assyrian inscriptions also speak of Armenia as 'Urartu'. Mount Ararat is 17,000 feet high.

5. The waters continued to decrease for a further period of 73 days, and then the tops of ordinary mountains, as contrasted with Ararat, became visible.

6–14. The Raven and the Dove

6. *at the end of forty days. i.e.* after the first day of the tenth month, referred to in the last verse.

window. lit. 'aperture.' The Heb. is a different word from that used in VI, 16.

7. *a raven.* He selected the raven because, as a bird of prey, the raven would sustain itself by feeding on carrion which would abound if the earth were dry.

8. *sent forth a dove.* Rashi explains that between the sending forth of the raven and the sending forth of the dove there was an interval of seven days, since in *v.* 10 it is stated 'he stayed *yet another* seven days'. Noah changed his scout, because the action of the dove would give more reliable information. The dove fed on vegetation; and should it find food, Noah would have the sign for which he was waiting.

11. *at eventide.* Noah had presumably let the dove out in the morning. It must therefore have flown a considerable distance if it did not return until the evening. The inference was that the earth all around was covered by water.

olive-leaf. Since the olive tree grew to no great height, Noah understood that the waters had almost disappeared, though not completely. He, therefore, waited another week. The Rabbis have a beautiful comment on the fact that the dove comes back to Noah with the bitter olive leaf in its mouth. 'Better,' it seemed to say, 'bitter food that comes from God than the sweetest food at the hands of man.'

that the waters were abated from off the earth. 12. And he stayed yet other seven days; and sent forth the dove; and she returned not again unto him any more. ¶ 13. And it came to pass in the six hundred and first year, in the first month, the first day of the month, the waters were dried up from off the earth; and Noah removed the covering of the ark, and looked, and, behold, the face of the ground was dried. 14. And in the second month, on the seven and twentieth day of the month, was the earth dry.* iv. ¶ 15. And God spoke unto Noah, saying: 16. 'Go forth from the ark, thou, and thy wife, and thy sons, and thy sons' wives with thee. 17. Bring forth with thee every living thing that is with thee of all flesh, both fowl, and cattle, and every creeping thing that creepeth upon the earth; that they may swarm in the earth, and be fruitful, and multiply upon the earth.' 18. And Noah went forth, and his sons, and his wife, and his sons' wives with him; 19. every beast, every creeping thing, and every fowl, whatsoever moveth upon the earth, after their families, went forth out of the ark. ¶ 20. And Noah builded an altar unto the LORD; and took of every clean beast, and of every clean fowl, and offered burnt-offerings on the altar. 21. And the LORD smelled the sweet savour; and the LORD said in His heart: 'I will not again curse the ground any more for man's sake; for the imagination of man's heart is evil from his youth; neither will I again smite any more every thing

12 נֹחַ כִּי־קַלּוּ הַמַּיִם מֵעַל הָאָרֶץ׃ וַיִּיָּחֶל עוֹד שִׁבְעַת יָמִים
13 אֲחֵרִים וַיְשַׁלַּח אֶת־הַיּוֹנָה וְלֹא־יָסְפָה שׁוּב־אֵלָיו עוֹד׃ וַיְהִי
בְּאַחַת וְשֵׁשׁ־מֵאוֹת שָׁנָה בָּרִאשׁוֹן בְּאֶחָד לַחֹדֶשׁ חָרְבוּ
הַמַּיִם מֵעַל הָאָרֶץ וַיָּסַר נֹחַ אֶת־מִכְסֵה הַתֵּבָה וַיַּרְא וְהִנֵּה
14 חָרְבוּ פְּנֵי הָאֲדָמָה׃ וּבַחֹדֶשׁ הַשֵּׁנִי בְּשִׁבְעָה וְעֶשְׂרִים יוֹם
רביעי טו לַחֹדֶשׁ יָבְשָׁה הָאָרֶץ׃ * ס וַיְדַבֵּר אֱלֹהִים אֶל־נֹחַ לֵאמֹר׃
16 צֵא מִן־הַתֵּבָה אַתָּה וְאִשְׁתְּךָ וּבָנֶיךָ וּנְשֵׁי־בָנֶיךָ אִתָּךְ׃
17 כָּל־הַחַיָּה אֲשֶׁר־אִתְּךָ מִכָּל־בָּשָׂר בָּעוֹף וּבַבְּהֵמָה וּבְכָל־
הָרֶמֶשׂ הָרֹמֵשׂ עַל־הָאָרֶץ הַוְצֵא אִתָּךְ וְשָׁרְצוּ בָאָרֶץ וּפָרוּ
18 וְרָבוּ עַל־הָאָרֶץ׃ וַיֵּצֵא־נֹחַ וּבָנָיו וְאִשְׁתּוֹ וּנְשֵׁי־בָנָיו אִתּוֹ׃
19 כָּל־הַחַיָּה כָּל־הָרֶמֶשׂ וְכָל־הָעוֹף כֹּל רוֹמֵשׂ עַל־הָאָרֶץ
כ לְמִשְׁפְּחֹתֵיהֶם יָצְאוּ מִן־הַתֵּבָה׃ וַיִּבֶן נֹחַ מִזְבֵּחַ לַיהוָה
וַיִּקַּח מִכֹּל ׀ הַבְּהֵמָה הַטְּהֹרָה וּמִכֹּל הָעוֹף הַטָּהֹר וַיַּעַל
21 עֹלֹת בַּמִּזְבֵּחַ׃ וַיָּרַח יְהוָה אֶת־רֵיחַ הַנִּיחֹחַ וַיֹּאמֶר יְהוָה
אֶל־לִבּוֹ לֹא אֹסִף לְקַלֵּל עוֹד אֶת־הָאֲדָמָה בַּעֲבוּר
הָאָדָם כִּי יֵצֶר לֵב הָאָדָם רַע מִנְּעֻרָיו וְלֹא־אֹסִף עוֹד

v. 17. היצא קרי   v. 18. במקף ובנגינה

13. *first month.* Two months after the tops of the mountains had become visible (*v.* 5).

removed the covering. He took off part of the roof so as to get a view of what was outside.

the ground was dried. i.e. the water had drained away from the surface of the ground; but the surrounding earth must have been a mass of marsh and bog, and it was unsafe to step upon the ground.

14. *dry.* A different Heb. word from that used in the previous verse. It denotes that the ground had become hard, and could bear the weight of the inhabitants of the ark.

15–22. LEAVING THE ARK, AND BUILDING AN ALTAR

17. *swarm.* 'Breed abundantly' (RV). The Heb. word denotes a moving about from place to place.

19. *families. i.e.* species, as in Jer. XV, 3.

20. *builded an altar.* Noah feels moved to express his gratitude to God. He is the pioneer of all the altar-builders of the Bible.

burnt-offerings. A burnt-offering was entirely consumed by fire on the altar, and no part eaten by the priest or the bringer of the sacrifice.

21. *the sweet savour.* The sacrifice offered by Noah was as agreeable to the Deity, humanly speaking, as sweet odours are to a man. To avoid the anthropomorphism, the Targum renders 'And the Lord accepted with pleasure the sweet savour'.

in His heart. The Heb. is 'to His heart', *i.e.* to Himself. The phrase means simply, 'God resolved.'

I will not again curse. There will be no repetition of the curse pronounced in the days of Adam (see III, 17). In all probability, the 'curse' of the Flood is also implied. A world-catastrophe will in such measure never recur.

for man's sake. Better, *for Adam's sake.*

of man's heart. Better, *of Adam's heart.*

imagination. The Evil Inclination in man, *Yetzer hara,* which too often gains the mastery over the Good Inclination, *Yetzer tob.*

from his youth. i.e. from the dawn of his knowledge of good and evil.

as I have done. In the future, God will punish the individual sinners, and not the human family as a body.

living, as I have done. 22. While the earth remaineth, seedtime and harvest, and cold and heat, and summer and winter, and day and night shall not cease.'

9

Chapter IX

1. And God blessed Noah and his sons, and said unto them: 'Be fruitful, and multiply, and replenish the earth. 2. And the fear of you and the dread of you shall be upon every beast of the earth, and upon every fowl of the air, and upon all wherewith the ground teemeth, and upon all the fishes of the sea: into your hand are they delivered. 3. Every moving thing that liveth shall be for food for you; as the green herb have I given you all. 4. Only flesh with the life thereof, which is the blood thereof, shall ye not eat. 5. And surely your blood of your lives will I require; at the hand of every beast will I require it; and at the hand of man, even at the hand of every man's brother, will I require the life of man. 6. Whoso sheddeth man's

22 לְהַכּוֹת אֶת־כׇּל־חַי כַּאֲשֶׁר עָשִׂיתִי׃ עֹד כׇּל־יְמֵי הָאָרֶץ
זֶרַע וְקָצִיר וְקֹר וָחֹם וְקַיִץ וָחֹרֶף וְיוֹם וָלַיְלָה לֹא
יִשְׁבֹּתוּ׃

ט

Cap. IX. ט

א וַיְבָרֶךְ אֱלֹהִים אֶת־נֹחַ וְאֶת־בָּנָיו וַיֹּאמֶר לָהֶם פְּרוּ וּרְבוּ
2 וּמִלְאוּ אֶת־הָאָרֶץ׃ וּמוֹרַאֲכֶם וְחִתְּכֶם יִהְיֶה עַל כׇּל־חַיַּת
הָאָרֶץ וְעַל כׇּל־עוֹף הַשָּׁמָיִם בְּכֹל אֲשֶׁר תִּרְמֹשׂ הָאֲדָמָה
3 וּבְכׇל־דְּגֵי הַיָּם בְּיֶדְכֶם נִתָּנוּ׃ כׇּל־רֶמֶשׂ אֲשֶׁר הוּא־חַי לָכֶם
4 יִהְיֶה לְאׇכְלָה כְּיֶרֶק עֵשֶׂב נָתַתִּי לָכֶם אֶת־כֹּל׃ אַךְ־בָּשָׂר
ה בְּנַפְשׁוֹ דָמוֹ לֹא תֹאכֵלוּ׃ וְאַךְ אֶת־דִּמְכֶם לְנַפְשֹׁתֵיכֶם
אֶדְרֹשׁ מִיַּד כׇּל־חַיָּה אֶדְרְשֶׁנּוּ וּמִיַּד הָאָדָם מִיַּד אִישׁ אָחִיו
6 אֶדְרֹשׁ אֶת־נֶפֶשׁ הָאָדָם׃ שֹׁפֵךְ דַּם הָאָדָם בָּאָדָם דָּמוֹ

22. The regular change of the seasons will not again be suspended. According to the Talmud, these six terms here enumerated mark the actual divisions of the year, each being of two months.

Chapter IX, 1–17. The Covenant with Noah. The Seven Commandments of Man

1–2. The blessing which was bestowed on Adam (I, 28) is repeated, since Noah and his sons were the heads of a new race. The Divine benediction would hearten them to undertake the task of rebuilding a ruined world.

3. *every moving thing.* The term is here used in a wide sense to include beast, fish and fowl.

as the green herb. The meaning is that just as the green herb was granted to man as food by God (I, 29), so now permission is given him to partake of the flesh of animals.

4. *blood.* In the Biblical conception, the blood is identified with life; cf. Deut. XII, 23, 'for the blood is the life.' This thought was the obvious deduction from the fact that as the blood is drained from the body, the vitality weakens until it ceases altogether. Life, in every form, has in it an element of holiness, since God is the source of all life. Therefore, although permission was given to eat the flesh of an animal, this was done with one special restriction; *viz.* life must altogether have departed from the animal before man partakes of its flesh. According to Rashi, the restriction was of a twofold nature. It, firstly, forbade אבר מן החי 'cutting a limb from a live animal'—a barbarous practice common among primitive races; and secondly, the blood must not on any account be eaten, since it was the seat of life. This double prohibition of cruelty to animals and the partaking of blood, is the basis of most of the rules of the Jewish slaughter of animals (Shechitah) and of the preparation (koshering) of meats, that have been observed by Jews from time immemorial.

5. *your blood of your lives.* lit. 'your blood, according to your own souls.' The Rabbis understood these words literally, *i.e. your* life-blood, and based on them the prohibition of suicide.

will I require. i.e. will I exact punishment for it.

beast. If an animal killed a man, it must be put to death; see Exod. XXI, 28–32 for the law concerning an ox which gored a man.

at the hand of every man's brother. Better, *at the hand of his brother-man* (M. Friedländer). This clause emphasizes the preceding phrase, 'and at the hand of man.' If God seeks the blood of a man at the hand of a beast which kills him, how much more will He exact vengeance from a human being who murders his brother-man!

6. *by man.* This is usually understood, as the Targum has it, through the agency of man, *viz.* by judges or by an avenger.

for in the image of God. See I, 27. We have here a declaration of the native dignity of man, irrespective of his race or creed. Because man is created in the image of God, he can never be reduced to the level of a thing or chattel; he remains a *personality*, with inalienable human rights. To rob a man of these inalienable rights constitutes an outrage against God. It is upon this thought that the Jewish conception of Justice, as respect for human personality, rests; see on Deut. XVI, 20.

blood, by man shall his blood be shed; for in the image of God made He man. 7. And you, be ye fruitful, and multiply; swarm in the earth, and multiply therein.' *v. ¶ 8. And God spoke unto Noah, and to his sons with him, saying: 9. 'As for Me, behold, I establish My covenant with you, and with your seed after you; 10. and with every living creature that is with you, the fowl, the cattle, and every beast of the earth with you; of all that go out of the ark, even every beast of the earth. 11. And I will establish My covenant with you; neither shall all flesh be cut off any more by the waters of the flood; neither shall there any more be a flood to destroy the earth.' 12. And God said: 'This is the token of the covenant which I make between Me and you and every living creature that is with you, for perpetual generations: 13. I have set My bow in the cloud, and it shall be for a token of a covenant between Me and the earth. 14. And it shall come to pass, when I bring clouds over the earth, and the bow is seen in the cloud, 15. that I will remember My covenant, which is between Me and you and every living creature of all flesh; and the waters shall no more become a flood to destroy all flesh. 16. And the bow shall be in the cloud; and I will look upon it, that I may remember the everlasting covenant between God and every living creature of all flesh that is upon the earth.' 17. And God said unto Noah: 'This is the token of the covenant which

7 יִשָּׁפֵךְ כִּי בְּצֶלֶם אֱלֹהִים עָשָׂה אֶת־הָאָדָם׃ וְאַתֶּם פְּרוּ
חמישי
8 וּרְבוּ שִׁרְצוּ בָאָרֶץ וּרְבוּ־בָהּ׃* ס וַיֹּאמֶר אֱלֹהִים אֶל־
9 נֹחַ וְאֶל־בָּנָיו אִתּוֹ לֵאמֹר׃ וַאֲנִי הִנְנִי מֵקִים אֶת־בְּרִיתִי
י אִתְּכֶם וְאֶת־זַרְעֲכֶם אַחֲרֵיכֶם׃ וְאֵת כָּל־נֶפֶשׁ הַחַיָּה אֲשֶׁר
אִתְּכֶם בָּעוֹף בַּבְּהֵמָה וּבְכָל־חַיַּת הָאָרֶץ אִתְּכֶם מִכֹּל יֹצְאֵי
11 הַתֵּבָה לְכֹל חַיַּת הָאָרֶץ׃ וַהֲקִמֹתִי אֶת־בְּרִיתִי אִתְּכֶם
וְלֹא־יִכָּרֵת כָּל־בָּשָׂר עוֹד מִמֵּי הַמַּבּוּל וְלֹא־יִהְיֶה עוֹד
12 מַבּוּל לְשַׁחֵת הָאָרֶץ׃ וַיֹּאמֶר אֱלֹהִים זֹאת אוֹת־הַבְּרִית
אֲשֶׁר־אֲנִי נֹתֵן בֵּינִי וּבֵינֵיכֶם וּבֵין כָּל־נֶפֶשׁ חַיָּה אֲשֶׁר אִתְּכֶם
13 לְדֹרֹת עוֹלָם׃ אֶת־קַשְׁתִּי נָתַתִּי בֶּעָנָן וְהָיְתָה לְאוֹת בְּרִית
14 בֵּינִי וּבֵין הָאָרֶץ׃ וְהָיָה בְּעַנְנִי עָנָן עַל־הָאָרֶץ וְנִרְאֲתָה
טו הַקֶּשֶׁת בֶּעָנָן׃ וְזָכַרְתִּי אֶת־בְּרִיתִי אֲשֶׁר בֵּינִי וּבֵינֵיכֶם וּבֵין
כָּל־נֶפֶשׁ חַיָּה בְּכָל־בָּשָׂר וְלֹא־יִהְיֶה עוֹד הַמַּיִם לְמַבּוּל
16 לְשַׁחֵת כָּל־בָּשָׂר׃ וְהָיְתָה הַקֶּשֶׁת בֶּעָנָן וּרְאִיתִיהָ לִזְכֹּר
בְּרִית עוֹלָם בֵּין אֱלֹהִים וּבֵין כָּל־נֶפֶשׁ חַיָּה בְּכָל־בָּשָׂר
17 אֲשֶׁר עַל־הָאָרֶץ׃ וַיֹּאמֶר אֱלֹהִים אֶל־נֹחַ זֹאת אוֹת־הַבְּרִית

7. This verse is not a superfluous repetition of v. 1. It gives a further reason why God holds bloodshed in such abhorrence. It is His desire that life should be multiplied, and not diminished through murder. The Talmud founded on this verse its strong condemnation of him who does not fulfil the command to found a family.

Rabbinic interpretation of these verses deduced seven fundamental laws from them: *viz.* (1) the establishment of courts of justice; (2) the prohibition of blasphemy; (3) of idolatry; (4) of incest; (5) of bloodshed; (6) of robbery; (7) of eating flesh cut from a living animal. The Rabbis called these seven laws the 'Seven Commandments given to the descendants of Noah'. These constitute what we might call Natural Religion, as they are vital to the existence of human society. Whereas an Israelite was to carry out all the precepts of the Torah, obedience to these Seven Commandments alone was in ancient times required of non-Jews living among Israelites, or attaching themselves to the Jewish community.

9. *as for Me.* If man, by avoiding homicide, will do his part not to destroy human life, God will never send another Flood.

establish. i.e. confirm. The covenant is that mentioned in VI, 18.

12. *token.* The visible sign of the permanence of the covenant.

13. *I have set My bow.* This does not imply that the rainbow was then for the first time instituted; it merely assumed a new role as a token of the Divine pledge that there would never again be a world-devastating Deluge. 'We must explain the verse as saying, The bow which I have set in the clouds from the day of creation shall henceforth be a token of the covenant between Me and you . . . a covenant of peace' (Nachmanides). The same commentator further asserts, 'We must accept the view of the Greeks that the rainbow is the result of the reflection of the sun in the moist atmosphere,' *i.e.* the refraction and reflection of light.

16. *I will look upon it.* The Midrashic comment is: 'When the attribute of Justice will come to accuse you and hold you guilty of offending, then I will look upon the bow and remember the covenant.'

17. This concluding verse of the paragraph stresses the idea that the covenant was not only with Noah but with 'all flesh that is upon the earth'.

I have established between Me and all flesh that is upon the earth.'* vi. ¶ 18. And the sons of Noah, that went forth from the ark, were Shem, and Ham, and Japheth; and Ham is the father of Canaan. 19. These three were the sons of Noah, and of these was the whole earth overspread. ¶ 20. And Noah the husbandman began, and planted a vineyard. 21. And he drank of the wine, and was drunken; and he was uncovered within his tent. 22. And Ham, the father of Canaan, saw the nakedness of his father, and told his two brethren without. 23. And Shem and Japheth took a garment, and laid it upon both their shoulders, and went backward, and covered the nakedness of their father; and their faces were backward, and they saw not their father's nakedness. 24. And Noah

ששי אֲשֶׁר הֲקִמֹתִי בֵּינִי וּבֵין כָּל־בָּשָׂר אֲשֶׁר עַל־הָאָרֶץ׃ פ
18 וַיִּהְיוּ בְנֵי־נֹחַ הַיֹּצְאִים מִן־הַתֵּבָה שֵׁם וְחָם וָיָפֶת וְחָם הוּא
19 אֲבִי כְנָעַן׃ שְׁלֹשָׁה אֵלֶּה בְּנֵי־נֹחַ וּמֵאֵלֶּה נָפְצָה כָל־הָאָרֶץ׃
כ 21 וַיָּחֶל נֹחַ אִישׁ הָאֲדָמָה וַיִּטַּע כָּרֶם׃ וַיֵּשְׁתְּ מִן־הַיַּיִן וַיִּשְׁכָּר
22 וַיִּתְגַּל בְּתוֹךְ אָהֳלֹה׃ וַיַּרְא חָם אֲבִי כְנַעַן אֵת עֶרְוַת אָבִיו
23 וַיַּגֵּד לִשְׁנֵי־אֶחָיו בַּחוּץ׃ וַיִּקַּח שֵׁם וָיֶפֶת אֶת־הַשִּׂמְלָה
וַיָּשִׂימוּ עַל־שְׁכֶם שְׁנֵיהֶם וַיֵּלְכוּ אֲחֹרַנִּית וַיְכַסּוּ אֵת עֶרְוַת
24 אֲבִיהֶם וּפְנֵיהֶם אֲחֹרַנִּית וְעֶרְוַת אֲבִיהֶם לֹא רָאוּ׃ וַיִּיקֶץ

18–29. PLANTING A VINEYARD

18. The historical thread of the main narrative—which is the story of the Human Family—is now resumed, after the digression on the symbolic meaning of the rainbow. Shem, Ham and Japheth are the fathers of the races from which the whole of mankind has descended.

Canaan. This is mentioned because of the narrative which follows. From a father showing such a fundamental lack of moral sense as Ham, it is not surprising that a wicked people like the Canaanites sprang.

19. *overspread.* Heb. 'the whole earth was dispersed'; the word 'earth' here meaning 'the population of the earth' as in VI, 11 f; XI, 1.

20. *began.* The Heb. word has also the meaning of 'being profane'. Hence, Rashi's comment:—'Noah made himself profane, degraded himself. He should have planted anything but the vine,' which is the source of so much sin and crime among the children of men.

21. *uncovered.* 'Scripture shows in this narrative what shame and evil can through drunkenness befall even a man like Noah who was otherwise found righteous and blameless before God. Some commentators, however, explain that as Noah was the first to cultivate the vine, he was ignorant of the intoxicating effect of its fruit. What happened to him is therefore a warning to mankind' (Luzzatto).

22. *Ham, the father of Canaan.* This vague narrative refers to some abominable deed in which Canaan seems to have been implicated.

told his two brethren. Instead of showing filial respect and covering his father, Ham deemed the occasion food for laughter, and mockingly repeated the incident to his brothers.

23. *garment.* Heb. 'an outer cloak.'

Some Jewish and non-Jewish teachers omit this story in children's Bible classes. Yet, it is of deep significance in a child's moral training. An intelligent child cannot help now and then detecting a fault or something to laugh at in his parents; but instead of mockery or callous exposure, it is for him to throw the mantle of filial love over the fault and turn away his face. 'Am I the one to judge my parents?' a child should ask himself (F. Adler). Few Jewish children have parents who are drunkards, but there is a great number whose fathers and mothers do not, *e.g.*, speak the language of the land as fluently as they do. Instead of laughing at them, Jewish children should be taught to feel: 'Have my parents had the opportunities in life that they have given *me?*'

24. *youngest son.* Heb. *beno hak-katan*, which might also mean 'grandson', like the French *petit fils* (Wogue). The reference is evidently to Canaan.

25. *cursed be Canaan.* It was firmly held in ancient time (cf. XLVIII and XLIX) that the blessing or curse which a father pronounced upon a child affected the latter's descendants. We, therefore, have here in effect a forecast of the future, that the Canaanites would be a servile and degraded race.

servant of servants. A Hebraism expressing the superlative degree; the meanest, most degraded, servant; cf. 'Song of Songs'; *i.e.* the most beautiful song.

awoke from his wine, and knew what his youngest son had done unto him. 25. And he said: Cursed be Canaan;
A servant of servants shall he be unto his brethren.
26. And he said:
Blessed be the LORD, the God of Shem;
And let Canaan be their servant.
27. God [1]enlarge Japheth,
And he shall dwell in the tents of Shem;
And let Canaan be their servant.
¶ 28. And Noah lived after the flood three hundred and fifty years. 29. And all the days of Noah were nine hundred and fifty years; and he died.

כה נֹחַ מִיֵּינוֹ וַיֵּדַע אֵת אֲשֶׁר־עָשָׂה לוֹ בְּנוֹ הַקָּטָן: וַיֹּאמֶר
26 אָרוּר כְּנָעַן עֶבֶד עֲבָדִים יִהְיֶה לְאֶחָיו: וַיֹּאמֶר בָּרוּךְ יְהוָה
27 אֱלֹהֵי שֵׁם וִיהִי כְנַעַן עֶבֶד לָמוֹ: יַפְתְּ אֱלֹהִים לְיֶפֶת וְיִשְׁכֹּן
28 בְּאָהֳלֵי־שֵׁם וִיהִי כְנַעַן עֶבֶד לָמוֹ: וַיְחִי־נֹחַ אַחַר הַמַּבּוּל
29 שְׁלֹשׁ מֵאוֹת שָׁנָה וַחֲמִשִּׁים שָׁנָה: וַיְהִי כָּל־יְמֵי־נֹחַ תְּשַׁע
מֵאוֹת שָׁנָה וַחֲמִשִּׁים שָׁנָה וַיָּמֹת: פ

10

CHAPTER X

1. Now these are the generations of the sons of Noah: Shem, Ham, and Japheth; and unto them were sons born after the flood. ¶ 2. The sons of Japheth: Gomer, and Magog, and Madai, and Javan, and Tubal, and Meshech, and Tiras. 3. And the sons of Gomer: Ashkenaz, and Riphath, and Togarmah. 4. And the sons of Javan: Elishah, and Tarshish, Kittim, and

CAP. X. י

י
א וְאֵלֶּה תּוֹלְדֹת בְּנֵי־נֹחַ שֵׁם חָם וָיָפֶת וַיִּוָּלְדוּ לָהֶם בָּנִים
2 אַחַר הַמַּבּוּל: בְּנֵי יֶפֶת גֹּמֶר וּמָגוֹג וּמָדַי וְיָוָן וְתֻבָל וּמֶשֶׁךְ
3 4 וְתִירָס: וּבְנֵי גֹּמֶר אַשְׁכְּנַז וְרִיפַת וְתֹגַרְמָה: וּבְנֵי יָוָן

[1] Heb. *japhth.*

ט׳ v. 29. כצ״ל

26. *the God of Shem.* The meaning is, Blessed be the God who will, in the days to come, keep His promise to the descendants of Shem—the Israelites—the promise to give unto them the land of Canaan for a possession, and to be their God and their Guide.

27. *God enlarge Japheth.* A play on the root-meaning of the name, which may mean 'enlargement'. Japheth, the progenitor of the Indo-European or Aryan peoples, receives the blessing of worldly prosperity and widespread dominion, but he was to dwell 'in the tents of Shem'. Friendly relations should subsist between the Semitic and Japhetic races. This is the first of the universalist forecasts in Scripture of the day when enmity between nations will be forgotten, and they unite in acknowledgment of the God of Israel.

The word Japheth may also mean 'beauty'. The Rabbis conceived of beauty under the category of purity; and longed for Japheth, *i.e.* the beauty of Greece, to dwell in the tents of Shem.

CHAPTER X. THE FAMILY OF THE NATIONS

This chapter traces the nations of the earth to the sons of Noah. The principal races and peoples known to the Israelites are arranged as if they were different branches of one great family. Thus, all the nations are represented as having sprung from the same ancestry. All men are therefore brothers. This sublime conception of the *Unity of the Human Race* logically follows from the belief in the Unity of God, and like it, forms one of the corner-stones of the edifice of Judaism. Polytheism could never rise to the idea of Humanity; heathen society 'was vitiated by failure to recognize the moral obligation involved in our common humanity' (Elmslie). There is, therefore, no parallel to this chapter in the literature of any other ancient people. It has been rightly called a Messianic document.

While the surpassing importance of this wonderful chapter is *religious*, 'the so-called table of the nations remains, according to all results of archæological exploration, an ethnographic original document of the first rank which nothing can replace' (Kautzsch). In all essential details, its trustworthiness has been strikingly vindicated by the new light from ancient monuments.

2. Contains the names of peoples in Asia Minor.

Gomer. The Cimmerians, on the shores of the Caspian Sea.

Magog. The Scythians whose territory lay on the borders of the Caucasus.

Madai. The Medes.

Javan. The Greeks; (Ionians, in the older language, Iawones).

3. *Ashkenaz.* They lived in the neighbourhood of Ararat, Armenia. In later Jewish literature, Ashkenaz is used to denote Germany; hence, *Ashkenazim*, Jews hailing from Germanic countries. For *Sephardim*, see p. 140.

Riphath and Togarmah. Peoples of Asia Minor.

Dodanim. 5. Of these were the isles of the
nations divided in their lands, every one
after his tongue, after their families, in
their nations. ¶ 6. And the sons of Ham:
Cush, and Mizraim, and Put, and Canaan.
7. And the sons of Cush: Seba, and Havilah,
and Sabtah, and Raamah, and Sabteca; and
the sons of Raamah: Sheba, and Dedan.
8. And Cush begot Nimrod; he began to
be a mighty one in the earth. 9. He was
a mighty hunter before the LORD; wherefore
it is said: 'Like Nimrod a mighty hunter
before the LORD.' 10. And the beginning
of his kingdom was Babel, and Erech, and
Accad, and Calneh, in the land of Shinar.

ה אֱלִישָׁה וְתַרְשִׁישׁ כִּתִּים וְדֹדָנִים׃ מֵאֵלֶּה נִפְרְדוּ אִיֵּי הַגּוֹיִם
6 בְּאַרְצֹתָם אִישׁ לִלְשֹׁנוֹ לְמִשְׁפְּחֹתָם בְּגוֹיֵהֶם׃ וּבְנֵי חָם
7 כּוּשׁ וּמִצְרַיִם וּפוּט וּכְנָעַן׃ וּבְנֵי כוּשׁ סְבָא וַחֲוִילָה וְסַבְתָּה
8 וְרַעְמָה וְסַבְתְּכָא וּבְנֵי רַעְמָה שְׁבָא וּדְדָן׃ וְכוּשׁ יָלַד אֶת־
9 נִמְרֹד הוּא הֵחֵל לִהְיוֹת גִּבֹּר בָּאָרֶץ׃ הוּא־הָיָה גִבֹּר־צַיִד
לִפְנֵי יְהוָה עַל־כֵּן יֵאָמַר כְּנִמְרֹד גִּבּוֹר צַיִד לִפְנֵי יְהוָה׃
י וַתְּהִי רֵאשִׁית מַמְלַכְתּוֹ בָּבֶל וְאֶרֶךְ וְאַכַּד וְכַלְנֵה בְּאֶרֶץ

4. *Elishah.* Most scholars see the word 'Hellas' in the name. Others identify it with Southern Italy, Sicily or Cyprus.

Tarshish. Frequently mentioned in the Bible as a flourishing and wealthy seaport. It is generally identified with Tartessus in ancient Spain.

Kittim. A race inhabiting part of the island of Cyprus, of Phœnician extraction.

Dodanim. In I Chron. I, 4–25 (with which this chapter should be compared) it is written *Rodanim, i.e.* the inhabitants of the Rhodian islands in the Ægean Sea. Both forms, **רודנים** and **דודנים**, are shortened forms of **דרדנים** as given in Targum Jonathan, and referring to Dardania in the region of Troy (Luzzatto).

5. *of these.* From these, *i.e.* the sons of Javan enumerated in the preceding verse.

divided. As separate countries, because of their distinctive populations.

after his tongue. The differentiation of language is accounted for in the next chapter. The Rabbis explain that the narratives in Scripture are not always in strict chronological order. Sometimes an event is anticipated, at other times it is told in connection with a later event. **אין מוקדם ומאוחר בתורה**.

6. *Ham.* The most ancient name for Egypt was 'Chem', meaning 'black', alluding no doubt to the dark colour of the Egyptian soil.

Cush. Ethiopia.

Mizraim. The most common name for Egypt. The Heb. form of the name is dual, and refers to the division into Upper and Lower Egypt.

Put. Lybia.

Canaan. The word is probably derived from a root meaning 'to be low'; and Canaan was the term originally applied to the lowland of the coast of Phœnicia and the land of the Philistines. The name was afterwards extended to the whole of Western Palestine. According to this verse, Mizraim and Canaan were 'brothers'; *i.e.* Palestine and Egypt were provinces of the same Empire. This was the case only in the time of the Nineteenth Dynasty, the age of Moses (Sayce). It was quite untrue of the time of the Exile when the alleged author of 'P' (see p. 198) is said to have lived. The name 'Persians' does not occur in the chapter, because in the days of Moses, these did not yet exist.

7. Tribes and places on the African coast of the Red Sea, or on the opposite shore of Arabia.

Sheba. A great commercial state in Southern Arabia. The Queen of Sheba visited King Solomon (I Kings x).

8. *Nimrod.* Nimrod is a descendant of Ham. It is now established that the original founders of Babylonian civilization, the Sumerians, were a people of non-Semitic stock.

a mighty one. He acquired dominion and ascendancy by conquest and by the terror he inspired.

9. *a mighty hunter.* lit. 'a hero of the chase.' The Assyrian monuments often depict monarchs and nobles in the act of hunting.

before the LORD. This phrase is an expression of emphasis, 'a very great hunter'; cf. Jonah III, 5, 'Nineveh was a city great unto God,' meaning, Nineveh was an exceeding great city.

wherefore it is said. A formula introducing a proverb; cf. XXII, 14, Num. XXXI, 14, etc. Nimrod's exploits became proverbial.

10. *beginning of his kingdom.* When he commenced to reign, his dominion extended over the cities here enumerated.

Babel. Babylon; its building is described in the next chapter. It was the centre of the ancient Orient, and for many centuries, the mistress of the world.

Erech. The Babylonian city 'Uruk', now called 'Warka', on the left bank of the lower Euphrates.

Accad. Name of a city, Agade; also of the land of Accad, Northern Babylonia.

Shinar. A Heb. name for Babylonia; cf. XIV, 1, 9; Joshua VII, 21, etc. Some identify Shinar with 'Sumir', the land of the Sumerians (Delitzsch, Jampel).

11. Out of that land went forth Asshur, and builded Nineveh, and Rehoboth-ir, and Calah, 12. and Resen between Nineveh and Calah—the same is the great city. 13. And Mizraim begot Ludim, and Anamim, and Lehabim, and Naphtuhim, 14. and Pathrusim, and Casluhim—whence went forth the Philistines—and Caphtorim. ¶15. And Canaan begot Zidon his first-born, and Heth; 16. and the Jebusite, and the Amorite, and the Girgashite; 17. and the Hivite, and the Arkite, and the Sinite; 18. and the Arvadite, and the Zemarite, and the Hamathite; and afterward were the families of the Canaanite spread abroad. 19. And the border of the Canaanite was from Zidon, as thou goest toward Gerar, unto Gaza; as thou goest toward Sodom and Gomorrah and Admah and Zeboiim, unto Lasha. 20. These are the sons of Ham, after their families, after their tongues, in their lands, in their nations. ¶ 21. And unto Shem, the father of all the children of Eber, the elder brother of Japheth, to him also were children born. 22. The sons

11 שִׁנְעָר׃ מִן־הָאָרֶץ הַהִוא יָצָא אַשּׁוּר וַיִּבֶן אֶת־נִינְוֵה וְאֶת־
12 רְחֹבֹת עִיר וְאֶת־כָּלַח׃ וְאֶת־רֶסֶן בֵּין נִינְוֵה וּבֵין כָּלַח
13 הִוא הָעִיר הַגְּדֹלָה׃ וּמִצְרַיִם יָלַד אֶת־לוּדִים וְאֶת־עֲנָמִים
14 וְאֶת־לְהָבִים וְאֶת־נַפְתֻּחִים׃ וְאֶת־פַּתְרֻסִים וְאֶת־כַּסְלֻחִים
טו אֲשֶׁר יָצְאוּ מִשָּׁם פְּלִשְׁתִּים וְאֶת־כַּפְתֹּרִים׃ ס וּכְנַעַן
16 יָלַד אֶת־צִידֹן בְּכֹרוֹ וְאֶת־חֵת׃ וְאֶת־הַיְבוּסִי וְאֶת־הָאֱמֹרִי
17 18 וְאֵת הַגִּרְגָּשִׁי׃ וְאֶת־הַחִוִּי וְאֶת־הָעַרְקִי וְאֶת־הַסִּינִי׃ וְאֶת־
הָאַרְוָדִי וְאֶת־הַצְּמָרִי וְאֶת־הַחֲמָתִי וְאַחַר נָפֹצוּ מִשְׁפְּחוֹת
19 הַכְּנַעֲנִי׃ וַיְהִי גְּבוּל הַכְּנַעֲנִי מִצִּידֹן בֹּאֲכָה גְרָרָה עַד־עַזָּה
כ בֹּאֲכָה סְדֹמָה וַעֲמֹרָה וְאַדְמָה וּצְבֹיִם עַד־לָשַׁע׃ אֵלֶּה
בְנֵי־חָם לְמִשְׁפְּחֹתָם לִלְשֹׁנֹתָם בְּאַרְצֹתָם בְּגוֹיֵהֶם׃ ס
21 וּלְשֵׁם יֻלַּד גַּם־הוּא אֲבִי כָּל־בְּנֵי־עֵבֶר אֲחִי יֶפֶת הַגָּדוֹל׃

v. 17. הה״א בקמץ   v. 19. וצבוים קרי

11. *went forth Asshur.* Archæology confirms the Biblical statement that the cities of Assyria owed their existence to the development of Babylonian power by conquest and colonization.
Nineveh. The capital of Assyria.

12. *great city. i.e.* Nineveh together with the other three places constituted one great city (Jonah III, 3).

13. *Lehabim.* The Lybians.
Naphtuhim. The dwellers of the Nile Delta.

14. *Pathrusim.* The population of Upper Egypt, Pathros.
whence went forth the Philistines. A difficulty arises from the fact that in Deut. II, 23, Amos IX, 7, the Philistines are spoken of as coming from Caphtor, *i.e.* Crete. The explanation may be that there were two immigrations of Philistines, one by way of the Egyptian sea-coast and the other from Crete. They have given their name to the land, 'Palestine.'
Caphtorim. The inhabitants of Crete.

15. *Zidon his first-born.* 'First-born,' the oldest settlement of the Canaanites. Zidon, the capital of ancient Phœnicia, stands for the whole country.
Heth. The Hittites, a powerful and warlike nation who held sway in Syria and Asia Minor from 1800 to 900 B.C.E. Wonderful remains of their civilization have been unearthed since the beginning of this century, and their language is now deciphered.

16. *Jebusite.* This tribe dwelt in and around Jerusalem, which was originally known as Jebus.
Amorite. This term is sometimes used to denote all the inhabitants of Canaan before the coming of the Israelites, and sometimes one particular warlike tribe amongst the Canaanites.
Girgashite. One of the peoples driven from Canaan by the Israelites (XV, 21).

17. These tribes, mentioned in this and in the following verse, lived in greater or less proximity to Mt. Lebanon.

18. *Hamathite.* Hamath, in Syria, was at one time the capital of a strong kingdom (Is. XXXVII, 13).
spread abroad. They extended into the territory mentioned in the next verse.

19. The border of the Canaanites was originally within the limits stated in this verse—from Zidon in the North to Gaza in the South, and from Sodom and Gomorrah in the South-east to Lasha in the North-east of Palestine.

22–24. According to this genealogical table, Eber was the great-grandson of Shem; but he was the ancestor of Abram who is called *Ha-ibri* (XIV, 13). From 'Eber' is formed the word 'Hebrew', the name by which the Israelites were known to foreign peoples. Special stress is here laid on Eber because he is, through Abram, the ancestor of the people of Israel.

22. *Elam.* The name of a land and people beyond Babylonia and the Persian Gulf—the easternmost people with which the descendants of Shem were brought into contact. As the Elam of history is Aryan, the correctness of of Shem: Elam, and Asshur, and Arpachshad, and Lud, and Aram. 23. And the sons of Aram: Uz, and Hul, and Gether, and Mash. 24. And Arpachshad begot Shelah; and Shelah begot Eber. 25. And unto Eber were born two sons; the name of the one was [1]Peleg; for in his days was the earth divided; and his brother's name was Joktan. 26. And Joktan begot Almodad, and Sheleph, and Hazarmaveth, and Jerah; 27. and Hadoram, and Uzal, and Diklah; 28. and Obal, and Abimael, and Sheba; 29. and Ophir, and Havilah, and Jobab; all these were the sons of Joktan. 30. And their dwelling was from Mesha, as thou goest toward Sephar, unto the mountain of the east. 31. These are the sons of Shem, after their families, after their tongues, in their lands, after their nations. ¶ 32. These are the families of the sons of Noah, after their generations, in their nations; and of these were the nations divided in the earth after the flood.* vii.

11

CHAPTER XI

1. And the whole earth was of one language and of one speech. 2. And it came to pass,

[1] That is, *Division*.

22 בְּנֵי שֵׁם עֵילָם וְאַשּׁוּר וְאַרְפַּכְשַׁד וְלוּד וַאֲרָם׃ וּבְנֵי אֲרָם
23
24 עוּץ וְחוּל וְגֶתֶר וָמַשׁ׃ וְאַרְפַּכְשַׁד יָלַד אֶת־שָׁלַח וְשֶׁלַח
כה יָלַד אֶת־עֵבֶר׃ וּלְעֵבֶר יֻלַּד שְׁנֵי בָנִים שֵׁם הָאֶחָד פֶּלֶג
26 כִּי בְיָמָיו נִפְלְגָה הָאָרֶץ וְשֵׁם אָחִיו יָקְטָן׃ וְיָקְטָן יָלַד אֶת־
27 אַלְמוֹדָד וְאֶת־שָׁלֶף וְאֶת־חֲצַרְמָוֶת וְאֶת־יָרַח׃ וְאֶת־הֲדוֹרָם
28 וְאֶת־אוּזָל וְאֶת־דִּקְלָה׃ וְאֶת־עוֹבָל וְאֶת־אֲבִימָאֵל וְאֶת־
29 שְׁבָא׃ וְאֶת־אוֹפִר וְאֶת־חֲוִילָה וְאֶת־יוֹבָב כָּל־אֵלֶּה בְּנֵי
ל יָקְטָן׃ וַיְהִי מוֹשָׁבָם מִמֵּשָׁא בֹּאֲכָה סְפָרָה הַר הַקֶּדֶם׃
31 אֵלֶּה בְנֵי־שֵׁם לְמִשְׁפְּחֹתָם לִלְשֹׁנֹתָם בְּאַרְצֹתָם לְגוֹיֵהֶם׃
32 אֵלֶּה מִשְׁפְּחֹת בְּנֵי־נֹחַ לְתוֹלְדֹתָם בְּגוֹיֵהֶם וּמֵאֵלֶּה נִפְרְדוּ
הַגּוֹיִם בָּאָרֶץ אַחַר הַמַּבּוּל׃* פ שביעי

CAP. XI. יא

יא

א 2 וַיְהִי כָל־הָאָרֶץ שָׂפָה אֶחָת וּדְבָרִים אֲחָדִים׃ וַיְהִי בְּנָסְעָם
3 מִקֶּדֶם וַיִּמְצְאוּ בִקְעָה בְּאֶרֶץ שִׁנְעָר וַיֵּשְׁבוּ שָׁם׃ וַיֹּאמְרוּ

ו׳ v. 23. פתח בס״פ

the Biblical view that Elam is a son of Shem was questioned. The French exploration at Susa, however, has shown that the oldest Elamite inscriptions are written in Babylonian, which proves that early Elam was peopled by Semites. Bible critics did not relish the idea of being robbed of one of their stock arguments against the trustworthiness of this chapter. But as they are forced to admit that the statement in regard to Elam is correct, they add: 'The fact [that his statement is correct] is not one which the writer of the verse is very likely to have known' (Driver). No clearer proof is needed of the negative dogmatism of Bible critics.

Asshur. Assyria, the most powerful of the Semitic peoples.

Arpachshad. Sayce explains the name as 'the territory of the Chasd' (cf. Ur of the Casdim, *i.e.* Chaldæans).

Lud. The Lydians of Asia Minor.

Aram. The Aramæan or Syrian people whose territory included Mesopotamia ('Aram of the two Rivers'). Both the Aramæan people and language were destined to exert great influence in Jewish history.

23. *Uz*. The land where Job lived (Job, I). In Lam. IV, 21, the Edomites are mentioned as dwelling in the land of Uz.

Hul, Gether, Mash. Unidentified localities in Syria.

25. *divided*. By 'earth' is meant the population of the earth. The allusion is probably to the scattering of the peoples described in the next chapter.

Peleg. In Assyrian, *palgu* means 'canal'; and Sayce believes the 'division of the land' to refer to the introduction of a system of canals into Babylonia.

26. *Joktan*. Regarded as the progenitor of the Southern Arabs.

Hazarmaveth. The land of Hadramaut, in Southern Arabia.

29. *Ophir*. Famed for its gold (I Kings IX, 28 and XII).

30. The identification of these Arabian landmarks is uncertain.

CHAPTER XI, 1–9. THE BUILDING OF THE TOWER

For an explanation of this difficult Chapter, see p. 197.

1. *one speech*. Better, '*few words*.' *i.e.* they had but a small vocabulary (Malbim).

2. *plain*. The territory of Babylon consisted of an almost unbroken plain.

Shinar. Cf. X, 10. It is more and more coming to be regarded as the cradle of the earliest civilization.

as they journeyed east, that they found a
plain in the land of Shinar; and they dwelt
there. 3. And they said one to another:
'Come, let us make brick, and burn them
thoroughly.' And they had brick for stone,
and slime had they for mortar. 4. And they
said: 'Come, let us build us a city, and a
tower, with its top in heaven, and let us
make us a name; lest we be scattered
abroad upon the face of the whole earth.'
5. And the LORD came down to see the
city and the tower, which the children of
men builded. 6. And the LORD said: 'Behold,
they are one people, and they have all one
language; and this is what they begin to do;
and now nothing will be withholden from
them, which they purpose to do. 7. Come,
let us go down, and there confound their
language, that they may not understand
one another's speech.' 8. So the LORD
scattered them abroad from thence upon
the face of all the earth; and they left off
to build the city. 9. Therefore was the
name of it called Babel; because the LORD
did there [1]confound the language of all the
earth; and from thence did the LORD scatter
them abroad upon the face of all the earth.
¶ 10. These are the generations of Shem.
Shem was a hundred years old, and begot
Arpachshad two years after the flood.
11. And Shem lived after he begot Arpach-
shad five hundred years, and begot sons
and daughters. ¶ 12. And Arpachshad lived
five and thirty years, and begot Shelah.
13. And Arpachshad lived after he begot
Shelah four hundred and three years, and
begot sons and daughters. ¶ 14. And Shelah
lived thirty years, and begot Eber. 15.
And Shelah lived after he begot Eber four
hundred and three years, and begot sons

[1] Heb. *balal*, to confound.

אִישׁ אֶל־רֵעֵהוּ הָבָה נִלְבְּנָה לְבֵנִים וְנִשְׂרְפָה לִשְׂרֵפָה
וַתְּהִי לָהֶם הַלְּבֵנָה לְאָבֶן וְהַחֵמָר הָיָה לָהֶם לַחֹמֶר׃
4 וַיֹּאמְרוּ הָבָה ׀ נִבְנֶה־לָּנוּ עִיר וּמִגְדָּל וְרֹאשׁוֹ בַשָּׁמַיִם
ה וְנַעֲשֶׂה־לָּנוּ שֵׁם פֶּן־נָפוּץ עַל־פְּנֵי כָל־הָאָרֶץ׃ וַיֵּרֶד יְהוָה
לִרְאֹת אֶת־הָעִיר וְאֶת־הַמִּגְדָּל אֲשֶׁר בָּנוּ בְּנֵי הָאָדָם׃
6 וַיֹּאמֶר יְהוָה הֵן עַם אֶחָד וְשָׂפָה אַחַת לְכֻלָּם וְזֶה הַחִלָּם
לַעֲשׂוֹת וְעַתָּה לֹא־יִבָּצֵר מֵהֶם כֹּל אֲשֶׁר יָזְמוּ לַעֲשׂוֹת׃
7 הָבָה נֵרְדָה וְנָבְלָה שָׁם שְׂפָתָם אֲשֶׁר לֹא יִשְׁמְעוּ אִישׁ
8 שְׂפַת רֵעֵהוּ׃ וַיָּפֶץ יְהוָה אֹתָם מִשָּׁם עַל־פְּנֵי כָל־הָאָרֶץ
9 וַיַּחְדְּלוּ לִבְנֹת הָעִיר׃ עַל־כֵּן קָרָא שְׁמָהּ בָּבֶל כִּי־שָׁם
בָּלַל יְהוָה שְׂפַת כָּל־הָאָרֶץ וּמִשָּׁם הֱפִיצָם יְהוָה עַל־פְּנֵי
כָּל־הָאָרֶץ׃ פ
י אֵלֶּה תּוֹלְדֹת שֵׁם שֵׁם בֶּן־מְאַת שָׁנָה וַיּוֹלֶד אֶת־אַרְפַּכְשָׁד
11 שְׁנָתַיִם אַחַר הַמַּבּוּל׃ וַיְחִי־שֵׁם אַחֲרֵי הוֹלִידוֹ אֶת־אַרְפַּכְשָׁד
12 חֲמֵשׁ מֵאוֹת שָׁנָה וַיּוֹלֶד בָּנִים וּבָנוֹת׃ ס וְאַרְפַּכְשַׁד
13 חַי חָמֵשׁ וּשְׁלֹשִׁים שָׁנָה וַיּוֹלֶד אֶת־שָׁלַח׃ וַיְחִי אַרְפַּכְשַׁד
אַחֲרֵי הוֹלִידוֹ אֶת־שֶׁלַח שָׁלֹשׁ שָׁנִים וְאַרְבַּע מֵאוֹת שָׁנָה
14 וַיּוֹלֶד בָּנִים וּבָנוֹת׃ ס וְשֶׁלַח חַי שְׁלֹשִׁים שָׁנָה וַיּוֹלֶד
טו אֶת־עֵבֶר׃ וַיְחִי־שֶׁלַח אַחֲרֵי הוֹלִידוֹ אֶת־עֵבֶר שָׁלֹשׁ שָׁנִים
16 וְאַרְבַּע מֵאוֹת שָׁנָה וַיּוֹלֶד בָּנִים וּבָנוֹת׃ ס וַיְחִי־

v. 3. קמץ בז״ק   v. 11. קמץ בז״ק

3. *brick.* In Babylon, clay-bricks were the material for building.

burn them thoroughly. Bricks were usually sun-dried; but in order to make these more durable, they were put through a process of burning by fire.

slime. Bitumen.

4. *with its top in heaven.* An exaggerated statement; cf. Deut. I, 28, 'the cities are great and walled up to heaven.'

a name. If they all dwelt together, they would be powerful and become renowned.

5. *came down.* So again XVIII, 21. An anthropomorphic expression. The Rabbis deduce from this the rule that a judge should never condemn an offender without first seeing for himself both him and the nature of the offence.

6. *begin to do.* At this early stage in human history, men are led to combine by an unworthy motive. If their design is not frustrated, they might employ their united strength for outrageous purposes. All human effort is both futile and empty, if dictated by self-exaltation, and divorced from acknowledgement of God.

7. *let us go down.* The plural of Majesty, as in I, 26.

9. *Babel.* This is an instance of popular etymology based on resemblance of sound and is frequently found in Scripture. The Assyrian name for Babel means, 'Gate of God.'

10–32. FROM SHEM TO ABRAHAM

10. *these are the generations.* This new section, leaving Universal History behind, reverts to the main purpose of the First Book of the Torah, which is that of giving a complete account of the founders of the Hebrew race, *viz.* Abraham, Isaac, and Jacob and their children. Abram is traced back through ten successive generations to Shem, the son of Noah.

16. *Peleg.* See X, 25. The descendants of

and daughters. ¶ 16. And Eber lived four and thirty years, and begot Peleg. 17. And Eber lived after he begot Peleg four hundred and thirty years, and begot sons and daughters. ¶ 18. And Peleg lived thirty years, and begot Reu. 19. And Peleg lived after he begot Reu two hundred and nine years, and begot sons and daughters. ¶ 20. And Reu lived two and thirty years, and begot Serug. 21. And Reu lived after he begot Serug two hundred and seven years, and begot sons and daughters. ¶ 22. And Serug lived thirty years, and begot Nahor. 23. And Serug lived after he begot Nahor two hundred years, and begot sons and daughters. ¶ 24. And Nahor lived nine and twenty years, and begot Terah. 25. And Nahor lived after he begot Terah a hundred and nineteen years, and begot sons and daughters. ¶ 26. And Terah lived seventy years, and begot Abram, Nahor, and Haran. ¶ 27. Now these are the generations of Terah. Terah begot Abram, Nahor, and Haran; and Haran begot Lot. 28. And Haran died in the presence of his father Terah in the land of his nativity, in Ur of the Chaldees. *m. 29. And Abram and Nahor took them wives: the name of Abram's wife was Sarai; and the name of Nahor's wife, Milcah, the daughter of Haran, the father of Milcah, and the father of Iscah. 30. And Sarai was barren; she had no child. 31. And Terah took Abram his son, and Lot the son of Haran, his son's son, and Sarai his daughter-in-law, his son Abram's wife; and they went forth with them from Ur of the Chaldees, to go into the land of Canaan; and they came unto Haran, and dwelt there. 32. And the days of Terah were two hundred and five years; and Terah died in Haran.

17 עֵבֶר אַרְבַּע וּשְׁלשִׁים שָׁנָה וַיּוֹלֶד אֶת־פָּלֶג: וַיְחִי־עֵבֶר
אַחֲרֵי הוֹלִידוֹ אֶת־פֶּלֶג שְׁלשִׁים שָׁנָה וְאַרְבַּע מֵאוֹת שָׁנָה
18 וַיּוֹלֶד בָּנִים וּבָנוֹת: ס וַיְחִי־פֶלֶג שְׁלשִׁים שָׁנָה וַיּוֹלֶד
19 אֶת־רְעוּ: וַיְחִי־פֶלֶג אַחֲרֵי הוֹלִידוֹ אֶת־רְעוּ תֵּשַׁע שָׁנִים
כ וּמָאתַיִם שָׁנָה וַיּוֹלֶד בָּנִים וּבָנוֹת: ס וַיְחִי רְעוּ שְׁתַּיִם
21 וּשְׁלשִׁים שָׁנָה וַיּוֹלֶד אֶת־שְׂרוּג: וַיְחִי רְעוּ אַחֲרֵי הוֹלִידוֹ
אֶת־שְׂרוּג שֶׁבַע שָׁנִים וּמָאתַיִם שָׁנָה וַיּוֹלֶד בָּנִים וּבָנוֹת:
22 23 ס וַיְחִי שְׂרוּג שְׁלשִׁים שָׁנָה וַיּוֹלֶד אֶת־נָחוֹר: וַיְחִי שְׂרוּג
אַחֲרֵי הוֹלִידוֹ אֶת־נָחוֹר מָאתַיִם שָׁנָה וַיּוֹלֶד בָּנִים וּבָנוֹת:
24 כה ס וַיְחִי נָחוֹר תֵּשַׁע וְעֶשְׂרִים שָׁנָה וַיּוֹלֶד אֶת־תָּרַח: וַיְחִי
נָחוֹר אַחֲרֵי הוֹלִידוֹ אֶת־תֶּרַח תְּשַׁע־עֶשְׂרֵה שָׁנָה וּמְאַת
26 שָׁנָה וַיּוֹלֶד בָּנִים וּבָנוֹת: ס וַיְחִי־תֶרַח שִׁבְעִים שָׁנָה
27 וַיּוֹלֶד אֶת־אַבְרָם אֶת־נָחוֹר וְאֶת־הָרָן: וְאֵלֶּה תּוֹלְדֹת תֶּרַח
תֶּרַח הוֹלִיד אֶת־אַבְרָם אֶת־נָחוֹר וְאֶת־הָרָן וְהָרָן הוֹלִיד
28 אֶת־לוֹט: וַיָּמָת הָרָן עַל־פְּנֵי תֶּרַח אָבִיו בְּאֶרֶץ מוֹלַדְתּוֹ
מפטיר 29 בְּאוּר כַּשְׂדִּים: * וַיִּקַּח אַבְרָם וְנָחוֹר לָהֶם נָשִׁים שֵׁם אֵשֶׁת־
אַבְרָם שָׂרָי וְשֵׁם אֵשֶׁת־נָחוֹר מִלְכָּה בַּת־הָרָן אֲבִי־מִלְכָּה
ל 31 וַאֲבִי יִסְכָּה: וַתְּהִי שָׂרַי עֲקָרָה אֵין לָהּ וָלָד: וַיִּקַּח תֶּרַח
אֶת־אַבְרָם בְּנוֹ וְאֶת־לוֹט בֶּן־הָרָן בֶּן־בְּנוֹ וְאֵת שָׂרַי כַּלָּתוֹ
אֵשֶׁת אַבְרָם בְּנוֹ וַיֵּצְאוּ אִתָּם מֵאוּר כַּשְׂדִּים לָלֶכֶת אַרְצָה
32 כְּנַעַן וַיָּבֹאוּ עַד־חָרָן וַיֵּשְׁבוּ שָׁם: וַיִּהְיוּ יְמֵי־תֶרַח חָמֵשׁ
שָׁנִים וּמָאתַיִם שָׁנָה וַיָּמָת תֶּרַח בְּחָרָן:

v. 32. נון גזורה

Peleg were omitted from the former chapter because they were to be mentioned here.

26. *Abram.* The name was in common use at Babylon. 'Abi-rama' is a witness to a Babylonian deed long before the days of Abraham.

28. *in the presence of.* During his father's lifetime.

Ur of the Chaldees. Usually identified with Mugheir, a town on the Euphrates some distance east of its junction with the Tigris. The name Ur occurs in the inscriptions in the form Uru, which was one of the old Babylonian royal towns and a centre of the moon-god worship. Astounding discoveries have in recent years been made, and are still being made, in its ruins. These enable us to have a vivid picture of contemporary life in the native city of Abraham; see *Abraham,* by C. Leonard Woolley, 1936.

Chaldees. Is often used in the Bible as a synonym for Babylonians.

29. *Sarai.* The personal names 'Sarai' and 'Nahor' also occur in Babylonian inscriptions.

Milcah. The importance of mentioning her lies in the fact that she was the ancestress of Rebekah, the wife of Isaac (XXIII, 20; XXIV, 15).

Iscah. This name is the basis for the Shakespearian name Jessica.

31. *Haran.* A town on the highway from Mesopotamia to the West; the converging point of the commercial routes from Babylon in the South, Nineveh in the East, and Damascus in the West.

32. The death of Terah did not take place till sixty years after Abram had left Haran; but it is recorded here to complete the story of Terah and thus concentrate on the life of Abram.

For Additional Notes on THE FLOOD, THE DELUGE AND ITS BABYLONIAN PARALLEL, see pp. 196–198.

HAFTORAH NOACH הפטרת נח

ISAIAH LIV LV, 5

Chapter LIV

1. Sing, O barren, thou that didst not bear,
Break forth into singing, and cry aloud, thou that didst not travail;
For more are the children of the desolate
Than the children of the married wife, saith the Lord.

2. Enlarge the place of thy tent,
And let them stretch forth the curtains of thy habitations, spare not;
Lengthen thy cords, and strengthen thy stakes.

3. For thou shalt spread abroad on the right hand and on the left;
And thy seed shall possess the nations,
And make the desolate cities to be inhabited.

4. Fear not, for thou shalt not be ashamed.
Neither be thou confounded, for thou shalt not be put to shame;
For thou shalt forget the shame of thy youth,
And the reproach of thy widowhood shalt thou remember no more.

Cap. LIV. נד

א רָנִּי עֲקָרָה לֹא יָלָדָה פִּצְחִי רִנָּה וְצַהֲלִי לֹא־חָלָה כִּי־
2 רַבִּים בְּנֵי־שׁוֹמֵמָה מִבְּנֵי בְעוּלָה אָמַר יְהוָה׃ הַרְחִיבִי ׀
מְקוֹם אָהֳלֵךְ וִירִיעוֹת מִשְׁכְּנוֹתַיִךְ יַטּוּ אַל־תַּחְשֹׂכִי הַאֲרִיכִי
3 מֵיתָרַיִךְ וִיתֵדֹתַיִךְ חַזֵּקִי׃ כִּי־יָמִין וּשְׂמֹאול תִּפְרֹצִי וְזַרְעֵךְ
4 גּוֹיִם יִירָשׁ וְעָרִים נְשַׁמּוֹת יוֹשִׁיבוּ׃ אַל־תִּירְאִי כִּי־לֹא
תֵבוֹשִׁי וְאַל־תִּכָּלְמִי כִּי־לֹא תַחְפִּירִי כִּי בֹשֶׁת עֲלוּמַיִךְ
ה תִּשְׁכָּחִי וְחֶרְפַּת אַלְמְנוּתַיִךְ לֹא תִזְכְּרִי־עוֹד׃ כִּי בֹעֲלַיִךְ
עֹשַׂיִךְ יְהוָה צְבָאוֹת שְׁמוֹ וְגֹאֲלֵךְ קְדוֹשׁ יִשְׂרָאֵל אֱלֹהֵי כָל־

5. For thy Maker is thy husband,
The Lord of hosts is His name;
And the Holy One of Israel is thy Redeemer,
The God of the whole earth shall He be called.

v. 3. מלא ו ibid. קמץ בז״ק v. 4. קמץ בז״ק

Isaiah LIV–LV, 5

The Haftorah, like the preceding one, forms a portion of the glowing prophetic Rhapsody, 'Israel Redeemed,' which is the main theme of the second half of the Book of Isaiah.

The reference in *v.* 9 to 'the waters of Noah', provides a literal connection with the Sedrah. But the connection is deeper. The Flood was apparently an act of destruction; yet, by wiping out a corrupt world, it paved the way for a new humanity. So Israel's Exile. From its suffering, declares the Prophet, Israel is issuing stronger in loyalty to God and in the conception of his vocation. Again, God's covenant with Noah ('I will establish My covenant with you . . . neither shall there be any more flood to destroy the earth') is paralleled by the 'Covenant of Peace' into which, in God's everlasting mercy, Israel now enters.

Chapter LIV. Jerusalem Rebuilt

1. *more are the children.* Zion's cities shall be repopulated; Jerusalem desolate was like a woman forsaken. Now with her exiles returned, she is like the wife reunited with husband and children.

2. *enlarge.* Because of the increase of her children, *i.e.* Zion's population.

tent. i.e. Jerusalem.

thy habitations. The other cities of Israel. All of Zion's children who have become estranged from her, wherever they may be dispersed, shall renew their allegiance and return to her leading.

3. *possess. i.e.* dispossess those of alien race who have occupied the desolate Jewish cities during the Exile.

4. *the shame of thy youth.* The defeats and humiliations in Israel's earlier history.

thy widowhood. i.e. the Exile, when God, 'Zion's husband,' seemed to have withdrawn from her. 'Widowhood' has a wider significance than in ordinary English, being used to denote a woman abandoned by her husband.

6 הָאָרֶץ יִקָּרֵא׃ כִּי־כְאִשָּׁה עֲזוּבָה וַעֲצוּבַת רוּחַ קְרָאָךְ
7 יְהוָה וְאֵשֶׁת נְעוּרִים כִּי תִמָּאֵס אָמַר אֱלֹהָיִךְ׃ בְּרֶגַע קָטֹן
8 עֲזַבְתִּיךְ וּבְרַחֲמִים גְּדוֹלִים אֲקַבְּצֵךְ׃ בְּשֶׁצֶף קֶצֶף הִסְתַּרְתִּי
פָנַי רֶגַע מִמֵּךְ וּבְחֶסֶד עוֹלָם רִחַמְתִּיךְ אָמַר גֹּאֲלֵךְ יְהוָה׃
9 כִּי־מֵי נֹחַ זֹאת לִי אֲשֶׁר נִשְׁבַּעְתִּי מֵעֲבֹר מֵי־נֹחַ עוֹד
י עַל־הָאָרֶץ כֵּן נִשְׁבַּעְתִּי מִקְּצֹף עָלַיִךְ וּמִגְּעָר־בָּךְ׃ כִּי הֶהָרִים
יָמוּשׁוּ וְהַגְּבָעוֹת תְּמוּטֶינָה וְחַסְדִּי מֵאִתֵּךְ לֹא־יָמוּשׁ וּבְרִית
11 שְׁלוֹמִי לֹא תָמוּט אָמַר מְרַחֲמֵךְ יְהוָה׃ • עֲנִיָּה סֹעֲרָה
לֹא נֻחָמָה הִנֵּה אָנֹכִי מַרְבִּיץ בַּפּוּךְ אֲבָנַיִךְ וִיסַדְתִּיךְ
12 בַּסַּפִּירִים׃ וְשַׂמְתִּי כַּדְכֹד שִׁמְשֹׁתַיִךְ וּשְׁעָרַיִךְ לְאַבְנֵי אֶקְדָּח
13 וְכָל־גְּבוּלֵךְ לְאַבְנֵי־חֵפֶץ׃ וְכָל־בָּנַיִךְ לִמּוּדֵי יְהוָה וְרַב

6. For the LORD hath called thee
As a wife forsaken and grieved in spirit;
And a wife of youth, can she be rejected?
Saith thy God.

7. For a small moment have I forsaken thee;
But with great compassion will I gather thee.

8. In a little wrath I hid My face from thee for a moment;
But with everlasting kindness will I have compassion on thee,
Saith the LORD thy Redeemer.

9. For this is as the waters of Noah unto Me;
For as I have sworn that the waters of Noah
Should no more go over the earth,
So have I sworn that I would not be wroth with thee,
Nor rebuke thee.

10. For the mountains may depart,
And the hills be removed;
But My kindness shall not depart from thee,
Nether shall My covenant of peace be removed,
Saith the LORD that hath compassion on thee.*

11. O thou afflicted, tossed with tempest,
And not comforted,
Behold, I will set thy stones in fair colours,
And lay thy foundations with sapphires.

12. And I will make thy pinnacles of rubies,
And thy gates of carbuncles,
And all thy border of precious stones.

13. And all thy children shall be taught of the LORD;
And great shall be the peace of thy children.

* Sephardim conclude here.

v. 9. נ"א כימי   * כאן מסיימין הספרדים

7–8. God's anger is but momentary; cf. Psalm xxx, 5. Although the years of the Exile seemed interminably long, they will prove but a brief space in the vast sweep of Israel's history.

9–10. Yet another utterance of comfort.

9. *for this. i.e.* the Exile and the comfort. The Exile is compared to the Flood; and the comfort, to the Divine promise that the Flood should never again occur.

11-17. OUTER AND INNER SPLENDOUR OF ZION

13. *taught of the LORD.* Or, 'disciples of the LORD.' Zion's peace will be based not on armed force, but on the God-fearing lives of all its inhabitants. In some ancient manuscripts, it seems, the second word for 'thy children' (*banayich*) in this verse was read as *bonayich*, 'thy builders.' In other words, the children of a nation are the builders of its future. And every Jewish child must be reared to become such a builder of his People's better future; every Jewish child must be fortified by a knowledge of Judaism and trained for a life of beneficence for Israel and humanity. This verse ('All thy children shall be taught of the LORD') is an important landmark in the history of civilization. In obedience to it, Israel led the way in universal education. Thus, in his *History of the World*, H. G. Wells records, 'The Jewish religion, because it was a literature-sustained religion, led to the first efforts to provide elementary instruction for all the children of the community.'

14 שְׁלוֹם בָּנָיִךְ׃ בִּצְדָקָה תִּכּוֹנָנִי רַחֲקִי מֵעֹשֶׁק כִּי־לֹא תִירָאִי
טו וּמִמְּחִתָּה כִּי לֹא־תִקְרַב אֵלָיִךְ׃ הֵן גּוֹר יָגוּר אֶפֶס מֵאוֹתִי
16 מִי־גָר אִתָּךְ עָלַיִךְ יִפּוֹל׃ הֵן אָנֹכִי בָּרָאתִי חָרָשׁ נֹפֵחַ
בְּאֵשׁ פֶּחָם וּמוֹצִיא כְלִי לְמַעֲשֵׂהוּ וְאָנֹכִי בָּרָאתִי מַשְׁחִית
17 לְחַבֵּל׃ כָּל־כְּלִי יוּצַר עָלַיִךְ לֹא יִצְלָח וְכָל־לָשׁוֹן תָּקוּם־
אִתָּךְ לַמִּשְׁפָּט תַּרְשִׁיעִי זֹאת נַחֲלַת עַבְדֵי יְהוָה וְצִדְקָתָם
מֵאִתִּי נְאֻם־יְהוָה׃

14. In righteousness shalt thou be established;
Be thou far from oppression, for thou shalt not fear,
And from ruin, for it shall not come near thee.

15. Behold, they may gather together, but not by Me;
Whosoever shall gather together against thee shall fall because of thee.

16. Behold, I have created the smith
That bloweth the fire of coals,
And bringeth forth a weapon for his work;
And I have created the waster to destroy.

17. No weapon that is formed against thee shall prosper;
And every tongue that shall rise against thee in judgment thou shalt condemn.
This is the heritage of the servants of the LORD,
And their due reward from Me, saith the LORD.

CAP. LV. נה

א הוֹי כָּל־צָמֵא לְכוּ לַמַּיִם וַאֲשֶׁר אֵין־לוֹ כָּסֶף לְכוּ שִׁבְרוּ
וֶאֱכֹלוּ וּלְכוּ שִׁבְרוּ בְּלוֹא־כֶסֶף וּבְלוֹא מְחִיר יַיִן וְחָלָב׃
2 לָמָּה תִשְׁקְלוּ־כֶסֶף בְּלוֹא־לֶחֶם וִיגִיעֲכֶם בְּלוֹא לְשָׂבְעָה
שִׁמְעוּ שָׁמוֹעַ אֵלַי וְאִכְלוּ־טוֹב וְתִתְעַנַּג בַּדֶּשֶׁן נַפְשְׁכֶם׃

CHAPTER LV

1. Ho, every one that thirsteth, come ye for water,
And he that hath no money;
Come ye, buy, and eat;
Yea, come, buy wine and milk
Without money and without price.

2. Wherefore do ye spend money for that which is not bread?
And your gain for that which satisfieth not?
Hearken diligently unto Me, and eat ye that which is good,
And let your soul delight itself in fatness.

נד׳ v. 16. הנה ק׳ v. 17. קמץ בז״ק

14. *be thou far from oppression.* Be steadfast in righteousness, and panic ('terror') shall not touch thee. The discharge of duty is a great moral tonic.

15. *not by Me.* All those who now stir up strife with thee shall shatter themselves against thee.

17. Israel's vindication in history is assured: neither might nor malice can destroy the Servant of the Lord.

condemn. Overthrow in argument.

this. i.e. no weapon forged against Israel shall succeed.

the servants. The worshippers.

their due reward from Me. צדקה means both 'righteousness' (*i.e.* holiness of life in the individual) and 'victory' (*i.e.* the triumph of right in the world).

CHAPTER LV. THE RETURN TO ZION SHOULD ALSO BE A RETURN TO GOD

1. A call to rich and poor alike to participate in the blessings of the new era, by coming to the source whence the knowledge of duty springs—the word of God. The cry is like that of the water-carrier in Eastern cities, and blessings are expressed in Oriental imagery, in terms of quickening water, nourishing milk, and gladdening wine. 'One cannot fail to perceive the note of wistfulness in the appeal, suggestive of the dread of an unspeakable disappointment' (Elmslie and Skinner).

2. Why spend time and labour and money on material pursuits that cannot in the end satisfy the soul created for holiness and righteousness?

fatness. Spiritual well-being. Its contrast is, 'leanness of soul,' Ps. CVI, 15.

3. Incline your ear, and come unto Me;
Hear, and your soul shall live;
And I will make an everlasting covenant with you,
Even the sure mercies of David.
4. Behold, I have given him for a witness to the peoples,
A prince and commander to the peoples.
5. Behold, thou shalt call a nation that thou knowest not,
And a nation that knew not thee shall run unto thee;
Because of the LORD thy God,
And for the Holy One of Israel, for He hath glorified thee.

3 הַטּוּ אָזְנְכֶם וּלְכוּ אֵלַי שִׁמְעוּ וּתְחִי נַפְשְׁכֶם וְאֶכְרְתָה
4 לָכֶם בְּרִית עוֹלָם חַסְדֵי דָוִד הַנֶּאֱמָנִים׃ הֵן עֵד לְאוּמִּים
ה נְתַתִּיו נָגִיד וּמְצַוֵּה לְאֻמִּים׃ הֵן גּוֹי לֹא־תֵדַע תִּקְרָא וְגוֹי
לֹא־יְדָעוּךָ אֵלֶיךָ יָרוּצוּ לְמַעַן יְהוָה אֱלֹהֶיךָ וְלִקְדוֹשׁ יִשְׂרָאֵל
כִּי פֵאֲרָךְ׃

v. 4. דגש אחר שורק

3. *the sure mercies of David.* The new covenant shall be the fulfilment of the promise that the Davidic Kingdom would endure (II Sam. VIII, 8–16).

4. *I have given him.* David or the representative of David's family. Zerubbabel, the leader of the returning exiles, was a descendant of David.

5. *thou shalt call.* A return to the description of the unconscious influence which Israel's loyalty to his Divinely-appointed mission is sure to effect.

12 CHAPTER XII

1. Now the LORD said unto Abram: 'Get thee out of thy country, and from thy kindred, and from thy father's house, unto the land that I will show thee. 2. And I will make of thee a great nation, and I will bless thee, and make thy name great; and be thou a blessing. 3. And I will bless them that bless thee, and him that curseth thee will I curse; and in thee shall all the families of the earth be blessed.' 4. So Abram went, as the LORD had spoken unto

CAP. XII. יב יב

פ פ פ ג 3

א וַיֹּאמֶר יְהוָה אֶל־אַבְרָם לֶךְ־לְךָ מֵאַרְצְךָ וּמִמּוֹלַדְתְּךָ וּמִבֵּית
2 אָבִיךָ אֶל־הָאָרֶץ אֲשֶׁר אַרְאֶךָּ׃ וְאֶעֶשְׂךָ לְגוֹי גָּדוֹל וַאֲבָרֶכְךָ
3 וַאֲגַדְּלָה שְׁמֶךָ וֶהְיֵה בְּרָכָה׃ וַאֲבָרְכָה מְבָרְכֶיךָ וּמְקַלֶּלְךָ
4 אָאֹר וְנִבְרְכוּ בְךָ כֹּל מִשְׁפְּחֹת הָאֲדָמָה׃ וַיֵּלֶךְ אַבְרָם כַּאֲשֶׁר

III. LECH LECHA

(CHAPTERS XII–XVII)

HISTORY OF THE PATRIARCHS

(*a*) ABRAHAM (CHAPTERS XII, 1–XXV, 18)

CHAPTER XII. THE CALL OF ABRAHAM, V. 1–9

1. *out of thy country.* 'In this land of idol worship thou art not worthy to rear sons to the service of God' (Rashi)—the evil surroundings would contaminate them. The Midrash explains that the command was issued for the benefit of his fellow-men. 'When a flask of balsam is sealed and stored away, its fragrance is not perceptible; but, opened and moved about, its sweet odour is widely diffused.'

thy country . . . thy kindred . . . thy father's house. These are the main influences which mould a person's thoughts and actions. The words also indicate the severity of the trial which was being imposed upon him. He was to cut himself completely adrift from all associations that could possibly hinder his mission. A similar 'call' comes to Abraham's descendants in every age and clime, to separate themselves from all associations and influences that are inimical to their Faith and Destiny.

thy country. Babylonia, which was then the most powerful empire in the world, with a highly developed city-civilization, commercial society, and literary culture.

land that I will show thee. The destination of the journey is not specified, to increase the test of Abram's faith in the Divine call. He was to follow whithersoever the will of God would direct him.

2. *I will bless thee.* With all good.

make thy name great. Although at first he would be unknown, a stranger in a strange land.

be thou a blessing. These words contain the ideal which Abram was to set himself, to become a blessing to humanity by the beneficent influence of his godly life and by turning others to a knowledge of God. With the change of one vowel, says the Midrash, the Hebrew word for 'blessing' means 'spring of water'. Even as a spring purifies the defiled, so do thou attract those who are far from the knowledge of God and purify them for their Heavenly Father. And such has indeed been the role played by the children of Abraham on the stage of human history. 'The Jew is that sacred being,' says Tolstoy, 'who has brought down from heaven the everlasting fire, and has illumined with it the entire world. He is the religious source, spring, and fountain out of which all the rest of the peoples have drawn their beliefs and their religions.'

3. *I will bless.* They who follow Abram's teachings will, like him, enjoy God's favour.

him that curseth thee. 'The story of European history during the past centuries teaches one uniform lesson. That the nations which have received and in any way dealt fairly and mercifully with the Jew have prospered—and that the nations that have tortured and oppressed him have written out their own curse' (Olive Schreiner).

all the families of the earth be blessed. Israel shall be 'a light of the nations' (Isa. XLII, 6). Through him, all men were to be taught the existence of the Most High God, and the love of righteousness, thereby opening for themselves the same treasury of blessings which he enjoyed. 'The germ of the idea underlying the fuller conception of a Messianic Age was in existence from the time of the founders of the race of Israel. *In thy seed shall all the families of the earth be blessed*, was the promise given both to Abraham and Isaac. It was a promise that reached far beyond the lifetime of each, farther than the limits of the temporal kingdom their descendants founded; that has obtained but partial fulfilment up to our time, and looks for fullest realization to that future towards which each of us in his measure may contribute his share' (S. Singer).

4. *as the LORD had spoken.* In obedience to the Heavenly voice, he leaves the land of his birth him; and Lot went with him; and Abram was seventy and five years old when he departed out of Haran. 5. And Abram took Sarai his wife, and Lot his brother's son, and all their substance that they had gathered, and the souls that they had gotten in Haran; and they went forth to go into the land of Canaan; and into the land of Canaan they came. 6. And Abram passed through the land unto the place of Shechem, unto the terebinth of Moreh. And the Canaanite was then in the land. 7. And the LORD appeared unto Abram, and said: 'Unto thy seed will I give this land'; and he builded there an altar unto the LORD, who appeared unto him. 8. And he removed from thence unto the mountain on the east of Beth-el, and pitched his tent, having Beth-el on the west, and Ai on the east; and he builded there an altar unto the LORD, and called upon the name of the LORD. 9. And Abram journeyed, going on still toward the South. ¶ 10. And there was a famine in the land; and Abram went

דִּבֶּר אֵלָיו יְהוָֹה וַיֵּלֶךְ אִתּוֹ לוֹט וְאַבְרָם בֶּן־חָמֵשׁ שָׁנִים
ה וְשִׁבְעִים שָׁנָה בְּצֵאתוֹ מֵחָרָן׃ וַיִּקַּח אַבְרָם אֶת־שָׂרַי אִשְׁתּוֹ
וְאֶת־לוֹט בֶּן־אָחִיו וְאֶת־כָּל־רְכוּשָׁם אֲשֶׁר רָכָשׁוּ וְאֶת־
הַנֶּפֶשׁ אֲשֶׁר־עָשׂוּ בְחָרָן וַיֵּצְאוּ לָלֶכֶת אַרְצָה כְּנַעַן וַיָּבֹאוּ
6 אַרְצָה כְּנָעַן׃ וַיַּעֲבֹר אַבְרָם בָּאָרֶץ עַד מְקוֹם שְׁכֶם עַד
7 אֵלוֹן מוֹרֶה וְהַכְּנַעֲנִי אָז בָּאָרֶץ׃ וַיֵּרָא יְהוָֹה אֶל־אַבְרָם
וַיֹּאמֶר לְזַרְעֲךָ אֶתֵּן אֶת־הָאָרֶץ הַזֹּאת וַיִּבֶן שָׁם מִזְבֵּחַ לַידוָֹה
8 הַנִּרְאֶה אֵלָיו׃ וַיַּעְתֵּק מִשָּׁם הָהָרָה מִקֶּדֶם לְבֵית־אֵל וַיֵּט
אָהֳלֹה בֵּית־אֵל מִיָּם וְהָעַי מִקֶּדֶם וַיִּבֶן־שָׁם מִזְבֵּחַ לַידוָֹה
9 וַיִּקְרָא בְּשֵׁם יְהוָֹה׃ וַיִּסַּע אַבְרָם הָלוֹךְ וְנָסוֹעַ הַנֶּגְבָּה׃ פ
י וַיְהִי רָעָב בָּאָרֶץ וַיֵּרֶד אַבְרָם מִצְרַיְמָה לָגוּר שָׁם כִּי־כָבֵד

v. 5. קמץ בז״ק

and all the glamour and worldly prosperity of his native place; he becomes a pilgrim for life, enduring trials, famines, privations; wandering into Canaan as a sojourner, into Egypt as a refugee, and back again into Canaan—all for the sake of humanity, that it might share the blessing of his knowledge of God and Righteousness.

Lot went with him. Lot was a mere follower, and does not seem to have been inspired with the same ideals as prompted Abram's departure.

5. *their substance.* Their worldly goods, movable property.

the souls. *i.e.* their slaves and dependents. The Rabbis take the word 'souls' to mean the proselytes whom Abram made among the men, and Sarai among the women. These converts became subservient to God's law and followed their master in his spiritual adventure.

gotten. lit. 'made'; for, declare the Rabbis, he who wins over an idolater to the service of God is as though he had created him anew.

6. *Shechem.* The modern Nablus, 30 miles N. of Jerusalem. It is one of the oldest cities of Palestine.

terebinth of Moreh. Some translate, 'the directing terebinth,' *i.e.* the oracular tree held sacred by the tree-worshipping Canaanites. Such trees were attended by priests, who interpreted the answers of the oracle to those who came to consult it. The terebinth (or turpentine-tree) grows to a height of from twenty to forty feet, and may therefore well have served as a landmark.

the Canaanite was then in the land. *i.e.* was already in the land. 'Before the age of Abraham, the Canaanites had already settled in the lowlands of Palestine—Canaan, be it noted, signified Lowlands' (Sayce). The interpretation of this verse as meaning that the Canaanites were *at that time* in the land, but were no longer so at the time when Genesis was written (an interpretation which misled even Ibn Ezra), is quite impossible. The Canaanites formed part of the population down to the days of the later Kings.

7. *unto thy seed.* In spite of its possession by the warlike and racially alien Canaanites (x, 6).

8. *Beth-el.* In Central Palestine, the modern Beitin, 10 miles N. of Jerusalem. The place is here called by the name given to it by Jacob, XXVIII, 19.

Ai. Probably the modern Haiyan, about two miles E. of Bethel.

called upon the name of the LORD. The Targum renders, 'and prayed in the name of the LORD.' He proclaimed the knowledge of the true God (Talmud). He had the moral courage to preach his conception of God and duty in the very face of the soul-degrading ideas of divine worship and human duty held by the peoples then inhabiting Canaan.

9. *going on still.* The Hebrew indicates travelling by stages, after the manner of nomads.

the South. Or, 'the Negeb,' the name by which the Southern district of Judah is known. The Midrash explains that Abram was being drawn towards the city of Jerusalem, which is in the south of Palestine.

10–20. ABRAM IN EGYPT

10. *a famine in the land.* Owing to the scarcity of rivers and lack of irrigation, the country was down into Egypt to sojourn there; for the famine was sore in the land. 11. And it came to pass, when he was come near to enter into Egypt, that he said unto Sarai his wife: 'Behold now, I know that thou art a fair woman to look upon. 12. And it will come to pass, when the Egyptians shall see thee, that they will say: This is his wife; and they will kill me, but thee they will keep alive. 13. Say, I pray thee, thou art my sister; that it may be well with me for thy sake, and that my soul may live because of thee.' *ii. 14. And it came to pass, that, when Abram was come into Egypt, the Egyptians beheld the woman that she was very fair. 15. And the princes of Pharaoh saw her, and praised her to Pharaoh; and the woman was taken into Pharaoh's house. 16. And he dealt well with Abram for her sake; and he had sheep, and oxen, and he-asses, and men-servants, and maid-servants, and she-asses, and camels. 17. And the LORD plagued Pharaoh and his house with great plagues because of Sarai Abram's wife. 18. And Pharaoh called Abram, and said: 'What is

11 הָרָעָב בָּאָרֶץ׃ וַיְהִי כַּאֲשֶׁר הִקְרִיב לָבוֹא מִצְרָיְמָה וַיֹּאמֶר
אֶל־שָׂרַי אִשְׁתּוֹ הִנֵּה־נָא יָדַעְתִּי כִּי אִשָּׁה יְפַת־מַרְאֶה אָתְּ׃
12 וְהָיָה כִּי־יִרְאוּ אֹתָךְ הַמִּצְרִים וְאָמְרוּ אִשְׁתּוֹ זֹאת וְהָרְגוּ
13 אֹתִי וְאֹתָךְ יְחַיּוּ׃ אִמְרִי־נָא אֲחֹתִי אָתְּ לְמַעַן יִיטַב־לִי
שני
14 בַעֲבוּרֵךְ וְחָיְתָה נַפְשִׁי בִּגְלָלֵךְ׃ * וַיְהִי כְּבוֹא אַבְרָם מִצְרָיְמָה
טו וַיִּרְאוּ הַמִּצְרִים אֶת־הָאִשָּׁה כִּי־יָפָה הִוא מְאֹד׃ וַיִּרְאוּ
אֹתָהּ שָׂרֵי פַרְעֹה וַיְהַלְלוּ אֹתָהּ אֶל־פַּרְעֹה וַתֻּקַּח הָאִשָּׁה
16 בֵּית פַּרְעֹה׃ וּלְאַבְרָם הֵיטִיב בַּעֲבוּרָהּ וַיְהִי־לוֹ צֹאן־וּבָקָר
17 וַחֲמֹרִים וַעֲבָדִים וּשְׁפָחֹת וַאֲתֹנֹת וּגְמַלִּים׃ וַיְנַגַּע יְהוָה ׀
אֶת־פַּרְעֹה נְגָעִים גְּדֹלִים וְאֶת־בֵּיתוֹ עַל־דְּבַר שָׂרַי אֵשֶׁת
18 אַבְרָם׃ וַיִּקְרָא פַרְעֹה לְאַבְרָם וַיֹּאמֶר מַה־זֹּאת עָשִׂיתָ לִּי
19 לָמָּה לֹא־הִגַּדְתָּ לִּי כִּי אִשְׁתְּךָ הִוא׃ לָמָה אָמַרְתְּ אֲחֹתִי

subject to famine if the rainy seasons failed. Palestine nomads would then seek safety in Egypt. A famine drove Abram to Egypt, and the same cause was again to bring his descendants to that land. As the Rabbis say, 'The lives of the Patriarchs foreshadow the story of their descendants.'

to sojourn there. For a temporary stay only.

12. *they will kill me.* To kill the husband in order to possess himself of his wife seems to have been a common royal custom in those days. A papyrus tells of a Pharaoh who, acting on the advice of one of his princes, sent armed men to fetch a beautiful woman and make away with her husband. Another Pharaoh is promised by his priest on his tombstone, that even after death he will kill Palestinian sheiks and include their wives in his harem.

13. Once or twice Abram falls a prey to fear and plays with the truth in order to preserve his life. Though merely an episode with him, natural enough in an ordinary man, it is quite unworthy of his majestic soul. It is the glory of the Bible that it shows no partiality towards its heroes; they are *not* superhuman, sinless beings. And when they err—for 'there is no man on earth who doeth good always and sinneth never'—Scripture does not gloss over their faults. The great Jewish commentator Nachmanides refers to Abram's action as 'a great sin'.

my sister. The statement was partly true; see on XX, 12.

that it may be well with me. He would escape death. The same thought is repeated in the following clause.

my soul may live. The Heb. idiomatic way of saying, 'I may live.'

14. *very fair.* Sarai was then in middle age, and apparently had retained her youthful beauty.

15. *Pharaoh.* The Heb. transcription of *Pr-'o*, the Egyptian title of the king of the country. It signifies 'Great House'. The statement of some writers that the title did not come into use till much later is inaccurate. In the days of the Nineteenth Dynasty, the age of Moses, the word is the usual reverential designation of the King.

16. *and he had.* And he came to have. In this verse we have enumerated what was then considered true wealth. Note the omission of silver and gold; cf. Job I, 3.

17. *plagued.* A mysterious sickness fell upon Pharaoh and his house, which aroused suspicion and led to enquiries that resulted in the discovery of the truth (Driver). According to the Rabbis, the nature of the plague was such as to constitute a safeguard to Sarai's honour.

and his house. i.e. his household.

18. *what is this that thou hast done unto me?* 'Pharaoh, justly incensed with Abram, sternly reproves him and dismisses him with abruptness.' This is the usual non-Jewish comment on this that thou hast done unto me? why didst thou not tell me that she was thy wife? 19. Why saidst thou: She is my sister? so that I took her to be my wife; now therefore behold thy wife, take her, and go thy way.' 20. And Pharaoh gave men charge concerning him; and they brought him on the way, and his wife, and all that he had.

13 CHAPTER XIII

1. And Abram went up out of Egypt, he, and his wife, and all that he had, and Lot with him, into the South. 2. And Abram was very rich in cattle, in silver, and in gold. 3. And he went on his journeys from the South even to Beth-el, unto the place where his tent had been at the beginning, between Beth-el and Ai; 4. unto the place of the altar, which he had made there at the first; and Abram called there on the name of the Lord.* iii. 5. And Lot also, who went with Abram, had flocks, and herds, and tents. 6. And the land was not able to bear them, that they might dwell together; for their substance was great, so that they could not dwell together. 7. And there was a strife between the herdmen of Abram's cattle and the herdmen of Lot's cattle. And the Canaanite and the Perizzite dwelt then in the land. 8. And Abram said unto Lot: 'Let there be no strife, I pray thee, between me and thee, and between my herdmen and thy herdmen; for we are brethren. 9. Is not the whole land before thee? separate thyself, I pray thee, from me; if thou wilt take the left hand, then I will go to the right; or if thou take the right hand, then I will go to the left.' 10. And

הוּא וָאֶקַּח אֹתָהּ לִי לְאִשָּׁה וְעַתָּה הִנֵּה אִשְׁתְּךָ קַח וָלֵךְ׃
כ וַיְצַו עָלָיו פַּרְעֹה אֲנָשִׁים וַיְשַׁלְּחוּ אֹתוֹ וְאֶת־אִשְׁתּוֹ וְאֶת־
כָּל־אֲשֶׁר־לוֹ׃

יג CAP. XIII. יג

א וַיַּעַל אַבְרָם מִמִּצְרַיִם הוּא וְאִשְׁתּוֹ וְכָל־אֲשֶׁר־לוֹ וְלוֹט עִמּוֹ
2 3 הַנֶּגְבָּה׃ וְאַבְרָם כָּבֵד מְאֹד בַּמִּקְנֶה בַּכֶּסֶף וּבַזָּהָב׃ וַיֵּלֶךְ
לְמַסָּעָיו מִנֶּגֶב וְעַד־בֵּית־אֵל עַד־הַמָּקוֹם אֲשֶׁר־הָיָה שָׁם
4 אָהֳלֹה בַּתְּחִלָּה בֵּין בֵּית־אֵל וּבֵין הָעָי׃ אֶל־מְקוֹם הַמִּזְבֵּחַ
שלישי אֲשֶׁר־עָשָׂה שָׁם בָּרִאשֹׁנָה וַיִּקְרָא שָׁם אַבְרָם בְּשֵׁם יְהוָה׃
ה וְגַם־לְלוֹט הַהֹלֵךְ אֶת־אַבְרָם הָיָה צֹאן־וּבָקָר וְאֹהָלִים׃
6 וְלֹא־נָשָׂא אֹתָם הָאָרֶץ לָשֶׁבֶת יַחְדָּו כִּי־הָיָה רְכוּשָׁם רָב
7 וְלֹא־יָכְלוּ לָשֶׁבֶת יַחְדָּו׃ וַיְהִי־רִיב בֵּין רֹעֵי מִקְנֵה־אַבְרָם
וּבֵין רֹעֵי מִקְנֵה־לוֹט וְהַכְּנַעֲנִי וְהַפְּרִזִּי אָז יֹשֵׁב בָּאָרֶץ׃
8 וַיֹּאמֶר אַבְרָם אֶל־לוֹט אַל־נָא תְהִי מְרִיבָה בֵּינִי וּבֵינֶךָ וּבֵין
9 רֹעַי וּבֵין רֹעֶיךָ כִּי־אֲנָשִׁים אַחִים אֲנָחְנוּ׃ הֲלֹא כָל־הָאָרֶץ
לְפָנֶיךָ הִפָּרֶד נָא מֵעָלָי אִם־הַשְּׂמֹאל וְאֵימִנָה וְאִם־הַיָּמִין

this verse. Yet Pharaoh, in whose land the husband of a beautiful wife was in danger of being murdered so that the wife be taken into the royal harem, was hardly justified in his moral indignation towards Abraham. Pharaoh's was largely the blame for the shortcoming on the part of the Patriarch.

CHAPTER XIII. ABRAM AND LOT

1. *Lot with him.* Lot is here explicitly named because of the incident which follows.

2. *rich.* Lit. 'heavy,' *i.e.* laden with possessions.

3. *and he went on his journeys.* The Heb. implies that he travelled by stages, covering much the same ground as on the outward journey.

4. *at the first.* Rashi renders: 'Unto the place of the altar which he had made there at the first, and where Abram had called on the name of the Lord.' See XII, 8.

6. *not able to bear them.* *i.e.* there was insufficient pasturage and water for their numerous herds.

7. *the Canaanite and the Perizzite dwelt then in the land.* This seemingly superfluous clause explains how so large a tract of country could not supply sufficient pasturage for the flocks of Abram and Lot. The older inhabitants would naturally have taken possession of the fertile districts.

8. *no strife.* Abram's conduct is both self-denying and peace-loving.

for we are brethren. *i.e.* kinsmen. Strife would be especially unseemly among relations.

9. *the whole land before thee.* Although the Canaanites and the Perizzites inhabit the country, there are several unoccupied sites available. In the interests of peace, Abram waives his right, as the elder, to make the selection, and allows Lot to choose in which direction he will go.

10. *the plain of the Jordan.* Lit. 'the circle of the Jordan,' is the specific name for the land on both sides of the lower Jordan valley. 'A large part of this valley is of exuberant fertility . . . Wherever water comes, the flowers rise to the

י וְאַשְׁמְאִילָה: וַיִּשָּׂא־לוֹט אֶת־עֵינָיו וַיַּרְא אֶת־כָּל־כִּכַּר הַיַּרְדֵּן
כִּי כֻלָּהּ מַשְׁקֶה לִפְנֵי ׀ שַׁחֵת יְהוָה אֶת־סְדֹם וְאֶת־עֲמֹרָה
11 כְּגַן־יְהוָה כְּאֶרֶץ מִצְרַיִם בֹּאֲכָה צֹעַר: וַיִּבְחַר־לוֹ לוֹט אֵת
כָּל־כִּכַּר הַיַּרְדֵּן וַיִּסַּע לוֹט מִקֶּדֶם וַיִּפָּרְדוּ אִישׁ מֵעַל אָחִיו:
12 אַבְרָם יָשַׁב בְּאֶרֶץ־כְּנָעַן וְלוֹט יָשַׁב בְּעָרֵי הַכִּכָּר וַיֶּאֱהַל
13 14 עַד־סְדֹם: וְאַנְשֵׁי סְדֹם רָעִים וְחַטָּאִים לַיהוָה מְאֹד: וַיהוָה
אָמַר אֶל־אַבְרָם אַחֲרֵי הִפָּרֶד־לוֹט מֵעִמּוֹ שָׂא נָא עֵינֶיךָ
וּרְאֵה מִן־הַמָּקוֹם אֲשֶׁר־אַתָּה שָׁם צָפֹנָה וָנֶגְבָּה וָקֵדְמָה
טו וָיָמָּה: כִּי אֶת־כָּל־הָאָרֶץ אֲשֶׁר־אַתָּה רֹאֶה לְךָ אֶתְּנֶנָּה
16 וּלְזַרְעֲךָ עַד־עוֹלָם: וְשַׂמְתִּי אֶת־זַרְעֲךָ כַּעֲפַר הָאָרֶץ אֲשֶׁר ׀
אִם־יוּכַל אִישׁ לִמְנוֹת אֶת־עֲפַר הָאָרֶץ גַּם זַרְעֲךָ יִמָּנֶה:
17 קוּם הִתְהַלֵּךְ בָּאָרֶץ לְאָרְכָּהּ וּלְרָחְבָּהּ כִּי לְךָ אֶתְּנֶנָּה:

Lot lifted up his eyes, and beheld all the plain of the Jordan, that it was well watered every where, before the LORD destroyed Sodom and Gomorrah, like the garden of the LORD, like the land of Egypt, as thou goest unto Zoar. 11. So Lot chose him all the plain of the Jordan; and Lot journeyed east; and they separated themselves the one from the other. 12. Abram dwelt in the land of Canaan, and Lot dwelt in the cities of the Plain, and moved his tent as far as Sodom. 13. Now the men of Sodom were wicked and sinners against the LORD exceedingly. 14. And the LORD said unto Abram, after that Lot was separated from him: 'Lift up now thine eyes, and look from the place where thou art, northward and southward and eastward and westward; 15. for all the land which thou seest, to thee will I give it, and to thy seed for ever. 16. And I will make thy seed as the dust of the earth; so that if a man can number the dust of the earth, then shall thy seed also be numbered. 17. Arise, walk through the land in the length of it and in the breadth of it; for unto thee

knee, and the herbage to the shoulder' (G. A. Smith).

well watered. By the Jordan and its tributaries.

like the garden of the LORD. *i.e.* Eden and its river (II, 10).

like the land of Egypt. Watered by the Nile.

as thou goest unto Zoar. Better, *as thou camest unto Zoar.* This is one of the Mosaic 'touches' in Genesis (Naville). Zoar is *not* the town near Sodom. It is the name of an ancient Egyptian frontier fortress. *Speaking to men who had come out of Egypt,* Scripture compares the fertility of the Plain of Jordan to the verdure and richness of Egypt 'as thou camest unto Zoar', on the edge of the barren desert and sands.

11. *Lot chose him all the plain of the Jordan.* 'He chose the rich soil, and with it the corrupt civilization which had grown up in the rank climate of that deep descent; and left to Abraham, the hardship, the glory, and the virtues of the rugged hills, the sea-breezes, and the inexhaustible future of Western Palestine' (Stanley).

12. *in the land of Canaan.* *i.e.* the remainder of the land.

13. *men of Sodom.* The fertility of the soil, with the luxurious and enervating character of the climate, rapidly developed the sensual vices of this early civilized but depraved race; cf. Ezek. XVI, 49 f. For all that, Lot was willing to dwell amongst them. The material attractions of the locality overbore his fear of moral contamination. This statement also prepares us for their destruction narrated in Chap. XIX.

wicked and sinners. Wicked—heartless and inhuman in their dealings with their fellowmen; and sinners—abandoning themselves to nameless abominations and depravities.

against the LORD. Their immoral conduct was an offence to God.

14. *Lot was separated from him.* God chose that moment to renew His assurance to Abram, because he may then have been depressed by the departure of his nephew whom, in default of a son, he had regarded as his probable heir, through whom the Divine promise was to be fulfilled.

from the place where thou art. The spot near Bethel where he was standing commands a wonderful view of the whole country. Travellers speak in glowing terms of the panorama which this holy place affords.

15. *for ever.* 'It will be theirs for ever, even though they may not always be in possession of it; even as it was given to Abraham, without his being in actual possession of it' (S. R. Hirsch).

16. *as the dust.* 'As the dust of the earth extends from one end of the world to the other, so will thy seed be dispersed throughout all lands. And as the dust causes even metals to decay but itself endures, so will all worshippers of idolatry perish, but Israel will continue forever' (Midrash).

17. *arise, walk through the land.* The act of walking through the land was a legal formality denoting acquisition.

will I give it.' 18. And Abram moved his tent, and came and dwelt by the terebinths of Mamre, which are in Hebron, and built there an altar unto the LORD.* iv.

14

CHAPTER XIV

1. And it came to pass in the days of Amraphel king of Shinar, Arioch king of Ellasar, Chedorlaomer king of Elam, and Tidal king of Goiim, 2. that they made war with Bera king of Sodom, and with Birsha king of Gomorrah, Shinab king of Admah, and Shemeber king of Zeboiim, and the king of Bela—the same is Zoar. 3. All these came as allies unto the vale of Siddim—the same is the Salt Sea. 4. Twelve years they served Chedorlaomer, and in the thirteenth year they rebelled. 5. And in the fourteenth year came Chedorlaomer and the kings that were with him, and smote the Rephaim in Ashteroth-karnaim, and the Zuzim in Ham, and the Emim in

18 וַיֶּאֱהַל אַבְרָם וַיָּבֹא וַיֵּשֶׁב בְּאֵלֹנֵי מַמְרֵא אֲשֶׁר בְּחֶבְרוֹן
וַיִּבֶן־שָׁם מִזְבֵּחַ לַיהוָה׃* פ רביעי

יד

CAP. XIV. יד

א וַיְהִי בִּימֵי אַמְרָפֶל מֶלֶךְ־שִׁנְעָר אַרְיוֹךְ מֶלֶךְ אֶלָּסָר
2 כְּדָרְלָעֹמֶר מֶלֶךְ עֵילָם וְתִדְעָל מֶלֶךְ גּוֹיִם׃ עָשׂוּ מִלְחָמָה
אֶת־בֶּרַע מֶלֶךְ סְדֹם וְאֶת־בִּרְשַׁע מֶלֶךְ עֲמֹרָה שִׁנְאָב ׀ מֶלֶךְ
3 אַדְמָה וְשֶׁמְאֵבֶר מֶלֶךְ צְבֹיִים וּמֶלֶךְ בֶּלַע הִיא־צֹעַר׃ כָּל־
4 אֵלֶּה חָבְרוּ אֶל־עֵמֶק הַשִּׂדִּים הוּא יָם הַמֶּלַח׃ שְׁתֵּים
עֶשְׂרֵה שָׁנָה עָבְדוּ אֶת־כְּדָרְלָעֹמֶר וּשְׁלֹשׁ־עֶשְׂרֵה שָׁנָה
ה מָרָדוּ׃ וּבְאַרְבַּע עֶשְׂרֵה שָׁנָה בָּא כְדָרְלָעֹמֶר וְהַמְּלָכִים
אֲשֶׁר אִתּוֹ וַיַּכּוּ אֶת־רְפָאִים בְּעַשְׁתְּרֹת קַרְנַיִם וְאֶת־הַזּוּזִים

יג׳ v. 18. בתביר יד׳ v. 2. צבוים ק׳

18. *Hebron.* Josephus speaks of it as a 'more ancient city than Memphis in Egypt'. Of the oak-tree he says, 'Report goes, that this tree has continued since the creation of the world.'

CHAPTER XIV. THE WAR OF THE KINGS

Much has been written on this chapter during the last sixty years. This chapter does not fit in with any of the so-called 'sources' of the Bible critics; hence their determined attacks on its veracity. Its historical accuracy has, however, been strikingly confirmed by recent discoveries, which conclusively show that the age of Abraham was a literary age with a developed historic sense (Sayce).

1–17. ABRAM RESCUES LOT

1. *Amraphel.* Usually identified with Hammurabi, a great and enlightened king of Babylon. He finally united all the city-states of North and South Babylonia into one strong centralized empire, defeated the Elamites and extended his rule to the shores of the Mediterranean. He undertook the codification of Babylonian law, and his Code was rediscovered at the beginning of this century. The date of his reign is 1945–1902 before the Christian era. The final consonant in the Heb. form of the name probably corresponds to the ending *el,* 'God,' in Biblical names.

Shinar. The Targum reads 'Babylon'; it seems to have been one of the Egyptian names for Babylonia. The word may possibly be identical with Sumir; see on x, 10.

Arioch king of Ellasar. i.e. Eriaku, king of Larsa, midway between Babylon and the mouth of the Euphrates.

Chedorlaomer. A Hebraized form of Kudur, 'servant of,' and Lagamar, the name of an Elamite deity.

Elam. See on x, 22. It was at this time in possession of Babylonia, and therefore, also of Canaan which was under Babylonian supremacy.

Tidal king of Goiim. Tudghula of the cuneiform texts, who was king of the 'hordes' of Northern Kurdish nations mentioned from time to time in the inscriptions as invading Assyria (Sayce). Some explain Goiim as the Heb. form of Gutium, Kurdistan.

2. *Bera, etc.* The names of these kings (like the 'kings' in Joshua, petty princes of Canaanite towns) are discussed in W. T. Pilter's monumental work on Genesis xiv, '*The Pentateuch, a Historical Record*, 1928,' chap. x.

3. *vale of Siddim.* The name does not occur elsewhere.

Salt Sea. Deservedly so called. Whereas ordinary seawater contains six per cent of salt, its waters have four times that quantity. The Church Fathers named it 'the Dead Sea'.

4. *they served. i.e.* they paid tribute; withholding the annual payment was the act of rebellion.

5. The peoples named in this verse—Rephaim, Zuzim, Emim, Horites—are the aboriginal inhabitants of the regions afterwards occupied by Edom, Moab and Ammon; see Deut. II, 9 f.

Ashteroth-karnaim. A hill 21 miles E. of the Sea of Galilee. The name means 'Astarte of the two horns', derived in all probability from a local Sanctuary of that goddess, whose symbol was the crescent or two-horned moon.

Ham. The primitive name of the Ammonite capital, Rabbah, 25 miles N.E. of the upper end of the Dead Sea.

Shaveh-kiriathaim, 6. and the Horites in their mount Seir, unto El-paran, which is by the wilderness. 7. And they turned back, and came to En-mishpat—the same is Kadesh—and smote all the country of the Amalekites, and also the Amorites, that dwelt in Hazazon-tamar. 8. And there went out the king of Sodom, and the king of Gomorrah, and the king of Admah, and the king of Zeboiim, and the king of Bela—the same is Zoar; and they set the battle in array against them in the vale of Siddim; 9. against Chedorlaomer king of Elam, and Tidal king of Goiim, and Amraphel king of Shinar, and Arioch king of Ellasar; four kings against the five. 10. Now the vale of Siddim was full of slime pits; and the kings of Sodom and Gomorrah fled, and they fell there, and they that remained fled to the mountain. 11. And they took all the goods of Sodom and Gomorrah, and all their victuals, and went their way. 12. And they took Lot, Abram's brother's son, who dwelt in Sodom, and his goods, and departed. 13.

6 בְּהָם וְאֵת הָאֵימִים בְּשָׁוֵה קִרְיָתָיִם׃ וְאֶת־הַחֹרִי בְּהַרְרָם
7 שֵׂעִיר עַד אֵיל פָּארָן אֲשֶׁר עַל־הַמִּדְבָּר׃ וַיָּשֻׁבוּ וַיָּבֹאוּ
אֶל־עֵין מִשְׁפָּט הִוא קָדֵשׁ וַיַּכּוּ אֶת־כָּל־שְׂדֵה הָעֲמָלֵקִי וְגַם
8 אֶת־הָאֱמֹרִי הַיֹּשֵׁב בְּחַצֲצֹן תָּמָר׃ וַיֵּצֵא מֶלֶךְ־סְדֹם וּמֶלֶךְ
עֲמֹרָה וּמֶלֶךְ אַדְמָה וּמֶלֶךְ צְבֹיִים וּמֶלֶךְ בֶּלַע הִוא־צֹעַר
9 וַיַּעַרְכוּ אִתָּם מִלְחָמָה בְּעֵמֶק הַשִּׂדִּים׃ אֵת כְּדָרְלָעֹמֶר
מֶלֶךְ עֵילָם וְתִדְעָל מֶלֶךְ גּוֹיִם וְאַמְרָפֶל מֶלֶךְ שִׁנְעָר וְאַרְיוֹךְ
י מֶלֶךְ אֶלָּסָר אַרְבָּעָה מְלָכִים אֶת־הַחֲמִשָּׁה׃ וְעֵמֶק הַשִּׂדִּים
בֶּאֱרֹת בֶּאֱרֹת חֵמָר וַיָּנֻסוּ מֶלֶךְ־סְדֹם וַעֲמֹרָה וַיִּפְּלוּ־שָׁמָּה
11 וְהַנִּשְׁאָרִים הֶרָה נָּסוּ׃ וַיִּקְחוּ אֶת־כָּל־רְכֻשׁ סְדֹם וַעֲמֹרָה
12 וְאֶת־כָּל־אָכְלָם וַיֵּלֵכוּ׃ וַיִּקְחוּ אֶת־לוֹט וְאֶת־רְכֻשׁוֹ בֶּן־אֲחִי
13 אַבְרָם וַיֵּלֵכוּ וְהוּא יֹשֵׁב בִּסְדֹם׃ וַיָּבֹא הַפָּלִיט וַיַּגֵּד

v. 8. צבוים ק'

Shaveh-kiriathaim. Lit. 'the plain of the two towns'. Usually identified with the modern Kureyat, 10 miles E. of the Dead Sea.

6. *Seir.* The mountainous district S.E. of the Dead Sea.

El-paran. Probably the port at the Northern extremity of the Gulf of Akaba, Red Sea.

the wilderness. The bare plateau of limestone between Canaan and Egypt.

7. *they turned back.* Their march had hitherto been towards the South; but they now turned to the N.W.

En-mishpat. That is, 'the well of judgment,' probably the seat of an oracle to which disputants resorted for the settlement of their claims.

the same is Kadesh. Usually 'Kadesh-Barnea' (cf. Deut. I, 2, 46). It is situated on the S.E. frontier of Judah.

all the country of the Amalekites. More accurately, 'the field of the Amalekites,' a nomad people living between Palestine and Egypt, and later on attempting to prevent the Israelites from entering the peninsula of Sinai (Exod. XVII, 8 ff.). The phrase, 'all the country of the Amalekites,' must be understood to mean, 'the country afterwards inhabited by the Amalekites' (Midrash, Rashi). Esau's grandson was named after a chieftain Amalek who had founded the Amalekite people (Nachmanides).

the Amorites. Denoting generally the pre-Israelite population of Canaan.

Hazazon-tamar. At the mouth of the deep gorge which runs into the Dead Sea, about half-way down the western shore.

10. *full of slime pits.* *i.e.* wells of bitumen. These pits hampered the flight of the defeated army.

and they fell there, etc. The subject of the verb is vaguely expressed. The kings of Sodom and Gomorrah fell into the pits, whereas the remainder (*i.e.* the other three kings) made good their escape. From *v.* 17 we learn that the king of Sodom must have been rescued from the slime pits.

to the mountain. Of Moab, to the E. of the Dead Sea.

12. *who dwelt in Sodom.* It was because of Lot's willingness to live with evil-doers, that this misfortune befell him (Rashi).

13. *the Hebrew.* This is the first time this word occurs in the Bible, where it is a title used of Israelites either by foreigners or in speaking of them to foreigners, or in contrast to foreigners. After the exile of the Ten Tribes, when the tribe of Judah (Yehudah) remained the principal branch of Israel, the name *Yehudim* (translated Judaioi, Judaei, Juden, Jews) came into general use. The Rabbis, also modern scholars, are divided as to the origin of the name Hebrew. Either the word is to be connected with Eber (see X, 21; XI, 16 f) and signifies 'a descendant of Eber'; or it means 'one from the other side', in accordance with the statement, 'And I took your father Abraham from the other side of the River (Euphrates)' (Josh. XXIV, 3). It is also claimed that the name is identical with that of the *Habiri*, a nomad people mentioned in the Tell-el-Amarna Tablets (see on *v.* 18 below), as making war upon the Canaanite towns and population.

And there came one that had escaped, and told Abram the Hebrew—now he dwelt by the terebinths of Mamre the Amorite, brother of Eshcol, and brother of Aner; and these were confederate with Abram. 14. And when Abram heard that his brother was taken captive, he led forth his trained men, born in his house, three hundred and eighteen, and pursued as far as Dan. 15. And he divided himself against them by night, he and his servants, and smote them, and pursued them unto Hobah, which is on the left hand of Damascus. 16. And he brought back all the goods, and also brought back his brother Lot, and his goods, and the women also, and the people. 17. And the king of Sodom went out to meet him, after his return from the slaughter of Chedorlaomer and the kings that were with him, at the vale of Shaveh—the same is the King's Vale. 18. And Melchizedek king of Salem brought forth bread and

לְאַבְרָם הָעִבְרִי וְהוּא שֹׁכֵן בְּאֵלֹנֵי מַמְרֵא הָאֱמֹרִי אֲחִי
14 אֶשְׁכֹּל וַאֲחִי עָנֵר וְהֵם בַּעֲלֵי בְרִית־אַבְרָם׃ וַיִּשְׁמַע אַבְרָם
כִּי נִשְׁבָּה אָחִיו וַיָּרֶק אֶת־חֲנִיכָיו יְלִידֵי בֵיתוֹ שְׁמֹנָה עָשָׂר
טו וּשְׁלֹשׁ מֵאוֹת וַיִּרְדֹּף עַד־דָּן׃ וַיֵּחָלֵק עֲלֵיהֶם ׀ לַיְלָה הוּא
וַעֲבָדָיו וַיַּכֵּם וַיִּרְדְּפֵם עַד־חוֹבָה אֲשֶׁר מִשְּׂמֹאל לְדַמָּשֶׂק׃
16 וַיָּשֶׁב אֵת כָּל־הָרְכֻשׁ וְגַם אֶת־לוֹט אָחִיו וּרְכֻשׁוֹ הֵשִׁיב
17 וְגַם אֶת־הַנָּשִׁים וְאֶת־הָעָם׃ וַיֵּצֵא מֶלֶךְ־סְדֹם לִקְרָאתוֹ
אַחֲרֵי שׁוּבוֹ מֵהַכּוֹת אֶת־כְּדָרְלָעֹמֶר וְאֶת־הַמְּלָכִים אֲשֶׁר
18 אִתּוֹ אֶל־עֵמֶק שָׁוֵה הוּא עֵמֶק הַמֶּלֶךְ׃ וּמַלְכִּי־צֶדֶק מֶלֶךְ
19 שָׁלֵם הוֹצִיא לֶחֶם וָיָיִן וְהוּא כֹהֵן לְאֵל עֶלְיוֹן׃ וַיְבָרְכֵהוּ

14. *when Abram heard.* The Midrash describes his emotions on hearing the news, in the words of Psalm CXII, 7, 'He shall not be afraid of evil tidings; his heart is steadfast, trusting in the Lord.' With gentleness and reasonableness of disposition, there were united in Abraham the most conspicuous courage and decision.

his brother. *i.e.* his kinsman, as in XIII, 8.

he led forth. 'He emptied'; it therefore signifies that he called upon every one of his dependents to aid him in the attempt to rescue Lot.

born in his house. *i.e.* slaves reared in the Patriarch's home; and, therefore, feeling a greater attachment to their master.

Dan. The name is given to the place by anticipation. Formerly it was called Leshem (Josh. XIX 47) or Laish (Judg. XVIII, 29). It is in the extreme North of Palestine.

15. *divided himself.* He formed his men into several bodies which attacked the enemy in the dark from different directions. The suddenness of the onslaught, and the assault in several places simultaneously, would enable small bands of men to throw a far larger force into panic. The same strategy was used by Gideon (Judg. VII, 16 f).

Hobah. 50 miles N. of Damascus.

Damascus. An important political and commercial city from the earliest times; mentioned in Egyptian inscriptions of the sixteenth century B.C.E.

16. *all the goods.* As the captor, Abram could have taken undisputed possession of the spoils. The manner of their disposal affords fresh illustration of his magnanimous nature.

17. *the king of Sodom.* See on *v.* 10.

from the slaughter of. Better, *'from the smiting of.'* The Heb. only signifies the defeat of the enemy.

King's Vale. Mentioned in II Sam. XVIII, 18, in connection with Absalom.

18–20. ABRAM AND MELCHIZEDEK

18. This name (which may mean 'My King is righteousness') is mentioned elsewhere in the Bible only in Psalm CX, 4, 'Thou art a priest for ever after the manner of Melchizedek,' the reference being to the offices of king and priest combined in one man. In the light of recent excavations, every reasonable doubt as to the authenticity of the account of Melchizedek is removed. Among the Tell-el-Amarna tablets are letters to the Egyptian government, written in the fifteenth pre-Christian century by the vassal king of Jerusalem, or 'Urusalim'. Like Melchizedek, he was a priest-king. For the name, cf. 'Adonizedek, king of Jerusalem' (Josh. x, 1). (As repeated reference is made to the Tell-el-Amarna tablets or letters, a few words must be said of this most remarkable archæological find. The last Pharaoh of the powerful and mighty 18th Dynasty was Amenophis IV or Ikhnaten, the so-called Heretic King, who undertook to replace the Egyptian religion by a monotheism in which the sun was to be worshipped as the sole god. He moved his capital from Thebes to the modern Tell-el-Amarna in Middle Egypt. His reformation was a failure; he died *circa* 1350 B.C.E. amidst the curses of his subjects. The capital returned to Thebes, and the place where he dwelt was abandoned because it was regarded as haunted by evil demons. And as a result of this belief, the complete royal archives, his own and his father's diplomatic correspondence, were preserved in the ruins of Tell-el-Amarna, where they were found 3,200 years later in 1887).

wine; and he was priest of God the Most
High. 19. And he blessed him, and said:
'Blessed be Abram of God Most High,
Maker of heaven and earth; 20. and blessed
be God the Most High, who hath delivered
thine enemies into thy hand.' And he gave
him a tenth of all.* ה׳ 21. And the king of
Sodom said unto Abram: 'Give me the
persons, and take the goods to thyself.'
22. And Abram said to the king of Sodom:
'I have lifted up my hand unto the LORD,
God Most High, Maker of heaven and
earth, 23. that I will not take a thread
nor a shoe-latchet nor aught that is thine,
lest thou shouldest say: I have made Abram
rich; 24. save only that which the young
men have eaten, and the portion of the
men which went with me, Aner, Eshcol,
and Mamre, let them take their portion.'

ב וַיֹּאמַר בָּרוּךְ אַבְרָם לְאֵל עֶלְיוֹן קֹנֵה שָׁמַיִם וָאָרֶץ׃ וּבָרוּךְ
חמישי אֵל עֶלְיוֹן אֲשֶׁר־מִגֵּן צָרֶיךָ בְּיָדֶךָ וַיִּתֶּן־לוֹ מַעֲשֵׂר מִכֹּל׃
21 וַיֹּאמֶר מֶלֶךְ־סְדֹם אֶל־אַבְרָם תֶּן־לִי הַנֶּפֶשׁ וְהָרְכֻשׁ קַח־לָךְ׃
22 וַיֹּאמֶר אַבְרָם אֶל־מֶלֶךְ סְדֹם הֲרִמֹתִי יָדִי אֶל־יְהוָה אֵל
23 עֶלְיוֹן קֹנֵה שָׁמַיִם וָאָרֶץ׃ אִם־מִחוּט וְעַד שְׂרוֹךְ־נַעַל וְאִם־
אֶקַּח מִכָּל־אֲשֶׁר־לָךְ וְלֹא תֹאמַר אֲנִי הֶעֱשַׁרְתִּי אֶת־אַבְרָם׃
24 בִּלְעָדַי רַק אֲשֶׁר אָכְלוּ הַנְּעָרִים וְחֵלֶק הָאֲנָשִׁים אֲשֶׁר הָלְכוּ
אִתִּי עָנֵר אֶשְׁכֹּל וּמַמְרֵא הֵם יִקְחוּ חֶלְקָם׃ ס

15 טו

CHAPTER XV

1. After these things the word of the LORD
came unto Abram in a vision, saying:
'Fear not, Abram, I am thy shield, thy
reward shall be exceeding great.' 2. And
Abram said: 'O Lord GOD, what wilt Thou
give me, seeing I go hence childless, and

CAP. XV. טו

א אַחַר ׀ הַדְּבָרִים הָאֵלֶּה הָיָה דְבַר־יְהוָה אֶל־אַבְרָם בַּמַּחֲזֶה
לֵאמֹר אַל־תִּירָא אַבְרָם אָנֹכִי מָגֵן לָךְ שְׂכָרְךָ הַרְבֵּה
2 מְאֹד׃ וַיֹּאמֶר אַבְרָם אֲדֹנָי יֱהוִה מַה־תִּתֶּן־לִי וְאָנֹכִי

Salem. An earlier, or poetic, designation for Jerusalem.

bread and wine. A token of friendship and hospitality.

God the Most High. Heb. *El Elyon.* The phrase occurs again in Scripture only in Psalm LXXVIII, 35, but the Ras Shamra tablets show that it was quite a familiar appellation of Deity in pre-Mosaic Canaan. Melchizedek was evidently a convert of Abraham's. A Talmudic tradition makes Melchizedek the head of a school for the propagation of the knowledge of God.

maker. lit. 'possessor'. The word combines the ideas of making, creating, and owning. The phrase, 'Maker of heaven and earth,' has been embodied in the Liturgy.

19. *and he blessed him.* In his capacity as priest, Melchizedek invokes the Divine blessing upon Abram for his chivalrous action.

20. *and he gave him a tenth.* Abram acknowledges Melchizedek as priest of the Most High, and gives him tithe of the spoil as a thanksgiving offering.

21. *give me the persons.* As the victor, Abram had the right to dispose of the people he had rescued, in any manner he desired. He could have retained them as his slaves, sold them into bondage, or demanded a ransom. But he spurns the doctrine, To the victor belong the spoils.

22. *I have lifted up my hand unto the LORD.* Malbim explains that the purpose of this act was to declare that 'the victory is His, and the spoil therefore does not belong to me, . . . and *it* (my hand) shall not say: I have made Abraham rich'; cf. Deut. VIII, 17, 'and thou say in thy heart, my power and the might of my hand had gotten me this wealth.'

23. *nor a shoe-latchet.* His fine sense of independence would not permit him to benefit in the slightest degree by the rescue of his kinsmen.

24. He felt, however, that he had no right to penalize those who had shared the dangers of the campaign with him. His followers should receive their rations, and an equitable share of the spoil should go to his confederates.

CHAPTER XV. PROMISE OF AN HEIR TO ABRAM

1. *after these things.* This phrase commonly joins a new chapter with the preceding. It does not necessarily imply an immediate sequence.

in a vision. A frequent medium through which God communicated with man. Nachmanides points out that the vision happened during the day time.

fear not. The possibility of reprisals, because of his intervention in the war. Or, it may refer to the Patriarch's anxiety with regard to his childlessness.

thy shield. A symbol of defence and protection, often used in the Psalms.

thy reward. For obedience to God's call and for uprightness of life.

2. *what wilt Thou give me?* This agonizing cry

he that shall be possessor of my house is Eliezer of Damascus?' 3. And Abram said: 'Behold, to me Thou hast given no seed, and, lo, one born in my house is to be mine heir.' 4. And, behold, the word of the LORD came unto him, saying: 'This man shall not be thine heir; but he that shall come forth out of thine own bowels shall be thine heir.' 5. And He brought him forth abroad, and said: 'Look now toward heaven, and count the stars, if thou be able to count them'; and He said unto him: 'So shall thy seed be.' 6. And he believed in the LORD; and He counted it to him for righteousness.* vi. 7. And He said unto him: 'I am the LORD that brought thee out of Ur of the Chaldees, to give thee this land to inherit it.' 8. And he said: 'O Lord GOD, whereby shall I know that I shall inherit it?' 9. And He said unto him: 'Take Me a heifer of three years old, and a she-goat of three years old, and a ram of three years old, and a turtle-dove, and a young pigeon.' 10. And he took

3 הוֹלֵךְ עֲרִירִי וּבֶן־מֶשֶׁק בֵּיתִי הוּא דַּמֶּשֶׂק אֱלִיעֶזֶר׃ וַיֹּאמֶר
אַבְרָם הֵן לִי לֹא נָתַתָּה זָרַע וְהִנֵּה בֶן־בֵּיתִי יוֹרֵשׁ אֹתִי׃
4 וְהִנֵּה דְבַר־יְהוָה אֵלָיו לֵאמֹר לֹא יִירָשְׁךָ זֶה כִּי־אִם אֲשֶׁר
ה יֵצֵא מִמֵּעֶיךָ הוּא יִירָשֶׁךָ׃ וַיּוֹצֵא אֹתוֹ הַחוּצָה וַיֹּאמֶר
הַבֶּט־נָא הַשָּׁמַיְמָה וּסְפֹר הַכּוֹכָבִים אִם־תּוּכַל לִסְפֹּר
6 אֹתָם וַיֹּאמֶר לוֹ כֹּה יִהְיֶה זַרְעֶךָ׃ וְהֶאֱמִן בַּיהוָה וַיַּחְשְׁבֶהָ
ששי
7 לּוֹ צְדָקָה׃* וַיֹּאמֶר אֵלָיו אֲנִי יְהוָה אֲשֶׁר הוֹצֵאתִיךָ מֵאוּר
8 כַּשְׂדִּים לָתֶת לְךָ אֶת־הָאָרֶץ הַזֹּאת לְרִשְׁתָּהּ׃ וַיֹּאמַר
9 אֲדֹנָי יֱהוִה בַּמָּה אֵדַע כִּי אִירָשֶׁנָּה׃ וַיֹּאמֶר אֵלָיו קְחָה
לִי עֶגְלָה מְשֻׁלֶּשֶׁת וְעֵז מְשֻׁלֶּשֶׁת וְאַיִל מְשֻׁלָּשׁ וְתֹר וְגוֹזָל׃
י וַיִּקַּח־לוֹ אֶת־כָּל־אֵלֶּה וַיְבַתֵּר אֹתָם בַּתָּוֶךְ וַיִּתֵּן אִישׁ־בִּתְרוֹ

enables us to look into the soul of the Patriarch. Of what value were earthly possessions to him if a worthy child who would continue his work after him was denied him? This attitude of the Father of the Jewish people towards the child, that it is the highest of human treasures, has remained that of his descendants to the present day. Among the most enlightened nations of antiquity, the child had no rights, no protection, no dignity of any sort. In Greece, for example, weak children were generally *exposed* on a lonely mountain to perish. The Roman historian (Tacitus) deemed it a contemptible prejudice of the Jews that 'it is a crime among them to kill any child!' The Rabbis, on the other hand, spoke of little children as 'the Messiahs of mankind', *i.e.* the child is the perennial regenerative force in humanity, because, in the child, God continually gives mankind a chance to make good its mistakes.

of Damascus. Chap. XXIV shows the important position which he occupied in Abram's household. But, if he was to be Abram's heir, what of the great mission that was the motive of Abram's call from Ur of the Chaldees? The incident which follows allays these anxieties.

3. *one born in my house. i.e.* my servant. It is noteworthy that Abram does not think of Lot as his possible heir; *he* had returned to Sodom.

5. Since the words which follow, 'Look now toward heaven, etc.,' are part of the vision, we are not to suppose that Abram was actually led into the open. He imagined himself as gazing up at the stars.

6. *believed. i.e.* trusted. The childless Abram had faith in God's promise that his descendants would be countless like the stars of heaven. He was ready to wait God's time, without doubting God's truth. That is the mark of true faith—*steadfast trust* in God, despite darkness and disappointment, and despite the fact that circumstances all point in the opposite direction. True faith 'discovers through the mists of the present the sunshine of the future; and recognizes in the discordant strife of the world the traces of the Eternal Mind that leads it to an unceasing harmony' (Kalisch).

and He counted it to him for righteousness. 'Counted his trust as real religion' (Moffatt). Trustful surrender to the loving Will and Wisdom of God is the proof, as it is the basis, of true religion. Such spiritual faithfulness is a great spiritual virtue, and cannot be found where there is unrighteousness.

8. *whereby shall I know?* He does not doubt God, but desires confirmation of the vision that had been granted him.

9. *three years old.* Possibly because the number three has a sacred signification.

10. *and he took him.* 'Him' means, to himself.

and divided them in the midst. The ancient method of making a covenant was to cut an animal in half, and the contracting parties to pass through the portions of the slain animal. Thereby the parties were thought to be united by the bond of a common blood.

but the birds divided he not. Cf. Lev. I, 17.

him all these, and divided them in the midst, and laid each half over against the other; but the birds divided he not. 11. And the birds of prey came down upon the carcasses, and Abram drove them away. 12. And it came to pass, that, when the sun was going down, a deep sleep fell upon Abram, and, lo, a dread, even a great darkness, fell upon him. 13. And He said unto Abram: 'Know of a surety that thy seed shall be a stranger in a land that is not theirs, and shall serve them; and they shall afflict them four hundred years; 14. and also that nation, whom they shall serve, will I judge; and afterward shall they come out with great substance. 15. But thou shalt go to thy fathers in peace; thou shalt be buried in a good old age. 16. And in the fourth generation they shall come back hither; for the iniquity of the Amorite is not yet full.' 17. And it came to pass, that, when the sun went down, and there was thick darkness, behold a smoking furnace, and a flaming torch that passed between these pieces. 18. In that day the LORD made a covenant with Abram,

11 לִקְרַאת רֵעֵהוּ וְאֶת־הַצִּפֹּר לֹא בָתָר׃ וַיֵּרֶד הָעַיִט עַל־
12 הַפְּגָרִים וַיַּשֵּׁב אֹתָם אַבְרָם׃ וַיְהִי הַשֶּׁמֶשׁ לָבוֹא וְתַרְדֵּמָה
נָפְלָה עַל־אַבְרָם וְהִנֵּה אֵימָה חֲשֵׁכָה גְדֹלָה נֹפֶלֶת עָלָיו׃
13 וַיֹּאמֶר לְאַבְרָם יָדֹעַ תֵּדַע כִּי־גֵר ׀ יִהְיֶה זַרְעֲךָ בְּאֶרֶץ לֹא
14 לָהֶם וַעֲבָדוּם וְעִנּוּ אֹתָם אַרְבַּע מֵאוֹת שָׁנָה׃ וְגַם אֶת־
הַגּוֹי אֲשֶׁר יַעֲבֹדוּ דָּן אָנֹכִי וְאַחֲרֵי־כֵן יֵצְאוּ בִּרְכֻשׁ גָּדוֹל׃
טו וְאַתָּה תָּבוֹא אֶל־אֲבֹתֶיךָ בְּשָׁלוֹם תִּקָּבֵר בְּשֵׂיבָה טוֹבָה׃
16 וְדוֹר רְבִיעִי יָשׁוּבוּ הֵנָּה כִּי לֹא־שָׁלֵם עֲוֹן הָאֱמֹרִי עַד־
17 הֵנָּה׃ וַיְהִי הַשֶּׁמֶשׁ בָּאָה וַעֲלָטָה הָיָה וְהִנֵּה תַנּוּר עָשָׁן
18 וְלַפִּיד אֵשׁ אֲשֶׁר עָבַר בֵּין הַגְּזָרִים הָאֵלֶּה׃ בַּיּוֹם הַהוּא
כָּרַת יְהוָה אֶת־אַבְרָם בְּרִית לֵאמֹר לְזַרְעֲךָ נָתַתִּי אֶת־
הָאָרֶץ הַזֹּאת מִנְּהַר מִצְרַיִם עַד־הַנָּהָר הַגָּדֹל נְהַר־פְּרָת׃

11. *and the birds of prey came down.* Symbolically foreshadowing the obstacles in the way of the taking possession of the land.

Abram drove them away. The attempts to frustrate God's design would not succeed.

12. *a deep sleep.* The same word is used of Adam in II, 21.

a dread, even a great darkness. The nation which was to issue from him would have to pass through bitter times of oppression.

13. *a stranger.* Better, '*a sojourner.*' The word means a temporary resident. The reference is, of course, to the stay of the Israelites in Egypt.

four hundred years. A round number; Exod. XII, 40, gives the more precise number, 430 years.

14. *with great substance.* Referring to the gifts of the Egyptians, Exod. XII, 35 f.

15. *shalt go to thy fathers.* 'The death of Abram is predicted in one of those remarkable phrases which seem to prove that the Hebrews were not unacquainted with the doctrine of immortality. Here the return of the soul to the eternal abodes of the fathers is, with some distinctness, separated from the interment of the body. That both cannot be identical is evident; for while Abraham was entombed in Canaan, all his forefathers died and were buried in Mesopotamia' (Kalisch).

in peace. Thou wilt not witness any of the tribulations that will befall thy children (Kimchi).

16. *and in the fourth generation.* 'The Arabic *dahr* (corresponding to the Hebrew דור) is also used for a hundred years and over' (Burckhardt); thus, the 400 years mentioned in *v.* 13 are referred to here as four generations. Or, these four generations are not to be computed from the time of the vision of Abram, but from the time when his posterity first came into Egypt (Rashi).

the iniquity of the Amorite. 'Amorite' denotes the inhabitants of Canaan generally. Some of their abominations are enumerated in Leviticus XVIII, 21-30. The postponement of the penalty indicates Divine forbearance. God would give the Canaanites full time to repent. Hence he sent Abraham who 'proclaimed the Lord', and, with his disciples and descendants, taught by precept and example 'the way of the Lord to do justice and mercy'. Meanwhile, the gradually accumulating guilt of the Amorites rendered dire punishment inevitable. God's prescience was certain that their hearts were forever turned from Him.

17. *a smoking furnace, and a flaming torch.* This symbol of the Godhead was seen to pass between the pieces, to ratify the covenant which was being made.

18. *have I given.* The perfect tense is used, although it refers to the future, in order to denote the certainty of the event.

river of Egypt. 'Brook of Egypt' (Num. XXXIV, 5), the Wady-el-Arish, which is the boundary between Egypt and Palestine.

Euphrates. The ideal limit of Israelite territory, reached in the days of Solomon (I Kings V, 1).

saying: 'Unto thy seed have I given this land, from the river of Egypt unto the great river, the river Euphrates; 19. the Kenite, and the Kenizzite, and the Kadmonite, 20. and the Hittite, and the Perizzite, and the Rephaim, 21. and the Amorite, and the Canaanite, and the Girgashite, and the Jebusite.'

16

Chapter XVI

1. Now Sarai Abram's wife bore him no children; and she had a handmaid, an Egyptian, whose name was Hagar. 2. And Sarai said unto Abram: 'Behold now, the Lord hath restrained me from bearing; go in, I pray thee, unto my handmaid; it may be that I shall be builded up through her.' And Abram hearkened to the voice of Sarai. 3. And Sarai Abram's wife took Hagar the Egyptian, her handmaid, after Abram had dwelt ten years in the land of Canaan, and gave her to Abram her husband to be his wife. 4. And he went in unto Hagar, and she conceived; and when she saw that she had conceived, her mistress was despised in her eyes. 5. And Sarai said unto Abram: 'My wrong be upon thee: I gave my handmaid into thy bosom; and when she saw that she had conceived, I was despised in her eyes: the Lord judge between me and thee.' 6. But Abram said unto Sarai: 'Behold, thy maid is in thy hand; do to her that which is good in thine eyes.' And Sarai dealt harshly with her, and she fled from her face. 7. And the angel of the Lord found her by a fountain of water

19 אֶת־הַקֵּינִי וְאֶת־הַקְּנִזִּי וְאֵת הַקַּדְמֹנִי׃ וְאֶת־הַחִתִּי וְאֶת־
כ
21 הַפְּרִזִּי וְאֶת־הָרְפָאִים׃ וְאֶת־הָאֱמֹרִי וְאֶת־הַכְּנַעֲנִי וְאֶת־
הַגִּרְגָּשִׁי וְאֶת־הַיְבוּסִי׃ ס

Cap. XVI. טז

טז

א וְשָׂרַי אֵשֶׁת אַבְרָם לֹא יָלְדָה לוֹ וְלָהּ שִׁפְחָה מִצְרִית
2 וּשְׁמָהּ הָגָר׃ וַתֹּאמֶר שָׂרַי אֶל־אַבְרָם הִנֵּה־נָא עֲצָרַנִי
יְהוָה מִלֶּדֶת בֹּא־נָא אֶל־שִׁפְחָתִי אוּלַי אִבָּנֶה מִמֶּנָּה
3 וַיִּשְׁמַע אַבְרָם לְקוֹל שָׂרָי׃ וַתִּקַּח שָׂרַי אֵשֶׁת־אַבְרָם
אֶת־הָגָר הַמִּצְרִית שִׁפְחָתָהּ מִקֵּץ עֶשֶׂר שָׁנִים לְשֶׁבֶת
אַבְרָם בְּאֶרֶץ כְּנָעַן וַתִּתֵּן אֹתָהּ לְאַבְרָם אִישָׁהּ לוֹ לְאִשָּׁה׃
4 וַיָּבֹא אֶל־הָגָר וַתַּהַר וַתֵּרֶא כִּי הָרָתָה וַתֵּקַל גְּבִרְתָּהּ
ה בְּעֵינֶיהָ׃ וַתֹּאמֶר שָׂרַי אֶל־אַבְרָם חֲמָסִי עָלֶיךָ אָנֹכִי נָתַתִּי
שִׁפְחָתִי בְּחֵיקֶךָ וַתֵּרֶא כִּי הָרָתָה וָאֵקַל בְּעֵינֶיהָ יִשְׁפֹּט
6 יְהוָה בֵּינִי וּבֵינֶיךָ׃ וַיֹּאמֶר אַבְרָם אֶל־שָׂרַי הִנֵּה שִׁפְחָתֵךְ
בְּיָדֵךְ עֲשִׂי־לָהּ הַטּוֹב בְּעֵינָיִךְ וַתְּעַנֶּהָ שָׂרַי וַתִּבְרַח מִפָּנֶיהָ׃
7 וַיִּמְצָאָהּ מַלְאַךְ יְהוָה עַל־עֵין הַמַּיִם בַּמִּדְבָּר עַל־הָעַיִן

טז׳ v. 5. נקוד על י׳ בתרא

19. *Kenite, and the Kenizzite.* Friendly tribes inhabiting the S. of Palestine, which merged with the Israelites.

Kadmonite. Not mentioned elsewhere.

20. *Perizzite.* See on xiii, 7.

Rephaim. See on xiv, 5.

21. For the peoples enumerated in this verse, see on x, 16.

Chapter XVI. Hagar and Ishmael

1. *no children.* In the ancient Orient, childlessness was a calamity and a disgrace to a woman.

an Egyptian. Sarai probably acquired her during the stay in Egypt described in Chap. xii. Such female slaves remained the property of the wife solely.

2. *the LORD hath restrained me.* In Scripture the hand of God is traced in every occurrence of life. Even what we should call 'natural phenomena' are ascribed to Divine agency.

unto my handmaid. It was the legalized custom in Babylon, the home-land of Abram and Sarai, that if a man's wife was childless, he was allowed to take a concubine, but he was not to place her upon an equal footing with his first wife.

be builded up through her. By the adoption of Hagar's children as her own. The literal translation of the phrase is, 'be builded by her.' The family was pictured by the Hebrews under the image of a house; and the Rabbis speak of the wife as the husband's 'house'.

4. *her mistress was despised in her eyes.* Hagar, who was still a slave, behaved in a disrespectful and ungrateful manner towards her mistress.

5. *my wrong be upon thee. i.e.* thine is the responsibility for the wrong done to me by Hagar. Sarai's reproach is that he did not check Hagar's haughtiness towards her.

6. *in thy hand.* In thy power. From his knowledge of Sarai, he thought she would aim merely to bring Hagar back to proper behaviour.

harshly. Sarai probably imposed heavy tasks upon her. 'Sarah our Mother acted sinfully in thus ill-treating Hagar, and also Abram in permitting it; therefore, God heard her affliction and gave her a son who became the ancestor of a ferocious race that was destined to deal harshly with the descendants of Abram and Sarai' (Nachmanides). Some modern commentators, however, admit that 'few women would have borne the insolence of Hagar'.

in the wilderness, by the fountain in the way to Shur. 8. And he said: 'Hagar, Sarai's handmaid, whence camest thou? and whither goest thou?' And she said: 'I flee from the face of my mistress Sarai.' 9. And the angel of the LORD said unto her: 'Return to thy mistress, and submit thyself under her hands.' 10. And the angel of the LORD said unto her: 'I will greatly multiply thy seed, that it shall not be numbered for multitude.' 11. And the angel of the LORD said unto her: 'Behold, thou art with child, and shalt bear a son; and thou shalt call his name [1]Ishmael, because the LORD hath heard thy affliction. 12. And he shall be a wild ass of a man: his hand shall be against every man, and every man's hand against him; and he shall dwell in the face of all his brethren.' 13. And she called the name of the LORD that spoke unto her, Thou art [2]a God of seeing; for she said: 'Have I even here seen Him that seeth me?' 14. Wherefore the well was called [3]Beer-lahai-roi; behold, it is between Kadesh and Bered. 15. And Hagar bore Abram a son; and Abram called the name of his son, whom Hagar bore, Ishmael. 16. And Abram was fourscore and six years old, when Hagar bore Ishmael to Abram.

8 בְּדֶרֶךְ שׁוּר׃ וַיֹּאמַר הָגָר שִׁפְחַת שָׂרַי אֵי־מִזֶּה בָאת וְאָנָה
9 תֵלֵכִי וַתֹּאמֶר מִפְּנֵי שָׂרַי גְּבִרְתִּי אָנֹכִי בֹּרַחַת׃ וַיֹּאמֶר
לָהּ מַלְאַךְ יְהוָה שׁוּבִי אֶל־גְּבִרְתֵּךְ וְהִתְעַנִּי תַּחַת יָדֶיהָ׃
י וַיֹּאמֶר לָהּ מַלְאַךְ יְהוָה הַרְבָּה אַרְבֶּה אֶת־זַרְעֵךְ וְלֹא
11 יִסָּפֵר מֵרֹב׃ וַיֹּאמֶר לָהּ מַלְאַךְ יְהוָה הִנָּךְ הָרָה וְיֹלַדְתְּ
בֵּן וְקָרָאת שְׁמוֹ יִשְׁמָעֵאל כִּי־שָׁמַע יְהוָה אֶל־עָנְיֵךְ׃
12 וְהוּא יִהְיֶה פֶּרֶא אָדָם יָדוֹ בַכֹּל וְיַד כֹּל בּוֹ וְעַל־פְּנֵי כָל־
13 אֶחָיו יִשְׁכֹּן׃ וַתִּקְרָא שֵׁם־יְהוָה הַדֹּבֵר אֵלֶיהָ אַתָּה אֵל
14 רֳאִי כִּי אָמְרָה הֲגַם הֲלֹם רָאִיתִי אַחֲרֵי רֹאִי׃ עַל־כֵּן קָרָא
טו לַבְּאֵר בְּאֵר לַחַי רֹאִי הִנֵּה בֵין־קָדֵשׁ וּבֵין בָּרֶד׃ וַתֵּלֶד
הָגָר לְאַבְרָם בֵּן וַיִּקְרָא אַבְרָם שֶׁם־בְּנוֹ אֲשֶׁר־יָלְדָה הָגָר
16 יִשְׁמָעֵאל׃ וְאַבְרָם בֶּן־שְׁמֹנִים שָׁנָה וְשֵׁשׁ שָׁנִים בְּלֶדֶת־
הָגָר אֶת־יִשְׁמָעֵאל לְאַבְרָם׃ ס

17

CHAPTER XVII

1. And when Abram was ninety years old and nine, the LORD appeared to Abram,

CAP. XVII. יז

יז

א וַיְהִי אַבְרָם בֶּן־תִּשְׁעִים שָׁנָה וְתֵשַׁע שָׁנִים וַיֵּרָא יְהוָה

[1] That is, *God heareth.* [2] Heb. *El roi.* [3] That is, *The well of the Living One who seeth me.*

טז' v. 8. פתח בס"פ

7. *the angel of the LORD found her.* 'The narrative, like XXI, 16–19, illustrates beautifully the Divine regard for the forlorn and desolate soul' (Driver). This is the first time that an 'angel' is mentioned in the Bible. The Hebrew word, like the English 'angel', originally means 'messenger', and is applied to any agent or missioner of God. The phrase 'angel of the Lord', however, is sometimes used to denote God Himself.

Shur. lit. 'the wall', or fortification which protected Egypt on the East from the incursion of raiding Bedouins. Hagar, in her flight through the wilderness, wanders in the direction of her native land.

8. *Hagar, Sarai's handmaid.* Reminding Hagar of the duty she owed her mistress.

whence camest thou? A leading question, not seeking for information, but giving Hagar an opportunity of unburdening her heart.

11. *affliction.* The use of this word clearly indicates the Divine disapproval of Sarah's treatment of Hagar. In ancient Israel, the servant is quite other from the 'helot' in Greece, or the 'slave' in Rome. Underlying the Hagar narrative is the assumption that fair and friendly treatment should be shown even to an alien bondwoman; cf. the position of Eliezer in Abraham's household.

12. *a wild ass of a man.* A vivid description of 'the sons of the desert, owning no authority save that of their own chief, reckless of life, treacherous towards strangers, ever ready for war or pillage' (Driver).

13. *a God of seeing. i.e.* a God who deigns to take notice of the plight of His creatures, and sends them succour in the hour of their need.

even here. In the desert, a 'God-forsaken place'!

15. *and Abram called.* On Hagar's return to her mistress, Abram learned all that had occurred; and he accordingly gave the child the name ordained for him.

CHAPTER XVII. THE COVENANT OF ABRAHAM

1. *I am God Almighty.* Heb. *El Shaddai*; cf. Exod. VI, 3, 'and I appeared unto Abraham, unto Isaac, and unto Jacob, as God Almighty.' The derivation of the Divine Name, *Shaddai*, is

and said unto him: 'I am God Almighty; walk before Me, and be thou whole-hearted. 2. And I will make My covenant between Me and thee, and will multiply thee exceedingly.' 3. And Abram fell on his face; and God talked with him, saying: 4. 'As for Me, behold, My covenant is with thee, and thou shalt be [1]the father of a multitude of nations. 5. Neither shall thy name any more be called Abram, but thy name shall be Abraham; for the father of a multitude of nations have I made thee. 6. And I will make thee exceeding fruitful, and I will make nations of thee, and kings shall come out of thee.* vii. 7. And I will establish My covenant between Me and thee and thy seed after thee throughout their generations for an everlasting covenant, to be a God unto thee and to thy seed after thee. 8. And I will give unto thee, and to thy seed after thee, the land of thy sojournings, all the land of Canaan, for an everlasting possession; and I will be their God.' 9. And God said unto Abraham: 'And as for thee, thou shalt keep My covenant, thou, and thy seed after thee throughout their generations. 10. This is

אֶל־אַבְרָם וַיֹּאמֶר אֵלָיו אֲנִי־אֵל שַׁדַּי הִתְהַלֵּךְ לְפָנַי וֶהְיֵה
2 תָמִים׃ וְאֶתְּנָה בְרִיתִי בֵּינִי וּבֵינֶךָ וְאַרְבֶּה אוֹתְךָ בִּמְאֹד
3 מְאֹד׃ וַיִּפֹּל אַבְרָם עַל־פָּנָיו וַיְדַבֵּר אִתּוֹ אֱלֹהִים לֵאמֹר׃
4 ה אֲנִי הִנֵּה בְרִיתִי אִתָּךְ וְהָיִיתָ לְאַב הֲמוֹן גּוֹיִם׃ וְלֹא־יִקָּרֵא
עוֹד אֶת־שִׁמְךָ אַבְרָם וְהָיָה שִׁמְךָ אַבְרָהָם כִּי אַב־הֲמוֹן
6 גּוֹיִם נְתַתִּיךָ׃ וְהִפְרֵתִי אֹתְךָ בִּמְאֹד מְאֹד וּנְתַתִּיךָ לְגוֹיִם
שביעי
7 וּמְלָכִים מִמְּךָ יֵצֵאוּ׃* וַהֲקִמֹתִי אֶת־בְּרִיתִי בֵּינִי וּבֵינֶךָ
וּבֵין זַרְעֲךָ אַחֲרֶיךָ לְדֹרֹתָם לִבְרִית עוֹלָם לִהְיוֹת לְךָ
8 לֵאלֹהִים וּלְזַרְעֲךָ אַחֲרֶיךָ׃ וְנָתַתִּי לְךָ וּלְזַרְעֲךָ אַחֲרֶיךָ
אֵת ׀ אֶרֶץ מְגֻרֶיךָ אֵת כָּל־אֶרֶץ כְּנַעַן לַאֲחֻזַּת עוֹלָם וְהָיִיתִי
9 לָהֶם לֵאלֹהִים׃ וַיֹּאמֶר אֱלֹהִים אֶל־אַבְרָהָם וְאַתָּה אֶת־
י בְּרִיתִי תִשְׁמֹר אַתָּה וְזַרְעֲךָ אַחֲרֶיךָ לְדֹרֹתָם׃ זֹאת בְּרִיתִי

[1] Heb. *Ab hamon.*

uncertain. The usual translation, 'Almighty,' is due to the Vulgate (the Latin version of the Bible). The realization of Abram's hopes must often have appeared dim and distant to him. Here he is reassured: nothing is impossible to God Almighty. *Shaddai* has also been derived from a root 'to heap benefits'; and it would then mean 'Dispenser of benefits', the Friend who shepherds the Patriarchs and preserves them from all harm; see on Numbers I, 4.

whole-hearted. i.e. place implicit and undivided confidence in God alone. The Rabbis connect this exhortation with the Covenant of Circumcision, which was about to be instituted, and thus indicate the moral ideal which underlies the ritual act.

make My covenant. lit. 'I will give (*i.e.* grant) My covenant.' What follows is not a compact between God and the Patriarch, but a statement of the plans which He had designed for Abram and his descendants.

3. *and Abram fell on his face.* The Oriental mode of expressing gratitude.

4. *as for Me.* Introducing God's part of the covenant, as contrasted with 'And as for thee' in *v.* 9.

a multitude of nations. The Israelites; the Arabs, descended from Ishmael; and the tribes enumerated in XXV, 1 f.

5. *Abraham . . . multitude of nations. Ab* means 'father'; and *raham,* the second half of the new name, is an Arabic word for 'multitude'. The change of name emphasizes the mission of Abraham, which is 'To bring all the peoples under the wings of the Shechinah'.

8. *the land of thy sojournings.* The land in which Abraham dwelt only as 'a sojourner'.

10. *this is My covenant which ye shall keep.* The meaning is not that the Covenant is to consist in the rite of circumcision, but that circumcision is to be the external sign of the Covenant. As the following verse declares, 'it shall be a token of a covenant,' just as the rainbow was the token of the covenant with Noah. And even as the rainbow had existed before Noah, this rite had been practised among other peoples before Israel. To whatever origin and purpose it might be traced—whether as a measure safeguarding cleanliness and health (Philo), or to counteract excessive lust (Maimonides), or as a sacrificial symbol—for Abraham and his descendants all these conceptions are supplanted, and the rite is the abiding symbol of the consecration of the Children of Abraham to the God of Abraham. It is the *rite of the covenant;* and unbounded has been the loyalty and devotion with which this vital and fundamental institution of the Jewish Faith has been and is being observed. Jewish men and women have in all ages been ready to lay down their lives in its defence. The Maccabean martyrs died for it. The officers of King Antiochus put to death the mothers who initiated their children into the Covenant—'and they hanged their babes about their necks' (I Maccabees I, 61). The same readiness for self-immolation in defence of this sacred rite

My covenant, which ye shall keep, between Me and you and thy seed after thee: every male among you shall be circumcised. 11. And ye shall be circumcised in the flesh of your foreskin; and it shall be a token of a covenant betwixt Me and you. 12. And he that is eight days old shall be circumcised among you, every male throughout your generations, he that is born in the house, or bought with money of any foreigner, that is not of thy seed. 13. He that is born in thy house, and he that is bought with thy money, must needs be circumcised; and My covenant shall be in your flesh for an everlasting covenant. 14. And the uncircumcised male who is not circumcised in the flesh of his foreskin, that soul shall be cut off from his people; he hath broken My covenant.' ¶ 15. And God said unto Abraham: 'As for Sarai thy wife, thou shalt not call her name Sarai, but [1]Sarah shall her name be. 16. And I will bless her, and moreover I will give thee a son of her; yea, I will bless her, and she shall be a mother of nations; kings of peoples shall be of her.' 17. Then Abraham fell upon his face, and laughed, and said in his heart: 'Shall a child be born unto him that is a hundred years old? and shall Sarah, that is ninety years old, bear?' 18. And Abraham said unto God: 'Oh that Ishmael might live before Thee!' 19. And God said: 'Nay, but Sarah thy wife shall bear thee a son; and thou shalt call his name [2]Isaac; and I will establish My covenant with him for an everlasting covenant for his seed after him. 20. And as for Ishmael, I have heard thee; behold, I have blessed him, and will make him fruitful, and will multiply him exceedingly; twelve princes shall he beget, and I will make him a great nation. 21. But My covenant will I establish with Isaac, whom

אֲשֶׁר תִּשְׁמְרוּ בֵּינִי וּבֵינֵיכֶם וּבֵין זַרְעֲךָ אַחֲרֶיךָ הִמּוֹל
11 לָכֶם כָּל־זָכָר׃ וּנְמַלְתֶּם אֵת בְּשַׂר עָרְלַתְכֶם וְהָיָה לְאוֹת
12 בְּרִית בֵּינִי וּבֵינֵיכֶם׃ וּבֶן־שְׁמֹנַת יָמִים יִמּוֹל לָכֶם כָּל־זָכָר
לְדֹרֹתֵיכֶם יְלִיד בָּיִת וּמִקְנַת־כֶּסֶף מִכֹּל בֶּן־נֵכָר אֲשֶׁר לֹא
13 מִזַּרְעֲךָ הוּא׃ הִמּוֹל ׀ יִמּוֹל יְלִיד בֵּיתְךָ וּמִקְנַת כַּסְפֶּךָ
14 וְהָיְתָה בְרִיתִי בִּבְשַׂרְכֶם לִבְרִית עוֹלָם׃ וְעָרֵל ׀ זָכָר אֲשֶׁר
לֹא־יִמּוֹל אֶת־בְּשַׂר עָרְלָתוֹ וְנִכְרְתָה הַנֶּפֶשׁ הַהִוא מֵעַמֶּיהָ
טו אֶת־בְּרִיתִי הֵפַר׃ ס וַיֹּאמֶר אֱלֹהִים אֶל־אַבְרָהָם שָׂרַי
16 אִשְׁתְּךָ לֹא־תִקְרָא אֶת־שְׁמָהּ שָׂרָי כִּי שָׂרָה שְׁמָהּ׃ וּבֵרַכְתִּי
אֹתָהּ וְגַם נָתַתִּי מִמֶּנָּה לְךָ בֵּן וּבֵרַכְתִּיהָ וְהָיְתָה לְגוֹיִם
17 מַלְכֵי עַמִּים מִמֶּנָּה יִהְיוּ׃ וַיִּפֹּל אַבְרָהָם עַל־פָּנָיו וַיִּצְחָק
וַיֹּאמֶר בְּלִבּוֹ הַלְּבֶן מֵאָה־שָׁנָה יִוָּלֵד וְאִם־שָׂרָה הֲבַת־
18 תִּשְׁעִים שָׁנָה תֵּלֵד׃ וַיֹּאמֶר אַבְרָהָם אֶל־הָאֱלֹהִים לוּ
19 יִשְׁמָעֵאל יִחְיֶה לְפָנֶיךָ׃ וַיֹּאמֶר אֱלֹהִים אֲבָל שָׂרָה אִשְׁתְּךָ
יֹלֶדֶת לְךָ בֵּן וְקָרָאתָ אֶת־שְׁמוֹ יִצְחָק וַהֲקִמֹתִי אֶת־בְּרִיתִי
כ אִתּוֹ לִבְרִית עוֹלָם לְזַרְעוֹ אַחֲרָיו׃ וּלְיִשְׁמָעֵאל שְׁמַעְתִּיךָ
הִנֵּה ׀ בֵּרַכְתִּי אֹתוֹ וְהִפְרֵיתִי אֹתוֹ וְהִרְבֵּיתִי אֹתוֹ בִּמְאֹד
21 מְאֹד שְׁנֵים־עָשָׂר נְשִׂיאִם יוֹלִיד וּנְתַתִּיו לְגוֹי גָּדוֹל׃ וְאֶת־
בְּרִיתִי אָקִים אֶת־יִצְחָק אֲשֶׁר תֵּלֵד לְךָ שָׂרָה לַמּוֹעֵד הַזֶּה

[1] That is, *Princess*. [2] From the Heb. root meaning *to laugh*.

v. 14. פתח בס"פ

we find in the times of the Hadrianic persecution, in the dread days of the Inquisition, yea, whenever and wherever tyrants undertook to uproot the Jewish Faith. Even an excommunicated semi-apostate like Benedict Spinoza declares: 'Such great importance do I attach to the sign of the Covenant, that I am persuaded that it is sufficient by itself to maintain the separate existence of the nation for ever.'

12. *he that is born in the house. i.e.* the child of a slave; see on XIV, 14. Slaves were regarded as part of the household.

14. *cut off from his people.* Either through punishment at the hands of God; or through expulsion from the community.

15. *Sarah.* Brings out more forcibly the meaning 'Princess' than the archaic form *Sarai.*

17. *and laughed.* The Targum renders 'and rejoiced', to imply that he laughed for joy, not from incredulity. What follows would accordingly not be a question, but an exclamation of surprise.

18. *Ishmael might live.* Abraham, despairing of the possibility of having issue by Sarah, expresses the hope that Ishmael 'might live before Thee', in order that the promises made to Abraham might be fulfilled through him. It is also possible to understand it as a prayer that, though Ishmael is excluded from the spiritual heritage, he may yet live under the Divine care and blessing.

20. *twelve princes.* They are enumerated in XXV, 13–16.

Sarah shall bear unto thee at this set time in the next year.' 22. And He left off talking with him, and God went up from Abraham. 23. And Abraham took Ishmael his son, and all that were born in his house, and all that were bought with his money, every male among the men of Abraham's house, and circumcised the flesh of their foreskin in the selfsame day, as God had said unto him.* m. 24. And Abraham was ninety years old and nine, when he was circumcised in the flesh of his foreskin. 25. And Ishmael his son was thirteen years old, when he was circumcised in the flesh of his foreskin. 26. In the selfsame day was Abraham circumcised, and Ishmael his son. 27. And all the men of his house, those born in the house, and those bought with money of a foreigner, were circumcised with him.

22 בַּשָּׁנָה הָאַחֶרֶת׃ וַיְכַל לְדַבֵּר אִתּוֹ וַיַּעַל אֱלֹהִים מֵעַל
23 אַבְרָהָם׃ וַיִּקַּח אַבְרָהָם אֶת־יִשְׁמָעֵאל בְּנוֹ וְאֵת כָּל־יְלִידֵי
בֵיתוֹ וְאֵת כָּל־מִקְנַת כַּסְפּוֹ כָּל־זָכָר בְּאַנְשֵׁי בֵּית אַבְרָהָם
וַיָּמָל אֶת־בְּשַׂר עָרְלָתָם בְּעֶצֶם הַיּוֹם הַזֶּה כַּאֲשֶׁר דִּבֶּר
מפטיר
24 אִתּוֹ אֱלֹהִים׃* וְאַבְרָהָם בֶּן־תִּשְׁעִים וָתֵשַׁע שָׁנָה בְּהִמֹּלוֹ
כה בְּשַׂר עָרְלָתוֹ׃ וְיִשְׁמָעֵאל בְּנוֹ בֶּן־שְׁלֹשׁ עֶשְׂרֵה שָׁנָה בְּהִמֹּלוֹ
26 אֵת בְּשַׂר עָרְלָתוֹ׃ בְּעֶצֶם הַיּוֹם הַזֶּה נִמּוֹל אַבְרָהָם
27 וְיִשְׁמָעֵאל בְּנוֹ׃ וְכָל־אַנְשֵׁי בֵיתוֹ יְלִיד בָּיִת וּמִקְנַת־כֶּסֶף
מֵאֵת בֶּן־נֵכָר נִמֹּלוּ אִתּוֹ׃

23. *in the selfsame day.* An indication of Abraham's readiness to perform his obligations without delay.

HAFTORAH LECH LECHA הפטרת לך לך

ISAIAH XL, 27–XLI, 16

CHAPTER XL

27. Why sayest thou, O Jacob,
And speakest, O Israel:
'My way is hid from the LORD,
And my right is passed over from my God'?
28. Hast thou not known? hast thou not heard
That the everlasting God, the LORD,
The Creator of the ends of the earth,
Fainteth not, neither is weary?
His discernment is past searching out.

CAP. XL. מ

27 לָמָּה תֹאמַר יַעֲקֹב וּתְדַבֵּר יִשְׂרָאֵל נִסְתְּרָה
28 דַרְכִּי מֵיְהוָה וּמֵאֱלֹהַי מִשְׁפָּטִי יַעֲבוֹר׃ הֲלוֹא יָדַעְתָּ אִם־
לֹא שָׁמַעְתָּ אֱלֹהֵי עוֹלָם ׀ יְהוָה בּוֹרֵא קְצוֹת הָאָרֶץ לֹא

29. He giveth power to the faint;
And to him that hath no might He increaseth strength.

ISAIAH XL, 27–XLI, 16

The Sedrah opens with the call of Abraham, and the Divine bidding, 'Be thou a blessing' unto all the families of the earth. Such likewise declares the great Prophet of Consolation is the Divine charge to the Children of Abraham. Israel, suffering in Exile, might well despair of the fulfilment of that Divine promise, nay, even of God's remembrance of that promise. The Prophet here stills such questionings. In God, Israel has the source of inexhaustible strength. The everlasting God will not fail to carry through His great purposes for mankind through Israel His servant, the child of 'Abraham, My friend'.

27. *my way is hid.* 'My lot is unnoticed by God. He passes over my right to be protected from intolerable oppression,' such is the despairing complaint of many in the Exile. Israel fears that it is forgotten by God.

28. Gives the answer of the Prophet.

everlasting God. The God of eternity.

His discernment is past searching out. He therefore must have good reason for delaying the Redemption.

29 ייעף ולא ייגע אין חקר לתבונתו׃ נתן ליעף כח ולאין
ל אונים עצמה ירבה׃ ויעפו נערים ויגעו ובחורים כשול
31 יכשלו׃ וקוי יהוה יחליפו כח יעלו אבר כנשרים ירוצו
ולא ייגעו ילכו ולא ייעפו׃

30. Even the youths shall faint and be weary,
And the young men shall utterly fall;
31. But they that wait for the LORD shall renew their strength;
They shall mount up with wings as eagles;
They shall run, and not be weary;
They shall walk, and not faint.

CAP. XLI. מא

א החרישו אלי איים ולאמים יחליפו כח יגשו אז ידברו
2 יחדו למשפט נקרבה׃ מי העיר ממזרח צדק יקראהו
לרגלו יתן לפניו גוים ומלכים ירד יתן כעפר חרבו כקש
3 נדף קשתו׃ ירדפם יעבור שלום ארח ברגליו לא יבוא׃
4 מי־פעל ועשה קרא הדרות מראש אני יהוה ראשון
ה ואת־אחרנים אני־הוא׃ ראו איים וייראו קצות הארץ
6 יחרדו קרבו ויאתיון׃ איש את־רעהו יעזרו ולאחיו יאמר
7 חזק׃ ויחזק חרש את־צרף מחליק פטיש את־הולם
פעם אמר לדבק טוב הוא ויחזקהו במסמרים לא ימוט׃

מא׳ v. 7. כצ״ל

CHAPTER XLI

1. Keep silence before Me, O islands,
And let the peoples renew their strength;
Let them draw near, then let them speak;
Let us come near together to judgment.
2. Who hath raised up one from the east,
At whose steps victory attendeth?
He giveth nations before him,
And maketh him rule over kings;
His sword maketh them as the dust,
His bow as the driven stubble.
3. He pursueth them, and passeth on safely;
The way with his feet he treadeth not.
4. Who hath wrought and done it?
He that called the generations from the beginning.
I, the Lord, who am the first,
And with the last am the same.
5. The isles saw, and feared;
The ends of the earth trembled;
They drew near, and came.
6. They helped every one his neighbour;
And every one said to his brother:
'Be of good courage.'
7. So the carpenter encouraged the goldsmith,
And he that smootheth with the hammer him that smiteth the anvil,

31. *they that wait.* They who hope in the Lord are borne aloft on wings of faith above all earthly cares. The phrases 'mount up with wings as eagles', 'run', and 'walk' do not form an anti-climax. Under a wave of enthusiasm we are all capable of an isolated act of heroism, *i.e.* to 'soar' or 'to run' for a time. It is far harder to follow the monotonous round of everyday duty when the vision has faded and the splendour seems gone, undeterred by trials and hindrances, meeting them in the spirit of faith and conquering them by steadfastness. This is the achievement of those who 'wait for the LORD'. Day by day, they shall renew their strength.

CHAPTER XLI. GOD, ISRAEL AND THE HEATHENS

1–5. A summons to the nations to assemble for a process at law before the tribunal of the Almighty.

1. *islands.* Habitable lands.

renew their strength. Pluck up courage to speak.

2. *who hath raised up one from the east.* Since Ibn Ezra, it has been recognized that this refers to Cyrus. In the victorious career of this magnanimous conqueror and Liberator which had at that time commenced, the Prophet beheld the instrument of God for the release of Israel from Exile.

3. *the way with his feet he treadeth not. i.e.* so swift is his victorious progress that he seems scarcely to touch the ground, but to fly over it.

4. *called generations from the beginning. i.e.* He who from the first knew all future times and events, and summons each to appear at its right moment. This verse is one of the sublimest in the Bible: 'Human history is the thought of God,' the 'counsel' of the Almighty. God is 'the First and the Last', initiating all movements—calling the generations from the beginning—and bringing them to a close. Prediction and fulfilment are thus manifestations of His universal Wisdom and Power (Davidson).

5. *the isles saw.* These victories of Cyrus.

6–7. The nations thereupon frantically set

8 וְאַתָּה יִשְׂרָאֵל עַבְדִּי יַעֲקֹב אֲשֶׁר בְּחַרְתִּיךָ זֶרַע
9 אַבְרָהָם אֹהֲבִי׃ אֲשֶׁר הֶחֱזַקְתִּיךָ מִקְצוֹת הָאָרֶץ וּמֵאֲצִילֶיהָ
קְרָאתִיךָ וָאֹמַר לְךָ עַבְדִּי־אַתָּה בְּחַרְתִּיךָ וְלֹא מְאַסְתִּיךָ׃
י אַל־תִּירָא כִּי־עִמְּךָ אָנִי אַל־תִּשְׁתָּע כִּי־אֲנִי אֱלֹהֶיךָ אִמַּצְתִּיךָ
11 אַף־עֲזַרְתִּיךָ אַף־תְּמַכְתִּיךָ בִּימִין צִדְקִי׃ הֵן יֵבֹשׁוּ וְיִכָּלְמוּ
כֹּל הַנֶּחֱרִים בָּךְ יִהְיוּ כְאַיִן וְיֹאבְדוּ אַנְשֵׁי רִיבֶךָ׃
12 תְּבַקְשֵׁם וְלֹא תִמְצָאֵם אַנְשֵׁי מַצֻּתֶךָ יִהְיוּ כְאַיִן וּכְאֶפֶס
13 אַנְשֵׁי מִלְחַמְתֶּךָ׃ כִּי אֲנִי יְהוָה אֱלֹהֶיךָ מַחֲזִיק יְמִינֶךָ
14 הָאֹמֵר לְךָ אַל־תִּירָא אֲנִי עֲזַרְתִּיךָ׃ אַל־תִּירְאִי תּוֹלַעַת
יַעֲקֹב מְתֵי יִשְׂרָאֵל אֲנִי עֲזַרְתִּיךְ נְאֻם־יְהוָה וְגֹאֲלֵךְ קְדוֹשׁ
טו יִשְׂרָאֵל׃ הִנֵּה שַׂמְתִּיךְ לְמוֹרַג חָרוּץ חָדָשׁ בַּעַל פִּיפִיּוֹת
16 תָּדוּשׁ הָרִים וְתָדֹק וּגְבָעוֹת כַּמֹּץ תָּשִׂים׃ תִּזְרֵם וְרוּחַ
תִּשָּׂאֵם וּסְעָרָה תָּפִיץ אֹתָם וְאַתָּה תָּגִיל בַּיהוָה בִּקְדוֹשׁ
יִשְׂרָאֵל תִּתְהַלָּל׃

Saying of the soldering: 'It is good';
And he fastened it with nails, that it should not be moved.

8. But thou, Israel, My servant,
Jacob whom I have chosen,
The seed of Abraham My friend;

9. Thou whom I have taken hold of from the ends of the earth,
And called thee from the uttermost parts thereof,
And said unto thee: 'Thou art My servant,
I have chosen thee and not cast thee away';

10. Fear thou not, for I am with thee,
Be not dismayed, for I am thy God;
I strengthen thee, yea, I help thee;
Yea, I uphold thee with My victorious right hand.

11. Behold, all they that were incensed against thee
Shall be ashamed and confounded;
They that strove with thee
Shall be as nothing, and shall perish.

12. Thou shalt seek them, and shalt not find them,
Even them that contended with thee;
They that warred against thee
Shall be as nothing, and as a thing of nought.

13. For I the LORD thy God
Hold thy right hand,
Who say unto thee: 'Fear not,
I help thee.'

14. Fear not, thou worm Jacob,
And ye men of Israel;
I help thee, saith the LORD,
And thy Redeemer, the Holy One of Israel.

15. Behold, I make thee a new threshing-sledge
Having sharp teeth;
Thou shalt thresh the mountains, and beat them small,
And shalt make the hills as chaff.

16. Thou shalt fan them, and the wind shall carry them away,
And the whirlwind shall scatter them;
And thou shalt rejoice in the LORD,
Thou shalt glory in the Holy One of Israel.

themselves to the fashioning of new and strong idols to deliver them from the conqueror.

8–14. In contrast to these other nations, Israel is the Servant of God, and need not fear.

8. *My servant.* My worshipper.
My friend. Or, 'who loved me.' Abraham was not merely passively but actively the 'friend of God'. His love was obedience. This striking title recurs in II Chron. xx, 7.

9. *ends of the earth.* Ur of the Chaldees.

10. *dismayed.* lit. 'gaze not anxiously around you.'

11–14. ISRAEL'S ENEMIES WILL BE CONFOUNDED

14. *worm Jacob.* Worm as a symbol of weakness, and of Israel's condition in captivity.

Redeemer. Heb. '*Goel*', the technical term for the relative whose duty it was to redeem the person or property of a kinsman, or to avenge him if murdered. It is a favourite title of God in Isaiah.

15–16. *a new threshing-sledge.* The mountains and the hills represent the powerful, worldly forces that seek to block the spiritual and ethical ideals in Israel's message and work. These shall be reduced to powder and scattered by the whirlwind, and Israel shall rejoice in the vindication of his faith in God.

18

CHAPTER XVIII

1. And the LORD appeared unto him by the terebinths of Mamre, as he sat in the tent door in the heat of the day; 2. and he lifted up his eyes and looked, and, lo, three men stood over against him; and when he saw them, he ran to meet them from the tent door, and bowed down to the earth, 3. and said: 'My lord, if now I have found favour in thy sight, pass not away, I pray thee, from thy servant. 4. Let now a little water be fetched, and wash your feet, and recline yourselves under the tree. 5. And I will fetch a morsel of bread, and stay ye your heart; after that ye shall pass on; forasmuch as ye are come to your servant.' And they said: 'So do, as thou hast said.' 6. And Abraham hastened into the tent unto Sarah, and said: 'Make ready quickly three measures of fine meal, knead it, and make cakes.' 7. And Abraham ran unto the herd, and fetched a calf tender and good, and gave it unto the servant; and he hastened to dress it. 8. And he took curd, and milk, and the calf which he had dressed, and set it before them; and he

יח

CAP. XVIII. יח

פ פ פ ד 4

א וַיֵּרָא אֵלָיו יְהוָה בְּאֵלֹנֵי מַמְרֵא וְהוּא יֹשֵׁב פֶּתַח־הָאֹהֶל
2 כְּחֹם הַיּוֹם׃ וַיִּשָּׂא עֵינָיו וַיַּרְא וְהִנֵּה שְׁלֹשָׁה אֲנָשִׁים נִצָּבִים
עָלָיו וַיַּרְא וַיָּרָץ לִקְרָאתָם מִפֶּתַח הָאֹהֶל וַיִּשְׁתַּחוּ אָרְצָה׃
3 וַיֹּאמַר אֲדֹנָי אִם־נָא מָצָאתִי חֵן בְּעֵינֶיךָ אַל־נָא תַעֲבֹר מֵעַל
4 עַבְדֶּךָ׃ יֻקַּח־נָא מְעַט־מַיִם וְרַחֲצוּ רַגְלֵיכֶם וְהִשָּׁעֲנוּ תַּחַת
ה הָעֵץ׃ וְאֶקְחָה פַת־לֶחֶם וְסַעֲדוּ לִבְּכֶם אַחַר תַּעֲבֹרוּ כִּי־
עַל־כֵּן עֲבַרְתֶּם עַל־עַבְדְּכֶם וַיֹּאמְרוּ כֵּן תַּעֲשֶׂה כַּאֲשֶׁר
6 דִּבַּרְתָּ׃ וַיְמַהֵר אַבְרָהָם הָאֹהֱלָה אֶל־שָׂרָה וַיֹּאמֶר מַהֲרִי
7 שְׁלֹשׁ סְאִים קֶמַח סֹלֶת לוּשִׁי וַעֲשִׂי עֻגוֹת׃ וְאֶל־הַבָּקָר
רָץ אַבְרָהָם וַיִּקַּח בֶּן־בָּקָר רַךְ וָטוֹב וַיִּתֵּן אֶל־הַנַּעַר וַיְמַהֵר
8 לַעֲשׂוֹת אֹתוֹ׃ וַיִּקַּח חֶמְאָה וְחָלָב וּבֶן־הַבָּקָר אֲשֶׁר עָשָׂה

v. 3. קדש v. 6. חנ׳ רפה

IV. VAYYERA

(CHAPTERS XVIII–XXII)

THE DESTRUCTION OF SODOM AND GOMORRAH (CHAPTERS XVIII–XIX)

CHAPTER XVIII, 1–16. VISIT OF THE ANGELS

1. *and the LORD appeared unto him.* The Rabbis connect this chapter with the preceding, and declare that God visited the Patriarch during the indisposition which resulted from his circumcision. From this passage they deduce the duty of visiting the sick.

in the tent door. Abraham was watching for passers by to offer them hospitality, an occupation in which he delighted.

2. *three men.* One to announce the tidings of the birth of Isaac; the second to destroy Sodom; and the third to rescue Lot. 'An angel is never sent on more than one errand at a time' (Midrash).

3. *my lord.* Abraham speaks to the one who appeared to be the chief of the three men.

4. *wash your feet.* A refreshing comfort to travellers who wore sandals; cf. XIX, 2; XXIV, 32; XLIII, 24.

recline yourselves. While the meal was being prepared for them, they could enjoy the shade of the tree in front of his tent (see *v.* 1).

5. *and I will fetch a morsel of bread.* It is a mark of the good man, declare the Rabbis, to perform more than he promises. The Patriarch belittles the fare he offers to provide for his guests, but gives them of his best.

stay ye your heart. Refresh your strength.

forasmuch as. Seeing that you are in haste, for otherwise you would not be passing my tent in the heat of the day.

6. *and Abraham hastened.* Note also the instruction to Sarah, 'make ready *quickly*.'

7. *unto the servant.* lit. 'the lad', Ishmael, whom Abraham was thus instructing in the duties of hospitality (Midrash). Such instruction in the duty of hospitality to strangers may appear superfluous in the eyes of some parents and teachers to-day. They are in error. In Western countries, the old Bible command, *Love ye the stranger* (Deut. x, 19), is honoured more in the breach than in the observance. The vulgar, high and low, deem it 'patriotic' to despise aliens, and find their foreign manners and language contemptible.

8. The verse may be understood as meaning that the guests were given curd and milk to slake their thirst and refresh them (cf. Judges IV, 19), and then followed the meal proper which consisted of the calf. This procedure would be quite in accord with the dietary laws.

and he stood by them. In the East, the host does not sit with his guests, but stands and attends to their needs.

and they did eat. This is the only place in the

stood by them under the tree, and they did eat. 9. And they said unto him: 'Where is Sarah thy wife?' And he said: 'Behold, in the tent.' 10. And He said: 'I will certainly return unto thee when the season cometh round; and, lo, Sarah thy wife shall have a son.' And Sarah heard in the tent door, which was behind him.—11. Now Abraham and Sarah were old, and well stricken in age; it had ceased to be with Sarah after the manner of women.—12. And Sarah laughed within herself, saying: 'After I am waxed old shall I have pleasure, my lord being old also?' 13. And the LORD said unto Abraham: 'Wherefore did Sarah laugh, saying: Shall I of a surety bear a child, who am old? 14. Is any thing too hard for the LORD? At the set time I will return unto thee, when the season cometh round, and Sarah shall have a son.'* ii. 15. Then Sarah denied, saying: 'I laughed not'; for she was afraid. And He said: 'Nay; but thou didst laugh.' ¶ 16. And the men rose up from thence, and looked out toward Sodom; and Abraham went with them to bring them on the way. 17. And the LORD said: 'Shall I hide from Abraham that which I am doing; 18. seeing that Abraham shall surely become a great and mighty nation, and all the nations of the earth shall be blessed in him? 19. For I have known him, to the end that he may command his children and his household after him, that they may keep the way of

ויתן לפניהם והוא־עמד עליהם תחת העץ ויאכלו:
9 ויאמרו אליו איה שרה אשתך ויאמר הנה באהל:
י ויאמר שוב אשוב אליך כעת חיה והנה־בן לשרה
11 אשתך ושרה שמעת פתח האהל והוא אחריו: ואברהם
ושרה זקנים באים בימים חדל להיות לשרה ארח
12 כנשים: ותצחק שרה בקרבה לאמר אחרי בלתי
13 היתה־לי עדנה ואדני זקן: ויאמר יהוה אל־אברהם
למה זה צחקה שרה לאמר האף אמנם אלד ואני זקנתי:
14 היפלא מיהוה דבר למועד אשוב אליך כעת חיה
שני
טו ולשרה בן: ותכחש שרה | לאמר לא צחקתי כי |
16 יראה ויאמר | לא כי צחקת: ויקמו משם האנשים
וישקפו על־פני סדם ואברהם הלך עמם לשלחם:
17 ויהוה אמר המכסה אני מאברהם אשר אני עשה:
18 ואברהם היו יהיה לגוי גדול ועצום ונברכו־בו כל גויי
19 הארץ: כי ידעתיו למען אשר יצוה את־בניו ואת־ביתו

v. 9. נקוד על איו v. 13. פתח בס"פ

Bible where celestial beings are mentioned as partaking of food, or as appearing to do so (see Tobit XII, 19). The Rabbis deduced from this, that it is necessary to conform to the social habits of the people in whose midst one lives.

9. *in the tent.* The Talmud sees herein praise of Sarah, the highest excellence of a wife being her domesticity.

10. *and He said.* One of the angels.

cometh round. lit. 'reviveth'—this time next year.

and Sarah heard in the tent door. More accurately, 'now Sarah was listening at the entrance of the tent.'

11. *well stricken.* 'Advanced.'

12. *and Sarah laughed.* Incredulous at the news.

waxed old. lit. 'withered'.

13. *shall I . . . who am old?* Sarah had referred both to her and to Abraham's extreme age. God only mentioned the reference to herself. This was done so as not to give cause for quarrel between husband and wife, say the Rabbis.

14. *is anything too hard for the LORD?* Or, 'Is anything too wonderful for the LORD?'

16. *to bring them on the way.* The final act of courtesy of a gracious host.

17–33. ABRAHAM'S INTERCESSION FOR SODOM

17. *the LORD said.* Equivalent to 'the Lord thought'—a usage often found in the Bible.

18. *blessed in him.* See on XII, 3.

19. *for I have known him. i.e.* regarded and chosen him; cf. Amos III, 2, 'You only have I known of all the families of the earth'; Psalm I, 6, 'the Lord knoweth the way of the righteous.' God's choice of Abraham is no arbitrary election.

command his children. Or, 'charge his children.' An important doctrine is here taught in connection with the word 'command' יצוה, which has played a conspicuous part in Jewish life. It is the sacred duty of the Israelite to transmit the Jewish heritage to his children after him. The last injunction of the true Jewish father to his children is that they walk in 'the way of the LORD' and live lives of probity and goodness. These injunctions were often put in writing; and this custom has given rise to a distinct type of literary production, the Jewish Ethical Will (**צוואה**).

the LORD, to do righteousness and justice; to the end that the LORD may bring upon Abraham that which He hath spoken of him.' 20. And the LORD said: 'Verily, the cry of Sodom and Gomorrah is great, and, verily, their sin is exceeding grievous. 21. I will go down now, and see whether they have done altogether according to the cry of it, which is come unto Me; and if not, I will know.' 22. And the men turned from thence, and went toward Sodom; but Abraham stood yet before the LORD. 23. And Abraham drew near, and said: 'Wilt Thou indeed sweep away the righteous with the wicked? 24. Peradventure there are fifty righteous within the city; wilt Thou indeed sweep away and not forgive the place for the fifty righteous that are therein? 25. That be far from Thee to do after this manner, to slay the righteous with the wicked, that so the righteous should be as the wicked; that be far from

אַחֲרָיו וְשָׁמְרוּ דֶּרֶךְ יְהוָה לַעֲשׂוֹת צְדָקָה וּמִשְׁפָּט לְמַעַן
כ הָבִיא יְהוָה עַל־אַבְרָהָם אֵת אֲשֶׁר־דִּבֶּר עָלָיו׃ וַיֹּאמֶר
יְהוָה זַעֲקַת סְדֹם וַעֲמֹרָה כִּי־רָבָּה וְחַטָּאתָם כִּי כָבְדָה
21 מְאֹד׃ אֵרְדָה־נָּא וְאֶרְאֶה הַכְּצַעֲקָתָהּ הַבָּאָה אֵלַי עָשׂוּ ׀
22 כָּלָה וְאִם־לֹא אֵדָעָה׃ וַיִּפְנוּ מִשָּׁם הָאֲנָשִׁים וַיֵּלְכוּ סְדֹמָה
23 וְאַבְרָהָם עוֹדֶנּוּ עֹמֵד לִפְנֵי יְהוָה׃ וַיִּגַּשׁ אַבְרָהָם וַיֹּאמַר
24 הַאַף תִּסְפֶּה צַדִּיק עִם־רָשָׁע׃ אוּלַי יֵשׁ חֲמִשִּׁים צַדִּיקִם
בְּתוֹךְ הָעִיר הַאַף תִּסְפֶּה וְלֹא־תִשָּׂא לַמָּקוֹם לְמַעַן חֲמִשִּׁים
כה הַצַּדִּיקִם אֲשֶׁר בְּקִרְבָּהּ׃ חָלִלָה לְּךָ מֵעֲשֹׂת ׀ כַּדָּבָר
הַזֶּה לְהָמִית צַדִּיק עִם־רָשָׁע וְהָיָה כַצַּדִּיק כָּרָשָׁע חָלִלָה

v. 21. מלעיל

20. *the cry of Sodom.* The cries of those who suffered from the atrocious wickedness of the inhabitants of Sodom and who implored Heaven's vengeance against their cruel oppressors (Ezek. XVI, 49). The following legend graphically describes their hatred of all strangers and their fiendish punishment of all who departed from their ways. A girl, overcome by pity, supplied food to a poor stranger. On detection, she was stripped, bound, daubed with honey and placed on the roof under the burning sun to be devoured by the bees.

their sin. Exemplified in the narrative of the next chapter.

21. *I will go down now.* An anthropomorphic expression, as in XI, 7, to convey the idea that before God decided to punish the dwellers of the cities, 'He descended,' as it were, to obtain ocular proof of, or extenuating circumstances for, their crimes.

22. *from thence.* From the place to which Abraham had accompanied them.

23. The remainder of the chapter forms one of the sublimest passages in the Bible or out of the Bible. Abraham's plea for Sodom is a signal illustration of his nobility of character. Amid the hatreds and feuds of primitive tribes who glorified brute force and despised pity, Abraham proves true to his new name and embraces in his sympathy all the children of men. Even the wicked inhabitants of Sodom were his brothers, and his heart overflows with sorrow over their doom. The unique dialogue between God and Abraham teaches two vital lessons; first, the supreme value of righteousness; and, secondly, God's readiness to pardon (Ezek. XXXIII, 11), if only He can do so consistently with justice.

drew near. By the act of prayer (Abarbanel).

righteous . . . wicked. i.e. 'innocent . . . guilty.' Abraham rests his case on the conviction that the action of God cannot be arbitrary but only in accordance with perfect justice. In an indiscriminate destruction, however, all the inhabitants, whether good or wicked, would share the same fate. Abraham pleads that as it would not be just to destroy the righteous, therefore, in order to save the righteous, the judgment which had been pronounced over the cities should be stayed (Ryle). This intercession on behalf of Sodom and Gomorrah—Abraham arguing with God, yea, bargaining with Him, to save their depraved inhabitants from merited destruction—is the highest spiritual pinnacle reached by the Patriarch. Its grandeur exceeds even the willingness to sacrifice his son at the Divine bidding. Within his breast there was a conflict between his sense of justice that the wicked must pay the penalty of their misdeeds, and his anguish at the thought that human beings were about to perish.

25. *far from Thee. i.e.* it would be unworthy of Thee (Mendelssohn).

shall not the Judge of all the earth do justly? These words have been well described as an 'epochal sentence in the Bible' (Zangwill). They make Justice the main pillar of God's Throne; without it, the whole idea of the Divine totters. Justice, it is true, is not the only ethical quality in God or man, nor is it the highest quality; but it is the basis for all the others. 'That which is

Thee; shall not the Judge of all the earth do justly?' 26. And the LORD said: 'If I find in Sodom fifty righteous within the city, then I will forgive all the place for their sake.' 27. And Abraham answered and said: 'Behold now, I have taken upon me to speak unto the LORD, who am but dust and ashes. 28. Peradventure there shall lack five of the fifty righteous; wilt Thou destroy all the city for lack of five?' And He said: 'I will not destroy it, if I find there forty and five.' 29. And he spoke unto Him yet again, and said: 'Peradventure there shall be forty found there.' And He said: 'I will not do it for the forty's sake.' 30. And he said: 'Oh, let not the LORD be angry, and I will speak. Peradventure there shall thirty be found there.' And He said: 'I will not do it, if I find thirty there.' 31. And he said: 'Behold now, I have taken upon me to speak unto the LORD. Peradventure there shall be twenty found there.' And He said: 'I will not destroy it for the twenty's sake.' 32. And he said: 'Oh, let not the LORD be angry, and I will speak yet but this once. Peradventure ten shall be found there.' And He said: 'I will not destroy it for the ten's sake.' 33. And the LORD went His way, as soon as He had left off speaking to Abraham; and Abraham returned unto his place.* iii.

26 לָךְ הֲשֹׁפֵט כָּל־הָאָרֶץ לֹא יַעֲשֶׂה מִשְׁפָּט׃ וַיֹּאמֶר יְהוָה
אִם־אֶמְצָא בִסְדֹם חֲמִשִּׁים צַדִּיקִם בְּתוֹךְ הָעִיר וְנָשָׂאתִי
27 לְכָל־הַמָּקוֹם בַּעֲבוּרָם׃ וַיַּעַן אַבְרָהָם וַיֹּאמַר הִנֵּה־נָא
28 הוֹאַלְתִּי לְדַבֵּר אֶל־אֲדֹנָי וְאָנֹכִי עָפָר וָאֵפֶר׃ אוּלַי יַחְסְרוּן
חֲמִשִּׁים הַצַּדִּיקִם חֲמִשָּׁה הֲתַשְׁחִית בַּחֲמִשָּׁה אֶת־כָּל־
הָעִיר וַיֹּאמֶר לֹא אַשְׁחִית אִם־אֶמְצָא שָׁם אַרְבָּעִים וַחֲמִשָּׁה׃
29 וַיֹּסֶף עוֹד לְדַבֵּר אֵלָיו וַיֹּאמַר אוּלַי יִמָּצְאוּן שָׁם אַרְבָּעִים
ל וַיֹּאמֶר לֹא אֶעֱשֶׂה בַּעֲבוּר הָאַרְבָּעִים׃ וַיֹּאמֶר אַל־נָא יִחַר
לַאדֹנָי וַאֲדַבֵּרָה אוּלַי יִמָּצְאוּן שָׁם שְׁלֹשִׁים וַיֹּאמֶר לֹא
31 אֶעֱשֶׂה אִם־אֶמְצָא שָׁם שְׁלֹשִׁים׃ וַיֹּאמֶר הִנֵּה־נָא הוֹאַלְתִּי
לְדַבֵּר אֶל־אֲדֹנָי אוּלַי יִמָּצְאוּן שָׁם עֶשְׂרִים וַיֹּאמֶר לֹא
32 אַשְׁחִית בַּעֲבוּר הָעֶשְׂרִים׃ וַיֹּאמֶר אַל־נָא יִחַר לַאדֹנָי
וַאֲדַבְּרָה אַךְ־הַפַּעַם אוּלַי יִמָּצְאוּן שָׁם עֲשָׂרָה וַיֹּאמֶר לֹא
33 אַשְׁחִית בַּעֲבוּר הָעֲשָׂרָה׃ וַיֵּלֶךְ יְהוָה כַּאֲשֶׁר כִּלָּה לְדַבֵּר
שלישי אֶל־אַבְרָהָם וְאַבְרָהָם שָׁב לִמְקֹמוֹ׃ *

19

CHAPTER XIX

1. And the two angels came to Sodom at even; and Lot sat in the gate of Sodom; and Lot saw them, and rose up to meet them; and he fell down on his face to the earth; 2. and he said: 'Behold now, my lords, turn aside, I pray you, into your servant's house, and tarry all night, and wash your feet, and ye shall rise up early, and go on your way.' And they said:

CAP. XIX. יט

יט

א וַיָּבֹאוּ שְׁנֵי הַמַּלְאָכִים סְדֹמָה בָּעֶרֶב וְלוֹט יֹשֵׁב בְּשַׁעַר־
סְדֹם וַיַּרְא־לוֹט וַיָּקָם לִקְרָאתָם וַיִּשְׁתַּחוּ אַפַּיִם אָרְצָה׃
2 וַיֹּאמֶר הִנֶּה נָּא־אֲדֹנַי סוּרוּ נָא אֶל־בֵּית עַבְדְּכֶם וְלִינוּ
וְרַחֲצוּ רַגְלֵיכֶם וְהִשְׁכַּמְתֶּם וַהֲלַכְתֶּם לְדַרְכְּכֶם וַיֹּאמְרוּ

יט' v. 2. חול

above justice must be based on justice, and include justice, and be reached through justice' (Henry George). Only Israel, the Justice-intoxicated people, in time became רחמנים בני רחמנים, 'merciful children of merciful ancestors.' The boldness of the Patriarch's ringing challenge, the universality of the phrase 'all the earth', and the absolute conviction that the infinite might of God must be controlled by the decrees of Justice —that, in fact, an unjust God would be a contradiction in terms—are truly extraordinary. Despite the lapse of thousands of years, mankind has not yet fully grasped this lofty conception of God and its ethical consequences in human society. 'When Abraham could not find fifty righteous men in Sodom, and pleaded on behalf of forty, thirty, twenty, ten, that the great city might be spared, do you think God did not know all the time that there were not even ten righteous men in Sodom? But God wanted our father Abraham to show whether he was a man or no; and didn't he show himself a man!' (Arnold Zweig).

33. *returned unto his place.* From where he prayed, unto his own abode, Mamre; see *v.* 1.

CHAPTER XIX. THE ANGELS, SODOM AND LOT

1. *angels.* This is the first time the visitors are referred to by this term.

in the gate of Sodom. i.e. the passage beneath the city-wall, where people congregate in the East to converse, transact business, or have their disputes adjudicated.

2. *your servant's house.* Being a resident of a

'Nay; but we will abide in the broad place all night.' 3. And he urged them greatly; and they turned in unto him, and entered into his house; and he made them a feast, and did bake unleavened bread, and they did eat. 4. But before they lay down, the men of the city, even the men of Sodom, compassed the house round, both young and old, all the people from every quarter. 5. And they called unto Lot, and said unto him: 'Where are the men that came in to thee this night? bring them out unto us, that we may know them.' 6. And Lot went out unto them to the door, and shut the door after him. 7. And he said: 'I pray you, my brethren, do not so wickedly. 8. Behold now, I have two daughters that have not known man; let me, I pray you, bring them out unto you, and do ye to them as is good in your eyes; only unto these men do nothing; forasmuch as they are come under the shadow of my roof.' 9. And they said: 'Stand back.' And they said: 'This one fellow came in to sojourn, and he will needs play the judge; now will we deal worse with thee, than with them.' And they pressed sore upon the man, even Lot, and drew near to break the door. 10. But the men put forth their hand, and brought Lot into the house to them, and the door they shut. 11. And they smote the men that were at the door of the house with blindness, both small and great; so that they wearied themselves to find the door. 12. And the men said unto Lot: 'Hast thou here any besides? son-in-law, and thy sons, and thy daughters, and whomsoever thou hast in the city; bring them out of the place; 13. for we will destroy this place, because the cry of them is waxed great before the LORD; and the LORD hath sent us to destroy it.' 14. And Lot went out, and spoke unto his sons-in-law, who married his daughters, and said: 'Up, get you out of this place; for the LORD will destroy the city.' But he seemed unto his sons-in-law as one that jested. 15. And

3 לֹּא כִּי בָרְחוֹב נָלִין׃ וַיִּפְצַר־בָּם מְאֹד וַיָּסֻרוּ אֵלָיו וַיָּבֹאוּ
4 אֶל־בֵּיתוֹ וַיַּעַשׂ לָהֶם מִשְׁתֶּה וּמַצּוֹת אָפָה וַיֹּאכֵלוּ׃ טֶרֶם
יִשְׁכָּבוּ וְאַנְשֵׁי הָעִיר אַנְשֵׁי סְדֹם נָסַבּוּ עַל־הַבַּיִת מִנַּעַר
ה וְעַד־זָקֵן כָּל־הָעָם מִקָּצֶה׃ וַיִּקְרְאוּ אֶל־לוֹט וַיֹּאמְרוּ לוֹ
אַיֵּה הָאֲנָשִׁים אֲשֶׁר־בָּאוּ אֵלֶיךָ הַלָּיְלָה הוֹצִיאֵם אֵלֵינוּ
6 וְנֵדְעָה אֹתָם׃ וַיֵּצֵא אֲלֵהֶם לוֹט הַפֶּתְחָה וְהַדֶּלֶת סָגַר
7 8 אַחֲרָיו׃ וַיֹּאמַר אַל־נָא אַחַי תָּרֵעוּ׃ הִנֵּה־נָא לִי שְׁתֵּי בָנוֹת
אֲשֶׁר לֹא־יָדְעוּ אִישׁ אוֹצִיאָה־נָּא אֶתְהֶן אֲלֵיכֶם וַעֲשׂוּ לָהֶן
כַּטּוֹב בְּעֵינֵיכֶם רַק לָאֲנָשִׁים הָאֵל אַל־תַּעֲשׂוּ דָבָר כִּי־עַל־
9 כֵּן בָּאוּ בְּצֵל קֹרָתִי׃ וַיֹּאמְרוּ ׀ גֶּשׁ־הָלְאָה וַיֹּאמְרוּ הָאֶחָד
בָּא־לָגוּר וַיִּשְׁפֹּט שָׁפוֹט עַתָּה נָרַע לְךָ מֵהֶם וַיִּפְצְרוּ בָאִישׁ
י בְּלוֹט מְאֹד וַיִּגְּשׁוּ לִשְׁבֹּר הַדָּלֶת׃ וַיִּשְׁלְחוּ הָאֲנָשִׁים אֶת־
יָדָם וַיָּבִיאוּ אֶת־לוֹט אֲלֵיהֶם הַבָּיְתָה וְאֶת־הַדֶּלֶת סָגָרוּ׃
11 וְאֶת־הָאֲנָשִׁים אֲשֶׁר־פֶּתַח הַבַּיִת הִכּוּ בַּסַּנְוֵרִים מִקָּטֹן
12 וְעַד־גָּדוֹל וַיִּלְאוּ לִמְצֹא הַפָּתַח׃ וַיֹּאמְרוּ הָאֲנָשִׁים אֶל־
לוֹט עֹד מִי־לְךָ פֹה חָתָן וּבָנֶיךָ וּבְנֹתֶיךָ וְכֹל אֲשֶׁר־לְךָ בָּעִיר
13 הוֹצֵא מִן־הַמָּקוֹם׃ כִּי־מַשְׁחִתִים אֲנַחְנוּ אֶת־הַמָּקוֹם הַזֶּה
כִּי־גָדְלָה צַעֲקָתָם אֶת־פְּנֵי יְהוָה וַיְשַׁלְּחֵנוּ יְהוָה לְשַׁחֲתָהּ׃
14 וַיֵּצֵא לוֹט וַיְדַבֵּר ׀ אֶל־חֲתָנָיו ׀ לֹקְחֵי בְנֹתָיו וַיֹּאמֶר קוּמוּ
צְּאוּ מִן־הַמָּקוֹם הַזֶּה כִּי־מַשְׁחִית יְהוָה אֶת־הָעִיר וַיְהִי
טו כִמְצַחֵק בְּעֵינֵי חֲתָנָיו׃ וּכְמוֹ הַשַּׁחַר עָלָה וַיָּאִיצוּ הַמַּלְאָכִים

v. 2. ל' דגושה   v. 4. קמץ בסגולתא   v. 8. סבירין האלה   v. 14. צ' דגושה

city, Lot dwelt in a 'house', whereas Abraham's abode was a 'tent'.

broad place. The 'square' of the city; and the climate being warm, it would be a natural place where a homeless visitor would spend the night.

3. *unleavened bread.* Which could be baked rapidly.

4. *all the people.* Emphasis is here laid on the fact that the inhabitants were all addicted to unnatural depravity. The rejection of Abraham's plea was, therefore, justified.

8. *my roof.* The duty of protecting a guest is sacred in the East. As soon as a stranger had touched the tent-rope, he could claim guest-right. But the price which Lot was prepared to pay is unthinkable in our eyes, though a different view would present itself to the Oriental in those times.

9. *this one fellow.* An expression of contempt.

to sojourn. i.e. this newcomer presumes to judge our actions, and interfere with our customs!

11. *blindness.* The Heb. word occurs again only in II Kings VI, 18, and denotes a temporary loss of vision.

12. *any besides.* Lot's household is to be saved with him.

15. *iniquity.* As in IV, 13, the Heb. word for

when the morning arose, then the angels hastened Lot, saying: 'Arise, take thy wife, and thy two daughters that are here; lest thou be swept away in the iniquity of the city.' 16. But he lingered; and the men laid hold upon his hand, and upon the hand of his wife, and upon the hand of his two daughters; the LORD being merciful unto him. And they brought him forth, and set him without the city. 17. And it came to pass, when they had brought them forth abroad, that he said: 'Escape for thy life; look not behind thee, neither stay thou in all the Plain; escape to the mountain, lest thou be swept away.' 18. And Lot said unto them: 'Oh, not so, my lord; 19. behold now, thy servant hath found grace in thy sight, and thou hast magnified thy mercy, which thou hast shown unto me in saving my life; and I cannot escape to the mountain, lest the evil overtake me, and I die. 20. Behold now, this city is near to flee unto, and it is a little one; oh, let me escape thither—is it not a little one?—and my soul shall live.'* iv. 21. And he said unto him: 'See, I have accepted thee concerning this thing also, that I will not overthrow the city of which thou hast spoken. 22. Hasten thou, escape thither; for I cannot do anything till thou be come thither.'—Therefore the name of the city was called [1]Zoar.—23. The sun was risen upon the earth when Lot came unto Zoar. 24. Then the LORD caused to rain upon Sodom and upon Gomorrah brimstone and fire from the LORD out of heaven; 25. and He overthrew those cities, and all the Plain, and all the inhabitants of the cities, and that which grew upon the ground. 26. But his wife looked back from behind him, and she became a pillar of salt. 27. And Abraham got up early in the morning to the place where he had stood before the LORD. 28. And he looked out toward

[1] That is, *Little*, see verse 20.

בְּלוֹט לֵאמֹר קוּם קַח אֶת־אִשְׁתְּךָ וְאֶת־שְׁתֵּי בְנֹתֶיךָ
16 הַנִּמְצָאֹת פֶּן־תִּסָּפֶה בַּעֲוֺן הָעִיר׃ וַיִּתְמַהְמָהּ ׀ וַיַּחֲזִקוּ
הָאֲנָשִׁים בְּיָדוֹ וּבְיַד־אִשְׁתּוֹ וּבְיַד שְׁתֵּי בְנֹתָיו בְּחֶמְלַת
17 יְהוָה עָלָיו וַיֹּצִאֻהוּ וַיַּנִּחֻהוּ מִחוּץ לָעִיר׃ וַיְהִי כְהוֹצִיאָם
אֹתָם הַחוּצָה וַיֹּאמֶר הִמָּלֵט עַל־נַפְשֶׁךָ אַל־תַּבִּיט אַחֲרֶיךָ
18 וְאַל־תַּעֲמֹד בְּכָל־הַכִּכָּר הָהָרָה הִמָּלֵט פֶּן־תִּסָּפֶה׃ וַיֹּאמֶר
19 לוֹט אֲלֵהֶם אַל־נָא אֲדֹנָי׃ הִנֵּה־נָא מָצָא עַבְדְּךָ חֵן בְּעֵינֶיךָ
וַתַּגְדֵּל חַסְדְּךָ אֲשֶׁר עָשִׂיתָ עִמָּדִי לְהַחֲיוֹת אֶת־נַפְשִׁי
וְאָנֹכִי לֹא אוּכַל לְהִמָּלֵט הָהָרָה פֶּן־תִּדְבָּקַנִי הָרָעָה וָמַתִּי׃
כ הִנֵּה־נָא הָעִיר הַזֹּאת קְרֹבָה לָנוּס שָׁמָּה וְהִוא מִצְעָר
רביעי
21 אִמָּלְטָה נָּא שָׁמָּה הֲלֹא מִצְעָר הִוא וּתְחִי נַפְשִׁי׃* וַיֹּאמֶר
אֵלָיו הִנֵּה נָשָׂאתִי פָנֶיךָ גַּם לַדָּבָר הַזֶּה לְבִלְתִּי הָפְכִּי אֶת־
22 הָעִיר אֲשֶׁר דִּבַּרְתָּ׃ מַהֵר הִמָּלֵט שָׁמָּה כִּי לֹא אוּכַל
לַעֲשׂוֹת דָּבָר עַד־בֹּאֲךָ שָׁמָּה עַל־כֵּן קָרָא שֵׁם־הָעִיר
23 24 צוֹעַר׃ הַשֶּׁמֶשׁ יָצָא עַל־הָאָרֶץ וְלוֹט בָּא צֹעֲרָה׃ וַיהוָה
הִמְטִיר עַל־סְדֹם וְעַל־עֲמֹרָה גָּפְרִית וָאֵשׁ מֵאֵת יְהוָה מִן
כה הַשָּׁמָיִם׃ וַיַּהֲפֹךְ אֶת־הֶעָרִים הָאֵל וְאֵת כָּל־הַכִּכָּר וְאֵת
26 כָּל־יֹשְׁבֵי הֶעָרִים וְצֶמַח הָאֲדָמָה׃ וַתַּבֵּט אִשְׁתּוֹ מֵאַחֲרָיו
27 וַתְּהִי נְצִיב מֶלַח׃ וַיַּשְׁכֵּם אַבְרָהָם בַּבֹּקֶר אֶל־הַמָּקוֹם
28 אֲשֶׁר־עָמַד שָׁם אֶת־פְּנֵי יְהוָה׃ וַיַּשְׁקֵף עַל־פְּנֵי סְדֹם

v. 18. קדש v. 19. פתח בס״פ v. 21. פתח בס״פ v. 25. סבירין האלה

'iniquity' means also its consequence, 'punishment.'

16. *but he lingered.* Either to collect his valuables, or he was reluctant to leave. All that Scripture tells of Lot is characteristic of a weak, irresolute character.

17. *that he said.* The angel whose mission it was to rescue Lot.

the Plain. See on XIII, 10.

the mountain. See on XIV, 10.

19. *the evil.* The disaster.

20. *a little one.* It is so insignificant in size; and, therefore, it is a small favour he is asking for, when pleading that it be spared.

and my soul shall live. i.e. my life be spared.

26. *a pillar of salt.* She looked back and lingered behind, to be overtaken by the brimstone and fire from which the others escaped. A similar fate befell lingering refugees at Pompeii. 'Her body became encrusted and saturated with a nitrous and saline substance, that very likely preserved it for some time from decay' (De Sola). Ancient writers refer to this pillar as being still in existence. Josephus claims to have seen it.

27. *Abraham.* After a restless night, his heart heavy with the knowledge of what was about to befall the five cities, he rises early in the morning to gaze with compassionate eyes upon the fulfilment of the Divine decree.

28. Archæological exploration has established the existence of an early Canaanite civilization in

Sodom and Gomorrah, and toward all the land of the Plain, and beheld, and, lo, the smoke of the land went up as the smoke of a furnace. ¶ 29. And it came to pass, when God destroyed the cities of the Plain, that God remembered Abraham, and sent Lot out of the midst of the overthrow, when He overthrew the cities in which Lot dwelt. ¶ 30. And Lot went up out of Zoar, and dwelt in the mountain, and his two daughters with him; for he feared to dwell in Zoar; and he dwelt in a cave, he and his two daughters. 31. And the first-born said unto the younger: 'Our father is old, and there is not a man in the earth to come in unto us after the manner of all the earth. 32. Come, let us make our father drink wine, and we will lie with him, that we may preserve seed of our father.' 33. And they made their father drink wine that night. And the first-born went in, and lay with her father; and he knew not when she lay down, nor when she arose. 34. And it came to pass on the morrow, that the first-born said unto the younger: 'Behold, I lay yesternight with my father. Let us make him drink wine this night also; and go thou in, and lie with him, that we may preserve seed of our father.' 35. And they made their father drink wine that night also. And the younger arose, and lay with him; and he knew not when she lay down, nor when she arose. 36. Thus were both the daughters of Lot with child by their father. 37. And the first-born bore a son, and called his name Moab—the same is the father of the Moabites unto this day. 38. And the younger, she also bore a son, and called his name Ben-ammi—the same is the father of the children of Ammon unto this day.

וַעֲמֹרָה וְעַל כָּל־פְּנֵי אֶרֶץ הַכִּכָּר וַיַּרְא וְהִנֵּה עָלָה קִיטֹר
29 הָאָרֶץ כְּקִיטֹר הַכִּבְשָׁן׃ וַיְהִי בְּשַׁחֵת אֱלֹהִים אֶת־עָרֵי
הַכִּכָּר וַיִּזְכֹּר אֱלֹהִים אֶת־אַבְרָהָם וַיְשַׁלַּח אֶת־לוֹט מִתּוֹךְ
ל הַהֲפֵכָה בַּהֲפֹךְ אֶת־הֶעָרִים אֲשֶׁר־יָשַׁב בָּהֵן לוֹט׃ וַיַּעַל
לוֹט מִצּוֹעַר וַיֵּשֶׁב בָּהָר וּשְׁתֵּי בְנֹתָיו עִמּוֹ כִּי יָרֵא לָשֶׁבֶת
31 בְּצוֹעַר וַיֵּשֶׁב בַּמְּעָרָה הוּא וּשְׁתֵּי בְנֹתָיו׃ וַתֹּאמֶר הַבְּכִירָה
אֶל־הַצְּעִירָה אָבִינוּ זָקֵן וְאִישׁ אֵין בָּאָרֶץ לָבוֹא עָלֵינוּ
32 כְּדֶרֶךְ כָּל־הָאָרֶץ׃ לְכָה נַשְׁקֶה אֶת־אָבִינוּ יַיִן וְנִשְׁכְּבָה
33 עִמּוֹ וּנְחַיֶּה מֵאָבִינוּ זָרַע׃ וַתַּשְׁקֶיןָ אֶת־אֲבִיהֶן יַיִן בַּלַּיְלָה
הוּא וַתָּבֹא הַבְּכִירָה וַתִּשְׁכַּב אֶת־אָבִיהָ וְלֹא־יָדַע בְּשִׁכְבָהּ
34 וּבְקוּמָהּ׃ וַיְהִי מִמָּחֳרָת וַתֹּאמֶר הַבְּכִירָה אֶל־הַצְּעִירָה
הֵן־שָׁכַבְתִּי אֶמֶשׁ אֶת־אָבִי נַשְׁקֶנּוּ יַיִן גַּם־הַלַּיְלָה וּבֹאִי
לה שִׁכְבִי עִמּוֹ וּנְחַיֶּה מֵאָבִינוּ זָרַע׃ וַתַּשְׁקֶיןָ גַּם בַּלַּיְלָה הַהוּא
אֶת־אֲבִיהֶן יָיִן וַתָּקָם הַצְּעִירָה וַתִּשְׁכַּב עִמּוֹ וְלֹא־יָדַע
36 37 בְּשִׁכְבָהּ וּבְקֻמָהּ׃ וַתַּהֲרֶיןָ שְׁתֵּי בְנוֹת־לוֹט מֵאֲבִיהֶן׃ וַתֵּלֶד
הַבְּכִירָה בֵּן וַתִּקְרָא שְׁמוֹ מוֹאָב הוּא אֲבִי־מוֹאָב עַד־
38 הַיּוֹם׃ וְהַצְּעִירָה גַם־הִוא יָלְדָה בֵּן וַתִּקְרָא שְׁמוֹ בֶּן־עַמִּי
הוּא אֲבִי בְנֵי־עַמּוֹן עַד־הַיּוֹם׃ ס

20 CHAPTER XX

1\. And Abraham journeyed from thence toward the land of the South, and dwelt between Kadesh and Shur; and he

CAP. XX. כ כ

א וַיִּסַּע מִשָּׁם אַבְרָהָם אַרְצָה הַנֶּגֶב וַיֵּשֶׁב בֵּין־קָדֵשׁ וּבֵין

יט' v. 33. סבירין ההוא ibid. נקוד על ו'

the Plain. Many scholars to-day locate Sodom four miles north-east of the Dead Sea; formerly they located it to the south of the Dead Sea (Albright).

29. *remembered Abraham.* Gives the reason why Lot had been spared.

30. *he feared.* That God might yet include Zoar in the general destruction originally intended for all the five cities; and it seems that after his departure it was likewise destroyed by fire.

31. *there is not a man.* Some commentators state that Lot's daughters believed that the destruction had been universal, and that but for them the world would be completely depopulated. This explanation is untenable, seeing that they had just left Zoar. Their conduct does not admit of any extenuation: they were true children of Sodom.

32. *wine.* The mountainous country of Moab is full of caves; and the Midrash states that the inhabitants used to store their wines in such caves.

37. *Moab.* The name is explained as though it were the equivalent of *me-ab*, 'from a father.'

38. *Ben-ammi.* 'The son of my people,' or, 'the son of my father's kin.'

sojourned in Gerar. 2. And Abraham said of Sarah his wife: 'She is my sister.' And Abimelech king of Gerar sent, and took Sarah. 3. But God came to Abimelech in a dream of the night, and said to him: 'Behold, thou shalt die, because of the woman whom thou hast taken; for she is a man's wife.' 4. Now Abimelech had not come near her; and he said: 'LORD, wilt Thou slay even a righteous nation? 5. Said he not himself unto me: She is my sister? and she, even she herself said: He is my brother. In the simplicity of my heart and the innocency of my hands have I done this.' 6. And God said unto him in the dream: 'Yea, I know that in the simplicity of thy heart thou hast done this, and I also withheld thee from sinning against Me. Therefore suffered I thee not to touch her. 7. Now therefore restore the man's wife; for he is a prophet, and he shall pray for thee, and thou shalt live; and if thou restore her not, know thou that thou shalt surely die, thou, and all that are thine.' 8. And Abimelech rose early in the morning, and called all his servants, and told all these things in their ears; and the men were sore afraid. 9. Then Abimelech called Abraham, and said unto him: 'What hast thou done unto us? and wherein have I sinned against thee, that thou hast brought on me and on my kingdom a great sin? thou hast done deeds unto me that ought not to be done.' 10. And Abimelech said unto Abraham: 'What sawest thou, that thou hast done this thing?' 11. And Abraham said: 'Because I thought: Surely the fear of God is not in this place; and they will slay me for my wife's sake. 12. And moreover she is indeed my sister, the daughter of my father, but not the daughter of my mother;

2 שׁוּר וַיָּגָר בִּגְרָר׃ וַיֹּאמֶר אַבְרָהָם אֶל־שָׂרָה אִשְׁתּוֹ אֲחֹתִי
3 הִוא וַיִּשְׁלַח אֲבִימֶלֶךְ מֶלֶךְ גְּרָר וַיִּקַּח אֶת־שָׂרָה׃ וַיָּבֹא
אֱלֹהִים אֶל־אֲבִימֶלֶךְ בַּחֲלוֹם הַלָּיְלָה וַיֹּאמֶר לוֹ הִנְּךָ מֵת
4 עַל־הָאִשָּׁה אֲשֶׁר־לָקַחְתָּ וְהִוא בְּעֻלַת בָּעַל׃ וַאֲבִימֶלֶךְ
ה לֹא קָרַב אֵלֶיהָ וַיֹּאמַר אֲדֹנָי הֲגוֹי גַּם־צַדִּיק תַּהֲרֹג׃ הֲלֹא
הוּא אָמַר־לִי אֲחֹתִי הִוא וְהִיא־גַם־הִוא אָמְרָה אָחִי הוּא
6 בְּתָם־לְבָבִי וּבְנִקְיֹן כַּפַּי עָשִׂיתִי זֹאת׃ וַיֹּאמֶר אֵלָיו הָאֱלֹהִים
בַּחֲלֹם גַּם אָנֹכִי יָדַעְתִּי כִּי בְתָם־לְבָבְךָ עָשִׂיתָ זֹּאת וָאֶחְשֹׂךְ
גַּם־אָנֹכִי אוֹתְךָ מֵחֲטוֹ־לִי עַל־כֵּן לֹא־נְתַתִּיךָ לִנְגֹּעַ אֵלֶיהָ׃
7 וְעַתָּה הָשֵׁב אֵשֶׁת־הָאִישׁ כִּי־נָבִיא הוּא וְיִתְפַּלֵּל בַּעַדְךָ
וֶחְיֵה וְאִם־אֵינְךָ מֵשִׁיב דַּע כִּי־מוֹת תָּמוּת אַתָּה וְכָל־אֲשֶׁר־
8 לָךְ׃ וַיַּשְׁכֵּם אֲבִימֶלֶךְ בַּבֹּקֶר וַיִּקְרָא לְכָל־עֲבָדָיו וַיְדַבֵּר
אֶת־כָּל־הַדְּבָרִים הָאֵלֶּה בְּאָזְנֵיהֶם וַיִּירְאוּ הָאֲנָשִׁים מְאֹד׃
9 וַיִּקְרָא אֲבִימֶלֶךְ לְאַבְרָהָם וַיֹּאמֶר לוֹ מֶה־עָשִׂיתָ לָּנוּ וּמֶה־
חָטָאתִי לָךְ כִּי־הֵבֵאתָ עָלַי וְעַל־מַמְלַכְתִּי חֲטָאָה גְדֹלָה
י מַעֲשִׂים אֲשֶׁר לֹא־יֵעָשׂוּ עָשִׂיתָ עִמָּדִי׃ וַיֹּאמֶר אֲבִימֶלֶךְ
11 אֶל־אַבְרָהָם מָה רָאִיתָ כִּי עָשִׂיתָ אֶת־הַדָּבָר הַזֶּה׃ וַיֹּאמֶר
אַבְרָהָם כִּי אָמַרְתִּי רַק אֵין־יִרְאַת אֱלֹהִים בַּמָּקוֹם הַזֶּה
12 וַהֲרָגוּנִי עַל־דְּבַר אִשְׁתִּי׃ וְגַם־אָמְנָה אֲחֹתִי בַת־אָבִי הוּא

v. 6. חסר א׳

CHAPTER XX. ABIMELECH

The promise and hope of a son seems to have rejuvenated Sarah. She is taken into the harem of the king of Gerar.

1. *from thence.* From the terebinths of Mamre; see XVIII, 1.

South. The Negeb; see on XII, 9.

Kadesh and Shur. See on XIV, 7 and XVI, 7.

Gerar. Probably the Wady Jerur, 13 miles S.W. of Kadesh.

2. *my sister.* Abraham adopts the same precautions as when he was in Egypt; cf. XII, 13 f.

Abimelech. Abimilki is the name of the Egyptian governor of Tyre in the Tell-el-Amarna tablets.

and took Sarah. Had her brought to his harem.

4. *A righteous nation.* 'Innocent folk' (Moffatt).

7. *a prophet.* This is the first time the word occurs in the Bible. It is here used to denote a man who stands in a specially near relationship to God, and is consequently under the Divine protection.

10. *what sawest thou? i.e.* what hadst thou in view?

12. *daughter of my father.* The Bible sometimes uses 'son' and 'daughter' to denote a grandson or granddaughter (cf. IX, 24). Sarah may well have been Terah's granddaughter and Abraham's niece. Nachmanides, in his Commentary, severely denounces the Patriarch's conduct on the ground that it again imperilled his wife; and he adds that it makes no difference whether Abraham told Abimelech the truth in calling Sarah his 'sister', inasmuch as he suppressed the all-important fact that she was also his wife. Scripture impartially relates both the failings and the virtues of its heroes.

and so she became my wife. 13. And it came to pass, when God caused me to wander from my father's house, that I said unto her: This is thy kindness which thou shalt show unto me; at every place whither we shall come, say of me: He is my brother.' 14. And Abimelech took sheep and oxen, and men-servants and women-servants, and gave them unto Abraham, and restored him Sarah his wife. 15. And Abimelech said: 'Behold, my land is before thee: dwell where it pleaseth thee.' 16. And unto Sarah he said: 'Behold, I have given thy brother a thousand pieces of silver; behold, it is for thee a covering of the eyes to all that are with thee; and before all men thou art righted.' 17. And Abraham prayed unto God; and God healed Abimelech, and his wife, and his maid-servants; and they bore children. 18. For the LORD had fast closed up all the wombs of the house of Abimelech, because of Sarah Abraham's wife.

21

CHAPTER XXI

1. And the LORD remembered Sarah as He had said, and the LORD did unto Sarah as He had spoken. 2. And Sarah conceived, and bore Abraham a son in his old age, at the set time of which God had spoken to him. 3. And Abraham called the name of his son that was born unto him, whom Sarah bore to him, Isaac. 4. And Abraham circumcised his son Isaac when he was eight days old, as God had commanded him.* v. 5. And Abraham was a hundred years old, when his son Isaac was born unto him. 6. And Sarah said: 'God hath made laughter for me; every one that heareth will laugh on account of me.' 7. And she said: 'Who would have said unto Abraham, that Sarah should give children suck? for I have borne him a son in his old age.' ¶ 8. And the child grew, and was weaned. And Abraham made a great feast on the day that Isaac was weaned. 9. And Sarah saw the son of Hagar the

13 אַךְ לֹא בַת־אִמִּי וַתְּהִי־לִי לְאִשָּׁה׃ וַיְהִי כַּאֲשֶׁר הִתְעוּ
אֹתִי אֱלֹהִים מִבֵּית אָבִי וָאֹמַר לָהּ זֶה חַסְדֵּךְ אֲשֶׁר תַּעֲשִׂי
עִמָּדִי אֶל כָּל־הַמָּקוֹם אֲשֶׁר נָבוֹא שָׁמָּה אִמְרִי־לִי אָחִי
14 הוּא׃ וַיִּקַּח אֲבִימֶלֶךְ צֹאן וּבָקָר וַעֲבָדִים וּשְׁפָחֹת וַיִּתֵּן
טו לְאַבְרָהָם וַיָּשֶׁב לוֹ אֵת שָׂרָה אִשְׁתּוֹ׃ וַיֹּאמֶר אֲבִימֶלֶךְ
16 הִנֵּה אַרְצִי לְפָנֶיךָ בַּטּוֹב בְּעֵינֶיךָ שֵׁב׃ וּלְשָׂרָה אָמַר
הִנֵּה נָתַתִּי אֶלֶף כֶּסֶף לְאָחִיךְ הִנֵּה הוּא־לָךְ כְּסוּת עֵינַיִם
17 לְכֹל אֲשֶׁר אִתָּךְ וְאֵת כֹּל וְנֹכָחַת׃ וַיִּתְפַּלֵּל אַבְרָהָם אֶל־
הָאֱלֹהִים וַיִּרְפָּא אֱלֹהִים אֶת־אֲבִימֶלֶךְ וְאֶת־אִשְׁתּוֹ וְאַמְהֹתָיו
18 וַיֵּלֵדוּ׃ כִּי־עָצֹר עָצַר יְהוָה בְּעַד כָּל־רֶחֶם לְבֵית אֲבִימֶלֶךְ
עַל־דְּבַר שָׂרָה אֵשֶׁת אַבְרָהָם׃ ס

CAP. XXI. כא

כא

א וַיהוָה פָּקַד אֶת־שָׂרָה כַּאֲשֶׁר אָמָר וַיַּעַשׂ יְהוָה לְשָׂרָה
2 כַּאֲשֶׁר דִּבֵּר׃ וַתַּהַר וַתֵּלֶד שָׂרָה לְאַבְרָהָם בֵּן לִזְקֻנָיו
3 לַמּוֹעֵד אֲשֶׁר־דִּבֶּר אֹתוֹ אֱלֹהִים׃ וַיִּקְרָא אַבְרָהָם אֶת־
4 שֶׁם־בְּנוֹ הַנּוֹלַד־לוֹ אֲשֶׁר־יָלְדָה־לּוֹ שָׂרָה יִצְחָק׃ וַיָּמָל
אַבְרָהָם אֶת־יִצְחָק בְּנוֹ בֶּן־שְׁמֹנַת יָמִים כַּאֲשֶׁר צִוָּה אֹתוֹ
חמישי ה אֱלֹהִים׃ וְאַבְרָהָם בֶּן־מְאַת שָׁנָה בְּהִוָּלֶד לוֹ אֵת יִצְחָק
6 בְּנוֹ׃ וַתֹּאמֶר שָׂרָה צְחֹק עָשָׂה לִי אֱלֹהִים כָּל־הַשֹּׁמֵעַ
7 יִצְחַק־לִי׃ וַתֹּאמֶר מִי מִלֵּל לְאַבְרָהָם הֵינִיקָה בָנִים שָׂרָה
8 כִּי־יָלַדְתִּי בֵן לִזְקֻנָיו׃ וַיִּגְדַּל הַיֶּלֶד וַיִּגָּמַל וַיַּעַשׂ אַבְרָהָם

כ' v. 13. קדש כא' v. 8. פתח באתנח

13. *God caused me to wander.* The verb is in the plural, which is sometimes used when an Israelite speaks to a heathen; cf. also XXXI, 53 and Isa. XXIV, 9. It may also be the 'plural of Majesty', cf. I, 26.

15. *my land.* This offer is to be contrasted with the action of Pharaoh in XII, 19 f.

16. *a thousand pieces of silver.* This is not mentioned in *v.* 14; probably an additional personal gift.

a covering of the eyes. Figurative for 'justification'; to make them blind to the wrong which had been done her.

CHAPTER XXI, 1–21. ISAAC AND ISHMAEL

1. *as He had said.* See XV, 4; XVIII, 10.

2. *at the set time.* See XVIII, 14.

3. *Isaac.* See XVII, 19.

6. *laughter. i.e.* joy; an additional reason why the name Isaac was appropriate for the child.

laugh . . . me. i.e. rejoice with me.

8. *the child . . . was weaned.* Usually at two or even three years; cf. II Maccabees, VII, 26. Weaning a child is in the East still made the occasion of a family feast.

Egyptian, whom she had borne unto Abraham, making sport. 10. Wherefore she said unto Abraham: 'Cast out this bondwoman and her son; for the son of this bondwoman shall not be heir with my son, even with Isaac.' 11. And the thing was very grievous in Abraham's sight on account of his son. 12. And God said unto Abraham: 'Let it not be grievous in thy sight because of the lad, and because of thy bondwoman; in all that Sarah saith unto thee, hearken unto her voice; for in Isaac shall seed be called to thee. 13. And also of the son of the bondwoman will I make a nation, because he is thy seed.' 14. And Abraham rose up early in the morning, and took bread and a bottle of water, and gave it unto Hagar, putting it on her shoulder, and the child, and sent her away; and she departed, and strayed in the wilderness of Beer-sheba. 15. And the water in the bottle was spent, and she cast the child under one of the shrubs. 16. And she went, and sat her down over against him a good way off, as it were a bowshot; for she said: 'Let me not look upon the death of the child.' And she sat over against him, and lifted up her voice, and wept. 17. And God heard the voice of the lad; and the angel of God called to Hagar out of heaven, and said unto her: 'What aileth thee, Hagar? fear not; for God hath heard the voice of the lad where he is. 18. Arise, lift up the lad, and hold him fast by thy hand; for I will make him a great nation.' 19. And God opened her eyes, and she saw a well of water; and she went, and filled the bottle with water, and gave the lad drink. 20. And God was with the lad, and he grew; and he dwelt in the wilderness, and became an archer. 21. And he dwelt

9 מִשְׁתֶּה גָדוֹל בְּיוֹם הִגָּמֵל אֶת־יִצְחָק׃ וַתֵּרֶא שָׂרָה אֶת־
י בֶּן־הָגָר הַמִּצְרִית אֲשֶׁר־יָלְדָה לְאַבְרָהָם מְצַחֵק׃ וַתֹּאמֶר
לְאַבְרָהָם גָּרֵשׁ הָאָמָה הַזֹּאת וְאֶת־בְּנָהּ כִּי לֹא יִירַשׁ בֶּן־
11 הָאָמָה הַזֹּאת עִם־בְּנִי עִם־יִצְחָק׃ וַיֵּרַע הַדָּבָר מְאֹד בְּעֵינֵי
12 אַבְרָהָם עַל אוֹדֹת בְּנוֹ׃ וַיֹּאמֶר אֱלֹהִים אֶל־אַבְרָהָם אַל־
יֵרַע בְּעֵינֶיךָ עַל־הַנַּעַר וְעַל־אֲמָתֶךָ כֹּל אֲשֶׁר תֹּאמַר אֵלֶיךָ
13 שָׂרָה שְׁמַע בְּקֹלָהּ כִּי בְיִצְחָק יִקָּרֵא לְךָ זָרַע׃ וְגַם אֶת־
14 בֶּן־הָאָמָה לְגוֹי אֲשִׂימֶנּוּ כִּי זַרְעֲךָ הוּא׃ וַיַּשְׁכֵּם אַבְרָהָם ׀
בַּבֹּקֶר וַיִּקַּח־לֶחֶם וְחֵמַת מַיִם וַיִּתֵּן אֶל־הָגָר שָׂם עַל־
שִׁכְמָהּ וְאֶת־הַיֶּלֶד וַיְשַׁלְּחֶהָ וַתֵּלֶךְ וַתֵּתַע בְּמִדְבַּר בְּאֵר
טו שָׁבַע׃ וַיִּכְלוּ הַמַּיִם מִן־הַחֵמֶת וַתַּשְׁלֵךְ אֶת־הַיֶּלֶד תַּחַת
16 אַחַד הַשִּׂיחִם׃ וַתֵּלֶךְ וַתֵּשֶׁב לָהּ מִנֶּגֶד הַרְחֵק כִּמְטַחֲוֵי
קֶשֶׁת כִּי אָמְרָה אַל־אֶרְאֶה בְּמוֹת הַיָּלֶד וַתֵּשֶׁב מִנֶּגֶד
17 וַתִּשָּׂא אֶת־קֹלָהּ וַתֵּבְךְּ׃ וַיִּשְׁמַע אֱלֹהִים אֶת־קוֹל הַנַּעַר
וַיִּקְרָא מַלְאַךְ אֱלֹהִים ׀ אֶל־הָגָר מִן־הַשָּׁמַיִם וַיֹּאמֶר לָהּ
מַה־לָּךְ הָגָר אַל־תִּירְאִי כִּי־שָׁמַע אֱלֹהִים אֶל־קוֹל הַנַּעַר
18 בַּאֲשֶׁר הוּא־שָׁם׃ קוּמִי שְׂאִי אֶת־הַנַּעַר וְהַחֲזִיקִי אֶת־
19 יָדֵךְ בּוֹ כִּי־לְגוֹי גָּדוֹל אֲשִׂימֶנּוּ׃ וַיִּפְקַח אֱלֹהִים אֶת־עֵינֶיהָ
וַתֵּרֶא בְּאֵר מָיִם וַתֵּלֶךְ וַתְּמַלֵּא אֶת־הַחֵמֶת מַיִם וַתַּשְׁק
כ אֶת־הַנָּעַר׃ וַיְהִי אֱלֹהִים אֶת־הַנַּעַר וַיִּגְדָּל וַיֵּשֶׁב בַּמִּדְבָּר
21 וַיְהִי רֹבֶה קַשָּׁת׃ וַיֵּשֶׁב בְּמִדְבַּר פָּארָן וַתִּקַּח־לוֹ אִמּוֹ אִשָּׁה

9. *making sport.* 'Mocking' (RV). The Heb. term usually refers to an act of impurity or idolatry. Or, 'Ishmael laughed derisively at the feasting and rejoicing over the child Isaac, inasmuch as he was the elder son and the heir to his father's estate. Hence Sarah's natural desire to drive him out of the house' (Ehrlich).

11. *the thing was very grievous.* For Abraham was attached to Ishmael; see XVII, 18.

12. *God said unto Abraham.* Probably in a dream during the night; cf. *v.* 14.

in Isaac shall seed be called to thee. Isaac was to be the Patriarch's heir; and consequently Abraham might act upon Sarah's wish, and send Ishmael away, thus avoiding any dispute later on concerning the inheritance.

14. *Bottle of water.* Still used in the East.

and the child. Abarbanel shows that the Heb. text can be translated to mean that both Hagar and the lad carried the food and water.

wilderness of Beer-sheba. The town Beer-sheba, in the extreme South of Palestine, is situated on the border of the desert.

15. *one of the shrubs.* To protect him from the fierce sun.

16. *as it were a bowshot. i.e.* within hearing.

17. *heard the voice of the lad.* God has pity on the anguish of the alien slave mother, and hears her prayer no less than that of an Abraham.

where he is. lit. 'as he now is'. The Rabbis deduce from this the doctrine that God, in answering prayer, judges the penitent worshipper *as he is at that moment of his penitence.*

19. *and God opened her eyes. i.e.* she now perceived the well of water which was quite near her, in the wilderness of Paran; and his mother took him a wife out of the land of Egypt.* vi. ¶ 22. And it came to pass at that time, that Abimelech and Phicol the captain of his host spoke unto Abraham, saying: 'God is with thee in all that thou doest. 23. Now therefore swear unto me here by God that thou wilt not deal falsely with me, nor with my son, nor with my son's son; but according to the kindness that I have done unto thee, thou shalt do unto me, and to the land wherein thou hast sojourned.' 24. And Abraham said: 'I will swear.' 25. And Abraham reproved Abimelech because of the well of water, which Abimelech's servants had violently taken away. 26. And Abimelech said: 'I know not who hath done this thing; neither didst thou tell me, neither yet heard I of it, but to-day.' 27. And Abraham took sheep and oxen, and gave them unto Abimelech; and they two made a covenant. 28. And Abraham set seven ewe-lambs of the flock by themselves. 29. And Abimelech said unto Abraham: 'What mean these seven ewe-lambs which thou hast set by themselves?' 30. And he said: 'Verily, these seven ewe-lambs shalt thou take of my hand, that it may be a witness unto me, that I have digged this well.' 31. Wherefore that place was called Beer-sheba; because there they swore both of them. 32. So they made a covenant at Beer-sheba; and Abimelech rose up, and Phicol the captain of his host, and they returned into the land of the Philistines. 33. And Abraham planted

מֵאֶרֶץ מִצְרָיִם׃ * פ ששי
22 וַיְהִי בָּעֵת הַהִוא וַיֹּאמֶר אֲבִימֶלֶךְ וּפִיכֹל שַׂר־צְבָאוֹ אֶל־
אַבְרָהָם לֵאמֹר אֱלֹהִים עִמְּךָ בְּכֹל אֲשֶׁר־אַתָּה עֹשֶׂה׃
23 וְעַתָּה הִשָּׁבְעָה לִּי בֵאלֹהִים הֵנָּה אִם־תִּשְׁקֹר לִי וּלְנִינִי
וּלְנֶכְדִּי כַּחֶסֶד אֲשֶׁר עָשִׂיתִי עִמְּךָ תַּעֲשֶׂה עִמָּדִי וְעִם־
24 הָאָרֶץ אֲשֶׁר־גַּרְתָּה בָּהּ׃ וַיֹּאמֶר אַבְרָהָם אָנֹכִי אִשָּׁבֵעַ׃
כה וְהוֹכִחַ אַבְרָהָם אֶת־אֲבִימֶלֶךְ עַל־אֹדוֹת בְּאֵר הַמַּיִם אֲשֶׁר
26 גָּזְלוּ עַבְדֵי אֲבִימֶלֶךְ׃ וַיֹּאמֶר אֲבִימֶלֶךְ לֹא יָדַעְתִּי מִי
עָשָׂה אֶת־הַדָּבָר הַזֶּה וְגַם־אַתָּה לֹא־הִגַּדְתָּ לִּי וְגַם אָנֹכִי
27 לֹא שָׁמַעְתִּי בִּלְתִּי הַיּוֹם׃ וַיִּקַּח אַבְרָהָם צֹאן וּבָקָר וַיִּתֵּן
28 לַאֲבִימֶלֶךְ וַיִּכְרְתוּ שְׁנֵיהֶם בְּרִית׃ וַיַּצֵּב אַבְרָהָם אֶת־
29 שֶׁבַע כִּבְשֹׂת הַצֹּאן לְבַדְּהֶן׃ וַיֹּאמֶר אֲבִימֶלֶךְ אֶל־אַבְרָהָם
מָה הֵנָּה שֶׁבַע כְּבָשֹׂת הָאֵלֶּה אֲשֶׁר הִצַּבְתָּ לְבַדָּנָה׃
ל וַיֹּאמֶר כִּי אֶת־שֶׁבַע כְּבָשֹׂת תִּקַּח מִיָּדִי בַּעֲבוּר תִּהְיֶה־לִּי
31 לְעֵדָה כִּי חָפַרְתִּי אֶת־הַבְּאֵר הַזֹּאת׃ עַל־כֵּן קָרָא לַמָּקוֹם
32 הַהוּא בְּאֵר שָׁבַע כִּי שָׁם נִשְׁבְּעוּ שְׁנֵיהֶם׃ וַיִּכְרְתוּ בְרִית
בִּבְאֵר שָׁבַע וַיָּקָם אֲבִימֶלֶךְ וּפִיכֹל שַׂר־צְבָאוֹ וַיָּשֻׁבוּ אֶל־
33 אֶרֶץ פְּלִשְׁתִּים׃ וַיִּטַּע אֶשֶׁל בִּבְאֵר שָׁבַע וַיִּקְרָא־שָׁם בְּשֵׁם

but which in her anguish of mind she had overlooked. 'The Hebrew phrase *to open the eyes* is exclusively employed in the figurative sense of receiving new sources of knowledge, not in that of regaining the sense of sight' (Maimonides).

21. *wilderness of Paran.* See on XIV, 6.

his mother took him a wife. It was usually the concern of parent to find a wife for the son, cf. XXIV, 3 f; XXXIV, 4.

out of the land of Egypt. Her native land.

V. 22–34. ALLIANCE BETWEEN ABRAHAM AND ABIMELECH

22. *God is with thee.* Evidenced by the birth of a son to the Patriarch in his old age.

23. *here.* In this place, *i.e.* Beer-sheba.

kindness. Referring to gifts and permission to dwell in the land, see XX, 14 f.

25. *reproved.* While agreeing to the suggested alliance, Abraham stated a grievance; cf. Lev. XIX, 17, 'Thou shalt not hate thy brother in thy heart; thou shalt surely reprove thy neighbour.'

27. *sheep and oxen.* The exchange of gifts on making a treaty.

30. *witness.* The acceptance of the lambs would be equivalent to acknowledging Abraham's right to the possession of the well.

31. *Beer-sheba.* The name is given a double etymology; 'the well of seven (lambs)' and 'the well of swearing'.

33. *and called there on the name of the LORD.* See on XII, 8.

It is noteworthy that the story of Hagar and Ishmael is the Reading for the First Day of Rosh Hashanah; while the next chapter, the intended Sacrifice of Isaac is read on the Second Day. The highest manifestation of the Divine is not to be found in the calling into existence of Nature's elemental forces; far higher are God's ways manifest in the hearts and souls of men, in the home life of those who do justice, love mercy, and walk humbly with their God.

a tamarisk-tree in Beer-sheba, and called there on the name of the LORD, the Everlasting God. 34. And Abraham sojourned in the land of the Philistines many days.* vii.

34 יְהוָה אֵל עוֹלָם׃ וַיָּגָר אַבְרָהָם בְּאֶרֶץ פְּלִשְׁתִּים יָמִים רַבִּים׃ פ
שביעי

22

CHAPTER XXII

1. And it came to pass after these things, that God did prove Abraham, and said unto him: 'Abraham'; and he said: 'Here am I.' 2. And He said: 'Take now thy son, thine only son, whom thou lovest, even Isaac, and get thee into the land of Moriah; and offer him there for a burnt-offering upon one of the mountains which I will tell thee of.' 3. And Abraham rose early in the morning, and saddled his ass, and took two of his young men with him, and Isaac his son; and he cleaved the wood for the burnt-offering, and rose up, and went unto the place of which God had told him. 4. On the third day Abraham lifted up his eyes, and saw the place afar off. 5. And Abraham said unto his young men: 'Abide ye here with the ass, and I and the lad will go yonder; and we will worship, and come back to you.' 6. And Abraham took the wood of the burnt-offering, and laid it upon Isaac his son; and he took in his hand the fire and the knife; and they went both of them together. 7. And Isaac spoke unto Abraham his father, and said: 'My father.' And he said:

CAP. XXII. כב

כב

א וַיְהִי אַחַר הַדְּבָרִים הָאֵלֶּה וְהָאֱלֹהִים נִסָּה אֶת־אַבְרָהָם
2 וַיֹּאמֶר אֵלָיו אַבְרָהָם וַיֹּאמֶר הִנֵּנִי׃ וַיֹּאמֶר קַח־נָא אֶת־
בִּנְךָ אֶת־יְחִידְךָ אֲשֶׁר־אָהַבְתָּ אֶת־יִצְחָק וְלֶךְ־לְךָ אֶל־אֶרֶץ
הַמֹּרִיָּה וְהַעֲלֵהוּ שָׁם לְעֹלָה עַל אַחַד הֶהָרִים אֲשֶׁר אֹמַר
3 אֵלֶיךָ׃ וַיַּשְׁכֵּם אַבְרָהָם בַּבֹּקֶר וַיַּחֲבֹשׁ אֶת־חֲמֹרוֹ וַיִּקַּח
אֶת־שְׁנֵי נְעָרָיו אִתּוֹ וְאֵת יִצְחָק בְּנוֹ וַיְבַקַּע עֲצֵי עֹלָה וַיָּקָם
4 וַיֵּלֶךְ אֶל־הַמָּקוֹם אֲשֶׁר־אָמַר־לוֹ הָאֱלֹהִים׃ בַּיּוֹם הַשְּׁלִישִׁי
ה וַיִּשָּׂא אַבְרָהָם אֶת־עֵינָיו וַיַּרְא אֶת־הַמָּקוֹם מֵרָחֹק׃ וַיֹּאמֶר
אַבְרָהָם אֶל־נְעָרָיו שְׁבוּ־לָכֶם פֹּה עִם־הַחֲמוֹר וַאֲנִי וְהַנַּעַר
6 נֵלְכָה עַד־כֹּה וְנִשְׁתַּחֲוֶה וְנָשׁוּבָה אֲלֵיכֶם׃ וַיִּקַּח אַבְרָהָם
אֶת־עֲצֵי הָעֹלָה וַיָּשֶׂם עַל־יִצְחָק בְּנוֹ וַיִּקַּח בְּיָדוֹ אֶת־הָאֵשׁ
7 וְאֶת־הַמַּאֲכֶלֶת וַיֵּלְכוּ שְׁנֵיהֶם יַחְדָּו׃ וַיֹּאמֶר יִצְחָק אֶל־
אַבְרָהָם אָבִיו וַיֹּאמֶר אָבִי וַיֹּאמֶר הִנֶּנִּי בְנִי וַיֹּאמֶר הִנֵּה

כב׳ v. 6. סגול באתנח

CHAPTER XXII

THE BINDING OF ISAAC

On the great importance of this chapter, see "THE AKEDAH", p. 201.

1. *prove.* The Authorised Version has the older English 'tempt', *i.e.* test; a trial (in older English, 'a temptation') is that which puts to the test. A test is never employed for the purpose of injury, but to certify the power of resistance. All his other trials of faith were to be crowned by Abraham's willingness to sacrifice his dearest hope to the will of God. The Rabbis speak of it as the tenth and the greatest of the trials to which he was exposed.

and said unto him. From *v.* 3 we may deduce that God communicated with Abraham during the night, perhaps in a vision.

2. *take now.* The Heb. is peculiar: the imperative 'take' is followed by the Heb. particle נא which means, 'I pray thee'—God was speaking to Abraham 'as friend to friend'.

thy son, thine only son, whom thou lovest, even Isaac. The repetition indicates the intense strain that was being placed upon Abraham's faith, and the greatness of the sacrifice demanded.

the land of Moriah. Jewish Tradition identifies the locality with the Temple Mount (II Chron. III, 1).

and offer him there. lit. 'lift him up' (upon the altar). God, in His command, did not use the word which signifies the *slaying* of the sacrificial victim. From the outset, therefore, there was no intention of accepting a human sacrifice, although Abraham was at first not aware of this.

3. *and Abraham rose early in the morning.* There is no response in words on the part of Abraham. His answer is in deeds. He lost no time in obeying the will of God.

cleaved the wood. This task, usually left to a servant to perform, he now did himself.

5. *abide ye here.* Desiring to be alone with Isaac at the dread moment of sacrifice.

and come back. Was there an undercurrent of conviction that God would not exact His demand of him? The Rabbis declare that at the moment the Spirit of Prophecy entered into him, and he spoke more truly than he knew.

6. *the fire.* *i.e.* the vessel containing glowing embers, by means of which the wood on the altar was to be kindled.

7. *the lamb for a burnt offering.* This simple expression of boyish curiosity heightens the intense pathos of the situation.

'Here am I, my son.' And he said: 'Behold
the fire and the wood; but where is the
lamb for a burnt-offering?' 8. And Abraham
said: 'God will [1]provide Himself the lamb
for a burnt-offering, my son.' So they
went both of them together. 9. And they
came to the place which God had told
him of; and Abraham built the altar there,
and laid the wood in order, and bound
Isaac his son, and laid him on the altar,
upon the wood. 10. And Abraham stretched
forth his hand, and took the knife to slay
his son. 11. And the angel of the LORD
called unto him out of heaven, and said:
'Abraham, Abraham.' And he said:
'Here am I.' 12. And he said: 'Lay not
thy hand upon the lad, neither do thou
any thing unto him; for now I know that
thou art a God-fearing man, seeing thou
hast not withheld thy son, thine only son,
from Me.' 13. And Abraham lifted up
his eyes, and looked, and behold behind
him a ram caught in the thicket by his
horns. And Abraham went and took the
ram, and offered him up for a burnt-offering
in the stead of his son. 14. And Abraham
called the name of that place [2]Adonaijireh;
as it is said to this day: 'In the mount
where the LORD is seen.' 15. And the angel
of the LORD called unto Abraham a second
time out of heaven, 16. and said: 'By
Myself have I sworn, saith the LORD,
because thou hast done this thing, and hast
not withheld thy son, thine only son, 17.
that in blessing I will bless thee, and in
multiplying I will multiply thy seed as the
stars of the heaven, and as the sand which
is upon the sea-shore; and thy seed shall
possess the gate of his enemies; 18. and
in thy seed shall all the nations of the
earth be blessed; because thou hast heark-
ened to My voice.' 19. So Abraham returned

8 הָאֵשׁ וְהָעֵצִים וְאַיֵּה הַשֶּׂה לְעֹלָה׃ וַיֹּאמֶר אַבְרָהָם אֱלֹהִים
9 יִרְאֶה־לּוֹ הַשֶּׂה לְעֹלָה בְּנִי וַיֵּלְכוּ שְׁנֵיהֶם יַחְדָּו׃ וַיָּבֹאוּ
אֶל־הַמָּקוֹם אֲשֶׁר אָמַר־לוֹ הָאֱלֹהִים וַיִּבֶן שָׁם אַבְרָהָם
אֶת־הַמִּזְבֵּחַ וַיַּעֲרֹךְ אֶת־הָעֵצִים וַיַּעֲקֹד אֶת־יִצְחָק בְּנוֹ וַיָּשֶׂם
י אֹתוֹ עַל־הַמִּזְבֵּחַ מִמַּעַל לָעֵצִים׃ וַיִּשְׁלַח אַבְרָהָם אֶת־
11 יָדוֹ וַיִּקַּח אֶת־הַמַּאֲכֶלֶת לִשְׁחֹט אֶת־בְּנוֹ׃ וַיִּקְרָא אֵלָיו
מַלְאַךְ יְהוָה מִן־הַשָּׁמַיִם וַיֹּאמֶר אַבְרָהָם ׀ אַבְרָהָם וַיֹּאמֶר
12 הִנֵּנִי׃ וַיֹּאמֶר אַל־תִּשְׁלַח יָדְךָ אֶל־הַנַּעַר וְאַל־תַּעַשׂ לוֹ
מְאוּמָה כִּי ׀ עַתָּה יָדַעְתִּי כִּי־יְרֵא אֱלֹהִים אַתָּה וְלֹא חָשַׂכְתָּ
13 אֶת־בִּנְךָ אֶת־יְחִידְךָ מִמֶּנִּי׃ וַיִּשָּׂא אַבְרָהָם אֶת־עֵינָיו וַיַּרְא
וְהִנֵּה־אַיִל אַחַר נֶאֱחַז בַּסְּבַךְ בְּקַרְנָיו וַיֵּלֶךְ אַבְרָהָם וַיִּקַּח
14 אֶת־הָאַיִל וַיַּעֲלֵהוּ לְעֹלָה תַּחַת בְּנוֹ׃ וַיִּקְרָא אַבְרָהָם שֵׁם־
הַמָּקוֹם הַהוּא יְהוָה ׀ יִרְאֶה אֲשֶׁר יֵאָמֵר הַיּוֹם בְּהַר יְהוָה
טו יֵרָאֶה׃ וַיִּקְרָא מַלְאַךְ יְהוָה אֶל־אַבְרָהָם שֵׁנִית מִן־הַשָּׁמָיִם׃
16 וַיֹּאמֶר בִּי נִשְׁבַּעְתִּי נְאֻם־יְהוָה כִּי יַעַן אֲשֶׁר עָשִׂיתָ אֶת־
17 הַדָּבָר הַזֶּה וְלֹא חָשַׂכְתָּ אֶת־בִּנְךָ אֶת־יְחִידֶךָ׃ כִּי־בָרֵךְ
אֲבָרֶכְךָ וְהַרְבָּה אַרְבֶּה אֶת־זַרְעֲךָ כְּכוֹכְבֵי הַשָּׁמַיִם וְכַחוֹל
18 אֲשֶׁר עַל־שְׂפַת הַיָּם וְיִרַשׁ זַרְעֲךָ אֵת שַׁעַר אֹיְבָיו׃ וְהִתְבָּרְכוּ
19 בְזַרְעֲךָ כֹּל גּוֹיֵי הָאָרֶץ עֵקֶב אֲשֶׁר שָׁמַעְתָּ בְּקֹלִי׃ וַיָּשָׁב
אַבְרָהָם אֶל־נְעָרָיו וַיָּקֻמוּ וַיֵּלְכוּ יַחְדָּו אֶל־בְּאֵר שָׁבַע

[1] Heb. *jireh*; that is, *see for Himself*. [2] That is, *The LORD seeth.*

סגול באתנח v. 10.

8. *so they went both of them together.* This phrase is repeated from *v.* 6. Abraham's answer caused the truth to dawn upon Isaac's mind that *he* was to be the offering.

9. *bound.* Tied together the limbs.

11. *Abraham, Abraham.* This exclamation (Abraham, Abraham!) shows the anxiety of the angel of the Lord to hold Abraham back at the very last moment.

12. *now I know.* All that God desires was proof of Abraham's *willingness* to obey His command; and the moral surrender had been complete.

14. *to this day. i.e.* it has become a proverbial expression.

where the LORD is seen. i.e. where He reveals himself—referring to the Temple which was afterwards erected on this mount.

16. *by Myself have I sworn.* Moses referred to this oath when he pleaded for Israel; see Exod. XXXII, 13. The expression is the equivalent of, 'as I live, saith the Lord,' Num. XIV, 28, and elsewhere.

17. *as the sand which is upon the sea-shore.* 'As the sand has been placed as a boundary for the sea, and though the waves thereof roar and toss themselves, yet can they not prevail (Jer. V, 22), so would multitudes of enemies strive in vain to destroy Abraham's descendants; *but thy seed shall possess, etc.*' (Malbim); cf. XXXII, 13.

possess the gate of his enemies. Cf. XXIV, 60. The 'gate' of the city was its most important site (see on XIX, 1), and its capture gave one command of the city.

18. *be blessed.* See on XII, 2.

unto his young men, and they rose up and went together to Beer-sheba; and Abraham dwelt at Beer-sheba.*m. ¶ 20. And it came to pass after these things, that it was told Abraham, saying: 'Behold, Milcah, she also hath borne children unto thy brother Nahor: 21. Uz his first-born, and Buz his brother, and Kemuel the father of Aram; 22. and Chesed, and Hazo, and Pildash, and Jidlaph, and Bethuel.' 23. And Bethuel begot Rebekah; these eight did Milcah bear to Nahor, Abraham's brother. 24. And his concubine, whose name was Reumah, she also bore Tebah, and Gaham, and Tahash, and Maacah.

וַיֵּשֶׁב אַבְרָהָם בִּבְאֵר שָׁבַע׃* פ מפטיר
כ וַיְהִי אַחֲרֵי הַדְּבָרִים הָאֵלֶּה וַיֻּגַּד לְאַבְרָהָם לֵאמֹר הִנֵּה
21 יָלְדָה מִלְכָּה גַם־הִוא בָּנִים לְנָחוֹר אָחִיךָ׃ אֶת־עוּץ בְּכֹרוֹ
22 וְאֶת־בּוּז אָחִיו וְאֶת־קְמוּאֵל אֲבִי אֲרָם׃ וְאֶת־כֶּשֶׂד וְאֶת־חֲזוֹ
23 וְאֶת־פִּלְדָּשׁ וְאֶת־יִדְלָף וְאֵת בְּתוּאֵל׃ וּבְתוּאֵל יָלַד אֶת־
רִבְקָה שְׁמֹנָה אֵלֶּה יָלְדָה מִלְכָּה לְנָחוֹר אֲחִי אַבְרָהָם׃
24 וּפִילַגְשׁוֹ וּשְׁמָהּ רְאוּמָה וַתֵּלֶד גַּם־הִוא אֶת־טֶבַח וְאֶת־
גַּחַם וְאֶת־תַּחַשׁ וְאֶת־מַעֲכָה׃

20–24. These verses are inserted to give the genealogy of Rebekah, whose life was to be linked with Isaac's.

20. *Milcah and Nahor.* See XI, 29.

22. *Bethuel.* Mentioned again in Chap. XXIV.

HAFTORAH VAYYERA הפטרת וירא

II KINGS IV, 1–37

CHAPTER IV

1. Now there cried a certain woman of the wives of the sons of the prophets unto Elisha, saying: 'Thy servant my husband is dead; and thou knowest that thy servant did fear the LORD; and the creditor is come to take unto him my two children to be bondmen.' 2. And Elisha said unto her: 'What shall I do for thee? tell me; what hast thou in the house?' And she said: 'Thy handmaid hath not any thing in the house, save a pot of oil.' 3. Then he said: 'Go,

CAP. IV. ד

א וְאִשָּׁה אַחַת מִנְּשֵׁי בְנֵי־הַנְּבִיאִים צָעֲקָה אֶל־אֱלִישָׁע
לֵאמֹר עַבְדְּךָ אִישִׁי מֵת וְאַתָּה יָדַעְתָּ כִּי עַבְדְּךָ הָיָה יָרֵא
אֶת־יְהוָה וְהַנֹּשֶׁה בָּא לָקַחַת אֶת־שְׁנֵי יְלָדַי לוֹ לַעֲבָדִים׃
2 וַיֹּאמֶר אֵלֶיהָ אֱלִישָׁע מָה אֶעֱשֶׂה־לָּךְ הַגִּידִי לִי מַה־יֶּשׁ־
לָכִי בַּבָּיִת וַתֹּאמֶר אֵין לְשִׁפְחָתְךָ כֹל בַּבַּיִת כִּי אִם־אָסוּךְ
3 שָׁמֶן׃ וַיֹּאמֶר לְכִי שַׁאֲלִי־לָךְ כֵּלִים מִן־הַחוּץ מֵאֵת כָּל־

ד׳ v. 2. לך קרי

II KINGS IV, 1–37

The parallel between the Sedrah and Haftorah is clear. The Prophet Elisha, like Abraham, seeks every opportunity to practise lovingkindness and bring relief and blessing wherever he goes in the course of his ministrations. Even more does the story of the Shunammite and her child recall the story of Sarah. Both occurrences were 'Providential' happenings. The Haftorah teaches that there is Divine control of human conditions, and that many humanly unaccountable things happen in life.

1–7. THE WIDOW'S POT OF OIL

This story is one of a cycle of miraculous tales that relate the activities of Elisha, the disciple of the great Prophet Elijah.

1. *a certain woman.* According to tradition, she was the widow of Obadiah (I Kings XVII, 3) the god-fearing minister of king Ahab, who fed and sheltered the Prophets when Jezebel persecuted them. Was her poverty due to the burden of debt with which Obadiah had loaded himself in order to save the Prophets of the LORD from the hands of the murderous Jezebel?

sons of the prophets. i.e. members of a guild, or company, of disciples of the Prophets.

creditor. Throughout antiquity the children of the debtor could be 'collected' instead of the debt.

borrow thee vessels abroad of all thy neighbours, even empty vessels; borrow not a few. 4. And thou shalt go in, and shut the door upon thee and upon thy sons, and pour out into all those vessels; and thou shalt set aside that which is full.' 5. So she went from him, and shut the door upon her and upon her sons; they brought the vessels to her, and she poured out. 6. And it came to pass, when the vessels were full, that she said unto her son: 'Bring me yet a vessel.' And he said unto her: 'There is not a vessel more.' And the oil stayed. 7. Then she came and told the man of God. And he said: 'Go, sell the oil, and pay thy debt, and live thou and thy sons of the rest.' ¶ 8. And it fell on a day, that Elisha passed to Shunem, where was a great woman; and she constrained him to eat bread. And so it was, that as oft as he passed by, he turned in thither to eat bread. 9. And she said unto her husband: 'Behold now, I perceive that this is a holy man of God, that passeth by us continually. 10. Let us make, I pray thee, a little chamber on the roof; and let us set for him there a bed, and a table, and a stool, and a candlestick; and it shall be, when he cometh to us, that he shall turn in thither.' 11. And it fell on a day, that he came thither, and he turned into the upper chamber and lay there. 12. And he said to Gehazi his servant: 'Call this Shunammite.' And when he had called her, she stood before him. 13. And he said unto him: 'Say now unto her: Behold, thou hast been careful for us with all this care; what is to be done for thee? wouldest thou be spoken for to the king, or to the captain of the host?' And she answered: 'I dwell among mine own people.' 14. And he said: 'What then is to be done for her?' And Gehazi answered: 'Verily she hath no son, and her husband is old.' 15. And he said: 'Call her.' And when he had called her, she stood in the door. 16. And he said: 'At this season, when the time cometh round, thou shalt embrace a son.' And she said: 'Nay, my lord, thou man of God, do not lie unto thy handmaid.' 17. And the woman conceived, and bore a son at that season, when the time came round, as Elisha had said unto her. ¶ 18. And when the child was grown, it fell on

4 שְׁכֵנָ֑כְיִ כֵּלִים רֵקִים אַל־תַּמְעִיטִי׃ וּבָאת וְסָגַרְתְּ הַדֶּלֶת
בַּעֲדֵךְ וּבְעַד־בָּנַיִךְ וְיָצַקְתְּ עַל כָּל־הַכֵּלִים הָאֵלֶּה וְהַמָּלֵא
ה תַּסִּיעִי׃ וַתֵּלֶךְ מֵאִתּוֹ וַתִּסְגֹּר הַדֶּלֶת בַּעֲדָהּ וּבְעַד בָּנֶיהָ
6 הֵם מַגִּשִׁים אֵלֶיהָ וְהִיא מֹיצָקֶת׃ וַיְהִי ׀ כִּמְלֹאת הַכֵּלִים
וַתֹּאמֶר אֶל־בְּנָהּ הַגִּישָׁה אֵלַי עוֹד כֶּלִי וַיֹּאמֶר אֵלֶיהָ אֵין
7 עוֹד כֶּלִי וַיַּעֲמֹד הַשָּׁמֶן׃ וַתָּבֹא וַתַּגֵּד לְאִישׁ הָאֱלֹהִים
וַיֹּאמֶר לְכִי מִכְרִי אֶת־הַשֶּׁמֶן וְשַׁלְּמִי אֶת־נִשְׁיֵכְיְ וְאַתְּ
8 בָּנַיִכְיְ תִּחְיִי בַּנּוֹתָר׃ וַיְהִי הַיּוֹם וַיַּעֲבֹר אֱלִישָׁע
אֶל־שׁוּנֵם וְשָׁם אִשָּׁה גְדוֹלָה וַתַּחֲזֶק־בּוֹ לֶאֱכָל־לָחֶם וַיְהִי
9 מִדֵּי עָבְרוֹ יָסֻר שָׁמָּה לֶאֱכָל־לָחֶם׃ וַתֹּאמֶר אֶל־אִישָׁהּ
הִנֵּה־נָא יָדַעְתִּי כִּי אִישׁ אֱלֹהִים קָדוֹשׁ הוּא עֹבֵר עָלֵינוּ
י תָּמִיד׃ נַעֲשֶׂה־נָּא עֲלִיַּת־קִיר קְטַנָּה וְנָשִׂים לוֹ שָׁם מִטָּה
וְשֻׁלְחָן וְכִסֵּא וּמְנוֹרָה וְהָיָה בְּבֹאוֹ אֵלֵינוּ יָסוּר שָׁמָּה׃
11 וַיְהִי הַיּוֹם וַיָּבֹא שָׁמָּה וַיָּסַר אֶל־הָעֲלִיָּה וַיִּשְׁכַּב־שָׁמָּה׃
12 וַיֹּאמֶר אֶל־גֵּיחֲזִי נַעֲרוֹ קְרָא לַשּׁוּנַמִּית הַזֹּאת וַיִּקְרָא־
13 לָהּ וַתַּעֲמֹד לְפָנָיו׃ וַיֹּאמֶר לוֹ אֱמָר־נָא אֵלֶיהָ הִנֵּה
חָרַדְתְּ ׀ אֵלֵינוּ אֶת־כָּל־הַחֲרָדָה הַזֹּאת מֶה לַעֲשׂוֹת לָךְ
הֲיֵשׁ לְדַבֶּר־לָךְ אֶל־הַמֶּלֶךְ אוֹ אֶל־שַׂר הַצָּבָא וַתֹּאמֶר
14 בְּתוֹךְ עַמִּי אָנֹכִי יֹשָׁבֶת׃ וַיֹּאמֶר וּמֶה לַעֲשׂוֹת לָהּ וַיֹּאמֶר
טו גֵּיחֲזִי אֲבָל בֵּן אֵין־לָהּ וְאִישָׁהּ זָקֵן׃ וַיֹּאמֶר קְרָא־לָהּ
16 וַיִּקְרָא־לָהּ וַתַּעֲמֹד בַּפָּתַח׃ וַיֹּאמֶר לַמּוֹעֵד הַזֶּה כָּעֵת
חַיָּה אַתְּי חֹבֶקֶת בֵּן וַתֹּאמֶר אַל־אֲדֹנִי אִישׁ הָאֱלֹהִים
17 אַל־תְּכַזֵּב בְּשִׁפְחָתֶךָ׃ וַתַּהַר הָאִשָּׁה וַתֵּלֶד בֵּן לַמּוֹעֵד
18 הַזֶּה כָּעֵת חַיָּה אֲשֶׁר־דִּבֶּר אֵלֶיהָ אֱלִישָׁע׃ וַיִּגְדַּל הַיָּלֶד

v. 3. שכניך ק׳ v. 5. מוצקת קרי v. 7. נשיך ק׳ ibid. ובניך ק׳ v. 16. את ק׳

7. *man of God.* Popular term for 'Prophet'.

go, sell the oil, and pay thy debt. An ethical rule of Jewish conduct: first pay thy debts, afterwards minister to thine own needs.

8–37. The Shunammite's Son

8. *a great woman. i.e.* a woman of substance and worth. She joyfully extended hospitality to the Prophet on his frequent journeys through that district.

13. *careful for us with all this care.* 'Showed us all this reverence' (RV Margin).

I dwell among mine own people. Among her own relatives; and she wished so to continue. She had no need for influence to be used on her behalf with the king or his officers (Rashi).

a day, that he went out to his father to the reapers. 19. And he said unto his father: 'My head, my head.' And he said to his servant: 'Carry him to his mother.' 20. And when he had taken him, and brought him to his mother, he sat on her knees till noon, and then died. 21. And she went up, and laid him on the bed of the man of God, and shut the door upon him, and went out. 22. And she called unto her husband, and said: 'Send me, I pray thee, one of the servants, and one of the asses, that I may run to the man of God, and come back.' 23. And he said: 'Wherefore wilt thou go to him to-day? it is neither new moon nor sabbath.' And she said: 'It shall be well.'[1] 24. Then she saddled an ass, and said to her servant: 'Drive, and go forward; slacken me not the riding, except I bid thee.' 25. So she went, and came unto the man of God to mount Carmel. ¶ And it came to pass, when the man of God saw her afar off, that he said to Gehazi his servant: 'Behold, yonder is that Shunammite. 26. Run, I pray thee, now to meet her, and say unto her: Is it well with thee? is it well with thy husband? is it well with the child?' And she answered: 'It is well.' 27. And when she came to the man of God to the hill, she caught hold of his feet. And Gehazi came near to thrust her away; but the man of God said: 'Let her alone; for her soul is bitter within her; and the LORD hath hid it from me, and hath not told me.' 28. Then she said: 'Did I desire a son of my lord? did I not say: Do not deceive me?' 29. Then he said to Gehazi: 'Gird up thy loins, and take my staff in thy hand, and go thy way; if thou meet any man, salute him not; and if any salute thee, answer him not; and lay my staff upon the face of the child.' 30. And the

[1] Sephardim conclude here.

19 וַיְהִי הַיּוֹם וַיֵּצֵא אֶל־אָבִיו אֶל־הַקֹּצְרִים׃ וַיֹּאמֶר אֶל־אָבִיו
כ רֹאשִׁי ׀ רֹאשִׁי וַיֹּאמֶר אֶל־הַנַּעַר שָׂאֵהוּ אֶל־אִמּוֹ׃ וַיִּשָּׂאֵהוּ
וַיְבִיאֵהוּ אֶל־אִמּוֹ וַיֵּשֶׁב עַל־בִּרְכֶּיהָ עַד־הַצָּהֳרַיִם וַיָּמֹת׃
21 וַתַּעַל וַתַּשְׁכִּבֵהוּ עַל־מִטַּת אִישׁ הָאֱלֹהִים וַתִּסְגֹּר בַּעֲדוֹ
22 וַתֵּצֵא׃ וַתִּקְרָא אֶל־אִישָׁהּ וַתֹּאמֶר שִׁלְחָה נָא לִי אֶחָד
מִן־הַנְּעָרִים וְאַחַת הָאֲתֹנוֹת וְאָרוּצָה עַד־אִישׁ הָאֱלֹהִים
23 וְאָשׁוּבָה׃ וַיֹּאמֶר מַדּוּעַ אַתְּי הֹלֶכְתִּי אֵלָיו הַיּוֹם לֹא־
24 חֹדֶשׁ וְלֹא שַׁבָּת וַתֹּאמֶר שָׁלוֹם׃ · וַתַּחֲבֹשׁ הָאָתוֹן וַתֹּאמֶר
אֶל־נַעֲרָהּ נְהַג וָלֵךְ אַל־תַּעֲצָר־לִי לִרְכֹּב כִּי אִם־אָמַרְתִּי
כה לָךְ׃ וַתֵּלֶךְ וַתָּבוֹא אֶל־אִישׁ הָאֱלֹהִים אֶל־הַר הַכַּרְמֶל
וַיְהִי כִּרְאוֹת אִישׁ־הָאֱלֹהִים אוֹתָהּ מִנֶּגֶד וַיֹּאמֶר אֶל־גֵּיחֲזִי
26 נַעֲרוֹ הִנֵּה הַשּׁוּנַמִּית הַלָּז׃ עַתָּה רוּץ־נָא לִקְרָאתָהּ וֶאֱמָר־
לָהּ הֲשָׁלוֹם לָךְ הֲשָׁלוֹם לְאִישֵׁךְ הֲשָׁלוֹם לַיָּלֶד וַתֹּאמֶר
27 שָׁלוֹם׃ וַתָּבֹא אֶל־אִישׁ הָאֱלֹהִים אֶל־הָהָר וַתַּחֲזֵק בְּרַגְלָיו
וַיִּגַּשׁ גֵּיחֲזִי לְהָדְפָהּ וַיֹּאמֶר אִישׁ הָאֱלֹהִים הַרְפֵּה־לָהּ
כִּי־נַפְשָׁהּ מָרָה־לָהּ וַיהוָה הֶעְלִים מִמֶּנִּי וְלֹא הִגִּיד לִי׃
28 וַתֹּאמֶר הֲשָׁאַלְתִּי בֵן מֵאֵת אֲדֹנִי הֲלֹא אָמַרְתִּי לֹא תַשְׁלֶה
29 אֹתִי׃ וַיֹּאמֶר לְגֵיחֲזִי חֲגֹר מָתְנֶיךָ וְקַח מִשְׁעַנְתִּי בְיָדְךָ
וָלֵךְ כִּי־תִמְצָא אִישׁ לֹא תְבָרְכֶנּוּ וְכִי־יְבָרֶכְךָ אִישׁ לֹא

v. 23. את קרי ibid. הולכת ק׳ כאן מסיימין הספרדים

19. *my head, my head.* Heb. *roshi, roshi.* A marvellously vivid description of the child's sunstroke, and in two Heb. words!

23. *new moon.* This points to a custom of the time to make pilgrimages to the Prophet or to the sanctuary on Sabbaths and New Moons.

it shall be well. Expressed in one Heb. word, '*Shalom.*' We have no sound of wailing: with perfect self-control and vivid faith the Shunammite woman hastens to the Prophet.

25. *yonder is that Shunammite.* He is surprised at her unexpected visit.

26. *Is it well with thee?* All mothers and fathers might well ask themselves these three soul-searching questions. השלום לך *Is it well with thee?* lit. 'Is peace thine?' Are you at peace with yourself, your conscience, your God? *Is it well with thy husband? i.e.* is it well with your home? Is it still a Jewish home, a sanctuary? *Is it well with the child?* In the Sedrah, Abraham and Isaac are called upon to tread the path of supreme sacrifice; yet, Scripture records of father and son, 'And they walked both of them together.' Is there similar unity of heart and soul between you and *your* child? Education is the shibboleth of the hour; but in Judaism the word for 'education' (חינוך) is the same as for 'consecration'. Is your child being *consecrated* for a life of beneficence for Israel and humanity?

'The object of education is not merely to enable our children to gain their daily bread and to acquire pleasant means of recreation, but that they should know God and serve Him with earnestness and devotion. Are you thus training your children? Is it your care that they be mother of the child said: 'As the LORD liveth, and as thy soul liveth, I will not leave thee.' And he arose, and followed her. 31. And Gehazi passed on before them, and laid the staff upon the face of the child; but there was neither voice, nor hearing. Wherefore he returned to meet him, and told him, saying: 'The child is not awaked.' ¶ 32. And when Elisha was come into the house, behold, the child was dead, and laid upon his bed. 33. He went in therefore, and shut the door upon them twain, and prayed unto the LORD. 34. And he went up, and lay upon the child, and put his mouth upon his mouth, and his eyes upon his eyes, and his hands upon his hands; and he stretched himself upon him; and the flesh of the child waxed warm. 35. Then he returned, and walked in the house once to and fro; and went up, and stretched himself upon him; and the child sneezed seven times, and the child opened his eyes. 36. And he called Gehazi, and said: 'Call this Shunammite.' So he called her. And when she was come in unto him, he said: 'Take up thy son.' 37. Then she went in, and fell at his feet, and bowed down to the ground; and she took up her son, and went out.

ל תַּעֲנֶנּוּ וְשַׂמְתָּ מִשְׁעַנְתִּי עַל־פְּנֵי הַנָּעַר׃ וַתֹּאמֶר אֵם הַנַּעַר
31 חַי־יְהוָה וְחֵי־נַפְשְׁךָ אִם־אֶעֶזְבֶךָּ וַיָּקָם וַיֵּלֶךְ אַחֲרֶיהָ׃ וְגֵחֲזִי
עָבַר לִפְנֵיהֶם וַיָּשֶׂם אֶת־הַמִּשְׁעֶנֶת עַל־פְּנֵי הַנַּעַר וְאֵין
קוֹל וְאֵין קָשֶׁב וַיָּשָׁב לִקְרָאתוֹ וַיַּגֶּד־לוֹ לֵאמֹר לֹא הֵקִיץ
32 הַנָּעַר׃ וַיָּבֹא אֱלִישָׁע הַבַּיְתָה וְהִנֵּה הַנַּעַר מֵת מֻשְׁכָּב
33 עַל־מִטָּתוֹ׃ וַיָּבֹא וַיִּסְגֹּר הַדֶּלֶת בְּעַד שְׁנֵיהֶם וַיִּתְפַּלֵּל
34 אֶל־יְהוָה׃ וַיַּעַל וַיִּשְׁכַּב עַל־הַיֶּלֶד וַיָּשֶׂם פִּיו עַל־פִּיו
וְעֵינָיו עַל־עֵינָיו וְכַפָּיו עַל־כַּפָּו וַיִּגְהַר עָלָיו וַיָּחָם בְּשַׂר
לה הַיָּלֶד׃ וַיָּשָׁב וַיֵּלֶךְ בַּבַּיִת אַחַת הֵנָּה וְאַחַת הֵנָּה וַיַּעַל
וַיִּגְהַר עָלָיו וַיְזוֹרֵר הַנַּעַר עַד־שֶׁבַע פְּעָמִים וַיִּפְקַח הַנַּעַר
36 אֶת־עֵינָיו׃ וַיִּקְרָא אֶל־גֵּיחֲזִי וַיֹּאמֶר קְרָא אֶל־הַשֻּׁנַמִּית
37 הַזֹּאת וַיִּקְרָאֶהָ וַתָּבוֹא אֵלָיו וַיֹּאמֶר שְׂאִי בְנֵךְ׃ וַתָּבֹא
וַתִּפֹּל עַל־רַגְלָיו וַתִּשְׁתַּחוּ אָרְצָה וַתִּשָּׂא אֶת־בְּנָהּ וַתֵּצֵא׃

v. 34. כפיו קרי

educated as Jews and Jewesses?' (Hermann Adler).

it is well. A mere affirmative; she will lay bare her grief only when she is alone with the Prophet.

29. *salute him not.* To avoid waste of time.

31. *voice, nor hearing.* No sign of life.

35. We may find deep suggestion in the restoration of the Shunammite's child to life. The child was revived by contact with the living warmth of the Prophet's body. Thus has Israel throughout the ages survived a thousand deaths, because his soul was ever quickened into life by direct contact with the Divine teaching of Israel's Lawgiver, Prophets, and Sages.

23

CHAPTER XXIII

1. And the life of Sarah was a hundred and seven and twenty years; these were the years of the life of Sarah. 2. And Sarah died in Kiriath-arba—the same is Hebron—in the land of Canaan; and Abraham came to mourn for Sarah, and to weep for her. 3. And Abraham rose up from before his dead, and spoke unto the children of Heth, saying: 4. 'I am a stranger and a sojourner with you; give me a possession of a burying-place with you, that I may bury my dead out of my sight.' 5. And the children of Heth answered Abraham, saying unto him: 6. 'Hear us, my lord: thou art a mighty prince among us; in the choice of our sepulchres bury thy dead; none of us shall withhold from thee his sepulchre, but that thou mayest bury thy dead.' 7. And Abraham rose up, and bowed down to the people of the land, even to the children of Heth. 8. And he spoke with them, saying: 'If it be your mind that I should bury my dead out of my sight,

CAP. XXIII. כג

כג

פ פ פ ה 5

א וַיִּהְיוּ חַיֵּי שָׂרָה מֵאָה שָׁנָה וְעֶשְׂרִים שָׁנָה וְשֶׁבַע שָׁנִים
2 שְׁנֵי חַיֵּי שָׂרָה׃ וַתָּמָת שָׂרָה בְּקִרְיַת אַרְבַּע הִוא חֶבְרוֹן
בְּאֶרֶץ כְּנָעַן וַיָּבֹא אַבְרָהָם לִסְפֹּד לְשָׂרָה וְלִבְכֹּתָהּ׃
3 וַיָּקָם אַבְרָהָם מֵעַל פְּנֵי מֵתוֹ וַיְדַבֵּר אֶל־בְּנֵי־חֵת לֵאמֹר׃
4 גֵּר־וְתוֹשָׁב אָנֹכִי עִמָּכֶם תְּנוּ לִי אֲחֻזַּת־קֶבֶר עִמָּכֶם וְאֶקְבְּרָה
ה 6 מֵתִי מִלְּפָנָי׃ וַיַּעֲנוּ בְנֵי־חֵת אֶת־אַבְרָהָם לֵאמֹר לוֹ׃ שְׁמָעֵנוּ ׀
אֲדֹנִי נְשִׂיא אֱלֹהִים אַתָּה בְּתוֹכֵנוּ בְּמִבְחַר קְבָרֵינוּ קְבֹר
אֶת־מֵתֶךָ אִישׁ מִמֶּנּוּ אֶת־קִבְרוֹ לֹא־יִכְלֶה מִמְּךָ מִקְּבֹר
7 מֵתֶךָ׃ וַיָּקָם אַבְרָהָם וַיִּשְׁתַּחוּ לְעַם־הָאָרֶץ לִבְנֵי־חֵת׃
8 וַיְדַבֵּר אִתָּם לֵאמֹר אִם־יֵשׁ אֶת־נַפְשְׁכֶם לִקְבֹּר אֶת־מֵתִי

v. 2. כ״ף זעירא

V. CHAYYE SARAH

(CHAPTERS XXIII–XXV, 18)

CHAPTER XXIII. DEATH AND BURIAL OF SARAH

1. *a hundred and seven and twenty years.* lit. 'a hundred years, and twenty years, and seven years'; and since the word 'year' is inserted after every figure, the Rabbis comment: 'She was as handsome at one hundred as at the age of twenty; and as sinless at twenty as at seven.' (This, according to Luzzatto and Berliner, was the original form of the saying.)

2. *Kiriath-arba.* lit. 'the city of four'. In Judges I, 10, it is stated that Kiriath-arba was the old name of Hebron, and in that city the Israelites slew three giant chieftains, the sons of a man named Arba (see Josh. XV, 13). Hence the city was named after Arba; or it signified the city of these *four* giants.

Hebron. See on XIII, 18.

to mourn. The Hebrew word indicates the loud wailing still usual in the East as a manifestation of grief.

3. *rose up.* This verb is used because the mourner sat and slept on the ground; see II Sam. XII, 16; Lam. II, 10.

children of Heth. i.e. the Hittites; see on X, 15.

4. *stranger and a sojourner.* A proverbial phrase describing one whose origin is foreign, and whose period of residence is uncertain (Ryle).

out of my sight. Better, '*from before me.*'

This is the first reference in the Bible to burial; and the reverential concern which the Patriarch shows to give honourable sepulchre to his dead has been a distinguishing feature among his descendants. *Meth mitzvah,* care of the unburied body of a friendless man, takes precedence over all other commandments. Burial is the Jewish method of disposal of the dead. Tacitus (Hist. v, 5) remarked upon the fact that the Jews buried their dead, instead of burning them. Cremation has always been repugnant to Jewish feeling, and is in total variance with the law and custom of Israel.

6–18. The bargaining which follows, with grandiloquent phrases and lavish offers, not to be taken too seriously by the person addressed, is still typically Oriental.

6. *a mighty prince.* lit. 'a prince of God'; similarly, 'mountains of God' means 'great mountains'.

in the choice of our sepulchres. Family or tribal vaults were common in ancient times, and the Hittites gave Abraham permission to select any one of these vaults; but the Patriarch insists on a separate resting-place for his wife. He probably had the intention of being buried there himself. If such was his intention, it was fulfilled; see XLIX, 29 f.

7. *people of the land.* Heb. *Am ha-aretz,* which elsewhere means 'the people of the land', and in later Hebrew, 'an ignorant person,' here means the Council of the Hittites in session. Abraham desired to secure a burial place that should for ever hear me, and entreat for me to Ephron the son of Zohar, 9. that he may give me the cave of Machpelah, which he hath, which is in the end of his field; for the full price let him give it to me in the midst of you for a possession of a burying-place.' 10. Now Ephron was sitting in the midst of the children of Heth; and Ephron the Hittite answered Abraham in the hearing of the children of Heth, even of all that went in at the gate of his city, saying: 11. 'Nay, my lord, hear me: the field give I thee, and the cave that is therein, I give it thee; in the presence of the sons of my people give I it thee; bury thy dead.' 12. And Abraham bowed down before the people of the land. 13. And he spoke unto Ephron in the hearing of the people of the land, saying: 'But if thou wilt, I pray thee, hear me: I will give the price of the field; take it of me, and I will bury my dead there.' 14. And Ephron answered Abraham, saying unto him: 15. 'My lord, hearken unto me: a piece of land worth four hundred shekels of silver, what is that betwixt me and thee? bury therefore thy dead.' 16. And Abraham hearkened unto Ephron; and Abraham weighed to Ephron the silver, which he had named in the hearing of the children of Heth, four hundred shekels of silver, current money with the merchant.* ii. 17. So the field of Ephron, which was in Machpelah, which was before Mamre, the field, and the cave

9 מִלְּפָנַי שְׁמָעוּנִי וּפִגְעוּ־לִי בְּעֶפְרוֹן בֶּן־צֹחַר׃ וְיִתֶּן־לִי אֶת־
מְעָרַת הַמַּכְפֵּלָה אֲשֶׁר־לוֹ אֲשֶׁר בִּקְצֵה שָׂדֵהוּ בְּכֶסֶף
י מָלֵא יִתְּנֶנָּה לִּי בְּתוֹכְכֶם לַאֲחֻזַּת־קָבֶר׃ וְעֶפְרוֹן יֹשֵׁב בְּתוֹךְ
בְּנֵי־חֵת וַיַּעַן עֶפְרוֹן הַחִתִּי אֶת־אַבְרָהָם בְּאָזְנֵי בְנֵי־חֵת
11 לְכֹל בָּאֵי שַׁעַר־עִירוֹ לֵאמֹר׃ לֹא־אֲדֹנִי שְׁמָעֵנִי הַשָּׂדֶה
נָתַתִּי לָךְ וְהַמְּעָרָה אֲשֶׁר־בּוֹ לְךָ נְתַתִּיהָ לְעֵינֵי בְנֵי־עַמִּי
12 נְתַתִּיהָ לָּךְ קְבֹר מֵתֶךָ׃ וַיִּשְׁתַּחוּ אַבְרָהָם לִפְנֵי עַם־הָאָרֶץ׃
13 וַיְדַבֵּר אֶל־עֶפְרוֹן בְּאָזְנֵי עַם־הָאָרֶץ לֵאמֹר אַךְ אִם־אַתָּה
לוּ שְׁמָעֵנִי נָתַתִּי כֶּסֶף הַשָּׂדֶה קַח מִמֶּנִּי וְאֶקְבְּרָה אֶת־
14 טו מֵתִי שָׁמָּה׃ וַיַּעַן עֶפְרוֹן אֶת־אַבְרָהָם לֵאמֹר לוֹ׃ אֲדֹנִי
שְׁמָעֵנִי אֶרֶץ אַרְבַּע מֵאֹת שֶׁקֶל־כֶּסֶף בֵּינִי וּבֵינְךָ מַה־
16 הִוא וְאֶת־מֵתְךָ קְבֹר׃ וַיִּשְׁמַע אַבְרָהָם אֶל־עֶפְרוֹן וַיִּשְׁקֹל
שני אַבְרָהָם לְעֶפְרֹן אֶת־הַכֶּסֶף אֲשֶׁר דִּבֶּר בְּאָזְנֵי בְנֵי־חֵת
17 אַרְבַּע מֵאוֹת שֶׁקֶל כֶּסֶף עֹבֵר לַסֹּחֵר׃ *וַיָּקָם ׀ שְׂדֵה עֶפְרוֹן
אֲשֶׁר בַּמַּכְפֵּלָה אֲשֶׁר לִפְנֵי מַמְרֵא הַשָּׂדֶה וְהַמְּעָרָה אֲשֶׁר־

remain a possession of his family. Such 'freehold' purchase was impossible without the assent of the local Hittite national Council. 'The expression *am ha-aretz* occurs 49 times in Scripture. In 42 of these instances it means neither the nation nor an individual boor, but is simply a technical term of Hebrew Politics and signifies what we would call Parliament.' Judge Mayer Sulzberger, *The Am ha-aretz, the Ancient Hebrew Parliament*, Philadelphia, 1910.

9. *the cave of Machpelah.* It was a common practice to bury in caves. The word which is the name of the cave and of the locality denotes 'double'; possibly because it consisted of two storeys.

full price. lit. 'full silver'; Abraham wished to establish an unassailable right to the land by the payment of its value.

10. *Ephron was sitting.* Presiding over the session of the Assembly.

in the hearing. *i.e.* publicly; cf. 'all the goers-out of the gate of his city,' XXXIV, 24.

11. *give I thee.* An expression of conventional politeness, neither intended nor taken literally.

15. *what is that betwixt me and thee?* What can such a sum as that just mentioned matter to persons such as we? In this apparently unconcerned tone, the seller indicates the price he wants. The sum demanded, four hundred shekels of silver, is a very substantial sum, perhaps equivalent in purchasing power to from £1,000 to £2,000 in our time. In the contemporary Code of Hammurabi (see on XIV, 1) the wages of a working-man for a year are fixed at six or eight shekels (Bennett).

16. *weighed.* There were no coins of standard size and shape; therefore the pieces of silver had to be weighed before their value could be ascertained.

current money with the merchant. The phrase probably denotes that the silver was in convenient-sized pieces, readily usable in business transactions.

17. *were made sure.* *i.e.* were assured to Abraham. This verse and the following may well be a citation from the deed of assignment which was drawn up at the purchase. Contracts of this kind, dating from very early Semitic times, have been discovered in large numbers.

which was therein, and all the trees that were in the field, that were in all the border thereof round about, were made sure 18. unto Abraham for a possession in the presence of the children of Heth, before all that went in at the gate of his city. 19. And after this, Abraham buried Sarah his wife in the cave of the field of Machpelah before Mamre—the same is Hebron—in the land of Canaan. 20. And the field, and the cave that is therein, were made sure unto Abraham for a possession of a burying-place by the children of Heth.

18 בּוֹ וְכָל־הָעֵץ אֲשֶׁר בַּשָּׂדֶה אֲשֶׁר בְּכָל־גְּבֻלוֹ סָבִיב׃ לְאַבְרָהָם
19 לְמִקְנָה לְעֵינֵי בְנֵי־חֵת בְּכֹל בָּאֵי שַׁעַר־עִירוֹ׃ וְאַחֲרֵי־כֵן
קָבַר אַבְרָהָם אֶת־שָׂרָה אִשְׁתּוֹ אֶל־מְעָרַת שְׂדֵה הַמַּכְפֵּלָה
כ עַל־פְּנֵי מַמְרֵא הִוא חֶבְרוֹן בְּאֶרֶץ כְּנָעַן׃ וַיָּקָם הַשָּׂדֶה
וְהַמְּעָרָה אֲשֶׁר־בּוֹ לְאַבְרָהָם לַאֲחֻזַּת־קָבֶר מֵאֵת בְּנֵי־חֵת׃ ס

24 CHAPTER XXIV

כד

CAP. XXIV. כד

1. And Abraham was old, well stricken in age; and the LORD had blessed Abraham in all things. 2. And Abraham said unto his servant, the elder of his house, that ruled over all that he had: 'Put, I pray thee, thy hand under my thigh. 3. And I will make thee swear by the LORD, the God of heaven and the God of the earth, that thou shalt not take a wife for my son of the daughters of the Canaanites, among whom I dwell. 4. But thou shalt go unto my country, and to my kindred, and take a wife for my son, even for Isaac.' 5. And the servant said unto him: 'Peradventure the woman will not be willing to follow me unto this land; must I needs bring thy son back unto the land from whence thou camest?' 6. And Abraham said unto him: 'Beware thou that thou bring not my son back thither. 7. The LORD, the God of heaven, who took me from my father's house, and from the land of my nativity, and who spoke unto me, and who swore

א וְאַבְרָהָם זָקֵן בָּא בַּיָּמִים וַיהוָה בֵּרַךְ אֶת־אַבְרָהָם בַּכֹּל׃
2 וַיֹּאמֶר אַבְרָהָם אֶל־עַבְדּוֹ זְקַן בֵּיתוֹ הַמֹּשֵׁל בְּכָל־אֲשֶׁר־
3 לוֹ שִׂים־נָא יָדְךָ תַּחַת יְרֵכִי׃ וְאַשְׁבִּיעֲךָ בַּיהוָה אֱלֹהֵי
הַשָּׁמַיִם וֵאלֹהֵי הָאָרֶץ אֲשֶׁר לֹא־תִקַּח אִשָּׁה לִבְנִי מִבְּנוֹת
4 הַכְּנַעֲנִי אֲשֶׁר אָנֹכִי יוֹשֵׁב בְּקִרְבּוֹ׃ כִּי אֶל־אַרְצִי וְאֶל־
ה מוֹלַדְתִּי תֵּלֵךְ וְלָקַחְתָּ אִשָּׁה לִבְנִי לְיִצְחָק׃ וַיֹּאמֶר אֵלָיו
הָעֶבֶד אוּלַי לֹא־תֹאבֶה הָאִשָּׁה לָלֶכֶת אַחֲרַי אֶל־הָאָרֶץ
הַזֹּאת הֶהָשֵׁב אָשִׁיב אֶת־בִּנְךָ אֶל־הָאָרֶץ אֲשֶׁר־יָצָאתָ
6 מִשָּׁם׃ וַיֹּאמֶר אֵלָיו אַבְרָהָם הִשָּׁמֶר לְךָ פֶּן־תָּשִׁיב אֶת־
7 בְּנִי שָׁמָּה׃ יְהוָה ׀ אֱלֹהֵי הַשָּׁמַיִם אֲשֶׁר לְקָחַנִי מִבֵּית

18. *in the presence of.* The sale was duly witnessed; cf. Jer. xxxii, 12.

For generations, nay centuries, the children of Israel were to have no point of fixity save the sepulchre of the Patriarchs. The Cave of Machpelah is regarded with immense veneration by the Mohammedans, who built a large mosque over it, and until recently altogether excluded both Jews and Christians from viewing it. A visit is still connected with considerable difficulty to a Jew.

CHAPTER XXIV. REBEKAH

1. *well stricken in age.* See on xviii, 11.

2. *the elder of his house.* The one who possessed the greatest authority. Although the servant is not named here, it is clear from what was stated in xv, 2 that Eliezer is intended.

put thy hand under my thigh. According to the Biblical idiom, children are said to issue from the 'thigh' or 'loins' of their father (cf. xlvi, 26). Therefore the formality of placing the hand upon the thigh was taken to signify that if the oath were violated, the children who have issued, or might issue, from the 'thigh' would avenge the act of disloyalty.

3. *God of heaven.* Abraham makes his servant swear in the name of the God he himself worshipped; he had converted his servant to the true Faith (see on xii, 5), evidenced by Eliezer's devout conduct throughout the narrative which follows.

daughters of the Canaanites. Who might divert Isaac from the path which his father had mapped out for him; cf. xxviii, 1. This fear of the evil consequences which would result from intermarriage with heathens is frequently expressed in the Bible; *e.g.* Deut. vii, 3 f.

4. *my country . . . kindred.* Here the reference is to Haran and to the family of his brother Nahor.

5. The meaning is, If I find a suitable wife for Isaac in Haran but the woman is not willing to leave her home, am I to take Isaac to Haran?

6. On no account is Isaac to return to Haran, lest he abandon the Land of Promise.

7. Abraham felt strongly that Isaac's marriage would be an important factor in the fulfilment of the Divine promise. Hence God would help

unto me, saying: Unto thy seed will I give
this land; He will send His angel before
thee, and thou shalt take a wife for my
son from thence. 8. And if the woman
be not willing to follow thee, then thou
shalt be clear from this my oath; only
thou shalt not bring my son back thither.'
9. And the servant put his hand under the
thigh of Abraham his master, and swore
to him concerning this matter.* iii. 10.
And the servant took ten camels, of the
camels of his master, and departed; having
all goodly things of his master's in his
hand; and he arose, and went to [1]Aram-
naharaim, unto the city of Nahor. 11.
And he made the camels to kneel down
without the city by the well of water at
the time of evening, the time that women
go out to draw water. 12. And he said:
'O LORD, the God of my master Abraham,
send me, I pray Thee, good speed this day,
and show kindness unto my master Abra-
ham. 13. Behold, I stand by the fountain
of water; and the daughters of the men
of the city come out to draw water. 14.
So let it come to pass, that the damsel to
whom I shall say: Let down thy pitcher,
I pray thee, that I may drink; and she
shall say: Drink, and I will give thy camels
drink also; let the same be she that Thou
hast appointed for Thy servant, even for
Isaac; and thereby shall I know that Thou
hast shown kindness unto my master.' 15.
And it came to pass, before he had done
speaking, that, behold, Rebekah came out,
who was born to Bethuel the son of Milcah,
the wife of Nahor, Abraham's brother,
with her pitcher upon her shoulder. 16.
And the damsel was very fair to look upon,
a virgin, neither had any man known her;

[1] That is, *Mesopotamia.*

אָבִי וּמֵאֶרֶץ מוֹלַדְתִּי וַאֲשֶׁר דִּבֶּר־לִי וַאֲשֶׁר נִשְׁבַּע־לִי
לֵאמֹר לְזַרְעֲךָ אֶתֵּן אֶת־הָאָרֶץ הַזֹּאת הוּא יִשְׁלַח מַלְאָכוֹ
8 לְפָנֶיךָ וְלָקַחְתָּ אִשָּׁה לִבְנִי מִשָּׁם׃ וְאִם־לֹא תֹאבֶה הָאִשָּׁה
לָלֶכֶת אַחֲרֶיךָ וְנִקִּיתָ מִשְּׁבֻעָתִי זֹאת רַק אֶת־בְּנִי לֹא תָשֵׁב
9 שָׁמָּה׃ וַיָּשֶׂם הָעֶבֶד אֶת־יָדוֹ תַּחַת יֶרֶךְ אַבְרָהָם אֲדֹנָיו
שלישי י וַיִּשָּׁבַע לוֹ עַל־הַדָּבָר הַזֶּה׃ וַיִּקַּח הָעֶבֶד עֲשָׂרָה גְמַלִּים
מִגְּמַלֵּי אֲדֹנָיו וַיֵּלֶךְ וְכָל־טוּב אֲדֹנָיו בְּיָדוֹ וַיָּקָם וַיֵּלֶךְ אֶל־
11 אֲרַם נַהֲרַיִם אֶל־עִיר נָחוֹר׃ וַיַּבְרֵךְ הַגְּמַלִּים מִחוּץ לָעִיר
12 אֶל־בְּאֵר הַמָּיִם לְעֵת עֶרֶב לְעֵת צֵאת הַשֹּׁאֲבֹת׃ וַיֹּאמַר ׀
יְהוָה אֱלֹהֵי אֲדֹנִי אַבְרָהָם הַקְרֵה־נָא לְפָנַי הַיּוֹם וַעֲשֵׂה־
13 חֶסֶד עִם אֲדֹנִי אַבְרָהָם׃ הִנֵּה אָנֹכִי נִצָּב עַל־עֵין הַמָּיִם
14 וּבְנוֹת אַנְשֵׁי הָעִיר יֹצְאֹת לִשְׁאֹב מָיִם׃ וְהָיָה הַנַּעֲרָ אֲשֶׁר
אֹמַר אֵלֶיהָ הַטִּי־נָא כַדֵּךְ וְאֶשְׁתֶּה וְאָמְרָה שְׁתֵה וְגַם־
גְּמַלֶּיךָ אַשְׁקֶה אֹתָהּ הֹכַחְתָּ לְעַבְדְּךָ לְיִצְחָק וּבָהּ אֵדַע
טו כִּי־עָשִׂיתָ חֶסֶד עִם־אֲדֹנִי׃ וַיְהִי־הוּא טֶרֶם כִּלָּה לְדַבֵּר
וְהִנֵּה רִבְקָה יֹצֵאת אֲשֶׁר יֻלְּדָה לִבְתוּאֵל בֶּן־מִלְכָּה אֵשֶׁת
16 נָחוֹר אֲחִי אַבְרָהָם וְכַדָּהּ עַל־שִׁכְמָהּ׃ וְהַנַּעֲרָ טֹבַת מַרְאֶה
מְאֹד בְּתוּלָה וְאִישׁ לֹא יְדָעָהּ וַתֵּרֶד הָעַיְנָה וַתְּמַלֵּא כַדָּהּ

v. 14. הנערה קרי v. 16. והנערה קרי

Eliezer in his mission to find a worthy wife for Isaac.

He will send His angel before thee. An expression denoting that God's protection and aid would be given him; cf. Exod. XXIII, 20.

9. *concerning this matter.* lit. 'in accordance with this word,' *i.e.* on the terms just laid down; namely, if the woman declines to follow him, Eliezer should be free from his obligation.

10. *and the servant took.* Gifts for the bride and her family.

Aram-naharaim. *i.e.* Aram of the two rivers, Euphrates and Tigris, Mesopotamia.

the city of Nahor. *i.e.* the city in which Nahor and his family dwelt, Haran.

11. *by the well of water.* The place where a stranger would naturally wait who required information concerning an inhabitant of the city.

12. *send me good speed.* lit. 'make it happen before me' (as I desire).

14. *camels drink also.* Eliezer would only ask a drink of water for himself. The maiden on her own initiative was to suggest water for the camels. Her doing so would be evidence of a tender heart. Kindness to animals is a virtue upon which Judaism lays stress. The Talmud declares that a man must not sit down to his meal before giving food to his animals. It is noteworthy that Eliezer decided to make beauty of character the criterion in his selection of a wife for Isaac. He anticipated the writer of Prov. XXXI, 30, who declared, 'Favour is deceitful and beauty is vain; but a woman that feareth the Lord, she shall be praised.'

15. *Bethuel.* See XXII, 20 f.

16. *very fair to look upon.* Rebekah possessed physical beauty as well as goodness of heart.

and she went down to the fountain, and filled her pitcher, and came up. 17. And the servant ran to meet her, and said: 'Give me to drink, I pray thee, a little water of thy pitcher.' 18. And she said: 'Drink, my lord'; and she hastened, and let down her pitcher upon her hand, and gave him drink. 19. And when she had done giving him drink, she said: 'I will draw for thy camels also, until they have done drinking.' 20. And she hastened, and emptied her pitcher into the trough, and ran again unto the well to draw, and drew for all his camels. 21. And the man looked steadfastly on her; holding his peace, to know whether the LORD had made his journey prosperous or not. 22. And it came to pass, as the camels had done drinking, that the man took a golden ring of half a shekel weight, and two bracelets for her hands of ten shekels weight of gold; 23. and said: 'Whose daughter art thou? tell me, I pray thee. Is there room in thy father's house for us to lodge in?' 24. And she said unto him: 'I am the daughter of Bethuel the son of Milcah, whom she bore unto Nahor.' 25. She said moreover unto him: 'We have both straw and provender enough, and room to lodge in.' 26. And the man bowed his head, and prostrated himself before the LORD.* iv. 27. And he said: 'Blessed be the LORD, the God of my master Abraham, who hath not forsaken His mercy and His truth toward my master; as for me, the LORD hath led me in the way to the house of my master's brethren.' 28. And the damsel ran, and told her mother's house according to these words. 29. And Rebekah had a brother, and his name was Laban; and Laban ran out unto the man, unto the fountain. 30. And it came to pass, when he saw the ring, and the bracelets upon his sister's hands, and when he heard the words of Rebekah his sister, saying: 'Thus spoke the man unto me,' that he came unto the man; and, behold, he stood by the camels at the fountain. 31. And he said: 'Come

17 וַתָּעַל׃ וַיָּרָץ הָעֶבֶד לִקְרָאתָהּ וַיֹּאמֶר הַגְמִיאִינִי נָא מְעַט־
18 מַיִם מִכַּדֵּךְ׃ וַתֹּאמֶר שְׁתֵה אֲדֹנִי וַתְּמַהֵר וַתֹּרֶד כַּדָּהּ עַל־
19 יָדָהּ וַתַּשְׁקֵהוּ׃ וַתְּכַל לְהַשְׁקֹתוֹ וַתֹּאמֶר גַּם לִגְמַלֶּיךָ אֶשְׁאָב
כ עַד אִם־כִּלּוּ לִשְׁתֹּת׃ וַתְּמַהֵר וַתְּעַר כַּדָּהּ אֶל־הַשֹּׁקֶת וַתָּרָץ
21 עוֹד אֶל־הַבְּאֵר לִשְׁאֹב וַתִּשְׁאַב לְכָל־גְּמַלָּיו׃ וְהָאִישׁ
מִשְׁתָּאֵה לָהּ מַחֲרִישׁ לָדַעַת הַהִצְלִיחַ יְהוָה דַּרְכּוֹ אִם־
22 לֹא׃ וַיְהִי כַּאֲשֶׁר כִּלּוּ הַגְּמַלִּים לִשְׁתּוֹת וַיִּקַּח הָאִישׁ נֶזֶם
זָהָב בֶּקַע מִשְׁקָלוֹ וּשְׁנֵי צְמִידִים עַל־יָדֶיהָ עֲשָׂרָה זָהָב
23 מִשְׁקָלָם׃ וַיֹּאמֶר בַּת־מִי אַתְּ הַגִּידִי נָא לִי הֲיֵשׁ בֵּית־
24 אָבִיךְ מָקוֹם לָנוּ לָלִין׃ וַתֹּאמֶר אֵלָיו בַּת־בְּתוּאֵל אָנֹכִי בֶּן־
כה מִלְכָּה אֲשֶׁר יָלְדָה לְנָחוֹר׃ וַתֹּאמֶר אֵלָיו גַּם־תֶּבֶן גַּם־
26 מִסְפּוֹא רַב עִמָּנוּ גַּם־מָקוֹם לָלוּן׃ וַיִּקֹּד הָאִישׁ וַיִּשְׁתַּחוּ
רביעי
27 לַיהוָה׃ * וַיֹּאמֶר בָּרוּךְ יְהוָה אֱלֹהֵי אֲדֹנִי אַבְרָהָם אֲשֶׁר
לֹא־עָזַב חַסְדּוֹ וַאֲמִתּוֹ מֵעִם אֲדֹנִי אָנֹכִי בַּדֶּרֶךְ נָחַנִי יְהוָה
28 בֵּית אֲחֵי אֲדֹנִי׃ וַתָּרָץ הַנַּעֲרָ וַתַּגֵּד לְבֵית אִמָּהּ כַּדְּבָרִים
29 הָאֵלֶּה׃ וּלְרִבְקָה אָח וּשְׁמוֹ לָבָן וַיָּרָץ לָבָן אֶל־הָאִישׁ
ל הַחוּצָה אֶל־הָעָיִן׃ וַיְהִי ׀ כִּרְאֹת אֶת־הַנֶּזֶם וְאֶת־הַצְּמִדִים
עַל־יְדֵי אֲחֹתוֹ וּכְשָׁמְעוֹ אֶת־דִּבְרֵי רִבְקָה אֲחֹתוֹ לֵאמֹר
כֹּה־דִבֶּר אֵלַי הָאִישׁ וַיָּבֹא אֶל־הָאִישׁ וְהִנֵּה עֹמֵד עַל־
31 הַגְּמַלִּים עַל־הָעָיִן׃ וַיֹּאמֶר בּוֹא בְּרוּךְ יְהוָה לָמָּה תַעֲמֹד

v. 19. קמץ בז״ק v. 28. הנערה קרי

21. *holding his peace. i.e.* wondering in silence.

22. *ring. i.e.* nose-ring; see *v.* 47.

half a shekel weight. The shekel weighed about half an ounce. These gifts were both a token of gratitude and a means of obtaining the maiden's favourable opinion.

27. *mercy.* Better, '*kindness*.' The phrase 'kindness and truth' is the Heb. idiom for 'true kindness'.

brethren. i.e. kinsfolk.

28. *her mother's house. i.e.* the part of Bethuel's house reserved for the women.

30. *he saw the ring.* Laban lacked the true spirit of hospitality, and was actuated solely by sordid motives.

31. *blessed of the LORD.* An expression denoting profound respect. So again XXVI, 39. Rebekah had heard Eliezer use the Divine Name (see *v.* 27), and had probably repeated it in her narrative (*v.* 28).

32. *he gave straw.* The pronouns, as often in Hebrew, are vaguely used. It was probably Laban who ungirded the camels; and it was certainly he who provided the water.

in, thou blessed of the LORD; wherefore standest thou without? for I have cleared the house, and made room for the camels.' 32. And the man came into the house, and he ungirded the camels; and he gave straw and provender for the camels, and water to wash his feet and the feet of the men that were with him. 33. And there was set food before him to eat; but he said: 'I will not eat, until I have told mine errand.' And he said: 'Speak on.' 34. And he said: 'I am Abraham's servant. 35. And the LORD hath blessed my master greatly; and he is become great; and He hath given him flocks and herds, and silver and gold, and men-servants and maid-servants, and camels and asses. 36. And Sarah my master's wife bore a son to my master when she was old; and unto him hath he given all that he hath. 37. And my master made me swear, saying: Thou shalt not take a wife for my son of the daughters of the Canaanites, in whose land I dwell. 38. But thou shalt go unto my father's house, and to my kindred, and take a wife for my son. 39. And I said unto my master: Peradventure the woman will not follow me. 40. And he said unto me: The LORD, before whom I walk, will send His angel with thee, and prosper thy way; and thou shalt take a wife for my son of my kindred, and of my father's house; 41. then shalt thou be clear from my oath, when thou comest to my kindred; and if they give her not to thee, thou shalt be clear from my oath. 42. And I came this day unto the fountain, and said: O LORD, the God of my master Abraham, if now Thou do prosper my way which I go: 43. behold, I stand by the fountain of water; and let it come to pass, that the maiden that cometh forth to draw, to whom I shall say: Give me, I pray thee, a little water from thy pitcher to drink; 44. and she shall say to me: Both drink thou, and I will also draw for thy camels; let the same be the woman whom the LORD hath appointed for my master's son. 45. And before I had done speaking to my heart, behold, Rebekah came forth with her pitcher on her shoulder; and she went down unto the fountain, and drew. And I said unto her: Let me drink, I pray thee.

32 בַּחוּץ וְאָנֹכִי פִּנִּיתִי הַבַּיִת וּמָקוֹם לַגְּמַלִּים׃ וַיָּבֹא הָאִישׁ
הַבַּיְתָה וַיְפַתַּח הַגְּמַלִּים וַיִּתֵּן תֶּבֶן וּמִסְפּוֹא לַגְּמַלִּים
33 וּמַיִם לִרְחֹץ רַגְלָיו וְרַגְלֵי הָאֲנָשִׁים אֲשֶׁר אִתּוֹ׃ וַיּוּשַׂם
לְפָנָיו לֶאֱכֹל וַיֹּאמֶר לֹא אֹכַל עַד אִם־דִּבַּרְתִּי דְּבָרָי וַיֹּאמֶר
34 לה דַּבֵּר׃ וַיֹּאמַר עֶבֶד אַבְרָהָם אָנֹכִי׃ וַיהוָֹה בֵּרַךְ אֶת־אֲדֹנִי
מְאֹד וַיִּגְדָּל וַיִּתֶּן־לוֹ צֹאן וּבָקָר וְכֶסֶף וְזָהָב וַעֲבָדִם וּשְׁפָחֹת
36 וּגְמַלִּים וַחֲמֹרִים׃ וַתֵּלֶד שָׂרָה אֵשֶׁת אֲדֹנִי בֵן לַאדֹנִי
37 אַחֲרֵי זִקְנָתָהּ וַיִּתֶּן־לוֹ אֶת־כָּל־אֲשֶׁר־לוֹ׃ וַיַּשְׁבִּעֵנִי אֲדֹנִי
לֵאמֹר לֹא־תִקַּח אִשָּׁה לִבְנִי מִבְּנוֹת הַכְּנַעֲנִי אֲשֶׁר אָנֹכִי
38 יֹשֵׁב בְּאַרְצוֹ׃ אִם־לֹא אֶל־בֵּית־אָבִי תֵּלֵךְ וְאֶל־מִשְׁפַּחְתִּי
39 וְלָקַחְתָּ אִשָּׁה לִבְנִי׃ וָאֹמַר אֶל־אֲדֹנִי אֻלַי לֹא־תֵלֵךְ הָאִשָּׁה
מ אַחֲרָי׃ וַיֹּאמֶר אֵלָי יְהוָֹה אֲשֶׁר־הִתְהַלַּכְתִּי לְפָנָיו יִשְׁלַח
מַלְאָכוֹ אִתָּךְ וְהִצְלִיחַ דַּרְכֶּךָ וְלָקַחְתָּ אִשָּׁה לִבְנִי מִמִּשְׁפַּחְתִּי
41 וּמִבֵּית אָבִי׃ אָז תִּנָּקֶה מֵאָלָתִי כִּי תָבוֹא אֶל־מִשְׁפַּחְתִּי
42 וְאִם־לֹא יִתְּנוּ לָךְ וְהָיִיתָ נָקִי מֵאָלָתִי׃ וָאָבֹא הַיּוֹם אֶל־
הָעָיִן וָאֹמַר יְהוָֹה אֱלֹהֵי אֲדֹנִי אַבְרָהָם אִם־יֶשְׁךָ־נָּא
43 מַצְלִיחַ דַּרְכִּי אֲשֶׁר אָנֹכִי הֹלֵךְ עָלֶיהָ׃ הִנֵּה אָנֹכִי נִצָּב
עַל־עֵין הַמָּיִם וְהָיָה הָעַלְמָה הַיֹּצֵאת לִשְׁאֹב וְאָמַרְתִּי
44 אֵלֶיהָ הַשְׁקִינִי־נָא מְעַט־מַיִם מִכַּדֵּךְ׃ וְאָמְרָה אֵלַי גַּם־
אַתָּה שְׁתֵה וְגַם לִגְמַלֶּיךָ אֶשְׁאָב הִוא הָאִשָּׁה אֲשֶׁר־הֹכִיחַ
מה יְהוָֹה לְבֶן־אֲדֹנִי׃ אֲנִי טֶרֶם אֲכַלֶּה לְדַבֵּר אֶל־לִבִּי וְהִנֵּה
רִבְקָה יֹצֵאת וְכַדָּהּ עַל־שִׁכְמָהּ וַתֵּרֶד הָעַיְנָה וַתִּשְׁאָב

v. 33. ויושם קרי

34. *I am Abraham's servant.* The Arab host does not ask his guest's name, at any rate till the latter has eaten of his food, lest there should prove to be a blood-feud between them or their tribes. After the guest has eaten with his host, he is safe (Bennett).

39. *peradventure the woman will not follow me.* From this and *v.* 57 below, it is evident that whatever the preliminary negotiations in the 'arrangement' of the marriage, the whole matter was contingent on the consent of the maiden.

40. *my kindred.* lit. 'my family'.

43. *maiden.* A different Hebrew word from that rendered 'damsel' in *v.* 14. It denotes a girl of marriageable age, and is the word which occurs in Isaiah VII, 14.

46. And she made haste, and let down her pitcher from her shoulder, and said: Drink, and I will give thy camels drink also. So I drank, and she made the camels drink also. 47. And I asked her, and said: Whose daughter art thou? And she said: The daughter of Bethuel, Nahor's son, whom Milcah bore unto him. And I put the ring upon her nose, and the bracelets upon her hands. 48. And I bowed my head, and prostrated myself before the LORD, and blessed the LORD, the God of my master Abraham, who had led me in the right way to take my master's brother's daughter for his son. 49. And now if ye will deal kindly and truly with my master, tell me; and if not, tell me; that I may turn to the right hand, or to the left.' 50. Then Laban and Bethuel answered and said: 'The thing proceedeth from the LORD; we cannot speak unto thee bad or good. 51. Behold, Rebekah is before thee, take her, and go, and let her be thy master's son's wife, as the LORD hath spoken.' 52. And it came to pass, that, when Abraham's servant heard their words, he bowed himself down to the earth unto the LORD.* v. 53. And the servant brought forth jewels of silver, and jewels of gold, and raiment, and gave them to Rebekah; he gave also to her brother and to her mother precious things. 54. And they did eat and drink, he and the men that were with him, and tarried all night; and they rose up in the morning, and he said: 'Send me away unto my master.' 55. And her brother and her mother said: 'Let the damsel abide with us a few days, at the least ten; after that she shall go.' 56. And he said unto them: 'Delay me not, seeing the LORD hath prospered my way; send me away that

46 וָאֹמַר אֵלֶיהָ הַשְׁקִינִי נָא׃ וַתְּמַהֵר וַתּוֹרֶד כַּדָּהּ מֵעָלֶיהָ
וַתֹּאמֶר שְׁתֵה וְגַם־גְּמַלֶּיךָ אַשְׁקֶה וָאֵשְׁתְּ וְגַם הַגְּמַלִּים
47 הִשְׁקָתָה׃ וָאֶשְׁאַל אֹתָהּ וָאֹמַר בַּת־מִי אַתְּ וַתֹּאמֶר בַּת־
בְּתוּאֵל בֶּן־נָחוֹר אֲשֶׁר יָלְדָה־לּוֹ מִלְכָּה וָאָשִׂם הַנֶּזֶם עַל־
48 אַפָּהּ וְהַצְּמִידִים עַל־יָדֶיהָ׃ וָאֶקֹּד וָאֶשְׁתַּחֲוֶה לַיהוָה
וָאֲבָרֵךְ אֶת־יְהוָה אֱלֹהֵי אֲדֹנִי אַבְרָהָם אֲשֶׁר הִנְחַנִי בְּדֶרֶךְ
49 אֱמֶת לָקַחַת אֶת־בַּת־אֲחִי אֲדֹנִי לִבְנוֹ׃ וְעַתָּה אִם־יֶשְׁכֶם
עֹשִׂים חֶסֶד וֶאֱמֶת אֶת־אֲדֹנִי הַגִּידוּ לִי וְאִם־לֹא הַגִּידוּ
נ לִי וְאֶפְנֶה עַל־יָמִין אוֹ עַל־שְׂמֹאל׃ וַיַּעַן לָבָן וּבְתוּאֵל
וַיֹּאמְרוּ מֵיְהוָה יָצָא הַדָּבָר לֹא נוּכַל דַּבֵּר אֵלֶיךָ רַע אוֹ־
51 טוֹב׃ הִנֵּה־רִבְקָה לְפָנֶיךָ קַח וָלֵךְ וּתְהִי אִשָּׁה לְבֶן־אֲדֹנֶיךָ
52 כַּאֲשֶׁר דִּבֶּר יְהוָה׃ וַיְהִי כַּאֲשֶׁר שָׁמַע עֶבֶד אַבְרָהָם אֶת־
חמישי
53 דִּבְרֵיהֶם וַיִּשְׁתַּחוּ אַרְצָה לַיהוָה׃ * וַיּוֹצֵא הָעֶבֶד כְּלֵי־כֶסֶף
וּכְלֵי זָהָב וּבְגָדִים וַיִּתֵּן לְרִבְקָה וּמִגְדָּנֹת נָתַן לְאָחִיהָ
54 וּלְאִמָּהּ׃ וַיֹּאכְלוּ וַיִּשְׁתּוּ הוּא וְהָאֲנָשִׁים אֲשֶׁר־עִמּוֹ וַיָּלִינוּ
נה וַיָּקוּמוּ בַבֹּקֶר וַיֹּאמֶר שַׁלְּחֻנִי לַאדֹנִי׃ וַיֹּאמֶר אָחִיהָ וְאִמָּהּ
56 תֵּשֵׁב הַנַּעֲרָ אִתָּנוּ יָמִים אוֹ עָשׂוֹר אַחַר תֵּלֵךְ׃ וַיֹּאמֶר
אֲלֵהֶם אַל־תְּאַחֲרוּ אֹתִי וַיהוָה הִצְלִיחַ דַּרְכִּי שַׁלְּחוּנִי
57 וְאֵלְכָה לַאדֹנִי׃ וַיֹּאמְרוּ נִקְרָא לַנַּעֲרָ וְנִשְׁאֲלָה אֶת־פִּיהָ׃

v. 55. הנערה קרי   v. 57. לנערה קרי

47. In point of fact, he had given her the presents before asking who she was; see *v.* 22 f.

48. *brother's daughter. i.e.* kinsman's daughter. 'Brother' is used here, as in XIV, 14, 16; XXIX, 12, to denote 'nephew'.

49. *that I may turn. i.e.* that he may consider what course he is next to pursue.

50. *Laban and Bethuel answered.* It is to be noted that Laban is mentioned first. He disrespectfully answered before his father.

bad or good. An idiomatic expression meaning 'anything at all'; cf. III, 22. They cannot act against the manifest decree of God.

51. *take her, and go.* As is usual in the Orient, the preliminary negotiations in regard to the marriage take place without consultation with the maiden; but see *v.* 39, 57.

53. Eliezer hands her mother and brother the *mohar*, or compensation for her loss to the family.

54. Only after he had discharged his duty to his master, does Eliezer think of himself and partake of the food offered to him.

55. *her brother and her mother.* Again Laban interposes before his parent; see *v.* 50. We might have expected mention of the father instead of the mother. He was in all probability quite satisfied to let Rebekah go immediately.

a few days, at the least ten. Or, 'a full year or ten months.' This is the rendering of Onkelos and other ancient Jewish versions and is quite justified by Heb. idiom. Rebekah's mother and relatives were loth suddenly to part from her, as they might never see her again.

57. *inquire at her mouth. i.e.* consult her, as to

I may go to my master.' 57. And they said:
'We will call the damsel, and inquire at
her mouth.' 58. And they called Rebekah,
and said unto her: 'Wilt thou go with
this man?' And she said: 'I will go.' 59.
And they sent away Rebekah their sister,
and her nurse, and Abraham's servant,
and his men. 60. And they blessed Rebekah,
and said unto her: 'Our sister, be thou
the mother of thousands of ten thousands,
and let thy seed possess the gate of those
that hate them.' 61. And Rebekah arose,
and her damsels, and they rode upon the
camels, and followed the man. And the
servant took Rebekah, and went his way.
62. And Isaac came from the way of
Beer-lahai-roi; for he dwelt in the land of
the South. 63. And Isaac went out to
meditate in the field at the eventide; and
he lifted up his eyes, and saw, and, behold,
there were camels coming. 64. And
Rebekah lifted up her eyes, and when she
saw Isaac, she alighted from the camel.
65. And she said unto the servant: 'What
man is this that walketh in the field to
meet us?' And the servant said: 'It is my
master.' And she took her veil, and covered
herself. 66. And the servant told Isaac all
the things that he had done. 67. And Isaac
brought her into his mother Sarah's tent,
and took Rebekah, and she became his
wife; and he loved her. And Isaac was
comforted for his mother.* vi.

58 וַיִּקְרְאוּ לְרִבְקָה וַיֹּאמְרוּ אֵלֶיהָ הֲתֵלְכִי עִם־הָאִישׁ הַזֶּה
59 וַתֹּאמֶר אֵלֵךְ׃ וַיְשַׁלְּחוּ אֶת־רִבְקָה אֲחֹתָם וְאֶת־מֵנִקְתָּהּ
ס וְאֶת־עֶבֶד אַבְרָהָם וְאֶת־אֲנָשָׁיו׃ וַיְבָרְכוּ אֶת־רִבְקָה וַיֹּאמְרוּ
לָהּ אֲחֹתֵנוּ אַתְּ הֲיִי לְאַלְפֵי רְבָבָה וְיִירַשׁ זַרְעֵךְ אֵת שַׁעַר
61 שֹׂנְאָיו׃ וַתָּקָם רִבְקָה וְנַעֲרֹתֶיהָ וַתִּרְכַּבְנָה עַל־הַגְּמַלִּים
וַתֵּלַכְנָה אַחֲרֵי הָאִישׁ וַיִּקַּח הָעֶבֶד אֶת־רִבְקָה וַיֵּלַךְ׃
62 וְיִצְחָק בָּא מִבּוֹא בְּאֵר לַחַי רֹאִי וְהוּא יוֹשֵׁב בְּאֶרֶץ הַנֶּגֶב׃
63 וַיֵּצֵא יִצְחָק לָשׂוּחַ בַּשָּׂדֶה לִפְנוֹת עָרֶב וַיִּשָּׂא עֵינָיו וַיַּרְא
64 וְהִנֵּה גְמַלִּים בָּאִים׃ וַתִּשָּׂא רִבְקָה אֶת־עֵינֶיהָ וַתֵּרֶא אֶת־
סה יִצְחָק וַתִּפֹּל מֵעַל הַגָּמָל׃ וַתֹּאמֶר אֶל־הָעֶבֶד מִי־הָאִישׁ
הַלָּזֶה הַהֹלֵךְ בַּשָּׂדֶה לִקְרָאתֵנוּ וַיֹּאמֶר הָעֶבֶד הוּא אֲדֹנִי
66 וַתִּקַּח הַצָּעִיף וַתִּתְכָּס׃ וַיְסַפֵּר הָעֶבֶד לְיִצְחָק אֵת כָּל־
67 הַדְּבָרִים אֲשֶׁר עָשָׂה׃ וַיְבִאֶהָ יִצְחָק הָאֹהֱלָה שָׂרָה אִמּוֹ
וַיִּקַּח אֶת־רִבְקָה וַתְּהִי־לוֹ לְאִשָּׁה וַיֶּאֱהָבֶהָ וַיִּנָּחֵם יִצְחָק
אַחֲרֵי אִמּוֹ׃ * פ ששי

the time of her going. The Rabbis take it to mean, as to whether she wishes to follow Eliezer, and deduce from this text the rule that a woman cannot legally be given away in marriage without her consent.

59. *their sister.* Laban had throughout been most prominent in the negotiations.

her nurse. Her name was Deborah; see xxxv, 8.

60. *be thou the mother of.* The Heb. is simply 'become', as in xvii, 16.

let thy seed possess. See on xxii, 17.

61. *and followed the man.* In the East it is still the custom for the woman to walk or ride in the rear.

62. *Beer-lahai-roi.* The well associated with the story of Hagar.

the South. i.e. the Negeb; see on xii, 9.

63. *to meditate.* The Targums and the Rabbis understood the word to mean 'pray', and declared that Isaac instituted the Afternoon Service (מנחה), as Abraham had instituted the Morning Service (derived from xix, 27), and Jacob later on instituted the Evening Service (deduced from xxviii, 11).

64. *alighted from.* A mark of respect; cf. Joshua, xv, 18; i Sam. xxv, 23. In the East men and women dismount on the approach of a person of importance.

65. *took her veil.* Rebekah again acted in accordance with Eastern etiquette. It was not necessary for her to have her face veiled in the presence of Eliezer, since he was only a servant.

67. *into his mother Sarah's tent.* He installed her as mistress of the household.

The order of the words, *He took Rebekah, she became his wife, and he loved her,* calls for comment. In modern life we would place 'he loved her' first, and write: 'He loved Rebekah, he took her, and she became his wife.' But, however important it is that love shall precede marriage, it is far more important that it shall continue *after* marriage. The modern attitude lays all the stress on the romance before marriage; the olden Jewish view emphasizes the life-long devotion and affection after marriage (S. R. Hirsch).

comforted. Rebekah filled the gap caused in Isaac's life by the death of his mother. The Rabbis explain that on the death of Sarah the blessings which had attended the household of the Patriarch and the pious customs which distinguished it, came to an end; but when Rebekah was brought to the tent, they were restored. 'The Sabbath lamp once more illumined the home of the Patriarch,' and Rebekah continued as well all the other religious rites which Sarah had initiated.

25

CHAPTER XXV

1. And Abraham took another wife, and her name was Keturah. 2. And she bore him Zimram, and Jokshan, and Medan, and Midian, and Ishbak, and Shuah. 3. And Jokshan begot Sheba, and Dedan. And the sons of Dedan were Asshurim, and Letushim, and Leummim. 4. And the sons of Midian: Ephah, and Epher, and Hanoch, and Abida, and Eldaah. All these were the children of Keturah. 5. And Abraham gave all that he had unto Isaac. 6. But unto the sons of the concubines, that Abraham had, Abraham gave gifts; and he sent them away from Isaac his son, while he yet lived, eastward, unto the east country. 7. And these are the days of the years of Abraham's life which he lived, a hundred threescore and fifteen years. 8. And Abraham expired, and died in a good old age, an old man, and full of years; and was gathered to his people. 9. And Isaac and Ishmael his sons buried him in the cave of Machpelah, in the field of Ephron the son of Zohar the Hittite, which is before Mamre; 10. the field which Abraham purchased of the children of Heth; there was Abraham buried, and Sarah his wife. 11. And it came to pass after the death of Abraham, that God blessed Isaac his son; and Isaac dwelt by Beer-lahai-roi.* vii. ¶ 12. Now these

CAP. XXV. כה

כה

א 2 וַיֹּסֶף אַבְרָהָם וַיִּקַּח אִשָּׁה וּשְׁמָהּ קְטוּרָה׃ וַתֵּלֶד לוֹ אֶת־
זִמְרָן וְאֶת־יָקְשָׁן וְאֶת־מְדָן וְאֶת־מִדְיָן וְאֶת־יִשְׁבָּק וְאֶת־
3 שׁוּחַ׃ וְיָקְשָׁן יָלַד אֶת־שְׁבָא וְאֶת־דְּדָן וּבְנֵי דְדָן הָיוּ
4 אַשּׁוּרִם וּלְטוּשִׁם וּלְאֻמִּים׃ וּבְנֵי מִדְיָן עֵיפָה וָעֵפֶר וַחֲנֹךְ
ה וַאֲבִידָע וְאֶלְדָּעָה כָּל־אֵלֶּה בְּנֵי קְטוּרָה׃ וַיִּתֵּן אַבְרָהָם
6 אֶת־כָּל־אֲשֶׁר־לוֹ לְיִצְחָק׃ וְלִבְנֵי הַפִּילַגְשִׁים אֲשֶׁר
לְאַבְרָהָם נָתַן אַבְרָהָם מַתָּנֹת וַיְשַׁלְּחֵם מֵעַל יִצְחָק בְּנוֹ
7 בְּעוֹדֶנּוּ חַי קֵדְמָה אֶל־אֶרֶץ קֶדֶם׃ וְאֵלֶּה יְמֵי שְׁנֵי־חַיֵּי
אַבְרָהָם אֲשֶׁר־חָי מְאַת שָׁנָה וְשִׁבְעִים שָׁנָה וְחָמֵשׁ שָׁנִים׃
8 וַיִּגְוַע וַיָּמָת אַבְרָהָם בְּשֵׂיבָה טוֹבָה זָקֵן וְשָׂבֵעַ וַיֵּאָסֶף אֶל־
9 עַמָּיו׃ וַיִּקְבְּרוּ אֹתוֹ יִצְחָק וְיִשְׁמָעֵאל בָּנָיו אֶל־מְעָרַת הַמַּכְפֵּלָה
אֶל־שְׂדֵה עֶפְרֹן בֶּן־צֹחַר הַחִתִּי אֲשֶׁר עַל־פְּנֵי מַמְרֵא׃
י הַשָּׂדֶה אֲשֶׁר־קָנָה אַבְרָהָם מֵאֵת בְּנֵי־חֵת שָׁמָּה קֻבַּר
11 אַבְרָהָם וְשָׂרָה אִשְׁתּוֹ׃ וַיְהִי אַחֲרֵי מוֹת אַבְרָהָם וַיְבָרֶךְ

CHAPTER XXV. DEATH OF ABRAHAM AND DESCENDANTS OF ISHMAEL

1. *and Abraham took another wife.* It does not necessarily mean that it was not until after the death of Sarah that he married again. It is quite possible that he took his secondary wife (in I Chron. I, 32 Keturah is called a 'concubine') during her lifetime; and it is only mentioned here in connection with the disposal of the Patriarch's property.

2. The domestic tradition in these verses preserves the recollection of the early relationship between the ancestors of Israel and the tribes of the North Arabian desert (Ryle).

Medan. The 'Medanites' are referred to in XXXVII as traders with Egypt.

Midian. The name of a nomad tribe frequently occurring in the Bible.

Shuah. One of Job's friends is described as a Shuhite (Job II, 11).

3. *Sheba and Dedan.* Mentioned in X, 7. The other names are found on Arabian inscriptions.

5. Cf. XXIV, 36.

6. *concubines. i.e.* Hagar and Keturah.

while he yet lived. i.e. in his lifetime, a wise precaution to ensure the safety of Isaac and prevent disputes amongst the members of the family.

eastward. i.e. to Arabia. The Arabs are sometimes described as 'children of the East'; see Judges VI, 3; Job I, 3.

7. *a hundred threescore and fifteen years.* Abraham must have lived to see his grandchildren. Isaac was born when his father was a hundred (XXI, 5), and was sixty at the birth of Esau and Jacob (see *v.* 26); hence they were fifteen when the Patriarch died.

8. *was gathered to his people.* Not to be understood literally, as his people were buried in Mesopotamia. It is a parallel phrase to 'thou shalt go to thy fathers' in XVI, 15; and, like it, is an intimation of immortality.

9. *Isaac and Ishmael.* At the graveside of their father, the half-brothers were reconciled (Midrash).

Machpelah. See XXIII, 9 f.

11. *God blessed Isaac. i.e.* the promises made to Abraham were now transferred to him.

12–18. DESCENDANTS OF ISHMAEL

12. *generations.* Descendants. Some of the names that follow are found in Assyrian and Arabian inscriptions.

are the generations of Ishmael, Abraham's son, whom Hagar the Egyptian, Sarah's handmaid, bore unto Abraham. 13. And these are the names of the sons of Ishmael, by their names, according to their generations: the first-born of Ishmael, Nebaioth; and Kedar, and Adbeel, and Mibsam, 14. and Mishma, and Dumah, and Massa; 15. Hadad and Tema, Jetur, Naphish, and Kedem;*m. 16. these are the sons of Ishmael, and these are their names, by their villages, and by their encampments; twelve princes according to their nations. 17. And these are the years of the life of Ishmael, a hundred and thirty and seven years; and he expired and died; and was gathered unto his people. 18. And they dwelt from Havilah unto Shur, that is before Egypt, as thou goest toward Asshur: over against all his brethren he did settle.

שביעי אֱלֹהִים אֶת־יִצְחָק בְּנוֹ וַיֵּשֶׁב יִצְחָק עִם־בְּאֵר לַחַי רֹאִי׃ פ
12 וְאֵלֶּה תֹּלְדֹת יִשְׁמָעֵאל בֶּן־אַבְרָהָם אֲשֶׁר יָלְדָה הָגָר
13 הַמִּצְרִית שִׁפְחַת שָׂרָה לְאַבְרָהָם׃ וְאֵלֶּה שְׁמוֹת בְּנֵי
יִשְׁמָעֵאל בִּשְׁמֹתָם לְתוֹלְדֹתָם בְּכֹר יִשְׁמָעֵאל נְבָיֹת וְקֵדָר
14 טו מפטיר וְאַדְבְּאֵל וּמִבְשָׂם׃ וּמִשְׁמָע וְדוּמָה וּמַשָּׂא׃ חֲדַד וְתֵימָא
16 יְטוּר נָפִישׁ וָקֵדְמָה׃ *אֵלֶּה הֵם בְּנֵי יִשְׁמָעֵאל וְאֵלֶּה שְׁמֹתָם
17 בְּחַצְרֵיהֶם וּבְטִירֹתָם שְׁנֵים־עָשָׂר נְשִׂיאִם לְאֻמֹּתָם׃ וְאֵלֶּה
שְׁנֵי חַיֵּי יִשְׁמָעֵאל מְאַת שָׁנָה וּשְׁלֹשִׁים שָׁנָה וְשֶׁבַע שָׁנִים
18 וַיִּגְוַע וַיָּמָת וַיֵּאָסֶף אֶל־עַמָּיו׃ וַיִּשְׁכְּנוּ מֵחֲוִילָה עַד־שׁוּר
אֲשֶׁר עַל־פְּנֵי מִצְרַיִם בֹּאֲכָה אַשּׁוּרָה עַל־פְּנֵי כָל־אֶחָיו נָפָל׃

13. *Nebaioth.* Later known as Nabatæans.

Kedar. In Ps. CXX, 5, they are taken as a type of hostile neighbours.

15. *Tema.* An important station on the trade-route from Yemen to Syria.

16. *encampments.* Probably a technical term to denote the circular enclosure used by a nomad people.

princes. Sheikhs of clans.

17. *was gathered.* See on *v.* 8.

18. *Havilah.* See II, 11; situated in N.E. Arabia.

Shur. See on XVI, 7; cf. also I Sam. XV, 7.

Asshur. The reference is probably to the land of Asshurim mentioned in *v.* 3.

did settle. lit. 'fell.' For this sense of the word, cf. Judges VII, 12.

This chapter concludes the Biblical account of the first of the Patriarchs. It is difficult, indeed, because of our lifelong familiarity with the story, rightly to estimate the nobility and grandeur of the personality revealed in these chapters.

He was the pioneer of the monotheistic faith. Undazzled by the heathen splendour of a Nimrod or a Hammurabi, he broke away from the debasing idol-worship of his contemporaries, and devoted his life to the spread of the world-redeeming truth of the One God of Justice and Mercy. He forsook home and family to brave unknown dangers because the Voice of God bade him do so; and, throughout his days, he showed that faith in God must manifest itself in implicit and joyful surrender to the Divine will. He set an example to his children to sacrifice the dearest things in life and, if need be, life itself, in defence of the spiritual heritage entrusted to their care. While he preached renunciation in the service of God, he practised lovingkindness and truth towards his fellow men. Witness his magnanimity in his treatment of Lot; his fine independence in the refusal to accept any of the spoils won by the men of his household; his benevolence in the reception of strangers; his stand for justice, when pleading for the doomed cities; and his all-embracing human pity which extended even to those who had forfeited all claim to human pity. Finally, the closing stage of his life shows his anxiety that the spiritual treasures he has acquired should be transmitted unimpaired through his son to future generations. Verily, he is the prototype of what the Jew should aim at being. 'Look unto the rock whence ye were digged, look unto Abraham, your father,' is the Divine exhortation addressed to Israel (Isaiah LI, 1).

HAFTORAH CHAYYE SARAH הפטרת חיי שרה

I KINGS I, 1–31

Chapter I

1. Now king David was old and stricken in years; and they covered him with clothes, but he could get no heat. 2. Wherefore his servants said unto him: 'Let there be sought for my lord the king a young virgin; and let her stand before the king, and be a companion unto him; and let her lie in thy bosom, that my lord the king may get heat.' 3. So they sought for a fair damsel throughout all the borders of Israel, and found Abishag the Shunammite, and brought her to the king. 4. And the damsel was very fair; and she became a companion unto the king, and ministered to him; but the king knew her not. ¶ 5. Now Adonijah the son of Haggith exalted himself, saying: 'I will be king'; and he prepared him chariots and horsemen, and fifty men to run before him. 6. And his father had not grieved him all his life in saying: 'Why hast thou done so?' and he was also a very goodly man; and he was born after Absalom. 7. And he conferred with Joab the son of Zeruiah, and with Abiathar the priest; and they following Adonijah helped him. 8. But Zadok the priest, and Benaiah

Cap. I. א

א וְהַמֶּלֶךְ דָּוִד זָקֵן בָּא בַּיָּמִים וַיְכַסֻּהוּ בַּבְּגָדִים וְלֹא יִחַם לוֹ׃
2 וַיֹּאמְרוּ לוֹ עֲבָדָיו יְבַקְשׁוּ לַאדֹנִי הַמֶּלֶךְ נַעֲרָה בְתוּלָה
וְעָמְדָה לִפְנֵי הַמֶּלֶךְ וּתְהִי־לוֹ סֹכֶנֶת וְשָׁכְבָה בְחֵיקֶךָ וְחַם
3 לַאדֹנִי הַמֶּלֶךְ׃ וַיְבַקְשׁוּ נַעֲרָה יָפָה בְּכֹל גְּבוּל יִשְׂרָאֵל
4 וַיִּמְצְאוּ אֶת־אֲבִישַׁג הַשּׁוּנַמִּית וַיָּבִאוּ אֹתָהּ לַמֶּלֶךְ׃ וְהַנַּעֲרָה
יָפָה עַד־מְאֹד וַתְּהִי לַמֶּלֶךְ סֹכֶנֶת וַתְּשָׁרְתֵהוּ וְהַמֶּלֶךְ לֹא
ה יְדָעָהּ׃ וַאֲדֹנִיָּה בֶן־חַגִּית מִתְנַשֵּׂא לֵאמֹר אֲנִי אֶמְלֹךְ וַיַּעַשׂ
6 לוֹ רֶכֶב וּפָרָשִׁים וַחֲמִשִּׁים אִישׁ רָצִים לְפָנָיו׃ וְלֹא־עֲצָבוֹ
אָבִיו מִיָּמָיו לֵאמֹר מַדּוּעַ כָּכָה עָשִׂיתָ וְגַם־הוּא טוֹב־תֹּאַר
7 מְאֹד וְאֹתוֹ יָלְדָה אַחֲרֵי אַבְשָׁלוֹם׃ וַיִּהְיוּ דְבָרָיו עִם יוֹאָב
8 בֶּן־צְרוּיָה וְעִם אֶבְיָתָר הַכֹּהֵן וַיַּעְזְרוּ אַחֲרֵי אֲדֹנִיָּה׃ וְצָדוֹק
הַכֹּהֵן וּבְנָיָהוּ בֶן־יְהוֹיָדָע וְנָתָן הַנָּבִיא וְשִׁמְעִי וְרֵעִי וְהַגִּבּוֹרִים

I Kings I, 1–31

The Book of Kings (the division into two books occurs only in *printed* Hebrew Bibles) gives the history of the Monarchy from the last days of David to the Babylonian exile.

This opening chapter portrays the struggle for the Crown among David's surviving sons.

The connection between Sedrah and Haftorah is readily seen. The one portrays Abraham's old age, and the other David's; the one depicts Abraham's solicitude for the piety of his house, and the other, David's for the right succession in his.

There is contrast in the character of the two sons. Isaac allows himself to be guided by his father in a great decision, in spite of his forty years; Adonijah in the Haftorah cannot wait for the death of his father to proclaim himself king. In violent contrast to the simple life in Abraham's tent, we have, in David's palace, conspiracy and all the intrigues of an Oriental Court, 'told with a convincing realism which conveys the impression of first-hand information derived from the evidence of eye-witnesses' (Skinner).

1. *old.* Seventy years.

clothes. Bed-clothes.

2. *stand before the king.* Serve him.

3. *the Shunammite.* Shunem, 3 miles N. of Jezreel, not far from Mt. Carmel.

5. *Adonijah.* The fourth son of David, see II Sam. III, 4. Two of his elder brothers (Amnon and Absalom) being dead, he regards himself as heir.

fifty men. A royal bodyguard.

6. *also a very goodly.* See II Sam. XIV, 25. It gives the reason of Adonijah's disobedience—his father's reluctance to rebuke the handsome, self-willed boy. What a warning to parents against the son of Jehoiada, and Nathan the prophet, and Shimei, and Rei, and the mighty men that belonged to David, were not with Adonijah. 9. And Adonijah slew sheep and oxen and fatlings by the stone of Zoheleth, which is beside En-rogel; and he called all his brethren the king's sons, and all the men of Judah the king's servants; 10. but Nathan the prophet, and Benaiah, and the mighty men, and Solomon his brother, he called not. ¶ 11. Then Nathan spoke unto Bath-sheba the mother of Solomon, saying: 'Hast thou not heard that Adonijah the son of Haggith doth reign, and David our lord knoweth it not? 12. Now therefore come, let me, I pray thee, give thee counsel, that thou mayest save thine own life, and the life of thy son Solomon. 13. Go and get thee in unto king David, and say unto him: Didst not thou, my lord, O king, swear unto thy handmaid, saying: Assuredly Solomon thy son shall reign after me, and he shall sit upon my throne? why then doth Adonijah reign? 14. Behold, while thou yet talkest there with the king, I also will come in after thee, and confirm thy words.' ¶ 15. And Bath-sheba went in unto the king into the chamber.—Now the king was very old; and Abishag the Shunammite ministered unto the king.—16. And Bath-sheba bowed, and prostrated herself unto the king. And the king said: 'What wouldest thou?' 17. And she said unto him: 'My lord, thou didst swear by the LORD thy God unto thy handmaid: Assuredly Solomon thy son shall reign after me, and he shall sit upon my throne. 18. And now, behold, Adonijah reigneth; and thou, my lord the king, knowest it not. 19. And he hath slain oxen and fatlings and sheep in abundance, and hath called all the sons of the king, and

9 אֲשֶׁר לְדָוִד לֹא הָיוּ עִם־אֲדֹנִיָּהוּ׃ וַיִּזְבַּח אֲדֹנִיָּהוּ צֹאן וּבָקָר
וּמְרִיא עִם אֶבֶן הַזֹּחֶלֶת אֲשֶׁר־אֵצֶל עֵין רֹגֵל וַיִּקְרָא אֶת־
כָּל־אֶחָיו בְּנֵי הַמֶּלֶךְ וּלְכָל־אַנְשֵׁי יְהוּדָה עַבְדֵי הַמֶּלֶךְ׃
י וְאֶת־נָתָן הַנָּבִיא וּבְנָיָהוּ וְאֶת־הַגִּבּוֹרִים וְאֶת־שְׁלֹמֹה אָחִיו
11 לֹא קָרָא׃ וַיֹּאמֶר נָתָן אֶל־בַּת־שֶׁבַע אֵם־שְׁלֹמֹה לֵאמֹר
הֲלוֹא שָׁמַעַתְּ כִּי מָלַךְ אֲדֹנִיָּהוּ בֶן־חַגִּית וַאֲדֹנֵינוּ דָוִד לֹא
12 יָדָע׃ וְעַתָּה לְכִי אִיעָצֵךְ נָא עֵצָה וּמַלְּטִי אֶת־נַפְשֵׁךְ וְאֶת־
13 נֶפֶשׁ בְּנֵךְ שְׁלֹמֹה׃ לְכִי וּבֹאִי ׀ אֶל־הַמֶּלֶךְ דָּוִד וְאָמַרְתְּ אֵלָיו
הֲלֹא־אַתָּה אֲדֹנִי הַמֶּלֶךְ נִשְׁבַּעְתָּ לַאֲמָתְךָ לֵאמֹר כִּי־שְׁלֹמֹה
בְנֵךְ יִמְלֹךְ אַחֲרַי וְהוּא יֵשֵׁב עַל־כִּסְאִי וּמַדּוּעַ מָלַךְ
14 אֲדֹנִיָּהוּ׃ הִנֵּה עוֹדָךְ מְדַבֶּרֶת שָׁם עִם־הַמֶּלֶךְ וַאֲנִי אָבוֹא
טו אַחֲרַיִךְ וּמִלֵּאתִי אֶת־דְּבָרָיִךְ׃ וַתָּבֹא בַת־שֶׁבַע אֶל־הַמֶּלֶךְ
הַחַדְרָה וְהַמֶּלֶךְ זָקֵן מְאֹד וַאֲבִישַׁג הַשּׁוּנַמִּית מְשָׁרַת אֶת־
16 הַמֶּלֶךְ׃ וַתִּקֹּד בַּת־שֶׁבַע וַתִּשְׁתַּחוּ לַמֶּלֶךְ וַיֹּאמֶר הַמֶּלֶךְ
17 מַה־לָּךְ׃ וַתֹּאמֶר לוֹ אֲדֹנִי אַתָּה נִשְׁבַּעְתָּ בַּיהוָה אֱלֹהֶיךָ
לַאֲמָתֶךָ כִּי־שְׁלֹמֹה בְנֵךְ יִמְלֹךְ אַחֲרָי וְהוּא יֵשֵׁב עַל־כִּסְאִי׃
18 וְעַתָּה הִנֵּה אֲדֹנִיָּה מָלָךְ וְעַתָּה אֲדֹנִי הַמֶּלֶךְ לֹא יָדָעְתָּ׃
19 וַיִּזְבַּח שׁוֹר וּמְרִיא־וְצֹאן לָרֹב וַיִּקְרָא לְכָל־בְּנֵי הַמֶּלֶךְ
וּלְאֶבְיָתָר הַכֹּהֵן וּלְיֹאָב שַׂר הַצָּבָא וְלִשְׁלֹמֹה עַבְדְּךָ לֹא

favouritism and indulgence to children! It is the road to unhappiness for themselves, and ruin for their children.

7. *Joab.* David's commander-in-chief.

Abiathar. A descendant of Aaron's youngest son, Ithamar.

8. *Zadok.* A descendant of Aaron's son Eleazar.

Benaiah. Succeeded Joab as commander-in-chief.

Nathan. The fearless Prophet; see II Sam. XII, 1–12.

the mighty men. Heb. *Gibborim.* David's army of picked warriors; II Sam. X, 7.

9. *En-rogel.* 'The Fuller's spring,' near Siloam, close to Jerusalem.

11. *Bath-sheba.* The note on Gen. XXVI, 33, throws light on the meaning of this name, which is 'Fortune's daughter', Fortunata, Glueckel. She was apparently the favourite wife of David.

12. Unless Adonijah's plot is defeated, his first act after the death of David would be to remove opposition by slaying Solomon, his rival to the throne, and Bath-sheba. Thus the successor to Alexander the Great put to death his widow, in addition to slaying his young son.

14. *confirm.* Supplement.

Abiathar the priest, and Joab the captain
of the host; but Solomon thy servant hath
he not called. 20. And thou, my lord the
king, the eyes of all Israel are upon thee,
that thou shouldest tell them who shall sit
on the throne of my lord the king after
him. 21. Otherwise it will come to pass,
when my lord the king shall sleep with his
fathers, that I and my son Solomon shall
be counted offenders.' ¶ 22. And, lo, while
she yet talked with the king, Nathan the
prophet came in. 23. And they told the
king, saying: 'Behold Nathan the prophet.'
And when he was come in before the king,
he bowed down before the king with his
face to the ground. 24. And Nathan said:
'My lord, O king, hast thou said: Adonijah
shall reign after me, and he shall sit upon
my throne? 25. For he is gone down this
day, and hath slain oxen and fatlings and
sheep in abundance, and hath called all the
king's sons, and the captains of the host,
and Abiathar the priest; and, behold, they
eat and drink before him, and say: Long
live king Adonijah. 26. But me, even me
thy servant, and Zadok the priest, and
Benaiah the son of Jehoiada, and thy
servant Solomon, hath he not called. 27.
Is this thing done by my lord the king, and
thou hast not declared unto thy servant
who should sit on the throne of my lord
the king after him?' ¶ 28. Then king David
answered and said: 'Call me Bath-sheba.'
And she came into the king's presence, and
stood before the king. 29. And the king
swore and said: 'As the LORD liveth, who
hath redeemed my soul out of all adversity,
30. verily as I swore unto thee by the LORD,
the God of Israel, saying: Assuredly
Solomon thy son shall reign after me, and
he shall sit upon my throne in my stead;
verily so will I do this day.' 31. Then Bath-
sheba bowed with her face to the earth, and
prostrated herself to the king, and said:
'Let my lord king David live for ever.'

כ קָרָא׃ וְאַתָּה אֲדֹנִי הַמֶּלֶךְ עֵינֵי כָל־יִשְׂרָאֵל עָלֶיךָ לְהַגִּיד
21 לָהֶם מִי יֵשֵׁב עַל־כִּסֵּא אֲדֹנִי־הַמֶּלֶךְ אַחֲרָיו׃ וְהָיָה
כִּשְׁכַב אֲדֹנִי־הַמֶּלֶךְ עִם־אֲבֹתָיו וְהָיִיתִי אֲנִי וּבְנִי שְׁלֹמֹה
22 חַטָּאִים׃ וְהִנֵּה עוֹדֶנָּה מְדַבֶּרֶת עִם־הַמֶּלֶךְ וְנָתָן הַנָּבִיא
23 בָּא׃ וַיַּגִּידוּ לַמֶּלֶךְ לֵאמֹר הִנֵּה נָתָן הַנָּבִיא וַיָּבֹא לִפְנֵי
24 הַמֶּלֶךְ וַיִּשְׁתַּחוּ לַמֶּלֶךְ עַל־אַפָּיו אָרְצָה׃ וַיֹּאמֶר נָתָן
אֲדֹנִי הַמֶּלֶךְ אַתָּה אָמַרְתָּ אֲדֹנִיָּהוּ יִמְלֹךְ אַחֲרָי וְהוּא
כה יֵשֵׁב עַל־כִּסְאִי׃ כִּי ׀ יָרַד הַיּוֹם וַיִּזְבַּח שׁוֹר וּמְרִיא־וְצֹאן
לָרֹב וַיִּקְרָא לְכָל־בְּנֵי הַמֶּלֶךְ וּלְשָׂרֵי הַצָּבָא וּלְאֶבְיָתָר
הַכֹּהֵן וְהִנָּם אֹכְלִים וְשֹׁתִים לְפָנָיו וַיֹּאמְרוּ יְחִי הַמֶּלֶךְ
26 אֲדֹנִיָּהוּ׃ וְלִי אֲנִי־עַבְדֶּךָ וּלְצָדֹק הַכֹּהֵן וְלִבְנָיָהוּ בֶן
27 יְהוֹיָדָע וְלִשְׁלֹמֹה עַבְדְּךָ לֹא קָרָא׃ אִם מֵאֵת אֲדֹנִי הַמֶּלֶךְ
נִהְיָה הַדָּבָר הַזֶּה וְלֹא הוֹדַעְתָּ אֶת־עַבְדְּיךָ מִי יֵשֵׁב עַל־
28 כִּסֵּא אֲדֹנִי־הַמֶּלֶךְ אַחֲרָיו׃ וַיַּעַן הַמֶּלֶךְ דָּוִד וַיֹּאמֶר קִרְאוּ־
לִי לְבַת־שָׁבַע וַתָּבֹא לִפְנֵי הַמֶּלֶךְ וַתַּעֲמֹד לִפְנֵי הַמֶּלֶךְ׃
29 וַיִּשָּׁבַע הַמֶּלֶךְ וַיֹּאמַר חַי־יְהוָה אֲשֶׁר־פָּדָה אֶת־נַפְשִׁי
ל מִכָּל־צָרָה׃ כִּי כַּאֲשֶׁר נִשְׁבַּעְתִּי לְךָ בַּיהוָה אֱלֹהֵי יִשְׂרָאֵל
לֵאמֹר כִּי־שְׁלֹמֹה בְנֵךְ יִמְלֹךְ אַחֲרַי וְהוּא יֵשֵׁב עַל־כִּסְאִי
31 תַּחְתָּי כִּי כֵּן אֶעֱשֶׂה הַיּוֹם הַזֶּה׃ וַתִּקֹּד בַּת־שֶׁבַע אַפַּיִם
אֶרֶץ וַתִּשְׁתַּחוּ לַמֶּלֶךְ וַתֹּאמֶר יְחִי אֲדֹנִי הַמֶּלֶךְ דָּוִד לְעֹלָם׃

v. 27. עבדך קרי

20. *tell them.* She presses for a public pronouncement as to the succession.

21. *counted offenders. i.e.* shall be put to death.

25. *eat and drink before him.* Thus sealing their allegiance to him.

long live king Adonijah. 'God save king Adonijah' (RV).

26. *not called.* Because standing outside the conspiracy.

29. With a firm hand, David now safeguards the destinies of his House.

25 19. And these are the generations of Isaac, Abraham's son: Abraham begot Isaac. 20. And Isaac was forty years old when he took Rebekah, the daughter of Bethuel the Aramean, of Paddan-aram, the sister of Laban the Aramean, to be his wife. 21. And Isaac entreated the LORD for his wife, because she was barren; and the LORD let Himself be entreated of him, and Rebekah his wife conceived. 22. And the children struggled together within her; and she said: 'If it be so, wherefore do I live?' And she went to inquire of the LORD. 23. And the LORD said unto her:

Two nations are in thy womb,
And two peoples shall be separated from thy bowels;
And the one people shall be stronger than the other people;
And the elder shall serve the younger.

24. And when her days to be delivered were fulfilled, behold, there were twins in her womb. 25. And the first came forth ruddy, all over like a hairy mantle; and they called his name Esau. 26. And after that came forth his brother, and his hand had

כה

פ פ פ ו 6

19 וְאֵלֶּה תּוֹלְדֹת יִצְחָק בֶּן־אַבְרָהָם אַבְרָהָם הוֹלִיד אֶת־
כ יִצְחָק׃ וַיְהִי יִצְחָק בֶּן־אַרְבָּעִים שָׁנָה בְּקַחְתּוֹ אֶת־רִבְקָה
בַּת־בְּתוּאֵל הָאֲרַמִּי מִפַּדַּן אֲרָם אֲחוֹת לָבָן הָאֲרַמִּי לוֹ
21 לְאִשָּׁה׃ וַיֶּעְתַּר יִצְחָק לַיהוָה לְנֹכַח אִשְׁתּוֹ כִּי עֲקָרָה
22 הִוא וַיֵּעָתֶר לוֹ יְהוָה וַתַּהַר רִבְקָה אִשְׁתּוֹ׃ וַיִּתְרֹצְצוּ
הַבָּנִים בְּקִרְבָּהּ וַתֹּאמֶר אִם־כֵּן לָמָּה זֶּה אָנֹכִי וַתֵּלֶךְ לִדְרֹשׁ
23 אֶת־יְהוָה׃ וַיֹּאמֶר יְהוָה לָהּ שְׁנֵי גֹיִים בְּבִטְנֵךְ וּשְׁנֵי
לְאֻמִּים מִמֵּעַיִךְ יִפָּרֵדוּ וּלְאֹם מִלְאֹם יֶאֱמָץ וְרַב יַעֲבֹד
24 כה צָעִיר׃ וַיִּמְלְאוּ יָמֶיהָ לָלֶדֶת וְהִנֵּה תוֹמִם בְּבִטְנָהּ׃ וַיֵּצֵא
הָרִאשׁוֹן אַדְמוֹנִי כֻּלּוֹ כְּאַדֶּרֶת שֵׂעָר וַיִּקְרְאוּ שְׁמוֹ עֵשָׂו׃
26 וְאַחֲרֵי־כֵן יָצָא אָחִיו וְיָדוֹ אֹחֶזֶת בַּעֲקֵב עֵשָׂו וַיִּקְרָא

v. 23. גוים ק׳ ibid. קמץ בז״ק v. 24. חסר

VI. TOLEDOTH

(CHAPTERS XXV, 19–XXVIII, 9)

(*b*) JACOB (CHAPTERS XXV–XXXVI)

CHAPTER XXV, 19–34. THE BIRTHRIGHT

19. With this verse, a new section of the Book of Genesis commences, which extends to the end of Chapter XXXVI. Therefore, we are given a brief summary of what has gone before, to prepare us for the new events to be described.

Abraham's son. i.e. his son and heir, to distinguish him from the children of Hagar and Keturah.

Abraham begot Isaac. It was not until the Patriarch's name was altered from Abram to Abraham, 'father of a multitude of nations' (XVII, 5), that Isaac was born.

20. *Paddan-aram.* Identical with Aram-Naharaim, or Mesopotamia; cf. XXIV, 10.

21. *she was barren.* Like Sarah before her (XVI, 1) and Rachel after her (XXX, 31). This sterility may have been intended to emphasize that the children who were eventually born were a gift of grace from God for the fulfilment of His purpose.

22. *struggled together.* A premonition of the rivalry which was to exist between the brothers and their descendants.

if it be so, wherefore do I live? Life was unbearable for her, and she wished to die (Nachmanides).

to inquire of the LORD. A technical term for seeking an answer from a Divine source. According to the Midrash, she went to the School of Shem, where the knowledge of God was taught. It is very probable that she went to 'inquire of the Lord' through Abraham, who was still alive at this time (see on *v.* 7 above).

23. *two nations. i.e.* the founders of two nations. The oracular answer is in four poetic lines.

shall be separated. Shall be mutually antagonistic from birth.

the elder shall serve the younger. This prophecy was fulfilled when David defeated Edom. See II Sam. VIII, 14.

25. *ruddy.* Heb. *admoni.* The Midrash explains the ruddiness as a premonition of his love for hunting and the shedding of blood.

Esau. Some authorities derive it from a Semitic root meaning 'thick-haired'.

26. *his hand had hold on Esau's heel.* As it were to pull him back and prevent him from being the firstborn; cf. Hosea XII, 4.

hold on Esau's heel; and his name was called [1]Jacob. And Isaac was threescore years old when she bore them. 27. And the boys grew; and Esau was a cunning hunter, a man of the field; and Jacob was a quiet man, dwelling in tents. 28. Now Isaac loved Esau, because he did eat of his venison; and Rebekah loved Jacob. 29. And Jacob sod pottage; and Esau came in from the field, and he was faint. 30. And Esau said to Jacob: 'Let me swallow, I pray thee, some of this red, red pottage; for I am faint.' Therefore was his name called [2]Edom. 31. And Jacob said: 'Sell me first thy birthright.' 32. And Esau said: 'Behold, I am at the point to die; and what profit shall the birthright do to me?' 33. And Jacob said: 'Swear to me first'; and he swore unto him; and he sold his birthright unto Jacob. 34. And Jacob gave Esau bread and pottage of lentils; and he did eat and drink, and rose up, and went his way. So Esau despised his birthright.

27 שמו יעקב ויצחק בן־ששים שנה בלדת אתם: ויגדלו
הנערים ויהי עשו איש ידע ציד איש שדה ויעקב איש
28 תם ישב אהלים: ויאהב יצחק את־עשו כי־ציד בפיו
29 ורבקה אהבת את־יעקב: ויזד יעקב נזיד ויבא עשו
ל מן־השדה והוא עיף: ויאמר עשו אל־יעקב הלעיטני
נא מן־האדם האדם הזה כי עיף אנכי על־כן קרא־
31 שמו אדום: ויאמר יעקב מכרה כיום את־בכרתך לי:
32 ויאמר עשו הנה אנכי הולך למות ולמה־זה לי בכרה:
33 ויאמר יעקב השבעה לי כיום וישבע לו וימכר את־
34 בכרתו ליעקב: ויעקב נתן לעשו לחם ונזיד עדשים
ויאכל וישת ויקם וילך ויבז עשו את־הבכרה: פ

26

CHAPTER XXVI

CAP. XXVI. כו

כו

1. And there was a famine in the land, beside the first famine that was in the days of

א ויהי רעב בארץ מלבד הרעב הראשון אשר היה בימי

[1] That is, *One that takes by the heel*, or, *supplants*. [2] That is, *Red*.

27. *a cunning hunter.* lit. 'knowing hunting.' The word 'cunning' is used in its old meaning, 'skilful.'

quiet. lit. 'perfect'; *i.e.* quiet, harmless.

dwelling in tents. i.e. a shepherd. The Midrash explains 'tents' to mean 'schools of religious study'; cf. on *v.* 22.

28. *now Isaac loved Esau.* Although in Rabbinic literature, Esau the roving huntsman is, like Nimrod, depicted as a bad character because of the bloodshed and cruelty to animals that the hunter's life entails, yet he is praised for his devotion to Isaac. To have merited his father's love is regarded as the consequence of Esau's filial piety.

and Rebekah loved Jacob. Each parent had a favourite child, which was to lead to the break-up of the household. 'Love thy children with an impartial love,' is the wise admonition of a medieval Jewish teacher.

30. *swallow.* The Heb. word, which does not occur elsewhere in the Bible, implies animal-like voracity.

Edom. 'The Hebrews saw in the name of the rival nation, a standing reminder of the impulsive shortsightedness of its ancestor' (Driver). The term 'mess of pottage', used proverbially of this transaction, does not occur in the Authorised Version of the Bible.

31. *sell me first thy birthright.* At first sight, Jacob's conduct appears indeed reprehensible. On closer examination, however, we learn that the privileges of the birthright so coveted by Jacob were purely spiritual. In primitive times, the head of the clan or the firstborn acted as the priest. Esau's general behaviour hardly accorded with what was due from one who was to serve the Supreme God; and Jacob suspected that his brother did not value the dignity and privilege of being the firstborn as they should be valued. When, therefore, an opportunity suggested itself, Jacob determined to put his brother to the test. He knew full well that the withholding of the pottage would not have fatal consequences. He would, however, find out what Esau really thought of his birthright. 'As to power and command, Jacob never exercised any over Esau; but on the contrary, humbly and submissively addresses him as "my Lord"' (Abarbanel).

32. *I am at the point to die.* The exaggeration of a hungry man of uncontrolled appetite.

34. *So Esau despised his birthright.* Which he would not have done had it carried with it material advantages. The spiritual inheritance of Abraham, which would normally have passed into the hands of Esau, was not worth to him as much as a dish of pottage. Like the true sensualist, this fickle and impulsive hunter readily sacrifices to the gratification of the moment that which to a man of nobler build would be of transcendent worth.

CHAPTER XXVI. ISAAC AND THE PHILISTINES

1. *the first famine.* Mentioned in XII, 10.

Abimelech. See on XX, 2. Possibly the dynastic name of the Philistine rulers.

Gerar. See on XX, 1.

אַבְרָהָם וַיֵּלֶךְ יִצְחָק אֶל־אֲבִימֶלֶךְ מֶלֶךְ־פְּלִשְׁתִּים גְּרָרָה׃
2 וַיֵּרָא אֵלָיו יְהוָה וַיֹּאמֶר אַל־תֵּרֵד מִצְרָיְמָה שְׁכֹן בָּאָרֶץ
3 אֲשֶׁר אֹמַר אֵלֶיךָ׃ גּוּר בָּאָרֶץ הַזֹּאת וְאֶהְיֶה עִמְּךָ וַאֲבָרְכֶךָּ
כִּי־לְךָ וּלְזַרְעֲךָ אֶתֵּן אֶת־כָּל־הָאֲרָצֹת הָאֵל וַהֲקִמֹתִי אֶת־
4 הַשְּׁבֻעָה אֲשֶׁר נִשְׁבַּעְתִּי לְאַבְרָהָם אָבִיךָ׃ וְהִרְבֵּיתִי אֶת־
זַרְעֲךָ כְּכוֹכְבֵי הַשָּׁמַיִם וְנָתַתִּי לְזַרְעֲךָ אֵת כָּל־הָאֲרָצֹת
ה הָאֵל וְהִתְבָּרְכוּ בְזַרְעֲךָ כֹּל גּוֹיֵי הָאָרֶץ׃ עֵקֶב אֲשֶׁר־שָׁמַע
שני אַבְרָהָם בְּקֹלִי וַיִּשְׁמֹר מִשְׁמַרְתִּי מִצְוֹתַי חֻקּוֹתַי וְתוֹרֹתָי׃
6 7 וַיֵּשֶׁב יִצְחָק בִּגְרָר׃ וַיִּשְׁאֲלוּ אַנְשֵׁי הַמָּקוֹם לְאִשְׁתּוֹ וַיֹּאמֶר
אֲחֹתִי הִוא כִּי יָרֵא לֵאמֹר אִשְׁתִּי פֶּן־יַהַרְגֻנִי אַנְשֵׁי הַמָּקוֹם
8 עַל־רִבְקָה כִּי־טוֹבַת מַרְאֶה הִוא׃ וַיְהִי כִּי אָרְכוּ־לוֹ שָׁם
הַיָּמִים וַיַּשְׁקֵף אֲבִימֶלֶךְ מֶלֶךְ פְּלִשְׁתִּים בְּעַד הַחַלּוֹן וַיַּרְא
9 וְהִנֵּה יִצְחָק מְצַחֵק אֵת רִבְקָה אִשְׁתּוֹ׃ וַיִּקְרָא אֲבִימֶלֶךְ
לְיִצְחָק וַיֹּאמֶר אַךְ הִנֵּה אִשְׁתְּךָ הִוא וְאֵיךְ אָמַרְתָּ אֲחֹתִי
הִוא וַיֹּאמֶר אֵלָיו יִצְחָק כִּי אָמַרְתִּי פֶּן־אָמוּת עָלֶיהָ׃
י וַיֹּאמֶר אֲבִימֶלֶךְ מַה־זֹּאת עָשִׂיתָ לָּנוּ כִּמְעַט שָׁכַב אַחַד
11 הָעָם אֶת־אִשְׁתֶּךָ וְהֵבֵאתָ עָלֵינוּ אָשָׁם׃ וַיְצַו אֲבִימֶלֶךְ אֶת־
כָּל־הָעָם לֵאמֹר הַנֹּגֵעַ בָּאִישׁ הַזֶּה וּבְאִשְׁתּוֹ מוֹת יוּמָת׃
12 וַיִּזְרַע יִצְחָק בָּאָרֶץ הַהִוא וַיִּמְצָא בַּשָּׁנָה הַהִוא מֵאָה

v. 3. v. 4. סבירין האלה

Abraham. And Isaac went unto Abimelech king of the Philistines unto Gerar. 2. And the LORD appeared unto him, and said: 'Go not down into Egypt; dwell in the land which I shall tell thee of. 3. Sojourn in this land, and I will be with thee, and will bless thee; for unto thee, and unto thy seed, I will give all these lands, and I will establish the oath which I swore unto Abraham thy father; 4. and I will multiply thy seed as the stars of heaven, and will give unto thy seed all these lands; and by thy seed shall all the nations of the earth bless themselves; 5. because that Abraham hearkened to My voice, and kept My charge, My commandments, My statutes, and My laws.'* ii. 6. And Isaac dwelt in Gerar. 7. And the men of the place asked him of his wife; and he said: 'She is my sister'; for he feared to say: 'My wife'; 'lest the men of the place should kill me for Rebekah, because she is fair to look upon.' 8. And it came to pass, when he had been there a long time, that Abimelech king of the Philistines looked out at a window, and saw, and, behold, Isaac was sporting with Rebekah his wife. 9. And Abimelech called Isaac, and said: 'Behold, of a surety she is thy wife; and how saidst thou: She is my sister?' And Isaac said unto him: 'Because I said: Lest I die because of her.' 10. And Abimelech said: 'What is this thou hast done unto us? one of the people might easily have lain with thy wife, and thou wouldest have brought guiltiness upon us.' 11. And Abimelech charged all the people, saying: 'He that toucheth this man or his wife shall surely be put to death.' 12. And Isaac sowed in that land, and found in the same year a hundredfold; and the LORD blessed him.*iii.

2. *go not down into Egypt.* Isaac would naturally resolve to do what his father had done in similar circumstances, as described in XII, 10.

3. *sojourn.* Stay for the time being; cf. on XII, 10.

4. *as the stars of heaven.* Cf. XV, 5.
bless themselves. See on XII, 3.

5. *because that Abraham.* Emphasizing the unity and continuity of Abraham and his descendants.
commandments. Laws dictated by the moral sense, *e.g.* against the crimes of robbery, bloodshed, etc. (מצוות).
statutes. Laws ordained by God which we are to observe although reason cannot assign an explanation, *e.g.* the prohibition of swine's flesh (חוקים).
laws. Customs and traditional ordinances orally transmitted from generation to generation (תורות). These definitions are given in the Midrash.

7. Isaac meets with the same experience as his father (XII, 13; XX, 5), and unwisely adopts the same plan for safeguarding his person.

8. Abimelech had not taken Rebekah into his household as had been done with Sarah.

at a window. Or, 'through the window.'

sporting. The same word as used in XXI, 8, but having here a different meaning. Their conduct was such that Abimelech suspected they were husband and wife.

12. *in the same year. i.e.* in the year of famine. That is why his prosperity was regarded as not a natural thing but a Divine blessing.

a hundredfold. 'In the rich lava-soil of Hauran, wheat is said to yield on an average 80 fold, and barley, 100 fold' (Wetzstein).

13. And the man waxed great, and grew more and more until he became very great. 14. And he had possessions of flocks, and possessions of herds, and a great household; and the Philistines envied him. 15. Now all the wells which his father's servants had digged in the days of Abraham his father, the Philistines had stopped them, and filled them with earth. 16. And Abimelech said unto Isaac: 'Go from us; for thou art much mightier than we.' 17. And Isaac departed thence, and encamped in the valley of Gerar, and dwelt there. 18. And Isaac digged again the wells of water, which they had digged in the days of Abraham his father; for the Philistines had stopped them after the death of Abraham; and he called their names after the names by which his father had called them. 19. And Isaac's servants digged in the valley, and found there a well of living water. 20. And the herdmen of Gerar strove with Isaac's herdmen, saying: 'The water is ours.' And he called the name of the well [1]Esek; because they contended with him. 21. And they digged another well, and they strove for that also. And he called the name of it [2]Sitnah. 22. And he removed from thence, and digged another well; and for that they strove not. And he called the name of it [3]Rehoboth; and he said: 'For now the LORD hath made room for us, and we shall be fruitful in the land.'* iv. 23. And he went up from thence to Beer-sheba. 24. And the LORD appeared unto him the same night, and said: 'I am the God of Abraham thy father. Fear not, for I am with thee, and will bless thee, and multiply thy seed for My servant Abraham's sake.' 25. And he builded an altar there, and called upon the name of the LORD, and pitched his tent there; and there Isaac's servants digged a well. 26. Then Abimelech went to him from Gerar, and Ahuzzath his friend, and Phicol the captain of his host. 27. And Isaac said unto them: 'Wherefore are ye come unto me, seeing ye hate me, and have

שלישי
13 שְׁעָרִים וַיְבָרְכֵהוּ יְהוָה: * וַיִּגְדַּל הָאִישׁ וַיֵּלֶךְ הָלוֹךְ וְגָדֵל
14 עַד כִּי־גָדַל מְאֹד: וַיְהִי־לוֹ מִקְנֵה־צֹאן וּמִקְנֵה בָקָר וַעֲבֻדָּה
טו רַבָּה וַיְקַנְאוּ אֹתוֹ פְּלִשְׁתִּים: וְכָל־הַבְּאֵרֹת אֲשֶׁר חָפְרוּ
עַבְדֵי אָבִיו בִּימֵי אַבְרָהָם אָבִיו סִתְּמוּם פְּלִשְׁתִּים
16 וַיְמַלְאוּם עָפָר: וַיֹּאמֶר אֲבִימֶלֶךְ אֶל־יִצְחָק לֵךְ מֵעִמָּנוּ
17 כִּי־עָצַמְתָּ מִמֶּנּוּ מְאֹד: וַיֵּלֶךְ מִשָּׁם יִצְחָק וַיִּחַן בְּנַחַל־גְּרָר
18 וַיֵּשֶׁב שָׁם: וַיָּשָׁב יִצְחָק וַיַּחְפֹּר | אֶת־בְּאֵרֹת הַמַּיִם אֲשֶׁר
חָפְרוּ בִּימֵי אַבְרָהָם אָבִיו וַיְסַתְּמוּם פְּלִשְׁתִּים אַחֲרֵי מוֹת
אַבְרָהָם וַיִּקְרָא לָהֶן שֵׁמוֹת כַּשֵּׁמֹת אֲשֶׁר־קָרָא לָהֶן אָבִיו:
19 וַיַּחְפְּרוּ עַבְדֵי־יִצְחָק בַּנָּחַל וַיִּמְצְאוּ־שָׁם בְּאֵר מַיִם חַיִּים:
כ וַיָּרִיבוּ רֹעֵי גְרָר עִם־רֹעֵי יִצְחָק לֵאמֹר לָנוּ הַמָּיִם וַיִּקְרָא
21 שֵׁם־הַבְּאֵר עֵשֶׂק כִּי הִתְעַשְּׂקוּ עִמּוֹ: וַיַּחְפְּרוּ בְּאֵר אַחֶרֶת
22 וַיָּרִיבוּ גַּם־עָלֶיהָ וַיִּקְרָא שְׁמָהּ שִׂטְנָה: וַיַּעְתֵּק מִשָּׁם
וַיַּחְפֹּר בְּאֵר אַחֶרֶת וְלֹא רָבוּ עָלֶיהָ וַיִּקְרָא שְׁמָהּ רְחֹבוֹת
רביעי
23 וַיֹּאמֶר כִּי־עַתָּה הִרְחִיב יְהוָה לָנוּ וּפָרִינוּ בָאָרֶץ: * וַיַּעַל
24 מִשָּׁם בְּאֵר שָׁבַע: וַיֵּרָא אֵלָיו יְהוָה בַּלַּיְלָה הַהוּא וַיֹּאמֶר
אָנֹכִי אֱלֹהֵי אַבְרָהָם אָבִיךָ אַל־תִּירָא כִּי־אִתְּךָ אָנֹכִי
וּבֵרַכְתִּיךָ וְהִרְבֵּיתִי אֶת־זַרְעֲךָ בַּעֲבוּר אַבְרָהָם עַבְדִּי:
כה וַיִּבֶן שָׁם מִזְבֵּחַ וַיִּקְרָא בְּשֵׁם יְהוָה וַיֶּט־שָׁם אָהֳלוֹ וַיִּכְרוּ־
26 שָׁם עַבְדֵי־יִצְחָק בְּאֵר: וַאֲבִימֶלֶךְ הָלַךְ אֵלָיו מִגְּרָר וַאֲחֻזַּת
27 מֵרֵעֵהוּ וּפִיכֹל שַׂר־צְבָאוֹ: וַיֹּאמֶר אֲלֵהֶם יִצְחָק מַדּוּעַ
בָּאתֶם אֵלָי וְאַתֶּם שְׂנֵאתֶם אֹתִי וַתְּשַׁלְּחוּנִי מֵאִתְּכֶם:

[1] That is, *Contention.* [2] That is, *Enmity.* [3] That is, *Room.*

v. 15. ל׳ רפה v. 22. מלרע

16. The prosperity of the Patriarch creates envy among his neighbours. Modern anti-Semitism is, likewise, largely dictated by envy, thus illustrating the Rabbinic saying, 'What happened to the Patriarchs, repeats itself in the life of their descendants.'

17. *valley.* The Heb. word *nahal* means a *wady* or river-bed, which in the winter, or even after a storm, is a rushing stream, but in summer is usually reduced to a mere thread of water, or may even be entirely dry. In the bed of such wadys, water may often be found by digging (Driver).

19 *living water.* Or, 'springing water'; the opposite of stagnant water.

22. *Rehoboth. i.e.* 'Room', latitude; lit. 'broad places'. In Heb. the word denoting 'spaciousness' is used to express comfort and security. Twenty miles S.W. of Beer-sheba there is a well known as *Ruhaibeh.*

24. *fear not.* In view of the hostility recently shown him.

25. *called upon the name of the* LORD. See on XII, 18.

26. *his friend. i.e.* his intimate counsellor.

Phicol. The same as in XXI, 22. If the Abimelech and Phicol are identical with those mentioned in Chap. XXI, they must have been old men in the time of Isaac.

sent me away from you?' 28. And they said: 'We saw plainly that the LORD was with thee; and we said: Let there now be an oath betwixt us, even betwixt us and thee, and let us make a covenant with thee; 29. that thou wilt do us no hurt, as we have not touched thee, and as we have done unto thee nothing but good, and have sent thee away in peace; thou art now the blessed of the LORD.'* v. 30. And he made them a feast, and they did eat and drink. 31. And they rose up betimes in the morning, and swore one to another; and Isaac sent them away, and they departed from him in peace. 32. And it came to pass the same day, that Isaac's servants came, and told him concerning the well which they had digged, and said unto him: 'We have found water.' 33. And he called it Shibah. Therefore the name of the city is Beer-sheba unto this day. ¶ 34. And when Esau was forty years old, he took to wife Judith the daughter of Beeri the Hittite, and Basemath the daughter of Elon the Hittite. 35. And they were a bitterness of spirit unto Isaac and to Rebekah.

28 ויאמרו ראו ראינו כי־היה יהוה ׀ עמך ונאמר תהי נא
29 אלה בינותינו בינינו ובינך ונכרתה ברית עמך׃ אם־
חמישי תעשה עמנו רעה כאשר לא נגענוך וכאשר עשינו עמך
ל רק־טוב ונשלחך בשלום אתה עתה ברוך יהוה׃ ויעש
31 להם משתה ויאכלו וישתו׃ וישכימו בבקר וישבעו
32 איש לאחיו וישלחם יצחק וילכו מאתו בשלום׃ ויהי ׀
ביום ההוא ויבאו עבדי יצחק ויגדו לו על־אדות הבאר
33 אשר חפרו ויאמרו לו מצאנו מים׃ ויקרא אתה שבעה
34 על־כן שם־העיר באר שבע עד היום הזה׃ ס ויהי
עשו בן־ארבעים שנה ויקח אשה את־יהודית בת־בארי
לה החתי ואת־בשמת בת־אילן החתי׃ ותהיין מרת רוח
ליצחק ולרבקה׃ ס

27

CHAPTER XXVII

1. And it came to pass, that when Isaac was old, and his eyes were dim, so that he could not see, he called Esau his elder son, and said unto him: 'My son'; and he said unto him: 'Here am I.' 2. And he said: 'Behold now, I am old, I know not the day of my death. 3. Now therefore take, I pray thee, thy weapons, thy quiver and thy bow, and go out to the field, and take me venison; 4. and make me savoury food, such as I love, and bring it to me, that I may eat; that my soul may bless thee before I die.' 5. And Rebekah heard when Isaac

CAP. XXVII. כז

כז

א ויהי כי־זקן יצחק ותכהין עיניו מראת ויקרא את־עשו ׀
2 בנו הגדל ויאמר אליו בני ויאמר אליו הנני׃ ויאמר
3 הנה־נא זקנתי לא ידעתי יום מותי׃ ועתה שא־נא כליך
4 תליך וקשתך וצא השדה וצודה לי צידה׃ ועשה־לי
מטעמים כאשר אהבתי והביאה לי ואכלה בעבור
ה תברכך נפשי בטרם אמות׃ ורבקה שמעת בדבר יצחק

כו׳ v. 29. הש׳ בצירי כז׳ v. 2. פתח באתנח v. 3. ה׳ יתירה

28. *the LORD was with thee.* The same motive for seeking friendship as in XXI, 22.

oath. A compact sealed by an oath.

29. *we have not touched thee.* Cf. *v.* 11.

33. *Shibah.* Better, *Good Fortune.* The Semitic root שבע—in addition to its other meanings and because of those other meanings—denotes 'to be fortunate'. Thus the Samaritan Targum for באשרי in Gen. XXX, 13 is במשבעי (Oppenheim in Berliner's Magazin, 1875).

Beer-sheba. i.e. Fortune's Well.

34. *Judith.* It is not found again in the Bible, but is the name of the heroine of one of the books of the Apocrypha.

Basemath. In XXXVI, 2 f, we are given the names of more wives of Esau.

35. *a bitterness of spirit.* Or, 'a grief of mind.' It was against the family tradition to intermarry with these races; see XXIV, 3; XXVII, 46. The mention of Esau's wives is introduced here to show how faithless he was to the teachings and example of Abraham and Isaac, and therefore unworthy to be regarded as their spiritual heir and to receive his father's blessing.

CHAPTER XXVII. THE BLESSING OF ISAAC

2. *I know not the day of my death.* 'I know not how soon I may die' (Moffatt).

4. *my soul may bless thee.* Only an emphatic form of 'I may bless thee'; see on XII, 13. The dying utterance was deemed prophetic.

5. *heard.* More accurately, 'was listening.' To understand Rebekah's action, it is necessary to bear in mind what had been stated in XXV, 23. When she had inquired of the LORD about her unborn children, she had been told, 'the elder spoke to Esau his son. And Esau went to the field to hunt for venison, and to bring it. 6. And Rebekah spoke unto Jacob her son, saying: 'Behold, I heard thy father speak unto Esau thy brother, saying: 7. Bring me venison, and make me savoury food, that I may eat, and bless thee before the LORD before my death. 8. Now therefore, my son, hearken to my voice according to that which I command thee. 9. Go now to the flock, and fetch me from thence two good kids of the goats; and I will make them savoury food for thy father, such as he loveth; 10. and thou shalt bring it to thy father, that he may eat, so that he may bless thee before his death.' 11. And Jacob said to Rebekah his mother: 'Behold, Esau my brother is a hairy man, and I am a smooth man. 12. My father peradventure will feel me, and I shall seem to him as a mocker; and I shall bring a curse upon me, and not a blessing.' 13. And his mother said unto him: 'Upon me be thy curse, my son; only hearken to my voice, and go fetch me them.' 14. And he went, and fetched, and brought them to his mother; and his mother made savoury food, such as his father loved. 15. And Rebekah took the choicest garments of Esau her elder son, which were with her in the house, and put them upon Jacob her younger son. 16. And she put the skins of the kids of the goats upon his hands, and upon the smooth of his neck. 17. And she gave the savoury food and the bread, which she had prepared, into the hand of her son Jacob. 18. And he came unto his father, and said: 'My father'; and he said: 'Here am I; who art thou, my son?' 19. And Jacob said unto his father: 'I am Esau thy first-born; I have done according as thou badest me. Arise, I pray thee, sit and eat of my venison, that thy soul may bless me.' 20. And Isaac said unto his son: 'How is it that thou hast found it so quickly, my son?' And he said: 'Because the LORD thy God sent me good

6 אֶל־עֵשָׂו בְּנוֹ וַיֵּלֶךְ עֵשָׂו הַשָּׂדֶה לָצוּד צַיִד לְהָבִיא׃ וְרִבְקָה
אָמְרָה אֶל־יַעֲקֹב בְּנָהּ לֵאמֹר הִנֵּה שָׁמַעְתִּי אֶת־אָבִיךָ
7 מְדַבֵּר אֶל־עֵשָׂו אָחִיךָ לֵאמֹר׃ הָבִיאָה לִּי צַיִד וַעֲשֵׂה־לִי
8 מַטְעַמִּים וְאֹכֵלָה וַאֲבָרֶכְכָה לִפְנֵי יְהוָה לִפְנֵי מוֹתִי׃ וְעַתָּה
9 בְנִי שְׁמַע בְּקֹלִי לַאֲשֶׁר אֲנִי מְצַוָּה אֹתָךְ׃ לֶךְ־נָא אֶל־הַצֹּאן
וְקַח־לִי מִשָּׁם שְׁנֵי גְּדָיֵי עִזִּים טֹבִים וְאֶעֱשֶׂה אֹתָם מַטְעַמִּים
י לְאָבִיךָ כַּאֲשֶׁר אָהֵב׃ וְהֵבֵאתָ לְאָבִיךָ וְאָכָל בַּעֲבֻר אֲשֶׁר
11 יְבָרֶכְךָ לִפְנֵי מוֹתוֹ׃ וַיֹּאמֶר יַעֲקֹב אֶל־רִבְקָה אִמּוֹ הֵן
12 עֵשָׂו אָחִי אִישׁ שָׂעִר וְאָנֹכִי אִישׁ חָלָק׃ אוּלַי יְמֻשֵּׁנִי אָבִי
וְהָיִיתִי בְעֵינָיו כִּמְתַעְתֵּעַ וְהֵבֵאתִי עָלַי קְלָלָה וְלֹא בְרָכָה׃
13 וַתֹּאמֶר לוֹ אִמּוֹ עָלַי קִלְלָתְךָ בְּנִי אַךְ שְׁמַע בְּקֹלִי וְלֵךְ
14 קַח־לִי׃ וַיֵּלֶךְ וַיִּקַּח וַיָּבֵא לְאִמּוֹ וַתַּעַשׂ אִמּוֹ מַטְעַמִּים
טו כַּאֲשֶׁר אָהֵב אָבִיו׃ וַתִּקַּח רִבְקָה אֶת־בִּגְדֵי עֵשָׂו בְּנָהּ
הַגָּדֹל הַחֲמֻדֹת אֲשֶׁר אִתָּהּ בַּבָּיִת וַתַּלְבֵּשׁ אֶת־יַעֲקֹב בְּנָהּ
16 הַקָּטָן׃ וְאֵת עֹרֹת גְּדָיֵי הָעִזִּים הִלְבִּישָׁה עַל־יָדָיו וְעַל
17 חֶלְקַת צַוָּארָיו׃ וַתִּתֵּן אֶת־הַמַּטְעַמִּים וְאֶת־הַלֶּחֶם אֲשֶׁר
18 עָשָׂתָה בְּיַד יַעֲקֹב בְּנָהּ׃ וַיָּבֹא אֶל־אָבִיו וַיֹּאמֶר אָבִי
19 וַיֹּאמֶר הִנֶּנִּי מִי אַתָּה בְּנִי׃ וַיֹּאמֶר יַעֲקֹב אֶל־אָבִיו אָנֹכִי
עֵשָׂו בְּכֹרֶךָ עָשִׂיתִי כַּאֲשֶׁר דִּבַּרְתָּ אֵלָי קוּם־נָא שְׁבָה

shall serve the younger.' This prophecy appeared on the point of being falsified by Isaac's intention to bestow his chief blessing upon Esau. Knowing how attached Isaac was to the elder son, she must have felt that it would be useless to try and dissuade her husband from his intention. She, therefore, in desperation, decided to circumvent him.

12. *mocker.* Or, 'deceiver.'

15. *choicest garments.* His choicest garments, as distinct from the rough and blood-stained garments he wore when hunting.

which were with her in the house. Though Esau was married and presumably had a home of his own, he would keep some of his clothes at his father's house which he would don during his visits from hunting, after removing his soiled garments.

19. *I am Esau thy first-born.* These words misled Isaac, and were spoken with the intention of inducing his father to believe that it was Esau who stood before him. Jacob, having been persuaded to adopt his mother's plan, is forced to play his part to the end (Ibn Ezra).

20. *so quickly.* This was not an oversight of Rebekah's. She was obliged to hurry lest Esau should return and upset the plot.

the LORD thy God sent me good speed. Such words were not of the kind likely to have been spoken by the rough Esau. The name of God was probably rare on his lips. Hence Jacob's

כ וְאָכְלָה מִצֵּידִי בַּעֲבוּר תְּבָרֲכַנִּי נַפְשֶׁךָ׃ וַיֹּאמֶר יִצְחָק אֶל־
בְּנוֹ מַה־זֶּה מִהַרְתָּ לִמְצֹא בְּנִי וַיֹּאמֶר כִּי הִקְרָה יְהוָה
21 אֱלֹהֶיךָ לְפָנָי׃ וַיֹּאמֶר יִצְחָק אֶל־יַעֲקֹב גְּשָׁה־נָּא וַאֲמֻשְׁךָ
22 בְּנִי הַאַתָּה זֶה בְּנִי עֵשָׂו אִם־לֹא׃ וַיִּגַּשׁ יַעֲקֹב אֶל־יִצְחָק
אָבִיו וַיְמֻשֵּׁהוּ וַיֹּאמֶר הַקֹּל קוֹל יַעֲקֹב וְהַיָּדַיִם יְדֵי עֵשָׂו׃
23 וְלֹא הִכִּירוֹ כִּי־הָיוּ יָדָיו כִּידֵי עֵשָׂו אָחִיו שְׂעִרֹת וַיְבָרְכֵהוּ׃
24 כה וַיֹּאמֶר אַתָּה זֶה בְּנִי עֵשָׂו וַיֹּאמֶר אָנִי׃ וַיֹּאמֶר הַגִּשָׁה לִּי
וְאֹכְלָה מִצֵּיד בְּנִי לְמַעַן תְּבָרֶכְךָ נַפְשִׁי וַיַּגֶּשׁ־לוֹ וַיֹּאכַל
26 וַיָּבֵא לוֹ יַיִן וַיֵּשְׁתְּ׃ וַיֹּאמֶר אֵלָיו יִצְחָק אָבִיו גְּשָׁה־נָּא
27 ששי וּשְׁקָה־לִּי בְּנִי׃ וַיִּגַּשׁ וַיִּשַּׁק־לוֹ וַיָּרַח אֶת־רֵיחַ בְּגָדָיו וַיְבָרְכֵהוּ
28 וַיֹּאמֶר רְאֵה רֵיחַ בְּנִי כְּרֵיחַ שָׂדֶה אֲשֶׁר בֵּרְכוֹ יְהוָה׃ וְיִתֶּן־
לְךָ הָאֱלֹהִים מִטַּל הַשָּׁמַיִם וּמִשְׁמַנֵּי הָאָרֶץ וְרֹב דָּגָן וְתִירֹשׁ׃
29 יַעַבְדוּךָ עַמִּים וְיִשְׁתַּחֲוֻ לְךָ לְאֻמִּים הֱוֵה גְבִיר לְאַחֶיךָ
וְיִשְׁתַּחֲווּ לְךָ בְּנֵי אִמֶּךָ אֹרְרֶיךָ אָרוּר וּמְבָרְכֶיךָ בָּרוּךְ׃
ל וַיְהִי כַּאֲשֶׁר כִּלָּה יִצְחָק לְבָרֵךְ אֶת־יַעֲקֹב וַיְהִי אַךְ יָצֹא
יָצָא יַעֲקֹב מֵאֵת פְּנֵי יִצְחָק אָבִיו וְעֵשָׂו אָחִיו בָּא מִצֵּידוֹ׃
31 וַיַּעַשׂ גַּם־הוּא מַטְעַמִּים וַיָּבֵא לְאָבִיו וַיֹּאמֶר לְאָבִיו יָקֻם
32 אָבִי וְיֹאכַל מִצֵּיד בְּנוֹ בַּעֲבֻר תְּבָרֲכַנִּי נַפְשֶׁךָ׃ וַיֹּאמֶר לוֹ
33 יִצְחָק אָבִיו מִי־אָתָּה וַיֹּאמֶר אֲנִי בִּנְךָ בְכֹרְךָ עֵשָׂו׃ וַיֶּחֱרַד

v. 29. וישתחוו קרי

speed.' 21. And Isaac said unto Jacob: 'Come near, I pray thee, that I may feel thee, my son, whether thou be my very son Esau or not.' 22. And Jacob went near unto Isaac his father; and he felt him, and said: 'The voice is the voice of Jacob, but the hands are the hands of Esau.' 23. And he discerned him not, because his hands were hairy, as his brother Esau's hands; so he blessed him. 24. And he said: 'Art thou my very son Esau?' And he said: 'I am.' 25. And he said: 'Bring it near to me, and I will eat of my son's venison, that my soul may bless thee.' And he brought it near to him, and he did eat; and he brought him wine, and he drank. 26. And his father Isaac said unto him: 'Come near now, and kiss me, my son.' 27. And he came near, and kissed him. And he smelled the smell of his raiment, and blessed him, and said:

See, the smell of my son
Is as the smell of a field which the Lord hath blessed.* vi.
28. So God give thee of the dew of heaven,
And of the fat places of the earth,
And plenty of corn and wine.
29. Let peoples serve thee,
And nations bow down to thee.
Be lord over thy brethren,
And let thy mother's sons bow down to thee.
Cursed be every one that curseth thee,
And blessed be every one that blesseth thee.

30. And it came to pass, as soon as Isaac had made an end of blessing Jacob, and Jacob was yet scarce gone out from the presence of Isaac his father, that Esau his brother came in from his hunting. 31. And he also made savoury food, and brought it unto his father; and he said unto his father: 'Let my father arise, and eat of his son's venison, that thy soul may bless me.' 32. And Isaac his father said unto him: 'Who art thou?' And he said: 'I am thy son, thy first-born, Esau.' 33. And

statement arouses his father's suspicions, who requires to be assured by the very test which Jacob dreaded, in *v.* 12.

23. *so he blessed him.* If that be the meaning of the Hebrew, we should expect the wording of the blessing to follow immediately. We do not, however, have that until *v.* 28. It is therefore possible that the Hebrew should here be rendered: 'he greeted him.'

28. *the dew of heaven.* In those countries where the days are hot and the nights are cold, the dew is very abundant and drenches the ground. It is essential to vegetation during the rainless summer, and was therefore regarded as a Divine blessing.

29. *peoples.* Refers to foreign nations, like the Canaanites.

brethren. Kindred peoples.

thy mother's sons. 'Sons' is here used in the sense of descendants.

cursed . . . blessed. Jacob was thus to inherit the Divine promise made to Abraham in XII, 3.

33. *yea, and he shall be blessed.* The benediction, having been uttered, was irrevocable. It may also imply that Isaac saw in what had happened the will of God.

Isaac trembled very exceedingly, and said: 'Who then is he that hath taken venison, and brought it me, and I have eaten of all before thou camest, and have blessed him? yea, and he shall be blessed.' 34. When Esau heard the words of his father, he cried with an exceeding great and bitter cry, and said unto his father: 'Bless me, even me also, O my father.' 35. And he said: 'Thy brother came with guile, and hath taken away thy blessing.' 36. And he said: 'Is not he rightly named Jacob? for he hath supplanted me these two times: he took away my birthright; and, behold, now he hath taken away my blessing.' And he said: 'Hast thou not reserved a blessing for me?' 37. And Isaac answered and said unto Esau: 'Behold, I have made him thy lord, and all his brethren have I given to him for servants; and with corn and wine have I sustained him; and what then shall I do for thee, my son?' 38. And Esau said unto his father: 'Hast thou but one blessing, my father? bless me, even me also, O my father.' And Esau lifted up his voice, and wept. 39. And Isaac his father answered and said unto him:

Behold, of the fat places of the earth
shall be thy dwelling,
And of the dew of heaven from above;
40. And by thy sword shalt thou live,
and thou shalt serve thy brother;
And it shall come to pass when thou
shalt break loose,
That thou shalt shake his yoke from off
thy neck.

41. And Esau hated Jacob because of the blessing wherewith his father blessed him. And Esau said in his heart: 'Let the days of mourning for my father be at hand; then will I slay my brother Jacob.' 42. And the words of Esau her elder son were told to Rebekah; and she sent and called Jacob her younger son, and said unto him:

יִצְחָק חֲרָדָה גְּדֹלָה עַד־מְאֹד וַיֹּאמֶר מִי־אֵפוֹא הוּא הַצָּד־
צַיִד וַיָּבֵא לִי וָאֹכַל מִכֹּל בְּטֶרֶם תָּבוֹא וָאֲבָרְכֵהוּ גַּם־בָּרוּךְ
34 יִהְיֶה׃ כִּשְׁמֹעַ עֵשָׂו אֶת־דִּבְרֵי אָבִיו וַיִּצְעַק צְעָקָה גְּדֹלָה
לה וּמָרָה עַד־מְאֹד וַיֹּאמֶר לְאָבִיו בָּרְכֵנִי גַם־אָנִי אָבִי׃ וַיֹּאמֶר
36 בָּא אָחִיךָ בְּמִרְמָה וַיִּקַּח בִּרְכָתֶךָ׃ וַיֹּאמֶר הֲכִי קָרָא שְׁמוֹ
יַעֲקֹב וַיַּעְקְבֵנִי זֶה פַעֲמַיִם אֶת־בְּכֹרָתִי לָקָח וְהִנֵּה עַתָּה
37 לָקַח בִּרְכָתִי וַיֹּאמַר הֲלֹא־אָצַלְתָּ לִּי בְּרָכָה׃ וַיַּעַן יִצְחָק
וַיֹּאמֶר לְעֵשָׂו הֵן גְּבִיר שַׂמְתִּיו לָךְ וְאֶת־כָּל־אֶחָיו נָתַתִּי
לוֹ לַעֲבָדִים וְדָגָן וְתִירֹשׁ סְמַכְתִּיו וּלְכָה אֵפוֹא מָה אֶעֱשֶׂה
38 בְּנִי׃ וַיֹּאמֶר עֵשָׂו אֶל־אָבִיו הַבְרָכָה אַחַת הִוא־לְךָ אָבִי
39 בָּרְכֵנִי גַם־אָנִי אָבִי וַיִּשָּׂא עֵשָׂו קֹלוֹ וַיֵּבְךְּ׃ וַיַּעַן יִצְחָק אָבִיו
וַיֹּאמֶר אֵלָיו הִנֵּה מִשְׁמַנֵּי הָאָרֶץ יִהְיֶה מוֹשָׁבֶךָ וּמִטַּל
מ הַשָּׁמַיִם מֵעָל׃ וְעַל־חַרְבְּךָ תִחְיֶה וְאֶת־אָחִיךָ תַּעֲבֹד וְהָיָה
41 כַּאֲשֶׁר תָּרִיד וּפָרַקְתָּ עֻלּוֹ מֵעַל צַוָּארֶךָ׃ וַיִּשְׂטֹם עֵשָׂו אֶת־
יַעֲקֹב עַל־הַבְּרָכָה אֲשֶׁר בֵּרְכוֹ אָבִיו וַיֹּאמֶר עֵשָׂו בְּלִבּוֹ
42 יִקְרְבוּ יְמֵי אֵבֶל אָבִי וְאַהַרְגָה אֶת־יַעֲקֹב אָחִי׃ וַיֻּגַּד
לְרִבְקָה אֶת־דִּבְרֵי עֵשָׂו בְּנָהּ הַגָּדֹל וַתִּשְׁלַח וַתִּקְרָא
לְיַעֲקֹב בְּנָהּ הַקָּטָן וַתֹּאמֶר אֵלָיו הִנֵּה עֵשָׂו אָחִיךָ מִתְנַחֵם
43 לְךָ לְהָרְגֶךָ׃ וְעַתָּה בְנִי שְׁמַע בְּקֹלִי וְקוּם בְּרַח־לְךָ אֶל־

v. 36. קמץ בו"ק v. 40. חצי הספר בפסוקים

36. *supplanted. i.e.* outwitted.

my birthright. In his passionate anger, he blames Jacob for 'taking away' that which he sold and ratified with an oath.

38. *wept.* 'Those tears of Esau, the sensuous, wild impulsive man, almost like the cry of some "trapped creature", are among the most pathetic in the Bible' (Davidson). The Rabbis declare that bitter retribution was in later years exacted from Jacob for having caused these tears of Esau.

39. *of the fat places of the earth . . . the dew of heaven,* etc. The soil will not furnish his means of sustenance—he will live in waste, arid regions.

40. *by thy sword shalt thou live. i.e.* by campaigns of plunder. The life of marauders dwelling in mountain fastnesses will be his. He will raid his brother's borders, and cut off the merchants travelling with caravans (Ryle).

thou shalt serve thy brother. The promise of lordship made to Jacob could not be recalled; but Isaac foretells that it will be of limited duration. We read of revolts on the part of the Edomites in I Kings XI, 14 f, and II Kings VIII, 20 f.

41. *mourning for my father.* It is at least to Esau's credit that he decided to spare his father's feelings, and wait for his death before avenging himself on Jacob (Midrash).

'Behold, thy brother Esau, as touching thee, doth comfort himself, purposing to kill thee. 43. Now therefore, my son, hearken to my voice; and arise, flee thou to Laban my brother to Haran; 44. and tarry with him a few days, until thy brother's fury turn away; 45. until thy brother's anger turn away from thee, and he forget that which thou hast done to him; then I will send, and fetch thee from thence; why should I be bereaved of you both in one day?' ¶ 46. And Rebekah said to Isaac: 'I am weary of my life because of the daughters of Heth. If Jacob take a wife of the daughters of Heth, such as these, of the daughters of the land, what good shall my life do me?'

44 לבן אחי חרנה׃ וישבת עמו ימים אחדים עד אשר־
מה תשוב חמת אחיך׃ עד־שוב אף־אחיך ממך ושכח את
אשר־עשית לו ושלחתי ולקחתיך משם למה אשכל גם־
46 שניכם יום אחד׃ ותאמר רבקה אל־יצחק קצתי בחיי
מפני בנות חת אם־לקח יעקב אשה מבנות־חת כאלה
מבנות הארץ למה לי חיים׃

28

Chapter XXVIII

1. And Isaac called Jacob, and blessed him, and charged him, and said unto him: 'Thou shalt not take a wife of the daughters of Canaan. 2. Arise, go to Paddan-aram, to the house of Bethuel thy mother's father; and take thee a wife from thence of the daughters of Laban thy mother's brother. 3. And God Almighty bless thee, and make thee fruitful, and multiply thee, that thou mayest be a congregation of peoples; 4. and give thee the blessing of Abraham, to thee, and to thy seed with thee; that thou mayest inherit the land of thy sojournings, which God gave unto Abraham.'* vii. 5. And Isaac sent away Jacob; and he went to Paddan-aram unto Laban, son of Bethuel the Aramean, the brother of Rebekah, Jacob's and Esau's mother. 6. Now Esau saw that Isaac had blessed Jacob and sent him away to Paddan-aram, to take him a wife from thence; and that as he blessed him he gave him a charge, saying: 'Thou shalt not take a wife of the daughters of Canaan';* m. 7. and that Jacob hearkened to his father and his mother, and was gone to Paddan-aram; 8. and Esau saw that the daughters of Canaan pleased not Isaac his father; 9. so Esau went unto Ishmael, and took unto the wives that he had Mahalath the daughter of Ishmael Abraham's son, the sister of Nebaioth, to be his wife.

Cap. XXVIII. כח

כח

א ויקרא יצחק אל־יעקב ויברך אתו ויצוהו ויאמר לו לא־
2 תקח אשה מבנות כנען׃ קום לך פדנה ארם ביתה
בתואל אבי אמך וקח־לך משם אשה מבנות לבן אחי
3 אמך׃ ואל שדי יברך אתך ויפרך וירבך והיית לקהל
4 עמים׃ ויתן־לך את־ברכת אברהם לך ולזרעך אתך
שביעי לרשתך את־ארץ מגריך אשר־נתן אלהים לאברהם׃*
ה וישלח יצחק את־יעקב וילך פדנה ארם אל־לבן בן־
6 בתואל הארמי אחי רבקה אם יעקב ועשו׃ וירא עשו
כי־ברך יצחק את־יעקב ושלח אתו פדנה ארם לקחת־
לו משם אשה בברכו אתו ויצו עליו לאמר לא־תקח
7 אשה מבנות כנען׃ וישמע יעקב אל־אביו ואל־אמו
8 וילך פדנה ארם׃ וירא עשו כי רעות בנות כנען בעיני
9 יצחק אביו׃ וילך עשו אל־ישמעאל ויקח את־מחלת בת־
ישמעאל בן־אברהם אחות נביות על־נשיו לו לאשה׃

כז׳ v. 46. ק׳ זעירא כח׳ v. 2. v. 5. v. 6. v. 7. פדנה כצ״ל בהעמדה תחת הגנון

44. *a few days.* It was the mother's hope that the difference between the brothers would soon be smoothed over, and the pain of separation be quickly succeeded by the joy of reunion. But she was fated never to see him again.

45. *bereaved of you both.* Isaac and Jacob; the death of the former being the signal for the murder of the latter.

46. *daughters of Heth.* See xxvi, 34 f. To save Isaac from the knowledge of the true reason why Jacob was leaving his home, Rebekah pretends that he is going to Haran in search of a wife.

Chapter XXVIII

2. *Paddan-aram.* See on xxv, 20.

3. *God Almighty.* See on xvii, 1.

4. *the blessing of Abraham.* Cf. xxv, 20.

9. *unto the wives.* In addition to those mentioned in xxvi, 24. It seems that he married his cousin in order to propitiate his parents, who were grieved at his alien wives.

HAFTORAH TOLEDOTH הפטרת תולדת

MALACHI I–II, 7

Chapter I

1. The burden of the word of the Lord to Israel by Malachi.

2. I have loved you, saith the Lord.
Yet ye say: 'Wherein hast Thou loved us?'
Was not Esau Jacob's brother?
Saith the Lord;
Yet I loved Jacob;

3. But Esau I hated,
And made his mountains a desolation,
And gave his heritage to the jackals of the wilderness.

4. Whereas Edom saith:
'We are beaten down,
But we will return and build the waste places';
Thus saith the Lord of hosts:
They shall build, but I will throw down;
And they shall be called The border of wickedness,
And The people whom the Lord execrateth for ever.

Cap. I. א

א 2 מַשָּׂא דְבַר־יְהוָה אֶל־יִשְׂרָאֵל בְּיַד מַלְאָכִי׃ אָהַבְתִּי אֶתְכֶם
אָמַר יְהוָה וַאֲמַרְתֶּם בַּמָּה אֲהַבְתָּנוּ הֲלוֹא־אָח עֵשָׂו
3 לְיַעֲקֹב נְאֻם־יְהוָה וָאֹהַב אֶת־יַעֲקֹב׃ וְאֶת־עֵשָׂו שָׂנֵאתִי
4 וָאָשִׂים אֶת־הָרָיו שְׁמָמָה וְאֶת־נַחֲלָתוֹ לְתַנּוֹת מִדְבָּר׃ כִּי־
תֹאמַר אֱדוֹם רֻשַּׁשְׁנוּ וְנָשׁוּב וְנִבְנֶה חֳרָבוֹת כֹּה אָמַר יְהוָה
צְבָאוֹת הֵמָּה יִבְנוּ וַאֲנִי אֶהֱרוֹס וְקָרְאוּ לָהֶם גְּבוּל רִשְׁעָה
ה וְהָעָם אֲשֶׁר־זָעַם יְהוָה עַד־עוֹלָם׃ וְעֵינֵיכֶם תִּרְאֶינָה וְאַתֶּם

5. And your eyes shall see,
And ye shall say:
'The Lord is great beyond the border of Israel.'

Malachi I–II, 7

Malachi was the last of the Prophets. Nothing is known of his life, except what can be gathered from his prophecies, which seem to have been spoken sometime about the year 450 before the Common Era.

The Second Temple had been rebuilt, but the high hopes of the returned exiles had not been fulfilled. The lamp of religious enthusiasm burned but dimly in that age, and both priest and people treated sacred things with a weary indifference. Though from the rising of the sun until the going down of the same, God's name was revered among the nations, it was Israel that began to doubt whether there was a righteous Governor of the universe, and was losing Israel's belief in Israel. 'I have loved you, saith the Lord. Yet ye say, "Wherein hast Thou loved us?" Your words have been stout against Me. Ye have said, "it is vain to serve God, and what profit is it that we have kept His charge?" '

It is to such a generation that Malachi brings his 'burden', *i.e.* utterance, message. He reaffirms and boldly proclaims the Divine election and the deathlessness of Israel. Confronted by sordid irreligion and cruel selfishness, he preaches the reality of the Unseen, and gives eternal expression to the brotherhood of man. 'Have we not all one father, hath not one God created us all? Why, then, do we deal faithlessly every man against his brother?' he asks. These words alone should endear him to every human heart.

The connection with the Sedrah lies chiefly in the opening verses.

The difference in the treatment of the two nations descended from Jacob and Esau is due to the difference in the character and life of these nations. The Edomites were a fierce and cruel people, 'a turbulent and unruly race, always hovering on the verge of revolution, rushing to battle as if going to a feast' (Josephus). In the Rabbinical writings, Edom became the name, the veiled name for tyrannous Imperial Rome, and in later times for the persecuting Christian Church.

3. *Esau I hated.* 'Loved' and 'hated' in this and the preceding verse are relative terms only, denoting that one has been preferred to another; cf. the similar phraseology applied to Leah and Rachel, and in Deut. xxi, 15.

4. Some disaster has recently befallen the Edomites; but for them, there is no hope of restoration such as Israel has enjoyed.

6 תֹּאמְרוּ יִגְדַּל יְהוָה מֵעַל לִגְבוּל יִשְׂרָאֵל׃ בֵּן יְכַבֵּד אָב
וְעֶבֶד אֲדֹנָיו וְאִם־אָב אָנִי אַיֵּה כְבוֹדִי וְאִם־אֲדוֹנִים אָנִי
אַיֵּה מוֹרָאִי אָמַר ׀ יְהוָה צְבָאוֹת לָכֶם הַכֹּהֲנִים בּוֹזֵי שְׁמִי
7 וַאֲמַרְתֶּם בַּמֶּה בָזִינוּ אֶת־שְׁמֶךָ׃ מַגִּישִׁים עַל־מִזְבְּחִי לֶחֶם
מְגֹאָל וַאֲמַרְתֶּם בַּמֶּה גֵאַלְנוּךָ בֶּאֱמָרְכֶם שֻׁלְחַן יְהוָה
8 נִבְזֶה הוּא׃ וְכִי־תַגִּשׁוּן עִוֵּר לִזְבֹּחַ אֵין רָע וְכִי תַגִּישׁוּ
פִּסֵּחַ וְחֹלֶה אֵין רָע הַקְרִיבֵהוּ נָא לְפֶחָתֶךָ הֲיִרְצְךָ אוֹ
9 הֲיִשָּׂא פָנֶיךָ אָמַר יְהוָה צְבָאוֹת׃ וְעַתָּה חַלּוּ־נָא פְנֵי־אֵל
וִיחָנֵנוּ מִיֶּדְכֶם הָיְתָה זֹּאת הֲיִשָּׂא מִכֶּם פָּנִים אָמַר יְהוָה
י צְבָאוֹת׃ מִי גַם־בָּכֶם וְיִסְגֹּר דְּלָתַיִם וְלֹא־תָאִירוּ מִזְבְּחִי
חִנָּם אֵין־לִי חֵפֶץ בָּכֶם אָמַר יְהוָה צְבָאוֹת וּמִנְחָה לֹא־
11 אֶרְצֶה מִיֶּדְכֶם׃ כִּי מִמִּזְרַח שֶׁמֶשׁ וְעַד־מְבוֹאוֹ גָּדוֹל
שְׁמִי בַּגּוֹיִם וּבְכָל־מָקוֹם מֻקְטָר מֻגָּשׁ לִשְׁמִי וּמִנְחָה
12 טְהוֹרָה כִּי־גָדוֹל שְׁמִי בַּגּוֹיִם אָמַר יְהוָה צְבָאוֹת׃ וְאַתֶּם
מְחַלְּלִים אוֹתוֹ בֶּאֱמָרְכֶם שֻׁלְחַן אֲדֹנָי מְגֹאָל הוּא וְנִיבוֹ

6. A son honoureth his father,
And a servant his master;
If then I be a father,
Where is My honour?
And if I be a master,
Where is My fear?
Saith the LORD of hosts
Unto you, O priests, that despise My name.
And ye say: 'Wherein have we despised Thy name?'

7. Ye offer polluted bread upon Mine altar.
And ye say: 'Wherein have we polluted Thee?'
In that ye say: 'The table of the LORD is contemptible.'

8. And when ye offer the blind for sacrifice, it is no evil!
And when ye offer the lame and sick, it is no evil!
Present it now unto thy governor;
Will he be pleased with thee?
Or will he accept thy person?
Saith the LORD of hosts.

9. And now, I pray you, entreat the favour of God
That He may be gracious unto us!—
This hath been of your doing.—
Will He accept any of your persons?
Saith the LORD of hosts.

10. Oh that there were even one among you that would shut the doors,
That ye might not kindle fire on Mine altar in vain!
I have no pleasure in you,
Saith the LORD of hosts,
Neither will I accept an offering at your hand.

11. For from the rising of the sun even unto the going down of the same
My name is great among the nations;
And in every place offerings are presented unto My name,
Even pure oblations;
For My name is great among the nations,
Saith the LORD of hosts.

12. But ye profane it,
In that ye say:

6–8. The Prophet rebukes the degenerate priests who are bringing the service of God into contempt.

7. *polluted bread.* In their indifference, they accepted blemished animals and did not rebuke the people who presented them.

8. *accept thy person.* *i.e.* receive thee favourably. Would you treat your earthly ruler as you treat God?

9. The office of the true priest was to supplicate God on behalf of the people: could He receive prayers at their hands when they were responsible for such wrong?

10. It were better that the altar fires go out altogether, than that sacrifices should be offered in such spirit.

11. *great among the nations.* *i.e.* even the heathen nations that worship the heavenly hosts pay tribute to a Supreme Being, and in this way honour My Name; and the offerings which they thus present (indirectly) unto Me are animated by a pure spirit, God looking to the heart of the worshipper. This wonderful thought was further developed by the Rabbis, and is characteristic of the universalism of Judaism; see on Deut. IV, 19.

12. *in that ye say.* Not literally—their actions speak.

'The table of the LORD is polluted,
And the fruit thereof, even the food thereof, is contemptible.'

13. Ye say also:
'Behold, what a weariness is it!'
And ye have snuffed at it,
Saith the LORD of hosts;
And ye have brought that which was taken by violence,
And the lame, and the sick;
Thus ye bring the offering;
Should I accept this of your hand?
Saith the LORD.

14. But cursed be he that dealeth craftily,
Whereas he hath in his flock a male,
And voweth, and sacrificeth unto the LORD a blemished thing;
For I am a great King,
Saith the LORD of hosts,
And My name is feared among the nations.

CHAPTER II

1. And now, this commandment
Is for you, O ye priests.

2. If ye will not hearken, and if ye will not lay it to heart,
To give glory unto My name,
Saith the LORD of hosts,
Then will I send the curse upon you,
And I will curse your blessings;
Yea, I curse them,
Because ye do not lay it to heart.

3. Behold, I will rebuke the seed for your hurt,
And will spread dung upon your faces,
Even the dung of your sacrifices;
And ye shall be taken away unto it.

4. Know then that I have sent
This commandment unto you,
That My covenant might be with Levi,
Saith the LORD of hosts.

13 נִבְזֶה אָכְלוֹ׃ וַאֲמַרְתֶּם הִנֵּה מַתְּלָאָה וְהִפַּחְתֶּם אוֹתוֹ
אָמַר יְהוָה צְבָאוֹת וַהֲבֵאתֶם גָּזוּל וְאֶת־הַפִּסֵּחַ וְאֶת־
הַחוֹלֶה וַהֲבֵאתֶם אֶת־הַמִּנְחָה הַאֶרְצֶה אוֹתָהּ מִיֶּדְכֶם
14 אָמַר יְהוָה׃ וְאָרוּר נוֹכֵל וְיֵשׁ בְּעֶדְרוֹ זָכָר וְנֹדֵר וְזֹבֵחַ
מָשְׁחָת לַאדֹנָי כִּי מֶלֶךְ גָּדוֹל אָנִי אָמַר יְהוָה צְבָאוֹת
וּשְׁמִי נוֹרָא בַגּוֹיִם׃

CAP. II. ב

א 2 וְעַתָּה אֲלֵיכֶם הַמִּצְוָה הַזֹּאת הַכֹּהֲנִים׃ אִם־לֹא תִשְׁמְעוּ
וְאִם־לֹא תָשִׂימוּ עַל־לֵב לָתֵת כָּבוֹד לִשְׁמִי אָמַר יְהוָה
צְבָאוֹת וְשִׁלַּחְתִּי בָכֶם אֶת־הַמְּאֵרָה וְאָרוֹתִי אֶת־בִּרְכוֹתֵיכֶם
3 וְגַם אָרוֹתִיהָ כִּי אֵינְכֶם שָׂמִים עַל־לֵב׃ הִנְנִי גֹעֵר לָכֶם
אֶת־הַזֶּרַע וְזֵרִיתִי פֶרֶשׁ עַל־פְּנֵיכֶם פֶּרֶשׁ חַגֵּיכֶם וְנָשָׂא
4 אֶתְכֶם אֵלָיו׃ וִידַעְתֶּם כִּי שִׁלַּחְתִּי אֲלֵיכֶם אֵת הַמִּצְוָה
ה הַזֹּאת לִהְיוֹת בְּרִיתִי אֶת־לֵוִי אָמַר יְהוָה צְבָאוֹת׃ בְּרִיתִי ׀
הָיְתָה אִתּוֹ הַחַיִּים וְהַשָּׁלוֹם וָאֶתְּנֵם־לוֹ מוֹרָא וַיִּירָאֵנִי

5. My covenant was with him
Of life and peace, and I gave them to him,
And of fear, and he feared Me,
And was afraid of My name.

13. *that which was taken by violence.* Even 'wild animals' were not to be brought as sacrifices, because a person must not offer anything which costs nothing; how much the more heinous was it to offer a robbed thing as a sacrifice! It is adding blasphemy to crime.

CHAPTER II, 1–7

A charge to the priests to be worthy of their vocation, or dire suffering and indignity will be the result.

2. *curse your blessings.* Those to whom you should be a source of blessing will suffer grave injury through you and your example.

3. *rebuke the seed.* That it will not sprout and thrive—to your loss.

upon your faces. i.e. in your presence. An act of insult. Malachi means that the priests will be utterly despised by the people.

4. *Levi.* The tribe of Levi, as the priestly tribe.

5. *covenant of life and peace.* Life, in the highest sense, and peace would be the result of the priest's faithfulness to his vocation; but the fear of God, *i.e.* the reverential awe for the God of Holiness, is the first essential.

6. The law of truth was in his mouth,
And unrighteousness was not found in his lips;
He walked with Me in peace and uprightness,
And did turn many away from iniquity.
7. For the priest's lips should keep knowledge,
And they should seek the law at his mouth;
For he is the messenger of the LORD of hosts.

6 וּמִפְּנֵי שְׁמִי נִחַת הוּא׃ תּוֹרַת אֱמֶת הָיְתָה בְּפִיהוּ וְעַוְלָה
לֹא־נִמְצָא בִשְׂפָתָיו בְּשָׁלוֹם וּבְמִישׁוֹר הָלַךְ אִתִּי וְרַבִּים
7 הֵשִׁיב מֵעָוֹן׃ כִּי־שִׂפְתֵי כֹהֵן יִשְׁמְרוּ־דַעַת וְתוֹרָה יְבַקְשׁוּ
מִפִּיהוּ כִּי מַלְאַךְ יְהוָה־צְבָאוֹת הוּא׃

6. The spiritual results that had been achieved through the faithful priests in whom this true fear of God was found.

turn many away from iniquity. His influence was seen in the lives of men; cf. Daniel XII, 3.

7. Completes with *v.* 6 the ideal of the true priest, as the spokesman of God, never more beautifully expressed.

law. lit. 'instruction', in God's commands.

28 10. And Jacob went out from Beer-sheba, and went toward Haran. 11. And he lighted upon the place, and tarried there all night, because the sun was set; and he took one of the stones of the place, and put it under his head, and lay down in that place to sleep. 12. And he dreamed, and behold a ladder set up on the earth, and the top of it reached to heaven; and behold the angels of God ascending and descending on it. 13. And, behold, the LORD stood beside him, and said: 'I am the LORD, the God of Abraham thy father, and the God of Isaac. The land whereon thou liest, to thee will I give it, and to thy seed. 14. And thy seed shall be as the dust of the earth, and thou shalt spread abroad to the west, and to the east, and to the north, and to the south. And in thee and in thy seed shall all the families of the earth be blessed. 15. And, behold, I am with thee, and will keep thee withersoever thou goest, and will bring thee back into this land; for I will not leave thee, until I have done that which I have spoken to thee of.' 16. And Jacob awaked out of his sleep, and he said:

כח ס ס ס ז 7

11 וַיֵּצֵא יַעֲקֹב מִבְּאֵר שָׁבַע וַיֵּלֶךְ חָרָנָה׃ וַיִּפְגַּע בַּמָּקוֹם וַיָּלֶן
שָׁם כִּי־בָא הַשֶּׁמֶשׁ וַיִּקַּח מֵאַבְנֵי הַמָּקוֹם וַיָּשֶׂם מְרַאֲשֹׁתָיו
12 וַיִּשְׁכַּב בַּמָּקוֹם הַהוּא׃ וַיַּחֲלֹם וְהִנֵּה סֻלָּם מֻצָּב אַרְצָה
וְרֹאשׁוֹ מַגִּיעַ הַשָּׁמָיְמָה וְהִנֵּה מַלְאֲכֵי אֱלֹהִים עֹלִים וְיֹרְדִים
13 בּוֹ׃ וְהִנֵּה יְהוָה נִצָּב עָלָיו וַיֹּאמַר אֲנִי יְהוָה אֱלֹהֵי אַבְרָהָם
אָבִיךָ וֵאלֹהֵי יִצְחָק הָאָרֶץ אֲשֶׁר אַתָּה שֹׁכֵב עָלֶיהָ לְךָ
14 אֶתְּנֶנָּה וּלְזַרְעֶךָ׃ וְהָיָה זַרְעֲךָ כַּעֲפַר הָאָרֶץ וּפָרַצְתָּ יָמָּה
וָקֵדְמָה וְצָפֹנָה וָנֶגְבָּה וְנִבְרְכוּ בְךָ כָּל־מִשְׁפְּחֹת הָאֲדָמָה
טו וּבְזַרְעֶךָ׃ וְהִנֵּה אָנֹכִי עִמָּךְ וּשְׁמַרְתִּיךָ בְּכֹל אֲשֶׁר־תֵּלֵךְ
וַהֲשִׁבֹתִיךָ אֶל־הָאֲדָמָה הַזֹּאת כִּי לֹא אֶעֱזָבְךָ עַד אֲשֶׁר אִם־
16 עָשִׂיתִי אֵת אֲשֶׁר־דִּבַּרְתִּי לָךְ׃ וַיִּיקַץ יַעֲקֹב מִשְּׁנָתוֹ וַיֹּאמֶר
17 אָכֵן יֵשׁ יְהוָה בַּמָּקוֹם הַזֶּה וְאָנֹכִי לֹא יָדָעְתִּי׃ וַיִּירָא וַיֹּאמַר

VII. VAYYETZE

(CHAPTERS XXVIII, 10–XXXII, 3)

CHAPTER XXVIII, 10–22. JACOB'S DREAM

10. *went out from Beer-sheba.* Why is this mentioned—ask the Rabbis—since it would have been sufficient to state, 'Jacob went towards Haran'? They reply that the departure of a righteous man from any place diminishes its importance, and should be keenly felt by its inhabitants.

11. *and he lighted.* Since the same Heb. word signifies 'to entreat', the Talmud deduces from this passage that Jacob prayed there for Divine protection, and thus instituted the Evening Prayer (see on XXIV, 63).

the place. lit. 'upon the place'. The Rabbis stress the definite article in the Heb. idiom, and state that it was Mount Moriah.

12. The description of Jacob's dream is among the most beautiful in literature (Hazlitt). We have here wonderful imagery which, in its symbolism, speaks to each man according to his mental and spiritual outlook. Its message to Jacob is its message to all men in all ages—that the earth is full of the glory of God, that He is not far off in His heavenly abode and heedless of what men do on earth. Every spot on earth may be for man 'the gate of heaven'.

ascending and descending. It is to be noted that the angels are first mentioned as ascending, as though they had been accompanying the Patriarch on his journey. He may have been without human friends; but, unseen, there had been angels by his side to protect and encourage him.

13. *beside him.* Or, 'above it,' *i.e.* the ladder. The translation, 'beside him,' is supported by many Jewish commentators and is to be preferred.

thy father. i.e. thy ancestor. Jacob's relationship with Abraham is referred to because it was to him that the original promise had been made which Jacob was now told he would inherit.

14. *spread abroad.* lit. 'break forth', *i.e.* burst the narrow boundaries.

be blessed. See on XII, 3.

15. *I am with thee.* Therefore Jacob need have no fear of the threats of Esau.

16. *I knew it not.* In popular belief the presence of God was restricted to 'sacred places'. Many people still confine religion to sacred occasions and the sacred locality which is their place of worship, instead of looking upon religion as a continuously active influence and regulative principle in their daily life.

'Surely the LORD is in this place; and I knew it not.' 17. And he was afraid, and said: 'How full of awe is this place! this is none other than the house of God, and this is the gate of heaven.' 18. And Jacob rose up early in the morning, and took the stone that he had put under his head, and set it up for a pillar, and poured oil upon the top of it. 19. And he called the name of that place [1]Beth-el, but the name of the city was Luz at the first. 20. And Jacob vowed a vow, saying: 'If God will be with me, and will keep me in this way that I go, and will give me bread to eat, and raiment to put on, 21. so that I come back to my father's house in peace, then shall the LORD be my God, 22. and this stone, which I have set up for a pillar, shall be God's house; and of all that Thou shalt give me I will surely give the tenth unto Thee.'* ii.

מַה־נּוֹרָא הַמָּקוֹם הַזֶּה אֵין זֶה כִּי אִם־בֵּית אֱלֹהִים וְזֶה
18 שַׁעַר הַשָּׁמָיִם׃ וַיַּשְׁכֵּם יַעֲקֹב בַּבֹּקֶר וַיִּקַּח אֶת־הָאֶבֶן אֲשֶׁר־
שָׂם מְרַאֲשֹׁתָיו וַיָּשֶׂם אֹתָהּ מַצֵּבָה וַיִּצֹק שֶׁמֶן עַל־רֹאשָׁהּ׃
19 וַיִּקְרָא אֶת־שֵׁם־הַמָּקוֹם הַהוּא בֵּית־אֵל וְאוּלָם לוּז שֵׁם־
כ הָעִיר לָרִאשֹׁנָה׃ וַיִּדַּר יַעֲקֹב נֶדֶר לֵאמֹר אִם־יִהְיֶה
אֱלֹהִים עִמָּדִי וּשְׁמָרַנִי בַּדֶּרֶךְ הַזֶּה אֲשֶׁר אָנֹכִי הוֹלֵךְ וְנָתַן
21 לִי לֶחֶם לֶאֱכֹל וּבֶגֶד לִלְבֹּשׁ׃ וְשַׁבְתִּי בְשָׁלוֹם אֶל־בֵּית אָבִי
22 וְהָיָה יְהוָה לִי לֵאלֹהִים׃ וְהָאֶבֶן הַזֹּאת אֲשֶׁר־שַׂמְתִּי מַצֵּבָה
שני יִהְיֶה בֵּית אֱלֹהִים וְכֹל אֲשֶׁר תִּתֶּן־לִי עַשֵּׂר אֲעַשְּׂרֶנּוּ לָךְ׃

29

CHAPTER XXIX

1. Then Jacob went on his journey, and came to the land of the children of the east. 2. And he looked, and behold a well in the field, and lo three flocks of sheep lying there by it.—For out of that well they watered the flocks. And the stone upon the well's mouth was great. 3. And thither were all the flocks gathered; and they rolled the stone from the well's mouth, and watered the sheep, and put the stone back upon the well's mouth in its place.—4. And Jacob said unto them: 'My brethren, whence are ye?' And they said: 'Of Haran are we.' 5. And he said unto them: 'Know

CAP. XXIX. כט

כט

א 2 וַיִּשָּׂא יַעֲקֹב רַגְלָיו וַיֵּלֶךְ אַרְצָה בְנֵי־קֶדֶם׃ וַיַּרְא וְהִנֵּה
בְאֵר בַּשָּׂדֶה וְהִנֵּה־שָׁם שְׁלֹשָׁה עֶדְרֵי־צֹאן רֹבְצִים עָלֶיהָ
כִּי מִן־הַבְּאֵר הַהִוא יַשְׁקוּ הָעֲדָרִים וְהָאֶבֶן גְּדֹלָה עַל־
3 פִּי הַבְּאֵר׃ וְנֶאֶסְפוּ־שָׁמָּה כָל־הָעֲדָרִים וְגָלְלוּ אֶת־הָאֶבֶן
מֵעַל פִּי הַבְּאֵר וְהִשְׁקוּ אֶת־הַצֹּאן וְהֵשִׁיבוּ אֶת־הָאֶבֶן עַל־
4 פִּי הַבְּאֵר לִמְקֹמָהּ׃ וַיֹּאמֶר לָהֶם יַעֲקֹב אַחַי מֵאַיִן אַתֶּם
ה וַיֹּאמְרוּ מֵחָרָן אֲנָחְנוּ׃ וַיֹּאמֶר לָהֶם הַיְדַעְתֶּם אֶת־לָבָן

[1] That is, *The house of God.*

כח׳ v. 18. צ׳ רפה

17. *full of awe.* The Heb. word *nora* signifies, inspiring reverential awe.

18. *for a pillar.* Not intended as an altar or as an act of worship, but to mark the spot where he had had the fateful dream-vision. He hopes, however, at a later time to erect a Sanctuary on the spot (see *v.* 22).

poured oil. To distinguish that stone from the rest, so that Jacob might recognize it on his return (Ibn Ezra).

19. *Luz.* The holy place Beth-el was outside the old city of Luz. Jacob did not spend the night in Luz but on its outskirts. We learn from Chap. XIX of the dangers which might attend a traveller who entered a strange town at night.

20. *vowed.* Jacob resolved to devote a part of the prosperity which God had promised him to His service. This is the first mention of a vow in the Bible.

21. *then shall the LORD be my God.* *i.e.* in gratitude for His care and protection, I shall dedicate my life to Him.

22. *tenth.* Cf. XIV, 20. The tithe figures later in the laws of the Israelite people. To this day pious Jews spend a tenth of their earnings in charity.

CHAPTER XXIX. JACOB AND LABAN

1. *children of the east.* A term to denote generally the Arab tribes located E. and N.E. of Palestine.

2. *the stone upon the well's mouth.* In the East, wells are still covered over with a large boulder to prevent the water from becoming polluted.

3. *gathered.* The verbs are 'frequentative', and should be rendered, 'All the flocks used to gather together . . . used to roll . . . and water' (Rashi).

4. *my brethren.* Evidently a common form of address.

5. *the son of Nahor.* Laban was Nahor's grandson; but see on XX, 12.

we know him. There is no word in Biblical Hebrew corresponding to our 'yes'; consequently the answer to a question is a repetition of the word or words in the affirmative or negative.

ye Laban the son of Nahor?' And they said: 'We know him.' 6. And he said unto them: 'Is it well with him?' And they said: 'It is well; and, behold, Rachel his daughter cometh with the sheep.' 7. And he said: 'Lo, it is yet high day, neither is it time that the cattle should be gathered together; water ye the sheep, and go and feed them.' 8. And they said: 'We cannot, until all the flocks be gathered together, and they roll the stone from the well's mouth; then we water the sheep.' 9. While he was yet speaking with them, Rachel came with her father's sheep; for she tended them. 10. And it came to pass, when Jacob saw Rachel the daughter of Laban his mother's brother, and the sheep of Laban his mother's brother, that Jacob went near, and rolled the stone from the well's mouth, and watered the flock of Laban his mother's brother. 11. And Jacob kissed Rachel, and lifted up his voice, and wept. 12. And Jacob told Rachel that he was her father's brother, and that he was Rebekah's son; and she ran and told her father. 13. And it came to pass, when Laban heard the tidings of Jacob his sister's son, that he ran to meet him, and embraced him, and kissed him, and brought him to his house. And he told Laban all these things. 14. And Laban said to him: 'Surely thou art my bone and my flesh.' And he abode with him the space of a month. 15. And Laban said unto Jacob: 'Because thou art my brother, shouldest thou therefore serve me for nought? tell me, what shall thy wages be?' 16. Now Laban had two daughters: the name of the elder was Leah, and the name of the younger was Rachel. 17. And Leah's eyes were weak; but Rachel was of

6 בֶּן־נָחוֹר וַיֹּאמְרוּ יָדָעְנוּ׃ וַיֹּאמֶר לָהֶם הֲשָׁלוֹם לוֹ וַיֹּאמְרוּ
7 שָׁלוֹם וְהִנֵּה רָחֵל בִּתּוֹ בָּאָה עִם־הַצֹּאן׃ וַיֹּאמֶר הֵן עוֹד
הַיּוֹם גָּדוֹל לֹא־עֵת הֵאָסֵף הַמִּקְנֶה הַשְׁקוּ הַצֹּאן וּלְכוּ
8 רְעוּ׃ וַיֹּאמְרוּ לֹא נוּכַל עַד אֲשֶׁר יֵאָסְפוּ כָּל־הָעֲדָרִים
9 וְגָלְלוּ אֶת־הָאֶבֶן מֵעַל פִּי הַבְּאֵר וְהִשְׁקִינוּ הַצֹּאן׃ עוֹדֶנּוּ
מְדַבֵּר עִמָּם וְרָחֵל ׀ בָּאָה עִם־הַצֹּאן אֲשֶׁר לְאָבִיהָ כִּי רֹעָה
י הִוא׃ וַיְהִי כַּאֲשֶׁר רָאָה יַעֲקֹב אֶת־רָחֵל בַּת־לָבָן אֲחִי
אִמּוֹ וְאֶת־צֹאן לָבָן אֲחִי אִמּוֹ וַיִּגַּשׁ יַעֲקֹב וַיָּגֶל אֶת־הָאֶבֶן
11 מֵעַל פִּי הַבְּאֵר וַיַּשְׁקְ אֶת־צֹאן לָבָן אֲחִי אִמּוֹ׃ וַיִּשַּׁק יַעֲקֹב
12 לְרָחֵל וַיִּשָּׂא אֶת־קֹלוֹ וַיֵּבְךְּ׃ וַיַּגֵּד יַעֲקֹב לְרָחֵל כִּי אֲחִי
13 אָבִיהָ הוּא וְכִי בֶן־רִבְקָה הוּא וַתָּרָץ וַתַּגֵּד לְאָבִיהָ׃ וַיְהִי
כִשְׁמֹעַ לָבָן אֶת־שֵׁמַע ׀ יַעֲקֹב בֶּן־אֲחֹתוֹ וַיָּרָץ לִקְרָאתוֹ
וַיְחַבֶּק־לוֹ וַיְנַשֶּׁק־לוֹ וַיְבִיאֵהוּ אֶל־בֵּיתוֹ וַיְסַפֵּר לְלָבָן אֵת
14 כָּל־הַדְּבָרִים הָאֵלֶּה׃ וַיֹּאמֶר לוֹ לָבָן אַךְ עַצְמִי וּבְשָׂרִי
טו אָתָּה וַיֵּשֶׁב עִמּוֹ חֹדֶשׁ יָמִים׃ וַיֹּאמֶר לָבָן לְיַעֲקֹב הֲכִי־
אָחִי אַתָּה וַעֲבַדְתַּנִי חִנָּם הַגִּידָה לִּי מַה־מַּשְׂכֻּרְתֶּךָ׃
16 וּלְלָבָן שְׁתֵּי בָנוֹת שֵׁם הַגְּדֹלָה לֵאָה וְשֵׁם הַקְּטַנָּה רָחֵל׃
שלישי
17 וְעֵינֵי לֵאָה רַכּוֹת וְרָחֵל הָיְתָה יְפַת־תֹּאַר וִיפַת מַרְאֶה׃

6. *is it well with him?* lit. 'is there peace to him?'

cometh. lit. 'is coming'.

8. They wait for others to arrive, so that by their combined effort they remove the stone; or, possibly, because it would be unwise to remove the stone until all the flocks were there, lest in the interval the wind blew dust and sand into the well.

9. *tended them.* To this day it would not be considered derogatory for an Arab Sheikh's daughter to be his shepherdess.

10. Jacob disregards the local custom, and by a feat of great personal strength, removes the stone. The phrase 'his mother's brother' is used three times in this verse, to denote the joy Jacob felt in meeting and helping a member of his mother's family.

11. *kissed.* When the Heb. verb is, as here, not followed by the accusative case, it denotes kissing the hand as a respectful salutation (Ibn Ezra).

and wept. 'The demonstrative display of feeling is Homeric in its simplicity' (Ryle).

12. *her father's brother. i.e.* her relative.

told her father. Her mother having died (Midrash).

13. *embraced him.* The effusive welcome stands in sharp contrast to Laban's later treatment of Jacob. The Rabbis doubted its genuineness.

all these things. i.e. that Rebekah had sent him because of the wrath of Esau.

14. *my bone and my flesh.* As his near kinsman, he is welcome to his home.

15. *wages.* Jacob from the outset seems to have decided not to be indebted to his uncle, but to earn his maintenance.

17. *weak.* Better, *tender*, which the Targum understands in the sense of 'beautiful'.

beautiful form and fair to look upon.* iii. 18. And Jacob loved Rachel; and he said: 'I will serve thee seven years for Rachel thy younger daughter.' 19. And Laban said: 'It is better that I give her to thee, than that I should give her to another man; abide with me.' 20. And Jacob served seven years for Rachel; and they seemed unto him but a few days, for the love he had to her. 21. And Jacob said unto Laban: 'Give me my wife, for my days are fulfilled, that I may go in unto her.' 22. And Laban gathered together all the men of the place, and made a feast. 23. And it came to pass in the evening, that he took Leah his daughter, and brought her to him; and he went in unto her. 24. And Laban gave Zilpah his handmaid unto his daughter Leah for a handmaid. 25. And it came to pass in the morning that, behold, it was Leah; and he said to Laban: 'What is this thou hast done unto me? did not I serve with thee for Rachel? wherefore then hast thou beguiled me?' 26. And Laban said: 'It is not so done in our place, to give the younger before the first-born. 27. Fulfil the week of this one, and we will give thee the other also for the service which thou shalt serve with me yet seven other years.' 28. And Jacob did so, and fulfilled her week; and he gave him Rachel his daughter to wife. 29. And Laban gave to Rachel his daughter Bilhah his handmaid to be her handmaid. 30. And he went in also unto Rachel, and he loved Rachel more than Leah, and served with him yet seven other years. ¶ 31. And the LORD saw that Leah was hated, and He opened her womb;

18 וַיֶּאֱהַב יַעֲקֹב אֶת־רָחֵל וַיֹּאמֶר אֶעֱבָדְךָ שֶׁבַע שָׁנִים בְּרָחֵל
19 בִּתְּךָ הַקְּטַנָּה׃ וַיֹּאמֶר לָבָן טוֹב תִּתִּי אֹתָהּ לָךְ מִתִּתִּי
כ אֹתָהּ לְאִישׁ אַחֵר שְׁבָה עִמָּדִי׃ וַיַּעֲבֹד יַעֲקֹב בְּרָחֵל שֶׁבַע
21 שָׁנִים וַיִּהְיוּ בְעֵינָיו כְּיָמִים אֲחָדִים בְּאַהֲבָתוֹ אֹתָהּ׃ וַיֹּאמֶר
יַעֲקֹב אֶל־לָבָן הָבָה אֶת־אִשְׁתִּי כִּי מָלְאוּ יָמָי וְאָבוֹאָה
22 אֵלֶיהָ׃ וַיֶּאֱסֹף לָבָן אֶת־כָּל־אַנְשֵׁי הַמָּקוֹם וַיַּעַשׂ מִשְׁתֶּה׃
23 וַיְהִי בָעֶרֶב וַיִּקַּח אֶת־לֵאָה בִתּוֹ וַיָּבֵא אֹתָהּ אֵלָיו וַיָּבֹא
24 אֵלֶיהָ׃ וַיִּתֵּן לָבָן לָהּ אֶת־זִלְפָּה שִׁפְחָתוֹ לְלֵאָה בִתּוֹ שִׁפְחָה׃
כה וַיְהִי בַבֹּקֶר וְהִנֵּה־הִוא לֵאָה וַיֹּאמֶר אֶל־לָבָן מַה־זֹּאת
26 עָשִׂיתָ לִּי הֲלֹא בְרָחֵל עָבַדְתִּי עִמָּךְ וְלָמָּה רִמִּיתָנִי׃ וַיֹּאמֶר
לָבָן לֹא־יֵעָשֶׂה כֵן בִּמְקוֹמֵנוּ לָתֵת הַצְּעִירָה לִפְנֵי הַבְּכִירָה׃
27 מַלֵּא שְׁבֻעַ זֹאת וְנִתְּנָה לְךָ גַּם־אֶת־זֹאת בַּעֲבֹדָה אֲשֶׁר
28 תַּעֲבֹד עִמָּדִי עוֹד שֶׁבַע־שָׁנִים אֲחֵרוֹת׃ וַיַּעַשׂ יַעֲקֹב כֵּן
29 וַיְמַלֵּא שְׁבֻעַ זֹאת וַיִּתֶּן־לוֹ אֶת־רָחֵל בִּתּוֹ לוֹ לְאִשָּׁה׃ וַיִּתֵּן
ל לָבָן לְרָחֵל בִּתּוֹ אֶת־בִּלְהָה שִׁפְחָתוֹ לָהּ לְשִׁפְחָה׃ וַיָּבֹא
גַּם אֶל־רָחֵל וַיֶּאֱהַב גַּם־אֶת־רָחֵל מִלֵּאָה וַיַּעֲבֹד עִמּוֹ עוֹד
31 שֶׁבַע־שָׁנִים אֲחֵרוֹת׃ וַיַּרְא יְהוָה כִּי־שְׂנוּאָה לֵאָה וַיִּפְתַּח

v. 28. במקצת ספרים אין מלת לו

18. *for Rachel.* See on XXIV, 53. It is still the custom in the East for a man who cannot provide money or cattle, to offer his labour as a substitute for such compensation.

19. *to thee.* A relative; it was considered preferable for husband and wife to belong to the same family.

20. *and they seemed unto him but a few days, for the love he had to her.* The six Heb. words of which this is the translation condense a world of affection and tenderest love. They are unsurpassed in the whole literature of romantic love.

21. *my wife. i.e.* the woman who was betrothed to him as his wife.

23. *he took Leah.* Heavily veiled and in the dark. This fraud may be regarded as a retribution for the deception which Jacob himself practised upon his father.

26. *give the younger.* A feigned excuse, since the feast was for the maiden for whom Jacob had served.

27. *fulfil the week of this one. i.e.* do not repudiate the marriage with Leah. The wedding celebrations usually lasted a week; cf. Judges XIV, 12.

we will give thee. i.e. Laban and his family will give; cf. XXIV, 50.

28. *and he gave him Rachel.* Eight days after Leah, on the understanding that Jacob was to serve Laban for another seven years. After the Giving of the Law at Sinai, the marrying of two sisters was forbidden.

30. *seven other years.* The Midrash comments that Jacob served the second term as conscientiously as the first, although he was labouring under a sense of grievance against his uncle.

CHAPTER XXIX, 31–XXX, 24. THE BIRTH OF JACOB'S CHILDREN

31. *hated.* The word here only means 'less loved'—not that Jacob had an aversion to her, but that he preferred Rachel; cf. Deut. XXI, 15.

but Rachel was barren. 32. And Leah conceived, and bore a son, and she called his name Reuben; for she said: 'Because the LORD [1]hath looked upon my affliction; for now my husband will love me.' 33. And she conceived again, and bore a son; and said: 'Because the LORD [2]hath heard that I am hated, He hath therefore given me this son also.' And she called his name [3]Simeon. 34. And she conceived again, and bore a son; and said: 'Now this time will my husband be [4]joined unto me, because I have borne him three sons.' Therefore was his name called Levi. 35. And she conceived again, and bore a son; and she said: 'This time will I [5]praise the LORD.' Therefore she called his name [6]Judah; and she left off bearing.

30

CHAPTER XXX

1. And when Rachel saw that she bore Jacob no children, Rachel envied her sister; and she said unto Jacob: 'Give me children, or else I die.' 2. And Jacob's anger was kindled against Rachel; and he said: 'Am I in God's stead, who hath withheld from thee the fruit of the womb?' 3. And she said: 'Behold my maid Bilhah, go in unto her; that she may bear upon my knees, and I also may be builded up through her.' 4. And she gave him Bilhah her handmaid to wife; and Jacob went in unto her. 5. And Bilhah conceived and bore Jacob a son. 6. And Rachel said: 'God hath [7]judged me, and hath also heard my voice, and hath given me a son.' Therefore called she his name Dan. 7. And Bilhah Rachel's handmaid conceived again, and bore Jacob a second son. 8. And Rachel said: 'With mighty wrestlings have I [8]wrestled with my sister, and have prevailed.' And she called his name Naphtali. 9. When Leah saw that she had left off bearing, she took Zilpah her handmaid, and gave her to Jacob to wife. 10. And Zilpah Leah's handmaid bore Jacob

32 אֶת־רַחְמָהּ וְרָחֵל עֲקָרָה׃ וַתַּהַר לֵאָה וַתֵּלֶד בֵּן וַתִּקְרָא
שְׁמוֹ רְאוּבֵן כִּי אָמְרָה כִּי־רָאָה יְהוָה בְּעָנְיִי כִּי עַתָּה
33 יֶאֱהָבַנִי אִישִׁי׃ וַתַּהַר עוֹד וַתֵּלֶד בֵּן וַתֹּאמֶר כִּי־שָׁמַע
יְהוָה כִּי־שְׂנוּאָה אָנֹכִי וַיִּתֶּן־לִי גַּם־אֶת־זֶה וַתִּקְרָא שְׁמוֹ
34 שִׁמְעוֹן׃ וַתַּהַר עוֹד וַתֵּלֶד בֵּן וַתֹּאמֶר עַתָּה הַפַּעַם יִלָּוֶה
אִישִׁי אֵלַי כִּי־יָלַדְתִּי לוֹ שְׁלֹשָׁה בָנִים עַל־כֵּן קָרָא־שְׁמוֹ
לה לֵוִי׃ וַתַּהַר עוֹד וַתֵּלֶד בֵּן וַתֹּאמֶר הַפַּעַם אוֹדֶה אֶת־
יְהוָה עַל־כֵּן קָרְאָה שְׁמוֹ יְהוּדָה וַתַּעֲמֹד מִלֶּדֶת׃

CAP. XXX. ל

ל

א וַתֵּרֶא רָחֵל כִּי לֹא יָלְדָה לְיַעֲקֹב וַתְּקַנֵּא רָחֵל בַּאֲחֹתָהּ
וַתֹּאמֶר אֶל־יַעֲקֹב הָבָה־לִּי בָנִים וְאִם־אַיִן מֵתָה אָנֹכִי׃
2 וַיִּחַר־אַף יַעֲקֹב בְּרָחֵל וַיֹּאמֶר הֲתַחַת אֱלֹהִים אָנֹכִי אֲשֶׁר־
3 מָנַע מִמֵּךְ פְּרִי־בָטֶן׃ וַתֹּאמֶר הִנֵּה אֲמָתִי בִלְהָה בֹּא אֵלֶיהָ
4 וְתֵלֵד עַל־בִּרְכַּי וְאִבָּנֶה גַם־אָנֹכִי מִמֶּנָּה׃ וַתִּתֶּן־לוֹ אֶת־
ה בִּלְהָה שִׁפְחָתָהּ לְאִשָּׁה וַיָּבֹא אֵלֶיהָ יַעֲקֹב׃ וַתַּהַר בִּלְהָה
6 וַתֵּלֶד לְיַעֲקֹב בֵּן׃ וַתֹּאמֶר רָחֵל דָּנַנִּי אֱלֹהִים וְגַם שָׁמַע
7 בְּקֹלִי וַיִּתֶּן־לִי בֵּן עַל־כֵּן קָרְאָה שְׁמוֹ דָּן׃ וַתַּהַר עוֹד
8 וַתֵּלֶד בִּלְהָה שִׁפְחַת רָחֵל בֵּן שֵׁנִי לְיַעֲקֹב׃ וַתֹּאמֶר רָחֵל
נַפְתּוּלֵי אֱלֹהִים ׀ נִפְתַּלְתִּי עִם־אֲחֹתִי גַּם־יָכֹלְתִּי וַתִּקְרָא
9 שְׁמוֹ נַפְתָּלִי׃ וַתֵּרֶא לֵאָה כִּי עָמְדָה מִלֶּדֶת וַתִּקַּח אֶת־
י זִלְפָּה שִׁפְחָתָהּ וַתִּתֵּן אֹתָהּ לְיַעֲקֹב לְאִשָּׁה׃ וַתֵּלֶד זִלְפָּה

[1] Heb. *raah beonji.* [2] Heb. *shama.* [3] Heb. *Shimeon.* [4] From the Heb. root *lavah.* [5] From the Heb. *hodah.* [6] Heb. *Jehudah.* [7] Heb. *dan,* he judged. [8] Heb. *niphtal,* he wrestled.

32. *Reuben.* In this and the following names, the meaning is derived by the resemblance of the name in sound to the words which explain it.

will love me. The birth of a son raised the wife in the esteem of her husband.

33. *hath heard.* Better, *knows.*

35. *Judah.* Heb. *Yehudah.* The name of the members of his tribe was later extended to all the descendants of Jacob, *Yehudim.*

CHAPTER XXX

1. *else I die.* Of grief and shame.

2. *am I in God's stead?* In His hands alone are the issues of life and death.

3. *behold my maid.* Rachel resorts to the same expedient as Sarah.

upon my knees. A figurative expression denoting the adoption of a child.

be builded up. As in XVI, 2. She can thus have 'sons whom I may nurse and rear as my own' (Targum).

6. *judged me.* God has decided in her favour.

8. *mighty wrestlings.* lit. 'wrestlings of God', where 'of God' is merely the Heb. idiom for the superlative.

a son. 11. And Leah said: 'Fortune is
come!' And she called his name [1]Gad.
12. And Zilpah Leah's handmaid bore
Jacob a second son. 13. And Leah said:
'Happy am I! for the daughters will call
me happy.' And she called his name
[2]Asher. *iv. 14. And Reuben went in the
days of wheat harvest, and found man-
drakes in the field, and brought them unto
his mother Leah. Then Rachel said to
Leah: 'Give me, I pray thee, of thy son's
mandrakes.' 15. And she said unto her:
'Is it a small matter that thou hast taken
away my husband? and wouldest thou take
away my son's mandrakes also?' And
Rachel said: 'Therefore he shall lie with
thee to-night for thy son's mandrakes.'
16. And Jacob came from the field in the
evening, and Leah went out to meet him,
and said: 'Thou must come in unto me;
for I have surely hired thee with my son's
mandrakes.' And he lay with her that
night. 17. And God hearkened unto Leah,
and she conceived, and bore Jacob a fifth
son. 18. And Leah said: 'God hath given
me my [3]hire, because I gave my handmaid
to my husband.' And she called his name
Issachar. 19. And Leah conceived again,
and bore a sixth son to Jacob. 20. And
Leah said: 'God hath endowed me with
a good dowry; now will my husband
[4]dwell with me, because I have borne
him six sons.' And she called his name
Zebulun. 21. And afterwards she bore a
daughter, and called her name Dinah. 22.
And God remembered Rachel, and God
hearkened to her, and opened her womb.
23. And she conceived, and bore a son,
and said: 'God [5]hath taken away my
reproach.' 24. And she called his name
Joseph, saying: 'The LORD [6]add to me
another son.' ¶ 25. And it came to pass,
when Rachel had borne Joseph, that Jacob
said unto Laban: 'Send me away, that I
may go unto mine own place, and to my
country. 26. Give me my wives and my
children for whom I have served thee, and
let me go; for thou knowest my service

11 שִׁפְחַת לֵאָה לְיַעֲקֹב בֵּן׃ וַתֹּאמֶר לֵאָה בָּגָד וַתִּקְרָא אֶת־
12 שְׁמוֹ גָּד׃ וַתֵּלֶד זִלְפָּה שִׁפְחַת לֵאָה בֵּן שֵׁנִי לְיַעֲקֹב׃
13 וַתֹּאמֶר לֵאָה בְּאָשְׁרִי כִּי אִשְּׁרוּנִי בָּנוֹת וַתִּקְרָא אֶת־שְׁמוֹ רביעי
14 אָשֵׁר׃ * וַיֵּלֶךְ רְאוּבֵן בִּימֵי קְצִיר־חִטִּים וַיִּמְצָא דוּדָאִים
בַּשָּׂדֶה וַיָּבֵא אֹתָם אֶל־לֵאָה אִמּוֹ וַתֹּאמֶר רָחֵל אֶל־לֵאָה
טו תְּנִי־נָא לִי מִדּוּדָאֵי בְּנֵךְ׃ וַתֹּאמֶר לָהּ הַמְעַט קַחְתֵּךְ אֶת־
אִישִׁי וְלָקַחַת גַּם אֶת־דּוּדָאֵי בְּנִי וַתֹּאמֶר רָחֵל לָכֵן יִשְׁכַּב
16 עִמָּךְ הַלַּיְלָה תַּחַת דּוּדָאֵי בְנֵךְ׃ וַיָּבֹא יַעֲקֹב מִן־הַשָּׂדֶה
בָּעֶרֶב וַתֵּצֵא לֵאָה לִקְרָאתוֹ וַתֹּאמֶר אֵלַי תָּבוֹא כִּי שָׂכֹר
17 שְׂכַרְתִּיךָ בְּדוּדָאֵי בְּנִי וַיִּשְׁכַּב עִמָּהּ בַּלַּיְלָה הוּא׃ וַיִּשְׁמַע
18 אֱלֹהִים אֶל־לֵאָה וַתַּהַר וַתֵּלֶד לְיַעֲקֹב בֵּן חֲמִישִׁי׃ וַתֹּאמֶר
לֵאָה נָתַן אֱלֹהִים שְׂכָרִי אֲשֶׁר־נָתַתִּי שִׁפְחָתִי לְאִישִׁי וַתִּקְרָא
19 שְׁמוֹ יִשָּׂשכָר׃ וַתַּהַר עוֹד לֵאָה וַתֵּלֶד בֵּן־שִׁשִּׁי לְיַעֲקֹב׃
כ וַתֹּאמֶר לֵאָה זְבָדַנִי אֱלֹהִים ׀ אֹתִי זֵבֶד טוֹב הַפַּעַם יִזְבְּלֵנִי
אִישִׁי כִּי־יָלַדְתִּי לוֹ שִׁשָּׁה בָנִים וַתִּקְרָא אֶת־שְׁמוֹ זְבֻלוּן׃
21 22 וְאַחַר יָלְדָה בַּת וַתִּקְרָא אֶת־שְׁמָהּ דִּינָה׃ וַיִּזְכֹּר אֱלֹהִים
אֶת־רָחֵל וַיִּשְׁמַע אֵלֶיהָ אֱלֹהִים וַיִּפְתַּח אֶת־רַחְמָהּ׃
23 24 וַתַּהַר וַתֵּלֶד בֵּן וַתֹּאמֶר אָסַף אֱלֹהִים אֶת־חֶרְפָּתִי׃ וַתִּקְרָא
כה אֶת־שְׁמוֹ יוֹסֵף לֵאמֹר יֹסֵף יְהוָה לִי בֵּן אַחֵר׃ וַיְהִי כַּאֲשֶׁר
יָלְדָה רָחֵל אֶת־יוֹסֵף וַיֹּאמֶר יַעֲקֹב אֶל־לָבָן שַׁלְּחֵנִי וְאֵלְכָה
26 אֶל־מְקוֹמִי וּלְאַרְצִי׃ תְּנָה אֶת־נָשַׁי וְאֶת־יְלָדַי אֲשֶׁר עָבַדְתִּי
אֹתְךָ בָּהֵן וְאֵלֵכָה כִּי אַתָּה יָדַעְתָּ אֶת־עֲבֹדָתִי אֲשֶׁר עֲבַדְתִּיךָ׃

[1] That is, *Fortune*. [2] That is, *Happy*. [3] Heb. *sachar*. [4] Heb. *zabal*, he dwelt. [5] Heb. *asaph*. [6] Heb. *joseph*.

v. 11. בא גד קרי v. 16. סבירין ההוא v. 19. צירי בסמוך ובמקף

11. *Fortune is come.* This translation is according to the traditional Reading, the *Kre*.

14. *mandrakes.* Or, as the RV Margin translates, 'love-apples.' The fruit is of the size of a large plum, quite round, yellow and full of soft pulp. The fruit is still considered in the East as a love-charm. This explains Rachel's anxiety to obtain it.

15. *thou hast taken away.* By holding first place in his affections.

22. *God hearkened.* To her prayers.

23. *my reproach.* Of being left childless. The Heb. name has the double sense of 'taking away' (the reproach) and of 'adding' (to her another son).

25–43. JACOB'S WAGES

25. *send me away.* It would thus seem that the fourteen years' service terminated shortly after Joseph's birth.

26. *give me my wives.* In spite of Jacob's completed years of service the wives and children were in the *legal* power of Laban, who could refuse to hand them over to Jacob; see XXXI, 43.

wherewith I have served thee.' 27. And Laban said unto him: 'If now I have found favour in thine eyes—I have observed the signs, and the LORD hath blessed me for thy sake.* v. 28. And he said: 'Appoint me thy wages, and I will give it.' 29. And he said unto him: 'Thou knowest how I have served thee, and how thy cattle have fared with me. 30. For it was little which thou hadst before I came, and it hath increased abundantly; and the LORD hath blessed thee whithersoever I turned. And now when shall I provide for mine own house also?' 31. And he said: 'What shall I give thee?' And Jacob said: 'Thou shalt not give me aught; if thou wilt do this thing for me, I will again feed thy flock and keep it. 32. I will pass through all thy flock to-day, removing from thence every speckled and spotted one, and every dark one among the sheep, and the spotted and speckled among the goats; and of such shall be my hire. 33. So shall my righteousness witness against me hereafter, when thou shalt come to look over my hire that is before thee: every one that is not speckled and spotted among the goats, and dark among the sheep, that if found with me shall be counted stolen.' 34. And Laban said: 'Behold, would it might be according to thy word.' 35. And he removed that day the he-goats that were streaked and spotted, and all the she-goats that were speckled and spotted, every one that had white in it, and all the dark ones among the sheep, and gave them into the hand of his sons. 36.

27 וַיֹּאמֶר אֵלָיו לָבָן אִם־נָא מָצָאתִי חֵן בְּעֵינֶיךָ נִחַשְׁתִּי
חמישי
28 וַיְבָרְכֵנִי יְהוָה בִּגְלָלֶךָ׃ *וַיֹּאמַר נָקְבָה שְׂכָרְךָ עָלַי וְאֶתֵּנָה׃
29 וַיֹּאמֶר אֵלָיו אַתָּה יָדַעְתָּ אֵת אֲשֶׁר עֲבַדְתִּיךָ וְאֵת אֲשֶׁר־
ל הָיָה מִקְנְךָ אִתִּי׃ כִּי מְעַט אֲשֶׁר־הָיָה לְךָ לְפָנַי וַיִּפְרֹץ
לָרֹב וַיְבָרֶךְ יְהוָה אֹתְךָ לְרַגְלִי וְעַתָּה מָתַי אֶעֱשֶׂה גַם־
31 אָנֹכִי לְבֵיתִי׃ וַיֹּאמֶר מָה אֶתֶּן־לָךְ וַיֹּאמֶר יַעֲקֹב לֹא־תִתֶּן־
לִי מְאוּמָה אִם־תַּעֲשֶׂה־לִּי הַדָּבָר הַזֶּה אָשׁוּבָה אֶרְעֶה
32 צֹאנְךָ אֶשְׁמֹר׃ אֶעֱבֹר בְּכָל־צֹאנְךָ הַיּוֹם הָסֵר מִשָּׁם כָּל־
שֶׂה ׀ נָקֹד וְטָלוּא וְכָל־שֶׂה־חוּם בַּכְּשָׂבִים וְטָלוּא וְנָקֹד
33 בָּעִזִּים וְהָיָה שְׂכָרִי׃ וְעָנְתָה־בִּי צִדְקָתִי בְּיוֹם מָחָר כִּי־
תָבוֹא עַל־שְׂכָרִי לְפָנֶיךָ כֹּל אֲשֶׁר־אֵינֶנּוּ נָקֹד וְטָלוּא בָּעִזִּים
34 וְחוּם בַּכְּשָׂבִים גָּנוּב הוּא אִתִּי׃ וַיֹּאמֶר לָבָן הֵן לוּ יְהִי
לה כִדְבָרֶךָ׃ וַיָּסַר בַּיּוֹם הַהוּא אֶת־הַתְּיָשִׁים הָעֲקֻדִּים וְהַטְּלֻאִים
וְאֵת כָּל־הָעִזִּים הַנְּקֻדּוֹת וְהַטְּלֻאֹת כֹּל אֲשֶׁר־לָבָן בּוֹ וְכָל־
36 חוּם בַּכְּשָׂבִים וַיִּתֵּן בְּיַד־בָּנָיו׃ וַיָּשֶׂם דֶּרֶךְ שְׁלֹשֶׁת יָמִים
37 בֵּינוֹ וּבֵין יַעֲקֹב וְיַעֲקֹב רֹעֶה אֶת־צֹאן לָבָן הַנּוֹתָרֹת׃ וַיִּקַּח

27. *found favour in thine eyes.* Laban wishes to retain Jacob.

29. *with me.* Under my care.

30. *whithersoever I turned.* lit. 'at my foot', *i.e.* either 'at every step I took'; or (so the Midrash), 'at my coming' into thy house.

provide for mine own house. His wives and children now belong to him, and he feels the responsibility of making provision for their future.

31. Jacob, still feeling sore at the way he had been outwitted by Laban over the matter of Rachel, determines to put to good use his exceptional knowledge and skill as a shepherd.

32. The sheep in Syria are white and the goats black. Jacob asks as his wages the sheep which are not white and the goats which are not black. Laban considers the request fair and, to him, profitable.

of such shall be my hire. These, and the lambs and kids subsequently born with the same peculiarity, should belong to him.

33. *righteousness.* 'In this way my honesty will tell, when you come to cast your eye over my share; any goat in my lot that is not speckled or spotted, any sheep that is not black, you may consider to have been stolen' (Moffatt).

The compact is all in Laban's favour; but, crafty, selfish and grasping, he starts to circumvent Jacob, by preventing the increase of any speckled or brown cattle.

36. *three days' journey.* A phrase denoting a considerable distance; cf. Exod. III, 18.

37. *streaks.* Jacob devises three plans for the purpose of frustrating Laban. He placed streaked rods over against the ewes. The sight of these rods would affect the colouring of the young about to be born. 'He did not resort to this device the first year, and thereafter only in connection with his own flock; otherwise it would have been flagrant dishonesty' (Kimchi).

And he set three days' journey betwixt himself and Jacob. And Jacob fed the rest of Laban's flocks. 37. And Jacob took him rods of fresh poplar, and of the almond and of the plane-tree; and peeled white streaks in them, making the white appear which was in the rods. 38. And he set the rods which he had peeled over against the flocks in the gutters in the watering-troughs where the flocks came to drink; and they conceived when they came to drink. 39. And the flocks conceived at the sight of the rods, and the flocks brought forth streaked, speckled, and spotted. 40. And Jacob separated the lambs—he also set the faces of the flocks toward the streaked and all the dark in the flock of Laban—and put his own droves apart, and put them not unto Laban's flock. 41. And it came to pass, whensoever the stronger of the flock did conceive, that Jacob laid the rods before the eyes of the flock in the gutters, that they might conceive among the rods; 42. but when the flock were feeble, he put them not in; so the feebler were Laban's, and the stronger Jacob's. 43. And the man increased exceedingly, and had large flocks, and maidservants and men-servants, and camels and asses.

לוֹ יַעֲקֹב מַקַּל לִבְנֶה לַח וְלוּז וְעַרְמוֹן וַיְפַצֵּל בָּהֵן פְּצָלוֹת
38 לְבָנוֹת מַחְשֹׂף הַלָּבָן אֲשֶׁר עַל־הַמַּקְלוֹת׃ וַיַּצֵּג אֶת־
הַמַּקְלוֹת אֲשֶׁר פִּצֵּל בָּרְהָטִים בְּשִׁקְתוֹת הַמָּיִם אֲשֶׁר
תָּבֹאןָ הַצֹּאן לִשְׁתּוֹת לְנֹכַח הַצֹּאן וַיֵּחַמְנָה בְּבֹאָן לִשְׁתּוֹת׃
39 וַיֶּחֱמוּ הַצֹּאן אֶל־הַמַּקְלוֹת וַתֵּלַדְןָ הַצֹּאן עֲקֻדִּים נְקֻדִּים
מ וּטְלֻאִים׃ וְהַכְּשָׂבִים הִפְרִיד יַעֲקֹב וַיִּתֵּן פְּנֵי הַצֹּאן אֶל־עָקֹד
וְכָל־חוּם בְּצֹאן לָבָן וַיָּשֶׁת לוֹ עֲדָרִים לְבַדּוֹ וְלֹא שָׁתָם
41 עַל־צֹאן לָבָן׃ וְהָיָה בְּכָל־יַחֵם הַצֹּאן הַמְקֻשָּׁרוֹת וְשָׂם
יַעֲקֹב אֶת־הַמַּקְלוֹת לְעֵינֵי הַצֹּאן בָּרְהָטִים לְיַחְמֵנָּה
42 בַּמַּקְלוֹת׃ וּבְהַעֲטִיף הַצֹּאן לֹא יָשִׂים וְהָיָה הָעֲטֻפִים
43 לְלָבָן וְהַקְּשֻׁרִים לְיַעֲקֹב׃ וַיִּפְרֹץ הָאִישׁ מְאֹד מְאֹד וַיְהִי־
לוֹ צֹאן רַבּוֹת וּשְׁפָחוֹת וַעֲבָדִים וּגְמַלִּים וַחֲמֹרִים׃

31

CHAPTER XXXI

1. And he heard the words of Laban's sons, saying: 'Jacob hath taken away all that was our father's; and of that which was our father's hath he gotten all this wealth.' 2. And Jacob beheld the countenance of Laban, and, behold, it was not toward him as beforetime. 3. And the LORD said unto Jacob: 'Return unto the land of thy fathers, and to thy kindred; and I will be with thee.' 4. And Jacob sent and called Rachel and Leah to the field unto his flock, 5. and said unto them: 'I see your father's countenance, that it is not toward me as beforetime; but the God of my father hath been with me. 6. And ye

לא CAP. XXXI. לא

א וַיִּשְׁמַע אֶת־דִּבְרֵי בְנֵי־לָבָן לֵאמֹר לָקַח יַעֲקֹב אֵת כָּל־
אֲשֶׁר לְאָבִינוּ וּמֵאֲשֶׁר לְאָבִינוּ עָשָׂה אֵת כָּל־הַכָּבֹד הַזֶּה׃
2 וַיַּרְא יַעֲקֹב אֶת־פְּנֵי לָבָן וְהִנֵּה אֵינֶנּוּ עִמּוֹ כִּתְמוֹל שִׁלְשׁוֹם׃
3 וַיֹּאמֶר יְהוָה אֶל־יַעֲקֹב שׁוּב אֶל־אֶרֶץ אֲבוֹתֶיךָ וּלְמוֹלַדְתֶּךָ
4 וְאֶהְיֶה עִמָּךְ׃ וַיִּשְׁלַח יַעֲקֹב וַיִּקְרָא לְרָחֵל וּלְלֵאָה הַשָּׂדֶה
ה אֶל־צֹאנוֹ׃ וַיֹּאמֶר לָהֶן רֹאֶה אָנֹכִי אֶת־פְּנֵי אֲבִיכֶן כִּי־
6 אֵינֶנּוּ אֵלַי כִּתְמֹל שִׁלְשֹׁם וֵאלֹהֵי אָבִי הָיָה עִמָּדִי׃ וְאַתֵּנָה
7 יְדַעְתֶּן כִּי בְּכָל־כֹּחִי עָבַדְתִּי אֶת־אֲבִיכֶן׃ וַאֲבִיכֶן הֵתֶל בִּי

ל׳ v. 42. ף׳ רבתי בנ״א הף׳ לא רבתי

40. The second plan was, Jacob separates the newly-born spotted lambs and kids from the rest of the flock, but so arranges them that there should be a further tendency to bear spotted young.

41. He devises to secure for his own share the young of the strongest animals.

CHAPTER XXXI, 1–21. THE FLIGHT OF JACOB

1. *Laban's sons.* See XXX, 35. Jacob's prosperity bred jealousy among his relatives.

3. *said unto Jacob.* In a dream, see *v.* 11.

the land of thy fathers. Canaan.

4. *Rachel and Leah.* Another instance of the dignified position of woman in ancient Israel. The Patriarchs do nothing without consulting their wives, whom they regard as their equals.

to the field. To speak with them in private. As the Midrash states, 'Walls have ears.'

5. *hath been with me.* Hence my great increase in wealth.

7. *my wages.* See on XXIX, 15.

ten times. The phrase only means 'several times'. Laban would naturally make attempt after attempt to alter the conditions in his favour when he found they were against him. The story here supplements what was related in the last chapter.

know that with all my power I have served your father. 7. And your father hath mocked me, and changed my wages ten times; but God suffered him not to hurt me. 8. If he said thus: The speckled shall be thy wages; then all the flock bore speckled; and if he said thus: The streaked shall be thy wages; then bore all the flock streaked. 9. Thus God hath taken away the cattle of your father, and given them to me. 10. And it came to pass at the time that the flock conceived, that I lifted up mine eyes, and saw in a dream, and, behold, the he-goats which leaped upon the flock were streaked, speckled, and grizzled. 11. And the angel of God said unto me in the dream: Jacob; and I said: Here am I. 12. And he said: Lift up now thine eyes, and see, all the he-goats which leap upon the flock are streaked, speckled, and grizzled; for I have seen all that Laban doeth unto thee. 13. I am the God of Beth-el, where thou didst anoint a pillar, where thou didst vow a vow unto Me. Now arise, get thee out from this land, and return unto the land of thy nativity.' 14. And Rachel and Leah answered and said unto him: 'Is there yet any portion or inheritance for us in our father's house? 15. Are we not accounted by him strangers? for he hath sold us, and hath also quite devoured our price. 16. For all the riches which God hath taken away from our father, that is ours and our children's. Now then, whatsoever God hath said unto thee, do.'* vi. 17. Then Jacob rose up, and set his sons and his wives upon the camels; 18. and he carried away all his cattle, and all his substance which he had gathered, the cattle of his getting, which he had gathered in Paddan-aram, to go to Isaac his father unto the land of Canaan. 19. Now Laban was gone to shear his sheep. And Rachel stole the teraphim that were her father's. 20. And Jacob outwitted Laban the Aramean, in that he told him not that he fled. 21. So he fled with all that he had; and he rose up, and passed over the [1]River,

[1] That is, the Euphrates.

וְהֶחֱלִף אֶת־מַשְׂכֻּרְתִּי עֲשֶׂרֶת מֹנִים וְלֹא־נְתָנוֹ אֱלֹהִים לְהָרַע
8 עִמָּדִי׃ אִם־כֹּה יֹאמַר נְקֻדִּים יִהְיֶה שְׂכָרֶךָ וְיָלְדוּ כָל־הַצֹּאן
נְקֻדִּים וְאִם־כֹּה יֹאמַר עֲקֻדִּים יִהְיֶה שְׂכָרֶךָ וְיָלְדוּ כָל־
9 הַצֹּאן עֲקֻדִּים׃ וַיַּצֵּל אֱלֹהִים אֶת־מִקְנֵה אֲבִיכֶם וַיִּתֶּן־לִי׃
י וַיְהִי בְּעֵת יַחֵם הַצֹּאן וָאֶשָּׂא עֵינַי וָאֵרֶא בַּחֲלוֹם וְהִנֵּה
הָעַתֻּדִים הָעֹלִים עַל־הַצֹּאן עֲקֻדִּים נְקֻדִּים וּבְרֻדִּים׃
11 וַיֹּאמֶר אֵלַי מַלְאַךְ הָאֱלֹהִים בַּחֲלוֹם יַעֲקֹב וָאֹמַר הִנֵּנִי׃
12 וַיֹּאמֶר שָׂא־נָא עֵינֶיךָ וּרְאֵה כָּל־הָעַתֻּדִים הָעֹלִים עַל־
הַצֹּאן עֲקֻדִּים נְקֻדִּים וּבְרֻדִּים כִּי רָאִיתִי אֵת כָּל־אֲשֶׁר לָבָן
13 עֹשֶׂה לָּךְ׃ אָנֹכִי הָאֵל בֵּית־אֵל אֲשֶׁר מָשַׁחְתָּ שָּׁם מַצֵּבָה
אֲשֶׁר נָדַרְתָּ לִּי שָׁם נֶדֶר עַתָּה קוּם צֵא מִן־הָאָרֶץ הַזֹּאת
14 וְשׁוּב אֶל־אֶרֶץ מוֹלַדְתֶּךָ׃ וַתַּעַן רָחֵל וְלֵאָה וַתֹּאמַרְנָה לוֹ
טו הַעוֹד לָנוּ חֵלֶק וְנַחֲלָה בְּבֵית אָבִינוּ׃ הֲלוֹא נָכְרִיּוֹת
16 נֶחְשַׁבְנוּ לוֹ כִּי מְכָרָנוּ וַיֹּאכַל גַּם־אָכוֹל אֶת־כַּסְפֵּנוּ׃ כִּי
כָל־הָעֹשֶׁר אֲשֶׁר הִצִּיל אֱלֹהִים מֵאָבִינוּ לָנוּ הוּא וּלְבָנֵינוּ
ששי
17 וְעַתָּה כֹּל אֲשֶׁר אָמַר אֱלֹהִים אֵלֶיךָ עֲשֵׂה׃* וַיָּקָם יַעֲקֹב
18 וַיִּשָּׂא אֶת־בָּנָיו וְאֶת־נָשָׁיו עַל־הַגְּמַלִּים׃ וַיִּנְהַג אֶת־כָּל־
מִקְנֵהוּ וְאֶת־כָּל־רְכֻשׁוֹ אֲשֶׁר רָכָשׁ מִקְנֵה קִנְיָנוֹ אֲשֶׁר
רָכַשׁ בְּפַדַּן אֲרָם לָבוֹא אֶל־יִצְחָק אָבִיו אַרְצָה כְּנָעַן׃
19 וְלָבָן הָלַךְ לִגְזֹז אֶת־צֹאנוֹ וַתִּגְנֹב רָחֵל אֶת־הַתְּרָפִים אֲשֶׁר
כ לְאָבִיהָ׃ וַיִּגְנֹב יַעֲקֹב אֶת־לֵב לָבָן הָאֲרַמִּי עַל־בְּלִי הִגִּיד
21 לוֹ כִּי בֹרֵחַ הוּא׃ וַיִּבְרַח הוּא וְכָל־אֲשֶׁר־לוֹ וַיָּקָם וַיַּעֲבֹר

v. 9. בם״ם v. 18. קמץ בז״ק

11. *angel of God.* In *v.* 3 it is 'The LORD said'. The interchange of 'God' and 'angel of God' is frequent.

13. *The God of Beth-el.* The God who appeared unto thee at Beth-el, see XXVIII.

15. *strangers.* He has not allowed us and our children to enjoy some of the prosperity which accrued during Jacob's fourteen years of labour for us. And now he begrudges what our husband has gained by his toil.

17. *his sons.* The word should be rendered here, '*his children.*'

18. *the cattle of his getting.* *i.e.* which he had purchased; viz. camels and asses, XXX, 43.

19. *gone to shear his sheep.* The occasion of sheep-shearing was a time of feasting, and lasted several days.

ter phim. Images kept in the house, perhaps corresponding to the Roman *penates*, to bring protection and good fortune. Laban calls them 'my gods' (*v.* 30). Why did Rachel carry them off? The Midrash answers, to prevent her father from worshipping them.

21. *passed over the River.* Euphrates.

and set his face toward the mountain of Gilead. ¶ 22. And it was told Laban on the third day that Jacob was fled. 23. And he took his brethren with him, and pursued after him seven days' journey; and he overtook him in the mountain of Gilead. 24. And God came to Laban the Aramean in a dream of the night, and said unto him: 'Take heed to thyself that thou speak not to Jacob either good or bad.' 25. And Laban came up with Jacob. Now Jacob had pitched his tent in the mountain; and Laban with his brethren pitched in the mountain of Gilead. 26. And Laban said to Jacob: 'What hast thou done, that thou hast outwitted me, and carried away my daughters as though captives of the sword? 27. Wherefore didst thou flee secretly, and outwit me; and didst not tell me, that I might have sent thee away with mirth and with songs, with tabret and with harp; 28. and didst not suffer me to kiss my sons and my daughters? now hast thou done foolishly. 29. It is in the power of my hand to do you hurt; but the God of your father spoke unto me yesternight, saying: Take heed to thyself that thou speak not to Jacob either good or bad. 30. And now that thou art surely gone, because thou sore longest after thy father's house, wherefore hast thou stolen my gods?' 31. And Jacob answered and said to Laban: 'Because I was afraid; for I said: Lest thou shouldest take thy daughters from me by force. 32. With whomsoever thou findest thy gods, he shall not live; before our brethren discern thou what is thine with me, and take it to thee.'—For Jacob knew not that Rachel had stolen them.—33. And Laban went into Jacob's tent, and into Leah's tent, and into the tent of the two maid-servants; but he found them not. And he went out of Leah's tent, and entered into Rachel's tent. 34. Now Rachel had taken the teraphim, and put

22 אֶת־הַנָּהָר וַיָּשֶׂם אֶת־פָּנָיו הַר הַגִּלְעָד׃ וַיֻּגַּד לְלָבָן בַּיּוֹם
23 הַשְּׁלִישִׁי כִּי בָרַח יַעֲקֹב׃ וַיִּקַּח אֶת־אֶחָיו עִמּוֹ וַיִּרְדֹּף
24 אַחֲרָיו דֶּרֶךְ שִׁבְעַת יָמִים וַיַּדְבֵּק אֹתוֹ בְּהַר הַגִּלְעָד׃ וַיָּבֹא
אֱלֹהִים אֶל־לָבָן הָאֲרַמִּי בַּחֲלֹם הַלָּיְלָה וַיֹּאמֶר לוֹ הִשָּׁמֶר
כה לְךָ פֶּן־תְּדַבֵּר עִם־יַעֲקֹב מִטּוֹב עַד־רָע׃ וַיַּשֵּׂג לָבָן אֶת־
יַעֲקֹב וְיַעֲקֹב תָּקַע אֶת־אָהֳלוֹ בָּהָר וְלָבָן תָּקַע אֶת־אֶחָיו
26 בְּהַר הַגִּלְעָד׃ וַיֹּאמֶר לָבָן לְיַעֲקֹב מֶה עָשִׂיתָ וַתִּגְנֹב אֶת־
27 לְבָבִי וַתְּנַהֵג אֶת־בְּנֹתַי כִּשְׁבֻיוֹת חָרֶב׃ לָמָּה נַחְבֵּאתָ
לִבְרֹחַ וַתִּגְנֹב אֹתִי וְלֹא־הִגַּדְתָּ לִּי וָאֲשַׁלֵּחֲךָ בְּשִׂמְחָה
28 וּבְשִׁרִים בְּתֹף וּבְכִנּוֹר׃ וְלֹא נְטַשְׁתַּנִי לְנַשֵּׁק לְבָנַי וְלִבְנֹתָי
29 עַתָּה הִסְכַּלְתָּ עֲשׂוֹ׃ יֶשׁ־לְאֵל יָדִי לַעֲשׂוֹת עִמָּכֶם רָע וֵאלֹהֵי
אֲבִיכֶם אֶמֶשׁ ׀ אָמַר אֵלַי לֵאמֹר הִשָּׁמֶר לְךָ מִדַּבֵּר עִם־
ל יַעֲקֹב מִטּוֹב עַד־רָע׃ וְעַתָּה הָלֹךְ הָלַכְתָּ כִּי־נִכְסֹף נִכְסַפְתָּה
31 לְבֵית אָבִיךָ לָמָּה גָנַבְתָּ אֶת־אֱלֹהָי׃ וַיַּעַן יַעֲקֹב וַיֹּאמֶר
לְלָבָן כִּי יָרֵאתִי כִּי אָמַרְתִּי פֶּן־תִּגְזֹל אֶת־בְּנוֹתֶיךָ מֵעִמִּי׃
32 עִם אֲשֶׁר תִּמְצָא אֶת־אֱלֹהֶיךָ לֹא יִחְיֶה נֶגֶד אַחֵינוּ הַכֶּר־
לְךָ מָה עִמָּדִי וְקַח־לָךְ וְלֹא־יָדַע יַעֲקֹב כִּי רָחֵל גְּנָבָתַם׃
33 וַיָּבֹא לָבָן בְּאֹהֶל־יַעֲקֹב ׀ וּבְאֹהֶל לֵאָה וּבְאֹהֶל שְׁתֵּי
הָאֲמָהֹת וְלֹא מָצָא וַיֵּצֵא מֵאֹהֶל לֵאָה וַיָּבֹא בְּאֹהֶל רָחֵל׃
34 וְרָחֵל לָקְחָה אֶת־הַתְּרָפִים וַתְּשִׂמֵם בְּכַר הַגָּמָל וַתֵּשֶׁב

the mountain of Gilead. Or, 'the hill-country of Gilead,' the region E. of Jordan.

23. *brethren.* Men of his clan.

22–54. LABAN'S PURSUIT

24. *either good or bad.* *i.e.* anything, as in XXIV, 50. The phrase is the same Heb. phrase and idiom as in II, 17, III, 5 and 22, where it means, 'all things.' Here it is in negative form and means, 'not anything.' Laban was neither to entice him by offers of kindness, nor force him to return by threats.

26. *as though captives of the sword.* Without allowing them an opportunity of taking farewell of their father and brothers. Laban strikes the note of injured innocence.

28. *sons.* *i.e.* grandsons (see on XX, 12), and *daughters* may include Rachel, Leah and Laban's granddaughters.

29. *to do you hurt.* It would thus seem that Laban was accompanied by a large band which outnumbered Jacob and his servants.

31. This verse answers the first point mentioned by Laban, viz. the secrecy with which Jacob left him.

32. *shall not live.* The Patriarch does not mean that he will himself kill the culprit, but the wrongdoer's life will be placed in Laban's hands; cf. XLIV, 9.

33. Nachmanides explains that Laban's search was in the following order: Jacob, Leah, Rachel, and lastly the handmaids. The narrative, however, reserves the mention of Rachel for the last, because it is upon her that interest is centred.

them in the saddle of the camel, and sat upon them. And Laban felt about all the tent, but found them not. 35. And she said to her father: 'Let not my lord be angry that I cannot rise up before thee; for the manner of women is upon me.' And he searched, but found not the teraphim. 36. And Jacob was wroth, and strove with Laban. And Jacob answered and said to Laban: 'What is my trespass? what is my sin, that thou hast hotly pursued after me? 37. Whereas thou hast felt about all my stuff, what hast thou found of all thy household stuff? Set it here before my brethren and thy brethren, that they may judge betwixt us two. 38. These twenty years have I been with thee; thy ewes and thy she-goats have not cast their young, and the rams of thy flocks have I not eaten. 39. That which was torn of beasts I brought not unto thee; I bore the loss of it; of my hand didst thou require it, whether stolen by day or stolen by night. 40. Thus I was: in the day the drought consumed me, and the frost by night; and my sleep fled from mine eyes. 41. These twenty years have I been in thy house: I served thee fourteen years for thy two daughters, and six years for thy flock; and thou hast changed my wages ten times. 42. Except the God of my father, the God of Abraham, and the Fear of Isaac, had been on my side, surely now hadst thou sent me away empty. God hath seen mine affliction and the labour of my hands, and gave judgment yesternight.'* vii. 43. And Laban answered and said unto Jacob: 'The daughters are my

לה עֲלֵיהֶם וַיְמַשֵּׁשׁ לָבָן אֶת־כָּל־הָאֹהֶל וְלֹא מָצָא׃ וַתֹּאמֶר
אֶל־אָבִיהָ אַל־יִחַר בְּעֵינֵי אֲדֹנִי כִּי לוֹא אוּכַל לָקוּם מִפָּנֶיךָ
36 כִּי־דֶרֶךְ נָשִׁים לִי וַיְחַפֵּשׂ וְלֹא מָצָא אֶת־הַתְּרָפִים׃ וַיִּחַר
לְיַעֲקֹב וַיָּרֶב בְּלָבָן וַיַּעַן יַעֲקֹב וַיֹּאמֶר לְלָבָן מַה־פִּשְׁעִי
37 מַה חַטָּאתִי כִּי דָלַקְתָּ אַחֲרָי׃ כִּי־מִשַּׁשְׁתָּ אֶת־כָּל־כֵּלַי
מַה־מָּצָאתָ מִכֹּל כְּלֵי־בֵיתֶךָ שִׂים כֹּה נֶגֶד אַחַי וְאַחֶיךָ
38 וְיוֹכִיחוּ בֵּין שְׁנֵינוּ׃ זֶה עֶשְׂרִים שָׁנָה אָנֹכִי עִמָּךְ רְחֵלֶיךָ
39 וְעִזֶּיךָ לֹא שִׁכֵּלוּ וְאֵילֵי צֹאנְךָ לֹא אָכָלְתִּי׃ טְרֵפָה לֹא־
הֵבֵאתִי אֵלֶיךָ אָנֹכִי אֲחַטֶּנָּה מִיָּדִי תְּבַקְשֶׁנָּה גְּנֻבְתִי יוֹם
מ וּגְנֻבְתִי לָיְלָה׃ הָיִיתִי בַיּוֹם אֲכָלַנִי חֹרֶב וְקֶרַח בַּלָּיְלָה
41 וַתִּדַּד שְׁנָתִי מֵעֵינָי׃ זֶה־לִּי עֶשְׂרִים שָׁנָה בְּבֵיתֶךָ עֲבַדְתִּיךָ
אַרְבַּע־עֶשְׂרֵה שָׁנָה בִּשְׁתֵּי בְנֹתֶיךָ וְשֵׁשׁ שָׁנִים בְּצֹאנֶךָ
42 וַתַּחֲלֵף אֶת־מַשְׂכֻּרְתִּי עֲשֶׂרֶת מֹנִים׃ לוּלֵי אֱלֹהֵי אָבִי
אֱלֹהֵי אַבְרָהָם וּפַחַד יִצְחָק הָיָה לִי כִּי עַתָּה רֵיקָם שִׁלַּחְתָּנִי
שביעי
43 אֶת־עָנְיִי וְאֶת־יְגִיעַ כַּפַּי רָאָה אֱלֹהִים וַיּוֹכַח אָמֶשׁ׃ * וַיַּעַן
לָבָן וַיֹּאמֶר אֶל־יַעֲקֹב הַבָּנוֹת בְּנֹתַי וְהַבָּנִים בָּנַי וְהַצֹּאן
צֹאנִי וְכֹל אֲשֶׁר־אַתָּה רֹאֶה לִי־הוּא וְלִבְנֹתַי מָה־אֶעֱשֶׂה

v. 35. מלא וא"ו

34. *saddle.* The word is better translated 'palanquin'—a sort of compartment, tied on to the saddle, covered with an awning and surrounded with curtains, in which Oriental women travel.

35. *rise.* A child had to stand up when the father entered the room.

36. *wroth.* The Patriarch's indignation is aroused when his innocence is established; and he accuses Laban of fabricating the charge of stealing the teraphim as a pretext to search his possessions.

answered. i.e. replied to Laban's accusations.

38. *have not cast their young.* Due to the skill and assiduity of the shepherd.

39. *or by night.* In these words lies the bitterness of reproach. A shepherd was entitled to his rest at night, and he could not in justice be held responsible if damage was then done by prowling beasts, provided reasonable precautions had been taken.

According to the Code of Hammurabi, which was the Common Law in Mesopotamia at the time, the shepherd gave a receipt for the animals entrusted to him, and was bound to return them with reasonable increase. He was allowed to use a certain number for food, and was not responsible for those killed by lion or lightning. Any loss due to his carelessness he had to repay tenfold. All this throws wonderful light on the relations between Jacob and Laban.

42. *Fear of Isaac.* Or, 'Awe of Isaac'; *i.e.* He whom Isaac feared. The noun, in this special use as a Divine appellation, occurs again in *v.* 53. See Isaiah VIII, 13, where a synonymous word is used.

gave judgment. See *v.* 29.

43. Laban is unable to answer Jacob's reproaches, and therefore repeats the claim based on primitive usage, whereby the head of the family is the nominal possessor of all that belonged to its members. He then pretends to be solicitous for the welfare of his daughters and grandchildren.

daughters, and the children are my children, and the flocks are my flocks, and all that thou seest is mine; and what can I do this day for these my daughters, or for their children whom they have borne? 44. And now come, let us make a covenant, I and thou; and let it be for a witness between me and thee.' 45. And Jacob took a stone, and set it up for a pillar. 46. And Jacob said unto his brethren: 'Gather stones'; and they took stones, and made a heap. And they did eat there by the heap. 47. And Laban called it [1]Jegar-sahadutha; but Jacob called it [2]Galeed. 48. And Laban said: 'This heap is witness between me and thee this day.' Therefore was the name of it called Galeed; 49. and [3]Mizpah, for he said: 'The LORD watch between me and thee, when we are absent one from another. 50. If thou shalt afflict my daughters, and if thou shalt take wives beside my daughters, no man being with us; see, God is witness betwixt me and thee.' 51. And Laban said to Jacob: 'Behold this heap, and behold the pillar, which I have set up betwixt me and thee. 52. This heap be witness, and the pillar be witness, that I will not pass over this heap to thee, and that thou shalt not pass over this heap and this pillar unto me, for harm. 53. The God of Abraham, and the God of Nahor, the God of their father, judge betwixt us.' And Jacob swore by the Fear of his father Isaac. 54. And Jacob offered a sacrifice in the mountain, and called his brethren to eat bread; and they did eat bread, and tarried all night in the mountain. *m.

44 לָאֵלֶּה הַיּוֹם אוֹ לִבְנֵיהֶן אֲשֶׁר יָלָדוּ׃ וְעַתָּה לְכָה נִכְרְתָה
מה בְרִית אֲנִי וָאָתָּה וְהָיָה לְעֵד בֵּינִי וּבֵינֶךָ׃ וַיִּקַּח יַעֲקֹב אָבֶן
46 וַיְרִימֶהָ מַצֵּבָה׃ וַיֹּאמֶר יַעֲקֹב לְאֶחָיו לִקְטוּ אֲבָנִים וַיִּקְחוּ
47 אֲבָנִים וַיַּעֲשׂוּ־גָל וַיֹּאכְלוּ שָׁם עַל־הַגָּל׃ וַיִּקְרָא־לוֹ לָבָן
48 יְגַר שָׂהֲדוּתָא וְיַעֲקֹב קָרָא לוֹ גַּלְעֵד׃ וַיֹּאמֶר לָבָן הַגַּל
הַזֶּה עֵד בֵּינִי וּבֵינְךָ הַיּוֹם עַל־כֵּן קָרָא־שְׁמוֹ גַּלְעֵד׃
49 וְהַמִּצְפָּה אֲשֶׁר אָמַר יִצֶף יְהוָה בֵּינִי וּבֵינֶךָ כִּי נִסָּתֵר אִישׁ
נ מֵרֵעֵהוּ׃ אִם־תְּעַנֶּה אֶת־בְּנֹתַי וְאִם־תִּקַּח נָשִׁים עַל־בְּנֹתַי
51 אֵין אִישׁ עִמָּנוּ רְאֵה אֱלֹהִים עֵד בֵּינִי וּבֵינֶךָ׃ וַיֹּאמֶר לָבָן
לְיַעֲקֹב הִנֵּה ׀ הַגַּל הַזֶּה וְהִנֵּה הַמַּצֵּבָה אֲשֶׁר יָרִיתִי בֵּינִי
52 וּבֵינֶךָ׃ עֵד הַגַּל הַזֶּה וְעֵדָה הַמַּצֵּבָה אִם־אָנִי לֹא־אֶעֱבֹר
אֵלֶיךָ אֶת־הַגַּל הַזֶּה וְאִם־אַתָּה לֹא־תַעֲבֹר אֵלַי אֶת־הַגַּל
53 הַזֶּה וְאֶת־הַמַּצֵּבָה הַזֹּאת לְרָעָה׃ אֱלֹהֵי אַבְרָהָם וֵאלֹהֵי
נָחוֹר יִשְׁפְּטוּ בֵינֵינוּ אֱלֹהֵי אֲבִיהֶם וַיִּשָּׁבַע יַעֲקֹב בְּפַחַד
54 אָבִיו יִצְחָק׃ וַיִּזְבַּח יַעֲקֹב זֶבַח בָּהָר וַיִּקְרָא לְאֶחָיו לֶאֱכָל־
לָחֶם וַיֹּאכְלוּ לֶחֶם וַיָּלִינוּ בָּהָר׃ מפטיר

32

CHAPTER XXXII

1. And early in the morning Laban rose up, and kissed his sons and his daughters, and blessed them. And Laban departed, and returned unto his place. 2. And Jacob went on his way, and the angels of God met him. 3. And Jacob said when he saw them: 'This is God's camp.' And he called the name of that place [4]Mahanaim.

CAP. XXXII. לב לב

א וַיַּשְׁכֵּם לָבָן בַּבֹּקֶר וַיְנַשֵּׁק לְבָנָיו וְלִבְנוֹתָיו וַיְבָרֶךְ אֶתְהֶם
2 וַיֵּלֶךְ וַיָּשָׁב לָבָן לִמְקֹמוֹ׃ וְיַעֲקֹב הָלַךְ לְדַרְכּוֹ וַיִּפְגְּעוּ־בוֹ
3 מַלְאֲכֵי אֱלֹהִים׃ וַיֹּאמֶר יַעֲקֹב כַּאֲשֶׁר רָאָם מַחֲנֵה אֱלֹהִים
זֶה וַיִּקְרָא שֵׁם־הַמָּקוֹם הַהוּא מַחֲנָיִם׃

[1] That is, *The heap of witness*, in Aramaic. [2] That is, *The heap of witness*, in Hebrew. [3] *The watch-post.* [4] *Two camps.* לא׳ v. 53. חול

46. *heap.* Or, 'cairn.'

they did eat. The meal was part of the ceremony of the covenant of friendship.

50. Laban still keeps up the pretext that the pact made between him and Jacob is for the protection of his daughters; but he immediately proceeds to set up another heap and pillar to safeguard himself from any aggression on Jacob's part in the future.

53. Laban, being a descendant of Nahor (XXII, 20 f), calls upon the deity worshipped by his family as well as upon the God worshipped by Jacob's family to witness the covenant; but Jacob, who refuses to acknowledge the 'god of Nahor', swears only by the 'Fear' of Isaac.

God of their father. Each one swears by the God of his father (Nachmanides).

54. *offered a sacrifice.* Of thanksgiving to God.

CHAPTER XXXII

1. *his sons. i.e.* his grandchildren.

2. *went on his way.* To Beth-el, whither God had sent him to fulfil his vow. This vision assured him that God was mindful of His promises.

3. *Mahanaim. i.e.* two camps; the company of the angels and Laban's camp.

HOSEA XII, 13–XIV, 10

Chapter XII

13. And Jacob fled into the field of Aram,
And Israel served for a wife,
And for a wife he kept sheep.
14. And by a prophet the Lord brought Israel up out of Egypt,
And by a prophet was he kept.
15. Ephraim hath provoked most bitterly;
Therefore shall his blood be cast upon him,
And his reproach shall his Lord return unto him.

Chapter XIII

1. When Ephraim spoke, there was trembling,
He exalted himself in Israel;
But when he became guilty through Baal, he died.
2. And now they sin more and more,
And have made them molten images of their silver,
According to their own understanding, even idols,
All of them the work of the craftsmen;
Of them they say:
'They that sacrifice men kiss calves.'

Cap. XII. יב

וַיִּבְרַח 13
יַעֲקֹב שְׂדֵה אֲרָם וַיַּעֲבֹד יִשְׂרָאֵל בְּאִשָּׁה וּבְאִשָּׁה שָׁמָר׃
14 וּבְנָבִיא הֶעֱלָה יְהוָה אֶת־יִשְׂרָאֵל מִמִּצְרָיִם וּבְנָבִיא נִשְׁמָר׃
טו הִכְעִיס אֶפְרַיִם תַּמְרוּרִים וְדָמָיו עָלָיו יִטּוֹשׁ וְחֶרְפָּתוֹ יָשִׁיב
לוֹ אֲדֹנָיו׃

Cap. XIII. יג

א כְּדַבֵּר אֶפְרַיִם רְתֵת נָשָׂא הוּא בְּיִשְׂרָאֵל וַיֶּאְשַׁם בַּבַּעַל
2 וַיָּמֹת׃ וְעַתָּה ׀ יוֹסִפוּ לַחֲטֹא וַיַּעֲשׂוּ לָהֶם מַסֵּכָה מִכַּסְפָּם
כִּתְבוּנָם עֲצַבִּים מַעֲשֵׂה חָרָשִׁים כֻּלֹּה לָהֶם הֵם אֹמְרִים

יג' v. 2. נ"א בתבונם

Like his older contemporary, Amos, Hosea is the Prophet of the Decline and Fall of the Northern Israel.

The reign of Jeroboam II—a time of prosperity, luxury and idolatry in Northern Israel—closed in the year 740, before the Common Era. And very soon thereafter came 'the beginning of the end'. A succession of usurpers and adventurers occupied the throne, and the land was swiftly drifting towards social and political disintegration. Instead of obeying the law of God, Israel amused itself with international intrigues, and imitated the morals and idolatries of her allies. But the world-power of Assyria had appeared on the horizon, and was soon destined to engulf everything. 'Let Israel come back to God, and call upon Him in their anguish. Let Israel seek the Lord, it is still time,' such is the burden of Hosea. 'His sensitive soul is full of sympathy and love for his people; and his keen perception of the destruction towards which they are hastening produces a conflict of emotions which is reflected in the pathos, and force, and artless rhythm of sighs and sobs which characterize his prophecy' (Driver).

13. *Jacob fled.* The Prophet takes the people back to their beginnings, to their ancestor Jacob. (This connects the Sedrah with the Haftorah.) Did not the Patriarch, in his hard life, find God his support, guide and Redeemer? And Israel in Egypt was freed by Divine power, just as later he was 'guarded' (and guided) by God's chosen Prophet (Moses) whose successors the people were now disregarding and despising. Hosea bids the people remember that God is their only Saviour, even as His hand is manifest in all their history.

15. *Ephraim.* The Northern Kingdom is so called from the name of its most prominent tribe.

Chapter XIII. The Last Judgment of Ephraim

1. *when Ephraim spoke.* A rapid résumé of the history of the Northern Kingdom. At first Ephraim's power was great, and he was feared by surrounding tribes. Jeroboam, the first king of the Ten Tribes, was an Ephraimite. 'He sinned and led Israel to sin,' through the calf-worship which he had set up at Dan and Beersheba.

Baal. See I Kings XVI, 31.

died. Spiritually; yet literally too, for Baal-worship was a cause of the national decay and final downfall. 'It could no more inspire courage than love of goodness' (Cheyne).

2. *kiss calves.* See I Kings XIX, 18. Kissing a calf as an act of religious homage!

3 זֹבְחֵי אָדָם עֲגָלִים יִשָּׁקוּן׃ לָכֵן יִהְיוּ כַּעֲנַן־בֹּקֶר וְכַטַּל
4 מַשְׁכִּים הֹלֵךְ כְּמֹץ יְסֹעֵר מִגֹּרֶן וּכְעָשָׁן מֵאֲרֻבָּה׃ וְאָנֹכִי
יְהוָה אֱלֹהֶיךָ מֵאֶרֶץ מִצְרָיִם וֵאלֹהִים זוּלָתִי לֹא תֵדָע
ה וּמוֹשִׁיעַ אַיִן בִּלְתִּי׃ אֲנִי יְדַעְתִּיךָ בַּמִּדְבָּר בְּאֶרֶץ תַּלְאֻבוֹת׃
6 כְּמַרְעִיתָם וַיִּשְׂבָּעוּ שָׂבְעוּ וַיָּרָם לִבָּם עַל־כֵּן שְׁכֵחוּנִי׃
7 8 וָאֱהִי לָהֶם כְּמוֹ־שָׁחַל כְּנָמֵר עַל־דֶּרֶךְ אָשׁוּר׃ אֶפְגְּשֵׁם
כְּדֹב שַׁכּוּל וְאֶקְרַע סְגוֹר לִבָּם וְאֹכְלֵם שָׁם כְּלָבִיא חַיַּת
9 הַשָּׂדֶה תְּבַקְּעֵם׃ שִׁחֶתְךָ יִשְׂרָאֵל כִּי־בִי בְעֶזְרֶךָ׃ אֱהִי
מַלְכְּךָ אֵפוֹא וְיוֹשִׁיעֲךָ בְּכָל־עָרֶיךָ וְשֹׁפְטֶיךָ אֲשֶׁר אָמַרְתָּ
11 תְּנָה־לִּי מֶלֶךְ וְשָׂרִים׃ אֶתֶּן־לְךָ מֶלֶךְ בְּאַפִּי וְאֶקַּח בְּעֶבְרָתִי׃
12 13 צָרוּר עֲוֺן אֶפְרָיִם צְפוּנָה חַטָּאתוֹ׃ חֶבְלֵי יוֹלֵדָה יָבֹאוּ
לוֹ הוּא־בֵן לֹא חָכָם כִּי־עֵת לֹא־יַעֲמֹד בְּמִשְׁבַּר בָּנִים׃
14 מִיַּד שְׁאוֹל אֶפְדֵּם מִמָּוֶת אֶגְאָלֵם אֱהִי דְבָרֶיךָ מָוֶת אֱהִי

3. Therefore they shall be as the morning cloud,
And as the dew that early passeth away,
As the chaff that is driven with the wind out of the threshing-floor,
And as the smoke out of the window.

4. Yet I am the LORD thy God
From the land of Egypt;
And thou knowest no God but Me,
And beside Me there is no saviour.

5. I did know thee in the wilderness,
In the land of great drought.

6. When they were fed, they became full,
They were filled, and their heart was exalted;
Therefore have they forgotten Me.

7. Therefore am I become unto them as a lion;
As a leopard will I watch by the way;

8. I will meet them as a bear that is bereaved of her whelps,
And will rend the enclosure of their heart;
And there will I devour them like a lioness,
The wild beast shall tear them.

9. It is thy destruction, O Israel,
That thou art against Me, against thy help.

10. Ho, now, thy king,
That he may save thee in all thy cities!
And thy judges, of whom thou saidst:
'Give me a king and princes!'

11. I give thee a king in Mine anger,
And take him away in My wrath.

12. The iniquity of Ephraim is bound up;
His sin is laid up in store.

13. The throes of a travailing woman shall come upon him;
He is an unwise son;
For it is time he should not tarry
In the place of the breaking forth of children.

14. Shall I ransom them from the power of the nether-world?

4. v קמץ בז״ק v. 12. קמץ בז״ק

3. *morning cloud.* Figures of speech to represent the swift and complete extinction of the Northern Kingdom. The morning cloud which passes as one observes it, the chaff scattered by the whirlwind, the smoke of the chimney—all leave no trace behind. So shall it be with the Kingdom of Israel. The prophecy was fulfilled within 20 years.

7–9. God, who is and would be their help, they have turned to be their destroyer; and they have brought ruin on themselves.

11. *a king in Mine anger.* Jeroboam I, who became king of Israel when the Ten Tribes broke away from Solomon's incompetent son.

take him away in My wrath. Refers to the list of usurping kings on the eve of the destruction of the kingdom by Assyria.

12. *bound up.* It is not forgotten; it is tied up as in a bag.

13. Israel is compared to a travailing woman, and also to the child imperilled by its weak will.

14. *I will ransom.* 'A father cannot long endure to contemplate the prospect of his child's ruin' (Cheyne).

repentance be hid. Suddenly the tone of the prophecy changes, and the thought in verses 12 and 13 is resumed.

טו קֹטָבְךָ שְׁאוֹל נֹחַם יִסָּתֵר מֵעֵינָי׃ כִּי הוּא בֵּין אַחִים יַפְרִיא
יָבוֹא קָדִים רוּחַ יְהוָה מִמִּדְבָּר עֹלֶה וְיֵבוֹשׁ מְקוֹרוֹ וְיֶחֱרַב
מַעְיָנוֹ הוּא יִשְׁסֶה אוֹצַר כָּל־כְּלִי חֶמְדָּה׃

Shall I redeem them from death?
Ho, thy plagues, O death!
Ho, thy destruction, O nether-world!
Repentance be hid from Mine eyes!

15. For though he be fruitful among the reed-plants,
An east wind shall come, the wind of the LORD coming up from the wilderness,
And his spring shall become dry, and his fountain shall be dried up;
He shall spoil the treasure of all precious vessels.

CAP. XIV. יד

א תֶּאְשַׁם שֹׁמְרוֹן כִּי מָרְתָה בֵּאלֹהֶיהָ בַּחֶרֶב יִפֹּלוּ עֹלְלֵיהֶם
2 יְרֻטָּשׁוּ וְהָרִיּוֹתָיו יְבֻקָּעוּ׃ שׁוּבָה יִשְׂרָאֵל עַד יְהוָה
3 אֱלֹהֶיךָ כִּי כָשַׁלְתָּ בַּעֲוֺנֶךָ׃ קְחוּ עִמָּכֶם דְּבָרִים וְשׁוּבוּ אֶל־
יְהוָה אִמְרוּ אֵלָיו כָּל־תִּשָּׂא עָוֺן וְקַח־טוֹב וּנְשַׁלְּמָה פָרִים
4 שְׂפָתֵינוּ׃ אַשּׁוּר ׀ לֹא יוֹשִׁיעֵנוּ עַל־סוּס לֹא נִרְכָּב וְלֹא־
נֹאמַר עוֹד אֱלֹהֵינוּ לְמַעֲשֵׂה יָדֵינוּ אֲשֶׁר־בְּךָ יְרֻחַם יָתוֹם׃
ה 6 אֶרְפָּא מְשׁוּבָתָם אֹהֲבֵם נְדָבָה כִּי שָׁב אַפִּי מִמֶּנּוּ׃ אֶהְיֶה
7 כַטַּל לְיִשְׂרָאֵל יִפְרַח כַּשּׁוֹשַׁנָּה וְיַךְ שָׁרָשָׁיו כַּלְּבָנוֹן׃ יֵלְכוּ

CHAPTER XIV

1. Samaria shall bear her guilt,
For she hath rebelled against her God;
They shall fall by the sword;
Their infants shall be dashed in pieces,
And their women with child shall be ripped up.

2. Return, O Israel, unto the LORD thy God;
For thou hast stumbled in thine iniquity.

3. Take with you words,
And return unto the LORD;
Say unto Him: 'Forgive all iniquity,
And accept that which is good;
So will we render for bullocks the offering of our lips.

4. Asshur shall not save us;
We will not ride upon horses;
Neither will we call any more the work of our hands our gods;
For in Thee the fatherless findeth mercy.'

5. I will heal their backsliding,
I will love them freely;
For Mine anger is turned away from him.

6. I will be as the dew unto Israel;
He shall blossom as the lily,
And cast forth his roots as Lebanon.

7. His branches shall spread,
And his beauty shall be as the olive-tree,
And his fragrance as Lebanon.

יד׳ v. 4. קמץ בז״ק

15. *he shall spoil.* *i.e.* the enemy who is to destroy Israel, symbolized here by the evil wind.

CHAPTER XIV

1. *Samaria.* The capital of Northern Kingdom, standing here for the whole land. The savage inhumanities of ancient barbaric warfare recall the atrocities of modern pogroms.

2–10. A DESPERATE CALL TO REPENTANCE

2. *return unto the LORD.* God's love and mercy are unending. Even after the pronouncement of doom, there is Hope and Forgiveness to repentant Israel.

3. *take with you words.* God does not require gifts or sacrifices, but sincere confession and penitent words expressing the resolve to amend (Midrash).

4. *Asshur shall not save us.* The people will no longer put their trust in alliances with foreign idol-worshipping nations—Assyria or Egypt.
will not ride upon horses. A reference to the help looked for from Egypt. (See I Kings x, 28; Isaiah xxx and xxxi).

5–7. God's gracious and loving reply to those words of repentance and faith. The blessings that will follow Israel's spiritual regeneration.

6. *blossom as the lily.* Israel shall be as the lily, a symbol of beauty and fruitfulness; but his roots shall be deep and unmovable as Lebanon.

7. *his fragrance as Lebanon.* On the lower slopes of Lebanon are aromatic shrubs, lavender and myrtle (Song of Songs IV, 4).

8 יֹנְקוֹתָיו וִיהִי כַזַּיִת הוֹדוֹ וְרֵיחַ לוֹ כַּלְּבָנוֹן׃ יָשֻׁבוּ יֹשְׁבֵי
9 בְצִלּוֹ יְחַיּוּ דָגָן וְיִפְרְחוּ כַגָּפֶן זִכְרוֹ כְּיֵין לְבָנוֹן׃ אֶפְרַיִם
מַה־לִּי עוֹד לָעֲצַבִּים אֲנִי עָנִיתִי וַאֲשׁוּרֶנּוּ אֲנִי כִּבְרוֹשׁ רַעֲנָן
י מִמֶּנִּי פֶּרְיְךָ נִמְצָא׃ מִי חָכָם וְיָבֵן אֵלֶּה נָבוֹן וְיֵדָעֵם כִּי־
יְשָׁרִים דַּרְכֵי יְהוָה וְצַדִּקִים יֵלְכוּ בָם וּפֹשְׁעִים יִכָּשְׁלוּ בָם׃

8. They that dwell under his shadow shall again
Make corn to grow,
And shall blossom as the vine;
The scent thereof shall be as the wine of Lebanon.

9. Ephraim [shall say]:
'What have I to do any more with idols?'
As for Me, I respond and look on him;
I am like a leafy cypress-tree;
From Me is thy fruit found.

10. Whoso is wise, let him understand these things,
Whoso is prudent, let him know them.
For the ways of the LORD are right,
And the just do walk in them;
But transgressors do stumble therein.

10. v. כצ״ל

9. *from Me is thy fruit found.* 'From Me all thy good cometh.'

10. *stumble therein.* They stumble as if the ways were actually crooked, because their wrong thoughts and desires pervert the meaning of the Divine commands. Thus they do wrong and stumble, even when they would claim to be walking in the ways of the LORD.

Chapter XIV, 2–10, is appropriately enough the Haftorah for the Sabbath of Penitence, שבת שובה, lit. 'The Sabbath of *O Israel, return unto the LORD*'. The very term, *Teshubah*, *i.e.* 'a turning away from sin and a turning towards God', is taken from the word שובה in its opening verse. The doctrine of Repentance which is founded on it, is of fundamental importance in Judaism.

32 4. And Jacob sent messengers before him to Esau his brother unto the land of Seir, the field of Edom. 5. And he commanded them, saying: 'Thus shall ye say unto my lord Esau: Thus saith thy servant Jacob: I have sojourned with Laban, and stayed until now. 6. And I have oxen, and asses and flocks, and men-servants and maid-servants; and I have sent to tell my lord, that I may find favour in thy sight.' 7. And the messengers returned to Jacob, saying: 'We came to thy brother Esau, and moreover he cometh to meet thee, and four hundred men with him.' 8. Then Jacob was greatly afraid and was distressed. And he divided the people that was with him, and the flocks, and the herds, and the camels, into two camps. 9. And he said: 'If Esau come to the one camp, and smite it, then the camp which is left shall escape.' 10. And Jacob said: 'O God of my father Abraham, and God of my father Isaac, O LORD, who saidst unto me: Return unto thy country, and to thy kindred, and I will do thee good; 11. I am not worthy of all the mercies, and of all the truth, which

לב פ פ פ ח 8
4 וַיִּשְׁלַח יַעֲקֹב מַלְאָכִים לְפָנָיו אֶל־עֵשָׂו אָחִיו אַרְצָה שֵׂעִיר
ה שְׂדֵה אֱדוֹם׃ וַיְצַו אֹתָם לֵאמֹר כֹּה תֹאמְרוּן לַאדֹנִי לְעֵשָׂו
כֹּה אָמַר עַבְדְּךָ יַעֲקֹב עִם־לָבָן גַּרְתִּי וָאֵחַר עַד־עָתָּה׃
6 וַיְהִי־לִי שׁוֹר וַחֲמוֹר צֹאן וְעֶבֶד וְשִׁפְחָה וָאֶשְׁלְחָה לְהַגִּיד
7 לַאדֹנִי לִמְצֹא־חֵן בְּעֵינֶיךָ׃ וַיָּשֻׁבוּ הַמַּלְאָכִים אֶל־יַעֲקֹב
לֵאמֹר בָּאנוּ אֶל־אָחִיךָ אֶל־עֵשָׂו וְגַם הֹלֵךְ לִקְרָאתְךָ וְאַרְבַּע־
8 מֵאוֹת אִישׁ עִמּוֹ׃ וַיִּירָא יַעֲקֹב מְאֹד וַיֵּצֶר לוֹ וַיַּחַץ אֶת־
הָעָם אֲשֶׁר־אִתּוֹ וְאֶת־הַצֹּאן וְאֶת־הַבָּקָר וְהַגְּמַלִּים לִשְׁנֵי
9 מַחֲנוֹת׃ וַיֹּאמֶר אִם־יָבוֹא עֵשָׂו אֶל־הַמַּחֲנֶה הָאַחַת וְהִכָּהוּ
י וְהָיָה הַמַּחֲנֶה הַנִּשְׁאָר לִפְלֵיטָה׃ וַיֹּאמֶר יַעֲקֹב אֱלֹהֵי
אָבִי אַבְרָהָם וֵאלֹהֵי אָבִי יִצְחָק יְהוָה הָאֹמֵר אֵלַי שׁוּב
11 לְאַרְצְךָ וּלְמוֹלַדְתְּךָ וְאֵיטִיבָה עִמָּךְ׃ קָטֹנְתִּי מִכֹּל הַחֲסָדִים

VIII. VAYYISHLACH

(CHAPTERS XXXII, 4–XXXVI)

CHAPTERS XXXII, 4–XXXIII, 17. THE FEAR OF ESAU

4. As Jacob approaches his home land, the fear of his brother revives in him. Twenty years had passed, but Esau might still wreak vengeance on Jacob and his dependants. Jacob well knew that some men nurse their anger, so that it should not die down or out.

field. i.e. territory.

5. Jacob frames his message in the most humble and conciliatory words.

I have sojourned. Rashi takes these words to mean: 'I have not become a prince but am only a "sojourner"; therefore thou hast no cause to hate me because of my father's blessing, in which I was promised to be made greater than thou. It has not been fulfilled.' Since the letters of the Hebrew word גרתי 'I have sojourned' correspond to the numerals denoting 'six hundred and thirteen', the number of Pentateuchal commandments (תרי"ג מצוות), the Midrash comments: 'With Laban I sojourned, but the 613 Commandments I observed'—an exhortation to Jacob's descendants to be faithful to the Torah even when living in a non-Jewish environment.

6. *to tell my lord.* That I am on my way home, and am desirous of finding 'favour in thy sight'.

7. *to thy brother Esau.* lit. 'to thy brother, to Esau'; which the Rabbis explain to mean, 'We came to him whom thou hast called "brother", but we found that we had come to "Esau", to one who still hates thee.'

four hundred men. A considerable following; which naturally alarmed Jacob as to his brother's intentions.

8. *greatly afraid.* Lest he and his be slain.

and was distressed. Even greater anguish possessed him at the thought that he might be compelled *to slay* (Midrash). He does not, however, give way to despair, but takes all possible steps to safeguard himself and those with him. He adopted three methods for overcoming the evil intentions of his brother. His first defence was prayer to God for His protection (*v.* 10–13); the second was to turn Esau's hate into goodwill by gifts (*v.* 14–22); his third and last resource was to stand his ground and fight (XXXIII, 1–3).

10. Jacob's prayer, showing his humility and gratitude, is proof that misfortune had developed the nobler impulses of his heart. Twenty years of fixed principle, steadfast purpose, and of resolute sacrifice of present for future, purify and ennoble. It proves that even from the first, though he may appear self-centred, Jacob is yet delicately sensitive to spiritual realities and capable of genuine reformation. And the truly penitent—declare the Rabbis—come nearer unto God than even those who have never stumbled or fallen into sin.

who saidst unto me. See XXXI, 3.

Thou hast shown unto Thy servant; for with my staff I passed over this Jordan; and now I am become two camps. 12. Deliver me, I pray Thee, from the hand of my brother, from the hand of Esau; for I fear him, lest he come and smite me, the mother with the children. 13. And Thou saidst: I will surely do thee good, and make thy seed as the sand of the sea, which cannot be numbered for multitude.'* ii. 14. And he lodged there that night; and took of that which he had with him a present for Esau his brother: 15. two hundred she-goats and twenty he-goats, two hundred ewes and twenty rams, 16. thirty milch camels and their colts, forty kine and ten bulls, twenty she-asses and ten foals. 17. And he delivered them into the hand of his servants, every drove by itself; and said unto his servants: 'Pass over before me, and put a space betwixt drove and drove.' 18. And he commanded the foremost, saying: 'When Esau my brother meeteth thee, and asketh thee, saying: Whose art thou? and whither goest thou? and whose are these before thee? 19. then thou shalt say: They are thy servant Jacob's; it is a present sent unto my lord, even unto Esau; and, behold, he also is behind us.' 20. And he commanded also the second, and the third, and all that followed the droves, saying: 'In this manner shall ye speak unto Esau, when ye find him; 21. and ye shall say: Moreover, behold, thy servant Jacob is behind us.' For he said: 'I will appease him with the present that goeth before me, and afterward I will see his face; peradventure he will accept me.' 22. So the present passed over before him; and he himself lodged that night in the

וּמִכָּל־הָאֱמֶת אֲשֶׁר עָשִׂיתָ אֶת־עַבְדֶּךָ כִּי בְמַקְלִי עָבַרְתִּי
12 אֶת־הַיַּרְדֵּן הַזֶּה וְעַתָּה הָיִיתִי לִשְׁנֵי מַחֲנוֹת׃ הַצִּילֵנִי נָא
מִיַּד אָחִי מִיַּד עֵשָׂו כִּי־יָרֵא אָנֹכִי אֹתוֹ פֶּן־יָבוֹא וְהִכַּנִי אֵם
13 עַל־בָּנִים׃ וְאַתָּה אָמַרְתָּ הֵיטֵב אֵיטִיב עִמָּךְ וְשַׂמְתִּי אֶת־
שני
14 זַרְעֲךָ כְּחוֹל הַיָּם אֲשֶׁר לֹא־יִסָּפֵר מֵרֹב׃ *וַיָּלֶן שָׁם בַּלַּיְלָה
טו הַהוּא וַיִּקַּח מִן־הַבָּא בְיָדוֹ מִנְחָה לְעֵשָׂו אָחִיו׃ עִזִּים
מָאתַיִם וּתְיָשִׁים עֶשְׂרִים רְחֵלִים מָאתַיִם וְאֵילִים עֶשְׂרִים׃
16 גְּמַלִּים מֵינִיקוֹת וּבְנֵיהֶם שְׁלֹשִׁים פָּרוֹת אַרְבָּעִים וּפָרִים
17 עֲשָׂרָה אֲתֹנֹת עֶשְׂרִים וַעְיָרִם עֲשָׂרָה׃ וַיִּתֵּן בְּיַד־עֲבָדָיו
עֵדֶר עֵדֶר לְבַדּוֹ וַיֹּאמֶר אֶל־עֲבָדָיו עִבְרוּ לְפָנַי וְרֶוַח
18 תָּשִׂימוּ בֵּין עֵדֶר וּבֵין עֵדֶר׃ וַיְצַו אֶת־הָרִאשׁוֹן לֵאמֹר כִּי
יִפְגָּשְׁךָ עֵשָׂו אָחִי וּשְׁאֵלְךָ לֵאמֹר לְמִי־אַתָּה וְאָנָה תֵלֵךְ
19 וּלְמִי אֵלֶּה לְפָנֶיךָ׃ וְאָמַרְתָּ לְעַבְדְּךָ לְיַעֲקֹב מִנְחָה הִוא
כ שְׁלוּחָה לַאדֹנִי לְעֵשָׂו וְהִנֵּה גַם־הוּא אַחֲרֵינוּ׃ וַיְצַו גַּם
אֶת־הַשֵּׁנִי גַּם אֶת־הַשְּׁלִישִׁי גַּם אֶת־כָּל־הַהֹלְכִים אַחֲרֵי
הָעֲדָרִים לֵאמֹר כַּדָּבָר הַזֶּה תְּדַבְּרוּן אֶל־עֵשָׂו בְּמֹצַאֲכֶם
21 אֹתוֹ׃ וַאֲמַרְתֶּם גַּם הִנֵּה עַבְדְּךָ יַעֲקֹב אַחֲרֵינוּ כִּי־אָמַר
אֲכַפְּרָה פָנָיו בַּמִּנְחָה הַהֹלֶכֶת לְפָנָי וְאַחֲרֵי־כֵן אֶרְאֶה
22 פָנָיו אוּלַי יִשָּׂא פָנָי׃ וַתַּעֲבֹר הַמִּנְחָה עַל־פָּנָיו וְהוּא לָן

v. 21. קמץ בז"ק

11. *truth. i.e.* faithfulness.

staff. Such as a lonely wanderer would use on his journey.

12. *the mother with the children.* lit. 'the mother *upon* the children'—a vivid picture of the mother placing herself in front of her children to shield them, so that she is slain *upon* them. The phrase is apparently a proverbial expression to describe a pitiless massacre; like a pogrom in our own times, not sparing the weak and helpless.

13. *as the sand of the sea.* Jacob was thinking of the promise to his forefathers (XXII, 17).

15–21. Jacob hopes by the succession of gifts to pacify Esau's wrath against him.

21. *appease him.* lit. 'cover his face'; so that he no longer sees any cause for being angry with me; cf. the phrase used in XX, 16.

accept me. lit. 'lift up my face', *i.e.* receive me favourably.

23–33. Jacob becomes Israel

This passage represents the crisis in Jacob's spiritual history. It records his meeting with a Heavenly Being, the change of his name to Israel, the blessing of the Being that wrestled with him, and the consequent transformation of his character. Maimonides is of opinion that the whole incident was a 'prophetic vision'; and other commentators likewise have in all ages regarded the contest as symbolic, the outward manifestation of the struggle within the Patriarch, as in every mortal, between his baser passions and his nobler ideals. In the dead of night he had sent his wives and sons and all that he had across the river. Jacob was left alone—with God. There, in the darkness, given over to anxious fears, God's camp. ¶ 23. And he rose up that night, and took his two wives, and his two handmaids, and his eleven children, and passed over the ford of the Jabbok. 24. And he took them, and sent them over the stream, and sent over that which he had. 25. And Jacob was left alone; and there wrestled a man with him until the breaking of the day. 26. And when he saw that he prevailed not against him, he touched the hollow of his thigh; and the hollow of Jacob's thigh was strained, as he wrestled with him. 27. And he said: 'Let me go, for the day breaketh.' And he said: 'I will not let thee go, except thou bless me.' 28. And he said unto him: 'What is thy name?' And he said: 'Jacob.' 29. And he said: 'Thy name shall be called no more Jacob, but [1]Israel; for thou hast striven with God and with men, and hast prevailed.' 30. And Jacob asked him, and said: 'Tell me, I pray thee, thy name.' And he said: 'Wherefore is it that thou dost ask after my name?' And he blessed him there. * iii. 31. And Jacob called the name of the place [2]Peniel: 'for I have seen God face to face, and my life is preserved.' 32. And the sun rose upon him as he passed over [3]Peniel, and he limped upon his thigh. 33. Therefore the children of Israel eat not the sinew of the thigh-vein which is

23 בַּלַּיְלָה־הַהוּא בַּמַּחֲנֶה׃ וַיָּקָם ׀ בַּלַּיְלָה הוּא וַיִּקַּח אֶת־
שְׁתֵּי נָשָׁיו וְאֶת־שְׁתֵּי שִׁפְחֹתָיו וְאֶת־אַחַד עָשָׂר יְלָדָיו
24 וַיַּעֲבֹר אֵת מַעֲבַר יַבֹּק׃ וַיִּקָּחֵם וַיַּעֲבִרֵם אֶת־הַנָּחַל וַיַּעֲבֵר
כה אֶת־אֲשֶׁר־לוֹ׃ וַיִּוָּתֵר יַעֲקֹב לְבַדּוֹ וַיֵּאָבֵק אִישׁ עִמּוֹ עַד
26 עֲלוֹת הַשָּׁחַר׃ וַיַּרְא כִּי לֹא יָכֹל לוֹ וַיִּגַּע בְּכַף־יְרֵכוֹ וַתֵּקַע
27 כַּף־יֶרֶךְ יַעֲקֹב בְּהֵאָבְקוֹ עִמּוֹ׃ וַיֹּאמֶר שַׁלְּחֵנִי כִּי עָלָה
28 הַשָּׁחַר וַיֹּאמֶר לֹא אֲשַׁלֵּחֲךָ כִּי אִם־בֵּרַכְתָּנִי׃ וַיֹּאמֶר אֵלָיו
29 מַה־שְּׁמֶךָ וַיֹּאמֶר יַעֲקֹב׃ וַיֹּאמֶר לֹא יַעֲקֹב יֵאָמֵר עוֹד
שִׁמְךָ כִּי אִם־יִשְׂרָאֵל כִּי־שָׂרִיתָ עִם־אֱלֹהִים וְעִם־אֲנָשִׁים
ל וַתּוּכָל׃ וַיִּשְׁאַל יַעֲקֹב וַיֹּאמֶר הַגִּידָה־נָּא שְׁמֶךָ וַיֹּאמֶר
שלישי
31 לָמָּה זֶּה תִּשְׁאַל לִשְׁמִי וַיְבָרֶךְ אֹתוֹ שָׁם׃ * וַיִּקְרָא יַעֲקֹב
שֵׁם הַמָּקוֹם פְּנִיאֵל כִּי־רָאִיתִי אֱלֹהִים פָּנִים אֶל־פָּנִים
32 וַתִּנָּצֵל נַפְשִׁי׃ וַיִּזְרַח־לוֹ הַשֶּׁמֶשׁ כַּאֲשֶׁר עָבַר אֶת־פְּנוּאֵל
33 וְהוּא צֹלֵעַ עַל־יְרֵכוֹ׃ עַל־כֵּן לֹא יֹאכְלוּ בְנֵי־יִשְׂרָאֵל אֶת־

[1] That is, *He who striveth with God.* [2] That is, *The face of God.* [3] Heb. *Penuel.*

סבירין ההוא v. 23.

Messenger was wrestling with him who had so often wrestled with men and had won by sheer energy, persistency and superior wit. In the words of the Prophet chosen as the Haftorah for this Sedrah, 'He (Jacob) had power over the angel, and prevailed: he (Jacob) wept, and made supplication unto him.' That supplication for mercy, forgiveness and Divine protection is heard. Jacob the Supplanter, becomes Israel, Prince of God. 'This mysterious encounter of the Patriarch has become the universal human allegory of the struggles and wrestlings on the eve of some dreadful crisis, in the solitude and darkness of some overhanging trial' (Stanley).

23. *Jabbok.* A tributary of the Jordan, halfway between the Dead Sea and the Sea of Galilee.

26. *touched the hollow of his thigh.* This is usually interpreted as a final effort of the assailant to overcome Jacob.

27. The opponent's anxiety to escape before 'the day breaketh' suggested to the Patriarch's mind that he was a supernatural Being. Jacob, therefore, demanded a blessing as the price of release.

28. *what is thy name?* A rhetorical question, not seeking information. As explained on XVII, 5, a name in Scripture is more than a label; it possesses significance.

29. *no more Jacob.* That is, 'the Supplanter,' prevailing over opponents by deceit.

Israel. The name is clearly a title of victory; probably 'a champion of God'. The children of the Patriarch are *Israelites,* Champions of God, Contenders for the Divine, conquering by strength from Above.

striven. The Septuagint and Vulgate translate, 'Thou didst prevail with God, and thou shalt prevail against men.'

with God. Cf. Hosea XII, 4. We have here another instance of 'God' interchanging with 'angel of God', as in XVI, 7, XXXI, 11.

with men. Laban and Esau.

30. As in Judg. XIII, 17 f, the angel refuses to disclose his name, because it was something mysterious.

31. *I have seen God face to face.* The Targum translates, 'I have seen angels of God face to face.'

my life is preserved. Jacob had seen an angel, a Divine Being, and yet lives; cf. Exod. XXXIII, 20.

32. *limped.* The struggle left its mark, but Jacob issued from the contest victor, redeemed and transformed by the contest. So it has ever been with the People called by his name.

33. *thigh-vein.* The sciatic nerve. This, together with other arteries and tendons, must be removed from the slaughtered animal, before upon the hollow of the thigh, unto this day; because he touched the hollow of Jacob's thigh, even in the sinew of the thigh-vein.

גִּיד הַנָּשֶׁה אֲשֶׁר עַל־כַּף הַיָּרֵךְ עַד הַיּוֹם הַזֶּה כִּי נָגַע בְּכַף־
יֶרֶךְ יַעֲקֹב בְּגִיד הַנָּשֶׁה׃

33

CHAPTER XXXIII

1. And Jacob lifted up his eyes, and looked, and, behold, Esau came, and with him four hundred men. And he divided the children unto Leah, and unto Rachel, and unto the two handmaids. 2. And he put the handmaids and their children foremost, and Leah and her children after, and Rachel and Joseph hindermost. 3. And he himself passed over before them, and bowed himself to the ground seven times, until he came near to his brother. 4. And Esau ran to meet him, and embraced him, and fell on his neck, and kissed him; and they wept. 5. And he lifted up his eyes, and saw the women and the children; and said: 'Who are these with thee?' And he said: 'The children whom God hath graciously given thy servant.'* iv. 6. Then the handmaids came near, they and their children, and they bowed down. 7. And Leah also and her children came near, and bowed down; and after came Joseph near and Rachel, and they bowed down. 8. And he said: 'What meanest thou by all this camp which I met?' And he said: 'To find favour in the sight of my lord.' 9. And Esau said: 'I have enough; my brother, let that which thou hast be thine.' 10. And Jacob said: 'Nay, I pray thee, if now I have found favour in

לג CAP. XXXIII. לג

א וַיִּשָּׂא יַעֲקֹב עֵינָיו וַיַּרְא וְהִנֵּה עֵשָׂו בָּא וְעִמּוֹ אַרְבַּע מֵאוֹת
אִישׁ וַיַּחַץ אֶת־הַיְלָדִים עַל־לֵאָה וְעַל־רָחֵל וְעַל שְׁתֵּי
2 הַשְּׁפָחוֹת׃ וַיָּשֶׂם אֶת־הַשְּׁפָחוֹת וְאֶת־יַלְדֵיהֶן רִאשֹׁנָה וְאֶת־
לֵאָה וִילָדֶיהָ אַחֲרֹנִים וְאֶת־רָחֵל וְאֶת־יוֹסֵף אַחֲרֹנִים׃
3 וְהוּא עָבַר לִפְנֵיהֶם וַיִּשְׁתַּחוּ אַרְצָה שֶׁבַע פְּעָמִים עַד־
4 גִּשְׁתּוֹ עַד־אָחִיו׃ וַיָּרָץ עֵשָׂו לִקְרָאתוֹ וַיְחַבְּקֵהוּ וַיִּפֹּל עַל־
ה צַוָּארָו וַיִּשָּׁקֵהוּ וַיִּבְכּוּ׃ וַיִּשָּׂא אֶת־עֵינָיו וַיַּרְא אֶת־הַנָּשִׁים
וְאֶת־הַיְלָדִים וַיֹּאמֶר מִי־אֵלֶּה לָּךְ וַיֹּאמַר הַיְלָדִים אֲשֶׁר־
רביעי
6 חָנַן אֱלֹהִים אֶת־עַבְדֶּךָ׃ וַתִּגַּשְׁןָ הַשְּׁפָחוֹת הֵנָּה וְיַלְדֵיהֶן
7 וַתִּשְׁתַּחֲוֶיןָ׃ וַתִּגַּשׁ גַּם־לֵאָה וִילָדֶיהָ וַיִּשְׁתַּחֲווּ וְאַחַר נִגַּשׁ
8 יוֹסֵף וְרָחֵל וַיִּשְׁתַּחֲווּ׃ וַיֹּאמֶר מִי לְךָ כָּל־הַמַּחֲנֶה הַזֶּה
9 אֲשֶׁר פָּגָשְׁתִּי וַיֹּאמֶר לִמְצֹא־חֵן בְּעֵינֵי אֲדֹנִי׃ וַיֹּאמֶר עֵשָׂו
י יֶשׁ־לִי רָב אָחִי יְהִי לְךָ אֲשֶׁר־לָךְ׃ וַיֹּאמֶר יַעֲקֹב אַל־נָא

לג׳ v. 4. צואריו ק׳ ibid. נקוד על וישקהו

that portion of the animal can be ritually prepared for Jewish consumption. This precept is a constant reminder of the Divine Providence to Israel as exemplified in the experience of the Patriarch.

CHAPTER XXXIII. THE MEETING OF JACOB AND ESAU

1. *came.* Or, 'was coming.'

2. *hindermost.* Placing those he loved best in as secure a position as possible.

3. *passed over before them.* To conciliate his brother if possible, or to bear the brunt of the attack, and thus help his wives and children to escape.

seven times. In ancient inscriptions, the phrase, 'at the feet of my lord, seven times and seven times I fall,' frequently occurs.

4. *kissed him.* Esau proved both good-natured and forgiving. He fell on Jacob's neck, kissed Jacob, and they wept with the strong emotion of Orientals. Yet, the word for 'and kissed him' וישקהו is marked in the Heb. text with dots on every letter. The Rabbis doubted whether the kiss of Esau was genuine or not. Esau's conduct is certainly strange. If his intentions were friendly from the first, why was he accompanied by so considerable a force as four hundred armed men? And if he had started out with a resolve to injure his brother, how account for the warm greeting immediately on coming face to face with him? This was in answer to Jacob's prayer, the Rabbis say. God had turned Esau's hate to love. Be that as it may, we have here another instance of the splendid impartiality of Scripture. The ancestor of Israel's hereditary enemy, the Edomites, is presented as chivalrous and dignified, full of magnanimity and generosity.

8. *camp. i.e.* the droves sent ahead as a gift to Esau. See XXXII, 17.

9. *I have enough.* lit. 'I have much.' Esau's reluctance to accept the gift was probably only another illustration of Oriental courtesy; see Chap. XXIII.

10. *seen thy face.* The phrase, 'to see the face,' expresses the idea of being favourably received. Jacob accordingly meant, 'I have been graciously pardoned by you, as I would have received forgiveness from God, had I appeared before Him in the humble spirit and with the tokens of contrition wherewith I approach you. Regard, then, my gift as a *minchah*, an offering.'

אִם־נָא מָצָאתִי חֵן בְּעֵינֶיךָ וְלָקַחְתָּ מִנְחָתִי מִיָּדִי כִּי עַל־
11 כֵּן רָאִיתִי פָנֶיךָ כִּרְאֹת פְּנֵי אֱלֹהִים וַתִּרְצֵנִי׃ קַח־נָא אֶת־
בִּרְכָתִי אֲשֶׁר הֻבָאת לָךְ כִּי־חַנַּנִי אֱלֹהִים וְכִי יֶשׁ־לִי־כֹל
12 וַיִּפְצַר־בּוֹ וַיִּקָּח׃ וַיֹּאמֶר נִסְעָה וְנֵלֵכָה וְאֵלְכָה לְנֶגְדֶּךָ׃
13 וַיֹּאמֶר אֵלָיו אֲדֹנִי יֹדֵעַ כִּי־הַיְלָדִים רַכִּים וְהַצֹּאן וְהַבָּקָר
14 עָלוֹת עָלָי וּדְפָקוּם יוֹם אֶחָד וָמֵתוּ כָּל־הַצֹּאן׃ יַעֲבָר־נָא
אֲדֹנִי לִפְנֵי עַבְדּוֹ וַאֲנִי אֶתְנַהֲלָה לְאִטִּי לְרֶגֶל הַמְּלָאכָה
אֲשֶׁר־לְפָנַי וּלְרֶגֶל הַיְלָדִים עַד אֲשֶׁר־אָבֹא אֶל־אֲדֹנִי
טו שֵׂעִירָה׃ וַיֹּאמֶר עֵשָׂו אַצִּיגָה־נָּא עִמְּךָ מִן־הָעָם אֲשֶׁר אִתִּי
16 וַיֹּאמֶר לָמָּה זֶּה אֶמְצָא־חֵן בְּעֵינֵי אֲדֹנִי׃ וַיָּשָׁב בַּיּוֹם הַהוּא
17 עֵשָׂו לְדַרְכּוֹ שֵׂעִירָה׃ וְיַעֲקֹב נָסַע סֻכֹּתָה וַיִּבֶן לוֹ בָּיִת
וּלְמִקְנֵהוּ עָשָׂה סֻכֹּת עַל־כֵּן קָרָא שֵׁם־הַמָּקוֹם סֻכּוֹת׃ ס
18 וַיָּבֹא יַעֲקֹב שָׁלֵם עִיר שְׁכֶם אֲשֶׁר בְּאֶרֶץ כְּנַעַן בְּבֹאוֹ

thy sight, then receive my present at my hand; forasmuch as I have seen thy face, as one seeth the face of God, and thou wast pleased with me. 11. Take, I pray thee, my gift that is brought to thee; because God hath dealt graciously with me, and because I have enough.' And he urged him, and he took it. 12. And he said: 'Let us take our journey, and let us go, and I will go before thee.' 13. And he said unto him: 'My lord knoweth that the children are tender, and that the flocks and herds giving suck are a care to me; and if they overdrive them one day, all the flocks will die. 14. Let my lord, I pray thee, pass over before his servant; and I will journey on gently, according to the pace of the cattle that are before me and according to the pace of the children, until I come unto my lord unto Seir.' 15. And Esau said: 'Let me now leave with thee some of the folk that are with me.' And he said: 'What needeth it? let me find favour in the sight of my lord.' 16. So Esau returned that day on his way unto Seir. 17. And Jacob journeyed to Succoth, and built him a house, and made booths for his cattle. Therefore the name of the place is called [1]Succoth. ¶ 18. And Jacob came in peace

[1] That is, *Booths*.

11. *my gift.* lit. 'my blessing', the gift being the outward manifestation of the goodwill in the giver's heart.

I have enough. Esau has 'much'; therefore, he is quite willing to have 'more'. Jacob has 'all' now that the danger of being slain by a brother, *or of slaying a brother*, is over; see on XXXII, 8.

12. *I will go before thee.* Esau offers him his armed men.

13. Jacob, knowing the unstable character of Esau, is anxious that they should part company as quickly as possible.

tender. i.e. unequal to the fatigues of travel.

14. *the cattle.* lit. 'the work'; cf. the use of the word in Gen. II, 2, where it refers to, among other things, the creatures that God had made. The Heb. word for 'work' might here also mean 'property', as in Exod. XXII, 7, 10.

unto Seir. There is no record that Jacob went to Seir to see his brother. But, add the Rabbis, Jacob will yet visit Esau in the day of the Messiah when the reconciliation between Israel and Edom will be complete.

15. Jacob prudently declines the offer.

17. *Succoth.* The exact site is unknown. It was part of the territory of the tribe of Gad, West of the Jordan (Josh. XIII, 27). Jacob must have stayed some years in Succoth.

18–20. AT SHECHEM

18. *in peace. i.e.* peaceably, with peaceable intentions. Since the word also has the meaning 'complete, whole', we have various Midrashic interpretations; such as, *recovered* from his lameness; and *perfect* in his knowledge of Torah, which he had not forgotten during his stay with Laban.

Shechem. See on XII, 6.

before the city. i.e. to the east of the city; cf. on XVI, 12. About a mile from the city there is still shown Jacob's well.

19. *he bought.* The Patriarchs display their independent spirit by establishing an inalienable right to their land by means of purchase. See Chap. XXIII.

children of Hamor. People of the clan of Hamor.

Shechem's father. The founder, or chieftain, of the city of Shechem.

20. *altar.* In gratitude to God who had permitted him to return in safety to the land of his fathers.

El-elohe-Israel. A profession of faith in the one true God made at the moment when Jacob comes to dwell among the heathen Canaanites (Ryle).

to the city of Shechem, which is in the land of Canaan, when he came from Paddan-aram; and encamped before the city. 19. And he bought the parcel of ground, where he had spread his tent, at the hand of the children of Hamor, Shechem's father, for a hundred pieces of money. 20. And he erected there an altar, and called it [1]El-elohe-Israel.* v.

34

Chapter XXXIV

1. And Dinah the daughter of Leah, whom she had borne unto Jacob, went out to see the daughters of the land. 2. And Shechem the son of Hamor the Hivite, the prince of the land, saw her; and he took her, and lay with her, and humbled her. 3. And his soul did cleave unto Dinah the daughter of Jacob, and he loved the damsel, and spoke comfortingly unto the damsel. 4. And Shechem spoke unto his father Hamor, saying: 'Get me this damsel to wife.' 5. Now Jacob heard that he had defiled Dinah his daughter; and his sons were with his cattle in the field; and Jacob held his peace until they came. 6. And Hamor the father of Shechem went out unto Jacob to speak with him. 7. And the sons of Jacob came in from the field when they heard it; and the men were grieved, and they were very wroth, because he had wrought a vile deed in Israel in lying with Jacob's daughter; which thing ought not to be done. 8. And Hamor spoke with them, saying: 'The soul of my son Shechem longeth for your daughter. I pray you give her unto him to wife. 9. And make ye marriages with us; give your daughters unto us, and take our daughters unto you. 10. And ye shall dwell with us; and the land shall be before you; dwell and trade ye therein, and get you

[1] That is, *God, the God of Israel.*

19 מפדן ארם ויחן את־פני העיר: ויקן את־חלקת השדה
אשר נטה־שם אהלו מיד בני־חמור אבי שכם במאה
חמישי
כ קשיטה: ויצב־שם מזבח ויקרא־לו אל אלהי ישראל:* ס

לד CAP. XXXIV. לד

א ותצא דינה בת־לאה אשר ילדה ליעקב לראות בבנות
2 הארץ: וירא אתה שכם בן־חמור החוי נשיא הארץ
3 ויקח אתה וישכב אתה ויענה: ותדבק נפשו בדינה
4 בת־יעקב ויאהב את־הנער וידבר על־לב הנער: ויאמר
שכם אל־חמור אביו לאמר קח־לי את־הילדה הזאת
ה לאשה: ויעקב שמע כי טמא את־דינה בתו ובניו היו
6 את־מקנהו בשדה והחרש יעקב עד־באם: ויצא חמור
7 אבי־שכם אל־יעקב לדבר אתו: ובני יעקב באו מן־
השדה כשמעם ויתעצבו האנשים ויחר להם מאד כי
נבלה עשה בישראל לשכב את־בת־יעקב וכן לא יעשה:
8 וידבר חמור אתם לאמר שכם בני חשקה נפשו בבתכם
9 תנו נא אתה לו לאשה: והתחתנו אתנו בנתיכם תתנו־
י לנו ואת־בנתינו תקחו לכם: ואתנו תשבו והארץ תהיה

לד' v. 3. הנערה ק' הנערה קרי

Chapter XXXIV. Dinah

This chapter is an exception to the series of peaceful scenes from Patriarchal life and character—a tale of dishonour, wild revenge, and indiscriminate slaughter.

1. *to see.* 'and be seen,' is added in the Samaritan text. The Heb. idiom 'to see, to look upon' means 'to make friendship with'. It was wrong of Jacob to suffer his daughter alone and unprotected to visit the daughters of the land (Adam Clarke).

2. *humbled. i.e.* dishonoured; the Heb. implies by force.

3. *comfortingly.* lit. 'spoke to the heart' of the damsel; cf. Isaiah XL, 2. He tried to console her by his words of love, and his declared wish to make her his wife.

4. *get me this damsel.* It was the parent's duty to secure a wife for the son; cf. XXI, 21.

7. *vile deed.* Or, 'folly' (RV). The Heb. word translated by 'folly' means, senseless wickedness, total insensibility to moral distinctions.

in Israel. Since the word means 'the people of Israel', it is strictly an anachronism because the nation was not yet in existence. The latter part of this sentence must therefore be regarded not as spoken by Jacob's sons, but as the reflection of Scripture on the incident, wherein it points out that in the homes of the Patriarchs high conceptions of morality were entertained, and the defilement of a daughter was looked upon as an outrage against family honour and morality that demanded stern retribution.

10. The cordiality of Hamor's invitation is to be contrasted with what he told his townsmen in *v.* 23. To induce them to adopt his suggestion, he promises that it would be profitable to them, and they would gradually absorb the rich possessions of Jacob's household.

possessions therein.' 11. And Shechem said unto her father and unto her brethren: 'Let me find favour in your eyes, and what ye shall say unto me I will give. 12. Ask me never so much dowry and gift, and I will give according as ye shall say unto me; but give me the damsel to wife.' 13. And the sons of Jacob answered Shechem and Hamor his father with guile, and spoke, because he had defiled Dinah, their sister, 14. and said unto them: 'We cannot do this thing, to give our sister to one that is uncircumcised; for that were a reproach unto us. 15. Only on this condition will we consent unto you: if ye will be as we are, that every male of you be circumcised; 16. then will we give our daughters unto you, and we will take your daughters to us, and we will dwell with you, and we will become one people. 17. But if ye will not hearken unto us, to be circumcised; then will we take our daughter, and we will be gone.' 18. And their words pleased Hamor, and Shechem Hamor's son. 19. And the young man deferred not to do the thing, because he had delight in Jacob's daughter. And he was honoured above all the house of his father. 20. And Hamor and Shechem his son came unto the gate of their city, and spoke with the men of their city, saying: 21. 'These men are peaceable with us; therefore let them dwell in the land, and trade therein; for, behold, the land is large enough for them; let us take their daughters to us for wives, and let us give them our daughters. 22. Only on this condition will the men consent unto us to dwell with us, to become one people, if every male among us be circumcised, as they are circumcised. 23. Shall not their cattle and their substance and all their beasts be ours? only let us consent unto them, and they will dwell with us.' 24. And unto Hamor and unto Shechem his son hearkened all that went out of the gate of his city; and every male was circumcised, all that went out of the gate

11 לפניכם שבו וסחרוה והאחזו בה: ויאמר שכם אל־
אביה ואל־אחיה אמצא־חן בעיניכם ואשר תאמרו אלי
12 אתן: הרבו עלי מאד מהר ומתן ואתנה כאשר תאמרו
13 אלי ותנו־לי את־הנער לאשה: ויענו בני־יעקב את־שכם
ואת־חמור אביו במרמה וידברו אשר טמא את דינה
14 אחתם: ויאמרו אליהם לא נוכל לעשות הדבר הזה
לתת את־אחתנו לאיש אשר־לו ערלה כי־חרפה הוא
טו לנו: אך־בזאת נאות לכם אם תהיו כמנו להמל לכם
16 כל־זכר: ונתנו את־בנתינו לכם ואת־בנתיכם נקח־לנו
17 וישבנו אתכם והיינו לעם אחד: ואם־לא תשמעו אלינו
18 להמול ולקחנו את־בתנו והלכנו: וייטבו דבריהם בעיני
19 חמור ובעיני שכם בן־חמור: ולא־אחר הנער לעשות
הדבר כי־חפץ בבת־יעקב והוא נכבד מכל בית אביו:
כ ויבא חמור ושכם בנו אל־שער עירם וידברו אל־אנשי
21 עירם לאמר: האנשים האלה שלמים הם אתנו וישבו
בארץ ויסחרו אתה והארץ הנה רחבת־ידים לפניהם
22 את־בנתם נקח־לנו לנשים ואת־בנתינו נתן להם: אך־
בזאת יאתו לנו האנשים לשבת אתנו להיות לעם אחד
23 בהמול לנו כל־זכר כאשר הם נמלים: מקנהם וקנינם
וכל־בהמתם הלוא לנו הם אך נאותה להם וישבו
24 אתנו: וישמעו אל־חמור ואל־שכם בנו כל־יצאי שער

v. 12. הנערה ק'

12. *dowry*. The purchase price, *mohar*, given to the father and brothers of the bride; see on XXIV, 53, XXIX, 18.

gift. Personal presents to the bride.

13. *with guile*. Knowing that they were outnumbered by the citizens of Shechem, Jacob's sons resort to devious methods to carry out their determination to avenge their sister's dishonour. Their proposal would, if adopted, render the male population weak and helpless for a time; and this would give them the opportunity of making a successful attack. But why should all the men of the city suffer for the misdeed of one of their number? The sons of Jacob certainly acted in a treacherous and godless manner. Jacob did not forgive them to his dying day; see XLIX, 7.

14. *reproach*. Cf. Josh. v, 9.

20. *unto the gate*. The usual place of assembly. See on XIX, 1.

23. *be ours*. This argument proves Hamor's disingenuousness.

24. *all that went out of the gate*. Cf. on XXIII, 10. Probably the able-bodied men, to the exclusion of the old men and boys who would not be affected by the proposal of inter-marriage.

of his city. 25. And it came to pass on the third day, when they were in pain, that two of the sons of Jacob, Simeon and Levi, Dinah's brethren, took each man his sword, and came upon the city unawares, and slew all the males. 26. And they slew Hamor and Shechem his son with the edge of the sword, and took Dinah out of Shechem's house, and went forth. 27. The sons of Jacob came upon the slain, and spoiled the city, because they had defiled their sister. 28. They took their flocks and their herds and their asses, and that which was in the city and that which was in the field; 29. and all their wealth, and all their little ones and their wives, took they captive and spoiled, even all that was in the house. 30. And Jacob said to Simeon and Levi: 'Ye have troubled me, to make me odious unto the inhabitants of the land, even unto the Canaanites and the Perizzites; and, I being few in number, they will gather themselves together against me and smite me; and I shall be destroyed, I and my house.' 31. And they said: 'Should one deal with our sister as with a harlot?'

כה עירו וימלו כל־זכר כל־יצאי שער עירו: ויהי ביום
השלישי בהיותם כאבים ויקחו שני־בני־יעקב שמעון
ולוי אחי דינה איש חרבו ויבאו על־העיר בטח ויהרגו
26 כל־זכר: ואת־חמור ואת־שכם בנו הרגו לפי־חרב ויקחו
27 את־דינה מבית שכם ויצאו: בני יעקב באו על־החללים
28 ויבזו העיר אשר טמאו אחותם: את־צאנם ואת־בקרם
ואת־חמריהם ואת אשר־בעיר ואת־אשר בשדה לקחו:
29 ואת־כל־חילם ואת־כל־טפם ואת־נשיהם שבו ויבזו ואת
ל כל־אשר בבית: ויאמר יעקב אל־שמעון ואל־לוי עכרתם
אתי להבאישני בישב הארץ בכנעני ובפרזי ואני מתי
31 מספר ונאספו עלי והכוני ונשמדתי אני וביתי: ויאמרו
הכזונה יעשה את־אחותנו: פ

35

CHAPTER XXXV

CAP. XXXV. לה

לה

1. And God said unto Jacob: 'Arise, go up to Beth-el, and dwell there; and make there an altar unto God, who appeared unto thee when thou didst flee from the face of Esau thy brother.' 2. Then Jacob said unto his household, and to all that were with him: 'Put away the strange gods that are among you, and purify yourselves, and change your garments; 3. and let us arise, and go up to Beth-el; and I will make there an altar unto God, who answered me in the day of my distress, and was with me in the way

א ויאמר אלהים אל־יעקב קום עלה בית־אל ושב־שם
ועשה־שם מזבח לאל הנראה אליך בברחך מפני עשו
2 אחיך: ויאמר יעקב אל־ביתו ואל כל־אשר עמו הסרו
את־אלהי הנכר אשר בתככם והטהרו והחליפו
3 שמלתיכם: ונקומה ונעלה בית־אל ואעשה־שם מזבח
לאל הענה אתי ביום צרתי ויהי עמדי בדרך אשר

לד׳ v. 25. סגול באתנח v. 31. זין רבתי

25. *Dinah's brethren.* These words are added to emphasize that Simeon, Levi and Dinah were children of the same mother, and therefore they felt the more acutely the insult and the desire for revenge.

30. Jacob has been criticized for merely rebuking his sons because their action might cause him personal danger, and not pointing out the heinous crime they had done in taking advantage of the helplessness of men with whom they had made a pact of friendship. Scripture, however, often lets facts speak for themselves, and does not always append the moral or the warning to a tale. Moreover, this chapter is supplemented by Jacob's Blessing in XLIX, 5 f. In reference to Simeon and Levi, the dying Patriarch there exclaims: 'Simeon and Levi are brethren; weapons of violence their kinship. Cursed be their anger, for it was fierce, and their wrath, for it was cruel.'

31. Jacob's sons reply that the dishonour of their sister had to be avenged, and there was only one course of action to follow. High-spirited and martial men have among all nations and throughout history often yielded to blind cruelty when dealing with an outrage of this nature.

CHAPTER XXXV. THE RETURN TO BETH-EL. DEATH OF ISAAC

1. *go up to Beth-el.* Shechem is situated 1,880 ft. above sea-level, and Beth-el 2,890 ft. From the former place to the latter is a continuous ascent.

an altar. Alluding to the Patriarch's vow in XXVIII, 22.

2. *the strange gods. i.e.* gods worshipped by foreign tribes. According to Rashi, the reference is to the images which were included in the spoil of Shechem.

purify yourselves. By bathing, and abstaining from any act that would render them ceremonially unclean; cf. Exod. XIX, 10 ff.

which I went.' 4. And they gave unto Jacob all the foreign gods which were in their hand, and the rings which were in their ears; and Jacob hid them under the terebinth which was by Shechem. 5. And they journeyed; and a terror of God was upon the cities that were round about them, and they did not pursue after the sons of Jacob. 6. So Jacob came to Luz, which is in the land of Canaan—the same is Beth-el—he and all the people that were with him. 7. And he built there an altar, and called the place [1]El-beth-el, because there God was revealed unto him, when he fled from the face of his brother. 8. And Deborah Rebekah's nurse died, and she was buried below Beth-el under the oak; and the name of it was called [2]Allon-bacuth. ¶ 9. And God appeared unto Jacob again, when he came from Paddan-aram, and blessed him. 10. And God said unto him: 'Thy name is Jacob; thy name shall not be called any more Jacob, but Israel shall be thy name'; and He called his name Israel. 11. And God said unto him: 'I am God Almighty. Be fruitful and multiply; a nation and a company of nations shall be of thee, and kings shall come out of thy loins;* vi a. 12. and the land which I gave unto Abraham and Isaac, to thee I will give it, and to thy seed after thee will I give the land.' 13. And God went up from him in the place where He spoke with him. * vi s. 14. And Jacob set up a pillar in the place where He spoke with him, a pillar of stone, and he poured out a drink-offering thereon, and poured oil thereon. 15. And Jacob called the name of the place where God spoke with him, Beth-el. 16. And they journeyed from Beth-el; and there was still some way to come to Ephrath; and Rachel travailed, and she had hard labour. 17. And

4 הָלָכְתִּי׃ וַיִּתְּנוּ אֶל־יַעֲקֹב אֵת כָּל־אֱלֹהֵי הַנֵּכָר אֲשֶׁר בְּיָדָם
וְאֶת־הַנְּזָמִים אֲשֶׁר בְּאָזְנֵיהֶם וַיִּטְמֹן אֹתָם יַעֲקֹב תַּחַת
ה הָאֵלָה אֲשֶׁר עִם־שְׁכֶם׃ וַיִּסָּעוּ וַיְהִי ׀ חִתַּת אֱלֹהִים עַל־
הֶעָרִים אֲשֶׁר סְבִיבוֹתֵיהֶם וְלֹא רָדְפוּ אַחֲרֵי בְּנֵי יַעֲקֹב׃
6 וַיָּבֹא יַעֲקֹב לוּזָה אֲשֶׁר בְּאֶרֶץ כְּנַעַן הִוא בֵּית־אֵל הוּא
7 וְכָל־הָעָם אֲשֶׁר־עִמּוֹ׃ וַיִּבֶן שָׁם מִזְבֵּחַ וַיִּקְרָא לַמָּקוֹם
אֵל בֵּית־אֵל כִּי שָׁם נִגְלוּ אֵלָיו הָאֱלֹהִים בְּבָרְחוֹ מִפְּנֵי
8 אָחִיו׃ וַתָּמָת דְּבֹרָה מֵינֶקֶת רִבְקָה וַתִּקָּבֵר מִתַּחַת לְבֵית־
אֵל תַּחַת הָאַלּוֹן וַיִּקְרָא שְׁמוֹ אַלּוֹן בָּכוּת׃ פ
9 וַיֵּרָא אֱלֹהִים אֶל־יַעֲקֹב עוֹד בְּבֹאוֹ מִפַּדַּן אֲרָם וַיְבָרֶךְ
י אֹתוֹ׃ וַיֹּאמֶר־לוֹ אֱלֹהִים שִׁמְךָ יַעֲקֹב לֹא־יִקָּרֵא שִׁמְךָ עוֹד
יַעֲקֹב כִּי אִם־יִשְׂרָאֵל יִהְיֶה שְׁמֶךָ וַיִּקְרָא אֶת־שְׁמוֹ יִשְׂרָאֵל׃
11 וַיֹּאמֶר לוֹ אֱלֹהִים אֲנִי אֵל שַׁדַּי פְּרֵה וּרְבֵה גּוֹי וּקְהַל גּוֹיִם
ששי
12 יִהְיֶה מִמֶּךָּ וּמְלָכִים מֵחֲלָצֶיךָ יֵצֵאוּ׃* וְאֶת־הָאָרֶץ אֲשֶׁר
נָתַתִּי לְאַבְרָהָם וּלְיִצְחָק לְךָ אֶתְּנֶנָּה וּלְזַרְעֲךָ אַחֲרֶיךָ אֶתֵּן (ששי לספ׳)
13 אֶת־הָאָרֶץ׃ וַיַּעַל מֵעָלָיו אֱלֹהִים בַּמָּקוֹם אֲשֶׁר־דִּבֶּר אִתּוֹ׃*
14 וַיַּצֵּב יַעֲקֹב מַצֵּבָה בַּמָּקוֹם אֲשֶׁר־דִּבֶּר אִתּוֹ מַצֶּבֶת אָבֶן
טו וַיַּסֵּךְ עָלֶיהָ נֶסֶךְ וַיִּצֹק עָלֶיהָ שָׁמֶן׃ וַיִּקְרָא יַעֲקֹב אֶת־שֵׁם
16 הַמָּקוֹם אֲשֶׁר דִּבֶּר אִתּוֹ שָׁם אֱלֹהִים בֵּית־אֵל׃ וַיִּסְעוּ
מִבֵּית אֵל וַיְהִי־עוֹד כִּבְרַת־הָאָרֶץ לָבוֹא אֶפְרָתָה וַתֵּלֶד

[1] That is, *The God of Beth-el.* [2] That is, *The oak of weeping.*

קדש v. 7.

4. *rings.* In their ears. They were more than ornaments; they were also amulets and charms (Targum Jonathan).

terebinth. See on XII, 6.

5. *a terror of God.* A fear inspired by God.

6. *Luz.* See on XXVIII, 19.

7. *El-beth-el.* Rashi explains, 'God who manifested Himself in Beth-el.'

8. *Deborah Rebekah's nurse died.* Cf. XXIV, 59. She had accompanied Jacob all this while.

9. *again.* As God had appeared to him on the outward journey, He once more manifested Himself on the return journey, to renew the promises.

Paddan-aram. See on XXV, 20.

10. God confirms the change of name made by the Angel in the heat of the contest (XXXII, 29).

11. *God Almighty.* Heb. '*El Shaddai*'. For the promise which follows, cf. Isaac's blessing to Jacob in XXVIII, 3.

13. *and God went up from him.* The same phrase in XVII, 22.

14. *poured oil thereon.* Cf. on XXVIII, 18.

16. *some way to come.* *i.e.* a distance of no great length.

Ephrath. A place south of Beth-el.

17. *also is a son.* 'So the nurse cheers the dying woman by recalling her prayer at the birth of Joseph, XXX, 24' (Skinner).

it came to pass, when she was in hard labour, that the midwife said unto her: 'Fear not; for this also is a son for thee.' 18. And it came to pass, as her soul was in departing—for she died—that she called his name [1]Ben-oni; but his father called him [2]Benjamin. 19. And Rachel died, and was buried in the way to Ephrath—the same is Beth-lehem. 20. And Jacob set up a pillar upon her grave; the same is the pillar of Rachel's grave unto this day. 21. And Israel journeyed, and spread his tent beyond Migdal-eder. 22. And it came to pass, while Israel dwelt in that land, that Reuben went and lay with Bilhah his father's concubine; and Israel heard of it. ¶ Now the sons of Jacob were twelve: 23. the sons of Leah: Reuben, Jacob's first-born, and Simeon, and Levi, and Judah, and Issachar, and Zebulun; 24. the sons of Rachel: Joseph and Benjamin; 25. and the sons of Bilhah, Rachel's handmaid: Dan and Naphtali; 26. and the sons of Zilpah, Leah's handmaid: Gad and Asher. These are the sons of Jacob, that were born to him in Paddan-aram. 27. And Jacob came unto Isaac his father to Mamre, to Kiriath-arba—the same is Hebron—where Abraham and Isaac sojourned. 28. And the days of Isaac were a hundred and fourscore years. 29. And Isaac expired, and died, and was gathered unto his people, old and full of days; and Esau and Jacob his sons buried him.

17 רָחֵל וַתְּקַשׁ בְּלִדְתָּהּ׃ וַיְהִי בְהַקְשֹׁתָהּ בְּלִדְתָּהּ וַתֹּאמֶר
18 לָהּ הַמְיַלֶּדֶת אַל־תִּירְאִי כִּי־גַם־זֶה לָךְ בֵּן׃ וַיְהִי בְּצֵאת
נַפְשָׁהּ כִּי מֵתָה וַתִּקְרָא שְׁמוֹ בֶּן־אוֹנִי וְאָבִיו קָרָא־לוֹ
19 בִנְיָמִין׃ וַתָּמָת רָחֵל וַתִּקָּבֵר בְּדֶרֶךְ אֶפְרָתָה הִוא בֵּית
כ לָחֶם׃ וַיַּצֵּב יַעֲקֹב מַצֵּבָה עַל־קְבֻרָתָהּ הִוא מַצֶּבֶת קְבֻרַת־
21 רָחֵל עַד־הַיּוֹם׃ וַיִּסַּע יִשְׂרָאֵל וַיֵּט אָהֳלֹה מֵהָלְאָה לְמִגְדַּל־
22 עֵדֶר׃ וַיְהִי בִּשְׁכֹּן יִשְׂרָאֵל בָּאָרֶץ הַהִוא וַיֵּלֶךְ רְאוּבֵן וַיִּשְׁכַּב
אֶת־בִּלְהָה פִּילֶגֶשׁ אָבִיו וַיִּשְׁמַע יִשְׂרָאֵל ס פ
23 וַיִּהְיוּ בְנֵי־יַעֲקֹב שְׁנֵים עָשָׂר׃ בְּנֵי לֵאָה בְּכוֹר יַעֲקֹב
24 רְאוּבֵן וְשִׁמְעוֹן וְלֵוִי וִיהוּדָה וְיִשָּׂשכָר וּזְבֻלוּן׃ בְּנֵי רָחֵל
כה יוֹסֵף וּבִנְיָמִן׃ וּבְנֵי בִלְהָה שִׁפְחַת רָחֵל דָּן וְנַפְתָּלִי׃ וּבְנֵי 26
זִלְפָּה שִׁפְחַת לֵאָה גָּד וְאָשֵׁר אֵלֶּה בְּנֵי יַעֲקֹב אֲשֶׁר יֻלַּד־
27 לוֹ בְּפַדַּן אֲרָם׃ וַיָּבֹא יַעֲקֹב אֶל־יִצְחָק אָבִיו מַמְרֵא
קִרְיַת הָאַרְבַּע הִוא חֶבְרוֹן אֲשֶׁר־גָּר־שָׁם אַבְרָהָם וְיִצְחָק׃
28 29 וַיִּהְיוּ יְמֵי יִצְחָק מְאַת שָׁנָה וּשְׁמֹנִים שָׁנָה׃ וַיִּגְוַע יִצְחָק
וַיָּמָת וַיֵּאָסֶף אֶל־עַמָּיו זָקֵן וּשְׂבַע יָמִים וַיִּקְבְּרוּ אֹתוֹ עֵשָׂו
וְיַעֲקֹב בָּנָיו׃ פ

[1] That is, *The son of my sorrow.* [2] That is, *The son of the right hand.*

v. 22. ב׳ טעמים: פסקא באמצע פסוק

18.* *Benjamin.* The correct translation is, 'the son of my old age' (Hoffmann). The Samaritan Targum rightly transliterates בנימין by בן ימים.

19. *Rachel died.* Nothing is said of Jacob's grief. Another instance of the marvellous reserve of the Scriptural narrative. His grief for her, on whose behalf he rendered patient service for fourteen years, is indicated by a pathetic reference in XLVIII, 7.

20. *pillar.* The Heb. word מצבה is that which was in later use for 'tombstone'. Rachel's Tomb is one of the Jewish 'Holy Places' in Palestine.

21. *Migdal-eder.* The site has not been identified.

22. *Reuben.* It was the practice among Eastern heirs-apparent to take possession of their father's wives, as an assertion of their right to the succession; cf. on Lev. XVIII, 8. But whatever the reason, the memory of this repulsive incident lingered in the Patriarch's mind; it influenced the 'blessing' which on his death-bed he imparted to his eldest son (XLIX, 4).

and Israel heard of it. 'Of it' is not represented in the Hebrew. The ancient editors of the Hebrew text, the Massoretes, indicated 'A pause in the middle of a verse'. This means that the subject is abruptly dropped; it being too distasteful to continue so revolting a theme.

26. *born to him in Paddan-aram.* A generalization, disregarding the one exception, Benjamin, who was born in Canaan.

27. *Mamre.* See on XIII, 18.

Kiriath-arba. See on XXIII, 2. Since Rebekah is not mentioned here, we may infer that she died before Jacob's return.

29. *expired.* As Rashi points out, the Bible does not follow the chronological order here. It is only for the sake of convenience that his death is recorded at this point.

was gathered unto his people. See on XXV, 8.

Esau and Jacob. Similarly Isaac and Ishmael had jointly performed the last rites for Abraham (XXV, 8). Isaac is a less active character than either Abraham or Jacob. 'Abraham was an epoch-maker; his life, therefore, was an eventful one. Jacob closes the Patriarchal period, and his life was both rough and eventful. Not so Isaac. He inherits the true belief in God; his is merely the task of loyally transmitting it. No wonder that we hear little of him, and that he repeats some of his father's experiences' (Hoffmann). 'Isaac, a

* *Benjamin* (last line) Text reads 72.

36

CHAPTER XXXVI

1. Now these are the generations of Esau—the same is Edom. 2. Esau took his wives of the daughters of Canaan; Adah the daughter of Elon the Hittite, and Oholibamah the daughter of Anah, the daughter of Zibeon the Hivite, 3. and Basemath Ishmael's daughter, sister of Nebaioth. 4. And Adah bore to Esau Eliphaz; and Basemath bore Reuel; 5. and Oholibamah bore Jeush, and Jalam, and Korah. These are the sons of Esau, that were born unto him in the land of Canaan. 6. And Esau took his wives, and his sons, and his daughters, and all the souls of his house, and his cattle, and all his beasts, and all his possessions, which he had gathered in the land of Canaan; and went into a land away from his brother Jacob. 7. For their substance was too great for them to dwell together; and the land of their sojournings could not bear them because of their cattle. 8. And Esau dwelt in the mountain-land of Seir—Esau is Edom. 9. And these are the generations of Esau the father of [1]the Edomites in the mountain-land of Seir. 10. These are the names of Esau's sons: Eliphaz the son of Adah the wife of Esau, Reuel the son of Basemath the wife of Esau. 11. And the sons of Eliphaz were Teman, Omar, Zepho, and Gatam, and Kenaz. 12. And Timna was concubine to Eliphaz Esau's son; and she bore to Eliphaz Amalek. These are the sons of Adah Esau's wife. 13. And these are the sons of Reuel: Nahath, and Zerah, Shammah, and Mizzah. These were the sons of Basemath Esau's wife. 14. And these were the sons of Oholibamah the daughter of Anah, the daughter of Zibeon, Esau's wife; and she bore to Esau Jeush, and Jalam, and Korah. 15. These are the chiefs of the sons of Esau: the sons of Eliphaz the first-born of Esau: the chief of Teman, the chief of Omar, the chief of Zepho, the chief of Kenaz, 16. the chief of Korah, the chief of Gatam, the chief of Amalek. These are the chiefs that came of Eliphaz in the land of Edom. These

[1] Heb. *Edom.*

CAP. XXXVI. לו

לו

א 2 וְאֵלֶּה תֹּלְדוֹת עֵשָׂו הוּא אֱדוֹם׃ עֵשָׂו לָקַח אֶת־נָשָׁיו מִבְּנוֹת
כְּנָעַן אֶת־עָדָה בַּת־אֵילוֹן הַחִתִּי וְאֶת־אָהֳלִיבָמָה בַּת־עֲנָה
3 בַּת־צִבְעוֹן הַחִוִּי׃ וְאֶת־בָּשְׂמַת בַּת־יִשְׁמָעֵאל אֲחוֹת נְבָיוֹת׃
4 וַתֵּלֶד עָדָה לְעֵשָׂו אֶת־אֱלִיפָז וּבָשְׂמַת יָלְדָה אֶת־רְעוּאֵל׃
ה וְאָהֳלִיבָמָה יָלְדָה אֶת־יְעִישׁ וְאֶת־יַעְלָם וְאֶת־קֹרַח אֵלֶּה
6 בְּנֵי עֵשָׂו אֲשֶׁר יֻלְּדוּ־לוֹ בְּאֶרֶץ כְּנָעַן׃ וַיִּקַּח עֵשָׂו אֶת־נָשָׁיו
וְאֶת־בָּנָיו וְאֶת־בְּנֹתָיו וְאֶת־כָּל־נַפְשׁוֹת בֵּיתוֹ וְאֶת־מִקְנֵהוּ
וְאֶת־כָּל־בְּהֶמְתּוֹ וְאֵת כָּל־קִנְיָנוֹ אֲשֶׁר רָכַשׁ בְּאֶרֶץ כְּנָעַן
7 וַיֵּלֶךְ אֶל־אֶרֶץ מִפְּנֵי יַעֲקֹב אָחִיו׃ כִּי־הָיָה רְכוּשָׁם רָב
מִשֶּׁבֶת יַחְדָּו וְלֹא יָכְלָה אֶרֶץ מְגוּרֵיהֶם לָשֵׂאת אֹתָם
8 מִפְּנֵי מִקְנֵיהֶם׃ וַיֵּשֶׁב עֵשָׂו בְּהַר שֵׂעִיר עֵשָׂו הוּא אֱדוֹם׃
9 וְאֵלֶּה תֹּלְדוֹת עֵשָׂו אֲבִי אֱדוֹם בְּהַר שֵׂעִיר׃ אֵלֶּה שְׁמוֹת
בְּנֵי־עֵשָׂו אֱלִיפַז בֶּן־עָדָה אֵשֶׁת עֵשָׂו רְעוּאֵל בֶּן־בָּשְׂמַת
11 אֵשֶׁת עֵשָׂו׃ וַיִּהְיוּ בְּנֵי אֱלִיפָז תֵּימָן אוֹמָר צְפוֹ וְגַעְתָּם
12 וּקְנַז׃ וְתִמְנַע ׀ הָיְתָה פִילֶגֶשׁ לֶאֱלִיפַז בֶּן־עֵשָׂו וַתֵּלֶד
13 לֶאֱלִיפַז אֶת־עֲמָלֵק אֵלֶּה בְּנֵי עָדָה אֵשֶׁת עֵשָׂו׃ וְאֵלֶּה בְּנֵי
רְעוּאֵל נַחַת וָזֶרַח שַׁמָּה וּמִזָּה אֵלֶּה הָיוּ בְּנֵי בָשְׂמַת אֵשֶׁת
14 עֵשָׂו׃ וְאֵלֶּה הָיוּ בְּנֵי אָהֳלִיבָמָה בַת־עֲנָה בַּת־צִבְעוֹן אֵשֶׁת
טו עֵשָׂו וַתֵּלֶד לְעֵשָׂו אֶת־יְעִישׁ וְאֶת־יַעְלָם וְאֶת־קֹרַח׃ אֵלֶּה
אַלּוּפֵי בְנֵי־עֵשָׂו בְּנֵי אֱלִיפַז בְּכוֹר עֵשָׂו אַלּוּף תֵּימָן אַלּוּף

v. 5. יעוש ק׳ v. 14. יעוש ק׳

patient, meditative man, strong in affection and love, typical of the domestic virtues for which his descendants have throughout the ages been remarkable. He stands as a type of the passive virtues, which have a strength of their own.' (The Study Bible.)

CHAPTER XXXVI. THE GENERATIONS OF ESAU

1. *the same is Edom.* Cf. XXV, 30.

2. *Esau took.* More accurately, 'had taken.' On the names of Esau's wives, see on XXVI, 34.

6. *into a land.* 'Unto another land' (Targum), as distinctive from 'the land of Canaan'.

7. The same cause induced Abraham to separate from his nephew Lot (XIII, 6).

8. *Seir.* See on XIV, 6.

10. *Eliphaz.* In Rabbinic legend he is the worthiest of Esau's descendants; he was trained to pious living under the eyes of Isaac; the Lord had even endowed him with the spirit of prophecy, for he was none other than Eliphaz the friend of Job.

12. *Amalek.* Cf. on XIV, 7.

are the sons of Adah. 17. And these are the sons of Reuel Esau's son: the chief of Nahath, the chief of Zerah, the chief of Shammah, the chief of Mizzah. These are the chiefs that came of Reuel in the land of Edom. These are the sons of Basemath Esau's wife. 18. And these are the sons of Oholibamah Esau's wife: the chief of Jeush, the chief of Jalam, the chief of Korah. These are the chiefs that came of Oholibamah the daughter of Anah, Esau's wife. 19. These are the sons of Esau, and these are their chiefs; the same is Edom.* vii. ¶ 20. These are the sons of Seir the Horite, the inhabitants of the land: Lotan and Shobal and Zibeon and Anah, 21. and Dishon and Ezer and Dishan. These are the chiefs that came of the Horites, the children of Seir in the land of Edom. 22. And the children of Lotan were Hori and Hemam; and Lotan's sister was Timna. 23. And these are the children of Shobal: Alvan and Manahath and Ebal, Shepho and Onam. 24. And these are the children of Zibeon: Aiah and Anah—this is Anah who found the hot springs in the wilderness, as he fed the asses of Zibeon his father. 25. And these are the children of Anah: Dishon and Oholibamah the daughter of Anah. 26. And these are the children of [1]Dishon: Hemdan and Eshban and Ithran and Cheran. 27. These are the children of Ezer: Bilhan and Zaavan and Akan. 28. These are the children of Dishan: Uz and Aran. 29. These are the chiefs that came of the Horites: the chief of Lotan, the chief of Shobal, the chief of Zibeon, the chief of Anah, 30. the chief of Dishon, the chief of Ezer, the chief of Dishan. These are the chiefs that came of the Horites, according to their chiefs in the land of Seir. ¶ 31. And these are the kings that

16 אוֹמָר אַלּוּף צְפוֹ אַלּוּף קְנַז׃ אַלּוּף קֹרַח אַלּוּף גַּעְתָּם
אַלּוּף עֲמָלֵק אֵלֶּה אַלּוּפֵי אֱלִיפַז בְּאֶרֶץ אֱדוֹם אֵלֶּה בְּנֵי
17 עָדָה׃ וְאֵלֶּה בְּנֵי רְעוּאֵל בֶּן־עֵשָׂו אַלּוּף נַחַת אַלּוּף זֶרַח
אַלּוּף שַׁמָּה אַלּוּף מִזָּה אֵלֶּה אַלּוּפֵי רְעוּאֵל בְּאֶרֶץ אֱדוֹם
18 אֵלֶּה בְּנֵי בָשְׂמַת אֵשֶׁת עֵשָׂו׃ וְאֵלֶּה בְּנֵי אָהֳלִיבָמָה אֵשֶׁת
עֵשָׂו אַלּוּף יְעוּשׁ אַלּוּף יַעְלָם אַלּוּף קֹרַח אֵלֶּה אַלּוּפֵי
19 אָהֳלִיבָמָה בַּת־עֲנָה אֵשֶׁת עֵשָׂו׃ אֵלֶּה בְנֵי־עֵשָׂו וְאֵלֶּה
שביעי
כ אַלּוּפֵיהֶם הוּא אֱדוֹם׃ * ס אֵלֶּה בְנֵי־שֵׂעִיר הַחֹרִי
21 יֹשְׁבֵי הָאָרֶץ לוֹטָן וְשׁוֹבָל וְצִבְעוֹן וַעֲנָה׃ וְדִשׁוֹן וְאֵצֶר
22 וְדִישָׁן אֵלֶּה אַלּוּפֵי הַחֹרִי בְּנֵי שֵׂעִיר בְּאֶרֶץ אֱדוֹם׃ וַיִּהְיוּ
23 בְנֵי־לוֹטָן חֹרִי וְהֵימָם וַאֲחוֹת לוֹטָן תִּמְנָע׃ וְאֵלֶּה בְּנֵי
24 שׁוֹבָל עַלְוָן וּמָנַחַת וְעֵיבָל שְׁפוֹ וְאוֹנָם׃ וְאֵלֶּה בְנֵי־צִבְעוֹן
וְאַיָּה וַעֲנָה הוּא עֲנָה אֲשֶׁר מָצָא אֶת־הַיֵּמִם בַּמִּדְבָּר בִּרְעֹתוֹ
כה אֶת־הַחֲמֹרִים לְצִבְעוֹן אָבִיו׃ וְאֵלֶּה בְנֵי־עֲנָה דִּשֹׁן וְאָהֳלִיבָמָה
26 בַּת־עֲנָה׃ וְאֵלֶּה בְּנֵי דִישָׁן חֶמְדָּן וְאֶשְׁבָּן וְיִתְרָן וּכְרָן׃
27 28 אֵלֶּה בְּנֵי־אֵצֶר בִּלְהָן וְזַעֲוָן וַעֲקָן׃ אֵלֶּה בְנֵי־דִישָׁן עוּץ וַאֲרָן׃
29 אֵלֶּה אַלּוּפֵי הַחֹרִי אַלּוּף לוֹטָן אַלּוּף שׁוֹבָל אַלּוּף צִבְעוֹן
ל אַלּוּף עֲנָה׃ אַלּוּף דִּשֹׁן אַלּוּף אֵצֶר אַלּוּף דִּישָׁן אֵלֶּה
אַלּוּפֵי הַחֹרִי לְאַלֻּפֵיהֶם בְּאֶרֶץ שֵׂעִיר׃ פ

[1] Heb. *Dishan.*

20. *the inhabitants of the land.* The original settlers before the arrival of Esau's clans. The Horites seem to have been cave-dwellers. Some consider them to have been the cultural ancestors of the Hittites; see on Deut. II, 12.

24. *hot springs.* The Heb. word occurs only here. The older Jewish commentators understood it to mean 'mules'.

31. This verse raises an obvious difficulty. Ibn Ezra understands the 'king' to refer to Moses, the ruler of the Children of Israel. A more satisfactory explanation of the verse is the following. In the last chapter (XXXV, 11) there had been an emphatic promise from God Almighty to Jacob that 'kings shall come out of thy loins'. The Israelites, no doubt, cherished a constant hope of such a kingdom and such a kingly race. Moses himself (Deut. XXVIII, 36) prophesied concerning the king whom the Israelites would set over them; and hence it was not unnatural that, when recording the eight kings who had reigned in the family of Esau up to his own time, Scripture should go out of its way to reassure the Israelites that their history was not yet complete. The words in the Hebrew are, 'before the reigning of a king to the sons of Israel'; and might be rendered 'whilst as yet the Children of Israel have no king'; there being nothing in the words expressive of past tense, or indicating that, before they were written, a king had reigned in Israel.

31 וְאֵלֶּה הַמְּלָכִים אֲשֶׁר מָלְכוּ בְּאֶרֶץ אֱדוֹם לִפְנֵי מְלָךְ־מֶלֶךְ
32 לִבְנֵי יִשְׂרָאֵל׃ וַיִּמְלֹךְ בֶּאֱדוֹם בֶּלַע בֶּן־בְּעוֹר וְשֵׁם עִירוֹ
33 דִּנְהָבָה׃ וַיָּמָת בָּלַע וַיִּמְלֹךְ תַּחְתָּיו יוֹבָב בֶּן־זֶרַח מִבָּצְרָה׃
34 לה וַיָּמָת יוֹבָב וַיִּמְלֹךְ תַּחְתָּיו חֻשָׁם מֵאֶרֶץ הַתֵּימָנִי׃ וַיָּמָת
חֻשָׁם וַיִּמְלֹךְ תַּחְתָּיו הֲדַד בֶּן־בְּדַד הַמַּכֶּה אֶת־מִדְיָן
36 בִּשְׂדֵה מוֹאָב וְשֵׁם עִירוֹ עֲוִית׃ וַיָּמָת הֲדָד וַיִּמְלֹךְ תַּחְתָּיו
37 שַׂמְלָה מִמַּשְׂרֵקָה׃ וַיָּמָת שַׂמְלָה וַיִּמְלֹךְ תַּחְתָּיו שָׁאוּל
38 מֵרְחֹבוֹת הַנָּהָר׃ וַיָּמָת שָׁאוּל וַיִּמְלֹךְ תַּחְתָּיו בַּעַל חָנָן
39 בֶּן־עַכְבּוֹר׃ וַיָּמָת בַּעַל חָנָן בֶּן־עַכְבּוֹר וַיִּמְלֹךְ תַּחְתָּיו
הֲדַר וְשֵׁם עִירוֹ פָּעוּ וְשֵׁם אִשְׁתּוֹ מְהֵיטַבְאֵל בַּת־מַטְרֵד
מפטיר מ בַּת מֵי זָהָב׃ * וְאֵלֶּה שְׁמוֹת אַלּוּפֵי עֵשָׂו לְמִשְׁפְּחֹתָם
לִמְקֹמֹתָם בִּשְׁמֹתָם אַלּוּף תִּמְנָע אַלּוּף עַלְוָה אַלּוּף יְתֵת׃
41 42 אַלּוּף אָהֳלִיבָמָה אַלּוּף אֵלָה אַלּוּף פִּינֹן׃ אַלּוּף קְנַז
43 אַלּוּף תֵּימָן אַלּוּף מִבְצָר׃ אַלּוּף מַגְדִּיאֵל אַלּוּף עִירָם
אֵלֶּה ׀ אַלּוּפֵי אֱדוֹם לְמֹשְׁבֹתָם בְּאֶרֶץ אֲחֻזָּתָם הוּא עֵשָׂו
אֲבִי אֱדוֹם׃

reigned in the land of Edom, before there reigned any king over the children of Israel. 32. And Bela the son of Beor reigned in Edom; and the name of his city was Dinhabah. 33. And Bela died, and Jobab the son of Zerah of Bozrah reigned in his stead. 34. And Jobab died, and Husham of the land of the Temanites reigned in his stead. 35. And Husham died, and Hadad the son of Bedad, who smote Midian in the field of Moab, reigned in his stead; and the name of his city was Avith. 36. And Hadad died, and Samlah of Masrekah reigned in his stead. 37. And Samlah died, and Shaul of Rehoboth by the River reigned in his stead. 38. And Shaul died, and Baal-hanan the son of Achbor reigned in his stead. 39. And Baal-hanan the son of Achbor died, and Hadar reigned in his stead; and the name of his city was Pau; and his wife's name was Mehetabel, the daughter of Matred, the daughter of Mezahab.* m. 40. And these are the names of the chiefs that came of Esau, according to their families, after their places, by their names: the chief of Timna, the chief of Alvah, the chief of Jetheth; 41. the chief of Oholibamah, the chief of Elah, the chief of Pinon; 42. the chief of Kenaz, the chief of Teman, the chief of Mibzar; 43. the chief of Magdiel, the chief of Iram. These are the chiefs of Edom, according to their habitations in the land of their possession. This is Esau the father of the Edomites.

35. *Hadad.* The name of the Syrian storm-god, and common in Edomite names.

38. *Baal-hanan.* The same name as Hannibal, *i.e.* 'Baal is favourable'.

40. *chiefs.* The clan-chiefs (as their title indicates) were not sovereigns of the whole of Edom, but rulers of tribes or provinces. The RV calls them 'dukes'.

HOSEA XI, 7–XII, 12

Cap. XI. יא

7 וְעַמִּי
8 תְלוּאִים לִמְשׁוּבָתִי וְאֶל־עַל יִקְרָאֻהוּ יַחַד לֹא יְרוֹמֵם׃ אֵיךְ
אֶתֶּנְךָ אֶפְרַיִם אֲמַגֶּנְךָ יִשְׂרָאֵל אֵיךְ אֶתֶּנְךָ כְאַדְמָה אֲשִׂימְךָ
9 כִּצְבֹאיִם נֶהְפַּךְ עָלַי לִבִּי יַחַד נִכְמְרוּ נִחוּמָי׃ לֹא אֶעֱשֶׂה
חֲרוֹן אַפִּי לֹא אָשׁוּב לְשַׁחֵת אֶפְרָיִם כִּי אֵל אָנֹכִי וְלֹא־
י אִישׁ בְּקִרְבְּךָ קָדוֹשׁ וְלֹא אָבוֹא בְּעִיר׃ אַחֲרֵי יְהוָה יֵלְכוּ
11 כְּאַרְיֵה יִשְׁאָג כִּי־הוּא יִשְׁאַג וְיֶחֶרְדוּ בָנִים מִיָּם׃ יֶחֶרְדוּ
כְצִפּוֹר מִמִּצְרַיִם וּכְיוֹנָה מֵאֶרֶץ אַשּׁוּר וְהוֹשַׁבְתִּים עַל־
בָּתֵּיהֶם נְאֻם־יְהוָה׃

Cap. XII. יב

א סְבָבֻנִי בְכַחַשׁ אֶפְרַיִם וּבְמִרְמָה בֵּית יִשְׂרָאֵל וִיהוּדָה עֹד

Chapter XI

7. And My people are in suspense about returning to Me;
And though they call them upwards,
None at all will lift himself up.

8. How shall I give thee up, Ephraim?
How shall I surrender thee, Israel?
How shall I make thee as Admah?
How shall I set thee as Zeboim?
My heart is turned within Me,
My compassions are kindled together.

9. I will not execute the fierceness of Mine anger,
I will not return to destroy Ephraim;
For I am God, and not man,
The Holy One in the midst of thee,
And I will not come in fury.

10. They shall walk after the Lord,
Who shall roar like a lion;
For He shall roar,
And the children shall come trembling from the west.

11. They shall come trembling as a bird out of Egypt,
And as a dove out of the land of Assyria;
And I will make them to dwell in their houses,
Saith the Lord.

Chapter XII

1. Ephraim compasseth Me about with lies,
And the house of Israel with deceit;
And Judah is yet wayward towards God,
And towards the Holy One who is faithful.

יא׳ v. 8. א׳ נחח

Hosea's is the message of God's unwearying love to Israel, a message which reached its fullest expression in the cry 'O Israel, return unto the Lord thy God'. In this Haftorah, he interweaves incidents from the life of Jacob in the Sedrah, in order to recall what Israel was intended to be, in contrast with the degeneracy of his contemporaries. The Prophet's whole soul goes out in sympathy for his People; he would give his all to reclaim it, if only it were possible. Hosea's is a deeply affectionate nature; and his sentences of doom against his people read like short, disconnected sobs. The connection between the parts of his discourse, or even between his sentences, is not always distinct. But 'ever and anon, the tossing restless discourse begins again, like the wild cry of an anguish that can hardly be mastered' (Ewald).

7. *in suspense about returning to Me.* Uncertain, swaying to and fro like a door on its hinges.

And though they call them. 'They,' *i.e.* the Prophets.

8. Hosea portrays God's yearning, unending love for His people.

Admah, Zeboim. Cities of the Plain, destroyed together with Sodom and Gomorrah (Gen. XIX).

9. *for I am God.* Therefore, merciful and gracious, slow to anger, and abounding in mercy.

10. God's message shall stir the hearts of Israel. The figure of the lion, roaring to call his young, represents God calling His people out of captivity.

trembling. With contrition and joy.

11. *as a dove.* Noted for its swiftness, which shall characterize Israel's return.

Chapter XII

From this vision of a happier future the Prophet returns to the sad conditions of the present.

2 רָד עִם־אֵל וְעִם־קְדוֹשִׁים נֶאֱמָן׃ אֶפְרַיִם רֹעֶה רוּחַ וְרֹדֵף
קָדִים כָּל־הַיּוֹם כָּזָב וָשֹׁד יַרְבֶּה וּבְרִית עִם־אַשּׁוּר יִכְרֹתוּ
3 וְשֶׁמֶן לְמִצְרַיִם יוּבָל׃ וְרִיב לַיהוָה עִם־יְהוּדָה וְלִפְקֹד עַל־
4 יַעֲקֹב כִּדְרָכָיו כְּמַעֲלָלָיו יָשִׁיב לוֹ׃ בַּבֶּטֶן עָקַב אֶת־אָחִיו
ה וּבְאוֹנוֹ שָׂרָה אֶת־אֱלֹהִים׃ וַיָּשַׂר אֶל־מַלְאָךְ וַיֻּכָל בָּכָה
6 וַיִּתְחַנֶּן־לוֹ בֵּית־אֵל יִמְצָאֶנּוּ וְשָׁם יְדַבֵּר עִמָּנוּ׃ וַיהוָה
7 אֱלֹהֵי הַצְּבָאוֹת יְהוָה זִכְרוֹ׃ וְאַתָּה בֵּאלֹהֶיךָ תָשׁוּב חֶסֶד
8 וּמִשְׁפָּט שְׁמֹר וְקַוֵּה אֶל־אֱלֹהֶיךָ תָּמִיד׃ כְּנַעַן בְּיָדוֹ מֹאזְנֵי
9 מִרְמָה לַעֲשֹׁק אָהֵב׃ וַיֹּאמֶר אֶפְרַיִם אַךְ עָשַׁרְתִּי מָצָאתִי

2. Ephraim striveth after wind, and followeth after the east wind;
All the day he multiplieth lies and desolation;
And they make a covenant with Assyria,
And oil is carried into Egypt.

3. The LORD hath also a controversy with Judah,
And will punish Jacob according to his ways,
According to his doings will He recompense him.

4. In the womb he took his brother by the heel,
And by his strength he strove with a godlike being;

5. So he strove with an angel, and prevailed;
He wept, and made supplication unto him;
At Beth-el he would find him,
And there he would speak with us.

6. But the LORD, the God of hosts,
The LORD is His name.

7. Therefore turn thou to thy God;
Keep mercy and justice,
And wait for thy God continually.

8. As for the trafficker, the balances of deceit are in his hand,
He loveth to oppress.

9. And Ephraim said: 'Surely I am become rich,
I have found me wealth;
In all my labours they shall find in me
No iniquity that were sin.'

v. 5. קמץ בז"ק

2. *striveth after wind.* Vain and fruitless efforts, resulting in 'lies and desolation'; a telling summary of the results of the foreign alliances.

oil. Representing the wealth which the last king, Hoshea, sent to Egypt for help against Assyria.

4. In order to move them to repentance, the Prophet reminds the people of the wrestling in prayer of their ancestor Jacob, and of God's acceptance of him.

with a godlike being. An angel, as is evident from the very next verse.

5. *he wept.* The subject is Jacob.

he would find him. God found Jacob at Beth-el.

would speak with us. In speaking to Jacob, God as it were spake also to his descendants.

6. *the LORD is His name.* The same now as then. As He received Jacob, so will He receive Israel; therefore, 'turn to thy God.'

7. *keep mercy and justice.* This sums up the teaching of Hosea. 'Justice' (judgement) alone is not sufficient. Mercy, loving sympathy towards our fellowmen, must go with it; *and mercy must precede it.*

8. *trafficker.* lit. 'Canaanite'. From the call to repentance, the Prophet again returns to the evil-doing of his day. Israel's ideal is now Canaan's—to get rich. 'Canaanite' had become a synonym for 'trafficker', from the low repute of the Phœnician (Canaanitish) merchant for honesty.

9. Ephraim's answer. He boasts of his wealth, and callously maintains it has been obtained honestly—and that any trifling lapses in his methods cannot be accounted as sins. He does not perceive that, apart from his methods of acquisition, his reliance on material possessions and absorption in amassing them, have blinded the moral and spiritual sense within him. Israel had become Canaan, and yet was quite unconscious of it!

10. But I am the LORD thy God
From the land of Egypt;
I will yet again make thee to dwell in tents,
As in the days of the appointed season.
11. I have also spoken unto the prophets,
And I have multiplied visions;
And by the ministry of the prophets have I used similitudes.
12. If Gilead be given to iniquity
Becoming altogether vanity,
In Gilgal they sacrifice unto bullocks;
Yea, their altars shall be as heaps
In the furrows of the field.

י אוֹן לִי כָּל־יְגִיעַי לֹא יִמְצְאוּ־לִי עָוֹן אֲשֶׁר־חֵטְא׃ וְאָנֹכִי
יְהוָה אֱלֹהֶיךָ מֵאֶרֶץ מִצְרָיִם עֹד אוֹשִׁיבְךָ בָאֳהָלִים כִּימֵי
11 מוֹעֵד׃ וְדִבַּרְתִּי עַל־הַנְּבִיאִים וְאָנֹכִי חָזוֹן הִרְבֵּיתִי וּבְיַד
12 הַנְּבִיאִים אֲדַמֶּה׃ אִם־גִּלְעָד אָוֶן אַךְ־שָׁוְא הָיוּ בַּגִּלְגָּל
שְׁוָרִים זִבֵּחוּ גַּם מִזְבְּחוֹתָם כְּגַלִּים עַל תַּלְמֵי שָׂדָי׃

10. *to dwell in tents.* 'The tent-life of the wilderness was a trial and pain for which the settlement in the Promised Land was readily exchanged. But it was also a blessing and a revelation, a walking in mystery and wonder, the Divine Presence always felt and often manifest. The Feast of Tabernacles was the yearly remembrance of this wonderful pilgrim experience' (Horton). Israel must go back to captivity and begin his discipline over again, as when he came out of Egypt.

11. In vain did the Prophets convey the Divine will in visions and similitudes. They failed to bring Israel to repentance.

12. References to the heathen practices at Gilgal following the ill example of neighbouring Gilead on the other side of the Jordan. The meaning seems to be: 'In Gilead there are iniquity and falsehood; they sacrifice to demons in Gilgal; their altars shall become stone-heaps in the furrows of the fields.' They that make the idols become like unto them.

HAFTORAH VAYYISHLACH (FOR SEPHARDIM) הפטרת וישלח

THE BOOK OF OBADIAH

1. The vision of Obadiah.
Thus saith the LORD God concerning Edom:
We have heard a message from the LORD,
And an ambassador is sent among the nations:
'Arise ye, and let us rise up against her in battle.'
2. Behold, I make thee small among the nations;
Thou art greatly despised.

א חֲזוֹן עֹבַדְיָה כֹּה־אָמַר אֲדֹנָי יֱהוִה לֶאֱדוֹם שְׁמוּעָה שָׁמַעְנוּ
מֵאֵת יְהוָה וְצִיר בַּגּוֹיִם שֻׁלָּח קוּמוּ וְנָקוּמָה עָלֶיהָ
2 לַמִּלְחָמָה׃ הִנֵּה קָטֹן נְתַתִּיךָ בַּגּוֹיִם בָּזוּי אַתָּה מְאֹד׃

קמץ בז״ק ibid. v. 1.

The prophecy of Obadiah is directed against Edom, the nation descended from Esau. It thus connects with the Sedrah, reflecting the opposition between the two brothers in the story of Jacob and Esau. The bitter enmity of the Edomites to Israel was particularly inexcusable, because of their common descent. The Prophet instances the cruelty of the Edomites in the day of Israel's ruin. Apart, however, from the denunciation of unbrotherliness wherever exhibited, the book has a wider application. Other nations in later times played the cruel role of Edom towards Israel. Against these too, according to our commentators, Obadiah prophetically inveighs and predicts Israel's triumph over them. The forces of evil will never destroy Israel, because Israel's Faith, and the Truth enshrined in it, are eternal.

1. *we have heard.* 'We,' *i.e.* other Prophets, who also denounced Edom; see especially Jer. XLIX, 7–12.

3 זְדוֹן לִבְּךָ הִשִּׁיאֶךָ שֹׁכְנִי בְחַגְוֵי־סֶלַע מְרוֹם שִׁבְתּוֹ אֹמֵר
4 בְּלִבּוֹ מִי יוֹרִדֵנִי אָרֶץ׃ אִם־תַּגְבִּיהַּ כַּנֶּשֶׁר וְאִם־בֵּין כּוֹכָבִים
ה שִׂים קִנֶּךָ מִשָּׁם אוֹרִידְךָ נְאֻם־יְהוָה׃ אִם־גַּנָּבִים בָּאוּ־לְךָ
אִם־שׁוֹדְדֵי לַיְלָה אֵיךְ נִדְמֵיתָה הֲלוֹא יִגְנְבוּ דַּיָּם אִם־
6 בֹּצְרִים בָּאוּ לָךְ הֲלוֹא יַשְׁאִירוּ עֹלֵלוֹת׃ אֵיךְ נֶחְפְּשׂוּ עֵשָׂו
7 נִבְעוּ מַצְפֻּנָיו׃ עַד־הַגְּבוּל שִׁלְּחוּךָ כֹּל אַנְשֵׁי בְרִיתֶךָ
הִשִּׁיאוּךָ יָכְלוּ לְךָ אַנְשֵׁי שְׁלֹמֶךָ לַחְמְךָ יָשִׂימוּ מָזוֹר תַּחְתֶּיךָ
8 אֵין תְּבוּנָה בּוֹ׃ הֲלוֹא בַּיּוֹם הַהוּא נְאֻם־יְהוָה וְהַאֲבַדְתִּי
9 חֲכָמִים מֵאֱדוֹם וּתְבוּנָה מֵהַר עֵשָׂו׃ וְחַתּוּ גִבּוֹרֶיךָ תֵּימָן
י לְמַעַן יִכָּרֶת־אִישׁ מֵהַר עֵשָׂו מִקָּטֶל׃ מֵחֲמַס אָחִיךָ יַעֲקֹב
11 תְּכַסְּךָ בוּשָׁה וְנִכְרַתָּ לְעוֹלָם׃ בְּיוֹם עֲמָדְךָ מִנֶּגֶד בְּיוֹם
שְׁבוֹת זָרִים חֵילוֹ וְנָכְרִים בָּאוּ שְׁעָרָו וְעַל־יְרוּשָׁלַם יַדּוּ

3. The pride of thy heart hath beguiled thee,
O thou that dwellest in the clefts of the rock,
Thy habitation on high;
That sayest in thy heart:
'Who shall bring me down to the ground?'

4. Though thou make thy nest as high as the eagle,
And though thou set it among the stars,
I will bring thee down from thence, saith the LORD.

5. If thieves came to thee, if robbers by night—
How art thou cut off!—
Would they not steal till they had enough?
If grape-gatherers came to thee,
Would they not leave some gleaning grapes?

6. How is Esau searched out!
How are his hidden places sought out!

7. All the men of thy confederacy
Have conducted thee to the border;
The men that were at peace with thee
Have beguiled thee, and prevailed against thee;
They that eat thy bread lay a snare under thee,
In whom there is no discernment.

8. Shall I not in that day, saith the LORD,
Destroy the wise men out of Edom,
And discernment out of the mount of Esau?

9. And thy mighty men, O Teman, shall be dismayed,
To the end that every one may be cut off from the mount of Esau by slaughter.

10. For the violence done to thy brother Jacob shame shall cover thee,
And thou shalt be cut off for ever.

11. In the day that thou didst stand aloof,
In the day that strangers carried away his substance,
And foreigners entered into his gates,
And cast lots upon Jerusalem,
Even thou wast as one of them.

v. 11. שעריו ק׳

3. *pride of thy heart.* Their previous successes, and their belief that they could not be dislodged from their impregnable position.

clefts of the rock. Edom occupied a mountainous strip to the South of Palestine. Its rocky valleys were fertile and difficult of access to outsiders. The ruins of its capital, Petra, the mysterious, secluded city with its thousand caves, have come down to our day.

4. Their pride defies God. So does all pride.

5. The meaning is that ordinary thieves and grape-gleaners will leave something behind. Not so those who will fall upon Edom. They will destroy everything.

7. Not merely enemies—but their own familiar friends shall be against them.

8. *wise men out of Edom.* Edom's reputation for wisdom and shrewdness was proverbial. The story of Job was enacted in Edom.

9. *Teman.* Probably the north part of Edom; used for Edom as a whole.

10–15. The crowning cruelty of Edom to his brother Jacob, his malice when Jerusalem fell. Instead of helping his brother, or at least standing aside, Edom took part in the looting, and in the slaughter of the inhabitants (Ps. CXXXVII, 3).

11. *thou wast as one of them.* As one of the pitiless enemies. A brief but biting indictment.

12 גּוֹרָל גַּם־אַתָּה כְּאַחַד מֵהֶם׃ וְאַל־תֵּרֶא בְיוֹם־אָחִיךָ בְּיוֹם
נָכְרוֹ וְאַל־תִּשְׂמַח לִבְנֵי־יְהוּדָה בְּיוֹם אָבְדָם וְאַל־תַּגְדֵּל
13 פִּיךָ בְּיוֹם צָרָה׃ אַל־תָּבוֹא בְשַׁעַר־עַמִּי בְּיוֹם אֵידָם אַל־
תֵּרֶא גַם־אַתָּה בְּרָעָתוֹ בְּיוֹם אֵידוֹ וְאַל־תִּשְׁלַחְנָה בְחֵילוֹ
14 בְּיוֹם אֵידוֹ׃ וְאַל־תַּעֲמֹד עַל־הַפֶּרֶק לְהַכְרִית אֶת־פְּלִיטָיו
טו וְאַל־תַּסְגֵּר שְׂרִידָיו בְּיוֹם צָרָה׃ כִּי־קָרוֹב יוֹם־יְהוָה עַל־
כָּל־הַגּוֹיִם כַּאֲשֶׁר עָשִׂיתָ יֵעָשֶׂה לָּךְ גְּמֻלְךָ יָשׁוּב בְּרֹאשֶׁךָ׃
16 כִּי כַּאֲשֶׁר שְׁתִיתֶם עַל־הַר קָדְשִׁי יִשְׁתּוּ כָל־הַגּוֹיִם תָּמִיד
17 וְשָׁתוּ וְלָעוּ וְהָיוּ כְּלוֹא הָיוּ׃ וּבְהַר צִיּוֹן תִּהְיֶה פְלֵיטָה
18 וְהָיָה קֹדֶשׁ וְיָרְשׁוּ בֵּית יַעֲקֹב אֵת מוֹרָשֵׁיהֶם׃ וְהָיָה בֵית־
יַעֲקֹב אֵשׁ וּבֵית יוֹסֵף לֶהָבָה וּבֵית עֵשָׂו לְקַשׁ וְדָלְקוּ בָהֶם
וַאֲכָלוּם וְלֹא־יִהְיֶה שָׂרִיד לְבֵית עֵשָׂו כִּי יְהוָה דִּבֵּר׃
19 וְיָרְשׁוּ הַנֶּגֶב אֶת־הַר עֵשָׂו וְהַשְּׁפֵלָה אֶת־פְּלִשְׁתִּים וְיָרְשׁוּ
אֶת־שְׂדֵה אֶפְרַיִם וְאֵת שְׂדֵה שֹׁמְרוֹן וּבִנְיָמִן אֶת־הַגִּלְעָד׃

12. But thou shouldest not have gazed on the day of thy brother
In the day of his disaster,
Neither shouldest thou have rejoiced over the children of Judah
In the day of their destruction;
Neither shouldest thou have spoken proudly
In the day of distress.

13. Thou shouldest not have entered into the gate of My people
In the day of their calamity;
Yea, thou shouldest not have gazed on their affliction
In the day of their calamity,
Nor have laid hands on their substance
In the day of their calamity.

14. Neither shouldest thou have stood in the crossway,
To cut off those of his that escape;
Neither shouldest thou have delivered up those of his
That did remain in the day of distress.

15. For the day of the LORD is near upon all the nations;
As thou hast done, it shall be done unto thee;
Thy dealing shall return upon thine own head.

16. For as ye have drunk upon My holy mountain,
So shall all the nations drink continually,
Yea, they shall drink, and swallow down,
And shall be as though they had not been.

17. But in mount Zion there shall be those that escape,
And it shall be holy;
And the house of Jacob shall possess their possessions.

18. And the house of Jacob shall be a fire,
And the house of Joseph a flame,
And the house of Esau for stubble,
And they shall kindle in them, and devour them;
And there shall not be any remaining of the house of Esau;
For the LORD hath spoken.

19. And they of the South shall possess the mount of Esau,
And they of the Lowland the Philistines;
And they shall possess the field of Ephraim,
And the field of Samaria;
And Benjamin shall possess Gilead.

12. *Thou shouldest not have gazed.* With malicious pleasure, with *Schadenfreude*.
disaster. lit. 'strange, unwonted fortune'.

15. *day of the LORD.* God's triumphant vindication of His people against their cruel enemies.

16. *ye have drunk. i.e.* the Israelites, have drunk of the cup of suffering.
shall be as though they had not been. This verse is an indictment of the 'gospel of hate' wherever held, whether by nations or individuals. They who nourish and practise it are, in the end, self-destroyers.

17. *possess their possessions.* The house of Jacob shall not finally lack anything which is rightly theirs. The Heb. word for 'possessions' is rare; the national and religious values of Israel are singularly precious.

19–20. Generally meaning that the returning exiles shall occupy a territory enlarged on all sides.

20. And the captivity of this host of the children of Israel,
That are among the Canaanites, even unto Zarephath,
And the captivity of Jerusalem, that is in Sepharad,
Shall possess the cities of the South.
21. And saviours shall come up on mount Zion
To judge the mount of Esau;
And the kingdom shall be the LORD's.

כ וְגָלֻת הַחֵל־הַזֶּה לִבְנֵי יִשְׂרָאֵל אֲשֶׁר־כְּנַעֲנִים עַד־צָרְפַת
21 וְגָלֻת יְרוּשָׁלַם אֲשֶׁר בִּסְפָרַד יִרְשׁוּ אֵת עָרֵי הַנֶּגֶב׃ וְעָלוּ
מוֹשִׁעִים בְּהַר צִיּוֹן לִשְׁפֹּט אֶת־הַר עֵשָׂו וְהָיְתָה לַיהוָה
הַמְּלוּכָה׃

v. 20. הר' בפתח

20. *Sepharad.* Some locality in Babylonia or Asia Minor. Targum Jonathan, however, and all subsequent Jewish writers, understand by that name, Spain; ḥence Jews hailing from the Iberian Peninsula are called *Sephardim.*

21. *saviours.* A wider sweep here than even Israel's triumphant vindication. For it is not merely Israel's supremacy that the Prophet sees in his vision of saviours climbing Mount Zion but the supremacy of God. There shall be no more causeless enmity (שנאת חנם) between nation and nation, between man and man. Such causeless enmity Edom stands for. It shall cease. And then humanity will be nearer the time when 'the kingdom shall be the LORD's'.

37

CHAPTER XXXVII — CAP. XXXVII. לז

1. And Jacob dwelt in the land of his father's sojournings, in the land of Canaan. 2. These are the generations of Jacob. Joseph, being seventeen years old, was feeding the flock with his brethren, being still a lad, even with the sons of Bilhah, and with the sons of Zilpah, his father's wives; and Joseph brought evil report of them unto their father. 3. Now Israel loved Joseph more than all his children, because he was the son of his old age; and he made him a coat of many colours. 4. And when his brethren saw that their father loved him more than all his brethren, they hated him, and could not speak peaceably unto him. 5. And Joseph dreamed a dream, and he told it to his brethren; and they hated him yet the more. 6. And he said unto them: 'Hear, I pray you, this dream which I have

לז פ פ פ ט 9

א 2 וַיֵּשֶׁב יַעֲקֹב בְּאֶרֶץ מְגוּרֵי אָבִיו בְּאֶרֶץ כְּנָעַן׃ אֵלֶּה ׀ תֹּלְדוֹת
יַעֲקֹב יוֹסֵף בֶּן־שְׁבַע־עֶשְׂרֵה שָׁנָה הָיָה רֹעֶה אֶת־אֶחָיו
בַּצֹּאן וְהוּא נַעַר אֶת־בְּנֵי בִלְהָה וְאֶת־בְּנֵי זִלְפָּה נְשֵׁי אָבִיו
3 וַיָּבֵא יוֹסֵף אֶת־דִּבָּתָם רָעָה אֶל־אֲבִיהֶם׃ וְיִשְׂרָאֵל אָהַב
אֶת־יוֹסֵף מִכָּל־בָּנָיו כִּי־בֶן־זְקֻנִים הוּא לוֹ וְעָשָׂה לוֹ כְּתֹנֶת
4 פַּסִּים׃ וַיִּרְאוּ אֶחָיו כִּי־אֹתוֹ אָהַב אֲבִיהֶם מִכָּל־אֶחָיו
ה וַיִּשְׂנְאוּ אֹתוֹ וְלֹא יָכְלוּ דַּבְּרוֹ לְשָׁלֹם׃ וַיַּחֲלֹם יוֹסֵף חֲלוֹם
6 וַיַּגֵּד לְאֶחָיו וַיּוֹסִפוּ עוֹד שְׂנֹא אֹתוֹ׃ וַיֹּאמֶר אֲלֵיהֶם שִׁמְעוּ

IX. VAYYESHEV

(CHAPTERS XXXVII–XL)

(*c*) JOSEPH AND HIS BRETHREN

CHAPTER XXXVII. JOSEPH'S DREAMS

1. After a brief enumeration of Esau's descendants, without giving their history, Scripture resumes the account of the fortunes of Jacob and his sons.

2. *the generations.* Joseph alone is mentioned because he is the centre of the narrative which fills the remainder of Genesis, and forms its notable climax.

The stories of Genesis, and especially the story of Joseph, have at all times called forth the admiration of mankind. Dealing with the profoundest thoughts in terms of everyday life, a child can grasp the outline of the story; yet the greatest thinkers are continually finding in it fresh depths of unexpected meaning (Ryle). Like summer and the starry skies, like joy and childhood, these stories touch and enthral the human soul with their sublime simplicity, high seriousness and marvellous beauty. And they are absolutely irreplaceable in the moral and religious training of children. The fact that, after having been repeated for three thousand years and longer, these stories still possess an eternal freshness to children of all races and climes, proves that there is in them something of imperishable worth. There is no other literature in the world which offers that something. This is recognized even in educational circles that are far removed not only from the Traditional attitude towards the Bible, but even from the religious outlook. The uniqueness of these stories consists in the fact that there is in them a sense of overruling Divine Providence realizing its purpose through the complex interaction of human motives. They are saturated with the moral spirit. Duty, guilt and its punishment, the conflict of conscience with inclination, the triumph of moral and spiritual forces amidst the vicissitudes of human affairs—are the leading themes. And what is pre-eminently true of Genesis, applies to the whole of Bible history. Not by means of abstract formulae does it bring God and duty to the soul of man, but by means of *lives* of human beings who feel and fail, who stumble and sin as we do; yet who in their darkest groping, remain conscious of the one true way—and rise again. Witness the conduct of the brothers of Joseph when they had fully grasped the enormity of their crime. 'By the study of what other book,' asked the agnostic T. H. Huxley, 'could children be so much humanized and made to feel that each figure in the vast procession of history fills, like themselves, but a momentary space in the interval between the Eternities; and earns the blessings or the curses of all time according to its effort to do good and hate evil?'

feeding. Or, 'supervising.' The picture of Joseph doing the same work as his brothers is out of accord with what is told in the next verse. Ehrlich therefore translates: 'Joseph, being seventeen years old, used to supervise—although only a lad—his brethren, *viz.*, the sons of Bilhah and the sons of Zilpah (when they were) with the sheep.' Joseph would thus be placed in charge of only the sons of the handmaids.

evil report of them. Probably, their inattention to duty.

3. *he was the son of his old age.* At this time

dreamed: 7. for, behold, we were binding sheaves in the field, and, lo, my sheaf arose, and also stood upright; and, behold, your sheaves came round about, and bowed down to my sheaf.' 8. And his brethren said to him: 'Shalt thou indeed reign over us? or shalt thou indeed have dominion over us?' And they hated him yet the more for his dreams, and for his words. 9. And he dreamed yet another dream, and told it to his brethren, and said: 'Behold, I have dreamed yet a dream: and, behold, the sun and the moon and eleven stars bowed down to me.' 10. And he told it to his father, and to his brethren; and his father rebuked him, and said unto him: 'What is this dream that thou hast dreamed? Shall I and thy mother and thy brethren indeed come to bow down to thee to the earth?' 11. And his brethren envied him; but his father kept the saying in mind. *ii. ¶ 12. And his brethren went to feed their father's flock in Shechem. 13. And Israel said unto Joseph: 'Do not thy brethren feed the flock in Shechem? come, and I will send thee unto them.' And he said to him: 'Here am I.' 14. And he said to him: 'Go now, see whether it is well with thy brethren, and well with the flock; and bring me back word.' So he sent him out of the vale of Hebron, and he came to Shechem. 15. And a certain man found him, and, behold, he

7 נָא הַחֲלוֹם הַזֶּה אֲשֶׁר חָלָמְתִּי׃ וְהִנֵּה אֲנַחְנוּ מְאַלְּמִים
אֲלֻמִּים בְּתוֹךְ הַשָּׂדֶה וְהִנֵּה קָמָה אֲלֻמָּתִי וְגַם־נִצָּבָה וְהִנֵּה
8 תְסֻבֶּינָה אֲלֻמֹּתֵיכֶם וַתִּשְׁתַּחֲוֶיןָ לַאֲלֻמָּתִי׃ וַיֹּאמְרוּ לוֹ אֶחָיו
הֲמָלֹךְ תִּמְלֹךְ עָלֵינוּ אִם־מָשׁוֹל תִּמְשֹׁל בָּנוּ וַיּוֹסִפוּ עוֹד
9 שְׂנֹא אֹתוֹ עַל־חֲלֹמֹתָיו וְעַל־דְּבָרָיו׃ וַיַּחֲלֹם עוֹד חֲלוֹם
אַחֵר וַיְסַפֵּר אֹתוֹ לְאֶחָיו וַיֹּאמֶר הִנֵּה חָלַמְתִּי חֲלוֹם עוֹד
וְהִנֵּה הַשֶּׁמֶשׁ וְהַיָּרֵחַ וְאַחַד עָשָׂר כּוֹכָבִים מִשְׁתַּחֲוִים לִי׃
י וַיְסַפֵּר אֶל־אָבִיו וְאֶל־אֶחָיו וַיִּגְעַר־בּוֹ אָבִיו וַיֹּאמֶר לוֹ מָה
הַחֲלוֹם הַזֶּה אֲשֶׁר חָלָמְתָּ הֲבוֹא נָבוֹא אֲנִי וְאִמְּךָ וְאַחֶיךָ
11 לְהִשְׁתַּחֲוֺת לְךָ אָרְצָה׃ וַיְקַנְאוּ־בוֹ אֶחָיו וְאָבִיו שָׁמַר אֶת־
שני
12 הַדָּבָר׃ וַיֵּלְכוּ אֶחָיו לִרְעוֹת אֶת־צֹאן אֲבִיהֶם בִּשְׁכֶם׃
13 וַיֹּאמֶר יִשְׂרָאֵל אֶל־יוֹסֵף הֲלוֹא אַחֶיךָ רֹעִים בִּשְׁכֶם לְכָה
14 וְאֶשְׁלָחֲךָ אֲלֵיהֶם וַיֹּאמֶר לוֹ הִנֵּנִי׃ וַיֹּאמֶר לוֹ לֶךְ־נָא רְאֵה
אֶת־שְׁלוֹם אַחֶיךָ וְאֶת־שְׁלוֹם הַצֹּאן וַהֲשִׁבֵנִי דָּבָר וַיִּשְׁלָחֵהוּ
טו מֵעֵמֶק חֶבְרוֹן וַיָּבֹא שְׁכֶמָה׃ וַיִּמְצָאֵהוּ אִישׁ וְהִנֵּה תֹעֶה

v. 12. נקוד על את

Benjamin was but an infant, and the father's affections were centred in Joseph. However, when the latter was sold, Jacob's whole life was bound up with Benjamin (XLIV, 20).

coat of many colours. This translation is based on the Septuagint, Targum Jonathan and Kimchi. People have often wondered why a trifle like this gaudy garment should have provoked the murderous hatred of all the brethren. We now know from the painted Tombs of the Bene Hassein in Egypt that, in the Patriarchal age, Semitic chiefs wore coats of many colours as insignia of rulership. Joseph had made himself disliked by his brothers for reporting on them; and Jacob, in giving him a coat of many colours, *marked him for the chieftainship of the tribes at his father's death.* Add to this the lad's vanity in telling his dreams, and the rage of the brethren becomes intelligible. This sign of rulership and royalty was still in use in the household of King David, as is seen from II Sam. XIII, 18, though the chronicler must explain this strange fashion in dress. The fact that in the Joseph story no such explanatory gloss is given is proof of the antiquity of the narrative. When it was first written its implications were perfectly intelligible (M. G. Kyle).

10. *to his father.* Joseph is at first the clever child of a large family, too untutored in life to veil his superiority (Moulton).

rebuked him. Because his words were deepening the ill-will against him among his brothers.

thy mother. Who was dead.

11. *envied.* The repetition of the dream was a sign to them that it was more than a dream. They envied him his assured greatness. And now that envy was added to hatred, they were in a mental state to do him violence. One of the hardest things to learn is to recognize without envy the superiority of a younger brother.

kept the saying in mind. He noted with satisfaction that his designation of Joseph as the future ruler of the family seemed to have the Divine approval.

12. *in Shechem.* Meaning in the region of Shechem, which was a fertile plain. It would appear hazardous for Jacob's sons to venture thither after what is narrated in Chap. XXXIV. But we are expressly told in XXXV, 5, that God inspired fear in the peoples, which caused Jacob to be unmolested.

14. *Hebron.* The residence of Jacob, XXXV, 27. The city lies low down on the sloping sides of a narrow valley of its mountainous setting.

was wandering in the field. And the man asked him, saying: 'What seekest thou?' 16. And he said: 'I seek my brethren. Tell me, I pray thee, where they are feeding the flock.' 17. And the man said: 'They are departed hence; for I heard them say: Let us go to Dothan.' And Joseph went after his brethren, and found them in Dothan. 18. And they saw him afar off, and before he came near unto them, they conspired against him to slay him. 19. And they said one to another: 'Behold, this dreamer cometh. 20. Come now therefore, and let us slay him, and cast him into one of the pits, and we will say: An evil beast hath devoured him; and we shall see what will become of his dreams.' 21. And Reuben heard it, and delivered him out of their hand; and said: 'Let us not take his life.' 22. And Reuben said unto them: 'Shed no blood; cast him into this pit that is in the wilderness, but lay no hand upon him'—that he might deliver him out of their hand, to restore him to his father.* iii. 23. And it came to pass, when Joseph was come unto his brethren, that they stripped Joseph of his coat, the coat of many colours that was on him; 24. and they took him, and cast him into the pit—and the pit was empty, there was no water in it. 25. And they sat down to eat bread; and they lifted up their eyes and looked, and, behold, a caravan of Ishmaelites came from Gilead, with their camels bearing spicery and balm and

16 בַּשָּׂדֶה וַיִּשְׁאָלֵהוּ הָאִישׁ לֵאמֹר מַה־תְּבַקֵּשׁ׃ וַיֹּאמֶר אֶת־
17 אַחַי אָנֹכִי מְבַקֵּשׁ הַגִּידָה־נָּא לִי אֵיפֹה הֵם רֹעִים׃ וַיֹּאמֶר
הָאִישׁ נָסְעוּ מִזֶּה כִּי שָׁמַעְתִּי אֹמְרִים נֵלְכָה דֹּתָיְנָה וַיֵּלֶךְ
18 יוֹסֵף אַחַר אֶחָיו וַיִּמְצָאֵם בְּדֹתָן׃ וַיִּרְאוּ אֹתוֹ מֵרָחֹק
19 וּבְטֶרֶם יִקְרַב אֲלֵיהֶם וַיִּתְנַכְּלוּ אֹתוֹ לַהֲמִיתוֹ׃ וַיֹּאמְרוּ
כ אִישׁ אֶל־אָחִיו הִנֵּה בַּעַל הַחֲלֹמוֹת הַלָּזֶה בָּא׃ וְעַתָּה ׀
לְכוּ וְנַהַרְגֵהוּ וְנַשְׁלִכֵהוּ בְּאַחַד הַבֹּרוֹת וְאָמַרְנוּ חַיָּה רָעָה
21 אֲכָלָתְהוּ וְנִרְאֶה מַה־יִּהְיוּ חֲלֹמֹתָיו׃ וַיִּשְׁמַע רְאוּבֵן וַיַּצִּלֵהוּ
22 מִיָּדָם וַיֹּאמֶר לֹא נַכֶּנּוּ נָפֶשׁ׃ וַיֹּאמֶר אֲלֵהֶם ׀ רְאוּבֵן אַל־
תִּשְׁפְּכוּ־דָם הַשְׁלִיכוּ אֹתוֹ אֶל־הַבּוֹר הַזֶּה אֲשֶׁר בַּמִּדְבָּר
וְיָד אַל־תִּשְׁלְחוּ־בוֹ לְמַעַן הַצִּיל אֹתוֹ מִיָּדָם לַהֲשִׁיבוֹ שלישי
23 אֶל־אָבִיו׃ *וַיְהִי כַּאֲשֶׁר־בָּא יוֹסֵף אֶל־אֶחָיו וַיַּפְשִׁיטוּ אֶת־
24 יוֹסֵף אֶת־כֻּתָּנְתּוֹ אֶת־כְּתֹנֶת הַפַּסִּים אֲשֶׁר עָלָיו׃ וַיִּקָּחֻהוּ
כה וַיַּשְׁלִכוּ אֹתוֹ הַבֹּרָה וְהַבּוֹר רֵק אֵין בּוֹ מָיִם׃ וַיֵּשְׁבוּ
לֶאֱכָל־לֶחֶם וַיִּשְׂאוּ עֵינֵיהֶם וַיִּרְאוּ וְהִנֵּה אֹרְחַת יִשְׁמְעֵאלִים
בָּאָה מִגִּלְעָד וּגְמַלֵּיהֶם נֹשְׂאִים נְכֹאת וּצְרִי וָלֹט הוֹלְכִים

17. *Dothan.* The modern name is Tel-Dothan. It has a rich pasturage.

19. *dreamer.* lit. 'master of dreams'; this is only the Heb. idiom for 'dreamer'.

The brothers speak of him with a bitter derision which bodes ill for him.

20. *pits.* Or, 'cisterns,' where water was stored; these are still in common use in the East. The opening is narrow, so that any one imprisoned in them could not get out unassisted.

and we shall see. The Midrash regards these words as the comment of God upon the brother's declaration, 'let us slay him.' The Divine reply is to the effect: We shall see whose counsel will stand, Mine or theirs. The Midrash furthermore states that it was Simeon who first made the fratricidal proposal. This explains Joseph's procedure later in XLII, 24.

22. *shed no blood.* Reuben's first appeal of 'No murder' fell on deaf ears (see XLII, 22); he then hopes to outwit them by a stratagem. He appeals to them that at least they need not shed any blood, hoping later to rescue Joseph and bring him back to Jacob, against whom he had previously so grievously sinned (Nachmanides, Abarbanel).

23. *stripped.* Tore off with violence. What Joseph's words were in connection with this unnatural conduct of his brethren, we only indirectly know from XLII, 21; just as we are left to gather Jacob's feelings at the death of Rachel from the pathetic reference in XLVIII, 7. The reserve of the Scripture narrative in this chapter, as in XXII, represents the acme of literary art (Steinthal).

24. *no water in it.* But it did contain serpents and scorpions (Rashi).

25. *to eat bread.* While the piercing cries of their doomed brother were still ringing in their ears. Nothing can more forcibly paint the callousness to all human feeling which comes from slavery to hate.

caravan. Such a caravan would in the clear air of Palestine be seen many miles away. It might take two or three hours before it came up to the brothers. Dothan lay on the trade-route from Gilead, the country east of the Jordan, across the Valley of Jezreel, along the Philistine coast to Egypt.

balm. For which Gilead was proverbially famous.

ladanum, going to carry it down to Egypt. 26. And Judah said unto his brethren: 'What profit is it if we slay our brother and conceal his blood? 27. Come, and let us sell him to the Ishmaelites, and let not our hand be upon him; for he is our brother, our flesh.' And his brethren hearkened unto him. 28. And there passed by Midianites, merchantmen; and they drew and lifted up Joseph out of the pit, and sold Joseph to the Ishmaelites for twenty shekels of silver. And they brought Joseph into Egypt. 29. And Reuben returned unto the pit; and, behold, Joseph was not in the pit; and he rent his clothes. 30. And he returned unto his brethren, and said: 'The child is not; and as for me, whither shall I go?' 31. And they took Joseph's coat, and killed a he-goat, and dipped the coat in the blood; 32. and they sent the coat of many colours, and they brought it to their father; and said: 'This have we found. Know now whether it is thy son's coat or not.' 33. And he knew it, and said: 'It is my son's coat; an evil beast hath devoured him; Joseph is without doubt torn in pieces.' 34. And Jacob rent his garments, and put sackcloth upon his loins, and mourned for his son many days. 35. And all his sons and all his daughters rose up to comfort him; but he refused to be comforted; and he said: 'Nay, but I will go down to the grave to my son mourning.' And his father wept for him. 36. And the

26 לְהוֹרִיד מִצְרָיְמָה׃ וַיֹּאמֶר יְהוּדָה אֶל־אֶחָיו מַה־בֶּצַע כִּי
27 נַהֲרֹג אֶת־אָחִינוּ וְכִסִּינוּ אֶת־דָּמוֹ׃ לְכוּ וְנִמְכְּרֶנּוּ לַיִּשְׁמְעֵאלִים
וְיָדֵנוּ אַל־תְּהִי־בוֹ כִּי־אָחִינוּ בְשָׂרֵנוּ הוּא וַיִּשְׁמְעוּ אֶחָיו׃
28 וַיַּעַבְרוּ אֲנָשִׁים מִדְיָנִים סֹחֲרִים וַיִּמְשְׁכוּ וַיַּעֲלוּ אֶת־יוֹסֵף
מִן־הַבּוֹר וַיִּמְכְּרוּ אֶת־יוֹסֵף לַיִּשְׁמְעֵאלִים בְּעֶשְׂרִים כָּסֶף
29 וַיָּבִיאוּ אֶת־יוֹסֵף מִצְרָיְמָה׃ וַיָּשָׁב רְאוּבֵן אֶל־הַבּוֹר וְהִנֵּה
ל אֵין־יוֹסֵף בַּבּוֹר וַיִּקְרַע אֶת־בְּגָדָיו׃ וַיָּשָׁב אֶל־אֶחָיו וַיֹּאמַר
31 הַיֶּלֶד אֵינֶנּוּ וַאֲנִי אָנָה אֲנִי־בָא׃ וַיִּקְחוּ אֶת־כְּתֹנֶת יוֹסֵף
32 וַיִּשְׁחֲטוּ שְׂעִיר עִזִּים וַיִּטְבְּלוּ אֶת־הַכֻּתֹּנֶת בַּדָּם׃ וַיְשַׁלְּחוּ
אֶת־כְּתֹנֶת הַפַּסִּים וַיָּבִיאוּ אֶל־אֲבִיהֶם וַיֹּאמְרוּ זֹאת מָצָאנוּ
33 הַכֶּר־־נָא הַכְּתֹנֶת בִּנְךָ הִוא אִם־לֹא׃ וַיַּכִּירָהּ וַיֹּאמֶר
34 כְּתֹנֶת בְּנִי חַיָּה רָעָה אֲכָלָתְהוּ טָרֹף טֹרַף יוֹסֵף׃ וַיִּקְרַע
יַעֲקֹב שִׂמְלֹתָיו וַיָּשֶׂם שַׂק בְּמָתְנָיו וַיִּתְאַבֵּל עַל־בְּנוֹ יָמִים
לה רַבִּים׃ וַיָּקֻמוּ כָל־בָּנָיו וְכָל־בְּנֹתָיו לְנַחֲמוֹ וַיְמָאֵן לְהִתְנַחֵם
וַיֹּאמֶר כִּי־אֵרֵד אֶל־בְּנִי אָבֵל שְׁאֹלָה וַיֵּבְךְּ אֹתוֹ אָבִיו׃

27. *hearkened unto him.* The horror of their contemplated murder by starvation dawns upon them; they agree to a less violent scheme. Reuben keeps his counsel.

28. *Midianites.* In the meantime, while the brethren were at the meal, some Midianite merchants, casually passing by and hearing human cries from the pit near the roadside, carry off Joseph and sell him to the caravan going to Egypt. The brothers did not thus actually sell Joseph. He was 'stolen away', as he himself says in XL, 15 (Rashbam, Luzzatto).

29. Reuben who, it seems, did not participate in the meal, *v.* 25, had intended to remove Joseph from the pit and bring him back to his father. He finds the pit empty and no trace of Joseph. Some wild beast, he thinks, has carried him off.

30. *whither shall I go?* As the first-born, the father would hold him morally responsible. 'Whither shall I flee from my father's woe' (Rashi).

31. *they took.* The brothers, however, were not displeased to be rid of Joseph.

32. *they sent.* Through others; *i.e.* they arranged that people should bring the coat to Jacob (Rashbam).

they said. Those who brought the coat.

33. The lit. translation of the Heb. is 'My son's coat! a wild beast hath eaten him! torn, torn is Joseph!'—a reproduction of the father's anguish that is as natural as nature.

34. *rent his garments.* The traditional mourning rite on the loss of a near relative, *Keriah.*

many days. A long time; two and twenty years.

35. *daughters.* Includes granddaughters and daughters-in-law, as 'sons' may include grandsons.

grave. Heb. '*Sheol*', the name of the abode of the dead. Jacob's words mean either that he will mourn his son all his life, or that even in the grave he will continue to mourn him.

36. *into Egypt.* Through the Ishmaelite caravan.

Potiphar. The name means, 'The gift of Ra,' the sun-god.

officer. The Heb. word came to have the general significance of 'court official'.

[1]Midianites sold him into Egypt unto Potiphar, an officer of Pharaoh's, the captain of the guard.*iv.

38 CHAPTER XXXVIII

1. And it came to pass at that time, that Judah went down from his brethren, and turned in to a certain Adullamite, whose name was Hirah. 2. And Judah saw there a daughter of a certain Canaanite whose name was Shua; and he took her, and went in unto her. 3. And she conceived, and bore a son; and he called his name Er. 4. And she conceived again, and bore a son; and she called his name Onan. 5. And she yet again bore a son, and called his name Shelah; and he was at Chezib, when she bore him. 6. And Judah took a wife for Er his first-born, and her name was Tamar. 7. And Er, Judah's first-born, was wicked in the sight of the LORD; and the LORD slew him. 8. And Judah said unto Onan: 'Go in unto thy brother's wife, and perform the duty of a husband's brother unto her, and raise up seed to thy brother.' 9. And Onan knew that the seed would not be his; and it came to pass, when he went in unto his brother's wife, that he spilled it on the ground, lest he should give seed to his brother. 10. And the thing which he did was evil in the sight of the LORD; and He slew him also. 11. Then said Judah to Tamar his daughter-in-law: 'Remain a widow in thy father's house, till Shelah my son be grown up'; for he said: 'Lest he also die, like his brethren.' And Tamar

[1] Heb. *Medanites.*

36 וְהַמְּדָנִים מָכְרוּ אֹתוֹ אֶל־מִצְרָיִם לְפוֹטִיפַר סְרִיס פַּרְעֹה
שַׂר הַטַּבָּחִים׃ פ רביעי

לח CAP. XXXVIII. לח

א וַיְהִי בָּעֵת הַהִוא וַיֵּרֶד יְהוּדָה מֵאֵת אֶחָיו וַיֵּט עַד־אִישׁ
2 עֲדֻלָּמִי וּשְׁמוֹ חִירָה׃ וַיַּרְא־שָׁם יְהוּדָה בַּת־אִישׁ כְּנַעֲנִי
3 וּשְׁמוֹ שׁוּעַ וַיִּקָּחֶהָ וַיָּבֹא אֵלֶיהָ׃ וַתַּהַר וַתֵּלֶד בֵּן וַיִּקְרָא
4 אֶת־שְׁמוֹ עֵר׃ וַתַּהַר עוֹד וַתֵּלֶד בֵּן וַתִּקְרָא אֶת־שְׁמוֹ אוֹנָן׃
ה וַתֹּסֶף עוֹד וַתֵּלֶד בֵּן וַתִּקְרָא אֶת־שְׁמוֹ שֵׁלָה וְהָיָה בִכְזִיב
6 בְּלִדְתָּהּ אֹתוֹ׃ וַיִּקַּח יְהוּדָה אִשָּׁה לְעֵר בְּכוֹרוֹ וּשְׁמָהּ
7 תָּמָר׃ וַיְהִי עֵר בְּכוֹר יְהוּדָה רַע בְּעֵינֵי יְהוָה וַיְמִתֵהוּ
8 יְהוָה׃ וַיֹּאמֶר יְהוּדָה לְאוֹנָן בֹּא אֶל־אֵשֶׁת אָחִיךָ וְיַבֵּם
9 אֹתָהּ וְהָקֵם זֶרַע לְאָחִיךָ׃ וַיֵּדַע אוֹנָן כִּי לֹּא לוֹ יִהְיֶה
הַזָּרַע וְהָיָה אִם־בָּא אֶל־אֵשֶׁת אָחִיו וְשִׁחֵת אַרְצָה לְבִלְתִּי
י נְתָן־זֶרַע לְאָחִיו׃ וַיֵּרַע בְּעֵינֵי יְהוָה אֲשֶׁר עָשָׂה וַיָּמֶת גַּם־
11 אֹתוֹ׃ וַיֹּאמֶר יְהוּדָה לְתָמָר כַּלָּתוֹ שְׁבִי אַלְמָנָה בֵית־
אָבִיךְ עַד־יִגְדַּל שֵׁלָה בְנִי כִּי אָמַר פֶּן־יָמוּת גַּם־הוּא

Pharaoh. The *title* of the Egyptian Sovereign.

captain of the guard. Or, 'chief of the executioners'.

CHAPTER XXXVIII. JUDAH AND TAMAR

In the history of Jacob's family the two central persons are Judah and Joseph. The former became the leader of his brethren and the ancestor of David; the latter, from his noble character and personal influence on the future destinies of Jacob's children, is regarded as next in importance. Before recounting Joseph's fortunes in Egypt, Scripture records the following incident in the life of Judah, so as to draw a contrast between his conduct and that of Joseph in the hour of temptation.

1. *at that time.* An indefinite phrase used sometimes of events which occurred several years earlier or later. In this instance, the marriage took place prior to the sale of Joseph (Ibn Ezra).

went down. From the rocky hills around Hebron to Adullam, in the Lowland, 17 miles S.W. of Jerusalem.

2. *Canaanite.* Following Esau's evil example (cf. XXVI, 34 f), and reaping an abundant harvest of sin and shame. Many commentators, however, take the word in the sense used in Zech. XIV, 21, and translate 'merchant' (Targum, Rashi, Mendelssohn).

6. *Judah took.* Such was the custom for the parent to select the son's bride.

Tamar. lit. 'a date palm'. The name occurs later in the family of David.

7. *slew him.* lit. 'caused him to die'.

8. *perform the duty of a husband's brother.* This refers to the custom of the levirate marriage by which a surviving brother-in-law (in Latin, *levir*) marries the childless widow, see Deut. XXV, 5 and cf. Ruth IV, 5 f. The eldest son of such marriage inherited the name and property of the deceased.

9. *would not be his.* *i.e.* would not bear his name.

11. *daughter-in-law.* Tamar. The childless widow went back to her father's house. Judah believed that the deaths of Er and Onan were due to Tamar. He, therefore, fears to have Shelah perform the levirate duty.

went and dwelt in her father's house. 12. And in process of time Shua's daughter, the wife of Judah, died; and Judah was comforted, and went up unto his sheep-shearers to Timnah, he and his friend Hirah the Adullamite. 13. And it was told Tamar, saying: 'Behold, thy father-in-law goeth up to Timnah to shear his sheep.' 14. And she put off from her the garments of her widowhood, and covered herself with her veil, and wrapped herself, and sat in the entrance of Enaim, which is by the way to Timnah; for she saw that Shelah was grown up, and she was not given unto him to wife. 15. When Judah saw her, he thought her to be a harlot; for she had covered her face. 16. And he turned unto her by the way, and said: 'Come, I pray thee, let me come in unto thee'; for he knew not that she was his daughter-in-law. And she said: 'What wilt thou give me, that thou mayest come in unto me?' 17. And he said: 'I will send thee a kid of the goats from the flock.' And she said: 'Wilt thou give me a pledge, till thou send it?' 18. And he said: 'What pledge shall I give thee?' And she said: 'Thy signet and thy cord, and thy staff that is in thy hand.' And he gave them to her, and came in unto her, and she conceived by him. 19. And she arose, and went away, and put off her veil from her, and put on the garments of her widowhood. 20. And Judah sent the kid of the goats by the hand of his friend the Adullamite, to receive the pledge from the woman's hand; but he found her not. 21. Then he asked the men of her place, saying: 'Where is the harlot, that was at Enaim by the wayside?' And they said: 'There hath been no harlot here.' 22. And he returned to Judah, and said: 'I have not found her; and also the men of the place said: There hath been no harlot here.' 23. And Judah said: 'Let her take it, lest we be put to shame; behold, I sent this kid, and thou hast not found her.' 24. And it came to pass about three months after, that it was told Judah, saying: 'Tamar thy daughter-in-law hath played the harlot;

12 כְּאֶחָיו וַתֵּלֶךְ תָּמָר וַתֵּשֶׁב בֵּית אָבִיהָ׃ וַיִּרְבּוּ הַיָּמִים וַתָּמָת
בַּת־שׁוּעַ אֵשֶׁת־יְהוּדָה וַיִּנָּחֶם יְהוּדָה וַיַּעַל עַל־גֹּזְזֵי צֹאנוֹ
13 הוּא וְחִירָה רֵעֵהוּ הָעֲדֻלָּמִי תִּמְנָתָה׃ וַיֻּגַּד לְתָמָר לֵאמֹר
14 הִנֵּה חָמִיךְ עֹלֶה תִמְנָתָה לָגֹז צֹאנוֹ׃ וַתָּסַר בִּגְדֵי אַלְמְנוּתָהּ
מֵעָלֶיהָ וַתְּכַס בַּצָּעִיף וַתִּתְעַלָּף וַתֵּשֶׁב בְּפֶתַח עֵינַיִם אֲשֶׁר
עַל־דֶּרֶךְ תִּמְנָתָה כִּי רָאֲתָה כִּי־גָדַל שֵׁלָה וְהִוא לֹא־נִתְּנָה
טו לוֹ לְאִשָּׁה׃ וַיִּרְאֶהָ יְהוּדָה וַיַּחְשְׁבֶהָ לְזוֹנָה כִּי כִסְּתָה
16 פָּנֶיהָ׃ וַיֵּט אֵלֶיהָ אֶל־הַדֶּרֶךְ וַיֹּאמֶר הָבָה־נָּא אָבוֹא אֵלַיִךְ
כִּי לֹא יָדַע כִּי כַלָּתוֹ הִוא וַתֹּאמֶר מַה־תִּתֶּן־לִי כִּי תָבוֹא
17 אֵלָי׃ וַיֹּאמֶר אָנֹכִי אֲשַׁלַּח גְּדִי־עִזִּים מִן־הַצֹּאן וַתֹּאמֶר
18 אִם־תִּתֵּן עֵרָבוֹן עַד שָׁלְחֶךָ׃ וַיֹּאמֶר מָה הָעֵרָבוֹן אֲשֶׁר
אֶתֶּן־לָךְ וַתֹּאמֶר חֹתָמְךָ וּפְתִילֶךָ וּמַטְּךָ אֲשֶׁר בְּיָדֶךָ וַיִּתֶּן
19 לָהּ וַיָּבֹא אֵלֶיהָ וַתַּהַר לוֹ׃ וַתָּקָם וַתֵּלֶךְ וַתָּסַר צְעִיפָהּ
כ מֵעָלֶיהָ וַתִּלְבַּשׁ בִּגְדֵי אַלְמְנוּתָהּ׃ וַיִּשְׁלַח יְהוּדָה אֶת־גְּדִי
הָעִזִּים בְּיַד רֵעֵהוּ הָעֲדֻלָּמִי לָקַחַת הָעֵרָבוֹן מִיַּד הָאִשָּׁה
21 וְלֹא מְצָאָהּ׃ וַיִּשְׁאַל אֶת־אַנְשֵׁי מְקֹמָהּ לֵאמֹר אַיֵּה הַקְּדֵשָׁה
הִוא בָעֵינַיִם עַל־הַדָּרֶךְ וַיֹּאמְרוּ לֹא־הָיְתָה בָזֶה קְדֵשָׁה׃
22 וַיָּשָׁב אֶל־יְהוּדָה וַיֹּאמֶר לֹא מְצָאתִיהָ וְגַם אַנְשֵׁי הַמָּקוֹם
23 אָמְרוּ לֹא־הָיְתָה בָזֶה קְדֵשָׁה׃ וַיֹּאמֶר יְהוּדָה תִּקַּח־לָהּ
פֶּן נִהְיֶה לָבוּז הִנֵּה שָׁלַחְתִּי הַגְּדִי הַזֶּה וְאַתָּה לֹא מְצָאתָהּ׃

12. *Shua's daughter.* Her own name is not known. Some time after the death, Judah found it becoming to attend the Canaanite festivities in connection with the sheep-shearing.

Timnah. A few miles S. of Hebron.

14. *garments of her widowhood.* To prevent detection by Judah. She resorts to a disguise and stratagem that must have appeared quite honourable in her Canaanite eyes. She assumes the veil of a votary of Astarte. Her intention was to force Judah himself to perform the levirate duty. In pre-Mosaic times, it seems, every member of the late husband's family was under that obligation.

15. *harlot.* In *v.* 21 she is described as a *kedeshah*; that is, a woman dedicated to impure heathen worship. This repulsive custom was common in ancient Phœnicia and Babylonia and survives in many forms of Hindu worship. No *kedeshah* was permitted in Israel; see Deut. XXIII, 17.

16. *and he turned unto her.* He left his path to go to her (Rashi).

18. Tamar thus secured a pledge which rendered the identification of the owner absolutely certain. Signet, cord and staff were the insignia of a sheikh in Canaan, as of a man of rank among the Babylonians and Egyptians.

cord. Used to suspend the seal.

and moreover, behold, she is with child by harlotry.' And Judah said: 'Bring her forth, and let her be burnt.' 25. When she was brought forth, she sent to her father-in-law, saying: 'By the man, whose these are, am I with child'; and she said: 'Discern, I pray thee, whose are these, the signet, and the cords, and the staff.' 26. And Judah acknowledged them, and said: 'She is more righteous than I; forasmuch as I gave her not to Shelah my son.' And he knew her again no more. 27. And it came to pass in the time of her travail, that, behold, twins were in her womb. 28. And it came to pass, when she travailed, that one put out a hand; and the midwife took and bound upon his hand a scarlet thread, saying: 'This came out first.' 29. And it came to pass, as he drew back his hand, that, behold, his brother came out; and she said: 'Wherefore hast thou made a breach for thyself?' Therefore his name was called [1]Perez. 30. And afterward came out his brother, that had the scarlet thread upon his hand; and his name was called Zerah.* v.

24 וַיְהִי ׀ כְּמִשְׁלֹשׁ חֳדָשִׁים וַיֻּגַּד לִיהוּדָה לֵאמֹר זָנְתָה תָּמָר
כַּלָּתֶךָ וְגַם הִנֵּה הָרָה לִזְנוּנִים וַיֹּאמֶר יְהוּדָה הוֹצִיאוּהָ
כה וְתִשָּׂרֵף׃ הִוא מוּצֵאת וְהִיא שָׁלְחָה אֶל־חָמִיהָ לֵאמֹר
לְאִישׁ אֲשֶׁר־אֵלֶּה לּוֹ אָנֹכִי הָרָה וַתֹּאמֶר הַכֶּר־נָא לְמִי
26 הַחֹתֶמֶת וְהַפְּתִילִים וְהַמַּטֶּה הָאֵלֶּה׃ וַיַּכֵּר יְהוּדָה וַיֹּאמֶר
צָדְקָה מִמֶּנִּי כִּי־עַל־כֵּן לֹא־נְתַתִּיהָ לְשֵׁלָה בְנִי וְלֹא־יָסַף
27 עוֹד לְדַעְתָּהּ׃ וַיְהִי בְּעֵת לִדְתָּהּ וְהִנֵּה תְאוֹמִים בְּבִטְנָהּ׃
28 וַיְהִי בְלִדְתָּהּ וַיִּתֶּן־יָד וַתִּקַּח הַמְיַלֶּדֶת וַתִּקְשֹׁר עַל־יָדוֹ
29 שָׁנִי לֵאמֹר זֶה יָצָא רִאשֹׁנָה׃ וַיְהִי ׀ כְּמֵשִׁיב יָדוֹ וְהִנֵּה יָצָא
אָחִיו וַתֹּאמֶר מַה־פָּרַצְתָּ עָלֶיךָ פָּרֶץ וַיִּקְרָא שְׁמוֹ פָּרֶץ׃
חמישי
ל וְאַחַר יָצָא אָחִיו אֲשֶׁר עַל־יָדוֹ הַשָּׁנִי וַיִּקְרָא שְׁמוֹ זָרַח׃ ס

39

Chapter XXXIX

1. And Joseph was brought down to Egypt; and Potiphar, an officer of Pharaoh's, the captain of the guard, an Egyptian, bought him of the hand of the Ishmaelites, that had brought him down thither. 2. And the Lord was with Joseph, and he was a prosperous man; and he was in the house of his master the Egyptian. 3. And his master saw that the Lord was with him, and that the Lord made all that he did to prosper

Cap. XXXIX. לט

לט

א וְיוֹסֵף הוּרַד מִצְרָיְמָה וַיִּקְנֵהוּ פּוֹטִיפַר סְרִיס פַּרְעֹה שַׂר
הַטַּבָּחִים אִישׁ מִצְרִי מִיַּד הַיִּשְׁמְעֵאלִים אֲשֶׁר הוֹרִדֻהוּ
2 שָׁמָּה׃ וַיְהִי יְהוָה אֶת־יוֹסֵף וַיְהִי אִישׁ מַצְלִיחַ וַיְהִי בְּבֵית
3 אֲדֹנָיו הַמִּצְרִי׃ וַיַּרְא אֲדֹנָיו כִּי יְהוָה אִתּוֹ וְכֹל אֲשֶׁר־

[1] That is, *A breach.*

23. *let her take it.* Let her keep the pledges, lest, if they search further, he be exposed to shame. Even before מתן תורה, the revelation of a higher ideal of personal conduct at Sinai and the promulgation of the Holiness code (Lev. XIX), some moral turpitude attached to such conduct.

sent this kid. He feels he could do no more.

24. *let her be burnt.* Judah, as head of the family, has power of life and death; cf. XXXI, 32. Tamar was the betrothed of Shelah, and betrothal was considered to be as binding as marriage.

25. *by the man.* Tamar acts nobly in withholding the name of the betrayer. Judah also shows his better side by confessing his sin. The Rabbis dwell on this act of contrition.

26. Scripture does not hide the sins of its heroes and heroines.

28. *a scarlet thread.* To secure his right as the first-born.

Chapter XXXIX. Potiphar's Wife

The story of Joseph is resumed in this chapter. Amid the new and trying circumstances of his new existence, Joseph's winsome personality and innate nobility of character are revealed. He gains the confidence of his master and emerges unscathed from sinful temptation.

1. *was brought down.* Better, '*had been brought down.*'

an Egyptian. The story of Joseph took place during the reign of the Hyksos kings, the Bedouin conquerors of Egypt. Exceptionally, 'an Egyptian' was entrusted with a high Government post.

2. *prosperous man.* All that he did prospered.

in his hand. 4. And Joseph found favour in his sight, and he ministered unto him. And he appointed him overseer over his house, and all that he had he put into his hand. 5. And it came to pass from the time that he appointed him overseer in his house, and over all that he had, that the LORD blessed the Egyptian's house for Joseph's sake; and the blessing of the LORD was upon all that he had, in the house and in the field. 6. And he left all that he had in Joseph's hand; and, having him, he knew not aught save the bread which he did eat. And Joseph was of beautiful form, and fair to look upon.* vi. ¶ 7. And it came to pass after these things, that his master's wife cast her eyes upon Joseph; and she said: 'Lie with me.' 8. But he refused, and said unto his master's wife: 'Behold, my master, having me, knoweth not what is in the house, and he hath put all that he hath into my hand; 9. he is not greater in this house than I; neither hath he kept back any thing from me but thee, because thou art his wife. How then can I do this great wickedness, and sin against God?' 10. And it came to pass, as she spoke to Joseph day by day, that he hearkened not unto her, to lie by her, or to be with her. 11. And it came to pass on a certain day, when he went into the house to do his work, and there was none of the men of the house there within, 12. that she caught him by his garment, saying: 'Lie with me.' And he left his garment in her hand, and fled, and got him out. 13. And it came to pass, when she saw that he had left his garment in her hand, and was fled forth, 14. that she called unto the men of her house, and spoke unto them, saying: 'See, he hath brought

4 הוּא עֹשֶׂה יְהוָה מַצְלִיחַ בְּיָדוֹ׃ וַיִּמְצָא יוֹסֵף חֵן בְּעֵינָיו
וַיְשָׁרֶת אֹתוֹ וַיַּפְקִדֵהוּ עַל־בֵּיתוֹ וְכָל־יֶשׁ־לוֹ נָתַן בְּיָדוֹ׃
ה וַיְהִי מֵאָז הִפְקִיד אֹתוֹ בְּבֵיתוֹ וְעַל כָּל־אֲשֶׁר יֶשׁ־לוֹ וַיְבָרֶךְ
יְהוָה אֶת־בֵּית הַמִּצְרִי בִּגְלַל יוֹסֵף וַיְהִי בִּרְכַּת יְהוָה
6 בְּכָל־אֲשֶׁר יֶשׁ־לוֹ בַּבַּיִת וּבַשָּׂדֶה׃ וַיַּעֲזֹב כָּל־אֲשֶׁר־לוֹ בְּיַד
יוֹסֵף וְלֹא־יָדַע אִתּוֹ מְאוּמָה כִּי אִם־הַלֶּחֶם אֲשֶׁר־הוּא
ששי 7 אוֹכֵל וַיְהִי יוֹסֵף יְפֵה־תֹאַר וִיפֵה מַרְאֶה׃ וַיְהִי אַחַר
הַדְּבָרִים הָאֵלֶּה וַתִּשָּׂא אֵשֶׁת־אֲדֹנָיו אֶת־עֵינֶיהָ אֶל־יוֹסֵף
8 וַתֹּאמֶר שִׁכְבָה עִמִּי׃ וַיְמָאֵן וַיֹּאמֶר אֶל־אֵשֶׁת אֲדֹנָיו הֵן
אֲדֹנִי לֹא־יָדַע אִתִּי מַה־בַּבָּיִת וְכֹל אֲשֶׁר־יֶשׁ־לוֹ נָתַן בְּיָדִי׃
9 אֵינֶנּוּ גָדוֹל בַּבַּיִת הַזֶּה מִמֶּנִּי וְלֹא־חָשַׂךְ מִמֶּנִּי מְאוּמָה
כִּי אִם־אוֹתָךְ בַּאֲשֶׁר אַתְּ־אִשְׁתּוֹ וְאֵיךְ אֶעֱשֶׂה הָרָעָה הַגְּדֹלָה
י הַזֹּאת וְחָטָאתִי לֵאלֹהִים׃ וַיְהִי כְּדַבְּרָהּ אֶל־יוֹסֵף יוֹם ׀ יוֹם
11 וְלֹא־שָׁמַע אֵלֶיהָ לִשְׁכַּב אֶצְלָהּ לִהְיוֹת עִמָּהּ׃ וַיְהִי כְּהַיּוֹם
הַזֶּה וַיָּבֹא הַבַּיְתָה לַעֲשׂוֹת מְלַאכְתּוֹ וְאֵין אִישׁ מֵאַנְשֵׁי
12 הַבַּיִת שָׁם בַּבָּיִת׃ וַתִּתְפְּשֵׂהוּ בְּבִגְדוֹ לֵאמֹר שִׁכְבָה עִמִּי
13 וַיַּעֲזֹב בִּגְדוֹ בְּיָדָהּ וַיָּנָס וַיֵּצֵא הַחוּצָה׃ וַיְהִי כִּרְאוֹתָהּ
14 כִּי־עָזַב בִּגְדוֹ בְּיָדָהּ וַיָּנָס הַחוּצָה׃ וַתִּקְרָא לְאַנְשֵׁי בֵיתָהּ

4. *ministered unto him.* As his personal attendant. Then he is advanced to the position of overseer, or controller of the household and estate generally.

6. *having him, he knew not aught. i.e.* having him, he troubled himself about nothing, and left all his affairs to the care of Joseph, except his food. This could not be left to a non-Egyptian; see XLIII, 32.

of beautiful form. Like his mother Rachel (Ibn Ezra).

7. *after these things. i.e.* after the twofold advancement of Joseph when he was no longer a slave, but had become overseer and trusted confidant, his master's wife makes advances to him. The immorality of the ancient Egyptians, both men and women, was notorious.

9. *and sin against God.* Joseph would not betray his master's confidence, neither would he sin against God. As a God-fearing man, he knows that the thing is wrong in the sight of God; and that is enough for him. Potiphar might never know of the sin, but God would know.

12. *and fled.* Some sins can only be avoided by flight. Ecclesiasticus XXI, 2. 'Flee from sin, as from the face of a serpent; for if thou come too near it will bite thee: the teeth thereof are as the teeth of a lion, slaying the souls of men.' The Rabbis say, 'At the moment of temptation, his father's image appeared to him and gave him strength to resist.'

14. *she called.* Filled with vindictive malice because of thwarted desire, she calls aloud to the men of the house, who would be envious of their master's favour towards Joseph.

a Hebrew. See *v.* 1 and XXXIII, 32. Being of ancient Egyptian stock (see *v.* 1), she appeals to Egyptian racial prejudice. The admission of this Asiatic alien into her home is an insult to her and to every race-pure Egyptian!

to mock us. To attempt the greatest outrage against us.

in a Hebrew unto us to mock us; he came in unto me to lie with me, and I cried with a loud voice. 15. And it came to pass, when he heard that I lifted up my voice and cried, that he left his garment by me, and fled, and got him out.' 16. And she laid up his garment by her, until his master came home. 17. And she spoke unto him according to these words, saying: 'The Hebrew servant, whom thou hast brought unto us, came in unto me to mock me. 18. And it came to pass, as I lifted up my voice and cried, that he left his garment by me, and fled out.' 19. And it came to pass, when his master heard the words of his wife, which she spoke unto him, saying: 'After this manner did thy servant to me'; that his wrath was kindled. 20. And Joseph's master took him, and put him into the prison, the place where the king's prisoners were bound; and he was there in the prison. 21. But the LORD was with Joseph, and showed kindness unto him, and gave him favour in the sight of the keeper of the prison. 22. And the keeper of the prison committed to Joseph's hand all the prisoners that were in the prison; and whatsoever they did there, he was the doer of it. 23. The keeper of the prison looked not to any thing that was under his hand, because the LORD was with him; and that which he did, the LORD made it to prosper.* vii.

40

CHAPTER XL

1. And it came to pass after these things, that the butler of the king of Egypt and his baker offended their lord the king of Egypt. 2. And Pharaoh was wroth against his two officers, against the chief of the butlers, and against the chief of the bakers.

וַתֹּאמֶר לָהֶם לֵאמֹר רְאוּ הֵבִיא לָנוּ אִישׁ עִבְרִי לְצַחֶק
טו בָּנוּ בָּא אֵלַי לִשְׁכַּב עִמִּי וָאֶקְרָא בְּקוֹל גָּדוֹל׃ וַיְהִי כְשָׁמְעוֹ
כִּי־הֲרִימֹתִי קוֹלִי וָאֶקְרָא וַיַּעֲזֹב בִּגְדוֹ אֶצְלִי וַיָּנָס וַיֵּצֵא
16 הַחוּצָה׃ וַתַּנַּח בִּגְדוֹ אֶצְלָהּ עַד־בּוֹא אֲדֹנָיו אֶל־בֵּיתוֹ׃
17 וַתְּדַבֵּר אֵלָיו כַּדְּבָרִים הָאֵלֶּה לֵאמֹר בָּא אֵלַי הָעֶבֶד
18 הָעִבְרִי אֲשֶׁר־הֵבֵאתָ לָּנוּ לְצַחֶק בִּי׃ וַיְהִי כַּהֲרִימִי קוֹלִי
19 וָאֶקְרָא וַיַּעֲזֹב בִּגְדוֹ אֶצְלִי וַיָּנָס הַחוּצָה׃ וַיְהִי כִשְׁמֹעַ
אֲדֹנָיו אֶת־דִּבְרֵי אִשְׁתּוֹ אֲשֶׁר דִּבְּרָה אֵלָיו לֵאמֹר כַּדְּבָרִים
כ הָאֵלֶּה עָשָׂה לִי עַבְדֶּךָ וַיִּחַר אַפּוֹ׃ וַיִּקַּח אֲדֹנֵי יוֹסֵף אֹתוֹ
וַיִּתְּנֵהוּ אֶל־בֵּית הַסֹּהַר מְקוֹם אֲשֶׁר־אֲסוּרֵי הַמֶּלֶךְ אֲסוּרִים
21 וַיְהִי־שָׁם בְּבֵית הַסֹּהַר׃ וַיְהִי יְהוָה אֶת־יוֹסֵף וַיֵּט אֵלָיו
22 חָסֶד וַיִּתֵּן חִנּוֹ בְּעֵינֵי שַׂר בֵּית־הַסֹּהַר׃ וַיִּתֵּן שַׂר בֵּית־
הַסֹּהַר בְּיַד־יוֹסֵף אֵת כָּל־הָאֲסִירִם אֲשֶׁר בְּבֵית הַסֹּהַר
23 וְאֵת כָּל־אֲשֶׁר עֹשִׂים שָׁם הוּא הָיָה עֹשֶׂה׃ אֵין ׀ שַׂר בֵּית־
הַסֹּהַר רֹאֶה אֶת־כָּל־מְאוּמָה בְּיָדוֹ בַּאֲשֶׁר יְהוָה אִתּוֹ
וַאֲשֶׁר־הוּא עֹשֶׂה יְהוָה מַצְלִיחַ׃ פ שביעי

CAP. XL. מ

מ
א וַיְהִי אַחַר הַדְּבָרִים הָאֵלֶּה חָטְאוּ מַשְׁקֵה מֶלֶךְ־מִצְרַיִם
2 וְהָאֹפֶה לַאֲדֹנֵיהֶם לְמֶלֶךְ מִצְרָיִם׃ וַיִּקְצֹף פַּרְעֹה עַל שְׁנֵי

לט' v. 20. אסירי ק'

16. *laid up.* *i.e.* put by.
his garment. As evidence to convict Joseph, and convince Potiphar of her own innocence.

20. *the prison.* The Heb. word occurs only here, and seems to be Egyptian. The Midrash explains that Potiphar had some doubt as to the truth of the accusation against Joseph; otherwise he would have put him to death, instead of putting him to prison. To this episode in Joseph's life, there is an interesting parallel in the Egyptian 'Tale of the two Brothers'. In the Tale, the wicked wife is slain by her husband.

21. *but the LORD was with Joseph.* In the prison, giving him comfort and strength to endure the suffering and the shame. He wins the confidence of the keeper, as he did of his master. The light of a superior mind and soul cannot be hidden even in a prison.

22. *committed to Joseph's hand.* *i.e.* he is made superintendent of the other prisoners.
he was the doer of it. All was done at the suggestion of Joseph.

23. *looked not to any thing.* Just as Potiphar had done. Joseph enjoyed full confidence.

CHAPTER XL. JOSEPH AND THE PRISONERS

Joseph interprets the dreams of Pharaoh's two officers. The scene faithfully reflects Egyptian conditions in the age of Joseph.

1. *after these things.* Recounted in the preceding chapter.

2. *the butlers . . . the bakers.* The Egyptian court had a 'scribe of the sideboard' and a 'superintendent of the bakehouse' (Erman).

3 סָרִיסָיו עַל שַׂר הַמַּשְׁקִים וְעַל שַׂר הָאוֹפִים׃ וַיִּתֵּן אֹתָם
בְּמִשְׁמַר בֵּית שַׂר הַטַּבָּחִים אֶל־בֵּית הַסֹּהַר מְקוֹם אֲשֶׁר
4 יוֹסֵף אָסוּר שָׁם׃ וַיִּפְקֹד שַׂר הַטַּבָּחִים אֶת־יוֹסֵף אִתָּם
ה וַיְשָׁרֶת אֹתָם וַיִּהְיוּ יָמִים בְּמִשְׁמָר׃ וַיַּחַלְמוּ חֲלוֹם שְׁנֵיהֶם
אִישׁ חֲלֹמוֹ בְּלַיְלָה אֶחָד אִישׁ כְּפִתְרוֹן חֲלֹמוֹ הַמַּשְׁקֶה
וְהָאֹפֶה אֲשֶׁר לְמֶלֶךְ מִצְרַיִם אֲשֶׁר אֲסוּרִים בְּבֵית הַסֹּהַר׃
6 וַיָּבֹא אֲלֵיהֶם יוֹסֵף בַּבֹּקֶר וַיַּרְא אֹתָם וְהִנָּם זֹעֲפִים׃
7 וַיִּשְׁאַל אֶת־סְרִיסֵי פַרְעֹה אֲשֶׁר אִתּוֹ בְמִשְׁמַר בֵּית אֲדֹנָיו
8 לֵאמֹר מַדּוּעַ פְּנֵיכֶם רָעִים הַיּוֹם׃ וַיֹּאמְרוּ אֵלָיו חֲלוֹם
חָלַמְנוּ וּפֹתֵר אֵין אֹתוֹ וַיֹּאמֶר אֲלֵהֶם יוֹסֵף הֲלוֹא לֵאלֹהִים
9 פִּתְרֹנִים סַפְּרוּ־נָא לִי׃ וַיְסַפֵּר שַׂר־הַמַּשְׁקִים אֶת־חֲלֹמוֹ
י לְיוֹסֵף וַיֹּאמֶר לוֹ בַּחֲלוֹמִי וְהִנֵּה־גֶפֶן לְפָנָי׃ וּבַגֶּפֶן שְׁלֹשָׁה
שָׂרִיגִם וְהִוא כְפֹרַחַת עָלְתָה נִצָּהּ הִבְשִׁילוּ אַשְׁכְּלֹתֶיהָ
11 עֲנָבִים׃ וְכוֹס פַּרְעֹה בְּיָדִי וָאֶקַּח אֶת־הָעֲנָבִים וָאֶשְׂחַט
אֹתָם אֶל־כּוֹס פַּרְעֹה וָאֶתֵּן אֶת־הַכּוֹס עַל־כַּף פַּרְעֹה׃
12 וַיֹּאמֶר לוֹ יוֹסֵף זֶה פִּתְרֹנוֹ שְׁלֹשֶׁת הַשָּׂרִגִים שְׁלֹשֶׁת יָמִים
13 הֵם׃ בְּעוֹד ׀ שְׁלֹשֶׁת יָמִים יִשָּׂא פַרְעֹה אֶת־רֹאשֶׁךָ וַהֲשִׁיבְךָ

3. And he put them in ward in the house of the captain of the guard, into the prison, the place where Joseph was bound. 4. And the captain of the guard charged Joseph to be with them, and he ministered unto them; and they continued a season in ward. 5. And they dreamed a dream both of them, each man his dream, in one night, each man according to the interpretation of his dream, the butler and the baker of the king of Egypt, who were bound in the prison. 6. And Joseph came in unto them in the morning, and saw them, and, behold, they were sad. 7. And he asked Pharaoh's officers that were with him in the ward of his master's house, saying: 'Wherefore look ye so sad to-day?' 8. And they said unto him: 'We have dreamed a dream, and there is none that can interpret it.' And Joseph said unto them: 'Do not interpretations belong to God? tell it me, I pray you.' 9. And the chief butler told his dream to Joseph, and said to him: 'In my dream, behold, a vine was before me; 10. and in the vine were three branches; and as it was budding, its blossoms shot forth, and the clusters thereof brought forth ripe grapes; 11. and Pharaoh's cup was in my hand; and I took the grapes, and pressed them into Pharaoh's cup, and I gave the cup into Pharaoh's hand.' 12. And Joseph said unto him: 'This is the interpretation of it: the three branches are three days; 13. within yet three days shall Pharaoh lift up thy head, and restore thee unto thine office; and thou shalt give Pharaoh's cup

These officers had to taste the food for the king before the royal meal began. The word for butler may also be rendered, 'cup-bearer.' It is conjectured that these officials were accused of plotting to poison Pharaoh.

3. *in ward.* In confinement, pending their trial.

captain of the guard. i.e. Potiphar. In the prison, the keeper was in charge and was responsible to Potiphar.

4. Potiphar appoints Joseph to be with the imprisoned officers. He is not appointed over them, but he is deputed to be their attendant—a mark of courtesy on the part of Potiphar to his unfortunate colleagues.

a season. lit. 'days'; implying a considerable time.

5. *according to the interpretation.* As the future verified.

8. *none that can interpret it.* No professional interpreter was available, and they had in vain consulted others in the prison as to the possible meaning of their dreams. The interpreter was a professional man of importance in Egypt and Babylon, belonging to the class of soothsayers, magicians and 'wise men'.

do not interpretations belong to God. i.e. it may be that God who sent the dreams will give me the interpretation of them. 'Man cannot by his own wisdom interpret dreams. God alone can reveal their true meaning. Pray tell me the dream, perhaps He will favour me with wisdom to explain its import' (Chizkuni).

11. *pressed them.* Grape juice mixed with water is mentioned as a refreshing drink on the Egyptian inscriptions.

13. *lift up thy head.* In honour, by restoring thee to thy post.

14. *have me in thy remembrance.* All he asks is that the chief butler should not forget him, but try to secure his freedom.

עַל־כַּנֶּךָ וְנָתַתָּ כוֹס־פַּרְעֹה בְּיָדוֹ כַּמִּשְׁפָּט הָרִאשׁוֹן אֲשֶׁר
14 הָיִיתָ מַשְׁקֵהוּ׃ כִּי אִם־זְכַרְתַּנִי אִתְּךָ כַּאֲשֶׁר יִיטַב לָךְ
וְעָשִׂיתָ־נָּא עִמָּדִי חָסֶד וְהִזְכַּרְתַּנִי אֶל־פַּרְעֹה וְהוֹצֵאתַנִי
טו מִן־הַבַּיִת הַזֶּה׃ כִּי־גֻנֹּב גֻּנַּבְתִּי מֵאֶרֶץ הָעִבְרִים וְגַם־פֹּה
16 לֹא־עָשִׂיתִי מְאוּמָה כִּי־שָׂמוּ אֹתִי בַּבּוֹר׃ וַיַּרְא שַׂר־הָאֹפִים
כִּי־טוֹב פָּתָר וַיֹּאמֶר אֶל־יוֹסֵף אַף־אֲנִי בַּחֲלוֹמִי וְהִנֵּה
17 שְׁלֹשָׁה סַלֵּי חֹרִי עַל־רֹאשִׁי׃ וּבַסַּל הָעֶלְיוֹן מִכֹּל מַאֲכַל
פַּרְעֹה מַעֲשֵׂה אֹפֶה וְהָעוֹף אֹכֵל אֹתָם מִן־הַסַּל מֵעַל
18 רֹאשִׁי׃ וַיַּעַן יוֹסֵף וַיֹּאמֶר זֶה פִּתְרֹנוֹ שְׁלֹשֶׁת הַסַּלִּים
19 שְׁלֹשֶׁת יָמִים הֵם׃ בְּעוֹד ׀ שְׁלֹשֶׁת יָמִים יִשָּׂא פַרְעֹה אֶת־
רֹאשְׁךָ מֵעָלֶיךָ וְתָלָה אוֹתְךָ עַל־עֵץ וְאָכַל הָעוֹף אֶת־
מפטיר
כ בְּשָׂרְךָ מֵעָלֶיךָ׃ וַיְהִי ׀ בַּיּוֹם הַשְּׁלִישִׁי יוֹם הֻלֶּדֶת אֶת־
פַּרְעֹה וַיַּעַשׂ מִשְׁתֶּה לְכָל־עֲבָדָיו וַיִּשָּׂא אֶת־רֹאשׁ ׀ שַׂר
21 הַמַּשְׁקִים וְאֶת־רֹאשׁ שַׂר הָאֹפִים בְּתוֹךְ עֲבָדָיו׃ וַיָּשֶׁב
אֶת־שַׂר הַמַּשְׁקִים עַל־מַשְׁקֵהוּ וַיִּתֵּן הַכּוֹס עַל־כַּף פַּרְעֹה׃
22 23 וְאֵת שַׂר הָאֹפִים תָּלָה כַּאֲשֶׁר פָּתַר לָהֶם יוֹסֵף׃ וְלֹא־זָכַר
שַׂר־הַמַּשְׁקִים אֶת־יוֹסֵף וַיִּשְׁכָּחֵהוּ׃

v. 15. טלרע

into his hand, after the former manner when thou wast his butler. 14. But have me in thy remembrance when it shall be well with thee, and show kindness, I pray thee, unto me, and make mention of me unto Pharaoh, and bring me out of this house. 15. For indeed I was stolen away out of the land of the Hebrews; and here also have I done nothing that they should put me into the dungeon.' 16. When the chief baker saw that the interpretation was good, he said unto Joseph: 'I also saw in my dream, and, behold, three baskets of white bread were on my head; 17. and in the uppermost basket there was of all manner of baked food for Pharaoh; and the birds did eat them out of the basket upon my head.' 18. And Joseph answered and said: 'This is the interpretation thereof: the three baskets are three days; 19. within yet three days shall Pharaoh lift up thy head from off thee, and shall hang thee on a tree; and the birds shall eat thy flesh from off thee.'* m. 20. And it came to pass the third day, which was Pharaoh's birthday, that he made a feast unto all his servants; and he lifted up the head of the chief butler and the head of the chief baker among his servants. 21. And he restored the chief butler back unto his butlership; and he gave the cup into Pharaoh's hand. 22. But he hanged the chief baker, as Joseph had interpreted to them. 23. Yet did not the chief butler remember Joseph, but forgot him.

15. *stolen away.* See XXXVII, 28, implying that he was not a slave by birth.

land of the Hebrews. The land where Jacob was dwelling. Some identify the word 'Hebrews' in this verse with the *Habiri*, the invaders of Palestine in the 14th pre-Christian century, who are mentioned in the Tell-el-Amarna tablets.

16. *that the interpretation was good.* *i.e.* favourable. This encourages him to relate his dream.

baskets of white bread. For the king (cf. Neh. V, 18); or, 'baskets of open wicker-work,' enabling the birds to peck at the contents (Rashbam).

17. *baked food.* Confectionery.

and the birds. The butler dreamed that he actually performed the duties of his office, whereas the baker only sought to do so, but was prevented. The further ominous circumstance was the birds darting down upon the food, he being powerless to drive them away.

19. *hang thee.* Impale thee. The decapitated corpse of malefactors was allowed to hang exposed to the public view, and to become the prey of the birds. In Israel, this barbarous custom was prohibited (Deut. XXI, 23).

20. *Pharaoh's birthday.* On that day he reviewed the prisoners or considered their petitions.

23. *not . . . remember Joseph.* On that day.

but forgot him. Afterwards (Rashi). As Joseph had put his trust in the butler, God caused him to wait two years for his freedom (Midrash). The chief butler's forgetfulness, in the enjoyment of his own good fortune, is sadly natural. Nothing alas is more common than ingratitude. Man forgets; but God does not forget his own. And when the night is darkest, the dawn is near.

AMOS II, 6–III, 8

CHAPTER II

6. Thus saith the LORD:
For three transgressions of Israel,
Yea, for four, I will not reverse it:
Because they sell the righteous for silver,
And the needy for a pair of shoes;
7. That pant after the dust of the earth on the head of the poor,
And turn aside the way of the humble;
And a man and his father go unto the same maid,
To profane My holy name;
8. And they lay themselves down beside every altar
Upon clothes taken in pledge,
And in the house of their God they drink
The wine of them that have been fined.

CAP. II. ב

6 כֹּה אָמַר יְהוָה עַל־שְׁלֹשָׁה
פִּשְׁעֵי יִשְׂרָאֵל וְעַל־אַרְבָּעָה לֹא אֲשִׁיבֶנּוּ עַל־מִכְרָם בַּכֶּסֶף
7 צַדִּיק וְאֶבְיוֹן בַּעֲבוּר נַעֲלָיִם׃ הַשֹּׁאֲפִים עַל־עֲפַר־אֶרֶץ
בְּרֹאשׁ דַּלִּים וְדֶרֶךְ עֲנָוִים יַטּוּ וְאִישׁ וְאָבִיו יֵלְכוּ אֶל־
8 הַנַּעֲרָה לְמַעַן חַלֵּל אֶת־שֵׁם קָדְשִׁי׃ וְעַל־בְּגָדִים חֲבֻלִים
יַטּוּ אֵצֶל כָּל־מִזְבֵּחַ וְיֵין עֲנוּשִׁים יִשְׁתּוּ בֵּית אֱלֹהֵיהֶם׃

Amos, a herdsman and dresser of sycamore trees, felt the stirring of the spirit of the LORD while pursuing his lonely calling amid the hills of Judea. He is an older contemporary of Hosea, and is the first of the literary Prophets. The master-word of existence to Amos is Righteousness—which to him, as to his successors, means holiness of life in the individual and the triumph of right in the world. Righteousness is the basis of national as of individual life. Without it, all else crumbles to ruin. For God is righteousness. He is the God of all families of the earth; and all of them alike He judges according to their humane dealings towards their fellowmen. Man's inhumanity to man, Amos proclaims to be *the* cardinal sin. As to Israel, it is God's chosen people; but this great privilege carried no immunity against Divine punishment for wrong-doing. On the contrary. Just because Israel is God's people, the higher must be its standard of life; and the greater its guilt and punishment, if and when it falls away from righteousness.

After pronouncing judgment on the surrounding peoples for their violation of the dictates of universal morality and their participation in barbarous practices, Amos turns to the Northern Kingdom of Israel, judging its inhabitants with the same standard and in the very same words as he did the heathens.

6–8. Israel's crimes are no less heinous. It sins against justice, mercy and purity.

6. *For three transgressions of Israel, yea, for four, I will not reverse it. i.e.* turn away the punishment. Three or four—a phrase signifying an indefinite number, and illustrating the mercy of God. For the first, second, and even third transgression, He holds His hand, waiting for the transgressor to cease wrong-doing. It is not till the fourth sin, that His long-suffering is at an end (Kimchi).

sell the righteous. The innocent are declared guilty for a bribe; and rich men sell into slavery poor honest people whose only crime was that they were in debt to them, sometimes only to the value of a pair of shoes. This sale of the innocent man (צדיק) gives the connection with the story of Joseph, spoken of by the Rabbis as הצדיק, the innocent victim of hatred and slander.

7. *that pant.* So great is the cupidity of the rich and powerful that they covet the most insignificant possession still left to the poor, even the dust on the poor man's head sprinkled there as a sign of mourning—ironically adds the Prophet.

turn aside the way of the humble. 'Humble souls they harry' (Moffatt). The word 'way' here means the right. They pervert the justice of those who are too weak to defend themselves against their cunning.

the same maid. With callousness to human suffering goes lust. And their unchastity is abominable, devoid of all human shame.

profane My holy name. Their life and actions constitute a *chillul hashem*, a profanation of the Name of God and Israel—an unpardonable sin; cf. Lev. XXII, 24; Ezek. XX, 9, 14.

8. *clothes taken in pledge.* They make the necessities of the poor serve their heartless luxury during their religious feasts. For the sin against the poor, see Exod. XXII, 25, and Deut. XXIV, 12–13.

9. Yet destroyed I the Amorite before them,
Whose height was like the height of the cedars,
And he was strong as the oaks;
Yet I destroyed his fruit from above,
And his roots from beneath.
10. Also I brought you up out of the land of Egypt,
And led you forty years in the wilderness,
To possess the land of the Amorite.
11. And I raised up of your sons for prophets,
And of your young men for Nazirites.
Is it not even thus, O ye children of Israel?
Saith the LORD.
12. But ye gave the Nazirites wine to drink;
And commanded the prophets, saying: 'Prophesy not.'
13. Behold, I will make it creak under you,
As a cart creaketh that is full of sheaves.
14. And flight shall fail the swift,
And the strong shall not exert his strength,
Neither shall the mighty deliver himself;
15. Neither shall he stand that handleth the bow;
And he that is swift of foot shall not deliver himself;
Neither shall he that rideth the horse deliver himself;
16. And he that is courageous among the mighty
Shall flee away naked in that day,
Saith the LORD.

CHAPTER III

1. Hear this word that the LORD hath spoken against you, O children of Israel, against the whole family which I brought up out of the land of Egypt, saying:

2. You only have I known of all the families of the earth;
Therefore I will visit upon you all your iniquities.

9 וְאָנֹכִי הִשְׁמַדְתִּי אֶת־הָאֱמֹרִי מִפְּנֵיהֶם אֲשֶׁר כְּגֹבַהּ אֲרָזִים
גָּבְהוֹ וְחָסֹן הוּא כָּאַלּוֹנִים וָאַשְׁמִיד פִּרְיוֹ מִמַּעַל וְשָׁרָשָׁיו
י מִתָּחַת׃ וְאָנֹכִי הֶעֱלֵיתִי אֶתְכֶם מֵאֶרֶץ מִצְרָיִם וָאוֹלֵךְ
אֶתְכֶם בַּמִּדְבָּר אַרְבָּעִים שָׁנָה לָרֶשֶׁת אֶת־אֶרֶץ הָאֱמֹרִי׃
11 וָאָקִים מִבְּנֵיכֶם לִנְבִיאִים וּמִבַּחוּרֵיכֶם לִנְזִרִים הַאַף אֵין
12 זֹאת בְּנֵי יִשְׂרָאֵל נְאֻם־יְהוָה׃ וַתַּשְׁקוּ אֶת־הַנְּזִרִים יָיִן
13 וְעַל־הַנְּבִיאִים צִוִּיתֶם לֵאמֹר לֹא תִּנָּבְאוּ׃ הִנֵּה אָנֹכִי מֵעִיק
14 תַּחְתֵּיכֶם כַּאֲשֶׁר תָּעִיק הָעֲגָלָה הַמְלֵאָה לָהּ עָמִיר׃ וְאָבַד
מָנוֹס מִקָּל וְחָזָק לֹא־יְאַמֵּץ כֹּחוֹ וְגִבּוֹר לֹא־יְמַלֵּט נַפְשׁוֹ׃
טו וְתֹפֵשׂ הַקֶּשֶׁת לֹא יַעֲמֹד וְקַל בְּרַגְלָיו לֹא יְמַלֵּט וְרֹכֵב
16 הַסּוּס לֹא יְמַלֵּט נַפְשׁוֹ׃ וְאַמִּיץ לִבּוֹ בַּגִּבּוֹרִים עָרוֹם יָנוּס
בַּיּוֹם־הַהוּא נְאֻם־יְהוָה׃

CAP. III. ג

א שִׁמְעוּ אֶת־הַדָּבָר הַזֶּה אֲשֶׁר דִּבֶּר יְהוָה עֲלֵיכֶם בְּנֵי יִשְׂרָאֵל
עַל כָּל־הַמִּשְׁפָּחָה אֲשֶׁר הֶעֱלֵיתִי מֵאֶרֶץ מִצְרַיִם לֵאמֹר׃
2 רַק אֶתְכֶם יָדַעְתִּי מִכֹּל מִשְׁפְּחוֹת הָאֲדָמָה עַל־כֵּן אֶפְקֹד

ב׳ v. 14. קמץ בז״ק

9. *the Amorite.* Representing the previous inhabitants of Palestine, as the Amorite was the most powerful tribe. The Prophet points to the monstrous ingratitude of Israel.

11. *Nazirites.* True and inspired men are among a nation's most precious possessions. The Nazirite, who vowed to refrain from wine (Numbers VI, 2–21), stood for self-control, and by his very existence rebuked the intemperance of the day. So he was basely urged to break his vow.

12. *prophesy not.* The experience of Amos himself, VIII, 13.

13. As a cart overloaded with its harvest creaks under the weight; so a people overladen with sin cannot escape the consequences of its sins. The prophecy was fulfilled by the invasion of Assyria.

CHAPTER III

2. *therefore.* The most famous 'therefore' in history. Israel is the chosen of God. *Therefore*, God demands higher, not lower, standards of goodness from Israel, and will punish lapses more severely. The higher the privilege, the graver the responsibility. The greater the opportunity, the more inexcusable the failure to use it.

3–8. These verses give the ground on which Amos claims to be heard.

3 עֲלֵיכֶם אֵת כָּל־עֲוֺנֹתֵיכֶם׃ הֲיֵלְכוּ שְׁנַיִם יַחְדָּו בִּלְתִּי אִם־
4 נוֹעָדוּ׃ הֲיִשְׁאַג אַרְיֵה בַּיַּעַר וְטֶרֶף אֵין לוֹ הֲיִתֵּן כְּפִיר
ה קוֹלוֹ מִמְּעֹנָתוֹ בִּלְתִּי אִם־לָכָד׃ הֲתִפֹּל צִפּוֹר עַל־פַּח
הָאָרֶץ וּמוֹקֵשׁ אֵין לָהּ הֲיַעֲלֶה־פַּח מִן־הָאֲדָמָה וְלָכוֹד לֹא
6 יִלְכּוֹד׃ אִם־יִתָּקַע שׁוֹפָר בְּעִיר וְעָם לֹא יֶחֱרָדוּ אִם־תִּהְיֶה
7 רָעָה בְּעִיר וַיהוָה לֹא עָשָׂה׃ כִּי לֹא יַעֲשֶׂה אֲדֹנָי יֱהוִה
8 דָּבָר כִּי אִם־גָּלָה סוֹדוֹ אֶל־עֲבָדָיו הַנְּבִיאִים׃ אַרְיֵה שָׁאָג
מִי לֹא יִירָא אֲדֹנָי יֱהוִה דִּבֶּר מִי לֹא יִנָּבֵא׃

3. Will two walk together,
Except they have agreed?

4. Will a lion roar in the forest,
When he hath no prey?
Will a young lion give forth his voice out of his den,
If he have taken nothing?

5. Will a bird fall in a snare upon the earth,
Where there is no lure for it?
Will a snare spring up from the ground,
And have taken nothing at all?

6. Shall the horn be blown in a city,
And the people not tremble?
Shall evil befall a city,
And the LORD hath not done it?

7. For the LORD God will do nothing,
But He revealeth His counsel unto His servants the prophets.

8. The lion hath roared,
Who will not fear?
The LORD God hath spoken,
Who can but prophesy?

v. 8. קמץ בלא אס״ף

3. A declaration of the Prophet's Divine authority. The Prophet has spoken, only because God has inspired him. God and the Prophet are met on this sad task.

4–6. Figures of speech illustrating the cause and effect stated in the previous verse, drawn from experiences in the Prophet's earlier calling as herdsman. If the roar of the lion is heard in the desert, it is because he has seized his prey. The bird has fallen, because the snare has caught it. The tocsin is sounded in the city, because the enemy is at the gate. So likewise disaster does not overwhelm a people without a cause.

7. *He revealeth His counsel.* The watcher on the tower at the entrance of the city who sees attacking troops advancing will sound the alarm that arouses and terrifies the people. Israel cannot plead lack of warning. The Prophet is the true Watcher on the tower who would deliver from threatening evils by his summons to repentance. And he speaks because God is acting within, and irresistibly compels him.

8. *who can but prophesy?* To us the voice of God speaks through the pages of Scripture; and, if we would listen and understand and perform its precepts, surely would 'all the LORD's people be prophets'.

41

CHAPTER XLI

1. And it came to pass at the end of two full years, that Pharaoh dreamed: and, behold, he stood by the [1]river. 2. And, behold, there came up out of the river seven kine, well-favoured and fat-fleshed; and they fed in the reed-grass. 3. And, behold, seven other kine came up after them out of the river, ill-favoured and lean-fleshed; and stood by the other kine upon the brink of the river. 4. And the ill-favoured and lean-fleshed kine did eat up the seven well-favoured and fat kine. So Pharaoh awoke. 5. And he slept and dreamed a second time: and, behold, seven ears of corn came up upon one stalk, rank and good. 6. And, behold, seven ears, thin and blasted with the east wind, sprung up after them. 7. And the thin ears swallowed up the seven rank and full ears. And Pharaoh awoke, and, behold, it was a dream. 8. And it came to pass in the morning that his spirit was troubled; and he sent and called for all the magicians of Egypt, and all the wise men thereof; and Pharaoh told them his dream; but there was none that could interpret them unto Pharaoh. 9. Then spoke the chief butler unto Pharaoh, saying: 'I make mention of my faults this day: 10. Pharaoh was wroth with his servants, and put me in the ward of the house of the captain of the guard, me and the chief baker. 11. And we dreamed a dream in one night, I and he; we dreamed each man according to the interpretation of his dream. 12. And there was with us there a young man, a Hebrew, servant to the captain of the guard; and we told him, and he interpreted to us our dreams; to each man according to his dream he did interpret. 13. And it came to pass, as he interpreted to us, so it was: I was restored unto mine office,

[1] That is, the Nile.

CAP. XLI. מא

מא פ פ פ י 10

א ויהי מקץ שנתים ימים ופרעה חלם והנה עמד על־
2 היאר: והנה מן־היאר עלת שבע פרות יפות מראה
3 ובריאת בשר ותרעינה באחו: והנה שבע פרות אחרות
עלות אחריהן מן־היאר רעות מראה ודקות בשר
4 ותעמדנה אצל הפרות על־שפת היאר: ותאכלנה הפרות
רעות המראה ודקת הבשר את שבע הפרות יפת
ה המראה והבריאת וייקץ פרעה: ויישן ויחלם שנית
והנה ׀ שבע שבלים עלות בקנה אחד בריאות וטבות:
6 והנה שבע שבלים דקות ושדופת קדים צמחות אחריהן:
7 ותבלענה השבלים הדקות את שבע השבלים הבריאות
8 והמלאות וייקץ פרעה והנה חלום: ויהי בבקר ותפעם
רוחו וישלח ויקרא את־כל־חרטמי מצרים ואת־כל־
חכמיה ויספר פרעה להם את־חלמו ואין־פותר אותם
9 לפרעה: וידבר שר המשקים את־פרעה לאמר את־
י חטאי אני מזכיר היום: פרעה קצף על־עבדיו ויתן אתי
במשמר בית שר הטבחים אתי ואת שר האפים:
11 ונחלמה חלום בלילה אחד אני והוא איש כפתרון
12 חלמו חלמנו: ושם אתנו נער עברי עבד לשר הטבחים
ונספר־לו ויפתר־לנו את־חלמתינו איש כחלמו פתר:
13 ויהי כאשר פתר־לנו כן היה אתי השיב על־כני ואתו

v. 5. קמץ בז״ק

X. MIKKETZ

(CHAPTERS XLI–XLIV, 17)

CHAPTER XLI. JOSEPH AND PHARAOH

1. *two full years.* After the events recounted in the previous chapter.

2. *reed-grass.* Heb. *achu*, another Egyptian loan-word. The Nile-grass is meant here.

5. *rank.* Heb. 'fat', *i.e.* rich.

6. *east wind.* The dreaded sirocco coming from Arabia. It lasts at times fifty days and destroys the vegetation.

8. *his spirit was troubled.* The double dream convinced him of its significance. The Heb. verb for 'was troubled' suggests the violent beating of the heart in excitement.

magicians. Or, 'sacred scribes'; Heb. *chartumim*—probably an Egyptian word.

none that could interpret. The complete failure of heathen magic is here contrasted with the perfect wisdom of the God-inspired Hebrew slave; cf. Exod. VII–IX, 2, and Daniel II and V.

9. *I make mention of my faults.* Not only his offence against the king, but also his sin against Joseph in forgetting him.

12. *to each man according to his dream.* The dream was appropriate to each one, and the interpretation was equally appropriate.

and he was hanged.' 14. Then Pharaoh sent and called Joseph, and they brought him hastily out of the dungeon. And he shaved himself, and changed his raiment, and came in unto Pharaoh.* ii a. 15. And Pharaoh said unto Joseph: 'I have dreamed a dream, and there is none that can interpret it; and I have heard say of thee, that when thou hearest a dream thou canst interpret it.' 16. And Joseph answered Pharaoh, saying: 'It is not in me; God will give Pharaoh an answer of peace.'* ii s. 17. And Pharaoh spoke unto Joseph: 'In my dream, behold, I stood upon the brink of the river. 18. And, behold, there came up out of the river seven kine, fat-fleshed and well-favoured; and they fed in the reed-grass. 19. And, behold, seven other kine came up after them, poor and very ill-favoured and lean-fleshed, such as I never saw in all the land of Egypt for badness. 20. And the lean and ill-favoured kine did eat up the first seven fat kine. 21. And when they had eaten them up, it could not be known that they had eaten them; but they were still ill-favoured as at the beginning. So I awoke. 22. And I saw in my dream, and, behold, seven ears came up upon one stalk, full and good. 23. And, behold, seven ears, withered, thin, and blasted with the east wind, sprung up after them. 24. And the thin ears swallowed up the seven good ears. And I told it unto the magicians; but there was none that could declare it to me.' 25. And Joseph said unto Pharaoh: 'The dream of Pharaoh is one; what God is about to do He hath declared unto Pharaoh. 26. The seven good kine are seven years; and the seven good ears are seven years: the dream is one. 27. And the seven lean and ill-favoured kine that came up after them are seven years, and also the seven empty ears blasted with the east wind; they shall be seven years of famine. 28. That is the thing which I spoke unto Pharaoh: what God is about to do He hath shown unto Pharaoh. 29. Behold, there come seven years of great plenty throughout all

14 תָּלָה: וַיִּשְׁלַח פַּרְעֹה וַיִּקְרָא אֶת־יוֹסֵף וַיְרִיצֻהוּ מִן־הַבּוֹר
שני
טו וַיְגַלַּח וַיְחַלֵּף שִׂמְלֹתָיו וַיָּבֹא אֶל־פַּרְעֹה: וַיֹּאמֶר פַּרְעֹה
אֶל־יוֹסֵף חֲלוֹם חָלַמְתִּי וּפֹתֵר אֵין אֹתוֹ וַאֲנִי שָׁמַעְתִּי
16 עָלֶיךָ לֵאמֹר תִּשְׁמַע חֲלוֹם לִפְתֹּר אֹתוֹ: וַיַּעַן יוֹסֵף אֶת־
שני לספ') פַּרְעֹה לֵאמֹר בִּלְעָדָי אֱלֹהִים יַעֲנֶה אֶת־שְׁלוֹם פַּרְעֹה:
17 וַיְדַבֵּר פַּרְעֹה אֶל־יוֹסֵף בַּחֲלֹמִי הִנְנִי עֹמֵד עַל־שְׂפַת הַיְאֹר:
18 וְהִנֵּה מִן־הַיְאֹר עֹלֹת שֶׁבַע פָּרוֹת בְּרִיאוֹת בָּשָׂר וִיפֹת
19 תֹּאַר וַתִּרְעֶינָה בָּאָחוּ: וְהִנֵּה שֶׁבַע־פָּרוֹת אֲחֵרוֹת עֹלוֹת
אַחֲרֵיהֶן דַּלּוֹת וְרָעוֹת תֹּאַר מְאֹד וְרַקּוֹת בָּשָׂר לֹא־רָאִיתִי
כ כָהֵנָּה בְּכָל־אֶרֶץ מִצְרַיִם לָרֹעַ: וַתֹּאכַלְנָה הַפָּרוֹת הָרַקּוֹת
21 וְהָרָעוֹת אֵת שֶׁבַע הַפָּרוֹת הָרִאשֹׁנוֹת הַבְּרִיאֹת: וַתָּבֹאנָה
אֶל־קִרְבֶּנָה וְלֹא נוֹדַע כִּי־בָאוּ אֶל־קִרְבֶּנָה וּמַרְאֵיהֶן רַע
22 כַּאֲשֶׁר בַּתְּחִלָּה וָאִיקָץ: וָאֵרֶא בַּחֲלֹמִי וְהִנֵּה ׀ שֶׁבַע שִׁבֳּלִים
23 עֹלֹת בְּקָנֶה אֶחָד מְלֵאֹת וְטֹבוֹת: וְהִנֵּה שֶׁבַע שִׁבֳּלִים
24 צְנֻמוֹת דַּקּוֹת שְׁדֻפוֹת קָדִים צֹמְחוֹת אַחֲרֵיהֶם: וַתִּבְלַעְןָ
הַשִּׁבֳּלִים הַדַּקֹּת אֵת שֶׁבַע הַשִּׁבֳּלִים הַטֹּבוֹת וָאֹמַר אֶל־
כה הַחַרְטֻמִּים וְאֵין מַגִּיד לִי: וַיֹּאמֶר יוֹסֵף אֶל־פַּרְעֹה חֲלוֹם
פַּרְעֹה אֶחָד הוּא אֵת אֲשֶׁר הָאֱלֹהִים עֹשֶׂה הִגִּיד לְפַרְעֹה:
26 שֶׁבַע פָּרֹת הַטֹּבֹת שֶׁבַע שָׁנִים הֵנָּה וְשֶׁבַע הַשִּׁבֳּלִים
27 הַטֹּבֹת שֶׁבַע שָׁנִים הֵנָּה חֲלוֹם אֶחָד הוּא: וְשֶׁבַע הַפָּרוֹת
הָרַקּוֹת וְהָרָעֹת הָעֹלֹת אַחֲרֵיהֶן שֶׁבַע שָׁנִים הֵנָּה וְשֶׁבַע
הַשִּׁבֳּלִים הָרֵקוֹת שְׁדֻפוֹת הַקָּדִים יִהְיוּ שֶׁבַע שְׁנֵי רָעָב:
28 הוּא הַדָּבָר אֲשֶׁר דִּבַּרְתִּי אֶל־פַּרְעֹה אֲשֶׁר הָאֱלֹהִים עֹשֶׂה

16. *it is not in me.* Pharaoh assumed that Joseph was a professional interpreter of dreams. Joseph's answer is a fine combination of religious sincerity and courtly deference.

an answer of peace. i.e. an answer that will correspond to the needs of Pharaoh and his people.

19. *such as I never saw.* Pharaoh colours the recital by giving expression to the feelings which the dream excited.

25. *is one.* The two dreams have the same meaning. They are a foreboding of what God is about to do.

30. *shall consume the land. i.e.* the people of the land (Onkelos).

33–36. Joseph explains how God gives Pharaoh the answer of peace (*v.* 16). The interpretation of the dream is supplemented by the practical advice as to how the coming crisis should be met. Joseph the dreamer and saint proves himself in an eminent degree a man of practical affairs.

the land of Egypt. 30. And there shall arise after them seven years of famine; and all the plenty shall be forgotten in the land of Egypt; and the famine shall consume the land; 31. and the plenty shall not be known in the land by reason of that famine which followeth; for it shall be very grievous. 32. And for that the dream was doubled unto Pharaoh twice, it is because the thing is established by God, and God will shortly bring it to pass. 33. Now therefore let Pharaoh look out a man discreet and wise, and set him over the land of Egypt. 34. Let Pharaoh do this, and let him appoint overseers over the land, and take up the fifth part of the land of Egypt in the seven years of plenty. 35. And let them gather all the food of these good years that come, and lay up corn under the hand of Pharaoh for food in the cities, and let them keep it. 36. And the food shall be for a store to the land against the seven years of famine, which shall be in the land of Egypt; that the land perish not through the famine.' 37. And the thing was good in the eyes of Pharaoh, and in the eyes of all his servants. 38. And Pharaoh said unto his servants: 'Can we find such a one as this, a man in whom the spirit of God is?' * iii. 39. And Pharaoh said unto Joseph: 'Forasmuch as God hath shown thee all this, there is none so discreet and wise as thou. 40. Thou shalt be over my house, and according unto thy word shall all my people be ruled; only in the throne will I be greater than thou.' 41. And Pharaoh said unto Joseph: 'See, I have set thee over all the land of Egypt.' 42. And Pharaoh took off his signet ring from his hand, and put it upon Joseph's hand, and arrayed him in vestures of fine linen, and put a gold chain about his neck. 43. And he made him to ride in the second chariot which he had; and they cried before

29 הִרְאָה אֶת־פַּרְעֹה׃ הִנֵּה שֶׁבַע שָׁנִים בָּאוֹת שָׂבָע גָּדוֹל
ל בְּכָל־אֶרֶץ מִצְרָיִם׃ וְקָמוּ שֶׁבַע שְׁנֵי רָעָב אַחֲרֵיהֶן וְנִשְׁכַּח
31 כָּל־הַשָּׂבָע בְּאֶרֶץ מִצְרָיִם וְכִלָּה הָרָעָב אֶת־הָאָרֶץ׃ וְלֹא־
יִוָּדַע הַשָּׂבָע בָּאָרֶץ מִפְּנֵי הָרָעָב הַהוּא אַחֲרֵי־כֵן כִּי־כָבֵד
32 הוּא מְאֹד׃ וְעַל הִשָּׁנוֹת הַחֲלוֹם אֶל־פַּרְעֹה פַּעֲמָיִם כִּי־
נָכוֹן הַדָּבָר מֵעִם הָאֱלֹהִים וּמְמַהֵר הָאֱלֹהִים לַעֲשֹׂתוֹ׃
33 וְעַתָּה יֵרֶא פַרְעֹה אִישׁ נָבוֹן וְחָכָם וִישִׁיתֵהוּ עַל־אֶרֶץ
34 מִצְרָיִם׃ יַעֲשֶׂה פַרְעֹה וְיַפְקֵד פְּקִדִים עַל־הָאָרֶץ וְחִמֵּשׁ
לה אֶת־אֶרֶץ מִצְרַיִם בְּשֶׁבַע שְׁנֵי הַשָּׂבָע׃ וְיִקְבְּצוּ אֶת־כָּל־
אֹכֶל הַשָּׁנִים הַטֹּבוֹת הַבָּאֹת הָאֵלֶּה וְיִצְבְּרוּ־בָר תַּחַת יַד־
36 פַּרְעֹה אֹכֶל בֶּעָרִים וְשָׁמָרוּ׃ וְהָיָה הָאֹכֶל לְפִקָּדוֹן לָאָרֶץ
לְשֶׁבַע שְׁנֵי הָרָעָב אֲשֶׁר תִּהְיֶיןָ בְּאֶרֶץ מִצְרָיִם וְלֹא־תִכָּרֵת
37 הָאָרֶץ בָּרָעָב׃ וַיִּיטַב הַדָּבָר בְּעֵינֵי פַרְעֹה וּבְעֵינֵי כָּל־
38 עֲבָדָיו׃ וַיֹּאמֶר פַּרְעֹה אֶל־עֲבָדָיו הֲנִמְצָא כָזֶה אִישׁ אֲשֶׁר
שלישי 39 רוּחַ אֱלֹהִים בּוֹ׃ וַיֹּאמֶר פַּרְעֹה אֶל־יוֹסֵף אַחֲרֵי הוֹדִיעַ
מ אֱלֹהִים אוֹתְךָ אֶת־כָּל־זֹאת אֵין־נָבוֹן וְחָכָם כָּמוֹךָ׃ אַתָּה
תִּהְיֶה עַל־בֵּיתִי וְעַל־פִּיךָ יִשַּׁק כָּל־עַמִּי רַק הַכִּסֵּא אֶגְדַּל
41 מִמֶּךָּ׃ וַיֹּאמֶר פַּרְעֹה אֶל־יוֹסֵף רְאֵה נָתַתִּי אֹתְךָ עַל כָּל־
42 אֶרֶץ מִצְרָיִם׃ וַיָּסַר פַּרְעֹה אֶת־טַבַּעְתּוֹ מֵעַל יָדוֹ וַיִּתֵּן
אֹתָהּ עַל־יַד יוֹסֵף וַיַּלְבֵּשׁ אֹתוֹ בִּגְדֵי־שֵׁשׁ וַיָּשֶׂם רְבִד
43 הַזָּהָב עַל־צַוָּארוֹ׃ וַיַּרְכֵּב אֹתוֹ בְּמִרְכֶּבֶת הַמִּשְׁנֶה אֲשֶׁר־

35. *the hand of Pharaoh. i.e.* in the royal granaries.

in the cities. Where the royal granaries were.

36. *store.* A reserve.

38. *in whom the spirit of God is. i.e.* combining the supernatural power of interpreting dreams with the practical sagacity of a statesman.

40. *over my house.* He makes him Grand Vizier.
be ruled. Or, 'do homage.'

42. *signet ring.* Thereby symbolically endowing him with royal authority.

fine linen. The Heb. word comes from the Egyptian. It is the material worn by the royal family and the highest officials of the kingdom.

a gold chain. The gold collar appertaining to the office of Grand Vizier. This is another instance of the remarkable historical exactness of the Joseph narrative. 'No ancient civilization was more distinct and unique than that of Egypt. Her customs, her language, and her system of writing were shared by no other people; and yet, at every point, the narrative reveals a thorough familiarity with Egyptian life. Peculiar Egyptian customs are also reflected in the stories; as, for example, the giving of the much-prized golden collar, which was bestowed upon a public servant for distinguished achievement' (F. C. Kent).

43. *second chariot.* Next to Pharaoh's. Horses and chariots were introduced into Egypt during the Hyksos period.

abrech. 'Probably an Egyptian word similar in sound to the Hebrew word meaning "to kneel"' (RV Margin).

him: 'Abrech'; and he set him over all the land of Egypt. 44. And Pharaoh said unto Joseph: 'I am Pharaoh, and without thee shall no man lift up his hand or his foot in all the land of Egypt.' 45. And Pharaoh called Joseph's name Zaphenath-paneah; and he gave him to wife Asenath the daughter of Poti-phera priest of On. And Joseph went out over the land of Egypt.—46. And Joseph was thirty years old when he stood before Pharaoh king of Egypt.—And Joseph went out from the presence of Pharaoh, and went throughout all the land of Egypt. 47. And in the seven years of plenty the earth brought forth in heaps. 48. And he gathered up all the food of the seven years which were in the land of Egypt, and laid up the food in the cities; the food of the field, which was round about every city, laid he up in the same. 49. And Joseph laid up corn as the sand of the sea, very much, until they left off numbering; for it was without number. 50. And unto Joseph were born two sons before the year of famine came, whom Asenath the daughter of Poti-phera priest of On bore unto him. 51. And Joseph called the name of the first-born [1]Manasseh: 'for God hath made me forget all my toil, and all my father's house.' 52. And the name of the second called he [2]Ephraim: 'for God hath made me fruitful in the land of my affliction.'* iv. 53. And the seven years of plenty, that was in the land of Egypt, came to an end. 54. And the seven years of famine began to come, according as Joseph had said; and there was famine in all lands; but in all the land of Egypt there was bread. 55. And when all the land of Egypt was famished, the people cried to Pharaoh for bread; and Pharaoh said unto all the Egyptians: 'Go unto Joseph; what he saith to you, do.' 56. And the famine was over all the face of

לו ויקראו לפניו אברך ונתון אתו על כל־ארץ מצרים׃
44 ויאמר פרעה אל־יוסף אני פרעה ובלעדיך לא־ירים
מה איש את־ידו ואת־רגלו בכל־ארץ מצרים׃ ויקרא פרעה
שם־יוסף צפנת פענח ויתן־לו את־אסנת בת־פוטי פרע
46 כהן אן לאשה ויצא יוסף על־ארץ מצרים׃ ויוסף בן־
שלשים שנה בעמדו לפני פרעה מלך־מצרים ויצא
47 יוסף מלפני פרעה ויעבר בכל־ארץ מצרים׃ ותעש
48 הארץ בשבע שני השבע לקמצים׃ ויקבץ את־כל־אכל
שבע שנים אשר היו בארץ מצרים ויתן־אכל בערים
49 אכל שדה־העיר אשר סביבתיה נתן בתוכה׃ ויצבר
יוסף בר כחול הים הרבה מאד עד כי־חדל לספר כי־
נ אין מספר׃ וליוסף ילד שני בנים בטרם תבוא שנת
הרעב אשר ילדה־לו אסנת בת־פוטי פרע כהן און׃
51 ויקרא יוסף את־שם הבכור מנשה כי־נשני אלהים את־
52 כל־עמלי ואת כל־בית אבי׃ ואת שם השני קרא אפרים
רביעי
53 כי־הפרני אלהים בארץ עניי׃ ותכלינה שבע שני השבע
54 אשר היה בארץ מצרים׃ ותחלינה שבע שני הרעב
לבוא כאשר אמר יוסף ויהי רעב בכל־הארצות ובכל־
נה ארץ מצרים היה לחם׃ ותרעב כל־ארץ מצרים ויצעק
העם אל־פרעה ללחם ויאמר פרעה לכל־מצרים לכו
56 אל־יוסף אשר־יאמר לכם תעשו׃ והרעב היה על כל־

[1] That is, *Making to forget.* [2] From a Hebrew word signifying *to be fruitful.*

v. 50. למ"ד קמוצה

44. *lift up his hand or his foot. i.e.* do anything.

45. *Zaphenath-paneah.* Joseph receives a new name on his state appointment. This is both an Egyptian and a Hebrew custom; *e.g.* Num. XIII, 16. Egyptologists explain that *Zaphenath* means 'food-man', and *paneah*, 'of the life,' *i.e.* the Chief Steward in the realm in face of Famine (Kyle). The importance of the change of name in the story lies in the fact that it helps to conceal the identity of Joseph when his brethren come to Egypt.

Asenath. i.e. belonging to the goddess Neith.

Poti-phera. To be distinguished from Potiphar, the former master of Joseph.

On. Later known as Heliopolis, near Cairo. On was the centre of Sun worship in Egypt. Cleopatra's Needle on the Thames Embankment originally stood in On.

46. *thirty years old.* He had spent about twelve years in prison.

47. *in heaps.* The produce was most abundant. Some Jewish commentators render, 'for the storehouses.'

51. *all my toil, and all my father's house.* His position had made him forget his toil as a bondman, and the ill-will of his brethren that was the cause of that bondage. Or, the phrase can be viewed as the Heb. idiom for 'all the suffering caused to me by my father's house', *i.e.* my brethren (Wogue).

54. *all lands.* All the neighbouring lands.

56. *the storehouses.* The granaries.

the earth; and Joseph opened all the storehouses, and sold unto the Egyptians; and the famine was sore in the land of Egypt. 57. And all countries came into Egypt to Joseph to buy corn; because the famine was sore in all the earth.

42

Chapter XLII

1. Now Jacob saw that there was corn in Egypt, and Jacob said unto his sons: 'Why do ye look one upon another?' 2. And he said: 'Behold, I have heard that there is corn in Egypt. Get you down thither, and buy for us from thence; that we may live, and not die.' 3. And Joseph's ten brethren went down to buy corn from Egypt. 4. But Benjamin, Joseph's brother, Jacob sent not with his brethren; for he said: 'Lest peradventure harm befall him.' 5. And the sons of Israel came to buy among those that came; for the famine was in the land of Canaan. 6. And Joseph was the governor over the land; he it was that sold to all the people of the land. And Joseph's brethren came, and bowed down to him with their faces to the earth. 7. And Joseph saw his brethren, and he knew them, but made himself strange unto them, and spoke roughly with them; and he said unto them: 'Whence come ye?' And they said: 'From the land of Canaan to buy food.' 8. And Joseph knew his brethren, but they knew not him. 9. And Joseph remembered the dreams which he dreamed of them, and said unto them: 'Ye are spies; to see the nakedness of the land ye are come.' 10. And they said unto him: 'Nay, my lord, but to buy food are thy servants come. 11. We are all one man's sons; we are upright men, thy

פְּנֵי הָאָרֶץ וַיִּפְתַּח יוֹסֵף אֶת־כָּל־אֲשֶׁר בָּהֶם וַיִּשְׁבֹּר לְמִצְרַיִם
57 וַיֶּחֱזַק הָרָעָב בְּאֶרֶץ מִצְרָיִם׃ וְכָל־הָאָרֶץ בָּאוּ מִצְרַיְמָה
לִשְׁבֹּר אֶל־יוֹסֵף כִּי־חָזַק הָרָעָב בְּכָל־הָאָרֶץ׃

מב

Cap. XLII. מב

א וַיַּרְא יַעֲקֹב כִּי יֶשׁ־שֶׁבֶר בְּמִצְרָיִם וַיֹּאמֶר יַעֲקֹב לְבָנָיו
2 לָמָּה תִּתְרָאוּ׃ וַיֹּאמֶר הִנֵּה שָׁמַעְתִּי כִּי יֶשׁ־שֶׁבֶר בְּמִצְרָיִם
3 רְדוּ־שָׁמָּה וְשִׁבְרוּ־לָנוּ מִשָּׁם וְנִחְיֶה וְלֹא נָמוּת׃ וַיֵּרְדוּ
4 אֲחֵי־יוֹסֵף עֲשָׂרָה לִשְׁבֹּר בָּר מִמִּצְרָיִם׃ וְאֶת־בִּנְיָמִין אֲחִי
יוֹסֵף לֹא־שָׁלַח יַעֲקֹב אֶת־אֶחָיו כִּי אָמַר פֶּן־יִקְרָאֶנּוּ אָסוֹן׃
ה וַיָּבֹאוּ בְּנֵי יִשְׂרָאֵל לִשְׁבֹּר בְּתוֹךְ הַבָּאִים כִּי־הָיָה הָרָעָב
6 בְּאֶרֶץ כְּנָעַן׃ וְיוֹסֵף הוּא הַשַּׁלִּיט עַל־הָאָרֶץ הוּא הַמַּשְׁבִּיר
לְכָל־עַם הָאָרֶץ וַיָּבֹאוּ אֲחֵי יוֹסֵף וַיִּשְׁתַּחֲווּ־לוֹ אַפַּיִם
7 אָרְצָה׃ וַיַּרְא יוֹסֵף אֶת־אֶחָיו וַיַּכִּרֵם וַיִּתְנַכֵּר אֲלֵיהֶם
וַיְדַבֵּר אִתָּם קָשׁוֹת וַיֹּאמֶר אֲלֵהֶם מֵאַיִן בָּאתֶם וַיֹּאמְרוּ
8 מֵאֶרֶץ כְּנַעַן לִשְׁבָּר־אֹכֶל׃ וַיַּכֵּר יוֹסֵף אֶת־אֶחָיו וְהֵם
9 לֹא הִכִּרֻהוּ׃ וַיִּזְכֹּר יוֹסֵף אֵת הַחֲלֹמוֹת אֲשֶׁר חָלַם לָהֶם
וַיֹּאמֶר אֲלֵהֶם מְרַגְּלִים אַתֶּם לִרְאוֹת אֶת־עֶרְוַת הָאָרֶץ
י בָּאתֶם׃ וַיֹּאמְרוּ אֵלָיו לֹא אֲדֹנִי וַעֲבָדֶיךָ בָּאוּ לִשְׁבָּר־אֹכֶל׃
11 כֻּלָּנוּ בְּנֵי אִישׁ־אֶחָד נָחְנוּ כֵּנִים אֲנַחְנוּ לֹא־הָיוּ עֲבָדֶיךָ

57. *all countries. i.e.* 'the whole world', everybody. This verse prepares for the next scene of the drama (chap. XLII).

Chapter XLII. Joseph's Brethren in Egypt

1. *saw.* He had probably seen the corn brought by caravans.

why do ye look one upon another? Paralysed by doubt and helplessness (Luzzatto).

2. *get you down.* Cf. XII, 10.

6. *he it was that sold.* He superintended the sales, and foreign purchasers would be brought to him to be interrogated. His dreams were being fulfilled, see XXXVII, 7–10. The brothers 'bowed themselves down before him'.

7. *spoke roughly with them.* The brother who had been shamefully and pitilessly sold into slavery now had his opportunity for revenge. The greatness of Joseph lies in the fact that for all time he showed men a better way. He tests his brethren, holding his own natural feelings in check until convinced of their filial piety to their father, their love for Benjamin, and their sincere contrition for their crime towards him. Then he forgives them freely, fully, and lovingly.

8. *his brethren.* Recognized, but not recognizing the Grand Vizier, who in dress, name, language, and bearing was an Egyptian, as their brother.

9. *and Joseph remembered the dreams.* Not in a spirit of pride and hatred, but as the revealed will of the good God whose ways are inscrutable.

ye are spies. The most natural accusation to bring against strangers in Egypt, or anywhere.

nakedness of the land. The weak spots in the line of defence along the border. The North-East of Egypt was its weak side, and strangers entering from this direction were jealously watched.

11. *one man's sons.* A sufficient answer to the charge of being spies, for no man would risk the lives of ten sons in so dangerous an undertaking.

servants are no spies.' 12. And he said unto them: 'Nay, but to see the nakedness of the land ye are come.' 13. And they said: 'We thy servants are twelve brethren, the sons of one man in the land of Canaan; and, behold, the youngest is this day with our father, and one is not.' 14. And Joseph said unto them: 'That is it that I spoke unto you, saying: Ye are spies. 15. Hereby ye shall be proved: as Pharaoh liveth, ye shall not go forth hence, except your youngest brother come hither. 16. Send one of you, and let him fetch your brother, and ye shall be bound, that your words may be proved, whether there be truth in you; or else, as Pharaoh liveth, surely ye are spies.' 17. And he put them all together into ward three days. 18. And Joseph said unto them the third day: 'This do, and live; for I fear God:* v. 19. if ye be upright men, let one of your brethren be bound in your prison-house; but go ye, carry corn for the famine of your houses; 20. and bring your youngest brother unto me; so shall your words be verified, and ye shall not die.' And they did so. 21. And they said one to another: 'We are verily guilty concerning our brother, in that we saw the distress of his soul, when he besought us, and we would not hear; therefore is this distress come upon us.' 22. And Reuben answered them, saying: 'Spoke I not unto you, saying: Do not sin against the child; and ye would not hear? therefore also, behold, his blood is required.' 23. And they knew not that Joseph understood them; for the interpreter was between them. 24. And he turned himself about from them, and wept; and he returned to them, and spoke to them,

12 מְרַגְּלִים׃ וַיֹּאמֶר אֲלֵהֶם לֹא כִּי־עֶרְוַת הָאָרֶץ בָּאתֶם
13 לִרְאוֹת׃ וַיֹּאמְרוּ שְׁנֵים עָשָׂר עֲבָדֶיךָ אַחִים ׀ אֲנַחְנוּ בְּנֵי
אִישׁ־אֶחָד בְּאֶרֶץ כְּנָעַן וְהִנֵּה הַקָּטֹן אֶת־אָבִינוּ הַיּוֹם
14 וְהָאֶחָד אֵינֶנּוּ׃ וַיֹּאמֶר אֲלֵהֶם יוֹסֵף הוּא אֲשֶׁר דִּבַּרְתִּי
טו אֲלֵכֶם לֵאמֹר מְרַגְּלִים אַתֶּם׃ בְּזֹאת תִּבָּחֵנוּ חֵי פַרְעֹה אִם־
16 תֵּצְאוּ מִזֶּה כִּי אִם־בְּבוֹא אֲחִיכֶם הַקָּטֹן הֵנָּה׃ שִׁלְחוּ
מִכֶּם אֶחָד וְיִקַּח אֶת־אֲחִיכֶם וְאַתֶּם הֵאָסְרוּ וְיִבָּחֲנוּ דִּבְרֵיכֶם
הַאֱמֶת אִתְּכֶם וְאִם־לֹא חֵי פַרְעֹה כִּי מְרַגְּלִים אַתֶּם׃
17 18 וַיֶּאֱסֹף אֹתָם אֶל־מִשְׁמָר שְׁלֹשֶׁת יָמִים׃ וַיֹּאמֶר אֲלֵהֶם
חמישי יוֹסֵף בַּיּוֹם הַשְּׁלִישִׁי זֹאת עֲשׂוּ וִחְיוּ אֶת־הָאֱלֹהִים אֲנִי
19 יָרֵא׃* אִם־כֵּנִים אַתֶּם אֲחִיכֶם אֶחָד יֵאָסֵר בְּבֵית מִשְׁמַרְכֶם
כ וְאַתֶּם לְכוּ הָבִיאוּ שֶׁבֶר רַעֲבוֹן בָּתֵּיכֶם׃ וְאֶת־אֲחִיכֶם
הַקָּטֹן תָּבִיאוּ אֵלַי וְיֵאָמְנוּ דִבְרֵיכֶם וְלֹא תָמוּתוּ וַיַּעֲשׂוּ־כֵן׃
21 וַיֹּאמְרוּ אִישׁ אֶל־אָחִיו אֲבָל אֲשֵׁמִים ׀ אֲנַחְנוּ עַל־אָחִינוּ
אֲשֶׁר רָאִינוּ צָרַת נַפְשׁוֹ בְּהִתְחַנְנוֹ אֵלֵינוּ וְלֹא שָׁמָעְנוּ עַל־
22 כֵּן בָּאָה אֵלֵינוּ הַצָּרָה הַזֹּאת׃ וַיַּעַן רְאוּבֵן אֹתָם לֵאמֹר
הֲלוֹא אָמַרְתִּי אֲלֵיכֶם ׀ לֵאמֹר אַל־תֶּחֶטְאוּ בַיֶּלֶד וְלֹא
23 שְׁמַעְתֶּם וְגַם־דָּמוֹ הִנֵּה נִדְרָשׁ׃ וְהֵם לֹא יָדְעוּ כִּי שֹׁמֵעַ
24 יוֹסֵף כִּי הַמֵּלִיץ בֵּינֹתָם׃ וַיִּסֹּב מֵעֲלֵיהֶם וַיֵּבְךְּ וַיָּשָׁב

12. *nay.* Joseph repeats his accusation. This throws them off their guard, and they seek to disarm his suspicions by volunteering information about their father and youngest brother, of which Joseph at once takes advantage.

13. *one is not.* Refers of course to Joseph. They did not say that he was dead, because they did not really know what became of him.

15. *ye shall be proved.* Their story is improbable. It must be verified. Let them bring Benjamin down to Egypt. In this way, Joseph would test their loyalty to their youngest brother. Did they also hate Benjamin as they had hated him? He delicately refrains from cross-questioning them about the brother who 'is not'.

as Pharaoh liveth. A form of oath, or strong asseveration. The oath by the life of the king is found in an Egyptian inscription of the twentieth pre-Christian century.

18. *this do, and live.* Better, '*this do in order that ye may live.*' The brethren claimed to be upright, honest men. Profession was not enough. Let them bring the youngest brother, 'so shall your words be verified and ye shall not die' (*v.* 20).

for I fear God. And so am unwilling to treat you with unnecessary severity on mere suspicion. I will keep one of you as a hostage, the rest shall convey food for your families. '*Fear of God* is the universal element in religion which humanizes our dealings with "foreigners", even when national interests are involved' (Procksch); cf. xx, 11.

21. *we are verily guilty.* Joseph had at last awakened remorse in their hearts. They had been blind to the distress of their brother, and deaf to his entreaties. They were guilty, and their misfortune was a just retribution for their cruelty. It is only now, in the mirror of their repentance, that we see reflected the agonizing scene when the lad was thrown into the pit many years before.

and took Simeon from among them, and bound him before their eyes. 25. Then Joseph commanded to fill their vessels with corn, and to restore every man's money into his sack, and to give them provision for the way; and thus was it done unto them. 26. And they laded their asses with their corn, and departed thence. 27. And as one of them opened his sack to give his ass provender in the lodging-place, he espied his money; and, behold, it was in the mouth of his sack. 28. And he said unto his brethren: 'My money is restored; and, lo, it is even in my sack.' And their heart failed them, and they turned trembling one to another, saying: 'What is this that God hath done unto us?' 29. And they came unto Jacob their father unto the land of Canaan, and told him all that had befallen them, saying: 30. 'The man, the lord of the land, spoke roughly with us, and took us for spies of the country. 31. And we said unto him: We are upright men; we are no spies. 32. We are twelve brethren, sons of our father; one is not, and the youngest is this day with our father in the land of Canaan. 33. And the man, the lord of the land, said unto us: Hereby shall I know that ye are upright men: leave one of your brethren with me, and take corn for the famine of your houses, and go your way. 34. And bring your youngest brother unto me; then shall I know that ye are no spies, but that ye are upright men; so will I deliver you your brother, and ye shall traffic in the land.' 35. And it came to pass as they emptied their sacks, that, behold,

אֲלֵהֶם וַיְדַבֵּר אֲלֵהֶם וַיִּקַּח מֵאִתָּם אֶת־שִׁמְעוֹן וַיֶּאֱסֹר אֹתוֹ
כה לְעֵינֵיהֶם׃ וַיְצַו יוֹסֵף וַיְמַלְאוּ אֶת־כְּלֵיהֶם בָּר וּלְהָשִׁיב
כַּסְפֵּיהֶם אִישׁ אֶל־שַׂקּוֹ וְלָתֵת לָהֶם צֵדָה לַדָּרֶךְ וַיַּעַשׂ
26 לָהֶם כֵּן׃ וַיִּשְׂאוּ אֶת־שִׁבְרָם עַל־חֲמֹרֵיהֶם וַיֵּלְכוּ מִשָּׁם׃
27 וַיִּפְתַּח הָאֶחָד אֶת־שַׂקּוֹ לָתֵת מִסְפּוֹא לַחֲמֹרוֹ בַּמָּלוֹן וַיַּרְא
28 אֶת־כַּסְפּוֹ וְהִנֵּה־הוּא בְּפִי אַמְתַּחְתּוֹ׃ וַיֹּאמֶר אֶל־אֶחָיו
הוּשַׁב כַּסְפִּי וְגַם הִנֵּה בְאַמְתַּחְתִּי וַיֵּצֵא לִבָּם וַיֶּחֶרְדוּ אִישׁ
29 אֶל־אָחִיו לֵאמֹר מַה־זֹּאת עָשָׂה אֱלֹהִים לָנוּ׃ וַיָּבֹאוּ אֶל־
יַעֲקֹב אֲבִיהֶם אַרְצָה כְּנָעַן וַיַּגִּידוּ לוֹ אֵת כָּל־הַקֹּרֹת אֹתָם
ל לֵאמֹר׃ דִּבֶּר הָאִישׁ אֲדֹנֵי הָאָרֶץ אִתָּנוּ קָשׁוֹת וַיִּתֵּן אֹתָנוּ
31 כִּמְרַגְּלִים אֶת־הָאָרֶץ׃ וַנֹּאמֶר אֵלָיו כֵּנִים אֲנָחְנוּ לֹא הָיִינוּ
32 מְרַגְּלִים׃ שְׁנֵים־עָשָׂר אֲנַחְנוּ אַחִים בְּנֵי אָבִינוּ הָאֶחָד אֵינֶנּוּ
33 וְהַקָּטֹן הַיּוֹם אֶת־אָבִינוּ בְּאֶרֶץ כְּנָעַן׃ וַיֹּאמֶר אֵלֵינוּ הָאִישׁ
אֲדֹנֵי הָאָרֶץ בְּזֹאת אֵדַע כִּי כֵנִים אַתֶּם אֲחִיכֶם הָאֶחָד
34 הַנִּיחוּ אִתִּי וְאֶת־רַעֲבוֹן בָּתֵּיכֶם קְחוּ וָלֵכוּ׃ וְהָבִיאוּ אֶת־
אֲחִיכֶם הַקָּטֹן אֵלַי וְאֵדְעָה כִּי לֹא מְרַגְּלִים אַתֶּם כִּי כֵנִים
לה אַתֶּם אֶת־אֲחִיכֶם אֶתֵּן לָכֶם וְאֶת־הָאָרֶץ תִּסְחָרוּ׃ וַיְהִי
הֵם מְרִיקִים שַׂקֵּיהֶם וְהִנֵּה־אִישׁ צְרוֹר־כַּסְפּוֹ בְּשַׂקּוֹ

See on XXXVII, 23. With broken and contrite hearts, they now recall their inhuman callousness —all in the hearing of Joseph.

22. *his blood is required.* Reuben assumes that Joseph's death, whatever form it took, was due to them. They were morally guilty of his death. His blood is 'required', *i.e.* is now being avenged (see IX, 5).

23. *interpreter.* Joseph throughout spoke to them as the Viceroy, in Egyptian.

24. *and wept.* He is touched to tears by their penitence and contrition.

Simeon. As the next in age to Reuben, who as the eldest was to report to Jacob. According to Rabbinic tradition, it was Simeon who had counselled that Joseph be slain.

27. *lodging-place.* Wayside shelter.

28. *they turned trembling.* They wonder what such an unusual occurrence may portend. Will they be accused of theft?

29–34. They recount their experience to their father.

30. *the lord of.* The Heb. is in the plural, often used to express power or greatness.

33. *corn for the famine.* The words 'corn for' are supplied from the context.

34. *traffic in the land.* Joseph did not say this, but 'and ye shall not die' (*v.* 20). This could only be by allowing the brethren to come to Egypt and buy corn.

35. *they were afraid. i.e.* Jacob and his sons. They looked upon it as a deliberate act on the part of the Egyptian lord to bring a charge of theft against them.

36. *upon me are all these things come.* The point of the reproach is that it is his children, not their own, that they are endangering: to which Reuben's offer is the rejoinder.

every man's bundle of money was in his sack; and when they and their father saw their bundles of money, they were afraid. 36. And Jacob their father said unto them: 'Me have ye bereaved of my children: Joseph is not, and Simeon is not, and ye will take Benjamin away; upon me are all these things come.' 37. And Reuben spoke unto his father, saying: 'Thou shalt slay my two sons, if I bring him not to thee; deliver him into my hand, and I will bring him back to thee.' 38. And he said: 'My son shall not go down with you; for his brother is dead, and he only is left; if harm befall him by the way in which ye go, then will ye bring down my gray hairs with sorrow to the grave.'

43 CHAPTER XLIII

1. And the famine was sore in the land. 2. And it came to pass, when they had eaten up the corn which they had brought out of Egypt, that their father said unto them: 'Go again, buy us a little food.' 3. And Judah spoke unto him, saying: 'The man did earnestly forewarn us, saying: Ye shall not see my face, except your brother be with you. 4. If thou wilt send our brother with us, we will go down and buy thee food; 5. but if thou wilt not send him, we will not go down, for the man said unto us: Ye shall not see my face, except your brother be with you.' 6. And Israel said: 'Wherefore dealt ye so ill with me, as to tell the man whether ye had yet a brother?' 7. And they said: 'The man asked straitly concerning ourselves, and concerning our kindred, saying: Is your father yet alive? have ye another brother? and we told him according to the tenor of these words; could we in any wise know that he would say: Bring your brother down?' 8. And Judah said unto Israel his father: 'Send the lad with me, and we will arise and go, that we may live, and not die, both we, and thou, and also our little ones. 9. I will be surety for him; of my hand shalt thou require him; if

36 וַיִּרְאוּ אֶת־צְרֹרוֹת כַּסְפֵּיהֶם הֵמָּה וַאֲבִיהֶם וַיִּירָאוּ׃ וַיֹּאמֶר
אֲלֵהֶם יַעֲקֹב אֲבִיהֶם אֹתִי שִׁכַּלְתֶּם יוֹסֵף אֵינֶנּוּ וְשִׁמְעוֹן
37 אֵינֶנּוּ וְאֶת־בִּנְיָמִן תִּקָּחוּ עָלַי הָיוּ כֻלָּנָה׃ וַיֹּאמֶר רְאוּבֵן
אֶל־אָבִיו לֵאמֹר אֶת־שְׁנֵי בָנַי תָּמִית אִם־לֹא אֲבִיאֶנּוּ
38 אֵלֶיךָ תְּנָה אֹתוֹ עַל־יָדִי וַאֲנִי אֲשִׁיבֶנּוּ אֵלֶיךָ׃ וַיֹּאמֶר לֹא־
יֵרֵד בְּנִי עִמָּכֶם כִּי־אָחִיו מֵת וְהוּא לְבַדּוֹ נִשְׁאָר וּקְרָאָהוּ
אָסוֹן בַּדֶּרֶךְ אֲשֶׁר תֵּלְכוּ־בָהּ וְהוֹרַדְתֶּם אֶת־שֵׂיבָתִי בְּיָגוֹן
שְׁאוֹלָה׃

CAP. XLIII. מג

מג

א 2 וְהָרָעָב כָּבֵד בָּאָרֶץ׃ וַיְהִי כַּאֲשֶׁר כִּלּוּ לֶאֱכֹל אֶת־הַשֶּׁבֶר
אֲשֶׁר הֵבִיאוּ מִמִּצְרָיִם וַיֹּאמֶר אֲלֵיהֶם אֲבִיהֶם שֻׁבוּ שִׁבְרוּ־
3 לָנוּ מְעַט־אֹכֶל׃ וַיֹּאמֶר אֵלָיו יְהוּדָה לֵאמֹר הָעֵד הֵעִד
בָּנוּ הָאִישׁ לֵאמֹר לֹא־תִרְאוּ פָנַי בִּלְתִּי אֲחִיכֶם אִתְּכֶם׃
4 אִם־יֶשְׁךָ מְשַׁלֵּחַ אֶת־אָחִינוּ אִתָּנוּ נֵרְדָה וְנִשְׁבְּרָה לְךָ
ה אֹכֶל׃ וְאִם־אֵינְךָ מְשַׁלֵּחַ לֹא נֵרֵד כִּי־הָאִישׁ אָמַר אֵלֵינוּ
6 לֹא־תִרְאוּ פָנַי בִּלְתִּי אֲחִיכֶם אִתְּכֶם׃ וַיֹּאמֶר יִשְׂרָאֵל לָמָה
7 הֲרֵעֹתֶם לִי לְהַגִּיד לָאִישׁ הַעוֹד לָכֶם אָח׃ וַיֹּאמְרוּ שָׁאוֹל
שָׁאַל־הָאִישׁ לָנוּ וּלְמוֹלַדְתֵּנוּ לֵאמֹר הַעוֹד אֲבִיכֶם חַי הֲיֵשׁ
לָכֶם אָח וַנַּגֶּד־לוֹ עַל־פִּי הַדְּבָרִים הָאֵלֶּה הֲיָדוֹעַ נֵדַע כִּי
8 יֹאמַר הוֹרִידוּ אֶת־אֲחִיכֶם׃ וַיֹּאמֶר יְהוּדָה אֶל־יִשְׂרָאֵל
אָבִיו שִׁלְחָה הַנַּעַר אִתִּי וְנָקוּמָה וְנֵלֵכָה וְנִחְיֶה וְלֹא נָמוּת
9 גַּם־אֲנַחְנוּ גַם־אַתָּה גַּם־טַפֵּנוּ׃ אָנֹכִי אֶעֶרְבֶנּוּ מִיָּדִי תְּבַקְשֶׁנּוּ

מב' v. 36. קמץ בז"ק

37. *slay my two sons.* The impetuous nature of Reuben is seen here. 'Two sons,' one for Benjamin and one for Joseph—of whose death he *feels* that he shares the guilt with his brothers.

CHAPTER XLIII. THE SECOND VISIT OF JOSEPH'S BRETHREN TO EGYPT

1–14. Judah prevails upon Jacob to allow Benjamin to accompany the brethren. Judah now takes the lead in the place of Reuben, in whom his father had little confidence.

2. *eaten up the corn.* Not in its entirety; they must have left sufficient for their father and the household during their absence in Egypt.

5. *we will not go down.* Judah's decisive language has the desired effect with Jacob.

6. *dealt ye so ill with me.* This is not a question, but a reproach. He blames them for volunteering statements.

7. *straitly.* Closely, particularly.

according to the tenor of these words. i.e. we gave the answers which his questions called for.

9. *I will be surety for him.* I guarantee to bring him back. Jacob is more impressed by his words than by Reuben's wild offer.

bear the blame. lit. 'I shall have sinned against thee for ever'.

I bring him not unto thee, and set him before thee, then let me bear the blame for ever. 10. For except we had lingered, surely we had now returned a second time.' 11. And their father Israel said unto them: 'If it be so now, do this: take of the choice fruits of the land in your vessels, and carry down the man a present, a little balm, and a little honey, spicery and ladanum, nuts, and almonds; 12. and take double money in your hand; and the money that was returned in the mouth of your sacks carry back in your hand; peradventure it was an oversight; 13. take also your brother, and arise, go again unto the man; 14. and God Almighty give you mercy before the man, that he may release unto you your other brother and Benjamin. And as for me, if I be bereaved of my children, I am bereaved.' ¶ 15. And the men took that present, and they took double money in their hand, and Benjamin; and rose up, and went down to Egypt, and stood before Joseph.* vi. 16. And when Joseph saw Benjamin with them, he said to the steward of his house: 'Bring the men into the house, and kill the beasts, and prepare the meat; for the men shall dine with me at noon.' 17. And the man did as Joseph bade; and the man brought the men into Joseph's house. 18. And the men were afraid, because they were brought into Joseph's house; and they said: 'Because of the money that was returned in our sacks at the first time are we brought in; that he may seek occasion against us, and fall upon us, and take us for bondmen, and our asses.' 19. And they came near to the steward of Joseph's house, and they spoke unto him at the door of the house,

אִם־לֹא הֲבִיאֹתִיו אֵלֶיךָ וְהִצַּגְתִּיו לְפָנֶיךָ וְחָטָאתִי לְךָ
י כָּל־הַיָּמִים׃ כִּי לוּלֵא הִתְמַהְמָהְנוּ כִּי־עַתָּה שַׁבְנוּ זֶה
11 פַעֲמָיִם׃ וַיֹּאמֶר אֲלֵהֶם יִשְׂרָאֵל אֲבִיהֶם אִם־כֵּן ׀ אֵפוֹא
זֹאת עֲשׂוּ קְחוּ מִזִּמְרַת הָאָרֶץ בִּכְלֵיכֶם וְהוֹרִידוּ לָאִישׁ
מִנְחָה מְעַט צֳרִי וּמְעַט דְּבַשׁ נְכֹאת וָלֹט בָּטְנִים וּשְׁקֵדִים׃
12 וְכֶסֶף מִשְׁנֶה קְחוּ בְיֶדְכֶם וְאֶת־הַכֶּסֶף הַמּוּשָׁב בְּפִי
13 אַמְתְּחֹתֵיכֶם תָּשִׁיבוּ בְיֶדְכֶם אוּלַי מִשְׁגֶּה הוּא׃ וְאֶת־
14 אֲחִיכֶם קָחוּ וְקוּמוּ שׁוּבוּ אֶל־הָאִישׁ׃ וְאֵל שַׁדַּי יִתֵּן לָכֶם
רַחֲמִים לִפְנֵי הָאִישׁ וְשִׁלַּח לָכֶם אֶת־אֲחִיכֶם אַחֵר וְאֶת־
טו בִּנְיָמִין וַאֲנִי כַּאֲשֶׁר שָׁכֹלְתִּי שָׁכָלְתִּי׃ וַיִּקְחוּ הָאֲנָשִׁים אֶת־
הַמִּנְחָה הַזֹּאת וּמִשְׁנֶה־כֶּסֶף לָקְחוּ בְיָדָם וְאֶת־בִּנְיָמִן
ששי 16 וַיָּקֻמוּ וַיֵּרְדוּ מִצְרַיִם וַיַּעַמְדוּ לִפְנֵי יוֹסֵף׃ וַיַּרְא יוֹסֵף
אִתָּם אֶת־בִּנְיָמִין וַיֹּאמֶר לַאֲשֶׁר עַל־בֵּיתוֹ הָבֵא אֶת־הָאֲנָשִׁים
הַבָּיְתָה וּטְבֹחַ טֶבַח וְהָכֵן כִּי אִתִּי יֹאכְלוּ הָאֲנָשִׁים
17 בַּצָּהֳרָיִם׃ וַיַּעַשׂ הָאִישׁ כַּאֲשֶׁר אָמַר יוֹסֵף וַיָּבֵא הָאִישׁ
18 אֶת־הָאֲנָשִׁים בֵּיתָה יוֹסֵף׃ וַיִּירְאוּ הָאֲנָשִׁים כִּי הוּבְאוּ
בֵּית יוֹסֵף וַיֹּאמְרוּ עַל־דְּבַר הַכֶּסֶף הַשָּׁב בְּאַמְתְּחֹתֵינוּ
בַּתְּחִלָּה אֲנַחְנוּ מוּבָאִים לְהִתְגֹּלֵל עָלֵינוּ וּלְהִתְנַפֵּל עָלֵינוּ
19 וְלָקַחַת אֹתָנוּ לַעֲבָדִים וְאֶת־חֲמֹרֵינוּ׃ וַיִּגְּשׁוּ אֶל־הָאִישׁ

v. 12. הש' בפתח

10. *except we had lingered.* And wasted time in discussion.

11. *if it be so now, do this.* 'Since it must be so, do this.' Jacob yields to the inevitable, and offers his children prudent counsel.

honey. *i.e.* the date-honey, rarely found in Egypt.

nuts. *i.e.* pistachio nuts. Still considered a delicacy in the East.

12. *double money . . . and the money.* They were now to take double money, as they were returning the money that had been placed in their sacks.

14. *God Almighty.* Heb. *El Shaddai.* 'The God of Abraham can alone now help him, an old man trembling for the life of his two children' (Procksch).

mercy. Divine pity for the helpless misery of the weak and the defenceless.

if I be bereaved. An expression of mournful acquiescence in the Divine will, like the exclamation of Esther IV, 16, 'and if I perish, I perish.'

15–34. The brethren in Joseph's palace.

15. *before Joseph.* At his government office, where the people came to purchase corn.

16. *the steward of his house.* lit. 'him that was over his house'.

bring the men into the house. *i.e.* Joseph's private residence.

dine with me at noon. This is interesting as indicating the time when meat was eaten in the house of the upper classes in ancient Egypt.

18. *money that was returned.* The brethren fear that they are entrapped and about to be punished.

take us for bondmen. As detected thieves; cf. Ex. XXII, 3.

19. *at the door of the house.* Before crossing the threshold, they would clear themselves of the suspicion against them.

20. and said: 'Oh my lord, we came indeed down at the first time to buy food. 21. And it came to pass, when we came to the lodging-place, that we opened our sacks, and, behold, every man's money was in the mouth of his sack, our money in full weight; and we have brought it back in our hand. 22. And other money have we brought down in our hand to buy food. We know not who put our money in our sacks.' 23. And he said: 'Peace be to you, fear not; your God, and the God of your father, hath given you treasure in your sacks; I had your money.' And he brought Simeon out unto them. 24. And the man brought the men into Joseph's house, and gave them water, and they washed their feet; and he gave their asses provender. 25. And they made ready the present against Joseph's coming at noon; for they heard that they should eat bread there. 26. And when Joseph came home, they brought him the present which was in their hand into the house, and bowed down to him to the earth. 27. And he asked them of their welfare, and said: 'Is your father well, the old man of whom ye spoke? Is he yet alive?' 28. And they said: 'Thy servant our father is well, he is yet alive.' And they bowed the head, and made obeisance. 29. And he lifted up his eyes, and saw Benjamin his brother, his mother's son, and said: 'Is this your youngest brother of whom ye spoke unto me?' And he said: 'God be gracious unto thee, my son.'* vii. 30. And Joseph made haste; for his heart yearned toward his brother; and he sought where to weep; and he entered into his chamber, and wept there. 31. And he washed his face, and came out; and he refrained himself, and said: 'Set on bread.' 32. And they set on for him by himself, and for them by themselves, and for the Egyptians, that did eat with him, by themselves; because the Egyptians might not eat bread with the Hebrews; for that is an abomination

כ אֲשֶׁר עַל־בֵּית יוֹסֵף וַיְדַבְּרוּ אֵלָיו פֶּתַח הַבָּיִת׃ וַיֹּאמְרוּ
21 בִּי אֲדֹנִי יָרֹד יָרַדְנוּ בַּתְּחִלָּה לִשְׁבָּר־אֹכֶל׃ וַיְהִי כִּי־בָאנוּ
אֶל־הַמָּלוֹן וַנִּפְתְּחָה אֶת־אַמְתְּחֹתֵינוּ וְהִנֵּה כֶסֶף־אִישׁ בְּפִי
22 אַמְתַּחְתּוֹ כַּסְפֵּנוּ בְּמִשְׁקָלוֹ וַנָּשֶׁב אֹתוֹ בְּיָדֵנוּ׃ וְכֶסֶף אַחֵר
הוֹרַדְנוּ בְיָדֵנוּ לִשְׁבָּר־אֹכֶל לֹא יָדַעְנוּ מִי־שָׂם כַּסְפֵּנוּ
23 בְּאַמְתְּחֹתֵינוּ׃ וַיֹּאמֶר שָׁלוֹם לָכֶם אַל־תִּירָאוּ אֱלֹהֵיכֶם
וֵאלֹהֵי אֲבִיכֶם נָתַן לָכֶם מַטְמוֹן בְּאַמְתְּחֹתֵיכֶם כַּסְפְּכֶם
24 בָּא אֵלָי וַיּוֹצֵא אֲלֵהֶם אֶת־שִׁמְעוֹן׃ וַיָּבֵא הָאִישׁ אֶת־
הָאֲנָשִׁים בֵּיתָה יוֹסֵף וַיִּתֶּן־מַיִם וַיִּרְחֲצוּ רַגְלֵיהֶם וַיִּתֵּן
כה מִסְפּוֹא לַחֲמֹרֵיהֶם׃ וַיָּכִינוּ אֶת־הַמִּנְחָה עַד־בּוֹא יוֹסֵף
26 בַּצָּהֳרָיִם כִּי שָׁמְעוּ כִּי־שָׁם יֹאכְלוּ לָחֶם׃ וַיָּבֹא יוֹסֵף הַבַּיְתָה
וַיָּבִיאּוּ לוֹ אֶת־הַמִּנְחָה אֲשֶׁר־בְּיָדָם הַבָּיְתָה וַיִּשְׁתַּחֲווּ־לוֹ
27 אָרְצָה׃ וַיִּשְׁאַל לָהֶם לְשָׁלוֹם וַיֹּאמֶר הֲשָׁלוֹם אֲבִיכֶם
28 הַזָּקֵן אֲשֶׁר אֲמַרְתֶּם הַעוֹדֶנּוּ חָי׃ וַיֹּאמְרוּ שָׁלוֹם לְעַבְדְּךָ
29 לְאָבִינוּ עוֹדֶנּוּ חָי וַיִּקְּדוּ וַיִּשְׁתַּחֲוֻּ׃ וַיִּשָּׂא עֵינָיו וַיַּרְא אֶת־
בִּנְיָמִין אָחִיו בֶּן־אִמּוֹ וַיֹּאמֶר הֲזֶה אֲחִיכֶם הַקָּטֹן אֲשֶׁר
שביעי
ל אֲמַרְתֶּם אֵלָי וַיֹּאמַר אֱלֹהִים יָחְנְךָ בְּנִי׃* וַיְמַהֵר יוֹסֵף כִּי־
נִכְמְרוּ רַחֲמָיו אֶל־אָחִיו וַיְבַקֵּשׁ לִבְכּוֹת וַיָּבֹא הַחַדְרָה
31 וַיֵּבְךְּ שָׁמָּה׃ וַיִּרְחַץ פָּנָיו וַיֵּצֵא וַיִּתְאַפַּק וַיֹּאמֶר שִׂימוּ
32 לָחֶם׃ וַיָּשִׂימוּ לוֹ לְבַדּוֹ וְלָהֶם לְבַדָּם וְלַמִּצְרִים הָאֹכְלִים
אִתּוֹ לְבַדָּם כִּי לֹא יוּכְלוּן הַמִּצְרִים לֶאֱכֹל אֶת־הָעִבְרִים

v. 26. א׳ דגושה v. 28. וישתחוו קרי

21. *we have brought it back.* They say this to forestall the suspicion of theft.

22. *we know not who put.* They emphasize their ignorance of the entire transaction.

23. *I had your money.* Doubtless on the instruction of Joseph, the steward reassures them that what they found in their sacks was God's gift.

25. *against Joseph's coming.* Here means, 'so as to be ready when Joseph arrived.' This is the old use of 'against', in the sense of 'in readiness for the time when'.

27. *of whom ye spoke.* Joseph carefully avoids betraying himself to his brethren.

29. *his mother's son.* These words augment the pathos of the situation.

30. *Joseph made haste.* To close the interview and to retire.

his heart yearned toward. Seeing his own mother's son, he felt unable to restrain his tears.

31. *set on bread. i.e.* let the food be served.

32. *for him by himself.* As an Egyptian noble he would have his food apart from his retinue, and, of course, apart from the Hebrews, who were foreigners in the eyes of the Egyptians. The Hyksos conquerors soon adopted the old Egyptian exclusiveness in intercourse with foreigners.

unto the Egyptians. 33. And they sat before him, the first-born according to his birthright, and the youngest according to his youth; and the men marvelled one with another. 34. And portions were taken unto them from before him; but Benjamin's portion was five times so much as any of theirs. And they drank, and were merry with him.

33 לָחֶם כִּי־תוֹעֵבָה הִוא לְמִצְרָיִם׃ וַיֵּשְׁבוּ לְפָנָיו הַבְּכֹר
כִּבְכֹרָתוֹ וְהַצָּעִיר כִּצְעִרָתוֹ וַיִּתְמְהוּ הָאֲנָשִׁים אִישׁ אֶל־
34 רֵעֵהוּ׃ וַיִּשָּׂא מַשְׂאֹת מֵאֵת פָּנָיו אֲלֵהֶם וַתֵּרֶב מַשְׂאַת בִּנְיָמִן
מִמַּשְׂאֹת כֻּלָּם חָמֵשׁ יָדוֹת וַיִּשְׁתּוּ וַיִּשְׁכְּרוּ עִמּוֹ׃

44

Chapter XLIV

1. And he commanded the steward of his house, saying: 'Fill the men's sacks with food, as much as they can carry, and put every man's money in his sack's mouth. 2. And put my goblet, the silver goblet, in the sack's mouth of the youngest, and his corn money.' And he did according to the word that Joseph had spoken. 3. As soon as the morning was light, the men were sent away, they and their asses. 4. And when they were gone out of the city, and were not yet far off, Joseph said unto his steward: 'Up, follow after the men; and when thou dost overtake them, say unto them: Wherefore have ye rewarded evil for good? 5. Is not this it in which my lord drinketh, and whereby he indeed divineth? ye have done evil in so doing.' 6. And he overtook them, and he spoke unto them these words. 7. And they said unto him: 'Wherefore speaketh my lord such words as these? Far be it from thy servants that they should do such a thing. 8. Behold, the money, which we found in our sacks' mouths, we brought back unto thee out of the land of Canaan; how then should we steal out of thy lord's house silver

מד

Cap. XLIV. מד

א וַיְצַו אֶת־אֲשֶׁר עַל־בֵּיתוֹ לֵאמֹר מַלֵּא אֶת־אַמְתְּחֹת הָאֲנָשִׁים
אֹכֶל כַּאֲשֶׁר יוּכְלוּן שְׂאֵת וְשִׂים כֶּסֶף־אִישׁ בְּפִי אַמְתַּחְתּוֹ׃
2 וְאֶת־גְּבִיעִי גְּבִיעַ הַכֶּסֶף תָּשִׂים בְּפִי אַמְתַּחַת הַקָּטֹן וְאֵת
3 כֶּסֶף שִׁבְרוֹ וַיַּעַשׂ כִּדְבַר יוֹסֵף אֲשֶׁר דִּבֵּר׃ הַבֹּקֶר אוֹר
4 וְהָאֲנָשִׁים שֻׁלְּחוּ הֵמָּה וַחֲמֹרֵיהֶם׃ הֵם יָצְאוּ אֶת־הָעִיר
לֹא הִרְחִיקוּ וְיוֹסֵף אָמַר לַאֲשֶׁר עַל־בֵּיתוֹ קוּם רְדֹף אַחֲרֵי
הָאֲנָשִׁים וְהִשַּׂגְתָּם וְאָמַרְתָּ אֲלֵהֶם לָמָּה שִׁלַּמְתֶּם רָעָה
ה תַּחַת טוֹבָה׃ הֲלוֹא זֶה אֲשֶׁר יִשְׁתֶּה אֲדֹנִי בּוֹ וְהוּא נַחֵשׁ
6 יְנַחֵשׁ בּוֹ הֲרֵעֹתֶם אֲשֶׁר עֲשִׂיתֶם׃ וַיַּשִּׂגֵם וַיְדַבֵּר אֲלֵהֶם
7 אֶת־הַדְּבָרִים הָאֵלֶּה׃ וַיֹּאמְרוּ אֵלָיו לָמָּה יְדַבֵּר אֲדֹנִי
8 כַּדְּבָרִים הָאֵלֶּה חָלִילָה לַעֲבָדֶיךָ מֵעֲשׂוֹת כַּדָּבָר הַזֶּה׃ הֵן
כֶּסֶף אֲשֶׁר מָצָאנוּ בְּפִי אַמְתְּחֹתֵינוּ הֱשִׁיבֹנוּ אֵלֶיךָ מֵאֶרֶץ

33. *the men marvelled.* How could the Egyptian know their ages? They looked at one another in astonishment.

34. *were merry.* lit. 'drank largely'. Joseph wishes to divert their attention from his table, whence his goblet was about to be removed. The extra portion given to Benjamin was a special mark of respect.

Chapter XLIV

The chapter sets forth Joseph's device to test still further the sincerity and loyalty of his brethren.

1–17. The Divining Cup

1. *as much as they can carry.* More than they were entitled to by their purchase. This act of kindness on Joseph's part was intentional, so as to increase the apparent baseness of their conduct; see *v.* 4.

put every man's money. This was done to prevent the brethren from suspecting Benjamin of having really stolen the goblet. When they again found their money returned, they could not but believe that the goblet had in the selfsame unaccountable manner come into Benjamin's sack (Abarbanel).

2. *the silver goblet.* Divining goblets were much used in Egypt. Pieces of gold or silver were thrown into the water or liquid in the goblet and caused movements, which were supposed to represent coming events.

4. *rewarded evil for good.* Joseph's steward assumes that they are aware of the theft of this valuable and wonderful goblet.

5. *whereby he indeed divineth.* The cup is a sacred one, by which their host obtains oracles.

8. *how then should we steal?* Their argument is sound. They had brought back from Canaan the money which they had found in their sacks. Would they then think of robbing the Egyptian lord, who had treated them with so much consideration?

or gold? 9. With whomsoever of thy servants it be found, let him die, and we also will be my lord's bondmen.' 10. And he said: 'Now also let it be according unto your words: he with whom it is found shall be my bondman; and ye shall be blameless.' 11. Then they hastened, and took down every man his sack to the ground, and opened every man his sack. 12. And he searched, beginning at the eldest, and leaving off at the youngest; and the goblet was found in Benjamin's sack. 13. Then they rent their clothes, and laded every man his ass, and returned to the city.* m a. 14. And Judah and his brethren came to Joseph's house, and he was yet there; and they fell before him on the ground.* m s. 15. And Joseph said unto them: 'What deed is this that ye have done? know ye not that such a man as I will indeed divine?' 16. And Judah said: 'What shall we say unto my lord? what shall we speak? or how shall we clear ourselves? God hath found out the iniquity of thy servants; behold, we are my lord's bondmen, both we, and he also in whose hand the cup is found.' 17. And he said: 'Far be it from me that I should do so; the man in whose hand the goblet is found, he shall be my bondman; but as for you, get you up in peace unto your father.'

9 כְּנַעַן וְאֵיךְ נִגְנֹב מִבֵּית אֲדֹנֶיךָ כֶּסֶף אוֹ זָהָב׃ אֲשֶׁר יִמָּצֵא
אִתּוֹ מֵעֲבָדֶיךָ וָמֵת וְגַם־אֲנַחְנוּ נִהְיֶה לַאדֹנִי לַעֲבָדִים׃
י וַיֹּאמֶר גַּם־עַתָּה כְדִבְרֵיכֶם כֶּן־הוּא אֲשֶׁר יִמָּצֵא אִתּוֹ יִהְיֶה־
11 לִּי עָבֶד וְאַתֶּם תִּהְיוּ נְקִיִּם׃ וַיְמַהֲרוּ וַיּוֹרִדוּ אִישׁ אֶת־
12 אַמְתַּחְתּוֹ אָרְצָה וַיִּפְתְּחוּ אִישׁ אַמְתַּחְתּוֹ׃ וַיְחַפֵּשׂ בַּגָּדוֹל
הֵחֵל וּבַקָּטֹן כִּלָּה וַיִּמָּצֵא הַגָּבִיעַ בְּאַמְתַּחַת בִּנְיָמִן׃
מפטיר 13 וַיִּקְרְעוּ שִׂמְלֹתָם וַיַּעֲמֹס אִישׁ עַל־חֲמֹרוֹ וַיָּשֻׁבוּ הָעִירָה׃*
מפטיר לספ') 14 וַיָּבֹא יְהוּדָה וְאֶחָיו בֵּיתָה יוֹסֵף וְהוּא עוֹדֶנּוּ שָׁם וַיִּפְּלוּ
טו לְפָנָיו אָרְצָה׃* וַיֹּאמֶר לָהֶם יוֹסֵף מָה־הַמַּעֲשֶׂה הַזֶּה אֲשֶׁר
עֲשִׂיתֶם הֲלוֹא יְדַעְתֶּם כִּי־נַחֵשׁ יְנַחֵשׁ אִישׁ אֲשֶׁר כָּמֹנִי׃
16 וַיֹּאמֶר יְהוּדָה מַה־נֹּאמַר לַאדֹנִי מַה־נְּדַבֵּר וּמַה־נִּצְטַדָּק
הָאֱלֹהִים מָצָא אֶת־עֲוֹן עֲבָדֶיךָ הִנֶּנּוּ עֲבָדִים לַאדֹנִי גַּם־
17 אֲנַחְנוּ גַּם אֲשֶׁר־נִמְצָא הַגָּבִיעַ בְּיָדוֹ׃ וַיֹּאמֶר חָלִילָה לִּי
מֵעֲשׂוֹת זֹאת הָאִישׁ אֲשֶׁר נִמְצָא הַגָּבִיעַ בְּיָדוֹ הוּא יִהְיֶה־לִּי
עָבֶד וְאַתֶּם עֲלוּ לְשָׁלוֹם אֶל־אֲבִיכֶם׃

v. 10. קמץ בז"ק v. 17. קמץ בז"ק

9. *let him die.* Convinced of their absolute innocence, they propose the penalty of death as the punishment to be inflicted on the thief. They add to this, slavery for all the other brothers.

10. The steward asks only for the guilty one to be his bondman. According to Rashi the verse means: 'Verily it should be as ye have said (for ye are all accessories, and, therefore, all guilty; but I will be more lenient) he alone with whom it is found shall be my bondman.'

11. *Then they hastened.* This agitated zeal wonderfully depicts their confident innocence (Procksch).

12. *beginning at the eldest.* To prevent suspicion of his knowledge of the affair. It is also a dramatic touch adding to the excitement of the scene described.

13. *then they rent their clothes.* In their grief at the thought of the loss of Benjamin, mourning him as if he were dead.

14. *and Judah.* Who assumes the leadership, having undertaken the responsibility of bringing Benjamin home again.

and they fell. The Heb. word denotes a prostration in utter despair.

15. *will indeed divine.* And thereby discover the thief.

16. *or how shall we clear ourselves? i.e.* prove our innocence; the goblet condemns us.

God hath found out the iniquity. The exclamation does not imply admission of that particular sin: it is the wrong done to their father and to Joseph in the olden days which is behind Judah's confession. The work of the moral regeneration of the brothers is complete.

HAFTORAH MIKKETZ הפטרת מקץ

I KINGS III, 15–IV, 1

Chapter III

15. And Solomon awoke, and, behold, it
was a dream; and he came to Jerusalem,
and stood before the ark of the covenant
of the Lord, and offered up burnt-offerings,
and offered peace-offerings, and made a
feast to all his servants. ¶ 16. Then came
there two women, that were harlots, unto
the king, and stood before him. 17. And
the one woman said: 'Oh, my lord, I and
this woman dwell in one house; and I was
delivered of a child with her in the house.
18. And it came to pass the third day after
I was delivered, that this woman was
delivered also; and we were together;
there was no stranger with us in the house,
save we two in the house. 19. And this
woman's child died in the night; because
she overlay it. 20. And she arose at mid-
night, and took my son from beside me,
while thy handmaid slept, and laid it in
her bosom, and laid her dead child in my
bosom. 21. And when I rose in the morning
to give my child suck, behold, it was dead;
but when I had looked well at it in the
morning, behold, it was not my son, whom
I did bear.' 22. And the other woman said:
'Nay; but the living is my son, and the dead
is thy son.' And this said: 'No; but the
dead is thy son, and the living is my son.'
Thus they spoke before the king. ¶ 23. Then
said the king: 'The one saith: This is my
son that liveth, and thy son is the dead;
and the other saith: Nay; but thy son is
the dead, and my son is the living.' 24. And
the king said: 'Fetch me a sword.' And
they brought a sword before the king. 25.
And the king said: 'Divide the living child
in two, and give half to the one, and half
to the other.' 26. Then spoke the woman

Cap. III. ג

טו וַיִּקַץ
שְׁלֹמֹה וְהִנֵּה חֲלוֹם וַיָּבוֹא יְרוּשָׁלַ͏ִם וַיַּעֲמֹד ׀ לִפְנֵי ׀ אֲרוֹן
בְּרִית־אֲדֹנָי וַיַּעַל עֹלוֹת וַיַּעַשׂ שְׁלָמִים וַיַּעַשׂ מִשְׁתֶּה לְכָל־
16 עֲבָדָיו׃ אָז תָּבֹאנָה שְׁתַּיִם נָשִׁים זֹנוֹת אֶל־הַמֶּלֶךְ
17 וַתַּעֲמֹדְנָה לְפָנָיו׃ וַתֹּאמֶר הָאִשָּׁה הָאַחַת בִּי אֲדֹנִי אֲנִי
18 וְהָאִשָּׁה הַזֹּאת יֹשְׁבֹת בְּבַיִת אֶחָד וָאֵלֵד עִמָּהּ בַּבָּיִת׃ וַיְהִי
בַּיּוֹם הַשְּׁלִישִׁי לְלִדְתִּי וַתֵּלֶד גַּם־הָאִשָּׁה הַזֹּאת וַאֲנַחְנוּ יַחְדָּו
19 אֵין־זָר אִתָּנוּ בַּבַּיִת זוּלָתִי שְׁתַּיִם אֲנַחְנוּ בַּבָּיִת׃ וַיָּמָת בֶּן־
כ הָאִשָּׁה הַזֹּאת לָיְלָה אֲשֶׁר שָׁכְבָה עָלָיו׃ וַתָּקָם בְּתוֹךְ
הַלַּיְלָה וַתִּקַּח אֶת־בְּנִי מֵאֶצְלִי וַאֲמָתְךָ יְשֵׁנָה וַתַּשְׁכִּיבֵהוּ
21 בְּחֵיקָהּ וְאֶת־בְּנָהּ הַמֵּת הִשְׁכִּיבָה בְחֵיקִי׃ וָאָקֻם בַּבֹּקֶר
לְהֵינִיק אֶת־בְּנִי וְהִנֵּה־מֵת וָאֶתְבּוֹנֵן אֵלָיו בַּבֹּקֶר וְהִנֵּה
22 לֹא־הָיָה בְנִי אֲשֶׁר יָלָדְתִּי׃ וַתֹּאמֶר הָאִשָּׁה הָאַחֶרֶת
לֹא כִי בְּנִי הַחַי וּבְנֵךְ הַמֵּת וְזֹאת אֹמֶרֶת לֹא כִי בְּנֵךְ הַמֵּת
23 וּבְנִי הֶחָי וַתְּדַבֵּרְנָה לִפְנֵי הַמֶּלֶךְ׃ וַיֹּאמֶר הַמֶּלֶךְ זֹאת
אֹמֶרֶת זֶה־בְּנִי הַחַי וּבְנֵךְ הַמֵּת וְזֹאת אֹמֶרֶת לֹא כִי בְּנֵךְ
24 הַמֵּת וּבְנִי הֶחָי׃ וַיֹּאמֶר הַמֶּלֶךְ קְחוּ־לִי חָרֶב וַיָּבִאוּ הַחֶרֶב
כה לִפְנֵי הַמֶּלֶךְ׃ וַיֹּאמֶר הַמֶּלֶךְ גִּזְרוּ אֶת־הַיֶּלֶד הַחַי לִשְׁנָיִם
26 וּתְנוּ אֶת־הַחֲצִי לְאַחַת וְאֶת־הַחֲצִי לְאֶחָת׃ וַתֹּאמֶר הָאִשָּׁה

In both Sedrah and Haftorah, kings have dreams which are more than dreams. In the Sedrah, Joseph unravels the mystery to the Egyptian sovereign, first humbly ascribing his power of understanding to God, the Source of all wisdom. In the Haftorah, all Israel join the king in acknowledging that the wisdom which the youthful monarch possesses is of God. In the spirit of reverence, Solomon had asked not for long life or riches or honour, but for power to serve others, for an understanding heart to discharge the duties and responsibilities of his position, and to advance the welfare of the great people entrusted to him while so young and inexperienced.

16–28. Solomon the wise judge.

16. *two women.* The meanest of his subjects had access to the king for justice.

harlots. The word may also be translated 'innkeepers' (Ralbag).

18. *no stranger.* None but they could ever know the truth. Observation on the part of a judge must in a case of this nature be supplemented by extraordinary intuition.

whose the living child was unto the king, for her heart yearned upon her son, and she said: 'Oh, my lord, give her the living child, and in no wise slay it.' But the other said: 'It shall be neither mine nor thine; divide it.' 27. Then the king answered and said: 'Give her the living child, and in no wise slay it: she is the mother thereof.' 28. And all Israel heard of the judgment which the king had judged; and they feared the king; for they saw that the wisdom of God was in him, to do justice.

אֲשֶׁר־בְּנָהּ הַחַי אֶל־הַמֶּלֶךְ כִּֽי־נִכְמְרוּ רַחֲמֶיהָ עַל־בְּנָהּ
וַתֹּאמֶר ׀ בִּי אֲדֹנִי תְּנוּ־לָהּ אֶת־הַיָּלוּד הַחַי וְהָמֵת אַל־
27 תְּמִיתֻהוּ וְזֹאת אֹמֶרֶת גַּם־לִי גַם־לָךְ לֹא יִהְיֶה גְּזֹרוּ׃ וַיַּעַן
הַמֶּלֶךְ וַיֹּאמֶר תְּנוּ־לָהּ אֶת־הַיָּלוּד הַחַי וְהָמֵת לֹא תְמִיתֻהוּ
28 הִיא אִמּוֹ׃ וַיִּשְׁמְעוּ כָל־יִשְׂרָאֵל אֶת־הַמִּשְׁפָּט אֲשֶׁר שָׁפַט
הַמֶּלֶךְ וַיִּרְאוּ מִפְּנֵי הַמֶּלֶךְ כִּי רָאוּ כִּי־חָכְמַת אֱלֹהִים
בְּקִרְבּוֹ לַעֲשׂוֹת מִשְׁפָּט׃

CHAPTER IV.

CAP. IV. ד

1. And king Solomon was king over all Israel.

א וַיְהִי הַמֶּלֶךְ שְׁלֹמֹה מֶלֶךְ עַל־כָּל־יִשְׂרָאֵל׃

27. *she is the mother.* A Heavenly Voice (בת קול) resounded in his ears, and told him, '*She* is the mother thereof' (Targum Jonathan, Talmud).

28. *heard of the judgment.* His decision arrived at by his keen-sighted appeal to the instincts of human nature, his shrewd insight into the workings of the human heart.

they feared the king. Revered him; or, fear possessed evil-doers because of the certainty of punishment.

CHAPTER IV

1. *over all Israel.* The display of such a Divine gift of Wisdom established his sway over all Israel.

'To be the successor of David was a great inheritance, but a much greater responsibility. Solomon was eighteen years old when he ascended the throne. The fact that, in spite of this, he maintained his dominion for forty years under the most trying conditions, is of itself evidence of his great qualities. If David created an Israelitish nation, Solomon created an Israelitish state. He extended immensely the intellectual horizon of Israel. He placed Israel in the rank of the great nations' (Cornill).

44

18. Then Judah came near unto him, and said: Oh my lord, let thy servant, I pray thee, speak a word in my lord's ears, and let not thine anger burn against thy servant; for thou art even as Pharaoh. 19. My lord asked his servants, saying: Have ye a father, or a brother? 20. And we said unto my lord: We have a father, an old man, and a child of his old age, a little one; and his brother is dead, and he alone is left of his mother, and his father loveth him. 21. And thou saidst unto thy servants: Bring him down unto me, that I may set mine eyes upon him. 22. And we said unto my lord: The lad cannot leave his father; for if he should leave his father, his father would die. 23. And thou saidst unto thy servants: Except your youngest brother come down with you, ye shall see my face no more. 24. And it came to pass when we came up unto thy servant my father, we told him the words of my lord. 25. And our father said: Go again, buy us a little food. 26. And we said: We cannot go down; if our youngest brother be with us, then will we go down; for we may not see the man's face, except our youngest brother be with us. 27. And thy servant my father said unto us: Ye know that my wife bore me two sons; 28. and the one went out from me, and I said: Surely he is torn in pieces; and I have not seen him since; 29. and if ye take this one also from me, and harm befall him, ye

מד ס ס ס יא 11

18 ויגש אליו יהודה ויאמר בי אדני ידבר־נא עבדך דבר
באזני אדני ואל־יחר אפך בעבדך כי כמוך כפרעה׃
19 אדני שאל את־עבדיו לאמר היש־לכם אב או־אח׃
כ ויאמר אל־אדני יש־לנו אב זקן וילד זקנים קטן ואחיו
21 מת ויותר הוא לבדו לאמו ואביו אהבו׃ ותאמר אל־
22 עבדיך הורדהו אלי ואשימה עיני עליו׃ ונאמר אל־
אדני לא־יוכל הנער לעזב את־אביו ועזב את־אביו ומת׃
23 ותאמר אל־עבדיך אם־לא ירד אחיכם הקטן אתכם לא
24 תספון לראות פני׃ ויהי כי עלינו אל־עבדך אבי ונגד־
כה לו את דברי אדני׃ ויאמר אבינו שבו שברו־לנו מעט־
26 אכל׃ ונאמר לא נוכל לרדת אם־יש אחינו הקטן אתנו
וירדנו כי־לא נוכל לראות פני האיש ואחינו הקטן
27 איננו אתנו׃ ויאמר עבדך אבי אלינו אתם ידעתם כי
28 שנים ילדה־לי אשתי׃ ויצא האחד מאתי ואמר אך
29 טרף טרף ולא ראיתיו עד־הנה׃ ולקחתם גם־את־זה

XI. VAYYIGGASH

(CHAPTERS XLIV, 18–XLVII, 27)

CHAPTER XLIV

18–34. The pathos and beauty of Judah's plea on behalf of Benjamin have retained their appeal to man's heart throughout the ages. Sir Walter Scott called it 'the most complete pattern of genuine natural eloquence extant in any language. When we read this generous speech, we forgive Judah all the past, and cannot refuse to say "Thou art he whom thy brethren shall praise" '. The spirit of self-sacrifice which Judah's speech reveals, offering to remain as a slave in Benjamin's place, has its parallel in the life-story of Moses, who besought God to blot out his name from the Book of Life, unless his people, Israel, is saved with him (Exod. XXXII, 32).

18. *came near.* Not in fear, but conscious of the vital issues at stake. Benjamin's servitude would involve the death of Jacob and the shame of Judah.

speak a word. He asks pardon for venturing to continue the conversation after Joseph had decided their case. Just because Joseph is like Pharaoh in authority, it behoves him to listen to the appeal which Judah is about to make.

19. *my lord asked.* See XLIII, 7. Judah wishes to divert the sympathy of Joseph towards the unhappy position of the old father bereft of his youngest son, whom Judah refers to as 'a child of his old age, a little one'.

20. *his brother is dead.* Joseph is now spoken of before his eleven brethren as dead. Dead, but still remembered by father and brothers.

28. *torn in pieces; and I have not seen him since.* Joseph now learns the manner of his supposed death. Do these last words imply a lurking disbelief in Jacob's mind as to the story of Joseph's death? Perhaps they give expression to Jacob's unquenchable longing for his beloved Joseph. The words must have touched the very core of Joseph's heart.

will bring down my gray hairs with sorrow to the grave. 30. Now therefore when I come to thy servant my father, and the lad is not with us; seeing that his soul is bound up with the lad's soul;* ii. 31. it will come to pass, when he seeth that the lad is not with us, that he will die; and thy servants will bring down the gray hairs of thy servant our father with sorrow to the grave. 32. For thy servant became surety for the lad unto my father, saying: If I bring him not unto thee, then shall I bear the blame to my father for ever. 33. Now therefore, let thy servant, I pray thee, abide instead of the lad a bondman to my lord; and let the lad go up with his brethren. 34. For how shall I go up to my father, if the lad be not with me? lest I look upon the evil that shall come on my father.'

מֵעִם פָּנַי וְקָרָהוּ אָסוֹן וְהֽוֹרַדְתֶּם אֶת־שֵׂיבָתִי בְּרָעָה
ל שְׁאֹֽלָה׃ וְעַתָּה כְּבֹאִי אֶל־עַבְדְּךָ אָבִי וְהַנַּעַר אֵינֶנּוּ אִתָּנוּ
שני
31 וְנַפְשׁוֹ קְשׁוּרָה בְנַפְשֽׁוֹ׃ וְהָיָה כִּרְאוֹתוֹ כִּי־אֵין הַנַּעַר וָמֵת
וְהוֹרִידוּ עֲבָדֶיךָ אֶת־שֵׂיבַת עַבְדְּךָ אָבִינוּ בְּיָגוֹן שְׁאֹֽלָה׃
32 כִּי עַבְדְּךָ עָרַב אֶת־הַנַּעַר מֵעִם אָבִי לֵאמֹר אִם־לֹא אֲבִיאֶנּוּ
33 אֵלֶיךָ וְחָטָאתִי לְאָבִי כָּל־הַיָּמִֽים׃ וְעַתָּה יֵֽשֶׁב־נָא עַבְדְּךָ
34 תַּחַת הַנַּעַר עֶבֶד לַֽאדֹנִי וְהַנַּעַר יַעַל עִם־אֶחָֽיו׃ כִּי־אֵיךְ
אֶֽעֱלֶה אֶל־אָבִי וְהַנַּעַר אֵינֶנּוּ אִתִּי פֶּן אֶרְאֶה בָרָע אֲשֶׁר
יִמְצָא אֶת־אָבִֽי׃

45

CHAPTER XLV

1. Then Joseph could not refrain himself before all them that stood by him; and he cried: 'Cause every man to go out from me.' And there stood no man with him, while Joseph made himself known unto his brethren. 2. And he wept aloud; and the Egyptians heard, and the house of Pharaoh heard. 3. And Joseph said unto his brethren: 'I am Joseph; doth my father yet live?' And his brethren could not answer him; for they were affrighted at his presence. 4. And Joseph said unto his brethren: 'Come near to me, I pray you.' And they came near. And he said: 'I am Joseph your brother, whom ye sold into Egypt. 5. And now be not grieved, nor angry with yourselves, that ye sold

CAP. XLV. מה

מה

א וְלֹֽא־יָכֹל יוֹסֵף לְהִתְאַפֵּק לְכֹל הַנִּצָּבִים עָלָיו וַיִּקְרָא
הוֹצִיאוּ כָל־אִישׁ מֵעָלָי וְלֹא־עָמַד אִישׁ אִתּוֹ בְּהִתְוַדַּע יוֹסֵף
2 אֶל־אֶחָֽיו׃ וַיִּתֵּן אֶת־קֹלוֹ בִּבְכִי וַיִּשְׁמְעוּ מִצְרַיִם וַיִּשְׁמַע
3 בֵּית פַּרְעֹֽה׃ וַיֹּאמֶר יוֹסֵף אֶל־אֶחָיו אֲנִי יוֹסֵף הַעוֹד אָבִי
4 חָי וְלֹֽא־יָכְלוּ אֶחָיו לַעֲנוֹת אֹתוֹ כִּי נִבְהֲלוּ מִפָּנָֽיו׃ וַיֹּאמֶר
יוֹסֵף אֶל־אֶחָיו גְּשׁוּ־נָא אֵלַי וַיִּגָּשׁוּ וַיֹּאמֶר אֲנִי יוֹסֵף אֲחִיכֶם
ה אֲשֶׁר־מְכַרְתֶּם אֹתִי מִצְרָֽיְמָה׃ וְעַתָּה ׀ אַל־תֵּעָצְבוּ וְאַל־

30. *his soul is bound up with the lad's soul.* The same phrase is used of the intertwined souls of David and Jonathan, I Sam. XVIII, 1. The beauty and conciseness of the three Hebrew words cannot be reproduced in translation.

31. *with sorrow to the grave.* The skilful repetition of the phrase by Judah is poignantly pathetic.

33. *abide instead of the lad a bondman.* Judah became surety (*v.* 32) and now offers himself as a substitute. He prefers bondage to freedom, so as to save his brother. He once saw the anguish of his old father when Joseph was gone; he cannot endure to see a repetition.

CHAPTER XLV. JOSEPH REVEALS HIMSELF

1. *could not refrain himself.* The repeated references to the misfortune of his aged father overwhelm him; and as he does not wish his retinue to hear of the old crime of his brethren, he orders every man to depart. He is now alone with his eleven brothers. There is no interpreter present, and Joseph uses the language of his brethren.

2. *wept aloud.* lit. 'gave forth his voice in weeping'.

the house of Pharaoh heard. From the retinue of Joseph. The news of the coming of Joseph's brethren travelled fast.

3. *doth my father yet live?* The question seems to ask, 'Is it really true that our father, so old, so sorely tried, is still alive?' The wonder of it seems to urge the question from Joseph's lips as the first word in revealing himself to his brethren. The thought of his father is uppermost in his mind. He does not wait for an answer.

they were affrighted. Consternation made them dumb. They do not believe their eyes and ears.

4. *come near to me.* The better to convince themselves.

5. *be not grieved.* 'With singular generosity Joseph reassures them by pointing out the Providential purpose which had overruled their crime for good' (Skinner).

me hither; for God did send me before you to preserve life. 6. For these two years hath the famine been in the land; and there are yet five years, in which there shall be neither plowing nor harvest. 7. And God sent me before you to give you a remnant on the earth, and to save you alive for a great deliverance.* iii. 8. So now it was not you that sent me hither, but God; and He hath made me a father to Pharaoh, and lord of all his house, and ruler over all the land of Egypt. 9. Hasten ye, and go up to my father, and say unto him: Thus saith thy son Joseph: God hath made me lord of all Egypt; come down unto me, tarry not. 10. And thou shalt dwell in the land of Goshen, and thou shalt be near unto me, thou, and thy children, and thy children's children, and thy flocks, and thy herds, and all that thou hast; 11. and there will I sustain thee; for there are yet five years of famine; lest thou come to poverty, thou, and thy household, and all that thou hast. 12. And, behold, your eyes see, and the eyes of my brother Benjamin, that it is my mouth that speaketh unto you. 13. And ye shall tell my father of all my glory in Egypt, and of all that ye have seen; and ye shall hasten and bring down my father hither.' 14. And he fell upon his brother Benjamin's neck, and wept; and Benjamin wept upon his neck. 15. And he kissed all his brethren, and wept upon them; and after that his brethren talked with him. ¶ 16. And the report thereof was heard in Pharaoh's house, saying: 'Joseph's brethren are come'; and it pleased Pharaoh well, and his servants. 17. And Pharaoh said unto Joseph: 'Say unto thy brethren: This do ye: lade your beasts, and go, get you unto the land of Canaan; 18. and take your father and your households, and come unto me; and I will give you the good of

יִחַר בְּעֵינֵיכֶם כִּי־מְכַרְתֶּם אֹתִי הֵנָּה כִּי לְמִחְיָה שְׁלָחַנִי
6 אֱלֹהִים לִפְנֵיכֶם׃ כִּי־זֶה שְׁנָתַיִם הָרָעָב בְּקֶרֶב הָאָרֶץ
7 וְעוֹד חָמֵשׁ שָׁנִים אֲשֶׁר אֵין־חָרִישׁ וְקָצִיר׃ וַיִּשְׁלָחֵנִי
אֱלֹהִים לִפְנֵיכֶם לָשׂוּם לָכֶם שְׁאֵרִית בָּאָרֶץ וּלְהַחֲיוֹת לָכֶם
8 לִפְלֵיטָה גְּדֹלָה׃ * וְעַתָּה לֹא־אַתֶּם שְׁלַחְתֶּם אֹתִי הֵנָּה כִּי שלישי
הָאֱלֹהִים וַיְשִׂימֵנִי לְאָב לְפַרְעֹה וּלְאָדוֹן לְכָל־בֵּיתוֹ וּמֹשֵׁל
9 בְּכָל־אֶרֶץ מִצְרָיִם׃ מַהֲרוּ וַעֲלוּ אֶל־אָבִי וַאֲמַרְתֶּם אֵלָיו
כֹּה אָמַר בִּנְךָ יוֹסֵף שָׂמַנִי אֱלֹהִים לְאָדוֹן לְכָל־מִצְרָיִם
י רְדָה אֵלַי אַל־תַּעֲמֹד׃ וְיָשַׁבְתָּ בְאֶרֶץ־גֹּשֶׁן וְהָיִיתָ קָרוֹב
אֵלַי אַתָּה וּבָנֶיךָ וּבְנֵי בָנֶיךָ וְצֹאנְךָ וּבְקָרְךָ וְכָל־אֲשֶׁר־לָךְ׃
11 וְכִלְכַּלְתִּי אֹתְךָ שָׁם כִּי־עוֹד חָמֵשׁ שָׁנִים רָעָב פֶּן־תִּוָּרֵשׁ
12 אַתָּה וּבֵיתְךָ וְכָל־אֲשֶׁר־לָךְ׃ וְהִנֵּה עֵינֵיכֶם רֹאוֹת וְעֵינֵי
13 אָחִי בִנְיָמִין כִּי־פִי הַמְדַבֵּר אֲלֵיכֶם׃ וְהִגַּדְתֶּם לְאָבִי
אֶת־כָּל־כְּבוֹדִי בְּמִצְרַיִם וְאֵת כָּל־אֲשֶׁר רְאִיתֶם וּמִהַרְתֶּם
14 וְהוֹרַדְתֶּם אֶת־אָבִי הֵנָּה׃ וַיִּפֹּל עַל־צַוְּארֵי בִנְיָמִן־אָחִיו וַיֵּבְךְּ
טו וּבִנְיָמִן בָּכָה עַל־צַוָּארָיו׃ וַיְנַשֵּׁק לְכָל־אֶחָיו וַיֵּבְךְּ עֲלֵהֶם
16 וְאַחֲרֵי כֵן דִּבְּרוּ אֶחָיו אִתּוֹ׃ וְהַקֹּל נִשְׁמַע בֵּית פַּרְעֹה
לֵאמֹר בָּאוּ אֲחֵי יוֹסֵף וַיִּיטַב בְּעֵינֵי פַרְעֹה וּבְעֵינֵי עֲבָדָיו׃
17 וַיֹּאמֶר פַּרְעֹה אֶל־יוֹסֵף אֱמֹר אֶל־אַחֶיךָ זֹאת עֲשׂוּ טַעֲנוּ
18 אֶת־בְּעִירְכֶם וּלְכוּ־בֹאוּ אַרְצָה כְּנָעַן׃ וּקְחוּ אֶת־אֲבִיכֶם

sold me hither. i.e. caused me to be sold hither.

7. *a remnant.* Offspring, descendants.

8. *but God.* Joseph again ascribes his presence in Egypt to the intervention of God.

a father. Heb. *Ab*, which is the exact transliteration of an Egyptian title of state rank, corresponding to 'vizier'.

9. *tarry not.* The anxiety to see his father is revealed by this request.

10. *Goshen.* The railway from Alexandria to Suez now runs through the district where Joseph's father and family settled. It was the best pasture-land in Egypt.

thou shalt be near unto me. This was possibly spoken with a view of inducing Jacob to come to Egypt.

12. *your eyes see.* This is spoken to his dazed and still incredulous brethren.

15. *after that.* The brethren did not talk with him until he had shown the same fraternal love to them as he had done to Benjamin. Then they knew 'that his heart was with them' (Kimchi).

16–20. Pharaoh seconds Joseph's invitation and orders wagons to be sent for the conveyance of Jacob and his family.

17. *beasts.* Of burden.

18. *the good of the land.* Seems to be parallel to the next phrase, 'the fat of the land'; wherever the word *fat* is used, it means the best, the most desirable part of anything (Rashi).

the land of Egypt, and ye shall eat the fat of the land.* iv. 19. Now thou art commanded, this do ye: take your wagons out of the land of Egypt for your little ones, and for your wives, and bring your father, and come. 20. Also regard not your stuff; for the good things of all the land of Egypt are yours.' 21. And the sons of Israel did so; and Joseph gave them wagons, according to the commandment of Pharaoh, and gave them provision for the way. 22. To all of them he gave each man changes of raiment; but to Benjamin he gave three hundred shekels of silver, and five changes of raiment. 23. And to his father he sent in like manner ten asses laden with the good things of Egypt, and ten she-asses laden with corn and bread and victual for his father by the way. 24. So he sent his brethren away, and they departed; and he said unto them: 'See that ye fall not out by the way.' 25. And they went up out of Egypt, and came into the land of Canaan unto Jacob their father. 26. And they told him, saying: 'Joseph is yet alive, and he is ruler over all the land of Egypt.' And his heart fainted, for he believed them not. 27. And they told him all the words of Joseph, which he had said unto them; and when he saw the wagons which Joseph had sent to carry him, the spirit of Jacob their father revived.* v. 28. And Israel said: 'It is enough; Joseph my son is yet alive; I will go and see him before I die.'

46

Chapter XLVI

1. And Israel took his journey with all that he had, and came to Beer-sheba, and offered sacrifices unto the God of his father Isaac. 2. And God spoke unto Israel in the visions of the night, and said:

וְאֶת־בָּתֵּיכֶם וּבֹאוּ אֵלָי וְאֶתְּנָה לָכֶם אֶת־טוּב אֶרֶץ מִצְרַיִם
רביעי
19 וְאִכְלוּ אֶת־חֵלֶב הָאָרֶץ׃* וְאַתָּה צֻוֵּיתָה זֹאת עֲשׂוּ קְחוּ־
לָכֶם מֵאֶרֶץ מִצְרַיִם עֲגָלוֹת לְטַפְּכֶם וְלִנְשֵׁיכֶם וּנְשָׂאתֶם
כ אֶת־אֲבִיכֶם וּבָאתֶם׃ וְעֵינְכֶם אַל־תָּחֹס עַל־כְּלֵיכֶם כִּי־
21 טוּב כָּל־אֶרֶץ מִצְרַיִם לָכֶם הוּא׃ וַיַּעֲשׂוּ־כֵן בְּנֵי יִשְׂרָאֵל
וַיִּתֵּן לָהֶם יוֹסֵף עֲגָלוֹת עַל־פִּי פַרְעֹה וַיִּתֵּן לָהֶם צֵדָה
22 לַדָּרֶךְ׃ לְכֻלָּם נָתַן לָאִישׁ חֲלִפוֹת שְׂמָלֹת וּלְבִנְיָמִן נָתַן
23 שְׁלֹשׁ־מֵאוֹת כֶּסֶף וְחָמֵשׁ חֲלִפֹת שְׂמָלֹת׃ וּלְאָבִיו שָׁלַח
כְּזֹאת עֲשָׂרָה חֲמֹרִים נֹשְׂאִים מִטּוּב מִצְרָיִם וְעֶשֶׂר אֲתֹנֹת
24 נֹשְׂאֹת בָּר וָלֶחֶם וּמָזוֹן לְאָבִיו לַדָּרֶךְ׃ וַיְשַׁלַּח אֶת־אֶחָיו
כה וַיֵּלֵכוּ וַיֹּאמֶר אֲלֵהֶם אַל־תִּרְגְּזוּ בַּדָּרֶךְ׃ וַיַּעֲלוּ מִמִּצְרָיִם
26 וַיָּבֹאוּ אֶרֶץ כְּנַעַן אֶל־יַעֲקֹב אֲבִיהֶם׃ וַיַּגִּדוּ לוֹ לֵאמֹר עוֹד
יוֹסֵף חַי וְכִי־הוּא מֹשֵׁל בְּכָל־אֶרֶץ מִצְרָיִם וַיָּפָג לִבּוֹ כִּי לֹא־
27 הֶאֱמִין לָהֶם׃ וַיְדַבְּרוּ אֵלָיו אֵת כָּל־דִּבְרֵי יוֹסֵף אֲשֶׁר דִּבֶּר
אֲלֵהֶם וַיַּרְא אֶת־הָעֲגָלוֹת אֲשֶׁר־שָׁלַח יוֹסֵף לָשֵׂאת אֹתוֹ
חמישי
28 וַתְּחִי רוּחַ יַעֲקֹב אֲבִיהֶם׃* וַיֹּאמֶר יִשְׂרָאֵל רַב עוֹד־יוֹסֵף
בְּנִי חָי אֵלְכָה וְאֶרְאֶנּוּ בְּטֶרֶם אָמוּת׃

Cap. XLVI. מו

מו

א וַיִּסַּע יִשְׂרָאֵל וְכָל־אֲשֶׁר־לוֹ וַיָּבֹא בְּאֵרָה שָּׁבַע וַיִּזְבַּח זְבָחִים

מח׳ v. 25. סבירין ארצה

19. *now thou art commanded, this do ye.* The phrase is elliptical, it means: 'Now thou art commanded by me to tell them, this do ye' (Rashi).

20. *also regard not your stuff.* They would have to leave much of their property in the land of Canaan, and would be able to transport only part of their movable property, but they should pay no regard to this.

for the good things of all the land of Egypt are yours. Thus Jacob and his family came to Egypt at the express invitation of the king. There was even a promise of good treatment to the immigrants as guests of the State, which one of their family had saved. As free men they were subsequently entitled to return at their pleasure to their old home in Canaan.

21. *according to the commandment of Pharaoh. i.e.* provided by the king.

24. *fall not out by the way.* This is usually interpreted as meaning, 'Do not quarrel owing to mutual recriminations.'

26. *his heart fainted. i.e.* his heart stood still, unable to beat for astonishment.

for he believed them not. The news was too good to be true.

28. *it is enough.* 'What care I for all his glory? Joseph, my son, is still alive!'

Chapter XLVI. Jacob's Journey to Egypt

1. *came to Beer-sheba.* From Hebron, to offer sacrifice where God had appeared to Abraham. Jacob desired God's sanction, prior to his leaving the land of Promise.

his father Isaac. Who had built the altar and fixed his home at Beer-sheba.

'Jacob, Jacob.' And he said: 'Here am I.' 3. And He said: 'I am God, the God of thy father; fear not to go down into Egypt; for I will there make of thee a great nation. 4. I will go down with thee into Egypt; and I will also surely bring thee up again; and Joseph shall put his hand upon thine eyes.' 5. And Jacob rose up from Beer-sheba; and the sons of Israel carried Jacob their father, and their little ones, and their wives, in the wagons which Pharaoh had sent to carry him. 6. And they took their cattle, and their goods, which they had gotten in the land of Canaan, and came into Egypt, Jacob, and all his seed with him; 7. his sons, and his sons' sons with him, his daughters, and his sons' daughters, and all his seed brought he with him into Egypt. ¶ 8. And these are the names of the children of Israel, who came into Egypt, Jacob and his sons: Reuben, Jacob's first-born. 9. And the sons of Reuben: Hanoch, and Pallu, and Hezron, and Carmi. 10. And the sons of Simeon: Jemuel, and Jamin, and Ohad, and Jachin, and Zohar, and Shaul the son of a Canaanitish woman. 11. And the sons of Levi: Gershon, Kohath, and Merari. 12. And the sons of Judah: Er, and Onan, and Shelah, and Perez, and Zerah; but Er and Onan died in the land of Canaan. And the sons of Perez were Hezron and Hamul. 13. And the sons of Issachar: Tola, and Puvah, and Iob, and Shimron. 14. And the sons of Zebulun: Sered, and Elon, and Jahleel. 15. These are the sons of Leah, whom she bore unto

2 לאלהי אביו יצחק: ויאמר אלהים | לישראל במראת
3 הלילה ויאמר יעקב | יעקב ויאמר הנני: ויאמר אנכי
האל אלהי אביך אל-תירא מרדה מצרימה כי-לגוי גדול
4 אשימך שם: אנכי ארד עמך מצרימה ואנכי אעלך
ה גם-עלה ויוסף ישית ידו על-עיניך: ויקם יעקב מבאר
שבע וישאו בני-ישראל את-יעקב אביהם ואת-טפם
ואת-נשיהם בעגלות אשר-שלח פרעה לשאת אתו:
6 ויקחו את-מקניהם ואת-רכושם אשר רכשו בארץ כנען
7 ויבאו מצרימה יעקב וכל-זרעו אתו: בניו ובני בניו אתו
בנתיו ובנות בניו וכל-זרעו הביא אתו מצרימה: ס
8 ואלה שמות בני-ישראל הבאים מצרימה יעקב ובניו
9 בכר יעקב ראובן: ובני ראובן חנוך ופלוא וחצרן וכרמי:
י ובני שמעון ימואל וימין ואהד ויכין וצחר ושאול בן
11 12 הכנענית: ובני לוי גרשון קהת ומררי: ובני יהודה ער
ואונן ושלה ופרץ וזרח וימת ער ואונן בארץ כנען ויהיו בני-
13 פרץ חצרן וחמול: ובני יששכר תולע ופוה ויוב ושמרן:
14 טו ובני זבלון סרד ואלון ויחלאל: אלה | בני לאה אשר ילדה

2. *in the visions of the night.* In a dream.

3. *fear not to go down.* Isaac had intended to migrate to Egypt, but God had forbidden it. Now permission is granted to Jacob. 'It was a sleepless night in which God brought the peace of certainty to the aged man whose being had been stirred to its foundations. We should feel with the Patriarch that we are at the turning-point of his history, which we to-day may well call a turning-point in the history of mankind. It was in Egypt that Israel's greatest religious genius was to arise' (Procksch).

4. *I will go down with thee.* God's words here imply His promise to protect Jacob in Egypt and to achieve the Divine will concerning him and his offspring (cf. XXVIII, 15).

bring thee up again. i.e. thy descendants. Some commentators explain the phrase as referring to the burial of Jacob, L, 13 (Rashi and Kimchi).

put his hand upon thine eyes. At thy death; it is customary that the living do this to the dead (Ibn Ezra).

5. *Pharaoh had sent to carry him.* This is repeated with a view of showing how Pharaoh had invited the family of Jacob to come to Egypt.

7. *his daughters.* Includes the daughters-in-law.

all his seed. i.e. his great-grandchildren.

8–27. The list of Jacob's descendants who came into Egypt. Compare the lists in Num. XXVI and I Chron. II–VIII which show slight variations in the forms of the names.

10. *Jachin.* For this name in Solomon's Temple, see I Kings VII, 21.

a Canaanitish woman. Luzzatto explains that she was the daughter of Dinah, and because of her father, Shechem, she is called a 'Canaanite woman'.

15. *thirty and three.* This number included Jacob, see *v.* 8. The actual number of the descendants of Jacob in *v.* 9–14 is thirty-two. The Rabbis add Jochebed, the daughter of Levi, who was born exactly at the time of the entrance into Egypt.

Jacob in Paddan-aram, with his daughter Dinah; all the souls of his sons and his daughters were thirty and three. 16. And the sons of Gad: Ziphion, and Haggi, Shuni, and Ezbon, Eri, and Arodi, and Areli. 17. And the sons of Asher: Imnah, and Ishvah, and Ishvi, and Beriah, and Serah their sister; and the sons of Beriah: Heber, and Malchiel. 18. These are the sons of Zilpah, whom Laban gave to Leah his daughter, and these she bore unto Jacob, even sixteen souls. 19. The sons of Rachel Jacob's wife: Joseph and Benjamin. 20. And unto Joseph in the land of Egypt were born Manasseh and Ephraim, whom Asenath the daughter of Poti-phera priest of On bore unto him. 21. And the sons of Benjamin: Bela, and Becher, and Ashbel, Gera, and Naaman, Ehi, and Rosh, Muppim, and Huppim, and Ard. 22. These are the sons of Rachel, who were born to Jacob; all the souls were fourteen. 23. And the sons of Dan: Hushim. 24. And the sons of Naphtali: Jahzeel, and Guni, and Jezer, and Shillem. 25. These are the sons of Bilhah, whom Laban gave unto Rachel his daughter, and these she bore unto Jacob; all the souls were seven. 26. All the souls belonging to Jacob that came into Egypt, that came out of his loins, besides Jacob's sons' wives, all the souls were threescore and six. 27. And the sons of Joseph, who were born to him in Egypt, were two souls; all the souls of the house of Jacob, that came into Egypt, were threescore and ten.* vi. ¶ 28. And he sent Judah before him unto Joseph, to show the way before him unto Goshen; and they came into the land of Goshen. 29. And Joseph made ready his chariot, and went up to meet Israel his father, to Goshen; and he presented himself unto him, and fell on his neck, and wept on his neck a good while. 30. And Israel said unto Joseph: 'Now let me die, since I have seen thy face, that thou art yet alive.'

לְיַעֲקֹב בְּפַדַּן אֲרָם וְאֵת דִּינָה בִתּוֹ כָּל־נֶפֶשׁ בָּנָיו וּבְנוֹתָיו
16 שְׁלֹשִׁים וְשָׁלֹשׁ׃ וּבְנֵי גָד צִפְיוֹן וְחַגִּי שׁוּנִי וְאֶצְבֹּן עֵרִי
17 וַאֲרוֹדִי וְאַרְאֵלִי׃ וּבְנֵי אָשֵׁר יִמְנָה וְיִשְׁוָה וְיִשְׁוִי וּבְרִיעָה
18 וְשֶׂרַח אֲחֹתָם וּבְנֵי בְרִיעָה חֶבֶר וּמַלְכִּיאֵל׃ אֵלֶּה בְּנֵי זִלְפָּה
אֲשֶׁר־נָתַן לָבָן לְלֵאָה בִתּוֹ וַתֵּלֶד אֶת־אֵלֶּה לְיַעֲקֹב שֵׁשׁ
19 כ עֶשְׂרֵה נָפֶשׁ׃ בְּנֵי רָחֵל אֵשֶׁת יַעֲקֹב יוֹסֵף וּבִנְיָמִן׃ וַיִּוָּלֵד
לְיוֹסֵף בְּאֶרֶץ מִצְרַיִם אֲשֶׁר יָלְדָה־לּוֹ אָסְנַת בַּת־פּוֹטִי פֶרַע
21 כֹּהֵן אֹן אֶת־מְנַשֶּׁה וְאֶת־אֶפְרָיִם׃ וּבְנֵי בִנְיָמִן בֶּלַע וָבֶכֶר
22 וְאַשְׁבֵּל גֵּרָא וְנַעֲמָן אֵחִי וָרֹאשׁ מֻפִּים וְחֻפִּים וָאָרְדְּ׃ אֵלֶּה
בְּנֵי רָחֵל אֲשֶׁר יֻלַּד לְיַעֲקֹב כָּל־נֶפֶשׁ אַרְבָּעָה עָשָׂר׃
23 24 וּבְנֵי־דָן חֻשִׁים׃ וּבְנֵי נַפְתָּלִי יַחְצְאֵל וְגוּנִי וְיֵצֶר וְשִׁלֵּם׃
כה אֵלֶּה בְּנֵי בִלְהָה אֲשֶׁר־נָתַן לָבָן לְרָחֵל בִּתּוֹ וַתֵּלֶד אֶת־
26 אֵלֶּה לְיַעֲקֹב כָּל־נֶפֶשׁ שִׁבְעָה׃ כָּל־הַנֶּפֶשׁ הַבָּאָה לְיַעֲקֹב
מִצְרַיְמָה יֹצְאֵי יְרֵכוֹ מִלְּבַד נְשֵׁי בְנֵי־יַעֲקֹב כָּל־נֶפֶשׁ שִׁשִּׁים
27 וָשֵׁשׁ׃ וּבְנֵי יוֹסֵף אֲשֶׁר־יֻלַּד־לוֹ בְמִצְרַיִם נֶפֶשׁ שְׁנָיִם כָּל־
ששי 28 הַנֶּפֶשׁ לְבֵית־יַעֲקֹב הַבָּאָה מִצְרַיְמָה שִׁבְעִים׃ ס וְאֶת־
יְהוּדָה שָׁלַח לְפָנָיו אֶל־יוֹסֵף לְהוֹרֹת לְפָנָיו גֹּשְׁנָה וַיָּבֹאוּ
29 אַרְצָה גֹּשֶׁן׃ וַיֶּאְסֹר יוֹסֵף מֶרְכַּבְתּוֹ וַיַּעַל לִקְרַאת־יִשְׂרָאֵל
אָבִיו גֹּשְׁנָה וַיֵּרָא אֵלָיו וַיִּפֹּל עַל־צַוָּארָיו וַיֵּבְךְּ עַל־צַוָּארָיו
ל עוֹד׃ וַיֹּאמֶר יִשְׂרָאֵל אֶל־יוֹסֵף אָמוּתָה הַפָּעַם אַחֲרֵי רְאוֹתִי
31 אֶת־פָּנֶיךָ כִּי עוֹדְךָ חָי׃ וַיֹּאמֶר יוֹסֵף אֶל־אֶחָיו וְאֶל־בֵּית

21. *Naaman.* Is here one of the sons of Benjamin, but in Num. XXVI, 40, the same name occurs as that of a grandson. Ibn Ezra suggests that the same name is applied to two different persons. The supposed difficulty of Benjamin having sons and grandsons when coming to Egypt, and at the same time being referred to as 'a little one' (XLIV, 20), is to be explained by comparing Jacob's age with that of Benjamin, his youngest son.

26. *threescore and six.* The descendants of Leah numbered 33, of Zilpah 16, of Rachel 14, and of Bilhah 7. The sum of these figures gives a total of 70; but if Jacob, Joseph, and his two sons be excluded, the result is 66.

28. *to show the way.* For Joseph to direct Judah as to the place where Jacob should dwell. The Midrash explains the Heb. phrase literally, 'to establish a house of teaching.' Such has remained the first care of Jews whenever migrating to a new land—to provide for the religious teaching of their children.

29. *a good while. i.e.* at first neither of them can speak, being overpowered by emotion.

30. *now let me die.* Having once more seen Joseph, there was nothing more for him to live for. He had attained the highest joy in life.

31. And Joseph said unto his brethren, and unto his father's house: 'I will go up, and tell Pharaoh, and will say unto him: My brethren, and my father's house, who were in the land of Canaan, are come unto me; 32. and the men are shepherds, for they have been keepers of cattle; and they have brought their flocks, and their herds, and all that they have. 33. And it shall come to pass, when Pharaoh shall call you, and shall say: What is your occupation? 34. that ye shall say: Thy servants have been keepers of cattle from our youth even until now, both we, and our fathers; that ye may dwell in the land of Goshen; for every shepherd is an abomination unto the Egyptians.'

47

CHAPTER XLVII

1. Then Joseph went in and told Pharaoh, and said: 'My father and my brethren, and their flocks, and their herds, and all that they have, are come out of the land of Canaan; and, behold, they are in the land of Goshen.' 2. And from among his brethren he took five men, and presented them unto Pharaoh. 3. And Pharaoh said unto his brethren: 'What is your occupation?' And they said unto Pharaoh: 'Thy servants are shepherds, both we, and our fathers.' 4. And they said unto Pharaoh: 'To sojourn in the land are we come; for there is no pasture for thy servants' flocks; for the famine is sore in the land of Canaan. Now therefore, we pray thee, let thy servants dwell in the land of Goshen.' 5. And Pharaoh spoke unto Joseph, saying: 'Thy father and thy brethren are come unto thee; 6. the land of Egypt is before thee; in the best of the land make thy father and thy brethren to dwell; in the land of Goshen let them dwell. And if thou knowest any able men among them, then make them rulers over my cattle.' 7. And Joseph brought in Jacob his father, and set him before Pharaoh. And Jacob blessed

אָבִיו אֶעֱלֶה וְאַגִּידָה לְפַרְעֹה וְאֹמְרָה אֵלָיו אַחַי וּבֵית־אָבִי
32 אֲשֶׁר בְּאֶרֶץ־כְּנַעַן בָּאוּ אֵלָי׃ וְהָאֲנָשִׁים רֹעֵי צֹאן כִּי־אַנְשֵׁי
33 מִקְנֶה הָיוּ וְצֹאנָם וּבְקָרָם וְכָל־אֲשֶׁר לָהֶם הֵבִיאוּ׃ וְהָיָה
34 כִּי־יִקְרָא לָכֶם פַּרְעֹה וְאָמַר מַה־מַּעֲשֵׂיכֶם׃ וַאֲמַרְתֶּם
אַנְשֵׁי מִקְנֶה הָיוּ עֲבָדֶיךָ מִנְּעוּרֵינוּ וְעַד־עַתָּה גַּם־אֲנַחְנוּ גַּם־
אֲבֹתֵינוּ בַּעֲבוּר תֵּשְׁבוּ בְּאֶרֶץ גֹּשֶׁן כִּי־תוֹעֲבַת מִצְרַיִם כָּל־
רֹעֵה צֹאן׃

CAP. XLVII. מז

מז

א וַיָּבֹא יוֹסֵף וַיַּגֵּד לְפַרְעֹה וַיֹּאמֶר אָבִי וְאַחַי וְצֹאנָם וּבְקָרָם
2 וְכָל־אֲשֶׁר לָהֶם בָּאוּ מֵאֶרֶץ כְּנָעַן וְהִנָּם בְּאֶרֶץ גֹּשֶׁן׃ וּמִקְצֵה
3 אֶחָיו לָקַח חֲמִשָּׁה אֲנָשִׁים וַיַּצִּגֵם לִפְנֵי פַרְעֹה׃ וַיֹּאמֶר
פַּרְעֹה אֶל־אֶחָיו מַה־מַּעֲשֵׂיכֶם וַיֹּאמְרוּ אֶל־פַּרְעֹה רֹעֵה
4 צֹאן עֲבָדֶיךָ גַּם־אֲנַחְנוּ גַּם־אֲבוֹתֵינוּ׃ וַיֹּאמְרוּ אֶל־פַּרְעֹה
לָגוּר בָּאָרֶץ בָּאנוּ כִּי־אֵין מִרְעֶה לַצֹּאן אֲשֶׁר לַעֲבָדֶיךָ כִּי־
כָבֵד הָרָעָב בְּאֶרֶץ כְּנָעַן וְעַתָּה יֵשְׁבוּ־נָא עֲבָדֶיךָ בְּאֶרֶץ
ה גֹּשֶׁן׃ וַיֹּאמֶר פַּרְעֹה אֶל־יוֹסֵף לֵאמֹר אָבִיךָ וְאַחֶיךָ בָּאוּ
6 אֵלֶיךָ׃ אֶרֶץ מִצְרַיִם לְפָנֶיךָ הִוא בְּמֵיטַב הָאָרֶץ הוֹשֵׁב
אֶת־אָבִיךָ וְאֶת־אַחֶיךָ יֵשְׁבוּ בְּאֶרֶץ גֹּשֶׁן וְאִם־יָדַעְתָּ וְיֶשׁ־
7 בָּם אַנְשֵׁי־חַיִל וְשַׂמְתָּם שָׂרֵי מִקְנֶה עַל־אֲשֶׁר־לִי׃ וַיָּבֵא
יוֹסֵף אֶת־יַעֲקֹב אָבִיו וַיַּעֲמִדֵהוּ לִפְנֵי פַרְעֹה וַיְבָרֶךְ יַעֲקֹב

מו׳ v. 34. הע׳ בצרי

34. *every shepherd.* The Hyksos, or alien Shepherd-kings, thus seem to have acquired the native Egyptian dislike of foreigners in general and herdsmen in particular.

CHAPTER XLVII, 1–10. JACOB AND HIS SONS BEFORE PHARAOH

This is the crucial test of Joseph's character. For the Viceroy of Egypt to acknowledge as his own brothers the rude Canaanite shepherds, who had besides given him every reason for repudiating them, called for the highest loyalty and devotion. 'Many men resist the temptations of youth, and attain to positions of eminence, and then fail to pay the debt which they owe to their own humble kinsmen who have helped them to success. With Joseph the debt, if any, was small. There was also no absolute necessity of revealing his identity, much less of inviting his uncouth kinsmen to the land of Egypt. His action, therefore, shows a simple nobility of character rarely equalled in the past or present' (C. F. Kent).

6. *the best of the land.* Is to be placed at their disposal. This was Pharaoh's gratitude to Joseph for his eminent services to Egypt.

make them rulers over my cattle. A further sign of the king's gratitude. Joseph's relatives are to be appointed royal officers, superintendents of the king's herdsmen.

7–11. Joseph presents his father to the king.

8 אֶת־פַּרְעֹה: וַיֹּאמֶר פַּרְעֹה אֶל־יַעֲקֹב כַּמָּה יְמֵי שְׁנֵי חַיֶּיךָ:
9 וַיֹּאמֶר יַעֲקֹב אֶל־פַּרְעֹה יְמֵי שְׁנֵי מְגוּרַי שְׁלֹשִׁים וּמְאַת
שָׁנָה מְעַט וְרָעִים הָיוּ יְמֵי שְׁנֵי חַיַּי וְלֹא הִשִּׂיגוּ אֶת־יְמֵי שְׁנֵי
י חַיֵּי אֲבֹתַי בִּימֵי מְגוּרֵיהֶם: וַיְבָרֶךְ יַעֲקֹב אֶת־פַּרְעֹה וַיֵּצֵא
שביעי
11 מִלִּפְנֵי פַרְעֹה: * וַיּוֹשֵׁב יוֹסֵף אֶת־אָבִיו וְאֶת־אֶחָיו וַיִּתֵּן לָהֶם
אֲחֻזָּה בְּאֶרֶץ מִצְרַיִם בְּמֵיטַב הָאָרֶץ בְּאֶרֶץ רַעְמְסֵס כַּאֲשֶׁר
12 צִוָּה פַרְעֹה: וַיְכַלְכֵּל יוֹסֵף אֶת־אָבִיו וְאֶת־אֶחָיו וְאֵת כָּל־
13 בֵּית אָבִיו לֶחֶם לְפִי הַטָּף: וְלֶחֶם אֵין בְּכָל־הָאָרֶץ כִּי־
כָבֵד הָרָעָב מְאֹד וַתֵּלַהּ אֶרֶץ מִצְרַיִם וְאֶרֶץ כְּנַעַן מִפְּנֵי
14 הָרָעָב: וַיְלַקֵּט יוֹסֵף אֶת־כָּל־הַכֶּסֶף הַנִּמְצָא בְאֶרֶץ־מִצְרַיִם
וּבְאֶרֶץ כְּנַעַן בַּשֶּׁבֶר אֲשֶׁר־הֵם שֹׁבְרִים וַיָּבֵא יוֹסֵף אֶת־
טו הַכֶּסֶף בֵּיתָה פַרְעֹה: וַיִּתֹּם הַכֶּסֶף מֵאֶרֶץ מִצְרַיִם וּמֵאֶרֶץ
כְּנַעַן וַיָּבֹאוּ כָל־מִצְרַיִם אֶל־יוֹסֵף לֵאמֹר הָבָה־לָּנוּ לֶחֶם
16 וְלָמָּה נָמוּת נֶגְדֶּךָ כִּי אָפֵס כָּסֶף: וַיֹּאמֶר יוֹסֵף הָבוּ מִקְנֵיכֶם
17 וְאֶתְּנָה לָכֶם בְּמִקְנֵיכֶם אִם־אָפֵס כָּסֶף: וַיָּבִיאוּ אֶת־מִקְנֵיהֶם
אֶל־יוֹסֵף וַיִּתֵּן לָהֶם יוֹסֵף לֶחֶם בַּסּוּסִים וּבְמִקְנֵה הַצֹּאן
וּבְמִקְנֵה הַבָּקָר וּבַחֲמֹרִים וַיְנַהֲלֵם בַּלֶּחֶם בְּכָל־מִקְנֵהֶם
18 בַּשָּׁנָה הַהִוא: וַתִּתֹּם הַשָּׁנָה הַהִוא וַיָּבֹאוּ אֵלָיו בַּשָּׁנָה

Pharaoh. 8. And Pharaoh said unto Jacob: 'How many are the days of the years of thy life?' 9. And Jacob said unto Pharaoh: 'The days of the years of my sojournings are a hundred and thirty years; few and evil have been the days of the years of my life, and they have not attained unto the days of the years of the life of my fathers in the days of their sojournings.' 10. And Jacob blessed Pharaoh, and went out from the presence of Pharaoh.* vii. 11. And Joseph placed his father and his brethren, and gave them a possession in the land of Egypt, in the best of the land, in the land of Rameses, as Pharaoh had commanded. 12. And Joseph sustained his father, and his brethren, and all his father's household, with bread, according to the want of their little ones. ¶ 13. And there was no bread in all the land; for the famine was very sore, so that the land of Egypt and the land of Canaan languished by reason of the famine. 14. And Joseph gathered up all the money that was found in the land of Egypt, and in the land of Canaan, for the corn which they bought; and Joseph brought the money into Pharaoh's house. 15. And when the money was all spent in the land of Egypt, and in the land of Canaan, all the Egyptians came unto Joseph, and said: 'Give us bread; for why should we die in thy presence? for our money faileth.' 16. And Joseph said: 'Give your cattle, and I will give you [bread] for your cattle, if money fail.' 17. And they brought their cattle unto Joseph. And Joseph gave them bread in exchange for the horses, and for the flocks, and for the herds, and for the asses; and he fed them with bread in exchange for all

7. *set him.* Or, 'presented him.'
Jacob blessed Pharaoh. The aged Patriarch asks the blessing of God for the king who had befriended his beloved son.

9. *sojournings.* Jacob does not say 'my life'. 'All the days of my life I have been a sojourner' (Rashi). To the Patriarch this earthly life is but a pilgrimage, the real life is Beyond; cf. Ps. XXXIX, 13.
few and evil. 'Few,' as compared with the long life of his father and grandfather; 'evil,' sad or unhappy.

11. *and Joseph placed.* Or, 'settled.'
in the land of Rameses. i.e. the district round the town Rameses. This town is mentioned in Ex. I, 11. Its name was given to it in the reign of Rameses II, who is held by some to be the Pharaoh of the Oppression.

12. *sustained.* Supported.

13–27. The famine in Egypt.

13. *in all the land.* lit. 'in all the earth'.
languished. Dean Stanley recalls the descriptions of similar famines in Egypt, which enable us to realize the calamity from which Joseph delivered the country. 'The eating of human flesh became so common as to excite no surprise,' writes a medieval eye-witness of one of these famines; 'the road between Syria and Egypt was like a vast field sown with human bodies.'

14. *Pharaoh's house. i.e.* the royal treasury.

15. *faileth.* lit. 'is at an end'.

16. *for your cattle.* In exchange for your cattle.

17. *horses.* As articles of luxury, the horses are mentioned first.

18. *the second year.* The year following the year after the five years, *i.e.* the seventh year (Luzzatto).

their cattle for that year. 18. And when that year was ended, they came unto him the second year, and said unto him: 'We will not hide from my lord, how that our money is all spent; and the herds of cattle are my lord's; there is nought left in the sight of my lord, but our bodies, and our lands. 19. Wherefore should we die before thine eyes, both we and our land? buy us and our land for bread, and we and our land will be bondmen unto Pharaoh; and give us seed, that we may live, and not die, and that the land be not desolate.' 20. So Joseph bought all the land of Egypt for Pharaoh; for the Egyptians sold every man his field, because the famine was sore upon them; and the land became Pharaoh's. 21. And as for the people, he removed them city by city, from one end of the border of Egypt even to the other end thereof. 22. Only the land of the priests bought he not, for the priests had a portion from Pharaoh, and did eat their portion which Pharaoh gave them; wherefore they sold not their land. 23. Then Joseph said unto the people: 'Behold, I have bought you this day and your land for Pharaoh. Lo, here is seed for you, and ye shall sow the land. 24. And it shall come to pass at the ingatherings, that ye shall give a fifth unto Pharaoh, and four parts shall be your own, for seed of the field, and for your food, and for them of your households, and for food for your little ones.'* m. 25. And they said: 'Thou hast saved our lives. Let us find favour in the sight of my lord, and we will be Pharaoh's bondmen.' 26. And Joseph made it a statute concerning the land of Egypt unto this day, that Pharaoh should have the fifth; only the land of the priests alone became not Pharaoh's. 27. And Israel dwelt in the land of Egypt, in the land of Goshen; and they got them possessions therein, and were fruitful, and multiplied exceedingly.

הַשֵּׁנִית וַיֹּאמְרוּ לוֹ לֹא־נְכַחֵד מֵאֲדֹנִי כִּי אִם־תַּם הַכֶּסֶף
וּמִקְנֵה הַבְּהֵמָה אֶל־אֲדֹנִי לֹא נִשְׁאַר לִפְנֵי אֲדֹנִי בִּלְתִּי אִם־
19 גְּוִיָּתֵנוּ וְאַדְמָתֵנוּ׃ לָמָּה נָמוּת לְעֵינֶיךָ גַּם־אֲנַחְנוּ גַּם־אַדְמָתֵנוּ
קְנֵה־אֹתָנוּ וְאֶת־אַדְמָתֵנוּ בַּלָּחֶם וְנִהְיֶה אֲנַחְנוּ וְאַדְמָתֵנוּ
עֲבָדִים לְפַרְעֹה וְתֶן־זֶרַע וְנִחְיֶה וְלֹא נָמוּת וְהָאֲדָמָה לֹא
כ תֵשָׁם׃ וַיִּקֶן יוֹסֵף אֶת־כָּל־אַדְמַת מִצְרַיִם לְפַרְעֹה כִּי־מָכְרוּ
מִצְרַיִם אִישׁ שָׂדֵהוּ כִּי־חָזַק עֲלֵהֶם הָרָעָב וַתְּהִי הָאָרֶץ
21 לְפַרְעֹה׃ וְאֶת־הָעָם הֶעֱבִיר אֹתוֹ לֶעָרִים מִקְצֵה גְבוּל־
22 מִצְרַיִם וְעַד־קָצֵהוּ׃ רַק אַדְמַת הַכֹּהֲנִים לֹא קָנָה כִּי חֹק
לַכֹּהֲנִים מֵאֵת פַּרְעֹה וְאָכְלוּ אֶת־חֻקָּם אֲשֶׁר נָתַן לָהֶם
23 פַּרְעֹה עַל־כֵּן לֹא מָכְרוּ אֶת־אַדְמָתָם׃ וַיֹּאמֶר יוֹסֵף אֶל־
הָעָם הֵן קָנִיתִי אֶתְכֶם הַיּוֹם וְאֶת־אַדְמַתְכֶם לְפַרְעֹה הֵא־
24 לָכֶם זֶרַע וּזְרַעְתֶּם אֶת־הָאֲדָמָה׃ וְהָיָה בַּתְּבוּאֹת וּנְתַתֶּם
חֲמִישִׁית לְפַרְעֹה וְאַרְבַּע הַיָּדֹת יִהְיֶה לָכֶם לְזֶרַע הַשָּׂדֶה
מפטיר
כה וּלְאָכְלְכֶם וְלַאֲשֶׁר בְּבָתֵּיכֶם וְלֶאֱכֹל לְטַפְּכֶם׃ וַיֹּאמְרוּ
הֶחֱיִתָנוּ נִמְצָא־חֵן בְּעֵינֵי אֲדֹנִי וְהָיִינוּ עֲבָדִים לְפַרְעֹה׃
26 וַיָּשֶׂם אֹתָהּ יוֹסֵף לְחֹק עַד־הַיּוֹם הַזֶּה עַל־אַדְמַת מִצְרַיִם
לְפַרְעֹה לַחֹמֶשׁ רַק אַדְמַת הַכֹּהֲנִים לְבַדָּם לֹא הָיְתָה
27 לְפַרְעֹה׃ וַיֵּשֶׁב יִשְׂרָאֵל בְּאֶרֶץ מִצְרַיִם בְּאֶרֶץ גֹּשֶׁן וַיֵּאָחֲזוּ
בָהּ וַיִּפְרוּ וַיִּרְבּוּ מְאֹד׃

our bodies, and our lands. Which they offer in exchange for bread.

19. *both we and our land.* 'The old feudal nobility of Egypt disappeared in the Hyksos period, and from the time of the eighteenth Dynasty onward we find the land, which had formerly been held by local proprietors, belonging either to the Pharaoh or to the temples. At the same time public granaries make their appearance, the superintendent of which became one of the most important of Egyptian officials' (Sayce).

seed. See *v.* 23.

20. *bought all the land of Egypt.* In this manner Pharaoh became the feudal lord of all Egypt.

21. *city by city.* The cities became 'concentration camps' for facilitating the distribution of food.

22. *only the land of the priests.* The priests had a fixed portion from the royal granaries; so there was no occasion for them to sell their lands.

24. *a fifth.* This tax was not excessive. The Jews, in the time of the Maccabees, paid the Syrian government one-third of the seed (I Macc. x, 30).

25. *Pharaoh's bondmen.* To pay the tax as ordained (Rashi).

26. *unto this day.* In the days of Moses, the arrangement described was still in force.

27. *got them possessions.* Acquired property by purchase (Kimchi).

HAFTORAH VAYYIGGASH הפטרת ויגש

EZEKIEL XXXVII, 15–28

Chapter XXXVII

15. And the word of the Lord came unto me, saying: 16. 'And thou, son of man, take thee one stick, and write upon it: For Judah, and for the children of Israel his companions; then take another stick, and write upon it: For Joseph, the stick of Ephraim, and of all the house of Israel his companions; 17. and join them for thee one to another into one stick, that they may become one in thy hand. 18. And when the children of thy people shall speak unto thee, saying: Wilt thou not tell us what thou meanest by these? 19. say unto them: Thus saith the Lord God: Behold, I will take the stick of Joseph, which is in the hand of Ephraim, and the tribes of Israel his companions; and I will put them unto him together with the stick of Judah, and make them one stick, and they shall be one in My hand. 20. And the sticks whereon thou writest shall be in thy hand before their eyes. 21. And say unto them: Thus saith the Lord God: Behold, I will take the children of Israel from among the nations, whither they are gone, and will gather them on every side, and bring them into their own land; 22. and I will make them one nation in the land, upon the mountains of Israel, and one king shall be king to them all; and they shall be no more two nations, neither shall they be divided into two kingdoms any more at all; 23. neither shall

Cap. XXXVII. לז

טו 16 וַיְהִי דְבַר־יְהוָה אֵלַי לֵאמֹר׃ וְאַתָּה
בֶן־אָדָם קַח־לְךָ עֵץ אֶחָד וּכְתֹב עָלָיו לִיהוּדָה וְלִבְנֵי
יִשְׂרָאֵל חֲבֵרָו וּלְקַח עֵץ אֶחָד וּכְתוֹב עָלָיו לְיוֹסֵף עֵץ
17 אֶפְרַיִם וְכָל־בֵּית יִשְׂרָאֵל חֲבֵרָו׃ וְקָרַב אֹתָם אֶחָד אֶל־
18 אֶחָד לְךָ לְעֵץ אֶחָד וְהָיוּ לַאֲחָדִים בְּיָדֶךָ׃ וְכַאֲשֶׁר יֹאמְרוּ
אֵלֶיךָ בְּנֵי עַמְּךָ לֵאמֹר הֲלוֹא־תַגִּיד לָנוּ מָה־אֵלֶּה לָּךְ׃
19 דַּבֵּר אֲלֵהֶם כֹּה־אָמַר אֲדֹנָי יְהוִה הִנֵּה אֲנִי לֹקֵחַ אֶת־עֵץ
יוֹסֵף אֲשֶׁר בְּיַד־אֶפְרַיִם וְשִׁבְטֵי יִשְׂרָאֵל חֲבֵרָו וְנָתַתִּי אוֹתָם
עָלָיו אֶת־עֵץ יְהוּדָה וַעֲשִׂיתִם לְעֵץ אֶחָד וְהָיוּ אֶחָד בְּיָדִי׃
כ 21 וְהָיוּ הָעֵצִים אֲשֶׁר תִּכְתֹּב עֲלֵיהֶם בְּיָדְךָ לְעֵינֵיהֶם׃ וְדַבֵּר
אֲלֵהֶם כֹּה־אָמַר אֲדֹנָי יְהוִה הִנֵּה אֲנִי לֹקֵחַ אֶת־בְּנֵי
יִשְׂרָאֵל מִבֵּין הַגּוֹיִם אֲשֶׁר הָלְכוּ־שָׁם וְקִבַּצְתִּי אֹתָם
22 מִסָּבִיב וְהֵבֵאתִי אוֹתָם אֶל־אַדְמָתָם׃ וְעָשִׂיתִי אֹתָם לְגוֹי
אֶחָד בָּאָרֶץ בְּהָרֵי יִשְׂרָאֵל וּמֶלֶךְ אֶחָד יִהְיֶה לְכֻלָּם לְמֶלֶךְ
וְלֹא יִהְיֶה־עוֹד לִשְׁנֵי גוֹיִם וְלֹא יֵחָצוּ עוֹד לִשְׁתֵּי מַמְלָכוֹת

v. 16, 19. חבריו ק׳ v. 22. יהיו קרי

Ezekiel, the son of a priest, was among those who were carried off into exile in Babylon. He became one of the spiritual agencies that kept Israel's soul alive in those years of despair. He is at once priest and prophet, preacher and writer, inspirer of the nation and pastor of individual souls. A characteristic feature of his teaching is his insistence on *individual responsibility*. He is the great preacher of Repentance, and of the Divine Forgiveness to those who in sincerity seek God's pardon. 'When the wicked man turneth away from his wickedness that he hath committed, and doeth that which is lawful and right, he shall save his soul alive.' When the members of the House of Israel shall thus be purified, Israel would be restored, and become a Holy People amid whom God would be seen to dwell.

More than any other Prophet, Ezekiel makes vivid use of allegory, symbol and parable to illustrate his message. The first half of this chapter (*v.* 1–14) is his Vision of the Valley of Dry Bones. The Prophet sees the nation dead, as it were, with all fires extinct in the dreary winter of Exile; and then beholds Israel revived through the Spirit of Prophecy, rising to renewed life and glory. In the second half of the chapter, *v.* 15–28, which constitutes our Haftorah, the Prophet pictures the continuation of this national resurrection by the definite announcement of the reunion of the two kingdoms of Judah and Joseph (the Northern Kingdom of Israel). This is symbolized by the union of the two sticks and is a reflex of the picture given in the Sedrah, of Joseph and his Brethren united after long years of estrangement.

16. The symbolic action of the Prophet is intended to secure attention to his message. One stick, to represent the Kingdom of Judah (two tribes); the other, to represent the Kingdom of Israel (ten tribes). As here, the latter kingdom is often called Ephraim (the name of one of the two sons of Joseph).

18–22. The people ask the meaning of Ezekiel's action, which is the reunion of the two kingdoms into one, as they were under Saul, David and Solomon.

they defile themselves any more with their idols, nor with their detestable things, nor with any of their transgressions; but I will save them out of all their dwelling-places, wherein they have sinned, and will cleanse them; so shall they be My people, and I will be their God. 24. And My servant David shall be king over them, and they all shall have one shepherd; they shall also walk in Mine ordinances, and observe My statutes, and do them. 25. And they shall dwell in the land that I have given unto Jacob My servant, wherein your fathers dwelt; and they shall dwell therein, they, and their children, and their children's children, for ever; and David My servant shall be their prince for ever. 26. Moreover I will make a covenant of peace with them—it shall be an everlasting covenant with them; and I will establish them, and multiply them, and will set My sanctuary in the midst of them for ever. 27. My dwelling-place also shall be over them; and I will be their God, and they shall be My people. 28. And the nations shall know that I am the LORD that sanctify Israel, when My sanctuary shall be in the midst of them for ever.'

23 עוֹד׃ וְלֹא יִטַּמְּאוּ עוֹד בְּגִלּוּלֵיהֶם וּבְשִׁקּוּצֵיהֶם וּבְכֹל
פִּשְׁעֵיהֶם וְהוֹשַׁעְתִּי אֹתָם מִכֹּל מוֹשְׁבֹתֵיהֶם אֲשֶׁר חָטְאוּ
בָהֶם וְטִהַרְתִּי אוֹתָם וְהָיוּ־לִי לְעָם וַאֲנִי אֶהְיֶה לָהֶם
24 לֵאלֹהִים׃ וְעַבְדִּי דָוִד מֶלֶךְ עֲלֵיהֶם וְרוֹעֶה אֶחָד יִהְיֶה
כה לְכֻלָּם וּבְמִשְׁפָּטַי יֵלֵכוּ וְחֻקֹּתַי יִשְׁמְרוּ וְעָשׂוּ אוֹתָם׃ וְיָשְׁבוּ
עַל־הָאָרֶץ אֲשֶׁר נָתַתִּי לְעַבְדִּי לְיַעֲקֹב אֲשֶׁר יָשְׁבוּ־בָהּ
אֲבוֹתֵיכֶם וְיָשְׁבוּ עָלֶיהָ הֵמָּה וּבְנֵיהֶם וּבְנֵי בְנֵיהֶם עַד־
26 עוֹלָם וְדָוִד עַבְדִּי נָשִׂיא לָהֶם לְעוֹלָם׃ וְכָרַתִּי לָהֶם בְּרִית
שָׁלוֹם בְּרִית עוֹלָם יִהְיֶה אוֹתָם וּנְתַתִּים וְהִרְבֵּיתִי אוֹתָם
27 וְנָתַתִּי אֶת־מִקְדָּשִׁי בְּתוֹכָם לְעוֹלָם׃ וְהָיָה מִשְׁכָּנִי עֲלֵיהֶם
28 וְהָיִיתִי לָהֶם לֵאלֹהִים וְהֵמָּה יִהְיוּ־לִי לְעָם׃ וְיָדְעוּ הַגּוֹיִם
כִּי אֲנִי יְהוָה מְקַדֵּשׁ אֶת־יִשְׂרָאֵל בִּהְיוֹת מִקְדָּשִׁי בְּתוֹכָם
לְעוֹלָם׃

23. The result is not merely political reunion, but spiritual regeneration. Israel united—but united in a return to God and in faithful performance of His Law. Then would they deserve the name of 'God's People'.

24. *David. i.e.* the ideal ruler in the future kingdom; one who, like David, would be the leader in the Messianic time.

27. The Shechinah (שכינה). God's Divine Presence will be clearly among them when they are true to their vocation as a Holy People. And thus too will Israel be the means of revealing God to the nations.

47 28. And Jacob lived in the land of Egypt seventeen years; so the days of Jacob, the years of his life, were a hundred forty and seven years. 29. And the time drew near that Israel must die; and he called his son Joseph, and said unto him: 'If now I have found favour in thy sight, put, I pray thee, thy hand under my thigh, and deal kindly and truly with me; bury me not, I pray thee, in Egypt. 30. But when I sleep with my fathers, thou shalt carry me out of Egypt, and bury me in their burying-place.' And he said: 'I will do as thou hast said.' 31. And he said: 'Swear unto me.' And he swore unto him. And Israel bowed down upon the bed's head.

28 ויחי* יעקב בארץ מצרים שבע עשרה שנה ויהי ימי־
29 יעקב שני חייו שבע שנים וארבעים ומאת שנה: ויקרבו
ימי־ישראל למות ויקרא | לבנו ליוסף ויאמר לו אם־נא
מצאתי חן בעיניך שים־נא ידך תחת ירכי ועשית עמדי
ל חסד ואמת אל־נא תקברני במצרים: ושכבתי עם־אבתי
ונשאתני ממצרים וקברתני בקברתם ויאמר אנכי אעשה
31 כדברך: ויאמר השבעה לי וישבע לו וישתחו ישראל
על־ראש המטה: פ

48 Chapter XLVIII

1. And it came to pass after these things, that one said to Joseph: 'Behold, thy father is sick.' And he took with him his two sons, Manasseh and Ephraim. 2. And one told Jacob, and said: 'Behold, thy son

מח Cap. XLVIII. מח

א ויהי אחרי הדברים האלה ויאמר ליוסף הנה אביך
חלה ויקח את־שני בניו עמו את־מנשה ואת־אפרים:

מז׳ v. 28. אין כאן פסקא כלל כי אם רוח אות אחת

XII. VAYYECHI
(Chapters XLVII, 28–L, 26)

Chapter XLVII

In this concluding Sedrah of Genesis, we see the sunset of Jacob's career. We behold this storm-tossed soul on his death-bed, blessing his children. He is not afraid to die: 'I will sleep with my fathers,' he says. He is at peace with God. 'For thy salvation do I hope, O Lord,' are among the last words he utters. He knows that he can never travel beyond God's care. He is at peace with man. Esau, Dinah, Joseph—what a world of strife and suffering and anguish, did each of these tragedies bring him—and yet he dies blessing. Though starting as 'a plain man dwelling in tents', his is no cloistered virtue, and he certainly is no sinless being. But he possesses the rare art of extracting good from every buffeting of Destiny. He errs and he stumbles, but he ever rises again; and on the anvil of affliction his soul is forged.

28. *And Jacob lived.* Heb. **ויחי יעקב**. Of how few men, asks a famous modern Jewish preacher, can we repeat a phrase like, 'And Jacob *lived*'? When many a man dies, a death-notice appears in the Press. In reality, it is a life-notice; because but for it, the world would never have known that that man had ever been alive. Only he who has been a force for human goodness, and abides in hearts and souls made better by his presence during his pilgrimage on earth, can be said to have *lived*, only such a one is heir to immortality.

29. *and the time drew near.* lit. 'and the days of Israel drew near to die'. The 'days' play an important part in the story of Jacob. He lived every day; every moment counted.

thy hand under my thigh. See on xxiv, 2.

kindly and truly. Heb. '*chesed ve-emess*'. 'Deal in true kindness with me even after my death by carrying out my wishes as regards my burial.' 'Which is the highest form of loving-kindness?' ask the Rabbis. 'The kindness shown to one who is dead,' חסד של אמת.

bury me not, I pray thee, in Egypt. His one thought, oftentimes repeated, was that his bones should not rest in that strange land; not in pyramid or painted chamber, but in the cell that he had digged for himself in the primitive sepulchre of his fathers (Stanley).

30. *but when I sleep with my fathers.* Better, *so that I sleep with my fathers.* His burial in Canaan would keep alive the wish of his descendants to return to the Promised Land.

31. *swear unto me.* The actual oath seems to be independent of the ceremony of placing the hand under the thigh, in *v.* 29. The oath was to enable Joseph to overcome any objections that might be raised by Pharaoh.

bowed down upon the bed's head. i.e. he worshipped God on the pillow of the bed. During the taking of the oath, Jacob was sitting up in bed. He now lies down again in his bed, and thanks God for the assurance given by Joseph to bury him in Canaan (Ibn Ezra, Sforno).

Chapter XLVIII. Ephraim and Manasseh

1. *took with him his two sons.* That Jacob might bless them before his death.

2 ויגד ליעקב ויאמר הנה בנך יוסף בא אליך ויתחזק
3 ישראל וישב על־המטה: ויאמר יעקב אל־יוסף אל שדי
4 נראה־אלי בלוז בארץ כנען ויברך אתי: ויאמר אלי
הנני מפרך והרביתך ונתתיך לקהל עמים ונתתי את־
ה הארץ הזאת לזרעך אחריך אחזת עולם: ועתה שני־
בניך הנולדים לך בארץ מצרים עד־באי אליך מצרימה
6 לי־הם אפרים ומנשה כראובן ושמעון יהיו־לי: ומולדתך
אשר־הולדת אחריהם לך יהיו על שם אחיהם יקראו
7 בנחלתם: ואני בבאי מפדן מתה עלי רחל בארץ כנען
בדרך בעוד כברת־ארץ לבא אפרתה ואקברה שם
8 בדרך אפרת הוא בית לחם: וירא ישראל את־בני
9 יוסף ויאמר מי־אלה: ויאמר יוסף אל־אביו בני הם
שני אשר־נתן־לי אלהים בזה ויאמר קחם־נא אלי ואברכם:
י ועיני ישראל כבדו מזקן לא יוכל לראות ויגש אתם
11 אליו וישק להם ויחבק להם: ויאמר ישראל אל־יוסף
ראה פניך לא פללתי והנה הראה אתי אלהים גם
12 את־זרעך: ויוצא יוסף אתם מעם ברכיו וישתחו לאפיו

Joseph cometh unto thee.' And Israel strengthened himself, and sat upon the bed. 3. And Jacob said unto Joseph: 'God Almighty appeared unto me at Luz in the land of Canaan, and blessed me, 4. and said unto me: Behold, I will make thee fruitful, and multiply thee, and I will make of thee a company of peoples; and will give this land to thy seed after thee for an everlasting possession. 5. And now thy two sons, who were born unto thee in the land of Egypt before I came unto thee into Egypt, are mine; Ephraim and Manasseh, even as Reuben and Simeon, shall be mine. 6. And thy issue, that thou begettest after them, shall be thine; they shall be called after the name of their brethren in their inheritance. 7. And as for me, when I came from Paddan, Rachel died unto me in the land of Canaan in the way, when there was still some way to come unto Ephrath; and I buried her there in the way to Ephrath—the same is Beth-lehem.' 8. And Israel beheld Joseph's sons, and said: 'Who are these?' 9. And Joseph said unto his father: 'They are my sons, whom God hath given me here.' And he said: 'Bring them, I pray thee, unto me, and I will bless them.'* ii. 10. Now the eyes of Israel were dim for age, so that he could not see. And he brought them near unto him; and he kissed them, and embraced them. 11. And Israel said unto Joseph: 'I had not thought to see thy face; and, lo, God hath let me see thy seed also.' 12. And Joseph brought

2. *Israel strengthened himself.* He exerted himself and sat up, with his feet on the ground.

3. *God Almighty.* Heb. '*El Shaddai*'.
Luz. i.e. Beth-el, see XXVIII, 19.

4. *an everlasting possession.* In spite of temporary loss, the children of Israel have an inalienable right to the Land of Promise.

5. *and now.* Jacob adopts the two sons of Joseph, Ephraim and Manasseh, born before he came to Egypt, thus making them equal to any of his other sons. By giving him a double portion of his inheritance, he transferred to Joseph the rights of the true firstborn.

6. *called after the name of their brethren.* They will be included in the tribe of Ephraim or in the tribe of Manasseh.

7. *Rachel.* These words, it seems, Jacob spoke to himself; otherwise he would have said, 'thy mother.' It was to honour Rachel, the sorrow of whose loss haunts him all his life, that Jacob adopts her grandchildren as his own sons. Instead of being the mother of only two tribes, she will now be accounted the ancestress of three, her honour and esteem increasing accordingly (Herxheimer, S. R. Hirsch).

unto me. Or, 'to my sorrow' (RV); cf. XXXIII, 13.

8. *beheld.* He is on his death-bed with eyes dimmed by the mist that would soon close them for ever. He does not know his grandchildren who accompany their father. He discerned faintly the figures of the young men, but could not distinguish their features; see *v.* 10.

10. *could not see.* Clearly; hence his question when seeing Joseph's sons, 'Who are these?'

12. *from between his knees.* To place a child upon the knees was the symbol of adoption. Joseph's sons had thus been placed upon or between the knees of Jacob. This having been done, Joseph removes them.

fell down on his face. In gratitude to his father.

13 אָֽרְצָה׃ וַיִּקַּ֣ח יוֹסֵף֮ אֶת־שְׁנֵיהֶם֒ אֶֽת־אֶפְרַ֤יִם בִּֽימִינוֹ֙ מִשְּׂמֹ֣אל
יִשְׂרָאֵ֔ל וְאֶת־מְנַשֶּׁ֥ה בִשְׂמֹאל֖וֹ מִימִ֣ין יִשְׂרָאֵ֑ל וַיַּגֵּ֖שׁ אֵלָֽיו׃
14 וַיִּשְׁלַח֩ יִשְׂרָאֵ֨ל אֶת־יְמִינ֜וֹ וַיָּ֨שֶׁת עַל־רֹ֤אשׁ אֶפְרַ֙יִם֙ וְה֣וּא
הַצָּעִ֔יר וְאֶת־שְׂמֹאל֖וֹ עַל־רֹ֣אשׁ מְנַשֶּׁ֑ה שִׂכֵּל֙ אֶת־יָדָ֔יו כִּ֥י
טו מְנַשֶּׁ֖ה הַבְּכֽוֹר׃ וַיְבָ֥רֶךְ אֶת־יוֹסֵ֖ף וַיֹּאמַ֑ר הָֽאֱלֹהִ֡ים אֲשֶׁר֩
הִתְהַלְּכ֨וּ אֲבֹתַ֤י לְפָנָיו֙ אַבְרָהָ֣ם וְיִצְחָ֔ק הָֽאֱלֹהִים֙ הָרֹעֶ֣ה
16 אֹתִ֔י מֵעוֹדִ֖י עַד־הַיּ֥וֹם הַזֶּֽה׃ הַמַּלְאָךְ֩ הַגֹּאֵ֨ל אֹתִ֜י מִכָּל־
רָ֗ע יְבָרֵךְ֮ אֶת־הַנְּעָרִים֒ וְיִקָּרֵ֤א בָהֶם֙ שְׁמִ֔י וְשֵׁ֥ם אֲבֹתַ֖י
שלישי
17 אַבְרָהָ֣ם וְיִצְחָ֑ק וְיִדְגּ֥וּ לָרֹ֖ב בְּקֶ֥רֶב הָאָֽרֶץ׃ וַיַּ֣רְא יוֹסֵ֗ף כִּֽי־
יָשִׁ֨ית אָבִ֧יו יַד־יְמִינ֛וֹ עַל־רֹ֥אשׁ אֶפְרַ֖יִם וַיֵּ֣רַע בְּעֵינָ֑יו וַיִּתְמֹ֣ךְ
יַד־אָבִ֗יו לְהָסִ֥יר אֹתָ֛הּ מֵעַ֥ל רֹאשׁ־אֶפְרַ֖יִם עַל־רֹ֥אשׁ מְנַשֶּֽׁה׃
18 וַיֹּ֧אמֶר יוֹסֵ֛ף אֶל־אָבִ֖יו לֹא־כֵ֣ן אָבִ֑י כִּי־זֶ֣ה הַבְּכֹ֔ר שִׂ֥ים יְמִינְךָ֖
19 עַל־רֹאשֽׁוֹ׃ וַיְמָאֵ֣ן אָבִ֗יו וַיֹּ֙אמֶר֙ יָדַ֤עְתִּֽי בְנִי֙ יָדַ֔עְתִּי גַּם־ה֥וּא
יִֽהְיֶה־לְּעָ֖ם וְגַם־ה֣וּא יִגְדָּ֑ל וְאוּלָ֗ם אָחִ֤יו הַקָּטֹן֙ יִגְדַּ֣ל מִמֶּ֔נּוּ

them out from between his knees; and he fell down on his face to the earth. 13. And Joseph took them both, Ephraim in his right hand toward Israel's left hand, and Manasseh in his left hand toward Israel's right hand, and brought them near unto him. 14. And Israel stretched out his right hand, and laid it upon Ephraim's head, who was the younger, and his left hand upon Manasseh's head, guiding his hands wittingly; for Manasseh was the first-born. 15. And he blessed Joseph, and said: 'The God before whom my fathers Abraham and Isaac did walk, the God who hath been my shepherd all my life long unto this day, 16. the angel who hath redeemed me from all evil, bless the lads; and let my name be named in them, and the name of my fathers Abraham and Isaac; and let them grow into a multitude in the midst of the earth.'* iii. 17. And when Joseph saw that his father was laying his right hand upon the head of Ephraim, it displeased him, and he held up his father's hand, to remove it from Ephraim's head unto Manasseh's head. 18. And Joseph said unto his father: 'Not so, my father, for this is the first-born; put thy right hand upon his head.' 19. And his father refused, and said: 'I know it, my son, I know it; he also shall become a people, and he also shall be great; howbeit his younger brother shall be greater than he, and his seed shall become a multitude of nations.' 20. And

13. Jacob was now to bless the lads. Joseph places Manasseh, the first-born, opposite to Jacob's right hand. This position was the station of honour.

14. *guiding his hands wittingly.* Jacob, against Joseph's wish, places the younger above the elder. This is the first instance in Scripture of the laying on of the hands in blessing.

15. *blessed Joseph.* By blessing his children (Rashbam).

16. *the angel.* This verse is connected with the preceding verse. The Jonathan Targum paraphrases: 'The God whom my fathers Abraham and Isaac worshipped, the God who hath nourished me all my life long unto this day—may it be Thy will that the angel whom Thou didst appoint to redeem me from all evil, bless the lads.'

let my name be named in them. i.e. 'may they be worthy of having their names coupled with my own, and those of my ancestors Abraham and Isaac' (Sforno).

17. *it displeased him.* Seeing his father place the younger son above the older. What is narrated in *v.* 17–19 happened before the blessing was given (Rashbam).

he held up. He grasped.

19. *I know it.* 'That Manasseh is the firstborn' (Rashi).

his younger brother shall be greater. Just as if he had been endowed with the birthright. The younger brother in Scripture is at times preferred to the elder. Abel, Abraham, Isaac, Moses and David afford striking instances of this fact.

a multitude. lit. 'fullness'.

20. *By thee shall Israel bless.* To this day, every pious Jewish father on Sabbath eve places his hand on the head of his son, and blesses him in the words: 'God make thee as Ephraim and Manasseh' (Authorised Prayer Book, p. 122). Ephraim and Manasseh would not barter away their 'Jewishness' for the most exalted social position, or the most enviable political career, in the Egyptian state. They voluntarily gave up their place in the higher Egyptian aristocracy, and openly identified themselves with their 'alien' kinsmen, the despised shepherd-immigrants. Every Jewish parent may well pray that his children show the same loyalty to their father and their father's God as did Ephraim and Manasseh.

he blessed them that day, saying: 'By thee shall Israel bless, saying: God make thee as Ephraim and as Manasseh.' And he set Ephraim before Manasseh. 21. And Israel said unto Joseph: 'Behold, I die; but God will be with you, and bring you back unto the land of your fathers. 22. Moreover I have given to thee one [1]portion above thy brethren, which I took out of the hand of the Amorite with my sword and with my bow.'* iv.

49 CHAPTER XLIX

1. And Jacob called unto his sons, and said: 'Gather yourselves together, that I may tell you that which shall befall you in the end of days.

2. Assemble yourselves, and hear, ye sons of Jacob;
And hearken unto Israel your father.

3. Reuben, thou art my first-born,
My might, and the first-fruits of my strength;
The excellency of dignity, and the excellency of power.

[1] Heb. *schechem*, shoulder.

כ וְזַרְעוֹ יִהְיֶה מְלֹא־הַגּוֹיִם׃ וַיְבָרְכֵם בַּיּוֹם הַהוּא לֵאמוֹר בְּךָ
יְבָרֵךְ יִשְׂרָאֵל לֵאמֹר יְשִׂמְךָ אֱלֹהִים כְּאֶפְרַיִם וְכִמְנַשֶּׁה
21 וַיָּשֶׂם אֶת־אֶפְרַיִם לִפְנֵי מְנַשֶּׁה׃ וַיֹּאמֶר יִשְׂרָאֵל אֶל־יוֹסֵף
הִנֵּה אָנֹכִי מֵת וְהָיָה אֱלֹהִים עִמָּכֶם וְהֵשִׁיב אֶתְכֶם אֶל־
22 אֶרֶץ אֲבֹתֵיכֶם׃ וַאֲנִי נָתַתִּי לְךָ שְׁכֶם אַחַד עַל־אַחֶיךָ אֲשֶׁר
לָקַחְתִּי מִיַּד הָאֱמֹרִי בְּחַרְבִּי וּבְקַשְׁתִּי׃ פ רביעי

מט

CAP. XLIX. מט

א וַיִּקְרָא יַעֲקֹב אֶל־בָּנָיו וַיֹּאמֶר הֵאָסְפוּ וְאַגִּידָה לָכֶם אֵת
2 אֲשֶׁר־יִקְרָא אֶתְכֶם בְּאַחֲרִית הַיָּמִים׃ הִקָּבְצוּ וְשִׁמְעוּ בְּנֵי
3 יַעֲקֹב וְשִׁמְעוּ אֶל־יִשְׂרָאֵל אֲבִיכֶם׃ רְאוּבֵן בְּכֹרִי אַתָּה כֹּחִי

מח' v. 20. מלא ו'

22. This verse is the blessing addressed to Joseph personally.

portion. Heb. *shechem.* The reference is to the plot of ground purchased by Jacob from Hamor at Shechem; see XXXIII, 19. It seems from the context that this plot of land had fallen into the hands of the Amorites, and had been retaken from them by force of arms. Jacob's military exploit is not elsewhere mentioned.

above thy brethren. i.e. more than thy brethren. Some commentators explain the extra portion bestowed upon Joseph as referring to the privilege accorded to his two sons in being accounted equals of the other tribes.

CHAPTER XLIX. THE BLESSING OF JACOB

1. *Jacob called unto his sons.* His other sons who were not present when Jacob blessed Ephraim and Manasseh.

shall befall you. Jacob's words are prophetic anticipations of the future destinies of his children. The counsel and benediction which Israel imparts to them are such that their descendants have remained 'Children of Israel' for all time.

in the end of days. i.e. in the distant future. In the Prophets, this phrase is used to express the Messianic age.

2. The Blessing is in poetic form, and therefore marked by *parallelism*, or 'thought rhythm', which is a characteristic of all Heb. poetry. This verse forms an introduction to the main theme of the chapter. Jacob demands their earnest attention because of the fateful message he has to convey to them.

3–4. REUBEN

3. *my first-born.* Reuben's natural rights have been forfeited. He has birth, dignity, opportunity; but no strength of character. In the Scripture narrative, he appears as a man who begins good actions, but does not complete them. Thus, he plans to save Joseph and he actually prevents the murder, but Joseph is sold nevertheless. Reuben's descendants in Jewish history remain true to ancestral type. When Deborah unfurled the banner of Israelitish independence in the days of the Judges, the tribes rallied round her. In the camp of Reuben, however, there were great deliberations and mighty searchings of heart, but no action; see Judges V, 15. Subsequently, the tribe of Reuben is rarely mentioned in Israel's history.

my might. 'As the first-born, Reuben is endowed with a superabundant vitality, which is the cause at once of his pre-eminence and his undoing' (Skinner).

the excellency of dignity. A Hebraism for 'superior in dignity'. Superiority in dignity and power belonged to the first-born. Onkelos renders, 'For thee it was provided to receive three portions, the right of first born, the priesthood, and the kingdom.' The first of these was given to Joseph, I Chron. V, 1; the priesthood was given to Levi, Num. III, 41; the kingly power or headship was allotted to Judah, see *v.* 8.

4. *unstable as water.* Any breeze can ruffle its surface. Or, 'bubbling over like water,' in uncontrolled vehemence of passion. Reuben's cardinal sin, says Jacob, was weakness of will, lack of self-control and firmness of purpose.

4. Unstable as water, have not thou the excellency;
Because thou wentest up to thy father's bed;
Then defiledst thou it—he went up to my couch.

5. Simeon and Levi are brethren;
Weapons of violence their kinship.

6. Let my soul not come into their council;
Unto their assembly let my glory not be united;
For in their anger they slew men,
And in their self-will they houghed oxen.

7. Cursed be their anger, for it was fierce,
And their wrath, for it was cruel;
I will divide them in Jacob,
And scatter them in Israel.

4 וְרֵאשִׁית אוֹנִי יֶתֶר שְׂאֵת וְיֶתֶר עָז׃ פַּחַז כַּמַּיִם אַל־תּוֹתַר
כִּי עָלִיתָ מִשְׁכְּבֵי אָבִיךָ אָז חִלַּלְתָּ יְצוּעִי עָלָה׃ פ
ה 6 שִׁמְעוֹן וְלֵוִי אַחִים כְּלֵי חָמָס מְכֵרֹתֵיהֶם׃ בְּסֹדָם אַל־תָּבֹא
נַפְשִׁי בִּקְהָלָם אַל־תֵּחַד כְּבֹדִי כִּי בְאַפָּם הָרְגוּ אִישׁ וּבִרְצֹנָם
7 עִקְּרוּ־שׁוֹר׃ אָרוּר אַפָּם כִּי עָז וְעֶבְרָתָם כִּי קָשָׁתָה אֲחַלְּקֵם
בְּיַעֲקֹב וַאֲפִיצֵם בְּיִשְׂרָאֵל׃ פ
8 יְהוּדָה אַתָּה יוֹדוּךָ אַחֶיךָ יָדְךָ בְּעֹרֶף אֹיְבֶיךָ יִשְׁתַּחֲווּ לְךָ

8. Judah, thee shall thy brethren praise;
Thy hand shall be on the neck of thine enemies;
Thy father's sons shall bow down before thee.

v. 8. בראש עמוד סימן בי״ה שמ״ו

The Heb. word for 'unstable', *pachaz*, means recklessness; the same root in Aramaic means 'to be lascivious'.

have not thou the excellency. i.e. 'thou shalt forfeit thy privileges' as the first-born. None of the descendants of Reuben ever became Judge, Prophet, or leader. Here Scripture stresses the idea that moral character is a more important factor than hereditary right.

he went up to my couch. The sudden change from the second to the third person is due to Jacob's loathing at the mere memory of Reuben's offence; see on XXXV, 22.

5–7. SIMEON AND LEVI

5. *Simeon and Levi are brethren.* In violence. See XXXIV, 26 f. Moffatt translates: 'Simeon and Levi are a pair.'

weapons of violence their kinship. The phrase is also rendered, 'instruments of cruelty are in their habitations' (Onkelos, Kimchi, and AV). The reference is evidently to their dealings in Shechem; see XXXIV.

6. *council.* Or, 'secret'; *i.e.* secret confederacy.

my glory. i.e. my soul; as in Psalm XVI, 9. What lofty conception of both glory and soul, to make them synonymous as the Heb. language does!

men. The Heb. is in the singular, the word being used collectively.

they houghed oxen. A figure of vindictive destructiveness, such as is recounted in XXXIV, 28, 29. To 'hough' is to sever certain sinews which render the animal helpless. The mutilation of animals is not recorded in that chapter. Many Versions therefore render, 'they digged down a wall,' referring to the destruction of Shechem. The Heb. words for 'ox' and 'wall' differ only in one dot—שור and שזר.

7. *cursed be their anger.* Jacob does not curse them but their sin, of which he could not have given a stronger condemnation. It is characteristic of the untrustworthiness of the Samaritan Text that instead of the reading ארור, 'Cursed be their anger,' it has אדיר, 'How splendid is their anger'!

I will divide them in Jacob. Fulfilled by the intermingling of the Simeonites in the inheritance of Judah (see Josh. XIX, 1), and by the dispersion of the tribe of Levi among the other tribes of Israel.

8–12. JUDAH

Contrast the characterization of Reuben with Jacob's jubilant praise of Judah. Unlike Reuben, Judah has neither birthright nor the dignity or opportunity of the first-born, but he has both strength and consistency of purpose. He knows his enemy, and—whether it be a person, an evil, or a cause—his hand is upon that enemy's neck. Capable indeed of falling into grievous error and sin, he is yet true at heart. Judah's character fits him to take the lead and rule. He is the worthy ancestor of David, Isaiah and Nehemiah, the father of the royal tribe that led in the conquest of the Promised Land.

8. *Judah, thee shall thy brethren praise.* Foretells Judah's miltary glory in subduing the enemies of his brethren, the Philistines and Edomites, resulting in the acknowledgment of Judah as the national leader, or king.

9 בְּנֵי אָבִיךָ׃ גּוּר אַרְיֵה יְהוּדָה מִטֶּרֶף בְּנִי עָלִיתָ כָּרַע רָבַץ
י כְּאַרְיֵה וּכְלָבִיא מִי יְקִימֶנּוּ׃ לֹא־יָסוּר שֵׁבֶט מִיהוּדָה וּמְחֹקֵק
11 מִבֵּין רַגְלָיו עַד כִּי־יָבֹא שִׁילֹה וְלוֹ יִקְּהַת עַמִּים׃ אֹסְרִי
לַגֶּפֶן עִירֹה וְלַשֹּׂרֵקָה בְּנִי אֲתֹנוֹ כִּבֵּס בַּיַּיִן לְבֻשׁוֹ וּבְדַם־
12 עֲנָבִים סוּתֹה׃ חַכְלִילִי עֵינַיִם מִיָּיִן וּלְבֶן־שִׁנַּיִם מֵחָלָב׃ פ
13 זְבוּלֻן לְחוֹף יַמִּים יִשְׁכֹּן וְהוּא לְחוֹף אֳנִיֹּת וְיַרְכָתוֹ עַל־צִידֹן׃ פ
14 טו יִשָּׂשכָר חֲמֹר גָּרֶם רֹבֵץ בֵּין הַמִּשְׁפְּתָיִם׃ וַיַּרְא מְנֻחָה

9. Judah is a lion's whelp;
From the prey, my son, thou art gone up.
He stooped down, he couched as a lion,
And as a lioness; who shall rouse him up?

10. The sceptre shall not depart from Judah,
Nor the ruler's staff from between his feet,
As long as men come to Shiloh;
And unto him shall the obedience of the peoples be.

11. Binding his foal unto the vine,
And his ass's colt unto the choice vine;
He washeth his garments in wine,
And his vesture in the blood of grapes;

12. His eyes shall be red with wine,
And his teeth white with milk.

13. Zebulun shall dwell at the shore of the sea,
And he shall be a shore for ships,
And his flank shall be upon Zidon.

14. Issachar is a large-boned ass,
Couching down between the sheepfolds.

v. 10. ק׳ דגושה v. 11. עירו ק׳ ibid. סותו ק׳

9. *lion's whelp.* According to the Midrash, the emblem of the tribe of Judah was a lion. The metaphor suggests the vigour and nobility of Judah and his offspring; and the habitual swiftness and force of their military movements.

thou art gone up. To the security of the Judean hills, after the victorious conflicts in the Plain below.

10. *the sceptre.* The emblem of kingship.

from between his feet. The figure is that of an Oriental king sitting, with the ruler's staff between his knees; as can be seen on Assyrian and Persian monuments.

as long as men come to Shiloh. Heb. *ad ki yabo shiloh;* lit. 'until Shiloh come'; or, 'until that which is his shall come'; *i.e.* Judah's rule shall continue till he comes to his own, and the obedience of all the tribes is his. This translation may also mean that when the tribe of Judah has come into its own, the sceptre shall be taken out of its hands.

The explanation of this verse, especially of the Hebrew words עד כי יבא שילה, is very difficult. Some Jewish commentators have given it a Messianic meaning. For the interpretation that it has been given in the Church, see the Additional Note, p. 201.

the peoples. i.e. the tribes of Israel, as in Deut. XXXIII, 3, 19.

11. Instead of the translation, 'Binding his foal unto the vine' (also AV and RV), which would make Judah out to be a fool, render:

'*Harnessing his foal for* (the produce of) *one vine,*
'*And his ass's colt for* (the produce of) *one choice vine*'—

which brings out in a striking figure the fruitfulness of Judah's land: one ass is required to carry away the produce of one vine; and even one choice vine yields enough fruit for the load of an ass's colt. This translation, founded on the interpretation of the Rabbis, is plainly indicated in Rashi and Rashbam; yet it has been overlooked by subsequent commentators (Marcus Jastrow).

choice vine. Heb. *sorek,* produced sweet grapes of superior quality. Grapes are to be so abundant that the people of Judah might wash their garments in them.

12. *his eyes shall be red with wine.* This rendering is absurd. According to it, Judah's eyes are red from excessive drinking, and Jacob's blessing is that Judah should be a drunkard! The word rendered 'red', however, means 'sparkling' (Septuagint, Gunkel, Gressmann); and the correct translation of the verse is: '*his eyes are more sparkling than wine.*'

his teeth white with milk. Does drinking milk produce white teeth? The correct translation (Septuagint, Vulgate, Saadyah, Jastrow) is, '*his teeth are whiter than milk.*'

13. Zebulun

13. The favourable geographical position of Zebulun's territory is described.

a shore for ships. To which they may come in safety.

Zidon. The actual territory of Zebulun stretched from the Sea of Galilee to Mt. Carmel, close under Tyre and Zidon.

14–15. Issachar

14. *large-boned ass.* Indicating great physical power.

כִּי טוֹב וְאֶת־הָאָרֶץ כִּי נָעֵמָה וַיֵּט שִׁכְמוֹ לִסְבֹּל וַיְהִי לְמַס־
16 עֹבֵד׃ ס דָּן יָדִין עַמּוֹ כְּאַחַד שִׁבְטֵי יִשְׂרָאֵל׃ יְהִי־
17 דָן נָחָשׁ עֲלֵי־דֶרֶךְ שְׁפִיפֹן עֲלֵי־אֹרַח הַנֹּשֵׁךְ עִקְּבֵי־סוּס
חמישי 18 וַיִּפֹּל רֹכְבוֹ אָחוֹר׃ לִישׁוּעָתְךָ קִוִּיתִי יְהוָה׃ ס גָּד גְּדוּד
19
כ יְגוּדֶנּוּ וְהוּא יָגֻד עָקֵב׃ ס מֵאָשֵׁר שְׁמֵנָה לַחְמוֹ וְהוּא
21 יִתֵּן מַעֲדַנֵּי־מֶלֶךְ׃ ס נַפְתָּלִי אַיָּלָה שְׁלֻחָה הַנֹּתֵן אִמְרֵי־

15. For he saw a resting-place that it was good,
And the land that it was pleasant;
And he bowed his shoulder to bear,
And became a servant under taskwork.

16. Dan shall judge his people,
As one of the tribes of Israel.

17. Dan shall be a serpent in the way,
A horned snake in the path,
That biteth the horse's heels,
So that his rider falleth backward.

18. I wait for Thy salvation, O LORD.* ▼.

19. Gad, [1]a troop [2]shall troop upon him;
But he shall troop upon their heel.

20. As for Asher, his bread shall be fat,
And he shall yield royal dainties.

21. Naphtali is a hind let loose:
He giveth goodly words.

[1] Heb. *gedud*. [2] From the Heb. root *gadad*.

v. 17. ק' הנושה

15. *A resting-place.* As opposed to the wandering life of nomads (Ryle).

taskwork. Or, 'tribute.' Issachar, possessed of rich territory, preferred rather to submit to tribute than to leave his ploughshare and take up the sword. See Deut. XXXIII, 18. Zunz translates, 'and yieldeth himself to the service of the labourer.'

16–18. DAN

16. *shall judge.* Or, 'shall defend,' or, 'avenge.' Onkelos understood this to refer to the tribe of Dan in the days of Samson (Judg. XV, 20).

his people. The tribe of Dan.

17. *a horned snake.* Is small, but highly venomous; it coils itself in the sand and, if disturbed, darts out upon any passing animal. Dan will prove dangerous to his foes by ambuscades and guerilla warfare.

18. *I wait for Thy salvation.* Is probably intended as part of the blessing bestowed upon Dan, who was in the most exposed position among all the tribes of Israel.

Thy salvation. i.e. deliverance wrought by Thee.

19. GAD

19. *a troop shall troop.* There is here, as in previous verses, a play upon the name. Perhaps the translation should be 'a raiding band raids him, but he will band himself against their heel'.

Gad succeeded in repelling the Ammonites, Moabites and Aramæans, who were constantly raiding his borders. Jephthah was of this tribe.

20. ASHER

20. *Asher.* The name Asher means, 'happy' or 'fortunate' (see XXX, 13); and this meaning is reflected in the blessing bestowed upon him. The land of Asher was prosperous or happy; cf. Arabia Felix.

royal dainties. Delicacies fit for the table of kings. The allusion is probably to an export trade carried on by the men of Asher.

21. NAPHTALI

21. *hind let loose.* An image of swiftness and grace in movement.

he giveth goodly words. Refers to the tribe's reputation for eloquence, and the great victory of Barak, a Naphtalite, which was followed by the glorious Song of Deborah (Kimchi). Another translation is, 'Naphtali is a slender terebinth, which putteth forth goodly branches.' Joseph, too (next verse), is compared to a vine.

22–26. JOSEPH

Jacob reserves his softest and most loving accents for Joseph, who united whatever is best and noblest in both Reuben and Judah. He is the man of vision, the man of dreams; but to this he joins moral and spiritual strength in all the vicissitudes of life. He is the ideal son, the ideal brother, the ideal servant, the ideal administrator. His character and story have from of old been held to be typical of the character and story of Israel. Like Joseph, the Jew has been the dreamer of the ages, dreaming Israel's dream of universal justice and peace and brotherhood. Like Joseph, he has everywhere been the helpless victim of the hatred of his step-brethren, hatred that drove him from home and doomed him to Exile. In that Exile, he has, like Joseph, times without number resisted the Great Temptation of disloyalty to the God of his fathers. In the dreams of Joseph, the sun, moon and eleven stars bowed down to him. It is the stars that bow to *him*, and not he to the stars. This is characteristic of both Joseph and Israel. **אין מזל לישראל**, says

22 שָׁפֶר׃ ס בֵּן פֹּרָת יוֹסֵף בֵּן פֹּרָת עֲלֵי־עָיִן בָּנוֹת צָעֲדָה
23 24 עֲלֵי־שׁוּר׃ וַיְמָרֲרֻהוּ וָרֹבּוּ וַיִּשְׂטְמֻהוּ בַּעֲלֵי חִצִּים׃ וַתֵּשֶׁב
בְּאֵיתָן קַשְׁתּוֹ וַיָּפֹזּוּ זְרֹעֵי יָדָיו מִידֵי אֲבִיר יַעֲקֹב מִשָּׁם
כה רֹעֶה אֶבֶן יִשְׂרָאֵל׃ מֵאֵל אָבִיךָ וְיַעְזְרֶךָּ וְאֵת שַׁדַּי וִיבָרְכֶךָּ
בִּרְכֹת שָׁמַיִם מֵעָל בִּרְכֹת תְּהוֹם רֹבֶצֶת תָּחַת בִּרְכֹת
26 שָׁדַיִם וָרָחַם׃ בִּרְכֹת אָבִיךָ גָּבְרוּ עַל־בִּרְכֹת הוֹרַי עַד־
ששי תַּאֲוַת גִּבְעֹת עוֹלָם תִּהְיֶיןָ לְרֹאשׁ יוֹסֵף וּלְקָדְקֹד נְזִיר אֶחָיו׃ פ
27 בִּנְיָמִין זְאֵב יִטְרָף בַּבֹּקֶר יֹאכַל עַד וְלָעֶרֶב יְחַלֵּק שָׁלָל׃
28 כָּל־אֵלֶּה שִׁבְטֵי יִשְׂרָאֵל שְׁנֵים עָשָׂר וְזֹאת אֲשֶׁר־דִּבֶּר

22. Joseph is a fruitful vine,
A fruitful vine by a fountain;
Its branches run over the wall.

23. The archers have dealt bitterly with him,
And shot at him, and hated him;

24. But his bow abode firm,
And the arms of his hands were made supple,
By the hands of the Mighty One of Jacob,
From thence, from the Shepherd, the Stone of Israel,

25. Even by the God of thy father, who shall help thee,
And by the Almighty, who shall bless thee,
With blessings of heaven above,
Blessings of the deep that coucheth beneath,
Blessings of the breasts, and of the womb.

26. The blessings of thy father
Are mighty beyond the blessings of my progenitors
Unto the utmost bound of the everlasting hills;
They shall be on the head of Joseph,
And on the crown of the head of the prince among his brethren.* vi.

27. Benjamin is a wolf that raveneth;
In the morning he devoureth the prey,
And at even he divideth the spoil.'

28. All these are the twelve tribes of Israel,

v. 25. קמץ בז״ק v. 27. קמץ בז״ק

Rabbi Yochanan. An Israelite should be ashamed to blame his star, his environment, or any outward circumstance for his moral downfall or his religious apostasy. Man is captain of his own soul; and wherever there is a will to Judaism, there is a way to lead the Jewish life.

22. *by a fountain.* Cf. Psalm I, 3; the proximity of water is a necessary condition, if the tree is to grow and bear fruit.

23. *the archers.* His brethren.

dealt bitterly. Harassed by hostile action. In spite of attack, the strength of Joseph and his descendants is unimpaired, because the Almighty is with him.

24. *abode firm. i.e.* continued strong.

made supple. Or, 'active.' This verse suggests a fine picture; the bow held steadily in position, while the hand that discharges the arrows in quick succession moves nimbly to and fro (Gunkel).

by the hands. Indicating the source of Joseph's salvation.

the Mighty One of Jacob. A title of God, see Is. I, 24.

from thence. From the Mighty One of Jacob.

the Stone of Israel. A rare parallel to the better known 'Rock of Israel'.

25. Three blessings are mentioned.

blessings of heaven. Rain and dew, sunshine and wind.

the deep. The subterranean reservoir of waters beneath, from which springs the fertility to soil.

the breasts. The fruitfulness of the family.

26. *are mighty beyond.* The verse states that the blessings received by Jacob surpass the blessings vouchsafed to Jacob's fathers. Jacob now bestows these enhanced blessings upon Joseph, thereby making him the heir both of himself and of his ancestors.

unto the utmost bound of the everlasting hills. As high above the blessings bestowed on Jacob's father as the hills are above the plains.

prince. lit. 'that is separate from his brethren', *i.e.* apart from, eminent, among his brethren.

27. Benjamin

27. *a wolf that raveneth.* Or, 'that teareth,' referring to the warlike character of the tribe; see Judg. v, 14 and xx, 16.

28. *twelve tribes.* Joseph, and not his sons, receives the blessings. Jacob in blessing his sons was at the same time blessing the future tribes.

every one. Received his appropriate blessing. The future would prove the prophetic nature of their father's benediction.

and this is it that their father spoke unto them and blessed them; every one according to his blessing he blessed them. 29. And he charged them, and said unto them: 'I am to be gathered unto my people; bury me with my fathers in the cave that is in the field of Ephron the Hittite, 30. in the cave that is in the field of Machpelah, which is before Mamre, in the land of Canaan, which Abraham bought with the field from Ephron the Hittite for a possession of a burying-place. 31. There they buried Abraham and Sarah his wife; there they buried Isaac and Rebekah his wife; and there I buried Leah. 32. The field and the cave that is therein, which was purchased from the children of Heth.' 33. And when Jacob made an end of charging his sons, he gathered up his feet into the bed, and expired, and was gathered unto his people.

50

Chapter L

1. And Joseph fell upon his father's face, and wept upon him, and kissed him. 2. And Joseph commanded his servants the physicians to embalm his father. And the physicians embalmed Israel. 3. And forty days were fulfilled for him; for so are fulfilled the days of embalming. And the Egyptians wept for him threescore and ten days. ¶ 4. And when the days of weeping for him were past, Joseph spoke unto the house of Pharaoh, saying: 'If now I have found favour in your eyes, speak, I pray you, in the ears of Pharaoh, saying: 5. My father made me swear, saying: Lo, I die; in my grave which I have digged for me in the land of Canaan, there shalt thou bury me. Now therefore let me go up, I pray thee, and bury my father, and I will come back.' 6. And Pharaoh said: 'Go up, and bury thy father, according as he

לָהֶם אֲבִיהֶם וַיְבָרֶךְ אוֹתָם אִישׁ אֲשֶׁר כְּבִרְכָתוֹ בֵּרַךְ
29 אֹתָם׃ וַיְצַו אוֹתָם וַיֹּאמֶר אֲלֵהֶם אֲנִי נֶאֱסָף אֶל־עַמִּי קִבְרוּ
אֹתִי אֶל־אֲבֹתָי אֶל־הַמְּעָרָה אֲשֶׁר בִּשְׂדֵה עֶפְרוֹן הַחִתִּי׃
ל בַּמְּעָרָה אֲשֶׁר בִּשְׂדֵה הַמַּכְפֵּלָה אֲשֶׁר־עַל־פְּנֵי מַמְרֵא
בְּאֶרֶץ כְּנָעַן אֲשֶׁר קָנָה אַבְרָהָם אֶת־הַשָּׂדֶה מֵאֵת עֶפְרֹן
31 הַחִתִּי לַאֲחֻזַּת־קָבֶר׃ שָׁמָּה קָבְרוּ אֶת־אַבְרָהָם וְאֵת שָׂרָה
אִשְׁתּוֹ שָׁמָּה קָבְרוּ אֶת־יִצְחָק וְאֵת רִבְקָה אִשְׁתּוֹ וְשָׁמָּה
32 קָבַרְתִּי אֶת־לֵאָה׃ מִקְנֵה הַשָּׂדֶה וְהַמְּעָרָה אֲשֶׁר־בּוֹ מֵאֵת
33 בְּנֵי־חֵת׃ וַיְכַל יַעֲקֹב לְצַוֹּת אֶת־בָּנָיו וַיֶּאֱסֹף רַגְלָיו אֶל־
הַמִּטָּה וַיִּגְוַע וַיֵּאָסֶף אֶל־עַמָּיו׃

נ CAP. L. נ

א 2 וַיִּפֹּל יוֹסֵף עַל־פְּנֵי אָבִיו וַיֵּבְךְּ עָלָיו וַיִּשַּׁק־לוֹ׃ וַיְצַו יוֹסֵף
אֶת־עֲבָדָיו אֶת־הָרֹפְאִים לַחֲנֹט אֶת־אָבִיו וַיַּחַנְטוּ הָרֹפְאִים
3 אֶת־יִשְׂרָאֵל׃ וַיִּמְלְאוּ־לוֹ אַרְבָּעִים יוֹם כִּי כֵּן יִמְלְאוּ יְמֵי
4 הַחֲנֻטִים וַיִּבְכּוּ אֹתוֹ מִצְרַיִם שִׁבְעִים יוֹם׃ וַיַּעַבְרוּ יְמֵי
בְכִיתוֹ וַיְדַבֵּר יוֹסֵף אֶל־בֵּית פַּרְעֹה לֵאמֹר אִם־נָא מָצָאתִי
ה חֵן בְּעֵינֵיכֶם דַּבְּרוּ־נָא בְּאָזְנֵי פַרְעֹה לֵאמֹר׃ אָבִי הִשְׁבִּיעַנִי
לֵאמֹר הִנֵּה אָנֹכִי מֵת בְּקִבְרִי אֲשֶׁר כָּרִיתִי לִי בְּאֶרֶץ כְּנַעַן
שָׁמָּה תִּקְבְּרֵנִי וְעַתָּה אֶעֱלֶה־נָּא וְאֶקְבְּרָה אֶת־אָבִי וְאָשׁוּבָה׃

32. *purchased from the children of Heth.* With their knowledge and consent (Abarbanel). Joseph having been away from Canaan for so many years, receives explicit directions as to the spot where his father is to be buried. This verse implies a deed of purchase.

33. *gathered up his feet.* He had been sitting; he now lay down in bed.

and was gathered unto his people. This passage shows that not burial of the body is meant, but the soul's departure to join the souls of those who had gone before.

Chapter L. Jacob's Burial. The Death of Joseph

1. *and Joseph.* This does not imply that the other children of Jacob did not do even as Joseph did.

2. *to embalm his father.* Not in imitation of the custom of the Egyptians who took care to preserve the body after death and keep it ready for occupation by the soul. Joseph's purpose was merely to preserve it from dissolution before it reached the Cave of Machpelah.

3. *the Egyptians wept for him.* Out of respect for Joseph. Probably the forty days of embalming formed part of the seventy days (Rashi).

4. *unto the house of Pharaoh.* Joseph, as a mourner, would not approach the king in person.

5. *which I have digged.* 'Which I have prepared' (Onkelos). It is quite likely that Jacob had prepared the grave for his own interment, next to the grave of Leah in the Cave of Machpelah.

and I will come back. Joseph assures Pharaoh that he intends to return to Egypt.

made thee swear.' 7. And Joseph went up to bury his father; and with him went up all the servants of Pharaoh, the elders of his house, and all the elders of the land of Egypt, 8. and all the house of Joseph, and his brethren, and his father's house; only their little ones, and their flocks, and their herds, they left in the land of Goshen. 9. And there went up with him both chariots and horsemen; and it was a very great company. 10. And they came to the threshing-floor of Atad, which is beyond the Jordan, and there they wailed with a very great and sore wailing; and he made a mourning for his father seven days. 11. And when the inhabitants of the land, the Canaanites, saw the mourning in the floor of Atad, they said: 'This is a grievous [1]mourning to the Egyptians.' Wherefore the name of it was called Abel-mizraim, which is beyond the Jordan. 12. And his sons did unto him according as he commanded them. 13. For his sons carried him into the land of Canaan, and buried him in the cave of the field of Machpelah, which Abraham bought with the field, for a possession of a burying-place, of Ephron the Hittite, in front of Mamre. ¶ 14. And Joseph returned into Egypt, he, and his brethren, and all that went up with him to bury his father, after he had buried his father.* 15. And when Joseph's brethren saw that their father was dead, they said: 'It may be that Joseph will hate us, and will fully requite us all the evil which we did unto him.' 16. And they sent a message unto Joseph, saying: 'Thy father did command before he died, saying: 17. So shall ye say unto Joseph: Forgive, I pray thee now, the transgression of thy brethren,

[1] Heb. *ebel.*

6 וַיֹּאמֶר פַּרְעֹה עֲלֵה וּקְבֹר אֶת־אָבִיךָ כַּאֲשֶׁר הִשְׁבִּיעֶךָ׃
7 וַיַּעַל יוֹסֵף לִקְבֹּר אֶת־אָבִיו וַיַּעֲלוּ אִתּוֹ כָּל־עַבְדֵי פַרְעֹה
8 זִקְנֵי בֵיתוֹ וְכֹל זִקְנֵי אֶרֶץ־מִצְרָיִם׃ וְכֹל בֵּית יוֹסֵף וְאֶחָיו
וּבֵית אָבִיו רַק טַפָּם וְצֹאנָם וּבְקָרָם עָזְבוּ בְּאֶרֶץ גֹּשֶׁן׃
9 וַיַּעַל עִמּוֹ גַּם־רֶכֶב גַּם־פָּרָשִׁים וַיְהִי הַמַּחֲנֶה כָּבֵד מְאֹד׃
י וַיָּבֹאוּ עַד־גֹּרֶן הָאָטָד אֲשֶׁר בְּעֵבֶר הַיַּרְדֵּן וַיִּסְפְּדוּ־שָׁם
מִסְפֵּד גָּדוֹל וְכָבֵד מְאֹד וַיַּעַשׂ לְאָבִיו אֵבֶל שִׁבְעַת יָמִים׃
11 וַיַּרְא יוֹשֵׁב הָאָרֶץ הַכְּנַעֲנִי אֶת־הָאֵבֶל בְּגֹרֶן הָאָטָד וַיֹּאמְרוּ
אֵבֶל־כָּבֵד זֶה לְמִצְרָיִם עַל־כֵּן קָרָא שְׁמָהּ אָבֵל מִצְרַיִם
12 אֲשֶׁר בְּעֵבֶר הַיַּרְדֵּן׃ וַיַּעֲשׂוּ בָנָיו לוֹ כֵּן כַּאֲשֶׁר צִוָּם׃
13 וַיִּשְׂאוּ אֹתוֹ בָנָיו אַרְצָה כְּנַעַן וַיִּקְבְּרוּ אֹתוֹ בִּמְעָרַת שְׂדֵה
הַמַּכְפֵּלָה אֲשֶׁר קָנָה אַבְרָהָם אֶת־הַשָּׂדֶה לַאֲחֻזַּת־קֶבֶר
14 מֵאֵת עֶפְרֹן הַחִתִּי עַל־פְּנֵי מַמְרֵא׃ וַיָּשָׁב יוֹסֵף מִצְרַיְמָה
הוּא וְאֶחָיו וְכָל־הָעֹלִים אִתּוֹ לִקְבֹּר אֶת־אָבִיו אַחֲרֵי קָבְרוֹ
טו אֶת־אָבִיו׃ וַיִּרְאוּ אֲחֵי־יוֹסֵף כִּי־מֵת אֲבִיהֶם וַיֹּאמְרוּ לוּ
יִשְׂטְמֵנוּ יוֹסֵף וְהָשֵׁב יָשִׁיב לָנוּ אֵת כָּל־הָרָעָה אֲשֶׁר גָּמַלְנוּ
16 אֹתוֹ׃ וַיְצַוּוּ אֶל־יוֹסֵף לֵאמֹר אָבִיךָ צִוָּה לִפְנֵי מוֹתוֹ לֵאמֹר׃
17 כֹּה־תֹאמְרוּ לְיוֹסֵף אָנָּא שָׂא נָא פֶּשַׁע אַחֶיךָ וְחַטָּאתָם

v. 17. ב' טעמים

7. *the elders.* The respect shown to Jacob is evidently due to the great position occupied by Joseph in Egypt. Such processions as described in our text are frequently represented on Egyptian tombs.

8. *only their little ones . . . they left in the land of Goshen.* Because unable to endure the fatigue of travel to Canaan.

9. *chariots and horsemen.* To protect the procession.

10. *the threshing-floor of Atad.* The place Atad has not been identified.

beyond the Jordan. This cannot mean east of the Jordan, as it is unthinkable that in going to the cave of Machpelah at Hebron the company would take the circuitous route round the Dead Sea. All difficulties disappear when we remember that to Moses and the Israelites in the land of Moab, the words 'beyond Jordan' meant *west* of Jordan. This phrase therefore is another incidental confirmation of the Mosaic authorship of Genesis (W. H. Green).

seven days. This is still the Jewish period of mourning for the dead. The sacred institution of *Shivah* in its essence thus goes back to Patriarchal times.

11. *a grievous mourning.* Or, 'an honourable mourning.'

15. *Joseph will hate us.* A notable example of the never-to-be-silenced voice of the guilty conscience.

16. *thy father did command.* An unrecorded message.

17. *servants of the God of thy father.* Though thy father is dead, the God of thy father liveth (Rashi). They ask for his forgiveness, basing their plea on the claims of brotherhood of Faith. A fine religious appeal.

Joseph wept. Because of their want of confidence in him.

כִּי־רָעָה גְמָלוּךָ וְעַתָּה שָׂא נָא לְפֶשַׁע עַבְדֵי אֱלֹהֵי אָבִיךָ
18 וַיֵּבְךְּ יוֹסֵף בְּדַבְּרָם אֵלָיו׃ וַיֵּלְכוּ גַּם־אֶחָיו וַיִּפְּלוּ לְפָנָיו
19 וַיֹּאמְרוּ הִנֶּנּוּ לְךָ לַעֲבָדִים׃ וַיֹּאמֶר אֲלֵהֶם יוֹסֵף אַל־
כ תִּירָאוּ כִּי הֲתַחַת אֱלֹהִים אָנִי׃ וְאַתֶּם חֲשַׁבְתֶּם עָלַי רָעָה
אֱלֹהִים חֲשָׁבָהּ לְטֹבָה לְמַעַן עֲשֹׂה כַּיּוֹם הַזֶּה לְהַחֲיֹת
שביעי
21 עַם־רָב׃ וְעַתָּה אַל־תִּירָאוּ אָנֹכִי אֲכַלְכֵּל אֶתְכֶם וְאֶת־
22 טַפְּכֶם וַיְנַחֵם אוֹתָם וַיְדַבֵּר עַל־לִבָּם׃ וַיֵּשֶׁב יוֹסֵף בְּמִצְרַיִם
מפטיר
23 הוּא וּבֵית אָבִיו וַיְחִי יוֹסֵף מֵאָה וָעֶשֶׂר שָׁנִים׃ וַיַּרְא
יוֹסֵף לְאֶפְרַיִם בְּנֵי שִׁלֵּשִׁים גַּם בְּנֵי מָכִיר בֶּן־מְנַשֶּׁה יֻלְּדוּ
24 עַל־בִּרְכֵּי יוֹסֵף׃ וַיֹּאמֶר יוֹסֵף אֶל־אֶחָיו אָנֹכִי מֵת וֵאלֹהִים
פָּקֹד יִפְקֹד אֶתְכֶם וְהֶעֱלָה אֶתְכֶם מִן־הָאָרֶץ הַזֹּאת אֶל־
כה הָאָרֶץ אֲשֶׁר נִשְׁבַּע לְאַבְרָהָם לְיִצְחָק וּלְיַעֲקֹב׃ וַיַּשְׁבַּע

v. 23. ם׳ רבתי

and their sin, for that they did unto thee evil. And now, we pray thee, forgive the transgression of the servants of the God of thy father.' And Joseph wept when they spoke unto him. 18. And his brethren also went and fell down before his face; and they said: 'Behold, we are thy bondmen.' 19. And Joseph said unto them: 'Fear not; for am I in the place of God? 20. And as for you, ye meant evil against me; but God meant it for good, to bring to pass, as it is this day, to save much people alive. * vii. 21. Now therefore fear ye not; I will sustain you, and your little ones.' And he comforted them, and spoke kindly unto them. ¶ 22. And Joseph dwelt in Egypt, he, and his father's house; and Joseph lived a hundred and ten years.* m. 23. And Joseph saw Ephraim's children of the third generation; the children also of Machir the son of Manasseh were born upon Joseph's knees. 24. And Joseph said unto his brethren: 'I die; but God will surely remember you, and bring you up out of this land unto the land which He swore to Abraham, to Isaac, and to Jacob.' 25.

18. *and his brethren also went.* Having originally sent others on their behalf, see *v.* 16, they now come in person to plead with Joseph.
behold, we are thy bondmen. Again fulfilling the old dreams, see XXXVII, 6 f.

19. It is quite impossible for any man to counteract the Divine plan.

20. *ye meant evil.* Man proposes, but God disposes. 'To me it appears that the sale of Joseph was the work of Providence, not only for him who was to be advanced to an exalted station, but also in the benign care that resulted from it for the whole people of Israel. Therefore, Joseph's brethren were not deserving punishment; on the contrary, Joseph repeatedly declares that in whatever they had done, they were unwittingly carrying out the design of Providence' (Abarbanel).
save much people alive. Not only the Egyptians and the children of Israel, but other people who came to Egypt to buy corn in the time of famine.

21. *spoke kindly unto them.* lit. 'and he spoke to their heart'.

22. *a hundred and ten years.* He survived his father fifty-four years. In Egyptian writings, the age of 110 years is spoken of as an ideal lifetime.

23. *Machir.* The most powerful of the clans of Manasseh; see Judg. V, 14.
born upon Joseph's knees. The symbolical act of adoption.

24. *brethren.* Not necessarily brothers; near relatives is the meaning in our context.
which He swore. See XXII, 16; XXVI, 3.

25. *and ye shall carry up my bones from hence.* He has faith in the Divine promise to redeem His people. Joseph's bones are to participate in the return to Canaan, and to rest there. The promise was fulfilled; see Exod. XIII, 19, and Josh. XXIV, 32.

26. *coffin.* Heb. *aron.* The same Heb. word is used of the receptacle of the Tables of the Law. This is significant. Judaism preaches respect for human personality as a duty, because man has it in his power to become a living embodiment of the Moral Law. The Rabbis tell: The nations wondered why the Children of Israel in their wanderings through the desert, carried with them the bones of Joseph in a similar ark and in the same reverential manner as they did the Tables of the Covenant. 'He whose remains are preserved in the one ark,' they answered, 'loyally obeyed the Divine commands enshrined in the other.'
in Egypt. These last words prepare the mind for the new era that awaits Israel in Egypt, and for the eventful story of the Exodus.

According to Jewish custom, the completion of any of the Five Books of the Torah is marked in the Synagogue by the congregation exclaiming חזק חזק ונתחזק, 'Be strong, be strong, and let us strengthen one another'—an echo of the words

And Joseph took an oath of the children of Israel, saying: 'God will surely remember you, and ye shall carry up my bones from hence.' 26. So Joseph died, being a hundred and ten years old. And they embalmed him, and he was put in a coffin in Egypt.

יוֹסֵף אֶת־בְּנֵי יִשְׂרָאֵל לֵאמֹר פָּקֹד יִפְקֹד אֱלֹהִים אֶתְכֶם
26 וְהַעֲלִתֶם אֶת־עַצְמֹתַי מִזֶּה׃ וַיָּמָת יוֹסֵף בֶּן־מֵאָה וָעֶשֶׂר
שָׁנִים וַיַּחַנְטוּ אֹתוֹ וַיִּישֶׂם בָּאָרוֹן בְּמִצְרָיִם׃

חזק

סכום פסוקי דספר בראשית אלף וחמש מאות ושלשים וארבעה. א״ך ל״ד סימן: וחציו ועל חרבך תחיה: ופרשיותיו י״ב. זה שמי לעלם סימן: וסדריו מ״ג. גם ברוך יהיה סימן: ופרקיו נ׳. יי׳ חננו לך קוינו סימן: מניין הפתוחות שלשה וארבעים והסתומות שמנה וארבעים. הכל תשעים ואחת פרשיות. צא אתה וכל העם אשר ברגליך סימן:

The Massoretic Note states the number of verses in Genesis to be 1,534; its Sedrahs (*parshiyyoth*) 12; its Sedarim, smaller divisions according to the Triennial Cycle, 43; and its Chapters 50.

of the ancient warrior, 'Be of good courage, and let us play the men, for our people and the cities of our God' (II Sam. x, 12). *Be strong. i.e.* to carry out the teaching contained in the Book just completed.

HAFTORAH VAYYECHI — הפטרת ויחי

I KINGS II, 1–12

CHAPTER II

1. Now the days of David drew nigh that he should die; and he charged Solomon his son, saying: 2. 'I go the way of all the earth; be thou strong therefore, and show thyself a man; 3. and keep the charge of the LORD thy God, to walk in His ways, to keep His statutes, and His commandments, and His ordinances, and His testimonies, according to that which is written in the law of Moses, that thou mayest prosper in all that thou doest, and whithersoever thou turnest thyself; 4. that the LORD may establish His word which He spoke concerning me, saying: If thy children take heed to their way, to walk before Me in truth with all their heart and with all their soul, there shall not fail thee, said He, a man on the throne of Israel. 5. Moreover thou knowest also what Joab the son of Zeruiah did unto me, even what he did to the two captains of the hosts of Israel, unto Abner the son of Ner and unto Amasa the son of Jether, whom he slew, and shed the blood of war in peace, and put the blood of war upon his girdle that was about his loins,

CAP. II. ב

א וַיִּקְרְבוּ יְמֵי־דָוִד לָמוּת וַיְצַו אֶת־שְׁלֹמֹה בְנוֹ לֵאמֹר׃
2 3 אָנֹכִי הֹלֵךְ בְּדֶרֶךְ כָּל־הָאָרֶץ וְחָזַקְתָּ וְהָיִיתָ לְאִישׁ׃ וְשָׁמַרְתָּ
אֶת־מִשְׁמֶרֶת יְהוָה אֱלֹהֶיךָ לָלֶכֶת בִּדְרָכָיו לִשְׁמֹר חֻקֹּתָיו
מִצְוֹתָיו וּמִשְׁפָּטָיו וְעֵדְוֹתָיו כַּכָּתוּב בְּתוֹרַת מֹשֶׁה לְמַעַן
תַּשְׂכִּיל אֵת כָּל־אֲשֶׁר תַּעֲשֶׂה וְאֵת כָּל־אֲשֶׁר תִּפְנֶה שָׁם׃
4 לְמַעַן יָקִים יְהוָה אֶת־דְּבָרוֹ אֲשֶׁר דִּבֶּר עָלַי לֵאמֹר אִם־
יִשְׁמְרוּ בָנֶיךָ אֶת־דַּרְכָּם לָלֶכֶת לְפָנַי בֶּאֱמֶת בְּכָל־לְבָבָם
וּבְכָל־נַפְשָׁם לֵאמֹר לֹא־יִכָּרֵת לְךָ אִישׁ מֵעַל כִּסֵּא יִשְׂרָאֵל׃
ה וְגַם אַתָּה יָדַעְתָּ אֵת אֲשֶׁר־עָשָׂה לִי יוֹאָב בֶּן־צְרוּיָה אֲשֶׁר
עָשָׂה לִשְׁנֵי־שָׂרֵי צִבְאוֹת יִשְׂרָאֵל לְאַבְנֵר בֶּן־נֵר וְלַעֲמָשָׂא
בֶן־יֶתֶר וַיַּהַרְגֵם וַיָּשֶׂם דְּמֵי־מִלְחָמָה בְּשָׁלֹם וַיִּתֵּן דְּמֵי

1–4. In the Sedrah, the dying Patriarch, assembling his sons, speaks to them last words of guidance and admonition, and 'blesses them each one according to his blessing'. In the Haftorah, David feeling his end near, gives his son the best of blessings in words which point the way of life for every son of Israel. 'Be thou strong, therefore, and show thyself a man; and keep the charge of the LORD thy God, to walk in His ways, to keep His statutes and His commandments.'

and in his shoes that were on his feet. 6. Do therefore according to thy wisdom, and let not his hoar head go down to the grave in peace. 7. But show kindness unto the sons of Barzillai the Gileadite, and let them be of those that eat at thy table; for so they drew nigh unto me when I fled from Absalom thy brother. 8. And, behold, there is with thee Shimei the son of Gera, the Benjamite, of Bahurim, who cursed me with a grievous curse in the day when I went to Mahanaim; but he came down to meet me at the Jordan, and I swore to him by the LORD, saying: I will not put thee to death with the sword. 9. Now therefore hold him not guiltless, for thou art a wise man; and thou wilt know what thou oughtest to do unto him, and thou shalt bring his hoar head down to the grave with blood.' ¶ 10. And David slept with his fathers, and was buried in the city of David. 11. And the days that David reigned over Israel were forty years: seven years reigned he in Hebron, and thirty and three years reigned he in Jerusalem. 12. And Solomon sat upon the throne of David his father; and his kingdom was established firmly.

מִלְחָמָה בַּחֲגֹרָתוֹ אֲשֶׁר בְּמָתְנָיו וּבְנַעֲלוֹ אֲשֶׁר בְּרַגְלָיו׃
6 וְעָשִׂיתָ כְּחָכְמָתֶךָ וְלֹא־תוֹרֵד שֵׂיבָתוֹ בְּשָׁלֹם שְׁאֹל׃
7 וְלִבְנֵי בַרְזִלַּי הַגִּלְעָדִי תַּעֲשֶׂה־חֶסֶד וְהָיוּ בְּאֹכְלֵי שֻׁלְחָנֶךָ
8 כִּי־כֵן קָרְבוּ אֵלַי בְּבָרְחִי מִפְּנֵי אַבְשָׁלוֹם אָחִיךָ׃ וְהִנֵּה
עִמְּךָ שִׁמְעִי בֶן־גֵּרָא בֶן־הַיְמִינִי מִבַּחֻרִים וְהוּא קִלְלַנִי
קְלָלָה נִמְרֶצֶת בְּיוֹם לֶכְתִּי מַחֲנָיִם וְהוּא־יָרַד לִקְרָאתִי
הַיַּרְדֵּן וָאֶשָּׁבַע לוֹ בַיהוָה לֵאמֹר אִם־אֲמִיתְךָ בֶּחָרֶב׃
9 וְעַתָּה אַל־תְּנַקֵּהוּ כִּי אִישׁ חָכָם אָתָּה וְיָדַעְתָּ אֵת אֲשֶׁר
י תַּעֲשֶׂה־לּוֹ וְהוֹרַדְתָּ אֶת־שֵׂיבָתוֹ בְּדָם שְׁאוֹל׃ וַיִּשְׁכַּב דָּוִד
11 עִם־אֲבֹתָיו וַיִּקָּבֵר בְּעִיר דָּוִד׃ וְהַיָּמִים אֲשֶׁר מָלַךְ דָּוִד
עַל־יִשְׂרָאֵל אַרְבָּעִים שָׁנָה בְּחֶבְרוֹן מָלַךְ שֶׁבַע שָׁנִים
12 וּבִירוּשָׁלַם מָלַךְ שְׁלֹשִׁים וְשָׁלֹשׁ שָׁנִים׃ וּשְׁלֹמֹה יָשַׁב
עַל־כִּסֵּא דָּוִד אָבִיו וַתִּכֹּן מַלְכֻתוֹ מְאֹד׃

5. *Abner.* He was treacherously slain by Joab; II Sam. III, 27.

Amasa. Similarly murdered, II Sam. XX, 10.

shed the blood of war in peace. Joab's unpardonable crime consisted in having avenged, in time of peace, blood justifiably shed in self-defence in time of war.

6. *do therefore according to thy wisdom.* Solomon need not act precipitately. Both men, true to their nature, would sooner or later commit themselves, and for that reason give Solomon just cause for dealing effectively with them.

7. The dying king cherishes tender gratitude for kindnesses shown him.

5–9. The difficulty created by these verses cannot be ignored. As part of a last charge, they shock one's finer feelings. No admirer of David's otherwise magnanimous character can read without a pang that he passes into eternity with vengeance in his heart and on his lips.

Is there any extenuation or explanation? David charges his son to carry out the Divine laws. The thought then flashes through his mind that, as the guardian of justice in the land, he had grievously failed inasmuch as he allowed the perpetration of treacherous murders committed by Joab to go unpunished. It was a blot on his government, and the thought weighed on him at this hour. Unless justice, even-handed and impartial, was seen to rule in the highest quarter, no kingdom could be established.

A note of warning must be uttered. Whatever *reasons of state* may be advanced in mitigation of David's action, it is not an act for imitation in the life of the ordinary individual. The temptation to take vengeance is never so insiduous as when it comes cloaked under high-sounding names; as when, for example, we say that it is in the interests of justice that we satisfy those feelings of vindictiveness. The Divine command 'Thou shalt not take vengeance nor bear any grudge' (Lev. XIX, 18) is the safest guiding principle for prince and people.

There is recorded another Farewell Speech of David (I Chron. XXVIII and XXIX) and we take our leave of him with a few verses from that nobler utterance. He lays the solemn charge upon his son to complete the Temple which *he* was not permitted to begin, and in a prayer of fine humility and faith he commends his son and his children to the eternal God of Israel. 'As for me, it was in mine heart to build an house of rest for the Ark of the Covenant of the LORD . . . and I had made ready for the building. But God said to me, Thou shalt not build an house for My name, because thou art a man of war, and hast shed blood. . . . Thine, O LORD, is the greatness, and the power, and the glory, and the victory, and the majesty . . . all things come of Thee, and of Thine own have we given Thee. For we are strangers before Thee, and sojourners, as all our fathers were: our days on the earth are as a shadow, and there is no abiding.'

ADDITIONAL NOTES TO GENESIS

A

THE CREATION CHAPTER

Genesis I–II, 3, is a worthy opening of Israel's Sacred Scriptures, and ranks among the most important chapters of the Bible. Even in form it is pre-eminent in the literature of religion. No other ancient account of creation (cosmogony) will bear a second reading. Most of them not only describe the origin of the world, but begin by describing how the gods emerged out of pre-existent chaos (theogony). In contrast with the simplicity and sublimity of Genesis I, we find all ancient cosmogonies, whether it be the Babylonian or the Phœnician, the Greek or the Roman, alike unrelievedly wild, cruel, even foul.

Thus, the Assyro-Babylonian mythology tells how, before what we call earth or heaven had come into being, there existed a primeval watery chaos—Tiamat—out of which the gods were evolved:—

'When, in the height, heaven was not yet named,
And the earth beneath did not bear a name,
And the primeval Apsu (the Abyss), their begetter,
And Chaos (Tiamat), the mother of them both,
Their waters were mingled together,
Then were created the gods in the midst of heaven.'

Apsu, the Abyss, disturbed at finding his domain invaded by the new gods, induced Tiamat and Chaos to join him in contesting their supremacy; he was, however, subdued by the cunning of Ea; and Tiamat, left to carry on the struggle alone, provides herself with a brood of hideous allies. The alarmed gods thereupon appoint Marduk as their champion. With winds and lightnings, Marduk advances; he seizes Tiamat in a huge net, and 'with his merciless club he crushed her skull'. The carcase of the monster he split into two halves, one of which he fixed on high, to form a firmament supporting the waters above it. In the same grotesque way, the story continues to describe the formation of sun, moon, plants, animals and man. Many moderns feign to believe that this is the source from which Genesis I is taken. But a thorough-going Bible critic like the late Dr. Driver admits, 'It is incredible that the monotheistic author of Genesis I could have borrowed any detail, however slight, from the polytheistic epic of the conflict of Marduk and Tiamat.'

The infinite importance, however, of the first page of the Bible consists in the fact that it enshrines some of the fundamental beliefs of Judaism. Among these are:—

I. GOD IS THE CREATOR OF THE UNIVERSE. Each religion has certain specific teachings, convictions, dogmas. Such a dogma of Judaism is its belief that the world was called into existence at the will of the One, Almighty and All-good God. And nowhere does this fundamental conviction of Israel's Faith find clearer expression than in Genesis I. When neighbouring peoples deified the sun, moon and stars, or worshipped stocks and stones and beasts, the sacred river Nile, the crocodile that swam in its waters, and the very beetles that crawled along its banks, the opening page of Scripture proclaimed in language of majestic simplicity that the universe, and all that therein is, are the product of one supreme directing Intelligence; of an eternal, spiritual Being, prior to them and independent of them.

Now, while the *fact* of creation has to this day remained the first of the articles of the Jewish Creed, there is no uniform and binding belief as to the *manner* of creation, *i.e.* as to the process whereby the universe came into existence. The manner of the Divine creative activity is presented in varying forms and under differing metaphors by Prophet, Psalmist and Sage; by the Rabbis in Talmudic times, as well as by our medieval Jewish thinkers. In the Bible itself we have at least three modes of representing the overwhelming fact of Divine Creation. Genesis I gives us the story of Creation in the form of a Divine drama set out in six acts of a day each, with a similar refrain (*And there was evening, and there was morning, etc.*) closing the creative work of each day. The Psalmist, to whom Nature was a continual witness of its Divine Author (Ps. XIX), gives in Psalm CIV a purely poetic representation of the Creation story:—

'O LORD my God, Thou art very great;
Thou art clothed with honour and majesty.
Who coverest Thyself with light as with a garment;
Who stretchest out the heavens like a curtain . . .
Who maketh the clouds his chariot;
Who walketh upon the wings of the wind:
Who maketh winds his messengers . . .'

Again, Proverbs VIII, 22–31, shows forth Divine Wisdom presiding at the birth of Nature.

The mode of creation continued to engage Jewish minds after the close of the Bible and throughout the Rabbinic period, even though the Mishnah warns against all speculation concerning the beginning of things. To some, the relation of God to the universe was that of a mason to his work, and they accordingly spoke of God's 'architect's plans'; others lost themselves in heretic fancies as to what constituted the raw material, so to speak, of Creation; while to Philo of Alexandria, Creation was altogether outside time. Several of the ancient Rabbis, followed by the later Mystics, believed in successive creations. Prior to the existence of the present universe, they held, certain formless worlds issued from the Fountain of Existence and then vanished, like sparks which fly from a red-hot iron beaten by a hammer, that are extinguished as they separate themselves from the burning mass. In contrast to these abortive creations, the medieval Jewish Mystics maintain, ours is the best of all possible worlds. It is the outcome of a series of emanations and eradiations from God, the Infinite, *En Sof.* Furthermore, Rashi, the greatest Jewish commentator of all times, taught that the purpose of Scripture was not to give a strict chronology of Creation; while no less an authority than Maimonides declared: 'The account given in Scripture of the Creation is not, as is generally believed, intended to be in all its parts literal.' Later Jewish philosophers (Levi ben Gerson, Crescas, Albalag) made dangerous concessions to the Aristotelian doctrine of the eternity of matter; which doctrine Yehudah Hallevi, among others, strongly opposed as both contrary to Reason and as limiting God's Omnipotence.

Jewish Attitude towards Evolution

In face of this great diversity of views as to the *manner* of creation, there is, therefore, nothing inherently un-Jewish in the evolutionary conception of the origin and growth of forms of existence from the simple to the complex, and from the lowest to the highest. The Biblical account itself gives expression to the same general truth of gradual ascent from amorphous chaos to order, from inorganic to organic, from lifeless matter to vegetable, animal and man; *insisting, however, that each stage is no product of chance, but is an act of Divine will,* realizing the Divine purpose, and receiving the seal of the Divine approval. Such, likewise, is in effect the evolutionary position. Behind the orderly development of the universe there must be a Cause, at once controlling and permeating the process. Allowing for all the evidence in favour of interpreting existence in terms of the evolutionary doctrine, there still remain facts—tremendous facts—to be explained; *viz.* the origin of life, mind, conscience, human personality. For each of these, we must look back to the Creative Omnipotence of the Eternal Spirit. Nor is that all. Instead of evolution ousting design and purpose from nature, 'almost every detail is now found to have a purpose and a use' (A. R. Wallace). In brief, evolution is conceivable only as the activity of a creative Mind purposing, by means of physical and biological laws, that wonderful organic development which has reached its climax in a being endowed with rational and moral faculties and capable of high ethical and spiritual achievement; in other words, as the activity of a supreme, directing Intelligence that has planned out, far back in the recesses of time, the ultimate goal of creation—'last in production, first in thought' סוף מעשה במחשבה תחלה. Thus evolution, far from destroying the *religious* teaching of Gen. I, is its profound confirmation.

As a noted scientist well remarks:—

> 'Slowly and by degrees, Science is being brought to recognize in the universe the existence of One Power, which is of no beginning and no end; which has existed before all things were formed, and will remain in its integrity when all is gone—the Source and Origin of all, in Itself beyond any conception or image that man can form and set up before his eye or mind. This sum total of the scientific discoveries of all lands and times is the approach of the world's thought to our *Adon Olam*, the sublime chant, by means of which the Jew has wrought and will further work the most momentous changes in the world' (Haffkine).

II. The second teaching of this chapter is, MAN IS THE GOAL AND CROWN OF CREATION—he is fundamentally distinguished from the lower creation, and is akin to the Divine. Man, modern scientists declare, is cousin to the anthropoid ape. But it is not so much the descent, as the *ascent* of man, which is decisive. Furthermore, it is not the resemblance, but the *difference* between man and the ape, that are of infinite importance. It is the differences between them that constitute the humanity of man, the God-likeness of man. The qualities that distinguish the lowest man from the highest brute make the differences between them differences in kind rather than in degree; so much so that, whatever man might have inherited from his animal ancestors, his advent can truly be spoken of as a specific Divine act, whereby a new being had arisen with God-like possibilities within him, and *conscious* of these God-like possibilities within him. Man is of God, declared Rabbi Akiba; and what is far more, he *knows* he is of God.

Nor is the Biblical account of the creation of man irreconcilable with the view that certain forms of organized being have been endowed with the capacity of developing, in God's good time and under the action of suitable environment, the attributes distinctive of man. 'God formed man of the dust of the ground' (Gen. II, 7). Whence that dust was taken is not, and cannot be, of fundamental importance. Science holds that man was formed from the lower animals; are they not too 'dust of the ground'? 'And God said, *Let the earth bring forth the living creature*'—this command, says the Midrash, includes Adam as well, תוצא הארץ נפש חיה, זו רוחו של אדם הראשון. The thing that eternally matters is the breath of Divine and everlasting life that He breathed into the being coming from the dust. By virtue of that Divine impact, a new and distinctive creature made its appearance—man, dowered with an immortal soul. The sublime revelation of the unique worth and dignity of man, contained in Gen. I, 27 ('And God created man in His own image, in the image of God created He him'), may well be called the Magna Charta of humanity. Its purpose is not to explain the biological origins of the human race, but *its spiritual kinship with God.* There is much force in the view expressed by a modern thinker: '(The Bible) neither provides, nor, in the nature of things, could provide, faultless anticipations of sciences still unborn. If by a miracle it had provided them, without a miracle they could not have been understood' (Balfour). And fully to grasp the eternal power and infinite beauty of these words—'And God created man in His own image'—we need but compare them with the genealogy of man, condensed from the pages of one of the leading biologists of the age (Haeckel):—

> 'Monera begat Amoeba, Amoeba begat Synamoebae, Synamoebae begat Ciliated Larva, Ciliated Larva begat Primeval Stomach Animals, Primeval Stomach Animals begat Gliding Worms, Gliding Worms begat Skull-less Animals, Skull-less Animals begat Single-nostrilled Animals, Single-nostrilled Animals begat Primeval Fish, Primeval Fish begat Mud-fish, Mud-fish begat Gilled Amphibians, Gilled Amphibians begat Tailed Amphibians, Tailed Amphibians begat Primary Mammals, Primary Mammals begat Pouched Animals, Pouched Animals begat Semi-Apes, Semi-Apes begat Tailed Apes, Tailed Apes begat Man-like Apes, Man-like Apes begat Ape-like Men, Ape-like Men begat Men.'

Let anyone who is disturbed by the fact that Scripture does not include the latest scientific doctrine, try to imagine such information provided in a Biblical chapter.

III. Judaism is optimism, is the third teaching of this chapter. No less than five times is the refrain, 'And God saw that it was good' repeated in the Creation Chapter. The world is not something hostile to God or independent of Him. All comes from God and all is His handiwork; all is in its essence good, nor is there anything absolutely evil. Israel acclaims God as the sole 'King of the universe, who formest light and createst darkness, who makest peace and createst all things' (Authorised Prayer Book, p. 37). Though Nature seems to be indifferent to man's sense of compassion, the world is good, since goodness is its final aim: without struggle, there would be no natural selection or adaptation to changing surroundings, and therefore no progress from lower to higher. 'And God saw everything that He had made, and, behold it was *very* good'—even suffering, evil, nay death itself, have a rightful and beneficent place in the Divine scheme, is the Rabbinic comment on this verse.

IV. The Sabbath consecrates work and hallows man's life, is the culminating teaching of the Chapter. The institution of the Sabbath is part of the cosmic plan, and therefore intended for all humanity. The Sabbath is a specifically Jewish contribution to human civilization. 'The actual Jewish Sabbath as we know it is without any point of contact in Babylonian institutions' (Skinner). The ancient Babylonians had 'a day of cessation', which they called by a name somewhat similar to 'Sabbath', and it was observed on the 7th, 14th, 19th, 21st, and 28th days of the months Ellul and Marcheshvan. These were considered unlucky days, and on them the king was not to offer sacrifice, nor consult an oracle, nor invoke curses on his enemies. Quite other is the Jewish Sabbath. It is not merely a day of cessation from toil. On the one hand, it has its positive aspect as a day of spiritual recreation; and, on the other hand, it is a day of joy, and is greeted in the Synagogue in the words לכה דודי לקראת כלה ('Come, my Beloved, to meet the Bride, Queen Sabbath'). It banishes toil and sorrow—a symbol of immortality, of that Life which is wholly a Sabbath; see on Exod. xx, 9-11.

God the Creator and Lord of the Universe, which is the work of His goodness and wisdom; and Man, made in His image, who is to hallow his week-day labours by the blessedness of Sabbath-rest—such are the teachings of the Creation chapter. Its purpose is to reveal these teachings to the children of men—and not to serve as a textbook of astronomy, geology or anthropology. Its object is not to teach scientific facts; but to proclaim highest religious truths respecting God, Man, and the Universe. The 'conflict' between the fundamental realities of Religion and the established facts of Science, is seen to be unreal as soon as Religion and Science each recognizes the true borders of its dominion.

B

THE GARDEN OF EDEN

Chapter iii is one of the most beautiful in the Bible. It has been called the 'pearl of Genesis', and men read with wonder its profound psychology of temptation and conscience. With unsurpassable art, it shows the beginning, the progress and the culmination of temptation and the consequences of sin. It depicts the earliest tragedy in the life of each human soul—the loss of man's happy, natural relation with God, through deliberate disobedience of the voice of conscience, the voice of God. 'Every man who knows his own heart, knows that the story is true; it is the story of his own fall. Adam אדם is man, and his story is ours' (McFadyen).

Is the narrative literal or figurative, and is the Serpent an animal, a demon or merely the symbolic representation of Sin? Various have been the answers to these questions; and none of them are of cardinal importance to the Faith of the Jew. There is nothing in Judaism against the belief that the Bible attempts to convey deep truths of life and conduct by means of allegory. The Rabbis often taught by parable; and such method of instruction is, as is well known, the immemorial way among Oriental peoples. Eminent Jewish thinkers, like Maimonides and Nachmanides, have accordingly understood this chapter as a parable; and Saadyah regarded the Serpent as the personification of the sinful tendencies in man, the *Yetzer hara,* the Evil Imagination.

Two fundamental religious truths are reflected in this Chapter. One of them is, *the seriousness of sin.* There is an everlasting distinction between right and wrong, between good and evil. There have always been voices—Serpent voices—deriding all moral do's and don'ts, proclaiming instinct and inclination to be the truest guides to human happiness, and bluntly denying that any evil consequences follow defiance of God's commands. This Chapter for all time warns mankind against these insidious and fateful voices. In the words of Isaiah it seems to say, 'Woe unto them that call evil good, and good evil; that put darkness for light, and light for darkness; that put bitter for sweet, and sweet for bitter! Woe unto them that are wise in their own eyes.'

The other vital teaching of this chapter is, *Free will has been given to man,* and it is in his power either to work with or against God. It is not the knowledge of evil, but the succumbing to it, which is deadly; man may see the forbidden fruit, he need not eat of it. Man himself can make or mar his destiny. In all ages and in all conditions, man has shown the power to resist the suggestions of sin and proved himself superior to the power of evil. And if a man stumble and fall on the pathway of life, Judaism bids him rise again and seek the face of his Heavenly Father in humility, contrition and repentance. 'If a man sin, what is his punishment?' ask the Rabbis. The answer of the Prophet is, 'The soul that sinneth, it shall die'—the wages of sin is death. The answer of the Sage is, 'Evil pursueth the evil-doer'—the wages of sin is sin. The answer of the Almighty is, 'Let a man repent, and his sin will be forgiven him'—*the wages of sin is repentance.*

Jewish View of the 'Fall of Man'

Strange and sombre doctrines have been built on this chapter of the Garden of Eden, such as the Christian doctrine of Original Sin (*e.g.* 'In Adam's fall, we sinned all'—New England Primer. 'The condition of man after the fall of Adam is such that he cannot turn and prepare himself by his own natural strength and good works to faith and calling upon God'—Art x, Free Will, of the Thirty-nine Articles). This Christian dogma of Original Sin is throughout the Middle Ages accompanied by an unbelievable vilification of Woman, as the authoress of death and all our earthly woe. Judaism rejects these doctrines. Man was mortal from the first, and death did not enter the world through the transgression of Eve. Stray Rabbinic utterances to the contrary are merely homiletic, and possess no binding authority in Judaism. There is no loss of the God-likeness of man, nor of man's ability to do right in the eyes of God; and no such loss has been transmitted to his latest descendants. Although a few of the Rabbis occasionally lament Eve's share in the poisoning of the human race by the Serpent, even they declare that the antidote to such poison has been found at Sinai; rightly holding that the Law of God is the bulwark against the devastations of animalism and godlessness. The Psalmists often speak of sin and guilt; but never is there a reference to this chapter or to what Christian Theology calls 'The Fall'. One searches in vain the Prayer Book, of even the Days of Penitence, for the slightest echo of the doctrine of the Fall of man. 'My God, the soul which Thou hast given me is pure,' is the Jew's daily morning prayer. 'Even as the soul is pure when entering upon its earthly career, so can man return it pure to his Maker' (Midrash).

Instead of the Fall of man (in the sense of humanity as a whole), Judaism preaches the Rise of man; and instead of Original Sin, it stresses Original Virtue (זכות אבות), the beneficent hereditary influence of righteous ancestors upon their descendants. 'There is no generation without its Abraham, Moses or Samuel,' says the Midrash; *i.e.* each age is capable of realizing the highest potentialities of the moral and spiritual life. Judaism clings to the idea of Progress. The Golden Age of Humanity is not in the past, but in the future (Isaiah II and XI); and all the children of men are destined to help in the establishment of that Kingdom of God on earth.

C

THE FLOOD

The primeval traditions recorded in the early chapters of Genesis stretch away into prehistoric times, and enshrine in outline, great universal truths that touch the origin and meaning of Life and Man. The Rabbis tell us that the Patriarch Jacob spent fourteen years in the centres of ancient Semitic learning, the 'academies of Shem and Eber' (בבית מדרשו של שם ועבר), acquiring the ancient traditions which he handed on to his descendants. Among these was the memory of a fearful upheaval with an all-destroying Flood that caused a complete breach in the continuity of civilization in the primitive dwelling-place of mankind. Striking evidence is now at hand that the Bible story of the Flood is an event in historic times, approximately about the year 3800 before the Common Era. 'New discoveries have brought history so close to the Flood period and have produced so many phenomena requiring for their explanation just such an event as the Flood is supposed to have been, that the *a priori* denial of the Flood becomes thoroughly unscientific. We are justified in asking for more evidence, but there can be little doubt which way that evidence will trend' (L. Woolley). As it was recounted in the families of the Patriarchs, the story of that Flood is of great ethical and religious value. The Deluge was a Divine judgment upon an age in which might was right, and depravity degraded and enslaved the children of men. There were giants on earth in those days; *they* were the 'men of renown'; and life to these super-men meant unscrupulous selfishness and the deification of power and pleasure.

Among these men of violence, one man alone was upright and blameless, Noah, who believed in justice and practised mercy. He preached to the men of his generation—the Rabbis tell us—and warned them that a Deluge was coming, peradventure they might desist from iniquity and turn to righteousness. In vain. He saw that entire generation swept away; but he also lived to see the Rainbow of Promise, and the beginnings of a better world that was eventually to gain in strength, and to find lasting expression in Abraham and his descendants.

D

THE TOWER OF BABEL AND THE DIVERSITY OF LANGUAGES

One explanation of Genesis, chapter XI, is that it continues the theme of the preceding section and indicates that the Divine ideal was One Humanity united by one universal language. In view of the division of mankind by diversity of tongue, which has ever been a source of misunderstanding, hostility and war, this chapter answers the question how the original Divinely-ordained unity of language, that indispensable link for the unity of mankind, was lost. Only a great transgression—an enterprise colossal in its insolent impiety and evidencing an open revolt against God—could account for such a moral catastrophe to humanity (Steinthal). Standing symbols of such heathen impiety to the Hebrew mind were the *ziggurats*, the Mesopotamian temple-towers, rising to an immense height as if intended to scale Heaven.

The building of the greatest of these towers was associated with Babylon, the centre of ancient luxury and power. The Rabbis assert that the builders of this Tower of Babel wished to storm the heavens in order to wage war against the Deity; and 'as the highest stage in an Assyrian or Babylonian ziggurat was surmounted by a shrine of the Deity, there is perhaps less fancifulness in these words than is often suspected' (Ryle). Jewish legend tells of the godlessness and inhumanity of these tower-builders. If, in the course of the construction of the Tower, a man fell down and met his death, none paid heed to it; but if a brick fell down and broke into fragments, they were grieved and even shed tears—a graphic summing up of heathen civilization, ancient or modern. Such an enterprise provoked Divine punishment; and that insolence and power were broken by lasting division occasioned by diversity of language.

Quite a different interpretation of this chapter is given by Ibn Ezra: 'The purpose of the builders was simply to prevent their becoming separated, and to secure their dwelling together. But as this purpose was contrary to the design of Providence (IX, 1; I, 28) that the whole earth should be inhabited, it was frustrated. The expression 'whose top may reach unto heaven' must accordingly be interpreted that that tower was to be of very great height so that it would be visible at a considerable distance and become a rallying point to all people.

E

THE DELUGE AND ITS BABYLONIAN PARALLEL

Flood stories are very numerous, and are found in every part of the world. But these are of little or no interest to the Bible student or to the modern reader. The Babylonian parallel to the Biblical account of the Deluge, however, stands in a class by itself. Both the resemblances and the differences of the two accounts are of great importance for the understanding and proper appreciation of the Bible narrative.

The Babylonian story is as follows: The gods in council decide to send a Flood upon the earth. One of the gods, Ea, who was present at the council, resolves to save his favourite Utnapishtim—this is the name of the Babylonian Noah. He warns him of the impending danger and at the same time commands him to build a ship. He also furnishes the 'superlatively clever one', Utnapishtim, with a misleading pretext to offer his contemporaries when questioned as to the reason for his building the ship. (In the Rabbinical legend, Noah during the years of the ship's construction, is a preacher of repentance. 'Turn from your evil ways and live,' is his admonition to his fellow men.) When the ship is built, Utnapishtim fills it with his possessions, his family, dependants, including artisans, together with domestic and wild animals. He then enters it himself and closes the door behind him. The storm rages for six days and nights, till all mankind are destroyed, and the very gods 'cowered in terror like dogs'. On the seventh day, he sends out a dove, which comes back to him. And then he lets go a raven which does not return. On this, Utnapishtim released all the animals; and leaving the ship, offered a sacrifice. 'The gods gathered like flies over the sacrifice.' The deities then began to quarrel; but eventually Utnapishtim is blessed, and is received into the society of the gods.

The resemblances between this Babylonian story and the Biblical account lie on the surface. To mention only a few features common to both: the whole human race is doomed to destruction; one man with his dependants and animals is saved in a ship; the episode of the dove and raven; and after leaving the ship, the man offers sacrifices and receives Divine blessings.

Of far greater significance, however, are the differences between the two accounts. The Babylonian story is unethical and polytheistic, devoid of any uniform or exalted purpose, and lacking in reverence and restraint. Not so the terse, direct, and simple Hebrew narrative. Instead of the quarrelsome, deceitful, vindictive pack of Babylonian deities, false to one another and false to men, we have in the Hebrew account, the One and Supreme God—holy and righteous in His dealings with man. Unlike its Babylonian counterpart, the Hebrew Deluge is a proclamation of the eternal truth that the basis of human society is justice, and that any society which is devoid of justice deserves to perish, and will inevitably perish. Noah is saved, not through celestial caprice or favouritism, not because he was 'superlatively clever', but because he was righteous and blameless in a perverse generation; a man who was worthy of God's approval, as well as of inaugurating a new era for humanity. An impassable gulf separates the Biblical and the Babylonian Deluge stories. This infinite ethical *difference* between them is recognized even by those who are otherwise hostile to the Bible. 'The Biblical story of the Deluge possesses an intrinsic power to stir the conscience of the world, and it was written with this educational and moral end in view. Of this end, there is no trace in the Deluge records outside the Bible' (A. Jeremias).

In its Babylonian form, Assyriologists tell us, the story seems to have been reduced to writing as early as the days of Abraham. It must have been known in substance to the children of Israel in Canaan and later in Egypt. But in the form in which, under God's Providence, the Patriarchs transmitted it to their descendants, it was free from all degrading elements, and became an assertion of the everlasting righteousness of the One God. 'The Babylonian parallel only serves to bring out the unique grandeur of Israel's God-idea, which could thus purify and transform the most uncongenial and repugnant features of the ancient Deluge tradition' (Gunkel).

F

ARE THERE TWO CONFLICTING ACCOUNTS OF CREATION AND THE DELUGE IN THE *GENESIS*?

All those scholars who are followers of what is called 'Higher Criticism' maintain that the account of the Flood in the Bible was written much later than Moses. In the face of all archæological evidence to the contrary, they maintain that the art of writing was not known in Israel before the days of David. Like all primitive nations, Israel had bards and singers who recited and composed legends and tales concerning the exploits of the ancestral heroes; and in the course of centuries, these early legends and tales of Israel assumed a fixed literary form in two distinct collections. They call one of these supposed 'collections' E, because the Divine Name used in it is *Elohim* (rendered in English by GOD), and allege that it arose in the Prophetic circles of Northern Israel in the ninth pre-Christian century. The other collection they call J, because, they say, it regularly employs the Divine Name which is read as *Adonay* (translated into English by the word LORD), and they declare it arose in the Prophetic circles of Judea in the eighth pre-Christian century. A third document (Deuteronomy), they tell us, arose in the reign of King Josiah; and on the return from Exile, a fourth portion of the Torah came into existence, the Priestly Document, which they call P. As these distinct documents, however, E, J, D, and P, do not exist separately or even side by side, we are asked to believe that at various stages in Israel's history, these different parts have been combined and edited by a succession of 'redactors' We shall elsewhere in the course of this commentary show the utter baselessness of this revolutionary view of Israel's history and religion. At this place, we shall examine the principal reasons which the critics assign for the division of the text of the Torah into what they call its 'original elements'. These reasons are: (*a*) the alleged diversity in the use of Divine Names; and (*b*) supposed discrepancies in statement between the various 'sources'. And nowhere in the Pentateuch, they hold, are these differences in Divine Names and in details of statement more evident than in the chapters dealing with the Creation and the Deluge. These sections, therefore, should afford the best test to prove the tenability, or otherwise, of the claims of the Bible critics.

A. Genesis, chapters I and II are supposed to contain two distinct accounts of Creation. Genesis, chapter I–II, 3 is called P—the Priestly account, and is supposed to be post-exilic; whereas Genesis, chapter II, 4–25 is the Prophetic account, J, and is stated to be some two centuries earlier.

But, *are* there two accounts of Creation? Can Genesis II, 4–25, honestly be considered as such? Unlike chapter I, it does not describe the coming into existence of the sun, moon and stars, of the seas and their inhabitants. Even Heaven and earth are mentioned only indirectly, in an introductory phrase. Genesis II, 4–25, pre-supposes Gen. I, supplements it, and is unintelligible without it. The proposed distinguishing of the two sources by the use of the different Divine

Names fails at the very start. *Elohim* they declare to be exclusively used by the Priestly writer of Gen. I; and *Adonay* to be the Divine Name used only by the supposed Prophetic writer to whom they assign Gen. II, 4–15; *and yet Elohim occurs* 20 *times together with Adonay in Gen.* II, 4–25 and in Chap. III, which is also held by them to be Prophetic. The Critics attempt to get over this difficulty by stating that Elohim has been here interpolated by the 'redactor' 20 times in one chapter. But then, in the conversation between Eve and the serpent, Elohim without Adonay is used! Is this, too, an interpolation?

As explained in the comment on II, 4, the alternate, or combined, use of Elohim and Adonay for the Name of God presents no difficulty whatsoever. Their employment varies according to the nature of the context. Thus, in connection with the creation of the Universe at large (Genesis I), the Divine Name employed is *Elohim*. In God's merciful relations with human beings, however (Gen. II, 4–25), He is spoken of as *Adonay*, Lord. There is nothing strange or out of the way in such usage. In English, we choose words like Deity, Supreme Being, Almighty, God, Lord, according as the subject and occasion demand. *One and the same writer*, may at various times use any one of these English terms for the Divine Being. The nature of the context decides what Divine Name is employed. In the same way, different Divine Names in the Hebrew text do not argue a diversity of writers, but simply that the Divine Name has each time been selected in accordance with the idea to be expressed. David Hoffmann, W. H. Green, and B. Jacob have examined each and every instance of the use of these Names throughout Genesis, and have shown the exact appropriateness of each Name to the subject matter in which it occurs.

B. No more are there two distinct accounts of the Deluge than there are two accounts of Creation. Here, too, the Divine Name 'test' fails completely. One example will suffice. 'And they that went in, went in male and female of all flesh, as God (Elohim) commanded him; and the LORD (Adonay) shut him in' (VII, 16). As the Bible critics declare this verse to be written by P, it ought to contain only Elohim; and yet we have Elohim followed by *Adonay!* The critics are compelled by their theory to assign the 'offending' words to J, although the whole context belongs to P. Those who are not critics find, of course, no difficulty here: Adonay is used, because 'the LORD (Adonay) shut him in' describes a merciful action. In face of such a combined use of both Elohim and Adonay as we have here, and in Genesis II, the test of the Divine Name surely breaks down.

Equally baseless is the argument triumphantly brought forward that there is a striking discrepancy of statement in the directions given to Noah, which discrepancy compels the assumption of two distinct accounts. Noah is first told (VI, 19) to take into the ark two each of all animals; whereas, in the next chapter, he is told to take two of all animals, but *seven* of all clean beasts! The answer is plain: VI, 19 does not say that *only* two shall be taken from each kind. The first is a general command; whereas the second command at the moment of entering the ark is more specific, and directs that of the clean domestic animals of Noah that were to serve him for food and later for sacrifices, he was to take seven of each. Such general statements (כלל) followed by a statement giving specific details (פרט) is the rule in Scripture. Thus, the opening verse of Gen. I, 'In the beginning God created the heavens and the earth,' is a general statement. This is followed by a whole series of supplementary specific statements, giving the details of creation. Yet there certainly is no contradiction between the general statement that back of the whole Universe is a Creator, and the remainder of the chapter describing the various creative acts. The same rule of general and specific statement obtains in connection with the command to Noah.

But the utter falsity of the critical theory is proved by the Babylonian version itself. The Babylonian version is in agreement with the Bible account *as an undivided whole*. There are special points of agreement between it and the portions assigned to P; such as, the precise instructions for building the ark, and the statement that the ark rested on a mountain, etc. There are also special points of agreement between it and the portions assigned to J, such as, the sending forth of birds, and the later building of an altar and the offering of sacrifices. This is unanswerable testimony to the unity of the Scriptural Deluge account.

The procedure of the critics in connection with the Creation and Deluge chapters is typical of their method throughout. It justifies the protest of the late Lord Chancellor of England, the Earl of Halsbury—an excellent judge of evidence—who in 1915 found himself impelled to declare:—'For my own part I consider the assignment of different fragments of Genesis to a number of wholly imaginary authors great rubbish. I do not understand the attitude of those men who base a whole theory of this kind on hypotheses for which there is no evidence whatsoever.' A generation before the Earl of Halsbury, the historian Lecky gave expression to a similar judgment, in the following words: 'I may be pardoned for expressing my belief that this kind of investigation is often pursued with an exaggerated confidence. Plausible conjecture is too easily mistaken for positive proof. Undue significance is attached to what may be mere casual coincidence, and a minuteness of accuracy is professed in discriminating between different elements in a narrative which cannot be attained by mere internal evidence.'

Whenever *external* evidence comes to light, as in the case of the Babylonian version of the

Deluge, or, as we shall see later, in the case of the discovery of the Babylonian Code of Laws—the arbitrary and purely fictitious nature of the critical theories becomes patent to all.

G

ABRAHAM

I

Mankind descending from Adam became hopelessly corrupt and was swept away by the Deluge. Noah alone was spared. But before many generations pass away, mankind once again becomes arrogant and impious, and moral darkness overspreads the earth. 'And God said *Let Abraham be*—and there was light,' is the profound saying of the Midrash. In many a beautiful legend, the Rabbis recount how Abraham refused to walk in the way of the Tower-builders, and broke away from the debasing heathenism of his contemporaries. In his early childhood one night, he looked at the stars under the clear Mesopotamian sky, and felt, 'These are the gods!' But the dawn came, and soon the stars could be seen no longer when the sun rose. 'This is my god, him will I adore!' he exclaimed. But then the sun set, and he hailed the moon as his deity. When in turn the moon was obscured, he cried out: 'This, too, is no god! There must be One who is the Maker of Sun, Moon and Stars.' Having gradually reached the momentous conviction that the Universe is the work of One Supreme Being who is the God of righteousness, he endeavours to open the eyes of others to the folly of idol-worship, and becomes the Preacher of the True Faith. In his father's house, the legend continues, there stood one great idol and a large number of smaller ones. Abraham broke all the smaller ones and then placed the hammer in the hand of the big idol. 'They quarrelled among themselves,' he later explained to his dumb-founded father, 'and the big one thereupon took a hammer and shattered them all. Behold, it is still in his hands!' 'But there is no life and power in them to do such things,' his father answered in rage. 'Why then dost thou serve them? Can they hear thy prayers when thou callest upon them?' was the reply. Abraham was thereupon haled before the ruler of Babylon, Nimrod, who cast him into a fiery furnace (whence the name of the city 'Ur', which means *fire*). An angel of God rescues him unhurt from its devouring flames (Midrash). Abraham the idol-wrecker is the father of that People which was to shatter all idolatries; which was to suffer all things, endure all things, and survive all things in its defiance of despotisms of the body and soul; which was to succeed in turning the course of history by the perpetuation of true religion for the children of men. The call of Abraham is the beginning of the higher spiritual life of humanity.

II

With Abraham, the nature of the Book of Genesis changes. Hitherto, in its first eleven chapters, it gave an account of the dawn of the world and of human society. The remainder of the Book is the story of the founders of the People whose destiny, in the light of God's purpose, forms the main theme of Scripture. These founders of the Jewish People are not divine or semi-divine beings, as is the case with the mythical heroes of Greece, Rome or the Teutonic nations. They are purely human personalities, just normal men, of like passions with ourselves, having their faults and excellencies. 'Abraham is the "Friend of God". He is nothing more; but he is nothing less. In him was exemplified the fundamental truth of all religion, that God has not deserted the world; that His work is carried on by His own chosen instruments; that good men are not only His creatures and His servants, but His friends' (Stanley).

With the Patriarchs, we leave the dim, Primeval world and enter the full daylight of historical times. Even a generation ago, Bible critics looked upon the Patriarchal stories in Genesis as a tissue of fabrications, at best as legends, but in no case as authentic history. No theory was too fantastic, or too blasphemous, to be put forward as a serious explanation of the narrative. One critic declared Abraham to be a 'free creation of unconscious art'; another turned him into a 'fetish stone'; a third identified him with the 'starry heavens'; and a fourth made of him 'a sacred locality'. One of the greatest of these Bible critics (Dillmann), who at one time shared those preposterous views, eventually felt himself impelled to state 'we have no right to explain these Genesis narratives as pure fiction. They rest in essentials on sound historical recollection'. This view is now that of all responsible students of the Bible. 'The patriarchal period has been so illumined by recent discoveries,' says the author of the commentary on 'Genesis' in the *International Critical Series*, 'that it is no longer possible to doubt its substantial historicity. Contemporary documents reveal a set of conditions into which the patriarchal narratives fit perfectly, and which are so different from those prevailing under the monarchy that the situation could not possibly have been imagined by an Israelite of that age' (John Skinner). The words of the Psalmist, 'Truth shall spring out of the earth,' have become literally fulfilled, and the very stones of the Nile and the Euphrates valleys, of Palestine, and Asia Minor, have given their decisive testimony in vindication of the Torah. 'We have travelled far from the time when scholars attempted to turn the Patriarchs into mythical beings. To-day that attempt itself almost appears mythical' (Professor D. H. Müller).

H

THE BINDING OF ISAAC (AKEDAH)

This Chapter is of great importance both in the life of Abraham and in the life of Israel. The aged Patriarch who had longed for a rightful heir ('O Lord God, what wilt Thou give me, seeing I go hence childless?') and who had had his longing fulfilled in the birth of Isaac, is now bidden offer up this child as a burnt offering unto the Lord. The purpose of the command was to apply a supreme test to Abraham's faith, thus strengthening his faith by the heroic exercise of it. The proofs of a man's love of God are his willingness to serve Him with all his heart, all his soul and all his might; as well as his readiness to sacrifice unto Him what is even dearer than life. It was a test safe only in a Divine hand, capable of intervening as He did intervene, and as it was His purpose from the first to intervene, as soon as the spiritual end of the trial was accomplished.

So much for what may be called the *positive* lesson of the Akedah. We shall now examine another side, the great *negative* teaching of this trial of Abraham. The story of the Binding of Isaac opens the age-long warfare of Israel against the abominations of child sacrifice which was rife among the Semitic peoples, as well as their Egyptian and Aryan neighbours. In that age, it was astounding that Abraham's God should have interposed *to prevent* the sacrifice, not that He should have asked for it. A primary purpose of this command, therefore, was to demonstrate to Abraham and his descendants after him that God abhorred human sacrifice with an infinite abhorrence. Unlike the cruel heathen deities, *it was the spiritual surrender alone that God required.* Moses warns his people not to serve God in the manner of the surrounding nations. 'For every abomination to the LORD which He hateth have they done unto their gods; for even their sons and their daughters they have burnt in the fire to their gods' (Deuteronomy XII, 31). All the Prophets alike shudder at this hideous aberration of man's sense of worship, and they do not rest till all Israel shares their horror of this savage custom. It is due to the influence of their teaching that the name *Ge-Hinnom*, the valley where the wicked kings practised this horrible rite, became a synonym for 'Hell'.

A new meaning and influence begin for the Akedah and its demand for man's unconditional surrender to God's will and the behests of God's law, with the Maccabean revolt, when Jews were first called upon to die for their Faith. Abraham's readiness to sacrifice his most sacred affections on the altar of his God, evoked and developed a new ideal in Israel, *the ideal of martyrdom.* The story of Hannah and her seven sons, immortalized in the Second Book of Maccabees, has come down to us in many forms. In one of these, the martyr mother says to her youngest child, 'Go to Abraham our Father, and tell him that I have bettered his instruction. He offered one child to God; I offered seven. He merely bound the sacrifice; I performed it' (Midrash). As persecution deepened during later centuries, the Binding of Isaac was ever in the mind of men and women who might at any moment be given the dread alternative of apostasy or death. Allusions to the Akedah early found their way into the Liturgy; and in time a whole cycle of synagogue hymns (*piyyutim*) grew round it. In the Middle Ages, it gave fathers and mothers the superhuman courage to immolate themselves and their children, rather than see them fall away to idolatry or baptism. English Jews need but think of the soul-stirring tragedy enacted at York Castle in the year 1190 to understand the lines of the modern Jewish poet:—

'We have sacrificed all. We have given our wealth,
Our homes, our honours, our land, our health,
Our lives—like Hannah her children seven—
For the sake of the Torah that came from Heaven' (J. L. Gordon).

Many to-day have no understanding of martyrdom. They fail to see that it represents the highest moral triumph of humanity—unwavering steadfastness to principle, even at the cost of life. They equally fail to see the lasting influence of such martyrdoms upon the life and character of the nation whose history they adorn. Those who are thus blind to unconquerable courage and endurance naturally display hostility to the whole idea of the Akedah and its place and associations in Jewish thought. 'Only a Moloch requires human sacrifices' (Geiger), they exclaim. But in all human history, there is not a single noble cause, movement or achievement that did not call for sacrifice, nay sacrifice of life itself. Science, Liberty, Humanity, all took their toll of martyrs; and so did and does Judaism. Israel is the classical people of martyrdom. No other people has made similar sacrifices for Truth, Conscience, Human Honour and Human Freedom (Martin Schreiner). Even in our own day, Jewish parents in Eastern and Central European lands have refused, and refuse, fortune and honours for the sake of conscience. What is far harder, they sacrifice the careers of their children whenever these involve disloyalty to the God of their Fathers. Few chapters of the Bible have had a more potent and more lasting influence on the lives and souls of men than the Akedah.

I

ALLEGED CHRISTOLOGICAL REFERENCES IN SCRIPTURE

The first of these references is alleged to be in the words often translated by 'Until Shiloh come', in Gen. XLIX, 10. Most of the ancient and modern explanations of this verse turn upon the Heb. word rendered by *Shiloh.*

I. It is a strange circumstance that the older Jewish Versions and commentators (Septuagint, Targums, Saadyah and Rashi) read this word without a *yod*, as if written שִׁלֹה, the archaic form for 'his'; or, as if it were a poetic form for 'peace'.

(*a*) The translation, 'until that which is his shall come,' is derived from the Septuagint. Its meaning is, The sceptre shall not depart from Judah till all that is reserved for him shall have been fulfilled.

(*b*) 'Till he come whose it (the kingdom) is' (Onkelos and Jerusalem Targum, Saadyah, Rashi and other Jewish commentators).

(*c*) 'Till peace cometh' (M. Friedlander).

II. Most commentators, however, take the word שילה as the name of a place or person.

(*a*) 'As long as men come to Shiloh' (to worship). Shiloh was the location of the sanctuary in the days of the Prophet Samuel, before Jerusalem became the centre of Jewish worship. As the outstanding superiority of the tribe of Judah only began after the Temple was built at Jerusalem, this interpretation is unsatisfactory.

(*b*) 'Till he of Shiloh cometh, and the obedience of the peoples be turned to him.' Mendelssohn and Zunz see in the verse a prediction of the event described in I Kings XI, 29 f. Ahijah, the Prophet of Shiloh, foretold to Jeroboam that a part of the Kingdom would be taken from Solomon and transferred to him; that ten tribes of Israel (here called 'peoples', see Gen. XLVIII, 4) would break away from the House of David, and submit to his rule. This ingenious explanation fails to satisfy for various reasons. 'He of Shiloh' would be in Heb. not שילה but השילוני; the tribes were not turned to the Prophet of Shiloh but to Jeroboam; and the utterance would have been quite unintelligible to Judah.

(*c*) 'Till Shiloh come.' This is the rendering of the Authorised Version, and assumes that *Shiloh* is a personal name or a Messianic title. Although this assumption finds support in Rabbinic literature, it is there only a homiletic comment without official and binding authority. Despite the fact that nowhere in Scripture is that term applied to the Messiah, Christian theologians assume that Shiloh is a name of the Founder of Christianity. In this sense, 'Till Shiloh come' is a favourite text of Christian missionaries in attempting to convert illiterate Jews or those ignorant of Scripture. It is noteworthy that this translation only dates from the year 1534, and is found for the first time in the German Bible of Sebastian Munster. Although it is retained in the text of the Revised Version, it is now rejected by all those who have a scholarly acquaintance with the subject. Even a loyal Bishop of the Church of England, the late Dean of Westminster, wrote, 'The improbability of this later interpretation is so great that it may be dismissed from consideration' (Ryle).

Such likewise is the judgment which must be passed on the translations of all the other alleged Christological passages which missionaries to the Jews are fond of quoting. Christian scholars of repute are gradually giving up such partisan interpretations. Thus Psalm II, 12 is translated in the Authorised Version as, 'Kiss the Son,' with the obvious Christian reference. In the Revised Version text, however, this is softened to 'Kiss the son'; while the Margin gives, 'Worship in purity.' The latter is in agreement with Jewish authorities.

Similarly, in connection with Isaiah VII, 14, 'A virgin shall conceive,' Christian scholars today admit that 'virgin' is a mistranslation for the Heb. word *almah*, in that verse. A 'maid' or unmarried woman is expressed in Hebrew by *bethulah*. The word *almah* in Isaiah VII, 14 means no more than a young woman of age to be a mother, whether she be married or not.

The most famous passage of this class is the Fifty-third chapter of Isaiah. For eighteen hundred years Christian theologians have passionately maintained that it is a Prophetic anticipation of the life of the Founder of their Faith. An impartial examination of the chapter, however, shows that the Prophet is speaking of *a past historical fact*, and is describing one who had already been smitten to death. Consequently, a reference to an event which is said to have happened many centuries later is excluded.

These three instances may be taken as typical. Modern scholarship has shattered the arguments from the Scriptures which missionaries have tried, and are still trying, to impose upon ignorant Jews.

ספר שמות

THE BOOK OF EXODUS

ספר שמות

THE BOOK OF EXODUS

NAME. The Second Book of Moses was originally called ספר יציאת מצרים, 'the Book of the Going out of Egypt.' At an early date, however, it came to be known as שמות, from its opening phrase, *Ve-eleh shemoth* ('And these are the names'). Its current designation in Western countries is Exodus—from the Greek term *exodos*, 'The Departure' (of the children of Israel out of Egypt), a name applied to it in the Septuagint, the ancient Greek translation of Scripture.

CONTENTS. The Book of Exodus is the natural continuation of Genesis. Genesis describes the lives of the Fathers of the Hebrew People: Exodus tells the beginning of the People itself. It records Israel's enslavement in Egypt, and the deliverance from the House of Bondage. It describes the institution of the Passover, the Covenant at Mount Sinai, and the organization of Public Worship that was to make Israel into 'a kingdom of priests and an holy nation'. It recounts the murmurings and backslidings of Israel as well as the Divine guidance and instruction, vouchsafed to it; the apostasy of the Golden Calf, as well as the supreme Revelation that followed it—the revelation of the Divine Being as a 'God, full of compassion and gracious, slow to anger, and plenteous in mercy and truth; keeping mercy for thousands, forgiving iniquity and transgression and sin; and who will by no means clear the guilty'.

IMPORTANCE. Nearly all the foundations on which Jewish life is built—the Ten Commandments, the historic Festivals, the leading principles of civil law—are contained in the Book of Exodus. And the importance of this Book is not confined to Israel. In its epic account of Israel's redemption from slavery, mankind learned that God is a God of Freedom; that, even as in Egypt He espoused the cause of brick-making slaves against the royal tyrant, Providence ever exalts righteousness and freedom, and humbles iniquity and oppression. And the Ten Commandments spoken at Sinai, form the Magna Charta of religion and morality, linking them for the first time, and for all time, in indissoluble union.

DIVISIONS. The Book may be divided into five parts. The first part (chaps. I–XV) relates the story of the Oppression and Redemption. The second part (chaps. XVI–XXIV) describes the journey to Sinai, and embodies the Decalogue and the civil laws and judgments that were to have such a profound influence on human society. Then follow, in chaps. XXV–XXXI, the directions for the building of the Sanctuary. Chaps. XXXII–XXXIV detail Israel's apostasy in connection with the Golden Calf; and chaps. XXXV–XL describe the construction of the Sanctuary, and thus prepare the way for the Third Book of Moses, the Book of Leviticus.

CHAPTER I

1. Now these are the names of the sons of Israel, who came into Egypt with Jacob; every man came with his household: 2. Reuben, Simeon, Levi, and Judah; 3. Issachar, Zebulun, and Benjamin; 4. Dan and Naphtali, Gad and Asher. 5. And all the souls that came out of the loins of Jacob were seventy souls; and Joseph was in Egypt already. 6. And Joseph died, and all his brethren, and all that generation. 7. And the children of Israel were fruitful, and increased abundantly, and multiplied, and waxed exceeding mighty; and the land was filled with them. ¶ 8. Now there arose a new king over Egypt, who knew not Joseph. 9. And he said unto his people: 'Behold, the people of the children of Israel are too many and too

CAP. I. א

א

13 יג

א וְאֵלֶּה שְׁמוֹת בְּנֵי יִשְׂרָאֵל הַבָּאִים מִצְרָיְמָה אֵת יַעֲקֹב אִישׁ
2 3 וּבֵיתוֹ בָּאוּ׃ רְאוּבֵן שִׁמְעוֹן לֵוִי וִיהוּדָה׃ יִשָּׂשכָר זְבוּלֻן
4 ה וּבִנְיָמִן׃ דָּן וְנַפְתָּלִי גָּד וְאָשֵׁר׃ וַיְהִי כָּל־נֶפֶשׁ יֹצְאֵי יֶרֶךְ־
6 יַעֲקֹב שִׁבְעִים נָפֶשׁ וְיוֹסֵף הָיָה בְמִצְרָיִם׃ וַיָּמָת יוֹסֵף וְכָל־
7 אֶחָיו וְכֹל הַדּוֹר הַהוּא׃ וּבְנֵי יִשְׂרָאֵל פָּרוּ וַיִּשְׁרְצוּ וַיִּרְבּוּ
וַיַּעַצְמוּ בִּמְאֹד מְאֹד וַתִּמָּלֵא הָאָרֶץ אֹתָם׃ פ
8 וַיָּקָם מֶלֶךְ־חָדָשׁ עַל־מִצְרָיִם אֲשֶׁר לֹא־יָדַע אֶת־יוֹסֵף׃

I. SHEMOTH

(CHAPTERS I–VI, 1)

ISRAEL IN EGYPT: THE OPPRESSION AND THE REDEMPTION

THE OPPRESSION OF THE ISRAELITES. CHAPTER I

1. *now these.* lit. 'and these', which better indicates the close connection between the first two books of the Pentateuch, since the whole Torah is one continuous narrative.

5. *seventy souls.* Jacob himself is included in the number; see Gen. XLVI, 8–27. Of the seventy, sixty-eight were males. If to these we add the wives of the sons and grandsons, and the husbands of the daughters and granddaughters, and all their servants and their families, the total number of those who entered Egypt must have been several hundreds, if not thousands.

6. *and Joseph died.* This verse resumes the thread of the narrative of the last verse of Gen. (L, 26) where we read, 'So Joseph died.'

all that generation. Both Israelites and Egyptians.

7. *increased abundantly.* lit. 'swarmed.' Note the accumulation of the synonyms—were fruitful, increased abundantly, multiplied, and waxed exceeding mighty. The extraordinary increase of the Israelites in Egypt presents a difficulty that is more apparent than real. As we have seen, the seventy souls who went down to Egypt did so accompanied by extensive households whom they eventually incorporated into their families (cf. Gen. XVII, 12, 27). Prof. Orr recalls from personal knowledge the case of a golden wedding where the original couple had multiplied to 69. If, he says, one bears this in mind in connection with the descendants of Jacob in Egypt, and 'reckons the result of a similar rate of increase for 300 or 400 years, the figures may surprise him'.

the land was filled. Not only Goshen, the eastern Delta of the Nile, the abode originally assigned to the Israelites. In time, they were found everywhere in Egypt as well as outside Egypt, in territories under Egyptian control; see *v.* 12.

8. *a new king.* A monarch of a new dynasty, with a 'nationalist' policy; probably Rameses II. Joseph served one of the Hyksos (Shepherd) kings, an Asiatic dynasty whose rule in Egypt began some centuries before him; see note on Gen. XXXIX, 1. Their rule came to an end not long after the death of Joseph, when the Hyksos were driven back into Asia, and a descendant of the native dynasty regained the throne. See Additional Note A, 'Israel in Egypt,' p. 394.

who knew not Joseph. He feigned to know nothing of Joseph's merits (Rashi). The immemorial ingratitude of rulers and commonwealths is proverbial. Especially common is ingratitude to Israel—the People that has achieved so much of eternal worth, but has rarely succeeded in winning gratitude.

With the death of Joseph, a large portion of the Israelites in time forgot the religious traditions and the religious practices of the Fathers (Josh. XXIV, 14; Ezek. XX, 8). The greater portion of the people, however, must have kept alive in their hearts the memory and hope of Israel. Otherwise it is quite impossible to understand how they maintained their separate existence during generations of oppression, and still more during centuries of prosperity, in a highly civilized society like the Egyptian. Foremost among the loyalists were the tribe of Levi, who alone maintained the covenant of Abraham. Of those who had abandoned Israel's hope, many reverted to heathen Semitic practices; while others, the Midrash tells us, adopted the motto, 'Let us be Egyptians in all things.'

mighty for us; 10. come, let us deal wisely with them, lest they multiply, and it come to pass, that, when there befalleth us any war, they also join themselves unto our enemies, and fight against us, and get them up out of the land.' 11. Therefore they did set over them taskmasters to afflict them with their burdens. And they built for Pharaoh store-cities, Pithom and Raamses. 12. But the more they afflicted them, the more they multiplied and the

9 וַיֹּאמֶר אֶל־עַמּוֹ הִנֵּה עַם בְּנֵי יִשְׂרָאֵל רַב וְעָצוּם מִמֶּנּוּ׃
י הָבָה נִתְחַכְּמָה לוֹ פֶּן־יִרְבֶּה וְהָיָה כִּי־תִקְרֶאנָה מִלְחָמָה
וְנוֹסַף גַּם־הוּא עַל־שֹׂנְאֵינוּ וְנִלְחַם־בָּנוּ וְעָלָה מִן־הָאָרֶץ׃
11 וַיָּשִׂימוּ עָלָיו שָׂרֵי מִסִּים לְמַעַן עַנֹּתוֹ בְּסִבְלֹתָם וַיִּבֶן עָרֵי
12 מִסְכְּנוֹת לְפַרְעֹה אֶת־פִּתֹם וְאֶת־רַעַמְסֵס׃ וְכַאֲשֶׁר יְעַנּוּ

9. *too many and too mighty for us.* The exaggeration of hatred, jealousy and fear. The land, it seemed to them, was full of Israelites; they were *everywhere!* 'They filled the theatres and all the places of amusements,' is the comment of the Midrash. The fact that their increase is their only crime and that no activity inimical to society could be charged against them, is striking testimony to the blameless civic life of our ancestors in Egypt.

10. *come, let us deal.* The king plans the means of crushing the Israelites in common deliberation with his counsellors. 'This first instance of *rishus* on a large scale is noteworthy also for the fact that it arises *not from the Egyptian people*, but from the ruling classes. It is the king who stirs it up, and assigns high reasons of state for making it a national policy. This has often repeated itself in history' (Hirsch).

wisely. i.e. craftily.

join themselves. Living in Goshen, the Israelites might assist the enemy and make common cause with the Hittites, whose power Rameses could not break; or with any Semitic invaders of Egypt from the East. It is at all times a common stratagem of 'patriots' to suspect the loyalty of the envied alien who is living peacefully and prosperously among them. One of the first laws the children of Israel were to learn on leaving Egypt was: 'And a stranger shalt thou not wrong, neither shalt thou oppress him; for ye were strangers in the land of Egypt' (XXII, 21; see p. 63, note on XVIII, 7).

and get them. Mendelssohn here translates the conjunction *vav* by *or* (as in XXI, 15); 'and fight against us'—in case of invasion; '*or* get them out of the land' and strengthen the enemy peoples who are threatening us. Hence the anxiety of the Egyptian rulers both to *retain* the Israelites, and at the same time to decimate, and eventually destroy, them through forced labour.

up out of the land. Heb. idiom speaks of 'going *down* to Egypt' and 'going *up* to Canaan', because Egypt lies lower than Palestine.

11. *taskmasters.* Or, 'gang-overseers.' This was the first move in the scheme of checking the increase of the Israelites. The free and independent settlers in Goshen, who had been invited to Egypt (Gen. XLV, 16–20), were now subjected to the corvée, *i.e.* compelled to labour on public works without pay. 'Their labour was a sort of tribal tax which they had to render, and for which their own head-men were responsible' (Petrie). The Egyptian and Assyrian monuments show us gangs of slaves working at brick-making, stone-breaking, and other severe labours, under the lash of their overseers.

to afflict them. i.e. to break their spirit.

burdens. Heavy burdens, carried out under compulsion. *store-cities.* Fortresses to protect the kingdom against possible invasion from the Asiatic side; and, at the same time, arsenals and granaries for Egyptian armies about to cross into Asia.

Pithom. In Egyptian Pi-Tum, 'the dwelling of the God Tum'; was identified by Naville in 1883 with the ruins in the Wady Tumilat about 60 miles N.E. of Cairo. He found a number of thick-walled rectangular chambers not communicating with one another, but filled from above, as required in the case of granaries. A. H. Gardiner places it eight miles farther west, at the modern Tell-er-Retabeh.

Raamses. The site on which later the Roman city Pelusium stood, at the mouth of the ancient Eastern branch of the Nile Delta on the Mediterranean (Gardiner). It was the capital of the Hyksos kings, and was enlarged and renamed at this time. In an inscription of Rameses II, recently found at Beisan, Palestine, he boasts that he built the city called after his name with *Semitic* slaves (Naville).

12. Pharaoh's first plan to destroy Israel—the first, too, known to history—had failed.

spread abroad. lit. 'breaking over limits'. They spread not only beyond the confines of Goshen, but beyond the borders of Egypt itself, into S. Palestinian territory, which was then under Egyptian sovereignty; see p. 395.

adread. Or, 'had an horror of.' They loathed the Israelites.

more they spread abroad. And they were adread because of the children of Israel. 13. And the Egyptians made the children of Israel to serve with rigour. 14. And they made their lives bitter with hard service, in mortar and in brick, and in all manner of service in the field; in all their service, wherein they made them serve with rigour. ¶ 15. And the king of Egypt spoke to the Hebrew midwives, of whom the name of the one was Shiphrah, and the name of the other Puah; 16. and he said: 'When ye do the office of a midwife to the Hebrew women, ye shall look upon the birthstool: if it be a son, then ye shall kill him; but if it be a daughter, then she shall live.' 17. But the midwives feared God, and did not as the king of Egypt commanded them, but saved the men-children alive.* ii. 18. And the king of Egypt called for the midwives, and said unto them: 'Why have ye done this thing, and have saved the men-children alive?' 19. And the midwives said unto Pharaoh: 'Because the Hebrew women are not as the Egyptian women;

13 אֹתוֹ כֵּן יִרְבֶּה וְכֵן יִפְרֹץ וַיָּקֻצוּ מִפְּנֵי בְּנֵי יִשְׂרָאֵל׃ וַיַּעֲבִדוּ
14 מִצְרַיִם אֶת־בְּנֵי יִשְׂרָאֵל בְּפָרֶךְ׃ וַיְמָרְרוּ אֶת־חַיֵּיהֶם
בַּעֲבֹדָה קָשָׁה בְּחֹמֶר וּבִלְבֵנִים וּבְכָל־עֲבֹדָה בַּשָּׂדֶה אֵת
טו כָּל־עֲבֹדָתָם אֲשֶׁר־עָבְדוּ בָהֶם בְּפָרֶךְ׃ וַיֹּאמֶר מֶלֶךְ
מִצְרַיִם לַמְיַלְּדֹת הָעִבְרִיֹּת אֲשֶׁר שֵׁם הָאַחַת שִׁפְרָה וְשֵׁם
16 הַשֵּׁנִית פּוּעָה׃ וַיֹּאמֶר בְּיַלֶּדְכֶן אֶת־הָעִבְרִיּוֹת וּרְאִיתֶן עַל־
הָאָבְנָיִם אִם־בֵּן הוּא וַהֲמִתֶּן אֹתוֹ וְאִם־בַּת הִוא וָחָיָה׃
17 וַתִּירֶאןָ הַמְיַלְּדֹת אֶת־הָאֱלֹהִים וְלֹא עָשׂוּ כַּאֲשֶׁר דִּבֶּר אֲלֵיהֶן
שני 18 מֶלֶךְ מִצְרָיִם וַתְּחַיֶּיןָ אֶת־הַיְלָדִים׃ וַיִּקְרָא מֶלֶךְ־מִצְרַיִם
לַמְיַלְּדֹת וַיֹּאמֶר לָהֶן מַדּוּעַ עֲשִׂיתֶן הַדָּבָר הַזֶּה וַתְּחַיֶּיןָ
19 אֶת־הַיְלָדִים׃ וַתֹּאמַרְןָ הַמְיַלְּדֹת אֶל־פַּרְעֹה כִּי לֹא כַנָּשִׁים
הַמִּצְרִיֹּת הָעִבְרִיֹּת כִּי־חָיוֹת הֵנָּה בְּטֶרֶם תָּבוֹא אֲלֵהֶן

13. *with rigour.* Or, 'with crushing oppression,' to annihilate both the energies and the spirit of the labourer, and calculated to bring about the degeneration of the Hebrew race. Sir H. H. Johnston, in his account of slavery in Africa, has shown that the horrible traffic in human beings, as in fact all slavery, often created in the master a deliberate love of cruelty, even when it entailed considerable commercial loss.

14. *in brick.* Bricks, stamped with the name of Rameses II, are in the British Museum.

in the field. For the difficult works of irrigation (see Deut. XI, 10). The water had to be brought to the high-lying fields artificially, by a series of buckets attached to long poles, worked on axles. Nothing was, and still is, as tiring in the daily life of the Egyptian as this irrigation of the fields (Erman).

15–22. Failing to weaken the Israelites by the corvée, Pharaoh now proposes infanticide.

15. *Hebrew midwives. i.e.* the Egyptian women who served as midwives to the Hebrews (Septuagint, Josephus, Abarbanel). It is hardly probable that the king would have expected Hebrew women to slay the children of their own people.

Shiphrah . . . Puah. The names are probably Egyptian. They were the two midwives in the capital, where Hebrew women would seek the services of a midwife (Strack). In the capital, furthermore, dwelt the 'better classes' of the children of Israel—their natural leaders. If Pharaoh could only succeed in exterminating these, he would experience little difficulty in rendering the slave portion harmless.

16. *then ye shall kill him.* The purpose of the king is to make an end of the Israelites altogether.

a daughter . . . shall live. These could not prove dangerous in time of war, and would be serviceable as slaves. The remnant of the Israelite people would thus be absorbed in the native population.

17. *feared God.* And would not be parties to a monstrous crime. The expression *fearing God* in Scripture is used in connection with heathens to denote the feeling which humanizes man's dealings with foreigners, even where national interests are supposed to be at stake; see note on Gen. XLII, 18. Thus, when Amalek attacked Israel, not in open warfare but stealthily, from the rear, slaying the old and the feeble, showing himself devoid of this natural piety and fundamental humanity, Scripture says of him, 'and he feared not God' (Deut. XXV, 18). The midwives were required by their king to act barbarously towards 'aliens'. But they preferred to obey the voice of human kindliness, the voice of conscience: 'the midwives feared God.' See also Gen. XX, 11.

19. *lively.* Better, *vigorous* (Ibn Ezra); *i.e.* the Hebrew women had greater vitality than the Egyptian women, and—like most Arabian women, ancient and modern—did not require the services of midwives; it would therefore be impossible to slay the child unperceived by the mother. The Heb. word *chayoth* may, however, be taken as a noun, meaning 'animals' (Talmud). The midwives would then have said to the king, 'The Hebrew women are not human; they are *animals*, and do not need a midwife.' Their loathing of the Hebrew women would disarm the suspicions of the king (Ehrlich, Yahuda).

for they are lively, and are delivered ere the midwife come unto them.' 20. And God dealt well with the midwives; and the people multiplied, and waxed very mighty. 21. And it came to pass, because the midwives feared God, that He made them houses. 22. And Pharaoh charged all his people, saying: 'Every son that is born ye shall cast into the river, and every daughter ye shall save alive.'

כ הַמְיַלֶּדֶת וְיָלָדוּ׃ וַיֵּיטֶב אֱלֹהִים לַמְיַלְּדֹת וַיִּרֶב הָעָם וַיַּעַצְמוּ
21 מְאֹד׃ וַיְהִי כִּי־יָרְאוּ הַמְיַלְּדֹת אֶת־הָאֱלֹהִים וַיַּעַשׂ לָהֶם
22 בָּתִּים׃ וַיְצַו פַּרְעֹה לְכָל־עַמּוֹ לֵאמֹר כָּל־הַבֵּן הַיִּלּוֹד הַיְאֹרָה
תַּשְׁלִיכֻהוּ וְכָל־הַבַּת תְּחַיּוּן׃ פ

2

Chapter II

1. And there went a man of the house of Levi, and took to wife a daughter of Levi. 2. And the woman conceived, and bore a son; and when she saw him that he was a goodly child, she hid him three months.

ב CAP. II. ב

א 2 וַיֵּלֶךְ אִישׁ מִבֵּית לֵוִי וַיִּקַּח אֶת־בַּת־לֵוִי׃ וַתַּהַר הָאִשָּׁה
וַתֵּלֶד בֵּן וַתֵּרֶא אֹתוֹ כִּי־טוֹב הוּא וַתִּצְפְּנֵהוּ שְׁלֹשָׁה יְרָחִים׃

21. *made them houses.* God built up their families or increased their prosperity. The verse may also be translated, 'And it came to pass, that because the midwives feared God, He made them (the Israelites) houses'; *i.e.* the people multiplied and increased abundantly.

22. *charged all his people.* In consequence of this continuous increase of the Israelites, and having failed in his measures with the midwives, Pharaoh now orders his people generally to drown the male children born to the Israelites. 'The whole people were now let loose against the Hebrews; spying and informing were made acts of loyalty, and compassion stamped as high treason' (Kalisch). While many would still, like the midwives, 'fear God,' others would now take a special delight in carrying out the command of the king.

cast into the river. The Spartans practised similar barbarities upon their helot population.

the river. i.e. the Nile. The longest river in the Old World, starting in the heart of Africa, and flowing northward, over 3,000 miles, into the Mediterranean. Egypt is by nature a rainless desert which the Nile, and the Nile only, converts into a garden every year. As most of the Israelites, however, lived away from the Nile such a savage decree could not have been strictly carried out, and must in time have become a dead letter. Rabbinic tradition states that the edict was in force some three years.

Chapter II

THE BIRTH AND EDUCATION OF MOSES

Providence overrules the despotic plans of men, and Israel's future deliverer is being prepared for his task in the very court of the merciless tyrant. The marvellous and unique emergence of a people from the midst of another land and people would be both impossible and inexplicable, apart from a great directing genius. This chapter opens the story of the Father of the Prophets, the Liberator and Teacher of Israel, the man who not only led the children of Israel from the Egyptian house of bondage, but brought them to Sinai and trained them to become a free people consecrated unto God and righteousness. 'Moses was a great artist, and possessed the true artistic spirit. But this spirit was directed by him, as by his Egyptian compatriots, to colossal and indestructible undertakings. He built human pyramids, carved human obelisks; he took a poor shepherd family and made a nation of it—a great, eternal, holy people: a people of God, destined to outlive the centuries, and to serve as a pattern to all other nations, a prototype to the whole of mankind. He created Israel' (Heine).

Even in its literary form this chapter is noteworthy. Few portions of Scripture condense so many dramatic incidents into a few verses. The power of the narrative only gains thereby.

1. *the house of Levi. i.e.* tribe of Levi. His name and that of his wife are given in VI, 20. Here the narrative *hastens on* to the story of the Redemption.

took to wife. The explicit language in these two verses brings out an important characteristic of Judaism. In other religions, the founders are represented as of supernatural birth. Not so in Judaism. Even Moses is human as to birth, as also in regard to death (Deut. XXXIV, 5).

2. *bore a son.* Two children had already been born to them—Miriam, the elder, was a young woman at the time of the birth of Moses; and Aaron, who was born three years before Moses. The king's order to drown the Israelite children must have been promulgated after the birth of Aaron, as his life had not been in peril.

when she saw. Better, *and she saw that he was a goodly child, and she hid,* etc.; because the mother would in any case have been anxious to preserve his life.

a goodly child. i.e. a 'good' child; not betraying his presence by crying, so that she could hide him for a space of three months (Luzzatto).

3. And when she could not longer hide him, she took for him an ark of bulrushes, and daubed it with slime and with pitch; and she put the child therein, and laid it in the flags by the river's brink. 4. And his sister stood afar off, to know what would be done to him. 5. And the daughter of Pharaoh came down to bathe in the river; and her maidens walked along by the river-side; and she saw the ark among the flags, and sent her handmaid to fetch it. 6. And she opened it, and saw it, even the child; and behold a boy that wept. And she had compassion on him, and said: 'This is one of the Hebrews' children.' 7. Then said his sister to Pharaoh's daughter: 'Shall I go and call thee a nurse of the Hebrew women, that she may nurse the child for thee?' 8. And Pharaoh's daughter said to her: 'Go.' And the maiden went and called the child's mother. 9. And Pharaoh's daughter said unto her: 'Take this child away, and nurse it for me, and I will give thee thy wages.' And the woman took the child, and nursed it. 10. And the child grew, and she brought him unto

3 וְלֹא־יָכְלָה עוֹד הַצְּפִינוֹ וַתִּקַּח־לוֹ תֵּבַת גֹּמֶא וַתַּחְמְרָה
בַחֵמָר וּבַזָּפֶת וַתָּשֶׂם בָה אֶת־הַיֶּלֶד וַתָּשֶׂם בַּסּוּף עַל־
4 שְׂפַת הַיְאֹר׃ וַתֵּתַצַּב אֲחֹתוֹ מֵרָחֹק לְדֵעָה מַה־יֵּעָשֶׂה
ה לוֹ׃ וַתֵּרֶד בַּת־פַּרְעֹה לִרְחֹץ עַל־הַיְאֹר וְנַעֲרֹתֶיהָ הֹלְכֹת
עַל־יַד הַיְאֹר וַתֵּרֶא אֶת־הַתֵּבָה בְּתוֹךְ הַסּוּף וַתִּשְׁלַח אֶת־
6 אֲמָתָהּ וַתִּקָּחֶהָ׃ וַתִּפְתַּח וַתִּרְאֵהוּ אֶת־הַיֶּלֶד וְהִנֵּה־נַעַר
7 בֹּכֶה וַתַּחְמֹל עָלָיו וַתֹּאמֶר מִיַּלְדֵי הָעִבְרִים זֶה׃ וַתֹּאמֶר
אֲחֹתוֹ אֶל־בַּת־פַּרְעֹה הַאֵלֵךְ וְקָרָאתִי לָךְ אִשָּׁה מֵינֶקֶת
8 מִן הָעִבְרִיֹּת וְתֵינִק לָךְ אֶת־הַיָּלֶד׃ וַתֹּאמֶר־לָהּ בַּת־פַּרְעֹה
9 לֵכִי וַתֵּלֶךְ הָעַלְמָה וַתִּקְרָא אֶת־אֵם הַיָּלֶד׃ וַתֹּאמֶר לָהּ
בַּת־פַּרְעֹה הֵילִיכִי אֶת־הַיֶּלֶד הַזֶּה וְהֵינִקִהוּ לִי וַאֲנִי אֶתֵּן
י אֶת־שְׂכָרֵךְ וַתִּקַּח הָאִשָּׁה הַיֶּלֶד וַתְּנִיקֵהוּ׃ וַיִּגְדַּל הַיֶּלֶד

v. 3. ה' בלא מפיק

3. *an ark.* A chest. The Heb. for 'ark' is elsewhere used only for Noah's ark.

bulrushes. The Heb. is an Egyptian loan-word. It denotes the paper-reed (called papyrus), growing ten to twelve feet high. Its leaves were used for making boats, mats, ropes and paper.

slime. i.e. bitumen—to make it watertight.

flags. A kind of reed, of smaller growth than the papyrus.

4. *stood.* Better, '*took her stand,*' not far from the place reserved for bathing.

5. *came down.* From her palace, probably at Zoan (Tanis), one of the chief royal residences in the Delta.

by the river-side. To give warning of an intrusion upon the privacy of the princess.

handmaid. Her personal attendant at the moment of bathing.

6. *a boy that wept.* lit. 'a weeping boy'.

she had compassion. Despite Pharaoh's orders, she is moved to spare the child. She 'feared God'.

one of the Hebrews' children. Only a Hebrew mother, in desperation to save her child from destruction, would thus expose it on the River.

7. *sister.* When she saw that the ark was found, she ventured to join the princess's attendants to see what would happen to her brother.

a nurse of the Hebrew women. lit. 'a woman giving suck'. A native Egyptian woman would not have undertaken to nurse a Hebrew child (Driver).

9. *give thee thy wages.* Pharaoh's plans for the annihilation of the Israelite children are defeated by women—the human feelings of the midwives, the tender sympathy of a woman of royal birth, and a sister's watchfulness and resource in extremity. 'It was to the merit of pious women, that Israel owed its redemption in Egypt,' say the Rabbis.

10. *the child grew.* He remained under his mother's care till he was quite a lad. During these most impressionable years of his life, his mother must have instilled into him the belief in one God, the Creator of heaven and earth, an Eternal Spirit without any shape or form that the mind of man could devise; and imparted to him the sacred traditions of Israel, the story of the Fathers in Canaan, of Joseph in Egypt, and of the Divine promise of deliverance from Egyptian bondage. When Moses returned to the Palace, he received, as the adopted child of the princess, the education of boys of the highest rank, probably at Heliopolis—'the Oxford of Ancient Egypt' (Stanley). There he 'must have learnt many things which from a Hebrew point of view would be extremely undesirable for him to know' (Driver). But whenever the priests undertook to initiate him into their fantastic idolatry, he remembered the teachings of his childhood; and he remained a Hebrew.

he became her son. He was adopted by the princess, and life at the Egyptian court gave him the training which was essential for a leader of men. 'Deep are the ways of Providence! It was His inscrutable intention that Moses should be reared in a Palace, that his spirit might remain

Pharaoh's daughter, and he became her son. And she called his name [1]Moses, and said: 'Because I [2]drew him out of the water.'* iii. ¶ 11. And it came to pass in those days, when Moses was grown up, that he went out unto his brethren, and looked on their burdens; and he saw an Egyptian smiting a Hebrew, one of his brethren. 12. And he looked this way and that way, and when he saw that there was no man, he smote the Egyptian, and hid him in the sand. 13. And he went out the second day, and, behold, two men of the Hebrews were striving together; and he said to him that did the wrong: 'Wherefore smitest thou thy fellow?' 14. And he said: 'Who made thee a ruler and a judge over us? thinkest thou to kill me, as thou didst kill

[1] Heb. *Mosheh*. [2] Heb. *mashah*, to draw out.

שלישי
וַתְּבִאֵהוּ לְבַת־פַּרְעֹה וַיְהִי־לָהּ לְבֵן וַתִּקְרָא שְׁמוֹ מֹשֶׁה
11 וַתֹּאמֶר כִּי מִן־הַמַּיִם מְשִׁיתִהוּ׃ * וַיְהִי ׀ בַּיָּמִים הָהֵם וַיִּגְדַּל
מֹשֶׁה וַיֵּצֵא אֶל־אֶחָיו וַיַּרְא בְּסִבְלֹתָם וַיַּרְא אִישׁ מִצְרִי
12 מַכֶּה אִישׁ־עִבְרִי מֵאֶחָיו׃ וַיִּפֶן כֹּה וָכֹה וַיַּרְא כִּי־אֵין אִישׁ
13 וַיַּךְ אֶת־הַמִּצְרִי וַיִּטְמְנֵהוּ בַּחוֹל׃ וַיֵּצֵא בַּיּוֹם הַשֵּׁנִי וְהִנֵּה
שְׁנֵי־אֲנָשִׁים עִבְרִים נִצִּים וַיֹּאמֶר לָרָשָׁע לָמָּה תַכֶּה רֵעֶךָ׃
14 וַיֹּאמֶר מִי שָׂמְךָ לְאִישׁ שַׂר וְשֹׁפֵט עָלֵינוּ הַלְהָרְגֵנִי אַתָּה
אֹמֵר כַּאֲשֶׁר הָרַגְתָּ אֶת־הַמִּצְרִי וַיִּירָא מֹשֶׁה וַיֹּאמַר אָכֵן

uncurbed by the oppressive and enervating influence of slavery. Thus he slew the Egyptian because his heart could not see violence and injustice, and from the same generous motive he took the part of the daughters of Reuel against the shepherds. It served another purpose also. Had he always lived amongst his own people, they would not so readily have accepted him as their leader, nor would they have shown him the respect and deference which were essential for the accomplishment of his great mission' (Ibn Ezra).

Moses. Heb. *Mosheh*, the Hebraised reproduction of an Egyptian word which probably means, 'child of the Nile' (Yahuda). The explanation of the name given in the text ('because I drew him out of the water') rests upon the similarity of sound, as is repeatedly seen in Genesis; the word *Mosheh* resembling the word for, 'the one who is drawn out.'

11. *when Moses was grown up.* lit. 'when Moses became great', he went out *to* his brethren. In later ages it must alas be said of many a son of Israel who had become great, that he went away *from* his brethren. Not so Moses. He went out of the Palace into the brick-fields where his brethren toiled and agonized in cruel bondage. It was lovingkindness to his people that impelled him to do so. There are ten strong things in the world, say the Rabbis: rock is strong but iron cleaves it; fire melts iron; water extinguishes fire; the clouds bear aloft the water; the wind drives away the clouds; man withstands the wind; fear unmans man; wine dispels fear; sleep overcomes wine; and death sweeps away even sleep. But strongest of all is lovingkindness, for it defies and survives death. Now Moses was filled with lovingkindness. Full of pity, he watched his brethren groaning beneath their burdens. 'What has Israel done to deserve such wretchedness?' he wondered.

an Egyptian smiting. Probably one of the taskmasters applying the lash to an Israelite. We know only too well from ancient writings and paintings what the flogging of slaves was like. Moses for the first time saw a poor Hebrew flogged, and it was more than he could bear. His loyalty to his kin had not been destroyed by his Egyptian upbringing.

12. *he smote.* Moses resembles 'the great patriots of the past and the present, who have taken the sword to deliver their people from the hands of tyrants. His act may be condemned as hasty. In its immediate results it was fruitless, as is every intemperate attempt to right a wrong by violence. However, it allied Moses definitely with his kinsmen' (Kent).

13. *to him that did the wrong. i.e.* to the man who was in the wrong.

14. *who made thee a ruler.* A typical attitude of a small but persistent Jewish minority towards anyone working for Israel. The Rabbis speak of it as the Dathan-and-Abiram type of mind (cf. Num. XVI).

surely the thing is known. Referring to the death of the Egyptian. The Midrash takes these words as an answer to his question why Israel should suffer such slavery. Now he knew the reason: they deserved it. 'It is characteristic of the faithfulness of the Sacred Record that his flight is occasioned rather by the malignity of his countrymen than by the enmity of the Egyptians' (Stanley).

The first action of Moses shows him swept away by fierce indignation against the oppressor; the second, anxious to restore harmony among the oppressed. In both these acts, Moses is seen burning with patriotic ardour. His nature, however, requires to be freed from impetuous passion. In the desert whither he is now fleeing, his spirit will be purified and deepened, and he will return as the destined Liberator of his brethren.

the Egyptian?' And Moses feared, and said: 'Surely the thing is known.' 15. Now when Pharaoh heard this thing, he sought to slay Moses. But Moses fled from the face of Pharaoh, and dwelt in the land of Midian; and he sat down by a well. 16. Now the priest of Midian had seven daughters; and they came and drew water, and filled the troughs to water their father's flock. 17. And the shepherds came and drove them away; but Moses stood up and helped them, and watered their flock. 18. And when they came to Reuel their father, he said: 'How is it that ye are come so soon to-day?' 19. And they said: 'An Egyptian delivered us out of the hand of the shepherds, and moreover he drew water for us, and watered the flock.' 20. And he said unto his daughters: 'And where is he? why is it that ye have left the man? call him, that he may eat bread.' 21. And Moses was content to dwell with the man; and he gave Moses Zipporah his daughter. 22. And she bore a son, and he called his name Gershom; for he said: 'I have been [1]a stranger in a strange land.' ¶ 23. And it came to pass in the course of those many days that the king of Egypt died; and the children of Israel sighed by reason of the bondage, and they cried,

טו נוֹדַע הַדָּבָר׃ וַיִּשְׁמַע פַּרְעֹה אֶת־הַדָּבָר הַזֶּה וַיְבַקֵּשׁ לַהֲרֹג
אֶת־מֹשֶׁה וַיִּבְרַח מֹשֶׁה מִפְּנֵי פַרְעֹה וַיֵּשֶׁב בְּאֶרֶץ־מִדְיָן
16 וַיֵּשֶׁב עַל־הַבְּאֵר׃ וּלְכֹהֵן מִדְיָן שֶׁבַע בָּנוֹת וַתָּבֹאנָה
וַתִּדְלֶנָה וַתְּמַלֶּאנָה אֶת־הָרְהָטִים לְהַשְׁקוֹת צֹאן אֲבִיהֶן׃
17 וַיָּבֹאוּ הָרֹעִים וַיְגָרְשׁוּם וַיָּקָם מֹשֶׁה וַיּוֹשִׁעָן וַיַּשְׁקְ אֶת־
18 צֹאנָם׃ וַתָּבֹאנָה אֶל־רְעוּאֵל אֲבִיהֶן וַיֹּאמֶר מַדּוּעַ מִהַרְתֶּן
19 בֹּא הַיּוֹם׃ וַתֹּאמַרְןָ אִישׁ מִצְרִי הִצִּילָנוּ מִיַּד הָרֹעִים וְגַם־
כ דָּלֹה דָלָה לָנוּ וַיַּשְׁקְ אֶת־הַצֹּאן׃ וַיֹּאמֶר אֶל־בְּנֹתָיו וְאַיּוֹ
21 לָמָּה זֶּה עֲזַבְתֶּן אֶת־הָאִישׁ קִרְאֶן לוֹ וְיֹאכַל לָחֶם׃ וַיּוֹאֶל
מֹשֶׁה לָשֶׁבֶת אֶת־הָאִישׁ וַיִּתֵּן אֶת־צִפֹּרָה בִתּוֹ לְמֹשֶׁה׃
22 וַתֵּלֶד בֵּן וַיִּקְרָא אֶת־שְׁמוֹ גֵּרְשֹׁם כִּי אָמַר גֵּר הָיִיתִי
בְּאֶרֶץ נָכְרִיָּה׃ פ
23 וַיְהִי בַיָּמִים הָרַבִּים הָהֵם וַיָּמָת מֶלֶךְ מִצְרַיִם וַיֵּאָנְחוּ בְנֵי־
יִשְׂרָאֵל מִן־הָעֲבֹדָה וַיִּזְעָקוּ וַתַּעַל שַׁוְעָתָם אֶל־הָאֱלֹהִים מִן־

[1] Heb. *ger.*

15–22. Moses in Midian

15. *Midian.* In the south-eastern part of the Sinai peninsula. Here he would be beyond Egyptian jurisdiction. The main home of the Midianites appears to have been on the east side of the Gulf of Akabah.

16. *priest of Midian.* Heb. *kohen*, which does not necessarily mean *priest.* It may also mean 'chief'. And so Onkelos and Rashi translate it here. The sons of David are likewise termed *kohanim* in II Sam. VIII, 18, where it only means, nobles or officers.

to water their father's flock. Even to this day the young women tend the sheep among the Bedouin of the Sinai peninsula.

17. *drove them away.* These 'chivalrous' Arabs wished to water their own sheep first, although the women had already filled the troughs. Moses again takes the part of the injured side, but this time without violence.

18. *Reuel their father.* Reuel seems to have been their father, while Jethro was the father-in-law of Moses. The word Jethro means, 'His Excellence,' and may be regarded as a title borne by the priest or chief of Midian, whose proper name is given in Num. X, 28, as Hobab. Reuel, therefore, was the grandfather (often called 'father' in Scripture; see Gen. XXVII, 13 and XXXII, 10) of the shepherdesses. If Jethro and Reuel are taken as one person, there is nothing unusual in one man having two names (*e.g.* Jacob, Israel); and South Arabian inscriptions show many chieftains having two names.

ye are come so soon. Reuel was familiar with the usual delay caused by the interference of the shepherds.

19. *an Egyptian.* Moses' dress and speech would be Egyptian.

drew water for us. lit. 'he actually drew water for us'; they are surprised at the kindness of his action in helping them to draw water.

20. *where is he?* Expresses displeasure that they had failed in hospitality towards the stranger who had befriended them.

21. *was content.* Or, 'agreed.' One cannot help contrasting the breadth with which the wooing of both Isaac and Jacob is recounted, with the extraordinary, nay irreducible, brevity with which the wooing of Moses is told. What we would call the 'romantic' element in the story of Moses disappears like a bubble; it is the woe of his People that engrosses his mind.

Zipporah. The meaning of this name is 'bird'. The Midianites spoke a language kindred to Hebrew.

22. *Gershom.* Heb. *ger*, 'a stranger,' and *sham*, 'there,' in a strange land. His heart was with his suffering brethren in Egypt.

strange land. i.e. foreign land.

23–25. Transition to the Call and Commission of Moses.

and their cry came up unto God by reason of the bondage. 24. And God heard their groaning, and God remembered His covenant with Abraham, with Isaac, and with Jacob. 25. And God saw the children of Israel, and God took cognizance of them.* iv.

3

Chapter III

1. Now Moses was keeping the flock of Jethro his father-in-law, the priest of Midian; and he led the flock to the farthest end of the wilderness, and came to the mountain of God, unto Horeb. 2. And the angel of the LORD appeared unto him in a flame of fire out of the midst of a bush; and he looked, and, behold, the bush burned with fire, and the bush was not consumed. 3. And Moses said: 'I will turn aside now, and see this great sight, why the bush is not burnt.' 4. And when the LORD saw that he turned aside to see,

24 הָעֲבֹדָה: וַיִּשְׁמַע אֱלֹהִים אֶת־נַאֲקָתָם וַיִּזְכֹּר אֱלֹהִים אֶת־
כה בְּרִיתוֹ אֶת־אַבְרָהָם אֶת־יִצְחָק וְאֶת־יַעֲקֹב: וַיַּרְא אֱלֹהִים
אֶת־בְּנֵי יִשְׂרָאֵל וַיֵּדַע אֱלֹהִים:* ס רביעי

Cap. III. ג

ג

א וּמֹשֶׁה הָיָה רֹעֶה אֶת־צֹאן יִתְרוֹ חֹתְנוֹ כֹּהֵן מִדְיָן וַיִּנְהַג
אֶת־הַצֹּאן אַחַר הַמִּדְבָּר וַיָּבֹא אֶל־הַר הָאֱלֹהִים חֹרֵבָה:
2 וַיֵּרָא מַלְאַךְ יְהוָה אֵלָיו בְּלַבַּת־אֵשׁ מִתּוֹךְ הַסְּנֶה וַיַּרְא
3 וְהִנֵּה הַסְּנֶה בֹּעֵר בָּאֵשׁ וְהַסְּנֶה אֵינֶנּוּ אֻכָּל: וַיֹּאמֶר מֹשֶׁה
אָסֻרָה־נָּא וְאֶרְאֶה אֶת־הַמַּרְאֶה הַגָּדֹל הַזֶּה מַדּוּעַ לֹא־
4 יִבְעַר הַסְּנֶה: וַיַּרְא יְהוָה כִּי סָר לִרְאוֹת וַיִּקְרָא אֵלָיו

ג׳ v. 1. בתביר

23. *many days.* Rabbinic tradition assigns 40 years to the period spent by Moses in exile from Egypt.

the king of Egypt died. Probably Rameses II, who reigned 67 years. The Israelites evidently hoped that his successor, Meremptah, might offer them some relief; but they were disappointed. The regime of ruthless oppression towards Israel would now become the *status quo.* They realize the hopelessness of their bondage. Therefore, 'they cried unto God.'

24. *remembered His covenant.* Not that He had forgotten it, but that now the opportunity had come for the fulfilment of His merciful purposes.

25. *took cognizance of them.* God did not close His eyes to their suffering (Rashi), but He chose His own time when to send deliverance and cause Israel to go forth from Egypt. See also Additional Note B, 'Israel and Egypt: the Spiritual Contrast,' p. 396.

Chapters III and IV. The Call of Moses

1. *keeping the flock.* God never gives an exalted office to a man unless He has first tested him in small things, say the Rabbis. When feeding the flocks of Jethro, they tell us, Moses saw a little lamb escape from the flock, and when he followed it, he overtook it at a brook quenching its thirst. 'Had I known that thou wast thirsty, I would have taken thee in my arms and carried thee hither,' he said. 'As thou livest,' a Heavenly Voice resounded, 'thou art fit to shepherd Israel' (Midrash).

to the farthest end of the wilderness. Behind or beyond the wilderness, as the scanty shrubs in the wilderness itself were insufficient for the flock. 'The solemn solitude of the dreary desert was to prepare his mind for the sublime commission for which Providence had selected him' (Kalisch).

mountain of God. So called because the Glory of God was later manifested there. The spot chosen by God to announce the physical redemption of Israel was also chosen by Him as the place of their spiritual redemption.

Horeb. Horeb is the mountain and district, Sinai the summit itself; or, the two names refer to two peaks of the same mountain range, which some identify with Jebel Musa (7,636 feet), others with Mount Serbal (6,734 feet), in the Sinai Peninsula. The aridity and dryness of this region have been much exaggerated. In the highest region, fertile valleys are found, with fruit trees and water in plenty.

2. *angel of the* LORD. The angel in Scripture is not to be identified with God. The angel is the messenger of God and speaks in His name, and is often called by the Name of Him who sent him (see *v.* 4). The speech and action are the work of the angel, but the thought or will is God's.

in a flame of fire. Or, 'in the heart of the fire'; *i.e.* in the midst of fire (Maimonides).

bush. *i.e.* the thorn-bush, the wild acacia which is the characteristic shrub of that region.

was not consumed. The burning bush has often been taken as a symbol of Israel—small and lowly among the nations, and yet indestructible; because of the Divine Spirit that dwelleth within Israel.

4. *God called unto him.* *i.e.* the angel of God, mentioned in *v.* 2. The angel is here spoken of as

God called unto him out of the midst of the bush, and said: 'Moses, Moses.' And he said: 'Here am I.' 5. And He said: 'Draw not nigh hither; put off thy shoes from off thy feet, for the place whereon thou standest is holy ground.' 6. Moreover He said: 'I am the God of thy father, the God of Abraham, the God of Isaac, and the God of Jacob.' And Moses hid his face; for he was afraid to look upon God. 7. And the LORD said: 'I have surely seen the affliction of My people that are in Egypt and have heard their cry by reason of their taskmasters; for I know their pains; 8. and I am come down to deliver them out of the hand of the Egyptians, and to bring them up out of that land unto a good land and a large, unto a land flowing with milk and honey; unto the place of the Canaanite, and the Hittite, and the Amorite, and the Perizzite, and the Hivite, and the Jebusite. 9. And now, behold, the cry of the children of Israel is come unto Me; moreover I have seen the oppression wherewith the Egyptians oppress them. 10. Come now therefore,

אֱלֹהִים מִתּוֹךְ הַסְּנֶה וַיֹּאמֶר מֹשֶׁה מֹשֶׁה וַיֹּאמֶר הִנֵּנִי׃
ה וַיֹּאמֶר אַל־תִּקְרַב הֲלֹם שַׁל־נְעָלֶיךָ מֵעַל רַגְלֶיךָ כִּי הַמָּקוֹם
6 אֲשֶׁר אַתָּה עוֹמֵד עָלָיו אַדְמַת־קֹדֶשׁ הוּא׃ וַיֹּאמֶר אָנֹכִי
אֱלֹהֵי אָבִיךָ אֱלֹהֵי אַבְרָהָם אֱלֹהֵי יִצְחָק וֵאלֹהֵי יַעֲקֹב
7 וַיַּסְתֵּר מֹשֶׁה פָּנָיו כִּי יָרֵא מֵהַבִּיט אֶל־הָאֱלֹהִים׃ וַיֹּאמֶר
יְהוָה רָאֹה רָאִיתִי אֶת־עֳנִי עַמִּי אֲשֶׁר בְּמִצְרָיִם וְאֶת־
צַעֲקָתָם שָׁמַעְתִּי מִפְּנֵי נֹגְשָׂיו כִּי יָדַעְתִּי אֶת־מַכְאֹבָיו׃
8 וָאֵרֵד לְהַצִּילוֹ ׀ מִיַּד מִצְרַיִם וּלְהַעֲלֹתוֹ מִן־הָאָרֶץ הַהִוא
אֶל־אֶרֶץ טוֹבָה וּרְחָבָה אֶל־אֶרֶץ זָבַת חָלָב וּדְבָשׁ אֶל־
מְקוֹם הַכְּנַעֲנִי וְהַחִתִּי וְהָאֱמֹרִי וְהַפְּרִזִּי וְהַחִוִּי וְהַיְבוּסִי׃
9 וְעַתָּה הִנֵּה צַעֲקַת בְּנֵי־יִשְׂרָאֵל בָּאָה אֵלָי וְגַם־רָאִיתִי אֶת־
י הַלַּחַץ אֲשֶׁר מִצְרַיִם לֹחֲצִים אֹתָם׃ וְעַתָּה לְכָה וְאֶשְׁלָחֲךָ

v. 4. משה משה בלא פסיק ביניהן

God, because he represents the Almighty (Ibn Ezra).

Moses, Moses. God here addresses Moses by his name. 'The repetition of the name is an expression of affection intended to encourage him' (Mechilta); cf. *Abraham, Abraham,* in Gen. XXII, 11; and *Jacob, Jacob,* in Gen. XLVI, 2. God's choice is never groundless or arbitrary. Moses' warm heart for his brethren, and his burning indignation against all injustice, made him worthy of God's love and choice.

5. *holy ground.* Every spot where God manifests Himself is holy ground.

6. *thy father. i.e.* thy fathers; the word is here used collectively (Onkelos), and is explained by the words, 'the God of Abraham, Isaac and Jacob'; see XV, 2. The Midrash, however, refers the word 'father' to Amram, the father of Moses. It was with his father's voice that the angel of God addressed him, 'I am the God of thy father, *i.e.* the God of whom thy father spake, the unchangeable God of eternity, who is now about to fulfil the promise given to Israel's ancestors.'

hid his face. Or, 'covered his face' (Jerusalem Targum) in reverence (cf. I Kings XIX, 13). In the presence of the All-holy, an instant and irresistible feeling of human nothingness overpowers him. In sacred awe before the majesty of the Godhead, he hides his face. No mortal eye is worthy of beholding God. Even the angels are not pure in His sight; and, therefore, in the vision of Isaiah VI, 2, they are spoken of as covering their faces and bodies; see p. 302.

7. *My people.* This is the first time Israel is so called: God had made their cause His own. 'God always takes the side of the persecuted,' say the Rabbis.

heard their cry. See II, 23–25. The cry of the Israelites was the cry of human beings who were being inhumanly treated, a cry of despair that ascends to the very throne of the Almighty.

for I know their pains. Better, *indeed, I know their sorrows.*

8. *I am come down.* A similar human way of speaking of the Divine (*anthropomorphism*) occurs in XIX, 11.

flowing with milk and honey. A proverbial expression, often applied to Canaan, see XIII, 5; Num. XIII, 27. The description of the Promised Land is here required, because Moses does not know it from personal observation.

the Canaanite. The general name for all the peoples inhabiting ancient Palestine. Originally Canaan, meaning *the Lowland,* was applied only to the coast of Phœnicia and the land of the Philistines; see Gen. X, 6.

the Hittite. A powerful and warlike nation whose seat was Asia Minor; an offshoot of this people lived in Southern Palestine; see Gen. XXIII.

Amorite. Originally a warlike tribe inhabiting the hill country, behind Phœnicia. Later, it was the name for all pre-Israelitish inhabitants of Canaan (Amos II, 9).

Perizzite, Hivite. Seem to have lived in Central Palestine.

Jebusite. This tribe inhabited Jerusalem.

and I will send thee unto Pharaoh, that thou mayest bring forth My people the children of Israel out of Egypt.' 11. And Moses said unto God: 'Who am I, that I should go unto Pharaoh, and that I should bring forth the children of Israel out of Egypt?' 12. And He said: 'Certainly I will be with thee; and this shall be the token unto thee, that I have sent thee: when thou hast brought forth the people out of Egypt, ye shall serve God upon this mountain.' 13. And Moses said unto God: 'Behold, when I come unto the children of Israel, and shall say unto them: The God of your fathers hath sent me unto you: and they shall say to me: What is His name? what shall I say unto them?' 14. And God said unto Moses: 'I AM THAT I AM'; and He said: 'Thus shalt thou say unto the children of Israel: I AM hath sent me unto you.' 15. And God said moreover unto Moses: 'Thus shalt thou say unto the children of Israel: The LORD, the God of your fathers, the God of Abraham, the

11 אֶל־פַּרְעֹה וְהוֹצֵא אֶת־עַמִּי בְנֵי־יִשְׂרָאֵל מִמִּצְרָיִם׃ וַיֹּאמֶר
מֹשֶׁה אֶל־הָאֱלֹהִים מִי אָנֹכִי כִּי אֵלֵךְ אֶל־פַּרְעֹה וְכִי
12 אוֹצִיא אֶת־בְּנֵי יִשְׂרָאֵל מִמִּצְרָיִם׃ וַיֹּאמֶר כִּי־אֶהְיֶה
עִמָּךְ וְזֶה־לְּךָ הָאוֹת כִּי אָנֹכִי שְׁלַחְתִּיךָ בְּהוֹצִיאֲךָ אֶת־
הָעָם מִמִּצְרַיִם תַּעַבְדוּן אֶת־הָאֱלֹהִים עַל הָהָר הַזֶּה׃
13 וַיֹּאמֶר מֹשֶׁה אֶל־הָאֱלֹהִים הִנֵּה אָנֹכִי בָא אֶל־בְּנֵי יִשְׂרָאֵל
וְאָמַרְתִּי לָהֶם אֱלֹהֵי אֲבוֹתֵיכֶם שְׁלָחַנִי אֲלֵיכֶם וְאָמְרוּ־לִי
14 מַה־שְּׁמוֹ מָה אֹמַר אֲלֵהֶם׃ וַיֹּאמֶר אֱלֹהִים אֶל־מֹשֶׁה אֶהְיֶה
אֲשֶׁר אֶהְיֶה וַיֹּאמֶר כֹּה תֹאמַר לִבְנֵי יִשְׂרָאֵל אֶהְיֶה שְׁלָחַנִי
טו אֲלֵיכֶם׃ וַיֹּאמֶר עוֹד אֱלֹהִים אֶל־מֹשֶׁה כֹּה תֹאמַר אֶל־
בְּנֵי יִשְׂרָאֵל יְהוָה אֱלֹהֵי אֲבֹתֵיכֶם אֱלֹהֵי אַבְרָהָם אֱלֹהֵי

11–12. MOSES' FIRST DIFFICULTY: HE IS UNSUITED FOR HIS MISSION

11. *who am I.* How different was Moses' attitude in his youth! With age, Moses can only think of his own unfitness for the gigantic undertaking; cf. Jeremiah's diffidence to assume the Prophet's office, Jer. I, 6 f; see p. 229.

12. *I will be with thee.* This tremendous fact of the reality of the Divine help would make it possible for Moses, an old man of eighty years, to face Pharaoh and demand the emancipation of his enslaved brethren. Moses' humility, therefore, is here out of place; and, when persisted in, earns him a Divine rebuke (IV, 14).

this shall be the token. i.e. the proof that thou art sent by God will be that in this very place, where thou art now doubting the possibility of redemption, the children of Israel will worship, in thanksgiving, the God who will have brought them out of the land of bondage.

serve God upon this mountain. See XIX, 3 f.

13–22. MOSES' SECOND DIFFICULTY: THE 'NAME' OF GOD

13. *when I come. i.e.* assuming that I come.

what is His name? Heb. מה שמו. Not an inquiry for information as to what God is *called*. Moses comes to Israel with the words, 'the God of your fathers hath sent me unto you.' It is, therefore, hardly conceivable that he should proclaim a God quite unknown unto them, as the God of their Fathers (G. B. Gray). They must have known what He was *called*, 'since nothing is more un-Biblical than the idea of an "Unknown God"' (B. Jacob). But since *name* means fame, 'record,' and in IX, 16 is the synonym of 'power', *What is His name?* means 'What are the mighty deeds which thou canst recount of Him—what is His power—that we should listen to thy message from Him?'

14. I AM THAT I AM. Heb. *Ehyeh asher ehyeh*—the self-existent and eternal God; a declaration of the unity and spirituality of the Divine Nature, the exact opposite of all the forms of idolatry, human, animal, and celestial, that prevailed everywhere else. *I am that I am* is, however, not merely a philosophical phrase; the emphasis is on *the active manifestation* of the Divine existence; cf. the explanation of the Midrash, אהיה אשר אהיה אני נקרא לפי מעשי. To the Israelites in bondage, the meaning would be, 'Although He has not yet displayed His power towards you, He will do so; He is eternal and will certainly redeem you.'

Most moderns follow Rashi in rendering '*I will be what I will be*'; *i.e.* no words can sum up all that He will be to His people, but His everlasting faithfulness and unchanging mercy will more and more manifest themselves in the guidance of Israel. The answer which Moses receives in these words is thus equivalent to, 'I shall save in the way that I shall save.' It is to assure the Israelites of the *fact* of deliverance, but does not disclose the *manner*. It must suffice the Israelites to learn that, 'Ehyeh, I WILL BE (with you), hath sent me unto you.'

15. *the LORD.* This is the translation of the Divine Name written in the four Hebrew letters Y H W H and always pronounced 'Adonay' (see *Genesis*, p. 6). This Divine Name of four letters—the Tetragrammaton—comes from the same Heb. root (*hayah*) as *Ehyeh;* viz. 'to be'. It gives expression to the fact that He was, He

God of Isaac, and the God of Jacob, hath sent me unto you; this is My name for ever, and this is My memorial unto all generations.* v. 16. Go, and gather the elders of Israel together, and say unto them: The LORD, the God of your fathers, the God of Abraham, of Isaac, and of Jacob, hath appeared unto me, saying: I have surely remembered you, and seen that which is done to you in Egypt. 17. And I have said: I will bring you up out of the affliction of Egypt unto the land of the Canaanite, and the Hittite, and the Amorite, and the Perizzite, and the Hivite, and the Jebusite, unto a land flowing with milk and honey. 18. And they shall hearken to thy voice. And thou shalt come, thou and the elders of Israel, unto the king of Egypt, and ye shall say unto him: The LORD, the God of the Hebrews, hath met with us. And now let us go, we pray thee, three days' journey into the wilderness, that we may sacrifice to the LORD our God. 19. And I know that the king of Egypt will not give you leave to go, except by a mighty hand. 20. And I will put forth My hand, and smite Egypt with all My wonders which I will do in the midst thereof. And after that he will let you go. 21. And

יִצְחָק וֵאלֹהֵי יַעֲקֹב שְׁלָחַנִי אֲלֵיכֶם זֶה־שְּׁמִי לְעֹלָם וְזֶה
חמישי
16 זִכְרִי לְדֹר דֹּר׃* לֵךְ וְאָסַפְתָּ אֶת־זִקְנֵי יִשְׂרָאֵל וְאָמַרְתָּ
אֲלֵהֶם יְהוָה אֱלֹהֵי אֲבֹתֵיכֶם נִרְאָה אֵלַי אֱלֹהֵי אַבְרָהָם
יִצְחָק וְיַעֲקֹב לֵאמֹר פָּקֹד פָּקַדְתִּי אֶתְכֶם וְאֶת־הֶעָשׂוּי
17 לָכֶם בְּמִצְרָיִם׃ וָאֹמַר אַעֲלֶה אֶתְכֶם מֵעֳנִי מִצְרַיִם אֶל־
אֶרֶץ הַכְּנַעֲנִי וְהַחִתִּי וְהָאֱמֹרִי וְהַפְּרִזִּי וְהַחִוִּי וְהַיְבוּסִי אֶל־
18 אֶרֶץ זָבַת חָלָב וּדְבָשׁ׃ וְשָׁמְעוּ לְקֹלֶךָ וּבָאתָ אַתָּה וְזִקְנֵי
יִשְׂרָאֵל אֶל־מֶלֶךְ מִצְרַיִם וַאֲמַרְתֶּם אֵלָיו יְהוָה אֱלֹהֵי
הָעִבְרִיִּים נִקְרָה עָלֵינוּ וְעַתָּה נֵלְכָה־נָּא דֶּרֶךְ שְׁלֹשֶׁת יָמִים
19 בַּמִּדְבָּר וְנִזְבְּחָה לַיהוָה אֱלֹהֵינוּ׃ וַאֲנִי יָדַעְתִּי כִּי לֹא־יִתֵּן
כ אֶתְכֶם מֶלֶךְ מִצְרַיִם לַהֲלֹךְ וְלֹא בְּיָד חֲזָקָה׃ וְשָׁלַחְתִּי
אֶת־יָדִי וְהִכֵּיתִי אֶת־מִצְרַיִם בְּכֹל נִפְלְאֹתַי אֲשֶׁר אֶעֱשֶׂה
21 בְּקִרְבּוֹ וְאַחֲרֵי־כֵן יְשַׁלַּח אֶתְכֶם׃ וְנָתַתִּי אֶת־חֵן הָעָם־

is, and He ever will be. Here, too, the words must not be understood in the philosophical sense of mere 'being', but as active manifestation of the Divine existence. According to the Rabbis, this Name stresses the lovingkindness and faithfulness of God in relation to His creatures: He who educates, punishes, and guides; He who hears the cry of the oppressed, and makes known His ways of righteousness unto the children of men. He is the great Living God who reveals Himself in the Providential care of His people.

the LORD, the God of your fathers. Not a deity discovered by Moses in Midian, but the same God who had revealed Himself to their fathers, the Creator of the world and the righteous Judge of all the earth—*Adonay*—the ever-living God of faithfulness and lovingkindness, hath sent him unto them.

this is My memorial. The designation by which I will be remembered. 'Memorial' is a synonym of 'Name'; Hos. XII, 6 (*Genesis*, p. 136).

16. *the elders of Israel.* It seems that the Israelites had a representative national organization consisting of the elders or leading men in each family; see v, 5.

the LORD, the God of your fathers. This shows that the elders, as well as the people, are acquainted with the Name of God. 'What impression could Moses have possibly hoped to make upon them with an altogether new Name?' (B. Jacob).

Remembered you. i.e. borne you in mind.

18. *shall hearken.* Better, *will hearken.*

the God of the Hebrews. As distinct from the gods of the Egyptians.

hath met with us. Through Moses, who represented the whole people.

three days' journey. A current expression for a considerable distance; Gen. XXX, 36; Num. X, 33. 'The Israelites were to ask what could not reasonably be refused, being a demand quite in accordance with Egyptian customs. . . . It is important to observe that the first request which Pharaoh rejected could have been granted without any damage to Egypt, or any risk of the Israelites passing the strongly fortified frontier' (Speaker's Bible). The request was *not* granted; and so it resolved itself in the end into a demand for the unconditional release of the people and their actual departure.

20. *with all My wonders. i.e.* the plagues.

21. *will give this people favour.* The Egyptian people are throughout far friendlier to the Israelites than the hard-hearted king. Not only will they let the Israelites go, but God will dispose them favourably towards the Israelites.

when ye go, ye shall not go empty. To understand this phrase and the promise it contains, we must recall Deut. XV, 12 f, which ordains that when a faithful servant leaves his master after many years' service, he is to be liberally equipped from his owner's property. 'When thou lettest

הַזֶּ֖ה בְּעֵינֵ֣י מִצְרָ֑יִם וְהָיָה֙ כִּ֣י תֵֽלֵכ֔וּן לֹ֥א תֵלְכ֖וּ רֵיקָֽם׃
22 וְשָׁאֲלָ֨ה אִשָּׁ֤ה מִשְּׁכֶנְתָּהּ֙ וּמִגָּרַ֣ת בֵּיתָ֔הּ כְּלֵי־כֶ֛סֶף וּכְלֵ֥י
זָהָ֖ב וּשְׂמָלֹ֑ת וְשַׂמְתֶּ֗ם עַל־בְּנֵיכֶם֙ וְעַל־בְּנֹ֣תֵיכֶ֔ם וְנִצַּלְתֶּ֖ם
אֶת־מִצְרָֽיִם׃

I will give this people favour in the sight of the Egyptians. And it shall come to pass, that, when ye go, ye shall not go empty; 22. but every woman shall ask of her neighbour, and of her that sojourneth in her house, jewels of silver, and jewels of gold, and raiment; and ye shall put them upon your sons, and upon your daughters; and ye shall spoil the Egyptians.'

him go free from thee, thou shalt not let him go empty; thou shalt furnish him liberally out of thy flock, out of thy threshing-floor, and out of thy wine-press.' The phrase, 'Thou shalt furnish him liberally,' is a paraphrase of the Heb. העניק תעניק לו, which means lit. 'make him a necklace'—the metaphor being that of ornamenting and embellishing, of giving some striking gift as from a man who wishes to show his lasting regard for the servant who had served him faithfully through many years. Such—God announces unto Moses—will be the farewell which the Egyptian people will accord unto the departing Israelites.

22. *shall ask.* For the mere asking, they will be given in gladness and friendliness precious and valuable gifts. The Heb. שאל means to ask as a gift (see Ps. II, 8), with no idea of giving back the object thus received. AV translates, 'every woman shall borrow of her neighbour.' This translation is thoroughly mischievous and misleading. 'If there was any borrowing, it was on the part of the Egyptians, who had been taking the labour of the Israelites without recompense' (Dummelow).

that sojourneth in her house. It is most unlikely that the households of the oppressed Israelites included Egyptian dependants. Therefore, Ehrlich, following Rashi and in strict accordance with Semitic idiom, rightly translates, *in whose house she sojourneth.*

jewels. Heb. 'articles'. These articles were not asked for to be used for festive wear when worshipping God. Worship requires purification, sanctification on the part of the worshipper (cf. Gen. XXXV, 2), not ornamentation (B. Jacob); see following note.

upon your sons, and upon your daughters. The striking manifestation of kindliness and goodwill on the side of the Egyptian people is to be remembered by the Israelites throughout the generations; and, therefore, they are bidden to put these gifts and ornaments upon their children, who will ask concerning that great Day when the Lord saved Israel out of the hands of Pharaoh. These jewels, tokens of friendship and repentance, were fittingly employed later in the adornment and enrichment of the Sanctuary.

ye shall spoil the Egyptians. This rendering should be replaced by *ye shall save the Egyptians* (B. Jacob). 'Spoil the Egyptians' (or, 'strip Egypt') is an incorrect, nay impossible, rendering of the Heb. text. The root נצל, which is here translated 'spoil' or 'strip', occurs 212 times in Scripture; and in 210 instances its meaning is admitted by all to be, to snatch (from danger), to rescue (from a wild beast), to recover (property), also to plunder (booty). Its direct object is never the person or thing *from whom* the saving or the rescuing or the snatching has taken place, but always the person or thing rescued. The usual translation, both here and in XII, 36, 'ye shall spoil the Egyptians,' is, therefore, unwarranted, for two reasons. It takes the persons from whom things are snatched as the direct object; and, furthermore, it necessitates an entire reversal of the meaning of נצל from *save* into *despoil!* There is no justification for departing, in this verse, or in XII, 36, from the rendering which is absolutely unchallenged in the 210 other places where it occurs. The words ונצלתם את מצרים can only be translated, '*and ye shall save the Egyptians,*' *i.e.* clear the name, and vindicate the humanity, of the Egyptians. Bitter memories and associations would have clung to the word 'Egyptians' in the mind of the Israelites, as the hereditary enslavers and oppressors of Israel. A friendly parting, and generous gifts, however, would banish that feeling. The Israelites would come to see that the oppressors were Pharaoh and his courtiers, not the Egyptian people. They would be enabled thereby to carry out the command to be given to them forty years later, 'Thou shalt not abhor an Egyptian' (Deut. XXIII, 8). It is for such reasons that the Israelites are bidden to *ask* their neighbours for these gifts, in order to ensure such a parting in friendship and goodwill, with its consequent clearing of the name, and vindication of the honour, of the Egyptian people (B. Jacob).

v. 21 and 22 lend a poetic and unforgettable touch of beauty to the going out of Egypt; and yet these verses, as few others, have been misunderstood and been looked upon as a 'blot' on the moral teaching of Scripture. The Talmud records a formal claim for indemnity put forward by the Egyptians before Alexander the Great for the vessels of gold and silver which the Israelites had taken with them at the Exodus! The Jewish spokesman, however, had little difficulty in proving to Alexander that, if any indemnity was to be paid, it was the Egyptians who were the debtors, seeing that they had enslaved and exploited the Israelites for many centuries without any pay for their labours.

In modern times, enemies of the Bible vie with one another in finding terms strong enough in which to condemn the 'deceit' practised on the

4

CHAPTER IV

1. And Moses answered and said: 'But, behold, they will not believe me, nor hearken unto my voice; for they will say: The LORD hath not appeared unto thee.' 2. And the LORD said unto him: 'What is that in thy hand?' And he said: 'A rod.' 3. And He said: 'Cast it on the ground.' And he cast it on the ground, and it became a serpent; and Moses fled from before it. 4. And the LORD said unto Moses: 'Put forth thy hand, and take it by the tail—and he put forth his hand, and laid hold of it, and it became a rod in his hand— 5. that they may believe that the LORD, the God of their fathers, the God of Abraham, the God of Isaac, and the God of Jacob, hath appeared unto thee.' 6. And the LORD said furthermore unto him: 'Put now thy hand into thy bosom.' And he put his hand into his bosom; and when he took it out, behold, his hand was leprous, as white as snow. 7. And He said: 'Put

CAP. IV. ד

ד
א וַיַּעַן מֹשֶׁה וַיֹּאמֶר וְהֵן לֹא־יַאֲמִינוּ לִי וְלֹא יִשְׁמְעוּ בְּקֹלִי
2 כִּי יֹאמְרוּ לֹא־נִרְאָה אֵלֶיךָ יְהוָה׃ וַיֹּאמֶר אֵלָיו יְהוָה מַזֶּה
3 בְיָדֶךָ וַיֹּאמֶר מַטֶּה׃ וַיֹּאמֶר הַשְׁלִיכֵהוּ אַרְצָה וַיַּשְׁלִכֵהוּ
4 אַרְצָה וַיְהִי לְנָחָשׁ וַיָּנָס מֹשֶׁה מִפָּנָיו׃ וַיֹּאמֶר יְהוָה אֶל־
מֹשֶׁה שְׁלַח יָדְךָ וֶאֱחֹז בִּזְנָבוֹ וַיִּשְׁלַח יָדוֹ וַיַּחֲזֶק בּוֹ וַיְהִי
ה לְמַטֶּה בְּכַפּוֹ׃ לְמַעַן יַאֲמִינוּ כִּי־נִרְאָה אֵלֶיךָ יְהוָה אֱלֹהֵי
6 אֲבֹתָם אֱלֹהֵי אַבְרָהָם אֱלֹהֵי יִצְחָק וֵאלֹהֵי יַעֲקֹב׃ וַיֹּאמֶר
יְהוָה לוֹ עוֹד הָבֵא־נָא יָדְךָ בְּחֵיקֶךָ וַיָּבֵא יָדוֹ בְּחֵיקוֹ
7 וַיּוֹצִאָהּ וְהִנֵּה יָדוֹ מְצֹרַעַת כַּשָּׁלֶג׃ וַיֹּאמֶר הָשֵׁב יָדְךָ אֶל־
חֵיקֶךָ וַיָּשֶׁב יָדוֹ אֶל־חֵיקוֹ וַיּוֹצִאָהּ מֵחֵיקוֹ וְהִנֵּה־שָׁבָה

v. 2. מה זה ק'

Egyptians. Apologists, both Jewish and non-Jewish, usually reply that this silver and gold was in exchange for the property the Israelites left behind them (Malbim); or they repeat the reply of the Alexandrian Jews: 'Through God's providence, the Israelites were enriched at the expense of their oppressors, and gained as it were a prize of victory in compensation for their long oppression' (Dillmann). Far better than any of these current explanations is that given by Rabbiner Dr. B. Jacob, which we have adopted. It meets all the apparent difficulties, and brings out unexpected beauties in the Divine command. Thus, the phrase, *spoiling the Egyptians*, which has become a proverbial expression, is like the phrase, *brand of Cain* (*Genesis*, p. 15), due to a complete misunderstanding of the text.

CHAPTER IV

1–9. MOSES' THIRD DIFFICULTY: THE ISRAELITES MAY NOT BELIEVE HIS MESSAGE OF FREEDOM

1. *the LORD hath not appeared unto thee.* How could this be answered? Argument would be of little avail. Their uneblief must be swept aside by something that would carry conviction to men whose religious memories are dimmed and whose spirit is crushed.

2–5. The first sign.

2. *a rod.* Jewish legend has woven marvellous tales round the Rod of Moses. 'It was probably only a shepherd's crook. What a history, however, awaited it! It was to be stretched out over the Red Sea, pointing a pathway through its depths; to smite the flinty rock; to win victory over the hosts of Amalek; to be known as the rod of God' (Meyer).

3. *a serpent.* Heb. *nachash;* the basilisk, the symbol of royal and divine power in the diadem worn by Pharaoh. 'The meaning of this miracle seems to be, Pharaoh's own power shall become an instrument of punishment, and his enslaved enemy shall triumph' (Hirsch).

4. *put forth thy hand.* Snake-charmers usually take hold of snakes by the neck to prevent them biting. It is much more dangerous to seize them by the tail. The living serpent becomes a staff by the will of God. Pharaoh can be overcome, like the serpent.

6–8. The second sign.

6. *his hand was leprous.* Moses' ability to produce, and to heal, that most malignant disease would be to them an even more convincing proof of his Divine commission.

as white as snow. Leprosy was common in Egypt. In its worst form, the whole skin becomes glossy white, dry and ulcerous.

7. *it was turned.* Old English for, 'it turned.'

as his other flesh. This miracle was the greater, as white leprosy, when fully developed, is rarely curable (Kalisch).

8 כִּבְשָׂרוֹ׃ וְהָיָה אִם־לֹא יַאֲמִינוּ לָךְ וְלֹא יִשְׁמְעוּ לְקֹל הָאֹת
9 הָרִאשׁוֹן וְהֶאֱמִינוּ לְקֹל הָאֹת הָאַחֲרוֹן׃ וְהָיָה אִם־לֹא
יַאֲמִינוּ גַּם לִשְׁנֵי הָאֹתוֹת הָאֵלֶּה וְלֹא יִשְׁמְעוּן לְקֹלֶךָ
וְלָקַחְתָּ מִמֵּימֵי הַיְאֹר וְשָׁפַכְתָּ הַיַּבָּשָׁה וְהָיוּ הַמַּיִם אֲשֶׁר
10 תִּקַּח מִן־הַיְאֹר וְהָיוּ לְדָם בַּיַּבָּשֶׁת׃ וַיֹּאמֶר מֹשֶׁה אֶל־
יְהוָה בִּי אֲדֹנָי לֹא אִישׁ דְּבָרִים אָנֹכִי גַּם מִתְּמוֹל גַּם
מִשִּׁלְשֹׁם גַּם מֵאָז דַּבֶּרְךָ אֶל־עַבְדֶּךָ כִּי כְבַד־פֶּה וּכְבַד
11 לָשׁוֹן אָנֹכִי׃ וַיֹּאמֶר יְהוָה אֵלָיו מִי שָׂם פֶּה לָאָדָם אוֹ
מִי־יָשׂוּם אִלֵּם אוֹ חֵרֵשׁ אוֹ פִקֵּחַ אוֹ עִוֵּר הֲלֹא אָנֹכִי יְהוָה׃
12 וְעַתָּה לֵךְ וְאָנֹכִי אֶהְיֶה עִם־פִּיךָ וְהוֹרֵיתִיךָ אֲשֶׁר תְּדַבֵּר׃
13 14 וַיֹּאמֶר בִּי אֲדֹנָי שְׁלַח־נָא בְּיַד־תִּשְׁלָח׃ וַיִּחַר־אַף יְהוָה
בְּמֹשֶׁה וַיֹּאמֶר הֲלֹא אַהֲרֹן אָחִיךָ הַלֵּוִי יָדַעְתִּי כִּי־דַבֵּר
יְדַבֵּר הוּא וְגַם הִנֵּה־הוּא יֹצֵא לִקְרָאתֶךָ וְרָאֲךָ וְשָׂמַח

thy hand back into thy bosom.—And he put his hand back into his bosom; and when he took it out of his bosom, behold, it was turned again as his other flesh.— 8. And it shall come to pass, if they will not believe thee, neither hearken to the voice of the first sign, that they will believe the voice of the latter sign. 9. And it shall come to pass, if they will not believe even these two signs, neither hearken unto thy voice, that thou shalt take of the water of the river, and pour it upon the dry land; and the water which thou takest out of the river shall become blood upon the dry land.' 10. And Moses said unto the LORD: 'Oh Lord, I am not a man of words, neither heretofore, nor since Thou hast spoken unto Thy servant; for I am slow of speech, and of a slow tongue.' 11. And the LORD said unto him: 'Who hath made man's mouth? or who maketh a man dumb, or deaf, or seeing, or blind? is it not I the LORD? 12. Now therefore go, and I will be with thy mouth, and teach thee what thou shalt speak.' 13. And he said: 'Oh Lord, send, I pray Thee, by the hand of him whom Thou wilt send.' 14. And the anger of the LORD was kindled against Moses, and He said: 'Is there not Aaron

8. *if they will not believe.* God full well knows whether they will believe or not; but Moses is to be fortified by the information that if a portion of the people refuse to be convinced by the first miracle, they will be convinced by the second miracle (Ibn Ezra).

the voice of the first sign. The lesson or purport of the sign.

9. The third sign.

take of the water. Moses is thus given three signs to attest his Divine commission to the Israelites, the third being similar to the first of the ten plagues.

the river. i.e. the Nile.

10–17. MOSES STILL HESITATES: HE IS NOT ELOQUENT

10. *a man of words.* Or, 'eloquent.' He had spent the years of his manhood in the great silent spaces of the desert, and he could only stammer forth the message of freedom. Leadership, it seemed to him, was impossible to a man unskilled in forensic eloquence with which to win the Council of Elders to his way of thinking, or to state his case fluently and convincingly before Pharaoh.

neither heretofore. lit. 'neither from yesterday nor from before yesterday'.

slow of speech, and of a slow tongue. lit. 'heavy of speech and heavy of tongue'. He may have had an actual impediment in his speech. Rabbinic legend tells that Moses when a child was one day taken by Pharaoh on his knee. He thereupon grasped Pharaoh's crown and placed it on his head. The astrologers were horror-struck. 'Let two braziers be brought'—they counselled; 'one filled with gold, the other with glowing coals; and set them before him. If he grasps the gold, it will be safer for Pharaoh to put the possible usurper to death.' When the braziers were brought, the hand of Moses was stretching for the gold, but the angel Gabriel guided it to the coals. The child plucked out a burning coal and put it to his lips, and for life remained 'heavy of speech and heavy of tongue'.

12. *and teach thee.* The fluent expression of the right thought.

13. *of him whom Thou wilt send. i.e.* by anyone but myself (Rashbam). Discouraged by the failure of his first blow for freedom in his youth, he is unwilling to undertake the mission.

14. *was kindled.* Because of his obstinate reluctance in accepting the charge, despite the Divine promise of help. Another anthropomorphic phrase.

is there not . . . speak well. Or, 'Do I not know that Aaron the Levite thy brother can speak well?' (Kalisch).

the Levite. This description is not superfluous. Heb. usage for indicating affection is by giving the full name of the person in question; cf. 'Take now thy son, thine only son, whom thou lovest, even Isaac,' Gen. XXII, 2.

טו בְּלִבּוֹ׃ וְדִבַּרְתָּ אֵלָיו וְשַׂמְתָּ אֶת־הַדְּבָרִים בְּפִיו וְאָנֹכִי
אֶהְיֶה עִם־פִּיךָ וְעִם־פִּיהוּ וְהוֹרֵיתִי אֶתְכֶם אֵת אֲשֶׁר תַּעֲשׂוּן׃
16 וְדִבֶּר־הוּא לְךָ אֶל־הָעָם וְהָיָה הוּא יִהְיֶה־לְּךָ לְפֶה וְאַתָּה
17 תִּהְיֶה־לּוֹ לֵאלֹהִים׃ וְאֶת־הַמַּטֶּה הַזֶּה תִּקַּח בְּיָדֶךָ אֲשֶׁר
תַּעֲשֶׂה־בּוֹ אֶת־הָאֹתֹת׃* פ ששי
18 וַיֵּלֶךְ מֹשֶׁה וַיָּשָׁב ׀ אֶל־יֶתֶר חֹתְנוֹ וַיֹּאמֶר לוֹ אֵלְכָה נָּא
וְאָשׁוּבָה אֶל־אַחַי אֲשֶׁר־בְּמִצְרַיִם וְאֶרְאֶה הַעוֹדָם חַיִּים
19 וַיֹּאמֶר יִתְרוֹ לְמֹשֶׁה לֵךְ לְשָׁלוֹם׃ וַיֹּאמֶר יְהוָה אֶל־מֹשֶׁה
בְּמִדְיָן לֵךְ שֻׁב מִצְרָיִם כִּי־מֵתוּ כָּל־הָאֲנָשִׁים הַמְבַקְשִׁים
כ אֶת־נַפְשֶׁךָ׃ וַיִּקַּח מֹשֶׁה אֶת־אִשְׁתּוֹ וְאֶת־בָּנָיו וַיַּרְכִּבֵם
עַל־הַחֲמֹר וַיָּשָׁב אַרְצָה מִצְרָיִם וַיִּקַּח מֹשֶׁה אֶת־מַטֵּה
21 הָאֱלֹהִים בְּיָדוֹ׃ וַיֹּאמֶר יְהוָה אֶל־מֹשֶׁה בְּלֶכְתְּךָ לָשׁוּב

thy brother the Levite? I know that he can speak well. And also, behold, he cometh forth to meet thee; and when he seeth thee, he will be glad in his heart. 15. And thou shalt speak unto him, and put the words in his mouth; and I will be with thy mouth, and with his mouth, and will teach you what ye shall do. 16. And he shall be thy spokesman unto the people; and it shall come to pass, that he shall be to thee a mouth, and thou shalt be to him in God's stead. 17. And thou shalt take in thy hand this rod, wherewith thou shalt do the signs.' *** vi.** ¶ 18. And Moses went and returned to [1]Jethro his father-in-law, and said unto him: 'Let me go, I pray thee, and return unto my brethren that are in Egypt, and see whether they be yet alive.' And Jethro said to Moses: 'Go in peace.' 19. And the LORD said unto Moses in Midian: 'Go, return into Egypt; for all the men are dead that sought thy life.' 20. And Moses took his wife and his sons, and set them upon an ass, and he returned to the land of Egypt; and Moses took the rod of God in his hand. 21. And the LORD said unto Moses: 'When thou

[1] Heb. *Jether.*

16. *in God's stead.* Moses receives his inspiration direct from God; and becomes the inspirer of his brother, who acts as his interpreter to Pharaoh and Israel.

18–31. MOSES RETURNS TO EGYPT

18. *brethren.* To my kinsfolk; see Gen. XIII, 8.

19. *go, return into Egypt.* There were still some hesitancies and fears in the mind of Moses. Hence the distinct assurance that all his enemies were dead.

20. *sons.* The birth of the elder is mentioned in II, 22; the second seems to have been a mere infant.

ass. 'The animal is of a far superior quality in Arabia and Egypt than in Northern countries. It is livelier, quicker, more courageous and robust' (Kalisch).

the rod of God. Called thus by reason of the miracle performed in connection therewith; *v.* 2 and 3.

21. *harden his heart.* Or, *make his heart strong; i.e.* stubborn. This does not mean that God on purpose made Pharaoh sinful. For God to make it impossible for a man to obey Him, and then punish him for his disobedience, would be both unjust and contrary to the fundamental Jewish belief in Freedom of the Will.

The phrase most often translated 'hardening of the heart' occurs nineteen times; ten times it is said that Pharaoh hardened his heart; and nine times the hardening of Pharaoh's heart is ascribed to God. There thus seem to be two sides to this hardening. When the Divine command came to Pharaoh, 'Set the slaves free,' and his reply was, 'I will not,' each repetition of Pharaoh's persistent obstinacy made it less likely that he would eventually listen to the word of God. For such is the law of conscience: every time the voice of conscience is disobeyed, it becomes duller and feebler, and the heart grows harder. Man cannot remain 'neutral' in the presence of Duty or of any direct command of God. He either obeys the Divine command, and it becomes unto him a blessing; or he defies God, and such command then becomes unto him a curse. 'It is part of the Divinely ordered scheme of things that if a man deliberately chooses evil, it proceeds to enslave him; it blinds and stupefies him, making for him repentance well-nigh impossible' (Riehm). Thus, every successive refusal on the part of Pharaoh to listen to the message of Moses froze up his better nature more and more, until it seemed as if God had hardened his heart. But this is only so because Pharaoh had first hardened it himself, and continued doing so. The Omniscient God knew beforehand whither his obstinacy would lead Pharaoh, and prepared Moses for initial failure by warning him that Pharaoh's heart would become 'hardened'.

The modern mind whilst agreeing that all things are ultimately controlled by God's will, does not attribute results to the *immediate* action of God. Not so the Biblical idiom. Events, whether physical or moral, which are the inevitable result of the Divine ordering of the universe, are spoken of as the direct work of God (Dillmann, Driver, Jacob). See also note on Isa. VI, 9, p. 303.

goest back into Egypt, see that thou do before Pharaoh all the wonders which I have put in thy hand; but I will harden his heart, and he will not let the people go. 22. And thou shalt say unto Pharaoh: Thus saith the LORD: Israel is My son, My first-born. 23. And I have said unto thee: Let My son go, that he may serve Me; and thou hast refused to let him go. Behold, I will slay thy son, thy first-born.'—24. And it came to pass on the way at the lodging-place, that the LORD met him, and sought to kill him. 25. Then Zipporah took a flint and cut off the foreskin of her son, and cast it at his feet; and she said: 'Surely a bridegroom of blood art thou to me.' 26. So He let him alone. Then she said: 'A bridegroom of blood in regard of the circumcision.' ¶ 27. And the LORD said to Aaron: 'Go into the wilderness to meet Moses.' And he went, and met him in the mountain of God, and kissed him. 28. And Moses told Aaron all the words of the LORD wherewith He had sent him, and all the signs wherewith He had charged him. 29. And Moses and Aaron went and

מִצְרַיְמָה רְאֵה כָּל־הַמֹּפְתִים אֲשֶׁר־שַׂמְתִּי בְיָדֶךָ וַעֲשִׂיתָם
לִפְנֵי פַרְעֹה וַאֲנִי אֲחַזֵּק אֶת־לִבּוֹ וְלֹא יְשַׁלַּח אֶת־הָעָם׃
22 וְאָמַרְתָּ אֶל־פַּרְעֹה כֹּה אָמַר יְהוָה בְּנִי בְכֹרִי יִשְׂרָאֵל׃
23 וָאֹמַר אֵלֶיךָ שַׁלַּח אֶת־בְּנִי וְיַעַבְדֵנִי וַתְּמָאֵן לְשַׁלְּחוֹ הִנֵּה אָנֹכִי
24 הֹרֵג אֶת־בִּנְךָ בְּכֹרֶךָ׃ וַיְהִי בַדֶּרֶךְ בַּמָּלוֹן וַיִּפְגְּשֵׁהוּ יְהוָה
כה וַיְבַקֵּשׁ הֲמִיתוֹ׃ וַתִּקַּח צִפֹּרָה צֹר וַתִּכְרֹת אֶת־עָרְלַת בְּנָהּ
26 וַתַּגַּע לְרַגְלָיו וַתֹּאמֶר כִּי חֲתַן־דָּמִים אַתָּה לִי׃ וַיִּרֶף מִמֶּנּוּ
אָז אָמְרָה חֲתַן דָּמִים לַמּוּלֹת׃ פ
27 וַיֹּאמֶר יְהוָה אֶל־אַהֲרֹן לֵךְ לִקְרַאת מֹשֶׁה הַמִּדְבָּרָה וַיֵּלֶךְ
28 וַיִּפְגְּשֵׁהוּ בְּהַר הָאֱלֹהִים וַיִּשַּׁק־לוֹ׃ וַיַּגֵּד מֹשֶׁה לְאַהֲרֹן
אֵת כָּל־דִּבְרֵי יְהוָה אֲשֶׁר שְׁלָחוֹ וְאֵת כָּל־הָאֹתֹת אֲשֶׁר
29 צִוָּהוּ׃ וַיֵּלֶךְ מֹשֶׁה וְאַהֲרֹן וַיַּאַסְפוּ אֶת־כָּל־זִקְנֵי בְּנֵי יִשְׂרָאֵל׃

22. *Israel is My son.* This expression is here applied for the first time to Israel as a nation.

first-born. Implying the universal fatherhood of God. The other nations, too, are God's children; and in Abraham's seed, spiritually the first-born among them, all the families of the earth are to be blessed (Gen. XII, 3).

23. *thou hast refused.* Better, '*and if thou refusest . . . I shall slay.*'

24. *at the lodging-place.* The verse can also be translated: 'On the way, he tarried in a lodging-place.' Moses was still distrusting himself in regard to his mission, hesitating, tarrying in the inn. This brings down the Divine displeasure upon him (Wogue).

sought to kill him. An anthropomorphic way of saying that Moses fell suddenly into a serious illness. Many commentators connect this sudden illness of Moses with his postponing, for some reason, the circumcision of his son. Tradition ascribes the omission to the influence of Jethro and Zipporah, who may have desired the circumcision postponed to the 13th year, as was customary among the Bedouin tribes. However, in the previous verse Moses had warned Pharaoh that disobedience of God's will carried dire punishment with it; and he himself should, therefore, on no account have permitted any postponement of a duty incumbent upon him.

25. *Zipporah.* Moses being disabled by illness, Zipporah performed the ceremony.

a flint. A sharp, stone instrument; see Josh. v, 2.

cast it at his feet. i.e. the feet of Moses—to connect him with what she had done.

bridegroom of blood. This is the literal translation of the Heb. *chathan damim.* Since circumcision is the symbol of the covenant between God and the child, the child was spoken of as the *bridegroom* of the covenant; in the same way as the 'hero' of *Simchath Torah*, the Festival of the Rejoicing of the Law, came in medieval times to be called *chathan Torah*, the 'bridegroom' of the Torah.

According to Ibn Ezra, the words, 'Surely a bridegroom of blood art thou to me,' were addressed to the child: 'Indeed, thee I might call literally a *bridegroom of blood*, because thou didst nearly cause the death of my husband.'

26. *So He let him alone.* The illness of Moses abated, and he was soon restored to health.

then she said, A bridegroom, etc. i.e. Zipporah was the first to use the term *chathan damim* in connection with circumcision (Rosin, Baentsch).

27. *the mountain of God. i.e.* Horeb, see III, 1. The 'wilderness' is the one between Horeb and Egypt.

28. *He had charged him.* To perform.

29. *elders.* See note on III, 16.

'Now after all these years comes a vague rumour through the brick-fields and along the great canal, about the two old men from far-off Midian with a most startling message. One, it was said, was that Moses whose exciting story their aged elders still talked about, the story that had so stirred the slave settlements long ago—

gathered together all the elders of the children of Israel. 30. And Aaron spoke all the words which the LORD had spoken unto Moses, and did the signs in the sight of the people. 31. And the people believed; and when they heard that the LORD had remembered the children of Israel, and that He had seen their affliction, then they bowed their heads and worshipped.* vii.

5 CHAPTER V

1. And afterward Moses and Aaron came, and said unto Pharaoh: 'Thus saith the LORD, the God of Israel: Let My people go, that they may hold a feast unto Me in the wilderness.' 2. And Pharaoh said: 'Who is the LORD, that I should hearken unto His voice to let Israel go? I know not the LORD, and moreover I will not let Israel go.' 3. And they said: 'The God of the Hebrews hath met with us. Let us go, we pray thee, three days' journey into the wilderness

ל וַיְדַבֵּר אַהֲרֹן אֵת כָּל־הַדְּבָרִים אֲשֶׁר־דִּבֶּר יְהוָה אֶל־
31 מֹשֶׁה וַיַּעַשׂ הָאֹתֹת לְעֵינֵי הָעָם׃ וַיַּאֲמֵן הָעָם וַיִּשְׁמְעוּ כִּי־
פָקַד יְהוָה אֶת־בְּנֵי יִשְׂרָאֵל וְכִי רָאָה אֶת־עָנְיָם וַיִּקְּדוּ
וַיִּשְׁתַּחֲוּוּ׃ * שביעי

CAP. V. ה

ה

א וְאַחַר בָּאוּ מֹשֶׁה וְאַהֲרֹן וַיֹּאמְרוּ אֶל־פַּרְעֹה כֹּה־אָמַר
יְהוָה אֱלֹהֵי יִשְׂרָאֵל שַׁלַּח אֶת־עַמִּי וְיָחֹגּוּ לִי בַּמִּדְבָּר׃
2 וַיֹּאמֶר פַּרְעֹה מִי יְהוָה אֲשֶׁר אֶשְׁמַע בְּקֹלוֹ לְשַׁלַּח אֶת־
יִשְׂרָאֵל לֹא יָדַעְתִּי אֶת־יְהוָה וְגַם אֶת־יִשְׂרָאֵל לֹא אֲשַׁלֵּחַ׃
3 וַיֹּאמְרוּ אֱלֹהֵי הָעִבְרִים נִקְרָא עָלֵינוּ נֵלֲכָה נָּא דֶּרֶךְ
שְׁלֹשֶׁת יָמִים בַּמִּדְבָּר וְנִזְבְּחָה לַיהוָה אֱלֹהֵינוּ פֶּן־יִפְגָּעֵנוּ

when a prince of Egypt, who was one of themselves, had, for their sakes, refused to be called the son of Pharaoh's daughter. Then came the secret messages from Moses and Aaron to the heads of families. Before going to Pharaoh, they must first be sure that their leadership will be accepted by the people. You can imagine the secret gatherings along the canals, the midnight meetings of desperate men assembling at risk of their lives, such as one reads of in *Uncle Tom's Cabin*—the old slaves, the elders of the tribes, with the first dawn of hope in their eyes. Ah, poor wretches, one needs to have suffered like them to understand the goodness of finding out that God cared after all' (Smyth).

30. *Aaron spoke.* Acting as the spokesman of Moses; see *v.* 15.

and did the signs. Jewish commentators assume that this means that Aaron performed the signs; others hold that it was Moses.

31. *the people.* As represented by the elders. It is also reasonable to assume that the elders called the people together to hear the message brought by Moses and Aaron. Already the word of God, 'They shall hearken to thy voice' (III, 18), was being fulfilled.

worshipped. lit. 'they prostrated themselves', in prayer and gratitude to God.

CHAPTER V–VI, 1. UNSUCCESSFUL APPEAL TO PHARAOH AND INCREASE OF THE OPPRESSION

1. *and afterward.* Only after the confidence of the Israelites had been assured by means of the signs, could Moses and Aaron approach Pharaoh.

Pharaoh. Probably Merenptah, see p. 395.

a feast. Heb. *hag*, the common Semitic word for a pilgrimage to a sanctuary, where pilgrims took part in religious processions and ritual dances. Sacrifice was an essential part of such a festival.

in the wilderness. The Israelites could not offer sacrifices in the presence of the Egyptians, in view of the fact that the animals to be sacrificed were held sacred by the Egyptians; just as Mohammedans in India cannot with impunity slaughter cows in sight of a Hindu mob. Hence the request to go to the wilderness to celebrate the feast.

2. *who is the LORD.* An expression of contempt; Pharaoh does not know *Adonay*, and does not acknowledge His right to command him. The Rabbis say that he turned to his seventy scribes who knew all the tongues spoken on earth, and asked them: 'Know ye a god who is called *Adonay*, the God of Eternity?' They answered, 'We have sought in all the books of all the peoples among the names of all the gods; but we have not found *Adonay* among them.' They spake the truth. It was a new revelation, a new conception of God that Moses brought to the children of men. None of the heathen empires or emperors of old knew the God of Freedom, Holiness and Righteousness. He was not in their pantheon.

3. *the God of the Hebrews hath met with us.* Moses and Aaron now use language which Pharaoh is more likely to understand. Instead of speaking of *Adonay*, they tell him that the God who had manifested Himself to Moses is the God of the Hebrews.

three days' journey. See III, 18.

with the sword. Even Pharaoh could understand that for a people to neglect the worship of its god, rendered it liable to divine punishment by sword or pestilence.

and sacrifice unto the LORD our God;
lest He fall upon us with pestilence, or with
the sword.' 4. And the king of Egypt
said unto them: 'Wherefore do ye, Moses
and Aaron, cause the people to break loose
from their work? get you unto your
burdens.' 5. And Pharaoh said: 'Behold,
the people of the land are now many, and
will ye make them rest from their burdens?'
6. And the same day Pharaoh commanded
the taskmasters of the people, and their
officers, saying: 7. 'Ye shall no more give
the people straw to make brick, as here-
tofore. Let them go and gather straw for
themselves. 8. And the tale of the bricks,
which they did make heretofore, ye shall
lay upon them; ye shall not diminish aught
thereof; for they are idle, therefore they
cry, saying: Let us go and sacrifice to our
God. 9. Let heavier work be laid upon the
men, that they may labour therein; and
let them not regard lying words.' 10. And
the taskmasters of the people went out, and
their officers, and they spoke to the people,
saying: 'Thus saith Pharaoh: I will not
give you straw. 11. Go yourselves, get you
straw where ye can find it; for nought
of your work shall be diminished.' 12. So
the people were scattered abroad through-
out all the land of Egypt to gather stubble
for straw. 13. And the taskmasters were
urgent, saying: 'Fulfil your work, your
daily task, as when there was straw.' 14.
And the officers of the children of Israel,

4 בַּדֶּבֶר אוֹ בֶחָרֶב׃ וַיֹּאמֶר אֲלֵהֶם מֶלֶךְ מִצְרַיִם לָמָּה מֹשֶׁה
וְאַהֲרֹן תַּפְרִיעוּ אֶת־הָעָם מִמַּעֲשָׂיו לְכוּ לְסִבְלֹתֵיכֶם׃
ה וַיֹּאמֶר פַּרְעֹה הֵן־רַבִּים עַתָּה עַם הָאָרֶץ וְהִשְׁבַּתֶּם אֹתָם
6 מִסִּבְלֹתָם׃ וַיְצַו פַּרְעֹה בַּיּוֹם הַהוּא אֶת־הַנֹּגְשִׂים בָּעָם
7 וְאֶת־שֹׁטְרָיו לֵאמֹר׃ לֹא תֹאסִפוּן לָתֵת תֶּבֶן לָעָם לִלְבֹּן
הַלְּבֵנִים כִּתְמוֹל שִׁלְשֹׁם הֵם יֵלְכוּ וְקֹשְׁשׁוּ לָהֶם תֶּבֶן׃
8 וְאֶת־מַתְכֹּנֶת הַלְּבֵנִים אֲשֶׁר הֵם עֹשִׂים תְּמוֹל שִׁלְשֹׁם
תָּשִׂימוּ עֲלֵיהֶם לֹא תִגְרְעוּ מִמֶּנּוּ כִּי־נִרְפִּים הֵם עַל־כֵּן
9 הֵם צֹעֲקִים לֵאמֹר נֵלְכָה נִזְבְּחָה לֵאלֹהֵינוּ׃ תִּכְבַּד הָעֲבֹדָה
י עַל־הָאֲנָשִׁים וְיַעֲשׂוּ־בָהּ וְאַל־יִשְׁעוּ בְּדִבְרֵי־שָׁקֶר׃ וַיֵּצְאוּ
נֹגְשֵׂי הָעָם וְשֹׁטְרָיו וַיֹּאמְרוּ אֶל־הָעָם לֵאמֹר כֹּה אָמַר
11 פַּרְעֹה אֵינֶנִּי נֹתֵן לָכֶם תֶּבֶן׃ אַתֶּם לְכוּ קְחוּ לָכֶם תֶּבֶן
12 מֵאֲשֶׁר תִּמְצָאוּ כִּי אֵין נִגְרָע מֵעֲבֹדַתְכֶם דָּבָר׃ וַיָּפֶץ הָעָם
13 בְּכָל־אֶרֶץ מִצְרָיִם לְקֹשֵׁשׁ קַשׁ לַתֶּבֶן׃ וְהַנֹּגְשִׂים אָצִים
לֵאמֹר כַּלּוּ מַעֲשֵׂיכֶם דְּבַר־יוֹם בְּיוֹמוֹ כַּאֲשֶׁר בִּהְיוֹת
14 הַתֶּבֶן׃ וַיֻּכּוּ שֹׁטְרֵי בְּנֵי יִשְׂרָאֵל אֲשֶׁר־שָׂמוּ עֲלֵהֶם נֹגְשֵׂי

4. *cause the people to break loose from the work.* Why do you unsettle the people in their work with all this talk of a pilgrimage, which is only an excuse for a holiday? Back, to your labours!

5. *people of the land.* Better, *Council of Elders* (see page 80, note on Gen. XXIII, 7), Heb. *am ha-aretz,* refers to the elders who, as representatives of the people, accompanied Moses (III, 18). 'Why, asked Pharaoh, should *all these elders*—and there are so many of them—rest from their labours, in order to listen to the talk of Moses and Aaron?'

6. *the same day.* Pharaoh lost no time in devising a plan by which to crush the aspirations of the Hebrew leaders.

taskmasters. Heb. *nogesim,* not the same word as in I, 11 (*sare missim*). The *nogesim* were probably subordinate to them.

their officers. Who were Hebrews; see *v.* 14.

7. *straw.* Necessary for holding the clay together and to prevent it from cracking.

let them go and gather straw. They would have to seek it in the fields of the Egyptians.

8. *tale.* Number; the same quantity was to be required of them under the new regulations as before. The demand was, as Pharaoh well knew, impossible, and increased the task of his Hebrew subjects beyond the point of human performance.

they are idle. In two papyrus documents found in Egyptian tombs of the time of the Exodus, one passage says: 'I have no one to help me in making bricks, no straw, etc.'; and another tells of twelve labourers punished for failing to make up their daily tale of bricks.

9. *let heavier work be laid.* He is determined to leave his slaves no time to think of freedom or worship.

let them not regard lying words. The 'lying words' refer to the promised redemption, which in his eyes is merely a pretext for seeking a holiday.

10–12. The taskmasters communicate Pharaoh's orders to the people.

12. *stubble.* All kinds of field rubbish, small twigs, stems, roots of withered plants. This had to be chopped and sorted.

for straw. i.e. to make into straw.

14. *yesterday and to-day.* Heb. idiom for *recently.*

whom Pharaoh's taskmasters had set over them, were beaten, saying: 'Wherefore have ye not fulfilled your appointed task in making brick both yesterday and to-day as heretofore?' 15. Then the officers of the children of Israel came and cried unto Pharaoh, saying: 'Wherefore dealest thou thus with thy servants? 16. There is no straw given unto thy servants, and they say to us: Make brick: and, behold, thy servants are beaten, but the fault is in thine own people.' 17. But he said: 'Ye are idle, ye are idle; therefore ye say: Let us go and sacrifice to the LORD. 18. Go therefore now, and work; for there shall no straw be given you, yet shall ye deliver the tale of bricks.' 19. And the officers of the children of Israel did see that they were set on mischief, when they said: 'Ye shall not diminish aught from your bricks, your daily task.' 20. And they met Moses and Aaron, who stood in the way, as they came forth from Pharaoh; 21. and they said unto them: 'The LORD look upon you, and judge; because ye have made our savour to be abhorred in the eyes of Pharaoh, and in the eyes of his servants, to put a sword in their hand to slay us.'* m. 22. And Moses returned unto the LORD, and said: 'Lord, wherefore hast Thou dealt ill with this people? why is it that Thou hast sent me? 23. For since I came to Pharaoh to speak in Thy name, he hath dealt ill with this people; neither hast Thou delivered Thy people at all.'

6 CHAPTER VI

1. And the LORD said unto Moses: 'Now shalt thou see what I will do to Pharaoh; for by a strong hand shall he let them go, and by a strong hand shall he drive them out of his land.'

פַּרְעֹה לֵאמֹר מַדּוּעַ לֹא כִלִּיתֶם חָקְכֶם לִלְבֹּן כִּתְמוֹל
טו שִׁלְשֹׁם גַּם־תְּמוֹל גַּם־הַיּוֹם׃ וַיָּבֹאוּ שֹׁטְרֵי בְּנֵי יִשְׂרָאֵל
16 וַיִּצְעֲקוּ אֶל־פַּרְעֹה לֵאמֹר לָמָּה תַעֲשֶׂה כֹה לַעֲבָדֶיךָ׃ תֶּבֶן
אֵין נִתָּן לַעֲבָדֶיךָ וּלְבֵנִים אֹמְרִים לָנוּ עֲשׂוּ וְהִנֵּה עֲבָדֶיךָ
17 מֻכִּים וְחָטָאת עַמֶּךָ׃ וַיֹּאמֶר נִרְפִּים אַתֶּם נִרְפִּים עַל־כֵּן
18 אַתֶּם אֹמְרִים נֵלְכָה נִזְבְּחָה לַיהוָה׃ וְעַתָּה לְכוּ עִבְדוּ
19 וְתֶבֶן לֹא־יִנָּתֵן לָכֶם וְתֹכֶן לְבֵנִים תִּתֵּנוּ׃ וַיִּרְאוּ שֹׁטְרֵי בְנֵי־
יִשְׂרָאֵל אֹתָם בְּרָע לֵאמֹר לֹא־תִגְרְעוּ מִלִּבְנֵיכֶם דְּבַר־יוֹם
כ בְּיוֹמוֹ׃ וַיִּפְגְּעוּ אֶת־מֹשֶׁה וְאֶת־אַהֲרֹן נִצָּבִים לִקְרָאתָם
21 בְּצֵאתָם מֵאֵת פַּרְעֹה׃ וַיֹּאמְרוּ אֲלֵהֶם יֵרֶא יְהוָה עֲלֵיכֶם
וְיִשְׁפֹּט אֲשֶׁר הִבְאַשְׁתֶּם אֶת־רֵיחֵנוּ בְּעֵינֵי פַרְעֹה וּבְעֵינֵי
מפטיר 22 עֲבָדָיו לָתֶת־חֶרֶב בְּיָדָם לְהָרְגֵנוּ׃ וַיָּשָׁב מֹשֶׁה אֶל־יְהוָה
וַיֹּאמַר אֲדֹנָי לָמָה הֲרֵעֹתָה לָעָם הַזֶּה לָמָּה זֶּה שְׁלַחְתָּנִי׃
23 וּמֵאָז בָּאתִי אֶל־פַּרְעֹה לְדַבֵּר בִּשְׁמֶךָ הֵרַע לָעָם הַזֶּה וְהַצֵּל
לֹא־הִצַּלְתָּ אֶת־עַמֶּךָ׃

ו CAP. VI. ו

א וַיֹּאמֶר יְהוָה אֶל־מֹשֶׁה עַתָּה תִרְאֶה אֲשֶׁר אֶעֱשֶׂה לְפַרְעֹה
כִּי בְיָד חֲזָקָה יְשַׁלְּחֵם וּבְיָד חֲזָקָה יְגָרְשֵׁם מֵאַרְצוֹ׃

15–19. The officers of the Israelites cry in vain to the king.

15. *unto Pharaoh.* 'Direct access to the ruler on the part of petitioners of humble rank is comparatively easy in the East' (Bennett).

16. *they say. i.e.* the Egyptian taskmasters.

the fault is in thine own people. lit. 'but thy people sins'. A hint that the tyrannical conduct of the overseers constitutes a sin, and will call down the punishment of Heaven (Kalisch).

19. *they were set on mischief.* The word *they* refers to the Egyptian taskmasters.

20–21. The Hebrew officers blame Moses and Aaron for the plight of the Hebrews.

20. *stood in the way.* lit. 'standing to meet them'. Moses and Aaron were waiting to learn the reply of the king (Luzzatto).

21. *the LORD look upon you, and judge.* May God requite you for the evil you have brought upon the Israelites!

a sword. A pretext to ruin us.

22–23. Moses complains to God that the bondage had become more cruel than ever.

22. *returned.* 'The expression is beautiful in its simplicity, implying his constant communion with God' (McNeile).

23. *neither hast Thou.* Fulfilled Thy promise of deliverance, III, 8. 'He could not understand this long-suffering delay of the Eternal Judge to afford time for the hardened tyrant to repent. The desponding complaint of Moses was the effort of a pious soul struggling after a deeper penetration into the mysteries of the Almighty' (Kalisch).

CHAPTER VI

1. *now shalt thou see.* God calms Moses by renewing the promise of redemption.

by a strong hand. Compelled by the power of God.

ISAIAH XXVII, 6–XXVIII, 13 AND XXIX, 22, 23

CHAPTER XXVII

CAP. XXVII. כז

הַבָּאִים יַשְׁרֵשׁ יַעֲקֹב יָצִיץ וּפָרַח 6
יִשְׂרָאֵל וּמָלְאוּ פְנֵי־תֵבֵל תְּנוּבָה׃ הַכְּמַכַּת מַכֵּהוּ 7
הִכָּהוּ אִם־כְּהֶרֶג הֲרֻגָיו הֹרָג׃ בְּסַאסְּאָה בְּשַׁלְחָהּ תְּרִיבֶנָּה 8
הָגָה בְּרוּחוֹ הַקָּשָׁה בְּיוֹם קָדִים׃ לָכֵן בְּזֹאת יְכֻפַּר עֲוֹן־ 9

6. In days to come shall Jacob take root,
Israel shall blossom and bud;
And the face of the world shall be filled
with fruitage.

7. Hath He smitten him as He smote
those that smote him?
Or is he slain according to the slaughter
of them that were slain by Him?

8. In full measure, when Thou sendest
her away, Thou dost contend with her;
He hath removed her with His rough
blast in the day of the east wind.

9. Therefore by this shall the iniquity of
Jacob be expiated,
And this is all the fruit of taking away
his sin:

Isaiah the son of Amoz was a native of Jerusalem. His family seems to have been one of rank, and he moved in royal circles. His Prophetic ministry extended for close upon 40 years, from 740–701 B.C.E. These years were the most stirring that the kingdom of Judah had yet passed through; and, throughout that entire period, he was the dominant figure in the land. The momentous event of his time was the rise of Assyria. From being a mere garrison province of Babylon in northern Mesopotamia, Assyria had become a world power. The kingdoms of Syria and Israel fell before the Assyrians in 721; and only as by a miracle was Jerusalem delivered from their grasp in 701.

With the downfall of the kingdom of Israel, Judah became the sole representative and repository of true Religion; and in the fate of that tiny land, the moral destinies of the whole world were involved. In this time of upheaval and spiritual travail, Isaiah brought to King and People the message of the holiness, omnipotence, and sovereignty of God ('Holy, holy, holy, is the LORD of hosts: the whole earth is full of His glory'). With passionate fervour he sought to instil his own vital faith in God and Providence into the hearts of his brethren, and interpret for them the crises of history in the light of Divine guidance and Righteousness. His efforts brought him into violent conflict with the war party of his day; and, throughout his life, he remained an implacable enemy of shallow 'patriots' and opportunist politicians. According to one tradition, he perished in the heathen reaction under King Manasseh.

Great in thought and great in action, Isaiah united the profoundest religious insight with wide knowledge of men and affairs. The princely personality of the man is reflected in his style. His words are instinct with power, and he is the master of the sublime in universal literature. His moral passion, moreover, marks him as one of the world's greatest orators. See also p. 302.

The connection between the Sedrah and Haftorah is apparent. Israel had suffered in Egypt, but Israel's taskmasters had received adequate punishment; and Israel's affliction in Isaiah's day was as nothing compared with the fate that would befall its foes. Israel in Egypt chafed at Redemption's delay, tiring of the visits of Moses and Aaron; Israel of Isaiah's age gibed at the monotony of Prophetical teaching, and doubted the validity of Divine promise. The Egyptian Deliverance revealed that Justice triumphs in God's universe; so would the men of a later age see that the hand of God moves in the destinies of men.

6. *in days to come.* The word for 'days' must be supplied in the Heb. text.

the face of the world shall be filled with fruitage. Israel is saved, and saving the world. The prophet dreams for Israel the ascendancy of noble example to the other nations; as in Isa. II, 2 f.

7. *smitten him. i.e.* Israel. Severely as Israel had been punished, its punishment was mild in comparison to that meted out to Israel's enemies (Kimchi). The implied answer is No.

8. *in full measure.* According to their sins, but tempered with mercy.

when Thou sendest her away. The reference is to Samaria, representing Israel, *i.e.* the Northern Kingdom (Ibn Ezra).

the east wind. The Assyrians, who would lead the Kingdom into captivity.

9. *therefore.* God had only banished, not destroyed, Israel; hence repentance is still possible.

Jacob. The poetical name for Israel.

the fruit of taking away his sin. Penitence is at once the condition and the 'fruit' of Israel's forgiveness.

when he maketh. Better, *that he should make.*

Asherim and the sun-images. The Asherah was probably the sacred pole, or symbol of fertility, found in ancient shrines. The sun-images were pillars dedicated to the worship of the sun-god.

When he maketh all the stones of the altar as chalkstones that are beaten in pieces,
So that the Asherim and the sun-images shall rise no more.

10. For the fortified city is solitary,
A habitation abandoned and forsaken, like the wilderness;
There shall the calf feed, and there shall he lie down,
And consume the branches thereof.

11. When the boughs thereof are withered, they shall be broken off;
The women shall come, and set them on fire;
For it is a people of no understanding;
Therefore He that made them will not have compassion upon them,
And He that formed them will not be gracious unto them.

12. And it shall come to pass in that day,
That the LORD will beat off [His fruit]
From the flood of the River unto the Brook of Egypt,
And ye shall be gathered one by one, O ye children of Israel.

13. And it shall come to pass in that day,
That a great horn shall be blown;
And they shall come that were lost in the land of Assyria,
And they that were dispersed in the land of Egypt;
And they shall worship the LORD in the holy mountain at Jerusalem.

יַעֲקֹב וְזֶה כָּל־פְּרִי הָסִר חַטָּאתוֹ בְּשׂוּמוֹ ׀ כָּל־אַבְנֵי מִזְבֵּחַ
י כְּאַבְנֵי־גִר מְנֻפָּצוֹת לֹא־יָקֻמוּ אֲשֵׁרִים וְחַמָּנִים׃ כִּי עִיר
בְּצוּרָה בָּדָד נָוֶה מְשֻׁלָּח וְנֶעֱזָב כַּמִּדְבָּר שָׁם יִרְעֶה עֵגֶל
11 וְשָׁם יִרְבָּץ וְכִלָּה סְעִפֶיהָ׃ בִּיבֹשׁ קְצִירָהּ תִּשָּׁבַרְנָה
נָשִׁים בָּאוֹת מְאִירוֹת אוֹתָהּ כִּי לֹא עַם־בִּינוֹת הוּא עַל־כֵּן
12 לֹא־יְרַחֲמֶנּוּ עֹשֵׂהוּ וְיֹצְרוֹ לֹא יְחֻנֶּנּוּ׃ וְהָיָה בַּיּוֹם
הַהוּא יַחְבֹּט יְהוָה מִשִּׁבֹּלֶת הַנָּהָר עַד־נַחַל מִצְרָיִם וְאַתֶּם
13 תְּלֻקְּטוּ לְאַחַד אֶחָד בְּנֵי יִשְׂרָאֵל׃ וְהָיָה ׀ בַּיּוֹם הַהוּא
יִתָּקַע בְּשׁוֹפָר גָּדוֹל וּבָאוּ הָאֹבְדִים בְּאֶרֶץ אַשּׁוּר וְהַנִּדָּחִים
בְּאֶרֶץ מִצְרָיִם וְהִשְׁתַּחֲווּ לַיהוָה בְּהַר הַקֹּדֶשׁ בִּירוּשָׁלִָם׃

CAP. XXVIII. כח

א הוֹי עֲטֶרֶת גֵּאוּת שִׁכֹּרֵי אֶפְרַיִם וְצִיץ נֹבֵל צְבִי תִפְאַרְתּוֹ

CHAPTER XXVIII

1. Woe to the crown of pride of the drunkards of Ephraim,
And to the fading flower of his glorious beauty,
Which is on the head of the fat valley of them that are smitten down with wine!

כז׳ v. 10. קמץ בטרחא

10, 11. Repentance can bring forgiveness, but it does not imply immunity from punishment. The 'solitary city' is Jerusalem, deserted and forsaken, with grass and boughs growing in the streets, food for calves and fuel for its needy inhabitants. They are 'a people of no understanding'. The time of punishment, in shape of exile must, therefore, inevitably come.

12, 13. But there will be a Return from that exile, and it will include even those who are scattered in distant lands.

12. *in that day.* The day of salvation; see the opening verse of the Haftorah and *v.* 1 of the chapter.

beat off His fruit. As one beats the olives from the leaves (or the grain from the chaff) and goes back again and again and collects all the fruit, so that all is gathered in (Rashi).

one by one. With such loving care for each individual Israelite, that not a single soul shall be lost.

13. *horn.* Heb. *shofar.* But even those who seem to be lost in distant Assyria or the interior of Egypt, will be ingathered. This verse is employed with soul-stirring effect in the Mussaph Prayers for the New Year.

lost. To Israel.

CHAPTER XXVIII

The date of this denunciation of the luxury and dissoluteness of the aristocracy of Samaria, the capital of Israel, the northern Kingdom, must be before the capture of Samaria by the Assyrians, which took place in 722. In Judah, an influential party favoured resistance to Assyria and an alliance with Egypt for that purpose—a course of action opposed by Isaiah as both foolish and fatal.

1. *Woe to.* Or, 'alas for.'

crown of pride. Samaria, a city of great strength and beauty, on a hill overlooking a rich valley, is likened to a chaplet of flowers on the head of a reveller. But the wearer is a drunkard, and the flowers are fading (Skinner).

2 אֲשֶׁר עַל־רֹאשׁ גֵּיא־שְׁמָנִים הֲלוּמֵי יָיִן׃ הִנֵּה חָזָק וְאַמִּץ
לַאדֹנָי כְּזֶרֶם בָּרָד שַׂעַר קָטֶב כְּזֶרֶם מַיִם כַּבִּירִים שֹׁטְפִים
3 הִנִּיחַ לָאָרֶץ בְּיָד׃ בְּרַגְלַיִם תֵּרָמַסְנָה עֲטֶרֶת גֵּאוּת שִׁכּוֹרֵי
4 אֶפְרָיִם׃ וְהָיְתָה צִיצַת נֹבֵל צְבִי תִפְאַרְתּוֹ אֲשֶׁר עַל־רֹאשׁ
גֵּיא שְׁמָנִים כְּבִכּוּרָהּ בְּטֶרֶם קַיִץ אֲשֶׁר יִרְאֶה הָרֹאֶה
ה אוֹתָהּ בְּעוֹדָהּ בְּכַפּוֹ יִבְלָעֶנָּה׃ בַּיּוֹם הַהוּא יִהְיֶה
יְהוָה צְבָאוֹת לַעֲטֶרֶת צְבִי וְלִצְפִירַת תִּפְאָרָה לִשְׁאָר
6 עַמּוֹ׃ וּלְרוּחַ מִשְׁפָּט לַיּוֹשֵׁב עַל־הַמִּשְׁפָּט וְלִגְבוּרָה
7 מְשִׁיבֵי מִלְחָמָה שָׁעְרָה׃ וְגַם־אֵלֶּה בַּיַּיִן שָׁגוּ וּבַשֵּׁכָר תָּעוּ
כֹּהֵן וְנָבִיא שָׁגוּ בַשֵּׁכָר נִבְלְעוּ מִן־הַיַּיִן תָּעוּ מִן־הַשֵּׁכָר שָׁגוּ
8 בָּרֹאֶה פָּקוּ פְּלִילִיָּה׃ כִּי כָּל־שֻׁלְחָנוֹת מָלְאוּ קִיא צֹאָה
9 בְּלִי מָקוֹם׃ אֶת־מִי יוֹרֶה דֵעָה וְאֶת־מִי יָבִין שְׁמוּעָה

2. Behold, the LORD hath a mighty and strong one,
As a storm of hail, a tempest of destruction,
As a storm of mighty waters overflowing,
That casteth down to the earth with violence.

3. The crown of pride of the drunkards of Ephraim
Shall be trodden under foot;

4. And the fading flower of his glorious beauty,
Which is on the head of the fat valley,
Shall be as the first-ripe fig before the summer,
Which when one looketh upon it,
While it is yet in his hand he eateth it up.

5. In that day shall the LORD of hosts be
For a crown of glory, and for a diadem of beauty,
Unto the residue of His people;

6. And for a spirit of judgment to him that sitteth in judgment,
And for strength to them that turn back the battle at the gate.

7. But these also reel through wine,
And stagger through strong drink;
The priest and the prophet reel through strong drink,
They are confused because of wine,
They stagger because of strong drink;
They reel in vision, they totter in judgment.

8. For all tables are full of filthy vomit,
And no place is clean.

9. Whom shall one teach knowledge?
And whom shall one make to understand the message?
Them that are weaned from the milk,
Them that are drawn from the breasts?

2. *a mighty and strong one. i.e.* the coming Assyrian invasion, compared to a devastating storm and flood.

4. *as the first-ripe fig.* A delicacy eagerly coveted and devoured. Thus would the enemy pounce upon Samaria with avidity (Kimchi).

5. *crown of glory.* Isaiah denounces, but never fails to bring a message of comfort. Samaria, 'the crown of pride,' will fall; but a faithful residue of Israel shall survive the storm, and to them God Himself will be 'the crown of glory'.

6. *spirit of judgment.* To the faithful remnant of Israel, God will be the source of justice within, and of strength to withstand the enemy already pouring in through the gate of the almost captured city.

7. *these also.* The prophet now turns from Samaria to Jerusalem, and finds the ruling classes in Jerusalem are those of Samaria over again. Why should Judah escape Samaria's fate, if she too remain deaf to the Divine Voice?

they reel in vision . . . judgment. Through intemperance the 'prophets' lack the capacity to discern the real significance of their own visions, or to understand and convey the teachings of their great predecessors. The priests, who were forbidden while on duty to take any wine or strong drink, from the same cause give feeble and irresolute guidance.

8. *all tables.* This verse is either a figurative description of the debasement of the national intelligence and conscience (Kay); or, 'of an actual banquet at which priests, prophets, and nobles were carousing. When the orgy is at its height, Isaiah enters and expresses his abhorrence of the scene' (Skinner).

9. *whom shall one teach.* The revellers, who resent the monotonous lessons of this Prophetic pedagogue, as they think him, are mocking Isaiah over their cups. 'Does he take us for mere children, that he gives us these platitudes and repetitions?'

י גְּמוּלֵי מֵחָלָב עַתִּיקֵי מִשָּׁדָיִם׃ כִּי צַו לָצָו צַו לָצָו קַו
11 לָקָו קַו לָקָו זְעֵיר שָׁם זְעֵיר שָׁם׃ כִּי בְּלַעֲגֵי שָׂפָה וּבְלָשׁוֹן
12 אַחֶרֶת יְדַבֵּר אֶל־הָעָם הַזֶּה׃ אֲשֶׁר ׀ אָמַר אֲלֵיהֶם זֹאת
הַמְּנוּחָה הָנִיחוּ לֶעָיֵף וְזֹאת הַמַּרְגֵּעָה וְלֹא אָבוּא שְׁמוֹעַ׃
13 וְהָיָה לָהֶם דְּבַר־יְהוָה צַו לָצָו צַו לָצָו קַו לָקָו קַו לָקָו
זְעֵיר שָׁם זְעֵיר שָׁם לְמַעַן יֵלְכוּ וְכָשְׁלוּ אָחוֹר וְנִשְׁבָּרוּ
וְנוֹקְשׁוּ וְנִלְכָּדוּ׃

CAP. XXIX. כט

22 לָכֵן כֹּה־אָמַר יְהוָה אֶל־
בֵּית יַעֲקֹב אֲשֶׁר פָּדָה אֶת־אַבְרָהָם לֹא־עַתָּה יֵבוֹשׁ יַעֲקֹב
23 וְלֹא עַתָּה פָּנָיו יֶחֱוָרוּ׃ כִּי בִרְאֹתוֹ יְלָדָיו מַעֲשֵׂה יָדַי
בְּקִרְבּוֹ יַקְדִּישׁוּ שְׁמִי וְהִקְדִּישׁוּ אֶת־קְדוֹשׁ יַעֲקֹב וְאֶת־
אֱלֹהֵי יִשְׂרָאֵל יַעֲרִיצוּ׃

10. For it is precept by precept, precept by precept,
Line by line, line by line;
Here a little, there a little.

11. For with stammering lips and with a strange tongue
Shall it be spoken to this people;

12. To whom it was said: 'This is the rest,
Give ye rest to the weary;
And this is the refreshing';
Yet they would not hear.

13. And so the word of the LORD is unto them
Precept by precept, precept by precept,
Line by line, line by line;
Here a little, there a little;
That they may go, and fall backward, and be broken,
And snared, and taken.

CHAPTER XXIX

22. Therefore thus saith the LORD, who redeemed Abraham, concerning the house of Jacob:

Jacob shall not now be ashamed,
Neither shall his face now wax pale;

23. When he seeth his children, the work of My hands, in the midst of him,
That they sanctify My name;
Yea, they shall sanctify the Holy One of Jacob,
And shall stand in awe of the God of Israel.

כח' v. 12. כצ"ל v. 13. קמץ בז"ק

10. *precept . . . a little.* Heb. *tzav latzav . . . kav lakav.* The Heb. words are purposely of one syllable and made to rhyme, so as to convey the idea of childish instruction, what they deem the Prophet's unnecessary repetition of elementary truths.

11. *with strange tongue.* Isaiah's reply is, You stammer out mocking words; God will soon 'talk Assyrian' to you. Through the harsh, laconic speech of the merciless invader, you will be fittingly chastised.

12. *to whom it was said.* God had pointed out the way of peace and recovery for the nation; but the politicians in Judah were preparing further trouble for the suffering people by seeking alliance with Egypt (Dummelow).

to the weary. The plain man of the people who would bear the brunt of the privation in any war.

13. *precept by precept.* Their contempt, even their caricature, of the Prophet's plain teachings will come bitterly home to them when God speaks to them through 'line upon line', in punishment upon punishment, for 'every precept upon precept' they have defied and broken (Rashi).

CHAPTER XXIX, 22, 23

The Prophetic message must not end in despair. These verses hark back to Israel's early history; they look forward to the future as a time of restoration, when the people shall by their lives sanctify the Holy One of Jacob.

HAFTORAH SHEMOTH (FOR SEPHARDIM) הפטרת שמות לספרדים

JEREMIAH I–II, 3

CHAPTER I

1. The words of Jeremiah the son of Hilkiah, of the priests that were in Anathoth in the land of Benjamin, 2. to whom the word of the Lord came in the days of Josiah the son of Amon, king of Judah, in the thirteenth year of his reign. 3. It came also in the days of Jehoiakim the son of Josiah, king of Judah, unto the end of the eleventh year of Zedekiah the son of Josiah, king of Judah, unto the carrying away of Jerusalem captive in the fifth month. 4. And the word of the LORD came unto me, saying:

5. Before I formed thee in the belly I knew thee,
And before thou camest forth out of the womb I sanctified thee;
I have appointed thee a prophet unto the nations.

6. Then said I: 'Ah, Lord GOD! behold, I cannot speak; for I am a child.' 7. But the LORD said unto me:

Say not: I am a child;
For to whomsoever I shall send thee thou shalt go,
And whatsoever I shall command thee thou shalt speak.

8. Be not afraid of them;
For I am with thee to deliver thee,
Saith the LORD.

CAP. I. א

א דִּבְרֵי יִרְמְיָהוּ בֶּן־חִלְקִיָּהוּ מִן־הַכֹּהֲנִים אֲשֶׁר בַּעֲנָתוֹת
2 בְּאֶרֶץ בִּנְיָמִן׃ אֲשֶׁר הָיָה דְבַר־יְהוָה אֵלָיו בִּימֵי יֹאשִׁיָּהוּ
3 בֶן־אָמוֹן מֶלֶךְ יְהוּדָה בִּשְׁלֹשׁ־עֶשְׂרֵה שָׁנָה לְמָלְכוֹ׃ וַיְהִי
בִּימֵי יְהוֹיָקִים בֶּן־יֹאשִׁיָּהוּ מֶלֶךְ יְהוּדָה עַד־תֹּם עַשְׁתֵּי־
עֶשְׂרֵה שָׁנָה לְצִדְקִיָּהוּ בֶן־יֹאשִׁיָּהוּ מֶלֶךְ יְהוּדָה עַד־גְּלוֹת
4 יְרוּשָׁלַםִ בַּחֹדֶשׁ הַחֲמִישִׁי׃ וַיְהִי דְבַר־יְהוָה אֵלַי
ה לֵאמֹר׃ בְּטֶרֶם אֶצָּורְךָ בַבֶּטֶן יְדַעְתִּיךָ וּבְטֶרֶם תֵּצֵא
6 מֵרֶחֶם הִקְדַּשְׁתִּיךָ נָבִיא לַגּוֹיִם נְתַתִּיךָ׃ וָאֹמַר אֲהָהּ
7 אֲדֹנָי יֱהוִה הִנֵּה לֹא־יָדַעְתִּי דַּבֵּר כִּי־נַעַר אָנֹכִי׃ וַיֹּאמֶר
יְהוָה אֵלַי אַל־תֹּאמַר נַעַר אָנֹכִי כִּי עַל־כָּל־אֲשֶׁר אֶשְׁלָחֲךָ
8 תֵּלֵךְ וְאֵת כָּל־אֲשֶׁר אֲצַוְּךָ תְּדַבֵּר׃ אַל־תִּירָא מִפְּנֵיהֶם

v. 5. ו׳ יתירה

The call of Jeremiah has been aptly chosen by the Sephardim as the Haftorah for the Sedrah dealing with the call of Moses: diffidence and hesitancy in assuming the well-nigh superhuman task that Heaven assigned to them, are common to both. The final verses of the Haftorah (II, 2, 3), poetically recalling the wanderings in the Wilderness, form another link with the Sedrah.

Jeremiah was born of a priestly family about the year 650 B.C.E. His Prophetic call came to him in the reign of Josiah, king of Judah, in the year 626. He witnessed the fall of Nineveh and the annihilation of the Assyrian Empire in 606; the death of Josiah, Judah's righteous king, in 605; and lived through the two sieges of Jerusalem in 597 and 586, with the attendant destruction of the Jewish state and the consequent transportation of the greater portion of his people to 'the rivers of Babylon'. We last hear of him in Egypt, carried thither by fugitive Judeans; and legend relates that he died a martyr's death at the hands of his brethren. Whatever basis there may be for this legend, it is but too true that Jeremiah the Prophet lived a martyr's life. For the greater part of his career, he was one man against the whole nation. By nature timid and shrinking, he proclaimed the Divine message fearlessly to ruler, noble, priest, and people alike.

Jeremiah is the spiritual heir of the great Prophets that preceded him. He combines the tenderness of Hosea, the fearlessness of Amos, and the stern majesty of Isaiah. Like them, he is first of all a preacher of repentance; threatening judgment and, at the same time, holding out the promise of restoration. But even in his darkest moments, when he utterly despairs of the future of the Jewish state, his faith and trust in God do not forsake him. 'Though all be lost,' he seems to say to Israel, 'turn to God in perfect trust, call Him your Father, and His love will regenerate you.' To Jeremiah, Religion is an inward thing, a personal relation between the individual and his Maker, a relation that is untouched by national prosperity and can only be deepened by national ruin. 'The history of Israel begins with the migration of Abraham from the Euphrates to the Jordan; its classical period closes with the compulsory migration of the exiles from the Jordan back to the Euphrates. If Israel had been merely a race like others it would never have survived this fearful catastrophe, and would have disappeared in the Babylonian exile' (Cornill). That it did not so disappear was due to the activity of two men—Jeremiah and his disciple Ezekiel. Jeremiah's message to his despairing brethren in Babylon, 'Seek the welfare of the city wherein ye dwell, and pray unto the LORD for it: for in its welfare shall be your peace,' has been of incalculable influence in the civic life of all Jews throughout the world.

9. Then the LORD put forth His hand, and touched my mouth; and the LORD said unto me:

Behold, I have put My words in thy mouth;
10. See, I have this day set thee over the nations and over the kingdoms,
To root out and to pull down,
And to destroy and to overthrow;
To build, and to plant.

11. Moreover the word of the LORD came unto me, saying: 'Jeremiah, what seest thou?' And I said: 'I see a rod of an [1]almond-tree.' 12. Then said the LORD unto me: 'Thou hast well seen; for I [2]watch over My word to perform it.' ¶ 13. And the word of the LORD came unto me the second time, saying: 'What seest thou?' And I said: 'I see a seething pot; and the face thereof is from the north.' 14. Then the LORD said unto me: 'Out of the north the evil shall break forth upon all the inhabitants of the land. 15. For, lo, I will call all the families of the kingdoms of the north, saith the LORD; and they shall come, and they shall set every one his throne at the entrance of the gates of Jerusalem, and against all the walls thereof round about, and against all the cities of Judah. 16. And I will utter my judgments against them touching all their wickedness; in that they have forsaken Me, and have offered unto other gods, and worshipped the work of their own hands. 17. Thou therefore gird up thy loins, and arise, and speak unto them all that I com-

[1] Heb. *shaked*. [2] Heb. *shoked*.

9 כִּֽי־אִתְּךָ֥ אֲנִ֛י לְהַצִּלֶ֖ךָ נְאֻם־יְהוָֽה׃ וַיִּשְׁלַ֤ח יְהוָה֙ אֶת־יָד֔וֹ
וַיַּגַּ֖ע עַל־פִּ֑י וַיֹּ֤אמֶר יְהוָה֙ אֵלַ֔י הִנֵּ֛ה נָתַ֥תִּי דְבָרַ֖י בְּפִֽיךָ׃
י רְאֵ֞ה הִפְקַדְתִּ֣יךָ ׀ הַיּ֣וֹם הַזֶּ֗ה עַל־הַגּוֹיִם֙ וְעַל־הַמַּמְלָכ֔וֹת
לִנְת֥וֹשׁ וְלִנְת֖וֹץ וּלְהַאֲבִ֣יד וְלַהֲר֑וֹס לִבְנ֖וֹת וְלִנְטֽוֹעַ׃
11 וַיְהִ֤י דְבַר־יְהוָה֙ אֵלַ֣י לֵאמֹ֔ר מָה־אַתָּ֥ה רֹאֶ֖ה יִרְמְיָ֑הוּ וָאֹמַ֕ר
12 מַקֵּ֥ל שָׁקֵ֖ד אֲנִ֥י רֹאֶֽה׃ וַיֹּ֧אמֶר יְהוָ֛ה אֵלַ֖י הֵיטַ֣בְתָּ לִרְא֑וֹת
13 כִּֽי־שֹׁקֵ֥ד אֲנִ֛י עַל־דְּבָרִ֖י לַעֲשֹׂתֽוֹ׃ וַיְהִ֨י דְבַר־יְהוָ֥ה ׀
אֵלַי֙ שֵׁנִ֣ית לֵאמֹ֔ר מָ֖ה אַתָּ֣ה רֹאֶ֑ה וָאֹמַ֗ר סִ֤יר נָפ֙וּחַ֙ אֲנִ֣י
14 רֹאֶ֔ה וּפָנָ֖יו מִפְּנֵ֥י צָפֽוֹנָה׃ וַיֹּ֥אמֶר יְהוָ֖ה אֵלָ֑י מִצָּפוֹן֙ תִּפָּתַ֣ח
טו הָֽרָעָ֔ה עַ֥ל כָּל־יֹשְׁבֵ֖י הָאָֽרֶץ׃ כִּ֣י ׀ הִנְנִ֣י קֹרֵ֗א לְכָל־
מִשְׁפְּח֛וֹת מַמְלְכ֥וֹת צָפ֖וֹנָה נְאֻם־יְהוָ֑ה וּבָ֡אוּ וְנָתְנוּ֩ אִ֨ישׁ
כִּסְא֜וֹ פֶּ֣תַח ׀ שַׁעֲרֵ֣י יְרוּשָׁלִַ֗ם וְעַ֤ל כָּל־חוֹמֹתֶ֙יהָ֙ סָבִ֔יב וְעַ֖ל
16 כָּל־עָרֵ֥י יְהוּדָֽה׃ וְדִבַּרְתִּ֤י מִשְׁפָּטַי֙ אוֹתָ֔ם עַ֖ל כָּל־רָעָתָ֑ם
אֲשֶׁ֣ר עֲזָב֗וּנִי וַֽיְקַטְּרוּ֙ לֵאלֹהִ֣ים אֲחֵרִ֔ים וַיִּֽשְׁתַּחֲו֖וּ לְמַעֲשֵׂ֥י
17 יְדֵיהֶֽם׃ וְאַתָּה֙ תֶּאְזֹ֣ר מָתְנֶ֔יךָ וְקַמְתָּ֙ וְדִבַּרְתָּ֣ אֲלֵיהֶ֔ם אֵ֛ת

1. *Hilkiah.* Not the priest of that name.
Anathoth. Four miles north-east of Jerusalem.
land of Benjamin. This hilly territory was 26 miles by 12 miles, about the size of Middlesex.

2. *Josiah.* He reigned from 626–605. He put down the idolatries, abominations and immoralities that had been introduced by Manasseh, and led a great religious revival in Israel.

3. *Zedekiah.* The youngest son of Josiah, and the last king of Judah.

4–10. JEREMIAH'S CALL

5. *knew thee. i.e.* chose thee; cf. Gen. XVIII, 19.
sanctified thee. Consecrated thee; *i.e.* set thee apart for My service. 'In the very moment of his call, Jeremiah learnt that he was a child of destiny. God had planned his life, even before he was born. The riddle and purpose of existence were thus solved for Jeremiah' (Duhm).
unto the nations. As Amos and Isaiah before him, but more so. Israel was now caught in the current of universal politics and its career was inextricably bound up with Assyria, Babylon and Egypt (Peake).

6. *I am a child.* These words express the shrinking self-distrust of a sensitive nature, and the humility that characterizes truly great minds; cf. the reply of Moses in the Sedrah, IV, 10.

7. *say not.* Whatever his limitations may be, they matter not, for he is to be God's messenger; and, whatever opposition or even persecution may be his lot, he would be Divinely supported.

9. *touched my mouth.* Symbolic of Divine inspiration.

10. *set thee.* lit. 'made thee My deputy'.
to root out. Because the Word of God, which the Prophet proclaims, determines the fate of nations and kingdoms.
to plant. Jeremiah's activity would also be to prepare the way for the work of restoration.

11, 12. THE SYMBOL OF THE ALMOND-TREE

11. *an almond-tree.* Heb. *shaked*, and the Heb. for 'watching' is *shoked.* There is more than a play on words here. The almond-tree is so named in Hebrew, because, blossoming early in January, it is the first to awake from winter's sleep. On seeing it, the thought flashes across mand thee; be not dismayed at them, lest I dismay thee before them. 18. For, behold, I have made thee this day a fortified city, and an iron pillar, and brazen walls, against the whole land, against the kings of Judah, against the princes thereof, against the priests thereof, and against the people of the land. 19. And they shall fight against thee; but they shall not prevail against thee; For I am with thee, saith the LORD, to deliver thee.'

CHAPTER II

1. And the word of the LORD came to me, saying: 2. Go, and cry in the ears of Jerusalem, saying: Thus saith the LORD:

I remember for thee the affection of thy youth,
The love of thine espousals;
How thou wentest after Me in the wilderness,
In a land that was not sown.

3. Israel is the LORD's hallowed portion,
His first-fruits of the increase;
All that devour him shall be held guilty,
Evil shall come upon them,
Saith the LORD.

כָּל־אֲשֶׁר אָנֹכִי אֲצַוֶּךָּ אַל־תֵּחַת מִפְּנֵיהֶם פֶּן־אֲחִתְּךָ
18 לִפְנֵיהֶם׃ וַאֲנִי הִנֵּה נְתַתִּיךָ הַיּוֹם לְעִיר מִבְצָר וּלְעַמּוּד
בַּרְזֶל וּלְחֹמוֹת נְחֹשֶׁת עַל־כָּל־הָאָרֶץ לְמַלְכֵי יְהוּדָה לְשָׂרֶיהָ
19 לְכֹהֲנֶיהָ וּלְעַם הָאָרֶץ׃ וְנִלְחֲמוּ אֵלֶיךָ וְלֹא־יוּכְלוּ לָךְ כִּי־
אִתְּךָ אֲנִי נְאֻם־יְהוָה לְהַצִּילֶךָ׃

CAP. II. ב

א 2 וַיְהִי דְבַר־יְהוָה אֵלַי לֵאמֹר׃ הָלֹךְ וְקָרָאתָ בְאָזְנֵי יְרוּשָׁלִַם
לֵאמֹר כֹּה אָמַר יְהוָה זָכַרְתִּי לָךְ חֶסֶד נְעוּרַיִךְ אַהֲבַת
3 כְּלוּלֹתָיִךְ לֶכְתֵּךְ אַחֲרַי בַּמִּדְבָּר בְּאֶרֶץ לֹא זְרוּעָה׃ קֹדֶשׁ
יִשְׂרָאֵל לַיהוָה רֵאשִׁית תְּבוּאָתֹה כָּל־אֹכְלָיו יֶאְשָׁמוּ רָעָה
תָּבֹא אֲלֵיהֶם נְאֻם־יְהוָה׃

ב׳ v. 3. קמץ בז״ק

the Prophet's mind that God is awake and watches over His word to fulfil it, without delay.

13–16. THE SYMBOL OF THE CALDRON

14. *out of the north.* From the North had come the Assyrian invasions, and into the North the Ten Tribes had been led captive. And Babylon, which was to take Judah into exile, also lay to the North.

the evil. Foretold by all the prophets as the result of the nation's sinning.

15. *shall set every one his throne.* The neighbourhood of the city gate was the place where trials were ordinarily held. Here the rulers of the invading army will sit in judgment on the conquered people. This was literally fulfilled; see Jer. XXXIX, 3.

17–19. ENCOURAGEMENT TO JEREMIAH

17. *gird up thy loins.* Prepare thyself for a strenuous task.

lest I dismay thee before them. If thou fearest them, thou wilt fail before them (Kimchi). Jeremiah can only conquer if he does not for one moment lose courage—a warning needed by the Prophet whose life would be full of anguish and martyrdom.

18. *the people of the land.* Heb. *am ha-aretz*; probably the National Assembly; see p. 80, note 7.

19. *shall not prevail.* *i.e.* shall not finally prevail (Streane). Before the Prophet's death, his warnings would be justified, and his cause vindicated.

CHAPTER II

1–3. The opening verses of the first prophecy of Jeremiah. God reminds Israel of her loyalty and affection in the Wilderness. Jeremiah pictures Israel's loyalty to God as that of an affectionate bride, who follows the chosen of her heart even into a wilderness.

2. *affection.* Heb. *chesed.* A very rich and beautiful word, here meaning unquestioned and whole-hearted devotion and total forgetfulness of self, a love more than filial, like that of a youthful, loving bride.

how thou wentest after Me. It was only such love, thought the Prophet, that could account for Israel's willingness to forget the grandeur of Egypt, and brave the terrors of the Wilderness—its hardships, perils and treacherous foes. It was only such love that could cause them gladly to follow the call of God into the Unknown, on a novel quest of the Divine, that was to fill man's earthly existence with new hopes; on an unheard-of adventure in Religion, that was to turn the current of history and humanize mankind.

3. *the LORD'S hallowed portion.* All the nations are the LORD's harvest; but Israel is set apart for Him alone, even as the first-fruits are set apart for the use of the priest. In the Sedrah, IV, 21, Israel is called God's firstborn son.

evil shall come upon them. Woe to anyone who violates that sanctity, and assails Israel.

6 2. And God spoke unto Moses, and said unto him: 'I am the LORD; 3. and I appeared unto Abraham, unto Isaac, and unto Jacob, as God Almighty, but by My name [1]יהוה I made Me not known to them. 4. And I have also established My covenant with them, to give them the land of Canaan, the land of their sojournings, wherein they sojourned. 5. And moreover I have heard the groaning of the children of Israel, whom the Egyptians keep in bondage; and I have

[1] The ineffable name, read *Adonai*, which means, *the Lord*.

פ פ פ יד 14

2 וַיְדַבֵּר אֱלֹהִים אֶל־מֹשֶׁה וַיֹּאמֶר אֵלָיו אֲנִי יְהוָה׃ וָאֵרָא 3
אֶל־אַבְרָהָם אֶל־יִצְחָק וְאֶל־יַעֲקֹב בְּאֵל שַׁדָּי וּשְׁמִי יְהוָה
4 לֹא נוֹדַעְתִּי לָהֶם׃ וְגַם הֲקִמֹתִי אֶת־בְּרִיתִי אִתָּם לָתֵת
לָהֶם אֶת־אֶרֶץ כְּנָעַן אֵת אֶרֶץ מְגֻרֵיהֶם אֲשֶׁר־גָּרוּ בָהּ׃
ה וְגַם ׀ אֲנִי שָׁמַעְתִּי אֶת־נַאֲקַת בְּנֵי יִשְׂרָאֵל אֲשֶׁר מִצְרַיִם

II. VA-AYRA

(CHAPTERS VI, 2–IX)

RENEWED PROMISE OF REDEMPTION. CHAPTER VI, 2–13

These verses are the concluding portion of the Call of Moses, and can only be understood in connection with Chaps. III–V.

In view of the despair and despondency of both Moses and the People recorded in the last chapter, and in reply to the reproach of Moses, 'Thou hast not delivered Thy people,' God repeats the promises of redemption made at Horeb.

2. *I am the LORD.* Or, *I am ADONAY.*

The emphasis is on the words *I am the LORD.* They are not intended to inform Moses what God is *called*, but to impress upon him that *the guarantee of the fulfilment of the Divine promises lay in the nature of the Being who had given the promises.* Even as the phrase, 'I am Pharaoh' (Gen. XLI, 44) is merely an assertion of royal authority and power, in the same manner, 'I am Adonay,' means, 'I am He who has the power and the faithfulness to fulfil any promise vouchsafed by Me. I have promised Redemption, and I shall fulfil that promise; I will and can do it. Israel shall yet know that I am the LORD; and Pharaoh, who had contemptuously declared, I know not the LORD!—he too shall know it.' This is also the explanation given by Rashi: 'God says unto Moses, I have not sent thee in vain as thou complainest, but in order to fulfil My words to the Fathers. *I am the LORD* is often used as a reminder of Divine retribution both in connection with rewards and with punishments.'

3. *as God Almighty.* Heb. *El Shaddai*; see Gen. XVII, 1 (p. 57, note 1). Note that the text reads, 'as God Almighty' and not, '*with my name* God Almighty.' There is here no question of contrasting an old Name with any new Name about to be disclosed.

but by My name ADONAY I made Me not known to them. Better, '*but as to My name ADONAY, I was not known to them.*' Although the Patriarchs were familiar with, and freely used, the Name *Adonay*, its import *as the everlasting God of faithfulness whose promises, even though they extend over centuries and millennia, are invariably fulfilled*, was not fully understood by them. 'Scripture does not state, My Name Adonay *I did not make known* to them (הודעתי); but, By My Name Adonay *I was not known* to them (נודעתי); *i.e.* I was not recognized by them in my attribute of Faithfulness, which is the essential part of the Name *Adonay*, signifying One who is faithful to give reality of His word; seeing that I had promised them possession of Canaan, but had not in their day fulfilled that promise' (Rashi). God was now to make the full signification of that Name known to the children of Israel by redeeming them from slavery. Thus would He manifest Himself to the children in a manner that He had not done to the Fathers. See Additional Note C, p. 397.

4. *of their sojournings.* The land of their temporary abode, in which they resided as strangers, but which was promised to their descendants as a permanent possession.

5. *I have heard.* The pronoun is emphatic; *i.e.* the same Being who established the Covenant. The context of the passage implying: 'I am unchangeable and My plans are unalterable. I have promised to your ancestors the possession of Canaan after a certain time of trial and misery; this period of oppression is now drawing near its close; and I shall therefore fulfil My promise by rescuing you with great judgments from your oppressors' (Kalisch).

remembered My covenant. 6. Wherefore say unto the children of Israel: I am the LORD, and I will bring you out from under the burdens of the Egyptians, and I will deliver you from their bondage, and I will redeem you with an outstretched arm, and with great judgments; 7. and I will take you to Me for a people, and I will be to you a God; and ye shall know that I am the LORD your God, who brought you out from under the burdens of the Egyptians. 8. And I will bring you in unto the land concerning which I lifted up My hand to give it to Abraham, to Isaac, and to Jacob; and I will give it you for a heritage: I am the LORD.' 9. And Moses spoke so unto the children of Israel; but they hearkened not unto Moses for impatience of spirit, and for cruel bondage. ¶ 10. And the LORD spoke unto Moses, saying: 11. 'Go in, speak unto Pharaoh king of Egypt, that he let the children of Israel go out of his land.' 12. And Moses spoke before the LORD, saying: 'Behold, the children of Israel have not hearkened unto me; how then shall Pharaoh hear me, who am of uncircumcised lips?' ¶ 13. And the LORD spoke unto Moses and unto Aaron, and gave them a charge unto the children of Israel, and unto Pharaoh king of Egypt, to bring the children

6 מַעֲבִדִים אֹתָם וָאֶזְכֹּר אֶת־בְּרִיתִי׃ לָכֵן אֱמֹר לִבְנֵי־יִשְׂרָאֵל
אֲנִי יְהוָה וְהוֹצֵאתִי אֶתְכֶם מִתַּחַת סִבְלֹת מִצְרַיִם וְהִצַּלְתִּי
אֶתְכֶם מֵעֲבֹדָתָם וְגָאַלְתִּי אֶתְכֶם בִּזְרוֹעַ נְטוּיָה וּבִשְׁפָטִים
7 גְּדֹלִים׃ וְלָקַחְתִּי אֶתְכֶם לִי לְעָם וְהָיִיתִי לָכֶם לֵאלֹהִים
וִידַעְתֶּם כִּי אֲנִי יְהוָה אֱלֹהֵיכֶם הַמּוֹצִיא אֶתְכֶם מִתַּחַת
8 סִבְלוֹת מִצְרָיִם׃ וְהֵבֵאתִי אֶתְכֶם אֶל־הָאָרֶץ אֲשֶׁר נָשָׂאתִי
אֶת־יָדִי לָתֵת אֹתָהּ לְאַבְרָהָם לְיִצְחָק וּלְיַעֲקֹב וְנָתַתִּי אֹתָהּ
9 לָכֶם מוֹרָשָׁה אֲנִי יְהוָה׃ וַיְדַבֵּר מֹשֶׁה כֵּן אֶל־בְּנֵי יִשְׂרָאֵל
וְלֹא שָׁמְעוּ אֶל־מֹשֶׁה מִקֹּצֶר רוּחַ וּמֵעֲבֹדָה קָשָׁה׃ פ
11 וַיְדַבֵּר יְהוָה אֶל־מֹשֶׁה לֵּאמֹר׃ בֹּא דַבֵּר אֶל־פַּרְעֹה מֶלֶךְ
12 מִצְרָיִם וִישַׁלַּח אֶת־בְּנֵי־יִשְׂרָאֵל מֵאַרְצוֹ׃ וַיְדַבֵּר מֹשֶׁה
לִפְנֵי יְהוָה לֵאמֹר הֵן בְּנֵי־יִשְׂרָאֵל לֹא־שָׁמְעוּ אֵלַי וְאֵיךְ
יִשְׁמָעֵנִי פַרְעֹה וַאֲנִי עֲרַל שְׂפָתָיִם׃ פ
13 וַיְדַבֵּר יְהוָה אֶל־מֹשֶׁה וְאֶל־אַהֲרֹן וַיְצַוֵּם אֶל־בְּנֵי יִשְׂרָאֵל
וְאֶל־פַּרְעֹה מֶלֶךְ מִצְרָיִם לְהוֹצִיא אֶת־בְּנֵי־יִשְׂרָאֵל מֵאֶרֶץ

6. *I will redeem you.* Heb. *gaal* means, 'to reclaim, redeem'; hence *goel*, the technical term for the kinsman whose duty it was to ransom or, if need be, avenge the person or property of his relative. God intervenes in order to ransom His helpless and suffering People from slavery; and in mercy and faithfulness, He becomes their Redeemer (*goel*).

with an outstretched arm. With manifestation of My power.

judgments. Wherewith to punish the oppressing tyrant.

7. *I will take you to Me for a people.* After the redemption from Egypt, God will take Israel to Mount Sinai to receive His revealed Teaching. The covenant at Mount Sinai was the higher spiritual purpose of Israel's deliverance.

ye shall know. Here again it is not a question of learning a new Name of God, but of feeling His power in actual experiences of life.

8. *lifted up My hand. i.e.* sware. The expression is taken from the custom of lifting up the hand to heaven when taking an oath.

heritage. Heb. *morashah*, the same word used in Deut. XXXIII, 4 of the Torah. This is significant. Israel has been offered two heritages: the one spiritual—the Torah—is unconditional and eternal. Not so the other heritage, the Land of Promise. Its possession depends upon Israel's appreciation of, and obedience to, its God-given Law (Hirsch).

I am the LORD. Or, 'I am ADONAY.' The message to Moses closes with the same Divine assertion with which it opens—God is a God of faithfulness, and His promises are unfailingly realized.

9. *impatience of spirit.* The people were utterly crushed by their disappointment, and they paid no heed to fresh promises of redemption.

cruel bondage. lit. 'hard labour'.

12. *who am. i.e.* especially since I am.

of uncircumcised lips. i.e. with lips closed or impeded, not properly prepared to deliver an all-important message; see IV, 9. The same metaphor is used of the heart (Lev. XXVI, 41) and of the ear (Jer. VI, 10). He believes that his effort had failed owing to his stammering and hesitating speech.

13. *unto Moses and unto Aaron.* God replies by charging Aaron to take part with Moses in the emancipation of Israel (Rashi).

CHAPTER VI, 14–VII, 7

THE GENEALOGY OF MOSES AND AARON

14–27. At this point the narrative gives the genealogical tree of Moses and Aaron, who now assume leadership of the People. In giving the chiefs of the families of the tribe of Levi, the of Israel out of the land of Egypt.* ii. ¶ 14. These are the heads of their fathers' houses: the sons of Reuben the first-born of Israel: Hanoch, and Pallu, Hezron, and Carmi. These are the families of Reuben. 15. And the sons of Simeon: Jemuel, and Jamin, and Ohad, and Jachin, and Zohar, and Shaul the son of a Canaanitish woman. These are the families of Simeon. 16. And these are the names of the sons of Levi according to their generations: Gershon and Kohath, and Merari. And the years of the life of Levi were a hundred thirty and seven years. 17. The sons of Gershon: Libni and Shimei, according to their families. 18. And the sons of Kohath: Amram, and Izhar, and Hebron, and Uzziel. And the years of the life of Kohath were a hundred thirty and three years. 19. And the sons of Merari: Mahli and Mushi. These are the families of the Levites according to their generations. 20. And Amram took him Jochebed his father's sister to wife; and she bore him Aaron and Moses. And the years of the life of Amram were a hundred and thirty and seven years. 21. And the sons of Izhar: Korah, and Nepheg, and Zichri. 22. And the sons of Uzziel: Mishael, and Elzaphan, and Sithri. 23. And

שני
14 מִצְרָיִם׃ ס אֵלֶּה רָאשֵׁי בֵית־אֲבֹתָם בְּנֵי רְאוּבֵן
בְּכֹר יִשְׂרָאֵל חֲנוֹךְ וּפַלּוּא חֶצְרֹן וְכַרְמִי אֵלֶּה מִשְׁפְּחֹת
טו רְאוּבֵן׃ וּבְנֵי שִׁמְעוֹן יְמוּאֵל וְיָמִין וְאֹהַד וְיָכִין וְצֹחַר
16 וְשָׁאוּל בֶּן־הַכְּנַעֲנִית אֵלֶּה מִשְׁפְּחֹת שִׁמְעוֹן׃ וְאֵלֶּה שְׁמוֹת
בְּנֵי־לֵוִי לְתֹלְדֹתָם גֵּרְשׁוֹן וּקְהָת וּמְרָרִי וּשְׁנֵי חַיֵּי לֵוִי שֶׁבַע
17 וּשְׁלֹשִׁים וּמְאַת שָׁנָה׃ בְּנֵי גֵרְשׁוֹן לִבְנִי וְשִׁמְעִי לְמִשְׁפְּחֹתָם׃
18 וּבְנֵי קְהָת עַמְרָם וְיִצְהָר וְחֶבְרוֹן וְעֻזִּיאֵל וּשְׁנֵי חַיֵּי קְהָת
19 שָׁלֹשׁ וּשְׁלֹשִׁים וּמְאַת שָׁנָה׃ וּבְנֵי מְרָרִי מַחְלִי וּמוּשִׁי אֵלֶּה
כ מִשְׁפְּחֹת הַלֵּוִי לְתֹלְדֹתָם׃ וַיִּקַּח עַמְרָם אֶת־יוֹכֶבֶד דֹּדָתוֹ
לוֹ לְאִשָּׁה וַתֵּלֶד לוֹ אֶת־אַהֲרֹן וְאֶת־מֹשֶׁה וּשְׁנֵי חַיֵּי עַמְרָם
21 שֶׁבַע וּשְׁלֹשִׁים וּמְאַת שָׁנָה׃ וּבְנֵי יִצְהָר קֹרַח וָנֶפֶג וְזִכְרִי׃
22 23 וּבְנֵי עֻזִּיאֵל מִישָׁאֵל וְאֶלְצָפָן וְסִתְרִי׃ וַיִּקַּח אַהֲרֹן אֶת־
אֱלִישֶׁבַע בַּת־עַמִּינָדָב אֲחוֹת נַחְשׁוֹן לוֹ לְאִשָּׁה וַתֵּלֶד לוֹ

names of the families of the two elder tribes are included, possibly to show that even as Moses was not the eldest son of Amram, Kohath was not the eldest son of Levi. The firstborn according to nature is not always the 'first-born' in the sight of God. This thought is general in Scripture. Abel, Shem, Isaac, Jacob, Levi, Judah, Joseph, Ephraim, Moses, David, were none of them eldest sons in their families.

14. *fathers' houses.* A technical term for 'clans' or 'families'—the 'heads' are the acknowledged chiefs and founders of families. For the names enumerated, see Gen. XLVI, 9 and I Chron. V, 3.

15. *the sons of Simeon.* The list corresponds with that given in Gen. XLVI, 10.

16. *according to their generations.* This phrase is introduced here because in regard to Levi, the grandsons, great-grandsons, and other descendants are also given.

20. *Amram.* Referred to, but not mentioned, in II, 1.

Jochebed. As later in the case of royal persons, *e.g.* I Kings XV, 2, the name of the mothers of Moses and Aaron, Eleasar and Phineas, are given. The name means, '*Adonay* is my glory' (which shows that, contrary to the belief of Bible critics, even according to 'P', the name *Adonay* was used *before* the days of Moses. Some scholars maintain that it was known in Abraham's home, long before Abraham. There is nothing contrary to Jewish tradition in such a belief).

his father's sister. Marriage with an aunt is prohibited in Lev. XVIII, 12. Such marriages were not unlawful before the Giving of the Torah. That such a circumstance is not suppressed in regard to the family of the Lawgiver is eloquent testimony to the unsparing veracity of Scripture.

Aaron and Moses. Miriam is not mentioned, as the descent in the male line only is traced.

21. *Korah.* See Num. XVI, 1 and I Chron. VI, 38.

23. *Aaron took.* Aaron's children are enumerated because of their later prominence in Israel's history.

Elisheba. This name is better known under the form given in the Septuagint, 'Elizabeth.'

Nadab and Abihu. They died before the altar for offering 'strange fire'; see Lev. X, 1, 2.

25. *Eleazar.* Became high-priest upon the death of Aaron; see Num. XX, 23–28.

Phinehas. Became high-priest on the death of Eleazar; see Judg. XX, 28. The name Phinehas

Aaron took him Elisheba, the daughter of Amminadab, the sister of Nahshon, to wife; and she bore him Nadab and Abihu, Eleazar and Ithamar. 24. And the sons of Korah: Assir, and Elkanah, and Abiasaph; these are the families of the Korahites. 25. And Eleazar Aaron's son took him one of the daughters of Putiel to wife; and she bore him Phinehas. These are the heads of the fathers' houses of the Levites according to their families. 26. These are that Aaron and Moses, to whom the LORD said: 'Bring out the children of Israel from the land of Egypt according to their hosts.' 27. These are they that spoke to Pharaoh king of Egypt, to bring out the children of Israel from Egypt. These are that Moses and Aaron. 28. And it came to pass on the day when the LORD spoke unto Moses in the land of Egypt,* iii. 29. that the LORD spoke unto Moses, saying: 'I am the LORD; speak thou unto Pharaoh king of Egypt all that I speak unto thee.' 30. And Moses said before the LORD: 'Behold, I am of uncircumcised lips, and how shall Pharaoh hearken unto me?'

24 אֶת־נָדָב וְאֶת־אֲבִיהוּא אֶת־אֶלְעָזָר וְאֶת־אִיתָמָר׃ וּבְנֵי קֹרַח
כה אַסִּיר וְאֶלְקָנָה וַאֲבִיאָסָף אֵלֶּה מִשְׁפְּחֹת הַקָּרְחִי׃ וְאֶלְעָזָר
בֶּן־אַהֲרֹן לָקַח־לוֹ מִבְּנוֹת פּוּטִיאֵל לוֹ לְאִשָּׁה וַתֵּלֶד לוֹ
26 אֶת־פִּינְחָס אֵלֶּה רָאשֵׁי אֲבוֹת הַלְוִיִּם לְמִשְׁפְּחֹתָם׃ הוּא
אַהֲרֹן וּמֹשֶׁה אֲשֶׁר אָמַר יְהוָה לָהֶם הוֹצִיאוּ אֶת־בְּנֵי
27 יִשְׂרָאֵל מֵאֶרֶץ מִצְרַיִם עַל־צִבְאֹתָם׃ הֵם הַמְדַבְּרִים אֶל־
פַּרְעֹה מֶלֶךְ־מִצְרַיִם לְהוֹצִיא אֶת־בְּנֵי־יִשְׂרָאֵל מִמִּצְרָיִם
28 הוּא מֹשֶׁה וְאַהֲרֹן׃ וַיְהִי בְּיוֹם דִּבֶּר יְהוָה אֶל־מֹשֶׁה בְּאֶרֶץ
שלישי 29 מִצְרָיִם׃* ס וַיְדַבֵּר יְהוָה אֶל־מֹשֶׁה לֵּאמֹר אֲנִי יְהוָה
דַּבֵּר אֶל־פַּרְעֹה מֶלֶךְ מִצְרַיִם אֵת כָּל־אֲשֶׁר אֲנִי דֹּבֵר אֵלֶיךָ׃
ל וַיֹּאמֶר מֹשֶׁה לִפְנֵי יְהוָה הֵן אֲנִי עֲרַל שְׂפָתַיִם וְאֵיךְ יִשְׁמַע
אֵלַי פַּרְעֹה׃ פ

7

CHAPTER VII

1. And the LORD said unto Moses: 'See, I have set thee in God's stead to Pharaoh; and Aaron thy brother shall be thy prophet. 2. Thou shalt speak all that I command thee; and Aaron thy brother shall speak unto Pharaoh, that he let the children of Israel go out of his land. 3. And I will harden Pharaoh's heart, and multiply My signs and My wonders in the land of Egypt. 4. But Pharaoh will not hearken unto you, and I will lay My hand upon Egypt, and bring forth My hosts, My people the children of Israel, out of the land of

ז

CAP. VII. ז

א וַיֹּאמֶר יְהוָה אֶל־מֹשֶׁה רְאֵה נְתַתִּיךָ אֱלֹהִים לְפַרְעֹה וְאַהֲרֹן
2 אָחִיךָ יִהְיֶה נְבִיאֶךָ׃ אַתָּה תְדַבֵּר אֵת כָּל־אֲשֶׁר אֲצַוֶּךָּ
וְאַהֲרֹן אָחִיךָ יְדַבֵּר אֶל־פַּרְעֹה וְשִׁלַּח אֶת־בְּנֵי־יִשְׂרָאֵל
3 מֵאַרְצוֹ׃ וַאֲנִי אַקְשֶׁה אֶת־לֵב פַּרְעֹה וְהִרְבֵּיתִי אֶת־אֹתֹתַי
4 וְאֶת־מוֹפְתַי בְּאֶרֶץ מִצְרָיִם׃ וְלֹא־יִשְׁמַע אֲלֵכֶם פַּרְעֹה
וְנָתַתִּי אֶת־יָדִי בְּמִצְרָיִם וְהוֹצֵאתִי אֶת־צִבְאֹתַי אֶת־עַמִּי

is common in Egyptian and signifies, 'the child of dark complexion.'

26. *Aaron and Moses.* Mentioned here in the order of age.

according to their hosts. Or, 'armies.' The Israelites did not leave Egypt as a disorderly mob; they were divided into tribes, clans and families, with leaders and elders.

VI, 28–VII, 7, are a continuation of VI, 2–12, at the point where the narrative gives place to the genealogical list.

29 and 30. These verses are, in effect, identical with *v.* 11 and 12, and the repetition serves merely to resume the story of the Redemption.

CHAPTER VII

1. *I have set thee in God's stead to Pharaoh.* Moses would give the Divine message as the direct representative of God; see IV, 16.

prophet. Spokesman; this is the *original* meaning of the Semitic root of the Heb. *nabi*, prophet. Aaron would give utterance to the words communicated by God to Moses, or to the thoughts which God put into the mind of Moses, with reference to Pharaoh. The Prophets are inspired spokesmen of God's will. They warn the people of the consequences of disobedience, and they often foretell events; but the latter is not their primary function.

3. *I will harden.* See on IV, 21. The phrase predicts what is likely to be Pharaoh's attitude.

signs, wonders, judgments. Terms describing the same acts from different points of view.

4. *lay My hand.* *i.e.* display My almighty power.

by great judgments. *i.e.* punishments; see VI, 6.

Egypt by great judgments. 5. And the Egyptians shall know that I am the LORD, when I stretch forth My hand upon Egypt and bring out the children of Israel from among them.' 6. And Moses and Aaron did so; as the LORD commanded them, so did they. 7. And Moses was fourscore years old, and Aaron fourscore and three years old, when they spoke unto Pharaoh.* iv. ¶ 8. And the LORD spoke unto Moses and unto Aaron, saying: 9. 'When Pharaoh shall speak unto you, saying: Show a wonder for you; then thou shalt say unto Aaron: Take thy rod, and cast it down before Pharaoh, that it become a serpent.' 10. And Moses and Aaron went in unto Pharaoh, and they did so, as the LORD had commanded; and Aaron cast down his rod before Pharaoh and before his servants, and it became a serpent. 11. Then Pharaoh also called for the wise men and the sorcerers; and they also, the magicians of Egypt, did in like manner with their secret arts. 12. For they cast down every man his rod, and they became serpents; but Aaron's rod swallowed up their rods. 13. And Pharaoh's heart was hardened, and he hearkened not unto them; as the LORD had

ה בְּנֵי־יִשְׂרָאֵל מֵאֶרֶץ מִצְרַיִם בִּשְׁפָטִים גְּדֹלִים׃ וְיָדְעוּ מִצְרַיִם
כִּי־אֲנִי יְהוָה בִּנְטֹתִי אֶת־יָדִי עַל־מִצְרָיִם וְהוֹצֵאתִי אֶת־
6 בְּנֵי־יִשְׂרָאֵל מִתּוֹכָם׃ וַיַּעַשׂ מֹשֶׁה וְאַהֲרֹן כַּאֲשֶׁר צִוָּה יְהוָה
7 אֹתָם כֵּן עָשׂוּ׃ וּמֹשֶׁה בֶּן־שְׁמֹנִים שָׁנָה וְאַהֲרֹן בֶּן־שָׁלֹשׁ
וּשְׁמֹנִים שָׁנָה בְּדַבְּרָם אֶל־פַּרְעֹה׃* פ רביעי
8 9 וַיֹּאמֶר יְהוָה אֶל־מֹשֶׁה וְאֶל־אַהֲרֹן לֵאמֹר׃ כִּי יְדַבֵּר
אֲלֵכֶם פַּרְעֹה לֵאמֹר תְּנוּ לָכֶם מוֹפֵת וְאָמַרְתָּ אֶל־אַהֲרֹן
י קַח אֶת־מַטְּךָ וְהַשְׁלֵךְ לִפְנֵי־פַרְעֹה יְהִי לְתַנִּין׃ וַיָּבֹא מֹשֶׁה
וְאַהֲרֹן אֶל־פַּרְעֹה וַיַּעֲשׂוּ כֵן כַּאֲשֶׁר צִוָּה יְהוָה וַיַּשְׁלֵךְ
אַהֲרֹן אֶת־מַטֵּהוּ לִפְנֵי פַרְעֹה וְלִפְנֵי עֲבָדָיו וַיְהִי לְתַנִּין׃
11 וַיִּקְרָא גַּם־פַּרְעֹה לַחֲכָמִים וְלַמְכַשְּׁפִים וַיַּעֲשׂוּ גַם־הֵם
12 חַרְטֻמֵּי מִצְרַיִם בְּלַהֲטֵיהֶם כֵּן׃ וַיַּשְׁלִיכוּ אִישׁ מַטֵּהוּ
13 וַיִּהְיוּ לְתַנִּינִם וַיִּבְלַע מַטֵּה־אַהֲרֹן אֶת־מַטֹּתָם׃ וַיֶּחֱזַק לֵב

5. *I am the LORD.* Or, 'I am ADONAY'; see VI, 3. When God led His people forth from the brickfields of Egypt into freedom, there would be such a display of His mercy and power, that Egypt, and all the surrounding nations, would know that only a Being of such attributes as are implied in His holy Name (ADONAY) could have wrought that redemption.

6. *Moses and Aaron did so.* Henceforth all diffidence ceased, and they applied themselves in confidence and zeal to their charge (Kalisch).

7. *fourscore years old.* The age of Joseph is similarly indicated (Gen. XLI, 46) on his appointment as Viceroy by the king. That appointment is made with the formula, 'I am Pharaoh,' and is followed by the statement, 'and Joseph was thirty years old.' Then his official activity begins. The appointment of Moses to be 'in God's stead to Pharaoh' is announced with a similar formula, 'I am Adonay'; and his official activity, like that of Joseph, is prefaced by the statement of his age. This disposes of the belief that *I am Adonay* in VI, 2 is any revelation of a new Name of God.

8–13. Moses, Aaron and the Magicians.

9. *show a wonder.* Display some portent as the credential of being God's messengers; see IV, 21.

serpent. Heb. *tannin*, denotes any large reptile, sea or river monster, and more especially the crocodile, as the symbol of Egypt.

10. *Aaron cast down his rod.* *i.e.* the rod of Moses used by Aaron at the bidding of Moses.

before his servants. Pharaoh's ministers of state were present.

11. *wise men.* Wizards, who possessed a knowledge of many secrets of nature which were unknown to the people.

sorcerers. 'Men who are adept in altering the external appearance of things by their arts' (Ibn Ezra).

magicians. 'Sacred scribes,' versed in magic lore and practice; jugglers of marvellous skill; see Gen. XLI, 8.

secret arts. Their spells and sleight-of-hand. Snake-charming is widespread in the East, ancient and modern; and is to-day a professional secret with many families in Egypt. Dr. A. Macalister says that he has 'seen both a snake and a crocodile thrown by hypnotism into the condition of rigidity in which they could be held up as rods by the tip of the tail'.

12. *they became serpents.* Through their 'secret arts' they produced the illusion of converting them into serpents (Ibn Ezra, Maimonides and Abarbanel).

13. *Pharaoh's heart was hardened.* *i.e.* the sign failed to make any impression on him. The fact that Moses and Aaron had done so more easily than his own magicians, only served to increase his stubbornness; see note on IV, 21.

14 פַּרְעֹה וְלֹא שָׁמַע אֲלֵהֶם כַּאֲשֶׁר דִּבֶּר יְהוָה׃ ס וַיֹּאמֶר
טו יְהוָה אֶל־מֹשֶׁה כָּבֵד לֵב פַּרְעֹה מֵאֵן לְשַׁלַּח הָעָם׃ לֵךְ
אֶל־פַּרְעֹה בַּבֹּקֶר הִנֵּה יֹצֵא הַמַּיְמָה וְנִצַּבְתָּ לִקְרָאתוֹ עַל־
שְׂפַת הַיְאֹר וְהַמַּטֶּה אֲשֶׁר־נֶהְפַּךְ לְנָחָשׁ תִּקַּח בְּיָדֶךָ׃
16 וְאָמַרְתָּ אֵלָיו יְהוָה אֱלֹהֵי הָעִבְרִים שְׁלָחַנִי אֵלֶיךָ לֵאמֹר
שַׁלַּח אֶת־עַמִּי וְיַעַבְדֻנִי בַּמִּדְבָּר וְהִנֵּה לֹא־שָׁמַעְתָּ עַד־כֹּה׃
17 כֹּה אָמַר יְהוָה בְּזֹאת תֵּדַע כִּי אֲנִי יְהוָה הִנֵּה אָנֹכִי מַכֶּה ׀
בַּמַּטֶּה אֲשֶׁר־בְּיָדִי עַל־הַמַּיִם אֲשֶׁר בַּיְאֹר וְנֶהֶפְכוּ לְדָם׃
18 וְהַדָּגָה אֲשֶׁר־בַּיְאֹר תָּמוּת וּבָאַשׁ הַיְאֹר וְנִלְאוּ מִצְרַיִם
19 לִשְׁתּוֹת מַיִם מִן־הַיְאֹר׃ ס וַיֹּאמֶר יְהוָה אֶל־מֹשֶׁה
אֱמֹר אֶל־אַהֲרֹן קַח מַטְּךָ וּנְטֵה־יָדְךָ עַל־מֵימֵי מִצְרַיִם
עַל־נַהֲרֹתָם ׀ עַל־יְאֹרֵיהֶם וְעַל־אַגְמֵיהֶם וְעַל כָּל־מִקְוֵה
מֵימֵיהֶם וְיִהְיוּ־דָם וְהָיָה דָם בְּכָל־אֶרֶץ מִצְרַיִם וּבָעֵצִים
כ וּבָאֲבָנִים׃ וַיַּעֲשׂוּ־כֵן מֹשֶׁה וְאַהֲרֹן כַּאֲשֶׁר ׀ צִוָּה יְהוָה
וַיָּרֶם בַּמַּטֶּה וַיַּךְ אֶת־הַמַּיִם אֲשֶׁר בַּיְאֹר לְעֵינֵי פַרְעֹה וּלְעֵינֵי
21 עֲבָדָיו וַיֵּהָפְכוּ כָּל־הַמַּיִם אֲשֶׁר־בַּיְאֹר לְדָם׃ וְהַדָּגָה אֲשֶׁר־

spoken. ¶ 14. And the LORD said unto Moses: 'Pharaoh's heart is stubborn, he refuseth to let the people go. 15. Get thee unto Pharaoh in the morning; lo, he goeth out unto the water; and thou shalt stand by the river's brink to meet him; and the rod which was turned to a serpent shalt thou take in thy hand. 16. And thou shalt say unto him: The LORD, the God of the Hebrews, hath sent me unto thee, saying: Let My people go, that they may serve Me in the wilderness; and, behold, hitherto thou hast not hearkened; 17. thus saith the LORD: In this thou shalt know that I am the LORD—behold, I will smite with the rod that is in my hand upon the waters which are in the river, and they shall be turned to blood. 18. And the fish that are in the river shall die, and the river shall become foul; and the Egyptians shall loathe to drink water from the river.' ¶ 19. And the LORD said unto Moses: 'Say unto Aaron: Take thy rod and stretch out thy hand over the waters of Egypt, over their rivers, over their streams, and over their pools, and over all their ponds of water, that they may become blood; and there shall be blood throughout all the land of Egypt, both in vessels of wood and in vessels of stone.' 20. And Moses and Aaron did so, as the LORD commanded; and he lifted up the rod, and smote the waters that were in the river, in the sight of Pharaoh, and in the sight of his servants; and all the waters that were in the river were turned to blood. 21. And the fish that were in the river died, and the

CHAPTERS VII, 14–XII, 36. THE TEN PLAGUES

For a general explanation of the Ten Plagues, see Additional Note, p. 398.

14–25. THE FIRST PLAGUE: THE WATER TURNED INTO BLOOD

15. *unto the water.* To learn how many degrees it had risen (Ibn Ezra); or, to offer worship to the god of the River. The Nile, as the source of Egypt's 'fertility', was venerated under various names and symbols. In honour of the Nile-god, religious festivals were held, at which Pharaoh himself sometimes officiated. Hymns addressed to the Nile are extant.

17. *know that I am the LORD.* Pharaoh had boldly and wantonly said at his first interview with Moses, 'I know not the LORD' (v, 2). He is now told that he shall soon *know* the LORD.

I will smite. The speaker is Moses. Aaron performed the act at the bidding of Moses.

be turned to blood. They shall have the appearance of blood (cf. Joel III, 4. 'The sun shall be turned into darkness, and the moon into blood'). The plague spoke its own message: 'At the sight of the bloody Nile, the Egyptians were with horror reminded of Pharaoh's murderous command against the Hebrew children' (Wisdom of Solomon XI, 6, 7).

18. *the fish that are in the river.* The Nile possesses abundant fish, whose death would be a national calamity, as fish was one of the principal articles of food in ancient Egypt.

loathe to drink water. The word here translated 'loathe' may be rendered 'weary themselves'; see Gen. XIX, 19. 'They will exert themselves in vain to find a remedy to make the water of the Nile palatable' (Rashi).

19. *rivers.* The arms of the Nile flowing into the Mediterranean. The Nile has no tributary rivers.

streams. Dug by human hands from the Nile to fertilize the fields (Rashi).

pools. Caused by the inundation of the Nile (see Isa. XLII, 15).

ponds. Wells, cisterns and reservoirs.

20. *he lifted up. i.e.* Aaron.

river became foul, and the Egyptians could not drink water from the river; and the blood was throughout all the land of Egypt. 22. And the magicians of Egypt did in like manner with their secret arts; and Pharaoh's heart was hardened, and he hearkened not unto them; as the LORD had spoken. 23. And Pharaoh turned and went into his house, neither did he lay even this to heart. 24. And all the Egyptians digged round about the river for water to drink; for they could not drink of the water of the river. 25. And seven days were fulfilled, after that the LORD had smitten the river. ¶ 26. And the LORD spoke unto Moses: 'Go in unto Pharaoh, and say unto him: Thus saith the LORD: Let My people go, that they may serve Me. 27. And if thou refuse to let them go, behold, I will smite all thy borders with frogs. 28. And the river shall swarm with frogs, which shall go up and come into thy house, and into thy bed-chamber, and upon thy bed, and into the house of thy servants, and upon thy people, and into thine ovens, and into thy kneading-troughs. 29. And the frogs shall come up both upon thee, and upon thy people, and upon all thy servants.'

8

CHAPTER VIII

1. And the LORD said unto Moses: 'Say unto Aaron: Stretch forth thy hand with thy rod over the rivers, over the canals, and over the pools, and cause frogs to come up upon the land of Egypt.' 2. And Aaron stretched out his hand over the waters of Egypt; and the frogs came up, and covered the land of Egypt. 3. And the magicians did in like manner with their secret arts, and brought up frogs upon the land of Egypt. 4. Then Pharaoh called for Moses and Aaron, and said: 'Entreat the

בַּיְאֹר מֵתָה וַיִּבְאַשׁ הַיְאֹר וְלֹא־יָכְלוּ מִצְרַיִם לִשְׁתּוֹת מַיִם
22 מִן־הַיְאֹר וַיְהִי הַדָּם בְּכָל־אֶרֶץ מִצְרָיִם׃ וַיַּעֲשׂוּ־כֵן חַרְטֻמֵּי
מִצְרַיִם בְּלָטֵיהֶם וַיֶּחֱזַק לֵב־פַּרְעֹה וְלֹא־שָׁמַע אֲלֵהֶם כַּאֲשֶׁר
23 דִּבֶּר יְהוָה׃ וַיִּפֶן פַּרְעֹה וַיָּבֹא אֶל־בֵּיתוֹ וְלֹא־שָׁת לִבּוֹ
24 גַּם־לָזֹאת׃ וַיַּחְפְּרוּ כָל־מִצְרַיִם סְבִיבֹת הַיְאֹר מַיִם לִשְׁתּוֹת
כה כִּי לֹא יָכְלוּ לִשְׁתֹּת מִמֵּימֵי הַיְאֹר׃ וַיִּמָּלֵא שִׁבְעַת יָמִים
אַחֲרֵי הַכּוֹת־יְהוָה אֶת־הַיְאֹר׃ פ
26 וַיֹּאמֶר יְהוָה אֶל־מֹשֶׁה בֹּא אֶל־פַּרְעֹה וְאָמַרְתָּ אֵלָיו כֹּה
27 אָמַר יְהוָה שַׁלַּח אֶת־עַמִּי וְיַעַבְדֻנִי׃ וְאִם־מָאֵן אַתָּה לְשַׁלֵּחַ
28 הִנֵּה אָנֹכִי נֹגֵף אֶת־כָּל־גְּבוּלְךָ בַּצְפַרְדְּעִים׃ וְשָׁרַץ הַיְאֹר
צְפַרְדְּעִים וְעָלוּ וּבָאוּ בְּבֵיתֶךָ וּבַחֲדַר מִשְׁכָּבְךָ וְעַל־מִטָּתֶךָ
29 וּבְבֵית עֲבָדֶיךָ וּבְעַמֶּךָ וּבְתַנּוּרֶיךָ וּבְמִשְׁאֲרוֹתֶיךָ׃ וּבְכָה
וּבְעַמְּךָ וּבְכָל־עֲבָדֶיךָ יַעֲלוּ הַצְפַרְדְּעִים׃

CAP. VIII. ח

ח

א וַיֹּאמֶר יְהוָה אֶל־מֹשֶׁה אֱמֹר אֶל־אַהֲרֹן נְטֵה אֶת־יָדְךָ
בְּמַטֶּךָ עַל־הַנְּהָרֹת עַל־הַיְאֹרִים וְעַל־הָאֲגַמִּים וְהַעַל אֶת־
2 הַצְפַרְדְּעִים עַל־אֶרֶץ מִצְרָיִם׃ וַיֵּט אַהֲרֹן אֶת־יָדוֹ עַל
מֵימֵי מִצְרָיִם וַתַּעַל הַצְּפַרְדֵּעַ וַתְּכַס אֶת־אֶרֶץ מִצְרָיִם׃
3 וַיַּעֲשׂוּ־כֵן הַחַרְטֻמִּים בְּלָטֵיהֶם וַיַּעֲלוּ אֶת־הַצְפַרְדְּעִים

ז' v. 29. יתיר ה'

22. *in like manner.* From where did the magicians obtain water for their experiment, as *all* the water had been turned into blood? asks Ibn Ezra. They took rain (Midrash), or they obtained the water from Goshen, or they dug for it (*v.* 24).

23. *neither did he lay even this to heart.* Referring to the first miracle of Aaron's serpent to which he paid no attention. To make an apparent change of small quantities of water into blood, was one of the common tricks of Egyptian magic. Pharaoh, therefore, disregarding the universality and completeness of Moses' miracle, thought it nothing more than what he had often seen done by his magicians.

25. *seven days were fulfilled.* Evidently referring to the duration of the plague. Nothing is said about the restoration of the Nile to its natural state. The flow of fresh water from the Upper Nile would cleanse the Nile in Egypt.

CHAPTERS VII, 26–VIII, 11. THE SECOND PLAGUE: FROGS

27. *thy borders.* But not the land of Goshen. *frogs.* This plague, like the preceding, was in general accordance with natural phenomena, but marvellous both for its extent and intensity.

28. *upon thy bed.* The extreme cleanliness of the Egyptians rendered this plague peculiarly disagreeable to them.

CHAPTER VIII

4–10. At Pharaoh's request the plague ceases. He promises to let the Israelites go.

4. *entreat the LORD.* Pharaoh hereby acknow-

4 עַל־אֶרֶץ מִצְרָיִם׃ וַיִּקְרָא פַרְעֹה לְמֹשֶׁה וּלְאַהֲרֹן וַיֹּאמֶר
הַעְתִּירוּ אֶל־יְהוָה וְיָסֵר הַצְפַרְדְּעִים מִמֶּנִּי וּמֵעַמִּי וַאֲשַׁלְּחָה
ה אֶת־הָעָם וְיִזְבְּחוּ לַיהוָה׃ וַיֹּאמֶר מֹשֶׁה לְפַרְעֹה הִתְפָּאֵר
עָלַי לְמָתַי ׀ אַעְתִּיר לְךָ וְלַעֲבָדֶיךָ וּלְעַמְּךָ לְהַכְרִית
6 הַצְפַרְדְּעִים מִמְּךָ וּמִבָּתֶּיךָ רַק בַּיְאֹר תִּשָּׁאַרְנָה׃ וַיֹּאמֶר
חמישי לְמָחָר וַיֹּאמֶר כִּדְבָרְךָ לְמַעַן תֵּדַע כִּי־אֵין כַּיהוָה אֱלֹהֵינוּ׃
7 וְסָרוּ הַצְפַרְדְּעִים מִמְּךָ וּמִבָּתֶּיךָ וּמֵעֲבָדֶיךָ וּמֵעַמֶּךָ רַק
8 בַּיְאֹר תִּשָּׁאַרְנָה׃ וַיֵּצֵא מֹשֶׁה וְאַהֲרֹן מֵעִם פַּרְעֹה וַיִּצְעַק
מֹשֶׁה אֶל־יְהוָה עַל־דְּבַר הַצְפַרְדְּעִים אֲשֶׁר־שָׂם לְפַרְעֹה׃
9 וַיַּעַשׂ יְהוָה כִּדְבַר מֹשֶׁה וַיָּמֻתוּ הַצְפַרְדְּעִים מִן־הַבָּתִּים
י מִן־הַחֲצֵרֹת וּמִן־הַשָּׂדֹת׃ וַיִּצְבְּרוּ אֹתָם חֳמָרִם חֳמָרִם
11 וַתִּבְאַשׁ הָאָרֶץ׃ וַיַּרְא פַּרְעֹה כִּי הָיְתָה הָרְוָחָה וְהַכְבֵּד
12 אֶת־לִבּוֹ וְלֹא שָׁמַע אֲלֵהֶם כַּאֲשֶׁר דִּבֶּר יְהוָה׃ ס וַיֹּאמֶר
יְהוָה אֶל־מֹשֶׁה אֱמֹר אֶל־אַהֲרֹן נְטֵה אֶת־מַטְּךָ וְהַךְ
13 אֶת־עֲפַר הָאָרֶץ וְהָיָה לְכִנִּם בְּכָל־אֶרֶץ מִצְרָיִם׃ וַיַּעֲשׂוּ־
כֵן וַיֵּט אַהֲרֹן אֶת־יָדוֹ בְמַטֵּהוּ וַיַּךְ אֶת־עֲפַר הָאָרֶץ וַתְּהִי
הַכִּנָּם בָּאָדָם וּבַבְּהֵמָה כָּל־עֲפַר הָאָרֶץ הָיָה כִנִּים בְּכָל־
14 אֶרֶץ מִצְרָיִם׃ וַיַּעֲשׂוּ־כֵן הַחַרְטֻמִּים בְּלָטֵיהֶם לְהוֹצִיא אֶת־

מלרע v. 7.

LORD, that He take away the frogs from me, and from my people; and I will let the people go, that they may sacrifice unto the LORD.' 5. And Moses said unto Pharaoh: 'Have thou this glory over me; against what time shall I entreat for thee, and for thy servants, and for thy people, that the frogs be destroyed from thee and thy houses, and remain in the river only?' 6. And he said: 'Against to-morrow.' And he said: 'Be it according to thy word; that thou mayest know that there is none like unto the LORD our God.* v. 7. And the frogs shall depart from thee, and from thy houses, and from thy servants, and from thy people; they shall remain in the river only.' 8. And Moses and Aaron went out from Pharaoh; and Moses cried unto the LORD concerning the frogs, which He had brought upon Pharaoh. 9. And the LORD did according to the word of Moses; and the frogs died out of the houses, out of the courts, and out of the fields. 10. And they gathered them together in heaps; and the land stank. 11. But when Pharaoh saw that there was respite, he hardened his heart, and hearkened not unto them; as the LORD had spoken. ¶ 12. And the LORD said unto Moses: 'Say unto Aaron: Stretch out thy rod, and smite the dust of the earth, that it may become gnats throughout all the land of Egypt.' 13. And they did so; and Aaron stretched out his hand with his rod, and smote the dust of the earth, and there were gnats upon man, and upon beast; all the dust of the earth became gnats throughout all the land of Egypt. 14. And the magicians did so with their secret arts to bring forth gnats, but they could not; and there were gnats upon man, and upon

ledges that this plague had been sent by the God of the Hebrews.

5. *have thou this glory over me. i.e.* 'assume the honour of deciding when the plague shall cease'; or, 'have this glory over me, in fixing the time when the plague shall cease at my entreaty' (Luzzatto). The words are a polite address to the king.

6. *against to-morrow.* 'To-morrow' (AV).
none like unto the LORD. The removal of the plague at a time fixed by Pharaoh himself, should be conclusive evidence to him that it was sent by God (Driver).

7. *in the river only.* Where they would naturally be at any time.

8. *Moses cried.* The expression is a strong one. Moses had ventured to allow Pharaoh to fix a time for the removal of the plague, without the Divine approval. Hence earnest prayer was necessary (Ibn Ezra).

9. *courts.* Belonging to the private houses.

10. *they gathered them.* Better, *they piled them.*

11. *respite.* Relief.
he hardened his heart. He again breaks his promise.
hearkened not unto them. When they demanded the promised freedom.

12–15. THE THIRD PLAGUE: GNATS

12. *gnats.* Heb. *kinnim.* RV Margin has 'sand flies', or, 'fleas.'

13. *dust of the earth became gnats.* Thus it appeared to the people, owing to the multitude of the insects (Luzzatto).

14. *to bring forth.* Or, 'to remove' the gnats (Chizkuni, Hirsch).

beast. 15. Then the magicians said unto Pharaoh: 'This is the finger of God'; and Pharaoh's heart was hardened, and he hearkened not unto them; as the LORD had spoken. ¶ 16. And the LORD said unto Moses: 'Rise up early in the morning, and stand before Pharaoh; lo, he cometh forth to the water; and say unto him: Thus saith the LORD: Let My people go, that they may serve Me. 17. Else, if thou wilt not let My people go, behold, I will send swarms of flies upon thee, and upon thy servants, and upon thy people, and into thy houses; and the houses of the Egyptians shall be full of swarms of flies, and also the ground whereon they are. 18. And I will set apart in that day the land of Goshen, in which My people dwell, that no swarms of flies shall be there; to the end that thou mayest know that I am the LORD in the midst of the earth.* vi. 19. And I will put a division between My people and thy people—by to-morrow shall this sign be.' 20. And the LORD did so; and there came grievous swarms of flies into the house of Pharaoh, and into his servants' houses; and in all the land of Egypt the land was ruined by reason of the swarms of flies. 21. And Pharaoh called for Moses and for Aaron, and said: 'Go ye, sacrifice to your God in the land.' 22. And Moses said: 'It is not meet so to do; for we shall sacrifice the abomination of the Egyptians to the LORD our God; lo, if we sacrifice the abomination of the Egyptians before their eyes, will they not

טו הַכִּנִּם וְלֹא יָכֹלוּ וַתְּהִי הַכִּנָּם בָּאָדָם וּבַבְּהֵמָה׃ וַיֹּאמְרוּ
הַחַרְטֻמִּם אֶל־פַּרְעֹה אֶצְבַּע אֱלֹהִים הִוא וַיֶּחֱזַק לֵב־פַּרְעֹה
16 וְלֹא־שָׁמַע אֲלֵהֶם כַּאֲשֶׁר דִּבֶּר יְהוָה׃ ס וַיֹּאמֶר יְהוָה
אֶל־מֹשֶׁה הַשְׁכֵּם בַּבֹּקֶר וְהִתְיַצֵּב לִפְנֵי פַרְעֹה הִנֵּה יוֹצֵא
הַמָּיְמָה וְאָמַרְתָּ אֵלָיו כֹּה אָמַר יְהוָה שַׁלַּח עַמִּי וְיַעַבְדֻנִי׃
17 כִּי אִם־אֵינְךָ מְשַׁלֵּחַ אֶת־עַמִּי הִנְנִי מַשְׁלִיחַ בְּךָ וּבַעֲבָדֶיךָ
וּבְעַמְּךָ וּבְבָתֶּיךָ אֶת־הֶעָרֹב וּמָלְאוּ בָּתֵּי מִצְרַיִם אֶת־
18 הֶעָרֹב וְגַם הָאֲדָמָה אֲשֶׁר־הֵם עָלֶיהָ׃ וְהִפְלֵיתִי בַיּוֹם
הַהוּא אֶת־אֶרֶץ גֹּשֶׁן אֲשֶׁר עַמִּי עֹמֵד עָלֶיהָ לְבִלְתִּי הֱיוֹת־
ששי
19 שָׁם עָרֹב לְמַעַן תֵּדַע כִּי אֲנִי יְהוָה בְּקֶרֶב הָאָרֶץ׃ וְשַׂמְתִּי
כ פְדֻת בֵּין עַמִּי וּבֵין עַמֶּךָ לְמָחָר יִהְיֶה הָאֹת הַזֶּה׃ וַיַּעַשׂ
יְהוָה כֵּן וַיָּבֹא עָרֹב כָּבֵד בֵּיתָה פַרְעֹה וּבֵית עֲבָדָיו וּבְכָל־
21 אֶרֶץ מִצְרַיִם תִּשָּׁחֵת הָאָרֶץ מִפְּנֵי הֶעָרֹב׃ וַיִּקְרָא פַרְעֹה
אֶל־מֹשֶׁה וּלְאַהֲרֹן וַיֹּאמֶר לְכוּ זִבְחוּ לֵאלֹהֵיכֶם בָּאָרֶץ׃
22 וַיֹּאמֶר מֹשֶׁה לֹא נָכוֹן לַעֲשׂוֹת כֵּן כִּי תּוֹעֲבַת מִצְרַיִם
נִזְבַּח לַיהוָה אֱלֹהֵינוּ הֵן נִזְבַּח אֶת־תּוֹעֲבַת מִצְרַיִם לְעֵינֵיהֶם

v. 20. סבירין ובבית

15. *finger of God.* The magicians had encouraged Pharaoh in his defiance of the Divine will; hence, their confessed failure now is the more complete. They discern the hand or work of God in the plague.

16–28. THE FOURTH PLAGUE: BEETLES

17. *swarms of flies.* Heb. *ha-arob*, a collective singular, from a root meaning 'to mix'. The authorities again differ as to the exact interpretation; some render, 'a mixture of noxious animals' (Rashi); others, 'beetles' (Kalisch). 'The beetle, or scarab, was sacred and was regarded as the emblem of the Sun-god. It was sculptured on monuments, painted on tombs, engraved on gems, worn round the neck as an amulet and honoured in ten thousand images' (Geikie).

18. *set apart.* Dividing and miraculously distinguishing Goshen from the rest of Egypt. 'Such swarms may advance along particular lines, and so spare a given district' (Dillmann).

the LORD in the midst of the earth. Although My glory is in Heaven, My will is omnipotent on earth (Rashi).

19. *I will put a division.* Or, 'set a sign of deliverance.'

to-morrow. Allowing time for repentance.

20. *grievous.* Burdensome, severe, numerous.

the land was ruined. Not only did the Egyptians and their cattle suffer, but the daily occupations of the people were interrupted.

21. *in the land.* But not in the wilderness, as demanded by Moses. At last the king begins to yield.

22. *abomination of the Egyptians.* The sacrifice of these animals, sacred to the Egyptians, would be an abominable crime in their eyes. The ancient historian Diodorus tells of a Roman ambassador who was put to death in Egypt for killing a cat. We need only think of Hindu riots at the slaughtering of cows by Moslems in our own days.

23. *three days' journey.* Idiomatic expression for a long distance; see III, 18.

as He shall command us. See X, 26. The manner of sacrificial worship had not yet been laid down to the Israelites.

stone us? 23. We will go three days' journey into the wilderness, and sacrifice to the LORD our God, as He shall command us.' 24. And Pharaoh said: 'I will let you go, that ye may sacrifice to the LORD your God in the wilderness; only ye shall not go very far away; entreat for me.' 25. And Moses said: 'Behold, I go out from thee, and I will entreat the LORD that the swarms of flies may depart from Pharaoh, from his servants, and from his people, to-morrow; only let not Pharaoh deal deceitfully any more in not letting the people go to sacrifice to the LORD.' 26. And Moses went out from Pharaoh and entreated the LORD. 27. And the LORD did according to the word of Moses; and He removed the swarms of flies from Pharaoh, from his servants, and from his people; there remained not one. 28. And Pharaoh hardened his heart this time also, and he did not let the people go.

23 וְלֹא יִסְקְלֻנוּ׃ דֶּרֶךְ שְׁלֹשֶׁת יָמִים נֵלֵךְ בַּמִּדְבָּר וְזָבַחְנוּ
24 לַיהוָה אֱלֹהֵינוּ כַּאֲשֶׁר יֹאמַר אֵלֵינוּ׃ וַיֹּאמֶר פַּרְעֹה אָנֹכִי
אֲשַׁלַּח אֶתְכֶם וּזְבַחְתֶּם לַיהוָה אֱלֹהֵיכֶם בַּמִּדְבָּר רַק
כה הַרְחֵק לֹא־תַרְחִיקוּ לָלֶכֶת הַעְתִּירוּ בַּעֲדִי׃ וַיֹּאמֶר מֹשֶׁה
הִנֵּה אָנֹכִי יוֹצֵא מֵעִמָּךְ וְהַעְתַּרְתִּי אֶל־יְהוָה וְסָר הֶעָרֹב
מִפַּרְעֹה מֵעֲבָדָיו וּמֵעַמּוֹ מָחָר רַק אַל־יֹסֵף פַּרְעֹה הָתֵל
26 לְבִלְתִּי שַׁלַּח אֶת־הָעָם לִזְבֹּחַ לַיהוָה׃ וַיֵּצֵא מֹשֶׁה מֵעִם
27 פַּרְעֹה וַיֶּעְתַּר אֶל־יְהוָה׃ וַיַּעַשׂ יְהוָה כִּדְבַר מֹשֶׁה וַיָּסַר
28 הֶעָרֹב מִפַּרְעֹה מֵעֲבָדָיו וּמֵעַמּוֹ לֹא נִשְׁאַר אֶחָד׃ וַיַּכְבֵּד
פַּרְעֹה אֶת־לִבּוֹ גַּם בַּפַּעַם הַזֹּאת וְלֹא שִׁלַּח אֶת־הָעָם׃ פ

9

CHAPTER IX

1. Then the LORD said unto Moses: 'Go in unto Pharaoh, and tell him: Thus saith the LORD, the God of the Hebrews: Let My people go, that they may serve Me. 2. For if thou refuse to let them go, and wilt hold them still, 3. behold, the hand of the LORD is upon thy cattle which are in the field, upon the horses, upon the asses, upon the camels, upon the herds, and upon the flocks; there shall be a very grievous murrain. 4. And the LORD shall make a division between the cattle of Israel and the cattle of Egypt; and there shall nothing die of all that belongeth to the children of Israel.' 5. And the LORD appointed a set time, saying: 'To-morrow the LORD shall do this thing in the land.' 6. And the LORD did that thing on the morrow, and all the cattle of Egypt died; but of the cattle of the children of Israel died not one. 7. And

ט

CAP. IX. ט

א וַיֹּאמֶר יְהוָה אֶל־מֹשֶׁה בֹּא אֶל־פַּרְעֹה וְדִבַּרְתָּ אֵלָיו כֹּה־
2 אָמַר יְהוָה אֱלֹהֵי הָעִבְרִים שַׁלַּח אֶת־עַמִּי וְיַעַבְדֻנִי׃ כִּי
3 אִם־מָאֵן אַתָּה לְשַׁלֵּחַ וְעוֹדְךָ מַחֲזִיק בָּם׃ הִנֵּה יַד־יְהוָה
הוֹיָה בְּמִקְנְךָ אֲשֶׁר בַּשָּׂדֶה בַּסּוּסִים בַּחֲמֹרִים בַּגְּמַלִּים
4 בַּבָּקָר וּבַצֹּאן דֶּבֶר כָּבֵד מְאֹד׃ וְהִפְלָה יְהוָה בֵּין מִקְנֵה
יִשְׂרָאֵל וּבֵין מִקְנֵה מִצְרָיִם וְלֹא יָמוּת מִכָּל־לִבְנֵי יִשְׂרָאֵל
ה דָּבָר׃ וַיָּשֶׂם יְהוָה מוֹעֵד לֵאמֹר מָחָר יַעֲשֶׂה יְהוָה הַדָּבָר
6 הַזֶּה בָּאָרֶץ׃ וַיַּעַשׂ יְהוָה אֶת־הַדָּבָר הַזֶּה מִמָּחֳרָת וַיָּמָת
כֹּל מִקְנֵה מִצְרָיִם וּמִמִּקְנֵה בְנֵי־יִשְׂרָאֵל לֹא־מֵת אֶחָד׃
7 וַיִּשְׁלַח פַּרְעֹה וְהִנֵּה לֹא־מֵת מִמִּקְנֵה יִשְׂרָאֵל עַד־אֶחָד

25. *deal deceitfully.* Or, 'mock.' Moses fears Pharaoh will once more prove faithless, as in *v.* 11 after the promise to let the people go.

28. *this time also.* As he had done before. On this occasion he had given a more definite promise (*v.* 24).

CHAPTER IX, 1–7. THE FIFTH PLAGUE: THE MURRAIN ON CATTLE

3. *a very grievous murrain.* A 'rinderpest'; see *v.* 15.

camels. Traders who brought merchandise across the Arabian desert early introduced the camel into Egypt; see Gen. XXXVII, 25. Horses, which are said to have been unknown there prior to the Hyksos invasion, became common under the Eighteenth Dynasty, when they were used in war.

4. *shall make a division.* See VIII, 18; the land of Goshen is again to be immune from the plague.

6. *all the cattle.* In the field. The word 'all' need not be pressed, but understood (as often in Hebrew and other languages) merely to denote such a large number that those which remained may be disregarded (Keil); cf. the English phrase, '*all* the world knows.'

7. *Pharaoh sent.* To see if it was even so; but the very knowledge embittered his heart the more.

וַיִּכְבַּד לֵב פַּרְעֹה וְלֹא שִׁלַּח אֶת־הָעָם׃ פ
8 וַיֹּאמֶר יְהוָה אֶל־מֹשֶׁה וְאֶל־אַהֲרֹן קְחוּ לָכֶם מְלֹא חָפְנֵיכֶם
9 פִּיחַ כִּבְשָׁן וּזְרָקוֹ מֹשֶׁה הַשָּׁמַיְמָה לְעֵינֵי פַרְעֹה׃ וְהָיָה
לְאָבָק עַל כָּל־אֶרֶץ מִצְרָיִם וְהָיָה עַל־הָאָדָם וְעַל־הַבְּהֵמָה
י לִשְׁחִין פֹּרֵחַ אֲבַעְבֻּעֹת בְּכָל־אֶרֶץ מִצְרָיִם׃ וַיִּקְחוּ אֶת־
פִּיחַ הַכִּבְשָׁן וַיַּעַמְדוּ לִפְנֵי פַרְעֹה וַיִּזְרֹק אֹתוֹ מֹשֶׁה
הַשָּׁמָיְמָה וַיְהִי שְׁחִין אֲבַעְבֻּעֹת פֹּרֵחַ בָּאָדָם וּבַבְּהֵמָה׃
11 וְלֹא־יָכְלוּ הַחַרְטֻמִּים לַעֲמֹד לִפְנֵי מֹשֶׁה מִפְּנֵי הַשְּׁחִין כִּי־
12 הָיָה הַשְּׁחִין בַּחַרְטֻמִּם וּבְכָל־מִצְרָיִם׃ וַיְחַזֵּק יְהוָה אֶת־
לֵב פַּרְעֹה וְלֹא שָׁמַע אֲלֵהֶם כַּאֲשֶׁר דִּבֶּר יְהוָה אֶל־
13 מֹשֶׁה׃ ס וַיֹּאמֶר יְהוָה אֶל־מֹשֶׁה הַשְׁכֵּם בַּבֹּקֶר
וְהִתְיַצֵּב לִפְנֵי פַרְעֹה וְאָמַרְתָּ אֵלָיו כֹּה־אָמַר יְהוָה אֱלֹהֵי
14 הָעִבְרִים שַׁלַּח אֶת־עַמִּי וְיַעַבְדֻנִי׃ כִּי ׀ בַּפַּעַם הַזֹּאת אֲנִי
שֹׁלֵחַ אֶת־כָּל־מַגֵּפֹתַי אֶל־לִבְּךָ וּבַעֲבָדֶיךָ וּבְעַמֶּךָ בַּעֲבוּר
טו תֵּדַע כִּי אֵין כָּמֹנִי בְּכָל־הָאָרֶץ׃ כִּי עַתָּה שָׁלַחְתִּי אֶת־
יָדִי וָאַךְ אוֹתְךָ וְאֶת־עַמְּךָ בַּדָּבֶר וַתִּכָּחֵד מִן־הָאָרֶץ׃
16 וְאוּלָם בַּעֲבוּר זֹאת הֶעֱמַדְתִּיךָ בַּעֲבוּר הַרְאֹתְךָ אֶת־כֹּחִי
שביעי 17 וּלְמַעַן סַפֵּר שְׁמִי בְּכָל־הָאָרֶץ׃ * עוֹדְךָ מִסְתּוֹלֵל בְּעַמִּי
18 לְבִלְתִּי שַׁלְּחָם׃ הִנְנִי מַמְטִיר כָּעֵת מָחָר בָּרָד כָּבֵד מְאֹד

Pharaoh sent, and, behold, there was not so much as one of the cattle of the Israelites dead. But the heart of Pharaoh was stubborn, and he did not let the people go. ¶ 8. And the LORD said unto Moses and unto Aaron: 'Take to you handfuls of soot of the furnace, and let Moses throw it heavenward in the sight of Pharaoh. 9. And it shall become small dust over all the land of Egypt, and shall be a boil breaking forth with blains upon man and upon beast, throughout all the land of Egypt.' 10. And they took soot of the furnace, and stood before Pharaoh; and Moses threw it up heavenward; and it became a boil breaking forth with blains upon man and upon beast. 11. And the magicians could not stand before Moses because of the boils; for the boils were upon the magicians, and upon all the Egyptians. 12. And the LORD hardened the heart of Pharaoh, and he hearkened not unto them; as the LORD had spoken unto Moses. ¶ 13. And the LORD said unto Moses: 'Rise up early in the morning, and stand before Pharaoh, and say unto him: Thus saith the LORD, the God of the Hebrews: Let My people go, that they may serve Me. 14. For I will this time send all My plagues upon thy person, and upon thy servants, and upon thy people; that thou mayest know that there is none like Me in all the earth. 15. Surely now I had put forth My hand, and smitten thee and thy people with pestilence, and thou hadst been cut off from the earth. 16. But in very deed for this cause have I made thee to stand, to show thee My power, and that My name may be declared throughout all the earth.* vii. 17. As yet exaltest thou thyself against My people, that thou wilt not let them go? 18. Behold, to-morrow about this

8–12. SIXTH PLAGUE: BOILS

9. *small dust.* The disease would be carried through Egypt by the air.

11. *the magicians could not stand.* Not only were they unable to imitate it, but they were themselves included in the affliction.

12. *hardened the heart.* 'Pharaoh's sin preceded and provoked God's punishments, which, however, far from moving his stubborn heart, tended to harden it still more, and to bring him into a self-conscious opposition to the God of Israel' (Kalisch). See note on IV, 21.

14 and **15.** These two verses are interdependent. Moffatt translates *v.* 15: 'Otherwise, I would have exerted my force and struck you and your people with pestilence, till you were swept off the earth.'

14. *this time. i.e.* at one time, and without delay.

plagues. Heb. *maggephah*; is not the word for the ten plagues, but means a fatal chastisement; cf. Num. XIV, 37.

16. *to show thee. i.e.* to make thee experience My power, which *might* have had the effect of softening Pharaoh's heart, and did in fact lead him more than once to give God the glory, *v.* 27; X, 16 (Driver).

17–35. THE SEVENTH PLAGUE: HAIL

17. *exaltest thou thyself.* lit. 'thou raisest thyself as an obstacle' against My people, and opposest their emancipation. Targum and Rashi translate: 'thou treadest down (*i.e.* oppressest) My people.'

18. *since the day it was founded. i.e.* since it was inhabited.

time I will cause it to rain a very grievous hail, such as hath not been in Egypt since the day it was founded even until now. 19. Now therefore send, hasten in thy cattle and all that thou hast in the field; for every man and beast that shall be found in the field, and shall not be brought home, the hail shall come down upon them, and they shall die.' 20. He that feared the word of the LORD among the servants of Pharaoh made his servants and his cattle flee into the houses; 21. and he that regarded not the word of the LORD left his servants and his cattle in the field. ¶ 22. And the LORD said unto Moses: 'Stretch forth thy hand toward heaven, that there may be hail in all the land of Egypt, upon man, and upon beast, and upon every herb of the field, throughout the land of Egypt.' 23. And Moses stretched forth his rod toward heaven; and the LORD sent thunder and hail, and fire ran down unto the earth; and the LORD caused to hail upon the land of Egypt. 24. So there was hail, and fire flashing up amidst the hail, very grievous, such as had not been in all the land of Egypt since it became a nation. 25. And the hail smote throughout all the land of Egypt all that was in the field, both man and beast; and the hail smote every herb of the field, and broke every tree of the field. 26. Only in the land of Goshen, where the children of Israel were, was there no hail. 27. And Pharaoh sent, and called for Moses and Aaron, and said unto them: 'I have sinned this time; the LORD is righteous, and I and my people are wicked. 28. Entreat the LORD, and let there be enough of these mighty thunderings and hail; and I will let you go, and ye shall stay no longer.' 29. And Moses said unto him: 'As soon as I am gone out of the city, I will spread forth my hands unto the LORD; the thunders shall cease, neither shall there be any more hail;

אֲשֶׁר לֹא־הָיָה כָמֹהוּ בְּמִצְרַיִם לְמִן־הַיּוֹם הִוָּסְדָה וְעַד־
19 עָתָּה׃ וְעַתָּה שְׁלַח הָעֵז אֶת־מִקְנְךָ וְאֵת כָּל־אֲשֶׁר לְךָ
בַּשָּׂדֶה כָּל־הָאָדָם וְהַבְּהֵמָה אֲשֶׁר־יִמָּצֵא בַשָּׂדֶה וְלֹא יֵאָסֵף
כ הַבַּיְתָה וְיָרַד עֲלֵהֶם הַבָּרָד וָמֵתוּ׃ הַיָּרֵא אֶת־דְּבַר יְהוָה
מֵעַבְדֵי פַּרְעֹה הֵנִיס אֶת־עֲבָדָיו וְאֶת־מִקְנֵהוּ אֶל־הַבָּתִּים׃
21 וַאֲשֶׁר לֹא־שָׂם לִבּוֹ אֶל־דְּבַר יְהוָה וַיַּעֲזֹב אֶת־עֲבָדָיו וְאֶת־
מִקְנֵהוּ בַּשָּׂדֶה׃ פ
22 וַיֹּאמֶר יְהוָה אֶל־מֹשֶׁה נְטֵה אֶת־יָדְךָ עַל־הַשָּׁמַיִם וִיהִי
בָרָד בְּכָל־אֶרֶץ מִצְרָיִם עַל־הָאָדָם וְעַל־הַבְּהֵמָה וְעַל כָּל־
23 עֵשֶׂב הַשָּׂדֶה בְּאֶרֶץ מִצְרָיִם׃ וַיֵּט מֹשֶׁה אֶת־מַטֵּהוּ עַל־
הַשָּׁמַיִם וַיהוָה נָתַן קֹלֹת וּבָרָד וַתִּהֲלַךְ־אֵשׁ אָרְצָה וַיַּמְטֵר
24 יְהוָה בָּרָד עַל־אֶרֶץ מִצְרָיִם׃ וַיְהִי בָרָד וְאֵשׁ מִתְלַקַּחַת
בְּתוֹךְ הַבָּרָד כָּבֵד מְאֹד אֲשֶׁר לֹא־הָיָה כָמֹהוּ בְּכָל־אֶרֶץ
כה מִצְרַיִם מֵאָז הָיְתָה לְגוֹי׃ וַיַּךְ הַבָּרָד בְּכָל־אֶרֶץ מִצְרַיִם
אֵת כָּל־אֲשֶׁר בַּשָּׂדֶה מֵאָדָם וְעַד־בְּהֵמָה וְאֵת כָּל־עֵשֶׂב
26 הַשָּׂדֶה הִכָּה הַבָּרָד וְאֶת־כָּל־עֵץ הַשָּׂדֶה שִׁבֵּר׃ רַק בְּאֶרֶץ
27 גֹּשֶׁן אֲשֶׁר־שָׁם בְּנֵי יִשְׂרָאֵל לֹא הָיָה בָּרָד׃ וַיִּשְׁלַח פַּרְעֹה
וַיִּקְרָא לְמֹשֶׁה וּלְאַהֲרֹן וַיֹּאמֶר אֲלֵהֶם חָטָאתִי הַפָּעַם יְהוָה
28 הַצַּדִּיק וַאֲנִי וְעַמִּי הָרְשָׁעִים׃ הַעְתִּירוּ אֶל־יְהוָה וְרַב מִהְיֹת
קֹלֹת אֱלֹהִים וּבָרָד וַאֲשַׁלְּחָה אֶתְכֶם וְלֹא תֹסִפוּן לַעֲמֹד׃
29 וַיֹּאמֶר אֵלָיו מֹשֶׁה כְּצֵאתִי אֶת־הָעִיר אֶפְרֹשׂ אֶת־כַּפַּי אֶל־

19. *hasten in.* Or, 'bring in safety'.
they shall die. God had compassion on man and beast, in order to save the sinners and deliver them from death (Nachmanides).

20. *feared the word of the LORD.* This is the first indication that the warnings had a salutary effect upon the Egyptians.

22. *upon man, and upon beast.* Of those who disregarded the Divine warning; see the preceding verses.

23. *fire ran down unto the earth.* Probably lightning is implied. Luzzatto suggests thunderbolts.

24. *fire flashing up amidst the hail.* Perhaps forked or zigzag lightning is meant.

25. *every herb of the field.* lit. 'all the grass of the field'; *all*, according to the Heb. usage meaning *a great part.*

26. *only in the land of Goshen.* See VIII, 22; IX, 4, 7.

27–33. Pharaoh craves a third time for the cessation of the Plague (see VIII, 8, 28).

27. *sinned this time.* Pharaoh this time confesses his fault as he had never done before. His penitence, however, as the sequel shows, is not very deep (Driver).
is righteous. i.e. is the one in the right.
are wicked. Are in the wrong.

29. *gone out of the city.* Which was full of idols (Midrash).
spread forth my hands. i.e. in prayer.

that thou mayest know that the earth is the LORD's. 30. But as for thee and thy servants, I know that ye will not yet fear the LORD God.'—31. And the flax and the barley were smitten; for the barley was in the ear, and the flax was in bloom. 32. But the wheat and the spelt were not smitten; for they ripen late.*m. 33. And Moses went out of the city from Pharaoh, and spread forth his hands unto the LORD; and the thunders and hail ceased, and the rain was not poured upon the earth. 34. And when Pharaoh saw that the rain and the hail and the thunders were ceased, he sinned yet more, and hardened his heart, he and his servants. 35. And the heart of Pharaoh was hardened, and he did not let the children of Israel go; as the LORD had spoken by Moses.

יְהוָה הַקֹּלוֹת יֶחְדָּלוּן וְהַבָּרָד לֹא יִהְיֶה־עוֹד לְמַעַן תֵּדַע
ל כִּי לַיהוָה הָאָרֶץ׃ וְאַתָּה וַעֲבָדֶיךָ יָדַעְתִּי כִּי טֶרֶם תִּירְאוּן
31 מִפְּנֵי יְהוָה אֱלֹהִים׃ וְהַפִּשְׁתָּה וְהַשְּׂעֹרָה נֻכָּתָה כִּי הַשְּׂעֹרָה
32 אָבִיב וְהַפִּשְׁתָּה גִּבְעֹל׃ וְהַחִטָּה וְהַכֻּסֶּמֶת לֹא נֻכּוּ כִּי
מפטיר
33 אֲפִילֹת הֵנָּה׃* וַיֵּצֵא מֹשֶׁה מֵעִם פַּרְעֹה אֶת־הָעִיר וַיִּפְרֹשׂ
כַּפָּיו אֶל־יְהוָה וַיַּחְדְּלוּ הַקֹּלוֹת וְהַבָּרָד וּמָטָר לֹא־נִתַּךְ
34 אָרְצָה׃ וַיַּרְא פַּרְעֹה כִּי־חָדַל הַמָּטָר וְהַבָּרָד וְהַקֹּלֹת
לה וַיֹּסֶף לַחֲטֹא וַיַּכְבֵּד לִבּוֹ הוּא וַעֲבָדָיו׃ וַיֶּחֱזַק לֵב פַּרְעֹה
וְלֹא שִׁלַּח אֶת־בְּנֵי יִשְׂרָאֵל כַּאֲשֶׁר דִּבֶּר יְהוָה בְּיַד־מֹשֶׁה׃

the earth is the LORD'S. The imaginary sway of the idols was limited to a single land or part thereof. The God of the Hebrews is living Ruler of the whole earth.

30. *not yet fear. i.e.* you do not yet stand in awe of Him, so as to set Israel free.

31. *flax and the barley were smitten.* The time indicated is the end of January or the beginning of February. Flax was much esteemed by the Egyptians, and Egypt was the great linen market of the ancient world. Barley was used for making a coarse bread eaten by the poor.

32. *wheat and the spelt.* Wheat was the most cultivated grain in Egypt. Spelt, see Isa. XXVIII, 25 and Ezek. IV, 9, is a kind of wild wheat.

for they ripen late. And, therefore, being then tender and flexible, they yielded to the stroke of the hail without any hurt.

33. *not poured upon the earth.* At the prayer of Moses, the lightning and the hail ceased.

34. *he sinned yet more.* Having acknowledged that God was righteous (*v.* 27), he continues to resist His commands. He now becomes a rebel. The ministers of state are associated with the king in the obstinate resistance to God.

35. *was hardened.* Repeating his sin by again breaking his promise.

HAFTORAH VA-AYRA הפטרת וארא

EZEKIEL XXVIII, 25–XXIX, 21

CHAPTER XXVIII

25. Thus saith the Lord GOD: When I shall have gathered the house of Israel from the peoples among whom they are scattered, and shall be sanctified in them in the sight of the nations, then shall they dwell in their own land which I gave to My servant Jacob. 26. And they shall dwell safely therein, and shall build houses, and plant vineyards; yea, they shall dwell safely; when I have executed judgments

CAP. XXVIII. כח

כה כֹּה־אָמַר אֲדֹנָי
יֱהוִה בְּקַבְּצִי ׀ אֶת־בֵּית יִשְׂרָאֵל מִן־הָעַמִּים אֲשֶׁר נָפֹצוּ
בָם וְנִקְדַּשְׁתִּי בָם לְעֵינֵי הַגּוֹיִם וְיָשְׁבוּ עַל־אַדְמָתָם אֲשֶׁר
26 נָתַתִּי לְעַבְדִּי לְיַעֲקֹב׃ וְיָשְׁבוּ עָלֶיהָ לָבֶטַח וּבָנוּ בָתִּים

The section is chiefly a prophecy against Egypt and thus forms the link with the Sedrah.

For Ezekiel's life and message, see p. 178, as well as the introductory notes to the Haftorah of Tetzaveh, Parah and Hachodesh. He and the flower of the nation were deported to Babylon in 597 B.C.E. He seems to have lived a peaceful and honoured life in Chaldea. The exiles had their own houses and lands, and their own government by Elders. They seem readily to have entered into the upon all those that have them in disdain round about them; and they shall know that I am the LORD their God.

וְנָטְעוּ כְרָמִים וְיָשְׁבוּ לָבֶטַח בַּעֲשׂוֹתִי שְׁפָטִים בְּכֹל הַשָּׁאטִים
אֹתָם מִסְּבִיבֹתָם וְיָדְעוּ כִּי אֲנִי יְהוָה אֱלֹהֵיהֶם׃

CHAPTER XXIX

1. In the tenth year, in the tenth month, in the twelfth day of the month, the word of the LORD came unto me, saying: 2. 'Son of man, set thy face against Pharaoh king of Egypt, and prophesy against him, and against all Egypt; 3. speak, and say: Thus saith the Lord GOD:

Behold, I am against thee, Pharaoh
King of Egypt,
The great dragon that lieth
In the midst of his rivers,
That hath said: My river is mine own,
And I have made it for myself.

4. And I will put hooks in thy jaws, and I will cause the fish of thy rivers to stick unto thy scales; and I will bring thee up out of the midst of thy rivers, and all the fish of thy rivers shall stick unto thy scales. 5. And I will cast thee into the wilderness,

Thee and all the fish of thy rivers;
Thou shalt fall upon the open field;
Thou shalt not be brought together, nor
gathered;

CAP. XXIX. כט

א בַּשָּׁנָה הָעֲשִׂרִית בָּעֲשִׂרִי בִּשְׁנֵים עָשָׂר לַחֹדֶשׁ הָיָה דְבַר־
2 יְהוָה אֵלַי לֵאמֹר׃ בֶּן־אָדָם שִׂים פָּנֶיךָ עַל־פַּרְעֹה מֶלֶךְ
3 מִצְרָיִם וְהִנָּבֵא עָלָיו וְעַל־מִצְרַיִם כֻּלָּהּ׃ דַּבֵּר וְאָמַרְתָּ
כֹּה־אָמַר ׀ אֲדֹנָי יֱהוִה הִנְנִי עָלֶיךָ פַּרְעֹה מֶלֶךְ־מִצְרַיִם
הַתַּנִּים הַגָּדוֹל הָרֹבֵץ בְּתוֹךְ יְאֹרָיו אֲשֶׁר אָמַר לִי יְאֹרִי
4 וַאֲנִי עֲשִׂיתִנִי׃ וְנָתַתִּי חַחִיִּים בִּלְחָיֶיךָ וְהִדְבַּקְתִּי דְגַת־
יְאֹרֶיךָ בְּקַשְׂקְשֹׂתֶיךָ וְהַעֲלִיתִיךָ מִתּוֹךְ יְאֹרֶיךָ וְאֵת כָּל־
ה דְּגַת יְאֹרֶיךָ בְּקַשְׂקְשֹׂתֶיךָ תִּדְבָּק׃ וּנְטַשְׁתִּיךָ הַמִּדְבָּרָה
אוֹתְךָ וְאֵת כָּל־דְּגַת יְאֹרֶיךָ עַל־פְּנֵי הַשָּׂדֶה תִּפּוֹל לֹא
תֵאָסֵף וְלֹא תִקָּבֵץ לְחַיַּת הָאָרֶץ וּלְעוֹף הַשָּׁמַיִם נְתַתִּיךָ

כ"ט v. 4. חחים קרי

'modern' life of Babylon, under the firm and not unjust rule of Nebuchadnezzar. In common with Jeremiah, he held that the future of the nation lay with the exiles, and he devoted his extraordinary genius to saving these exiles, as Israelites, for Israel. He follows events in the Holy Land with feverish anxiety, and warns his brethren against the alliance with Egypt.

25. *shall have gathered.* A leading doctrine in Ezekiel's message is that God will restore and purify His people.
shall be sanctified. i.e. be recognized as holy. Through Israel, God will be recognized as the God of Holiness by all the nations.

26. *they shall know that I am the LORD.* The result of such restoration and purification of Israel will vindicate the supreme power of the God of Israel. A repentant and restored Israel would reveal to all the nations the 'Name' of God; *i.e.* the real character and majesty of the God of Israel. On the meaning of this phrase, see p. 398.

CHAPTER XXIX. THE ORACLE AGAINST EGYPT

Egypt, the house of bondage and oppression for Israel in the days of its youth, was again the enemy during the last years of the Jewish state. It was 'a broken reed', and was as perfidious as it was decadent.

1. *in the tenth year.* Of the reign of Zedekiah, the last king of Judah; 587 B.C.E.
tenth month. i.e. Tebeth (January–February), about seven months before the destruction of Jerusalem.

2. *son of man.* A favourite expression of Ezekiel, and equivalent to *man* or *mortal.*
Pharaoh. Pharaoh Hophra.

3. *the great dragon.* The crocodile; which infested the Nile and was worshipped as a god. It is here the symbol of Egypt.
his rivers. The Nile and its branches.
my river is mine own. It is this insolent pride of Egypt in its land and River, this self-deification on the part of the Pharaohs, that was an assured forerunner of its fall.

4. *hooks in thy jaws.* The crocodile is really less formidable than he appears to be, and is an easy prey to such as assail him with skill; the same will be true of Egypt.
fish of thy rivers. The subjects or allies of Egypt will be involved in its ruin.

6 לְאָכְלָה׃ וְיָדְעוּ כָּל־יֹשְׁבֵי מִצְרַיִם כִּי אֲנִי יְהוָה יַעַן הֱיוֹתָם
7 מִשְׁעֶנֶת קָנֶה לְבֵית יִשְׂרָאֵל׃ בְּתָפְשָׂם בְּךָ בַכַּפְּךָ תֵּרוֹץ
וּבָקַעְתָּ לָהֶם כָּל־כָּתֵף וּבְהִשָּׁעֲנָם עָלֶיךָ תִּשָּׁבֵר וְהַעֲמַדְתָּ
8 לָהֶם כָּל־מָתְנָיִם׃ לָכֵן כֹּה אָמַר אֲדֹנָי יֱהוִה הִנְנִי
9 מֵבִיא עָלַיִךְ חָרֶב וְהִכְרַתִּי מִמֵּךְ אָדָם וּבְהֵמָה׃ וְהָיְתָה
אֶרֶץ־מִצְרַיִם לִשְׁמָמָה וְחָרְבָּה וְיָדְעוּ כִּי־אֲנִי יְהוָה יַעַן
י אָמַר יְאֹר לִי וַאֲנִי עָשִׂיתִי׃ לָכֵן הִנְנִי אֵלֶיךָ וְאֶל־יְאֹרֶיךָ
וְנָתַתִּי אֶת־אֶרֶץ מִצְרַיִם לְחָרְבוֹת חֹרֶב שְׁמָמָה מִמִּגְדֹּל
11 סְוֵנֵה וְעַד־גְּבוּל כּוּשׁ׃ לֹא תַעֲבָר־בָּהּ רֶגֶל אָדָם וְרֶגֶל
12 בְּהֵמָה לֹא תַעֲבָר־בָּהּ וְלֹא תֵשֵׁב אַרְבָּעִים שָׁנָה׃ וְנָתַתִּי
אֶת־אֶרֶץ מִצְרַיִם שְׁמָמָה בְּתוֹךְ ׀ אֲרָצוֹת נְשַׁמּוֹת וְעָרֶיהָ
בְּתוֹךְ עָרִים מָחֳרָבוֹת תִּהְיֶיןָ שְׁמָמָה אַרְבָּעִים שָׁנָה וַהֲפִצֹתִי
13 אֶת־מִצְרַיִם בַּגּוֹיִם וְזֵרִיתִים בָּאֲרָצוֹת׃ כִּי כֹה אָמַר
אֲדֹנָי יֱהוִה מִקֵּץ אַרְבָּעִים שָׁנָה אֲקַבֵּץ אֶת־מִצְרַיִם מִן־
14 הָעַמִּים אֲשֶׁר־נָפֹצוּ שָׁמָּה׃ וְשַׁבְתִּי אֶת־שְׁבוּת מִצְרַיִם
וַהֲשִׁבֹתִי אֹתָם אֶרֶץ פַּתְרוֹס עַל־אֶרֶץ מְכוּרָתָם וְהָיוּ שָׁם
טו מַמְלָכָה שְׁפָלָה׃ מִן־הַמַּמְלָכוֹת תִּהְיֶה שְׁפָלָה וְלֹא־
תִתְנַשֵּׂא עוֹד עַל־הַגּוֹיִם וְהִמְעַטְתִּים לְבִלְתִּי רְדוֹת בַּגּוֹיִם׃

To the beasts of the earth and to the fowls of the heaven
Have I given thee for food.

6. And all the inhabitants of Egypt shall know
That I am the LORD,
Because they have been a staff of reed
To the house of Israel.

7. When they take hold of thee with the hand, thou dost break,
And rend all their shoulders;
And when they lean upon thee, thou breakest,
And makest all their loins to be at a stand.

8. Therefore thus saith the Lord GOD: Behold, I will bring a sword upon thee, and will cut off from thee man and beast. 9. And the land of Egypt shall be desolate and waste, and they shall know that I am the LORD; because he hath said: The river is mine, and I have made it. 10. Therefore, behold, I am against thee, and against thy rivers, and I will make the land of Egypt utterly waste and desolate, from Migdol to Syene even unto the border of Ethiopia. 11. No foot of man shall pass through it, nor foot of beast shall pass through it, neither shall it be inhabited forty years. 12. And I will make the land of Egypt desolate in the midst of the countries that are desolate, and her cities among the cities that are laid waste shall be desolate forty years; and I will scatter the Egyptians among the nations, and will disperse them through the countries. ¶ 13. For thus saith the Lord GOD: At the end of forty years will I gather the Egyptians from the peoples whither they were scattered; 14. and I will turn the captivity of Egypt, and will cause them to return into the land of Pathros, into the land of their origin; and they shall be there a lowly kingdom. 15. It shall be the lowliest of the kingdoms, neither shall it any more lift itself up above the nations; and I will

v. 7. בכף קרי

6. *a staff of reed to the house of Israel.* An exact picture of the deceptive character of Egypt's relationship with Israel. By promises of assistance she incited Israel to rebel against Assyria and Babylon, but always failed at the critical hour to redeem her promise.

7. *to be at a stand. i.e.* to stand alone, without the support on which the tired body could lean in time of strain.

10. *Migdol to Syene. i.e.* the whole of Egypt. Migdol is in the North, and Syene, the modern Assouan, in the South. (In 1904, a large quantity of Aramaic documents were found at Assouan, dating from the years 471–411 B.C.E. They reveal the existence of a large and prosperous Jewish community, probably the descendants of the Jewish refugees from Jerusalem; Jer. XLI.)

Ethiopia. The land and people of the southern Nile-valley, towards the Sudan and Abyssinia.

11. *forty years.* A round number, indicating a generation.

13. *will I gather.* Isaiah and Jeremiah also foretell a restored Egypt.

14. *Pathros.* In Upper (*i.e.* South) Egypt, the original seat of Egyptian rule.

16 וְלֹא יִהְיֶה־עוֹד לְבֵית יִשְׂרָאֵל לְמִבְטָח מַזְכִּיר עָוֺן בִּפְנוֹתָם
17 אַחֲרֵיהֶם וְיָדְעוּ כִּי אֲנִי אֲדֹנָי יְהוִה׃ וַיְהִי בְּעֶשְׂרִים
וָשֶׁבַע שָׁנָה בָּרִאשׁוֹן בְּאֶחָד לַחֹדֶשׁ הָיָה דְבַר־יְהוָה אֵלַי
18 לֵאמֹר׃ בֶּן־אָדָם נְבוּכַדְרֶאצַּר מֶלֶךְ־בָּבֶל הֶעֱבִיד אֶת־חֵילוֹ
עֲבֹדָה גְדוֹלָה אֶל־צֹר כָּל־רֹאשׁ מֻקְרָח וְכָל־כָּתֵף מְרוּטָה
וְשָׂכָר לֹא־הָיָה לוֹ וּלְחֵילוֹ מִצֹּר עַל־הָעֲבֹדָה אֲשֶׁר־עָבַד
19 עָלֶיהָ׃ לָכֵן כֹּה אָמַר אֲדֹנָי יְהוִה הִנְנִי נֹתֵן לִנְבוּכַדְרֶאצַּר
מֶלֶךְ־בָּבֶל אֶת־אֶרֶץ מִצְרָיִם וְנָשָׂא הֲמֹנָהּ וְשָׁלַל שְׁלָלָהּ
כ וּבָזַז בִּזָּהּ וְהָיְתָה שָׂכָר לְחֵילוֹ׃ פְּעֻלָּתוֹ אֲשֶׁר־עָבַד בָּהּ נָתַתִּי
21 לוֹ אֶת־אֶרֶץ מִצְרָיִם אֲשֶׁר עָשׂוּ לִי נְאֻם אֲדֹנָי יְהוִה׃ בַּיּוֹם
הַהוּא אַצְמִיחַ קֶרֶן לְבֵית יִשְׂרָאֵל וּלְךָ אֶתֵּן פִּתְחוֹן־פֶּה
בְּתוֹכָם וְיָדְעוּ כִּי־אֲנִי יְהוָה׃

diminish them, that they shall no more rule over the nations. 16. And it shall be no more the confidence of the house of Israel, bringing iniquity to remembrance, when they turn after them; and they shall know that I am the Lord GOD.' ¶ 17. And it came to pass in the seven and twentieth year, in the first month, in the first day of the month, the word of the LORD came unto me, saying: 18. 'Son of man, Nebuchadrezzar king of Babylon caused his army to serve a great service against Tyre; every head was made bald, and every shoulder was peeled; yet had he no wages, nor his army, from Tyre, for the service that he had served against it; 19. therefore thus saith the Lord GOD: Behold, I will give the land of Egypt unto Nebuchadrezzar king of Babylon; and he shall carry off her abundance, and take her spoil, and take her prey; and it shall be the wages for his army. 20. I have given him the land of Egypt as his hire for which he served, because they wrought for Me, saith the Lord GOD. ¶ 21. In that day will I cause a horn to shoot up unto the house of Israel, and I will give thee the opening of the mouth in the midst of them; and they shall know that I am the LORD.'

16. *no more the confidence.* Too weak to help, and no longer able either to harm or tempt Israel into trusting Egypt. After its conquest by the Babylonians, Egypt never again became really independent.

bringing iniquity to remembrance. 'Every alliance with Egypt brings the headstrong folly of Israel into fresh prominence' (Lofthouse).

17–20. THE CONQUEST OF EGYPT BY NEBUCHADNEZZAR

17. *the seven and twentieth year.* 570 B.C.E. This is Ezekiel's latest prophecy.

18. *Nebuchadrezzar.* The original and more correct form of the name.

every shoulder was peeled. From the constant carrying of burdens. As Nebuchadnezzar had no fleet, the arm of the sea between Tyre and the mainland had to be filled up. Hence the arduous toil of his army.

no wages. He was disappointed in the spoil he expected from Tyre.

20. *they wrought for Me.* Nebuchadnezzar and his army who are God's instruments against Egypt, which is now given to the Babylonian king as compensation for Tyre.

21. *in that day.* The humiliation of Egypt would open the way for Israel's restoration. Israel would see 'the finger of God' in all this upheaval.

horn. Symbol of power and prosperity.

opening of the mouth. The Prophet's prediction having been fulfilled, the people would believe in the efficacy of his teaching and message.

10

CHAPTER X

1. And the LORD said unto Moses: 'Go in unto Pharaoh; for I have hardened his heart, and the heart of his servants, that I might show these My signs in the midst of them; 2. and that thou mayest tell in the ears of thy son, and of thy son's son, what I have wrought upon Egypt, and My signs which I have done among them; that ye may know that I am the LORD.' 3. And Moses and Aaron went in unto Pharaoh, and said unto him: 'Thus saith the LORD, the God of the Hebrews: How long wilt thou refuse to humble thyself before Me? let My people go, that they may serve Me. 4. Else, if thou refuse to let My people go, behold, to-morrow will I bring locusts into thy border; 5. and they shall cover the face of the earth, that one shall not be able to see the earth; and they shall eat the residue of that which is escaped, which remaineth unto you from the hail, and shall

CAP. X. י

פ פ פ טו 15

י

א וַיֹּאמֶר יְהוָה אֶל־מֹשֶׁה בֹּא אֶל־פַּרְעֹה כִּי־אֲנִי הִכְבַּדְתִּי
אֶת־לִבּוֹ וְאֶת־לֵב עֲבָדָיו לְמַעַן שִׁתִי אֹתֹתַי אֵלֶּה בְּקִרְבּוֹ׃
2 וּלְמַעַן תְּסַפֵּר בְּאָזְנֵי בִנְךָ וּבֶן־בִּנְךָ אֵת אֲשֶׁר הִתְעַלַּלְתִּי
בְּמִצְרַיִם וְאֶת־אֹתֹתַי אֲשֶׁר־שַׂמְתִּי בָם וִידַעְתֶּם כִּי־אֲנִי
3 יְהוָה׃ וַיָּבֹא מֹשֶׁה וְאַהֲרֹן אֶל־פַּרְעֹה וַיֹּאמְרוּ אֵלָיו כֹּה־
אָמַר יְהוָה אֱלֹהֵי הָעִבְרִים עַד־מָתַי מֵאַנְתָּ לֵעָנֹת מִפָּנָי
4 שַׁלַּח עַמִּי וְיַעַבְדֻנִי׃ כִּי אִם־מָאֵן אַתָּה לְשַׁלֵּחַ אֶת־עַמִּי
ה הִנְנִי מֵבִיא מָחָר אַרְבֶּה בִּגְבֻלֶךָ׃ וְכִסָּה אֶת־עֵין הָאָרֶץ
וְלֹא יוּכַל לִרְאֹת אֶת־הָאָרֶץ וְאָכַל ׀ אֶת־יֶתֶר הַפְּלֵטָה

III. BO

(CHAPTERS X–XIII, 16)

CHAPTER X, 1–20

THE EIGHTH PLAGUE: LOCUSTS

1. *go in unto Pharaoh.* And caution him (Rashi).

hardened his heart. See note on IV, 21.

2. *that thou. i.e.* Moses, as the representative of the Israelites.

mayest tell. 'This phrase is appropriate in regard to the plague of locusts, which constantly recurs in those lands; and men on such occasions would compare their visitation with preceding ones, and thus be reminded of the unparalleled visitation in the days of Moses' (Bechor Shor).

wrought upon Egypt. The Heb. verb is uncommon. It implies an action which brings shame and disgrace upon its objects, making them, so to speak, playthings of Divine power.

know that I am the LORD. See notes on VI, 3–7. The object of the plagues is the education of men in the knowledge of God. Ps. LXXVIII and CV are instances of the instruction of later generations in the meaning of the wonders wrought by God for the Israelites of old.

3. *refuse to humble thyself.* This was now the real cause of Pharaoh's sin after all these plagues—refusal to humble himself before God. And Pharaoh would not really humble himself, until he made God's will his own, and fulfilled his oft-given promise to permit the Israelites to leave Egypt. His heart was hardened, but his will was still free, and he could repent if he chose.

4. *to-morrow.* Again another opportunity is given to the king to submit himself to the Divine command.

5. *they shall cover the face of the earth.* This is literally true of locusts. Lord Bryce thus describes a swarm of locusts:—

> 'It is a strange sight, beautiful if you can forget the destruction it brings with it. The whole air, to twelve or even eighteen feet above the ground, is filled with the insects, reddish-brown in body, with bright, gauzy wings. When the sun's rays catch them, it is like the seas sparkling with light. When you see them against a cloud, they are like the dense flakes of a driving snowstorm. You feel as if you had never before realized immensity in number. . . . They blot out the sun above, and cover the ground beneath, and fill the air whichever way one looks. The breeze carries them swiftly past, but they come on in fresh clouds, a host of which there is no end, each of them a harmless creature which you can catch and crush in your hand, but appalling in their power of collective devastation.'

eat the residue. Their voracity is incredible; see Joel II, 20 (Haftorah Sabbath Shuvah). Not only the leaves, but the branches and even the wood are attacked and devoured. The residue here refers to the wheat and the spelt (IX, 32), which escaped the havoc wrought by the hail (Malbim).

eat every tree which groweth for you out of the field; 6. and thy houses shall be filled, and the houses of all thy servants, and the houses of all the Egyptians; as neither thy fathers nor thy fathers' fathers have seen, since the day that they were upon the earth unto this day.' And he turned, and went out from Pharaoh. 7. And Pharaoh's servants said unto him: 'How long shall this man be a snare unto us? let the men go, that they may serve the LORD their God; knowest thou not yet that Egypt is destroyed?' 8. And Moses and Aaron were brought again unto Pharaoh; and he said unto them: 'Go, serve the LORD your God; but who are they that shall go?' 9. And Moses said: 'We will go with our young and with our old, with our sons and with our daughters, with our flocks and with our herds we will go; for we must hold a feast unto the LORD.' 10. And he said unto them: 'So be the LORD with you, as I will let you go, and your little ones; see ye that evil is before your face. 11. Not so; go now ye that are men, and serve the LORD; for that is what ye desire.' And they were driven out from Pharaoh's presence.*ii. ¶ 12. And the LORD said unto Moses: 'Stretch out thy hand over the land of Egypt for the

הַנִּשְׁאֶרֶת לָכֶם מִן־הַבָּרָד וְאָכַל אֶת־כָּל־הָעֵץ הַצֹּמֵחַ לָכֶם
6 מִן־הַשָּׂדֶה׃ וּמָלְאוּ בָתֶּיךָ וּבָתֵּי כָל־עֲבָדֶיךָ וּבָתֵּי כָל־
מִצְרַיִם אֲשֶׁר לֹא־רָאוּ אֲבֹתֶיךָ וַאֲבוֹת אֲבֹתֶיךָ מִיּוֹם
הֱיוֹתָם עַל־הָאֲדָמָה עַד הַיּוֹם הַזֶּה וַיִּפֶן וַיֵּצֵא מֵעִם פַּרְעֹה׃
7 וַיֹּאמְרוּ עַבְדֵי פַרְעֹה אֵלָיו עַד־מָתַי יִהְיֶה זֶה לָנוּ לְמוֹקֵשׁ
שַׁלַּח אֶת־הָאֲנָשִׁים וְיַעַבְדוּ אֶת־יְהֹוָה אֱלֹהֵיהֶם הֲטֶרֶם תֵּדַע
8 כִּי אָבְדָה מִצְרָיִם׃ וַיּוּשַׁב אֶת־מֹשֶׁה וְאֶת־אַהֲרֹן אֶל־
פַּרְעֹה וַיֹּאמֶר אֲלֵהֶם לְכוּ עִבְדוּ אֶת־יְהֹוָה אֱלֹהֵיכֶם מִי וָמִי
9 הַהֹלְכִים׃ וַיֹּאמֶר מֹשֶׁה בִּנְעָרֵינוּ וּבִזְקֵנֵינוּ נֵלֵךְ בְּבָנֵינוּ
י וּבִבְנוֹתֵנוּ בְּצֹאנֵנוּ וּבִבְקָרֵנוּ נֵלֵךְ כִּי חַג־יְהֹוָה לָנוּ׃ וַיֹּאמֶר
אֲלֵהֶם יְהִי כֵן יְהֹוָה עִמָּכֶם כַּאֲשֶׁר אֲשַׁלַּח אֶתְכֶם וְאֶת־
11 טַפְּכֶם רְאוּ כִּי רָעָה נֶגֶד פְּנֵיכֶם׃ לֹא כֵן לְכוּ־נָא הַגְּבָרִים
וְעִבְדוּ אֶת־יְהֹוָה כִּי אֹתָהּ אַתֶּם מְבַקְשִׁים וַיְגָרֶשׁ אֹתָם מֵאֵת
שני
12 פְּנֵי פַרְעֹה׃ ס וַיֹּאמֶר יְהֹוָה אֶל־מֹשֶׁה נְטֵה יָדְךָ עַל־אֶרֶץ

6. *thy houses shall be filled.* If part of a swarm alights on a house, the locusts enter its innermost recesses, and fill every corner.

since the day. Cf. IX, 24.

and he turned. i.e. Moses, and Aaron followed; see *v.* 3.

7–11. For the first time the servants intervene before the plague is inflicted, showing at once their belief in Moses' threat and their dread of the affliction. They suggest that Pharaoh should come to terms with Moses, who demands that the entire people must go to worship God.

7. *Pharaoh's servants.* Their hearts were not so hard as their master's; see VIII, 19, and IX, 20.

this man. i.e. Moses.

a snare. fig. for any cause of destruction.

destroyed. i.e. ruined through all the plagues.

8. *who are they that shall go.* lit. 'who and who are those who are going?' *i.e.* who exactly is to go?

9. *go with our young.* There was nothing extraordinary in Moses' demand, as great festivals in Egypt were kept by the whole population.

10. *so be the LORD with you.* Pharaoh replies ironically, 'May God be with you as assuredly as I will let you go.'

evil is before your face. Or, 'evil is what ye purpose.' The evil intention which you harbour, to leave Egypt for good with all your belongings, is standing plainly before your face; it is evident to all (Bechor Shor).

11. *not so.* As ye have said, to take your little ones with you (Rashi).

ye that are men. This policy of Pharaoh has more than once been imitated by Israel's oppressors. After the expulsion from Spain, 80,000 Jews took refuge in Portugal, 'relying on the promise of the king. Spanish priests lashed the Portuguese into fury, and the king was persuaded to issue an edict which threw even that of Isabella into the shade. All the adult Jews were banished from Portugal; but first of all their children below the age of fourteen were taken from them to be educated as Christians. Then, indeed, the serene fortitude with which the exiled people had borne so many and such grievous calamities gave way, and was replaced by the wildest paroxysms of despair' (Lecky). And in our own day, the Soviet rulers extend considerable religious freedom *to adults;* religious instruction *to children,* however, is rigorously suppressed.

that is what ye desire. This is what you asked for hitherto, to hold a sacrificial feast unto God; and for this men alone suffice. Moses, however, demanded from the first 'Let my people go'—the entire people, and not the men only.

locusts, that they may come up upon the land of Egypt, and eat every herb of the land, even all that the hail hath left.' 13. And Moses stretched forth his rod over the land of Egypt, and the LORD brought an east wind upon the land all that day, and all the night; and when it was morning, the east wind brought the locusts. 14. And the locusts went up over all the land of Egypt, and rested in all the borders of Egypt; very grievous were they; before them there were no such locusts as they, neither after them shall be such. 15. For they covered the face of the whole earth, so that the land was darkened; and they did eat every herb of the land, and all the fruit of the trees which the hail had left; and there remained not any green thing, either tree or herb of the field, through all the land of Egypt. 16. Then Pharaoh called for Moses and Aaron in haste; and he said: 'I have sinned against the LORD your God, and against you. 17. Now therefore forgive, I pray thee, my sin only this once, and entreat the LORD your God, that He may take away from me this death only.' 18. And he went out from Pharaoh, and entreated the LORD. 19. And the LORD turned an exceeding strong west wind, which took up the locusts, and drove them into the Red Sea; there remained not one locust in all the border of Egypt. 20. But the LORD hardened Pharaoh's heart, and he did not let the children of Israel go. ¶ 21. And the

מִצְרַיִם בָּאַרְבֶּה וְיַעַל עַל־אֶרֶץ מִצְרָיִם וְיֹאכַל אֶת־כָּל־
13 עֵשֶׂב הָאָרֶץ אֵת כָּל־אֲשֶׁר הִשְׁאִיר הַבָּרָד׃ וַיֵּט מֹשֶׁה אֶת־
מַטֵּהוּ עַל־אֶרֶץ מִצְרַיִם וַיהוָה נִהַג רוּחַ־קָדִים בָּאָרֶץ כָּל־
הַיּוֹם הַהוּא וְכָל־הַלָּיְלָה הַבֹּקֶר הָיָה וְרוּחַ הַקָּדִים נָשָׂא
14 אֶת־הָאַרְבֶּה׃ וַיַּעַל הָאַרְבֶּה עַל כָּל־אֶרֶץ מִצְרַיִם וַיָּנַח בְּכֹל
גְּבוּל מִצְרָיִם כָּבֵד מְאֹד לְפָנָיו לֹא־הָיָה כֵן אַרְבֶּה כָּמֹהוּ
טו וְאַחֲרָיו לֹא יִהְיֶה־כֵּן׃ וַיְכַס אֶת־עֵין כָּל־הָאָרֶץ וַתֶּחְשַׁךְ
הָאָרֶץ וַיֹּאכַל אֶת־כָּל־עֵשֶׂב הָאָרֶץ וְאֵת כָּל־פְּרִי הָעֵץ אֲשֶׁר
הוֹתִיר הַבָּרָד וְלֹא־נוֹתַר כָּל־יֶרֶק בָּעֵץ וּבְעֵשֶׂב הַשָּׂדֶה
16 בְּכָל־אֶרֶץ מִצְרָיִם׃ וַיְמַהֵר פַּרְעֹה לִקְרֹא לְמֹשֶׁה וּלְאַהֲרֹן
17 וַיֹּאמֶר חָטָאתִי לַיהוָה אֱלֹהֵיכֶם וְלָכֶם׃ וְעַתָּה שָׂא נָא חַטָּאתִי
אַךְ הַפַּעַם וְהַעְתִּירוּ לַיהוָה אֱלֹהֵיכֶם וְיָסֵר מֵעָלַי רַק אֶת־
18 19 הַמָּוֶת הַזֶּה׃ וַיֵּצֵא מֵעִם פַּרְעֹה וַיֶּעְתַּר אֶל־יְהוָה׃ וַיַּהֲפֹךְ
יְהוָה רוּחַ־יָם חָזָק מְאֹד וַיִּשָּׂא אֶת־הָאַרְבֶּה וַיִּתְקָעֵהוּ יָמָּה
כ סוּף לֹא נִשְׁאַר אַרְבֶּה אֶחָד בְּכֹל גְּבוּל מִצְרָיִם׃ וַיְחַזֵּק יְהוָה
אֶת־לֵב פַּרְעֹה וְלֹא שִׁלַּח אֶת־בְּנֵי יִשְׂרָאֵל׃ פ

14. *the borders. i.e.* the territory.

very grievous were they. See VIII, 20. The reference here is to the tremendous quantities of the locusts.

no such locusts. In Egypt.

neither after them shall be such. In Egypt. The last two phrases are to be taken as proverbial, hyperbolical expressions (Luzzatto); cf. II Kings XVIII, 5 and XXIII, 25. See also IX, 24.

15. *was darkened.* The expression is exact and graphic. Afar off the locusts appear like a heavy cloud hanging over the land. As they approach, they completely hide the sun.

not any green thing. Where such a swarm appears, they eat the land bare and everything green vanishes from the fields.

16. *and against you.* See IX, 27. Here the king confesses his double sin against God and against Israel.

17. *this death. i.e.* this pestilence, destructive of all food and sustenance.

19. *into the Red Sea.* A swarm of locusts floats upon an easy breeze, but is beaten down by a storm; and if it touches water it perishes. Pliny also speaks of swarms of locusts carried away by the wind and cast into the sea.

Red Sea. lit. 'the sea of reeds'. It may also originally have been the name of the fresh-water lake lying immediately to the North of the Red Sea. The name, Red Sea (Septuagint), has been variously derived from the corals within its waters, the colour of the mountains bordering its coasts, or the glow of the sky reflected on it.

20. After the removal of the plague, Pharaoh once again breaks faith.

21–23. NINTH PLAGUE: DARKNESS

21. *darkness over the land.* 'Like the third and sixth plagues, it is inflicted unannounced; and the parleying, the driving of a bargain and then breaking it, by which the eighth was attended, is quite enough to account for this' (Chadwick).

This plague would especially affect the spirits of the Egyptians, whose chief object of worship was Ra, the sun-God. Merenphtah is depicted in a sculptured effigy with the inscription, 'He adores the sun.'

darkness which may be felt. Explained as an aggravation of the *khamsin*, or 'wind of the desert', which is not uncommon in Egypt, and is accompanied by weird darkness, beyond that of our worst fogs (Rawlinson). The following

LORD said unto Moses: 'Stretch out thy hand toward heaven, that there may be darkness over the land of Egypt, even darkness which may be felt.' 22. And Moses stretched forth his hand toward heaven; and there was a thick darkness in all the land of Egypt three days; 23. they saw not one another, neither rose any from his place for three days; but all the children of Israel had light in their dwellings.* iii. 24. And Pharaoh called unto Moses, and said: 'Go ye, serve the LORD; only let your flocks and your herds be stayed; let your little ones also go with you.' 25. And Moses said: 'Thou must also give into our hand sacrifices and burnt-offerings, that we may sacrifice unto the LORD our God. 26. Our cattle also shall go with us; there shall not a hoof be left behind; for thereof must we take to serve the LORD our God; and we know not with what we must serve the LORD, until we come thither.' 27. But the LORD hardened Pharaoh's heart, and he would not let them go. 28. And Pharaoh

21 וַיֹּאמֶר יְהוָה אֶל־מֹשֶׁה נְטֵה יָדְךָ עַל־הַשָּׁמַיִם וִיהִי חֹשֶׁךְ עַל־
22 אֶרֶץ מִצְרָיִם וְיָמֵשׁ חֹשֶׁךְ׃ וַיֵּט מֹשֶׁה אֶת־יָדוֹ עַל־הַשָּׁמָיִם
23 וַיְהִי חֹשֶׁךְ־אֲפֵלָה בְּכָל־אֶרֶץ מִצְרַיִם שְׁלֹשֶׁת יָמִים׃ לֹא־רָאוּ
אִישׁ אֶת־אָחִיו וְלֹא־קָמוּ אִישׁ מִתַּחְתָּיו שְׁלֹשֶׁת יָמִים וּלְכָל־
שלישי 24 בְּנֵי יִשְׂרָאֵל הָיָה אוֹר בְּמוֹשְׁבֹתָם׃* וַיִּקְרָא פַרְעֹה אֶל־מֹשֶׁה
וַיֹּאמֶר לְכוּ עִבְדוּ אֶת־יְהוָה רַק צֹאנְכֶם וּבְקַרְכֶם יֻצָּג גַּם־
כה טַפְּכֶם יֵלֵךְ עִמָּכֶם׃ וַיֹּאמֶר מֹשֶׁה גַּם־אַתָּה תִּתֵּן בְּיָדֵנוּ זְבָחִים
26 וְעֹלֹת וְעָשִׂינוּ לַיהוָה אֱלֹהֵינוּ׃ וְגַם־מִקְנֵנוּ יֵלֵךְ עִמָּנוּ לֹא
תִשָּׁאֵר פַּרְסָה כִּי מִמֶּנּוּ נִקַּח לַעֲבֹד אֶת־יְהוָה אֱלֹהֵינוּ
27 וַאֲנַחְנוּ לֹא־נֵדַע מַה־נַּעֲבֹד אֶת־יְהוָה עַד־בֹּאֵנוּ שָׁמָּה׃ וַיְחַזֵּק
28 יְהוָה אֶת־לֵב פַּרְעֹה וְלֹא אָבָה לְשַׁלְּחָם׃ וַיֹּאמֶר־לוֹ פַרְעֹה

verses are from the wonderful description of the plague of Darkness in Wisdom of Solomon XVII.

'No force of fire prevailed to give them light, neither were the bright flames of the stars strong enough to illumine that gloomy night;

'For wickedness, condemned by a witness within, is a coward thing; and being pressed hard by conscience, always forecasteth the worst lot;

'Whether there were a whistling wind, or a melodious noise of birds among the spreading branches, or a measured fall of water running violently:

'All these things paralysed them with terror; but for thy saints there was great light.'

23. *they saw not one another.* lit. 'man did not see his brother'.

neither rose any from his place. Too terrified to move.

had light in their dwellings. i.e. in the land of Goshen. Prof. Mahler identifies the ninth plague with the solar eclipse of March 13, 1335 B.C.E., which darkened Egypt proper but did not extend *as a total eclipse* to Goshen; hence, 'all the children of Israel had light in their habitations.' (Thus, the eclipse of the sun on January 24, 1925, was not visible in the lower half of New York City—96th Street marking the southern limit of the path of totality.) Tradition states that the darkness took place on the first of Nisan, which then fell on a Thursday. If Mahler's identification is correct, we would know the exact date—Thursday, March 27, 1335 B.C.E.—of the Exodus. Prof. Mahler, furthermore, takes the words 'three days' at the end of *v.* 22, and joins them to *v.* 23; thus, 'Three days they saw not one another, neither rose any from his place three days.' Accordingly, the eclipse was on one day only, but its terrifying effects—the blank, utter paralysis of dread—lasted three days. Greek writers have left us graphic descriptions of the effects of eclipses, 'when sore fear comes upon men.' Herodotus tells us that a total eclipse of the sun in 585 B.C.E., during a battle between the Lydians and Medes, so terrified the combatants that they ceased fighting and concluded peace. When the spectators are 'natives', a total eclipse of the sun is the occasion of remarkable scenes in which alarm and despair and anger are intermingled.

24. *called unto Moses.* After the darkness had passed away.

your little ones also. Pharaoh offers a greater concession than before, a step further on the way to complete capitulation. The entire people may now go. Their cattle, however, he desires them to leave behind as a security for their return. Moses refuses to listen to compromise.

25. *sacrifices.* Part of which was consumed on the altar, and part eaten by the worshippers.

burnt-offerings. Were wholly burnt on the altar.

26. *not a hoof be left behind.* Moses emphasizes his intention of not bringing Israel back to Egypt.

with what we must serve the LORD. We do not know what kind of animals are to be used for the sacrifice, neither do we know how many (Ibn Ezra).

28. *see my face no more.* Seek no more admittance to my presence; cf. II Sam. XIV, 24, 28; II Kings XXV, 19. When they once more met, it was the king that changed his purpose; and said unto him: 'Get thee from me, take heed to thyself, see my face no more; for in the day thou seest my face thou shalt die.' 29. And Moses said: 'Thou hast spoken well; I will see thy face again no more.'

11

CHAPTER XI

1. And the LORD said unto Moses: 'Yet one plague more will I bring upon Pharaoh, and upon Egypt; afterwards he will let you go hence; when he shall let you go, he shall surely thrust you out hence altogether. 2. Speak now in the ears of the people, and let them ask every man of his neighbour, and every woman of her neighbour, jewels of silver, and jewels of gold.' 3. And the LORD gave the people favour in the sight of the Egyptians. Moreover the man Moses was very great in the land of Egypt, in the sight of Pharaoh's servants, and in the sight of the people.* iv. ¶ 4. And Moses said: 'Thus saith the LORD: About midnight will I go out into the midst of Egypt; 5. and all the first-born in the land of Egypt shall die, from the first-born of Pharaoh that

לֵךְ מֵעָלָי הִשָּׁמֶר לְךָ אַל־תֹּסֶף רְאוֹת פָּנַי כִּי בְּיוֹם
29 רְאֹתְךָ פָנַי תָּמוּת׃ וַיֹּאמֶר מֹשֶׁה כֵּן דִּבַּרְתָּ לֹא־אֹסִף עוֹד
רְאוֹת פָּנֶיךָ׃ פ

יא

CAP. XI. יא

א וַיֹּאמֶר יְהוָה אֶל־מֹשֶׁה עוֹד נֶגַע אֶחָד אָבִיא עַל־פַּרְעֹה
וְעַל־מִצְרַיִם אַחֲרֵי־כֵן יְשַׁלַּח אֶתְכֶם מִזֶּה כְּשַׁלְּחוֹ כָּלָה
2 גָּרֵשׁ יְגָרֵשׁ אֶתְכֶם מִזֶּה׃ דַּבֶּר־נָא בְּאָזְנֵי הָעָם וְיִשְׁאֲלוּ
אִישׁ ׀ מֵאֵת רֵעֵהוּ וְאִשָּׁה מֵאֵת רְעוּתָהּ כְּלֵי־כֶסֶף וּכְלֵי
3 זָהָב׃ וַיִּתֵּן יְהוָה אֶת־חֵן הָעָם בְּעֵינֵי מִצְרָיִם גַּם ׀ הָאִישׁ
מֹשֶׁה גָּדוֹל מְאֹד בְּאֶרֶץ מִצְרַיִם בְּעֵינֵי עַבְדֵי־פַרְעֹה וּבְעֵינֵי
רביעי
4 הָעָם׃ ס וַיֹּאמֶר מֹשֶׁה כֹּה אָמַר יְהוָה כַּחֲצֹת הַלַּיְלָה אֲנִי
ה יוֹצֵא בְּתוֹךְ מִצְרָיִם׃ וּמֵת כָּל־בְּכוֹר בְּאֶרֶץ מִצְרַיִם

י׳ v. 29. פתח באתנח

on *his* face, not on that of Moses, was the pallor of impending death. In his negotiations with Pharaoh, Moses was ever ready to intercede; he never 'reviles the ruler', nor transgresses the limits of courtesy towards the king; yet he never falters nor compromises. Throughout, the dignified bearing is with Moses, the meanness and shame with Pharaoh who begins by insulting him, goes on to impose on him, and ends by an ignominious surrender, to be followed by treachery and abject defeat on the shores of the Red Sea (Chadwick).

29. *spoken well.* Further interviews would be useless.

see thy face again no more. But before Moses leaves the king's presence, he announces to him the tenth plague (XI, 4), and then leaves him for the last time (XI, 8).

CHAPTER XI. THE WARNING OF THE LAST PLAGUE

1. *the LORD said.* Or, 'had said' (Ibn Ezra). The tense is pluperfect and *v.* 1–3 are parenthetical, having been communicated to Moses on a previous occasion.

thrust you out. Moses thus learns that the last plague would be followed by an immediate departure; and this gave him time to devise measures of preparing the Israelites for the journey.

2. *let them ask.* They were, however, to leave Egypt where they had lived for so many centuries without any bitter memories of the Egyptian people. See note on III, 21.

3. *gave the people favour.* And, therefore, the Egyptians were most generous and friendly in the way they parted with the Israelites; see the explanation of Deut. XV, 14 in note on III, 21.

was very great. i.e. had gained a great reputation, because of the visitations; and, especially, by the care he had taken to warn them, and, so far as was possible, to save them from suffering. This conduct elicited their kindliest feelings towards the people of Moses.

4. *Moses said.* To Pharaoh, in answer to his ultimatum, X, 28.

will I go out. Onkelos renders, 'I will reveal Myself.'

5. *that sitteth upon his throne.* This phrase refers to Pharaoh, and not to the eldest son.

first-born of the maidservant. The meanest person in the kingdom is contrasted with the noblest. Grinding the corn, the lowest drudgery, was the work of women, slaves and captives. The hand-mill is still in daily use in practically every Eastern or East European village.

first-born of cattle. The plague of the cattle described in IX, 6 was limited to the 'cattle which are in the field'. The Heb. word for cattle in IX, 6 is *mikneh*, whereas here the word *behemah* is used. The Egyptians paid Divine honours to various animals; and the first-born of all these beasts were to be doomed.

sitteth upon his throne, even unto the first-born of the maid-servant that is behind the mill; and all the first-born of cattle. 6. And there shall be a great cry throughout all the land of Egypt, such as there hath been none like it, nor shall be like it any more. 7. But against any of the children of Israel shall not a dog whet his tongue, against man or beast; that ye may know how that the LORD doth put a difference between the Egyptians and Israel. 8. And all these thy servants shall come down unto me, and bow down unto me, saying: Get thee out, and all the people that follow thee; and after that I will go out.' And he went out from Pharaoh in hot anger. ¶ 9. And the LORD said unto Moses: 'Pharaoh will not hearken unto you; that My wonders may be multiplied in the land of Egypt.' 10. And Moses and Aaron did all these wonders before Pharaoh; and the LORD hardened Pharaoh's heart, and he did not let the children of Israel go out of his land.

מִבְּכ֤וֹר פַּרְעֹה֙ הַיֹּשֵׁ֣ב עַל־כִּסְא֔וֹ עַ֚ד בְּכ֣וֹר הַשִּׁפְחָ֔ה אֲשֶׁ֖ר
6 אַחַ֣ר הָרֵחָ֑יִם וְכֹ֖ל בְּכ֥וֹר בְּהֵמָֽה׃ וְהָֽיְתָ֛ה צְעָקָ֥ה גְדֹלָ֖ה
בְּכָל־אֶ֣רֶץ מִצְרָ֑יִם אֲשֶׁ֤ר כָּמֹ֙הוּ֙ לֹ֣א נִהְיָ֔תָה וְכָמֹ֖הוּ לֹ֥א
7 תֹסִֽף׃ וּלְכֹ֣ל ׀ בְּנֵ֣י יִשְׂרָאֵ֗ל לֹ֤א יֶחֱרַץ־כֶּ֙לֶב֙ לְשֹׁנ֔וֹ לְמֵאִ֖ישׁ
וְעַד־בְּהֵמָ֑ה לְמַ֙עַן֙ תֵּֽדְע֔וּן אֲשֶׁר֙ יַפְלֶ֣ה יְהוָ֔ה בֵּ֥ין מִצְרַ֖יִם
8 וּבֵ֥ין יִשְׂרָאֵֽל׃ וְיָרְד֣וּ כָל־עֲבָדֶיךָ֩ אֵ֨לֶּה אֵלַ֜י וְהִשְׁתַּֽחֲווּ־לִ֣י
לֵאמֹ֗ר צֵ֤א אַתָּה֙ וְכָל־הָעָ֣ם אֲשֶׁר־בְּרַגְלֶ֔יךָ וְאַחֲרֵי־כֵ֖ן אֵצֵ֑א
9 וַיֵּצֵ֥א מֵֽעִם־פַּרְעֹ֖ה בָּחֳרִי־אָֽף׃ ס וַיֹּ֤אמֶר יְהוָה֙ אֶל־מֹשֶׁ֔ה
לֹא־יִשְׁמַ֥ע אֲלֵיכֶ֖ם פַּרְעֹ֑ה לְמַ֛עַן רְב֥וֹת מוֹפְתַ֖י בְּאֶ֥רֶץ
10 מִצְרָֽיִם׃ וּמֹשֶׁ֣ה וְאַהֲרֹ֗ן עָשׂ֛וּ אֶת־כָּל־הַמֹּפְתִ֥ים הָאֵ֖לֶּה
לִפְנֵ֣י פַרְעֹ֑ה וַיְחַזֵּ֤ק יְהוָה֙ אֶת־לֵ֣ב פַּרְעֹ֔ה וְלֹֽא־שִׁלַּ֥ח אֶת־
בְּנֵֽי־יִשְׂרָאֵ֖ל מֵאַרְצֽוֹ׃ ס

12 CHAPTER XII

1. And the LORD spoke unto Moses and Aaron in the land of Egypt, saying: 2. 'This month shall be unto you the beginning of months; it shall be the first month of the

יב CAP. XII. יב

א וַיֹּ֤אמֶר יְהוָה֙ אֶל־מֹשֶׁ֣ה וְאֶֽל־אַהֲרֹ֔ן בְּאֶ֥רֶץ מִצְרַ֖יִם לֵאמֹֽר׃
2 הַחֹ֧דֶשׁ הַזֶּ֛ה לָכֶ֖ם רֹ֣אשׁ חֳדָשִׁ֑ים רִאשׁ֥וֹן הוּא֙ לָכֶ֔ם לְחָדְשֵׁ֖י

יא׳ v. 6. ב׳ סבירין כמוה בענין

6. *a great cry.* The freedom with which Orientals give vent to their emotions is well known.

7. *a dog whet his tongue.* A proverbial expression indicating safety and peace.

8. *shall come down.* The courtiers will be sent in haste to Moses to grant all that he had demanded.

in hot anger. Because of the words 'see my face no more' that the king had addressed to him (x, 28).

9. *the LORD said.* All that had hitherto happened to Pharaoh, as well as the effect of the miracles upon him, is here briefly restated. This summary marks the close of one principal division of the Book of Exodus.

CHAPTER XII

THE INSTITUTION OF THE PASSOVER

The deliverance from Egypt is to be not only from physical but also from spiritual slavery. Israel is to be freed from all heathen influences and consecrated to the service of God. These commandments concerning the Passover open the religious legislation of the Torah. The occasion when they were given, and the manner in which they were enjoined, emphasize the basic importance of that Festival in the life and history of Israel. 'The Exodus from Egypt is not only one of the greatest events and epochs in the history of the Jews, but one of the greatest events and epochs in the history of the world. To that successful escape, Europe, America, and Australia are as much indebted as the Jews themselves. And the men of Europe, the men of America, and the men of Australia might join with us Jews in celebrating that feast of the Passover' (C. G. Montefiore).

2. *this month.* The month of 'Abib', or Nisan, in which the deliverance was about to take place.

the beginning of months. 'The first month of your Freedom shall be made the first in reckoning the months, so that you reckon your time from the hour of Freedom. In this way will ye remember the hour of Freedom, and also My beneficent dealings with you and you will be heedful to fear, love, and serve Me' (Bechor Shor). The redemption from Egypt is to be both in deed and in word 'epoch-making'. The Exodus was to mark the beginning of a new era; and not only the years in the national history were to be counted from it (see XVI, 1; XIX, 1; Num. I, 1; I Kings VI, 1), but also the months of each year were to be counted from the first month of Israel's Freedom. Israel is now given a new Calendar, thus making the break with Egypt complete.

The ordinary Jewish year consists of twelve lunar months of a little more than 29½ days each, with every new moon (Rosh Chodesh) a minor

3 הַשָּׁנָה׃ דַּבְּרוּ אֶל־כָּל־עֲדַת יִשְׂרָאֵל לֵאמֹר בֶּעָשֹׂר לַחֹדֶשׁ
4 הַזֶּה וְיִקְחוּ לָהֶם אִישׁ שֶׂה לְבֵית־אָבֹת שֶׂה לַבָּיִת׃ וְאִם־
יִמְעַט הַבַּיִת מִהְיוֹת מִשֶּׂה וְלָקַח הוּא וּשְׁכֵנוֹ הַקָּרֹב אֶל־
בֵּיתוֹ בְּמִכְסַת נְפָשֹׁת אִישׁ לְפִי אָכְלוֹ תָּכֹסּוּ עַל־הַשֶּׂה׃
ה שֶׂה תָמִים זָכָר בֶּן־שָׁנָה יִהְיֶה לָכֶם מִן־הַכְּבָשִׂים וּמִן־
6 הָעִזִּים תִּקָּחוּ׃ וְהָיָה לָכֶם לְמִשְׁמֶרֶת עַד אַרְבָּעָה עָשָׂר
יוֹם לַחֹדֶשׁ הַזֶּה וְשָׁחֲטוּ אֹתוֹ כֹּל קְהַל עֲדַת־יִשְׂרָאֵל בֵּין

year to you. 3. Speak ye unto all the congregation of Israel, saying: In the tenth day of this month they shall take to them every man a lamb, according to their fathers' houses, a lamb for a household; 4. and if the household be too little for a lamb, then shall he and his neighbour next unto his house take one according to the number of the souls; according to every man's eating ye shall make your count for the lamb. 5. Your lamb shall be without blemish, a male of the first year; ye shall take it from the sheep, or from the goats; 6. and ye shall keep it until the fourteenth

festival. As, on the one hand, twelve lunar months total only a little more than $354\frac{1}{3}$ days, eleven days less than the solar year which consists, roughly, of $365\frac{1}{4}$ days; and, on the other hand, the Festivals had to be celebrated in their seasons according to the solar year—Passover in spring, Pentecost in summer, and Tabernacles in autumn—it was essential to harmonize the lunar and solar years. This was done by the 'intercalation', or introduction, of an extra month Adar, which made that year a leap year. There are seven such leap years, of thirteen months each, in every cycle of nineteen years. But years, whether ordinary years or leap years, have not a uniform duration in the Jewish reckoning. According as the months of Kislev and Cheshvan have 29 or 30 days, ordinary years vary between 353, 354, and 355 days, and leap years between 383, 384, and 385 days. By these means the mathematical exactness of the Jewish Calendar was secured. A renowned non-Jewish scholar declared, 'There is nothing more perfect than the calculation of the Jewish year' (Scaliger).

unto you. Heb. לכם. The Rabbis emphasize this word, and deduce from it that the exact fixation of the Festivals is in the hands of Israel and his ancient religious guides. In Biblical and early Talmudic times, the Sanhedrin fixed the new moons by actual observation, and the dates were announced by messengers from Jerusalem to surrounding countries. Later, the dates were determined by astronomical calculation. Religious considerations decided which year was to be a leap year, and when the months of Kislev and Chesvan were to be 'long' (having 30 days) or 'short' (29 days). Furthermore, Rosh Hashanah could never be a Sunday, Wednesday, or Friday (לא אדו ראש השנה), which rule secured, among other things, that the Day of Atonement did not either immediately precede or immediately follow the Sabbath.

3. *all the congregation.* Hitherto Moses and Aaron had been God's ambassadors to Pharaoh; they now become God's ambassadors to Israel. The 'congregation of Israel', *adath Yisrael*, is the term for the community as a religious entity.

tenth day of this month. Only on this occasion was the paschal lamb to be chosen on the tenth of the month.

according to their fathers' houses. A 'father's house' is here synonymous with *mishpachah*, a family. The Passover is to be the specific *family* festival of Israel. And it is noteworthy that the first ordinance of the Jewish religion was a domestic service. A nation is strong in so far as it cherishes the domestic sanctities.

4. *too little for a lamb. i.e.* too few to consume it at a sitting. 'If, however, the men of the house are less than ten' (Jerusalem Targum). Had a family of two or three been compelled to take a lamb, a considerable quantity would have been wasted; see *v.* 10.

souls. Persons.

according to every man's eating. Small children and the very aged who cannot eat even the small obligatory quantity (כזית) were not to be reckoned among the number.

5. *without blemish.* Faultless, like all animals for sacrifice; Lev. XXII, 19, 21.

male. As in the case of a burnt-offering; Lev. I, 3, 10.

of the first year. lit. 'the son of a year'. The Rabbis take this to mean, within the first year of its birth; Lev. IX, 3. 'This tender age, the type of innocence, made it peculiarly adapted for a sacrifice of the Covenant to be concluded between God and Israel as a nation' (Kalisch).

6. *at dusk.* Better, *towards even* (M. Friedlander); lit. 'between the two evenings'. According to the Talmud the 'first evening' is the time in the afternoon when the heat of the sun begins to decrease, about 3 o'clock; and the 'second evening' commences with sunset. Josephus relates that the Passover sacrifice 'was offered from the ninth to the eleventh hour', *i.e.* between 3 and 5 p.m.

day of the same month; and the whole assembly of the congregation of Israel shall kill it at dusk. 7. And they shall take of the blood, and put it on the two side-posts and on the lintel, upon the houses wherein they shall eat it. 8. And they shall eat the flesh in that night, roast with fire, and unleavened bread; with bitter herbs they shall eat it. 9. Eat not of it raw, nor sodden at all with water, but roast with fire; its head with its legs and with the inwards thereof. 10. And ye shall let nothing of it remain until the morning; but that which remaineth of it until the morning ye shall burn with fire. 11. And thus shall ye eat it: with your loins girded, your shoes on your feet, and your staff in your hand; and ye shall eat it in haste—it is the LORD's passover. 12. For I will go through the land of Egypt in that night, and will smite all the first-born in the land of Egypt, both man and beast; and against all the gods of Egypt I will execute judgments: I am the LORD. 13. And the blood shall be to you for

7 הָעַרְבָּיִם׃ וְלָקְחוּ מִן־הַדָּם וְנָתְנוּ עַל־שְׁתֵּי הַמְּזוּזֹת וְעַל־
8 הַמַּשְׁקוֹף עַל הַבָּתִּים אֲשֶׁר־יֹאכְלוּ אֹתוֹ בָּהֶם׃ וְאָכְלוּ
אֶת־הַבָּשָׂר בַּלַּיְלָה הַזֶּה צְלִי־אֵשׁ וּמַצּוֹת עַל־מְרֹרִים
9 יֹאכְלֻהוּ׃ אַל־תֹּאכְלוּ מִמֶּנּוּ נָא וּבָשֵׁל מְבֻשָּׁל בַּמָּיִם כִּי
י אִם־צְלִי־אֵשׁ רֹאשׁוֹ עַל־כְּרָעָיו וְעַל־קִרְבּוֹ׃ וְלֹא־תוֹתִירוּ
11 מִמֶּנּוּ עַד־בֹּקֶר וְהַנֹּתָר מִמֶּנּוּ עַד־בֹּקֶר בָּאֵשׁ תִּשְׂרֹפוּ׃ וְכָכָה
תֹּאכְלוּ אֹתוֹ מָתְנֵיכֶם חֲגֻרִים נַעֲלֵיכֶם בְּרַגְלֵיכֶם וּמַקֶּלְכֶם
12 בְּיֶדְכֶם וַאֲכַלְתֶּם אֹתוֹ בְּחִפָּזוֹן פֶּסַח הוּא לַיהוָה׃ וְעָבַרְתִּי
בְאֶרֶץ־מִצְרַיִם בַּלַּיְלָה הַזֶּה וְהִכֵּיתִי כָל־בְּכוֹר בְּאֶרֶץ
מִצְרַיִם מֵאָדָם וְעַד־בְּהֵמָה וּבְכָל־אֱלֹהֵי מִצְרַיִם אֶעֱשֶׂה
13 שְׁפָטִים אֲנִי יְהוָה׃ וְהָיָה הַדָּם לָכֶם לְאֹת עַל הַבָּתִּים

v. 7. ב׳ טעמים v. 11. מלעיל

7. *lintel.* The beam across the top of the doorway; or, possibly the latticed window which was commonly placed over a doorway in an Egyptian house (Rawlinson).

8. *the flesh.* Of the paschal lamb.

in that night. Following the fourteenth day of Nisan.

roast with fire. Because of the haste when they would leave Egypt.

unleavened bread. 'Because they could prepare it hastily' (Maimonides); symbolic of the haste with which the Israelites left Egypt when there was no time for their dough to leaven. In Deut. XVI, 3, the 'unleavened bread' (Heb. *matzoth,* plural of *matzah*) is called the 'bread of affliction'.

bitter herbs. Heb. *merorim,* plural of *maror.* To symbolize the bitterness of the Egyptian bondage; I, 14.

9. *eat not of it raw.* As was the custom of many heathen peoples at their sacrifices.

nor sodden at all with water. The lamb was not to be boiled, because this would make the dismemberment of the animal indispensable. It is not to be divided, but to be roasted whole. This rite was probably intended to represent the perfect unity of Israel as a nation. One meal, at one table, eaten whole and eaten entirely (nothing left till the morning).

10. *remaineth of it.* Was not to be used for an ordinary meal, and was not to be thrown away disrespectfully; it was to be burned instead.

11. *loins girded.* The long and loose robes worn by the people of the East were fastened up round the waist with a girdle when proceeding on a journey. These and the following instructions apply only to the Passover in Egypt, not to any succeeding Passover celebration.

shoes on your feet. Ready for travel. The shoe or sandal was not generally worn in the house.

staff in your hand. Essential for the traveller in the desert.

eat it in haste. As they might have to commence their journey at any moment.

the LORD's passover. Better, *a passover unto the LORD* (M. Friedlander); *i.e.* a paschal sacrifice in honour of the LORD (Mendelssohn). The word *pesach,* 'passover,' here means the paschal lamb; and is derived from the verb *pasach,* 'to pass over,' to protect and deliver; see *v.* 13.

12. *go through the land of Egypt.* Cf. XI, 4. 'The power of God will fearfully manifest itself in the land; His majesty will create terror; His justice will produce awe and veneration—and *thus* He will pass through the land' (Kalisch).

against all the gods of Egypt. In smiting the firstborn of all living beings, man and beast, God smote objects of Egyptian worship. Not a single deity of Egypt was unrepresented by some beast.

I am the LORD. Further evidence that this phrase in VI, 2 means an assertion of power, and not the revelation of a new Name.

13. *to you.* For you, in your interest.

a token. A pledge of mercy. The sight of the blood will strengthen your hearts, when ye hear the cry of the Egyptians as their firstborn die by the hand of the angel of destruction (Ibn Ezra and Reggio).

when I see the blood. 'Everything is revealed before Him, but the Holy One, blessed be He,

אֲשֶׁר אַתֶּם שָׁם וְרָאִיתִי אֶת־הַדָּם וּפָסַחְתִּי עֲלֵכֶם וְלֹא־
14 יִהְיֶה בָכֶם נֶגֶף לְמַשְׁחִית בְּהַכֹּתִי בְּאֶרֶץ מִצְרָיִם׃ וְהָיָה
הַיּוֹם הַזֶּה לָכֶם לְזִכָּרוֹן וְחַגֹּתֶם אֹתוֹ חַג לַיהוָה לְדֹרֹתֵיכֶם
טו חֻקַּת עוֹלָם תְּחָגֻּהוּ׃ שִׁבְעַת יָמִים מַצּוֹת תֹּאכֵלוּ אַךְ בַּיּוֹם
הָרִאשׁוֹן תַּשְׁבִּיתוּ שְׂאֹר מִבָּתֵּיכֶם כִּי ׀ כָּל־אֹכֵל חָמֵץ
וְנִכְרְתָה הַנֶּפֶשׁ הַהִוא מִיִּשְׂרָאֵל מִיּוֹם הָרִאשֹׁן עַד־יוֹם
16 הַשְּׁבִעִי׃ וּבַיּוֹם הָרִאשׁוֹן מִקְרָא־קֹדֶשׁ וּבַיּוֹם הַשְּׁבִיעִי
מִקְרָא־קֹדֶשׁ יִהְיֶה לָכֶם כָּל־מְלָאכָה לֹא־יֵעָשֶׂה בָהֶם
אַךְ אֲשֶׁר יֵאָכֵל לְכָל־נֶפֶשׁ הוּא לְבַדּוֹ יֵעָשֶׂה לָכֶם׃
17 וּשְׁמַרְתֶּם אֶת־הַמַּצּוֹת כִּי בְּעֶצֶם הַיּוֹם הַזֶּה הוֹצֵאתִי אֶת־
צִבְאוֹתֵיכֶם מֵאֶרֶץ מִצְרָיִם וּשְׁמַרְתֶּם אֶת־הַיּוֹם הַזֶּה
18 לְדֹרֹתֵיכֶם חֻקַּת עוֹלָם׃ בָּרִאשֹׁן בְּאַרְבָּעָה עָשָׂר יוֹם לַחֹדֶשׁ
בָּעֶרֶב תֹּאכְלוּ מַצֹּת עַד יוֹם הָאֶחָד וְעֶשְׂרִים לַחֹדֶשׁ
19 בָּעָרֶב׃ שִׁבְעַת יָמִים שְׂאֹר לֹא יִמָּצֵא בְּבָתֵּיכֶם כִּי ׀ כָּל־
אֹכֵל מַחְמֶצֶת וְנִכְרְתָה הַנֶּפֶשׁ הַהִוא מֵעֲדַת יִשְׂרָאֵל בַּגֵּר

a token upon the houses where ye are; and when I see the blood, I will pass over you, and there shall no plague be upon you to destroy you, when I smite the land of Egypt. 14. And this day shall be unto you for a memorial, and ye shall keep it a feast to the LORD; throughout your generations ye shall keep it a feast by an ordinance for ever. 15. Seven days shall ye eat unleavened bread; howbeit the first day ye shall put away leaven out of your houses; for whosoever eateth leavened bread from the first day until the seventh day, that soul shall be cut off from Israel. 16. And in the first day there shall be to you a holy convocation, and in the seventh day a holy convocation; no manner of work shall be done in them, save that which every man must eat, that only may be done by you. 17. And ye shall observe the feast of unleavened bread; for in this selfsame day have I brought your hosts out of the land of Egypt; therefore shall ye observe this day throughout your generations by an ordinance for ever. 18. In the first month, on the fourteenth day of the month at even, ye shall eat unleavened bread, until the one and twentieth day of the month at even. 19. Seven days shall there be no leaven found in your houses; for whosoever eateth that which is leavened, that soul shall be cut off from the congregation of Israel,

said: I will direct My eye to see whether you are occupied in obeying My precepts, and then I will spare you' (Rashi).

I will pass over you. Or, 'I will spare you' (Targum); 'I will protect you' (Septuagint). The Heb. verb. פסח combines the idea of passing over and sparing.

no plague be upon you. The angel of destruction will not have permission to bring the plague upon you (Reggio).

14–20. REGULATIONS FOR THE PASSOVER FESTIVAL

14. *for a memorial.* In the future. The regulations so far concerned the Passover in Egypt (*v.* 1–13); now (*v.* 14–20) the precepts for its future celebration are given.

ye shall keep it. *i.e.* the anniversary of the paschal sacrifice as an annual festival of seven days marked by eating unleavened bread.

for ever. Israel still keeps it.

15. *howbeit the first day . . . leaven out of your houses.* Better, *Of a surety on the first day ye shall have removed the leaven from your houses* (Mendelssohn). The leaven is therefore removed and symbolically destroyed by fire (ביעור חמץ) on the forenoon of the day before Passover. The Rabbis have also instituted a search for leaven (בדיקת חמץ) on the preceding evening. Leaven is the symbol of corruption, passion and sin.

soul. Person.

cut off from Israel. See Gen. XVII, 14. Not put to death, but cast out from the congregation of Israel, becoming like one of the heathens.

16. *holy convocation.* A holy festival. The term is no doubt derived from the fact that originally the worshippers were called together for the celebration of a festival.

which every man must eat. The preparation of food for man or beast is permitted on the Festival when it occurs on a week day. This constitutes the main difference between Sabbath and Festival.

17. *have I brought.* Better, *I shall have brought out* (Mendelssohn).

18. *at even.* The Jewish day begins with the preceding evening, and terminates at evening.

19. *that which is leavened.* Heb. *machmetzeth; i.e.* anything which leavens; not merely *chametz*, leavened food.

sojourner. Heb. *ger.* The resident alien. 'He was not directed or compelled to assume a religious duty of Israel, but he was prevented from interfering with the religious practices of

כ וּבְאֶזְרַח הָאָרֶץ׃ כָּל־מַחְמֶצֶת לֹא תֹאכֵלוּ בְּכֹל מוֹשְׁבֹתֵיכֶם
תֹּאכְלוּ מַצּוֹת׃ פ חמישי
21 וַיִּקְרָא מֹשֶׁה לְכָל־זִקְנֵי יִשְׂרָאֵל וַיֹּאמֶר אֲלֵהֶם מִשְׁכוּ וּקְחוּ
22 לָכֶם צֹאן לְמִשְׁפְּחֹתֵיכֶם וְשַׁחֲטוּ הַפָּסַח׃ וּלְקַחְתֶּם אֲגֻדַּת
אֵזוֹב וּטְבַלְתֶּם בַּדָּם אֲשֶׁר־בַּסַּף וְהִגַּעְתֶּם אֶל־הַמַּשְׁקוֹף
וְאֶל־שְׁתֵּי הַמְּזוּזֹת מִן־הַדָּם אֲשֶׁר בַּסָּף וְאַתֶּם לֹא תֵצְאוּ
23 אִישׁ מִפֶּתַח־בֵּיתוֹ עַד־בֹּקֶר׃ וְעָבַר יְהוָה לִנְגֹּף אֶת־מִצְרַיִם
וְרָאָה אֶת־הַדָּם עַל־הַמַּשְׁקוֹף וְעַל שְׁתֵּי הַמְּזוּזֹת וּפָסַח
יְהוָה עַל־הַפֶּתַח וְלֹא יִתֵּן הַמַּשְׁחִית לָבֹא אֶל־בָּתֵּיכֶם לִנְגֹּף׃
24 וּשְׁמַרְתֶּם אֶת־הַדָּבָר הַזֶּה לְחָק־לְךָ וּלְבָנֶיךָ עַד־עוֹלָם׃
כה וְהָיָה כִּי־תָבֹאוּ אֶל־הָאָרֶץ אֲשֶׁר יִתֵּן יְהוָה לָכֶם כַּאֲשֶׁר
26 דִּבֵּר וּשְׁמַרְתֶּם אֶת־הָעֲבֹדָה הַזֹּאת׃ וְהָיָה כִּי־יֹאמְרוּ

v. 22. קמץ בסגולתא

whether he be a sojourner, or one that is born in the land. 20. Ye shall eat nothing leavened; in all your habitations shall ye eat unleavened bread.'*v. ¶ 21. Then Moses called for all the elders of Israel, and said unto them: 'Draw out, and take you lambs according to your families, and kill the passover lamb. 22. And ye shall take a bunch of hyssop, and dip it in the blood that is in the basin, and strike the lintel and the two side-posts with the blood that is in the basin; and none of you shall go out of the door of his house until the morning. 23. For the LORD will pass through to smite the Egyptians; and when He seeth the blood upon the lintel, and on the two side-posts, the LORD will pass over the door, and will not suffer the destroyer to come in unto your houses to smite you. 24. And ye shall observe this thing for an ordinance to thee and to thy sons for ever. 25. And it shall come to pass, when ye be come to the land which the LORD will give you, according as He hath promised, that ye shall keep this service. 26. And it shall come to pass,

Israel' (Sulzberger). In later Hebrew law, the resident alien is either a *ger tzedek*, a righteous proselyte, who has been received into the covenant of Abraham, and thereby enjoys the same privileges and obligations as the born Israelite; or *ger toshab* or *sha'ar*, 'the stranger of the gate,' the alien squatter who remains outside the religious life of Israel, but who has undertaken to adhere to the seven Noachic laws that are binding upon all men who desire to live in human society; see p. 33.

20. *in all your habitations.* Even out of Palestine, where there was no paschal lamb offered up, the observance of the Passover festival is obligatory.

21–28. Moses communicates the laws of Passover to the elders.

21. *draw out.* The elders should tell the people to draw the lamb out of the fold.

take you. If you have none, buy your lamb (Rashi).

according to your families. i.e. a lamb for a household; see *v.* 3 and 4.

22. *hyssop.* Heb. *ezob.* A few bunches of this plant could be used as a sponge to take up a liquid. It became a symbol for spiritual purification from sin (Ps. LI, 7).

strike. lit. 'make it touch'.

none of you shall go out. But ye shall all be ready to answer the call to Freedom.

23. *smite the Egyptians.* Their firstborn.

will pass over the door. Sparing those within; see *v.* 13.

the destroyer. The destroying angel; as in II Sam. XXIV, 16.

24. *observe this thing.* Cf. *v.* 17. The reference here is to the Passover celebration, and not to the sprinkling of the blood, which was restricted to the Passover in Egypt at the time of the Exodus.

25. *come to the land. i.e.* of Canaan. The sacrifice of the paschal lamb was to be a regular institution in the land of Canaan, after its conquest by Israel.

as He hath promised. To Abraham; Gen. XII, 1, 7.

keep this service. In connection with the paschal lamb.

26. *your children shall say.* The children of successive generations are to be instructed at Passover as to the origin and significance of the Festival. In the Seder service on the first two nights of Passover, this command has found its solemn realization. In it we have history raised to religion. The youngest child present asks the Questions, which are answered by a recitation of the events that culminated in the original institution of Passover. Education in the home is thus as old as the Hebrew people; see Gen. XVIII, 19.

what mean ye by this service? By the religious rites and ceremonies in connection with the Passover, intended to keep the memory of the wonderful deliverance alive in the hearts of the Israelites. Since the destruction of the Temple, the Questions of the child are concerned with the distinctive features of the Sedar meal.

when your children shall say unto you: What mean ye by this service? 27. that ye shall say: It is the sacrifice of the LORD's passover, for that He passed over the houses of the children of Israel in Egypt, when He smote the Egyptians, and delivered our houses.' And the people bowed the head and worshipped. 28. And the children of Israel went and did so; as the LORD had commanded Moses and Aaron, so did they.* vi. ¶ 29. And it came to pass at midnight, that the LORD smote all the first-born in the land of Egypt, from the first-born of Pharaoh that sat on his throne unto the first-born of the captive that was in the dungeon; and all the first-born of cattle. 30. And Pharaoh rose up in the night, he, and all his servants, and all the Egyptians; and there was a great cry in Egypt; for there was not a house where there was not one dead. 31. And he called for Moses and Aaron by night, and said: 'Rise up, get you forth from among my people, both ye and the children of Israel; and go, serve the LORD, as ye have said. 32. Take both your flocks and your herds, as ye have said, and be gone; and bless me also.' 33. And the Egyptians were urgent upon the people, to send them out of the land in haste; for they said: 'We are all dead men.' 34. And the people took their dough before it was leavened, their kneading-troughs being bound up in their clothes upon their shoulders. 35. And the children of Israel did according to the word of Moses; and they asked of the Egyptians jewels of silver, and jewels of gold, and raiment. 36. And the LORD gave the people favour in the sight of the Egyptians, so that they let them have what they asked.

27 אֲלֵיכֶם בְּנֵיכֶם מָה הָעֲבֹדָה הַזֹּאת לָכֶם׃ וַאֲמַרְתֶּם זֶבַח־
פֶּסַח הוּא לַיהוָה אֲשֶׁר פָּסַח עַל־בָּתֵּי בְנֵי־יִשְׂרָאֵל בְּמִצְרַיִם
בְּנָגְפּוֹ אֶת־מִצְרַיִם וְאֶת־בָּתֵּינוּ הִצִּיל וַיִּקֹּד הָעָם וַיִּשְׁתַּחֲווּ׃
28 וַיֵּלְכוּ וַיַּעֲשׂוּ בְּנֵי יִשְׂרָאֵל כַּאֲשֶׁר צִוָּה יְהוָה אֶת־מֹשֶׁה
ששי
29 וְאַהֲרֹן כֵּן עָשׂוּ׃ ס וַיְהִי ׀ בַּחֲצִי הַלַּיְלָה וַיהוָה הִכָּה כָל־בְּכוֹר
בְּאֶרֶץ מִצְרַיִם מִבְּכֹר פַּרְעֹה הַיֹּשֵׁב עַל־כִּסְאוֹ עַד בְּכוֹר
ל הַשְּׁבִי אֲשֶׁר בְּבֵית הַבּוֹר וְכֹל בְּכוֹר בְּהֵמָה׃ וַיָּקָם פַּרְעֹה
לַיְלָה הוּא וְכָל־עֲבָדָיו וְכָל־מִצְרַיִם וַתְּהִי צְעָקָה גְדֹלָה
31 בְּמִצְרָיִם כִּי־אֵין בַּיִת אֲשֶׁר אֵין־שָׁם מֵת׃ וַיִּקְרָא לְמֹשֶׁה
וּלְאַהֲרֹן לַיְלָה וַיֹּאמֶר קוּמוּ צְּאוּ מִתּוֹךְ עַמִּי גַּם־אַתֶּם גַּם־
32 בְּנֵי יִשְׂרָאֵל וּלְכוּ עִבְדוּ אֶת־יְהוָה כְּדַבֶּרְכֶם׃ גַּם־צֹאנְכֶם
גַּם־בְּקַרְכֶם קְחוּ כַּאֲשֶׁר דִּבַּרְתֶּם וָלֵכוּ וּבֵרַכְתֶּם גַּם־אֹתִי׃
33 וַתֶּחֱזַק מִצְרַיִם עַל־הָעָם לְמַהֵר לְשַׁלְּחָם מִן־הָאָרֶץ כִּי
34 אָמְרוּ כֻּלָּנוּ מֵתִים׃ וַיִּשָּׂא הָעָם אֶת־בְּצֵקוֹ טֶרֶם יֶחְמָץ
לה מִשְׁאֲרֹתָם צְרֻרֹת בְּשִׂמְלֹתָם עַל־שִׁכְמָם׃ וּבְנֵי־יִשְׂרָאֵל
עָשׂוּ כִּדְבַר מֹשֶׁה וַיִּשְׁאֲלוּ מִמִּצְרַיִם כְּלֵי־כֶסֶף וּכְלֵי זָהָב
36 וּשְׂמָלֹת׃ וַיהוָה נָתַן אֶת־חֵן הָעָם בְּעֵינֵי מִצְרַיִם וַיַּשְׁאִלוּם
וַיְנַצְּלוּ אֶת־מִצְרָיִם׃ פ

v. 27. הפ׳ דגושה v. 31. צ׳ דגושה

27. *delivered our houses.* The children of future generations are to consider that their freedom is associated with that of their ancestors in Egypt.

the people bowed . . . worshipped. When they heard the promise of Redemption and of the future inheritance of Canaan (Rashi).

28. *went and did so.* They prepared for the Passover celebration.

29–36. THE LAST PLAGUE, AND ISRAEL'S DEPARTURE

29. *the captive that was in the dungeon.* In XI, 5, 'the maidservant that is behind the mill.'

30. *a great cry.* A frantic wail of agony, the wild cry of Eastern bereavement, through the whole land.

not a house. Of the Egyptians.

31. *and he called.* *i.e* Pharaoh; cf. x, 28.

from among my people. Even in Goshen the Israelites were in Pharaoh's land and among his people. Many Israelites, however, were doing slave-labour in various parts of Egypt.

32. *and bless me also.* Pray on my behalf that no further plague come upon me.

33. *were urgent upon the people.* Fearing that new plagues might follow, unless the Israelites were sent away without further delay.

34. *kneading-troughs.* These would soon be a necessity in the wilderness.

clothes. Or, 'mantles.'

35. *asked of the Egyptians.* See III, 22. The command had been given to the people some time before their departure.

36. *and they despoiled the Egyptians.* Render, 'and they *saved* the Egyptians,' from hatred and revengeful feelings. See, and read carefully, note on III, 22.

And they despoiled the Egyptians. ¶ 37. And the children of Israel journeyed from Rameses to Succoth, about six hundred thousand men on foot, beside children. 38. And a mixed multitude went up also with them; and flocks, and herds, even very much cattle. 39. And they baked unleavened cakes of the dough which they brought forth out of Egypt, for it was not leavened; because they were thrust out of Egypt, and could not tarry, neither had they prepared for themselves any victual. 40. Now the time that the children of Israel dwelt in Egypt was four hundred and thirty years. 41. And it came to pass at the end of four hundred and thirty years, even the selfsame day it came to pass, that all the hosts of the LORD went out from the land of Egypt. 42. It was a night of watching unto the LORD for bringing them out from the land of Egypt; this same night is a night of watching unto the LORD for all the children of Israel throughout their generations. ¶ 43. And the LORD said unto Moses and Aaron: 'This is the ordinance of the pass-

37 וַיִּסְעוּ בְנֵי־יִשְׂרָאֵל מֵרַעְמְסֵס סֻכֹּתָה כְּשֵׁשׁ־מֵאוֹת אֶלֶף
38 רַגְלִי הַגְּבָרִים לְבַד מִטָּף׃ וְגַם־עֵרֶב רַב עָלָה אִתָּם וְצֹאן
39 וּבָקָר מִקְנֶה כָּבֵד מְאֹד׃ וַיֹּאפוּ אֶת־הַבָּצֵק אֲשֶׁר הוֹצִיאוּ
מִמִּצְרַיִם עֻגֹת מַצּוֹת כִּי לֹא חָמֵץ כִּי־גֹרְשׁוּ מִמִּצְרַיִם וְלֹא
מ יָכְלוּ לְהִתְמַהְמֵהַּ וְגַם־צֵדָה לֹא־עָשׂוּ לָהֶם׃ וּמוֹשַׁב בְּנֵי
יִשְׂרָאֵל אֲשֶׁר יָשְׁבוּ בְּמִצְרָיִם שְׁלֹשִׁים שָׁנָה וְאַרְבַּע מֵאוֹת
41 שָׁנָה׃ וַיְהִי מִקֵּץ שְׁלֹשִׁים שָׁנָה וְאַרְבַּע מֵאוֹת שָׁנָה וַיְהִי
בְּעֶצֶם הַיּוֹם הַזֶּה יָצְאוּ כָּל־צִבְאוֹת יְהוָה מֵאֶרֶץ מִצְרָיִם׃
42 לֵיל שִׁמֻּרִים הוּא לַיהוָה לְהוֹצִיאָם מֵאֶרֶץ מִצְרָיִם הוּא־
הַלַּיְלָה הַזֶּה לַיהוָה שִׁמֻּרִים לְכָל־בְּנֵי יִשְׂרָאֵל לְדֹרֹתָם׃ פ
43 וַיֹּאמֶר יְהוָה אֶל־מֹשֶׁה וְאַהֲרֹן זֹאת חֻקַּת הַפָּסַח כָּל־בֶּן

v. 39. הנ׳ רפה

37–51. OUT OF EGYPT

37. *Rameses.* See I, 11.

Succoth. The place has been identified with Thuku, either another name for Pithom or in its immediate neighbourhood.

six hundred thousand. A round number, representing the 603,550 of Num. I, 46. There are no doubt difficulties in conceiving the departure at one time and in one place of such a large body of men; but the event has its parallels in history. At the close of the 18th century, 400,000 Tartars started in a single night from the confines of Russia towards the Chinese borders.

men on foot. All the males who could march.

38. *a mixed multitude.* The mass of non-Israelite strangers, including slaves and prisoners of war, who took advantage of the panic to escape from Egypt. They were not a desirable class of associates, as appears from Num. XI, 4, 5.

flocks, and herds. The Israelites were not all slave-labourers, but also nomad tribes possessing cattle.

39. *any victual.* Other than the dough.

40. *four hundred and thirty years.* In Gen. XV, 13, the period of affliction is foretold, and was to be four hundred years, beginning—according to Rabbinic tradition—with the birth of Isaac. The thirty years not accounted for, are supposed to refer to the years that elapsed between the vision when the affliction was foretold and the birth of Isaac (Luzzatto). Others refer these thirty years to the exploit of the Ephraimites who, according to the Book of Chronicles, made a raid out of Egypt a generation before the Exodus. Of these four hundred and thirty years, the Rabbis state, the Israelites were in Egypt for a period of 210 years. This accords with the narrative of Exodus, and with the genealogies given in chap. VI.

41. *the selfsame day.* The fifteenth of Nisan.

42. *of watching. i.e.* of keeping in mind. Heb. *shimmurim;* 'of celebration,' and, 'of vigilance'—are alternative translations. 'Because God shielded them, and did not suffer destruction to approach their houses, He ordered that the night be observed by all Israelites as a night of watching, a memorial of the night of redemption' (Ibn Ezra). It was the birthnight of the Israelite nation, and the whole history of Israel is stamped with its memory.

43–51. FURTHER REGULATIONS REGARDING THE PASSOVER

43. *ordinance of the passover.* Introduced here in consequence of what is said concerning the mixed multitude in *v.* 38 (Abarbanel).

no alien eat thereof. The non-Israelite, who has not chosen to enter the Covenant of Abraham, as well as the man whose deeds have alienated him from his Father in Heaven (Rashi), was not to partake of the paschal meal. It is to be a distinctly Israelitish observance.

over: there shall no alien eat thereof; **44.** but every man's servant that is bought for money, when thou hast circumcised him, then shall he eat thereof. 45. A sojourner and a hired servant shall not eat thereof. 46. In one house shall it be eaten; thou shalt not carry forth aught of the flesh abroad out of the house; neither shall ye break a bone thereof. 47. All the congregation of Israel shall keep it. 48. And when a stranger shall sojourn with thee, and will keep the passover to the LORD, let all his males be circumcised, and then let him come near and keep it; and he shall be as one that is born in the land; but no uncircumcised person shall eat thereof. **49.** One law shall be to him that is homeborn, and unto the stranger that sojourneth among you.' 50. Thus did all the children of Israel; as the LORD commanded Moses and Aaron, so did they.* vii. ¶ 51. And it came to pass the selfsame day that the LORD did bring the children of Israel out of the land of Egypt by their hosts.

44 נֵכָר לֹא־יֹאכַל בּוֹ׃ וְכָל־עֶבֶד אִישׁ מִקְנַת־כָּסֶף וּמַלְתָּה
מה 46 אֹתוֹ אָז יֹאכַל בּוֹ׃ תּוֹשָׁב וְשָׂכִיר לֹא־יֹאכַל בּוֹ׃ בְּבַיִת אֶחָד
יֵאָכֵל לֹא־תוֹצִיא מִן־הַבַּיִת מִן־הַבָּשָׂר חוּצָה וְעֶצֶם לֹא־
47 48 תִשְׁבְּרוּ־בוֹ׃ כָּל־עֲדַת יִשְׂרָאֵל יַעֲשׂוּ אֹתוֹ׃ וְכִי־יָגוּר אִתְּךָ
גֵּר וְעָשָׂה פֶסַח לַיהוָה הִמּוֹל לוֹ כָל־זָכָר וְאָז יִקְרַב
49 לַעֲשֹׂתוֹ וְהָיָה כְּאֶזְרַח הָאָרֶץ וְכָל־עָרֵל לֹא־יֹאכַל בּוֹ׃ תּוֹרָה
נ אַחַת יִהְיֶה לָאֶזְרָח וְלַגֵּר הַגָּר בְּתוֹכְכֶם׃ וַיַּעֲשׂוּ כָּל־בְּנֵי
יִשְׂרָאֵל כַּאֲשֶׁר צִוָּה יְהוָה אֶת־מֹשֶׁה וְאֶת־אַהֲרֹן כֵּן עָשׂוּ׃
51 ס וַיְהִי בְּעֶצֶם הַיּוֹם הַזֶּה הוֹצִיא יְהוָה אֶת־בְּנֵי יִשְׂרָאֵל
מֵאֶרֶץ מִצְרַיִם עַל־צִבְאֹתָם׃ פ שביעי

13 CHAPTER XIII

CAP. XIII. יג

1. And the LORD spoke unto Moses, saying: **2.** 'Sanctify unto Me all the first-born, whatsoever openeth the womb among the children of Israel, both of man and of beast, it

א 2 וַיְדַבֵּר יְהוָה אֶל־מֹשֶׁה לֵּאמֹר׃ קַדֶּשׁ־לִי כָל־בְּכוֹר פֶּטֶר
3 כָּל־רֶחֶם בִּבְנֵי יִשְׂרָאֵל בָּאָדָם וּבַבְּהֵמָה לִי הוּא׃ וַיֹּאמֶר

44. *servant.* However, a foreigner who as a bought servant permanently enters the family circle of an Israelite, may become a full member of Israel, and, therefore, partake of the Passover.
hast circumcised him. 'With his consent' (Ibn Ezra). He cannot be forced to embrace the faith of Israel. Circumcision and Passover belong together; the former is the sign of Israel's election, and of God's covenant with His people; the latter is a sign of the fulfilment of the covenant on God's part (Talmud).

45. *a sojourner. i.e.* an alien who is his own master; as distinguished from 'an hired servant' who, as a rule, is also merely a temporary resident in Israel. The bought slave, however, who has consented to circumcision shares the religious privileges of the born Israelite.

46. *in one house. i.e.* in one company (Rashi).

49. *the stranger that sojourneth among you.* See *v.* 19. According to Ibn Ezra, the stranger referred to here is the *ger tzedek*, the 'righteous proselyte'. The principle of this injunction—*one law shall be to him that is homeborn, and unto the stranger that sojourneth among you*—has an application in Jewry beyond the sphere of ritual practice. (See especially Lev. XXIV, 22.) It is dominant not only in Jewish moral conduct, but also in the civil legislation of Israel; and, in consequence, Jewish law recognizes no distinction in civil rights between native and alien. Only recently this verse was recommended for selection as the motto of the Congress for the Protection of Minority Populations in European Countries.

50. *thus did all the children of Israel.* A repetition of *v.* 28, because new precepts regarding the Passover have been introduced.

51. *the selfsame day.* The fifteenth of Nisan, after the night of the Passover.

CHAPTER XIII. CONSECRATION OF THE FIRST-BORN

2. *sanctify unto Me.* Dedicate, devote unto Me; see Num. III, 13 and XVIII, 17, 18.
all the first-born. Just as the annual celebration of the Passover served to remind the Israelites of the great Redemption, so the sanctification of every male first-born would keep the memory fresh in every home blessed with a first-born son. The rite is still remembered in Israel in the ceremony of 'Redeeming the son' (*pidyon habben*) which is solemnized on the thirty-first day of the child's birth; see Authorised Prayer Book, p. 308. First-born Israelites keep the fourteenth day of Nisan as a fast, in commemoration of the miracle wrought for their ancestors.

3–9. Repeated exhortation concerning the Passover Festival.

מֹשֶׁה אֶל־הָעָם זָכוֹר אֶת־הַיּוֹם הַזֶּה אֲשֶׁר יְצָאתֶם מִמִּצְרַיִם
מִבֵּית עֲבָדִים כִּי בְּחֹזֶק יָד הוֹצִיא יְהוָה אֶתְכֶם מִזֶּה וְלֹא
4 ה יֵאָכֵל חָמֵץ׃ הַיּוֹם אַתֶּם יֹצְאִים בְּחֹדֶשׁ הָאָבִיב׃ וְהָיָה
כִי־יְבִיאֲךָ יְהוָה אֶל־אֶרֶץ הַכְּנַעֲנִי וְהַחִתִּי וְהָאֱמֹרִי וְהַחִוִּי
וְהַיְבוּסִי אֲשֶׁר נִשְׁבַּע לַאֲבֹתֶיךָ לָתֶת לָךְ אֶרֶץ זָבַת חָלָב
6 וּדְבָשׁ וְעָבַדְתָּ אֶת־הָעֲבֹדָה הַזֹּאת בַּחֹדֶשׁ הַזֶּה׃ שִׁבְעַת
7 יָמִים תֹּאכַל מַצֹּת וּבַיּוֹם הַשְּׁבִיעִי חַג לַיהוָה׃ מַצּוֹת
יֵאָכֵל אֵת שִׁבְעַת הַיָּמִים וְלֹא־יֵרָאֶה לְךָ חָמֵץ וְלֹא־יֵרָאֶה
8 לְךָ שְׂאֹר בְּכָל־גְּבֻלֶךָ׃ וְהִגַּדְתָּ לְבִנְךָ בַּיּוֹם הַהוּא לֵאמֹר
9 בַּעֲבוּר זֶה עָשָׂה יְהוָה לִי בְּצֵאתִי מִמִּצְרָיִם׃ וְהָיָה לְךָ
לְאוֹת עַל־יָדְךָ וּלְזִכָּרוֹן בֵּין עֵינֶיךָ לְמַעַן תִּהְיֶה תּוֹרַת יְהוָה
י בְּפִיךָ כִּי בְּיָד חֲזָקָה הוֹצִאֲךָ יְהוָה מִמִּצְרָיִם׃ וְשָׁמַרְתָּ
אֶת־הַחֻקָּה הַזֹּאת לְמוֹעֲדָהּ מִיָּמִים יָמִימָה׃ פ
11 וְהָיָה כִּי־יְבִאֲךָ יְהוָה אֶל־אֶרֶץ הַכְּנַעֲנִי כַּאֲשֶׁר נִשְׁבַּע לְךָ
12 וְלַאֲבֹתֶיךָ וּנְתָנָהּ לָךְ׃ וְהַעֲבַרְתָּ כָל־פֶּטֶר־רֶחֶם לַיהוָה

is Mine.' ¶ 3. And Moses said unto the people: 'Remember this day, in which ye came out from Egypt, out of the house of bondage; for by strength of hand the LORD brought you out from this place; there shall no leavened bread be eaten. 4. This day ye go forth in the month Abib. 5. And it shall be when the LORD shall bring thee into the land of the Canaanite, and the Hittite, and the Amorite, and the Hivite, and the Jebusite, which He swore unto thy fathers to give thee, a land flowing with milk and honey, that thou shalt keep this service in this month. 6. Seven days thou shalt eat unleavened bread, and in the seventh day shall be a feast to the LORD. 7. Unleavened bread shall be eaten throughout the seven days; and there shall no leavened bread be seen with thee, neither shall there be leaven seen with thee, in all thy borders. 8. And thou shalt tell thy son in that day, saying: It is because of that which the LORD did for me when I came forth out of Egypt. 9. And it shall be for a sign unto thee upon thy hand, and for a memorial between thine eyes, that the law of the LORD may be in thy mouth; for with a strong hand hath the LORD brought thee out of Egypt. 10. Thou shalt therefore keep this ordinance in its season from year to year. ¶ 11. And it shall be when the LORD shall bring thee into the land of the Canaanite, as He swore unto thee and to thy fathers, and shall give it thee, 12. that thou shalt set apart unto the LORD all that openeth the womb; every firstling that is a

3. *remember this day.* Every year.

the house of bondage. lit. 'the house of bondmen', *i.e.* the land where they were treated like slaves.

from this place. This phrase could only have been used at the exact stage when they were emancipated and as yet upon Egyptian soil.

8. *tell thy son.* The Rabbis derive from this verse the law that every father should relate on the evening of Passover the story of the Deliverance to his children. The story itself, as formulated for recitation during the domestic service on the eve of Passover, is called *Haggadah shel Pesach.*

9. *for a sign unto thee.* The Exodus is to be more than a mere annual celebration. Its eternal lessons are to be ever before the mind of the Israelite, by means of a 'sign' upon the hand, and of a 'memento' between the eyes. The reminders on arm and forehead are called *tephillin*, a late Heb. plural of תפלה, prayer. Four sections from the Torah (Ex. XIII, 1–10, 11–16; Deut. VI, 4–9; and XI, 13–21) are in the tephillin; and 'these four sections have been chosen in preference to all the other passages of the Torah, because they embrace the acceptance of the Kingdom of Heaven, the unity of the Creator, and the exodus from Egypt—fundamental doctrines of Judaism'. (Sefer ha-Chinuch.) The purpose of the tephillin is given in the Meditation recited before putting on the tephillin (Authorised Prayer Book, p. 15):—

'Within these Tephillin are placed four sections of the Law, that declare the absolute unity of God, and that remind us of the miracles and wonders which he wrought for us when he brought us forth from Egypt, even he who hath power over the highest and lowest to deal with them according to his will. He hath commanded us to lay the Tephillin on the hand as a memorial of his outstretched arm; opposite the heart, to indicate the duty of subjecting the longings and designs of our heart to his service, blessed be he; and upon the head over against the brain, thereby teaching that the mind, whose seat is in the brain, together with all senses and faculties, is to be subjected to his service, blessed be he.'

The tephillin are not worn at night, nor on

male, which thou hast coming of a beast, shall be the LORD's. 13. And every firstling of an ass thou shalt redeem with a lamb; and if thou wilt not redeem it, then thou shalt break its neck; and all the first-born of man among thy sons shalt thou redeem.* m. 14. And it shall be when thy son asketh thee in time to come, saying: What is this? that thou shalt say unto him: By strength of hand the LORD brought us out from Egypt, from the house of bondage; 15. and it came to pass, when Pharaoh would hardly let us go, that the LORD slew all the first-born in the land of Egypt, both the first-born of man, and the first-born of beast; therefore I sacrifice to the LORD all that openeth the womb, being males; but all the first-born of my sons I redeem. 16. And it shall be for a sign upon thy hand, and for frontlets between thine eyes; for by strength of hand the LORD brought us forth out of Egypt.'

וכל־פטר ׀ שגר בהמה אשר יהיה לך הזכרים ליהוה׃
13 וכל־פטר חמר תפדה בשה ואם־לא תפדה וערפתו וכל
מפטיר
14 בכור אדם בבניך תפדה׃ והיה כי־ישאלך בנך מחר
לאמר מה־זאת ואמרת אליו בחזק יד הוציאנו יהוה
טו ממצרים מבית עבדים׃ ויהי כי־הקשה פרעה לשלחנו
ויהרג יהוה כל־בכור בארץ מצרים מבכר אדם ועד־
בכור בהמה על־כן אני זבח ליהוה כל־פטר רחם
16 הזכרים וכל־בכור בני אפדה׃ והיה לאות על־ידכה
ולטוטפת בין עיניך כי בחזק יד הוציאנו יהוה ממצרים׃

Sabbaths or Festivals, as these are themselves called 'a sign' of the great truths symbolized by the tephillin. The commandment of tephillin applies to all male persons from their thirteenth birthday, when they attain their religious majority (*Barmitzvah*). On the Sabbath following that birthday, the Barmitzvah is called to the Law, publicly to acknowledge God as the Giver of the Torah.

10. *this ordinance.* Of the Passover.

in its season. Or, 'appointed time,' *i.e.* at the full moon of the month of Nisan.

from year to year. lit. 'from days to days'. The same Heb. idiom is found in Judges XI, 40.

11. *land of the Canaanite.* The term is general, and includes all the tribes of the land. The law of the redemption of the firstborn was to be obligatory after the conquest of the Holy Land.

12. *thou shalt set apart.* Heb. 'cause to pass over', to the LORD; *i.e.* thou shalt put it aside for the LORD, lest it be mixed with other beasts (Ibn Ezra).

13. *firstling of an ass.* The ass is an unclean animal and could not be sacrificed.

redeem with a lamb. The priest received the lamb, and then the Israelite could retain the firstborn ass for his own use.

break its neck. This requirement ensured the scrupulous execution of the law of redemption in regard to unclean animals, as every one would prefer parting with a lamb to losing an ass.

thy sons shalt thou redeem. With 'five shekels apiece'; Num. III, 45-47. This law is in direct opposition to the practice of the heathen Semitic peoples of sacrificing their first-born. Even Wellhausen admits that of this abomination there is no trace in the religion of Israel. Driver writes: 'The instances of child-sacrifice which occur are either altogether abnormal, or, as in the reigns of Ahaz and Manasseh, due to the importation of Phœnician customs into Judah.'

14. *what is this? i.e.* what is the meaning of the precept concerning the first-born.

15. *would hardly let us go. i.e.* hardened himself *not* to let us go.

slew all the first-born. And spared our first-born.

therefore I sacrifice. In gratitude for sparing the first-born of our cattle.

of my sons I redeem. In memory of the preservation of those of the Israelites.

16. *frontlets.* Heb. '*totafoth*', phylacteries; see Deut. VI, 8.

This verse, with the preceding two verses, is to form the answer of the father to the question put by his son. The religious education of the children is a Divine command, and the future of religion depends upon this precept being loyally obeyed. In addition to these signs and observances, both the Sabbath, and even those Festivals that have other historic associations, are all spoken of in the Liturgy as זכר ליציאת מצרים 'memorials of the Going forth out of Egypt'.

HAFTORAH BO הפטרת בא

JEREMIAH XLVI, 13–28

CHAPTER XLVI

13. The word that the LORD spoke to Jeremiah the prophet, how that Nebuchadrezzar king of Babylon should come and smite the land of Egypt.

14. Declare ye in Egypt, and announce in Migdol,
And announce in Noph and in Tahpanhes;
Say ye: 'Stand forth, and prepare thee,
For the sword hath devoured round about thee.'

15. Why is thy strong one overthrown?
He stood not, because the LORD did thrust him down.

16. He made many to stumble;
Yea, they fell one upon another,
And said: 'Arise, and let us return to our own people,
And to the land of our birth,
From the oppressing sword.'

17. They cried there: 'Pharaoh king of Egypt is but a noise;
He hath let the appointed time pass by.'

18. As I live, saith the King,
Whose name is the LORD of hosts,
Surely like Tabor among the mountains,
And like Carmel by the sea, so shall he come.

CAP. XLVI. מו

13 הַדָּבָר אֲשֶׁר דִּבֶּר
יְהוָה אֶל־יִרְמְיָהוּ הַנָּבִיא לָבוֹא נְבוּכַדְרֶאצַּר מֶלֶךְ בָּבֶל
14 לְהַכּוֹת אֶת־אֶרֶץ מִצְרָיִם׃ הַגִּידוּ בְמִצְרַיִם וְהַשְׁמִיעוּ
בְמִגְדּוֹל וְהַשְׁמִיעוּ בְנֹף וּבְתַחְפַּנְחֵס אִמְרוּ הִתְיַצֵּב וְהָכֵן
טו לָךְ כִּי־אָכְלָה חֶרֶב סְבִיבֶיךָ׃ מַדּוּעַ נִסְחַף אַבִּירֶיךָ לֹא
עָמַד כִּי יְהוָה הֲדָפוֹ׃ הִרְבָּה כּוֹשֵׁל גַּם־נָפַל אִישׁ אֶל־רֵעֵהוּ
16 וַיֹּאמְרוּ קוּמָה ׀ וְנָשֻׁבָה אֶל־עַמֵּנוּ וְאֶל־אֶרֶץ מוֹלַדְתֵּנוּ מִפְּנֵי
17 חֶרֶב הַיּוֹנָה׃ קָרְאוּ שָׁם פַּרְעֹה מֶלֶךְ־מִצְרַיִם שָׁאוֹן הֶעֱבִיר
18 הַמּוֹעֵד׃ חַי־אָנִי נְאֻם־הַמֶּלֶךְ יְהוָה צְבָאוֹת שְׁמוֹ כִּי כְּתָבוֹר
19 בֶּהָרִים וּכְכַרְמֶל בַּיָּם יָבוֹא׃ כְּלֵי גוֹלָה עֲשִׂי לָךְ יוֹשֶׁבֶת
בַּת־מִצְרָיִם כִּי־נֹף לְשַׁמָּה תִהְיֶה וְנִצְּתָה מֵאֵין יוֹשֵׁב׃

19. O thou daughter that dwellest in Egypt,
Furnish thyself to go into captivity;
For Noph shall become a desolation,
And shall be laid waste, without inhabitant.

For Jeremiah's life and message, see p. 229.

Like the previous Haftorah, this also is a prophecy against Egypt, and is thus connected with the Sedrah. Jeremiah was the older contemporary of Ezekiel; and during the last days of the Jewish state, both of them, the one in Jerusalem, and the other in Babylon, denounced the sin and folly of seeking help from Egypt. This is one of the last prophecies uttered by Jeremiah. It forms part of his Ode of Triumph upon the humiliating defeat of Pharaoh at the great battle of Charchemish in 605 B.C.E., and foretells the total collapse of Egypt before the power of Babylon.

14. *declare ye.* All Egypt is called upon to stand forth and prepare to repel the coming invader. Migdol is a frontier town in the north, also Tahpanhes; and Noph (Memphis) is the capital of Upper Egypt.

15. *why is thy strong one overthrown?* The Heb. for 'strong one' is in the plural, 'the plural of majesty,' and refers to the king, not to the people. The Septuagint divides the Heb. word for 'overthrown' into two, reading 'Why is Apis fled? The mighty one stood not, etc.' Apis was the sacred bull, the symbol of Osiris, the chief Egyptian deity worshipped at Memphis, and was called *the mighty one.*

16. *they fell one upon another.* The Egyptian armies in the panic of defeat.

and said. Either the mercenaries from other countries brought in to help Egypt; or, the foreign traders who prepare to flee to their several countries.

17. *they cried.* The mercenaries and traders.

a noise . . . pass by. Pharaoh's name is but an empty noise; the time when he might have saved himself and them is past.

18. *like Tabor.* As surely as Tabor is among the mountains and Carmel is by the sea, so surely shall the conqueror come (Rashi and Kimchi). Others explain, just as Tabor stands out among mountains, and Carmel rises sheer out of the sea, so shall the coming foe—Nebuchadnezzar—overtop other conquerors.

19. *daughter.* Heb. poetical expression for 'population'; cf. *daughter of Zion.*

21 כ עֶגְלָה יְפֵה־פִיָּה מִצְרָיִם קֶרֶץ מִצָּפוֹן בָּא בָא׃ גַּם־שְׂכִרֶיהָ
בְקִרְבָּהּ כְּעֶגְלֵי מַרְבֵּק כִּי־גַם־הֵמָּה הִפְנוּ נָסוּ יַחְדָּיו לֹא
22 עָמָדוּ כִּי יוֹם אֵידָם בָּא עֲלֵיהֶם עֵת פְּקֻדָּתָם׃ קוֹלָהּ כַּנָּחָשׁ
יֵלֵךְ כִּי־בְחַיִל יֵלֵכוּ וּבְקַרְדֻּמּוֹת בָּאוּ לָהּ כְּחֹטְבֵי עֵצִים׃
23 כָּרְתוּ יַעְרָהּ נְאֻם־יְהוָה כִּי לֹא יֵחָקֵר כִּי רַבּוּ מֵאַרְבֶּה
24 וְאֵין לָהֶם מִסְפָּר׃ הֹבִישָׁה בַּת־מִצְרָיִם נִתְּנָה בְּיַד עַם־
כה צָפוֹן׃ אָמַר יְהוָה צְבָאוֹת אֱלֹהֵי יִשְׂרָאֵל הִנְנִי פוֹקֵד אֶל־
אָמוֹן מִנֹּא וְעַל־פַּרְעֹה וְעַל־מִצְרַיִם וְעַל־אֱלֹהֶיהָ וְעַל־מְלָכֶיהָ
26 וְעַל־פַּרְעֹה וְעַל הַבֹּטְחִים בּוֹ׃ וּנְתַתִּים בְּיַד מְבַקְשֵׁי נַפְשָׁם
וּבְיַד נְבוּכַדְרֶאצַּר מֶלֶךְ־בָּבֶל וּבְיַד עֲבָדָיו וְאַחֲרֵי־כֵן תִּשְׁכֹּן
27 כִּימֵי־קֶדֶם נְאֻם־יְהוָה׃ וְאַתָּה אַל־תִּירָא עַבְדִּי יַעֲקֹב
וְאַל־תֵּחַת יִשְׂרָאֵל כִּי הִנְנִי מוֹשִׁעֲךָ מֵרָחוֹק וְאֶת־זַרְעֲךָ
28 מֵאֶרֶץ שִׁבְיָם וְשָׁב יַעֲקוֹב וְשָׁקַט וְשַׁאֲנַן וְאֵין מַחֲרִיד׃ אַתָּה
אַל־תִּירָא עַבְדִּי יַעֲקֹב נְאֻם־יְהוָה כִּי אִתְּךָ אָנִי כִּי אֶעֱשֶׂה
כָלָה בְּכָל־הַגּוֹיִם ׀ אֲשֶׁר הִדַּחְתִּיךָ שָׁמָּה וְאֹתְךָ לֹא־אֶעֱשֶׂה
כָלָה וְיִסַּרְתִּיךָ לַמִּשְׁפָּט וְנַקֵּה לֹא אֲנַקֶּךָּ׃

20. Egypt is a very fair heifer;
But the gadfly out of the north is come, it is come.

21. Also her mercenaries in the midst of her
Are like calves of the stall,
For they also are turned back, they are fled away together,
They did not stand;
For the day of their calamity is come upon them,
The time of their visitation.

22. The sound thereof shall go like the serpent's;
For they march with an army,
And come against her with axes,
As hewers of wood.

23. They cut down her forest, saith the LORD,
Though it cannot be searched;
Because they are more than the locusts,
And are innumerable.

24. The daughter of Egypt is put to shame;
She is delivered into the hand of the people of the north.

25. The LORD of hosts, the God of Israel, saith: Behold, I will punish Amon of No, and Pharaoh, and Egypt, with her gods, and her kings; even Pharaoh, and them that trust in him; 26. and I will deliver them into the hand of those that seek their lives, and into the hand of Nebuchadrezzar king of Babylon, and into the hand of his servants; and afterwards it shall be inhabited, as in the days of old, saith the LORD.

27. But fear not thou, O Jacob My servant,
Neither be dismayed, O Israel;
For, lo, I will save thee from afar,
And thy seed from the land of their captivity;
And Jacob shall again be quiet and at ease,
And none shall make him afraid.

28. Fear not thou, O Jacob My servant, saith the LORD,
For I am with thee;
For I will make a full end of all the nations whither I have driven thee,
But I will not make a full end of thee;
And I will correct thee in measure,
But will not utterly destroy thee.

מלא ו׳ v. 27.

20–26. THE OVERTHROW WOULD NOT BE FINAL

20. *fair heifer.* Well-nourished; the figure is chosen in allusion to her spouse, the bull Apis. *the gadfly. i.e.* the foe, is stinging her to flight. *out of the north.* Babylon was, of course, north of Egypt.

21. *like calves.* They were well-fed but cowardly, proving useless in the hour of danger.

22. *the sound.* The voice of Egypt as she flees from the enemy shall be like a serpent hissing impotently at the wood-cutters who attack her (Streane).

25. *Amon.* The god worshipped at No (Thebes, now Luxor, in South Egypt).

26. *and afterwards it shall be inhabited.* A promise of restoration to Egypt; cf. previous Haftorah, *v.* 12.

27–28. WORDS OF HOPE FOR ISRAEL

27. *fear not.* In contrast with all the foregoing, the Prophet closes with a message of hope and restoration, addressed to the Jewish exiles in Egypt and Chaldea.

28. *will not utterly destroy thee.* Other nations shall be blotted out of existence; not so shall it be with Israel.

13 17. And it came to pass, when Pharaoh had let the people go, that God led them not by the way of the land of the Philistines, although that was near; for God said: 'Lest peradventure the people repent when they see war, and they return to Egypt.' 18. But God led the people about, by the way of the wilderness by the Red Sea; and the children of Israel went up armed out of the land of Egypt. 19. And Moses took the bones of Joseph with him; for he had straitly sworn the children of Israel, saying: 'God will surely remember you; and ye shall carry up my bones hence with you.' 20. And they took their journey from Succoth, and encamped in Etham, in the edge of the wilderness. 21. And the LORD went before them by day

יג ס ס ס יו 16

17 וַיְהִי בְּשַׁלַּח פַּרְעֹה אֶת־הָעָם וְלֹא־נָחָם אֱלֹהִים דֶּרֶךְ אֶרֶץ
פְּלִשְׁתִּים כִּי קָרוֹב הוּא כִּי ׀ אָמַר אֱלֹהִים פֶּן־יִנָּחֵם הָעָם
18 בִּרְאֹתָם מִלְחָמָה וְשָׁבוּ מִצְרָיְמָה׃ וַיַּסֵּב אֱלֹהִים ׀ אֶת־הָעָם
דֶּרֶךְ הַמִּדְבָּר יַם־סוּף וַחֲמֻשִׁים עָלוּ בְנֵי־יִשְׂרָאֵל מֵאֶרֶץ
19 מִצְרָיִם׃ וַיִּקַּח מֹשֶׁה אֶת־עַצְמוֹת יוֹסֵף עִמּוֹ כִּי הַשְׁבֵּעַ
הִשְׁבִּיעַ אֶת־בְּנֵי יִשְׂרָאֵל לֵאמֹר פָּקֹד יִפְקֹד אֱלֹהִים אֶתְכֶם
כ וְהַעֲלִיתֶם אֶת־עַצְמֹתַי מִזֶּה אִתְּכֶם׃ וַיִּסְעוּ מִסֻּכֹּת וַיַּחֲנוּ
21 בְאֵתָם בִּקְצֵה הַמִּדְבָּר׃ וַיהוָה הֹלֵךְ לִפְנֵיהֶם יוֹמָם בְּעַמּוּד

v. 18. חש' רפה

IV. BESHALLACH

(CHAPTERS XIII, 17–XVII)

THE REDEMPTION FROM EGYPT

XIII, 17–XIV, 31. THE PASSAGE OF THE RED SEA

17. *had let the people go.* God did not lead His people toward Canaan by the shorter way through the land of the Philistines, the direct caravan route to Canaan along the coast to Gaza, but by the opposite route towards the Red Sea.

the Philistines. A strongly intrenched and warlike people, who gave their name Philistia, *i.e.* Palestine, to all the land of Canaan; see p. 37, note 14. They are probably to be identified with the Purasati or Pulsata, one of a group of piratical tribes from the coast of Asia Minor or the Aegean Islands, who are known to have raided Egypt in the times of Rameses III, after the Exodus. There is no reason to assume that that was their first emergence from the place of their origin.

although that was near. It would have enabled them to reach the Land of Promise in about eleven days.

repent. 'Have regrets' (Moffatt), and change their mind and go back to Egypt. They required training and teaching and disciplining. 'It is like that king who wished to give his son his inheritance. He thought to himself, My son is young; he hardly knows how to read and write. If I give him all my possessions now, will he be able to keep them? I will wait until he has grown in strength and wisdom. In the same way God thought, The children of Israel are verily still children; first let Me teach them to understand and practise My precepts and commandments, then will I give them the Promised Land' (Talmud).

18. *by the way of the wilderness. i.e.* in the direction of the Egyptian wilderness, west of the northern end of the Gulf of Suez.

Red Sea. lit. 'the sea of reeds', see II, 3, 5. Denotes the northern part of our Red Sea; see on X, 19. Reeds have been found on spots N. of Suez, and they abound in Lake Timsah, exactly at the entrance of Goshen. In those days, there was a shallow extension of the Gulf of Suez, reaching to Lake Timsah; see note on *v.* 2 in next chapter.

armed. Better, *armed with lances.* Heb. *chamushim,* which probably comes from the Egyptian word *chams,* 'lance' (Yahuda).

19. *Moses took the bones of Joseph with him.* Joseph had caused his brethren to swear that they would carry his bones with them from Egypt. Moses, in performing this solemn duty, set an example of noble piety towards the dead; see on Gen. L, 26.

straitly. Strictly.

20. *Succoth.* See note on XII, 37.

Etham, in the edge of the wilderness. Where their route crossed the Egyptian frontier, *i.e.* in the neighbourhood of the modern Ismailia (Naville). At the frontier, the green land of Egypt would be cut off as with a knife from the hard desert tract on which they entered.

21. *a pillar of cloud.* The pillar of cloud by day and the pillar of fire by night were symbols of, and witnesses to, God's watching providence (Abarbanel). Sir Walter Scott has based on this in a pillar of cloud, to lead them the way; and by night in a pillar of fire, to give them light; that they might go by day and by night: 22. the pillar of cloud by day, and the pillar of fire by night, departed not from before the people.

4

CHAPTER XIV

1. And the LORD spoke unto Moses, saying: 2. 'Speak unto the children of Israel, that they turn back and encamp before Pi-hahiroth, between Migdol and the sea, before Baal-zephon, over against it shall ye encamp by the sea. 3. And Pharaoh will say of the children of Israel: They are entangled in the land, the wilderness hath shut them in. 4. And I will harden Pharaoh's heart, and he shall follow after

עָנָן לַנְחֹתָם הַדֶּרֶךְ וְלַיְלָה בְּעַמּוּד אֵשׁ לְהָאִיר לָהֶם
22 לָלֶכֶת יוֹמָם וָלָיְלָה׃ לֹא־יָמִישׁ עַמּוּד הֶעָנָן יוֹמָם וְעַמּוּד
הָאֵשׁ לָיְלָה לִפְנֵי הָעָם׃ פ

יד CAP. XIV. יד

א 2 וַיְדַבֵּר יְהוָה אֶל־מֹשֶׁה לֵּאמֹר׃ דַּבֵּר אֶל־בְּנֵי יִשְׂרָאֵל וְיָשֻׁבוּ
וְיַחֲנוּ לִפְנֵי פִּי הַחִירֹת בֵּין מִגְדֹּל וּבֵין הַיָּם לִפְנֵי בַּעַל
3 צְפֹן נִכְחוֹ תַחֲנוּ עַל־הַיָּם׃ וְאָמַר פַּרְעֹה לִבְנֵי יִשְׂרָאֵל
4 נְבֻכִים הֵם בָּאָרֶץ סָגַר עֲלֵיהֶם הַמִּדְבָּר׃ וְחִזַּקְתִּי אֶת־לֵב־

verse one of the most beautiful religious songs in English literature, *Rebecca's Hymn.*

Luzzatto and Kalisch refer to the Oriental custom of fire-signals in front of armies, or of a brazier filled with burning wood borne along at the head of a caravan, as the natural basis of the miracle. In that case, we should have in this narrative of the guiding Cloud and Pillar another instance of the interweaving of the supernatural and the natural in Scripture.

CHAPTER XIV

2. *that they turn back.* The march was no sooner begun than it was checked. The people were ordered to return. They were now in great danger, in case the king of Egypt wished to pursue them. His chariots would soon have overtaken this multitude, and his host would have made a slaughter of the fugitives. This seemed to be the reason why they received a command which they must have considered as very extraordinary, and of a nature to shake their confidence in their leader (Naville). Instead of continuing to march to the north of the northern end of the Gulf of Suez, they were bidden to turn south or south-west, keeping the Sea, *i.e.* the Gulf of Suez, on their left. It is probable that the Gulf of Suez then extended much further north than it does now, and that the modern Lake Timsah and the Bitter Lakes were connected with each other and the Gulf of Suez by necks of shallow water, which would in a tornado be swept almost dry.

The landmarks mentioned in this verse have long ago disappeared, and cannot be identified with certainty. The precision, however, with which they are designated, guarantees that the spots were once well known. No portion of the world outside of Palestine was more familiar to the Israelites than the western border of Egypt; and no event in Bible history more perennially popular than the story of the Deliverance from Egypt.

Pi-hahiroth. Has been identified by Naville with Pi-kerehet, which he argues was on the S.W. edge of Lake Timsah. It was a sanctuary of Osiris. Cf. Num. XXXIII, 7.

Baal-zephon. The place of worship of a Semitic deity, on the opposite, Asiatic side, of the Sea which was in front of them.

3. *entangled.* Or, 'perplexed,' not knowing which way to turn in order to escape.

in the land. They are now back on Egyptian territory.

the wilderness. i.e. the Egyptian wilderness, a tract of desert land between the Nile and the Red Sea. The southern boundary of that wilderness was a high mountain range. With mountains to the south and the Sea to the west, they are 'shut in'.

4. *I will harden Pharaoh's heart.* After an interval of several days, during which the king gradually recovered from his panic, and reflected on his loss through the dismissal of so many scores of thousands of labourers, his innate obstinacy returned. His blindness to the right of the Israelites to their freedom became a malady of the mind with him, that was to drive him to destruction. His obdurate impiety was encouraged by the report that the Hebrew army was now between Migdol and the Sea, patently ignorant of the trap in which they now found themselves.

follow after. Pursue.

I will get Me honour upon Pharaoh. Better, *through Pharaoh.* By shielding the righteous and overthrowing the wicked, God manifests His justice and might. Thus, the Egyptians and all humanity come to know that there is a God of righteousness in the world.

they did so. The Israelites turned back and encamped before Pi-hahiroth.

פַּרְעֹה֙ וְרָדַ֣ף אַחֲרֵיהֶ֔ם וְאִכָּבְדָ֤ה בְּפַרְעֹה֙ וּבְכָל־חֵיל֔וֹ וְיָדְע֥וּ
ה מִצְרַ֖יִם כִּֽי־אֲנִ֣י יְהוָ֑ה וַיַּֽעֲשׂוּ־כֵֽן׃ וַיֻּגַּד֙ לְמֶ֣לֶךְ מִצְרַ֔יִם כִּ֥י
בָרַ֖ח הָעָ֑ם וַ֠יֵּהָפֵךְ לְבַ֨ב פַּרְעֹ֤ה וַעֲבָדָיו֙ אֶל־הָעָ֔ם וַיֹּֽאמְרוּ֙
6 מַה־זֹּ֣את עָשִׂ֔ינוּ כִּֽי־שִׁלַּ֥חְנוּ אֶת־יִשְׂרָאֵ֖ל מֵעָבְדֵֽנוּ׃ וַיֶּאְסֹ֖ר
7 אֶת־רִכְבּ֑וֹ וְאֶת־עַמּ֖וֹ לָקַ֥ח עִמּֽוֹ׃ וַיִּקַּ֗ח שֵׁשׁ־מֵא֤וֹת רֶ֙כֶב֙
8 בָּח֔וּר וְכֹ֖ל רֶ֣כֶב מִצְרָ֑יִם וְשָֽׁלִשִׁ֖ם עַל־כֻּלּֽוֹ׃ וַיְחַזֵּ֣ק יְהוָ֗ה
אֶת־לֵ֤ב פַּרְעֹה֙ מֶ֣לֶךְ מִצְרַ֔יִם וַיִּרְדֹּ֕ף אַחֲרֵ֖י בְּנֵ֣י יִשְׂרָאֵ֑ל וּבְנֵ֣י
שני 9 יִשְׂרָאֵ֔ל יֹצְאִ֖ים בְּיָ֥ד רָמָֽה׃* וַיִּרְדְּפ֨וּ מִצְרַ֜יִם אַחֲרֵיהֶ֗ם וַיַּשִּׂ֤יגוּ
אוֹתָם֙ חֹנִ֣ים עַל־הַיָּ֔ם כָּל־סוּס֙ רֶ֣כֶב פַּרְעֹ֔ה וּפָרָשָׁ֖יו וְחֵיל֑וֹ
י עַל־פִּי֙ הַחִירֹ֔ת לִפְנֵ֖י בַּ֥עַל צְפֹֽן׃ וּפַרְעֹ֖ה הִקְרִ֑יב וַיִּשְׂא֩וּ
בְנֵֽי־יִשְׂרָאֵ֨ל אֶת־עֵינֵיהֶ֜ם וְהִנֵּ֥ה מִצְרַ֣יִם ׀ נֹסֵ֣עַ אַחֲרֵיהֶ֗ם
11 וַיִּֽירְאוּ֙ מְאֹ֔ד וַיִּצְעֲק֥וּ בְנֵֽי־יִשְׂרָאֵ֖ל אֶל־יְהוָֽה׃ וַיֹּאמְרוּ֮ אֶל־
מֹשֶׁה֒ הֲֽמִבְּלִ֤י אֵין־קְבָרִים֙ בְּמִצְרַ֔יִם לְקַחְתָּ֖נוּ לָמ֣וּת בַּמִּדְבָּ֑ר
12 מַה־זֹּאת֙ עָשִׂ֣יתָ לָּ֔נוּ לְהוֹצִיאָ֖נוּ מִמִּצְרָֽיִם׃ הֲלֹא־זֶ֣ה הַדָּבָ֗ר
אֲשֶׁ֣ר דִּבַּ֣רְנוּ אֵלֶ֣יךָ בְמִצְרַיִם֮ לֵאמֹר֒ חֲדַ֥ל מִמֶּ֖נּוּ וְנַעַבְדָ֣ה

them; and I will get Me honour upon Pharaoh, and upon all his host; and the Egyptians shall know that I am the LORD.' And they did so.
5. And it was told the king of Egypt that the people were fled; and the heart of Pharaoh and of his servants was turned towards the people, and they said: 'What is this we have done, that we have let Israel go from serving us?'
6. And he made ready his chariots, and took his people with him.
7. And he took six hundred chosen chariots, and all the chariots of Egypt, and captains over all of them.
8. And the LORD hardened the heart of Pharaoh king of Egypt, and he pursued after the children of Israel; for the children of Israel went out with a high hand.*ii.
9. And the Egyptians pursued after them, all the horses and chariots of Pharaoh, and his horsemen, and his army, and overtook them encamping by the sea, beside Pi-hahiroth, in front of Baal-zephon.
10. And when Pharaoh drew nigh, the children of Israel lifted up their eyes, and, behold, the Egyptians were marching after them; and they were sore afraid; and the children of Israel cried out unto the LORD.
11. And they said unto Moses: 'Because there were no graves in Egypt, hast thou taken us away to die in the wilderness? wherefore hast thou dealt thus with us, to bring us forth out of Egypt?
12. Is not this the word that we spoke unto thee in Egypt, saying: Let us alone, that we may serve the

5–14. The epic story of Israel's Redemption is now swiftly approaching its climax. The last chapters described Israel's final night in Egypt, with its panic for the Egyptians and rejoicing for the Israelites, when monarch and people alike hurried the children of Israel out of the land of bondage. But no sooner had Israel gone, than Pharaoh and his court regretted the act of emancipation. 'What have we done!' they exclaimed. There followed a swift marshalling of the cavalry and chariots of Egypt; and only a few days after being thrust out into freedom, the children of Israel beheld the hosts of Egypt in hot pursuit after them.

5. *turned toward the people.* They saw Goshen empty, the brickfields deserted, great works of Egypt stopped for want of slaves, and they regretted that the Israelites had been allowed to depart; see XII, 31 f.

6. *made ready.* lit. 'bound', *i.e.* attached the chariots to the horses; cf. Gen. XLVI, 29.
his people with him. *i.e.* his warriors; cf. Num. XXI, 23.

8. *with a high hand.* *i.e.* confidently and fearlessly.

9. *horsemen.* Probably charioteers. Rameses II is said to have had a force of 2,400 cavalry, independent of his chariots. Isaiah (XXX, 1) makes the same distinction between the chariots and horsemen of Egypt.

10. *they were sore afraid.* 'It is very surprising that such a large host should be so terrified by an approaching enemy. But our astonishment ceases if we consider that the Egyptians had been the lords of the Hebrews, and that that generation had learned from their youth patiently to endure all insults which the Egyptians inflicted upon them. Thus had their minds become depressed and servile' (Ibn Ezra).

11. *because there were no graves in Egypt.* Is the bitter taunt of the Israelites. 'These words show the hand of the eye-witness of the events he relates' (Naville). Similar taunts were flung at their leader every time anything went wrong in regard to food, water or comfort.

12. *let us alone.* The Midrash indicates that not only were the people distracted by fear, but they were further demoralized by divided counsels. One group, frantic with despair, cried, Let us cast ourselves into the sea. Another group said, Let us go back to Egypt and submit to slavery. Other groups were for giving battle to the enemy.

Egyptians? For it were better for us to serve the Egyptians, than that we should die in the wilderness.' 13. And Moses said unto the people: 'Fear ye not, stand still, and see the salvation of the LORD, which He will work for you to-day; for whereas ye have seen the Egyptians to-day, ye shall see them again no more for ever. 14. The LORD will fight for you, and ye shall hold your peace.'*iii a. ¶ 15. And the LORD said unto Moses: 'Wherefore criest thou unto Me? speak unto the children of Israel, that they go forward. 16. And lift thou up thy rod, and stretch out thy hand over the sea, and divide it; and the children of Israel shall go into the midst of the sea on dry ground. 17. And I, behold, I will harden the hearts of the Egyptians, and they shall go in after them; and I will get Me honour upon Pharaoh, and upon all his host, upon his chariots, and upon his horsemen. 18. And the Egyptians shall know that I am the LORD, when I have gotten Me honour upon Pharaoh, upon his chariots, and upon his horsemen.' 19. And the angel of God, who went before the camp of Israel, removed and went behind them: and the pillar of cloud removed from before them, and stood behind them; 20. and it came between the camp of Egypt and the camp of Israel; and there was the cloud and the darkness here, yet gave it light by night there; and the one came not near the other all the night. 21. And Moses stretched out his

אֶת־מִצְרַיִם כִּי טוֹב לָנוּ עֲבֹד אֶת־מִצְרַיִם מִמֻּתֵנוּ בַּמִּדְבָּר׃
13 וַיֹּאמֶר מֹשֶׁה אֶל־הָעָם אַל־תִּירָאוּ הִתְיַצְּבוּ וּרְאוּ אֶת־
יְשׁוּעַת יְהוָה אֲשֶׁר־יַעֲשֶׂה לָכֶם הַיּוֹם כִּי אֲשֶׁר רְאִיתֶם אֶת־
14 מִצְרַיִם הַיּוֹם לֹא תֹסִפוּ לִרְאֹתָם עוֹד עַד־עוֹלָם׃ יְהוָה
יִלָּחֵם לָכֶם וְאַתֶּם תַּחֲרִשׁוּן׃* פ שלישי
טו וַיֹּאמֶר יְהוָה אֶל־מֹשֶׁה מַה־תִּצְעַק אֵלָי דַּבֵּר אֶל־בְּנֵי־
16 יִשְׂרָאֵל וְיִסָּעוּ׃ וְאַתָּה הָרֵם אֶת־מַטְּךָ וּנְטֵה אֶת־יָדְךָ עַל־
הַיָּם וּבְקָעֵהוּ וְיָבֹאוּ בְנֵי־יִשְׂרָאֵל בְּתוֹךְ הַיָּם בַּיַּבָּשָׁה׃
17 וַאֲנִי הִנְנִי מְחַזֵּק אֶת־לֵב מִצְרַיִם וְיָבֹאוּ אַחֲרֵיהֶם וְאִכָּבְדָה
18 בְּפַרְעֹה וּבְכָל־חֵילוֹ בְּרִכְבּוֹ וּבְפָרָשָׁיו׃ וְיָדְעוּ מִצְרַיִם
19 כִּי־אֲנִי יְהוָה בְּהִכָּבְדִי בְּפַרְעֹה בְּרִכְבּוֹ וּבְפָרָשָׁיו׃ וַיִּסַּע
מַלְאַךְ הָאֱלֹהִים הַהֹלֵךְ לִפְנֵי מַחֲנֵה יִשְׂרָאֵל וַיֵּלֶךְ מֵאַחֲרֵיהֶם
כ וַיִּסַּע עַמּוּד הֶעָנָן מִפְּנֵיהֶם וַיַּעֲמֹד מֵאַחֲרֵיהֶם׃ וַיָּבֹא בֵּין ׀
מַחֲנֵה מִצְרַיִם וּבֵין מַחֲנֵה יִשְׂרָאֵל וַיְהִי הֶעָנָן וְהַחֹשֶׁךְ וַיָּאֶר
21 אֶת־הַלַּיְלָה וְלֹא־קָרַב זֶה אֶל־זֶה כָּל־הַלָּיְלָה׃ וַיֵּט מֹשֶׁה

v. 13. סבירין כאשר

13. *the salvation of the LORD.* A great expression, implying help, deliverance, welfare, and blessings Divine.

14. *ye shall hold your peace.* This was no time for giving wild expression to fear, but to await God's deliverance in quiet confidence.

15. *wherefore criest thou.* That moment of anguish called not for prayer but for action.
go forward. To the shore of the sea.

16. *and divide it.* 'We know that the rod did not divide the sea, but as soon as Moses stretched out his hand over the sea, God caused the sea to go back by a strong east wind' (Ibn Ezra).

17. *get Me honour.* See *v.* 4.

18. *Egyptians shall know.* The Egyptians who remain in Egypt will acknowledge Me as God, for I do not delight in the death of the sinner, but that he turn from his evil ways and live (Sforno).

19. *angel of God.* See note on XIII, 21.
before the camp of Israel. That is, the angel of God and the pillar of cloud, instead of being in front of the Israelites, as hitherto, now stand behind them. The pillar is the instrument of the angel. The second half of the verse, 'the pillar of cloud removed from before them and stood behind them,' is synonymous with the first half of the verse.

20. *cloud and the darkness.* Heb. idiom for, 'the dark cloud.'
light by night. To the Israelites. If there was a pillar of light and another of darkness, then the one enabled the Israelites to pass through the sea during that night, whilst the pillar of darkness stood before the Egyptians and hindered their movement. On the other hand, if we assume that there was only one pillar, then it was dark to the Egyptians and gave light to the Israelites.

21. *caused the sea to go back.* A strong east wind, blowing all night and acting with the ebbing tide, may have laid bare the neck of water joining the Bitter Lakes to the Red Sea, allowing the Israelites to cross in safety. 'As in all the wonders of Egypt, this also, the greatest of all, is based upon a natural cause; and in this the boundless power of God, who, by an insignificant change, knows how to convert the natural and common course of things into extraordinary and marvellous events, is sublimely manifest' (Kalisch).

hand over the sea; and the LORD caused the sea to go back by a strong east wind all the night, and made the sea dry land, and the waters were divided. 22. And the children of Israel went into the midst of the sea upon the dry ground; and the waters were a wall unto them on their right hand, and on their left. 23. And the Egyptians pursued, and went in after them into the midst of the sea, all Pharaoh's horses, his chariots, and his horsemen. 24. And it came to pass in the morning watch, that the LORD looked forth upon the host of the Egyptians through the pillar of fire and of cloud, and discomfited the host of the Egyptians. 25. And He took off their chariot wheels, and made them to drive heavily; so that the Egyptians said: 'Let us flee from the face of Israel; for the LORD fighteth for them against the Egyptians.' *iii s, iv a. ¶ 26. And the LORD said unto Moses: 'Stretch out thy hand over the sea, that the waters may come back upon the Egyptians, upon their chariots, and upon their horsemen.' 27. And Moses stretched forth his hand over the sea, and the sea returned to its strength when the morning appeared; and the Egyptians fled

אֶת־יָדוֹ עַל־הַיָּם וַיּוֹלֶךְ יְהוָה ׀ אֶת־הַיָּם בְּרוּחַ קָדִים עַזָּה
22 כָּל־הַלַּיְלָה וַיָּשֶׂם אֶת־הַיָּם לֶחָרָבָה וַיִּבָּקְעוּ הַמָּיִם׃ וַיָּבֹאוּ
בְנֵי־יִשְׂרָאֵל בְּתוֹךְ הַיָּם בַּיַּבָּשָׁה וְהַמַּיִם לָהֶם חוֹמָה מִימִינָם
23 וּמִשְּׂמֹאלָם׃ וַיִּרְדְּפוּ מִצְרַיִם וַיָּבֹאוּ אַחֲרֵיהֶם כֹּל סוּס
24 פַּרְעֹה רִכְבּוֹ וּפָרָשָׁיו אֶל־תּוֹךְ הַיָּם׃ וַיְהִי בְּאַשְׁמֹרֶת הַבֹּקֶר
וַיַּשְׁקֵף יְהוָה אֶל־מַחֲנֵה מִצְרַיִם בְּעַמּוּד אֵשׁ וְעָנָן וַיָּהָם אֵת
כה מַחֲנֵה מִצְרָיִם׃ וַיָּסַר אֵת אֹפַן מַרְכְּבֹתָיו וַיְנַהֲגֵהוּ בִּכְבֵדֻת
וַיֹּאמֶר מִצְרַיִם אָנוּסָה מִפְּנֵי יִשְׂרָאֵל כִּי יְהוָה נִלְחָם לָהֶם
בְּמִצְרָיִם׃ * פ רביעי (שלישי לספ׳)
26 וַיֹּאמֶר יְהוָה אֶל־מֹשֶׁה נְטֵה אֶת־יָדְךָ עַל־הַיָּם וְיָשֻׁבוּ הַמַּיִם
27 עַל־מִצְרַיִם עַל־רִכְבּוֹ וְעַל־פָּרָשָׁיו׃ וַיֵּט מֹשֶׁה אֶת־יָדוֹ
עַל־הַיָּם וַיָּשָׁב הַיָּם לִפְנוֹת בֹּקֶר לְאֵיתָנוֹ וּמִצְרַיִם נָסִים

22. *a wall unto them. i.e.* a protection and a defence. Pharaoh could not attack them on either flank, on account of the two bodies of water between which their march lay. He could only come at them by following after them (Rawlinson).

24. *in the morning watch.* From two to six in the morning. The night was divided into three 'watches'. The passage across the Red Sea was thus not effected in broad daylight but in the depth of the night.

the LORD looked forth. Metaphorical for lightning. One glance of God's eye sufficed to throw into hopeless confusion the enemies of His redeemed firstborn. An anthropomorphic expression, but most forcible. For a similar metaphor, see Amos IX, 4; Ps. CIV, 32.

discomfited. Threw into confusion. The text does not allude to the means whereby the panic of the Egyptians was produced. The Psalmist supplies this omission. 'The clouds poured out water; the skies sent out a sound; thine arrows also went abroad. The voice of thy thunder was in the whirlwind; the lightnings lighted up the world; the earth trembled and shook. Thou leddest thy people like a flock by the hand of Moses and Aaron' (LXXVII, 17, 18–20). There was a hurricane raging with tornado force, causing the sea to go back, amidst a darkness lit up only by the glare of lightning, as 'the LORD looked out' from the black skies.

25. *and He took off.* The Egyptians were hindered in their pursuit, because the lightning struck the chariot-wheels, and slew the Egyptian warriors who commanded the chariots (Rashi).

drive heavily. The wheels stuck fast in the loose wet sand.

the Egyptians said. One to another. The Heb. is in the singular, 'And Egypt said.'

the LORD fighteth for them. At last the Egyptians realize against Whom they are fighting.

26. *may come back.* 'A sudden cessation of the wind, possibly coinciding with a spring tide (it was full moon), would immediately convert the low flat sandbanks first into a quicksand, and then into a mass of waters, in a time far less than would suffice for the escape of a single chariot' (F. C. Cook).

27. *its strength.* Or, 'its wonted flow.'

fled against it. Better, *were fleeing towards it* (Rashi). Terror maddened them, and instead of fleeing from the waters, they ran towards them.

28. *after them. i.e.* the Israelites.

not so much as one of them. Escape was impossible; see Ps. CXXVI, 15. According to some Rabbis, Pharaoh alone escaped. Later Jewish legend adds that 'he never died, and never will die. He stands at the portals of against it; and the LORD overthrew the Egyptians in the midst of the sea. 28. And the waters returned, and covered the chariots, and the horsemen, even all the host of Pharaoh that went in after them into the sea; there remained not so much as one of them. 29. But the children of Israel walked upon dry land in the midst of the sea; and the waters were a wall unto them on their right hand, and on their left. 30. Thus the LORD saved Israel that day out of the hand of the Egyptians; and Israel saw the Egyptians dead upon the sea-shore. 31. And Israel saw the great work which the LORD did upon the Egyptians, and the people feared the LORD; and they believed in the LORD, and in His servant Moses.

28 לִקְרָאתוֹ וַיְנַעֵר יְהוָה אֶת־מִצְרַיִם בְּתוֹךְ הַיָּם׃ וַיָּשֻׁבוּ
הַמַּיִם וַיְכַסּוּ אֶת־הָרֶכֶב וְאֶת־הַפָּרָשִׁים לְכֹל חֵיל פַּרְעֹה
29 הַבָּאִים אַחֲרֵיהֶם בַּיָּם לֹא־נִשְׁאַר בָּהֶם עַד־אֶחָד׃ וּבְנֵי
יִשְׂרָאֵל הָלְכוּ בַיַּבָּשָׁה בְּתוֹךְ הַיָּם וְהַמַּיִם לָהֶם חֹמָה מִימִינָם
ל וּמִשְּׂמֹאלָם׃ וַיּוֹשַׁע יְהוָה בַּיּוֹם הַהוּא אֶת־יִשְׂרָאֵל מִיַּד
31 מִצְרָיִם וַיַּרְא יִשְׂרָאֵל אֶת־מִצְרַיִם מֵת עַל־שְׂפַת הַיָּם׃ וַיַּרְא
יִשְׂרָאֵל אֶת־הַיָּד הַגְּדֹלָה אֲשֶׁר עָשָׂה יְהוָה בְּמִצְרַיִם וַיִּירְאוּ
הָעָם אֶת־יְהוָה וַיַּאֲמִינוּ בַּיהוָה וּבְמֹשֶׁה עַבְדּוֹ׃ פ

15

CHAPTER XV

1. Then sang Moses and the children of Israel this song unto the LORD, and spoke, saying:

I will sing unto the LORD, for He is highly exalted;
The horse and his rider hath He thrown into the sea.

CAP. XV. טו

טו

א אָז יָשִׁיר־מֹשֶׁה וּבְנֵי יִשְׂרָאֵל אֶת־הַשִּׁירָה הַזֹּאת לַיהוָה וַיֹּאמְרוּ
לֵאמֹר אָשִׁירָה לַיהוָה כִּי־גָאֹה גָּאָה סוּס

יד׳ v. 28. בראש עמוד סימן בי״ה שמ״ו טו׳ v. 1. ג׳ דגושה

Gehinnom and, when heathen tyrants enter, he greets them with the words: 'Why have ye not profited by my example?'

29. *dry land.* Dry ground.

30. *the LORD saved Israel.* It was not a victory in which a feeling of pride or self-exaltation could enter. Unlike any other nation that has thrown off the yoke of slavery, neither Israel nor its leader claimed any merit of glory for the victory. In the *Haggadah shel Pesach*, the story of the Redemption is told without any reference to the Leader. *Once* only, indirectly in a quotation, does the name Moses occur at all in the whole Seder Service!

Egyptians dead upon the sea-shore. The fact that the Egyptains had to perish mars the completeness of Israel's victory. 'When the Egyptian hosts were drowning in the Red Sea,' say the Rabbis, 'the angels in heaven were about to break forth into songs of jubilation. But the Holy One, blessed be He, silenced them with the words, "My creatures are perishing, and ye are ready to sing!"' In the same spirit, a medieval rabbi explained why a drop of wine is poured out of the wine-cup on Seder eve at the mention of each of the plagues that were inflicted on the Egyptians. Israel's cup of joy, he said, cannot be full if Israel's triumph involves suffering even to its enemies.

31. *the great work.* lit. 'the great hand', *i.e.* power, achievement.

believed in the LORD, and in His servant Moses. 'An experience such as the Exodus, and the passage through the Red Sea, must have been reckoned by all who participated in them as a direct act of God. Moses was thereby authenticated in the eyes of his people' (Kittel). Their new-born faith in God, and their witnessing of His marvellous help, led to the wonderful outburst of song in the next chapter. Whenever Israel has faith in God and in the Divine Mission of Moses, Israel sings.

CHAPTER XV. THE SONG AT THE RED SEA

1–21. This Song, notable for poetic fire, vivid imagery and quick movement, gives remarkable expression to the mingled horror, triumph and gratitude that the hosts of Israel had lived through during the fateful hours when they were in sight of Pharaoh's pursuing hosts. In Jewish literature it is spoken of as the Song שירה and the Sabbath on which it is read in the Synagogue as שבת שירה.

1. *Moses and the children of Israel.* Moses composed the Song, and the Israelites joined their Leader in praising God. From *v.* 20 and 21, it appears that there was musical accompaniment, with male and female choruses. It is probably the oldest song of national triumph extant.

unto the LORD. In His honour.

for He is highly exalted. Or, 'for He hath triumphed gloriously.'

the horse and his rider hath He thrown into the sea. In four Heb. words is the complete ruin of the military power of Egypt described. 'Its chariots and horses, the mainstay of its strength, are, by Divine might, cast irretrievably into the sea' (Driver).

2 וְרֹכְבוֹ רָמָה בַיָּם׃ עָזִּי וְזִמְרָת יָהּ וַיְהִי־לִי
לִישׁוּעָה זֶה אֵלִי וְאַנְוֵהוּ אֱלֹהֵי
3 אָבִי וַאֲרֹמְמֶנְהוּ׃ יְהוָה אִישׁ מִלְחָמָה יְהוָה
4 שְׁמוֹ׃ מַרְכְּבֹת פַּרְעֹה וְחֵילוֹ יָרָה בַיָּם וּמִבְחַר
ה שָׁלִשָׁיו טֻבְּעוּ בְיַם־סוּף׃ תְּהֹמֹת יְכַסְיֻמוּ יָרְדוּ בִמְצוֹלֹת כְּמוֹ־
6 אָבֶן׃ יְמִינְךָ יְהוָה נֶאְדָּרִי בַּכֹּחַ יְמִינְךָ
7 יְהוָה תִּרְעַץ אוֹיֵב׃ וּבְרֹב גְּאוֹנְךָ תַּהֲרֹס
8 קָמֶיךָ תְּשַׁלַּח חֲרֹנְךָ יֹאכְלֵמוֹ כַּקַּשׁ׃ וּבְרוּחַ
אַפֶּיךָ נֶעֶרְמוּ מַיִם נִצְּבוּ כְמוֹ־נֵד
9 נֹזְלִים קָפְאוּ תְהֹמֹת בְּלֶב־יָם׃ אָמַר
אוֹיֵב אֶרְדֹּף אַשִּׂיג אֲחַלֵּק שָׁלָל תִּמְלָאֵמוֹ

2. The LORD is my strength and song,
And He is become my salvation;
This is my God, and I will glorify Him;
My father's God, and I will exalt Him.

3. The LORD is a man of war,
The LORD is His name.

4. Pharaoh's chariots and his host hath He cast into the sea,
And his chosen captains are sunk in the Red Sea.

5. The deeps cover them—
They went down into the depths like a stone.

6. Thy right hand, O LORD, glorious in power,
Thy right hand, O LORD, dasheth in pieces the enemy.

7. And in the greatness of Thine excellency Thou overthrowest them that rise up against Thee;
Thou sendest forth Thy wrath, it consumeth them as stubble.

8. And with the blast of Thy nostrils the waters were piled up—
The floods stood upright as a heap;
The deeps were congealed in the heart of the sea.

9. The enemy said:
'I will pursue, I will overtake, I will divide the spoil;
My lust shall be satisfied upon them;
I will draw my sword, my hand shall destroy them.'

2. *the LORD.* Heb. *Yah*, the shortened form of the Tetragrammaton, as in *Hallelujah* (lit. 'praise ye Yah').

my strength and song. He is the source of my strength and the theme of my song.

and He is become my salvation. lit. 'and He is become to me a salvation', *i.e.* the source of deliverance.

this is my God. Who has saved me. The redeemed at the Red Sea had a unique realization of the Presence and of the present help of God. The Rabbis say, 'A maidservant at the Red Sea had a more vivid and vitalizing experience of the Divine than many a prophet.'

and I will glorify Him. The rendering, 'I will prepare him an habitation' (AV), follows Onkelos and the Rabbis, who translate, 'I shall build Thee a sanctuary.'

my father's God. The continuity of worship among the children of the Patriarchs is emphasized here. The God of tradition has justified Himself by redeeming Israel. The promises made to the forefathers have now been fulfilled. 'My father's God' stands here for 'the God of my fathers'; see III, 6.

3. *the LORD is a man of war.* God has fought the battle of His persecuted children and overthrown the cruel oppressor.

the LORD is His name. 'For He has wrought justice' (Rashbam); see note on VI, 3.

4. *his chosen captains.* lit. 'the choice of his captains', *i.e.* the flower of his warriors.

5. *cover them.* lit. 'are covering them'. The Heb. verb is in the imperfect tense, and graphically describes the event as if taking place before the eyes of the singers.

6. *Thy right hand.* *i.e.* the power of God.

7. *excellency.* Better, *majesty.*

8. *blast of Thy nostrils.* Is the poetical version of XIV, 22. Used figuratively for the wind.

stood upright as a heap. See XIV, 22. The fine poetic image is sustained throughout the verse. The effect of the wind was to pile up the waters into a wall-like formation.

9. *I will pursue, I will overtake, I will divide the spoil.* A magnificent specimen of Hebrew poetry. The short crisp words express the eagerness of the exultant foe, and his assurance of complete victory.

my lust. lit. 'my soul', which in Heb. psychology is the seat of *desire*, here for vengeance and plunder.

10. Thou didst blow with Thy wind, the sea covered them;
They sank as lead in the mighty waters.

11. Who is like unto Thee, O LORD, among the mighty?
Who is like unto Thee, glorious in holiness,
Fearful in praises, doing wonders?

12. Thou stretchedst out Thy right hand—
The earth swallowed them.

13. Thou in Thy love has led the people that Thou hast redeemed;
Thou hast guided them in Thy strength to Thy holy habitation.

14. The peoples have heard, they tremble;
Pangs have taken hold on the inhabitants of Philistia.

15. Then were the chiefs of Edom affrighted;
The mighty men of Moab, trembling taketh hold upon them;
All the inhabitants of Canaan are melted away.

י נַפְשִׁי   אָרִיק חַרְבִּי תּוֹרִישֵׁמוֹ יָדִי׃   נָשַׁפְתָּ
בְרוּחֲךָ כִּסָּמוֹ יָם   צָלְלוּ כַּעוֹפֶרֶת בְּמַיִם
11 אַדִּירִים׃   מִי־כָמֹכָה בָּאֵלִם יְהוָה   מִי
כָּמֹכָה נֶאְדָּר בַּקֹּדֶשׁ   נוֹרָא תְהִלֹּת עֹשֵׂה־
12 13 פֶלֶא׃   נָטִיתָ יְמִינְךָ תִּבְלָעֵמוֹ אָרֶץ׃   נָחִיתָ
בְחַסְדְּךָ עַם־זוּ גָּאָלְתָּ   נֵהַלְתָּ בְעָזְּךָ אֶל־נְוֵה
14 קָדְשֶׁךָ׃   שָׁמְעוּ עַמִּים יִרְגָּזוּן   חִיל
טו אָחַז יֹשְׁבֵי פְּלָשֶׁת׃   אָז נִבְהֲלוּ אַלּוּפֵי
אֱדוֹם   אֵילֵי מוֹאָב יֹאחֲזֵמוֹ רָעַד   נָמֹגוּ

16. Terror and dread falleth upon them;
By the greatness of Thine arm they are as still as a stone;
Till Thy people pass over, O LORD,
Till the people pass over that Thou hast gotten.

v. 11. כ׳ דגושה   v. 13. ג׳ דגושה

11. *glorious in holiness.* Exalted in the majesty of holiness, which is the essential, distinguishing attribute of the God of Israel.

fearful in praises. Or, 'revered in praises,' *i.e.* praiseworthy acts; inspiring awe by the mighty deeds for which His people are to praise Him.

12. *Thou stretchedst out Thy right hand.* As a man puts forth his hand to indicate his will to his servants (Luzzatto).

13. *Thou in Thy love.* God at the same time shows His abounding love to those who had been persecuted by the Egyptians.

hast led. Better, *leadest.* The verbs of this and the following verses are, according to the sense, futures. In *v.* 16 the text itself passes over into future forms.

Thou hast guided. Better, *thou guidest them,* gently as a shepherd leads his flock. 'The following part of the Song describes in prophetic images the providence of God for the Israelites, shielding them till they have overcome the dangers of the desert, conquered the nations of Canaan, and erected the sanctuary on Zion' (Kalisch).

Thy holy habitation. Mount Sinai, on which God's glory abode when Moses received the Torah (Ibn Ezra); or the Temple on Mount Moriah. Rashbam considers that Canaan is meant here, as it is sometimes called, 'the habitation of God'; see Ps. CXXXII, 13.

14. *peoples have heard.* The story of God's miracles on behalf of Israel. The defeat of the Egyptians would be a source of terror to the heathens who hear the report; see Josh. II, 9–11.
they tremble. lit. 'are trembling'. The poet sees the nations trembling at the approach of God's people (Luzzatto).
pangs. As of childbirth.
Philistia. See XIII, 17.

15. *chiefs of Edom affrighted.* Edom embraced the ranges of Mount Seir on either side of the Arabah, or depression which runs southward from the Dead Sea to the head of the Gulf of Akabah.
mighty men of Moab. Moab was the high tableland east of the Dead Sea and the southernmost section of the Jordan.
are melted away. fig. for, 'are helpless through terror and despair'; cf. Josh. II, 9, 24.

16. *terror and dread falleth upon them.* Or, 'let terror and dread fall upon them . . . let them be still as a stone' (Septuagint).
of Thine arm. Of Thy power.
pass over. On their way to Canaan.
hast gotten. lit. 'hast purchased'; God acquired Israel by redeeming them from the power of Pharaoh.

17. Thou bringest them in, and plantest them in the mountain of Thine inheritance,
The place, O LORD, which Thou hast made for Thee to dwell in,
The sanctuary, O LORD, which Thy hands have established.

18. The LORD shall reign for ever and ever.

19. For the horses of Pharaoh went in with his chariots and with his horsemen into the sea, and the LORD brought back the waters of the sea upon them; but the children of Israel walked on dry land in the midst of the sea. ¶ 20. And Miriam the prophetess, the sister of Aaron, took a timbrel in her hand; and all the women went out after her with timbrels and with dances. 21. And Miriam sang unto them:

Sing ye to the LORD, for He is highly exalted:
The horse and his rider hath He thrown into the sea.

¶ 22. And Moses led Israel onward from the Red Sea, and they went out into the wilderness of Shur; and they went three days in

16 כֹּל יֹשְׁבֵי כְנָעַן׃ תִּפֹּל עֲלֵיהֶם אֵימָתָה
וָפַחַד בִּגְדֹל זְרוֹעֲךָ יִדְּמוּ כָּאָבֶן עַד־
יַעֲבֹר עַמְּךָ יְהוָה עַד־יַעֲבֹר עַם־זוּ
17 קָנִיתָ׃ תְּבִאֵמוֹ וְתִטָּעֵמוֹ בְּהַר נַחֲלָתְךָ מָכוֹן
לְשִׁבְתְּךָ פָּעַלְתָּ יְהוָה מִקְּדָשׁ אֲדֹנָי כּוֹנְנוּ
18 19 יָדֶיךָ׃ יְהוָה ׀ יִמְלֹךְ לְעֹלָם וָעֶד׃ כִּי
בָא סוּס פַּרְעֹה בְּרִכְבּוֹ וּבְפָרָשָׁיו בַּיָּם וַיָּשֶׁב יְהוָה עֲלֵהֶם
אֶת־מֵי הַיָּם וּבְנֵי יִשְׂרָאֵל הָלְכוּ בַיַּבָּשָׁה בְּתוֹךְ הַיָּם׃ פ
כ וַתִּקַּח מִרְיָם הַנְּבִיאָה אֲחוֹת אַהֲרֹן אֶת־הַתֹּף בְּיָדָהּ וַתֵּצֶאןָ
21 כָל־הַנָּשִׁים אַחֲרֶיהָ בְּתֻפִּים וּבִמְחֹלֹת׃ וַתַּעַן לָהֶם מִרְיָם
שִׁירוּ לַיהוָה כִּי־גָאֹה גָּאָה סוּס וְרֹכְבוֹ רָמָה בַיָּם׃ ס
22 וַיַּסַּע מֹשֶׁה אֶת־יִשְׂרָאֵל מִיַּם־סוּף וַיֵּצְאוּ אֶל־מִדְבַּר־שׁוּר

v. 16. כ׳ דגושה v. 17. ק׳ דגושה v. 21. ג׳ דגושה

17. *Thou bringest them in.* The final goal of Israel's triumphant progress was to be the land of Canaan, promised to the forefathers.
mountain of Thine inheritance. i.e. Canaan, and thus spoken of owing to the mountainous character of many of its most important parts; cf. Deut. III, 25; Is. XI, 9; Ps. LXXVIII, 54 (with allusion to this passage).
the sanctuary. Mount Moriah is probably referred to here.
have established. To stand firm; see Ps. LXVIII, 9.

18. *the LORD shall reign for ever and ever.* The Song closes, not with the conquest of material domains, but with the promise of the Kingdom of God. This is the climax. The redemption from Egypt was to be followed by the Revelation on Mount Sinai, when God's Kingdom on earth was inaugurated. That Kingdom is eternal.

19. This verse does not belong to the Song. It is a summary of the great event culminating in the Song of victory, and forms the transition to the following narrative.
for the horses of Pharaoh. It is better to combine this and the following verse; thus, *when the horses of Pharaoh went in . . . but the children of Israel walked on dry land in the midst of the sea, Miriam the prophetess . . . took* (Rashi, Mendelssohn).

20. *the prophetess.* See Num. XII, 2, and cf. Judg. IV, 4.
sister of Aaron. Miriam being more closely associated with Aaron than with Moses; see Num. XII, 1 f.
went out after her. She led the women in the praise of God.
dances. See II Sam. VI, 14 and Ps. CXLIX, 3. In the East, dancing was, and is, part of the language of religion.

21. *sang unto them. i.e.* answered as a chorus; see I Sam. XVIII, 7. Miriam sang, and the women responded (Luzzatto).

THE JOURNEY TO SINAI

22–27. Israel at Marah and Elim.

22. *led Israel onward.* lit. 'made Israel to journey'; see XII, 7.
the wilderness of Shur. The district of the N.E. frontier of Egypt; see Gen. XVI, 7 and XXV, 18. Along the coast of the Gulf of Suez is a strip of level country: the northern part is called the wilderness of Shur; the southern, the wilderness of Sin.
The station where Moses and the Israelites halted after their passage of the Red Sea, is regarded by the Arabs to be Ayun Musa, 'the springs of Moses,' 9 miles below Suez, on the east side of the Gulf, and 1½ miles from the coast.
three days. About 45 miles would thus be covered by a caravan, travelling with baggage.

the wilderness, and found no water. 23. And when they came to Marah, they could not drink of the waters of Marah, for they were bitter. Therefore the name of it was called [1]Marah. 24. And the people murmured against Moses, saying: 'What shall we drink?' 25. And he cried unto the LORD; and the LORD showed him a tree, and he cast it into the waters, and the waters were made sweet. There He made for them a statute and an ordinance, and there He proved them; 26. and He said: 'If thou wilt diligently hearken to the voice of the LORD thy God, and wilt do that which is right in His eyes, and wilt give ear to His commandments, and keep all His statutes, I will put none of the diseases upon thee, which I have put upon the Egyptians; for I am the LORD that healeth thee.'* iv s, v a. ¶ 27. And they came to Elim, where were twelve springs of water, and three score and ten palm-trees; and they encamped there by the waters.

23 וַיֵּלְכוּ שְׁלֹשֶׁת־יָמִים בַּמִּדְבָּר וְלֹא־מָצְאוּ מָיִם׃ וַיָּבֹאוּ
מָרָתָה וְלֹא יָכְלוּ לִשְׁתֹּת מַיִם מִמָּרָה כִּי מָרִים הֵם עַל־
24 כֵּן קָרָא־שְׁמָהּ מָרָה׃ וַיִּלֹּנוּ הָעָם עַל־מֹשֶׁה לֵּאמֹר מַה־
כה נִּשְׁתֶּה׃ וַיִּצְעַק אֶל־יְהוָה וַיּוֹרֵהוּ יְהוָה עֵץ וַיַּשְׁלֵךְ אֶל־
הַמַּיִם וַיִּמְתְּקוּ הַמָּיִם שָׁם שָׂם לוֹ חֹק וּמִשְׁפָּט וְשָׁם נִסָּהוּ׃
26 וַיֹּאמֶר אִם־שָׁמוֹעַ תִּשְׁמַע לְקוֹל ׀ יְהוָה אֱלֹהֶיךָ וְהַיָּשָׁר בְּעֵינָיו
תַּעֲשֶׂה וְהַאֲזַנְתָּ לְמִצְוֺתָיו וְשָׁמַרְתָּ כָּל־חֻקָּיו כָּל־הַמַּחֲלָה
חמישי (רביעי לספ׳) אֲשֶׁר־שַׂמְתִּי בְמִצְרַיִם לֹא־אָשִׂים עָלֶיךָ כִּי אֲנִי יְהוָה
27 רֹפְאֶךָ׃ ס וַיָּבֹאוּ אֵילִמָה וְשָׁם שְׁתֵּים עֶשְׂרֵה עֵינֹת מַיִם
וְשִׁבְעִים תְּמָרִים וַיַּחֲנוּ־שָׁם עַל־הַמָּיִם׃

16

CHAPTER XVI

1. And they took their journey from Elim, and all the congregation of the children of Israel came unto the wilderness of Sin, which is between Elim and Sinai, on the fifteenth day of the second month after their departing out of the land of Egypt. 2. And the whole congregation of the children of Israel murmured against Moses

CAP. XVI. טז

טז

א וַיִּסְעוּ מֵאֵילִם וַיָּבֹאוּ כָּל־עֲדַת בְּנֵי־יִשְׂרָאֵל אֶל־מִדְבַּר־סִין
אֲשֶׁר בֵּין־אֵילִם וּבֵין סִינָי בַּחֲמִשָּׁה עָשָׂר יוֹם לַחֹדֶשׁ
2 הַשֵּׁנִי לְצֵאתָם מֵאֶרֶץ מִצְרָיִם׃ וַיִּלּוֹנוּ כָּל־עֲדַת בְּנֵי־יִשְׂרָאֵל

[1] That is, *Bitterness.*

טז׳ v. 2. וילונו ק׳

23. *Marah.* Has been identified by some with Bir Huwara, about 47 miles S.E. of Ayun Musa, and 7 miles from the coast, on the usual route to Mt. Sinai. Others identify Marah with 'Ain Naba' (also called el-Churkudeh) a fountain with a considerable supply of brackish water, about 10 miles S.E. of Suez, and 50 miles from Lake Timsah.

25. *the LORD showed him a tree.* There are certain shrubs that sweeten bitter water.

a statute and an ordinance. The moral and social basis of the Hebrew Law is here taught the people in connection with the sweetening of the bitter waters. God set before them the fundamental principle of implicit faith in His providence, to be shown by willing obedience to His will. The healing of the bitter waters was a symbol of the Divine deliverance from all evils.

there He proved them. Man is tried by the gifts of God, and also by the lack of them.

26. *diligently hearken.* At Marah the Israelites found themselves threatened with one of the plagues of Egypt, undrinkable water. God delivered them from this; and similarly, if they were obedient, He would protect them from the diseases which had afflicted the Egyptians.

that healeth thee. lit. 'thy physician'. 'A master demands obedience in order to assert his own authority. A physician likewise demands obedience, but only for the purpose of securing the patient's welfare. Such are the statutes of the Lord, our Physician' (Malbim).

27. *Elim.* lit. 'terebinths'. Often identified with Wady Gherandel which is situated two and a half miles north of Tor, in a very beautiful valley, with excellent fountains and many palm trees.

CHAPTER XVI, 1–36. THE MANNA

1. *the wilderness of Sin.* See on xv, 22.

fifteenth day of the second month. i.e. one month after the departure from Egypt.

2. *murmured.* The moment that the want of food was felt. The fact that these constant murmurings of the people are recorded is evidence for 'the historic truthfulness of the narratives of the wanderings. A purely ideal picture of the Chosen People would have omitted them. They also serve to display the wonderful personality of Moses, who could control, pacify, and lead such a collection of rude nomad tribes' (McNeile).

and against Aaron in the wilderness; 3. and the children of Israel said unto them: 'Would that we had died by the hand of the LORD in the land of Egypt, when we sat by the flesh-pots, when we did eat bread to the full; for ye have brought us forth into this wilderness, to kill this whole assembly with hunger.' ¶ 4. Then said the LORD unto Moses: 'Behold, I will cause to rain bread from heaven for you; and the people shall go out and gather a day's portion every day, that I may prove them, whether they will walk in My law or not. 5. And it shall come to pass on the sixth day that they shall prepare that which they bring in, and it shall be twice as much as they gather daily.' 6. And Moses and Aaron said unto all the children of Israel: 'At even, then ye shall know that the LORD hath brought you out from the land of Egypt; 7. and in the morning, then ye shall see the glory of the LORD; for that He hath heard your murmurings against the LORD; and what are we, that ye murmur against us?' 8. And Moses said: 'This shall be, when the LORD shall give you in the evening flesh to eat, and in the morning bread to the full; for that the LORD heareth your murmurings which ye murmur against Him; and what are we? your murmurings are not against us, but against the LORD.' 9. And Moses said unto Aaron: 'Say unto all the congregation of the children of Israel: Come near before the LORD; for He hath heard your murmurings.' 10. And it came to pass, as Aaron spoke unto the whole congregation of the children of Israel, that they looked toward the wilderness,

3 עַל־מֹשֶׁה וְעַל־אַהֲרֹן בַּמִּדְבָּר׃ וַיֹּאמְרוּ אֲלֵהֶם בְּנֵי יִשְׂרָאֵל
מִי־יִתֵּן מוּתֵנוּ בְיַד־יְהוָה בְּאֶרֶץ מִצְרַיִם בְּשִׁבְתֵּנוּ עַל־סִיר
הַבָּשָׂר בְּאָכְלֵנוּ לֶחֶם לָשֹׂבַע כִּי־הוֹצֵאתֶם אֹתָנוּ אֶל־
הַמִּדְבָּר הַזֶּה לְהָמִית אֶת־כָּל־הַקָּהָל הַזֶּה בָּרָעָב׃ ס
4 וַיֹּאמֶר יְהוָה אֶל־מֹשֶׁה הִנְנִי מַמְטִיר לָכֶם לֶחֶם מִן־הַשָּׁמָיִם
וְיָצָא הָעָם וְלָקְטוּ דְּבַר־יוֹם בְּיוֹמוֹ לְמַעַן אֲנַסֶּנּוּ הֲיֵלֵךְ
ה בְּתוֹרָתִי אִם־לֹא׃ וְהָיָה בַּיּוֹם הַשִּׁשִּׁי וְהֵכִינוּ אֵת אֲשֶׁר־
6 יָבִיאוּ וְהָיָה מִשְׁנֶה עַל אֲשֶׁר־יִלְקְטוּ יוֹם ׀ יוֹם׃ וַיֹּאמֶר
מֹשֶׁה וְאַהֲרֹן אֶל־כָּל־בְּנֵי יִשְׂרָאֵל עֶרֶב וִידַעְתֶּם כִּי יְהוָה
7 הוֹצִיא אֶתְכֶם מֵאֶרֶץ מִצְרָיִם׃ וּבֹקֶר וּרְאִיתֶם אֶת־כְּבוֹד
יְהוָה בְּשָׁמְעוֹ אֶת־תְּלֻנֹּתֵיכֶם עַל־יְהוָה וְנַחְנוּ מָה כִּי תַלּוֹנוּ
8 עָלֵינוּ׃ וַיֹּאמֶר מֹשֶׁה בְּתֵת יְהוָה לָכֶם בָּעֶרֶב בָּשָׂר לֶאֱכֹל
וְלֶחֶם בַּבֹּקֶר לִשְׂבֹּעַ בִּשְׁמֹעַ יְהוָה אֶת־תְּלֻנֹּתֵיכֶם אֲשֶׁר־
אַתֶּם מַלִּינִם עָלָיו וְנַחְנוּ מָה לֹא־עָלֵינוּ תְלֻנֹּתֵיכֶם כִּי עַל־
9 יְהוָה׃ וַיֹּאמֶר מֹשֶׁה אֶל־אַהֲרֹן אֱמֹר אֶל־כָּל־עֲדַת בְּנֵי
י יִשְׂרָאֵל קִרְבוּ לִפְנֵי יְהוָה כִּי שָׁמַע אֵת תְּלֻנֹּתֵיכֶם׃ וַיְהִי
כְּדַבֵּר אַהֲרֹן אֶל־כָּל־עֲדַת בְּנֵי־יִשְׂרָאֵל וַיִּפְנוּ אֶל־הַמִּדְבָּר

v. 7. תלינו ק׳

3. *sat by the flesh-pots.* They remembered the bread and the flesh-pots, but not the slavery. Some commentators infer from this that the Israelites in Egypt must have had a good and full diet. Such inference is quite unwarranted. The pangs of hunger cause them to look back upon their slave-fare, served to them from pots large enough to supply a whole gang, as the height of luxury.

4. *prove them.* The food that God will send will save them from hunger, but the manner in which it will be given will test their faith and obedience.

5. *the sixth day.* Of the week, *i.e.* Friday.

they shall prepare. As no cooking was to take place on the Sabbath.

twice as much. As the supply will be more abundant on the sixth day, so every one will gather more, and when they come to prepare it, they will find that it is just twice as much as they gather usually.

6. *the LORD hath brought you out.* And not Moses and Aaron, as you have falsely said; see *v.* 3.

at even. The gifts of the quails would take place; see *v.* 8.

7. *and in the morning.* They would have the bread from heaven.

see the glory of the LORD. Manifested by the wonderful gift of the manna (Rashi, Luzzatto).

murmurings against the LORD. Really against Moses and Aaron, but they were merely the servants of God.

8. *this shall be.* *i.e.* the fulfilment of the promise referred to in *v.* 6 and 7, is about to take place.

10. *toward the wilderness.* In the direction of the impending journey (Strack).

the glory of the LORD. Cf. XIII, 21 f. The Glory of God was 'a certain light', also called 'Divine light' (Maimonides). Perhaps the cloud shrouded the full brilliancy of the Divine Light.

and, behold, the glory of the LORD appeared in the cloud.* v s, vi a. 11. And the LORD spoke unto Moses, saying: 12. 'I have heard the murmurings of the children of Israel. Speak unto them, saying: At dusk ye shall eat flesh, and in the morning ye shall be filled with bread; and ye shall know that I am the LORD your God.' 13. And it came to pass at even, that the quails came up, and covered the camp; and in the morning there was a layer of dew round about the camp. 14. And when the layer of dew was gone up, behold upon the face of the wilderness a fine, scale-like thing, fine as the hoar-frost on the ground. 15. And when the children of Israel saw it, they said one to another: [1]'What is it?'—for they knew not what it was. And Moses said unto them: 'It is the bread which the LORD hath given you to eat. 16. This is the thing which the LORD hath commanded: Gather ye of it every man according to his eating; an omer a head, according to the number of your persons, shall ye take it, every man for them that are in his tent.' 17. And the children of Israel did so, and gathered some more, some less. 18. And when they did mete it with an omer, he that gathered much had nothing over, and he that gathered little had no lack; they gathered every man according to his eating. 19. And Moses said unto them: 'Let no man leave of it till the morning.' 20. Notwithstanding they

[1] Heb. *Man hu.*

וְהִנֵּה כְּבוֹד יְהוָה נִרְאָה בֶּעָנָן׃ פ ששי (חמישי לספ׳)
11 וַיְדַבֵּר יְהוָה אֶל־מֹשֶׁה לֵּאמֹר׃ 12 שָׁמַעְתִּי אֶת־תְּלוּנֹּת בְּנֵי
יִשְׂרָאֵל דַּבֵּר אֲלֵהֶם לֵאמֹר בֵּין הָעַרְבַּיִם תֹּאכְלוּ בָשָׂר
וּבַבֹּקֶר תִּשְׂבְּעוּ־לָחֶם וִידַעְתֶּם כִּי אֲנִי יְהוָה אֱלֹהֵיכֶם׃
13 וַיְהִי בָעֶרֶב וַתַּעַל הַשְּׂלָו וַתְּכַס אֶת־הַמַּחֲנֶה וּבַבֹּקֶר הָיְתָה
14 שִׁכְבַת הַטַּל סָבִיב לַמַּחֲנֶה׃ וַתַּעַל שִׁכְבַת הַטָּל וְהִנֵּה
עַל־פְּנֵי הַמִּדְבָּר דַּק מְחֻסְפָּס דַּק כַּכְּפֹר עַל־הָאָרֶץ׃
טו וַיִּרְאוּ בְנֵי־יִשְׂרָאֵל וַיֹּאמְרוּ אִישׁ אֶל־אָחִיו מָן הוּא כִּי לֹא
יָדְעוּ מַה־הוּא וַיֹּאמֶר מֹשֶׁה אֲלֵהֶם הוּא הַלֶּחֶם אֲשֶׁר נָתַן
16 יְהוָה לָכֶם לְאָכְלָה׃ זֶה הַדָּבָר אֲשֶׁר צִוָּה יְהוָה לִקְטוּ
מִמֶּנּוּ אִישׁ לְפִי אָכְלוֹ עֹמֶר לַגֻּלְגֹּלֶת מִסְפַּר נַפְשֹׁתֵיכֶם
17 אִישׁ לַאֲשֶׁר בְּאָהֳלוֹ תִּקָּחוּ׃ וַיַּעֲשׂוּ־כֵן בְּנֵי יִשְׂרָאֵל וַיִּלְקְטוּ
18 הַמַּרְבֶּה וְהַמַּמְעִיט׃ וַיָּמֹדּוּ בָעֹמֶר וְלֹא הֶעְדִּיף הַמַּרְבֶּה
19 וְהַמַּמְעִיט לֹא הֶחְסִיר אִישׁ לְפִי־אָכְלוֹ לָקָטוּ׃ וַיֹּאמֶר
כ מֹשֶׁה אֲלֵהֶם אִישׁ אַל־יוֹתֵר מִמֶּנּוּ עַד־בֹּקֶר׃ וְלֹא־שָׁמְעוּ

v. 12. דגש אחר ת״נ v. 13. השליו ק׳

12. *that I am the LORD your God.* Who not only hears your murmuring, but who can supply all your wants.

13. *the quails came up.* Quails are migratory birds, coming in the spring in immense numbers from Arabia and other southern countries. They are nowhere more common than in the neighbourhood of the Red Sea. They always fly with the wind; and when exhausted after a long flight, they are easily captured even with the hand. 'The gift of quails, unlike the gift of manna, was limited to the one occasion here mentioned' (Abarbanel).

in the morning. Following the night when the quails appeared.

14. *was gone up.* Had risen or evaporated.

a fine, scale-like thing. i.e. the manna. According to Rashi, and other Jewish commentators, first dew had fallen, then manna over the dew, and then dew again over the manna. Consequently the manna was enclosed between two layers of dew.

15. *what is it?* Or, 'It is manna' (RV Margin). The Heb. word *man* may really be Egyptian (Rashbam, Ebers); the translation would then be, 'They said one to another, It is *man*, for they knew not what it was'; *i.e.* they called it by the name of the substance that resembled it most in appearance, and was well known to them in Egypt. The Arabs give the name *man* to a sweet, sticky, honey-like juice, exuding in heavy drops, in May or June, from a shrub found in the Sinai peninsula. This, however, is found in only small quantities and does not correspond to the description given in our text, where the manna is clearly a miraculous substance. God in His ever-sustaining providence fed Israel's hosts during the weary years of wandering in His own unsearchable way.

the bread. The food.

16. *this is the thing.* The commandment concerning the manna.

an omer. A measure, less than two quarts.

18. *when they did mete it.* However much or little the individual gathered, when he measured it in his tent, he found that there was just an *omer* apiece for his family.

20. *Moses was wroth.* Because of their disobedience and lack of faith in God's loving providence.

hearkened not unto Moses; but some of them left of it until the morning, and it bred worms, and rotted; and Moses was wroth with them. 21. And they gathered it morning by morning, every man according to his eating; and as the sun waxed hot, it melted. 22. And it came to pass that on the sixth day they gathered twice as much bread, two omers for each one; and all the rulers of the congregation came and told Moses. 23. And he said unto them: 'This is that which the LORD hath spoken: To-morrow is a solemn rest, a holy sabbath unto the LORD. Bake that which ye will bake, and seethe that which ye will seethe; and all that remaineth over lay up for you to be kept until the morning.' 24. And they laid it up till the morning, as Moses bade; and it did not rot, neither was there any worm therein. 25. And Moses said: 'Eat that to-day; for to-day is a sabbath unto the LORD; to-day ye shall not find it in the field. 26. Six days ye shall gather it; but on the seventh day is the sabbath, in it there shall be none.' 27. And it came to pass on the seventh day, that there went out some of the people to gather, and they found none. 28. And the LORD said unto Moses: 'How long refuse ye to keep My commandments and My laws? 29. See that the LORD hath given you the sabbath; therefore He giveth you on the sixth day the bread of two days; abide ye every man in his place, let no man go out of his place on the seventh day.' 30. So the people rested on the seventh day.* vi s. 31. And the house of Israel called the name thereof [1]Manna; and it was like coriander seed, white; and the

[1] Heb. *Man*.

אֶל־מֹשֶׁה וַיּוֹתִרוּ אֲנָשִׁים מִמֶּנּוּ עַד־בֹּקֶר וַיָּרֻם תּוֹלָעִים
21 וַיִּבְאַשׁ וַיִּקְצֹף עֲלֵהֶם מֹשֶׁה׃ וַיִּלְקְטוּ אֹתוֹ בַּבֹּקֶר בַּבֹּקֶר אִישׁ
22 כְּפִי אָכְלוֹ וְחַם הַשֶּׁמֶשׁ וְנָמָס׃ וַיְהִי ׀ בַּיּוֹם הַשִּׁשִּׁי לָקְטוּ
לֶחֶם מִשְׁנֶה שְׁנֵי הָעֹמֶר לָאֶחָד וַיָּבֹאוּ כָּל־נְשִׂיאֵי הָעֵדָה
23 וַיַּגִּידוּ לְמֹשֶׁה׃ וַיֹּאמֶר אֲלֵהֶם הוּא אֲשֶׁר דִּבֶּר יְהוָה
שַׁבָּתוֹן שַׁבַּת־קֹדֶשׁ לַיהוָה מָחָר אֵת אֲשֶׁר־תֹּאפוּ אֵפוּ
וְאֵת אֲשֶׁר־תְּבַשְּׁלוּ בַּשֵּׁלוּ וְאֵת כָּל־הָעֹדֵף הַנִּיחוּ לָכֶם
24 לְמִשְׁמֶרֶת עַד־הַבֹּקֶר׃ וַיַּנִּיחוּ אֹתוֹ עַד־הַבֹּקֶר כַּאֲשֶׁר צִוָּה
כה מֹשֶׁה וְלֹא הִבְאִישׁ וְרִמָּה לֹא־הָיְתָה בּוֹ׃ וַיֹּאמֶר מֹשֶׁה
אִכְלֻהוּ הַיּוֹם כִּי־שַׁבָּת הַיּוֹם לַיהוָה הַיּוֹם לֹא תִמְצָאֻהוּ
26 בַּשָּׂדֶה׃ שֵׁשֶׁת יָמִים תִּלְקְטֻהוּ וּבַיּוֹם הַשְּׁבִיעִי שַׁבָּת לֹא
27 יִהְיֶה־בּוֹ׃ וַיְהִי בַּיּוֹם הַשְּׁבִיעִי יָצְאוּ מִן־הָעָם לִלְקֹט וְלֹא
28 מָצָאוּ׃ ס וַיֹּאמֶר יְהוָה אֶל־מֹשֶׁה עַד־אָנָה מֵאַנְתֶּם
29 לִשְׁמֹר מִצְוֹתַי וְתוֹרֹתָי׃ רְאוּ כִּי־יְהוָה נָתַן לָכֶם הַשַּׁבָּת
עַל־כֵּן הוּא נֹתֵן לָכֶם בַּיּוֹם הַשִּׁשִּׁי לֶחֶם יוֹמָיִם שְׁבוּ ׀ אִישׁ
(ששי) ל תַּחְתָּיו אַל־יֵצֵא אִישׁ מִמְּקֹמוֹ בַּיּוֹם הַשְּׁבִיעִי׃ וַיִּשְׁבְּתוּ הָעָם
(לספ׳) 31 בַּיּוֹם הַשְּׁבִעִי׃ * וַיִּקְרְאוּ בֵית־יִשְׂרָאֵל אֶת־שְׁמוֹ מָן וְהוּא

v. 20. פתח באתנח

23. *the LORD hath spoken.* With reference to the Sabbath.

holy sabbath unto the LORD. The seventh day must have been known to the people as a special day, distinct from the other days of the week. The children of the Patriarchs had brought with them to Egypt the tradition that God had completed His work of creation in six days, and that He had sanctified the seventh day. At Mt. Sinai, therefore, the children of Israel are bidden, '*Remember* the Sabbath day.'

bake that which ye will bake. On the Friday. What was not eaten on the Friday was to be kept for the Sabbath day.

27. *there went out some of the people.* Not because they were lacking food, for they had gathered a double portion on the previous day; but because they doubted the word of Moses.

28. *how long refuse ye.* The rebuke is addressed to Moses as the representative of the people.

29. *abide ye. i.e.* do not go out in order to gather manna.

go out of his place. To gather manna on the Sabbath. Rabbinical tradition has deduced from this context the prohibition, that no Israelite shall go more than 2,000 yards from the place of his abode. This is called the תחום שבת 'the Sabbath journey'. Travelling interrupts the rest both of man and his beast, and was therefore to be avoided on the Sabbath day.

31. *house of Israel.* An unusual expression for, 'the children of Israel'; see XI, 38; Num. XX, 29.

like coriander seed, white. The coriander plant grows wild in Palestine and Egypt, producing small greyish-white seeds, with a pleasant spicy flavour.

wafers made with honey. Cf. Num. XI, 8, 'the taste of it was as the taste of cake baked with oil.' Jewish tradition says that the manna contained the ingredients of every delicious food, and suited the taste of all who partook thereof.

32–36. Various commands relating to the manna.

taste of it was like wafers made with honey. 32. And Moses said: 'This is the thing which the LORD hath commanded: Let an omerful of it be kept throughout your generations; that they may see the bread wherewith I fed you in the wilderness, when I brought you forth from the land of Egypt.' 33. And Moses said unto Aaron: 'Take a jar, and put an omerful of manna therein, and lay it up before the LORD, to be kept throughout your generations.' 34. As the LORD commanded Moses, so Aaron laid it up before the Testimony, to be kept. 35. And the children of Israel did eat the manna forty years, until they came to a land inhabited; they did eat the manna, until they came unto the borders of the land of Canaan. 36. Now an omer is the tenth part of an ephah.* vii.

17

CHAPTER XVII

1. And all the congregation of the children of Israel journeyed from the wilderness of Sin, by their stages, according to the commandment of the LORD, and encamped in Rephidim; and there was no water for the people to drink. 2. Wherefore the people strove with Moses, and said: 'Give us water

32 כְּזֶרַע גַּד לָבָן וְטַעְמוֹ כְּצַפִּיחִת בִּדְבָשׁ׃ וַיֹּאמֶר מֹשֶׁה זֶה
הַדָּבָר אֲשֶׁר צִוָּה יְהֹוָה מְלֹא הָעֹמֶר מִמֶּנּוּ לְמִשְׁמֶרֶת
לְדֹרֹתֵיכֶם לְמַעַן ׀ יִרְאוּ אֶת־הַלֶּחֶם אֲשֶׁר הֶאֱכַלְתִּי אֶתְכֶם
33 בַּמִּדְבָּר בְּהוֹצִיאִי אֶתְכֶם מֵאֶרֶץ מִצְרָיִם׃ וַיֹּאמֶר מֹשֶׁה אֶל־
אַהֲרֹן קַח צִנְצֶנֶת אַחַת וְתֶן־שָׁמָּה מְלֹא־הָעֹמֶר מָן וְהַנַּח
34 אֹתוֹ לִפְנֵי יְהֹוָה לְמִשְׁמֶרֶת לְדֹרֹתֵיכֶם׃ כַּאֲשֶׁר צִוָּה יְהֹוָה
לה אֶל־מֹשֶׁה וַיַּנִּיחֵהוּ אַהֲרֹן לִפְנֵי הָעֵדֻת לְמִשְׁמָרֶת׃ וּבְנֵי יִשְׂרָאֵל
אָכְלוּ אֶת־הַמָּן אַרְבָּעִים שָׁנָה עַד־בֹּאָם אֶל־אֶרֶץ נוֹשָׁבֶת
36 אֶת־הַמָּן אָכְלוּ עַד־בֹּאָם אֶל־קְצֵה אֶרֶץ כְּנָעַן׃ וְהָעֹמֶר
עֲשִׂרִית הָאֵיפָה הוּא׃ פ שביעי

CAP. XVII. יז

יז
א וַיִּסְעוּ כָּל־עֲדַת בְּנֵי־יִשְׂרָאֵל מִמִּדְבַּר־סִין לְמַסְעֵיהֶם עַל־
2 פִּי יְהֹוָה וַיַּחֲנוּ בִּרְפִידִים וְאֵין מַיִם לִשְׁתֹּת הָעָם׃ וַיָּרֶב

32. *throughout your generations.* i.e. for posterity.

they may see the bread. And derive the spiritual lessons connected therewith; *e.g.* trust in God, belief in the providence and mercy of God.

33. *take a jar.* Of earthenware (Rashi).

lay it up before the LORD. i.e. before the Ark of the Testimony, in the Tabernacle. Ibn Ezra says that this section should come after the story of the erection of the Tabernacle; and Luzzatto suggests that Moses wrote *v.* 33–35 in the fortieth year of the wandering in the wilderness. It is well to keep in mind the Rabbinical saying, that the events in Scripture are not always arranged in strict chronological order. אין מוקדם ומאוחר בתורה. Sometimes an *inner connection* causes events wide apart in time to be mentioned together in one chapter.

34. *the Testimony.* i.e. the Ark, so called because of the Tables on which the Ten Commandments (spoken of as 'the Testimony' in XXV, 22, XXXI, 18) were engraved.

35. *forty years.* This does not lead the narrative beyond the time of Moses, and there is no reason why Moses could not have written it just before his death.

to a land inhabited. Canaan, so called in contrast to the desert.

unto the borders of the land of Canaan. This was the limit of the wanderings under the leadership of Moses. Moses gives the complete history of the manna up to the end of his own life. He does not state that the manna ceased; because the manna was not withheld until after the death of Moses, when the Israelites had passed the Jordan under Joshua (Josh. v, 12).

36. *an ephah.* The name of a measure well known to the people, whereas the name *omer* was not known (Abarbanel). This seems to be supported by the fact that the Torah does not employ the name *omer* as a measure anywhere outside this chapter.

CHAPTER XVII

1–7. WATER FROM THE ROCK IN HOREB

1. *by their stages.* Or, 'journeys.' The route was as follows: the wilderness of Sin, Dophkah, Alush, Rephidim: see Num. XXXIII, 14. The various stages are omitted, as it is not the intention of Scripture here to enumerate the different places where the Israelites halted. Its purpose is to narrate the occasions when the people murmured (Biur).

Rephidim. Either the upper part of the broad and long oasis of Feiran, the most fertile part of the Peninsula of Sinai, or the narrow defile el-Watiyeh, 27 miles beyond Feiran.

2. *give us water.* The Heb. for 'give' is in the plural, and refers to Moses and Aaron.

try the LORD. Heb. *nissah* means to *test* or *prove* a person, to see *whether* he will act in a particular way, or *whether* the character he bears is well established (Driver).

that we may drink.' And Moses said unto them: 'Why strive ye with me? wherefore do ye try the LORD?' 3. And the people thirsted there for water; and the people murmured against Moses, and said: 'Wherefore hast thou brought us up out of Egypt, to kill us and our children and our cattle with thirst?' 4. And Moses cried unto the LORD, saying: 'What shall I do unto this people? they are almost ready to stone me.' 5. And the LORD said unto Moses: 'Pass on before the people, and take with thee of the elders of Israel; and thy rod, wherewith thou smotest the river, take in thy hand, and go. 6. Behold, I will stand before thee there upon the rock in Horeb; and thou shalt smite the rock, and there shall come water out of it, that the people may drink.' And Moses did so in the sight of the elders of Israel. 7. And the name of the place was called [1]Massah, and [2]Meribah, because of the striving of the children of Israel, and because they tried the LORD, saying: 'Is the LORD among us, or not?' ¶ 8. Then came Amalek, and fought

הָעָם עִם־מֹשֶׁה וַיֹּאמְרוּ תְּנוּ־לָנוּ מַיִם וְנִשְׁתֶּה וַיֹּאמֶר לָהֶם
3 מֹשֶׁה מַה־תְּרִיבוּן עִמָּדִי מַה־תְּנַסּוּן אֶת־יְהוָה׃ וַיִּצְמָא שָׁם
הָעָם לַמַּיִם וַיָּלֶן הָעָם עַל־מֹשֶׁה וַיֹּאמֶר לָמָּה זֶּה הֶעֱלִיתָנוּ
4 מִמִּצְרַיִם לְהָמִית אֹתִי וְאֶת־בָּנַי וְאֶת־מִקְנַי בַּצָּמָא׃ וַיִּצְעַק
מֹשֶׁה אֶל־יְהוָה לֵאמֹר מָה אֶעֱשֶׂה לָעָם הַזֶּה עוֹד מְעַט
ה וּסְקָלֻנִי׃ וַיֹּאמֶר יְהוָה אֶל־מֹשֶׁה עֲבֹר לִפְנֵי הָעָם וְקַח
אִתְּךָ מִזִּקְנֵי יִשְׂרָאֵל וּמַטְּךָ אֲשֶׁר הִכִּיתָ בּוֹ אֶת־הַיְאֹר קַח
6 בְּיָדְךָ וְהָלָכְתָּ׃ הִנְנִי עֹמֵד לְפָנֶיךָ שָּׁם ׀ עַל־הַצּוּר בְּחֹרֵב
וְהִכִּיתָ בַצּוּר וְיָצְאוּ מִמֶּנּוּ מַיִם וְשָׁתָה הָעָם וַיַּעַשׂ כֵּן מֹשֶׁה
7 לְעֵינֵי זִקְנֵי יִשְׂרָאֵל׃ וַיִּקְרָא שֵׁם הַמָּקוֹם מַסָּה וּמְרִיבָה
עַל־רִיב ׀ בְּנֵי יִשְׂרָאֵל וְעַל נַסֹּתָם אֶת־יְהוָה לֵאמֹר הֲיֵשׁ
יְהוָה בְּקִרְבֵּנוּ אִם־אָיִן׃ פ

[1] That is, *Trying*. [2] That is, *Strife*.

3. *to kill us . . . with thirst.* lit. 'to kill me and my sons and my cattle with thirst', as if each one had cried out separately. The reaction from the mood of exultation at the Red Sea is complete. 'It is the nature of man,' says Macaulay, 'to overrate present evil. A hundred generations have passed away since the first great national emancipation of which an account has come down to us. We read in the most ancient of books that a people bowed to the dust under a cruel yoke, scourged to toil by hard taskmasters, not supplied with straw, yet compelled to furnish the daily tale of bricks, became sick of life, and raised such a cry of misery as pierced the heavens. The slaves were wonderfully set free; at the moment of their liberation they raised a song of gratitude and triumph; but in a few hours they began to regret their slavery, and to reproach the leader who had decoyed them away from the savoury fare of the house of bondage to the dreary waste which still separated them from the land flowing with milk and honey. Since that time the history of every great deliverer has been the history of Moses retold. Down to the present hour, rejoicings like those on the shore of the Red Sea have ever been speedily followed by murmurings like those at the Waters of Strife.'

4. *what shall I do unto this people?* To save them from despair and sin.

5. *take with thee of the elders.* To witness the wonder that was to be done. They were the people's representatives.

thy rod. The rod which could make the waters of the Nile undrinkable for the Egyptians (VII, 17), could produce water to satisfy the thirst of the Israelites. Although Aaron performed the symbolic action preceding the first plague, it is attributed to Moses, and therefore termed his rod. Aaron acted on his behalf.

and go. To the rock in Horeb.

6. *I will stand before thee.* I will be present with My omnipotence (Dillmann).

upon the rock in Horeb. The rock known to Moses, where he had already seen the Glory of God (Abarbanel).

that the people may drink. The people were at Rephidim, some distance away from Horeb. The water from the rock flowed down to them.

7. *Meribah.* There they had murmured against Moses; see Ps. XCV, 8.

tried the LORD. Better, '*put the* LORD *to the proof*' (Driver).

is the LORD *among us, or not? i.e.* can He help us in our need or not?

8–16. THE BATTLE WITH THE AMALEKITES

The Amalekites were a predatory tribe, who are spoken of as having their home in the desert of Palestine. At the same time, a nomad tribe is quite capable of raids at a distance from its usual home (*e.g.* it was with some difficulty that the Transjordan Arabs were prevented from taking part in the loot and murder of Palestine Jews in August, 1929); or, the Amalekites may in the summer months have led their flocks up into the cooler and fresher pastures in the mountains of the Sinai Peninsula.

with Israel in Rephidim. 9. And Moses said unto Joshua: 'Choose us out men, and go out, fight with Amalek; to-morrow I will stand on the top of the hill with the rod of God in my hand.' 10. So Joshua did as Moses had said to him, and fought with Amalek; and Moses, Aaron, and Hur went up to the top of the hill. 11. And it came to pass, when Moses held up his hand, that Israel prevailed; and when he let down his hand, Amalek prevailed. 12. But Moses' hands were heavy; and they took a stone, and put it under him, and he sat thereon; and Aaron and Hur stayed up his hands, the one on the one side, and the other on the other side; and his hands were steady until the going down of the sun. 13. And Joshua discomfited Amalek and his people with the edge of the sword.*m. ¶ 14. And the LORD said unto Moses: 'Write this for a memorial in the book, and rehearse it in the ears of Joshua: for I will utterly blot out the remembrance of Amalek from under heaven.' 15. And Moses built an altar, and

8 9 וַיָּבֹא עֲמָלֵק וַיִּלָּחֶם עִם־יִשְׂרָאֵל בִּרְפִידִם׃ וַיֹּאמֶר מֹשֶׁה
אֶל־יְהוֹשֻׁעַ בְּחַר־לָנוּ אֲנָשִׁים וְצֵא הִלָּחֵם בַּעֲמָלֵק מָחָר
אָנֹכִי נִצָּב עַל־רֹאשׁ הַגִּבְעָה וּמַטֵּה הָאֱלֹהִים בְּיָדִי׃ וַיַּעַשׂ
יְהוֹשֻׁעַ כַּאֲשֶׁר אָמַר־לוֹ מֹשֶׁה לְהִלָּחֵם בַּעֲמָלֵק וּמֹשֶׁה
11 אַהֲרֹן וְחוּר עָלוּ רֹאשׁ הַגִּבְעָה׃ וְהָיָה כַּאֲשֶׁר יָרִים מֹשֶׁה
12 יָדוֹ וְגָבַר יִשְׂרָאֵל וְכַאֲשֶׁר יָנִיחַ יָדוֹ וְגָבַר עֲמָלֵק׃ וִידֵי
מֹשֶׁה כְּבֵדִים וַיִּקְחוּ־אֶבֶן וַיָּשִׂימוּ תַחְתָּיו וַיֵּשֶׁב עָלֶיהָ וְאַהֲרֹן
וְחוּר תָּמְכוּ בְיָדָיו מִזֶּה אֶחָד וּמִזֶּה אֶחָד וַיְהִי יָדָיו אֱמוּנָה
13 עַד־בֹּא הַשָּׁמֶשׁ׃ וַיַּחֲלֹשׁ יְהוֹשֻׁעַ אֶת־עֲמָלֵק וְאֶת־עַמּוֹ
לְפִי־חָרֶב׃ * פ מפטיר
14 וַיֹּאמֶר יְהוָה אֶל־מֹשֶׁה כְּתֹב זֹאת זִכָּרוֹן בַּסֵּפֶר וְשִׂים בְּאָזְנֵי
יְהוֹשֻׁעַ כִּי־מָחֹה אֶמְחֶה אֶת־זֵכֶר עֲמָלֵק מִתַּחַת הַשָּׁמָיִם׃

8. *then came Amalek.* As an immediate sequence of the murmuring on the part of the Israelites, say the Rabbis. It is the invariable lesson of Jewish history that whenever Israel begins to doubt God and Israel, asking, *Is the LORD among us or not?* that an Amalek unexpectedly assails it.

fought with Israel. Deut. xxv, 18 records that Amalek cut off, at the rear of Israel, all that were feeble and weary.

9. *Joshua.* His name was originally Hoshea (Num. XIII, 8). This is the first mention of the great captain and successor of Moses. By anticipation, he is here called by his latter name.

to-morrow. When the battle is waged.

with the rod of God. The victory over their enemies was to be attributed altogether to God.

10. *Hur.* The son of Miriam and Caleb (Talmud).

11. *Moses held up his hand.* The Talmud remarks, 'Can the hands of Moses really cause victory, if they are raised; or defeat, if they are lowered? Scripture teaches here, that, when the Israelites looked up to God, and humbled themselves before their Father in Heaven, they were victorious; when they did not, they were defeated.' Some commentators explain that Moses raised his staff like a banner. When the Israelites saw this banner, they were courageous and victorious; when they did not see it, they were despondent and fled; and, therefore, the place was called Adonai-nissi, *i.e.* 'The LORD is my banner' (*v.* 15).

12. *heavy.* With weariness, after the exertion of holding them up a long time.

they took. i.e. Aaron and Hur.

a stone. 'Could they not have given him a chair or a cushion? But he said, Since the Israelites are in trouble, lo, I will bear my part with them; for he who bears his share in the troubles of Israel, will live to enjoy the hour of consolation' (Talmud).

Aaron and Hur stayed up his hands. This is another trait which no legend would have created for the first martial exploit of Israel. Moses plays but a secondary part; and even as intercessor his arms have to be held up! Everything is as prosaic as the *real course of events* in this poor world is wont to be (Chadwick).

steady. Heb. *emunah*; lit. steadiness, steadfastness, faithfulness, faith.

until the going down of the sun. It was no mere raid, but a fierce battle.

13. *discomfited.* lit. 'weakened'.

Amalek and his people. Heb. idiom for, 'the people of the Amalekites.'

14. *write this.* The attack of the Amalekites.

in the book. In the Torah, the Book written by Moses; cf. XXIV, 4, 7, and XXXIV, 27.

rehearse it in the ears of. i.e. impress it upon.

Joshua. Who would have to fight the kings of Canaan, and was destined to lead the Israelites into the Holy Land.

I will utterly blot out. On account of the unprovoked and inhuman attack on the people of God; see Deut. XXV, 17 f.

15. *built an altar.* On Horeb.

Adonai-nissi. God had again saved His people. He is Israel's victorious Banner.

called the name of it [1]Adonai-nissi. 16. And he said: 'The hand upon the throne of the LORD: the LORD will have war with Amalek from generation to generation.'

טו וַיִּבֶן מֹשֶׁה מִזְבֵּחַ וַיִּקְרָא שְׁמוֹ יְהוָה ׀ נִסִּי׃ וַיֹּאמֶר כִּי־יָד עַל־
16 כֵּס יָהּ מִלְחָמָה לַיהוָה בַּעֲמָלֵק מִדֹּר דֹּר׃

[1] That is, *The LORD is my banner*.

16. *the hand upon the throne of the LORD. i.e.* the hand of Amalek was against Israel, the host of God. The text is difficult, and can also be translated, 'The LORD hath sworn, the LORD will have war with Amalek from generation to generation' (Onkelos, Rashi, Ibn Ezra, Luzzatto, RV Text).

war with Amalek. See I Sam. xv, 2 f; Deut. **xxv,** 17–19. 'As Amalek was the first to attack Israel with the sword, Israel was commanded to blot out his name by means of the sword' (Maimonides). Amalek has disappeared from under heaven, but his spirit still walks the earth. In the battle of the LORD against the Amalekites in the realm of the Spirit, the only successful weapons are courage and conviction, truth and righteousness.

HAFTORAH BESHALLACH הפטרת בשלח

JUDGES IV, 4–V, 31

CHAPTER IV

CAP. IV. ד

4. Now Deborah, a prophetess, the wife of Lappidoth, she judged Israel at that time. 5. And she sat under the palm-tree of Deborah between Ramah and Beth-el in the hill-country of Ephraim; and the children of Israel came up to her for judgment. 6. And she sent and called Barak the son of Abinoam out of Kedesh-naphtali,

4 וּדְבוֹרָה* אִשָּׁה נְבִיאָה אֵשֶׁת לַפִּידוֹת הִיא שֹׁפְטָה אֶת־
ה יִשְׂרָאֵל בָּעֵת הַהִיא׃ וְהִיא יוֹשֶׁבֶת תַּחַת־תֹּמֶר דְּבוֹרָה
בֵּין הָרָמָה וּבֵין בֵּית־אֵל בְּהַר אֶפְרָיִם וַיַּעֲלוּ אֵלֶיהָ בְּנֵי
6 יִשְׂרָאֵל לַמִּשְׁפָּט׃ וַתִּשְׁלַח וַתִּקְרָא לְבָרָק בֶּן־אֲבִינֹעַם

v. 4. יש מתחילין ותשר דבורה

In both Sedrah and Haftorah we have the story of a deliverance from oppression celebrated in a Song of triumph and praise.

These chapters of the Book of Judges take us back to an early period in Israel's history, the days after the death of Joshua, when the tribes were compelled to wage a hard and often desperate struggle against the remaining warlike Canaanites. It was a barbaric period, without national unity and devoid of religious authority. 'In those days there was no king of Israel: every man did that which was right in his own eyes.' But God does not utterly forsake His people. An overwhelming national calamity, or foreign oppression, would bring forth a Champion, who would repel or destroy the foe, or rescue the people from the threatened calamity. Such Champions, known as *Shofetim* ('Judges'), were Gideon, Jephthah, Samson, and the most remarkable of all, Deborah. The story of her achievement has come down to us in two versions, in prose and in verse. From them we can reconstruct the mortal danger from which her victory saved Israel. That victory was one of the 'decisive battles' of the world. It settled the destiny of Palestine, and a great many other things, for all time. Moreover, under the inspiration of Deborah's lofty patriotism, most of the tribes for the first time combined in face of a common danger. Those wild years forged the bonds of a nationality that has survived unprecedented shocks throughout the ages.

4. *prophetess.* Although she did not foretell the future she is described as a prophetess, because she was inspired to grapple with the great difficulties of the hour (Kimchi).

5. *sat.* To decide disputes brought to her for judgment.

6. *Kedesh-naphtali.* About four miles from the north end of the 'waters of Merom'.

mount Tabor. The conical shaped hill commanding the Plain of Esdraelon. The Plain runs like a wedge from the coast to within 10 miles of the Jordan, and is dominated by hills on all sides. It is to-day known as 'the Emek'.

of Naphtali . . . Zebulun. These two tribes bordering on the Plain suffered most under the oppression of the heathens.

and said unto him: 'Hath not the LORD, the God of Israel, commanded, saying: Go and draw toward mount Tabor, and take with thee ten thousand men of the children of Naphtali and of the children of Zebulun? 7. And I will draw unto thee to the brook Kishon Sisera, the captain of Jabin's army, with his chariots and his multitude; and I will deliver him into thy hand.' 8. And Barak said unto her: 'If thou wilt go with me, then I will go; but if thou wilt not go with me, I will not go.' 9. And she said: 'I will surely go with thee; notwithstanding the journey that thou takest shall not be for thy honour; for the LORD will give Sisera over into the hand of a woman.' And Deborah arose, and went with Barak to Kedesh. 10. And Barak called Zebulun and Naphtali together to Kedesh; and there went up ten thousand men at his feet; and Deborah went up with him. ¶ 11. Now Heber the Kenite had severed himself from the Kenites, even from the children of Hobab the father-in-law of Moses, and had pitched his tent as far as Elon-bezaanannim, which is by Kedesh. ¶ 12. And they told Sisera that Barak the son of Abinoam was gone up to mount Tabor. 13. And Sisera gathered together all his chariots, even nine hundred chariots of iron, and all the people that were with him, from Harosheth-goiim, unto the brook Kishon. 14. And Deborah said unto Barak: 'Up; for this is the day in which the LORD hath delivered Sisera into thy hand; is not the LORD gone out before thee?' So Barak went down from mount Tabor, and ten thousand men after him. 15. And the LORD discomfited Sisera, and all his chariots, and all his host, with the edge of the sword before Barak; and Sisera alighted from his chariot, and fled away on his feet. 16. But Barak pursued after the chariots, and after the host, unto Harosheth-goiim; and all the host of Sisera fell by the edge of the

מִקֶּדֶשׁ נַפְתָּלִי וַתֹּאמֶר אֵלָיו הֲלֹא־צִוָּה ׀ יְהוָה אֱלֹהֵי־
יִשְׂרָאֵל לֵךְ וּמָשַׁכְתָּ בְּהַר תָּבוֹר וְלָקַחְתָּ עִמְּךָ עֲשֶׂרֶת
7 אֲלָפִים אִישׁ מִבְּנֵי נַפְתָּלִי וּמִבְּנֵי זְבֻלוּן׃ וּמָשַׁכְתִּי אֵלֶיךָ
אֶל־נַחַל קִישׁוֹן אֶת־סִיסְרָא שַׂר־צְבָא יָבִין וְאֶת־רִכְבּוֹ
8 וְאֶת־הֲמוֹנוֹ וּנְתַתִּיהוּ בְּיָדֶךָ׃ וַיֹּאמֶר אֵלֶיהָ בָּרָק אִם־תֵּלְכִי
9 עִמִּי וְהָלָכְתִּי וְאִם־לֹא תֵלְכִי עִמִּי לֹא אֵלֵךְ׃ וַתֹּאמֶר הָלֹךְ
אֵלֵךְ עִמָּךְ אֶפֶס כִּי לֹא תִהְיֶה תִּפְאַרְתְּךָ עַל־הַדֶּרֶךְ אֲשֶׁר־
אַתָּה הוֹלֵךְ כִּי בְיַד אִשָּׁה יִמְכֹּר יְהוָה אֶת־סִיסְרָא וַתָּקָם
י דְּבוֹרָה וַתֵּלֶךְ עִם־בָּרָק קֶדְשָׁה׃ וַיַּזְעֵק בָּרָק אֶת־זְבוּלֻן
וְאֶת־נַפְתָּלִי קֶדְשָׁה וַיַּעַל בְּרַגְלָיו עֲשֶׂרֶת אַלְפֵי אִישׁ וַתַּעַל
11 עִמּוֹ דְּבוֹרָה׃ וְחֶבֶר הַקֵּינִי נִפְרָד מִקַּיִן מִבְּנֵי חֹבָב חֹתֵן
12 מֹשֶׁה וַיֵּט אָהֳלוֹ עַד־אֵלוֹן בְּצַעֲנַּיִם אֲשֶׁר אֶת־קֶדֶשׁ׃ וַיַּגִּדוּ
13 לְסִיסְרָא כִּי עָלָה בָּרָק בֶּן־אֲבִינֹעַם הַר־תָּבוֹר׃ וַיַּזְעֵק
סִיסְרָא אֶת־כָּל־רִכְבּוֹ תְּשַׁע מֵאוֹת רֶכֶב בַּרְזֶל וְאֶת־כָּל־
14 הָעָם אֲשֶׁר אִתּוֹ מֵחֲרֹשֶׁת הַגּוֹיִם אֶל־נַחַל קִישׁוֹן׃ וַתֹּאמֶר
דְּבֹרָה אֶל־בָּרָק קוּם כִּי זֶה הַיּוֹם אֲשֶׁר נָתַן יְהוָה אֶת־
סִיסְרָא בְּיָדֶךָ הֲלֹא יְהוָה יָצָא לְפָנֶיךָ וַיֵּרֶד בָּרָק מֵהַר
טו תָּבוֹר וַעֲשֶׂרֶת אֲלָפִים אִישׁ אַחֲרָיו׃ וַיָּהָם יְהוָה אֶת־
סִיסְרָא וְאֶת־כָּל־הָרֶכֶב וְאֶת־כָּל־הַמַּחֲנֶה לְפִי־חֶרֶב לִפְנֵי
16 בָרָק וַיֵּרֶד סִיסְרָא מֵעַל הַמֶּרְכָּבָה וַיָּנָס בְּרַגְלָיו׃ וּבָרָק
רָדַף אַחֲרֵי הָרֶכֶב וְאַחֲרֵי הַמַּחֲנֶה עַד חֲרֹשֶׁת הַגּוֹיִם וַיִּפֹּל

v. 11. הר׳ בקמץ ibid. בצעננים קרי

7. *Jabin.* The king of Canaan who oppressed Israel. He had 900 chariots of iron; and against these 'armoured cars', the Israelite peasants were powerless.

8. *if thou wilt go with me.* Indicates the remarkable confidence that Deborah's wisdom and work had inspired.

9. *for thy honour.* The word *thy* is emphatic: the chief glory of the victory shall not be his. *give.* Deliver.

10. *went up. i.e.* to Mount Tabor.

11. *the Kenites.* A nomadic tribe in close league with Israel; see Num. XXIV, 22. Heber had branched off from the main clan, in Southern Palestine, and wandered as far north as Kedesh. This information is necessary for the understanding of *v.* 17.

13. *Harosheth-goiim.* Near Megiddo.
Kishon. The river rises in the S.E. of the Plain of Esdraelon, and flows through it into the sea of Haifa. It is the second river of Palestine.

14. *went down.* From Mt. Tabor; the Israelites dashed down, and drove the Canaanites back upon the banks of the river Kishon. Its overflowing waters swollen by a rain-storm, had turned the Plain into a morass, rendering any use of the chariots impossible.

15. *discomfited.* Confused, threw into a panic; cf. the Sedrah, XIV, 24.

sword; there was not a man left. ¶ 17. Howbeit Sisera fled away on his feet to the tent of Jael the wife of Heber the Kenite; for there was peace between Jabin the king of Hazor and the house of Heber the Kenite. 18. And Jael went out to meet Sisera, and said unto him: 'Turn in, my lord, turn in to me; fear not.' And he turned in unto her into the tent, and she covered him with a rug. 19. And he said unto her: 'Give me, I pray thee, a little water to drink; for I am thirsty.' And she opened a bottle of milk, and gave him drink, and covered him. 20. And he said unto her: 'Stand in the door of the tent, and it shall be, when any man doth come and inquire of thee, and say: Is there any man here? that thou shalt say: No.' 21. Then Jael Heber's wife took a tent-pin, and took a hammer in her hand, and went softly unto him, and smote the pin into his temples, and it pierced through into the ground; for he was in a deep sleep; so he swooned and died. 22. And, behold, as Barak pursued Sisera, Jael came out to meet him, and said unto him: 'Come, and I will show thee the man whom thou seekest.' And he came unto her; and, behold, Sisera lay dead, and the tent-pin was in his temples. 23. So God subdued on that day Jabin the king of Canaan before the children of Israel. 24. And the hand of the children of Israel prevailed more and more against Jabin the king of Canaan, until they had destroyed Jabin king of Canaan.

17 כָּל־מַחֲנֵה סִֽיסְרָא לְפִי־חֶרֶב לֹא נִשְׁאַר עַד־אֶחָֽד׃ וְסִֽיסְרָא
נָס בְּרַגְלָיו אֶל־אֹהֶל יָעֵל אֵשֶׁת חֶבֶר הַקֵּינִי כִּי שָׁלוֹם בֵּין
18 יָבִין מֶלֶךְ־חָצוֹר וּבֵין בֵּית חֶבֶר הַקֵּינִֽי׃ וַתֵּצֵא יָעֵל לִקְרַאת
סִֽיסְרָא וַתֹּאמֶר אֵלָיו סוּרָה אֲדֹנִי סוּרָה אֵלַי אַל־תִּירָא
19 וַיָּסַר אֵלֶיהָ הָאֹהֱלָה וַתְּכַסֵּהוּ בַּשְּׂמִיכָֽה׃ וַיֹּאמֶר אֵלֶיהָ
הַשְׁקִֽינִי־נָא מְעַט־מַיִם כִּי צָמֵאתִי וַתִּפְתַּח אֶת־נֹאוד הֶחָלָב
כ וַתַּשְׁקֵהוּ וַתְּכַסֵּֽהוּ׃ וַיֹּאמֶר אֵלֶיהָ עֲמֹד פֶּתַח הָאֹהֶל וְהָיָה
אִם־אִישׁ יָבֹא וּשְׁאֵלֵךְ וְאָמַר הֲיֵשׁ־פֹּה אִישׁ וְאָמַרְתְּ אָֽיִן׃
21 וַתִּקַּח יָעֵל אֵֽשֶׁת־חֶבֶר אֶת־יְתַד הָאֹהֶל וַתָּשֶׂם אֶת־הַמַּקֶּבֶת
בְּיָדָהּ וַתָּבוֹא אֵלָיו בַּלָּאט וַתִּתְקַע אֶת־הַיָּתֵד בְּרַקָּתוֹ
22 וַתִּצְנַח בָּאָרֶץ וְהֽוּא־נִרְדָּם וַיָּעַף וַיָּמֹֽת׃ וְהִנֵּה בָרָק רֹדֵף
אֶת־סִֽיסְרָא וַתֵּצֵא יָעֵל לִקְרָאתוֹ וַתֹּאמֶר לוֹ לֵךְ וְאַרְאֶךָּ
אֶת־הָאִישׁ אֲשֶׁר־אַתָּה מְבַקֵּשׁ וַיָּבֹא אֵלֶיהָ וְהִנֵּה סִֽיסְרָא
23 נֹפֵל מֵת וְהַיָּתֵד בְּרַקָּתֽוֹ׃ וַיַּכְנַע אֱלֹהִים בַּיּוֹם הַהוּא אֵת
24 יָבִין מֶלֶךְ־כְּנָעַן לִפְנֵי בְּנֵי יִשְׂרָאֵֽל׃ וַתֵּלֶךְ יַד בְּנֵֽי־יִשְׂרָאֵל
הָלוֹךְ וְקָשָׁה עַל יָבִין מֶלֶךְ־כְּנָעַן עַד אֲשֶׁר הִכְרִיתוּ אֵת
יָבִין מֶֽלֶךְ־כְּנָֽעַן׃

Chapter V

1. Then sang Deborah and Barak the son of Abinoam on that day, saying:

2. When men let grow their hair in Israel,
When the people offer themselves willingly,
Bless ye the Lord.
3. Hear, O ye kings; give ear, O ye princes;
I, unto the Lord will I sing;
I will sing praise to the Lord, the God of Israel.

Cap. V. ה

א וַתָּשַׁר דְּבוֹרָה וּבָרָק בֶּן־אֲבִינֹעַם בַּיּוֹם הַהוּא
2 לֵאמֹֽר׃ בִּפְרֹעַ פְּרָעוֹת בְּיִשְׂרָאֵל בְּהִתְנַדֵּב
3 עָם בָּרְכוּ יְהוָֽה׃ שִׁמְעוּ מְלָכִים הַאֲזִינוּ
רֹזְנִים אָֽנֹכִי לַיהוָה אָנֹכִי אָשִׁירָה אֲזַמֵּר

ד' v. 18. מלרע v. 19. חסר א' ibid. מלא וא"ו v. 21. א' נחת

17. *Jael the wife of Heber.* This family had taken no part in the battle.

21. *tent-pin.* On the morality of the action, see note on *v.* 24 of next chapter.

24. *prevailed more and more.* This staggering success was the beginning of a series of crushing victories over Jabin.

Chapter V. Deborah's Song of Deliverance and Praise

'The Song of Deborah holds a high place among Triumphal Odes in the literature of the world. It is a work of that highest art which is not studied and artificial, but spontaneous and inevitable. It shows a development and command of the resources of the language for ends of poetical expression, which prove that poetry had long been cultivated among the Hebrews' (Moore).

2. *when men let grow their hair in Israel. i.e.* when men took the vow and consecrated themselves to the war of liberation. 'Wearing the hair long was the mark of a vow not to do certain things until a specified object had been attained' (Cooke); cf. Num. vi, 5.

4. LORD, when Thou didst go forth out of Seir,
When Thou didst march out of the field of Edom,
The earth trembled, the heavens also dropped,
Yea, the clouds dropped water.

5. The mountains quaked at the presence of the LORD,
Even yon Sinai at the presence of the LORD, the God of Israel.

6. In the days of Shamgar the son of Anath,
In the days of Jael, the highways ceased,
And the travellers walked through byways.

7. The rulers ceased in Israel, they ceased,
Until that thou didst arise, Deborah,
That thou didst arise a mother in Israel.

8. They chose new gods;
Then was war in the gates;
Was there a shield or spear seen
Among forty thousand in Israel?

9. My heart is toward the governors of Israel,
That offered themselves willingly among the people.
Bless ye the LORD.

10. Ye that ride on white asses,
Ye that sit on rich cloths,
And ye that walk by the way, tell of it;

11. Louder than the voice of archers, by the watering-troughs!
There shall they rehearse the righteous acts of the LORD,
Even the righteous acts of His rulers in Israel.
Then the people of the LORD went down to the gates.

4 לַיהוָה אֱלֹהֵי יִשְׂרָאֵל׃ יְהוָה בְּצֵאתְךָ
מִשֵּׂעִיר בְּצַעְדְּךָ מִשְּׂדֵה אֱדוֹם אֶרֶץ
רָעָשָׁה גַּם־שָׁמַיִם נָטָפוּ גַּם־עָבִים נָטְפוּ
ה מָיִם׃ הָרִים נָזְלוּ מִפְּנֵי יְהוָה זֶה
6 סִינַי מִפְּנֵי יְהוָה אֱלֹהֵי יִשְׂרָאֵל׃ בִּימֵי שַׁמְגַּר בֶּן
עֲנָת בִּימֵי יָעֵל חָדְלוּ אֳרָחוֹת וְהֹלְכֵי
7 נְתִיבוֹת יֵלְכוּ אֳרָחוֹת עֲקַלְקַלּוֹת׃ חָדְלוּ פְרָזוֹן בְּיִשְׂרָאֵל
חָדֵלּוּ עַד שַׁקַּמְתִּי דְּבוֹרָה שַׁקַּמְתִּי
8 אֵם בְּיִשְׂרָאֵל׃ יִבְחַר אֱלֹהִים
חֲדָשִׁים אָז לָחֶם שְׁעָרִים מָגֵן
אִם־יֵרָאֶה וָרֹמַח בְּאַרְבָּעִים אֶלֶף
9 בְּיִשְׂרָאֵל׃ לִבִּי לְחוֹקְקֵי יִשְׂרָאֵל הַמִּתְנַדְּבִים
י בָּעָם בָּרְכוּ יְהוָה׃ רֹכְבֵי אֲתֹנוֹת
צְחֹרוֹת יֹשְׁבֵי עַל־מִדִּין וְהֹלְכֵי
11 עַל־דֶּרֶךְ שִׂיחוּ׃ מִקּוֹל מְחַצְצִים בֵּין
מַשְׁאַבִּים שָׁם יְתַנּוּ צִדְקוֹת יְהוָה צִדְקֹת
פִּרְזוֹנוֹ בְּיִשְׂרָאֵל אָז יָרְדוּ לַשְּׁעָרִים עַם־
12 יְהוָה׃ עוּרִי עוּרִי דְּבוֹרָה עוּרִי
עוּרִי דַּבְּרִי־שִׁיר קוּם בָּרָק וּשְׁבֵה שֶׁבְיְךָ בֶּן

12. Awake, awake, Deborah;
Awake, awake, utter a song;
Arise, Barak, and lead thy captivity captive, thou son of Abinoam.

v. 4. קמץ בז״ק v. 7. הש׳ בפתח v. 12. מלרע

4. *LORD, when Thou didst go forth.* A bringing to remembrance of God's might in the days of old, at the Revelation at Sinai, as an encouragement in the present distress.

6–11. THE OPPRESSION

6. *Shamgar.* The previous judge; see Judges III, 31.
highways ceased. Israel was in hiding, and all travel on the highways was stopped. The people had to abandon their villages because of the harrying armed bands of Canaanites.

7. *thou didst arise a mother in Israel.* The Heb. is as an old grammatical form, and has also been translated, 'till I arose a mother in Israel.'

8. *was there a shield or spear.* The people had no proper weapons with which to defend themselves.

9. *governors.* Commanders; they are praised for their instant response to her clarion call.

10. *tell of it.* All should now join in praising God—the leaders and magistrates, the men of wealth as well as the plain people. They could now travel in safety on the high-roads, in contrast to *v.* 6.

11. *righteous.* With the additional meaning, 'victorious.'
went down to the gates. Prepared to assault the strongholds of the enemy.

12–23. THE GATHERING OF THE TRIBES

12. *utter a song.* The war-song which roused the clans to battle.
lead thy captivity captive. An idiomatic phrase for *turn the tables* in war.

13. Then made He a remnant to have dominion over the nobles and the people;
The LORD made me have dominion over the mighty.

14. Out of Ephraim came they whose root is in Amalek;
After thee, Benjamin, among thy peoples;
Out of Machir came down governors,
And out of Zebulun they that handle the marshal's staff.

15. And the princes of Issachar were with Deborah;
As was Issachar, so was Barak;
Into the valley they rushed forth at his feet.
Among the divisions of Reuben
There were great resolves of heart.

16. Why sattest thou among the sheepfolds,
To hear the pipings for the flocks?
At the divisions of Reuben
There were great searchings of heart.

17. Gilead abode beyond the Jordan;
And Dan, why doth he sojourn by the ships?
Asher dwelt at the shore of the sea,
And abideth by its bays.

18. Zebulun is a people that jeoparded their lives unto the death,
And Naphtali, upon the high places of the field.

19. The kings came, they fought;
Then fought the kings of Canaan,
In Taanach by the waters of Megiddo;
They took no gain of money.

20. They fought from heaven,
The stars in their courses fought against Sisera.

13 אֲבִינֹעַם׃ אָז יְרַד שָׂרִיד לְאַדִּירִים עָם יְהוָה
14 יְרַד־לִי בַּגִּבּוֹרִים׃ מִנִּי אֶפְרַיִם שָׁרְשָׁם
בַּעֲמָלֵק אַחֲרֶיךָ בִנְיָמִין בַּעֲמָמֶיךָ מִנִּי
מָכִיר יָרְדוּ מְחֹקְקִים וּמִזְּבוּלֻן מֹשְׁכִים בְּשֵׁבֶט
טו סֹפֵר׃ וְשָׂרַי בְּיִשָּׂשכָר עִם־דְּבֹרָה וְיִשָּׂשכָר
כֵּן בָּרָק בָּעֵמֶק שֻׁלַּח
בְּרַגְלָיו בִּפְלַגּוֹת רְאוּבֵן גְּדֹלִים
16 חִקְקֵי־לֵב׃ לָמָּה יָשַׁבְתָּ בֵּין
הַמִּשְׁפְּתַיִם לִשְׁמֹעַ שְׁרִקוֹת עֲדָרִים לִפְלַגּוֹת
17 רְאוּבֵן גְּדוֹלִים חִקְרֵי־לֵב׃ גִּלְעָד בְּעֵבֶר הַיַּרְדֵּן
שָׁכֵן וְדָן לָמָּה יָגוּר אֳנִיּוֹת אָשֵׁר
יָשַׁב לְחוֹף יַמִּים וְעַל־מִפְרָצָיו
18 יִשְׁכּוֹן׃ זְבֻלוּן עַם חֵרֵף נַפְשׁוֹ לָמוּת וְנַפְתָּלִי
19 עַל מְרוֹמֵי שָׂדֶה׃ בָּאוּ מְלָכִים
נִלְחָמוּ אָז נִלְחֲמוּ מַלְכֵי כְנַעַן בְּתַעְנַךְ
עַל־מֵי מְגִדּוֹ בֶּצַע כֶּסֶף לֹא
כ לָקָחוּ׃ מִן־שָׁמַיִם נִלְחָמוּ הַכּוֹכָבִים

v. 19. קמץ בז״ק

14. *root is in Amalek.* This suggests that Ephraim possessed land formerly held by Amalekites (see Judges XII, 5).

after thee. i.e. Ephraim. The largest and the smallest tribes are mentioned together. Others are included in the words, 'among thy peoples' (Kimchi).

Machir. On the other side of the Jordan.

governors. Commanders.

the marshal's staff. lit. 'the staff of the scribe', who enrols the muster of troops.

15. *great resolves of heart.* There was much discussion of the situation, but they did not join their brethren in their life-and-death struggle. Reuben remains true to his character as delineated in Jacob's blessing; see *Genesis*, p. 183.

16. *searchings.* Mighty deliberations, but no action. They preferred to listen to the pipings of the shepherds.

17. Gilead, Dan and Asher are similarly branded. The latter had established themselves on the sea-coast with the Phœnicians.

bays. Landing-places at the mouth of a river.

18. The shining example of Zebulun and Naphtali contrasted with cowardice or indifference of the above.

19–22. THE BATTLE

19. *the kings.* The rulers of the districts united under Sisera.

no gain of money. They got no booty from the Israelites: they themselves were vanquished.

20. *the stars in their courses.* One of the most beautiful figures in literature. The powers of heaven themselves were arrayed against the heathen, and the victory was not won by Israel unaided. The reference is to torrential rain which swept away the Canaanite chariots; cf. in the Sedrah, XIV, 25. 'In 1799, at the battle of Mt. Tabor between the army of Napoleon and the Turks, many of the latter were drowned when attempting to escape across the Plain inundated by the Kishon' (Cooke).

21 מִמְּסִלּוֹתָם נִלְחֲמוּ עִם סִֽיסְרָא׃ נַחַל קִישׁוֹן
גְּרָפָם נַחַל קְדוּמִים נַחַל קִישׁוֹן תִּדְרְכִי
22 נַפְשִׁי עֹז׃ אָז הָלְמוּ עִקְּבֵי־
23 סוּס מִדַּהֲרוֹת דַּהֲרוֹת אַבִּירָֽיו׃ אוֹרוּ
מֵרוֹז אָמַר מַלְאַךְ יְהוָה אֹרוּ אָרוֹר
יֹשְׁבֶיהָ כִּי לֹא־בָאוּ לְעֶזְרַת יְהוָה לְעֶזְרַת
24 יְהוָה בַּגִּבּוֹרִֽים׃ תְּבֹרַךְ מִנָּשִׁים
יָעֵל אֵשֶׁת חֶבֶר הַקֵּינִי מִנָּשִׁים
כה בָּאֹהֶל תְּבֹרָֽךְ׃ מַיִם שָׁאַל חָלָב
26 נָתָנָה בְּסֵפֶל אַדִּירִים הִקְרִיבָה חֶמְאָֽה׃ יָדָהּ
לַיָּתֵד תִּשְׁלַחְנָה וִימִינָהּ לְהַלְמוּת
עֲמֵלִים וְהָלְמָה סִֽיסְרָא מָחֲקָה רֹאשׁוֹ וּמָחֲצָה
27 וְחָלְפָה רַקָּתֽוֹ׃ בֵּין רַגְלֶיהָ כָּרַע נָפַל
שָׁכָב בֵּין רַגְלֶיהָ כָּרַע נָפָל בַּאֲשֶׁר
28 כָּרַע שָׁם נָפַל שָׁדֽוּד׃ בְּעַד הַחַלּוֹן נִשְׁקְפָה
וַתְּיַבֵּב אֵם סִֽיסְרָא בְּעַד הָאֶשְׁנָב מַדּוּעַ
בֹּשֵׁשׁ רִכְבּוֹ לָבוֹא מַדּוּעַ אֶחֱרוּ פַּעֲמֵי
29 מַרְכְּבוֹתָֽיו׃ חַכְמוֹת שָׂרוֹתֶיהָ תַּעֲנֶנָּה אַף־

21. The brook Kishon swept them away,
That ancient brook, the brook Kishon.
O my soul, tread them down with strength.

22. Then did the horsehoofs stamp
By reason of the prancings, the prancings of their mighty ones.

23. 'Curse ye Meroz,' said the angel of the LORD,
'Curse ye bitterly the inhabitants thereof,
Because they came not to the help of the LORD,
To the help of the LORD against the mighty.'

24. Blessed above women shall Jael be,
The wife of Heber the Kenite,
Above women in the tent shall she be blessed.

25. Water he asked, milk she gave him;
On a lordly bowl she brought him curd.

26. Her hand she put to the tent-pin,
And her right hand to the workmen's hammer;
And with the hammer she smote Sisera, she smote through his head,
Yea, she pierced and struck through his temples.

27. At her feet he sunk, he fell, he lay;
At her feet he sunk, he fell;
Where he sunk, there he fell down dead.

28. Through the window she looked forth, and peered,
The mother of Sisera, through the lattice:
'Why is his chariot so long in coming?
Why tarry the wheels of his chariots?'

29. The wisest of her princesses answer her,
Yea, she returneth answer to herself:

v. 27. קמץ בז״ק

22. *horsehoofs stamp.* A picture of the confusion of flight.

23–31. The Defeat of the Enemy

23. *Meroz.* An Israelite town near the scene of the battle that refused to help in following up the victory.

against the mighty. Or, 'among the brave'; as brave men who rallied to the LORD's banner.

24. *Jael.* The resource and 'pro-Israelite' action of this heathen, Kenite woman is contrasted with the cowardice and perfidy of the inhabitants of Meroz. Jael's murder is viewed as an act of national deliverance, without which the victory might have been fruitless; it, therefore, receives high praise. Judged by standards of peace, her act was one of treacherous cruelty; but every nation glorifies similar, and worse, deeds in its history. Our own age, in which the most enlightened nations have, for reasons of policy or patriotism, committed or condoned crimes and inhumanities on an immeasurably greater scale, is not entitled to condemn the praise bestowed upon the fierce deed of this wild Bedouin woman.

women in the tent. Or, 'Bedouin women' (Moore), tenting women.

25. *lordly bowl.* A bowl fit for nobles.

29. *the wisest of her princesses.* Comfort her by their certainty that Sisera is bringing back rich booty. His delay, they tell her, is being caused by his collecting, and apportioning this booty.

she returneth answer to herself. Or, 'keeps repeating to herself.' She silences her presentiments of evil by the same kind of answer which her companions give her (Rashi).

30. 'Are they not finding, are they not dividing the spoil?
A damsel, two damsels to every man;
To Sisera a spoil of dyed garments,
A spoil of dyed garments of embroidery,
Two dyed garments of broidery for the neck of every spoiler?'

31. So perish all Thine enemies, O LORD;
But they that love Him be as the sun when he goeth forth in his might.
And the land had rest forty years.

ל הִיא תָּשִׁיב אֲמָרֶיהָ לָהּ׃ הֲלֹא יִמְצְאוּ יְחַלְּקוּ
שָׁלָל רַחַם רַחֲמָתַיִם לְרֹאשׁ גֶּבֶר שְׁלַל
צְבָעִים לְסִיסְרָא שְׁלַל צְבָעִים
31 רִקְמָה צֶבַע רִקְמָתַיִם לְצַוְּארֵי שָׁלָל׃ כֵּן
יֹאבְדוּ כָל־אוֹיְבֶיךָ יְהוָה וְאֹהֲבָיו כְּצֵאת הַשֶּׁמֶשׁ
בִּגְבֻרָתוֹ וַתִּשְׁקֹט הָאָרֶץ אַרְבָּעִים שָׁנָה׃

30. ***are they not finding.*** The Heb. phrase means, 'no doubt they are finding.'

damsel. The Heb. is a rare, and, it seems, an insulting word. It is intentionally used to show her contempt for the Israelite women.

dyed garments of embroidery. Or, 'embroidered garments of divers colours'—a picturesque touch that betrays the hand of the feminine author of this ode. Its climax 'is as weird as it is fantastic, the figure of Sisera's mother mumbling to herself of the "spoil of damsels, divers colours and embroidery", which her son is to bring home, and which we already know he never will' (George A. Smith).

31. *so.* 'With consummate art the poet breaks off, leaving to the imagination of the reader, who knows all, the terrible revelation of the truth' (Moore).

as the sun when he goeth forth in his might. Invincible, annihilating the darkness of the night—a marvellously effective ending to one of the most magnificent lyrical poems in any language. The Rabbis based the following teaching on this verse: 'Whosoever does not persecute them that persecute him, whosoever takes an offence in silence, he who does good for its own sake, he who is cheerful under his sufferings—they are the friends of God; and of them Scripture says, "They that love Him shall be as the sun, when he goeth forth in his might."'

and the land had rest forty years. 'These words are not by Deborah, but by the writer of the Book of Judges' (Rashi).

18 CHAPTER XVIII

1. Now Jethro, the priest of Midian, Moses' father-in-law, heard of all that God had done for Moses, and for Israel His people, how that the LORD had brought Israel out of Egypt. 2. And Jethro, Moses' father-in-law, took Zipporah, Moses' wife, after he had sent her away, 3. and her two sons; of whom the name of the one was Gershom; for he said: 'I have been a stranger in a strange land'; 4. and the name of the other was [1]Eliezer: 'for the God of my father was my help, and delivered me from the sword of Pharaoh.' 5. And Jethro, Moses' father-in-law, came with his sons and his wife unto Moses into the wilderness where he was encamped, at the mount of God; 6. and he said unto Moses: 'I thy father-in-law Jethro am coming unto thee, and thy wife, and her two sons with her.' 7. And Moses went out to meet his father-in-law, and bowed down and kissed him; and they asked each other of their welfare; and they came into the tent. 8. And Moses told his father-in-law all that the LORD had done unto Pharaoh and to the Egyptians for Israel's sake, all the travail that had come upon them by the way, and how the LORD delivered them. 9. And Jethro rejoiced for all the goodness which the LORD had done to Israel, in that He had delivered them out of the hand of the Egyptians. 10. And Jethro said: 'Blessed

[1] Heb. *El*, God, and *ezer*, help.

CAP. XVIII. יח

יח פ פ פ 17 יז

א וַיִּשְׁמַע יִתְרוֹ כֹהֵן מִדְיָן חֹתֵן מֹשֶׁה אֵת כָּל־אֲשֶׁר עָשָׂה
אֱלֹהִים לְמֹשֶׁה וּלְיִשְׂרָאֵל עַמּוֹ כִּי־הוֹצִיא יְהוָה אֶת־יִשְׂרָאֵל
2 מִמִּצְרָיִם׃ וַיִּקַּח יִתְרוֹ חֹתֵן מֹשֶׁה אֶת־צִפֹּרָה אֵשֶׁת מֹשֶׁה
3 אַחַר שִׁלּוּחֶיהָ׃ וְאֵת שְׁנֵי בָנֶיהָ אֲשֶׁר שֵׁם הָאֶחָד גֵּרְשֹׁם
4 כִּי אָמַר גֵּר הָיִיתִי בְּאֶרֶץ נָכְרִיָּה׃ וְשֵׁם הָאֶחָד אֱלִיעֶזֶר
ה כִּי־אֱלֹהֵי אָבִי בְּעֶזְרִי וַיַּצִּלֵנִי מֵחֶרֶב פַּרְעֹה׃ וַיָּבֹא יִתְרוֹ
חֹתֵן מֹשֶׁה וּבָנָיו וְאִשְׁתּוֹ אֶל־מֹשֶׁה אֶל־הַמִּדְבָּר אֲשֶׁר־הוּא
6 חֹנֶה שָׁם הַר הָאֱלֹהִים׃ וַיֹּאמֶר אֶל־מֹשֶׁה אֲנִי חֹתֶנְךָ
7 יִתְרוֹ בָּא אֵלֶיךָ וְאִשְׁתְּךָ וּשְׁנֵי בָנֶיהָ עִמָּהּ׃ וַיֵּצֵא מֹשֶׁה
לִקְרַאת חֹתְנוֹ וַיִּשְׁתַּחוּ וַיִּשַּׁק־לוֹ וַיִּשְׁאֲלוּ אִישׁ־לְרֵעֵהוּ
8 לְשָׁלוֹם וַיָּבֹאוּ הָאֹהֱלָה׃ וַיְסַפֵּר מֹשֶׁה לְחֹתְנוֹ אֵת כָּל־
אֲשֶׁר עָשָׂה יְהוָה לְפַרְעֹה וּלְמִצְרַיִם עַל אוֹדֹת יִשְׂרָאֵל
9 אֵת כָּל־הַתְּלָאָה אֲשֶׁר מְצָאָתַם בַּדֶּרֶךְ וַיַּצִּלֵם יְהוָה׃ וַיִּחַדְּ
יִתְרוֹ עַל כָּל־הַטּוֹבָה אֲשֶׁר־עָשָׂה יְהוָה לְיִשְׂרָאֵל אֲשֶׁר
י הִצִּילוֹ מִיַּד מִצְרָיִם׃ וַיֹּאמֶר יִתְרוֹ בָּרוּךְ יְהוָה אֲשֶׁר הִצִּיל

V. YITHRO

(CHAPTERS XVIII–XX)

CHAPTER XVIII. THE VISIT OF JETHRO

1. *Jethro.* See III, 1 and II, 16 f. This chapter is one of the few passages in Exodus that are reminiscent of Patriarchal scenes in Genesis.

2. *he had sent her.* Back to Jethro in Midian, after the incident related in IV, 24–26.

3. *Gershom.* See on II, 22.

4. *the God of my father.* See III, 6; XV, 2.
from the sword of Pharaoh. See II, 15. One may assume that when Moses named his second son, he said, 'For the God of my father was my help,' etc.

5. *at the mount of God.* Sinai, or Horeb. Moses had there struck the rock in order to procure water for the people, XVII, 6. Rephidim lies in the vicinity of Horeb.

6. *and he said unto Moses.* *i.e.* through a messenger; see VII, 17.

7. *went out to meet.* And to pay respect to his father-in-law, his guest. This was the usual etiquette; see Gen. XXIII, 7–12.

8. *travail.* lit. 'weariness'; the pursuit of the Israelites on the part of the Egyptians, and the events associated with Marah, Massah, Meribah and Rephidim.

9. *Jethro rejoiced.* Not because the Egyptians had been punished, but because of all the goodness shown by God to Israel.

10. *delivered you.* *i.e.* Moses and Aaron.
delivered the people. By defeating the Egyptians at the crossing of the Red Sea.
hand. Power.

be the LORD, who hath delivered you out of the hand of the Egyptians, and out of the hand of Pharaoh; who hath delivered the people from under the hand of the Egyptians. 11. Now I know that the LORD is greater than all gods; yea, for that they dealt proudly against them.' 12. And Jethro, Moses' father-in-law, took a burnt-offering and sacrifices for God; and Aaron came, and all the elders of Israel, to eat bread with Moses' father-in-law before God.* ii. 13. And it came to pass on the morrow, that Moses sat to judge the people; and the people stood about Moses from the morning unto the evening. 14. And when Moses' father-in-law saw all that he did to the people, he said: 'What is this thing that thou doest to the people? why sittest thou thyself alone, and all the people stand about thee from morning unto even?' 15. And Moses said unto his father-in-law: 'Because the people come unto me to inquire of God; 16. when they have a matter, it cometh unto me; and I judge between a man and his neighbour, and I make them know the statutes of God, and His laws.' 17. And Moses' father-in-law said unto him: 'The thing that thou doest is not good. 18. Thou wilt surely wear away, both thou, and this people that is with thee; for the thing is too heavy for thee; thou art not able to perform it thyself alone. 19. Hearken now unto my voice, I will give thee counsel, and God be with thee: be thou for the people before God, and bring thou the causes unto God. 20. And thou

אֶתְכֶם מִיַּד מִצְרַיִם וּמִיַּד פַּרְעֹה אֲשֶׁר הִצִּיל אֶת־הָעָם
11 מִתַּחַת יַד־מִצְרָיִם׃ עַתָּה יָדַעְתִּי כִּי־גָדוֹל יְהוָה מִכָּל־
12 הָאֱלֹהִים כִּי בַדָּבָר אֲשֶׁר זָדוּ עֲלֵיהֶם׃ וַיִּקַּח יִתְרוֹ חֹתֵן
שני מֹשֶׁה עֹלָה וּזְבָחִים לֵאלֹהִים וַיָּבֹא אַהֲרֹן וְכֹל ׀ זִקְנֵי יִשְׂרָאֵל
13 לֶאֱכָל־לֶחֶם עִם־חֹתֵן מֹשֶׁה לִפְנֵי הָאֱלֹהִים׃ וַיְהִי מִמָּחֳרָת
וַיֵּשֶׁב מֹשֶׁה לִשְׁפֹּט אֶת־הָעָם וַיַּעֲמֹד הָעָם עַל־מֹשֶׁה מִן־
14 הַבֹּקֶר עַד־הָעָרֶב׃ וַיַּרְא חֹתֵן מֹשֶׁה אֵת כָּל־אֲשֶׁר־הוּא
עֹשֶׂה לָעָם וַיֹּאמֶר מָה־הַדָּבָר הַזֶּה אֲשֶׁר אַתָּה עֹשֶׂה לָעָם
מַדּוּעַ אַתָּה יוֹשֵׁב לְבַדֶּךָ וְכָל־הָעָם נִצָּב עָלֶיךָ מִן־בֹּקֶר
טו עַד־עָרֶב׃ וַיֹּאמֶר מֹשֶׁה לְחֹתְנוֹ כִּי־יָבֹא אֵלַי הָעָם לִדְרֹשׁ
16 אֱלֹהִים׃ כִּי־יִהְיֶה לָהֶם דָּבָר בָּא אֵלַי וְשָׁפַטְתִּי בֵּין אִישׁ
וּבֵין רֵעֵהוּ וְהוֹדַעְתִּי אֶת־חֻקֵּי הָאֱלֹהִים וְאֶת־תּוֹרֹתָיו׃
17 וַיֹּאמֶר חֹתֵן מֹשֶׁה אֵלָיו לֹא־טוֹב הַדָּבָר אֲשֶׁר אַתָּה עֹשֶׂה׃
18 נָבֹל תִּבֹּל גַּם־אַתָּה גַּם־הָעָם הַזֶּה אֲשֶׁר עִמָּךְ כִּי־כָבֵד
19 מִמְּךָ הַדָּבָר לֹא־תוּכַל עֲשֹׂהוּ לְבַדֶּךָ׃ עַתָּה שְׁמַע בְּקֹלִי
אִיעָצְךָ וִיהִי אֱלֹהִים עִמָּךְ הֱיֵה אַתָּה לָעָם מוּל הָאֱלֹהִים
כ וְהֵבֵאתָ אַתָּה אֶת־הַדְּבָרִים אֶל־הָאֱלֹהִים׃ וְהִזְהַרְתָּה

11. *they dealt proudly against them.* Because the Egyptians had dealt proudly and obstinately with Israel, God felt the need of using His power to humble the Egyptians (Rashbam). God made use of their very pride and defiance to bring about their doom, and at the same time, the salvation of Israel. By this, Jethro realizes that God is 'greater than all other gods'. According to the Rabbis, Jethro thereupon forsook idolatry and became a proselyte.

12. *Aaron came, and all the elders.* Though Moses is not mentioned, he was naturally present, as the meeting took place in his tent (Ibn Ezra).
to eat bread . . . before God. To take part in the sacrificial meal.
before God. Before the altar built by Moses in honour of God; see XVII, 15.

13–23. Jethro's advice to Moses. This section is of the greatest interest: it presents a picture of Moses legislating, and deciding cases as they arose.

13. *on the morrow.* After his arrival.
judge the people. In primitive Semitic society, the ruler was both leader in war and arbiter in disputes.

14. *all that he did.* Acting single-handed as leader and judge.

15. *to inquire of God.* See Gen. XXV, 22. The phrase may mean to obtain from God a legal decision; see Num. IX, 8. In Israel, justice was considered as belonging to God; see Deut. I, 17.

16. *a matter.* A cause of dispute.
statutes of God. Naturally, the Israelites, like every group constituting a human society, had such definite rules (*e.g.* against theft and violence) long before the promulgation of the Decalogue.
His laws. Heb. *toroth.* Directions delivered for special circumstances.

18. *this people that is with thee.* Because they will not all receive the attention they require.

19. *God be with thee.* God will help thee, if thou wilt follow this advice (Ibn Ezra).
before God. God's representative to the people.
bring thou the causes. The difficult cases. This refers to the occasions when the people come to Moses to inquire of God (see *v.* 15).

20. *they must do.* Their conduct in any given case. Jethro conceives the activity of Moses as that of instructor.

shalt teach them the statutes and the laws, and shalt show them the way wherein they must walk, and the work that they must do. 21. Moreover, thou shalt provide out of all the people able men, such as fear God, men of truth, hating unjust gain; and place such over them, to be rulers of thousands, rulers of hundreds, rulers of fifties, and rulers of tens. 22. And let them judge the people at all seasons; and it shall be, that every great matter they shall bring unto thee, but every small matter they shall judge themselves; so shall they make it easier for thee and bear the burden with thee. 23. If thou shalt do this thing, and God command thee so, then thou shalt be able to endure, and all this people also shall go to their place in peace.'* iii. 24. So Moses hearkened to the voice of his father-in-law, and did all that he had said. 25. And Moses chose able men out of all Israel, and made them heads over the people, rulers of thousands, rulers of hundreds, rulers of fifties, and rulers of tens. 26. And they judged the people at all seasons: the hard causes they brought unto Moses, but every small matter they judged themselves. 27. And Moses let his father-in-law depart; and he went his way into his own land.* iv.

19

Chapter XIX

1. In the third month after the children of Israel were gone forth out of the land of Egypt, the same day came they into the

אֶתְהֶם אֶת־הַחֻקִּים וְאֶת־הַתּוֹרֹת וְהוֹדַעְתָּ לָהֶם אֶת־הַדֶּרֶךְ
21 יֵלְכוּ בָהּ וְאֶת־הַמַּעֲשֶׂה אֲשֶׁר יַעֲשׂוּן׃ וְאַתָּה תֶחֱזֶה מִכָּל־
הָעָם אַנְשֵׁי־חַיִל יִרְאֵי אֱלֹהִים אַנְשֵׁי אֱמֶת שֹׂנְאֵי בָצַע
וְשַׂמְתָּ עֲלֵהֶם שָׂרֵי אֲלָפִים שָׂרֵי מֵאוֹת שָׂרֵי חֲמִשִּׁים וְשָׂרֵי
22 עֲשָׂרֹת׃ וְשָׁפְטוּ אֶת־הָעָם בְּכָל־עֵת וְהָיָה כָּל־הַדָּבָר הַגָּדֹל
יָבִיאוּ אֵלֶיךָ וְכָל־הַדָּבָר הַקָּטֹן יִשְׁפְּטוּ־הֵם וְהָקֵל מֵעָלֶיךָ
23 וְנָשְׂאוּ אִתָּךְ׃ אִם אֶת־הַדָּבָר הַזֶּה תַּעֲשֶׂה וְצִוְּךָ אֱלֹהִים
שלישי וְיָכָלְתָּ עֲמֹד וְגַם כָּל־הָעָם הַזֶּה עַל־מְקֹמוֹ יָבֹא בְשָׁלוֹם׃ *
24 כה וַיִּשְׁמַע מֹשֶׁה לְקוֹל חֹתְנוֹ וַיַּעַשׂ כֹּל אֲשֶׁר אָמָר׃ וַיִּבְחַר
מֹשֶׁה אַנְשֵׁי־חַיִל מִכָּל־יִשְׂרָאֵל וַיִּתֵּן אֹתָם רָאשִׁים עַל־
הָעָם שָׂרֵי אֲלָפִים שָׂרֵי מֵאוֹת שָׂרֵי חֲמִשִּׁים וְשָׂרֵי עֲשָׂרֹת׃
26 וְשָׁפְטוּ אֶת־הָעָם בְּכָל־עֵת אֶת־הַדָּבָר הַקָּשֶׁה יְבִיאוּן אֶל־
27 מֹשֶׁה וְכָל־הַדָּבָר הַקָּטֹן יִשְׁפּוּטוּ הֵם׃ וַיְשַׁלַּח מֹשֶׁה אֶת־
חֹתְנוֹ וַיֵּלֶךְ לוֹ אֶל־אַרְצוֹ׃* פ רביעי

יט

CAP. XIX. יט

א בַּחֹדֶשׁ הַשְּׁלִישִׁי לְצֵאת בְּנֵי־יִשְׂרָאֵל מֵאֶרֶץ מִצְרָיִם בַּיּוֹם

יח' v. 26. מלרע

21. *provide.* The Heb. is an unusual word for 'look out', select, appoint. It is used of prophetic vision; 'select by the prophetic insight which God has given thee' (Rashi).

such as fear God. And not man; men of fundamental piety and humanity; cf. I, 17.

hating unjust gain. Incorruptible and above the suspicion of bribery.

rulers of thousands. An elaborate system of judges, and assistant judges is here indicated. Gersonides suggests that the ruler of tens controlled several such subdivisions, but less than a hundred; the ruler of hundreds, several hundreds, but less than a thousand; and so on.

22. *at all seasons. i.e.* as cases arise.

every great matter. Extraordinary cases.

23. *and God command thee so.* Jethro's suggestions required Divine sanction.

go to their place in peace. After having their cases settled quickly, the parties will return to their tents satisfied. No longer will the people have to stand all day waiting for their turn before Moses (see *v.* 14). Moreover, by the new institution the people would be able to obtain justice in their own part of the camp.

27. *his own land.* Midian, see II, 15 and cf. Num. X, 30.

'The wise plan devised by Jethro has never become antiquated. The statesman-like principle of decentralization—the delegation of responsibility—is as important to-day as in the time of Moses' (McNeile).

Chapter XIX. Preparations for the Covenant at Sinai

The arrival at the foot of Mt. Sinai marks the beginning of Israel's spiritual history. We reach what was the kernel and core of the nation's life, the Covenant by which all the tribes were united in allegiance to One God, the Covenant by which a priest-people was created, and a Kingdom of God on earth inaugurated among the children of men.

1. *in the third month.* The month of Sivan.

the same day. lit. 'in that day', *i.e.* the first of the month (Mechilta).

into the wilderness of Sinai. As foretold when God first revealed Himself to Moses at the Burning Bush (see IV, 29). Moses is bringing his wilderness of Sinai. 2. And when they were departed from Rephidim, and were come to the wilderness of Sinai, they encamped in the wilderness; and there Israel encamped before the mount. 3. And Moses went up unto God, and the LORD called unto him out of the mountain, saying: 'Thus shalt thou say to the house of Jacob, and tell the children of Israel: 4. Ye have seen what I did unto the Egyptians, and how I bore you on eagles' wings, and brought you unto Myself. 5. Now therefore, if ye will hearken unto My voice indeed, and keep My covenant, then ye shall be Mine own treasure from among all peoples; for all the earth is Mine; 6. and ye shall be unto Me a kingdom of priests, and a

2 הַזֶּה בָּאוּ מִדְבַּר סִינָי: וַיִּסְעוּ מֵרְפִידִים וַיָּבֹאוּ מִדְבַּר
3 סִינַי וַיַּחֲנוּ בַּמִּדְבָּר וַיִּחַן־שָׁם יִשְׂרָאֵל נֶגֶד הָהָר: וּמֹשֶׁה
עָלָה אֶל־הָאֱלֹהִים וַיִּקְרָא אֵלָיו יְהוָה מִן־הָהָר לֵאמֹר כֹּה
4 תֹאמַר לְבֵית יַעֲקֹב וְתַגֵּיד לִבְנֵי יִשְׂרָאֵל: אַתֶּם רְאִיתֶם
אֲשֶׁר עָשִׂיתִי לְמִצְרָיִם וָאֶשָּׂא אֶתְכֶם עַל־כַּנְפֵי נְשָׁרִים
ה וָאָבִא אֶתְכֶם אֵלָי: וְעַתָּה אִם־שָׁמוֹעַ תִּשְׁמְעוּ בְּקֹלִי וּשְׁמַרְתֶּם
אֶת־בְּרִיתִי וִהְיִיתֶם לִי סְגֻלָּה מִכָּל־הָעַמִּים כִּי־לִי כָּל־
6 הָאָרֶץ: וְאַתֶּם תִּהְיוּ־לִי מַמְלֶכֶת כֹּהֲנִים וְגוֹי קָדוֹשׁ אֵלֶּה

v. 5. מלעיל

People to acknowledge and worship the God of their Fathers at that Mount.

The *wilderness* is the wide plain in front of Mt. Sinai. This mountain is generally identified with Jebel Musa; and accordingly, the wilderness is in all probability the plain of Er-Rahah, situated 5,000 feet above the sea. By careful local investigation, Robinson arrived at the conviction that there was space enough in the plain Er-Rahah to satisfy all the requirements of the Scripture narrative, so far as it relates to the assembling of the people for the Divine revelation. The plain is one-and-half miles long and one mile broad; while the adjacent valleys afford ample space for tents, animals and baggage.

2. *departed from Rephidim.* Or, 'For they had journeyed from Rephidim' (Mendelssohn, Benisch); see XVII, 8 f. This supplies the link in the narrative, interrupted by the story of Jethro's visit in the preceding chapter.

they encamped. In the wilderness of Sinai.

3. *Moses went up unto God. i.e.* he ascended the mountain. On the day when the Israelites came to Mt. Sinai, the cloud of God's glory covered the mountain; see XXIV, 16.

out of the mountain. Out of the cloud on the summit; see *v.* 20.

house of Jacob . . . children of Israel. Israel has an exalted future in store for it; it is called to become the priest-people of the God of Holiness and Righteousness. *House of Jacob* occurs only here in the Pentateuch, and is a poetical synonym of 'house of Israel'. The Rabbis understood by the 'house of Jacob' the women of the nation. Moses is bidden to approach the women first, as it is they who rear the children in the ways of Religion. God asked Israel, 'What sureties have you to give that you will keep My Covenant?' They offered the Patriarchs, the Prophets and their righteous Rulers as their guarantors. But all of them were rejected. It was only when they offered their children as sureties for the permanence of the Covenant, that these were accepted.

4. *ye have seen.* They were eye-witnesses, and not listening merely to the recital of old traditions (Rashi).

how I bore you. 'As though I bare you' (Ibn Ezra, Luzzatto).

on eagles' wings. This verse is a magnificent and beautiful example of Heb. poetry, expressing God's relations with Israel. The Jewish commentators point out that the eagle carried its young upon its wings, offering its own body as a shield to protect the fledglings from the arrows of the archer. This strong tenderness of the eagle towards its young is a symbol of God's love in taking His people out of the reach of danger to His own abode.

brought you unto Myself. To Sinai, where My Kingdom is to be proclaimed.

5. *Mine own treasure.* 'A peculiar treasure' (RV). Heb. *segullah*, a term used to denote a precious object or treasure that is one's special possession; I Chron. XXIX, 3. 'These words, *a peculiar treasure*, sound more partial than they really are. If I have chosen an instrument for a peculiar purpose, that instrument may be to me a peculiar treasure, but the purpose is greater than the instrument. So with the Jews. They are God's instrument, and as such a peculiar treasure; but the work is far greater than the instrument' (C. G. Montefiore).

for all the earth is Mine. See VI, 7. God is the Creator of all things and the Father of all mankind. Israel, in common with every other nation, forms part of God's possession; but He has chosen Israel to be His in a special degree, to be 'a light unto the nations' and a blessing to all humanity. There is no thought of favouritism in God's choice. Israel's call has not been to privilege and rulership, but to martyrdom and service.

6. *a kingdom of priests.* Or, 'a priestly kingdom'; a kingdom whose citizens are all priests (cf. Isa. LXI, 6), living wholly in God's service and ever enjoying the right of access to Him. As it is the duty of the priest to bring man nearer

חמישי
7 הַדְּבָרִים אֲשֶׁר תְּדַבֵּר אֶל־בְּנֵי יִשְׂרָאֵל׃ *וַיָּבֹא מֹשֶׁה וַיִּקְרָא
לְזִקְנֵי הָעָם וַיָּשֶׂם לִפְנֵיהֶם אֵת כָּל־הַדְּבָרִים הָאֵלֶּה אֲשֶׁר
8 צִוָּהוּ יְהוָה׃ וַיַּעֲנוּ כָל־הָעָם יַחְדָּו וַיֹּאמְרוּ כֹּל אֲשֶׁר־דִּבֶּר
9 יְהוָה נַעֲשֶׂה וַיָּשֶׁב מֹשֶׁה אֶת־דִּבְרֵי הָעָם אֶל־יְהוָה׃ וַיֹּאמֶר
יְהוָה אֶל־מֹשֶׁה הִנֵּה אָנֹכִי בָּא אֵלֶיךָ בְּעַב הֶעָנָן בַּעֲבוּר
יִשְׁמַע הָעָם בְּדַבְּרִי עִמָּךְ וְגַם־בְּךָ יַאֲמִינוּ לְעוֹלָם וַיַּגֵּד
10 מֹשֶׁה אֶת־דִּבְרֵי הָעָם אֶל־יְהוָה׃ וַיֹּאמֶר יְהוָה אֶל־מֹשֶׁה
11 לֵךְ אֶל־הָעָם וְקִדַּשְׁתָּם הַיּוֹם וּמָחָר וְכִבְּסוּ שִׂמְלֹתָם׃ וְהָיוּ
נְכֹנִים לַיּוֹם הַשְּׁלִישִׁי כִּי ׀ בַּיּוֹם הַשְּׁלִשִׁי יֵרֵד יְהוָה לְעֵינֵי
12 כָל־הָעָם עַל־הַר סִינָי׃ וְהִגְבַּלְתָּ אֶת־הָעָם סָבִיב לֵאמֹר

holy nation. These are the words which thou shalt speak unto the children of Israel.'* v. 7. And Moses came and called for the elders of the people, and set before them all these words which the LORD commanded him. 8. And all the people answered together, and said: 'All that the LORD hath spoken we will do.' And Moses reported the words of the people unto the LORD. 9. And the LORD said unto Moses: 'Lo, I come unto thee in a thick cloud, that the people may hear when I speak with thee, and may also believe thee for ever.' And Moses told the words of the people unto the LORD. 10. And the LORD said unto Moses: 'Go unto the people, and sanctify them to-day and to-morrow, and let them wash their garments, 11. and be ready against the third day; for the third day the LORD will come down in the sight of all the people upon mount Sinai. 12. And thou shalt set bounds unto the people

to God, so Israel has been called to play the part of a priest to other nations; *i.e.* to bring them closer to God and Righteousness. This spiritual Kingdom constitutes the highest mission of Israel.

and a holy nation. 'Holy' here means, 'separated' from the false beliefs and the idolatry of the other nations. Israel becomes holy by cleaving unto God and by obeying His Torah; see also on XXII, 30.

7–9. Moses informs the Israelites of God's purpose.

7. *Moses came.* From the mount to the elders.

called for the elders. Who reported to the people.

set before them. Giving the entire nation the choice of accepting or rejecting the Divine message; cf. Ex. XXIV, 3 and Deut. IV, 44. Religion in Israel was not to be a secret doctrine of one favoured class, not a body of 'mysteries' entrusted to the keeping of priests, as in Egypt. At Sinai, the Divine Message comes to rich and poor, old and young, learned and unlearned alike.

8. *all that the LORD hath spoken.* They gladly and freely expressed their willingness to enter God's Covenant; cf. XXIV, 3. They thereby become in a special sense, God's People. The conviction of having entered upon such a Covenant—a conviction that henceforth remains imprinted for all time in the consciousness of Israel—cannot have arisen of itself. Its historicity is as unassailable as that of the sojourn in Egypt.

Moses reported. He returned to the mountain. God knew their reply, and immediately declared His intention of revealing Himself in the hearing of the people.

9. *that the people may hear.* Directly and not through a messenger or an intermediary; see XX, 16. The actual witnessing by the entire nation of the redemption from Egypt, and their direct perception of the Divine Manifestation at Sinai, these *religious experiences*, form, according to Yehudah Hallevi, the Foundations of Belief in Israel.

also believe thee. The pronoun *thee* is emphatic. Having heard the Voice from the cloud and fire, the people would nevermore doubt the Divine mission of Moses. 'Henceforth the people knew that Moses held direct communication with God, that his words were not creations of his own mind' (Hallevi).

for ever. 'The Law of Moses will not be changed, and there will never be any other Torah from the Creator, blessed be His name' (IXth article of the Jewish Creed, as formulated by Maimonides).

10–15. The People were to be rendered fit for the approaching Revelation. These ceremonies and warnings were to impress God's holiness upon their untutored minds.

10. *sanctify them.* Bid them sanctify themselves. Prepare them to meet God. The exceptional solemnity of the Divine Manifestation demanded sanctification; cf. Gen. XXXV, 2.

to-day and to-morrow. The fourth and fifth of Sivan.

let them wash their garments. An outward symbol implying purification by bathing and abstention from bodily pleasure; cf. Isa. I, 16; Ps. LI, 9.

11. *against the third day.* Not of the month, but of 'the three days of preparation', and, therefore, the sixth of Sivan.

will come down. His glory will be revealed in fire.

round about, saying: Take heed to yourselves, that ye go not up into the mount, or touch the border of it; whosoever toucheth the mount shall be surely put to death; 13. no hand shall touch him, but he shall surely be stoned, or shot through; whether it be beast or man, it shall not live; when the ram's horn soundeth long, they shall come up to the mount.'* vi s. 14. And Moses went down from the mount unto the people, and sanctified the people; and they washed their garments. 15. And he said unto the people; 'Be ready against the third day; come not near a woman.' 16. And it came to pass on the third day, when it was morning, that there were thunders and lightnings and a thick cloud upon the mount, and the voice of a horn exceeding loud; and all the people that were in the camp trembled. 17. And Moses brought forth the people out of the camp to meet God; and they stood at the nether part of the mount. 18. Now mount Sinai was altogether on smoke, because the LORD

הִשָּׁמְרוּ לָכֶם עֲלוֹת בָּהָר וּנְגֹעַ בְּקָצֵהוּ כָּל־הַנֹּגֵעַ בָּהָר
13 מוֹת יוּמָת׃ לֹא־תִגַּע בּוֹ יָד כִּי־סָקוֹל יִסָּקֵל אוֹ־יָרֹה יִיָּרֶה
(ששי לספ') אִם־בְּהֵמָה אִם־אִישׁ לֹא יִחְיֶה בִּמְשֹׁךְ הַיֹּבֵל הֵמָּה יַעֲלוּ
14 בָהָר׃* וַיֵּרֶד מֹשֶׁה מִן־הָהָר אֶל־הָעָם וַיְקַדֵּשׁ אֶת־הָעָם
טו וַיְכַבְּסוּ שִׂמְלֹתָם׃ וַיֹּאמֶר אֶל־הָעָם הֱיוּ נְכֹנִים לִשְׁלֹשֶׁת
16 יָמִים אַל־תִּגְּשׁוּ אֶל־אִשָּׁה׃ וַיְהִי בַיּוֹם הַשְּׁלִישִׁי בִּהְיֹת
הַבֹּקֶר וַיְהִי קֹלֹת וּבְרָקִים וְעָנָן כָּבֵד עַל־הָהָר וְקֹל שֹׁפָר
17 חָזָק מְאֹד וַיֶּחֱרַד כָּל־הָעָם אֲשֶׁר בַּמַּחֲנֶה׃ וַיּוֹצֵא מֹשֶׁה
אֶת־הָעָם לִקְרַאת הָאֱלֹהִים מִן־הַמַּחֲנֶה וַיִּתְיַצְּבוּ בְּתַחְתִּית
18 הָהָר׃ וְהַר סִינַי עָשַׁן כֻּלּוֹ מִפְּנֵי אֲשֶׁר יָרַד עָלָיו יְהוָה
בָּאֵשׁ וַיַּעַל עֲשָׁנוֹ כְּעֶשֶׁן הַכִּבְשָׁן וַיֶּחֱרַד כָּל־הָהָר מְאֹד׃

12. *set bounds unto the people. i.e.* confine them within certain marked limits (Rashi). The mount where God's glory was about to be revealed would for the time being be a Sanctuary, and endowed with the unapproachable sacredness of the Ark or the Holy of Holies in the later Tabernacle.

the border. i.e. even its border (Rashi).

13. *no hand shall touch him. i.e.* the trespasser; as this would necessitate another touching at least the edge of the mountain.

soundeth long. i.e. drawing out the same tone for a long time. This would be the signal that the Manifestation was at an end, and the mountain had resumed its ordinary character.

they. The people.

shall come up. Better, *may come up.*

16–19. NATURAL ACCOMPANIMENTS OF THE REVELATION

16. *thick cloud.* lit. 'heavy', *i.e.* dense cloud. No mortal can gaze on the unveiled majesty of God. The cloud is the symbol and vehicle of the Divine Presence; see XIII, 21. The Revelation takes place in a thunderstorm of exceptional impressiveness and grandeur, amid overwhelming natural phenomena—lightning, thunder, earthquake and fire; cf. the revelation to Elijah, I Kings XIX, 11–13.

the voice of a horn. Heb. *shofar*, see *v.* 19 and XX, 18. The shofar was used to signalize, or accompany, important public events, such as the proclamation of a king. At Sinai, God's Kingdom was inaugurated by the voice of the shofar. On the New Year, the shofar is used to proclaim God's sovereignty; and, at the conclusion of the Day of Atonement, it is sounded to announce Israel's emancipation from sin obtained through the Day of Atonement, just as, in ancient times, the blowing of the shofar on that Day proclaimed freedom for the slave (Lev. XXV, 9 and 10).

17. *to meet God.* Or, 'toward God.'

they stood. Or, 'they took their stand.'

at the nether part of the mount. i.e. within the bounds, see *v.* 13.

18. *on smoke. i.e.* in smoke.

of a furnace. Cf. Gen. XV, 17, and Isa. VI, 4.

19. *God answered him by a voice.* This does not refer to the Ten Commandments, but to what took place in *v.* 21–24; Moses spoke to God, and God answered with voice loud enough to surpass the ever increasing sound of the horn.

20–25. The final directions before the Revelation.

20. *the LORD came down.* 'The Torah employs the language of man,' so that the listener or reader may understand the narrative.

21. *charge. i.e.* warn them not to go up the mountain (Rashi).

break through. The barriers (*v.* 12).

to gaze. Beyond the barriers, to see more closely the Divine Manifestation.

19 וַיְהִי קוֹל הַשֹּׁפָר הוֹלֵךְ וְחָזֵק מְאֹד מֹשֶׁה יְדַבֵּר וְהָאֱלֹהִים
(שביעי לספ') כ יַעֲנֶנּוּ בְקוֹל׃ וַיֵּרֶד יְהוָה עַל־הַר סִינַי אֶל־רֹאשׁ הָהָר
21 וַיִּקְרָא יְהוָה לְמֹשֶׁה אֶל־רֹאשׁ הָהָר וַיַּעַל מֹשֶׁה׃ וַיֹּאמֶר
יְהוָה אֶל־מֹשֶׁה רֵד הָעֵד בָּעָם פֶּן־יֶהֶרְסוּ אֶל־יְהוָה לִרְאוֹת
22 וְנָפַל מִמֶּנּוּ רָב׃ וְגַם הַכֹּהֲנִים הַנִּגָּשִׁים אֶל־יְהוָה יִתְקַדָּשׁוּ
23 פֶּן־יִפְרֹץ בָּהֶם יְהוָה׃ וַיֹּאמֶר מֹשֶׁה אֶל־יְהוָה לֹא־יוּכַל
הָעָם לַעֲלֹת אֶל־הַר סִינָי כִּי־אַתָּה הַעֵדֹתָה בָּנוּ לֵאמֹר
24 הַגְבֵּל אֶת־הָהָר וְקִדַּשְׁתּוֹ׃ וַיֹּאמֶר אֵלָיו יְהוָה לֶךְ־רֵד
וְעָלִיתָ אַתָּה וְאַהֲרֹן עִמָּךְ וְהַכֹּהֲנִים וְהָעָם אַל־יֶהֶרְסוּ
כה לַעֲלֹת אֶל־יְהוָה פֶּן־יִפְרָץ־בָּם׃ וַיֵּרֶד מֹשֶׁה אֶל־הָעָם
וַיֹּאמֶר אֲלֵהֶם׃ ס

descended upon it in fire; and the smoke thereof ascended as the smoke of a furnace, and the whole mount quaked greatly. 19. And when the voice of the horn waxed louder and louder, Moses spoke, and God answered him by a voice.* vi a, vii s. 20. And the LORD came down upon mount Sinai, to the top of the mount; and the LORD called Moses to the top of the mount; and Moses went up. 21. And the LORD said unto Moses: 'Go down, charge the people, lest they break through unto the LORD to gaze, and many of them perish. 22. And let the priests also, that come near to the LORD, sanctify themselves, lest the LORD break forth upon them.' 23. And Moses said unto the LORD: 'The people cannot come up to mount Sinai; for thou didst charge us, saying: Set bounds about the mount, and sanctify it.' 24. And the LORD said unto him: 'Go, get thee down, and thou shalt come up, thou, and Aaron with thee; but let not the priests and the people break through to come up unto the LORD, lest He break forth upon them.' 25. So Moses went down unto the people, and told them.

20 CHAPTER XX

כ CAP. XX. כ

א 2 וַיְדַבֵּר אֱלֹהִים אֵת כָּל־הַדְּבָרִים הָאֵלֶּה לֵאמֹר׃ ס אָנֹכִי

1. And God spake all these words, saying: ¶ 2. I am the LORD thy God, who brought thee out of the land of Egypt, out of the

22. *priests.* The first-born (Rashi, Ibn Ezra); cf. XIII, 2 and XXIV, 5. Even the 'priests', who are privileged to come nigh to God, require sanctification on this occasion.

come near. To the barrier of the Mount.

break forth. Or, 'make a breach in them.'

23. *the people cannot come.* Moses makes bold 'to question the need of such precaution, urging that the people are already debarred from trespassing by the bounds. God's answer in *v.* 24 shows a deeper knowledge of the human heart. His commands are never unnecessary' (H. F. Stewart).

25. *and told them.* He repeated the warning (Rashi).

In the next chapter, the Ten Commandments have a double accentuation in the Hebrew text—one for use in public reading in the Synagogue, and one for use in private devotion or study. The latter alone is given in the Authorized Prayer Book, p. 87.

THE TEN COMMANDMENTS

CHAPTER XX, 1–14

The 'Ten Words' or Commandments, the עשרת הדברות or the Decalogue (from *deka*, ten, and *logos*, word), are supreme among the precepts of the Torah, both on account of their fundamental and far-reaching importance, and on account of the awe-inspiring manner in which they were revealed to the whole nation. Amid thunder and lightning and the sounding of the shofar, amid flames of fire that enveloped the smoking mountain, a Majestic Voice pronounced the Words which from that day to this have been the guide of conduct to mankind. That Revelation was the most remarkable event in the history of humanity. It was the birth-hour of the Religion of the Spirit, which was destined in time to illumine the souls, and order the lives, of all the children of men. The Decalogue is a sublime summary of human duties binding upon all mankind; a summary unequalled for simplicity, comprehensiveness and solemnity; a summary which bears divinity on its face, and cannot be antiquated as long as the world endures. It is at the same time a Divine epitome of the fundamentals of Israel's Creed and Life; and Jewish teachers, ancient and modern, have looked upon it as the fountain-head from which all Jewish truth and Jewish teaching could be derived. 'These Commandments are written on the walls of Synagogue and Church; they are the world's laws for all time. Never will their empire cease. The prophetic cry is true: the word of our God house of bondage. ¶ 3. Thou shalt have no other gods before Me. 4. Thou shalt not make unto thee a graven image, nor any manner of likeness, of any thing that is in heaven above, or that is in the earth beneath, or that is in the water under the earth; 5. thou shalt not bow down unto them, nor serve them; for I the LORD thy God am a jealous God, visiting the iniquity

יְהוָה אֱלֹהֶיךָ אֲשֶׁר הוֹצֵאתִיךָ מֵאֶרֶץ מִצְרַיִם מִבֵּית עֲבָדִים׃
לֹא־יִהְיֶה לְךָ אֱלֹהִים אֲחֵרִים עַל־פָּנָי׃ לֹא־תַעֲשֶׂה לְךָ 3 4
פֶּסֶל ׀ וְכָל־תְּמוּנָה אֲשֶׁר בַּשָּׁמַיִם ׀ מִמַּעַל וַאֲשֶׁר בָּאָרֶץ
מִתַּחַת וַאֲשֶׁר בַּמַּיִם ׀ מִתַּחַת לָאָרֶץ׃ לֹא־תִשְׁתַּחֲוֶה לָהֶם ה

shall stand for ever' (M. Joseph). See Additional Note E, 'The Decalogue,' p. 400.

The most natural division of the Ten Commandments is into *man's duties towards God* (בין אדם למקום), the opening five Commandments engraved on the First Table; and into *man's duties to his fellow-man* (בין אדם לחברו), the five Commandments engraved on the Second Table.

FIRST TABLE: DUTIES TOWARDS GOD

First Commandment: Recognition of the Sovereignty of God

2. *I am the LORD thy God.* Jewish Tradition considers this verse as the first of the Ten Words, and deduces from it the positive precept, *To believe in the existence of God.*

I. Heb. *anochi.* The God adored by Judaism is not an impersonal Force, an It, whether spoken of as 'Nature' or 'World-Reason'. The God of Israel is the Source not only of power and life, but of consciousness, personality, moral purpose and ethical action (M. Joël).

thy God. The emphasis is on *thy.* He is the God not merely of the past generations, but of every individual soul in each generation.

who brought thee out of the land of Egypt. God is not here designated, 'Creator of heaven and earth.' Israel's God is seen not merely in Nature, but in the destinies of man. He had revealed Himself to Israel in a great historic deed, the greatest in the life of any people: the God who saved Israel from slavery had a moral claim, as their Benefactor and Redeemer, on their gratitude and obedience. 'The foundation of Jewish life is not merely that there is only one God, but the conviction that this One, Only and True God is *my* God, my sole Ruler and Guide in all that I do' (Hirsch). The first Commandment is thus an exhortation to acknowledge the sovereignty of God (קבלת עול מלכות שמים, lit. 'the taking upon ourselves the yoke of the Kingdom of Heaven').

The reference to the redemption of Egypt is of deepest significance, not only to the Israelites, but to all mankind. The primal word of Israel's Divine Message is the proclamation of the One God as the God of Freedom. The recognition of God as the God of Freedom illumines the whole of human history for us. In the light of this truth, history becomes one continuous Divine revelation of the gradual growth of freedom and justice on earth.

Second Commandment: The Unity and Spirituality of God

Jewish Tradition (based on Talmud, Midrash and Targum) makes *v.* 3 the beginning of the Second Commandment.

3. *thou shalt have no other gods.* Because there are no other gods besides God. The fundamental dogma of Israel's religion, as of all higher religion, is the Unity of God.

before Me. Or, 'besides Me'; or, 'to My face' (Koenig). Nothing shall receive the worship due to Him. Neither angels nor saintly men or women, are to receive adoration as Divine beings; and the Jew is forbidden to pray to them. This Commandment also forbids belief in evil spirits, witchcraft, and similar evil superstition. Furthermore, he who believes in God will not put his trust in Chance or 'luck'.

4. *a graven image.* This verse forbids the worship of the One God in the wrong way. Judaism alone, from the very beginning, taught that God was a Spirit; and made it an unpardonable sin to worship God under any external form that human hands can fashion. No doubt this law hindered the free development of plastic arts in ancient Israel; but it was of incalculable importance for the purity of the conception of God.

nor any manner of likeness. Nor is He to be worshipped under any image, though such be not graven, which the human mind can conceive.

in heaven above. i.e. of the heavenly bodies; such as the ancestors of the Hebrews in Babylonia adored.

in the earth beneath. e.g. of animals, such as the Israelites saw the Egyptians worshipping.

in the water under the earth. The monsters of the deep.

5. *a jealous God.* The Heb. root for 'jealous', *kanna,* designates the just indignation of one injured; used here of the all-requiting righteousness of God. God desires to be all in all to His children, and claims an exclusive right to their love and obedience. He hates cruelty and unrighteousness, and loathes impurity and vice; and, even as a mother is jealous of all evil influences that rule her children, He is jealous of the fathers upon the children unto the third and fourth generation of them that hate Me; 6. and showing mercy unto the thousandth generation of them that love Me and keep My commandments. ¶ 7. Thou shalt not take the name of the LORD thy

וְלֹא תָעָבְדֵם כִּי אָנֹכִי יְהוָה אֱלֹהֶיךָ אֵל קַנָּא פֹּקֵד עֲוֺן
6 אָבֹת עַל־בָּנִים עַל־שִׁלֵּשִׁים וְעַל־רִבֵּעִים לְשֹׂנְאָי׃ וְעֹשֶׂה
7 חֶסֶד לַאֲלָפִים לְאֹהֲבַי וּלְשֹׁמְרֵי מִצְוֺתָי׃ ס לֹא תִשָּׂא

when, instead of purity and righteousness, it is idolatry and unholiness that command their heart-allegiance. It is, of course, evident that terms like 'jealousy' or 'zeal' are applied to God in an anthropomorphic sense. It is also evident that this jealousy of God is of the very essence of His holiness. Outside Israel, the ancients believed that the more gods the better; the richer the pantheon of a people, the greater its power. It is because the heathen deities were free from 'jealousy' and, therefore, tolerant of one another and all their abominations, that heathenism was spiritually so degrading and morally so devastating; see on Deut. IV, 24.

visiting the iniquity of the fathers upon the children. The Torah does not teach here or elsewhere that the sins of the guilty fathers shall be visited upon their innocent children. *The soul that sinneth, it shall die* proclaims the Prophet Ezekiel. And in the administration of justice by the state, the Torah distinctly lays down, 'The fathers shall not be put to death for the children, neither shall the children be put to death for the fathers; every man shall be put to death for his own sin' (Deut. XXIV, 16). However, human experience all too plainly teaches the moral interdependence of parents and children. The bad example set by a father frequently corrupts those that come after him. His most dreadful bequest to his children is not a liability to punishment, but a liability to the commission of fresh offences. In every parent, therefore, the love of God, as a restraining power from evil actions, should be reinforced by love for his children; that they should not inherit the tendency to commit, and suffer the consequences of, *his* transgressions.

Another translation is, '*remembering* the sins of the fathers unto the children'; *i.e.* God *remembers* the sins of the fathers when about to punish the children. He distinguishes between the moral responsibility which falls exclusively upon the sinful parents, and the natural consequences and predisposition to sin, inherited by the descendants. He takes into account the evil environment and influence. He, therefore, tempers justice with mercy; and He does so to the third and fourth generation.

of them that hate Me. The Rabbis refer these words to the children. The sins of the fathers will be visited upon them, only if they too transgress God's commandments.

6. *unto the thousandth generation.* Contrast the narrow limits, three or four generations, within which the sin is visited, with the thousand generations that His mercy is shown to those who love God and keep His commandments. 'History and experience alike teach how often, and under what varied conditions, it happens that the misdeeds of a parent result in bitter consequence for the children. In His providence, the beneficent consequences of a life of goodness extend indefinitely further than the retribution which is the penalty of persistence in sin' (Driver).

that love Me. Note the verb 'love', used to designate the right attitude to God; cf. 'Thou shalt love the Lord thy God with all thy heart, with all thy soul, and with all thy might' (Deut. VI, 5). Love of God is the essence of Judaism, and from love of God springs obedience to His will.

THIRD COMMANDMENT: AGAINST PERJURY AND PROFANE SWEARING

The Second Commandment lays down the duty of worshipping God alone, and worshipping Him in spirit and not through images. The Third Commandment forbids us to dishonour God by invoking His name to attest what is untrue, or by joining His name to anything frivolous or insincere.

7. *take the name of the LORD.* Upon the lips; *i.e.* to utter.

in vain. lit. 'for vanity', or 'falsehood'; for anything that is unreal or groundless.

God is holy and His Name is holy. His Name, therefore, must not be used profanely to testify to anything that is untrue, insincere or empty. We are to swear by God's Name, only when we are fully convinced of the truth of our declaration, and then only when we are required to do so in a Court of law. This verse, according to the Rabbis, forbids using the Name of God in false oaths (*e.g.* that wood is stone); as well as using the Name of God in vain and flippant oaths (*e.g.* that stone is stone). God's Name is, moreover, not to be uttered unnecessarily in common conversation.

will not hold him guiltless. i.e. will not leave him unpunished. Perjury is an unpardonable offence, which, unless repressed by severest penalties, would destroy human society. The Rabbis ordained a special solemn warning to be administered to anyone about to take an oath in a Court of law. In various ages, saintly men have avoided swearing altogether. The Essenes, a Jewish Sect in the days of the Second Temple, held that 'he who cannot be believed without swearing is already condemned'. 'Let thy yea be yea, and thy nay, nay,' says the Talmud.

God in vain; for the LORD will not hold him guiltless that taketh His name in vain. ¶ 8. Remember the sabbath day, to keep it holy. 9. Six days shalt thou labour, and do all thy work; 10. but the seventh day is a sabbath unto the LORD thy God, in it thou shalt not do any manner of work, thou, nor thy son, nor thy daughter, nor thy man-servant, nor thy maid-servant, nor thy cattle, nor thy stranger that is within

אֶת־שֵׁם־יְהוָה אֱלֹהֶיךָ לַשָּׁוְא כִּי לֹא יְנַקֶּה יְהוָה אֵת אֲשֶׁר־
יִשָּׂא אֶת־שְׁמוֹ לַשָּׁוְא׃ פ
8 9 זָכוֹר אֶת־יוֹם הַשַּׁבָּת לְקַדְּשׁוֹ׃ שֵׁשֶׁת יָמִים תַּעֲבֹד וְעָשִׂיתָ
י כָּל־מְלַאכְתֶּךָ׃ וְיוֹם הַשְּׁבִיעִי שַׁבָּת ׀ לַיהוָה אֱלֹהֶיךָ לֹא־
תַעֲשֶׂה כָל־מְלָאכָה אַתָּה ׀ וּבִנְךָ־וּבִתֶּךָ עַבְדְּךָ וַאֲמָתְךָ

FOURTH COMMANDMENT : THE SABBATH

8. *remember.* The use of the word 'remember' may indicate that the institution was well known to the Israelites, long before their manna experiences; that it was a treasured and sacred institution inherited from the days of the Patriarchs; see also Note IV, p. 195. The Rabbis, however, explain 'Remember the Sabbath day' to mean, Bear it in mind and prepare for its advent; think of it day by day, and speak of its holiness and sanctifying influence. They instituted the Kiddush prayer, praising God for the gift of the Sabbath, to celebrate its coming in; and the Havdalah blessing, praising God for the distinction between the Sabbath and the six weekdays, to mark its going out.

sabbath day. Heb. *shabbath*, from a root meaning desisting from work.

to keep it holy. To treat it as a day unprofaned by workaday purposes. In addition to being a day of rest, the Sabbath is to be 'a holy day, set apart for the building up of the spiritual element in man' (Philo). Religious worship and religious instruction—the renewal of man's spiritual life in God—form an essential part of Sabbath observance. We, therefore, sanctify the Sabbath by a special Sabbath liturgy, by statutory Lessons from the Torah and the Prophets, and by attention to discourse and instruction by religious teachers. The Sabbath has thus proved the great educator of Israel in the highest education of all; namely the laws governing human conduct. The effect of these Sabbath prayers and Synagogue homilies upon the Jewish people has been incalculable. Leopold Zunz, the founder of the New Jewish Learning, has shown that almost the whole of Israel's inner history since the close of Bible times, can be traced in following the development of these Sabbath discourses on the Torah. Sabbath worship is still the chief bond which unites Jews into a *religious* Brotherhood. Neglect of such worship injures the spiritual life of both the individual and the community.

9. *shalt thou labour.* Work during the six days of the week is as essential to man's welfare as is rest on the seventh. No man or woman, howsoever rich, is freed from the obligation of doing some work, say the Rabbis, as idleness invariably leads to evil thoughts and evil deeds. The proportion of one day's rest in seven has been justified by the experience of the last 3,000 years. Physical health suffers without such relief. The first French Republic rejected the one day in seven, and ordained a rest of one day in ten. The experiment was a complete failure.

work. Heb. מלאכה, that which man produces by his thought, effort and will.

10. *a sabbath unto the LORD.* A day specially devoted to God.

thou shalt not do any manner of work. Scripture does not give a list of labours forbidden on Sabbath; but it incidentally mentions field-labour, buying and selling, travelling, cooking, etc., as forbidden work. The Mishna enumerates under thirty-nine different heads all such acts as are in Jewish Law defined as 'work', and, therefore, not to be performed on the Sabbath day; such as ploughing, reaping, carrying loads, kindling a fire, writing, sewing, etc. Certain other things which cannot be brought under any of these 39 Categories are also prohibited, because they lead to a breach of Sabbath laws (שבות); as well as all acts that would tend to change the Sabbath into an ordinary day. Whatever we are not allowed to do ourselves, we must not have done for us by a fellow-Jew, even by one who is a Sabbath-breaker. All these Sabbath laws, however, are suspended as soon as there is the least danger to human life; פקוח נפש דוחה את השבת say the Rabbis. The Commandments of God are to promote life and well-being, a principle based on Lev. XVIII, 5, 'and these are the precepts of the LORD by which *ye shall live* וחי בהם.'

thou. The head of the house, responsible for all that dwell therein.

manservant . . . maidservant. Or, 'bondman' . . . 'bondmaid'; cf. Deut. v, 14. Not only the children but also the servants, whether Israelite or heathen, nay even the beasts of burden, are to share in the rest of the Sabbath day; see note on XXIII, 12. 'The Sabbath is a boundless boon for mankind and the greatest wonder of religion. Nothing can appear more simple than this institution, to rest on the seventh day after six days of work. And yet no legislator in the world hit upon this idea! To the Greeks and the Romans it was an object of derision, a superthy gates; 11. for in six days the LORD made heaven and earth, the sea, and all that in them is, and rested on the seventh day; wherefore the LORD blessed the sabbath day, and hallowed it. ¶ 12. Honour thy father and thy mother, that thy days may be

11 וּבְהֶמְתֶּ֔ךָ וְגֵרְךָ֖ אֲשֶׁ֥ר בִּשְׁעָרֶֽיךָ׃ כִּ֣י שֵֽׁשֶׁת־יָמִים֩ עָשָׂ֨ה
יְהוָ֜ה אֶת־הַשָּׁמַ֣יִם וְאֶת־הָאָ֗רֶץ אֶת־הַיָּם֙ וְאֶת־כָּל־אֲשֶׁר־בָּ֔ם
וַיָּ֖נַח בַּיּ֣וֹם הַשְּׁבִיעִ֑י עַל־כֵּ֗ן בֵּרַ֧ךְ יְהוָ֛ה אֶת־י֥וֹם הַשַּׁבָּ֖ת

stitious usage. But it has removed with one stroke the contrast between slaves who must labour incessantly, and their masters who may celebrate continuously' (B. Jacob).

thy cattle. It is one of the glories of Judaism that, thousands of years before anyone else, it so fully recognized our duties to the dumb friends and helpers of man; see on Deut. v, 14.

thy stranger. The non-Israelite, who agrees to keep the seven Noachic precepts; see XII, 48. Though the Sabbath was not included in these precepts, he too is to enjoy the Sabbath rest for his own sake as a human being.

within thy gates. Within the borders of the town.

11. *rested.* See on Gen. II, 1–3.

By keeping the Sabbath, the Rabbis tell us, we testify to our belief in God as the Creator of the Universe; in a God who is not identical with Nature, but is a *free Personality*, the creator and ruler of Nature. The Talmudic mystics tell that when the heavens and earth were being called into existence, matter was getting out of hand, and the Divine Voice had to resound, 'Enough! So far and no further!' Man, made in the image of God, has been endowed by Him with the power of creating. But in his little universe, too, matter is constantly getting out of hand, threatening to overwhelm and crush out soul. By means of the Sabbath, called זכרון למעשה בראשית, 'a memorial of Creation,' we are endowed with the Divine power of saying 'Enough!' to all rebellious claims of our environment, and are reminded of our potential victory over all material forces that would drag us down.

blessed the sabbath. Made it a day of blessing to those who observe it. See note on Gen. II, 3. The Sabbath was something quite new, which had never before existed in any nation or in any religion—a standing reminder that man can emancipate himself from the slavery of his worldly cares; that man was made for spiritual freedom, peace and joy (Ewald). 'The Sabbath is one of the glories of our humanity. For if to labour is noble, of our own free will to pause in that labour which may lead to success, to money, to fame is nobler still. To dedicate one day a week to rest and to God, this is the prerogative and the privilege of man alone' (C. G. Montefiore).

and hallowed it. Endowed it with sanctifying powers. The sanctity of the Sabbath is seen in its traces upon the Jewish soul. Isaiah speaks of the Sabbath as 'a delight'; and the Liturgy describes Sabbath rest as 'voluntary and congenial, happy and cheerful'. 'The Sabbath planted a heaven in every Jewish home, filling it with long-expected and blissfully-greeted peace; making each home a sanctuary, the father a priest, and the mother who lights the Sabbath candles an angel of light' (B. Jacob). The Sabbath banishes care and toil, grief and sorrow. All fasting (except on the Day of Atonement, which as the Sabbath of Sabbaths transcends this rule of the ordinary Sabbath) is forbidden; and mourning is suspended on the Sabbath day. Each of the three Sabbath-meals is an obligatory religious act (מצוה); and is in the olden Jewish home accompanied by זמירות, Table Songs. The spiritual effect of the Sabbath is termed by the Rabbis the 'extra soul', which the Israelite enjoys on that day.

Ignorant and unsympathetic critics, condemn the Rabbinic Sabbath-laws with their numberless minutiæ as an intolerable 'burden'. These restrictions justify themselves in that the Jew who actually and strictly obeys these injunctions, *and only such a Jew*, has a Sabbath. And in regard to the alleged formalism of all these Sabbath laws, a German Protestant theologian of anti-Semitic tendencies has recently confessed: 'Anyone who has had the opportunity of knowing in our own day the inner life of Jewish families that observe the Law of the fathers with sincere piety and in all strictness, will have been astonished at the wealth of joyfulness, gratitude and sunshine, undreamt of by the outsider, which the Law animates in the Jewish home. The whole household rejoices on the Sabbath, which they celebrate with rare satisfaction not only as the day of rest, but rather as the day of rejoicing. Jewish prayers term the Sabbath a "joy of the soul" to him who hallows it; *he* "enjoys the abundance of Thy goodness". Such expressions are not mere words; they are the outcome of pure and genuine happiness and enthusiasm' (Kittel).

Without the observance of the Sabbath, of the olden Sabbath, of the Sabbath as perfected by the Rabbis, the whole of Jewish life would in time disappear.

FIFTH COMMANDMENT: HONOUR OF PARENTS

This Commandment follows the Sabbath command, because the Sabbath is the source and the guarantor of the family life; and it is among the Commandments engraved on the First Tablet, the laws of piety towards God, because parents stand in the place of God, so far as their children are concerned. Elsewhere in Scripture, the duty to one's parents stands likewise next to the duties towards God (Lev. XIX, 3).

long upon the land which the LORD thy God giveth thee.

¶ 13. Thou shalt not murder.
Thou shalt not commit adultery.
Thou shalt not steal.
Thou shalt not bear false witness against thy neighbour.

12 וַיְקַדְּשֵׁהוּ׃ ס כַּבֵּד אֶת־אָבִיךָ וְאֶת־אִמֶּךָ לְמַעַן יַאֲרִכוּן
13 יָמֶיךָ עַל הָאֲדָמָה אֲשֶׁר־יְהוָה אֱלֹהֶיךָ נֹתֵן לָךְ׃ ס לֹא
תִּרְצָח׃ ס לֹא תִּנְאָף׃ ס לֹא תִּגְנֹב׃ ס לֹא־
14 תַעֲנֶה בְרֵעֲךָ עֵד שָׁקֶר׃ ס לֹא תַחְמֹד בֵּית רֵעֶךָ

12. *honour thy father and thy mother.* By showing them respect, obedience and love. Each parent alike is entitled to these. For although 'father' is here mentioned first, in Lev. XIX, 3 we read, 'each one shall fear (*i.e.* reverence) *his mother* and his father.' And this obligation extends beyond the grave. The child must revere the memory of the departed parent in act and feeling. Respect to parents is among the primary human duties; and no excellence can atone for the lack of such respect. Only in cases of extreme rarity (*e.g.* where Godless parents would guide children towards crime) can disobedience be justified. Proper respect to parents may at times involve immeasurable hardship; yet the duty remains. Shem and Japhet throw the mantle of charity over their father's shame: only an unnatural child gloats over a parent's disgrace or dishonour. See note on Gen. IX, 23 (p. 34) and Prov. XXX, 17. The greatest achievement open to parents is to be ever fully worthy of their children's reverence and trust and love.

that thy days may be long. i.e. the honouring one's parents will be rewarded by happiness and blessing. This is not always seen in the life of the individual; but the Commandment is addressed to the individual as a member of society, as the child of a people. The home is infinitely more important to a people than the schools, the professions or its political life; and filial respect is the ground of national permanence and prosperity. If a nation thinks of its past with contempt, it may well contemplate its future with despair; it perishes through moral suicide.

SECOND TABLE: DUTIES TOWARDS FELLOW-MEN

The first five Commandments have each an explanatory addition; the last five are brief and emphatic Thou shalt not's. Our relation to our neighbours requires no eludication; since we feel the wrongs which others do to us, we have a clear guide how we ought to act towards others. These duties have their root in the principle 'Thou shalt love thy neighbour as thyself', applied to life, house, property and honour.

THE SIXTH COMMANDMENT: THE SANCTITY OF HUMAN LIFE

13. *thou shalt not murder.* The infinite worth of human life is based on the fact that man is created 'in the image of God'. God alone gives life, and He alone may take it away. The intentional killing of any human being, apart from capital punishment legally imposed by a judicial tribunal, or in a war for the defence of national and human rights, is absolutely forbidden. Child-life is as sacred as that of an adult. In Greece, weak children were *exposed;* that is, abandoned on a lonely mountain to perish. Jewish horror of child-murder was long looked upon as a contemptible prejudice. 'It is a crime among the Jews to kill any child,' sneered the Roman historian Tacitus.

Hebrew law carefully distinguishes homicide from wilful murder. It saves the involuntary slayer of his fellow-man from vendetta; and does not permit composition, or money-fine, for the life of the murderer. Jewish ethics enlarges the notion of murder so as to include both the doing of anything by which the health and well-being of a fellow-man is undermined, as well as the omission of any act by which a fellow-man could be saved in peril, distress or despair. For the prohibition of suicide, see note on Gen. IX, 5.

SEVENTH COMMANDMENT: THE SANCTITY OF MARRIAGE

adultery. 'Is an execrable and God-detested wrong-doing' (Philo). This Commandment against infidelity warns husband and wife alike against profaning the sacred Covenant of Marriage. It involves the prohibition of immoral speech, immodest conduct, or association with persons who scoff at the sacredness of purity. Among no people has there been a purer home-life than among the Jewish people. No woman enjoyed greater respect than the Jewish woman; and she fully merited that respect.

EIGHTH COMMANDMENT: THE SANCTITY OF PROPERTY

thou shalt not steal. Property represents the fruit of industry and intelligence. Any aggression on the property of our neighbour is, therefore, an assault on his human personality. This Commandment also has a wider application than theft and robbery; and it forbids every illegal acquisition of property by cheating, by embezzlement or forgery. 'There are transactions which are legal and do not involve any breach of law, which are yet base and disgraceful. Such are all transactions in which a person takes advantage of the ignorance or embarrassment of his neighbour for the purposes of increasing his own property' (M. Friedländer).

¶ 14. Thou shalt not covet thy neighbour's house; thou shalt not covet thy neighbour's wife, nor his man-servant, nor his maid-servant, nor his ox, nor his ass, nor any thing that is thy neighbour's. *vii a. ¶ 15. And all the people perceived the thunderings, and the lightnings, and the voice of the horn, and the mountain smoking; and when the people saw it, they trembled, and stood afar off. 16. And they said unto Moses: 'Speak thou with us, and we will hear; but let not God speak with us, lest we die.' 17. And Moses said unto the people: 'Fear not; for God is come to prove you, and that His fear may be before you, that ye

ס לֹא תַחְמֹד אֵשֶׁת רֵעֶךָ וְעַבְדּוֹ וַאֲמָתוֹ וְשׁוֹרוֹ וַחֲמֹרוֹ
וְכֹל אֲשֶׁר לְרֵעֶךָ׃ פ שביעי
טו וְכָל־הָעָם רֹאִים אֶת־הַקּוֹלֹת וְאֶת־הַלַּפִּידִם וְאֵת קוֹל
הַשֹּׁפָר וְאֶת־הָהָר עָשֵׁן וַיַּרְא הָעָם וַיָּנֻעוּ וַיַּעַמְדוּ מֵרָחֹק׃
16 וַיֹּאמְרוּ אֶל־מֹשֶׁה דַּבֵּר־אַתָּה עִמָּנוּ וְנִשְׁמָעָה וְאַל־יְדַבֵּר
17 עִמָּנוּ אֱלֹהִים פֶּן־נָמוּת׃ וַיֹּאמֶר מֹשֶׁה אֶל־הָעָם אַל־תִּירָאוּ
כִּי לְבַעֲבוּר נַסּוֹת אֶתְכֶם בָּא הָאֱלֹהִים וּבַעֲבוּר תִּהְיֶה
18 יִרְאָתוֹ עַל־פְּנֵיכֶם לְבִלְתִּי תֶחֱטָאוּ׃ וַיַּעֲמֹד הָעָם מֵרָחֹק

Ninth Commandment: Against Bearing False Witness

The three preceding Commandments are concerned with wrongs inflicted upon our neighbour by actual deed: this Commandment is concerned with wrong inflicted by word of mouth.

thou shalt not bear false witness. The prohibition embraces all forms of slander, defamation and misrepresentation, whether of an individual, a group, a people, a race, or a Faith. None have suffered so much from slander, defamation and misrepresentation as the Jew and Judaism. Thus, modernist theologians still repeat that, according to this Commandment, the Israelite is prohibited only from slandering a fellow-Israelite; because, they allege, the Heb. word for 'neighbour' (רע) here, and in 'Thou shalt love *thy neighbour* as thyself' (Lev. xix), does not mean fellow-man, but only fellow-Israelite. This is a glaring instance of bearing false witness against Judaism; and is proved to be so by xi, 2 ('Let every man ask of his neighbour, jewels of silver, etc.'), where the word *neighbour* cannot possibly mean an Israelite, but distinctly refers to the Egyptian. In this Commandment, as in all moral precepts in the Torah, the Heb. word *neighbour* is equivalent to *fellow-man.*

Tenth Commandment: Against Covetous Desires

14. *covet. i.e.* to long for the possession of anything that we cannot get in an honest and legal manner. This Commandment goes to the root of all evil actions—the unholy instincts and impulses of predatory desire, which are the spring of nearly every sin against a neighbour. The man who does not covet his neighbour's goods will not bear false witness against him; he will neither rob nor murder, nor will he commit adultery. It commands self-control; for every man has it in his power to determine whether his desires are to master him, or he is to master his desires. Without such self-control, there can be no worthy human life; it alone is the measure of true manhood or womanhood. 'Who is strong'? ask the Rabbis. 'He who controls his passions,' is their reply.

thy neighbour's house. i.e. his household. The examples enumerated are the objects most likely to be coveted.

This Commandment is somewhat differently worded in the Decalogue which is repeated by Moses in his Farewell Addresses to Israel. That difference, together with the other slight variations in that Decalogue from the original in this chapter of Exodus, is dealt with in the Commentary on *Deuteronomy.*

15–18. The Effect of the Revelation

15. *perceived the thunderings, and the lightnings.* An example of the rhetorical figure called *zeugma*, by which a verb is used with two or more objects, some of which should strictly be governed by another verb. As soon as the people heard the thunder and saw the lightning (xix, 16, 19) they trembled, even before the Commandments were given; see Deut. v, 15, 19.

trembled. Or, 'reeled,' fell in panic.

16. *we will hear.* And obey; see Deut. v, 24.

but let not God speak with us. Prior to the promulgation of the Decalogue.

lest we die. See Deut. v, 22.

17. *to prove you.* Moses pacifies the people. The object of the terrors of Sinai was to 'prove' them; *i.e.* to put them to the proof (xvi, 4) whether they were inclined to submit themselves to God. Luzzatto takes the expression in the sense of testing a person desiring to be initiated, with a view of determining his fitness.

that His fear may be before you. The fear of God means the fear or dread of offending God; and since this prevents sin, the 'fear of God' becomes the 'love of God'.

that ye sin not. God desires that righteousness shall be the rule of man's life.

sin not.' 18. And the people stood afar off; but Moses drew near unto the thick darkness where God was.* m a. ¶ 19. And the LORD said unto Moses: Thus thou shalt say unto the children of Israel: Ye yourselves have seen that I have talked with you from heaven. 20. Ye shall not make with Me—gods of silver, or gods of gold, ye shall not make unto you.* m s. 21. An altar of earth thou shalt make unto Me, and shalt sacrifice thereon thy burnt-offerings, and thy peace-offerings, thy sheep, and thine oxen; in every place where I cause My name to be mentioned I will come unto thee and bless thee. 22. And if thou make Me an altar of stone, thou shalt not build it of hewn stones; for if thou lift up thy tool upon it, thou hast profaned it. 23. Neither shalt thou go up by steps unto Mine altar, that thy nakedness be not uncovered thereon.

מפטיר וּמֹשֶׁה נִגַּשׁ אֶל־הָעֲרָפֶל אֲשֶׁר־שָׁם הָאֱלֹהִים׃ ס
19 וַיֹּאמֶר יְהוָה אֶל־מֹשֶׁה כֹּה תֹאמַר אֶל־בְּנֵי יִשְׂרָאֵל אַתֶּם
(מפטיר לספ׳) כ רְאִיתֶם כִּי מִן־הַשָּׁמַיִם דִּבַּרְתִּי עִמָּכֶם׃ לֹא תַעֲשׂוּן אִתִּי
21 אֱלֹהֵי כֶסֶף וֵאלֹהֵי זָהָב לֹא תַעֲשׂוּ לָכֶם׃ * מִזְבַּח אֲדָמָה
תַּעֲשֶׂה־לִּי וְזָבַחְתָּ עָלָיו אֶת־עֹלֹתֶיךָ וְאֶת־שְׁלָמֶיךָ אֶת־
צֹאנְךָ וְאֶת־בְּקָרֶךָ בְּכָל־הַמָּקוֹם אֲשֶׁר אַזְכִּיר אֶת־שְׁמִי
22 אָבוֹא אֵלֶיךָ וּבֵרַכְתִּיךָ׃ וְאִם־מִזְבַּח אֲבָנִים תַּעֲשֶׂה־לִּי
לֹא־תִבְנֶה אֶתְהֶן גָּזִית כִּי חַרְבְּךָ הֵנַפְתָּ עָלֶיהָ וַתְּחַלְלֶהָ׃
23 וְלֹא־תַעֲלֶה בְמַעֲלֹת עַל־מִזְבְּחִי אֲשֶׁר לֹא־תִגָּלֶה
עֶרְוָתְךָ עָלָיו׃

18. The people remained standing afar off (see *v.* 15), whilst Moses approached the thick darkness.

where God was. 'Where the Glory of God was' (Onkelos).

THE BOOK OF THE COVENANT

CHAPTERS XX, 19–XXIII, 33

This section is a body of miscellaneous laws—civil, criminal, moral and religious. Nothing could be more appropriate for the opening of such a collection of laws than regulations for public worship.

19–23. HOW GOD IS TO BE WORSHIPPED

19. *ye yourselves have seen.* You have been eye-witnesses, and know the reality of My revelation.

from heaven. In an overwhelming and incomparable manner (Strack).

20. *make with Me—gods.* The regulations concerning worship begin by repeating the prohibition of idol-worship, even if the idol be of silver or gold. The incident of the Golden Calf shows that such repetition was far from unnecessary.

21. *an altar of earth.* Not even an altar of stone is essential for worshipping God; see *v.* 22.

thereon. Better, '*thereby*,' for the animal was not to be slain on the altar.

in every place. Refers to the different places at which the Tabernacle rested, from the entry of the Israelites into Canaan to the erection of the Temple by Solomon (Hoffmann); see Additional Notes on Deuteronomy, *Centralization of Worship*.

to be mentioned. i.e. wherever I command thee to build an altar or sanctuary unto Me. To *mention* or *remember* the name of God, means to worship Him; cf. Ps. XX, 8 and Isa. XXVI, 13.

22. *an altar of stone.* Is permissible; but the stones must be of unhewn natural rock, with the stamp of God's handiwork alone.

tool. lit. 'sword' or, 'iron instrument.' The Talmud explains this prohibition as follows, 'Iron shortens life, whilst the altar prolongs it. The sword, or weapon of iron, is the symbol of strife; whereas the altar is the symbol of reconciliation and peace between God and man, and between man and his fellow.'

23. *uncovered.* Lest the clothes of the priest be disturbed and his limbs uncovered. It is a warning not only against the frantic indecencies of pagan rituals, but against all infractions of propriety in worship.

HAFTORAH YITHRO הפטרת יתרו

ISAIAH VI–VII, 6 AND IX, 5, 6

CHAPTER VI

1. In the year that king Uzziah died I saw the Lord sitting upon a throne high and lifted up, and His train filled the temple. 2. Above Him stood the seraphim; each one had six wings: with twain he covered his face, and with twain he covered his feet, and with twain he did fly. 3. And one called unto another, and said:

Holy, holy, holy, is the LORD of hosts;
The whole earth is full of His glory.

4. And the posts of the door were moved at the voice of them that called, and the house was filled with smoke. 5. Then said I:

CAP. VI. ו

א בִּשְׁנַת־מוֹת הַמֶּלֶךְ עֻזִּיָּהוּ וָאֶרְאֶה אֶת־אֲדֹנָי יֹשֵׁב עַל־כִּסֵּא
2 רָם וְנִשָּׂא וְשׁוּלָיו מְלֵאִים אֶת־הַהֵיכָל׃ שְׂרָפִים עֹמְדִים ׀
מִמַּעַל לוֹ שֵׁשׁ כְּנָפַיִם שֵׁשׁ כְּנָפַיִם לְאֶחָד בִּשְׁתַּיִם ׀ יְכַסֶּה
3 פָנָיו וּבִשְׁתַּיִם יְכַסֶּה רַגְלָיו וּבִשְׁתַּיִם יְעוֹפֵף׃ וְקָרָא זֶה
אֶל־זֶה וְאָמַר קָדוֹשׁ ׀ קָדוֹשׁ קָדוֹשׁ יְהוָה צְבָאוֹת מְלֹא
4 כָל־הָאָרֶץ כְּבוֹדוֹ׃ וַיָּנֻעוּ אַמּוֹת הַסִּפִּים מִקּוֹל הַקּוֹרֵא

For the life and message of Isaiah, see p. 225.

The Sedrah describes the Revelation on Sinai that was to turn Israel into a Holy Nation, and guide the children of men in the paths of Reverence and Righteousness. The Haftorah brings the revelation that came to Isaiah in his early manhood, when, one day in the Temple, he heard the Seraphim sing, 'Holy, holy, holy is the LORD of hosts, the whole earth is full of His glory.' This cry out of eternity, proclaiming the ineffable holiness, the supreme majesty, and universal sovereignty of God, has been called the quintessence of all the teachings of the Prophets. It is the quintessence of the teachings of all true Religion.

1–5. THE CALL OF ISAIAH

1. *in the year that king Uzziah died.* After a prosperous reign of over a half-century (790–740 B.C.E.). He had greatly increased the wealth and power of the kingdom of Judah (II Chron. XXVI, 1–15); and his death filled all minds with misgivings. 'What will become of Judah now that Uzziah is gone?' was on the lips of all. In that year Isaiah 'saw the LORD', and realized that though mortal rulers come and go, God is in His heaven. This vision marks the beginning of Isaiah's ministry.

I saw the Lord. In prophetic ecstasy (Kimchi). The unseen spiritual world opens to Isaiah's inner eye; the Temple walls seem to him to expand into a Heavenly Palace; and he beholds God enthroned as the Sovereign of every being on earth or in heaven. '*How* God reveals Himself to His chosen messengers will scarcely ever be understood. It is the greatest of mysteries; although *that* He reveals Himself is the greatest of certainties' (Marti).

2. *above Him stood the seraphim.* Better, *seraphim were standing over Him; i.e.* angelic beings were in attendance upon Him.

covered his face. In reverence (Exod. III, 6).

covered his feet. In humility, unworthy to meet directly the Divine glance.

he did fly. To perform the will of the Creator.

3. *holy, holy, holy.* Threefold repetition in Heb. poetry indicates the superlative degree: God is the highest Holiness. 'Holy—in the highest Heaven, the place of His Divine abode; holy—upon earth, the work of His might; holy—for ever and ever unto all eternity' (Targum Jonathan).

'The Holy One of Israel,' is the title of God in Isaiah's writings. In Rabbinical literature, the most frequent Name used for God is הקדוש ברוך הוא 'The Holy One, blessed be He.' *Holy* denotes the awe-ful and august ethical majesty of God (R. Otto), His moral perfectness and complete freedom from all that makes men imperfect and impure. It denotes 'more than goodness, more than purity, more than righteousness: it embraces all these in their ideal completeness, but it expresses besides the recoil from everything which is their opposite' (Driver). Holiness is the *essential* attribute of God. Because of this holiness, inherent in Himself, His power is absolute and infinite.

the whole earth is full of His glory. All that is sublime in nature and human history is the outward expression and eradiation of the Divine Spirit.

4. *Posts.* Though the vision is seen with his inner eye, it is none the less actual. In the agitation of such a soul-experience, the pillars shake and the House becomes blurred before his physical eyes.

5. *I am undone.* God's holiness is, as it were, 'a devouring fire' of all impurity. The Prophet, therefore, is overwhelmed by the sense of his own unworthiness, and of the unworthiness of his people. Like Abraham of old, he feels that

Woe is me! for I am undone;
Because I am a man of unclean lips,
And I dwell in the midst of a people of unclean lips;
For mine eyes have seen the King,
The LORD of hosts.

6. Then flew unto me one of the seraphim, with a glowing stone in his hand, which he had taken with the tongs from off the altar; 7. and he touched my mouth with it, and said:

Lo, this hath touched thy lips;
And thine iniquity is taken away,
And thy sin expiated.

8. And I heard the voice of the Lord, saying:

Whom shall I send,
And who will go for us?

Then I said: 'Here am I; send me.' 9. And He said: 'Go, and tell this people:

Hear ye indeed, but understand not;
And see ye indeed, but perceive not.

10. Make the heart of this people fat,
And make their ears heavy,
And shut their eyes;
Lest they, seeing with their eyes,
And hearing with their ears,
And understanding with their heart,
Return, and be healed.'

ה וְהַבַּיִת יִמָּלֵא עָשָׁן׃ וָאֹמַר אוֹי־לִי כִי־נִדְמֵיתִי כִּי אִישׁ טְמֵא־
שְׂפָתַיִם אָנֹכִי וּבְתוֹךְ עַם־טְמֵא שְׂפָתַיִם אָנֹכִי יֹשֵׁב כִּי אֶת־
6 הַמֶּלֶךְ יְהוָה צְבָאוֹת רָאוּ עֵינָי׃ וַיָּעָף אֵלַי אֶחָד מִן־הַשְּׂרָפִים
7 וּבְיָדוֹ רִצְפָּה בְּמֶלְקַחַיִם לָקַח מֵעַל הַמִּזְבֵּחַ׃ וַיַּגַּע עַל־פִּי
וַיֹּאמֶר הִנֵּה נָגַע זֶה עַל־שְׂפָתֶיךָ וְסָר עֲוֺנֶךָ וְחַטָּאתְךָ תְּכֻפָּר׃
8 וָאֶשְׁמַע אֶת־קוֹל אֲדֹנָי אֹמֵר אֶת־מִי אֶשְׁלַח וּמִי יֵלֶךְ־לָנוּ
9 וָאֹמַר הִנְנִי שְׁלָחֵנִי׃ וַיֹּאמֶר לֵךְ וְאָמַרְתָּ לָעָם הַזֶּה שִׁמְעוּ
י שָׁמוֹעַ וְאַל־תָּבִינוּ וּרְאוּ רָאוֹ וְאַל־תֵּדָעוּ׃ הַשְׁמֵן לֵב־הָעָם
הַזֶּה וְאָזְנָיו הַכְבֵּד וְעֵינָיו הָשַׁע פֶּן־יִרְאֶה בְעֵינָיו וּבְאָזְנָיו
11 יִשְׁמָע וּלְבָבוֹ יָבִין וָשָׁב וְרָפָא לוֹ׃ וָאֹמַר עַד־מָתַי אֲדֹנָי
וַיֹּאמֶר עַד אֲשֶׁר אִם־שָׁאוּ עָרִים מֵאֵין יוֹשֵׁב וּבָתִּים מֵאֵין

11. Then said I: 'Lord, how long?' And He answered:

'Until cities be waste without inhabitant,
And houses without man,
And the land become utterly waste,

v. 10. קמץ ברביע

he and his people and all existence are but 'dust and ashes' in the presence of the Divine Holiness (R. Otto).

mine eyes have seen the King. No vision of any form or appearance is meant, but a revelation of His transcendent holiness and might.

6–13. ISAIAH'S PURIFICATION AND MISSION

6. *from off the altar.* Where the fire is holy; and where there is no 'strange fire' (Ibn Ezra). Man must be sanctified, *i.e.* purged of impurity, before he can hear God. 'As earthly fire burns away the outward impurity, so the heavenly fire burns away the defilement of sin, first from the lips, but through them from the whole man' (Dillmann).

8. *who will go for us.* The plural is the so-called plural of majesty; as in Gen. I, 26.

here am I; send me. Isaiah answers the call not out of compulsion, but out of freedom. His eager response rushes from heart and lips cleansed of human impurity.

9. *hear ye indeed.* The great failing of the inhabitants of Judah and Jerusalem during the prosperous reign of Uzziah was an insensibility to God and Divine things; they did not *miss* God, and therefore they were not prepared to *seek* Him. To such a generation, the first effect of Isaiah's message of the holiness of God and His absolute sovereignty over their lives, would be to *increase* their blindness and obduracy. It would tend to 'harden their hearts'; see on Exod. IV, 21. Most of his hearers will stubbornly reject his message; they will harden their hearts; and the fuller the teachings imparted to them, the deeper will be the guilt of rejecting them. This tragic effect of his message, Isaiah is clearly shown on the very threshold of his ministry; and the '*result* of the prophet's ministration is described as though it were its purpose' (Skinner).

11. *Lord, how long?* How long shall this spiritual blindness and unwillingness to repent endure? This question is wrung from the Prophet by his compassion for his people. The answer is given in *v.* 11–13. The perseverance in unbelief will continue until national disasters and exile have swept away the idolatrous majority and enabled the Remnant, the indestructible germ of spiritual Israel, to flourish and blossom under God's care.

12. And the LORD have removed men far away,
And the forsaken places be many in the midst of the land.

13. And if there be yet a tenth in it, it shall again be eaten up; as a terebinth, and as an oak, whose stock remaineth, when they cast their leaves, so the holy seed shall be the stock thereof.'

12 אָדָם וְהָאֲדָמָה תִּשָּׁאֶה שְׁמָמָה׃ וְרִחַק יְהוָה אֶת־הָאָדָם
13 וְרַבָּה הָעֲזוּבָה בְּקֶרֶב הָאָרֶץ׃ וְעוֹד בָּהּ עֲשִׂירִיָּה וְשָׁבָה
וְהָיְתָה לְבָעֵר כָּאֵלָה וְכָאַלּוֹן אֲשֶׁר בְּשַׁלֶּכֶת מַצֶּבֶת בָּם
זֶרַע קֹדֶשׁ מַצַּבְתָּהּ׃

CHAPTER VII

1. And it came to pass in the days of Ahaz the son of Jotham, the son of Uzziah, king of Judah, that Rezin the king of Aram, and Pekah the son of Remaliah, king of Israel, went up to Jerusalem to war against it; but could not prevail against it. 2. And it was told the house of David, saying: 'Aram is confederate with Ephraim.' And his heart was moved, and the heart of his people, as the trees of the forest are moved with the wind. ¶ 3. Then said the LORD unto Isaiah: 'Go forth now to meet Ahaz, thou, and [1]Shear-jashub thy son, at the end of the conduit of the upper pool, in the highway of the fullers' field; 4. and say unto him: Keep calm, and be quiet; fear not, neither let thy heart be faint, because of these two tails of smoking firebrands, for the fierce anger of Rezin and Aram, and of the son of Remaliah. 5. Because Aram hath counselled evil against thee, Ephraim also, and the son of Remaliah, saying: 6. Let us go up against Judah, and vex it, and let us make a breach therein for us, and set up a king in the midst of it, even the son of Tabeel.

[1] That is, *A remnant shall return.*

CAP. VII. ז

א וַיְהִי בִּימֵי אָחָז בֶּן־יוֹתָם בֶּן־עֻזִּיָּהוּ מֶלֶךְ יְהוּדָה עָלָה רְצִין
מֶלֶךְ־אֲרָם וּפֶקַח בֶּן־רְמַלְיָהוּ מֶלֶךְ־יִשְׂרָאֵל יְרוּשָׁלַםִ
2 לַמִּלְחָמָה עָלֶיהָ וְלֹא יָכֹל לְהִלָּחֵם עָלֶיהָ׃ וַיֻּגַּד לְבֵית דָּוִד
לֵאמֹר נָחָה אֲרָם עַל־אֶפְרָיִם וַיָּנַע לְבָבוֹ וּלְבַב עַמּוֹ כְּנוֹעַ
3 עֲצֵי־יַעַר מִפְּנֵי־רוּחַ׃ וַיֹּאמֶר יְהוָה אֶל־יְשַׁעְיָהוּ צֵא־
נָא לִקְרַאת אָחָז אַתָּה וּשְׁאָר יָשׁוּב בְּנֶךָ אֶל־קְצֵה תְּעָלַת
4 הַבְּרֵכָה הָעֶלְיוֹנָה אֶל־מְסִלַּת שְׂדֵה כוֹבֵס׃ וְאָמַרְתָּ אֵלָיו
הִשָּׁמֵר וְהַשְׁקֵט אַל־תִּירָא וּלְבָבְךָ אַל־יֵרַךְ מִשְּׁנֵי זַנְבוֹת
הָאוּדִים הָעֲשֵׁנִים הָאֵלֶּה בָּחֳרִי־אַף רְצִין וַאֲרָם וּבֶן־
ה רְמַלְיָהוּ׃ יַעַן כִּי־יָעַץ עָלֶיךָ אֲרָם רָעָה אֶפְרַיִם וּבֶן־רְמַלְיָהוּ
6 לֵאמֹר׃ נַעֲלֶה בִיהוּדָה וּנְקִיצֶנָּה וְנַבְקִעֶנָּה אֵלֵינוּ וְנַמְלִיךְ
מֶלֶךְ בְּתוֹכָהּ אֵת בֶּן־טָבְאַל׃

ז׳ v. 2. מלעיל

13. *if there be yet a tenth.* After the exile of the ten tribes of the Northern Kingdom, Judah maintained its existence for 134 years.

it shall again be eaten up. The kingdom of Judah too shall go into exile.

whose stock remaineth. As when a tree is cut down, the stump retains the vitality from which new shoots may grow, so there is a kernel of Israel, a Remnant of faithful and godly men, that form the indestructible 'stock' of the Tree of Judaism.

CHAPTER VII

From the vision of the future, the prophet returns to events of his day. The kings of Israel, having failed to induce Ahaz, king of Judah, to join them in their alliance against Assyria, advanced upon Jerusalem, and were determined to dethrone Ahaz. Isaiah bids the despairing king have faith in God and fear nought.

2. *the house of David. i.e.* Ahaz.

Ephraim. The poetical name for the kingdom of Israel.

3. *Shear-jashub.* lit. 'A remnant shall return'. Isaiah gave significant and prophetic names to his sons, as did Hosea (I, 6, 9).

conduit of the upper pool. Identified with recently discovered reservoirs near to the pool of Siloam. Ahaz had gone there to assure himself of an adequate water supply in the event of a siege.

4. *tails of smoking firebrands.* Incapable of more mischief; the strength of the advance of the two allies is exhausted; they do not know that they are two dying nations already doomed. The Assyrian hordes were at that moment hastening on to descend upon Syria and Israel.

son of Remaliah. i.e. Pekah, king of Israel.

6. *a breach.* In its walls; *i.e.* capture its capital city.

son of Tabeel. One of their own puppets, amenable to their plans.

The Prophet assures Ahaz that the campaign against him will utterly fail, and exhorts him to have confidence in God's care and guidance.

CHAPTER IX

5. For a child is born unto us,
A son is given unto us;
And the government is upon his shoulder;
And his name is called
[1]Pele-joez-el-gibbor-
Abi-ad-sar-shalom;

6. That the government may be increased,
And of peace there be no end,
Upon the throne of David, and upon his kingdom,
To establish it, and to uphold it
Through justice and through righteousness
From henceforth even for ever.
The zeal of the LORD of hosts doth perform this.

CAP. IX. ט

ה כִּי־יֶלֶד יֻלַּד־לָנוּ
בֵּן נִתַּן־לָנוּ וַתְּהִי הַמִּשְׂרָה עַל־שִׁכְמוֹ וַיִּקְרָא שְׁמוֹ פֶּלֶא
6 יוֹעֵץ אֵל גִּבּוֹר אֲבִי־עַד שַׂר־שָׁלוֹם׃ לְםַרְבֵּה הַמִּשְׂרָה
וּלְשָׁלוֹם אֵין־קֵץ עַל־כִּסֵּא דָוִד וְעַל־מַמְלַכְתּוֹ לְהָכִין אֹתָהּ
וּלְסַעֲדָהּ בְּמִשְׁפָּט וּבִצְדָקָה מֵעַתָּה וְעַד־עוֹלָם קִנְאַת יְהוָה
צְבָאוֹת תַּעֲשֶׂה־זֹּאת׃

[1] That is, *Wonderful in counsel is God the mighty, the Everlasting Father, the Ruler of peace.*

v. 6. מ' סתומה באמצע תיבה

CHAPTER IX, 5, 6

The Haftorah breaks off here and continues with two verses from a later prophecy, concerning Hezekiah, the son of Ahaz, then but a lad. His righteous reign will lift Judah from the degenerate condition into which it had sunk. Hezekiah will be the leader of the 'holy seed', the indestructible faithful Remnant in Israel.

5. *a child is born unto us.* The correct rendering of the Heb. is: unto us a child *has been* born—unto us a son *has been* given. The reference is not to any future Messiah, nor to any one yet unborn (see p. 202). Hezekiah had already given promise of the qualities of heart and mind that pointed to him as the future regenerator of his people.

the government is upon his shoulder. This clearly indicates that the 'crown prince' is the person referred to.

pele-joez-el-gibbor-abi-ad-sar-shalom. i.e. Wonderful in counsel is God the mighty, the Everlasting Father, the Ruler of peace (Rashi and Luzzatto). This is the significant name by which the child will be known; it is, therefore, left untranslated; in the same way as *Shear-jashub* (*v.* 3), *Immanuel* (*v.* 14) and *Maher-shalal-hash-baz* (VIII, 3) are all given in the Hebrew form.

The RV gives 'Wonderful, Counsellor, Mighty God, Everlasting Father, Prince of Peace'. This is quite impossible. No true Prophet—indeed, no true Israelite—would apply a term like 'Mighty God' or 'Everlasting Father' to any mortal prince. What is equally decisive against the RV rendering (which is followed by all Christian translators and, with some modifications, by many Jewish ones; *e.g.* Zunz, Leeser, Philippson) is the fact that the significant names of the children of the Prophets never describe the child, but in each case embody some religious message to the Prophet's contemporaries. Thus, *Shear-jashub* proclaimed that a faithful Remnant would survive the successive calamities that would befall Israel. This is true of all the other significant names in Isaiah; as well as of Hosea's names, like Lo-ruhammah and Lo-ammi.

6. *the throne of David.* The kingdom of Israel, devastated by the Assyrians in the days of Ahaz, fell into the hands of Hezekiah by reason of the weakening of Assyria in his days. For the first time since the days of Solomon, the national unity was re-established, and Hezekiah was the first ruler once more to occupy the throne of David; hence the Prophet speaks of the *increase of his government.*

for ever. i.e. during the days of Hezekiah (Rashi).

through justice and through righteousness. Characteristics of true government—and of Hezekiah's reign.

the zeal of the LORD of hosts. The love of God for His people, and His passion for Righteousness guarantee the promised deliverance.

21

CHAPTER XXI

1. Now these are the ordinances which thou shalt set before them. ¶ 2. If thou buy a Hebrew servant, six years he shall serve; and in the seventh he shall go out free for nothing. 3. If he come in by himself, he shall go out by himself; if he be married, then his wife shall go out with him. 4. If his master give him a wife, and she bear him sons or daughters; the wife and her children shall be her master's, and he shall go out by himself. 5. But if the servant shall

כא

CAP. XXI. כא

פ פ יח 18

א 2 וְאֵלֶּה הַמִּשְׁפָּטִים אֲשֶׁר תָּשִׂים לִפְנֵיהֶם׃ כִּי תִקְנֶה עֶבֶד
3 עִבְרִי שֵׁשׁ שָׁנִים יַעֲבֹד וּבַשְּׁבִעִת יֵצֵא לַחָפְשִׁי חִנָּם׃ אִם־
בְּגַפּוֹ יָבֹא בְּגַפּוֹ יֵצֵא אִם־בַּעַל אִשָּׁה הוּא וְיָצְאָה אִשְׁתּוֹ
4 עִמּוֹ׃ אִם־אֲדֹנָיו יִתֶּן־לוֹ אִשָּׁה וְיָלְדָה־לוֹ בָנִים אוֹ בָנוֹת

VI. MISHPATIM

(CHAPTERS XXI–XXIV)

CIVIL LEGISLATION

CHAPTER XXI, 1–32. THE RIGHT OF PERSONS

1. *now these are.* lit. '*and* these are.' '*And* links together the preceding commandments with those that follow. As the preceding commandments were revealed on Sinai, so were the succeeding regulations also communicated there' (Mechilta). The Torah recognizes no strong line of demarcation between the Decalogue and the civil laws in the chapters that follow it. All alike disclose the will of God. His Torah treats of every phase of human and national life—civil as well as religious, physical as well as spiritual.

set before them. Rehearse and explain to them.

2–11. THE HEBREW SERVANT

2. *servant.* Or, 'bondman.' The very first civil ordinance secures the personal rights of the lowliest in the social scale, the bondman.

The Rabbis limit this provision to the thief who is sold to make restitution for his theft. The case of the Hebrew who sells himself into bondage because of poverty is dealt with in Lev. xxv, 39.

Hebrew servant. Slavery as permitted by the Torah was quite different from Greek and Roman slavery, or even the cruel system in some modern countries down to our own times. In Hebrew law, the slave was not a thing, but a human being; he was not the chattel of a master who had unlimited power over him. In the Hebrew language, there is only one word for slave and servant. Brutal treatment of any slave, whether Hebrew or heathen, secured his immediate liberty; see on *v.* 26 f.

in the seventh. From the time that he was sold. If, however, the year of Jubilee occurred during the six years, the slave goes free without completing the time (Lev. xxv, 10).

for nothing. Without paying for his release.

3. *by himself.* And not with wife or children.

go out by himself. See *v.* 4.

married. To an Israelitish woman. The master is obliged to provide lodging and maintenance for the family of his bondman, the wife and older children doubtless paying for their keep by their labour. Both the wife and the children accompanied their father when he acquired his freedom.

4. *give him.* The slave had not the right of contracting a marriage for himself.

a wife. A non-Israelite slave. There was a saying current among ancient peoples to the effect that there was no morality among slaves. To prevent such promiscuity, the Torah makes a concession to human frailty and permits a temporary marriage.

the wife and her children. In Jewish law, the children share the status of the mother. If the Israelite had been permitted to take them into freedom with him, it would have impaired the purity of the race, and created a body of half-castes.

5. *plainly say.* Or, 'firmly say.' The master attempts to dissuade the Israelite slave from preferring bondage to freedom, but the latter is resolute in his intention.

my wife, and my children. Although it is natural for a man to become attached to his wife and offspring even in the circumstances here described, yet such conduct must have highly injurious results to the Hebrew state. It would tend to produce a class of dependent slaves; and, instead of the community consisting of free and equal citizens, it would be divided into a ruling and a servile class (Kalisch).

plainly say: I love my master, my wife, and my children; I will not go out free: 6. then his master shall bring him unto [1]God, and shall bring him to the door, or unto the door-post; and his master shall bore his ear through with an awl; and he shall serve him for ever. ¶ 7. And if a man sell his daughter to be a maid-servant, she shall not go out as the men-servants do. 8. If she please not her master, who hath espoused her to himself, then shall he let her be redeemed; to sell her unto a foreign people he shall have no power, seeing he hath dealt deceitfully with her. 9. And if he espouse her unto his son, he shall deal with her after the manner of daughters. 10. If he take him another wife, her food, her raiment, and her conjugal rights, shall he not diminish. 11. And if he do not these three unto her, then shall she go out for nothing, without money. ¶ 12. He that smiteth a man, so that he dieth, shall surely be put to death. 13. And if a man lie not

[1] That is, the judges.

ה הָאִשָּׁה וִילָדֶיהָ תִּהְיֶה לַאדֹנֶיהָ וְהוּא יֵצֵא בְגַפּוֹ׃ וְאִם־
אָמֹר יֹאמַר הָעֶבֶד אָהַבְתִּי אֶת־אֲדֹנִי אֶת־אִשְׁתִּי וְאֶת־בָּנָי
6 לֹא אֵצֵא חָפְשִׁי׃ וְהִגִּישׁוֹ אֲדֹנָיו אֶל־הָאֱלֹהִים וְהִגִּישׁוֹ אֶל־
הַדֶּלֶת אוֹ אֶל־הַמְּזוּזָה וְרָצַע אֲדֹנָיו אֶת־אָזְנוֹ בַּמַּרְצֵעַ
7 וַעֲבָדוֹ לְעֹלָם׃ ס וְכִי־יִמְכֹּר אִישׁ אֶת־בִּתּוֹ לְאָמָה
8 לֹא תֵצֵא כְּצֵאת הָעֲבָדִים׃ אִם־רָעָה בְּעֵינֵי אֲדֹנֶיהָ אֲשֶׁר־
לֹא יְעָדָהּ וְהֶפְדָּהּ לְעַם נָכְרִי לֹא־יִמְשֹׁל לְמָכְרָהּ בְּבִגְדוֹ־
9 בָהּ׃ וְאִם־לִבְנוֹ יִיעָדֶנָּה כְּמִשְׁפַּט הַבָּנוֹת יַעֲשֶׂה־לָּהּ׃ אִם־
11 אַחֶרֶת יִקַּח־לוֹ שְׁאֵרָהּ כְּסוּתָהּ וְעֹנָתָהּ לֹא יִגְרָע׃ וְאִם־
שְׁלָשׁ־אֵלֶּה לֹא יַעֲשֶׂה לָהּ וְיָצְאָה חִנָּם אֵין כָּסֶף׃ ס
12 13 מַכֵּה אִישׁ וָמֵת מוֹת יוּמָת׃ וַאֲשֶׁר לֹא צָדָה וְהָאֱלֹהִים

v. 8. לו ק'

6. *unto God.* Or, 'unto the judges.' The judges pronounce sentence in the name of God (Deut. I, 17).

The slave's declaration had to be made publicly before the judges, in order to prevent the master from boring his servant's ear by force, and alleging that it was by the servant's desire.

door. Of the house belonging to the master.

bore his ear. 'Why was the ear, among all the organs of the body, selected for perforation?' asked the pupils of Rabban Yochanan ben Zakkai. He answered 'The ear that heard the Divine utterance, *for unto Me the children of Israel are servants* (Lev. XXV, 55), and had yet preferred a human master, let that ear be bored.' The drilling of the ear to the door of the house may also have symbolized the attaching of the slave to the household, and may have served as permanent evidence that the slave had remained in service of his own free will. This boring of the ear was thus something altogether different from the inhuman custom in modern times of branding slaves by a red-hot iron, marked with certain letters, and then pouring ink into the furrows to make the inscription more conspicuous.

for ever. All the days of his life (Rashbam). The Rabbis, however, understood the Heb. word לעלם as signifying 'until the year of Jubilee' (Lev. XXV, 10). This Rabbinic interpretation is confirmed by Josephus.

7. *a maidservant.* Or, 'a bondwoman'; to be the secondary wife for the master or his son. In an age of polygamy, the position of concubine, or second wife, was not a degraded one. Her offspring had equal rights in matters of inheritance with the children of the first wife (Deut. XXI, 10–14).

as the menservants. i.e. not only after six years, but even earlier, according to the circumstances as given in the succeeding verse.

8. *espoused.* Or, 'designated.' The master had intended her for himself, not for his son (*v.* 9); but finding her displeasing to himself, he must allow her father or relatives to buy her back.

a foreign people. The master must either allow her to be redeemed by her relatives, or he must keep her. The abominable practice against which this law is directed was not confined to Hebrew masters or to ancient times. Thus, William of Malmesbury, speaking of the days before the Norman Conquest, complains of the horrible custom of Saxon masters who, after associating with the maid servants on their estates, sold them to a life of shame or into foreign slavery.

he shall have no power. The Talmud refers 'he' to both the master and the father: the master has acted deceitfully in that he has not kept faith with her; the father in that he sold her at all.

dealt deceitfully with her. By not carrying out the purpose for which he had acquired her.

9. *deal with her after the manner of daughters.* 'Treat her as a daughter' (Moffatt). Whether as wife to the father or to the son, the bondwoman is to be treated like a freeborn girl who marries. The rights due to her are enumerated in the next verse.

11. *these three.* The three obligations mentioned in the preceding verse (Abarbanel).

in wait, but God cause it to come to hand; then I will appoint thee a place whither he may flee. ¶ 14. And if a man come presumptuously upon his neighbour, to slay him with guile: thou shalt take him from Mine altar, that he may die. ¶ 15. And he that smiteth his father, or his mother, shall be surely put to death. ¶ 16. And he that stealeth a man, and selleth him, or if he be found in his hand, he shall surely be put to death. ¶ 17. And he that curseth his father or his mother, shall surely be put to death. ¶ 18. And if men contend, and one smite the other with a stone, or with his fist, and he die not, but keep his bed; 19. if he rise again, and walk abroad upon his staff, then shall he that smote him be quit; only he shall pay for the loss of his time, and shall cause him to be thoroughly healed.* ii. ¶ 20. And if a man smite his bondman, or

14 אִנָּ֣ה לְיָד֑וֹ וְשַׂמְתִּ֤י לְךָ֙ מָק֔וֹם אֲשֶׁ֥ר יָנ֖וּס שָֽׁמָּה׃ ס וְכִֽי־
יָזִ֥ד אִ֛ישׁ עַל־רֵעֵ֖הוּ לְהָרְג֣וֹ בְעָרְמָ֑ה מֵעִ֣ם מִזְבְּחִ֔י תִּקָּחֶ֖נּוּ
טו 16 לָמֽוּת׃ ס וּמַכֵּ֥ה אָבִ֛יו וְאִמּ֖וֹ מ֥וֹת יוּמָֽת׃ ס וְגֹנֵ֨ב
17 אִ֧ישׁ וּמְכָר֛וֹ וְנִמְצָ֥א בְיָד֖וֹ מ֥וֹת יוּמָֽת׃ ס וּמְקַלֵּ֥ל אָבִ֛יו
18 וְאִמּ֖וֹ מ֥וֹת יוּמָֽת׃ ס וְכִֽי־יְרִיבֻ֣ן אֲנָשִׁ֔ים וְהִכָּה־אִישׁ֙
אֶת־רֵעֵ֔הוּ בְּאֶ֖בֶן א֣וֹ בְאֶגְרֹ֑ף וְלֹ֥א יָמ֖וּת וְנָפַ֥ל לְמִשְׁכָּֽב׃
19 אִם־יָק֞וּם וְהִתְהַלֵּ֥ךְ בַּח֛וּץ עַל־מִשְׁעַנְתּ֖וֹ וְנִקָּ֣ה הַמַּכֶּ֑ה רַ֥ק
שני כ שִׁבְתּ֛וֹ יִתֵּ֖ן וְרַפֹּ֥א יְרַפֵּֽא׃ * ס וְכִֽי־יַכֶּה֩ אִ֨ישׁ אֶת־עַבְדּ֜וֹ
21 א֤וֹ אֶת־אֲמָתוֹ֙ בַּשֵּׁ֔בֶט וּמֵ֖ת תַּ֣חַת יָד֑וֹ נָקֹ֖ם יִנָּקֵֽם׃ אַ֥ךְ אִם־

12–14. Laws concerning Murder

13. *lie not in wait.* The Torah draws a distinction between intentional and accidental homicide.

God cause it to come to hand. The modern mind, whilst agreeing that all things are ultimately controlled by God's will, does not attribute results to the *immediate* action of God. Not so the Biblical idiom. Nothing happens except by God's will; so if the murderer had no intention of killing his victim, the death must be due to His decree. English law retains the same idea, and uses the term 'act of God'; cf. note on the hardening of Pharaoh's heart, p. 220.

a place. Of shelter from the vengeance of the next-of-kin. Special cities were to be set apart for this purpose when the Israelites had settled in Canaan (Num. xxxv, Deut. xix).

14. *from Mine altar.* Even if it was a priest who officiated at the altar, he was not to escape his punishment, if his act was other than unintentional homicide (Talmud). Among the Greeks, an altar gave asylum to every murderer. In the Middle Ages, the Church offered 'sanctuary' to criminals of every description.

15–17. Crimes against Parents; Kidnapping

15. *smiteth.* The Rabbis rule that only when the blow left a bruise was the death penalty incurred.

16. *stealeth a man.* Kidnapping for the purpose of selling the victim into slavery in a foreign land (cf. the story of Joseph). It, therefore, meant both loss of liberty and spiritual death to the victim, if an Israelite. It was only towards the end of the eighteenth century that the slave trade, *i.e.* organized kidnapping on a vast scale, with the hideous cruelties attendant on it, began to be recognized in Western European countries as something unspeakably vile.

or if he be found. lit. '*and* he be found.' Prompted by the desire to reduce capital punishment as much as possible, the Rabbis cling to the *literal* translation of these words. The victim must have been seen by witnesses in the hands of the kidnapper *and* also have been sold, before the crime was punishable by death.

17. *curseth.* The Rabbis declared that for capital punishment to be incurred, the son must have used the Divine Name itself in cursing his parents.

put to death. By a court of law, and after judicial trial not by the parents themselves. In Rome, a father was allowed to put to death a grown-up son, even for no reason whatsoever.

18–27. Personal Injuries

18. *he die not.* If the blow proved fatal, then *v.* 12 applied.

19. *be quit.* As soon as the injured person walks abroad, there can be no possibility of manslaughter.

loss of his time. lit. 'his ceasing' from work. However, the Rabbis permitted him to claim compensation also on other grounds; *viz.* for the pain he had suffered, the 'shame' he had incurred by his disfigurement, etc.

to be thoroughly healed. Pay the doctor's bill (Talmud).

20. *bondman. i.e.* a heathen slave, because he only could be described as 'his money' (see on *v.* 21).

with a rod. Better, *with the rod, i.e.* the

22 יוֹם אוֹ יוֹמַיִם יַעֲמֹד לֹא יֻקַּם כִּי כַסְפּוֹ הוּא׃ ס וְכִי־
יִנָּצוּ אֲנָשִׁים וְנָגְפוּ אִשָּׁה הָרָה וְיָצְאוּ יְלָדֶיהָ וְלֹא יִהְיֶה אָסוֹן
עָנוֹשׁ יֵעָנֵשׁ כַּאֲשֶׁר יָשִׁית עָלָיו בַּעַל הָאִשָּׁה וְנָתַן בִּפְלִלִים׃
23 24 וְאִם־אָסוֹן יִהְיֶה וְנָתַתָּה נֶפֶשׁ תַּחַת נָפֶשׁ׃ עַיִן תַּחַת עַיִן שֵׁן
כה תַּחַת שֵׁן יָד תַּחַת יָד רֶגֶל תַּחַת רָגֶל׃ כְּוִיָּה תַּחַת כְּוִיָּה
26 פֶּצַע תַּחַת פָּצַע חַבּוּרָה תַּחַת חַבּוּרָה׃ ס וְכִי־יַכֶּה אִישׁ
אֶת־עֵין עַבְדּוֹ אוֹ־אֶת־עֵין אֲמָתוֹ וְשִׁחֲתָהּ לַחָפְשִׁי יְשַׁלְּחֶנּוּ
27 תַּחַת עֵינוֹ׃ וְאִם־שֵׁן עַבְדּוֹ אוֹ־שֵׁן אֲמָתוֹ יַפִּיל לַחָפְשִׁי יְשַׁלְּחֶנּוּ
תַּחַת שִׁנּוֹ׃ פ

his bondwoman, with a rod, and he die under his hand, he shall surely be punished. 21. Notwithstanding, if he continue a day or two, he shall not be punished; for he is his money. ¶ 22. And if men strive together, and hurt a woman with child, so that her fruit depart, and yet no harm follow, he shall be surely fined, according as the woman's husband shall lay upon him; and he shall pay as the judges determine. 23. But if any harm follow, then thou shalt give life for life, 24. eye for eye, tooth for tooth, hand for hand, foot for foot, 25. burning for burning, wound for wound, stripe for stripe. ¶ 26. And if a man smite the eye of his bondman, or the eye of his bondwoman, and destroy it, he shall let him go free for his eye's sake. 27. And if he smite out his bondman's tooth, or his bondwoman's tooth, he shall let him go free

instrument customarily used (Prov. x, 13; xiii, 24) and sufficient to secure obedience from the rebellious slave, but not to injure him severely. The master was allowed to chastise his slave, but not in a brutal manner so as to endanger his life.

surely be punished. There was no fixed penalty; the judges had to determine each case on its own merits. The Mechilta declares that the master was to be beheaded for such brutality.

21. *a day or two.* The master is not then punished, as it is clear that he had intended only to chastise the slave. Similar considerations have in all ages weighed in judging a parent whose child died in consequence of a correction. The death is then looked upon as an unfortunate accident, nothing more.

he is his money. 'This bare fact was presumptive evidence that the master had not intended to inflict serious injury, inasmuch as that would have involved pecuniary loss to himself' (H. Adler). In the circumstances, therefore, the financial loss was sufficient punishment for him.

22. *a woman.* Either she was near the men who were fighting, or she had endeavoured to separate them.

no harm. i.e. no fatal injury (Mechilta).

as the judges determine. If the husband makes an exorbitant claim, the sum to be paid was to be fixed by the court.

23. *life for life.* The Rabbis ruled that since no homicide was here intended it was a case for monetary compensation. That the words 'life for life' are merely a *legal term* meaning 'fair compensation', is seen from the parallel passage in Lev. xxiv, 18, which says: 'Whoever kills an animal shall pay for it: life for life.' This only means 'fair compensation'; otherwise, any man who slew an animal would have to forfeit his own life in return! To remove all doubt as to the meaning of the legal term 'life for life', the same paragraph (Lev. xxiv, 21) states, 'He that killeth a beast, shall make it good; and he that killeth a man shall be put to death.'

24. *eye for eye.* This law of retaliation—'measure for measure'—existed among ancient peoples, and persists to our own day in capital punishment. In the Torah, likewise, this law of 'measure for measure' is carried out literally only in the case of murder. 'Ye shall take no ransom for the life of a manslayer which is guilty of death: but he shall surely be put to death,' says Scripture (Num. xxxv, 31). Hence, it is evident that other physical injuries which are not fatal are a matter of *monetary compensation* for the injured party. Such monetary compensation, however, had to be equitable, and as far as possible *equivalent.* This is the significance of the *legal technical terms,* 'life for life, eye for eye, and tooth for tooth.' See Additional Note, p. 405.

25. *wound.* When blood is drawn.

stripe. When there is only a bruise. In computing compensation, the actual damage, the loss of time, the cost of the cure, the pain and the disfigurement, are all taken into consideration.

26. *bondman.* The loss of any limb from the most essential down to the least indispensable gave the slave immediate freedom, if that loss was due to brutal treatment of the master. According to the Rabbinic interpretation, *v.* 26 and 27 apply only to a heathen slave. If the slave was a Hebrew, he was treated entirely like the free Hebrew citizen, and received the same indemnification, but could not *ipso facto* claim his release.

eye. The Rabbis regard 'eye' and 'tooth' as typical, and enumerate twenty-four organs of the body which come within the operation of this law.

28 וְכִי־יִגַּח שׁוֹר אֶת־אִישׁ אוֹ אֶת־אִשָּׁה וָמֵת סָקוֹל יִסָּקֵל
29 הַשּׁוֹר וְלֹא יֵאָכֵל אֶת־בְּשָׂרוֹ וּבַעַל הַשּׁוֹר נָקִי: וְאִם שׁוֹר
נַגָּח הוּא מִתְּמֹל שִׁלְשֹׁם וְהוּעַד בִּבְעָלָיו וְלֹא יִשְׁמְרֶנּוּ
וְהֵמִית אִישׁ אוֹ אִשָּׁה הַשּׁוֹר יִסָּקֵל וְגַם־בְּעָלָיו יוּמָת:
ל אִם־כֹּפֶר יוּשַׁת עָלָיו וְנָתַן פִּדְיֹן נַפְשׁוֹ כְּכֹל אֲשֶׁר־יוּשַׁת
31 עָלָיו: אוֹ־בֵן יִגָּח אוֹ־בַת יִגָּח כַּמִּשְׁפָּט הַזֶּה יֵעָשֶׂה לּוֹ:
32 אִם־עֶבֶד יִגַּח הַשּׁוֹר אוֹ אָמָה כֶּסֶף ׀ שְׁלֹשִׁים שְׁקָלִים יִתֵּן
33 לַאדֹנָיו וְהַשּׁוֹר יִסָּקֵל: ס וְכִי־יִפְתַּח אִישׁ בּוֹר אוֹ כִּי־
יִכְרֶה אִישׁ בֹּר וְלֹא יְכַסֶּנּוּ וְנָפַל־שָׁמָּה שּׁוֹר אוֹ חֲמוֹר:
34 בַּעַל הַבּוֹר יְשַׁלֵּם כֶּסֶף יָשִׁיב לִבְעָלָיו וְהַמֵּת יִהְיֶה־לּוֹ:
לה ס וְכִי־יִגֹּף שׁוֹר־אִישׁ אֶת־שׁוֹר רֵעֵהוּ וָמֵת וּמָכְרוּ אֶת־
36 הַשּׁוֹר הַחַי וְחָצוּ אֶת־כַּסְפּוֹ וְגַם אֶת־הַמֵּת יֶחֱצוּן: אוֹ נוֹדַע
כִּי שׁוֹר נַגָּח הוּא מִתְּמוֹל שִׁלְשֹׁם וְלֹא יִשְׁמְרֶנּוּ בְּעָלָיו
37 שַׁלֵּם יְשַׁלֵּם שׁוֹר תַּחַת הַשּׁוֹר וְהַמֵּת יִהְיֶה־לּוֹ: ס כִּי
יִגְנֹב־אִישׁ שׁוֹר אוֹ־שֶׂה וּטְבָחוֹ אוֹ מְכָרוֹ חֲמִשָּׁה בָקָר יְשַׁלֵּם
תַּחַת הַשּׁוֹר וְאַרְבַּע־צֹאן תַּחַת הַשֶּׂה:

for his tooth's sake. ¶ 28. And if an ox gore a man or a woman, that they die, the ox shall be surely stoned, and its flesh shall not be eaten; but the owner of the ox shall be quit. 29. But if the ox was wont to gore in time past, and warning hath been given to its owner, and he hath not kept it in, but it hath killed a man or a woman; the ox shall be stoned, and its owner also shall be put to death. 30. If there be laid on him a ransom, then he shall give for the redemption of his life whatsoever is laid upon him. 31. Whether it have gored a son, or have gored a daughter, according to this judgment shall it be done unto him. 32. If the ox gore a bondman or a bondwoman, he shall give unto their master thirty shekels of silver, and the ox shall be stoned. ¶ 33. And if a man shall open a pit, or if a man shall dig a pit and not cover it, and an ox or an ass fall therein, 34. the owner of the pit shall make it good; he shall give money unto the owner of them, and the dead beast shall be his. ¶ 35. And if one man's ox hurt another's, so that it dieth; then they shall sell the live ox, and divide the price of it; and the dead also they shall divide. 36. Or if it be known that the ox was wont to gore in time past, and its owner hath not kept it in; he shall surely pay ox for ox, and the dead beast shall be his own. ¶ 37. If a man steal an ox, or a sheep, and kill it, or sell it, he shall pay five oxen for an ox, and four sheep for a sheep.

28–32. Injury caused by a Beast

28. *ox.* Or any other animal.

stoned. In order to implant horror against murder, even the beast, although it had not a moral sense, was to be removed from existence, since it was the cause of the destruction of a human being, made in the image of God.

29. *put to death.* Not by the hand of a human tribunal, but 'death by the hand of God' (Mechilta). Nachmanides quotes as a parallel, 'And the stranger that cometh nigh shall be put to death' (Num. I, 51), where the punishment for sacrilege is left to God.

30. *laid on him.* By a tribunal.

ransom. lit. 'covering'; a payment for the next of kin to forgive such intentional bloodshed.

31. *son . . . daughter.* For the explanation of this puzzling verse, and the light it throws on the true meaning of the *lex talionis* ('measure for measure'), as well as on the immeasurable moral difference between the civil legislation of the Torah and the Code of Hammurabi, see Additional Note F, p. 403.

32. *bondman.* A heathen slave (Mechilta). The valuation of an adult Israelite slave was fifty shekels (Lev. XXVII, 3).

OFFENCES AGAINST PROPERTY

XXI, 33–XXII, 14

33–36. Through Neglect or through an Animal

33. *open a pit.* For the storage of water. Where rivers are few and the rain falls only at certain periods, water has to be stored and covered. To 'open' a pit, therefore, means to remove the covering and fail to replace it.

ox or an ass. i.e. any animal. The law excludes the human being, because it assumes that a human being looks where he is walking.

34. *owner of the pit.* The man concerned in connection with the pit. It need not be his property; if he left it open, he is liable for his heedlessness.

shall be his. i.e. the man's who incurred the loss (Mechilta).

36. *wont to gore.* See on *v.* 29.

shall be his own. The Heb. is identical with the wording in *v.* 34, where 'own' is omitted.

37–XXII, 3. Theft

37. *five oxen.* Multiple restitution, but in far heavier ratios, is the penalty prescribed in the Hammurabi Code. In most European countries

22 CHAPTER XXII

CAP. XXII. כב

1. If a thief be found breaking in, and be smitten so that he dieth, there shall be no bloodguiltiness for him. 2. If the sun be risen upon him, there shall be bloodguiltiness for him—he shall make restitution; if he have nothing, then he shall be sold for his theft. 3. If the theft be found in his hand alive, whether it be ox, or ass, or sheep, he shall pay double.* iii. ¶ 4. If a man cause a field or vineyard to be eaten, and shall let his beast loose, and it feed in another man's field; of the best of his own field, and of the best of his own vineyard, shall he make restitution. ¶ 5. If fire break out, and catch in thorns, so that the shocks of corn, or the standing corn, or the field are consumed; he that kindled the fire shall surely make restitution. ¶ 6. If a man deliver unto his neighbour money or stuff to keep, and it be stolen out of the man's house; if the thief be found, he shall pay double. 7. If the thief be not found, then the master of the house shall come near unto [1]God, to see whether he have not put his hand unto his neighbour's goods. 8. For every matter of trespass, whether it be for ox, for ass, for

[1] That is, the judges.

א אם־במחתרת ימצא הגנב והכה ומת אין לו דמים׃
2 אם־זרחה השמש עליו דמים לו שלם ישלם אם־אין
3 לו ונמכר בגנבתו׃ אם־המצא תמצא בידו הגנבה
ישי 4 משור עד־חמור עד־שה חיים שנים ישלם׃ * ס כי
יבער־איש שדה או־כרם ושלח את־בעירה ובער בשדה
ה אחר מיטב שדהו ומיטב כרמו ישלם׃ ס כי־תצא
אש ומצאה קצים ונאכל גדיש או הקמה או השדה
6 שלם ישלם המבער את־הבערה׃ ס כי־יתן איש
אל־רעהו כסף או־כלים לשמר וגנב מבית האיש אם־
7 ימצא הגנב ישלם שנים׃ אם־לא ימצא הגנב ונקרב
בעל־הבית אל־האלהים אם־לא שלח ידו במלאכת
8 רעהו׃ על־כל־דבר־פשע על־שור על־חמור על־שה

v. 4. בעירו ק'

death was meted out for offences against property well into the nineteenth century. In Israel, however, the death penalty was not inflicted for an offence against property.

CHAPTER XXII

1. *breaking in.* lit. 'digging through.' The houses were built of clay and cross-beams, and the thief dug a hole in the wall.

no bloodguiltiness. The thief would only do this in the dead of night, and it could not be considered murder if the owner killed the intruder who, it is assumed in both ancient and modern codes of law, would not hesitate to take life.

2. *be risen upon him.* *i.e.* upon the thief. If the burglary takes place after daybreak (Ibn Ezra, Nachmanides), the slaying of the thief is murder, because it is not absolutely necessary to take his life.

for him. The murdered thief.

he shall make restitution. He who steals in the daytime; likewise, the thief in the night who is caught in the act and not slain (Herxheimer).

for his theft. The Rabbis add that if the value of the stolen animal was less than the price of a slave, the thief may not be sold. If the thief is sold, it can only be for the 'theft'; *i.e.* the price of the stolen article, and not for the four-fold or five-fold fine which is imposed.

3. *double.* He must return the stolen animal and give the owner another as a fine. This rule was extended to all stolen articles.

4–14. DAMAGE BY CATTLE OR FIRE, AND LAWS OF SAFE-KEEPING

4. *eaten.* By cattle.

let his beast loose. Wilfully sending his cattle to graze in a field which did not belong to him. If they wandered there, without any culpable negligence on his part, he is not liable.

of the best. When estimating the damage, the best of the injured man's field is to be taken as the basis of calculation of the value of the whole.

5. *fire break out.* *i.e.* a man kindles a fire in his own field, and the wind carries sparks into a neighbouring field and a conflagration is caused.

6. *deliver.* A man asks his neighbour to take charge of valuables as a favour. He may wish to go on a journey, and in his own interest requests a person to safeguard his property.

it be stolen. *i.e.* the trustee affirms that there has been a theft.

7. *unto God.* As in XXI, 6. Having solemnly sworn that he had not embezzled what had been entrusted to him, the trustee is free from all obligation. In the event of his having perjured himself, his punishment would come from God Himself.

8. *trespass.* Here the equivalent of embezzlement.

whereof one saith. Either the owner or a witness comes forward and identifies something which is in the possession of the trustee or the thief as the lost property.

this is it. The thing lost.

sheep, for raiment, or for any manner of lost thing, whereof one saith: 'This is it,' the cause of both parties shall come before God; he whom God shall condemn shall pay double unto his neighbour. ¶ 9. If a man deliver unto his neighbour an ass, or an ox, or a sheep, or any beast, to keep, and it die, or be hurt, or driven away, no man seeing it; 10. the oath of the LORD shall be between them both, to see whether he have not put his hand unto his neighbour's goods; and the owner thereof shall accept it, and he shall not make restitution. 11. But if it be stolen from him, he shall make restitution unto the owner thereof. 12. If it be torn in pieces, let him bring it for witness; he shall not make good that which was torn. ¶ 13. And if a man borrow aught of his neighbour, and it be hurt, or die, the owner thereof not being with it, he shall surely make restitution. 14. If the owner thereof be with it, he shall not make it good; if it be a hireling he loseth his hire. ¶ 15. And if a man entice a virgin that is not betrothed, and lie with her, he shall surely pay a dowry for her to be his wife. 16. If her father utterly refuse to give her unto

עַל־שַׂלְמָה עַל־כָּל־אֲבֵדָה אֲשֶׁר יֹאמַר כִּי־הוּא זֶה עַד
הָאֱלֹהִים יָבֹא דְּבַר־שְׁנֵיהֶם אֲשֶׁר יַרְשִׁיעֻן אֱלֹהִים יְשַׁלֵּם
9 שְׁנַיִם לְרֵעֵהוּ׃ ס כִּי־יִתֵּן אִישׁ אֶל־רֵעֵהוּ חֲמוֹר אוֹ־שׁוֹר
אוֹ־שֶׂה וְכָל־בְּהֵמָה לִשְׁמֹר וּמֵת אוֹ־נִשְׁבַּר אוֹ־נִשְׁבָּה אֵין
י רֹאֶה׃ שְׁבֻעַת יְהוָה תִּהְיֶה בֵּין שְׁנֵיהֶם אִם־לֹא שָׁלַח יָדוֹ
11 בִּמְלֶאכֶת רֵעֵהוּ וְלָקַח בְּעָלָיו וְלֹא יְשַׁלֵּם׃ וְאִם־גָּנֹב
12 יִגָּנֵב מֵעִמּוֹ יְשַׁלֵּם לִבְעָלָיו׃ אִם־טָרֹף יִטָּרֵף יְבִאֵהוּ עֵד
הַטְּרֵפָה לֹא יְשַׁלֵּם׃ פ
13 וְכִי־יִשְׁאַל אִישׁ מֵעִם רֵעֵהוּ וְנִשְׁבַּר אוֹ־מֵת בְּעָלָיו אֵין
14 עִמּוֹ שַׁלֵּם יְשַׁלֵּם׃ אִם־בְּעָלָיו עִמּוֹ לֹא יְשַׁלֵּם אִם־שָׂכִיר
טו הוּא בָּא בִּשְׂכָרוֹ׃ ס וְכִי־יְפַתֶּה אִישׁ בְּתוּלָה אֲשֶׁר
16 לֹא־אֹרָשָׂה וְשָׁכַב עִמָּהּ מָהֹר יִמְהָרֶנָּה לּוֹ לְאִשָּׁה׃ אִם־

condemn. Convict. If it is the trustee, he refunds the article and another of the same value. If the trustee is acquitted the witnesses who falsely accused him must pay him double the value of the lost article.

9. *be hurt*. By a fall, or an attack by another animal.

driven away. *i.e.* carried off by raiders.

10. *shall be between them both*. Shall decide between them. The trustee swears as to how the animal was hurt.

put his hand. To make an improper use of the animal, against the wishes of the owner, whereby it received its injury.

accept it. The oath, as fully acquitting the suspected trustee.

11. *stolen*. As distinct from its being carried off by a band of marauders, against whom he was powerless. In the case of theft, it was assumed that the trustee, who was paid to take care of the animal, had not done so sufficiently.

12. *bring it for witness*. Produce the torn flesh as evidence.

13. *aught*. An animal.

14. *be with it*. It is then the duty of the owner to take care of his animal.

he loseth his hire. Or, 'it is reckoned in its hire.' In accepting money for the use of the animal, the owner must take the risk.

MORAL OFFENCES

XXII, 15–XXIII, 9

15, 16. SEDUCTION

15. *entice*. Induces her to be a consenting party. If he violates her against her will, he pays her father fifty shekels of silver and is obliged to marry her, without the possibility of a subsequent divorce (Deut. XXII, 28 f).

not betrothed. If the girl was betrothed, their crime is on a par with adultery, should the offence have taken place within a city. If it happened in a field, the man alone suffers capital punishment (Deut. 23 f). On betrothal, see note on Lev. XXI, 3.

pay a dowry. Or, 'endow her,' to be his wife. 'In this way virgins were shielded from permanent ignominy in consequence of a momentary crime' (Kalisch). The monetary payment prescribed in this verse would provide against the seducer escaping his obligations. Without it, he might demand her in marriage without paying the dowry (*mohar*), thinking that, in the circumstances, the father would be anxious to grant the request. Originally this *mohar* was paid to the father; cf. Gen. XXXIV, 12. In later times, it was received not by the father but by the bride, in order to enable her to enter with proper dignity into the house of her future husband.

16. *refuse*. According to the Rabbis, the same law applies if the girl declines to marry him.

dowry of virgins. Fifty shekels (Deut. XXII, 29).

מָאֵן יְמָאֵן אָבִיהָ לְתִתָּהּ לוֹ כֶּסֶף יִשְׁקֹל כְּמֹהַר הַבְּתוּלֹת׃
17 18 ס מְכַשֵּׁפָה לֹא תְחַיֶּה׃ כָּל־שֹׁכֵב עִם־בְּהֵמָה מוֹת
19 יוּמָת׃ ס זֹבֵחַ לָאֱלֹהִים יָחֳרָם בִּלְתִּי לַיהוָה לְבַדּוֹ׃
כ וְגֵר לֹא־תוֹנֶה וְלֹא תִלְחָצֶנּוּ כִּי־גֵרִים הֱיִיתֶם בְּאֶרֶץ מִצְרָיִם׃

him, he shall pay money according to the dowry of virgins. ¶ 17. Thou shalt not suffer a sorceress to live. ¶ 18. Whosoever lieth with a beast shall surely be put to death. ¶ 19. He that sacrificeth unto the gods save unto the LORD only, shall be utterly destroyed. ¶ 20. And a stranger shalt thou not wrong, neither shalt thou oppress him; for ye were strangers in the land of Egypt.

17. WITCHCRAFT

17. *sorceress to live.* Not because there was any reality to witchcraft, but because it was a negation of the unity of God and an abominable form of idolatry. It is noteworthy that the Septuagint translates the Heb. word for *sorceress* by 'poisoner'. Ancient witchcraft was steeped in crime, immorality and imposture; and it debased the populace by hideous practices and superstitions. Hence the place of this command in this chapter. It is preceded by provisions against sexual licence (*v.* 15) and followed by condemnation of unnatural vice and idolatry (*v.* 18 and 19). The wording of the command is in an unusual form. We should have expected, 'A sorcerer shall surely be put to death.' Some commentators, therefore, explain it as a prohibition of resorting to the sorceress, and thus enabling her to thrive in her nefarious avocation. The law applied to the sorcerer as well (Lev. XX, 27).

It is fashionable to trace all the horrors of the persecution of witches in medieval times to this verse. There is no justification for this. Witchcraft as a sinister danger in Jewish social life ceases to count long before the Destruction of the Second Temple. (The incident in connection with Simon ben Shetach is no proof to the contrary. Both Jewish and non-Jewish scholars —Derenbourg, *Essai*, 69; Israel Lévi, *Revue des Etudes Juives*, XXXV, 213; and Strack, *Einleitung*[5], 118—have made it the subject of investigation, and are agreed that it is merely Haggadic). Later Jewish teachers (Samuel Ibn Chofni and Ibn Ezra) are among the earliest to deny the existence of demons or the efficacy of witchcraft. The hideous cruelties in the medieval trials of witches would have been impossible in Jewish judicial procedure. Torture to extort confession was unknown in Jewish law; and no confession on the part of the accused, that would have involved capital punishment, was allowable. 'No man can in law brand himself a criminal' (אין אדם משים עצמו רשע) is a principle in Jewish criminal law. Christianity, furthermore, which disregarded portions of the Decalogue (*e.g.* the Second Commandment, with respect to the prohibition of image-worship; and the Fourth Commandment, with respect to the Seventh day as the Sabbath) would certainly not have been guided in its attitude towards witchcraft by any single verse in the 'Old' Testament, if the New Testament had not been a demon-haunted book. Down to quite modern times the Church ascribed reality to the works of witches. In Germany alone, no less than 100,000 women and children are said to have suffered a cruel death during the horrible hunt of witches that disgraced the sixteenth century. So late as 1716, a woman and her daughter of nine years were hanged at Huntingdon for raising storms by witchcraft.

18. SODOMY

18. The law against witchcraft leads to the prohibition of kindred monstrous abominations, which formed part of many ancient heathen cults. See also Lev. XVIII, 23; XX, 15 f; Deut. XXVII, 21.

19. POLYTHEISM

19. *sacrificeth.* 'As the offering of sacrifices was the chief part of divine service, all other branches of unlawful worship were contained therein' (Rosenmüller). The warning against sacrificing to other deities was for many ages, alas, not a superfluous one in Israel.

the LORD only. Not even to angels as His ministers, or to an intermediary between Him and man.

utterly destroyed. Or, 'devoted'; *i.e.* doomed to extirpation; see Lev. XXVIII, 29.

20–23. OPPRESSION OF THE WEAK

20. *stranger.* Heb. *ger.* A resident alien; see XII. He was not required to adopt the Jewish Faith, as little as the Israelites, with whose position in Egypt he is compared, were worshippers of Isis or Apis.

shalt thou not wrong. The Rabbis explain this term to mean that nothing must be done to injure or annoy him, or even by word to wound his feelings. The fact that a man is a stranger should in no way justify treatment other than that enjoyed by brethren in race. 'This law of shielding the alien from all wrong is of vital significance in the history of religion. With it, alone, true Religion begins. The alien was to be protected, not because he was a member of one's family, clan, religious community, or people; but because he was a human being. *In the alien, therefore, man discovered the idea of humanity*' (Hermann Cohen).

for ye were strangers. In the next chapter, *v.* 9, this phrase is preceded by the words, 'for ye know the heart of the stranger'; *i.e.* you know

21. Ye shall not afflict any widow, or fatherless child. 22. If thou afflict them in any wise—for if they cry at all unto Me, I will surely hear their cry—23. My wrath shall wax hot, and I will kill you with the sword; and your wives shall be widows, and your children fatherless. ¶ 24. If thou lend money to any of My people, even to the poor with thee, thou shalt not be to him as a creditor; neither shall ye lay upon him interest. 25. If thou at all take thy neighbour's garment to pledge, thou shalt restore it unto him by that the sun goeth

21 22 כָּל־אַלְמָנָה וְיָתוֹם לֹא תְעַנּוּן׃ אִם־עַנֵּה תְעַנֶּה אֹתוֹ כִּי
23 אִם־צָעֹק יִצְעַק אֵלַי שָׁמֹעַ אֶשְׁמַע צַעֲקָתוֹ׃ וְחָרָה אַפִּי
וְהָרַגְתִּי אֶתְכֶם בֶּחָרֶב וְהָיוּ נְשֵׁיכֶם אַלְמָנוֹת וּבְנֵיכֶם יְתֹמִים׃ פ
24 אִם־כֶּסֶף ׀ תַּלְוֶה אֶת־עַמִּי אֶת־הֶעָנִי עִמָּךְ לֹא־תִהְיֶה לוֹ
כה כְּנֹשֶׁה לֹא־תְשִׂימוּן עָלָיו נֶשֶׁךְ׃ אִם־חָבֹל תַּחְבֹּל שַׂלְמַת
26 רֵעֶךָ עַד־בֹּא הַשֶּׁמֶשׁ תְּשִׁיבֶנּוּ לוֹ׃ כִּי הִוא כְסוּתֹה לְבַדָּהּ

v. 22. הנון בצירי v. 24. סגול בס"פ v. 26. כסותו ק'

from bitter experience what such a position means, and how it feels to be a stranger. Love of the alien is something unknown in ancient times. 'The Egyptians frankly hated strangers' (Holzinger); and the Greeks coined the infamous term 'barbarian' for all non-Greeks. The love of alien is still universally unheeded in modern times. Lev. XIX, 24, expressly demands in regard to the stranger, 'Thou shalt love him as thyself.' The Talmud mentions that the precept to love, or not to oppress, the stranger occurs thirty-six times in the Torah. The reason for this constantly-repeated exhortation is due to the fact that those who have been downtrodden frequently prove to be the worst oppressors when they acquire power over anyone.

21. *widow, or fatherless child.* Who are bereft of their human protector and destitute of the physical force to defend their rights.

22. *thou afflict.* The verb is changed from the plural in the preceding verse to the singular in this verse; and Ibn Ezra makes the fine comment. If a single individual afflict the widow and orphan, and the community does not intervene to protect them, punishment will fall on all.

23. *My wrath shall wax hot.* The punishment of hard-heartedness against the weak is pronounced with extraordinary emphasis, and a severe 'measure for measure' is threatened (Kalisch).

24–26. LOANS AND PLEDGES

24. *if.* Better, *when*, as it is an obligation on an Israelite to assist his neighbour with a *free* loan (Mechilta).

any of My people. See comments on Lev. XXV, 35, and Deut. XXIII, 20 f.

even to the poor. A loan to prevent a poor man falling into destitution is considered one of man's most meritorious deeds, and among the greatest of lovingkindnesses that can be shown to the living. This feeling towards the poor has led to the Institution of a Free Loan (Gemillus Chasodim) Society in every well-organized Jewish community.

creditor. viz., by seizing the debtor's land, or selling him or his family into slavery, to recover payment; see II Kings IV, 1. 'If you know he cannot pay, do not press him and so put him to shame' (Rashi).

interest. All interest is forbidden on loans to the poor. 'In modern times money is commonly lent for *commercial* purposes, to enable the borrower to increase his capital and develop his business; and it is as natural and proper that a reasonable payment should be made for this accommodation, as that it should be made for the loan (*i.e.* the hire) of a house, or any other commodity. But this use of loans is a modern development: in ancient times money was commonly lent for the relief of poverty brought about by misfortune or debt; it partook thus of the nature of charity; to take interest on money thus lent was felt to be making gain out of a neighbour's need' (Driver).

25. *pledge.* In Deut. XXIV, 6, it is forbidden to take a handmill or a mill-stone as security, because it is an indispensable article in a house. It is precepts like these that caused Huxley to declare: 'There is no code of legislation, ancient or modern, at once so just and so merciful, so tender to the weak and poor, as the Jewish law.'

26. *I will hear.* Just as God hears the cry of the widow and orphan (*v.* 22). The chivalry to the poor ordained in these verses will appear even more striking when we recall the barbarous treatment of the debtor in ancient Rome. If the debtor was unable to make repayment within thirty days after the expiration of the term agreed upon, the Law of the Twelve Tables permitted the creditor to keep him in chains for 60 days, publicly exposing the debtor and proclaiming his debt. If no person came forward to pay the debt the creditor might sell him into slavery or put him to death. If there were several creditors they might cut him to pieces, and take their share of the body in proportion to their debt.

down; 26. for that is his only covering, it is his garment for his skin; wherein shall he sleep? and it shall come to pass, when he crieth unto Me, that I will hear; for I am gracious.*iv. ¶ 27. Thou shalt not revile [1]God, nor curse a ruler of thy people. 28. Thou shalt not delay to offer of the fulness of thy harvest, and of the outflow of thy presses. The first-born of thy sons shalt thou give unto Me. 29. Likewise shalt thou do with thine oxen, and with thy sheep; seven days it shall be with its dam; on the eighth day thou shalt give it Me. 30. And ye shall be holy men unto Me; therefore ye shall not eat any flesh that is torn of beasts in the field; ye shall cast it to the dogs.

23

CHAPTER XXIII

1. Thou shalt not utter a false report; put not thy hand with the wicked to be an

הִוא שִׂמְלָתוֹ לְעֹרוֹ בַּמֶּה יִשְׁכָּב וְהָיָה כִּי־יִצְעַק אֵלַי וְשָׁמַעְתִּי
רביעי
27 כִּי־חַנּוּן אָנִי׃ ס אֱלֹהִים לֹא תְקַלֵּל וְנָשִׂיא בְעַמְּךָ לֹא
28 תָאֹר׃ מְלֵאָתְךָ וְדִמְעֲךָ לֹא תְאַחֵר בְּכוֹר בָּנֶיךָ תִּתֶּן־לִי׃
29 כֵּן־תַּעֲשֶׂה לְשֹׁרְךָ לְצֹאנֶךָ שִׁבְעַת יָמִים יִהְיֶה עִם־אִמּוֹ בַּיּוֹם
ל הַשְּׁמִינִי תִּתְּנוֹ־לִי׃ וְאַנְשֵׁי־קֹדֶשׁ תִּהְיוּן לִי וּבָשָׂר בַּשָּׂדֶה
טְרֵפָה לֹא תֹאכֵלוּ לַכֶּלֶב תַּשְׁלִכוּן אֹתוֹ׃ ס

CAP. XXIII. כג

כג

א לֹא תִשָּׂא שֵׁמַע שָׁוְא אַל־תָּשֶׁת יָדְךָ עִם־רָשָׁע לִהְיֹת עֵד

[1] That is, the judges.

כב' v. 26. קמץ בז"ק v. 27. חצי הספר בפסוקים

27. RESPECT TOWARDS GOD AND RULERS

27. *thou shalt not revile God.* Some of the Rabbis interpreted this as referring to blasphemy, others understand *elohim* as 'judges' (cf. XXI, 6; XXII, 7). Josephus and Philo explain thus, 'Let no one blaspheme those gods which other citizens esteem as such'; *i.e.* do not speak disrespectfully of the religious beliefs of the followers of other faiths.

a ruler. The authorities of the State must be spoken of with respect. As to the connection of this with the preceding verse, Philippsohn remarks: 'The last verses treat of the poor. They are warned, even in their most desperate need, not to blaspheme God or entertain and give utterance to feelings of revolt against their rulers.'

28, 29. OFFERINGS OF FIRST-FRUITS

28. *fulness.* The law concerning firstlings is given more fully in Lev. XIX; Num. XV, XVIII; and Deut. XXVI.

first-born. For the sanctification of the first-born among men and beasts, see note on XIII, 2 f.

29. *seven days.* Maimonides explains that the animal is 'as if it had no vitality before the end of that period; and not until the eighth day can it be counted among those that enjoy the light of the world'.

30. UNLAWFUL MEAT

30. *holy men.* On the association of the idea of holiness with forbidden food, see on Lev. XI, 44. All the preceding laws, as well as those following, are in the singular: this verse alone is in the plural. The philosopher Moritz Lazarus calls attention to the fact that whenever the duty or ideal of holiness is spoken of in the Torah, the plural is invariably used (*e.g.* 'Ye shall be holy,' Lev. XIX, 2), because mortal man can only attain to holiness when co-operating with others in the service of a great Cause or Ideal, as a member of a Community, Society, or 'Kingdom'. Of God alone can we say, the Holy One.

torn of beasts. Heb. *terefah;* which term originally was applied only to the meat of an animal torn by beasts in the field, but is now applied to any meats that are not ritually fit for Jewish consumption (kosher). The aim of Kashruth is the sanctification of life.

to the dogs. Such flesh is only fit to be eaten by dogs (Ibn Ezra).

CHAPTER XXIII, 1–3. TRUTH IN JUSTICE

1. *utter a false report.* *i.e.* utter a groundless report; forbids originating a calumny. The Rabbis explain it as a warning not to listen to a calumny, or join others in spreading it. Slander, they say, kills three—the person slandered, the slanderer, and the person who takes up and passes on the slander. They also apply the words of the text to evidence given at a trial. Such evidence must not include a statement of which the witness is not absolutely certain. The Talmud, on the basis of this verse, rules that a litigant must not state his case to the Court in the absence of the other litigant.

the wicked. Better, *a guilty person*; the Heb. word denotes the party who is in the wrong.

unrighteous witness. lit. 'a witness of violence'. The meaning is, Do not make common cause with the guilty person to give evidence which will bring about his acquittal.

unrighteous witness. 2. Thou shalt not follow a multitude to do evil; neither shalt thou bear witness in a cause to turn aside after a multitude to pervert justice; 3. neither shalt thou favour a poor man in his cause. ¶ 4. If thou meet thine enemy's ox or his ass going astray, thou shalt surely bring it back to him again. ¶ 5. If thou see the ass of him that hateth thee lying under its burden, thou shalt forbear to pass by him; thou shalt surely release it with him.*v. ¶ 6. Thou shalt not wrest the judgment of thy poor in his cause. 7. Keep thee far from a false matter; and the in-

2 חָמָֽס׃ לֹא־תִהְיֶה אַחֲרֵֽי־רַבִּים לְרָעֹת וְלֹא־תַעֲנֶה עַל־רִב
3 לִנְטֹת אַחֲרֵי רַבִּים לְהַטֹּת׃ וְדָל לֹא תֶהְדַּר בְּרִיבוֹ׃ ס
4 כִּי תִפְגַּע שׁוֹר אֹיִבְךָ אוֹ חֲמֹרוֹ תֹּעֶה הָשֵׁב תְּשִׁיבֶנּוּ לוֹ׃
ה ס כִּֽי־תִרְאֶה חֲמוֹר שֹׂנַאֲךָ רֹבֵץ תַּחַת מַשָּׂאוֹ וְחָדַלְתָּ
חמישי 6 מֵעֲזֹב לוֹ עָזֹב תַּעֲזֹב עִמּוֹ׃ • ס לֹא תַטֶּה מִשְׁפַּט אֶבְיֹנְךָ
7 בְּרִיבוֹ׃ מִדְּבַר־שֶׁקֶר תִּרְחָק וְנָקִי וְצַדִּיק אַל־תַּהֲרֹג

2. *a multitude.* This verse is a warning not to follow a majority blindly for evil purposes, especially to pervert justice. Because the majority of judges or witnesses are agreed on an opinion, which opinion he knows to be unjust, he should not abandon his own view in order to fall into line with the others. One with God and the Right, are the true majority.

bear witness. For this use of the Heb. verb, see xx, 16.

pervert justice. The Rabbis disregarded the literal meaning of the last three Heb. words, and took them to imply that, except when it is 'to do evil', one should follow the majority.

3. *favour a poor man.* Out of false sympathy, or antipathy to the rich and powerful (Driver). The Biblical view of justice is remarkable for its unbending insistence on the strictest impartiality. If the matter in dispute is a question of money between a rich and a poor man, the judge is not to give a wrongful verdict in favour of the poor man on the plea that the rich man would not miss the sum involved. 'Sympathy and compassion are great virtues, but even these feelings must be silenced in the presence of Justice' (Geiger).

4, 5. Love of Enemy

4. *thine enemy's ox.* Or any other animal belonging to him (Mechilta). This law is connected with the precepts concerning justice which immediately precede. Because your neighbour has done you an injury, so that you entertain a grievance against him, it is not right for you to allow it to influence your action when your duty towards him is clear. He has not ceased to be your fellowman, because he violates the law of neighbourly love towards you. Therefore, all envy or ill-will towards him is forbidden. No thought of vengeance (see on Lev. xix, 18) must be permitted to rise in your heart: *his* actions towards you must not be the standard of your conduct towards him. For the sake of your own human dignity there must be readiness to help him in his need, as in the typical instances adduced in the text.

Genuine, practical love of enemy is inculcated in this and following verse. As to the partisan statement in the New Testament, 'ye have heard that it was said, Thou shalt love thy neighbour *and hate thine enemy*,' that statement is absolutely baseless. 'Thou shalt hate thine enemy' is nowhere found in the Torah. C. G. Montefiore rightly observes that we cannot think very highly of the morality of that New Testament author in inventing a sentence unknown to the Torah in order to depreciate the Torah. Canon Rawlinson admits that '*hate thine enemy*' was no injunction of the Mosaic Law, but maintains that it is a conclusion which Rabbinical teachers unwarrantably drew from it. This charge against the Rabbis is utterly false. It is Christian teachers who rarely preached, and still more rarely practised, love of those whom they branded as 'enemies'. C. G. Montefiore has given an excellent summary of Jewish opinion on this matter: 'The adherents of no religion have hated their enemies more than Christians. The atrocities which they have committed in the name of religion, both inside and outside their own pale, are unexampled in the world's history. And even to-day it cannot be said that the various sects of Christians love one another, while anti-Semitism is a proof that they do not love those who are not Christians.'

5. *surely release it with him.* The general sense is clear. 'If you see the ass of a man who hates you lying helpless under its load, you must not leave it all to him, you must help him to release the animal' (Moffatt). This injunction has both the humanitarian motive towards the animal and the charitable motive towards the enemy. The greatest hero, say the Rabbis, is he who turns an enemy into a friend; and this can only be done by deeds of loving-kindness. 'If thine enemy be hungry give him bread to eat, and if he be thirsty, give him water to drink . . . and the Lord shall reward thee' (Prov. xxv, 21, 22).

6–9. Impartiality in Justice

6. *wrest the judgment.* 'As is well known, the maladministration of justice is, and always has been, a crying evil among Oriental nations' (Driver); but nowhere has there been such ringing denunciation of oppression of the poor and of denying justice to the victims of violence, as in Israel.

8 כִּי לֹא־אַצְדִּיק רָשָׁע׃ וְשֹׁחַד לֹא תִקָּח כִּי הַשֹּׁחַד יְעַוֵּר
9 פִּקְחִים וִיסַלֵּף דִּבְרֵי צַדִּיקִים׃ וְגֵר לֹא תִלְחָץ וְאַתֶּם
יְדַעְתֶּם אֶת־נֶפֶשׁ הַגֵּר כִּי־גֵרִים הֱיִיתֶם בְּאֶרֶץ מִצְרָיִם׃
10 וְשֵׁשׁ שָׁנִים תִּזְרַע אֶת־אַרְצֶךָ וְאָסַפְתָּ אֶת־תְּבוּאָתָהּ׃
11 וְהַשְּׁבִיעִת תִּשְׁמְטֶנָּה וּנְטַשְׁתָּהּ וְאָכְלוּ אֶבְיֹנֵי עַמֶּךָ וְיִתְרָם
12 תֹּאכַל חַיַּת הַשָּׂדֶה כֵּן־תַּעֲשֶׂה לְכַרְמְךָ לְזֵיתֶךָ׃ שֵׁשֶׁת יָמִים
תַּעֲשֶׂה מַעֲשֶׂיךָ וּבַיּוֹם הַשְּׁבִיעִי תִּשְׁבֹּת לְמַעַן יָנוּחַ שׁוֹרְךָ
13 וַחֲמֹרֶךָ וְיִנָּפֵשׁ בֶּן־אֲמָתְךָ וְהַגֵּר׃ וּבְכֹל אֲשֶׁר־אָמַרְתִּי
אֲלֵיכֶם תִּשָּׁמֵרוּ וְשֵׁם אֱלֹהִים אֲחֵרִים לֹא תַזְכִּירוּ לֹא

nocent and righteous slay thou not; for I will not justify the wicked. 8. And thou shalt take no gift; for a gift blindeth them that have sight, and perverteth the words of the righteous. 9. And a stranger shalt thou not oppress; for ye know the heart of a stranger, seeing ye were strangers in the land of Egypt. ¶ 10. And six years thou shalt sow thy land, and gather in the increase thereof; 11. but the seventh year thou shalt let it rest and lie fallow, that the poor of thy people may eat; and what they leave the beast of the field shall eat. In like manner thou shalt deal with thy vineyard, and with thy oliveyard. 12. Six days thou shalt do thy work, but on the seventh day thou shalt rest; that thine ox and thine ass may have rest, and the son of thy handmaid, and the stranger, may be refreshed. 13. And in all things that I have said unto you take ye heed; and make no mention of the name

7. *a false matter.* In the administration of justice; but this warning has the wider application as a rule of life of the highest importance.

innocent and righteous. Take every possible precaution so as not to condemn an innocent person to death. According to Talmudical law, a condemned man must have a re-trial whenever new evidence is forthcoming; but if there has been an acquittal, there cannot be a fresh hearing of the case.

justify the wicked. Better, *acquit a guilty person.* The guilty will not escape punishment at the hand of God, even if the human tribunal fails to inflict it.

8. *gift.* Better, *bribe.*

blindeth. A judge must not accept a gift even if he proposes to give a verdict in favour of the man who attempts to bribe him. A bribe has an insidious power; it will tend to shut the eyes of the judge to what he would otherwise have seen, and will inevitably corrupt him.

perverteth. Or, 'subverteth.' 'Destroys the case of a good man' (Moffatt).

9. *stranger.* See on XXII, 20–26. Like the poor, he was liable to become a victim of injustice. The alien was to receive the same treatment as the native Israelite; Deut. I, 16.

ye were strangers. See on XXII, 20.

10–12. The Sabbath Year and Sabbath Day

The institution of the Sabbatical year is fully treated in Lev. XXV and Deut. XV. It is included here because, in one aspect, it reinforced the teaching of humanity to the poor and helpless (Ibn Ezra, Luzzatto).

11. *shalt let it rest.* Or, 'release it.' Heb. *shamat* from which comes the name, *shemittah*, for the Sabbatical year, the Sabbath of the fields. 'The soil enjoyed a regular rest, doubly necessary in the imperfect state of agriculture of those ages, and calculated considerably to enhance its fertility in the other years' (Kalisch).

may eat. In an ordinary year, the poor could gather up the gleanings of the field, and also take from the 'corner' which had to be left unreaped (Lev. XIX, 9 f). In the Sabbatical year, there was no harvesting. Proprietor, servants, the poor and the stranger, all had equal rights to the produce (Lev. XXV, 6). Even the beasts of the field are not forgotten.

12. 'Even though the entire year be one of "rest", the weekly Sabbath day must be observed' (Mechilta). And as with the Sabbatical year, so with the Sabbath day; the law is restated here in order to emphasize its humanitarian teaching of affording complete rest to the servant, the stranger and the domestic animals.

be refreshed. Equivalent to the colloquial, 'catch their breath.' The word translated 'refreshed' (וינפש) is connected with the word נפש 'soul'; even the lowliest in Israel is to be reminded by the Sabbath day that he has a soul, that there is a higher life than mere drudgery; he is to receive spiritual refreshment on the Sabbath day.

13. *make no mention.* The Israelites could not serve God and any other deity at the same time; the very mention of the name of other gods is forbidden to them.

14 טו יִשָּׁמַע עַל־פִּיךָ׃ שָׁלֹשׁ רְגָלִים תָּחֹג לִי בַּשָּׁנָה׃ אֶת־חַג
הַמַּצּוֹת תִּשְׁמֹר שִׁבְעַת יָמִים תֹּאכַל מַצּוֹת כַּאֲשֶׁר צִוִּיתִךָ
לְמוֹעֵד חֹדֶשׁ הָאָבִיב כִּי־בוֹ יָצָאתָ מִמִּצְרָיִם וְלֹא־יֵרָאוּ
16 פָנַי רֵיקָם׃ וְחַג הַקָּצִיר בִּכּוּרֵי מַעֲשֶׂיךָ אֲשֶׁר תִּזְרַע בַּשָּׂדֶה
וְחַג הָאָסִף בְּצֵאת הַשָּׁנָה בְּאָסְפְּךָ אֶת־מַעֲשֶׂיךָ מִן־הַשָּׂדֶה׃
17 שָׁלֹשׁ פְּעָמִים בַּשָּׁנָה יֵרָאֶה כָּל־זְכוּרְךָ אֶל־פְּנֵי הָאָדֹן ׀
18 יְהוָה׃ לֹא־תִזְבַּח עַל־חָמֵץ דַּם־זִבְחִי וְלֹא־יָלִין חֵלֶב־חַגִּי
19 עַד־בֹּקֶר׃ רֵאשִׁית בִּכּוּרֵי אַדְמָתְךָ תָּבִיא בֵּית יְהוָה
אֱלֹהֶיךָ לֹא־תְבַשֵּׁל גְּדִי בַּחֲלֵב אִמּוֹ׃ פ ששי

of other gods, neither let it be heard out of thy mouth. ¶ 14. Three times thou shalt keep a feast unto Me in the year. 15. The feast of unleavened bread shalt thou keep; seven days thou shalt eat unleavened bread, as I commanded thee, at the time appointed in the month of Abib—for in it thou camest out from Egypt; and none shall appear before Me empty; 16. and the feast of harvest, the first-fruits of thy labours, which thou sowest in the field; and the feast of ingathering, at the end of the year, when thou gatherest in thy labours out of the field. 17. Three times in the year all thy males shall appear before the Lord GOD. ¶ 18. Thou shalt not offer the blood of My sacrifice with leavened bread: neither shall the fat of My feast remain all night until the morning. 19. The choicest first-fruits of thy land thou shalt bring into the house of the LORD thy God. Thou shalt not seethe

14–18. THE THREE ANNUAL PILGRIM FESTIVALS

The three pilgrimages which every adult Israelite had to make to the Sanctuary are more fully treated in Lev. XXIII and Deut. XVI.

15. *as I commanded thee.* In XII, 15.

Abib. lit. 'in the ear'; see IX, 31.

empty. This is explained in Deut. XVI, 17, 'every man shall give as he is able, according to the blessing of the LORD thy God which He hath given thee.' The pilgrim should bring with him offerings expressive of his gratitude for God's bounty.

16. *feast of harvest. i.e.* the feast of the first harvest. This is the festival of Pentecost. In Num. XXVIII, 26, it is called יום הבכורים, the day on which the first loaves made from the new corn were offered. In Deut. XVI, 10, it is called חג שבעות, the Feast of Weeks, because it is kept seven complete weeks after the first day of Passover. Jewish Tradition describes it as זמן מתן תורתנו, the anniversary of the Giving of the Torah, the revelation of the Decalogue having taken place on the sixth day of Sivan.

feast of ingathering. The Festival of Tabernacles; see Lev. XXIII, 34, 39 f.

the end of the year. i.e. of the agricultural year; see on Lev. XXIII, 24.

17. *all thy males. i.e.* adult males. Women are freed from all positive commandments depending on time, מצוות עשה שהזמן גרמא. Women could not be expected to leave their children unattended. Though it was not obligatory for them to do so, women were in the habit of accompanying their husbands to the Sanctuary; *e.g.* Elkanah and Hannah and Peninnah in I Sam. I; see further on XXXIV, 24.

the LORD. Heb. *adon*, master, overlord. These pilgrimages are marks of homage to the Sovereign of the land.

18. *leavened bread.* The Passover lamb was not to be slain until all the leaven had been removed.

the fat. This part of the sacrificial animal had to be burned on the altar (XXIX, 13).

My feast. Better, *My festival sacrifice, i.e.* the offering brought by the pilgrim.

until the morning. Cf. XII, 10.

19. *first-fruits.* The mode of presentation is described in Deut. XXVI, 2 f.

thou shalt not seethe. This command is repeated in XXXIV, 26, and Deut. XIV, 21. Upon these words, the Rabbis based the prohibition against eating meat and milk together in any way or form whatever. This prohibition was doubtless observed long before the age of the Rabbis; and in connecting it with this text, they merely sought a support in the Torah for an immemorial Jewish practice. Thus, Onkelos, who usually keeps close to the Hebrew text, renders, 'ye shall not eat flesh and milk.'

As to the original purpose of this law, opinions are divided. Some explain it that the command is levelled against idolatry and superstition (Maimonides); others state that it is a humanitarian ordinance intended to discourage a practice that would tend to harden the heart (Abarbanel, Luzzatto). 'We no longer know by what revolting sight this prohibition may have been called forth, but evidently that phrase became a kind of memorial by which Israel should always be reminded of that considerate humanity which was to distinguish it from the barbarous nations' (Ewald). Ibn Ezra writes: 'the reason of this prohibition is concealed from the eyes of even the wise.' Mendelssohn's comment on this law is, 'The benefit arising from the many inexplicable laws of God is in their practice, and not in the understanding of their motives.'

כ הִנֵּה אָנֹכִי שֹׁלֵחַ מַלְאָךְ לְפָנֶיךָ לִשְׁמָרְךָ בַּדָּרֶךְ וְלַהֲבִיאֲךָ
21 אֶל־הַמָּקוֹם אֲשֶׁר הֲכִנֹתִי׃ הִשָּׁמֶר מִפָּנָיו וּשְׁמַע בְּקֹלוֹ
22 אַל־תַּמֵּר בּוֹ כִּי לֹא יִשָּׂא לְפִשְׁעֲכֶם כִּי שְׁמִי בְּקִרְבּוֹ׃ כִּי
אִם־שָׁמוֹעַ תִּשְׁמַע בְּקֹלוֹ וְעָשִׂיתָ כֹּל אֲשֶׁר אֲדַבֵּר וְאָיַבְתִּי
23 אֶת־אֹיְבֶיךָ וְצַרְתִּי אֶת־צֹרְרֶיךָ׃ כִּי־יֵלֵךְ מַלְאָכִי לְפָנֶיךָ
וֶהֱבִיאֲךָ אֶל־הָאֱמֹרִי וְהַחִתִּי וְהַפְּרִזִּי וְהַכְּנַעֲנִי הַחִוִּי וְהַיְבוּסִי
24 וְהִכְחַדְתִּיו׃ לֹא־תִשְׁתַּחֲוֶה לֵאלֹהֵיהֶם וְלֹא תָעָבְדֵם וְלֹא
תַעֲשֶׂה כְּמַעֲשֵׂיהֶם כִּי הָרֵס תְּהָרְסֵם וְשַׁבֵּר תְּשַׁבֵּר
כה מַצֵּבֹתֵיהֶם׃ וַעֲבַדְתֶּם אֵת יְהוָה אֱלֹהֵיכֶם וּבֵרַךְ אֶת־
שביעי
26 לַחְמְךָ וְאֶת־מֵימֶיךָ וַהֲסִרֹתִי מַחֲלָה מִקִּרְבֶּךָ׃ ס לֹא
תִהְיֶה מְשַׁכֵּלָה וַעֲקָרָה בְּאַרְצֶךָ אֶת־מִסְפַּר יָמֶיךָ אֲמַלֵּא׃

a kid in its mother's milk.*vi. ¶ 20. Behold, I send an angel before thee, to keep thee by the way, and to bring thee into the place which I have prepared. 21. Take heed of him, and hearken unto his voice; be not rebellious against him; for he will not pardon your transgression; for My name is in him. 22. But if thou shalt indeed hearken unto his voice, and do all that I speak; then I will be an enemy unto thine enemies, and an adversary unto thine adversaries. 23. For Mine angel shall go before thee, and bring thee in unto the Amorite, and the Hittite, and the Perizzite, and the Canaanite, the Hivite, and the Jebusite; and I will cut them off. 24. Thou shalt not bow down to their gods, nor serve them, nor do after their doings; but thou shalt utterly overthrow them, and break in pieces their pillars. 25. And ye shall serve the LORD your God, and He will bless thy bread, and thy water; and I will take sickness away from the midst of thee.* vii. 26. None shall miscarry, nor be barren, in thy land; the number of thy days I will fulfil.

20–23. An Exhortation

The summary of the entire Divine legislation—the Decalogue—has been followed by an outline of the most necessary moral, religious, and civil precepts. An exhortation is now added, as is usual throughout the Torah, faithfully to adhere to these laws, with the promise of the special Providential guidance to the Holy Land, and a happy existence in it, as rewards of such obedience.

20. *an angel.* The Heb. word does not of necessity imply a supernatural being. It denotes, as does also the English word in its original signification, a messenger; and it is evident that an actual person is meant. Consequently, it is most natural to understand the word as a reference to Moses, with whom God had spoken 'face to face', and who was able to communicate His will to the people (Ralbag and Luzzatto). Moses would only command what God had ordained; therefore, loyalty to him would mean obedience of God. The prophets and priests are also sometimes called God's 'angels'; cf. Mal. II, 7.

the place. The Promised Land.

21. *he will not pardon.* Because *he* cannot pardon. Although he may desire to be lenient with you and overlook your faults, God will punish disobedience.

My name. God's 'name', *i.e.* His Divine authority, was vested in His messenger; see on III, 13.

22. *I will be an enemy.* God would help them against their foes who stood in the way of their taking possession of Canaan.

23. *Mine angel.* Not necessarily identical with the 'angel' of *v.* 20. In point of fact, it was Joshua who completed this task; but he, like Moses, was divinely appointed to the leadership (Deut. XXXI, 23).

Amorite. Cf. III, 17.

I will cut them off. God, and not the 'angel', will assure the victory to them. The Israelites were ever to remember to Whom alone they owed their success. Ehrlich connects *v.* 23 and 24 and translates, 'When mine angel shall go before thee . . . and I cut them off, thou shalt not bow down to their gods.'

24. *do after their doings.* Construct images similar to those which the inhabitants had made (Ehrlich).

overthrow them. So long as idols remain, there will be temptation to worship them. Therefore, every trace of idolatry must be uprooted.

pillars. Either a natural boulder, or an artificial construction, which was considered to be the abode of a deity.

25. *bless thy bread and thy water.* God will secure for them the necessities of life; or, He will ensure that their food be a blessing to them; *i.e.* it will invigorate them.

sickness. Cf. XV, 26.

26. *I will fulfil.* God will allow the individual to reach old age and not come to a premature end. It is analogous to 'that thy days may be long' (XX, 12).

27. I will send My terror before thee, and will discomfit all the people to whom thou shalt come, and I will make all thine enemies turn their backs unto thee. 28. And I will send the hornet before thee, which shall drive out the Hivite, the Canaanite, and the Hittite, from before thee. 29. I will not drive them out from before thee in one year, lest the land become desolate, and the beasts of the field multiply against thee. 30. By little and little I will drive them out from before thee, until thou be increased, and inherit the land. 31. And I will set thy border from the Red Sea even unto the sea of the Philistines, and from the wilderness unto [1]the River; for I will deliver the inhabitants of the land into your hand; and thou shalt drive them out before thee. 32. Thou shalt make no covenant with them, nor with their gods. 33. They shall not dwell in thy land—lest they make thee sin against Me, for thou wilt serve their gods—for they will be a snare unto thee.

27 אֶת־אֵימָתִי אֲשַׁלַּח לְפָנֶיךָ וְהַמֹּתִי אֶת־כָּל־הָעָם אֲשֶׁר
28 תָּבֹא בָּהֶם וְנָתַתִּי אֶת־כָּל־אֹיְבֶיךָ אֵלֶיךָ עֹרֶף׃ וְשָׁלַחְתִּי
אֶת־הַצִּרְעָה לְפָנֶיךָ וְגֵרְשָׁה אֶת־הַחִוִּי אֶת־הַכְּנַעֲנִי וְאֶת־
29 הַחִתִּי מִלְּפָנֶיךָ׃ לֹא אֲגָרְשֶׁנּוּ מִפָּנֶיךָ בְּשָׁנָה אֶחָת פֶּן־
ל תִּהְיֶה הָאָרֶץ שְׁמָמָה וְרַבָּה עָלֶיךָ חַיַּת הַשָּׂדֶה׃ מְעַט
מְעַט אֲגָרְשֶׁנּוּ מִפָּנֶיךָ עַד אֲשֶׁר תִּפְרֶה וְנָחַלְתָּ אֶת־הָאָרֶץ׃
31 וְשַׁתִּי אֶת־גְּבֻלְךָ מִיַּם־סוּף וְעַד־יָם פְּלִשְׁתִּים וּמִמִּדְבָּר
עַד־הַנָּהָר כִּי ׀ אֶתֵּן בְּיֶדְכֶם אֵת יֹשְׁבֵי הָאָרֶץ וְגֵרַשְׁתָּמוֹ
32 33 מִפָּנֶיךָ׃ לֹא־תִכְרֹת לָהֶם וְלֵאלֹהֵיהֶם בְּרִית׃ לֹא יֵשְׁבוּ
בְּאַרְצְךָ פֶּן־יַחֲטִיאוּ אֹתְךָ לִי כִּי תַעֲבֹד אֶת־אֱלֹהֵיהֶם כִּי־
יִהְיֶה לְךָ לְמוֹקֵשׁ׃ פ

24

CHAPTER XXIV

CAP. XXIV. כד

כד

1. And unto Moses He said: 'Come up unto the LORD, thou, and Aaron, Nadab,

א וְאֶל־מֹשֶׁה אָמַר עֲלֵה אֶל־יְהוָֹה אַתָּה וְאַהֲרֹן נָדָב וַאֲבִיהוּא

[1] That is, the Euphrates.

27. *My terror. i.e.* terror of Me. The nations, hearing that God is helping His people, will be panic-stricken at the approach of the Israelites. For historical instances, see Num. XXII, 2 f; Josh. IX, 3 f.

turn their backs. In flight.

28. *hornet.* Cf. Deut. VII, 20; Josh. XXIV, 12. The Israelites would be assisted in their campaign by a plague of stinging insects, which would harry and weaken the enemy. Some commentators take the Heb. word for 'hornet' as a reference to Egyptian invasions that would reduce the fighting power of the Canaanites. See on Deut. VII, 20.

29. *beasts of the field multiply.* The same thought occurs again in Deut. VII, 22. If the Canaanites had been swept from the land in a single, continuous campaign, the Israelites would not have been sufficiently numerous to inhabit the whole country. In consequence the large areas left desolate would swarm with wild beasts. Thus, after the deportation of the Ten Tribes to Assyria, lions infested the desolate district; see II Kings XVII, 25.

30. *by little and little.* The conquest of Canaan was not completed until the end of David's reign.

31. *Red Sea.* See on X, 19.

sea of the Philistines. i.e. the S.E. coast of the Mediterranean, which was the territory of the Philistines.

wilderness. At the south of Palestine, through which they were passing.

the River. Does not here mean the Nile, but the Euphrates. The boundaries extended to the Euphrates in the reigns of David and Solomon.

32. *no covenant.* The warning against forming an alliance with the inhabitants of Canaan, lest Israel be seduced by them into idolatry, is frequently repeated; and, as the whole later history of Israel proves, was sorely needed; cf. XXXIV, 12 f, and Deut. VII, 2 f.

33. *a snare.* A lure to destruction.

CHAPTER XXIV. RATIFICATION OF THE COVENANT

1. *And unto Moses He said.* After the Decalogue had been proclaimed in the hearing of the entire people, Moses again ascended the mountain (XX, 18), and received the commandments which form the Book of the Covenant (XX, 19–XXIII, 33). God commanded Moses to place these laws before the people, and then come to the mountain with Aaron, Nadab, and Abihu, and seventy elders (XXIV, 1), though he alone was to ascend the mountain (*v.* 2). Moses did so. He communicated to the people the words of God (*v.* 3) and after having ratified the covenant with a sacrifice, he went up with the men named (*v.* 9), when they were shown a Divine vision. Then Moses was commanded to ascend further with Joshua (*v.* 12 f) while the others either stayed

2 וְשִׁבְעִים מִזִּקְנֵי יִשְׂרָאֵל וְהִשְׁתַּחֲוִיתֶם מֵרָחֹק׃ וְנִגַּשׁ מֹשֶׁה
3 לְבַדּוֹ אֶל־יְהוָה וְהֵם לֹא יִגָּשׁוּ וְהָעָם לֹא יַעֲלוּ עִמּוֹ׃ וַיָּבֹא
מֹשֶׁה וַיְסַפֵּר לָעָם אֵת כָּל־דִּבְרֵי יְהוָה וְאֵת כָּל־הַמִּשְׁפָּטִים
וַיַּעַן כָּל־הָעָם קוֹל אֶחָד וַיֹּאמְרוּ כָּל־הַדְּבָרִים אֲשֶׁר־דִּבֶּר
4 יְהוָה נַעֲשֶׂה׃ וַיִּכְתֹּב מֹשֶׁה אֵת כָּל־דִּבְרֵי יְהוָה וַיַּשְׁכֵּם
בַּבֹּקֶר וַיִּבֶן מִזְבֵּחַ תַּחַת הָהָר וּשְׁתֵּים עֶשְׂרֵה מַצֵּבָה
ה לִשְׁנֵים עָשָׂר שִׁבְטֵי יִשְׂרָאֵל׃ וַיִּשְׁלַח אֶת־נַעֲרֵי בְּנֵי יִשְׂרָאֵל
6 וַיַּעֲלוּ עֹלֹת וַיִּזְבְּחוּ זְבָחִים שְׁלָמִים לַיהוָה פָּרִים׃ וַיִּקַּח
מֹשֶׁה חֲצִי הַדָּם וַיָּשֶׂם בָּאַגָּנֹת וַחֲצִי הַדָּם זָרַק עַל־
7 הַמִּזְבֵּחַ׃ וַיִּקַּח סֵפֶר הַבְּרִית וַיִּקְרָא בְּאָזְנֵי הָעָם וַיֹּאמְרוּ
8 כֹּל אֲשֶׁר־דִּבֶּר יְהוָה נַעֲשֶׂה וְנִשְׁמָע׃ וַיִּקַּח מֹשֶׁה אֶת־הַדָּם
וַיִּזְרֹק עַל־הָעָם וַיֹּאמֶר הִנֵּה דַם־הַבְּרִית אֲשֶׁר כָּרַת יְהוָה

and Abihu, and seventy of the elders of Israel; and worship ye afar off; 2. and Moses alone shall come near unto the LORD; but they shall not come near; neither shall the people go up with him.' 3. And Moses came and told the people all the words of the LORD, and all the ordinances; and all the people answered with one voice, and said: 'All the words which the LORD hath spoken will we do.' 4. And Moses wrote all the words of the LORD, and rose up early in the morning, and builded an altar under the mount, and twelve pillars, according to the twelve tribes of Israel. 5. And he sent the young men of the children of Israel, who offered burnt-offerings, and sacrificed peace-offerings of oxen unto the LORD. 6. And Moses took half of the blood, and put it in basins; and half of the blood he dashed against the altar. 7. And he took the book of the covenant, and read in the hearing of the people; and they said: 'All that the LORD hath spoken will we do, and obey.' 8. And Moses took the blood, and sprinkled it on the people, and said: 'Be-

where they were, or, more probably, returned to the camp; see the note on *v.* 14. After six days of waiting, during which the cloud covered the Mount, Moses alone was summoned to penetrate within the cloud (*v.* 16) and he remained there forty days (*v.* 18).

come up. This command was addressed to Moses as he was about to descend; and we are to supply before these words, 'Place my laws before the people and then.'

Nadab, and Abihu. Sons of Aaron.

seventy of the elders. Acting as representatives of the people.

worship ye. Prepare yourselves for the Divine vision which you are about to behold (*v.* 10).

afar off. At a distance from the summit which Moses was alone to reach.

2. *and Moses alone.* The abrupt change from the second to the third person is common in Hebrew; but its purpose here is to make it perfectly explicit that only Moses was to 'come near unto the Lord', *i.e.* go within the cloud (*v.* 15).

3. *and Moses came.* Ibn Ezra observes it is not mentioned that he descended the mountain because there was no necessity to do so.

words . . . ordinances. As contained in the Book of the Covenant (*v.* 7).

answered with one voice. As in XIX, 8. 'The unanimity with which the Israelites here pledge themselves to the Divine worship partakes of the sublime; and we willingly forget for a moment how little they remained faithful to this promise even in the time immediately following' (Kalisch).

4. *pillars.* These were to serve as a symbol that the twelve tribes had accepted the Covenant; cf. Gen. XXXI, 45 f; Josh. XXIV, 27.

5. *the young men.* Onkelos renders, 'the firstborn,' in agreement with the Talmudical statement that before the institution of the priesthood, the duty of offering sacrifice devolved upon the firstborn. 'Only the firstborn sons of the seventy elders can here be intended' (Ibn Ezra).

6. *half of the blood.* Was to be sprinkled upon the people, and the other half poured against the altar, which symbolized God. The two contracting parties to the Covenant were by this ceremony united by a solemn bond.

7. *book of the covenant.* According to Rashi, this means Genesis and the first half of Exodus. More probably it was the Decalogue and chapters XX, 19–XXIII, 33. They are the Torah in epitome.

read. Before sprinkling the blood, which would formally constitute the ratification of the Covenant, Moses read to the people what he had written, so that there could be no misunderstanding or doubt as to what they were undertaking.

the people. Not the elders only. Every Israelite was personally involved, and assumed individual responsibility.

will we do, and obey. Heb. נעשה ונשמע; instant and instinctive response to carry out the will of God. The Rabbis see in these words the utmost submission to God and self-consecration to His Covenant.

hold the blood of the covenant, which the LORD hath made with you in agreement with all these words.' 9. Then went up Moses, and Aaron, Nadab, and Abihu, and seventy of the elders of Israel; 10. and they saw the God of Israel; and there was under His feet the like of a paved work of sapphire stone, and the like of the very heaven for clearness. 11. And upon the nobles of the children of Israel He laid not His hand; and they beheld God, and did eat and drink. ¶ 12. And the LORD said unto Moses: 'Come up to Me into the mount, and be there; and I will give thee the tables of stone, and the law and the commandment, which I have written, that thou mayest teach them.' 13. And Moses rose up, and Joshua his minister; and Moses went up into the mount of God. 14. And unto the elders he said: 'Tarry ye here for us, until we come back unto you; and, behold, Aaron and Hur are with you; whosoever hath a cause, let him come near unto them.' 15. And Moses went up into the mount, and the cloud covered the mount.*m. 16. And the glory of the LORD abode upon mount Sinai, and the cloud covered it six days; and the seventh day He called unto Moses out of the midst of the cloud. 17. And the appearance of the glory of the LORD was like devouring fire on the top of the mount in the eyes of the children of Israel. 18. And Moses entered into the midst of the cloud, and went up into the mount; and Moses was in the mount forty days and forty nights.

9 עִמָּכֶם עַל כָּל־הַדְּבָרִים הָאֵלֶּה׃ וַיַּעַל מֹשֶׁה וְאַהֲרֹן נָדָב
י וַאֲבִיהוּא וְשִׁבְעִים מִזִּקְנֵי יִשְׂרָאֵל׃ וַיִּרְאוּ אֵת אֱלֹהֵי יִשְׂרָאֵל
וְתַחַת רַגְלָיו כְּמַעֲשֵׂה לִבְנַת הַסַּפִּיר וּכְעֶצֶם הַשָּׁמַיִם
11 לָטֹהַר׃ וְאֶל־אֲצִילֵי בְּנֵי יִשְׂרָאֵל לֹא שָׁלַח יָדוֹ וַיֶּחֱזוּ אֶת־
12 הָאֱלֹהִים וַיֹּאכְלוּ וַיִּשְׁתּוּ׃ ס וַיֹּאמֶר יְהוָה אֶל־מֹשֶׁה
עֲלֵה אֵלַי הָהָרָה וֶהְיֵה־שָׁם וְאֶתְּנָה לְךָ אֶת־לֻחֹת הָאֶבֶן
13 וְהַתּוֹרָה וְהַמִּצְוָה אֲשֶׁר כָּתַבְתִּי לְהוֹרֹתָם׃ וַיָּקָם מֹשֶׁה
14 וִיהוֹשֻׁעַ מְשָׁרְתוֹ וַיַּעַל מֹשֶׁה אֶל־הַר הָאֱלֹהִים׃ וְאֶל־
הַזְּקֵנִים אָמַר שְׁבוּ־לָנוּ בָזֶה עַד אֲשֶׁר־נָשׁוּב אֲלֵיכֶם וְהִנֵּה (מפטיר
טו אַהֲרֹן וְחוּר עִמָּכֶם מִי־בַעַל דְּבָרִים יִגַּשׁ אֲלֵהֶם׃ * וַיַּעַל לספ')
16 מֹשֶׁה אֶל־הָהָר וַיְכַס הֶעָנָן אֶת־הָהָר׃ * וַיִּשְׁכֹּן כְּבוֹד־יְהוָה מפטיר
עַל־הַר סִינַי וַיְכַסֵּהוּ הֶעָנָן שֵׁשֶׁת יָמִים וַיִּקְרָא אֶל־מֹשֶׁה
17 בַּיּוֹם הַשְּׁבִיעִי מִתּוֹךְ הֶעָנָן׃ וּמַרְאֵה כְּבוֹד יְהוָה כְּאֵשׁ
18 אֹכֶלֶת בְּרֹאשׁ הָהָר לְעֵינֵי בְּנֵי יִשְׂרָאֵל׃ וַיָּבֹא מֹשֶׁה
בְּתוֹךְ הֶעָנָן וַיַּעַל אֶל־הָהָר וַיְהִי מֹשֶׁה בָּהָר אַרְבָּעִים יוֹם
וְאַרְבָּעִים לָיְלָה׃

9–11. Moses and Aaron, Nadab and Abihu, and seventy elders go up into the Mount, and are vouchsafed a mystic vision of the Divine Glory.

10. *and they saw.* 'And they beheld the majesty of the God of Israel, and beneath His majestic throne was work of precious stones, etc.' (Onkelos). What these men actually experienced is, of course, beyond human ken; but it is supposed that they fell into a trance in which this mystic vision was seen by them.

11. *nobles.* Moses, Aaron and his sons, and the seventy elders.

laid not His hand. They remained uninjured, because they were worthy to see the vision (Nachmanides).

did eat and drink. They brought with them the flesh of the peace-offerings, and consumed it as a sacred sacrificial meal, which formed part of the ceremony of ratification; see on Gen. XXXI, 46.

12. *come up to Me.* See on *v.* 1.

tables of stone. On which the Ten Commandments were inscribed.

and the law. Better, *even the law.* The Rabbis explain that the words, 'that thou mayest teach them,' refer to the Talmud. Every interpretation of the Law given by a universally recognized authority is regarded as given on Sinai; for every shade of meaning which Divinely inspired interpreters discover in the Law merely states *explicitly* what is implicitly and organically contained in it from the very beginning.

13. *Joshua.* See XVII, 9. He accompanied Moses from the camp and remained in the lower part of the Mount (Ibn Ezra).

14. *for us.* Moses and Joshua.

Hur. See on XVII, 10.

hath a cause. Moses had appointed magistrates to adjudicate disputes; but the difficult cases (XVIII, 26), which would have been reserved for his decision were, in the absence of Moses, to be referred to Aaron and Hur.

15. *the cloud.* A similar cloud had made its appearance before the revelation at Sinai (XIX, 16).

16. *glory of the LORD.* See on XVI, 7, 10.

seventh day. The six days were apparently spent by Moses in preparing himself for communion with God.

17. *devouring fire.* Blazing fire. The people in the camp beheld flames of fire appearing above the cloud.

18. *into the mount.* To the top of the Mount.

forty days. Cf. XXXIV, 28; Deut. IX, 9.

JEREMIAH XXXIV, 8–22, AND XXXIII, 25, 26

CHAPTER XXXIV — CAP. XXXIV. לד

8. The word that came unto Jeremiah from the LORD, after that the king Zedekiah had made a covenant with all the people that were at Jerusalem, to proclaim liberty unto them; 9. that every man should let his man-servant, and every man his maid-servant, being a Hebrew man or a Hebrew woman, go free; that none should make bondmen of them, even of a Jew his brother; 10. and all the princes and all the people hearkened, that had entered into the covenant to let every one his man-servant, and every one his maid-servant, go free, and not to make bondmen of them any more; they hearkened, and let them go; 11. but afterwards they turned, and caused the servants and the handmaids, whom they had let go free, to return, and brought them into subjection for servants and for handmaids; 12. therefore the word of the LORD came to Jeremiah from the LORD, saying: ¶ 13. Thus saith the LORD, the God of Israel: I made a covenant with your fathers in the day that I brought them forth out of the land of Egypt, out of the house of bondage, saying: 14. 'At the end of seven years ye shall let go every man his brother that is a Hebrew, that hath been sold unto thee, and hath served thee six years, thou shalt let him go free from thee'; but your fathers hearkened not unto Me, neither inclined their ear. 15. And ye were now turned, and had done that which is right in Mine eyes, in proclaiming liberty every man to his neighbour; and ye had

8 הַדָּבָר אֲשֶׁר־הָיָה אֶל־יִרְמְיָהוּ מֵאֵת יְהוָה
אַחֲרֵי כְּרֹת הַמֶּלֶךְ צִדְקִיָּהוּ בְּרִית אֶת־כָּל־הָעָם אֲשֶׁר
9 בִּירוּשָׁלִַם לִקְרֹא לָהֶם דְּרוֹר׃ לְשַׁלַּח אִישׁ אֶת־עַבְדּוֹ
וְאִישׁ אֶת־שִׁפְחָתוֹ הָעִבְרִי וְהָעִבְרִיָּה חָפְשִׁים לְבִלְתִּי עֲבָד־
י בָּם בִּיהוּדִי אָחִיהוּ אִישׁ׃ וַיִּשְׁמְעוּ כָל־הַשָּׂרִים וְכָל־הָעָם
אֲשֶׁר־בָּאוּ בַבְּרִית לְשַׁלַּח אִישׁ אֶת־עַבְדּוֹ וְאִישׁ אֶת־
שִׁפְחָתוֹ חָפְשִׁים לְבִלְתִּי עֲבָד־בָּם עוֹד וַיִּשְׁמְעוּ וַיְשַׁלֵּחוּ׃
11 וַיָּשׁוּבוּ אַחֲרֵי־כֵן וַיָּשִׁבוּ אֶת־הָעֲבָדִים וְאֶת־הַשְּׁפָחוֹת
אֲשֶׁר שִׁלְּחוּ חָפְשִׁים וַיִּכְבִּישׁוּם לַעֲבָדִים וְלִשְׁפָחוֹת׃
12 וַיְהִי דְבַר־יְהוָה אֶל־יִרְמְיָהוּ מֵאֵת יְהוָה לֵאמֹר׃ כֹּה־אָמַר 13
יְהוָה אֱלֹהֵי יִשְׂרָאֵל אָנֹכִי כָּרַתִּי בְרִית אֶת־אֲבוֹתֵיכֶם בְּיוֹם
14 הוֹצִאִי אוֹתָם מֵאֶרֶץ מִצְרַיִם מִבֵּית עֲבָדִים לֵאמֹר׃ מִקֵּץ
שֶׁבַע שָׁנִים תְּשַׁלְּחוּ אִישׁ אֶת־אָחִיו הָעִבְרִי אֲשֶׁר־יִמָּכֵר
לְךָ וַעֲבָדְךָ שֵׁשׁ שָׁנִים וְשִׁלַּחְתּוֹ חָפְשִׁי מֵעִמָּךְ וְלֹא־שָׁמְעוּ
טו אֲבוֹתֵיכֶם אֵלַי וְלֹא הִטּוּ אֶת־אָזְנָם׃ וַתָּשֻׁבוּ אַתֶּם הַיּוֹם

v. 11. יתיר י'

For the life and teachings of Jeremiah, see introduction to the Haftorah, p. 229.

The Sedrah opens with the enactment to free a Hebrew bondman after six years' service. The Haftorah records a grave breach of this regulation at a critical hour of Israel's history. In the face of the disaster threatening the Nation at the hands of the Babylonian besiegers, the last king of Judah had induced the ruling classes to bind themselves by oath to release their slaves, so that no Jew should any longer be a bondman to a fellow-Jew. They did so; but subsequently, when the danger had passed, they impiously broke their oath, and forced their emancipated brethren back into bondage. Jeremiah is outraged at this base conduct, and announces that the enemy would soon return; when fire, war, hunger and pestilence would rage in the city.

8. *with all the people.* With their representatives. Possibly, the Heb. term for 'all the people' stands for the National Assembly; see *v.* 19.

to proclaim liberty unto them. i.e. to the slaves.

9. *of a Jew.* This is the earliest mention of the word *Yehudi* ('Jew') in Scripture.

10. *princes . . . people hearkened.* Impending danger quickened their conscience into a course of action that might render them more worthy of deliverance.

14. *at the end of seven years . . . and hath served thee six years.* In English we would say, 'at the end of six years' service' (Moffatt). A similar Heb. idiom says 'And on the *seventh* day God finished his work' (Gen. II, 2). Cf. the French 'quinze jours' for the English 'fourteen days'; or the German 'nach acht Tagen' for the English 'in a week's time'.

hath been sold. Or, 'hath sold himself.'

16. *ye turned and profaned My name.* The Holy One of Israel is sanctified *by justice*, and profaned *by inhumanity.*

at their pleasure. Better, *to be their own masters* (Biur).

17–22. THE PUNISHMENT

17. *I proclaim for you a liberty. i.e.* from Me, from the Divine protection.

18. *cut the calf in twain.* A reference to the ancient method of ratifying a covenant, as in Gen. XV, 10.

made a covenant before Me in the house whereon My name is called; 16. but ye turned and profaned My name, and caused every man his servant, and every man his handmaid, whom ye had let go free at their pleasure, to return; and ye brought them into subjection, to be unto you for servants and for handmaids. 17. Therefore thus saith the LORD: Ye have not hearkened unto Me, to proclaim liberty, every man to his brother, and every man to his neighbour; behold, I proclaim for you a liberty, saith the LORD, unto the sword, unto the pestilence, and unto the famine; and I will make you a horror unto all the kingdoms of the earth. 18. And I will give the men that have transgressed My covenant, that have not performed the words of the covenant which they made before Me, when they cut the calf in twain and passed between the parts thereof; 19. the princes of Judah, and the princes of Jerusalem, the officers, and the priests, and all the people of the land, that passed between the parts of the calf; 20. I will even give them into the hand of their enemies, and into the hand of them that seek their life; and their dead bodies shall be for food unto the fowls of the heaven, and to the beasts of the earth. 21. And Zedekiah king of Judah and his princes will I give into the hand of their enemies, and into the hand of them that seek their life, and into the hand of the king of Babylon's army, that are gone up from you. 22. Behold, I will command, saith the LORD, and cause them to return to this city; and they shall fight against it, and take it, and burn it with fire; and I will make the cities of Judah a desolation, without inhabitant.

CHAPTER XXXIII

25. Thus saith the LORD: If My covenant be not with day and night, if I have not appointed the ordinances of heaven and earth; 26. then will I also cast away the seed of Jacob, and of David My servant, so that I will not take of his seed to be rulers over the seed of Abraham, Isaac, and Jacob; for I will cause their captivity to return, and will have compassion on them.

וַתַּעֲשׂוּ אֶת־הַיָּשָׁר בְּעֵינַי לִקְרֹא דְרוֹר אִישׁ לְרֵעֵהוּ וַתִּכְרְתוּ
16 בְרִית לְפָנַי בַּבַּיִת אֲשֶׁר־נִקְרָא שְׁמִי עָלָיו׃ וַתָּשֻׁבוּ וַתְּחַלְּלוּ
אֶת־שְׁמִי וַתָּשִׁבוּ אִישׁ אֶת־עַבְדּוֹ וְאִישׁ אֶת־שִׁפְחָתוֹ אֲשֶׁר־
שִׁלַּחְתֶּם חָפְשִׁים לְנַפְשָׁם וַתִּכְבְּשׁוּ אֹתָם לִהְיוֹת לָכֶם
17 לַעֲבָדִים וְלִשְׁפָחוֹת׃ לָכֵן כֹּה־אָמַר יְהוָה אַתֶּם
לֹא־שְׁמַעְתֶּם אֵלַי לִקְרֹא דְרוֹר אִישׁ לְאָחִיו וְאִישׁ לְרֵעֵהוּ
הִנְנִי קֹרֵא לָכֶם דְּרוֹר נְאֻם־יְהוָה אֶל־הַחֶרֶב אֶל־הַדֶּבֶר
וְאֶל־הָרָעָב וְנָתַתִּי אֶתְכֶם לְזַוְעָה לְכֹל מַמְלְכוֹת הָאָרֶץ׃
18 וְנָתַתִּי אֶת־הָאֲנָשִׁים הָעֹבְרִים אֶת־בְּרִתִי אֲשֶׁר לֹא־הֵקִימוּ
אֶת־דִּבְרֵי הַבְּרִית אֲשֶׁר כָּרְתוּ לְפָנָי הָעֵגֶל אֲשֶׁר כָּרְתוּ
19 לִשְׁנַיִם וַיַּעַבְרוּ בֵּין בְּתָרָיו׃ שָׂרֵי יְהוּדָה וְשָׂרֵי יְרוּשָׁלִַם
הַסָּרִסִים וְהַכֹּהֲנִים וְכֹל עַם הָאָרֶץ הָעֹבְרִים בֵּין בִּתְרֵי
כ הָעֵגֶל׃ וְנָתַתִּי אוֹתָם בְּיַד אֹיְבֵיהֶם וּבְיַד מְבַקְשֵׁי נַפְשָׁם
וְהָיְתָה נִבְלָתָם לְמַאֲכָל לְעוֹף הַשָּׁמַיִם וּלְבֶהֱמַת הָאָרֶץ׃
21 וְאֶת־צִדְקִיָּהוּ מֶלֶךְ־יְהוּדָה וְאֶת־שָׂרָיו אֶתֵּן בְּיַד אֹיְבֵיהֶם
וּבְיַד מְבַקְשֵׁי נַפְשָׁם וּבְיַד חֵיל מֶלֶךְ בָּבֶל הָעֹלִים מֵעֲלֵיכֶם׃
22 הִנְנִי מְצַוֶּה נְאֻם־יְהוָה וַהֲשִׁבֹתִים אֶל־הָעִיר הַזֹּאת וְנִלְחֲמוּ
עָלֶיהָ וּלְכָדוּהָ וּשְׂרָפֻהָ בָאֵשׁ וְאֶת־עָרֵי יְהוּדָה אֶתֵּן שְׁמָמָה
מֵאֵין יֹשֵׁב׃

CAP. XXXIII. לג

כה כֹּה אָמַר יְהוָה
אִם־לֹא בְרִיתִי יוֹמָם וָלָיְלָה חֻקּוֹת שָׁמַיִם וָאָרֶץ לֹא־
26 שָׂמְתִּי׃ גַּם־זֶרַע יַעֲקוֹב וְדָוִד עַבְדִּי אֶמְאַס מִקַּחַת מִזַּרְעוֹ
מֹשְׁלִים אֶל־זֶרַע אַבְרָהָם יִשְׂחָק וְיַעֲקֹב כִּי־אָשׁוּב אֶת־
שְׁבוּתָם וְרִחַמְתִּים׃

לד' v. 17. לזועה קרי v. 18. חסר י' לג' v. 26. מלא ו' ibid. אשיב קרי

19. *all the people of the land.* Better, *the National Council*, who, with the rulers, were parties to the solemn covenant; cf. p. 80.

20. *dead bodies.* Shall remain unburied.

21. *that are gone up from you. i.e.* the Babylonian army, which had temporarily raised the siege. This led to premature rejoicing on the part of the princes and people, and was responsible for the gross breach of faith which is the subject of the prophet's denunciation.

22. *to return.* They have forced the slaves to return to bondage; therefore, the Babylonians shall return and be the instrument of the Divine punishment. Jerusalem was taken by them in 586, the Temple was burned, and the larger portion of the population carried away into exile.

CHAPTER XXXIII, 25, 26

These verses foretell the Return from Babylonian captivity, and declare that this Divine promise of mercy is as sure as the ordinances of Nature.

VII. TERUMAH

(Chapters XXV–XXVII, 19)

THE SANCTUARY

With the exception of chaps. xxxii–xxxiv, which tell the story of the Golden Calf, the remainder of the Book of Exodus is concerned with the construction of the Sanctuary.

Israel had been redeemed from bondage, and God had proclaimed His laws unto them at Sinai. The communion of God with Moses and Israel was not, however, to cease with Israel's departure from Sinai. Moses is bidden to erect a Sanctuary that shall be a visible emblem to the people that God dwelleth among them.

In form, the Sanctuary was a portable structure, as it was to accompany the Israelites on their wanderings. It was primarily a tent, with a wooden frame-work to give it greater stability and security than ordinary tent-poles could give. The entire Sanctuary consisted of three parts:—

(1) There was the outer *Court*, enclosed by curtains supported on pillars. It was oblong in shape, 100 cubits by 50, and the entrance was on the eastern side.

(2) Within the Court facing the entrance, was the *Altar of Sacrifice;* and, behind it, towards the West, was the *Laver* for the Priests.

(3) In the western portion of the Court was the Sanctuary proper, the Tabernacle. This was divided by a 'Veil', or hanging curtain, into two chambers. The first of these, which only the priests might enter, was the *Holy Place*, containing the Table, the Candlestick and the Altar of Incense. The second of the chambers was called the *Holy of Holies*, and contained the Ark of the Covenant. This was entered once a year by the High Priest on the Day of Atonement. Precious metals and finely woven coloured materials were employed in its construction. The nearer an object was to the Holy of Holies, the rarer and costlier the material; the objects further off being made of bronze and ordinary woven cloths.

The northern, western and southern sides of the Tabernacle were a wooden framework; the eastern side, *i.e.* the front, consisted of a screen. The entire Tabernacle was covered by a tent, and over the tent there were further coverings.

Practically all commentators are agreed that the Sanctuary was a symbol; and its purpose, to impress the children of men with spiritual teachings. What, however, were the spiritual teachings which the Tabernacle symbolized? This question offered full scope to the ingenuity of mystic interpreters, ancient and modern, Jewish and non-Jewish, who declared the Sanctuary to be an epitome of that which is presented on a larger scale in the Universe as a whole, and an emblem of Religion's profoundest teachings on Life and Eternity.

Their interpretations, however, are too remote from the spirit of the plain narrative to carry conviction. Much more helpful is the view of Maimonides that the main purpose of the Sanctuary was to wean the Israelites from idolatrous worship and turn them towards God. The Sanctuary and its ritual occupy so large a place both in the Torah and in the life of ancient Israel, because they formed part of the Divine scheme in moulding the Chosen People for its spiritual mission. The Sanctuary re-inforced the laws which Moses had been commanded to set before the children of Israel. It kept before them the thought that God was in their midst; and their life, individually and collectively, had to be influenced by that knowledge. As God was holy and as the Sanctuary was holy, so must the Israelites make the sanctification of their lives the aim of all their endeavours. The Sanctuary thus embodies the principle which is the central thought of the whole of the Divine revelation to Moses.

25

CHAPTER XXV

1. And the LORD spoke unto Moses, saying: 2. 'Speak unto the children of Israel, that they take for Me an offering; of every man whose heart maketh him willing ye shall take My offering. 3. And this is the offering which ye shall take of them: gold, and silver, and brass; 4. and blue, and purple, and scarlet, and fine linen, and goats' hair; 5. and rams' skins dyed red, and sealskins, and acacia-wood; 6. oil for the light, spices for the anointing oil, and for the sweet incense; 7. onyx stones, and stones to be set, for the ephod, and for the breastplate. 8. And let them make Me a sanctuary, that I may dwell among them. 9. According to all that I show thee, the pattern of the tabernacle, and the pattern of

כה

CAP. XXV. כה

פ פ פ יט 19

א 2 וַיְדַבֵּר יְהֹוָה אֶל־מֹשֶׁה לֵּאמֹר׃ דַּבֵּר אֶל־בְּנֵי יִשְׂרָאֵל
וְיִקְחוּ־לִי תְּרוּמָה מֵאֵת כָּל־אִישׁ אֲשֶׁר יִדְּבֶנּוּ לִבּוֹ תִּקְחוּ
3 אֶת־תְּרוּמָתִי׃ וְזֹאת הַתְּרוּמָה אֲשֶׁר תִּקְחוּ מֵאִתָּם זָהָב
4 וָכֶסֶף וּנְחֹשֶׁת׃ וּתְכֵלֶת וְאַרְגָּמָן וְתוֹלַעַת שָׁנִי וְשֵׁשׁ וְעִזִּים׃
ה 6 וְעֹרֹת אֵילִם מְאָדָּמִים וְעֹרֹת תְּחָשִׁים וַעֲצֵי שִׁטִּים׃ שֶׁמֶן
7 לַמָּאֹר בְּשָׂמִים לְשֶׁמֶן הַמִּשְׁחָה וְלִקְטֹרֶת הַסַּמִּים׃ אַבְנֵי־
8 שֹׁהַם וְאַבְנֵי מִלֻּאִים לָאֵפֹד וְלַחֹשֶׁן׃ וְעָשׂוּ לִי מִקְדָּשׁ

VII. TERUMAH

(CHAPTERS XXV–XXVII, 19)

CHAPTER XXV

2–7. MATERIALS FOR THE SANCTUARY

2. *an offering.* Heb. *terumah;* 'that which is lifted off,' or separated; that which the Israelite sets apart from his possessions as a contribution to the requirements of the Sanctuary.

maketh him willing. Whosoever is stirred by a spontaneous desire to participate in the holy work. The beauty of the Tabernacle and the donation of material objects of value rendered necessary thereby called forth the spirit of self-sacrifice. The construction of the Tabernacle with its demands for all treasures of the thought that invents and of the hand that labours; of wisdom and beauty; of wealth of wood and weight of stone; of the strength of iron, and the light of gold—thus became an external sign of love and gratitude and surrender to God's will (Ruskin).

3. *gold.* For the ark, the Cherubim, the table of showbread, the candlestick and the altar of incense.

silver. Was the only material not obtained by voluntary contribution, but by a levy of a half-shekel upon each adult Israelite; XXXVIII, 25.

brass. The Heb. means 'copper' or 'bronze', as is evident from Deut. VIII, 9, where the metal is said to be hewn out of mountains. This metal was used for the altar of burnt-offerings.

4. *blue. i.e.* threads dyed a very dark blue, perhaps violet, derived, according to the Rabbis, from the blood of a shell-fish found in the Mediterranean Sea.

purple. i.e. a reddish purple; a dye likewise obtained from a species of shell-fish (I Macc. IV, 23).

scarlet. lit. 'worm of shining', from its brilliant hue. The worm referred to is the cochineal insect. The Arabs called it 'kirmiz', whence is derived the English word 'crimson'.

fine linen. 'A kind of linen which was only produced in Egypt' (Ibn Ezra), and worn by the royal family and the highest officials; see on Gen. XLI, 42.

goats' hair. This hair was woven by women into yarn (XXXV, 26) making a hard-wearing material most suitable as a tent-covering.

5. *rams' skins.* Dyed red, after they had been prepared.

sealskins. Or, 'badgers' skins.' Heb. *tachash;* possibly a species of sea-animal common in the Red Sea. Jewish legend explains it as a unique animal, which existed only in the time of Moses.

acacia-wood. lit. 'wood of Shittim', the Arabic name of the acacia tree. This tree grows abundantly in the Sinai Peninsula, but not farther north. It is a most durable wood.

6. *oil. i.e.* olive oil (XXVII, 20).

spices. See XXX, 22 f.

sweet incense. See XXX, 34 f.

7. *stones to be set.* See XXVIII, 17 f.

ephod . . . breastplate. See XXVIII, 6 f, and ibid., 14 f.

8, 9. PURPOSE OF THE SANCTUARY

8. *make Me. i.e.* 'For My Name' (Rashi). It would only be a Sanctuary so long as it remained dedicated to the service of God.

sanctuary. Heb. *mikdash.* The same word occurs in the Song of Moses (XV, 13 and 17), and

9 וְשָׁכַנְתִּי בְּתוֹכָם׃ כְּכֹל אֲשֶׁר אֲנִי מַרְאֶה אוֹתְךָ אֵת תַּבְנִית
י הַמִּשְׁכָּן וְאֵת תַּבְנִית כָּל־כֵּלָיו וְכֵן תַּעֲשׂוּ׃ ס וְעָשׂוּ
אֲרוֹן עֲצֵי שִׁטִּים אַמָּתַיִם וָחֵצִי אָרְכּוֹ וְאַמָּה וָחֵצִי רָחְבּוֹ
11 וְאַמָּה וָחֵצִי קֹמָתוֹ׃ וְצִפִּיתָ אֹתוֹ זָהָב טָהוֹר מִבַּיִת וּמִחוּץ
12 תְּצַפֶּנּוּ וְעָשִׂיתָ עָלָיו זֵר זָהָב סָבִיב׃ וְיָצַקְתָּ לּוֹ אַרְבַּע
טַבְּעֹת זָהָב וְנָתַתָּה עַל אַרְבַּע פַּעֲמֹתָיו וּשְׁתֵּי טַבָּעֹת עַל־
13 צַלְעוֹ הָאֶחָת וּשְׁתֵּי טַבָּעֹת עַל־צַלְעוֹ הַשֵּׁנִית׃ וְעָשִׂיתָ בַדֵּי
14 עֲצֵי שִׁטִּים וְצִפִּיתָ אֹתָם זָהָב׃ וְהֵבֵאתָ אֶת־הַבַּדִּים בַּטַּבָּעֹת
טו עַל צַלְעֹת הָאָרֹן לָשֵׂאת אֶת־הָאָרֹן בָּהֶם׃ בְּטַבְּעֹת הָאָרֹן

all the furniture thereof, even so shall ye make it. ¶ 10. And they shall make an ark of acacia-wood: two cubits and a half shall be the length thereof, and a cubit and a half the breadth thereof, and a cubit and a half the height thereof. 11. And thou shalt overlay it with pure gold, within and without shalt thou overlay it, and shalt make upon it a crown of gold round about. 12. And thou shalt cast four rings of gold for it, and put them in the four feet thereof; and two rings shall be on the one side of it, and two rings on the other side of it. 13. And thou shalt make staves of acacia-wood, and overlay them with gold. 14. And thou shalt put the staves into the rings on the sides of the ark, wherewith to bear the ark. 15. The staves shall be in the rings of the ark;

Ibn Ezra refers those phrases ('Thou hast guided them . . . to Thy holy habitation . . . the sanctuary which Thy hands have established') to Mt. Sinai, which is indeed treated as a sanctuary in XIX and XX. 'God, who on Sinai dwelt in a Sanctuary which His hands have made is now to dwell in a Sanctuary which Israel would make; and the Tabernacle would be a wandering Sinai' (B. Jacob).

that I may dwell. Heb. ושכנתי; the verb is the one from which *Shechinah*, the Rabbinic term for the Divine Presence, is derived.

dwell among them. Note that the Torah does not say, 'that I may dwell *in it*,' but '*among them*', *i.e.* in the midst of the people. The Sanctuary was not the dwelling-place of God; cf. I Kings VIII, 27. It was the symbol of that holiness which was to be the rule of life for the Israelites, if His Spirit was to abide with the community. They were to hold themselves aloof from everything that was defiling, because God was amongst them (Lev. XV, 31). The Sanctuary was, therefore, the fountain of holiness for the congregation of Israel.

9. *the pattern.* Moses was given detailed instructions in his Vision. He was shown a model, as it were, of the construction, from which he was not to deviate.

tabernacle. Better, *dwelling*. Heb. *mishkan*, the noun formed from the verb 'dwell' used in the preceding verse. The English word 'tabernacle' is the usual translation of the Heb. *ohel* ('tent'), and designates that part of the Sanctuary which was protected by a tent, *viz.* the Holy Place and the Holy of Holies.

furniture. All the articles, vessels and utensils in connection with the tabernacle.

10–16. THE ARK

The articles for the Holy of Holies are described first; and the beginning is made with the Ark, the most important article in the whole Sanctuary: the tabernacle was the edifice constructed to contain the Ark (see on *v.* 16).

10. *they shall make.* As in *v.* 8. The following verses have 'thou shalt'; *i.e.* Moses was to see that the command was duly carried out by others.

an ark. Also called, 'ark of the covenant,' of the testimony', 'of God', and 'of the LORD'.

cubit. lit. 'the fore-arm', from the elbow to the tip of the middle finger—roughly eighteen inches; so that the Ark measured 3 feet 9 inches in length, and 2 feet 3 inches in width and depth.

11. *pure gold.* Only the purest and most precious metal was used in connection with the Holy of Holies. The Ark was overlaid with gold inside, where it was not visible to the eye, as well as outside where it was visible; to teach us that man must be as pure in mind and heart as he appears pure in outward manner and bearing. Especially is it the duty of a scholar, continue the Rabbis, to be inwardly what he pretends to be outwardly (תוכו כברו).

upon it. Running around the edge of the top surface.

crown. *i.e.* an ornamental rim or moulding.

12. *two rings.* For the purpose of transportation in the Israelites' wanderings in the Wilderness the Ark was provided with four rings at its four feet, two on each side, through which two gilded poles of acacia wood were passed.

13. *staves.* Poles, by means of which the Ark was carried.

overlay them with gold. May mean either gilding, an art well-known in Egypt, or plating.

16 יִהְיוּ הַבַּדִּים לֹא יָסֻרוּ מִמֶּנּוּ׃ וְנָתַתָּ אֶל־הָאָרֹן אֵת הָעֵדֻת
שני
17 אֲשֶׁר אֶתֵּן אֵלֶיךָ׃ וְעָשִׂיתָ כַפֹּרֶת זָהָב טָהוֹר אַמָּתַיִם וָחֵצִי
18 אָרְכָּהּ וְאַמָּה וָחֵצִי רָחְבָּהּ׃ וְעָשִׂיתָ שְׁנַיִם כְּרֻבִים זָהָב
19 מִקְשָׁה תַּעֲשֶׂה אֹתָם מִשְּׁנֵי קְצוֹת הַכַּפֹּרֶת׃ וַעֲשֵׂה כְּרוּב
אֶחָד מִקָּצָה מִזֶּה וּכְרוּב־אֶחָד מִקָּצָה מִזֶּה מִן־הַכַּפֹּרֶת
כ תַּעֲשׂוּ אֶת־הַכְּרֻבִים עַל־שְׁנֵי קְצוֹתָיו׃ וְהָיוּ הַכְּרֻבִים
פֹּרְשֵׂי כְנָפַיִם לְמַעְלָה סֹכְכִים בְּכַנְפֵיהֶם עַל־הַכַּפֹּרֶת
וּפְנֵיהֶם אִישׁ אֶל־אָחִיו אֶל־הַכַּפֹּרֶת יִהְיוּ פְּנֵי הַכְּרֻבִים׃
21 וְנָתַתָּ אֶת־הַכַּפֹּרֶת עַל־הָאָרֹן מִלְמָעְלָה וְאֶל־הָאָרֹן תִּתֵּן
22 אֶת־הָעֵדֻת אֲשֶׁר אֶתֵּן אֵלֶיךָ׃ וְנוֹעַדְתִּי לְךָ שָׁם וְדִבַּרְתִּי
אִתְּךָ מֵעַל הַכַּפֹּרֶת מִבֵּין שְׁנֵי הַכְּרֻבִים אֲשֶׁר עַל־אֲרוֹן
הָעֵדֻת אֵת כָּל־אֲשֶׁר אֲצַוֶּה אוֹתְךָ אֶל־בְּנֵי יִשְׂרָאֵל׃ פ

they shall not be taken from it. 16. And thou shalt put into the ark the testimony which I shall give thee. *ii. 17. And thou shalt make an ark-cover of pure gold: two cubits and a half shall be the length thereof, and a cubit and a half the breadth thereof. 18. And thou shalt make two cherubim of gold; of beaten work shalt thou make them, at the two ends of the ark-cover. 19. And make one cherub at the one end, and one cherub at the other end; of one piece with the ark-cover shall ye make the cherubim of the two ends thereof. 20. And the cherubim shall spread out their wings on high, screening the ark-cover with their wings, with their faces one to another; toward the ark-cover shall the faces of the cherubim be. 21. And thou shalt put the ark-cover above upon the ark; and in the ark thou shalt put the testimony that I shall give thee. 22. And there I will meet with thee, and I will speak with thee from above the ark-cover, from between the two cherubim which are upon the ark of the testimony, of all things which I will give thee in commandment unto the children of Israel.

16. *the testimony. i.e.* the two Tables of the Law which were evidence of the Divine Covenant concluded with Israel. Cf. I Kings VIII, 9, 'there was nothing in the ark save the two tables of stone.' The imageless inmost shrine was a continuous proclamation of the spirituality of God. The knowledge that in the holiest part of the Sanctuary was deposited nothing but the original Tables of the Law would ever impress the Israelites with the thought that the moral laws engraved on them constituted the conditions of that Covenant between God and Israel.

17–22. THE MERCY-SEAT AND CHERUBIM

17. *ark-cover.* RV has 'mercy-seat', first used by Tindale. Heb. *kapporeth.* It was a slab of gold, of the same dimensions as the top surface of the Ark, and was set upon it. According to the Talmud, it was a handbreath in thickness. So much importance was attached to it that, in I Chron. XXVIII, 11, the Holy of Holies is called 'the house of the *kapporeth*'. The root of the word means not only 'to cover', but also to 'atone'. It is, therefore, doubtful whether the *kaporeth* served no other purpose than that of a cover to the Ark. It figures prominently in the ritual of the Day of Atonement (Lev. XVI, 2, 14 f).

18. *cherubim.* Apart from the mention of wings, there is no description offered of these emblematic figures. The Talmud, by a popular derivation of the Hebrew word, asserts that the cherubim had the faces of children. In Biblical poetry, the cherubim are an emblem of God's nearness to man. Thus the Psalmist speaks of God as 'enthroned upon the cherubim' (Ps. LXXX, 2), when he invokes Him to help his people: that is, He is not far off in the heavens, and not powerless to aid, but a very present Helper in the day of distress and trouble.

beaten work. i.e. hammered out of one piece.

19. *of one piece with.* Heb. is simply 'out of'. The figures were not made separately and fastened to the mercy-seat, but both were fashioned out of the same mass of gold (Rashi).

20. *screening the ark-cover.* The wings would thus veil the sight of the mercy-seat from the eyes of the High Priest when he entered the Holy of Holies on the Day of Atonement; and teach that no human being, even one who penetrated into the Holy of Holies, could attain to a full comprehension of God. There have been several mystical applications of the symbolism of the cherubim ('who had the faces of children') to educational problems. Children should be taught to aspire upwards ('spread out their wings on high'); to become protectors of the Ark of the Covenant ('covering the mercy-seat with their wings'); their faces towards their fellow-man ('their faces one to another'); and their eyes towards the mercy-seat of God.

21. See *v.* 16.

22. *I will meet with thee.* Heb. ונועדתי; hence the whole sanctuary is called אהל מועד 'the Tent of Meeting', *i.e.* the place where God reveals His will, through Moses, to Israel.

¶ 23. And thou shalt make a table of acacia-wood: two cubits shall be the length thereof, and a cubit the breadth thereof, and a cubit and a half the height thereof. 24. And thou shalt overlay it with pure gold, and make thereto a crown of gold round about. 25. And thou shalt make unto it a border of a handbreadth round about, and thou shalt make a golden crown to the border thereof round about. 26. And thou shalt make for it four rings of gold, and put the rings in the four corners that are on the four feet thereof. 27. Close by the border shall the rings be, for places for the staves to bear the table. 28. And thou shalt make the staves of acacia-wood, and overlay them with gold, that the table may be borne with them. 29. And thou shalt make the dishes thereof, and the pans thereof, and the jars thereof, and the bowls thereof, wherewith to pour out; of pure gold shalt thou make them. 30. And thou shalt set upon the table showbread before Me alway.*iii s. ¶ 31. And thou shalt make a candlestick of pure gold: of beaten work shall the candlestick be made, even its base, and its shaft; its cups, its knops, and its flowers, shall be of one piece with it. 32. And there shall be six

23 וְעָשִׂיתָ שֻׁלְחָן עֲצֵי שִׁטִּים אַמָּתַיִם אָרְכּוֹ וְאַמָּה רָחְבּוֹ וְאַמָּה
24 וָחֵצִי קֹמָתוֹ׃ וְצִפִּיתָ אֹתוֹ זָהָב טָהוֹר וְעָשִׂיתָ לּוֹ זֵר זָהָב
כה סָבִיב׃ וְעָשִׂיתָ לּוֹ מִסְגֶּרֶת טֹפַח סָבִיב וְעָשִׂיתָ זֵר־זָהָב
26 לְמִסְגַּרְתּוֹ סָבִיב׃ וְעָשִׂיתָ לּוֹ אַרְבַּע טַבְּעֹת זָהָב וְנָתַתָּ
אֶת־הַטַּבָּעֹת עַל אַרְבַּע הַפֵּאֹת אֲשֶׁר לְאַרְבַּע רַגְלָיו׃ לְעֻמַּת
27 הַמִּסְגֶּרֶת תִּהְיֶיןָ הַטַּבָּעֹת לְבָתִּים לְבַדִּים לָשֵׂאת אֶת־
28 הַשֻּׁלְחָן׃ וְעָשִׂיתָ אֶת־הַבַּדִּים עֲצֵי שִׁטִּים וְצִפִּיתָ אֹתָם
29 זָהָב וְנִשָּׂא־בָם אֶת־הַשֻּׁלְחָן׃ וְעָשִׂיתָ קְּעָרֹתָיו וְכַפֹּתָיו
וּקְשׂוֹתָיו וּמְנַקִּיֹּתָיו אֲשֶׁר יֻסַּךְ בָּהֵן זָהָב טָהוֹר תַּעֲשֶׂה אֹתָם׃
ל וְנָתַתָּ עַל־הַשֻּׁלְחָן לֶחֶם פָּנִים לְפָנַי תָּמִיד׃ פ (שלישי) (לספ׳)
31 וְעָשִׂיתָ מְנֹרַת זָהָב טָהוֹר מִקְשָׁה תֵּעָשֶׂה הַמְּנוֹרָה יְרֵכָהּ
32 וְקָנָהּ גְּבִיעֶיהָ כַּפְתֹּרֶיהָ וּפְרָחֶיהָ מִמֶּנָּה יִהְיוּ׃ וְשִׁשָּׁה
קָנִים יֹצְאִים מִצִּדֶּיהָ שְׁלֹשָׁה ׀ קְנֵי מְנֹרָה מִצִּדָּהּ הָאֶחָד

v. 29. ק׳ דגושה v. 31. מלא יו״ד

23–30. THE TABLE OF SHOWBREAD

23. *table.* A representation of this table is on the Arch of Titus.

24. *a crown.* An ornamental moulding, as in *v.* 11.

25. *border.* Either on the top surface of the table or attached to the legs half-way down, so as to keep them together, like rungs of a chair. The illustration on the Arch of Titus favours the latter view.

handbreath. i.e. the four fingers of the hand joined together; about three inches.

crown. Rashi makes this identical with the crown mentioned in the last verse, but on the Arch of Titus this central border has traces of decorative work.

26. *four rings.* For purposes of transportation, as in *v.* 12.

29. *dishes.* In which the loaves were brought to and from the table.

pans. Better, *cups,* for the frankincense which was set upon the two piles of loaves; see Lev. XXIV, 7.

jars . . . bowls. Jars and chalices used for the libation of wine which accompanied the burning of the incense. The former would be the large flagons in which the wine was stored; the latter, the bowls used in the actual libation.

30. *showbread.* lit. 'bread of the Presence'. It is described in Lev. XXIV, 5–9, where it is said to have consisted of twelve loaves of wheaten flour, corresponding in number to the tribes of Israel. It was placed on the table on the Sabbath, arranged in two rows, and left there until the following Sabbath. When the loaves were removed, they were eaten by the priests. The symbolic meaning of the showbread is a matter of conjecture. Maimonides confesses, 'I do not know the object of the table with the bread upon it continually, and up to this day I have not been able to assign any reason to this commandment.' Most commentators understand the Presence-bread as an expression of thankfulness and standing acknowledgment on the part of the children of Israel that God was the Giver of man's daily necessities.

31. *candlestick.* A lampstand. Among the spoils of the Temple depicted on the Arch of Titus the candlestick is conspicuous.

beaten work. See on *v.* 18.

shaft. The central stem.

cups. These were formed in the shape of an opened almond-blossom, the exterior being the 'knops', and the interior the 'flowers'; *i.e.* the outer and inner petals.

32. *six branches.* They curved to the same height as the central shaft, so that all the seven lamps were in a straight line. Seven represents the idea of completeness; and seven lamps therefore symbolize perfect life. See further on XXVII, 20 f.

branches going out of the sides thereof: three branches of the candlestick out of the one side thereof, and three branches of the candlestick out of the other side thereof; 33. three cups made like almond-blossoms in one branch, a knop and a flower; and three cups made like almond-blossoms in the other branch, a knop and a flower; so for the six branches going out of the candlestick. 34. And in the candlestick four cups made like almond-blossoms, the knops thereof, and the flowers thereof. 35. And a knop under two branches of one piece with it, and a knop under two branches of one piece with it, and a knop under two branches of one piece with it, for the six branches going out of the candlestick. 36. Their knops and their branches shall be of one piece with it; the whole of it one beaten work of pure gold. 37. And thou shalt make the lamps thereof, seven; and they shall light the lamps thereof, to give light over against it. 38. And the tongs thereof, and the snuffdishes thereof, shall be of pure gold. 39. Of a talent of pure gold shall it be made, with all these vessels. 40. And see that thou make them after their pattern, which is being shown thee in the mount.* iii a.

26

CHAPTER XXVI

1. Moreover thou shalt make the tabernacle with ten curtains: of fine twined linen, and

33 וּשְׁלֹשָׁה קָנֵי מְנֹרָה מִצִּדָּהּ הַשֵּׁנִי׃ שְׁלֹשָׁה גְבִעִים מְשֻׁקָּדִים
בַּקָּנֶה הָאֶחָד כַּפְתֹּר וָפֶרַח וּשְׁלֹשָׁה גְבִעִים מְשֻׁקָּדִים
בַּקָּנֶה הָאֶחָד כַּפְתֹּר וָפָרַח כֵּן לְשֵׁשֶׁת הַקָּנִים הַיֹּצְאִים
34 מִן־הַמְּנֹרָה׃ וּבַמְּנֹרָה אַרְבָּעָה גְבִעִים מְשֻׁקָּדִים כַּפְתֹּרֶיהָ
לה וּפְרָחֶיהָ׃ וְכַפְתֹּר תַּחַת שְׁנֵי הַקָּנִים מִמֶּנָּה וְכַפְתֹּר תַּחַת
שְׁנֵי הַקָּנִים מִמֶּנָּה וְכַפְתֹּר תַּחַת־שְׁנֵי הַקָּנִים מִמֶּנָּה לְשֵׁשֶׁת
36 הַקָּנִים הַיֹּצְאִים מִן־הַמְּנֹרָה׃ כַּפְתֹּרֵיהֶם וּקְנֹתָם מִמֶּנָּה
37 יִהְיוּ כֻּלָּהּ מִקְשָׁה אַחַת זָהָב טָהוֹר׃ וְעָשִׂיתָ אֶת־נֵרֹתֶיהָ
38 שִׁבְעָה וְהֶעֱלָה אֶת־נֵרֹתֶיהָ וְהֵאִיר עַל־עֵבֶר פָּנֶיהָ׃ וּמַלְקָחֶיהָ
39 וּמַחְתֹּתֶיהָ זָהָב טָהוֹר׃ כִּכָּר זָהָב טָהוֹר יַעֲשֶׂה אֹתָהּ אֵת
מ כָּל־הַכֵּלִים הָאֵלֶּה׃ וּרְאֵה וַעֲשֵׂה בְּתַבְנִיתָם אֲשֶׁר־אַתָּה
מָרְאֶה בָּהָר׃ * ס שלישי

כו CAP. XXVI. כו

א וְאֶת־הַמִּשְׁכָּן תַּעֲשֶׂה עֶשֶׂר יְרִיעֹת שֵׁשׁ מָשְׁזָר וּתְכֵלֶת
וְאַרְגָּמָן וְתֹלַעַת שָׁנִי כְּרֻבִים מַעֲשֵׂה חֹשֵׁב תַּעֲשֶׂה אֹתָם׃
2 אֹרֶךְ ׀ הַיְרִיעָה הָאַחַת שְׁמֹנֶה וְעֶשְׂרִים בָּאַמָּה וְרֹחַב

כה' v. 39. סבירין תעשה

33. *three cups.* Each branch was divided into three parts by having a 'cup' placed at the top end, and a third, and two-thirds of the way down towards the central shaft.

34–36. It is not quite certain from this description how these ornaments were arranged on the central shaft.

37. *lamps.* Receptacles for the oil and wick, probably shaped like elongated shells.
over against it. Or, 'in front of it.' According to Rashi, the lamps were so arranged that the wick-mouths from which the flame burned were directed towards the central shaft.

38. *tongs.* For drawing out the wick.
snuffdishes. Receptacles in which the burnt wicks are placed.

39. *talent of pure gold.* Josephus gives the weight as one hundred pounds, and that is approximately correct. The value would be about six thousand pounds sterling.

40. *which is being shown.* The Rabbis declare that Moses found it so difficult to grasp the verbal instruction in connection with the candlestick, that God constructed for him a model of fire. But from the text, it is not necessarily to be inferred that an actual model was shown to Moses. As Luzzatto remarks, the verb, 'to see,' may signify mental perception as well as ocular vision.

CHAPTER XXVI

1–6. THE CURTAINS OF THE TABERNACLE

1. *the tabernacle. i.e.* Holy Place and the Holy of Holies. The interior is to be covered with a fabric of curtains, supported upon a wooden framework.
fine twined linen. Linen of exceptional fineness on which the figures of cherubim were worked in coloured threads.
work of the skilful workman. Or, 'work of a designer,' or 'pattern-weaver'; work requiring exceptional skill. The traditional explanation is that in this class of work a design appeared on both sides of the fabric.

אַרְבַּע בָּאַמָּה הַיְרִיעָה הָאֶחָת מִדָּה אַחַת לְכָל־הַיְרִיעֹת׃
3 חֲמֵשׁ הַיְרִיעֹת תִּהְיֶיןָ חֹבְרֹת אִשָּׁה אֶל־אֲחֹתָהּ וְחָמֵשׁ יְרִיעֹת
4 חֹבְרֹת אִשָּׁה אֶל־אֲחֹתָהּ׃ וְעָשִׂיתָ לֻלְאֹת תְּכֵלֶת עַל שְׂפַת
הַיְרִיעָה הָאֶחָת מִקָּצָה בַּחֹבָרֶת וְכֵן תַּעֲשֶׂה בִּשְׂפַת הַיְרִיעָה
ה הַקִּיצוֹנָה בַּמַּחְבֶּרֶת הַשֵּׁנִית׃ חֲמִשִּׁים לֻלָאֹת תַּעֲשֶׂה
בַּיְרִיעָה הָאֶחָת וַחֲמִשִּׁים לֻלָאֹת תַּעֲשֶׂה בִּקְצֵה הַיְרִיעָה
אֲשֶׁר בַּמַּחְבֶּרֶת הַשֵּׁנִית מַקְבִּילֹת הַלֻּלָאֹת אִשָּׁה אֶל־
6 אֲחֹתָהּ׃ וְעָשִׂיתָ חֲמִשִּׁים קַרְסֵי זָהָב וְחִבַּרְתָּ אֶת־הַיְרִיעֹת
7 אִשָּׁה אֶל־אֲחֹתָהּ בַּקְּרָסִים וְהָיָה הַמִּשְׁכָּן אֶחָד׃ וְעָשִׂיתָ
יְרִיעֹת עִזִּים לְאֹהֶל עַל־הַמִּשְׁכָּן עַשְׁתֵּי־עֶשְׂרֵה יְרִיעֹת
8 תַּעֲשֶׂה אֹתָם׃ אֹרֶךְ ׀ הַיְרִיעָה הָאַחַת שְׁלֹשִׁים בָּאַמָּה
וְרֹחַב אַרְבַּע בָּאַמָּה הַיְרִיעָה הָאֶחָת מִדָּה אַחַת לְעַשְׁתֵּי
9 עֶשְׂרֵה יְרִיעֹת׃ וְחִבַּרְתָּ אֶת־חֲמֵשׁ הַיְרִיעֹת לְבָד וְאֶת־
שֵׁשׁ הַיְרִיעֹת לְבָד וְכָפַלְתָּ אֶת־הַיְרִיעָה הַשִּׁשִּׁית אֶל־מוּל
י פְּנֵי הָאֹהֶל׃ וְעָשִׂיתָ חֲמִשִּׁים לֻלָאֹת עַל שְׂפַת הַיְרִיעָה
הָאֶחָת הַקִּיצֹנָה בַּחֹבָרֶת וַחֲמִשִּׁים לֻלָאֹת עַל שְׂפַת

v. 9. קמץ בז״ק

blue, and purple, and scarlet, with cherubim the work of the skilful workman shalt thou make them. 2. The length of each curtain shall be eight and twenty cubits, and the breadth of each curtain four cubits; all the curtains shall have one measure. 3. Five curtains shall be coupled together one to another; and the other five curtains shall be coupled one to another. 4. And thou shalt make loops of blue upon the edge of the one curtain that is outmost in the first set; and likewise shalt thou make in the edge of the curtain that is outmost in the second set. 5. Fifty loops shalt thou make in the one curtain, and fifty loops shalt thou make in the edge of the curtain that is in the second set; the loops shall be opposite one to another. 6. And thou shalt make fifty clasps of gold, and couple the curtains one to another with the clasps, that the tabernacle may be one whole. 7. And thou shalt make curtains of goats' hair for a tent over the tabernacle; eleven curtains shalt thou make them. 8. The length of each curtain shall be thirty cubits, and the breadth of each curtain four cubits; the eleven curtains shall have one measure. 9. And thou shalt couple five curtains by themselves, and six curtains by themselves, and shalt double over the sixth curtain in the forefront of the tent. 10. And thou shalt make fifty loops on the edge of the one curtain that is outmost in the first set, and fifty loops upon the edge of the curtain

2. *length.* The curtains were arranged in two sets of five, each set being 28 cubits in length and 20 cubits in breadth. The Tabernacle was 30 cubits long and 10 cubits in width and height. Consequently, as Josephus declares, the curtains 'covered all the top and parts of the walls, on the sides and behind, so far as within one cubit of the ground'; because the two walls and top of the structure measured 30 cubits and the curtain only 28 cubits, leaving 2 cubits exposed. The length of the structure 30 cubits, and the western side, 10 cubits, would be exactly covered by the two sets of curtains, 20 cubits each in breadth. The eastern side, the entrance, was provided with a special screen; *v.* 36.

4. *loops.* Five curtains formed 'a set', and at the edge of each set there were to be fifty loops, so that they could be coupled together by means of clasps.

6. *that the tabernacle may be one.* They were formed of separate pieces, yet they were so arranged that when they formed the covering of the Tabernacle they were a single whole. Similarly the community of Israel, comprising different tribes and families, must be linked together in peace and solidarity (Ibn Ezra).

7–14. THE CURTAINS AND COVERINGS OF THE TENT

7. *of goats' hair.* To protect the finely-spun curtains of the Tabernacle from dust and rain there was a tent erected as an outer covering, and the sides of the tent were made of goats' hair cloth. There were eleven of these curtains. Why an additional one was required is explained in *v.* 9.

8. *length.* The goats' hair curtains were of the same breadth as the linen, but were two cubits longer to make up the deficiency of a cubit on each side (see on 2 f).

9. *double over.* Two cubits' length of the curtain was folded back at the entrance on the east side, so as to form a kind of portal above the entrance.

10. Similar to *v.* 4 f. It is not stated of what material the loops were to be made. They were probably of woven goats' hair. The clasps were of copper or bronze, because this outer covering was not part of the actual Tabernacle, like the curtains of linen, but only a protection against rain, dust and sun.

11 הַיְרִיעָה הַחֹבֶרֶת הַשֵּׁנִית׃ וְעָשִׂיתָ קַרְסֵי נְחֹשֶׁת חֲמִשִּׁים
וְהֵבֵאתָ אֶת־הַקְּרָסִים בַּלֻּלָאֹת וְחִבַּרְתָּ אֶת־הָאֹהֶל וְהָיָה
12 אֶחָד׃ וְסֶרַח הָעֹדֵף בִּירִיעֹת הָאֹהֶל חֲצִי הַיְרִיעָה הָעֹדֶפֶת
13 תִּסְרַח עַל אֲחֹרֵי הַמִּשְׁכָּן׃ וְהָאַמָּה מִזֶּה וְהָאַמָּה מִזֶּה
בָּעֹדֵף בְּאֹרֶךְ יְרִיעֹת הָאֹהֶל יִהְיֶה סָרוּחַ עַל־צִדֵּי הַמִּשְׁכָּן
14 מִזֶּה וּמִזֶּה לְכַסֹּתוֹ׃ וְעָשִׂיתָ מִכְסֶה לָאֹהֶל עֹרֹת אֵילִם
מְאָדָּמִים וּמִכְסֵה עֹרֹת תְּחָשִׁים מִלְמָעְלָה׃ * פ רביעי
טו 16 וְעָשִׂיתָ אֶת־הַקְּרָשִׁים לַמִּשְׁכָּן עֲצֵי שִׁטִּים עֹמְדִים׃ עֶשֶׂר
אַמּוֹת אֹרֶךְ הַקָּרֶשׁ וְאַמָּה וַחֲצִי הָאַמָּה רֹחַב הַקֶּרֶשׁ
17 הָאֶחָד׃ שְׁתֵּי יָדוֹת לַקֶּרֶשׁ הָאֶחָד מְשֻׁלָּבֹת אִשָּׁה אֶל־
18 אֲחֹתָהּ כֵּן תַּעֲשֶׂה לְכֹל קַרְשֵׁי הַמִּשְׁכָּן׃ וְעָשִׂיתָ אֶת־הַקְּרָשִׁים
19 לַמִּשְׁכָּן עֶשְׂרִים קֶרֶשׁ לִפְאַת נֶגְבָּה תֵימָנָה׃ וְאַרְבָּעִים
אַדְנֵי־כֶסֶף תַּעֲשֶׂה תַּחַת עֶשְׂרִים הַקָּרֶשׁ שְׁנֵי אֲדָנִים תַּחַת־
הַקֶּרֶשׁ הָאֶחָד לִשְׁתֵּי יְדֹתָיו וּשְׁנֵי אֲדָנִים תַּחַת־הַקֶּרֶשׁ
כ הָאֶחָד לִשְׁתֵּי יְדֹתָיו׃ וּלְצֶלַע הַמִּשְׁכָּן הַשֵּׁנִית לִפְאַת צָפוֹן
21 עֶשְׂרִים קָרֶשׁ׃ וְאַרְבָּעִים אַדְנֵיהֶם כָּסֶף שְׁנֵי אֲדָנִים תַּחַת

which is outmost in the second set. 11. And thou shalt make fifty clasps of brass, and put the clasps into the loops, and couple the tent together, that it may be one. 12. And as for the overhanging part that remaineth of the curtains of the tent, the half curtain that remaineth over shall hang over the back of the tabernacle. 13. And the cubit on the one side, and the cubit on the other side, of that which remaineth over in the length of the curtains of the tent, shall hang over the sides of the tabernacle on this side and on that side, to cover it. 14. And thou shalt make a covering for the tent of rams' skins dyed red, and a covering of sealskins above.*iv. ¶ 15. And thou shalt make the boards for the tabernacle of acacia-wood, standing up. 16. Ten cubits shall be the length of a board, and a cubit and a half the breadth of each board. 17. Two tenons shall there be in each board, joined one to another; thus shalt thou make for all the boards of the tabernacle. 18. And thou shalt make the boards for the tabernacle, twenty boards for the south side southward. 19. And thou shalt make forty sockets of silver under the twenty boards: two sockets under one board for its two tenons, and two sockets under another board for its two tenons; 20. and for the second side of the tabernacle, on the north side, twenty boards. 21. And their forty sockets of silver: two sockets under one board, and two sockets under another

12. Since there were eleven hair curtains as against ten of linen, and two cubits of the eleventh curtain had been accounted for in *v.* 9, the remaining two cubits were allowed to trail on the ground at the back of the edifice, on the west side.

13. The hair curtains were two cubits longer than the linen, and this extra length provided for the cubit of the boards on either side which was left exposed by the other curtains (2 f). The sides were thus completely protected by the outer curtains.

14. As a further protection to the precious fabrics of the Tabernacle, there were two additional coverings of skin spread over the roof, and hanging down at the sides. According to some Rabbis, there was only one additional covering of rams' skins, with patches of porpoise-skins.

15–30. The Boards of the Tabernacle

15. *boards.* Either solid boards, or, as some have suggested, 'frames'; *i.e.* two planks of wood joined by a cross-piece at the top and bottom.

standing up. The boards are to be placed vertically in position. The length of the board, ten cubits (15 feet), represents the height of the Tabernacle.

17. *tenons. i.e.* projecting pegs, which fitted into sockets. These tenons were 'joined one to another', which may mean that they were fixed on to a plate of metal whereby they were held together.

18. *twenty boards.* Formed the length of the Tabernacle, each a cubit and a half in breadth. The total length was thus 30 cubits (45 feet).

south side. lit. 'towards the Negeb', *i.e.* the arid Southern part of Palestine. Likewise in *v.* 22, 'westward' is lit. 'sea-ward', as the Mediterranean formed the Western horizon in Palestine. Bible critics deduce from the use of such terms in this narrative that it was written after Israel had lived long enough in Canaan for the words to have acquired this sense. The argument is absurd; because it overlooks the fact that the Hebrew language did not originate in Egypt during the bondage, but that it had been in existence many many centuries before the Children of Israel ever went down to Egypt.

19. *sockets.* To receive the tenons or projecting pegs. These sockets were on the bases or pedestals which kept the boards erect.

22 הַקֶּרֶשׁ הָאֶחָד וּשְׁנֵי אֲדָנִים תַּחַת הַקֶּרֶשׁ הָאֶחָד׃ וּלְיַרְכְּתֵי
23 הַמִּשְׁכָּן יָמָּה תַּעֲשֶׂה שִׁשָּׁה קְרָשִׁים׃ וּשְׁנֵי קְרָשִׁים תַּעֲשֶׂה
24 לִמְקֻצְעֹת הַמִּשְׁכָּן בַּיַּרְכָתָיִם׃ וְיִהְיוּ תֹאֲמִם מִלְּמַטָּה וְיַחְדָּו
יִהְיוּ תַמִּים עַל־רֹאשׁוֹ אֶל־הַטַּבַּעַת הָאֶחָת כֵּן יִהְיֶה
כה לִשְׁנֵיהֶם לִשְׁנֵי הַמִּקְצֹעֹת יִהְיוּ׃ וְהָיוּ שְׁמֹנָה קְרָשִׁים
וְאַדְנֵיהֶם כֶּסֶף שִׁשָּׁה עָשָׂר אֲדָנִים שְׁנֵי אֲדָנִים תַּחַת
26 הַקֶּרֶשׁ הָאֶחָד וּשְׁנֵי אֲדָנִים תַּחַת הַקֶּרֶשׁ הָאֶחָד׃ וְעָשִׂיתָ
בְרִיחִם עֲצֵי שִׁטִּים חֲמִשָּׁה לְקַרְשֵׁי צֶלַע־הַמִּשְׁכָּן הָאֶחָד׃
27 וַחֲמִשָּׁה בְרִיחִם לְקַרְשֵׁי צֶלַע־הַמִּשְׁכָּן הַשֵּׁנִית וַחֲמִשָּׁה
28 בְרִיחִם לְקַרְשֵׁי צֶלַע הַמִּשְׁכָּן לַיַּרְכָתַיִם יָמָּה׃ וְהַבְּרִיחַ
הַתִּיכֹן בְּתוֹךְ הַקְּרָשִׁים מַבְרִחַ מִן־הַקָּצֶה אֶל־הַקָּצֶה׃
29 וְאֶת־הַקְּרָשִׁים תְּצַפֶּה זָהָב וְאֶת־טַבְּעֹתֵיהֶם תַּעֲשֶׂה זָהָב
ל בָּתִּים לַבְּרִיחִם וְצִפִּיתָ אֶת־הַבְּרִיחִם זָהָב׃ וַהֲקֵמֹתָ אֶת־
חמישי 31 הַמִּשְׁכָּן כְּמִשְׁפָּטוֹ אֲשֶׁר הָרְאֵיתָ בָּהָר׃ ס וְעָשִׂיתָ
פָרֹכֶת תְּכֵלֶת וְאַרְגָּמָן וְתוֹלַעַת שָׁנִי וְשֵׁשׁ מָשְׁזָר מַעֲשֵׂה
32 חֹשֵׁב יַעֲשֶׂה אֹתָהּ כְּרֻבִים׃ וְנָתַתָּה אֹתָהּ עַל־אַרְבָּעָה
עַמּוּדֵי שִׁטִּים מְצֻפִּים זָהָב וָוֵיהֶם זָהָב עַל־אַרְבָּעָה אַדְנֵי־
33 כָסֶף׃ וְנָתַתָּה אֶת־הַפָּרֹכֶת תַּחַת הַקְּרָסִים וְהֵבֵאתָ שָׁמָּה

v. 31. סבירין תעשה

board. 22. And for the hinder part of the tabernacle westward thou shalt make six boards. 23. And two boards shalt thou make for the corners of the tabernacle in the hinder part. 24. And they shall be double beneath, and in like manner they shall be complete unto the top thereof unto the first ring; thus shall it be for them both; they shall be for the two corners. 25. Thus there shall be eight boards, and their sockets of silver, sixteen sockets: two sockets under one board, and two sockets under another board. 26. And thou shalt make bars of acacia-wood: five for the boards of the one side of the tabernacle, 27. and five bars for the boards of the other side of the tabernacle, and five bars for the boards of the side of the tabernacle, for the hinder part westward; 28. and the middle bar in the midst of the boards, which shall pass through from end to end. 29. And thou shalt overlay the boards with gold, and make their rings of gold for holders for the bars; and thou shalt overlay the bars with gold. 30. And thou shalt rear up the tabernacle according to the fashion thereof which hath been shown thee in the mount.*v. ¶ 31. And thou shalt make a veil of blue, and purple, and scarlet, and fine twined linen; with cherubim the work of the skilful workman shall it be made. 32. And thou shalt hang it upon four pillars of acacia overlaid with gold, their hooks being of gold, upon four sockets of silver. 33. And thou shalt hang up the veil under the clasps, and shalt bring in thither within the veil the ark of the testimony; and the veil shall divide unto you between the holy

22. *westward.* There were only six boards to form the western wall, and these would occupy a space of nine cubits. It is certain that the width of the edifice was ten cubits, the same as the height. There is consequently still one cubit to be accounted for.

24. *double.* The remaining cubit (*v.* 22) was filled in by two boards, one fitted into each corner. These additional boards would naturally not protrude outside the building, but inside, and in this way they would be 'double', since they overlapped the last of the twenty boards on each side. They would serve as buttresses and strengthen the corners.

the first ring. See *v.* 29.

26. *bars.* Along each of the three walls of the Tabernacle bars were fixed in three rows. The central bar was the entire length of the structure; but on the top and bottom rows the bars were shorter.

29. *holders for the bars.* These bars fitted into rings. The rings and bars were to join the walls fast together, 'that the Tabernacle might not be shaken, either by the winds or by any other means, but that it might preserve itself quiet and immovable continually' (Josephus).

30. This verse (cf. xxv, 9, 40) perhaps implies that more detailed directions were given to Moses than are recorded in this Book; and this supplementary instruction filled in the gaps which occur in the written account, and explained its obscurities.

31–33. The Veil

31. *veil.* Its purpose was to form a partition between the Holy of Holies and the remaining part of the Tabernacle.

32. *pillars.* The veil was held up by four wooden posts with golden hooks. The posts fitted into silver sockets similar to those places under the boards (*v.* 19).

33. *most holy.* The Holy of Holies formed a perfect cube, being 10 cubits in height, length and breadth.

ark of the testimony. i.e. the Ark containing the two tables of stone (xxv, 10 f).

מִבֵּית לַפָּרֹכֶת אֵת אֲרוֹן הָעֵדוּת וְהִבְדִּילָה הַפָּרֹכֶת לָכֶם
34 בֵּין הַקֹּדֶשׁ וּבֵין קֹדֶשׁ הַקֳּדָשִׁים׃ וְנָתַתָּ אֶת־הַכַּפֹּרֶת עַל
לה אֲרוֹן הָעֵדֻת בְּקֹדֶשׁ הַקֳּדָשִׁים׃ וְשַׂמְתָּ אֶת־הַשֻּׁלְחָן מִחוּץ
לַפָּרֹכֶת וְאֶת־הַמְּנֹרָה נֹכַח הַשֻּׁלְחָן עַל צֶלַע הַמִּשְׁכָּן תֵּימָנָה
36 וְהַשֻּׁלְחָן תִּתֵּן עַל־צֶלַע צָפוֹן׃ וְעָשִׂיתָ מָסָךְ לְפֶתַח הָאֹהֶל
תְּכֵלֶת וְאַרְגָּמָן וְתוֹלַעַת שָׁנִי וְשֵׁשׁ מָשְׁזָר מַעֲשֵׂה רֹקֵם׃
37 וְעָשִׂיתָ לַמָּסָךְ חֲמִשָּׁה עַמּוּדֵי שִׁטִּים וְצִפִּיתָ אֹתָם זָהָב וָוֵיהֶם
זָהָב וְיָצַקְתָּ לָהֶם חֲמִשָּׁה אַדְנֵי נְחֹשֶׁת׃ * ס ששי

place and the most holy. 34. And thou shalt put the ark-cover upon the ark of the testimony in the most holy place. 35. And thou shalt set the table without the veil, and the candlestick over against the table on the side of the tabernacle toward the south; and thou shalt put the table on the north side. 36. And thou shalt make a screen for the door of the Tent, of blue, and purple, and scarlet, and fine twined linen, the work of the weaver in colours. 37. And thou shalt make for the screen five pillars of acacia, and overlay them with gold; their hooks shall be of gold; and thou shalt cast five sockets of brass for them.* vi.

כז Cap. XXVII. כז

א וְעָשִׂיתָ אֶת־הַמִּזְבֵּחַ עֲצֵי שִׁטִּים חָמֵשׁ אַמּוֹת אֹרֶךְ וְחָמֵשׁ
אַמּוֹת רֹחַב רָבוּעַ יִהְיֶה הַמִּזְבֵּחַ וְשָׁלֹשׁ אַמּוֹת קֹמָתוֹ׃
2 וְעָשִׂיתָ קַרְנֹתָיו עַל אַרְבַּע פִּנֹּתָיו מִמֶּנּוּ תִּהְיֶיןָ קַרְנֹתָיו
3 וְצִפִּיתָ אֹתוֹ נְחֹשֶׁת׃ וְעָשִׂיתָ סִּירֹתָיו לְדַשְּׁנוֹ וְיָעָיו וּמִזְרְקֹתָיו

27 Chapter XXVII

1. And thou shalt make the altar of acacia-wood, five cubits long, and five cubits broad; the altar shall be four-square; and the height thereof shall be three cubits. 2. And thou shalt make the horns of it upon the four corners thereof; the horns thereof shall be of one piece with it; and thou shalt overlay it with brass. 3. And thou shalt make its pots to take away its ashes, and its shovels, and its basins, and its flesh-hooks, and its fire-pans; all the vessels thereof

כו׳ v. 33. מלרע כז׳ v. 3. הס׳ דגושה

35. *thou shalt set.* Rashi gives the traditional account of the arrangement of the furniture in the Tabernacle. The table of showbread was set in the north, two and a half cubits from the wall; the candlestick in the south, an equal distance from the wall; and between the two was the golden altar of incense.

36. *screen.* Instead of the curtains, a special screen was made for the entrance. Its material was similar to the veil, except that no cherubim were embroidered thereon.

37. *five pillars.* The screen, unlike the veil, which had four pillars, was supported by five. It would require this additional support because of the frequency with which it would be drawn aside to allow the priests to enter.

Chapter XXVII

1–8. The Altar of Burnt-Offerings

1. *altar.* The Rabbis explained the symbolism of the altar by making each letter of the Heb. name for altar (מזבח) the initial of a word, thus: מחילה 'forgiveness'—the altar was the channel whereby the Israelite could seek reconciliation with God from Whom he had become estranged by sin; זכות 'merit'—gratitude, humility, contrition found an outlet on the altar, and by the exercise of these virtues, life was ennobled and 'merit' acquired; ברכה 'blessing'—by being true to the teachings that centred round the altar, man earns the Divine blessings and himself becomes a blessing to his fellowmen; חיים 'life'—the altar points the way of the life everlasting, to the things that abide for evermore, truth, righteousness, holiness.

2. *horns.* There were projections at each of the four corners of the altar. The commonly accepted view is that they were pointed at the top. Josephus, describing the altar in the Second Temple, says, 'it had corners like horns.' The purpose of these horns can only be conjectured. The horn was the symbol of power, glory, salvation; and these horns no doubt typified to the worshipper the might of God and His ability to protect those who resorted to His altar. Consequently, a fugitive, unless he was a murderer, obtained safety by seizing hold of the altar-horns (see on XXI, 14).

of one piece with it. Cf. XXV, 19, 31.

overlay it with brass. Since fires would be constantly burning upon the altar.

3. *ashes.* Of the burnt animals and fuels.

shovels. To remove the ashes from the altar.

basins. Receptacles for the blood of the slain animals.

flesh-hooks. Forks for handling the flesh of the sacrifices.

fire-pans. In which burning coal was carried from the altar of burnt-offering to the altar of incense.

thou shalt make of brass. 4. And thou shalt make for it a grating of network of brass; and upon the net shalt thou make four brazen rings in the four corners thereof. 5. And thou shalt put it under the ledge round the altar beneath, that the net may reach halfway up the altar. 6. And thou shalt make staves for the altar, staves of acacia-wood, and overlay them with brass. 7. And the staves thereof shall be put into the rings, and the staves shall be upon the two sides of the altar, in bearing it. 8. Hollow with planks shalt thou make it; as it hath been shown thee in the mount, so shall they make it.* vii. ¶ 9. And thou shalt make the court of the tabernacle: for the south side southward there shall be hangings for the court of fine twined linen a hundred cubits long for one side. 10. And the pillars thereof shall be twenty, and their sockets twenty, of brass; the hooks of the pillars and their fillets shall be of silver. 11. And likewise for the north side in length there shall be hangings a hundred cubits long, and the pillars thereof twenty, and their sockets twenty, of brass; the hooks of the pillars and their fillets of silver. 12. And for the breadth of the court on the west side shall be hangings of fifty cubits: their pillars ten, and their sockets ten. 13. And the breadth of the court on the east side eastward shall be fifty cubits. 14. The hangings for the one side [of the gate] shall be fifteen cubits: their pillars three, and their sockets three. 15. And for the other side shall be hangings of fifteen cubits: their pillars three, and their sockets three. 16. And for the gate of the court shall be a screen of twenty cubits, of blue, and purple, and scarlet, and fine twined linen, the work of the weaver in

4 וּמִזְלְגֹתָיו וּמַחְתֹּתָיו לְכָל־כֵּלָיו תַּעֲשֶׂה נְחֹשֶׁת׃ וְעָשִׂיתָ
לּוֹ מִכְבָּר מַעֲשֵׂה רֶשֶׁת נְחֹשֶׁת וְעָשִׂיתָ עַל־הָרֶשֶׁת אַרְבַּע
ה טַבְּעֹת נְחֹשֶׁת עַל אַרְבַּע קְצוֹתָיו׃ וְנָתַתָּה אֹתָהּ תַּחַת
כַּרְכֹּב הַמִּזְבֵּחַ מִלְּמָטָּה וְהָיְתָה הָרֶשֶׁת עַד חֲצִי הַמִּזְבֵּחַ׃
6 וְעָשִׂיתָ בַדִּים לַמִּזְבֵּחַ בַּדֵּי עֲצֵי שִׁטִּים וְצִפִּיתָ אֹתָם נְחֹשֶׁת׃
7 וְהוּבָא אֶת־בַּדָּיו בַּטַּבָּעֹת וְהָיוּ הַבַּדִּים עַל־שְׁתֵּי צַלְעֹת
8 הַמִּזְבֵּחַ בִּשְׂאֵת אֹתוֹ׃ נְבוּב לֻחֹת תַּעֲשֶׂה אֹתוֹ כַּאֲשֶׁר
שביעי 9 הֶרְאָה אֹתְךָ בָּהָר כֵּן יַעֲשׂוּ׃ * ס וְעָשִׂיתָ אֵת חֲצַר
הַמִּשְׁכָּן לִפְאַת נֶגֶב־תֵּימָנָה קְלָעִים לֶחָצֵר שֵׁשׁ מָשְׁזָר
י מֵאָה בָאַמָּה אֹרֶךְ לַפֵּאָה הָאֶחָת׃ וְעַמֻּדָיו עֶשְׂרִים וְאַדְנֵיהֶם
11 עֶשְׂרִים נְחֹשֶׁת וָוֵי הָעַמֻּדִים וַחֲשֻׁקֵיהֶם כָּסֶף׃ וְכֵן לִפְאַת
צָפוֹן בָּאֹרֶךְ קְלָעִים מֵאָה אֹרֶךְ וְעַמֻּדָו עֶשְׂרִים וְאַדְנֵיהֶם
12 עֶשְׂרִים נְחֹשֶׁת וָוֵי הָעַמֻּדִים וַחֲשֻׁקֵיהֶם כָּסֶף׃ וְרֹחַב הֶחָצֵר
לִפְאַת־יָם קְלָעִים חֲמִשִּׁים אַמָּה עַמֻּדֵיהֶם עֲשָׂרָה וְאַדְנֵיהֶם
13 עֲשָׂרָה׃ וְרֹחַב הֶחָצֵר לִפְאַת קֵדְמָה מִזְרָחָה חֲמִשִּׁים
14 אַמָּה׃ וַחֲמֵשׁ עֶשְׂרֵה אַמָּה קְלָעִים לַכָּתֵף עַמֻּדֵיהֶם
טו שְׁלֹשָׁה וְאַדְנֵיהֶם שְׁלֹשָׁה׃ וְלַכָּתֵף הַשֵּׁנִית חֲמֵשׁ עֶשְׂרֵה
16 קְלָעִים עַמֻּדֵיהֶם שְׁלֹשָׁה וְאַדְנֵיהֶם שְׁלֹשָׁה׃ וּלְשַׁעַר הֶחָצֵר
מָסָךְ ׀ עֶשְׂרִים אַמָּה תְּכֵלֶת וְאַרְגָּמָן וְתוֹלַעַת שָׁנִי וְשֵׁשׁ

v. 11. ועמודיו קרי

5. *ledge.* Half-way round the altar there ran a ledge, probably made of copper, and this rested upon a brazen grating, 2½ feet in height. According to Tradition, this ledge was a cubit in width, and seems to have been used by the priests to stand on. Attached to the grating were rings to enable the altar to be carried.

8. *hollow with planks.* The altar consisted of wooden planks covered with metal, so that the inside was hollow. Rashi explains that the command in xx, 21, 'an altar of earth thou shalt make unto Me,' signifies that a mound of earth, equal to the dimensions of the hollow of the altar, was heaped up, and the casing of the altar set over it.

9–19. THE COURT OF THE TABERNACLE

9. *court.* *i.e.* an enclosure, but without a roof. It marked off the limits of the Sanctuary-precincts. Any Israelite, who was not ritually unclean, could enter the court. The material used for the enclosure was 'fine twisted linen' (see on XXVI, 1), and the length was 100 cubits (150 feet).

10. The hangings were supported by twenty pillars, set five cubits apart; and, since the height was five cubits (*v.* 18), the spaces created by the pillars were square.

sockets. See on XXVI, 19.

fillets. Narrow strips of binding material; binding-rods, connecting the pillars.

12. *breadth.* The court was twice as long as it was broad. There were twenty pillars along the length, and ten along the breadth.

16. *screen.* On the east side, there were hangings, as on the other three sides, but only for fifteen cubits from each corner. This left an open space in the middle, measuring twenty cubits which was filled in by a screen. This screen was of the same fabric as that of the Tabernacle (XXVI, 36).

colours: their pillars four, and their sockets four.* m. 17. All the pillars of the court round about shall be filleted with silver; their hooks of silver, and their sockets of brass. 18. The length of the court shall be a hundred cubits, and the breadth fifty every where, and the height five cubits, of fine twined linen, and their sockets of brass. 19. All the instruments of the tabernacle in all the service thereof, and all the pins thereof, and all the pins of the court, shall be of brass.

מפטיר מָשְׁזָר מַעֲשֵׂה רֹקֵם עַמֻּדֵיהֶם אַרְבָּעָה וְאַדְנֵיהֶם אַרְבָּעָה׃*
17 כָּל־עַמּוּדֵי הֶחָצֵר סָבִיב מְחֻשָּׁקִים כֶּסֶף וָוֵיהֶם כָּסֶף
18 וְאַדְנֵיהֶם נְחֹשֶׁת׃ אֹרֶךְ הֶחָצֵר מֵאָה בָאַמָּה וְרֹחַב ׀ חֲמִשִּׁים
בַּחֲמִשִּׁים וְקֹמָה חָמֵשׁ אַמּוֹת שֵׁשׁ מָשְׁזָר וְאַדְנֵיהֶם נְחֹשֶׁת׃
19 לְכֹל כְּלֵי הַמִּשְׁכָּן בְּכֹל עֲבֹדָתוֹ וְכָל־יְתֵדֹתָיו וְכָל־יִתְדֹת
הֶחָצֵר נְחֹשֶׁת׃

17. *filleted. i.e.* bound round, as in *v.* 10.

18. *every where.* A difficult phrase. Its literal meaning is 'fifty by fifty', which the Talmud explains by supposing that on the East side the court was fifty cubits square.

19. *instruments.* Tools used in setting up the tabernacle; such as hammers for driving the pins into the ground.

tabernacle. The word is here used in its widest sense, to include the Court as well as the Holy Place and Holy of Holies.

service thereof. Its workmanship.

pins. Tent-pegs.

HAFTORAH TERUMAH — הפטרת תרומה

I KINGS V, 26–VI, 13

CHAPTER V

26. And the LORD gave Solomon wisdom, as He promised him; and there was peace between Hiram and Solomon; and they two made a league together. ¶27. And king Solomon raised a levy out of all Israel; and the levy was thirty thousand men. 28. And he sent them to Lebanon, ten thousand a month by courses: a month they were in Lebanon, and two months at home; and

CAP. V. ה

26 וַיהוָה נָתַן חָכְמָה לִשְׁלֹמֹה כַּאֲשֶׁר דִּבֶּר־
לוֹ וַיְהִי שָׁלֹם בֵּין חִירָם וּבֵין שְׁלֹמֹה וַיִּכְרְתוּ בְרִית
27 שְׁנֵיהֶם׃ וַיַּעַל הַמֶּלֶךְ שְׁלֹמֹה מַס מִכָּל־יִשְׂרָאֵל וַיְהִי
28 הַמַּס שְׁלֹשִׁים אֶלֶף אִישׁ׃ וַיִּשְׁלָחֵם לְבָנוֹנָה עֲשֶׂרֶת אֲלָפִים

The Sedrah describes the Tabernacle in the wilderness. This is paralleled in the Haftorah by the description of the Temple of Solomon at Jerusalem.

It was King David's yearning desire to build a Temple unto God—a central Sanctuary that was to be the symbol of Israel's obedience to God's Law, of Israel's unity and Israel's peace. He was not destined to see his life-dream realized; but Solomon his son makes its fulfilment almost the first care of his reign.

26. *as He promised him.* See I Kings III, 12.

Hiram. King of Tyre, the principal city of Phœnicia, on the coast, north of Palestine. Hiram was a friend of David, and helped him to build his own house (II Sam. v, 11). He now agrees, on Solomon's request, to supply timber and skilled labour for the building of the Temple, in return for an annual payment of wheat and oil.

THE PREPARATION FOR THE WORK

27. *a levy.* Heb. *mas.* the same word as in Exod. I, 11, and denoting a body of men set to forced labour for a definite time. 'It was perhaps from his Egyptian father-in-law that Solomon, to his own cost, learnt the secret of forced labour. In their Egyptian bondage the forefathers of Israel had been fatally familiar with the ugly word *mas*, the labour wrung from them by hard task-masters' (Farrar). See I Sam. VIII, 11–18. Discontent with this practice eventually rent Solomon's kingdom in twain. In contrast to this forced labour, the Tabernacle of old was the result of the free-will offerings of the entire People.

28. *to Lebanon.* To cut down the trees there. The mountain range of Lebanon, to the north of Palestine, is still noted for its magnificent cedar trees.

Adoniram was over the levy. 29. And Solomon had threescore and ten thousand that bore burdens, and fourscore thousand that were hewers in the mountains; 30. besides Solomon's chief officers that were over the work, three thousand and three hundred, who bore rule over the people that wrought in the work. 31. And the king commanded, and they quarried great stones, costly stones, to lay the foundation of the house with hewn stone. 32. And Solomon's builders and Hiram's builders and the Gebalites did fashion them, and prepared the timber and the stones to build the house.

בַּחֹדֶשׁ חֲלִיפוֹת חֹדֶשׁ יִהְיוּ בַלְּבָנוֹן שְׁנַיִם חֳדָשִׁים בְּבֵיתוֹ
29 וַאֲדֹנִירָם עַל־הַמַּס׃ וַיְהִי לִשְׁלֹמֹה שִׁבְעִים אֶלֶף נֹשֵׂא
ל סַבָּל וּשְׁמֹנִים אֶלֶף חֹצֵב בָּהָר׃ לְבַד מִשָּׂרֵי הַנִּצָּבִים
לִשְׁלֹמֹה אֲשֶׁר עַל־הַמְּלָאכָה שְׁלֹשֶׁת אֲלָפִים וּשְׁלֹשׁ מֵאוֹת
31 הָרֹדִים בָּעָם הָעֹשִׂים בַּמְּלָאכָה׃ וַיְצַו הַמֶּלֶךְ וַיַּסִּעוּ אֲבָנִים
32 גְּדֹלוֹת אֲבָנִים יְקָרוֹת לְיַסֵּד הַבָּיִת אַבְנֵי גָזִית׃ וַיִּפְסְלוּ
בֹּנֵי שְׁלֹמֹה וּבֹנֵי חִירוֹם וְהַגִּבְלִים וַיָּכִינוּ הָעֵצִים וְהָאֲבָנִים
לִבְנוֹת הַבָּיִת׃

Chapter VI

1. And it came to pass in the four hundred and eightieth year after the children of Israel were come out of the land of Egypt, in the fourth year of Solomon's reign over Israel, in the month Ziv, which is the second month, that he began to build the house of the LORD. 2. And the house which king Solomon built for the LORD, the length thereof was threescore cubits, and the breadth thereof twenty cubits, and the height thereof thirty cubits. 3. And the porch before [1]the temple of the house, twenty cubits was the length thereof, according to the breadth of the house; and ten cubits was the breadth thereof before the house. 4. And for the house he made windows broad within, and narrow without. 5. And against the wall of the house he built a side-structure round about, against the walls of the house round about, both of the temple and of [2]the Sanctuary;

Cap. VI. ו

א וַיְהִי בִשְׁמוֹנִים שָׁנָה וְאַרְבַּע מֵאוֹת שָׁנָה לְצֵאת בְּנֵי־
יִשְׂרָאֵל מֵאֶרֶץ־מִצְרַיִם בַּשָּׁנָה הָרְבִיעִית בְּחֹדֶשׁ זִו הוּא
הַחֹדֶשׁ הַשֵּׁנִי לִמְלֹךְ שְׁלֹמֹה עַל־יִשְׂרָאֵל וַיִּבֶן הַבַּיִת לַיהוָה׃
2 וְהַבַּיִת אֲשֶׁר בָּנָה הַמֶּלֶךְ שְׁלֹמֹה לַיהוָה שִׁשִּׁים־אַמָּה
3 אָרְכּוֹ וְעֶשְׂרִים רָחְבּוֹ וּשְׁלֹשִׁים אַמָּה קוֹמָתוֹ׃ וְהָאוּלָם עַל־
פְּנֵי הֵיכַל הַבַּיִת עֶשְׂרִים אַמָּה אָרְכּוֹ עַל־פְּנֵי רֹחַב הַבָּיִת
4 עֶשֶׂר בָּאַמָּה רָחְבּוֹ עַל־פְּנֵי הַבָּיִת׃ וַיַּעַשׂ לַבַּיִת חַלּוֹנֵי
ה שְׁקֻפִים אֲטֻמִים׃ וַיִּבֶן עַל־קִיר הַבַּיִת יָצוּעַ סָבִיב אֶת־

[1] That is, the holy place.
[2] Heb. *debir*, that is, the hindmost or innermost room, the most holy place.

ה׳ v. 31. קמץ בטרחא ו׳ v. 4. קמץ בז"ק v. 5. יציע ק׳

by courses. i.e. in relays, or shifts. There were ten thousand at work each month; the others were resting in their homes for two months.

Adoniram. Was the overseer over the levy.

29. *hewers in the mountains. i.e.* sent to quarry stones in the hill-country of Palestine.

30. *bore rule.* As taskmasters.

32. *the Gebalites.* Inhabitants of Gebal, a maritime town north of Beyrout.

Chapter VI. A General Description of the Temple

The Temple buildings stood within a large court in which the worshippers could assemble. The Temple proper was a rectangular hall 60 by 20 by 30 cubits. Its entrance, in shape of a porch, was ten cubits long; and as it extended over the whole front, it was 20 cubits wide. On the three sides of the House were built a number of chambers in three stories. Within, the building was divided into two parts; the larger, to the East, being the Holy Place; and the smaller, the Most Holy Place.

1. *the month Ziv.* The ancient name of the second month, now called Iyyar.

3. *temple of the house. i.e.* the Holy Place.

4. *broad within, and narrow without.* This translation follows the Targum. The Rabbis, however, explain that the windows were *narrow within* and, cut obliquely through the wall, *widening towards the exterior*—teaching that the Sanctuary required no outward light, rather was its spiritual radiance to spread abroad and illumine the world outside.

5. *side-structure.* It enclosed the whole of three sides of the building; and, within it on different stories, he built the side-chambers mentioned below.

and he made side-chambers round about; 6. the nethermost story of the side-structure was five cubits broad, and the middle was six cubits broad, and the third was seven cubits broad; for on the outside he made rebatements in the wall of the house round about, that the beams should not have hold in the walls of the house.—7. For the house, when it was in building, was built of stone made ready at the quarry; and there was neither hammer nor axe nor any tool of iron heard in the house, while it was in building. —8. The door for the [1]lowest row of chambers was in the right side of the house; and they went up by winding stairs into the middle row, and out of the middle into the third. 9. So he built the house, and finished it; and he covered in the house with planks of cedar over beams. 10. And he built the stories of the side-structure against all the house, each five cubits high; and they rested on the house with timber of cedar. ¶ 11. And the word of the LORD came to Solomon, saying: 12. 'As for this house which thou art building, if thou wilt walk in My statutes, and execute Mine ordinances, and keep all My commandments to walk in them; then will I establish My word with thee, which I spoke unto David thy father; 13. in that I will dwell therein among the children of Israel, and will not forsake My people Israel.'

קִירוֹת הַבַּיִת סָבִיב לַהֵיכָל וְלַדְּבִיר וַיַּעַשׂ צְלָעוֹת סָבִיב׃
6 הַיָּצוּעַ הַתַּחְתֹּנָה חָמֵשׁ בָּאַמָּה רָחְבָּהּ וְהַתִּיכֹנָה שֵׁשׁ
בָּאַמָּה רָחְבָּהּ וְהַשְּׁלִישִׁית שֶׁבַע בָּאַמָּה רָחְבָּהּ כִּי מִגְרָעוֹת
נָתַן לַבַּיִת סָבִיב חוּצָה לְבִלְתִּי אֲחֹז בְּקִירוֹת הַבָּיִת׃
7 וְהַבַּיִת בְּהִבָּנֹתוֹ אֶבֶן שְׁלֵמָה מַסָּע נִבְנָה וּמַקָּבוֹת וְהַגַּרְזֶן
8 כָּל־כְּלִי בַרְזֶל לֹא־נִשְׁמַע בַּבַּיִת בְּהִבָּנֹתוֹ׃ פֶּתַח הַצֵּלָע
הַתִּיכֹנָה אֶל־כֶּתֶף הַבַּיִת הַיְמָנִית וּבְלוּלִּים יַעֲלוּ עַל־
9 הַתִּיכֹנָה וּמִן־הַתִּיכֹנָה אֶל־הַשְּׁלִשִׁים׃ וַיִּבֶן אֶת־הַבַּיִת
י וַיְכַלֵּהוּ וַיִּסְפֹּן אֶת־הַבַּיִת גֵּבִים וּשְׂדֵרֹת בָּאֲרָזִים׃ וַיִּבֶן
אֶת־הַיָּצוּעַ עַל־כָּל־הַבַּיִת חָמֵשׁ אַמּוֹת קוֹמָתוֹ וַיֶּאֱחֹז אֶת־
11 הַבַּיִת בַּעֲצֵי אֲרָזִים׃ וַיְהִי דְּבַר־יְהוָה אֶל־שְׁלֹמֹה
12 לֵאמֹר׃ הַבַּיִת הַזֶּה אֲשֶׁר־אַתָּה בֹנֶה אִם־תֵּלֵךְ בְּחֻקֹּתַי
וְאֶת־מִשְׁפָּטַי תַּעֲשֶׂה וְשָׁמַרְתָּ אֶת־כָּל־מִצְוֺתַי לָלֶכֶת בָּהֶם
וַהֲקִמֹתִי אֶת־דְּבָרִי אִתָּךְ אֲשֶׁר דִּבַּרְתִּי אֶל־דָּוִד אָבִיךָ׃
13 וְשָׁכַנְתִּי בְּתוֹךְ בְּנֵי יִשְׂרָאֵל וְלֹא אֶעֱזֹב אֶת־עַמִּי יִשְׂרָאֵל׃

[1] Heb. *middle*.

v. 6. היציע קרי v. 8. דגש אחר שורק v. 10. היציע קרי

the sanctuary. Heb. *debir.* That is, the Most Holy Place (RV Margin); the hindmost, or innermost room.

side-chambers. They were probably for the accommodation of the priests, and for storing the treasure of the Sanctuary.

6. *rebatements in the wall.* There were successive reductions in the thickness of the walls in the second and third story. The chambers thus *increased* somewhat in size in the upper stories, each of these resting on a recess, or rebatement, in the thick wall of the Temple.

the beams should not have hold in the walls. Thus the walls were not pierced in order to give support to the beams, and these were not fixed into the actual building of the Temple.

7. *at the quarry.* The stones were squared, dressed and finished at the quarries, before being sent to Jerusalem.

neither hammer . . . heard in the house. The Temple rose *silently and peacefully.* Jewish Legend wove its magic web around this striking verse. If neither hammer nor axe was used in the building of the House, how then were the stones fitted together? the people asked. Solomon in his wisdom, was the answer, had come into possession of a wonderful worm, one of the marvels of creation, the *Shamir*, which, if placed upon the hardest stones, would instantly and noiselessly cleave them as desired. The great moral truth enshrined in this verse and legend is this: a Temple of the LORD cannot be where there is discord, violence or revolt.

9. *covered. i.e.* roofed it.

10. *the stories.* See *v.* 5.

11–13. CHARGE TO SOLOMON

12. *as for this house.* The erection of the Temple was only an external sign of the allegiance of Solomon and Israel to the LORD. To win Divine favour, they must submit their life and conduct to the guidance of the Divine Law.

27 20. And thou shalt command the children of Israel, that they bring unto thee pure olive oil beaten for the light, to cause a lamp to burn continually. 21. In the tent of meeting, without the veil which is before the testimony, Aaron and his sons shall set it in order, to burn from evening to morning before the LORD; it shall be a statute for ever throughout their generations on the behalf of the children of Israel.

28 CHAPTER XXVIII

1. And bring thou near unto thee Aaron thy brother, and his sons with him, from among the children of Israel, that they may minister unto Me in the priest's office, even Aaron, Nadab and Abihu, Eleazar and Ithamar, Aaron's sons. 2. And thou shalt make holy garments for Aaron thy brother, for splendour and for beauty. 3. And thou

כז ס ס ס כ 20

כ וְאַתָּה תְּצַוֶּה ׀ אֶת־בְּנֵי יִשְׂרָאֵל וְיִקְחוּ אֵלֶיךָ שֶׁמֶן זַיִת זָךְ
21 כָּתִית לַמָּאוֹר לְהַעֲלֹת נֵר תָּמִיד: בְּאֹהֶל מוֹעֵד מִחוּץ
לַפָּרֹכֶת אֲשֶׁר עַל־הָעֵדֻת יַעֲרֹךְ אֹתוֹ אַהֲרֹן וּבָנָיו מֵעֶרֶב עַד־
בֹּקֶר לִפְנֵי יְהוָה חֻקַּת עוֹלָם לְדֹרֹתָם מֵאֵת בְּנֵי יִשְׂרָאֵל: ס

כח CAP. XXVIII. כח

א וְאַתָּה הַקְרֵב אֵלֶיךָ אֶת־אַהֲרֹן אָחִיךָ וְאֶת־בָּנָיו אִתּוֹ מִתּוֹךְ
בְּנֵי יִשְׂרָאֵל לְכַהֲנוֹ־לִי אַהֲרֹן נָדָב וַאֲבִיהוּא אֶלְעָזָר וְאִיתָמָר
2 בְּנֵי אַהֲרֹן: וְעָשִׂיתָ בִגְדֵי־קֹדֶשׁ לְאַהֲרֹן אָחִיךָ לְכָבוֹד
3 וּלְתִפְאָרֶת: וְאַתָּה תְּדַבֵּר אֶל־כָּל־חַכְמֵי־לֵב אֲשֶׁר מִלֵּאתִיו

VIII. TETZAVEH

(CHAPTERS XXVII, 20–XXX, 10)

20, 21. THE OIL FOR THE LAMP

After the description of the Sanctuary, Scripture proceeds to deal with the requirements of those who were to minister therein.

20. *for the light.* That was to be kept burning in the Sanctuary every night.

pure olive oil. Used for all sacred purposes.

beaten. The olives were gently pounded in a mortar, and the first drops of oil obtained were of the purest quality.

continually. *i.e.* regularly, as a standing practice. Because no sunlight fell into the Sanctuary, there had always to be one light (cf. I Sam. III, 3). The lamp of the Sanctuary is represented in the Synagogue by the perpetual lamp burning before the Ark (the *Ner Tamid*). The Rabbis interpret the lamp as a symbol of Israel, whose mission it was to become 'a light of the nations' (Isa. XLII, 7).

21. *tent of meeting.* *i.e.* the Holy Place, not the Holy of Holies; see XXV, 22.

without the veil. Outside the veil.

the testimony. See XXV, 21.

from evening to morning. Cf. XXX, 7, where it is stated that it was Aaron's duty in the morning to remove the burnt wick, replace it with a fresh one and fill the lamp with oil. He was to light it in the evening.

CHAPTER XXVIII. THE VESTMENTS OF THE PRIESTS

After the instructions as to the building of the Sanctuary, Moses receives directions concerning the men who are to serve as priests. That sacred office was reserved for Aaron, his sons and their descendants. This chapter describes the garments which were to be worn by the priests when ministering in the Sanctuary. These garments distinguished the priest from the lay Israelite, and reminded him that even more than the layman he must make the ideal of holiness the constant guide of his life. These vestments also added to the solemnity and awe of the service of the Sanctuary.

1. *that he may minister.* The verb is in the singular, referring to the principal person in the group, Aaron.

2. *holy garments.* *i.e.* garments to be worn by the priests when discharging their holy functions.

for splendour and for beauty. Or, 'for splendour and distinction.'

3. *wise-hearted.* In Bible psychology, the heart is the seat of intellect, not of feeling.

whom I have filled. Not that God had endowed certain men with extraordinary skill for this special occasion. Whatever gifts a man possesses are an endowment from God. Those, therefore, who are exceptionally skilful in craftsmanship are to offer their artistic skill for the making of the vestments.

sanctify him. The investiture in the priestly garments was part of the ceremony of induction into the priest's office, described in the next chapter.

רוּחַ חָכְמָה וְעָשׂוּ אֶת־בִּגְדֵי אַהֲרֹן לְקַדְּשׁוֹ לְכַהֲנוֹ־לִי׃
4 וְאֵלֶּה הַבְּגָדִים אֲשֶׁר יַעֲשׂוּ חֹשֶׁן וְאֵפוֹד וּמְעִיל וּכְתֹנֶת
תַּשְׁבֵּץ מִצְנֶפֶת וְאַבְנֵט וְעָשׂוּ בִגְדֵי־קֹדֶשׁ לְאַהֲרֹן אָחִיךָ
ה וּלְבָנָיו לְכַהֲנוֹ־לִי׃ וְהֵם יִקְחוּ אֶת־הַזָּהָב וְאֶת־הַתְּכֵלֶת
וְאֶת־הָאַרְגָּמָן וְאֶת־תּוֹלַעַת הַשָּׁנִי וְאֶת־הַשֵּׁשׁ׃ פ
6 וְעָשׂוּ אֶת־הָאֵפֹד זָהָב תְּכֵלֶת וְאַרְגָּמָן תּוֹלַעַת שָׁנִי וְשֵׁשׁ
7 מָשְׁזָר מַעֲשֵׂה חֹשֵׁב׃ שְׁתֵּי כְתֵפֹת חֹבְרֹת יִהְיֶה־לּוֹ אֶל־
8 שְׁנֵי קְצוֹתָיו וְחֻבָּר׃ וְחֵשֶׁב אֲפֻדָּתוֹ אֲשֶׁר עָלָיו כְּמַעֲשֵׂהוּ
מִמֶּנּוּ יִהְיֶה זָהָב תְּכֵלֶת וְאַרְגָּמָן וְתוֹלַעַת שָׁנִי וְשֵׁשׁ
9 מָשְׁזָר׃ וְלָקַחְתָּ אֶת־שְׁתֵּי אַבְנֵי־שֹׁהַם וּפִתַּחְתָּ עֲלֵיהֶם
י שְׁמוֹת בְּנֵי יִשְׂרָאֵל׃ שִׁשָּׁה מִשְּׁמֹתָם עַל הָאֶבֶן הָאֶחָת
וְאֶת־שְׁמוֹת הַשִּׁשָּׁה הַנּוֹתָרִים עַל־הָאֶבֶן הַשֵּׁנִית כְּתוֹלְדֹתָם׃
11 מַעֲשֵׂה חָרַשׁ אֶבֶן פִּתּוּחֵי חֹתָם תְּפַתַּח אֶת־שְׁתֵּי הָאֲבָנִים
עַל־שְׁמֹת בְּנֵי יִשְׂרָאֵל מֻסַבֹּת מִשְׁבְּצוֹת זָהָב תַּעֲשֶׂה
12 אֹתָם׃ וְשַׂמְתָּ אֶת־שְׁתֵּי הָאֲבָנִים עַל כִּתְפֹת הָאֵפֹד אַבְנֵי
זִכָּרֹן לִבְנֵי יִשְׂרָאֵל וְנָשָׂא אַהֲרֹן אֶת־שְׁמוֹתָם לִפְנֵי יְהוָה

shalt speak unto all that are wise-hearted, whom I have filled with the spirit of wisdom, that they make Aaron's garments to sanctify him, that he may minister unto Me in the priest's office. 4. And these are the garments which they shall make: a breastplate, and an ephod, and a robe, and a tunic of chequer work, a mitre, and a girdle; and they shall make holy garments for Aaron thy brother, and his sons, that he may minister unto Me in the priest's office. 5. And they shall take the gold, and the blue, and the purple, and the scarlet, and the fine linen. ¶ 6. And they shall make the ephod of gold, of blue, and purple, scarlet, and fine twined linen, the work of the skilful workman. 7. It shall have two shoulder-pieces joined to the two ends thereof, that it may be joined together. 8. And the skilfully woven band, which is upon it, wherewith to gird it on, shall be like the work thereof and of the same piece: of gold, of blue, and purple, and scarlet, and fine twined linen. 9. And thou shalt take two onyx stones, and grave on them the names of the children of Israel: 10. six of their names on the one stone, and the names of the six that remain on the other stone, according to their birth. 11. With the work of an engraver in stone, like the engravings of a signet, shalt thou engrave the two stones, according to the names of the children of Israel; thou shalt make them to be inclosed in settings of gold. 12. And thou shalt put the two stones upon the shoulder-pieces of the ephod, to be stones of memorial for the children of Israel; and Aaron shall bear their names before the

4. *breastplate.* This and the other garments of the High Priest, described later, were additional to the garments of the priests.

5. *they shall take.* *i.e.* the workmen shall receive the materials (xxv, 3) from those who give them.

6–12. The Ephod

6. *ephod.* A short close-fitting coat, worn round the body under the arms, and having straps over the shoulders to keep it in place.

skilful workman. See on xxvi, 1. The fabric of the ephod was the same as the curtains and veil of the Tabernacle, indicating the intimate connection between the High Priest and the Sanctuary. But in addition, there were gold threads woven into the material, probably as a symbol of royal power, because of the High Priest's position as the spiritual head of the community.

8. *band.* Around the waist, at the bottom of the ephod, was an artistically woven band, part of the ephod.

9. *onyx stones.* 'To fasten it, after the manner of buttons' (Josephus).

children of Israel. Better, '*sons of Israel*'; *i.e.* the twelve sons of Jacob who gave their names to the tribes. The name of Joseph was used here instead of Manasseh and Ephraim.

11. *engraver.* Tut-an-khamen's Tomb and the discoveries in regard to the goldsmith's art and precious jewellery at Ur, have shown that the art of engraving, such as here described, was common in the ancient world.

12. *stones of memorial.* To remind the children of Israel of their unity of descent, and unity of service to the God of Holiness.

Aaron shall bear. The names denoted in concrete form that the High Priest was the messenger and representative of the entire community.

LORD upon his two shoulders for a memorial.* ii. ¶ 13. And thou shalt make settings of gold; 14. and two chains of pure gold; of plaited thread shalt thou make them, of wreathen work; and thou shalt put the wreathen chains on the settings. ¶ 15. And thou shalt make a breastplate of judgment, the work of the skilful workman; like the work of the ephod thou shalt make it: of gold, of blue, and purple, and scarlet and fine twined linen, shalt thou make it. 16. Four-square it shall be and double: a span shall be the length thereof, and a span the breadth thereof. 17. And thou shalt set in it settings of stones, four rows of stones: a row of carnelian, topaz, and smaragd shall be the first row; 18. and the second row a carbuncle, a sapphire, and an emerald; 19. and the third row a jacinth, an agate, and an amethyst; 20. and the fourth row a beryl, and an onyx, and a jasper; they shall be inclosed in gold in their settings. 21. And the stones shall be according to the names of the children of Israel, twelve, according to their names; like the engravings of a signet, every one according to his name, they shall be for the twelve tribes. 22. And thou shalt make upon the breastplate plaited chains of wreathen work of pure gold. 23. And thou shalt make upon the breastplate two rings of gold, and shalt put the two rings on the two ends of the breastplate. 24. And thou shalt put the two wreathen chains of gold on the two rings at the ends of the breastplate. 25. And the other two ends of the two wreathen chains thou shalt put on the two settings, and put them on the shoulder-pieces of the

שני
13 עַל־שְׁתֵּי כְתֵפָיו לְזִכָּרֹן׃ ס וְעָשִׂיתָ מִשְׁבְּצֹת זָהָב׃
14 וּשְׁתֵּי שַׁרְשְׁרֹת זָהָב טָהוֹר מִגְבָּלֹת תַּעֲשֶׂה אֹתָם מַעֲשֵׂה
עֲבֹת וְנָתַתָּה אֶת־שַׁרְשְׁרֹת הָעֲבֹתֹת עַל־הַמִּשְׁבְּצֹת׃ ס
טו וְעָשִׂיתָ חֹשֶׁן מִשְׁפָּט מַעֲשֵׂה חֹשֵׁב כְּמַעֲשֵׂה אֵפֹד תַּעֲשֶׂנּוּ
זָהָב תְּכֵלֶת וְאַרְגָּמָן וְתוֹלַעַת שָׁנִי וְשֵׁשׁ מָשְׁזָר תַּעֲשֶׂה
16 17 אֹתוֹ׃ רָבוּעַ יִהְיֶה כָּפוּל זֶרֶת אָרְכּוֹ וְזֶרֶת רָחְבּוֹ׃ וּמִלֵּאתָ
בוֹ מִלֻּאַת אֶבֶן אַרְבָּעָה טוּרִים אָבֶן טוּר אֹדֶם פִּטְדָה
18 וּבָרֶקֶת הַטּוּר הָאֶחָד׃ וְהַטּוּר הַשֵּׁנִי נֹפֶךְ סַפִּיר וְיָהֲלֹם׃
19 כ וְהַטּוּר הַשְּׁלִישִׁי לֶשֶׁם שְׁבוֹ וְאַחְלָמָה׃ וְהַטּוּר הָרְבִיעִי
תַּרְשִׁישׁ וְשֹׁהַם וְיָשְׁפֵה מְשֻׁבָּצִים זָהָב יִהְיוּ בְּמִלּוּאֹתָם׃
21 וְהָאֲבָנִים תִּהְיֶיןָ עַל־שְׁמֹת בְּנֵי־יִשְׂרָאֵל שְׁתֵּים עֶשְׂרֵה עַל־
שְׁמֹתָם פִּתּוּחֵי חוֹתָם אִישׁ עַל־שְׁמוֹ תִּהְיֶיןָ לִשְׁנֵי עָשָׂר
22 שָׁבֶט׃ וְעָשִׂיתָ עַל־הַחֹשֶׁן שַׁרְשֹׁת גַּבְלֻת מַעֲשֵׂה עֲבֹת זָהָב
23 טָהוֹר׃ וְעָשִׂיתָ עַל־הַחֹשֶׁן שְׁתֵּי טַבְּעוֹת זָהָב וְנָתַתָּ אֶת־
24 שְׁתֵּי הַטַּבָּעוֹת עַל־שְׁנֵי קְצוֹת הַחֹשֶׁן׃ וְנָתַתָּה אֶת־שְׁתֵּי
כה עֲבֹתֹת הַזָּהָב עַל־שְׁתֵּי הַטַּבָּעֹת אֶל־קְצוֹת הַחֹשֶׁן׃ וְאֵת

13–30. THE BREASTPLATE

14. *pure gold.* The same metal as used in the Holy of Holies.

15. *breastplate.* The breastplate was double, open on all sides except the bottom. It is called 'the breastplate of judgment', because it was to contain the Urim and the Thummim, by means of which the High Priest was to seek the judgment of God on difficult questions affecting the welfare of the community (*v.* 30).

like the work of the ephod. i.e. of the same material as the ephod.

16. *double.* The piece of cloth was a cubit in length, and a half cubit in breadth; doubled over, so as to form a bag or pouch.

17. *settings of stones.* The distinguishing feature of the breastplate was that it was set with twelve precious stones, each engraved with the name of one of the tribes of Israel; the stones being arranged in gold settings in four rows, three stones in a row.

carnelian. Or, 'ruby.'

topaz. Its colour is yellowish green.

smaragd. Some authorities suggest the rock-crystal, a colourless stone used in ancient Egypt for engravings.

18. *carbuncle.* Or, 'red garnet.'

19. *jacinth.* A clear yellow stone.

agate. A red, opaque stone.

20. *beryl.* Or, 'chalcedony.' Its colour is green to yellow.

jasper. The colour is bright green.

22. The chains referred to in this verse are the same as those mentioned in *v.* 14.

23. *and shalt put. i.e.* and shall fasten.

25. *two ends. i.e.* the corners at the top of the breastplate.

שְׁתֵּי קְצוֹת שְׁתֵּי הָעֲבֹתֹת תִּתֵּן עַל־שְׁתֵּי הַמִּשְׁבְּצוֹת וְנָתַתָּה
26 עַל־כִּתְפוֹת הָאֵפֹד אֶל־מוּל פָּנָיו׃ וְעָשִׂיתָ שְׁתֵּי טַבְּעוֹת זָהָב
וְשַׂמְתָּ אֹתָם עַל־שְׁנֵי קְצוֹת הַחֹשֶׁן עַל־שְׂפָתוֹ אֲשֶׁר אֶל־
27 עֵבֶר הָאֵפוֹד בָּיְתָה׃ וְעָשִׂיתָ שְׁתֵּי טַבְּעוֹת זָהָב וְנָתַתָּה
אֹתָם עַל־שְׁתֵּי כִתְפוֹת הָאֵפוֹד מִלְמַטָּה מִמּוּל פָּנָיו לְעֻמַּת
28 מַחְבַּרְתּוֹ מִמַּעַל לְחֵשֶׁב הָאֵפוֹד׃ וְיִרְכְּסוּ אֶת־הַחֹשֶׁן
מִטַּבְּעֹתָו אֶל־טַבְּעֹת הָאֵפוֹד בִּפְתִיל תְּכֵלֶת לִהְיוֹת עַל־
29 חֵשֶׁב הָאֵפוֹד וְלֹא־יִזַּח הַחֹשֶׁן מֵעַל הָאֵפוֹד׃ וְנָשָׂא אַהֲרֹן
אֶת־שְׁמוֹת בְּנֵי־יִשְׂרָאֵל בְּחֹשֶׁן הַמִּשְׁפָּט עַל־לִבּוֹ בְּבֹאוֹ אֶל־
ל הַקֹּדֶשׁ לְזִכָּרֹן לִפְנֵי־יְהוָה תָּמִיד׃ וְנָתַתָּ אֶל־חֹשֶׁן הַמִּשְׁפָּט
אֶת־הָאוּרִים וְאֶת־הַתֻּמִּים וְהָיוּ עַל־לֵב אַהֲרֹן בְּבֹאוֹ לִפְנֵי
יְהוָה וְנָשָׂא אַהֲרֹן אֶת־מִשְׁפַּט בְּנֵי־יִשְׂרָאֵל עַל־לִבּוֹ לִפְנֵי
שלישי
31 יְהוָה תָּמִיד׃ * ס וְעָשִׂיתָ אֶת־מְעִיל הָאֵפוֹד כְּלִיל תְּכֵלֶת׃

v. 28. מטבעתיו ק׳

ephod, in the forepart thereof. 26. And thou shalt make two rings of gold, and thou shalt put them upon the two ends of the breastplate, upon the edge thereof, which is toward the side of the ephod inward. 27. And thou shalt make two rings of gold, and shalt put them on the two shoulder-pieces of the ephod underneath, in the forepart thereof, close by the coupling thereof, above the skilfully woven band of the ephod. 28. And they shall bind the breastplate by the rings thereof unto the rings of the ephod with a thread of blue, that it may be upon the skilfully woven band of the ephod, and that the breastplate be not loosed from the ephod. 29. And Aaron shall bear the names of the children of Israel in the breastplate of judgment upon his heart, when he goeth in unto the holy place, for a memorial before the LORD continually. 30. And thou shalt put in the breastplate of judgment the Urim and the Thummim; and they shall be upon Aaron's heart, when he goeth in before the LORD; and Aaron shall bear the judgment of the children of Israel upon his heart before the LORD continually.*iii. ¶ 31. And thou shalt make the robe of the ephod all of blue. 32. And it shall have a hole for the head in the midst thereof: it shall

26–28. Two rings were to be attached to the inner lower corners of the breastplate. Two other rings were to be placed on the lower part of the shoulder-straps. Threads of blue passing through the rings tied them together. By these means the breastplate was kept firmly in its place on the breast of the High Priest.

29. *for a memorial.* 'The stones on his heart are Aaron's silent prayer to God on behalf of his entire people' (B. Jacob).

30. *the Urim and the Thummim.* lit. 'the Lights and the Perfections'; which may mean, in accordance with Heb. idiom, 'perfect lights.' Were the Urim and the Thummim identical with the breastplate and the twelve brilliant stones, or were they distinct from it? At first view, the wording of this verse, 'thou shalt put in the breastplate of judgment, the Urim and the Thummim,' seems to favour the latter alternative; and many moderns think, 'they were two sacred lots, used for the purpose of ascertaining the Divine Will on questions of national importance' (Driver). Rashi, likewise, supposes that it was some material upon which the Name of God was engraven, which the High Priest carried in the breastplate. Against this opinion it is urged that in chap. XXXIX, where the making of the breastplate is given in detail, nothing is said in regard to the fashioning of the Urim and the Thummim. Thus, it seems that 'the Urim and the Thummim' was the term whereby the twelve stones were denoted. The fact that the breastplate is called 'the breastplate of judgment', indicates that the breastplate itself, and not something distinct from it, was the medium of the Divine communications. In Lev. VIII, 8, the Urim and the Thummim alone are mentioned, not the precious stones—a strong proof of the identity of both.

Scripture records that in times of doubt and national crisis during the earlier period of Israel's history, the people consulted the Urim and the Thummim for information and guidance (Num. XXVII, 21; I Sam. XXVIII, 6); but what the procedure was is nowhere explained. No recourse to the Urim and the Thummim is mentioned after the days of David. They remain one of the most obscure subjects connected with the High Priesthood.

31–35. THE ROBE

31. *robe.* A long garment worn by men of high rank. Whether the 'robe' was always sleeveless is uncertain, but that of the High Priest was so. It is called 'robe of the ephod', because the ephod was worn over it.

all of blue. The garment was woven of one kind of thread only; the colour *blue* was significant; cf. the thread of blue on the 'fringes' (Num. XV, 38).

32 וְהָיָה פִי־רֹאשׁוֹ בְּתוֹכוֹ שָׂפָה יִהְיֶה לְפִיו סָבִיב מַעֲשֵׂה
33 אֹרֵג כְּפִי תַחְרָא יִהְיֶה־לּוֹ לֹא יִקָּרֵעַ׃ וְעָשִׂיתָ עַל־שׁוּלָיו
רִמֹּנֵי תְּכֵלֶת וְאַרְגָּמָן וְתוֹלַעַת שָׁנִי עַל־שׁוּלָיו סָבִיב וּפַעֲמֹנֵי
34 זָהָב בְּתוֹכָם סָבִיב׃ פַּעֲמֹן זָהָב וְרִמּוֹן פַּעֲמֹן זָהָב וְרִמּוֹן
לה עַל־שׁוּלֵי הַמְּעִיל סָבִיב׃ וְהָיָה עַל־אַהֲרֹן לְשָׁרֵת וְנִשְׁמַע
קוֹלוֹ בְּבֹאוֹ אֶל־הַקֹּדֶשׁ לִפְנֵי יְהוָה וּבְצֵאתוֹ וְלֹא יָמוּת׃ ס
36 וְעָשִׂיתָ צִּיץ זָהָב טָהוֹר וּפִתַּחְתָּ עָלָיו פִּתּוּחֵי חֹתָם קֹדֶשׁ
37 לַיהוָה׃ וְשַׂמְתָּ אֹתוֹ עַל־פְּתִיל תְּכֵלֶת וְהָיָה עַל־הַמִּצְנָפֶת
38 אֶל־מוּל פְּנֵי־הַמִּצְנֶפֶת יִהְיֶה׃ וְהָיָה עַל־מֵצַח אַהֲרֹן וְנָשָׂא
אַהֲרֹן אֶת־עֲוֺן הַקֳּדָשִׁים אֲשֶׁר יַקְדִּישׁוּ בְּנֵי יִשְׂרָאֵל לְכָל־
מַתְּנֹת קָדְשֵׁיהֶם וְהָיָה עַל־מִצְחוֹ תָּמִיד לְרָצוֹן לָהֶם לִפְנֵי
39 יְהוָה׃ וְשִׁבַּצְתָּ הַכְּתֹנֶת שֵׁשׁ וְעָשִׂיתָ מִצְנֶפֶת שֵׁשׁ וְאַבְנֵט

have a binding of woven work round about the hole of it, as it were the hole of a coat of mail, that it be not rent.
33. And upon the skirts of it thou shalt make pomegranates of blue, and of purple, and of scarlet, round about the skirts thereof; and bells of gold between them round about:
34. a golden bell and a pomegranate, a golden bell and a pomegranate, upon the skirts of the robe round about.
35. And it shall be upon Aaron to minister; and the sound thereof shall be heard when he goeth in unto the holy place before the LORD, and when he cometh out, that he die not. ¶
36. And thou shalt make a plate of pure gold, and engrave upon it, like the engravings of a signet: HOLY TO THE LORD.
37. And thou shalt put it on a thread of blue, and it shall be upon the mitre; upon the forefront of the mitre it shall be.
38. And it shall be upon Aaron's forehead, and Aaron shall bear the iniquity committed in the holy things, which the children of Israel shall hallow, even in all their holy gifts; and it shall be always upon his forehead, that they may be accepted before the LORD.
39. And thou shalt weave the tunic in chequer work

32. *for the head.* The robe had an opening only on top. It had, therefore, to be drawn over the head; and to prevent the material from tearing, the edge was strengthened by means of additional weaving.

33–35. The hem of the robe was adorned with balls of richly coloured material, of pomegranate shape. Between each pair of pomegranates was a golden bell. The Talmud states that there were 72 ornaments around the hem. The High Priest was on no account to officiate without donning his garments. The bells attached to the robe indicated to the congregation in the Court when he was performing his duties. Kalisch explains: 'The whole people gave themselves up to prayer and repentance, whilst the High Priest stepped into the Holy of Holies to officiate in their name. It was therefore most appropriate that they should all know the moment when he entered the Holy of Holies.'

36–43. THE PLATE, MITRE AND OTHER PRIESTLY GARMENTS

36. *plate of gold.* According to Tradition, it was two fingers in depth, and extended right across the forehead.

HOLY TO THE LORD. lit. 'Holiness to the LORD.' This inscription not only marked the dedication of the High Priest to the service of God, but also crystallized the aim and purpose of that service. It proclaimed the spiritual ideal of which the Sanctuary was the concrete emblem.

37. *thread of blue.* A thread of blue, attached to the extremities of the gold plate, kept it in position upon the forehead of the High Priest; but between the skin and the plate was the linen of the mitre (see *v.* 39).

38. *Aaron shall bear.* The meaning is probably this: What is presented to God must be without blemish, and the mode of presentation must be in agreement with the prescribed rites. Should there, however, be any imperfection in the sacrifice, or any error in the manner of offering, the High Priest assumes the responsibility. He is the custodian of the Sanctuary; and, by virtue of his sacred office, exemplified by the gold plate on his forehead, he can secure Divine acceptance of the offerings brought to the altar of God.

always upon his forehead. Whenever he officiates as High Priest.

39. *tunic.* 'This garment reached down to the feet, and was close to the body, and had sleeves that were tied fast to the arms' (Josephus).

fine linen. Or, 'silk'; the colour was no doubt white, the colour of purity and holiness.

mitre. This is a doubtful translation. The root signifies, 'to wind round'; and what is intended is possibly a kind of turban.

girdle. A sash.

מ תַּעֲשֶׂה מַעֲשֵׂה רֹקֵם׃ וְלִבְנֵי אַהֲרֹן תַּעֲשֶׂה כֻתֳּנֹת וְעָשִׂיתָ
לָהֶם אַבְנֵטִים וּמִגְבָּעוֹת תַּעֲשֶׂה לָהֶם לְכָבוֹד וּלְתִפְאָרֶת׃
41 וְהִלְבַּשְׁתָּ אֹתָם אֶת־אַהֲרֹן אָחִיךָ וְאֶת־בָּנָיו אִתּוֹ וּמָשַׁחְתָּ
42 אֹתָם וּמִלֵּאתָ אֶת־יָדָם וְקִדַּשְׁתָּ אֹתָם וְכִהֲנוּ־לִי׃ וַעֲשֵׂה
לָהֶם מִכְנְסֵי־בָד לְכַסּוֹת בְּשַׂר עֶרְוָה מִמָּתְנַיִם וְעַד־יְרֵכַיִם
43 יִהְיוּ׃ וְהָיוּ עַל־אַהֲרֹן וְעַל־בָּנָיו בְּבֹאָם ׀ אֶל־אֹהֶל מוֹעֵד אוֹ
בְגִשְׁתָּם אֶל־הַמִּזְבֵּחַ לְשָׁרֵת בַּקֹּדֶשׁ וְלֹא־יִשְׂאוּ עָוֹן וָמֵתוּ
חֻקַּת עוֹלָם לוֹ וּלְזַרְעוֹ אַחֲרָיו׃ * ס רביעי

of fine linen, and thou shalt make a mitre of fine linen, and thou shalt made a girdle, the work of the weaver in colours. 40. And for Aaron's sons thou shalt make tunics, and thou shalt make for them girdles, and head-tires shalt thou make for them, for splendour and for beauty. 41. And thou shalt put them upon Aaron thy brother, and upon his sons with him; and shalt anoint them, and consecrate them, and sanctify them, that they may minister unto Me in the priest's office. 42. And thou shalt make them linen breeches to cover the flesh of their nakedness; from the loins even unto the thighs they shall reach. 43. And they shall be upon Aaron, and upon his sons, when they go in unto the tent of meeting, or when they come near unto the altar to minister in the holy place; that they bear not iniquity, and die; it shall be a statute for ever unto him and unto his seed after him.* iv.

כט CAP. XXIX. כט

א וְזֶה הַדָּבָר אֲשֶׁר־תַּעֲשֶׂה לָהֶם לְקַדֵּשׁ אֹתָם לְכַהֵן לִי לְקַח
2 פַּר אֶחָד בֶּן־בָּקָר וְאֵילִם שְׁנַיִם תְּמִימִם׃ וְלֶחֶם מַצּוֹת
וְחַלֹּת מַצֹּת בְּלוּלֹת בַּשֶּׁמֶן וּרְקִיקֵי מַצּוֹת מְשֻׁחִים בַּשָּׁמֶן
3 סֹלֶת חִטִּים תַּעֲשֶׂה אֹתָם׃ וְנָתַתָּ אוֹתָם עַל־סַל אֶחָד
4 וְהִקְרַבְתָּ אֹתָם בַּסָּל וְאֶת־הַפָּר וְאֵת שְׁנֵי הָאֵילִם׃ וְאֶת־
אַהֲרֹן וְאֶת־בָּנָיו תַּקְרִיב אֶל־פֶּתַח אֹהֶל מוֹעֵד וְרָחַצְתָּ
ה אֹתָם בַּמָּיִם׃ וְלָקַחְתָּ אֶת־הַבְּגָדִים וְהִלְבַּשְׁתָּ אֶת־אַהֲרֹן

v. 42. כח׳ קמץ בז״ק

29

CHAPTER XXIX

1. And this is the thing that thou shalt do unto them to hallow them, to minister unto Me in the priest's office: take one young bullock and two rams without blemish, 2. and unleavened bread, and cakes unleavened mingled with oil, and wafers unleavened spread with oil; of fine wheaten flour shalt thou make them. 3. And thou shalt put them into one basket, and bring them in the basket, with the bullock and the two rams. 4. And Aaron and his sons thou shalt bring unto the door of the tent of meeting, and shalt wash them with water. 5. And thou shalt take the garments, and

40. *Aaron's sons.* The ordinary priests were to have a coat and girdle, similar to the High Priest. Instead of a mitre, they were to wear a cap on their heads.

41. *put them upon Aaron.* This ceremony of induction will be described in the next chapter. *consecrate them.* lit. 'fill their hand' (with the first sacrifices)—the technical term for installing a priest into his office.

42. *breeches.* These reached to the knees. There is no mention of covering for the feet.

43. *altar.* Of burnt-offerings.
holy place. Here this phrase denotes the Sanctuary in general, including the Court.
and die. God ruthlessly punishes any desecration of the Tabernacle by its ministers; cf. the fate of Nadab and Abihu, Lev. x, 1 f.

CHAPTER XXIX. CONSECRATION OF THE PRIESTHOOD

The fulfilment of the regulations here laid down are given more fully in Lev. VIII, with which this chapter should be compared.

1. *bullock.* Of the sin-offering (Lev. VIII, 2). The priests must themselves have undergone atonement for their transgressions before they could perform the ceremonies that would help others to gain purification from sin.
two rams. One served as a burnt-offering (*v.* 18), and the other was the 'ram of consecration' (*v.* 22).

2. *unleavened bread.* This, together with the cakes and wafers, constituted a 'meal offering' (see on Lev. II).

3. *bring them.* To the court of the Sanctuary.

4. *shalt wash them.* See that they undergo ablution of entire body. The moral symbolism of the act of washing, as the first stage in the ceremony of induction, is obvious. 'Clean hands and pure heart,' according to the Psalmist (XXIV, 4), are an essential qualification in those who would draw near to God.

אֶת־הַכֻּתֹּנֶת וְאֵת מְעִיל הָאֵפֹד וְאֶת־הָאֵפֹד וְאֶת־הַחֹשֶׁן
6 וְאָפַדְתָּ לוֹ בְּחֵשֶׁב הָאֵפֹד: וְשַׂמְתָּ הַמִּצְנֶפֶת עַל־רֹאשׁוֹ וְנָתַתָּ
7 אֶת־נֵזֶר הַקֹּדֶשׁ עַל־הַמִּצְנָפֶת: וְלָקַחְתָּ אֶת־שֶׁמֶן הַמִּשְׁחָה
8 וְיָצַקְתָּ עַל־רֹאשׁוֹ וּמָשַׁחְתָּ אֹתוֹ: וְאֶת־בָּנָיו תַּקְרִיב
9 וְהִלְבַּשְׁתָּם כֻּתֳּנֹת: וְחָגַרְתָּ אֹתָם אַבְנֵט אַהֲרֹן וּבָנָיו
וְחָבַשְׁתָּ לָהֶם מִגְבָּעֹת וְהָיְתָה לָהֶם כְּהֻנָּה לְחֻקַּת עוֹלָם
י וּמִלֵּאתָ יַד־אַהֲרֹן וְיַד־בָּנָיו: וְהִקְרַבְתָּ אֶת־הַפָּר לִפְנֵי אֹהֶל
מוֹעֵד וְסָמַךְ אַהֲרֹן וּבָנָיו אֶת־יְדֵיהֶם עַל־רֹאשׁ הַפָּר:
11 12 וְשָׁחַטְתָּ אֶת־הַפָּר לִפְנֵי יְהוָה פֶּתַח אֹהֶל מוֹעֵד: וְלָקַחְתָּ
מִדַּם הַפָּר וְנָתַתָּה עַל־קַרְנֹת הַמִּזְבֵּחַ בְּאֶצְבָּעֶךָ וְאֶת־כָּל־
13 הַדָּם תִּשְׁפֹּךְ אֶל־יְסוֹד הַמִּזְבֵּחַ: וְלָקַחְתָּ אֶת־כָּל־הַחֵלֶב
הַמְכַסֶּה אֶת־הַקֶּרֶב וְאֵת הַיֹּתֶרֶת עַל־הַכָּבֵד וְאֵת שְׁתֵּי
14 הַכְּלָיֹת וְאֶת־הַחֵלֶב אֲשֶׁר עֲלֵיהֶן וְהִקְטַרְתָּ הַמִּזְבֵּחָה: וְאֶת־
בְּשַׂר הַפָּר וְאֶת־עֹרוֹ וְאֶת־פִּרְשׁוֹ תִּשְׂרֹף בָּאֵשׁ מִחוּץ לַמַּחֲנֶה
טו חַטָּאת הוּא: וְאֶת־הָאַיִל הָאֶחָד תִּקָּח וְסָמְכוּ אַהֲרֹן וּבָנָיו

put upon Aaron the tunic, and the robe of the ephod, and the ephod, and the breastplate, and gird him with the skilfully woven band of the ephod. 6. And thou shalt set the mitre upon his head, and put the holy crown upon the mitre. 7. Then shalt thou take the anointing oil, and pour it upon his head, and anoint him. 8. And thou shalt bring his sons, and put tunics upon them. 9. And thou shalt gird them with girdles, Aaron and his sons, and bind head-tires on them; and they shall have the priesthood by a perpetual statute; and thou shalt consecrate Aaron and his sons. 10. And thou shalt bring the bullock before the tent of meeting; and Aaron and his sons shall lay their hands upon the head of the bullock. 11. And thou shalt kill the bullock before the LORD, at the door of the tent of meeting. 12. And thou shalt take of the blood of the bullock, and put it upon the horns of the altar with thy finger; and thou shalt pour out all the remaining blood at the base of the altar. 13. And thou shalt take all the fat that covereth the inwards, and the lobe above the liver, and the two kidneys, and the fat that is upon them, and make them smoke upon the altar. 14. But the flesh of the bullock, and its skin, and its dung, shalt thou burn with fire without the camp; it is a sin-offering. 15. Thou shalt also take the one ram; and Aaron and his sons shall lay their hands upon the head of

5. *put upon Aaron the tunic.* The clothing of Aaron, and his sons, invested them with the visible emblems of their holiness and their functions, and marked them as distinct from the rest of the nation. 'When the priests are clothed in their garments,' says the Talmud, 'their priesthood is upon them; when they are not clothed in their garments, their priesthood is not upon them.' This Rabbinic dictum teaches the important truth that the priests did not differ from the rest of Israel. Only when they functioned in the Sanctuary were they, for the time being, distinct from the remainder of the community.

6. *mitre.* Or, 'diadem'; the gold plate (XXVIII, 36).

7. *anointing oil.* Its composition is described in XXX, 22 f. The soothing effect of oil on the skin scorched by the burning sun in the Orient made it to be regarded as a symbol of comfort and happiness. Hence, its place in the ceremony of the anointing of kings and priests. It became synonymous with the imparting of the Divine blessing.

pour it upon his head. Only in case of the High Priest. For an ordinary priest the oil was not poured, but smeared with the finger upon the head (see on Lev. VIII, 12).

9. *a perpetual statute.* The priesthood was for all time to be restricted to the house of Aaron.

10–14. The sin-offering of Aaron and his sons.

10. *lay their hands.* Each shall lay his hand to designate the animal as the representative of the person who brought the sacrifice; see on Lev. I, 4. Aaron and his sons no doubt make a confession of sins while their hands are upon the head of the animal.

11. *thou shalt kill.* The slaying of the sacrifice need not of necessity be done by a priest (see on Lev. I, 5).

12. The ritual which is now described is that which normally accompanied the sacrifice of a sin-offering (see Lev. IV, 4).

13. *make them smoke.* Heb. *hiktir*, the technical term for burning a sacrifice or incense.

15. *the one ram.* After the sin-offering which brought purification from sin, there was the burnt-offering which symbolized communion with God. The ritual of the burnt-offering is detailed in Lev. I and VIII, and will be explained in the notes on those chapters.

16 אֶת־יְדֵיהֶם עַל־רֹאשׁ הָאָיִל׃ וְשָׁחַטְתָּ אֶת־הָאָיִל וְלָקַחְתָּ
17 אֶת־דָּמוֹ וְזָרַקְתָּ עַל־הַמִּזְבֵּחַ סָבִיב׃ וְאֶת־הָאַיִל תְּנַתֵּחַ
לִנְתָחָיו וְרָחַצְתָּ קִרְבּוֹ וּכְרָעָיו וְנָתַתָּ עַל־נְתָחָיו וְעַל־
18 רֹאשׁוֹ׃ וְהִקְטַרְתָּ אֶת־כָּל־הָאַיִל הַמִּזְבֵּחָה עֹלָה הוּא לַיהוָה
חמישי 19 רֵיחַ נִיחוֹחַ אִשֶּׁה לַיהוָה הוּא׃ וְלָקַחְתָּ אֵת הָאַיִל הַשֵּׁנִי
כ וְסָמַךְ אַהֲרֹן וּבָנָיו אֶת־יְדֵיהֶם עַל־רֹאשׁ הָאָיִל׃ וְשָׁחַטְתָּ
אֶת־הָאַיִל וְלָקַחְתָּ מִדָּמוֹ וְנָתַתָּה עַל־תְּנוּךְ אֹזֶן אַהֲרֹן וְעַל־
תְּנוּךְ אֹזֶן בָּנָיו הַיְמָנִית וְעַל־בֹּהֶן יָדָם הַיְמָנִית וְעַל־בֹּהֶן
21 רַגְלָם הַיְמָנִית וְזָרַקְתָּ אֶת־הַדָּם עַל־הַמִּזְבֵּחַ סָבִיב׃ וְלָקַחְתָּ
מִן־הַדָּם אֲשֶׁר עַל־הַמִּזְבֵּחַ וּמִשֶּׁמֶן הַמִּשְׁחָה וְהִזֵּיתָ עַל־
אַהֲרֹן וְעַל־בְּגָדָיו וְעַל־בָּנָיו וְעַל־בִּגְדֵי בָנָיו אִתּוֹ וְקָדַשׁ
22 הוּא וּבְגָדָיו וּבָנָיו וּבִגְדֵי בָנָיו אִתּוֹ׃ וְלָקַחְתָּ מִן־הָאַיִל
הַחֵלֶב וְהָאַלְיָה וְאֶת־הַחֵלֶב ׀ הַמְכַסֶּה אֶת־הַקֶּרֶב וְאֵת
יֹתֶרֶת הַכָּבֵד וְאֵת ׀ שְׁתֵּי הַכְּלָיֹת וְאֶת־הַחֵלֶב אֲשֶׁר עֲלֵיהֶן
23 וְאֵת שׁוֹק הַיָּמִין כִּי אֵיל מִלֻּאִים הוּא׃ וְכִכַּר לֶחֶם אַחַת
וַחַלַּת לֶחֶם שֶׁמֶן אַחַת וְרָקִיק אֶחָד מִסַּל הַמַּצּוֹת אֲשֶׁר
24 לִפְנֵי יְהוָה׃ וְשַׂמְתָּ הַכֹּל עַל כַּפֵּי אַהֲרֹן וְעַל כַּפֵּי בָנָיו
כה וְהֵנַפְתָּ אֹתָם תְּנוּפָה לִפְנֵי יְהוָה׃ וְלָקַחְתָּ אֹתָם מִיָּדָם
וְהִקְטַרְתָּ הַמִּזְבֵּחָה עַל־הָעֹלָה לְרֵיחַ נִיחוֹחַ לִפְנֵי יְהוָה
26 אִשֶּׁה הוּא לַיהוָה׃ וְלָקַחְתָּ אֶת־הֶחָזֶה מֵאֵיל הַמִּלֻּאִים
אֲשֶׁר לְאַהֲרֹן וְהֵנַפְתָּ אֹתוֹ תְּנוּפָה לִפְנֵי יְהוָה וְהָיָה לְךָ

the ram. 16. And thou shalt slay the ram, and thou shalt take its blood, and dash it round about against the altar. 17. And thou shalt cut the ram into its pieces, and wash its inwards, and its legs, and put them with its pieces, and with its head. 18. And thou shalt make the whole ram smoke upon the altar; it is a burnt-offering unto the LORD; it is a sweet savour, an offering made by fire unto the LORD.* v. 19. And thou shalt take the other ram; and Aaron and his sons shall lay their hands upon the head of the ram. 20. Then shalt thou kill the ram, and take of its blood, and put it upon the tip of the right ear of Aaron, and upon the tip of the right ear of his sons, and upon the thumb of their right hand, and upon the great toe of their right foot, and dash the blood against the altar round about. 21. And thou shalt take of the blood that is upon the altar, and of the anointing oil, and sprinkle it upon Aaron, and upon his garments, and upon his sons, and upon the garments of his sons with him; and he and his garments shall be hallowed, and his sons and his sons' garments with him. 22. Also thou shalt take of the ram the fat, and the fat tail, and the fat that covereth the inwards, and the lobe of the liver, and the two kidneys, and the fat that is upon them, and the right thigh; for it is a ram of consecration; 23. and one loaf of bread, and one cake of oiled bread, and one wafer, out of the basket of unleavened bread that is before the LORD. 24. And thou shalt put the whole upon the hands of Aaron, and upon the hands of his sons; and shalt wave them for a wave-offering before the LORD. 25. And thou shalt take them from their hands, and make them smoke on the altar upon the burnt-offering, for a sweet savour before the LORD; it is an offering made by fire unto the LORD. 26. And thou shalt take the breast of Aaron's ram of consecration, and wave it for a wave-offering before the LORD; and it shall be thy

18. *a sweet savour. i.e.* a savour agreeable to God. 'The burning of the offering is called "a sweet savour unto the LORD"; and so it undoubtedly is, since it serves to remove sinful thoughts from our hearts. The *effect of the offering upon the man* who sacrificed it, is pleasant unto the LORD' (Maimonides).

19. *the other ram.* For the consecration sacrifice. All that has preceded is only preparatory to the rites of induction.

20. *ear . . . thumb . . . toe.* The ear was touched with the blood, that it may be consecrated to hear the word of God; the hand, to perform the duties connected with the priesthood; and the foot, to walk in the path of righteousness. In a 'kingdom of priests', the consecration of ear, hand and foot, should be extended to every member of that kingdom.

21. *sprinkle.* The double sprinkling of blood and oil typified the two main functions of the priesthood; to diffuse the light and joy of godliness, and impress upon the people the truth that atonement can be found for human wrong-doing.

22–30. Symbolized investiture of the priests with the authority to offer sacrifice. Typical offerings are to be placed upon their hands and waved before the altar, and finally burnt.

portion. 27. And thou shalt sanctify the breast of the wave-offering, and the thigh of the heave-offering, which is waved, and which is heaved up, of the ram of consecration, even of that which is Aaron's, and of that which is his sons'. 28. And it shall be for Aaron and his sons as a due for ever from the children of Israel; for it is a heave-offering; and it shall be a heave-offering from the children of Israel of their sacrifices of peace-offerings, even their heave-offering unto the LORD. 29. And the holy garments of Aaron shall be for his sons after him, to be anointed in them, and to be consecrated in them. 30. Seven days shall the son that is priest in his stead put them on, even he who cometh into the tent of meeting to minister in the holy place. 31. And thou shalt take the ram of consecration, and seethe its flesh in a holy place. 32. And Aaron and his sons shall eat the flesh of the ram, and the bread that is in the basket, at the door of the tent of meeting. 33. And they shall eat those things wherewith atonement was made, to consecrate and to sanctify them; but a stranger shall not eat thereof, because they are holy. 34. And if aught of the flesh of the consecration, or of the bread, remain unto the morning, then thou shalt burn the remainder with fire; it shall not be eaten, because it is holy. 35. And thus shalt thou do unto Aaron, and to his sons, according to all that I have commanded thee; seven days shalt thou consecrate them. 36. And every day shalt thou offer the bullock of sin-offering, beside the other offerings of

27 לְמָנֶה׃ וְקִדַּשְׁתָּ֞ אֵ֣ת ׀ חֲזֵ֣ה הַתְּנוּפָ֗ה וְאֵת֙ שׁ֣וֹק הַתְּרוּמָ֔ה
אֲשֶׁ֥ר הוּנַ֖ף וַאֲשֶׁ֣ר הוּרָ֑ם מֵאֵיל֙ הַמִּלֻּאִ֔ים מֵאֲשֶׁ֥ר לְאַהֲרֹ֖ן
28 וּמֵאֲשֶׁ֥ר לְבָנָֽיו׃ וְהָיָה֩ לְאַהֲרֹ֨ן וּלְבָנָ֜יו לְחָק־עוֹלָ֗ם מֵאֵת֙
בְּנֵ֣י יִשְׂרָאֵ֔ל כִּ֥י תְרוּמָ֖ה ה֑וּא וּתְרוּמָ֞ה יִהְיֶ֨ה מֵאֵ֤ת בְּנֵֽי־
29 יִשְׂרָאֵל֙ מִזִּבְחֵ֣י שַׁלְמֵיהֶ֔ם תְּרוּמָתָ֖ם לַיהוָֽה׃ וּבִגְדֵ֤י הַקֹּ֙דֶשׁ֙
אֲשֶׁ֣ר לְאַהֲרֹ֔ן יִהְי֥וּ לְבָנָ֖יו אַחֲרָ֑יו לְמָשְׁחָ֣ה בָהֶ֔ם וּלְמַלֵּא־
ל בָ֖ם אֶת־יָדָֽם׃ שִׁבְעַ֣ת יָמִ֗ים יִלְבָּשָׁ֧ם הַכֹּהֵ֛ן תַּחְתָּ֖יו מִבָּנָ֑יו
31 אֲשֶׁ֨ר יָבֹ֛א אֶל־אֹ֥הֶל מוֹעֵ֖ד לְשָׁרֵ֥ת בַּקֹּֽדֶשׁ׃ וְאֵ֛ת אֵ֥יל הַמִּלֻּאִ֖ים
32 תִּקָּ֑ח וּבִשַּׁלְתָּ֥ אֶת־בְּשָׂר֖וֹ בְּמָקֹ֥ם קָדֹֽשׁ׃ וְאָכַ֨ל אַהֲרֹ֤ן וּבָנָיו֙
אֶת־בְּשַׂ֣ר הָאַ֔יִל וְאֶת־הַלֶּ֖חֶם אֲשֶׁ֣ר בַּסָּ֑ל פֶּ֖תַח אֹ֥הֶל מוֹעֵֽד׃
33 וְאָכְל֤וּ אֹתָם֙ אֲשֶׁ֣ר כֻּפַּ֣ר בָּהֶ֔ם לְמַלֵּ֥א אֶת־יָדָ֖ם לְקַדֵּ֣שׁ אֹתָ֑ם
34 וְזָ֥ר לֹא־יֹאכַ֖ל כִּי־קֹ֥דֶשׁ הֵֽם׃ וְאִם־יִוָּתֵ֞ר מִבְּשַׂ֧ר הַמִּלֻּאִ֛ים
וּמִן־הַלֶּ֖חֶם עַד־הַבֹּ֑קֶר וְשָׂרַפְתָּ֤ אֶת־הַנּוֹתָר֙ בָּאֵ֔שׁ לֹ֥א יֵאָכֵ֖ל
לה כִּי־קֹ֥דֶשׁ הֽוּא׃ וְעָשִׂ֜יתָ לְאַהֲרֹ֤ן וּלְבָנָיו֙ כָּ֔כָה כְּכֹ֖ל אֲשֶׁר־
36 צִוִּ֣יתִי אֹתָ֑כָה שִׁבְעַ֥ת יָמִ֖ים תְּמַלֵּ֥א יָדָֽם׃ וּפַ֨ר חַטָּ֜את תַּעֲשֶׂ֤ה
לַיּוֹם֙ עַל־הַכִּפֻּרִ֔ים וְחִטֵּאתָ֙ עַל־הַמִּזְבֵּ֔חַ בְּכַפֶּרְךָ֖ עָלָ֑יו

24. *wave them.* Turn the offering to all the four parts of heaven and earth, as a symbol that it was offered to the God of heaven and earth.

26. *the breast.* Was allowed to be retained by the officiating priests for food (Lev. VII, 34); hence, it is allocated to Moses who on this occasion filled the priests' office.

27. *sanctify.* Consecrate; *i.e.* set apart as the due of Aaron and his sons; see Lev. VII, 34 f.

heave-offering. Or, 'contribution,' by the worshipper to the priest.

30. *seven days.* See on *v.* 35 below.

even he who cometh. i.e. when he first cometh.

31–34. A continuation of *v.* 27, describing the sacrificial meal of Aaron and his sons in connection with their installation.

32. *shall eat.* A characteristic feature of the peace-offering was that it was a symbolic meal, in which, so to speak, God and the Israelite shared (see on XXIV, 11).

33. *atonement. i.e.* at-one-ment, setting at one, reconciliation.

a stranger. A non-priest.

34. *remain.* Cf. XII, 10. This law applied to all peace-offerings and sin-offerings.

it is holy. Sacred to God.

35. *seven days.* The rites of consecration were to be repeated daily for seven days.

36. *do the purification of the altar.* On the Day of Atonement, the High Priest purified the Sanctuary and its contents of any defilement which may have been contracted during the year (Lev. XVI, 20). Consequently, before the altar was used for the public offerings, a ceremony of purification was performed.

37. *whatsoever toucheth.* Or, 'whosoever toucheth'; anyone approaching the altar must be pure (Ibn Ezra, Rashbam). Most modern commentators explain the words to mean, Whatsoever touched the altar, became thereby 'holy'; *i.e.* the property of the Sanctuary, and had to be sacrificed.

atonement; and thou shalt do the purification upon the altar when thou makest atonement for it; and thou shalt anoint it, to sanctify it. 37. Seven days thou shalt make atonement for the altar, and sanctify it; thus shall the altar be most holy; whatsoever toucheth the altar shall be holy.* vi. ¶ 38. Now this is that which thou shalt offer upon the altar: two lambs of the first year day by day continually. 39. The one lamb thou shalt offer in the morning; and the other lamb thou shalt offer at dusk. 40. And with the one lamb a tenth part of an ephah of fine flour mingled with the fourth part of a hin of beaten oil; and the fourth part of a hin of wine for a drink-offering. 41. And the other lamb thou shalt offer at dusk, and shalt do thereto according to the meal-offering of the morning, and according to the drink-offering thereof, for a sweet savour, an offering made by fire unto the LORD. 42. It shall be a continual burnt-offering throughout your generations at the door of the tent of meeting before the LORD, where I will meet with you, to speak there unto thee. 43. And there I will meet with the children of Israel; and [the Tent] shall be sanctified by My glory. 44. And I will sanctify the tent of meeting, and the altar; Aaron also and his sons will I sanctify, to minister to Me in the priest's office. 45. And I will dwell among the children of Israel, and will be their God. 46. And they shall know that I am the LORD their God, that brought them forth out of the land of Egypt, that I may dwell among them. I am the LORD their God.* vii.

37 וּמִשַׁחְתָּ אֹתוֹ לְקַדְּשׁוֹ: שִׁבְעַת יָמִים תְּכַפֵּר עַל־הַמִּזְבֵּחַ
ששי וְקִדַּשְׁתָּ אֹתוֹ וְהָיָה הַמִּזְבֵּחַ קֹדֶשׁ קָדָשִׁים כָּל־הַנֹּגֵעַ בַּמִּזְבֵּחַ
38 יִקְדָּשׁ: ס וְזֶה אֲשֶׁר תַּעֲשֶׂה עַל־הַמִּזְבֵּחַ כְּבָשִׂים בְּנֵי־
39 שָׁנָה שְׁנַיִם לַיּוֹם תָּמִיד: אֶת־הַכֶּבֶשׂ הָאֶחָד תַּעֲשֶׂה
מ בַבֹּקֶר וְאֵת הַכֶּבֶשׂ הַשֵּׁנִי תַּעֲשֶׂה בֵּין הָעַרְבָּיִם: וְעִשָּׂרֹן
סֹלֶת בָּלוּל בְּשֶׁמֶן כָּתִית רֶבַע הַהִין וְנֵסֶךְ רְבִיעִת הַהִין
41 יָיִן לַכֶּבֶשׂ הָאֶחָד: וְאֵת הַכֶּבֶשׂ הַשֵּׁנִי תַּעֲשֶׂה בֵּין הָעַרְבָּיִם
כְּמִנְחַת הַבֹּקֶר וּכְנִסְכָּהּ תַּעֲשֶׂה־לָּהּ לְרֵיחַ נִיחֹחַ אִשֶּׁה
42 לַיהוָה: עֹלַת תָּמִיד לְדֹרֹתֵיכֶם פֶּתַח אֹהֶל־מוֹעֵד לִפְנֵי
43 יְהוָה אֲשֶׁר אִוָּעֵד לָכֶם שָׁמָּה לְדַבֵּר אֵלֶיךָ שָׁם: וְנֹעַדְתִּי
44 שָׁמָּה לִבְנֵי יִשְׂרָאֵל וְנִקְדַּשׁ בִּכְבֹדִי: וְקִדַּשְׁתִּי אֶת־אֹהֶל
מוֹעֵד וְאֶת־הַמִּזְבֵּחַ וְאֶת־אַהֲרֹן וְאֶת־בָּנָיו אֲקַדֵּשׁ לְכַהֵן
מה לִי: וְשָׁכַנְתִּי בְּתוֹךְ בְּנֵי יִשְׂרָאֵל וְהָיִיתִי לָהֶם לֵאלֹהִים:
46 וְיָדְעוּ כִּי אֲנִי יְהוָה אֱלֹהֵיהֶם אֲשֶׁר הוֹצֵאתִי אֹתָם מֵאֶרֶץ
מִצְרַיִם לְשָׁכְנִי בְתוֹכָם אֲנִי יְהוָה אֱלֹהֵיהֶם: פ שביעי

30

CHAPTER XXX

1. And thou shalt make an altar to burn incense upon; of acacia-wood shalt thou make it. 2. A cubit shall be the length thereof, and a cubit the breadth thereof; four-square shall it be; and two cubits shall

ל CAP. XXX. ל

א וְעָשִׂיתָ מִזְבֵּחַ מִקְטַר קְטֹרֶת עֲצֵי שִׁטִּים תַּעֲשֶׂה אֹתוֹ:
2 אַמָּה אָרְכּוֹ וְאַמָּה רָחְבּוֹ רָבוּעַ יִהְיֶה וְאַמָּתַיִם קֹמָתוֹ

כט׳ v. 43. ד׳ קמוצה

38–42. THE DAILY SACRIFICES

A summary of the daily sacrifices to be offered for the community as a whole, and the chief duty of the priests just consecrated; cf. Num. XXVIII, 3–8.

40. *fine flour.* With the burnt-offering were to be brought a meal-offering and drink-offering.

42. *I will meet with you.* See XXV, 22.

43–46. The sacred purpose of the Sanctuary.

43. *with the children of Israel.* The Sanctuary is not the exclusive possession of the priests, nor will God manifest Himself there only to the High Priest.

by My glory. i.e. the Manifestation of God in the cloud; see XL, 34 f.

44. *I will sanctify.* God is the only source of holiness, and He alone can sanctify.

45. *dwell among.* Cf. XXV, 8.
will be their God. See VI, 7.

46. *and they shall know.* That the same God who rescued them from Egypt selected them as His people, and consecrated them to His service.

CHAPTER XXX, 1–10. THE ALTAR OF INCENSE

1. *altar.* No sacrifices were offered on it, and was only so called because of its resemblance to the altar of burnt-offerings.

3 מִמֶּנּוּ קַרְנֹתָיו׃ וְצִפִּיתָ אֹתוֹ זָהָב טָהוֹר אֶת־גַּגּוֹ וְאֶת־
קִירֹתָיו סָבִיב וְאֶת־קַרְנֹתָיו וְעָשִׂיתָ לּוֹ זֵר זָהָב סָבִיב׃
4 וּשְׁתֵּי טַבְּעֹת זָהָב תַּעֲשֶׂה־לּוֹ ׀ מִתַּחַת לְזֵרוֹ עַל שְׁתֵּי
צַלְעֹתָיו תַּעֲשֶׂה עַל־שְׁנֵי צִדָּיו וְהָיָה לְבָתִּים לְבַדִּים לָשֵׂאת
ה אֹתוֹ בָּהֵמָּה׃ וְעָשִׂיתָ אֶת־הַבַּדִּים עֲצֵי שִׁטִּים וְצִפִּיתָ אֹתָם
6 זָהָב׃ וְנָתַתָּה אֹתוֹ לִפְנֵי הַפָּרֹכֶת אֲשֶׁר עַל־אֲרֹן הָעֵדֻת לִפְנֵי
7 הַכַּפֹּרֶת אֲשֶׁר עַל־הָעֵדֻת אֲשֶׁר אִוָּעֵד לְךָ שָׁמָּה׃ וְהִקְטִיר
עָלָיו אַהֲרֹן קְטֹרֶת סַמִּים בַּבֹּקֶר בַּבֹּקֶר בְּהֵיטִיבוֹ אֶת־הַנֵּרֹת
מפטיר 8 יַקְטִירֶנָּה׃ וּבְהַעֲלֹת אַהֲרֹן אֶת־הַנֵּרֹת בֵּין הָעַרְבַּיִם יַקְטִירֶנָּה
9 קְטֹרֶת תָּמִיד לִפְנֵי יְהוָה לְדֹרֹתֵיכֶם׃ לֹא־תַעֲלוּ עָלָיו קְטֹרֶת
י זָרָה וְעֹלָה וּמִנְחָה וְנֶסֶךְ לֹא תִסְּכוּ עָלָיו׃ וְכִפֶּר אַהֲרֹן עַל־
קַרְנֹתָיו אַחַת בַּשָּׁנָה מִדַּם חַטַּאת הַכִּפֻּרִים אַחַת בַּשָּׁנָה
יְכַפֵּר עָלָיו לְדֹרֹתֵיכֶם קֹדֶשׁ־קָדָשִׁים הוּא לַיהוָה׃

be the height thereof; the horns thereof shall be of one piece with it. 3. And thou shalt overlay it with pure gold, the top thereof, and the sides thereof round about, and the horns thereof; and thou shalt make unto it a crown of gold round about. 4. And two golden rings shalt thou make for it under the crown thereof, upon the two ribs thereof, upon the two sides of it shalt thou make them; and they shall be for places for staves wherewith to bear it. 5. And thou shalt make the staves of acacia-wood, and overlay them with gold. 6. And thou shalt put it before the veil that is by the ark of the testimony, before the ark-cover that is over the testimony, where I will meet with thee. 7. And Aaron shall burn thereon incense of sweet spices; every morning, when he dresseth the lamps, he shall burn it.* m. 8. And when Aaron lighteth the lamps at dusk, he shall burn it, a perpetual incense before the LORD throughout your generations. 9. Ye shall offer no strange incense thereon, nor burnt-offering, nor meal-offering; and ye shall pour no drink-offering thereon. 10. And Aaron shall make atonement upon the horns of it once in the year; with the blood of the sin-offering of atonement once in the year shall he make atonement for it throughout your generations; it is most holy unto the LORD.'

3. *pure gold.* Since the altar of incense was located in the Holy Place, and not in the Court with the altar of burnt-offering, the metal was gold; see p. 325.
crown of gold. See on xxv, 11.

4. *ribs.* Flanks. It has to have rings and acacia wood poles for transport, like the Ark, table and the other altar.

6. *before the veil.* *i.e.* from the standpoint of one entering the Sanctuary. The altar of incense (or 'inner altar') was about half-way between the altar of burnt-offerings and the Holy of Holies.
by the ark. *i.e.* before the Ark.
testimony. See xxv, 16.
where I will meet. See xxv, 22.

7. *dresseth the lamps.* See xxvii, 21.
Incense had a symbolic significance, as is evident from Ps. cxli, 2, 'Let my prayer be set forth as incense before Thee.' It became a metaphor for fervent and contrite Prayer. The Rabbis explained that the four letters of the Heb. word for incense קטרת stood for קדושה, holiness; טהרה, purity; רחמים, pity; and תקוה, hope—a wonderful summary of the prerequisites of Prayer and of its spiritual results in the lives of men.

8. *at dusk.* Towards even.
perpetual incense. Better, *continual incense.*

9. *strange incense.* *i.e.* not prepared in the manner prescribed in *v.* 23, or offered in an irregular manner. This altar is to be reserved exclusively for incense.

10. *upon the horns.* By an application of the blood of the sin-offering (Lev. xvi, 18).
once in the year. On the Day of Atonement.
for it. To preserve it in its ideal holiness.

EZEKIEL XLIII, 10–27

CHAPTER XLIII

10. Thou, son of man, show the house to the house of Israel, that they may be ashamed of their iniquities; and let them measure accurately. 11. And if they be ashamed of all that they have done, make known unto them the form of the house, and the fashion thereof, and the goings out thereof, and the comings in thereof, and all the forms thereof, and all the ordinances thereof, and all the forms thereof, and all the laws thereof, and write it in their sight; that they may keep the whole form thereof, and all the ordinances thereof, and do them. ¶ 12. This is the law of the house: upon the top of the mountain the whole limit thereof round about shall be most holy. Behold, this is the law of the house. ¶ 13. And these are the measures of the altar by cubits—the cubit is a cubit and a handbreadth: the bottom shall be a cubit, and the breadth a cubit, and the border thereof by the edge thereof round about a span; and this shall be the base of the altar. 14. And from the bottom upon the ground to the lower settle shall be two cubits, and the breadth one cubit; and from the lesser settle to the

CAP. XLIII. מג

אַתָּה בֶן־אָדָם הַגֵּד אֶת־
בֵּית־יִשְׂרָאֵל אֶת־הַבַּיִת וְיִכָּלְמוּ מֵעֲוֺנוֹתֵיהֶם וּמָדְדוּ אֶת־
11 תָּכְנִית׃ וְאִם־נִכְלְמוּ מִכֹּל אֲשֶׁר־עָשׂוּ צוּרַת הַבַּיִת וּתְכוּנָתוֹ
וּמוֹצָאָיו וּמוֹבָאָיו וְכָל־צוּרֹתָו וְאֵת כָּל־חֻקֹּתָיו וְכָל־צוּרֹתָו
וְכָל־תּוֹרֹתָו הוֹדַע אוֹתָם וּכְתֹב לְעֵינֵיהֶם וְיִשְׁמְרוּ אֶת־כָּל־
12 צוּרָתוֹ וְאֶת־כָּל־חֻקֹּתָיו וְעָשׂוּ אוֹתָם׃ זֹאת תּוֹרַת הַבָּיִת
עַל־רֹאשׁ הָהָר כָּל־גְּבֻלוֹ סָבִיב ׀ סָבִיב קֹדֶשׁ קָדָשִׁים הִנֵּה־
13 זֹאת תּוֹרַת הַבָּיִת׃ וְאֵלֶּה מִדּוֹת הַמִּזְבֵּחַ בָּאַמּוֹת אַמָּה
אַמָּה וָטֹפַח וְחֵיק הָאַמָּה וְאַמָּה־רֹחַב וּגְבוּלָהּ אֶל־שְׂפָתָהּ
14 סָבִיב זֶרֶת הָאֶחָד וְזֶה גַּב הַמִּזְבֵּחַ׃ וּמֵחֵיק הָאָרֶץ עַד־
הָעֲזָרָה הַתַּחְתּוֹנָה שְׁתַּיִם אַמּוֹת וְרֹחַב אַמָּה אֶחָת

v. 11. צורתיו קרי ibid. תורתיו קרי

The Sedrah concludes with a description of the altar of incense. The Haftorah describes the altar of burnt-offering in the restored Temple of Ezekiel's vision, and its consecration. For Ezekiel's life and message, see pp. 178 and 245, and the introductory remarks to Haftorahs Parah and Hachodesh.

The last portion of the Book of Ezekiel, chaps. XL–XLVIII, is a Vision of the New Jerusalem that is to arise when the Exile is over. In his vision the Prophet is in Palestine on Mount Zion, and he sees the Temple building arising and extending like a city. No detail is too small to be delineated with passionate care. Chapter XLIII describes God's return to the Temple and His directions as to the construction and dedication of the altar of burnt-offering. This new Temple was also to symbolize and embody in concrete form the teachings of Holiness and Purity preached by the Prophet in the preceding 39 chapters of his book. He, therefore, lays the greatest stress on correctness of Temple ritual and service. In this way alone can the aberrations and idolatries be prevented that so often disgraced the destroyed Temple. 'For Ezekiel the Law is the means of preserving religious freedom from contamination; without it, the prophetic ideas would hardly have survived. The real hope of the future for Ezekiel lies in perfect and willing obedience to the Law' (Lofthouse).

10. *son of man.* This expression is found almost exclusively in Ezekiel.

show . . . ashamed of their iniquities. The plan of the Holy House would awaken remorse for the past iniquities that had brought about the destruction of the Temple and the Exile, and implant a resolve to be worthy of a Restoration.

11. *if they be ashamed.* Then let them know the great future in store for them (Rashi).

form of the house. The picture of the Temple in its entirety.

fashion thereof. The courts and other parts of the Temple, showing their inter-connection.

goings out . . . comings in. The entrances and exits.

and all the forms thereof. The plans of the divisions of the Temple.

the ordinances thereof. The purpose of the different divisions.

13–17. THE ALTAR OF BURNT-OFFERING

The altar was to have a base, and upon it three square slabs of stone, one above the other, each decreasing in length, but increasing in thickness. The height of the altar, excluding the horns, would be 11 cubits (about 20 feet), and the top of the altar was to be reached by stairs on the east side (*v.* 17).

13. *the cubit is a cubit and an handbreadth. i.e.* one handbreadth longer than the common cubit (thus seven handbreadths in all).

14. *settle.* Or, 'ledge.'

greater settle shall be four cubits, and the breadth a cubit. 15. And the hearth shall be four cubits; and from the hearth and upward there shall be four horns. 16. And the hearth shall be twelve cubits long by twelve broad, square in the four sides thereof. 17. And the settle shall be fourteen cubits long by fourteen broad in the four sides thereof; and the border about it shall be half a cubit; and the bottom thereof shall be a cubit about; and the steps thereof shall look toward the east. ¶ 18. And He said unto me: 'Son of man, thus saith the Lord GOD: These are the ordinances of the altar in the day when they shall make it, to offer burnt-offerings thereon, and to dash blood against it. 19. Thou shalt give to the priests the Levites that are of the seed of Zadok, who are near unto Me, to minister unto Me, saith the Lord GOD, a young bullock for a sin-offering. 20. And thou shalt take of the blood thereof, and put it on the four horns of it, and on the four corners of the settle, and upon the border round about; thus shalt thou purify it and make atonement for it. 21. Thou shalt also take the bullock of the sin-offering, and it shall be burnt in the appointed place of the house, without the sanctuary. 22. And on the second day thou shalt offer a he-goat without blemish for a sin-offering; and they shall purify the altar, as they did purify it with the bullock. 23. When thou hast made an end of purifying it, thou shalt offer a young bullock without blemish, and a ram out of the flock without blemish. 24. And thou shalt present them before the LORD, and the priests shall cast salt upon them, and they shall offer them up for a burnt-offering unto the LORD. 25. Seven days shalt thou prepare every day a goat for a sin-offering; they shall also prepare a young bullock, and a ram out of the flock, without blemish. 26. Seven days shall they make atonement for the altar and cleanse it; so shall they consecrate it. 27. And when they have accomplished the days, it shall be that upon the eighth day, and forward, the priests shall make your burnt-offerings upon the altar, and your peace-offerings; and I will accept you, saith the Lord GOD.'

וּמֵהָעֲזָרָה הַקְּטַנָּה עַד־הָעֲזָרָה הַגְּדוֹלָה אַרְבַּע אַמּוֹת
טו וְרֹחַב הָאַמָּה׃ וְהַהַרְאֵל אַרְבַּע אַמּוֹת וּמֵהָאֲרִאֵיל וּלְמַעְלָה
16 הַקְּרָנוֹת אַרְבַּע׃ וְהָאֲרִאֵיל שְׁתֵּים עֶשְׂרֵה אֹרֶךְ בִּשְׁתֵּים
17 עֶשְׂרֵה רֹחַב רָבוּעַ אֶל אַרְבַּעַת רְבָעָיו׃ וְהָעֲזָרָה אַרְבַּע
עֶשְׂרֵה אֹרֶךְ בְּאַרְבַּע עֶשְׂרֵה רֹחַב אֶל אַרְבַּעַת רְבָעֶיהָ
וְהַגְּבוּל סָבִיב אוֹתָהּ חֲצִי הָאַמָּה וְהַחֵיק־לָהּ אַמָּה סָבִיב
18 וּמַעֲלֹתֵהוּ פְּנוֹת קָדִים׃ וַיֹּאמֶר אֵלַי בֶּן־אָדָם כֹּה אָמַר
אֲדֹנָי יֱהוִה אֵלֶּה חֻקּוֹת הַמִּזְבֵּחַ בְּיוֹם הֵעָשׂוֹתוֹ לְהַעֲלוֹת
19 עָלָיו עוֹלָה וְלִזְרֹק עָלָיו דָּם׃ וְנָתַתָּה אֶל־הַכֹּהֲנִים הַלְוִיִּם
אֲשֶׁר הֵם מִזֶּרַע צָדוֹק הַקְּרֹבִים אֵלַי נְאֻם אֲדֹנָי יֱהוִה
כ לְשָׁרְתֵנִי פַּר בֶּן־בָּקָר לְחַטָּאת׃ וְלָקַחְתָּ מִדָּמוֹ וְנָתַתָּה עַל־
אַרְבַּע קַרְנֹתָיו וְאֶל־אַרְבַּע פִּנּוֹת הָעֲזָרָה וְאֶל־הַגְּבוּל
21 סָבִיב וְחִטֵּאתָ אוֹתוֹ וְכִפַּרְתָּהוּ׃ וְלָקַחְתָּ אֵת הַפָּר הַחַטָּאת
22 וּשְׂרָפוֹ בְּמִפְקַד הַבַּיִת מִחוּץ לַמִּקְדָּשׁ׃ וּבַיּוֹם הַשֵּׁנִי תַּקְרִיב
שְׂעִיר־עִזִּים תָּמִים לְחַטָּאת וְחִטְּאוּ אֶת־הַמִּזְבֵּחַ כַּאֲשֶׁר
23 חִטְּאוּ בַּפָּר׃ בְּכַלּוֹתְךָ מֵחַטֵּא תַּקְרִיב פַּר בֶּן־בָּקָר תָּמִים
24 וְאַיִל מִן־הַצֹּאן תָּמִים׃ וְהִקְרַבְתָּם לִפְנֵי יְהוָה וְהִשְׁלִיכוּ
כה הַכֹּהֲנִים עֲלֵיהֶם מֶלַח וְהֶעֱלוּ אוֹתָם עֹלָה לַיהוָה׃ שִׁבְעַת
יָמִים תַּעֲשֶׂה שְׂעִיר־חַטָּאת לַיּוֹם וּפַר בֶּן־בָּקָר וְאַיִל מִן־
26 הַצֹּאן תְּמִימִים יַעֲשׂוּ׃ שִׁבְעַת יָמִים יְכַפְּרוּ אֶת־הַמִּזְבֵּחַ
27 וְטִהֲרוּ אֹתוֹ וּמִלְאוּ יָדָו׃ וִיכַלּוּ אֶת־הַיָּמִים וְהָיָה בַיּוֹם
הַשְּׁמִינִי וָהָלְאָה יַעֲשׂוּ הַכֹּהֲנִים עַל־הַמִּזְבֵּחַ אֶת־עוֹלוֹתֵיכֶם
וְאֶת־שַׁלְמֵיכֶם וְרָצָאתִי אֶתְכֶם נְאֻם אֲדֹנָי יֱהוִה׃

v. 15. ומהאריאל קרי v. 16. והאריאל קרי v. 26. למדנחאי וכפרו כתיב יכפרו ק' ibid. ידיו ק' v. 27. א' במקום י'

15. *the hearth.* The topmost stone, 4 cubits high, with a square surface of 12 square cubits.

hearth. Heb. *ariel* (see Isa. XXIX, 1); lit. 'hearth of God.'

four horns. At the corners.

17. *the steps.* By which the priests ascend to the altar hearth.

18–27. THE CONSECRATION OF THE ALTAR

18. *and He said.* The angel who is God's spokesman to Ezekiel in his vision.

19. *the priests the Levites.* The priests, who were the tribe of Levi.

Zadok. A priest loyal to David during Absolom's rebellion. His descent is traced back to Aaron in I Chron. The high-priesthood remained in the hands of the descendants of Zadok till the times of the Maccabees.

30 11. And the LORD spoke unto Moses, saying: 12. 'When thou takest the sum of the children of Israel, according to their number, then shall they give every man a ransom for his soul unto the LORD, when thou numberest them; that there be no plague among them, when thou numberest them. 13. This they shall give, every one that passeth among them that are numbered, half a shekel after the shekel of the sanctuary—the shekel is twenty gerahs—half a shekel for an offering to the LORD. 14. Every one that passeth among them that are numbered, from twenty years old and upward, shall give the offering of the LORD. 15. The rich shall not give more, and the poor shall not give less, than the

ל פ פ פ כא 21

11 וַיְדַבֵּר יְהוָה אֶל־מֹשֶׁה לֵּאמֹר׃ כִּי תִשָּׂא אֶת־רֹאשׁ בְּנֵֽי־
12 יִשְׂרָאֵל לִפְקֻדֵיהֶם וְנָתְנוּ אִישׁ כֹּפֶר נַפְשׁוֹ לַיהוָה בִּפְקֹד
13 אֹתָם וְלֹא־יִהְיֶה בָהֶם נֶגֶף בִּפְקֹד אֹתָם׃ זֶה ׀ יִתְּנוּ כָּל־
הָעֹבֵר עַל־הַפְּקֻדִים מַחֲצִית הַשֶּׁקֶל בְּשֶׁקֶל הַקֹּדֶשׁ עֶשְׂרִים
14 גֵּרָה הַשֶּׁקֶל מַחֲצִית הַשֶּׁקֶל תְּרוּמָה לַיהוָה׃ כֹּל הָעֹבֵר
עַל־הַפְּקֻדִים מִבֶּן עֶשְׂרִים שָׁנָה וָמָעְלָה יִתֵּן תְּרוּמַת יְהוָה׃
טו הֶעָשִׁיר לֹא־יַרְבֶּה וְהַדַּל לֹא יַמְעִיט מִמַּחֲצִית הַשָּׁקֶל

IX. KI THISSA

(CHAPTERS XXX, 11–XXXIV)

CHAPTER XXX

11–16. THE LAW OF THE SHEKEL

Whenever a census of the warriors was taken, every adult Israelite was to pay a half-shekel.

12. *their number.* Their mustering, as an army before going to war.

a ransom. Heb. כפר. This technical expression for 'ransom' occurs three times in the Torah, and each time it refers to the money paid by one who is guilty of taking human life in circumstances that do not constitute murder. Thus, the owner of the ox that had killed a man after the owner had received warning that the animal was dangerous, was charged with the death of a man; but as his crime was not intentional he was permitted to pay a *ransom* (כפר). Such a ransom was forbidden in the case of deliberate murder. This is the conception that underlies the law of the half-shekel in this chapter. The soldier who is ready to march into battle is in the eyes of Heaven a potential taker of life, though not a deliberate murderer. Hence, he requires 'a ransom for his life' (B. Jacob).

when thou numberest them. The soldier is to be impressed with the fact that, high as the aims for which he goes to battle may be, war remains a necessary *evil.* The ransom is, therefore, to be paid at the time of the mustering, long before the actual fighting begins.

plague. Heb. *negeph.* This word comes from the same root as the Heb. word for 'slaughter in battle'; and a noted Karaite commentator translates the phrase, 'that they suffer not defeat in battle.'

when thou numberest them. According to the above explanation, this phrase would begin *v.* 13.

13. *every one that passeth among.* Before the officers mustering the forces for battle.

shekel of the sanctuary. The full weight shekel used in connection with sacred things.

offering to the LORD. Heb. *terumah,* 'contribution'; the same phrase is used in Num. XXXI, 52.

14. *twenty years.* The Israelite's military age.

15. *and the poor shall not give less.* All souls are of equal value in the eyes of God. Hence, all are to give the same ransom.

to make atonement for your souls. Heb. לכפר על נפשתיכם. This phrase is an amplification of כפר, and is repeated in the next verse. Even a rationalist commentator like Ehrlich, rightly sees in the use of this last phrase one of the sublimest teachings of Scripture, unparalleled in any other sacred Book, ancient or modern. The same phrase is used in connection with the Midianite battle in Num. XXXI, 52. After signally defeating the Midianites, the victorious warriors come to the Tabernacle, bringing jewels and other valuable booty as an offering in order *to make atonement for their souls before the LORD.* 'Other peoples sing songs of triumph after a victory over their enemies; why then did these warriors offer sacrifices of atonement for their souls at such an hour?' asks Ehrlich; 'it is another indication of the horror of shedding human blood that the Torah inculcates. It is the same feeling that prompted the Jewish Sages to tell that the angels when about to break forth in song over the Egyptian hosts drowning in the Red Sea, were silenced by God in the words, "My creatures are perishing, and ye are ready to sing!" '

16 לָתֵת אֶת־תְּרוּמַת יְהוָה לְכַפֵּר עַל־נַפְשֹׁתֵיכֶם׃ וְלָקַחְתָּ אֶת־
כֶּסֶף הַכִּפֻּרִים מֵאֵת בְּנֵי יִשְׂרָאֵל וְנָתַתָּ אֹתוֹ עַל־עֲבֹדַת
אֹהֶל מוֹעֵד וְהָיָה לִבְנֵי יִשְׂרָאֵל לְזִכָּרוֹן לִפְנֵי יְהוָה לְכַפֵּר
עַל־נַפְשֹׁתֵיכֶם׃ פ
17 18 וַיְדַבֵּר יְהוָה אֶל־מֹשֶׁה לֵּאמֹר׃ וְעָשִׂיתָ כִּיּוֹר נְחֹשֶׁת וְכַנּוֹ
נְחֹשֶׁת לְרָחְצָה וְנָתַתָּ אֹתוֹ בֵּין־אֹהֶל מוֹעֵד וּבֵין הַמִּזְבֵּחַ
19 וְנָתַתָּ שָׁמָּה מָיִם׃ וְרָחֲצוּ אַהֲרֹן וּבָנָיו מִמֶּנּוּ אֶת־יְדֵיהֶם
כ וְאֶת־רַגְלֵיהֶם׃ בְּבֹאָם אֶל־אֹהֶל מוֹעֵד יִרְחֲצוּ־מַיִם וְלֹא
יָמֻתוּ אוֹ בְגִשְׁתָּם אֶל־הַמִּזְבֵּחַ לְשָׁרֵת לְהַקְטִיר אִשֶּׁה
21 לַיהוָה׃ וְרָחֲצוּ יְדֵיהֶם וְרַגְלֵיהֶם וְלֹא יָמֻתוּ וְהָיְתָה לָהֶם
חָק־עוֹלָם לוֹ וּלְזַרְעוֹ לְדֹרֹתָם׃ פ
22 23 וַיְדַבֵּר יְהוָה אֶל־מֹשֶׁה לֵּאמֹר׃ וְאַתָּה קַח־לְךָ בְּשָׂמִים

half shekel, when they give the offering of the LORD, to make atonement for your souls. 16. And thou shalt take the atonement money from the children of Israel, and shalt appoint it for the service of the tent of meeting, that it may be a memorial for the children of Israel before the LORD, to make atonement for your souls.' ¶ 17. And the LORD spoke unto Moses, saying: 18. 'Thou shalt also make a laver of brass, and the base thereof of brass, whereat to wash; and thou shalt put it between the tent of meeting and the altar, and thou shalt put water therein. 19. And Aaron and his sons shall wash their hands and their feet thereat; 20. when they go into the tent of meeting, they shall wash with water, that they die not; or when they come near to the altar to minister, to cause an offering made by fire to smoke unto the LORD; 21. so they shall wash their hands and their feet, that they die not; and it shall be a statute for ever to them, even to him and to his seed throughout their generations.' ¶ 22. Moreover the LORD spoke unto Moses,

16. *for the service.* The silver of the shekels was used for the bases of the pillars of the Sanctuary, and also for the hooks to keep the boards together (XXXVIII, 27).

a memorial. i.e. that the Lord remember the children of Israel in grace, and grant them atonement for the blood shed in battle.

In later ages, the half-shekel became an annual tax devoted to maintaining the public services of the Temple; the daily worship was thus carried on by the entire People and not by the gifts of a few rich donors. The fact that the rich were not to give more, nor the poor less, than a half shekel taught that, 'weighed in the balance of the Sanctuary' (which is the lit. meaning of בשקל הקדש), differences of rank and wealth do not exist. The fact, furthermore, that only a *half*-shekel was to be paid, taught that an individual's contribution to the community was but a fragment. For any complete work to be achieved on behalf of the Sanctuary, the efforts of all, high and low, rich and poor alike, are required.

The Jews outside Palestine were, throughout the ancient world, as zealous in their contribution of this Temple tax as the inhabitants of Judea. Anti-Semites, in consequence, even raised the cry that the Jews 'were sending too much money out of the country'. One of the Roman Provincial Governors who seized these offerings, was defended by Cicero in an anti-Jewish speech. After the destruction of the Temple, the Jews of the Empire were compelled to pay this contribution to the Temple of Jupiter at Rome! When this iniquitous tax was eventually abolished, the contribution from the Jews in the Diaspora was used for the support of the Rabbinical Academies in Palestine.

At the present day, the memory of the half-shekel is still alive by the reading of Exodus XXX, 11–17, on the Sabbath before the month of Adar, with a special Haftorah, Shekalim; as well as by donating on Purim half the current silver coin of the country for any worthy charitable cause. With the rise of the Jewish Nationalist Movement, the payment of the shekel has been revived as a token of sympathy with the aims of that movement.

17–21. THE LAVER

18. *base.* A pedestal.

the altar. Of burnt-offerings.

20. *that they die not.* To enter the Sanctuary with soiled hands and feet would have been a desecration of its holiness.

to the altar. Although the altar was situate in the Court and not in the Holy Sanctuary, the same penalty would be incurred.

21. *they shall wash.* The repetition of the preceding words is to stress that the ordinance was for ever.

throughout their generations. This rule has been observed by the pious in all ages, who wash their hands before beginning any of the statutory services, which the Rabbis declare to be the present-day equivalents of the sacrifices. Many synagogues arrange lavers at the entrance for such a ceremonial washing of the hands by the worshippers.

22–23. THE ANOINTING OIL

Olive oil was to be mixed with the essences of four aromatic herbs for use in the symbolic act of anointing; *i.e.* consecrating the Tent of Meeting and those that minister therein.

saying: 23. 'Take thou also unto thee the chief spices, of flowing myrrh five hundred shekels, and of sweet cinnamon half so much, even two hundred and fifty, and of sweet calamus two hundred and fifty, 24. and of cassia five hundred, after the shekel of the sanctuary, and of olive oil a hin. 25. And thou shalt make it a holy anointing oil, a perfume compounded after the art of the perfumer; it shall be a holy anointing oil. 26. And thou shalt anoint therewith the tent of meeting, and the ark of the testimony, 27. and the table and all the vessels thereof, and the candlestick and the vessels thereof, and the altar of incense, 28. and the altar of burnt-offering with all the vessels thereof, and the laver and the base thereof. 29. And thou shalt sanctify them, that they may be most holy; whatsoever toucheth them shall be holy. 30. And thou shalt anoint Aaron and his sons, and sanctify them, that they may minister unto Me in the priest's office. 31. And thou shalt speak unto the children of Israel, saying: This shall be a holy anointing oil unto Me throughout your generations. 32. Upon the flesh of man shall it not be poured, neither shall ye make any like it, according to the composition thereof; it is holy, and it shall be holy unto you. 33. Whosoever com-

רֹאשׁ מָר־דְּרוֹר חֲמֵשׁ מֵאוֹת וְקִנְּמָן־בֶּשֶׂם מַחֲצִיתוֹ חֲמִשִּׁים
24 וּמָאתָיִם וּקְנֵה־בֹשֶׂם חֲמִשִּׁים וּמָאתָיִם׃ וְקִדָּה חֲמֵשׁ
כה מֵאוֹת בְּשֶׁקֶל הַקֹּדֶשׁ וְשֶׁמֶן זַיִת הִין׃ וְעָשִׂיתָ אֹתוֹ שֶׁמֶן
מִשְׁחַת־קֹדֶשׁ רֹקַח מִרְקַחַת מַעֲשֵׂה רֹקֵחַ שֶׁמֶן מִשְׁחַת־
26 קֹדֶשׁ יִהְיֶה׃ וּמָשַׁחְתָּ בוֹ אֶת־אֹהֶל מוֹעֵד וְאֵת אֲרוֹן הָעֵדֻת׃
27 וְאֶת־הַשֻּׁלְחָן וְאֶת־כָּל־כֵּלָיו וְאֶת־הַמְּנֹרָה וְאֶת־כֵּלֶיהָ וְאֵת
28 מִזְבַּח הַקְּטֹרֶת׃ וְאֶת־מִזְבַּח הָעֹלָה וְאֶת־כָּל־כֵּלָיו וְאֶת־
29 הַכִּיֹּר וְאֶת־כַּנּוֹ׃ וְקִדַּשְׁתָּ אֹתָם וְהָיוּ קֹדֶשׁ קָדָשִׁים כָּל־
ל הַנֹּגֵעַ בָּהֶם יִקְדָּשׁ׃ וְאֶת־אַהֲרֹן וְאֶת־בָּנָיו תִּמְשָׁח וְקִדַּשְׁתָּ
31 אֹתָם לְכַהֵן לִי׃ וְאֶל־בְּנֵי יִשְׂרָאֵל תְּדַבֵּר לֵאמֹר שֶׁמֶן
32 מִשְׁחַת־קֹדֶשׁ יִהְיֶה זֶה לִי לְדֹרֹתֵיכֶם׃ עַל־בְּשַׂר אָדָם
לֹא יִיסָךְ וּבְמַתְכֻּנְתּוֹ לֹא תַעֲשׂוּ כָּמֹהוּ קֹדֶשׁ הוּא קֹדֶשׁ
33 יִהְיֶה לָכֶם׃ אִישׁ אֲשֶׁר יִרְקַח כָּמֹהוּ וַאֲשֶׁר יִתֵּן מִמֶּנּוּ עַל־
34 זָר וְנִכְרַת מֵעַמָּיו׃ ס וַיֹּאמֶר יְהוָה אֶל־מֹשֶׁה קַח־לְךָ

23. *chief spices.* lit. 'finest spices'.

flowing myrrh. Of the purest kind, which either exuded spontaneously from the plant or was obtained by tapping.

five hundred shekels. In weight; about sixteen pounds.

24. *cassia.* The inner bark of a species of cinnamon tree, peeled off and dried in the sun (Driver).

a hin. About ten pints.

25. *perfumer.* Great skill was required in obtaining the best compound of these ingredients. The work was, therefore, handed over to experts. In later times, certain 'sons of the priests' were trained for this work (I Chron. IX, 30).

29. *shall be holy.* Cf. XXIX, 37.

30. *anoint Aaron.* Cf. XXIX, 7, 29.

32. *man. i.e.* a non-priest. This holy oil was not to be utilized for secular purposes.

neither shall ye make any like it. For ordinary use.

33. *stranger.* One not authorized to be anointed with it.

shall be cut off. See on XII, 15.

34–38. The Holy Incense

Incense forms part of all forms of ancient ceremonial worship. On its symbolic significance see note on XXX, 7. The Jewish mystics declare, 'If men knew the sublime importance of the Holy Incense, they would set a crown of gold on each of the ingredients.' Incense possesses antiseptic properties; and it has a marked effect both on the nervous system as well as on the emotions of the worshippers. In the sayings of the Rabbis on the incense we can discern their recognition of these qualities.

34. *stacte.* A fragrant oil or resin. The Rabbis identified it with 'balm of Gilead'.

onycha. Obtained from certain shell-fish found in the Red Sea.

galbanum. Heb. חלבנה the gum of a shrub, growing in Asia Minor and Persia. In contrast with the foregoing ingredients it did not have an agreeable odour. Its inclusion was intentional say the Rabbis. As the galbanum is an essential ingredient of the sacred incense, even so is the prayer of the Congregation of Israel most acceptable to God when it includes the prayers of sinners and transgressors.

35. *art of the perfumer.* Special skill was also demanded for the compounding of the incense, secrets which were transmitted from generation to generation in the family of Abtinas, who were entrusted with its manufacture.

seasoned with salt. Or, 'tempered together.'

pounded any like it, or whosoever putteth any of it upon a stranger, he shall be cut off from his people.' ¶ 34. And the LORD said unto Moses: 'Take unto thee sweet spices, stacte, and onycha, and galbanum; sweet spices with pure frankincense; of each shall there be a like weight. 35. And thou shalt make of it incense, a perfume after the art of the perfumer, seasoned with salt, pure and holy. 36. And thou shalt beat some of it very small, and put of it before the testimony in the tent of meeting, where I will meet with thee; it shall be unto you most holy. 37. And the incense which thou shalt make, according to the composition thereof ye shall not make for yourselves; it shall be unto thee holy for the LORD. 38. Whosoever shall make like unto that, to smell thereof, he shall be cut off from his people.'

סַמִּים נָטָף ׀ וּשְׁחֵלֶת וְחֶלְבְּנָה סַמִּים וּלְבֹנָה זַכָּה בַּד בְּבַד
לה יִהְיֶה׃ וְעָשִׂיתָ אֹתָהּ קְטֹרֶת רֹקַח מַעֲשֵׂה רוֹקֵחַ מְמֻלָּח
36 טָהוֹר קֹדֶשׁ׃ וְשָׁחַקְתָּ מִמֶּנָּה הָדֵק וְנָתַתָּה מִמֶּנָּה לִפְנֵי
הָעֵדֻת בְּאֹהֶל מוֹעֵד אֲשֶׁר אִוָּעֵד לְךָ שָׁמָּה קֹדֶשׁ קָדָשִׁים
37 תִּהְיֶה לָכֶם׃ וְהַקְּטֹרֶת אֲשֶׁר תַּעֲשֶׂה בְּמַתְכֻּנְתָּהּ לֹא
38 תַעֲשׂוּ לָכֶם קֹדֶשׁ תִּהְיֶה לְךָ לַיהוָה׃ אִישׁ אֲשֶׁר־יַעֲשֶׂה
כָמוֹהָ לְהָרִיחַ בָּהּ וְנִכְרַת מֵעַמָּיו׃ ס

31

CHAPTER XXXI

1. And the LORD spoke unto Moses, saying: 2. 'See, I have called by name Bezalel the son of Uri, the son of Hur, of the tribe of Judah; 3. and I have filled him with the spirit of God, in wisdom, and in understanding, and in knowledge, and in all manner of workmanship, 4. to devise skilful works, to work in gold, and in silver, and in brass, 5. and in cutting of stones for setting, and in carving of wood, to work in all manner of workmanship. 6. And I, behold, I have appointed with him Oholiab, the son of Ahisamach, of the tribe of Dan; and in the hearts of all that are wise-hearted I have put wisdom, that they may make all that I have commanded thee: 7. the tent of meeting, and the ark of the testimony, and the ark-cover that is thereupon, and all the furniture of the Tent; 8. and the table and its vessels, and the pure candlestick with all its vessels, and the altar of incense; 9. and the altar of burnt-offering with all its vessels, and the laver and its base; 10. and the plaited garments, and the holy garments for Aaron the priest, and the garments of his sons, to minister in the priest's office; 11. and the anointing oil, and the incense of sweet spices for the holy place; according to all that I have commanded thee shall they do.' ¶ 12. And the LORD spoke unto Moses, saying: 13. 'Speak thou also unto the children of Israel,

לא

CAP. XXXI. לא

א 2 וַיְדַבֵּר יְהוָה אֶל־מֹשֶׁה לֵּאמֹר׃ רְאֵה קָרָאתִי בְשֵׁם בְּצַלְאֵל
3 בֶּן־אוּרִי בֶן־חוּר לְמַטֵּה יְהוּדָה׃ וָאֲמַלֵּא אֹתוֹ רוּחַ אֱלֹהִים
4 בְּחָכְמָה וּבִתְבוּנָה וּבְדַעַת וּבְכָל־מְלָאכָה׃ לַחְשֹׁב מַחֲשָׁבֹת
ה לַעֲשׂוֹת בַּזָּהָב וּבַכֶּסֶף וּבַנְּחֹשֶׁת׃ וּבַחֲרֹשֶׁת אֶבֶן לְמַלֹּאת
6 וּבַחֲרֹשֶׁת עֵץ לַעֲשׂוֹת בְּכָל־מְלָאכָה׃ וַאֲנִי הִנֵּה נָתַתִּי אִתּוֹ
אֵת אָהֳלִיאָב בֶּן־אֲחִיסָמָךְ לְמַטֵּה־דָן וּבְלֵב כָּל־חֲכַם־לֵב
7 נָתַתִּי חָכְמָה וְעָשׂוּ אֵת כָּל־אֲשֶׁר צִוִּיתִךָ׃ אֵת ׀ אֹהֶל מוֹעֵד
וְאֶת־הָאָרֹן לָעֵדֻת וְאֶת־הַכַּפֹּרֶת אֲשֶׁר עָלָיו וְאֵת כָּל־כְּלֵי
8 הָאֹהֶל׃ וְאֶת־הַשֻּׁלְחָן וְאֶת־כֵּלָיו וְאֶת־הַמְּנֹרָה הַטְּהֹרָה
9 וְאֶת־כָּל־כֵּלֶיהָ וְאֵת מִזְבַּח הַקְּטֹרֶת׃ וְאֶת־מִזְבַּח הָעֹלָה
י וְאֶת־כָּל־כֵּלָיו וְאֶת־הַכִּיּוֹר וְאֶת־כַּנּוֹ׃ וְאֵת בִּגְדֵי הַשְּׂרָד וְאֶת־
11 בִּגְדֵי הַקֹּדֶשׁ לְאַהֲרֹן הַכֹּהֵן וְאֶת־בִּגְדֵי בָנָיו לְכַהֵן׃ וְאֵת
שֶׁמֶן הַמִּשְׁחָה וְאֶת־קְטֹרֶת הַסַּמִּים לַקֹּדֶשׁ כְּכֹל אֲשֶׁר־
צִוִּיתִךָ יַעֲשׂוּ׃ פ
12 13 וַיֹּאמֶר יְהוָה אֶל־מֹשֶׁה לֵּאמֹר׃ וְאַתָּה דַּבֵּר אֶל־בְּנֵי יִשְׂרָאֵל

37. *holy for the LORD.* Preparation of incense from similar ingredients and in similar proportions for private or profane use is forbidden.

CHAPTER XXXI

1–11. THE CHIEF ARTIFICERS AND THEIR TASK

See the commentary on xxxv, 30–xxxvi, 2.

13–17. THE SABBATH

13. *My sabbaths.* The work of constructing the Tabernacle that was now to commence was of the highest importance, and was work in the service of God; but it was not of greater importance than the Divinely-ordained Sabbath, and was not to be permitted to supersede it.

saying: Verily ye shall keep My sabbaths, for it is a sign between Me and you throughout your generations, that ye may know that I am the LORD who sanctify you. 14. Ye shall keep the sabbath therefore, for it is holy unto you; every one that profaneth it shall surely be put to death; for whosoever doeth any work therein, that soul shall be cut off from among his people. 15. Six days shall work be done; but on the seventh day is a sabbath of solemn rest, holy to the LORD; whosoever doeth any work in the sabbath day, he shall surely be put to death. 16. Wherefore the children of Israel shall keep the sabbath, to observe the sabbath throughout their generations, for a perpetual covenant. 17. It is a sign between Me and the children of Israel for ever; for in six days the LORD made heaven and earth, and on the seventh day He ceased from work and rested.' * ii. ¶ 18. And He gave unto Moses, when He had made an end of speaking with him upon mount Sinai, the two tables of the testimony, tables of stone, written with the finger of God.

לֵאמֹר אַךְ אֶת־שַׁבְּתֹתַי תִּשְׁמֹרוּ כִּי אוֹת הִוא בֵּינִי וּבֵינֵיכֶם
14 לְדֹרֹתֵיכֶם לָדַעַת כִּי אֲנִי יְהוָה מְקַדִּשְׁכֶם׃ וּשְׁמַרְתֶּם אֶת־
הַשַּׁבָּת כִּי קֹדֶשׁ הִוא לָכֶם מְחַלְלֶיהָ מוֹת יוּמָת כִּי כָּל־
הָעֹשֶׂה בָהּ מְלָאכָה וְנִכְרְתָה הַנֶּפֶשׁ הַהִוא מִקֶּרֶב עַמֶּיהָ׃
טו שֵׁשֶׁת יָמִים יֵעָשֶׂה מְלָאכָה וּבַיּוֹם הַשְּׁבִיעִי שַׁבַּת שַׁבָּתוֹן
קֹדֶשׁ לַיהוָה כָּל־הָעֹשֶׂה מְלָאכָה בְּיוֹם הַשַּׁבָּת מוֹת יוּמָת׃
16 וְשָׁמְרוּ בְנֵי־יִשְׂרָאֵל אֶת־הַשַּׁבָּת לַעֲשׂוֹת אֶת־הַשַּׁבָּת
17 לְדֹרֹתָם בְּרִית עוֹלָם׃ בֵּינִי וּבֵין בְּנֵי יִשְׂרָאֵל אוֹת הִוא
לְעֹלָם כִּי־שֵׁשֶׁת יָמִים עָשָׂה יְהוָה אֶת־הַשָּׁמַיִם וְאֶת־הָאָרֶץ
שני
18 וּבַיּוֹם הַשְּׁבִיעִי שָׁבַת וַיִּנָּפַשׁ׃ ס וַיִּתֵּן אֶל־מֹשֶׁה כְּכַלֹּתוֹ
לְדַבֵּר אִתּוֹ בְּהַר סִינַי שְׁנֵי לֻחֹת הָעֵדֻת לֻחֹת אֶבֶן כְּתֻבִים
בְּאֶצְבַּע אֱלֹהִים׃

32

CHAPTER XXXII

1. And when the people saw that Moses delayed to come down from the mount, the people gathered themselves together unto Aaron, and said unto him: 'Up, make us a

לב CAP. XXXII. לב

א וַיַּרְא הָעָם כִּי־בֹשֵׁשׁ מֹשֶׁה לָרֶדֶת מִן־הָהָר וַיִּקָּהֵל הָעָם

לא׳ v. 14. קמץ בז״ק

Hence the repetition of the law of the Sabbath; cf. xxxv, 2.

a sign. The Sabbath was more than a day of rest. Its observance by the Israelites was a constantly recurring acknowledgment of God as the Creator of the Universe. It would be an open denial of God for an Israelite to desecrate the Sabbath, even in the construction of the Tabernacle; as well as a contradiction of the essential purpose of the Sanctuary, the sanctification of Israel's life in the service of God.

that ye may know. lit. 'to know,' and the subject has to be supplied. Rashi and Maimonides explain it to mean 'that all nations shall know'. Similarly Driver comments: 'that all the world may recognize, by means of the Sabbath, that it is God Who sanctifies Israel, or provides it with the means of becoming a holy People.' The Sabbath was recognized throughout the ancient world as the peculiar and distinctive festival of the Jewish people.

14. *be put to death.* This extreme penalty was only to be inflicted if the culprit desecrated the Sabbath in the presence of two witnesses who had previously warned him of the punishment that awaited him.

15. *sabbath of solemn rest. i.e.* a complete cessation of work.

16. *a perpetual covenant.* The weekly hallowing of the Sabbath by the Israelites, being a proclamation of belief in God and obedience to His law, effects a perennial renewal of the covenant of God with the Patriarchs.

17. *in six days.* As in the fourth commandment (xx, 11).

18. MOSES RECEIVES THE TABLES OF STONE

18. *tables of the testimony. i.e.* the Decalogue.

finger of God. An expression for the ineffable sanctity of the Tables, and for the Divine source of their Message to the children of men.

v. 18 connects this chapter with the narrative of the Golden Calf in the chapter following. xxxii, 15 relates that Moses had the Tables in his hands, and this verse tells how he received them.

CHAPTER XXXII

THE GOLDEN CALF AND THE IDOLATRY OF THE PEOPLE

1. *delayed.* The Rabbis explain that the people expected Moses to return on the fortieth day, inclusive of the day of his ascent; but he remained forty clear days on Mount Sinai. When he did not appear on the day they expected him, the people concluded that he was dead, and a feeling of utter helplessness possessed them. They demanded a visible god.

עַל־אַהֲרֹן וַיֹּאמְרוּ אֵלָיו קוּם ׀ עֲשֵׂה־לָנוּ אֱלֹהִים אֲשֶׁר
יֵלְכוּ לְפָנֵינוּ כִּי־זֶה ׀ מֹשֶׁה הָאִישׁ אֲשֶׁר הֶעֱלָנוּ מֵאֶרֶץ
2 מִצְרַיִם לֹא יָדַעְנוּ מֶה־הָיָה לוֹ׃ וַיֹּאמֶר אֲלֵהֶם אַהֲרֹן
פָּרְקוּ נִזְמֵי הַזָּהָב אֲשֶׁר בְּאָזְנֵי נְשֵׁיכֶם בְּנֵיכֶם וּבְנֹתֵיכֶם
3 וְהָבִיאוּ אֵלָי׃ וַיִּתְפָּרְקוּ כָּל־הָעָם אֶת־נִזְמֵי הַזָּהָב אֲשֶׁר
4 בְּאָזְנֵיהֶם וַיָּבִיאוּ אֶל־אַהֲרֹן׃ וַיִּקַּח מִיָּדָם וַיָּצַר אֹתוֹ בַּחֶרֶט
וַיַּעֲשֵׂהוּ עֵגֶל מַסֵּכָה וַיֹּאמְרוּ אֵלֶּה אֱלֹהֶיךָ יִשְׂרָאֵל אֲשֶׁר
ה הֶעֱלוּךָ מֵאֶרֶץ מִצְרָיִם׃ וַיַּרְא אַהֲרֹן וַיִּבֶן מִזְבֵּחַ לְפָנָיו וַיִּקְרָא
6 אַהֲרֹן וַיֹּאמַר חַג לַיהוָה מָחָר׃ וַיַּשְׁכִּימוּ מִמָּחֳרָת וַיַּעֲלוּ עֹלֹת
וַיַּגִּשׁוּ שְׁלָמִים וַיֵּשֶׁב הָעָם לֶאֱכֹל וְשָׁתוֹ וַיָּקֻמוּ לְצַחֵק׃ פ
7 וַיְדַבֵּר יְהוָה אֶל־מֹשֶׁה לֶךְ־רֵד כִּי שִׁחֵת עַמְּךָ אֲשֶׁר הֶעֱלֵיתָ
8 מֵאֶרֶץ מִצְרָיִם׃ סָרוּ מַהֵר מִן־הַדֶּרֶךְ אֲשֶׁר צִוִּיתִם עָשׂוּ

god who shall go before us; for as for this Moses, the man that brought us up out of the land of Egypt, we know not what is become of him.' 2. And Aaron said unto them: 'Break off the golden rings, which are in the ears of your wives, of your sons, and of your daughters, and bring them unto me.' 3. And all the people broke off the golden rings which were in their ears, and brought them unto Aaron. 4. And he received it at their hand, and fashioned it with a graving tool, and made it a molten calf; and they said: 'This is thy god, O Israel, which brought thee up out of the land of Egypt.' 5. And when Aaron saw this, he built an altar before it; and Aaron made proclamation, and said: 'To-morrow shall be a feast to the LORD.' 6. And they rose up early on the morrow, and offered burnt-offerings, and brought peace-offerings; and the people sat down to eat and to drink, and rose up to make merry. ¶ 7. And the LORD spoke unto Moses: 'Go, get thee down; for thy people, that thou broughtest up out of the land of Egypt, have dealt corruptly; 8. they have turned

unto Aaron. When Moses departed from the camp, he left Aaron and Hur in charge (XXIV, 14). Why, then, is Aaron alone mentioned here? Tradition relates that Hur resisted the people's demand, and was put to death by them. Aaron, seeing the determination of the people, decided to work for gaining time till the arrival of Moses.

make us a god. RV Text translates, 'make us gods.'

who shall go before us. The 'god' was to replace Moses as their leader.

2. *break off.* Aaron's intention may have been to cool their ardour, thinking they would hesitate to sacrifice their ornaments.

3. *broke off.* To Aaron's astonishment, the people at once complied with his request. 'What a fickle people!' say the Rabbis: 'one day they give their silver and gold for the Sanctuary of God; and on the morrow, they do the same for a Golden Calf.'

4. *fashioned it.* The golden articles were first melted, so that a mass of metal was formed, and this was shaped by Aaron into the semblance of a calf. The latter was the object of worship among Israel's Semitic kinsmen (see on I, 7).

this is thy god. The RV Text translates, 'These be thy gods.'

5. *to-morrow.* The postponement, the Rabbis say, was due to Aaron's confident hope that Moses would appear by then, and the feast in honour of the calf would be changed into 'a feast to the LORD.' Yehudah Hallevi declares, 'the people did not intend to give up their allegiance to God.' They desired a *visible symbolic representation* of the God who brought them out of Egypt. Their sin was not a breach of the First, but of the Second Commandment.

The conduct of Aaron throughout this incident is difficult to understand. There is, however, an explanation, though no excuse, for his behaviour. Tradition makes love of peace the outstanding trait of his nature. Always a lover of peace and a pursuer of peace, and thinking that resistance was futile, he acquiesced in the people's demand. There would doubtless have been many to side with him, but he feared division that might result in bloodshed.

6. *on the morrow.* After the altar had been erected.

burnt offerings. Cf. XX, 24.

to eat and to drink. Possibly a sacramental meal is intended (see on XXIV, 11).

to play. Or, 'to make merry.' By dancing and singing (cf. *v.* 18 f), which usually figured in the religious celebrations of heathen peoples.

7. *thy people.* God disowns the sinful Israelites. He refuses to acknowledge them as His people. The Rabbis, on the other hand, understand '*thy* people which thou broughtest up out of the land of Egypt' as an allusion to the mixed multitude. It was not God who had brought these out of Egypt, but Moses had allowed them to accompany the Israelites.

8. *quickly.* It was less than six weeks since they had heard the Voice of God declaring, 'Thou shalt not make unto thee a graven image.'

aside quickly out of the way which I commanded them; they have made them a molten calf, and have worshipped it, and have sacrificed unto it, and said: This is thy god, O Israel, which brought thee up out of the land of Egypt.' 9. And the LORD said unto Moses: 'I have seen this people, and, behold, it is a stiffnecked people. 10. Now therefore let Me alone, that My wrath may wax hot against them, and that I may consume them; and I will make of thee a great nation.' 11. And Moses besought the LORD his God, and said: 'LORD, why doth Thy wrath wax hot against Thy people, that Thou hast brought forth out of the land of Egypt with great power and with a mighty hand? 12. Wherefore should the Egyptians speak, saying: For evil did He bring them forth, to slay them in the mountains, and to consume them from the face of the earth? Turn from Thy fierce wrath, and repent of this evil against Thy people. 13. Remember Abraham, Isaac, and Israel, Thy servants, to whom Thou didst swear by Thine own self, and saidst unto them: I will multiply your seed as the stars of heaven, and all this land that I have spoken of will I give unto your seed, and they shall inherit it for ever.' 14. And the LORD repented of the evil which He said He would do unto His people. ¶ 15. And Moses turned, and went down from the mount, with the two tables of the testimony in his hand; tables that were written on both their sides; on the one side and on the other were they written. 16. And the tables were the work of God, and the writing was the writing of God, graven upon the tables. 17. And when Joshua heard the noise of the people as they shouted, he said unto Moses: 'There is a noise of war in the camp.' 18. And he said: 'It is not the voice of them that shout for mastery,

לָהֶם עֵגֶל מַסֵּכָה וַיִּשְׁתַּחֲווּ־לוֹ וַיִּזְבְּחוּ־לוֹ וַיֹּאמְרוּ אֵלֶּה
9 אֱלֹהֶיךָ יִשְׂרָאֵל אֲשֶׁר הֶעֱלוּךָ מֵאֶרֶץ מִצְרָיִם׃ וַיֹּאמֶר יְהוָה
אֶל־מֹשֶׁה רָאִיתִי אֶת־הָעָם הַזֶּה וְהִנֵּה עַם־קְשֵׁה־עֹרֶף הוּא׃
י וְעַתָּה הַנִּיחָה לִּי וְיִחַר־אַפִּי בָהֶם וַאֲכַלֵּם וְאֶעֱשֶׂה אוֹתְךָ
11 לְגוֹי גָּדוֹל׃ וַיְחַל מֹשֶׁה אֶת־פְּנֵי יְהוָה אֱלֹהָיו וַיֹּאמֶר לָמָה
יְהוָה יֶחֱרֶה אַפְּךָ בְּעַמֶּךָ אֲשֶׁר הוֹצֵאתָ מֵאֶרֶץ מִצְרַיִם בְּכֹחַ
12 גָּדוֹל וּבְיָד חֲזָקָה׃ לָמָּה יֹאמְרוּ מִצְרַיִם לֵאמֹר בְּרָעָה
הוֹצִיאָם לַהֲרֹג אֹתָם בֶּהָרִים וּלְכַלֹּתָם מֵעַל פְּנֵי הָאֲדָמָה
13 שׁוּב מֵחֲרוֹן אַפֶּךָ וְהִנָּחֵם עַל־הָרָעָה לְעַמֶּךָ׃ זְכֹר לְאַבְרָהָם
לְיִצְחָק וּלְיִשְׂרָאֵל עֲבָדֶיךָ אֲשֶׁר נִשְׁבַּעְתָּ לָהֶם בָּךְ וַתְּדַבֵּר
אֲלֵהֶם אַרְבֶּה אֶת־זַרְעֲכֶם כְּכוֹכְבֵי הַשָּׁמָיִם וְכָל־הָאָרֶץ
14 הַזֹּאת אֲשֶׁר אָמַרְתִּי אֶתֵּן לְזַרְעֲכֶם וְנָחֲלוּ לְעֹלָם׃ וַיִּנָּחֶם
יְהוָה עַל־הָרָעָה אֲשֶׁר דִּבֶּר לַעֲשׂוֹת לְעַמּוֹ׃ פ
טו וַיִּפֶן וַיֵּרֶד מֹשֶׁה מִן־הָהָר וּשְׁנֵי לֻחֹת הָעֵדֻת בְּיָדוֹ לֻחֹת
16 כְּתֻבִים מִשְּׁנֵי עֶבְרֵיהֶם מִזֶּה וּמִזֶּה הֵם כְּתֻבִים׃ וְהַלֻּחֹת
מַעֲשֵׂה אֱלֹהִים הֵמָּה וְהַמִּכְתָּב מִכְתַּב אֱלֹהִים הוּא חָרוּת
17 עַל־הַלֻּחֹת׃ וַיִּשְׁמַע יְהוֹשֻׁעַ אֶת־קוֹל הָעָם בְּרֵעֹה וַיֹּאמֶר
18 אֶל־מֹשֶׁה קוֹל מִלְחָמָה בַּמַּחֲנֶה׃ וַיֹּאמֶר אֵין קוֹל עֲנוֹת

v. 17. ברעו ק'

9. *stiffnecked.* Obstinate; here, persisting in its idolatry. The figure is taken from a stubborn ox that refuses to submit to the yoke.

10. *let Me alone.* The Rabbis explain this to mean that Moses understood from these Divine words that his intercession alone could save the the Israelites from the extermination which threatened them.

12. *for evil.* With evil intent. Such would be the mockery of the Egyptians, if Israel were now to perish; cf. x, 10.

the mountains. Of the Peninsula of Sinai.

repent. Heb. idiom often attributes to God the feelings or emotions of man. God is thus said to 'repent', when, in consequence of a change in the character and conduct of men, He makes a corresponding change in the purpose towards them which he had previously announced (Driver).

13. *by Thine own self.* By the great Name which endures for all eternity.

15–20. MOSES RETURNS TO THE CAMP

16. *the work of God.* In his horror at the conduct of the Israelites Moses shattered the Tablets, although they were made by God Himself.

17. *Joshua.* Moses had left him on the lower slope of the mountain (XXIV, 13) ; and, consequently, Joshua was in ignorance of what had transpired.

18. *sing. i.e.* answer in song; the answering voices of singers.

19 גְבוּרָה וְאֵין קוֹל עֲנוֹת חֲלוּשָׁה קוֹל עַנּוֹת אָנֹכִי שֹׁמֵעַ׃ וַיְהִי
כַּאֲשֶׁר קָרַב אֶל־הַמַּחֲנֶה וַיַּרְא אֶת־הָעֵגֶל וּמְחֹלֹת וַיִּחַר־
אַף מֹשֶׁה וַיַּשְׁלֵךְ מִיָּדָו אֶת־הַלֻּחֹת וַיְשַׁבֵּר אֹתָם תַּחַת
כ הָהָר׃ וַיִּקַּח אֶת־הָעֵגֶל אֲשֶׁר עָשׂוּ וַיִּשְׂרֹף בָּאֵשׁ וַיִּטְחַן עַד
אֲשֶׁר־דָּק וַיִּזֶר עַל־פְּנֵי הַמַּיִם וַיַּשְׁקְ אֶת־בְּנֵי יִשְׂרָאֵל׃
21 וַיֹּאמֶר מֹשֶׁה אֶל־אַהֲרֹן מֶה־עָשָׂה לְךָ הָעָם הַזֶּה כִּי־הֵבֵאתָ
22 עָלָיו חֲטָאָה גְדֹלָה׃ וַיֹּאמֶר אַהֲרֹן אַל־יִחַר אַף אֲדֹנִי אַתָּה
23 יָדַעְתָּ אֶת־הָעָם כִּי בְרָע הוּא׃ וַיֹּאמְרוּ לִי עֲשֵׂה־לָנוּ אֱלֹהִים
אֲשֶׁר יֵלְכוּ לְפָנֵינוּ כִּי־זֶה ׀ מֹשֶׁה הָאִישׁ אֲשֶׁר הֶעֱלָנוּ מֵאֶרֶץ
24 מִצְרַיִם לֹא יָדַעְנוּ מֶה־הָיָה לוֹ׃ וָאֹמַר לָהֶם לְמִי זָהָב
הִתְפָּרָקוּ וַיִּתְּנוּ־לִי וָאַשְׁלִכֵהוּ בָאֵשׁ וַיֵּצֵא הָעֵגֶל הַזֶּה׃
כה וַיַּרְא מֹשֶׁה אֶת־הָעָם כִּי פָרֻעַ הוּא כִּי־פְרָעֹה אַהֲרֹן
26 לְשִׁמְצָה בְּקָמֵיהֶם׃ וַיַּעֲמֹד מֹשֶׁה בְּשַׁעַר הַמַּחֲנֶה וַיֹּאמֶר
27 מִי לַיהוָה אֵלָי וַיֵּאָסְפוּ אֵלָיו כָּל־בְּנֵי לֵוִי׃ וַיֹּאמֶר לָהֶם

v. 19. מידיו ק׳ v. 25. ק׳ דבוקה

neither is it the voice of them that cry for being overcome, but the noise of them that sing do I hear.' 19. And it came to pass, as soon as he came nigh unto the camp, that he saw the calf and the dancing; and Moses' anger waxed hot, and he cast the tables out of his hands, and broke them beneath the mount. 20. And he took the calf which they had made, and burnt it with fire, and ground it to powder, and strewed it upon the water, and made the children of Israel drink of it. 21. And Moses said unto Aaron: 'What did this people unto thee, that thou hast brought a great sin upon them?' 22. And Aaron said: 'Let not the anger of my lord wax hot; thou knowest the people, that they are set on evil. 23. So they said unto me: Make us a god, which shall go before us; for as for this Moses, the man that brought us up out of the land of Egypt, we know not what is become of him. 24. And I said unto them: Whosoever hath any gold, let them break it off; so they gave it me; and I cast it into the fire, and there came out this calf.' 25. And when Moses saw that the people were broken loose—for Aaron had let them loose for a derision among their enemies—26. then Moses stood in the gate of the camp, and said: 'Whoso is on the LORD's side, let him come unto me.' And all the sons of Levi gathered themselves together unto him. 27. And he said unto

19. *Moses' anger waxed hot . . . and broke them.* The Heb. term translated by 'anger' covers both *anger* and *indignation*. Now, it was not *anger* that caused him to shatter the Tables. 'He who breaks anything in anger is as if he were an idolater,' say the Rabbis. Anger is selfish and blind, and a purely emotional reaction against an injury received. Thus, when a child hurts its foot against a stone, it is often so unreasonably angry as to strike the stone. Altogether different is the moral feeling of *indignation* that sweeps over us whenever we see a great wrong committed; not because it injures *us*, as is always the case in anger, but because the wrong is an outrage against justice and right. Such a feeling of righteous indignation filled Moses when he beheld a People that had been at Sinai, dancing before a golden calf! A mob guilty of such base and senseless ingratitude to God was, he felt, unworthy of the Divine Tables of the Law.

beneath the mount. At its foot.

20. *which they had made.* By contributing the gold, the Israelites were co-makers of the calf with Aaron.

strewed it upon the water. An emblem of perfect annihilation. In Deut. IX, 21, it is mentioned that a brook 'descended out of the mount'.

made the children of Israel drink. The Talmud compares this act with the ordeal imposed upon a suspected wife (Num. V); the drink harmfully affecting anyone who had been guilty; and leaving the innocent immune.

21. *brought a great sin upon them.* The participation of Aaron in such an offence fills Moses with amazement; and he demands an explanation.

22. *set on evil.* Aaron puts the whole blame on others.

24. *there came out this calf.* As if it happened by itself! Aaron's two pleas of compulsion and accident are the usual excuses in palliation of wrongdoing. His want of moral courage evoked the Divine displeasure; Deut. IX, 20.

25. *broken loose.* From their loyalty to God.

a derision. God's punishment of their sin would render them ignominious in the eyes of the neighbouring hostile peoples.

26. *whoso is on the LORD'S side.* By not having had any share in the idolatry.

27. *thus saith the LORD.* The Mechilta explains that Moses applied the law of XXII, 19. 'He that sacrificeth unto any god, save unto the LORD only, shall be utterly destroyed.'

them: 'Thus saith the LORD, the God of Israel: Put ye every man his sword upon his thigh, and go to and fro from gate to gate throughout the camp, and slay every man his brother, and every man his companion, and every man his neighbour.' 28. And the sons of Levi did according to the word of Moses; and there fell of the people that day about three thousand men. 29. And Moses said: 'Consecrate yourselves to-day to the LORD, for every man hath been against his son and against his brother; that He may also bestow upon you a blessing this day.' 30. And it came to pass on the morrow, that Moses said unto the people: 'Ye have sinned a great sin; and now I will go up unto the LORD, peradventure I shall make atonement for your sin.' 31. And Moses returned unto the LORD, and said: 'Oh, this people have sinned a great sin, and have made them a god of gold. 32. Yet now, if Thou wilt forgive their sin—; and if not, blot me, I pray Thee, out of Thy book which Thou hast written.' 33. And the LORD said unto Moses: 'Whosoever hath sinned against Me, him will I blot out of My book. 34. And now go, lead the people unto the place of which I have spoken unto thee; behold, Mine angel shall go before thee; nevertheless in the day when I visit, I will visit their sin upon them.' 35. And the LORD smote the people, because they made the calf, which Aaron made.

כֹּה־אָמַר יְהוָה אֱלֹהֵי יִשְׂרָאֵל שִׂימוּ אִישׁ־חַרְבּוֹ עַל־יְרֵכוֹ
עִבְרוּ וָשׁוּבוּ מִשַּׁעַר לָשַׁעַר בַּמַּחֲנֶה וְהִרְגוּ אִישׁ־אֶת־אָחִיו
28 וְאִישׁ אֶת־רֵעֵהוּ וְאִישׁ אֶת־קְרֹבוֹ׃ וַיַּעֲשׂוּ בְנֵי־לֵוִי כִּדְבַר
מֹשֶׁה וַיִּפֹּל מִן־הָעָם בַּיּוֹם הַהוּא כִּשְׁלֹשֶׁת אַלְפֵי אִישׁ׃
29 וַיֹּאמֶר מֹשֶׁה מִלְאוּ יֶדְכֶם הַיּוֹם לַיהוָה כִּי אִישׁ בִּבְנוֹ
ל וּבְאָחִיו וְלָתֵת עֲלֵיכֶם הַיּוֹם בְּרָכָה׃ וַיְהִי מִמָּחֳרָת וַיֹּאמֶר
מֹשֶׁה אֶל־הָעָם אַתֶּם חֲטָאתֶם חֲטָאָה גְדֹלָה וְעַתָּה אֶעֱלֶה
31 אֶל־יְהוָה אוּלַי אֲכַפְּרָה בְּעַד חַטַּאתְכֶם׃ וַיָּשָׁב מֹשֶׁה אֶל־
יְהוָה וַיֹּאמַר אָנָּא חָטָא הָעָם הַזֶּה חֲטָאָה גְדֹלָה וַיַּעֲשׂוּ
32 לָהֶם אֱלֹהֵי זָהָב׃ וְעַתָּה אִם־תִּשָּׂא חַטָּאתָם וְאִם־אַיִן מְחֵנִי
33 נָא מִסִּפְרְךָ אֲשֶׁר כָּתָבְתָּ׃ וַיֹּאמֶר יְהוָה אֶל־מֹשֶׁה מִי אֲשֶׁר
34 חָטָא־לִי אֶמְחֶנּוּ מִסִּפְרִי׃ וְעַתָּה לֵךְ ׀ נְחֵה אֶת־הָעָם אֶל
אֲשֶׁר־דִּבַּרְתִּי לָךְ הִנֵּה מַלְאָכִי יֵלֵךְ לְפָנֶיךָ וּבְיוֹם פָּקְדִי
לה וּפָקַדְתִּי עֲלֵיהֶם חַטָּאתָם׃ וַיִּגֹּף יְהוָה אֶת־הָעָם עַל אֲשֶׁר
עָשׂוּ אֶת־הָעֵגֶל אֲשֶׁר עָשָׂה אַהֲרֹן׃ ס

v. 31. ב׳ טעמים

from gate to gate. From one end of the camp to the other.

his brother. He summoned the Levites to kill the criminals with the sword, and not even to spare their nearest relatives if among the criminals. 'Brother' is often used in Heb. in the sense of 'relative'.

29. *consecrate yourselves to the LORD.* lit. 'fill your hand to the LORD,' see on XXVIII, 41; usually taken to mean that as a reward for fidelity and zeal, the tribe of Levi was to be given the charge of the Sanctuary.

a blessing. The privilege of being His servant.

30. *make atonement.* By intercession, win God's forgiveness for the people.

32. *if Thou wilt forgive.* Words as, 'I am content to live,' must be supplied. This suppressing of part of a conditional sentence, is not unusual in Hebrew.

blot me. Moses lived only for his people. If they were destroyed, he had no desire for life. 'This verse is one of the most beautiful and impressive in the whole of Scripture, strikingly depicting Moses' affection and self-devotion for his people' (Driver).

Thy book. In which the destinies of human beings are recorded; cf. Mal. III, 16, and Psalm CXXXIX, 16.

33. *him will I blot out of My book.* God will not permit Moses to suffer vicariously for others. Judaism recognizes neither vicarious punishment nor vicarious atonement. 'The soul that sinneth, *it* shall die'—unless by repentance and good deeds it gains the Divine forgiveness.

34. *Mine angel.* Not God Himself, because He cannot overlook what the people had done. For the 'angel', see on XXIII, 20.

when I visit. Moffatt, 'Yet when I am punishing, I will punish them for their sin.' The day of reckoning is only postponed; but, for the sake of Moses, the people shall, nevertheless, be led to the Land of Promise.

35. *smote.* A note confirming the words of the last sentence. Punishment was subsequently exacted from the people (Ibn Ezra).

33

Chapter XXXIII

1. And the Lord spoke unto Moses: 'Depart, go up hence, thou and the people that thou hast brought up out of the land of Egypt, unto the land of which I swore unto Abraham, to Isaac, and to Jacob, saying: Unto thy seed will I give it—2. and I will send an angel before thee; and I will drive out the Canaanite, the Amorite, and the Hittite, and the Perizzite, the Hivite, and the Jebusite—3. unto a land flowing with milk and honey; for I will not go up in the midst of thee; for thou art a stiffnecked people; lest I consume thee in the way.' 4. And when the people heard these evil tidings, they mourned; and no man did put on him his ornaments. 5. And the Lord said unto Moses: 'Say unto the children of Israel: Ye are a stiffnecked people; if I go up into the midst of thee for one moment, I shall consume thee; therefore now put off thy ornaments from thee, that I may know what to do unto thee.' 6. And the children of Israel stripped themselves of their ornaments from mount Horeb onward. ¶ 7. Now Moses used to take the tent and to pitch it without the camp, afar off from the camp; and he called it The tent of meeting. And it came to pass, that every one that sought the Lord went out unto the tent of meeting, which was without the camp. 8. And it came to pass, when Moses went out unto the Tent, that all the people rose up, and stood, every man at his tent door, and looked after Moses, until he was gone into the Tent. 9. And it came to pass, when Moses entered into the Tent, the pillar of cloud descended, and stood at the door of the Tent; and [the Lord] spoke

Cap. XXXIII. לג

לג

א וַיְדַבֵּר יְהוָה אֶל־מֹשֶׁה לֵךְ עֲלֵה מִזֶּה אַתָּה וְהָעָם אֲשֶׁר
הֶעֱלִיתָ מֵאֶרֶץ מִצְרָיִם אֶל־הָאָרֶץ אֲשֶׁר נִשְׁבַּעְתִּי לְאַבְרָהָם
2 לְיִצְחָק וּלְיַעֲקֹב לֵאמֹר לְזַרְעֲךָ אֶתְּנֶנָּה׃ וְשָׁלַחְתִּי לְפָנֶיךָ
מַלְאָךְ וְגֵרַשְׁתִּי אֶת־הַכְּנַעֲנִי הָאֱמֹרִי וְהַחִתִּי וְהַפְּרִזִּי הַחִוִּי
3 וְהַיְבוּסִי׃ אֶל־אֶרֶץ זָבַת חָלָב וּדְבָשׁ כִּי לֹא אֶעֱלֶה בְּקִרְבְּךָ
4 כִּי עַם־קְשֵׁה־עֹרֶף אַתָּה פֶּן־אֲכֶלְךָ בַּדָּרֶךְ׃ וַיִּשְׁמַע הָעָם
אֶת־הַדָּבָר הָרָע הַזֶּה וַיִּתְאַבָּלוּ וְלֹא־שָׁתוּ אִישׁ עֶדְיוֹ עָלָיו׃
ה וַיֹּאמֶר יְהוָה אֶל־מֹשֶׁה אֱמֹר אֶל־בְּנֵי־יִשְׂרָאֵל אַתֶּם עַם־
קְשֵׁה־עֹרֶף רֶגַע אֶחָד אֶעֱלֶה בְקִרְבְּךָ וְכִלִּיתִיךָ וְעַתָּה הוֹרֵד
6 עֶדְיְךָ מֵעָלֶיךָ וְאֵדְעָה מָה אֶעֱשֶׂה־לָּךְ׃ וַיִּתְנַצְּלוּ בְנֵי־
7 יִשְׂרָאֵל אֶת־עֶדְיָם מֵהַר חוֹרֵב׃ וּמֹשֶׁה יִקַּח אֶת־הָאֹהֶל
וְנָטָה־לוֹ ׀ מִחוּץ לַמַּחֲנֶה הַרְחֵק מִן־הַמַּחֲנֶה וְקָרָא לוֹ
אֹהֶל מוֹעֵד וְהָיָה כָּל־מְבַקֵּשׁ יְהוָה יֵצֵא אֶל־אֹהֶל מוֹעֵד
8 אֲשֶׁר מִחוּץ לַמַּחֲנֶה׃ וְהָיָה כְּצֵאת מֹשֶׁה אֶל־הָאֹהֶל
יָקוּמוּ כָּל־הָעָם וְנִצְּבוּ אִישׁ פֶּתַח אָהֳלוֹ וְהִבִּיטוּ אַחֲרֵי
9 מֹשֶׁה עַד־בֹּאוֹ הָאֹהֱלָה׃ וְהָיָה כְּבֹא מֹשֶׁה הָאֹהֱלָה יֵרֵד

Chapter XXXIII

1–6. The Contrition of the People

1. *thou and the people.* Not 'thy people', as in xxxii, 7. God no longer utterly repudiates them.

2. *before thee. i.e.* before Israel, to whom this message was to be delivered.

3. *consume thee.* Another act of treason on their part might well bring about their utter destruction.

4. *these evil tidings.* That God's spirit would not dwell with them (Rashi).

5. *that I may know.* They had shown their remorse by stripping themselves of their ornaments. If they persevered in this chastened frame of mind, God would show mercy.

7–11. Moses and his Tent of Meeting

7. *used to take.* From the time of the sin of the Golden Calf onwards (Rashi), until the Sanctuary had been erected.

the tent. Despite the use of the definite article, the allusion cannot be to the 'Tent of Meeting' mentioned in xxvii, 21, as that was not yet in existence. It may point back to Moses' tent, which is referred to in xviii, 7, where Moses used to receive the people who came to him with their disputes.

sought the LORD. Through the medium of Moses.

without the camp. Because the camp had been defiled by the Golden Calf, and the sins of the people had removed the Divine Presence from their midst; but Moses, who was innocent of guilt, was not for that reason debarred from communion with God.

8. *rose up.* In reverence.

looked after Moses. Followed him reverently with their eyes.

9. *pillar of cloud.* The visible representation of the Shechinah (xiii, 21).

stood. i.e. remained.

spoke. The subject, 'the Lord,' is not stated; cf. Ezek. ii, 1.

with Moses. 10. And when all the people saw the pillar of cloud stand at the door of the Tent, all the people rose up and worshipped, every man at his tent door. 11. And the LORD spoke unto Moses face to face, as a man speaketh unto his friend. And he would return into the camp; but his minister Joshua, the son of Nun, a young man, departed not out of the Tent.* iii. ¶ 12. And Moses said unto the LORD: 'See, Thou sayest unto me: Bring up this people; and Thou hast not let me know whom Thou wilt send with me. Yet Thou hast said: I know thee by name, and thou hast also found grace in My sight. 13. Now therefore, I pray Thee, if I have found grace in Thy sight, show me now Thy ways, that I may know Thee, to the end that I may find grace in Thy sight; and consider that this nation is Thy people.' 14. And He said: 'My presence shall go with thee, and I will give thee rest.' 15. And he said unto Him: 'If Thy presence go not with me, carry us not up hence. 16. For wherein now shall

י עַמּוּד הֶעָנָן וְעָמַד פֶּתַח הָאֹהֶל וְדִבֶּר עִם־מֹשֶׁה׃ וְרָאָה
כָּל־הָעָם אֶת־עַמּוּד הֶעָנָן עֹמֵד פֶּתַח הָאֹהֶל וְקָם כָּל־הָעָם
11 וְהִשְׁתַּחֲווּ אִישׁ פֶּתַח אָהֳלוֹ׃ וְדִבֶּר יְהוָה אֶל־מֹשֶׁה פָּנִים
אֶל־פָּנִים כַּאֲשֶׁר יְדַבֵּר אִישׁ אֶל־רֵעֵהוּ וְשָׁב אֶל־הַמַּחֲנֶה
שלישי וּמְשָׁרְתוֹ יְהוֹשֻׁעַ בִּן־נוּן נַעַר לֹא יָמִישׁ מִתּוֹךְ הָאֹהֶל׃ * פ
12 וַיֹּאמֶר מֹשֶׁה אֶל־יְהוָה רְאֵה אַתָּה אֹמֵר אֵלַי הַעַל אֶת־
הָעָם הַזֶּה וְאַתָּה לֹא הוֹדַעְתַּנִי אֵת אֲשֶׁר־תִּשְׁלַח עִמִּי וְאַתָּה
13 אָמַרְתָּ יְדַעְתִּיךָ בְשֵׁם וְגַם־מָצָאתָ חֵן בְּעֵינָי׃ וְעַתָּה אִם־
נָא מָצָאתִי חֵן בְּעֵינֶיךָ הוֹדִעֵנִי נָא אֶת־דְּרָכֶךָ וְאֵדָעֲךָ לְמַעַן
14 אֶמְצָא־חֵן בְּעֵינֶיךָ וּרְאֵה כִּי עַמְּךָ הַגּוֹי הַזֶּה׃ וַיֹּאמַר פָּנַי
טו יֵלֵכוּ וַהֲנִחֹתִי לָךְ׃ וַיֹּאמֶר אֵלָיו אִם־אֵין פָּנֶיךָ הֹלְכִים אַל־

10. *worshipped.* Prostrated themselves to the ground.

11. *face to face. i.e.* not in obscure visions and dreams, nor in enigmatical allusions, but distinctly. 'As in a clear mirror was the Divine message reflected in Moses' mind,' say the Rabbis; see p. 402.

he would return. He only left them when it was essential to consult God, and then he would return into the camp.

his minister. His attendant; cf. XXIV, 13.

a young man. So called because he performed for Moses humble services, such as are generally given only by a youthful follower (Ibn Ezra). The Heb. term *naar* may also denote an unmarried man (Ehrlich); he was, therefore, able permanently to remain in charge of the tent. No children of Joshua are mentioned in the genealogical table in I Chron. VII, 27.

12–XXXIV, 7. MOSES' PRAYER, THE SECOND TABLES, AND THE THIRTEEN ATTRIBUTES OF GOD'S NATURE

After Israel had danced before the Golden Calf, and the Tables of the Law lay shattered at the foot of Sinai, Moses again ascended the mountain, and prostrated himself in prayer before God. After forty days, he returns unto Israel, when, in addition to new Tables of the Law, he brings a Heavenly commentary on that Law, the thirteen attributes of the Divine Nature, שלוש עשרה מדות, each a synonym of the everlasting mercy of God.

12. *whom Thou wilt send.* Moses, deprived of the assurance of God's Presence, feels that the task imposed upon him, 'Bring up this people,' is far too difficult to undertake. He, therefore, pleads for the Divine assistance.

Thou hast said. The Torah has not recorded the circumstances in which the words that follow were spoken by God: but they might well have been uttered when He desired to destroy the Israelites and make 'a great nation' of Moses (XXXII, 10).

I know thee by name. i.e. selected thee to fulfil My commission. Moses recalls these words of graciousness, for the purpose of contrasting them with the hopeless position in which he now finds himself.

13. *show me.* lit. 'make me to know.'

Thy ways. The Talmud understands Moses' request as a desire to know the principles on which God deals with human beings, granting prosperity to some and adversity to others; to understand God's nature, in order that he might lead and govern the people in accordance with the Divine will.

this nation is Thy people. And should not be left without the inspiration of God's Presence.

14. *My presence.* Heb. *panai.* The expression is synonymous with 'I' (cf. II Sam. XVII, 11). Onkelos renders by, 'My Shechinah.'

give thee rest. In the Promised Land. 'Thee' refers to the people, as in *v.* 2 f above.

15. *carry us not up hence.* Unless the Divine Presence be in their midst when they proceed on their journey, Moses begs that they stay at Sinai—a spot which had been hallowed by the Revelation.

it be known that I have found grace in Thy sight, I and Thy people? is it not in that Thou goest with us, so that we are distinguished, I and Thy people, from all the people that are upon the face of the earth?'*iv. ¶ 17. And the LORD said unto Moses: 'I will do this thing also that thou hast spoken, for thou hast found grace in My sight, and I know thee by name.' 18. And he said: 'Show me, I pray Thee, Thy glory.' 19. And He said: 'I will make all My goodness pass before thee, and will proclaim the name of the LORD before thee; and I will be gracious to whom I will be gracious, and will show mercy on whom I will show mercy.' 20. And He said: 'Thou canst not see My face, for man shall not see Me and live.' 21. And the LORD said: 'Behold, there is a place by Me, and thou shalt stand upon the rock. 22. And it shall come to pass, while My glory passeth by, that I will put thee in a cleft of the rock, and will cover thee with My hand until I have passed by. 23. And I will take away My hand, and thou shalt see My back; but My face shall not be seen.'*v.

16 תַּעֲלֵנוּ מִזֶּה׃ וּבַמֶּה ׀ יִוָּדַע אֵפוֹא כִּי־מָצָאתִי חֵן בְּעֵינֶיךָ אֲנִי
וְעַמֶּךָ הֲלוֹא בְּלֶכְתְּךָ עִמָּנוּ וְנִפְלֵינוּ אֲנִי וְעַמְּךָ מִכָּל־הָעָם
אֲשֶׁר עַל־פְּנֵי הָאֲדָמָה׃ * פ רביעי
17 וַיֹּאמֶר יְהוָה אֶל־מֹשֶׁה גַּם אֶת־הַדָּבָר הַזֶּה אֲשֶׁר דִּבַּרְתָּ
18 אֶעֱשֶׂה כִּי־מָצָאתָ חֵן בְּעֵינַי וָאֵדָעֲךָ בְּשֵׁם׃ וַיֹּאמַר הַרְאֵנִי
19 נָא אֶת־כְּבֹדֶךָ׃ וַיֹּאמֶר אֲנִי אַעֲבִיר כָּל־טוּבִי עַל־פָּנֶיךָ
וְקָרָאתִי בְשֵׁם יְהוָה לְפָנֶיךָ וְחַנֹּתִי אֶת־אֲשֶׁר אָחֹן וְרִחַמְתִּי
כ אֶת־אֲשֶׁר אֲרַחֵם׃ וַיֹּאמֶר לֹא תוּכַל לִרְאֹת אֶת־פָּנָי כִּי
21 לֹא־יִרְאַנִי הָאָדָם וָחָי׃ וַיֹּאמֶר יְהוָה הִנֵּה מָקוֹם אִתִּי וְנִצַּבְתָּ
22 עַל־הַצּוּר׃ וְהָיָה בַּעֲבֹר כְּבֹדִי וְשַׂמְתִּיךָ בְּנִקְרַת הַצּוּר
23 וְשַׂכֹּתִי כַפִּי עָלֶיךָ עַד־עָבְרִי׃ וַהֲסִרֹתִי אֶת־כַּפִּי וְרָאִיתָ
אֶת־אֲחֹרָי וּפָנַי לֹא יֵרָאוּ׃ * פ חמישי

16. *distinguished.* Israel's distinctiveness consisted solely in the Divine nearness to Israel.

17. *this thing also.* Better, *even this thing that thou hast spoken will I do.*

18. *Thy glory.* Emboldened by the success of his plea on behalf of the people, Moses begs the privilege of being acquainted with 'the glory of God', *i.e.* with His eternal qualities.

19. *My goodness.* God's moral attributes. The revelation of these Attributes of love and mercy is the source of the sublime principle of the *Imitation of God*, הדבקת במדותיו של הקב׳׳ה. This Jewish ideal, 'one of the most advanced triumphs of Religion,' goes back to the Divine demand in Lev. XIX, 2. 'Ye shall be holy: for I the LORD your God am holy.' Israel is not only to serve God, but to imitate Him. Mortal man, however, cannot imitate God's infinity, omnipotence or eternity. That side of His nature, which is beyond human comprehension, is also beyond human imitation. But we *can* know His 'goodness', and we can follow *His ways of mercy and forgiveness.* Thus, pity is a Divine attribute; and man is never nearer to the Divine than in his compassionate moments. God's merciful qualities are, therefore, the most real links between God and Man. 'Even as I am merciful, be thou merciful; even as I am gracious, be thou gracious,' is the Rabbinic translation of the great commandment of the Imitation of God.

proclaim the name of the LORD. The term 'Name' has here the same significance as in III, 13 f, and denotes the Divine essence, nature and character.

I will be gracious. God will show mercy to those who deserve it. Who these are, is not expressly stated; but fallen and penitent Israel is intended (Driver). The Heb. idiom employed here, is the same as in 'send by the hand of him whom thou wilt send' (IV. 13).

20. *see My face.* Moses desires to know what no human being can fathom, what no human language can express. His request, however, is not due to curiosity, but in order to confirm the promise in *v.* 14.

and live. The expression that a mortal cannot see God and live is frequently found in Scripture.

21. *upon the rock.* Of Sinai.

23. *My face shall not be seen.* When God passes by, presumably in the form of fire (see XXIV, 17), Moses will be sheltered in 'a cleft of the rock'. He will thus not see 'the face', the full Manifestation of the Divine radiance; but only its afterglow, 'the back,' so to speak. It is, of course, quite impossible to penetrate the full mystery of these words, conveying sublime truths concerning the Divine nature in the ordinary language of man. Many interpreters deduce from this passage the teaching that no living being can see God's face, *i.e.* penetrate His eternal essence. It is only from the *rearward* that we can know Him. Even as a ship sails through the waters of ocean and leaves its wake behind, so God may be known by His Divine 'footprints' in human history, by His traces in the human soul.

34

CHAPTER XXXIV

1. And the LORD said unto Moses: 'Hew thee two tables of stone like unto the first; and I will write upon the tables the words that were on the first tables, which thou didst break. 2. And be ready by the morning, and come up in the morning unto mount Sinai, and present thyself there to Me on the top of the mount. 3. And no man shall come up with thee, neither let any man be seen throughout all the mount; neither let the flocks nor herds feed before that mount.' 4. And he hewed two tables of stone like unto the first; and Moses rose up early in the morning, and went up unto mount Sinai, as the LORD had commanded him, and took in his hand two tables of stone. 5. And the LORD descended in the cloud, and stood with him there, and proclaimed the name of the LORD. 6. And the LORD passed by before him, and proclaimed: 'The LORD, the LORD, God, merciful and gracious, long-suffering, and abundant in goodness and truth; 7. keeping

CAP. XXXIV. לד

לד

א וַיֹּאמֶר יְהוָה אֶל־מֹשֶׁה פְּסָל־לְךָ שְׁנֵי־לֻחֹת אֲבָנִים כָּרִאשֹׁנִים
וְכָתַבְתִּי עַל־הַלֻּחֹת אֶת־הַדְּבָרִים אֲשֶׁר הָיוּ עַל־הַלֻּחֹת
2 הָרִאשֹׁנִים אֲשֶׁר שִׁבַּרְתָּ׃ וֶהְיֵה נָכוֹן לַבֹּקֶר וְעָלִיתָ בַבֹּקֶר
3 אֶל־הַר סִינַי וְנִצַּבְתָּ לִי שָׁם עַל־רֹאשׁ הָהָר׃ וְאִישׁ לֹא־
יַעֲלֶה עִמָּךְ וְגַם־אִישׁ אַל־יֵרָא בְּכָל־הָהָר גַּם־הַצֹּאן וְהַבָּקָר
4 אַל־יִרְעוּ אֶל־מוּל הָהָר הַהוּא׃ וַיִּפְסֹל שְׁנֵי לֻחֹת אֲבָנִים
כָּרִאשֹׁנִים וַיַּשְׁכֵּם מֹשֶׁה בַבֹּקֶר וַיַּעַל אֶל־הַר סִינַי כַּאֲשֶׁר
ה צִוָּה יְהוָה אֹתוֹ וַיִּקַּח בְּיָדוֹ שְׁנֵי לֻחֹת אֲבָנִים׃ וַיֵּרֶד יְהוָה
6 בֶּעָנָן וַיִּתְיַצֵּב עִמּוֹ שָׁם וַיִּקְרָא בְשֵׁם יְהוָה׃ וַיַּעֲבֹר יְהוָה ׀

CHAPTER XXXIV

1. *hew thee two tables.* The vision of God which was now to be granted to Moses marks the re-establishment of the Covenant between God and Israel that had been annulled by the apostasy in connection with the Golden Calf. Therefore, the broken Tables of the Law are replaced by new Tables.

2. *be ready.* Even a man living a life so consecrated as Moses must 'prepare to meet his God' by self-purification; cf. XIX, 10.

top of the mount. From whence God had proclaimed the Ten Words (XIX, 20).

3. *no man.* Neither Aaron (XIX, 17), nor the elders (XXIV, 9) were to be with him on the mountain. Moses alone was this time to witness the Revelation. The Rabbis remark that the first Tables were given amid great pomp and upheaval, physical and psychic; and they were destroyed. The Second Revelation was given in silence, to one human soul alone in mystic communion with His Maker; and these Tables endured, for the salvation of Israel and mankind.

4. *went up.* Tradition relates that Moses ascended on the first day of Ellul, and remaining on the Mount forty days, descended on the tenth of Tishri, the Day of Atonement, on which day he brought the tidings of God's perfect pardon unto the sinful people.

5–7. THE REVELATION OF GOD'S NATURE IN THE THIRTEEN ATTRIBUTES

God's 'ways' are now proclaimed unto Moses in the thirteen characteristic qualities of the Divine Nature, enumerated in *v.* 6 and 7. Judaism has been very chary of definitions of God. He is the *En sof*, the Infinite, the Undefinable. However, the Thirteen Attributes give us a definition of God in ethical terms. All schools of Jewish thought agree that these momentous and sublime attributes enshrine some of the most distinctive doctrines of Judaism. The Rabbis made *v.* 6 and 7, containing the Thirteen Attributes of Divine Mercy, the dominant refrain in all prayers of repentance.

5. *stood.* The subject is 'the LORD' (Ibn Ezra, Nachmanides).

6. *proclaimed.* God reveals the 'name of the LORD', *i.e.* His characteristic qualities, to Moses. The Rabbis held that there are thirteen distinct attributes in these two verses; though there are differences as to their precise enumeration. The enumeration in the following comments is in accordance with the views of Rabbenu Tam, Ibn Ezra, Mendelssohn and Reggio.

the LORD, the LORD. Heb. *Adonay, Adonay* (I and II). ADONAY denotes God in His attribute of mercy; and the repetition is explained in the Talmud as meaning, 'I am the merciful God before a man commits a sin, and I am the same merciful and forgiving God after a man has sinned. Whatever change has to be wrought, must be in the heart of the sinner; not in the nature of the Deity. He is the same after a man has sinned, as He was before a man has sinned.'

God. Heb. *el* (III). The all-mighty Lord of the Universe, Ruler of Nature and mankind.

merciful. Heb. *rachum* (IV); full of affectionate sympathy for the sufferings and miseries of human frailty.

and gracious. Heb. *ve-channun* (V); assisting

mercy unto the thousandth generation, forgiving iniquity and transgression and sin; and that will by no means clear the guilty; visiting the iniquity of the fathers upon the children, and upon the children's children, unto the third and unto the fourth generation.' 8. And Moses made haste, and bowed his head toward the earth, and worshipped. 9. And he said: 'If now I have found grace in Thy sight, O Lord, let the Lord, I pray Thee, go in the midst of us; for it is a stiffnecked people; and pardon our iniquity and our sin, and take us for Thine inheritance.'* vi. 10. And He said: 'Behold, I make a covenant; before all thy people I

עַל־פָּנָיו וַיִּקְרָא יְהוָה ׀ יְהוָה אֵל רַחוּם וְחַנּוּן אֶרֶךְ אַפַּיִם
7 וְרַב־חֶסֶד וֶאֱמֶת׃ נֹצֵר חֶסֶד לָאֲלָפִים נֹשֵׂא עָוֺן וָפֶשַׁע
וְחַטָּאָה וְנַקֵּה לֹא יְנַקֶּה פֹּקֵד ׀ עֲוֺן אָבוֹת עַל־בָּנִים וְעַל־
8 בְּנֵי בָנִים עַל־שִׁלֵּשִׁים וְעַל־רִבֵּעִים׃ וַיְמַהֵר מֹשֶׁה וַיִּקֹּד
9 אַרְצָה וַיִּשְׁתָּחוּ׃ וַיֹּאמֶר אִם־נָא מָצָאתִי חֵן בְּעֵינֶיךָ אֲדֹנָי
יֵלֶךְ־נָא אֲדֹנָי בְּקִרְבֵּנוּ כִּי עַם־קְשֵׁה־עֹרֶף הוּא וְסָלַחְתָּ
ששי
י לַעֲוֺנֵנוּ וּלְחַטָּאתֵנוּ וּנְחַלְתָּנוּ׃ * וַיֹּאמֶר הִנֵּה אָנֹכִי כֹּרֵת

v. 7. נון רבתי

and helping; consoling the afflicted and raising up the oppressed. 'In man these two qualities manifest themselves fitfully and temporarily; he is מרחם וחונן. It is otherwise in God: in Him, compassion and grace are permanent, inherent and necessary emanations of His nature. Hence, He alone can be spoken of as *rachun ve-channun*' (Mendelssohn).

long-suffering. Or, 'slow to anger.' Heb. *erech appayim* (VI); not hastening to punish the sinner, but affording him opportunities to retrace his evil courses.

abundant in goodness. Or, plenteous in mercy. Heb. *rav chesed* (VII); granting His gifts and blessings beyond the deserts of man.

and truth. Heb. *ve-emess* (VIII); eternally rue to Himself, pursuing His inscrutable plans for the salvation of mankind, and rewarding those who are obedient to His will. Note that 'chesed,' lovingkindness, precedes 'emess,' truth, both here and generally throughout Scripture; as if to say, 'Speak the truth by all means; but be quite sure that you speak the truth *in love*.'

7. *keeping mercy unto the thousandth generation.* Heb. *notzer chesed la-alafim* (IX). Remembering the good deeds of the ancestors to the thousandth generation, and reserving reward and recompense to the remotest descendants.

forgiving iniquity. Heb. *noseh avon* (X); bearing with indulgence the failings of man, and by forgiveness restoring him to the original purity of his soul. The Heb. for 'iniquity' is *avon;* sins committed from evil disposition.

transgression. Heb. *pesha* (XI); evil deeds springing from malice and rebellion against the Divine.

sin. Heb. *chattaah* (XII); shortcomings due to heedlessness and error.

will by no means clear the guilty. i.e. He will not allow the guilty to pass unpunished. Heb. *venakkeh lo yenakkeh* (XIII). The Rabbis explain: *venakkeh* 'acquitting—the penitent; *lo yenakkeh,* but not acquitting—the impenitent.' He is merciful and gracious and forgiving; but He will never obliterate the eternal and unbridgeable distinction between light and darkness, between good and evil. God cannot leave repeated wickedness and obstinate persistence in evil entirely unpunished. His goodness cannot destroy His justice. The sinner must suffer the consequences of his misdeeds. The unfailing and impartial consequences of sin help man to perceive that there is no 'chance' in morals. The punishments of sin are thus not vindictive, but remedial.

visiting . . . upon the children. See XX, 5. This law relates only to the consequences of sin. Pardon is not the remission of the *penalty*, but the forgiveness of the guilt and the removal of the sinfulness. The misdeeds of those who are God's enemies are visited only to the third and fourth generation, whereas His mercy to those who love Him is unto a thousand generations.

8–9. Moses' Prayer

8. *made haste.* Upon learning the prominent place that mercy held in the Divine Nature, Moses immediately supplicates God to exercise His quality of mercy in favour of Israel.

9. *our iniquity.* Moses identified himself with his people. He speaks of 'our' iniquity. Similarly in the Liturgy of the Synagogue, especially in the Confession of the Day of Atonement, the prayers are composed in the plural ('*we* have sinned,' etc.); for the Rabbis exhort, 'The individual should associate himself with the Community in all his supplications.'

for Thine inheritance. i.e. by Thy presence in Israel's midst, acknowledge the people as Thine.

10–26. The Renewal and Conditions of the Covenant

10. *I make a covenant.* In answer to Moses' petition, God will go in the midst of Israel.

thy people. God will manifest wondrous deeds on their behalf, to convince them that He is desirous of leading them to their destination.

בְּרִית נֶגֶד כָּל־עַמְּךָ֙ אֶעֱשֶׂ֣ה נִפְלָאֹ֔ת אֲשֶׁ֛ר לֹא־נִבְרְא֥וּ בְכָל־
הָאָ֖רֶץ וּבְכָל־הַגּוֹיִ֑ם וְרָאָ֣ה כָל־הָ֠עָם אֲשֶׁר־אַתָּ֨ה בְקִרְבּ֜וֹ
אֶת־מַעֲשֵׂ֤ה יְהוָה֙ כִּֽי־נוֹרָ֣א ה֔וּא אֲשֶׁ֥ר אֲנִ֖י עֹשֶׂ֥ה עִמָּֽךְ׃
11 שְׁמָר־לְךָ֔ אֵ֛ת אֲשֶׁ֥ר אָנֹכִ֖י מְצַוְּךָ֣ הַיּ֑וֹם הִנְנִ֧י גֹרֵ֣שׁ מִפָּנֶ֗יךָ
אֶת־הָֽאֱמֹרִי֙ וְהַכְּנַעֲנִ֔י וְהַֽחִתִּי֙ וְהַפְּרִזִּ֔י וְהַחִוִּ֖י וְהַיְבוּסִֽי׃
12 הִשָּׁ֣מֶר לְךָ֗ פֶּן־תִּכְרֹ֤ת בְּרִית֙ לְיוֹשֵׁ֣ב הָאָ֔רֶץ אֲשֶׁ֥ר אַתָּ֖ה בָּ֣א
13 עָלֶ֑יהָ פֶּן־יִהְיֶ֥ה לְמוֹקֵ֖שׁ בְּקִרְבֶּֽךָ׃ כִּ֤י אֶת־מִזְבְּחֹתָם֙ תִּתֹּצ֔וּן
14 וְאֶת־מַצֵּבֹתָ֖ם תְּשַׁבֵּר֑וּן וְאֶת־אֲשֵׁרָ֖יו תִּכְרֹתֽוּן׃ כִּ֛י לֹ֥א
תִשְׁתַּחֲוֶ֖ה לְאֵ֣ל אַחֵ֑ר כִּ֤י יְהוָה֙ קַנָּ֣א שְׁמ֔וֹ אֵ֥ל קַנָּ֖א הֽוּא׃
טו פֶּן־תִּכְרֹ֥ת בְּרִ֖ית לְיוֹשֵׁ֣ב הָאָ֑רֶץ וְזָנ֣וּ ׀ אַחֲרֵ֣י אֱלֹֽהֵיהֶ֗ם
16 וְזָבְחוּ֙ לֵאלֹ֣הֵיהֶ֔ם וְקָרָ֣א לְךָ֔ וְאָכַלְתָּ֖ מִזִּבְחֽוֹ׃ וְלָקַחְתָּ֥
מִבְּנֹתָ֖יו לְבָנֶ֑יךָ וְזָנ֣וּ בְנֹתָ֗יו אַחֲרֵי֙ אֱלֹ֣הֵיהֶ֔ן וְהִזְנוּ֙ אֶת־
17 18 בָּנֶ֔יךָ אַחֲרֵ֖י אֱלֹהֵיהֶֽן׃ אֱלֹהֵ֥י מַסֵּכָ֖ה לֹ֥א תַעֲשֶׂה־לָּֽךְ׃ אֶת־
חַ֣ג הַמַּצּוֹת֮ תִּשְׁמֹר֒ שִׁבְעַ֨ת יָמִ֜ים תֹּאכַ֤ל מַצּוֹת֙ אֲשֶׁ֣ר צִוִּיתִ֔ךָ

v. 14. ר' רבתי

will do marvels, such as have not been wrought in all the earth, nor in any nation; and all the people among which thou art shall see the work of the LORD that I am about to do with thee, that it is tremendous. 11. Observe thou that which I am commanding thee this day; behold, I am driving out before thee the Amorite, and the Canaanite, and the Hittite, and the Perizzite, and the Hivite, and the Jebusite. 12. Take heed to thyself, lest thou make a covenant with the inhabitants of the land whither thou goest, lest they be for a snare in the midst of thee. 13. But ye shall break down their altars, and dash in pieces their pillars, and ye shall cut down their Asherim. 14. For thou shalt bow down to no other god; for the LORD, whose name is Jealous, is a jealous God; 15. lest thou make a covenant with the inhabitants of the land, and they go astray after their gods, and do sacrifice unto their gods, and they call thee, and thou eat of their sacrifice; 16. and thou take of their daughters unto thy sons, and their daughters go astray after their gods, and make thy sons go astray after their gods. 17. Thou shalt make thee no molten gods. 18. The feast of unleavened bread shalt thou keep. Seven days thou shalt eat unleavened bread, as I commanded thee, at the time appointed in the month

11. *commanding thee. i.e.* Israel, as in XXXIII, 2 f.

12. *a snare.* Fraternization with the heathen would inevitably lead to idol-worship, and bring disaster upon the Israelites, as was proved abundantly in the time of the Judges.

13. *break down.* All forms of heathenish worship are to be obliterated.

altars. On which human sacrifice was not uncommon.

pillars. See on XXIII, 24. Wooden poles, around which immoral orgies were carried on.

Asherim. 'Probably wooden symbols of a goddess Ashera' (RV Margin), the Venus of the Phœnicians, Ashtoreth, Astarte. Immoral rites were practised at these shrines.

14. *name. i.e.* character (cf. XXXIII, 19).

a jealous God. See on XX, 5.

15. *call thee. i.e.* invite thee.

eat of their sacrifice. To partake of the flesk of a heathen sacrifice would be tantamount to apostasy, since religious ideas were associated with a sacrificial meal.

16. *take of their daughters.* The dangers of intermarriage from the spiritual point of view were recognized by the Patriarchs (Gen. XXIV and XXVIII). They are emphasized by Moses (Deut. VII, 3 f) and by Joshua (Josh. XXIII, 12). The danger, though of a different character, is just as real to-day. The training of every Jewish child should be such that he remain part of Israel, that he continue the work of Israel, and that he make the building of a home *in* Israel the ambition of his youth and manhood. Intermarriage would then be out of the question for any son or daughter of Israel. Unlike other peoples, Israel does not wage any wars; and rarely, therefore, does it require its children to lay down their lives in its defence; but Judaism expects that its sons and daughters should feel themselves bound, even though the duty involve the sacrifice of precious affections, to refrain from courses of conduct that undermine the stability of Israel. 'Every Jew who contemplates marriage outside the pale must regard himself as paving the way to a disruption which would be the final, as it would be the culminating, disaster in the history of his people' (M. Joseph).

17. *molten gods.* The 'pillars' and 'asherim' having been condemned as objects of worship, the warning against molten gods of silver and gold is repeated (XX, 23).

18–26. The commands in these verses concern exclusively the relation between God and man. For these verses speak of the Covenant which had been broken, not by any neglect of duties towards fellow-men, but of Israel's duty toward God.

לְמוֹעֵד חֹדֶשׁ הָאָבִיב כִּי בְּחֹדֶשׁ הָאָבִיב יָצָאתָ מִמִּצְרָיִם׃
19 כָּל־פֶּטֶר רֶחֶם לִי וְכָל־מִקְנְךָ תִּזָּכָר פֶּטֶר שׁוֹר וָשֶׂה׃
כ וּפֶטֶר חֲמוֹר תִּפְדֶּה בְשֶׂה וְאִם־לֹא תִפְדֶּה וַעֲרַפְתּוֹ כֹּל
21 בְּכוֹר בָּנֶיךָ תִּפְדֶּה וְלֹא־יֵרָאוּ פָנַי רֵיקָם׃ שֵׁשֶׁת יָמִים
תַּעֲבֹד וּבַיּוֹם הַשְּׁבִיעִי תִּשְׁבֹּת בֶּחָרִישׁ וּבַקָּצִיר תִּשְׁבֹּת׃
22 וְחַג שָׁבֻעֹת תַּעֲשֶׂה לְךָ בִּכּוּרֵי קְצִיר חִטִּים וְחַג הָאָסִיף
23 תְּקוּפַת הַשָּׁנָה׃ שָׁלֹשׁ פְּעָמִים בַּשָּׁנָה יֵרָאֶה כָּל־זְכוּרְךָ
24 אֶת־פְּנֵי הָאָדֹן ׀ יְהוָה אֱלֹהֵי יִשְׂרָאֵל׃ כִּי־אוֹרִישׁ גּוֹיִם
מִפָּנֶיךָ וְהִרְחַבְתִּי אֶת־גְּבֻלֶךָ וְלֹא־יַחְמֹד אִישׁ אֶת־אַרְצְךָ
בַּעֲלֹתְךָ לֵרָאוֹת אֶת־פְּנֵי יְהוָה אֱלֹהֶיךָ שָׁלֹשׁ פְּעָמִים בַּשָּׁנָה׃
כה לֹא־תִשְׁחַט עַל־חָמֵץ דַּם־זִבְחִי וְלֹא־יָלִין לַבֹּקֶר זֶבַח חַג
26 הַפָּסַח׃ רֵאשִׁית בִּכּוּרֵי אַדְמָתְךָ תָּבִיא בֵּית יְהוָה אֱלֹהֶיךָ
לֹא־תְבַשֵּׁל גְּדִי בַּחֲלֵב אִמּוֹ׃ פ שביעי
27 וַיֹּאמֶר יְהוָה אֶל־מֹשֶׁה כְּתָב־לְךָ אֶת־הַדְּבָרִים הָאֵלֶּה כִּי
עַל־פִּי ׀ הַדְּבָרִים הָאֵלֶּה כָּרַתִּי אִתְּךָ בְּרִית וְאֶת־יִשְׂרָאֵל׃

v. 19. קמץ בז"ק

Abib, for in the month Abib thou camest out from Egypt. 19. All that openeth the womb is Mine; and of all thy cattle thou shalt sanctify the males, the firstlings of ox and sheep. 20. And the firstling of an ass thou shalt redeem with a lamb; and if thou wilt not redeem it, then thou shalt break its neck. All the first-born of thy sons thou shalt redeem. And none shall appear before Me empty. 21. Six days thou shalt work, but on the seventh day thou shalt rest; in plowing time and in harvest thou shalt rest. 22. And thou shalt observe the feast of weeks, even of the first-fruits of wheat harvest, and the feast of ingathering at the turn of the year. 23. Three times in the year shall all thy males appear before the Lord GOD, the God of Israel. 24. For I will cast out nations before thee, and enlarge thy borders; neither shall any man covet thy land, when thou goest up to appear before the LORD thy God three times in the year. 25. Thou shalt not offer the blood of My sacrifice with leavened bread; neither shall the sacrifice of the feast of the passover be left unto the morning. 26. The choicest first-fruits of thy land thou shalt bring unto the house of the LORD thy God. Thou shalt not seethe a kid in its mother's milk.'* vii. ¶ 27. And the LORD said unto Moses: 'Write thou these words, for after the tenor of these words I have made a covenant with thee and with Israel.' 28. And he was there

18. *feast of unleavened bread.* The reminder that Israel owes freedom and national existence to the redemptive power of God. Its due observance would prevent Israel's going astray after other gods.

19. *firstlings.* See XIII, 12 and XXII, 28 f. Ibn Ezra rightly explains that this law is mentioned here because it is connected with the Exodus from Egypt. The sparing of the firstborn of the Israelites (XII, 13) was commemorated by the dedication of the firstborn, human and animal, to God; see XIII, 2 f, 15.

20. *a lamb.* See XIII, 13.
none shall appear. Cf. XXIII, 15. These words are taken to refer to the Feast of Unleavened Bread, and also to the Feast of Weeks and of Ingathering (*v.* 22 f).

21. *seventh day.* See XX, 8, XXIII, 12. The observance of the Sabbath would likewise be a reminder of God, both as Creator of the Universe, and Deliverer of Israel from Egypt.
in plowing time. Even during the periods of the year when there is urgent pressure in the field, and the Israelite feels that his livelihood demands continuous work, without a break on the Sabbath, he must nevertheless not desecrate the holy day.

22. *feast of weeks.* See on XXIII, 16. This name is given also in Deut. XVI, 10, and the reason for it stated, 'seven weeks shalt thou number unto thee.'
at the turn of the year. The year being reckoned according to the agricultural seasons, the gathering of the harvest marks its end.

24. *covet thy land.* God will shield their homes against enemies who might seize such a favourable opportunity to attack the women and children.

25. *with leavened bread.* See XXIII, 18.

26. *seethe a kid.* See XXIII, 19.

27, 28. THE SECOND TABLES

27. *these words.* The contents of *v.* 11–26, which were the conditions of the renewal of the Covenant.

28. *forty days.* This period is reckoned from his ascent mentioned in *v.* 4.
the words of the covenant. Better, *with the words of the covenant* (Ibn Ezra). Moses wrote

with the LORD forty days and forty nights; he did neither eat bread, nor drink water. And he wrote upon the tables the words of the covenant, the ten words. 29. And it came to pass, when Moses came down from mount Sinai with the two tables of the testimony in Moses' hand, when he came down from the mount, that Moses knew not that the skin of his face sent forth [1]beams while He talked with him. 30. And when Aaron and all the children of Israel saw Moses, behold, the skin of his face sent forth beams; and they were afraid to come nigh him. 31. And Moses called unto them; and Aaron and all the rulers of the congregation returned unto him; and Moses spoke to them. 32. And afterward all the children of Israel came nigh, and he gave them in commandment all that the LORD had spoken with him in mount Sinai.* m. 33. And when Moses had done speaking with them, he put a veil on his face. 34. But when Moses went in before the LORD that He might speak with him, he took the veil off, until he came out; and he came out, and spoke unto the children of Israel that which he was commanded. 35. And the children of Israel saw the face of Moses, that the skin of Moses' face sent forth beams; and Moses put the veil back upon his face, until he went in to speak with Him.

[1] Heb. *horns.*

28 וַיְהִי־שָׁם עִם־יְהוָה אַרְבָּעִים יוֹם וְאַרְבָּעִים לַיְלָה לֶחֶם
לֹא אָכַל וּמַיִם לֹא שָׁתָה וַיִּכְתֹּב עַל־הַלֻּחֹת אֵת דִּבְרֵי
29 הַבְּרִית עֲשֶׂרֶת הַדְּבָרִים׃ וַיְהִי בְּרֶדֶת מֹשֶׁה מֵהַר סִינַי
וּשְׁנֵי לֻחֹת הָעֵדֻת בְּיַד־מֹשֶׁה בְּרִדְתּוֹ מִן־הָהָר וּמֹשֶׁה לֹא־
ל יָדַע כִּי קָרַן עוֹר פָּנָיו בְּדַבְּרוֹ אִתּוֹ׃ וַיַּרְא אַהֲרֹן וְכָל־בְּנֵי
יִשְׂרָאֵל אֶת־מֹשֶׁה וְהִנֵּה קָרַן עוֹר פָּנָיו וַיִּירְאוּ מִגֶּשֶׁת
31 אֵלָיו׃ וַיִּקְרָא אֲלֵהֶם מֹשֶׁה וַיָּשֻׁבוּ אֵלָיו אַהֲרֹן וְכָל־
32 הַנְּשִׂאִים בָּעֵדָה וַיְדַבֵּר מֹשֶׁה אֲלֵהֶם׃ וְאַחֲרֵי־כֵן נִגְּשׁוּ כָּל־
בְּנֵי יִשְׂרָאֵל וַיְצַוֵּם אֵת כָּל־אֲשֶׁר דִּבֶּר יְהוָה אִתּוֹ בְּהַר
מפטיר
33 34 סִינָי׃ *וַיְכַל מֹשֶׁה מִדַּבֵּר אִתָּם וַיִּתֵּן עַל־פָּנָיו מַסְוֶה׃ וּבְבֹא
מֹשֶׁה לִפְנֵי יְהוָה לְדַבֵּר אִתּוֹ יָסִיר אֶת־הַמַּסְוֶה עַד־צֵאתוֹ
לה וְיָצָא וְדִבֶּר אֶל־בְּנֵי יִשְׂרָאֵל אֵת אֲשֶׁר יְצֻוֶּה׃ וְרָאוּ בְנֵי־
יִשְׂרָאֵל אֶת־פְּנֵי מֹשֶׁה כִּי קָרַן עוֹר פְּנֵי מֹשֶׁה וְהֵשִׁיב מֹשֶׁה
אֶת־הַמַּסְוֶה עַל־פָּנָיו עַד־בֹּאוֹ לְדַבֵּר אִתּוֹ׃

down all these commands, whilst God Himself inscribed the Decalogue upon the second Tables; see *v.* 1 and Deut. x, 1. The Heb. particle את here means 'with'; otherwise it would have been repeated before each of the two phrases.

Starting from this verse, the German poet Goethe conjectured in 1773 that the regulations in *v.* 14–26 could be grouped as ten laws, and these ten laws were the original Ten Commandments! In his later and riper years (*Wahrheit und Dichtung*, Book XII), he spoke of this alleged discovery of his as 'a freakish notion', due to his insufficient knowledge. Since his day, however, Wellhausen and other Bible Critics, have revived the preposterous idea of the youthful poet as to a Second Decalogue, the 'moral' Decalogue as they call it, as distinct from the alleged 'ritual' Decalogue in this chapter. Leading Bible scholars, however, see the obvious intention of the narrative indicated in *v.* 1 ('I will write upon the tables of stone the words which were upon the first tables, which thou brakest'). They, furthermore, recognize that it is only by arbitrary and baseless *guesswork* that the precepts in *v.* 14–26 can be arranged so as to make ten.

29–35. SHINING OF MOSES' FACE

29. *two tables of the testimony.* As in XXXI, 18.
knew not. Unconscious that the Divine lustre was reflected upon his face. The greatest are unconscious of their greatness.

sent forth beams. Of light. The Heb. קרן either means, 'a ray of light' or, more commonly, 'a horn.' The Latin translation of the Bible, the Vulgate, translates, 'his face sent out horns of light.' The medieval artists, therefore, including Michael Angelo, were thus misled into representing Moses as with horns protruding from his forehead!

while He talked . . . with him. Communion with God illumines the soul with a Divine radiance.

31. *called.* To reassure them.

returned. The verb implies that they had retreated in terror.

spoke to them. He repeated to them what God had commanded him in the Mount.

32. *all that the LORD had spoken. viz.* the Covenant, upon the fulfilment of which, His presence would accompany the people.

33. *veil.* The radiance was something that appertained to the Divine, and for that reason must not be put to a profane use.

34. *when Moses went in . . . he took.* Better, *Whenever Moses went in . . . he would take . . .*

35. *children of Israel saw.* The People were the more deeply impressed by his message when they beheld the radiance of his countenance.

HAFTORAH KI THISSA הפטרת כי תשא

I KINGS XVIII, 1–39

Chapter XVIII

1. And it came to pass after many days, that the word of the Lord came to Elijah, in the third year, saying: 'Go, show thyself unto Ahab, and I will send rain upon the land.' 2. And Elijah went to show himself unto Ahab. ¶ And the famine was sore in Samaria. 3. And Ahab called Obadiah, who was over the household.—Now Obadiah feared the Lord greatly; 4. for it was so, when Jezebel cut off the prophets of the Lord, that Obadiah took a hundred prophets, and hid them fifty in a cave, and fed them with bread and water.—5. And Ahab said unto Obadiah: 'Go through the land, unto all the springs of water, and unto all the brooks; peradventure we may find grass and save the horses and mules alive, that we lose not all the beasts.' 6. So they divided the land between them to pass throughout it: Ahab went one way by himself, and Obadiah went another way by himself. ¶ 7. And as Obadiah was in the way, behold, Elijah met him; and he knew him, and fell on his face, and said: 'Is it thou, my lord Elijah?' 8. And he answered him: 'It is I; go, tell thy lord: Behold, Elijah is here.' 9. And he said: 'Wherein have I sinned, that thou wouldest deliver thy servant into the hand of Ahab, to slay me? 10. As the Lord thy God liveth, there is no nation or kingdom, whither my lord hath not sent to seek thee; and when they said: He is not here, he took an oath of the kingdom and nation, that they found thee

Cap. XVIII. יח

א וַיְהִי יָמִים רַבִּים וּדְבַר יְהֹוָה הָיָה אֶל־אֵלִיָּהוּ בַּשָּׁנָה
הַשְּׁלִישִׁית לֵאמֹר לֵךְ הֵרָאֵה אֶל־אַחְאָב וְאֶתְּנָה מָטָר
2 עַל־פְּנֵי הָאֲדָמָה׃ וַיֵּלֶךְ אֵלִיָּהוּ לְהֵרָאוֹת אֶל־אַחְאָב
3 וְהָרָעָב חָזָק בְּשֹׁמְרוֹן׃ וַיִּקְרָא אַחְאָב אֶל־עֹבַדְיָהוּ אֲשֶׁר
4 עַל־הַבָּיִת וְעֹבַדְיָהוּ הָיָה יָרֵא אֶת־יְהֹוָה מְאֹד׃ וַיְהִי
בְּהַכְרִית אִיזֶבֶל אֵת נְבִיאֵי יְהֹוָה וַיִּקַּח עֹבַדְיָהוּ מֵאָה
נְבִיאִים וַיַּחְבִּיאֵם חֲמִשִּׁים אִישׁ בַּמְּעָרָה וְכִלְכְּלָם לֶחֶם
ה וָמָיִם׃ וַיֹּאמֶר אַחְאָב אֶל־עֹבַדְיָהוּ לֵךְ בָּאָרֶץ אֶל־כָּל־
מַעְיְנֵי הַמַּיִם וְאֶל כָּל־הַנְּחָלִים אוּלַי ׀ נִמְצָא חָצִיר וּנְחַיֶּה
6 סוּס וָפֶרֶד וְלוֹא נַכְרִית מֵהַבְּהֵמָה׃ וַיְחַלְּקוּ לָהֶם אֶת־
הָאָרֶץ לַעֲבָר־בָּהּ אַחְאָב הָלַךְ בְּדֶרֶךְ אֶחָד לְבַדּוֹ וְעֹבַדְיָהוּ
7 הָלַךְ בְּדֶרֶךְ־אֶחָד לְבַדּוֹ׃ וַיְהִי עֹבַדְיָהוּ בַּדֶּרֶךְ וְהִנֵּה
אֵלִיָּהוּ לִקְרָאתוֹ וַיַּכִּרֵהוּ וַיִּפֹּל עַל־פָּנָיו וַיֹּאמֶר הַאַתָּה זֶה
8 אֲדֹנִי אֵלִיָּהוּ׃ וַיֹּאמֶר לוֹ אָנִי לֵךְ אֱמֹר לַאדֹנֶיךָ הִנֵּה אֵלִיָּהוּ׃
9 וַיֹּאמֶר מֶה חָטָאתִי כִּי־אַתָּה נֹתֵן אֶת־עַבְדְּךָ בְּיַד אַחְאָב
י לַהֲמִיתֵנִי׃ חַי ׀ יְהֹוָה אֱלֹהֶיךָ אִם־יֶשׁ־גּוֹי וּמַמְלָכָה אֲשֶׁר

v. 5. כצ״ל כתיב וקרי

In the Sedrah, the people worship the Golden Calf. In the Haftorah, centuries later, their descendants in the time of King Ahab are wavering between God and Baal. Ahab was a generous ruler, but weak-willed and dominated by his Phœnician wife, who pursued the prophets with murderous cruelty. It was high treason to proclaim the God of Israel. Against this dark setting, the figure of Elijah stands out in all its greatness. He meets and confronts the king and queen, and fearlessly pronounces the doom that will follow upon their apostasy and their outrage of justice. On Mt. Carmel, though he is alone and defenceless, his titanic personality overawes the multitude at that historic scene. He brings the people back to God in an overwhelming act of surrender. Their confession: *Adonay, hu ha-elohim*, 'The Lord, He is God,' has become, alongside the declaration of the Unity, Israel's watchword. Elijah, the timeless and deathless Prophet, is the champion of Purity of Worship and Justice to fellow-man. He is a type of Israel.

1. *in the third year. i.e.* of the drought; see I Kings xvii, 1.

Elijah. To him the conflict between the worship of God and Baal was 'a conflict between two diametrically opposite religious principles which could not exist side by side; *i.e.* an immoral Nature-religion and the ethical Religion of Israel' (Skinner).

2. *Samaria.* The capital of the kingdom of Israel.

4. *Jezebel cut off.* Summarizes the persecution of the Prophets, *i.e.* members of the Prophetical schools, who aroused her murderous wrath because their activity was directed against her paganizing influence.

hid them fifty. In separate bands of 50 each, to save them from extermination by Jezebel.

fed them with bread and water. Water was scarce and more precious than gold during those days of the drought; but he procured it for them at all costs—a striking testimony of his loyalty to the cause of God.

7. *fell on his face.* In reverence.

9. *to slay me.* He feared that, after Ahab had received the message, Elijah would vanish

not. 11. And now thou sayest: Go, tell thy lord: Behold, Elijah is here. 12. And it will come to pass, as soon as I am gone from thee, that the spirit of the LORD will carry thee whither I know not; and so when I come and tell Ahab, and he cannot find thee, he will slay me; but I thy servant fear the LORD from my youth. 13. Was it not told my lord what I did when Jezebel slew the prophets of the LORD, how I hid a hundred men of the LORD's prophets by fifty in a cave, and fed them with bread and water? 14. And now thou sayest: Go, tell thy lord: Behold, Elijah is here; and he will slay me.' 15. And Elijah said: 'As the LORD of hosts liveth, before whom I stand, I will surely show myself unto him to-day.' ¶ 16. So Obadiah went to meet Ahab, and told him; and Ahab went to meet Elijah. 17. And it came to pass, when Ahab saw Elijah, that Ahab said unto him: 'Is it thou, thou troubler of Israel?' 18. And he answered: 'I have not troubled Israel; but thou, and thy father's house, in that ye have forsaken the commandments of the LORD, and thou hast followed the Baalim. 19. Now therefore send, and gather to me all Israel unto mount Carmel, and the prophets of Baal four hundred and fifty, and the prophets of the Asherah four hundred, that eat at Jezebel's table.' ¶ 20. And Ahab sent unto all the children of Israel, and gathered the prophets together unto mount Carmel. 21. And Elijah came near unto all the people, and said: 'How long halt ye between two opinions? if the LORD be God, follow Him; but if Baal, follow him.' And the people answered him not a word. 22. Then said Elijah unto the people: 'I, even I only, am left a prophet of the LORD; but Baal's prophets are four hundred and fifty men. 23. Let them therefore give us two bullocks; and let them choose one bullock for themselves, and cut it in pieces, and lay it on the wood, and put no fire under; and I will dress the other bullock, and lay it on the

לֹא־שָׁלַח אֲדֹנִי שָׁם לְבַקֶּשְׁךָ וְאָמְרוּ אָיִן וְהִשְׁבִּיעַ אֶת־
11 הַמַּמְלָכָה וְאֶת־הַגּוֹי כִּי לֹא יִמְצָאֶכָּה׃ וְעַתָּה אַתָּה אֹמֵר
12 לֵךְ אֱמֹר לַאדֹנֶיךָ הִנֵּה אֵלִיָּהוּ׃ וְהָיָה אֲנִי ׀ אֵלֵךְ מֵאִתָּךְ
וְרוּחַ יְהוָה ׀ יִשָּׂאֲךָ עַל־אֲשֶׁר לֹא־אֵדָע וּבָאתִי לְהַגִּיד לְאַחְאָב
13 וְלֹא יִמְצָאֲךָ וַהֲרָגָנִי וְעַבְדְּךָ יָרֵא אֶת־יְהוָה מִנְּעֻרָי׃ הֲלֹא־
הֻגַּד לַאדֹנִי אֵת אֲשֶׁר־עָשִׂיתִי בַּהֲרֹג אִיזֶבֶל אֵת נְבִיאֵי
יְהוָה וָאַחְבִּא מִנְּבִיאֵי יְהוָה מֵאָה אִישׁ חֲמִשִּׁים חֲמִשִּׁים
14 אִישׁ בַּמְּעָרָה וָאֲכַלְכְּלֵם לֶחֶם וָמָיִם׃ וְעַתָּה אַתָּה אֹמֵר
טו לֵךְ אֱמֹר לַאדֹנֶיךָ הִנֵּה אֵלִיָּהוּ וַהֲרָגָנִי׃ וַיֹּאמֶר אֵלִיָּהוּ
חַי יְהוָה צְבָאוֹת אֲשֶׁר עָמַדְתִּי לְפָנָיו כִּי הַיּוֹם אֵרָאֶה
16 אֵלָיו׃ וַיֵּלֶךְ עֹבַדְיָהוּ לִקְרַאת אַחְאָב וַיַּגֶּד־לוֹ וַיֵּלֶךְ אַחְאָב
17 לִקְרַאת אֵלִיָּהוּ׃ וַיְהִי כִּרְאוֹת אַחְאָב אֶת־אֵלִיָּהוּ וַיֹּאמֶר
18 אַחְאָב אֵלָיו הַאַתָּה זֶה עֹכֵר יִשְׂרָאֵל׃ וַיֹּאמֶר לֹא עָכַרְתִּי
אֶת־יִשְׂרָאֵל כִּי אִם־אַתָּה וּבֵית אָבִיךָ בַּעֲזָבְכֶם אֶת־מִצְוֹת
19 יְהוָה וַתֵּלֶךְ אַחֲרֵי הַבְּעָלִים׃ וְעַתָּה שְׁלַח קְבֹץ אֵלַי אֶת־
כָּל־יִשְׂרָאֵל אֶל־הַר הַכַּרְמֶל וְאֶת־נְבִיאֵי הַבַּעַל אַרְבַּע־
מֵאוֹת וַחֲמִשִּׁים וּנְבִיאֵי הָאֲשֵׁרָה אַרְבַּע מֵאוֹת אֹכְלֵי שֻׁלְחַן
כ אִיזָבֶל׃ וַיִּשְׁלַח אַחְאָב בְּכָל־בְּנֵי יִשְׂרָאֵל וַיִּקְבֹּץ אֶת־
21 הַנְּבִיאִים אֶל־הַר הַכַּרְמֶל׃ וַיִּגַּשׁ אֵלִיָּהוּ אֶל־כָּל־הָעָם
וַיֹּאמֶר עַד־מָתַי אַתֶּם פֹּסְחִים עַל־שְׁתֵּי הַסְּעִפִּים אִם־יְהוָה
הָאֱלֹהִים לְכוּ אַחֲרָיו וְאִם־הַבַּעַל לְכוּ אַחֲרָיו וְלֹא־עָנוּ
22 הָעָם אֹתוֹ דָּבָר׃ וַיֹּאמֶר אֵלִיָּהוּ אֶל־הָעָם אֲנִי נוֹתַרְתִּי
נָבִיא לַיהוָה לְבַדִּי וּנְבִיאֵי הַבַּעַל אַרְבַּע־מֵאוֹת וַחֲמִשִּׁים

v. 12. קמץ בז"ק v. 20. כאן מתחילין הספרדים v. 21. הפ' דגושה

as suddenly as he now appeared, and that he (Obadiah) would have to meet the king's fierce anger.

10. *there is no nation.* The exaggeration of fear.

12. *whither I know not.* Elijah's movements had made them accustomed to sudden disappearances to localities unknown to them (Rashi).

15. *the LORD of hosts.* A solemn description of the universal character of God, *i.e.* LORD and Ruler of all men and nations and all the forces of existence.

17. *thou troubler of Israel.* Alluding to Elijah's prediction of the drought.

18. *Baalim.* The plural of Baal, the name of the principal god of the Canaanites.

19. *Asherah.* The female counterpart of Baal, the Astarte of the Phœnicians.

20–39. THE DAY OF DECISION: THE LORD OR BAAL?

20. *mount Carmel.* The only mountain on the Palestine coast, rising to nearly 1,800 ft. above the sea level.

21. *how long halt ye between two opinions?* lit. 'how long will ye go limping, resting now on one foot, now on another?' Or, 'hopping between two branches,' like birds; *i.e.* at one time serving Baal, at another, the LORD.

wood, and put no fire under. 24. And call ye on the name of your god, and I will call on the name of the LORD; and the God that answereth by fire, let him be God.' And all the people answered and said: 'It is well spoken.' ¶ 25. And Elijah said unto the prophets of Baal: 'Choose you one bullock for yourselves, and dress it first; for ye are many; and call on the name of your god, but put no fire under.' 26. And they took the bullock which was given them, and they dressed it, and called on the name of Baal from morning even until noon, saying: 'O Baal, answer us.' But there was no voice, nor any that answered. And they danced in halting wise about the altar which was made. 27. And it came to pass at noon, that Elijah mocked them, and said: 'Cry aloud; for he is a god; either he is musing, or he is gone aside, or he is in a journey, or peradventure he sleepeth, and must be awaked.' 28. And they cried aloud, and cut themselves after their manner with swords and lances, till the blood gushed out upon them. 29. And it was so, when midday was past, that they prophesied until the time of the offering of the evening offering; but there was neither voice, nor any to answer, nor any that regarded. ¶ 30. And Elijah said unto all the people: 'Come near unto me'; and all the people came near unto him. And he repaired the altar of the LORD that was thrown down. 31. And Elijah took twelve stones, according to the number of the tribes of the sons of Jacob, unto whom the word of the LORD came, saying: 'Israel shall be thy name.' 32. And with the stones he built an altar in the name of the LORD; and he made a trench about the altar, as great as would contain two measures of seed. 33. And he put the wood in order, and cut the bullock in pieces, and laid it on the wood. 34. And he said: 'Fill four jars with water, and pour it on the burnt-offering, and on the wood.' And he said: 'Do it the second

23 איש׃ ויתנו־לנו שנים פרים ויבחרו להם הפר האחד
וינתחהו וישימו על־העצים ואש לא ישימו ואני אעשה ׀
את־הפר האחד ונתתי על־העצים ואש לא אשים׃
24 וקראתם בשם אלהיכם ואני אקרא בשם־יהוה והיה
האלהים אשר־יענה באש הוא האלהים ויען כל־העם
כה ויאמרו טוב הדבר׃ ויאמר אליהו לנביאי הבעל בחרו
לכם הפר האחד ועשו ראשנה כי אתם הרבים וקראו
26 בשם אלהיכם ואש לא תשימו׃ ויקחו את־הפר אשר־
נתן להם ויעשו ויקראו בשם־הבעל מהבקר ועד־
הצהרים לאמר הבעל עננו ואין קול ואין ענה ויפסחו
27 על־המזבח אשר עשה׃ ויהי בצהרים ויהתל בהם
אליהו ויאמר קראו בקול־גדול כי־אלהים הוא כי־שיח
28 וכי־שיג לו וכי־דרך לו אולי ישן הוא ויקץ׃ ויקראו
בקול גדול ויתגדדו כמשפטם בחרבות וברמחים עד־
29 שפך־דם עליהם׃ ויהי כעבר הצהרים ויתנבאו עד
ל לעלות המנחה ואין־קול ואין־ענה ואין קשב׃ ויאמר
אליהו לכל־העם גשו אלי ויגשו כל־העם אליו וירפא
31 את־מזבח יהוה ההרוס׃ ויקח אליהו שתים עשרה
אבנים כמספר שבטי בני־יעקב אשר היה דבר־יהוה
32 אליו לאמר ישראל יהיה שמך׃ ויבנה את־האבנים
מזבח בשם יהוה ויעש תעלה כבית סאתים זרע סביב
33 למזבח׃ ויערך את־העצים וינתח את־הפר וישם על־
34 העצים׃ ויאמר מלאו ארבעה כדים מים ויצקו על־

v. 27. הק׳ רפה

22. *am left a prophet of the LORD.* The other Prophets of the LORD were either killed, or in hiding.

26. *danced in halting wise.* Performed uncouth religious dances about the altar, as was customary in their ceremonies.

27. *for he is a god.* Spoke mockingly.

28. *cut themselves.* To excite the pity of their gods Elijah's taunts stir them to a condition of frenzy.

29. *prophesied.* The word is used here in its original sense; meaning, they worked themselves into a frenzy by ecstatic cries and convulsive contortions.

30. *the altar.* It was the site of an altar in the days of Saul (Rashi).

31. *twelve stones.* Although the ten tribes of the kingdom of Israel had broken away from Judah, in the eyes of the Prophets the nation was an undivided unity.

32. *he built an altar.* To build an altar and offer sacrifices outside the Temple Mount, after the central Sanctuary at Jerusalem had been erected, was an action contrary to the Torah; but was permitted as an exceptional measure to meet an exceptional situation—*horaath shaah.*

time'; and they did it the second time. And he said: 'Do it the third time'; and they did it the third time. 35. And the water ran round about the altar; and he filled the trench also with water. 36. And it came to pass at the time of the offering of the evening offering, that Elijah the prophet came near, and said: 'O LORD, the God of Abraham, of Isaac, and of Israel, let it be known this day that Thou art God in Israel, and that I am Thy servant, and that I have done all these things at Thy word. 37. Hear me, O LORD, hear me, that this people may know that Thou, LORD, art God, for Thou didst turn their heart backward.' 38. Then the fire of the LORD fell, and consumed the burnt-offering, and the wood, and the stones, and the dust, and licked up the water that was in the trench. 39. And when all the people saw it, they fell on their faces; and they said: 'The LORD, He is God; the LORD, He is God.'

הָעֹלָה וְעַל־הָעֵצִים וַיֹּאמֶר שְׁנוּ וַיִּשְׁנוּ וַיֹּאמֶר שַׁלֵּשׁוּ
לה וַיְשַׁלֵּשׁוּ׃ וַיֵּלְכוּ הַמַּיִם סָבִיב לַמִּזְבֵּחַ וְגַם אֶת־הַתְּעָלָה
36 מִלֵּא־מָיִם׃ וַיְהִי ׀ בַּעֲלוֹת הַמִּנְחָה וַיִּגַּשׁ אֵלִיָּהוּ הַנָּבִיא
וַיֹּאמַר יְהוָה אֱלֹהֵי אַבְרָהָם יִצְחָק וְיִשְׂרָאֵל הַיּוֹם יִוָּדַע כִּי־
אַתָּה אֱלֹהִים בְּיִשְׂרָאֵל וַאֲנִי עַבְדֶּךָ וּבִדְבָרֶיךָ עָשִׂיתִי אֵת
37 כָּל־הַדְּבָרִים הָאֵלֶּה׃ עֲנֵנִי יְהוָה עֲנֵנִי וְיֵדְעוּ הָעָם הַזֶּה
כִּי־אַתָּה יְהוָה הָאֱלֹהִים וְאַתָּה הֲסִבֹּתָ אֶת־לִבָּם אֲחֹרַנִּית׃
38 וַתִּפֹּל אֵשׁ־יְהוָה וַתֹּאכַל אֶת־הָעֹלָה וְאֶת־הָעֵצִים וְאֶת־
הָאֲבָנִים וְאֶת־הֶעָפָר וְאֶת־הַמַּיִם אֲשֶׁר־בַּתְּעָלָה לִחֵכָה׃
39 וַיַּרְא כָּל־הָעָם וַיִּפְּלוּ עַל־פְּנֵיהֶם וַיֹּאמְרוּ יְהוָה הוּא
הָאֱלֹהִים יְהוָה הוּא הָאֱלֹהִים׃

v. 36. נ"א לישראל ibid. יתיר י'

36. *let it be known . . . at Thy word.* That all Elijah's actions, even his prophecy of drought, were in accordance with the will of God. His prayer is that the people shall recognize this, and be brought back to faith in God alone.

39. *the LORD, He is God.* Not Baal, or any other. These words form the conclusion of the Day of Atonement Service, and are the last words uttered by the dying Israelite.

The contest on Mt. Carmel is typical of every conflict in which opposite principles of conduct with vital consequences to the individual or the nation stand face to face; in which conflict prompt decision is both urgent and, as in the days of Elijah, can alone ensure the victory of Right (Dummelow).

35

CHAPTER XXXV

1. And Moses assembled all the congregation of the children of Israel, and said unto them: 'These are the words which the LORD hath commanded, that ye should do them. 2. Six days shall work be done, but on the seventh day there shall be to you a holy day, a sabbath of solemn rest to the LORD; whosoever doeth any work therein shall be put to death. 3. Ye shall kindle no fire throughout your habitations upon the sabbath day.' ¶ 4. And Moses spoke unto all the congregation of the children of Israel, saying: 'This is the thing which the LORD commanded, saying: 5. Take ye from among you an offering unto the LORD, whosoever is of a willing heart, let him bring it, the LORD's offering: gold, and silver, and brass; 6. and blue, and purple, and scarlet, and fine linen, and goats' hair; 7. and rams' skins dyed red, and sealskins, and acacia-wood; 8. and oil for the light, and spices for the anointing oil, and for the sweet incense; 9. and onyx stones, and stones to be set, for the ephod, and for the breastplate. 10. And let every wise-hearted man among you come, and make all that the LORD hath commanded: 11. the tabernacle, its tent, and its covering, its clasps, and its boards, its bars, its pillars, and its sockets; 12. the ark, and the staves thereof, the ark-cover, and the veil of the screen; 13. the

לה

CAP. XXXV. לה

ס ס ס כב 22

א וַיַּקְהֵל מֹשֶׁה אֶת־כָּל־עֲדַת בְּנֵי יִשְׂרָאֵל וַיֹּאמֶר אֲלֵהֶם

2 אֵלֶּה הַדְּבָרִים אֲשֶׁר־צִוָּה יְהוָה לַעֲשֹׂת אֹתָם׃ שֵׁשֶׁת יָמִים

תֵּעָשֶׂה מְלָאכָה וּבַיּוֹם הַשְּׁבִיעִי יִהְיֶה לָכֶם קֹדֶשׁ שַׁבַּת

3 שַׁבָּתוֹן לַיהוָה כָּל־הָעֹשֶׂה בוֹ מְלָאכָה יוּמָת׃ לֹא־תְבַעֲרוּ

אֵשׁ בְּכֹל מֹשְׁבֹתֵיכֶם בְּיוֹם הַשַּׁבָּת׃ פ

4 וַיֹּאמֶר מֹשֶׁה אֶל־כָּל־עֲדַת בְּנֵי־יִשְׂרָאֵל לֵאמֹר זֶה הַדָּבָר

ה אֲשֶׁר־צִוָּה יְהוָה לֵאמֹר׃ קְחוּ מֵאִתְּכֶם תְּרוּמָה לַיהוָה כֹּל

נְדִיב לִבּוֹ יְבִיאֶהָ אֵת תְּרוּמַת יְהוָה זָהָב וָכֶסֶף וּנְחֹשֶׁת׃

6 7 וּתְכֵלֶת וְאַרְגָּמָן וְתוֹלַעַת שָׁנִי וְשֵׁשׁ וְעִזִּים׃ וְעֹרֹת אֵילִם

8 מְאָדָּמִים וְעֹרֹת תְּחָשִׁים וַעֲצֵי שִׁטִּים׃ וְשֶׁמֶן לַמָּאוֹר

9 וּבְשָׂמִים לְשֶׁמֶן הַמִּשְׁחָה וְלִקְטֹרֶת הַסַּמִּים׃ וְאַבְנֵי־שֹׁהַם

י וְאַבְנֵי מִלֻּאִים לָאֵפוֹד וְלַחֹשֶׁן׃ וְכָל־חֲכַם־לֵב בָּכֶם יָבֹאוּ

11 וְיַעֲשׂוּ אֵת כָּל־אֲשֶׁר צִוָּה יְהוָה׃ אֶת־הַמִּשְׁכָּן אֶת־אָהֳלוֹ

וְאֶת־מִכְסֵהוּ אֶת־קְרָסָיו וְאֶת־קְרָשָׁיו אֶת־בְּרִיחָו אֶת־עַמֻּדָיו

v. 11. בריחיו ק'

X. VAYYAKHEL

(CHAPTERS XXXV–XXXVIII, 20)

CHAPTER XXXV

We now enter upon the final section of the Book of Exodus dealing with the actual construction of the Sanctuary. Instead of giving a brief notice announcing the execution of the Divine command, Scripture describes in detail how every instruction was faithfully and lovingly carried out.

1. *assembled.* The Rabbis, assuming that Moses would lose no time in starting upon the work, declare that the assembly occurred on the 11th of Tishri, immediately after his descent from Sinai on the day which was to become the Day of Atonement (see on XXXIV, 4).

all the congregation. The Sanctuary was the concern of every individual in Israel.

2, 3. THE SABBATH

2. *a holy day.* lit. 'holiness.' The exhortation which God had given to Moses concerning the holiness of the Sabbath which must not be violated even for the sacred purpose of building the Tabernacle (XXXI, 13 f), is repeated by Moses to the Congregation.

3. *kindle no fire.* This command has been understood by certain Jewish sects to prohibit even the *enjoyment* of light or fire on the Sabbath; the Rabbis, however, apply it only to cooking and baking. In connection with the Manna, it had already been pointed out that there must be no preparation of food by fire on the Sabbath (XVI, 23).

your habitations. This excludes the Sanctuary. Lamps and the fire on the altar were there attended to on the Sabbath.

upon the sabbath day. On Festivals (barring the Day of Atonement, which is the 'Sabbath of Sabbaths') kindling of fire is permitted.

4. *commanded, saying.* 'Saying' is not here the equivalent of 'namely', but of 'to say'; *i.e.* that I should say to you.

5. *from among you.* Better, *from you.*

brass. Better, *bronze.*

6–9. Corresponding to XXV, 4–7.

10. *wise-hearted.* See on XXVIII, 3.

11. *tabernacle.* See on XXVI, 1.

covering. See XXVI, 14.

table, and its staves, and all its vessels, and the showbread; 14. the candlestick also for the light, and its vessels, and its lamps, and the oil for the light; 15. and the altar of incense, and its staves, and the anointing oil, and the sweet incense, and the screen for the door, at the door of the tabernacle; 16. the altar of burnt-offering, with its grating of brass, its staves, and all its vessels, the laver and its base; 17. the hangings of the court, the pillars thereof, and their sockets, and the screen for the gate of the court; 18. the pins of the tabernacle, and the pins of the court, and their cords; 19. the plaited garments, for ministering in the holy place, the holy garments for Aaron the priest, and the garments of his sons, to minister in the priest's office.' ¶ 20. And all the congregation of the children of Israel departed from the presence of Moses.* ii. 21. And they came, every one whose heart stirred him up, and every one whom his spirit made willing, and brought the LORD's offering, for the work of the tent of meeting, and for all the service thereof, and for the holy garments. 22. And they came, both men and women, as many as were willing-hearted, and brought nose-rings, and ear-rings, and signet-rings, and girdles, all jewels of gold; even every man that brought an offering of gold unto the LORD. 23. And every man, with whom was found blue, and purple, and scarlet, and fine linen, and goats' hair, and rams' skins dyed red, and sealskins, brought them. 24. Every one that did set apart an offering of silver and brass brought the LORD's offering; and every man, with whom was found acacia-wood for any work of the service, brought it. 25. And all the women that were wise-hearted did spin with their hands, and brought that which they had spun, the blue,

12 וְאֶת־אֲדָנָיו׃ אֶת־הָאָרֹן וְאֶת־בַּדָּיו אֶת־הַכַּפֹּרֶת וְאֵת פָּרֹכֶת
13 הַמָּסָךְ׃ אֶת־הַשֻּׁלְחָן וְאֶת־בַּדָּיו וְאֶת־כָּל־כֵּלָיו וְאֵת לֶחֶם
14 הַפָּנִים׃ וְאֶת־מְנֹרַת הַמָּאוֹר וְאֶת־כֵּלֶיהָ וְאֶת־נֵרֹתֶיהָ וְאֵת
טו שֶׁמֶן הַמָּאוֹר׃ וְאֶת־מִזְבַּח הַקְּטֹרֶת וְאֶת־בַּדָּיו וְאֵת שֶׁמֶן
הַמִּשְׁחָה וְאֵת קְטֹרֶת הַסַּמִּים וְאֶת־מָסַךְ הַפֶּתַח לְפֶתַח
16 הַמִּשְׁכָּן׃ אֵת ׀ מִזְבַּח הָעֹלָה וְאֶת־מִכְבַּר הַנְּחֹשֶׁת אֲשֶׁר־
17 לוֹ אֶת־בַּדָּיו וְאֶת־כָּל־כֵּלָיו אֶת־הַכִּיֹּר וְאֶת־כַּנּוֹ׃ אֵת קַלְעֵי
הֶחָצֵר אֶת־עַמֻּדָיו וְאֶת־אֲדָנֶיהָ וְאֵת מָסַךְ שַׁעַר הֶחָצֵר׃
18 אֶת־יִתְדֹת הַמִּשְׁכָּן וְאֶת־יִתְדֹת הֶחָצֵר וְאֶת־מֵיתְרֵיהֶם׃
19 אֶת־בִּגְדֵי הַשְּׂרָד לְשָׁרֵת בַּקֹּדֶשׁ אֶת־בִּגְדֵי הַקֹּדֶשׁ לְאַהֲרֹן
כ הַכֹּהֵן וְאֶת־בִּגְדֵי בָנָיו לְכַהֵן׃ וַיֵּצְאוּ כָּל־עֲדַת בְּנֵי־יִשְׂרָאֵל
שני 21 מִלִּפְנֵי מֹשֶׁה׃ וַיָּבֹאוּ כָּל־אִישׁ אֲשֶׁר־נְשָׂאוֹ לִבּוֹ וְכֹל אֲשֶׁר
נָדְבָה רוּחוֹ אֹתוֹ הֵבִיאוּ אֶת־תְּרוּמַת יְהוָה לִמְלֶאכֶת אֹהֶל
22 מוֹעֵד וּלְכָל־עֲבֹדָתוֹ וּלְבִגְדֵי הַקֹּדֶשׁ׃ וַיָּבֹאוּ הָאֲנָשִׁים
עַל־הַנָּשִׁים כֹּל ׀ נְדִיב לֵב הֵבִיאוּ חָח וָנֶזֶם וְטַבַּעַת וְכוּמָז
כָּל־כְּלִי זָהָב וְכָל־אִישׁ אֲשֶׁר הֵנִיף תְּנוּפַת זָהָב לַיהוָה׃
23 וְכָל־אִישׁ אֲשֶׁר־נִמְצָא אִתּוֹ תְּכֵלֶת וְאַרְגָּמָן וְתוֹלַעַת שָׁנִי
וְשֵׁשׁ וְעִזִּים וְעֹרֹת אֵילִם מְאָדָּמִים וְעֹרֹת תְּחָשִׁים הֵבִיאוּ׃
24 כָּל־מֵרִים תְּרוּמַת כֶּסֶף וּנְחֹשֶׁת הֵבִיאוּ אֵת תְּרוּמַת יְהוָה
וְכֹל אֲשֶׁר נִמְצָא אִתּוֹ עֲצֵי שִׁטִּים לְכָל־מְלֶאכֶת הָעֲבֹדָה
כה הֵבִיאוּ׃ וְכָל־אִשָּׁה חַכְמַת־לֵב בְּיָדֶיהָ טָווּ וַיָּבִיאוּ מַטְוֶה

12. *ark.* See xxv, 10–22.
veil of the screen. In front of the Holy of Holies (xxvi, 31).

13. *table.* See xxv, 23.
showbread. See xxv, 30.

14. *candlestick.* See xxv, 31.
oil. See xxvii, 20.

15. *altar of incense.* See xxx, 1.
anointing oil. See xxx, 23 f.
sweet incense. See xxx, 34 f.
screen. See xxvi, 36.

16. *altar of burnt-offering.* See xxvii, 1.
the laver. See xxx, 18.

17. *hangings.* See xxvii, 9.
screen for the gate. See xxvii, 16.

18. *pins.* See xxvii, 19.
cords. These were not specified in the earlier chapters, but the mention of 'pins' presupposes the use of cords to which they were fastened.

19. *plaited garments.* See xxxi, 10.
holy garments. See chap. xxviii.

20–29. THE RESPONSE OF THE PEOPLE

20. *all the congregation.* All were ready and eager to share in the erection of the Sanctuary.

21. *whom his spirit made willing.* Cf. xxv, 2. Moses depended upon the enthusiasm of the people for freewill offerings; he had no need to resort to a levy.

22. *women.* Although nothing was asked of them, they freely contributed their ornaments.
ear-rings. Or, 'bracelets' (Rashi).
girdles. The Heb. *kumaz* occurs again only in Num. xxxi, 50.

and the purple, the scarlet, and the fine linen. 26. And all the women whose heart stirred them up in wisdom spun the goats' hair. 27. And the rulers brought the onyx stones, and the stones to be set, for the ephod, and for the breastplate; 28. and the spice, and the oil, for the light, and for the anointing oil, and for the sweet incense. 29. The children of Israel brought a freewill-offering unto the LORD; every man and woman, whose heart made them willing to bring for all the work, which the LORD had commanded by the hand of Moses to be made. *iii(**ii). ¶ 30. And Moses said unto the children of Israel: 'See, the LORD hath called by name Bezalel the son of Uri, the son of Hur, of the tribe of Judah. 31. And He hath filled him with the spirit of God, in wisdom, in understanding, and in knowledge, and in all manner of workmanship. 32. And to devise skilful works, to work in gold, and in silver, and in brass, 33. and in cutting of stones for setting, and in carving of wood, to work in all manner of skilful workmanship. 34. And He hath put in his heart that he may teach, both he, and Oholiab, the son of Ahisamach, of the tribe of Dan. 35. Them hath He filled with

אֶת־הַתְּכֵלֶת וְאֶת־הָֽאַרְגָּמָן אֶת־תּוֹלַעַת הַשָּׁנִי וְאֶת־הַשֵּׁשׁ׃
26 וְכָל־הַנָּשִׁים אֲשֶׁר נָשָׂא לִבָּן אֹתָנָה בְּחָכְמָה טָווּ אֶת־
27 הָֽעִזִּים׃ וְהַנְּשִׂאִם הֵבִיאוּ אֵת אַבְנֵי הַשֹּׁהַם וְאֵת אַבְנֵי
28 הַמִּלֻּאִים לָֽאֵפוֹד וְלַחֹשֶׁן׃ וְאֶת־הַבֹּשֶׂם וְאֶת־הַשָּׁמֶן לְמָאוֹר
29 וּלְשֶׁמֶן הַמִּשְׁחָה וְלִקְטֹרֶת הַסַּמִּים׃ כָּל־אִישׁ וְאִשָּׁה אֲשֶׁר
שי נָדַב לִבָּם אֹתָם לְהָבִיא לְכָל־הַמְּלָאכָה אֲשֶׁר צִוָּה יְהוָה
(כשהן חוב׳) לַעֲשׂוֹת בְּיַד־מֹשֶׁה הֵבִיאוּ בְנֵי־יִשְׂרָאֵל נְדָבָה לַיהוָה׃ * פ
ל וַיֹּאמֶר מֹשֶׁה אֶל־בְּנֵי יִשְׂרָאֵל רְאוּ קָרָא יְהוָה בְּשֵׁם
31 בְּצַלְאֵל בֶּן־אוּרִי בֶן־חוּר לְמַטֵּה יְהוּדָה׃ וַיְמַלֵּא אֹתוֹ
רוּחַ אֱלֹהִים בְּחָכְמָה בִּתְבוּנָה וּבְדַעַת וּבְכָל־מְלָאכָה׃
32 33 וְלַחְשֹׁב מַחֲשָׁבֹת לַעֲשֹׂת בַּזָּהָב וּבַכֶּסֶף וּבַנְּחֹשֶׁת׃ וּבַחֲרֹשֶׁת
אֶבֶן לְמַלֹּאת וּבַחֲרֹשֶׁת עֵץ לַעֲשׂוֹת בְּכָל־מְלֶאכֶת מַחֲשָׁבֶת׃
34 וּלְהוֹרֹת נָתַן בְּלִבּוֹ הוּא וְאָהֳלִיאָב בֶּן־אֲחִיסָמָךְ לְמַטֵּה־דָן׃
לה מִלֵּא אֹתָם חָכְמַת־לֵב לַעֲשׂוֹת כָּל־מְלֶאכֶת חָרָשׁ ׀ וְחֹשֵׁב

27. *rulers.* The leading men of the tribes.

30–XXXVI, 2

The appointment of the artificers of the Sanctuary. These sections are almost identical with XXXI, 1–6.

30. *the LORD hath called by name.* The artist is 'called'; *i.e.* specially endowed by native gift for his task; predestined, in a sense, for his artistic mission. The Rabbis explain the opening words, 'See, the LORD hath called, etc.' to mean that the nomination of Bezalel for his important task should be ratified by the community, as no leader may be set over a congregation without its approval.

Hur. The Rabbis identified him with the Hur of XVII, 10, XXIV, 14; and held that he was killed by the people for resisting their demand for the golden calf.

31. *the spirit of God.* Is regarded in Scripture as the source of any exceptional gift, power or activity of man; *e.g.*, Gen. XLI, 38, of administrative ability, and here of Bezalel's artistic capacity.

in wisdom . . . understanding . . . knowledge. i.e. displaying itself in artistic skill, whether that skill be the result of imitation, or the artist's own initiative and inspiration.

32. *to devise skilful works.* lit. 'to think thoughts.' In all true art, there is a vital underlying *thought*, and artists have accordingly been among the great thinkers of mankind. An eminent painter of the nineteenth century has well expressed it: 'My intention has not been so much to paint pictures that will charm the eye as to suggest great thoughts that will appeal to the imagination and the heart, and kindle all that is best and noblest in humanity. I even think, that in the future, art may yet speak, as great poetry itself, with the solemn and majestic ring in which the Hebrew prophets spoke to the Jews of old, demanding noble aspirations, condemning in the most trenchant manner private vices, and warning us in deep tones against lapses from morals and duties' (F. W. Watts).

33. *skilful workmanship.* We are accustomed to limit Divine inspiration to thoughts expressed in words. This is not the Scriptural view. The worker in metals, the cutter of precious stones, and the carver of wood can likewise produce work that is inspired.

34. *that he may teach. i.e.* direct and train others. The true artist possesses the power to inspire others. A light that cannot kindle other lights, is but a feeble flame. But להורת, 'to teach,' has also a wider meaning. The core of art is its teaching and ennobling influence not only on other artists, but on humanity.

wisdom of heart, to work all manner of workmanship, of the craftsman, and of the skilful workman, and of the weaver in colours, in blue, and in purple, in scarlet, and in fine linen, and of the weaver, even of them that do any workmanship, and of those that devise skilful works.

36

Chapter XXXVI

1. And Bezalel and Oholiab shall work, and every wise-hearted man, in whom the LORD hath put wisdom and understanding to know how to work all the work for the service of the sanctuary, according to all that the LORD hath commanded.' ¶ 2. And Moses called Bezalel and Oholiab, and every wise-hearted man, in whose heart the LORD had put wisdom, even every one whose heart stirred him up to come unto the work to do it. 3. And they received of Moses all the offering, which the children of Israel had brought for the work of the service of the sanctuary, wherewith to make it. And they brought yet unto him freewill-offerings every morning. 4. And

וְרֹקֵם בַּתְּכֵלֶת וּבָאַרְגָּמָן בְּתוֹלַעַת הַשָּׁנִי וּבַשֵּׁשׁ וְאֹרֵג
עֹשֵׂי כָּל־מְלָאכָה וְחֹשְׁבֵי מַחֲשָׁבֹת׃

לו

CAP. XXXVI. לו

א וְעָשָׂה בְצַלְאֵל וְאָהֳלִיאָב וְכֹל ׀ אִישׁ חֲכַם־לֵב אֲשֶׁר נָתַן
יְהוָה חָכְמָה וּתְבוּנָה בָּהֵמָּה לָדַעַת לַעֲשֹׂת אֶת־כָּל־
2 מְלֶאכֶת עֲבֹדַת הַקֹּדֶשׁ לְכֹל אֲשֶׁר־צִוָּה יְהוָה׃ וַיִּקְרָא מֹשֶׁה
אֶל־בְּצַלְאֵל וְאֶל־אָהֳלִיאָב וְאֶל כָּל־אִישׁ חֲכַם־לֵב אֲשֶׁר
נָתַן יְהוָה חָכְמָה בְּלִבּוֹ כֹּל אֲשֶׁר נְשָׂאוֹ לִבּוֹ לְקָרְבָה אֶל־
3 הַמְּלָאכָה לַעֲשֹׂת אֹתָהּ׃ וַיִּקְחוּ מִלִּפְנֵי מֹשֶׁה אֵת כָּל־
הַתְּרוּמָה אֲשֶׁר הֵבִיאוּ בְּנֵי יִשְׂרָאֵל לִמְלֶאכֶת עֲבֹדַת הַקֹּדֶשׁ
לַעֲשֹׂת אֹתָהּ וְהֵם הֵבִיאוּ אֵלָיו עוֹד נְדָבָה בַּבֹּקֶר בַּבֹּקֶר׃
4 וַיָּבֹאוּ כָּל־הַחֲכָמִים הָעֹשִׂים אֵת כָּל־מְלֶאכֶת הַקֹּדֶשׁ אִישׁ־

tribe of Dan. Bezalel belonged to Judah, the leading tribe: Oholiab, to one of the smaller tribes. The selection, declares the Midrash, was significant. In the service of God, the great and the small should be united.

Proper understanding and appreciation of these verses should modify current views on Judaism and its relation to Art. The opinion is often expressed that there is no art in Judaism; that the Jew lacks the æsthetic sense; and that this is largely due to the influence of the Second Commandment which prohibited plastic art in Israel. Defenders of the Jew and Judaism usually reply that Judaism was determined to lift the God-idea above the sensual, and to represent the Divine as spirit only; that Art was not Israel's predestined province; that whereas the legacy of Greece was Beauty, the mission of Israel was Righteousness. Neither friend nor foe do full justice to the facts of the case. There is not such a clear-cut difference between the races as is generally assumed. Greek Art itself is now seen to be of Semitic origin; and Semites have produced many a monument of surpassing beauty in the world of Art. And is not poetry, too, a province of Art? Surely, the Books of Psalms, Isaiah and Job need fear no comparison with any literary product of man. And the above applies not merely to the Bible age. The Rabbis, too, had a passionate love of beauty. They prescribed a special Benediction at the sight of a beautiful tree or animal, as well as on beholding the first blossoms of spring (Authorized Prayer Book, p. 291). Some of them conceived the whole of Creation as a process of unfolding beauty; and spoke of God as the Incomparable Artist (אין צור כאלהינו—אין צייר כאלהינו). The highest artist, in the eyes of Jewish teachers of all generations, is not the greatest master in self-expression, but in self-control; he who fashions *himself* into a sanctuary. Such a view sounds strange in modern ears. One of the saddest phenomena of the age is the misuse of Art for the perversion of Youth. Art is a divine gift, and must be divinely used. 'When the Hebrew spirit prevails over the Greek, he strips it of its pagan sensuality, so that its beauty stands revealed untarnished by barbaric or ungodly association' (Solomon J. Solomon).

Chapter XXXVI

1. *hath put wisdom.* 'God gives wisdom to him only who possesses wisdom,' is a paradoxical saying of the Rabbis. They were already wise-hearted; *i.e.* possessed of the necessary artistic aptitude, and God further endowed them with the requisite skill.

the service. i.e. the construction.

according to all. Better, '*with respect to all.*'

2. *to come unto.* lit. 'to draw near unto,' in order to participate in the construction.

3–7. The People's Liberality

3. *of Moses.* lit. 'from before Moses.' The donations of the people are represented as lying in a heap before Moses, and the artificers took what they required.

4. *which they wrought.* More accurately, 'which they were doing.'

all the wise men, that wrought all the work of the sanctuary, came every man from his work which they wrought. 5. And they spoke unto Moses, saying: 'The people bring much more than enough for the service of the work, which the LORD commanded to make.' 6. And Moses gave commandment, and they caused it to be proclaimed throughout the camp, saying: 'Let neither man nor woman make any more work for the offering of the sanctuary.' So the people were restrained from bringing. 7. For the stuff they had was sufficient for all the work to make it, and too much.*iv. ¶ 8. And every wise-hearted man among them that wrought the work made the tabernacle with ten curtains: of fine twined linen, and blue, and purple, and scarlet, with cherubim the work of the skilful workman made he them. 9. The length of each curtain was eight and twenty cubits, and the breadth of each curtain four cubits; all the curtains had one measure. 10. And he coupled five curtains one to another; and the other five curtains he coupled one to another. 11. And he made loops of blue upon the edge of the one curtain that was outmost in the first set; likewise he made in the edge of the curtain that was outmost in the second set. 12. Fifty loops made he in the one curtain, and fifty loops made he in the edge of the curtain that was in the second set; the loops were opposite one to another. 13. And he made fifty clasps of gold, and coupled the curtains one to another with the clasps: so the tabernacle was one. ¶ 14. And he made curtains of goats' hair for a tent over the tabernacle; eleven curtains he made them. 15. The length of each curtain was thirty cubits, and four cubits the breadth of each curtain; the eleven curtains had one measure. 16. And he coupled five curtains by themselves, and six curtains by themselves. 17. And he made fifty loops on the edge of the curtain that was outmost in the first set, and fifty loops made he upon the edge of the curtain which was outmost in the second set. 18. And he made fifty clasps of brass to couple the tent together, that it might be one. 19. And he made a covering for the tent of rams' skins dyed red, and a covering of sealskins above.* v. ¶ 20. And he made the boards for the tabernacle of acacia-wood, standing up. 21. Ten cubits was the length of a board, and a cubit and a half the breadth of each board. 22. Each board had two tenons, joined one to another. Thus did he make for all the

ה אִישׁ מִמְּלַאכְתּוֹ אֲשֶׁר־הֵמָּה עֹשִׂים׃ וַיֹּאמְרוּ אֶל־מֹשֶׁה
לֵּאמֹר מַרְבִּים הָעָם לְהָבִיא מִדֵּי הָעֲבֹדָה לַמְּלָאכָה אֲשֶׁר־
6 צִוָּה יְהוָה לַעֲשֹׂת אֹתָהּ׃ וַיְצַו מֹשֶׁה וַיַּעֲבִירוּ קוֹל בַּמַּחֲנֶה
לֵאמֹר אִישׁ וְאִשָּׁה אַל־יַעֲשׂוּ־עוֹד מְלָאכָה לִתְרוּמַת הַקֹּדֶשׁ
7 וַיִּכָּלֵא הָעָם מֵהָבִיא׃ וְהַמְּלָאכָה הָיְתָה דַיָּם לְכָל־הַמְּלָאכָה
רביעי 8 לַעֲשׂוֹת אֹתָהּ וְהוֹתֵר׃ ס וַיַּעֲשׂוּ כָל־חֲכַם־לֵב בְּעֹשֵׂי
הַמְּלָאכָה אֶת־הַמִּשְׁכָּן עֶשֶׂר יְרִיעֹת שֵׁשׁ מָשְׁזָר וּתְכֵלֶת
וְאַרְגָּמָן וְתוֹלַעַת שָׁנִי כְּרֻבִים מַעֲשֵׂה חֹשֵׁב עָשָׂה אֹתָם׃
9 אֹרֶךְ הַיְרִיעָה הָאַחַת שְׁמֹנֶה וְעֶשְׂרִים בָּאַמָּה וְרֹחַב אַרְבַּע
י בָּאַמָּה הַיְרִיעָה הָאֶחָת מִדָּה אַחַת לְכָל־הַיְרִיעֹת׃ וַיְחַבֵּר
אֶת־חֲמֵשׁ הַיְרִיעֹת אַחַת אֶל־אֶחָת וְחָמֵשׁ יְרִיעֹת חִבַּר אַחַת
11 אֶל־אֶחָת׃ וַיַּעַשׂ לֻלְאֹת תְּכֵלֶת עַל שְׂפַת הַיְרִיעָה הָאֶחָת
מִקָּצָה בַּמַּחְבָּרֶת כֵּן עָשָׂה בִּשְׂפַת הַיְרִיעָה הַקִּיצוֹנָה
12 בַּמַּחְבֶּרֶת הַשֵּׁנִית׃ חֲמִשִּׁים לֻלָאֹת עָשָׂה בַּיְרִיעָה הָאֶחָת
וַחֲמִשִּׁים לֻלָאֹת עָשָׂה בִּקְצֵה הַיְרִיעָה אֲשֶׁר בַּמַּחְבֶּרֶת
13 הַשֵּׁנִית מַקְבִּילֹת הַלֻּלָאֹת אַחַת אֶל־אֶחָת׃ וַיַּעַשׂ חֲמִשִּׁים
קַרְסֵי זָהָב וַיְחַבֵּר אֶת־הַיְרִיעֹת אַחַת אֶל־אַחַת בַּקְּרָסִים
וַיְהִי הַמִּשְׁכָּן אֶחָד׃ פ
14 וַיַּעַשׂ יְרִיעֹת עִזִּים לְאֹהֶל עַל־הַמִּשְׁכָּן עַשְׁתֵּי־עֶשְׂרֵה יְרִיעֹת
טו עָשָׂה אֹתָם׃ אֹרֶךְ הַיְרִיעָה הָאַחַת שְׁלֹשִׁים בָּאַמָּה וְאַרְבַּע
אַמּוֹת רֹחַב הַיְרִיעָה הָאֶחָת מִדָּה אַחַת לְעַשְׁתֵּי עֶשְׂרֵה
16 יְרִיעֹת׃ וַיְחַבֵּר אֶת־חֲמֵשׁ הַיְרִיעֹת לְבָד וְאֶת־שֵׁשׁ הַיְרִיעֹת
17 לְבָד׃ וַיַּעַשׂ לֻלָאֹת חֲמִשִּׁים עַל שְׂפַת הַיְרִיעָה הַקִּיצֹנָה
בַּמַּחְבָּרֶת וַחֲמִשִּׁים לֻלָאֹת עָשָׂה עַל־שְׂפַת הַיְרִיעָה הַחֹבֶרֶת
18 הַשֵּׁנִית׃ וַיַּעַשׂ קַרְסֵי נְחֹשֶׁת חֲמִשִּׁים לְחַבֵּר אֶת־הָאֹהֶל
19 לִהְיֹת אֶחָד׃ וַיַּעַשׂ מִכְסֶה לָאֹהֶל עֹרֹת אֵילִם מְאָדָּמִים
חמישי כ וּמִכְסֵה עֹרֹת תְּחָשִׁים מִלְמָעְלָה׃ ס וַיַּעַשׂ אֶת־הַקְּרָשִׁים
21 לַמִּשְׁכָּן עֲצֵי שִׁטִּים עֹמְדִים׃ עֶשֶׂר אַמֹּת אֹרֶךְ הַקָּרֶשׁ
22 וְאַמָּה וַחֲצִי הָאַמָּה רֹחַב הַקֶּרֶשׁ הָאֶחָד׃ שְׁתֵּי יָדֹת לַקֶּרֶשׁ

v. 10. קמץ בז״ק

7. *sufficient . . . and too much.* Young and old, noble and commoner, were all aglow with holy enthusiasm, and cheerfully consecrated their diversity of gifts to the Sanctuary.

8–19. THE CURTAINS

Corresponding to XXVI, 1–11, 14.

הָאֶחָד מְשֻׁלָּבֹת אַחַת אֶל־אֶחָת כֵּן עָשָׂה לְכֹל קַרְשֵׁי
23 הַמִּשְׁכָּן׃ וַיַּעַשׂ אֶת־הַקְּרָשִׁים לַמִּשְׁכָּן עֶשְׂרִים קְרָשִׁים
24 לִפְאַת נֶגֶב תֵּימָנָה׃ וְאַרְבָּעִים אַדְנֵי־כֶסֶף עָשָׂה תַּחַת
עֶשְׂרִים הַקְּרָשִׁים שְׁנֵי אֲדָנִים תַּחַת־הַקֶּרֶשׁ הָאֶחָד לִשְׁתֵּי
יְדֹתָיו וּשְׁנֵי אֲדָנִים תַּחַת־הַקֶּרֶשׁ הָאֶחָד לִשְׁתֵּי יְדֹתָיו׃
כה וּלְצֶלַע הַמִּשְׁכָּן הַשֵּׁנִית לִפְאַת צָפוֹן עָשָׂה עֶשְׂרִים קְרָשִׁים׃
26 וְאַרְבָּעִים אַדְנֵיהֶם כָּסֶף שְׁנֵי אֲדָנִים תַּחַת הַקֶּרֶשׁ הָאֶחָד
27 וּשְׁנֵי אֲדָנִים תַּחַת הַקֶּרֶשׁ הָאֶחָד׃ וּלְיַרְכְּתֵי הַמִּשְׁכָּן יָמָּה
28 עָשָׂה שִׁשָּׁה קְרָשִׁים׃ וּשְׁנֵי קְרָשִׁים עָשָׂה לִמְקֻצְעֹת הַמִּשְׁכָּן
29 בַּיַּרְכָתָיִם׃ וְהָיוּ תוֹאֲמִם מִלְּמַטָּה וְיַחְדָּו יִהְיוּ תַמִּים אֶל־
רֹאשׁוֹ אֶל־הַטַּבַּעַת הָאֶחָת כֵּן עָשָׂה לִשְׁנֵיהֶם לִשְׁנֵי
ל הַמִּקְצֹעֹת׃ וְהָיוּ שְׁמֹנָה קְרָשִׁים וְאַדְנֵיהֶם כֶּסֶף שִׁשָּׁה עָשָׂר
31 אֲדָנִים שְׁנֵי אֲדָנִים תַּחַת הַקֶּרֶשׁ הָאֶחָד׃ וַיַּעַשׂ
בְרִיחֵי עֲצֵי שִׁטִּים חֲמִשָּׁה לְקַרְשֵׁי צֶלַע־הַמִּשְׁכָּן הָאֶחָת׃
32 וַחֲמִשָּׁה בְרִיחִם לְקַרְשֵׁי צֶלַע־הַמִּשְׁכָּן הַשֵּׁנִית וַחֲמִשָּׁה
33 בְרִיחִם לְקַרְשֵׁי הַמִּשְׁכָּן לַיַּרְכָתַיִם יָמָּה׃ וַיַּעַשׂ אֶת־הַבְּרִיחַ
34 הַתִּיכֹן לִבְרֹחַ בְּתוֹךְ הַקְּרָשִׁים מִן־הַקָּצֶה אֶל־הַקָּצֶה׃ וְאֶת־
הַקְּרָשִׁים צִפָּה זָהָב וְאֶת־טַבְּעֹתָם עָשָׂה זָהָב בָּתִּים לַבְּרִיחִם
לה וַיְצַף אֶת־הַבְּרִיחִם זָהָב׃ וַיַּעַשׂ אֶת־הַפָּרֹכֶת תְּכֵלֶת וְאַרְגָּמָן
וְתוֹלַעַת שָׁנִי וְשֵׁשׁ מָשְׁזָר מַעֲשֵׂה חֹשֵׁב עָשָׂה אֹתָהּ כְּרֻבִים׃
36 וַיַּעַשׂ לָהּ אַרְבָּעָה עַמּוּדֵי שִׁטִּים וַיְצַפֵּם זָהָב וָוֵיהֶם זָהָב
37 וַיִּצֹק לָהֶם אַרְבָּעָה אַדְנֵי־כָסֶף׃ וַיַּעַשׂ מָסָךְ לְפֶתַח הָאֹהֶל
תְּכֵלֶת וְאַרְגָּמָן וְתוֹלַעַת שָׁנִי וְשֵׁשׁ מָשְׁזָר מַעֲשֵׂה רֹקֵם׃
38 וְאֶת־עַמּוּדָיו חֲמִשָּׁה וְאֶת־וָוֵיהֶם וְצִפָּה רָאשֵׁיהֶם וַחֲשֻׁקֵיהֶם
זָהָב וְאַדְנֵיהֶם חֲמִשָּׁה נְחֹשֶׁת׃ פ

boards of the tabernacle. 23. And he made the boards for the tabernacle; twenty boards for the south side southward. 24. And he made forty sockets of silver under the twenty boards: two sockets under one board for its two tenons, and two sockets under another board for its two tenons. 25. And for the second side of the tabernacle, on the north side, he made twenty boards, 26. and their forty sockets of silver: two sockets under one board, and two sockets under another board. 27. And for the hinder part of the tabernacle westward he made six boards. 28. And two boards made he for the corners of the tabernacle in the hinder part; 29. that they might be double beneath, and in like manner they should be complete unto the top thereof unto the first ring. Thus he did to both of them in the two corners. 30. And there were eight boards, and their sockets of silver, sixteen sockets: under every board two sockets. 31. And he made bars of acacia-wood: five for the boards of the one side of the tabernacle, 32. and five bars for the boards of the other side of the tabernacle, and five bars for the boards of the tabernacle for the hinder part westward. 33. And he made the middle bar to pass through in the midst of the boards from the one end to the other. 34. And he overlaid the boards with gold, and made their rings of gold for holders for the bars, and overlaid the bars with gold. ¶ 35. And he made the veil of blue, and purple, and scarlet, and fine twined linen; with cherubim the work of the skilful workman made he it. 36. And he made thereunto four pillars of acacia, and overlaid them with gold, their hooks being of gold; and he cast for them four sockets of silver. 37. And he made a screen for the door of the Tent, of blue, and purple, and scarlet, and fine twined linen, the work of the weaver in colours; 38. and the five pillars of it with their hooks; and he overlaid their capitals and their fillets with gold; and their five sockets were of brass.

20–34. The Wooden Framework

Corresponding to xxvi, 15–29.

35–38. The Veil and Screen

Corresponding to xxvi, 31 f, 36 f.

38. *their fillets.* Better, *their sockets.* In the parallel passage (xxvi, 37), it is, 'overlay them (*i.e.* the pillars) with gold.' In addition to the verbal instructions given on Sinai, Moses was granted a vision wherein he saw a pattern of what was required. Hence many of the directions are not given in full detail. We have, therefore, to assume that the word 'them' is used vaguely, and Moses understood that not the whole of the pillars, but only the tops, were to be overlaid with gold.

37

CHAPTER XXXVII

1. And Bezalel made the ark of acacia-wood: two cubits and a half was the length of it, and a cubit and a half the breadth of it, and a cubit and a half the height of it. 2. And he overlaid it with pure gold within and without, and made a crown of gold to it round about. 3. And he cast for it four rings of gold, in the four feet thereof: even two rings on the one side of it, and two rings on the other side of it. 4. And he made staves of acacia-wood, and overlaid them with gold. 5. And he put the staves into the rings on the sides of the ark, to bear the ark. 6. And he made an ark-cover of pure gold: two cubits and a half was the length thereof, and a cubit and a half the breadth thereof. 7. And he made two cherubim of gold: of beaten work made he them, at the two ends of the ark-cover: 8. one cherub at the one end, and one cherub at the other end; of one piece with the ark-cover made he the cherubim at the two ends thereof. 9. And the cherubim spread out their wings on high, screening the ark-cover with their wings, with their faces one to another; toward the ark-cover were the faces of the cherubim. ¶ 10. And he made the table of acacia-wood: two cubits was the length thereof, and a cubit the breadth thereof, and a cubit and a half the height thereof. 11. And he overlaid it with pure gold, and made thereto a crown of gold round about. 12. And he made unto it a border of a handbreadth round about, and made a golden crown to the border thereof round about. 13. And he cast for it four rings of gold, and put the rings in the four corners that were on the four feet thereof. 14. Close by the border were the rings, the holders for the staves to bear the table. 15. And he made the staves of acacia-wood, and overlaid them with gold, to bear the table. 16. And he made the vessels which were upon the table, the dishes thereof, and the pans thereof, and the bowls thereof, and the jars thereof, wherewith to pour out, of pure gold.*vi (**iii). ¶ 17. And he made the candlestick of pure gold: of beaten work made he the candlestick, even its base, and its shaft; its cups, its knops, and its flowers, were of one piece with it. 18. And there were six branches going out of the sides thereof: three branches of the candlestick out of the one side thereof, and three branches of the

CAP. XXXVII. לז

לז

א וַיַּעַשׂ בְּצַלְאֵל אֶת־הָאָרֹן עֲצֵי שִׁטִּים אַמָּתַיִם וָחֵצִי אָרְכּוֹ
2 וְאַמָּה וָחֵצִי רָחְבּוֹ וְאַמָּה וָחֵצִי קֹמָתוֹ׃ וַיְצַפֵּהוּ זָהָב טָהוֹר
3 מִבַּיִת וּמִחוּץ וַיַּעַשׂ לוֹ זֵר זָהָב סָבִיב׃ וַיִּצֹק לוֹ אַרְבַּע
טַבְּעֹת זָהָב עַל אַרְבַּע פַּעֲמֹתָיו וּשְׁתֵּי טַבָּעֹת עַל־צַלְעוֹ
4 הָאֶחָת וּשְׁתֵּי טַבָּעֹת עַל־צַלְעוֹ הַשֵּׁנִית׃ וַיַּעַשׂ בַּדֵּי עֲצֵי
ה שִׁטִּים וַיְצַף אֹתָם זָהָב׃ וַיָּבֵא אֶת־הַבַּדִּים בַּטַּבָּעֹת עַל
6 צַלְעֹת הָאָרֹן לָשֵׂאת אֶת־הָאָרֹן׃ וַיַּעַשׂ כַּפֹּרֶת זָהָב טָהוֹר
7 אַמָּתַיִם וָחֵצִי אָרְכָּהּ וְאַמָּה וָחֵצִי רָחְבָּהּ׃ וַיַּעַשׂ שְׁנֵי כְרֻבִים
8 זָהָב מִקְשָׁה עָשָׂה אֹתָם מִשְּׁנֵי קְצוֹת הַכַּפֹּרֶת׃ כְּרוּב אֶחָד
מִקָּצָה מִזֶּה וּכְרוּב־אֶחָד מִקָּצָה מִזֶּה מִן־הַכַּפֹּרֶת עָשָׂה
9 אֶת־הַכְּרֻבִים מִשְּׁנֵי קְצוֹוֹתָו׃ וַיִּהְיוּ הַכְּרֻבִים פֹּרְשֵׂי כְנָפַיִם
לְמַעְלָה סֹכְכִים בְּכַנְפֵיהֶם עַל־הַכַּפֹּרֶת וּפְנֵיהֶם אִישׁ אֶל־
אָחִיו אֶל־הַכַּפֹּרֶת הָיוּ פְּנֵי הַכְּרֻבִים׃ פ
י וַיַּעַשׂ אֶת־הַשֻּׁלְחָן עֲצֵי שִׁטִּים אַמָּתַיִם אָרְכּוֹ וְאַמָּה רָחְבּוֹ
11 וְאַמָּה וָחֵצִי קֹמָתוֹ׃ וַיְצַף אֹתוֹ זָהָב טָהוֹר וַיַּעַשׂ לוֹ זֵר זָהָב
12 סָבִיב׃ וַיַּעַשׂ לוֹ מִסְגֶּרֶת טֹפַח סָבִיב וַיַּעַשׂ זֵר־זָהָב
13 לְמִסְגַּרְתּוֹ סָבִיב׃ וַיִּצֹק לוֹ אַרְבַּע טַבְּעֹת זָהָב וַיִּתֵּן אֶת־
14 הַטַּבָּעֹת עַל אַרְבַּע הַפֵּאֹת אֲשֶׁר לְאַרְבַּע רַגְלָיו׃ לְעֻמַּת
הַמִּסְגֶּרֶת הָיוּ הַטַּבָּעֹת בָּתִּים לַבַּדִּים לָשֵׂאת אֶת־הַשֻּׁלְחָן׃
טו וַיַּעַשׂ אֶת־הַבַּדִּים עֲצֵי שִׁטִּים וַיְצַף אֹתָם זָהָב לָשֵׂאת אֶת־
16 הַשֻּׁלְחָן׃ וַיַּעַשׂ אֶת־הַכֵּלִים ׀ אֲשֶׁר עַל־הַשֻּׁלְחָן אֶת־קְעָרֹתָיו
וְאֶת־כַּפֹּתָיו וְאֵת מְנַקִּיֹּתָיו וְאֶת־הַקְּשָׂוֹת אֲשֶׁר יֻסַּךְ בָּהֵן
זָהָב טָהוֹר׃ * פ ששי (שלישי כשהן מחוב׳)
17 וַיַּעַשׂ אֶת־הַמְּנֹרָה זָהָב טָהוֹר מִקְשָׁה עָשָׂה אֶת־הַמְּנֹרָה
18 יְרֵכָהּ וְקָנָהּ גְּבִיעֶיהָ כַּפְתֹּרֶיהָ וּפְרָחֶיהָ מִמֶּנָּה הָיוּ׃ וְשִׁשָּׁה
קָנִים יֹצְאִים מִצִּדֶּיהָ שְׁלֹשָׁה ׀ קְנֵי מְנֹרָה מִצִּדָּהּ הָאֶחָד

v. 8. קצותיו ק׳

CHAPTER XXXVII

1–9. THE ARK

Corresponding to xxv, 10–15, 18–20.

10–16. THE TABLE

Corresponding to xxv, 23–29.

17–24. THE CANDLESTICK

Corresponding to xxv, 31–39.

candlestick out of the other side thereof; 19. three cups made like almond-blossoms in one branch, a knop and a flower; and three cups made like almond-blossoms in the other branch, a knop and a flower. So for the six branches going out of the candlestick. 20. And in the candlestick were four cups made like almond-blossoms, the knops thereof, and the flowers thereof; 21. and a knop under two branches of one piece with it, and a knop under two branches of one piece with it, and a knop under two branches of one piece with it, for the six branches going out of it. 22. Their knops and their branches were of one piece with it; the whole of it was one beaten work of pure gold. 23. And he made the lamps thereof, seven, and the tongs thereof, and the snuffdishes thereof, of pure gold. 24. Of a talent of pure gold made he it, and all the vessels thereof. ¶ 25. And he made the altar of incense of acacia-wood: a cubit was the length thereof, and a cubit the breadth thereof, four-square; and two cubits was the height thereof; the horns thereof were of one piece with it. 26. And he overlaid it with pure gold, the top thereof, and the sides thereof round about, and the horns of it; and he made unto it a crown of gold round about. 27. And he made for it two golden rings under the crown thereof, upon the two ribs thereof, upon the two sides of it, for holders for staves wherewith to bear it. 28. And he made the staves of acacia-wood, and overlaid them with gold. 29. And he made the holy anointing oil, and the pure incense of sweet spices, after the art of the perfumer.* vii (** iv).

19 וּשְׁלֹשָׁה קְנֵי מְנֹרָה מִצִּדָּהּ הַשֵּׁנִי׃ שְׁלֹשָׁה גְבִעִים מְשֻׁקָּדִים
בַּקָּנֶה הָאֶחָד כַּפְתֹּר וָפֶרַח וּשְׁלֹשָׁה גְבִעִים מְשֻׁקָּדִים
בְּקָנֶה אֶחָד כַּפְתֹּר וָפָרַח כֵּן לְשֵׁשֶׁת הַקָּנִים הַיֹּצְאִים מִן
כ הַמְּנֹרָה׃ וּבַמְּנֹרָה אַרְבָּעָה גְבִעִים מְשֻׁקָּדִים כַּפְתֹּרֶיהָ
21 וּפְרָחֶיהָ׃ וְכַפְתֹּר תַּחַת שְׁנֵי הַקָּנִים מִמֶּנָּה וְכַפְתֹּר תַּחַת
שְׁנֵי הַקָּנִים מִמֶּנָּה וְכַפְתֹּר תַּחַת־שְׁנֵי הַקָּנִים מִמֶּנָּה
22 לְשֵׁשֶׁת הַקָּנִים הַיֹּצְאִים מִמֶּנָּה׃ כַּפְתֹּרֵיהֶם וּקְנֹתָם מִמֶּנָּה
23 הָיוּ כֻּלָּהּ מִקְשָׁה אַחַת זָהָב טָהוֹר׃ וַיַּעַשׂ אֶת־נֵרֹתֶיהָ
24 שִׁבְעָה וּמַלְקָחֶיהָ וּמַחְתֹּתֶיהָ זָהָב טָהוֹר׃ כִּכָּר זָהָב טָהוֹר
עָשָׂה אֹתָהּ וְאֵת כָּל־כֵּלֶיהָ׃ פ
כה וַיַּעַשׂ אֶת־מִזְבַּח הַקְּטֹרֶת עֲצֵי שִׁטִּים אַמָּה אָרְכּוֹ וְאַמָּה
26 רָחְבּוֹ רָבוּעַ וְאַמָּתַיִם קֹמָתוֹ מִמֶּנּוּ הָיוּ קַרְנֹתָיו׃ וַיְצַף אֹתוֹ
זָהָב טָהוֹר אֶת־גַּגּוֹ וְאֶת־קִירֹתָיו סָבִיב וְאֶת־קַרְנֹתָיו וַיַּעַשׂ
27 לוֹ זֵר זָהָב סָבִיב׃ וּשְׁתֵּי טַבְּעֹת זָהָב עָשָׂה־לוֹ ׀ מִתַּחַת
לְזֵרוֹ עַל שְׁתֵּי צַלְעֹתָיו עַל שְׁנֵי צִדָּיו לְבָתִּים לְבַדִּים לָשֵׂאת
28 אֹתוֹ בָּהֶם׃ וַיַּעַשׂ אֶת־הַבַּדִּים עֲצֵי שִׁטִּים וַיְצַף אֹתָם
29 זָהָב׃ וַיַּעַשׂ אֶת־שֶׁמֶן הַמִּשְׁחָה קֹדֶשׁ וְאֶת־קְטֹרֶת הַסַּמִּים
טָהוֹר מַעֲשֵׂה רֹקֵחַ׃ * שביעי ס (רביעי כשהן מחובר׳)

38

CHAPTER XXXVIII

CAP. XXXVIII. לח

לח

1. And he made the altar of burnt-offering of acacia-wood: five cubits was the length thereof, and five cubits the breadth thereof, four-square, and three cubits the height thereof. 2. And he made the horns thereof upon the four corners of it; the horns thereof were of one piece with it; and he overlaid it with brass. 3. And he made all the vessels of the altar, the pots, and the shovels, and the basins, the flesh-hooks, and the fire-pans; all the vessels thereof made he of brass. 4. And he made for the altar a grating of network of brass, under the ledge round it beneath, reaching halfway up. 5. And he cast four rings for the four ends of the grating of brass, to be holders for the staves. 6. And he made the staves

א וַיַּעַשׂ אֶת־מִזְבַּח הָעֹלָה עֲצֵי שִׁטִּים חָמֵשׁ אַמּוֹת אָרְכּוֹ
2 וְחָמֵשׁ אַמּוֹת רָחְבּוֹ רָבוּעַ וְשָׁלֹשׁ אַמּוֹת קֹמָתוֹ׃ וַיַּעַשׂ
קַרְנֹתָיו עַל אַרְבַּע פִּנֹּתָיו מִמֶּנּוּ הָיוּ קַרְנֹתָיו וַיְצַף אֹתוֹ
3 נְחֹשֶׁת׃ וַיַּעַשׂ אֶת־כָּל־כְּלֵי הַמִּזְבֵּחַ אֶת־הַסִּירֹת וְאֶת־הַיָּעִים
וְאֶת־הַמִּזְרָקֹת אֶת־הַמִּזְלָגֹת וְאֶת־הַמַּחְתֹּת כָּל־כֵּלָיו עָשָׂה
4 נְחֹשֶׁת׃ וַיַּעַשׂ לַמִּזְבֵּחַ מִכְבָּר מַעֲשֵׂה רֶשֶׁת נְחֹשֶׁת תַּחַת
ה כַּרְכֻּבּוֹ מִלְּמַטָּה עַד־חֶצְיוֹ׃ וַיִּצֹק אַרְבַּע טַבָּעֹת בְּאַרְבַּע
6 הַקְּצָוֹת לְמִכְבַּר הַנְּחֹשֶׁת בָּתִּים לַבַּדִּים׃ וַיַּעַשׂ אֶת־הַבַּדִּים

25–27. THE ALTAR OF INCENSE AND ANOINTING OIL

Corresponding to xxx, 1–5.

CHAPTER XXXVIII

1–8. THE ALTAR OF BURNT-OFFERING AND LAVER

Corresponding to xxvii, 1–8, and xxx, 18–21.

of acacia-wood, and overlaid them with brass. 7. And he put the staves into the rings on the sides of the altar, wherewith to bear it; he made it hollow with planks. ¶ 8. And he made the laver of brass, and the base thereof of brass, of the mirrors of the serving women that did service at the door of the tent of meeting. ¶ 9. And he made the court; for the south side southward the hangings of the court were of fine twined linen, a hundred cubits. 10. Their pillars were twenty, and their sockets twenty, of brass; the hooks of the pillars and their fillets were of silver. 11. And for the north side a hundred cubits, their pillars twenty, and their sockets twenty, of brass; the hooks of the pillars and their fillets of silver. 12. And for the west side were hangings of fifty cubits, their pillars ten, and their sockets ten; the hooks of the pillars and their fillets of silver. 13. And for the east side eastward fifty cubits. 14. The hangings for the one side [of the gate] were fifteen cubits; their pillars three, and their sockets three. 15. And so for the other side; on this hand and that hand by the gate of the court were hangings of fifteen cubits; their pillars three, and their sockets three. 16. All the hangings of the court round about were of fine twined linen. 17. And the sockets for the pillars were of brass; the hooks of the pillars and their fillets of silver; and the overlaying of their capitals of silver; and all the pillars of the court were filleted with silver.*m. 18. And the screen for the gate of the court was the work of the weaver in colours, of blue, and purple, and scarlet, and fine twined linen; and twenty cubits was the length, and the height in the breadth was five cubits, answerable to the hangings of the court. 19. And their pillars were four, and their sockets four, of brass; their hooks of silver, and the overlaying of their capitals and their fillets of silver. 20. And all the pins of the tabernacle, and of the court round about, were of brass.

7 עצי שטים ויצף אתם נחשת: ויבא את־הבדים בטבעת
על צלעת המזבח לשאת אתו בהם נבוב לחת עשה
8 אתו: ס ויעש את הכיור נחשת ואת כנו נחשת
במראת הצבאת אשר צבאו פתח אהל מועד: ס
9 ויעש את־החצר לפאת | נגב תימנה קלעי החצר שש
י משזר מאה באמה: עמודיהם עשרים ואדניהם עשרים
11 נחשת ווי העמודים וחשקיהם כסף: ולפאת צפון מאה
באמה עמודיהם עשרים ואדניהם עשרים נחשת ווי
12 העמודים וחשקיהם כסף: ולפאת־ים קלעים חמשים
באמה עמודיהם עשרה ואדניהם עשרה ווי העמדים
13 וחשוקיהם כסף: ולפאת קדמה מזרחה חמשים אמה:
14 קלעים חמש־עשרה אמה אל־הכתף עמודיהם שלשה
טו ואדניהם שלשה: ולכתף השנית מזה ומזה לשער
החצר קלעים חמש עשרה אמה עמדיהם שלשה
16 ואדניהם שלשה: כל־קלעי החצר סביב שש משזר:
17 והאדנים לעמדים נחשת ווי העמודים וחשוקיהם כסף
וצפוי ראשיהם כסף והם מחשקים כסף כל עמדי
מפטיר 18 החצר: ומסך שער החצר מעשה רקם תכלת וארגמן
ותולעת שני ושש משזר ועשרים אמה ארך וקומה ברחב
19 חמש אמות לעמת קלעי החצר: ועמדיהם ארבעה
ואדניהם ארבעה נחשת וויהם כסף וצפוי ראשיהם
כ וחשקיהם כסף: וכל־היתדת למשכן ולחצר סביב נחשת:

8. *the mirrors.* These were made of burnished copper. According to a Rabbinic tradition, Moses at first wished to reject the offering of the mirrors because they ministered to feminine vanity; but God reminded him how the Israelite woman had shared the bitterness of her husband's bondage in Egypt and done her utmost to cheer him. Moses, thereupon, agreed to accept the mirrors, but utilized the metal for the laver, and not for the structure of the actual Tabernacle.

did service. Or, 'that come to pray' (Onkelos). A number of devout women who yielded up their mirrors as a token of self-dedication to God, assembled at the entrance of the Tabernacle for prayer (Ibn Ezra).

tent of meeting. This may either mean the tent of Moses (XXXIII, 7) or the Sanctuary. If the latter, it is mentioned here by anticipation, since the Tent of Meeting had not yet been erected. They were the women who resolved to be in attendance there, and afterwards did so.

9–20. THE COURT

Corresponding to XXVII, 9–19.

18. *answerable to.* Better, *corresponding to.*

HAFTORAH VAYYAKHEL (FOR ASHKENAZIM) הפטרת ויקהל לאשכנזים

HAFTORAH PEKUDEY (FOR SEPHARDIM) הפטרת פקודי לספרדים

I KINGS VII, 40–50

CHAPTER VII

40. And [1]Hiram made the pots, and the shovels, and the basins. ¶ So Hiram made an end of doing all the work that he wrought for king Solomon in the house of the LORD: 41. the two pillars, and the two bowls of the capitals that were on the top of the pillars; and the two networks to cover the two bowls of the capitals that were on the top of the pillars; 42. and the four hundred pomegranates for the two networks, two rows of pomegranates for each network, to cover the two bowls of the capitals that were upon the top of the pillars; 43. and the ten bases, and the ten lavers on the bases; 44. and the one sea, and the twelve oxen under the sea; 45. and the pots, and the shovels, and the basins; even all these vessels, which Hiram made for king Solomon, in the house of the LORD, were of burnished brass. 46. In the plain of the Jordan did the king cast them, in the clay ground between Succoth and Zarethan. 47. And Solomon left all the vessels unweighed, because they were exceeding many; the weight of the brass could not be found out. 48. And Solomon made all the vessels that were in the house of the LORD: the golden altar, and the table whereupon the showbread was, of gold; 49. and the candlesticks, five on the right side, and five on the left, be-

[1] Heb. *Hirom.*

CAP. VII. ז

מ וַיַּעַשׂ חִירוֹם אֶת־הַכִּיֹּרוֹת
וְאֶת־הַיָּעִים וְאֶת־הַמִּזְרָקוֹת וַיְכַל חִירָם לַעֲשׂוֹת אֶת־כָּל־
41 הַמְּלָאכָה אֲשֶׁר עָשָׂה לַמֶּלֶךְ שְׁלֹמֹה בֵּית יְהוָה׃ עַמֻּדִים
שְׁנַיִם וְגֻלֹּת הַכֹּתָרֹת אֲשֶׁר־עַל־רֹאשׁ הָעַמּוּדִים שְׁתָּיִם
וְהַשְּׂבָכוֹת שְׁתַּיִם לְכַסּוֹת אֶת־שְׁתֵּי גֻּלּוֹת הַכֹּתָרֹת אֲשֶׁר
42 עַל־רֹאשׁ הָעַמּוּדִים׃ וְאֶת־הָרִמֹּנִים אַרְבַּע מֵאוֹת לִשְׁתֵּי
הַשְּׂבָכוֹת שְׁנֵי־טוּרִים רִמֹּנִים לַשְּׂבָכָה הָאֶחָת לְכַסּוֹת אֶת־
43 שְׁתֵּי גֻּלּוֹת הַכֹּתָרֹת אֲשֶׁר עַל־פְּנֵי הָעַמּוּדִים׃ וְאֶת־הַמְּכֹנוֹת
44 עֶשֶׂר וְאֶת־הַכִּיֹּרֹת עֲשָׂרָה עַל־הַמְּכֹנוֹת׃ וְאֶת־הַיָּם הָאֶחָד
מה וְאֶת־הַבָּקָר שְׁנֵים־עָשָׂר תַּחַת הַיָּם׃ וְאֶת־הַסִּירוֹת וְאֶת־
הַיָּעִים וְאֶת־הַמִּזְרָקוֹת וְאֵת כָּל־הַכֵּלִים הָאֹהֶל* אֲשֶׁר עָשָׂה
46 חִירָם לַמֶּלֶךְ שְׁלֹמֹה בֵּית יְהוָה נְחֹשֶׁת מְמֹרָט׃ בְּכִכַּר
הַיַּרְדֵּן יְצָקָם הַמֶּלֶךְ בְּמַעֲבֵה הָאֲדָמָה בֵּין סֻכּוֹת וּבֵין
47 צָרְתָן׃ וַיַּנַּח שְׁלֹמֹה אֶת־כָּל־הַכֵּלִים מֵרֹב מְאֹד לֹא
48 נֶחְקַר מִשְׁקַל הַנְּחֹשֶׁת׃ וַיַּעַשׂ שְׁלֹמֹה אֵת כָּל־הַכֵּלִים
אֲשֶׁר בֵּית יְהוָה אֵת מִזְבַּח הַזָּהָב וְאֶת־הַשֻּׁלְחָן אֲשֶׁר עָלָיו
49 לֶחֶם הַפָּנִים זָהָב׃ וְאֶת־הַמְּנֹרוֹת חָמֵשׁ מִיָּמִין וְחָמֵשׁ מִשְּׂמֹאול

v. 45. האלה קרי

With the same care as in the Sedrah, we have in the Haftorah a description of the appurtenances for the Temple.

40. *Hiram.* A famous brass-worker, the son of a Tyrian father, who was also a skilled artist, and an Israelitish mother; see note on *v.* 14, p. 383.

44. *and the one sea.* An enormous circular vessel ten cubits (about 18 feet) in diameter and five cubits (about 9 feet) in depth. It was richly decorated, and was supported on the backs of twelve brazen oxen, three looking towards each of the cardinal points of the compass. See *v.* 23–26 of this chapter, p. 384.

45. *in the house of the LORD.* For use in the house of the LORD.

46. *between Succoth and Zarethan.* Succoth was on the other, the east side of the river, in Gad. Zarethan was on the west side of Jordan, about 24 miles north of the Dead Sea.

47. The amount of brass used was so great that no attempt was made to keep an account of it.

48. *the golden altar.* The altar of incense.

49. *the flowers.* The flower-like ornaments of the candlesticks.

To appreciate the significance of the Temple in the life of ancient Israel, we must continue reading the next chapter of the First Book of Kings, Solomon's Prayer of Dedication (set aside as the Haftorah for the first and eighth days of Tabernacles).

The Temple was the forum, the fortress, the 'university', as well as the Central Sanctuary, of Israel. The People *loved* it; the pomp and ceremony, the music and song of the Levites, the ministrations of the priests, the high priest as he stood and blessed the prostrate worshippers amid fore the Sanctuary, of pure gold; and the flowers, and the lamps, and the tongs, of gold; 50. and the cups, and the snuffers, and the basins, and the pans, and the fire-pans, of pure gold; and the hinges, both for the doors of the inner house, the most holy place, and for the doors of the house, that is, of the temple, of gold.

לִפְנֵי הַדְּבִיר זָהָב סָגוּר וְהַפֶּרַח וְהַנֵּרֹת וְהַמֶּלְקַחַיִם זָהָב׃
נ וְהַסִּפּוֹת וְהַמְזַמְּרוֹת וְהַמִּזְרָקוֹת וְהַכַּפּוֹת וְהַמַּחְתּוֹת זָהָב
סָגוּר וְהַפֹּתוֹת לְדַלְתוֹת הַבַּיִת הַפְּנִימִי לְקֹדֶשׁ הַקֳּדָשִׁים
לְדַלְתֵי הַבַּיִת לַהֵיכָל זָהָב׃

profound silence on the Atonement Day. As for the choicer spirits, their passionate devotion found expression in words like those of the Psalmist:

'How lovely are thy tabernacles,
O LORD of Hosts!
'My soul longeth, yea, fainteth for the courts of the LORD . . . .
'Blessed are they that dwell in thy house.'

The destruction of the Sanctuary could not drown Israel's undying love of its 'House of Holiness'. Throughout the ages down to this day, the sole relic of its ancient glory—the so-called Wailing Wall—has remained for millions of Jews the most sacred memento of their national sanctities, a 'Holy Place' from which the Shechinah has never departed.

HAFTORAH VAYYAKHEL (FOR SEPHARDIM) הפטרת ויקהל לספרדים

I KINGS VII, 13–26

CHAPTER VII

13. And king Solomon sent and fetched Hiram out of Tyre. 14. He was the son of a widow of the tribe of Naphtali, and his father was a man of Tyre, a worker in brass; and he was filled with wisdom and understanding and skill, to work all works in brass. And he came to king Solomon, and wrought all his work. ¶ 15. Thus he fashioned the two pillars of brass, of eighteen cubits high each; and a line of twelve cubits did compass it about; [and so] the other pillar. 16. And he made two capitals of molten brass, to set upon the tops of the pillars; the height of the one capital was five cubits, and the height of the

CAP. VII. ז

13 וַיִּשְׁלַח הַמֶּלֶךְ שְׁלֹמֹה וַיִּקַּח אֶת־חִירָם
14 מִצֹּר׃ בֶּן־אִשָּׁה אַלְמָנָה הוּא מִמַּטֵּה נַפְתָּלִי וְאָבִיו אִישׁ־
צֹרִי חֹרֵשׁ נְחֹשֶׁת וַיִּמָּלֵא אֶת־הַחָכְמָה וְאֶת־הַתְּבוּנָה
וְאֶת־הַדַּעַת לַעֲשׂוֹת כָּל־מְלָאכָה בַּנְּחֹשֶׁת וַיָּבוֹא אֶל־
טו הַמֶּלֶךְ שְׁלֹמֹה וַיַּעַשׂ אֶת־כָּל־מְלַאכְתּוֹ׃ וַיָּצַר אֶת־שְׁנֵי
הָעַמּוּדִים נְחֹשֶׁת שְׁמֹנֶה עֶשְׂרֵה אַמָּה קוֹמַת הָעַמּוּד
הָאֶחָד וְחוּט שְׁתֵּים־עֶשְׂרֵה אַמָּה יָסֹב אֶת־הָעַמּוּד הַשֵּׁנִי׃
16 וּשְׁתֵּי כֹתָרֹת עָשָׂה לָתֵת עַל־רָאשֵׁי הָעַמּוּדִים מֻצַק

The Sedrah continues the description of the skilled work lavished on the Tabernacle. Corresponding to this, the Haftorah describes the artistry of Hiram of Tyre on the pillars and the brass ornamental work in King Solomon's Temple.

13. *Solomon sent.* To the King of Tyre, for permission for his famous artist in brass and precious metals, to assist in the work for the Temple.

14. *of Naphtali.* In II Chron. XI, 14, his mother is called a daughter of Dan; and, according to Jewish tradition, the father and not the mother (as might appear from the text) was of the tribe of Naphtali.

his father was a man of Tyre. i.e. he had settled in Tyre, though born in Israel.

15. *he fashioned. i.e.* he cast. Moulds were made in the earth into which the molten brass was poured.

a line of twelve cubits. i.e. they were 12 cubits (about 20 feet) in circumference. According to Jer. LII, 21, the pillars were hollow.

16. *capitals.* The upper parts of the columns. They were spherical in shape (*v.* 42).

other capital was five cubits. 17. He also made nets of checker-work, and wreaths of chain-work, for the capitals which were upon the top of the pillars: seven for the one capital, and seven for the other capital. 18. And he made the pillars; and there were two rows round about upon the one network, to cover the capitals that were upon the top of the pomegranates; and so did he for the other capital. 19. And the capitals that were upon the top of the pillars in the porch were of lily-work, four cubits. 20. And there were capitals above also upon the two pillars, close by the belly which was beside the network; and the pomegranates were two hundred, in rows round about upon each capital. 21. And he set up the pillars at the porch of the temple; and he set up the right pillar, and called the name thereof Jachin; and he set up the left pillar, and called the name thereof Boaz. 22. And upon the top of the pillars was lily-work; so was the work of the pillars finished. ¶ 23. And he made the molten sea of ten cubits from brim to brim, round the compass, and the height thereof was five cubits; and a line of thirty cubits did compass it round about. 24. And under the brim of it round about there were knops which did compass it, for ten cubits, compassing the sea round about; the knops were in two rows, cast when it was cast. 25. It stood upon twelve oxen, three looking toward the north, and three looking toward the west, and three looking toward the south, and three looking toward the east; and the sea was set upon them above, and all the hinder parts were inward. 26. And it was a handbreadth thick; and the brim thereof was wrought like the brim of a cup, like the flower of a lily; it held two thousand baths.

נְחֹשֶׁת חָמֵשׁ אַמּוֹת קוֹמַת הַכֹּתֶרֶת הָאֶחָת וְחָמֵשׁ אַמּוֹת
17 קוֹמַת הַכֹּתֶרֶת הַשֵּׁנִית׃ שְׂבָכִים מַעֲשֵׂה שְׂבָכָה גְּדִלִים
מַעֲשֵׂה שַׁרְשְׁרוֹת לַכֹּתָרֹת אֲשֶׁר עַל־רֹאשׁ הָעַמּוּדִים שִׁבְעָה
18 לַכֹּתֶרֶת הָאֶחָת וְשִׁבְעָה לַכֹּתֶרֶת הַשֵּׁנִית׃ וַיַּעַשׂ אֶת־
הָעַמּוּדִים וּשְׁנֵי טוּרִים סָבִיב עַל־הַשְּׂבָכָה הָאֶחָת לְכַסּוֹת
אֶת־הַכֹּתָרֹת אֲשֶׁר עַל־רֹאשׁ הָרִמֹּנִים וְכֵן עָשָׂה לַכֹּתֶרֶת
19 הַשֵּׁנִית׃ וְכֹתָרֹת אֲשֶׁר עַל־רֹאשׁ הָעַמּוּדִים מַעֲשֵׂה שׁוּשַׁן
כ בָּאוּלָם אַרְבַּע אַמּוֹת׃ וְכֹתָרֹת עַל־שְׁנֵי הָעַמּוּדִים גַּם־
מִמַּעַל מִלְּעֻמַּת הַבֶּטֶן אֲשֶׁר לְעֵבֶר שְׂבָכָה וְהָרִמּוֹנִים
21 מָאתַיִם טֻרִים סָבִיב עַל הַכֹּתֶרֶת הַשֵּׁנִית׃ וַיָּקֶם אֶת־
הָעַמֻּדִים לְאֻלָם הַהֵיכָל וַיָּקֶם אֶת־הָעַמּוּד הַיְמָנִי וַיִּקְרָא
אֶת־שְׁמוֹ יָכִין וַיָּקֶם אֶת־הָעַמּוּד הַשְּׂמָאלִי וַיִּקְרָא אֶת־
22 שְׁמוֹ בֹּעַז׃ וְעַל רֹאשׁ הָעַמּוּדִים מַעֲשֵׂה שׁוֹשָׁן וַתִּתֹּם
23 מְלֶאכֶת הָעַמּוּדִים׃ וַיַּעַשׂ אֶת־הַיָּם מוּצָק עֶשֶׂר
בָּאַמָּה מִשְּׂפָתוֹ עַד־שְׂפָתוֹ עָגֹל ׀ סָבִיב וְחָמֵשׁ בָּאַמָּה
24 קוֹמָתוֹ וקוה שְׁלֹשִׁים בָּאַמָּה יָסֹב אֹתוֹ סָבִיב׃ וּפְקָעִים
מִתַּחַת לִשְׂפָתוֹ ׀ סָבִיב סֹבְבִים אֹתוֹ עֶשֶׂר בָּאַמָּה מַקִּפִים
אֶת־הַיָּם סָבִיב שְׁנֵי טוּרִים הַפְּקָעִים יְצֻקִים בִּיצֻקָתוֹ׃
כה עֹמֵד עַל־שְׁנֵי עָשָׂר בָּקָר שְׁלֹשָׁה פֹנִים ׀ צָפוֹנָה וּשְׁלֹשָׁה
פֹּנִים יָמָּה וּשְׁלֹשָׁה ׀ פֹּנִים נֶגְבָּה וּשְׁלֹשָׁה פֹּנִים מִזְרָחָה
26 וְהַיָּם עֲלֵיהֶם מִלְמָעְלָה וְכָל־אֲחֹרֵיהֶם בָּיְתָה׃ וְעָבְיוֹ טֶפַח
וּשְׂפָתוֹ כְּמַעֲשֵׂה שְׂפַת־כּוֹס פֶּרַח שׁוֹשָׁן אַלְפַּיִם בַּת יָכִיל׃

v. 18. קמץ ברביע v. 20. השבכה ק' v. 22. כצ"ל v. 23. וקו קרי v. 26. כצ"ל

17. *nets . . . chain work.* The capitals were decorated with tracery.

18. *two rows.* Of pomegranates hung in festoons.

to cover the capitals. Referring to the network, which fitted closely to, and covered, the capitals.

19. *lily work.* The rim curving outwards. The capitals rested on a border of lily work on top of the pillars (see *v.* 22).

21. *the pillars.* They stood in the porchway, not supporting but clear of it. Detached pillars of this kind were a feature of temples in the East.

Jachin. That is, 'He shall establish,' *i.e.* the Temple, for ever.

Boaz. A union of two words: *bo* and *oz*; that is, 'In it is strength.' Through the services of the Temple, strength should come to Israel (Rashi).

23. *molten sea.* See on *v.* 44, p. 382.

a line of thirty cubits. Its circumference, about 52 feet.

24. *knops.* Egg-shaped (Targum); probably gourds which adorned the circumference of the bowl.

ten cubits. Ten in a cubit (Ralbag).

cast when it was cast. In the same mould as the basin.

26. *a handbreadth thick. i.e.* the casting, about 3 inches.

two thousand baths. A 'bath' was about 8 gallons.

38 21. These are the accounts of the tabernacle, even the tabernacle of the testimony, as they were rendered according to the commandment of Moses, through the service of the Levites, by the hand of Ithamar, the son of Aaron the priest.— 22. And Bezalel the son of Uri, the son of Hur, of the tribe of Judah, made all that the LORD commanded Moses. 23. And with him was Oholiab, the son of Ahisamach, of the tribe of Dan, a craftsman, and a skilful workman, and a weaver in colours, in blue, and in purple, and in scarlet, and fine linen. ¶ 24. All the gold that was used for the work in all the work of the sanctuary, even the gold of the offering, was twenty and nine talents, and seven hundred and thirty shekels, after the shekel of the sanctuary. 25. And the silver of them that were numbered of the congregation was a hundred talents, and a thousand seven hundred and three-score and fifteen shekels, after the shekel of the sanctuary: 26. a beka a head, that is, half a shekel, after the shekel of the sanctuary, for every one that passed over to them that are numbered, from twenty years old and upward, for six hundred thousand and three thousand and five hundred and fifty men. 27. And the hundred talents of silver were for casting the sockets of the sanctuary, and the sockets of the veil: a hundred sockets for the hundred talents, a talent for a socket. 28. And of the thousand seven hundred seventy and five shekels he made hooks for the pillars, and overlaid their

לח ס ס ס כג 23

21 אֵלֶּה פְקוּדֵי הַמִּשְׁכָּן מִשְׁכַּן הָעֵדֻת אֲשֶׁר פֻּקַּד עַל־פִּי
22 מֹשֶׁה עֲבֹדַת הַלְוִיִּם בְּיַד אִיתָמָר בֶּן־אַהֲרֹן הַכֹּהֵן׃ וּבְצַלְאֵל
בֶּן־אוּרִי בֶן־חוּר לְמַטֵּה יְהוּדָה עָשָׂה אֵת כָּל־אֲשֶׁר־צִוָּה
23 יְהוָה אֶת־מֹשֶׁה׃ וְאִתּוֹ אָהֳלִיאָב בֶּן־אֲחִיסָמָךְ לְמַטֵּה־דָן
חָרָשׁ וְחֹשֵׁב וְרֹקֵם בַּתְּכֵלֶת וּבָאַרְגָּמָן וּבְתוֹלַעַת הַשָּׁנִי
24 וּבַשֵּׁשׁ׃ ס כָּל־הַזָּהָב הֶעָשׂוּי לַמְּלָאכָה בְּכֹל מְלֶאכֶת
הַקֹּדֶשׁ וַיְהִי ׀ זְהַב הַתְּנוּפָה תֵּשַׁע וְעֶשְׂרִים כִּכָּר וּשְׁבַע
כה מֵאוֹת וּשְׁלֹשִׁים שֶׁקֶל בְּשֶׁקֶל הַקֹּדֶשׁ׃ וְכֶסֶף פְּקוּדֵי הָעֵדָה
מְאַת כִּכָּר וְאֶלֶף וּשְׁבַע מֵאוֹת וַחֲמִשָּׁה וְשִׁבְעִים שֶׁקֶל
26 בְּשֶׁקֶל הַקֹּדֶשׁ׃ בֶּקַע לַגֻּלְגֹּלֶת מַחֲצִית הַשֶּׁקֶל בְּשֶׁקֶל
הַקֹּדֶשׁ לְכֹל הָעֹבֵר עַל־הַפְּקֻדִים מִבֶּן עֶשְׂרִים שָׁנָה וָמַעְלָה
לְשֵׁשׁ־מֵאוֹת אֶלֶף וּשְׁלֹשֶׁת אֲלָפִים וַחֲמֵשׁ מֵאוֹת וַחֲמִשִּׁים׃
27 וַיְהִי מְאַת כִּכַּר הַכֶּסֶף לָצֶקֶת אֵת אַדְנֵי הַקֹּדֶשׁ וְאֵת אַדְנֵי
28 הַפָּרֹכֶת מְאַת אֲדָנִים לִמְאַת הַכִּכָּר כִּכָּר לָאָדֶן׃ וְאֶת־
הָאֶלֶף וּשְׁבַע הַמֵּאוֹת וַחֲמִשָּׁה וְשִׁבְעִים עָשָׂה וָוִים לָעַמּוּדִים
29 וְצִפָּה רָאשֵׁיהֶם וְחִשַּׁק אֹתָם׃ וּנְחֹשֶׁת הַתְּנוּפָה שִׁבְעִים

XI. PEKUDEY

(CHAPTER XXXVIII, 21–XL)

With minute care these chapters of Exodus describe the concluding stages of the construction of the Sanctuary. *v.* 21–31 of this chapter give the total amount of the precious metals used.

21. *tabernacle of the testimony.* So called because of the Tables of the Decalogue that were deposited there; cf. xxv, 16.

through the service of the Levites. Or, 'being the work of the Levites, under the hand, etc.'

Ithamar. The superintendent of the Tabernacle (Num. IV, 28).

22. *Bezalel.* Tribute is paid in this and the following verse to the faithful manner in which the two principal architects executed their work.

24. *talents.* See on xxv, 39. A talent equalled 3,000 shekels.

shekel of the sanctuary. See on xxx, 13. It has been computed that the total quantity of gold was worth about £160,000.

25. *that were numbered.* Cf. xxx, 12 f. The silver weighed 301,775 shekels; and since each male adult contributed half a shekel, the census showed a total of 603,000; cf. Num. I, 46. This suggests that the computations recorded here were not made at this time, but after the erection of the Tabernacle.

27. *for casting the sockets.* See on XXVI, 19.

29. *brass of the offering.* The quantity of copper was about three tons.

capitals, and made fillets for them. 29. And the brass of the offering was seventy talents, and two thousand and four hundred shekels. 30. And therewith he made the sockets to the door of the tent of meeting, and the brazen altar, and the brazen grating for it, and all the vessels of the altar, 31. and the sockets of the court round about, and the sockets of the gate of the court, and all the pins of the tabernacle, and all the pins of the court round about.

39

CHAPTER XXXIX

1. And of the blue, and purple, and scarlet, they made plaited garments, for ministering in the holy place, and made the holy garments for Aaron, as the LORD commanded Moses.*ii (**v). ¶ 2. And he made the ephod of gold, blue, and purple, and scarlet, and fine twined linen. 3. And they did beat the gold into thin plates, and cut it into threads, to work it in the blue, and in the purple, and in the scarlet, and in the fine linen, the work of the skilful workman. 4. They made shoulder-pieces for it, joined together; at the two ends was it joined together. 5. And the skilfully woven band, that was upon it, wherewith to gird it on, was of the same piece and like the work thereof: of gold, of blue, and purple, and scarlet, and fine twined linen, as the LORD commanded Moses. ¶ 6. And they wrought the onyx stones, inclosed in settings of gold, graven with the engravings of a signet, according to the names of the children of Israel. 7. And he put them on the shoulder-pieces of the ephod, to be stones of memorial for the children of Israel, as the LORD commanded Moses. ¶ 8. And he made the breastplate, the work of the skilful workman, like the work of the ephod: of gold, of blue, and purple, and scarlet, and fine twined linen. 9. It was four-square; they made the breastplate double: a span was the length thereof, and a span the breadth thereof, being double. 10. And they set in it four rows of stones: a row of carnelian, topaz, and smaragd was the first row. 11. And the second row, a carbuncle, a sapphire, and an emerald. 12. And the third row, a jacinth, an agate, and an amethyst. 13. And the

ל כִּכָּר וְאַלְפַּיִם וְאַרְבַּע־מֵאוֹת שָׁקֶל׃ וַיַּעַשׂ בָּהּ אֶת־אַדְנֵי
פֶּתַח אֹהֶל מוֹעֵד וְאֵת מִזְבַּח הַנְּחֹשֶׁת וְאֶת־מִכְבַּר הַנְּחֹשֶׁת
31 אֲשֶׁר־לוֹ וְאֵת כָּל־כְּלֵי הַמִּזְבֵּחַ׃ וְאֶת־אַדְנֵי הֶחָצֵר סָבִיב
וְאֶת־אַדְנֵי שַׁעַר הֶחָצֵר וְאֵת כָּל־יִתְדֹת הַמִּשְׁכָּן וְאֶת־כָּל־
יִתְדֹת הֶחָצֵר סָבִיב׃

CAP. XXXIX. לט

לט

א וּמִן־הַתְּכֵלֶת וְהָאַרְגָּמָן וְתוֹלַעַת הַשָּׁנִי עָשׂוּ בִגְדֵי־שְׂרָד
לְשָׁרֵת בַּקֹּדֶשׁ וַיַּעֲשׂוּ אֶת־בִּגְדֵי הַקֹּדֶשׁ אֲשֶׁר לְאַהֲרֹן כַּאֲשֶׁר
צִוָּה יְהוָה אֶת־מֹשֶׁה׃ * שני פ (חמישי כשהן מחוב׳)
2 וַיַּעַשׂ אֶת־הָאֵפֹד זָהָב תְּכֵלֶת וְאַרְגָּמָן וְתוֹלַעַת שָׁנִי וְשֵׁשׁ
3 מָשְׁזָר׃ וַיְרַקְּעוּ אֶת־פַּחֵי הַזָּהָב וְקִצֵּץ פְּתִילִם לַעֲשׂוֹת
בְּתוֹךְ הַתְּכֵלֶת וּבְתוֹךְ הָאַרְגָּמָן וּבְתוֹךְ תּוֹלַעַת הַשָּׁנִי
4 וּבְתוֹךְ הַשֵּׁשׁ מַעֲשֵׂה חֹשֵׁב׃ כְּתֵפֹת עָשׂוּ־לוֹ חֹבְרֹת עַל־שְׁנֵי
ה קְצוֹוֹתָו חֻבָּר׃ וְחֵשֶׁב אֲפֻדָּתוֹ אֲשֶׁר עָלָיו מִמֶּנּוּ הוּא
כְּמַעֲשֵׂהוּ זָהָב תְּכֵלֶת וְאַרְגָּמָן וְתוֹלַעַת שָׁנִי וְשֵׁשׁ מָשְׁזָר
6 כַּאֲשֶׁר צִוָּה יְהוָה אֶת־מֹשֶׁה׃ ס וַיַּעֲשׂוּ אֶת־אַבְנֵי הַשֹּׁהַם
מֻסַבֹּת מִשְׁבְּצֹת זָהָב מְפֻתָּחֹת פִּתּוּחֵי חוֹתָם עַל־שְׁמוֹת
7 בְּנֵי יִשְׂרָאֵל׃ וַיָּשֶׂם אֹתָם עַל כִּתְפֹת הָאֵפֹד אַבְנֵי זִכָּרוֹן
לִבְנֵי יִשְׂרָאֵל כַּאֲשֶׁר צִוָּה יְהוָה אֶת־מֹשֶׁה׃ פ
8 וַיַּעַשׂ אֶת־הַחֹשֶׁן מַעֲשֵׂה חֹשֵׁב כְּמַעֲשֵׂה אֵפֹד זָהָב תְּכֵלֶת
9 וְאַרְגָּמָן וְתוֹלַעַת שָׁנִי וְשֵׁשׁ מָשְׁזָר׃ רָבוּעַ הָיָה כָּפוּל עָשׂוּ
י אֶת־הַחֹשֶׁן זֶרֶת אָרְכּוֹ וְזֶרֶת רָחְבּוֹ כָּפוּל׃ וַיְמַלְאוּ־בוֹ
אַרְבָּעָה טוּרֵי אָבֶן טוּר אֹדֶם פִּטְדָה וּבָרֶקֶת הַטּוּר הָאֶחָד׃
11 12 וְהַטּוּר הַשֵּׁנִי נֹפֶךְ סַפִּיר וְיָהֲלֹם׃ וְהַטּוּר הַשְּׁלִישִׁי לֶשֶׁם
13 שְׁבוֹ וְאַחְלָמָה׃ וְהַטּוּר הָרְבִיעִי תַּרְשִׁישׁ שֹׁהַם וְיָשְׁפֵה

לט׳ v. 4. קצותיו ק׳

30. *brazen altar.* There is no mention of the laver, which was likewise made of copper. The reason is that the material for this came from a special source; see *v.* 8 above.

CHAPTER XXXIX

1–31. THE PRIESTS' VESTMENTS

2–7. THE EPHOD

Corresponding to XXVIII, 6–12.

3. *beat the gold.* This verse does not occur in the parallel passage; it explains how the gold was utilized in making the vestments.

8–21. THE BREASTPLATE

Corresponding to XXVIII, 15–28.

fourth row, a beryl, an onyx, and a jasper; they were inclosed in fittings of gold in their settings. 14. And the stones were according to the names of the children of Israel, twelve, according to their names, like the engravings of a signet, every one according to his name, for the twelve tribes. 15. And they made upon the breastplate plaited chains, of wreathen work of pure gold. 16. And they made two settings of gold, and two gold rings; and put the two rings on the two ends of the breastplate. 17. And they put the two wreathen chains of gold on the two rings at the ends of the breastplate. 18. And the other two ends of the two wreathen chains they put on the two settings, and put them on the shoulder-pieces of the ephod, in the forepart thereof. 19. And they made two rings of gold, and put them upon the two ends of the breastplate, upon the edge thereof, which was toward the side of the ephod inward. 20. And they made two rings of gold, and put them on the two shoulder-pieces of the ephod underneath, in the forepart thereof, close by the coupling thereof, above the skilfully woven band of the ephod. 21. And they did bind the breastplate by the rings thereof unto the rings of the ephod with a thread of blue, that it might be upon the skilfully woven band of the ephod, and that the breastplate might not be loosed from the ephod; as the LORD commanded Moses.*iii (**vi). ¶ 22. And he made the robe of the ephod of woven work, all of blue; 23. and the hole of the robe in the midst thereof, as the hole of a coat of mail, with a binding round about the hole of it, that it should not be rent. 24. And they made upon the skirts of the robe pomegranates of blue, and purple, and scarlet, and twined linen. 25. And they made bells of pure gold, and put the bells between the pomegranates upon the skirts of the robe round about, between the pomegranates: 26. a bell and a pomegranate, a bell and a pomegranate, upon the skirts of the robe round about, to minister in; as the LORD commanded Moses. ¶ 27. And they made the tunics of fine linen of woven work for Aaron, and for his sons,

14 מוּסַבֹּת מִשְׁבְּצֹת זָהָב בְּמִלֻּאֹתָם׃ וְהָאֲבָנִים עַל־שְׁמֹת
בְּנֵי־יִשְׂרָאֵל הֵנָּה שְׁתֵּים עֶשְׂרֵה עַל־שְׁמֹתָם פִּתּוּחֵי חֹתָם
טו אִישׁ עַל־שְׁמוֹ לִשְׁנֵים עָשָׂר שָׁבֶט׃ וַיַּעֲשׂוּ עַל־הַחֹשֶׁן
16 שַׁרְשְׁרֹת גַּבְלֻת מַעֲשֵׂה עֲבֹת זָהָב טָהוֹר׃ וַיַּעֲשׂוּ שְׁתֵּי
מִשְׁבְּצֹת זָהָב וּשְׁתֵּי טַבְּעֹת זָהָב וַיִּתְּנוּ אֶת־שְׁתֵּי הַטַּבָּעֹת
17 עַל־שְׁנֵי קְצוֹת הַחֹשֶׁן׃ וַיִּתְּנוּ שְׁתֵּי הָעֲבֹתֹת הַזָּהָב עַל־
18 שְׁתֵּי הַטַּבָּעֹת עַל־קְצוֹת הַחֹשֶׁן׃ וְאֵת שְׁתֵּי קְצוֹת שְׁתֵּי
הָעֲבֹתֹת נָתְנוּ עַל־שְׁתֵּי הַמִּשְׁבְּצֹת וַיִּתְּנֻם עַל־כִּתְפֹת
19 הָאֵפֹד אֶל־מוּל פָּנָיו׃ וַיַּעֲשׂוּ שְׁתֵּי טַבְּעֹת זָהָב וַיָּשִׂימוּ עַל־
שְׁנֵי קְצוֹת הַחֹשֶׁן עַל־שְׂפָתוֹ אֲשֶׁר אֶל־עֵבֶר הָאֵפֹד בָּיְתָה׃
כ וַיַּעֲשׂוּ שְׁתֵּי טַבְּעֹת זָהָב וַיִּתְּנֻם עַל־שְׁתֵּי כִתְפֹת הָאֵפֹד
מִלְּמַטָּה מִמּוּל פָּנָיו לְעֻמַּת מַחְבַּרְתּוֹ מִמַּעַל לְחֵשֶׁב הָאֵפֹד׃
21 וַיִּרְכְּסוּ אֶת־הַחֹשֶׁן מִטַּבְּעֹתָיו אֶל־טַבְּעֹת הָאֵפֹד בִּפְתִיל
תְּכֵלֶת לִהְיֹת עַל־חֵשֶׁב הָאֵפֹד וְלֹא־יִזַּח הַחֹשֶׁן מֵעַל הָאֵפֹד
כַּאֲשֶׁר צִוָּה יְהוָה אֶת־מֹשֶׁה׃ * שלישי פ (ששי כשהן מחוב')
22 23 וַיַּעַשׂ אֶת־מְעִיל הָאֵפֹד מַעֲשֵׂה אֹרֵג כְּלִיל תְּכֵלֶת׃ וּפִי־
הַמְּעִיל בְּתוֹכוֹ כְּפִי תַחְרָא שָׂפָה לְפִיו סָבִיב לֹא יִקָּרֵעַ׃
24 וַיַּעֲשׂוּ עַל־שׁוּלֵי הַמְּעִיל רִמּוֹנֵי תְּכֵלֶת וְאַרְגָּמָן וְתוֹלַעַת
כה שָׁנִי מָשְׁזָר׃ וַיַּעֲשׂוּ פַעֲמֹנֵי זָהָב טָהוֹר וַיִּתְּנוּ אֶת־הַפַּעֲמֹנִים
בְּתוֹךְ הָרִמֹּנִים עַל־שׁוּלֵי הַמְּעִיל סָבִיב בְּתוֹךְ הָרִמֹּנִים׃
26 פַּעֲמֹן וְרִמֹּן פַּעֲמֹן וְרִמֹּן עַל־שׁוּלֵי הַמְּעִיל סָבִיב לְשָׁרֵת
27 כַּאֲשֶׁר צִוָּה יְהוָה אֶת־מֹשֶׁה׃ ס וַיַּעֲשׂוּ אֶת־הַכָּתְנֹת
28 שֵׁשׁ מַעֲשֵׂה אֹרֵג לְאַהֲרֹן וּלְבָנָיו׃ וְאֵת הַמִּצְנֶפֶת שֵׁשׁ
וְאֶת־פַּאֲרֵי הַמִּגְבָּעֹת שֵׁשׁ וְאֶת־מִכְנְסֵי הַבָּד שֵׁשׁ מָשְׁזָר׃

22–26. THE ROBE OF THE EPHOD

Corresponding to XXVIII, 31–34.

27–29. THE TUNICS AND HEADGEAR

Corresponding to XXVIII, 39–42.

28. *goodly headtires.* lit. 'ornaments of caps', *i.e.* ornamental caps. These were for the priests, whereas the mitre was for the High Priest.

30, 31. THE HOLY CROWN

Corresponding to XXVIII, 36 f.

30. *holy crown.* Not mentioned in the parallel passage, but in XXIX, 6. It is identical with the golden plate.

32–43. SUMMARY OF THE WORK

33. *brought . . . unto Moses.* The sectional pieces. The task of fitting them together and

28. and the mitre of fine linen, and the goodly head-tires of fine linen, and the linen breeches of fine twined linen, 29. and the girdle of fine twined linen, and blue, and purple, and scarlet, the work of the weaver in colours; as the LORD commanded Moses. ¶ 30. And they made the plate of the holy crown of pure gold, and wrote upon it a writing, like the engravings of a signet: HOLY TO THE LORD. 31. And they tied unto it a thread of blue, to fasten it upon the mitre above; as the LORD commanded Moses. ¶ 32. Thus was finished all the work of the tabernacle of the tent of meeting; and the children of Israel did according to all that the LORD commanded Moses, so did they.*iv. ¶ 33. And they brought the tabernacle unto Moses, the Tent, and all its furniture, its clasps, its boards, its bars, and its pillars, and its sockets; 34. and the covering of rams' skins dyed red, and the covering of sealskins, and the veil of the screen; 35. the ark of the testimony, and the staves thereof, and the ark-cover; 36. the table, all the vessels thereof, and the showbread; 37. the pure candlestick, the lamps thereof, even the lamps to be set in order, and all the vessels thereof, and the oil for the light; 38. and the golden altar, and the anointing oil, and the sweet incense, and the screen for the door of the Tent; 39. the brazen altar, and its grating of brass, its staves, and all its vessels, the laver and its base; 40. the hangings of the court, its pillars, and its sockets, and the screen for the gate of the court, the cords thereof, and the pins thereof, and all the instruments of the service of the tabernacle of the tent of meeting; 41. the plaited garments for ministering in the holy place; the holy garments for Aaron the priest, and the garments of his sons, to minister in the priest's office. 42. According to all that the LORD commanded Moses, so the children of Israel did all the work. 43. And Moses saw all the work, and, behold, they had done it; as the LORD had commanded, even so had they done it. And Moses blessed them.* v (** vii).

29 וְאֶת־הָאַבְנֵט שֵׁשׁ מָשְׁזָר וּתְכֵלֶת וְאַרְגָּמָן וְתוֹלַעַת שָׁנִי
ל מַעֲשֵׂה רֹקֵם כַּאֲשֶׁר צִוָּה יְהוָה אֶת־מֹשֶׁה׃ ס וַיַּעֲשׂוּ אֶת־
צִיץ נֵזֶר־הַקֹּדֶשׁ זָהָב טָהוֹר וַיִּכְתְּבוּ עָלָיו מִכְתַּב פִּתּוּחֵי
31 חוֹתָם קֹדֶשׁ לַיהוָה׃ וַיִּתְּנוּ עָלָיו פְּתִיל תְּכֵלֶת לָתֵת עַל־
32 הַמִּצְנֶפֶת מִלְמָעְלָה כַּאֲשֶׁר צִוָּה יְהוָה אֶת־מֹשֶׁה׃ ס וַתֵּכֶל
כָּל־עֲבֹדַת מִשְׁכַּן אֹהֶל מוֹעֵד וַיַּעֲשׂוּ בְּנֵי יִשְׂרָאֵל כְּכֹל
אֲשֶׁר צִוָּה יְהוָה אֶת־מֹשֶׁה כֵּן עָשׂוּ׃ * פ רביעי
33 וַיָּבִיאוּ אֶת־הַמִּשְׁכָּן אֶל־מֹשֶׁה אֶת־הָאֹהֶל וְאֶת־כָּל־כֵּלָיו
34 קְרָסָיו קְרָשָׁיו בְּרִיחָו וְעַמֻּדָיו וַאֲדָנָיו׃ וְאֶת־מִכְסֵה עוֹרֹת
הָאֵילִם הַמְאָדָּמִים וְאֶת־מִכְסֵה עֹרֹת הַתְּחָשִׁים וְאֵת פָּרֹכֶת
לה 36 הַמָּסָךְ׃ אֶת־אֲרוֹן הָעֵדֻת וְאֶת־בַּדָּיו וְאֵת הַכַּפֹּרֶת׃ אֶת־
37 הַשֻּׁלְחָן אֶת־כָּל־כֵּלָיו וְאֵת לֶחֶם הַפָּנִים׃ אֶת־הַמְּנֹרָה
הַטְּהֹרָה אֶת־נֵרֹתֶיהָ נֵרֹת הַמַּעֲרָכָה וְאֶת־כָּל־כֵּלֶיהָ וְאֵת
38 שֶׁמֶן הַמָּאוֹר׃ וְאֵת מִזְבַּח הַזָּהָב וְאֵת שֶׁמֶן הַמִּשְׁחָה וְאֵת
39 קְטֹרֶת הַסַּמִּים וְאֵת מָסַךְ פֶּתַח הָאֹהֶל׃ אֵת ׀ מִזְבַּח
הַנְּחֹשֶׁת וְאֶת־מִכְבַּר הַנְּחֹשֶׁת אֲשֶׁר־לוֹ אֶת־בַּדָּיו וְאֶת־כָּל־
מ כֵּלָיו אֶת־הַכִּיֹּר וְאֶת־כַּנּוֹ׃ אֵת קַלְעֵי הֶחָצֵר אֶת־עַמֻּדֶיהָ
וְאֶת־אֲדָנֶיהָ וְאֶת־הַמָּסָךְ לְשַׁעַר הֶחָצֵר אֶת־מֵיתָרָיו וִיתֵדֹתֶיהָ
41 וְאֵת כָּל־כְּלֵי עֲבֹדַת הַמִּשְׁכָּן לְאֹהֶל מוֹעֵד׃ אֶת־בִּגְדֵי
הַשְּׂרָד לְשָׁרֵת בַּקֹּדֶשׁ אֶת־בִּגְדֵי הַקֹּדֶשׁ לְאַהֲרֹן הַכֹּהֵן
42 וְאֶת־בִּגְדֵי בָנָיו לְכַהֵן׃ כְּכֹל אֲשֶׁר־צִוָּה יְהוָה אֶת־מֹשֶׁה
43 כֵּן עָשׂוּ בְּנֵי יִשְׂרָאֵל אֵת כָּל־הָעֲבֹדָה׃ וַיַּרְא מֹשֶׁה אֶת־
כָּל־הַמְּלָאכָה וְהִנֵּה עָשׂוּ אֹתָהּ כַּאֲשֶׁר צִוָּה יְהוָה כֵּן עָשׂוּ
וַיְבָרֶךְ אֹתָם מֹשֶׁה׃ * חמישי פ (שביעי כשהן מחוב')

v. 33. בריחיו קרי

placing the articles of the Tabernacle in the right place, was to be done under the personal direction of Moses (XL, 1).

37. *lamps to be set in order.* *i.e.* to be arranged on it (Driver).

40. *all the instruments.* See on XXVII, 19.

42. *the children of Israel.* Credit is here given to the nameless donors and workers, who made the achievement of Bezalel and Oholiab possible.

43. *blessed them.* *i.e.* expressed his thanks by invoking a blessing upon them. The time had been short, the task great and arduous, but the labourers, fired by holy enthusiasm and zeal, had joyfully completed the work they had undertaken. Moses does not pronounce his blessing at the beginning of the sacred enterprise. Beginnings are easy; completions are as hard as they are rare. Tradition tells us that Moses composed Ps. XC, 'A Prayer of Moses,' for the occasion. Note its concluding words: 'Establish Thou the work of our hands upon us; yea, the work of our hands establish Thou it.'

40

Chapter XL

1. And the LORD spoke unto Moses, saying: 2. 'On the first day of the first month shalt thou rear up the tabernacle of the tent of meeting. 3. And thou shalt put therein the ark of the testimony, and thou shalt screen the ark with the veil. 4. And thou shalt bring in the table, and set in order the bread that is upon it; and thou shalt bring in the candlestick, and light the lamps thereof. 5. And thou shalt set the golden altar for incense before the ark of the testimony, and put the screen of the door to the tabernacle. 6. And thou shalt set the altar of burnt-offering before the door of the tabernacle of the tent of meeting. 7. And thou shalt set the laver between the tent of meeting and the altar, and shalt put water therein. 8. And thou shalt set up the court round about, and hang up the screen of the gate of the court. 9. And thou shalt take the anointing oil, and anoint the tabernacle, and all that is therein, and shalt hallow it, and all the furniture thereof; and it shall be holy. 10. And thou shalt anoint the altar of burnt-offering, and all its vessels, and sanctify the altar; and the altar shall be most holy. 11. And thou shalt anoint the laver and its base, and sanctify it. 12. And thou shalt bring Aaron and his sons unto the door of the tent of meeting, and shalt wash them with water. 13. And thou shalt put upon Aaron the holy garments; and thou shalt anoint him, and sanctify him, that he may minister unto Me in the priest's office. 14. And thou shalt bring his sons, and put tunics upon them. 15. And thou shalt anoint them, as thou didst anoint their father, that they may minister unto Me in the priest's office; and their anointing

מ

CAP. XL. מ

א 2 וַיְדַבֵּר יְהוָה אֶל־מֹשֶׁה לֵּאמֹר׃ בְּיוֹם־הַחֹדֶשׁ הָרִאשׁוֹן
3 בְּאֶחָד לַחֹדֶשׁ תָּקִים אֶת־מִשְׁכַּן אֹהֶל מוֹעֵד׃ וְשַׂמְתָּ שָׁם
4 אֵת אֲרוֹן הָעֵדוּת וְסַכֹּתָ עַל־הָאָרֹן אֶת־הַפָּרֹכֶת׃ וְהֵבֵאתָ
אֶת־הַשֻּׁלְחָן וְעָרַכְתָּ אֶת־עֶרְכּוֹ וְהֵבֵאתָ אֶת־הַמְּנֹרָה וְהַעֲלֵיתָ
ה אֶת־נֵרֹתֶיהָ׃ וְנָתַתָּה אֶת־מִזְבַּח הַזָּהָב לִקְטֹרֶת לִפְנֵי אֲרוֹן
6 הָעֵדֻת וְשַׂמְתָּ אֶת־מָסַךְ הַפֶּתַח לַמִּשְׁכָּן׃ וְנָתַתָּה אֵת
7 מִזְבַּח הָעֹלָה לִפְנֵי פֶּתַח מִשְׁכַּן אֹהֶל־מוֹעֵד׃ וְנָתַתָּ אֶת־
8 הַכִּיֹּר בֵּין־אֹהֶל מוֹעֵד וּבֵין הַמִּזְבֵּחַ וְנָתַתָּ שָׁם מָיִם׃ וְשַׂמְתָּ
9 אֶת־הֶחָצֵר סָבִיב וְנָתַתָּ אֶת־מָסַךְ שַׁעַר הֶחָצֵר׃ וְלָקַחְתָּ
אֶת־שֶׁמֶן הַמִּשְׁחָה וּמָשַׁחְתָּ אֶת־הַמִּשְׁכָּן וְאֶת־כָּל־אֲשֶׁר־בּוֹ
י וְקִדַּשְׁתָּ אֹתוֹ וְאֶת־כָּל־כֵּלָיו וְהָיָה קֹדֶשׁ׃ וּמָשַׁחְתָּ אֶת־
מִזְבַּח הָעֹלָה וְאֶת־כָּל־כֵּלָיו וְקִדַּשְׁתָּ אֶת־הַמִּזְבֵּחַ וְהָיָה
11 הַמִּזְבֵּחַ קֹדֶשׁ קָדָשִׁים׃ וּמָשַׁחְתָּ אֶת־הַכִּיֹּר וְאֶת־כַּנּוֹ וְקִדַּשְׁתָּ
12 אֹתוֹ׃ וְהִקְרַבְתָּ אֶת־אַהֲרֹן וְאֶת־בָּנָיו אֶל־פֶּתַח אֹהֶל מוֹעֵד
13 וְרָחַצְתָּ אֹתָם בַּמָּיִם׃ וְהִלְבַּשְׁתָּ אֶת־אַהֲרֹן אֵת בִּגְדֵי הַקֹּדֶשׁ
14 וּמָשַׁחְתָּ אֹתוֹ וְקִדַּשְׁתָּ אֹתוֹ וְכִהֵן לִי׃ וְאֶת־בָּנָיו תַּקְרִיב
טו וְהִלְבַּשְׁתָּ אֹתָם כֻּתֳּנֹת׃ וּמָשַׁחְתָּ אֹתָם כַּאֲשֶׁר מָשַׁחְתָּ אֶת־
אֲבִיהֶם וְכִהֲנוּ לִי וְהָיְתָה לִהְיֹת לָהֶם מָשְׁחָתָם לִכְהֻנַּת

CHAPTER XL

1–33. THE SETTING UP OF THE SANCTUARY

2. *the first month.* In the second year after the Exodus from Egypt (*v.* 17). Nine months had elapsed since the people's arrival at Sinai (XIX, 1). The actual work of construction occupied about four months.

3. *screen the ark.* See XXVI, 33.

4. *set in order.* Lit. 'thou shalt arrange its arrangement'; see XXV, 29 f.

5. *golden altar.* For the location of the contents of the Holy Place, see on XXVI, 35.

6. *before the door of the tabernacle. i.e.* in the court.

7. *laver.* See XXX, 18.

8. *the court.* See XXVII, 9 f.

9. *anointing oil.* See XXX, 26–28.

12. *bring Aaron.* See XXIX, 4 f, XXX, 30.

15. *an everlasting priesthood.* It was to be hereditary in the family of Aaron.

their anointing. Only the High Priest had in every case to be anointed when inducted into his office. For the other priests, the anointing of the first priests, the sons of Aaron, was held to suffice; and the consecration of the ordinary descendant of the sons of Aaron consisted merely in being clothed in the priestly garments.

16. *thus did Moses.* The fulfilment of the command, so far as the erection of the Tabernacle was concerned, is described in the verses that follow. The induction of Aaron and his sons is narrated in Lev. VIII.

shall be to them for an everlasting priesthood throughout their generations.' 16. Thus did Moses; according to all that the LORD commanded him, so did he.*vi. ¶ 17. And it came to pass in the first month in the second year, on the first day of the month, that the tabernacle was reared up. 18. And Moses reared up the tabernacle, and laid its sockets, and set up the boards thereof, and put in the bars thereof, and reared up its pillars. 19. And he spread the tent over the tabernacle, and put the covering of the tent above upon it; as the LORD commanded Moses. ¶ 20. And he took and put the testimony into the ark, and set the staves on the ark, and put the ark-cover above upon the ark. 21. And he brought the ark into the tabernacle, and set up the veil of the screen, and screened the ark of the testimony; as the LORD commanded Moses. ¶ 22. And he put the table in the tent of meeting, upon the side of the tabernacle northward, without the veil. 23. And he set a row of bread in order upon it before the LORD; as the LORD commanded Moses. ¶ 24. And he put the candlestick in the tent of meeting, over against the table, on the side of the tabernacle southward. 25. And he lighted the lamps before the LORD; as the LORD commanded Moses. ¶ 26. And he put the golden altar in the tent of meeting before the veil; 27. and he burnt thereon incense of sweet spices; as the LORD commanded Moses.*vii. ¶ 28. And he put the screen of the door to the tabernacle. 29. And the altar of burnt-offering he set at the door of the tabernacle of the tent of meeting, and offered upon it the burnt-offering and the meal-offering; as the LORD commanded Moses. ¶ 30. And he set the laver between the tent of meeting and the altar, and put water therein, wherewith to wash; 31. that Moses and Aaron and his sons might wash their hands and their feet thereat; 32. when they went into the tent of meeting, and when they came near unto the altar, they should wash; as the LORD commanded Moses. ¶ 33. And he reared up the court round about the tabernacle and the altar, and set up the screen of the gate of the court. So Moses finished the work.*m. ¶ 34. Then the cloud covered the tent of meeting, and the glory of the LORD filled the tabernacle.

16 עולם לדרתם: ויעש משה ככל אשר צוה יהוה אתו
ששי 17 כן עשה: ס ויהי בחדש הראשון בשנה השנית
18 באחד לחדש הוקם המשכן: ויקם משה את־המשכן
ויתן את־אדניו וישם את־קרשיו ויתן את־בריחיו ויקם
19 את־עמודיו: ויפרש את־האהל על־המשכן וישם את־
מכסה האהל עליו מלמעלה כאשר צוה יהוה את־משה:
כ ס ויקח ויתן את־העדת אל־הארן וישם את־הבדים על־
21 הארן ויתן את־הכפרת על־הארן מלמעלה: ויבא את־
הארן אל־המשכן וישם את פרכת המסך ויסך על ארון
22 העדות כאשר צוה יהוה את־משה: ס ויתן את־
השלחן באהל מועד על ירך המשכן צפנה מחוץ לפרכת:
23 ויערך עליו ערך לחם לפני יהוה כאשר צוה יהוה את־
24 משה: ס וישם את־המנרה באהל מועד נכח השלחן
כה על ירך המשכן נגבה: ויעל הנרת לפני יהוה כאשר
26 צוה יהוה את־משה: ס וישם את־מזבח הזהב באהל
27 מועד לפני הפרכת: ויקטר עליו קטרת סמים כאשר
שביעי 28 צוה יהוה את־משה: ס וישם את־מסך הפתח
29 למשכן: ואת מזבח העלה שם פתח משכן אהל־מועד
ויעל עליו את־העלה ואת־המנחה כאשר צוה יהוה
ל את־משה ס וישם את־הכיר בין־אהל מועד ובין
31 המזבח ויתן שמה מים לרחצה: ורחצו ממנו משה
32 ואהרן ובניו את־ידיהם ואת־רגליהם: בבאם אל־אהל
מועד ובקרבתם אל־המזבח ירחצו כאשר צוה יהוה
33 את־משה: ס ויקם את־החצר סביב למשכן ולמזבח
מפטיר ויתן את־מסך שער החצר ויכל משה את־המלאכה: פ
34 ויכס הענן את־אהל מועד וכבוד יהוה מלא את־

20. *the testimony.* *viz.* the Tables of the Decalogue. Tradition declares that the broken pieces of the First Tables were also deposited in the Ark.

set the staves on the ark. From which they were not to be removed (xxv, 15).

27. *burnt thereon incense.* Moses performed this and other priestly duties during the week of consecration, until the priests were installed.

34–38. THE CLOUD UPON THE TENT OF MEETING

34. *the cloud.* As in XIII, 21, and XXIV, 15, a cloud screened the 'glory of the LORD', and was a visible symbol to the people of His Presence.

glory of the LORD. See XXIX, 43. Since God is not corporeal, this can only imply a spiritual manifestation of His presence in the tent of meeting; *i.e.* the Shechinah.

35. And Moses was not able to enter into the tent of meeting, because the cloud abode thereon, and the glory of the LORD filled the tabernacle.—36. And whenever the cloud was taken up from over the tabernacle, the children of Israel went onward, throughout all their journeys. 37. But if the cloud was not taken up, then they journeyed not till the day that it was taken up. 38. For the cloud of the LORD was upon the tabernacle by day, and there was fire therein by night, in the sight of all the house of Israel, throughout all their journeys.

לה הַמִּשְׁכָּן׃ וְלֹא־יָכֹל מֹשֶׁה לָבוֹא אֶל־אֹהֶל מוֹעֵד כִּי־
36 שָׁכַן עָלָיו הֶעָנָן וּכְבוֹד יְהוָה מָלֵא אֶת־הַמִּשְׁכָּן׃ וּבְהֵעָלוֹת
הֶעָנָן מֵעַל הַמִּשְׁכָּן יִסְעוּ בְּנֵי יִשְׂרָאֵל בְּכֹל מַסְעֵיהֶם׃
37 38 וְאִם־לֹא יֵעָלֶה הֶעָנָן וְלֹא יִסְעוּ עַד־יוֹם הֵעָלֹתוֹ׃ כִּי עֲנַן
יְהוָה עַל־הַמִּשְׁכָּן יוֹמָם וְאֵשׁ תִּהְיֶה לַיְלָה בּוֹ לְעֵינֵי כָל־
בֵּית־יִשְׂרָאֵל בְּכָל־מַסְעֵיהֶם׃

חזק

סכום פסוקי דספר ואלה שמות אלף ומאתים ותשעה. אר״ט סימן: וחציו אלהים לא תקלל: ופרשיותיו אחד עשר. אי זה בית אשר תבנו לי סימן: וסדריו עשרים ותשעה. ולילה ללילה יחוה דעת סימן: ופרקיו ארבעים. תורת אלהיו בלבו סימן: מנין הפתוחות תשע וששים. והסתומות חמש ותשעים. הכל מאה וששים וארבע פרשיות: ישלח עורך מקדש ומציון יסעדך סימן:

35. *filled the tabernacle.* The seal of His approval was thus set on the work that was now completed.

36. *went onward.* Still another purpose was served by the cloud: it was a signal for the People when to halt and when to proceed on their journey.

38. *fire therein. i.e.* with fire shining in the cloud by night (cf. Num. IX, 15 f). Without this fire, the cloud would not have been perceptible at night.

The Book of Exodus thus closes with the fulfilment of the promise in XXIX, 43, 45. Moses' appeal had been effective, and God's protecting and sanctifying Presence in the midst of His people, would lead them to their appointed destination.

The Tabernacle, after it had accompanied the Israelites in their wanderings in the Wilderness, was most probably first set up in the Holy Land at Gilgal (Josh. IV, 19). Before the death of Joshua, it was erected at Shiloh (Josh. XVIII, 1). Here it remained as the national Sanctuary throughout the time of the Judges (Judg. XVIII, 31; I Sam. IV, 3). But its external construction was at this time somewhat changed, and doors seem to have taken the place of the entrance curtain (I Sam. III, 15). After the time of Eli, it was removed to Nob in the district of Benjamin, not far from Jerusalem (I Sam. XXI, 1–9). Thence, in the time of David, it was removed to Gibeon (I Kings III, 4). It was brought from Gibeon to Jerusalem by Solomon (I Kings VIII, 4). When the Temple of Solomon was built, the Tabernacle of the Wilderness had performed its work of protecting the Ark of the Covenant during all the migrations of Israel. The promise that the LORD would choose out a place for Himself in which His name should be preserved and His service should be maintained was then fulfilled.

* * * *

According to Jewish custom, the completion of any of the Five Books of the Torah is marked in the Synagogue by the congregation exclaiming *Be strong, be strong, and let us strengthen one another*—an echo of the words of the ancient warrior, 'Be of good courage and let us play the men, for our people and the cities of our God' (II Sam. X, 12). *Be strong, i.e.* to carry out the teaching contained in the Book just completed.

The Massoretic Note states the numbers of verses in Exodus to be 1,209; its Sedrahs (parshiyyoth), 11; its Sedarim, smaller divisions according to the Triennial Cycle, 29; and its Chapters, 40.

HAFTORAH PEKUDEY (FOR ASHKENAZIM) הפטרת פקודי לאשכנזים

I KINGS VII, 51–VIII, 21

CHAPTER VII

51. Thus all the work that king Solomon wrought in the house of the LORD was finished. And Solomon brought in the things which David his father had dedicated, the silver, and the gold, and the vessels, and put them in the treasuries of the house of the LORD.

CHAPTER VIII

1. Then Solomon assembled the elders of Israel, and all the heads of the tribes, the princes of the fathers' houses of the children of Israel, unto king Solomon in Jerusalem, to bring up the ark of the covenant of the LORD out of the city of David, which is Zion. 2. And all the men of Israel assembled themselves unto king Solomon at the feast, in the month Ethanim, which is the seventh month. 3. And all the elders of Israel came, and the priests took up the ark. 4. And they brought up the ark of the LORD, and the tent of meeting, and all the holy vessels that were in the Tent; even these did the priests and the Levites bring up. 5 And king Solomon and all the congregation of Israel, that were assembled unto him, were with him before the ark, sacrificing sheep and oxen, that could not be told nor numbered for multitude. 6. And the priests brought in the ark of the covenant of the LORD unto its place, into the Sanctuary of the house, to the most holy place, even under the wings of the cherubim. 7. For the cherubim spread forth their wings over the place of the ark, and the cherubim covered the ark and the staves thereof above. 8. And the staves were so long that the ends of the staves were seen from the holy place, even before the Sanctuary; but they could not be seen without; and there they are unto this day. 9. There was nothing in the ark save the two tables of stone which Moses put there at Horeb,

CAP. VII. ז

51 וַתִּשְׁלַם כָּל־הַמְּלָאכָה
אֲשֶׁר עָשָׂה הַמֶּלֶךְ שְׁלֹמֹה בֵּית יְהוָה וַיָּבֵא שְׁלֹמֹה אֶת־
קָדְשֵׁי ׀ דָּוִד אָבִיו אֶת־הַכֶּסֶף וְאֶת־הַזָּהָב וְאֶת־הַכֵּלִים נָתַן
בְּאֹצְרוֹת בֵּית יְהוָה׃

CAP. VIII. ח

א אָז יַקְהֵל שְׁלֹמֹה אֶת־זִקְנֵי יִשְׂרָאֵל וְאֶת־כָּל־רָאשֵׁי הַמַּטּוֹת
נְשִׂיאֵי הָאָבוֹת לִבְנֵי יִשְׂרָאֵל אֶל־הַמֶּלֶךְ שְׁלֹמֹה יְרוּשָׁלָם
לְהַעֲלוֹת אֶת־אֲרוֹן בְּרִית־יְהוָה מֵעִיר דָּוִד הִיא צִיּוֹן׃
2 וַיִּקָּהֲלוּ אֶל־הַמֶּלֶךְ שְׁלֹמֹה כָּל־אִישׁ יִשְׂרָאֵל בְּיֶרַח
3 הָאֵתָנִים בֶּחָג הוּא הַחֹדֶשׁ הַשְּׁבִיעִי׃ וַיָּבֹאוּ כֹּל זִקְנֵי
4 יִשְׂרָאֵל וַיִּשְׂאוּ הַכֹּהֲנִים אֶת־הָאָרוֹן׃ וַיַּעֲלוּ אֶת־אֲרוֹן יְהוָה
וְאֶת־אֹהֶל מוֹעֵד וְאֶת־כָּל־כְּלֵי הַקֹּדֶשׁ אֲשֶׁר בָּאֹהֶל וַיַּעֲלוּ
ה אֹתָם הַכֹּהֲנִים וְהַלְוִיִּם׃ וְהַמֶּלֶךְ שְׁלֹמֹה וְכָל־עֲדַת יִשְׂרָאֵל
הַנּוֹעָדִים עָלָיו אִתּוֹ לִפְנֵי הָאָרוֹן מְזַבְּחִים צֹאן וּבָקָר
6 אֲשֶׁר לֹא־יִסָּפְרוּ וְלֹא יִמָּנוּ מֵרֹב׃ וַיָּבִאוּ הַכֹּהֲנִים אֶת־
אֲרוֹן בְּרִית־יְהוָה אֶל־מְקוֹמוֹ אֶל־דְּבִיר הַבַּיִת אֶל־קֹדֶשׁ
7 הַקֳּדָשִׁים אֶל־תַּחַת כַּנְפֵי הַכְּרוּבִים׃ כִּי הַכְּרוּבִים פֹּרְשִׂים
כְּנָפַיִם אֶל־מְקוֹם הָאָרוֹן וַיָּסֹכּוּ הַכְּרֻבִים עַל־הָאָרוֹן וְעַל־
8 בַּדָּיו מִלְמָעְלָה׃ וַיַּאֲרִכוּ הַבַּדִּים וַיֵּרָאוּ רָאשֵׁי הַבַּדִּים
מִן־הַקֹּדֶשׁ עַל־פְּנֵי הַדְּבִיר וְלֹא יֵרָאוּ הַחוּצָה וַיִּהְיוּ שָׁם

ח׳ v. 1. נ״א את־

The Dedication of the Temple, and the first part of Solomon's Prayer of Consecration.

51. *and Solomon brought.* The Temple work completed, Solomon piously brings in the gifts his father David had given and consecrated for the House.

in the treasuries. Probably in the side-chambers referred to in I Kings VI, 5; see p. 338.

CHAPTER VIII

1. *the city of David.* Where David had placed it after bringing it from the house of Obed-Edom (II Sam. VI, 12). The city of David was built on the site of the old Jebusite fort captured by David (II Sam. V, 9). The Temple was built on a higher slope of the hill.

Zion. The name was originally applied to the Temple hill and the city generally.

2. *the feast.* Of Tabernacles, the Feast of Ingatherings. The people were assembled prior to the Feast, for the purpose of the dedication and rejoicings thereat (seven days), and afterwards observed the Festival according to *v.* 65.

Ethanim. The month later named Tishri.

4. *tent of meeting.* The Tabernacle built by Moses in the Wilderness.

when the LORD made a covenant with the children of Israel when they came out of the land of Egypt. 10. And it came to pass, when the priests were come out of the holy place, that the cloud filled the house of the LORD, 11. so that the priests could not stand to minister by reason of the cloud; for the glory of the LORD filled the house of the LORD.
12. Then spoke Solomon:

The LORD hath said that He would dwell
in the thick darkness.
13. I have surely built Thee a house of
habitation,
A place for Thee to dwell in for ever.

14. And the king turned his face about, and blessed all the congregation of Israel; and all the congregation of Israel stood. 15. And he said: 'Blessed be the LORD, the God of Israel, who spoke with His mouth unto David my father, and hath with His hand fulfilled it, saying: 16. Since the day that I brought forth My people Israel out of Egypt, I chose no city out of all the tribes of Israel to build a house, that My name might be there; but I chose David to be over My people Israel. 17. Now it was in the heart of David my father to build a house for the name of the LORD, the God of Israel. 18. But the LORD said unto David my father: Whereas it was in thy heart to build a house for My name, thou didst well that it was in thy heart; 19. nevertheless thou shalt not build the house; but thy son that shall come forth out of thy loins, he shall build the house for My name. 20. And the LORD hath established His word that He spoke; for I am risen up in the room of David my father, and sit on the throne of Israel, as the LORD promised, and have built the house for the name of the LORD, the God of Israel. 21. And there have I set a place for the ark, wherein is the covenant of the LORD, which He made with our fathers, when He brought them out of the land of Egypt.'

9 עַד הַיּוֹם הַזֶּה׃ אֵין בָּאָרוֹן רַק שְׁנֵי לֻחוֹת הָאֲבָנִים אֲשֶׁר
הִנִּחַ שָׁם מֹשֶׁה בְּחֹרֵב אֲשֶׁר כָּרַת יְהוָה עִם־בְּנֵי יִשְׂרָאֵל
י בְּצֵאתָם מֵאֶרֶץ מִצְרָיִם׃ וַיְהִי בְּצֵאת הַכֹּהֲנִים מִן־הַקֹּדֶשׁ
11 וְהֶעָנָן מָלֵא אֶת־בֵּית יְהוָה׃ וְלֹא־יָכְלוּ הַכֹּהֲנִים לַעֲמֹד
לְשָׁרֵת מִפְּנֵי הֶעָנָן כִּי־מָלֵא כְבוֹד־יְהוָה אֶת־בֵּית יְהוָה׃
12 13 אָז אָמַר שְׁלֹמֹה יְהוָה אָמַר לִשְׁכֹּן בָּעֲרָפֶל׃ בָּנֹה
14 בָנִיתִי בֵּית זְבֻל לָךְ מָכוֹן לְשִׁבְתְּךָ עוֹלָמִים׃ וַיַּסֵּב הַמֶּלֶךְ
אֶת־פָּנָיו וַיְבָרֶךְ אֵת כָּל־קְהַל יִשְׂרָאֵל וְכָל־קְהַל יִשְׂרָאֵל
טו עֹמֵד׃ וַיֹּאמֶר בָּרוּךְ יְהוָה אֱלֹהֵי יִשְׂרָאֵל אֲשֶׁר דִּבֶּר בְּפִיו
16 אֵת דָּוִד אָבִי וּבְיָדוֹ מִלֵּא לֵאמֹר׃ מִן־הַיּוֹם אֲשֶׁר הוֹצֵאתִי
אֶת־עַמִּי יִשְׂרָאֵל מִמִּצְרַיִם לֹא־בָחַרְתִּי בְעִיר מִכֹּל שִׁבְטֵי
יִשְׂרָאֵל לִבְנוֹת בַּיִת לִהְיוֹת שְׁמִי שָׁם וָאֶבְחַר בְּדָוִד לִהְיוֹת
17 עַל־עַמִּי יִשְׂרָאֵל׃ וַיְהִי עִם־לְבַב דָּוִד אָבִי לִבְנוֹת בַּיִת
18 לְשֵׁם יְהוָה אֱלֹהֵי יִשְׂרָאֵל׃ וַיֹּאמֶר יְהוָה אֶל־דָּוִד אָבִי יַעַן
אֲשֶׁר הָיָה עִם־לְבָבְךָ לִבְנוֹת בַּיִת לִשְׁמִי הֱטִיבֹתָ כִּי הָיָה
19 עִם־לְבָבֶךָ׃ רַק אַתָּה לֹא תִבְנֶה הַבָּיִת כִּי אִם־בִּנְךָ הַיֹּצֵא
כ מֵחֲלָצֶיךָ הוּא־יִבְנֶה הַבַּיִת לִשְׁמִי׃ וַיָּקֶם יְהוָה אֶת־דְּבָרוֹ
אֲשֶׁר דִּבֵּר וָאָקֻם תַּחַת דָּוִד אָבִי וָאֵשֵׁב ׀ עַל־כִּסֵּא יִשְׂרָאֵל
כַּאֲשֶׁר דִּבֶּר יְהוָה וָאֶבְנֶה הַבַּיִת לְשֵׁם יְהוָה אֱלֹהֵי יִשְׂרָאֵל׃
21 וָאָשִׂם שָׁם מָקוֹם לָאָרוֹן אֲשֶׁר־שָׁם בְּרִית יְהוָה אֲשֶׁר
כָּרַת עִם־אֲבֹתֵינוּ בְּהוֹצִיאוֹ אֹתָם מֵאֶרֶץ מִצְרָיִם׃

8. *the staves.* The poles by which the Ark was carried protruded from the Holy of Holies into the Holy Place.

9. *there was nothing in the ark . . . tables of stone.* The Ark contained no image or any mystic appurtenance of pagan worship.

12. *in the thick darkness.* In the heavy cloud (see Exod. xx, *v.* 18) which now filled the Temple was the visible sign of the Shechinah (God's Presence).

13. *to dwell in for ever.* The places where the Ark previously rested were only temporary Places of Worship until the Temple, Israel's permanent Sanctuary, was erected on the chosen site (Kimchi).

15–21. SOLOMON'S ADDRESS TO THE PEOPLE: THE CIRCUMSTANCES THAT LED TO HIS BUILDING THE TEMPLE

17. *in the heart of David.* To build the Temple was the cherished dream of David.

18. *the LORD said unto David.* Through the prophet Nathan; II Sam. VII, 8, 9.

thou didst well that it was in thine heart. Our own cherished high aims may not be fulfilled, but we are the better for striving for them.

21. *wherein is the covenant of the LORD.* The Tables of stone placed in the Ark.

ADDITIONAL NOTES TO EXODUS

A

ISRAEL IN EGYPT: THE HISTORICAL PROBLEMS

I

What Light does Egyptian History throw on Israel in Egypt?

The history of ancient Egypt is usually divided into three periods. The earliest period is that of the Old Kingdom, which comprises the first ten dynasties of pyramid builders, ending 2500 B.C.E. The second period, the Middle Kingdom, from the eleventh to the seventeenth dynasty of rulers (2500–1587 B.C.E.) is one of great obscurity, and covers the age during which the Hyksos, Bedouin invaders from the Arabian desert, ruled Egypt. They were expelled by the founder of the eighteenth dynasty in 1587. He opens the third period, the New Kingdom, which continues to the end of the twentieth dynasty in 1100 B.C.E. After that date, the country successively came under Lybian, Persian, Macedonian, and Roman rule.

Biblical interest in Egypt begins during the Middle Kingdom. Joseph served one of the Hyksos kings. These invaders, 'princes of the desert," as they called themselves, soon accommodated themselves to the system of Government they had found in Egypt; and their contribution to Egyptian culture was not inferior to that of the native kings. Their dominion was later described as one of desolation and ruin—which is quite untrue. The Hyksos kings restored and enlarged the temples, encouraged learning, and could not have destroyed any of the previous Egyptian monuments, seeing that these have come down to our own day. On the contrary, it is the native rulers who followed them that eradicated every trace of the Hyksos kings. This is responsible for the obscurity that overhangs the story of the whole Hyksos period, and the consequent uncertainty of so much of Egyptian chronology. Not long after the death of Joseph, the Hyksos were driven back into Asia; and a native ruler, the founder of the Eighteenth Dynasty, regained the throne.

The advent of this nationalist dynasty marked the turn of the tide in the fortunes of the descendants of Jacob. As friends of the overthrown Hyksos kings, they lost their favoured position, and their past services to the State were 'ignored'. From prosperous and honoured settlers in the Eastern Delta of the Nile, with freedom of movement and right of domicile throughout Egypt and her dominions, they were under the successive rulers of the Eighteenth Dynasty (1587–1350 B.C.E.) gradually reduced to a condition of serfdom. These rulers, as well as the kings of the Nineteenth Dynasty (1250–1200), were great architects and are famous for the number and magnificence of their monuments. That veritable frenzy for building which characterized all these rulers, naturally called for vast levies of forced labour. The feared and hated Israelites seemed to these Pharaohs to be at hand for just such a purpose. The Israelites were now condemned to cruel slave labour as bricklayers and navvies, both the kind and conditions of their labour being utterly alien to the nature and the traditions of free and independent shepherd folk.

It is difficult to determine the name of the 'new king' who initiated the Oppression. Scripture does not give us the name of the ruler in question, *Pharaoh* being merely the royal title of the reigning monarch. The one aim of the Scripture story is to describe God's Providential guidance of His people. The narrative is 'theocentric'; and events are viewed under the aspect of eternity. Details, such as the exact names of the impious heathen oppressors, are passed over, and all the emphasis is placed on the religious truths with which the narrative throbs (Boehl). And as to the hieroglyphic monuments, their information on this whole subject is most meagre. Possibly this is due to the fact that as yet little excavation has taken place in Goshen, *i.e.* the Eastern Delta, which was the main domicile of the Israelites. But even when ancient Goshen will have been revealed to us, it is well to remember that the true-born Egyptian chronicler took little notice of the fortunes of an alien serf-class like the Israelites, whose original occupation—keeping sheep—was, in his eyes, that of outcasts (Gen. XLVI, 34).

There are, therefore, but few casual references on the monuments to the *Aperu* or *Apuriu*, which is the Egyptian form of the name 'Hebrews'. Thus, in a report addressed to an official of the reign of Rameses II, there occur the words: 'I have obeyed the message of my lord, in which he said, "Give corn to the native soldiers, and also to the Apuriu, who are bringing up stones for the great tower of Pa-Ramessu" . . . I have given them their corn every month, according to the instructions of my lord.' In another report of the same age we read: 'I have hearkened to my lord's message, "Give provisions to the soldiers and to the *Aperu*, who bring up stones for Ra (the sun-god), viz. for Ra of Rameses, the beloved of Amon, in the southern quarter of Memphis."' So much for the nature of the few Egyptian references to the Hebrew serfs doing forced labour to the Pharaohs.

As to the exodus from Egypt, the Egyptian records pass it over in total silence—as was their invariable custom in connection with any defeat suffered by the ruler or nation. For instance, although the Hyksos conquest of Egypt is the most important political event in Egyptian history, yet almost no mention is made in the monuments of this catastrophe which shook the whole social structure to its foundations. The Egyptian records confine themselves to the boastful recounting of victories. The Biblical writers, alone, among all Oriental chroniclers, describe defeats of their kings and armies; nay more, they arraign ruler and people alike whensoever these are unfaithful to the aims and ideals of the nation. This is one of the reasons why of all Oriental chronicles, it is only the Biblical annals that deserve the name of history.

II

Who was the Pharaoh of the Oppression?

In view of the above, there are several candidates for the infamy of having been the 'Pharaoh of the Oppression', under whom the bondage of the Israelites ended in a systematic attempt at their extermination. The majority of scholars identify him with the splendour-loving and tyrannical Rameses II, whose dates are variously given as 1300–1234 B.C.E. (Petrie) and 1347–1280 (Mahler). 'He was a vain and boastful character who wished to dazzle posterity by covering the land with constructions whereon his name was engraved thousands of times, and who prided himself in his inscriptions upon great conquests which he never made' (Naville). The Exodus itself is held to have taken place under his son, Menremptah, with whom the decline of Egypt began. Menremptah (or Menephtah) was an obstinate and vain despot. He too had the habit of claiming as his own the achievements of others. 'He was one of the most unconscionable usurpers (and defacers) of the monuments of his predecessors, including those of his own father, who had set him the example . . . all due to a somewhat insane desire to perpetuate his own memory' (Prof. Griffith, *Encyclopædia Britannica*, 1929).

Some scholars, however, date the Oppression and the Exodus in the century preceding Rameses II, and connect it with the religious revolution of Amenophis IV, or Ikhnaton (1383–1365). This extraordinary personality abolished the multitudinous deities of the Egyptian Pantheon, and devoted himself exclusively to the worship of the Sun. These scholars hold that there was some relation between the faith of the Israelites and the solar monotheism of Ikhnaton, and that Israelite influence was partly responsible for this assault on the gross idolatry of Egypt. Ikhnaton was hated by the people as the 'heretic king', and his innovations were abandoned by his son-in-law Tut-an-khamen who succeeded him, eventually to be altogether uprooted by Haremrab the last Pharaoh of the Eighteenth Dynasty. When the native religion was restored—these scholars maintain—the Israelites suffered persecution and degradation; and the Oppression formed part of the extirpation of Ikhnaton's heresy.

Other Egyptologists go back still another century to Thotmes III (1503–1449), and declare him to have been the Pharaoh of the Oppression. They connect the Oppression and the departure of the Israelites from Egypt with the movements of the Habiri people in the Amarna age (see page 51, n. 13) and believe that the recently discovered inscriptions on the Sinai Peninsula likewise favour this theory.

One of the main reasons which induce both these groups of scholars to dissent from the general view that Rameses II was the Pharaoh of the Oppression, is the fact that the name 'Israel' is alleged to occur on an inscription of Menremptah. That Inscription (discovered in 1896) is a song of triumph of Menremptah, describing in grandiloquent language his victories in Canaan; and, among other conquests, he boasts that 'Canaan is seized with every evil; Ashkelon is carried away; Gezer is taken; Yenoam is annihilated; *Ysiraal is desolated, its seed is not*.' From the phrase, 'Ysiraal is desolated,' these scholars deduce that the Israelites must in those days have been in possession of Canaan; and that, therefore, the Exodus must have taken place long before the time of Menremptah. However, it is not at all certain that the words, 'Ysiraal is desolated,' refer to Israel at all. Thus, Prof. Kennett takes the phrase as analogous with that concerning Ashkelon and Gezer; and, therefore, as merely stating that Menremptah had devasted the district of 'Jezreel.' And if 'Ysiraal' *does* mean Israel, then it refers to the settlements in Palestine by Israelites from Egypt before the Exodus (Jampel). From various notices in I Chronicles we see that during the generations preceding the Oppression, the Israelites did not remain confined to Goshen or even to Egypt proper, but spread into the southern Palestinian territory, then under Egyptian control, and that they even engaged in skirmishes with the Philistines. When the bulk of the nation had left Egypt and was wandering in the Wilderness, these Israelite settlers had thrown off their Egyptian allegiance. And it is these settlements which Menremptah boasts of having devasted during his Canaanite campaign. There is, therefore, no cogent reason for dissenting from the current view that the Pharaoh of the Oppression was Rameses II, with his son Menremptah as the Pharaoh of the Exodus.

III

The 'Inconvenience' of Biblical Traditions

Little need be said in regard to the extreme and baseless scepticism, recently revived in Soviet anti-religious circles, that the Israelites never were in Egypt; and that, in consequence, there could not have been either an Oppression or an Exodus.

There is one conclusive answer to the doubts as to the historicity of the Exodus and other crucial events in Scriptural history; and that is, what has aptly been called *the 'inconvenience' of Biblical traditions*. One or two examples will both explain this argument and make clear its unanswerable force. The first example is taken from the story of Abraham. For centuries, the Hebrew tribes waged a life-and-death struggle with the native population for the possession of ancient Palestine. But instead of the Hebrews claiming that they too were natives of Canaan, or that they were the true aborigines of its soil, Bible Tradition concerning the beginnings of the Hebrew people is emphatic that its ancestors were *not* born in Canaan, but were nomads, immigrant shepherds, and had their origin in Ur of the Chaldees. Now, even the sceptical historian is forced to admit that such a tradition must be based on strict history, as no people would invent such an *inconvenient* tradition in regard to a matter of vital importance like its right and title to its national homeland. To take another example. The record in Genesis that Isaac and Jacob married Aramaean wives must be based on *fact*, and could not have arisen, as some Bible critics maintain, in the days of Monarchy. For throughout the days of the Monarchy, Aram was the hereditary enemy of Israel, and was guilty of the most hideous barbarities in its continued attempts to annihilate Israel. It is clear that here too the tradition that the 'Mothers' of the Israelite people were Aramaean women, was an *inconvenient* one—and cannot therefore be an invention of later legend (Cornill, Jirku).

All this applies with immeasurably greater force in regard to the historicity of the Oppression in Egypt. Compared with the Egyptian bondage and the deliverance therefrom, everything else in Bible history is of secondary importance. The memory of that bondage and deliverance is woven into the message of legislator, historian, psalmist, prophet and priest; and a large portion of Jewish life both in the Biblical and the post-Biblical ages is but a זכר ליציאת מצרים, an echo and reminder of that Divine event which meant the birth of Israel as a nation. Now, it is unthinkable that any nation, unless forced to do so by the overwhelming compulsion of unforgettable fact, would of its own account have wantonly affixed to its forefathers the stain and dishonour of slavery in a foreign country. No people has ever yet invented a *disgraceful* past for itself. The invention by a later age of a story so humiliating to national self-respect would be still more astounding in the case of Israel, when we consider that after the days of Menremptah the decline of Egypt began, and the invented national bondage would have been to a weak and waning Power. If, therefore, Israel's sojourn and bondage in Egypt were *merely* a fiction, such fiction would be quite inexplicable—in fact, a psychological miracle. Even a radical student of this question like Prof. Peet sums up his conclusions as follows: 'That Israel was in Egypt under one form or another no historian could possibly doubt; a legend of such tenacity representing the early fortunes of a people under so unfavourable an aspect, could not have arisen save as a reflection of real occurrences.'

B

ISRAEL AND EGYPT: THE SPIRITUAL CONTRAST

Israel and Egypt represent two world-conceptions, two ways of looking on God and Man that are not merely in conflict, but mutually exclusive.

For ages Egypt was the Land of Wonder, and men spoke in awe of the wisdom of the Egyptians. We know now that they were indeed a wonderful people; but that it is only in the arts and crafts and especially in their colossal and titanic architecture, that they attained truly astonishing results.

The real tests of a nation's civilization, however, are far other than these. The supreme test is its vision of God. Now what were the objects of Egyptian worship ? Stocks and stones, and, above all else, the beast. While there are traces, albeit faint traces, that the men of the Nile Valley were capable of learning both in religion and in conduct, they seem to have been quite incapable of *forgetting*. Egypt never discarded the low animism and savage fetishism of its prehistoric days, and remained always 'zoomorphic' in its conception of God: bulls, crocodiles, beetles, apes, cats, and goats—these were its gods. There were, it is true, stammerings of something nobler; glimpses of higher religious truth; but these remained only glimpses—like flashes of light for one brief moment in the night-time, leaving greater darkness, Egyptian darkness, behind. Once only was an attempt made by that remarkable man, Amenophis IV, to reform the barbarism of Egyptian worship and to put a kind of monotheism in its place. The sun was to be worshipped as the single deity under the name of Aton; and he changed his own name to Ikhnaton, 'Glory to the Sun.' But the reformation was a failure. He died amid the curses of his subjects, and the old confused polytheism returned stronger than ever. 'We have no grounds for holding the opinion,' says Prof. R. H. Hall, 'that the educated Egyptian priest, far less the man in the street, normally accepted any pious theories of a latent monotheism, underlying his blatant polytheism. Ikhnaton was branded as a criminal; and after his failure, we go back to the old spells and mumbo-jumbo again . . . till the death of the Egyptian religion in the days of Justinian. In religious matters, the Egyptians at all periods (except the educated at the end of the Eighteenth Dynasty) were in the mental condition of the blacks of the Gold Coast and Niger delta. They had "mysteries", of course, like the Ashantis or Ibos. It is a mistake, however, to think that these mysteries enshrined truth, and that there was an occult "faith" behind them. There is no more proof of it than in the case of the Ashantis or Ibos' (*Encyclopædia Britannica*, 1929).

Now where there is no vision of God there can be no vision of man. Hence the insignificance of man in the Egyptian world-conception. They bent the knee to the beast, but man throughout Egyptian history was in bondage. Human life had absolutely no value. The lives of vast multitudes of men were sacrificed in connection with the frenzied building schemes. Herodotus tells us that in the time of Pharaoh Necho II (609–588 B.C.E.), 120,000 labourers were worked to death in the construction of a canal connecting the Nile and the Red Sea. The pyramids, erected by the tyrant's unlimited command of human forces, remain everlasting monuments of human slavery—and of the national deification of reckless and irresponsible power.

In eternal contrast to Egypt, the whole story of Israel is one long protest against idolatry and inhumanity. A single incident in the life of a Jewish ruler will illustrate the world-wide difference between Israel and Egypt. King Jehoiakim, a contemporary of Pharaoh Necho II, tried to emulate his example, and he built himself palaces by means of forced labour. In Egypt, such a thing was taken as a matter of course, as the unquestioned prerogative of the king. In Israel, that enterprise was deemed an outrage against reason and human decency. Jeremiah the Prophet arose and came to the door of Jehoiakim's palace, crying: 'Woe unto him that buildeth his house by unrighteousness, and his chambers by injustice; that useth his neighbour's service without wages, and giveth him not his hire. . . . Thine eyes and thine heart are not but for thy covetousness, and for to shed innocent blood, and for oppression, and for violence, to do it. Therefore thus saith the LORD concerning Jehoiakim, the son of Josiah, king of Judah: They shall not lament for him. He shall be buried with the burial of an ass, drawn and cast forth beyond the gates of Jerusalem' (Jer. XXII, 13, 17–19). These words of Jeremiah are but a Prophetic echo of the Israelite's cry for freedom that pierced the heavens in the days of Moses: they are but the translation of the trumpet sounds of the Exodus and the Sinaitic Covenant with their Divine and everlasting proclamation of the rights of man.

Another characteristic element in the religious life of Egypt was Worship of the dead. I give a brief summary of that worship, taken from W. Max Müller's article in the *Encyclopædia Biblica*. The huge pyramids alone, says Prof. Müller, would be sufficient to testify that the Egyptians devoted greater zeal than any nation on earth to the abodes of their dead, and to the sustenance of their souls by sacrifices. The Bible of the Egyptians is the so-called 'Book of the Dead'. It contains magic formulæ for the guidance of man after death, warning him of the dangers he might expect to meet, and providing him with powerful spells—previously placed on the coffins for this purpose—to guarantee his safety. When the dead man reached the great Judgment Hall, of the god Osiris, his moral life was tested. In the course of that judgment, the deceased denied that he ever committed any of the 42 cardinal sins. (R. H. Hall rightly says: The Egyptian was never a humble person, either genuinely or hypocritically. When he confessed he did not say, 'I am guilty'; he said, 'I am not guilty'; his confession was negative, and the *onus probandi* lay on his judges). Simultaneously with the doctrine just stated, there existed the conflicting belief that the departed souls lived in darkness and misery in the nether world, persecuted by evil spirits, so that it was best for the dead person to become, by witchcraft, one of these evil monsters himself.

No wonder that the influence of the Egyptian religion on the lives of men was not very profound. In every respect the morality of the Egyptians seems to have been lax. One example will suffice. The tombs were almost invariably broken into soon after burial, and no military protection could prevent even the royal tombs from being plundered.

When we compare the Egyptian attitude towards death with that of the Pentateuch, we see in the latter what appears to be a deliberate aim to wean the Israelites from Egyptian superstition. In this way alone, can we explain the silence of Israel's Torah in regard to the Life after Death. On the one hand, there is not a word concerning immortality, or concerning reward and punishment in the Hereafter; and, on the other hand, there is rigorous proscription of all magic and sorcery, of sacrificing to the dead, as well as every form of alleged intercourse with the world of spirits. Israel's Faith is a religion *of life*, not of death; a religion that declares man's humanity to man as the most acceptable form of adoration of the One God, the Creator of heaven and earth, Who is from everlasting to everlasting.

Israel while in Egypt was yet but a child, and was not strong enough to withstand Egypt *in* Egypt. Only *out* of Egypt could it grow, uncontaminated by noxious influences of a decadent civilization. Only when liberated from the contagion of a nation of mere childish stammerers in the things of the Spirit, could it flourish, and fill the earth with the glad tidings of a God of holiness and pity, and the message of Righteousness to men and nations.

C

DOES EXODUS VI, 3, SUPPORT THE HIGHER CRITICAL THEORY?

This query, as well as the answer to it, may have little meaning and no interest to the general reader. In that case, he will be well advised to skip the next four pages. There is, however, a good number of laymen who are aware of the crucial significance that is attached to Exodus VI, 3 in modern Biblical study. For them it is of utmost importance that the question which forms the title of this Note be dealt with in a thoroughgoing way. Even the man who is not possessed of technical knowledge will then see how feeble, how insubstantial, is the Pillar on which so much of Bible Critical Theory rests.

I

Contrary to what we have seen to be the plain meaning of Exodus VI, 3, Bible Critics declare that, according to the author of this chapter, the Name Y H W H (Adonay) is here revealed for *the first time* to Moses. Therefore—they hold—all those chapters in Genesis and Exodus in which Adonay (or the LORD, in English) occurs, must have been written by another hand than Exodus VI, 3. They point to this verse as unanswerable proof of the alleged plurality of 'sources' in the Pentateuch (see p. 398; and Exodus VI, 3, is accordingly proclaimed in every learned and popular treatise on the Critical treatment of the Bible as *the* 'clue' to the various sources of the Pentateuch.

The current Critical explanation of this verse, however, rests on a total misunderstanding of Hebrew idiom. When Scripture states that Israel, or the nations, or Pharaoh, 'shall know that God is Adonay'—this does *not* mean that they shall be informed that His Name is Y H W H (Adonay), as the Critics would have it; but that they shall come to witness His power and comprehend those attributes of the Divine nature which that Name denotes. Thus, Jer. XVI, 21, 'I will cause them to know my hand and my might, and they shall know that my name is Adonay.' In Ezekiel the phrase, 'They shall know I am Adonay,' occurs more than sixty times. Nowhere does it mean, They will know Him by the four letters of His Name. Every time it means, They will know Him by His acts and the fulfilment of His promises (see, *e.g.*, the Haftorah of Va-ayra).

If a new Name indeed were here announced for the first time, Hebrew idiom would require the use of the verb הגיד (cf. Gen. XXXII, 30; Judges XIII, 6); and the actual phrase would be ושמי ד׳ לא הגדתי להם. B. Jacob has shown that the revelation of a *new* name of God would have been announced somewhat in the following manner:

הנה לא ידעת עד כה את שמי וגם אל אברהם אל יצחק ואל יעקב לא נודעתי כי אם בשם אל שדי ושמי ד׳ לא הגדתי להם : ועתה הנני מודיעך כי לא אל שדי יקרא עוד שמי כי אם ד׳ יהיה שמי :

'Behold, thou hast not hitherto known my Name; and even unto Abraham, unto Isaac, and unto Jacob I was known only by my Name El Shaddai, but my Name Adonay I did not tell them. Now I make known unto thee that my Name shall no longer be called Shaddai, but Adonay shall my Name be.'

As it is, the writer of VI, 3 could not possibly have meant what the Critics attempt to read into his words. Furthermore, the Critics themselves furnish a most awkward obstacle to their own theory. This is the 'Redactor'. Think of it. After supposedly combining the story of the Patriarchs from documents constantly using the name Adonay, he now introduces a statement that the Patriarchs had never heard of this Name! By such a statement, that Redactor would have stultified himself completely—if he had ever had any existence outside the imagination of modern Bible critics (W. H. Green).

One of these critics (Dr. J. Skinner) pleads that the Critical analysis of Scripture is a chain which is a good deal stronger than its weakest link. Whatever this may mean, no one will pretend that a chain can be stronger than its *strongest* link. And its strongest link—the alleged proof offered by Exodus VI, 3—consists not alone in disregarding the plain meaning of the text and attributing an absurdity to the Sacred Writer, but actually in sadly belittling the intelligence of the Critic's own creation, the 'Redactor'.

II

The so-called Analysis of Sources, with its series of non-existent authors and irresponsible 'Redactors', is unsupported by any external evidence whatsoever. None of these imaginary sources has come down to us in its original form, or in any form for that matter. 'The plurality of sources,' complains Naville, 'is *assumed* by the Critics as an indisputable fact. Unity of authorship is ruled out by them from the very first. They must at all costs discover diverse authors, in explanation of a perfectly simple narrative which unfolds itself in the most natural manner. It matters little that the text itself is altogether out of harmony with the conception of the Critics. The text must adjust itself to these conceptions. If it does not, what does it matter: *it* is at fault. They correct the text; with the result that it agrees with their theory.' Moreover, all this wanton tampering with the text leads nowhere. The varying use of the Divine Names does not indicate a difference of authorship, but is due to the different meanings of the Names, the choice of which is carefully considered in each case (see *Genesis*, pp. 17, 107). Differences of style and treatment are called forth by differences in the nature of the subjects treated, *e.g.* in Exodus, the story of the Deliverance from Egypt demands a strong, energetic narrative; while the account of the building of the Tabernacle calls for technical details. All suggestions of reduplications and contradictions are merely due to an insufficient insight into the spirit and intention of Scripture on the part of the Higher Critics.

Instead of the misleading term 'Higher Criticism' its followers now prefer to speak of their school as that of Historical Criticism. This, however, is even more misleading: for *nothing is more characteristic of the Higher Critic than the way he refuses to revise his views, in the face of historical discovery which disproves those views.* One example will suffice. The Critical theory starts from the assumption that, before the days of Solomon, the Hebrews lived in a state of savagery. Thus, it was one of the 'finalities of scholarship' that the art of writing was unknown in ancient Israel. As recently as 1892, an eminent exponent of that theory asserted deliberately, 'The time, of which the pre-Mosaic narratives treat, is a sufficient proof of their legendary character. It was a time prior to all knowledge of writing.' Others said the same thing of the Mosaic age. Whereas to-day, Professor Sellin—a leading exegete, excavator, and historian—says: 'That the question should ever have been raised whether Moses could have known how to write, appears to us now absurd. Every petty Canaanitish "king" of a city-state had his scribe, who conducted his correspondence and kept the necessary lists.' But though the main assumption on which the Critical speculations are based has been proved false, the Higher Critics remained as imperturbable as ever. An unimpeachable witness like Prof. Kittel, the eminent historian, recently wrote: 'The facts themselves had rendered a large portion of Wellhausen's hypothesis untenable. One would have thought that Wellhausen would have taken note of this new knowledge. But he never retracted or modified any of his theories; and his followers continued writing and building on his hypothesis, as if nothing had happened.' Wellhausen's devotees to-day still continue writing, as if nothing had happened; and his speculations are still proclaimed as truths which it is heresy to question, by the popularizers, hacks, and journeymen of theological literature, especially in English-speaking countries.

The leaders, however, are not as confident as they used to be in regard to the criterion of the Divine Names for the supposed separateness of the 'sources'. Jewish and Christian scholars like Hoffman and Wiener, Dahse and Eerdmans, W. H. Green and Naville have not laboured in vain; and the Critical structure begun in 1753, and completed with so much jubilation by Wellhausen, his forerunners and his disciples, is crumbling before our very eyes. Dr. B. Jacob recalls the fact that even as late as 1910, a Liberal-Jewish Critic had such an absolute faith in the Critical division of the Pentateuch according to the well-known symbols J, E, P, D, R, etc., that he permitted himself to declare: 'If one is to doubt the truth of the Critical analysis, one might just as well doubt the truth of Newton's law of gravitation!' In a statement of this nature, one sees mirrored the dogmatism of the entire school of Bible Criticism. Little did they dream of the Einsteins that were to arise, who, in the field of Physics, would restate the law of gravitation according to new categories of thought; and, in the field of Bible study, shatter the foundations of the Wellhausen hypothesis, and definitely declare its assumptions to be both unscientific and obsolete.

D

THE TEN PLAGUES

'Bible story is nowhere more vivid than in its picture of the Plagues of Egypt. Pharaoh is the incarnation of sullen force, yielding by inches, or for a single moment, only to harden his heart when the crisis is past. But it is human strength matching itself against the inexhaustible resources of nature, which Moses is permitted to wield. The river which is Egypt's pride runs with blood; from out its reed-grass, frogs invade the secret recesses of luxury; the dust of the ground takes life, to become loathsome vermin; indoors and outside, there is no escape from swarming flies and corruption. While all over the land of Egypt beasts are dying of murrain, in Israel's land of Goshen the cattle are intact. The royal magicians seeking to compete with the wonders of Moses, become themselves victims to the plague of boils. Now the heavens begin to play their part, and rain down wasting hail; while, to enhance the wonder, fire winds about the hailstones and melts them not. The land of Egypt is one mass of desolation; but from outside, the east wind blows steadily until the swarming locusts hide the ground; at a sign from the champion of Israel, the western hurricane succeeds, and the locust hosts are swept into the Red Sea. Then the whole scene dissolves into darkness that might be felt; every man a solitary prisoner where he stands. At last, midnight reveals the slain firstborn and Pharaoh and his people thrust Israel forth' (R. G. Moulton).

Who is the LORD that I should hearken unto his voice to let Israel go? I know not the LORD, and moreover I will not let Israel go, was the reply of Pharaoh to the message of the God of Righteousness who demanded justice for Israel, His firstborn son. Pharaoh, too, is a child of God, but 'a rebellious son' (Deut. XXI, 18) who must be chastised, before he will let his bondmen go free. The Plagues are disciplinary chastisements of God. Instead of annihilating the tyrant by one mighty stroke, God, in His Divine forbearance, inflicted ten successive plagues to break his pride. 'See how different are the ways of God from the ways of men,' say the Rabbis; 'when a mortal warrior would destroy his enemy, he attacks him by surprise; he spaces not out his blows; and when he has him beneath his feet, he makes an end of him. But God warned Pharaoh ten times, and ten times gave him respite to repent; and before punishing him, He ten times showed him His mercy.' For there is grace and merciful forgiveness for those who repent; but there is unsparing punishment for those who, hardening their hearts to the voice of God, continue to oppress their fellowmen.

The Ten Plagues form a symmetrical and regularly unfolding scheme. The first nine plagues consist of three series of three each: (*a*) blood, frogs, gnats; (*b*) fleas, murrain, boils; (*c*) hail, locusts, darkness. In each series the first plague is announced to Pharaoh beforehand at the brink of the Nile, the second is proclaimed by Moses at the Palace, and the third is sent without warning. Each series of plagues rises to a climax, the final series is the climax of all that preceded; and these are but the prelude to the tenth plague—the death of the firstborn, which seals the completeness of the whole. The first nine plagues, though often spoken of as wonders, are not fantastic miracles without any *basis* in natural phenomena. As everywhere else in Scripture, the supernatural is here interwoven with the natural; and the Plagues are but miraculously intensified forms of the diseases and other natural occurrences to which Egypt is more or less liable. Between June and August, the Nile usually turns to a dull red, owing to the presence of vegetable matter. Generally after this time, the slime of the river breeds a vast number of frogs; and the air is filled with swarms of tormenting insects. We can, therefore, understand that an *exceptional* defilement of the Nile would vastly increase the frogs which swarm in its waters; that the huge heaps of decaying frogs would inevitably breed great swarms of flies, which, in turn, would spread the disease-germs that attacked the animals and flocks in the pest-ridden region of the Nile. But, whether we place the greater emphasis on the natural or on the supernatural in the account of the Plagues, we must never forget the purpose for which they were recorded. As is true of every Scripture narrative, the purpose is not so much to give an exhaustive archæological or even historical chronicle, as it is moral and religious instruction. 'The story of the plagues is drawn with unfading colours, and its typical and didactic significance cannot be overrated. It depicts the impotence of man's strongest determination when it essays to contend with God, and the fruitlessness of all human efforts to frustrate His purposes' (Driver).

Moreover, the contest was far more than a dramatic humiliation of the unrepentant and infatuated tyrant. It was nothing less than a judgment on the gods of Egypt. The plagues fell on the principal divinities that were worshipped since times immemorial in the Nile Valley. The River was a god; it became loathsome to its worshippers. The frog was venerated as the sign of fruitfulness, and it was turned into a horror. The cattle—the sacred ram, the sacred goat, the sacred bull—were all smitten. The sacred beetle became a torment to those who put their trust in its divinity. When we add to these, the plague of darkness, which showed the eclipse of Ra, the Sun-god, we see that we have here a contrast between the God of Israel, the Lord of the Universe, and the senseless idols of a senile civilization; as it is written (XII, 12), 'against all the gods of Egypt I will execute judgments: I am the LORD.'

E

THE TEN COMMANDMENTS OR THE DECALOGUE

No religious document has exercised a greater influence on the moral and social life of man than the Divine Proclamation of Human Duty, known as the Decalogue. These few brief commands—only 120 Hebrew words in all—cover the whole sphere of conduct, not only of outer actions, but also of the secret thoughts of the heart. In simple, unforgettable form, this unique code of codes lays down the fundamental rules of Worship and of Right for all time and for all men.

I

THE DECALOGUE IN JUDAISM

From early times the basic importance of the Ten Commandments was duly recognized in Israel. The Teachers of the Talmud emphasized their eternal and universal significance by means of parable, metaphor, and all the rare poetic imagery of Rabbinic legend. The Tables on which the Ten Commandments were written, they said, were prepared at the eve of Creation—thus ante-dating humanity, and, therefore, independent of time or place or racial culture; and they were hewn from the sapphire Throne of Glory—and, therefore, of infinite worth and preciousness. The Revelation at Sinai, they taught, was given in desert territory, which belongs to no one nation exclusively; and it was heard not by Israel alone, but by the inhabitants of all the earth. The Divine Voice divided itself into the 70 tongues spoken on earth, so that all the children of men might understand its world-embracing and man-redeeming message. Each command, as it rang out from Sinai's top, filled the world with aroma. The dead in Sheol were revived, and betook themselves to Sinai; yea, even the souls of all the unborn generations in Israel were assembled there. As the Divine Commandments rang out from Sinai's height, no bird sang, no ox lowed, the ocean did not roar, and no creature stirred; all Nature was rapt in breathless silence at the sound of the Divine Voice asserting the supremacy of Conscience and Right in the Universe. The Rabbis held the sixth of Sivan, the day of the Revelation at Mount Sinai, to be as momentous as the day of Creation itself; for without the coming into existence of Moral Law, the creation of the material universe would have been incomplete, nay, meaningless. At the same time, the Teachers of the Talmud were most careful to emphasize that the Ten Commandments did not contain the Whole Duty of Man, as some Jewish sectaries in the days of the Second Temple contended. The Decalogue laid down the *foundations* of Religion and Morality, but was not in itself the entire structure of Human Duty.

The Rabbinic view of the Decalogue was shared by the religious teachers and philosophers in the Middle Ages, and is to-day held by the followers of all schools of Judaism. Saadyah and Yehudah Hallevi, Rashi and Aberbanel, the Karaites and the Cabalists, all agree in regarding the Ten Commandments as the Fundamentals of the Faith, as the Pillars of the Torah and its Roots. In modern times, various exponents of Judaism have shown that all the ritual observances prescribed in the Torah are visible embodiments of the general truths enshrined in the Decalogue; and that, in fact, the whole content of Judaism as Creed and Life can be arranged under the ten general headings of the Commandments.

II

The Decalogue outside Israel

It is interesting to note the place that the Decalogue held in the religious life of Humanity outside the Synagogue. One of the most renowned of the Church Fathers spoke of the Decalogue as 'the heart of the Law'; and this remained the opinion of Western Christendom for over 1,500 years. Luther's words—'Never will there be found a precept comparable or preferable to these commands, for they are so sublime that no man could attain to them by his own power'—are typical of thought in the Reformed Churches. The Humanists, the Deists and even the Freethinkers spoke in reverence of the Law of Sinai. Two generations ago, Renan wrote: 'The incomparable fortune which awaited this page of Exodus, namely, to become the code of universal ethics, was not unmerited. The Ten Words are for all peoples; and they will be, during all centuries, the commandments of God.' And historians of civilization are generally agreed that, low as the ethical standards of the world at present undoubtedly are, it is certain that they would be even lower, but for the supreme influence of the Ten Commandments.

Quite a different attitude towards the Decalogue began with the rise of Bible Criticism. Too often it has been one of undisguised hostility. This hostility is based on alleged historical and moral reasons. One example of each of these alleged reasons will suffice to show their groundlessness. Thus, during the greater part of the nineteenth century, Critics denied that the Decalogue was Mosaic, because of the prohibition of image-worship in the Second Commandment. The prevalence of image-worship during the period of the Judges and Monarchy, they maintained, proved that no prohibition of image-worship could have been promulgated in the days of Moses. Now it is quite true that the law against image-worship was for many centuries *disregarded* in large sections of ancient Israel; in the same way as throughout fourteen centuries after the rise of Christianity, the prohibition of image-worship was 'deliberately ignored by the *entire* Christian Church down to the Reformation, and is still treated as null and void by the major portion of Christendom' (Canon Charles). But it is never safe to argue that, because any law is openly broken or tacitly disregarded, such a law does not, therefore, exist. All experience, whether in ancient or modern societies, is against such an assumption. Eminent Bible Scholars fully recognize this; and men like Professors Burney and Sellin admit 'that no reasonable ground can be discovered against the Mosaic origin of the Decalogue'.

Not more convincing are the moral objections which Critics level against the Decalogue, *e.g.*, that it deals only with *outward* actions. They disregard the Tenth, the most inward of all the Commandments; or they deliberately deny that 'Thou shalt not covet' seeks to restrain the unlawful, inward desire for something that is another's. According to them, 'it emphasizes not so much the feelings, as the practical steps which might be taken to give effect to them' (Bennett). The reason for such an astounding explanation is given in the new Anglican Commentary as follows: 'A commandment which suggests so high a standard of morals as "Thou shalt not covet" is out of place in the Decalogue!' 'It is questionable,' adds the editor of that Commentary, 'whether the Decalogue should be so constantly and nakedly propounded as the summary of the Moral Law.' The motive behind this hostility of modernist ecclesiastics to the Decalogue, and to the whole of the Hebrew Scriptures, is a two-fold one. In the first place, if the Tenth Commandment is given its right and honest interpretation, *wherein is the superiority of the Gospels* over the Torah? And this alleged superiority of Christianity to Judaism they are determined to maintain at all costs. And in the second place, they believe they will save the New Testament by discrediting the 'Old'. A vain hope. Rejection of the Decalogue leads to rejection of all morality and religion.

III

The Moral Chaos of our Times

Attacks on the Decalogue are singularly inopportune at the present day. For our age and generation stand in especial need of a Divine Confirmation of the Moral Law. The nineteenth century loved to speak of itself as the Age of Science. Now 'Science equips men, but does not guide him. It illumines the world for him to the region of the most distant stars; but it leaves night in his heart. It is invincible; but indifferent, neutral, un-moral' (Darmesteter). That century widely heralded the discovery that man came from the beast; and very soon after that discovery, many of the literary and artistic leaders took it upon themselves to convince their contemporaries that it was only natural for man to return to the beast. A powerful Paganism began its assault against the ancient organized Morality. It dethroned God in the sphere of human conduct, derided all moral inhibitions, and declared instinct and inclination to be the true guides to human happiness. The twentieth century is bettering the instruction begun in the nineteenth. The so-called new Psychology preaches repression of instincts to be a danger to personality; and it regards as natural the unbridled gratification of impulses which civilized mankind has always been taught should be controlled or disciplined. A new ethic has arisen, as subversive as it is godless, which bids each man, woman or child do that which seems right in his or her own eyes. It teaches that *all* moral laws are man-made; and that *all* can, therefore, be unmade by man. There is, in consequence, on every side a questioning of the sacredness of human life, a scoffing at the holiness of purity, and an angry repudiation of the idea of property. In some lands, this has led to social and political upheavals, resulting in immemorial human institutions being torn up by the roots. Even in English-speaking countries there is to-day an impatience with moral authority; and men deny, at any rate, doubt, the reality of ethical distinctions. Things are tolerated, extenuated, nay encouraged—in fiction, on the stage, in everyday life—that only a generation ago would have been the subject of unqualified condemnation. The pilot's stars of moral guidance seem no longer to be fixed stars; and for the many voyagers over the ocean of life, the clouded heavens offer no guidance at all.

Amid this spiritual confusion and moral chaos, Judaism remains clear-eyed and unmoved. It clings unswervingly to the Divine origin of the Decalogue; and continues to proclaim that there is an everlasting distinction between right and wrong, an absolute 'Thou shalt' and 'Thou shalt not' in human life, a categorical imperative in religion—high above the promptings of passion, the peradventure of inclination, or the fashion of the hour. Weak and erring man needs an *authoritative* code in matters of right and wrong, laying down with unmistakable clearness the chief heads of duty, and denouncing the chief classes of sins. Such a Divine affirmation of the Moral Law was at all times a vital necessity for mankind, in order to set aside doubt, and to silence that preverse casuistry which is always ready to call good evil, and evil good. God is not only our Father. He is also our Law-giver; and in the Decalogue, He has made known to the children of men the foundations on which human welfare and happiness can be built.

IV

Revelation and the Decalogue

Judaism stands or falls with its belief in the historic actuality of the Revelation at Sinai.

Revelation, in the first instance, means the unveiling of the character and will of God to the children of men. This is implied in the Theistic position. If we think of the Universe as merely an aggregate of blind forces, then there is, of course, no room for *communication* of any kind between God and man. But the moment we assert the existence of a Supreme Mind as the Fountain and Soul of all the infinite forms of matter and life, revelation, or communication between God and man, becomes a logical and ethical necessity. The exact *manner* of this supernatural communication between God and man, will be conceived differently by different groups of believers. Some will follow the Biblical accounts of Revelation in their literal sense; others will accept the interpretation of these Biblical accounts by Rabbis of Talmudic days, Jewish philosophers of the Middle Ages, or Jewish religious thinkers of modern times. No interpretation, however, is valid or in consonance with the Jewish Theistic position, which makes human reason or the human personality the *source* of such revelation. A noted philosopher of religion has recently given expression to this truth in the words : '*All* Revelation is supernatural. There can be no such thing as a purely natural revelation. We cannot really know God except as He desires to be known and makes Himself apprehensible. No view of God that grew up "of itself" in the human mind, owing nothing to God's self-disclosing action, could have any value' (Wobbermin).

Revelation is thus but the obvious inference and corollary of the character of the Deity held by all who believe in a Personal God and Father in Heaven, in prayer to Whom, in worship of Whom, and in communion with Whom, the highest moments of our lives are passed and lived. This close spiritual relationship between God and man, this interplay of spiritual forces and energies, whereby the human soul responds to the Self-manifesting Life of all Worlds, attains in Israel's Prophets, that overmastering *certainty*, which enables them to declare, 'Thus saith the Lord.' Theirs is an absolute conviction that the thoughts which arose in their minds about Him and His will, and the commands and exhortations which they issued in His name, really came to them at His prompting and were invested with His authority. Maimonides compared revelation to illumination by lightning on a dark night. Some prophets were granted only one such lightning-flash from the Divine; in the case of others these lightning-flashes were oft repeated; whereas to Moses was accorded continuous, unintermittent Light. Not in dreams or visions or occasional flashes of Divine intuition was the manner of revelation in his case, but 'face to face'; *i.e.* in the form of self-luminous thought and complete self-consciousness. In his mind, the Rabbis say, the Divine Message was reflected as in a clear mirror (אספקלריה מאירה). The supreme revelation in the life of the Lawgiver, however, that of the Covenant at Mount Sinai, he shared with the whole of Israel. To all of them was then vouchsafed the psychic experience of a direct communion with God. Even at the shores of the Red Sea when, in the words of the Sages, an ordinary maidservant was able to perceive what an Ezekiel in his moments of ecstasy could not attain to—so, at Sinai, a mystic Vision gripped the spirit of the awe-struck People, filling their souls with reverence and certitude and Light.

V

Israel, the People of Revelation

A study of Israel's amazing story will strengthen any unbiased seeker of the Truth in the conviction that Israel's Vision of the Divine is different not only in degree *but in kind* from that of any other nation; and that, therefore, there has indeed been a unique impact of the Spirit of God upon the soul of Israel. In fact, from the very first there must have been a predisposition in the nature of the Jewish people to receive the Message of Sinai. The Rabbis point out that all the precepts of the Decalogue had been practised by the Patriarchs and had become the family tradition of their children. Before giving the Torah to Israel, Rabbinic legend furthermore tells us, God offered it to the other nations of the world; everyone of them, however, refused it for one reason or another. Thus, the children of Edom asked, 'What is written in this Torah?' When God named its principal commandment, *Thou shalt not kill*—their decisive answer was, 'We cannot accept it.' Other peoples objected to the seventh and eighth commandments—immorality and the appropriation of other men's possessions being the expression of their national bent. None of them, it seems, was against Religion as such, so long as Religion confined itself to general principles. What they all objected to was the definite, concrete 'do not's' of the Decalogue. 'We have no desire for the knowledge of Thy ways,' they exclaimed; 'give your Torah to Israel.' Then God came to Israel; and Israel's reply was, *All that the LORD hath spoken we will do and we will obey.*

So all-compelling has been the recognition of Israel's national genius for the Life of the Spirit that it has crystallized itself into the doctrine of the Election and Mission of Israel (I. Epstein). 'Israel is the People of Revelation,' says a modernist Jewish thinker. 'It must have had a native endowment to produce and rear the succession of Prophets. Hence we do not speak of the God of Moses, nor of the God of the Prophets, but of the God of Israel' (Geiger). 'Had there been no Israelites there would be no Torah,' said Yehudah Hallevi seven centuries before him. 'Israel's pre-eminence is not derived from Moses, it is Moses whose pre-eminence is due to Israel. The Divine love went out towards the descendants of the Patriarchs. Moses was merely the Divinely chosen instrument through whom God's Blessing was to be assured unto them.'

Medieval poet and modernist thinker alike agree that Israel was from its birth predestined to become a Kingdom of Priests. Its career as a Holy Nation dates from the historically actual, mystical experience at the foot of Sinai. *Without* the Covenant at Sinai, the Exodus would have had little meaning; the story of Israel, like that of other kindred Semitic tribes, would have lost itself in the sands of the desert. *With* the Covenant at Sinai, everlasting life was planted in Israel's soul; and the story of Israel issues in eternity.

F

IS THE CODE OF HAMMURABI THE SOURCE OF THE MOSAIC CIVIL LAW?

For nearly a century there has been continuous archæological rediscovery of ancient Civilizations that had for ages vanished from earth. To take one example: we possess to-day the actual originals of the code of laws, administrative orders and official letters of King Hammurabi, who was a contemporary of Abraham, and is mentioned in the early chapters of the Book of Genesis. This code of laws is one of the landmarks in world history, and has important bearings on the civil legislation of the Torah.

Mesopotamia. The original inhabitants of the Euphrates Valley—the domain of King Hammurabi—are generally spoken of as Sumerians. Thousands of years before any other people, they built brick houses, devised a strong family organization, and grouped themselves into city-states. The first schools in the world were established by them; and the Sumerians were the pioneers in alphabetic writing, architecture, weights and measures, and scientific irrigation. Their division of the circle into 360 degrees, and of the hour into sixty minutes of sixty seconds, has remained to this day.

The extraordinary fertility of their land made it the goal of invaders from the desert countries to the east and west. The vastest of these invading hordes in historic times, arrived about 2500 B.C.E. from the Arabian Peninsula. The invaders overwhelmed the country, and founded the city of Babylon in the year 2300—the city that was destined in time to become the emporium of the East and mistress of the world. The new population thoroughly assimilated, and immeasurably advanced, the religion and culture of the original Sumerians. The zenith of this

Babylonian civilization was reached under the sixth king of the Semitic dynasty, King Amraphel, better known as Hammurabi (1945–1902 B.C.E.), whose great achievement was the codification of Babylonian law. A generation ago this Code of Hammurabi was rediscovered for the modern world.

Babylonian Society. Nothing can give us such an insight into the cultural and social life of the Babylonians 3,900 years ago as this collection of laws. Society, in ancient Babylonia, consisted of certain definite castes; king, court and priests, men of gentle birth (aristocrats and officers), commoners and slaves. The differences between the social grades can been seen by various regulations; *e.g.* where capital punishment for theft was commuted for by payment, the thief had to pay thirtyfold if the theft was from the royal estate; tenfold, if from a gentleman; five-fold, if from a commoner. The commoner was a free man, but subject to *corvee*, or forced unpaid labour, and liable to be sold into slavery for debt or for crime.

The slave was merely a chattel, with his owner's name branded or tattooed on his arm, and could not go beyond the city gates without a written pass from his master. A strict fugitive slave law was in operation, which, in some respects, was as harsh as the American fugitive slave law of 'Uncle Tom' days. There were statutory rewards for the captor of the runaway slave; while anyone enticing a slave to escape, was punished by death. Contrast with this the commandment in Deuteronomy XXIII, 16, 'Thou shalt not deliver unto his master a bondman that is escaped from his master unto thee.'

If a slave married a free woman, the children were free. If a free man married a slave woman, even as a second wife, the children were free, and the slave woman also became free on her master's death. The first wife had the right to punish insolence, but only by degradation. Ishmael, the son of a free man and a bond-servant, Hagar, is free. When Hagar is insolent to Sarah, the latter may punish her as harshly as Abraham would permit, but she could no longer sell her.

The position of woman in Babylonian life was favourable. In marriage between different social grades, the wife maintained, and her children inherited, the higher status. On her marriage she brought a dowry to her husband, which remained tied to her for life. As wife, she could be witness, conduct business in her own name, and possess property which her husband's creditors could not take to pay any of his ante-nuptial debts.

Land laws and commerce. Land was private property, subject to an impost levied on the crop. Vast herds and flocks were owned. The shepherd gave a receipt for the animals entrusted to him, and was bound to return them with reasonable increase. He was allowed to use a certain number for food, and was not responsible for those killed by lion or lightning. Any loss due to his carelessness he had to repay tenfold. This illustrates Jacob's protest to Laban: 'This twenty years have I been with thee; thy ewes and thy she-goats have not cast their young, and the rams of thy flock have I not eaten. That which was torn of beasts I brought not unto thee; I bare the loss of it; of my hand didst thou require it, whether stolen by day or stolen by night' (Gen. XXXI, 38, 39).

In commerce, there was the all-pervading obligation of putting every business transaction in writing, signed, sealed, witnessed and in duplicate. There were detailed regulations for rent, lease and lease guarantees, administrators of property, safe-deposit, warehousing, partnership, commercial travellers and agents, transport shipping. There were fixed tariffs for various classes of labourers, ox-drivers, harvesters, veterinary surgeons, ship-builders, boatmen and branders. The physician's fee was fixed according to the social grade of the patient, the builder's according to the size of the house.

The value placed on human life in this Code is slight. Horrible mutilations abound—of eyes, ears, tongue, and hand; and there are thirty-four crimes for which the death penalty is inflicted; among these, every kind of theft, including receiving and buying from servants. It is well, however, to compare with this list, and the horrible forms of death prescribed, the exceedingly cruel modes of execution in European countries down to quite modern times. Even in England, pocket-picking was punishable by death till the year 1808, and sheep-stealing until 1832!

Moses and Hammurabi. Much more interesting than the examination of the detailed regulations of the Code is the question, What is the influence of this oldest code of laws in the world on the Mosaic civil law?

It is now admitted that some of the stories of the Patriarchs can only be fully understood in the light of Hammurabi family and shepherd law. This is so, as we have seen in the Sarah-Hagar incident; likewise, the complaint of Jacob against Laban is in strict conformity with sections 261 to 267 of the Code of Hammurabi. As for the legal portions of Exodus, Leviticus, and Deuteronomy, no feature can be definitely singled out as derived from Code Hammurabi. There are, however, some twenty-four instances of *analogies* and *resemblances* between the two Codes—in regard to the laws of kidnapping, burglary, deposit, assault, and various others; and especially in the *lex talionis*, life for life, eye for eye, tooth for tooth. Now, it is argued, in view of the fact that the Mosaic law is at least 400 years the younger of the two, these resemblances constitute strong evidence that the Hammurabi Code is the immediate or the remote source of the Mosaic civil and criminal legislation.

Many scholars, however, challenge this inference. They say that common laws are often due to common human experience, which is much the same everywhere. The history of the Patriarchs, they agree, has a Babylonian background; but this is so because they were of Babylonian descent. Abraham came from Ur of the Chaldees, a favourite city of his contemporary Hammurabi. Abraham, Isaac, and Jacob, all lived in Canaan, which was then under Babylonian sway. The Mosaic Law, however, is in no way indebted to the Babylonian. For it would be absolutely inexplicable why there are no Babylonian loan-words in its terminology, if the Babylonian law were the source of the Pentateuchal legislation. A higher culture always forces its use of language upon a primitive people which adopts that culture. Again, laws as the peculiar expression of a people's life, can only be imported where the habits of life of the two peoples are related, and where similar social and economic conditions exist. Now, Israel is the least Babylonian of peoples, being nomadic, rural, primitive; whereas Babylon has an intricate, highly industrialized, commercial city-civilization. In Israel, the people is in possession of sovereign rights; the king is under the law. In Babylon, a limited monarchy would have been deemed a contradiction in terms. In Israel, the death penalty for property crimes is abolished; and, whether the theft be from king, noble, commoner or slave, the fine is the same. The slave is considered a human being. He is to go free for the loss of an eye, or even a tooth, at the hands of his master. The Babylonian Code *closes* with the case of the slave whose ear is to be cut off for desiring freedom; whereas the Mosaic Civil law (Exodus XXI, 2–6) *opens* with the case of the slave whose ear is to be bored as a mark of disgrace for refusing to go free when his six years of servitude are at an end! There is not a trace of the Biblical ideal of personal holiness in the Babylonian Code, or of the beneficence and consideration to the poor and needy, which is so characteristic of the Mosaic legislation. Deeper still is the abyss between this Code and the Mosaic Law in their respective attitudes to human freedom. The words of Henry George, spoken fifty years ago, concerning the Mosaic Law, still hold good:

> 'The Hebrew commonwealth was based upon the individual—a commonwealth whose ideal it was that every man should sit under his own vine and fig-tree, with none to vex him or make him afraid; a commonwealth in which none should be condemned to ceaseless toil; in which for even the bond-slave there should be hope; in which for even the beast of burden there should be rest. It is not the protection of property, but the protection of humanity, that is the aim of the Mosaic Code. Its Sabbath day and Sabbath year secure, even to the lowliest, rest and leisure. With the blasts of the jubilee trumpets the slave goes free, and a re-division of the land secures again to the poorest his fair share in the bounty of the common Creator. The reaper must leave something for the gleaner; even the ox cannot be muzzled as he treadeth out the corn. Everywhere, in everything, the dominant idea is that of our homely phrase, "Live and let live." '

'Eye for eye' in Mosaic Law. Further, nothing can illustrate the fundamental difference of the legal systems of these two peoples better than their different application of the law of taliation, or the rule of 'measure for measure'. The enunciation of the principle of 'life for life, eye for eye, tooth for tooth', is to-day recognized as one of the most far-reaching steps in human progress. It means the substitution of legal punishment, and as far as possible the exact equivalent of the injury, in place of wild revenge. It is the spirit of equity. The Church Father, Augustine, was one of the first to declare that taliation was a law of justice, not of hatred; one eye, not two, for an eye; one tooth, not ten, for a tooth; one life, not a whole family, for a life. The founders of International Law—Hugo Grotius, Jean Bodin, and John Selden—all maintain that the rule 'eye for an eye' enjoins, on the one hand, that a fair and equitable relation must exist between the crime and the punishment; and, on the other hand, that all citizens are equal before the law, and that the injuries of *all* be valued according to the same standard. 'It is a law appropriate only for free peoples'—said one of the pioneers of modern Bible exegesis, John D. Michaelis—'in which the poorest inhabitant has the same rights as his most aristocratic assailant . . . It deems the tooth of the poorest peasant as valuable as that of the nobleman; strangely so, because the peasant must bite crust, while the nobleman eats cake.' Of course, in primitive society, there was great danger of this principle becoming petrified into a hard and fast rule of terrible cruelty. In the Mosaic Law, however, monetary commutation had already begun. This is seen from the prohibition of accepting money-compensation for malicious murder: 'Ye shall take no ransom for the life of a manslayer, which is guilty of death' (Numbers XXXV, 31). The literal application of 'eye for eye, tooth for tooth' was excluded in Rabbinic Law; and there is no instance in Jewish history of its literal application ever having been carried out.

'Son for son, and daughter for daughter' in Code Hammurabi. Very different is the way in which this principle was applied in the Code of Hammurabi. The whole Code seems to be built on it; and instead of being merely a general maxim, as in Hebrew jurisprudence, it is taken literally and translated into cold prose; *e.g.* 'If a man has caused the tooth of a man who is his equal to fall out, one shall make his tooth to fall out'; and similarly in fourteen other cases. It is true that here likewise the beginning of money-compensation appears; but not for the aristocrat or free-born, only for slaves. Furthermore, the taliation principle is extended and carried to grotesque extremes. For example, if the jerry-builder, by his faulty constructing of a house, causes the death of the owner, the jerry-builder

is killed; but if he causes the death of the son or daughter of the owner, then not the jerry-builder but his son or his daughter is killed! This illumines a passage in the Mosaic civil code which no one could ever explain till the discovery of the Hammurabi Code. In Exodus, XXI, 28–31, we read:—

'If an ox gore a man or a woman, that they die, the ox shall surely be stoned; but the owner of the ox shall be quit. But if the ox were wont to gore in time past, and it hath been testified to his owner, and he hath not kept him in, but that he hath killed a man or a woman; the ox shall be stoned, and his owner also shall be put to death. If there be laid on him a ransom, then he shall give for the redemption of his life whatsoever is laid upon him. Whether he have gored a son or have gored a daughter, according to this judgment shall it be done unto him.'

Now, what is the meaning of the last clause? Prof. David Mueller, whose treatise on the Code (Die Gesetze Hammurabis und ihr Verhaeltniss zur mosaischen Gesetzgebung, Vienna, 1903) is by far the best and most scholarly, reminds us that in the pre-Mosaic age if a goring ox killed a man, the owner of the ox was killed; if, however, he killed a son or daughter then not the owner of the ox, but his son or his daughter was killed. By this one unobtrusive clause, *Whether he have gored a son or have gored a daughter, according to this judgment shall it be done unto him*—the Torah sweeps away an infamous caricature of human justice. And that the meaning of this clause be for ever unmistakable, it again elsewhere declares (Deuteronomy XXIV, 6), 'The father shall not be put to death for the children, neither shall the children be put to death for the fathers. Every man shall be put to death for his own sin.'

No direct relation between the Codes. Now these differences certainly do away with the notion that Code Hammurabi is the source of the Mosaic Civil Law. The best authoritative opinion indeed holds that these two systems are independent codifications of ancient Semitic Common Law. The resemblances in two codes are due to the common usage of the Semitic ancestors of both Babylonians and Hebrews. This common element was in Babylon developed into the Code of Hammurabi; but in Israel it was, under Providence, sifted and transmuted in such a way as to include love of stranger, protection of slave, the Ten Commandments, and the law, 'Thou shalt love thy neighbour as thyself' (Leviticus XIX, 18, 34).

As to the influence of these Codes on the legislation of later ages, all traces of the Babylonian Code seems to have been lost with the passing of the Assyro-Babylonian Empire. It is far otherwise with Biblical Law. Woodrow Wilson called attention to the potent leaven of Judaic thought in the legislations of the Western peoples throughout the Christian era.

'It would be a mistake,' he writes, 'to ascribe to Roman legal conceptions an undivided sway over the development of law and institutions during the Middle Ages. The laws of Moses as well as the laws of Rome contributed suggestions and impulse to the men and institutions which were to prepare the modern world; and if we could but have the eyes to see the subtle elements of thought which constitute the gross substance of our present habit, both as regards the sphere of private life and as regards the action of the State, we should easily discover how very much besides religion we owe to the Jew.'

The discovery of the Hammurabi Code at the beginning of this century was most disturbing to Bible Critics. It had been to them one of the 'finalities of scholarship' that the Pentateuch came after the Prophets in time and was not, and could not have been, Mosaic. Now it was seen that as early as the days of Abraham there existed not only written laws, but a Code full of most remarkable detail which shed a new light on the Patriarchs and on the Torah. And though in Liberal Jewish circles the discovery of this Babylonian Code was hailed as 'a blow to Orthodoxy', because of its resemblances to the Mosaic Law, closer examination has made abundantly clear the everlasting difference between the two—in humanity, righteousness, and holiness.

That discovery, followed as it soon was by the finding of the Assyrian and Hittite Codes, has impressed a much-needed lesson on Bible Critics; and that is, Wisdom is not of yesterday! 'We must rid ourselves of the notion,' wrote the late Prof. Baentsch of Jena, one of the foremost Biblical scholars of our times, 'that the pre-Mosaic age in Israel was barbarous or semi-barbarous, with animistic tree, stone, and ancestor worship; with fetishism, totemism, witchcraft, and other such beautiful things. To-day, we know that the age of Abraham was the outcome of a religious development that goes back many thousands of years.' Verily, the horizon of human history has been widened by millennia; and the evolutionary view of history, the view which holds that progress is always in a straight line, is seen to be both fatalistic and false. There are ebb and flood-tides in the history of the human spirit; and periods of decline like the post-Homeric age in early Greece, or the barbarous period of the Judges in Israel, can no longer be used to disprove the existence of the Creative Epochs that preceded them. Once again we have seen that the words of the Psalmist, 'Truth shall spring from the earth,' have become literally fulfilled; and the very stones of the Euphrates and Tigris valleys have given their decisive testimony in vindication of the Torah.

ספר ויקרא

THE BOOK OF LEVITICUS

ספר ויקרא

THE BOOK OF LEVITICUS

NAME. The oldest name for the Third Book of Moses is תורת כהנים, 'The Law of the Priests,' *i.e.* the Book which describes the functions of the Priesthood and the duties of the priestly Nation. The Jewish name *Vayyikra* is from its opening Hebrew word. The current title, Leviticus, is derived from the Septuagint.

FUNDAMENTAL CONCEPTS. One half of the Book deals with sacrifice and the laws that safeguard the priestly character of Israel; and the other half with Holiness and the sanctification of human life.

I. SACRIFICE. The study of the origins of human worship has shown that animal sacrifice is an immemorial institution among virtually all races of men. It was therefore essential to raise this universal method of worship to a purely spiritual plane (Maimonides). This is done in Leviticus. All magic and incantation are banished from the sacrificial cult, and everything idolatrous or unholy is rigorously proscribed. With very few exceptions (Lev. v, 1, 20–26), deliberate sins are excluded from the sphere of sacrifice: and in all cases, repentance and restitution of the wrong done must precede the sacrificial act. And thus, while there are resemblances between sacrifice in Israel and sacrifice among other peoples, there are also fundamental differences that transform sacrifice as ordained in the Pentateuch into a vehicle of lofty religious communion and truth. The *burnt-offering* expressed the individual's self-surrender to God's will; the *peace-offering*, gratitude for His bounties and mercies; the *sin-offering*, sorrow at having erred from the way of God and the firm resolve to be reconciled with Him. The *congregational sacrifices*, furthermore, taught the vital lesson of the interdependence of all members of the congregation as a sacred Brotherhood, and kept alive within the nation the consciousness of its mission.

II. HOLINESS. The other fundamental thought of the Book is Holiness, *i.e.* purity of life, purity of action, purity of thought, befitting a priestly Nation. All the precepts in Leviticus are merely a translation into terms of daily life of the Divine call, 'Ye shall be holy; for I the LORD your God am holy' (XIX, 2). Holiness is an active principle, shaping and regulating every sphere of human life and activity. In Chap. XIX, the demand, 'Ye shall be holy,' is included in a series of sublime ethical doctrines; in Chap. XI, it is embodied in the dietary laws. The rule of Holiness governs the body as well as the soul, since the body is the instrument through which alone the soul acts. The Holy People of the Holy God was to keep itself free not only from moral transgressions, but also from ceremonial defilement which would weaken the barriers against the forces of heathenism and animalism that on all sides menaced Israel.

INFLUENCE. In ancient times, the Jewish child began the study of Scripture with Leviticus; 'because little children are pure and the sacrifices are pure, let those who are pure come and occupy themselves with pure things' (Midrash). And we may well judge this Book by its influence in the education of Israel. As a result of its stern legislation, Israel's sons and daughters were freed from the ignoble and the vile—from all brutality and bestiality. As a result of its sanctifying guidance, no people ever attained to a higher conception of God, or a saner appreciation of the vital significance of health and holiness in the life of men and nations.

DIVISIONS. Chaps. I–VII define the laws of sacrifice for the individual, for the congregation, and for the priests. Chaps. VIII–X describe the inauguration of worship in the completed Sanctuary. Chaps. XI–XVII deal with the laws of clean and unclean, of purity and purification, culminating in the institution of the Day of Atonement. Chaps. XVIII–XXVI legislate on marriage, personal and social ethics ('Thou shalt love thy neighbour as thyself'), the Sacred Festivals, land tenure, and conclude with a solemn exhortation on the connection between Religion and national welfare. Chap. XXVII is a supplementary chapter on vows and tithes.

1 **Chapter I**

1. And the Lord called unto Moses, and spoke unto him out of the tent of meeting, saying: 2. Speak unto the children of Israel, and say unto them: ¶ When any man of you bringeth an offering unto the Lord, ye shall

א **Cap. I. א**

א וַיִּקְרָא אֶל־מֹשֶׁה וַיְדַבֵּר יְהוָה אֵלָיו מֵאֹהֶל מוֹעֵד לֵאמֹר׃
2 דַּבֵּר אֶל־בְּנֵי יִשְׂרָאֵל וְאָמַרְתָּ אֲלֵהֶם אָדָם כִּי־יַקְרִיב מִכֶּם

v. 1. א' זעירא

I. VAYYIKRA

(Chapters I–V)

The Laws of Sacrifice (Chapters I–VII)

THE PRINCIPAL SACRIFICES

Chapter I. The Burnt-Offering

1. *And the LORD.* 'And' indicates the close connection between this and the preceding Book. Exodus, in its concluding chapter, records the completion of the Sanctuary. The opening of Leviticus, giving the commands concerning sacrifices and priestly functions to be performed in connection with the Sanctuary, continues the narrative of Exodus.

called. According to an ancient regulation, the last letter of the word ויקרא is in miniature. The Sacred Text was in ancient times written in a continuous row of letters, without any division between the words. When the last letter of a word was the same as the first of the next, as is here the case, one character would often serve for both (Luzzatto). When at a later time both letters were written out, one of them was in smaller size to show that it did not originally occur in the Text—an illustration of the profound reverence with which the Sacred Text was guarded by the Scribes.

tent of meeting. The Tent of Revelation; see Exod. xxv, 22, 'and there I will meet with thee, and I will commune with thee.' Before the Tabernacle had been built, Moses had to ascend Mount Sinai to receive instruction.

2. *unto the children of Israel.* Chaps. i–v form a manual of the ritual of sacrifice for the use of the laity; and deal with *voluntary* private sacrifices, for expression of gratitude, prayer, spiritual communion or desire for expiation, on the part of the individual. *v.* 2 is a general introduction, containing some essential principles of sacrifice. These laws closely affected the life of all the children of Israel, and were not of exclusive interest to the priests. The Sanctuary was the property of the entire people, who had all of them, men and women, young and old, voluntarily and generously contributed the materials for its construction.

any man. Heb. *adam.* Even a heathen may bring an offering, if he is moved to do so. A man's faith, not the accident of birth, is regarded by God. An apostate is therefore denied the privilege of bringing an offering at Israel's Sanctuary (Sifra). God would accept the offering of a heathen who turned to Him (i Kings viii, 41 f), but not the sacrifice of a disloyal Israelite.

bringeth an offering. The custom of sacrifice is here pre-supposed, and is not introduced as something novel and hitherto unheard of. Otherwise, terms like 'burnt offering' (*v.* 3) and 'meal offering' (ii, 1) would have been defined and their purpose stated, as was done in the case of the Passover sacrifice (Exod. xii), and of the sin and guilt-offering in Chaps. iv and v. Nowhere in the Hebrew Scriptures 'is the significance of sacrificial ritual formally explained; it is treated as self-evident and familiar to everyone . . . being the natural and, like prayer, universally current expression of religious homage' (Wellhausen). Sacrifice was thus an immemorial custom in Israel, and held to be coeval with mankind; Gen. iv, 3.

an offering. A voluntary, as distinct from the obligatory, sacrifice later to be described. The individual is left free, according to the occasion or according to his feelings, to decide the kind of prescribed sacrifice he wishes to bring. The Heb. word (*korban*) denotes 'that which is brought near' to God by presentation upon the Altar; but, 'alongside of this literal meaning, it likewise implies that the offering, if brought in the right spirit, is the medium whereby man attains to closer nearness to the Divine' (Abarbanel).

unto the LORD. A main purpose of the Levitical laws was to free the whole conception of sacrifice from all heathen associations (cf. xvii, 7). Hence, it was necessary clearly to indicate Who was to be the Israelite's sole object of devotion. The Name of God largely used in Leviticus is *Adonay*, the Deliverer and Guardian of Israel, and not *Elohim*, the term for 'God' used also by non-Israelites; cf. Exod. xxii, 19.

herd . . . flock. Domestic animals only are to be used, as these alone represent a real *sacrifice* to him who offers any of them. Wild animals, bring your offering of the cattle, even of the herd or of the flock. ¶ 3. If his offering be a burnt-offering of the herd, he shall offer it a male without blemish; he shall bring it to the door of the tent of meeting, that he may be accepted before the LORD. 4. And he shall lay his hand upon the head of the burnt-offering; and it shall be accepted for him to

קָרְבַּן לַיהוָה מִן־הַבְּהֵמָה מִן־הַבָּקָר וּמִן־הַצֹּאן תַּקְרִיבוּ
3 אֶת־קָרְבַּנְכֶם׃ אִם־עֹלָה קָרְבָּנוֹ מִן־הַבָּקָר זָכָר תָּמִים
יַקְרִיבֶנּוּ אֶל־פֶּתַח אֹהֶל מוֹעֵד יַקְרִיב אֹתוֹ לִרְצֹנוֹ לִפְנֵי
4 יְהוָה׃ וְסָמַךְ יָדוֹ עַל רֹאשׁ הָעֹלָה וְנִרְצָה לוֹ לְכַפֵּר עָלָיו׃

which cost nothing, are excluded; and the bringing of a stolen animal constituted a desecration (Isa. LXI, 8). Clean and domesticated animals, furthermore, neither prey on other creatures nor live by killing. Even as the use of iron was forbidden in the construction of the Sanctuary (Exod. XX, 25) because it was symbolic of the sword, so every animal that was associated with uncleanness or violence might not be offered on the Altar. A domestic animal that had mortally injured a human being was likewise declared by the Rabbis to be unfit as a sacrifice.

3. *burnt-offering*. Embodies the idea of the submission of the worshipper to the will of God in its most perfect form, as the entire animal was placed upon the Altar to be burnt. The Heb. name for burnt-offering, *olah*, signifies 'that which ascends', symbolizing the ascent of the soul in worship. 'By making the offering ascend to heaven, the one who offers it expresses his desire and intention to ascend himself to Heaven; *i.e.* to devote himself entirely to God and place his life in God's service' (Hoffmann). Some Semitic scholars derive עולה from עול, 'wrong,' and place it in the same class with חטאת and אשם, sin and guilt-offerings. Whatever its derivation, the burnt-offering is the oldest and commonest form of sacrifice for the community and individual, and it remained the chief spontaneous offering of the individual. It was brought whenever a man's conscience prompted him to do so from a feeling of estrangement from God, in expiation of evil thoughts or unwitting sins (Job I, 5). It was open to all men, even heathens from foreign countries (cf. Shekalim VII, 6, עכו"ם ששלח עולתו ממדינת הים), and was the most striking form of the Israelite's communion with God. But since communion with the Most High was impossible to anybody who was tainted with sin (cf. Isa. LIX, 2, 'your iniquities have separated between you and your God'), and since no man could be sure of being sinless, the rite of the burnt-offering first had an expiatory effect (see on next *v.*), before the worshipper's yearning for fellowship with God was fulfilled.

3–9. FROM THE HERD

of the herd. Burnt-offerings might also be taken from the flock (*v.* 10) or from fowls (*v.* 14). All alike are acceptable to God: He does not look to the quantity or cost of the sacrifice, but to the spirit in which it is offered (Talmud).

without blemish. As alone suitable for God's Altar.

to the door. lit. 'at the entrance'; in the Court, in front of the Sanctuary, where the Altar of sacrifice and the Laver were placed. In this way, centralization and unity of worship would be secured, and idolatrous rites rigorously banished. This injunction was, alas, too often disregarded in the course of Bible history, with calamitous spiritual and moral results. It is interesting to note that Plato likewise saw the danger of grave aberration if sacrifices and the erection of private temples were left to the caprice, or superstition, of every individual (Laws X).

that he may be accepted. Or, 'that it may be favourably received for him' (Leeser); see next *v.*

4. *lay his hand upon.* Press, or lean, his hands between the horns of the animal. By means of this act the animal was designated as the representative or substitute of the man who brought the sacrifice. This explanation is based on Num. XXVII, 18 and 23, where Moses placed his hands upon Joshua to denote that Joshua was to take the place of Moses as leader of the nation. Another explanation is that by laying his hands on the animal, the offerer indicates it to be his property, and hereby devotes it as *his* offering.

It does not seem probable that the sacrificial acts were ever performed altogether in silence. In Scripture, the Temple is spoken of as both 'a house of sacrifice' (II Chron. VII, 12) and 'a house of prayer' (Isa. LVI, 7). Prayer and confession accompanied the imposition of hands on the Day of Atonement (XVI, 21). There must, therefore, from the first have been prayer and confession in connection with every case of laying on of hands, such as have come down to us from the days of the Second Temple. To the Rabbis, sacrifice, without such prayer and confession, was devoid of all spiritual significance; and some applied to it the Scriptural verse, 'The sacrifice of the wicked is an abomination to the LORD' (Prov. XV, 8).

accepted . . . to make atonement. The Heb. word for 'atonement' usually derived from an Arabic root, meaning 'to cover' (the sin), is now connected with the Assyrian *kupparu*, 'to purge away sin.' In view of the yearning for God's favour manifested in the bringing of the offering, accompanied by confession and humble prayer, God would, as it were, wipe out the offence from make atonement for him. 5. And he shall kill the bullock before the LORD; and Aaron's sons, the priests, shall present the blood, and dash the blood round about against the altar that is at the door of the tent of meeting. 6. And he shall flay the burnt-offering, and cut it into its pieces. 7. And the sons of Aaron the priest shall put fire upon the altar, and lay wood in order upon the fire. 8. And Aaron's sons, the priests, shall lay the pieces, and the head, and the suet, in order upon the wood that is on the fire which is upon the altar; 9. but its inwards and its legs shall he wash with water; and the priest shall make the whole smoke on the altar, for a burnt-offering, an offering made by fire, of a sweet savour unto the LORD. ¶ 10. And if his offering be of the flock, whether of the sheep, or of the goats, for a burnt-offering, he shall offer it a male without blemish. 11. And he shall kill it on the side of the altar north-

ה וְשָׁחַט אֶת־בֶּן הַבָּקָר לִפְנֵי יְהוָה וְהִקְרִיבוּ בְּנֵי אַהֲרֹן
הַכֹּהֲנִים אֶת־הַדָּם וְזָרְקוּ אֶת־הַדָּם עַל־הַמִּזְבֵּחַ סָבִיב
6 אֲשֶׁר־פֶּתַח אֹהֶל מוֹעֵד׃ וְהִפְשִׁיט אֶת־הָעֹלָה וְנִתַּח אֹתָהּ
7 לִנְתָחֶיהָ׃ וְנָתְנוּ בְּנֵי אַהֲרֹן הַכֹּהֵן אֵשׁ עַל־הַמִּזְבֵּחַ וְעָרְכוּ
8 עֵצִים עַל־הָאֵשׁ׃ וְעָרְכוּ בְּנֵי אַהֲרֹן הַכֹּהֲנִים אֵת הַנְּתָחִים
אֶת־הָרֹאשׁ וְאֶת־הַפָּדֶר עַל־הָעֵצִים אֲשֶׁר עַל־הָאֵשׁ אֲשֶׁר
9 עַל־הַמִּזְבֵּחַ׃ וְקִרְבּוֹ וּכְרָעָיו יִרְחַץ בַּמָּיִם וְהִקְטִיר הַכֹּהֵן
אֶת־הַכֹּל הַמִּזְבֵּחָה עֹלָה אִשֵּׁה רֵיחַ־נִיחוֹחַ לַיהוָה׃ ס
י וְאִם־מִן־הַצֹּאן קָרְבָּנוֹ מִן הַכְּשָׂבִים אוֹ מִן־הָעִזִּים לְעֹלָה
11 זָכָר תָּמִים יַקְרִיבֶנּוּ׃ וְשָׁחַט אֹתוֹ עַל יֶרֶךְ הַמִּזְבֵּחַ צָפֹנָה

His sight. כפר thus means to reconcile; to restore by atonement that inward sense of close relationship with God which is lost through sin, evil desire, or constant brooding upon sinful things. In English, the word 'atone', which now means 'to make amends', originally meant 'to set at one, to reconcile, persons at variance'.

5. *he shall kill.* The subject is either the priest, or the offerer, or anyone deputed by them. The Heb. word used is not והמית 'put to death', but ושחט 'slaughter', in the swift and painless way of *Shechitah*, which brings with it greatest effusion of blood and instant unconsciousness.

before the LORD. *i.e.* at the entrance of the Tent of Meeting.

Aaron's sons, the priests. Those of Aaron's sons who are officiating as priests. Only the slaughtering might be done by one who was not a priest.

bring the blood. The priests receive the blood in one of the service-vessels and bring it up to the Altar. 'The blood is regarded as the seat of life, and is given back to God, who is the author of life' (Driver).

dash. The blood was thrown against the north-east and south-west corners of the Altar. For the association of the blood with the idea of atonement, see note on XVII, 11.

6. *and he shall flay.* From II Chron. XXIX, 24, XXXV, 9–11, it appears that priests and Levites performed these duties. The hide was not part of the burnt-offering.

cut it into its pieces. The animal was to be dismembered, but the limbs were not to be broken. The flame would thus pass *between* the pieces, and symbolize the covenant established between God and the offerer; see Gen. XV, 10.

7. *put fire upon the altar.* The regulations concerning the fire upon the Altar are given in VI, 2 f. Since the flame on the Altar must never be allowed to be extinguished, some fresh pieces of wood must be added for each sacrifice. Others refer it to the occasion when the fire was kindled for the first time. Malbim takes this verse to refer to the period of the Wandering in the Wilderness, when, according to Sifra, the fire was put out whenever the Altar was transmitted.

8. *the head.* Is mentioned separately, because it would have been severed from the body before the latter was flayed.

9. *made by fire.* To the mind of the Israelite, the sight of the sacrifice consumed by the flames would exemplify the ascent of the soul Godward.

a sweet savour. Like the term 'food' (Chap. III, 11), it is a survival in language of the early conception of sacrifice as affording physical pleasure to the deity. But this stage is long passed in Scripture, and nowhere are such phrases understood literally. 'The burning of the offering is called *a sweet savour unto the LORD*; and so it undoubtedly is, since it serves to remove sinful thoughts from our hearts. The effect of the offering upon the man who sacrificed it is pleasant unto the LORD' (Maimonides).

10–13. FROM THE FLOCK

10. *and if.* This and the preceding paragraph are closely connected, and the regulations in them supplement each other; thus, the rite of imposition of hands is not mentioned again, although it equally applied to sheep and oxen.

11. *side of the altar.* Its rear; *i.e.* the north side, the south being the side from which the Altar was ascended.

northward. *i.e.* the space between the rear of the Altar and the north wall of the Court.

ward before the LORD; and Aaron's sons, the priests, shall dash its blood against the altar round about. 12. And he shall cut it into its pieces; and the priest shall lay them, with its head and its suet, in order on the wood that is on the fire which is upon the altar. 13. But the inwards and the legs shall he wash with water; and the priest shall offer the whole, and make it smoke upon the altar; it is a burnt-offering, an offering made by fire, of a sweet savour unto the LORD.*ii. ¶ 14. And if his offering to the LORD be a burnt-offering of fowls, then he shall bring his offering of turtle-doves, or of young pigeons. 15. And the priest shall bring it unto the altar, and pinch off its head, and make it smoke on the altar; and the blood thereof shall be drained out on the side of the altar. 16. And he shall take away its crop with the feathers thereof, and cast it beside the altar on the east part, in the place of the ashes. 17. And he shall rend it by the wings thereof, but shall not divide it asunder; and the priest shall make it smoke upon the altar, upon the wood that is upon the fire; it is a burnt-offering, an offering made by fire, of a sweet savour unto the LORD.

לִפְנֵי יְהוָה וְזָרְקוּ בְּנֵי אַהֲרֹן הַכֹּהֲנִים אֶת־דָּמוֹ עַל־הַמִּזְבֵּחַ
12 סָבִיב׃ וְנִתַּח אֹתוֹ לִנְתָחָיו וְאֶת־רֹאשׁוֹ וְאֶת־פִּדְרוֹ וְעָרַךְ
הַכֹּהֵן אֹתָם עַל־הָעֵצִים אֲשֶׁר עַל־הָאֵשׁ אֲשֶׁר עַל־הַמִּזְבֵּחַ׃
13 וְהַקֶּרֶב וְהַכְּרָעַיִם יִרְחַץ בַּמָּיִם וְהִקְרִיב הַכֹּהֵן אֶת־הַכֹּל
שני וְהִקְטִיר הַמִּזְבֵּחָה עֹלָה הוּא אִשֵּׁה רֵיחַ נִיחֹחַ לַיהוָה׃ פ
14 וְאִם מִן־הָעוֹף עֹלָה קָרְבָּנוֹ לַיהוָה וְהִקְרִיב מִן־הַתֹּרִים
טו אוֹ מִן־בְּנֵי הַיּוֹנָה אֶת־קָרְבָּנוֹ׃ וְהִקְרִיבוֹ הַכֹּהֵן אֶל־הַמִּזְבֵּחַ
וּמָלַק אֶת־רֹאשׁוֹ וְהִקְטִיר הַמִּזְבֵּחָה וְנִמְצָה דָמוֹ עַל קִיר
16 הַמִּזְבֵּחַ׃ וְהֵסִיר אֶת־מֻרְאָתוֹ בְּנֹצָתָהּ וְהִשְׁלִיךְ אֹתָהּ אֵצֶל
17 הַמִּזְבֵּחַ קֵדְמָה אֶל־מְקוֹם הַדָּשֶׁן׃ וְשִׁסַּע אֹתוֹ בִכְנָפָיו לֹא
יַבְדִּיל וְהִקְטִיר אֹתוֹ הַכֹּהֵן הַמִּזְבֵּחָה עַל־הָעֵצִים אֲשֶׁר
עַל־הָאֵשׁ עֹלָה הוּא אִשֵּׁה רֵיחַ נִיחֹחַ לַיהוָה׃ ס

2

CHAPTER II

1. And when any one bringeth a meal-offering unto the LORD, his offering shall be of fine flour; and he shall pour oil upon

CAP. II. ב

ב

א וְנֶפֶשׁ כִּי־תַקְרִיב קָרְבַּן מִנְחָה לַיהוָה סֹלֶת יִהְיֶה קָרְבָּנוֹ

14–17. FOWL AS SACRIFICE

14. *turtle-doves . . . young pigeons.* The regulation that the sacrifice must be a male and without blemish did not apply to fowl, except that no limb must be missing. Birds were the poor man's offering (v, 7; XII, 8), and the Torah did not wish to place an undue burden upon him. The dove is the most inoffensive of birds; and, though attacked by other birds, it never attacks in return. It is a symbol of Israel, say the Rabbis; and teaches the offerer that he should rather be of the persecuted than of those that persecute.

15. *the priest shall bring it.* There was no rite of imposition of the hands when a bird was offered. 'Possibly in order to enhance the importance of the poor man's offering, the whole ceremonial was performed by the priest' (Kalisch).

16. *crop with the feathers thereof.* Unlike the entrails of the animal which are to be washed and offered on the Altar (*v.* 9, 13), those of the bird were to be thrown away. 'The ox or sheep is fed by its owner; but the bird obtains its food wherever it can. The undigested food in its stomach may be stolen property, and must, therefore, have no place on God's Altar' (Midrash).

17. *a sweet savour.* The same expression is used in connection with fowl, herd, and flock. 'It matters not whether one offer much or little, so long as the worshipper directs his heart to Heaven' (Talmud).

CHAPTER II. THE MEAL-OFFERING

Offerings of Flour, Wheat, or Barley, prepared with Oil and Frankincense.

1–3. OF FINE FLOUR

1. *any one.* Heb. *nefesh*, lit. 'soul'. 'Only a very poor man would bring a meal-offering instead of an animal or birds; and God views his sacrifice as though he had offered his very soul' (Talmud).

meal-offering. Heb. *minchah;* sacrifice, not involving the slaughter of an animal, but on that account not less ancient or important. Originally the term *minchah* was used in a wider sense and embraced any offering made to God, whether of animals or earth's produce; Gen. IV, 3. The two constituent parts of this offering—flour and oil—were the common articles of food. They are not natural products, but are obtained as the result of toil. The meal-offering typified the consecration of man's work to the service of God.

pour oil. Oil is used for sanctification.

frankincense. The emblem of devotion; Ps. CXLI, 2.

it, and put frankincense thereon. 2. And he shall bring it to Aaron's sons the priests; and he shall take thereout his handful of the fine flour thereof, and of the oil thereof, together with all the frankincense thereof; and the priest shall make the memorial-part thereof smoke upon the altar, an offering made by fire, of a sweet savour unto the LORD. 3. But that which is left of the meal-offering shall be Aaron's and his sons'; it is a thing most holy of the offerings of the LORD made by fire. ¶ 4. And when thou bringest a meal-offering baked in the oven, it shall be unleavened cakes of fine flour mingled with oil, or unleavened wafers spread with oil. ¶ 5. And if thy offering be a meal-offering baked on a griddle, it shall be of fine flour unleavened, mingled with oil. 6. Thou shalt break it in pieces, and pour oil thereon; it is a meal-offering.* iii. ¶ 7. And if thy offering be a meal-offering of the stewing-pan, it shall be made of fine flour with oil. 8. And thou shalt bring the meal-offering that is made of these things unto the LORD; and it shall be presented unto the priest, and he shall bring it unto the altar. 9. And the priest shall take off from the meal-offering the memorial-part thereof, and shall make it smoke upon the altar—an offering made by fire, of a sweet savour unto the LORD. 10. But that which is left of the meal-offering shall be Aaron's and his sons'; it is a thing most holy of the offerings of the LORD made by fire. 11. No meal-offering, which ye shall bring unto the LORD, shall be made with leaven; for ye shall make no leaven, nor any honey, smoke as an offering made by fire unto the LORD.

2 וְיָצַק עָלֶיהָ שֶׁמֶן וְנָתַן עָלֶיהָ לְבֹנָה׃ וֶהֱבִיאָהּ אֶל־בְּנֵי
אַהֲרֹן הַכֹּהֲנִים וְקָמַץ מִשָּׁם מְלֹא קֻמְצוֹ מִסָּלְתָּהּ וּמִשַּׁמְנָהּ
עַל כָּל־לְבֹנָתָהּ וְהִקְטִיר הַכֹּהֵן אֶת־אַזְכָּרָתָהּ הַמִּזְבֵּחָה
3 אִשֵּׁה רֵיחַ נִיחֹחַ לַיהוָה׃ וְהַנּוֹתֶרֶת מִן־הַמִּנְחָה לְאַהֲרֹן
4 וּלְבָנָיו קֹדֶשׁ קָדָשִׁים מֵאִשֵּׁי יְהוָה׃ ס וְכִי תַקְרִב
קָרְבַּן מִנְחָה מַאֲפֵה תַנּוּר סֹלֶת חַלּוֹת מַצֹּת בְּלוּלֹת בַּשֶּׁמֶן
ה וּרְקִיקֵי מַצּוֹת מְשֻׁחִים בַּשָּׁמֶן׃ ס וְאִם־מִנְחָה עַל־
6 הַמַּחֲבַת קָרְבָּנֶךָ סֹלֶת בְּלוּלָה בַשֶּׁמֶן מַצָּה תִהְיֶה׃ פָּתוֹת
שלישי 7 אֹתָהּ פִּתִּים וְיָצַקְתָּ עָלֶיהָ שָׁמֶן מִנְחָה הִוא׃ * ס וְאִם־
8 מִנְחַת מַרְחֶשֶׁת קָרְבָּנֶךָ סֹלֶת בַּשֶּׁמֶן תֵּעָשֶׂה׃ וְהֵבֵאתָ
אֶת־הַמִּנְחָה אֲשֶׁר יֵעָשֶׂה מֵאֵלֶּה לַיהוָה וְהִקְרִיבָהּ אֶל־
9 הַכֹּהֵן וְהִגִּישָׁהּ אֶל־הַמִּזְבֵּחַ׃ וְהֵרִים הַכֹּהֵן מִן־הַמִּנְחָה
אֶת־אַזְכָּרָתָהּ וְהִקְטִיר הַמִּזְבֵּחָה אִשֵּׁה רֵיחַ נִיחֹחַ לַיהוָה׃
י וְהַנּוֹתֶרֶת מִן־הַמִּנְחָה לְאַהֲרֹן וּלְבָנָיו קֹדֶשׁ קָדָשִׁים מֵאִשֵּׁי
11 יְהוָה׃ כָּל־הַמִּנְחָה אֲשֶׁר תַּקְרִיבוּ לַיהוָה לֹא תֵעָשֶׂה
חָמֵץ כִּי כָל־שְׂאֹר וְכָל־דְּבַשׁ לֹא־תַקְטִירוּ מִמֶּנּוּ אִשֶּׁה

2. *and he shall take.* One of the priests shall take; the previous acts might be done by the offerer or another.

the memorial-part thereof. The portion of the sacrifice which was actually used as an offering, as distinct from the part which became the property of the priests. It has been suggested that the Heb. *azkarah*, which is usually translated 'memorial', is an ancient Semitic sacrificial term, signifying the 'male', *i.e.* the best and finest, portion of the meal (Hommel).

3. *most holy.* The meal-offering would, therefore, be eaten only by the priests, and within the precincts of the Sanctuary; whereas ordinary 'holy things' (קדשים קלים) might be consumed by the priests and their households in any 'clean place'. In both cases it was necessary for the person who partook of that food to be ceremonially clean.

4–10. OF COOKED FLOUR

4. *unleavened wafers.* Similar to the unleavened bread used on Passover.

6. *break it in pieces.* The purpose of breaking up the cake may be the same as that of dissecting the animal of the burnt-offering; see on I, 6.

8. *of these things.* Enumerated in *v.* 4–7.

and it shall be presented. lit. 'and he (the offerer) shall bring it near'.

9. *the memorial-part thereof.* See *v.* 2. Although not here explicitly mentioned, incense accompanied every voluntary meal-offering.

11–13. LEAVEN, HONEY, AND SALT

11. *leaven . . . honey.* The prohibition extended only to their being burnt upon the Altar. Leaven was regarded as a symbol of fermentation and corruption; and man's tendency to sin was later viewed as a process of moral fermentation (שאור שבעיסה). Honey was deemed in heathen cults a favourite food of the gods, and its prohibition was intended to free the mind of the Israelite from any degrading notion that sacrifices might be the food of God (Maimonides, Hoffmann).

12 לַיהוָה׃ קָרְבַּן רֵאשִׁית תַּקְרִיבוּ אֹתָם לַיהוָה וְאֶל־הַמִּזְבֵּחַ
13 לֹא־יַעֲלוּ לְרֵיחַ נִיחֹחַ׃ וְכָל־קָרְבַּן מִנְחָתְךָ בַּמֶּלַח תִּמְלָח
וְלֹא תַשְׁבִּית מֶלַח בְּרִית אֱלֹהֶיךָ מֵעַל מִנְחָתֶךָ עַל כָּל־
14 קָרְבָּנְךָ תַּקְרִיב מֶלַח׃ ס וְאִם־תַּקְרִיב מִנְחַת בִּכּוּרִים
לַיהוָה אָבִיב קָלוּי בָּאֵשׁ גֶּרֶשׂ כַּרְמֶל תַּקְרִיב אֵת מִנְחַת
טו בִּכּוּרֶיךָ׃ וְנָתַתָּ עָלֶיהָ שֶׁמֶן וְשַׂמְתָּ עָלֶיהָ לְבֹנָה מִנְחָה
16 הִוא׃ וְהִקְטִיר הַכֹּהֵן אֶת־אַזְכָּרָתָהּ מִגִּרְשָׂהּ וּמִשַּׁמְנָהּ
עַל כָּל־לְבֹנָתָהּ אִשֶּׁה לַיהוָה׃ פ רביעי

12. As an offering of first-fruits ye may bring them unto the LORD; but they shall not come up for a sweet savour on the altar. 13. And every meal-offering of thine shalt thou season with salt; neither shalt thou suffer the salt of the covenant of thy God to be lacking from thy meal-offering; with all thine offerings thou shalt offer salt. ¶ 14. And if thou bring a meal-offering of first-fruits unto the LORD, thou shalt bring for the meal-offering of thy first-fruits corn in the ear parched with fire, even groats of the fresh ear. 15. And thou shalt put oil upon it, and lay frankincense thereon; it is a meal-offering. 16. And the priest shall make the memorial-part of it smoke, even of the groats thereof, and of the oil thereof, with all the frankincense thereof; it is an offering made by fire unto the LORD.* iv.

CAP. III. ג

ג

א וְאִם־זֶבַח שְׁלָמִים קָרְבָּנוֹ אִם מִן־הַבָּקָר הוּא מַקְרִיב אִם־
2 זָכָר אִם־נְקֵבָה תָּמִים יַקְרִיבֶנּוּ לִפְנֵי יְהוָה׃ וְסָמַךְ יָדוֹ
עַל־רֹאשׁ קָרְבָּנוֹ וּשְׁחָטוֹ פֶּתַח אֹהֶל מוֹעֵד וְזָרְקוּ בְּנֵי
3 אַהֲרֹן הַכֹּהֲנִים אֶת־הַדָּם עַל־הַמִּזְבֵּחַ סָבִיב׃ וְהִקְרִיב
מִזֶּבַח הַשְּׁלָמִים אִשֶּׁה לַיהוָה אֶת־הַחֵלֶב הַמְכַסֶּה אֶת־

3

CHAPTER III

1. And if his offering be a sacrifice of peace-offerings: if he offer of the herd, whether male or female, he shall offer it without blemish before the LORD. 2. And he shall lay his hand upon the head of his offering, and kill it at the door of the tent of meeting; and Aaron's sons the priests shall dash the blood against the altar round about. 3. And he shall present of the sacrifice of peace-offerings an offering made by fire unto the LORD: the fat that covereth the inwards, and

12. *as an offering of first-fruits.* Cf. XXIII, 17. Leaven and honey might be presented at the Sanctuary, though not on the Altar as a sacrifice, as were the ordinary first-fruits (Deut. XXVI, 2).

13. *salt.* Was to be used with every cereal offering: leaven and honey with none. Salt prevents putrefaction, while leaven and honey produce it. Salt is a preservative, and typifies that which is abiding; cf. 'an everlasting covenant of salt' (Num. XVIII, 19). Among most ancient peoples it was a sign of friendship 'to eat salt together'.

with all thine offerings. Also with animal and bird offerings. And as, according to the Rabbis, a man's table has the sacredness of the Altar, this law led to the custom of dipping bread in salt for the Grace before meals.

14–16. OF FIRST-FRUITS

14. *meal-offering of first-fruits.* A further instance of the class of meal-offerings. 'Parched ears' were a common article of food among the poor. The Rabbis identify this offering with the bringing of the Omer (XXIII, 10 f).

CHAPTER III. THE PEACE-OFFERING

1–5. FROM THE HERD

1. *peace-offerings.* Or, 'thank-offerings,' Heb. *zebach shelamim*, or merely *zebach* or *zebachim*, sacrifice made in fulfilment of a vow, or in gratitude for benefits received or expected. It would thus be an occasion when man seeks and obtains peace with his Creator. In the peace-offering there was inherent a feeling of joyousness, either in celebrating a happy occasion in the people's life (I Sam. XI, 15), or some important event in connection with a family or individual (Gen. XXXI, 54). Unlike a burnt-offering, a peace-offering could be either male or female; and only a small part of the peace-offering was burnt on the Altar. All the rest, with the exception of portions reserved for the priests, was eaten by the offerer, his kinsmen and guests, at a solemn meal which followed the offering of the sacrifice. 'It promoted the feeling of solidarity in the nation or family, and also pointed to dependence upon God for protection and for all the blessings of life' (Chapmann-Streane).

2. *dash the blood.* To obtain atonement for the offerer, in case he has done anything that rendered him unworthy to partake of the sacrificial meal. It was a rite of purification.

3. *the fat.* The fat which is attached to the stomach and extends over the intestines is forbidden to Jews as food, and has to be removed from the animal by 'porging'. It is here commanded to be devoted to the Altar.

4 הַקֶּרֶב וְאֵת כָּל־הַחֵלֶב אֲשֶׁר עַל־הַקֶּרֶב׃ וְאֵת שְׁתֵּי הַכְּלָיֹת
וְאֶת־הַחֵלֶב אֲשֶׁר עֲלֵהֶן אֲשֶׁר עַל־הַכְּסָלִים וְאֶת־הַיֹּתֶרֶת
ה עַל־הַכָּבֵד עַל־הַכְּלָיוֹת יְסִירֶנָּה׃ וְהִקְטִירוּ אֹתוֹ בְנֵי־
אַהֲרֹן הַמִּזְבֵּחָה עַל־הָעֹלָה אֲשֶׁר עַל־הָעֵצִים אֲשֶׁר עַל־
הָאֵשׁ אִשֵּׁה רֵיחַ נִיחֹחַ לַיהוָה׃ פ
6 וְאִם־מִן־הַצֹּאן קָרְבָּנוֹ לְזֶבַח שְׁלָמִים לַיהוָה זָכָר אוֹ נְקֵבָה
7 תָּמִים יַקְרִיבֶנּוּ׃ אִם־כֶּשֶׂב הוּא־מַקְרִיב אֶת־קָרְבָּנוֹ וְהִקְרִיב
8 אֹתוֹ לִפְנֵי יְהוָה׃ וְסָמַךְ אֶת־יָדוֹ עַל־רֹאשׁ קָרְבָּנוֹ וְשָׁחַט
אֹתוֹ לִפְנֵי אֹהֶל מוֹעֵד וְזָרְקוּ בְּנֵי אַהֲרֹן אֶת־דָּמוֹ עַל־
9 הַמִּזְבֵּחַ סָבִיב׃ וְהִקְרִיב מִזֶּבַח הַשְּׁלָמִים אִשֶּׁה לַיהוָה
חֶלְבּוֹ הָאַלְיָה תְמִימָה לְעֻמַּת הֶעָצֶה יְסִירֶנָּה וְאֶת־הַחֵלֶב
הַמְכַסֶּה אֶת־הַקֶּרֶב וְאֵת כָּל־הַחֵלֶב אֲשֶׁר עַל־הַקֶּרֶב׃
י וְאֵת שְׁתֵּי הַכְּלָיֹת וְאֶת־הַחֵלֶב אֲשֶׁר עֲלֵהֶן אֲשֶׁר עַל־
הַכְּסָלִים וְאֶת־הַיֹּתֶרֶת עַל־הַכָּבֵד עַל־הַכְּלָיֹת יְסִירֶנָּה׃
11 וְהִקְטִירוֹ הַכֹּהֵן הַמִּזְבֵּחָה לֶחֶם אִשֶּׁה לַיהוָה׃ פ
12 13 וְאִם עֵז קָרְבָּנוֹ וְהִקְרִיבוֹ לִפְנֵי יְהוָה׃ וְסָמַךְ אֶת־יָדוֹ עַל־
רֹאשׁוֹ וְשָׁחַט אֹתוֹ לִפְנֵי אֹהֶל מוֹעֵד וְזָרְקוּ בְּנֵי אַהֲרֹן אֶת־
14 דָּמוֹ עַל־הַמִּזְבֵּחַ סָבִיב׃ וְהִקְרִיב מִמֶּנּוּ קָרְבָּנוֹ אִשֶּׁה לַיהוָה
אֶת־הַחֵלֶב הַמְכַסֶּה אֶת־הַקֶּרֶב וְאֵת כָּל־הַחֵלֶב אֲשֶׁר עַל־
טו הַקֶּרֶב׃ וְאֵת שְׁתֵּי הַכְּלָיֹת וְאֶת־הַחֵלֶב אֲשֶׁר עֲלֵהֶן אֲשֶׁר
עַל־הַכְּסָלִים וְאֶת־הַיֹּתֶרֶת עַל־הַכָּבֵד עַל־הַכְּלָיֹת יְסִירֶנָּה׃
16 וְהִקְטִירָם הַכֹּהֵן הַמִּזְבֵּחָה לֶחֶם אִשֶּׁה לְרֵיחַ נִיחֹחַ כָּל־חֵלֶב

all the fat that is upon the inwards, 4. and the two kidneys, and the fat that is on them, which is by the loins, and the lobe above the liver, which he shall take away hard by the kidneys. 5. And Aaron's sons shall make it smoke on the altar upon the burnt-offering, which is upon the wood that is on the fire; it is an offering made by fire, of a sweet savour unto the LORD. ¶ 6. And if his offering for a sacrifice of peace-offerings unto the LORD be of the flock, male or female, he shall offer it without blemish. 7. If he bring a lamb for his offering, then shall he present it before the LORD. 8. And he shall lay his hand upon the head of his offering, and kill it before the tent of meeting; and Aaron's sons shall dash the blood thereof against the altar round about. 9. And he shall present of the sacrifice of peace-offerings an offering made by fire unto the LORD; the fat thereof, the fat tail entire, which he shall take away hard by the rump-bone; and the fat that covereth the inwards, and all the fat that is upon the inwards, 10. and the two kidneys, and the fat that is upon them, which is by the loins, and the lobe above the liver, which he shall take away by the kidneys. 11. And the priest shall make it smoke upon the altar; it is the food of the offering made by fire unto the LORD. ¶ 12. And if his offering be a goat, then he shall present it before the LORD. 13. And he shall lay his hand upon the head of it, and kill it before the tent of meeting; and the sons of Aaron shall dash the blood thereof against the altar round about. 14. And he shall present thereof his offering, even an offering made by fire unto the LORD: the fat that covereth the inwards, and all the fat that is upon the inwards, 15. and the two kidneys, and the fat that is upon them, which is by the loins, and the lobe above the liver, which he shall take away by the kidneys. 16. And the priest shall make them smoke upon the altar; it is the food of the offering made

4. *the lobe.* Attaching the liver to the kidneys.

5. *make it smoke. i.e.* all that has been mentioned in the preceding verses.

6–17. FROM THE FLOCK

9. *the fat tail.* Of certain breeds of sheep in the Orient.

11. *food of the offering.* lit. 'bread of the offering'. The phrase is identical in meaning with a similar phrase in *v.* 5 and 16. The Heb. לחם, 'bread,' has here its primitive Semitic meaning 'flesh'—another indication of the hoary age of the sacrificial system and its technical vocabulary.

12. *goat.* The treatment is the same as that of the lamb, with the exception of the fat tail. Birds were not accepted as a peace-offering, because they were not deemed sufficient to constitute a sacrificial meal.

17. *a perpetual statute.* The Sifra explains the verse thus: 'a perpetual statute'—the prohibition of eating fat and blood applied not only whilst the Israelites were in the Wilderness when the sacrificial fat was burnt on the Altar in the Tabernacle, but also during the period of the Temple. 'Throughout your generations'—the prohibition applies also to later times when

17 לַיהוָה׃ חֻקַּת עוֹלָם לְדֹרֹתֵיכֶם בְּכֹל מוֹשְׁבֹתֵיכֶם כָּל־חֵלֶב
וְכָל־דָּם לֹא תֹאכֵלוּ׃ פ חמישי

ד CAP. IV. ד

א 2 וַיְדַבֵּר יְהוָה אֶל־מֹשֶׁה לֵּאמֹר׃ דַּבֵּר אֶל־בְּנֵי יִשְׂרָאֵל
לֵאמֹר נֶפֶשׁ כִּי־תֶחֱטָא בִשְׁגָגָה מִכֹּל מִצְוֺת יְהוָה אֲשֶׁר
3 לֹא תֵעָשֶׂינָה וְעָשָׂה מֵאַחַת מֵהֵנָּה׃ אִם הַכֹּהֵן הַמָּשִׁיחַ
יֶחֱטָא לְאַשְׁמַת הָעָם וְהִקְרִיב עַל חַטָּאתוֹ אֲשֶׁר חָטָא
4 פַּר בֶּן־בָּקָר תָּמִים לַיהוָה לְחַטָּאת׃ וְהֵבִיא אֶת־הַפָּר
אֶל־פֶּתַח אֹהֶל מוֹעֵד לִפְנֵי יְהוָה וְסָמַךְ אֶת־יָדוֹ עַל־רֹאשׁ
ה הַפָּר וְשָׁחַט אֶת־הַפָּר לִפְנֵי יְהוָה׃ וְלָקַח הַכֹּהֵן הַמָּשִׁיחַ
6 מִדַּם הַפָּר וְהֵבִיא אֹתוֹ אֶל־אֹהֶל מוֹעֵד׃ וְטָבַל הַכֹּהֵן אֶת־
אֶצְבָּעוֹ בַּדָּם וְהִזָּה מִן־הַדָּם שֶׁבַע פְּעָמִים לִפְנֵי יְהוָה
7 אֶת־פְּנֵי פָּרֹכֶת הַקֹּדֶשׁ׃ וְנָתַן הַכֹּהֵן מִן־הַדָּם עַל־קַרְנוֹת
מִזְבַּח קְטֹרֶת הַסַּמִּים לִפְנֵי יְהוָה אֲשֶׁר בְּאֹהֶל מוֹעֵד וְאֵת
כָּל־דַּם הַפָּר יִשְׁפֹּךְ אֶל־יְסוֹד מִזְבַּח הָעֹלָה אֲשֶׁר־פֶּתַח
8 אֹהֶל מוֹעֵד׃ וְאֶת־כָּל־חֵלֶב פַּר הַחַטָּאת יָרִים מִמֶּנּוּ אֶת־
הַחֵלֶב הַמְכַסֶּה עַל־הַקֶּרֶב וְאֵת כָּל־הַחֵלֶב אֲשֶׁר עַל־

ד׳ v. 4. סבירין אשר לפני

by fire, for a sweet savour; all the fat is the LORD's. 17. It shall be a perpetual statute throughout your generations in all your dwellings, that ye shall eat neither fat nor blood.* v.

4

CHAPTER IV

1. And the LORD spoke unto Moses, saying: 2. Speak unto the children of Israel, saying: ¶ If any one shall sin through error, in any of the things which the LORD hath commanded not to be done, and shall do any one of them: 3. if the anointed priest shall sin so as to bring guilt on the people, then let him offer for his sin, which he hath sinned, a young bullock without blemish unto the LORD for a sin-offering. 4. And he shall bring the bullock unto the door of the tent of meeting before the LORD; and he shall lay his hand upon the head of the bullock, and kill the bullock before the LORD. 5. And the anointed priest shall take of the blood of the bullock, and bring it to the tent of meeting. 6. And the priest shall dip his finger in the blood, and sprinkle of the blood seven times before the LORD, in front of the veil of the sanctuary. 7. And the priest shall put of the blood upon the horns of the altar of sweet incense before the LORD, which is in the tent of meeting; and all the remaining blood of the bullock shall he pour out at the base of the altar of burnt-offering, which is at the door of the tent of meeting. 8. And all the fat of the bullock of the sin-offering he shall take off from it: the fat

sacrifices were no longer offered; 'in all your dwellings'—and it applies to all lands, even those outside Palestine where sacrifices could never be offered. See on XVII, 10.

CHAPTER IV, 1–V, 13. THE SIN-OFFERING

The animal sacrificed varied according to the rank of the offender, provision being made for simpler offerings on the part of the poor.

2. *sin.* This Heb. root חטא means in its simplest form, 'to miss the mark.' The sinner misses the true aim of human living.

through error. Or, 'unwittingly' (RV Text). The regulations here prescribed did not apply where the offence was committed deliberately; see, however, next chapter.

3–12. OF THE HIGH PRIEST

Details are now given as to whom the sin-offering applies.

3. *the anointed priest.* The High Priest. Upon his head alone anointing oil was poured at the ceremony of consecration (VIII, 12).

so as to bring guilt. By any involuntary offence. The High Priest was the teacher and leader of his community. Consequently any error he committed would tend 'to bring guilt on the people'.

a sin-offering. Heb. חטאת. Its real meaning is something that will purge, purify, and wash away the sin.

6. *the veil of the sanctuary. i.e.* the veil which separated the Holy Place from the Holy of Holies (Exod. XXVI, 33). The priest stood in the Holy Place and sprinkled the blood not on the veil, but in its direction.

7. *horns of the altar.* Of incense; see Exod. XXX, 2. They were corner-pieces rising upwards. Their significance lay in the fact that they pointed heavenward; and the application of the blood to these horns directed the thoughts of the sinner to God.

8. *fat of the bullock.* Removal of fat applied to every sin-offering.

that covereth the inwards, and all the fat that is upon the inwards, 9. and the two kidneys, and the fat that is upon them, which is by the loins, and the lobe above the liver, which he shall take away by the kidneys, 10. as it is taken off from the ox of the sacrifice of peace-offerings; and the priest shall make them smoke upon the altar of burnt-offering. 11. But the skin of the bullock, and all its flesh, with its head, and with its legs, and its inwards, and its dung, 12. even the whole bullock shall he carry forth without the camp unto a clean place, where the ashes are poured out, and burn it on wood with fire; where the ashes are poured out shall it be burnt. ¶ 13. And if the whole congregation of Israel shall err, the thing being hid from the eyes of the assembly, and do any of the things which the LORD hath commanded not to be done, and are guilty: 14. when the sin wherein they have sinned is known, then the assembly shall offer a young bullock for a sin-offering, and bring it before the tent of meeting. 15. And the elders of the congregation shall lay their hands upon the head of the bullock before the LORD; and the bullock shall be killed before the LORD. 16. And the anointed priest shall bring of the blood of the bullock to the tent of meeting. 17. And the priest shall dip his finger in the blood, and sprinkle it seven times before the LORD, in front of the veil. 18. And he shall put of the blood upon the horns of the altar which is before the LORD, that is in the tent of meeting, and all the remaining blood shall he pour out at the base of the altar of burnt-offering, which is at the door of the tent of meeting. 19. And all the fat thereof shall he take off from it, and make it smoke upon the altar. 20. Thus shall he do with the bullock; as he did with the bullock of the sin-offering, so shall he do

9 הַקֶּרֶב׃ וְאֵת שְׁתֵּי הַכְּלָיֹת וְאֶת־הַחֵלֶב אֲשֶׁר עֲלֵיהֶן אֲשֶׁר
עַל־הַכְּסָלִים וְאֶת־הַיֹּתֶרֶת עַל־הַכָּבֵד עַל־הַכְּלָיוֹת יְסִירֶנָּה׃
י כַּאֲשֶׁר יוּרַם מִשּׁוֹר זֶבַח הַשְּׁלָמִים וְהִקְטִירָם הַכֹּהֵן עַל
11 מִזְבַּח הָעֹלָה׃ וְאֶת־עוֹר הַפָּר וְאֶת־כָּל־בְּשָׂרוֹ עַל־רֹאשׁוֹ
12 וְעַל־כְּרָעָיו וְקִרְבּוֹ וּפִרְשׁוֹ׃ וְהוֹצִיא אֶת־כָּל־הַפָּר אֶל־
מִחוּץ לַמַּחֲנֶה אֶל־מָקוֹם טָהוֹר אֶל־שֶׁפֶךְ הַדֶּשֶׁן וְשָׂרַף
אֹתוֹ עַל־עֵצִים בָּאֵשׁ עַל־שֶׁפֶךְ הַדֶּשֶׁן יִשָּׂרֵף׃ פ
13 וְאִם כָּל־עֲדַת יִשְׂרָאֵל יִשְׁגּוּ וְנֶעְלַם דָּבָר מֵעֵינֵי הַקָּהָל
וְעָשׂוּ אַחַת מִכָּל־מִצְוֹת יְהוָה אֲשֶׁר לֹא־תֵעָשֶׂינָה וְאָשֵׁמוּ׃
14 וְנוֹדְעָה הַחַטָּאת אֲשֶׁר חָטְאוּ עָלֶיהָ וְהִקְרִיבוּ הַקָּהָל פַּר
טו בֶּן־בָּקָר לְחַטָּאת וְהֵבִיאוּ אֹתוֹ לִפְנֵי אֹהֶל מוֹעֵד׃ וְסָמְכוּ
זִקְנֵי הָעֵדָה אֶת־יְדֵיהֶם עַל־רֹאשׁ הַפָּר לִפְנֵי יְהוָה וְשָׁחַט
16 אֶת־הַפָּר לִפְנֵי יְהוָה׃ וְהֵבִיא הַכֹּהֵן הַמָּשִׁיחַ מִדַּם הַפָּר
17 אֶל־אֹהֶל מוֹעֵד׃ וְטָבַל הַכֹּהֵן אֶצְבָּעוֹ מִן־הַדָּם וְהִזָּה
18 שֶׁבַע פְּעָמִים לִפְנֵי יְהוָה אֶת־פְּנֵי הַפָּרֹכֶת׃ וּמִן־הַדָּם
יִתֵּן ׀ עַל־קַרְנֹת הַמִּזְבֵּחַ אֲשֶׁר לִפְנֵי יְהוָה אֲשֶׁר בְּאֹהֶל
מוֹעֵד וְאֵת כָּל־הַדָּם יִשְׁפֹּךְ אֶל־יְסוֹד מִזְבַּח הָעֹלָה אֲשֶׁר
19 פֶּתַח אֹהֶל מוֹעֵד׃ וְאֵת כָּל־חֶלְבּוֹ יָרִים מִמֶּנּוּ וְהִקְטִיר
כ הַמִּזְבֵּחָה׃ וְעָשָׂה לַפָּר כַּאֲשֶׁר עָשָׂה לְפַר הַחַטָּאת כֵּן
21 יַעֲשֶׂה־לּוֹ וְכִפֶּר עֲלֵהֶם הַכֹּהֵן וְנִסְלַח לָהֶם׃ וְהוֹצִיא אֶת־

12. *a clean place.* The sacrifice was not burnt on the Altar, lest the offerer imagine he was purchasing forgiveness from God by offering up the animal. It was removed outside the camp. The carcase had been used in the Sanctuary, and had to be treated reverently. The most appropriate place to which it could be removed was the ash-heap near the Sanctuary. Haupt and Ehrlich suggest that the phrase is an euphemism, and 'unclean place' is intended.

shall it be burnt. As the High Priest is himself one of those who have to be reconciled to God, he cannot, therefore, partake of the sacrifice. The holy meat must in consequence be destroyed by fire outside the camp, in a place free from ceremonial defilement.

13–21. OF THE COMMUNITY

13. *the whole congregation.* An error on the part of the High Priest could easily result in the entire community going astray.

the eyes of the assembly. Its leaders; *eye* being used in this sense in Rabbinic literature (Ehrlich).

17. *the veil.* Of the Inner Sanctuary; see *v.* 6.

18. *horns of the altar.* See *v.* 7.

20. *bullock of the sin-offering.* Of the High Priest, described in the first paragraph of this chapter.

make atonement. Or, 'make expiation for.'

shall be forgiven. Because God is plenteous in mercy, forgiving iniquity and transgression.

with this; and the priest shall make atone-
ment for them, and they shall be forgiven.
21. And he shall carry forth the bullock
without the camp, and burn it as he burned
the first bullock; it is the sin-offering for
the assembly. ¶ 22. When a ruler sinneth,
and doeth through error any one of all
the things which the LORD his God hath
commanded not to be done, and is guilty:
23. if his sin, wherein he hath sinned, be
known to him, he shall bring for his offering
a goat, a male without blemish. 24. And
he shall lay his hand upon the head of the
goat, and kill it in the place where they kill
the burnt-offering before the LORD; it is
a sin-offering. 25. And the priest shall
take of the blood of the sin-offering with
his finger, and put it upon the horns of the
altar of burnt-offering, and the remaining
blood thereof shall he pour out at the base
of the altar of burnt-offering. 26. And all
the fat thereof shall he make smoke upon
the altar, as the fat of the sacrifice of peace-
offerings; and the priest shall make atone-
ment for him as concerning his sin, and he
shall be forgiven.*vi. ¶ 27. And if any one of
the common people sin through error, in
doing any of the things which the LORD
hath commanded not to be done, and be
guilty: 28. if his sin, which he hath sinned,
be known to him, then he shall bring for
his offering a goat, a female without blemish,
for his sin which he hath sinned. 29. And
he shall lay his hand upon the head of the
sin-offering, and kill the sin-offering in the
place of burnt-offering. 30. And the priest
shall take of the blood thereof with his
finger, and put it upon the horns of the
altar of burnt-offering, and all the remain-
ing blood thereof shall he pour out at the
base of the altar. 31. And all the fat thereof
shall he take away, as the fat is taken away
from off the sacrifice of peace-offerings;
and the priest shall make it smoke upon
the altar for a sweet savour unto the LORD;
and the priest shall make atonement for
him, and he shall be forgiven. ¶ 32. And if
he bring a lamb as his offering for a sin-
offering, he shall bring it a female without
blemish. 33. And he shall lay his hand
upon the head of the sin-offering, and kill

הַפָּר אֶל־מִחוּץ לַמַּחֲנֶה וְשָׂרַף אֹתוֹ כַּאֲשֶׁר שָׂרַף אֵת הַפָּר
הָרִאשׁוֹן חַטַּאת הַקָּהָל הוּא׃ פ
22 אֲשֶׁר נָשִׂיא יֶחֱטָא וְעָשָׂה אַחַת מִכָּל־מִצְוֺת יְהוָה אֱלֹהָיו
23 אֲשֶׁר לֹא־תֵעָשֶׂינָה בִּשְׁגָגָה וְאָשֵׁם׃ אוֹ־הוֹדַע אֵלָיו חַטָּאתוֹ
אֲשֶׁר חָטָא בָּהּ וְהֵבִיא אֶת־קָרְבָּנוֹ שְׂעִיר עִזִּים זָכָר תָּמִים׃
24 וְסָמַךְ יָדוֹ עַל־רֹאשׁ הַשָּׂעִיר וְשָׁחַט אֹתוֹ בִּמְקוֹם אֲשֶׁר־
כה יִשְׁחַט אֶת־הָעֹלָה לִפְנֵי יְהוָה חַטָּאת הוּא׃ וְלָקַח הַכֹּהֵן
מִדַּם הַחַטָּאת בְּאֶצְבָּעוֹ וְנָתַן עַל־קַרְנֹת מִזְבַּח הָעֹלָה וְאֶת־
26 דָּמוֹ יִשְׁפֹּךְ אֶל־יְסוֹד מִזְבַּח הָעֹלָה׃ וְאֶת־כָּל־חֶלְבּוֹ יַקְטִיר
הַמִּזְבֵּחָה כְּחֵלֶב זֶבַח הַשְּׁלָמִים וְכִפֶּר עָלָיו הַכֹּהֵן מֵחַטָּאתוֹ
וְנִסְלַח לוֹ׃ פ ששי
27 וְאִם־נֶפֶשׁ אַחַת תֶּחֱטָא בִשְׁגָגָה מֵעַם הָאָרֶץ בַּעֲשֹׂתָהּ
28 אַחַת מִמִּצְוֺת יְהוָה אֲשֶׁר לֹא־תֵעָשֶׂינָה וְאָשֵׁם׃ אוֹ הוֹדַע
אֵלָיו חַטָּאתוֹ אֲשֶׁר חָטָא וְהֵבִיא קָרְבָּנוֹ שְׂעִירַת עִזִּים
29 תְּמִימָה נְקֵבָה עַל־חַטָּאתוֹ אֲשֶׁר חָטָא׃ וְסָמַךְ אֶת־יָדוֹ
עַל רֹאשׁ הַחַטָּאת וְשָׁחַט אֶת־הַחַטָּאת בִּמְקוֹם הָעֹלָה׃
ל וְלָקַח הַכֹּהֵן מִדָּמָהּ בְּאֶצְבָּעוֹ וְנָתַן עַל־קַרְנֹת מִזְבַּח הָעֹלָה
31 וְאֶת־כָּל־דָּמָהּ יִשְׁפֹּךְ אֶל־יְסוֹד הַמִּזְבֵּחַ׃ וְאֶת־כָּל־חֶלְבָּהּ
יָסִיר כַּאֲשֶׁר הוּסַר חֵלֶב מֵעַל זֶבַח הַשְּׁלָמִים וְהִקְטִיר
הַכֹּהֵן הַמִּזְבֵּחָה לְרֵיחַ נִיחֹחַ לַיהוָה וְכִפֶּר עָלָיו הַכֹּהֵן
וְנִסְלַח לוֹ׃ פ
32 וְאִם־כֶּבֶשׂ יָבִיא קָרְבָּנוֹ לְחַטָּאת נְקֵבָה תְמִימָה יְבִיאֶנָּה׃
33 וְסָמַךְ אֶת־יָדוֹ עַל רֹאשׁ הַחַטָּאת וְשָׁחַט אֹתָהּ לְחַטָּאת

22–26. OF A RULER

22. *ruler.* Or, 'a prince of a tribe' (Ibn Ezra). 'Happy is the generation whose prince publicly confesses a sin committed by him in error, for how much more would he do so in case of a deliberate sin,' is the comment of the Rabbis.

and is guilty. Or, 'and become guilty' (Leeser).

23. *a goat.* As the sinner descends in status, so his offering decreases in cost.

26. *as concerning his sin.* The meaning of this verse can thus be expressed: 'The priest shall perform the rites of expiation on his behalf, and he shall be purged from his sin, and so made capable of receiving, as he shall receive, the Divine forgiveness' (Kennedy).

27–35. OF A COMMONER

27. *of the common people.* Heb. *am-ha-aretz.* It has been urged that in view of the fact that this case comes immediately after the ruler, *am-ha-aretz* might here be the technical term for the Council of the People; see p. 80. In that case, however, there would here be no provision for the unwitting transgression of the commoner.

it for a sin-offering in the place where they kill the burnt-offering. 34. And the priest shall take of the blood of the sin-offering with his finger, and put it upon the horns of the altar of burnt-offering, and all the remaining blood thereof shall he pour out at the base of the altar. 35. And all the fat thereof shall he take away, as the fat of the lamb is taken away from the sacrifice of peace-offerings; and the priest shall make them smoke on the altar, upon the offerings of the LORD made by fire; and the priest shall make atonement for him as touching his sin that he hath sinned, and he shall be forgiven.

5

CHAPTER V

1. And if any one sin, in that he heareth the voice of adjuration, he being a witness, whether he hath seen or known, if he do not utter it, then he shall bear his iniquity; 2. or if any one touch any unclean thing, whether it be the carcass of an unclean beast, or the carcass of unclean cattle, or the carcass of unclean swarming things, and be guilty, it being hidden from him that he is unclean; 3. or if he touch the uncleanness of man, whatsoever his uncleanness be wherewith he is unclean, and it be hid from him; and, when he knoweth of it, be guilty; 4. or if any one swear clearly with his lips to do evil, or to do good, whatsoever it be that a man shall utter clearly with an oath, and it be hid from him; and, when he knoweth of it, be guilty in one of these things; 5. and it shall be, when he shall be guilty in one of these things, that he shall confess that wherein he hath sinned; 6. and he shall bring his forfeit unto the LORD for his sin which he

34 בִּמְקוֹם אֲשֶׁר יִשְׁחַט אֶת־הָעֹלָה׃ וְלָקַח הַכֹּהֵן מִדַּם
הַחַטָּאת בְּאֶצְבָּעוֹ וְנָתַן עַל־קַרְנֹת מִזְבַּח הָעֹלָה וְאֶת־כָּל־
לה דָּמָהּ יִשְׁפֹּךְ אֶל־יְסוֹד הַמִּזְבֵּחַ׃ וְאֶת־כָּל־חֶלְבָּהּ יָסִיר
כַּאֲשֶׁר יוּסַר חֵלֶב הַכֶּשֶׂב מִזֶּבַח הַשְּׁלָמִים וְהִקְטִיר הַכֹּהֵן
אֹתָם הַמִּזְבֵּחָה עַל אִשֵּׁי יְהוָה וְכִפֶּר עָלָיו הַכֹּהֵן עַל־
חַטָּאתוֹ אֲשֶׁר־חָטָא וְנִסְלַח לוֹ׃ פ

ה

CAP. V. ה

א וְנֶפֶשׁ כִּי־תֶחֱטָא וְשָׁמְעָה קוֹל אָלָה וְהוּא עֵד אוֹ רָאָה
2 אוֹ יָדָע אִם־לוֹא יַגִּיד וְנָשָׂא עֲוֺנוֹ׃ אוֹ נֶפֶשׁ אֲשֶׁר תִּגַּע בְּכָל־
דָּבָר טָמֵא אוֹ בְנִבְלַת חַיָּה טְמֵאָה אוֹ בְּנִבְלַת בְּהֵמָה
טְמֵאָה אוֹ בְּנִבְלַת שֶׁרֶץ טָמֵא וְנֶעְלַם מִמֶּנּוּ וְהוּא טָמֵא
3 וְאָשֵׁם׃ אוֹ כִי יִגַּע בְּטֻמְאַת אָדָם לְכֹל טֻמְאָתוֹ אֲשֶׁר יִטְמָא
4 בָּהּ וְנֶעְלַם מִמֶּנּוּ וְהוּא יָדַע וְאָשֵׁם׃ אוֹ נֶפֶשׁ כִּי תִשָּׁבַע
לְבַטֵּא בִשְׂפָתַיִם לְהָרַע ׀ אוֹ לְהֵיטִיב לְכֹל אֲשֶׁר יְבַטֵּא
הָאָדָם בִּשְׁבֻעָה וְנֶעְלַם מִמֶּנּוּ וְהוּא־יָדַע וְאָשֵׁם לְאַחַת
ה מֵאֵלֶּה׃ וְהָיָה כִי־יֶאְשַׁם לְאַחַת מֵאֵלֶּה וְהִתְוַדָּה אֲשֶׁר
6 חָטָא עָלֶיהָ׃ וְהֵבִיא אֶת־אֲשָׁמוֹ לַיהוָה עַל חַטָּאתוֹ אֲשֶׁר

CHAPTER V

1–13. OTHERS WHO BRING A SIN-OFFERING

1. *if any one sin.* The Torah proceeds to describe special cases in which a sin-offering is required, viz. a witness who fails to give testimony (*v.* 1); one who contracts impurity (*v.* 2 and 3); one who omits to fulfil his vow (*v.* 4). No distinction is here made between 'wittingly' and 'unwittingly'; see IV, 2.

heareth. Better, *had heard.*

adjuration. Addressed to a person in possession of evidence to come forward and offer testimony. This adjuration was known as an אלה, 'curse,' probably because it was accompanied by the pronouncement of a curse upon the person should he maintain silence. Having interfered with the execution of justice, he required expiation through a sin-offering.

bear his iniquity. *i.e.* incur guilt.

2. *unclean thing.* The law on this subject is given in chap. XI, 24–43.

be guilty. According to the Rabbis, only if, forgetting his impurity, he partakes of sacrificial food or enters the Sanctuary.

that he is unclean. Better, *that he became unclean.*

3. *uncleanness.* *e.g.* the dead body conveying impurity to those who touch it.

4. *clearly with his lips.* In contrast to a silent oath (Rashi).

to do evil, or to do good. To his advantage or otherwise (cf. Ps. XV, 4). It may also mean 'to do anything whatever' (see note on Gen. III, 22; XXXI, 29).

be hid from him. *i.e.* he forgot his oath.

5. *one of these things.* *i.e.* the offences stated in *v.* 1–4.

he shall confess. Confession was obligatory in the case of a sin-offering.

חָטָא נְקֵבָה מִן־הַצֹּאן כִּשְׂבָּה אוֹ־שְׂעִירַת עִזִּים לְחַטָּאת
7 וְכִפֶּר עָלָיו הַכֹּהֵן מֵחַטָּאתוֹ׃ וְאִם־לֹא תַגִּיעַ יָדוֹ דֵּי שֶׂה
וְהֵבִיא אֶת־אֲשָׁמוֹ אֲשֶׁר חָטָא שְׁתֵּי תֹרִים אוֹ־שְׁנֵי בְנֵי־
8 יוֹנָה לַיהוָה אֶחָד לְחַטָּאת וְאֶחָד לְעֹלָה׃ וְהֵבִיא אֹתָם
אֶל־הַכֹּהֵן וְהִקְרִיב אֶת־אֲשֶׁר לַחַטָּאת רִאשׁוֹנָה וּמָלַק אֶת־
9 רֹאשׁוֹ מִמּוּל עָרְפּוֹ וְלֹא יַבְדִּיל׃ וְהִזָּה מִדַּם הַחַטָּאת עַל־
קִיר הַמִּזְבֵּחַ וְהַנִּשְׁאָר בַּדָּם יִמָּצֵה אֶל־יְסוֹד הַמִּזְבֵּחַ חַטָּאת
י הוּא׃ וְאֶת־הַשֵּׁנִי יַעֲשֶׂה עֹלָה כַּמִּשְׁפָּט וְכִפֶּר עָלָיו הַכֹּהֵן
שביעי
11 מֵחַטָּאתוֹ אֲשֶׁר־חָטָא וְנִסְלַח לוֹ׃ ס וְאִם־לֹא תַשִּׂיג
יָדוֹ לִשְׁתֵּי תֹרִים אוֹ לִשְׁנֵי בְנֵי־יוֹנָה וְהֵבִיא אֶת־קָרְבָּנוֹ
אֲשֶׁר חָטָא עֲשִׂירִת הָאֵפָה סֹלֶת לְחַטָּאת לֹא־יָשִׂים עָלֶיהָ
12 שֶׁמֶן וְלֹא־יִתֵּן עָלֶיהָ לְבֹנָה כִּי חַטָּאת הִוא׃ וֶהֱבִיאָהּ אֶל־
הַכֹּהֵן וְקָמַץ הַכֹּהֵן ׀ מִמֶּנָּה מְלוֹא קֻמְצוֹ אֶת־אַזְכָּרָתָהּ
13 וְהִקְטִיר הַמִּזְבֵּחָה עַל אִשֵּׁי יְהוָה חַטָּאת הִוא׃ וְכִפֶּר
עָלָיו הַכֹּהֵן עַל־חַטָּאתוֹ אֲשֶׁר־חָטָא מֵאַחַת מֵאֵלֶּה וְנִסְלַח
14 לוֹ וְהָיְתָה לַכֹּהֵן כַּמִּנְחָה׃ ס וַיְדַבֵּר יְהוָה אֶל־מֹשֶׁה
טו לֵּאמֹר׃ נֶפֶשׁ כִּי־תִמְעֹל מַעַל וְחָטְאָה בִּשְׁגָגָה מִקָּדְשֵׁי
יְהוָה וְהֵבִיא אֶת־אֲשָׁמוֹ לַיהוָה אַיִל תָּמִים מִן־הַצֹּאן בְּעֶרְכְּךָ

hath sinned, a female from the flock, a lamb or a goat, for a sin-offering; and the priest shall make atonement for him as concerning his sin.
7. And if his means suffice not for a lamb, then he shall bring his forfeit for that wherein he hath sinned, two turtle-doves, or two young pigeons, unto the LORD: one for a sin-offering, and the other for a burnt-offering.
8. And he shall bring them unto the priest, who shall offer that which is for the sin-offering first, and pinch off its head close by its neck, but shall not divide it asunder.
9. And he shall sprinkle of the blood of the sin-offering upon the side of the altar; and the rest of the blood shall be drained out at the base of the altar; it is a sin-offering.
10. And he shall prepare the second for a burnt-offering, according to the ordinance; and the priest shall make atonement for him as concerning his sin which he hath sinned, and he shall be forgiven.*vii. ¶
11. But if his means suffice not for two turtle-doves, or two young pigeons, then he shall bring his offering for that wherein he hath sinned, the tenth part of an ephah of fine flour for a sin-offering; he shall put no oil upon it, neither shall he put any frankincense thereon; for it is a sin-offering.
12. And he shall bring it to the priest, and the priest shall take his handful of it as the memorial-part thereof, and make it smoke on the altar, upon the offerings of the LORD made by fire; it is a sin-offering.
13. And the priest shall make atonement for him as touching his sin that he hath sinned in any of these things, and he shall be forgiven; and the remnant shall be the priest's, as the meal-offering. ¶
14. And the LORD spoke unto Moses, saying:
15. If any one commit a trespass, and sin through error, in the holy things of the LORD, then he shall bring his forfeit unto the LORD, a ram without

8. *for the sin-offering first.* The sin-offering must precede the burnt-offering. There must be reconciliation between God and the sinner, before the latter's gift could be acceptable.

9. *side of the altar.* See on I, 15.

10. *according to the ordinance.* Described in I, 14 f.

12. *upon the offerings.* Better, *after the manner of the offerings* (RV Margin).

13. *any of these things.* As in *v.* 4. The poor were allowed to bring fine flour as a sin-offering only for the offences described in the beginning of the chapter.
as the meal-offering. See II, 4.

14–19. THE GUILT-OFFERING

This section deals with him who causes loss to the Sanctuary by unintentionally appropriating to his own use some 'holy thing'. He is to restore the value of the article and be fined.

15. *a trespass.* Heb. מעילה, lit. 'a breach of faith'; here, misappropriation of property of the Sanctuary.
the holy things of the LORD. Gifts to the Sanctuary and portions due to the priests.
according to thy valuation. The suffix 'thy' is invariably added to the word 'estimation', *i.e.* valuation, in Leviticus; so also in Num. XVIII, 16. That form had become the technical term reserved for sacred things.
shekel of the sanctuary. The shekel of full weight, twenty gerahs; Exod. XXX, 13.

16 כֶּסֶף־שְׁקָלִים בְּשֶׁקֶל־הַקֹּדֶשׁ לְאָשָׁם׃ וְאֵת אֲשֶׁר חָטָא
מִן־הַקֹּדֶשׁ יְשַׁלֵּם וְאֶת־חֲמִישִׁתוֹ יוֹסֵף עָלָיו וְנָתַן אֹתוֹ לַכֹּהֵן
וְהַכֹּהֵן יְכַפֵּר עָלָיו בְּאֵיל הָאָשָׁם וְנִסְלַח לוֹ׃ פ
17 וְאִם־נֶפֶשׁ כִּי תֶחֱטָא וְעָשְׂתָה אַחַת מִכָּל־מִצְוֺת יְהוָה אֲשֶׁר
18 לֹא תֵעָשֶׂינָה וְלֹא־יָדַע וְאָשֵׁם וְנָשָׂא עֲוֺנוֹ׃ וְהֵבִיא אַיִל
תָּמִים מִן־הַצֹּאן בְּעֶרְכְּךָ לְאָשָׁם אֶל־הַכֹּהֵן וְכִפֶּר עָלָיו הַכֹּהֵן
19 עַל שִׁגְגָתוֹ אֲשֶׁר־שָׁגָג וְהוּא לֹא־יָדַע וְנִסְלַח לוֹ׃ אָשָׁם הוּא
אָשֹׁם אָשַׁם לַיהוָה׃ פ
כ
21 וַיְדַבֵּר יְהוָה אֶל־מֹשֶׁה לֵּאמֹר׃ נֶפֶשׁ כִּי תֶחֱטָא וּמָעֲלָה
מַעַל בַּיהוָה וְכִחֵשׁ בַּעֲמִיתוֹ בְּפִקָּדוֹן אוֹ־בִתְשׂוּמֶת יָד אוֹ

v. 18. קמץ בתביר

blemish out of the flock, according to thy valuation in silver by shekels, after the shekel of the sanctuary, for a guilt-offering. 16. And he shall make restitution for that which he hath done amiss in the holy thing, and shall add the fifth part thereto, and give it unto the priest; and the priest shall make atonement for him with the ram of the guilt-offering, and he shall be forgiven. ¶ 17. And if any one sin, and do any of the things which the LORD hath commanded not to be done, though he know it not, yet is he guilty, and shall bear his iniquity. 18. And he shall bring a ram without blemish out of the flock, according to thy valuation, for a guilt-offering, unto the priest; and the priest shall make atonement for him concerning the error which he committed, though he knew it not, and he shall be forgiven. 19. It is a guilt-offering—he is certainly guilty before the LORD. ¶ 20. And the LORD spoke unto Moses, saying: 21. If any one sin, and commit a trespass against the LORD, and deal falsely with his neighbour

16. *add the fifth part.* One quarter of the original value, so that what he adds is a fifth of the repayment.

and the priest. Atonement could only be made *after* restitution.

17. *sin. i.e.* in error. Although these words are not added here, they occur in the next verse. This paragraph refers to what the Rabbis term אשם תלוי, the guilt-offering brought by one who is in doubt whether he has broken a law the infringement of which involves the bringing of a sin-offering.

18. *according to thy valuation.* As defined in *v.* 15.

though he knew it not. The meaning of the Hebrew phrase is, 'while not sure of it.' If at any time subsequently, the offence is recollected, then there must be a sin-offering.

19. *he is certainly guilty before the LORD.* Render, *he hath made complete restitution to the LORD.* That is to say, even if eventually guilty, so long as he is not certain, the trespass-offering secures atonement for him.

20–26. GUILT-OFFERING FOR BREACH OF TRUST

21. *against the LORD.* Rabbi Akiba considered these seemingly superfluous words to be of great significance. They teach that the man who falsely denied that he possessed his neighbour's property denied God who was witness to the deposit. Philo's comment on this phrase is similar: 'He who deposits anything with his neighbour depends upon the good faith alone of the man who receives it. There are no witnesses present except God, the most unerring and infallible witness who sees all the actions of men, whether they are willing that he should do so or not.'

deal falsely. A second class of מעילה, viz. embezzlement and misappropriation of property. The law here applies to cases which would not bring the offender within the jurisdiction of the civil courts. He had denied his guilt and sworn falsely. Later his awakened conscience caused him voluntarily to confess his wrongdoing. Though the Rabbis regarded a false oath as among the very gravest crimes, they accounted free confession of sin as a heroic moral act (Büchler).

neighbour. Fellow-man; see Additional Note D, p. 563.

deposit. He denies that any article had been deposited with him.

pledge. Security for a loan or the like. The rightful owner has no receipt to show that he had handed over the article. The accused, in the absence of witnesses, was only required to take an oath that he had not received the article, and then was exempt from repayment. Should he subsequently confess his guilt, the procedure described in this paragraph applies.

robbery. Includes theft. In the Prophets the word 'robbery' includes any injustice based on law, any legal pretext or trick by which the poor is deprived of what is his. The Rabbis gave an even wider application to the term 'robbery'. Thus, the owner of a field was not allowed to assign to his own poor relative the corner of the field that was to be left to all the poor, as he thereby would rob the other poor of their share.

in a matter of deposit, or of pledge, or of robbery, or have oppressed his neighbour; 22. or have found that which was lost, and deal falsely therein, and swear to a lie; in any of all these that a man doeth, sinning therein; 23. then it shall be, if he hath sinned, and is guilty, that he shall restore that which he took by robbery, or the thing which he hath gotten by oppression, or the deposit which was deposited with him, or the lost thing which he found,* m. 24. or any thing about which he hath sworn falsely, he shall even restore it in full, and shall add the fifth part more thereto; unto him to whom it appertaineth shall he give it, in the day of his being guilty. 25. And he shall bring his forfeit unto the LORD, a ram without blemish out of the flock, according to thy valuation, for a guilt-offering, unto the priest. 26. And the priest shall make atonement for him before the LORD, and he shall be forgiven, concerning whatsoever he doeth so as to be guilty thereby.

22 בְגָזֵל אוֹ עָשַׁק אֶת־עֲמִיתוֹ׃ אוֹ־מָצָא אֲבֵדָה וְכִחֶשׁ בָּהּ
וְנִשְׁבַּע עַל־שָׁקֶר עַל־אַחַת מִכֹּל אֲשֶׁר־יַעֲשֶׂה הָאָדָם לַחֲטֹא
23 בָהֵנָּה׃ וְהָיָה כִּי־יֶחֱטָא וְאָשֵׁם וְהֵשִׁיב אֶת־הַגְּזֵלָה אֲשֶׁר
גָּזָל אוֹ אֶת־הָעֹשֶׁק אֲשֶׁר עָשָׁק אוֹ אֶת־הַפִּקָּדוֹן אֲשֶׁר הָפְקַד
מפטיר 24 אִתּוֹ אוֹ אֶת־הָאֲבֵדָה אֲשֶׁר מָצָא׃ * אוֹ מִכֹּל אֲשֶׁר־יִשָּׁבַע
עָלָיו לַשֶּׁקֶר וְשִׁלַּם אֹתוֹ בְּרֹאשׁוֹ וַחֲמִשִׁתָיו יֹסֵף עָלָיו לַאֲשֶׁר
כה הוּא לוֹ יִתְּנֶנּוּ בְּיוֹם אַשְׁמָתוֹ׃ וְאֶת־אֲשָׁמוֹ יָבִיא לַיהוָה אַיִל
26 תָּמִים מִן־הַצֹּאן בְּעֶרְכְּךָ לְאָשָׁם אֶל־הַכֹּהֵן׃ וְכִפֶּר עָלָיו
הַכֹּהֵן לִפְנֵי יְהוָה וְנִסְלַח לוֹ עַל־אַחַת מִכֹּל אֲשֶׁר־יַעֲשֶׂה
לְאַשְׁמָה בָהּ׃

v. 23. קמץ ברביע

oppressed his neighbour. The withholding, on any pretext, of money due. Thus, the hired servant accuses the master of not having paid him his wages, and the latter asserts that he has paid.

23. *if he hath sinned. i.e.* the accusation brought against him is true. He acknowledges his guilt.
that which he took. When this was not possible, the payment was in money.

24. *in the day of his being guilty. i.e.* on the day when he makes voluntary acknowledgment of his guilt, or, on the day of his guilt-offering. He is to repay what it was worth at the time he misappropriated it, plus a fifth.

25. *bring his forfeit*. But only *after* the misappropriated article had been restored.
When, on the destruction of the Second Temple, all atoning sacrifices ceased, and repentance, confession, and prayer in connection with the Day of Atonement took their place, Rabbi Eleazar ben Azaryah formulated the same principle: 'The Day of Atonement atones for sins between man and God, but does not atone for sins between man and his neighbour, until the sinner has made restitution to his neighbour and conciliated him.'

26. *shall make atonement*. After confession of the sin during the imposition of hands upon the animal.
and he shall be forgiven. When the atonement of the offender's grave sin against God and his fellow man had been secured by confession, by full restitution and payment of the fine, by sprinkling the blood and the performance of all the rites of the guilt-offering, the stain of the sin was washed away and the offender felt relieved of the burden of his transgression. Man, having cleansed himself, is thereupon completely purified by God's loving forgiveness, which turns the gravest sinner, if repentant, into a new man, free from all the transgressions of the past, at peace with man, at peace with his Father Who is in Heaven (Büchler).

ISAIAH XLIII, 21–XLIV, 23

CAP. XLIII. מג

עַם־זוּ יָצַרְתִּי 21

22 לִי תְּהִלָּתִי יְסַפֵּרוּ׃ וְלֹא־אֹתִי קָרָאתָ יַעֲקֹב כִּי־יָגַעְתָּ בִּי

23 יִשְׂרָאֵל׃ לֹא־הֵבֵיאתָ לִּי שֵׂה עֹלֹתֶיךָ וּזְבָחֶיךָ לֹא כִבַּדְתָּנִי

24 לֹא הֶעֱבַדְתִּיךָ בְּמִנְחָה וְלֹא הוֹגַעְתִּיךָ בִּלְבוֹנָה׃ לֹא־קָנִיתָ

CHAPTER XLIII

21. The people which I formed for Myself,
That they might tell of My praise.

22. Yet thou hast not called upon Me, O Jacob,
Neither hast thou wearied thyself about Me, O Israel.

23. Thou hast not brought Me the small cattle of thy burnt-offerings;
Neither hast thou honoured Me with thy sacrifices.
I have not burdened thee with a meal-offering,
Nor wearied thee with frankincense.

The Sedrah presents detailed instructions of service in the Tabernacle leading to obedience to God. The Haftorah deplores Israel's neglect of all worship. It is addressed to the Jews deported to Babylon after the first destruction of Jerusalem. Israel has been utterly careless of God: but He, for his own sake, forgives Israel's iniquities, redeems Jacob, and will glorify Himself in Israel.

CHAPTER XLIII

21–25. THE MISSION OF ISRAEL

21. *the people which I formed for Myself.* Or, 'this people have I formed for myself' (Ibn Ezra; AV). Israel is an essential part of creation. By its life and history, Israel is to set forth the existence of spiritual values and a Divine purpose in the Universe: without which spiritual values, life would be meaningless; and without which Divine purpose, the material Universe would, morally speaking, be no better than primeval chaos, *tohu va-bohu.*

that they might tell of My praise. Through their righteousness to which worship of God should lead them, and through the Divine purpose revealed in their history. The proclamation and advancement of God's honour is the sole reason of Israel's existence.

22–25. But Israel failed to serve God, and showed ingratitude instead of thankful praise. Not as a reward for the offerings it has brought, but in spite of sins punished and now freely forgiven, is God's mercy to be shown to Israel.

22. *not called upon Me.* They did not seek God in prayer. As in many modern circles to-day, there was then an alarming subsidence of the sense of worship. 'The statement is of course general, and is doubtless true of the majority of exiles; it does not exclude the existence of a believing minority which poured out its heart in prayer to God' (Cheyne).

neither hast thou wearied thyself about Me. As in the days of Micah (VI, 3) and Malachi (I, 13), Israel became weary of its Faith and Law. There are epochs in Jewish history when men's souls are parched and dry, when Israel forgets God, and a weariness of everything appertaining to Jewish Duty and Destiny takes possession of Israel's spirit.

23. *the small cattle.* lit. 'the sheep'; the daily morning and evening sacrifice.

I have not burdened thee with a meal-offering. Though on Babylonian soil no sacrifice could be offered, yet the attitude of mind and heart of which the sacrifices were to be but the outward symbol is absent from the life of the people. This verse is often misunderstood. There is here no repudiation of sacrifice (Duhm); otherwise, it would destroy the whole sense of the Prophet's reproach (Marti). The Prophet addresses the people in Babylonian Exile, when the whole sacrificial system is suspended (Ibn Ezra). Though God does not there impose burdensome sacrifices upon Israel, *nevertheless* they do not call upon His Name. See Additional Note A, 'Do the Prophets Oppose Sacrifice?' p. 560.

frankincense. Generally accompanied meal-offerings; see Lev. II.

24. Thou hast bought Me no sweet cane with money,
Neither hast thou satisfied Me with the fat of thy sacrifices;
But thou hast burdened Me with thy sins,
Thou hast wearied Me with thine iniquities.
25. I, even I, am He that blotteth out thy transgressions for Mine own sake;
And thy sins I will not remember.
26. Put Me in remembrance, let us plead together;
Declare thou, that thou mayest be justified.
27. Thy first father sinned,
And thine intercessors have transgressed against Me.
28. Therefore I have profaned the princes of the sanctuary,
And I have given Jacob to condemnation,
And Israel to reviling.

לִי בַכֶּסֶף קָנֶה וְחֵלֶב זְבָחֶיךָ לֹא הִרְוִיתָנִי אַךְ הֶעֱבַדְתַּנִי
כה בְּחַטֹּאותֶיךָ הוֹגַעְתַּנִי בַּעֲוֹנֹתֶיךָ׃ אָנֹכִי אָנֹכִי הוּא מֹחֶה
26 פְשָׁעֶיךָ לְמַעֲנִי וְחַטֹּאתֶיךָ לֹא אֶזְכֹּר׃ הַזְכִּירֵנִי נִשָּׁפְטָה
27 יָחַד סַפֵּר אַתָּה לְמַעַן תִּצְדָּק׃ אָבִיךָ הָרִאשׁוֹן חָטָא
28 וּמְלִיצֶיךָ פָּשְׁעוּ בִי׃ וַאֲחַלֵּל שָׂרֵי קֹדֶשׁ וְאֶתְּנָה לַחֵרֶם
יַעֲקֹב וְיִשְׂרָאֵל לְגִדּוּפִים׃

CAP. XLIV. מד

א 2 וְעַתָּה שְׁמַע יַעֲקֹב עַבְדִּי וְיִשְׂרָאֵל בָּחַרְתִּי בוֹ׃ כֹּה־אָמַר

CHAPTER XLIV

1. Yet now hear, O Jacob My servant,
And Israel, whom I have chosen;

מג' v. 24. מלא ו'

24. *sweet cane.* A scented reed, probably a constituent of the anointing oil (Exod. xxx, 23).

satisfied Me with the fat. See Lev. III, 3. A bold anthropomorphism.

thou hast burdened Me with thy sins. An even bolder anthropomorphism. Instead of loyal obedience, Israel not only took its whole duty to God lightly, but laid on Him the load of its aggravated guilt. He was compelled to mete out punishment when He yearned to scatter salvation.

25. *I, even I, am He that blotteth out thy transgressions.* I, against whom ye have sinned, will forgive you spontaneously, and *unsought for.* 'A verse of perfect tenderness, which reveals the tragedy of all sin. The pathos of the situation is that Israel has despised love, a love which forgave and will still forgive' (Skinner).

for Mine own sake. Because God is merciful and gracious, forgiving iniquity, transgression and sin (Exod. xxxiv, 6 f), God Himself takes the initiative in blotting out Israel's transgressions. 'For Mine own sake' may have the additional meaning, 'that My Name be not profaned.' God will restore Israel, not because Israel deserved restoration, but because God's Glory demanded it. This restoration will, however, be accompanied by spiritual renewal; see the Haftorah of Sabbath Parah.

v. 25 embodies the fundamental proclamation of Judaism that there is no other Saviour beyond God. R. Akiba deepened this teaching in the words: 'Happy are ye, O Israel! Before Whom do you purify yourselves and Who is it that purifieth you? Your father Who is in Heaven.'

26–28. GOD OFFERS ISRAEL A FREE PARDON: ISRAEL HESITATES TO ADMIT THE NEED OF IT

26. *put Me in remembrance.* A touch of irony. 'Remind me of aught in your favour I have overlooked. Set forth any argument to justify your conduct.'

27. *thy first father.* Adam; or, more probably Jacob is meant (Hosea XII, 3 f).

thine intercessors. The Prophets and Teachers, the expounders of God's Word and Will; Jer. XXIII, 11 f; I Kings XXII, 10 f. If even patriarch and prophet have sinned, how much more the mass of the people! From first to last, Israel had fully deserved the punishment that finally overwhelmed it.

transgressed. lit. 'played the rebels.' This is still Israel's spiritual tragedy to-day. The very men who should show forth to the world its truth and beauty are often in rebellion against Jewish Teaching and the whole Jewish Life.

28. *I have profaned.* Or, 'I will profane' (Targum, RV Text); cause them to lose their sacred dignity with the destruction of the Temple.

the princes of the sanctuary. Consecrated leaders, both princes and priests, who suffered such humiliation at the capture of Jerusalem.

and Israel to reviling. Among the nations (Kimchi).

CHAPTER XLIV

1–5. PROMISE OF REVIVAL

Israel's weariness of God is only a passing phase in its history. Even as trees and plants, withered by drought, are restored and refreshed by rain, so will the Divine Spirit revive the parched soul of Israel, and awaken its children to the glory of belonging to Israel.

1. *now hear.* The good tidings of the Prophet.

יְהוָה עֹשֶׂךָ וְיֹצֶרְךָ מִבֶּטֶן יַעְזְרֶךָּ אַל־תִּירָא עַבְדִּי יַעֲקֹב
3 וִישֻׁרוּן בָּחַרְתִּי בוֹ׃ כִּי אֶצָּק־מַיִם עַל־צָמֵא וְנוֹזְלִים עַל־
4 יַבָּשָׁה אֶצֹּק רוּחִי עַל־זַרְעֶךָ וּבִרְכָתִי עַל־צֶאֱצָאֶיךָ׃ וְצָמְחוּ
ה בְּבֵין חָצִיר כַּעֲרָבִים עַל־יִבְלֵי־מָיִם׃ זֶה יֹאמַר לַיהוָה
אָנִי וְזֶה יִקְרָא בְשֵׁם־יַעֲקֹב וְזֶה יִכְתֹּב יָדוֹ לַיהוָה וּבְשֵׁם
6 יִשְׂרָאֵל יְכַנֶּה׃ כֹּה־אָמַר יְהוָה מֶלֶךְ־יִשְׂרָאֵל וְגֹאֲלוֹ
יְהוָה צְבָאוֹת אֲנִי רִאשׁוֹן וַאֲנִי אַחֲרוֹן וּמִבַּלְעָדַי אֵין אֱלֹהִים׃
7 וּמִי־כָמוֹנִי יִקְרָא וְיַגִּידֶהָ וְיַעְרְכֶהָ לִי מִשּׂוּמִי עַם־עוֹלָם

2. Thus saith the LORD that made thee,
And formed thee from the womb, who will help thee:
Fear not, O Jacob My servant,
And thou, Jeshurun, whom I have chosen.

3. For I will pour water upon the thirsty land,
And streams upon the dry ground;
I will pour My spirit upon thy seed,
And My blessing upon thine offspring;

4. And they shall spring up among the grass,
As willows by the watercourses.

5. One shall say: 'I am the LORD'S';
And another shall call himself by the name of Jacob;
And another shall subscribe with his hand unto the LORD,
And surname himself by the name of Israel.

6. Thus saith the LORD, the King of Israel,
And his Redeemer the LORD of hosts:
I am the first, and I am the last,
And beside Me there is no God.

7. And who, as I, can proclaim—
Let him declare it, and set it in order for Me—
Since I appointed the ancient people?
And the things that are coming, and that shall come to pass, let them declare.

2. *from the womb.* From the time when the nation was born, at the Red Sea, the fire of true Religion had never been altogether extinct in Israel.

fear not. On account of past failure, or present inability to visualize the blessed future predicted.

Jeshurun. lit. 'The Upright One'. A poetic title of affection and honour for Israel (Deut. XXXII, 15).

3. *upon the thirsty land.* As the thirsty land is thus made fertile, so will I pour My spirit upon you and make you fruitful in righteousness and service.

My spirit. i.e. knowledge and fear of God; Isa. XI, 2, 3; Joel II, 28. 'Exile to the ancients meant national death. The life-giving spirit must first of all reawaken an Israelitish feeling, so that the thought of belonging to Jacob or Israel, and to Israel's God, is a source of pride and happiness' (Cheyne).

4. *they . . . as willows.* Israel's offspring shall be regenerated, even as the withered plants are restored by rain.

5. *I am the LORD'S.* Showing sacred pride in Israel and the God of Israel.

shall call himself by the name of Jacob. Priding himself on belonging to the Holy People (Ibn Ezra).

another shall subscribe with his hand. A sign of public self-dedication to the service of the true God.

surname himself. Or, 'use for a title' (Cheyne). The name *Israelite* will be deemed the highest and most flattering of human titles.

6–23. GOD'S GREATNESS AND SUPREMACY ARE BEYOND CHALLENGE

6. *first, and . . . last.* There is no God before Him and none after Him. 'Grander than even His pre-eminence in space is His pre-eminence in time' (Duhm).

7. *who, as I, can proclaim.* He is the First and the Last, the God presiding over all history; He who from the first knew all future times and events, and summons each to appear at its right moment. He can therefore proclaim, *i.e.* foretell, them, which none of the lifeless idols can do.

ancient people. Heb. עם עולם; either to be translated, 'the everlasting People'—a fine and poetical description of Israel (Ewald), here used in reference to the impending fall of the idolatrous nations; or, 'the people of antiquity,' the first inhabitants of the world (Ibn Ezra). According to the first translation, prophecy is stated to have been continuous since Israel was formed into a nation; according to the latter, the succession of prophets goes back to the creation of man.

8 וְאֹתִיּוֹת וַאֲשֶׁר תָּבֹאנָה יַגִּידוּ לָמוֹ׃ אַל־תִּפְחֲדוּ וְאַל־
תִּרְהוּ הֲלֹא מֵאָז הִשְׁמַעְתִּיךָ וְהִגַּדְתִּי וְאַתֶּם עֵדָי הֲיֵשׁ
9 אֱלוֹהַּ מִבַּלְעָדַי וְאֵין צוּר בַּל־יָדָעְתִּי׃ יֹצְרֵי־פֶסֶל כֻּלָּם
תֹּהוּ וַחֲמוּדֵיהֶם בַּל־יוֹעִילוּ וְעֵדֵיהֶם הֵמָּה בַּל־יִרְאוּ וּבַל־
י יֵדְעוּ לְמַעַן יֵבֹשׁוּ׃ מִי־יָצַר אֵל וּפֶסֶל נָסָךְ לְבִלְתִּי הוֹעִיל׃
11 הֵן כָּל־חֲבֵרָיו יֵבֹשׁוּ וְחָרָשִׁים הֵמָּה מֵאָדָם יִתְקַבְּצוּ כֻלָּם
12 יַעֲמֹדוּ יִפְחֲדוּ יֵבֹשׁוּ יָחַד׃ חָרַשׁ בַּרְזֶל מַעֲצָד וּפָעַל
בַּפֶּחָם וּבַמַּקָּבוֹת יִצְּרֵהוּ וַיִּפְעָלֵהוּ בִּזְרוֹעַ כֹּחוֹ גַּם־רָעֵב
13 וְאֵין כֹּחַ לֹא־שָׁתָה מַיִם וַיִּיעָף׃ חָרַשׁ עֵצִים נָטָה קָו
יְתָאֲרֵהוּ בַשֶּׂרֶד יַעֲשֵׂהוּ בַּמַּקְצֻעוֹת וּבַמְּחוּגָה יְתָאֳרֵהוּ
וַיַּעֲשֵׂהוּ כְּתַבְנִית אִישׁ כְּתִפְאֶרֶת אָדָם לָשֶׁבֶת בָּיִת׃
14 לִכְרָת־לוֹ אֲרָזִים וַיִּקַּח תִּרְזָה וְאַלּוֹן וַיְאַמֶּץ־לוֹ בַּעֲצֵי־יָעַר

8. Fear ye not, neither be afraid;
Have I not announced unto thee of old, and declared it?
And ye are My witnesses.
Is there a God beside Me?
Yea, there is no Rock; I know not any.

9. They that fashion a graven image are all of them vanity,
And their delectable things shall not profit;
And their own witnesses see not, nor know;
That they may be ashamed.

10. Who hath fashioned a god, or molten an image
That is profitable for nothing?

11. Behold, all the fellows thereof shall be ashamed;
And the craftsmen skilled above men;
Let them all be gathered together, let them stand up;
They shall fear, they shall be ashamed together.

12. The smith maketh an axe,
And worketh in the coals, and fashioneth it with hammers,
And worketh it with his strong arm;
Yea, he is hungry, and his strength faileth;
He drinketh no water, and is faint.

13. The carpenter stretcheth out a line;
He marketh it out with a pencil;
He fitteth it with planes,
And he marketh it out with the compasses,
And maketh it after the figure of a man,
According to the beauty of a man, to dwell in the house.

14. He heweth him down cedars,
And taketh the ilex and the oak,
And strengtheneth for himself one among the trees of the forest;
He planteth a bay-tree, and the rain doth nourish it.

v. 9. נקוד על המה

8. *Rock.* Striking figure for God as Refuge and Shelter; cf. Isa. XXVI, 4.

9–20. THE ABSURDITY OF IDOL-MAKING

The prophet repeatedly returns to this theme because, it seems, idolatry had not yet altogether ceased among the exiles; or, readiness 'to come to terms' with idolatry 'began to make itself felt among the younger generation born in Babylon'.

9. *vanity.* Or, 'confusion.' They that fashion idols are faltering, confused men.

delectable things. i.e. the idols in which they delight.

shall not profit. Are of no avail.

their own witnesses. Their devotees.

that they may be ashamed. i.e. the idol-worshippers. The consequence of their folly is sarcastically stated as if it was the aim and object of their blind unintelligence (Skinner).

11. *all the fellows.* That join themselves in idol-worship.

let them all be gathered together. An ironical exhortation to unite for a combined effort.

12–17. The details of idol-manufacture. It is the description of an eye-witness of the activity in an idol-workshop.

12. *he is hungry.* The idol is produced by one who himself grows faint of hunger and thirst in making it!

13. *stretcheth out a line.* To mark off its dimensions on the block of wood.

marketh it out. Draws the outlines of the idol.

to dwell in the house. In a temple or in a private shrine.

14–17. The Prophet now traces the history of the idol back to the choosing of the wood. The workman uses part of the tree to make a fire, to warm himself and cook his meals, and with the remainder he makes a god!

14. *strengtheneth.* Reareth.

טו נָטַע אֹרֶן וְגֶשֶׁם יְגַדֵּל׃ וְהָיָה לְאָדָם לְבָעֵר וַיִּקַּח מֵהֶם
וַיָּחָם אַף־יַשִּׂיק וְאָפָה לָחֶם אַף־יִפְעַל־אֵל וַיִּשְׁתָּחוּ עָשָׂהוּ
16 פֶסֶל וַיִּסְגָּד־לָמוֹ׃ חֶצְיוֹ שָׂרַף בְּמוֹ־אֵשׁ עַל־חֶצְיוֹ בָּשָׂר
יֹאכֵל יִצְלֶה צָלִי וְיִשְׂבָּע אַף־יָחֹם וְיֹאמַר הֶאָח חַמּוֹתִי
17 רָאִיתִי אוּר׃ וּשְׁאֵרִיתוֹ לְאֵל עָשָׂה לְפִסְלוֹ יִסְגָּוד־לוֹ
18 וְיִשְׁתַּחוּ וְיִתְפַּלֵּל אֵלָיו וְיֹאמַר הַצִּילֵנִי כִּי אֵלִי אָתָּה׃ לֹא
יָדְעוּ וְלֹא יָבִינוּ כִּי טַח מֵרְאוֹת עֵינֵיהֶם מֵהַשְׂכִּיל לִבֹּתָם׃
19 וְלֹא־יָשִׁיב אֶל־לִבּוֹ וְלֹא דַעַת וְלֹא־תְבוּנָה לֵאמֹר חֶצְיוֹ
שָׂרַפְתִּי בְמוֹ־אֵשׁ וְאַף אָפִיתִי עַל־גֶּחָלָיו לֶחֶם אֶצְלֶה
בָשָׂר וְאֹכֵל וְיִתְרוֹ לְתוֹעֵבָה אֶעֱשֶׂה לְבוּל עֵץ אֶסְגּוֹד׃
כ רֹעֶה אֵפֶר לֵב הוּתַל הִטָּהוּ וְלֹא־יַצִּיל אֶת־נַפְשׁוֹ וְלֹא
21 יֹאמַר הֲלוֹא שֶׁקֶר בִּימִינִי׃ זְכָר־אֵלֶּה יַעֲקֹב וְיִשְׂרָאֵל
כִּי עַבְדִּי־אָתָּה יְצַרְתִּיךָ עֶבֶד־לִי אַתָּה יִשְׂרָאֵל לֹא תִנָּשֵׁנִי׃
22 מָחִיתִי כָעָב פְּשָׁעֶיךָ וְכֶעָנָן חַטֹּאותֶיךָ שׁוּבָה אֵלַי כִּי גְאַלְתִּיךָ׃
23 רָנּוּ שָׁמַיִם כִּי־עָשָׂה יְהוָה הָרִיעוּ תַּחְתִּיּוֹת אָרֶץ פִּצְחוּ
הָרִים רִנָּה יַעַר וְכָל־עֵץ בּוֹ כִּי־גָאַל יְהוָה יַעֲקֹב וּבְיִשְׂרָאֵל
יִתְפָּאָר׃

15. Then a man useth it for fuel;
And he taketh thereof, and warmeth himself;
Yea, he kindleth it, and baketh bread;
Yea, he maketh a god, and worshippeth it;
He maketh it a graven image, and falleth down thereto.

16. He burneth the half thereof in the fire;
With the half thereof he eateth flesh;
He roasteth roast, and is satisfied;
Yea, he warmeth himself, and saith: 'Aha,
I am warm, I have seen the fire';

17. And the residue thereof he maketh a god, even his graven image;
He falleth down unto it and worshippeth, and prayeth unto it,
And saith: 'Deliver me, for thou art my god.'

18. They know not, neither do they understand;
For their eyes are bedaubed, that they cannot see,
And their hearts, that they cannot understand.

19. And none considereth in his heart,
Neither is there knowledge nor understanding to say:
'I have burned the half of it in the fire;
Yea, also I have baked bread upon the coals thereof;
I have roasted flesh and eaten it;
And shall I make the residue thereof an abomination?
Shall I fall down to the stock of a tree?'

20. He striveth after ashes,
A deceived heart hath turned him aside,
That he cannot deliver his soul, nor say:
'Is there not a lie in my right hand?'

21. Remember these things, O Jacob,
And Israel, for thou art My servant;
I have formed thee, thou art Mine own servant;
O Israel, thou shouldest not forget Me.

22. I have blotted out, as a thick cloud, thy transgressions,
And, as a cloud, thy sins;
Return unto Me, for I have redeemed thee.

23. Sing, O ye heavens, for the LORD hath done it;
Shout, ye lowest parts of the earth;
Break forth into singing, ye mountains,
O forest, and every tree therein;
For the LORD hath redeemed Jacob,
And doth glorify Himself in Israel.

v. 14. נון זעירא. v. 15. קמץ בז״ק. v. 17. יתיר ו'. v. 23. קמץ בז״ק

18. *their eyes are bedaubed.* Only total intellectual blindness can account for such folly.

19. *abomination.* The contemptuous word for 'idol'.

20. *he striveth after ashes.* Or, 'feeding on ashes, a deceived heart, etc.' (Driver). Feeding on ashes is a proverbial phrase for resting content with what is essentially unreal, disappointing.

hath turned him aside. i.e. hath led him astray.

deliver his soul. Free himself from his error.

21–23. CONCLUSION

21. *these things.* The facts just enunciated, and the sublime words of *v.* 6–8, that God is Israel's Redeemer, and that there is none besides Him.

22. *as a thick cloud.* Which soon passes away because of winds and sun. Israel need only turn to God and become conscious of His unconditional, redeeming Love.

I have redeemed thee. The redemption is already accomplished in the decree of God.

23. *sing.* The redemption of Israel is of such profound meaning in the religious history of mankind that all creation utters a jubilant cry over it.

lowest parts. The abysses of earth.

doth glorify Himself. Israel shall become a crown of glory in His hands.

6

CHAPTER VI

1. And the LORD spoke unto Moses, saying: 2. Command Aaron and his sons, saying: ¶ This is the law of the burnt-offering: it is that which goeth up on its firewood upon the altar all night unto the morning; and the fire of the altar shall be kept burning thereby. 3. And the priest shall put on his linen garment, and his linen breeches shall he put upon his flesh; and he shall take up the ashes whereto the fire hath consumed the burnt-offering on the altar, and he shall put them beside the altar. 4. And he shall put off his garments, and put on other garments, and carry forth the ashes without the camp unto a clean place. 5. And the fire upon the altar shall be kept burning thereby, it shall not go out; and the priest shall kindle wood on it every morning; and he shall lay the burnt-offering in order upon it, and shall make smoke thereon the fat of the peace-offerings.

CAP. VI. ו

ו

25 כה פ פ פ

א 2 וַיְדַבֵּר יְהוָה אֶל־מֹשֶׁה לֵּאמֹר׃ צַו אֶת־אַהֲרֹן וְאֶת־בָּנָיו
לֵאמֹר זֹאת תּוֹרַת הָעֹלָה הִוא הָעֹלָה עַל מוֹקְדָה עַל־
הַמִּזְבֵּחַ כָּל־הַלַּיְלָה עַד־הַבֹּקֶר וְאֵשׁ הַמִּזְבֵּחַ תּוּקַד בּוֹ׃
3 וְלָבַשׁ הַכֹּהֵן מִדּוֹ בַד וּמִכְנְסֵי־בַד יִלְבַּשׁ עַל־בְּשָׂרוֹ
וְהֵרִים אֶת־הַדֶּשֶׁן אֲשֶׁר תֹּאכַל הָאֵשׁ אֶת־הָעֹלָה עַל־
4 הַמִּזְבֵּחַ וְשָׂמוֹ אֵצֶל הַמִּזְבֵּחַ׃ וּפָשַׁט אֶת־בְּגָדָיו וְלָבַשׁ
בְּגָדִים אֲחֵרִים וְהוֹצִיא אֶת־הַדֶּשֶׁן אֶל־מִחוּץ לַמַּחֲנֶה אֶל־
ה מָקוֹם טָהוֹר׃ וְהָאֵשׁ עַל־הַמִּזְבֵּחַ תּוּקַד־בּוֹ לֹא תִכְבֶּה
וּבִעֵר עָלֶיהָ הַכֹּהֵן עֵצִים בַּבֹּקֶר בַּבֹּקֶר וְעָרַךְ עָלֶיהָ הָעֹלָה

v. 2. מ׳ זעירא

II. TZAV

(CHAPTERS VI–VIII)

DIRECTIONS TO THE PRIESTS

CHAPTER VI, 1–6. FIRE FOR THE DAILY BURNT-OFFERING

2. *Aaron and his sons.* The first five chapters were addressed to 'the children of Israel', and concerned the whole people. Chapters VI and VII form a manual of sacrifice addressed to the priests.

law. Heb. *torah*; lit. 'direction, instruction'. The phrase, 'this is the *torah* of,' frequently heads a section in Lev. concerning a special law or group of allied laws.

burnt-offering. The sacrifice described in Chap. I is a free-will offering of an individual. Here the burnt-offering is the continual sacrifice brought every morning and evening in the name of the community (Exod. XXIX, 38–42). Hence its name *tamid*, the perpetual offering. The evening sacrifice is to be kept burning through the night until the flames can be used to kindle the wood for the morning burnt-offering.

In later times, this burnt-offering was regarded as an atoning sacrifice for the community, and hence a national institution. The Pharisees, therefore, insisted that the whole Jewish people, and not merely a few wealthy donors, should share in the privilege of defraying its cost. They, furthermore, arranged for direct spiritual participation of the entire nation in the actual offering of these daily sacrifices. For this purpose, Palestine Jewry was divided in 24 'Watches' (משמרות) of priests and Levites, each in turn to present itself for Temple service for one week. With each priestly Watch, there was also a corresponding delegation (מעמד) of Israelites, part of which stood by the priests, reciting prayers during the performance of the sacrificial rites. The remainder of the delegation would gather in their local synagogues and read the portions of the Torah relating to the sacrifice. 'Thus the spiritual danger that public and perpetual offerings would be looked upon as automatically securing atonement was averted' (Büchler).

thereby. By the firewood and sacrifice.

3. *shall he put upon his flesh.* The garments are described in Exod. XXVIII, 39, 42.

the ashes. Their removal (תרומת הדשן) completed the sacrifice of the preceding day, and therefore priestly garments were required.

beside the altar. The ashes of the burnt-offering were, according to Tradition, deposited daily on the east side of the incline leading to the Altar. When they accumulated they were carried forth outside the camp; see next *v.*

4. *other garments.* The holy priestly garments could be worn only in the Sanctuary.

a clean place. See on IV, 12.

5. *it shall not go out.* During the day also. Even on the Sabbath, fuel was to be placed on the Altar. The law, 'ye shall kindle no fire throughout your habitations upon the Sabbath day' (Exod. XXXV, 3) did not apply to the Sanctuary.

peace-offerings. Mentioned only as an example.

6. Fire shall be kept burning upon the altar continually; it shall not go out. ¶ 7. And this is the law of the meal-offering: the sons of Aaron shall offer it before the LORD, in front of the altar. 8. And he shall take up therefrom his handful, of the fine flour of the meal-offering, and of the oil thereof, and all the frankincense which is upon the meal-offering, and shall make the memorial-part thereof smoke upon the altar for a sweet savour unto the LORD. 9. And that which is left thereof shall Aaron and his sons eat; it shall be eaten without leaven in a holy place; in the court of the tent of meeting they shall eat it. 10. It shall not be baked with leaven. I have given it as their portion of My offerings made by fire; it is most holy, as the sin-offering, and as the guilt-offering. 11. Every male among the children of Aaron may eat of it, as a due for ever throughout your generations, from the offerings of the LORD made by fire; whatsoever toucheth them shall be holy.* ii. ¶ 12. And the LORD

6 וְהִקְטִיר עָלֶיהָ חֶלְבֵי הַשְּׁלָמִים׃ אֵשׁ תָּמִיד תּוּקַד עַל־
7 הַמִּזְבֵּחַ לֹא תִכְבֶּה׃ ס וְזֹאת תּוֹרַת הַמִּנְחָה הַקְרֵב
8 אֹתָהּ בְּנֵי־אַהֲרֹן לִפְנֵי יְהוָֹה אֶל־פְּנֵי הַמִּזְבֵּחַ׃ וְהֵרִים
מִמֶּנּוּ בְּקֻמְצוֹ מִסֹּלֶת הַמִּנְחָה וּמִשַּׁמְנָהּ וְאֵת כָּל־הַלְּבֹנָה
אֲשֶׁר עַל־הַמִּנְחָה וְהִקְטִיר הַמִּזְבֵּחַ רֵיחַ נִיחֹחַ אַזְכָּרָתָהּ
9 לַיהוָֹה׃ וְהַנּוֹתֶרֶת מִמֶּנָּה יֹאכְלוּ אַהֲרֹן וּבָנָיו מַצּוֹת תֵּאָכֵל
י בְּמָקוֹם קָדֹשׁ בַּחֲצַר אֹהֶל־מוֹעֵד יֹאכְלוּהָ׃ לֹא תֵאָפֶה
חָמֵץ חֶלְקָם נָתַתִּי אֹתָהּ מֵאִשָּׁי קֹדֶשׁ קָדָשִׁים הִוא כַּחַטָּאת
11 וְכָאָשָׁם׃ כָּל־זָכָר בִּבְנֵי אַהֲרֹן יֹאכְלֶנָּה חָק־עוֹלָם לְדֹרֹתֵיכֶם
מֵאִשֵּׁי יְהוָֹה כֹּל אֲשֶׁר־יִגַּע בָּהֶם יִקְדָּשׁ׃ * פ שני
12 13 וַיְדַבֵּר יְהוָֹה אֶל־מֹשֶׁה לֵּאמֹר׃ זֶה קָרְבַּן אַהֲרֹן וּבָנָיו

v. 8. סבירין ממנה

6. *continually.* By means of the two daily burnt-offerings a perpetual fire was kept burning on the Altar. A continuous fire was also maintained on some heathen altars. Their fire, however, was looked upon as either the symbol of the deity or as identical with it; whereas, on the Hebrew Altar, the perpetual fire, like the *Ner Tamid* (Exod. XXVII, 20), was but a witness of Israel's unremitting zeal in the service of God and typified its Religion, which embraces the whole of life and is not limited to certain special times or places. This principle, fundamental in Judaism, is translated by the Rabbinic codes into terms of everyday duty.

In the time of the Second Temple, there was a special day set apart 'when it was customary for everyone to bring wood for the Altar, that there might never be a want of fuel for that fire which was unquenchable and always burning' (Josephus). This is confirmed in the Talmud.

7–11. FURTHER DIRECTIONS CONCERNING THE MEAL-OFFERING

These verses repeat and supplement the regulations in Chap. II, having specially in view the daily meal-offering accompanying the *tamid* (Exod. XXIX, 41 f).

8. *his handful.* Not a fixed measure ; because each priest's handful varied slightly.

memorial-part thereof. See on II, 2.

9. The priests were to eat it, and they could not dispose of it in any other way.

without leaven. Better, *as unleavened bread.*

10. *their portion.* Leaven was prohibited in the part of the meal-offering burnt on the Altar (II, 4, 11), and likewise in the portion eaten by the priests.

most holy. See on II, 3. It could therefore be eaten only by the male descendants of Aaron.

11. *every male.* Even those disqualified by reason of a blemish; see XXI.

a due. Heb. חק; usually 'statute', but here as in Gen. XLVII, 22, meaning, 'portion,' 'due.'

whatsoever . . . shall be holy. As ritual impurity was infectious, even so could ritual holiness be conveyed from one thing to another. Any food, coming in contact with holy food, itself becomes 'holy', and is subject to all the regulations of קדשי קדשים or קדשים קלים (II, 3) as the case may be. Many modern commentators take the phrase 'shall be holy' to imply some form of consecration to the Sanctuary or obligation to do service at it. In that case, however, the Text should have been יתקדש, as in Exod. XIX, 22, instead of יקדש (Wessely).

12–16. THE HIGH PRIEST'S DAILY MEAL-OFFERING

13. *in the day when he is anointed.* This Heb. phrase (as again in VII, 35, 38) may mean, 'from the day when he is anointed onwards' (Ibn Ezra). After his ordination Aaron was to bring a daily meal-offering at his own expense, not on his behalf alone but for the priesthood as well (*minchath chabittim*). Likewise every priest, but only at the commencement of his ministry, offered a meal-offering (*minchath chinnuch*, 'the meal-offering of initiation') spoke unto Moses, saying: 13. This is the offering of Aaron and of his sons, which they shall offer unto the LORD in the day when he is anointed: the tenth part of an ephah of fine flour for a meal-offering perpetually, half of it in the morning, and half thereof in the evening. 14. On a griddle it shall be made with oil; when it is soaked, thou shalt bring it in; in broken pieces shalt thou offer the meal-offering for a sweet savour unto the LORD. ¶ 15. And the anointed priest that shall be in his stead from among his sons shall offer it, it is a due for ever; it shall be wholly made to smoke unto the LORD. 16. And every meal-offering of the priest shall be wholly made to smoke; it shall not be eaten. ¶ 17. And the LORD spoke unto Moses, saying: 18. Speak unto Aaron and to his sons, saying: ¶ This is the law of the sin-offering: in the place where the burnt-offering is killed shall the sin-offering be killed before the LORD; it is most holy. 19. The priest that offereth it for sin shall eat it; in a holy place shall it be eaten, in the court of the tent of meeting. 20. Whatsoever shall touch the flesh thereof shall be holy; and when there is sprinkled of the blood thereof upon any garment, thou shalt wash that whereon it was sprinkled in a holy place. 21. But the earthen vessel wherein it is sodden shall be broken; and if it be sodden in a brazen vessel, it shall be scoured, and rinsed in water. 22. Every male among the priests may eat thereof; it is most holy. 23. And no sin-offering, whereof any of the blood is brought into the tent of meeting to make atonement in the holy place, shall be eaten; it shall be burnt with fire.

7

CHAPTER VII

1. And this is the law of the guilt-offering; it is most holy. 2. In the place where they

אֲשֶׁר־יַקְרִיבוּ לַיהוָה בְּיוֹם הִמָּשַׁח אֹתוֹ עֲשִׂירִת הָאֵפָה
סֹלֶת מִנְחָה תָּמִיד מַחֲצִיתָהּ בַּבֹּקֶר וּמַחֲצִיתָהּ בָּעָרֶב׃
14 עַל־מַחֲבַת בַּשֶּׁמֶן תֵּעָשֶׂה מֻרְבֶּכֶת תְּבִיאֶנָּה תֻּפִינֵי מִנְחַת
טו פִּתִּים תַּקְרִיב רֵיחַ־נִיחֹחַ לַיהוָה׃ וְהַכֹּהֵן הַמָּשִׁיחַ תַּחְתָּיו
16 מִבָּנָיו יַעֲשֶׂה אֹתָהּ חָק־עוֹלָם לַיהוָה כָּלִיל תָּקְטָר׃ וְכָל־
מִנְחַת כֹּהֵן כָּלִיל תִּהְיֶה לֹא תֵאָכֵל׃ פ
17 18 וַיְדַבֵּר יְהוָה אֶל־מֹשֶׁה לֵּאמֹר׃ דַּבֵּר אֶל־אַהֲרֹן וְאֶל־
בָּנָיו לֵאמֹר זֹאת תּוֹרַת הַחַטָּאת בִּמְקוֹם אֲשֶׁר תִּשָּׁחֵט
הָעֹלָה תִּשָּׁחֵט הַחַטָּאת לִפְנֵי יְהוָה קֹדֶשׁ קָדָשִׁים הִוא׃
19 הַכֹּהֵן הַמְחַטֵּא אֹתָהּ יֹאכְלֶנָּה בְּמָקוֹם קָדֹשׁ תֵּאָכֵל
כ בַּחֲצַר אֹהֶל מוֹעֵד׃ כֹּל אֲשֶׁר־יִגַּע בִּבְשָׂרָהּ יִקְדָּשׁ
וַאֲשֶׁר יִזֶּה מִדָּמָהּ עַל־הַבֶּגֶד אֲשֶׁר יִזֶּה עָלֶיהָ תְּכַבֵּס בְּמָקוֹם
21 קָדֹשׁ׃ וּכְלִי־חֶרֶשׂ אֲשֶׁר תְּבֻשַּׁל־בּוֹ יִשָּׁבֵר וְאִם־בִּכְלִי
22 נְחֹשֶׁת בֻּשָּׁלָה וּמֹרַק וְשֻׁטַּף בַּמָּיִם׃ כָּל־זָכָר בַּכֹּהֲנִים
23 יֹאכַל אֹתָהּ קֹדֶשׁ קָדָשִׁים הִוא׃ וְכָל־חַטָּאת אֲשֶׁר
יוּבָא מִדָּמָהּ אֶל־אֹהֶל מוֹעֵד לְכַפֵּר בַּקֹּדֶשׁ לֹא תֵאָכֵל
בָּאֵשׁ תִּשָּׂרֵף׃ פ

ז

CAP. VII. ז

א 2 וְזֹאת תּוֹרַת הָאָשָׁם קֹדֶשׁ קָדָשִׁים הוּא׃ בִּמְקוֹם אֲשֶׁר
יִשְׁחֲטוּ אֶת־הָעֹלָה יִשְׁחֲטוּ אֶת־הָאָשָׁם וְאֶת־דָּמוֹ יִזְרֹק

14. *soaked.* lit. 'well mixed.'

in broken pieces. 'The meaning of the Hebrew word is uncertain' (RV Margin).

16. *every meal-offering.* *i.e.* not only that prescribed here by the Torah; but also when a priest voluntarily brought a meal-offering it was wholly consumed upon the Altar.

17–23. Holiness of the sin-offering (cf. IV–V, 13).

19. *shall eat it.* *i.e.* the portion left after the burning of the prescribed parts was to be eaten by the officiating priest and his fellows (see *v.* 22).

21. *shall be broken.* An earthen vessel would absorb and retain some of the contents, even after scouring and cleansing (see XI, 33).

23. *sin-offering.* As described in Chap. IV.

CHAPTER VII, 1–10. THE GUILT-OFFERING (cf. V, 14–26)

1. *guilt-offering.* Unlike the sin-offering, it did not bring complete expiation. It was brought either as penalty for a 'trespass' (see V, 14–16, 20–6), when it had to be offered besides the restitution; or in doubtful cases (see V, 17–19), where its purpose was to suspend the effects of sin.

most holy. See on II, 3.

2. *in the place where.* See I, 11.

shall be dashed. The blood of the sin-offering was sprinkled in the direction of the base of the Altar or applied to its horns (IV, 6 f) as a rite of complete expiation. But the guilt-offering served no such purpose, see on *v.* 1; hence the blood was simply dashed round the sides of the Altar.

3 עַל־הַמִּזְבֵּחַ סָבִיב׃ וְאֵת כָּל־חֶלְבּוֹ יַקְרִיב מִמֶּנּוּ אֵת
4 הָאַלְיָה וְאֶת־הַחֵלֶב הַמְכַסֶּה אֶת־הַקֶּרֶב׃ וְאֵת שְׁתֵּי
הַכְּלָיֹת וְאֶת־הַחֵלֶב אֲשֶׁר עֲלֵיהֶן אֲשֶׁר עַל־הַכְּסָלִים וְאֶת־
ה הַיֹּתֶרֶת עַל־הַכָּבֵד עַל־הַכְּלָיֹת יְסִירֶנָּה׃ וְהִקְטִיר אֹתָם
6 הַכֹּהֵן הַמִּזְבֵּחָה אִשֶּׁה לַיהוָה אָשָׁם הוּא׃ כָּל־זָכָר
בַּכֹּהֲנִים יֹאכְלֶנּוּ בְּמָקוֹם קָדוֹשׁ יֵאָכֵל קֹדֶשׁ קָדָשִׁים הוּא׃
7 כַּחַטָּאת כָּאָשָׁם תּוֹרָה אַחַת לָהֶם הַכֹּהֵן אֲשֶׁר יְכַפֶּר־בּוֹ
8 לוֹ יִהְיֶה׃ וְהַכֹּהֵן הַמַּקְרִיב אֶת־עֹלַת אִישׁ עוֹר הָעֹלָה אֲשֶׁר
9 הִקְרִיב לַכֹּהֵן לוֹ יִהְיֶה׃ וְכָל־מִנְחָה אֲשֶׁר תֵּאָפֶה בַּתַּנּוּר
וְכָל־נַעֲשָׂה בַמַּרְחֶשֶׁת וְעַל־מַחֲבַת לַכֹּהֵן הַמַּקְרִיב אֹתָהּ
י לוֹ תִהְיֶה׃ וְכָל־מִנְחָה בְלוּלָה־בַשֶּׁמֶן וַחֲרֵבָה לְכָל־בְּנֵי
אַהֲרֹן תִּהְיֶה אִישׁ כְּאָחִיו׃ * פ שלישי
11 12 וְזֹאת תּוֹרַת זֶבַח הַשְּׁלָמִים אֲשֶׁר יַקְרִיב לַיהוָה׃ אִם עַל־
תּוֹדָה יַקְרִיבֶנּוּ וְהִקְרִיב ׀ עַל־זֶבַח הַתּוֹדָה חַלּוֹת מַצּוֹת
בְּלוּלֹת בַּשֶּׁמֶן וּרְקִיקֵי מַצּוֹת מְשֻׁחִים בַּשָּׁמֶן וְסֹלֶת מֻרְבֶּכֶת
13 חַלֹּת בְּלוּלֹת בַּשָּׁמֶן׃ עַל־חַלֹּת לֶחֶם חָמֵץ יַקְרִיב קָרְבָּנוֹ
14 עַל־זֶבַח תּוֹדַת שְׁלָמָיו׃ וְהִקְרִיב מִמֶּנּוּ אֶחָד מִכָּל־קָרְבָּן

kill the burnt-offering shall they kill the guilt-offering; and the blood thereof shall be dashed against the altar round about. 3. And he shall offer of it all the fat thereof: the fat tail, and the fat that covereth the inwards, 4. and the two kidneys, and the fat that is on them, which is by the loins, and the lobe above the liver, which he shall take away by the kidneys. 5. And the priest shall make them smoke upon the altar for an offering made by fire unto the LORD; it is a guilt-offering. 6. Every male among the priests may eat thereof; it shall be eaten in a holy place; it is most holy. 7. As is the sin-offering, so is the guilt-offering; there is one law for them; the priest that maketh atonement therewith, he shall have it. 8. And the priest that offereth any man's burnt-offering, even the priest shall have to himself the skin of the burnt-offering which he hath offered. 9. And every meal-offering that is baked in the oven, and all that is dressed in the stewing-pan, and on the griddle, shall be the priest's that offereth it. 10. And every meal-offering, mingled with oil, or dry, shall all the sons of Aaron have, one as well as another.*iii. ¶ 11. And this is the law of the sacrifice of peace-offerings, which one may offer unto the LORD. 12. If he offer it for a thanksgiving, then he shall offer with the sacrifice of thanksgiving unleavened cakes mingled with oil, and unleavened wafers spread with oil, and cakes mingled with oil, of fine flour soaked. 13. With cakes of leavened bread he shall present his offering with the sacrifice of his peace-offerings for thanksgiving. 14. And of it he shall present one out of each offering for a gift unto the LORD; it shall be the priest's that dasheth the blood of

7. *that maketh atonement.* The officiating priest.

8. *skin.* The burnt-offering was to be flayed (I, 6).

10. *or dry.* Without oil; being the sin-offering of the poor man who brought fine flour instead of an animal (V, 11); see, however, Num. V, 15.

11–21. PEACE-OFFERING AND THANK-OFFERING (cf. Chap. III)

11. *peace-offerings.* See on III, 1. This class falls into three divisions: (1) thanksgiving-offerings for deliverance from sickness or danger (Ps. CVII); (2) those in fulfilment of a vow made in time of distress (Ps. CXVI); and (3) free-will offerings, when the heart is moved at the remembrance of God's tender mercies (Ps. CIII, 1–5).

12. *thanksgiving.* The Rabbis regarded the thank-offering as a supreme type of sacrifice; and they declare that, in the Messianic era, all sacrifices shall have completed their educational mission—all save the one inculcating the duty of gratitude. That sacrifice is to continue for ever. The Prophets rank ingratitude as a sin that reduces man below the level of a dumb animal (Isa. I, 3). Since the cessation of sacrifices, the Jew instead pronounces Benedictions of thanksgiving. Persons who have been in peril of life during journeys by sea or land, in captivity or sickness, upon their deliverance or recovery, publicly utter the *Gomel*-blessing (Authorised Prayer Book, p. 148) when called to the Reading of the Law.

unleavened cakes. See on II, 4.

soaked. See on VI, 14.

13. *leavened bread.* The accompaniment of an ordinary meal, and also of a sacrificial meal; it was not, of course, offered upon the Altar (see II, 11).

14. *one out of each offering.* One cake of each sort.

a gift. 'As a select portion' (Moffatt).

the peace-offerings against the altar. 15. And the flesh of the sacrifice of his peace-offerings for thanksgiving shall be eaten on the day of his offering; he shall not leave any of it until the morning. 16. But if the sacrifice of his offering be a vow, or a freewill-offering, it shall be eaten on the day that he offereth his sacrifice; and on the morrow that which remaineth of it may be eaten. 17. But that which remaineth of the flesh of the sacrifice on the third day shall be burnt with fire. 18. And if any of the flesh of the sacrifice of his peace-offerings be at all eaten on the third day, it shall not be accepted, neither shall it be imputed unto him that offereth it; it shall be an abhorred thing, and the soul that eateth of it shall bear his iniquity. 19. And the flesh that toucheth any unclean thing shall not be eaten; it shall be burnt with fire. And as for the flesh, every one that is clean may eat thereof. 20. But the soul that eateth of the flesh of the sacrifice of peace-offerings, that pertain unto the LORD, having his uncleanness upon him, that soul shall be cut off from his people. 21. And when any one shall touch any unclean thing, whether it be the uncleanness of man, or an unclean beast, or any unclean detestable thing, and eat of the flesh of the sacrifice of peace-offerings, which pertain unto the LORD, that soul shall be cut off from his people. ¶ 22. And the LORD spoke unto Moses, saying: 23. Speak unto the children of Israel,

תְּרוּמָה לַיהוָה לַכֹּהֵן הַזֹּרֵק אֶת־דַּם הַשְּׁלָמִים לוֹ יִהְיֶה׃
טו וּבְשַׂר זֶבַח תּוֹדַת שְׁלָמָיו בְּיוֹם קָרְבָּנוֹ יֵאָכֵל לֹא־יַנִּיחַ
16 מִמֶּנּוּ עַד־בֹּקֶר׃ וְאִם־נֶדֶר ׀ אוֹ נְדָבָה זֶבַח קָרְבָּנוֹ בְּיוֹם
הַקְרִיבוֹ אֶת־זִבְחוֹ יֵאָכֵל וּמִמָּחֳרָת וְהַנּוֹתָר מִמֶּנּוּ יֵאָכֵל׃
17 18 וְהַנּוֹתָר מִבְּשַׂר הַזָּבַח בַּיּוֹם הַשְּׁלִישִׁי בָּאֵשׁ יִשָּׂרֵף׃ וְאִם
הֵאָכֹל יֵאָכֵל מִבְּשַׂר־זֶבַח שְׁלָמָיו בַּיּוֹם הַשְּׁלִישִׁי לֹא
יֵרָצֶה הַמַּקְרִיב אֹתוֹ לֹא יֵחָשֵׁב לוֹ פִּגּוּל יִהְיֶה וְהַנֶּפֶשׁ
19 הָאֹכֶלֶת מִמֶּנּוּ עֲוֺנָהּ תִּשָּׂא׃ וְהַבָּשָׂר אֲשֶׁר יִגַּע בְּכָל־טָמֵא
לֹא יֵאָכֵל בָּאֵשׁ יִשָּׂרֵף וְהַבָּשָׂר כָּל־טָהוֹר יֹאכַל בָּשָׂר׃
כ וְהַנֶּפֶשׁ אֲשֶׁר־תֹּאכַל בָּשָׂר מִזֶּבַח הַשְּׁלָמִים אֲשֶׁר לַיהוָה
21 וְטֻמְאָתוֹ עָלָיו וְנִכְרְתָה הַנֶּפֶשׁ הַהִוא מֵעַמֶּיהָ׃ וְנֶפֶשׁ כִּי־
תִגַּע בְּכָל־טָמֵא בְּטֻמְאַת אָדָם אוֹ ׀ בִּבְהֵמָה טְמֵאָה אוֹ
בְּכָל־שֶׁקֶץ טָמֵא וְאָכַל מִבְּשַׂר־זֶבַח הַשְּׁלָמִים אֲשֶׁר לַיהוָה
22 וְנִכְרְתָה הַנֶּפֶשׁ הַהִוא מֵעַמֶּיהָ׃ וַיְדַבֵּר יְהוָה אֶל־מֹשֶׁה
23 לֵּאמֹר׃ דַּבֵּר אֶל־בְּנֵי יִשְׂרָאֵל לֵאמֹר כָּל־חֵלֶב שׁוֹר וְכֶשֶׂב

15. *on the day of his offering.* Cf. VIII, 32, 'that which remaineth of the flesh and of the bread shall ye burn with fire.'

16. *vow, or a freewill-offering.* When a man says, 'I take upon myself to bring an offering,' without specifying the animal, it is a 'vow'; a 'freewill' offering is, when he says, '*This* animal shall be an offering' (Talmud).

on the morrow. They were more frequently brought than the thank-offerings; and if the same law had applied to offerings for a vow as to peace-offerings, much of the flesh would have been wasted.

18. *neither shall it be imputed. i.e.* the sacrifice becomes null and void.

an abhorred thing. Heb. *piggul;* the technical term for stale sacrificial flesh.

bear his iniquity. Stated in XIX, 8, 'that soul shall be cut off from his people.' 'Death through Divine agency is meant, not punishment inflicted at the hands of the community' (Driver). Certain heinous offences, both moral and ceremonial, carried the sentence of כרת 'excision,' as their penalty. In some cases, however, כרת seems to be equivalent to outlawry. The man who refused to enter the covenant (Gen. XVII, 14), or the man who would not join in the celebration of the Passover—the Nation's birth-festival (Exod. XII, 15)—was looked upon as a traitor, and exile was not too severe a punishment for him (Sulzberger).

19. *and the flesh.* viz. of the peace-offerings.

20. *his uncleanness.* This refers to impurity due to physical causes in the man himself, such as enumerated in XI–XV.

21. *uncleanness of man.* See v, 2 f.

detestable thing. Heb. *sheketz ;* a creeping creature forbidden as food. It is here described as 'unclean', which means that it is dead.

22–27. PROHIBITION OF FAT AND BLOOD

23. *no fat.* The general law had been given in III, 17. Here the subject is treated in more detail.

ox, or sheep, or goat. The three sacrificial animals; their fat, called חלב, is forbidden, except when such fat is covered with flesh, when it does not come within the prohibition. The fat of other 'clean' animals is spoken of as שומן, and is permitted.

saying: ¶ Ye shall eat no fat, of ox, or sheep, or goat. 24. And the fat of that which dieth of itself, and the fat of that which is torn of beasts, may be used for any other service; but ye shall in no wise eat of it. 25. For whosoever eateth the fat of the beast, of which men present an offering made by fire unto the LORD, even the soul that eateth it shall be cut off from his people. 26. And ye shall eat no manner of blood, whether it be of fowl or of beast, in any of your dwellings. 27. Whosoever it be that eateth any blood, that soul shall be cut off from his people. ¶ 28. And the LORD spoke unto Moses, saying: ¶ 29. Speak unto the children of Israel, saying: He that offereth his sacrifice of peace-offerings unto the LORD shall bring his offering unto the LORD out of his sacrifice of peace-offerings. 30. His own hands shall bring the offerings of the LORD made by fire: the fat with the breast shall he bring, that the breast may be waved for a wave-offering before the LORD. 31. And the priest shall make the fat smoke upon the altar; but the breast shall be Aaron's and his sons'. 32. And the right thigh shall ye give unto the priest for a heave-offering out of your sacrifices of peace-offerings. 33. He among the sons of Aaron, that offereth the blood of the peace-offerings, and the fat, shall have the right thigh for a portion. 34. For the breast of waving and the thigh of heaving have I taken of the children of Israel out of their sacrifices of peace-offerings, and have given them unto Aaron the priest and unto his sons as a due for ever from the children of Israel. ¶ 35. This is the consecrated portion of Aaron, and the consecrated portion of his sons, out of the offerings of the LORD made by fire, in the day when they were presented to minister

24 וְעֵז לֹא תֹאכֵלוּ׃ וְחֵלֶב נְבֵלָה וְחֵלֶב טְרֵפָה יֵעָשֶׂה לְכָל־
כה מְלָאכָה וְאָכֹל לֹא תֹאכְלֻהוּ׃ כִּי כָּל־אֹכֵל חֵלֶב מִן־
הַבְּהֵמָה אֲשֶׁר יַקְרִיב מִמֶּנָּה אִשֶּׁה לַיהוָה וְנִכְרְתָה הַנֶּפֶשׁ
26 הָאֹכֶלֶת מֵעַמֶּיהָ׃ וְכָל־דָּם לֹא תֹאכְלוּ בְּכֹל מוֹשְׁבֹתֵיכֶם
27 לָעוֹף וְלַבְּהֵמָה׃ כָּל־נֶפֶשׁ אֲשֶׁר־תֹּאכַל כָּל־דָּם וְנִכְרְתָה
הַנֶּפֶשׁ הַהִוא מֵעַמֶּיהָ׃ פ
28 29 וַיְדַבֵּר יְהוָה אֶל־מֹשֶׁה לֵּאמֹר׃ דַּבֵּר אֶל־בְּנֵי יִשְׂרָאֵל
לֵאמֹר הַמַּקְרִיב אֶת־זֶבַח שְׁלָמָיו לַיהוָה יָבִיא אֶת־קָרְבָּנוֹ
ל לַיהוָה מִזֶּבַח שְׁלָמָיו׃ יָדָיו תְּבִיאֶינָה אֵת אִשֵּׁי יְהוָה אֶת־
הַחֵלֶב עַל־הֶחָזֶה יְבִיאֶנּוּ אֵת הֶחָזֶה לְהָנִיף אֹתוֹ תְּנוּפָה
31 לִפְנֵי יְהוָה׃ וְהִקְטִיר הַכֹּהֵן אֶת־הַחֵלֶב הַמִּזְבֵּחָה וְהָיָה
32 הֶחָזֶה לְאַהֲרֹן וּלְבָנָיו׃ וְאֵת שׁוֹק הַיָּמִין תִּתְּנוּ תְרוּמָה
33 לַכֹּהֵן מִזִּבְחֵי שַׁלְמֵיכֶם׃ הַמַּקְרִיב אֶת־דַּם הַשְּׁלָמִים וְאֶת־
34 הַחֵלֶב מִבְּנֵי אַהֲרֹן לוֹ תִהְיֶה שׁוֹק הַיָּמִין לְמָנָה׃ כִּי
אֶת־חֲזֵה הַתְּנוּפָה וְאֵת ׀ שׁוֹק הַתְּרוּמָה לָקַחְתִּי מֵאֵת
בְּנֵי־יִשְׂרָאֵל מִזִּבְחֵי שַׁלְמֵיהֶם וָאֶתֵּן אֹתָם לְאַהֲרֹן הַכֹּהֵן
לה וּלְבָנָיו לְחָק־עוֹלָם מֵאֵת בְּנֵי יִשְׂרָאֵל׃ זֹאת מִשְׁחַת אַהֲרֹן
וּמִשְׁחַת בָּנָיו מֵאִשֵּׁי יְהוָה בְּיוֹם הִקְרִיב אֹתָם לְכַהֵן
36 לַיהוָה׃ אֲשֶׁר צִוָּה יְהוָה לָתֵת לָהֶם בְּיוֹם מָשְׁחוֹ אֹתָם

v. 36. סבירין כאשר

24. *dieth of itself.* Heb. *nevelah;* is also the technical term for an animal that has not been correctly slaughtered.

26. *fowl or of beast.* Since the two species are named alone, the Rabbis deduced that the law did not apply to fish. Therefore the process of ritual *salting*, which is used for the purpose of extracting the blood, is unnecessary with the latter.

27. *eateth any blood.* See on XVII, 10.

28–34. PRIESTS' SHARE OF THE PEACE-OFFERINGS

30. *wave-offering.* The prescribed part of the offering being laid upon the offerer's hands, the priest placed his own hands beneath those of the offerer, and moved them first forward and backward, and then upward and downward—symbolizing the consecration of the gift to God, the Ruler of heaven and earth.

31. *the breast.* The fat only was for the Altar, the breast being the portion of the priests.

32. *right thigh.* Considered one of the best parts of the animal and was reserved for the most distinguished guest (I Sam. IX, 24).

34. *breast of waving . . . thigh of heaving.* The breast that is waved and the thigh that is 'heaved', *i.e.* set apart.

35–38. CONCLUDING SECTION ON OFFERINGS

35. *in the day when. i.e.* on the day and afterwards; cf. on VI, 13.

unto the LORD in the priest's office; 36. which the LORD commanded to be given them of the children of Israel, in the day that they were anointed. It is a due for ever throughout their generations. ¶ 37. This is the law of the burnt-offering, of the meal-offering, and of the sin-offering, and of the guilt-offering, and of the consecration-offering, and of the sacrifice of peace-offerings; 38. which the LORD commanded Moses in mount Sinai, in the day that he commanded the children of Israel to present their offerings unto the LORD, in the wilderness of Sinai.* iv.

8

CHAPTER VIII

1. And the LORD spoke unto Moses, saying: 2. 'Take Aaron and his sons with him, and the garments, and the anointing oil, and the bullock of the sin-offering, and the two rams, and the basket of unleavened bread; 3. and assemble thou all the congregation at the door of the tent of meeting.' 4. And Moses did as the LORD commanded him; and the congregation was assembled at the door of the tent of meeting. 5. And Moses said unto the congregation: 'This is the thing which the LORD hath commanded to be done.' 6. And Moses brought Aaron and his sons, and washed them with water. 7. And he put upon him the tunic, and girded him with the girdle, and clothed him

37 מֵאֵת בְּנֵי יִשְׂרָאֵל חֻקַּת עוֹלָם לְדֹרֹתָם׃ זֹאת הַתּוֹרָה
לָעֹלָה לַמִּנְחָה וְלַחַטָּאת וְלָאָשָׁם וְלַמִּלּוּאִים וּלְזֶבַח
38 הַשְּׁלָמִים׃ אֲשֶׁר צִוָּה יְהוָה אֶת־מֹשֶׁה בְּהַר סִינָי בְּיוֹם
צַוֺּתוֹ אֶת־בְּנֵי יִשְׂרָאֵל לְהַקְרִיב אֶת־קָרְבְּנֵיהֶם לַיהוָה
בְּמִדְבַּר סִינָי׃* פ רביעי

ח CAP. VIII. ח

א 2 וַיְדַבֵּר יְהוָה אֶל־מֹשֶׁה לֵּאמֹר׃ קַח אֶת־אַהֲרֹן וְאֶת־בָּנָיו
אִתּוֹ וְאֵת הַבְּגָדִים וְאֵת שֶׁמֶן הַמִּשְׁחָה וְאֵת ׀ פַּר הַחַטָּאת
3 וְאֵת שְׁנֵי הָאֵילִים וְאֵת סַל הַמַּצּוֹת׃ וְאֵת כָּל־הָעֵדָה
4 הַקְהֵל אֶל־פֶּתַח אֹהֶל מוֹעֵד׃ וַיַּעַשׂ מֹשֶׁה כַּאֲשֶׁר צִוָּה
ה יְהוָה אֹתוֹ וַתִּקָּהֵל הָעֵדָה אֶל־פֶּתַח אֹהֶל מוֹעֵד׃ וַיֹּאמֶר
מֹשֶׁה אֶל־הָעֵדָה זֶה הַדָּבָר אֲשֶׁר־צִוָּה יְהוָה לַעֲשׂוֹת׃
6 וַיַּקְרֵב מֹשֶׁה אֶת־אַהֲרֹן וְאֶת־בָּנָיו וַיִּרְחַץ אֹתָם בַּמָּיִם׃
7 וַיִּתֵּן עָלָיו אֶת־הַכֻּתֹּנֶת וַיַּחְגֹּר אֹתוֹ בָּאַבְנֵט וַיַּלְבֵּשׁ אֹתוֹ
אֶת־הַמְּעִיל וַיִּתֵּן עָלָיו אֶת־הָאֵפֹד וַיַּחְגֹּר אֹתוֹ בְּחֵשֶׁב

ז׳ v. 38. סבירין כאשר ibid. הב׳ בשוא

37. *consecration.* lit. 'filling.' The Heb. idiom for appointing to an office is 'to fill the hand'; probably alluding to the offerings placed in the hand, authorizing him to officiate as priest. This offering is described in Exod. XXIX.

38. *in the day.* 'At the time.'

CHAPTERS VIII–X. INAUGURATION OF THE SANCTUARY-SERVICE

CHAPTER VIII. CONSECRATION OF AARON AND HIS SONS

The appointment of Aaron and his sons to the priesthood is commanded in Exod. XXVIII; and directions are given in Exod. XXIX and XL as to their vestments and installation into their sacred office. The Torah first describes the different classes of offerings before recounting in Leviticus the institution of the Sanctuary-service and the consecration of the priesthood.

2. *basket of unleavened bread.* See Exod. XXIX, 2.

3. *all the congregation.* Some commentators (*e.g.* Ibn Ezra) understand the phrase to mean merely the heads of tribes and the elders; others, that every man was summoned. The vast majority would have had to stand outside, probably upon the slope of Mount Sinai, at the foot of which they were encamped.

5. *this is the thing.* The consecration which is to commence is by the expressed will of God. The purpose of the general assembly witnessing the consecration was, likewise, to avoid a revolt against the privileges of Aaron and his sons. An attempt to foment one was made later by Korah (Num. XVI).

6. *Moses brought. i.e.* to the entrance of the Tent of Meeting, where the Laver was placed.

washed. i.e. he commanded them to wash their hands and feet (Ibn Ezra). According to the Sifra, the priests were also to bathe first the entire body, as the High Priest did on the Day of Atonement (XVI, 4). Ordinarily they washed only the hands and feet on entering the Sanctuary (Exod. XXX, 19); but on the day of consecration complete immersion was required. The spiritual significance of the act of immersion, as the first stage of their consecration, is obvious.

7. *upon him.* Upon Aaron. The garments of Aaron and his sons are described in Exod. XXVIII, and the investment of the priests in Exod. XXIX. The clothing of Aaron and his sons was the next step in the actual induction into their sacred offices; it invested them with the visible emblems of their holiness and their functions; see p. 345.

with the robe, and put the ephod upon him, and he girded him with the skilfully woven band of the ephod, and bound it unto him therewith. 8. And he placed the breast-plate upon him; and in the breast-plate he put the Urim and the Thummim. 9. And he set the mitre upon his head; and upon the mitre, in front, did he set the golden plate, the holy crown; as the LORD commanded Moses. 10. And Moses took the anointing oil, and anointed the tabernacle and all that was therein, and sanctified them. 11. And he sprinkled thereof upon the altar seven times, and anointed the altar and all its vessels, and the laver and its base, to sanctify them. 12. And he poured of the anointing oil upon Aaron's head, and anointed him, to sanctify him. 13. And Moses brought Aaron's sons, and clothed them with tunics, and girded them with girdles, and bound head-tires upon them; as the LORD commanded Moses.* v. 14. And the bullock of the sin-offering was brought; and Aaron and his sons laid their hands upon the head of the bullock of the sin-offering. 15. And when it was slain, Moses took the blood, and put it upon the horns of the altar round about with his finger, and purified the altar, and poured out the remaining blood at the base of the altar, and sanctified it, to make atonement for it. 16. And he took all the fat that was upon the inwards, and the lobe of the liver, and the two kidneys, and their fat, and Moses made it smoke upon the altar. 17. But the bullock, and its skin, and its flesh, and its dung, were burnt with fire without the camp; as the LORD commanded Moses. 18. And the ram of the burnt-offering was presented; and Aaron and his sons laid their hands upon the head of the ram. 19. And when it was killed, Moses dashed

8 הָאֵפֹד וַיֶּאְפֹּד לוֹ בּוֹ׃ * וַיָּשֶׂם עָלָיו אֶת־הַחֹשֶׁן וַיִּתֵּן אֶל־
9 הַחֹשֶׁן אֶת־הָאוּרִים וְאֶת־הַתֻּמִּים׃ וַיָּשֶׂם אֶת־הַמִּצְנֶפֶת עַל־
רֹאשׁוֹ וַיָּשֶׂם עַל־הַמִּצְנֶפֶת אֶל־מוּל פָּנָיו אֵת צִיץ הַזָּהָב
י נֵזֶר הַקֹּדֶשׁ כַּאֲשֶׁר צִוָּה יְהוָה אֶת־מֹשֶׁה׃ וַיִּקַּח מֹשֶׁה
אֶת־שֶׁמֶן הַמִּשְׁחָה וַיִּמְשַׁח אֶת־הַמִּשְׁכָּן וְאֶת־כָּל־אֲשֶׁר־בּוֹ
11 וַיְקַדֵּשׁ אֹתָם׃ וַיַּז מִמֶּנּוּ עַל־הַמִּזְבֵּחַ שֶׁבַע פְּעָמִים וַיִּמְשַׁח
אֶת־הַמִּזְבֵּחַ וְאֶת־כָּל־כֵּלָיו וְאֶת־הַכִּיֹּר וְאֶת־כַּנּוֹ לְקַדְּשָׁם׃
12 וַיִּצֹק מִשֶּׁמֶן הַמִּשְׁחָה עַל רֹאשׁ אַהֲרֹן וַיִּמְשַׁח אֹתוֹ
13 לְקַדְּשׁוֹ׃ וַיַּקְרֵב מֹשֶׁה אֶת־בְּנֵי אַהֲרֹן וַיַּלְבִּשֵׁם כֻּתֳּנֹת
וַיַּחְגֹּר אֹתָם אַבְנֵט וַיַּחֲבֹשׁ לָהֶם מִגְבָּעוֹת כַּאֲשֶׁר צִוָּה
חמישי 14 יְהוָה אֶת־מֹשֶׁה׃ * וַיַּגֵּשׁ אֵת פַּר הַחַטָּאת וַיִּסְמֹךְ אַהֲרֹן
טו וּבָנָיו אֶת־יְדֵיהֶם עַל־רֹאשׁ פַּר הַחַטָּאת׃ וַיִּשְׁחָט וַיִּקַּח
מֹשֶׁה אֶת־הַדָּם וַיִּתֵּן עַל־קַרְנוֹת הַמִּזְבֵּחַ סָבִיב בְּאֶצְבָּעוֹ
וַיְחַטֵּא אֶת־הַמִּזְבֵּחַ וְאֶת־הַדָּם יָצַק אֶל־יְסוֹד הַמִּזְבֵּחַ
16 וַיְקַדְּשֵׁהוּ לְכַפֵּר עָלָיו׃ וַיִּקַּח אֶת־כָּל־הַחֵלֶב אֲשֶׁר עַל־
הַקֶּרֶב וְאֵת יֹתֶרֶת הַכָּבֵד וְאֶת־שְׁתֵּי הַכְּלָיֹת וְאֶת־חֶלְבְּהֶן
17 וַיַּקְטֵר מֹשֶׁה הַמִּזְבֵּחָה׃ וְאֶת־הַפָּר וְאֶת־עֹרוֹ וְאֶת־בְּשָׂרוֹ
וְאֶת־פִּרְשׁוֹ שָׂרַף בָּאֵשׁ מִחוּץ לַמַּחֲנֶה כַּאֲשֶׁר צִוָּה יְהוָה
18 אֶת־מֹשֶׁה׃ וַיַּקְרֵב אֵת אֵיל הָעֹלָה וַיִּסְמְכוּ אַהֲרֹן וּבָנָיו
19 אֶת־יְדֵיהֶם עַל־רֹאשׁ הָאָיִל׃ וַיִּשְׁחָט וַיִּזְרֹק מֹשֶׁה אֶת־

v. 8. חצי התורה בפסוקים v. 15. קמץ ברביע

8. *Urim and Thummim.* See on Exod. XXVIII, 30.

10. *anointing oil.* Its components are described in Exod. XXX, 23–5. The soothing effect of oil on skin scorched by the burning sun made it symbolize comfort and happiness; while its use for illumination suggested light and life.

11. *seven times.* The sanctification of the Altar was appointed for seven days, on each of which the Altar was to be anointed; Exod. XXIX, 36.

12. *he poured of the anointing oil.* In other passages (Exod. XXVIII, 41; XL, 15; Lev. VII, 36; X, 7) all the priests are referred to as having been anointed. Though Aaron and his sons alike were *sprinkled* with oil, the High Priest alone had oil *poured* upon his head.

13. *as the LORD commanded.* See Exod. XXIX, 8 f.

14. *sin-offering.* The first sacrifice to be offered was to cleanse the priests of any transgressions which they may have committed. They themselves must obtain atonement before they could help to secure it for others.

laid their hands. Making confession of their sins while doing so; see on I, 4.

15. *when it was slain.* By Moses. The procedure was that which normally followed the sin-offering (Chap. IV).

to make atonement for it. Better, *by making atonement for it.*

17. *as the LORD commanded.* See IV, 12.

18. *the ram.* After the sin-offering, they next brought a burnt-offering (see Exod. XXIX, 15 f) as an expression of whole-hearted submission to the will of God and desire for fellowship with Him. The usual procedure of the burnt-offering (Chap. I) was followed.

the blood against the altar round about. 20. And when the ram was cut into its pieces, Moses made the head, and the pieces, and the suet smoke. 21. And when the inwards and the legs were washed with water, Moses made the whole ram smoke upon the altar; it was a burnt-offering for a sweet savour; it was an offering made by fire unto the LORD; as the LORD commanded Moses.* vi. 22. And the other ram was presented, the ram of consecration, and Aaron and his sons laid their hands upon the head of the ram. 23. And when it was slain, Moses took of the blood thereof, and put it upon the tip of Aaron's right ear, and upon the thumb of his right hand, and upon the great toe of his right foot. 24. And Aaron's sons were brought, and Moses put of the blood upon the tip of their right ear, and upon the thumb of their right hand, and upon the great toe of their right foot; and Moses dashed the blood against the altar round about. 25. And he took the fat, and the fat tail, and all the fat that was upon the inwards, and the lobe of the liver, and the two kidneys, and their fat, and the right thigh. 26. And out of the basket of unleavened bread, that was before the LORD, he took one unleavened cake, and one cake of oiled bread, and one wafer, and placed them on the fat, and upon the right thigh. 27. And he put the whole upon the hands of Aaron, and upon the hands of his sons, and waved them for a wave-offering before the LORD. 28. And Moses took them from off their hands, and made them smoke on the altar upon the burnt-offering; they were a consecration-offering for a sweet savour; it was an offering made by fire unto the LORD. 29. And Moses took the breast, and waved it for a wave-offering before the LORD; it was Moses' portion of the ram of consecration; as the LORD commanded Moses.* vii. 30. And Moses took of

כ הַדָּם עַל־הַמִּזְבֵּחַ סָבִיב׃ וְאֶת־הָאַיִל נִתַּח לִנְתָחָיו וַיַּקְטֵר
21 מֹשֶׁה אֶת־הָרֹאשׁ וְאֶת־הַנְּתָחִים וְאֶת־הַפָּדֶר׃ וְאֶת־הַקֶּרֶב
וְאֶת־הַכְּרָעַיִם רָחַץ בַּמָּיִם וַיַּקְטֵר מֹשֶׁה אֶת־כָּל־הָאַיִל
הַמִּזְבֵּחָה עֹלָה הוּא לְרֵיחַ־נִיחֹחַ אִשֶּׁה הוּא לַיהוָה
ששי 22 כַּאֲשֶׁר צִוָּה יְהוָה אֶת־מֹשֶׁה׃* וַיַּקְרֵב אֶת־הָאַיִל הַשֵּׁנִי
אֵיל הַמִּלֻּאִים וַיִּסְמְכוּ אַהֲרֹן וּבָנָיו אֶת־יְדֵיהֶם עַל־רֹאשׁ
23 הָאָיִל׃ וַיִּשְׁחָט ׀ וַיִּקַּח מֹשֶׁה מִדָּמוֹ וַיִּתֵּן עַל־תְּנוּךְ אֹזֶן־
אַהֲרֹן הַיְמָנִית וְעַל־בֹּהֶן יָדוֹ הַיְמָנִית וְעַל־בֹּהֶן רַגְלוֹ
24 הַיְמָנִית׃ וַיַּקְרֵב אֶת־בְּנֵי אַהֲרֹן וַיִּתֵּן מֹשֶׁה מִן־הַדָּם עַל־
תְּנוּךְ אָזְנָם הַיְמָנִית וְעַל־בֹּהֶן יָדָם הַיְמָנִית וְעַל־בֹּהֶן רַגְלָם
כה הַיְמָנִית וַיִּזְרֹק מֹשֶׁה אֶת־הַדָּם עַל־הַמִּזְבֵּחַ סָבִיב׃ וַיִּקַּח
אֶת־הַחֵלֶב וְאֶת־הָאַלְיָה וְאֶת־כָּל־הַחֵלֶב אֲשֶׁר עַל־הַקֶּרֶב
וְאֵת יֹתֶרֶת הַכָּבֵד וְאֶת־שְׁתֵּי הַכְּלָיֹת וְאֶת־חֶלְבְּהֶן וְאֵת
26 שׁוֹק הַיָּמִין׃ וּמִסַּל הַמַּצּוֹת אֲשֶׁר ׀ לִפְנֵי יְהוָה לָקַח חַלַּת
מַצָּה אַחַת וְחַלַּת לֶחֶם שֶׁמֶן אַחַת וְרָקִיק אֶחָד וַיָּשֶׂם
27 עַל־הַחֲלָבִים וְעַל שׁוֹק הַיָּמִין׃ וַיִּתֵּן אֶת־הַכֹּל עַל כַּפֵּי
28 אַהֲרֹן וְעַל כַּפֵּי בָנָיו וַיָּנֶף אֹתָם תְּנוּפָה לִפְנֵי יְהוָה׃ וַיִּקַּח
מֹשֶׁה אֹתָם מֵעַל כַּפֵּיהֶם וַיַּקְטֵר הַמִּזְבֵּחָה עַל־הָעֹלָה
29 מִלֻּאִים הֵם לְרֵיחַ נִיחֹחַ אִשֶּׁה הוּא לַיהוָה׃ וַיִּקַּח מֹשֶׁה
אֶת־הֶחָזֶה וַיְנִיפֵהוּ תְנוּפָה לִפְנֵי יְהוָה מֵאֵיל הַמִּלֻּאִים
שביעי ל לְמֹשֶׁה הָיָה לְמָנָה כַּאֲשֶׁר צִוָּה יְהוָה אֶת־מֹשֶׁה׃* וַיִּקַּח

v. 23. ח' קמוצה

22. *ram of consecration.* This last sacrifice was the offering special to the consecration (Exod. XXIX, 19 f); see next *v.*

23. *ear . . . hand . . . foot.* Symbolic; representing consecration of the whole body. The priest must have consecrated ears ever to be attentive to the commands of God; consecrated hands at all times to do His will; and consecrated feet to walk evermore in holy ways (Dillmann); see Exod. XXIX, 20.

24. *Aaron's sons were brought.* This is not mentioned in Aaron's case, because he doubtless stood at the side of Moses throughout the ceremony.

25. *right thigh.* See on VII, 32.

27. *put the whole.* These parts of the different sacrifices were laid upon the priests' hands, reminding them of their trust on behalf of the people for the service of the Altar, and of their sacred obligation faithfully to discharge that trust.
waved them. See on VII, 30.

29. *Moses' portion.* Because he had temporarily filled the priestly office.

30. *of the anointing oil, and of the blood.* This act was the crowning point of the consecration ceremony; the double sprinkling 'sanctified' the

the anointing oil, and of the blood which was upon the altar, and sprinkled it upon Aaron, and upon his garments, and upon his sons, and upon his sons' garments with him, and sanctified Aaron, and his garments, and his sons, and his sons' garments with him. 31. And Moses said unto Aaron and to his sons: 'Boil the flesh at the door of the tent of meeting; and there eat it and the bread that is in the basket of consecration, as I commanded, saying: Aaron and his sons shall eat it. 32. And that which remaineth of the flesh and of the bread shall ye burn with fire.* m. 33. And ye shall not go out from the door of the tent of meeting seven days, until the days of your consecration be fulfilled; for He shall consecrate you seven days. 34. As hath been done this day, so the LORD hath commanded to do, to make atonement for you. 35. And at the door of the tent of meeting shall ye abide day and night seven days, and keep the charge of the LORD, that ye die not; for so I am commanded.' 36. And Aaron and his sons did all the things which the LORD commanded by the hand of Moses.

מֹשֶׁה מִשֶּׁמֶן הַמִּשְׁחָה וּמִן־הַדָּם אֲשֶׁר עַל־הַמִּזְבֵּחַ וַיַּז עַל־
אַהֲרֹן עַל־בְּגָדָיו וְעַל־בָּנָיו וְעַל־בִּגְדֵי בָנָיו אִתּוֹ וַיְקַדֵּשׁ
אֶת־אַהֲרֹן אֶת־בְּגָדָיו וְאֶת־בָּנָיו וְאֶת־בִּגְדֵי בָנָיו אִתּוֹ׃
31 וַיֹּאמֶר מֹשֶׁה אֶל־אַהֲרֹן וְאֶל־בָּנָיו בַּשְּׁלוּ אֶת־הַבָּשָׂר פֶּתַח
אֹהֶל מוֹעֵד וְשָׁם תֹּאכְלוּ אֹתוֹ וְאֶת־הַלֶּחֶם אֲשֶׁר בְּסַל
32 הַמִּלֻּאִים כַּאֲשֶׁר צִוֵּיתִי לֵאמֹר אַהֲרֹן וּבָנָיו יֹאכְלֻהוּ׃ וְהַנּוֹתָר
מפטיר
33 בַּבָּשָׂר וּבַלָּחֶם בָּאֵשׁ תִּשְׂרֹפוּ׃* וּמִפֶּתַח אֹהֶל מוֹעֵד לֹא
תֵצְאוּ שִׁבְעַת יָמִים עַד יוֹם מְלֹאת יְמֵי מִלֻּאֵיכֶם כִּי שִׁבְעַת
34 יָמִים יְמַלֵּא אֶת־יֶדְכֶם׃ כַּאֲשֶׁר עָשָׂה בַּיּוֹם הַזֶּה צִוָּה יְהוָה
לה לַעֲשֹׂת לְכַפֵּר עֲלֵיכֶם׃ וּפֶתַח אֹהֶל מוֹעֵד תֵּשְׁבוּ יוֹמָם
וָלַיְלָה שִׁבְעַת יָמִים וּשְׁמַרְתֶּם אֶת־מִשְׁמֶרֶת יְהוָה וְלֹא
36 תָמוּתוּ כִּי־כֵן צֻוֵּיתִי׃ וַיַּעַשׂ אַהֲרֹן וּבָנָיו אֵת כָּל־הַדְּבָרִים
אֲשֶׁר־צִוָּה יְהוָה בְּיַד־מֹשֶׁה׃

priests and their garments, and typified the two main duties of the priesthood—to diffuse the light of godliness, and proclaim the truth that God grants atonement for human wrong-doing.

upon his sons. See on *v.* 12.

31. *there eat it.* This meal sealed the covenant of the priests with God. For the custom of ratifying an agreement by means of a sacrificial meal, see Gen. XXXI, 46.

as I commanded. We must understand the subject to be God. Onkelos and Septuagint render the Heb. 'as I was commanded.' It involves no change of consonants in the Hebrew Text.

32. *remaineth.* Until the morning.

33. *ye shall not go out.* A precaution against contracting impurity, and to prevent their diversion by worldly matters. Throughout the week of consecration, mind and heart were to be concentrated upon the solemnity and importance of the office they were entering.

34. *as hath been done this day.* The rites performed on the first day were to be repeated on each of the seven days (Exod. XXXI, 35 f).

35. *that ye die not.* The warning was frequently given to the priests that any breaking of the Divine regulations involved them in the greatest danger.

36. *Aaron and his sons did.* Voluntarily underwent the consecration, testifying their readiness to enter upon the service of the Most High.

JEREMIAH VII, 21–VIII, 3; IX, 22, 23

CHAPTER VII

21. Thus saith the LORD of hosts, the God of Israel: Add your burnt-offerings unto your sacrifices, and eat ye flesh. 22. For I spoke not unto your fathers, nor commanded them in the day that I brought them out of the land of Egypt, concerning burnt-offerings or sacrifices; 23. but this thing I commanded them, saying: 'Hearken unto My voice, and I will be your God, and ye shall be My people; and walk ye in all the way that I command you, that it may be well with you.' 24. But they hearkened not, nor inclined their ear, but walked in their own counsels, even in the stubborn-

CAP. VII. ז

21 כֹּה אָמַר יְהוָה צְבָאוֹת אֱלֹהֵי יִשְׂרָאֵל
22 עֹלוֹתֵיכֶם סְפוּ עַל־זִבְחֵיכֶם וְאִכְלוּ בָשָׂר׃ כִּי לֹא־דִבַּרְתִּי
אֶת־אֲבוֹתֵיכֶם וְלֹא צִוִּיתִים בְּיוֹם הוֹצִיא* אוֹתָם מֵאֶרֶץ
23 מִצְרָיִם עַל־דִּבְרֵי עוֹלָה וָזָבַח׃ כִּי אִם־אֶת־הַדָּבָר הַזֶּה
צִוִּיתִי אוֹתָם לֵאמֹר שִׁמְעוּ בְקוֹלִי וְהָיִיתִי לָכֶם לֵאלֹהִים
וְאַתֶּם תִּהְיוּ־לִי לְעָם וַהֲלַכְתֶּם בְּכָל־הַדֶּרֶךְ אֲשֶׁר אֲצַוֶּה
24 אֶתְכֶם לְמַעַן יִיטַב לָכֶם׃ וְלֹא שָׁמְעוּ וְלֹא־הִטּוּ אֶת־אָזְנָם

v. 22. הוציאי קרי

For the life of Jeremiah, see p. 229.

The Sedrah continues the laws regulating sacrifice: the Haftorah reveals the object of sacrifice and of all outward worship; *i.e.* to deepen the inward sense of religion and to stimulate to a holy life. It proclaims the uselessness of worship when combined with unholiness and unrighteousness.

It was spoken by Jeremiah in the year 608 B.C.E. to some solemn gathering of the people in the Temple-area. His denunciation of mere mechanical performance of acts of worship; of the superstition that the Temple ritual could be a guarantee of security, while the people were divorced from obedience to the Moral Law; and his prediction of national disaster, which only whole-hearted repentance could avert, infuriated both priests and people, and placed him in imminent risk of death (see Jer. XXVI).

CHAPTER VII

21–28. God ever demanded obedience rather than sacrifice, but Israel has not taken to heart this teaching.

21. *add your burnt-offerings . . . and eat ye flesh.* Burnt-offerings were wholly consumed in the flames of the Altar and were not to be eaten by the worshipper (Lev. I, 9). The Prophet bids the people treat them as if, like peace-offerings, they could be eaten by the worshipper. 'For all God cares'—he in effect says to them—'you may eat the one along with the other, because both burnt-offerings and peace-offerings, when offered by guilty hands, have no value in His eyes!' They are then merely so much 'flesh', having no sacred significance whatsoever.

22. *I spoke not . . . concerning burnt-offerings.* The Prophet clearly and literally refers to Exod. XIX, 5, and wishes to say: At that moment I did not ask for sacrifices as a condition of my choice—I did not utter a single word about them—but only for the moral obedience towards Me and the Commandments which I was then to announce to you. Have you kept them?

The commandments that God gave to Israel at the Going out of Egypt were the laws at Sinai; and the laws of sacrifice are not among the laws of primary importance that constitute the Decalogue. עיקר המצוה לא היתה על דברי עולה וזבח אלא שמעו בקולי והייתם לי לעם (Kimchi). Others regard this verse as merely an extreme antithetical expression of the truth that 'to obey is better than sacrifice' (I Sam. XV, 22). The Prophet proclaims that sacrifice can be no substitute for justice and mercy, and that compared with the latter, it is altogether of minor importance. But Jeremiah by no means opposed sacrifice brought in the right spirit. In his picture of the Restoration (Jer. XXXIII, 18), due place is given to Temple worship and priestly sacrifices. See Additional Note, p. 561.

Jeremiah's passionate conviction that the moral laws should have precedence over ceremonial law was at no time altogether lost sight of in Israel. This is recognized even by some Christian commentators. 'In general it may be said the obedience to the Moral Law always ranked first, and sacrifices were, as is here taught, wholly worthless when offered by the immoral. The Jews read in their Services this portion of Jeremiah as the Lesson from the Prophets in connection with Lev. VI–VIII, thus supporting the view that sacrifices are but secondary' (Streane).

23. *hearken . . . well with you.* A free paraphrase of Exod. XIX, 3–6; Deut. V, 16.

24. *but they hearkened not.* Does not necessarily refer to the generation that went out of Egypt, whose lovingkindness the Prophet praises in Jer. II, 2.

backward and not forward. To desert the path of faithfulness and righteousness, no matter under what new or attractive name, is always *to go backward.*

וַיֵּלְכוּ בְּמֹעֵצוֹת בִּשְׁרִרוּת לִבָּם הָרָע וַיִּהְיוּ לְאָחוֹר וְלֹא
כה לְפָנִים׃ לְמִן־הַיּוֹם אֲשֶׁר יָצְאוּ אֲבוֹתֵיכֶם מֵאֶרֶץ מִצְרַיִם
עַד הַיּוֹם הַזֶּה וָאֶשְׁלַח אֲלֵיכֶם אֶת־כָּל־עֲבָדַי הַנְּבִיאִים
26 יוֹם הַשְׁכֵּם וְשָׁלֹחַ׃ וְלוֹא שָׁמְעוּ אֵלַי וְלֹא הִטּוּ אֶת־אָזְנָם
27 וַיַּקְשׁוּ אֶת־עָרְפָּם הֵרֵעוּ מֵאֲבוֹתָם׃ וְדִבַּרְתָּ אֲלֵיהֶם אֶת־
כָּל־הַדְּבָרִים הָאֵלֶּה וְלֹא יִשְׁמְעוּ אֵלֶיךָ וְקָרָאתָ אֲלֵיהֶם
28 וְלֹא יַעֲנוּכָה׃ וְאָמַרְתָּ אֲלֵיהֶם זֶה הַגּוֹי אֲשֶׁר לוֹא־שָׁמְעוּ
בְּקוֹל יְהוָה אֱלֹהָיו וְלֹא לָקְחוּ מוּסָר אָבְדָה הָאֱמוּנָה
29 וְנִכְרְתָה מִפִּיהֶם׃ גָּזִּי נִזְרֵךְ וְהַשְׁלִיכִי וּשְׂאִי עַל־
ל שְׁפָיִם קִינָה כִּי מָאַס יְהוָה וַיִּטֹּשׁ אֶת־דּוֹר עֶבְרָתוֹ׃ כִּי־
עָשׂוּ בְנֵי־יְהוּדָה הָרַע בְּעֵינַי נְאֻם־יְהוָה שָׂמוּ שִׁקּוּצֵיהֶם
31 בַּבַּיִת אֲשֶׁר־נִקְרָא שְׁמִי־עָלָיו לְטַמְּאוֹ׃ וּבָנוּ בָּמוֹת הַתֹּפֶת
אֲשֶׁר בְּגֵיא בֶן־הִנֹּם לִשְׂרֹף אֶת־בְּנֵיהֶם וְאֶת־בְּנֹתֵיהֶם בָּאֵשׁ
32 אֲשֶׁר לֹא צִוִּיתִי וְלֹא עָלְתָה עַל־לִבִּי׃ לָכֵן הִנֵּה־יָמִים
בָּאִים נְאֻם־יְהוָה וְלֹא־יֵאָמֵר עוֹד הַתֹּפֶת וְגֵיא בֶן־הִנֹּם

ness of their evil heart, and went backward and not forward, 25. even since the day that your fathers came forth out of the land of Egypt unto this day; and though I have sent unto you all My servants the prophets, sending them daily betimes and often, 26. yet they hearkened not unto Me, nor inclined their ear, but made their neck stiff; they did worse than their fathers. ¶ 27. And thou shalt speak all these words unto them, but they will not hearken to thee; thou shalt also call unto them, but they will not answer thee. 28. Therefore thou shalt say unto them:

This is the nation that hath not hearkened
To the voice of the LORD their God,
Nor received correction;
Faithfulness is perished,
And is cut off from their mouth.

29. Cut off thy hair, and cast it away,
And take up a lamentation on the high hills;
For the LORD hath rejected and forsaken the generation of His wrath.

30. For the children of Judah have done that which is evil in My sight, saith the LORD; they have set their detestable things in the house whereon My name is called, to defile it. 31. And they have built the high places of Topheth, which is in the valley of the son of Hinnom, to burn their sons and their daughters in the fire; which I commanded not, neither came it into My mind.

25. *sending them daily betimes.* Better, '*sending them early every day*' (Friedlander); 'daily in good time and often' (Rashi, Kimchi).

28. *from their mouth.* So hardened have they become that faithfulness not only is dead in their hearts, but they do not even make pretence to it in their speech (Kimchi). Hypocrisy is the tribute of vice to virtue; they do not recognize the necessity of even lip-homage to truth.

29–VIII, 3. The nation's hideous sin and its impending doom—destruction of the living and desecration of the dead.

29. *cut off thy hair.* As a sign of mourning.
generation of His wrath. Upon which His wrath is destined to be poured out.

30. *their detestable things.* The idols set up in the Temple by Manasseh (II Kings XXI, 3–7, XXIII, 4–12). During the long reign of that king, heathendom became the established religion in Jerusalem. All the foul impurities, gruesome rites, and unspeakable practices of ancient idolatry were fostered; the laws and precepts of Israel alone were proscribed. Shameful images were erected in the Temple itself.

31. *the high places of Topheth.* Where hideous cults with human sacrifices, especially of children, were carried on.
valley of the son of Hinnom. Heb. *Ge-Hinnom.* So called after a former owner. By reason of its evil repute as the place of human sacrifice, and later as the receptacle and burning place of the refuse of the city, the name Ge-Hinnom (afterwards Gehenna) became the term for the later conception of 'hell'.
to burn their sons. Moloch-worship was introduced. The fact that the neighbouring nations—Phœnicians and Moabites—sacrificed their first-born to their gods, was sufficient reason for Manasseh and the worldly-minded among the Israelites to imitate the horrors of religious savagery.
neither came it into My mind. It seems that the 'Progressives' of that day even quoted Scripture for their purpose, and distorted the ancient command concerning the first-born in order to support their hideous innovations.

32. Therefore, behold, the days come, saith the LORD, that it shall no more be called Topheth, nor The valley of the son of Hinnom, but The valley of slaughter; for they shall bury in Topheth, for lack of room. 33. And the carcasses of this people shall be food for the fowls of the heaven, and for the beasts of the earth; and none shall frighten them away. 34. Then will I cause to cease from the cities of Judah and from the streets of Jerusalem, the voice of mirth and the voice of gladness, the voice of the bridegroom and the voice of the bride; for the land shall be desolate.

CHAPTER VIII

1. At that time, saith the LORD, they shall bring out the bones of the kings of Judah, and the bones of his princes, and the bones of the priests, and the bones of the prophets, and the bones of the inhabitants of Jerusalem, out of their graves; 2. and they shall spread them before the sun, and the moon, and all the host of heaven, whom they have loved, and whom they have served, and after whom they have walked, and whom they have sought, and whom they have worshipped; they shall not be gathered, nor be buried, they shall be for dung upon the face of the earth. 3. And death shall be chosen rather than life by all the residue that remain of this evil family, that remain in all the places whither I have driven them, saith the LORD of hosts.

CHAPTER IX

22. Thus saith the LORD:

Let not the wise man glory in his wisdom,
Neither let the mighty man glory in his might,
Let not the rich man glory in his riches;

33 כִּי אִם־גֵּיא הַהֲרֵגָה וְקָבְרוּ בְתֹפֶת מֵאֵין מָקוֹם׃ וְהָיְתָה
נִבְלַת הָעָם הַזֶּה לְמַאֲכָל לְעוֹף הַשָּׁמַיִם וּלְבֶהֱמַת הָאָרֶץ
34 וְאֵין מַחֲרִיד׃ וְהִשְׁבַּתִּי ׀ מֵעָרֵי יְהוּדָה וּמֵחֻצוֹת יְרוּשָׁלִַם
קוֹל שָׂשׂוֹן וְקוֹל שִׂמְחָה קוֹל חָתָן וְקוֹל כַּלָּה כִּי לְחָרְבָּה
תִּהְיֶה הָאָרֶץ׃

CAP. VIII. ח

א בָּעֵת הַהִיא נְאֻם־יְהוָה ויוצִיאו אֶת־עַצְמוֹת מַלְכֵי־יְהוּדָה
וְאֶת־עַצְמוֹת שָׂרָיו וְאֶת־עַצְמוֹת הַכֹּהֲנִים וְאֵת ׀ עַצְמוֹת
2 הַנְּבִיאִים וְאֵת עַצְמוֹת יוֹשְׁבֵי־יְרוּשָׁלִָם מִקִּבְרֵיהֶם׃ וּשְׁטָחוּם
לַשֶּׁמֶשׁ וְלַיָּרֵחַ וּלְכֹל ׀ צְבָא הַשָּׁמַיִם אֲשֶׁר אֲהֵבוּם וַאֲשֶׁר
עֲבָדוּם וַאֲשֶׁר הָלְכוּ אַחֲרֵיהֶם וַאֲשֶׁר דְּרָשׁוּם וַאֲשֶׁר
הִשְׁתַּחֲווּ לָהֶם לֹא יֵאָסְפוּ וְלֹא יִקָּבֵרוּ לְדֹמֶן עַל־פְּנֵי הָאֲדָמָה
3 יִהְיוּ׃ וְנִבְחַר מָוֶת מֵחַיִּים לְכֹל הַשְּׁאֵרִית הַנִּשְׁאָרִים מִן
הַמִּשְׁפָּחָה הָרָעָה הַזֹּאת בְּכָל־הַמְּקֹמוֹת הַנִּשְׁאָרִים אֲשֶׁר
הִדַּחְתִּים שָׁם נְאֻם יְהוָה צְבָאוֹת׃

CAP. IX. ט

22 כֹּה ׀ אָמַר
יְהוָה אַל־יִתְהַלֵּל חָכָם בְּחָכְמָתוֹ וְאַל־יִתְהַלֵּל הַגִּבּוֹר

ח' v. 1. ויוציאו קרי ibid. קמץ בטרחא

32. *the valley of slaughter.* The place where they slaughtered their innocent children shall be the scene of their own slaughter.

for lack of room. The bodies will lie unburied.

33. *frighten.* The corpses will lie untended on the ground with none to scare away the birds.

CHAPTER VIII

1. *they shall bring out.* The enemies of Israel who are the instruments of the coming Divine punishment. The enemy will even open the tombs of the kings, not for the treasure buried with them, but to desecrate the bones of the dead rulers.

the bones of the priests. Of Baal.

2. *host of heaven.* The worship of sun, moon and stars was another Babylonian cult introduced by Manasseh.

whom they have loved. To regard as gods (Altschul). The heavenly hosts look down in cold indifference and powerlessness on the insults heaped upon their former worshippers!

3. *and death shall be chosen.* So great will be the misery of the generation that is exiled. Fortunately, the Prophet's worst apprehensions were not realized. Time softened the utter despair of the first exiles. Jeremiah himself was yet to advise them to build houses and rear families; Jer. XXIX, 5 f.

family. Poetically used for 'people'.

CHAPTER IX, 22, 23

In order that the Haftorah close on a note of encouragement, these verses are added, which give the practical conclusion drawn from God's righteous dealings with His people. The people have been trusting in false values. It is not the

23. But let him that glorieth glory in this,
That he understandeth, and knoweth Me,
That I am the LORD who exercise mercy,
Justice, and righteousness, in the earth;
For in these things I delight,
Saith the LORD.

23 בִּגְבוּרָתוֹ אַל־יִתְהַלֵּל עָשִׁיר בְּעָשְׁרוֹ׃ כִּי אִם־בְּזֹאת יִתְהַלֵּל
הַמִּתְהַלֵּל הַשְׂכֵּל וְיָדֹעַ אוֹתִי כִּי אֲנִי יְהוָה עֹשֶׂה חֶסֶד מִשְׁפָּט
וּצְדָקָה בָּאָרֶץ כִּי־בְאֵלֶּה חָפַצְתִּי נְאֻם־יְהוָה׃

v. 23. למדנחאי ומשפט

wiles of statecraft, strong battalions, or vast wealth that are the real and permanent foundations of a national life; as little as worldly wisdom, power, and riches, are in themselves the guarantors of happiness or peace in the life of the individual.

23. *let him that glorieth glory in this.* If one must glory one should at least glory not in ephemeral things but in things that are of eternal worth. Higher than all worldly wisdom and power is true knowledge of God, as the Fountain of Lovingkindness and Justice.

mercy. Precedes 'judgment and righteousness'. Elsewhere in Scriptures it even precedes 'truth' (חסד ואמת). Truth, justice and righteousness must all be spoken and acted in *lovingkindness*; otherwise, they cease to be truth, justice and righteousness.

for in these things I delight. God's delight is in those who train their hearts to imitate the Divine Attributes of Lovingkindness, Justice and Righteousness.

9

CHAPTER IX

1. And it came to pass on the eighth day, that Moses called Aaron and his sons, and the elders of Israel; 2. and he said unto Aaron: 'Take thee a bull-calf for a sin-offering, and a ram for a burnt-offering, without blemish, and offer them before the LORD. 3. And unto the children of Israel thou shalt speak, saying: Take ye a he-goat for a sin-offering; and a calf and a lamb, both of the first year, without blemish, for a burnt-offering; 4. and an ox and a ram for peace-offerings, to sacrifice before the LORD; and a meal-offering mingled with oil; for to-day the LORD appeareth unto you.' 5. And they brought that which Moses commanded before the tent of meeting; and all the congregation drew near and stood before the LORD. 6. And Moses said: 'This is the thing which the LORD commanded that ye should do; that the glory of the LORD may appear unto you.' 7. And Moses said unto Aaron: 'Draw near unto the altar, and offer thy sin-offering, and thy burnt-offering, and make atonement for thyself, and for the people; and present the offering of the people, and make atonement for them; as the LORD commanded.' 8. So Aaron drew near unto the altar, and slew the calf of the sin-offering, which was for himself. 9. And the sons of Aaron presented the blood unto him; and he dipped his finger in the blood, and put it upon the horns of the altar, and poured out the blood at

ט

CAP. IX. ט

ס ס ס כו 26

א וַיְהִי בַּיּוֹם הַשְּׁמִינִי קָרָא מֹשֶׁה לְאַהֲרֹן וּלְבָנָיו וּלְזִקְנֵי
2 יִשְׂרָאֵל׃ וַיֹּאמֶר אֶל־אַהֲרֹן קַח־לְךָ עֵגֶל בֶּן־בָּקָר לְחַטָּאת
3 וְאַיִל לְעֹלָה תְּמִימִם וְהַקְרֵב לִפְנֵי יְהוָה׃ וְאֶל־בְּנֵי יִשְׂרָאֵל
תְּדַבֵּר לֵאמֹר קְחוּ שְׂעִיר־עִזִּים לְחַטָּאת וְעֵגֶל וָכֶבֶשׂ בְּנֵי־
4 שָׁנָה תְּמִימִם לְעֹלָה׃ וְשׁוֹר וָאַיִל לִשְׁלָמִים לִזְבֹּחַ לִפְנֵי
יְהוָה וּמִנְחָה בְּלוּלָה בַשָּׁמֶן כִּי הַיּוֹם יְהוָה נִרְאָה
ה אֲלֵיכֶם׃ וַיִּקְחוּ אֵת אֲשֶׁר צִוָּה מֹשֶׁה אֶל־פְּנֵי אֹהֶל מוֹעֵד
6 וַיִּקְרְבוּ כָּל־הָעֵדָה וַיַּעַמְדוּ לִפְנֵי יְהוָה׃ וַיֹּאמֶר מֹשֶׁה
זֶה הַדָּבָר אֲשֶׁר־צִוָּה יְהוָה תַּעֲשׂוּ וְיֵרָא אֲלֵיכֶם כְּבוֹד
7 יְהוָה׃ וַיֹּאמֶר מֹשֶׁה אֶל־אַהֲרֹן קְרַב אֶל־הַמִּזְבֵּחַ וַעֲשֵׂה
אֶת־חַטָּאתְךָ וְאֶת־עֹלָתֶךָ וְכַפֵּר בַּעַדְךָ וּבְעַד הָעָם וַעֲשֵׂה
8 אֶת־קָרְבַּן הָעָם וְכַפֵּר בַּעֲדָם כַּאֲשֶׁר צִוָּה יְהוָה׃ וַיִּקְרַב
אַהֲרֹן אֶל־הַמִּזְבֵּחַ וַיִּשְׁחַט אֶת־עֵגֶל הַחַטָּאת אֲשֶׁר־לוֹ׃
9 וַיַּקְרִבוּ בְּנֵי אַהֲרֹן אֶת־הַדָּם אֵלָיו וַיִּטְבֹּל אֶצְבָּעוֹ בַּדָּם

III. SHEMINI

(CHAPTERS IX–XI)

CHAPTER IX. THE PRIESTS ENTER UPON THEIR OFFICE

1. *the eighth day.* The day after the seven days of consecration of the priests (VIII, 33).

2. *a bull-calf.* A two-year old animal.

a sin-offering. The newly-installed High Priest began his duties by sacrificing a sin-offering for himself and on behalf of his sons.

3–4. The offering brought for the people was of a comprehensive character, and included the principal types of sacrifices. The simplicity of this ceremony is in contrast with the holocausts which King Solomon slaughtered when he dedicated the Temple (I Kings VIII, 63). God does not require of His people more than they can bear.

3. *unto the children of Israel. i.e.* to the assembled elders as representatives of the community.

4. *appeareth.* The Heb. is in the perfect tense; the action is pictured as done, because it is sure to take place.

5. *before the LORD.* In His presence, as they were assembled before the Tent of Meeting.

6. *that ye should do.* Until the priests and the people had been purified, God would not manifest His approval of the Sanctuary.

glory of the LORD. They would not behold God Himself, only a manifestation of His Presence (*v.* 24).

7. *draw near.* Aaron was diffident and fearful of approaching the Altar; and therefore Moses had to reassure him (Sifra). Aaron did not enter upon his sacred duties with a feeling of self-exaltation or pride.

for thyself, and for the people. The High Priest's purity involved and reflected the purity of the nation.

9. *sons of Aaron.* Since Aaron himself did the slaughtering, he would require the assistance of the base of the altar. 10. But the fat, and the kidneys, and the lobe of the liver of the sin-offering, he made smoke upon the altar; as the LORD commanded Moses. 11. And the flesh and the skin were burnt with fire without the camp. 12. And he slew the burnt-offering; and Aaron's sons delivered unto him the blood, and he dashed it against the altar round about. 13. And they delivered the burnt-offering unto him, piece by piece, and the head; and he made them smoke upon the altar. 14. And he washed the inwards and the legs, and made them smoke upon the burnt-offering on the altar. 15. And the people's offering was presented; and he took the goat of the sin-offering which was for the people, and slew it, and offered it for sin, as the first. 16. And the burnt-offering was presented; and he offered it according to the ordinance.* ii. 17. And the meal-offering was presented; and he filled his hand therefrom, and made it smoke upon the altar, besides the burnt-offering of the morning. 18. He slew also the ox and the ram, the sacrifice of peace-offerings, which was for the people; and Aaron's sons delivered unto him the blood, and he dashed it against the altar round about, 19. and the fat of the ox, and of the ram, the fat tail, and that which covereth the inwards, and the kidneys, and the lobe of the liver. 20. And they put the fat upon the breasts, and he made the fat smoke upon the altar. 21. And the breasts and the right thigh Aaron waved for a wave-offering before the LORD; as Moses commanded. 22. And Aaron lifted up his hands toward the people, and blessed them; and he came down from offering

וַיִּתֵּן עַל־קַרְנוֹת הַמִּזְבֵּחַ וְאֶת־הַדָּם יָצַק אֶל־יְסוֹד הַמִּזְבֵּחַ׃
י וְאֶת־הַחֵלֶב וְאֶת־הַכְּלָיֹת וְאֶת־הַיֹּתֶרֶת מִן־הַכָּבֵד מִן־
הַחַטָּאת הִקְטִיר הַמִּזְבֵּחָה כַּאֲשֶׁר צִוָּה יְהוָה אֶת־
11 מֹשֶׁה׃ וְאֶת־הַבָּשָׂר וְאֶת־הָעוֹר שָׂרַף בָּאֵשׁ מִחוּץ לַמַּחֲנֶה׃
12 וַיִּשְׁחַט אֶת־הָעֹלָה וַיַּמְצִאוּ בְּנֵי אַהֲרֹן אֵלָיו אֶת־הַדָּם
13 וַיִּזְרְקֵהוּ עַל־הַמִּזְבֵּחַ סָבִיב׃ וְאֶת־הָעֹלָה הִמְצִיאוּ אֵלָיו
14 לִנְתָחֶיהָ וְאֶת־הָרֹאשׁ וַיַּקְטֵר עַל־הַמִּזְבֵּחַ׃ וַיִּרְחַץ אֶת־
טו הַקֶּרֶב וְאֶת־הַכְּרָעָיִם וַיַּקְטֵר עַל־הָעֹלָה הַמִּזְבֵּחָה׃ וַיַּקְרֵב
אֵת קָרְבַּן הָעָם וַיִּקַּח אֶת־שְׂעִיר הַחַטָּאת אֲשֶׁר לָעָם
16 וַיִּשְׁחָטֵהוּ וַיְחַטְּאֵהוּ כָּרִאשׁוֹן׃ וַיַּקְרֵב אֶת־הָעֹלָה וַיַּעֲשֶׂהָ
שני 17 כַּמִּשְׁפָּט׃ *וַיַּקְרֵב אֶת־הַמִּנְחָה וַיְמַלֵּא כַפּוֹ מִמֶּנָּה וַיַּקְטֵר
18 עַל־הַמִּזְבֵּחַ מִלְּבַד עֹלַת הַבֹּקֶר׃ וַיִּשְׁחַט אֶת־הַשּׁוֹר וְאֶת־
הָאַיִל זֶבַח הַשְּׁלָמִים אֲשֶׁר לָעָם וַיַּמְצִאוּ בְּנֵי אַהֲרֹן אֶת־
19 הַדָּם אֵלָיו וַיִּזְרְקֵהוּ עַל־הַמִּזְבֵּחַ סָבִיב׃ וְאֶת־הַחֲלָבִים
מִן־הַשּׁוֹר וּמִן־הָאַיִל הָאַלְיָה וְהַמְכַסֶּה וְהַכְּלָיֹת וְיֹתֶרֶת
כ הַכָּבֵד׃ וַיָּשִׂימוּ אֶת־הַחֲלָבִים עַל־הֶחָזוֹת וַיַּקְטֵר הַחֲלָבִים
21 הַמִּזְבֵּחָה׃ וְאֵת הֶחָזוֹת וְאֵת שׁוֹק הַיָּמִין הֵנִיף אַהֲרֹן
22 תְּנוּפָה לִפְנֵי יְהוָה כַּאֲשֶׁר צִוָּה מֹשֶׁה׃ וַיִּשָּׂא אַהֲרֹן אֶת־

his sons in the performance of the attendant rites.

horns of the altar. Of burnt-offering.

10. *of the sin-offering.* See IV, 8 f.

11. *and the flesh and the skin.* See IV, 12.

13. *piece by piece.* See I, 6.

15. *offered . . . as the first.* The purgation, *i.e.* the sprinkling of blood, was performed in the same manner as Aaron's own sin-offering, *v.* 8 f.

21. *waved.* Better, *had waved; i.e.* before the fat was burnt on the Altar. For the ceremony of waving, see on VII, 30. The order of the sacrifices described had religious significance. First there came the sin-offering, denoting purification; then the burnt-offering, indicating self-surrender to God; then the meal-offering, notifying consecration of labour; and finally the peace-offering symbolizing fellowship with God. Let the people rid themselves of sin, let them submit their will to the Divine will, let them consecrate their daily toil to His service, and they would enjoy that Divine communion which is the supreme experience of man.

22. *lifted up his hands.* In blessing.

blessed them. According to the Rabbinic explanation, he used the words of the Priestly Blessing, Num. VI, 22 f.

23. *blessed the people.* This phrase probably means, 'greeted the people,' with the joyful news that the priesthood was now able to discharge its sacred functions for the spiritual welfare of the community.

the sin-offering, and the burnt-offering, and the peace-offerings. 23. And Moses and Aaron went into the tent of meeting, and came out, and blessed the people; and the glory of the LORD appeared unto all the people.* iii. 24. And there came forth fire from before the LORD, and consumed upon the altar the burnt-offering and the fat; and when all the people saw it, they shouted, and fell on their faces.

10

CHAPTER X

1. And Nadab and Abihu, the sons of Aaron, took each of them his censer, and put fire therein, and laid incense thereon, and offered strange fire before the LORD, which He had not commanded them. 2. And there came forth fire from before the LORD, and devoured them, and they died before the LORD. 3. Then Moses said unto Aaron: 'This is it that the LORD spoke, saying: Through them that are nigh unto Me I will be sanctified, and before all the people I will be glorified.'

יָדָו אֶל־הָעָם וַיְבָרְכֵם וַיֵּרֶד מֵעֲשֹׂת הַחַטָּאת וְהָעֹלָה
23 וְהַשְּׁלָמִים׃ וַיָּבֹא מֹשֶׁה וְאַהֲרֹן אֶל־אֹהֶל מוֹעֵד וַיֵּצְאוּ וַיְבָרְכוּ
שלישי 24 אֶת־הָעָם וַיֵּרָא כְבוֹד־יְהוָה אֶל־כָּל־הָעָם׃ * וַתֵּצֵא אֵשׁ
מִלִּפְנֵי יְהוָה וַתֹּאכַל עַל־הַמִּזְבֵּחַ אֶת־הָעֹלָה וְאֶת־הַחֲלָבִים
וַיַּרְא כָּל־הָעָם וַיָּרֹנּוּ וַיִּפְּלוּ עַל־פְּנֵיהֶם׃

CAP. X. י

א וַיִּקְחוּ בְנֵי־אַהֲרֹן נָדָב וַאֲבִיהוּא אִישׁ מַחְתָּתוֹ וַיִּתְּנוּ בָהֵן
אֵשׁ וַיָּשִׂימוּ עָלֶיהָ קְטֹרֶת וַיַּקְרִיבוּ לִפְנֵי יְהוָה אֵשׁ זָרָה
2 אֲשֶׁר לֹא צִוָּה אֹתָם׃ וַתֵּצֵא אֵשׁ מִלִּפְנֵי יְהוָה וַתֹּאכַל
3 אוֹתָם וַיָּמֻתוּ לִפְנֵי יְהוָה׃ וַיֹּאמֶר מֹשֶׁה אֶל־אַהֲרֹן הוּא
אֲשֶׁר־דִּבֶּר יְהוָה ׀ לֵאמֹר בִּקְרֹבַי אֶקָּדֵשׁ וְעַל־פְּנֵי כָל־הָעָם

ט' v. 22. ידיו ק'

24. *came forth fire.* Portions of sacrificial flesh still upon the Altar-hearth were suddenly consumed by Divine fire—a sign that the sacrifice and what it denoted found favour in the sight of God; cf. I Kings XVIII, 38.

shouted. They broke into joyful song; 'they praised' (Targum).

fell on their faces. In gratitude and worship; cf. Gen. XXIV, 26, 52.

CHAPTER X

1–5. DEATH OF NADAB AND ABIHU

1. *Nadab and Abihu.* Aaron's eldest sons. Their death points the moral, 'Boast not thyself of to-morrow for thou knowest not what a day may bring forth!' That day promised to be the happiest in Aaron's life. As he, the High Priest, was moving about in his magnificent robes and performing the solemn duties of his exalted office, how elated he must have been! Yet soon his two sons were lying dead at his feet.

censer. A pan for carrying live coal.

strange fire. Unconsecrated fire, not from the Divinely kindled flames on the Altar. On the very day of the consecration of the Sanctuary they ventured to change an essential of the Service in obedience to a momentary whim. In the circumstances, and in view of their office, it constituted an unpardonable offence. The Rabbis, observing that the narrative is followed by an injunction that the priests were not to drink intoxicating liquor before performing their duties (*v.* 8 f), state that Nadab and Abihu had dared to enter the Sanctuary under the influence of drink. Another suggestion is that they had consulted neither Moses nor Aaron in taking the step they did; and that this deliberate disregard of their elders sprang from unfilial jealousy. They asked themselves, 'When will these old men die? How long must we wait to lead the congregation?' It was an impious ambition that led them to commit the unhallowed deed which called down terrible retribution upon them.

2. *devoured them.* Mysteriously—the Rabbis explain—only their souls were consumed; their bodies remained untouched. It is probable that the fire took the form of a lightning flash, killing them without destroying their garments.

3. *then Moses said.* To help the bereaved father understand the significance of what had happened.

this is it. The words which follow do not occur literally elsewhere, but their teaching is implied in such passages as Exod. XIX, 22, and XXIX, 1, 44, setting forth the duty of sanctification for the priesthood.

Through them that are nigh unto Me I will be sanctified. In sharp contrast to the common view that highly-placed or gifted men may disregard the laws of morality, Judaism teaches that the greater a man's knowledge or position, the stricter the standard by which he is to be judged, and the greater the consequent guilt and punishment, if there is a falling away from that standard (S. R. Hirsch). 'With the righteous, God is exacting even to a hair's breadth' (Talmud).

and before . . . glorified. Or, 'that before all the people I may be glorified.' When He is sanctified by those who are near to Him, the effect will be that He is glorified by the people who look to the priests for guidance and example.

held his peace. He found no answer to Moses' argument; or, he resigned himself to the just sentence which God had imposed upon his sons: cf. Ps. XXXIX, 10. 'I am dumb, I open not my mouth, because thou hast done it' (AJ).

And Aaron held his peace. 4. And Moses called Mishael and Elzaphan, the sons of Uzziel the uncle of Aaron, and said unto them: 'Draw near, carry your brethren from before the sanctuary out of the camp.' 5. So they drew near, and carried them in their tunics out of the camp, as Moses had said. 6. And Moses said unto Aaron, and unto Eleazar and unto Ithamar, his sons: 'Let not the hair of your heads go loose, neither rend your clothes, that ye die not, and that He be not wroth with all the congregation; but let your brethren, the whole house of Israel, bewail the burning which the LORD hath kindled. 7. And ye shall not go out from the door of the tent of meeting, lest ye die; for the anointing oil of the LORD is upon you.' And they did according to the word of Moses. ¶ 8. And the LORD spoke unto Aaron, saying: 9. 'Drink no wine nor strong drink, thou, nor thy sons with thee, when ye go into the tent of meeting, that ye die not; it shall be a statute for ever throughout your generations. 10. And that ye may put difference between the holy and the common, and between the unclean and the clean;

4 אֶכָּבֵד וַיִּדֹּם אַהֲרֹן׃ וַיִּקְרָא מֹשֶׁה אֶל־מִישָׁאֵל וְאֶל אֶלְצָפָן
בְּנֵי עֻזִּיאֵל דֹּד אַהֲרֹן וַיֹּאמֶר אֲלֵהֶם קִרְבוּ שְׂאוּ אֶת־אֲחֵיכֶם
ה מֵאֵת פְּנֵי־הַקֹּדֶשׁ אֶל־מִחוּץ לַמַּחֲנֶה׃ וַיִּקְרְבוּ וַיִּשָּׂאֻם
6 בְּכֻתֳּנֹתָם אֶל־מִחוּץ לַמַּחֲנֶה כַּאֲשֶׁר דִּבֶּר מֹשֶׁה׃ וַיֹּאמֶר
מֹשֶׁה אֶל־אַהֲרֹן וּלְאֶלְעָזָר וּלְאִיתָמָר ׀ בָּנָיו רָאשֵׁיכֶם אַל־
תִּפְרָעוּ ׀ וּבִגְדֵיכֶם לֹא־תִפְרֹמוּ וְלֹא תָמֻתוּ וְעַל כָּל־הָעֵדָה
יִקְצֹף וַאֲחֵיכֶם כָּל־בֵּית יִשְׂרָאֵל יִבְכּוּ אֶת־הַשְּׂרֵפָה אֲשֶׁר
7 שָׂרַף יְהוָה׃ וּמִפֶּתַח אֹהֶל מוֹעֵד לֹא תֵצְאוּ פֶּן־תָּמֻתוּ כִּי־
שֶׁמֶן מִשְׁחַת יְהוָה עֲלֵיכֶם וַיַּעֲשׂוּ כִּדְבַר מֹשֶׁה פ
8 וַיְדַבֵּר יְהוָה אֶל־אַהֲרֹן לֵאמֹר׃ 9 יַיִן וְשֵׁכָר אַל־תֵּשְׁתְּ ׀
אַתָּה ׀ וּבָנֶיךָ אִתָּךְ בְּבֹאֲכֶם אֶל־אֹהֶל מוֹעֵד וְלֹא תָמֻתוּ
י חֻקַּת עוֹלָם לְדֹרֹתֵיכֶם׃ וּלְהַבְדִּיל בֵּין הַקֹּדֶשׁ וּבֵין הַחֹל

v. 4. הקורא יטעים הגריש קודם התרסא

4. *Mishael and Elzaphan.* Aaron's first cousins, and the next-of-kin who were not priests. If the body had been touched by any of the priests, they would have become ritually defiled and unable to officiate in the Tabernacle.

brethren. Kinsfolk.

out of the camp. To bury them. Since the grave defiled whoever came in contact with it, the dead were buried outside the Israelite encampment.

5. *tunics.* See on *v.* 2.

6–7. The Priests Not to Mourn

6. *rend your clothes.* The commonest sign of grief (Gen. XXXVII, 29; XLIV, 13). Jews still rend the garment (*Keriah*) on hearing of the death of a near relative.

that ye die not. As the consequence of condoning the desecration of the Sanctuary of which the dead had been guilty.

be not wroth. An ancient Rabbinic interpretation connects the words 'be not wroth', with what follows. We should then render: 'And that he be not wroth with all the congregation, seeing that all your brethren, the whole house of Israel, will bewail, etc.' The meaning is: If the priests show signs of grief, the rest of the community will also lament the occurrence, and perhaps declaim against God for the calamity that marred the festivities of that day. His anger would then be roused against them.

7. *not go out.* Cf. VIII, 33, and XXI, 12.

8–11. Priests Warned Against Intoxicants

9. *wine nor strong drink.* As stated above, the Rabbis connected the incident of Nadab and Abihu with this injunction against intoxicating liquors before officiating in the Sanctuary. Mourners were encouraged to drink. ('Give wine unto the bitter in soul; let him drink . . . and remember his misery no more,' Prov. XXXI, 6 f). The prohibition against bewailing the dead is, therefore, followed by a further command against resorting to wine.

when ye go into the tent. Wine is a beneficent gift of God, when enjoyed in moderation. The priests need not abstain from it, except when discharging their sacred functions as priests or teachers. In those circumstances, the prohibition is made permanent.

10. *put difference.* As they would be called upon to decide questions affecting the life of the people, theirs must never be irresolute or confused guidance. 'They reel in vision, they totter in judgment,' is the terrible charge which Isaiah brings against the drunken spiritual guides of Judah; see p. 227.

the holy and the common. This has a wider than a merely levitical or ritual application. It is the sacred function of the priest to teach the children of men the everlasting distinction between holy and unholy, between light and darkness, between clean and unclean, between right and wrong; Deut. XXIV, 8.

11. and that ye may teach the children of Israel all the statutes which the LORD hath spoken unto them by the hand of Moses.' *iv. ¶ 12. And Moses spoke unto Aaron, and unto Eleazar and unto Ithamar, his sons that were left: 'Take the meal-offering that remaineth of the offerings of the LORD made by fire, and eat it without leaven beside the altar; for it is most holy. 13. And ye shall eat it in a holy place, because it is thy due, and thy sons' due, of the offerings of the LORD made by fire; for so I am commanded. 14. And the breast of waving and the thigh of heaving shall ye eat in a clean place; thou, and thy sons, and thy daughters with thee; for they are given as thy due, and thy sons' due, out of the sacrifices of the peace-offerings of the children of Israel. 15. The thigh of heaving and the breast of waving shall they bring with the offerings of the fat made by fire, to wave it for a wave-offering before the LORD, and it shall be thine, and thy sons' with thee, as a due for ever; as the LORD hath commanded.' *v. ¶16. And Moses diligently inquired for the goat of the sin-offering, and, behold, it was burnt; and he was angry with Eleazar and with Ithamar, the sons of Aaron that were left, saying: 17. 'Wherefore have ye not eaten the sin-offering in the place of the sanctuary, seeing it is most holy, and He hath given it you to bear the iniquity of the congregation, to make atonement for them before the LORD? 18. Behold, the blood of it was not brought into the sanctuary within; ye should certainly have eaten it in the sanctuary, as I commanded.' 19. And Aaron spoke unto Moses: 'Behold, this day have they offered their sin-offering

11 וּבֵ֥ין הַטָּמֵ֖א וּבֵ֥ין הַטָּהֽוֹר׃ וּלְהוֹרֹ֖ת אֶת־בְּנֵ֣י יִשְׂרָאֵ֑ל אֵ֚ת
רביעי כָּל־הַ֣חֻקִּ֔ים אֲשֶׁ֨ר דִּבֶּ֧ר יְהוָ֛ה אֲלֵיהֶ֖ם בְּיַד־מֹשֶֽׁה׃ פ
12 וַיְדַבֵּ֨ר מֹשֶׁ֜ה אֶֽל־אַהֲרֹ֗ן וְאֶ֣ל אֶ֠לְעָזָר וְאֶל־אִ֨יתָמָ֥ר ׀ בָּנָיו֮
הַנּֽוֹתָרִים֒ קְח֣וּ אֶת־הַמִּנְחָ֗ה הַנּוֹתֶ֙רֶת֙ מֵאִשֵּׁ֣י יְהוָ֔ה וְאִכְל֥וּהָ
13 מַצּ֖וֹת אֵ֣צֶל הַמִּזְבֵּ֑חַ כִּ֛י קֹ֥דֶשׁ קָֽדָשִׁ֖ים הִֽוא׃ וַאֲכַלְתֶּ֤ם
אֹתָהּ֙ בְּמָק֣וֹם קָדֹ֔שׁ כִּ֣י חָקְךָ֤ וְחָק־בָּנֶ֙יךָ֙ הִ֔וא מֵאִשֵּׁ֖י יְהוָ֑ה
14 כִּי־כֵ֖ן צֻוֵּֽיתִי׃ וְאֵת֩ חֲזֵ֨ה הַתְּנוּפָ֜ה וְאֵ֣ת ׀ שׁ֣וֹק הַתְּרוּמָ֗ה
תֹּֽאכְלוּ֙ בְּמָק֣וֹם טָה֔וֹר אַתָּ֕ה וּבָנֶ֥יךָ וּבְנֹתֶ֖יךָ אִתָּ֑ךְ כִּֽי־חָקְךָ֤
טו וְחָק־בָּנֶ֙יךָ֙ נִתְּנ֔וּ מִזִּבְחֵ֥י שַׁלְמֵ֖י בְּנֵ֥י יִשְׂרָאֵֽל׃ שׁ֣וֹק הַתְּרוּמָ֞ה
וַחֲזֵ֣ה הַתְּנוּפָ֗ה עַ֣ל אִשֵּׁ֤י הַחֲלָבִים֙ יָבִ֔יאוּ לְהָנִ֥יף תְּנוּפָ֖ה
לִפְנֵ֣י יְהוָ֑ה וְהָיָ֨ה לְךָ֜ וּלְבָנֶ֤יךָ אִתְּךָ֙ לְחָק־עוֹלָ֔ם כַּאֲשֶׁ֖ר
חמישי 16 צִוָּ֥ה יְהוָֽה׃ וְאֵ֣ת ׀ שְׂעִ֣יר הַֽחַטָּ֗את דָּרֹ֥שׁ דָּרַ֖שׁ מֹשֶׁ֑ה וְהִנֵּ֣ה
שֹׂרָ֔ף וַ֠יִּקְצֹף עַל־אֶלְעָזָ֤ר וְעַל־אִיתָמָר֙ בְּנֵ֣י אַהֲרֹ֔ן הַנּוֹתָרִ֖ם
17 לֵאמֹֽר׃ מַדּ֗וּעַ לֹא־אֲכַלְתֶּ֤ם אֶת־הַֽחַטָּאת֙ בִּמְק֣וֹם הַקֹּ֔דֶשׁ
כִּ֛י קֹ֥דֶשׁ קָֽדָשִׁ֖ים הִ֑וא וְאֹתָ֣הּ ׀ נָתַ֣ן לָכֶ֗ם לָשֵׂאת֙ אֶת־עֲוֺ֣ן
18 הָֽעֵדָ֔ה לְכַפֵּ֥ר עֲלֵיהֶ֖ם לִפְנֵ֥י יְהוָֽה׃ הֵ֚ן לֹֽא־הוּבָ֣א אֶת־
דָּמָ֔הּ אֶל־הַקֹּ֖דֶשׁ פְּנִ֑ימָה אָכ֨וֹל תֹּאכְל֥וּ אֹתָ֛הּ בַּקֹּ֖דֶשׁ כַּאֲשֶׁ֥ר
19 צִוֵּֽיתִי׃ וַיְדַבֵּ֨ר אַהֲרֹ֜ן אֶל־מֹשֶׁ֗ה הֵ֣ן הַ֠יּוֹם הִקְרִ֨יבוּ אֶת־

v. 16. דרש בראש שיטה והיא חצי התורה בתיבות

11. *ye may teach.* This duty of the priesthood is impressively formulated by the Prophet, 'For the priest's lips should keep knowledge, and they should seek the law at his mouth: for he is the messenger of the LORD of hosts' (Mal. II, 7).

12–19. DISPOSAL OF THE INITIATORY OFFERINGS

This paragraph continues Chap. IX.

12. *meal-offering that remaineth.* See IX, 4.

13. *for so I am commanded.* These words seem to refer to the special circumstances which were here involved. The priests were to eat their share of the meal-offering, although they were mourners.

14. *and thy daughters.* As the peace-offerings were not of the 'most holy' class, the portions could be eaten in any 'clean' place within the camp of Israel. The daughters were thus able to have a share.

16. *the goat of the sin-offering.* See IX, 15.
Eleazar and Ithamar. According to IX, 15, it is stated that Aaron had sacrificed this offering. Moses, however, addresses himself to the sons, in order to uphold the dignity of the High Priest's office (Rashi).

17. *in the place of the sanctuary.* Better, *in the holy place;* for the law regulating the sin-offering, see VI, 19.
to bear the iniquity. lit. 'to carry away the iniquity.' The Targum paraphrases, 'to obtain pardon.'

18. *as I commanded.* In VI, 19. We must understand, 'in the name of the LORD,' being implied here.

19. *Aaron spoke.* Although the rebuke had been addressed to the sons, it had been intended for him (see on *v.* 16). As on this day the priests had had to secure atonement for themselves, they

חַטָּאתָ֤ם וְאֶת־עֹֽלָתָם֙ לִפְנֵ֣י יְהוָ֔ה וַתִּקְרֶ֥אנָה אֹתִ֖י כָּאֵ֑לֶּה
כ וְאָכַ֤לְתִּי חַטָּאת֙ הַיּ֔וֹם הַיִּיטַ֖ב בְּעֵינֵ֥י יְהוָֽה׃ וַיִּשְׁמַ֣ע מֹשֶׁ֔ה
וַיִּיטַ֖ב בְּעֵינָֽיו׃ ׳ פ ששי

and their burnt-offering before the LORD, and there have befallen me such things as these; and if I had eaten the sin-offering to-day, would it have been well-pleasing in the sight of the LORD?' 20. And when Moses heard that, it was well-pleasing in his sight.* vi.

did not deem themselves in a state of purity to share in the solemn rite of eating the people's sin-offering. That feeling of imperfection became intensified when 'such things as these'—the death of Nadab and Abihu—had befallen them.

20. *it was well-pleasing.* He was convinced that the priests had acted as they did from praiseworthy motives.

CHAPTERS XI–XVI. THE LAWS OF PURITY

The first ten chapters of Leviticus contain The Law of the Sanctuary, in the stricter sense of the term. With the exception of paragraphs here and there, the remainder of the Book deals with matters other than priests and sacrifices, with what might be described as The Law of Daily Life. The Torah takes the whole of human life as its province; in the eyes of the Torah nothing human is secular. It penetrates into the home of the Israelite, and aims at controlling even the most intimate relations of his domestic existence. It is of the utmost importance to grasp this characteristic feature of the Torah. 'The Law of God embraces the whole of life with all its actions; and as none of these actions can be withdrawn from the unity of life, so can the Law be excluded from none of them' (Hermann Cohen). Many things, therefore, that affect only the physical life come under the purview of that Law. A healthy soul in a healthy body is clearly its ideal. The regulations prescribed in these chapters are means towards the attainment of that end, and have therefore a spiritual purpose and eternal worth.

CHAPTER XI. DIETARY LAWS

Among the laws of purity, first place is given to the subject of food, because the daily diet intimately affects man's whole being. The subscription to this chapter, *v.* 43 f, clearly reveals the object of the Dietary Laws. God brought Israel out of Egypt to be a 'holy people', a consecrated people, 'a people apart, distinguished from all others by outward rites which in themselves helped to constitute Holiness. Outward consecration was symbolically to express an inner sanctity.' This thought of being a 'holy people'—a light supernaturally kindled, lest darkness should become complete—a witness to God's sovereignty and purity, lest He become utterly unacknowledged in the world He had made—a 'kingdom of priests', sanctified in themselves, and sanctified for the rest of the world's sake—this sublime thought would be daily impressed on their minds by these Commandments which separated them from other nations. These would, furthermore, prevent that close and intimate association with heathens which would result in complete absorption. Indeed, the Dietary Laws have proved an important factor in the preservation of the Jewish race in the past, and are, in more than one respect, an irreplaceable agency for maintaining Jewish identity in the present. An illustrious Jewish scientist wrote: 'It may appear a minute matter to pronounce the Hebrew blessing over bread, and to accustom one's children to do so. Yet if a Jew, at the time of partaking of food, remembers the identical words used by his fellow Jews since time immemorial and the world over, he revives in himself, wherever he be at the moment, communion with his imperishable race. In contrast to not a few of our co-religionists who have no occasion for weeks and months together to bestow a thought on their Creed or their People, the Jew who keeps *Kashrus* has to think of his religious and communal allegiance on the occasion of every meal; and, on every such occasion, the observance of those laws constitutes a renewal of acquiescence in the fact that he is a Jew, and a deliberate acknowledgment of that fact' (Haffkine).

The Rabbis were content to say that these laws belong to the class called חוקים, 'statutes,' which must be obeyed, although the reason for them transcended human understanding, and although they provoke the derision of heathens, Jewish and non-Jewish. There have, however, at all times been those who have seen a hygienic purpose in these prohibitions, and have held that the forbidden meats were not prohibited arbitrarily, but were unwholesome and repulsive in themselves. Modern research, too, recognizes that certain animals harbour parasites that are both disease-creating and disease-spreading. Their flesh is consequently harmful to man. Such animals are excluded from the Hebrew dietary. Furthermore, as it is in the blood that the germs or spores of infectious disease circulate, the flesh of all animals must be thoroughly drained of blood before serving for food. This is most effectively done by the Jewish method of Shechitah, and especially by the Traditional koshering of the meat before it is prepared for food. Statistical investigation has demonstrated

11

Chapter XI

1. And the Lord spoke unto Moses and to Aaron, saying unto them: 2. Speak unto the children of Israel, saying: ¶ These are the living things which ye may eat among all the beasts that are on the earth. 3. Whatsoever parteth the hoof, and is wholly cloven-footed, and cheweth the cud, among the beasts, that may ye eat. 4. Nevertheless these shall ye not eat of them that only chew the cud, or of them that only part the hoof: the camel, because he cheweth the cud but parteth not the hoof, he is unclean unto you. 5. And the rock-badger, because he cheweth the cud but parteth not the hoof, he is unclean unto

יא

Cap. XI. יא

א 2 וַיְדַבֵּר יְהוָה אֶל־מֹשֶׁה וְאֶל־אַהֲרֹן לֵאמֹר אֲלֵהֶם׃ דַּבְּרוּ
אֶל־בְּנֵי יִשְׂרָאֵל לֵאמֹר זֹאת הַחַיָּה אֲשֶׁר תֹּאכְלוּ מִכָּל־
3 הַבְּהֵמָה אֲשֶׁר עַל־הָאָרֶץ׃ כֹּל ׀ מַפְרֶסֶת פַּרְסָה וְשֹׁסַעַת
4 שֶׁסַע פְּרָסֹת מַעֲלַת גֵּרָה בַּבְּהֵמָה אֹתָהּ תֹּאכֵלוּ׃ אַךְ אֶת־
זֶה לֹא תֹאכְלוּ מִמַּעֲלֵי הַגֵּרָה וּמִמַּפְרִסֵי הַפַּרְסָה אֶת־
הַגָּמָל כִּי־מַעֲלֵה גֵרָה הוּא וּפַרְסָה אֵינֶנּוּ מַפְרִיס טָמֵא הוּא
ה לָכֶם׃ וְאֶת־הַשָּׁפָן כִּי־מַעֲלֵה גֵרָה הוּא וּפַרְסָה לֹא יַפְרִיס

that Jews as a class are immune from, or less susceptible to, certain diseases; and their life-duration is frequently longer than that of their neighbours. Competent authorities have not hesitated to attribute these healthy characteristics to the influence of the Dietary Laws. In the Middle Ages, when epidemics devastated many a country, the Jews were far less affected than the rest of the population; and this immunity gave rise to the malicious accusation that the Jews had caused the plague by poisoning the wells! Although much remains to be discovered to explain in every detail the food-laws in Leviticus, sufficient is known to warrant the conviction that their observance produces beneficial effects upon the human body; cf. xviii, 5.

The supreme motive, however, of the Dietary Laws remains Holiness, not as an abstract idea but as a regulating principle in the everyday lives of men, women, and children. 'The Dietary Laws train us in the mastery over our appetites; they accustom us to restrain both the growth of desire and the disposition to consider pleasure of eating and drinking as the end of man's existence' (Maimonides). Whosoever eats forbidden foods becomes imbued with the spirit of impurity, and is cast out of the realm of Divine Holiness (Zohar). Rejection of the Dietary Laws has at various times been considered as equivalent to apostasy. The Maccabean martyrs died rather than transgress them. At the present day, the great majority of Jews continue to abstain from forbidden food, not only from personal aversion, but because 'our Father in Heaven has decreed that we should abstain from it' (Sifra). These laws constitute an invaluable training in self-mastery. 'Is there not something spiritually attractive in the idea of the Jew of this age voluntarily submitting to restrictions on his appetites for the sake of duty—forming one of a religious guild, whose special characteristic is its self-control? It ought to be the pride of the modern Jew and every child should be taught to feel it—that his religion demands from him a self-abnegation from which other religionists are absolved; that the price to be paid for the privilege of belonging to the hierarchy of Israel is continuous and conscious self-sacrifice. The Dietary Laws foster this spirit of self-surrender. Respect for them teaches and helps the Jew, in Rabbinic language, to abase his desires before the will of his Father in Heaven' (M. Joseph).

1–8. Clean and Unclean Quadrupeds

1. *and to Aaron.* It was the duty of the priests to 'put difference between the holy and the common, and between the unclean and the clean' (x, 10).

2. *speak unto the children of Israel.* The subject matter of this chapter is repeated in Deut. xiv. For the variations between the two accounts, see the commentary on Deuteronomy. A distinction between clean and unclean animals goes back to the earliest period of Biblical history; but whether the criteria were then the same as are indicated in this chapter is not known.

earth. Land; in contrast to *v.* 9 where the creatures that live in water are mentioned.

3. *whatsoever parteth the hoof.* Instead of enumerating the animals which may be eaten, as is done in Deut., the general rule is here given by which the individual species could be tested. The animal must possess three characteristics: (*a*) it must divide the hoof; (*b*) it must be wholly cloven-footed; and (*c*) it must chew the cud. It is probable that the three characteristics—divided hoof, cloven-footed, and chewing the cud—are named because they broadly demarcate beasts of prey and animals of obnoxious habits from those suitable for human consumption.

4. *camel.* At the bottom of the camel's hoof there is an elastic pad or cushion on which the camel gets its foothold in the sand. This pad prevents the hoof from being wholly divided.

5. *rock-badger.* Or, 'coney.' This animal, and likewise the hare, have the habit of working the jaws as though they were masticating food.

you. 6. And the hare, because she cheweth the cud but parteth not the hoof, she is unclean unto you. 7. And the swine, because he parteth the hoof, and is cloven-footed, but cheweth not the cud, he is unclean unto you. 8. Of their flesh ye shall not eat, and their carcasses ye shall not touch; they are unclean unto you. ¶ 9. These may ye eat of all that are in the waters: whatsoever hath fins and scales in the waters, in the seas, and in the rivers, them may ye eat. 10. And all that have not fins and scales in the seas, and in the rivers, of all that swarm in the waters, and of all the living creatures that are in the waters, they are a detestable thing unto you, 11. and they shall be a detestable thing unto you; ye shall not eat of their flesh, and their carcasses ye shall have in detestation. 12. Whatsoever hath no fins nor scales in the waters, that is a detestable thing unto you. ¶ 13. And these ye shall have in detestation among the fowls; they shall not be eaten, they are a detestable thing: the great vulture, and the bearded vulture, and the ospray; 14. and the kite, and the falcon after its kinds; 15. every raven after its kinds; 16. and the ostrich, and the night-hawk, and the sea-mew, and the hawk after its kinds; 17. and the little

6 טָמֵא הוּא לָכֶם׃ וְאֶת־הָאַרְנֶבֶת כִּי־מַעֲלַת גֵּרָה הִוא
7 וּפַרְסָה לֹא הִפְרִיסָה טְמֵאָה הִוא לָכֶם׃ וְאֶת־הַחֲזִיר כִּי־
מַפְרִיס פַּרְסָה הוּא וְשֹׁסַע שֶׁסַע פַּרְסָה וְהוּא גֵּרָה לֹא־
8 יִגָּר טָמֵא הוּא לָכֶם׃ מִבְּשָׂרָם לֹא תֹאכֵלוּ וּבְנִבְלָתָם לֹא
9 תִגָּעוּ טְמֵאִים הֵם לָכֶם׃ אֶת־זֶה תֹּאכְלוּ מִכֹּל אֲשֶׁר בַּמָּיִם
כֹּל אֲשֶׁר־לוֹ סְנַפִּיר וְקַשְׂקֶשֶׂת בַּמַּיִם בַּיַּמִּים וּבַנְּחָלִים
• אֹתָם תֹּאכֵלוּ׃ וְכֹל אֲשֶׁר אֵין־לוֹ סְנַפִּיר וְקַשְׂקֶשֶׂת בַּיַּמִּים
וּבַנְּחָלִים מִכֹּל שֶׁרֶץ הַמַּיִם וּמִכֹּל נֶפֶשׁ הַחַיָּה אֲשֶׁר בַּמָּיִם
11 שֶׁקֶץ הֵם לָכֶם׃ וְשֶׁקֶץ יִהְיוּ לָכֶם מִבְּשָׂרָם לֹא תֹאכֵלוּ
12 וְאֶת־נִבְלָתָם תְּשַׁקֵּצוּ׃ כֹּל אֲשֶׁר אֵין־לוֹ סְנַפִּיר וְקַשְׂקֶשֶׂת
13 בַּמָּיִם שֶׁקֶץ הוּא לָכֶם׃ וְאֶת־אֵלֶּה תְּשַׁקְּצוּ מִן־הָעוֹף לֹא
יֵאָכְלוּ שֶׁקֶץ הֵם אֶת־הַנֶּשֶׁר וְאֶת־הַפֶּרֶס וְאֵת הָעָזְנִיָּה׃
14 טו וְאֶת־הַדָּאָה וְאֶת־הָאַיָּה לְמִינָהּ׃ אֵת כָּל־עֹרֵב לְמִינוֹ׃
16 וְאֵת בַּת הַיַּעֲנָה וְאֶת־הַתַּחְמָס וְאֶת־הַשָּׁחַף וְאֶת־הַנֵּץ

7. *swine.* The aversion to the pig is not confined to Israel. The primary abhorrence was caused, in all probability, by its loathsome appearance and mode of living.

8. *their carcasses.* The carcass of a *clean* animal which had been slaughtered by the Traditional method, did not communicate defilement.

9–12. CLEAN AND UNCLEAN FISH

9. *in the waters.* 'The characteristics given in the Law of the permitted animals, *viz.* chewing the cud and divided hoofs for cattle, and fins and scales for fish, are in themselves neither the cause of the permission when they are present, nor of the prohibition when they are absent; but merely signs by which the recommended species of animals can be discerned from those that are forbidden' (Maimonides). In general, the Torah forbids every kind of shell-fish—which is disease-breeding, especially in hot countries.

10. *living creatures that are in the waters.* This alludes to the sea animals which do not come under the category of fish, such as seals and whales.

detestable thing. In the first paragraph, the forbidden species are described as 'unclean'; *i.e.* not only uneatable, but the touch of their carcass is defiling. With fish this was otherwise. They were 'detestable' and disallowed as food, but they were not defiling by touch.

12. *fins nor scales in the waters.* As long as they have the fins and scales *when in the water*, they are edible. The Rabbis were of the opinion that every fish which has scales also has fins, although these may be of a very rudimentary kind and not discernible to the eye. Therefore in actual practice they permit fish with scales only, but not fish with fins only.

13–19. UNCLEAN BIRDS

The birds prohibited all belong to the class denoted as birds of prey, and also those that live in dark ruins or marshy land. But since the Torah adds the words 'after its kind', the Rabbis enumerated various criteria by which a clean bird may be distinguished.

13. *in detestation.* See on *v.* 10.

great vulture. The Heb. word is often translated 'eagle', but it is very probable that the griffon-vulture is intended. It is the most powerful of the birds of prey; see Deut. XXXII, 11.

ospray. Possibly the sea-eagle is intended.

15. *raven.* The species including the crow, jackdaw, and rook.

16. *ostrich.* lit. 'daughter of wailing'. This bird is represented in the Bible as living in dreary ruins (Isa. XIII, 21) and constantly wailing (Micah I, 8).

night-hawk. Or, 'owl'; the meaning of the Heb. word is uncertain.

sea-mew. Or, 'sea-gull.'

owl, and the cormorant, and the great owl;
18. and the horned owl, and the pelican,
and the carrion-vulture; 19. and the stork,
and the heron after its kinds, and the
hoopoe, and the bat. ¶ 20. All winged
swarming things that go upon all fours are a
detestable thing unto you. 21. Yet these
may ye eat of all winged swarming things
that go upon all fours, which have jointed
legs above their feet, wherewith to leap upon
the earth; 22. even these of them ye may
eat: the locust after its kinds, and the bald
locust after its kinds, and the cricket after
its kinds, and the grasshopper after its
kinds. 23. But all winged swarming things,
which have four feet, are a detestable thing
unto you. ¶ 24. And by these ye shall be-
come unclean; whosoever toucheth the car-
cass of them shall be unclean until the even.
25. And whosoever beareth aught of the
carcass of them shall wash his clothes, and
be unclean until the even. 26. Every beast
which parteth the hoof, but is not cloven-
footed, nor cheweth the cud, is unclean
unto you; every one that toucheth them
shall be unclean. 27. And whatsoever
goeth upon its paws, among all beasts
that go on all fours, they are unclean unto
you; whoso toucheth their carcass shall
be unclean until the even. 28. And he
that beareth the carcass of them shall
wash his clothes, and be unclean until

17 18 לְמִינֵהוּ׃ וְאֶת־הַכּוֹס וְאֶת־הַשָּׁלָךְ וְאֶת־הַיַּנְשׁוּף׃ וְאֶת־
19 הַתִּנְשֶׁמֶת וְאֶת־הַקָּאָת וְאֶת־הָרָחָם׃ וְאֵת הַחֲסִידָה הָאֲנָפָה
כ לְמִינָהּ וְאֶת־הַדּוּכִיפַת וְאֶת־הָעֲטַלֵּף׃ כֹּל שֶׁרֶץ הָעוֹף
21 הַהֹלֵךְ עַל־אַרְבַּע שֶׁקֶץ הוּא לָכֶם׃ אַךְ אֶת־זֶה תֹּאכְלוּ
מִכֹּל שֶׁרֶץ הָעוֹף הַהֹלֵךְ עַל־אַרְבַּע אֲשֶׁר־לֹא כְרָעַיִם
22 מִמַּעַל לְרַגְלָיו לְנַתֵּר בָּהֵן עַל־הָאָרֶץ׃ אֶת־אֵלֶּה מֵהֶם
תֹּאכֵלוּ אֶת־הָאַרְבֶּה לְמִינוֹ וְאֶת־הַסָּלְעָם לְמִינֵהוּ וְאֶת־
23 הַחַרְגֹּל לְמִינֵהוּ וְאֶת־הֶחָגָב לְמִינֵהוּ׃ וְכֹל שֶׁרֶץ הָעוֹף
24 אֲשֶׁר־לוֹ אַרְבַּע רַגְלָיִם שֶׁקֶץ הוּא לָכֶם׃ וּלְאֵלֶּה תִּטַּמָּאוּ
כה כָּל־הַנֹּגֵעַ בְּנִבְלָתָם יִטְמָא עַד־הָעָרֶב׃ וְכָל־הַנֹּשֵׂא מִנִּבְלָתָם
26 יְכַבֵּס בְּגָדָיו וְטָמֵא עַד־הָעָרֶב׃ לְכָל־הַבְּהֵמָה אֲשֶׁר הִוא
מַפְרֶסֶת פַּרְסָה וְשֶׁסַע ׀ אֵינֶנָּה שֹׁסַעַת וְגֵרָה אֵינֶנָּה מַעֲלָה
27 טְמֵאִים הֵם לָכֶם כָּל־הַנֹּגֵעַ בָּהֶם יִטְמָא׃ וְכֹל ׀ הוֹלֵךְ עַל־
כַּפָּיו בְּכָל־הַחַיָּה הַהֹלֶכֶת עַל־אַרְבַּע טְמֵאִים הֵם לָכֶם
28 כָּל־הַנֹּגֵעַ בְּנִבְלָתָם יִטְמָא עַד־הָעָרֶב׃ וְהַנֹּשֵׂא אֶת־נִבְלָתָם

v. 21. לו קרי

17. *little owl.* Mentioned in Ps. CII, 7, as dwelling amidst ruins.

cormorant. lit. 'the hurler'; *i.e.* the bird which hurls itself from a height and snatches fish from the water.

great owl. The Heb. probably means, 'the bird which dwells in twilight,' an inhabiter of ruined places (Isa. XXXIV, 11).

18. *horned owl.* Or, 'swan.'

pelican. Mentioned several times in Scripture as leading a solitary life in desert places (Ps. CII, 7).

19. *stork.* The Heb. signifies a bird which is 'kind and affectionate' to its young.

heron. Or, 'ibis.'

hoopoe. An uncertain word. The Rabbis understood it to be a species of grouse.

bat. Named together with moles as being a bird which prefers dark places (Isa. II, 20).

20–23. Winged Swarming Things

20. *winged swarming things.* Insects that multiply rapidly and become a pest to man.

go upon all fours. The phrase used here cannot be taken to mean that the insects were possessed of only four legs. The words probably refer to their method of locomotion, and signify, 'that move like quadrupeds.'

21. *jointed legs.* Bending hind legs, higher than their other legs.

22. *locust.* None of the four kinds of locusts mentioned are certainly known (RV Margin). For this reason also, later Jewish authorities, realizing that it is impossible to avoid errors being made, declare every species of locust to be forbidden.

23. *which have four feet. i.e.* without the 'bending legs'.

24–28. Defilement Through Contact

24. *and by these.* The Sifra (and so Rashi) makes this paragraph a preface to *v.* 26 f.

shall be unclean. i.e. incapable of taking part in Sanctuary worship, or of touching 'holy' food.

until the even. When he had to bathe his body.

25. *beareth.* Carrying from one place to another. The impurity is passed on to the garments, and these also had to be purified.

the even; they are unclean unto you. ¶ 29. And these are they which are unclean unto you among the swarming things that swarm upon the earth: the weasel, and the mouse, and the great lizard after its kinds, 30. and the gecko, and the land-crocodile, and the lizard, and the sand-lizard, and the chameleon. 31. These are they which are unclean to you among all that swarm; whosoever doth touch them, when they are dead, shall be unclean until the even. 32. And upon whatsoever any of them, when they are dead, doth fall, it shall be unclean; whether it be any vessel of wood, or raiment, or skin, or sack, whatsoever vessel it be, wherewith any work is done, it must be put into water, and it shall be unclean until the even; then shall it be clean.* vii. 33. And every earthen vessel, whereinto any of them falleth, whatsoever is in it shall be unclean, and it ye shall break. 34. All food therein which may be eaten, that on which water cometh, shall be unclean; and all drink in every such vessel that may be drunk shall be unclean. 35. And every thing whereupon any part of their carcass falleth shall be unclean; whether oven, or range for pots, it shall be broken in pieces; they are unclean, and shall be unclean unto you. 36. Nevertheless a fountain or a cistern wherein is a gathering of water shall be clean; but he who toucheth their carcass shall be unclean. 37. And

יְכַבֵּס בְּגָדָיו וְטָמֵא עַד־הָעָרֶב טְמֵאִים הֵמָּה לָכֶם׃ ס
29 וְזֶה לָכֶם הַטָּמֵא בַּשֶּׁרֶץ הַשֹּׁרֵץ עַל־הָאָרֶץ הַחֹלֶד וְהָעַכְבָּר
ל וְהַצָּב לְמִינֵהוּ׃ וְהָאֲנָקָה וְהַכֹּחַ וְהַלְּטָאָה וְהַחֹמֶט וְהַתִּנְשָׁמֶת׃
31 אֵלֶּה הַטְּמֵאִים לָכֶם בְּכָל־הַשָּׁרֶץ כָּל־הַנֹּגֵעַ בָּהֶם בְּמֹתָם
32 יִטְמָא עַד־הָעָרֶב׃ וְכֹל אֲשֶׁר־יִפֹּל־עָלָיו מֵהֶם ׀ בְּמֹתָם
יִטְמָא מִכָּל־כְּלִי־עֵץ אוֹ בֶגֶד אוֹ־עוֹר אוֹ שָׂק כָּל־כְּלִי
אֲשֶׁר־יֵעָשֶׂה מְלָאכָה בָּהֶם בַּמַּיִם יוּבָא וְטָמֵא עַד־הָעֶרֶב
שביעי
33 וְטָהֵר׃ וְכָל־כְּלִי־חֶרֶשׂ אֲשֶׁר־יִפֹּל מֵהֶם אֶל־תּוֹכוֹ כֹּל
34 אֲשֶׁר בְּתוֹכוֹ יִטְמָא וְאֹתוֹ תִשְׁבֹּרוּ׃ מִכָּל־הָאֹכֶל אֲשֶׁר
יֵאָכֵל אֲשֶׁר יָבוֹא עָלָיו מַיִם יִטְמָא וְכָל־מַשְׁקֶה אֲשֶׁר יִשָּׁתֶה
לה בְּכָל־כְּלִי יִטְמָא׃ וְכֹל אֲשֶׁר־יִפֹּל מִנִּבְלָתָם ׀ עָלָיו יִטְמָא
36 תַּנּוּר וְכִירַיִם יֻתָּץ טְמֵאִים הֵם וּטְמֵאִים יִהְיוּ לָכֶם׃ אַךְ
מַעְיָן וּבוֹר מִקְוֵה־מַיִם יִהְיֶה טָהוֹר וְנֹגֵעַ בְּנִבְלָתָם יִטְמָא׃
37 וְכִי יִפֹּל מִנִּבְלָתָם עַל־כָּל־זֶרַע זֵרוּעַ אֲשֶׁר יִזָּרֵעַ טָהוֹר

29–43. UNCLEAN CREEPING THINGS

29. *unclean.* Prohibited as food, and whose dead bodies are defiling.

30. *gecko.* This and the succeeding three names are of uncertain meaning, probably denoting species of lizards.

31. *when they are dead.* Unclean creatures do not therefore defile by contact while alive.

32. *any vessel.* These creatures, which come in close contact with filth and when dead are covered with parasites, needed to be particularly guarded against.

33. *earthen vessel.* This is evidence that the concept of 'impurity' coincided to some extent with 'infection', and that different grades of impurity were different degrees of liability to infection; as, otherwise, the distinction between metal or glazed ware and earthenware would have no meaning. In the latter case, the infection could not be removed by washing; hence it had to be broken.

34. *all food therein.* The meaning is: If a dead creature fall into an earthen vessel wherein is food, the food becomes unclean only if it had at one time been moistened; the occasional moisture becoming a conductor of impurity for all times (cf. *v.* 38).

35. *oven, or range for pots.* The latter denotes a vessel in two compartments to receive two pots, the Heb. being in the dual. They were alike, usually made of earthenware; therefore they had to be broken if rendered unclean.

36. *a fountain.* This verse states the exceptional case where the carcase has no defiling effect. When it falls into water of a well, spring, or a large cistern in which the water is collected in a natural manner (*i.e.* not drawn by a vessel), then it does not render the water unclean. Such 'natural' waters are alone to be used for ritual purification. The minimum quantity for a ritual bath (Mikvah) is 24 cubic feet, so as to permit complete immersion.

but he who toucheth. Although it does not defile the water, it does affect anybody who touches it, even whilst it is in the cistern or pool.

37. *sowing seed.* *i.e.* seed to be planted. This does not contract impurity.

38 הוּא׃ וְכִי יֻתַּן־מַיִם עַל־זֶרַע וְנָפַל מִנִּבְלָתָם עָלָיו טָמֵא
39 הוּא לָכֶם׃ ס וְכִי יָמוּת מִן־הַבְּהֵמָה אֲשֶׁר־הִיא לָכֶם
מ לְאָכְלָה הַנֹּגֵעַ בְּנִבְלָתָהּ יִטְמָא עַד־הָעָרֶב׃ וְהָאֹכֵל מִנִּבְלָתָהּ
יְכַבֵּס בְּגָדָיו וְטָמֵא עַד־הָעָרֶב וְהַנֹּשֵׂא אֶת־נִבְלָתָהּ יְכַבֵּס
41 בְּגָדָיו וְטָמֵא עַד־הָעָרֶב׃ וְכָל־הַשֶּׁרֶץ הַשֹּׁרֵץ עַל־הָאָרֶץ
42 שֶׁקֶץ הוּא לֹא יֵאָכֵל׃ כֹּל הוֹלֵךְ עַל־גָּחוֹן וְכֹל ׀ הוֹלֵךְ
עַל־אַרְבַּע עַד כָּל־מַרְבֵּה רַגְלַיִם לְכָל־הַשֶּׁרֶץ הַשֹּׁרֵץ עַל־
43 הָאָרֶץ לֹא תֹאכְלוּם כִּי־שֶׁקֶץ הֵם׃ אַל־תְּשַׁקְּצוּ אֶת־
נַפְשֹׁתֵיכֶם בְּכָל־הַשֶּׁרֶץ הַשֹּׁרֵץ וְלֹא תִטַּמְּאוּ בָּהֶם וְנִטְמֵתֶם
44 בָּם׃ כִּי אֲנִי יְהוָה אֱלֹהֵיכֶם וְהִתְקַדִּשְׁתֶּם וִהְיִיתֶם קְדֹשִׁים
כִּי קָדוֹשׁ אָנִי וְלֹא תְטַמְּאוּ אֶת־נַפְשֹׁתֵיכֶם בְּכָל־הַשֶּׁרֶץ

v. 42. ו׳ רבתי והיא חצי התורה באותיות v. 43. חסר א׳

if aught of their carcass fall upon any sowing seed which is to be sown, it is clean.
38. But if water be put upon the seed, and aught of their carcass fall thereon, it is unclean unto you. ¶ 39. And if any beast, of which ye may eat, die, he that toucheth the carcass thereof shall be unclean until the even. 40. And he that eateth of the carcass of it shall wash his clothes, and be unclean until the even; he also that beareth the carcass of it shall wash his clothes, and be unclean until the even. ¶ 41. And every swarming thing that swarmeth upon the earth is a detestable thing; it shall not be eaten. 42. Whatsoever goeth upon the belly, and whatsoever goeth upon all fours, or whatsoever hath many feet, even all swarming things that swarm upon the earth, them ye shall not eat; for they are a detestable thing. 43. Ye shall not make yourselves detestable with any swarming thing that swarmeth, neither shall ye make yourselves unclean with them, that ye should be defiled thereby. 44. For I am the LORD your God; sanctify yourselves therefore, and be ye holy; for I am holy;

38. *be put upon the seed.* Better, *be poured upon seed; i.e.* grain stored for food.

39. *die.* A natural death. The carcass of even a clean beast causes uncleanness. *Touching* the carcass infects the person; but *carrying* it necessitates also the washing of clothes.

40. *eateth of the carcass.* Forbidden in Deut. XIV, 21.

41. *swarming thing.* This verse continues the exposition of the Dietary Laws which had been interrupted by the regulations concerning defilement. It follows on *v.* 23, which dealt with the larger class of 'swarming things', and refers to the smaller insects, like worms and slugs.

42. *belly.* The third letter of the word גחון is written in large character to make it stand out more boldly. It is the middle letter of the Pentateuch.

upon all fours. i.e. snake-like creatures which have legs, like the scorpion.

whatsoever hath many feet. e.g. spiders, caterpillars, centipedes.

43. *not make yourselves detestable.* By eating any of the forbidden things. The Rabbis widened this warning into a prohibition of any action or habit which is calculated to provoke disgust, such as eating from unclean plates or taking one's food with unwashed hands.

44–47. SPIRITUAL PURPOSE OF THE LAWS

44. *sanctify yourselves therefore, and be ye holy.* lit. 'strive after holiness and ye shall be holy'; *i.e.* the mere striving after holiness, in itself sanctifies (Hermann Cohen).

Israel is bidden to be holy. This demand has two aspects—one positive and the other negative. The positive aspect may be called the Imitation of God; see on XIX, 2. The negative aspect means the withdrawal from things impure and abominable. Even as nothing that suggested the least taint could be associated with God, so it was the duty of the Israelites to strive, so far as it was attainable by man, to avoid whatever would defile them, whether physically or spiritually. Wherever men and women honestly strive after holy living, such striving carries its own fulfilment with it. Rabbi Pinchas ben Yair said: 'Heedfulness leads to cleanness; cleanness to purity; purity to holiness; holiness to humility; humility to dread of sin; dread of sin to saintliness (chassiduth); saintliness to the possession of the Holy Spirit (רוח הקודש).'

The Rabbis, translating as ever general principles of religion into terms of life, based the precept of Washing the hands before Meals on והתקדשתם ('sanctify yourselves').

for I am holy. 'This constitutes the basis for your duty to sanctify yourselves, as well as the guarantee of your capacity to attain sanctification of life. Holiness is the very essence of the Divine being; and, in breathing His spirit into you, He made you the partaker of His Divine nature, and endowed you with the power to attain to holiness. "Because I am holy, you *shall* be holy, and you *can* be holy" ' (S. R. Hirsch).

neither shall ye defile yourselves with any manner of swarming thing that moveth upon the earth.*m. 45. For I am the LORD that brought you up out of the land of Egypt, to be your God; ye shall therefore be holy, for I am holy. ¶ 46. This is the law of the beast, and of the fowl, and of every living creature that moveth in the waters, and of every creature that swarmeth upon the earth; 47. to make a difference between the unclean and the clean, and between the living thing that may be eaten and the living thing that may not be eaten.

מפטיר מה הָרֹמֵשׂ עַל־הָאָרֶץ׃ כִּי ׀ אֲנִי יְהוָה הַמַּעֲלֶה אֶתְכֶם מֵאֶרֶץ
מִצְרַיִם לִהְיֹת לָכֶם לֵאלֹהִים וִהְיִיתֶם קְדֹשִׁים כִּי קָדוֹשׁ
46 אָנִי׃ זֹאת תּוֹרַת הַבְּהֵמָה וְהָעוֹף וְכֹל נֶפֶשׁ הַחַיָּה הָרֹמֶשֶׂת
47 בַּמָּיִם וּלְכָל־נֶפֶשׁ הַשֹּׁרֶצֶת עַל־הָאָרֶץ׃ לְהַבְדִּיל בֵּין
הַטָּמֵא וּבֵין הַטָּהֹר וּבֵין הַחַיָּה הַנֶּאֱכֶלֶת וּבֵין הַחַיָּה אֲשֶׁר
לֹא תֵאָכֵל׃

45. *that brought you up out of the land of Egypt.* To Him the Israelites owe their freedom; therefore, He has the authority to dictate His will to them. The verse also indicates that the purpose God had in delivering them from bondage was to bring them to His sanctifying service.

46–47. These verses form the epilogue to the chapter.

A brief résumé of the Dietary Laws and the rules of koshering are found in Dayan Lazarus, *The Ways of Her Household*, Part I, 1–37; and M. Friedländer, *The Jewish Religion*, 455–466.

HAFTORAH SHEMINI הפטרת שמיני

II SAMUEL VI, 1–VII, 17

CHAPTER VI

1. And David again gathered together all the chosen men of Israel, thirty thousand. 2. And David arose, and went with all the people that were with him, from Baale-judah, to bring up from thence the ark of God, whereupon is called the Name, even the name of the LORD of hosts that sitteth

CAP. VI. ו

א וַיֹּסֶף עוֹד דָּוִד אֶת־כָּל־בָּחוּר בְּיִשְׂרָאֵל שְׁלֹשִׁים אָלֶף׃
2 וַיָּקָם ׀ וַיֵּלֶךְ דָּוִד וְכָל־הָעָם אֲשֶׁר אִתּוֹ מִבַּעֲלֵי יְהוּדָה
לְהַעֲלוֹת מִשָּׁם אֵת אֲרוֹן הָאֱלֹהִים אֲשֶׁר־נִקְרָא שֵׁם שֵׁם

After restoring the unity of the nation, David consolidated it by establishing a capital, Jerusalem. But that impregnable natural fastness was destined to be far more than the royal residence of Judah and the political centre of the tribes of Israel. 'She was to be the City of God; and this sacred character, which has been hers ever since, was stamped upon her by David himself. His vision went beyond the immediate foundation to the issues that lay in time to come' (Marx-Margolis). It was his first care to bring back the sacred Ark from the out-of-the-way country town to which, a generation earlier, the Philistine conquerors had taken it, and to install it in his newly acquired capital.

The Sedrah describes the consecration of the Tabernacle in the Wilderness; the Haftorah tells of the transportation of the Ark of the Covenant. An untoward and tragic incident marks both Sedrah and Haftorah. The death of Nadab and Abihu in the Sedrah is a warning that no kind of caprice can be tolerated in the service of God. The same lesson is enforced in the Haftorah by the death of Uzzah, who was guilty of irreverence towards God's Majesty.

CHAPTER VI

1. *again.* Refers to the assembly at Hebron that was convened for David's coronation, described in II Sam. V, 1.

all the chosen men. David wished to interest the leading men of Israel in his sacred enterprise; cf. I Chron. XIII.

2. *from Baale-judah.* The phrase is an abbreviated one, meaning, 'They went from Baale-judah whither they had come to bring thence the Ark' (Kimchi). Baale-judah is another name for Kirjath-jearim (*i.e.* the City of Forests), about half-way between Jerusalem and Ashdod near the Mediterranean coast.

to bring up. Jerusalem is on higher ground than Kirjath-jearim.

sitteth upon the cherubim. See Exod. XXV, 22.

upon the cherubim. 3. And they set the ark of God upon a new cart, and brought it out of the house of Abinadab that was in the hill; and Uzzah and Ahio, the sons of Abinadab, drove the new cart. 4. And they brought it out of the house of Abinadab, which was in the hill, with the ark of God, and Ahio went before the ark. 5. And David and all the house of Israel played before the LORD with all manner of instruments made of cypress-wood, and with harps, and with psalteries, and with timbrels, and with sistra, and with cymbals. ¶ 6. And when they came to the threshing-floor of Nacon, Uzzah put forth his hand to the ark of God, and took hold of it; for the oxen stumbled. 7. And the anger of the LORD was kindled against Uzzah; and God smote him there for his error; and there he died by the ark of God. 8. And David was displeased, because the LORD had broken forth upon Uzzah; and that place was called [1]Perez-uzzah, unto this day. 9. And David was afraid of the LORD that day; and he said: 'How shall the ark of the LORD come unto me?' 10. So David would not remove the ark of the LORD unto him into the city of David; but David carried it aside into the house of Obed-edom the Gittite. 11. And the ark of the LORD remained in the house of Obed-edom the Gittite three months; and the LORD blessed Obed-edom, and all his house. ¶ 12. And it was told king David, saying: 'The LORD hath blessed the house of Obed-edom, and all that pertaineth unto him, because of the ark of God.' And David went and brought up the ark of God from the house of Obed-edom into the city of David with joy. 13. And it was so, that when they that bore the

[1] That is, *The breach of Uzzah.*

3 יְהוָה צְבָאוֹת יֹשֵׁב הַכְּרֻבִים עָלָיו׃ וַיַּרְכִּבוּ אֶת־אֲרוֹן
הָאֱלֹהִים אֶל־עֲגָלָה חֲדָשָׁה וַיִּשָּׂאֻהוּ מִבֵּית אֲבִינָדָב אֲשֶׁר
בַּגִּבְעָה וְעֻזָּא וְאַחְיוֹ בְּנֵי אֲבִינָדָב נֹהֲגִים אֶת־הָעֲגָלָה
4 חֲדָשָׁה׃ וַיִּשָּׂאֻהוּ מִבֵּית אֲבִינָדָב אֲשֶׁר בַּגִּבְעָה עִם אֲרוֹן
ה הָאֱלֹהִים וְאַחְיוֹ הֹלֵךְ לִפְנֵי הָאָרוֹן׃ וְדָוִד ׀ וְכָל־בֵּית
יִשְׂרָאֵל מְשַׂחֲקִים לִפְנֵי יְהוָה בְּכֹל עֲצֵי בְרוֹשִׁים וּבְכִנֹּרוֹת
6 וּבִנְבָלִים וּבְתֻפִּים וּבִמְנַעַנְעִים וּבְצֶלְצֶלִים׃ וַיָּבֹאוּ עַד־
גֹּרֶן נָכוֹן וַיִּשְׁלַח עֻזָּה אֶל־אֲרוֹן הָאֱלֹהִים וַיֹּאחֶז בּוֹ כִּי
7 שָׁמְטוּ הַבָּקָר׃ וַיִּחַר־אַף יְהוָה בְּעֻזָּה וַיַּכֵּהוּ שָׁם הָאֱלֹהִים
8 עַל־הַשַּׁל וַיָּמָת שָׁם עִם אֲרוֹן הָאֱלֹהִים׃ וַיִּחַר לְדָוִד עַל
אֲשֶׁר פָּרַץ יְהוָה פֶּרֶץ בְּעֻזָּה וַיִּקְרָא לַמָּקוֹם הַהוּא פֶּרֶץ
9 עֻזָּה עַד הַיּוֹם הַזֶּה׃ וַיִּרָא דָוִד אֶת־יְהוָה בַּיּוֹם הַהוּא
י וַיֹּאמֶר אֵיךְ יָבוֹא אֵלַי אֲרוֹן יְהוָה׃ וְלֹא־אָבָה דָוִד לְהָסִיר
אֵלָיו אֶת־אֲרוֹן יְהוָה עַל־עִיר דָּוִד וַיַּטֵּהוּ דָוִד בֵּית עֹבֵד־
11 אֱדֹם הַגִּתִּי׃ וַיֵּשֶׁב אֲרוֹן יְהוָה בֵּית עֹבֵד אֱדֹם הַגִּתִּי
שְׁלֹשָׁה חֳדָשִׁים וַיְבָרֶךְ יְהוָה אֶת־עֹבֵד אֱדֹם וְאֶת־כָּל־
12 בֵּיתוֹ׃ וַיֻּגַּד לַמֶּלֶךְ דָּוִד לֵאמֹר בֵּרַךְ יְהוָה אֶת־בֵּית עֹבֵד
אֱדֹם וְאֶת־כָּל־אֲשֶׁר־לוֹ בַּעֲבוּר אֲרוֹן הָאֱלֹהִים וַיֵּלֶךְ דָּוִד
וַיַּעַל אֶת־אֲרוֹן הָאֱלֹהִים מִבֵּית עֹבֵד אֱדֹם עִיר דָּוִד

v. 7. פתח באתנח

3. *a new cart.* The first attempt to bring the Ark to Mount Zion failed through want of reverence on the part of those transporting it. It should not have been carried in a common way on a waggon. It should have been borne on the shoulders of Levites (Num. III, 29 f).

in the hill. Better, *on the hill;* in or near the town of Kirjath-jearim.

7. *and God smote him there.* For this act of undue familiarity. The regulations surrounding Tabernacle and Temple were to deepen the sense of God's Holiness and of reverence for Him. The Ark was in especial degree the sign of His Presence. 'It has been surmised that Uzzah was crushed by a sudden and violent movement of the waggon bearing the Ark' (Ottley).

8. *and David was displeased.* Unlike Aaron who submitted to God's will in silence, David resented the judgment which God had inflicted, and in a petulant spirit abandoned the enterprise.

Perez-uzzah. That is, the breach of Uzzah.

10. *the Gittite.* So called, because he probably came from Gath-Rimmon, a Levitical city (Josh. XXI, 25).

13. *when they that bore the ark.* With staves on the shoulders of the Levites; see I Chron. XV. The requirements of the Law were now observed.

he sacrificed an ox. Because he saw his action now did not incur Divine displeasure. All were again swayed by religious joy. David himself flung aside all the ordinary restraints of royalty.

14-19. In a great popular celebration in which the king himself took a leading part, the Ark is brought to Jerusalem. Many are of opinion that the words of Psalm XXIV,

Lift up your heads, O ye gates;
And be ye lift up, ye everlasting doors:
That the King of Glory shall come in,

were composed and sung on the occasion of that great celebration.

ark of the LORD had gone six paces, he sacrificed an ox and a fatling. 14. And David danced before the LORD with all his might; and David was girded with a linen ephod. 15. So David and all the house of Israel brought up the ark of the LORD with shouting, and with the sound of the horn. ¶ 16. And it was so, as the ark of the LORD came into the city of David, that Michal the daughter of Saul looked out at the window, and saw king David leaping and dancing before the LORD; and she despised him in her heart. 17. And they brought in the ark of the LORD, and set it in its place, in the midst of the tent that David had pitched for it; and David offered burnt-offerings and peace-offerings before the LORD. 18. And when David had made an end of offering the burnt-offering and the peace-offerings, he blessed the people in the name of the LORD of hosts. 19. And he dealt among all the people, even among the whole multitude of Israel, both to men and women, to every one a cake of bread, and a cake made in a pan, and a sweet cake. So all the people departed every one to his house. ¶ 20. Then David returned to bless his household. And Michal the daughter of Saul came out to meet David, and said: 'How did the king of Israel get him honour to-day, who uncovered himself to-day in the eyes of the handmaids of his servants, as one of the vain fellows shamelessly uncovereth himself!' 21. And David said unto Michal: 'Before the LORD, who chose me above thy father, and above all his house, to appoint me prince over the people of the LORD, over Israel, before the LORD will I make merry. 22. And I will be yet more vile than thus, and will be base in mine own sight; and with the handmaids whom thou hast spoken of, with them will I get me honour.' 23. And Michal the daughter of Saul had no child unto the day of her death.

13 בְּשִׂמְחָה׃ וַיְהִי כִּי צָעֲדוּ נֹשְׂאֵי אֲרוֹן־יְהוָה שִׁשָּׁה צְעָדִים
14 וַיִּזְבַּח שׁוֹר וּמְרִיא׃ וְדָוִד מְכַרְכֵּר בְּכָל־עֹז לִפְנֵי יְהוָה
טו וְדָוִד חָגוּר אֵפוֹד בָּד׃ וְדָוִד וְכָל־בֵּית יִשְׂרָאֵל מַעֲלִים
16 אֶת־אֲרוֹן יְהוָה בִּתְרוּעָה וּבְקוֹל שׁוֹפָר׃ וְהָיָה אֲרוֹן יְהוָה
בָּא עִיר דָּוִד וּמִיכַל בַּת־שָׁאוּל נִשְׁקְפָה ׀ בְּעַד הַחַלּוֹן
וַתֵּרֶא אֶת־הַמֶּלֶךְ דָּוִד מְפַזֵּז וּמְכַרְכֵּר לִפְנֵי יְהוָה וַתִּבֶז
17 לוֹ בְּלִבָּהּ׃ וַיָּבִאוּ אֶת־אֲרוֹן יְהוָה וַיַּצִּגוּ אֹתוֹ בִּמְקוֹמוֹ
בְּתוֹךְ הָאֹהֶל אֲשֶׁר נָטָה־לוֹ דָּוִד וַיַּעַל דָּוִד עֹלוֹת לִפְנֵי
18 יְהוָה וּשְׁלָמִים׃ וַיְכַל דָּוִד מֵהַעֲלוֹת הָעוֹלָה וְהַשְּׁלָמִים
19 וַיְבָרֶךְ אֶת־הָעָם בְּשֵׁם יְהוָה צְבָאוֹת׃ וַיְחַלֵּק לְכָל־הָעָם
לְכָל־הֲמוֹן יִשְׂרָאֵל לְמֵאִישׁ וְעַד־אִשָּׁה לְאִישׁ חַלַּת לֶחֶם
אַחַת וְאֶשְׁפָּר אֶחָד וַאֲשִׁישָׁה אֶחָת וַיֵּלֶךְ כָּל־הָעָם אִישׁ
כ לְבֵיתוֹ׃ וַיָּשָׁב דָּוִד לְבָרֵךְ אֶת־בֵּיתוֹ * וַתֵּצֵא
מִיכַל בַּת־שָׁאוּל לִקְרַאת דָּוִד וַתֹּאמֶר מַה־נִּכְבַּד הַיּוֹם
מֶלֶךְ יִשְׂרָאֵל אֲשֶׁר נִגְלָה הַיּוֹם לְעֵינֵי אַמְהוֹת עֲבָדָיו
21 כְּהִגָּלוֹת נִגְלוֹת אַחַד הָרֵקִים׃ וַיֹּאמֶר דָּוִד אֶל־מִיכַל לִפְנֵי
יְהוָה אֲשֶׁר בָּחַר־בִּי מֵאָבִיךְ וּמִכָּל־בֵּיתוֹ לְצַוֹּת אֹתִי נָגִיד
22 עַל־עַם יְהוָה עַל־יִשְׂרָאֵל וְשִׂחַקְתִּי לִפְנֵי יְהוָה׃ וּנְקַלֹּתִי
עוֹד מִזֹּאת וְהָיִיתִי שָׁפָל בְּעֵינָי וְעִם־הָאֲמָהוֹת אֲשֶׁר אָמַרְתְּ
23 עִמָּם אִכָּבֵדָה׃ וּלְמִיכַל בַּת־שָׁאוּל לֹא־הָיָה לָהּ יָלֶד עַד
יוֹם מוֹתָהּ׃

* כאן מסיימין הספרדים v. 20. פסקא באמצע פסוק v. 23. כצ"ל

14. *with a linen ephod.* Not in his royal robes, but in the dress of a priest ministering before the Ark.

16. *Michal.* The only discordant note was the contemptuous greeting of his wife, the haughty daughter of Saul, who condemns his enthusiastic demeanour.

she despised him in her heart. Her pride revolted against the unseemliness, as she thought it, of a king breaking through conventional decorum to dance in front of a religious procession.

19. *dealt among all the people.* Divided among those who accompanied the Ark to its destination.

20. *to bless his household.* Or, 'to greet his family' (Moffatt).

vain fellows. Worthless fellows. She had the folly to despise, and the cruelty to ridicule, him.

21–22. David retorts that, for the sake of the Lord who had elevated him above her father's house, he would find honour in still humbler abasement.

23. *had no child.* The greatest cause of sorrow to an Eastern woman. Perhaps an explanation of her coldness and heartlessness.

Chapter VII

1. And it came to pass, when the king dwelt in his house, and the Lord had given him rest from all his enemies round about, 2. that the king said unto Nathan the prophet: 'See now, I dwell in a house of cedar, but the ark of God dwelleth within curtains.' 3. And Nathan said to the king: 'Go, do all that is in thy heart; for the Lord is with thee.' 4. And it came to pass the same night, that the word of the Lord came unto Nathan, saying: 5. 'Go and tell My servant David: Thus saith the Lord: Shalt thou build Me a house for Me to dwell in? 6. for I have not dwelt in a house since the day that I brought up the children of Israel out of Egypt, even to this day, but have walked in a tent and in a tabernacle. 7. In all places wherein I have walked among all the children of Israel, spoke I a word with any of the tribes of Israel, whom I commanded to feed My people Israel, saying: 'Why have ye not built Me a house of cedar? 8. Now therefore thus shalt thou say unto My servant David: Thus saith the Lord of hosts: I took thee from the sheepcote, from following the sheep, that thou shouldest be prince over My people, over Israel. 9. And I have been with thee whithersoever thou didst go, and have cut off all thine enemies from before thee; and I will make thee a great name, like unto the name of the great ones that are in the earth. 10. And I will appoint a place for My people Israel, and will plant them, that they may dwell in their own place, and be disquieted no more; neither shall the children of wickedness afflict them any more, as at the first, 11. even from the day that I commanded judges to be over My people Israel; and I will cause thee to rest from all

Cap. VII. ז

א וַיְהִי כִּי־יָשַׁב הַמֶּלֶךְ בְּבֵיתוֹ וַיהוָה הֵנִיחַ־לוֹ מִסָּבִיב מִכָּל־
2 אֹיְבָיו׃ וַיֹּאמֶר הַמֶּלֶךְ אֶל־נָתָן הַנָּבִיא רְאֵה נָא אָנֹכִי
יוֹשֵׁב בְּבֵית אֲרָזִים וַאֲרוֹן הָאֱלֹהִים יֹשֵׁב בְּתוֹךְ הַיְרִיעָה׃
3 וַיֹּאמֶר נָתָן אֶל־הַמֶּלֶךְ כֹּל אֲשֶׁר בִּלְבָבְךָ לֵךְ עֲשֵׂה כִּי
4 יְהוָה עִמָּךְ׃ וַיְהִי בַּלַּיְלָה הַהוּא • וַיְהִי דְּבַר־
ה יְהוָה אֶל־נָתָן לֵאמֹר׃ לֵךְ וְאָמַרְתָּ אֶל־עַבְדִּי אֶל־דָּוִד
6 כֹּה אָמַר יְהוָה הַאַתָּה תִּבְנֶה־לִּי בַיִת לְשִׁבְתִּי׃ כִּי לֹא
יָשַׁבְתִּי בְּבַיִת לְמִיּוֹם הַעֲלֹתִי אֶת־בְּנֵי יִשְׂרָאֵל מִמִּצְרַיִם
7 וְעַד הַיּוֹם הַזֶּה וָאֶהְיֶה מִתְהַלֵּךְ בְּאֹהֶל וּבְמִשְׁכָּן׃ בְּכֹל
אֲשֶׁר־הִתְהַלַּכְתִּי בְּכָל־בְּנֵי יִשְׂרָאֵל הֲדָבָר דִּבַּרְתִּי אֶת־אַחַד
שִׁבְטֵי יִשְׂרָאֵל אֲשֶׁר צִוִּיתִי לִרְעוֹת אֶת־עַמִּי אֶת־יִשְׂרָאֵל
8 לֵאמֹר לָמָּה לֹא־בְנִיתֶם לִי בֵּית אֲרָזִים׃ וְעַתָּה כֹּה־תֹאמַר
לְעַבְדִּי לְדָוִד כֹּה אָמַר יְהוָה צְבָאוֹת אֲנִי לְקַחְתִּיךָ מִן
הַנָּוֶה מֵאַחַר הַצֹּאן לִהְיוֹת נָגִיד עַל־עַמִּי עַל־יִשְׂרָאֵל׃
9 וָאֶהְיֶה עִמְּךָ בְּכֹל אֲשֶׁר הָלַכְתָּ וָאַכְרִתָה אֶת־כָּל־אֹיְבֶיךָ
מִפָּנֶיךָ וְעָשִׂתִי לְךָ שֵׁם גָּדוֹל כְּשֵׁם הַגְּדֹלִים אֲשֶׁר בָּאָרֶץ׃
י וְשַׂמְתִּי מָקוֹם לְעַמִּי לְיִשְׂרָאֵל וּנְטַעְתִּיו וְשָׁכַן תַּחְתָּיו וְלֹא
יִרְגַּז עוֹד וְלֹא־יֹסִיפוּ בְנֵי־עַוְלָה לְעַנּוֹתוֹ כַּאֲשֶׁר בָּרִאשׁוֹנָה׃
11 וּלְמִן־הַיּוֹם אֲשֶׁר צִוִּיתִי שֹׁפְטִים עַל־עַמִּי יִשְׂרָאֵל וַהֲנִיחֹתִי

v. 4. פסקא באמצע פסוק

Chapter VII

David's desire to build a Temple. The Prophet's message is that not David shall build a house unto God, but God shall build a 'house' (*i.e.* a dynasty) for David.

1. *had given him rest.* Recalling words in Deut. xii, 10–11. David felt that the duty now fell on him, to build a permanent Central Sanctuary.

2. *Nathan the prophet.* The fearless prophet who played such an important part in the lives of both David and Solomon.

within curtains. i.e. in a tent. He is struck by the contrast of his own palace of cedar with the simple tent which contained the Ark.

3. *go, do all that is in thine heart.* Nathan speaks here as a courtier, as one who saw that David was filled with a worthy desire to honour God. That same night he receives the Divine message to David.

5. *shalt thou build? i.e.* thou shalt not build. He was not the man to build; he had been, perforce, too much engaged in warfare, had shed too much human blood; i Chron. xxii, 8. Moreover, in spite of appearances, the kingdom was not yet sufficiently safe from hostile efforts to overthrow it, to justify the great undertaking of building a worthy national Temple.

8. *the sheepcote.* lit. 'the habitation,' *i.e.* of the sheep, and, therefore, the sheep-pen. But more likely the habitation of the shepherd, the shepherd's hut, is intended.

לְךָ מִכָּל־אֹיְבֶיךָ וְהִגִּיד לְךָ יְהוָה כִּי־בַיִת יַעֲשֶׂה־לְּךָ יְהוָה׃
12 כִּי ׀ יִמְלְאוּ יָמֶיךָ וְשָׁכַבְתָּ אֶת־אֲבֹתֶיךָ וַהֲקִימֹתִי אֶת־זַרְעֲךָ
13 אַחֲרֶיךָ אֲשֶׁר יֵצֵא מִמֵּעֶיךָ וַהֲכִינֹתִי אֶת־מַמְלַכְתּוֹ׃ הוּא
יִבְנֶה־בַּיִת לִשְׁמִי וְכֹנַנְתִּי אֶת־כִּסֵּא מַמְלַכְתּוֹ עַד־עוֹלָם׃
14 אֲנִי אֶהְיֶה־לּוֹ לְאָב וְהוּא יִהְיֶה־לִּי לְבֵן אֲשֶׁר בְּהַעֲוֺתוֹ
טו וְהֹכַחְתִּיו בְּשֵׁבֶט אֲנָשִׁים וּבְנִגְעֵי בְּנֵי אָדָם׃ וְחַסְדִּי לֹא־
יָסוּר מִמֶּנּוּ כַּאֲשֶׁר הֲסִרֹתִי מֵעִם שָׁאוּל אֲשֶׁר הֲסִרֹתִי
16 מִלְּפָנֶיךָ׃ וְנֶאְמַן בֵּיתְךָ וּמַמְלַכְתְּךָ עַד־עוֹלָם לְפָנֶיךָ כִּסְאֲךָ
17 יִהְיֶה נָכוֹן עַד־עוֹלָם׃ כְּכֹל הַדְּבָרִים הָאֵלֶּה וּכְכֹל הַחִזָּיוֹן
הַזֶּה כֵּן דִּבֶּר נָתָן אֶל־דָּוִד׃

thine enemies. Moreover the LORD telleth thee that the LORD will make thee a house. 12. When thy days are fulfilled, and thou shalt sleep with thy fathers, I will set up thy seed after thee, that shall proceed out of thy body, and I will establish his kingdom. 13. He shall build a house for my name, and I will establish the throne of his kingdom for ever. 14. I will be to him for a father, and he shall be to Me for a son; if he commit iniquity, I will chasten him with the rod of men, and with the stripes of the children of men; 15. but My mercy shall not depart from him, as I took it from Saul, whom I put away before thee. 16. And thy house and thy kingdom shall be made sure for ever before thee; thy throne shall be established for ever.' 17. According to all these words, and according to all this vision, so did Nathan speak unto David.

10. *I will appoint a place.* Better, *I have appointed . . . have planted . . . and they dwell in their own place.*

be disquieted no more. Better, *shall not be moved any more.*

11. *make thee a house.* Establish your family as a dynasty.

12. *thy seed.* This Divine promise was especially welcome in view of the insecurity of dynasties in Eastern countries, and the fearful tragedies that were often perpetrated to get rid of the old king's family (Blaikie).

13. *he shall build a house.* The word *he* is emphatic, and of course refers to Solomon.

14. *with the rod of men. i.e.* such chastisement as men inflict upon their children to correct and reclaim them, not to destroy them (Speaker's Bible).

16. *shall be made sure. i.e.* permanently established. The Davidic family reigned without interruption for 347 years. It was restored to rulership after the Exile, and continued to the end of the Maccabean dynasty. In the days of the Roman Empire and well into the Middle Ages, the 'Patriarchs' of Palestine and Exilarchs of Babylonia prided themselves on their Davidic descent.

'David is the most luminous figure and the most gifted personage in Israelitish history, surpassed in ethical greatness and general historical importance only by Moses, the man of God. He is one of those phenomenal men such as Providence gives but once to a people, in whom a whole nation and its history reaches once for all its climax. True, the picture of David does not lack the traits of human frailty, which Israelitish tradition, with a truly admirable sincerity, has neither suppressed not palliated; but the charm which this personality exercised over all contemporaries without exception has not yet faded for us of later day. The king, who did more for the worldly greatness and earthly power of Israel than any one else, was a genuine Israelite in that he appreciated also Israel's religious destiny; he was no soldier-king, no conqueror of common stamp, no ruler like any one of a hundred others, but he is the truest incorporation of the distinctive character of Israel—a unique personality in the history of the world' (Cornill).

THAZRIA

Laws of Purification (Chapters XII–XV)

Food laws were dealt with in the last chapter. We now have laws of purification in regard to (*a*) child-birth (XII); (*b*) leprosy (XIII, XIV); (*c*) bodily secretions (XV). (Another rite of purification, after contact with a human corpse, is expounded in Num. XIX.) There is abundant evidence that the laws of purity and impurity were from the earliest times faithfully observed in Israel. These laws, however, underwent various amplifications in the course of centuries; and not long after the Destruction of the Second Temple, disappeared, for the greater part, from Jewish life, even in Palestine. Only such comments as are essential to the understanding of the general meaning of the Text will here be given. The detailed exposition of this complex subject, with its successive expansions (the 'institutions' of Ezra, the modifications of the early Scribes and the Pharisees, and the deviating practice among later sects), must be sought for in specialist works, or in commentaries for the learned.

There are two distinct views in regard to the laws of purity and impurity: one, that they are hygienic; the other, that they are 'levitical', *i.e.* purely religious. Advocates of the hygienic view hold that the sources of impurity in Scripture—disease or death, the disintegrating corpse of man or beast, skin-diseases, and disorders in connection with sex-life—are in the main physical. In all these cases—they hold—impurity is equivalent to infection or the danger of infection; the rules of separation are intended to prevent the spread of infection; and the prescribed purification, whether by water or fire, is really *disinfection*. The procedure of purification bears out the character of disinfection. At no stage is there prescribed any prayer or formula to be recited; and the sacrifice, which invariably takes place *after* purification, is merely the token of re-admission into the camp (Katzenelsohn). The sanitary interpretation of the laws of purity is, however, contested by other authorities who, on their side, would rule out the hygienic motive altogether. They point to the Scripture passages which over and over again state that the supreme end of these laws is to lead men to holiness, and preserve them from anything that is defiling or that would exclude them from the Sanctuary. Strong arguments can thus be marshalled in favour of either view. However, while neither the hygienic nor the levitical motive can by itself account for all the facts, the two views are not mutually exclusive. Thus, in regard to Sabbath observance, Scripture assigns both a religious motive (Exod. XX, 11) and a social motive (Deut. V, 14). In the same manner, the eating of flesh of an animal torn in the fields is in one place forbidden for reasons of holiness (Exod. XXII, 30), and in another place plainly for reasons of hygiene (Lev. XI, 39, 40).

It is to be noted that most laws of purity and impurity apply only in reference to the Sanctuary and the holy objects connected with it. They did not apply in ordinary life, or to persons who did not intend to enter the Sanctuary.

Chapter XII. Purification after Child-birth

After the birth of a child, the mother brought a burnt-offering and a sin-offering at the Sanctuary, and thereby became ritually clean. Many non-Jewish commentators connect the regulation with the doom pronounced on Eve (Gen. III, 16). Life and death are in this way associated with the idea of the first sin in the Garden of Eden. Motherhood would thus in itself be a sinful thing, and its occurrence require purification and atonement. Such a thought, however, is utterly foreign to the general teaching of Scripture. 'Be fruitful and multiply, and replenish the earth' (Gen. I, 28), is the first command in the Torah; and childlessness was regarded as the worst calamity.

The more acceptable view is that the Law deals solely with the physical secretions attendant on child-birth. The mother becomes unclean through conditions attendant on parturition, but not the child. If impurity were associated with child-birth as a fact in nature, the child, who is the cause of the mother's defilement, would itself have been unclean.

12

CHAPTER XII

1. And the LORD spoke unto Moses, saying: 2. Speak unto the children of Israel, saying: ¶ If a woman be delivered, and bear a man-child, then she shall be unclean seven days; as in the days of the impurity of her sickness shall she be unclean. 3. And in the eighth day the flesh of his foreskin shall be circumcised. 4. And she shall continue in the blood of purification three and thirty days; she shall touch no hallowed thing, nor come into the sanctuary, until the days of her purification be fulfilled. 5. But if she bear a maid-child, then she shall be unclean two weeks, as in her impurity; and she shall continue in the blood of purification threescore and six days. 6. And when the days of her purification are fulfilled, for a son, or for a daughter, she shall bring a lamb of the first year for a burnt-offering, and a young pigeon, or a turtle-dove, for a sin-offering, unto the door of the tent of meeting, unto the priest. 7. And he shall offer it before the LORD, and make atonement for her; and she shall be cleansed from the fountain of her blood. This is the law for her that beareth, whether a male or a female. 8. And if her means suffice not for a lamb, then she shall take two turtle-doves, or two young pigeons:

CAP. XII. יב

יב פ פ פ כו 27

א 2 וַיְדַבֵּר יְהוָה אֶל־מֹשֶׁה לֵּאמֹר׃ דַּבֵּר אֶל־בְּנֵי יִשְׂרָאֵל
לֵאמֹר אִשָּׁה כִּי תַזְרִיעַ וְיָלְדָה זָכָר וְטָמְאָה שִׁבְעַת יָמִים
3 כִּימֵי נִדַּת דְּוֺתָהּ תִּטְמָא׃ וּבַיּוֹם הַשְּׁמִינִי יִמּוֹל בְּשַׂר
4 עָרְלָתוֹ׃ וּשְׁלֹשִׁים יוֹם וּשְׁלֹשֶׁת יָמִים תֵּשֵׁב בִּדְמֵי טָהֳרָה
בְּכָל־קֹדֶשׁ לֹא־תִגָּע וְאֶל־הַמִּקְדָּשׁ לֹא תָבֹא עַד־מְלֹאת
ה יְמֵי טָהֳרָהּ׃ וְאִם־נְקֵבָה תֵלֵד וְטָמְאָה שְׁבֻעַיִם כְּנִדָּתָהּ
6 וְשִׁשִּׁים יוֹם וְשֵׁשֶׁת יָמִים תֵּשֵׁב עַל־דְּמֵי טָהֳרָה׃ וּבִמְלֹאת ׀
יְמֵי טָהֳרָהּ לְבֵן אוֹ לְבַת תָּבִיא כֶּבֶשׂ בֶּן־שְׁנָתוֹ לְעֹלָה וּבֶן־
יוֹנָה אוֹ־תֹר לְחַטָּאת אֶל־פֶּתַח אֹהֶל־מוֹעֵד אֶל־הַכֹּהֵן׃
7 וְהִקְרִיבוֹ לִפְנֵי יְהוָה וְכִפֶּר עָלֶיהָ וְטָהֲרָה מִמְּקֹר דָּמֶיהָ
8 זֹאת תּוֹרַת הַיֹּלֶדֶת לַזָּכָר אוֹ לַנְּקֵבָה׃ וְאִם־לֹא תִמְצָא

v. 4. קמץ ברביע

IV. THAZRIA

(CHAPTERS XII AND XIII)

CHAPTER XII. PURIFICATION AFTER CHILDBIRTH (*Continued*)

2. *seven days.* Her uncleanness is of the same strict degree as that during menstruation (XVIII, 19). Seven days after that period, the ritual bath of purification is taken. During the remainder of the forty (or eighty) days she is only unclean as regards the Sanctuary (see *v.* 4).

3. *circumcised.* See Gen. XVII. This proves that the purification of the mother was solely from her physical condition. The circumcision is not a means of purifying the child; because in that case, we should have expected a ceremony of purification for a female child. The Rabbis deduced from the words 'the eighth *day*' that the rite must be performed on that day, even if it be the Sabbath; and during the daytime, not at night.

5. *two weeks.* There is no satisfactory explanation why the period is doubled when a female child is born. It cannot be because a female was regarded as more defiling than a male, since the mother's purification was the same for either sex.

6. *burnt-offering . . . sin-offering.* They are not here given in the usual order, which prescribes the sin-offering before the burnt-offering. The sin-offering was here merely a purgation offering, as with other cases of uncleanness (cf. XV, 30), where no sin had been committed (Sifra). The burnt-offering symbolized rededication to God, after the period of abstention from the Sanctuary.

unto the door. As it was only after the offerings had been sacrificed that she was again clean, she could not bring the animals beyond the entrance of the Tent of Meeting.

7. *he shall offer it.* *i.e.* each one of the two offerings.

make atonement. See on I, 4. The meaning is here that by virtue of the offerings, the cause which had made it impossible for her to come to the Sanctuary was *obliterated.*

the one for a burnt-offering, and the other for a sin-offering; and the priest shall make atonement for her, and she shall be clean.

יָדָהּ דֵּי שֶׂה וְלָקְחָה שְׁתֵּי־תֹרִים אוֹ שְׁנֵי בְּנֵי יוֹנָה אֶחָד
לְעֹלָה וְאֶחָד לְחַטָּאת וְכִפֶּר עָלֶיהָ הַכֹּהֵן וְטָהֵרָה׃ פ

13

Chapter XIII

1. And the Lord spoke unto Moses and unto Aaron, saying: ¶ 2. When a man shall have in the skin of his flesh a rising, or a scab, or a bright spot, and it become in the skin of his flesh the plague of leprosy, then he shall be brought unto Aaron the priest, or unto one of his sons the priests. 3. And the priest shall look on the plague in the skin of the flesh; and if the hair in the plague be turned white, and the appearance of the plague be deeper than the skin of his flesh, it is the plague of leprosy; and the priest shall look on him, and pronounce him unclean. 4. And if the bright spot be white in the skin of his

יג

Cap. XIII. יג

א וַיְדַבֵּר יְהוָה אֶל־מֹשֶׁה וְאֶל־אַהֲרֹן לֵאמֹר׃ 2 אָדָם כִּי־יִהְיֶה
בְעוֹר־בְּשָׂרוֹ שְׂאֵת אוֹ־סַפַּחַת אוֹ בַהֶרֶת וְהָיָה בְעוֹר־בְּשָׂרוֹ
לְנֶגַע צָרָעַת וְהוּבָא אֶל־אַהֲרֹן הַכֹּהֵן אוֹ אֶל־אַחַד מִבָּנָיו
3 הַכֹּהֲנִים׃ וְרָאָה הַכֹּהֵן אֶת־הַנֶּגַע בְּעוֹר־הַבָּשָׂר וְשֵׂעָר
בַּנֶּגַע הָפַךְ לָבָן וּמַרְאֵה הַנֶּגַע עָמֹק מֵעוֹר בְּשָׂרוֹ נֶגַע צָרַעַת
4 הוּא וְרָאָהוּ הַכֹּהֵן וְטִמֵּא אֹתוֹ׃ וְאִם־בַּהֶרֶת לְבָנָה הִוא

8. *two young pigeons.* As with the sin-offering of the poor in v, 7.

In our days, the mother visits the synagogue as soon as convalescence and circumstances permit, in order to render thanks for her recovery, and to offer prayer on behalf of the new-born child (Authorised Prayer Book, p. 312).

Chapters XIII–XIV

The Law of Leprosy

The prominence given to this subject must be due to the prevalence of this class of malady in the Near East; and this explanation is confirmed by the frequent reference to leprosy in the Bible.

As stated in the last chapter, many authorities regard these regulations as based only on sanitary principles. A suspected person was isolated for a period of time until the diagnosis became more certain; and when he was found to be afflicted, he was compelled to reside outside the camp.

It is to the ceremony of purification that we have to turn for the idea which underlies the treatment of the leper. That ceremony can bear only one interpretation; viz. the leper suffered from a *physical* impurity which debarred him from fulfilling his duty as an Israelite towards the Sanctuary. In the same manner that a priest who suffered from a bodily blemish could not officiate in the Sanctuary, so an Israelite, who was hideously disfigured, was disqualified from membership in 'a kingdom of priests'. During his leprosy, he was accounted as dead; when he recovered, he had to be formally rededicated as an Israelite to the service of God.

The Rabbis regard leprosy as a Providential affliction in punishment for slander or tale bearing (מצורע מוציא שם רע); thus teaching that the slanderer is a moral leper, and should find no place in the camp of Israel.

Chapter XIII

2–8. Early Symptoms of the Disease

1. *and unto Aaron.* To diagnose the disease—one of the functions of the priesthood.

2. *the skin of his flesh.* Possibly a technical term for the cuticle; see on *v.* 5.

rising. A tumor.

scab. A scurf which can fall off or be peeled away.

bright spot. A glossy patch.

the plague of leprosy. Lit. 'a stroke of leprosy'. It has been questioned whether the word צרעת corresponds to the English term 'leprosy'. In the latter, the most notable features are the swelling of organs and the rotting of the limbs. Nothing is here mentioned of these disfigurements. Moreover, leprosy is normally an incurable disease, whereas צרעת is deemed curable. In some of the paragraphs in this chapter a form of leprosy, known as elephantiasis, seems to be meant.

he shall be brought. Or, 'it (viz. the matter of the infection) shall be brought' (Ehrlich), to determine whether the malady was of such a character, or had so developed, as to make it necessary for the person to leave the camp.

3. *pronounce him unclean. i.e.* ritually defiled and unfit to enter the Sanctuary.

4. *shut up him.* The purpose of the period of isolation was to prevent him, during the time of doubt, from defiling others by contact, should he really be infected.

seven days. What is now called leprosy is a slow developing disease, and very little difference would be discernible in the space of a week.

flesh, and the appearance thereof be not deeper than the skin, and the hair thereof be not turned white, then the priest shall shut up him that hath the plague seven days. 5. And the priest shall look on him the seventh day; and, behold, if the plague stay in its appearance, and the plague be not spread in the skin, then the priest shall shut him up seven days more.*ii. 6. And the priest shall look on him again the seventh day; and, behold, if the plague be dim, and the plague be not spread in the skin, then the priest shall pronounce him clean: it is a scab; and he shall wash his clothes, and be clean. 7. But if the scab spread abroad in the skin, after that he hath shown himself to the priest for his cleansing, he shall show himself to the priest again. 8. And the priest shall look, and, behold, if the scab be spread in the skin, then the priest shall pronounce him unclean: it is leprosy. ¶ 9. When the plague of leprosy is in a man, then he shall be brought unto the priest. 10. And the priest shall look, and, behold, if there be a white rising in the skin, and it have turned the hair white, and there be quick raw flesh in the rising, 11. it is an old leprosy in the skin of his flesh, and the priest shall pronounce him unclean; he shall not shut him up; for he is unclean. 12. And if the leprosy break out abroad in the skin, and the leprosy cover all the skin of him that hath the plague from his head even to his feet, as far as appeareth to the priest; 13. then the priest shall look; and, behold, if the leprosy have covered all his flesh, he shall pronounce him clean that hath the plague;

בעור בשרו ועמק אין־מראה מן־העור ושערה לא־הפך
ה לבן והסגיר הכהן את־הנגע שבעת ימים: וראהו הכהן
ביום השביעי והנה הנגע עמד בעיניו לא־פשה הנגע
שני 6 בעור והסגירו הכהן שבעת ימים שנית: וראה הכהן
אתו ביום השביעי שנית והנה כהה הנגע ולא־פשה
הנגע בעור וטהרו הכהן מספחת הוא וכבס בגדיו וטהר:
7 ואם־פשה תפשה המספחת בעור אחרי הראתו אל־
8 הכהן לטהרתו ונראה שנית אל־הכהן: וראה הכהן
והנה פשתה המספחת בעור וטמאו הכהן צרעת הוא: פ
9 נגע צרעת כי תהיה באדם והובא אל־הכהן: וראה הכהן
והנה שאת־לבנה בעור והיא הפכה שער לבן ומחית
11 בשר חי בשאת: צרעת נושנת הוא בעור בשרו וטמאו
12 הכהן לא יסגרנו כי טמא הוא: ואם־פרוח תפרח הצרעת
בעור וכסתה הצרעת את כל־עור הנגע מראשו ועד־
13 רגליו לכל־מראה עיני הכהן: וראה הכהן והנה כסתה
הצרעת את־כל־בשרו וטהר את־הנגע כלו הפך לבן

v. 10. ש' רפה

5. *stay.* There has been no alteration for better or worse.

spread in the skin. i.e. deeper into the skin, attacking the cutis as well as the cuticle.

6. *dim. i.e.* fainter in appearance and, therefore, giving evidence of passing away (Ibn Ezra).

wash his clothes. An outward symbol that he was freed from suspicion, and could now associate with his brethren and join in the life of the Community. Several Jewish authorities, however, are of opinion that wherever Scripture enjoins washing of the garments, bathing the body is to be also understood.

7. *spread abroad in the skin.* Better, *spread into the skin.*

9–17. Diagnosing the Disease

This paragraph deals with the person who is suddenly attacked by the disease, or in whom it has developed rapidly, without the preliminary symptoms described above.

9. *he shall be brought.* See on *v.* 2.

10. *a white rising.* In the disease of elephantiasis one of the early manifestations is the growth of vesicles of a glistening white hue, which burst and discharge a whitish fluid.

in the skin. As in *v.* 5; the disease had penetrated to the cutis.

quick raw flesh. i.e. it is an open sore.

11. *old leprosy.* Confirmed leprosy; the malady is definitely established as rooted in the system by the presence of quick raw flesh and white hair. No preliminary isolation is necessary; it is a clear case of uncleanness.

12–17. These verses apparently refer to common white leprosy. It is less serious than elephantiasis or leprosy proper. The health of the person remains normal during the time the malady persists, and it generally passes off after a while. There is only discoloration of the skin in this milder form of infection.

it is all turned white: he is clean. 14. But whensoever raw flesh appeareth in him, he shall be unclean. 15. And the priest shall look on the raw flesh, and pronounce him unclean; the raw flesh is unclean: it is leprosy. 16. But if the raw flesh again be turned into white, then he shall come unto the priest; 17. and the priest shall look on him; and, behold, if the plague be turned into white, then the priest shall pronounce him clean that hath the plague: he is clean.* iii. ¶ 18. And when the flesh hath in the skin thereof a boil, and it is healed, 19. and in the place of the boil there is a white rising, or a bright spot, reddish-white, then it shall be shown to the priest. 20. And the priest shall look; and, behold, if the appearance thereof be lower than the skin, and the hair thereof be turned white, then the priest shall pronounce him unclean: it is the plague of leprosy, it hath broken out in the boil. 21. But if the priest look on it, and, behold, there be no white hairs therein, and it be not lower than the skin, but be dim, then the priest shall shut him up seven days. 22. And if it spread abroad in the skin, then the priest shall pronounce him unclean: it is a plague. 23. But if the bright spot stay in its place, and be not spread, it is the scar of the boil; and the priest shall pronounce him clean.* iv (** ii). ¶ 24. Or when the flesh hath in the skin thereof a burning by fire, and the quick flesh of the burning become a bright spot, reddish-white, or white; 25. then the priest shall look upon it; and, behold, if the hair in the bright spot be turned white, and the appearance thereof be deeper than the skin, it is leprosy, it hath broken out in the burning; and the priest shall pronounce him unclean: it is the plague of leprosy. 26. But if the priest look on it, and, behold, there be no white hair in the bright spot, and it be no lower than the skin, but be dim; then the priest shall shut him up seven days. 27. And the priest shall look upon him the seventh day; if it spread abroad in the skin, then the priest shall pronounce him unclean: it is the plague of leprosy. 28. And if the bright spot stay in its place, and be not spread in the skin, but be dim, it is the rising of the burning, and the priest shall pronounce him clean; for it is the scar of the burning.* v. ¶ 29. And when a man or woman hath a plague upon the head or upon the beard, 30. then the priest shall look on the plague;

14 טו טָהוֹר הוּא׃ וּבְיוֹם הֵרָאוֹת בּוֹ בָּשָׂר חַי יִטְמָא׃ וְרָאָה
הַכֹּהֵן אֶת־הַבָּשָׂר הַחַי וְטִמְּאוֹ הַבָּשָׂר הַחַי טָמֵא הוּא
16 צָרַעַת הוּא׃ אוֹ כִי יָשׁוּב הַבָּשָׂר הַחַי וְנֶהְפַּךְ לְלָבָן וּבָא
17 אֶל־הַכֹּהֵן׃ וְרָאָהוּ הַכֹּהֵן וְהִנֵּה נֶהְפַּךְ הַנֶּגַע לְלָבָן וְטִהַר
הַכֹּהֵן אֶת־הַנֶּגַע טָהוֹר הוּא׃ פ שלישי
18 19 וּבָשָׂר כִּי־יִהְיֶה בוֹ־בְעֹרוֹ שְׁחִין וְנִרְפָּא׃ וְהָיָה בִּמְקוֹם
הַשְּׁחִין שְׂאֵת לְבָנָה אוֹ בַהֶרֶת לְבָנָה אֲדַמְדָּמֶת וְנִרְאָה
כ אֶל־הַכֹּהֵן׃ וְרָאָה הַכֹּהֵן וְהִנֵּה מַרְאֶהָ שָׁפָל מִן־הָעוֹר
וּשְׂעָרָהּ הָפַךְ לָבָן וְטִמְּאוֹ הַכֹּהֵן נֶגַע־צָרַעַת הִוא בַּשְּׁחִין
21 פָּרָחָה׃ וְאִם ׀ יִרְאֶנָּה הַכֹּהֵן וְהִנֵּה אֵין־בָּהּ שֵׂעָר לָבָן וּשְׁפָלָה
אֵינֶנָּה מִן־הָעוֹר וְהִיא כֵהָה וְהִסְגִּירוֹ הַכֹּהֵן שִׁבְעַת יָמִים׃
22 23 וְאִם־פָּשֹׂה תִפְשֶׂה בָּעוֹר וְטִמֵּא הַכֹּהֵן אֹתוֹ נֶגַע הִוא׃ וְאִם־
רביעי (שני כשהן מחובר') תַּחְתֶּיהָ תַּעֲמֹד הַבַּהֶרֶת לֹא פָשָׂתָה צָרֶבֶת הַשְּׁחִין הִוא
24 וְטִהֲרוֹ הַכֹּהֵן׃ ס אוֹ בָשָׂר כִּי־יִהְיֶה בְעֹרוֹ מִכְוַת־אֵשׁ
וְהָיְתָה מִחְיַת הַמִּכְוָה בַּהֶרֶת לְבָנָה אֲדַמְדֶּמֶת אוֹ לְבָנָה׃
כה וְרָאָה אֹתָהּ הַכֹּהֵן וְהִנֵּה נֶהְפַּךְ שֵׂעָר לָבָן בַּבַּהֶרֶת וּמַרְאֶהָ
עָמֹק מִן־הָעוֹר צָרַעַת הִוא בַּמִּכְוָה פָּרָחָה וְטִמֵּא אֹתוֹ הַכֹּהֵן
26 נֶגַע צָרַעַת הִוא׃ וְאִם ׀ יִרְאֶנָּה הַכֹּהֵן וְהִנֵּה אֵין־בַּבַּהֶרֶת
שֵׂעָר לָבָן וּשְׁפָלָה אֵינֶנָּה מִן־הָעוֹר וְהִוא כֵהָה וְהִסְגִּירוֹ
27 הַכֹּהֵן שִׁבְעַת יָמִים׃ וְרָאָהוּ הַכֹּהֵן בַּיּוֹם הַשְּׁבִיעִי אִם־
פָּשֹׂה תִפְשֶׂה בָּעוֹר וְטִמֵּא הַכֹּהֵן אֹתוֹ נֶגַע צָרַעַת הִוא׃
28 וְאִם־תַּחְתֶּיהָ תַעֲמֹד הַבַּהֶרֶת לֹא־פָשְׂתָה בָעוֹר וְהִוא כֵהָה
חמישי שְׂאֵת הַמִּכְוָה הִוא וְטִהֲרוֹ הַכֹּהֵן כִּי־צָרֶבֶת הַמִּכְוָה הִוא׃ פ
29 ל וְאִישׁ אוֹ אִשָּׁה כִּי־יִהְיֶה בוֹ נָגַע בְּרֹאשׁ אוֹ בְזָקָן׃ וְרָאָה

v. 23. קמץ בז״ק

18–28. SPECIAL SYMPTOMS OF LEPROSY

18. *boil.* Probably a form of ulcer.

23. *scar.* Or, 'inflammation.'

29–44. LEPROSY ON HEAD AND FACE

29. *plague.* Here, a form of elephantiasis.

30. *scall.* The Heb. denotes, 'what one is inclined to scratch or tear away.'

and, behold, if the appearance thereof be deeper than the skin, and there be in it yellow thin hair, then the priest shall pronounce him unclean: it is a scall, it is leprosy of the head or of the beard. 31. And if the priest look on the plague of the scall, and, behold, the appearance thereof be not deeper than the skin, and there be no black hair in it, then the priest shall shut up him that hath the plague of the scall seven days. 32. And in the seventh day the priest shall look on the plague; and, behold, if the scall be not spread, and there be in it no yellow hair, and the appearance of the scall be not deeper than the skin, 33. then he shall be shaven, but the scall shall he not shave; and the priest shall shut up him that hath the scall seven days more. 34. And in the seventh day the priest shall look on the scall; and, behold, if the scall be not spread in the skin, and the appearance thereof be not deeper than the skin, then the priest shall pronounce him clean; and he shall wash his clothes, and be clean. 35. But if the scall spread abroad in the skin after his cleansing, 36. then the priest shall look on him; and, behold, if the scall be spread in the skin, the priest shall not seek for the yellow hair: he is unclean. 37. But if the scall stay in its appearance, and black hair be grown up therein; the scall is healed, he is clean; and the priest shall pronounce him clean. ¶ 38. And if a man or a woman have in the skin of their flesh bright spots, even white bright spots; 39. then the priest shall look; and, behold, if the bright spots in the skin of their flesh be of a dull white, it is a tetter, it hath broken out in the skin: he is clean. *vi(**iii). ¶ 40. And if a man's hair be fallen off his head, he is bald; yet is he clean. 41. And if his hair be fallen off from the front part of his head, he is forehead-bald; yet is he clean. 42. But if there be in the bald head, or the bald forehead, a reddish-white plague, it is leprosy breaking out in his bald head, or his bald forehead. 43. Then the priest shall look upon him; and, behold, if the rising of the plague be reddish-white in his bald head, or in his bald forehead,

הַכֹּהֵן אֶת־הַנֶּגַע וְהִנֵּה מַרְאֵהוּ עָמֹק מִן־הָעוֹר וּבוֹ שֵׂעָר
צָהֹב דָּק וְטִמֵּא אֹתוֹ הַכֹּהֵן נֶתֶק הוּא צָרַעַת הָרֹאשׁ אוֹ
31 הַזָּקָן הוּא׃ וְכִי־יִרְאֶה הַכֹּהֵן אֶת־נֶגַע הַנֶּתֶק וְהִנֵּה אֵין
מַרְאֵהוּ עָמֹק מִן־הָעוֹר וְשֵׂעָר שָׁחֹר אֵין בּוֹ וְהִסְגִּיר הַכֹּהֵן
32 אֶת־נֶגַע הַנֶּתֶק שִׁבְעַת יָמִים׃ וְרָאָה הַכֹּהֵן אֶת־הַנֶּגַע בַּיּוֹם
הַשְּׁבִיעִי וְהִנֵּה לֹא־פָשָׂה הַנֶּתֶק וְלֹא־הָיָה בוֹ שֵׂעָר צָהֹב
33 וּמַרְאֵה הַנֶּתֶק אֵין עָמֹק מִן־הָעוֹר׃ וְהִתְגַּלָּח וְאֶת־הַנֶּתֶק
לֹא יְגַלֵּחַ וְהִסְגִּיר הַכֹּהֵן אֶת־הַנֶּתֶק שִׁבְעַת יָמִים שֵׁנִית׃
34 וְרָאָה הַכֹּהֵן אֶת־הַנֶּתֶק בַּיּוֹם הַשְּׁבִיעִי וְהִנֵּה לֹא־פָשָׂה
הַנֶּתֶק בָּעוֹר וּמַרְאֵהוּ אֵינֶנּוּ עָמֹק מִן־הָעוֹר וְטִהַר אֹתוֹ
לה הַכֹּהֵן וְכִבֶּס בְּגָדָיו וְטָהֵר׃ וְאִם־פָּשֹׂה יִפְשֶׂה הַנֶּתֶק בָּעוֹר
36 אַחֲרֵי טָהֳרָתוֹ׃ וְרָאָהוּ הַכֹּהֵן וְהִנֵּה פָּשָׂה הַנֶּתֶק בָּעוֹר
37 לֹא־יְבַקֵּר הַכֹּהֵן לַשֵּׂעָר הַצָּהֹב טָמֵא הוּא׃ וְאִם־בְּעֵינָיו
עָמַד הַנֶּתֶק וְשֵׂעָר שָׁחֹר צָמַח־בּוֹ נִרְפָּא הַנֶּתֶק טָהוֹר הוּא
38 וְטִהֲרוֹ הַכֹּהֵן׃ ס וְאִישׁ אוֹ־אִשָּׁה כִּי־יִהְיֶה בְעוֹר־בְּשָׂרָם
39 בֶּהָרֹת בֶּהָרֹת לְבָנֹת׃ וְרָאָה הַכֹּהֵן וְהִנֵּה בְעוֹר־בְּשָׂרָם
בֶּהָרֹת כֵּהוֹת לְבָנֹת בֹּהַק הוּא פָּרַח בָּעוֹר טָהוֹר הוּא׃ ס שי (שלישי כשהן מחוב׳)
מ 41 וְאִישׁ כִּי יִמָּרֵט רֹאשׁוֹ קֵרֵחַ הוּא טָהוֹר הוּא׃ וְאִם מִפְּאַת
42 פָּנָיו יִמָּרֵט רֹאשׁוֹ גִּבֵּחַ הוּא טָהוֹר הוּא׃ וְכִי־יִהְיֶה בַקָּרַחַת
אוֹ בַגַּבַּחַת נֶגַע לָבָן אֲדַמְדָּם צָרַעַת פֹּרַחַת הִוא בְּקָרַחְתּוֹ
43 אוֹ בְגַבַּחְתּוֹ׃ וְרָאָה אֹתוֹ הַכֹּהֵן וְהִנֵּה שְׂאֵת־הַנֶּגַע לְבָנָה

v. 33. ג׳ רבתי

31. *no black hair.* So long as there was black hair on the infected spot, or it grew black hair (see *v.* 37), the man was not to be regarded as a leper.

38. *bright spots.* See *v.* 2.

39. *tetter.* Old English for, 'freckled spot,' a skin disease which is not leprous.

40. *fallen off.* The falling away of the hair was one of the symptoms that accompanied elephantiasis (see on *v.* 29); but in itself it was not a feature that rendered a person unclean, even if the head were left entirely bald.

42. *bald head.* Baldness from the crown backwards to the neck.

43. *in the skin of the flesh. i.e.* when the disease occurs in any other part of the body.

אֲדַמְדֶּמֶת בְּקָרַחְתּוֹ אוֹ בְגַבַּחְתּוֹ כְּמַרְאֵה צָרַעַת עוֹר בָּשָׂר׃
44 אִישׁ־צָרוּעַ הוּא טָמֵא הוּא טַמֵּא יְטַמְּאֶנּוּ הַכֹּהֵן בְּרֹאשׁוֹ
מה נִגְעוֹ׃ וְהַצָּרוּעַ אֲשֶׁר־בּוֹ הַנֶּגַע בְּגָדָיו יִהְיוּ פְרֻמִים וְרֹאשׁוֹ
46 יִהְיֶה פָרוּעַ וְעַל־שָׂפָם יַעְטֶה וְטָמֵא ׀ טָמֵא יִקְרָא׃ כָּל־יְמֵי
אֲשֶׁר הַנֶּגַע בּוֹ יִטְמָא טָמֵא הוּא בָּדָד יֵשֵׁב מִחוּץ לַמַּחֲנֶה
47 מוֹשָׁבוֹ׃ ס וְהַבֶּגֶד כִּי־יִהְיֶה בוֹ נֶגַע צָרָעַת בְּבֶגֶד צֶמֶר
48 אוֹ בְּבֶגֶד פִּשְׁתִּים׃ אוֹ בִשְׁתִי אוֹ בְעֵרֶב לַפִּשְׁתִּים וְלַצָּמֶר
49 אוֹ בְעוֹר אוֹ בְּכָל־מְלֶאכֶת עוֹר׃ וְהָיָה הַנֶּגַע יְרַקְרַק ׀ אוֹ
אֲדַמְדָּם בַּבֶּגֶד אוֹ בָעוֹר אוֹ־בַשְּׁתִי אוֹ־בָעֵרֶב אוֹ בְכָל־כְּלִי־
נ עוֹר נֶגַע צָרַעַת הוּא וְהָרְאָה אֶת־הַכֹּהֵן׃ וְרָאָה הַכֹּהֵן אֶת־
51 הַנָּגַע וְהִסְגִּיר אֶת־הַנֶּגַע שִׁבְעַת יָמִים׃ וְרָאָה אֶת־הַנֶּגַע
בַּיּוֹם הַשְּׁבִיעִי כִּי־פָשָׂה הַנֶּגַע בַּבֶּגֶד אוֹ־בַשְּׁתִי אוֹ־בָעֵרֶב
אוֹ בָעוֹר לְכֹל אֲשֶׁר־יֵעָשֶׂה הָעוֹר לִמְלָאכָה צָרַעַת מַמְאֶרֶת
52 הַנֶּגַע טָמֵא הוּא׃ וְשָׂרַף אֶת־הַבֶּגֶד אוֹ אֶת־הַשְּׁתִי ׀ אוֹ אֶת־
הָעֵרֶב בַּצֶּמֶר אוֹ בַפִּשְׁתִּים אוֹ אֶת־כָּל־כְּלִי הָעוֹר אֲשֶׁר־
53 יִהְיֶה בוֹ הַנָּגַע כִּי־צָרַעַת מַמְאֶרֶת הִוא בָּאֵשׁ תִּשָּׂרֵף׃ וְאִם
יִרְאֶה הַכֹּהֵן וְהִנֵּה לֹא־פָשָׂה הַנֶּגַע בַּבֶּגֶד אוֹ בַשְּׁתִי אוֹ
54 בָעֵרֶב אוֹ בְּכָל־כְּלִי־עוֹר׃ וְצִוָּה הַכֹּהֵן וְכִבְּסוּ אֵת אֲשֶׁר־
שביעי (רביעי כשהן מחוב')
נה בּוֹ הַנָּגַע וְהִסְגִּירוֹ שִׁבְעַת־יָמִים שֵׁנִית׃ וְרָאָה הַכֹּהֵן אַחֲרֵי ׀

as the appearance of leprosy in the skin of the flesh, 44. he is a leprous man, he is unclean; the priest shall surely pronounce him unclean: his plague is in his head. ¶ 45. And the leper in whom the plague is, his clothes shall be rent, and the hair of his head shall go loose, and he shall cover his upper lip, and shall cry: 'Unclean, unclean.' 46. All the days wherein the plague is in him he shall be unclean; he is unclean; he shall dwell alone; without the camp shall his dwelling be. ¶ 47. And when the plague of leprosy is in a garment, whether it be a woollen garment, or a linen garment; 48. or in the warp, or in the woof, whether they be of linen, or of wool; or in a skin, or in any thing made of skin: 49. if the plague be greenish or reddish in the garment, or in the skin, or in the warp, or in the woof, or in any thing of skin, it is the plague of leprosy, and shall be shown unto the priest. 50. And the priest shall look upon the plague, and shut up that which hath the plague seven days. 51. And he shall look on the plague on the seventh day: if the plague be spread in the garment, or in the warp, or in the woof, or in the skin, whatever service skin is used for, the plague is a malignant leprosy: it is unclean. 52. And he shall burn the garment, or the warp, or the woof, whether it be of wool or of linen, or any thing of skin, wherein the plague is; for it is a malignant leprosy; it shall be burnt in the fire. 53. And if the priest shall look, and, behold, the plague be not spread in the garment, or in the warp, or in the woof, or in any thing of skin; 54. then the priest shall command that they wash the thing wherein the plague is, and he shall shut it up seven days more.*vii (**iv). 55. And the priest shall look, after that the plague is washed; and, behold, if the plague have not changed its colour, and the plague be not spread, it is unclean;

45–46. Treatment of the Leper

45. *the leper.* The word is in the masculine; the female sufferer also left the camp and lived apart, but was not required to tear her garments and uncover her head (Sifra).

his clothes. The customs of the leper are those of a mourner. He was to regard himself as one upon whom death had laid its hand. His was a living death, not only in the physical sense, as suffering from a loathsome and lingering disease; but also in the spiritual sense, as cut off from the life of the Community of Israel.

unclean, unclean. To warn people from touching them. In later times, lepers wore a bell for the same purpose.

46. *alone.* Better, *apart.*

47–59. Leprosy of Garments

The materials could have become infected with the disease through contact with a leper or his sores. Some explain the spots on the garments as caused by mildew, or by some parasitic infection, analogous in its effects to leprosy of the body.

47. *garment.* The Heb. can refer to any cloth material, not necessarily an article of apparel.

48. *in the warp, or in the woof.* Or, 'woven or knitted stuff,' thou shalt burn it in the fire; it is a fret, whether the bareness be within or without. 56. And if the priest look, and, behold, the plague be dim after the washing thereof, then he shall rend it out of the garment, or out of the skin, or out of the warp, or out of the woof.*m. 57. And if it appear still in the garment, or in the warp, or in the woof, or in any thing of skin, it is breaking out, thou shalt burn that wherein the plague is with fire. 58. And the garment, or the warp, or the woof, or whatsoever thing of skin it be, which thou shalt wash, if the plague be departed from them, then it shall be washed the second time, and shall be clean. 59. This is the law of the plague of leprosy in a garment of wool or linen, or in the warp, or in the woof, or in any thing of skin, to pronounce it clean, or to pronounce it unclean.

הַכֻּבַּס אֶת־הַנֶּגַע וְהִנֵּה לֹא־הָפַךְ הַנֶּגַע אֶת־עֵינוֹ וְהַנֶּגַע לֹא
פָשָׂה טָמֵא הוּא בָּאֵשׁ תִּשְׂרְפֶנּוּ פְּחֶתֶת הִוא בְּקָרַחְתּוֹ אוֹ
56 בְגַבַּחְתּוֹ׃ וְאִם רָאָה הַכֹּהֵן וְהִנֵּה כֵּהָה הַנֶּגַע אַחֲרֵי הֻכַּבֵּס
אֹתוֹ וְקָרַע אֹתוֹ מִן־הַבֶּגֶד אוֹ מִן־הָעוֹר אוֹ מִן־הַשְּׁתִי אוֹ
מפטיר 57 מִן־הָעֵרֶב׃ וְאִם־תֵּרָאֶה עוֹד בַּבֶּגֶד אוֹ־בַשְּׁתִי אוֹ־בָעֵרֶב
אוֹ בְכָל־כְּלִי־עוֹר פֹּרַחַת הִוא בָּאֵשׁ תִּשְׂרְפֶנּוּ אֵת אֲשֶׁר־
58 בּוֹ הַנָּגַע׃ וְהַבֶּגֶד אוֹ־הַשְּׁתִי אוֹ־הָעֵרֶב אוֹ־כָל־כְּלִי הָעוֹר
59 אֲשֶׁר תְּכַבֵּס וְסָר מֵהֶם הַנָּגַע וְכֻבַּס שֵׁנִית וְטָהֵר׃ זֹאת
תּוֹרַת נֶגַע־צָרַעַת בֶּגֶד הַצֶּמֶר ׀ אוֹ הַפִּשְׁתִּים אוֹ הַשְּׁתִי אוֹ
הָעֵרֶב אוֹ כָּל־כְּלִי־עוֹר לְטַהֲרוֹ אוֹ לְטַמְּאוֹ׃

55. *it is a fret.* It has eaten into the cloth.
whether the bareness be within or without. lit. 'in its front-baldness or its back-baldness'; whether the threadbare appearance be on the right or on the reverse side.

59. *this is the law.* The purpose of this regulation is the same as that of the leprous body, viz. to remove from the camp of Israel everything which was unclean.

HAFTORAH THAZRIA — הפטרת תזריע

II KINGS IV, 42–V, 19

CHAPTER IV

42. And there came a man from Baal-shalishah, and brought the man of God bread of the first-fruits, twenty loaves of barley, and fresh ears of corn in his sack. And he said: 'Give unto the people, that they may eat.' 43. And his servant said: 'How should I set this before a hundred men?' But he said: 'Give the people, that they may eat; for thus saith the LORD: They shall eat, and shall leave thereof.'

CAP. IV. ד

42 וְאִישׁ בָּא מִבַּעַל שָׁלִשָׁה
וַיָּבֵא לְאִישׁ הָאֱלֹהִים לֶחֶם בִּכּוּרִים עֶשְׂרִים־לֶחֶם שְׂעֹרִים
43 וְכַרְמֶל בְּצִקְלֹנוֹ וַיֹּאמֶר תֵּן לָעָם וְיֹאכֵלוּ׃ וַיֹּאמֶר מְשָׁרְתוֹ
מָה אֶתֵּן זֶה לִפְנֵי מֵאָה אִישׁ וַיֹּאמֶר תֵּן לָעָם וְיֹאכֵלוּ כִּי

The Haftorah of this and of the succeeding Sedrah bring incidents from the cycle of tales describing the activities of the Prophet Elisha. There is little resemblance between him and the sublime, storm-compelling personality of his great Master. Unlike Elijah, 'he was the friend and counsellor of kings. His deeds were not of wild terror, but of gracious, soothing, homely beneficence, bound up with the ordinary tenor of human life' (Stanley). Many of these tales give us interesting glimpses into the social life of Israel in his day; *e.g.* the stories that form the Haftorah of Vayyera, see p. 76. Our Haftorah brings two stories—one in which, during the great famine, the scanty bread of a poor man's offering is multiplied, so that Elisha is enabled to feed a hundred of the 'sons of the prophets'; and the other, the story of the captain of Syria's host, who is cured of his leprosy by Elisha. This incident connects with the Sedrah which deals with the diagnosis and treatment of that disease.

CHAPTER IV

42. *Baal-shalishah.* In the country of Ephraim, to the north of Bethel. Fruits ripened there earlier than elsewhere in Palestine.
give unto the people. *i.e.* to the disciples, the 'sons of the prophets', who were with him (*v.* 38).

43. *should I set this.* *i.e.* is it not too little for them?

44. So he set it before them, and they did eat, and left thereof, according to the word of the LORD.

CHAPTER V

1. Now Naaman, captain of the host of the king of Aram, was a great man with his master, and held in esteem, because by him the LORD had given victory unto Aram; he was also a mighty man of valour, but he was a leper. 2. And the Arameans had gone out in bands, and had brought away captive out of the land of Israel a little maid; and she waited on Naaman's wife. 3. And she said unto her mistress: 'Would that my lord were with the prophet that is in Samaria! then would he recover him of his leprosy.' 4. And he went in, and told his lord, saying: 'Thus and thus said the maid that is of the land of Israel.' 5. And the king of Aram said: 'Go now, and I will send a letter unto the king of Israel.' And he departed, and took with him ten talents of silver, and six thousand pieces of gold, and ten changes of raiment. 6. And he brought the letter to the king of Israel, saying: 'And now when this letter is come unto thee, behold, I have sent Naaman my servant to thee, that thou mayest recover him of his leprosy.' 7. And it came to pass, when the king of Israel had read the letter, that he rent his clothes, and said: 'Am I God, to kill and to make alive, that this man doth send unto me to recover a man of his leprosy? but consider, I pray you, and see how he seeketh an occasion against me.' ¶ 8. And it was so, when Elisha the man of God heard that the king of Israel had rent his clothes, that he sent to the king, saying: 'Wherefore hast thou rent thy clothes? let him come now to me, and he shall know that there is a prophet in Israel.' 9. So Naaman came with his horses and with his chariots and stood at the door of the house of Elisha. 10. And Elisha sent a messenger unto him, saying: 'Go and wash in the Jordan seven

44 כֹּה אָמַר יְהוָה אָכֹל וְהוֹתֵר׃ וַיִּתֵּן לִפְנֵיהֶם וַיֹּאכְלוּ וַיּוֹתִרוּ
כִּדְבַר יְהוָה׃

CAP. V. ה

א וְנַעֲמָן שַׂר־צְבָא מֶלֶךְ־אֲרָם הָיָה אִישׁ גָּדוֹל לִפְנֵי אֲדֹנָיו
וּנְשֻׂא פָנִים כִּי־בוֹ נָתַן־יְהוָה תְּשׁוּעָה לַאֲרָם וְהָאִישׁ הָיָה
2 גִּבּוֹר חַיִל מְצֹרָע׃ וַאֲרָם יָצְאוּ גְדוּדִים וַיִּשְׁבּוּ מֵאֶרֶץ
3 יִשְׂרָאֵל נַעֲרָה קְטַנָּה וַתְּהִי לִפְנֵי אֵשֶׁת נַעֲמָן׃ וַתֹּאמֶר
אֶל־גְּבִרְתָּהּ אַחֲלֵי אֲדֹנִי לִפְנֵי הַנָּבִיא אֲשֶׁר בְּשֹׁמְרוֹן אָז
4 יֶאֱסֹף אֹתוֹ מִצָּרַעְתּוֹ׃ וַיָּבֹא וַיַּגֵּד לַאדֹנָיו לֵאמֹר כָּזֹאת
ה וְכָזֹאת דִּבְּרָה הַנַּעֲרָה אֲשֶׁר מֵאֶרֶץ יִשְׂרָאֵל׃ וַיֹּאמֶר מֶלֶךְ־
אֲרָם לֶךְ־בֹּא וְאֶשְׁלְחָה סֵפֶר אֶל־מֶלֶךְ יִשְׂרָאֵל וַיֵּלֶךְ וַיִּקַּח
בְּיָדוֹ עֶשֶׂר כִּכְּרֵי־כֶסֶף וְשֵׁשֶׁת אֲלָפִים זָהָב וְעֶשֶׂר חֲלִיפוֹת
6 בְּגָדִים׃ וַיָּבֵא הַסֵּפֶר אֶל־מֶלֶךְ יִשְׂרָאֵל לֵאמֹר וְעַתָּה כְּבוֹא
הַסֵּפֶר הַזֶּה אֵלֶיךָ הִנֵּה שָׁלַחְתִּי אֵלֶיךָ אֶת־נַעֲמָן עַבְדִּי
7 וַאֲסַפְתּוֹ מִצָּרַעְתּוֹ׃ וַיְהִי כִּקְרֹא מֶלֶךְ־יִשְׂרָאֵל אֶת־הַסֵּפֶר
וַיִּקְרַע בְּגָדָיו וַיֹּאמֶר הַאֱלֹהִים אָנִי לְהָמִית וּלְהַחֲיוֹת
כִּי־זֶה שֹׁלֵחַ אֵלַי לֶאֱסֹף אִישׁ מִצָּרַעְתּוֹ כִּי אַךְ־דְּעוּ־נָא
8 וּרְאוּ כִּי־מִתְאַנֶּה הוּא לִי׃ וַיְהִי כִּשְׁמֹעַ ׀ אֱלִישָׁע אִישׁ־
הָאֱלֹהִים כִּי־קָרַע מֶלֶךְ־יִשְׂרָאֵל אֶת־בְּגָדָיו וַיִּשְׁלַח אֶל־
הַמֶּלֶךְ לֵאמֹר לָמָּה קָרַעְתָּ בְּגָדֶיךָ יָבֹא־נָא אֵלַי וְיֵדַע כִּי
9 יֵשׁ נָבִיא בְּיִשְׂרָאֵל׃ וַיָּבֹא נַעֲמָן בְּסוּסָו וּבְרִכְבּוֹ וַיַּעֲמֹד
י פֶּתַח־הַבַּיִת לֶאֱלִישָׁע׃ וַיִּשְׁלַח אֵלָיו אֱלִישָׁע מַלְאָךְ לֵאמֹר

ה׳ v. 9. בסוסיו ק׳

CHAPTER V. THE HEALING OF NAAMAN

1. *but he was a leper.* A famous general, great and honoured in the land, but a leper; the *but's* of life can be even more grim and heart-breaking than its *if's*.

2. *in bands.* In marauding bands, raiding the territory of Israel even when no formal war existed between the two peoples. Since the death of Solomon, Syria had become a persistent and implacable foe to Israel.

3. *recover.* Cure; lit. 'receive him back'—as the cured leper was received back into the camp and city life from which he had been excluded (Kimchi).

5. *took with him.* As a gift to the Prophet who, as we learn later, would receive nothing at his hands.

ten talents of silver. A very large sum.

6. *recover him of his leprosy.* By using his influence with the Prophet. Only the main point of the letter is quoted. The king of Israel is addressed as a vassal.

7. *rent his clothes.* As at the receipt of bad news. The king trembles at the Syrian's demand, and thinks he is seeking a pretext for war.

times, and thy flesh shall come back to thee, and thou shalt be clean.' 11. But Naaman was wroth, and went away, and said: 'Behold, I thought: He will surely come out to me, and stand, and call on the name of the LORD his God, and wave his hand over the place, and recover the leper. 12. Are not Amanah and Pharpar, the rivers of Damascus, better than all the waters of Israel? may I not wash in them, and be clean?' So he turned, and went away in a rage. 13. And his servants came near, and spoke unto him, and said: 'My father, if the prophet had bid thee do some great thing, wouldest thou not have done it? how much rather then, when he saith to thee: Wash, and be clean?' 14. Then went he down, and dipped himself seven times in the Jordan, according to the saying of the man of God; and his flesh came back like unto the flesh of a little child, and he was clean. ¶ 15. And he returned to the man of God, he and all his company, and came, and stood before him; and he said: 'Behold now, I know that there is no God in all the earth, but in Israel; now therefore, I pray thee, take a present of thy servant.' 16. But he said: 'As the LORD liveth, before whom I stand, I will receive none.' And he urged him to take it; but he refused. 17. And Naaman said: 'If not, yet I pray thee let there be given to thy servant two mules' burden of earth; for thy servant will

הָלוֹךְ וְרָחַצְתָּ שֶׁבַע־פְּעָמִים בַּיַּרְדֵּן וְיָשֹׁב בְּשָׂרְךָ לְךָ וּטְהָר׃
11 וַיִּקְצֹף נַעֲמָן וַיֵּלַךְ וַיֹּאמֶר הִנֵּה אָמַרְתִּי אֵלַי ׀ יֵצֵא יָצוֹא
וְעָמַד וְקָרָא בְּשֵׁם־יְהוָה אֱלֹהָיו וְהֵנִיף יָדוֹ אֶל־הַמָּקוֹם
12 וְאָסַף הַמְּצֹרָע׃ הֲלֹא טוֹב אֲבָנָה וּפַרְפַּר נַהֲרוֹת דַּמֶּשֶׂק
מִכֹּל מֵימֵי יִשְׂרָאֵל הֲלֹא־אֶרְחַץ בָּהֶם וְטָהָרְתִּי וַיִּפֶן
13 וַיֵּלֶךְ בְּחֵמָה׃ וַיִּגְּשׁוּ עֲבָדָיו וַיְדַבְּרוּ אֵלָיו וַיֹּאמְרוּ אָבִי
דָּבָר גָּדוֹל הַנָּבִיא דִּבֶּר אֵלֶיךָ הֲלוֹא תַעֲשֶׂה וְאַף כִּי־אָמַר
14 אֵלֶיךָ רְחַץ וּטְהָר׃ וַיֵּרֶד וַיִּטְבֹּל בַּיַּרְדֵּן שֶׁבַע פְּעָמִים
כִּדְבַר אִישׁ הָאֱלֹהִים וַיָּשָׁב בְּשָׂרוֹ כִּבְשַׂר נַעַר קָטֹן וַיִּטְהָר׃
טו וַיָּשָׁב אֶל־אִישׁ הָאֱלֹהִים הוּא וְכָל־מַחֲנֵהוּ וַיָּבֹא וַיַּעֲמֹד
לְפָנָיו וַיֹּאמֶר הִנֵּה־נָא יָדַעְתִּי כִּי אֵין אֱלֹהִים בְּכָל־הָאָרֶץ
16 כִּי אִם־בְּיִשְׂרָאֵל וְעַתָּה קַח־נָא בְרָכָה מֵאֵת עַבְדֶּךָ׃ וַיֹּאמֶר
חַי־יְהוָה אֲשֶׁר־עָמַדְתִּי לְפָנָיו אִם־אֶקָּח וַיִּפְצַר־בּוֹ לָקַחַת
17 וַיְמָאֵן׃ וַיֹּאמֶר נַעֲמָן וָלֹא יֻתַּן־נָא לְעַבְדְּךָ מַשָּׂא צֶמֶד־
פְּרָדִים אֲדָמָה כִּי לוֹא־יַעֲשֶׂה עוֹד עַבְדְּךָ עֹלָה וָזֶבַח

v. 12. אמנה ק׳

11. *Naaman was wroth.* Elisha did not come out to him, and Naaman was enraged that the Prophet was no respecter of persons—in his case. He was especially annoyed at the *simplicity* of the remedy: he expected the Prophet to come out and play the wonder-worker.

12. *Amanah and Pharpar.* His patriotic pride is wounded: why was he bidden to wash in that wretched, turbid, tortuous stream—the Jordan—rather than in the pure and flowing waters of his own native Amanah and Pharpar?

The Prophet's bidding has a wider meaning than the ephemeral counsel to the ancient Syrian general. Whenever mankind seeks to be cured of moral leprosy, it can gain that cure only in Jordan, only in rivers of Jewish inspiration and teaching. The waters of India and Greece, of Italy and Germany, may be far greater, stronger, clearer; but they cannot restore moral health to the ailing soul of man. In the crises of life, whether of the individual or of humanity, we turn not to the Vedas or Homer, nor to Dante or Goethe, but to the Book of the Psalms.

15. *he returned.* Naaman was grateful. 'It is difficult to conceive the transport of a man cured of this most loathsome and humiliating of all earthly afflictions' (Farrar).

take a present. Accustomed to the ways of heathen priests, he could not imagine that so great a service would be rendered to a wealthy applicant without monetary reward.

16. *I will receive none.* Like Abraham, who would not take even a 'shoe-latchet' from the people he befriended (Gen. XIV, 23).

17. *two mules' burden of earth. i.e.* of the Holy Land, for constructing an altar to the God of Israel in Syria. Naaman held the heathen view that a deity was only powerful in the country which recognized him; and, therefore, that outside of Palestine, God could only be worshipped on *soil* from Israel's land!

henceforth offer neither burnt-offering nor sacrifice unto other gods, but unto the LORD. 18. In this thing the LORD pardon thy servant: when my master goeth into the house of Rimmon to worship there, and he leaneth on my hand, and I prostrate myself in the house of Rimmon, when I prostrate myself in the house of Rimmon, the LORD pardon thy servant in this thing.' 19. And he said unto him: 'Go in peace.' So he departed from him some way.

18 לֵאלֹהִים אֲחֵרִים כִּי אִם־לַיהוָה׃ לַדָּבָר הַזֶּה יִסְלַח
יְהוָה לְעַבְדֶּךָ בְּבוֹא אֲדֹנִי בֵית־רִמּוֹן לְהִשְׁתַּחֲוֹת שָׁמָּה
וְהוּא ׀ נִשְׁעָן עַל־יָדִי וְהִשְׁתַּחֲוֵיתִי בֵּית רִמֹּן בְּהִשְׁתַּחֲוָיָתִי
19 בֵּית רִמֹּן יִסְלַח־נא יְהוָה לְעַבְדְּךָ בַּדָּבָר הַזֶּה׃ וַיֹּאמֶר
לוֹ לֵךְ לְשָׁלוֹם וַיֵּלֶךְ מֵאִתּוֹ כִּבְרַת אָרֶץ׃

v. 18. כתיב ולא ק׳

18. *prostrate myself.* Or, 'bow myself.' Though he knows that the Lord God of Israel is the only living God, he must accompany his master on state occasions to the temple of *his* god Rimmon. The phrase, *to bow in the house of Rimmon*, has thus become proverbial to indicate unwilling and perfunctory homage, or dangerous and dishonest compromise.

19. *go in peace.* Elisha neither approves nor disapproves. Probably he did not wish to place too great a strain upon the devotion of the new convert. The phrase, 'go in peace' means lit. 'go *towards* peace.' In the ideology of our Sages the whole of life is a journey towards Peace; only when life is completed has man reached life's goal and entered into real peace. Hence the formula when the mortal remains are committed to the grave: 'May he come to his place *in* peace.'

14

CHAPTER XIV

CAP. XIV. יד

1. And the LORD spoke unto Moses, saying: ¶ 2. This shall be the law of the leper in the day of his cleansing: he shall be brought unto the priest. 3. And the priest shall go forth out of the camp; and the priest shall look, and, behold, if the plague of leprosy be healed in the leper; 4. then shall the priest command to take for him that is to be cleansed two living clean birds, and cedar-wood, and scarlet, and hyssop. 5. And the priest shall command to kill one of the birds in an earthen vessel over running water. 6. As for the living bird, he shall take it, and the cedar-wood, and the scarlet, and the hyssop, and shall dip them and the living bird in the blood of the bird that was killed over the running water. 7. And he shall sprinkle upon him that is to be cleansed from the leprosy seven times, and shall pronounce him clean, and shall let go the living bird into the open field. 8. And he that is to be cleansed shall wash his clothes, and shave off all his hair, and bathe himself in water, and he shall

יד פ פ פ כח 28

א 2 וַיְדַבֵּר יְהוָה אֶל־מֹשֶׁה לֵּאמֹר׃ זֹאת תִּהְיֶה תּוֹרַת הַמְּצֹרָע
3 בְּיוֹם טָהֳרָתוֹ וְהוּבָא אֶל־הַכֹּהֵן׃ וְיָצָא הַכֹּהֵן אֶל־מִחוּץ
לַמַּחֲנֶה וְרָאָה הַכֹּהֵן וְהִנֵּה נִרְפָּא נֶגַע־הַצָּרַעַת מִן־הַצָּרוּעַ׃
4 וְצִוָּה הַכֹּהֵן וְלָקַח לַמִּטַּהֵר שְׁתֵּי־צִפֳּרִים חַיּוֹת טְהֹרוֹת
ה וְעֵץ אֶרֶז וּשְׁנִי תוֹלַעַת וְאֵזֹב׃ וְצִוָּה הַכֹּהֵן וְשָׁחַט אֶת־
6 הַצִּפּוֹר הָאֶחָת אֶל־כְּלִי־חֶרֶשׂ עַל־מַיִם חַיִּים׃ אֶת־הַצִּפֹּר
הַחַיָּה יִקַּח אֹתָהּ וְאֶת־עֵץ הָאֶרֶז וְאֶת־שְׁנִי הַתּוֹלַעַת וְאֶת־
הָאֵזֹב וְטָבַל אוֹתָם וְאֵת ׀ הַצִּפֹּר הַחַיָּה בְּדַם הַצִּפֹּר הַשְּׁחֻטָה
7 עַל הַמַּיִם הַחַיִּים׃ וְהִזָּה עַל הַמִּטַּהֵר מִן־הַצָּרַעַת שֶׁבַע
פְּעָמִים וְטִהֲרוֹ וְשִׁלַּח אֶת־הַצִּפֹּר הַחַיָּה עַל־פְּנֵי הַשָּׂדֶה׃

V. METZORA

(CHAPTERS XIV–XV)

CHAPTER XIV, 1–32. PURIFICATION OF A LEPER

2. *day.* The Rabbis took this phrase literally, and ruled that the purification could not take place at night.

he shall be brought. To an appointed place outside the camp. Or, 'it (the news of the leper's recovery) shall be brought (*i.e.* reported) to the priest' (Ehrlich); see on XIII, 2.

3. *out of the camp.* To the leper.

shall look. The priest had to satisfy himself that the disease had completely passed away, before commencing the ceremony of purification.

4. *command to take.* The birds and articles required for the ceremony were not necessarily provided by the leper himself. This fact disposes of the idea that the birds were intended as a sacrifice. And further, no portion of the birds was placed on the Altar. The first part of the ceremony must be interpreted as a symbolic representation of the leper's restoration to life and his re-admission to the camp of Israel.

cedar-wood. The most durable of woods, with the strongest resisting power to decay; and, therefore, symbolical of the cured leper who overcame the purifying effects of his disease. Maimonides, however, declares, 'I do not know at present the reason of any of these things'; viz., the cedar-wood, hyssop and scarlet.

scarlet. According to Rabbinic tradition, a band of wool, dipped in scarlet, was used.

hyssop. See on Exod. XII, 22; it was a convenient instrument for sprinkling, as its leaves readily absorb the liquid and freely give it out when shaken. It was used in ceremonies of purification where sprinkling was included (Num. XIX, 6, 18), and therefore became later associated with the idea of cleanliness (Ps. LI, 9).

5. *kill one of the birds.* For the blood required in the ceremony; as a contrast to the other bird which was allowed to live, thus representing the state of death from which the leper has escaped and of the new life to which he could now look forward.

running water. lit. 'living water'; *i.e.* water fresh from a spring, or a stream; the natural symbol for life, freshness, and purity. The blood flowed into the vessel which contained the water.

7. *pronounce him clean.* He could now rejoin his brethren, although a further ceremony was necessary before he was permitted to approach the Sanctuary.

let go the living bird. In like manner, the leper had been spared from death, and was free to enter the camp.

8. *shave.* This is part of the rites of purification, since the disease specially attacked the hair; see next *v.*

be clean; and after that he may come into the camp, but shall dwell outside his tent seven days. 9. And it shall be on the seventh day, that he shall shave all his hair off his head and his beard and his eyebrows, even all his hair he shall shave off; and he shall wash his clothes, and he shall bathe his flesh in water, and he shall be clean. 10. And on the eighth day he shall take two he-lambs without blemish, and one ewe-lamb of the first year without blemish, and three tenth parts of an ephah of fine flour for a meal-offering, mingled with oil, and one log of oil. 11. And the priest that cleanseth him shall set the man that is to be cleansed, and those things, before the LORD, at the door of the tent of meeting. 12. And the priest shall take one of the he-lambs, and offer him for a guilt-offering, and the log of oil, and wave them for a wave-offering before the LORD.* ii. 13. And he shall kill the he-lamb in the place where they kill the sin-offering and the burnt-offering, in the place of the sanctuary; for as the sin-offering is the priest's, so is the guilt-offering; it is most holy. 14. And the priest shall take of the blood of the guilt-offering, and the priest shall put it upon the tip of the right ear of him that is to be cleansed, and upon the thumb of his right hand, and upon the great toe of his right foot. 15. And the priest shall take of the log of oil, and pour it into the palm of his own left hand. 16. And the priest shall dip his right finger in

8 וְכִבֶּס הַמִּטַּהֵר אֶת־בְּגָדָיו וְגִלַּח אֶת־כָּל־שְׂעָרוֹ וְרָחַץ בַּמַּיִם
וְטָהֵר וְאַחַר יָבוֹא אֶל־הַמַּחֲנֶה וְיָשַׁב מִחוּץ לְאָהֳלוֹ שִׁבְעַת
9 יָמִים׃ וְהָיָה בַיּוֹם הַשְּׁבִיעִי יְגַלַּח אֶת־כָּל־שְׂעָרוֹ אֶת־רֹאשׁוֹ
וְאֶת־זְקָנוֹ וְאֵת גַּבֹּת עֵינָיו וְאֶת־כָּל־שְׂעָרוֹ יְגַלֵּחַ וְכִבֶּס אֶת־
י בְּגָדָיו וְרָחַץ אֶת־בְּשָׂרוֹ בַּמַּיִם וְטָהֵר׃ וּבַיּוֹם הַשְּׁמִינִי יִקַּח
שְׁנֵי־כְבָשִׂים תְּמִימִם וְכַבְשָׂה אַחַת בַּת־שְׁנָתָהּ תְּמִימָה
וּשְׁלֹשָׁה עֶשְׂרֹנִים סֹלֶת מִנְחָה בְּלוּלָה בַשֶּׁמֶן וְלֹג אֶחָד
11 שָׁמֶן׃ וְהֶעֱמִיד הַכֹּהֵן הַמְטַהֵר אֵת הָאִישׁ הַמִּטַּהֵר וְאֹתָם
12 לִפְנֵי יְהוָה פֶּתַח אֹהֶל מוֹעֵד׃ וְלָקַח הַכֹּהֵן אֶת־הַכֶּבֶשׂ
הָאֶחָד וְהִקְרִיב אֹתוֹ לְאָשָׁם וְאֶת־לֹג הַשָּׁמֶן וְהֵנִיף אֹתָם
שני 13 תְּנוּפָה לִפְנֵי יְהוָה׃ וְשָׁחַט אֶת־הַכֶּבֶשׂ בִּמְקוֹם אֲשֶׁר
יִשְׁחַט אֶת־הַחַטָּאת וְאֶת־הָעֹלָה בִּמְקוֹם הַקֹּדֶשׁ כִּי כַּחַטָּאת
14 הָאָשָׁם הוּא לַכֹּהֵן קֹדֶשׁ קָדָשִׁים הוּא׃ וְלָקַח הַכֹּהֵן מִדַּם
הָאָשָׁם וְנָתַן הַכֹּהֵן עַל־תְּנוּךְ אֹזֶן הַמִּטַּהֵר הַיְמָנִית וְעַל־
טו בֹּהֶן יָדוֹ הַיְמָנִית וְעַל־בֹּהֶן רַגְלוֹ הַיְמָנִית׃ וְלָקַח הַכֹּהֵן
16 מִלֹּג הַשָּׁמֶן וְיָצַק עַל־כַּף הַכֹּהֵן הַשְּׂמָאלִית׃ וְטָבַל הַכֹּהֵן

outside his tent seven days. An intermediate stage between his complete isolation and his complete liberty which was to restore to him his religious privileges, and with them his full social rights (Kalisch).

9. *shave.* No longer to purify him of his former defilement, but to prepare him for the rite of consecration, even as the Levites should be shaven (Num. VIII, 7) before their induction to the service of the Sanctuary.

wash his clothes. Cf. the preparation of the Levites prior to their consecration (Num. VIII, 7).

10. *ephah.* Approximately a bushel.

log. About one pint.

11. *at the door of.* See on VII, 6. In the time of the Second Temple, he was brought to what was known as Nicanor's Gate which divided the Women's Court from the Court of the Israelites. The latter, but not the former Court, was regarded as part of the Sanctuary.

12. *guilt-offering.* This was the first of the three offerings sacrificed on behalf of the cleansed leper. He had been completely cut off from his people and, therefore, his first act was to renew his covenant, as an Israelite, with God. It was explained on VII, 1 that the guilt-offering was not an expiatory sacrifice, but a forfeit which was offered when a man had made restitution. By his severance from the life of the community, the leper had failed to bring his dues to the Sanctuary, and so took the earliest opportunity to place his forfeit on the Altar.

wave-offering. See on VII, 30; and Num. VIII, 11. The act of waving had the additional significance of dedicating the bringer of the sacrifice to the service of the Most High.

13. *is the priest's.* See VII, 6 f.

14. *ear . . . hand . . . foot.* This ceremony was identical with that of the consecration of the priests, and had the same significance; see on VIII, 23.

15. *of the log of oil. i.e.* some of the additional log, mentioned in *v.* 10. This was different from the anointing of the High Priest upon whose head the oil was poured (VIII, 12). Here the priest only 'put' it on the person's head.

the oil that is in his left hand, and shall
sprinkle of the oil with his finger seven
times before the LORD. 17. And of the
rest of the oil that is in his hand shall the
priest put upon the tip of the right ear
of him that is to be cleansed, and upon
the thumb of his right hand, and upon
the great toe of his right foot, upon the
blood of the guilt-offering. 18. And the
rest of the oil that is in the priest's hand
he shall put upon the head of him that
is to be cleansed; and the priest shall
make atonement for him before the LORD.
19. And the priest shall offer the sin-offering,
and make atonement for him that is to be
cleansed because of his uncleanness; and
afterward he shall kill the burnt-offering.
20. And the priest shall offer the burnt-
offering and the meal-offering upon the
altar; and the priest shall make atonement for
him, and he shall be clean.* iii (** v). ¶ 21.
And if he be poor, and his means suffice not,
then he shall take one he-lamb for a guilt-
offering to be waved, to make atonement
for him, and one tenth part of an ephah
of fine flour mingled with oil for a meal-
offering, and a log of oil; 22. and two
turtle-doves, or two young pigeons, such
as his means suffice for; and the one shall
be a sin-offering, and the other a burnt-
offering. 23. And on the eighth day he
shall bring them for his cleansing unto the
priest, unto the door of the tent of meeting,
before the LORD. 24. And the priest shall
take the lamb of the guilt-offering, and the
log of oil, and the priest shall wave them
for a wave-offering before the LORD. 25.
And he shall kill the lamb of the guilt-
offering, and the priest shall take of the
blood of the guilt-offering, and put it
upon the tip of the right ear of him that
is to be cleansed, and upon the thumb of
his right hand, and upon the great toe of
his right foot. 26. And the priest shall
pour of the oil into the palm of his own
left hand. 27. And the priest shall sprinkle
with his right finger some of the oil that
is in his left hand seven times before the
LORD. 28. And the priest shall put of the
oil that is in his hand upon the tip of the
right ear of him that is to be cleansed, and
upon the thumb of his right hand, and upon
the great toe of his right foot, upon the
place of the blood of the guilt-offering.
29. And the rest of the oil that is in the

אֶת־אֶצְבָּעוֹ הַיְמָנִית מִן־הַשֶּׁמֶן אֲשֶׁר עַל־כַּפּוֹ הַשְּׂמָאלִית
17 וְהִזָּה מִן־הַשֶּׁמֶן בְּאֶצְבָּעוֹ שֶׁבַע פְּעָמִים לִפְנֵי יְהוָה׃ וּמִיֶּתֶר
הַשֶּׁמֶן אֲשֶׁר עַל־כַּפּוֹ יִתֵּן הַכֹּהֵן עַל־תְּנוּךְ אֹזֶן הַמִּטַּהֵר
הַיְמָנִית וְעַל־בֹּהֶן יָדוֹ הַיְמָנִית וְעַל־בֹּהֶן רַגְלוֹ הַיְמָנִית עַל
18 דַּם הָאָשָׁם׃ וְהַנּוֹתָר בַּשֶּׁמֶן אֲשֶׁר עַל־כַּף הַכֹּהֵן יִתֵּן עַל־
19 רֹאשׁ הַמִּטַּהֵר וְכִפֶּר עָלָיו הַכֹּהֵן לִפְנֵי יְהוָה׃ וְעָשָׂה הַכֹּהֵן
אֶת־הַחַטָּאת וְכִפֶּר עַל־הַמִּטַּהֵר מִטֻּמְאָתוֹ וְאַחַר יִשְׁחַט
כ אֶת־הָעֹלָה׃ וְהֶעֱלָה הַכֹּהֵן אֶת־הָעֹלָה וְאֶת־הַמִּנְחָה הַמִּזְבֵּחָה
שלישי (חמישי כשהן מחובר׳)
21 וְכִפֶּר עָלָיו הַכֹּהֵן וְטָהֵר׃ ס וְאִם־דַּל הוּא וְאֵין יָדוֹ
מַשֶּׂגֶת וְלָקַח כֶּבֶשׂ אֶחָד אָשָׁם לִתְנוּפָה לְכַפֵּר עָלָיו וְעִשָּׂרוֹן
22 סֹלֶת אֶחָד בָּלוּל בַּשֶּׁמֶן לְמִנְחָה וְלֹג שָׁמֶן׃ וּשְׁתֵּי תֹרִים
אוֹ שְׁנֵי בְּנֵי יוֹנָה אֲשֶׁר תַּשִּׂיג יָדוֹ וְהָיָה אֶחָד חַטָּאת וְהָאֶחָד
23 עֹלָה׃ וְהֵבִיא אֹתָם בַּיּוֹם הַשְּׁמִינִי לְטָהֳרָתוֹ אֶל־הַכֹּהֵן
24 אֶל־פֶּתַח אֹהֶל־מוֹעֵד לִפְנֵי יְהוָה׃ וְלָקַח הַכֹּהֵן אֶת־כֶּבֶשׂ
הָאָשָׁם וְאֶת־לֹג הַשָּׁמֶן וְהֵנִיף אֹתָם הַכֹּהֵן תְּנוּפָה לִפְנֵי
כה יְהוָה׃ וְשָׁחַט אֶת־כֶּבֶשׂ הָאָשָׁם וְלָקַח הַכֹּהֵן מִדַּם הָאָשָׁם
וְנָתַן עַל־תְּנוּךְ אֹזֶן־הַמִּטַּהֵר הַיְמָנִית וְעַל־בֹּהֶן יָדוֹ הַיְמָנִית
26 וְעַל־בֹּהֶן רַגְלוֹ הַיְמָנִית׃ וּמִן־הַשֶּׁמֶן יִצֹק הַכֹּהֵן עַל־כַּף
27 הַכֹּהֵן הַשְּׂמָאלִית׃ וְהִזָּה הַכֹּהֵן בְּאֶצְבָּעוֹ הַיְמָנִית מִן־הַשֶּׁמֶן
28 אֲשֶׁר עַל־כַּפּוֹ הַשְּׂמָאלִית שֶׁבַע פְּעָמִים לִפְנֵי יְהוָה׃ וְנָתַן
הַכֹּהֵן מִן־הַשֶּׁמֶן ׀ אֲשֶׁר עַל־כַּפּוֹ עַל־תְּנוּךְ אֹזֶן הַמִּטַּהֵר
הַיְמָנִית וְעַל־בֹּהֶן יָדוֹ הַיְמָנִית וְעַל־בֹּהֶן רַגְלוֹ הַיְמָנִית עַל־
29 מְקוֹם דַּם הָאָשָׁם׃ וְהַנּוֹתָר מִן־הַשֶּׁמֶן אֲשֶׁר עַל־כַּף הַכֹּהֵן

19. *sin-offering.* viz. the ewe-lamb mentioned in *v.* 10. The sin-offering was, in this case, nothing more than a medium of purification; see on XII, 6.

20. *meal-offering.* The flour and the oil (see *v.* 10). This final sacrifice expressed the gratitude of the former leper.

21–32. In the case of poverty, the demand for the guilt-offering remains, but the other two

ל יִתֵּן עַל־רֹאשׁ הַמִּטַּהֵר לְכַפֵּר עָלָיו לִפְנֵי יְהוָה׃ וְעָשָׂה
אֶת־הָאֶחָד מִן־הַתֹּרִים אוֹ מִן־בְּנֵי הַיּוֹנָה מֵאֲשֶׁר תַּשִּׂיג יָדוֹ׃
31 אֵת אֲשֶׁר־תַּשִּׂיג יָדוֹ אֶת־הָאֶחָד חַטָּאת וְאֶת־הָאֶחָד עֹלָה
32 עַל־הַמִּנְחָה וְכִפֶּר הַכֹּהֵן עַל הַמִּטַּהֵר לִפְנֵי יְהוָה׃ זֹאת תּוֹרַת
רביעי (ששי כשהן מחוב׳) אֲשֶׁר־בּוֹ נֶגַע צָרָעַת אֲשֶׁר לֹא־תַשִּׂיג יָדוֹ בְּטָהֳרָתוֹ׃ פ
33 34 וַיְדַבֵּר יְהוָה אֶל־מֹשֶׁה וְאֶל־אַהֲרֹן לֵאמֹר׃ כִּי תָבֹאוּ אֶל־
אֶרֶץ כְּנַעַן אֲשֶׁר אֲנִי נֹתֵן לָכֶם לַאֲחֻזָּה וְנָתַתִּי נֶגַע צָרַעַת
לה בְּבֵית אֶרֶץ אֲחֻזַּתְכֶם׃ וּבָא אֲשֶׁר־לוֹ הַבַּיִת וְהִגִּיד לַכֹּהֵן
36 לֵאמֹר כְּנֶגַע נִרְאָה לִי בַּבָּיִת׃ וְצִוָּה הַכֹּהֵן וּפִנּוּ אֶת־הַבַּיִת
בְּטֶרֶם יָבֹא הַכֹּהֵן לִרְאוֹת אֶת־הַנֶּגַע וְלֹא יִטְמָא כָּל־אֲשֶׁר
37 בַּבָּיִת וְאַחַר כֵּן יָבֹא הַכֹּהֵן לִרְאוֹת אֶת־הַבָּיִת׃ וְרָאָה אֶת־
הַנֶּגַע וְהִנֵּה הַנֶּגַע בְּקִירֹת הַבַּיִת שְׁקַעֲרוּרֹת יְרַקְרַקֹּת אוֹ
38 אֲדַמְדַּמֹּת וּמַרְאֵיהֶן שָׁפָל מִן־הַקִּיר׃ וְיָצָא הַכֹּהֵן מִן־הַבַּיִת
39 אֶל־פֶּתַח הַבָּיִת וְהִסְגִּיר אֶת־הַבַּיִת שִׁבְעַת יָמִים׃ וְשָׁב
הַכֹּהֵן בַּיּוֹם הַשְּׁבִיעִי וְרָאָה וְהִנֵּה פָּשָׂה הַנֶּגַע בְּקִירֹת הַבָּיִת׃
מ וְצִוָּה הַכֹּהֵן וְחִלְּצוּ אֶת־הָאֲבָנִים אֲשֶׁר בָּהֵן הַנָּגַע וְהִשְׁלִיכוּ
41 אֶתְהֶן אֶל־מִחוּץ לָעִיר אֶל־מָקוֹם טָמֵא׃ וְאֶת־הַבַּיִת יַקְצִעַ
מִבַּיִת סָבִיב וְשָׁפְכוּ אֶת־הֶעָפָר אֲשֶׁר הִקְצוּ אֶל־מִחוּץ
42 לָעִיר אֶל־מָקוֹם טָמֵא׃ וְלָקְחוּ אֲבָנִים אֲחֵרוֹת וְהֵבִיאוּ

priest's hand he shall put upon the head of him that is to be cleansed, to make atonement for him before the LORD. 30. And he shall offer one of the turtle-doves, or of the young pigeons, such as his means suffice for; 31. even such as his means suffice for, the one for a sin-offering, and the other for a burnt-offering, with the meal-offering; and the priest shall make atonement for him that is to be cleansed before the LORD. 32. This is the law of him in whom is the plague of leprosy, whose means suffice not for that which pertaineth to his cleansing. *iv(**vi). ¶ 33. And the LORD spoke unto Moses and unto Aaron, saying: ¶ 34. When ye are come into the land of Canaan, which I give to you for a possession, and I put the plague of leprosy in a house of the land of your possession; 35. then he that owneth the house shall come and tell the priest, saying: 'There seemeth to me to be as it were a plague in the house.' 36. And the priest shall command that they empty the house, before the priest go in to see the plague, that all that is in the house be not made unclean; and afterward the priest shall go in to see the house. 37. And he shall look on the plague, and, behold, if the plague be in the walls of the house with hollow streaks, greenish or reddish, and the appearance thereof be lower than the wall; 38. then the priest shall go out of the house to the door of the house, and shut up the house seven days. 39. And the priest shall come again the seventh day, and shall look; and, behold, if the plague be spread in the walls of the house; 40. then the priest shall command that they take out the stones in which the plague is, and cast them into an unclean place without the city. 41. And he shall cause the house to be scraped within round about, and they shall pour out the mortar that they scrape off without the city into an unclean place. 42. And

animal sacrifices are replaced by turtle-doves or young pigeons, as in XII, 8.

33–53. LEPROSY IN A HOUSE

Caused by some fungus akin to that which produces dry rot. Others suppose that parasitic insects had nested in the house, or a nitrous incrustation had formed in the walls.

33. *saying.* We must understand some such words as, 'Speak unto the children of Israel.'

34. *when ye are come.* The Torah here legislates for the time when the Israelites shall have settled in their land and inhabit houses.

I put. This form of speech is used, because all phenomena are ultimately the consequence of the Divine will.

36. *empty the house.* Until the priest formally pronounced the house infected, its contents were not unclean. Similarly a man was not leprous, until the priest passed the verdict upon him. All the furniture was removed before the inspection, to save it from being defiled, should the house be condemned.

37. *streaks.* *i.e.* the plague had eaten into the material of the wall.

40. *take out the stones.* This is analogous to cutting out the infected part of a garment (XIII, 56).

unclean place. *i.e.* a place known to be unclean and used for such a purpose.

they shall take other stones, and put them in the place of those stones; and he shall take other mortar, and shall plaster the house. 43. And if the plague come again, and break out in the house, after that the stones have been taken out, and after the house hath been scraped, and after it is plastered; 44. then the priest shall come in and look; and, behold, if the plague be spread in the house, it is a malignant leprosy in the house: it is unclean. 45. And he shall break down the house, the stones of it, and the timber thereof, and all the mortar of the house; and he shall carry them forth out of the city into an unclean place. 46. Moreover he that goeth into the house all the while that it is shut up shall be unclean until the even. 47. And he that lieth in the house shall wash his clothes; and he that eateth in the house shall wash his clothes. 48. And if the priest shall come in, and look, and, behold, the plague hath not spread in the house, after the house was plastered; then the priest shall pronounce the house clean, because the plague is healed. 49. And he shall take to cleanse the house two birds, and cedar-wood, and scarlet, and hyssop. 50. And he shall kill one of the birds in an earthen vessel over running water. 51. And he shall take the cedar-wood, and the hyssop, and the scarlet, and the living bird, and dip them in the blood of the slain bird, and in the running water, and sprinkle the house seven times. 52. And he shall cleanse the house with the blood of the bird, and with the running water, and with the living bird, and with the cedar-wood, and with the hyssop, and with the scarlet. 53. But he shall let go the living bird out of the city into the open field; so shall he make atonement for the house; and it shall be clean.*v. ¶ 54. This is the law for all manner of plague of leprosy, and for a scall; 55. and for the leprosy of a garment, and for a house; 56. and for a rising, and for a scab, and for a bright spot; 57. to teach when it is unclean, and when it is clean; this is the law of leprosy.

43 אֶל־תַּחַת הָאֲבָנִים וְעָפָר אַחֵר יִקַּח וְטָח אֶת־הַבָּיִת׃ וְאִם־
יָשׁוּב הַנֶּגַע וּפָרַח בַּבַּיִת אַחַר חִלֵּץ אֶת־הָאֲבָנִים וְאַחֲרֵי
44 הִקְצוֹת אֶת־הַבַּיִת וְאַחֲרֵי הִטּוֹחַ׃ וּבָא הַכֹּהֵן וְרָאָה וְהִנֵּה
פָּשָׂה הַנֶּגַע בַּבָּיִת צָרַעַת מַמְאֶרֶת הִוא בַּבַּיִת טָמֵא הוּא׃
מה וְנָתַץ אֶת־הַבַּיִת אֶת־אֲבָנָיו וְאֶת־עֵצָיו וְאֵת כָּל־עֲפַר הַבָּיִת
46 וְהוֹצִיא אֶל־מִחוּץ לָעִיר אֶל־מָקוֹם טָמֵא׃ וְהַבָּא אֶל־הַבַּיִת
47 כָּל־יְמֵי הִסְגִּיר אֹתוֹ יִטְמָא עַד־הָעָרֶב׃ וְהַשֹּׁכֵב בַּבַּיִת
48 יְכַבֵּס אֶת־בְּגָדָיו וְהָאֹכֵל בַּבַּיִת יְכַבֵּס אֶת־בְּגָדָיו׃ וְאִם־בֹּא
יָבֹא הַכֹּהֵן וְרָאָה וְהִנֵּה לֹא־פָשָׂה הַנֶּגַע בַּבַּיִת אַחֲרֵי הִטֹּחַ
49 אֶת־הַבָּיִת וְטִהַר הַכֹּהֵן אֶת־הַבַּיִת כִּי נִרְפָּא הַנָּגַע׃ וְלָקַח
לְחַטֵּא אֶת־הַבַּיִת שְׁתֵּי צִפֳּרִים וְעֵץ אֶרֶז וּשְׁנִי תוֹלַעַת וְאֵזֹב׃
נ וְשָׁחַט אֶת־הַצִּפֹּר הָאֶחָת אֶל־כְּלִי־חֶרֶשׂ עַל־מַיִם חַיִּים׃
51 וְלָקַח אֶת־עֵץ־הָאֶרֶז וְאֶת־הָאֵזֹב וְאֵת ׀ שְׁנִי הַתּוֹלַעַת וְאֵת
הַצִּפֹּר הַחַיָּה וְטָבַל אֹתָם בְּדַם הַצִּפֹּר הַשְּׁחוּטָה וּבַמַּיִם
52 הַחַיִּים וְהִזָּה אֶל־הַבַּיִת שֶׁבַע פְּעָמִים׃ וְחִטֵּא אֶת־הַבַּיִת
בְּדַם הַצִּפּוֹר וּבַמַּיִם הַחַיִּים וּבַצִּפֹּר הַחַיָּה וּבְעֵץ הָאֶרֶז
53 וּבָאֵזֹב וּבִשְׁנִי הַתּוֹלָעַת׃ וְשִׁלַּח אֶת־הַצִּפֹּר הַחַיָּה אֶל־
חמישי 54 מִחוּץ לָעִיר אֶל־פְּנֵי הַשָּׂדֶה וְכִפֶּר עַל־הַבַּיִת וְטָהֵר׃ *וְזֹאת
נה הַתּוֹרָה לְכָל־נֶגַע הַצָּרַעַת וְלַנָּתֶק׃ וּלְצָרַעַת הַבֶּגֶד וְלַבָּיִת׃
56 57 וְלַשְׂאֵת וְלַסַּפַּחַת וְלַבֶּהָרֶת׃ לְהוֹרֹת בְּיוֹם הַטָּמֵא וּבְיוֹם
הַטָּהֹר זֹאת תּוֹרַת הַצָּרָעַת׃ פ

v. 56. ש׳ רפה

43–45. The reappearance of the plague in the house was analogous to the recurrence of the malady in a leper (XIII, 7 f) and demanded measures of the utmost stringency.

47. *lieth in the house.* This presupposes a longer stay in the house and, therefore, the garments are likewise defiled.

48. *shall come in.* After the house had been in quarantine for a week, or at the end of the second week.

53. *make atonement for the house.* Only purification is implied; cf. Exod. XXIX, 36, where the priests are told to make atonement for the Altar.

54. *this is the law.* These four concluding verses summarize the contents of the section, chaps. XIII–XIV.

57. *to teach.* The word is to be connected with, 'This is the law' (*v.* 54) and properly signifies 'to give a decision'. The meaning is: 'This is instruction concerning all manner . . . to decide when it is unclean.'

15

CHAPTER XV

1. And the LORD spoke unto Moses and to Aaron, saying: 2. Speak unto the children of Israel, and say unto them: ¶ When any man hath an issue out of his flesh, his issue is unclean. 3. And this shall be his uncleanness in his issue: whether his flesh run with his issue, or his flesh be stopped from his issue, it is his uncleanness. 4. Every bed whereon he that hath the issue lieth shall be unclean; and every thing whereon he sitteth shall be unclean. 5. And whosoever toucheth his bed shall wash his clothes, and bathe himself in water, and be unclean until the even. 6. And he that sitteth on any thing whereon he that hath the issue sat shall wash his clothes, and bathe himself in water, and be unclean until the even. 7. And he that toucheth the flesh of him that hath the issue shall wash his clothes, and bathe himself in water, and be unclean until the even. 8. And if he that hath the issue spit upon him that is clean, then he shall wash his clothes, and bathe himself in water, and be unclean until the even. 9. And what saddle soever he that hath the issue rideth upon shall be unclean. 10. And whosoever toucheth any thing that was under him shall be unclean until the even; and he that beareth those things shall wash his clothes, and bathe himself in water, and be unclean until the even. 11. And whomsoever he that hath the issue toucheth, without having rinsed his hands in water, he shall wash his clothes, and bathe himself in water, and be unclean until the even. 12. And the earthen vessel, which he that hath the issue toucheth, shall be broken; and every vessel of wood shall be rinsed in water. 13. And when he that hath an issue is cleansed of his issue, then he shall number to himself seven days for his cleansing, and wash his clothes; and he shall bathe his flesh in running water, and shall be clean. 14. And on the eighth

CAP. XV. טו

טו

א 2 וַיְדַבֵּר יְהוָה אֶל־מֹשֶׁה וְאֶל־אַהֲרֹן לֵאמֹר׃ דַּבְּרוּ אֶל־בְּנֵי
יִשְׂרָאֵל וַאֲמַרְתֶּם אֲלֵהֶם אִישׁ אִישׁ כִּי יִהְיֶה זָב מִבְּשָׂרוֹ
3 זוֹבוֹ טָמֵא הוּא׃ וְזֹאת תִּהְיֶה טֻמְאָתוֹ בְּזוֹבוֹ רָר בְּשָׂרוֹ
4 אֶת־זוֹבוֹ אוֹ־הֶחְתִּים בְּשָׂרוֹ מִזּוֹבוֹ טֻמְאָתוֹ הִוא׃ כָּל־
הַמִּשְׁכָּב אֲשֶׁר יִשְׁכַּב עָלָיו הַזָּב יִטְמָא וְכָל־הַכְּלִי אֲשֶׁר־
ה יֵשֵׁב עָלָיו יִטְמָא׃ וְאִישׁ אֲשֶׁר יִגַּע בְּמִשְׁכָּבוֹ יְכַבֵּס בְּגָדָיו
6 וְרָחַץ בַּמַּיִם וְטָמֵא עַד־הָעָרֶב׃ וְהַיֹּשֵׁב עַל־הַכְּלִי אֲשֶׁר־
יֵשֵׁב עָלָיו הַזָּב יְכַבֵּס בְּגָדָיו וְרָחַץ בַּמַּיִם וְטָמֵא עַד־הָעָרֶב׃
7 *וְהַנֹּגֵעַ בִּבְשַׂר הַזָּב יְכַבֵּס בְּגָדָיו וְרָחַץ בַּמַּיִם וְטָמֵא עַד־
8 הָעָרֶב׃ וְכִי־יָרֹק הַזָּב בַּטָּהוֹר וְכִבֶּס בְּגָדָיו וְרָחַץ בַּמַּיִם
9 וְטָמֵא עַד־הָעָרֶב׃ וְכָל־הַמֶּרְכָּב אֲשֶׁר יִרְכַּב עָלָיו הַזָּב
י יִטְמָא׃ וְכָל־הַנֹּגֵעַ בְּכֹל אֲשֶׁר יִהְיֶה תַחְתָּיו יִטְמָא עַד־
הָעָרֶב וְהַנּוֹשֵׂא אוֹתָם יְכַבֵּס בְּגָדָיו וְרָחַץ בַּמַּיִם וְטָמֵא עַד־
11 הָעָרֶב׃ וְכֹל אֲשֶׁר יִגַּע־בּוֹ הַזָּב וְיָדָיו לֹא־שָׁטַף בַּמָּיִם
12 וְכִבֶּס בְּגָדָיו וְרָחַץ בַּמַּיִם וְטָמֵא עַד־הָעָרֶב׃ וּכְלִי־חֶרֶשׂ
13 אֲשֶׁר־יִגַּע־בּוֹ הַזָּב יִשָּׁבֵר וְכָל־כְּלִי־עֵץ יִשָּׁטֵף בַּמָּיִם׃ וְכִי־
יִטְהַר הַזָּב מִזּוֹבוֹ וְסָפַר לוֹ שִׁבְעַת יָמִים לְטָהֳרָתוֹ וְכִבֶּס
14 בְּגָדָיו וְרָחַץ בְּשָׂרוֹ בְּמַיִם חַיִּים וְטָהֵר׃ וּבַיּוֹם הַשְּׁמִינִי

v. 7. חצי הספר בפסוקים

CHAPTER XV, 1–30. IMPURITY OF ISSUES

This chapter treats of physical secretions which render a person unclean, precluding him from coming into contact with anything appertaining to the Sanctuary. The gentile was excluded from these regulations, since he was exempt from all obligations in respect to the Holy Place. In *v.* 2 the reference is to a chronic discharge. The person thus is regarded as a source of ritual, no less than physical, infection. The uncleanness, described in *v.* 16–18, did not apply to laymen. It involved merely absence from the 'camp', which in Rabbinic exegesis was taken to mean the Sanctuary proper and the Levite encampment around the Sanctuary. It also involved abstention from sacrificial food (*terumah* and *maaser*). If the prescribed priestly ablutions had been taken, the prohibition ceased in regard to the Levite encampment and *maaser*.

A provision, ascribed to Ezra, to make *v.* 16–18 apply also outside the Sanctuary in the case of laymen reading in the Law, was in time disregarded; see Maimonides, *Yad* II, 1, 4.

v. 19–30 deal with menstruation; on which see XVIII, 19.

day he shall take to him two turtle-doves, or two young pigeons, and come before the LORD unto the door of the tent of meeting, and give them unto the priest. 15. And the priest shall offer them, the one for a sin-offering, and the other for a burnt-offering; and the priest shall make atonement for him before the LORD for his issue.*vi (**vii). ¶16. And if the flow of seed go out from a man, then he shall bathe all his flesh in water, and be unclean until the even. 17. And every garment, and every skin, whereon is the flow of seed, shall be washed with water, and be unclean until the even. 18. The woman also with whom a man shall lie carnally, they shall both bathe themselves in water, and be unclean until the even. ¶ 19. And if a woman have an issue, and her issue in her flesh be blood, she shall be in her impurity seven days; and whosoever toucheth her shall be unclean until the even. 20. And every thing that she lieth upon in her impurity shall be unclean; every thing also that she sitteth upon shall be unclean. 21. And whosoever toucheth her bed shall wash his clothes, and bathe himself in water, and be unclean until the even. 22. And whosoever toucheth any thing that she sitteth upon shall wash his clothes, and bathe himself in water, and be unclean until the even. 23. And if he be on the bed, or on any thing whereon she sitteth, when he toucheth it, he shall be unclean until the even. 24. And if any man lie with her, and her impurity be upon him, he shall be unclean seven days; and every bed whereon he lieth shall be unclean. ¶ 25. And if a woman have an issue of her blood many days not in the time of her impurity, or if she have an issue beyond the time of her impurity; all the days of the issue of her uncleanness she shall be as in the days of her impurity: she is unclean. 26. Every bed whereon she lieth all the days of her issue shall be unto her as the bed of her impurity; and every thing whereon she sitteth shall be unclean, as the uncleanness of her impurity. 27. And whosoever toucheth those things shall be unclean, and shall wash his clothes, and bathe himself in water, and be unclean until the even. 28. But if she be cleansed of her issue, then she shall number to herself seven days, and after that she shall be clean.* vii. 29. And on the eighth day she shall take unto her two turtle-doves, or two young pigeons, and bring them unto the priest, to the door of the tent of meeting. 30. And the priest shall offer the one for a sin-offering, and

יִקַּח־לוֹ שְׁתֵּי תֹרִים אוֹ שְׁנֵי בְּנֵי יוֹנָה וּבָא ׀ לִפְנֵי יְהוָה אֶל־
טו פֶּתַח אֹהֶל מוֹעֵד וּנְתָנָם אֶל־הַכֹּהֵן׃ וְעָשָׂה אֹתָם הַכֹּהֵן
אֶחָד חַטָּאת וְהָאֶחָד עֹלָה וְכִפֶּר עָלָיו הַכֹּהֵן לִפְנֵי יְהוָה ששי (שביעי כשהן מחוב׳)
16 מִזּוֹבוֹ׃ * ס וְאִישׁ כִּי־תֵצֵא מִמֶּנּוּ שִׁכְבַת־זָרַע וְרָחַץ
17 בַּמַּיִם אֶת־כָּל־בְּשָׂרוֹ וְטָמֵא עַד־הָעָרֶב׃ וְכָל־בֶּגֶד וְכָל־
עוֹר אֲשֶׁר־יִהְיֶה עָלָיו שִׁכְבַת־זָרַע וְכֻבַּס בַּמַּיִם וְטָמֵא עַד־
18 הָעָרֶב׃ וְאִשָּׁה אֲשֶׁר יִשְׁכַּב אִישׁ אֹתָהּ שִׁכְבַת־זָרַע וְרָחֲצוּ
בַמַּיִם וְטָמְאוּ עַד־הָעָרֶב׃ פ
19 וְאִשָּׁה כִּי־תִהְיֶה זָבָה דָּם יִהְיֶה זֹבָהּ בִּבְשָׂרָהּ שִׁבְעַת יָמִים
כ תִּהְיֶה בְנִדָּתָהּ וְכָל־הַנֹּגֵעַ בָּהּ יִטְמָא עַד־הָעָרֶב׃ וְכֹל אֲשֶׁר
תִּשְׁכַּב עָלָיו בְּנִדָּתָהּ יִטְמָא וְכֹל אֲשֶׁר־תֵּשֵׁב עָלָיו יִטְמָא׃
21 וְכָל־הַנֹּגֵעַ בְּמִשְׁכָּבָהּ יְכַבֵּס בְּגָדָיו וְרָחַץ בַּמַּיִם וְטָמֵא עַד־
22 הָעָרֶב׃ וְכָל־הַנֹּגֵעַ בְּכָל־כְּלִי אֲשֶׁר־תֵּשֵׁב עָלָיו יְכַבֵּס בְּגָדָיו
23 וְרָחַץ בַּמַּיִם וְטָמֵא עַד־הָעָרֶב׃ וְאִם עַל־הַמִּשְׁכָּב הוּא אוֹ
עַל־הַכְּלִי אֲשֶׁר־הִוא יֹשֶׁבֶת־עָלָיו בְּנָגְעוֹ־בוֹ יִטְמָא עַד־
24 הָעָרֶב׃ וְאִם שָׁכֹב יִשְׁכַּב אִישׁ אֹתָהּ וּתְהִי נִדָּתָהּ עָלָיו
וְטָמֵא שִׁבְעַת יָמִים וְכָל־הַמִּשְׁכָּב אֲשֶׁר־יִשְׁכַּב עָלָיו יִטְמָא׃
כה ס וְאִשָּׁה כִּי־יָזוּב זוֹב דָּמָהּ יָמִים רַבִּים בְּלֹא עֶת־נִדָּתָהּ
אוֹ כִי־תָזוּב עַל־נִדָּתָהּ כָּל־יְמֵי זוֹב טֻמְאָתָהּ כִּימֵי נִדָּתָהּ
26 תִּהְיֶה טְמֵאָה הִוא׃ כָּל־הַמִּשְׁכָּב אֲשֶׁר־תִּשְׁכַּב עָלָיו כָּל־
יְמֵי זוֹבָהּ כְּמִשְׁכַּב נִדָּתָהּ יִהְיֶה־לָּהּ וְכָל־הַכְּלִי אֲשֶׁר תֵּשֵׁב
27 עָלָיו טָמֵא יִהְיֶה כְּטֻמְאַת נִדָּתָהּ׃ וְכָל־הַנּוֹגֵעַ בָּם יִטְמָא
28 וְכִבֶּס בְּגָדָיו וְרָחַץ בַּמַּיִם וְטָמֵא עַד־הָעָרֶב׃ וְאִם־טָהֲרָה
29 מִזּוֹבָהּ וְסָפְרָה לָּהּ שִׁבְעַת יָמִים וְאַחַר תִּטְהָר׃ * וּבַיּוֹם שביעי
הַשְּׁמִינִי תִּקַּח־לָהּ שְׁתֵּי תֹרִים אוֹ שְׁנֵי בְּנֵי יוֹנָה וְהֵבִיאָה

v. 29. מלרע

31–33. CONCLUDING ADMONITION

31. *ye separate*. Or, 'ye warn.' The subject is Moses and Aaron, to whom these regulations had been addressed.

ל אֹתָם אֶל־הַכֹּהֵן אֶל־פֶּתַח אֹהֶל מוֹעֵד׃ וְעָשָׂה הַכֹּהֵן
אֶת־הָאֶחָד חַטָּאת וְאֶת־הָאֶחָד עֹלָה וְכִפֶּר עָלֶיהָ הַכֹּהֵן
מפטיר 31 לִפְנֵי יְהוָה מִזּוֹב טֻמְאָתָהּ׃ * וְהִזַּרְתֶּם אֶת־בְּנֵי־יִשְׂרָאֵל
מִטֻּמְאָתָם וְלֹא יָמֻתוּ בְּטֻמְאָתָם בְּטַמְּאָם אֶת־מִשְׁכָּנִי אֲשֶׁר
32 בְּתוֹכָם׃ זֹאת תּוֹרַת הַזָּב וַאֲשֶׁר תֵּצֵא מִמֶּנּוּ שִׁכְבַת־זֶרַע
33 לְטָמְאָה־בָהּ׃ וְהַדָּוָה בְּנִדָּתָהּ וְהַזָּב אֶת־זוֹבוֹ לַזָּכָר וְלַנְּקֵבָה
וּלְאִישׁ אֲשֶׁר יִשְׁכַּב עִם־טְמֵאָה׃

the other for a burnt-offering; and the priest shall make atonement for her before the LORD for the issue of her uncleanness.* m. ¶ 31. Thus shall ye separate the children of Israel from their uncleanness; that they die not in their uncleanness, when they defile My tabernacle that is in the midst of them. ¶ 32. This is the law of him that hath an issue, and of him from whom the flow of seed goeth out, so that he is unclean thereby; 33. and of her that is sick with her impurity, and of them that have an issue, whether it be a man, or a woman; and of him that lieth with her that is unclean.

defile My tabernacle. These words are the basis for the deduction of the Rabbis that these laws applied only to one about to enter the Sanctuary, or to come in contact with, or partake of, sacred things.

HAFTORAH METZORA הפטרת מצרע

II KINGS VII, 3-20

CHAPTER VII

CAP. VII. ז

3 וְאַרְבָּעָה אֲנָשִׁים הָיוּ מְצֹרָעִים פֶּתַח
הַשָּׁעַר וַיֹּאמְרוּ אִישׁ אֶל־רֵעֵהוּ מָה אֲנַחְנוּ יֹשְׁבִים פֹּה
4 עַד־מָתְנוּ׃ אִם־אָמַרְנוּ נָבוֹא הָעִיר וְהָרָעָב בָּעִיר וָמַתְנוּ
שָׁם וְאִם־יָשַׁבְנוּ פֹה וָמָתְנוּ וְעַתָּה לְכוּ וְנִפְּלָה אֶל־מַחֲנֵה
ה אֲרָם אִם־יְחַיֻּנוּ נִחְיֶה וְאִם־יְמִיתֻנוּ וָמָתְנוּ׃ וַיָּקֻמוּ בַנֶּשֶׁף

3. Now there were four leprous men at the entrance of the gate; and they said one to another: 'Why sit we here until we die? 4. If we say: We will enter into the city, then the famine is in the city, and we shall die there; and if we sit still here, we die also. Now therefore come, and let us fall unto the host of the Arameans; if they save us alive, we shall live; and if they kill us, we shall but die.' 5. And they rose up in the twilight, to go unto the camp of the

The theme of this Haftorah is again an incident in the life of Elisha during the siege of Samaria by the Syrians. It tells of four lepers who were facing death in that time of horror. All available food had been consumed, and even the refuse of the streets was sold at famine prices. The inhabitants were in the last stages of despair, and the king learns of women who had arranged to use their children for food! He blames the Prophet Elisha for all these calamities, as the Prophet no doubt encouraged the people to continue the resistance, and the king is determined to put him to death. However, when faced by the Prophet, he is overawed. Elisha then makes the astonishing announcement that the very next day God would send relief, and the famine would be at an end. A courtier standing by breaks out in mockery at the prediction. Signal punishment is announced to overtake him for this act of unbelief.

CHAPTER VII

3. *at the entrance of the gate.* Lepers were not permitted to live in the city. In the circumstances, they would naturally keep as near the entrance as possible.

4. *fall unto.* Desert to.

if they save us alive. If the Syrians killed them they would be no worse off; but the Syrians might spare their lives.

6. *the noise of a great host.* Thinking that mighty hosts were advancing against them. 'It was the result of one of those sudden unaccountable panics to which huge, unwieldy, heterogeneous Eastern armies, which have no organized system of sentries and no trained discipline, are constantly liable' (Farrar). The cradle of the Hittite power was in N. Syria, and Egypt was in the South. Accordingly the Syrians thought they were entrapped, and fled in confusion.

Arameans; and when they were come to
the outermost part of the camp of the
Arameans, behold, there was no man there.
6. For the LORD had made the host of the
Arameans to hear a noise of chariots, and a
noise of horses, even the noise of a great
host; and they said one to another: 'Lo,
the king of Israel hath hired against us the
kings of the Hittites, and the kings of the
Egyptians, to come upon us.' 7. Where-
fore they arose and fled in the twilight, and
left their tents, and their horses, and their
asses, even the camp as it was, and fled for
their life. 8. And when these lepers came to
the outermost part of the camp, they went
into one tent, and did eat and drink, and
carried thence silver, and gold, and raiment,
and went and hid it; and they came back,
and entered into another tent, and carried
thence also, and went and hid it. ¶ 9. Then
they said one to another: 'We do not well;
this day is a day of good tidings, and we
hold our peace; if we tarry till the morning
light, punishment will overtake us; now
therefore come, let us go and tell the king's
household.' 10. So they came and called
unto the porters of the city; and they told
them, saying: 'We came to the camp of the
Arameans, and, behold, there was no man
there, neither voice of man, but the horses
tied, and the asses tied, and the tents as
they were.' 11. And the porters called, and
they told it to the king's household within.
12. And the king arose in the night, and said
unto his servants: 'I will now tell you what
the Arameans have done to us. They know
that we are hungry; therefore are they gone
out of the camp to hide themselves in the
field, saying: When they come out of the
city, we shall take them alive, and get into
the city.' 13. And one of his servants
answered and said: 'Let some take, I pray
thee, five of the horses that remain, which
are left in the city—behold, they are as
all the multitude of Israel that are left in it;
behold, they are as all the multitude of
Israel that are consumed—and let us send
and see.' 14. They took therefore two
chariots with horses; and the king sent
after the host of the Arameans, saying:
'Go and see.' 15. And they went after

לָבוֹא אֶל־מַחֲנֵה אֲרָם וַיָּבֹאוּ עַד־קְצֵה מַחֲנֵה אֲרָם וְהִנֵּה
6 אֵין־שָׁם אִישׁ׃ וַאדֹנָי הִשְׁמִיעַ ׀ אֶת־מַחֲנֵה אֲרָם קוֹל
רֶכֶב וְקוֹל סוּס קוֹל חַיִל גָּדוֹל וַיֹּאמְרוּ אִישׁ אֶל־אָחִיו
הִנֵּה שָׂכַר־עָלֵינוּ מֶלֶךְ יִשְׂרָאֵל אֶת־מַלְכֵי הַחִתִּים וְאֶת־
7 מַלְכֵי מִצְרַיִם לָבוֹא עָלֵינוּ׃ וַיָּקוּמוּ וַיָּנוּסוּ בַנֶּשֶׁף וַיַּעַזְבוּ
אֶת־אָהֳלֵיהֶם וְאֶת־סוּסֵיהֶם וְאֶת־חֲמֹרֵיהֶם הַמַּחֲנֶה כַּאֲשֶׁר
8 הִיא וַיָּנֻסוּ אֶל־נַפְשָׁם׃ וַיָּבֹאוּ הַמְצֹרָעִים הָאֵלֶּה עַד־
קְצֵה הַמַּחֲנֶה וַיָּבֹאוּ אֶל־אֹהֶל אֶחָד וַיֹּאכְלוּ וַיִּשְׁתּוּ וַיִּשְׂאוּ
מִשָּׁם כֶּסֶף וְזָהָב וּבְגָדִים וַיֵּלְכוּ וַיַּטְמִנוּ וַיָּשֻׁבוּ וַיָּבֹאוּ
9 אֶל־אֹהֶל אַחֵר וַיִּשְׂאוּ מִשָּׁם וַיֵּלְכוּ וַיַּטְמִנוּ׃ וַיֹּאמְרוּ אִישׁ
אֶל־רֵעֵהוּ לֹא־כֵן ׀ אֲנַחְנוּ עֹשִׂים הַיּוֹם הַזֶּה יוֹם־בְּשֹׂרָה
הוּא וַאֲנַחְנוּ מַחְשִׁים וְחִכִּינוּ עַד־אוֹר הַבֹּקֶר וּמְצָאָנוּ
10 עָווֹן וְעַתָּה לְכוּ וְנָבֹאָה וְנַגִּידָה בֵּית הַמֶּלֶךְ׃ וַיָּבֹאוּ
וַיִּקְרְאוּ אֶל־שֹׁעֵר הָעִיר וַיַּגִּידוּ לָהֶם לֵאמֹר בָּאנוּ אֶל־
מַחֲנֵה אֲרָם וְהִנֵּה אֵין־שָׁם אִישׁ וְקוֹל אָדָם כִּי אִם־
הַסּוּס אָסוּר וְהַחֲמוֹר אָסוּר וְאֹהָלִים כַּאֲשֶׁר הֵמָּה׃
11 וַיִּקְרָא הַשֹּׁעֲרִים וַיַּגִּידוּ בֵּית הַמֶּלֶךְ פְּנִימָה׃ וַיָּקָם הַמֶּלֶךְ
12 לַיְלָה וַיֹּאמֶר אֶל־עֲבָדָיו אַגִּידָה־נָּא לָכֶם אֵת אֲשֶׁר־עָשׂוּ
לָנוּ אֲרָם יָדְעוּ כִּי־רְעֵבִים אֲנַחְנוּ וַיֵּצְאוּ מִן־הַמַּחֲנֶה
לְהֵחָבֵה בַהשָּׂדֶה לֵאמֹר כִּי־יֵצְאוּ מִן־הָעִיר וְנִתְפְּשֵׂם
13 חַיִּים וְאֶל־הָעִיר נָבֹא׃ וַיַּעַן אֶחָד מֵעֲבָדָיו וַיֹּאמֶר וְיִקְחוּ־
נָא חֲמִשָּׁה מִן־הַסּוּסִים הַנִּשְׁאָרִים אֲשֶׁר נִשְׁאֲרוּ־בָהּ
הִנָּם כְּכָל־הֶהָמוֹן יִשְׂרָאֵל אֲשֶׁר נִשְׁאֲרוּ־בָהּ הִנָּם כְּכָל־
14 הֲמוֹן יִשְׂרָאֵל אֲשֶׁר־תָּמּוּ וְנִשְׁלְחָה וְנִרְאֶה׃ וַיִּקְחוּ שְׁנֵי
רֶכֶב סוּסִים וַיִּשְׁלַח הַמֶּלֶךְ אַחֲרֵי מַחֲנֵה־אֲרָם לֵאמֹר

v. 11. נ"א ויקראו v. 12. בשדה ק' v. 13. המון ק'

9. *punishment will overtake us.* lit. 'guilt will find us,' for having delayed to bring the good news to their starving brethren in the city. The Heb. word *iniquity* (עון) connotes also *punishment* for iniquity.

10. *the porters.* The keepers of the city gate.

11. *the porters called.* The guardians of the city gate called the guardians of the king's gate who told the news within the royal household (Ralbag).

12. *we shall take them alive.* The king suspects a stratagem on the part of the Syrians to lure him and his army out of the city and capture them.

13. *behold . . . left in it; behold . . . consumed.* Whether they share the fate of those who are still alive in the city or those who have already perished, they are all destined to the same end—death by starvation. The few horses may, therefore, well be risked in the enterprise.

them unto the Jordan; and, lo, all the way was full of garments and vessels, which the Arameans had cast away in their haste. And the messengers returned, and told the king. ¶ 16. And the people went out, and spoiled the camp of the Arameans. So a measure of fine flour was sold for a shekel, and two measures of barley for a shekel, according to the word of the LORD. 17. And the king appointed the captain on whose hand he leaned to have the charge of the gate; and the people trod upon him in the gate, and he died as the man of God had said, who spoke when the king came down to him. 18. And it came to pass, as the man of God had spoken to the king, saying: 'Two measures of barley for a shekel, and a measure of fine flour for a shekel, shall be to-morrow about this time in the gate of Samaria'; 19. and that captain answered the man of God, and said: 'Now, behold, if the LORD should make windows in heaven, might such a thing be?' and he said: 'Behold, thou shalt see it with thine eyes, but shalt not eat thereof'; 20. it came to pass even so unto him; for the people trod upon him in the gate, and he died.

טו לְכוּ וּרְאוּ׃ וַיֵּלְכוּ אַחֲרֵיהֶם עַד־הַיַּרְדֵּן וְהִנֵּה כָל־הַדֶּרֶךְ
מְלֵאָה בְגָדִים וְכֵלִים אֲשֶׁר־הִשְׁלִיכוּ אֲרָם בְּהֵחָפְזָם וַיָּשֻׁבוּ
16 הַמַּלְאָכִים וַיַּגִּדוּ לַמֶּלֶךְ׃ וַיֵּצֵא הָעָם וַיָּבֹזּוּ אֵת מַחֲנֵה
אֲרָם וַיְהִי סְאָה־סֹלֶת בְּשֶׁקֶל וְסָאתַיִם שְׂעֹרִים בְּשֶׁקֶל
17 כִּדְבַר יְהוָה׃ וְהַמֶּלֶךְ הִפְקִיד אֶת־הַשָּׁלִישׁ אֲשֶׁר נִשְׁעָן
עַל־יָדוֹ עַל־הַשַּׁעַר וַיִּרְמְסֻהוּ הָעָם בַּשַּׁעַר וַיָּמֹת כַּאֲשֶׁר
18 דִּבֶּר אִישׁ הָאֱלֹהִים אֲשֶׁר דִּבֶּר בְּרֶדֶת הַמֶּלֶךְ אֵלָיו׃ וַיְהִי
כְּדַבֵּר אִישׁ הָאֱלֹהִים אֶל־הַמֶּלֶךְ לֵאמֹר סָאתַיִם שְׂעֹרִים
בְּשֶׁקֶל וּסְאָה־סֹלֶת בְּשֶׁקֶל יִהְיֶה כָּעֵת מָחָר בְּשַׁעַר
19 שֹׁמְרוֹן׃ וַיַּעַן הַשָּׁלִישׁ אֶת־אִישׁ הָאֱלֹהִים וַיֹּאמַר וְהִנֵּה
יְהוָה עֹשֶׂה אֲרֻבּוֹת בַּשָּׁמַיִם הֲיִהְיֶה כַּדָּבָר הַזֶּה וַיֹּאמֶר
כ הִנְּכָה רֹאֶה בְּעֵינֶיךָ וּמִשָּׁם לֹא תֹאכֵל׃ וַיְהִי־לוֹ כֵּן וַיִּרְמְסוּ
אֹתוֹ הָעָם בַּשַּׁעַר וַיָּמֹת׃

v. 15. בחפזם ק'

16. *according to the word of the LORD.* See *v.* 1 and 2 of this chapter.

17–20. The fulfilment of Elisha's prophecy against the king's officer and his punishment for the scoffing spirit in which he received the Prophet's hopeful words. Scoffing at matters sacred was always regarded by the Jewish Teachers as a heinous offence. 'Four classes shall not see God—the scoffer, the liar, the slanderer and the hypocrite' (Talmud).

17. *on whose hand he leaned.* The king's confidential counsellor.

19. *behold, if the LORD . . . thing be?* Better, *Behold, the LORD is about to make windows in heaven! Can this thing be?* The first utterance is a mocking assertion; the second, an unbelieving question.

20. *for the people trod upon him.* He was knocked down and trampled to death in the rush of the people who were maddened by famine, and hastening to the Syrian camp for food.

16

CHAPTER XVI

1. And the LORD spoke unto Moses, after the death of the two sons of Aaron, when they drew near before the LORD, and died; 2. and the LORD said unto Moses: 'Speak unto Aaron thy brother, that he come not at all times into the holy place within the veil, before the ark-cover which is upon the ark; that he die not; for I appear in the cloud upon the ark-cover. 3. Herewith shall Aaron come into the holy place: with a young bullock for a sin-offering, and a ram for a burnt-offering. 4. He shall put on the holy linen tunic, and he shall have the linen breeches upon his flesh, and shall be girdled with the linen girdle, and with

CAP. XVI. טז

טז פ פ כט 29

א וַיְדַבֵּר יְהוָה אֶל־מֹשֶׁה אַחֲרֵי מוֹת שְׁנֵי בְּנֵי אַהֲרֹן בְּקָרְבָתָם
2 לִפְנֵי־יְהוָה וַיָּמֻתוּ׃ וַיֹּאמֶר יְהוָה אֶל־מֹשֶׁה דַּבֵּר אֶל־אַהֲרֹן
אָחִיךָ וְאַל־יָבֹא בְכָל־עֵת אֶל־הַקֹּדֶשׁ מִבֵּית לַפָּרֹכֶת אֶל־
פְּנֵי הַכַּפֹּרֶת אֲשֶׁר עַל־הָאָרֹן וְלֹא יָמוּת כִּי בֶּעָנָן אֵרָאֶה
3 עַל־הַכַּפֹּרֶת׃ בְּזֹאת יָבֹא אַהֲרֹן אֶל־הַקֹּדֶשׁ בְּפַר בֶּן
4 בָּקָר לְחַטָּאת וְאַיִל לְעֹלָה׃ כְּתֹנֶת־בַּד קֹדֶשׁ יִלְבָּשׁ וּמִכְנְסֵי־

v. 4. קמץ ברביע

VI. ACHAREY MOS

(CHAPTERS XVI–XVIII)

THE DAY OF ATONEMENT

CHAPTER XVI, 1–28. THE RITUAL OF THE ANNUAL CEREMONY OF PURIFICATION IN THE SANCTUARY

1. *after the death.* The unfortunate incident narrated in x, 1–3 gave occasion for instructions as to time and manner in which the High Priest might enter the Holy Place. The death of Aaron's sons was a solemn warning addressed to the High Priest, that any desecration, whether it be on the part of the High Priest, or an ordinary priest, or the laity (see xv, 31), would be severely punished. See comment on x, 1 as to the reasons for the death of Aaron's sons—intoxication, unholy ambition, arbitrary tampering with the service, and introducing 'strange fire' into the Sanctuary. The story of Nadab and Abihu is a parable for Young Israel in every generation. 'He who is affected to tears while reading this portion of the Torah, taking its teaching to heart, will win forgiveness for his own sins and the blessing of old age for his children' (Zohar).

2. *that he come not at all times.* Only once a year, on the Day of Atonement, and with a due observance of prescribed rites.

the veil. Heb. *parocheth*, which separates the Holy Place from the Holy of Holies.

ark-cover. The solid gold plate which formed the cover for the Ark, on which the cherubim were fixed; see on Exod. xxv, 17.

the cloud. In which God manifests His presence; Exod. XL, 35; Isa. VI, 4.

3–10. HOW AARON IS TO COME INTO THE HOLY PLACE, HIS ATTIRE, AND THE OFFERING HE IS TO BRING

3. *herewith.* With the offerings and ceremonies set forth in the following verses. In later times the High Priest began to prepare himself for his functions seven days before the Sacred Day. During that time, he lived apart in a special portion of the Temple, and the elders read and expounded to him the ordinances of this chapter. The night prior to the Sacred Day he would pass sleepless, and be kept awake by readings from Job, Ezra, Chronicles and Daniel.

holy place. Not that he is to take the animals into the Holy Place, but their sacrifice is part of the prerequisite ceremony for entering there.

bullock . . . ram. These offerings are personal to the High Priest, and must be his own property. The atonement for his own sins was his first act on the Great Day. Only when purged of his own sin, was he fitted to secure forgiveness for the sins of others.

4. *holy garments.* In the Holy of Holies, he was not to be attired in his golden vestments, which on all other occasions he was to wear for 'splendour and distinction', but in simple garments of white linen—emblems of the lowliness and purity of thought demanded by the Sacred Day. For the same reason, white linen garments were for many centuries worn, and in some communities are still worn, by worshippers on the Day of Atonement. The Rabbis gave an additional reason for this custom. 'When men are summoned before an earthly ruler to defend themselves against some charge, they appear downcast and dressed in black like mourners. Israel appears before God arrayed in white, as if going to a feast, confident that all who return penitently to their Maker will receive not condemnation but pardon at His hands.'

the linen mitre shall he be attired; they are the holy garments; and he shall bathe his flesh in water, and put them on. 5. And he shall take of the congregation of the children of Israel two he-goats for a sin-offering, and one ram for a burnt-offering. 6. And Aaron shall present the bullock of the sin-offering, which is for himself, and make atonement for himself, and for his house. 7. And he shall take the two goats, and set them before the LORD at the door of the tent of meeting. 8. And Aaron shall cast lots upon the two goats: one lot for the LORD, and the other lot for Azazel. 9. And Aaron shall present the goat upon which the lot fell for the LORD, and offer him for a sin-offering. 10. But the goat, on which the lot fell for Azazel, shall be set alive before the LORD, to make atonement over him, to send him

בַּד יִהְיוּ עַל־בְּשָׂרוֹ וּבְאַבְנֵט בַּד יַחְגֹּר וּבְמִצְנֶפֶת בַּד יִצְנֹף
ה בִּגְדֵי־קֹדֶשׁ הֵם וְרָחַץ בַּמַּיִם אֶת־בְּשָׂרוֹ וּלְבֵשָׁם׃ וּמֵאֵת
עֲדַת בְּנֵי יִשְׂרָאֵל יִקַּח שְׁנֵי־שְׂעִירֵי עִזִּים לְחַטָּאת וְאַיִל
6 אֶחָד לְעֹלָה׃ וְהִקְרִיב אַהֲרֹן אֶת־פַּר הַחַטָּאת אֲשֶׁר־לוֹ
7 וְכִפֶּר בַּעֲדוֹ וּבְעַד בֵּיתוֹ׃ וְלָקַח אֶת־שְׁנֵי הַשְּׂעִירִם וְהֶעֱמִיד
8 אֹתָם לִפְנֵי יְהוָה פֶּתַח אֹהֶל מוֹעֵד׃ וְנָתַן אַהֲרֹן עַל־שְׁנֵי
הַשְּׂעִירִם גֹּרָלוֹת גּוֹרָל אֶחָד לַיהוָה וְגוֹרָל אֶחָד לַעֲזָאזֵל׃
9 וְהִקְרִיב אַהֲרֹן אֶת־הַשָּׂעִיר אֲשֶׁר עָלָה עָלָיו הַגּוֹרָל לַיהוָה
י וְעָשָׂהוּ חַטָּאת׃ וְהַשָּׂעִיר אֲשֶׁר עָלָה עָלָיו הַגּוֹרָל לַעֲזָאזֵל
יָעֳמַד־חַי לִפְנֵי יְהוָה לְכַפֵּר עָלָיו לְשַׁלַּח אֹתוֹ לַעֲזָאזֵל

v. 8. בראש עמוד סימן בי״ה שמו

5. *of the congregation.* Rites of purification were to be performed for the community as a body, and each individual was to regard himself as essentially a unit in the Brotherhood of Israel. The Confession on the Atonement Day is in the plural: '*We* have transgressed, *we* have dealt treacherously, etc.'; see on XXIII, 27.

6. *shall present.* The presentation is that alluded to in I, 3 f—at the entrance of the Tent of Meeting.

his house. The order of priests, who were sons of Aaron. The Rabbis, however, understood 'his house' to mean his wife; and the High Priest was not allowed to officiate on the Day of Atonement unless his wife was living at the time. In the traditional account of the rites of the Day of Atonement, preserved in the Mishnah, the High Priest made this confession: 'O God, I have sinned, I have committed iniquity, I have transgressed against Thee, I and my household. I beseech Thee by Thy Name, grant Thou atonement for the sins, and for the iniquities, and for the transgressions wherein I have sinned, and committed iniquity and transgressed against Thee, I and my household.' In his confession, the High Priest used the ineffable Name of God, the Tetragrammaton, in its true pronunciation; whereupon the assembled priests and people in the Court prostrated themselves to the ground, and exclaimed, 'Blessed be His Name, Whose glorious kingdom is for ever and ever.'

8. *lots.* By taking from an urn tablets, alike in size and shape, describing the destination of each animal (Mishnah).

Azazel. Better, *dismissal.* In the Septuagint this mysterious Hebrew word is rendered, 'the one to be sent away'; which agrees with the term used in the Mishnah. The Authorised Version, following the Vulgate, has 'scapegoat'; *i.e.* the goat driven, or escaping, into the wilderness. The Heb. *Azazel,* however, is not a proper name, but a rare Hebrew noun (עזלזל contracted to עזאזל) meaning, 'dismissal' or, 'entire removal' (RV Margin, Gesenius, Hoffmann, and the Oxford Hebrew Dictionary). It is the ancient technical term for the entire removal of the sin and guilt of the community, that was symbolized by the sending away of the goat into the wilderness.

In the Talmud, Azazel was translated by 'steep mountain', and was applied to the rock in the wilderness from which in later times the animal was hurled.

At an early period, however, the word עזאזל became personified, just as were the Hebrew words for the Underworld (Sheol) and Destruction (Abaddon). Thereupon, the strangest theories and legends grew up in connection with 'Azazel'. In certain Jewish traditions, for example, Azazel, or Azalzel, is foremost among the Fallen Angels who taught unrighteousness to the children of men (Book of Enoch). This view that the word *Azazel* is the name of a demon in the wilderness was shared by Ibn Ezra and Nachmanides, and is to-day adopted by most Bible critics. But it is quite untenable. The offering of sacrifices to 'satyrs' is spoken of as a heinous crime in the very next chapter, XVII, 7; homage to a demon of the wilderness cannot, therefore, be associated with the holiest of the Temple-rites in the chapter immediately preceding.

9. *offer him.* lit. 'make it,' *i.e.* appoint it. The offering of this goat is not mentioned until *v.* 15. The High Priest exclaimed over it, 'for the LORD, a sin offering' (Sifra).

10. *over him.* Refers to the confession of sins over the head of the animal.

away for Azazel into the wilderness. 11. And Aaron shall present the bullock of the sin-offering, which is for himself, and shall make atonement for himself, and for his house, and shall kill the bullock of the sin-offering which is for himself. 12. And he shall take a censer full of coals of fire from off the altar before the LORD, and his hands full of sweet incense beaten small, and bring it within the veil. 13. And he shall put the incense upon the fire before the LORD, that the cloud of the incense may cover the ark-cover that is upon the testimony, that he die not. 14. And he shall take of the blood of the bullock, and sprinkle it with his finger upon the ark-cover on the east; and before the ark-cover shall he sprinkle of the blood with his finger seven times. 15. Then shall he kill the goat of the sin-offering, that is for the people, and bring his blood within the veil, and do with his blood as he did with the blood of the bullock, and sprinkle it upon the ark-cover, and before the ark-cover. 16. And he shall make atonement for the holy place, because of the uncleannesses of the children of Israel, and because of their transgressions, even all their sins; and so shall he do for the tent of meeting, that dwelleth with them in the midst of their uncleannesses. 17. And there shall be no man in the tent of meeting when he goeth in to make atonement in the holy place, until he come out, and have made

11 הַמִּדְבָּרָה׃ וְהִקְרִיב אַהֲרֹן אֶת־פַּר הַחַטָּאת אֲשֶׁר־לוֹ
וְכִפֶּר בַּעֲדוֹ וּבְעַד בֵּיתוֹ וְשָׁחַט אֶת־פַּר הַחַטָּאת אֲשֶׁר־לוֹ׃
12 וְלָקַח מְלֹא־הַמַּחְתָּה גַּחֲלֵי־אֵשׁ מֵעַל הַמִּזְבֵּחַ מִלִּפְנֵי יְהוָה
וּמְלֹא חָפְנָיו קְטֹרֶת סַמִּים דַּקָּה וְהֵבִיא מִבֵּית לַפָּרֹכֶת׃
13 וְנָתַן אֶת־הַקְּטֹרֶת עַל־הָאֵשׁ לִפְנֵי יְהוָה וְכִסָּה ׀ עֲנַן הַקְּטֹרֶת
14 אֶת־הַכַּפֹּרֶת אֲשֶׁר עַל־הָעֵדוּת וְלֹא יָמוּת׃ וְלָקַח מִדַּם
הַפָּר וְהִזָּה בְאֶצְבָּעוֹ עַל־פְּנֵי הַכַּפֹּרֶת קֵדְמָה וְלִפְנֵי הַכַּפֹּרֶת
טו יַזֶּה שֶׁבַע־פְּעָמִים מִן־הַדָּם בְּאֶצְבָּעוֹ׃ וְשָׁחַט אֶת־שְׂעִיר
הַחַטָּאת אֲשֶׁר לָעָם וְהֵבִיא אֶת־דָּמוֹ אֶל־מִבֵּית לַפָּרֹכֶת
וְעָשָׂה אֶת־דָּמוֹ כַּאֲשֶׁר עָשָׂה לְדַם הַפָּר וְהִזָּה אֹתוֹ עַל־
16 הַכַּפֹּרֶת וְלִפְנֵי הַכַּפֹּרֶת׃ וְכִפֶּר עַל־הַקֹּדֶשׁ מִטֻּמְאֹת בְּנֵי
יִשְׂרָאֵל וּמִפִּשְׁעֵיהֶם לְכָל־חַטֹּאתָם וְכֵן יַעֲשֶׂה לְאֹהֶל מוֹעֵד
17 הַשֹּׁכֵן אִתָּם בְּתוֹךְ טֻמְאֹתָם׃ וְכָל־אָדָם לֹא־יִהְיֶה ׀ בְּאֹהֶל
מוֹעֵד בְּבֹאוֹ לְכַפֵּר בַּקֹּדֶשׁ עַד־צֵאתוֹ וְכִפֶּר בַּעֲדוֹ וּבְעַד

11–28. DETAILED ACCOUNT OF THE CEREMONIAL OF PURIFICATION

11. *present.* lit. 'bring it near,' to the Altar to be slain.

and for his house. According to the Rabbis, 'house' here refers to the order of priests; and the High Priest repeated his confession (as in *v.* 6), adding after 'my household' the words, 'and the sons of Aaron, Thy holy people.'

12. *a censer.* Heb. 'the censer'; a censer made of gold was, according to the Mishnah, used on this day.

the altar. The brazen Altar in the Fore-court.

before the LORD. See on I, 5.

within the veil. This is the first entrance of the High Priest into the innermost part of the Holy of Holies.

13. *cloud of the incense.* The purpose of the incense-smoke was to create a screen which would prevent the High Priest from gazing upon the Holy Presence.

On returning from the Holy of Holies, the High Priest in later times offered the following prayer: 'May it please Thee, O LORD our God, that this year may be a year of rain. Let there not be wanting a ruler belonging to the House of Judah. Let not Thy people Israel be in want, so that one Israelite may not be forced to beg his sustenance from another or from strangers; and hearken not to the prayer of travellers'—since they pray for rainless weather, which is a calamity in the Holy Land (Talmud).

14. *sprinkle . . . upon the ark-cover.* This act constituted the rite of expiation for the High Priest and the priestly order.

15. *then shall he kill.* The goat which had been designated by lot 'for the LORD' (*v.* 9).

16. *uncleannesses.* Besides the annual rite of atonement for the Community, there was also once a year a ceremonial cleansing of the Sanctuary from defilement through the presence of Israelites who were ritually unclean.

transgressions. This is defined by the Rabbis as alluding to the wilful entering of the holy precincts by a person who knew himself to be defiled. By 'sins' is meant those who entered without the knowledge that they were unclean.

17. *no man.* Not even the priests were to remain in the Tent while the ceremony of atonement was being performed. The awe of the occasion would be increased by the High Priest being quite alone in the Sanctuary.

atonement for himself, and for his household, and for all the assembly of Israel.* ii. 18. And he shall go out unto the altar that is before the LORD, and make atonement for it; and shall take of the blood of the bullock, and of the blood of the goat, and put it upon the horns of the altar round about. 19. And he shall sprinkle of the blood upon it with his finger seven times, and cleanse it, and hallow it from the uncleannesses of the children of Israel. 20. And when he hath made an end of atoning for the holy place, and the tent of meeting, and the altar, he shall present the live goat. 21. And Aaron shall lay both his hands upon the head of the live goat, and confess over him all the iniquities of the children of Israel, and all their transgressions, even all their sins; and he shall put them upon the head of the goat, and shall send him away by the hand of an appointed man into the wilderness. 22. And the goat shall bear upon him all their iniquities unto a land which is cut off; and he shall let go the goat in the wilderness. 23. And Aaron shall come into the tent of meeting, and shall put off the linen garments, which he put on when he went into the holy place, and shall leave them there. 24. And he shall bathe his flesh in water in a holy place, and put on

שני 18 בֵּיתוֹ וּבְעַד כָּל־קְהַל יִשְׂרָאֵל׃ וְיָצָא אֶל־הַמִּזְבֵּחַ אֲשֶׁר
לִפְנֵי־יְהוָה וְכִפֶּר עָלָיו וְלָקַח מִדַּם הַפָּר וּמִדַּם הַשָּׂעִיר
19 וְנָתַן עַל־קַרְנוֹת הַמִּזְבֵּחַ סָבִיב׃ וְהִזָּה עָלָיו מִן־הַדָּם
בְּאֶצְבָּעוֹ שֶׁבַע פְּעָמִים וְטִהֲרוֹ וְקִדְּשׁוֹ מִטֻּמְאֹת בְּנֵי יִשְׂרָאֵל׃
כ וְכִלָּה מִכַּפֵּר אֶת־הַקֹּדֶשׁ וְאֶת־אֹהֶל מוֹעֵד וְאֶת־הַמִּזְבֵּחַ
21 וְהִקְרִיב אֶת־הַשָּׂעִיר הֶחָי׃ וְסָמַךְ אַהֲרֹן אֶת־שְׁתֵּי יָדָו עַל־
רֹאשׁ הַשָּׂעִיר הַחַי וְהִתְוַדָּה עָלָיו אֶת־כָּל־עֲוֺנֹת בְּנֵי יִשְׂרָאֵל
וְאֶת־כָּל־פִּשְׁעֵיהֶם לְכָל־חַטֹּאתָם וְנָתַן אֹתָם עַל־רֹאשׁ
22 הַשָּׂעִיר וְשִׁלַּח בְּיַד־אִישׁ עִתִּי הַמִּדְבָּרָה׃ וְנָשָׂא הַשָּׂעִיר
עָלָיו אֶת־כָּל־עֲוֺנֹתָם אֶל־אֶרֶץ גְּזֵרָה וְשִׁלַּח אֶת־הַשָּׂעִיר
23 בַּמִּדְבָּר׃ וּבָא אַהֲרֹן אֶל־אֹהֶל מוֹעֵד וּפָשַׁט אֶת־בִּגְדֵי
24 הַבָּד אֲשֶׁר לָבַשׁ בְּבֹאוֹ אֶל־הַקֹּדֶשׁ וְהִנִּיחָם שָׁם׃ וְרָחַץ
אֶת־בְּשָׂרוֹ בַמַּיִם בְּמָקוֹם קָדוֹשׁ וְלָבַשׁ אֶת־בְּגָדָיו וְיָצָא

v. 21. ידיו קרי

18. *shall go out. i.e.* he shall go in the direction of the exit, towards the golden Altar of Incense.

19. *cleanse it.* From the defilement of the past year.
hallow it. Reconsecrate it for sacred use in the coming year.

20. *and the altar.* The golden Altar.
he shall present. Better, *he brings near to himself.* The ceremony of the 'scapegoat' took place in the Court.

21. *confess.* The High Priest placed his two hands on the goat to be sent away, and thereby, having confessed, symbolically transferred the people's sins to the head of the animal. The form of confession, as given in the Mishnah, was: 'O God, Thy people, the House of Israel, have sinned, they have committed iniquity, and they have transgressed against Thee.'
iniquities. The Heb. עון lit. means 'crookedness' and denotes a wilful departure from the law of God. Unlike the ordinary sacrifices which were limited in their expiatory power to *involuntary* transgressions, the Day of Atonement and its sacrifices purged away wilful iniquities as well as errors and involuntary sins.
transgressions. The Heb. פשע is stronger than 'transgression'; its lit. translation is 'rebellion'.
sins. The Heb. חטא denotes an unintentional deviation from the right path.
appointed. Or, 'in readiness' for that purpose.

22. *a land which is cut off.* A district effectually cut off from the encampment of Israel, so that the animal could not wander back. In later times the animal was cast down a precipice (see on *v.* 8), as it was no longer possible to send the goat to a place whence it would not return to inhabited parts. This chapter narrates the primitive custom in accordance with conditions in the Mosaic age, and is evidence of the antiquity of what is here described.
he shall let go. With this symbolic carrying away of the people's sins, cf. Micah VII, 19, 'Thou wilt cast all their sins into the depths of the sea.' These Prophetic words led to the institution of a similar rite—*Tashlich*—in connection with the New Year.

23. *Aaron shall come.* According to the Talmud, this verse refers to what happened after the sacrifice of the burnt-offerings described in *v.* 24 f.

24. *in a holy place.* A special chamber in the Court for the purpose.
his burnt-offering. The ram of the High Priest (*v.* 3) and the ram of the people (*v.* 5).

his other vestments, and come forth, and offer his burnt-offering and the burnt-offering of the people, and make atonement for himself and for the people.* iii (** ii). 25. And the fat of the sin-offering shall he make smoke upon the altar. 26. And he that letteth go the goat for Azazel shall wash his clothes, and bathe his flesh in water, and afterward he may come into the camp. 27. And the bullock of the sin-offering, and the goat of the sin-offering, whose blood was brought in to make atonement in the holy place, shall be carried forth without the camp; and they shall burn in the fire their skins, and their flesh, and their dung. 28. And he that burneth them shall wash his clothes, and bathe his flesh in water, and afterward he may come into the camp. ¶ 29. And it shall be a statute for ever unto you: in the seventh month, on the tenth day of the month, ye shall afflict your souls, and shall do no manner of work, the home-born, or the stranger that sojourneth among you. 30. For on this day shall atonement be made for you, to cleanse you; from all your sins shall ye

שלישי (שני שהן מחוב') וְעָשָׂה אֶת־עֹלָתוֹ וְאֶת־עֹלַת הָעָם וְכִפֶּר בַּעֲדוֹ וּבְעַד הָעָם׃*
כה 26 וְאֵת חֵלֶב הַחַטָּאת יַקְטִיר הַמִּזְבֵּחָה׃ וְהַמְשַׁלֵּחַ אֶת־
הַשָּׂעִיר לַעֲזָאזֵל יְכַבֵּס בְּגָדָיו וְרָחַץ אֶת־בְּשָׂרוֹ בַּמָּיִם
27 וְאַחֲרֵי־כֵן יָבוֹא אֶל־הַמַּחֲנֶה׃ וְאֵת פַּר הַחַטָּאת וְאֵת ׀
שְׂעִיר הַחַטָּאת אֲשֶׁר הוּבָא אֶת־דָּמָם לְכַפֵּר בַּקֹּדֶשׁ יוֹצִיא
אֶל־מִחוּץ לַמַּחֲנֶה וְשָׂרְפוּ בָאֵשׁ אֶת־עֹרֹתָם וְאֶת־בְּשָׂרָם
28 וְאֶת־פִּרְשָׁם׃ וְהַשֹּׂרֵף אֹתָם יְכַבֵּס בְּגָדָיו וְרָחַץ אֶת־בְּשָׂרוֹ
29 בַּמָּיִם וְאַחֲרֵי־כֵן יָבוֹא אֶל־הַמַּחֲנֶה׃ וְהָיְתָה לָכֶם לְחֻקַּת
עוֹלָם בַּחֹדֶשׁ הַשְּׁבִיעִי בֶּעָשׂוֹר לַחֹדֶשׁ תְּעַנּוּ אֶת־נַפְשֹׁתֵיכֶם
וְכָל־מְלָאכָה לֹא תַעֲשׂוּ הָאֶזְרָח וְהַגֵּר הַגָּר בְּתוֹכְכֶם׃
ל כִּי־בַיּוֹם הַזֶּה יְכַפֵּר עֲלֵיכֶם לְטַהֵר אֶתְכֶם מִכֹּל חַטֹּאתֵיכֶם
31 לִפְנֵי יְהוָה תִּטְהָרוּ׃ שַׁבַּת שַׁבָּתוֹן הִיא לָכֶם וְעִנִּיתֶם

26. *wash his clothes.* Since the 'scapegoat' bore upon itself the sins of the community, the man who had been in contact with it necessarily became defiled.

29–34. INSTITUTING THE DAY OF ATONEMENT

29. *it shall be.* Refers to what follows. Atonement is not automatically secured as a result of the ceremonies allotted to the High Priest. The people, too, had their part to perform in obtaining forgiveness.

seventh month. Cf. XXIII, 27 f.

afflict your souls. This Heb. phrase well indicates the spiritual aim of fasting. As the principal source of sin is the gratification of bodily appetites, the Fast is to demonstrate to the sinner that man can conquer all physical cravings, that the spirit can always master the body. The abstention from all food and from gratification of other bodily desires, however, must be accompanied by deep remorse at having fallen short of what it was in our power to be and to do as members of the House of Israel. Without such contrite confession accompanied by the solemn resolve to abandon the way of evil, fasting in itself is not the fulfilment of the Divine command and purpose of the Day of Atonement. תשובה תפלה וצדקה—Repentance, Prayer and Beneficence—these can change the whole current of a man's life and destiny, and lead to perfect atonement. 'Let the wicked forsake his way, and the unrighteous man his thoughts: and let him return unto the LORD, and He will have mercy upon him; and to our God, for He will abundantly pardon' (Isaiah LV, 7).

the stranger. Ibn Ezra points out that it is only work that the stranger is forbidden to do. He is not compelled to 'afflict his soul'.

30. *on this day.* Called in the Talmud יומא, *the* Day; see also on Exod. XXXIV, 4. For the name *Yom ha-kippurim*, see on XXIII, 27.

shall atonement be made for you. Heb. יכפר עליכם. As the preceding and following verses describe the duties of the people on the Day, the subject of יכפר עליכם cannot be the High Priest; otherwise, he would have been specially mentioned. Rabbi Akiba held the subject to be God. 'Happy Israel—he exclaimed—before Whom do ye purify yourselves, and Who is it that purifieth you? Your Father Who is in Heaven; as it is said (Ezek. XXXVI, 25) "I will sprinkle clean water upon you, and ye shall be clean".' Note that the initiative in atonement is with the sinner. He cleanses himself on the Day of Atonement by fearless self-examination, open confession, and the resolve not to repeat the transgressions of the past year. When our Heavenly Father sees the abasement of the penitent sinner, He—and not the High Priest or any other Mediator—sprinkles, as it were, the clean waters of pardon and forgiveness upon him. 'The whole philosophy of monotheism is contained in this rallying-cry of Rabbi Akiba' (Hermann Cohen).

all your sins. Not only involuntary transgressions; see the Confession, Authorised Prayer be clean before the LORD. 31. It is a sabbath of solemn rest unto you, and ye shall afflict your souls; it is a statute for ever. 32. And the priest, who shall be anointed and who shall be consecrated to be priest in his father's stead, shall make the atonement, and shall put on the linen garments, even the holy garments. 33. And he shall make atonement for the most holy place, and he shall make atonement for the tent of meeting and for the altar; and he shall make atonement for the priests and for all the people of the assembly. 34. And this shall be an everlasting statute unto you, to make atonement for the children of Israel because of all their sins once in the year.' And he did as the LORD commanded Moses.* iv.

32 אֶת־נַפְשֹׁתֵיכֶם חֻקַּת עוֹלָם׃ וְכִפֶּר הַכֹּהֵן אֲשֶׁר־יִמְשַׁח
אֹתוֹ וַאֲשֶׁר יְמַלֵּא אֶת־יָדוֹ לְכַהֵן תַּחַת אָבִיו וְלָבַשׁ אֶת־
33 בִּגְדֵי הַבָּד בִּגְדֵי הַקֹּדֶשׁ׃ וְכִפֶּר אֶת־מִקְדַּשׁ הַקֹּדֶשׁ וְאֶת־
אֹהֶל מוֹעֵד וְאֶת־הַמִּזְבֵּחַ יְכַפֵּר וְעַל הַכֹּהֲנִים וְעַל־כָּל־עַם
34 הַקָּהָל יְכַפֵּר׃ וְהָיְתָה־זֹּאת לָכֶם לְחֻקַּת עוֹלָם לְכַפֵּר עַל־
בְּנֵי יִשְׂרָאֵל מִכָּל־חַטֹּאתָם אַחַת בַּשָּׁנָה וַיַּעַשׂ כַּאֲשֶׁר צִוָּה
יְהוָה אֶת־מֹשֶׁה׃ * פ רביעי

17 CHAPTER XVII

1. And the LORD spoke unto Moses, saying: 2. Speak unto Aaron, and unto his sons,

יז CAP. XVII. יז

א 2 וַיְדַבֵּר יְהוָה אֶל־מֹשֶׁה לֵּאמֹר׃ דַּבֵּר אֶל־אַהֲרֹן וְאֶל־בָּנָיו

Book, p. 258b and 259. Repentance can give rebellious sins the character of 'errors'; *i.e.* by his penitence, the sinner shows that his wilful sins were largely due to ignorance, and hence are treated by God as if they were 'errors'. גדולה תשובה שזדונות נעשות כשגגות. A modern philosopher of religion finds the keynote of the Day in Num. xv, 26 ('And all the congregation of the children of Israel shall be forgiven and the stranger that sojourneth among them; for in respect of all the people it was done *in error*')—the verse recited before the opening of the evening service on Kol Nidré night.

before the LORD. From Whom alone, and not from the priest or the Altar, man is to seek atonement.

The order of the Heb. words is: 'from all your sins before the LORD shall ye be clean.' Thereon Rabbi Eleazar ben Azaryah founded the sublime teaching: 'For transgressions of man against God, the Day of Atonement atones (given repentance on the part of the sinner); but for transgressions against a fellow-man the Day of Atonement does not atone, unless and until he has conciliated his fellow-man and redressed the wrong he has done him.' The Confession (וידוי) deals almost exclusively with moral trespasses against our fellowmen. Especially numerous are the terms denoting sins committed with the tongue—falsehood, slander, frivolous and unclean speech. The Rabbis, who certainly did not underrate ritual offences, deemed moral shortcomings to be infinitely graver, and hence confined the Confession to them.

31–34. These verses explain that the ceremonies of the Day of Atonement are for all time. Although the Torah has been naming 'Aaron' as the atoning priest, whoever had been duly consecrated after him to the High Priest's office was eligible to perform the sacred functions prescribed in this chapter.

31. *sabbath of solemn rest.* The repetition is to impress the fact that cessation from labour and fasting must continue even when there are no longer priestly ceremonies (Wessely).

34. *everlasting statute.* The Day of Atonement survived the High Priesthood; nay, it gained in inwardness and spiritual power with the passing of the sacrificial system. 'The fasting and humiliation before God, the confession of sins and contrition for them, and fervent prayer for forgiveness, were even before the destruction of the Temple the reality in regard to the Day of Atonement, of which the rites in the Temple were but a dramatic symbol' (Moore). The Rabbis had stressed the Prophetic teaching that without repentance no sacrificial rites were of any avail. With the cessation of sacrifices, therefore, repentance was left as the sole condition of the remission of sins. 'In our time when there is no Temple and no Altar for atonement, there is repentance. Repentance atones for all iniquities' (Maimonides). The Day of Atonement, the Rabbis further declare, will never pass away, even if all other Festivals should pass away. And indeed as long as Israel does not lose its soul, so long shall the Day of Atonement remain. See also on XXIII, 27–32.

he did. The subject is Aaron.

CHAPTER XVII. HOLINESS IN MEAT FOODS

This chapter may be looked upon as supplementary to the first part of Leviticus. It ordains that meat-foods must be free from idolatrous taint. This taint assumed two forms: sacrificing to 'satyrs' (*v.* 7), and eating the blood (10–14).

and unto all the children of Israel, and say unto them: This is the thing which the LORD hath commanded, saying: ¶ 3. What man soever there be of the house of Israel, that killeth an ox, or lamb, or goat, in the camp, or that killeth it without the camp, 4. and hath not brought it unto the door of the tent of meeting, to present it as an offering unto the LORD before the tabernacle of the LORD, blood shall be imputed unto that man; he hath shed blood; and that man shall be cut off from among his people. 5. To the end that the children of Israel may bring their sacrifices, which they sacrifice in the open field, even that they may bring them unto the LORD, unto the door of the tent of meeting, unto the priest, and sacrifice them for sacrifices of peace-offerings unto the LORD. 6. And the priest shall dash the blood against the altar of the LORD at the door of the tent of meeting, and make the fat smoke for a sweet savour unto the LORD. 7. And they shall no more sacrifice their sacrifices unto the satyrs, after whom they go astray. This shall be a statute for ever unto them throughout their generations.* v (** iii). ¶ 8. And thou shalt say unto them: Whatsoever man there be of

וְאֶל כָּל־בְּנֵי יִשְׂרָאֵל וְאָמַרְתָּ אֲלֵיהֶם זֶה הַדָּבָר אֲשֶׁר־
3 צִוָּה יְהוָה לֵאמֹר׃ אִישׁ אִישׁ מִבֵּית יִשְׂרָאֵל אֲשֶׁר יִשְׁחַט
שׁוֹר אוֹ־כֶשֶׂב אוֹ־עֵז בַּמַּחֲנֶה אוֹ אֲשֶׁר יִשְׁחַט מִחוּץ
4 לַמַּחֲנֶה׃ וְאֶל־פֶּתַח אֹהֶל מוֹעֵד לֹא הֱבִיאוֹ לְהַקְרִיב
קָרְבָּן לַיהוָה לִפְנֵי מִשְׁכַּן יְהוָה דָּם יֵחָשֵׁב לָאִישׁ הַהוּא
5 דָּם שָׁפָךְ וְנִכְרַת הָאִישׁ הַהוּא מִקֶּרֶב עַמּוֹ׃ לְמַעַן אֲשֶׁר
יָבִיאוּ בְּנֵי יִשְׂרָאֵל אֶת־זִבְחֵיהֶם אֲשֶׁר הֵם זֹבְחִים עַל־
פְּנֵי הַשָּׂדֶה וֶהֱבִיאֻם לַיהוָה אֶל־פֶּתַח אֹהֶל מוֹעֵד אֶל־
6 הַכֹּהֵן וְזָבְחוּ זִבְחֵי שְׁלָמִים לַיהוָה אוֹתָם׃ וְזָרַק הַכֹּהֵן
אֶת־הַדָּם עַל־מִזְבַּח יְהוָה פֶּתַח אֹהֶל מוֹעֵד וְהִקְטִיר הַחֵלֶב
7 לְרֵיחַ נִיחֹחַ לַיהוָה׃ וְלֹא־יִזְבְּחוּ עוֹד אֶת־זִבְחֵיהֶם לַשְּׂעִירִם
חמישי (שלישי כשהן מחוב') אֲשֶׁר הֵם זֹנִים אַחֲרֵיהֶם חֻקַּת עוֹלָם תִּהְיֶה־זֹּאת לָהֶם
8 לְדֹרֹתָם׃ * וַאֲלֵהֶם תֹּאמַר אִישׁ אִישׁ מִבֵּית יִשְׂרָאֵל וּמִן־

v. 3. קמץ בז"ק v. 4. קמץ בז"ק

3–7. On Slaying Animals for Food

3. *killeth an ox.* Evidently refers to a time when the slaughtering of animals for food was rare, and only at a family festivity or other formal gathering was meat consumed. During the wandering in the Wilderness the people lived on manna; and only exceptionally would it happen that an animal was slaughtered for consumption. Every such slaughtering had to be a sacrificial act; it had to take place at the Sanctuary; and it was deemed a peace-offering. In Deut. XII, 20 f, the law is modified in anticipation of the fact that Israel would soon be spread over a large area; for the requirement that every animal killed for food should be brought to the Sanctuary could apply only when the entire Community lived in the closest proximity to it.

According to the Rabbis this section refers only to animals intended as sacrifices—that they must not be offered except at the door of the Tabernacle.

4. *an offering.* A peace-offering is meant; see next *v.*

before the tabernacle. On the Altar.

blood shall be imputed. 'Blood' is here used in the sense of 'the guilt of blood', as in Deut. XXI, 8. He is regarded as though he had shed blood, and thereby incurs a severe penalty.

be cut off. The offender was not to be punished by an earthly tribunal. The penalty was what the Rabbis term 'death by the hand of Heaven'.

5. *which they sacrifice. i.e.* which they had up to now sacrificed upon 'high places' in the open field.

peace-offerings. See on III, 1. In peace-offerings the offerer had a share of the sacrifice.

7. *satyrs.* lit. 'goats.' They were deemed to be sylvan gods or demons who inhabited waste places (Isa. XIII, 21; XXXIV, 14). The worship of the goat, accompanied by the foulest rites, prevailed in Lower Egypt. This was familiar to the Israelites, and God desired to wean them from it (cf. Josh. XXIV, 14; Ezek. XX, 7).

Some commentators point to this verse, as giving a main purpose of the sacrificial system in the Torah; *viz.* gradually to wean Israel away from primitive ideas and idolatrous practices. The *manner* of worship in use among the peoples of antiquity was retained, but that worship was now directed towards the One and Holy God. 'By this Divine plan, idolatry was eradicated, and the vital principle of our Faith, the existence and unity of God, was firmly established—without confusing the minds of the people by the abolition of sacrificial worship to which they were accustomed' (Maimonides).

for ever. That offerings to 'satyrs' are forbidden.

8–9. The actual offering of the sacrifice as well as its slaughtering must on no account be performed at any place except at that Sanctuary. This prohibition applies not only to Israelites, but also to those strangers (גרי צדק) who had been completely incorporated in Israel.

9 הַגֵּר אֲשֶׁר־יָגוּר בְּתוֹכָם אֲשֶׁר־יַעֲלֶה עֹלָה אוֹ־זָבַח׃ וְאֶל־
פֶּתַח אֹהֶל מוֹעֵד לֹא יְבִיאֶנּוּ לַעֲשׂוֹת אֹתוֹ לַיהוָה וְנִכְרַת
10 הָאִישׁ הַהוּא מֵעַמָּיו׃ וְאִישׁ אִישׁ מִבֵּית יִשְׂרָאֵל וּמִן־
הַגֵּר הַגָּר בְּתוֹכָם אֲשֶׁר יֹאכַל כָּל־דָּם וְנָתַתִּי פָנַי בַּנֶּפֶשׁ
11 הָאֹכֶלֶת אֶת־הַדָּם וְהִכְרַתִּי אֹתָהּ מִקֶּרֶב עַמָּהּ׃ כִּי־
נֶפֶשׁ הַבָּשָׂר בַּדָּם הִוא וַאֲנִי נְתַתִּיו לָכֶם עַל־הַמִּזְבֵּחַ
12 לְכַפֵּר עַל־נַפְשֹׁתֵיכֶם כִּי־הַדָּם הוּא בַּנֶּפֶשׁ יְכַפֵּר׃ עַל־כֵּן
אָמַרְתִּי לִבְנֵי יִשְׂרָאֵל כָּל־נֶפֶשׁ מִכֶּם לֹא־תֹאכַל דָּם וְהַגֵּר
13 הַגָּר בְּתוֹכְכֶם לֹא־יֹאכַל דָּם׃ וְאִישׁ אִישׁ מִבְּנֵי יִשְׂרָאֵל
וּמִן־הַגֵּר הַגָּר בְּתוֹכָם אֲשֶׁר יָצוּד צֵיד חַיָּה אוֹ־עוֹף אֲשֶׁר

the house of Israel, or of the strangers that sojourn among them, that offereth a burnt-offering or sacrifice, 9. and bringeth it not unto the door of the tent of meeting, to sacrifice it unto the LORD, even that man shall be cut off from his people. ¶ 10. And whatsoever man there be of the house of Israel, or of the strangers that sojourn among them, that eateth any manner of blood, I will set My face against that soul that eateth blood, and will cut him off from among his people. 11. For the life of the flesh is in the blood; and I have given it to you upon the altar to make atonement for your souls; for it is the blood that maketh atonement by reason of the life. 12. Therefore I said unto the children of Israel: No soul of you shall eat blood, neither shall any stranger that sojourneth among you eat blood. ¶ 13. And whatsoever man there be of the children of Israel, or of the strangers that sojourn

10–14. BLOOD NOT TO BE EATEN

10. *eateth any manner of blood.* The prohibition, which included the eating of flesh containing blood, has been stated in general terms in Lev. III, 17; VII, 26 f.

The reason for these repeated solemn injunctions is not given. The purpose may be to tame man's instincts of violence by weaning him from blood, and implanting within him a horror of all bloodshed. The slaying of animals for food was in time taken away altogether from the ordinary Israelite, and was relegated to a body of pious and specially trained men, *Shochetim.* These injunctions have undoubtedly contributed to render the Israelites a humane people. 'Consider the one circumstance that no Jewish mother ever killed a chicken with her own hand, and you will understand why homicide is rarer among Jews than among any other human group' (A. Leroy Beaulieu).

The Jewish method of slaughter (*Shechitah*) causes the maximum effusion of blood in the animal; and the remaining blood is extracted by means of the washing and salting of the meat. For the prescribed regulations, see Dayan Lazarus, *The Ways of Her Household*, Part I.

In regard to the terms *nevelah* and *terefah* in *v.* 15, the flesh of an animal that died of itself (nevelah), or was torn by beasts (terefah), is emphatically forbidden. The latter term (terefah) includes flesh of all animals ritually slaughtered but found to contain injuries or organic diseases, whether patent or determined by inspection of the animal after Shechitah. Animals not killed *strictly* in the prescribed Jewish manner, are technically also termed nevelah. The flesh of animals which are not found on Rabbinic inspection to be sound, is forbidden food.

11. *life of the flesh.* The vital principle of the animal was in the blood. While life and blood are not quite identical, the blood is the principal carrier of life. With heavy loss of blood, vital powers dwindle; and if the loss continues, they cease altogether. Blood is therefore something sacred. It is withdrawn from ordinary use as an article of food, and reserved for a sacred symbolic purpose.

I have given it to you. i.e. I have appointed it to be placed on the Altar on *your* behalf. These words effectually dispose of any idea that the life of the animal presented to God was intended as a bribe. The blood on the Altar was for the spiritual welfare of the worshipper, not for the gratification of God.

maketh atonement by reason of the life. Which it contains. The use of blood, representing life, in the rites of atonement symbolized the complete yielding up of the worshipper's life to God, and conveyed the thought that the surrender of a man to the will of God carried with it the assurance of Divine pardon.

12. *therefore I said. i.e.* because the life resides in the blood, for that reason is its consumption prohibited.

13. *cover it with dust.* The blood being the symbol of life, it had to be treated in a reverent manner, in the same way that a corpse must not be left exposed. The covering with dust was the equivalent of burial in the case of a dead body. According to Hoffmann, the exhortation to act reverently in regard to the blood of an animal was not liable to be forgotten in connection with animals that were admitted as sacrifices. But some reminder was necessary in the case of those other animals that could not be brought as sacrifices; hence, the command to cover the blood.

among them, that taketh in hunting any beast or fowl that may be eaten, he shall pour out the blood thereof, and cover it with dust. 14. For as to the life of all flesh, the blood thereof is all one with the life thereof; therefore I said unto the children of Israel: Ye shall eat the blood of no manner of flesh; for the life of all flesh is the blood thereof; whosoever eateth it shall be cut off. 15. And every soul that eateth that which dieth of itself, or that which is torn of beasts, whether he be home-born or a stranger, he shall wash his clothes, and bathe himself in water, and be unclean until the even; then shall he be clean. 16. But if he wash them not, nor bathe his flesh, then he shall bear his iniquity.

18

Chapter XVIII

1. And the Lord spoke unto Moses, saying: 2. Speak unto the children of Israel, and say unto them: ¶ I am the Lord your God.

14 יֵאָכֵל וְשָׁפַךְ אֶת־דָּמוֹ וְכִסָּהוּ בֶּעָפָר׃ כִּי־נֶפֶשׁ כָּל־בָּשָׂר
דָּמוֹ בְנַפְשׁוֹ הוּא וָאֹמַר לִבְנֵי יִשְׂרָאֵל דַּם כָּל־בָּשָׂר לֹא
תֹאכֵלוּ כִּי נֶפֶשׁ כָּל־בָּשָׂר דָּמוֹ הִוא כָּל־אֹכְלָיו יִכָּרֵת׃
טו וְכָל־נֶפֶשׁ אֲשֶׁר תֹּאכַל נְבֵלָה וּטְרֵפָה בָּאֶזְרָח וּבַגֵּר וְכִבֶּס
16 בְּגָדָיו וְרָחַץ בַּמַּיִם וְטָמֵא עַד־הָעֶרֶב וְטָהֵר׃ וְאִם לֹא יְכַבֵּס
וּבְשָׂרוֹ לֹא יִרְחָץ וְנָשָׂא עֲוֺנוֹ׃ פ

יח

Cap. XVIII. יח

א 2 וַיְדַבֵּר יְהוָה אֶל־מֹשֶׁה לֵּאמֹר׃ דַּבֵּר אֶל־בְּנֵי יִשְׂרָאֵל
3 וְאָמַרְתָּ אֲלֵהֶם אֲנִי יְהוָה אֱלֹהֵיכֶם׃ כְּמַעֲשֵׂה אֶרֶץ־מִצְרַיִם

15–16. Carcass which Causes Defilement

15. Cf. xi, 39 f.

a stranger. A full proselyte, גר צדק (Sifra); otherwise, he was not debarred from eating it; see Deut. xiv, 21.

16. *he shall bear his iniquity.* Should he enter the Sanctuary, or partake of sacred food.

Chapter XVIII

PROHIBITION OF UNLAWFUL MARRIAGES, UNCHASTITY AND MOLECH WORSHIP

Chapters xi–xvii, the subject of which is ritual uncleanness and its purification, are now followed by chapters xviii–xx, dealing with moral uncleanness and its punishments. The laws and precepts contained in xviii–xx lie at the very root of the life of purity and righteousness, and form the foundation principles of social morality. The first place among these is given to the institution of marriage (xviii). Marriage, the cornerstone of all human society, is here conceived in a purely ethical spirit; and any violation of the sacred character of marriage is deemed a heinous offence, calling down the punishment of Heaven both upon the offender and the society that condones the offence. Impurity in marriage, incestuous promiscuity among near relations, and other abominations are unpardonable sins, blighting the land and its inhabitants with defilement. 'In graphic brevity and comeliness, Lev. xviii surpasses all other passages of similar import; more delicately and at the same time more seriously, such matters cannot be spoken about' (Ewald).

If the cultural condition of any people can be measured by the purity of its home life, then Israel's is the primacy in moral culture among the peoples. In Israel, marriage is regarded as a Divine institution, under whose shadow alone there can be true reverence for the mystery, dignity, and sacredness of life. Marriage is a primary religious duty. He who has no wife—say the Rabbis—lives without comfort, help, joy, blessing, atonement (*i.e.* true religious communion with God). The Jewish husband—they declared—loves his wife as himself, and honours her more than himself. 'I will work for thee, I will honour thee, I will support thee, even as it beseemeth a Jewish husband to do,' is to this day the husband's vow in the Jewish marriage-contract. The affectionate consideration shown to the Jewish wife, however, as well as the domestic purity and devotion that are the glory of Jewish womanhood, are both largely the fruit of the laws and warnings in these chapters of Leviticus. They effectively prevented the submergence of Israel in the sea of heathen impurity that covered the whole ancient world. These laws proved the ramparts for a new human ideal—that of the Holiness of Home—an ideal that became one of the distinguishing features of the Jewish people throughout the ages.

Chapter xviii forms one of the Readings of the Day of Atonement. 'The selection was no doubt prompted by the desire to inculcate on the most solemn day in the Calendar the paramount duty of purity and self-control. And there is but little doubt that obedience to these behests has been, by Divine Providence, one of the most potent factors in the preservation of Israel' (Hermann Adler).

1–5. Introductory Exhortation

2. *I am the LORD your God.* These words proclaim the Source from which the precepts emanate, as well as the Power who will not brook the wanton violation of these fundamental laws.

3. After the doings of the land of Egypt, wherein ye dwelt, shall ye not do; and after the doings of the land of Canaan, whither I bring you, shall ye not do; neither shall ye walk in their statutes. 4. Mine ordinances shall ye do, and My statutes shall ye keep, to walk therein: I am the LORD your God. 5. Ye shall therefore keep My statutes, and Mine ordinances, which if a man do, he shall live by them: I am the LORD.* vi. ¶ 6. None of you shall approach to any that is near of kin to him, to uncover their naked-

אֲשֶׁר יְשַׁבְתֶּם־בָּהּ לֹא תַעֲשׂוּ וּכְמַעֲשֵׂה אֶרֶץ־כְּנַעַן אֲשֶׁר
אֲנִי מֵבִיא אֶתְכֶם שָׁמָּה לֹא תַעֲשׂוּ וּבְחֻקֹּתֵיהֶם לֹא תֵלֵכוּ׃
4 אֶת־מִשְׁפָּטַי תַּעֲשׂוּ וְאֶת־חֻקֹּתַי תִּשְׁמְרוּ לָלֶכֶת בָּהֶם אֲנִי
ה יְהוָה אֱלֹהֵיכֶם׃ וּשְׁמַרְתֶּם אֶת־חֻקֹּתַי וְאֶת־מִשְׁפָּטַי אֲשֶׁר
ששי 6 יַעֲשֶׂה אֹתָם הָאָדָם וָחַי בָּהֶם אֲנִי יְהוָה׃ * ס אִישׁ אִישׁ

3. *doings . . . Egypt . . . Canaan.* Neither the immoral practices of the land they left, nor the abominations of the land they were going to, should influence their religious life.

statutes. lit. 'laws engraven,' denotes the ordinances which control the life of the nation. The vicious practices of paganism, especially of Egypt and Canaan, were sanctioned by their national laws. 'Both the practices and the laws were contrary to Reason, Conscience, and the Divine Will' (Wogue).

4. *ordinances.* Israel was receiving a new code of laws that was to take the place of what they had seen in force in Egypt and would find in Canaan. *Judgments* are laws dictated by the moral sense, like the prohibition of theft: *statutes* are distinctive precepts addressed to the Israelite, like the prohibition of swine's flesh; see on Gen. XXVI, 5.

do . . . keep. The two verbs are complementary. *Do* is the mechanical performance; *keep* includes the idea of study and understanding of the principle underlying the command. Only where there is *intelligent* conformity to the letter of the Torah, does its spirit become a transforming power in the lives of men.

to walk therein. This phrase occurs only in two other places in the Torah (XX, 23; XXVI, 3). It means not merely to obey the behests of Religion once or twice, but to *walk* in them, to order life in accordance with them.

I am the LORD. i.e. I who command these precepts am the LORD your God. The refrain—'I am the LORD' gives peculiar solemnity to the demands which it accompanies in these chapters. Man must obey, because it is God who commands. 'The Divine imperative is its own self-sufficient motive' (Moore).

5. *if a man do.* The Rabbis emphasize the word *man*. Rabbi Meir used to say, 'Whence do we know that even a heathen, if he obeys the law of God, will thereby attain to the same spiritual communion with God as the High Priest? Scripture says, "which if a *man* do, he shall live by them"—not priest, Levite, or Israelite, but *man*' (Talmud).

he shall live by them. He will gain the life eternal in the world to come (Onkelos, Targum Jonathan, Rashi); yea, through it alone can he gain true life in this world, as the life of the wicked is not really Life (Hoffmann). The plain meaning is, that by adhering to the precepts of God, a man will enjoy well-being and length of days; cf. 'that thy days may be long' (Deut. XI, 21). 'No country was ever prosperous and strong in which the sanctity of family life and the value of personal purity were not upheld and practised' (W. R. Inge).

The Rabbis take the words 'he shall live by them' to mean that God's commandments are to be a means of life and not of destruction to His children, וחי בהם ולא שימות בהם. With the exception of three prohibitions, all commandments of the Law are, therefore, in abeyance whenever life is endangered. No man, however, is to save his life at the price of public idolatry, murder, or adultery. This was the decision of the Rabbis in the war of extermination which the Roman Emperor Hadrian waged against Judaism; see on XXII, 32.

6–18. FORBIDDEN MARRIAGES

All unions between the sexes that are repellent to the finer feelings of man, or would taint the natural affection between near relations, are sternly prohibited. Primary prohibited marriages are: — (*a*) blood - relations — mother, sister, daughter, grand-daughter, father's sister and mother's sister; and (*b*) cases of affinity—the wives of blood-relations and of the wife's blood-relations. All unions—whether temporary or permanent—between persons belonging to these groups are classed as 'incestuous' (עריות). They have no binding force whatsoever in Jewish Law, and can in no circumstance be deemed a 'marriage'; hence, no divorce (*Get*) is required for their dissolution. The issue are illegitimate (*mamzerim*).

The Rabbis have expanded the primary Prohibited Degrees in the ascending and descending line. These expansions are known as 'secondary Prohibited Marriages, שניות'; *e.g.* as the mother is forbidden, so is the grandmother and greatness: I am the LORD. ¶ 7. The nakedness of thy father, and the nakedness of thy mother, shalt thou not uncover: she is thy mother; thou shalt not uncover her nakedness. ¶ 8. The nakedness of thy father's wife shalt thou not uncover: it is thy father's nakedness. ¶ 9. The nakedness of thy sister, the daughter of thy father, or the daughter of thy mother, whether born at home, or born abroad, even their nakedness thou shalt not uncover. ¶ 10. The nakedness of thy son's daughter, or of thy daughter's daughter, even their nakedness thou shalt not uncover; for theirs is thine own naked-

אֶל־כָּל־שְׁאֵר בְּשָׂרוֹ לֹא תִקְרְבוּ לְגַלּוֹת עֶרְוָה אֲנִי יְהוָה׃
7 ס עֶרְוַת אָבִיךָ וְעֶרְוַת אִמְּךָ לֹא תְגַלֵּה אִמְּךָ הִוא לֹא
8 תְגַלֶּה עֶרְוָתָהּ׃ ס עֶרְוַת אֵשֶׁת־אָבִיךָ לֹא תְגַלֵּה
9 עֶרְוַת אָבִיךָ הִוא׃ ס עֶרְוַת אֲחוֹתְךָ בַת־אָבִיךָ אוֹ
בַת־אִמֶּךָ מוֹלֶדֶת בַּיִת אוֹ מוֹלֶדֶת חוּץ לֹא תְגַלֶּה עֶרְוָתָן׃
י ס עֶרְוַת בַּת־בִּנְךָ אוֹ בַת־בִּתְּךָ לֹא תְגַלֶּה עֶרְוָתָן כִּי

grandmother; as the step-mother so is the grandfather's wife; as the daughter-in-law, so is the grandson's wife. Marriages of the secondary Prohibited Degrees must be dissolved by a divorce, and the children are legitimate.

The above Prohibited Degrees of marriage, whether Biblical or Rabbinical, are based on instinctive abhorrence and natural decorum. Jewish sectaries, however, as well as various Christian Churches, largely under the influence of Roman Law, greatly extended these prohibitions, until even an alliance between the great-grandchildren of two brothers and sisters was by them deemed forbidden. The Church introduced further prohibitions in connection with 'spiritual kinship'; *e.g.* a godfather could not marry the child at whose baptism he was sponsor. The hardship resulting from such unbounded extension of Prohibited Degrees by the Roman Law and Church, was to some extent mitigated by *dispensation*, which the Church granted in certain circumstances; but this led to great abuses. Both dispensation and 'spiritual kinship' are, of course, unknown in Judaism.

The Rabbis explain that prior to the Revelation at Sinai, only the following marriages were prohibited: *viz.* mother, father's wife, married woman, and sister on mother's side. Hence Abraham was permitted to marry his half-sister; and Jacob, two sisters.

6. *none of you . . . nakedness.* No one shall contract a marriage with a blood-relation. The broad principle (כלל) is here stated, and then particulars are given in *v.* 7–18.

There was dire need for the legislation in this chapter. Many of the incestuous marriages herein mentioned were common among contemporary peoples, and were recognized in parts of the Roman world as late as the early Middle Ages. In Egypt, marriage with a sister was quite usual, especially in royal families. The Greeks countenanced marriage with a half-sister. Among the Persians, marriages with mother, sisters, and daughters were expressly recommended as meritorious and as most pleasing to the gods. Such were the usages, not of barbarous and reckless tribes unused to moral restrictions, but of the cultured nations of antiquity. 'It is evident that Mosaism brought the world a new message in the matter of marriage' (Dillmann). When we think of the influence of this Chapter on the Western and Near Eastern peoples, we realise that Judaism is indeed a religious civilization!

near of kin. lit. 'flesh of his flesh'; his flesh and blood. Within a certain degree of consanguinity two relatives are regarded as one flesh, and one person.

uncover their nakedness. Used for, 'to take to wife' in alliances which can never be regarded as 'marriage'. It is employed here, instead of the usual phrase, in order to bring out more strikingly the moral hideousness and animality of the transgression (S. R. Hirsch).

7. *of thy father.* Forbids a union between mother and son, as a dishonour both to father and mother.

8. *father's wife.* Forbids union with a step-mother. As marriage makes man and wife one (Gen. II, 24), a step-mother was regarded as a blood-relation of the nearest kind.

It was a practice among Eastern heirs-apparent to take possession of the father's wives, as an assertion of their right to the throne, that action identifying them with the late ruler's personality in the eyes of the people. This explains Reuben's conduct in Gen. XXXV, 22, and Absalom's in II Sam. XVI, 20–22.

9. *born at home.* A half-sister born of a legal marriage; see XX, 17.

born abroad. A half-sister born either of an illegal marriage or out of wedlock (Ibn Ezra).

10. *thy son's daughter.* As marriage with a step-grand-daughter is forbidden in *v.* 17, this verse seems superfluous. The Rabbis, however, understood it as referring to the daughter of an illegitimate son or daughter.

Marriage with a daughter is not expressly forbidden; because, in view of this prohibition of the grand-daughter, it is self-evident.

thine own nakedness. 'They are part of yourself' (Moffatt).

11 עֶרְוָתְךָ הֵנָּה׃ ס עֶרְוַת בַּת־אֵשֶׁת אָבִיךָ מוֹלֶדֶת
12 אָבִיךָ אֲחוֹתְךָ הִוא לֹא תְגַלֶּה עֶרְוָתָהּ׃ ס עֶרְוַת
13 אֲחוֹת־אָבִיךָ לֹא תְגַלֵּה שְׁאֵר אָבִיךָ הוּא׃ ס עֶרְוַת
14 אֲחוֹת־אִמְּךָ לֹא תְגַלֵּה כִּי־שְׁאֵר אִמְּךָ הוּא׃ ס עֶרְוַת
אֲחִי־אָבִיךָ לֹא תְגַלֵּה אֶל־אִשְׁתּוֹ לֹא תִקְרָב דֹּדָתְךָ הִוא׃
טו ס עֶרְוַת כַּלָּתְךָ לֹא תְגַלֵּה אֵשֶׁת בִּנְךָ הִוא לֹא תְגַלֶּה
16 עֶרְוָתָהּ׃ ס עֶרְוַת אֵשֶׁת־אָחִיךָ לֹא תְגַלֵּה עֶרְוַת
17 אָחִיךָ הוּא׃ ס עֶרְוַת אִשָּׁה וּבִתָּהּ לֹא תְגַלֵּה אֶת־
בַּת־בְּנָהּ וְאֶת־בַּת־בִּתָּהּ לֹא תִקַּח לְגַלּוֹת עֶרְוָתָהּ שַׁאֲרָה
18 הֵנָּה זִמָּה הִוא׃ וְאִשָּׁה אֶל־אֲחֹתָהּ לֹא תִקָּח לִצְרֹר לְגַלּוֹת
19 עֶרְוָתָהּ עָלֶיהָ בְּחַיֶּיהָ׃ וְאֶל־אִשָּׁה בְּנִדַּת טֻמְאָתָהּ לֹא תִקְרַב

v. 14. קמץ בז״ק

ness. ¶ 11. The nakedness of thy father's wife's daughter, begotten of thy father, she is thy sister, thou shalt not uncover her nakedness. ¶ 12. Thou shalt not uncover the nakedness of thy father's sister: she is thy father's near kinswoman. ¶ 13. Thou shalt not uncover the nakedness of thy mother's sister; for she is thy mother's near kinswoman. ¶ 14. Thou shalt not uncover the nakedness of thy father's brother, thou shalt not approach to his wife: she is thine aunt. ¶ 15. Thou shalt not uncover the nakedness of thy daughter-in-law: she is thy son's wife; thou shalt not uncover her nakedness. ¶ 16. Thou shalt not uncover the nakedness of thy brother's wife: it is thy brother's nakedness. 17. Thou shalt not uncover the nakedness of a woman and her daughter; thou shalt not take her son's daughter, or her daughter's daughter, to uncover her nakedness: they are near kinswomen; it is lewdness. 18. And thou shalt not take a woman to her sister, to be a rival to her, to uncover her nakedness, beside the other in her life-time. 19. And thou shalt not approach unto a woman to uncover her

11. *thy father's wife's daughter.* Descent from the same mother was long deemed a closer degree of relationship than descent from the same father (Gen. xx, 12). Consequently, *v.* 9 might have been misunderstood to apply to either 'thy sister (*viz.* of the same mother) who is the daughter of thy father,' *i.e.* a full sister; or, to 'the daughter of thy mother', *i.e.* a half-sister from the same mother but different father. Union with a half-sister from the same father but different mother might thus have been thought permissible. Hence the need of a clear prohibition of the daughter from the same father by another mother, as is here given (Hoffmann).

12. *thy father's sister.* This prohibition, too, was new to Israelites and contrary to their former usage (Exod. VI, 20).

14. *thy father's brother.* Union with the wife of a father's brother is an offence against two persons whom marriage had made '*one* flesh' (see *v.* 8). For that reason, her nephew could not marry her after his uncle's death. The Rabbis declare marriage with the wife of a mother's brother equally illegal.

15–18. Cases of affinity by marriage.

15. *daughter-in-law.* Forbids marriage between a man and his daughter-in-law after divorce or the husband's death. It was deemed a foul offence, almost on a plane with 'marriage' with a daughter.

16. *brother's wife.* An exception to this rule is given in Deut. xxv, 5 f, where the obligation is placed upon a man to marry his brother's widow, should his brother have died without issue.

17. *lewdness.* lit. 'harlotry'. The union of a man with both a woman and her daughter or grand-daughter, whether at the same time or after the death of one, is considered an execrable action, an 'enormity' (RV Margin).

18. *to be a rival to her.* Better, *as a fellow-wife.* Sisterly love would thereby turn to rivalry and hatred.

in her life-time. During the first wife's life-time, even if he had divorced her, he could not marry her sister. After her death it was permitted, and was even deemed by the Rabbis a praiseworthy thing to do, as no other woman would show the same affection to the orphaned children of the deceased sister.

19–23. Immoral Practices Forbidden

19. *impure.* In xv, 24, the same matter had been dealt with from the point of view of the ritual defilement that is thereby incurred. Here the practice is denounced as contrary to the principles of moral purity; see also xx, 18.

While recognizing the sacred nature of the estate of wedlock, Judaism prescribes continence even in marriage. 'The Jewish ideal of holiness is not confined to the avoidance of the illicit; its ideal includes the hallowing of the licit' (Moore). It categorically demands reserve, self-control, and moral freedom in the most intimate relations of life. It ordains the utmost consideration for the wife not only throughout the monthly period of separation (*niddah*), but also during the seven following days of convalescence and recovery (*taharah*), which are terminated by ritual purification through total immersion either in a fountain,

כ לְגַלּוֹת עֶרְוָתָהּ׃ וְאֶל־אֵשֶׁת עֲמִיתְךָ לֹא־תִתֵּן שְׁכָבְתְּךָ
21 לְזָרַע לְטָמְאָה־בָהּ׃ וּמִזַּרְעֲךָ לֹא־תִתֵּן לְהַעֲבִיר לַמֹּלֶךְ וְלֹא
22 תְחַלֵּל אֶת־שֵׁם אֱלֹהֶיךָ אֲנִי יְהוָה׃ ׳ וְאֶת־זָכָר לֹא תִשְׁכַּב (שביעי (רביעי כשהן מחוברין))
23 מִשְׁכְּבֵי אִשָּׁה תּוֹעֵבָה הִוא׃ וּבְכָל־בְּהֵמָה לֹא־תִתֵּן שְׁכָבְתְּךָ
לְטָמְאָה־בָהּ וְאִשָּׁה לֹא־תַעֲמֹד לִפְנֵי בְהֵמָה לְרִבְעָהּ תֶּבֶל
24 הוּא׃ אַל־תִּטַּמְּאוּ בְּכָל־אֵלֶּה כִּי בְכָל־אֵלֶּה נִטְמְאוּ הַגּוֹיִם

nakedness, as long as she is impure by her uncleanness. 20. And thou shalt not lie carnally with thy neighbour's wife, to defile thyself with her. 21. And thou shalt not give any of thy seed to set them apart to Molech, neither shalt thou profane the name of thy God: I am the LORD. *vii (** iv). 22. Thou shalt not lie with mankind, as with womankind; it is abomination. 23. And thou shalt not lie with any beast to defile thyself therewith; neither shall any woman stand before a beast, to lie down thereto; it is perversion. ¶ 24. Defile not ye yourselves

or a 'gathering of living water' (*mikweh*, in later Hebrew, *mikvah*; see on XI, 36). By the reverent guidance in these vital matters which these laws afford, Jewish men have been taught respect for womanhood, moral discipline, and ethical culture. As for Jewish women, they were, on the one hand, given protection from uncurbed passion; and, on the other hand, taught to view marital life under the aspect of holiness (קדושה).

Even apart from their purely religious side, the importance of these regulations, scrupulously observed throughout the generations in Israel, cannot be over-estimated. They have fostered racial sanity and well-being, and have proved as favourable to hygiene as to morals. The overwhelming majority of Jewish women still live, thank God, under the 'yoke' of these laws—to their own good and the biologic good of the Jewish people. Striking testimony has been given by scientists to the fact that, though health is not put forward as the primary purpose of these regulations, yet such is their indubitable result. These laws of marital continence are now held by some scientists to accord with the fundamental rhythm in woman's nature. While medical opinion is not unanimous on this difficult subject, there can be no doubt as to the significance of statistics like the following: an investigation, conducted over a number of years at Mount Sinai Hospital, New York, in connection with 80,000 Jewish women who observe *niddah* and *taharah* laws, showed that the proportion of those suffering from uterine cancer was one to fifteen of non-Jewish women of corresponding social and economic status. Even more noteworthy is the difference in the proportion of a certain form of cancer among Jewish and non-Jewish men respectively (Sorsby, *Cancer and Race*, 1931). 'The Mosaic Code again stands out as an astonishing example of inspired wisdom and foresight which should appeal with redoubled force to the enlightened minds of to-day. Discipline and self-restraint are perhaps the lessons most needed for the present times' (Lieut.-Col. F. E. Freemantle, Chairman, International Cancer Conference, London, July, 1928).

For a brief account of the traditional laws of *niddah* and *taharah*, see Dayan Lazarus, *The Ways of Her Household*, Part II (Myers and Co., 1923). See also Rabbi David Miller, *The Secret of the Jew; his Life—his Family* (Oakland, Calif.).

20. *thy neighbour's wife.* This prohibition is so vital to human society that it is included in the Ten Commandments, immediately after the protection of life, as being of equal importance with it (Ewald); see also note on XX, 10.

21. *set them apart.* Or, *pass through the fire.* We have here the first mention in the Bible of the dreadful practice of child-sacrifice to a deity of the surrounding heathen Semites. Israel's Teachers shudder at this hideous aberration of man's sense of worship, and they do not rest till all Israel shares their horror of it.

Sexual impurity, especially, when it is allied with, or elevated into, a form of worship, as it was in the cults of Baal and Astarte, dehumanizes, and leads to the deadening of the holiest human instincts.

neither shalt thou profane. Better, *that thou profane not;* such savage idolatry being an infamous travesty of all religion or adoration of God.

22. *with mankind.* Discloses the abyss of depravity from which the Torah saved the Israelite. This unnatural vice was also prevalent in Greece and Rome.

23. *perversion.* 'A violation of nature and of the Divine order' (Dillmann); cf. Exod. XXII, 18; Lev. XX, 15 f.

The almost incredible bestialities, revealing the hideous possibilities of corrupt human nature, enumerated in *v.* 21–23, are but too well attested in laws, customs, and legends of the ancient and medieval world. They are not unknown in modern societies. Nowhere in literature is there such an uncompromising condemnation of these offences as in XVIII and XX. It led to their extirpation in the midst of Israel, and eventually to their moral outlawry among all peoples that came under the sway of the Hebrew Scriptures.

24–30. An exhortation to lay to heart the fate of the Canaanites whose loathsome customs, disruptive of social morality, would bring about their annihilation.

in any of these things; for in all these the nations are defiled, which I cast out from before you. 25. And the land was defiled, therefore I did visit the iniquity thereof upon it, and the land vomited out her inhabitants. 26. Ye therefore shall keep My statutes and Mine ordinances, and shall not do any of these abominations; neither the home-born, nor the stranger that sojourneth among you—*m a. 27. for all these abominations have the men of the land done, that were before you, and the land is defiled—*m s. 28. that the land vomit not you out also, when ye defile it, as it vomited out the nation that was before you. 29. For whosoever shall do any of these abominations, even the souls that do them shall be cut off from among their people. 30. Therefore shall ye keep My charge, that ye do not any of these abominable customs, which were done before you, and that ye defile not yourselves therein: I am the LORD your God.

כה אֲשֶׁר־אֲנִי מְשַׁלֵּחַ מִפְּנֵיכֶם׃ וַתִּטְמָא הָאָרֶץ וָאֶפְקֹד עֲוֺנָהּ
26 עָלֶיהָ וַתָּקִא הָאָרֶץ אֶת־יֹשְׁבֶיהָ׃ וּשְׁמַרְתֶּם אַתֶּם אֶת־חֻקֹּתַי
וְאֶת־מִשְׁפָּטַי וְלֹא תַעֲשׂוּ מִכֹּל הַתּוֹעֵבֹת הָאֵלֶּה הָאֶזְרָח
מפטיר
27 וְהַגֵּר הַגָּר בְּתוֹכְכֶם׃ כִּי אֶת־כָּל־הַתּוֹעֵבֹת הָאֵל עָשׂוּ אַנְשֵׁי־
(מפטיר לספ')
28 הָאָרֶץ אֲשֶׁר לִפְנֵיכֶם וַתִּטְמָא הָאָרֶץ׃ וְלֹא־תָקִיא הָאָרֶץ
אֶתְכֶם בְּטַמַּאֲכֶם אֹתָהּ כַּאֲשֶׁר קָאָה אֶת־הַגּוֹי אֲשֶׁר
29 לִפְנֵיכֶם׃ כִּי כָּל־אֲשֶׁר יַעֲשֶׂה מִכֹּל הַתּוֹעֵבֹת הָאֵלֶּה וְנִכְרְתוּ
ל הַנְּפָשׁוֹת הָעֹשֹׂת מִקֶּרֶב עַמָּם׃ וּשְׁמַרְתֶּם אֶת־מִשְׁמַרְתִּי
לְבִלְתִּי עֲשׂוֹת מֵחֻקּוֹת הַתּוֹעֵבֹת אֲשֶׁר נַעֲשׂוּ לִפְנֵיכֶם וְלֹא
תִטַּמְּאוּ בָּהֶם אֲנִי יְהוָה אֱלֹהֵיכֶם׃

v. 27. סבירין האלה

24. *defile not ye yourselves.* Whenever sex is withdrawn from its place in marriage and separated from its function as the expression of reverent and lawful wedded love (whereby its quality is completely changed), the person concerned is defiled. The Rabbis deem sexual immorality the strongest of defilements (טומאה), cutting man off from God.

any of these things. The words refer to all the foregoing—the forbidden marriages, the neglect of marital restrictions, as well as unnatural abominations.

25. *the land was defiled.* Only moral offences, and not ceremonial transgressions, are said to defile the land. Every 'enormity' first defiles the person who commits it, be he Canaanite or an Israelite, and he in turn defiles the land (Büchler).

I did visit the iniquity thereof. The land (*i.e.* its inhabitants) is punished. Through pestilence and drought, its inhabitants are vomited out in the same manner as the human system rejects food which is disagreeable to it. The verbs in this verse visualize the future, as though it had actually come into being.

29. *shall be cut off.* In most of the offences mentioned, the penalty prescribed is death. With the remainder, the culprits were expelled from the Community and presumably from the country, since their presence contaminated the land.

30. *keep My charge.* The Rabbis understood this phrase in the sense of 'guard My charge'; *i.e.* it is the duty of the Religious Authorities to make a 'fence round the Law', in order to keep men far from sin, and to warn and instruct the people as to the seriousness and sacredness of these prohibitions.

I am the LORD your God. The former inhabitants indulged in unnatural vices because the worship of their gods was demoralizing. It is otherwise with Israel. The Lord is their God, and His service is elevating and spiritualizing. Hence there is here a natural transition to the next chapter with its opening command, 'Ye shall be holy; for I the LORD your God am holy.'

EZEKIEL XXII, 1–19

CHAPTER XXII

1. Moreover the word of the LORD came unto me, saying: 2. 'Now, thou, son of man, wilt thou judge, wilt thou judge the bloody city? then cause her to know all her abominations. 3. And thou shalt say: Thus saith the Lord GOD: O city that sheddest blood in the midst of thee, that thy time may come, and that makest idols unto thyself to defile thee; 4. thou art become guilty in thy blood that thou hast shed, and art defiled in thine idols which thou hast

CAP. XXII. כב

א 2 וַיְהִי דְבַר־יְהוָה אֵלַי לֵאמֹר׃ וְאַתָּה בֶן־אָדָם הֲתִשְׁפֹּט
הֲתִשְׁפֹּט אֶת־עִיר הַדָּמִים וְהוֹדַעְתָּהּ אֵת כָּל־תּוֹעֲבוֹתֶיהָ׃
3 וְאָמַרְתָּ כֹּה אָמַר אֲדֹנָי יֱהוִה עִיר שֹׁפֶכֶת דָּם בְּתוֹכָהּ
4 לָבוֹא עִתָּהּ וְעָשְׂתָה גִלּוּלִים עָלֶיהָ לְטָמְאָה׃ בְּדָמֵךְ אֲשֶׁר־

For Ezekiel's life and message, see pp. 178, 244, and 350; and the introductions to Haftorahs Parah and Hachodesh at the end of this volume.

The Sedrah ordains strict regulations for assuring the religious and moral purity of Israel; while the Haftorah is a terrible indictment of Jerusalem for callous violation of these regulations and prohibitions. 'The sins mentioned in Lev. XVIII were those which disgraced the heathen inhabitants of Canaan whom the Israelites were to cast out. The commission of like sins would ensure like judgment' (Speaker's Bible). This Haftorah forms part of a prophecy delivered in 590 B.C.E. Four years later, the Jewish State fell, Jerusalem was captured, the Temple burnt, and the larger portion of the People carried into Babylonian exile.

Ezekiel's role in those times that tried men's souls was a manifold one. He began as the denouncer of Israel, and ended as Israel's comforter. It was his task to utter a cry of doom, unrelenting and fierce, against Jerusalem and its inhabitants. With the destruction of the Temple, however, he opens wide the gates of hope, and prophesies an outpouring of the Divine Spirit that would lead to contrition and penitence, and the consequent resurrection of Israel in the Holy Land.

The Fall of Jerusalem and the Destruction of the Temple had left Israel spiritually stunned. Were the Israelites of that generation so morally degenerate—they asked—so especially godless as to have deserved nothing less than national annihilation and all the horrors of siege and exile? 'The way of the LORD is not just,' many were saying to themselves (Ezek. XVIII, 25). Israel was overwhelmed by doubt as to the existence of a Righteous Ruler of the Universe.

First of all, therefore, Ezekiel deemed it necessary to vindicate the ways of God with Israel. He passes in review the entire past of Israel; and, unlike the other Prophets, he declares it to have been one long chain of ingratitude and sin. The reason for the Prophet's pitiless vehemence is plain: it is only when Israel is *sincerely repentant* of its apostasies and abominations, it is only when Israel sees that its sufferings are the just chastisement of a holy God, that its redemption and resurrection can begin.

A great danger faces the Prophet; he may succeed too well in his denunciation of his people and condemnation of its entire past (Cornill). He may end in planting despair in the hearts of the exiles, and make them exclaim, 'If such has been Israel's past, Israel never deserved to live; and now that it is a valley of dry bones, Israel's story is at an end (Ezek. XXXVII, 11). "Our hope is lost, we are clean cut off".' He meets that danger by striking two notes; one is that God desires not the destruction, but the repentance, of Israel. 'Say unto them, As I live, saith the LORD God, I have no pleasure in the death of the wicked; but that the wicked turn from his way and live: turn ye, turn ye from your evil ways; for why will ye die, O house of Israel?' And the other note is, that God's glory is bound up with the resurrection of Israel. God will restore them, not because Israel deserved restoration, but because God's glory demanded it; see Haftorah Parah at the end of this volume.

The terrible earnestness of this great Preacher of Repentance wrought a wondrous change in Israel. The result of his ministry is, as C. G. Montefiore rightly says, unique in the history of humanity. A fragment of a small people, forcibly transplanted to an enemy's land, remains there for half-a-century without disintegrating or coalescing with its environment, and returns unimpaired to its own soil and resumes its own life, with national and religious identity heightened and strengthened!

CHAPTER XXII

1–12. THE SINS OF JERUSALEM

2. *wilt thou judge.* To rehearse the history of the fathers is to hold up the mirror to themselves (Davidson).

bloody city. Because of perversion of justice, murderous partisan conflicts, and chiefly the child-sacrifices during the reign of Manasseh.

3. *sheddest blood . . . makest idols.* Bloodshed and idolatry are the outstanding sins of the city.

that thy time may come. Her sins hasten the time of her destruction (Kimchi). She seems to be courting retribution.

unto thyself. Her idols are her real foes; crying out, as it were, for her punishment.

made; and thou hast caused thy days to draw near, and art come even unto thy years; therefore have I made thee a reproach unto the nations, and a mocking to all the countries! 5. Those that are near, and those that are far from thee, shall mock thee, thou defiled of name and full of tumult. ¶ 6. Behold, the princes of Israel, every one according to his might, have been in thee to shed blood. 7. In thee have they made light of father and mother; in the midst of thee have they dealt by oppression with the stranger; in thee have they wronged the fatherless and the widow. 8. Thou hast despised My holy things, and hast profaned My sabbaths. 9. In thee have been talebearers to shed blood; and in thee they have eaten upon the mountains; in the midst of thee they have committed lewdness. 10. In thee have they uncovered their fathers' nakedness; in thee have they humbled her that was unclean in her impurity. 11. And each hath committed abomination with his neighbour's wife;

שָׁפַכְתְּ אָשַׁמְתְּ וּבְגִלּוּלַיִךְ אֲשֶׁר־עָשִׂית טָמֵאת וַתַּקְרִיבִי
יָמַיִךְ וַתָּבוֹא עַד־שְׁנוֹתָיִךְ עַל־כֵּן נְתַתִּיךְ חֶרְפָּה לַגּוֹיִם
ה וְקַלָּסָה לְכָל־הָאֲרָצוֹת׃ הַקְּרֹבוֹת וְהָרְחֹקוֹת מִמֵּךְ יִתְקַלְּסוּ־
6 בָךְ טְמֵאַת הַשֵּׁם רַבַּת הַמְּהוּמָה׃ הִנֵּה נְשִׂיאֵי יִשְׂרָאֵל
7 אִישׁ לִזְרֹעוֹ הָיוּ בָךְ לְמַעַן שְׁפָךְ־דָּם׃ אָב וָאֵם הֵקַלּוּ בָךְ
8 לַגֵּר עָשׂוּ בַעֹשֶׁק בְּתוֹכֵךְ יָתוֹם וְאַלְמָנָה הוֹנוּ בָךְ׃ קָדָשַׁי
9 בָּזִית וְאֶת־שַׁבְּתֹתַי חִלָּלְתְּ׃ אַנְשֵׁי רָכִיל הָיוּ בָךְ לְמַעַן
י שְׁפָךְ־דָּם וְאֶל־הֶהָרִים אָכְלוּ בָךְ זִמָּה עָשׂוּ בְתוֹכֵךְ׃ עֶרְוַת־
11 אָב גִּלָּה־בָךְ טְמֵאַת הַנִּדָּה עִנּוּ־בָךְ׃ וְאִישׁ ׀ אֶת־אֵשֶׁת
רֵעֵהוּ עָשָׂה תּוֹעֵבָה וְאִישׁ אֶת־כַּלָּתוֹ טִמֵּא בְזִמָּה וְאִישׁ

v. 4. למדנ׳ אי עת כתיב עד ק׳ ibid. נ״א בגוים

4. *thy days.* Of judgment.

thy years. Of punishment and destruction.

therefore have I made. The judgment is as certain as though it had already taken place (Streane)—the Prophetic perfect tense.

5. *tumult.* Turbulence and disorder.

6. *princes of Israel.* Those to whom the people would look for an example of right living abandon themselves to evil. Everything most sacred in the Jewish life, and all that is the basis of human society, have been outraged—filial duty, justice, love of the stranger, compassion towards orphan and widow, observance of the Sabbath; and sins most sternly prohibited and regarded with utmost horror—usury and impure relationships—have been committed.

according to his might. They recognize no law but might.

to shed blood. By form of law; see I Kings XXI. These crimes were the order of the day among other ancient peoples, and were looked upon as part of the normal course of human events. In Israel alone did there arise teachers of religion who were dumbfounded at human ferocity, as at something against nature and reason; and whose cry of indignation at these inhumanities re-echoed the wrath of the Deity. 'Greece and Rome had their rich and poor, just as Israel had, and the various classes continued to slaughter one another for centuries; but no voice of justice and pity arose from the fierce tumult. Therefore, the words of the Prophets have more vitality at the present time, and answer better to the needs of modern souls, than all the classic masterpieces of antiquity' (Darmesteter).

7. *in thee.* In the Holy City.

8. *thou.* Jerusalem.

9. *talebearers.* Informers and false witnesses, the instruments of judicial murder.

in thee they have eaten upon the mountains. 'High places' were the seat of the heathen and impure rites. Participation in such Bacchanalian orgies is open idolatry.

10. *uncovered.* Marriage with the father's wife, though common among the surrounding heathens, was a heinous crime; Lev. XVIII, 7.

unclean. See Lev. XVIII, 19; XX, 18.

11. *defiled.* Idolatry, then as now, means sexual licence and the throwing overboard of all laws of holiness such as are given in Lev. XVIII.

12. *taken gifts . . . oppression.* These crimes have darkened Eastern societies since times immemorial; but Israel 'should have known better'.

hast forgotten Me. All their degeneracy is summed up in this crowning sin, 'They have forgotten Me, saith the LORD.' This was the root of their evil doing. Forgetting Him, they returned to the lower moral standards of heathenism—something that is seen over and over again in Jewish history.

and each hath lewdly defiled his daughter-in-law; and each in thee hath humbled his sister, his father's daughter. 12. In thee have they taken gifts to shed blood; thou hast taken interest and increase, and thou hast greedily gained of thy neighbours by oppression, and hast forgotten Me, saith the Lord GOD. ¶ 13. Behold, therefore, I have smitten My hand at thy dishonest gain which thou hast made, and at thy blood which hath been in the midst of thee. 14. Can thy heart endure, or can thy hands be strong, in the days that I shall deal with thee? I the LORD have spoken it, and will do it. 15. And I will scatter thee among the nations, and disperse thee through the countries; and I will consume thy filthiness out of thee. 16. And thou shalt be profaned in thyself, in the sight of the nations; and thou shalt know that I am the LORD.' ¶ 17. And the word of the LORD came unto me, saying: 18. 'Son of man, the house of Israel is become dross unto Me; all of them are brass and tin and iron and lead, in the midst of the furnace; they are the dross of silver. 19. Therefore thus saith the Lord GOD: Because ye are all become dross, therefore, behold, I will gather you into the midst of Jerusalem.'

12 אֶת־אֲחֹתוֹ בַת־אָבִיו עִנָּה־בָךְ׃ שֹׁחַד לָקְחוּ־בָךְ לְמַעַן
שְׁפָךְ־דָּם נֶשֶׁךְ וְתַרְבִּית לָקַחַתְּ וַתְּבַצְּעִי רֵעַיִךְ בַּעֹשֶׁק וְאֹתִי
13 שָׁכַחַתְּ נְאֻם אֲדֹנָי יֱהֹוִה׃ וְהִנֵּה הִכֵּיתִי כַפִּי אֶל־בִּצְעֵךְ
14 אֲשֶׁר עָשִׂית וְעַל־דָּמֵךְ אֲשֶׁר הָיוּ בְּתוֹכֵךְ׃ הֲיַעֲמֹד לִבֵּךְ
אִם־תֶּחֱזַקְנָה יָדַיִךְ לַיָּמִים אֲשֶׁר אֲנִי עֹשֶׂה אוֹתָךְ אֲנִי
טו יְהוָה דִּבַּרְתִּי וְעָשִׂיתִי׃ וַהֲפִיצוֹתִי אוֹתָךְ בַּגּוֹיִם וְזֵרִיתִיךְ
16 בָּאֲרָצוֹת וַהֲתִמֹּתִי טֻמְאָתֵךְ מִמֵּךְ׃ וְנִחַלְתְּ בָּךְ לְעֵינֵי גוֹיִם
17 וְיָדַעַתְּ כִּי־אֲנִי יְהוָה׃* וַיְהִי דְבַר־יְהוָה אֵלַי לֵאמֹר׃
18 בֶּן־אָדָם הָיוּ־לִי בֵית־יִשְׂרָאֵל לְסוּג כֻּלָּם נְחֹשֶׁת וּבְדִיל
19 וּבַרְזֶל וְעוֹפֶרֶת בְּתוֹךְ כּוּר סִגִים כֶּסֶף הָיוּ׃ לָכֵן כֹּה
אָמַר אֲדֹנָי יֱהֹוִה יַעַן הֱיוֹת כֻּלְּכֶם לְסִגִים לָכֵן הִנְנִי קֹבֵץ
אֶתְכֶם אֶל־תּוֹךְ יְרוּשָׁלִָם׃

*כאן מסיימין הספרדים v. 18. לסיג ק׳

13–19. THE PUNISHMENT

13. *I have smitten My hand.* In grief.

14. *can thy heart endure.* The suffering that will result from thy transgressions.

15. *consume thy filthiness out of thee.* The chastisements of God are not vindictive, but intended to purge the nation of its sin.

16. *thou shalt be profaned in thyself.* Or, 'thou shalt take thine inheritance' (AV; Kimchi), *i.e.* of punishment and shame.

and thou shalt know that I am the LORD. Punishment will purify you, and lead you to acknowledge Him as the God of Justice and Holiness.

18. *dross.* The people are to be tried in the furnace of affliction. Jerusalem, and all that it contains, will be subject to the fire of God's wrath. Only the dross will be burnt away. The purified remnant shall survive the fire.

19. *I will gather you.* The certainty of the siege approaches, and the people from the surrounding country take refuge within the walls of Jerusalem (Lofthouse). In brief, the end is at hand.

19 CHAPTER XIX

1. And the LORD spoke unto Moses, saying:
2. Speak unto all the congregation of the
children of Israel, and say unto them: ¶ Ye
shall be holy; for I the LORD your God am

CAP. XIX. יט יט

30 ל פ פ פ

א 2 וַיְדַבֵּר יְהוָה אֶל־מֹשֶׁה לֵּאמֹר׃ דַּבֵּר אֶל־כָּל־עֲדַת בְּנֵֽי־

VII. KEDOSHIM

(CHAPTERS XIX–XX)

CHAPTER XIX. A MANUAL OF MORAL INSTRUCTION

This remarkable chapter occupies the central position in Leviticus, and therefore in the Pentateuch. The Rabbis rightly regarded it as the kernel of the Law and declared that 'the essentials of the Torah (רוב גופי תורה) are summarized therein' (Sifra). This chapter has in fact been looked upon as a counterpart of the Decalogue itself, the Ten Commandments being in essence repeated in its verses (I and II in *v.* 4; III in *v.* 12; IV and V in *v.* 3; VI in *v.* 16; VII in *v.* 29; VIII and IX in *v.* 11–16; and X in *v.* 18). The precepts contained in the chapter may, at first sight, appear a medley of the spiritual and ceremonial—fundamental maxims and principles of justice and morality alongside of ritual laws and observances. The Torah, however, regards human life as an indivisible whole, and declines to exclude any phase thereof from its purview; see introductory note to chapters XI–XVI.

2. HOLINESS AND THE IMITATION OF GOD

As the command, 'ye shall be holy, for I the LORD your God am holy,' dominates not only this chapter but the whole ethical legislation in Leviticus, it is necessary to have a clear understanding of the word *holy* (קדוש) in its ethical, as distinct from its ritual, signification. Firstly, it denotes the sublime exaltedness and overpowering majesty of God: in the presence of that Divine holiness, mortal man feels 'but dust and ashes' and is crushed by the sense of his unworthiness (Isa. VI, 5). Secondly, *holy* expresses God's complete freedom from everything that makes men imperfect, and His recoil from everything impure and unrighteous; in the words of the Prophet, 'Thou art of purer eyes than to behold evil, and canst not look on iniquity' (Hab. I, 13). Thirdly, *holy* stands for the fulness of God's ethical qualities—for more than goodness (טוב), more than purity (טהור), more than righteousness (צדיק); it *embraces* all these in their ideal completeness. 'The Holy One, blessed be He!' (הקדוש ברוך הוא) is the most common Name for God in Rabbinical literature, as well as on the lips of the Jewish masses. In its ritual usage, the word 'holy' is applied to persons and things connected with the Sanctuary, or consecrated for religious purposes.

2. *all the congregation.* The Torah and its message of holiness is the heritage of the *congregation* of Israel. There was not to be a small class of 'specialists' in religion who dwelt apart, while the people were sunk in ignorance and superstition. Israel was to form a spiritual democracy; Deut. XXXIV; see note on Exod. XXII, 30.

ye shall be holy: for I the LORD your God am holy. Man is not only to worship God, but to imitate Him. By his deeds he must reveal the Divine that is implanted in him; and make manifest, by the purity and righteousness of his actions, that he is of God. Mortal man cannot imitate God's infinite majesty or His eternity; but he *can* strive towards a purity that is Divine, by keeping aloof from everything loathsome and defiling (XI, 44); and especially can he imitate God's merciful qualities. This 'imitation of God' is held forth by the Rabbis as the highest human ideal. 'Be like God; as He is merciful and gracious, so be thou merciful and gracious. Scripture commands, *Walk ye after the LORD your God.* But the LORD is a consuming fire; how can men walk after Him? But the meaning is, by being as He is—merciful, loving, longsuffering. Mark how, on the first page of the Torah, God clothed the naked—Adam; and on the last, He buried the dead—Moses. He heals the sick, frees the captives, does good even to His enemies, and is merciful both to the living and the dead' (Talmud). These merciful qualities, therefore, are real links between God and man; and man is never nearer the Divine than in his compassionate moments. Dr. Schechter has pointed out that the Imitation of God is confined by the Rabbis to His attributes of mercy and graciousness. 'The whole Rabbinic literature might be searched in vain for a single instance of the sterner Biblical attributes of God being set up as a model for a man to copy' (Abrahams).

Holiness is thus not so much an abstract or a mystic idea, as a regulative principle in the everyday lives of men and women. The words, 'ye shall be holy,' are the keynote of the *whole* chapter, and must be read in connection with its various precepts; reverence for parents, consideration for the needy, prompt wages for reasonable hours, honourable dealing, no talebearing or malice, love of one's neighbour and holy. 3. Ye shall fear every man his mother, and his father, and ye shall keep My sabbaths: I am the LORD your God. 4. Turn ye not unto the idols, nor make to yourselves molten gods: I am the LORD your God. ¶ 5. And when ye offer a sacrifice of peace-offerings unto the LORD, ye shall offer it that ye may be accepted. 6. It shall be eaten the same day ye offer it, and on the morrow; and if aught remain until the third day, it shall be burnt with

יִשְׂרָאֵל וְאָמַרְתָּ אֲלֵהֶם קְדֹשִׁים תִּהְיוּ כִּי קָדוֹשׁ אֲנִי יְהוָה
3 אֱלֹהֵיכֶם׃ אִישׁ אִמּוֹ וְאָבִיו תִּירָאוּ וְאֶת־שַׁבְּתֹתַי תִּשְׁמֹרוּ
4 אֲנִי יְהוָה אֱלֹהֵיכֶם׃ אַל־תִּפְנוּ אֶל־הָאֱלִילִם וֵאלֹהֵי מַסֵּכָה
ה לֹא תַעֲשׂוּ לָכֶם אֲנִי יְהוָה אֱלֹהֵיכֶם׃ וְכִי תִזְבְּחוּ זֶבַח
6 שְׁלָמִים לַיהוָה לִרְצֹנְכֶם תִּזְבָּחֻהוּ׃ בְּיוֹם זִבְחֲכֶם יֵאָכֵל

cordiality to the alien, equal justice to rich and poor, just measures and balances—together with abhorrence of everything unclean, irrational, or heathen. Holiness is thus attained not by flight from the world, nor by monk-like renunciation of human relationships of family or station, but by the spirit in which we fulfil the obligations of life in its simplest and commonest details: in this way—by doing justly, loving mercy, and walking humbly with our God—is everyday life transfigured. See also p. 315.

3–4. FUNDAMENTAL MORAL LAWS

3. *ye shall fear . . . his father.* The first precept stressed is reverence for parents. Neglect of filial duty vitiates a man's whole attitude to life, and places the ideal of holiness out of his reach; see p. 298. 'If we have failed in our duty towards our parents, we are not likely to succeed in our relations towards others' (Foerster).

fear . . . his mother. lit. 'stand in awe of . . . his mother'. In the Decalogue the father is mentioned before the mother, and the word used is *honour* instead of *fear*. The Rabbis suggest the following reason for the difference: the father is the parent who disciplines the child; the mother is richer in manifestations of affection and kindliness. The child would consequently have 'love' for the mother, but 'stand in awe' before the father. Therefore, the Torah insists on the child showing love and reverence to both. The term 'fear' in this verse is that used in reference to God. 'Dear to God is the ḥonouring of father and mother, for Scripture employs the same expressions about honouring and revering parents as about honouring and revering Himself' (Talmud). For the child, his father and mother are more than ordinary mortals; and, in fact, the Fifth Commandment is in the Decalogue the connecting link between our duties towards God and our fellowmen. Many are the beautiful sayings in Rabbinical literature in regard to this Commandment, but none more beautiful that the story of Dama. Dama, a heathen dealer in jewels in Ascalon, had a stone such as was required to replace one of the precious stones in the High Priest's breastplate. A deputation from Jerusalem came to him to negotiate for its purchase; and he agreed to sell it for one hundred *dinars*, but when he went into an inner room to fetch the stone, he found that his father was asleep in that room. Dama came back, and said he could not after all sell the stone. The deputation offered two hundred dinars, three hundred, a thousand dinars—but in vain. Soon after, his father having waked, Dama ran after the Temple emissaries with the jewel; but he refused to take more than the original one hundred dinars of the first offer. 'I will not make any profit from the honour which I paid to my father,' he said. Filial reverence, the Rabbis held, was a dictate of Natural Religion and, therefore, of universal application; and it is characteristic of their broad humanity that they selected the action of a contemporary heathen as a perfect example of filial piety.

ye shall keep My sabbaths. The connection of these two precepts is significant. Even as honouring of parents stands foremost among human duties, the sanctification of the Sabbath is the first step towards holiness in man's spiritual life. For the Sabbath is not only a day of cessation from work, but the weekly opportunity for communal worship and spiritual growth; see p. 297. These two commands are placed side by side in order to teach that the fear of parents must not exceed the fear of God. Should they demand anything that contravenes God's law, then the child must place his duty to God before that of his parents (Talmud).

I am the LORD your God. This phrase (often in the shorter form, *I am the LORD*) occurs sixteen times in this Chapter. It is the Divine seal set to the enactments of the law. It 'points to God at once as the Holy One and as the Judge; it is meant both to encourage and to awe; both to exhort to vigilance and to menace with punishment' (Kalisch).

4. *idols.* lit. 'things of nought, non-entities'; *i.e.* things that have no real existence; see Jer. XIV, 14.

5–8. RITUAL LAWS

5. *when ye offer.* Or 'if ye offer'. See III, 1 and VII, 15–20. Note that the form used is not the imperative—'ye shall offer'; sacrifices are voluntary (Kimchi). The main concern of Scripture seems to be not so much *that* a sacrifice shall be brought, as, if brought, *how* it shall be brought; *i.e.* that it be offered in strict accordance with the regulations prescribed for avoiding heathen associations.

fire. 7. And if it be eaten at all on the third day, it is a vile thing; it shall not be accepted. 8. But every one that eateth it shall bear his iniquity, because he hath profaned the holy thing of the LORD; and that soul shall be cut off from his people. ¶ 9. And when ye reap the harvest of your land, thou shalt not wholly reap the corner of thy field, neither shalt thou gather the gleaning of thy harvest. 10. And thou shalt not glean thy vineyard, neither shalt thou gather the fallen fruit of thy vineyard; thou shalt leave them for the poor and for the

7 וּמִמָּחֳרָת וְהַנּוֹתָר עַד־יוֹם הַשְּׁלִישִׁי בָּאֵשׁ יִשָּׂרֵף׃ וְאִם
8 הֵאָכֹל יֵאָכֵל בַּיּוֹם הַשְּׁלִישִׁי פִּגּוּל הוּא לֹא יֵרָצֶה׃ וְאֹכְלָיו
עֲוֺנוֹ יִשָּׂא כִּי־אֶת־קֹדֶשׁ יְהוָה חִלֵּל וְנִכְרְתָה הַנֶּפֶשׁ הַהִוא
9 מֵעַמֶּיהָ׃ וּבְקֻצְרְכֶם אֶת־קְצִיר אַרְצְכֶם לֹא תְכַלֶּה פְּאַת
י שָׂדְךָ לִקְצֹר וְלֶקֶט קְצִירְךָ לֹא תְלַקֵּט׃ וְכַרְמְךָ לֹא תְעוֹלֵל
וּפֶרֶט כַּרְמְךָ לֹא תְלַקֵּט לֶעָנִי וְלַגֵּר תַּעֲזֹב אֹתָם אֲנִי יְהוָה

9–10. CONSIDERATION FOR THE POOR

9. *corner of thy field.* What is here commanded is a statutory charge on one's harvest, to which the English poor rate is analogous. It does not exclude private and voluntary assistance, according to the generous impulse of the giver.

Consideration for the poor distinguishes the Mosaic Law from all other ancient legislations, such as the Roman Law. The object of the latter seems to be primarily to safeguard the rights of the possessing classes. In the Torah, the poor man is a *brother*, and when in need he is to be relieved ungrudgingly not only with an open hand but with an open heart. In his noble self-defence, Job (xxxi, 17–20) protests:

Never have I eaten my morsel alone,
Without sharing it with the fatherless;
Never saw I any perish for want of clothing
But I warmed him with fleece from my lambs,
And his loins gave me their blessing.

The Rabbis continued this doctrine, and declared pity to be a distinguishing trait of the Jewish character. If a Jew—they held—shows himself lacking in consideration for a fellowman in distress or suffering, we may well doubt the purity of his Jewish descent. 'There is no ethical quality more characteristic of Rabbinic Judaism than Rachmonuth—pity. The beggar whose point of view is that you are to thank him for allowing him to give you the opportunity for showing Rachmonuth, is a characteristically Jewish figure' (Montefiore).

gleaning. The ears of corn which fall to the ground at the time of reaping.

11–16. DUTIES TOWARDS OUR FELLOWMEN

These precepts restate the fundamental rules of life in human society that are contained in the Second Table of the Decalogue. These moral principles were expanded by the Rabbis and applied to every phase of civil and criminal law.

11. *ye shall not steal.* 'Even as a practical joke; or, in order to enable another to profit by the four- or five-fold restitution which thou shalt have to make; or, to reclaim by stealth thine own stolen property, lest thou seem a thief' (Sifra). Everything that has the appearance of stealing is strictly forbidden, lest a man become habituated to the act of stealing (Shulchan Aruch). Especially reprehensible is 'stealing the good opinion of others' (גניבת דעת)—by any manner of misrepresentation, 'publicity,' or flattery deceiving others into having a better opinion of him or his doings than he deserves. ראשון שבגנבים גונב דעת הבריות (Mechilta, Mishpatim). 'Let a man earn the good opinion of his fellowmen, but let him not steal it' (S. R. Hirsch). A classical example is afforded by Absalom's manner of ingratiating himself with all who felt discontent at 'the law's delay', suggesting that if *he* were king, things would be very different. 'And Absalom rose up early, and stood beside the way of the gate: and it was so, that when any man had a suit which should come to the king for judgment, then Absalom said unto him, . . . See, thy matters are good and right; but there is no man deputed of the king to hear thee. Absalom said moreover, Oh that I were made judge in the land, that every man which hath any suit or cause might come unto me, and I would do him justice! . . . So Absalom *stole the hearts* of the men of Israel' (II Sam. xv, 2–6).

deal falsely. lit. 'falsely deny'.

nor lie. 'Let your Yes be righteous and your No be righteous. He who exacted retribution from the generation of the Flood, will exact it of the man who does not stand by his word. Truth is one of the pillars of the Universe; it is God's own seal. The liar is an outcast from the Divine fellowship. Men too punish him, for he is not believed even when he speaks the truth. The good man is he who is what he seems' (Talmud). The truth, however, must be spoken *in love*. Truthfulness must be moral: it ceases to be truthfulness and becomes an abominable form of lying when it is used as a tool of revenge or malice in order to ruin another or for putting him to open shame.

'A truth that's told with bad intent
Beats all the lies you can invent' (Blake).

stranger: I am the LORD your God. 11. Ye shall not steal; neither shall ye deal falsely, nor lie one to another. 12. And ye shall not swear by My name falsely, so that thou profane the name of thy God: I am the LORD. 13. Thou shalt not oppress thy neighbour, nor rob him; the wages of a hired servant shall not abide with thee all night until the morning. 14. Thou shalt not curse the deaf, nor put a stumbling-block before the blind, but thou shalt fear thy God: I am the LORD.* ii (** v). 15. Ye shall do no unrighteousness in judgment; thou shalt not respect the person of the poor,

11 אֱלֹהֵיכֶם׃ לֹא תִּגְנֹבוּ וְלֹא־תְכַחֲשׁוּ וְלֹא־תְשַׁקְּרוּ אִישׁ
12 בַּעֲמִיתוֹ׃ וְלֹא־תִשָּׁבְעוּ בִשְׁמִי לַשָּׁקֶר וְחִלַּלְתָּ אֶת־שֵׁם
13 אֱלֹהֶיךָ אֲנִי יְהוָה׃ לֹא־תַעֲשֹׁק אֶת־רֵעֲךָ וְלֹא תִגְזֹל לֹא־
14 תָלִין פְּעֻלַּת שָׂכִיר אִתְּךָ עַד־בֹּקֶר׃ לֹא־תְקַלֵּל חֵרֵשׁ וְלִפְנֵי
שני (חמישי כשהן מחוב) טו עִוֵּר לֹא תִתֵּן מִכְשֹׁל וְיָרֵאתָ מֵּאֱלֹהֶיךָ אֲנִי יְהוָה׃ ׳ לֹא־תַעֲשׂוּ
עָוֶל בַּמִּשְׁפָּט לֹא־תִשָּׂא פְנֵי־דָל וְלֹא תֶהְדַּר פְּנֵי גָדוֹל

12. *and ye shall not swear. And* indicates that the verse is to be closely associated with the preceding one. 'If thou hast stolen, thou wilt end by falsely denying, lying, and swearing by My Name to a falsehood' (Sifra)—profaning the Name of God for the purpose of deceit and fraud.

13. *oppress.* 'Defraud' (Moffatt). In Deut. XXIV, 14, 'a hired servant' is substituted for 'thy neighbour'. 'Oppressing' a hired servant means taking advantage of his helplessness and paying him less than his due for his work.

rob him. By withholding from him that which is his.

abide with thee. If the labourer is hired by the day, his wages must be paid to him immediately after the day's work is done. The poor man lives from hand to mouth.

14. *curse the deaf.* Defame the deaf, or anyone who cannot hear, and so cannot vindicate his own character.

nor put a stumbling-block before the blind. 'Trip up a blind man' (Moffatt), either in sport or malice. Alas for the prevalence of human callousness and cruelty that render the formulation of such a precept necessary.

'Deaf' and 'blind' are typical figures of all misfortune, inexperience, and moral weakness. This verse is a warning against leading the young and morally weak into sin, or provoking them to commit irretrievable mistakes. The following are typical violations of this ethical precept: he who gives disingenuous advice to the inexperienced; he who tempts the Nazirite to break his oath not to drink wine; he who sells lethal weapons to weak or dangerous characters—all these transgress the command 'Thou shalt not put a stumbling-block before the blind'. Equally so does the man who administers corporal punishment to a grown-up son: it may make that son forgetful of filial duty, and in blind anger commit an unpardonable offence (Talmud).

fear thy God. Who is the avenger of the helpless; of the deaf or absent man who cannot protect himself from the reviling which he has not heard; of the 'blind' man who cannot avoid the stumbling-block of which he is not aware. Furthermore, the man who deliberately gives harmful advice may allege the noblest of intentions. But Scripture exhorts him to 'fear God', who searches the innermost recesses of the human heart and knows its secret thoughts. See the note of Exod. I, 17, showing that *fearing God* means natural piety and fundamental humanity.

15. *respect the person of the poor.* 'You shall not be partial to a poor man' (Moffatt). With all its sympathy for the poor and helpless, the Torah fears that justice might be outraged in favour of the poor man when he is in the wrong. Even sympathy and compassion must be silenced in the presence of Justice. In this Scriptural command, as in Exod. XXIII, 3 (Thou shalt not favour a poor man in his cause) 'there is a sublimity of moral view, which compels the reverence of all' (Geiger).

nor favour. The judge must not say, 'This man is rich and well connected; how can I put him to shame by deciding against him?' (Sifra).

in righteousness. There is to be neither prejudice in favour of the poor, nor dread of offending the great, but *justice;* see on Exod. XXIII, 3. Thus, one of the litigants is not to be permitted to state his case at length, and the other bidden 'to cut it short'. One litigant must not be allowed to be seated in court, and the other kept standing (Sifra). 'The judge should feel as though a sword were suspended above his head throughout the time he sits in judgment' (Talmud).

Another authoritative explanation of *in righteousness shalt thou judge thy neighbour* is, 'Judge every man in the scale of merit (לכף זכות); refuse to condemn by appearances, but put the best construction on the deeds of your fellowmen' (Talmud).

The teaching of this and the preceding verses is thus restated by the Prophet: 'Speak ye every man the truth with his neighbour; execute the judgment of truth and peace in your gates; and let none of you imagine evil in your hearts against his neighbour; and love no false oath: for all these are things that I hate, saith the LORD' (Zech. VIII, 16, 17).

16 בְּצֶדֶק תִּשְׁפֹּט עֲמִיתֶךָ׃ לֹא־תֵלֵךְ רָכִיל בְּעַמֶּיךָ לֹא תַעֲמֹד
17 עַל־דַּם רֵעֶךָ אֲנִי יְהוָה׃ לֹא־תִשְׂנָא אֶת־אָחִיךָ בִּלְבָבֶךָ
18 הוֹכֵחַ תּוֹכִיחַ אֶת־עֲמִיתֶךָ וְלֹא־תִשָּׂא עָלָיו חֵטְא׃ לֹא־
תִקֹּם וְלֹא־תִטֹּר אֶת־בְּנֵי עַמֶּךָ וְאָהַבְתָּ לְרֵעֲךָ כָּמוֹךָ אֲנִי

nor favour the person of the mighty; but in righteousness shalt thou judge thy neighbour.
16. Thou shalt not go up and down as a talebearer among thy people; neither shalt thou stand idly by the blood of thy neighbour: I am the LORD.
17. Thou shalt not hate thy brother in thy heart; thou shalt surely rebuke thy neighbour, and not bear sin because of him.
18.

16. *go up and down as a talebearer.* lit. 'go up and down as a pedlar'. This expressive idiom is here applied to a person who travels about dealing in scandal and malicious hearsay, getting the secrets of people and *retailing* them wherever he goes (Rashi). A mischievous business, even if the report is true and told without malice (Maimonides). 'A more despicable character exists not; such a person is a pest to society, and should be exiled from the habitation of men' (Adam Clarke). Injurious gossip may often do as much harm as slanderous defamation. Hence the prayer, three times daily, 'O my God, guard my tongue from evil and my lips from speaking guile' (Authorised Prayer Book, p. 54). The slanderer, the man of the evil tongue (לשון הרע), the calumniator, is worse than a murderer, since he destroys a man's reputation, which is more precious than his life (Talmud). Hence the informer (moser) was deemed the most abandoned creature among all evil-doers to their kind.

Stand idly by the blood of thy neighbour. I.e. when his life is in danger. Do not stand idly by, watching with indifference thy fellowman in mortal danger through drowning, or attacked by wild animals, or robbers, without hastening to his rescue (Talmud). In protecting the life of another, it is permitted to take the life of the assailant, even as in self-defence. The Sifra gives a further application to this verse: if thy fellowman is accused of a crime, and evidence that would clear him of it is in thy possession, thou art not at liberty to keep silent.

17–18. PROHIBITION OF HATRED AND VENGEANCE: LOVE OF NEIGHBOUR

17. *hate thy brother in thine heart.* Nursing your grievance against your fellowman. Most of the hating in the world is quite unjustified, groundless hating for its own sake (שנאת חנם). 'Thou shalt not hate thy brother *in thine heart.* Our Rabbis taught that if Scripture had merely said, "Thou shalt not hate thy brother," this precept might be explained to mean only that you must not injure him, nor insult him, nor vex him; and so the words "in thine heart" are added to forbid us even to feel hatred in our heart without giving it outward expression. Causeless hatred ranks with the three cardinal sins: Idolatry, Immorality, and Murder. The Second Temple, although in its time study of the Law and good works flourished and God's commandments were obeyed, was destroyed because of causeless hatred' (Achai Gaon). When it is fed by racial rivalry or religious bigotry, causeless hatred petrifies the heart and becomes organized malice. None has suffered, and is still suffering, from causeless hatred more than the Jewish People. The Talmud instances the Emperor Hadrian's conduct as typical of men swayed by such hatred. One day on Hadrian's journey in the East, a Jew passed the Imperial train and saluted the Emperor. Hadrian was beside himself with rage. 'You, a Jew, dare to greet the Emperor! You shall pay for this with your life.' In the course of the same day, another Jew passed him, and, warned by example, he did not greet Hadrian. 'You, a Jew, dare to pass the Emperor without a greeting,' he angrily exclaimed. 'You have forfeited your life.' To his astonished courtiers he replied: 'I hate the Jews. Whatever they do, I find intolerable. I, therefore, make use of any pretext to destroy them.' So are all anti-Semites; so, all slaves of 'causeless hatred'.

rebuke thy neighbour. A precept extremely difficult of fulfilment; it is as difficult to administer reproof with delicacy and tact, as it is to receive reproof. Reproof must, of course, be offered in all kindness, otherwise it fails of its purpose; and, if it entails putting a man to shame in public, it is mortal sin. No matter how much learning and good works the man who commits such a sin may possess, he has no share in the world to come—says a great Mishnah teacher.

sin because of him. Unless there is a frank statement from the aggrieved party, the hatred or dislike smouldering in his heart may lead him into sin.

18. *thou shalt not take vengeance.* Forbids repaying evil with evil. 'If a man finds both a friend and an enemy in distress, he should first assist his enemy, in order to subdue his evil inclination,' *i.e.* man's inborn passion for revenge (Talmud). Scripture inculcates this virtue both by precept and illustrious example. Joseph's conduct to his brethren, and David's to Saul, are among the noblest instances of forgiveness to be found in literature. Such examples are not confined to the Biblical period. Samuel ibn Nagrela was a Spanish-Jewish poet of the eleventh century, who was vizier to the king of Granada. He was one

Thou shalt not take vengeance, nor bear any grudge against the children of thy people, but thou shalt love thy neighbour as thyself: I am the LORD. 19. Ye shall keep My statutes. Thou shalt not let thy cattle gender with a diverse kind; thou shalt not sow thy field with two kinds of seed; neither shall there come upon thee a garment of two kinds of stuff mingled together. 20. And whosoever lieth carnally with a woman, that is a bondmaid, desig-

19 יְהוָה׃ אֶת־חֻקֹּתַי תִּשְׁמֹרוּ בְּהֶמְתְּךָ לֹא־תַרְבִּיעַ כִּלְאַיִם
שָׂדְךָ לֹא־תִזְרַע כִּלְאָיִם וּבֶגֶד כִּלְאַיִם שַׁעַטְנֵז לֹא יַעֲלֶה
כ עָלֶיךָ׃ וְאִישׁ כִּי־יִשְׁכַּב אֶת־אִשָּׁה שִׁכְבַת־זֶרַע וְהִוא שִׁפְחָה
נֶחֱרֶפֶת לְאִישׁ וְהָפְדֵּה לֹא נִפְדָּתָה אוֹ חֻפְשָׁה לֹא נִתַּן
21 לָהּ בִּקֹּרֶת תִּהְיֶה לֹא יוּמְתוּ כִּי־לֹא חֻפָּשָׁה׃ וְהֵבִיא אֶת־

day cursed in the presence of the king, who commanded Samuel to punish the offender by cutting out his tongue. The Jewish vizier, however, treated his enemy kindly, whereupon the curses became blessings. When the king next noticed the offender, he was astonished that Samuel had not carried out his command. Samuel replied, 'I have torn out his angry tongue, and given him instead a kind one.' The Rabbis rightly declare, 'Who is mighty? He who makes his enemy his friend.'

The Jew is not 'a good hater'. Shylock is 'the Jew that Shakespeare drew'. He is not the Jew of real life, even in the Middle Ages, stained as their story is with the hot tears—nay, the very heart's blood—of the martyred race. The medieval Jew did not take vengeance on his cruel foes. The Jews hunted out of Spain in 1492 were in turn cruelly expelled from Portugal. Some took refuge on the African coast. Eighty years later the descendants of the men who had thus inhumanly treated their Jewish fellowmen were defeated in Africa, whither they had been led by their king, Dom Sebastian. Those who were not slain were offered as slaves at Fez to the descendants of the Jewish exiles from Portugal. 'The humbled Portuguese nobles,' the historian narrates, 'were comforted when their purchasers proved to be Jews, for they knew that they had humane hearts' (M. Joseph).

nor bear any grudge. Waiting for an opportunity to repay evil with evil. The Rabbis give the following explanation of these two phrases: 'If a man says, I will not lend you the tool you require, because you did not lend it me when I asked for it—that is vengeance. If a man says, I will lend you the tool, although you refused to lend it when I asked for it—that is bearing grudge.' In an ancient Jewish book, that has come down to us probably from Maccabean times, known as *The Testaments of the Twelve Patriarchs*, we read: 'Love ye one another from the heart; and if a man sin against thee, cast forth the poison of hate and speak peaceably to him. If he confess and repent, forgive him. But if he be shameless and persist in his wrongdoing, even so forgive him from the heart, and leave to God the avenging. Beware of hatred; for it works lawlessness even against the Lord Himself. For it will not hear the words of the Commandments concerning the loving of one's neighbour. Love would quicken even the dead, and would call back them that are condemned to die; but hatred would slay the living.' The Rabbis declare, 'He who has a forgiving spirit is himself forgiven. Whosoever does not persecute them that persecute him, whosoever suffers wrong in silence and requites it not, they are deemed the *friends of God*.'

thou shalt love thy neighbour as thyself. Heb. ואהבת לרעך כמוך; *i.e.* let the honour and property of thy fellowman be as dear to thee as thine own. These three Heb. words were early recognized as the most comprehensive rule of conduct, as containing the essence of religion and applicable in every human relation and towards all men. Even the criminal condemned to die, say the Rabbis, has a claim on our brotherly love, and we must spare him unnecessary suffering. Hillel paraphrased this rule into 'Whatever is hateful unto thee do it not unto thy fellow'; and declared it to be the whole Law, the remainder being but a commentary on this fundamental principle of the Torah. See Additional Note 'Thou Shalt Love Thy Neighbour As Thyself', p. 563.

19–26. MISCELLANEOUS PRECEPTS

19. *statutes*. Laws for which the reason has not been revealed to us. However, the word may here mean, as in Jer. XXXIII, 25, fixed laws which God had instituted for the government of the physical universe. The purpose of the following regulations would then be: man must not deviate from the appointed order of things, nor go against the eternal laws of nature as established by Divine Wisdom. What God has ordained to be kept apart, man must not seek to mix together.

diverse kind. Josephus suggested as the reason for the prohibition of mixed breeding the fear that such unnatural union in the animal world might lead to moral perversion among human beings.

two kinds of seed. See Deut. XXII, 9.

mingled together. Heb. *shaatnez*. See Deut. XXII, 11, where the law is more explicitly stated: 'mingled stuff, wool and linen.' 'Nature does not rejoice in the union of things that are not in their nature alike' (Josephus).

20. *bondmaid*. Here we have an example of 'prohibited mixture in the sphere of moral relationship'—the union with a heathen bondmaid betrothed to a Hebrew slave. The offence is not as serious as in the case of a betrothed nated for a man, and not at all redeemed, nor was freedom given her; there shall be inquisition; they shall not be put to death, because she was not free. 21. And he shall bring his forfeit unto the LORD, unto the door of the tent of meeting, even a ram for a guilt-offering. 22. And the priest shall make atonement for him with the ram of the guilt-offering before the LORD for his sin which he hath sinned; and he shall be forgiven for his sin which he hath sinned.*iii. ¶23. And when ye shall come into the land, and shall have planted all manner of trees for food, then ye shall count the fruit thereof as forbidden; three years shall it be as forbidden unto you; it shall not be eaten. 24. And in the fourth year all the fruit thereof shall be holy, for giving praise unto the LORD. 25. But in the fifth year may ye eat of the fruit thereof, that it may yield unto you more richly the increase thereof: I am the LORD your God. 26. Ye shall not eat with the blood; neither shall ye practise divination nor soothsaying. 27. Ye shall not round the corners of your heads, neither shalt thou mar the corners of thy beard. 28. Ye shall not make any cuttings in your flesh for the dead, nor imprint any marks upon you: I am the LORD. 29. Profane not thy daugh-

22 אשמו ליהוה אל־פתח אהל מועד איל אשם׃ וכפר
עליו הכהן באיל האשם לפני יהוה על־חטאתו אשר
חטא ונסלח לו מחטאתו אשר חטא׃ פ שלישי
23 וכי־תבאו אל־הארץ ונטעתם כל־עץ מאכל וערלתם
ערלתו את־פריו שלש שנים יהיה לכם ערלים לא יאכל׃
24 ובשנה הרביעת יהיה כל־פריו קדש הלולים ליהוה׃
כה ובשנה החמישת תאכלו את־פריו להוסיף לכם תבואתו
26 אני יהוה אלהיכם׃ לא תאכלו על־הדם לא תנחשו
27 ולא תעוננו׃ לא תקפו פאת ראשכם ולא תשחית את
28 פאת זקנך׃ ושרט לנפש לא תתנו בבשרכם וכתבת
29 קעקע לא תתנו בכם אני יהוה׃ אל־תחלל את־בתך
ל להזנותה ולא־תזנה הארץ ומלאה הארץ זמה׃ את־

freewoman; nevertheless, the act is branded as immoral and one to be punished.

There shall be inquisition. Better, 'there shall be a lashing,' or corporal punishment. The Heb. בקרת means a lash made of ox-hide (Ibn Ezra).

23. *forbidden.* lit. you shall regard its fruit as defective. The fruit tree in its first three years is to be regarded as a male infant during his first eight days; *i.e.* as unconsecrated (Dillmann). Its fruit was then stunted in its growth and unfit as a first-fruit offering to God; and hence forbidden for human use.

25. *more richly.* The trees become more productive if they are stripped of the blossoms in the early years.

26–31. PROHIBITION OF CANAANITE CUSTOMS

The context suggests that the allusion is to a heathenish rite of divination, well-known to the Israelites.

26. *with the blood.* 'They killed a beast, received the blood in a vessel or pot, and ate of the flesh of that beast, whilst sitting round the blood. They imagined that in this manner, the spirits would come to partake of the blood which was their food; brotherhood and friendship would be established with the spirits' (Maimonides). It is, however, taken by the Rabbis both in a literal sense ('do not eat flesh from an animal whose blood is yet in it', *i.e.* whose life has not yet departed), and as an ethical injunction ('the members of a Court whose decree of capital punishment has been carried out shall on that day abstain from all food').

divination. Charms and incantations. Ancient life, whether in Egypt, Canaan, or Mesopotamia, was crushed under an intolerable weight of enchantment, magic, and demonology. The Israelite was freed from the incubus of superstition by these prohibitions, which constitute one of the great negations of Judaism; cf. Num. XXIII, 23.

soothsaying. Or, 'divination' by observing times and seasons and declaring one day 'lucky' and another 'unlucky'—a common practice among heathens.

27. *round the corners.* In this and the following verse, various mourning customs connected with the heathen worship of the dead are forbidden, as unbecoming the dignity of God's people and incompatible with loyalty to a God of holiness.

28. *cuttings . . . for the dead.* See on Deut. XIV, 1. Eastern peoples, in their excessive demonstration of grief at a bereavement, often gashed and mutilated themselves. The shedding of blood was also believed to have a sacrificial value for the dead person. Even aside from the prohibition of this idolatrous practice, the Torah inculcates reverence for the human body, as the work of God.

imprint any marks. By means of writing that sinks into the flesh. What is here forbidden is the custom of tattooing some part of the body. Often this was a representation of the deity worshipped by the bearer of that mark.

ter, to make her a harlot, lest the land fall into harlotry, and the land become full of lewdness. 30. Ye shall keep My sabbaths, and reverence My sanctuary: I am the LORD. 31. Turn ye not unto the ghosts, nor unto familiar spirits; seek them not out, to be defiled by them: I am the LORD your God. 32. Thou shalt rise up before the hoary head, and honour the face of the old man, and thou shalt fear thy God: I am the LORD.* iv (** vi). 33. And if a stranger sojourn with thee in your land, ye shall not do him wrong. 34. The stranger that sojourneth with you shall be unto you as the home-

31 שַׁבְּתֹתַי תִּשְׁמֹרוּ וּמִקְדָּשִׁי תִּירָאוּ אֲנִי יְהוָה׃ אַל־תִּפְנוּ
אֶל־הָאֹבֹת וְאֶל־הַיִּדְּעֹנִים אַל־תְּבַקְשׁוּ לְטָמְאָה בָהֶם אֲנִי
32 יְהוָה אֱלֹהֵיכֶם׃ מִפְּנֵי שֵׂיבָה תָּקוּם וְהָדַרְתָּ פְּנֵי זָקֵן וְיָרֵאתָ
רביעי (שני כשהן מחוב')
33 מֵּאֱלֹהֶיךָ אֲנִי יְהוָה׃ * ס וְכִי־יָגוּר אִתְּךָ גֵּר בְּאַרְצְכֶם לֹא
34 תוֹנוּ אֹתוֹ׃ כְּאֶזְרָח מִכֶּם יִהְיֶה לָכֶם הַגֵּר ׀ הַגָּר אִתְּכֶם
וְאָהַבְתָּ לוֹ כָּמוֹךָ כִּי־גֵרִים הֱיִיתֶם בְּאֶרֶץ מִצְרָיִם אֲנִי יְהוָה

29. *profane not thy daughter.* A prohibition for a father to hand over his daughter to a man without the previous rites of 'sanctification'—*i.e.* without a legal marriage; as well as prohibition for a woman of her own free will to consort with a man without such legal marriage (Sifra). The use of the word *profane* is noteworthy. It presupposes the sacredness of womanhood; and it brands such an action as a profanation and a desecration of the sacred personality of a human being.

the land. i.e. its inhabitants, as in XVIII, 25.

fall into harlotry. Looking upon the 'demand' for harlotry as a normal condition of things, and tolerating the consequent 'supply' of human beings for such life of shame.

30. *sabbaths . . . sanctuary.* The parenthetical insertion of this injunction may be intended to impress upon the Israelite that reverence for Sabbath and Sanctuary will keep him from the heathenish rites and immoralities mentioned in the preceding verses and that following.

31. *familiar spirits.* The English word 'familiar' here means 'attendant'. The wizard professes to know through the spirit attendant upon him, or residing within him, what is hidden from the ordinary person.

to be defiled. Physically, by coming into contact with the dead bones which were part of the paraphernalia of the wizard; and spiritually, by sinking into the mire of superstition inseparable from witchcraft and necromancy; see on XX, 6.

32–37. ETHICAL INJUNCTIONS

32. *rise up before the hoary head.* 'Hoary,' white with age. The ethical sublimity of this exhortation is not diminished by the fact that parallels exist among other ancient peoples, and that in the Orient reverence for old age is or was the rule until the present day.

honour the face of the old man. 'Honour the person of an old man' (Moffatt). The Rabbis enlarged the connotation of the word 'old' and made it include anyone who had acquired wisdom (זקן, זה שקנה חכמה). But even where there is no book-learning, there may be the matured wisdom of experience. A famous rabbi would stand up even before an aged heathen peasant, saying, 'What storms of fortune has this old man weathered in his life-time.'

thou shalt fear. Cf. on *v.* 14. Here, too, the inner motives of a man are involved, not only his outward acts.

33. *a stranger.* The duty of loving the stranger is stressed thirty-six times in Scripture and is placed on the same level as the duty of kindness to, and protection of, the widow or the orphan. 'The alien was to be protected, although he was not a member of one's family, clan, religious community, or people; simply *because he was a human being.* In the alien, therefore, man discovered the idea of humanity' (Hermann Cohen). See the comments on Exod. XXII, 20.

not do him wrong. Heb. לא תונו. Not only oppression by unrighteous deeds; such as, taking advantage of his ignorance to overreach him. The Rabbis take the word in sense of 'offend', and they emphasize the peculiar heinousness of wounding the alien's feelings by insulting speech (אונאת דברים). Few modern peoples, alas, can truthfully be said to have learned this ethical precept.

34. *as the home-born.* There was to be one law only, the same for home-born and alien alike (XXIV, 22; Num. XV, 16); see p. 260. The stranger is to share in the corners of the field, the forgotten sheaf, and every form of poor relief. The tremendous seriousness with which justice to the stranger is inculcated is seen from the fact that, among the covenant admonitions at Mount Ebal, we read 'Cursed is the man that perverteth the justice of the stranger' (Deut. XXVII, 19). Israel was not permitted to hate even the Egyptian, the people that enslaved him. It was to transform those memories of bitter oppression into feelings of compassion to all the friendless and downtrodden. In other ancient codes, the stranger was born among you, and thou shalt love him as thyself; for ye were strangers in the land of Egypt: I am the LORD your God. 35. Ye shall do no unrighteousness in judgment, in meteyard, in weight, or in measure. 36. Just balances, just weights, a just ephah, and a just hin, shall ye have: I am the LORD your God, who brought you out of the land of Egypt. 37. And ye shall observe all My statutes, and all Mine ordinances, and do them: I am the LORD.* v.

20

CHAPTER XX

1. And the LORD spoke unto Moses, saying: 2. Moreover, thou shalt say to the children of Israel: ¶ Whosoever he be of the children of Israel, or of the strangers that sojourn in Israel, that giveth of his seed unto Molech; he shall surely be put to death; the people of the land shall stone him with stones. 3. I also will set My face against that man, and will cut him off from among his people, because he hath given of his seed unto Molech, to defile My sanctuary,

לה אֱלֹהֵיכֶם׃ לֹא־תַעֲשׂוּ עָוֶל בַּמִּשְׁפָּט בַּמִּדָּה בַּמִּשְׁקָל
36 וּבַמְּשׂוּרָה׃ מֹאזְנֵי צֶדֶק אַבְנֵי־צֶדֶק אֵיפַת צֶדֶק וְהִין צֶדֶק
יִהְיֶה לָכֶם אֲנִי יְהוָה אֱלֹהֵיכֶם אֲשֶׁר־הוֹצֵאתִי אֶתְכֶם מֵאֶרֶץ
37 מִצְרָיִם׃ וּשְׁמַרְתֶּם אֶת־כָּל־חֻקֹּתַי וְאֶת־כָּל־מִשְׁפָּטַי
וַעֲשִׂיתֶם אֹתָם אֲנִי יְהוָה׃ * פ חמישי

CAP. XX. כ

כ

א 2 וַיְדַבֵּר יְהוָה אֶל־מֹשֶׁה לֵּאמֹר׃ וְאֶל־בְּנֵי יִשְׂרָאֵל תֹּאמַר
אִישׁ אִישׁ מִבְּנֵי יִשְׂרָאֵל וּמִן־הַגֵּר ׀ הַגָּר בְּיִשְׂרָאֵל אֲשֶׁר
יִתֵּן מִזַּרְעוֹ לַמֹּלֶךְ מוֹת יוּמָת עַם הָאָרֶץ יִרְגְּמֻהוּ בָאָבֶן׃
3 וַאֲנִי אֶתֵּן אֶת־פָּנַי בָּאִישׁ הַהוּא וְהִכְרַתִּי אֹתוֹ מִקֶּרֶב עַמּוֹ

rightless. Thus, the Romans had originally one word, hostis, for both stranger and enemy. According to Germanic Law the stranger was 'rechtsunfähig'. See on XXIV, 22.

thou shalt love him as thyself. Do to him what you would wish others to do unto you, if you were a stranger in a strange land. See Additional Note, 'Thou Shalt Love Thy Neighbour As Thyself,' p. 563.

35. *in judgment.* Not an unnecessary repetition of the same phrase in *v.* 15. God abhors unrighteousness, *i.e.* dishonesty, in business. 'For all that do such things, are an abomination unto the LORD' (Deut. XXV, 16).

36. *ephah.* The standard dry measure; somewhat larger than a bushel.

hin. A measure for liquids; a sixth of the ephah, about $1\frac{1}{4}$–$1\frac{1}{2}$ gallons.

brought you out. God had delivered the Israelites from a land where they had suffered from injustice; let them not practise injustice in their dealings with one another.

37. *I am the LORD.* Thus this remarkable series of precepts ends on the exalted note with which it opened; *v.* 2.

CHAPTER XX. PENALTIES FOR UNLAWFUL MARRIAGES, MOLECH WORSHIP AND NECROMANCY

This chapter is a natural pendant to XVIII and XIX, and enumerates the acts that would debase Israel's life, and altogether destroy its ideal of Holiness. In an organized society, it is essential to institute penalties for the violation of enactments that are vital to its existence. Ruthless measures were indispensable against the abominable vices and hideous practices which Israel was in danger of transplanting into its own life from its Canaanite and Egyptian neighbours. Flaming jealousy for Israel's mission of Holiness, and gigantic energy on the part of its ethical guides and religious teachers, could alone have overcome the bestialities of heathendom.

Unsparing condemnation of the crimes did not, however, invariably lead to the unsparing punishment of everyone suspected of them. In Jewish Law, the presumption of innocence is given to the accused, and capital punishments require two eye-witnesses to the *premeditated* commission of the crime. This alone rendered actual conviction in such cases a rare thing.

1–5. PENALTIES FOR MOLECH WORSHIP

2. *strangers.* Such horrors should not be permitted even to resident strangers on any false idea of toleration, or on the ground that it was no concern of the community what 'aliens' did.

Molech. See on XVIII, 21.

people of the land. Heb. *am ha-aretz.* Here again it is better to translate, *the National Council; i.e.* the national representatives, acting on behalf of the nation, shall stamp out this hideous idolatry.

stone him. Stoning goes back to hoary Semitic antiquity, and was prescribed for crimes that demanded punishments with a deterrent effect upon the people. In later ages, the original method was modified to render it more humane. The Talmud tells that, in capital offences, delinquents were drugged in order to deaden the senses before execution.

3. *set My face.* See XVII, 10.

will cut him off. This verse refers to the case of a man who performs the atrocity in private, so and to profane My holy name. 4. And if the people of the land do at all hide their eyes from that man, when he giveth of his seed unto Molech, and put him not to death; 5. then I will set My face against that man, and against his family, and will cut him off, and all that go astray after him, to go astray after Molech, from among their people. 6. And the soul that turneth unto the ghosts, and unto the familiar spirits, to go astray after them, I will even set My face against that soul, and will cut him off from among his people. 7. Sanctify yourselves therefore, and be ye holy; for I am the LORD your God. * vi (** vii). 8. And keep ye My statutes, and do them: I am the LORD who sanctify you. 9. For whatsoever man there be that curseth his father or his mother shall surely be put to death; he hath cursed his father or his mother; his blood shall be upon him. 10. And the man that committeth adultery

כִּֽי מִזַּרְעוֹ נָתַן לַמֹּלֶךְ לְמַעַן טַמֵּא אֶת־מִקְדָּשִׁי וּלְחַלֵּל אֶת־
4 שֵׁם קָדְשִׁי׃ וְאִם הַעְלֵם יַעְלִימוּ עַם הָאָרֶץ אֶת־עֵינֵיהֶם
מִן־הָאִישׁ הַהוּא בְּתִתּוֹ מִזַּרְעוֹ לַמֹּלֶךְ לְבִלְתִּי הָמִית אֹתוֹ׃
ה וְשַׂמְתִּי אֲנִי אֶת־פָּנַי בָּאִישׁ הַהוּא וּבְמִשְׁפַּחְתּוֹ וְהִכְרַתִּי
אֹתוֹ וְאֵת ׀ כָּל־הַזֹּנִים אַחֲרָיו לִזְנוֹת אַחֲרֵי הַמֹּלֶךְ מִקֶּרֶב
6 עַמָּם׃ וְהַנֶּפֶשׁ אֲשֶׁר תִּפְנֶה אֶל־הָאֹבֹת וְאֶל־הַיִּדְּעֹנִים
לִזְנֹת אַחֲרֵיהֶם וְנָתַתִּי אֶת־פָּנַי בַּנֶּפֶשׁ הַהִוא וְהִכְרַתִּי אֹתוֹ
7 מִקֶּרֶב עַמּוֹ׃ וְהִתְקַדִּשְׁתֶּם וִהְיִיתֶם קְדֹשִׁים כִּי אֲנִי יְהוָה
ששי (שביעי כשהן מחובר׳)
8 אֱלֹהֵיכֶם׃ * וּשְׁמַרְתֶּם אֶת־חֻקֹּתַי וַעֲשִׂיתֶם אֹתָם אֲנִי יְהוָה
9 מְקַדִּשְׁכֶם׃ כִּי־אִישׁ אִישׁ אֲשֶׁר יְקַלֵּל אֶת־אָבִיו וְאֶת־אִמּוֹ

that there are no witnesses of the act. In that event, God will Himself punish the evil-doer.

to defile My sanctuary. 'The community of Israel which is sanctified to God' (Rashi); or the soil would be defiled by such an enormity (XVII, 27), and the defilement conveyed to the Sanctuary established upon it.

to profane My holy name. See XVIII, 21.

4. *hide their eyes. i.e.* overlook it. For such an offence to be connived at and condoned by the authorities and nation is evidence of both religious demoralization and social decay. It furthermore proves that they too are on the threshold of succumbing to Molech worship (Strack).

5. *his family. i.e.* his sympathizers or accomplices. Ibn Ezra quotes an explanation which refers 'his family' to *am ha-aretz* in the preceding verse. They hide their eyes from his crime because they are of his family. Targum Jonathan renders this verse: 'And I shall choose My own time to attend to that man and to the members of the family who take him under their protection, and shall chasten them with painful trials; but the man himself I shall destroy.'

6. *familiar spirits.* See on XIX, 31. The punishment is left in the hands of God; but as for the necromancer himself, the penalty is death by stoning (*v.* 27 below), since to cause others to sin is worse than sinning. Here, too, ruthlessness—social surgery—was required, if true and ethical religion was not to perish from the earth. 'Not to realize the vital necessity of these laws concerning witchcraft and the vital duty of its extirpation, is to fall a victim to the superstition that witchcraft was mere harmless make-believe that did not call for any drastic punishment. At the bottom of this sceptical attitude towards the laws of witchcraft is indifference towards the unique value of monotheism. In a conflict of this nature—witchcraft *versus* monotheism—there can be no hesitancy or mutual tolerance of opposite points of view. It is a question of To be or not to be for the ethical life' (Hermann Cohen).

7–21. LAWS BEARING ON IMMORALITY

7. *sanctify yourselves.* This and the following verses are introductory to the laws which follow. The first section deals with idolatry and heathenish superstition. The motive that should guide the life of the Israelite and restrain him from wrong actions is solemnly repeated; cf. XI, 44.

8. *sanctify you.* By electing you from all the nations to be My people, and by giving you laws and institutions designed to lead to a holy life. Before the performance of any religious precept, the Israelite repeated the Blessing: 'Blessed art thou, O Lord our God, King of the universe, who hast *sanctified* us by thy commandments and hast commanded us . . .'

9. *curseth.* See Exod. XXI, 15, 17; Prov. XX, 20 ('Whoso curseth his father or his mother, his lamp shall be put out in the blackest darkness'). It was a capital offence; but the Rabbis, though they shared the horror with which the moral hideousness of such an action was viewed, endeavoured in various ways to render the carrying out of the penalty as rare as possible.

his blood shall be upon him. i.e. 'He has brought it upon himself that he should be killed' (Rashi). Some see in these Heb. words the formula used in pronouncing the condemnation.

י מוֹת יוּמָת אָבִיו וְאִמּוֹ קִלֵּל דָּמָיו בּוֹ׃ וְאִישׁ אֲשֶׁר יִנְאַף
אֶת־אֵשֶׁת אִישׁ אֲשֶׁר יִנְאַף אֶת־אֵשֶׁת רֵעֵהוּ מוֹת־יוּמַת
11 הַנֹּאֵף וְהַנֹּאָפֶת׃ וְאִישׁ אֲשֶׁר יִשְׁכַּב אֶת־אֵשֶׁת אָבִיו עֶרְוַת
12 אָבִיו גִּלָּה מוֹת־יוּמְתוּ שְׁנֵיהֶם דְּמֵיהֶם בָּם׃ וְאִישׁ אֲשֶׁר
יִשְׁכַּב אֶת־כַּלָּתוֹ מוֹת יוּמְתוּ שְׁנֵיהֶם תֶּבֶל עָשׂוּ דְּמֵיהֶם
13 בָּם׃ וְאִישׁ אֲשֶׁר יִשְׁכַּב אֶת־זָכָר מִשְׁכְּבֵי אִשָּׁה תּוֹעֵבָה
14 עָשׂוּ שְׁנֵיהֶם מוֹת יוּמָתוּ דְּמֵיהֶם בָּם׃ וְאִישׁ אֲשֶׁר יִקַּח
אֶת־אִשָּׁה וְאֶת־אִמָּהּ זִמָּה הִוא בָּאֵשׁ יִשְׂרְפוּ אֹתוֹ וְאֶתְהֶן
טו וְלֹא־תִהְיֶה זִמָּה בְּתוֹכְכֶם׃ וְאִישׁ אֲשֶׁר יִתֵּן שְׁכָבְתּוֹ
16 בִּבְהֵמָה מוֹת יוּמָת וְאֶת־הַבְּהֵמָה תַּהֲרֹגוּ׃ וְאִשָּׁה אֲשֶׁר
תִּקְרַב אֶל־כָּל־בְּהֵמָה לְרִבְעָה אֹתָהּ וְהָרַגְתָּ אֶת־הָאִשָּׁה
17 וְאֶת־הַבְּהֵמָה מוֹת יוּמָתוּ דְּמֵיהֶם בָּם׃ וְאִישׁ אֲשֶׁר־יִקַּח
אֶת־אֲחֹתוֹ בַּת־אָבִיו אוֹ־בַת־אִמּוֹ וְרָאָה אֶת־עֶרְוָתָהּ וְהִיא
תִרְאֶה אֶת־עֶרְוָתוֹ חֶסֶד הוּא וְנִכְרְתוּ לְעֵינֵי בְּנֵי עַמָּם
18 עֶרְוַת אֲחֹתוֹ גִּלָּה עֲוֹנוֹ יִשָּׂא׃ וְאִישׁ אֲשֶׁר־יִשְׁכַּב אֶת־אִשָּׁה
דָּוָה וְגִלָּה אֶת־עֶרְוָתָהּ אֶת־מְקֹרָהּ הֶעֱרָה וְהִוא גִּלְּתָה אֶת־
19 מְקוֹר דָּמֶיהָ וְנִכְרְתוּ שְׁנֵיהֶם מִקֶּרֶב עַמָּם׃ וְעֶרְוַת אֲחוֹת
אִמְּךָ וַאֲחוֹת אָבִיךָ לֹא תְגַלֵּה כִּי אֶת־שְׁאֵרוֹ הֶעֱרָה עֲוֹנָם

with another man's wife, even he that committeth adultery with his neighbour's wife, both the adulterer and the adulteress shall surely be put to death. 11. And the man that lieth with his father's wife—he hath uncovered his father's nakedness—both of them shall surely be put to death; their blood shall be upon them. 12. And if a man lie with his daughter-in-law, both of them shall surely be put to death; they have wrought corruption; their blood shall be upon them. 13. And if a man lie with mankind, as with womankind, both of them have committed abomination: they shall surely be put to death; their blood shall be upon them. 14. And if a man take with his wife also her mother, it is wickedness: they shall be burnt with fire, both he and they; that there be no wickedness among you. 15. And if a man lie with a beast, he shall surely be put to death; and ye shall slay the beast. 16. And if a woman approach unto any beast, and lie down thereto, thou shalt kill the woman, and the beast: they shall surely be put to death; their blood shall be upon them. 17. And if a man shall take his sister, his father's daughter, or his mother's daughter, and see her nakedness, and she see his nakedness: it is a shameful thing; and they shall be cut off in the sight of the children of their people: he hath uncovered his sister's nakedness; he shall bear his iniquity. 18. And if a man shall lie with a woman having her sickness, and shall uncover her nakedness—he hath made naked her fountain, and she hath uncovered the fountain of her blood—both of them shall be cut off from among their people. 19. And thou shalt not uncover

10. *committeth adultery.* The repetition of the phrase and the substitution of *neighbour's wife* for *another man's wife* stresses the heinousness of the offence. The consent of the husband is quite immaterial. Marriage is not merely a 'contract'; it is consecration, and adultery is far more than merely an offence against one of the parties to a contract. It is an offence against the Divine Command proclaimed at Sinai, and constitutes the annihilation of holiness in marriage (Z. Frankel).

11. *father's wife.* Stepmother; see XVIII, 7 f.

13. *mankind.* See XVIII, 22.

14. *wife also her mother.* Cf. XVIII, 17; brands as 'wickedness' (or 'enormity') the union with the two women at the same time.

15. *beast.* See XVIII, 23. Because it was the cause of the person's downfall, and would be a reminder to others of what had taken place.

17. *see.* Has the same meaning as 'uncover' in XVIII, 9, 11.

shameful thing. Or, 'impiousness,' unholiness. The Heb. term is an expression of strongest moral detestation. The vehement condemnation of this crime may be due to the fact that, in early times, marriage with a half-sister was deemed unobjectionable, a custom that lingered on for centuries after its proscription at Sinai.

cut off in the sight. The words signify that there was a public ceremony of excommunication.

he shall bear his iniquity. Ibn Ezra understands the second half of the verse to refer to the case where the sister was seduced against her will. He alone is then punished. According to Hoffmann, the repetition of the phrase is to indicate that his is a double turpitude, as it is a brother's part to defend his sister's honour.

18. *she hath uncovered.* See XVIII, 19.

19. *thy mother's sister.* See XVIII, 12 f.

כ יִשָּׂאוּ׃ וְאִישׁ אֲשֶׁר יִשְׁכַּב אֶת־דֹּדָתוֹ עֶרְוַת דֹּדוֹ גִּלָּה
21 חֶטְאָם יִשָּׂאוּ עֲרִירִים יָמֻתוּ׃ וְאִישׁ אֲשֶׁר יִקַּח אֶת־אֵשֶׁת
22 אָחִיו נִדָּה הִוא עֶרְוַת אָחִיו גִּלָּה עֲרִירִים יִהְיוּ׃ וּשְׁמַרְתֶּם
אֶת־כָּל־חֻקֹּתַי וְאֶת־כָּל־מִשְׁפָּטַי וַעֲשִׂיתֶם אֹתָם וְלֹא־תָקִיא
שביעי אֶתְכֶם הָאָרֶץ אֲשֶׁר אֲנִי מֵבִיא אֶתְכֶם שָׁמָּה לָשֶׁבֶת בָּהּ׃ *
23 וְלֹא תֵלְכוּ בְּחֻקֹּת הַגּוֹי אֲשֶׁר־אֲנִי מְשַׁלֵּחַ מִפְּנֵיכֶם כִּי
24 אֶת־כָּל־אֵלֶּה עָשׂוּ וָאָקֻץ בָּם׃ וָאֹמַר לָכֶם אַתֶּם תִּירְשׁוּ
אֶת־אַדְמָתָם וַאֲנִי אֶתְּנֶנָּה לָכֶם לָרֶשֶׁת אֹתָהּ אֶרֶץ זָבַת
חָלָב וּדְבָשׁ אֲנִי יְהוָה אֱלֹהֵיכֶם אֲשֶׁר־הִבְדַּלְתִּי אֶתְכֶם
מפטיר
כה מִן־הָעַמִּים׃ * וְהִבְדַּלְתֶּם בֵּין־הַבְּהֵמָה הַטְּהֹרָה לַטְּמֵאָה
וּבֵין־הָעוֹף הַטָּמֵא לַטָּהֹר וְלֹא־תְשַׁקְּצוּ אֶת־נַפְשֹׁתֵיכֶם
בַּבְּהֵמָה וּבָעוֹף וּבְכֹל אֲשֶׁר תִּרְמֹשׂ הָאֲדָמָה אֲשֶׁר־הִבְדַּלְתִּי
26 לָכֶם לְטַמֵּא׃ וִהְיִיתֶם לִי קְדֹשִׁים כִּי קָדוֹשׁ אֲנִי יְהוָה
27 וָאַבְדִּל אֶתְכֶם מִן־הָעַמִּים לִהְיוֹת לִי׃ וְאִישׁ אוֹ־אִשָּׁה כִּי־
יִהְיֶה בָהֶם אוֹב אוֹ יִדְּעֹנִי מוֹת יוּמָתוּ בָּאֶבֶן יִרְגְּמוּ אֹתָם
דְּמֵיהֶם בָּם׃

the nakedness of thy mother's sister, nor of thy father's sister; for he hath made naked his near kin; they shall bear their iniquity. 20. And if a man shall lie with his uncle's wife—he hath uncovered his uncle's nakedness—they shall bear their sin; they shall die childless. 21. And if a man shall take his brother's wife, it is impurity: he hath uncovered his brother's nakedness; they shall be childless. ¶ 22. Ye shall therefore keep all My statutes, and all Mine ordinances, and do them, that the land, whither I bring you to dwell therein, vomit you not out.*vii. 23. And ye shall not walk in the customs of the nation, which I am casting out before you; for they did all these things, and therefore I abhorred them. 24. But I have said unto you: 'Ye shall inherit their land, and I will give it unto you to possess it, a land flowing with milk and honey.' I am the LORD your God, who have set you apart from the peoples.*m. 25. Ye shall therefore separate between the clean beast and the unclean, and between the unclean fowl and the clean; and ye shall not make your souls detestable by beast, or by fowl, or by any thing wherewith the ground teemeth, which I have set apart for you to hold unclean. 26. And ye shall be holy unto Me; for I the LORD am holy, and have set you apart from the peoples, that ye should be Mine. ¶ 27. A man also or a woman that divineth by a ghost or a familiar spirit, shall surely be put to death; they shall stone them with stones; their blood shall be upon them.

20. *shall die childless.* See XVIII, 14. Childlessness was regarded as little less calamitous than death. 'It is evidently meant as a heavenly and supernatural retribution' (Kalisch).

21. *brother's wife.* See XVIII, 16.

22–26. EXHORTATION

From here to the end of the Chapter is the concluding exhortation of the Law of Holiness (XVIII–XX), or possibly of the whole section beginning with Chap. XI (cf. *v.* 25 below). This paragraph may be compared with XVIII, 24–30.

22. *vomit.* See on XVIII, 25.

23. *customs of the nation.* Cf. XVIII, 3. Heb. *chukoth ha-goy.* In later times, these Heb. words gave the name to the important principle in accordance with which Jewish life was jealously guarded against adopting the religious customs of surrounding nations.

24. *set you apart.* By means of distinctive laws and precepts.

25. *clean . . . unclean.* The inclusion of this verse is significant. It is a reminder, still required by the Jewish people, that the ideal of holiness for the Israelite consists in more than moral purity. The dietary laws have likewise their essential place in the scheme of the Torah, and form a necessary aid in the pursuit of the goal set by God.

26. *ye shall be holy.* Sums up the whole end and aim of the preceding laws. The people whom a holy God has chosen for His own must, like Him, be holy.

unto Me. 'If ye be separated from the heathen nations, then ye belong to Me; but if not, ye belong to Nebuchadnezzar and his colleagues,' *i.e.* you shall go into exile, become assimilated among the nations and lose your distinctive identity (Sifra).

27. *familiar spirit.* The position of this verse, after the exhortation, is intended as a final warning against superstition that was deadly to all higher religion. Unlike *v.* 6 the subject here is the person with 'the familiar spirit', and not he who consults the wizard.

HAFTORAH KEDOSHIM (FOR ASHKENAZIM) הפטרת קדשים לאשכנזים

AMOS IX, 7–15

CHAPTER IX

7. Are ye not as the children of the Ethiopians unto Me,
O children of Israel? saith the LORD.
Have not I brought up Israel out of the land of Egypt,
And the Philistines from Caphtor,
And Aram from Kir?

8. Behold, the eyes of the Lord GOD
Are upon the sinful kingdom,
And I will destroy it from off the face of the earth;
Saving that I will not utterly destroy the house of Jacob,
Saith the LORD.

9. For, lo, I will command, and I will sift the house of Israel among all the nations,
Like as corn is sifted in a sieve,
Yet shall not the least grain fall upon the earth.

10. All the sinners of My people shall die by the sword,
That say: 'The evil shall not overtake nor confront us.'

CAP. IX. ט

7 הֲלוֹא כִבְנֵי כֻשִׁיִּים אַתֶּם לִי בְּנֵי יִשְׂרָאֵל נְאֻם־יְהוָה
הֲלוֹא אֶת־יִשְׂרָאֵל הֶעֱלֵיתִי מֵאֶרֶץ מִצְרַיִם וּפְלִשְׁתִּיִּים
8 מִכַּפְתּוֹר וַאֲרָם מִקִּיר׃ הִנֵּה עֵינֵי ׀ אֲדֹנָי יֱהוִֹה בַּמַּמְלָכָה
הַחַטָּאָה וְהִשְׁמַדְתִּי אֹתָהּ מֵעַל פְּנֵי הָאֲדָמָה אֶפֶס כִּי לֹא
9 הַשְׁמֵיד אַשְׁמִיד אֶת־בֵּית יַעֲקֹב נְאֻם־יְהוָה׃ כִּי־הִנֵּה אָנֹכִי
מְצַוֶּה וַהֲנִעוֹתִי בְכָל־הַגּוֹיִם אֶת־בֵּית יִשְׂרָאֵל כַּאֲשֶׁר יִנּוֹעַ
י בַּכְּבָרָה וְלֹא־יִפּוֹל צְרוֹר אָרֶץ׃ בַּחֶרֶב יָמוּתוּ כֹּל חַטָּאֵי
11 עַמִּי הָאֹמְרִים לֹא־תַגִּישׁ וְתַקְדִּים בַּעֲדֵינוּ הָרָעָה׃ בַּיּוֹם
הַהוּא אָקִים אֶת־סֻכַּת דָּוִיד הַנֹּפֶלֶת וְגָדַרְתִּי אֶת־פִּרְצֵיהֶן

11. In that day will I raise up
The tabernacle of David that is fallen,
And close up the breaches thereof,
And I will raise up his ruins,
And I will build it as in the days of old;

Amos lived in the days of King Jeroboam II, about 750 B.C.E. The master-word of existence to Amos is Righteousness, which to him, as to his successors, means holiness of life in the individual and the triumph of right in the world. In His dealings with men and nations, he proclaims: God has but one test—their loyalty to the laws of righteousness; and He judges them accordingly. See p. 152.

The opening of the Sedrah strikes the note of consecration in the individual life; and the Haftorah in its earlier verses is an oracle against those who have rejected that high Jewish ideal, and thereby bring about the downfall of the Kingdom. But Israel will yet be true to its high and holy ideal, and worthy of the blessings that follow in the wake of such loyalty.

7. *as the children of the Ethiopians.* Two great teachings are here enunciated. The first is: God has guided other nations as well as the Israelites. All races are equally dear to Him; and the hand of Providence is seen not only in the migration of Israel, but in every historical movement. The second teaching is, God's special relationship to Israel rests on moral foundations. Degenerate Israel is no more to God than the despised inhabitants of distant Ethiopia, the descendants of Ham.

Caphtor. Probably the island of Crete.

Kir. A place in the remote North; II Kings XVI, 9.

8. *the sinful kingdom.* The Kingdom of Israel (*i.e.* that of the Ten Tribes), sinful in its royal house from beginning to end, will be destroyed.

the house of Jacob. A faithful and worthy 'Remnant' will survive the catastrophe, and form the nucleus of a purer community in the future. This thought, implicit in this verse, was adopted afterwards by Isaiah (I, 26–28) and became one of the most characteristic elements of his teaching (Driver).

9. *I will sift.* The whole nation will be subjected to a winnowing process, yet no good grain will be lost. Only the sinners will disappear (*v.* 10).

10. *confront.* Old English for 'meet' or 'come up to', 'catch'.

11. *in that day.* The day of Redemption which shall follow those other happenings of disaster.

12 וַהֲרִסֹתָיו אָקִים וּבְנִיתִיהָ כִּימֵי עוֹלָם׃ לְמַעַן יִירְשׁוּ אֶת־
שְׁאֵרִית אֱדוֹם וְכָל־הַגּוֹיִם אֲשֶׁר־נִקְרָא שְׁמִי עֲלֵיהֶם נְאֻם־
13 יְהוָה עֹשֶׂה זֹּאת׃ הִנֵּה יָמִים בָּאִים נְאֻם־יְהוָה וְנִגַּשׁ
חוֹרֵשׁ בַּקֹּצֵר וְדֹרֵךְ עֲנָבִים בְּמֹשֵׁךְ הַזָּרַע וְהִטִּיפוּ הֶהָרִים
14 עָסִיס וְכָל־הַגְּבָעוֹת תִּתְמוֹגַגְנָה׃ וְשַׁבְתִּי אֶת־שְׁבוּת עַמִּי
יִשְׂרָאֵל וּבָנוּ עָרִים נְשַׁמּוֹת וְיָשָׁבוּ וְנָטְעוּ כְרָמִים וְשָׁתוּ אֶת־
טו יֵינָם וְעָשׂוּ גַנּוֹת וְאָכְלוּ אֶת־פְּרִיהֶם׃ וּנְטַעְתִּים עַל־אַדְמָתָם
וְלֹא יִנָּתְשׁוּ עוֹד מֵעַל אַדְמָתָם אֲשֶׁר־נָתַתִּי לָהֶם אָמַר
יְהוָה אֱלֹהֶיךָ׃

12. That they may possess the remnant of Edom,
And all the nations, upon whom My name is called,
Saith the LORD that doeth this.

13. Behold, the days come, saith the LORD,
That the plowman shall overtake the reaper,
And the treader of grapes him that soweth seed;
And the mountains shall drop sweet wine,
And all the hills shall melt.

14. And I will turn the captivity of My people Israel,
And they shall build the waste cities, and inhabit them;
And they shall plant vineyards, and drink the wine thereof;
They shall also make gardens, and eat the fruit of them.

15. And I will plant them upon their land,
And they shall no more be plucked up
Out of their land which I have given them,
Saith the LORD thy God.

v. 14. קמץ בז"ק

will I raise up the tabernacle of David. The House of David, and revive the glories of the golden age of the Monarchy.

12. *possess the remnant of Edom.* That the empire of David may be restored to its former limits.

upon whom My name has been called. In token of ownership. Through their subjugation by David, they were deemed a part of Israel.

13–15. God's mercy will prevail, and will find a way of bringing back His banished ones to a state of prosperity as well as of purity. In these verses, 'the rigour relaxes, the voice softens, and the promise of restoration and blessing struggles up like a late winter dawn' (Horton).

13. *the plowman shall overtake the reaper . . . seed.* So fruitful will be the soil that the seasons will run into one another. Before they have ceased ploughing, the harvest will be ready for gathering in; cf. Lev. XXVI, 5, 10.

sweet wine. The newly pressed juice of the grape.

hills shall melt. As though the hills dissolved themselves in the rich streams which they poured down.

14. *turn the captivity.* Foretells the home-coming of the exiled Israelites. They shall rebuild the waste places for the fulfilment of their destined vocation in the uplifting of humanity. This promise is again being literally fulfilled in the New Judea that has come to life during the last fifty years.

Many Bible Critics maintain that the words of Amos end with the words, 'I will destroy it from off the face of the earth' (*v.* 8), and deem the remainder of the book to be from a later hand. This view fails to do justice to the idea of prophecy or of the prophet's office. 'For a prophet to close the entire volume of his prophecies without a single gleam of hope for a happier future, is very much opposed to the analogy of prophecy. Jeremiah and Ezekiel, for instance, blame Judah not less unsparingly than Amos blames Israel; but both nevertheless draw ideal pictures of the restored nation's future felicity' (Driver). 'If Amos had altogether despaired of Israel's future, he would not have had what to prophesy, nor to whom to prophesy. One does not moralize to the dead. Every preacher believes in the possibility of betterment, if the sinner repent; and he hopes that his words will lead to such repentance and consequent betterment. Thus also Amos' (Klausner).

EZEKIEL XX, 2–20

CHAPTER XX

2. And the word of the LORD came unto me, saying: 3. 'Son of man, speak unto the elders of Israel, and say unto them: Thus saith the Lord GOD: Are ye come to inquire of Me? As I live, saith the Lord GOD, I will not be inquired of by you. 4. Wilt thou judge them, son of man, wilt thou judge them? cause them to know the abominations of their fathers; 5. and say unto them: Thus saith the Lord GOD: In the day when I chose Israel, and lifted up My hand unto the seed of the house of Jacob, and made Myself known unto them in the land of Egypt, when I lifted up My hand unto them, saying: I am the LORD your God; 6. in that day I lifted up My hand unto them, to bring them forth out of the land of Egypt into a land that I had sought out for them, flowing with milk and honey, which is the beauty of all lands; 7. and I said unto them: Cast ye away every man the detestable things of his eyes, and defile not yourselves with the idols of Egypt; I am the LORD your God. 8. But they rebelled against Me, and would not hearken unto Me; they did not every man cast away the

CAP. XX. כ

2 3 וַיְהִי דְבַר־יְהוָה אֵלַי לֵאמֹר׃ בֶּן־אָדָם דַּבֵּר אֶת־זִקְנֵי
יִשְׂרָאֵל וְאָמַרְתָּ אֲלֵהֶם כֹּה אָמַר אֲדֹנָי יֱהוִה הֲלִדְרֹשׁ
אֹתִי אַתֶּם בָּאִים חַי־אָנִי אִם־אִדָּרֵשׁ לָכֶם נְאֻם אֲדֹנָי
4 יֱהוִה׃ הֲתִשְׁפֹּט אֹתָם הֲתִשְׁפּוֹט בֶּן־אָדָם אֶת־תּוֹעֲבֹת
ה אֲבוֹתָם הוֹדִיעֵם׃ וְאָמַרְתָּ אֲלֵיהֶם כֹּה־אָמַר אֲדֹנָי יֱהוִה
בְּיוֹם בָּחֳרִי בְיִשְׂרָאֵל וָאֶשָּׂא יָדִי לְזֶרַע בֵּית יַעֲקֹב וָאִוָּדַע
לָהֶם בְּאֶרֶץ מִצְרָיִם וָאֶשָּׂא יָדִי לָהֶם לֵאמֹר אֲנִי יְהוָה
6 אֱלֹהֵיכֶם׃ בַּיּוֹם הַהוּא נָשָׂאתִי יָדִי לָהֶם לְהוֹצִיאָם מֵאֶרֶץ
מִצְרָיִם אֶל־אֶרֶץ אֲשֶׁר־תַּרְתִּי לָהֶם זָבַת חָלָב וּדְבַשׁ צְבִי
7 הִיא לְכָל־הָאֲרָצוֹת׃ וָאֹמַר אֲלֵהֶם אִישׁ שִׁקּוּצֵי עֵינָיו
הַשְׁלִיכוּ וּבְגִלּוּלֵי מִצְרַיִם אַל־תִּטַּמָּאוּ אֲנִי יְהוָה אֱלֹהֵיכֶם׃
8 וַיַּמְרוּ־בִי וְלֹא אָבוּ לִשְׁמֹעַ אֵלַי אִישׁ אֶת־שִׁקּוּצֵי עֵינֵיהֶם
לֹא הִשְׁלִיכוּ וְאֶת־גִּלּוּלֵי מִצְרַיִם לֹא עָזָבוּ וָאֹמַר לִשְׁפֹּךְ

This retrospect of the early history of Israel in the Wilderness is the opening portion of the same prophecy from which the Haftorah of the preceding Sedrah is taken. It was spoken to the exiles who had been deported ten years earlier to Babylon, after the first capture of Jerusalem in 597 B.C.E. The impending destruction of the City is declared by the Prophet to be the wages for disloyalty to the 'statutes and judgments' of which the 19th chapter of Leviticus in the Sedrah is so outstanding a summary; see p. 494.

3. *son of man.* In the presence of the awful majesty of God, Ezekiel is ever conscious of his mortality. This phrase occurs nearly 100 times in Ezekiel.

to inquire of Me. To consult Him through His prophet; probably in 589 B.C.E., about three years before the fall of the Jewish State. The anxiety of the exiles was deepening over the ultimate fate of Judea and their own chance of returning to the Holy Land.

will not be inquired of by you. Because their act of inquiry was insincere, as the elders were themselves in secret sympathy with those of the exiles who were willing to become 'good Babylonians' and give up the Jewish Life and Faith. In *v.* 32 f of this same chapter, the Prophet exclaims: 'And that which cometh into your mind shall not be at all; in that ye say, We will be as the nations, as the families of the countries, to serve wood and stone. As I live, saith the LORD God, surely with a mighty hand . . . will I be king over you.'

4. *judge them.* Rehearsing the sins of the past with their consequences, as the people are still one in spirit and conduct with Israel in the past.

5–9. The iniquities in Egypt.

5. *lifted up My hand.* 'Sware.'
made Myself known. Through Moses.

6. *in that day.* At that period.
the beauty of all lands. See Jer. III, 19.

7. *detestable things.* Idols; the majority of the Israelites in Egypt adopted in time Egyptian religious practices.

8. *in the midst . . . Egypt.* The history of the Exodus is silent on the internal struggles in Israel itself. The efforts of Moses in educating the people are entirely passed over in the history (Davidson); see p. 206.

9. *but I wrought for My name's sake.* That the Divine nature—His justice, mercy and faithfulness—should be fully understood by Israel as well as the world.

חֲמָתִי עֲלֵיהֶם לְכַלּוֹת אַפִּי בָּהֶם בְּתוֹךְ אֶרֶץ מִצְרָיִם׃
9 וָאַעַשׂ לְמַעַן שְׁמִי לְבִלְתִּי הֵחֵל לְעֵינֵי הַגּוֹיִם אֲשֶׁר־הֵמָּה
בְתוֹכָם אֲשֶׁר נוֹדַעְתִּי אֲלֵיהֶם לְעֵינֵיהֶם לְהוֹצִיאָם מֵאֶרֶץ
י מִצְרָיִם׃ וָאוֹצִיאֵם מֵאֶרֶץ מִצְרָיִם וָאֲבִאֵם אֶל־הַמִּדְבָּר׃
11 וָאֶתֵּן לָהֶם אֶת־חֻקּוֹתַי וְאֶת־מִשְׁפָּטַי הוֹדַעְתִּי אוֹתָם אֲשֶׁר
12 יַעֲשֶׂה אוֹתָם הָאָדָם וָחַי בָּהֶם׃ וְגַם אֶת־שַׁבְּתוֹתַי נָתַתִּי
לָהֶם לִהְיוֹת לְאוֹת בֵּינִי וּבֵינֵיהֶם לָדַעַת כִּי אֲנִי יְהוָה
13 מְקַדְּשָׁם׃ וַיַּמְרוּ־בִי בֵית־יִשְׂרָאֵל בַּמִּדְבָּר בְּחֻקּוֹתַי לֹא־
הָלָכוּ וְאֶת־מִשְׁפָּטַי מָאָסוּ אֲשֶׁר יַעֲשֶׂה אֹתָם הָאָדָם וָחַי
בָּהֶם וְאֶת־שַׁבְּתֹתַי חִלְּלוּ מְאֹד וָאֹמַר לִשְׁפֹּךְ חֲמָתִי עֲלֵיהֶם
14 בַּמִּדְבָּר לְכַלּוֹתָם׃ וָאֶעֱשֶׂה לְמַעַן שְׁמִי לְבִלְתִּי הֵחֵל לְעֵינֵי
טו הַגּוֹיִם אֲשֶׁר הוֹצֵאתִים לְעֵינֵיהֶם׃ וְגַם־אֲנִי נָשָׂאתִי יָדִי
לָהֶם בַּמִּדְבָּר לְבִלְתִּי הָבִיא אוֹתָם אֶל־הָאָרֶץ אֲשֶׁר־נָתַתִּי
16 זָבַת חָלָב וּדְבַשׁ צְבִי הִיא לְכָל־הָאֲרָצוֹת׃ יַעַן בְּמִשְׁפָּטַי
מָאָסוּ וְאֶת־חֻקּוֹתַי לֹא־הָלְכוּ בָהֶם וְאֶת־שַׁבְּתוֹתַי חִלֵּלוּ כִּי
17 אַחֲרֵי גִלּוּלֵיהֶם לִבָּם הֹלֵךְ׃ וַתָּחָס עֵינִי עֲלֵיהֶם מִשַּׁחֲתָם
18 וְלֹא־עָשִׂיתִי אוֹתָם כָּלָה בַּמִּדְבָּר׃ וָאֹמַר אֶל־בְּנֵיהֶם
בַּמִּדְבָּר בְּחוּקֵּי אֲבוֹתֵיכֶם אַל־תֵּלֵכוּ וְאֶת־מִשְׁפְּטֵיהֶם
19 אַל־תִּשְׁמֹרוּ וּבְגִלּוּלֵיהֶם אַל־תִּטַּמָּאוּ׃ אֲנִי יְהוָה אֱלֹהֵיכֶם
כ בְּחֻקּוֹתַי לֵכוּ וְאֶת־מִשְׁפָּטַי שִׁמְרוּ וַעֲשׂוּ אוֹתָם׃ וְאֶת־
שַׁבְּתוֹתַי קַדֵּשׁוּ וְהָיוּ לְאוֹת בֵּינִי וּבֵינֵיכֶם לָדַעַת כִּי אֲנִי
יְהוָה אֱלֹהֵיכֶם׃

detestable things of their eyes, neither did they forsake the idols of Egypt; then I said I would pour out My fury upon them, to spend My anger upon them in the midst of the land of Egypt. 9. But I wrought for My name's sake, that it should not be profaned in the sight of the nations, among whom they were, in whose sight I made Myself known unto them, so as to bring them forth out of the land of Egypt. 10. So I caused them to go forth out of the land of Egypt, and brought them into the wilderness. 11. And I gave them My statutes, and taught them Mine ordinances, which if a man do, he shall live by them. 12. Moreover also I gave them My sabbaths, to be a sign between Me and them, that they might know that I am the LORD that sanctify them. 13. But the house of Israel rebelled against Me in the wilderness; they walked not in My statutes, and they rejected Mine ordinances, which if a man do, he shall live by them, and My sabbaths they greatly profaned; then I said I would pour out My fury upon them in the wilderness, to consume them. 14. But I wrought for My name's sake, that it should not be profaned in the sight of the nations, in whose sight I brought them out. 15. Yet also I lifted up My hand unto them in the wilderness, that I would not bring them into the land which I had given them, flowing with milk and honey, which is the beauty of all lands; 16. because they rejected Mine ordinances, and walked not in My statutes, and profaned My sabbaths—for their heart went after their idols. 17. Nevertheless Mine eye spared them from destroying them, neither did I make a full end of them in the wilderness. 18. And I said unto their children in the wilderness: Walk ye not in the statutes of your fathers, neither observe their ordinances, nor defile yourselves with their idols; 19. I am the LORD your God; walk in My statutes, and keep Mine ordinances, and do them; 20. and hallow My sabbaths, and they shall be a sign between Me and you, that ye may know that I am the LORD your God.

v. 13. הל׳ בקמץ v. 13, 16. קמץ ברביעי v. 18. דגש אחר שורק

10–20. The Generation in the Wilderness.

11. *he shall live by them.* As those laws are the foundations of all social life. Obedience to them ensures prosperity and stability in life; Lev. XVIII, 5; Deut. IV, 40.

12. *to be a sign.* The special sign of God's covenant with Israel (Exod. XXXI, 17). Since the observance of the Sabbath was not confined to Judea, its importance deepened in the eyes of the exiles, deprived of Temple and sacrifice.

14. *but I wrought for My name's sake.* See on *v.* 9. A sudden judgment upon Israel would have been misunderstood by the heathen.

17. *Mine eye spared them.* Another motive of God's long-suffering towards Israel—pity for the sinners; Ps. LXXVIII, 38 ('But he, being full of compassion, forgave their iniquity and destroyed them not; yea, many a time he turned his anger away').

20. *a sign.* Ezekiel again and again emphasizes the Sabbath as a constantly recurring reminder to Israel of their special relationship to God.

21 CHAPTER XXI

1. And the LORD said unto Moses: Speak unto the priests the sons of Aaron, and say unto them: ¶ There shall none defile himself for the dead among his people; 2. except for his kin, that is near unto him, for his mother, and for his father, and for his son, and for his daughter, and for his brother; 3. and for his sister a virgin, that is near unto him, that hath had no husband, for her may he defile himself. 4. He shall not defile himself, being a chief man among his people, to profane himself. 5. They shall not make baldness upon their head, neither shall they shave off the corners of their beard, nor make any cuttings in their flesh. 6. They shall be holy unto their God, and not profane the name of their God; for the offerings of the LORD made

CAP. XXI. כא

כא פ פ פ לא 31

א וַיֹּאמֶר יְהוָה אֶל־מֹשֶׁה אֱמֹר אֶל־הַכֹּהֲנִים בְּנֵי אַהֲרֹן
2 וְאָמַרְתָּ אֲלֵהֶם לְנֶפֶשׁ לֹא־יִטַּמָּא בְּעַמָּיו׃ כִּי אִם־לִשְׁאֵרוֹ
3 הַקָּרֹב אֵלָיו לְאִמּוֹ וּלְאָבִיו וְלִבְנוֹ וּלְבִתּוֹ וּלְאָחִיו׃ וְלַאֲחֹתוֹ
הַבְּתוּלָה הַקְּרוֹבָה אֵלָיו אֲשֶׁר לֹא־הָיְתָה לְאִישׁ לָהּ יִטַּמָּא׃
4 ה לֹא יִטַּמָּא בַּעַל בְּעַמָּיו לְהֵחַלּוֹ׃ לֹא־יִקְרְחָה קָרְחָה בְּרֹאשָׁם
וּפְאַת זְקָנָם לֹא יְגַלֵּחוּ וּבִבְשָׂרָם לֹא יִשְׂרְטוּ שָׂרָטֶת׃
6 קְדֹשִׁים יִהְיוּ לֵאלֹהֵיהֶם וְלֹא יְחַלְּלוּ שֵׁם אֱלֹהֵיהֶם כִּי

יקרחו ק׳ v. 5.

VIII. EMOR

(CHAPTERS XXI–XXIV)

REGULATIONS CONCERNING PRIESTS AND SANCTUARY

CHAPTER XXI

1–9. THE ORDINARY PRIEST

Whatever comes near, or is presented, to God must be perfect of its kind. Priests, therefore, must be free from physical defects or ceremonial impurity (XXI), and sacrifices must be without blemish (XXII).

The ideal of holiness, as expounded in the previous chapters, was intended for the whole Community of Israel. But since the priests were closely and constantly associated with the ritual of the Sanctuary, special laws were instituted for them and a higher standard was demanded.

1. *unto the priests.* To those performing sacerdotal functions, and not to such a one as had been rendered unfit for the priesthood on account of his father having contracted a marriage forbidden to a priest (see *v.* 7). The daughters of priestly families were not subject to these laws.

defile himself for the dead. Contact with the dead defiles (Num. XIX) and, for the time being, renders a priest unfit to perform his duties. The law only held good when the dead person was 'among his people'; *i.e.* if there were others who were not priests able and willing to attend to the burial (Sifra). In the case of an unattended dead body of a friendless man (מת מצוה), everyone, even a High Priest or a Nazirite, had to busy himself with the last rites.

2. *except for his kin.* A concession to the natural feelings of the priest as man. The word for 'kin' denotes the closest possible bond of relationship. The wife is not mentioned because, as throughout the Torah, man and wife are regarded as 'one flesh' (Gen. II, 24), and is here understood of itself. The mother is named before the father, because there is usually a deeper attachment between her and the son (see on XIX, 3), and the desire to be with her at the last would be more intense.

3. *sister . . . near unto him.* The Rabbis explain this to include a sister who is betrothed. Although betrothal was regarded almost as close a bond as marriage (Deut. XXII, 23 f), the priest may attend to the body in the event of her death. On her marriage, she became part of her husband; and in the same way that a priest was not allowed to defile himself for his brother-in-law, he was similarly forbidden to do so for his brother-in-law's wife, though she be his sister.

4. *being a chief man.* The translation is based on Onkelos. The reason why the priest is subjected to these special laws is that he is 'a chief man among his people; his is an honour which carried with it peculiar obligations. Instead of 'chief man', Sifra translates 'as a husband' (so also RV Margin) and takes it to mean that he is forbidden to attend to his dead wife, if she belonged to any of the classes named in *v.* 7.

to profane himself. To render himself unfit for the service of the Sanctuary.

5. *baldness . . . cuttings.* See on X, 6 f and XIX, 27 f.

6. *they shall be holy.* The motive for the special laws of the priests is the same as the motive for the laws of the Community (XX, 26). The sole reason why the restrictions on the priests were heavier was because they had the additional privilege of offering the sacrifices to God.

the bread of their God. See on III, 11.

by fire, the bread of their God, they do offer; therefore they shall be holy. 7. They shall not take a woman that is a harlot, or profaned; neither shall they take a woman put away from her husband; for he is holy unto his God. 8. Thou shalt sanctify him therefore; for he offereth the bread of thy God; he shall be holy unto thee; for I the LORD, who sanctify you, am holy. 9. And the daughter of any priest, if she profane herself by playing the harlot, she profaneth her father: she shall be burnt with fire. ¶ 10. And the priest that is highest among his brethren, upon whose head the anointing oil is poured, and that is consecrated to put on the garments, shall not let the hair of his head go loose, nor rend his clothes; 11. neither shall he go in to any dead body, nor defile himself for his father, or for his mother; 12. neither shall he go out of the sanctuary, nor profane the sanctuary of his God; for the consecration of the anointing oil of his God is upon him: I am the LORD. 13. And he shall take a wife in her virginity. 14. A widow, or one divorced, or a profaned woman, or a harlot, these shall he not take; but a virgin of his own people shall he take to wife. 15. And he shall not profane his seed among his people; for I am the LORD who sanctify him.*ii. ¶ 16. And the LORD spoke unto Moses, saying: 17. Speak unto Aaron, saying: ¶Whosoever he be of thy seed

אֶת־אִשֵּׁי יְהוָה לֶחֶם אֱלֹהֵיהֶם הֵם מַקְרִיבִם וְהָיוּ קֹדֶשׁ׃
7 אִשָּׁה זֹנָה וַחֲלָלָה לֹא יִקָּחוּ וְאִשָּׁה גְּרוּשָׁה מֵאִישָׁהּ לֹא
8 יִקָּחוּ כִּי־קָדֹשׁ הוּא לֵאלֹהָיו׃ וְקִדַּשְׁתּוֹ כִּי אֶת־לֶחֶם אֱלֹהֶיךָ
הוּא מַקְרִיב קָדֹשׁ יִהְיֶה־לָּךְ כִּי קָדוֹשׁ אֲנִי יְהוָה מְקַדִּשְׁכֶם׃
9 וּבַת אִישׁ כֹּהֵן כִּי תֵחֵל לִזְנוֹת אֶת־אָבִיהָ הִיא מְחַלֶּלֶת
י בָּאֵשׁ תִּשָּׂרֵף׃ ס וְהַכֹּהֵן הַגָּדוֹל מֵאֶחָיו אֲשֶׁר־יוּצַק
עַל־רֹאשׁוֹ ׀ שֶׁמֶן הַמִּשְׁחָה וּמִלֵּא אֶת־יָדוֹ לִלְבֹּשׁ אֶת־
11 הַבְּגָדִים אֶת־רֹאשׁוֹ לֹא יִפְרָע וּבְגָדָיו לֹא יִפְרֹם׃ וְעַל
12 כָּל־נַפְשֹׁת מֵת לֹא יָבֹא לְאָבִיו וּלְאִמּוֹ לֹא יִטַּמָּא׃ וּמִן־
הַמִּקְדָּשׁ לֹא יֵצֵא וְלֹא יְחַלֵּל אֵת מִקְדַּשׁ אֱלֹהָיו כִּי נֵזֶר
13 שֶׁמֶן מִשְׁחַת אֱלֹהָיו עָלָיו אֲנִי יְהוָה׃ וְהוּא אִשָּׁה בִבְתוּלֶיהָ
14 יִקָּח׃ אַלְמָנָה וּגְרוּשָׁה וַחֲלָלָה זֹנָה אֶת־אֵלֶּה לֹא יִקָּח
טו כִּי אִם־בְּתוּלָה מֵעַמָּיו יִקַּח אִשָּׁה׃ וְלֹא־יְחַלֵּל זַרְעוֹ בְּעַמָּיו
שני
16 כִּי אֲנִי יְהוָה מְקַדְּשׁוֹ׃ ס וַיְדַבֵּר יְהוָה אֶל־מֹשֶׁה
17 לֵּאמֹר׃ דַּבֵּר אֶל־אַהֲרֹן לֵאמֹר אִישׁ מִזַּרְעֲךָ לְדֹרֹתָם אֲשֶׁר

v. 7. קמץ בז"ק v. 10. קמץ בז"ק

7. *profaned.* Or, 'polluted' (RV Margin), 'dishonoured' (Driver). The Rabbis understand it as 'profaned'—the daughter of a forbidden marriage contracted by a priest, or a woman who had already entered into a marriage forbidden to a priest (*i.e.* a divorced woman whose previous husband, a priest, ought not to have married her).

put away. Better, *divorced.* There is no mention of a widow among the women whom a priest may not marry; see on Ezek. XLIV, 22, p. 529.

8. *thou shalt sanctify.* The Community as a body is addressed. The Israelites are to consider the priests as consecrated to God, and pay them the honour which is due to them. It is from this verse that the custom arose to give the *Kohen* precedence in such matters as the Reading of the Law.

9. *burnt with fire.* The Talmud maintains that the penalty of burning (see on XX, 14) was inflicted only if the priest's daughter became unchaste when betrothed or married—a crime which was in all cases considered a capital offence.

10–15. INCREASED RESTRICTIONS FOR THE HIGH PRIEST

10. *anointing oil.* See VIII, 12.

consecrated . . . garments. Or, 'consecrated by donning the vestments' (cf. XVI, 32). Nobody but a High Priest could wear the special garments; and his investiture in them was part of his consecration to his exalted office.

hair . . . go loose. See on x, 6.

11. *for his father.* Even for his father. But, according to the Rabbis, he must do so for the unattended body of a friendless man (see on *v.* 1).

12. *out of the sanctuary.* Cf. x, 7. He was dispensed from following even the funeral procession of his father or mother. It is probable that the High Priest had permanent quarters in the Temple-precincts (see I Sam. III, 2 f).

I am the LORD. These words are added to increase the solemnity of the warning.

14. *of his own people.* lit. 'of his kinsfolk'. The Septuagint and Philo limit his choice to the priestly families.

15. *profane his seed.* Impair the pure descent of the Aaronic family by an improper marriage.

16–24. PHYSICAL BLEMISHES IN A PRIEST

A physical defect in a priest disqualified him from officiating in the Sanctuary.

throughout their generations that hath a blemish, let him not approach to offer the bread of his God. 18. For whatsoever man he be that hath a blemish, he shall not approach: a blind man, or a lame, or he that hath any thing maimed, or any thing too long, 19. or a man that is broken-footed, or broken-handed, 20. or crook-backed, or a dwarf, or that hath his eye overspread, or is scabbed, or scurvy, or hath his stones crushed; 21. no man of the seed of Aaron the priest, that hath a blemish, shall come nigh to offer the offerings of the LORD made by fire; he hath a blemish; he shall not come nigh to offer the bread of his God. 22. He may eat the bread of his God, both of the most holy, and of the holy. 23. Only he shall not go in unto the veil, nor come nigh unto the altar, because he hath a blemish; that he profane not My holy places; for I am the LORD who sanctify them. ¶ 24. So Moses spoke unto Aaron, and to his sons, and unto all the children of Israel.

18 יִהְיֶה בוֹ מוּם לֹא יִקְרַב לְהַקְרִיב לֶחֶם אֱלֹהָיו׃ כִּי כָל־
אִישׁ אֲשֶׁר־בּוֹ מוּם לֹא יִקְרָב אִישׁ עִוֵּר אוֹ פִסֵּחַ אוֹ חָרֻם
19 אוֹ שָׂרוּעַ׃ אוֹ אִישׁ אֲשֶׁר־יִהְיֶה בוֹ שֶׁבֶר רָגֶל אוֹ שֶׁבֶר
כ יָד׃ אוֹ־גִבֵּן אוֹ־דַק אוֹ תְּבַלֻּל בְּעֵינוֹ אוֹ גָרָב אוֹ יַלֶּפֶת
21 אוֹ מְרוֹחַ אָשֶׁךְ׃ כָּל־אִישׁ אֲשֶׁר־בּוֹ מוּם מִזֶּרַע אַהֲרֹן
הַכֹּהֵן לֹא יִגַּשׁ לְהַקְרִיב אֶת־אִשֵּׁי יְהוָה מוּם בּוֹ אֵת לֶחֶם
22 אֱלֹהָיו לֹא יִגַּשׁ לְהַקְרִיב׃ לֶחֶם אֱלֹהָיו מִקָּדְשֵׁי הַקֳּדָשִׁים
23 וּמִן־הַקֳּדָשִׁים יֹאכֵל׃ אַךְ אֶל־הַפָּרֹכֶת לֹא יָבֹא וְאֶל־
הַמִּזְבֵּחַ לֹא יִגַּשׁ כִּי־מוּם בּוֹ וְלֹא יְחַלֵּל אֶת־מִקְדָּשַׁי כִּי
24 אֲנִי יְהוָה מְקַדְּשָׁם׃ וַיְדַבֵּר מֹשֶׁה אֶל־אַהֲרֹן וְאֶל־בָּנָיו
וְאֶל־כָּל־בְּנֵי יִשְׂרָאֵל׃ פ

22

CHAPTER XXII

1. And the LORD spoke unto Moses, saying: 2. Speak unto Aaron and to his sons, that they separate themselves from the holy things of the children of Israel, which they hallow unto Me, and that they profane not My holy name: I am the LORD. 3. Say unto them: ¶ Whosoever he be of all your seed throughout your generations, that approacheth unto the holy things,

CAP. XXII. כב

כב

א 2 וַיְדַבֵּר יְהוָה אֶל־מֹשֶׁה לֵּאמֹר׃ דַּבֵּר אֶל־אַהֲרֹן וְאֶל־בָּנָיו
וְיִנָּזְרוּ מִקָּדְשֵׁי בְנֵי־יִשְׂרָאֵל וְלֹא יְחַלְּלוּ אֶת־שֵׁם קָדְשִׁי
3 אֲשֶׁר הֵם מַקְדִּשִׁים לִי אֲנִי יְהוָה׃ אֱמֹר אֲלֵהֶם לְדֹרֹתֵיכֶם

20. *dwarf.* He was not to blame for being a dwarf, but only men without blemish and who had the full measure of manly power were permitted to exercise the functions of that holy office. Even so in the higher realms of the soul, a spiritual dwarf cannot offer the bread of his God to his fellows.

eye overspread. Probably, the white and black parts of the eye are not properly defined.

21. *that hath a blemish.* Any blemish not restricted to those just enumerated.

22. *he may eat.* Though he may not officiate, he is still a priest by birth; and he is, therefore, entitled to his share of the sacrificial dues.

most holy. *e.g.* the flesh of the sin-offering which could be eaten by male priests alone.

24. *all the children of Israel.* These laws, although they were the peculiar concern of the priests, were also addressed to the Community as a whole. The people must insist upon their being honoured.

CHAPTER XXII. HOLINESS OF THE SANCTUARY

1–9. REGULATIONS FOR PRIESTS WHO SHARE IN A SACRIFICIAL FEAST

The last Chapter dealt with the bodily defects that disqualify the priest from officiating in the Sanctuary: this section insists on physical purity as the condition in which alone he could handle the offerings.

2. *that they separate themselves.* The sacred foods may be eaten only by priests and the members of their family, and then only if they are ritually clean. We must add words like, 'in the time of impurity,' which are implied in the context.

holy things of. A comprehensive expression for all offerings presented at the Altar. Even the offerings which the priests themselves bring to the Altar on their own behalf, must not be sacrificed or eaten by them when they are ritually unclean (Rashi).

3. *approacheth.* To participate in the offering of the sacrifices or in the partaking of the sacred dues.

uncleanness. The term is defined in the next verses.

shall be cut off. Some understand this to mean

which the children of Israel hallow unto the LORD, having his uncleanness upon him, that soul shall be cut off from before Me: I am the LORD. 4. What man soever of the seed of Aaron is a leper, or hath an issue, he shall not eat of the holy things, until he be clean. And whoso toucheth any one that is unclean by the dead; or from whomsoever the flow of seed goeth out; 5. or whosoever toucheth any swarming thing, whereby he may be made unclean, or a man of whom he may take uncleanness, whatsoever uncleanness he hath; 6. the soul that toucheth any such shall be unclean until the even, and shall not eat of the holy things, unless he bathe his flesh in water. 7. And when the sun is down, he shall be clean; and afterward he may eat of the holy things, because it is his bread. 8. That which dieth of itself, or is torn of beasts, he shall not eat to defile himself therewith: I am the LORD. 9. They shall therefore keep My charge, lest they bear sin for it, and die therein, if they profane it: I am the LORD who sanctify them. 10. There shall no [1]common man eat of the holy thing; a tenant of a priest, or a hired servant, shall not eat of the holy thing. 11. But if a priest buy any soul, the purchase of his money, he may eat of it; and such as are born in his house, they may eat of his bread. 12. And if a priest's daughter be married unto a common man, she shall not eat of that which is set apart from the holy things. 13. But if a priest's daughter be a widow, or divorced, and have no child,

[1] That is, one who is not a priest.

כָּל־אִישׁ ׀ אֲשֶׁר־יִקְרַב מִכָּל־זַרְעֲכֶם אֶל־הַקֳּדָשִׁים אֲשֶׁר
יַקְדִּישׁוּ בְנֵי־יִשְׂרָאֵל לַיהוָה וְטֻמְאָתוֹ עָלָיו וְנִכְרְתָה הַנֶּפֶשׁ
4 הַהִוא מִלְּפָנַי אֲנִי יְהוָה׃ אִישׁ אִישׁ מִזֶּרַע אַהֲרֹן וְהוּא
צָרוּעַ אוֹ זָב בַּקֳּדָשִׁים לֹא יֹאכַל עַד אֲשֶׁר יִטְהָר וְהַנֹּגֵעַ
בְּכָל־טְמֵא־נֶפֶשׁ אוֹ אִישׁ אֲשֶׁר־תֵּצֵא מִמֶּנּוּ שִׁכְבַת־זָרַע׃
ה אוֹ־אִישׁ אֲשֶׁר יִגַּע בְּכָל־שֶׁרֶץ אֲשֶׁר יִטְמָא־לוֹ אוֹ בְאָדָם
6 אֲשֶׁר יִטְמָא־לוֹ לְכֹל טֻמְאָתוֹ׃ נֶפֶשׁ אֲשֶׁר תִּגַּע־בּוֹ וְטָמְאָה
עַד־הָעָרֶב וְלֹא יֹאכַל מִן־הַקֳּדָשִׁים כִּי אִם־רָחַץ בְּשָׂרוֹ
7 בַּמָּיִם׃ וּבָא הַשֶּׁמֶשׁ וְטָהֵר וְאַחַר יֹאכַל מִן־הַקֳּדָשִׁים
8 כִּי לַחְמוֹ הוּא׃ נְבֵלָה וּטְרֵפָה לֹא יֹאכַל לְטָמְאָה־בָהּ
9 אֲנִי יְהוָה׃ וְשָׁמְרוּ אֶת־מִשְׁמַרְתִּי וְלֹא־יִשְׂאוּ עָלָיו חֵטְא
י וּמֵתוּ בוֹ כִּי יְחַלְּלֻהוּ אֲנִי יְהוָה מְקַדְּשָׁם׃ וְכָל־זָר לֹא־
11 יֹאכַל קֹדֶשׁ תּוֹשַׁב כֹּהֵן וְשָׂכִיר לֹא־יֹאכַל קֹדֶשׁ׃ וְכֹהֵן
כִּי־יִקְנֶה נֶפֶשׁ קִנְיַן כַּסְפּוֹ הוּא יֹאכַל בּוֹ וִילִיד בֵּיתוֹ הֵם
12 יֹאכְלוּ בְלַחְמוֹ׃ וּבַת־כֹּהֵן כִּי תִהְיֶה לְאִישׁ זָר הִוא בִּתְרוּמַת
13 הַקֳּדָשִׁים לֹא תֹאכֵל׃ וּבַת־כֹּהֵן כִּי תִהְיֶה אַלְמָנָה וּגְרוּשָׁה

exclusion from the priestly service. It is, however, more likely that a sterner punishment is intended; see *v.* 9, and chap. x.

4. *unclean by the dead.* See Num. XIX. For the various forms of uncleanness and the manner of purification, see XI–XV.

whose seed. See XV, 16.

5. *swarming thing. i.e.* a dead insect or reptile; XI, 24, 29 f.

a man . . . uncleanness. See XV, 5, 7, 19.

6. *the soul.* Heb. idiom for 'the person'.

7. *bread.* Or, 'food.' Certain portions of the sacrifices were the prescriptive right of the priests, and they depended upon them for their sustenance (cf. x, 12 f).

8. *or is torn of beasts.* This prohibition is repeated here for the special warning of the priests, since the impurity thereby caused would incapacitate them for service at the Sanctuary (Ibn Ezra); see also Ezek. XLIV, 31, p. 530.

9. *for it.* Either for the Sanctuary (Ibn Ezra), or for the 'food' in *v.* 7, since the context speaks of the eating of the flesh of the sacrifices.

die therein. The Rabbis explain this as 'death by the hand of Heaven'.

10–16. No layman was to eat a sanctified thing; with a list of the exceptions to that rule.

10. *common man.* Not a priest; a layman.

tenant. One who dwells with the priest, or is his guest; or the Hebrew slave who refused his freedom in the seventh year and remained in his service.

hired servant. As distinct from a non-Israelite slave, who was considered a member of the household (see next *v.*). The Torah does not mention that the priest's wife may eat of the portion, as husband and wife were deemed one person; see note on XXI, 2.

11. *the purchase of his money.* The non-Israelite slave purchased by a priest became part of the family, and was allowed to share in the sacrificial portion.

12. *priest's daughter.* On marrying a layman, she no longer belonged to the priestly family (see on XXI, 3).

and is returned unto her father's house, as in her youth, she may eat of her father's bread; but there shall no common man eat thereof. 14. And if a man eat of the holy thing through error, then he shall put the fifth part thereof unto it, and shall give unto the priest the holy thing. 15. And they shall not profane the holy things of the children of Israel, which they set apart unto the LORD; 16. and so cause them to bear the iniquity that bringeth guilt, when they eat their holy things; for I am the LORD who sanctify them.*iii. ¶ 17. And the LORD spoke unto Moses, saying: 18. Speak unto Aaron, and to his sons, and unto all the children of Israel, and say unto them: ¶Whosoever he be of the house of Israel, or of the strangers in Israel, that bringeth his offering, whether it be any of their vows, or any of their freewill-offerings, which are brought unto the LORD for a burnt-offering; 19. that ye may be accepted, ye shall offer a male without blemish, of the beeves, of the sheep, or of the goats. 20. But whatsoever hath a blemish, that shall ye not bring; for it shall not be acceptable for you. 21. And whosoever bringeth a sacrifice of peace-offerings unto the LORD in fulfilment of a vow clearly uttered, or for a freewill-offering, of the herd or of the flock, it shall be perfect to be accepted; there shall be no blemish therein. 22. Blind, or broken, or maimed, or having a wen, or scabbed, or scurvy, ye shall not offer these unto the LORD, nor make an offering by fire of them upon the altar unto the LORD. 23. Either a bullock or a lamb that hath any thing too long or too short, that mayest thou

וְזֶ֙רַע֙ אֵ֣ין לָ֔הּ וְשָׁבָ֞ה אֶל־בֵּ֣ית אָבִ֗יהָ כִּנְעוּרֶ֔יהָ מִלֶּ֥חֶם
14 אָבִ֖יהָ תֹּאכֵ֑ל וְכָל־זָ֖ר לֹא־יֹ֥אכַל בּֽוֹ׃ וְאִ֕ישׁ כִּֽי־יֹאכַ֥ל קֹ֖דֶשׁ
טו בִּשְׁגָגָ֑ה וְיָסַ֤ף חֲמִֽשִׁיתוֹ֙ עָלָ֔יו וְנָתַ֥ן לַכֹּהֵ֖ן אֶת־הַקֹּֽדֶשׁ׃ וְלֹ֣א
יְחַלְּל֔וּ אֶת־קָדְשֵׁ֖י בְּנֵ֣י יִשְׂרָאֵ֑ל אֵ֥ת אֲשֶׁר־יָרִ֖ימוּ לַיהוָֽה׃
16 וְהִשִּׂ֤יאוּ אוֹתָם֙ עֲוֺ֣ן אַשְׁמָ֔ה בְּאָכְלָ֖ם אֶת־קָדְשֵׁיהֶ֑ם כִּ֛י אֲנִ֥י
יְהוָ֖ה מְקַדְּשָֽׁם׃ * פ שלישי
17 18 וַיְדַבֵּ֥ר יְהוָ֖ה אֶל־מֹשֶׁ֥ה לֵּאמֹֽר׃ דַּבֵּ֨ר אֶֽל־אַהֲרֹ֜ן וְאֶל־בָּנָ֗יו
וְאֶל֙ כָּל־בְּנֵ֣י יִשְׂרָאֵ֔ל וְאָמַרְתָּ֖ אֲלֵהֶ֑ם אִ֣ישׁ אִישׁ֩ מִבֵּ֨ית
יִשְׂרָאֵ֜ל וּמִן־הַגֵּ֣ר בְּיִשְׂרָאֵ֗ל אֲשֶׁ֨ר יַקְרִ֤יב קָרְבָּנוֹ֙ לְכָל־
נִדְרֵיהֶם֙ וּלְכָל־נִדְבוֹתָ֔ם אֲשֶׁר־יַקְרִ֥יבוּ לַיהוָ֖ה לְעֹלָֽה׃
19 כ לִֽרְצֹנְכֶ֑ם תָּמִ֣ים זָכָ֔ר בַּבָּקָ֕ר בַּכְּשָׂבִ֖ים וּבָעִזִּֽים׃ כֹּ֛ל אֲשֶׁר־
21 בּ֥וֹ מ֖וּם לֹ֣א תַקְרִ֑יבוּ כִּי־לֹ֥א לְרָצ֖וֹן יִהְיֶ֥ה לָכֶֽם׃ וְאִ֗ישׁ כִּֽי־
יַקְרִ֤יב זֶֽבַח־שְׁלָמִים֙ לַֽיהוָ֔ה לְפַלֵּא־נֶ֨דֶר֙ א֣וֹ לִנְדָבָ֔ה בַּבָּקָ֖ר
22 א֣וֹ בַצֹּ֑אן תָּמִ֤ים יִהְיֶה֙ לְרָצ֔וֹן כָּל־מ֖וּם לֹ֥א יִֽהְיֶה־בּֽוֹ׃ עַוֶּ֩רֶת֩
א֨וֹ שָׁב֜וּר אוֹ־חָר֣וּץ אֽוֹ־יַבֶּ֗לֶת א֤וֹ גָרָב֙ א֣וֹ יַלֶּ֔פֶת לֹא־
תַקְרִ֥יבוּ אֵ֖לֶּה לַיהוָ֑ה וְאִשֶּׁ֗ה לֹא־תִתְּנ֥וּ מֵהֶ֛ם עַל־הַמִּזְבֵּ֖חַ
23 לַיהוָֽה׃ וְשׁ֥וֹר וָשֶׂ֖ה שָׂר֣וּעַ וְקָל֑וּט נְדָבָה֙ תַּעֲשֶׂ֣ה אֹת֔וֹ וּלְנֵ֖דֶר

מלרע v. 13.

13. *have no child.* If there is issue of the marriage, she is still regarded as attached to her husband's family. If, however, the issue of the marriage died, she regained her former status as a priest's daughter.
bread. Food, as in *v.* 7 above.

14. *through error.* Cf. chap. v, 14–16.
the holy thing. *i.e.* its equivalent.

15. *they shall not profane.* The subject is the priests, and the profanation is the admission of unqualified persons to partake of the sacred dues (Rashi).

17–25. QUALITY OF OFFERINGS

After laws concerning the purity of the priesthood and the holiness of the sacrifices, there follow regulations concerning the faultlessness of the offerings. Jewish tradition demands of the Israelite such faultlessness in the case of any gift or offering set apart for sacred purposes, whether in the sphere of religion or of charity.

18. *the strangers.* Aliens who were residing in their midst; see on I, 2.

19. *male without blemish.* See on I, 3.
beeves. The same Heb. word is rendered 'herd' in I, 3.

20. *shall ye not bring.* The Rabbis extended the scope of this law and insisted that the oil, wine, flour, and wood offered and used in the Temple must likewise be of the best quality. Even the wood to be burnt on the Altar was to be carefully selected so as to contain no worm-eaten pieces.

22. *blind . . . scabbed.* The blemishes which disqualify the animal as an offering are very similar to those which render the priest unfit for service (XXI, 18 f).
wen. A running sore, an ulcer.

23. *mayest thou offer.* According to the Rabbinic interpretation, this means that the imperfect animal may not be sacrificed upon the Altar, but it may be donated to the Temple for working purposes.

offer for a freewill-offering; but for a vow it shall not be accepted. 24. That which hath its stones bruised, or crushed, or torn, or cut, ye shall not offer unto the LORD; neither shall ye do thus in your land. 25. Neither from the hand of a foreigner shall ye offer the bread of your God of any of these, because their corruption is in them, there is a blemish in them; they shall not be accepted for you. ¶ 26. And the LORD spoke unto Moses, saying: ¶ 27. When a bullock, or a sheep, or a goat, is brought forth, then it shall be seven days under the dam; but from the eighth day and thenceforth it may be accepted for an offering made by fire unto the LORD. 28. And whether it be cow or ewe, ye shall not kill it and its young both in one day. 29. And when ye sacrifice a sacrifice of thanksgiving unto the LORD, ye shall sacrifice it that ye may be accepted. 30. On the same day it shall be eaten; ye shall leave none of it until the morning: I am the LORD. 31. And ye shall keep My commandments, and do them: I am the LORD. 32. And ye shall not profane My holy name; but I will be hallowed among the children of Israel: I am the LORD who hallow you, 33. that brought you out of the land of Egypt, to be your God: I am the LORD.* iv.

24 לֹא יֵרָצֶה׃ וּמָעוּךְ וְכָתוּת וְנָתוּק וְכָרוּת לֹא תַקְרִיבוּ לַיהוָה
כה וּבְאַרְצְכֶם לֹא תַעֲשׂוּ׃ וּמִיַּד בֶּן־נֵכָר לֹא תַקְרִיבוּ אֶת־לֶחֶם
אֱלֹהֵיכֶם מִכָּל־אֵלֶּה כִּי מָשְׁחָתָם בָּהֶם מוּם בָּם לֹא יֵרָצוּ
26 27 לָכֶם׃ ס וַיְדַבֵּר יְהוָה אֶל־מֹשֶׁה לֵּאמֹר׃ שׁוֹר אוֹ־כֶשֶׂב
אוֹ־עֵז כִּי יִוָּלֵד וְהָיָה שִׁבְעַת יָמִים תַּחַת אִמּוֹ וּמִיּוֹם
28 הַשְּׁמִינִי וָהָלְאָה יֵרָצֶה לְקָרְבַּן אִשֶּׁה לַיהוָה׃ וְשׁוֹר אוֹ־
29 שֶׂה אֹתוֹ וְאֶת־בְּנוֹ לֹא תִשְׁחֲטוּ בְּיוֹם אֶחָד׃ וְכִי־תִזְבְּחוּ
ל זֶבַח־תּוֹדָה לַיהוָה לִרְצֹנְכֶם תִּזְבָּחוּ׃ בַּיּוֹם הַהוּא יֵאָכֵל
31 לֹא־תוֹתִירוּ מִמֶּנּוּ עַד־בֹּקֶר אֲנִי יְהוָה׃ וּשְׁמַרְתֶּם מִצְוֹתַי
32 וַעֲשִׂיתֶם אֹתָם אֲנִי יְהוָה׃ וְלֹא תְחַלְּלוּ אֶת־שֵׁם קָדְשִׁי
וְנִקְדַּשְׁתִּי בְּתוֹךְ בְּנֵי יִשְׂרָאֵל אֲנִי יְהוָה מְקַדִּשְׁכֶם׃
33 הַמּוֹצִיא אֶתְכֶם מֵאֶרֶץ מִצְרַיִם לִהְיוֹת לָכֶם לֵאלֹהִים
אֲנִי יְהוָה׃ * פ רביעי

24. *ye do thus.* The Heb. can bear two interpretations. It can mean, 'Ye shall not offer such mutilated animals'; or it may be taken, according to the Rabbis, as a general prohibition of emasculation in men and animals.

25. *foreigner.* Blemished animals are unacceptable even from a non-Israelite who 'comes out of a far country for Thy name's sake' (I Kings VIII, 41). The priest was not to think that he need not be so strict in such a case.

their corruption is in them. 'They are faulty' (Moffatt).

accepted for you. Who offer these animals on behalf of the foreigner.

26–33. FURTHER DIRECTIONS IN REGARD TO SACRIFICIAL ANIMALS

27. *eighth day.* See on Exod. XXII, 29.

28. *not kill it and its young.* Not only for sacrificial purposes, but also for ordinary consumption.

in one day. 'It is prohibited to kill an animal with its young on the same day, in order that people should be restrained and prevented from killing the two together in such a manner that the young is slain in the sight of the mother; for the pain of the animals under such circumstances is very great. There is no difference in this case between the pain of man and the pain of other living beings, since the love and the tenderness of the mother for her young ones is not produced by reasoning but by feeling, and this faculty exists not only in man but in most living things' (Maimonides); cf. the similar prohibition of the mother-bird being taken with her young (Deut. XXII, 6 f).

30. *on the same day.* See on VII, 15.

CHILLUL HASHEM AND KIDDUSH HASHEM

32. *ye shall not . . . Israel.* This verse has been called 'Israel's Bible in little' (Jellinek). It contains the solemn warning against the Profanation of the Divine Name (*Chillul Hashem*), and the positive injunction to every Israelite to hallow the Name of God (*Kiddush Hashem*) by his life and, if need be, by his death. Although spoken in reference to the priests as the appointed guardians of the Sanctuary, this commandment, both in its positive and negative forms, was early applied to the whole of Israel.

ye shall not profane My holy name. Be ye exceedingly guarded in your actions, say the Rabbis, so that ye do nothing that tarnishes the

23 כג

CHAPTER XXIII

1. And the LORD spoke unto Moses, saying:
2. Speak unto the children of Israel, and say unto them: ¶ The appointed seasons of the LORD, which ye shall proclaim to be holy convocations, even these are My

CAP. XXIII. כג

א 2 וַיְדַבֵּר יְהוָה אֶל־מֹשֶׁה לֵּאמֹר׃ דַּבֵּר אֶל־בְּנֵי יִשְׂרָאֵל
וְאָמַרְתָּ אֲלֵהֶם מוֹעֲדֵי יְהוָה אֲשֶׁר־תִּקְרְאוּ אֹתָם מִקְרָאֵי

honour of Judaism or of the Jew. Especially do they warn against any misdeed towards a non-Jew as an unpardonable sin, because it gives a false impression of the moral standard of Judaism. The Jew should remember that the glory of God is, as it were, entrusted to his care; and that *every Israelite holds the honour of his Faith and of his entire People in his hands.* A single Jew's offence can bring shame on the whole House of Israel. This has been the fate of Israel in all the ages; and nothing, it seems, will ever break the world of its habit of putting down the crimes, vices, or failings of a Jew, no matter how estranged from his people or his people's Faith he may be, to his Jewishness, and of fathering them upon the entire Jewish race. The Rabbis say: 'Wild beasts visit and afflict the world because of the profanation of the Divine Name' (Ethics of the Fathers, v, 11). And, indeed, wherever Jews are guilty of conduct unworthy of their Faith, there the wild beast in man—blind prejudice and causeless hatred—is unchained against Israel. No student of Jewish history will question the truth of this judgment. The Rabbis, in a striking apologue, picture a boat at sea, full of men. One of them begins to bore a hole in the bottom of the boat and, on being remonstrated with, urges that he is only boring under his own seat. 'Yes,' say his comrades, 'but when the sea rushes in we shall be drowned with you.' So it is with Israel. Its weal or its woe is in the hands of every one of its children.

I will be hallowed. Not to commit Chillul Hashem is only a negative virtue. Far more is required of the Israelite. He is bidden so to live as to shed lustre on the Divine Name and the Torah by his deeds and influence. Rabbi Simon ben Shetach one day commissioned his disciples to buy him a camel from an Arab. When they brought him the animal, they gleefully announced that they had found a precious stone in its collar. 'Did the seller know of this gem?' asked the Master. On being answered in the negative, he called out angrily, 'Do you think me a barbarian that I should take advantage of the letter of the law by which the gem is mine together with the camel? Return the gem to the Arab immediately.' When the heathen received it back he exclaimed: 'Blessed be the God of Simon ben Shatach! Blessed be the God of Israel!'

The highest form of hallowing God is martyrdom; and Jewish Law demands of every Israelite to surrender his life, rather than by public apostasy desecrate the Name of God (Shulchan Aruch, Yore Deah, CLVII). When during the war of annihilation which the Emperor Hadrian waged against Judaism, the readiness for martyrdom on the part of young and old began to imperil the existence of the Jewish nation, the Rabbis decreed that only with regard to three fundamental laws—idolatry, incest, and murder—should death be preferred to transgression. See also p. 201, on the Akedah, and the ideal of martyrdom in Jewish history. 'The Jewish martyrs of olden days, who bore witness to their God at the stake, are described as having yielded up their lives for the "sanctification of the Divine Name". Such testimony is within the power, and constitutes the duty of the Jew, in these times also. If he is not called upon to die for the sanctification of the Name, he has at least to live for it. His life must give glory to God, vindicate his God-given religion' (M. Joseph).

among the children of Israel. If it is a sacred duty to hallow the Name of God and Israel before the nations, it is even a more sacred duty to do so '*among the children of Israel*'. Moses could make Pharaoh fear God; the dukes of Edom, the mighty men of Moab, and the peoples of Canaan trembled before him; but he was far from uniformly successful in making his own people do so. Therefore he was to see the promised Land afar off, but he was not to enter it. 'Get thee up unto Mount Nebo, and die in the mount as Aaron thy brother died on Mount Hor, because ye sanctified me not *in the midst* of the children of Israel' (Deut. XXXII, 49–52). It is important to make non-Jews respect Judaism, but even more so to make Jews respect Judaism.

CHAPTER XXIII

THE HOLY DAYS

This chapter gives a comprehensive description of the sacred seasons in the Jewish year. There is no mention of the New Moon, because it was not necessarily a day of cessation from work, and was not ranked as one of the 'holy convocations'. The sacrifices for each Festival are given in Num. XXVIII.

2. *appointed seasons.* Or, 'appointed (or fixed) seasons.'

holy convocations. An assembly 'convoked' or called together, for worship at the Sanctuary. The calling together was done by means of sounding two silver trumpets (Num. x, 1–10). Although it was only on the three Pilgrimage Festivals that the Israelites were to appear before the Lord at the Sanctuary, many would no doubt also come for the Days of Memorial and Atonement.

appointed seasons. 3. Six days shall work be done; but on the seventh day is a sabbath of solemn rest, a holy convocation; ye shall do no manner of work; it is a sabbath unto the LORD in all your dwellings. ¶ 4. These are the appointed seasons of the LORD, even holy convocations, which ye shall proclaim in their appointed season. 5. In the first month, on the fourteenth day of the month at dusk, is the LORD's passover. 6. And on the fifteenth day of the same month is the feast of unleavened bread unto the LORD; seven days ye shall eat unleavened bread. 7. In the first day ye shall have a holy convocation; ye shall do no manner of servile work. 8. And ye shall bring an offering made by fire unto the LORD seven days; in the seventh day is a holy convocation; ye shall do no manner of servile work. ¶ 9. And the LORD spoke unto Moses, saying: 10. Speak unto the children of Israel, and say unto them: ¶ When ye are come into the land which I give unto you, and shall reap the harvest thereof, then ye shall bring the sheaf of the first-fruits of your harvest unto the priest. 11. And he shall wave the sheaf before the LORD, to be accepted for you; on the morrow after the sabbath the priest shall wave it. 12. And in the day when ye wave the sheaf, ye shall offer a he-lamb without blemish of the first year for a

3 קֹדֶשׁ אֵלֶּה הֵם מוֹעֲדָי: שֵׁשֶׁת יָמִים תֵּעָשֶׂה מְלָאכָה וּבַיּוֹם
הַשְּׁבִיעִי שַׁבַּת שַׁבָּתוֹן מִקְרָא־קֹדֶשׁ כָּל־מְלָאכָה לֹא תַעֲשׂוּ
שַׁבָּת הִוא לַיהוָה בְּכֹל מוֹשְׁבֹתֵיכֶם: פ
4 אֵלֶּה מוֹעֲדֵי יְהוָה מִקְרָאֵי קֹדֶשׁ אֲשֶׁר־תִּקְרְאוּ אֹתָם
5 בְּמוֹעֲדָם: בַּחֹדֶשׁ הָרִאשׁוֹן בְּאַרְבָּעָה עָשָׂר לַחֹדֶשׁ בֵּין
6 הָעַרְבָּיִם פֶּסַח לַיהוָה: וּבַחֲמִשָּׁה עָשָׂר יוֹם לַחֹדֶשׁ הַזֶּה
7 חַג הַמַּצּוֹת לַיהוָה שִׁבְעַת יָמִים מַצּוֹת תֹּאכֵלוּ: בַּיּוֹם
הָרִאשׁוֹן מִקְרָא־קֹדֶשׁ יִהְיֶה לָכֶם כָּל־מְלֶאכֶת עֲבֹדָה לֹא
8 תַעֲשׂוּ: וְהִקְרַבְתֶּם אִשֶּׁה לַיהוָה שִׁבְעַת יָמִים בַּיּוֹם
הַשְּׁבִיעִי מִקְרָא־קֹדֶשׁ כָּל־מְלֶאכֶת עֲבֹדָה לֹא תַעֲשׂוּ: פ
9 וַיְדַבֵּר יְהוָה אֶל־מֹשֶׁה לֵּאמֹר: דַּבֵּר אֶל־בְּנֵי יִשְׂרָאֵל
וְאָמַרְתָּ אֲלֵהֶם כִּי־תָבֹאוּ אֶל־הָאָרֶץ אֲשֶׁר אֲנִי נֹתֵן לָכֶם
וּקְצַרְתֶּם אֶת־קְצִירָהּ וַהֲבֵאתֶם אֶת־עֹמֶר רֵאשִׁית קְצִירְכֶם
11 אֶל־הַכֹּהֵן: וְהֵנִיף אֶת־הָעֹמֶר לִפְנֵי יְהוָה לִרְצֹנְכֶם
12 מִמָּחֳרַת הַשַּׁבָּת יְנִיפֶנּוּ הַכֹּהֵן: וַעֲשִׂיתֶם בְּיוֹם הֲנִיפְכֶם

3. *sabbath of solemn rest.* The reference to the Sabbath in this connection is, according to the Rabbis, to emphasize the fact that the seventh day of the week must always be 'a sabbath of solemn rest'—even when it coincides with a Festival, on which day, otherwise, only manual labour is prohibited, but not such as is necessary for the preparation of meals.

all your dwellings. See on III, 17.

5–8. THE PASSOVER

For the meaning and observance of this Festival, see on Exod. XII, 1–28.

5. *first month.* See on Exod. XII, 2.

at dusk is the LORD'S passover. Better, *towards even is a passover unto the LORD* (Friedländer); *i.e.* a paschal offering in honour of the LORD.

6. *feast of unleavened bread.* Only the 15th day of the month is 'the *feast* of unleavened bread', so called because the partaking of *matzah* (מצה של מצוה) is obligatory on the eve thereof, although unleavened bread is eaten for seven days and the seventh day is a 'holy convocation'.

7. *servile work.* lit. 'work of labour', the usual work which one does on an ordinary week day. It implies a less strict abstinence from labour than was demanded for the Sabbath (*v.* 3) and the Day of Atonement (*v.* 28), and does not include the prohibition of preparing food.

8. *offering.* This is defined in detail in Num. XXVIII, 19 f.

9–14. THE OMER

At the beginning of the barley harvest—barley ripens two or three weeks before the wheat—the first sheaf was presented at the Sanctuary; see Deut. XXVI, 2.

10. *when ye are come.* When the Israelites had begun to till the soil of their land.

11. *on the morrow after the sabbath.* Better, *on the morrow after the day of rest;* Heb. ממחרת השבת. The interpretation of this phrase was the subject of heated controversy in early Rabbinic times between the Pharisees and Sadducees. The latter took the word 'sabbath' in its usual sense, and maintained that the Omer was to be brought on the morrow of the first Saturday in Passover. The Pharisees argued that 'sabbath' (השבת) here means, 'the day of cessation from work'; and the context shows that the Feast of Unleavened Bread is intended: therefore, the Omer was to be brought on the 16th of Nisan. This is supported by the Septuagint which renders 'on the morrow of the first day', and by Josephus. 'The offerings of the sheaf took place on the 16th, the first busy work-day of the harvest, in relation to which the preceding day might well be called a *Sabbath* or rest-day, burnt-offering unto the LORD. 13. And the meal-offering thereof shall be two tenth parts of an ephah of fine flour mingled with oil, an offering made by fire unto the LORD for a sweet savour; and the drink-offering thereof shall be of wine, the fourth part of a hin. 14. And ye shall eat neither bread, nor parched corn, nor fresh ears, until this selfsame day, until ye have brought the offering of your God; it is a statute for ever throughout your generations in all your dwellings. ¶ 15. And ye shall count unto you from the morrow after the [1]day of rest, from the day that ye brought the sheaf of the waving; seven weeks shall there be complete; 16. even unto the morrow after the seventh week shall ye number fifty days; and ye shall present a new meal-offering unto the LORD. 17. Ye shall bring out of your dwellings two wave-loaves of two tenth parts of an ephah;

[1] Heb. *sabbath.*

13 אֶת־הָעֹמֶר כֶּבֶשׂ תָּמִים בֶּן־שְׁנָתוֹ לְעֹלָה לַיהוָה׃ וּמִנְחָתוֹ
שְׁנֵי עֶשְׂרֹנִים סֹלֶת בְּלוּלָה בַשֶּׁמֶן אִשֶּׁה לַיהוָה רֵיחַ
14 נִיחֹחַ וְנִסְכֹּה יַיִן רְבִיעִת הַהִין׃ וְלֶחֶם וְקָלִי וְכַרְמֶל לֹא
תֹאכְלוּ עַד־עֶצֶם הַיּוֹם הַזֶּה עַד הֲבִיאֲכֶם אֶת־קָרְבַּן
אֱלֹהֵיכֶם חֻקַּת עוֹלָם לְדֹרֹתֵיכֶם בְּכֹל מֹשְׁבֹתֵיכֶם׃ ס
טו וּסְפַרְתֶּם לָכֶם מִמָּחֳרַת הַשַּׁבָּת מִיּוֹם הֲבִיאֲכֶם אֶת־עֹמֶר
16 הַתְּנוּפָה שֶׁבַע שַׁבָּתוֹת תְּמִימֹת תִּהְיֶינָה׃ עַד מִמָּחֳרַת
הַשַּׁבָּת הַשְּׁבִיעִת תִּסְפְּרוּ חֲמִשִּׁים יוֹם וְהִקְרַבְתֶּם מִנְחָה
17 חֲדָשָׁה לַיהוָה׃ מִמּוֹשְׁבֹתֵיכֶם תָּבִיאּוּ ׀ לֶחֶם תְּנוּפָה
שְׁתַּיִם שְׁנֵי עֶשְׂרֹנִים סֹלֶת תִּהְיֶינָה חָמֵץ תֵּאָפֶינָה בִּכּוּרִים

v. 13. ונסכו ק' v. 17. א' דגושה

though not all labour was prohibited. This is alone compatible with the context, and is free from the objections to which all the other opinions are open' (Kalisch).

12. *ye shall offer.* The offering in connection with the bringing of the Omer is here specified, as it finds no mention in Num. XXVIII.

13. *ephah. . . hin.* See on XIX, 36.

14. *neither bread . . . day.* Josh. v, 11 contains a historical reference to this regulation.

15–21. FEAST OF WEEKS—SHAVUOS

One of the three agricultural festivals, the feast of the first harvest יום הבכורים. Jewish tradition, however, connects it with the Covenant on Mount Sinai, and speaks of the festival as זמן מתן תורתנו 'the Season of giving of our Torah'. The Israelites arrived at Sinai on the New Moon. On the second of the month, Moses ascended the mountain; on the third, he received the people's reply; on the fourth, he made the second ascent and was commanded to institute three days of preparation, at the conclusion of which the Revelation took place. Hence its association with the Feast of Weeks, which became the Festival of Revelation.

15. *and ye shall count.* The paragraph dealing with the Feast of Weeks has no introductory formula, 'The Lord spake unto Moses', such as we find in connection with the other Festivals, because it is conceived as the complement of the Passover, and not something independent of it. Its name in Talmudic literature is not *Shavuos*, but almost invariably עצרת, 'the concluding festival' to Passover. 'We count the days that pass since the preceding Festival, just as one who expects his most intimate friend on a certain day, counts the days and even the hours. This is the reason why we count the days that pass since the offering of the Omer, between the anniversary of our departure from Egypt and the anniversary of the Law-giving. The latter was the aim and object of the exodus from Egypt' (Maimonides). In other words, the Deliverance from bondage was not an end in itself; it was the prelude to Sinai (Exod. III, 12). Liberty without law is a doubtful boon, whether to men or nations.

unto you. From this addition, the Rabbis deduce that each Israelite had the duty of counting for himself; hence the 'counting of the days of the Omer' even after the Omer itself was no longer brought to the Temple. The season between Passover and Shavuos (or Pentecost, which in Greek means 'the fiftieth day' after the first day of Passover) is known as *Sephirah*, Period of Counting. It is a period of semi-mourning, because repeatedly dire calamities befell the Jewish people at this time.

day of rest. This is a departure from the RV which translates 'sabbath'; see on *v.* 11.

seven weeks. lit. 'seven sabbaths'. It is evident that here and in XXV, 8, the Heb. *shabbath* signifies 'week'. Hence the most common name for the Festival, חג השבועות, the Feast of Weeks; Deut. XVI, 10.

16. *seventh week.* Instead of, 'seventh sabbath' (RV).

new meal-offering. The cereal offering of the produce of the new wheat harvest; see next *v.*

'With the destruction of the Second Temple, the agricultural aspect of the Festival receded, and Shavuos became primarily the Feast of Revelation. An echo of nature, however, still lingers in the present custom of adorning the Synagogue with flowers' (H. M. Adler).

18 לַיהוָה: וְהִקְרַבְתֶּם עַל־הַלֶּחֶם שִׁבְעַת כְּבָשִׂים תְּמִימִם
בְּנֵי שָׁנָה וּפַר בֶּן־בָּקָר אֶחָד וְאֵילִם שְׁנָיִם יִהְיוּ עֹלָה
לַיהוָה וּמִנְחָתָם וְנִסְכֵּיהֶם אִשֵּׁה רֵיחַ־נִיחֹחַ לַיהוָה:
19 וַעֲשִׂיתֶם שְׂעִיר־עִזִּים אֶחָד לְחַטָּאת וּשְׁנֵי כְבָשִׂים בְּנֵי
כ שָׁנָה לְזֶבַח שְׁלָמִים: וְהֵנִיף הַכֹּהֵן | אֹתָם עַל לֶחֶם
הַבִּכֻּרִים תְּנוּפָה לִפְנֵי יְהוָה עַל־שְׁנֵי כְּבָשִׂים קֹדֶשׁ יִהְיוּ
21 לַיהוָה לַכֹּהֵן: וּקְרָאתֶם בְּעֶצֶם | הַיּוֹם הַזֶּה מִקְרָא־קֹדֶשׁ
יִהְיֶה לָכֶם כָּל־מְלֶאכֶת עֲבֹדָה לֹא תַעֲשׂוּ חֻקַּת עוֹלָם
22 בְּכָל־מוֹשְׁבֹתֵיכֶם לְדֹרֹתֵיכֶם: וּבְקֻצְרְכֶם אֶת־קְצִיר אַרְצְכֶם
לֹא־תְכַלֶּה פְּאַת שָׂדְךָ בְּקֻצְרֶךָ וְלֶקֶט קְצִירְךָ לֹא תְלַקֵּט
לֶעָנִי וְלַגֵּר תַּעֲזֹב אֹתָם אֲנִי יְהוָה אֱלֹהֵיכֶם: פ חמישי
23 24 וַיְדַבֵּר יְהוָה אֶל־מֹשֶׁה לֵּאמֹר: דַּבֵּר אֶל־בְּנֵי יִשְׂרָאֵל

they shall be of fine flour, they shall be baked with leaven, for first-fruits unto the LORD. 18. And ye shall present with the bread seven lambs without blemish of the first year, and one young bullock, and two rams; they shall be a burnt-offering unto the LORD, with their meal-offering, and their drink-offerings, even an offering made by fire, of a sweet savour unto the LORD. 19. And ye shall offer one he-goat for a sin-offering, and two he-lambs of the first year for a sacrifice of peace-offerings. 20. And the priest shall wave them with the bread of the first-fruits for a wave-offering before the LORD, with the two lambs; they shall be holy to the LORD for the priest. 21. And ye shall make proclamation on the selfsame day; there shall be a holy convocation unto you; ye shall do no manner of servile work; it is a statute for ever in all your dwellings throughout your generations. ¶ 22. And when ye reap the harvest of your land, thou shalt not wholly reap the corner of thy field, neither shalt thou gather the gleaning of thy harvest; thou shalt leave them for the poor, and for the stranger: I am the LORD your God.*v. ¶ 23. And the

17. *your dwellings.* The Rabbis explain this as meaning that the corn must have grown in the Holy Land.

baked with leaven. The loaves were made to represent the common food of the people, and symbolically mark their gratitude to the Provider of their sustenance. They were not offered upon the Altar (II, 11), but only 'waved'; they belonged to the priest.

19. *ye shall offer.* These offerings are additional to those mentioned in Num. XXVIII, 27.

20. *to the LORD for the priest. i.e.* they are devoted to God by being eaten by the priest; cf. Num. v, 8, for a similar usage.

22. *when ye reap.* A repetition of XIX, 9 f. A significant reminder to the Israelite that his thankfulness to God for the wheat-harvest was to be demonstrated by more than an offering on the Altar. If he failed to share God's bounty with the poor, his observance of the Festival would be unacceptable.

24–25. DAY OF MEMORIAL—ROSH HASHANAH

As the seventh day in the week was a holy day, so the seventh month was the holy month in the year. Each New Moon was made the occasion for additional offerings (Num. XXIII, 11 f). It is, therefore, not surprising that the New Moon of the seventh month should be a Festival of special solemnity. In later times, it was known as *Rosh Hashanah*, New Year's Day. But unlike the New Year celebrations of many ancient and modern nations, the Jewish New Year is not a time of revelry, but an occasion of the deepest religious import.

24. *a memorial.* In Num. XXIX, 1, the occasion is called 'a day of blowing the horn', *i.e.* Shofar, the ram's horn; Josh. VI, 4. This act must be differentiated from the sounding of the 'trumpet' (*not* the Shofar) which took place while the offerings were brought on all the Festivals and New Moons (Num. x, 10). The blowing of the Shofar had consequently quite a different significance, and was more awe-inspiring (see Amos III, 6) than the blowing of the silver trumpets, which generally was a joyous sound. The sound of Shofar consisting, as handed down by Tradition, of three distinctive Shofar-notes—tekiah, shevarim, teruah—has been looked upon from time immemorial as a call to contrition and penitence, as a reminder of the Shofar-sound of Sinai; and the Day of Memorial, the beginning of the Ten Days of Repentance (עשרת ימי תשובה) which culminate in the Day of Atonement, as a time of self-examination and humble petition for forgiveness. 'The Scriptural injunction of the Shofar for the New Year's Day has a profound meaning. It says: 'Awake, ye sleepers, and ponder over your deeds; remember your Creator and go back to Him in penitence. Be not of those who miss

LORD spoke unto Moses, saying: 24. Speak
unto the children of Israel, saying: ¶ In the
seventh month, in the first day of the
month, shall be a solemn rest unto you,
a memorial proclaimed with the blast of
horns, a holy convocation. 25. Ye shall
do no manner of servile work; and ye
shall bring an offering made by fire unto
the LORD. ¶ 26. And the LORD spoke unto
Moses, saying: ¶ 27. Howbeit on the tenth
day of this seventh month is the day of
atonement; there shall be a holy convocation
unto you, and ye shall afflict your souls;
and ye shall bring an offering made by fire
unto the LORD. 28. And ye shall do no
manner of work in that same day; for it
is a day of atonement, to make atonement
for you before the LORD your God. 29.
For whatever soul it be that shall not
be afflicted in that same day, he shall be
cut off from his people. 30. And whatsoever
soul it be that doeth any manner of work
in that same day, that soul will I destroy
from among his people. 31. Ye shall do
no manner of work; it is a statute for ever
throughout your generations in all your

לֵאמֹר בַּחֹדֶשׁ הַשְּׁבִיעִי בְּאֶחָד לַחֹדֶשׁ יִהְיֶה לָכֶם שַׁבָּתוֹן
כה זִכְרוֹן תְּרוּעָה מִקְרָא־קֹדֶשׁ׃ כָּל־מְלֶאכֶת עֲבֹדָה לֹא תַעֲשׂוּ
26 וְהִקְרַבְתֶּם אִשֶּׁה לַיהוָה׃ ס וַיְדַבֵּר יְהוָה אֶל־מֹשֶׁה
27 לֵּאמֹר׃ אַךְ בֶּעָשׂוֹר לַחֹדֶשׁ הַשְּׁבִיעִי הַזֶּה יוֹם הַכִּפֻּרִים
הוּא מִקְרָא־קֹדֶשׁ יִהְיֶה לָכֶם וְעִנִּיתֶם אֶת־נַפְשֹׁתֵיכֶם
28 וְהִקְרַבְתֶּם אִשֶּׁה לַיהוָה׃ וְכָל־מְלָאכָה לֹא תַעֲשׂוּ בְּעֶצֶם
הַיּוֹם הַזֶּה כִּי יוֹם כִּפֻּרִים הוּא לְכַפֵּר עֲלֵיכֶם לִפְנֵי יְהוָה
29 אֱלֹהֵיכֶם׃ כִּי כָל־הַנֶּפֶשׁ אֲשֶׁר לֹא־תְעֻנֶּה בְּעֶצֶם הַיּוֹם
ל הַזֶּה וְנִכְרְתָה מֵעַמֶּיהָ׃ וְכָל־הַנֶּפֶשׁ אֲשֶׁר תַּעֲשֶׂה כָּל־
מְלָאכָה בְּעֶצֶם הַיּוֹם הַזֶּה וְהַאֲבַדְתִּי אֶת־הַנֶּפֶשׁ הַהִוא
31 מִקֶּרֶב עַמָּהּ׃ כָּל־מְלָאכָה לֹא תַעֲשׂוּ חֻקַּת עוֹלָם

realities in their pursuit of shadows and waste their years in seeking after vain things which cannot profit or deliver. Look well to your souls and consider your acts; forsake each of you his evil ways and thoughts, and return to God so that He may have mercy upon you' (Maimonides).

25. *an offering.* Described in Num. XXIX, 2 f.

26–32. DAY OF ATONEMENT

On the subject of this the most solemn day in the Jewish year, see the commentary on XVI, 29–34. No other nation, ancient or modern, has an institution approaching the Day of Atonement in religious depth—'a day of purification and of turning from sins, for which forgiveness is granted through the grace of the merciful God, who holds penitence in as high an esteem as guiltlessness' (Philo).

27. *day of atonement.* Heb. *yom kippurim.* lit. 'Day of Atonements'. The name of this most sacred of Festivals is in the plural, 'because it represents two streams of love. As soon as the desire for reconciliation has awakened in the sinner's soul, and wings its way Heavenward, God's grace comes down to meet it, calming his breast with the assurance of Divine pardon and forgiveness' (Zohar).

afflict your souls. See on XVI, 29; this Day, set aside for penitence and moral regeneration, is the only one for which the Torah prescribes fasting —which is the intensest form of devotion and contrition. 'On that Day,' the Rabbis state, 'the Israelites resemble the angels, without human wants, without sins, and linked together in love and peace.' It is the only day of the year—they add—on which the accuser Satan is silenced before the Throne of Glory, and even becomes the defender of Israel. Confession of sin is the most essential and characteristic element in the services of the Day of Atonement; 'every one entreating pardon for his sins and hoping for God's mercy, not because of his own merits but through the compassionate nature of that Being who will have forgiveness rather than punishment' (Philo). The Confession is made by the whole Community collectively; and those who have not themselves committed the sins mentioned in the confession regret that they were unable to prevent them from being committed by others (Friedländer).

an offering. See Num. XXIX, 7 f.

28. *no manner of work.* The phrase is not qualified by the addition of the word 'servile'. With regard to work, the Day of Atonement is of the same strictness as the Sabbath (Exod. XX, 10), with similar exceptions where life might be endangered.

to make atonement for you. 'As I live, saith the Lord God, I have no pleasure in the death of the wicked; but that the wicked turn from his way and live: turn ye, turn ye from your evil ways' (Ezek. XXXIII, 11).

30. *will I destroy.* Synonymous with 'shall be cut off', showing that the punishment is not by a human Court.

31. *it is a statute.* As in III, 17.

dwellings. 32. It shall be unto you a sabbath of solemn rest, and ye shall afflict your souls; in the ninth day of the month at even, from even unto even, shall ye keep your sabbath. *vi. ¶ 33. And the LORD spoke unto Moses, saying: ¶ 34. Speak unto the children of Israel, saying: ¶ On the fifteenth day of this seventh month is the feast of tabernacles for seven days unto the LORD. 35. On the first day shall be a holy convocation; ye shall do no manner of servile work. 36. Seven days ye shall bring an offering made by fire unto the LORD; on the eighth day shall be a holy convocation unto you; and ye shall bring an offering made by fire unto the LORD; it is a day of solemn assembly; ye shall do no manner of servile work. ¶ 37. These are the appointed seasons of the LORD, which ye shall proclaim to be holy convocations, to bring an offering made by fire unto the LORD, a burnt-offering, and a meal-offering, a sacrifice, and drink-offerings, each on its own day; 38. beside the sabbaths of the LORD, and beside your gifts, and beside all your vows, and beside all your freewill-offerings, which ye give unto the LORD. ¶ 39. Howbeit on the fifteenth day of the seventh month, when ye have gathered in the fruits of the land, ye shall keep the feast of the LORD seven days; on the first day shall be a solemn rest, and on the eighth day shall be a solemn rest. 40.

32 לְדֹרֹתֵיכֶם בְּכֹל מֹשְׁבֹתֵיכֶם׃ שַׁבַּת שַׁבָּתוֹן הוּא לָכֶם
וְעִנִּיתֶם אֶת־נַפְשֹׁתֵיכֶם בְּתִשְׁעָה לַחֹדֶשׁ בָּעֶרֶב מֵעֶרֶב עַד־
עֶרֶב תִּשְׁבְּתוּ שַׁבַּתְּכֶם׃ פ ששי
33 34 וַיְדַבֵּר יְהוָה אֶל־מֹשֶׁה לֵּאמֹר׃ דַּבֵּר אֶל־בְּנֵי יִשְׂרָאֵל
לֵאמֹר בַּחֲמִשָּׁה עָשָׂר יוֹם לַחֹדֶשׁ הַשְּׁבִיעִי הַזֶּה חַג הַסֻּכּוֹת
לה שִׁבְעַת יָמִים לַיהוָה׃ בַּיּוֹם הָרִאשׁוֹן מִקְרָא־קֹדֶשׁ כָּל־
36 מְלֶאכֶת עֲבֹדָה לֹא תַעֲשׂוּ׃ שִׁבְעַת יָמִים תַּקְרִיבוּ אִשֶּׁה
לַיהוָה בַּיּוֹם הַשְּׁמִינִי מִקְרָא־קֹדֶשׁ יִהְיֶה לָכֶם וְהִקְרַבְתֶּם
אִשֶּׁה לַיהוָה עֲצֶרֶת הִוא כָּל־מְלֶאכֶת עֲבֹדָה לֹא תַעֲשׂוּ׃
37 אֵלֶּה מוֹעֲדֵי יְהוָה אֲשֶׁר־תִּקְרְאוּ אֹתָם מִקְרָאֵי קֹדֶשׁ לְהַקְרִיב
אִשֶּׁה לַיהוָה עֹלָה וּמִנְחָה זֶבַח וּנְסָכִים דְּבַר־יוֹם בְּיוֹמוֹ׃
38 מִלְּבַד שַׁבְּתֹת יְהוָה וּמִלְּבַד מַתְּנוֹתֵיכֶם וּמִלְּבַד כָּל־נִדְרֵיכֶם
39 וּמִלְּבַד כָּל־נִדְבֹתֵיכֶם אֲשֶׁר תִּתְּנוּ לַיהוָה׃ אַךְ בַּחֲמִשָּׁה
עָשָׂר יוֹם לַחֹדֶשׁ הַשְּׁבִיעִי בְּאָסְפְּכֶם אֶת־תְּבוּאַת הָאָרֶץ
תָּחֹגּוּ אֶת־חַג־יְהוָה שִׁבְעַת יָמִים בַּיּוֹם הָרִאשׁוֹן שַׁבָּתוֹן

32. *in the ninth day.* The Day commencing with the preceding eve (Gen. I, 5). Both the opening and closing evenings are marked by services (Kol Nidrê and Neilah) of special solemnity. The Neilah Amidah is one of the most masterly products of Israel's religious genius. It begins: 'Thou givest a hand to transgressors, and Thy right hand is stretched out to receive the penitent. Thou hast taught us, O LORD our God, to make confession unto Thee of all our sins, in order that we may cease from the violence of our hands and may return unto Thee who delightest in the repentance of the wicked.' These words contain, what has been called, 'the Jewish doctrine of salvation.'

33–43. FEAST OF TABERNACLES

34. *fifteenth day.* Like the Passover, this Feast commenced at full moon.

tabernacles. Heb. *Succoth.* lit. 'booths'. In Exod. XXIII, 16, it is called 'the Feast of Ingathering'. In Rabbinic literature, it is known as '*the* Feast', because, as the time of harvest, it would naturally be a period of rejoicing and holiday-making. It really consists of two groups: the first seven days, Tabernacles proper; and the eighth day, Atzeres. The seventh day of Tabernacles became in later times an echo of the Day of Atonement and was known as *Hoshanah Rabbah;* and the 'second day' of Atzeres assumed the nature of a separate Festival under the name of *Simchas Torah*, Rejoicing of the Law, the day on which the annual reading of the Torah was completed and restarted.

36. *an offering.* See Num. XXIX.

solemn assembly. Or, 'closing festival'. Heb. *atzereth*, the concluding day of a festival season, applied to the seventh day of Passover (Deut. XVI, 8), and, in Rabbinnc literature, to the Feast of Weeks (see on *v.* 15). Maimonides explains the purpose of this eighth day to be, 'in order to complete our rejoicings which cannot be perfect in booths, but in well-built houses.'

38. *the sabbaths. i.e.* the additional sacrifices offered on the Sabbaths (Num. XXVIII, 9 f).

gifts. The voluntary offerings that accompanied the Israelite on his pilgrimage to the Temple, when he was bidden not to appear before the LORD 'empty' (Deut. XVI, 16 f).

vows. See on VII, 16.

39–43. Additional directions in regard to Tabernacles for the time when, after the settlement in Canaan, the people would be tilling the soil and reaping the harvest.

39. *eighth day.* Which is deemed a Festival on its own account, distinct from the Feast of Tabernacles.

And ye shall take you on the first day the fruit of goodly trees, branches of palm-trees, and boughs of thick trees, and willows of the brook, and ye shall rejoice before the LORD your God seven days. 41. And ye shall keep it a feast unto the LORD seven days in the year; it is a statute for ever in your generations; ye shall keep it in the seventh month. 42. Ye shall dwell in booths seven days; all that are home-born in Israel shall dwell in booths; 43. that your generations may know that I made the children of Israel to dwell in booths, when I brought them out of the land of Egypt: I am the LORD your God. ¶ 44. And Moses declared unto the children of Israel the appointed seasons of the LORD.* vii.

24

CHAPTER XXIV

1. And the LORD spoke unto Moses, saying: 2. 'Command the children of Israel, that they bring unto thee pure olive oil beaten for the light, to cause a lamp to burn continually. 3. Without the veil of the testimony, in the tent of meeting, shall Aaron order it from evening to morning

מ וּבַיּוֹם הַשְּׁמִינִי שַׁבָּתוֹן׃ וּלְקַחְתֶּם לָכֶם בַּיּוֹם הָרִאשׁוֹן
פְּרִי עֵץ הָדָר כַּפֹּת תְּמָרִים וַעֲנַף עֵץ־עָבֹת וְעַרְבֵי־נָחַל
41 וּשְׂמַחְתֶּם לִפְנֵי יְהוָה אֱלֹהֵיכֶם שִׁבְעַת יָמִים׃ וְחַגֹּתֶם אֹתוֹ
חַג לַיהוָה שִׁבְעַת יָמִים בַּשָּׁנָה חֻקַּת עוֹלָם לְדֹרֹתֵיכֶם
42 בַּחֹדֶשׁ הַשְּׁבִיעִי תָּחֹגּוּ אֹתוֹ׃ בַּסֻּכֹּת תֵּשְׁבוּ שִׁבְעַת יָמִים
43 כָּל־הָאֶזְרָח בְּיִשְׂרָאֵל יֵשְׁבוּ בַּסֻּכֹּת׃ לְמַעַן יֵדְעוּ דֹרֹתֵיכֶם
כִּי בַסֻּכּוֹת הוֹשַׁבְתִּי אֶת־בְּנֵי יִשְׂרָאֵל בְּהוֹצִיאִי אוֹתָם
44 מֵאֶרֶץ מִצְרָיִם אֲנִי יְהוָה אֱלֹהֵיכֶם׃ וַיְדַבֵּר מֹשֶׁה אֶת־
מֹעֲדֵי יְהוָה אֶל־בְּנֵי יִשְׂרָאֵל׃ פ שביעי

כד CAP. XXIV. כד

א 2 וַיְדַבֵּר יְהוָה אֶל־מֹשֶׁה לֵּאמֹר׃ צַו אֶת־בְּנֵי יִשְׂרָאֵל וְיִקְחוּ
אֵלֶיךָ שֶׁמֶן זַיִת זָךְ כָּתִית לַמָּאוֹר לְהַעֲלֹת נֵר תָּמִיד׃
3 מִחוּץ לְפָרֹכֶת הָעֵדֻת בְּאֹהֶל מוֹעֵד יַעֲרֹךְ אֹתוֹ אַהֲרֹן

40. *fruit of goodly trees.* Tradition holds that this is the *ethrog*, the citron.

thick trees. Better, *thick-leaved trees;* myrtle branches. These traditional explanations are supported by the testimony of Josephus who writes: 'On this Festival we carry in our hands a branch of myrtle, and willow, and a bough of the palm-tree, with the addition of the citron.'

and ye shall rejoice before the LORD. This phrase was closely linked with the preceding, and gave rise to the joyous processions in the Temple. The pilgrims held the *lulav* and *esrog* in their hands and sang Psalms of praise to God.

42. *booths.* The Heb. *sukkah* represents a hastily-constructed and unsubstantial edifice, such as the Israelites must have set up during the wanderings in the Wilderness. In addition to its historical association reminding the Israelite of the Divine protection during the desert-journey, the command to dwell in booths has also a religious signification. 'Man ought to remember his evil days in his days of prosperity. He will thereby he induced to thank God repeatedly, to lead a modest and humble life. We, therefore, on Tabernacles leave our houses in order to dwell in booths. We shall thereby remember that this has once been our condition' (Maimonides). The Book of Ecclesiastes is aptly set aside for special reading during Tabernacles or Atzeres.

44. *Moses declared.* Cf. XXI, 24. Not only did he communicate the contents of the chapter to the people, but, as each Festival occurred, he took the opportunity of repeating the commands so that they were properly observed (Sifra).

CHAPTER XXIV

1–9. THE LAMPS AND THE SHEWBREAD

The Torah, before leaving the subject of the Sanctuary, alludes to the constant duty of the priests to see that the lamp is kept perpetually alight and the shewbread regularly arranged. These are outstanding obligations of priesthood, which must not be relaxed even at the special seasons of the year, when the attention and energies of the Temple-servants were otherwise taxed to the full.

2. *pure olive oil.* See on Exod. XXVII, 20 f.

3. *shall Aaron order it.* In Exod. the phrase 'and his sons' is added after 'Aaron'. In the first instance, the lamp was kindled by Aaron (Num. VIII, 3).

4. *the pure candlestick.* So called either because made of pure gold (Exod. XXV, 31 f), or because it was to be cleansed each time that the lamps are arranged upon it.

before the LORD. It must on no account be removed from the Sanctuary.

מֵעֶרֶב עַד־בֹּקֶר לִפְנֵי יְהוָה תָּמִיד חֻקַּת עוֹלָם לְדֹרֹתֵיכֶם׃
4 עַל הַמְּנֹרָה הַטְּהֹרָה יַעֲרֹךְ אֶת־הַנֵּרוֹת לִפְנֵי יְהוָה תָּמִיד׃ פ
ה וְלָקַחְתָּ סֹלֶת וְאָפִיתָ אֹתָהּ שְׁתֵּים עֶשְׂרֵה חַלּוֹת שְׁנֵי
6 עֶשְׂרֹנִים יִהְיֶה הַחַלָּה הָאֶחָת׃ וְשַׂמְתָּ אוֹתָם שְׁתַּיִם
מַעֲרָכוֹת שֵׁשׁ הַמַּעֲרָכֶת עַל הַשֻּׁלְחָן הַטָּהֹר לִפְנֵי יְהוָה׃
7 וְנָתַתָּ עַל־הַמַּעֲרֶכֶת לְבֹנָה זַכָּה וְהָיְתָה לַלֶּחֶם לְאַזְכָּרָה
8 אִשֶּׁה לַיהוָה׃ בְּיוֹם הַשַּׁבָּת בְּיוֹם הַשַּׁבָּת יַעַרְכֶנּוּ לִפְנֵי
9 יְהוָה תָּמִיד מֵאֵת בְּנֵי־יִשְׂרָאֵל בְּרִית עוֹלָם׃ וְהָיְתָה לְאַהֲרֹן
וּלְבָנָיו וַאֲכָלֻהוּ בְּמָקוֹם קָדֹשׁ כִּי קֹדֶשׁ קָדָשִׁים הוּא לוֹ
י מֵאִשֵּׁי יְהוָה חָק־עוֹלָם׃ ס וַיֵּצֵא בֶּן־אִשָּׁה יִשְׂרְאֵלִית
וְהוּא בֶּן־אִישׁ מִצְרִי בְּתוֹךְ בְּנֵי יִשְׂרָאֵל וַיִּנָּצוּ בַּמַּחֲנֶה
11 בֶּן הַיִּשְׂרְאֵלִית וְאִישׁ הַיִּשְׂרְאֵלִי׃ וַיִּקֹּב בֶּן־הָאִשָּׁה
הַיִּשְׂרְאֵלִית אֶת־הַשֵּׁם וַיְקַלֵּל וַיָּבִיאוּ אֹתוֹ אֶל־מֹשֶׁה וְשֵׁם
12 אִמּוֹ שְׁלֹמִית בַּת־דִּבְרִי לְמַטֵּה־דָן׃ וַיַּנִּיחֻהוּ בַּמִּשְׁמָר
לִפְרֹשׁ לָהֶם עַל־פִּי יְהוָה׃ פ
13 14 וַיְדַבֵּר יְהוָה אֶל־מֹשֶׁה לֵּאמֹר׃ הוֹצֵא אֶת־הַמְקַלֵּל אֶל־

v. 10. חב' בסגול

before the LORD continually; it shall be a statute for ever throughout your generations. 4. He shall order the lamps upon the pure candlestick before the LORD continually. ¶ 5. And thou shalt take fine flour, and bake twelve cakes thereof: two tenth parts of an ephah shall be in one cake. 6. And thou shalt set them in two rows, six in a row, upon the pure table before the LORD. 7. And thou shalt put pure frankincense with each row, that it may be to the bread for a memorial-part, even an offering made by fire unto the LORD. 8. Every sabbath day he shall set it in order before the LORD continually; it is from the children of Israel, an everlasting covenant. 9. And it shall be for Aaron and his sons; and they shall eat it in a holy place; for it is most holy unto him of the offerings of the LORD made by fire, a perpetual due.' ¶ 10. And the son of an Israelitish woman, whose father was an Egyptian, went out among the children of Israel; and the son of the Israelitish woman and a man of Israel strove together in the camp. 11. And the son of the Israelitish woman blasphemed the Name, and cursed; and they brought him unto Moses. And his mother's name was Shelomith, the daughter of Dibri, of the tribe of Dan. 12. And they put him in ward, that it might be declared unto them at the mouth of the LORD. ¶ 13. And the LORD spoke unto Moses, saying: 14. 'Bring forth him that hath cursed without the camp; and let all that heard him lay

5. *twelve cakes.* See on Exod. xxv, 30; see also *v.* 8.

6. *rows.* Or, 'piles.'

pure table. i.e. overlaid with pure gold (Exod. xxv, 24).

7. *memorial-part.* See on II, 2. The incense was put in two small golden cups, and one placed near each row of cakes. It symbolized prayer, and thus gave expression to the petition that God continue to grant food to the people of His covenant (Koenig).

8. *every sabbath day.* The bread remained on the table for a week, and was renewed each Sabbath.

an everlasting covenant. This phrase is applied to the Sabbath itself (Exod. XXXI, 16); and this weekly offering from the Children of Israel typified the regular renewal of the covenant between God and His people, of which the Sabbath was 'a sign'.

9. *holy place.* See II, 3.

10–23. THE PENALTY OF BLASPHEMY

The sole aim of all that is enjoined in the Book of Leviticus is to sanctify Israel, individually and collectively. When, therefore, anyone presumes to desecrate the Divine Name, the penalty must be ruthless.

10. *went out.* Or, 'had come forth' from Egypt, among the children of Israel (Ehrlich). The cause of the quarrel is not stated, because it is not of material importance. Note that the blasphemer is not 'an Israelite' but the 'son of the Israelitish woman'. Only one of the mixed multitude (Exod. XII, 38) could be guilty of so heinous an offence.

11. *blasphemed.* lit. 'to indicate by name', here with unholy contempt and dishonour.

the Name. The Divine Name of the four letters, Y H W H, which is never pronounced, but read as Adonay.

his mother's name. Rashi remarks that his genealogy is recorded to impress upon the Israelite that a man's life is not his own to do with as he pleased. His disgrace is also that of his parents, of his tribe, of his people.

12. *that it might be declared.* The Torah had ordained, 'Thou shalt not revile God' (Exod. XXII, 27); but no penalty had been mentioned in that connection.

their hands upon his head, and let all the congregation stone him. 15. And thou shalt speak unto the children of Israel, saying: Whosoever curseth his God shall bear his sin. 16. And he that blasphemeth the name of the LORD, he shall surely be put to death; all the congregation shall certainly stone him; as well the stranger, as the home-born, when he blasphemeth the Name, shall be put to death. 17. And he that smiteth any man mortally shall surely be put to death. 18. And he that smiteth a beast mortally shall make it good: life for life. 19. And if a man maim his neighbour; as he hath done, so shall it be done to him: 20. breach for breach, eye for eye, tooth for tooth; as he hath maimed a man, so shall it be rendered unto him.* m. 21. And he that killeth a beast shall make it good; and he that killeth a man shall be put to death. 22. Ye shall have one manner of law, as

מִחוּץ לַמַּחֲנֶה וְסָמְכוּ כָל־הַשֹּׁמְעִים אֶת־יְדֵיהֶם עַל־רֹאשׁוֹ
טו וְרָגְמוּ אֹתוֹ כָּל־הָעֵדָה׃ וְאֶל־בְּנֵי יִשְׂרָאֵל תְּדַבֵּר לֵאמֹר
16 אִישׁ אִישׁ כִּי־יְקַלֵּל אֱלֹהָיו וְנָשָׂא חֶטְאוֹ׃ וְנֹקֵב שֵׁם־יְהוָה
מוֹת יוּמָת רָגוֹם יִרְגְּמוּ־בוֹ כָּל־הָעֵדָה כַּגֵּר כָּאֶזְרָח בְּנָקְבוֹ
17 18 שֵׁם יוּמָת׃ וְאִישׁ כִּי יַכֶּה כָּל־נֶפֶשׁ אָדָם מוֹת יוּמָת׃ וּמַכֵּה
19 נֶפֶשׁ־בְּהֵמָה יְשַׁלְּמֶנָּה נֶפֶשׁ תַּחַת נָפֶשׁ׃ וְאִישׁ כִּי־יִתֵּן
כ מוּם בַּעֲמִיתוֹ כַּאֲשֶׁר עָשָׂה כֵּן יֵעָשֶׂה לּוֹ׃ שֶׁבֶר תַּחַת
שֶׁבֶר עַיִן תַּחַת עַיִן שֵׁן תַּחַת שֵׁן כַּאֲשֶׁר יִתֵּן מוּם בָּאָדָם
מפטיר 21 כֵּן יִנָּתֶן בּוֹ׃ *וּמַכֵּה בְהֵמָה יְשַׁלְּמֶנָּה וּמַכֵּה אָדָם יוּמָת׃
22 מִשְׁפַּט אֶחָד יִהְיֶה לָכֶם כַּגֵּר כָּאֶזְרָח יִהְיֶה כִּי אֲנִי

v. 16. קמץ בז"ק

14. *without the camp.* Where all executions took place, so as not to defile its holiness.

lay their hands. They thereby signified that they were personally concerned in the offence, inasmuch as the blasphemous words had fallen upon their ears. They were, therefore, discharging their duty by bringing the culprit to justice.

stone him. See on xx, 2.

15. *and thou shalt speak.* The incident became the opportunity of presenting to the Israelites a law on this and kindred offences.

16. *the stranger.* Although he is not subject to the precepts of the Torah and is to be allowed a large degree of tolerance, he yet may not be permitted to desecrate the holiness of the camp. If he does not wish to worship the God of Israel, he is not to be compelled to do so; but should he publicly revile the Holy Name, the offence is as serious with him as with the Israelite.

18. *life for life.* This phrase is a legal term equivalent to 'fair compensation'; for it cannot mean that anyone who slew an animal should forfeit his own life in return! In the same way, the phrase, 'as he hath done, so shall it be done to him' in *v.* 19, and 'eye for eye' and 'tooth for tooth' in *v.* 20, are merely technical phrases for the demand that adequate and equitable compensation, after due and judicial appraisement of the injury inflicted, is to be paid for the injury. There is in Jewish history no instance of the law of retaliation ever having been carried out *literally*—eye for an eye, tooth for a tooth. To the Talmudists the Biblical words *eye for eye* had become a mere expression of the law of equality. 'None of the later [Rabbinic] law books even suggest retaliation as a proper remedy, the example of contemporary European and Asiatic systems of jurisprudence to the contrary notwithstanding' (D. W. Amram). The last clause reminds us of one of the paradoxes of history. On the one hand, Judaism, the so-called religion of 'strict justice', rejected the literal application of the law of retaliation, and knew neither torture in legal procedure nor mutilation as a legal punishment. In Christian lands, on the other hand, mutilation and torture are well-nigh the indispensable accompaniments of justice from the middle of the thirteenth century down to the end of the eighteenth, and in some countries to the middle of the nineteenth century and beyond. See also pp. 309 and 405.

22. *ye shall have one manner of law . . . home-born.* One of the great texts of Scripture; cf. XIX, 33 f. Though in this connection, the application of the law may be, so to speak, disadvantageous to the alien, the general principle of equality between alien and native is only strengthened thereby. In no other code was there one and the same law for native-born and alien alike. Even in Roman Law, every alien was originally classed as an enemy, and therefore devoid of any rights. Only gradually was the protection of the law in a limited degree extended to him. It is not so very long ago that aliens in European states were incapable of owning landed property. In many countries, the denial by the dominant race of civic and political rights to 'aliens', though these may have lived for generations in the land of their sojourn, is a matter of contemporary history; see p. 260.

for I am the LORD your God. The reason given is noteworthy: show equal justice to all men, for I am your God, the God of Israel, the Father of all mankind. Once again, monotheism is the well for the stranger, as for the home-born; for I am the LORD your God.' 23. And Moses spoke to the children of Israel, and they brought forth him that had cursed out of the camp, and stoned him with stones. And the children of Israel did as the LORD commanded Moses.

23 יְהוָה אֱלֹהֵיכֶם׃ וַיְדַבֵּר מֹשֶׁה אֶל־בְּנֵי יִשְׂרָאֵל וַיּוֹצִיאוּ
אֶת־הַמְקַלֵּל אֶל־מִחוּץ לַמַּחֲנֶה וַיִּרְגְּמוּ אֹתוֹ אָבֶן וּבְנֵי־
יִשְׂרָאֵל עָשׂוּ כַּאֲשֶׁר צִוָּה יְהוָה אֶת־מֹשֶׁה׃

basis for the brotherhood of man (Hermann Cohen).

23. *stoned him.* For a later historical application of the law of blasphemy, see the story of Naboth in I Kings XXI.

HAFTORAH EMOR הפטרת אמר

EZEKIEL XLIV, 15–31

CHAPTER XLIV

15. But the priests the Levites, the sons of Zadok, that kept the charge of My sanctuary when the children of Israel went astray from Me, they shall come near to Me to minister unto Me; and they shall stand before Me to offer unto Me the fat and the blood, saith the LORD GOD; 16. they shall enter into My sanctuary, and they shall come near to My table, to minister unto Me, and they shall keep My charge. 17. And it shall be that when they enter in at the gates of the inner court, they shall be clothed with linen garments; and no wool shall come upon them, while they minister in the gates of the inner court, and within.

CAP. XLIV. מד

טו וְהַכֹּהֲנִים
הַלְוִיִּם בְּנֵי צָדוֹק אֲשֶׁר שָׁמְרוּ אֶת־מִשְׁמֶרֶת מִקְדָּשִׁי בִּתְעוֹת
בְּנֵי־יִשְׂרָאֵל מֵעָלַי הֵמָּה יִקְרְבוּ אֵלַי לְשָׁרְתֵנִי וְעָמְדוּ לְפָנַי
16 לְהַקְרִיב לִי חֵלֶב וָדָם נְאֻם אֲדֹנָי יְהוִה׃ הֵמָּה יָבֹאוּ אֶל־
מִקְדָּשִׁי וְהֵמָּה יִקְרְבוּ אֶל־שֻׁלְחָנִי לְשָׁרְתֵנִי וְשָׁמְרוּ אֶת־
17 מִשְׁמַרְתִּי׃ וְהָיָה בְּבוֹאָם אֶל־שַׁעֲרֵי הֶחָצֵר הַפְּנִימִית בִּגְדֵי
פִשְׁתִּים יִלְבָּשׁוּ וְלֹא־יַעֲלֶה עֲלֵיהֶם צֶמֶר בְּשָׁרְתָם בְּשַׁעֲרֵי

The Haftorah is taken from the last portion of the Book of Ezekiel (XL–XLVIII), which is a Vision of the New Jerusalem and the New Temple that are to arise when the Captivity is over. If, however, the new Temple is to be the embodiment in concrete form of Israel's ideals of Holiness and Purity, those that shall minister in the House of God must not, as in the past, permit any violations of those ideals. Therefore, only descendants of the loyal family of Zadok shall be the priests of the future. In this Haftorah, Ezekiel undertakes to define their duties and ministrations; and thus connects with the Sedrah which regulates the life and work of the priests.

15. *sons of Zadok.* The high priest appointed to that office by King Solomon (I Kings II, 35). Ezekiel was himself a priest, and in all probability spent his childhood and youth within the precincts of the Temple in Jerusalem. He therefore had a first-hand and sympathetic understanding of the better elements of the priestly class.

to minister unto Me. In distinction to the Levites mentioned in preceding verses, who had been unfaithful.

16. *come near to My table.* *i.e.* the Table of shewbread (Targum). The sacrifices named in the previous verses were offered in the outer Court. The service at the Table of shewbread was conducted in the Sanctuary, *i.e.* the inner Court.

they shall keep My charge. In all the remaining spheres of priestly service (Altschul).

17. *enter . . . the inner court.* *i.e.* on the Day of Atonement.

linen garments. The reason is given in the next verse: sweat was regarded as a form of uncleanness.

18. They shall have linen tires upon their heads, and shall have linen breeches upon their loins; they shall not gird themselves with any thing that causeth sweat. 19. And when they go forth into the outer court, even into the outer court to the people, they shall put off their garments wherein they minister, and lay them in the holy chambers, and they shall put on other garments, that they sanctify not the people with their garments. 20. Neither shall they shave their heads, nor suffer their locks to grow long; they shall only poll their heads. 21. Neither shall any priest drink wine, when they enter into the inner court. 22. Neither shall they take for their wives a widow, nor her that is put away; but they shall take virgins of the seed of the house of Israel, or a widow that is the widow of a priest. 23 And they shall teach My people the difference between the holy and the common, and cause them to discern between the unclean and the clean. 24. And in a controversy they shall stand to judge; according to Mine ordinances shall they judge it; and they shall keep My laws and My statutes in all My appointed seasons, and they shall hallow My sabbaths. 25. And they shall come near no dead person to defile themselves; but for father, or for mother, or for son, or for daughter, for brother, or for sister that hath had no husband, they may defile themselves. 26. And after he is cleansed, they shall reckon unto him seven days. 27. And in the day that he goeth into the sanctuary, into the inner court, to minister in the sanctuary, he shall offer his sin-offering,

18 הֶחָצֵר הַפְּנִימִית וָבָיְתָה׃ פַּאֲרֵי פִשְׁתִּים יִהְיוּ עַל־רֹאשָׁם
וּמִכְנְסֵי פִשְׁתִּים יִהְיוּ עַל־מָתְנֵיהֶם לֹא יַחְגְּרוּ בַּיָּזַע׃
19 וּבְצֵאתָם אֶל־הֶחָצֵר הַחִיצוֹנָה אֶל־הֶחָצֵר הַחִיצוֹנָה אֶל־
הָעָם יִפְשְׁטוּ אֶת־בִּגְדֵיהֶם אֲשֶׁר־הֵמָּה מְשָׁרְתִם בָּם
וְהִנִּיחוּ אוֹתָם בְּלִשְׁכֹת הַקֹּדֶשׁ וְלָבְשׁוּ בְּגָדִים אֲחֵרִים וְלֹא־
כ יְקַדְּשׁוּ אֶת־הָעָם בְּבִגְדֵיהֶם׃ וְרֹאשָׁם לֹא יְגַלֵּחוּ וּפֶרַע
21 לֹא יְשַׁלֵּחוּ כָּסוֹם יִכְסְמוּ אֶת־רָאשֵׁיהֶם׃ וְיַיִן לֹא־יִשְׁתּוּ
22 כָּל־כֹּהֵן בְּבוֹאָם אֶל־הֶחָצֵר הַפְּנִימִית׃ וְאַלְמָנָה וּגְרוּשָׁה
לֹא־יִקְחוּ לָהֶם לְנָשִׁים כִּי אִם־בְּתוּלֹת מִזֶּרַע בֵּית יִשְׂרָאֵל
23 וְהָאַלְמָנָה אֲשֶׁר־תִּהְיֶה אַלְמָנָה מִכֹּהֵן יִקָּחוּ׃ וְאֶת־עַמִּי
24 יוֹרוּ בֵּין קֹדֶשׁ לְחֹל וּבֵין־טָמֵא לְטָהוֹר יוֹדִיעֻם׃ וְעַל־רִיב
הֵמָּה יַעַמְדוּ לְ׳שְׁפֹּט בְּמִשְׁפָּטַי וּשְׁפָטֻהוּ וְאֶת־תּוֹרֹתַי
וְאֶת־חֻקֹּתַי בְּכָל־מוֹעֲדַי יִשְׁמֹרוּ וְאֶת־שַׁבְּתוֹתַי יְקַדֵּשׁוּ׃
כה וְאֶל־מֵת אָדָם לֹא יָבוֹא לְטָמְאָה כִּי אִם־לְאָב וּלְאֵם וּלְבֵן
26 וּלְבַת לְאָח וּלְאָחוֹת אֲשֶׁר־לֹא־הָיְתָה לְאִישׁ יִטַּמָּאוּ׃ וְאַחֲרֵי
27 טָהֳרָתוֹ שִׁבְעַת יָמִים יִסְפְּרוּ־לוֹ׃ וּבְיוֹם בֹּאוֹ אֶל־הַקֹּדֶשׁ
אֶל־הֶחָצֵר הַפְּנִימִית לְשָׁרֵת בַּקֹּדֶשׁ יַקְרִיב חַטָּאתוֹ נְאֻם

v. 24. למשפט קרי ibid. ישפטהו קרי

18. *linen tires on their heads.* Worn for ornament (Kimchi).

19. *sanctify not the people.* A precaution against confusion of the sacred and the common. They are not to mingle with the people in their sacred garments (Targum), lest the thoughtless among the people might consider themselves qualified to perform duties of the Temple Service.

20. *shave . . . grow long.* Both prohibitions in this verse are protests against customs of heathen worship that prevailed in one cult or another of the time.

poll their heads. i.e. keep it at a moderate and even length all round.

22. *neither shall they take . . . a widow.* In the Sedrah (Lev. XXI, 14) the prohibition is restricted to the High Priest. Although this is only a more stringent application of the principle underlying the original law—possibly in that decadent age, when the moral standards had lowered, it was found necessary to do so in order to protect the purity of the priestly families—it is one of Ezekiel's apparent divergencies from the Torah, and it raised doubts in the early Rabbinic period as to whether his Book should remain in the Canon of Scripture.

23. *teach.* Instruction, teaching the people the eternal difference between right and wrong, holy and unholy, 'Jewish' and heathen, has always been the main function and mission of priest, prophet, sage, rabbi or teacher in Judaism.

24. *to judge.* Cf. Deut. XVII, 8, on the judicial power given to the priests.

25. *but for father.* As in the Sedrah (XXI, 1–3) there is no mention of the wife, it being self-evident: cf. Ezek. XXIV, 15 f.

26. *and after he is cleansed.* The period before his cleansing seems likewise to have been seven days; Num. XIX, 11.

27. *he shall offer his sin-offering.* Contact with the dead was a technical, *i.e.* ritual, sin; the reference is not to any moral lapse.

saith the LORD GOD. 28. And it shall be unto them for an inheritance: I am their inheritance; and ye shall give them no possession in Israel: I am their possession. 29. The meal-offering, and the sin-offering, and the guilt-offering, they, even they, shall eat; and every devoted thing in Israel shall be theirs. 30. And the first of all the first-fruits of every thing, and every heave-offering of every thing, of all your offerings, shall be for the priests; ye shall also give unto the priest the first of your dough, to cause a blessing to rest on thy house. 31. The priests shall not eat of any thing that dieth of itself, or is torn, whether it be fowl or beast.

28 אֲדֹנָי יְהוִה׃ וְהָיְתָה לָהֶם לְנַחֲלָה אֲנִי נַחֲלָתָם וַאֲחֻזָּה
29 לֹא־תִתְּנוּ לָהֶם בְּיִשְׂרָאֵל אֲנִי אֲחֻזָּתָם׃ הַמִּנְחָה וְהַחַטָּאת
וְהָאָשָׁם הֵמָּה יֹאכְלוּם וְכָל־חֵרֶם בְּיִשְׂרָאֵל לָהֶם יִהְיֶה׃
ל וְרֵאשִׁית כָּל־בִּכּוּרֵי כֹל וְכָל־תְּרוּמַת כֹּל מִכֹּל תְּרוּמֹתֵיכֶם
לַכֹּהֲנִים יִהְיֶה וְרֵאשִׁית עֲרִיסוֹתֵיכֶם תִּתְּנוּ לַכֹּהֵן לְהָנִיחַ
31 בְּרָכָה אֶל־בֵּיתֶךָ׃ כָּל־נְבֵלָה וּטְרֵפָה מִן־הָעוֹף וּמִן־
הַבְּהֵמָה לֹא יֹאכְלוּ הַכֹּהֲנִים׃

28–31. Enumerate the dues for the maintenance of the priests. They had no possession in Israel—in contrast to the priests of the Babylonian temples who, besides stated tariffs for their services, often had large private estates (like medieval abbeys) and did much banking business (Lofthouse).

28. *I am their inheritance.* The priest's inheritance is a spiritual, not a material one.

29. *devoted thing.* Everything on which a ban had been placed; Lev. XXVII, 28.

30. *heave-offering.* Heb. *terumah*, 'contribution.'

31. *shall not eat.* The Rabbis explain that repetition of this law was required in the case of the priests, as the manner of the slaying (*e.g.* מליקה) of those sacrifices, of which the priests were permitted to partake, did not altogether coincide with the laws of Shechitah outside the Sanctuary.

In connection with this verse and *v.* 22, it is well to remember that this Haftorah is part of a half-ideal and half-allegorical programme of the New Jerusalem that is to follow the Captivity. The Prophet's symbolic picture was probably never intended for, and certainly never received, literal realization. A deeper study of his Vision shows that the account of the Temple, the City, the Prince, and the divisions of the land are as ideal as his vision of the stream that issues from under the threshold of the Temple and flows through the desert of southern Judea into the Dead Sea, fertilizing the one and transforming the other into a fresh-water lake swarming with life and surrounded by noble trees that bear fruit every month (XLVII, 1–12). Where all else is ideal, actuality is not to be affixed to the regulations alone concerning priests and their offerings. The Rabbis were therefore guided by highest spiritual wisdom (רוח הקודש) when, disregarding the apparent or real divergencies from the Torah which these chapters contain, they permitted the Book to remain part of Holy Scripture.

25

CHAPTER XXV

1. And the LORD spoke unto Moses in mount Sinai, saying: 2. Speak unto the children of Israel, and say unto them: ¶ When ye come into the land which I give you, then shall the land keep a sabbath unto the LORD. 3. Six years thou shalt sow thy field, and six years thou shalt prune thy vineyard, and gather in the produce thereof. 4. But in the seventh year shall be a sabbath of solemn rest for the land, a sabbath unto the LORD; thou shalt neither sow thy field, nor prune thy vineyard. 5. That which growth of itself of thy harvest thou shalt not reap, and the grapes of thy undressed vine thou shalt not gather; it shall be a

CAP. XXV. כה

כה

פ פ פ לב 32

א 2 וַיְדַבֵּר יְהוָה אֶל־מֹשֶׁה בְּהַר סִינַי לֵאמֹר׃ דַּבֵּר אֶל־בְּנֵי
יִשְׂרָאֵל וְאָמַרְתָּ אֲלֵהֶם כִּי תָבֹאוּ אֶל־הָאָרֶץ אֲשֶׁר אֲנִי
3 נֹתֵן לָכֶם וְשָׁבְתָה הָאָרֶץ שַׁבָּת לַיהוָה׃ שֵׁשׁ שָׁנִים תִּזְרַע
שָׂדֶךָ וְשֵׁשׁ שָׁנִים תִּזְמֹר כַּרְמֶךָ וְאָסַפְתָּ אֶת־תְּבוּאָתָהּ׃
4 וּבַשָּׁנָה הַשְּׁבִיעִת שַׁבַּת שַׁבָּתוֹן יִהְיֶה לָאָרֶץ שַׁבָּת לַיהוָה
ה שָׂדְךָ לֹא תִזְרָע וְכַרְמְךָ לֹא תִזְמֹר׃ אֵת סְפִיחַ קְצִירְךָ

v. 4. קמץ בז"ק

IX. BEHAR

(CHAPTERS XXV–XXVI, 2)

CHAPTER XXV. THE SABBATICAL YEAR AND THE YEAR OF JUBILEE

The cycle of sacred seasons begun in XXIII is here continued, and the system of sabbaths—the Sabbath at the end of the week; Pentecost at the end of seven weeks; the Seventh month, as the sacred month studded with Festivals—is here completed by the Sabbatical year and by the Jubilee, which came after a 'week' of Sabbatical years.

During the Sabbath-year the land was to lie fallow (Exod. XXIII, 10 f) and was to be 'released' from cultivation. The land is not the absolute possession of man; it belongs to God, and is to be held in trust for His purposes. The Sabbath-year does not seem to have been regularly observed in pre-exilic times, and, according to the Mishnah, the Sabbath-year was fully enforced only in Palestine. A promise to observe it in the future formed part of the covenant on the Return from Babylon; Neh. X, 32. Alexander the Great remitted to the Jews the tribute in every seventh year 'because then they did not sow their fields' (Josephus). Julius Caesar acted in the same manner.

Heathens did not trouble to understand the meaning of this unique law which, among other things, saved the soil from the danger of exhaustion. Thus, the Roman historian Tacitus attributes the Jews' observance of it to indolence.

1. *spoke unto Moses.* Better, *had spoken unto Moses.* As these laws are intended to meet the social problems that would arise in the Israelitish Commonwealth, they bring the legal part of Leviticus to an appropriate conclusion.

2. *the land keep a sabbath.* The land is personified. It should rest in the seventh year, as man rests on the seventh day. The Israelite may not during that year till it himself or allow anyone to do so on his behalf. 'Just as the freedom of the individual was a fundamental principle of the Torah, so was the freedom of the land from the absolute ownership of man' (F. Perles).

unto the LORD. As the Sabbath was more than a cessation of labour, and was a day dedicated to God—similarly during the Sabbatical year, the soil was to be devoted to Him by being placed at the service of the poor and the animal creation (Exod. XXIII, 10, 11). In Deut. XXXI, 10 f, we learn that the seventh year was, furthermore, to be utilized for national educational ends, and special measures were to be taken to acquaint the men and the women, the children as well as the resident aliens, with the teachings and duties of the Torah. Josephus rightly claims that while the best knowledge of olden times was usually treated as a secret doctrine, and confined to the few, it was the glory of Moses that he made it current coin. 'To place within the reach of the English worker, once in every seven years, a year's course at a University in science and law and literature and theology, would be something like the modern equivalent for one of the advantages which the Sabbath-year offered to the ancient Hebrew' (F. Verinder in *My Neighbour's Landmark*, Short Studies in Bible Land Laws, 1911).

4. *in the seventh year.* In the seventh month of that year, after the gathering of the harvest, the year of rest began.

sabbath of solemn rest. A Sabbath of the strictest kind. The same phrase is used of the Day of Atonement (XXIII, 32), as well as of the Sabbath day (XXIII, 3).

5. *undressed vine.* The Heb. is the word for a Nazirite whose hair was to remain unshorn (Num. VI, 5). Like him, the vines were not to be trimmed during the Sabbatical year. There was to be neither planting, pruning, nor gathering.

year of solemn rest for the land. 6. And the sabbath-produce of the land shall be for food for you: for thee, and for thy servant and for thy maid, and for thy hired servant and for the settler by thy side that sojourn with thee; 7. and for thy cattle, and for the beasts that are in thy land, shall all the increase thereof be for food. ¶ 8. And thou shalt number seven sabbaths of years unto thee, seven times seven years; and there shall be unto thee the days of seven sabbaths of years, even forty and nine years. 9. Then shalt thou make proclamation with the blast of the horn on the tenth day of the seventh month; in the day of atonement shall ye make

לֹא תִקְצוֹר וְאֶת־עִנְּבֵי נְזִירֶךָ לֹא תִבְצֹר שְׁנַת שַׁבָּתוֹן יִהְיֶה
6 לָאָרֶץ׃ וְהָיְתָה שַׁבַּת הָאָרֶץ לָכֶם לְאָכְלָה לְךָ וּלְעַבְדְּךָ
7 וְלַאֲמָתֶךָ וְלִשְׂכִירְךָ וּלְתוֹשָׁבְךָ הַגָּרִים עִמָּךְ׃ וְלִבְהֶמְתְּךָ
וְלַחַיָּה אֲשֶׁר בְּאַרְצֶךָ תִּהְיֶה כָל־תְּבוּאָתָהּ לֶאֱכֹל׃ ס
8 וְסָפַרְתָּ לְךָ שֶׁבַע שַׁבְּתֹת שָׁנִים שֶׁבַע שָׁנִים שֶׁבַע פְּעָמִים
וְהָיוּ לְךָ יְמֵי שֶׁבַע שַׁבְּתֹת הַשָּׁנִים תֵּשַׁע וְאַרְבָּעִים שָׁנָה׃
9 וְהַעֲבַרְתָּ שׁוֹפַר תְּרוּעָה בַּחֹדֶשׁ הַשְּׁבִעִי בֶּעָשׂוֹר לַחֹדֶשׁ

6. *the sabbath-produce of the land.* A poetic term for the chance, spontaneous produce during the Sabbath-year.

for you. The plural is used to comprehend all those that are to benefit by this provision. The fruit and grain which grew of itself in the Sabbatical year might be plucked and eaten, but not stored. Grain growing of itself—*i.e.* without regular ploughing and sowing—is not uncommon in Palestine; see on *v.* 22.

hired servant . . . settler. Non-Israelites are included (Sifra); see XIX, 10.

7. *cattle.* Heb. בהמה; domestic animals.

beasts. Heb. חיה; free beasts of the field or forest; sometimes used in contrast to חיה רעה 'evil beast' (XXVI, 6). The Divine promise in this verse is in accordance with the uniformly tender regard for animals throughout Scripture. They were part of God's creation, and as such were comprehended in His pity and love; see the concluding verse of Jonah. 'A righteous man regardeth the life of his beast' (Prov. XII, 10).

8–55. The Jubilee

In the fiftieth year, the Hebrew slaves with their families are emancipated, and property, except house property in a walled city, reverts to its original owner. The Jubilee institution was a marvellous safeguard against deadening poverty. By it, houses and lands were kept from accumulating in the hands of the few, pauperism was prevented, and a race of independent freeholders assured. It represented such a rare and striking introduction of morals into economics, that many have been inclined to question whether this wonderful institution was ever in actual force. However, 'nothing is more certain than that the Jubilee was once for centuries a reality in the national life of Israel' (Ewald). Ezekiel speaks of its non-observance as one of the signs that 'the end is come' upon the nation for its misdoings; and he mentions (see p. 964) 'the year of liberty', when a gift of land must return to the original owner. 'It is impossible to think that, as has sometimes been supposed, the institution of the Jubilee is a mere paper-law; at least as far as concerns the *land* (for the periodical redistribution of which there are analogies in other nations), it must date from ancient times in Israel' (Driver). According to the Talmud, the law of the Jubilee was observed as long as the entire territory of the Holy Land was inhabited by Israelites. When a portion of the tribes went into exile, the law lapsed.

8. *the days of.* Equivalent to 'the time of', as in Gen. XXV, 7; XLVII, 8 f.

9. *Horn.* Heb. *Shofar.*

in the day of atonement. Although the year commenced on the first of Tishri, Rosh Hashanah, it was not until the tenth of the month, Yom Kippur, that the proclamation of the Jubilee was made. The Day of Atonement and the Jubilee had much in common. The message of both was a 'new birth'. The Day of Atonement freed man from slavery to sin and enabled him to start life anew, at one with God and with his fellowmen. The Jubilee had for its aim the emancipation of the individual from the shackles of poverty, and the readjustment of the various strata in the commonwealth in accordance with social justice. No more appropriate day, therefore, for inaugurating such a year of rectification —as well as to attune the hearts of all to the sacrifices demanded by such rectification—than the day of Atonement; and no more suitable signal to inaugurate it than the blowing of the Shofar. Isa. LVIII, which forms the Haftorah for the Day of Atonement, seems to have been spoken on a Yom Kippur inaugurating a Jubilee year.

10. *the fiftieth year.* Some have held that the forty-ninth year itself was the Jubilee, as otherwise there would be two consecutive Sabbath-years. This opinion is not the traditional view,

י בְּיוֹם הַכִּפֻּרִים תַּעֲבִירוּ שׁוֹפָר בְּכָל־אַרְצְכֶם׃ וְקִדַּשְׁתֶּם
אֵת שְׁנַת הַחֲמִשִּׁים שָׁנָה וּקְרָאתֶם דְּרוֹר בָּאָרֶץ לְכָל־
יֹשְׁבֶיהָ יוֹבֵל הִוא תִּהְיֶה לָכֶם וְשַׁבְתֶּם אִישׁ אֶל־אֲחֻזָּתוֹ
11 וְאִישׁ אֶל־מִשְׁפַּחְתּוֹ תָּשֻׁבוּ׃ יוֹבֵל הִוא שְׁנַת הַחֲמִשִּׁים
שָׁנָה תִּהְיֶה לָכֶם לֹא תִזְרָעוּ וְלֹא תִקְצְרוּ אֶת־סְפִיחֶיהָ
12 וְלֹא תִבְצְרוּ אֶת־נְזִרֶיהָ׃ כִּי יוֹבֵל הִוא קֹדֶשׁ תִּהְיֶה לָכֶם
13 מִן־הַשָּׂדֶה תֹּאכְלוּ אֶת־תְּבוּאָתָהּ׃ בִּשְׁנַת הַיּוֹבֵל הַזֹּאת
שני 14 תָּשֻׁבוּ אִישׁ אֶל־אֲחֻזָּתוֹ׃ * וְכִי־תִמְכְּרוּ מִמְכָּר לַעֲמִיתֶךָ
טו אוֹ קָנֹה מִיַּד עֲמִיתֶךָ אַל־תּוֹנוּ אִישׁ אֶת־אָחִיו׃ בְּמִסְפַּר
שָׁנִים אַחַר הַיּוֹבֵל תִּקְנֶה מֵאֵת עֲמִיתֶךָ בְּמִסְפַּר שְׁנֵי־
16 תְבוּאֹת יִמְכָּר־לָךְ׃ לְפִי ׀ רֹב הַשָּׁנִים תַּרְבֶּה מִקְנָתוֹ וּלְפִי

v. 11. קמץ בז"ק

proclamation with the horn throughout all your land. 10. And ye shall hallow the fiftieth year, and proclaim liberty throughout the land unto all the inhabitants thereof; it shall be a jubilee unto you; and ye shall return every man unto his possession, and ye shall return every man unto his family. 11. A jubilee shall that fiftieth year be unto you; ye shall not sow, neither reap that which groweth of itself in it, nor gather the grapes in it of the undressed vines. 12 For it is a jubilee; it shall be holy unto you; ye shall eat the increase thereof out of the field. 13. In this year of jubilee ye shall return every man unto his possession.* ii. 14. And if thou sell aught unto thy neighbour, or buy of thy neighbour's hand, ye shall not wrong one another. 15. According to the number of years after the jubilee thou shalt buy of thy neighbour, and according unto the number of years of the crops he shall sell unto thee. 16. According to the multitude of the years thou shalt increase the price thereof, and according to the fewness of the years thou shalt diminish the price of

though it finds some support in Heb. idiom; see p. 323 (on Jer. XXXIV, 14).

proclaim liberty. The emancipation of the slaves, and the release of landed property from mortgage.

all the inhabitants thereof. Even to the man who had been sold into slavery and had refused to go out in the seventh year (Exod. XXI, 5).

a jubilee. Or, 'a year of jubilee'; the year is so named from the blast (Heb. *yobel*; lit. 'a ram's horn') by which it was announced.

every man unto his possession. In this way the original equal division of the land was restored. The permanent accumulation of land in the hands of a few was prevented, and those whom fault or misfortune had thrown into poverty were given a 'second chance'.

According to Scripture 'the earth is the LORD's'; and all the land was, as it were, held from God on lease (*v.* 23). The Israelite who voluntarily or through some compulsion sold his land to another, sold not the ownership of the land, but the remainder of the lease—till the next year of Jubilee, when all the leases fell in simultaneously. The land then came back to his family, all contracts of sale to the contrary notwithstanding. His children thus enjoyed the same advantage of a 'fair start' as their father had had before them (Verinder). Heine rightly remarks that the Torah does not aim at the impossible—the abolition of property, but at the *moralization* of property, striving to bring it into harmony with equity and the true law of Reason by means of the Jubilee-year. This institution forms a most striking contrast to 'prescription' among the Romans, according to which, the possessor of a piece of land could not, after the lapse of a certain period, be compelled to restore it to its real owner, so long as the latter was unable to show that he had during that period demanded restitution in due form. Far other is the spirit that we find in the Law of Moses. 'It is not the protection of property, but the protection of humanity, that is the aim of the Mosaic Code. Its Sabbath day and Sabbath year secure even to the lowliest, rest and leisure. With the blast of the jubilee trumpets the slave goes free, and a redivision of the land secures again to the poorest his fair share in the bounty of the common Creator' (Henry George).

11. *ye shall not sow.* The Jubilee year shares the features of the Sabbatical year.

12. *out of the field.* The Israelite may not store any of the produce, but whenever he required corn or fruit, he may go out into the field and gather it.

13. *unto his possession.* This repetition of *v.* 10 serves as an introduction to the exposition of the law of land-tenure.

14. *ye shall not wrong.* There is to be no rack-renting.

15. *according to the number of years.* What is really conveyed to the purchaser is *not the land*, but the number of harvests which the incoming tenant would enjoy.

16. *the number of the crops.* As the land itself belonged to God (*v.* 23), only the produce could be a matter of sale.

it; for the number of crops doth he sell unto thee. 17. And ye shall not wrong one another; but thou shalt fear thy God; for I am the LORD your God. 18. Wherefore ye shall do My statutes, and keep Mine ordinances and do them; and ye shall dwell in the land in safety.* iii (** ii). 19. And the land shall yield her fruit, and ye shall eat until ye have enough, and dwell therein in safety. 20. And if ye shall say: 'What shall we eat the seventh year? behold, we may not sow, nor gather in our increase'; 21. then I will command My blessing upon you in the sixth year, and it shall bring forth produce for the three years. 22. And ye shall sow the eighth year, and eat of the produce, the old store; until the ninth year, until her produce come in, ye shall eat the old store. 23. And the land shall not be sold in perpetuity; for the land is Mine; for ye are strangers and settlers with Me. 24. And in all the land of your possession ye shall grant a redemption for the land.*iv. ¶ 25. If thy brother be waxen poor, and sell some of his possession, then shall his kinsman that is next unto him come, and shall redeem that which his brother hath sold. 26. And if a man have no one to redeem it, and he be waxen rich and find sufficient means to redeem it; 27. then let him count the

מְעֹט הַשָּׁנִים תַּמְעִיט מִקְנָתוֹ כִּי מִסְפַּר תְּבוּאֹת הוּא
17 מֹכֵר לָךְ׃ וְלֹא תוֹנוּ אִישׁ אֶת־עֲמִיתוֹ וְיָרֵאתָ מֵאֱלֹהֶיךָ כִּי
18 אֲנִי יְהוָה אֱלֹהֵיכֶם׃ וַעֲשִׂיתֶם אֶת־חֻקֹּתַי וְאֶת־מִשְׁפָּטַי
שלישי (שני כשהן מחובר׳)
19 תִּשְׁמְרוּ וַעֲשִׂיתֶם אֹתָם וִישַׁבְתֶּם עַל־הָאָרֶץ לָבֶטַח׃ וְנָתְנָה
הָאָרֶץ פִּרְיָהּ וַאֲכַלְתֶּם לָשֹׂבַע וִישַׁבְתֶּם לָבֶטַח עָלֶיהָ׃
כ וְכִי תֹאמְרוּ מַה־נֹּאכַל בַּשָּׁנָה הַשְּׁבִיעִת הֵן לֹא נִזְרָע
21 וְלֹא נֶאֱסֹף אֶת־תְּבוּאָתֵנוּ׃ וְצִוִּיתִי אֶת־בִּרְכָתִי לָכֶם
בַּשָּׁנָה הַשִּׁשִּׁית וְעָשָׂת אֶת־הַתְּבוּאָה לִשְׁלֹשׁ הַשָּׁנִים׃
22 וּזְרַעְתֶּם אֵת הַשָּׁנָה הַשְּׁמִינִת וַאֲכַלְתֶּם מִן־הַתְּבוּאָה יָשָׁן
עַד ׀ הַשָּׁנָה הַתְּשִׁיעִת עַד־בּוֹא תְּבוּאָתָהּ תֹּאכְלוּ יָשָׁן׃
23 וְהָאָרֶץ לֹא תִמָּכֵר לִצְמִתֻת כִּי־לִי הָאָרֶץ כִּי־גֵרִים
24 וְתוֹשָׁבִים אַתֶּם עִמָּדִי׃ וּבְכֹל אֶרֶץ אֲחֻזַּתְכֶם גְּאֻלָּה תִּתְּנוּ
רביעי כה לָאָרֶץ׃ ס כִּי־יָמוּךְ אָחִיךָ וּמָכַר מֵאֲחֻזָּתוֹ וּבָא גֹאֲלוֹ

v. 20. קמץ בז״ק

17. *wrong.* Overreach; see on XIX, 33.

fear thy God. This principle of a fair deal in the leasing of landed property was to be acted upon in all relations between man and man. Hence the addition of, 'thou shalt fear thy God'; see on *v.* 43 and XIX, 14.

18–23. EXHORTATION

18. *dwell in . . . safety.* What follows must be understood of both the Sabbatical and Jubilee years. If the enactments are conscientiously carried out, the people, far from suffering because of the 'Sabbath' allowed to the land, would dwell in safety; *i.e.* secure from the perils of drought and famine (cf. XXVI, 5).

21. *for the three years.* The exceptional fertility in the sixth year might be compared with the double portion of manna which was to be gathered on the sixth day (Exod. XVI, 22).

22. *ninth year.* Until the Feast of Tabernacles; for then the produce of the eighth year is gathered in and stored (Rashi). 'The experience of the present day in Syria shows that, after lying fallow for a year, a field requires several ploughings before it can be sown. The consequence is that sowing cannot be begun till the following spring —the eighth year of *v.* 22—and the crop is not available till late autumn, when the ninth year has begun' (Kennedy).

23. *the land is Mine.* This verse enunciates the basic principle upon which all these enactments rest. 'The earth is the LORD's' (Ps. XXIV, 1), and His people hold their lands in fee from Him. The ground itself, then, was not a proper object of sale, but only the result of man's labour on the ground.

24–28. REDEMPTION OF LAND

25. *be waxen poor.* Only dire poverty would induce an Israelite to part with his family heritage. When Ahab asks Naboth to sell his vineyard, he answers the king, 'The LORD forbid it me, that I should give the inheritance of my fathers unto thee' (I Kings XXI, 3).

his kinsman. Heb. *goel,* lit. 'redeemer'; the technical term for him whose duty it was to avenge the person of his next-of-kin, or redeem his property that had been leased away. See Jer. XXXII, 8–12, the Haftorah to the Sedrah.

shall redeem. The next-of-kin is not under compulsion to do this; it is a moral obligation upon him, if his circumstances permit, to see that the property reverts to the family at the earliest opportunity. In that case, the purchaser cannot refuse to accept a just offer of repayment and return the land.

26. *waxen rich . . . redeem it.* 'Becomes rich enough to buy it back himself' (Moffatt).

years of the sale thereof, and restore the overplus unto the man to whom he sold it; and he shall return unto his possession. 28. But if he have not sufficient means to get it back for himself, then that which he hath sold shall remain in the hand of him that hath brought it until the year of jubilee; and in the jubilee it shall go out, and he shall return unto his possession.* v (** iii). ¶ 29. And if a man sell a dwelling-house in a walled city, then he may redeem it within a whole year after it is sold; for a full year shall he have the right of redemption. 30. And if it be not redeemed within the space of a full year, then the house that is in the walled city shall be made sure in perpetuity to him that bought it, throughout his generations; it shall not go out in the jubilee. 31. But the houses of the villages which have no wall round about them shall be reckoned with the fields of the country; they may be redeemed, and they shall go out in the jubilee. 32. But as for the cities of the Levites, the houses of the cities of their possession, the Levites shall have a perpetual right of redemption. 33. And if a man purchase of the Levites, then the house that was sold in the city of his possession, shall go out in the jubilee; for the houses of the cities of the Levites are their possession

26 הַקָּרֹב אֵלָיו וְגָאַל אֵת מִמְכַּר אָחִיו׃ וְאִישׁ כִּי לֹא יִהְיֶה־
27 לּוֹ גֹּאֵל וְהִשִּׂיגָה יָדוֹ וּמָצָא כְּדֵי גְאֻלָּתוֹ׃ וְחִשַּׁב אֶת־
שְׁנֵי מִמְכָּרוֹ וְהֵשִׁיב אֶת־הָעֹדֵף לָאִישׁ אֲשֶׁר מָכַר־לוֹ
28 וְשָׁב לַאֲחֻזָּתוֹ׃ וְאִם לֹא־מָצְאָה יָדוֹ דֵּי הָשִׁיב לוֹ וְהָיָה
חמישי (שלישי כשהן מחובר') מִמְכָּרוֹ בְּיַד הַקֹּנֶה אֹתוֹ עַד שְׁנַת הַיּוֹבֵל וְיָצָא בַּיֹּבֵל וְשָׁב
29 לַאֲחֻזָּתוֹ׃ ס וְאִישׁ כִּי־יִמְכֹּר בֵּית־מוֹשַׁב עִיר חוֹמָה
וְהָיְתָה גְּאֻלָּתוֹ עַד־תֹּם שְׁנַת מִמְכָּרוֹ יָמִים תִּהְיֶה גְאֻלָּתוֹ׃
ל וְאִם לֹא־יִגָּאֵל עַד־מְלֹאת לוֹ שָׁנָה תְמִימָה וְקָם הַבַּיִת
אֲשֶׁר־בָּעִיר אֲשֶׁר־לֹא חֹמָה לַצְּמִיתֻת לַקֹּנֶה אֹתוֹ לְדֹרֹתָיו
31 לֹא יֵצֵא בַּיֹּבֵל׃ וּבָתֵּי הַחֲצֵרִים אֲשֶׁר אֵין־לָהֶם חֹמָה
סָבִיב עַל־שְׂדֵה הָאָרֶץ יֵחָשֵׁב גְּאֻלָּה תִּהְיֶה־לּוֹ וּבַיֹּבֵל
32 יֵצֵא׃ וְעָרֵי הַלְוִיִּם בָּתֵּי עָרֵי אֲחֻזָּתָם גְּאֻלַּת עוֹלָם תִּהְיֶה
33 לַלְוִיִּם׃ וַאֲשֶׁר יִגְאַל מִן־הַלְוִיִּם וְיָצָא מִמְכַּר־בַּיִת וְעִיר

v. 30. לו ק'

27. *the overplus.* The amount by which the purchase money of the field exceeded the value of the crops reaped by the purchaser. In Rabbinic law, if the purchaser had resold the land to a second buyer, then the owner treats with the first purchaser, if he had sold it at a higher price than he paid; and with the second, if the price had been smaller. The purpose of this regulation was to give the advantage to the original owner, and also to discourage speculation in land values.

28. *it shall go out.* Into freedom. According to the testimony of Josephus there was due recognition of tenants' improvements. 'When the Jubilee is come, he that sold the land, and he that bought it, meet together, and make an estimate, on the one hand, of the fruits gathered; and, on the other hand, of the expenses laid out upon it. If the fruits gathered come to more than the expenses laid out, he that sold it takes the land again; but if the expenses prove more than the fruits, the present possessor receives of the former owner the difference that was wanting, and leaves the land to him; and if the fruits received and the expenses laid out prove equal to one another, the present possessor relinquishes it to the former owner.'

29–34. Redemption of Houses

29. *a dwelling-house.* A house in a walled city could be disposed of in perpetuity; but the owner had the right of re-purchase during the first year of the sale.

a walled city. In contrast to villages; see on *v.* 31.

30. *walled city.* The Written Text (Kethib) really is, 'unwalled city.' The Rabbis explain this anomalous Reading of the Text to indicate that this Law applies also to a city that was originally walled in, but is no longer so.

be made sure. That is, a house in the town could be sold 'out and out'; but not houses in the open country; see next *v.*

31. *reckoned with the fields.* Being indispensable to the man who had to work the land.

32. *Levites.* While Aaron and his sons were chosen for the priestly office, the menial services at the Sanctuary and Temple were assigned to the Levites—the rest of the tribe. In the Wilderness, they bore the furniture of the Sanctuary during the wanderings. At the Settlement in Canaan, the tribe of Levi received no definite domain, but scattered cities were assigned to them in territory belonging to other tribes. In these cities (see Num. xxxv, 2 f) the vendor has a perpetual right of redemption.

33. *if a man purchase of the Levites.* If one purchases a house in one of the Levitical cities, even if it be a walled city, the law of *v.* 30 does not apply; in the Jubilee, it reverts to the owner.

אֲחֻזָּתוֹ בַּיֹּבֵל כִּי בָתֵּי עָרֵי הַלְוִיִּם הִוא אֲחֻזָּתָם בְּתוֹךְ
34 בְּנֵי יִשְׂרָאֵל׃ וּשְׂדֵה מִגְרַשׁ עָרֵיהֶם לֹא יִמָּכֵר כִּי־אֲחֻזַּת
לה עוֹלָם הוּא לָהֶם׃ ס וְכִי־יָמוּךְ אָחִיךָ וּמָטָה יָדוֹ עִמָּךְ
36 וְהֶחֱזַקְתָּ בּוֹ גֵּר וְתוֹשָׁב וָחַי עִמָּךְ׃ אַל־תִּקַּח מֵאִתּוֹ נֶשֶׁךְ
37 וְתַרְבִּית וְיָרֵאתָ מֵאֱלֹהֶיךָ וְחֵי אָחִיךָ עִמָּךְ׃ אֶת־כַּסְפְּךָ
38 לֹא־תִתֵּן לוֹ בְּנֶשֶׁךְ וּבְמַרְבִּית לֹא־תִתֵּן אָכְלֶךָ׃ אֲנִי יְהוָה
ששי (רביעי כשהן מחוב׳) אֱלֹהֵיכֶם אֲשֶׁר־הוֹצֵאתִי אֶתְכֶם מֵאֶרֶץ מִצְרָיִם לָתֵת לָכֶם
39 אֶת־אֶרֶץ כְּנַעַן לִהְיוֹת לָכֶם לֵאלֹהִים׃ * ס וְכִי־יָמוּךְ
אָחִיךָ עִמָּךְ וְנִמְכַּר־לָךְ לֹא־תַעֲבֹד בּוֹ עֲבֹדַת עָבֶד׃
מ כְּשָׂכִיר כְּתוֹשָׁב יִהְיֶה עִמָּךְ עַד־שְׁנַת הַיֹּבֵל יַעֲבֹד עִמָּךְ׃

among the children of Israel. 34. But the fields of the open land about their cities may not be sold; for that is their perpetual possession. ¶ 35. And if thy brother be waxen poor, and his means fail with thee; then thou shalt uphold him: as a stranger and a settler shall he live with thee. 36. Take thou no interest of him or increase; but fear thy God; that thy brother may live with thee. 37. Thou shalt not give him thy money upon interest, nor give him thy victuals for increase. 38. I am the LORD your God, who brought you forth out of the land of Egypt, to give you the land of Canaan, to be your God.* vi (** iv). ¶39. And if thy brother be waxen poor with thee, and sell himself unto thee, thou shalt not make him to serve as a bondservant. 40. As a hired servant, and as a settler, he shall be with thee; he shall serve with thee unto the year of jubilee. 41. Then shall he go out from thee, he and his children with him, and shall return unto his own family, and unto the possession

35–38. PRACTICAL LOVE OF NEIGHBOUR

35. *if thy brother be waxen poor.* He still remains thy brother, and is to be treated in a brotherly and considerate manner. This is in strongest contrast to the treatment of the impoverished debtor in ancient Rome. The creditor could imprison him in his own private dungeon, chain him to a block, sell him into slavery, or even put him to death. If the debtor had several creditors, the Roman Law of the Twelve Tables ordained that they could hew him in pieces; and although one of them took a part of his body larger in proportion than his claim, the other creditors had no redress!

uphold him. Or, 'relieve him.' Do not suffer him to come down into the depths of misery, for then it is difficult to raise him; but come to his support at the time when his means *begin* to fail (Rashi).

as a stranger and a settler shall he live. Better, *yea though he be a stranger, or a sojourner; that he may live* (AV, Zunz, Benisch—following Rashi and Ibn Ezra). The great principle of 'Thou shalt love thy neighbour as thyself' must be a reality in Israelite life. The stranger and alien settler are explicitly included in the term *thy brother*, and are to be helped by timely loans, free of interest.

shall he live with thee. These words can be understood quite literally: it is the Israelite's *duty* to see to it that his fellowman does not die of starvation. It was centuries, millennia even, before the world outside Israel learned this elementary duty. Constantine in 315 is the first European ruler to have effected poor relief legislation, only to be repealed by Justinian two centuries later. It was not till the days of Queen Elizabeth that poor relief came to be recognized as a duty of the State. Other States followed England's example in the nineteenth century.

36. *interest.* This prohibition led to the establishment in every organized Jewish community, of a *Gemillus Chassodim* Society, for advancing loans free of interest to the poor; see also on Deut. XXIII, 19.

fear thy God. To take advantage of the dire need of the poor is contrary to all decent human feeling; for the Heb. idiom see on Exod. I, 17.

37. *victuals for increase.* Interest on foodstuffs, seed, and the like, which was paid in kind.

38. *brought . . . Egypt.* The Israelites, in their prosperity, were to remember the days when they were in bondage and needed the help that God had vouchsafed to them. Let them follow the Divine example and not imitate the callousness of their Egyptian masters, but deal with their fellowmen in a spirit of brotherhood and justice.

39–46. NO PERMANENT SERVITUDE FOR ANY ISRAELITE

When a man's ill fortune forces him to sell himself into bondage, his Hebrew master had definite obligations towards one who is of the same flesh and blood as himself. These regulations are unique in the respect for labour they inculcate and the manner in which the dignity of the labourer is safeguarded.

40. *as a hired servant.* He was not to be given any menial or degrading work, but only agricultural tasks or skilled labour, such as would be performed by a free labourer who is hired for a season.

of his fathers shall he return. 42. For they are My servants, whom I brought forth out of the land of Egypt; they shall not be sold as bondmen. 43. Thou shalt not rule over him with rigour; but shalt fear thy God. 44. And as for thy bondmen, and thy bondmaids, whom thou mayest have: of the nations that are round about you, of them shall ye buy bondmen and bondmaids. 45. Moreover of the children of the strangers that do sojourn among you, of them may ye buy, and of their families that are with you, which they have begotten in your land; and they may be your possession. 46. And ye may make them an inheritance for your children after you, to hold for a possession: of them may ye take your bondmen for ever; but over your brethren the children of Israel

41 וְיָצָא מֵעִמָּךְ הוּא וּבָנָיו עִמּוֹ וְשָׁב אֶל־מִשְׁפַּחְתּוֹ וְאֶל־
42 אֲחֻזַּת אֲבֹתָיו יָשׁוּב׃ כִּי־עֲבָדַי הֵם אֲשֶׁר־הוֹצֵאתִי אֹתָם
43 מֵאֶרֶץ מִצְרָיִם לֹא יִמָּכְרוּ מִמְכֶּרֶת עָבֶד׃ לֹא־תִרְדֶּה בוֹ
44 בְּפָרֶךְ וְיָרֵאתָ מֵאֱלֹהֶיךָ׃ וְעַבְדְּךָ וַאֲמָתְךָ אֲשֶׁר יִהְיוּ־לָךְ
מֵאֵת הַגּוֹיִם אֲשֶׁר סְבִיבֹתֵיכֶם מֵהֶם תִּקְנוּ עֶבֶד וְאָמָה׃
מה וְגַם מִבְּנֵי הַתּוֹשָׁבִים הַגָּרִים עִמָּכֶם מֵהֶם תִּקְנוּ וּמִמִּשְׁפַּחְתָּם
אֲשֶׁר עִמָּכֶם אֲשֶׁר הוֹלִידוּ בְּאַרְצְכֶם וְהָיוּ לָכֶם לַאֲחֻזָּה׃
46 וְהִתְנַחַלְתֶּם אֹתָם לִבְנֵיכֶם אַחֲרֵיכֶם לָרֶשֶׁת אֲחֻזָּה לְעֹלָם

unto the year of jubilee. This must be understood in connection with Exod. XXI, 2 f, and Deut. XV, 12 f, which ordain that the Hebrew who sells himself into slavery serves his master for six years, and goes free in the seventh. Should the Jubilee occur before his six years of service are over, the servant regains his personal freedom at the same time that his inheritance returns to him, in the year of Jubilee.

41. *his children.* Should the Hebrew be the father of a family when he sells himself into slavery, the master has to take the children into his care and maintain them.

his own family. The Rabbis taught that the freed slave must be received with cordiality and friendliness by his relatives, and no slight shown to him because of his former servitude.

42. *for they are My servants.* An Israelite therefore can never be more than nominally a slave to any human master.

they shall not be sold as bondmen. lit. 'they shall not be sold the sale of a slave'. The Rabbis ruled that a Hebrew is not to be sold publicly in the slave-market, but the sale is to be privately arranged.

43. *with rigour.* The same word is used to describe the hardship of Israel's bondage in Egypt (Exod. I, 13). In Rabbinic law, the rules that should regulate the relationship between a master and his Hebrew slave are given in great detail, and are based on the principle that master and man are kinsmen; *e.g.* the slave must not be given inferior food or accommodation to that of the master. Kindliness and chivalry are to characterize the bearing of the Israelite towards his less fortunate brother.

but shalt fear thy God. 'Whenever this phrase is used it refers to matters that are part of heart-religion,' דבר מסור ללב (Sifra); *i.e.* part of natural piety and fundamental humanity in our dealings with our fellowmen.

46. *of them may ye take your bondmen.* Better, *you may hold them to service* (Leeser); Heb. בהם תעבדו. 'You may hold them to service, but only to service, nothing more' (Sifra).

XXV, 46. SLAVERY

The system of slavery which is tolerated by the Torah was fundamentally different from the cruel systems of the ancient world, and even of Western countries down to the middle of the last century. The Code of Hammurabi has penalties only for the master who destroys the tooth or eye of *another man's* slave. It orders that a slave's ear be cut off, if he desires freedom; while to harbour a runaway slave was considered a capital offence. As to Greece, a slave was deemed 'an animated tool', and he could claim no more rights in his relationship to his master than a beast of burden. Agricultural labourers were chained. If at any time it was thought that there were too many slaves, they were exterminated, as wild beasts would be. Athens was an important slave market, and the State profited from it by a tax on the sales. So much for 'the glory that was Greece'. The 'grandeur that was Rome' was even more detestable. The slave was denied all human rights, and sentenced to horrible mutilation and even crucifixion at the whim of his master. Sick slaves were exposed to die of starvation, and there was *corporate* responsibility for slaves: Tacitus records that as late as the Empire the 400 slaves of one household were all put to death because they had been under their master's roof when he was murdered. Worlds asunder from these inhumanities and barbarities was the treatment accorded to the Hebrew slave. The position of Eliezer in Abraham's household (Gen. XXIV) enables us to realize the nature of servitude in the ancient Hebrew home. Kidnapping a man or selling him as a slave was a ye shall not rule, one over another, with rigour. *vii. ¶ 47. And if a stranger who is a settler with thee be waxen rich, and thy brother be waxen poor beside him, and sell himself unto the stranger who is a settler with thee, or to the offshoot of a stranger's family, 48. after that he is sold he may be redeemed; one of his brethren may redeem him; 49. or his uncle, or his uncle's son, may redeem him, or any that is nigh of kin unto him of his family may redeem him; or if he be waxen rich, he may redeem himself. 50. And he shall reckon with him that bought him from the year that he sold himself to him unto the year of jubilee; and the price of his sale shall be according unto the number of years; according to the time of a hired servant shall he be with him. 51. If there be yet many years, according unto them he shall give back the price of his redemption out of the money that he was bought for. 52. And if there remain but few years unto the year of jubilee, then he shall reckon with him; according unto his years shall he give back the price of his redemption. 53. As a servant hired year by year shall he be with him; he shall not rule with rigour over him in thy sight. 54. And if he be not redeemed by any of these means, then he shall go out in the year of jubilee,

בָּהֶם תַּעֲבֹדוּ וּבְאַחֵיכֶם בְּנֵי־יִשְׂרָאֵל אִישׁ בְּאָחִיו לֹא־
שביעי 47 תִרְדֶּה בּוֹ בְּפָרֶךְ׃ ס וְכִי תַשִּׂיג יַד גֵּר וְתוֹשָׁב עִמָּךְ
וּמָךְ אָחִיךָ עִמּוֹ וְנִמְכַּר לְגֵר תּוֹשָׁב עִמָּךְ אוֹ לְעֵקֶר
48 מִשְׁפַּחַת גֵּר׃ אַחֲרֵי נִמְכַּר גְּאֻלָּה תִּהְיֶה־לּוֹ אֶחָד מֵאֶחָיו
49 יִגְאָלֶנּוּ׃ אוֹ־דֹדוֹ אוֹ בֶן־דֹּדוֹ יִגְאָלֶנּוּ אוֹ־מִשְּׁאֵר בְּשָׂרוֹ
נ מִמִּשְׁפַּחְתּוֹ יִגְאָלֶנּוּ אוֹ־הִשִּׂיגָה יָדוֹ וְנִגְאָל׃ וְחִשַּׁב עִם־
קֹנֵהוּ מִשְּׁנַת הִמָּכְרוֹ לוֹ עַד שְׁנַת הַיֹּבֵל וְהָיָה כֶּסֶף מִמְכָּרוֹ
51 בְּמִסְפַּר שָׁנִים כִּימֵי שָׂכִיר יִהְיֶה עִמּוֹ׃ אִם־עוֹד רַבּוֹת
52 בַּשָּׁנִים לְפִיהֶן יָשִׁיב גְּאֻלָּתוֹ מִכֶּסֶף מִקְנָתוֹ׃ וְאִם־מְעַט
נִשְׁאַר בַּשָּׁנִים עַד־שְׁנַת הַיֹּבֵל וְחִשַּׁב־לוֹ כְּפִי שָׁנָיו יָשִׁיב
53 אֶת־גְּאֻלָּתוֹ׃ כִּשְׂכִיר שָׁנָה בְּשָׁנָה יִהְיֶה עִמּוֹ לֹא־יִרְדֶּנּוּ
54 בְּפֶרֶךְ לְעֵינֶיךָ׃ וְאִם לֹא יִגָּאֵל בְּאֵלֶּה וְיָצָא בִּשְׁנַת הַיֹּבֵל
מפטיר נה הוּא וּבָנָיו עִמּוֹ׃ כִּי־לִי בְנֵי־יִשְׂרָאֵל עֲבָדִים עֲבָדַי הֵם

capital offence. Cruelty on the part of the master that resulted in injury to an organ of the body, secured the slave's freedom (Exod. XXI, 26 f); and if the slave ran away, he must not be surrendered to his master (Deut. XXIII, 16 f). A Fugitive Slave Law, such as existed in America, with the tracking of runaway slaves by blood hounds, would have been unthinkable to the Israelite of old.

47–55. Israelites who are Slaves of Aliens

47. *offshoot.* Children of alien settlers would frequently join the Israelitish community; but the case dealt with here is that of a Hebrew selling himself into the service of an alien who remained aloof from the community.

48. *may be redeemed.* Forthwith.
may redeem him. For *may* substitute *shall*, here and in the next verse.

49. *if he be waxen rich.* lit. 'if he attaineth to power' (or 'means').

50. *unto the year of jubilee.* Hence it is to be deduced that, unlike the Hebrew slave who sells himself to a Hebrew master, his service does not automatically cease at the end of six years (Exod. XXI, 2). It is presupposed here that the man sold himself for an indefinite period, and unless redeemed would continue in bondage until the Jubilee.

a hired servant. The calculation is to be based on the assumption that the total sum paid was for a definite number of years till the Jubilee. This total sum is to be divided by the number of years, and it was to be considered that he had hired himself for the resulting amount per year (Rashi).

51. *yet many years.* To the Jubilee, and the amount required for the redemption accordingly high.

53. *servant.* He was to be treated like a workman hired by the year who belonged to a higher grade of labour.
in thy sight. If you see the alien master ill-treating him, you must intervene; but you have no right to enter his house to make investigation as to how he treats his slave (Sifra).

54. *by any of these means.* Lit. 'by those' which may refer to the kinsmen mentioned in *v.* 48, or to the method of regaining his freedom, described in *v.* 50 f.
and his children. See on *v.* 41 above.

55. *My servants.* Cf. *v.* 42.

he, and his children with him.* m. 55. For unto Me the children of Israel are servants; they are My servants whom I brought forth out of the land of Egypt; I am the LORD your God.

אֲשֶׁר־הוֹצֵאתִי אוֹתָם מֵאֶרֶץ מִצְרָיִם אֲנִי יְהוָה אֱלֹהֵיכֶם׃

26

CHAPTER XXVI

1. Ye shall make you no idols, neither shall ye rear you up a graven image, or a pillar, neither shall ye place any figured stone in your land, to bow down unto it; for I am the LORD your God. 2. Ye shall keep My sabbaths, and reverence My sanctuary: I am the LORD.

כו CAP. XXVI. כו

א לֹא־תַעֲשׂוּ לָכֶם אֱלִילִם וּפֶסֶל וּמַצֵּבָה לֹא־תָקִימוּ לָכֶם
וְאֶבֶן מַשְׂכִּית לֹא תִתְּנוּ בְּאַרְצְכֶם לְהִשְׁתַּחֲוֺת עָלֶיהָ כִּי
2 אֲנִי יְהוָה אֱלֹהֵיכֶם׃ אֶת־שַׁבְּתֹתַי תִּשְׁמֹרוּ וּמִקְדָּשִׁי תִּירָאוּ
אֲנִי יְהוָה׃

CHAPTER XXVI

The traditional Hebrew division of the Bible Text attaches the first two verses of this chapter to the preceding. The association of ideas is explained by the Sifra in this way: at the end of the last chapter, the Torah had treated of the case of an Israelite who had sold himself as a slave to a heathen master, and who might be tempted to follow the worship of his heathen master. Therefore, the warning of these verses is uttered. The words may, however, have a wider application. These two verses give 'the quintessence of the foregoing legislation' (Baentsch).

1–2. IDOLATRY FORBIDDEN, AND THE SABBATH TO BE OBSERVED

1. *idols.* See on XIX, 4.

pillar. Heb. *matzebah.* A memorial stone, as in Gen. XXVIII, 18, Exod. XXIV, 4; and also a stone or carved obelisk used for idolatrous worship (Exod. XXIII, 24, Deut. VII, 5).

figured stone. With some idolatrous representation carved on it.

unto it. Better, *thereon.*

2. *sabbaths . . . sanctuary.* Cf. XIX, 30. Not only have the Israelites to refrain from idol-worship, but God demands from them the due observance of 'Sabbaths'—which here includes the festive occasions as well as the Sabbatical years—and also the fulfilment of all obligations connected with the Sanctuary.

HAFTORAH BEHAR הפטרת בהר

JEREMIAH XXXII, 6–27

CHAPTER XXXII

6. And Jeremiah said: 'The word of the LORD came unto me, saying: 7. Behold, Hanamel, the son of Shallum thine uncle, shall come unto thee, saying: Buy thee my field that is in Anathoth; for the right of redemption is thine to buy it.' 8. So Hanamel mine uncle's son came to me in the court of the guard according to the word of the LORD, and said unto me: 'Buy my field, I pray thee, that is in Anathoth, which is

CAP. XXXII. לב

6 וַיֹּאמֶר
7 יִרְמְיָהוּ הָיָה דְבַר־יְהוָה אֵלַי לֵאמֹר׃ הִנֵּה חֲנַמְאֵל בֶּן
שַׁלֻּם דֹּדְךָ בָּא אֵלֶיךָ לֵאמֹר קְנֵה לְךָ אֶת־שָׂדִי אֲשֶׁר
8 בַּעֲנָתוֹת כִּי לְךָ מִשְׁפַּט הַגְּאֻלָּה לִקְנוֹת׃ וַיָּבֹא אֵלַי חֲנַמְאֵל

v. 7. הב׳ בקמץ

For a brief characterization of the life and message of Jeremiah see p. 229.

The Sedrah deals with the redemption of a family inheritance; and the Haftorah furnishes a striking instance of its observance at a great crisis in Israel's history. It was in the year 587, during the siege of Jerusalem, when Jeremiah was in prison because of his outspoken foretelling of the inevitable capture and destruction of the City by the Babylonians. At that dark hour, the Prophet 'redeemed' a piece of land, so that it shall not pass out of his family.

He looks beyond the storm of judgment to the hope of a brighter day. In the offer of redemp-

בֶּן־דֹּדִי כִּדְבַר יְהוָה אֶל־חֲצַר הַמַּטָּרָה וַיֹּאמֶר אֵלַי קְנֵה
נָא אֶת־שָׂדִי אֲשֶׁר־בַּעֲנָתוֹת אֲשֶׁר ׀ בְּאֶרֶץ בִּנְיָמִין כִּי לְךָ
מִשְׁפַּט הַיְרֻשָּׁה וּלְךָ הַגְּאֻלָּה קְנֵה־לָךְ וָאֵדַע כִּי דְבַר־
9 יְהוָה הוּא׃ וָאֶקְנֶה אֶת־הַשָּׂדֶה מֵאֵת חֲנַמְאֵל בֶּן־דֹּדִי
אֲשֶׁר בַּעֲנָתוֹת וָאֶשְׁקֲלָה־לּוֹ אֶת־הַכֶּסֶף שִׁבְעָה שְׁקָלִים
י וַעֲשָׂרָה הַכָּסֶף׃ וָאֶכְתֹּב בַּסֵּפֶר וָאֶחְתֹּם וָאָעֵד עֵדִים
11 וָאֶשְׁקֹל הַכֶּסֶף בְּמֹאזְנָיִם׃ וָאֶקַּח אֶת־סֵפֶר הַמִּקְנָה אֶת־
12 הֶחָתוּם הַמִּצְוָה וְהַחֻקִּים וְאֶת־הַגָּלוּי׃ וָאֶתֵּן אֶת־הַסֵּפֶר
הַמִּקְנָה אֶל־בָּרוּךְ בֶּן־נֵרִיָּה בֶּן־מַחְסֵיָה לְעֵינֵי חֲנַמְאֵל דֹּדִי
וּלְעֵינֵי הָעֵדִים הַכֹּתְבִים בְּסֵפֶר הַמִּקְנָה לְעֵינֵי כָּל־הַיְּהוּדִים
13 הַיֹּשְׁבִים בַּחֲצַר הַמַּטָּרָה׃ וָאֲצַוֶּה אֶת־בָּרוּךְ לְעֵינֵיהֶם
14 לֵאמֹר׃ כֹּה־אָמַר יְהוָה צְבָאוֹת אֱלֹהֵי יִשְׂרָאֵל לָקוֹחַ אֶת־
הַסְּפָרִים הָאֵלֶּה אֵת סֵפֶר הַמִּקְנָה הַזֶּה וְאֵת הֶחָתוּם וְאֵת
סֵפֶר הַגָּלוּי הַזֶּה וּנְתַתָּם בִּכְלִי־חָרֶשׂ לְמַעַן יַעַמְדוּ יָמִים
טו רַבִּים׃ כִּי כֹה אָמַר יְהוָה צְבָאוֹת אֱלֹהֵי יִשְׂרָאֵל

in the land of Benjamin; for the right of inheritance is thine, and the redemption is thine; buy it for thyself.' Then I knew that this was the word of the LORD. 9. And I bought the field that was in Anathoth of Hanamel mine uncle's son, and weighed him the money, even seventeen shekels of silver. 10. And I subscribed the deed, and sealed it, and called witnesses, and weighed him the money in the balances. 11. So I took the deed of the purchase, both that which was sealed, containing the terms and conditions, and that which was open; 12. and I delivered the deed of the purchase unto Baruch the son of Neriah, the son of Mahseiah, in the presence of Hanamel mine uncle['s son], and in the presence of the witnesses that subscribed the deed of the purchase, before all the Jews that sat in the court of the guard. 13. And I charged Baruch before them, saying: 14. 'Thus saith the LORD of hosts, the God of Israel: Take these deeds, this deed of the purchase, both that which is sealed, and this deed which is open, and put them in an earthen vessel; that they may continue many days. 15. For thus saith the LORD of hosts, the God of Israel: Houses and fields and vineyards shall yet again be bought in this land.' ¶ 16. Now after I had delivered the deed of

tion that is made to him by a kinsman, he sees a God-sent opportunity to show forth to his brethren a Divine pledge that the night of Captivity will be followed by the morn of Return, when houses and lands will once again be freely bought and sold. His action finds a parallel during Hannibal's invasion of Italy, when a Roman purchased, at full price in public auction, the ground on which the enemy's army was encamped.

7. *Anathoth.* Jeremiah's birthplace.

right of redemption. As next-of-kin, Jeremiah has the right of pre-emption to his relative's land, so that it shall not pass out of the family; Lev. XXV, 24 f.

8. *court of the guard.* A part of the court surrounding the Palace, railed off to guard prisoners whom it was not desired to throw into the common dungeon (Driver).

that I knew that this was the word of the LORD. He had previously (*v.* 7) had a mysterious premonition of the visit and of its purpose; but now he is convinced that God had inspired the visit. The purchase would illustrate in a most striking manner the certainty of Israel's restoration (see *v.* 15).

9–11. He bought the field, and sealed the purchase with all the legal formalities. The Jews had been vassals of Assyria and Babylon for about a century; and, it seems, transference of land was now performed according to the legal procedure of the Sovereign Power. As in all Babylonian documents of that nature, the deed was written on clay, and enclosed in a clay envelope which was sealed up. On the envelope, the *open* copy (*v.* 14) was inscribed a copy of the contract. Only in case of the writing on the envelope becoming obliterated or of suspicion that it had been tampered with, was the envelope broken and the text itself examined.

12. *Baruch.* Jeremiah's faithful secretary who, at the Prophet's dictation, wrote down his addresses (see Chap. XXXVI). It is to him that we owe the preservation of the Prophet's utterances.

14. *in an earthen vessel.* Similarly bottles are used nowadays to preserve documents placed in the memorial stones of public buildings (Bennett).

that they may continue many days. Though it would be a long time before the deed would be needed, yet the prophecy of which it is a sign would be fulfilled.

15. *houses . . . again be bought.* He who had been denounced as a deserter and traitor is now their best comforter and counsellor.

16–27. A wave of doubt surges over Jeremiah. He is himself overwhelmed by the darkness that is enveloping his People. From the court of the guard, he could see the works of the besiegers; and, within the City, famine and pestilence were the purchase unto Baruch the son of Neriah, I prayed unto the LORD, saying: 17. 'Ah Lord GOD! behold, Thou hast made the heaven and the earth by Thy great power and by Thy outstretched arm; there is nothing too hard for Thee; 18. who showest mercy unto thousands, and recompensest the iniquity of the fathers into the bosom of their children after them; the great, the mighty God, the LORD of hosts is His name; 19. great in counsel, and mighty in work; whose eyes are open upon all the ways of the sons of men, to give every one according to his ways, and according to the fruit of his doings; 20. who didst set signs and wonders in the land of Egypt, even unto this day, and in Israel and among other men; and madest Thee a name, as at this day; 21. and didst bring forth Thy people Israel out of the land of Egypt with signs, and with wonders, and with a strong hand, and with an outstretched arm, and with great terror; 22. and gavest them this land, which Thou didst swear to their fathers to give them, a land flowing with milk and honey; 23. and they came in, and possessed it; but they hearkened not to Thy voice, neither walked in Thy law; they have done nothing of all that Thou commandedst them to do; therefore Thou hast caused all this evil to befall them; 24. behold the mounds, they are come unto the city to take it; and the city is given into the hand of the Chaldeans that fight against it, because of the sword, and of the famine, and of the pestilence; and what Thou hast spoken is come to pass; and, behold, Thou seest it. 25. Yet Thou hast said unto me, O Lord GOD: Buy thee the field for money, and call witnesses; whereas the city is given into the hand of the Chaldeans.' ¶ 26. Then came the word of the LORD unto Jeremiah, saying: 27. 'Behold, I am the LORD, the God of all flesh; is there any thing too hard for Me?

עוֹד יִקָּנוּ בָתִּים וְשָׂדוֹת וּכְרָמִים בָּאָרֶץ הַזֹּאת׃
16 וָאֶתְפַּלֵּל אֶל־יְהוָה אַחֲרֵי תִתִּי אֶת־סֵפֶר הַמִּקְנָה אֶל־בָּרוּךְ
17 בֶּן־נֵרִיָּה לֵאמֹר׃ אֲהָהּ אֲדֹנָי יֱהוִה הִנֵּה ׀ אַתָּה עָשִׂיתָ
אֶת־הַשָּׁמַיִם וְאֶת־הָאָרֶץ בְּכֹחֲךָ הַגָּדוֹל וּבִזְרֹעֲךָ הַנְּטוּיָה
18 לֹא־יִפָּלֵא מִמְּךָ כָּל־דָּבָר׃ עֹשֶׂה חֶסֶד לַאֲלָפִים וּמְשַׁלֵּם
עֲוֺן אָבוֹת אֶל־חֵיק בְּנֵיהֶם אַחֲרֵיהֶם הָאֵל הַגָּדוֹל הַגִּבּוֹר
19 יְהוָה צְבָאוֹת שְׁמוֹ׃ גְּדֹל הָעֵצָה וְרַב הָעֲלִילִיָּה אֲשֶׁר־
עֵינֶיךָ פְקֻחוֹת עַל־כָּל־דַּרְכֵי בְּנֵי אָדָם לָתֵת לְאִישׁ כִּדְרָכָיו
כ וְכִפְרִי מַעֲלָלָיו׃ אֲשֶׁר שַׂמְתָּ אֹתוֹת וּמֹפְתִים בְּאֶרֶץ מִצְרַיִם
עַד־הַיּוֹם הַזֶּה וּבְיִשְׂרָאֵל וּבָאָדָם וַתַּעֲשֶׂה־לְּךָ שֵׁם כַּיּוֹם
21 הַזֶּה׃ וַתֹּצֵא אֶת־עַמְּךָ אֶת־יִשְׂרָאֵל מֵאֶרֶץ מִצְרָיִם בְּאֹתוֹת
וּבְמוֹפְתִים וּבְיָד חֲזָקָה וּבְאֶזְרוֹעַ נְטוּיָה וּבְמוֹרָא גָּדוֹל׃
22 וַתִּתֵּן לָהֶם אֶת־הָאָרֶץ הַזֹּאת אֲשֶׁר־נִשְׁבַּעְתָּ לַאֲבוֹתָם לָתֵת
23 לָהֶם אֶרֶץ זָבַת חָלָב וּדְבָשׁ׃ וַיָּבֹאוּ וַיִּרְשׁוּ אֹתָהּ וְלֹא־
שָׁמְעוּ בְקוֹלֶךָ וּבְתֹרוֹתְךָ לֹא־הָלָכוּ אֵת כָּל־אֲשֶׁר צִוִּיתָה
לָהֶם לַעֲשׂוֹת לֹא עָשׂוּ וַתַּקְרֵא אֹתָם אֵת כָּל־הָרָעָה
24 הַזֹּאת׃ הִנֵּה הַסֹּלְלוֹת בָּאוּ הָעִיר לְלָכְדָהּ וְהָעִיר נִתְּנָה
בְּיַד הַכַּשְׂדִּים הַנִּלְחָמִים עָלֶיהָ מִפְּנֵי הַחֶרֶב וְהָרָעָב וְהַדָּבֶר
כה וַאֲשֶׁר דִּבַּרְתָּ הָיָה וְהִנְּךָ רֹאֶה׃ וְאַתָּה אָמַרְתָּ אֵלַי אֲדֹנָי
יֱהוִה קְנֵה־לְךָ הַשָּׂדֶה בַּכֶּסֶף וְהָעֵד עֵדִים וְהָעִיר נִתְּנָה
26 בְּיַד הַכַּשְׂדִּים׃ וַיְהִי דְּבַר־יְהוָה אֶל־יִרְמְיָהוּ לֵאמֹר׃
27 הִנֵּה אֲנִי יְהוָה אֱלֹהֵי כָּל־בָּשָׂר הֲמִמֶּנִּי יִפָּלֵא כָּל־דָּבָר׃

v. 23. ובתורתך קרי ibid. קמץ בז״ק

raging. He, therefore, turns to God and seeks assurance for the faith and confidence which he has sought to implant in others by his symbolic action of purchase.

17–19. Jeremiah begins his prayer by declaring God's power in creation and history, and His righteous government of humanity.

18. *the iniquity of the fathers.* Recalling the words of the Second Commandment; Exod. xx, 5, 6.

20–23. He remembers the wonders of God wrought for Israel in Egypt, and the bounties bestowed on them after the Exodus.

20. *unto this day.* They are known and remembered to this day (Kimchi).

21. *great terror.* Struck into Egypt by the wonders He wrought at the Exodus.

24. *the mounds.* Embankments against the City walls, for the attacking soldiers to make their assaults.

Chaldeans. Chaldea at that time included the whole of Babylonia.

27. *Is there any thing too hard for Me?* One of the great answers—and facts of history; cf. Gen. XVIII, 14. God gives back to Jeremiah his own words 'There is nothing too hard for Thee' (*v.* 17). He had come to God with the best thoughts about Him, and God gives him the answer that his thoughts are true.

26 3. If ye walk in My statutes, and keep My commandments, and do them; 4. then I will give your rains in their season, and the land shall yield her produce, and the trees of the field shall yield their fruit. 5. And your threshing shall reach unto the vintage, and the vintage shall reach unto the sowing time; and ye shall eat your bread until ye have enough, and dwell in your land safely.* ii. 6. And I will give peace in the land, and ye shall lie down, and none shall make you afraid; and I will cause evil beasts

כו

פ פ פ לג 33

3 אִם־בְּחֻקֹּתַי תֵּלֵכוּ וְאֶת־מִצְוֺתַי תִּשְׁמְרוּ וַעֲשִׂיתֶם אֹתָם׃
4 וְנָתַתִּי גִשְׁמֵיכֶם בְּעִתָּם וְנָתְנָה הָאָרֶץ יְבוּלָהּ וְעֵץ הַשָּׂדֶה
ה יִתֵּן פִּרְיוֹ׃ וְהִשִּׂיג לָכֶם דַּיִשׁ אֶת־בָּצִיר וּבָצִיר יַשִּׂיג אֶת־
שני זָרַע וַאֲכַלְתֶּם לַחְמְכֶם לָשֹׂבַע וִישַׁבְתֶּם לָבֶטַח בְּאַרְצְכֶם׃
6 וְנָתַתִּי שָׁלוֹם בָּאָרֶץ וּשְׁכַבְתֶּם וְאֵין מַחֲרִיד וְהִשְׁבַּתִּי חַיָּה

X. BECHUKOSAI

(Chapters XXVI, 3–XXVII)

CONCLUDING ADMONITION

The Book of Leviticus has its sacerdotal chapters, its ceremonial parts, its ethical section; and, in its concluding portion, it strikes the note of Prophetic admonition and warning. This is not to be wondered at when we recall the fact that Moses is 'the Father of the Prophets'. The Jewish name for this chapter from *v.* 14–45 (as well as for the parallel section in Deut. xxviii) is *Tochacha*, תוכחה; lit. 'Warning', 'Admonition'.

After having declared the higher law and rooted all human duty, both to God and man, in the Holiness-ideal—'Ye shall be holy, for I the Lord your God am holy'—the Lawgiver endeavours to enlist man's natural fear and hope as allies of that sublime principle. In startling and indeed in terrifying form, he contrasts the blessings, in the event of faithfulness to God, with the dire calamities, if the people prove disloyal to Him. This fundamental thought, viz. that God rewards the righteous and punishes the wicked, is an essential doctrine of Judaism as of every higher religion. They may differ as to the nature and form of Divine retribution, but the belief that right is rewarded and wrong punished is part of an ethical faith, a belief vindicated and confirmed by the experience of humanity. 'One lesson, and only one, history may be said to repeat with distinctness, that the world is built somehow on moral foundations; that in the long run it is well with the good; in the long run it is ill with the wicked' (Froude). But, while there is general agreement with this truth underlying the Admonition, there has always been discontent with the manner in which it is presented in this chapter. 'Why,' it is asked, 'does Scripture enter into such dreadful details concerning the consequences of disobedience?' Two observations must be made in regard to this form of appeal. The first is, that it is a language which the people to whom this homiletic discourse on the Wages of Disobedience was originally addressed, could clearly understand. 'A wealth of bliss may be depicted in two or three concise phrases, but to cause the primitive mind to realize the awful consequences of sin and transgression, the words of denunciation must come swift and powerful as hammer blows, and must picture to their last terrible results, the dreadful devastation wrought by human perversity' (Drachmann). The second is that the *Tochacha*, though it may sound harsh, is true; and truth in its nakedness is not always pleasant. The promises and, alas, also the warnings in this chapter have abundantly been borne out by Jewish history. 'As a survey of the worldly blessings and tribulations employed by God in His education of Israel in Canaan, this chapter is fairly exhaustive, and is in line with what Prophecy proclaimed, and historical experience taught, in the course of the centuries' (Dillmann); see also on Deut. xxviii.

3–13. Blessings in the Wake of Obedience

3. *if ye walk in My statutes.* Heb. אם בחקתי תלכו; Sifra translates: 'Would that you walked in my statutes!'

statutes. See on xviii, 4.

4. *rains.* The rainfall is of supreme importance in the Holy Land. If it fails, the result is famine. Consequently, it comes first among the blessings.

5. *threshing.* Cf. Amos ix, 13. There will be so much corn to thresh, that the work will continue throughout the season until it is time to cut the vines.

safely. Without fear of famine; as in xxv, 19.

6. *I will give peace in the land.* Prosperity is valueless unless it can be enjoyed in tranquillity, without the dread of assault, robbery or devastation of war.

evil beasts. In the time of warfare, when the land is desolated, wild beasts multiply; cf. Exod. xxiii, 29; Isa. xxxv, 9.

sword. The symbol of an invading army; cf. Ezek. xiv, 17.

to cease out of the land, neither shall the sword go through your land. 7. And ye shall chase your enemies, and they shall fall before you by the sword. 8. And five of you shall chase a hundred, and a hundred of you shall chase ten thousand; and your enemies shall fall before you by the sword. 9. And I will have respect unto you, and make you fruitful, and multiply you; and will establish My covenant with you.*iii (**v). 10. And ye shall eat old store long kept, and ye shall bring forth the old from before the new. 11. And I will set My tabernacle among you, and My soul shall not abhor you. 12. And I will walk among you, and will be your God, and ye shall be My people. 13. I am the LORD your God, who brought you forth out of the land of Egypt, that ye should not be their bondmen; and I have broken the bars of your yoke, and made you go upright. ¶ 14. But if ye will not hearken unto Me, and will not do all these commandments; 15. and if ye shall reject My statutes, and if your soul abhor Mine ordinances, so that ye will not do all My commandments, but break My covenant; 16. I also will do this unto you: I will appoint terror over you, even consumption and fever, that shall make the eyes to fail, and the soul to languish; and ye shall sow your seed in vain, for your enemies shall eat it. 17.

7 רָעָה מִן־הָאָרֶץ וְחֶרֶב לֹא־תַעֲבֹר בְּאַרְצְכֶם׃ וּרְדַפְתֶּם
8 אֶת־אֹיְבֵיכֶם וְנָפְלוּ לִפְנֵיכֶם לֶחָרֶב׃ וְרָדְפוּ מִכֶּם חֲמִשָּׁה
מֵאָה וּמֵאָה מִכֶּם רְבָבָה יִרְדֹּפוּ וְנָפְלוּ אֹיְבֵיכֶם לִפְנֵיכֶם
9 לֶחָרֶב׃ וּפָנִיתִי אֲלֵיכֶם וְהִפְרֵיתִי אֶתְכֶם וְהִרְבֵּיתִי אֶתְכֶם שי׳(חמישי והן מחובר׳)
וַהֲקִימֹתִי אֶת־בְּרִיתִי אִתְּכֶם׃ * וַאֲכַלְתֶּם יָשָׁן נוֹשָׁן וְיָשָׁן
11 מִפְּנֵי חָדָשׁ תּוֹצִיאוּ׃ וְנָתַתִּי מִשְׁכָּנִי בְּתוֹכְכֶם וְלֹא־תִגְעַל
12 נַפְשִׁי אֶתְכֶם׃ וְהִתְהַלַּכְתִּי בְּתוֹכְכֶם וְהָיִיתִי לָכֶם לֵאלֹהִים
13 וְאַתֶּם תִּהְיוּ־לִי לְעָם׃ אֲנִי יְהוָה אֱלֹהֵיכֶם אֲשֶׁר הוֹצֵאתִי
אֶתְכֶם מֵאֶרֶץ מִצְרַיִם מִהְיֹת לָהֶם עֲבָדִים וָאֶשְׁבֹּר מֹטֹת
עֻלְּכֶם וָאוֹלֵךְ אֶתְכֶם קוֹמְמִיּוּת׃ פ
14 וְאִם־לֹא תִשְׁמְעוּ לִי וְלֹא תַעֲשׂוּ אֵת כָּל־הַמִּצְוֺת הָאֵלֶּה׃
טו וְאִם־בְּחֻקֹּתַי תִּמְאָסוּ וְאִם אֶת־מִשְׁפָּטַי תִּגְעַל נַפְשְׁכֶם
16 לְבִלְתִּי עֲשׂוֹת אֶת־כָּל־מִצְוֺתַי לְהַפְרְכֶם אֶת־בְּרִיתִי׃ אַף־
אֲנִי אֶעֱשֶׂה־זֹּאת לָכֶם וְהִפְקַדְתִּי עֲלֵיכֶם בֶּהָלָה אֶת־
הַשַּׁחֶפֶת וְאֶת־הַקַּדַּחַת מְכַלּוֹת עֵינַיִם וּמְדִיבֹת נָפֶשׁ וּזְרַעְתֶּם
17 לָרִיק זַרְעֲכֶם וַאֲכָלֻהוּ אֹיְבֵיכֶם׃ וְנָתַתִּי פָנַי בָּכֶם וְנִגַּפְתֶּם

v. 15. קמץ בז״ק

7. *ye shall chase.* Should they attempt to attack you.

8. *five . . . hundred.* These are round numbers, not to be taken literally. They express the idea that the Israelites, with God as their helper, will be able to overcome vastly superior forces; *e.g.* the victories of the Maccabees over armies of great numerical superiority.

9. *respect unto you.* lit. 'turn unto you'; *i.e.* be gracious, favourably inclined towards you.
establish. Carry out.

10. *the old.* *i.e.* of the previous years; cf. XXV, 22.

11. *My tabernacle.* Better, *My abiding presence* (cf. Exod. XXV, 8); God will be manifestly with His people, as evidenced by their extraordinary happiness.
abhor you. Withdraw My favour so as to expose you to misfortune; cf. Jer. XIV, 19.

12. *walk among you.* A forcible image to describe how intimately God will associate with Israel.

13. *brought you forth.* That God is able to fulfil His promises is proved by His mighty acts in overthrowing the power of Egypt and setting Israel free.
bars. With which the yoke was fastened to the animal's neck.

14–39. THE WAGES OF DISOBEDIENCE

In dealing with the consequences of faithfulness, the Torah speaks in general terms; but in regard to the wages of disobedience, this Prophetical warning describes in much detail the penalties and horrors that would befall the sinful people. These are arranged in a series of five groups of increasing severity—sickness and defeat, famine, wild beasts, siege and exile.

16–18. SICKNESS AND DEFEAT

16. *terror.* *i.e.* terrible things, defined by what follows. The diseases which are mentioned are such as would strike terror in the heart of a person afflicted with any of them; cf. Deut. XXVIII, 22.
consumption. Any disease which causes a wasting of the body.
fever. lit. 'a burning', internally.
sow your seed in vain. Toiling without enjoying the fruits of their labour is frequently given as a punishment for faithlessness; cf. Deut. XXVIII, 30.

17. *set My face.* See XVII, 10; XX, 3, 6.
ye shall flee. They will be so demoralized that panic will seize them without cause; cf. *v.* 36 below.

And I will set My face against you, and ye shall be smitten before your enemies; they that hate you shall rule over you; and ye shall flee when none pursueth you. 18. And if ye will not yet for these things hearken unto Me, then I will chastise you seven times more for your sins. 19. And I will break the pride of your power; and I will make your heaven as iron, and your earth as brass. 20. And your strength shall be spent in vain; for your land shall not yield her produce, neither shall the trees of the land yield their fruit. 21. And if ye walk contrary unto Me, and will not hearken unto Me; I will bring seven times more plagues upon you according to your sins. 22. And I will send the beast of the field among you, which shall rob you of your children, and destroy your cattle, and make you few in number; and your ways shall become desolate. 23. And if in spite of these things ye will not be corrected unto Me, but will walk contrary unto Me; 24. then will I also walk contrary unto you; and I will smite you, even I, seven times for your sins. 25. And I will bring a sword upon you, that shall execute the vengeance of the covenant; and ye shall be gathered together within your cities; and I will send the pestilence among you; and ye shall be delivered into the hand of the enemy. 26. When I break your staff of bread, ten women shall bake your bread in one oven, and they shall deliver your bread again by weight; and ye shall eat, and not be satisfied. ¶ 27. And if ye will not for all this hearken unto Me, but walk contrary unto Me; 28. then I will

לִפְנֵי אֹיְבֵיכֶם וְרָדוּ בָכֶם שֹׂנְאֵיכֶם וְנַסְתֶּם וְאֵין־רֹדֵף
18 אֶתְכֶם׃ וְאִם־עַד־אֵלֶּה לֹא תִשְׁמְעוּ לִי וְיָסַפְתִּי לְיַסְּרָה
19 אֶתְכֶם שֶׁבַע עַל־חַטֹּאתֵיכֶם׃ וְשָׁבַרְתִּי אֶת־גְּאוֹן עֻזְּכֶם
כ וְנָתַתִּי אֶת־שְׁמֵיכֶם כַּבַּרְזֶל וְאֶת־אַרְצְכֶם כַּנְּחֻשָׁה׃ וְתַם
לָרִיק כֹּחֲכֶם וְלֹא־תִתֵּן אַרְצְכֶם אֶת־יְבוּלָהּ וְעֵץ הָאָרֶץ לֹא
21 יִתֵּן פִּרְיוֹ׃ וְאִם־תֵּלְכוּ עִמִּי קֶרִי וְלֹא תֹאבוּ לִשְׁמֹעַ לִי
22 וְיָסַפְתִּי עֲלֵיכֶם מַכָּה שֶׁבַע כְּחַטֹּאתֵיכֶם׃ וְהִשְׁלַחְתִּי בָכֶם
אֶת־חַיַּת הַשָּׂדֶה וְשִׁכְּלָה אֶתְכֶם וְהִכְרִיתָה אֶת־בְּהֶמְתְּכֶם
23 וְהִמְעִיטָה אֶתְכֶם וְנָשַׁמּוּ דַּרְכֵיכֶם׃ וְאִם־בְּאֵלֶּה לֹא תִוָּסְרוּ
24 לִי וַהֲלַכְתֶּם עִמִּי קֶרִי׃ וְהָלַכְתִּי אַף־אֲנִי עִמָּכֶם בְּקֶרִי
כה וְהִכֵּיתִי אֶתְכֶם גַּם־אָנִי שֶׁבַע עַל־חַטֹּאתֵיכֶם׃ וְהֵבֵאתִי
עֲלֵיכֶם חֶרֶב נֹקֶמֶת נְקַם־בְּרִית וְנֶאֱסַפְתֶּם אֶל־עָרֵיכֶם
26 וְשִׁלַּחְתִּי דֶבֶר בְּתוֹכְכֶם וְנִתַּתֶּם בְּיַד־אוֹיֵב׃ בְּשִׁבְרִי לָכֶם
מַטֵּה־לֶחֶם וְאָפוּ עֶשֶׂר נָשִׁים לַחְמְכֶם בְּתַנּוּר אֶחָד וְהֵשִׁיבוּ
27 לַחְמְכֶם בַּמִּשְׁקָל וַאֲכַלְתֶּם וְלֹא תִשְׂבָּעוּ׃ ס וְאִם־
28 בְּזֹאת לֹא תִשְׁמְעוּ לִי וַהֲלַכְתֶּם עִמִּי בְּקֶרִי׃ וְהָלַכְתִּי

18. *seven times.* A round number, meaning, 'very much more.'

19–22. Famine and Wild Beasts

19. *pride of your power.* The power which is the cause of your pride. By 'power' is to be understood the feeling of independence that results from prosperity; cf. Deut. VIII, 11–18.

heaven as iron. A cloudless heaven in the rainy season and an unproductive soil would quickly humble the pride of the people, and make them realize their helplessness.

21. *contrary unto Me.* Heb. קרי acting perversely, and wilfully doing the opposite of what God wishes. The Heb. also means 'accident'. In defiant opposition to God, they would despise God's laws, and act as if *accident* ruled the moral and spiritual universe (S. R. Hirsch).

plagues. Strokes, smitings.

23–26. The Horrors of Siege

23. *corrected unto Me.* The purpose of God's chastisements is the moral discipline of His people.

25. *vengeance of the covenant. i.e.* retribution for disregarding My covenant with you.

within your cities. You will flee from the enemy and take refuge behind the fortifications of your cities (cf. Jer. IV, 5); but even there punishments, in the form of epidemics, will overtake you and weaken your powers of resistance.

26. *break your staff of bread.* An expression denoting the cutting off of the food-supply. Food being that upon which life is supported, it is symbolized as a staff; Isa. III, 1.

ten women. A round number. Although each household has its own oven, ten families will require the use of only one oven.

by weight. Food is so scarce that it is doled out by measure.

27–39. National Destruction and Exile

28. *in fury.* The continued stubbornness of the people will lead to direr and direr punishment. The warnings now reach the climax of horror.

עִמָּכֶם בַּחֲמַת־קֶרִי וְיִסַּרְתִּי אֶתְכֶם אַף־אָנִי שֶׁבַע עַל־
29 חַטֹּאתֵיכֶם׃ וַאֲכַלְתֶּם בְּשַׂר בְּנֵיכֶם וּבְשַׂר בְּנֹתֵיכֶם תֹּאכֵלוּ׃
ל וְהִשְׁמַדְתִּי אֶת־בָּמֹתֵיכֶם וְהִכְרַתִּי אֶת־חַמָּנֵיכֶם וְנָתַתִּי אֶת־
31 פִּגְרֵיכֶם עַל־פִּגְרֵי גִּלּוּלֵיכֶם וְגָעֲלָה נַפְשִׁי אֶתְכֶם׃ וְנָתַתִּי
אֶת־עָרֵיכֶם חָרְבָּה וַהֲשִׁמּוֹתִי אֶת־מִקְדְּשֵׁיכֶם וְלֹא אָרִיחַ
32 בְּרֵיחַ נִיחֹחֲכֶם׃ וַהֲשִׁמֹּתִי אֲנִי אֶת־הָאָרֶץ וְשָׁמְמוּ עָלֶיהָ
33 אֹיְבֵיכֶם הַיֹּשְׁבִים בָּהּ׃ וְאֶתְכֶם אֱזָרֶה בַגּוֹיִם וַהֲרִיקֹתִי
אַחֲרֵיכֶם חָרֶב וְהָיְתָה אַרְצְכֶם שְׁמָמָה וְעָרֵיכֶם יִהְיוּ חָרְבָּה׃
34 אָז תִּרְצֶה הָאָרֶץ אֶת־שַׁבְּתֹתֶיהָ כֹּל יְמֵי הֳשַּׁמָּה וְאַתֶּם
בְּאֶרֶץ אֹיְבֵיכֶם אָז תִּשְׁבַּת הָאָרֶץ וְהִרְצָת אֶת־שַׁבְּתֹתֶיהָ׃
לה כָּל־יְמֵי הָשַּׁמָּה תִּשְׁבֹּת אֵת אֲשֶׁר לֹא־שָׁבְתָה בְּשַׁבְּתֹתֵיכֶם
36 בְּשִׁבְתְּכֶם עָלֶיהָ׃ וְהַנִּשְׁאָרִים בָּכֶם וְהֵבֵאתִי מֹרֶךְ בִּלְבָבָם

walk contrary unto you in fury; and I also will chastise you seven times for your sins.
29. And ye shall eat the flesh of your sons, and the flesh of your daughters shall ye eat.
30. And I will destroy your high places, and cut down your sun-pillars, and cast your carcasses upon the carcasses of your idols; and My soul shall abhor you.
31. And I will make your cities a waste, and will bring your sanctuaries unto desolation, and I will not smell the savour of your sweet odours.
32. And I will bring the land into desolation; and your enemies that dwell therein shall be astonished at it.
33. And you will I scatter among the nations, and I will draw out the sword after you; and your land shall be a desolation, and your cities shall be a waste.
34. Then shall the land be paid her sabbaths, as long as it lieth desolate, and ye are in your enemies' land; even then shall the land rest, and repay her sabbaths.
35. As long as it lieth desolate it shall have rest; even the rest which it had not in your sabbaths, when ye dwelt upon it.
36. And as for them that are left of you, I will send a faintness into their heart in the lands of their enemies; and the sound of

30. *high places.* Heb. *bamoth;* the altars on the hilltops, or mounds, built by the Canaanites and taken over by idolatrous Israelites.

sun-pillars. Or, 'images of the sun-god.'

cast your carcasses. See II Kings XXIII, 14, 20, for a historical instance.

abhor you. In contrast to what was stated in *v.* 15.

31. *your sanctuaries.* God will not associate Himself with such a Temple; hence 'your sanctuaries', not 'My sanctuary' as in *v.* 2. The plural may refer to the different divisions of the Sanctuary.

I will not smell. Cf. Amos V, 21. Since the incense symbolized prayer (see on II, 1), the phrase means, 'I will ignore your petitions.' Sanctuary and sacrifice are valueless, if unaccompanied by moral obedience.

32. *astonished.* Amazement will seize them at the appalling desolation, and they will perceive that it is due to superhuman agency.

33. *you will I scatter among the nations.* 'There is a marvellous and grand display of the greatness of God in the fact that He holds out before the people whom He has just delivered from the hands of the heathen the prospect of being scattered again among the heathen, and that even before the land is taken by the Israelites, He predicts its return to desolation. These could only be spoken of by One who has the future really before His mind, who can destroy His own work, yet attain His end, certain of victory notwithstanding all opposing difficulties' (quoted in Keil-Delitzsch).

the sword after you. An expression for the hot pursuit of fugitives; cf. Ezek. XXI, 8–11. Malbim explains these words as an essential qualification of the first part of the verse, *scatter among the nations.* 'Israel's dispersion is not a curse in itself: it is a means of fulfilling God's purpose of spreading His word among the nations. The tragedy lies in being scattered because of the sword.'

34. *repay her sabbaths.* Better, *satisfy its sabbaths; i.e.* make compensation for the years of release which the Israelites did not observe according to the dictates of the law (Leeser). Driver explains that the Heb. word rendered 'enjoy' is the technical term in connection with the settlement of an account. When the people are exiled, the land, here personified, will receive payment of an overdue account on the long Sabbath-rest which it will then enjoy; see next *v.*

36. *left of you.* The two preceding verses are a parenthesis, describing the 'rest' which the land would have, when its inhabitants had been carried into captivity. This verse resumes *v.* 33, and alludes to the fate, with its resulting cowardice and 'spiritual slavery', that would be in store for those who escaped. 'The author possessed the imagination of a poet as well as the eloquence of an orator' (Kennedy).

בְּאַרְצֹת אֹיְבֵיהֶם וְרָדַף אֹתָם קוֹל עָלֶה נִדָּף וְנָסוּ מְנֻסַת־
37 חֶרֶב וְנָפְלוּ וְאֵין רֹדֵף׃ וְכָשְׁלוּ אִישׁ־בְּאָחִיו כְּמִפְּנֵי־חֶרֶב
38 וְרֹדֵף אָיִן וְלֹא־תִהְיֶה לָכֶם תְּקוּמָה לִפְנֵי אֹיְבֵיכֶם׃ וַאֲבַדְתֶּם
39 בַּגּוֹיִם וְאָכְלָה אֶתְכֶם אֶרֶץ אֹיְבֵיכֶם׃ וְהַנִּשְׁאָרִים בָּכֶם
יִמַּקּוּ בַּעֲוֺנָם בְּאַרְצֹת אֹיְבֵיכֶם וְאַף בַּעֲוֺנֹת אֲבֹתָם אִתָּם
מ יִמָּקּוּ׃ וְהִתְוַדּוּ אֶת־עֲוֺנָם וְאֶת־עֲוֺן אֲבֹתָם בְּמַעֲלָם אֲשֶׁר
41 מָעֲלוּ־בִי וְאַף אֲשֶׁר־הָלְכוּ עִמִּי בְּקֶרִי׃ אַף־אֲנִי אֵלֵךְ עִמָּם
בְּקֶרִי וְהֵבֵאתִי אֹתָם בְּאֶרֶץ אֹיְבֵיהֶם אוֹ־אָז יִכָּנַע לְבָבָם
42 הֶעָרֵל וְאָז יִרְצוּ אֶת־עֲוֺנָם׃ וְזָכַרְתִּי אֶת־בְּרִיתִי יַעֲקוֹב
וְאַף אֶת־בְּרִיתִי יִצְחָק וְאַף אֶת־בְּרִיתִי אַבְרָהָם אֶזְכֹּר
43 וְהָאָרֶץ אֶזְכֹּר׃ וְהָאָרֶץ תֵּעָזֵב מֵהֶם וְתִרֶץ אֶת־שַׁבְּתֹתֶיהָ
בָּהְשַׁמָּה מֵהֶם וְהֵם יִרְצוּ אֶת־עֲוֺנָם יַעַן וּבְיַעַן בְּמִשְׁפָּטַי
44 מָאָסוּ וְאֶת־חֻקֹּתַי גָּעֲלָה נַפְשָׁם׃ וְאַף גַּם־זֹאת בִּהְיוֹתָם
בְּאֶרֶץ אֹיְבֵיהֶם לֹא־מְאַסְתִּים וְלֹא־גְעַלְתִּים לְכַלֹּתָם לְהָפֵר

v. 42. מלא ו' v. 43. קמץ בז"ק

a driven leaf shall chase them; and they
shall flee, as one fleeth from the sword;
and they shall fall when none pursueth. 37.
And they shall stumble one upon another,
as it were before the sword, when none
pursueth; and ye shall have no power to
stand before your enemies. 38. And ye
shall perish among the nations, and the
land of your enemies shall eat you up.
39. And they that are left of you shall
pine away in their iniquity in your enemies'
lands; and also in the iniquities of their
fathers shall they pine away with them.
40. And they shall confess their iniquity,
and the iniquity of their fathers, in their
treachery which they committed against
Me, and also that they have walked con-
trary unto Me. 41. I also will walk con-
trary unto them, and bring them into the
land of their enemies; if then perchance
their uncircumcised heart be humbled,
and they then be paid the punishment of
their iniquity; 42. then will I remember
My covenant with Jacob, and also My
covenant with Isaac, and also My covenant
with Abraham will I remember; and I will
remember the land. 43. For the land shall
lie forsaken without them, and shall be
paid her sabbaths, while she lieth desolate
without them; and they shall be paid the
punishment of their iniquity; because,
even because they rejected Mine ordinances,
and their soul abhorred My statutes. 44.
And yet for all that, when they are in the

37. *stumble.* In their panic, caused by demoralization and not by a real enemy, they would forget the need for mutual help; and each would endeavour to escape, even at the cost of sacrificing his brother—true psychology of the Golus.

38. *eat you up.* For the image of a land consuming those who dwell upon its soil, see Num. XIII, 32.

39. *in their iniquity.* From the consequences of their guilt; *i.e.* their punishment. To this guilt (and punishment) their fathers have contributed.

with them. Refers to the fathers. There will be an added agony to the wretched lot of the sinful parents, that they will behold their children, who had followed their evil example, experiencing the hard fate which was so bitter to themselves. This explanation is supported by the Traditional accentuation of the words.

40–45. Repentance Shall Bring Restoration

40. *confess.* God desireth not the death of the sinner; and, therefore, every threat of punishment for disobedience is followed by a promise of mercy, if there is repentance and amendment. Divine discipline is for moral ends; and in truth the Exile proved a purifving furnace unto Israel.

treachery. Implying that faithlessness to the Covenant is a wrong committed directly against God; cf. *v.* 15.

41. *I also will walk.* Better, *I also walk.* They will acknowledge that the calamities which had overtaken them were God's method of humbling their arrogance.

uncircumcised. Unconsecrated, unclean; closed to the Divine call or appeal; cf. on XIX, 23.

be paid. Acknowledge that the punishment was deserved; see, however, *v.* 35 and 43.

42. *Jacob . . . Isaac . . . Abraham.* God is stirred to mercy by recalling the noble ancestors of Israel and the Covenant He entered into with each. In retrospect, the last comes first to mind.

the land. Which was itself a symbol of the Covenant with the Patriarchs, and prominently figured in the promises which God had made to them.

43. *shall lie forsaken without them.* Because the Israelites had failed to observe the Sabbatical year, they had wronged the soil of the Holy Land, and that wrong had to be expiated before they could return and resettle there; see XVIII, 25.

land of their enemies, I will not reject them, neither will I abhor them, to destroy them utterly, and to break My covenant with them; for I am the LORD their God. 45. But I will for their sakes remember the covenant of their ancestors, whom I brought forth out of the land of Egypt in the sight of the nations, that I might be their God: I am the LORD. ¶ 46. These are the statutes and ordinances and laws, which the LORD made between Him and the children of Israel in mount Sinai by the hand of Moses.* iv (** vi).

27

CHAPTER XXVII

1. And the LORD spoke unto Moses, saying: 2. Speak unto the children of Israel, and say unto them: ¶ When a man shall clearly utter a vow of persons unto the LORD according to thy valuation, 3. then thy valuation shall be for the male from twenty years old even unto sixty years old, even thy valuation shall be fifty shekels of silver, after the shekel of the sanctuary. 4. And if it be a female, then thy valuation shall be thirty shekels. 5. And if it be from five years old even unto twenty years old, then thy valuation shall be for the male twenty shekels, and for the female ten shekels. 6. And if it be from a month old even unto five years old, then thy valuation shall be for the male five shekels of silver, and for the female thy valuation shall be three shekels of silver. 7. And if it be from sixty years old and upward:

מה בְּרִיתִי אִתָּם כִּי אֲנִי יְהוָה אֱלֹהֵיהֶם׃ וְזָכַרְתִּי לָהֶם בְּרִית
רִאשֹׁנִים אֲשֶׁר הוֹצֵאתִי־אֹתָם מֵאֶרֶץ מִצְרַיִם לְעֵינֵי הַגּוֹיִם
46 לִהְיוֹת לָהֶם לֵאלֹהִים אֲנִי יְהוָה׃ אֵלֶּה הַחֻקִּים וְהַמִּשְׁפָּטִים
וְהַתּוֹרֹת אֲשֶׁר נָתַן יְהוָה בֵּינוֹ וּבֵין בְּנֵי יִשְׂרָאֵל בְּהַר סִינַי
בְּיַד־מֹשֶׁה׃ * פ רביעי (ששי כשהן מחוב׳)

CAP. XXVII. כז

כז
א 2 וַיְדַבֵּר יְהוָה אֶל־מֹשֶׁה לֵּאמֹר׃ דַּבֵּר אֶל־בְּנֵי יִשְׂרָאֵל
וְאָמַרְתָּ אֲלֵהֶם אִישׁ כִּי יַפְלִא נֶדֶר בְּעֶרְכְּךָ נְפָשֹׁת לַיהוָה׃
3 וְהָיָה עֶרְכְּךָ הַזָּכָר מִבֶּן עֶשְׂרִים שָׁנָה וְעַד בֶּן־שִׁשִּׁים שָׁנָה
4 וְהָיָה עֶרְכְּךָ חֲמִשִּׁים שֶׁקֶל כֶּסֶף בְּשֶׁקֶל הַקֹּדֶשׁ׃ וְאִם־
ה נְקֵבָה הִוא וְהָיָה עֶרְכְּךָ שְׁלֹשִׁים שָׁקֶל׃ וְאִם מִבֶּן־חָמֵשׁ
שָׁנִים וְעַד בֶּן־עֶשְׂרִים שָׁנָה וְהָיָה עֶרְכְּךָ הַזָּכָר עֶשְׂרִים
6 שְׁקָלִים וְלַנְּקֵבָה עֲשֶׂרֶת שְׁקָלִים׃ וְאִם מִבֶּן־חֹדֶשׁ וְעַד
בֶּן־חָמֵשׁ שָׁנִים וְהָיָה עֶרְכְּךָ הַזָּכָר חֲמִשָּׁה שְׁקָלִים כֶּסֶף
7 וְלַנְּקֵבָה עֶרְכְּךָ שְׁלֹשֶׁת שְׁקָלִים כָּסֶף׃ וְאִם מִבֶּן־שִׁשִּׁים

44. *yet for all that.* The chapter ends characteristically on a note of hope. God's anger may be severe, but it is not everlasting. He will grant His people every opportunity to renew the ancient Covenant. Israel—'a people who have been overthrown, crushed, scattered; who have been ground, as it were, to very dust, and flung to the four winds of heaven; yet who, though thrones have fallen, and empires have perished, and creeds have changed, and living tongues have become dead, still exist with a vitality seemingly unimpaired' (Henry George).

45. *their ancestors.* lit. 'the first' generations. It alludes not only to the Patriarchs, but the founders of the Twelve Tribes and their descendants who left Egypt; cf. Deut. XIX, 14; Isa. LXI, 4.

46. *these are the statutes.* This verse is the subscription not only to chaps. XVII–XXVI, but to the whole of Leviticus, the following chapter being an appendix to the Book.

CHAPTER XXVII

REDEMPTION OF VOWS AND TITHES

The Book of Levicitus concludes, as it opened, with a chapter of Sanctuary-regulations—voluntary contributions to the upkeep of the Sanctuary, such offerings being a true expression of devotion to the House of God.

2–8. VOWING AND VALUATION OF A PERSON

2. *clearly utter a vow.* By setting a valuation upon himself or any of his family, the money being paid unto the treasury of the Sanctuary.

3. *fifty shekels.* The equivalent of £7 of our money, but the true value in purchasing power is many times that sum (Kennedy). The form, *thy estimation,* is archaic; see on Exod. XXX, 13.

4. *thirty shekels.* The valuation seems to have been made on the basis of what might be called the market value of the individual's labour. A woman, not possessing the physical strength of a man, had a lower valuation set upon her.

6. *from a month old.* No valuation is placed in regard to a child under a month old. In Jewish law there are no mourning rites to be observed for a child who dies within a month of birth.

if it be a male, then thy valuation shall be fifteen shekels, and for the female ten shekels. 8. But if he be too poor for thy valuation, then he shall be set before the priest, and the priest shall value him; according to the means of him that vowed shall the priest value him. ¶ 9. And if it be a beast, whereof men bring an offering unto the LORD, all that any man giveth of such unto the LORD shall be holy. 10. He shall not alter it, nor change it, a good for a bad, or a bad for a good; and if he shall at all change beast for beast, then both it and that for which it is changed shall be holy. 11. And if it be any unclean beast, of which they may not bring an offering unto the LORD, then he shall set the beast before the priest. 12. And the priest shall value it, whether it be good or bad; as thou the priest valuest it, so shall it be. 13. But if he will indeed redeem it, then he shall add the fifth part thereof unto thy valuation. ¶ 14. And when a man shall sanctify his house to be holy unto the LORD, then the priest shall value it, whether it be good or bad; as the priest shall value it, so shall it stand. 15. And if he that sanctified it will redeem his house, then he shall add the fifth part of the money of thy valuation unto it, and it shall be his.*v(**vii). ¶ 16. And if a man shall sanctify unto the LORD part of the field of his possession, then thy valuation shall be according to the sowing thereof; the sowing of a homer of barley shall be valued at fifty shekels of silver. 17. If he sanctify

שָׁנָה וָמַעְלָה אִם־זָכָר וְהָיָה עֶרְכְּךָ חֲמִשָּׁה עָשָׂר שָׁקֶל
8 וְלַנְּקֵבָה עֲשָׂרָה שְׁקָלִים׃ וְאִם־מָךְ הוּא מֵעֶרְכֶּךָ וְהֶעֱמִידוֹ
לִפְנֵי הַכֹּהֵן וְהֶעֱרִיךְ אֹתוֹ הַכֹּהֵן עַל־פִּי אֲשֶׁר תַּשִּׂיג יַד הַנֹּדֵר
9 יַעֲרִיכֶנּוּ הַכֹּהֵן׃ ס וְאִם־בְּהֵמָה אֲשֶׁר יַקְרִיבוּ מִמֶּנָּה
י קָרְבָּן לַיהוָה כֹּל אֲשֶׁר יִתֵּן מִמֶּנּוּ לַיהוָה יִהְיֶה־קֹּדֶשׁ׃ לֹא
יַחֲלִיפֶנּוּ וְלֹא־יָמִיר אֹתוֹ טוֹב בְּרָע אוֹ־רַע בְּטוֹב וְאִם־הָמֵר
יָמִיר בְּהֵמָה בִּבְהֵמָה וְהָיָה־הוּא וּתְמוּרָתוֹ יִהְיֶה־קֹּדֶשׁ׃
11 וְאִם כָּל־בְּהֵמָה טְמֵאָה אֲשֶׁר לֹא־יַקְרִיבוּ מִמֶּנָּה קָרְבָּן
12 לַיהוָה וְהֶעֱמִיד אֶת־הַבְּהֵמָה לִפְנֵי הַכֹּהֵן׃ וְהֶעֱרִיךְ הַכֹּהֵן
13 אֹתָהּ בֵּין טוֹב וּבֵין רָע כְּעֶרְכְּךָ הַכֹּהֵן כֵּן יִהְיֶה׃ וְאִם־
14 גָּאֹל יִגְאָלֶנָּה וְיָסַף חֲמִישִׁתוֹ עַל־עֶרְכֶּךָ׃ וְאִישׁ כִּי־יַקְדִּשׁ
אֶת־בֵּיתוֹ קֹדֶשׁ לַיהוָה וְהֶעֱרִיכוֹ הַכֹּהֵן בֵּין טוֹב וּבֵין רָע
טו כַּאֲשֶׁר יַעֲרִיךְ אֹתוֹ הַכֹּהֵן כֵּן יָקוּם׃ וְאִם־הַמַּקְדִּישׁ יִגְאַל
חמישי (שביעי כשהן מחוברין) 16 אֶת־בֵּיתוֹ וְיָסַף חֲמִישִׁית כֶּסֶף־עֶרְכְּךָ עָלָיו וְהָיָה לוֹ׃ וְאִם
מִשְּׂדֵה אֲחֻזָּתוֹ יַקְדִּישׁ אִישׁ לַיהוָה וְהָיָה עֶרְכְּךָ לְפִי זַרְעוֹ

v. 9. סבירין ממנה v. 10. קמץ בטרחא

8. *according to the means.* 'If he (the person making the vow) be too poor to pay the valuation, then he shall set him (the person vowed) before the priest, and the priest shall value him.' The priest, in forming his estimate of what he could pay, must leave him sufficient means for his necessities (Talmud).

9–13. REDEMPTION OF AN ANIMAL

9. *if it be a beast.* If a 'clean' animal, that and none other had to be presented.

shall be holy. It became the property of the Sanctuary, and all profane use of it was interdicted.

10. *not alter it.* Even for one of greater value. *Alter* is to replace one species by another, *e.g.* a bull for a sheep; *change* refers to different members of the same species.

12. *good or bad. i.e.* whether it be of much value or little.

13. *fifth part.* See on *v.* 16.

14–15. REDEMPTION OF A HOUSE

14. *sanctify.* Dedicate.

15. *redeem.* As in *v.* 13. The law of xxv, 29 f applied to this case where the redeemer was not the owner. If the house was in a walled city, it could be redeemed by the owner within a year; and if not redeemed, it remained for ever in the possession of the buyer. In the case of a house situated in a village, the Jubilee-year brought its restitution to the owner.

16–25. REDEMPTION OF LAND

16. *possession.* An inherited field, as contrasted with a piece of land which he had bought (*v.* 22).

the sowing thereof. The value of the land was estimated by the quantity of seed required to sow it. For each *homer* of seed used in sowing barley, the valuation was placed at fifty shekels for the whole period of forty-nine years. A *homer* was ten ephahs (see on XIX, 36), and nearly six bushels in capacity.

17. *from the year of jubilee.* From the conclusion of the year.

it shall stand. At the valuation of fifty shekels for each *homer* of seed.

18. *an abatement.* A proportionate reduction in the price; cf. xxv, 50 f.

17 זֶרַע חֹמֶר שְׂעֹרִים בַּחֲמִשִּׁים שֶׁקֶל כָּסֶף׃ אִם־מִשְּׁנַת
18 הַיֹּבֵל יַקְדִּישׁ שָׂדֵהוּ כְּעֶרְכְּךָ יָקוּם׃ וְאִם־אַחַר הַיֹּבֵל
יַקְדִּישׁ שָׂדֵהוּ וְחִשַּׁב־לוֹ הַכֹּהֵן אֶת־הַכֶּסֶף עַל־פִּי הַשָּׁנִים
19 הַנּוֹתָרֹת עַד שְׁנַת הַיֹּבֵל וְנִגְרַע מֵעֶרְכֶּךָ׃ וְאִם־גָּאֹל יִגְאַל
אֶת־הַשָּׂדֶה הַמַּקְדִּישׁ אֹתוֹ וְיָסַף חֲמִשִׁית כֶּסֶף־עֶרְכְּךָ עָלָיו
כ וְקָם לוֹ׃ וְאִם־לֹא יִגְאַל אֶת־הַשָּׂדֶה וְאִם־מָכַר אֶת־הַשָּׂדֶה
21 לְאִישׁ אַחֵר לֹא־יִגָּאֵל עוֹד׃ וְהָיָה הַשָּׂדֶה בְּצֵאתוֹ בַיֹּבֵל
ששי 22 קֹדֶשׁ לַיהוָה כִּשְׂדֵה הַחֵרֶם לַכֹּהֵן תִּהְיֶה אֲחֻזָּתוֹ׃ וְאִם
אֶת־שְׂדֵה מִקְנָתוֹ אֲשֶׁר לֹא מִשְּׂדֵה אֲחֻזָּתוֹ יַקְדִּישׁ לַיהוָה׃
23 וְחִשַּׁב־לוֹ הַכֹּהֵן אֵת מִכְסַת הָעֶרְכְּךָ עַד שְׁנַת הַיֹּבֵל וְנָתַן
24 אֶת־הָעֶרְכְּךָ בַּיּוֹם הַהוּא קֹדֶשׁ לַיהוָה׃ בִּשְׁנַת הַיּוֹבֵל יָשׁוּב
כה הַשָּׂדֶה לַאֲשֶׁר קָנָהוּ מֵאִתּוֹ לַאֲשֶׁר־לוֹ אֲחֻזַּת הָאָרֶץ׃ וְכָל־
עֶרְכְּךָ יִהְיֶה בְּשֶׁקֶל הַקֹּדֶשׁ עֶשְׂרִים גֵּרָה יִהְיֶה הַשָּׁקֶל׃
26 אַךְ־בְּכוֹר אֲשֶׁר יְבֻכַּר לַיהוָה בִּבְהֵמָה לֹא־יַקְדִּישׁ אִישׁ
27 אֹתוֹ אִם־שׁוֹר אִם־שֶׂה לַיהוָה הוּא׃ וְאִם בַּבְּהֵמָה הַטְּמֵאָה
וּפָדָה בְעֶרְכֶּךָ וְיָסַף חֲמִשִׁתוֹ עָלָיו וְאִם־לֹא יִגָּאֵל וְנִמְכַּר
28 בְּעֶרְכֶּךָ׃ אַךְ כָּל־חֵרֶם אֲשֶׁר יַחֲרִם אִישׁ לַיהוָה מִכָּל־

his field from the year of jubilee, according to thy valuation it shall stand. 18. But if he sanctify his field after the jubilee, then the priest shall reckon unto him the money according to the years that remain unto the year of jubilee, and an abatement shall be made from thy valuation. 19. And if he that sanctified the field will indeed redeem it, then he shall add the fifth part of the money of thy valuation unto it, and it shall be assured to him. 20. And if he will not redeem the field, or if he have sold the field to another man, it shall not be redeemed any more. 21. But the field, when it goeth out in the jubilee, shall be holy unto the LORD, as a field devoted; the possession thereof shall be the priest's. *vi. 22. And if he sanctify unto the LORD a field which he hath bought, which is not of the field of his possession; 23. then the priest shall reckon unto him the worth of thy valuation unto the year of jubilee; and he shall give thy valuation in that day, as a holy thing unto the LORD. 24. In the year of jubilee the field shall return unto him of whom it was bought, even to him to whom the possession of the land belongeth. 25. And all thy valuations shall be according to the shekel of the sanctuary; twenty gerahs shall be the shekel. ¶ 26. Howbeit the firstling among beasts, which is born as a firstling to the LORD, no man shall sanctify it; whether it be ox or sheep, it is the LORD's. 27. And if it be an unclean beast, then he shall ransom it according to thy valuation, and shall add unto it the fifth part thereof; or if it be not redeemed, then it shall be sold according to thy valuation. ¶ 28. Notwithstanding, no devoted thing, that a man may devote

20. *if he will not redeem.* If the redeemer of the field is not the owner, the Sanctuary becomes the *de jure* owner of the field, which at the next Jubilee becomes the inalienable property of the Sanctuary.

21. *field devoted.* See on *v.* 28.

22. *bought.* Since he bought the field until the Jubilee only, it is clear that his gift to the Sanctuary is only temporary.

23. *in that day.* The price had to be paid in one sum and in full-weight shekels (see on Exod. XXX, 13).

26–27. REDEMPTION OF A FIRSTLING

26. *to the LORD.* As a firstling, it *ipso facto* belonged to God; see Exod. XIII, 2. Therefore, the owner cannot vow it again as a gift to the Sanctuary; it was not his to give away.

shall sanctify. *i.e.* devote, as a voluntary offering.

27 *an unclean beast.* *i.e.* a dedicated clean animal that became blemished; in which case the proceeds of the sale were to be used for Temple repair (Rashi).

28–29. LAW OF THE BAN

28. *devoted thing.* lit. 'cut-off, excluded', irrevocably given up. There were three varieties of the ban of differing degrees of stringency: the war ban, the justice ban, and the private ban. This verse deals with the last-named. The 'devoting' of anything to the Temple was a more solemn act than a mere presentation. The human being, animal, or field became 'most holy', *i.e.* remained the inalienable property of the Sanctuary, and passed into the possession of the priests.

field of his possession. Only an inheritance could be 'devoted', not a purchased field, since the latter only belonged to the owner temporarily, and passed out of his possession in the Jubilee. In the same manner, a Hebrew slave

unto the LORD of all that he hath, whether a man or beast, or of the field of his possession, shall be sold or redeemed; every devoted thing is most holy unto the LORD.* vii.
29. None devoted, that may be devoted of men, shall be ransomed; he shall surely be put to death. ¶ 30. And all the tithe of the land, whether of the seed of the land, or of the fruit of the tree, is the LORD'S; it is holy unto the LORD. 31. And if a man will redeem aught of his tithe, he shall add unto it the fifth part thereof.* m. 32. And all the tithe of the herd or the flock, whatsoever passeth under the rod, the tenth shall be holy unto the LORD. 33. He shall not inquire whether it be good or bad, neither shall he change it; and if he change it at all, then both it and that for which it is changed shall be holy; it shall not be redeemed. ¶ 34. These are the commandments, which the LORD commanded Moses for the children of Israel in mount Sinai.

אֲשֶׁר־לוֹ מֵאָדָם וּבְהֵמָה וּמִשְּׂדֵה אֲחֻזָּתוֹ לֹא יִמָּכֵר וְלֹא
שביעי
29 יִגָּאֵל כָּל־חֵרֶם קֹדֶשׁ־קָדָשִׁים הוּא לַיהוָה׃ * כָּל־חֵרֶם אֲשֶׁר
ל יָחֳרַם מִן־הָאָדָם לֹא יִפָּדֶה מוֹת יוּמָת׃ וְכָל־מַעְשַׂר הָאָרֶץ
31 מִזֶּרַע הָאָרֶץ מִפְּרִי הָעֵץ לַיהוָה הוּא קֹדֶשׁ לַיהוָה׃ וְאִם־
מפטיר
32 גָּאֹל יִגְאַל אִישׁ מִמַּעַשְׂרוֹ חֲמִשִׁיתוֹ יֹסֵף עָלָיו׃ * וְכָל־מַעְשַׂר
בָּקָר וָצֹאן כֹּל אֲשֶׁר־יַעֲבֹר תַּחַת הַשָּׁבֶט הָעֲשִׂירִי יִהְיֶה־
33 קֹּדֶשׁ לַיהוָה׃ לֹא יְבַקֵּר בֵּין־טוֹב לָרַע וְלֹא יְמִירֶנּוּ וְאִם־
הָמֵר יְמִירֶנּוּ וְהָיָה־הוּא וּתְמוּרָתוֹ יִהְיֶה־קֹּדֶשׁ לֹא יִגָּאֵל׃
34 אֵלֶּה הַמִּצְוֹת אֲשֶׁר צִוָּה יְהוָה אֶת־מֹשֶׁה אֶל־בְּנֵי יִשְׂרָאֵל
בְּהַר סִינָי׃

חזק

סכום פסוקי דספר ויקרא שמונה מאות וחמשים ותשעה. **נטף**
סימן: וחציו והנגע בבשר הזב: ופרשיותיו עשרה. **בא נד** סימן:
וסדריו **שלשה ועשרים.** ובתורתו **יהגה** יומם ולילה סימן:
ופרקיו **שבעה ועשרים.** ואהיה עמך ואברכך סימן: **מניין**
הפתוחות **שתים וחמשים.** והסתומות **ששה וארבעים. הכל**
שמנה ותשעים פרשיות. דודי **צח** ואדום סימן:

could not be 'devoted' because he regained his freedom in the seventh year.

sold. To another person.

redeemed. By the owner.

29. *devoted. i.e.* doomed.

of men. 'The reference here is to the justice-ban; in other words, to the judicial sentence by the proper authorities on such malefactors as the idolater (see Exod. XXII, 19), and the blasphemer' (Kennedy). The individual was not permitted to carry out such a ban. Deut. XII, 31, forbids human sacrifice, and the putting to death of a slave is forbidden in Exod. XXI, 29.

30–33. REDEMPTION OF THE TITHE

30. *tithe of the land.* This so-called 'second tithe', described in Deut. XIV, 22 f, was analogous to the firstling of sacrificial animals, and the same law of redemption applied.

is the LORD'S. Tithes belong to God as the real owner of the land; see on XXV, 1–7. They are a kind of rent paid by the people as His tenants. Being already God's, they cannot be made the subject of vows (Dummelow).

32. *tithe of the herd.* Every tenth animal born of the herd or flock had to be treated like the tenth of the produce of the field. The animals were sacrificed and the flesh consumed in Jerusalem.

passeth under the rod. The Mishnah thus describes the procedure: The new-born animals were herded in a pen with one narrow exit through which they could only pass in single file. As they came out, each tenth animal was touched on the back with a rod coated with red paint, and in this manner distinguished for the tithe.

33. *he shall not inquire.* The owner could not select which animals should form part of the tithe. If he substituted one of the designated animals for another, whether of better or inferior quality, he forfeited both.

34. *these are the commandments.* Cf. XXVI, 46. This verse seems to be the subscription of the concluding chapter only.

The Massoretic Note states the number of verses in Leviticus to be 859; its Sedrahs (parshiyoth) 10; its Sedarim, smaller divisions according to the Triennial Cycle, 23; and its Chapters 27.

HAFTORAH BECHUKOSAI הפטרת בחקתי

JEREMIAH XVI, 19–XVII, 14

CHAPTER XVI

19. O LORD, my strength, and my stronghold,
And my refuge, in the day of affliction,
Unto Thee shall the nations come
From the ends of the earth, and shall say:
'Our fathers have inherited nought but lies,
Vanity and things wherein there is no profit.'
20. Shall a man make unto himself gods,
And they are no gods?
21. Therefore, behold, I will cause them to know,
This once will I cause them to know
My hand and My might;
And they shall know that My name is the LORD.

CHAPTER XVII

1. The sin of Judah is written
With a pen of iron, and with the point of a diamond;
It is graven upon the tablet of their heart,
And upon the horns of your altars.

CAP. XVI. טז

19 יְהוָ֞ה עֻזִּ֧י וּמָֽעֻזִּ֛י
וּמְנוּסִ֖י בְּי֣וֹם צָרָ֑ה אֵלֶ֗יךָ גּוֹיִ֤ם יָבֹ֙אוּ֙ מֵֽאַפְסֵי־אָ֔רֶץ וְיֹאמְר֗וּ
כ אַךְ־שֶׁ֙קֶר֙ נָחֲל֣וּ אֲבוֹתֵ֔ינוּ הֶ֖בֶל וְאֵֽין־בָּ֥ם מוֹעִֽיל׃ הֲיַעֲשֶׂה־
21 לּ֥וֹ אָדָ֖ם אֱלֹהִ֑ים וְהֵ֖מָּה לֹ֥א אֱלֹהִֽים׃ לָכֵן֙ הִנְנִ֣י מֽוֹדִיעָ֔ם
בַּפַּ֣עַם הַזֹּ֔את אוֹדִיעֵ֥ם אֶת־יָדִ֖י וְאֶת־גְּבוּרָתִ֑י וְיָדְע֖וּ כִּֽי־
שְׁמִ֥י יְהוָֽה׃

CAP. XVII. יז

א חַטַּ֣את יְהוּדָ֔ה כְּתוּבָ֛ה בְּעֵ֥ט בַּרְזֶ֖ל בְּצִפֹּ֣רֶן שָׁמִ֑יר חֲרוּשָׁה֙

טז׳ v. 19. קמץ בז״ק

The Sedrah proclaims the happy result of national faithfulness, and the inevitable and disastrous consequences of national faithlessness to the Divine Law. The Haftorah is the utterance of the Prophet who witnessed the destruction of the Temple and State through the religious and moral degeneracy of the nation. His words, especially in the verses preceding this section, are thus an echo of the prophecy of Moses. But Jeremiah's message here is one of great hope. Even heathen nations shall yet acknowledge that truth and moral sanity are only to be found in the Revelation given to Israel. Let Israel trust—as he does—in God, the faithful Physician, who will heal them, and establish them on an eternal foundation.

19. *have inherited nought but lies.* The Prophet foresees that time when the heathen from the utmost ends of the earth will realize the vanity and falsehood of their hereditary gods, and come to acknowledge God's glorious Name.

That all mankind will at last grope their way out of the night of traditional ignorance towards the Truth, is a fundamental conviction of the Jewish spirit. This has found expression in the *Oleynu* prayer, with its culminating aspiration, taken from the Prophet (Zech. XIV, 9), *The LORD shall be King over all the earth: in that day shall the LORD be One and his name One* (Authorised Prayer Book, p. 77), and in the ויאתיו hymn of the New Year liturgy, dating from the early Middle Ages:—

'All the world shall come to serve Thee,
And bless Thy glorious Name,
And Thy righteousness triumphant
The islands shall acclaim.
And the peoples shall go seeking
Who knew thee not before;
And all the ends of the earth shall praise Thee,
And tell Thy greatness o'er.

They shall build for Thee their altars,
Their idols overthrown;
And their graven gods shall shame them,
As they turn to Thee alone.
They shall worship Thee at sunrise
And feel Thy Kingdom's might,
And impart their understanding
To those astray in night.'
(Trans. I. Zangwill.)

21. *that My name is the LORD.* They shall understand all that is implied in the Name *Adonay*—One God, who rules universally and eternally and fulfils His word (Rashi); see p. 232.

CHAPTER XVII

The action of the heathens only deepens the sin and folly of Israel, for resisting Divine teaching and sinking into the bog of the impure idolatry of Canaan.

1. *with a pen of iron, and with the point of a diamond.* Instruments used for cutting into hard substances; here, on the heart hardened by sin. Sin is indelibly ingrained in their nature, and their guilt is patent to all.

of your altars. A swift and effective change from the indirect (*their* heart) to the direct form of address (*your* altars). Other instances in the Scriptures are numerous (Kimchi).

2 עַל־לוּחַ לִבָּם וּלְקַרְנוֹת מִזְבְּחוֹתֵיכֶם׃ כִּזְכֹּר בְּנֵיהֶם
מִזְבְּחוֹתָם וַאֲשֵׁרֵיהֶם עַל־עֵץ רַעֲנָן עַל גְּבָעוֹת הַגְּבֹהוֹת׃
3 הֲרָרִי בַּשָּׂדֶה חֵילְךָ כָל־אוֹצְרוֹתֶיךָ לָבַז אֶתֵּן בָּמֹתֶיךָ
4 בְּחַטָּאת בְּכָל־גְּבוּלֶיךָ׃ וְשָׁמַטְתָּה וּבְךָ מִנַּחֲלָתְךָ אֲשֶׁר
נָתַתִּי לָךְ וְהַעֲבַדְתִּיךָ אֶת־אֹיְבֶיךָ בָּאָרֶץ אֲשֶׁר לֹא־יָדָעְתָּ
5 כִּי־אֵשׁ קְדַחְתֶּם בְּאַפִּי עַד־עוֹלָם תּוּקָד׃ כֹּה ׀ אָמַר
יְהוָה אָרוּר הַגֶּבֶר אֲשֶׁר יִבְטַח בָּאָדָם וְשָׂם בָּשָׂר זְרֹעוֹ
6 וּמִן־יְהוָה יָסוּר לִבּוֹ׃ וְהָיָה כְּעַרְעָר בָּעֲרָבָה וְלֹא יִרְאֶה
כִּי־יָבוֹא טוֹב וְשָׁכַן חֲרֵרִים בַּמִּדְבָּר אֶרֶץ מְלֵחָה וְלֹא
7 תֵשֵׁב׃ בָּרוּךְ הַגֶּבֶר אֲשֶׁר יִבְטַח בַּיהוָה וְהָיָה
8 יְהוָה מִבְטַחוֹ׃ וְהָיָה כְּעֵץ ׀ שָׁתוּל עַל־מַיִם וְעַל־יוּבַל
יְשַׁלַּח שָׁרָשָׁיו וְלֹא יִרְא כִּי־יָבֹא חֹם וְהָיָה עָלֵהוּ רַעֲנָן

2. Like the symbols of their sons are their altars.
And their Asherim are by the leafy trees,
Upon the high hills.
3. O thou that sittest upon the mountain in the field,
I will give thy substance and all thy treasures for a spoil,
And thy high places, because of sin, throughout all thy borders.
4. And thou, even of thyself, shalt discontinue from thy heritage
That I gave thee;
And I will cause thee to serve thine enemies
In the land which thou knowest not;
For ye have kindled a fire in My nostril,
Which shall burn for ever.

5. Thus saith the LORD:
Cursed is the man that trusteth in man,
And maketh flesh his arm,
And whose heart departeth from the LORD.
6. For he shall be like a tamarisk in the desert,
And shall not see when good cometh;
But shall inhabit the parched places in the wilderness,
A salt land and not inhabited.
7. Blessed is the man that trusteth in the LORD,
And whose trust the LORD is.
8. For he shall be as a tree planted by the waters,
And that spreadeth out its roots by the river,
And shall not see when heat cometh,
But its foliage shall be luxuriant;
And shall not be anxious in the year of drought,
Neither shall cease from yielding fruit.

v. 8. יראה קרי

2. *like the symbols of their sons.* Following Ehrlich who sees in these words a reference to the symbols of their immoral rites, symbols that correspond to the wooden poles of Asherah-worship.

Asherim. See Exod. XXXIV, 13. Poles set up near an altar for idol worship, generally for the worship of Astarte.

3. *O thou that sittest upon the mountain in the field.* Jerusalem, which was built on a hill, high above the surrounding plain or field (Rashi).

4. *shalt discontinue from thy heritage.* Shalt cease to retain thy land and be driven forth to foreign soil.

for ever. For a long time (Altschul); a frequent use of the phrase לעולם; cf. p. 305.

5–14. Passages of great beauty—on the Two Paths of life; the mystery and intricacy of the human heart; the fleetingness of ill-gotten gains; and God our Hope and our Physician.

5–8. The Two Paths—an epitome of the Blessings and Warnings of the Sedrah. These verses explain the doom just predicted.

5. *his arm. i.e.* his strength. Relies on flesh and blood with its inherent weakness for his help. Judah was looking to Egypt and Assyria for help in its troubles; hence this utterance (Kimchi).

6. *shall be like a tamarisk.* A small juniper tree, starved and stunted, and deprived of vivifying water, just hanging on to a miserable life. Such are those who rely entirely on human aid.

and shall not see when good cometh. Good, *i.e.* rain; the rain that refreshes other trees shall remain unknown to it.

8. *planted by the waters.* The tree planted by

9. The heart is deceitful above all things,
And it is exceeding weak—who can know it?

10. I the LORD search the heart,
I try the reins,
Even to give every man according to his ways,
According to the fruit of his doings.

11. As the partridge that broodeth over young which she hath not brought forth,
So is he that getteth riches, and not by right;
In the midst of his days he shall leave them,
And at his end he shall be a fool.

12. Thou throne of glory, on high from the beginning,
Thou place of our sanctuary,

13. Thou hope of Israel, the LORD!
All that forsake Thee shall be ashamed;
They that depart from Thee shall be written in the earth,
Because they have forsaken the LORD,
The fountain of living waters.

9 וּבִשְׁנַת בַּצֹּרֶת לֹא יִדְאָג וְלֹא יָמִישׁ מֵעֲשׂוֹת פֶּרִי׃ עָקֹב
· הַלֵּב מִכֹּל וְאָנֻשׁ הוּא מִי יֵדָעֶנּוּ׃ אֲנִי יְהוָה חֹקֵר לֵב בֹּחֵן
11 כְּלָיוֹת וְלָתֵת לְאִישׁ כִּדְרָכָו כִּפְרִי מַעֲלָלָיו׃ קֹרֵא
דָגַר וְלֹא יָלָד עֹשֶׂה עֹשֶׁר וְלֹא בְמִשְׁפָּט בַּחֲצִי יָמָו יַעַזְבֶנּוּ
12 וּבְאַחֲרִיתוֹ יִהְיֶה נָבָל׃ כִּסֵּא כָבוֹד מָרוֹם מֵרִאשׁוֹן מְקוֹם
13 מִקְדָּשֵׁנוּ׃ מִקְוֵה יִשְׂרָאֵל יְהוָה כָּל־עֹזְבֶיךָ יֵבֹשׁוּ יְסוּרַי
בָּאָרֶץ יִכָּתֵבוּ כִּי עָזְבוּ מְקוֹר מַיִם־חַיִּים אֶת־יְהוָה׃
14 רְפָאֵנִי יְהוָה וְאֵרָפֵא הוֹשִׁיעֵנִי וְאִוָּשֵׁעָה כִּי תְהִלָּתִי אָתָּה׃

14. Heal me, O LORD, and I shall be healed;
Save me, and I shall be saved;
For Thou art my praise.

v. 8. קמץ בז״ק v. 10. כדרכיו קרי v. 11. קמץ בז״ק ibid. ימיו קרי v. 13. וסורי קרי

the watercourse shall not perceive or feel the heat—a picture of the undisturbed heart and mind of him whose trust is in the LORD, the Fountain of Living Waters.

not be anxious. Because it is not dependent on rain.

9–10. The mystery of the human heart.

9. *deceitful.* Or, 'intricate.' Perhaps the ideal in the previous verse causes the Prophet to realize that his own heart has not always been true to that ideal. The Prophet recoils in amazement and dread at the sinful possibilities of human nature.

exceeding weak. AV renders 'And desperately wicked'. The Heb. אנש, however, means 'weak'; or, perhaps 'human', from אנוש man: 'the heart is deceitful above all things, and so very human!'

10. *I the LORD.* Answers the question in the preceding verse, 'Who can know it?' (*i.e.* the heart). The intricacies, windings, and subtleties of the human heart are all open to God.

reins. The seat of feeling in Bible psychology.

fruit of his doings. Good intentions are not sufficient. Man is judged by the outcome and unforeseen results of his actions.

11. Ill-gotten gains.

as the partridge . . . forth. It was a popular belief of the day that the partridge took possession of another bird's nest, and that the young which are thus nurtured, afterwards desert their false mother. So does wealth its unlawful possessor.

he shall be a fool. In the moral sense; he will be recognized by all as a 'wicked man', colour-blind in matters of religion and duty. A life of slavery to Mammon is essentially irrational. Some see in this verse a reference to King Jehoiakim; see p. 397.

12–14. God our Hope and our Physician.

12. *Thou throne of glory . . . hope of Israel.* It is an invocation to God. From the vanity of earthly thrones, the Prophet lifts his eyes to Him who is from everlasting.

the place of our sanctuary. These terms are used of God as we use the words 'the Throne', 'the Court', 'the Crown' for the actual ruler.

13. *written in the earth.* Unlike those engraved in some enduring material, they will be blotted out.

14. *heal me.* This petition has been taken over into the daily litany, the Shemoneh Esreh (Authorised Prayer Book, p. 47).

my praise. My boast and my glory.

ADDITIONAL NOTES TO LEVITICUS

A

THE BOOK OF LEVITICUS

Its Antiquity and Mosaic Authorship

Both the antiquity and the Mosaic authorship of the Book of Leviticus are denied by Bible Critics. They declare Leviticus to be part of that section of the Pentateuch which they call the 'Priestly code' and usually designate by the letter P. This 'Priestly code,' or P, is supposed to include, besides Leviticus, some portions of Genesis and Exodus (especially the chapters on the Tabernacle) and twenty-eight chapters of Numbers. They maintain that while some portions of P may be earlier than others, they were all edited, or written, by Ezra and his School and made an integral part of the Law of Moses in the year 444 before the Christian era, or very shortly thereafter.

It must be clearly understood that this idea of a 'Priestly code' and of its late origin is nothing more than pure hypothesis, and there is not a shred of evidence to show that it ever constituted a separate work. In fact, the whole Documentary theory as propounded by Julius Wellhausen and his followers—*i.e.* that the Pentateuch consists of separate 'documents' of different date and authorship—rests on unproved assumptions. It is easy to make any theory look plausible, if the facts are selected or trimmed judiciously; and Bible Critics are most judicious both in selecting the facts and in trimming them to suit their purpose. When the facts are against their theory, the facts are altered or pronounced to be a later gloss in the passage in which they occur, or the Critics declare the whole passage to be sheer forgery. Irreconcilable differences between the 'documents' are created, leading to a complete reversal of Israel's story. And the principal support for such a topsyturvy presentation of Bible history and religion is the alleged existence of these irreconcilable differences between the 'documents'. It is all reasoning in a vicious circle.

Outstanding scholars, like Prof. Sayce, have from the first pronounced the Documentary theory of the Pentateuch to be a 'baseless fabric of subjective imagination'. Others have come to share his view, realizing more and more the insuperable objections to the theory of the late origin of the Levitical legislation. The whole Critical theory is to-day being questioned on fundamental issues. Nevertheless, the popularizers of theological literature ignore altogether the existence of any other opinion than that of the Critics, and they continue to write as if the lateness of Leviticus were indeed one of the 'finalities of scholarship'. That nothing could be further from the truth will be plain to any student who will take the trouble to consult the following books:—

J. Robertson, *The Early Religion of Israel* (William Blackwood)—the first critical investigation of the Wellhausen hypothesis in English;

James Orr, *The Problem of the Old Testament* (James Nisbet)—gives a comprehensive survey of the weaknesses of the Critical position;

W. L. Baxter, *Sanctuary and Sacrifice* (Eyre and Spottiswoode)—demolishes the foundation pillars of Wellhausen's structure;

H. M. Wiener, *Essays in Pentateuchal Criticism* (Elliot Stock)—is a lawyer's examination of the Critical claims; and

D. Hoffmann, *Die Wichtigsten Instanzen gegen die Graf-Wellhausensche Hypothese* (Poppelauer, Berlin)—written over a generation ago, but still unanswered because unanswerable.

I

The Internal Evidence Against the Critical Theory

Leviticus merely continues the story of the departure from Egypt and of the Children of Israel in the Wilderness. The few incidents in Leviticus, as well as its legislation, point to a sojourn in the Desert of the Sinai Peninsula prior to the occupation of Canaan. A verse such as, 'After the doings of the land of Egypt, wherein ye dwelt, shall ye not do; and after the doings of the land of Canaan, whither I bring you, shall ye not do' (xviii, 3), is in itself decisive in favour of the Mosaic date.

In many passages of the Book, the going forth from Egypt and the manifestation of God's protecting power in the release, are spoken of as events of recent occurrence, fresh in the memory of those who had *experienced* the Divine mercy.

Israel is contemplated as living in tents, and the conditions of life which are presupposed are those of a *camp* (see on Lev. xvii, 3). The Sanctuary is depicted as a temporary structure of a portable nature, such as would be required while the people were wandering in the Wilderness. Leviticus assumes the people to be within reach of the religious centre, and in a position to attend the Sanctuary during the pilgrimage Festivals: in Ezra's time, this was impossible, as the bulk of the people was in Babylon, and another portion had drifted back to Egypt. The ritual of *Azazel* on the Day of Atonement is patently archaic, and had to be modified to meet the conditions of later times; see commentary on Lev. xvi, 21, p. 483.

The priests are always denoted as 'Aaron and his sons.' Their initial consecration to the priestly office is described (Lev. viii), to which ceremony 'all the congregation' was summoned (ibid. *v.* 3). This is meaningless on the supposition of the late origin of the Book. Furthermore, P exalts the High Priest. In Ezra's age, the High

Priests were not worthy of honour, and seem to have been among those that attempted to thwart the work of religious reformation.

Similarly, the story of the blasphemer in Leviticus (XXIV, 10–12) is inexplicable on the Critical theory. A son of an Israelitish woman blasphemes, he is put in ward, but no one knows what punishment is to be meted out for that offence. Compare with this the story of Naboth and his judicial murder for alleged blasphemy in I Kings XXI, which chapter the Critics declare to be centuries older than Leviticus. When Jezebel, by means of perjured witnesses, convicts Naboth of that grave offence, there is not the slightest doubt in the mind of the judges and the people—as little as in Jezebel's own mind—what his punishment is to be. Now, if we were to admit that the narrative of the blasphemer was indeed written, or even 'edited', for the benefit of the post-Exilic community, is it reasonable to assume that in those days there would be doubt as to the penalty for blasphemy?

The evidence of the *language* of Leviticus precludes a late date of composition. Reihn, Delitzsch, Dillmann, and Hoffmann have demonstrated that it cannot truthfully be said to show traces of Exilic or post-Exilic times. The technical terms of the sacrificial regulations point to hoary antiquity, and are linguistically derived from ancient Arabic and Minæan (Hommel). There is in Leviticus an entire absence of neo-Babylonian or Persian loan-words that would reflect the age of the Exile. Of course, the language, vocabulary, and style differ considerably from that of the historical parts of the Pentateuch. But this is due to the nature of the subjects treated in Leviticus; *e.g.* sacrifices, leprosy, land laws, as against stories of family life, national history, and moral admonition in the other books. One hundred years ago, Macaulay drafted the Penal Code for India. In that work, his whole manner of writing—vocabulary, sentence-formation, and style—is different from that used by him in his History, Essays, Speeches, or Ballads. Yet, would anyone question Macaulay's authorship of the Indian Code, or would anyone advance the hypothesis of the existence of five separate Macaulays—one each for the History, Essays, Speeches, Ballads, and Code—and living centuries apart from one another?

Bible Critics point to the *Tochacha*, the Admonition in Lev. XXVI, as proof that at any rate that chapter must have been written at a late date, because the punishments foreshadowed in that chapter (*v.* 14–45) were clearly realized in the time of the Babylonian Exile. Those who do not eliminate the Divine from history or from human life, regard the *Tochacha* as belonging to that unique mass of Bible predictions that have been fulfilled to the letter, and that are wholly inexplicable except on the Providential view of human history. But even quite apart from the predictive element in prophecy, there is no reason to doubt the Mosaic authorship of this chapter. Hoffmann has drawn attention to a parallel of the *Tochacha* in the far older code of Hammurabi. One thousand years before Moses, that code concludes with the promise of blessings of the god Shamash for obedience to his law, and with a detailed account of the calamities that would overtake those who are faithless to them. Leviticus XXVI is thus merely another instance of the principle דברה תורה כלשון בני אדם, which the Jewish exegetes of the Middle Ages translated to mean—Scripture chooses those forms of literary expression that would be most effective with the hearers to whom they are addressed.

One more striking circumstance. The Ten Commandments are given on Mt. Sinai, and the promulgation of the other laws takes place in the Wilderness and the plains of Moab. How came they to be attributed to lands *outside* the Holy Land, territories that had no sacred associations for the men of Ezra's age, or for that matter even for the heroes of the Patriarchal age? Surely such a strange, 'inconvenient,' unnatural tradition is not likely to have been *invented*, but is based on fact. And if so, the events associated with that tradition could only have taken place in Mosaic times.

II

Improbability of the Critical Theory

It is evident that if the Critical account of the origin and promulgation of the so-called Priestly code is accepted, it is necessary to attribute deliberate fraud to Ezra. The Critics do not feel this moral difficulty, because the avowed object of many of the Critics has for a long time been to 'deprive Israel of its halo', and to degrade its saints and heroes. But even those who do not recoil from attributing fraud to the sacred writers, should weigh the sheer *improbability* of the introduction of a new code in the manner put forward by the Critical theory.

> 'It is utterly out of the question, that a body of laws, never before heard of, could be imposed upon the people as though they had been given by Moses centuries before; and that they could have been accepted and obeyed by them, notwithstanding the fact that these laws imposed new and serious burdens, set aside established usages to which the people were devotedly attached, and conflicted with the interests of powerful classes of the people' (W. H. Green).

Thus, on the theory of the Critics, tithes of corn, oil, and cattle for the support of the Levitical order had never before been heard of; yet the people submit to the new burdens without dissent. The Book of Nehemiah shows that there was a strongly disaffected party and a religiously faithless party in Jerusalem; yet no one raises a doubt. The Book of Deuteronomy was in the hands of at least the priests; yet even the hostile members of that body do not attempt to ward off the alleged new legislation by appealing to Deuteronomy XIII, 1, 'What thing soever I command you, that shall ye observe to do; *thou shalt not add thereto*, nor diminish from it.' Even the Samaritans—then the bitterest enemies of Ezra and the Jews—are supposed to receive 'Ezra's Torah' as the undoubted work of Moses, and seem to keep on changing and enlarging it, as the followers of Ezra—on the assumption of the Critics—keep on making new additions to it for at least a century after his death!

The improbability of Ezra attempting to pass off his work as the work of Moses, or of his succeeding in such a hypothetical attempt, will be considerably increased, when we realize the lack of agreement between the 'Priestly code' and the conditions that confronted Ezra and his generation. P brings many things that could have been only of archæological interest. Its largest section deals with the portable Sanctuary in the Wilderness; but in Ezra's time, the Tabernacle, the Ark, the Urim and Thummim had long ceased to exist. The tithe-laws as given in P are intended for a large body of Levites and a small number of priests, in the proportion of ten Levites to one priest. But the Books of Ezra and Nehemiah tell us, that in the community under Ezra's spiritual guidance, there were, on the contrary, twelve *priests* to one Levite! And yet Ezra is alleged by the Critics to have spent fourteen years, from 458–444, in the adaptation of the older legal enactments to the conditions of the community in Palestine (Oxford Hexateuch, I, 137).

Even more strange, on the theory of the Critics, is the absence of *all* reference in the 'Priestly code' to the burning religious problems of the returned exiles, such as intermarriage. Ezra is crushed by grief and despair when he realizes the extent of the evil in the new community. 'And when I heard this thing, I rent my garments and my mantle, and plucked off the hair of my head and of my beard, and sat down. . . . I fell upon my knees and spread out my hands unto the LORD my God.' He then set about the work of reformation; he called upon the nobles and people to put away their strange wives. They answer with a loud voice, 'As thou hast said, so must we do'; and they enter upon the covenant, so fateful for the future of Israel and of monotheism. But to all this matter of intermarriage, which was of vital concern to Ezra and his School, there is not the slightest reference in the very legislation, which, we are asked to believe, was produced for the salvaging of the community from the mortal danger of absorption among the heathens. No less than two chapters in the 'Priestly code' (Lev. XVIII and XX) are devoted to the subject of prohibited marriages; but not a word to the question which shook the post-Exilic community to its foundations. Surely an unaccountable omission—if the Critics are right.

There is, furthermore, no provision in P for the singers, porters, Nethinim, and Levites of Ezra's day. 'The musical services of the Temple are as much beyond its line of vision as the worship of the Synagogue.' In view of the minute way in which Leviticus regulated worship for the Mosaic generation, is it conceivable that, if Levicitus were a product of Ezra's age, there would be in it nothing directly bearing on the manner of contemporary worship?

III

THE ARGUMENT FROM SILENCE

A favourite argument against the early date of Leviticus is the so-called argument from silence. It is somewhat as follows: Throughout the period of the Judges and Kings, we find that the precepts of the Book of Leviticus were violated; hence, they could not then have existed. Furthermore, it is alleged that there is no explicit reference to them in the historical books of Judges, Samuel, and Kings—another supposed proof that they could not have been known.

As to the first consideration, even cases of flagrant violation do not disprove the existence of the law as laid down in Leviticus. Neither a Jewish law, nor any other law, necessarily presupposes universal compliance with its terms. All historical experience is against it. It is unnecessary to point to modern laws of incontestable and universally acknowledged existence that are accompanied by open and organized violation. And the same is true of ancient laws, even of those believed to have Divine sanction. Take the prohibition of image-worship in the Ten Commandments. Canon Charles has aptly pointed out that for fifteen centuries the whole of Christendom disregarded it, and half of the Christian Church is still disregarding it. If violation of a law were proof of its non-existence, then the Second Commandment has to this day not yet been given! In fact, the Critics themselves note that the existence and the disregard of a law-book may very well go together. Deuteronomy became known—they hold—in the year 620, during the reign of king Josiah. It was observed during his lifetime; but immediately after his death, it was totally disregarded. The attitude of the Critics is therefore as follows:—non-observance of the Law in the ages after Moses is proof absolute that no such Law was ever promulgated in the days of Moses; but non-observance of the Law after the death of Josiah does not prove the non-existence of the Law in Josiah's time. In other words, 'witnesses are reliable when they testify in favour of the Critics; but their veracity is promptly impeached, if their testimony is on the other side' (Baxter). For departures from statutory law in exceptional circumstances, see p. 371.

And as for the second consideration, viz. the silence of the Historical books, that is an even feebler support for the Critical position. A few examples will illustrate its feebleness. Thus, none of the Prophets speaks of the Ten Commandments, and there are exceeding few references to Sabbath, New Moon, or circumcision outside the Pentateuch; and yet no responsible historian doubts the existence of these institutions in ancient Israel. As for the Day of Atonement, the first clear and unmistakable mention of it after the Pentateuch is in Roman times by Josephus! Furthermore, all Critics admit that the Passover and the Feast of Weeks existed in Israel since the earliest days. The Feast of Weeks, however, is nowhere named in the Historical books of the Bible; and Passover only twice, and then only in connection with exceptional conditions. An examination of the passages in which Passover is alluded to (Josh. v and II Kings XXIII) shows conclusively that, but for these exceptional conditions, viz. that the Festival had for a long time fallen into neglect, there would have been no record of its celebration. Would, in that case, the silence of the Bible have been valid evidence that Passover was unknown until after the Exile? Similarly, wherever the Sabbath is referred to outside the Pentateuch, it is nearly always in passages where the Israelites are rebuked for desecrating the holy day. Had the Sabbath been duly observed by the Israelites, none of the Prophets would have had occasion to mention it. The fact then, that the Day of Atonement is never alluded to in the Historical books is really *evidence in favour of its regular observance.*

Critics dwell on the fact that the Day of Atonement is not mentioned in I Kings VIII, 65, which describes the celebration of the dedication of Solomon's Temple. That celebration lasted a fortnight, during which period the tenth of the seventh month occurred, and there is no record that the festivities were suspended for that day. But neither is there in that chapter any indication that the popular rejoicings were moderated on the Sabbath day. Are we to argue that the Sabbath was unknown? We have here but another instance that, in regard to the feasts and fasts, Scripture does not record what is usual and normal, but only what is unusual and abnormal. This also explains Nehemiah VIII. That chapter describes the unusual events in the seventh month of the year 444, among them the observance of the Feast of Tabernacles on the 15th, 'for since the days of Joshua the son of Nun unto that day had not the children of Israel done so' (*v.* 17). It is silent in regard to the Day of Atonement, because evidently there had been no interruption in its observance, as it is quite unlikely that the priests ever allowed their supreme function in the Temple service on that day to fall into abeyance. The fast described in Nehemiah IX was not a substitute for the Day of Atonement. It was a special fast for special evils. It was a day of prayer and contrition, on which the people confessed the 'iniquities of their fathers' as well as their own. There is not the slightest analogy to the Day of Atonement. It was a fast supplementary to it, called forth by the uniqueness of the circumstances.

What we can deduce from the Biblical data is that past history is repeating itself at the present time. Just as many modern Jews who neglect the Sabbath and Festivals, adhere to Yom Kippur, so in the periods of religious decadence in the past, the Israelites seem to have hallowed the Day of Atonement while ignoring the other Festivals.

IV

'Evolution' in Sacrifice

'Those who advocate revolutionary ideas, either in government, in scholarship, or in religion, must show good cause and their arguments must possess overwhelming force. The proof must be clear, strong, and conclusive, without a shadow of suspicion in its reality or its sufficiency.' None can gainsay the reasonableness of this demand put forward by an impartial judge of the Critical views, nor the lamentable failure of those views to meet this reasonable demand. 'But,' it is said, 'these new views are in line with the principle of Evolution. In ritual, as in everything else, the more developed must be later than the less developed, out of which, on the principle of Evolution, it has gradually grown. As the Priestly code (Leviticus and Numbers) shows the most ramified sacrificial enactments, it must be the latest of all the documents of the Pentateuch.' We are even told that there is a clear evolution from the simple to the complex in sacrifice, a straight line of development from the Prophetic document (JE) to Deuteronomy (D), from Deuteronomy (D) to Ezekiel, and from Ezekiel to the Priestly Code (P).

If there ever was an instance when the saying was true that 'theories are vast soap-bubbles with which the grown-up children of Learning amuse themselves, while the ignorant public stand gazing on and dignify these vagaries by the name of Science', that instance is Evolution in sacrifice. In the first place, the straight line of evolution—JE, D, Ezekiel, and P—turns out to be anything but straight. It is now generally admitted by the Critics that the 'Priestly code'—or at any rate its most important constituent, the Holiness chapters—is far from being the latest of the series. Instead of being the culmination of the chain, it is the *source* of Ezekiel. Ezekiel is saturated with the phraseology of Leviticus XVII–XXVI, and he takes for granted an acquaintance therewith on the part of his Babylonian hearers. But Leviticus is not only older than Ezekiel's half-ideal and half-allegorical vision of the constitution of the New Jerusalem, it is older than Deuteronomy; for the law of leprosy in Lev. XIII is the basis of Deuteronomy XXIV, 8, and Deuteronomy XII presupposes Lev. XVII.

In the second place, the whole idea of evolution *does not apply to a field of human history like the institution of sacrifice.* In the realm of language, for example, it is not true to say that, on the one hand, the more simple the language, the more primitive it is; nor, on the other hand, the more complex it is, the later is its appearance in the life of any ethnic group. Thus, Anglo-Saxon, with its five cases and eight declensions of the noun, is immeasurably more complicated than its direct lineal descendant, modern English; even as Latin is far more complex than Italian. The same holds true in the development of ritual laws. Besides, the statement that Leviticus must be the latest sacrificial legislation, because its ritual laws are the most elaborate, is quite against the evidence of primitive cultures. 'It does not appear that very simple systems of law and observance do belong to very primitive societies, but rather the contrary' (Rawlinson).

The case for 'evolution' in Biblical sacrifice is furthermore based by its advocates on a series of dogmatic assumptions which are not only not borne out by the facts but are in direct contradiction to the facts. Among those unwarranted assumptions are the following: that in ancient Israel *every* slaughter for food was an act of sacrificial worship; that originally there was unlimited freedom of altar-building; that early sacrifices were all joyful feasts, with a total absence of any underlying reference to sin; and that sin and guilt offerings are late inventions, the fruit of the 'monotonous seriousness' of the so-called Priestly code.

Hoffmann, Wiener, and especially Baxter in his masterly *Sanctuary and Sacrifice*, have subjected these assumptions to an annihilating examination and shown their utter falsity.

As to sacrifice and slaughter being absolutely synonymous terms, Wiener refers to Exod. XXI, 37 ('If a man steal an ox, or a sheep, and kill it'), and he asks, Does the Legislator contemplate the *sacrifice* of stolen animals and of places made holy as the result? To ask the question is to reveal the utter absurdity of the Critical contention on this point.

To proceed to the next assumption of the Critics. The statement that there was unrestricted altar-building, and consequent multiplicity of sanctuaries in ancient Israel, rests upon a mistranslation of Exodus XX, 24. בכל המקום does not mean 'in every place', but 'in whatever place' (Graetz). That is, in whatever place God would designate for worship—Shiloh, Gibeon, Jerusalem—an altar might be erected, and sacrificial worship would there be considered legitimate. Such permission of *successive* places of worship, till the building of the Central Sanctuary in Jerusalem, is something quite different from a recognition of *simultaneous* sanctuaries in different places.

The charge that the strict regulations concerning the sacrificial cult killed all the spontaneous joy which characterized ancient Israelite worship, implies a partiality on the part of the Critics for the lawless licence, foul sensuality and unrestrained jollity of the heathen merry-makings—half-sacrifices, half-picnics—that were not infrequent in times of national apostasy. For nothing is further from the truth than to say that the Torah did, or does, kill joy. One commandment alone—that concerning Tabernacles, and found in the so-called Priestly code—would be sufficient to refute this. 'And ye shall take you on the first day the fruit of goodly trees, branches of palm trees, and boughs of thick trees, and willows of the brook: *and ye shall rejoice before the LORD your God seven days*' (Lev. XXIII, 40). The very men whom the Critics would turn into the makers of the 'Priestly code' soothe the people when weeping over their sins on that historic New Year's Day (Nehemiah VIII) with the words: 'This day is holy into the LORD your God; mourn not nor weep. Go your way, eat the fat and drink the sweet, and send portions to the poor: *for the joy of the LORD is your strength.*'

Even more astounding is the statement, in effect, that the sense of sin was unknown in Israel before the days of Ezra! It is sufficient to point to the agonized cry in Micah VI, 6 and 7—

'Wherewith shall I come before the LORD . . .
Shall I give my firstborn for my transgression,
The fruit of my body for the sin of my soul?'

Surely, if the semi-heathen worshipper of whom Micah speaks felt such a sense of guilt, the loyal Israelite did not have to wait for Ezra to invent sin and guilt offerings to ease his soul. And were not penitential psalms written in Babylon some two thousand years before Ezra's date? So far from sin and guilt offerings being of quite late date, they are distinctly mentioned in pre-Exilic times (*e.g.* II Kings XII, 17); and, for that matter, are never mentioned in any post-Exilic Prophet. There is no truth whatsoever in the statements that P assigns 'an enormous importance' to the sin offering, or that peace offerings were in post-Exilic times practically banished. In the most exhaustive sacrificial catalogue in the 'Priestly Code' (Numbers VII), the other sacrifices outnumber sin offerings in the proportion of seventeen to one!

Probably the strangest argument of all for the lateness of P is, that Ezekiel and his circle wrote down from memory the pre-existent Temple usage; for 'so long as the cult lasted, no sacrificial code was needed'. This is contrary both to reason and historical analogy. It is contrary to reason to maintain 'that the laws of sacrificial worship should have first been written down, or even invented, during the Exile in Babylon, when there was no longer any sacrificial worship' (Dillmann). It is also contrary to historical analogy. Written regulations for the existing sacrificial cult existed in Egypt, Babylonia, and Phœnicia.

One concluding consideration. The Critics themselves tell us that sacrifice was of old the natural and universal expression of religious homage; that religion without sacrificial cult was unthinkable throughout antiquity; and they admit that 'heathen sacrificial worship was a constant menace to morals and monotheism' (Wellhausen). If, therefore, there was any Divine choice of Israel at all, is it not of all things the most natural that Israel's manner of Divine Service should be freed from everything foul, cruel, immoral, and idolatrous? (Baxter). But for such regulation at the hand of Moses, banishing everything debasing either to morals or monotheism from what is admitted by all to have been the universal expression of religious homage, his mission would assuredly have failed, and his work would have disappeared.

B

TABLE OF PROHIBITED MARRIAGES

IN FORCE AMONG JEWS TO-DAY

A man may not marry :—

(*a*) His mother, grandmother, and ascendants; the mother of his grandfather; his stepmother, the wife of his paternal grandfather, and of his ascendants; and the wife of his maternal grandfather.

(*b*) His daughter, grand-daughter, great-grand-daughter and her descendants; his daughter-in-law; the wife of his son's son, and descendants; and the wife of his daughter's son.

(*c*) His wife's mother or grandmother; the mother of his father-in-law, and ascendants.

(*d*) His wife's daughter or her grand-daughter, and descendants.

(*e*) His sister, half-sister, his full- or half-brother's wife (divorced or widow; see, however, on Deut. xxv, 5, 9); and the full- or half-sister of his divorced wife in her lifetime.

(*f*) His aunt, and uncle's wife (divorced or widow), whether the uncle be the full- or half-brother of his father or mother.

(*g*) A married woman, unless Get has been given; and his divorced wife after her remarriage (her second husband having died or divorced her).

(*h*) Anyone who is not a member of the Jewish Faith ; the issue of an incestuous union (*mamzereth*); the married woman guilty of adultery with him; and the widow whose husband died childless, until Chalitzah has been performed. A *Kohen* may not marry a divorced woman, a Chalitzah widow, or a proselyte.

[A man may thus marry:—

(*a*) His stepsister, his stepfather's wife (divorced or widow), his [1]niece; and his full- or half-brother's or sister's daughter-in-law.

(*b*) His cousin; his stepson's wife (divorced or widow); and his deceased wife's sister.]

A woman may not marry :—

(*a*) Her father, grandfather, and ascendants; her stepfather; and the husband of her grand-mother, and of her ascendants.

(*b*) Her son, grandson, great-grandson; her son-in-law, and the husband of her grand-daughter and descendants.

(*c*) Her husband's father, or grandfather, and the father of her father-in-law—and ascendants; and the father of her mother-in-law.

(*d*) Her husband's son or grandson, and descendants.

(*e*) Her brother; half-brother; her full- or half-sister's divorced husband in her sister's lifetime; and her husband's brother and her nephew.

(*g*) A married man, unless Get has been given; and her divorced husband after the death or divorce of her second husband.

(*h*) Anyone who is not a member of the Jewish Faith; the issue of an incestuous union (*mamzer*); and the man guilty of adultery with her as a married woman.

[A woman may thus marry:—

(*a*) Her stepbrother; and her stepmother's former husband.

(*b*) Her cousin; and her deceased sister's husband, whether of a full- or half-sister.

(*c*) Her [1]uncle.]

[1] *In English law a man may marry the daughter of his wife's brother or his wife's sister; but not the daughter of his brother or sister.*

C

THE SACRIFICIAL CULT

I. Sacrifice: Hebrew and Heathen

According to Bible and Talmud, the institution of sacrifice is as old as the human race. The study of primitive man, likewise, traces its origins back to the very beginnings of human society, and declares sacrificial worship to be both an elementary and a universal fact in the history of Religion.

Apart from various unconvincing theories as to the rise of sacrifice, there are two simple explanations as to the fundamental meaning of sacrifice.

The first of these takes sacrifice to be an act of homage and submission to the Heavenly Ruler, or of thankfulness for God's bounties; even as the suppliant expresses his submissiveness and his gratitude to an earthly ruler by gifts. The other declares that sacrifice arose from primitive man's yearning for reconciliation with the Deity. If for some reason the worshipper feared that he had forfeited Divine favour, he sought to propitiate it; and the giving up of things dearest to him—his first-born, his cattle, his possessions—were intended to effect this propitiation.

The existence of animal sacrifice as a virtually universal custom of mankind from times immemorial proves that the expression of religious feeling in this form is an element of man's nature and, therefore, implanted in him by his Creator. To spiritualize this form of worship, free it from cruel practices and unholy associations, and so regulate the sacrificial cult that it makes for a life of righteousness and holiness, was the task of monotheism. In heathen Semitic religions, sacrificial worship was cruel, often requiring human victims. It was foul—licentious rites being an essential element in many kinds of sacrifice. It was immoral—covering crimes and deliberate iniquities against fellowmen. It was irrational—steeped in demonology and magic. In absolute contrast to this degrading heathenism, the Torah banishes everything cruel, foul and unholy from the sacrificial cult. Moreover, the sphere of the efficacy of sacrifice is strictly limited; and, with few specified exceptions (Lev. v, 1, 20–26), sacrifice atones only for sins committed unwittingly, if no human being suffers by them; viz., if restitution precedes the sacrifice. 'A deliberate moral obliquity is not to be obliterated by sacrifice. It must be punished under the penal law or forgiven by repentance, and for the individual there is no other means of atonement' (Montefiore).

Moderns do not always realize the genuine hold that the sacrificial service had upon the affections of the people in ancient Israel. It was for ages the main outward manifestation of religion, as well as the vehicle of supreme spiritual communion. The Central Sanctuary was the axis round which the national life revolved. The Temple was the forum, the fortress, the 'university' and, in the highest sense, the spiritual home of ancient Israel. The people *loved* the Temple, its pomp and ceremony, the music and song of the Levites and the ministrations of the priests, the High Priest as he stood and blessed the prostrate worshippers amid profound silence on the Atonement Day. As for the choicer spirits, their passionate devotion found expression in words like those of the Psalmist:—

'How lovely are thy tabernacles, O Lord of Hosts,
My soul longeth, yea, fainteth for the courts of the Lord. . . .
Blessed are they that dwell in thy house.'

'As the hart panteth after the water brooks,
So panteth my soul after thee, O God.
My soul thirsteth for God, for the living God:
When shall I come and appear before God?'

'O send out thy light and thy truth; let them lead me:
Let them bring me unto thy holy hill,
And to thy tabernacles.
Then will I go unto the altar of God,
Unto God, my exceeding joy.'

Religious ecstasy has rarely found nobler expression than in these lines of the Psalmist; and that words like these reflected the sincere and earnest faith of god-fearing men is beyond question. However, 'bad men also confided in sacrifice as an effective means of placating God, just as a gift might serve to corrupt a judge. This confidence in the efficacy of sacrifice involved an immoral idea of God and Religion. Against it, therefore, the Prophets direct their attack' (Moore).

II. Do the Prophets oppose Sacrifice?

Widespread misunderstanding exists in regard to the attitude of the Prophets to the sacrificial cult, which attitude is often represented as an uncompromisingly hostile one. This is far from being the case.

The Prophets do not seek to alter or abolish the externals of religion as such. They are not so unreasonable as to demand that men should worship without aid of any outward symbolism. What they protested against was the fatal tendency to make these outward symbols the whole of religion; the superstitious *over-estimate* of sacrifice as compared with justice, pity and purity; and especially the monstrous wickedness with which the offering of sacrifices was often accompanied.

Thus, Amos denounces the people for their oppressions and impurities, warning them that as long as these are adhered to, the multiplication of sacrifices will not avert God's threatened judgments.

> 'I hate, I despise your feasts, and I will take no delight in your solemn assemblies. Yea, though you offer me your burnt offerings and meal offerings, I will not accept them: neither will I regard the peace offerings of your fat beasts. Take thou away from me the noise of thy songs: for I will not hear the melody of thy viols. But let judgment roll down as waters, and righteousness as an everflowing stream' (v, 21–24).

God would not be the God of Holiness if He did not 'hate' and 'despise' sacrifices, hymns and songs of praise on the part of unholy and dishonourable worshippers. But there is no intimation that sacrifice, prayer and praise will continue to be 'hated', if the worshippers cast away their vile and oppressive deeds. In the same exhortation, he pleads:—

> 'Hate the evil, and love the good, and establish judgment in the gate; it may be that the LORD, the God of Hosts, will be gracious unto the remnant of Joseph' (v, 15).

Isaiah declares that the most elaborate ritual, if unaccompanied by righteous conduct, is both futile and blasphemous. In his opening arraignment of contemporary Israel, he proclaims:—

> 'Ah sinful nation, a people laden with iniquity. . . .
>
> 'To what purpose is the multitude of your sacrifices unto me? saith the LORD: I am full of the burnt offerings of rams, and the fat of fed beasts.
>
> 'When ye come to appear before me, who hath required this at your hand, to trample my courts?
>
> 'Bring no more vain oblations; incense is an abomination unto me; new moon and sabbath, the calling of assemblies—I cannot away with iniquity and the solemn meeting.
>
> 'Your new moons and your appointed feasts my soul hateth; they are a trouble unto me; I am weary to bear them.
>
> 'And when ye spread forth your hands, I will hide mine eyes from you: yea, when ye make many prayers, I will not hear: your hands are full of blood.
>
> 'Put away the evil of your doings from before mine eyes; cease to do evil; learn to do well; seek judgment, relieve the oppressed, judge the fatherless, plead for the widow' (Isa. I, 4, 11–17).

If this is to be taken as an absolute condemnation by Isaiah of all sacrifice, then that absolute condemnation must also include Sabbaths and Festivals; solemn Assemblies, *i.e.*, public gatherings for worship, and the appearing before the LORD in the Temple: for all these are classed by him with 'blood of bullocks' and 'fat of fed beasts'. But, of course, to Isaiah, prayers and Sabbaths and solemn assemblies and Temple were noble and sacred institutions, indispensable to religious life, and it was only their intolerable *abuse* which he condemned. The same thing applies to his view of sacrifices. The Prophet's call is not, Give up your sacrifices, but, Give up your evil-doing.

A fair examination of the above words of Amos, the first of the literary Prophets, and of Isaiah, who utters what is taken to be the most sustained condemnation of sacrifice, bears out the considered opinion that 'there was use, a seemly and beneficial use, of sacrifice, but there was also an abuse, a vile and God-dishonouring abuse. The Prophets made war upon the latter, but it does not follow that they objected to the former' (Baxter).

The Prophets were orators, and made occasional use of hyperbole, in order to drive home upon the conscience of their hearers a vital aspect of truth which those hearers were ignoring. And when they were confronted by the pernicious belief that God desired nothing but sacrifice, and saw sacrifice being held to excuse iniquity, heartlessness and impurity—they gave expression to their burning indignation in the impassioned language of vehement emotion (see on Jeremiah VII, 22, p. 439).

The lesson which the Prophets laboured to impress upon the soul of Israel was nevermore forgotten. It is repeated by the sacred singers to whom we owe the Book of Psalms, 'the hymnbook of the second Temple'; by the Sages, who teach that 'the sacrifice of the wicked is an abomination to the LORD' (Prov. XV, 8), that offerings made of goods wrung by extortion from the poor are like murder (Ecclesiasticus XXXIV, 20); as well as by the Rabbis, who declare that obedience to God and love to men are greater than sacrifice.

III. THE RABBIS AND THE SACRIFICIAL CULT

To the Rabbis, the institution of sacrifice is a mark of the Divine love unto Israel. Its purpose is to bring peace to the world. Nevertheless, the sacrificial cult is not to them of preeminent importance, but is co-ordinated with the knowledge and study of the Torah, with Prayer, and with the performance of good deeds. To the details of the sacrificial requirements they give symbolical meanings, and draw from them deep ethical and spiritual teachings. Thus, the sacrificial ordinances prove that God is with the persecuted. Cattle are chased by lions; goats, by panthers; sheep, by wolves; but God commanded, 'Not them that persecute, but them that are persecuted, offer ye up to Me.' In similar manner, Philo taught that 'the perfection of the victims indicates that the offerers should be irreproachable; that the Israelites should never bring with them to the altar weakness or evil passion in the soul, but should endeavour to make it wholly pure and clean; so that God may not turn away with aversion from the sight of it. The tribunal of God is inaccessible to bribes; it rejects the guilty, though they offer daily 100 oxen, and receives the guiltless though they offer no sacrifices at all. God delights in fireless altars, round which virtues form the choral dance.'

The Rabbis proclaim the cardinal importance, wellnigh the omnipotence, of Repentance in the spiritual life of man. 'Men asked Wisdom, "If a man sin what shall his punishment be?" Wisdom answered, "Evil pursueth the evil-doer." Men then asked Prophecy, the Torah, and God, "If a man sin what shall his punishment be?" Prophecy answered, "The soul that sinneth, it shall die." The Torah answered, "Let him bring a guilt-offering, and his sin shall be forgiven him " God answered, "Let him repent and it shall be forgiven him." ' Henceforth, Repentance becomes the sole condition of all expiation and Divine forgiveness of sins: 'Neither the sin-offering, nor trespass-offering, nor the Day of Atonement is of any avail, unless accompanied by Repentance.' With the cessation of sacrifices, study of the Torah, Prayer and Beneficence definitely take the place of the Temple Service. It is for this reason that the disappearance of the Temple did not in any way cripple Judaism. When the Temple fell, there still remained the Synagogue—with reading and exposition of the Torah, and congregational worship without priest or sacrificial ritual. The Temple was only in Jerusalem, while the Synagogue was in every village, the expression of the Jew's religion day by day and week by week. 'The Temple was the altar, the Synagogue was the hearth, and the sacred fire burned on each of them. With the fall of the Temple, the fire was quenched on the altar, stamped out under the heel of the conqueror; but it still glowed on the hearth. . . . In all their long history, the Jewish people have done scarcely anything more wonderful than to create the Synagogue. No human institution has a longer continuous history, and none has done more for the uplifting of the human race' (Herford).

IV. Jewish Interpretations of Sacrifice

Rabbinical Judaism accepted the law of sacrifices without presuming to find a satisfactory explanation of its details. 'The sacrificial institutions were an integral part of revealed religion, and had the obligation of statutory law. It was of no practical concern to inquire why the divine Lawgiver had ordained thus and not otherwise. It was enough that he had enjoined upon Israel the observance of them' (Moore). Sometimes, the Rabbis resorted to symbolism, though to a far lesser extent than Philo. Their attitude towards sacrifices has remained that of the main body of Jews in all generations, and has found eloquent expression in the writings of Yehudah Hallevi during the Middle Ages, and of S. R. Hirsch and D. Hoffmann in modern times. According to the last-named, sacrifices are symbols of man's gratitude to God and his dependence on Him; of the absolute devotion man owes to God, as well as of man's confidence in Him.

Alongside the symbolic interpretation of sacrifice is the so-called juridical. It is advocated by Ibn Ezra and to some extent by Nachmanides. Its essence is: As a sinner, the offender's life is forfeit to God; but by a gracious provision he is permitted to substitute a faultless victim to which his guilt is, as it were, transferred by the imposition of hands. Many Christian exegetes adopted this interpretation, and built the whole theological foundation of their Church upon it.

Quite otherwise is the rationalist view of sacrifice held by Maimonides and Abarbanel. Maimonides declares that the sacrificial cult was ordained as an accommodation to the conceptions of a primitive people, and for the purpose of weaning them away from the debased religious rites of their idolatrous neighbours. (See on Lev. XVII, 7.) Hence the restriction of the sacrifices to one locality by which means God kept this particular kind of service within bounds. By a circuitous road, Israel was thus to be led slowly and gradually up to a perception of the highest kind of service, which is spiritual. Abarbanel finds support for Maimonides' view in a striking parable of Rabbi Levi recorded in the Midrash. 'A king noticed that his son was wont to eat of the meat of animals that had died of themselves, or that had been torn by beasts. So the king said, "Let him eat constantly at my table, and he will rid himself of that gross habit." So it was with the Israelites who were sunk in Egyptian idolatry, and were wont to offer their sacrifices on the high places to the demons, and punishment used to come upon them. Thereupon the Holy One, blessed be He, said, "Let them at all times offer their sacrifices before Me in the Tabernacle, and they will be weaned from idolatry, and thus be saved." '

Notwithstanding these views, the Rabbis and such thinkers as Maimonides and Abarbanel did not cease to look forward to a restoration of the sacrificial cult in Messianic times. 'Even those laws which have been enacted by human authority remain in force till they are repealed in a regular and legal manner. Whether any of these laws of the Torah will ever be abrogated we do not know, but we are sure that in case of such abrogation taking place, it will be done by a revelation as convincing as that on Mount Sinai. On the other hand, the revival of the sacrificial Service must, likewise, be sanctioned by the divine voice of a prophet' (M. Friedländer).

The Rabbis, however, hoped that with the progress of time, human conduct would advance to higher standards, so that there would no longer be any need for expiatory sacrifices. Only the feeling of gratitude to God would remain. 'In the Messianic era, all offerings will cease, except the thanksgiving offering, which will continue forever' (Midrash).

D

THOU SHALT LOVE THY NEIGHBOUR AS THYSELF

LEVITICUS XIX, 18

The 'Golden Rule' in Judaism. The world at large is unaware of the fact that this comprehensive maxim of morality—the golden rule of human conduct—was first taught by Judaism. No less a thinker than John Stuart Mill expressed his surprise that it came from the Pentateuch. Not only is it Jewish in origin, but, long before the rise of Christianity, Israel's religious teachers quoted Leviticus XIX, 18 either verbally or in paraphrase, as expressing the essence of the moral life. Thus, Ben Sira says, 'Honour thy neighbour as thyself.' In the Testaments of the Twelve Patriarchs we read: 'A man should not do to his neighbour what a man does not desire for himself.' Tobit admonishes his son in the words, 'What is displeasing to thyself, that do not unto any other.' Philo and Josephus have sayings similar to the above. As to the Rabbis, there is the well-known story of Hillel and the heathen scoffer who asked Hillel to condense for him the whole Law in briefest possible form. Hillel's answer is, 'Whatever is hateful unto thee, do it not unto thy fellow: this is the whole Torah; the rest is explanation.' Targum Jonathan adds to its translation of Lev. XIX, 18 a paraphrase in words almost identical with those of Hillel. In the generation after the Destruction of the Temple, Rabbi Akiba declares '"Thou shalt love thy neighbour as thyself" is a fundamental rule in the Torah.' His contemporary Ben Azzai agrees that this law of love is such a fundamental rule, provided it is read in conjunction with Gen. V, 1 ('This is the book of the generations of man. In the day that God created man, in the likeness of God made He him'); for this latter verse teaches reverence for the Divine image in man, and proclaims the vital truth of the unity of mankind, and the consequent doctrine of the brotherhood of man. All men are created in the Divine image, says Ben Azzai; and, therefore, all are our fellowmen and entitled to human love.

And the command of Lev. XIX, 18 applies to classes and nations as well as to individuals. The Prophets in their day, on the one hand, arraigned the rich for their oppression of the poor; and, on the other hand, pilloried the nations that were guilty of inhumanity and breach of faith towards one another. Their sublime conception of international morality has found wonderful expression in the words of Judah the Pious, a medieval Jewish mystic, who said: 'On the Judgment Day, the Holy One, blessed be He, will call the nations to account for every violation of the command "Thou shalt love thy neighbour as thyself" of which they have been guilty in their dealings with one another.'

Modernist Depreciation of Lev. XIX, *18, 34.* Though the Founder of Christianity quotes 'Thou shalt love thy neighbour as thyself' as the old Biblical command of recognized central importance, many Christian theologians maintain that the Heb. word for 'neighbour' (*rea*) in this verse, refers only to the fellow-Israelite. Its morality therefore is only tribal. But the translation of the Heb. word *rea* by 'fellow-Israelite' is incorrect. One need not be a Hebrew scholar to convince oneself of the fact that *rea* means neighbour of whatever race or creed. Thus in Exodus XI, 2—'Let them ask every man of his neighbour and every woman of her neighbour, jewels of silver, etc.'—the Heb. word for *neighbour* cannot possibly mean 'fellow-Israelite', but distinctly refers to the Egyptians. As in all the moral precepts of Scripture, the word *neighbour* in Lev. XIX, 18, is equivalent to 'fellowman', and it includes in its range every human being by virtue of his humanity.

In order to prevent any possible misunderstanding, the command of love of neighbour is in *v.* 34 of this same nineteenth chapter of Leviticus extended to include the homeless alien.

> 'The stranger (*ger*) that sojourneth with you shall be unto you as the homeborn among you, and thou shalt love him as thyself; for ye were strangers (*gerim*) in the land of Egypt.'

But even this marvellous law, that is absolutely without parallel in any ancient or modern code of civil law, is cavilled at by modernist theologians and decried as 'narrow'. The Heb. word *ger*, they hold, denotes only an alien who had become a fellow-worshipper of the God of Israel. This is contrary to fact. The Israelites in Egypt are in this very verse spoken of as *gerim:* but they did not as a body adopt the worship of Isis or Apis; they were hated, suspected and enslaved 'strangers'. It is evident, therefore, that Lev. XIX, 34 likewise refers to the friendless and homeless foreigner. He was throughout antiquity the victim of injustice and oppression, as were the Israelites in Egypt; in Israel alone he was not obliged to struggle for recognition as a human being. (See further on love of alien and of enemy, pp. 313 and 316.)

The 'Negative' Golden Rule. There is one other argument that is resorted to in order to prove that the true Golden Rule was first promulgated by Christianity. The greatest stress is laid on the fact that both Tobit and Hillel paraphrase Lev. XIX, 18 in a negative way—'Whatever is hateful unto thee, do it not unto thy fellow.' This is contrasted, and unfavourably so, with the positive paraphrase in the New Testament, 'All things whatsoever ye would that men should do unto you, even so do ye unto them.' It is claimed that the former is only negative morality; and that in its positive restatement alone, as formulated in the Gospels, is the Rule a great imperative of moral enthusiasm.

This argument is now seen to be illusory. 'The delicate difference which has been thought to exist between the negative and positive form is due to modern reflection on the subject, and was quite unapparent to the men of antiquity' (G. Kittel). In the oldest Christian literature the two forms are recorded indiscriminately; and the negative Golden Rule occurs in the Western texts of Acts XV, 20, Romans XIII, 10, the Teaching of the Twelve Apostles, and the Apostolical Constitutions. And positive forms of the Rule have had a place in Judaism. Thus Hillel says, 'Love thy fellow-creatures'; and Eleazar ben Arach, 'Let the honour of thy neighbour be as dear to thee as thine own.' But the mere fact that Lev. XIX, 18 is positive, itself renders all talk of a negative Jewish morality in connection with the Golden Rule fatuous.

It is time that the attempt to rob Judaism of its title to having given the Golden Rule to humanity, as well as the dispute as to the superiority of the positive over the negative form came to an end.

As Thyself. 'Thou shalt love thy neighbour *as thyself.*' Regard for self has its legitimate place in the life of man. Unlimited self-surrender is impossible; and a sound morality takes account of our own interests equally with those of others. In the luminous words of Hillel: 'If I am not for myself, who will be for me? And if I am only for myself, what am I?' The Sifra, the oldest Rabbinic commentary on Leviticus, records the following: 'Two men are in the desert with a little water in possession of one of them. If the one drinks it, he will reach civilization; but if the two of them share it, both will die. Ben Petura said, Let the two of them drink, though both will die. Rabbi Akiba held that, in such a case, your own life has precedence over the life of your fellow-man.' Rabbi Akiba could not agree that two should perish where death demands but one as its toll. And, indeed, if the Torah had meant that a man must love his neighbour to the extent of sacrificing his life for him in all circumstances, it would have said: 'Thou shalt love thy neighbour *more than* thyself.'

There are those, both in ancient and in modern times, who do not agree with Rabbi Akiba, and who deem the view of Ben Petura the more altruistic, the more heroic. Such would have preferred that the words *as thyself* had not occurred in the Golden Rule. Others again preach the annihilation of self, or at any rate its total submergence, as the basic principle of human conduct. New formulations of the whole duty of man have in consequence been proposed by various thinkers. We need examine but one of these formulations—*Live for others.* Were such a rule seriously translated into practice, it would lead to absurdity. For *Live for others* necessarily entails that others live for you. You are to attend to everybody else's concerns, and everybody else is to attend to your concerns—except yourself. A moment's examination of this or any other proposed substitute for 'Thou shalt love thy neighbour as thyself' only brings out the more clearly the fundamental sanity of Judaism.

PENTATEUCH AND HAFTORAHS

ספר

חמשה חומשי תורה
עם הפטרות

נדפס על פי המסורה ומתורגם אַנגלית

עם פירוש קצר

מלאכת סיעת הוגי תורה ובראשם

יוסף צבי הערץ

רב הכולל דמלכות בריטאניה ומדינותיה

כרך שני

במדבר, דברים

THE

PENTATEUCH

AND

HAFTORAHS

HEBREW TEXT, ENGLISH TRANSLATION
AND COMMENTARY

EDITED BY

DR. J. H. HERTZ

CHIEF RABBI OF THE BRITISH EMPIRE

VOLUME II

NUMBERS, DEUTERONOMY

Printed in U. S. A.

TABLE OF CONTENTS

The Book of Numbers

The Book of Deuteronomy

Haftorahs for Special Sabbaths

ספר במדבר

THE BOOK OF NUMBERS

ספר במדבר

THE BOOK OF NUMBERS

NAME. The oldest name for the fourth book of the Pentateuch is חמש הפקודים 'the Fifth of the Musterings'; *i.e.* that one of the five books of Moses which describes the numbering of the Israelites. Later it came to be known by the fourth word in the opening sentence—במדבר *Bemidbar*, 'In the Wilderness'—a name that lends a unity of time and place to the varied happenings and laws in the Book. The current English designation *Numbers* is derived from the Septuagint.

CONTENTS. In contrast with Leviticus which is almost entirely legislative in character, Numbers, like Exodus, combines history and law. The greater portion of the Book is devoted to the vicissitudes of the Israelites in their wanderings after the exodus till, thirty-eight years later, they are about to enter the Holy Land. Numbers is no mere chronicle of the outstanding events during the journey in the wilderness. It interprets these events, and shows forth the faithful watchfulness of God in every distress and danger, as well as the stern severity of the Divine judgments against rebellion and apostasy. In addition to the story of this discipline, it records the laws and ordinances given during that journey; laws relating to the Sanctuary, the camp, and the purification of life; and such civil and political ordinances as would enable the Israelites to fulfil the task God assigned to them among the nations.

DIVISIONS. 1. Chapters I–X, 10 contain the laws and regulations given in the wilderness of Sinai: the first census, the choice of the Levites, the laws concerning the ordeal of jealousy, the Nazirites, the Menorah, and the Supplementary Passover. This section also includes the account of the consecration of the Altar and the Priestly Blessing.

2. Chapters X, 11–XXI cover the thirty-eight years' wanderings till the arrival at Moab. They bring the incidents of Taberah, the 'Graves of Lust', the appointment of the seventy elders, the punishment of Miriam, the mission of the Spies, the rebellion of Korah, the sin of Moses, and the conquest of the Amorite kingdoms. This section contains the command concerning Tzitzis and the ritual of the Red Heifer.

3. Chapters XXII–XXXVI describe the final happenings in Moab—the Testimony of Balaam to Israel's might, the zeal of Phinehas, the appointment of Joshua as the successor of Moses, the Midianite war, and the settlement East of the Jordan. Alongside these events, we have the commands concerning the second census, festival offerings, and vows; the itinerary from Egypt to Jordan; and a group of laws in connection with the impending occupation of Canaan. This section of Numbers forms the transition to Deuteronomy, the Fifth Book of Moses.

1

CHAPTER I

1. And the LORD spoke unto Moses in the wilderness of Sinai, in the tent of meeting, on the first day of the second month, in the second year after they were come out of the land of Egypt, saying: 2. 'Take ye the sum of all the congregation of the children of Israel, by their families, by their fathers' houses, according to the number of names, every male, by their polls; 3. from twenty years old and upward, all that are able to go forth to war in Israel: ye shall number them by their hosts, even thou and Aaron. 4. And with you there shall be a man of every tribe, every one

CAP. I. א

א

א וַיְדַבֵּר יְהוָה אֶל־מֹשֶׁה בְּמִדְבַּר סִינַי בְּאֹהֶל מוֹעֵד בְּאֶחָד
לַחֹדֶשׁ הַשֵּׁנִי בַּשָּׁנָה הַשֵּׁנִית לְצֵאתָם מֵאֶרֶץ מִצְרַיִם
2 לֵאמֹר׃ שְׂאוּ אֶת־רֹאשׁ כָּל־עֲדַת בְּנֵי־יִשְׂרָאֵל לְמִשְׁפְּחֹתָם
3 לְבֵית אֲבֹתָם בְּמִסְפַּר שֵׁמוֹת כָּל־זָכָר לְגֻלְגְּלֹתָם׃ מִבֶּן
עֶשְׂרִים שָׁנָה וָמַעְלָה כָּל־יֹצֵא צָבָא בְּיִשְׂרָאֵל תִּפְקְדוּ אֹתָם
4 לְצִבְאֹתָם אַתָּה וְאַהֲרֹן׃ וְאִתְּכֶם יִהְיוּ אִישׁ אִישׁ לַמַּטֶּה

A. AT SINAI

(CHAPTERS I–X, 10)

I. BEMIDBAR

(CHAPTERS I–IV, 20)

CHAPTER I. MUSTERING THE PEOPLE

One month after the erection of the Tabernacle, Moses is commanded to muster all the men of military age, *i.e.* those twenty years of age and upwards.

The total number of adult males is given in *v.* 46 as 603,550. This number is exactly the same as the number of individuals who paid the poll-tax six months previously—possibly because the census was taken *once only*, and that at the time of the taking of the poll-tax. All that is commanded in the present chapter may only be 'to prepare a classified return of the census already taken, with a view to the proper arrangement of the tribes in camps, as their wanderings were about to begin' (H. Adler).

1. *tent of meeting.* The Tabernacle ('the place where I will meet with you to speak there unto thee'; Exod. XXIX, 42), the Tent of revelation.

2. *take ye.* The plural is used because the command is to be carried out by both Moses and Aaron; see next *v.*

take ye the sum. Heb. שאו את ראש here equivalent to, Prepare a classified return of the census already taken. It is not quite synonymous with פקד, the root used in III, 15, 40, when the command is merely to *number* the first-born or the Levites.

all the congregation. Exclusive of the Levites; see *v.* 47 f.

their families. Their clans—subdivisions of a tribe.

fathers' houses. Their septs, subdivisions of the clan. Both 'family' (משפחה) and 'father's house' (בית אב) have each a wider and a narrower sense.

by their polls. lit. 'skulls'; individual persons, as in the English *poll*-tax or *head*-money.

3. *to go forth to war.* Or, *go forth to service.*

number them by their hosts. As military men: the march towards Canaan was to be that of a disciplined nation and not a rabble of runaway slaves (Luzzatto). The aged, infirm, and maimed were therefore exempted from the numbering, as were those under twenty years of age.

4. *a man of every tribe.* Twelve assessors, the head-man of each tribe, were to assist in the work of numbering.

5. *Elizur.* 'God is my rock.' Of the twenty-four proper names here given, nine contain the Divine name *El*, God; three, the name *Tzur*, Rock—a frequent appellation *for* God; and in three *Shaddai* occurs. Shaddai is usually translated 'Almighty' and derived from a Heb. root 'to overpower'. It has also been derived from the Arabic שדא which means 'to heap benefits', and 'to reconcile persons at enmity with one another'. This idea of beneficence and peace is amply borne out by the passages in Genesis in which *Shaddai* occurs (Gen. XVII, 1; XXVIII, 3; XLIII, 14). The meaning conveyed by them is that of a Friend and Protector, who watches over the Patriarchs, shepherds them and bestows upon them and their descendants great moral and material good. *Shaddai* can therefore be translated 'Dispenser of benefits' (Baron David Gunzburg in *Revue des Etudes Juives*, XLVII).

Shedeur. 'Shaddai is a light.'

ה אִישׁ רֹאשׁ לְבֵית־אֲבֹתָיו הוּא׃ וְאֵלֶּה שְׁמוֹת הָאֲנָשִׁים
6 אֲשֶׁר יַעַמְדוּ אִתְּכֶם לִרְאוּבֵן אֱלִיצוּר בֶּן־שְׁדֵיאוּר׃ לְשִׁמְעוֹן
7 שְׁלֻמִיאֵל בֶּן־צוּרִישַׁדָּי׃ לִיהוּדָה נַחְשׁוֹן בֶּן־עַמִּינָדָב׃
8 9 לְיִשָּׂשכָר נְתַנְאֵל בֶּן־צוּעָר׃ לִזְבוּלֻן אֱלִיאָב בֶּן־חֵלֹן׃
י לִבְנֵי יוֹסֵף לְאֶפְרַיִם אֱלִישָׁמָע בֶּן־עַמִּיהוּד לִמְנַשֶּׁה גַּמְלִיאֵל
11 12 בֶּן־פְּדָהצוּר׃ לְבִנְיָמִן אֲבִידָן בֶּן־גִּדְעֹנִי׃ לְדָן אֲחִיעֶזֶר בֶּן
13 14 עַמִּישַׁדָּי׃ לְאָשֵׁר פַּגְעִיאֵל בֶּן־עָכְרָן׃ לְגָד אֶלְיָסָף בֶּן
טו 16 דְּעוּאֵל׃ לְנַפְתָּלִי אֲחִירַע בֶּן־עֵינָן׃ אֵלֶּה קְרִיאֵי הָעֵדָה
17 נְשִׂיאֵי מַטּוֹת אֲבוֹתָם רָאשֵׁי אַלְפֵי יִשְׂרָאֵל הֵם׃ וַיִּקַּח
מֹשֶׁה וְאַהֲרֹן אֵת הָאֲנָשִׁים הָאֵלֶּה אֲשֶׁר נִקְּבוּ בְּשֵׁמוֹת׃
18 וְאֵת כָּל־הָעֵדָה הִקְהִילוּ בְּאֶחָד לַחֹדֶשׁ הַשֵּׁנִי וַיִּתְיַלְדוּ
עַל־מִשְׁפְּחֹתָם לְבֵית אֲבֹתָם בְּמִסְפַּר שֵׁמוֹת מִבֶּן עֶשְׂרִים
19 שָׁנָה וָמַעְלָה לְגֻלְגְּלֹתָם׃ כַּאֲשֶׁר צִוָּה יְהוָה אֶת־מֹשֶׁה

v. 16. קרואי ק׳

head of his fathers' house. 5. And these are the names of the men that shall stand with you: of Reuben, Elizur the son of Shedeur. 6. Of Simeon, Shelumiel the son of Zurishaddai. 7. Of Judah, Nahshon the son of Amminadab. 8. Of Issachar, Nethanel the son of Zuar. 9. Of Zebulun, Eliab the son of Helon. 10. Of the children of Joseph: of Ephraim, Elishama the son of Ammihud; of Manasseh, Gamaliel the son of Pedahzur. 11. Of Benjamin, Abidan the son of Gideoni. 12. Of Dan, Ahiezer the son of Ammishaddai. 13. Of Asher, Pagiel the son of Ochran. 14. Of Gad, Eliasaph the son of Deuel. 15. Of Naphtali, Ahira the son of Enan.' 16. These were the elect of the congregation, the princes of the tribes of their fathers; they were the heads of the thousands of Israel. 17. And Moses and Aaron took these men that are pointed out by name. 18. And they assembled all the congregation together on the first day of the second month, and they declared their pedigrees after their families, by their fathers' houses, according to the number of names, from twenty years old and upward, by their polls. 19. As the LORD commanded Moses, so did he number them

6. *Shelumiel.* Either, 'at peace with God,' or, 'my friend is God' (Hommel).
Zurishaddai. 'My Rock is Shaddai.'

7. *Nahshon.* 'Serpent.' Animal names are common in all lands; cf. the Germanic names, Wolf, Bear, etc.
Amminadab. 'The (divine) Kinsman is generous.'

8. *Nethanel.* 'God hath given.'

9. *Eliab.* 'God is Father.'

10. *Elishama.* 'God hath heard.'
Ammihud. 'The (divine) Kinsman is glorious.'
Gamaliel. 'God is my reward.' In later times, it was the name of many famous rabbis.
Pedahzur. 'The Rock hath redeemed.'

11. *Abidan.* 'The Father hath judged.'

12. *Ahiezer.* 'The (divine) Brother is a help.'
Ammishaddai. 'The people of Shaddai.'

13. *Pagiel.* 'The lot or fate of (*i.e.* given by) God.'

14. *Eliasaph.* 'God hath added.'
Deuel. Or, 'Reuel' (II, 14). 'God is a friend.' Both forms seem to be an abbreviation of Daruel (Luzzatto).

15. *Ahira.* Shortened form of Ahirea, 'the (divine) Brother is a friend.'

These names are invaluable documents of early life in Israel and throw light on the religious feelings of the ancient Israelite. They are genuine and trustworthy, as they can each be paralleled in Babylonian and Arabian inscriptions. If, as alleged by hostile critics, these names were merely made to pattern and the product of the age of Ezra, they should be met with in the Books of Ezra and Nehemiah. This, however, is not the case; and, in fact, such characteristic names as those compounded with Amm, Zur, and Shaddai are *never* found in post-Exilic times. 'It is quite certain that the names contained in the lists in the Book of Numbers cannot be rightly assigned to any other period than that of Moses' (Hommel).

16. *elect of the congregation.* Summoned as the congregation's representative men.
princes. Chiefs.
the thousands. A 'thousand' denotes a large division of the people for judicial or military purposes (II Sam. XVIII, 1; compare the similar use of the old English word 'hundred').

18. *on the first day.* The classifying of the returns began, but was not necessarily completed, on that one day.
they declared their pedigrees. Investigated the dates of their birth, to ascertain whether they were over twenty years of age; or, their pedigrees were written down (Ibn Ezra).

in the wilderness of Sinai.*ii. ¶ 20. And the
children of Reuben, Israel's first-born,
their generations, by their families, by
their fathers' houses, according to the
number of names, by their polls, every male
from twenty years old and upward, all
that were able to go forth to war; 21.
those that were numbered of them, of the
tribe of Reuben, were forty and six thousand
and five hundred. ¶ 22. Of the children of
Simeon, their generations, by their families,
by their fathers' houses, those that were
numbered thereof, according to the number
of names, by their polls, every male from
twenty years old and upward, all that were
able to go forth to war; 23. those that
were numbered of them, of the tribe of
Simeon, were fifty and nine thousand and
three hundred. ¶ 24. Of the children of Gad,
their generations, by their families, by their
fathers' houses, according to the number
of names, from twenty years old and
upward, all that were able to go forth
to war; 25. those that were numbered
of them, of the tribe of Gad, were forty
and five thousand six hundred and fifty.
¶ 26. Of the children of Judah, their genera-
tions, by their families, by their fathers'
houses, according to the number of names,
from twenty years old and upward, all
that were able to go forth to war; 27.
those that were numbered of them, of the
tribe of Judah, were threescore and fourteen
thousand and six hundred. ¶ 28. Of the
children of Issachar, their generations, by
their families, by their fathers' houses,
according to the number of names, from
twenty years old and upward, all that were
able to go forth to war; 29. those that
were numbered of them, of the tribe of
Issachar, were fifty and four thousand and
four hundred. ¶ 30. Of the children of
Zebulun, their generations, by their
families, by their fathers' houses, according
to the number of names, from twenty years
old and upward, all that were able to go
forth to war; 31. those that were numbered
of them, of the tribe of Zebulun, were fifty
and seven thousand and four hundred.
¶ 32. Of the children of Joseph, namely,
of the children of Ephraim, their genera-
tions, by their families, by their fathers'
houses, according to the number of names,
from twenty years old and upward, all
that were able to go forth to war; 33. those
that were numbered of them, of the tribe
of Ephraim, were forty thousand and five
hundred. ¶ 34. Of the children of Manasseh,
their generations, by their families, by their
fathers' houses, according to the number

שני
כ וַיִּפְקְדֵם בְּמִדְבַּר סִינָי׃ ס וַיִּהְיוּ בְנֵי־רְאוּבֵן בְּכֹר
יִשְׂרָאֵל תּוֹלְדֹתָם לְמִשְׁפְּחֹתָם לְבֵית אֲבֹתָם בְּמִסְפַּר
שֵׁמוֹת לְגֻלְגְּלֹתָם כָּל־זָכָר מִבֶּן עֶשְׂרִים שָׁנָה וָמַעְלָה כֹּל
21 יֹצֵא צָבָא׃ פְּקֻדֵיהֶם לְמַטֵּה רְאוּבֵן שִׁשָּׁה וְאַרְבָּעִים אֶלֶף
וַחֲמֵשׁ מֵאוֹת׃ פ
22 לִבְנֵי שִׁמְעוֹן תּוֹלְדֹתָם לְמִשְׁפְּחֹתָם לְבֵית אֲבֹתָם פְּקֻדָיו
בְּמִסְפַּר שֵׁמוֹת לְגֻלְגְּלֹתָם כָּל־זָכָר מִבֶּן עֶשְׂרִים שָׁנָה
23 וָמַעְלָה כֹּל יֹצֵא צָבָא׃ פְּקֻדֵיהֶם לְמַטֵּה שִׁמְעוֹן תִּשְׁעָה
וַחֲמִשִּׁים אֶלֶף וּשְׁלֹשׁ מֵאוֹת׃ פ
24 לִבְנֵי גָד תּוֹלְדֹתָם לְמִשְׁפְּחֹתָם לְבֵית אֲבֹתָם בְּמִסְפַּר שֵׁמוֹת
כה מִבֶּן עֶשְׂרִים שָׁנָה וָמַעְלָה כֹּל יֹצֵא צָבָא׃ פְּקֻדֵיהֶם לְמַטֵּה
גָד חֲמִשָּׁה וְאַרְבָּעִים אֶלֶף וְשֵׁשׁ מֵאוֹת וַחֲמִשִּׁים׃ פ
26 לִבְנֵי יְהוּדָה תּוֹלְדֹתָם לְמִשְׁפְּחֹתָם לְבֵית אֲבֹתָם בְּמִסְפַּר
27 שֵׁמֹת מִבֶּן עֶשְׂרִים שָׁנָה וָמַעְלָה כֹּל יֹצֵא צָבָא׃ פְּקֻדֵיהֶם
לְמַטֵּה יְהוּדָה אַרְבָּעָה וְשִׁבְעִים אֶלֶף וְשֵׁשׁ מֵאוֹת׃ פ
28 לִבְנֵי יִשָּׂשכָר תּוֹלְדֹתָם לְמִשְׁפְּחֹתָם לְבֵית אֲבֹתָם בְּמִסְפַּר
29 שֵׁמֹת מִבֶּן עֶשְׂרִים שָׁנָה וָמַעְלָה כֹּל יֹצֵא צָבָא׃ פְּקֻדֵיהֶם
לְמַטֵּה יִשָּׂשכָר אַרְבָּעָה וַחֲמִשִּׁים אֶלֶף וְאַרְבַּע מֵאוֹת׃ פ
ל לִבְנֵי זְבוּלֻן תּוֹלְדֹתָם לְמִשְׁפְּחֹתָם לְבֵית אֲבֹתָם בְּמִסְפַּר
31 שֵׁמֹת מִבֶּן עֶשְׂרִים שָׁנָה וָמַעְלָה כֹּל יֹצֵא צָבָא׃ פְּקֻדֵיהֶם
לְמַטֵּה זְבוּלֻן שִׁבְעָה וַחֲמִשִּׁים אֶלֶף וְאַרְבַּע מֵאוֹת׃ פ
32 לִבְנֵי יוֹסֵף לִבְנֵי אֶפְרַיִם תּוֹלְדֹתָם לְמִשְׁפְּחֹתָם לְבֵית
אֲבֹתָם בְּמִסְפַּר שֵׁמֹת מִבֶּן עֶשְׂרִים שָׁנָה וָמַעְלָה כֹּל
33 יֹצֵא צָבָא׃ פְּקֻדֵיהֶם לְמַטֵּה אֶפְרָיִם אַרְבָּעִים אֶלֶף
וַחֲמֵשׁ מֵאוֹת׃ פ

20–46. Details of the Census

20. *generations.* Descendants.

46. *six hundred . . . fifty.* See on III, 43.

of names, from twenty years old and upward, all that were able to go forth to war; 35. those that were numbered of them, of the tribe of Manasseh, were thirty and two thousand and two hundred. ¶ 36. Of the children of Benjamin, their generations, by their families, by their fathers' houses, according to the number of names, from twenty years old and upward, all that were able to go forth to war; 37. those that were numbered of them, of the tribe of Benjamin, were thirty and five thousand and four hundred. ¶ 38. Of the children of Dan, their generations, by their families, by their fathers' houses, according to the number of names, from twenty years old and upward, all that were able to go forth to war; 39. those that were numbered of them, of the tribe of Dan, were threescore and two thousand and seven hundred. ¶ 40. Of the children of Asher, their generations, by their families, by their fathers' houses, according to the number of names, from twenty years old and upward, all that were able to go forth to war; 41. those that were numbered of them, of the tribe of Asher, were forty and one thousand and five hundred. ¶ 42. Of the children of Naphtali, their generations, by their families, by their fathers' houses, according to the number of names, from twenty years old and upward, all that were able to go forth to war; 43. those that were numbered of them, of the tribe of Naphtali, were fifty and three thousand and four hundred. ¶ 44. These are those that were numbered, which Moses and Aaron numbered, and the princes of Israel, being twelve men; they were each one for his fathers' house. 45. And all those that were numbered of the children of Israel by their fathers' houses, from twenty years old and upward, all that were able to go forth to war in Israel; 46. even all those that were numbered were six hundred thousand and three thousand and five hundred and fifty. 47. But the Levites after the tribe of their fathers were not numbered among them. ¶ 48. And the LORD spoke unto Moses, saying: 49. 'Howbeit the tribe of Levi thou shalt not number, neither shalt thou take the sum of them among the children of Israel; 50. but appoint thou the Levites over the tabernacle of the testimony, and over all the furniture thereof, and over all that belongeth to it; they shall bear the

34 לִבְנֵי מְנַשֶּׁה תּוֹלְדֹתָם לְמִשְׁפְּחֹתָם לְבֵית אֲבֹתָם בְּמִסְפַּר
לה שֵׁמוֹת מִבֶּן עֶשְׂרִים שָׁנָה וָמַעְלָה כֹּל יֹצֵא צָבָא׃ פְּקֻדֵיהֶם
לְמַטֵּה מְנַשֶּׁה שְׁנַיִם וּשְׁלֹשִׁים אֶלֶף וּמָאתָיִם׃ פ
36 לִבְנֵי בִנְיָמִן תּוֹלְדֹתָם לְמִשְׁפְּחֹתָם לְבֵית אֲבֹתָם בְּמִסְפַּר
37 שֵׁמֹת מִבֶּן עֶשְׂרִים שָׁנָה וָמַעְלָה כֹּל יֹצֵא צָבָא׃ פְּקֻדֵיהֶם
לְמַטֵּה בִנְיָמִן חֲמִשָּׁה וּשְׁלֹשִׁים אֶלֶף וְאַרְבַּע מֵאוֹת׃ פ
38 לִבְנֵי דָן תּוֹלְדֹתָם לְמִשְׁפְּחֹתָם לְבֵית אֲבֹתָם בְּמִסְפַּר
39 שֵׁמֹת מִבֶּן עֶשְׂרִים שָׁנָה וָמַעְלָה כֹּל יֹצֵא צָבָא׃ פְּקֻדֵיהֶם
לְמַטֵּה דָן שְׁנַיִם וְשִׁשִּׁים אֶלֶף וּשְׁבַע מֵאוֹת׃ פ
מ לִבְנֵי אָשֵׁר תּוֹלְדֹתָם לְמִשְׁפְּחֹתָם לְבֵית אֲבֹתָם בְּמִסְפַּר
41 שֵׁמֹת מִבֶּן עֶשְׂרִים שָׁנָה וָמַעְלָה כֹּל יֹצֵא צָבָא׃ פְּקֻדֵיהֶם
לְמַטֵּה אָשֵׁר אֶחָד וְאַרְבָּעִים אֶלֶף וַחֲמֵשׁ מֵאוֹת׃ פ
42 בְּנֵי נַפְתָּלִי תּוֹלְדֹתָם לְמִשְׁפְּחֹתָם לְבֵית אֲבֹתָם בְּמִסְפַּר
43 שֵׁמֹת מִבֶּן עֶשְׂרִים שָׁנָה וָמַעְלָה כֹּל יֹצֵא צָבָא׃ פְּקֻדֵיהֶם
לְמַטֵּה נַפְתָּלִי שְׁלֹשָׁה וַחֲמִשִּׁים אֶלֶף וְאַרְבַּע מֵאוֹת׃ פ
44 אֵלֶּה הַפְּקֻדִים אֲשֶׁר פָּקַד מֹשֶׁה וְאַהֲרֹן וּנְשִׂיאֵי יִשְׂרָאֵל
מה שְׁנֵים עָשָׂר אִישׁ אִישׁ־אֶחָד לְבֵית־אֲבֹתָיו הָיוּ׃ וַיִּהְיוּ כָּל־
פְּקוּדֵי בְנֵי־יִשְׂרָאֵל לְבֵית אֲבֹתָם מִבֶּן עֶשְׂרִים שָׁנָה וָמַעְלָה
46 כָּל־יֹצֵא צָבָא בְּיִשְׂרָאֵל׃ וַיִּהְיוּ כָּל־הַפְּקֻדִים שֵׁשׁ־מֵאוֹת
47 אֶלֶף וּשְׁלֹשֶׁת אֲלָפִים וַחֲמֵשׁ מֵאוֹת וַחֲמִשִּׁים׃ וְהַלְוִיִּם
לְמַטֵּה אֲבֹתָם לֹא הָתְפָּקְדוּ בְּתוֹכָם׃ פ
48 49 וַיְדַבֵּר יְהוָה אֶל־מֹשֶׁה לֵּאמֹר׃ אַךְ אֶת־מַטֵּה לֵוִי לֹא תִפְקֹד
נ וְאֶת־רֹאשָׁם לֹא תִשָּׂא בְּתוֹךְ בְּנֵי יִשְׂרָאֵל׃ וְאַתָּה הַפְקֵד

47–54. The Levites, a summary of their duties and their place in the camp; see further III and IV.

47. *were not numbered.* 'The Levites are the Divine King's Legion, and are hence worthy to enjoy the distinction of a separate census' (Rashi).

50. *tabernacle of the testimony.* A fuller description for the Tabernacle or Dwelling (משכן) in which the 'tablets of the testimony' (Exod. XXXI, 18) were deposited; *i.e.* the two stone tablets of the Decalogue, that were placed inside the Ark, and were a testimony that the Divine Presence dwelt in Israel.

tabernacle, and all the furniture thereof; and they shall minister unto it, and shall encamp round about the tabernacle. 51. And when the tabernacle setteth forward, the Levites shall take it down; and when the tabernacle is to be pitched, the Levites shall set it up; and the common man that draweth nigh shall be put to death. 52. And the children of Israel shall pitch their tents, every man with his own camp, and every man with his own standard, according to their hosts. 53. But the Levites shall pitch round about the tabernacle of the testimony, that there be no wrath upon the congregation of the children of Israel; and the Levites shall keep the charge of the tabernacle of the testimony.' 54. Thus did the children of Israel; according to all that the LORD commanded Moses, so did they.* iii.

אֶת־הַלְוִיִּם עַל־מִשְׁכַּן הָעֵדֻת וְעַל כָּל־כֵּלָיו וְעַל כָּל־אֲשֶׁר־
לוֹ הֵמָּה יִשְׂאוּ אֶת־הַמִּשְׁכָּן וְאֶת־כָּל־כֵּלָיו וְהֵם יְשָׁרְתֻהוּ
51 וְסָבִיב לַמִּשְׁכָּן יַחֲנוּ׃ וּבִנְסֹעַ הַמִּשְׁכָּן יוֹרִידוּ אֹתוֹ הַלְוִיִּם
וּבַחֲנֹת הַמִּשְׁכָּן יָקִימוּ אֹתוֹ הַלְוִיִּם וְהַזָּר הַקָּרֵב יוּמָת׃
52 וְחָנוּ בְּנֵי יִשְׂרָאֵל אִישׁ עַל־מַחֲנֵהוּ וְאִישׁ עַל־דִּגְלוֹ לְצִבְאֹתָם׃
53 וְהַלְוִיִּם יַחֲנוּ סָבִיב לְמִשְׁכַּן הָעֵדֻת וְלֹא־יִהְיֶה קֶצֶף עַל־
עֲדַת בְּנֵי יִשְׂרָאֵל וְשָׁמְרוּ הַלְוִיִּם אֶת־מִשְׁמֶרֶת מִשְׁכַּן
54 הָעֵדוּת׃ וַיַּעֲשׂוּ בְּנֵי יִשְׂרָאֵל כְּכֹל אֲשֶׁר צִוָּה יְהוָה אֶת־
מֹשֶׁה כֵּן עָשׂוּ׃ * פ שלישי

2

CHAPTER II

1. And the LORD spoke unto Moses and unto Aaron, saying: 2. 'The children of Israel shall pitch by their fathers' houses; every man with his own standard, according to the ensigns; a good way off shall they pitch round about the tent of meeting. 3. Now those that pitch on the east side toward the sunrising shall be they of the

CAP. II. ב

ב

א 2 וַיְדַבֵּר יְהוָה אֶל־מֹשֶׁה וְאֶל־אַהֲרֹן לֵאמֹר׃ אִישׁ עַל־דִּגְלוֹ
בְאֹתֹת לְבֵית אֲבֹתָם יַחֲנוּ בְּנֵי יִשְׂרָאֵל מִנֶּגֶד סָבִיב לְאֹהֶל־

51. *common man. i.e.* a layman; here the word means, one who was not a Levite. In III, 10, the same term refers to one who does not belong to the priesthood.

draweth nigh. With the object of concerning himself with the service of the Levites, in connection with the Holy Tent and its furniture.

put to death. 'But not by a human tribunal' (Talmud).

53. *the Levites . . . round about the tabernacle.* Constituting a body-guard, to prevent the non-Levite from coming into contact with the holy vessels.

keep the charge . . . testimony. Perform the duties devolving upon them in connection with the Sanctuary.

CHAPTER II

ARRANGEMENT OF THE CAMP, AND ORDER OF THE MARCH

2. *with his own standard.* Or, *with his own division*. The Heb. *degel* may mean the larger field-sign of every division of three tribes, or the army corps itself. The latter is the meaning attached to the word in the recently discovered Jewish papyri at Elephantine.

ensigns. The smaller banners carried at the head of the different tribes.

According to the Talmud, a pictorial emblem was engraven on the ensign of each tribe. Thus, on that of Judah was depicted a young lion, as a mark of Judah's prowess and in accordance with Jacob's blessing (Gen. XLIX, 9).

round about the tent of meeting. The tribes differed as regards standards and ensigns, but they constituted one people whose common centre was the Tent of meeting.

The whole encampment was in the form of a quadrilateral, lying four-square with the Tabernacle in the centre. This central portion was called in the Talmud, the Camp of the Shechinah.

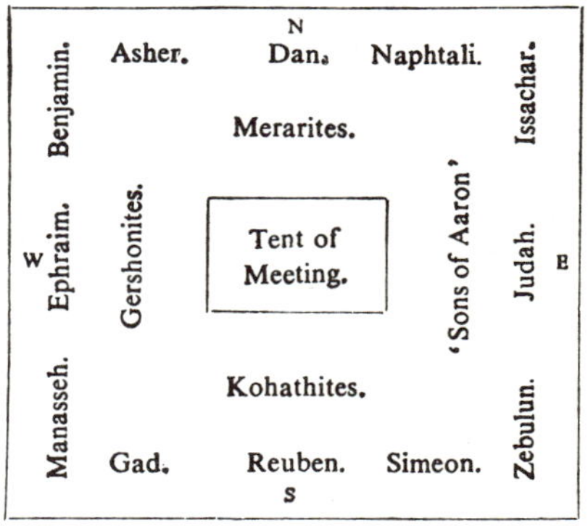

3 מוֹעֵד יַחֲנוּ׃ וְהַחֹנִים קֵדְמָה מִזְרָחָה דֶּגֶל מַחֲנֵה יְהוּדָה
4 לְצִבְאֹתָם וְנָשִׂיא לִבְנֵי יְהוּדָה נַחְשׁוֹן בֶּן־עַמִּינָדָב׃ וּצְבָאוֹ
ה וּפְקֻדֵיהֶם אַרְבָּעָה וְשִׁבְעִים אֶלֶף וְשֵׁשׁ מֵאוֹת׃ וְהַחֹנִים
עָלָיו מַטֵּה יִשָּׂשכָר וְנָשִׂיא לִבְנֵי יִשָּׂשכָר נְתַנְאֵל בֶּן־צוּעָר׃
6 וּצְבָאוֹ וּפְקֻדָיו אַרְבָּעָה וַחֲמִשִּׁים אֶלֶף וְאַרְבַּע מֵאוֹת׃
7 8 מַטֵּה זְבוּלֻן וְנָשִׂיא לִבְנֵי זְבוּלֻן אֱלִיאָב בֶּן־חֵלֹן׃ וּצְבָאוֹ
9 וּפְקֻדָיו שִׁבְעָה וַחֲמִשִּׁים אֶלֶף וְאַרְבַּע מֵאוֹת׃ כָּל־
הַפְּקֻדִים לְמַחֲנֵה יְהוּדָה מְאַת אֶלֶף וּשְׁמֹנִים אֶלֶף וְשֵׁשֶׁת־
י אֲלָפִים וְאַרְבַּע־מֵאוֹת לְצִבְאֹתָם רִאשֹׁנָה יִסָּעוּ׃ ס דֶּגֶל
מַחֲנֵה רְאוּבֵן תֵּימָנָה לְצִבְאֹתָם וְנָשִׂיא לִבְנֵי רְאוּבֵן אֱלִיצוּר
11 בֶּן־שְׁדֵיאוּר׃ וּצְבָאוֹ וּפְקֻדָיו שִׁשָּׁה וְאַרְבָּעִים אֶלֶף וַחֲמֵשׁ
12 מֵאוֹת׃ וְהַחוֹנִם עָלָיו מַטֵּה שִׁמְעוֹן וְנָשִׂיא לִבְנֵי שִׁמְעוֹן
13 שְׁלֻמִיאֵל בֶּן־צוּרִישַׁדָּי׃ וּצְבָאוֹ וּפְקֻדֵיהֶם תִּשְׁעָה וַחֲמִשִּׁים
14 אֶלֶף וּשְׁלֹשׁ מֵאוֹת׃ וּמַטֵּה גָּד וְנָשִׂיא לִבְנֵי גָד אֶלְיָסָף
טו בֶּן־רְעוּאֵל׃ וּצְבָאוֹ וּפְקֻדֵיהֶם חֲמִשָּׁה וְאַרְבָּעִים אֶלֶף
16 וְשֵׁשׁ מֵאוֹת וַחֲמִשִּׁים׃ כָּל־הַפְּקֻדִים לְמַחֲנֵה רְאוּבֵן מְאַת
אֶלֶף וְאֶחָד וַחֲמִשִּׁים אֶלֶף וְאַרְבַּע־מֵאוֹת וַחֲמִשִּׁים לְצִבְאֹתָם
17 וּשְׁנִיִּם יִסָּעוּ׃ ס וְנָסַע אֹהֶל־מוֹעֵד מַחֲנֵה הַלְוִיִּם בְּתוֹךְ
הַמַּחֲנֹת כַּאֲשֶׁר יַחֲנוּ כֵּן יִסָּעוּ אִישׁ עַל־יָדוֹ לְדִגְלֵיהֶם׃ ס
18 דֶּגֶל מַחֲנֵה אֶפְרַיִם לְצִבְאֹתָם יָמָּה וְנָשִׂיא לִבְנֵי אֶפְרָיִם

v. 17. קמץ בז״ק

standard of the camp of Judah, according to their hosts; the prince of the children of Judah being Nahshon the son of Amminadab, 4. and his host, and those that were numbered of them, threescore and fourteen thousand and six hundred; 5. and those that pitch next unto him shall be the tribe of Issachar; the prince of the children of Issachar being Nethanel the son of Zuar, 6. and his host, even those that were numbered thereof, fifty and four thousand and four hundred; 7. and the tribe of Zebulun; the prince of the children of Zebulun being Eliab the son of Helon, 8. and his host, and those that were numbered thereof, fifty and seven thousand and four hundred; 9. all that were numbered of the camp of Judah being a hundred thousand and fourscore thousand and six thousand and four hundred, according to their hosts; they shall set forth first. ¶ 10. On the south side shall be the standard of the camp of Reuben according to their hosts; the prince of the children of Reuben being Elizur the son of Shedeur, 11. and his host, and those that were numbered thereof, forty and six thousand and five hundred; 12. and those that pitch next unto him shall be the tribe of Simeon; the prince of the children of Simeon being Shelumiel the son of Zurishaddai, 13. and his host, and those that were numbered of them, fifty and nine thousand and three hundred, 14. and the tribe of Gad; the prince of the children of Gad being Eliasaph the son of Reuel, 15. and his host, even those that were numbered of them, forty and five thousand and six hundred and fifty; 16. all that were numbered of the camp of Reuben being a hundred thousand and fifty and one thousand and four hundred and fifty, according to their hosts; and they shall set forth second. ¶ 17. Then the tent of meeting, with the camp of the Levites, shall set forward in the midst of the camps; as they encamp, so shall they set forward, every man in his place, by their standards. ¶ 18. On the west side shall

Nearest to it, and surrounding it on all four sides as a protecting cordon, were the camps of the Levitical families. Beyond these and enclosing them was the camp of the Israelites—the tents of the twelve lay tribes, divided into four sections, each of which bore the name of its leading tribe.

9. *all that were numbered of the camp of Judah.* Judah, Issachar, and Zebulun are reckoned under the name of the leading tribe Judah, and similarly the other three divisions are named after Reuben, Ephraim, and Dan.

17. *with the camp of the Levites.* The Levites bearing the Tabernacle with all its parts and accessories are to have their position in the centre of the line of march. The Tabernacle, symbolizing the Divine Presence, should always be 'in the midst of the children of Israel'.

as they encamp, so shall they set forward. The repeated emphasis on discipline is noteworthy. Israel—God's army—however great in numbers, is nothing, unless order and discipline reign in the midst thereof. 'Order is heaven's first law.'

19 אֱלִישָׁמָע בֶּן־עַמִּיהוּד׃ וּצְבָאוֹ וּפְקֻדֵיהֶם אַרְבָּעִים אֶלֶף
כ וַחֲמֵשׁ מֵאוֹת׃ וְעָלָיו מַטֵּה מְנַשֶּׁה וְנָשִׂיא לִבְנֵי מְנַשֶּׁה
21 גַּמְלִיאֵל בֶּן־פְּדָהצוּר׃ וּצְבָאוֹ וּפְקֻדֵיהֶם שְׁנַיִם וּשְׁלֹשִׁים
22 אֶלֶף וּמָאתָיִם׃ וּמַטֵּה בִּנְיָמִן וְנָשִׂיא לִבְנֵי בִנְיָמִן אֲבִידָן
23 בֶּן־גִּדְעֹנִי׃ וּצְבָאוֹ וּפְקֻדֵיהֶם חֲמִשָּׁה וּשְׁלֹשִׁים אֶלֶף וְאַרְבַּע
24 מֵאוֹת׃ כָּל־הַפְּקֻדִים לְמַחֲנֵה אֶפְרַיִם מְאַת אֶלֶף וּשְׁמֹנַת־
כה אֲלָפִים וּמֵאָה לְצִבְאֹתָם וּשְׁלִשִׁים יִסָּעוּ׃ ס דֶּגֶל
מַחֲנֵה דָן צָפֹנָה לְצִבְאֹתָם וְנָשִׂיא לִבְנֵי דָן אֲחִיעֶזֶר בֶּן־
26 עַמִּישַׁדָּי׃ וּצְבָאוֹ וּפְקֻדֵיהֶם שְׁנַיִם וְשִׁשִּׁים אֶלֶף וּשְׁבַע
27 מֵאוֹת׃ וְהַחֹנִים עָלָיו מַטֵּה אָשֵׁר וְנָשִׂיא לִבְנֵי אָשֵׁר
28 פַּגְעִיאֵל בֶּן־עָכְרָן׃ וּצְבָאוֹ וּפְקֻדֵיהֶם אֶחָד וְאַרְבָּעִים אֶלֶף
29 וַחֲמֵשׁ מֵאוֹת׃ וּמַטֵּה נַפְתָּלִי וְנָשִׂיא לִבְנֵי נַפְתָּלִי אֲחִירַע
ל בֶּן־עֵינָן׃ וּצְבָאוֹ וּפְקֻדֵיהֶם שְׁלֹשָׁה וַחֲמִשִּׁים אֶלֶף וְאַרְבַּע
31 מֵאוֹת׃ כָּל־הַפְּקֻדִים לְמַחֲנֵה דָן מְאַת אֶלֶף וְשִׁבְעָה
וַחֲמִשִּׁים אֶלֶף וְשֵׁשׁ מֵאוֹת לָאַחֲרֹנָה יִסְעוּ לְדִגְלֵיהֶם׃ פ
32 אֵלֶּה פְּקוּדֵי בְנֵי־יִשְׂרָאֵל לְבֵית אֲבֹתָם כָּל־פְּקוּדֵי הַמַּחֲנֹת
לְצִבְאֹתָם שֵׁשׁ־מֵאוֹת אֶלֶף וּשְׁלֹשֶׁת אֲלָפִים וַחֲמֵשׁ מֵאוֹת
33 וַחֲמִשִּׁים׃ וְהַלְוִיִּם לֹא הָתְפָּקְדוּ בְּתוֹךְ בְּנֵי יִשְׂרָאֵל כַּאֲשֶׁר
34 צִוָּה יְהוָה אֶת־מֹשֶׁה׃ וַיַּעֲשׂוּ בְּנֵי יִשְׂרָאֵל כְּכֹל אֲשֶׁר־צִוָּה
יְהוָה אֶת־מֹשֶׁה כֵּן־חָנוּ לְדִגְלֵיהֶם וְכֵן נָסָעוּ אִישׁ לְמִשְׁפְּחֹתָיו
עַל־בֵּית אֲבֹתָיו׃ פ רביעי

CAP. III. ג

א וְאֵלֶּה תּוֹלְדֹת אַהֲרֹן וּמֹשֶׁה בְּיוֹם דִּבֶּר יְהוָה אֶת־מֹשֶׁה
2 בְּהַר סִינָי׃ וְאֵלֶּה שְׁמוֹת בְּנֵי־אַהֲרֹן הַבְּכֹר ׀ נָדָב וַאֲבִיהוּא
3 אֶלְעָזָר וְאִיתָמָר׃ אֵלֶּה שְׁמוֹת בְּנֵי אַהֲרֹן הַכֹּהֲנִים

ב' v. 34. קמץ בז״ק

be the standard of the camp of Ephraim according to their hosts; the prince of the children of Ephraim being Elishama the son of Ammihud, 19. and his host, and those that were numbered of them, forty thousand and five hundred; 20. and next unto him shall be the tribe of Manasseh; the prince of the children of Manasseh being Gamaliel the son of Pedahzur, 21. and his host, and those that were numbered of them, thirty and two thousand and two hundred; 22. and the tribe of Benjamin; the prince of the children of Benjamin being Abidan the son of Gideoni, 23. and his host, and those that were numbered of them, thirty and five thousand and four hundred; 24. all that were numbered of the camp of Ephraim being a hundred thousand and eight thousand and a hundred, according to their hosts; and they shall set forth third. ¶ 25. On the north side shall be the standard of the camp of Dan according to their hosts; the prince of the children of Dan being Ahiezer the son of Ammishaddai, 26. and his host, and those that were numbered of them, threescore and two thousand and seven hundred; 27. and those that pitch next unto him shall be the tribe of Asher; the prince of the children of Asher being Pagiel the son of Ochran, 28. and his host, and those that were numbered of them, forty and one thousand and five hundred; 29. and the tribe of Naphtali; the prince of the children of Naphtali being Ahira the son of Enan, 30. and his host, and those that were numbered of them, fifty and three thousand and four hundred; 31. all that were numbered of the camp of Dan being a hundred thousand and fifty and seven thousand and six hundred; they shall set forth hindmost by their standards.' ¶ 32. These are they that were numbered of the children of Israel by their fathers' houses; all that were numbered of the camps according to their hosts were six hundred thousand and three thousand and five hundred and fifty. 33. But the Levites were not numbered among the children of Israel; as the LORD commanded Moses. 34. This did the children of Israel: according to all that the LORD commanded Moses, so they pitched by their standards, and so they set forward, each one according to its families, and according to its fathers' houses.*iv.

CHAPTER III

1. Now these are the generations of Aaron and Moses in the day that the LORD spoke

CHAPTER III
THE LEVITES AND THEIR DUTIES

1. *generations.* As no descendants of Moses are named, 'generations' is here equivalent to happenings; *i.e.* the chapter relates what happened to Aaron and his sons at the hand of Moses, who

4 הַמְּשֻׁחִים אֲשֶׁר־מִלֵּא יָדָם לְכַהֵן׃ וַיָּמָת נָדָב וַאֲבִיהוּא
לִפְנֵי יְהוָה בְּהַקְרִבָם אֵשׁ זָרָה לִפְנֵי יְהוָה בְּמִדְבַּר סִינַי
וּבָנִים לֹא־הָיוּ לָהֶם וַיְכַהֵן אֶלְעָזָר וְאִיתָמָר עַל־פְּנֵי אַהֲרֹן
אֲבִיהֶם׃ פ
5 6 וַיְדַבֵּר יְהוָה אֶל־מֹשֶׁה לֵּאמֹר׃ הַקְרֵב אֶת־מַטֵּה לֵוִי
7 וְהַעֲמַדְתָּ אֹתוֹ לִפְנֵי אַהֲרֹן הַכֹּהֵן וְשֵׁרְתוּ אֹתוֹ׃ וְשָׁמְרוּ
אֶת־מִשְׁמַרְתּוֹ וְאֶת־מִשְׁמֶרֶת כָּל־הָעֵדָה לִפְנֵי אֹהֶל מוֹעֵד
8 לַעֲבֹד אֶת־עֲבֹדַת הַמִּשְׁכָּן׃ וְשָׁמְרוּ אֶת־כָּל־כְּלֵי אֹהֶל
מוֹעֵד וְאֶת־מִשְׁמֶרֶת בְּנֵי יִשְׂרָאֵל לַעֲבֹד אֶת־עֲבֹדַת הַמִּשְׁכָּן׃
9 וְנָתַתָּה אֶת־הַלְוִיִּם לְאַהֲרֹן וּלְבָנָיו נְתוּנִם נְתוּנִם הֵמָּה
10 לוֹ מֵאֵת בְּנֵי יִשְׂרָאֵל׃ וְאֶת־אַהֲרֹן וְאֶת־בָּנָיו תִּפְקֹד וְשָׁמְרוּ
אֶת־כְּהֻנָּתָם וְהַזָּר הַקָּרֵב יוּמָת׃ פ
11 12 וַיְדַבֵּר יְהוָה אֶל־מֹשֶׁה לֵּאמֹר׃ וַאֲנִי הִנֵּה לָקַחְתִּי אֶת־
הַלְוִיִּם מִתּוֹךְ בְּנֵי יִשְׂרָאֵל תַּחַת כָּל־בְּכוֹר פֶּטֶר רֶחֶם מִבְּנֵי
13 יִשְׂרָאֵל וְהָיוּ לִי הַלְוִיִּם׃ כִּי לִי כָּל־בְּכוֹר בְּיוֹם הַכֹּתִי כָל־
בְּכוֹר בְּאֶרֶץ מִצְרַיִם הִקְדַּשְׁתִּי לִי כָל־בְּכוֹר בְּיִשְׂרָאֵל
מֵאָדָם עַד־בְּהֵמָה לִי יִהְיוּ אֲנִי יְהוָה׃ פ חמישי

with Moses in mount Sinai. 2. And these are the names of the sons of Aaron: Nadab the first-born, and Abihu, Eleazar, and Ithamar. 3. These are the names of the sons of Aaron, the priests that were anointed, whom he consecrated to minister in the priest's office. 4. And Nadab and Abihu died before the LORD, when they offered strange fire before the LORD, in the wilderness of Sinai, and they had no children; and Eleazar and Ithamar ministered in the priest's office in the presence of Aaron their father. ¶ 5. And the LORD spoke unto Moses, saying: 6. 'Bring the tribe of Levi near, and set them before Aaron the priest, that they may minister unto him. 7. And they shall keep his charge, and the charge of the whole congregation before the tent of meeting, to do the service of the tabernacle. 8. And they shall keep all the furniture of the tent of meeting, and the charge of the children of Israel, to do the service of the tabernacle. 9. And thou shalt give the Levites unto Aaron and to his sons; they are wholly given unto him from the children of Israel. 10. And thou shalt appoint Aaron and his sons, that they may keep their priesthood; and the common man that draweth nigh shall be put to death.' ¶ 11. And the LORD spoke unto Moses, saying: 12. 'And I, behold, I have taken the Levites from among the children of Israel instead of every first-born that openeth the womb among the children of Israel; and the Levites shall be Mine; 13. for all the first-born are Mine: on the day that I smote all the first-born in the land of Egypt I hallowed unto Me all the first-born in Israel, both man and beast, Mine they shall be: I am the LORD.' *v.

appoints the Levites ministers unto them (Ehrlich).

in the day that the LORD spoke. 'When the LORD spoke.'

4. *offered strange fire.* See Lev. x, 1–7.

in the presence of Aaron. In his lifetime.

7. *keep his charge.* Do the bidding of Aaron and all the priests in the performance of their duties.

of the whole congregation. They are the messengers or agents representing the laity of Israel at the service of the Sanctuary.

9. *wholly given.* lit. 'given, given'; the repetition is emphatic, and expresses complete surrender.

from the children of Israel. i.e. from amongst the children of Israel. God had decreed that the Levites should be thus separated and distinguished from the main body of Israelites.

10. *keep their priesthood.* Not neglect the duties which are specifically theirs by falling back upon the Levites as substitutes.

12. *I have taken.* lit. 'I am taking'; cf. Gen. XXIII, 11 and 13.

instead of every first-born. The sacredness of the first-born, and the priestly functions which they are enjoined to perform, date from the time of the slaying of the first-born in the land of Egypt. At the worship of the Golden Calf, the first-born forfeited their special priestly privileges through their participation in that idolatrous worship. The Levites were chosen in their stead, in recognition of their firm and faithful stand at that hour of apostasy.

13. *Mine they shall be.* The Levites.

15. *every male from a month old and upward.* The Levites were numbered in this manner because they were substitutes for the first-born

¶14. And the LORD spoke unto Moses in the wilderness of Sinai, saying: 15. 'Number the children of Levi by their fathers' houses, by their families; every male from a month old and upward shalt thou number them.' 16. And Moses numbered them according to the word of the LORD, as he was commanded. 17. And these were the sons of Levi by their names: Gershon, and Kohath, and Merari. 18. And these are the names of the sons of Gershon by their families: Libni and Shimei. 19. And the sons of Kohath by their families: Amram and Izhar, Hebron and Uzziel. 20. And the sons of Merari by their families: Mahli and Mushi. These are the families of the Levites according to their fathers' houses. ¶ 21. Of Gershon was the family of the Libnites, and the family of the Shimeites; these are the families of the Gershonites. 22. Those that were numbered of them, according to the number of all the males, from a month old and upward, even those that were numbered of them were seven thousand and five hundred. 23. The families of the Gershonites were to pitch behind the tabernacle westward; 24. the prince of the fathers' house of the Gershonites being Eliasaph the son of Lael, 25. and the charge of the sons of Gershon in the tent of meeting the tabernacle, and the Tent, the covering thereof, and the screen for the door of the tent of meeting, 26. and the hangings of the court, and the screen for the door of the court—which is by the tabernacle, and by the altar, round about—and the cords of it, even whatsoever pertaineth to the service thereof. ¶ 27. And of Kohath was the family of the Amramites, and the family of the Izharites, and the family of the Hebronites, and the family of the Uzzielites; these are the families of the Kohathites: 28. according to the number of all the males, from a month old and upward, eight thousand and six hundred, keepers of the charge of the sanctuary. 29. The families of the sons of Kohath were to pitch on the side of the tabernacle southward; 30. the prince of the fathers' house of the families of the Kohathites being Elizaphan the son of Uzziel, 31. and their charge the ark, and the table, and the candlestick, and the altars, and

14 טו וַיְדַבֵּר יְהוָה אֶל־מֹשֶׁה בְּמִדְבַּר סִינַי לֵאמֹר: פְּקֹד אֶת־
בְּנֵי לֵוִי לְבֵית אֲבֹתָם לְמִשְׁפְּחֹתָם כָּל־זָכָר מִבֶּן־חֹדֶשׁ
16 וָמַעְלָה תִּפְקְדֵם: וַיִּפְקֹד אֹתָם מֹשֶׁה עַל־פִּי יְהוָה
17 כַּאֲשֶׁר צֻוָּה: וַיִּהְיוּ־אֵלֶּה בְנֵי־לֵוִי בִּשְׁמֹתָם גֵּרְשׁוֹן וּקְהָת
18 וּמְרָרִי: וְאֵלֶּה שְׁמוֹת בְּנֵי־גֵרְשׁוֹן לְמִשְׁפְּחֹתָם לִבְנִי
19 וְשִׁמְעִי: וּבְנֵי קְהָת לְמִשְׁפְּחֹתָם עַמְרָם וְיִצְהָר חֶבְרוֹן
כ וְעֻזִּיאֵל: וּבְנֵי מְרָרִי לְמִשְׁפְּחֹתָם מַחְלִי וּמוּשִׁי אֵלֶּה הֵם
21 מִשְׁפְּחֹת הַלֵּוִי לְבֵית אֲבֹתָם: לְגֵרְשׁוֹן מִשְׁפַּחַת הַלִּבְנִי
22 וּמִשְׁפַּחַת הַשִּׁמְעִי אֵלֶּה הֵם מִשְׁפְּחֹת הַגֵּרְשֻׁנִּי: פְּקֻדֵיהֶם
בְּמִסְפַּר כָּל־זָכָר מִבֶּן־חֹדֶשׁ וָמָעְלָה פְּקֻדֵיהֶם שִׁבְעַת
23 אֲלָפִים וַחֲמֵשׁ מֵאוֹת: מִשְׁפְּחֹת הַגֵּרְשֻׁנִּי אַחֲרֵי הַמִּשְׁכָּן
24 יַחֲנוּ יָמָּה: וּנְשִׂיא בֵית־אָב לַגֵּרְשֻׁנִּי אֶלְיָסָף בֶּן־לָאֵל:
כה וּמִשְׁמֶרֶת בְּנֵי־גֵרְשׁוֹן בְּאֹהֶל מוֹעֵד הַמִּשְׁכָּן וְהָאֹהֶל מִכְסֵהוּ
26 וּמָסַךְ פֶּתַח אֹהֶל מוֹעֵד: וְקַלְעֵי הֶחָצֵר וְאֶת־מָסַךְ פֶּתַח
הֶחָצֵר אֲשֶׁר עַל־הַמִּשְׁכָּן וְעַל־הַמִּזְבֵּחַ סָבִיב וְאֵת מֵיתָרָיו
27 לְכֹל עֲבֹדָתוֹ: ס וְלִקְהָת מִשְׁפַּחַת הָעַמְרָמִי וּמִשְׁפַּחַת
הַיִּצְהָרִי וּמִשְׁפַּחַת הַחֶבְרֹנִי וּמִשְׁפַּחַת הָעָזִּיאֵלִי אֵלֶּה הֵם
28 מִשְׁפְּחֹת הַקְּהָתִי: בְּמִסְפַּר כָּל־זָכָר מִבֶּן־חֹדֶשׁ וָמָעְלָה
שְׁמֹנַת אֲלָפִים וְשֵׁשׁ מֵאוֹת שֹׁמְרֵי מִשְׁמֶרֶת הַקֹּדֶשׁ:
29 ל מִשְׁפְּחֹת בְּנֵי־קְהָת יַחֲנוּ עַל יֶרֶךְ הַמִּשְׁכָּן תֵּימָנָה: וּנְשִׂיא
31 בֵית־אָב לְמִשְׁפְּחֹת הַקְּהָתִי אֱלִיצָפָן בֶּן־עֻזִּיאֵל: וּמִשְׁמַרְתָּם
הָאָרֹן וְהַשֻּׁלְחָן וְהַמְּנֹרָה וְהַמִּזְבְּחֹת וּכְלֵי הַקֹּדֶשׁ אֲשֶׁר

who, by Divine command, were to be redeemed 'from a month old' (Num. XVIII, 16).

21–26. The Gershonites were to encamp on the western side of the Tabernacle, and were charged with carrying its tapestry.

27–32. The Kohathites encamped to the south of the Tabernacle, and had charge of transporting its holy furniture—the Ark, the Table, the Candlestick, the Altars.

32. *Eleazar the son of Aaron the priest.* Eleaza was himself a Kohathite through his father Aaron and his grandfather Amram; Exod. VI, 18, 20, 23.

the vessels of the sanctuary wherewith the priests minister, and the screen, and all that pertaineth to the service thereof; 32. Eleazar the son of Aaron the priest being prince of the princes of the Levites, and having the oversight of them that keep the charge of the sanctuary. ¶ 33. Of Merari was the family of the Mahlites, and the family of the Mushites; these are the families of Merari. 34. And those that were numbered of them, according to the number of all the males, from a month old and upward, were six thousand and two hundred; 35. the prince of the fathers' house of the families of Merari being Zuriel the son of Abihail; they were to pitch on the side of the tabernacle northward; 36. the appointed charge of the sons of Merari being the boards of the tabernacle, and the bars thereof, and the pillars thereof, and the sockets thereof, and all the instruments thereof, and all that pertaineth to the service thereof; 37. and the pillars of the court round about, and their sockets, and their pins, and their cords. 38. And those that were to pitch before the tabernacle eastward, before the tent of meeting toward the sunrising, were Moses, and Aaron and his sons, keeping the charge of the sanctuary, even the charge for the children of Israel; and the common man that drew nigh was to be put to death. 39. All that were numbered of the Levites, whom Moses and Aaron numbered at the commandment of the LORD, by their families, all the males from a month old and upward, were twenty and two thousand. *vi. ¶ 40. And the LORD said unto Moses: 'Number all the first-born males of the children of Israel from a month old and upward, and take the number of their names. 41. And thou shalt take the Levites for Me, even the LORD, instead of all the first-born among the children of Israel; and the cattle of the Levites instead of all the firstlings among the cattle of the children of Israel.' 42. And Moses numbered, as the LORD commanded him, all the first-born among the children of Israel. 43. And all the first-born males according to the number

32 יְשָׁרְתוּ בָּהֶם וְהַמָּסָךְ וְכֹל עֲבֹדָתוֹ׃ וּנְשִׂיא נְשִׂיאֵי הַלֵּוִי
אֶלְעָזָר בֶּן־אַהֲרֹן הַכֹּהֵן פְּקֻדַּת שֹׁמְרֵי מִשְׁמֶרֶת הַקֹּדֶשׁ׃
33 לִמְרָרִי מִשְׁפַּחַת הַמַּחְלִי וּמִשְׁפַּחַת הַמּוּשִׁי אֵלֶּה הֵם
34 מִשְׁפְּחֹת מְרָרִי׃ וּפְקֻדֵיהֶם בְּמִסְפַּר כָּל־זָכָר מִבֶּן־חֹדֶשׁ
לה וָמָעְלָה שֵׁשֶׁת אֲלָפִים וּמָאתָיִם׃ וּנְשִׂיא בֵית־אָב לְמִשְׁפְּחֹת
מְרָרִי צוּרִיאֵל בֶּן־אֲבִיחָיִל עַל יֶרֶךְ הַמִּשְׁכָּן יַחֲנוּ צָפֹנָה׃
36 וּפְקֻדַּת מִשְׁמֶרֶת בְּנֵי מְרָרִי קַרְשֵׁי הַמִּשְׁכָּן וּבְרִיחָיו
37 וְעַמֻּדָיו וַאֲדָנָיו וְכָל־כֵּלָיו וְכֹל עֲבֹדָתוֹ׃ וְעַמֻּדֵי הֶחָצֵר
38 סָבִיב וְאַדְנֵיהֶם וִיתֵדֹתָם וּמֵיתְרֵיהֶם׃ וְהַחֹנִים לִפְנֵי הַמִּשְׁכָּן
קֵדְמָה לִפְנֵי אֹהֶל־מוֹעֵד ׀ מִזְרָחָה מֹשֶׁה ׀ וְאַהֲרֹן וּבָנָיו
שֹׁמְרִים מִשְׁמֶרֶת הַמִּקְדָּשׁ לְמִשְׁמֶרֶת בְּנֵי יִשְׂרָאֵל וְהַזָּר
39 הַקָּרֵב יוּמָת׃ כָּל־פְּקוּדֵי הַלְוִיִּם אֲשֶׁר פָּקַד מֹשֶׁה וְאַהֲרֹן
עַל־פִּי יְהוָה לְמִשְׁפְּחֹתָם כָּל־זָכָר מִבֶּן־חֹדֶשׁ וָמַעְלָה
ששי מ שְׁנַיִם וְעֶשְׂרִים אָלֶף׃ ס וַיֹּאמֶר יְהוָה אֶל־מֹשֶׁה פְּקֹד
כָּל־בְּכֹר זָכָר לִבְנֵי יִשְׂרָאֵל מִבֶּן־חֹדֶשׁ וָמָעְלָה וְשָׂא אֵת
41 מִסְפַּר שְׁמֹתָם׃ וְלָקַחְתָּ אֶת־הַלְוִיִּם לִי אֲנִי יְהוָה תַּחַת כָּל־
בְּכֹר בִּבְנֵי יִשְׂרָאֵל וְאֵת בֶּהֱמַת הַלְוִיִּם תַּחַת כָּל־בְּכוֹר
42 בְּבֶהֱמַת בְּנֵי יִשְׂרָאֵל׃ וַיִּפְקֹד מֹשֶׁה כַּאֲשֶׁר צִוָּה יְהוָה
43 אֹתוֹ אֶת־כָּל־בְּכוֹר בִּבְנֵי יִשְׂרָאֵל׃ וַיְהִי כָל־בְּכוֹר זָכָר
בְּמִסְפַּר שֵׁמֹת מִבֶּן־חֹדֶשׁ וָמַעְלָה לִפְקֻדֵיהֶם שְׁנַיִם וְעֶשְׂרִים
אֶלֶף שְׁלֹשָׁה וְשִׁבְעִים וּמָאתָיִם׃

v. 39. נקוד על ואהרן

Hence he ranks as the prince of Levi, and is invested with the supervision of all the other overseers.

33–37. The Merarites were to the north of the Sanctuary and were charged with transporting its boards, bolts, pillars, and sockets.

38. *those that were to pitch . . . eastward.* The most honourable place in the camp, and the most convenient for constant and direct access to the Sanctuary.

39. *twenty and two thousand.* This total of 22,000 Levites falls short by 300 of the separate totals of the divisions mentioned in this chapter. The Talmud explains the discrepancy by saying that the Levites were taken and counted instead of the first-born of the Israelites and as a 'redemption' for them. Hence, their own first-born, who amounted to 300, had to be excluded, as being ineligible for the purpose of redeeming other first-born.

40–51. The substitution of the Levites for the first-born.

of names, from a month old and upward, of those that were numbered of them, were twenty and two thousand two hundred and threescore and thirteen. ¶ 44. And the LORD spoke unto Moses, saying: 45. 'Take the Levites instead of all the first-born among the children of Israel, and the cattle of the Levites instead of their cattle; and the Levites shall be Mine, even the LORD's. 46. And as for the redemption of the two hundred and threescore and thirteen of the first-born of the children of Israel, that are over and above the number of the Levites, 47. thou shalt take five shekels apiece by the poll; after the shekel of the sanctuary shalt thou take them—the shekel is twenty gerahs. 48. And thou shalt give the money wherewith they that remain over of them are redeemed unto Aaron and to his sons.' 49. And Moses took the redemption-money from them that were over and above them that were redeemed by the Levites; 50. from the first-born of the children of Israel took he the money: a thousand three hundred and threescore and five shekels, after the shekel of the sanctuary. 51. And Moses gave the redemption-money unto Aaron and to his sons, according to the word of the LORD, as the LORD commanded Moses.*vii.

4

CHAPTER IV

1. And the LORD spoke unto Moses and unto Aaron, saying: 2. 'Take the sum of the sons of Kohath from among the sons

44 וַיְדַבֵּר יְהוָה אֶל־מֹשֶׁה לֵּאמֹר׃ קַח אֶת־הַלְוִיִּם תַּחַת כָּל־
מה
בְּכוֹר בִּבְנֵי יִשְׂרָאֵל וְאֶת־בֶּהֱמַת הַלְוִיִּם תַּחַת בְּהֶמְתָּם
46 וְהָיוּ־לִי הַלְוִיִּם אֲנִי יְהוָה׃ וְאֵת פְּדוּיֵי הַשְּׁלֹשָׁה וְהַשִּׁבְעִים
47 וְהַמָּאתָיִם הָעֹדְפִים עַל־הַלְוִיִּם מִבְּכוֹר בְּנֵי יִשְׂרָאֵל׃ וְלָקַחְתָּ
חֲמֵשֶׁת חֲמֵשֶׁת שְׁקָלִים לַגֻּלְגֹּלֶת בְּשֶׁקֶל הַקֹּדֶשׁ תִּקָּח
48 עֶשְׂרִים גֵּרָה הַשָּׁקֶל׃ וְנָתַתָּה הַכֶּסֶף לְאַהֲרֹן וּלְבָנָיו פְּדוּיֵי
49 הָעֹדְפִים בָּהֶם׃ וַיִּקַּח מֹשֶׁה אֵת כֶּסֶף הַפִּדְיוֹם מֵאֵת
נ הָעֹדְפִים עַל פְּדוּיֵי הַלְוִיִּם׃ מֵאֵת בְּכוֹר בְּנֵי יִשְׂרָאֵל לָקַח
אֶת־הַכָּסֶף חֲמִשָּׁה וְשִׁשִּׁים וּשְׁלֹשׁ מֵאוֹת וָאֶלֶף בְּשֶׁקֶל
51 הַקֹּדֶשׁ׃ וַיִּתֵּן מֹשֶׁה אֶת־כֶּסֶף הַפְּדֻיִם לְאַהֲרֹן וּלְבָנָיו עַל־
פִּי יְהוָה כַּאֲשֶׁר צִוָּה יְהוָה אֶת־מֹשֶׁה׃ פ שביעי

ד

CAP. IV. ד

א 2 וַיְדַבֵּר יְהוָה אֶל־מֹשֶׁה וְאֶל־אַהֲרֹן לֵאמֹר׃ נָשֹׂא אֶת־רֹאשׁ
3 בְּנֵי קְהָת מִתּוֹךְ בְּנֵי לֵוִי לְמִשְׁפְּחֹתָם לְבֵית אֲבֹתָם׃ מִבֶּן
שְׁלֹשִׁים שָׁנָה וָמַעְלָה וְעַד בֶּן־חֲמִשִּׁים שָׁנָה כָּל־בָּא לַצָּבָא

ג׳ v. 47. קמץ בז״ק v. 51. חסר ו׳

43. *twenty . . . and thirteen.* The first-born number 273 more than the Levites; and as no substitutes were available for the redemption of this extra 273, they had to be redeemed independently, by a payment of five shekels apiece, as the redemption price of a male child under five years old who has been vowed unto God; Lev. XXVII, 6.

At first sight, the numbers in these chapters present definite difficulties. Six hundred thousand adult males imply a total population of over two millions. How did such a large multitude live on the arid peninsula of Sinai, whose present population is under 10,000? But Scripture nowhere affirms that the Israelites lived for forty years upon the natural produce of the desert, but that they were fed miraculously with manna (Exod. XVI, 4, 35). And unless miracles are prejudged to be impossible, account must be taken of the miraculous provision made for the sustenance of the Israelites till the time that they entered Canaan. Moreover, the resources of the Wilderness must not be judged by present conditions. The word 'Wilderness' does not mean a barren tract, but an uninhabited country which may be very fertile. And traces exist to show that the 'Wilderness' not only could but did support at one time an extensive population. For a powerful presentation of evidence that this whole region had a higher rainfall, and was much more productive, at the time of the Exodus than now, see Huntington's 'The Climate of Ancient Palestine' (*Bulletin of The American Geographical Society*, vol. XL, 1908).

The other objection is that the number of first-born males is given as 22,273—a very small number in proportion to the total number of males. What is meant is the number of first-born males under twenty years of age at the time of the census. The law did not have retrospective force, so as to include all first-born sons throughout the nation who themselves were fathers or grandfathers at the time.

47. *shekel of the sanctuary.* Or, 'the sacred shekel'; as in לשון הקדש 'the Sacred Language'.

CHAPTER IV

NUMBERING OF THE LEVITES QUALIFIED FOR SERVICE AND RULES OF SERVICE

1–20. THE KOHATHITES AND THEIR DUTIES

A second mustering of the Levites for the

4 לַעֲשׂוֹת מְלָאכָה בְּאֹהֶל מוֹעֵד׃ זֹאת עֲבֹדַת בְּנֵי־קְהָת
ה בְּאֹהֶל מוֹעֵד קֹדֶשׁ הַקֳּדָשִׁים׃ וּבָא אַהֲרֹן וּבָנָיו בִּנְסֹעַ
הַמַּחֲנֶה וְהוֹרִדוּ אֵת פָּרֹכֶת הַמָּסָךְ וְכִסּוּ־בָהּ אֵת אֲרֹן
6 הָעֵדֻת׃ וְנָתְנוּ עָלָיו כְּסוּי עוֹר תַּחַשׁ וּפָרְשׂוּ בֶגֶד־כְּלִיל
7 תְּכֵלֶת מִלְמָעְלָה וְשָׂמוּ בַּדָּיו׃ וְעַל ׀ שֻׁלְחַן הַפָּנִים יִפְרְשׂוּ
בֶּגֶד תְּכֵלֶת וְנָתְנוּ עָלָיו אֶת־הַקְּעָרֹת וְאֶת־הַכַּפֹּת וְאֶת־
הַמְּנַקִּיֹּת וְאֵת קְשׂוֹת הַנָּסֶךְ וְלֶחֶם הַתָּמִיד עָלָיו יִהְיֶה׃
8 וּפָרְשׂוּ עֲלֵיהֶם בֶּגֶד תּוֹלַעַת שָׁנִי וְכִסּוּ אֹתוֹ בְּמִכְסֵה עוֹר
9 תָּחַשׁ וְשָׂמוּ אֶת־בַּדָּיו׃ וְלָקְחוּ ׀ בֶּגֶד תְּכֵלֶת וְכִסּוּ אֶת־
מְנֹרַת הַמָּאוֹר וְאֶת־נֵרֹתֶיהָ וְאֶת־מַלְקָחֶיהָ וְאֶת־מַחְתֹּתֶיהָ
· וְאֵת כָּל־כְּלֵי שַׁמְנָהּ אֲשֶׁר יְשָׁרְתוּ־לָהּ בָּהֶם׃ וְנָתְנוּ אֹתָהּ
וְאֶת־כָּל־כֵּלֶיהָ אֶל־מִכְסֵה עוֹר תָּחַשׁ וְנָתְנוּ עַל־הַמּוֹט׃
11 וְעַל ׀ מִזְבַּח הַזָּהָב יִפְרְשׂוּ בֶּגֶד תְּכֵלֶת וְכִסּוּ אֹתוֹ בְּמִכְסֵה
12 עוֹר תָּחַשׁ וְשָׂמוּ אֶת־בַּדָּיו׃ וְלָקְחוּ אֶת־כָּל־כְּלֵי הַשָּׁרֵת
אֲשֶׁר יְשָׁרְתוּ־בָם בַּקֹּדֶשׁ וְנָתְנוּ אֶל־בֶּגֶד תְּכֵלֶת וְכִסּוּ
13 אוֹתָם בְּמִכְסֵה עוֹר תָּחַשׁ וְנָתְנוּ עַל־הַמּוֹט׃ וְדִשְּׁנוּ אֶת־

of Levi, by their families, by their fathers' houses, 3. from thirty years old and upward even until fifty years old, all that enter upon the service, to do work in the tent of meeting. 4. This is the service of the sons of Kohath in the tent of meeting, about the most holy things: 5. when the camp setteth forward, Aaron shall go in, and his sons, and they shall take down the veil of the screen, and cover the ark of the testimony with it; 6. and shall put thereon a covering of sealskin, and shall spread over it a cloth all of blue, and shall set the staves thereof. 7. And upon the table of showbread they shall spread a cloth of blue, and put thereon the dishes, and the pans, and the bowls, and the jars wherewith to pour out; and the continual bread shall remain thereon. 8. And they shall spread upon them a cloth of scarlet, and cover the same with a covering of sealskin, and shall set the staves thereof. 9. And they shall take a cloth of blue, and cover the candlestick of the light, and its lamps, and its tongs, and its snuff-dishes, and all the oil vessels thereof, wherewith they minister unto it. 10. And they shall put it and all the vessels thereof within a covering of sealskin, and shall put it upon a bar. 11. And upon the golden altar they shall spread a cloth of blue, and cover it with a covering of sealskin, and shall set the staves thereof. 12. And they shall take all the vessels of ministry, wherewith they minister in the sanctuary, and put them in a cloth of blue, and cover them with a covering of sealskin, and shall put them on a bar. 13. And they shall take

service to be performed by those who were between the ages of 30 and 50.

2. *the sons of Kohath.* They are given priority because they were of the family of Moses and Aaron.

3. *the service.* lit. 'warfare'; perhaps implying that the Levites formed an organized body appointed for God's work under the command of superior officials, as were the rest of the Israelites who were numbered for war (McNeile).

to do work. In connection with the transport of the sacred objects.

4. *about the most holy things.* The Ark, the Table, the Candlestick, the Altars, the Veil, and 'the vessels of ministry' (*v.* 12).

5. *Aaron shall go in.* To cover up the holy vessels in the ways prescribed. The Kohathites would thus only have to carry the vessels, without actually touching them.

the veil of the screen. The Veil which acts as a screen.

6. *and shall put thereon.* Upon the Ark already covered with the Veil.

all of blue. Emblematic of the blue of the heavens—'the like of the very heaven for clearness'; Exod. XXIV, 10.

the staves thereof. The poles with which the Ark was furnished for the purpose of transport; Exod. XXV, 14.

7. *the table of showbread.* See Exod. XXV, 30.

10. *upon a bar.* As the Candelabrum possessed no staves it could not be carried in the same manner as the Ark and Table were. It was therefore placed with its appurtenances into a bag-like receptacle and this was then slung on a pole.

11. *and upon the golden altar.* The Altar of incense; Exod. XXX, 1.

13. *the ashes from the altar.* According to

away the ashes from the altar, and spread a purple cloth thereon. 14. And they shall put upon it all the vessels thereof, wherewith they minister about it, the fire-pans, the flesh-hooks, and the shovels, and the basins, all the vessels of the altar; and they shall spread upon it a covering of sealskin, and set the staves thereof. 15. And when Aaron and his sons have made an end of covering the holy furniture, and all the holy vessels, as the camp is to set forward—after that, the sons of Kohath shall come to bear them; but they shall not touch the holy things, lest they die. These things are the burden of the sons of Kohath in the tent of meeting. 16. And the charge of Eleazar the son of Aaron the priest shall be the oil for the light, and the sweet incense, and the continual meal-offering, and the anointing oil: he shall have the charge of all the tabernacle, and of all that therein is, whether it be the sanctuary, or the furniture thereof.'*m. ¶ 17. And the LORD spoke unto Moses and unto Aaron, saying: 18. 'Cut ye not off the tribe of the families of the Kohathites from among the Levites; 19. but thus do unto them, that they may live, and not die, when they approach unto the most holy things: Aaron and his sons shall go in, and appoint them every one to his service and to his burden; 20. but they shall not go in to see the holy things as they are being covered, lest they die.'

14 הַמִּזְבֵּחַ וּפָרְשׂוּ עָלָיו בֶּגֶד אַרְגָּמָן׃ וְנָתְנוּ עָלָיו אֶת־כָּל־
כֵּלָיו אֲשֶׁר יְשָׁרְתוּ עָלָיו בָּהֶם אֶת־הַמַּחְתֹּת אֶת־הַמִּזְלָגֹת
וְאֶת־הַיָּעִים וְאֶת־הַמִּזְרָקֹת כֹּל כְּלֵי הַמִּזְבֵּחַ וּפָרְשׂוּ עָלָיו
טו כְּסוּי עוֹר תַּחַשׁ וְשָׂמוּ בַדָּיו׃ וְכִלָּה אַהֲרֹן וּבָנָיו לְכַסֹּת
אֶת־הַקֹּדֶשׁ וְאֶת־כָּל־כְּלֵי הַקֹּדֶשׁ בִּנְסֹעַ הַמַּחֲנֶה וְאַחֲרֵי־כֵן
יָבֹאוּ בְנֵי־קְהָת לָשֵׂאת וְלֹא־יִגְּעוּ אֶל־הַקֹּדֶשׁ וָמֵתוּ אֵלֶּה
16 מַשָּׂא בְנֵי־קְהָת בְּאֹהֶל מוֹעֵד׃ וּפְקֻדַּת אֶלְעָזָר ׀ בֶּן
אַהֲרֹן הַכֹּהֵן שֶׁמֶן הַמָּאוֹר וּקְטֹרֶת הַסַּמִּים וּמִנְחַת הַתָּמִיד
וְשֶׁמֶן הַמִּשְׁחָה פְּקֻדַּת כָּל־הַמִּשְׁכָּן וְכָל־אֲשֶׁר־בּוֹ בְּקֹדֶשׁ
וּבְכֵלָיו׃ פ מפטיר
17 18 וַיְדַבֵּר יְהוָה אֶל־מֹשֶׁה וְאֶל־אַהֲרֹן לֵאמֹר׃ אַל־תַּכְרִיתוּ
19 אֶת־שֵׁבֶט מִשְׁפְּחֹת הַקְּהָתִי מִתּוֹךְ הַלְוִיִּם׃ וְזֹאת ׀ עֲשׂוּ
לָהֶם וְחָיוּ וְלֹא יָמֻתוּ בְּגִשְׁתָּם אֶת־קֹדֶשׁ הַקֳּדָשִׁים אַהֲרֹן
וּבָנָיו יָבֹאוּ וְשָׂמוּ אוֹתָם אִישׁ אִישׁ עַל־עֲבֹדָתוֹ וְאֶל־מַשָּׂאוֹ׃
כ וְלֹא־יָבֹאוּ לִרְאוֹת כְּבַלַּע אֶת־הַקֹּדֶשׁ וָמֵתוּ׃

Lev. VI, 5, 6, the fire on the Altar of sacrifice was never allowed to be extinguished. But in all probability the command concerning the perpetual fire did *not* apply to the period of transit. Rashi says that the heavenly fire which descended on the Altar used to crouch beneath the wrappings like the figure of a lion at the times of the journeyings, and was rendered innocuous by means of an intervening plate of bronze.

16. *the charge of Eleazar.* His was the duty of superintending the distribution for transport of the oil for light, the sweet incense, the continual meal-offering, and the anointing oil.

18. *cut ye not off. i.e.* take care that the Kohathites do not incur death through any negligence or want of consideration on your part.

20. *as they are being covered.* This translation of the Heb. כבלע את הקדש is quite uncertain and unsatisfactory. Better, *as the sanctuary is being taken apart* (Ehrlich). This explains the meaning of בלע to be, to divide, to take to pieces, to destroy; cf. Yoma 5*a*. The lower members of the priesthood are not to be present when the unity of the Sanctuary is being destroyed by being taken apart, as they would lose all reverence for the Sanctuary if they were to witness it.

HOSEA II, 1–22

The opening words of the Haftorah compare the future numbers of the nation to the sand of the sea, and thus connect with the Sedrah which gives the numbers of the Israelites in the wilderness. For the times and message of Hosea, see pp. 118 and 135.

The Parable of a Life's Tragedy

This Haftorah speaks in a strange imagery which is most puzzling to the ordinary reader. However, all difficulties disappear if we bear in mind that, in the opinion of the Rabbis, Hosea's domestic tragedy was ordained, and from the first intended, to make the Prophet realize, through personal suffering, Israel's unfaithfulness to God, and God's unending love of His people. Modern commentators (Ewald, W. R. Smith, Cheyne) similarly read our Haftorah in the light of the tragic experience of the Prophet, recorded in the opening chapter of the Book of Hosea which precedes our Haftorah, and in Chapter III which follows it.

Their interpretation is as follows. A heavy domestic sorrow darkened Hosea's life. He had married a woman called Gomer; and she rendered him deeply unhappy. He found that he had wasted his love on a profligate woman. She fled from the Prophet's house, and sank lower and lower until she became the slave-concubine of another. But Hosea's love was proof even against faithlessness and dishonour. He, the deeply aggrieved husband, buys her back from slavery, and brings her into his house—as a ward, pitied and sheltered, but subjected to a period of probation that shall show whether her better self can be awakened.

It seems that while this tragedy was taking place within his own home, Hosea began to feel as if his own individual experience was symbolic of the story of his nation. There, too, it might be said that a loving husband, as it were, had been deceived and abandoned by a wife—the wife being Israel and the husband God. God had chosen the poor down-trodden Israelites, the slaves of the Egyptians, to be His people; had allied Himself with them in love and faith; had showered His blessings upon them; had given them a national home, and made them a mighty people. And all these mercies Israel requited with blackest ingratitude. Instead of serving Him in purity and righteousness, they adopted the lascivious and cruel worship of the idolatrous Canaanites; and they forsook the true God, the Creator of heaven and earth, for the local godlings, the 'Baalim', of the heathens around them. But it is his *feelings* towards Gomer that led the Prophet to an overwhelming spiritual discovery:—if *he* could love a faithless wife so tenderly and patiently, what must the love of God be towards His people? And if *he* did not despair that love and patience would awaken Gomer's better nature, would not God's everlasting mercies redeem His sinning people and save it from the fate that would otherwise await it? Justice demanded that Israel suffer for his sins; and suffering and exile would inevitably overtake him. But God's dealings with His children were not guided by Justice alone. The suffering and exile, therefore, with which He visits Israel cannot be ends in themselves. The infinite love of God will, by means of this very suffering and exile, purify Israel, lead him to self-knowledge, and bring him back in perfect repentance to God. Israel's kingdom might fall, and all its outward structure totter into ruin; but Israel will live—because of the infinite love of God (Cassuto).

When the similarity between his wife's conduct and that of Israel dawned upon Hosea's mind, he felt that his marriage with the wayward Gomer must have been the will of God; nay, that his impulse to take this woman to wife was 'the *beginning* of God's speaking to him' (Hosea I, 2). He saw that it was God's will that he should come to realize Israel's faithlessness through the faithlessness of his wife; and God's love of Israel, through his own persistent love of Gomer. Hence, when he writes down this parable from his life, he represents it as if God had from the first ordered him to marry a woman who *was* 'light of love', and who *would be* faithless to her bond and her duty, in order by means of this parable to open the eyes of a blind and sinful people to their ingratitude and guilt (Montefiore). There is a perfect parallel to this in the Haftorah for Behar; see pp. 539 and 540.

Hosea tells us that of his unhappy marriage there were three children. When these children came, Hosea, it would appear, had already realized his wife's unworthiness, and the parable had already been borne in upon his soul. Hence, he feels constrained by a Divine command to give to their children symbolical names of terrible significance—names referring to that other wife's history and future, of which his own wife was the symbol and the image. The name of one is Jezreel (see on *v.* 2); of the second, Lo-Ruhammah ('Unpitied')—the dreadful message to his generation that the sin of Israel was too great to be forgiven; and the name of the third, Lo-Ammi, 'Not-my-people.' Israel was no longer God's covenant people.

HAFTORAH BEMIDBAR הפטרת במדבר

HOSEA II, 1–22

CHAPTER II

1. Yet the number of the children of Israel shall be as the sand of the sea, which cannot be measured nor numbered; and it shall come to pass that, instead of that which was said unto them: 'Ye are not My people,' it shall be said unto them: 'Ye are the children of the living God.' 2. And the children of Judah and the children of Israel shall be gathered together, and they shall appoint themselves one head, and shall go up out of the land; for great shall be the day of Jezreel. 3. Say ye unto your brethren: '[1]Ammi'; and to your sisters: '[2]Ruhamah.'

4. Plead with your mother, plead;
For she is not My wife, neither am I her husband;
And let her put away her harlotries from her face,
And her adulteries from between her breasts;

CAP. II. ב

א וְהָיָה מִסְפַּר בְּנֵי־יִשְׂרָאֵל כְּחוֹל הַיָּם אֲשֶׁר לֹא־יִמַּד וְלֹא
יִסָּפֵר וְהָיָה בִּמְקוֹם אֲשֶׁר־יֵאָמֵר לָהֶם לֹא־עַמִּי אַתֶּם
2 יֵאָמֵר לָהֶם בְּנֵי אֵל־חָי׃ וְנִקְבְּצוּ בְּנֵי־יְהוּדָה וּבְנֵי־יִשְׂרָאֵל
יַחְדָּו וְשָׂמוּ לָהֶם רֹאשׁ אֶחָד וְעָלוּ מִן־הָאָרֶץ כִּי גָדוֹל יוֹם
3 4 יִזְרְעֶאל׃ אִמְרוּ לַאֲחֵיכֶם עַמִּי וְלַאֲחוֹתֵיכֶם רֻחָמָה׃ רִיבוּ
בְאִמְּכֶם רִיבוּ כִּי־הִיא לֹא אִשְׁתִּי וְאָנֹכִי לֹא אִישָׁהּ וְתָסֵר

[1] That is, *My people.* [2] That is, *That hath obtained compassion.*

HOSEA II, 1–22

The background that is essential for the understanding of the Haftorah is given on the preceding page.

1–3. ISRAEL'S DESTINY AND GLORIOUS FUTURE

1. *yet the number. Yet, i.e.* in contrast to the severe judgment just pronounced in the names of the three children.

ye are not My people. lit. 'ye are Lo-Ammi.'

2. *gathered together.* By the union of the two divided kingdoms of Israel and of Judah.

one head. A king from the house of David; see III, 5.

out of the land. i.e. of their Exile (Targum and Kimchi).

Jezreel. The name of the Plain stretching from Mt. Carmel across the whole width of Palestine to the Jordan. In the preceding chapter (*v.* 4), *Jezreel* was the name given to the first son of Hosea to recall the massacre by Jehu in that Plain. It is an ominous sound, a knell rung in the ears of the house of Jehu to awaken the sense of guilt and the presentiment of retribution for the blood shed by its founder. But in the restoration now promised, Jezreel receives another and better significance based on its literal meaning: 'God will sow.' He will sow again His scattered people, and great will be that day of Israel's regeneration.

3. *say ye unto your brethren, Ammi.* The baleful names of the children are now reversed. Lo-Ammi becomes Ammi, My people; and Lo-Ruhammah becomes Ruhammah, *i.e.* she who obtains compassion.

4–15. ISRAEL'S DARK PRESENT

4–6. By one of those swift transitions that reflect the conflicting emotions by which his sensitive soul is torn—profound love for his people and anguish at their moral decay and the destruction it was precipitating—Hosea now arraigns Israel under the image of the faithless wife. Bright as is Israel's future, even so dark and despairing is the present. There must be a radical break with idolatries and disloyalties.

4. *plead with your mother.* The 'mother' is collective Israel, and since this is addressed to the Israelites individually, it is equivalent to saying, Plead with one another (Kimchi).

she is not My wife . . . husband. An ancient formula for divorcing a wife (Cassuto). God is casting Israel off, because she deserted Him for Baal-worship.

harlotries. The imagery appropriate to a dissolute woman is continued. The false teachers and corrupt worship of the surrounding nations are meant (Kimchi). Let her put these things away, and in repentance return to God.

ה זְנוּנֶיהָ מִפָּנֶיהָ וְנַאֲפוּפֶיהָ מִבֵּין שָׁדֶיהָ׃ פֶּן־אַפְשִׁיטֶנָּה
עֲרֻמָּה וְהִצַּגְתִּיהָ כְּיוֹם הִוָּלְדָהּ וְשַׂמְתִּיהָ כַמִּדְבָּר וְשַׁתִּהָ
6 כְּאֶרֶץ צִיָּה וַהֲמִתִּיהָ בַּצָּמָא׃ וְאֶת־בָּנֶיהָ לֹא אֲרַחֵם כִּי־
7 בְנֵי זְנוּנִים הֵמָּה׃ כִּי זָנְתָה אִמָּם הֹבִישָׁה הוֹרָתָם כִּי
אָמְרָה אֵלְכָה אַחֲרֵי מְאַהֲבַי נֹתְנֵי לַחְמִי וּמֵימַי צַמְרִי
8 וּפִשְׁתִּי שַׁמְנִי וְשִׁקּוּיָי׃ לָכֵן הִנְנִי־שָׂךְ אֶת־דַּרְכֵּךְ בַּסִּירִים
9 וְגָדַרְתִּי אֶת־גְּדֵרָהּ וּנְתִיבוֹתֶיהָ לֹא תִמְצָא׃ וְרִדְּפָה אֶת־
מְאַהֲבֶיהָ וְלֹא־תַשִּׂיג אֹתָם וּבִקְשָׁתַם וְלֹא תִמְצָא וְאָמְרָה
אֵלְכָה וְאָשׁוּבָה אֶל־אִישִׁי הָרִאשׁוֹן כִּי טוֹב לִי אָז מֵעָתָּה׃
י וְהִיא לֹא יָדְעָה כִּי אָנֹכִי נָתַתִּי לָהּ הַדָּגָן וְהַתִּירוֹשׁ
11 וְהַיִּצְהָר וְכֶסֶף הִרְבֵּיתִי לָהּ וְזָהָב עָשׂוּ לַבָּעַל׃ לָכֵן אָשׁוּב
וְלָקַחְתִּי דְגָנִי בְּעִתּוֹ וְתִירוֹשִׁי בְּמוֹעֲדוֹ וְהִצַּלְתִּי צַמְרִי
12 וּפִשְׁתִּי לְכַסּוֹת אֶת־עֶרְוָתָהּ׃ וְעַתָּה אֲגַלֶּה אֶת־נַבְלֻתָהּ

5\. Lest I strip her naked,
And set her as in the day that she was born,
And make her as a wilderness,
And set her like a dry land,
And slay her with thirst.

6\. And I will not have compassion upon her children;
For they are children of harlotry.

7\. For their mother hath played the harlot,
She that conceived them hath done shamefully;
For she said: 'I will go after my lovers,
That give me my bread and my water,
My wool and my flax, mine oil and my drink.'

8\. Therefore, behold, I will hedge up thy way with thorns,
And I will make a wall against her,
That she shall not find her paths.

9\. And she shall run after her lovers, but she shall not overtake them,
And she shall seek them, but shall not find them;
Then shall she say: 'I will go and return to my first husband;
For then was it better with me than now.'

10\. For she did not know that it was I that gave her
The corn, and the wine, and the oil,
And multiplied unto her silver and gold,
Which they used for Baal.

11\. Therefore will I take back My corn in the time thereof,
And My wine in the season thereof,
And will snatch away My wool and My flax
Given to cover her nakedness.

12\. And now will I uncover her shame in the sight of her lovers,
And none shall deliver her out of My hand.

5. *strip her.* In ancient societies, the woman convicted of faithlessness was stripped naked, and handed over to death. As applied to Israel, the simile means that the nation would be driven from its land and perish in the wilderness of exile.

the day that she was born. As in the beginning of her national history in Egypt, when she was without power or possessions.

6. *I will not have compassion.* Even as the innocent children suffer through their parents' faithlessness, so will the righteous in Israel be engulfed in the general calamity.

7. *hath done shamefully.* Through her worship of the Baalim, and the lascivious rites that accompanied such worship.

8–10. God separates Israel from the idols, so that Israel learns, through tribulation, their helplessness and vanity.

9. *run after her lovers . . . not find them.* Propitiation of the Baalim by supplication and sacrifices will not bring back her lost prosperity.

return to my first husband. i.e. God. Suffering will bring Israel back to Him. They will then realize that the great gifts they enjoyed were God's love tokens (Horton). But not till the Exile did genuine repentance come (Kimchi).

then was it better. When Israel trusted in and obeyed the God of his Fathers.

10. *she did not know.* During the years of apostasy.

they used for Baal. For making or beautifying images of Baal.

11–15. But repentance must be deep and lasting; a moral revolution, not merely an acknowledgment of God, or a desire for His benefits. *Therefore* (*v.* 11) dire punishment must first overtake the nation, and they must be deprived of all the good things they have abused.

11. *in the time thereof.* When the crop should ripen, it shall fail.

12. *her lovers.* The idols she worships.

13 לְעֵינֵי מְאַהֲבֶיהָ וְאִישׁ לֹא־יַצִּילֶנָּה מִיָּדִי׃ וְהִשְׁבַּתִּי כָּל־
14 מְשׂוֹשָׂהּ חַגָּהּ חָדְשָׁהּ וְשַׁבַּתָּהּ וְכֹל מוֹעֲדָהּ׃ וַהֲשִׁמֹּתִי
גַּפְנָהּ וּתְאֵנָתָהּ אֲשֶׁר אָמְרָה אֶתְנָה הֵמָּה לִי אֲשֶׁר נָתְנוּ־
טו לִי מְאַהֲבָי וְשַׂמְתִּים לְיַעַר וַאֲכָלָתַם חַיַּת הַשָּׂדֶה׃ וּפָקַדְתִּי
עָלֶיהָ אֶת־יְמֵי הַבְּעָלִים אֲשֶׁר תַּקְטִיר לָהֶם וַתַּעַד נִזְמָהּ
וְחֶלְיָתָהּ וַתֵּלֶךְ אַחֲרֵי מְאַהֲבֶיהָ וְאֹתִי שָׁכְחָה נְאֻם־יְהוָה׃
16 לָכֵן הִנֵּה אָנֹכִי מְפַתֶּיהָ וְהֹלַכְתִּיהָ הַמִּדְבָּר וְדִבַּרְתִּי עַל־
17 לִבָּהּ׃ וְנָתַתִּי לָהּ אֶת־כְּרָמֶיהָ מִשָּׁם וְאֶת־עֵמֶק עָכוֹר לְפֶתַח
תִּקְוָה וְעָנְתָה שָּׁמָּה כִּימֵי נְעוּרֶיהָ וּכְיוֹם עֲלוֹתָהּ מֵאֶרֶץ־
18 מִצְרָיִם׃ וְהָיָה בַיּוֹם־הַהוּא נְאֻם־יְהוָה תִּקְרְאִי אִישִׁי

13. I will also cause all her mirth to cease,
Her feasts, her new moons, and her sabbaths,
And all her appointed seasons.

14. And I will lay waste her vines and her fig-trees,
Whereof she hath said: 'These are my hire
That my lovers have given me';
And I will make them a forest,
And the beasts of the field shall eat them.

15. And I will visit upon her the days of the Baalim,
Wherein she offered unto them,
And decked herself with her earrings and her jewels,
And went after her lovers,
And forgot Me, saith the LORD.

16. Therefore, behold, I will allure her,
And bring her into the wilderness,
And speak tenderly unto her.

17. And I will give her her vineyards from thence,
And the valley of [1]Achor for a door of hope;
And she shall respond there, as in the days of her youth,
And as in the day when she came up out of the land of Egypt.

18. And it shall be at that day, saith the LORD,
That thou shalt call Me [2]Ishi,
And shalt call Me no more [3]Baali.

[1] That is, *Troubling.* [2] That is, *My husband.* [3] That is, *My master.*

13. *her feasts.* Passover, Pentecost, and Tabernacles; also any private occasion for rejoicing (Kimchi).

appointed seasons. To include New Year and the Day of Atonement.

14. *my lovers have given me.* As a reward for worshipping them.

15. *visit.* Remember for punishment.

the Baalim. The festivals kept in honour of the deities of the heathen Canaanites, or the adaptation of that cult by Jeroboam in the two golden calves he set up. These festivals were bacchanalian in character.

16–17. God's Love of Israel

The bright promise of the Divine undying love now takes the place of threats. Hosea's consciousness of the greatness of the Divine love was such that he never pronounced a doom on his people, but immediately the mercy of God broke in upon him like a new dawn. Israel, the erring wife, has been sent away from the home of her Husband, but not from His heart. The punishments were but God's *wooing* of the misguided spouse so that she seek Him again. He will never entirely repudiate her who gave Him the love of her youth. He will bring her into the wilderness, where they have loved each other; He will console her; she will sing there as she did in the days when she came out of Egypt, and the Valley of Sadness shall become the Door of Hope.

16. *I will allure her.* Entice her to return by the gentle discipline of love.

into the wilderness. Of the Exile, far from the distractions and temptations of the past.

tenderly. lit. 'to her heart.' God would woo His people in their distress.

17. *valley of Achor.* The reference is to Josh. VII, 26. *Achor* means, 'troubling.' The valley in which Achan was punished for his sin that brought down punishment upon Israel on entering the Holy Land, shall become a Door of Hope and shall bring deliverance. The punishment of exile would carry its hidden blessing: it would purge and purify the nation, and prove the door of hope leading to a better national future.

respond. i.e. to God's endearing call as in the days of the first espousals. Perhaps an allusion to the Songs of Moses and Miriam where the same word is used of Miriam's responding refrain to the chant of Moses.

18–22. The Fruits of Repentance

When Israel returns unto God, heathenish

19 וְלֹא־תִקְרְאִי־לִי עוֹד בַּעְלִי׃ וַהֲסִרֹתִי אֶת־שְׁמוֹת הַבְּעָלִים
כ מִפִּיהָ וְלֹא־יִזָּכְרוּ עוֹד בִּשְׁמָם׃ וְכָרַתִּי לָהֶם בְּרִית בַּיּוֹם
הַהוּא עִם־חַיַּת הַשָּׂדֶה וְעִם־עוֹף הַשָּׁמַיִם וְרֶמֶשׂ הָאֲדָמָה
וְקֶשֶׁת וְחֶרֶב וּמִלְחָמָה אֶשְׁבּוֹר מִן־הָאָרֶץ וְהִשְׁכַּבְתִּים
21 לָבֶטַח׃ וְאֵרַשְׂתִּיךְ לִי לְעוֹלָם וְאֵרַשְׂתִּיךְ לִי בְּצֶדֶק
22 וּבְמִשְׁפָּט וּבְחֶסֶד וּבְרַחֲמִים׃ וְאֵרַשְׂתִּיךְ לִי בֶּאֱמוּנָה וְיָדַעַתְּ
אֶת־יְהוָה׃

19. For I will take away the names of the Baalim out of her mouth,
And they shall no more be mentioned by their name.

20. And in that day will I make a covenant for them
With the beasts of the field, and with the fowls of heaven,
And with the creeping things of the ground;
And I will break the bow and the sword and the battle out of the land,
And will make them to lie down safely.

21. And I will betroth thee unto Me for ever;
Yea, I will betroth thee unto Me in righteousness, and in justice,
And in lovingkindness, and in compassion.

22. And I will betroth thee unto Me in faithfulness;
And thou shalt know the LORD.

worship will be done away with; there will be security from the ravages of beast and man; and the second betrothal of Israel unto God, being founded on righteousness and loyal love, will last for ever.

18. *Ishi.* 'My husband,' with the underlying idea of affection and endearment.
no more Baali. Also a term for husband, lit. 'my master'; but the word was debased through its use of heathen gods. Also it has the underlying idea of ownership, and corresponding subservience on the part of the wife. The bond between God and Israel is to be one of enduring love.

20. *will I make a covenant.* A reversal of *v.* 14. An assurance of the security awaiting both land and people under a striking poetical figure of immunity from hostile elements in Nature (cf. Isa. XI, 6–9), and from hostile man whose weapons of warfare would be broken for ever (cf. Isa. II, 4).

21. *I will betroth thee unto Me in righteousness . . . know the LORD.* Betrothal was always accompanied by a gift. God will endow Israel, His bride, with righteousness, lovingkindness, and faithfulness—that she had lost. The bride's gift will be 'knowledge of God'—recognition that God is a God of righteousness, lovingkindness and faithfulness, and that in these things He delights. Such a betrothal is everlasting.

4 21. And the LORD spoke unto Moses, saying: 22. 'Take the sum of the sons of Gershon also, by their fathers' houses, by their families; 23. from thirty years old and upward until fifty years old shalt thou number them: all that enter in to wait upon the service, to do service in the tent of meeting. 24. This is the service of the families of the Gershonites, in serving and in bearing burdens: 25. they shall bear the curtains of the tabernacle, and the tent of meeting, its covering, and the covering of sealskin that is above upon it, and the screen for the door of the tent of meeting; 26. and the hangings of the court, and the screen for the door of the gate of the court, which is by the tabernacle and by the altar round about, and their cords, and all the instruments of their service, and whatsoever there may be to do with them, therein shall they serve. 27. At the commandment of Aaron and his sons shall be all the service of the sons of the Gershonites, in all their burden, and in all their service; and ye shall appoint unto them in charge all their burden. 28. This is the service of the families of the sons of the Gershonites in the tent of meeting; and their charge shall be under the hand of Ithamar the son of Aaron the priest. ¶ 29. As for the sons of Merari, thou shalt number them by their families, by their fathers' houses; 30. from thirty years old and upward even unto fifty years old shalt thou number them, every one that entereth upon the service, to do the work of the tent of meeting. 31. And this is the charge of their burden, according to all their service in the tent of meeting: the boards of the tabernacle, and the bars thereof, and the

ד פ פ פ לה 35

21 22 וַיְדַבֵּר יְהוָה אֶל־מֹשֶׁה לֵּאמֹר׃ נָשֹׂא אֶת־רֹאשׁ בְּנֵי גֵרְשׁוֹן
23 גַּם־הֵם לְבֵית אֲבֹתָם לְמִשְׁפְּחֹתָם׃ מִבֶּן שְׁלֹשִׁים שָׁנָה
וָמַעְלָה עַד בֶּן־חֲמִשִּׁים שָׁנָה תִּפְקֹד אוֹתָם כָּל־הַבָּא לִצְבֹא
24 צָבָא לַעֲבֹד עֲבֹדָה בְּאֹהֶל מוֹעֵד׃ זֹאת עֲבֹדַת מִשְׁפְּחֹת
כה הַגֵּרְשֻׁנִּי לַעֲבֹד וּלְמַשָּׂא׃ וְנָשְׂאוּ אֶת־יְרִיעֹת הַמִּשְׁכָּן וְאֶת־
אֹהֶל מוֹעֵד מִכְסֵהוּ וּמִכְסֵה הַתַּחַשׁ אֲשֶׁר־עָלָיו מִלְמָעְלָה
26 וְאֶת־מָסַךְ פֶּתַח אֹהֶל מוֹעֵד׃ וְאֵת קַלְעֵי הֶחָצֵר וְאֶת־מָסַךְ ׀
פֶּתַח ׀ שַׁעַר הֶחָצֵר אֲשֶׁר עַל־הַמִּשְׁכָּן וְעַל־הַמִּזְבֵּחַ סָבִיב
וְאֵת מֵיתְרֵיהֶם וְאֶת־כָּל־כְּלֵי עֲבֹדָתָם וְאֵת כָּל־אֲשֶׁר יֵעָשֶׂה
27 לָהֶם וְעָבָדוּ׃ עַל־פִּי אַהֲרֹן וּבָנָיו תִּהְיֶה כָּל־עֲבֹדַת בְּנֵי
הַגֵּרְשֻׁנִּי לְכָל־מַשָּׂאָם וּלְכֹל עֲבֹדָתָם וּפְקַדְתֶּם עֲלֵהֶם
28 בְּמִשְׁמֶרֶת אֵת כָּל־מַשָּׂאָם׃ זֹאת עֲבֹדַת מִשְׁפְּחֹת בְּנֵי
הַגֵּרְשֻׁנִּי בְּאֹהֶל מוֹעֵד וּמִשְׁמַרְתָּם בְּיַד אִיתָמָר בֶּן־אַהֲרֹן
29 הַכֹּהֵן׃ ס בְּנֵי מְרָרִי לְמִשְׁפְּחֹתָם לְבֵית־אֲבֹתָם תִּפְקֹד
ל אֹתָם׃ מִבֶּן שְׁלֹשִׁים שָׁנָה וָמַעְלָה וְעַד בֶּן־חֲמִשִּׁים שָׁנָה
תִּפְקְדֵם כָּל־הַבָּא לַצָּבָא לַעֲבֹד אֶת־עֲבֹדַת אֹהֶל מוֹעֵד׃

II. NASO

(CHAPTERS IV, 21–VII)

IV, 21–49. CONTINUES THE NUMBERING OF THE LEVITICAL FAMILIES, AND DETAILS THEIR TRANSPORT DUTIES

21–28. Gershonites to carry all the hangings and coverings of the Dwelling and court of the Sanctuary.

26. *whatsoever there may be to do . . .* Whatsoever work may have to be done in connection with the vessels of the Tabernacle and the Altar, shall be done by the Gershonites.

27. *at the commandment . . . their burden.* Aaron and his sons were to have full authority over the Gershonites as attendants and bearers, specifying for them their duties in detail.

28. *under the hand of Ithamar.* He is personally to superintend the work done.

29–33. The Merarites and their duties. They had to carry the solid parts of the fabric of the Tabernacle and its court. This was the heaviest of the burdens, and hence wagons were assigned to them; see VII, 8.

32. *and by name ye shall appoint.* Each man shall be specifically named for his special task, in order to ensure a fair and equal distribution of these heavy burdens (Nachmanides).

their instruments. Their accessories.

the instruments of the charge of their burden. The articles committed to their charge to carry.

pillars thereof, and the sockets thereof; 32. and the pillars of the court round about, and their sockets, and their pins, and their cords, even all their appurtenance, and all that pertaineth to their service; and by name ye shall appoint the instruments of the charge of their burden. 33. This is the service of the families of the sons of Merari, according to all their service, in the tent of meeting, under the hand of Ithamar the son of Aaron the priest. *ii s. ¶ 34. And Moses and Aaron and the princes of the congregation numbered the sons of the Kohathites by their families, and by their fathers' houses, 35. from thirty years old and upward even unto fifty years old, every one that entered upon the service, for service in the tent of meeting. 36. And those that were numbered of them by their families were two thousand seven hundred and fifty. 37. These are they that were numbered of the families of the Kohathites, of all that did serve in the tent of meeting, whom Moses and Aaron numbered according to the commandment of the LORD by the hand of Moses. *ii a. ¶ 38. And those that were numbered of the sons of Gershon, by their families, and by their fathers' houses, 39. from thirty years old and upward even unto fifty years old, every one that entered upon the service, for service in the tent of meeting, 40. even those that were numbered of them, by their families, by their fathers' houses, were two thousand and six hundred and thirty. 41. These are they that were numbered of the families of the sons of Gershon, of all that did serve in the tent of meeting, whom Moses and Aaron numbered according to the commandment of the LORD. ¶ 42. And those that were numbered of the families of the sons of Merari, by their families, by their fathers' houses, 43. from thirty years old and upward even unto fifty years old, every one that entered upon the service, for service in the tent of meeting, 44. even those that were numbered of them by their families, were three thousand and two hundred. 45. These are they that were numbered of the families of the sons of Merari, whom Moses and Aaron numbered according to the commandment of the LORD by the hand of Moses. ¶ 46. All those that were numbered of the Levites, whom Moses and Aaron and the princes of Israel numbered, by their families, and by their fathers' houses, 47. from thirty years old and upward even unto fifty years old,

31 וְזֹאת מִשְׁמֶרֶת מַשָּׂאָם לְכָל־עֲבֹדָתָם בְּאֹהֶל מוֹעֵד קַרְשֵׁי
32 הַמִּשְׁכָּן וּבְרִיחָיו וְעַמּוּדָיו וַאֲדָנָיו׃ וְעַמּוּדֵי הֶחָצֵר סָבִיב
וְאַדְנֵיהֶם וִיתֵדֹתָם וּמֵיתְרֵיהֶם לְכָל־כְּלֵיהֶם וּלְכֹל עֲבֹדָתָם
33 וּבְשֵׁמֹת תִּפְקְדוּ אֶת־כְּלֵי מִשְׁמֶרֶת מַשָּׂאָם׃ זֹאת עֲבֹדַת
מִשְׁפְּחֹת בְּנֵי מְרָרִי לְכָל־עֲבֹדָתָם בְּאֹהֶל מוֹעֵד בְּיַד אִיתָמָר
שני לספ׳ 34 בֶּן־אַהֲרֹן הַכֹּהֵן׃ וַיִּפְקֹד מֹשֶׁה וְאַהֲרֹן וּנְשִׂיאֵי הָעֵדָה אֶת־
לה בְּנֵי הַקְּהָתִי לְמִשְׁפְּחֹתָם וּלְבֵית אֲבֹתָם׃ מִבֶּן שְׁלֹשִׁים
שָׁנָה וָמַעְלָה וְעַד בֶּן־חֲמִשִּׁים שָׁנָה כָּל־הַבָּא לַצָּבָא
36 לַעֲבֹדָה בְּאֹהֶל מוֹעֵד׃ וַיִּהְיוּ פְקֻדֵיהֶם לְמִשְׁפְּחֹתָם אַלְפָּיִם
37 שְׁבַע מֵאוֹת וַחֲמִשִּׁים׃ אֵלֶּה פְקוּדֵי מִשְׁפְּחֹת הַקְּהָתִי כָּל־
הָעֹבֵד בְּאֹהֶל מוֹעֵד אֲשֶׁר פָּקַד מֹשֶׁה וְאַהֲרֹן עַל־פִּי יְהוָה
שני 38 בְּיַד־מֹשֶׁה׃ ס וּפְקוּדֵי בְּנֵי גֵרְשׁוֹן לְמִשְׁפְּחוֹתָם וּלְבֵית
39 אֲבֹתָם׃ מִבֶּן שְׁלֹשִׁים שָׁנָה וָמַעְלָה וְעַד בֶּן־חֲמִשִּׁים
מ שָׁנָה כָּל־הַבָּא לַצָּבָא לַעֲבֹדָה בְּאֹהֶל מוֹעֵד׃ וַיִּהְיוּ
פְּקֻדֵיהֶם לְמִשְׁפְּחֹתָם לְבֵית אֲבֹתָם אַלְפַּיִם וְשֵׁשׁ מֵאוֹת
41 וּשְׁלֹשִׁים׃ אֵלֶּה פְקוּדֵי מִשְׁפְּחֹת בְּנֵי גֵרְשׁוֹן כָּל־הָעֹבֵד
בְּאֹהֶל מוֹעֵד אֲשֶׁר פָּקַד מֹשֶׁה וְאַהֲרֹן עַל־פִּי יְהוָה׃
42 וּפְקוּדֵי מִשְׁפְּחֹת בְּנֵי מְרָרִי לְמִשְׁפְּחֹתָם לְבֵית אֲבֹתָם׃
43 מִבֶּן שְׁלֹשִׁים שָׁנָה וָמַעְלָה וְעַד בֶּן־חֲמִשִּׁים שָׁנָה כָּל־הַבָּא
44 לַצָּבָא לַעֲבֹדָה בְּאֹהֶל מוֹעֵד׃ וַיִּהְיוּ פְקֻדֵיהֶם לְמִשְׁפְּחֹתָם
מה שְׁלֹשֶׁת אֲלָפִים וּמָאתָיִם׃ אֵלֶּה פְקוּדֵי מִשְׁפְּחֹת בְּנֵי
46 מְרָרִי אֲשֶׁר פָּקַד מֹשֶׁה וְאַהֲרֹן עַל־פִּי יְהוָה בְּיַד־מֹשֶׁה׃ כָּל־
הַפְּקֻדִים אֲשֶׁר פָּקַד מֹשֶׁה וְאַהֲרֹן וּנְשִׂיאֵי יִשְׂרָאֵל אֶת־
47 הַלְוִיִּם לְמִשְׁפְּחֹתָם וּלְבֵית אֲבֹתָם׃ מִבֶּן שְׁלֹשִׁים שָׁנָה וָמַעְלָה

34–49. TOTALS OF THE LEVITICAL CENSUS

47. *the work of service.* The work of setting up the Tabernacle at each encampment and of taking it down again for the march as given in I, 51.

and the work of bearing burdens. The transport duties of the Kohathites, Gershonites, and the sons of Merari.

every one that entered in to do the work of service, and the work of bearing burdens in the tent of meeting, 48. even those that were numbered of them, were eight thousand and five hundred and fourscore. 49. According to the commandment of the LORD they were appointed by the hand of Moses, every one to his service, and to his burden; they were also numbered, as the LORD commanded Moses.*iii.

וְעַד בֶּן־חֲמִשִּׁים שָׁנָה כָּל־הַבָּא לַעֲבֹד עֲבֹדַת עֲבֹדָה וַעֲבֹדַת
48 מַשָּׂא בְּאֹהֶל מוֹעֵד׃ וַיִּהְיוּ פְּקֻדֵיהֶם שְׁמֹנַת אֲלָפִים וַחֲמֵשׁ
49 מֵאוֹת וּשְׁמֹנִים׃ עַל־פִּי יְהוָה פָּקַד אוֹתָם בְּיַד־מֹשֶׁה אִישׁ אִישׁ
שלישי עַל־עֲבֹדָתוֹ וְעַל־מַשָּׂאוֹ וּפְקֻדָיו אֲשֶׁר־צִוָּה יְהוָה אֶת־מֹשֶׁה׃ *פ

5

CHAPTER V

1. And the LORD spoke unto Moses, saying: 2. Command the children of Israel, that they put out of the camp every leper, and every one that hath an issue, and whosoever is unclean by the dead; 3. both male and female shall ye put out, without the camp shall ye put them; that they defile not their camp, in the midst whereof I dwell.' 4. And the children of Israel did so, and put them out without the camp; as the LORD spoke unto Moses, so did the children of Israel. ¶ 5. And the LORD spoke unto Moses, saying: 6. Speak unto the children of Israel: ¶ When a man or woman shall commit any sin that men commit, to commit a trespass against the LORD, and that soul be guilty; 7. then they shall confess their sin which they have done; and he shall make restitution for his guilt in full, and add unto it the fifth part thereof, and give it unto him in respect of whom he hath been guilty.

ה

CAP. V. ה

א 2 וַיְדַבֵּר יְהוָה אֶל־מֹשֶׁה לֵּאמֹר׃ צַו אֶת־בְּנֵי יִשְׂרָאֵל
וִישַׁלְּחוּ מִן־הַמַּחֲנֶה כָּל־צָרוּעַ וְכָל־זָב וְכֹל טָמֵא לָנָפֶשׁ׃
3 מִזָּכָר עַד־נְקֵבָה תְּשַׁלֵּחוּ אֶל־מִחוּץ לַמַּחֲנֶה תְּשַׁלְּחוּם וְלֹא
4 יְטַמְּאוּ אֶת־מַחֲנֵיהֶם אֲשֶׁר אֲנִי שֹׁכֵן בְּתוֹכָם׃ וַיַּעֲשׂוּ־כֵן בְּנֵי
יִשְׂרָאֵל וַיְשַׁלְּחוּ אוֹתָם אֶל־מִחוּץ לַמַּחֲנֶה כַּאֲשֶׁר דִּבֶּר
יְהוָה אֶל־מֹשֶׁה כֵּן עָשׂוּ בְּנֵי יִשְׂרָאֵל׃ פ
ה 6 וַיְדַבֵּר יְהוָה אֶל־מֹשֶׁה לֵּאמֹר׃ דַּבֵּר אֶל־בְּנֵי יִשְׂרָאֵל אִישׁ
אוֹ־אִשָּׁה כִּי יַעֲשׂוּ מִכָּל־חַטֹּאת הָאָדָם לִמְעֹל מַעַל בַּיהוָה
7 וְאָשְׁמָה הַנֶּפֶשׁ הַהִוא׃ וְהִתְוַדּוּ אֶת־חַטָּאתָם אֲשֶׁר עָשׂוּ
וְהֵשִׁיב אֶת־אֲשָׁמוֹ בְּרֹאשׁוֹ וַחֲמִישִׁתוֹ יֹסֵף עָלָיו וְנָתַן לַאֲשֶׁר

ד׳ v. 49. סבירין כאשר

49. *according . . . Moses.* Keil translates this verse as follows: *According to the commandment of the LORD, they appointed them by the hand of Moses* (*i.e. under his direction*), *each one to his service and his burden, and his mustered things ; i.e.* the things assigned to him at the time of the mustering as his special charge (see Exod. XXXVIII, 21).

CHAPTER V

1–4. REMOVAL OF UNCLEAN PERSONS FROM THE CAMP

2. *put out of the camp every leper.* After detailing the arrangement of the camp and the ordering of the march, there follows the injunction that the ceremonial purity of the camp is to be safeguarded. Three classes of unclean persons are to be excluded: (1) the leper; (2) one that hath an 'issue' (see Lev. XV); and (3) one who has become polluted by contact with the dead (Num. XIX, 11–22). According to the Rabbis, the first was to be excluded from the whole camp. Those afflicted with issues were excluded from the Sanctuary proper (מחנה שכינה) and the Levite encampment (מחנה לויה) around the Sanctuary. One who had had contact with the dead was only excluded from the Sanctuary proper. Later in Canaan there were special houses outside the cities for lepers.

5–10. Restitution for Wrongs. The removal of physical impurities must be accompanied by the removal of moral wrongs.

6. *any sin . . . against the LORD. i.e.* any of the wrongs current amongst men. Bachya, the renowned Jewish moralist, takes these words to mean, 'Any wrong which a man commits against his fellow is at the same time treason against God.'

a trespass against the LORD. Breach of trust or wrongful misappropriation of the property of another; see Lev. VI, 2. The laws there laid down in regard to restitution and the bringing of guilt offering are here repeated, with further provisions in *v.* 7 regarding public confession, and in *v.* 8 regarding the property of a wronged person who died without leaving any kinsman to whom restitution might be made.

7. *shall make restitution for his guilt. i.e.* he shall restore that which he guiltily holds in his possession.

add . . . the fifth part. See Lev. VI, 5.

8. But if the man have no kinsman to whom restitution may be made for the guilt, the restitution for guilt which is made shall be the LORD's, even the priest's; besides the ram of the atonement, whereby atonement shall be made for him. 9. And every heave-offering of all the holy things of the children of Israel, which they present unto the priest, shall be his. 10. And every man's hallowed things shall be his: whatsoever any man giveth the priest, it shall be his.*iv a. ¶ 11. And the LORD spoke unto Moses, saying: 12. Speak unto the children of Israel, and say unto them: ¶ If any man's wife go aside, and act unfaithfully against him, 13. and a man lie with her carnally, and it be hid from the eyes of her husband, she being defiled secretly, and there be no witness against her, neither she be taken in the act; 14. and the spirit of jealousy come upon him, and he be jealous of his wife, and she be defiled; or if the spirit of jealousy come upon him, and he be jealous of his wife, and she be not defiled; 15. then shall the man bring his wife unto the priest, and shall bring her offering for

8 אָשָׁם לוֹ׃ וְאִם־אֵין לָאִישׁ גֹּאֵל לְהָשִׁיב הָאָשָׁם אֵלָיו הָאָשָׁם
הַמּוּשָׁב לַיהוָה לַכֹּהֵן מִלְּבַד אֵיל הַכִּפֻּרִים אֲשֶׁר יְכַפֶּר־
9 בּוֹ עָלָיו׃ וְכָל־תְּרוּמָה לְכָל־קָדְשֵׁי בְנֵי־יִשְׂרָאֵל אֲשֶׁר־
י יַקְרִיבוּ לַכֹּהֵן לוֹ יִהְיֶה׃ וְאִישׁ אֶת־קֳדָשָׁיו לוֹ יִהְיוּ אִישׁ
אֲשֶׁר־יִתֵּן לַכֹּהֵן לוֹ יִהְיֶה׃ פ רביעי
11 וַיְדַבֵּר יְהוָה אֶל־מֹשֶׁה לֵּאמֹר׃ 12 דַּבֵּר אֶל־בְּנֵי יִשְׂרָאֵל
וְאָמַרְתָּ אֲלֵהֶם אִישׁ אִישׁ כִּי־תִשְׂטֶה אִשְׁתּוֹ וּמָעֲלָה בוֹ
13 מָעַל׃ וְשָׁכַב אִישׁ אֹתָהּ שִׁכְבַת־זֶרַע וְנֶעְלַם מֵעֵינֵי אִישָׁהּ
וְנִסְתְּרָה וְהִיא נִטְמָאָה וְעֵד אֵין בָּהּ וְהִוא לֹא נִתְפָּשָׂה׃
14 וְעָבַר עָלָיו רוּחַ־קִנְאָה וְקִנֵּא אֶת־אִשְׁתּוֹ וְהִוא נִטְמָאָה אוֹ־
עָבַר עָלָיו רוּחַ־קִנְאָה וְקִנֵּא אֶת־אִשְׁתּוֹ וְהִיא לֹא נִטְמָאָה׃
טו וְהֵבִיא הָאִישׁ אֶת־אִשְׁתּוֹ אֶל־הַכֹּהֵן וְהֵבִיא אֶת־קָרְבָּנָהּ

8. *if the man have no kinsman.* According to the Talmud the reference is to the case of a proselyte who dies and leaves no heirs, as every Israelite would have some near or distant relative. For the meaning of the term *goel*, 'kinsman,' see on Lev. XXV, 25.

the priest's. He was to receive it as the representative of God; cf. Lev. XXIII, 20, 'they shall be holy to the LORD for the priest.'

ram of the atonement. See Lev. VI, 6.

9. *heave-offering of all the holy things.* The priest's due from any contribution brought to the Altar. It constituted his maintenance and was regarded as his legal property.

10. *every man's hallowed things shall be his.* Every man who brings a gift to the Altar may allocate it to any priest he chooses, and no fellow-priest may dispute his right to it.

11–31. ORDEAL OF JEALOUSY

This ordinance was intended to remove the very suspicion of marital unfaithfulness in the midst of Israel. As such crime is destructive of the foundations of social order, it was necessary to arrive at certainty in cases of doubt, and at the same time to afford protection to the innocent wife against unreasonable jealousies. If a husband suspect his wife of unfaithfulness, he may bring her to the Sanctuary for an oath of purgation and the drinking of 'the water of bitterness'. If she is innocent, no injuries result; if guilty, the combined oath and ordeal produce physical effects that proclaim her guilt to the world. This law is the only explicit instance in Scripture of trial by ordeal, an institution that was well-nigh universal in antiquity and a regular feature of Western European life down to the late Middle Ages. In Israel, the Ordeal of Jealousy was abolished by Johanan ben Zakkai soon after the Destruction of the Temple. From that time, divorce alone was customary in cases of well-proved faithlessness.

12. *if any man's wife go aside.* From the right path and become suspect in the eyes of her husband. By a slight change of punctuation the Heb. verb can be translated, 'if any man's wife commit folly,' and the Rabbis base thereon the saying, 'No one sinneth unless the spirit of folly has entered into him.'

13. *she being defiled secretly.* Even the presence of one witness to such defilement ruled out the Ordeal procedure. She was then tried on the evidence.

14. *spirit of jealousy. i.e.* an uncontrollable impulse. The Rabbis required the husband first to prohibit the woman, in the presence of witnesses, to hold any further communication with the man suspected; and then only, in case of the wife's disobedience, could the husband subject her to the Ordeal. The Ordeal could not be made use of if there was any connivance on the part of the husband; see also on *v.* 28.

15. *and shall bring her offering for her. i.e.* on her account; the offerings required in her case.

the tenth part of an ephah. A little under seven pints.

her, the tenth part of an ephah of barley meal; he shall pour no oil upon it, nor put frankincense thereon; for it is a meal-offering of jealousy, a meal-offering of memorial, bringing iniquity to remembrance. 16. And the priest shall bring her near, and set her before the LORD. 17. And the priest shall take holy water in an earthen vessel; and of the dust that is on the floor of the tabernacle the priest shall take, and put it into the water. 18. And the priest shall set the woman before the LORD, and let the hair of the woman's head go loose, and put the meal-offering of memorial in her hands, which is the meal-offering of jealousy; and the priest shall have in his hand the water of bitterness that causeth the curse. 19. And the priest shall cause her to swear, and shall say unto the woman: 'If no man have lain with thee, and if thou hast not gone aside to uncleanness, being under thy husband, be thou free from this water of bitterness that causeth the curse; 20. but if thou hast gone aside, being under thy husband, and if thou be defiled, and some man have lain with thee besides thy husband—21. then the priest shall cause the woman to swear with the oath of cursing, and the priest shall say unto the woman—the LORD make thee a curse and an oath among thy people, when the LORD doth make thy thigh to fall away, and thy belly to swell; 22. and this water that causeth the curse shall go into thy bowels, and make thy belly to swell,

עָלֶיהָ עֲשִׂירִת הָאֵיפָה קֶמַח שְׂעֹרִים לֹא־יִצֹק עָלָיו שֶׁמֶן
וְלֹא־יִתֵּן עָלָיו לְבֹנָה כִּי־מִנְחַת קְנָאֹת הוּא מִנְחַת זִכָּרוֹן
16 מַזְכֶּרֶת עָוֺן׃ וְהִקְרִיב אֹתָהּ הַכֹּהֵן וְהֶעֱמִדָהּ לִפְנֵי יְהוָה׃
17 וְלָקַח הַכֹּהֵן מַיִם קְדֹשִׁים בִּכְלִי־חָרֶשׂ וּמִן־הֶעָפָר אֲשֶׁר
18 יִהְיֶה בְּקַרְקַע הַמִּשְׁכָּן יִקַּח הַכֹּהֵן וְנָתַן אֶל־הַמָּיִם׃ וְהֶעֱמִיד
הַכֹּהֵן אֶת־הָאִשָּׁה לִפְנֵי יְהוָה וּפָרַע אֶת־רֹאשׁ הָאִשָּׁה וְנָתַן
עַל־כַּפֶּיהָ אֵת מִנְחַת הַזִּכָּרוֹן מִנְחַת קְנָאֹת הִוא וּבְיַד הַכֹּהֵן
19 יִהְיוּ מֵי הַמָּרִים הַמְאָרְרִים׃ וְהִשְׁבִּיעַ אֹתָהּ הַכֹּהֵן וְאָמַר
אֶל־הָאִשָּׁה אִם־לֹא שָׁכַב אִישׁ אֹתָךְ וְאִם־לֹא שָׂטִית
טֻמְאָה תַּחַת אִישֵׁךְ הִנָּקִי מִמֵּי הַמָּרִים הַמְאָרְרִים הָאֵלֶּה׃
כ וְאַתְּ כִּי שָׂטִית תַּחַת אִישֵׁךְ וְכִי נִטְמֵאת וַיִּתֵּן אִישׁ בָּךְ אֶת־
21 שְׁכָבְתּוֹ מִבַּלְעֲדֵי אִישֵׁךְ׃ וְהִשְׁבִּיעַ הַכֹּהֵן אֶת־הָאִשָּׁה
בִּשְׁבֻעַת הָאָלָה וְאָמַר הַכֹּהֵן לָאִשָּׁה יִתֵּן יְהוָה אוֹתָךְ לְאָלָה
וְלִשְׁבֻעָה בְּתוֹךְ עַמֵּךְ בְּתֵת יְהוָה אֶת־יְרֵכֵךְ נֹפֶלֶת וְאֶת־
22 בִּטְנֵךְ צָבָה׃ וּבָאוּ הַמַּיִם הַמְאָרְרִים הָאֵלֶּה בְּמֵעַיִךְ לַצְבּוֹת

of barley meal. Offerings usually consisted of fine rather than coarse meal, and the ingredient was wheat rather than barley. It was thus to indicate the abased condition of the suspected woman.

no oil . . . nor put frankincense thereon. These symbols of joy and festivity would not harmonize with the grievous nature of the occasion (Philo).

bringing iniquity to remembrance. Unlike other offerings it is a reminder not of Divine mercy, but of the guilt to be discovered and to be punished by God. Dillmann considers this phrase to be the technical term for accusation; see I Kings XVII, 18; Ezek. XXI, 23 f.

16. *before the LORD.* Near the Altar of burnt-offering; in later times, to the eastern gate of the Temple.

17. *holy water.* Taken from the brazen laver which stood near the Altar (Exod. xxx, 18).

dust. Also holy, in virtue of the place whence it was taken.

an earthen vessel. Cheap and coarse, like the offering itself.

18. *the hair . . . go loose.* As a sign of mourning (Lev. x, 6), or in token of her shame, as it was a sign of lack of morality for a woman to appear publicly with hair unloosed.

in her hands. To make her feel the severity of the ordeal to such an extent that she volunteer a confession of her guilt.

water of bitterness. Water which produces woeful results (Rashi).

that causeth the curse. Better, *that brings the guilt to light* (Luzzatto, following the Samaritan Version).

19–22. THE OATH OF PURGATION

19. *being under thy husband. i.e.* as a wife under the authority of her husband, and therefore bound to be faithful to him. The priest begins with the assumption of innocence.

be thou free from this water. Be unpunished by it.

21. *a curse and an oath.* So that people employ thy name both as a warning example and as an imprecation.

23 בֶּטֶן וְלַנְפִּל יָרֵךְ וְאָמְרָה הָאִשָּׁה אָמֵן ׀ אָמֵן׃ וְכָתַב אֶת־
24 הָאָלֹת הָאֵלֶּה הַכֹּהֵן בַּסֵּפֶר וּמָחָה אֶל־מֵי הַמָּרִים׃ וְהִשְׁקָה
אֶת־הָאִשָּׁה אֶת־מֵי הַמָּרִים הַמְאָרְרִים וּבָאוּ בָהּ הַמַּיִם
כה הַמְאָרְרִים לְמָרִים׃ וְלָקַח הַכֹּהֵן מִיַּד הָאִשָּׁה אֵת מִנְחַת
הַקְּנָאֹת וְהֵנִיף אֶת־הַמִּנְחָה לִפְנֵי יְהוָה וְהִקְרִיב אֹתָהּ אֶל־
26 הַמִּזְבֵּחַ׃ וְקָמַץ הַכֹּהֵן מִן־הַמִּנְחָה אֶת־אַזְכָּרָתָהּ וְהִקְטִיר
27 הַמִּזְבֵּחָה וְאַחַר יַשְׁקֶה אֶת־הָאִשָּׁה אֶת־הַמָּיִם׃ וְהִשְׁקָהּ
אֶת־הַמַּיִם וְהָיְתָה אִם־נִטְמְאָה וַתִּמְעֹל מַעַל בְּאִישָׁהּ וּבָאוּ
בָהּ הַמַּיִם הַמְאָרְרִים לְמָרִים וְצָבְתָה בִטְנָהּ וְנָפְלָה יְרֵכָהּ
28 וְהָיְתָה הָאִשָּׁה לְאָלָה בְּקֶרֶב עַמָּהּ׃ וְאִם־לֹא נִטְמְאָה
29 הָאִשָּׁה וּטְהֹרָה הִוא וְנִקְּתָה וְנִזְרְעָה זָרַע׃ זֹאת תּוֹרַת
ל הַקְּנָאֹת אֲשֶׁר תִּשְׂטֶה אִשָּׁה תַּחַת אִישָׁהּ וְנִטְמָאָה׃ אוֹ
אִישׁ אֲשֶׁר תַּעֲבֹר עָלָיו רוּחַ קִנְאָה וְקִנֵּא אֶת־אִשְׁתּוֹ
וְהֶעֱמִיד אֶת־הָאִשָּׁה לִפְנֵי יְהוָה וְעָשָׂה לָהּ הַכֹּהֵן אֵת כָּל־

and thy thigh to fall away'; and the woman
shall say: 'Amen, Amen.' 23. And the
priest shall write these curses in a scroll,
and he shall blot them out into the water
of bitterness. 24. And he shall make the
woman drink the water of bitterness that
causeth the curse; and the water that
causeth the curse shall enter into her and
become bitter. 25. And the priest shall
take the meal-offering of jealousy out of
the woman's hand, and shall wave the
meal-offering before the LORD, and bring
it unto the altar. 26. And the priest shall
take a handful of the meal-offering, as the
memorial-part thereof, and make it smoke
upon the altar, and afterward shall make
the woman drink the water. 27. And when
he hath made her drink the water, then it
shall come to pass, if she be defiled, and
have acted unfaithfully against her husband,
that the water that causeth the curse shall
enter into her and become bitter, and her
belly shall swell, and her thigh shall fall
away; and the woman shall be a curse
among her people. 28. And if the woman
be not defiled, but be clean; then she shall
be cleared, and shall conceive seed. 29.
This is the law of jealousy, when a wife,
being under her husband, goeth aside, and
is defiled; 30. or when the spirit of jealousy
cometh upon a man, and he be jealous
over his wife; then shall he set the woman
before the LORD, and the priest shall execute

22. *Amen.* Its original meaning is, 'So be it!' A solemn affirmation to a preceding statement. Whosoever answers Amen to an oath, it is as if he had himself pronounced that oath.

In later times, Amen becomes in the Synagogue—as distinct from the Temple—the regular liturgical response of the worshippers. It was often doubled at the end of a psalm or prayer. Great spiritual value was attached by the Rabbis to the reverent response of Amen in prayer. 'Whosoever says Amen with all his strength, to him the gates of Paradise shall be opened.' *Amen* is now one of the commonest words of human speech. Three great Religions have brought it into the daily lives of men of all races, climes, and cultures.

23. *in a scroll.* On anything that can receive writing (Mishnah). In Roman times, a royal proselyte to Judaism, Queen Helena, donated a tablet of gold to the Temple, with the chapter of the Ordeal of Jealousy written on it, and the priests would transcribe the oath from that tablet.

blot them out. Or, 'wash them into the bitter water.' A symbolical action to indicate that the curse is in this manner conveyed to the potion.

24. *make the woman drink.* This is said by anticipation, because she did not really drink it till after the offering; *v.* 26. The translation should read, 'and when he shall make the woman to drink the water that brings the guilt to light, the water that brings the guilt to light shall enter into her and become bitter.' The solemnity of the oath, and the awe-inspiring ritual which accompanied it, might of themselves deter a woman from taking it, unless she were supported by the consciousness of innocence (Speaker's Bible).

and become bitter. lit. 'for bitterness'; *i.e.* proving unpleasant and injurious.

26. *as the memorial-part thereof.* See Lev. II, 2.

27. *that causeth the curse.* Better, *that bringeth the guilt to light;* see on *v.* 18.

shall be a curse. The opposite of this phrase is seen in Gen. XII, 2.

28. *she shall be cleared.* Acquitted and proved innocent; and as Divine compensation for the suffering she had undergone, she would bear offspring—an indication of God's favour in Scripture.

upon her all this law. 31. And the man shall be clear from iniquity, and that woman shall bear her iniquity.

6

Chapter VI

1. And the Lord spoke unto Moses, saying: 2. Speak unto the children of Israel, and say unto them: ¶When either man or woman shall clearly utter a vow, the vow of a Nazirite, to consecrate himself unto the Lord, 3. he shall abstain from wine and strong drink: he shall drink no vinegar of wine, or vinegar of strong drink, neither shall he drink any liquor of grapes, nor eat fresh grapes or dried. 4. All the days of his Naziriteship shall he eat nothing that is made of the grape-vine, from the pressed grapes even to the grape-stone. 5. All the days of his vow of Naziriteship there shall no razor come upon his head; until the days be fulfilled, in which he consecrateth himself unto the Lord, he shall be holy, he shall let the locks of the hair of his head grow long. 6. All the days that he consecrateth himself unto the Lord he shall not come near to a dead body. 7. He shall not make himself unclean for his father, or for his mother, for his brother, or for his sister, when they die; because his consecration unto God is upon his head.

31 הַתּוֹרָה הַזֹּאת׃ וְנִקָּה הָאִישׁ מֵעָוֺן וְהָאִשָּׁה הַהִוא תִּשָּׂא
אֶת־עֲוֺנָהּ׃ פ

Cap. VI. ו

ו

א 2 וַיְדַבֵּר יְהוָה אֶל־מֹשֶׁה לֵּאמֹר׃ דַּבֵּר אֶל־בְּנֵי יִשְׂרָאֵל
וְאָמַרְתָּ אֲלֵהֶם אִישׁ אוֹ־אִשָּׁה כִּי יַפְלִא לִנְדֹּר נֶדֶר נָזִיר
3 לְהַזִּיר לַיהוָה׃ מִיַּיִן וְשֵׁכָר יַזִּיר חֹמֶץ יַיִן וְחֹמֶץ שֵׁכָר לֹא
יִשְׁתֶּה וְכָל־מִשְׁרַת עֲנָבִים לֹא יִשְׁתֶּה וַעֲנָבִים לַחִים וִיבֵשִׁים
4 לֹא יֹאכֵל׃ כֹּל יְמֵי נִזְרוֹ מִכֹּל אֲשֶׁר יֵעָשֶׂה מִגֶּפֶן הַיַּיִן
ה מֵחַרְצַנִּים וְעַד־זָג לֹא יֹאכֵל׃ כָּל־יְמֵי נֶדֶר נִזְרוֹ תַּעַר לֹא־
יַעֲבֹר עַל־רֹאשׁוֹ עַד־מְלֹאת הַיָּמִם אֲשֶׁר־יַזִּיר לַיהוָה קָדֹשׁ
6 יִהְיֶה גַּדֵּל פֶּרַע שְׂעַר רֹאשׁוֹ׃ כָּל־יְמֵי הַזִּירוֹ לַיהוָה עַל־
7 נֶפֶשׁ מֵת לֹא יָבֹא׃ לְאָבִיו וּלְאִמּוֹ לְאָחִיו וּלְאַחֹתוֹ לֹא־

31. *clear from iniquity.* Of having cast suspicion on one who is innocent (Sforno). The Rabbis, however, inferred from these Heb. words that the Ordeal proved ineffective if the husband was himself guilty of immorality.

shall bear her iniquity. Should she be proved guilty.

Chapter VI

The Law of the Nazirite

The previous chapter provided for the exclusion of certain forms of guilt and defilement from the pale of God's people. The present chapter offers an opening to the life of the devotee who, not content with observing what is obligatory, seeks austere modes of self-dedication. The Nazirite vow includes three things: (1) the hair to remain unshorn during the period of the vow; (2) abstinence from intoxicants; (3) avoidance of contact with a dead body. The Nazirite vow was often taken by men and women alike purely for personal reasons, such as thanksgiving for recovery from illness, or for the birth of a child. The minimum period of the vow was thirty days, but we have instances of Nazirite vows extending over repeated periods of seven years. Scripture records also life-long Nazirites who, however, were not bound by all the regulations of the temporary Nazirite. Mention is also made of the Rechabites, who abstained from wine (Jer. xxxv), and, in later times, the Essenes, whose life was semi-monastic. The institution disappeared in its entirety with the destruction of the Temple.

2. *Nazirite.* That is, one separated or consecrated. Heb. *Nazir;* cf. Judges xiii, 5, 7.

3. *wine.* The priest had to refrain from wine during service in the Sanctuary (Lev. x, 9), and the Nazirite's whole life was conceived as service of God; see, however, on *v.* 11.

strong drink. A comprehensive term for intoxicating liquors other than wine.

vinegar. Any preparation made from any intoxicant that has gone sour.

liquor of grapes. Made by soaking grape-skins in water.

4. *pressed grapes.* Pressed grapes from which the wine has already been extracted (Talmud).

5. *no razor come upon his head.* The hair was regarded as the symbol of the vital power at its full natural development; and the free growth of the hair on the head of the Nazirite represented the dedication of the man with all his strength and powers to the service of God.

holy. Here signifying separated, detached from ordinary mundane pursuits by leading a life of self-denial and self-dedication to God.

7. *unclean for his father.* In respect to contact with a dead body, the ordinary Nazirite was as

8. All the days of his Naziriteship he is holy unto the LORD. 9. And if any man die very suddenly beside him, and he defile his consecrated head, then he shall shave his head in the day of his cleansing, on the seventh day shall he shave it. 10. And on the eighth day he shall bring two turtle-doves, or two young pigeons, to the priest, to the door of the tent of meeting. 11. And the priest shall prepare one for a sin-offering, and the other for a burnt-offering, and make atonement for him, for that he sinned by reason of the dead; and he shall hallow his head that same day. 12. And he shall consecrate unto the LORD the days of his Naziriteship, and shall bring a he-lamb of the first year for a guilt-offering; but the former days shall be void, because his consecration was defiled. ¶ 13. And this is the law of the Nazirite, when the days of his consecration are fulfilled: he shall [1]bring it unto the door of the tent of meeting; 14. and he shall present his offering unto the LORD, one he-lamb of the first year without blemish for a burnt-offering, and one ewe-lamb of the first year without blemish for a sin-offering, and one ram without blemish for peace-offerings 15. and a basket of unleavened bread, cakes of fine flour mingled with oil, and unleavened wafers spread with oil, and their meal-offering, and their drink-offerings. 16. And the priest shall bring them before the LORD, and shall offer his sin-offering, and his burnt-offering. 17. And he shall offer the ram for a sacrifice of peace-offerings unto the LORD, with the basket of unleavened

8 יִטַּמָּא לָהֶם בְּמֹתָם כִּי נֵזֶר אֱלֹהָיו עַל־רֹאשׁוֹ׃ כֹּל יְמֵי
9 נִזְרוֹ קָדֹשׁ הוּא לַיהוָה׃ וְכִי־יָמוּת מֵת עָלָיו בְּפֶתַע פִּתְאֹם
וְטִמֵּא רֹאשׁ נִזְרוֹ וְגִלַּח רֹאשׁוֹ בְּיוֹם טָהֳרָתוֹ בַּיּוֹם הַשְּׁבִיעִי
י יְגַלְּחֶנּוּ׃ וּבַיּוֹם הַשְּׁמִינִי יָבִא שְׁתֵּי תֹרִים אוֹ שְׁנֵי בְּנֵי יוֹנָה
11 אֶל־הַכֹּהֵן אֶל־פֶּתַח אֹהֶל מוֹעֵד׃ וְעָשָׂה הַכֹּהֵן אֶחָד
לְחַטָּאת וְאֶחָד לְעֹלָה וְכִפֶּר עָלָיו מֵאֲשֶׁר חָטָא עַל־הַנָּפֶשׁ
12 וְקִדַּשׁ אֶת־רֹאשׁוֹ בַּיּוֹם הַהוּא׃ וְהִזִּיר לַיהוָה אֶת־יְמֵי נִזְרוֹ
וְהֵבִיא כֶּבֶשׂ בֶּן־שְׁנָתוֹ לְאָשָׁם וְהַיָּמִים הָרִאשֹׁנִים יִפְּלוּ כִּי
13 טָמֵא נִזְרוֹ׃ וְזֹאת תּוֹרַת הַנָּזִיר בְּיוֹם מְלֹאת יְמֵי נִזְרוֹ יָבִיא
14 אֹתוֹ אֶל־פֶּתַח אֹהֶל מוֹעֵד׃ וְהִקְרִיב אֶת־קָרְבָּנוֹ לַיהוָה
כֶּבֶשׂ בֶּן־שְׁנָתוֹ תָמִים אֶחָד לְעֹלָה וְכַבְשָׂה אַחַת בַּת־
טו שְׁנָתָהּ תְּמִימָה לְחַטָּאת וְאַיִל־אֶחָד תָּמִים לִשְׁלָמִים׃ וְסַל
מַצּוֹת סֹלֶת חַלֹּת בְּלוּלֹת בַּשֶּׁמֶן וּרְקִיקֵי מַצּוֹת מְשֻׁחִים
16 בַּשָּׁמֶן וּמִנְחָתָם וְנִסְכֵּיהֶם׃ וְהִקְרִיב הַכֹּהֵן לִפְנֵי יְהוָה וְעָשָׂה
17 אֶת־חַטָּאתוֹ וְאֶת־עֹלָתוֹ׃ וְאֶת־הָאַיִל יַעֲשֶׂה זֶבַח שְׁלָמִים
לַיהוָה עַל סַל הַמַּצּוֹת וְעָשָׂה הַכֹּהֵן אֶת־מִנְחָתוֹ וְאֶת־נִסְכּוֹ׃

[1] That is, bring his consecrated head (come with his consecrated hair unshaven).

stringently bound as the High Priest (Lev. XXI, 11). Not so another class of Nazirite, called by the Rabbis the Samson type of Nazirite.

his consecration unto God. lit. 'the crown of his God'; the sign and symbol of his special consecration unto God; the hair of the Nazirite being to him what the crown was to the king and what the mitre was to the High Priest.

9–12. INVOLUNTARY DEFILEMENT

9. *beside him.* In the tent wherein he is (Rashi).

day of his cleansing. The eighth day after his defilement.

11. *for that he sinned.* Although his defilement was involuntary, he should have avoided even the remotest possibility of defilement. The Talmud explains that he was ordered to make atonement for his vow to abstain from drinking wine, an unnecessary self-denial in regard to one of the permitted pleasures of life.

shall hallow . . . that same day. Renew his vow from the moment he has effected atonement.

12. *shall consecrate.* Resume his life under the Nazirite rule for the whole period which he had originally intended.

guilt-offering. For the sin committed unwittingly through which his defilement overtook him.

shall be void. Not be counted as part of the period during which the vow was valid.

13–21. RITES TO BE PERFORMED AT THE COMPLETION OF THE VOW

13. *he shall bring it.* *i.e.* he shall come with his consecrated head unshaven to the door of the Tent of Meeting; see further *v.* 18.

14. *he shall present his offering.* Which included all four ordinary sacrifices: (*a*) burnt-offering; (*b*) sin-offering; (*c*) peace-offering; and (*d*) meal-offering.

18 וְגִלַּח הַנָּזִיר פֶּתַח אֹהֶל מוֹעֵד אֶת־רֹאשׁ נִזְרוֹ וְלָקַח אֶת־
שְׂעַר רֹאשׁ נִזְרוֹ וְנָתַן עַל־הָאֵשׁ אֲשֶׁר־תַּחַת זֶבַח הַשְּׁלָמִים׃
19 וְלָקַח הַכֹּהֵן אֶת־הַזְּרֹעַ בְּשֵׁלָה מִן־הָאַיִל וְחַלַּת מַצָּה אַחַת
מִן־הַסַּל וּרְקִיק מַצָּה אֶחָד וְנָתַן עַל־כַּפֵּי הַנָּזִיר אַחַר
כ הִתְגַּלְּחוֹ אֶת־נִזְרוֹ׃ וְהֵנִיף אוֹתָם הַכֹּהֵן ׀ תְּנוּפָה לִפְנֵי יְהוָה
קֹדֶשׁ הוּא לַכֹּהֵן עַל חֲזֵה הַתְּנוּפָה וְעַל שׁוֹק הַתְּרוּמָה
21 וְאַחַר יִשְׁתֶּה הַנָּזִיר יָיִן׃ זֹאת תּוֹרַת הַנָּזִיר אֲשֶׁר יִדֹּר קָרְבָּנוֹ
לַיהוָה עַל־נִזְרוֹ מִלְּבַד אֲשֶׁר־תַּשִּׂיג יָדוֹ כְּפִי נִדְרוֹ אֲשֶׁר
יִדֹּר כֵּן יַעֲשֶׂה עַל תּוֹרַת נִזְרוֹ׃ פ
22 23 וַיְדַבֵּר יְהוָה אֶל־מֹשֶׁה לֵּאמֹר׃ דַּבֵּר אֶל־אַהֲרֹן וְאֶל־בָּנָיו
לֵאמֹר כֹּה תְבָרְכוּ אֶת־בְּנֵי יִשְׂרָאֵל אָמוֹר לָהֶם׃ ס

bread; the priest shall offer also the meal-offering thereof, and the drink-offering thereof. 18. And the Nazirite shall shave his consecrated head at the door of the tent of meeting, and shall take the hair of his consecrated head, and put it on the fire which is under the sacrifice of peace-offerings. 19. And the priest shall take the shoulder of the ram when it is sodden, and one unleavened cake out of the basket, and one unleavened wafer, and shall put them upon the hands of the Nazirite, after he hath shaven his consecrated head. 20. And the priest shall wave them for a wave-offering before the LORD; this is holy for the priest, together with the breast of waving and the thigh of heaving; and after that the Nazirite may drink wine. 21. This is the law of the Nazirite who voweth, and of his offering unto the LORD for his Naziriteship, beside that for which his means suffice; according to his vow which he voweth, so he must do after the law of his Naziriteship. ¶ 22. And the LORD spoke unto Moses, saying: 23. 'Speak unto Aaron and unto his sons, saying: On this wise ye shall bless the

18. *and shall take the hair.* As the Nazirite had during his vow worn his hair unshorn in honour of God, so when the time was complete it was natural that the hair, the symbol of his vow, should be cut off at the Sanctuary. In the times of the Mishnah, a special room was assigned to the Nazirites for that purpose in one of the Temple courts.

20. *the Nazirite may drink wine.* Presumably the other restrictions also fell away.

21. *beside that for which his means suffice.* Apart from whatever else he may be able to afford over and above the offerings laid down in this chapter.

according to his vow . . . so he must do. This warning concerning vows is clearly stated in Deut. XXIII, 24. 'That which is gone out of thy lips thou shalt observe and do; according as thou hast vowed unto the LORD thy God, a freewill offering, which thou hast promised with thy mouth.'

22–27. THE PRIESTLY BLESSING

The simple and beautiful threefold petition which follows in *v.* 24–26 is known as ברכת כהנים, 'The Priestly Blessing.' It is as it were the crown and seal of the whole sacred order by which Israel was now fully organized as the people of God, for the march to the Holy Land. The Heb. text consists of three short verses, of three, five, and seven words respectively. 'It mounts by gradual stages from the petition for material blessing and protection to that for Divine favour as a spiritual blessing, and in beautiful climax culminates in the petition for God's most consummate gift, *shalom*, peace, the welfare in which all material and spiritual well-being is comprehended' (Kautzsch). The fifteen words that constitute these three verses contain a world of trust in God and faith in God. They are clothed in a rhythmic form of great beauty, and they fall with majestic solemnity upon the ear of the worshipper. The Priestly Blessing was one of the most impressive features of the Service in the Temple at Jerusalem, and holds a prominent place in the worship of the Synagogue. In the Temple it was pronounced from a special tribune (*duchan;* hence the current name 'duchaning') after the sacrifice of the daily offering, morning and evening. In the Synagogue, it was early introduced into the daily Amidah (Authorised Prayer Book, p. 53). Its pronouncement by the Priests is in Ashkenazi communities limited, as a rule, to Festivals when not falling on Sabbaths. The ancient melody that accompanies its pronouncement by the Priests is in its original form weird and most impressive. Since the Reformation, the Priestly Blessing is a constituent of the service in many Protestant Churches.

23. *on this wise ye shall bless.* The Rabbis based on these words their specific regulations as to the manner in which alone the Blessing was to be pronounced. Only a priest, and not 'a stranger', was to pronounce it; it was to be done standing, and with outspread hands; the priest must be sober when blessing; and it must be given in the Hebrew tongue. These prescriptions have deep spiritual implications for all time. A stranger cannot bless; blessing requires knowledge and loving understanding of the person or cause to be blessed. Furthermore, to bless others is a difficult task, requiring children of Israel; ye shall say unto them: ¶ 24. The LORD bless thee, and keep thee; ¶ 25. The LORD make His face to shine upon thee, and be gracious unto thee; ¶ 26. The

24 כה יְבָרֶכְךָ יְהוָה וְיִשְׁמְרֶךָ׃ ס יָאֵר יְהוָה ׀ פָּנָיו אֵלֶיךָ
26 וִיחֻנֶּךָּ׃ ס יִשָּׂא יְהוָה ׀ פָּנָיו אֵלֶיךָ וְיָשֵׂם לְךָ שָׁלוֹם׃ ס

readiness for sacrifice and prayerfulness. And, unless the blessing is to prove a blight, he that blesses must be quite 'sober'—the fanatic or he whose judgment is beclouded by hatred or prejudice can never truly bless anyone. The requirement as to the language of the Blessing is as vital as any. As far as the Jew is concerned, every measure on his behalf must be in the Sacred Tongue—*i.e.* translatable into Hebrew terms, and in line with Jewish history and Jewish ideals.

24. The Guardianship of God

24. *the LORD bless thee.* With life, health, prosperity.

thee. Why is the singular used? A current explanation is, as the prerequisite of all blessing for Israel is unity, all Israel is to feel as one organic body.

and keep thee. Or, 'guard thee'; grant thee His Divine protection against evil, sickness, poverty, calamity. The LORD is the Keeper of Israel. He delivers our souls from death, keeps our eyes from tears, and our feet from stumbling. The Rabbis gave a wide application to these three Heb. words: May God bless thee, with possessions; and keep thee, from these possessions possessing thee. May God guard thee from sin, and shield thee from all destructive influences (מן המזיקין) that so often follow in the wake of earthly prosperity.

25. The Grace of God

25. *His face to shine upon thee.* Light in Scripture is the symbol not only of happiness and purity but also of friendship. To cause the face to shine upon one, is the Biblical idiom for to be friendly to him. When God's 'face' is said to be turned towards man and to shine upon him, it implies the outpouring of Divine love and salvation (Ps LXXX, 20). In contrast to this, we have the prayer, 'Hide not Thy face from me.'

The Rabbis interpret the words, 'make His face to shine upon thee,' in a purely spiritual sense, to imply the gift of knowledge and moral insight. 'May He give thee enlightenment of the eyes, the light of the Shechinah; may the fire of Prophecy burn in the souls of thy children; may the light of the Torah illumine thy home' (Sifri).

gracious unto thee. This is more than 'keep thee' in the preceding verse. May He be beneficent unto thee, and graciously fulfil thy petition. The Rabbis understand ויחנך in the sense of 'May He give thee grace in the eyes of thy fellowmen'; *i.e.* may He make thee lovable, and beloved in the eyes of others. Rabbi Chanina ben Dosa said, 'He in whom his fellow-creatures take delight, in him the All-present takes delight.'

26. The Peace of God

26. *lift up His countenance upon thee.* Or, 'turn His face unto thee'; turn His attention, His loving care unto thee.

give thee. lit. 'set thee,' establish for thee. The Heb. is not ויתן but וישם.

peace. 'Peace in thy coming in, peace in thy going out, peace with all men. Great is peace for it is the seal of all blessings' (Talmud). The Heb. *shalom* means not only freedom from all disaster; but health, welfare, security, and tranquillity; 'the peace which alone reconciles and strengthens, which calms us and clears our vision, which frees us from restlessness and from the bondage of unsatisfied desire, which gives us the consciousness of attainment, the consciousness of permanence even amid the transitoriness of ourselves and of outward things' (Montefiore).

'Peace, say the Rabbis, is one of the pillars of the world; without it the social order could not exist. Therefore let a man do his utmost to promote it. Thus it is that the greatest Sages made a point of being the first to salute passers-by in the street. Peace is the burthen of the prayer with which every service in the synagogue concludes: 'May He who maketh peace in His high heavens grant peace unto us!' And so a twofold duty is indicated. We are not only to be peaceful ourselves, but to help others to be peaceful also. Peace is not only a personal, but a national ideal. There are, doubtless, occasions when war is defensible as a less evil than a disastrous and dishonourable peace. There are worse things, it is true, than war; but the worst of them is the belief that war is indispensable. Such a belief is fatal to the ultimate establishment of universal peace. The Jew who is true to himself will labour with especial energy in the cause of peace. The war-loving Jew is a contradiction in terms. Only the peace-loving Jew is a true follower of his Prophets, who set universal brotherhood in the forefront of their pictures of coming happiness for mankind, predicting the advent of a Golden Age when nations should not lift up sword against nation, nor learn war any more' (Morris Joseph).

Peace is no negative conception and is not the equivalent of inactivity. Whether for the individual or for society, it is that harmonious co-operation of all human forces towards ethical and spiritual ends which men call the Kingdom of God. The Prophets longed for a Messianic peace that should pervade the universe, and include all men, all peoples—that should include also the beasts of the field; Isaiah XI, 6–10.

27 וְשָׂמוּ אֶת־שְׁמִי עַל־בְּנֵי יִשְׂרָאֵל וַאֲנִי אֲבָרְכֵם׃ ס
חמישי (רביעי לספ׳)

CAP. VII. ז

ז
א וַיְהִי בְּיוֹם כַּלּוֹת מֹשֶׁה לְהָקִים אֶת־הַמִּשְׁכָּן וַיִּמְשַׁח אֹתוֹ
וַיְקַדֵּשׁ אֹתוֹ וְאֶת־כָּל־כֵּלָיו וְאֶת־הַמִּזְבֵּחַ וְאֶת־כָּל־כֵּלָיו
2 וַיִּמְשָׁחֵם וַיְקַדֵּשׁ אֹתָם׃ וַיַּקְרִיבוּ נְשִׂיאֵי יִשְׂרָאֵל רָאשֵׁי
בֵּית אֲבֹתָם הֵם נְשִׂיאֵי הַמַּטֹּת הֵם הָעֹמְדִים עַל־הַפְּקֻדִים׃
3 וַיָּבִיאוּ אֶת־קָרְבָּנָם לִפְנֵי יְהוָה שֵׁשׁ־עֶגְלֹת צָב וּשְׁנֵי עָשָׂר
בָּקָר עֲגָלָה עַל־שְׁנֵי הַנְּשִׂאִים וְשׁוֹר לְאֶחָד וַיַּקְרִיבוּ אוֹתָם
4 ה לִפְנֵי הַמִּשְׁכָּן׃ וַיֹּאמֶר יְהוָה אֶל־מֹשֶׁה לֵּאמֹר׃ קַח מֵאִתָּם
וְהָיוּ לַעֲבֹד אֶת־עֲבֹדַת אֹהֶל מוֹעֵד וְנָתַתָּה אוֹתָם אֶל־
6 הַלְוִיִּם אִישׁ כְּפִי עֲבֹדָתוֹ׃ וַיִּקַּח מֹשֶׁה אֶת־הָעֲגָלֹת וְאֶת־
7 הַבָּקָר וַיִּתֵּן אוֹתָם אֶל־הַלְוִיִּם׃ אֵת ׀ שְׁתֵּי הָעֲגָלוֹת וְאֵת
8 אַרְבַּעַת הַבָּקָר נָתַן לִבְנֵי גֵרְשׁוֹן כְּפִי עֲבֹדָתָם׃ וְאֵת ׀
אַרְבַּע הָעֲגָלֹת וְאֵת שְׁמֹנַת הַבָּקָר נָתַן לִבְנֵי מְרָרִי כְּפִי
9 עֲבֹדָתָם בְּיַד אִיתָמָר בֶּן־אַהֲרֹן הַכֹּהֵן׃ וְלִבְנֵי קְהָת לֹא

ז׳ v. 2. ק׳ דבוקה

LORD lift up His countenance upon thee, and give thee peace. ¶ 27. So shall they put My name upon the children of Israel, and I will bless them.'*iv s, v a.

7

CHAPTER VII

1. And it came to pass on the day that Moses had made an end of setting up the tabernacle, and had anointed it and sanctified it, and all the furniture thereof, and the altar and all the vessels thereof, and had anointed them and sanctified them; 2. that the princes of Israel, the heads of their fathers' houses, offered—these were the princes of the tribes, these are they that were over them that were numbered. 3. And they brought their offering before the LORD, six covered wagons, and twelve oxen: a wagon for every two of the princes, and for each one an ox; and they presented them before the tabernacle. 4. And the LORD spoke unto Moses, saying: 5. 'Take it of them, that they may be to do the service of the tent of meeting; and thou shalt give them unto the Levites, to every man according to his service.' 6. And Moses took the wagons and the oxen, and gave them unto the Levites. 7. Two wagons and four oxen he gave unto the sons of Gershon, according to their service. 8. And four wagons and eight oxen he gave unto the sons of Merari,

27. *put My name.* Announce to the children of Israel the blessed and beneficent nearness of the living God. In this prayer on behalf of Israel, the priests pronounced over the people the Ineffable Name of God. Outside the Temple, *Adonay* was invariably substituted for the Tetragrammaton.

and I will bless them. i.e. the children of Israel. The Israelites say, Why didst Thou order the priest to bless us? We want Thy blessing only. And God replies, It is I who stand by the priests and bless you (Talmud). The priest was no Mediator; and no priest could say, *I* bless the children of Israel. God is the source of, and He alone can give effect to, the blessing pronounced by the priests. They were merely the channel through which the blessing was conveyed *to* the Israelites.

CHAPTER VII

THE OFFERINGS OF THE PRINCES

In this chapter we have the narrative of the presentation of identical gifts by the princes of each of the twelve tribes at the dedication of the Altar. This presentation took place at the time when Moses, after having completed the erection of the Tabernacle, anointed and sanctified it as well as the Altar and all the vessels connected with it (Lev. VIII, 10, 11). Chronologically the present chapter follows immediately after Lev. VIII. The offerings consist of gifts for the transport of the Tabernacle, and golden and silver vessels for the service of the Sanctuary, with sacrificial animals for the dedication ceremony. They were offered on twelve separate days. The narrative, describing each in unaltered language, reflects the stately solemnity that marked the repetition of the same ceremonial day by day. 'None among the princes wished to outrival the others, but such harmony reigned among them and such unity of spirit that God valued the service of each as if he had brought not only his own gifts but also those of his companions' (Midrash).

1. *on the day.* At the time when.

2. *over them that were numbered.* The leaders who were appointed to act with Moses in taking the census; see I, 4 f.

according unto their service, under the hand of Ithamar the son of Aaron the priest. 9. But unto the sons of Kohath he gave none, because the service of the holy things belonged unto them: they bore them upon their shoulders. 10. And the princes brought the dedication-offering of the altar in the day that it was anointed, even the princes brought their offering before the altar. 11. And the LORD said unto Moses: 'They shall present their offering, each prince on his day, for the dedication of the altar.'*vs. ¶ 12. And he that presented his offering the first day was Nahshon the son of Amminadab, of the tribe of Judah; 13. and his offering was one silver dish, the weight thereof was a hundred and thirty shekels, one silver basin of seventy shekels, after the shekel of the sanctuary; both of them full of fine flour mingled with oil for a meal-offering; 14. one golden pan of ten shekels, full of incense; 15. one young bullock, one ram, one he-lamb of the first year, for a burnt-offering; 16. one male of the goats for a sin-offering; 17. and for the sacrifice of peace-offerings, two oxen, five rams, five he-goats, five he-lambs of the first year. This was the offering of Nahshon the son of Amminadab. ¶ 18. On

י נָתָן כִּי־עֲבֹדַת הַקֹּדֶשׁ עֲלֵהֶם בַּכָּתֵף יִשָּׂאוּ׃ וַיַּקְרִיבוּ
הַנְּשִׂאִים אֵת חֲנֻכַּת הַמִּזְבֵּחַ בְּיוֹם הִמָּשַׁח אֹתוֹ וַיַּקְרִיבוּ
11 הַנְּשִׂיאִם אֶת־קָרְבָּנָם לִפְנֵי הַמִּזְבֵּחַ׃ וַיֹּאמֶר יְהוָה אֶל־
(חמישי לספ') מֹשֶׁה נָשִׂיא אֶחָד לַיּוֹם יַקְרִיבוּ אֶת־
12 קָרְבָּנָם לַחֲנֻכַּת הַמִּזְבֵּחַ׃ * ס וַיְהִי הַמַּקְרִיב בַּיּוֹם הָרִאשׁוֹן
13 אֶת־קָרְבָּנוֹ נַחְשׁוֹן בֶּן־עַמִּינָדָב לְמַטֵּה יְהוּדָה׃ וְקָרְבָּנוֹ
קַעֲרַת־כֶּסֶף אַחַת שְׁלֹשִׁים וּמֵאָה מִשְׁקָלָהּ מִזְרָק אֶחָד
כֶּסֶף שִׁבְעִים שֶׁקֶל בְּשֶׁקֶל הַקֹּדֶשׁ שְׁנֵיהֶם ׀ מְלֵאִים סֹלֶת
14 בְּלוּלָה בַשֶּׁמֶן לְמִנְחָה׃ כַּף אַחַת עֲשָׂרָה זָהָב מְלֵאָה
טו קְטֹרֶת׃ פַּר אֶחָד בֶּן־בָּקָר אַיִל אֶחָד כֶּבֶשׂ־אֶחָד בֶּן־שְׁנָתוֹ
16 17 לְעֹלָה׃ שְׂעִיר־עִזִּים אֶחָד לְחַטָּאת׃ וּלְזֶבַח הַשְּׁלָמִים בָּקָר
שְׁנַיִם אֵילִם חֲמִשָּׁה עַתֻּדִים חֲמִשָּׁה כְּבָשִׂים בְּנֵי־שָׁנָה
חֲמִשָּׁה זֶה קָרְבַּן נַחְשׁוֹן בֶּן־עַמִּינָדָב׃ פ
18 19 בַּיּוֹם הַשֵּׁנִי הִקְרִיב נְתַנְאֵל בֶּן־צוּעָר נְשִׂיא יִשָּׂשכָר׃ הִקְרִב

9. *they bore them upon their shoulders.* It was not seemly that the holiest vessels should be placed on wagons. Staves or poles had been provided so as to enable them to be borne on shoulders.

10. *dedication-offering of the altar.* After having presented the wagons and oxen for the conveyance of the Tabernacle and its appurtenances, the princes brought further sacrifices for the dedication of the Altar.

12. *Nahshon the son of Amminadab.* See I, 7 and II, 3. The names of the other princes and the order in which they are mentioned in the present chapter are the same as given previously in connection with the march. 'Nahshon was rewarded in this way for the devotion he had shown to God during the passage through the Red Sea. When Israel, beset by the Egyptians, reached the sea, the tribes hesitated to enter the sea and one urged the other to be the first to do so. At that moment Nahshon, the prince of Judah, fearlessly plunged in, firmly trusting that God would stand by Israel in their need' (Midrash).

13. *an hundred and thirty shekels.* About 60 oz. Troy.

seventy shekels. About 33 oz. Troy.

14. *pan.* Better, *cup.* Such incense-cups are to be seen in the representation of the Table of shewbread on the Arch of Titus.

17. *peace-offerings.* Were an expression of the joyous gratitude of the worshipper to God. Hence they were, in these instances, the most multiplied, as befitted an occasion of joy and of thankful communion with God.

The offerings of the princes were a favourite theme for the later Rabbinical homilists. They held that, though the offerings of all the princes were identical, these had a different significance for each tribe. From the time of Jacob, who foretold it to them, every tribe knew his future history to the time of the Messiah; hence, at the dedication of the Altar, each prince brought such offerings as symbolized the history of his tribe. Apart from the significance that the offerings had for each tribe respectively, they were held also to symbolize the history of the world from the time of Adam to the erection of the Tabernacle. The following comments on the gifts of the princes of Issachar (*v.* 18), of Reuben (*v.* 30), and on *v.* 84 f are fair samples of this symbolization.

18. *prince of Issachar.* 'The tribe of Issachar had good claims to be among the first to offer sacrifices, for this tribe devoted itself to the study of the Torah, so that the great scholars in Israel were among them; and then, too, it was this tribe that had proposed to the others the bringing of the dedication offerings. As this was the tribe of erudition, its gifts symbolized things appertaining to the Torah. The silver charger and the silver bowl corresponded to the Written and to the Oral Torah; and both vessels alike are filled

אֶת־קָרְבָּנוֹ קַעֲרַת־כֶּסֶף אַחַת שְׁלֹשִׁים וּמֵאָה מִשְׁקָלָהּ
מִזְרָק אֶחָד כֶּסֶף שִׁבְעִים שֶׁקֶל בְּשֶׁקֶל הַקֹּדֶשׁ שְׁנֵיהֶם ׀
כ מְלֵאִים סֹלֶת בְּלוּלָה בַשֶּׁמֶן לְמִנְחָה׃ כַּף אַחַת עֲשָׂרָה
21 זָהָב מְלֵאָה קְטֹרֶת׃ פַּר אֶחָד בֶּן־בָּקָר אַיִל אֶחָד כֶּבֶשׂ־
22 23 אֶחָד בֶּן־שְׁנָתוֹ לְעֹלָה׃ שְׂעִיר־עִזִּים אֶחָד לְחַטָּאת׃ וּלְזֶבַח
הַשְּׁלָמִים בָּקָר שְׁנַיִם אֵילִם חֲמִשָּׁה עַתֻּדִים חֲמִשָּׁה כְּבָשִׂים
בְּנֵי־שָׁנָה חֲמִשָּׁה זֶה קָרְבַּן נְתַנְאֵל בֶּן־צוּעָר׃ פ
24 כה בַּיּוֹם הַשְּׁלִישִׁי נָשִׂיא לִבְנֵי זְבוּלֻן אֱלִיאָב בֶּן־חֵלֹן׃ קָרְבָּנוֹ
קַעֲרַת־כֶּסֶף אַחַת שְׁלֹשִׁים וּמֵאָה מִשְׁקָלָהּ מִזְרָק אֶחָד
כֶּסֶף שִׁבְעִים שֶׁקֶל בְּשֶׁקֶל הַקֹּדֶשׁ שְׁנֵיהֶם ׀ מְלֵאִים סֹלֶת
26 בְּלוּלָה בַשֶּׁמֶן לְמִנְחָה׃ כַּף אַחַת עֲשָׂרָה זָהָב מְלֵאָה
27 קְטֹרֶת׃ פַּר אֶחָד בֶּן־בָּקָר אַיִל אֶחָד כֶּבֶשׂ־אֶחָד בֶּן־
28 29 שְׁנָתוֹ לְעֹלָה׃ שְׂעִיר־עִזִּים אֶחָד לְחַטָּאת׃ וּלְזֶבַח הַשְּׁלָמִים
בָּקָר שְׁנַיִם אֵילִם חֲמִשָּׁה עַתֻּדִים חֲמִשָּׁה כְּבָשִׂים בְּנֵי־שָׁנָה
חֲמִשָּׁה זֶה קָרְבַּן אֱלִיאָב בֶּן־חֵלֹן׃ פ
ל בַּיּוֹם הָרְבִיעִי נָשִׂיא לִבְנֵי רְאוּבֵן אֱלִיצוּר בֶּן־שְׁדֵיאוּר׃
31 קָרְבָּנוֹ קַעֲרַת־כֶּסֶף אַחַת שְׁלֹשִׁים וּמֵאָה מִשְׁקָלָהּ מִזְרָק
אֶחָד כֶּסֶף שִׁבְעִים שֶׁקֶל בְּשֶׁקֶל הַקֹּדֶשׁ שְׁנֵיהֶם ׀ מְלֵאִים
32 סֹלֶת בְּלוּלָה בַשֶּׁמֶן לְמִנְחָה׃ כַּף אַחַת עֲשָׂרָה זָהָב מְלֵאָה
33 קְטֹרֶת׃ פַּר אֶחָד בֶּן־בָּקָר אַיִל אֶחָד כֶּבֶשׂ־אֶחָד בֶּן־שְׁנָתוֹ
34 לה לְעֹלָה׃ שְׂעִיר־עִזִּים אֶחָד לְחַטָּאת׃ וּלְזֶבַח הַשְּׁלָמִים בָּקָר
שְׁנַיִם אֵילִם חֲמִשָּׁה עַתֻּדִים חֲמִשָּׁה כְּבָשִׂים בְּנֵי־שָׁנָה
חֲמִשָּׁה זֶה קָרְבַּן אֱלִיצוּר בֶּן־שְׁדֵיאוּר׃ פ
36 בַּיּוֹם הַחֲמִישִׁי נָשִׂיא לִבְנֵי שִׁמְעוֹן שְׁלֻמִיאֵל בֶּן־צוּרִישַׁדָּי׃
37 קָרְבָּנוֹ קַעֲרַת־כֶּסֶף אַחַת שְׁלֹשִׁים וּמֵאָה מִשְׁקָלָהּ מִזְרָק
אֶחָד כֶּסֶף שִׁבְעִים שֶׁקֶל בְּשֶׁקֶל הַקֹּדֶשׁ שְׁנֵיהֶם ׀ מְלֵאִים

the second day Nethanel the son of Zuar, prince of Issachar, did offer: 19. he presented for his offering one silver dish, the weight thereof was a hundred and thirty shekels, one silver basin of seventy shekels, after the shekel of the sanctuary; both of them full of fine flour mingled with oil for a meal-offering; 20. one golden pan of ten shekels, full of incense; 21. one young bullock, one ram one he-lamb of the first year, for a burnt-offering; 22. one male of the goats for a sin-offering; 23. and for the sacrifice of peace-offerings, two oxen, five rams, five he-goats, five he-lambs of the first year. This was the offering of Nethanel the son of Zuar. ¶ 24. On the third day Eliab the son of Helon, prince of the children of Zebulun: 25. his offering was one silver dish, the weight thereof was a hundred and thirty shekels, one silver basin of seventy shekels, after the shekel of the sanctuary; both of them full of fine flour mingled with oil for a meal-offering; 26. one golden pan of ten shekels, full of incense; 27. one young bullock, one ram, one he-lamb of the first year, for a burnt-offering; 28. one male of the goats for a sin-offering; 29. and for the sacrifice of peace-offerings, two oxen, five rams, five he-goats, five he-lambs of the first year. This was the offering of Eliab the son of Helon. ¶ 30. On the fourth day Elizur the son of Shedeur, prince of the children of Reuben: 31. his offering was one silver dish, the weight thereof was a hundred and thirty shekels, one silver basin of seventy shekels, after the shekel of the sanctuary; both of them full of fine flour mingled with oil for a meal-offering; 32. one golden pan of ten shekels, full of incense; 33. one young bullock, one ram, one he-lamb of the first year, for a burnt-offering; 34. one male of the goats for a sin-offering; 35. and for the sacrifice of peace-offerings, two oxen, five rams, five he-goats, five he-lambs of the first year. This was the offering of Elizur the son of Shedeur. ¶ 36. On the fifth day Shelumiel the son of Zurishaddai, prince of the children of Simeon: 37. his offering was one silver dish, the weight thereof was a hundred and thirty shekels, one silver basin of seventy shekels, after

with fine flour, for the two Laws are not antagonistic, but form a unity and contain the loftiest teachings. The fine flour was mingled with oil, just as knowledge of the Torah should be accompanied by good deeds; for he who occupies himself with the Torah, who works good deeds, and keeps himself aloof from sin, fills his Creator with delight. The golden spoon of ten shekels symbolizes the Two Tables on which God wrote the Ten Commandments, and which contained between the Commandments all the particulars of the Torah, just as the spoon was filled with incense. The three burnt offerings, the bullock, the ram, and the lamb, corresponded to the three groups of Priests, Levites, and Israelites; whereas the kid of the goats alluded to the proselytes, for the Torah was revealed not only for Israel but for all the world; and a proselyte who studies the Torah is no less than a high priest' (Midrash).

30. *prince of the children of Reuben.* 'The gifts

38 סֹלֶת בְּלוּלָה בַשֶּׁמֶן לְמִנְחָה׃ כַּף אַחַת עֲשָׂרָה זָהָב מְלֵאָה
39 קְטֹרֶת׃ פַּר אֶחָד בֶּן־בָּקָר אַיִל אֶחָד כֶּבֶשׂ־אֶחָד בֶּן־שְׁנָתוֹ
מ 41 לְעֹלָה׃ שְׂעִיר־עִזִּים אֶחָד לְחַטָּאת׃ וּלְזֶבַח הַשְּׁלָמִים בָּקָר
שְׁנַיִם אֵילִם חֲמִשָּׁה עַתֻּדִים חֲמִשָּׁה כְּבָשִׂים בְּנֵי־שָׁנָה
חֲמִשָּׁה זֶה קָרְבַּן שְׁלֻמִיאֵל בֶּן־צוּרִישַׁדָּי׃ פ ששי
42 43 בַּיּוֹם הַשִּׁשִּׁי נָשִׂיא לִבְנֵי גָד אֶלְיָסָף בֶּן־דְּעוּאֵל׃ קָרְבָּנוֹ
קַעֲרַת־כֶּסֶף אַחַת שְׁלֹשִׁים וּמֵאָה מִשְׁקָלָהּ מִזְרָק אֶחָד
כֶּסֶף שִׁבְעִים שֶׁקֶל בְּשֶׁקֶל הַקֹּדֶשׁ שְׁנֵיהֶם ׀ מְלֵאִים סֹלֶת
44 בְּלוּלָה בַשֶּׁמֶן לְמִנְחָה׃ כַּף אַחַת עֲשָׂרָה זָהָב מְלֵאָה קְטֹרֶת׃
מה פַּר אֶחָד בֶּן־בָּקָר אַיִל אֶחָד כֶּבֶשׂ־אֶחָד בֶּן־שְׁנָתוֹ לְעֹלָה׃
46 47 שְׂעִיר־עִזִּים אֶחָד לְחַטָּאת׃ וּלְזֶבַח הַשְּׁלָמִים בָּקָר שְׁנַיִם
אֵילִם חֲמִשָּׁה עַתֻּדִים חֲמִשָּׁה כְּבָשִׂים בְּנֵי־שָׁנָה חֲמִשָּׁה
זֶה קָרְבַּן אֶלְיָסָף בֶּן־דְּעוּאֵל׃ פ
48 בַּיּוֹם הַשְּׁבִיעִי נָשִׂיא לִבְנֵי אֶפְרָיִם אֱלִישָׁמָע בֶּן־עַמִּיהוּד׃
49 קָרְבָּנוֹ קַעֲרַת־כֶּסֶף אַחַת שְׁלֹשִׁים וּמֵאָה מִשְׁקָלָהּ מִזְרָק
אֶחָד כֶּסֶף שִׁבְעִים שֶׁקֶל בְּשֶׁקֶל הַקֹּדֶשׁ שְׁנֵיהֶם ׀ מְלֵאִים
נ סֹלֶת בְּלוּלָה בַשֶּׁמֶן לְמִנְחָה׃ כַּף אַחַת עֲשָׂרָה זָהָב מְלֵאָה
51 קְטֹרֶת׃ פַּר אֶחָד בֶּן־בָּקָר אַיִל אֶחָד כֶּבֶשׂ־אֶחָד בֶּן־שְׁנָתוֹ
52 53 לְעֹלָה׃ שְׂעִיר־עִזִּים אֶחָד לְחַטָּאת׃ וּלְזֶבַח הַשְּׁלָמִים בָּקָר
שְׁנַיִם אֵילִם חֲמִשָּׁה עַתֻּדִים חֲמִשָּׁה כְּבָשִׂים בְּנֵי־שָׁנָה
חֲמִשָּׁה זֶה קָרְבַּן אֱלִישָׁמָע בֶּן־עַמִּיהוּד׃ פ
54 בַּיּוֹם הַשְּׁמִינִי נָשִׂיא לִבְנֵי מְנַשֶּׁה גַּמְלִיאֵל בֶּן־פְּדָהצוּר׃
נה קָרְבָּנוֹ קַעֲרַת־כֶּסֶף אַחַת שְׁלֹשִׁים וּמֵאָה מִשְׁקָלָהּ מִזְרָק
אֶחָד כֶּסֶף שִׁבְעִים שֶׁקֶל בְּשֶׁקֶל הַקֹּדֶשׁ שְׁנֵיהֶם ׀ מְלֵאִים
56 סֹלֶת בְּלוּלָה בַשֶּׁמֶן לְמִנְחָה׃ כַּף אַחַת עֲשָׂרָה זָהָב מְלֵאָה
57 קְטֹרֶת׃ פַּר אֶחָד בֶּן־בָּקָר אַיִל אֶחָד כֶּבֶשׂ־אֶחָד בֶּן־שְׁנָתוֹ
58 59 לְעֹלָה׃ שְׂעִיר־עִזִּים אֶחָד לְחַטָּאת׃ וּלְזֶבַח הַשְּׁלָמִים בָּקָר
שְׁנַיִם אֵילִם חֲמִשָּׁה עַתֻּדִים חֲמִשָּׁה כְּבָשִׂים בְּנֵי־שָׁנָה

the shekel of the sanctuary; both of them full of fine flour mingled with oil for a meal-offering; 38. one golden pan of ten shekels, full of incense; 39. one young bullock, one ram, one he-lamb of the first year, for a burnt-offering; 40. one male of the goats for a sin-offering; 41. and for the sacrifice of peace-offerings, two oxen, five rams, five he-goats, five he-lambs of the first year. This was the offering of Shelumiel the son of Zurishaddai.*vi. ¶ 42. On the sixth day Eliasaph the son of Deuel, prince of the children of Gad: 43. his offering was one silver dish, the weight thereof was a hundred and thirty shekels, one silver basin of seventy shekels, after the shekel of the sanctuary; both of them full of fine flour mingled with oil for a meal-offering; 44. one golden pan of ten shekels, full of incense; 45. one young bullock, one ram, one he-lamb of the first year, for a burnt-offering; 46. one male of the goats for a sin-offering; 47. and for the sacrifice of peace-offerings, two oxen, five rams, five he-goats, five he-lambs of the first year. This was the offering of Eliasaph the son of Deuel. ¶ 48. On the seventh day Elishama the son of Ammihud, prince of the children of Ephraim: 49. his offering was one silver dish, the weight thereof was a hundred and thirty shekels, one silver basin of seventy shekels, after the shekel of the sanctuary; both of them full of fine flour mingled with oil for a meal-offering; 50. one golden pan of ten shekels, full of incense; 51. one young bullock, one ram, one he-lamb of the first year, for a burnt-offering; 52. one male of the goats for a sin-offering; 53. and for the sacrifice of peace-offerings, two oxen, five rams, five he-goats, five he-lambs of the first year. This was the offering of Elishama the son of Ammihud. ¶ 54. On the eighth day Gamaliel the son of Pedahzur, prince of the children of Manasseh: 55. his offering was one silver dish, the weight thereof was a hundred and thirty shekels, one silver basin of seventy shekels, after the shekel of the sanctuary; both of them full of fine flour mingled with oil for a meal-offering; 56. one golden pan of ten shekels, full of incense; 57. one young bullock, one ram, one he-lamb of the first year, for a burnt-offering; 58. one male of the goats for a sin-offering; 59. and for the sacrifice of

of the tribe of Reuben symbolized the events in the life of their forefather Reuben. The silver charger recalled Reuben's words when he saved the life of Joseph, whom his brothers wanted to kill, for "the tongue of the just is as choice silver". The silver bowl, from which was sprinkled the sacrificial blood, recalled the same incident, for it was Reuben who advised his brothers to throw Joseph into the pit rather than to kill him. The spoon of ten shekels of gold symbolized the deed of Reuben, who restrained Jacob's sons from bloodshed, hence the gold out of which the spoon peace-offerings, two oxen, five rams, five he-goats, five he-lambs of the first year. This was the offering of Gamaliel the son of Pedahzur. ¶ 60. On the ninth day Abidan the son of Gideoni, prince of the children of Benjamin: 61. his offering was one silver dish, the weight thereof was a hundred and thirty shekels, one silver basin of seventy shekels, after the shekel of the sanctuary; both of them full of fine flour mingled with oil for a meal-offering; 62. one golden pan of ten shekels, full of incense; 63. one young bullock, one ram, one he-lamb of the first year, for a burnt-offering; 64. one male of the goats for a sin-offering; 65. and for the sacrifice of peace-offerings, two oxen, five rams, five he-goats, five he-lambs of the first year. This was the offering of Abidan the son of Gideoni. ¶ 66. On the tenth day Ahiezer the son of Ammishaddai, prince of the children of Dan: 67. his offering was one silver dish, the weight thereof was a hundred and thirty shekels, one silver basin of seventy shekels, after the shekel of the sanctuary; both of them full of fine flour mingled with oil for a meal-offering; 68. one golden pan of ten shekels, full of incense; 69. one young bullock, one ram, one he-lamb of the first year, for a burnt-offering; 70. one male of the goats for a sin-offering; 71. and for the sacrifice of peace-offerings, two oxen, five rams, five he-goats, five he-lambs of the first year. This was the offering of Ahiezer the son of Ammishaddai.*vii. ¶ 72. On the eleventh day Pagiel the son of Ochran, prince of the children of Asher: 73. his offering was one silver dish, the weight thereof was a hundred and thirty shekels, one silver basin of seventy shekels, after the shekel of the sanctuary; both of them full of fine flour mingled with oil for a meal-offering; 74. one golden pan of ten shekels, full of incense; 75. one young bullock, one ram, one he-lamb of the first year, for a burnt-offering; 76. one male of the goats for a sin-offering; 77. and for the sacrifice of peace-offerings, two oxen, five rams, five he-goats, five he-lambs of the first year. This was the offering of Pagiel the son of Ochran. ¶ 78. On the twelfth day Ahira the son of Enan, prince of the children of Naphtali: 79. his offering was one silver dish, the weight thereof was a hundred and thirty shekels, one silver basin of seventy shekels, after the shekel of the sanctuary; both of them full of fine flour

חֲמִשָּׁה זֶה קָרְבַּן גַּמְלִיאֵל בֶּן־פְּדָהצוּר׃ פ
ס 61 בַּיּוֹם הַתְּשִׁיעִי נָשִׂיא לִבְנֵי בִנְיָמִן אֲבִידָן בֶּן־גִּדְעֹנִי׃ קָרְבָּנוֹ
קַעֲרַת־כֶּסֶף אַחַת שְׁלֹשִׁים וּמֵאָה מִשְׁקָלָהּ מִזְרָק אֶחָד
כֶּסֶף שִׁבְעִים שֶׁקֶל בְּשֶׁקֶל הַקֹּדֶשׁ שְׁנֵיהֶם ׀ מְלֵאִים סֹלֶת
62 בְּלוּלָה בַשֶּׁמֶן לְמִנְחָה׃ כַּף אַחַת עֲשָׂרָה זָהָב מְלֵאָה
63 קְטֹרֶת׃ פַּר אֶחָד בֶּן־בָּקָר אַיִל אֶחָד כֶּבֶשׂ־אֶחָד בֶּן־שְׁנָתוֹ
64 סה לְעֹלָה׃ שְׂעִיר־עִזִּים אֶחָד לְחַטָּאת׃ וּלְזֶבַח הַשְּׁלָמִים בָּקָר
שְׁנַיִם אֵילִם חֲמִשָּׁה עַתֻּדִים חֲמִשָּׁה כְּבָשִׂים בְּנֵי־שָׁנָה
חֲמִשָּׁה זֶה קָרְבַּן אֲבִידָן בֶּן־גִּדְעֹנִי׃ פ
66 67 בַּיּוֹם הָעֲשִׂירִי נָשִׂיא לִבְנֵי דָן אֲחִיעֶזֶר בֶּן־עַמִּישַׁדָּי׃ קָרְבָּנוֹ
קַעֲרַת־כֶּסֶף אַחַת שְׁלֹשִׁים וּמֵאָה מִשְׁקָלָהּ מִזְרָק אֶחָד
כֶּסֶף שִׁבְעִים שֶׁקֶל בְּשֶׁקֶל הַקֹּדֶשׁ שְׁנֵיהֶם ׀ מְלֵאִים סֹלֶת
68 בְּלוּלָה בַשֶּׁמֶן לְמִנְחָה׃ כַּף אַחַת עֲשָׂרָה זָהָב מְלֵאָה
69 קְטֹרֶת׃ פַּר אֶחָד בֶּן־בָּקָר אַיִל אֶחָד כֶּבֶשׂ־אֶחָד בֶּן־שְׁנָתוֹ
ע 71 לְעֹלָה׃ שְׂעִיר־עִזִּים אֶחָד לְחַטָּאת׃ וּלְזֶבַח הַשְּׁלָמִים בָּקָר
שְׁנַיִם אֵילִם חֲמִשָּׁה עַתֻּדִים חֲמִשָּׁה כְּבָשִׂים בְּנֵי־שָׁנָה
חֲמִשָּׁה זֶה קָרְבַּן אֲחִיעֶזֶר בֶּן־עַמִּישַׁדָּי׃ * פ שביעי
72 בְּיוֹם עַשְׁתֵּי עָשָׂר יוֹם נָשִׂיא לִבְנֵי אָשֵׁר פַּגְעִיאֵל בֶּן־עָכְרָן׃
73 קָרְבָּנוֹ קַעֲרַת־כֶּסֶף אַחַת שְׁלֹשִׁים וּמֵאָה מִשְׁקָלָהּ מִזְרָק
אֶחָד כֶּסֶף שִׁבְעִים שֶׁקֶל בְּשֶׁקֶל הַקֹּדֶשׁ שְׁנֵיהֶם ׀ מְלֵאִים
74 סֹלֶת בְּלוּלָה בַשֶּׁמֶן לְמִנְחָה׃ כַּף אַחַת עֲשָׂרָה זָהָב מְלֵאָה
עה קְטֹרֶת׃ פַּר אֶחָד בֶּן־בָּקָר אַיִל אֶחָד כֶּבֶשׂ־אֶחָד בֶּן־שְׁנָתוֹ
76 77 לְעֹלָה׃ שְׂעִיר־עִזִּים אֶחָד לְחַטָּאת׃ וּלְזֶבַח הַשְּׁלָמִים בָּקָר
שְׁנַיִם אֵילִם חֲמִשָּׁה עַתֻּדִים חֲמִשָּׁה כְּבָשִׂים בְּנֵי־שָׁנָה
חֲמִשָּׁה זֶה קָרְבַּן פַּגְעִיאֵל בֶּן־עָכְרָן׃ פ
78 בְּיוֹם שְׁנֵים עָשָׂר יוֹם נָשִׂיא לִבְנֵי נַפְתָּלִי אֲחִירַע בֶּן־עֵינָן׃
79 קָרְבָּנוֹ קַעֲרַת־כֶּסֶף אַחַת שְׁלֹשִׁים וּמֵאָה מִשְׁקָלָהּ מִזְרָק
אֶחָד כֶּסֶף שִׁבְעִים שֶׁקֶל בְּשֶׁקֶל הַקֹּדֶשׁ שְׁנֵיהֶם ׀ מְלֵאִים

was fashioned had a blood-red colour. The spoon was filled with incense, and so too did Reuben fill his days with fasting and prayer until God forgave his sin with Bilhah, and his "prayer was set forth before God as incense". As penance for this crime, Reuben offered the kid of the goats as a sin offering; whereas the two oxen of the peace offering corresponded to the two great deeds of Reuben, the deliverance of Joseph and the long penance for his sin' (Midrash).

mingled with oil for a meal-offering; 80. one golden pan of ten shekels, full of incense; 81. one young bullock, one ram, one he-lamb of the first year, for a burnt-offering; 82. one male of the goats for a sin-offering; 83. and for the sacrifice of peace-offerings, two oxen, five rams, five he-goats, five he-lambs of the first year. This was the offering of Ahira the son of Enan. ¶84. This was the dedication-offering of the altar, in the day when it was anointed, at the hands of the princes of Israel: twelve silver dishes, twelve silver basins, twelve golden pans; 85. each silver dish weighing a hundred and thirty shekels, and each basin seventy; all the silver of the vessels two thousand and four hundred shekels, after the shekel of the sanctuary; 86. twelve golden pans, full of incense, weighing ten shekels apiece, after the shekel of the sanctuary; all the gold of the pans a hundred and twenty shekels; *m. 87. all the oxen for the burnt-offering twelve bullocks, the rams twelve, the he-lambs of the first year twelve, and their meal-offering; and the males of the goats for a sin-offering twelve; 88. and all the oxen for the sacrifice of peace-offerings twenty and four bullocks, the rams sixty, the he-goats sixty, the he-lambs of the first year sixty. This was the dedication-offering of the altar, after that it was anointed. 89. And when Moses went into the tent of meeting that He might speak with him, then he heard the Voice speaking unto him from above the ark-cover that was upon the ark of the testimony, from between the two cherubim; and He spoke unto him.

פ סֹלֶת בְּלוּלָה בַשֶּׁמֶן לְמִנְחָה׃ כַּף אַחַת עֲשָׂרָה זָהָב מְלֵאָה
81 קְטֹרֶת׃ פַּר אֶחָד בֶּן־בָּקָר אַיִל אֶחָד כֶּבֶשׂ־אֶחָד בֶּן־שְׁנָתוֹ
82 83 לְעֹלָה׃ שְׂעִיר־עִזִּים אֶחָד לְחַטָּאת׃ וּלְזֶבַח הַשְּׁלָמִים בָּקָר
שְׁנַיִם אֵילִם חֲמִשָּׁה עַתֻּדִים חֲמִשָּׁה כְּבָשִׂים בְּנֵי־שָׁנָה
חֲמִשָּׁה זֶה קָרְבַּן אֲחִירַע בֶּן־עֵינָן׃ פ
84 זֹאת ׀ חֲנֻכַּת הַמִּזְבֵּחַ בְּיוֹם הִמָּשַׁח אֹתוֹ מֵאֵת נְשִׂיאֵי יִשְׂרָאֵל
קַעֲרֹת כֶּסֶף שְׁתֵּים עֶשְׂרֵה מִזְרְקֵי־כֶסֶף שְׁנֵים עָשָׂר כַּפּוֹת
פה זָהָב שְׁתֵּים עֶשְׂרֵה׃ שְׁלֹשִׁים וּמֵאָה הַקְּעָרָה הָאַחַת כֶּסֶף
וְשִׁבְעִים הַמִּזְרָק הָאֶחָד כֹּל כֶּסֶף הַכֵּלִים אַלְפַּיִם וְאַרְבַּע־
86 מֵאוֹת בְּשֶׁקֶל הַקֹּדֶשׁ׃ כַּפּוֹת זָהָב שְׁתֵּים־עֶשְׂרֵה מְלֵאֹת
קְטֹרֶת עֲשָׂרָה עֲשָׂרָה הַכַּף בְּשֶׁקֶל הַקֹּדֶשׁ כָּל־זְהַב הַכַּפּוֹת
מפטיר 87 עֶשְׂרִים וּמֵאָה׃ *כָּל־הַבָּקָר לָעֹלָה שְׁנֵים עָשָׂר פָּרִים אֵילִם
שְׁנֵים־עָשָׂר כְּבָשִׂים בְּנֵי־שָׁנָה שְׁנֵים עָשָׂר וּמִנְחָתָם וּשְׂעִירֵי
88 עִזִּים שְׁנֵים עָשָׂר לְחַטָּאת׃ וְכֹל בְּקַר ׀ זֶבַח הַשְּׁלָמִים עֶשְׂרִים
וְאַרְבָּעָה פָּרִים אֵילִם שִׁשִּׁים עַתֻּדִים שִׁשִּׁים כְּבָשִׂים בְּנֵי־
89 שָׁנָה שִׁשִּׁים זֹאת חֲנֻכַּת הַמִּזְבֵּחַ אַחֲרֵי הִמָּשַׁח אֹתוֹ׃ וּבְבֹא
מֹשֶׁה אֶל־אֹהֶל מוֹעֵד לְדַבֵּר אִתּוֹ וַיִּשְׁמַע אֶת־הַקּוֹל מִדַּבֵּר
אֵלָיו מֵעַל הַכַּפֹּרֶת אֲשֶׁר עַל־אֲרֹן הָעֵדֻת מִבֵּין שְׁנֵי הַכְּרֻבִים
וַיְדַבֵּר אֵלָיו׃

84. 'The gifts of the twelve princes of the tribes were equal in number as well as in the size and width of the objects bestowed. None among them wished to outrival the others; and such harmony and unity of spirit reigned among them, that God valued the service of each as if he had brought not only his own gifts but also those of his companions. The sum total of the gifts of the twelve princes of the tribes had also a symbolical significance. The twelve chargers correspond to the twelve constellations; the twelve bowls to the twelve months; the twelve spoons to the twelve guides of men, which are: the heart, the kidneys, the mouth, the palate, the windpipe, the esophagus, the lungs, the liver, the spleen, the crop, and the stomach. "All the silver of the vessels that weighed two thousand and four hundred shekels," corresponded to the years that had passed from the Creation of the World to the advent of Moses in the fortieth year of his life. All the gold of the spoons, the weight of which was an hundred and twenty shekels, corresponded to the years of Moses' life' (Midrash).

89. *that He might speak with him.* *i.e.* with God.

he heard the Voice speaking unto him. lit. 'he heard the Voice making itself as speaking'; *i.e.* Moses was audibly addressed by a Voice, not as before on the peak of Sinai far away, but in the Sanctuary that was now in the midst of Israel: Exod. xxv, 22.

'Moses in his humility felt that his mission as leader of the people ended with the erection of the Tabernacle, as Israel could now satisfy all their spiritual needs without his aid. But God said, As truly as thou livest, I have for thee a far greater task than any thou hast yet accomplished, for thou shalt instruct My children about "clean and unclean", and shalt teach them how to offer up offerings to Me. God hereupon called Moses to the Tabernacle, to reveal to him there the laws and teachings. The Voice that called Moses was as powerful as at the revelation at Sinai, still it was audible to none but Moses. Not even the angels heard it, for the words of God were destined exclusively for Moses' (Midrash).

HAFTORAH NASO הפטרת נשא

JUDGES XIII, 2–25

Chapter XIII

2. And there was a certain man of Zorah, of the family of the Danites, whose name was Manoah; and his wife was barren, and bore not. 3. And the angel of the Lord appeared unto the woman, and said unto her: 'Behold now, thou art barren, and hast not borne; but thou shalt conceive, and bear a son. 4. Now therefore beware, I pray thee, and drink no wine nor strong drink, and eat not any unclean thing. 5. For, lo, thou shalt conceive, and bear a son; and no razor shall come upon his head; for the child shall be a Nazirite unto God from the womb; and he shall begin to save Israel out of the hand of the Philistines.' 6. Then the woman came and told her husband, saying: 'A man of God came unto me, and his countenance was like the countenance of the angel of God, very

Cap. XIII. יג

2 וַיְהִי אִישׁ אֶחָד מִצָּרְעָה
מִמִּשְׁפַּחַת הַדָּנִי וּשְׁמוֹ מָנוֹחַ וְאִשְׁתּוֹ עֲקָרָה וְלֹא יָלָדָה׃
3 וַיֵּרָא מַלְאַךְ־יְהוָה אֶל־הָאִשָּׁה וַיֹּאמֶר אֵלֶיהָ הִנֵּה־נָא אַתְּ־
4 עֲקָרָה וְלֹא יָלַדְתְּ וְהָרִית וְיָלַדְתְּ בֵּן׃ וְעַתָּה הִשָּׁמְרִי נָא
ה וְאַל־תִּשְׁתִּי יַיִן וְשֵׁכָר וְאַל־תֹּאכְלִי כָּל־טָמֵא׃ כִּי הִנָּךְ
הָרָה וְיֹלַדְתְּ בֵּן וּמוֹרָה לֹא־יַעֲלֶה עַל־רֹאשׁוֹ כִּי־נְזִיר
אֱלֹהִים יִהְיֶה הַנַּעַר מִן־הַבָּטֶן וְהוּא יָחֵל לְהוֹשִׁיעַ אֶת־
6 יִשְׂרָאֵל מִיַּד פְּלִשְׁתִּים׃ וַתָּבֹא הָאִשָּׁה וַתֹּאמֶר לְאִישָׁהּ

Samson lived in the days of the Judges, that dark age in Bible history when there was no king in Israel and each one did that which was right in his own eyes. Deborah and Gideon and Jephthah were foremost amongst those 'Judges', *i.e.* champions who rescued their brethren from the slavery and degradation of the alien oppressor. And now the people had again been in bondage for over forty years to the Philistines, the most powerful and best organized of Israel's foes in the struggle for the possession of Canaan. They occupied the Maritime Plain and the hill-country between the sea and mountains of Judea, from Gaza northwards to Joppa. Unlike the Midianites and Moabites who merely came to plunder, the Philistines conquered in order to rule. They disarmed the Israelites, and reduced them to a condition of abject submission. They remained a mortal menace to Israel until their power was broken by David.

Samson, whose birth is foretold and announced in this Haftorah, brought a temporary deliverance from the Philistine yoke. But he was utterly alone, and he wrought his intermittent feats of private revenge and daring alone, supported neither by enthusiasm for the national cause nor by active help from his people. He was a man, strong physically but weak morally, who suffered shipwreck through following 'the desire of the eyes', and permitting himself to be ensnared by a heathen woman. His life came to nothing. Blinded by his enemies, he buried his enemies and himself in the ruins of the idolatrous temple in which the Philistines had gathered to feast over his miseries. 'The story of Samson and his vain struggles fitly closes the period of the Judges, while presaging the more ominous times when the tribes will seek and find, in union under a central monarchy, their freedom and their future' (Garstang).

Samson was to be a Nazirite from birth. Hence the selection of this chapter as Haftorah for the Sedrah which brings the regulations governing the life of the Nazirite.

2. *Zorah.* Identified with the modern Sur'ah, about 17 miles to the west of Jerusalem. Is it without religious significance that Israel's new champion was to arise from Dan, at that time the least powerful of the tribes?

Manoah. lit. 'rest', or 'place of rest'.

his wife. A woman of deep religious spirit, and worthy to be the mother of a deliverer of Israel.

was barren. 'The child in such a case was a special gift of God, and marked out for a special career' (Cooke).

4. *any unclean thing.* In order that self-control, which must distinguish all those consecrated to a higher service, might be implanted in him even during the pre-natal period (Ralbag). Samson was thus predestined for his career.

5. *begin to save Israel . . . Philistines.* No one before him attempted to shake their power. His exploits against them were the first steps towards their final subjugation by David. Samson *began* to save Israel.

6. *a man of God.* An inspired man; the designation of a prophet, for such she took him to be.

his countenance. His appearance.

very terrible. Awe-inspiring, so that she did not venture to question him.

terrible; and I asked him not whence he was, neither told he me his name; 7. but he said unto me: Behold, thou shalt conceive, and bear a son; and now drink no wine nor strong drink, and eat not any unclean thing; for the child shall be a Nazirite unto God from the womb to the day of his death.' ¶ 8. Then Manoah entreated the LORD, and said: 'Oh, Lord, I pray Thee, let the man of God whom Thou didst send come again unto us, and teach us what we shall do unto the child that shall be born.' 9. And God hearkened to the voice of Manoah; and the angel of God came again unto the woman as she sat in the field; but Manoah her husband was not with her. 10. And the woman made haste, and ran, and told her husband, and said unto him: 'Behold, the man hath appeared unto me, that came unto me that day.' 11. And Manoah arose, and went after his wife, and came to the man, and said unto him: 'Art thou the man that spokest unto the woman?' And he said: 'I am.' 12. And Manoah said: 'Now when thy word cometh to pass, what shall be the rule for the child, and what shall be done with him?' 13. And the angel of the LORD said unto Manoah: 'Of all that I said unto the woman let her beware. 14. She may not eat of any thing that cometh of the grape-vine, neither let her drink wine or strong drink, nor eat any unclean thing; all that I commanded her let her observe.' 15. And Manoah said unto the angel of the LORD: 'I pray thee, let us detain thee, that we may make ready a kid for thee.' 16. And the angel of the LORD said unto Manoah: 'Though thou detain me, I will not eat of thy bread; and if thou wilt make ready a burnt-offering, thou must offer it unto the LORD.' For Manoah knew not that he was the angel of the LORD. 17. And Manoah said unto the angel of the LORD: 'What is thy name, that when thy words come to pass we may do thee honour?' 18. And the angel of the LORD said unto him: 'Wherefore askest thou after my name, seeing it is hidden?' 19. So Manoah took the kid with the meal-offering, and offered it upon the rock unto the LORD; and [the angel] did wondrously, and Manoah and his wife looked on. 20. For it came to pass, when the flame went up toward heaven from off the altar, that the angel of the LORD ascended in the flame of

לֵאמֹר אִישׁ הָאֱלֹהִים בָּא אֵלַי וּמַרְאֵהוּ כְּמַרְאֵה מַלְאַךְ
הָאֱלֹהִים נוֹרָא מְאֹד וְלֹא שְׁאִלְתִּיהוּ אֵי־מִזֶּה הוּא וְאֶת־שְׁמוֹ
7 לֹא־הִגִּיד לִי׃ וַיֹּאמֶר לִי הִנָּךְ הָרָה וְיֹלַדְתְּ בֵּן וְעַתָּה אַל־
תִּשְׁתִּי ׀ יַיִן וְשֵׁכָר וְאַל־תֹּאכְלִי כָּל־טֻמְאָה כִּי־נְזִיר אֱלֹהִים
8 יִהְיֶה הַנַּעַר מִן־הַבֶּטֶן עַד־יוֹם מוֹתוֹ׃ וַיֶּעְתַּר מָנוֹחַ אֶל־
יְהוָה וַיֹּאמַר בִּי אֲדוֹנָי אִישׁ הָאֱלֹהִים אֲשֶׁר שָׁלַחְתָּ יָבוֹא־
9 נָא עוֹד אֵלֵינוּ וְיוֹרֵנוּ מַה־נַּעֲשֶׂה לַנַּעַר הַיּוּלָּד׃ וַיִּשְׁמַע
הָאֱלֹהִים בְּקוֹל מָנוֹחַ וַיָּבֹא מַלְאַךְ הָאֱלֹהִים עוֹד אֶל־
הָאִשָּׁה וְהִיא יוֹשֶׁבֶת בַּשָּׂדֶה וּמָנוֹחַ אִישָׁהּ אֵין עִמָּהּ׃
וַתְּמַהֵר הָאִשָּׁה וַתָּרָץ וַתַּגֵּד לְאִישָׁהּ וַתֹּאמֶר אֵלָיו הִנֵּה
11 נִרְאָה אֵלַי הָאִישׁ אֲשֶׁר־בָּא בַיּוֹם אֵלָי׃ וַיָּקָם וַיֵּלֶךְ מָנוֹחַ
אַחֲרֵי אִשְׁתּוֹ וַיָּבֹא אֶל־הָאִישׁ וַיֹּאמֶר לוֹ הַאַתָּה הָאִישׁ
12 אֲשֶׁר־דִּבַּרְתָּ אֶל־הָאִשָּׁה וַיֹּאמֶר אָנִי׃ וַיֹּאמֶר מָנוֹחַ עַתָּה
13 יָבֹא דְבָרֶיךָ מַה־יִּהְיֶה מִשְׁפַּט־הַנַּעַר וּמַעֲשֵׂהוּ׃ וַיֹּאמֶר
מַלְאַךְ יְהוָה אֶל־מָנוֹחַ מִכֹּל אֲשֶׁר־אָמַרְתִּי אֶל־הָאִשָּׁה
14 תִּשָּׁמֵר׃ מִכֹּל אֲשֶׁר־יֵצֵא מִגֶּפֶן הַיַּיִן לֹא תֹאכַל וְיַיִן וְשֵׁכָר
אַל־תֵּשְׁתְּ וְכָל־טֻמְאָה אַל־תֹּאכַל כֹּל אֲשֶׁר־צִוִּיתִיהָ
טו תִּשְׁמֹר׃ וַיֹּאמֶר מָנוֹחַ אֶל־מַלְאַךְ יְהוָה נַעְצְרָה־נָּא אוֹתָךְ
16 וְנַעֲשֶׂה לְפָנֶיךָ גְּדִי עִזִּים׃ וַיֹּאמֶר מַלְאַךְ יְהוָה אֶל־מָנוֹחַ
אִם־תַּעְצְרֵנִי לֹא־אֹכַל בְּלַחְמֶךָ וְאִם־תַּעֲשֶׂה עֹלָה לַיהוָה
17 תַּעֲלֶנָּה כִּי לֹא־יָדַע מָנוֹחַ כִּי־מַלְאַךְ יְהוָה הוּא׃ וַיֹּאמֶר
מָנוֹחַ אֶל־מַלְאַךְ יְהוָה מִי שְׁמֶךָ כִּי־יָבֹא דְבָרְךָ וְכִבַּדְנוּךָ׃
18 וַיֹּאמֶר לוֹ מַלְאַךְ יְהוָה לָמָּה זֶּה תִּשְׁאַל לִשְׁמִי וְהוּא־פֶלִאי׃
19 וַיִּקַּח מָנוֹחַ אֶת־גְּדִי הָעִזִּים וְאֶת־הַמִּנְחָה וַיַּעַל עַל־הַצּוּר
כ לַיהוָה וּמַפְלִא לַעֲשׂוֹת וּמָנוֹחַ וְאִשְׁתּוֹ רֹאִים׃ וַיְהִי בַעֲלוֹת
הַלַּהַב מֵעַל הַמִּזְבֵּחַ הַשָּׁמַיְמָה וַיַּעַל מַלְאַךְ־יְהוָה בְּלַהַב

v. 8. מלא ו׳ ibid. הל׳ ברגש v. 17. יתיר י׳ v. 18. יתיר א׳

12. *what shall be the rule for the child. i.e.* how shall we train him?

16. *thy bread.* Thy food.

thou must offer it. i.e. the kid which Manoah was ready to prepare (*v.* 15).

unto the LORD. And not to any strange gods.

18. *hidden.* lit. 'wonderful'; above your comprehension; cf. Gen. XXXII, 29.

19. *upon the rock.* As upon an altar.

the altar; and Manoah and his wife looked on; and they fell on their faces to the ground. 21. But the angel of the LORD did no more appear to Manoah or to his wife. Then Manoah knew that he was the angel of the LORD. 22. And Manoah said unto his wife: 'We shall surely die, because we have seen God.' 23. But his wife said unto him: 'If the LORD were pleased to kill us, He would not have received a burnt-offering and a meal-offering at our hand, neither would He have shown us all these things, nor would at this time have told such things as these.' ¶ 24. And the woman bore a son, and called his name Samson; and the child grew, and the LORD blessed him. 25. And the spirit of the LORD began to move him in Mahaneh-dan, between Zorah and Eshtaol.

הַמִּזְבֵּחַ וּמָנוֹחַ וְאִשְׁתּוֹ רֹאִים וַיִּפְּלוּ עַל־פְּנֵיהֶם אָרְצָה׃
21 וְלֹא־יָסַף עוֹד מַלְאַךְ יְהוָה לְהֵרָאֹה אֶל־מָנוֹחַ וְאֶל־אִשְׁתּוֹ
22 אָז יָדַע מָנוֹחַ כִּי־מַלְאַךְ יְהוָה הוּא׃ וַיֹּאמֶר מָנוֹחַ אֶל־
23 אִשְׁתּוֹ מוֹת נָמוּת כִּי אֱלֹהִים רָאִינוּ׃ וַתֹּאמֶר לוֹ אִשְׁתּוֹ
לוּ חָפֵץ יְהוָה לַהֲמִיתֵנוּ לֹא־לָקַח מִיָּדֵנוּ עֹלָה וּמִנְחָה
24 וְלֹא הֶרְאָנוּ אֶת־כָּל־אֵלֶּה וְכָעֵת לֹא הִשְׁמִיעָנוּ כָּזֹאת׃ וַתֵּלֶד
הָאִשָּׁה בֵּן וַתִּקְרָא אֶת־שְׁמוֹ שִׁמְשׁוֹן וַיִּגְדַּל הַנַּעַר וַיְבָרְכֵהוּ
כה יְהוָה׃ וַתָּחֶל רוּחַ יְהוָה לְפַעֲמוֹ בְּמַחֲנֵה־דָן בֵּין צָרְעָה
וּבֵין אֶשְׁתָּאֹל׃

23. *the LORD . . . he would not have received . . . at our hand.* The wisdom of her remark is noteworthy.

told such things as these. The message as to the birth and training of the child, which necessarily presupposed the continued life of the parents.

25. *to move him. i.e.* to great and powerful action from time to time (Rashi). 'The spirit of the LORD' is represented as an impulse stirring him from within. The Heb. root denotes the sounding of a bell. The story of Samson is full of sadness. It reveals a nation utterly deteriorated and disintegrated, and a man who through self-indulgence weakens and eventually loses his God-given power to deliver his people. The time was, alas, to come when Scripture would record of him, 'he wist not that the LORD was departed from him' (XVI, 20).

Milton's *Samson Agonistes* is a wonderful commentary on his life. So is Watts' *Samson.* 'Watts paints him in serious thoughtful mood, with a far-away look in his eyes that yet seem to see nothing, feeling how far short he has come of his great consecration; how the Spirit's power has been to him a gift endowing him at times with supernatural strength, but not a sanctifying grace always abiding in him and transforming his nature. And perhaps this was a more common mood with him, though he does not give way to it, than the joyousness which overflowed in mirthful tricks and plays upon words which is associated with him. His story, if we rightly consider it, was pathetic and tragic in the highest degree' (Macmillan).

8

CHAPTER VIII

1. And the LORD spoke unto Moses, saying: 2. 'Speak unto Aaron, and say unto him: When thou lightest the lamps, the seven lamps shall give light in front of the candlestick.' 3. And Aaron did so: he lighted the lamps thereof so as to give light in front of the candlestick, as the LORD commanded Moses. 4. And this was the work of the candlestick, beaten work of gold; unto the base thereof, and unto the flowers thereof, it was beaten work; according unto the pattern which the LORD had shown Moses, so he made the candlestick. ¶ 5. And the LORD spoke unto Moses, saying: 6. 'Take the Levites from among the

CAP. VIII. ח

ח פ פ פ לו 36

א 2 וַיְדַבֵּר יְהוָה אֶל־מֹשֶׁה לֵּאמֹר׃ דַּבֵּר אֶל־אַהֲרֹן וְאָמַרְתָּ
אֵלָיו בְּהַעֲלֹתְךָ אֶת־הַנֵּרֹת אֶל־מוּל פְּנֵי הַמְּנוֹרָה יָאִירוּ שִׁבְעַת
3 הַנֵּרוֹת׃ וַיַּעַשׂ כֵּן אַהֲרֹן אֶל־מוּל פְּנֵי הַמְּנוֹרָה הֶעֱלָה נֵרֹתֶיהָ
4 כַּאֲשֶׁר צִוָּה יְהוָה אֶת־מֹשֶׁה׃ וְזֶה מַעֲשֵׂה הַמְּנֹרָה מִקְשָׁה
זָהָב עַד־יְרֵכָהּ עַד־פִּרְחָהּ מִקְשָׁה הִוא כַּמַּרְאֶה אֲשֶׁר הֶרְאָה
יְהוָה אֶת־מֹשֶׁה כֵּן עָשָׂה אֶת־הַמְּנֹרָה׃ פ

III. BEHAALOSECHA

(CHAPTERS VIII–XII)

THE MENORAH

VIII, 1–4. The making of the Menorah is described in Exod. XXV. The command to light the lamps in the Tabernacle had been given briefly in Exod. XXV, 37; and in Exod. XXVII, 21 Aaron and his sons are specially entrusted with that duty.

2. *when thou lightest the lamps.* lit. 'when thou causest the lamps to go up'; *i.e.* when thou causest the flame of the lamps to go up.

'Why does this command follow immediately after the consecration of the Altar?' asks the Midrash. The answer is, when Aaron saw the rich gifts which the princes offered on that occasion, his heart grew faint that neither he nor his tribe had a part in that consecration. Thereupon the Holy One, blessed be He, reassured him in the words, 'By thy life, thine is greater glory than theirs, for thou lightest the Menorah.' There is a further rabbinical saying: 'The Sanctuary will on another occasion also be dedicated by kindling the lights, and then it will be done by thy descendants, the Hasmoneans. Thus greater glory is destined for thee than for the princes. Their offerings to the Sanctuary will be employed only as long as it endures, but the lights of the Chanukah festival shall shine for ever.'

give light in front of the candlestick. Aaron is here bidden to arrange the wicks of the seven lamps in such a way that they shall give out one combined blaze of light over against the central shaft of the candelabrum itself (Talmud). Israel said before God, 'LORD of the Universe, Thou commandest us to illumine before Thee; art Thou not the Light of the world, and with Whom light dwelleth?' 'Not that I require your light,' was the Divine reply, 'but that you may perpetuate the light which I conferred on you as an example to the nations of the world' (Talmud).

The Menorah is one of the favourite symbols of Judaism. Through its association with Chanukah, the Menorah has come to typify spiritual conquest, and that spiritual conquest is achieved neither by might nor by power but by God's spirit (see the Haftorah, which is the same as for the Sabbath of Chanukah). Israel, as the Servant of the LORD, is to perform his Divine task without violence: 'he is not to strive nor cry; the bruised reed he is not to break, nor quench the smoking flax' (Isa. XLII, 3). The image employed by Isaiah to describe Israel's mission is the gentle agency of light, with its irresistible illumination of the surrounding darkness. 'This is among the loftiest conceptions of all human thought. How new an idea it was, is measured by the length of time it has taken before the idea began slowly to make its way that force cannot conquer spirit' (Moulton).

5–26. DEDICATION OF THE LEVITES

The choice of the Levites for the service of the Sanctuary is given in III, 5–10 and their duties are detailed in IV. In view of the impending break-up of the camp, it was now necessary formally to dedicate them to their duties upon which they were about to enter.

6. *take the Levites.* 'With kind words. Say unto them, Happy are ye inasmuch as ye have been found worthy to be servants to the Omnipresent' (Rashi). 'For God elevates no man to an office unless He has tried him and found him worthy of his calling. He did not say, "and the Levites shall be Mine," before He had tried this

children of Israel, and cleanse them. 7.
And thus shalt thou do unto them, to
cleanse them: sprinkle the water of purifica-
tion upon them, and let them cause a razor
to pass over all their flesh, and let them
wash their clothes, and cleanse themselves.
8. Then let them take a young bullock,
and its meal-offering, fine flour mingled
with oil, and another young bullock shalt
thou take for a sin-offering. 9. And thou
shalt present the Levites before the tent
of meeting; and thou shalt assemble the
whole congregation of the children of
Israel. 10. And thou shalt present the
Levites before the LORD; and the children
of Israel shall lay their hands upon the
Levites. 11. And Aaron shall offer the
Levites before the LORD for a wave-offering
from the children of Israel, that they may
be to do the service of the LORD. 12. And
the Levites shall lay their hands upon the
heads of the bullocks; and offer thou the
one for a sin-offering, and the other for a
burnt-offering, unto the LORD, to make
atonement for the Levites. 13. And thou
shalt set the Levites before Aaron, and
before his sons, and offer them for a wave-
offering unto the LORD. 14. Thus shalt
thou separate the Levites from among the
children of Israel; and the Levites shall
be Mine.*ii. 15. And after that shall the
Levites go in to do the service of the tent
of meeting; and thou shalt cleanse them,

ה 6 וַיְדַבֵּר יְהוָה אֶל־מֹשֶׁה לֵּאמֹר׃ קַח אֶת־הַלְוִיִּם מִתּוֹךְ בְּנֵי
7 יִשְׂרָאֵל וְטִהַרְתָּ אֹתָם׃ וְכֹה־תַעֲשֶׂה לָהֶם לְטַהֲרָם הַזֵּה
עֲלֵיהֶם מֵי חַטָּאת וְהֶעֱבִירוּ תַעַר עַל־כָּל־בְּשָׂרָם וְכִבְּסוּ
8 בִגְדֵיהֶם וְהִטֶּהָרוּ׃ וְלָקְחוּ פַּר בֶּן־בָּקָר וּמִנְחָתוֹ סֹלֶת בְּלוּלָה
9 בַשָּׁמֶן וּפַר־שֵׁנִי בֶן־בָּקָר תִּקַּח לְחַטָּאת׃ וְהִקְרַבְתָּ אֶת־
הַלְוִיִּם לִפְנֵי אֹהֶל מוֹעֵד וְהִקְהַלְתָּ אֶת־כָּל־עֲדַת בְּנֵי
י יִשְׂרָאֵל׃ וְהִקְרַבְתָּ אֶת־הַלְוִיִּם לִפְנֵי יְהוָה וְסָמְכוּ בְנֵי־
11 יִשְׂרָאֵל אֶת־יְדֵיהֶם עַל־הַלְוִיִּם׃ וְהֵנִיף אַהֲרֹן אֶת־הַלְוִיִּם
תְּנוּפָה לִפְנֵי יְהוָה מֵאֵת בְּנֵי יִשְׂרָאֵל וְהָיוּ לַעֲבֹד אֶת־
12 עֲבֹדַת יְהוָה׃ וְהַלְוִיִּם יִסְמְכוּ אֶת־יְדֵיהֶם עַל רֹאשׁ הַפָּרִים
וַעֲשֵׂה אֶת־הָאֶחָד חַטָּאת וְאֶת־הָאֶחָד עֹלָה לַיהוָה לְכַפֵּר
13 עַל־הַלְוִיִּם׃ וְהַעֲמַדְתָּ אֶת־הַלְוִיִּם לִפְנֵי אַהֲרֹן וְלִפְנֵי בָנָיו
14 וְהֵנַפְתָּ אֹתָם תְּנוּפָה לַיהוָה׃ וְהִבְדַּלְתָּ אֶת־הַלְוִיִּם מִתּוֹךְ
שני טו בְּנֵי יִשְׂרָאֵל וְהָיוּ לִי הַלְוִיִּם׃ וְאַחֲרֵי־כֵן יָבֹאוּ הַלְוִיִּם

tribe, and found them worthy. In Egypt none but the tribe of Levi observed the Torah, and clung to the token of the Abrahamic convenant; while the other tribes, abandoning both Torah and token of covenant, like the Egyptians, practised idolatry. In the desert, also, it was this tribe alone that did not take part in the worship of the Golden Calf. Justly, therefore, did God's choice fall upon this godly tribe, who on this day were consecrated as the servants of God and His sanctuary' (Midrash).

cleanse them. Purify them from ritual uncleanness.

7. *sprinkle.* The Heb. is the infinitive. It does not, therefore, denote an act addressed to Moses which he himself must perform, an act that would have taken one person many months—but an action which he is to order to be performed (Ehrlich).

water of purification. lit. 'water of sin'; *i.e.* water which removes sin; according to Rashi, it was the water used in the rites connected with the ordinance of the Red Heifer (XIX, 9) for the removal of defilement due to contact with a dead body. Among the large number of Levites to be consecrated some must have required such purification.

and let them wash their clothes. An act enjoined in Scripture as a preparation for any special religious service; Gen. XXXV, 2; Exod. XIX, 10. This ceremonial cleansing symbolized the inward purity required of those who bore the vessels of the Sanctuary.

10. *before the LORD.* Before the Altar of sacrifice.

lay their hands upon the Levites. The representatives of the Israelites laid their hands upon the representatives of the Levites, in order to indicate that the whole community offered them to the service of God; cf. Lev. I, 4.

11. *offer.* lit. 'wave', so also in *v.* 13, 15, and 21.

a wave-offering. The Levites were probably led backwards and forwards by Aaron in the direction of the Holy of Holies, or he may have only waved his hand over them. The idea underlying was unmistakable. This is: having been given by the Israelites to God, the Levites were given back to the Israelites, whose servants they were to be in all matters appertaining to the Sanctuary.

12. *and the Levites. i.e.* the chosen representatives of the Levites.

and offer them for a wave-offering. 16. For they are wholly given unto Me from among the children of Israel; instead of all that openeth the womb, even the first-born of all the children of Israel, have I taken them unto Me. 17. For all the first-born among the children of Israel are Mine, both man and beast; on the day that I smote all the first-born in the land of Egypt I sanctified them for Myself. 18. And I have taken the Levites instead of all the first-born among the children of Israel. 19. And I have given the Levites—they are given to Aaron and to his sons from among the children of Israel, to do the service of the children of Israel in the tent of meeting, and to make atonement for the children of Israel, that there be no plague among the children of Israel, through the children of Israel coming nigh unto the sanctuary.' 20. Thus did Moses, and Aaron, and all the congregation of the children of Israel, unto the Levites; according unto all that the LORD commanded Moses touching the Levites, so did the children of Israel unto them. 21. And the Levites purified themselves, and they washed their clothes; and Aaron offered them for a sacred gift before the LORD; and Aaron made atonement for them to cleanse them. 22. And after that went the Levites in to do their service in the tent of meeting before Aaron, and before his sons; as the LORD had commanded Moses concerning the Levites, so did they unto them. ¶ 23. And the LORD spoke unto Moses, saying: 24. 'This is that which pertaineth unto the Levites: from twenty and five years old and upward they shall go in to perform the service in the work of the tent of meeting; 25. and from the age of fifty years they shall return from the service of the work, and shall

לַעֲבֹד אֶת־אֹהֶל מוֹעֵד וְטִהַרְתָּ אֹתָם וְהֵנַפְתָּ אֹתָם תְּנוּפָה׃
16 כִּי נְתֻנִים נְתֻנִים הֵמָּה לִי מִתּוֹךְ בְּנֵי יִשְׂרָאֵל תַּחַת פִּטְרַת
17 כָּל־רֶחֶם בְּכוֹר כֹּל מִבְּנֵי יִשְׂרָאֵל לָקַחְתִּי אֹתָם לִי׃ כִּי
לִי כָל־בְּכוֹר בִּבְנֵי יִשְׂרָאֵל בָּאָדָם וּבַבְּהֵמָה בְּיוֹם הַכֹּתִי
18 כָל־בְּכוֹר בְּאֶרֶץ מִצְרַיִם הִקְדַּשְׁתִּי אֹתָם לִי׃ וָאֶקַּח אֶת־
19 הַלְוִיִּם תַּחַת כָּל־בְּכוֹר בִּבְנֵי יִשְׂרָאֵל׃ וָאֶתְּנָה אֶת־
הַלְוִיִּם נְתֻנִים ׀ לְאַהֲרֹן וּלְבָנָיו מִתּוֹךְ בְּנֵי יִשְׂרָאֵל לַעֲבֹד
אֶת־עֲבֹדַת בְּנֵי־יִשְׂרָאֵל בְּאֹהֶל מוֹעֵד וּלְכַפֵּר עַל־בְּנֵי
יִשְׂרָאֵל וְלֹא יִהְיֶה בִּבְנֵי יִשְׂרָאֵל נֶגֶף בְּגֶשֶׁת בְּנֵי־יִשְׂרָאֵל
כ אֶל־הַקֹּדֶשׁ׃ וַיַּעַשׂ מֹשֶׁה וְאַהֲרֹן וְכָל־עֲדַת בְּנֵי־יִשְׂרָאֵל
לַלְוִיִּם כְּכֹל אֲשֶׁר־צִוָּה יְהוָה אֶת־מֹשֶׁה לַלְוִיִּם כֵּן־עָשׂוּ
21 לָהֶם בְּנֵי יִשְׂרָאֵל׃ וַיִּתְחַטְּאוּ הַלְוִיִּם וַיְכַבְּסוּ בִּגְדֵיהֶם
וַיָּנֶף אַהֲרֹן אֹתָם תְּנוּפָה לִפְנֵי יְהוָה וַיְכַפֵּר עֲלֵיהֶם אַהֲרֹן
22 לְטַהֲרָם׃ וְאַחֲרֵי־כֵן בָּאוּ הַלְוִיִּם לַעֲבֹד אֶת־עֲבֹדָתָם בְּאֹהֶל
מוֹעֵד לִפְנֵי אַהֲרֹן וְלִפְנֵי בָנָיו כַּאֲשֶׁר צִוָּה יְהוָה אֶת־מֹשֶׁה
23 עַל־הַלְוִיִּם כֵּן עָשׂוּ לָהֶם׃ ס וַיְדַבֵּר יְהוָה אֶל־מֹשֶׁה
24 לֵּאמֹר׃ זֹאת אֲשֶׁר לַלְוִיִּם מִבֶּן חָמֵשׁ וְעֶשְׂרִים שָׁנָה וָמַעְלָה
כה יָבוֹא לִצְבֹא צָבָא בַּעֲבֹדַת אֹהֶל מוֹעֵד׃ וּמִבֶּן חֲמִשִּׁים

16. *for they are wholly given.* lit. 'for they are given, given'; *given*, for carrying the Tabernacle and its furniture; and *given*, for singing the chants of the Sanctuary (Rashi).

the children of Israel. The five-fold repetition of these words in *v.* 19 indicates the love felt by God towards the bearers of the name of Israel (Midrash).

19. *atonement.* Here used not in the usual sense of making propitiation, but in the sense of 'covering', a meaning inherent in the Heb. root. The Levites were to form a sort of protective cordon for the Sanctuary.

no plague. The explanation is indicated in Rashi's comment, which in effect states, 'I have appointed the Levites to take over the service of the Sanctuary from the children of Israel upon whom it had hitherto devolved, and thereby to prevent a plague amongst the latter; because if *they* came near the Sanctuary there would certainly be a plague amongst them, since they have proved themselves unworthy of the priestly office.'

21. *purified themselves.* By having the 'water of expiation' sprinkled upon them; *v.* 7.

23–26. The Levites' Period of Service. Additional regulations to those in IV, including a probationary period from the age of 25 to 30, as well as the regulations for Levites over 50 years of age.

24. *twenty and five years old and upward.* 'The years of twenty-five to thirty were for initiation in connection with the lighter labours in the Sanctuary' (Sifri).

25. *return from the service.* Retire from active service in connection with the Sanctuary.

serve no more; 26. but shall minister with their brethren in the tent of meeting, to keep the charge, but they shall do no manner of service. Thus shalt thou do unto the Levites touching their charges.'*iii.

9

CHAPTER IX

1. And the LORD spoke unto Moses in the wilderness of Sinai, in the first month of the second year after they were come out of the land of Egypt, saying: 2. 'Let the children of Israel keep the passover in its appointed season. 3. In the fourteenth day of this month, at dusk, ye shall keep it in its appointed season; according to all the statutes of it, and according to all the ordinances thereof, shall ye keep it.' 4. And Moses spoke unto the children of Israel, that they should keep the passover. 5. And they kept the passover in the first month, on the fourteenth day of the month, at dusk, in the wilderness of Sinai; according to all that the LORD commanded Moses, so did the children of Israel. 6. But there were certain men, who were unclean by the dead body of a man, so that they could not keep the passover on that day; and they came before Moses and before Aaron on that day. 7. And those men said unto him: 'We are unclean by the dead body of a man; wherefore are we to be kept back, so as not to bring the offering of the LORD in its appointed season among the children of Israel?' 8. And Moses said unto them: 'Stay ye, that I may hear what the LORD will command concerning you.' ¶ 9. And the LORD spoke unto Moses, saying: 10. 'Speak unto the children of Israel, saying: If any man of you or of your generations shall

26 שָׁנָה יָשׁוּב מִצְּבָא הָעֲבֹדָה וְלֹא יַעֲבֹד עוֹד׃ וְשֵׁרֵת אֶת־
אֶחָיו בְּאֹהֶל מוֹעֵד לִשְׁמֹר מִשְׁמֶרֶת וַעֲבֹדָה לֹא יַעֲבֹד כָּכָה
תַּעֲשֶׂה לַלְוִיִּם בְּמִשְׁמְרֹתָם׃ פ שלישי

ט

CAP. IX. ט

א וַיְדַבֵּר יְהוָה אֶל־מֹשֶׁה בְמִדְבַּר־סִינַי בַּשָּׁנָה הַשֵּׁנִית
2 לְצֵאתָם מֵאֶרֶץ מִצְרַיִם בַּחֹדֶשׁ הָרִאשׁוֹן לֵאמֹר׃ וְיַעֲשׂוּ
3 בְנֵי־יִשְׂרָאֵל אֶת־הַפָּסַח בְּמוֹעֲדוֹ׃ בְּאַרְבָּעָה עָשָׂר־יוֹם
בַּחֹדֶשׁ הַזֶּה בֵּין הָעַרְבַּיִם תַּעֲשׂוּ אֹתוֹ בְּמֹעֲדוֹ כְּכָל־חֻקֹּתָיו
4 וּכְכָל־מִשְׁפָּטָיו תַּעֲשׂוּ אֹתוֹ׃ וַיְדַבֵּר מֹשֶׁה אֶל־בְּנֵי יִשְׂרָאֵל
ה לַעֲשֹׂת הַפָּסַח׃ וַיַּעֲשׂוּ אֶת־הַפֶּסַח בָּרִאשׁוֹן בְּאַרְבָּעָה עָשָׂר
יוֹם לַחֹדֶשׁ בֵּין הָעַרְבַּיִם בְּמִדְבַּר סִינָי כְּכֹל אֲשֶׁר צִוָּה יְהוָה
6 אֶת־מֹשֶׁה כֵּן עָשׂוּ בְּנֵי יִשְׂרָאֵל׃ וַיְהִי אֲנָשִׁים אֲשֶׁר הָיוּ
טְמֵאִים לְנֶפֶשׁ אָדָם וְלֹא־יָכְלוּ לַעֲשֹׂת־הַפֶּסַח בַּיּוֹם הַהוּא
7 וַיִּקְרְבוּ לִפְנֵי מֹשֶׁה וְלִפְנֵי אַהֲרֹן בַּיּוֹם הַהוּא׃ וַיֹּאמְרוּ
הָאֲנָשִׁים הָהֵמָּה אֵלָיו אֲנַחְנוּ טְמֵאִים לְנֶפֶשׁ אָדָם לָמָּה
נִגָּרַע לְבִלְתִּי הַקְרִיב אֶת־קָרְבַּן יְהוָה בְּמֹעֲדוֹ בְּתוֹךְ בְּנֵי
8 יִשְׂרָאֵל׃ וַיֹּאמֶר אֲלֵהֶם מֹשֶׁה עִמְדוּ וְאֶשְׁמְעָה מַה־יְצַוֶּה

ט' v. 2. קמץ בטרחא v. 6. סבירין ויהיו

26. *minister with their brethren.* Assist their younger fellow-Levites, but shall do no essential or responsible service. According to the Rabbis, their work was that of closing the gates of the Sanctuary and assisting in the choral singing.

keep the charge. Assist in dismantling and erecting the Tent of Meeting at the beginning or end of a journey (Rashi). A superannuated life need not be a useless life.

IX, 1–14. THE SECOND PASSOVER

A supplementary Passover on the same day in the second month for persons prevented by uncleanness and absence from participating in the Paschal sacrifice in Nisan.

1. *in the first month of the second year.* This date is earlier by one month than the date with which the Book of Numbers opens. 'You learn hereby that the narratives of Scripture are not given in strict chronological sequence' אין מוקדם ומאוחר בתורה (Sifri). From Exod. XII, 25, XIII, 5–10, it appears that the Passover there ordained was for celebration after the settlement in Canaan. Special direction was, therefore, required for a Passover in the Wilderness.

2. *in its appointed season.* 'Even if the Passover falls on the Sabbath' (Sifri).

3. *at dusk.* Better, *towards even* (Friedländer); lit. 'between the two evenings'; see on Exod. XII, 6.

5. *and they kept the passover.* According to Tradition, that was the only Paschal sacrifice offered in the Wilderness.

7. *wherefore are we to be kept back?* lit. 'why should we be made less?' Why should we, owing to accidental and temporary defilement, be made inferior to the rest of Israel by not being able to participate in the Festival celebration?

10. *or be in a journey afar off.* So that he cannot reach the Sanctuary in time for the slaughtering of the sacrifice.

be unclean by reason of a dead body, or be in a journey afar off, yet he shall keep the passover unto the LORD; 11. in the second month on the fourteenth day at dusk they shall keep it; they shall eat it with unleavened bread and bitter herbs; 12. they shall leave none of it unto the morning, nor break a bone thereof; according to all the statute of the passover they shall keep it. 13. But the man that is clean, and is not on a journey, and forbeareth to keep the passover, that soul shall be cut off from his people; because he brought not the offering of the LORD in its appointed season, that man shall bear his sin. 14. And if a stranger shall sojourn among you, and will keep the passover unto the LORD: according to the statute of the passover, and according to the ordinance thereof, so shall he do; ye shall have one statute, both for the stranger, and for him that is born in the land.' *iv. ¶15. And on the day that the tabernacle was reared up the cloud covered the tabernacle, even the tent of the testimony; and at even there was upon the tabernacle as it were the appearance of fire, until morning. 16. So it was alway: the cloud covered it, and the appearance of fire by night. 17. And whenever the cloud was taken up from over the Tent, then after that the children of Israel journeyed; and in the place where the cloud abode, there the children of Israel encamped. 18. At the commandment of the LORD the children of Israel journeyed, and at the commandment of the LORD they encamped: as long as the cloud abode upon the tabernacle they remained encamped. 19. And when the cloud tarried upon the tabernacle many days, then the children of Israel kept the charge of the LORD, and journeyed not. 20. And sometimes the cloud was a few days upon the tabernacle; according to the commandment of the LORD they remained encamped, and according to the commandment of the LORD they

יְהוָה לָכֶם׃ פ
9 וַיְדַבֵּר יְהוָה אֶל־מֹשֶׁה לֵּאמֹר׃ דַּבֵּר אֶל־בְּנֵי יִשְׂרָאֵל
לֵאמֹר אִישׁ אִישׁ כִּי־יִהְיֶה טָמֵא ׀ לָנֶפֶשׁ אוֹ בְדֶרֶךְ רְחֹקָה
11 לָכֶם אוֹ לְדֹרֹתֵיכֶם וְעָשָׂה פֶסַח לַיהוָה׃ בַּחֹדֶשׁ הַשֵּׁנִי
בְּאַרְבָּעָה עָשָׂר יוֹם בֵּין הָעַרְבַּיִם יַעֲשׂוּ אֹתוֹ עַל־מַצּוֹת
12 וּמְרֹרִים יֹאכְלֻהוּ׃ לֹא־יַשְׁאִירוּ מִמֶּנּוּ עַד־בֹּקֶר וְעֶצֶם לֹא
13 יִשְׁבְּרוּ־בוֹ כְּכָל־חֻקַּת הַפֶּסַח יַעֲשׂוּ אֹתוֹ׃ וְהָאִישׁ אֲשֶׁר־
הוּא טָהוֹר וּבְדֶרֶךְ לֹא־הָיָה וְחָדַל לַעֲשׂוֹת הַפֶּסַח וְנִכְרְתָה
הַנֶּפֶשׁ הַהִוא מֵעַמֶּיהָ כִּי ׀ קָרְבַּן יְהוָה לֹא הִקְרִיב בְּמֹעֲדוֹ
14 חֶטְאוֹ יִשָּׂא הָאִישׁ הַהוּא׃ וְכִי־יָגוּר אִתְּכֶם גֵּר וְעָשָׂה
פֶסַח לַיהוָה כְּחֻקַּת הַפֶּסַח וּכְמִשְׁפָּטוֹ כֵּן יַעֲשֶׂה חֻקָּה
רביעי טו אַחַת יִהְיֶה לָכֶם וְלַגֵּר וּלְאֶזְרַח הָאָרֶץ׃ ס וּבְיוֹם
הָקִים אֶת־הַמִּשְׁכָּן כִּסָּה הֶעָנָן אֶת־הַמִּשְׁכָּן לְאֹהֶל הָעֵדֻת
16 וּבָעֶרֶב יִהְיֶה עַל־הַמִּשְׁכָּן כְּמַרְאֵה־אֵשׁ עַד־בֹּקֶר׃ כֵּן יִהְיֶה
17 תָמִיד הֶעָנָן יְכַסֶּנּוּ וּמַרְאֵה־אֵשׁ לָיְלָה׃ וּלְפִי הֵעָלֹת
הֶעָנָן מֵעַל הָאֹהֶל וְאַחֲרֵי כֵן יִסְעוּ בְּנֵי יִשְׂרָאֵל וּבִמְקוֹם
18 אֲשֶׁר יִשְׁכָּן־שָׁם הֶעָנָן שָׁם יַחֲנוּ בְּנֵי יִשְׂרָאֵל׃ עַל־פִּי
יְהוָה יִסְעוּ בְּנֵי יִשְׂרָאֵל וְעַל־פִּי יְהוָה יַחֲנוּ כָּל־יְמֵי אֲשֶׁר
19 יִשְׁכֹּן הֶעָנָן עַל־הַמִּשְׁכָּן יַחֲנוּ׃ וּבְהַאֲרִיךְ הֶעָנָן עַל־הַמִּשְׁכָּן
יָמִים רַבִּים וְשָׁמְרוּ בְנֵי־יִשְׂרָאֵל אֶת־מִשְׁמֶרֶת יְהוָה וְלֹא
כ יִסָּעוּ׃ וְיֵשׁ אֲשֶׁר יִהְיֶה הֶעָנָן יָמִים מִסְפָּר עַל־הַמִּשְׁכָּן עַל־

v. 10. נקוד על ה'

13. *cut off.* Not by a human tribunal.

14. *a stranger.* Heb. *ger;* a resident non-Israelite who had become a convert to the religion of Israel, and had undertaken to conform to the laws and precepts of the Torah.

so shall he do. He must observe all the ordinances of the Passover, whether in regard to the first or to the supplementary Passover, even as does a homeborn Israelite.

15–23. The Fiery Cloud upon the Tabernacle

This section connects with Exod. XL, 34. It was the invariable custom to start on the march when the Cloud rose from the Tabernacle, and to halt when and as long as it rested.

15. *the cloud covered the tabernacle.* As the manifestation of the Divine Presence in the midst of Israel. It covered only that part of it in which the Ark was placed.

at even. The manifestation of the Divine Presence had the appearance of fire.

17. *and whenever the cloud was taken up.* This verse and the following to the end of the chapter are an amplification of Exod. XL, 36–8.

18. *at the commandment of the LORD.* The Israelites were uncertain as to the duration of their sojourn in any place; but, looking upon the Cloud as the symbol of the Divine Presence, they considered the Cloud's movements as orders from on High, which they invariably obeyed.

21 פִּי יְהוָה יַחֲנוּ וְעַל־פִּי יְהוָה יִסָּעוּ׃ וְיֵשׁ אֲשֶׁר יִהְיֶה הֶעָנָן
מֵעֶרֶב עַד־בֹּקֶר וְנַעֲלָה הֶעָנָן בַּבֹּקֶר וְנָסָעוּ אוֹ יוֹמָם וָלַיְלָה
22 וְנַעֲלָה הֶעָנָן וְנָסָעוּ׃ אוֹ־יֹמַיִם אוֹ־חֹדֶשׁ אוֹ־יָמִים בְּהַאֲרִיךְ
הֶעָנָן עַל־הַמִּשְׁכָּן לִשְׁכֹּן עָלָיו יַחֲנוּ בְנֵי־יִשְׂרָאֵל וְלֹא יִסָּעוּ
23 וּבְהֵעָלֹתוֹ יִסָּעוּ׃ עַל־פִּי יְהוָה יַחֲנוּ וְעַל־פִּי יְהוָה יִסָּעוּ אֶת־
מִשְׁמֶרֶת יְהוָה שָׁמָרוּ עַל־פִּי יְהוָה בְּיַד־מֹשֶׁה׃ פ

journeyed. 21. And sometimes the cloud was from evening until morning; and when the cloud was taken up in the morning, they journeyed; or if it continued by day and by night, when the cloud was taken up, they journeyed. 22. Whether it were two days, or a month, or a year, that the cloud tarried upon the tabernacle, abiding thereon, the children of Israel remained encamped, and journeyed not; but when it was taken up, they journeyed. 23. At the commandment of the LORD they encamped, and at the commandment of the LORD they journeyed; they kept the charge of the LORD, at the commandment of the LORD by the hand of Moses.

10

CAP. X. י

י

א 2 וַיְדַבֵּר יְהוָה אֶל־מֹשֶׁה לֵּאמֹר׃ עֲשֵׂה לְךָ שְׁתֵּי חֲצוֹצְרֹת
כֶּסֶף מִקְשָׁה תַּעֲשֶׂה אֹתָם וְהָיוּ לְךָ לְמִקְרָא הָעֵדָה וּלְמַסַּע
3 אֶת־הַמַּחֲנוֹת׃ וְתָקְעוּ בָּהֵן וְנוֹעֲדוּ אֵלֶיךָ כָּל־הָעֵדָה אֶל־
4 פֶּתַח אֹהֶל מוֹעֵד׃ וְאִם־בְּאַחַת יִתְקָעוּ וְנוֹעֲדוּ אֵלֶיךָ
ה הַנְּשִׂיאִים רָאשֵׁי אַלְפֵי יִשְׂרָאֵל׃ וּתְקַעְתֶּם תְּרוּעָה וְנָסְעוּ
6 הַמַּחֲנוֹת הַחֹנִים קֵדְמָה׃ וּתְקַעְתֶּם תְּרוּעָה שֵׁנִית וְנָסְעוּ
הַמַּחֲנוֹת הַחֹנִים תֵּימָנָה תְּרוּעָה יִתְקְעוּ לְמַסְעֵיהֶם׃
7 8 וּבְהַקְהִיל אֶת־הַקָּהָל תִּתְקְעוּ וְלֹא תָרִיעוּ׃ וּבְנֵי אַהֲרֹן
הַכֹּהֲנִים יִתְקְעוּ בַּחֲצֹצְרוֹת וְהָיוּ לָכֶם לְחֻקַּת עוֹלָם

CHAPTER X

1. And the LORD spoke unto Moses, saying: 2. 'Make thee two trumpets of silver; of beaten work shalt thou make them; and they shall be unto thee for the calling of the congregation, and for causing the camps to set forward. 3. And when they shall blow with them, all the congregation shall gather themselves unto thee at the door of the tent of meeting. 4. And if they blow but with one, then the princes, the heads of the thousands of Israel, shall gather themselves unto thee. 5. And when ye blow an alarm, the camps that lie on the east side shall take their journey. 6. And when ye blow an alarm the second time, the camps that lie on the south side shall set forward; they shall blow an alarm for their journeys. 7. But when the assembly is to be gathered together, ye shall blow, but ye shall not sound an alarm. 8. And the sons of Aaron, the priests, shall blow with the trumpets; and they shall be to you for a statute for ever throughout your generations. 9. And when ye go to war in

ט׳ v. 23. קמץ בז״ק

X, 1–10. CLARIONS OF SILVER

They were for summoning the congregation or the princes to the Sanctuary, as well as signals to begin the journey or in times of war. The clarions were long and narrow, with an expanded mouth, as distinct from the Shofar, or ram's horn of the Jubilee (Lev. xxv, 9). There is an illustration of these clarions among the spoils of the Temple, on the Arch of Titus.

2. *of beaten work.* Made out of a single plate of silver.

3. *all the congregation.* *i.e.* the representatives of the congregation, and the heads of families.

4. *but with one.* A blast on one clarion was the signal for an assembly of only the princes of the tribes; on both, for all the congregation.

5. *and when ye blow an alarm.* Heb. *teruah;* a succession of short, sharp, separate notes.

camps . . . east side. Judah, with Issachar and Zebulon.

6. *camps . . . south side.* Reuben, with Simeon and Gad.

an alarm for their journeys. *i.e.* a separate signal was to be blown for the startings on their journeys for each of the four groups of tribes (Nachmanides).

8. *statute for ever.* That only the priests may sound these sacred clarions.

your land against the adversary that oppresseth you, then ye shall sound an alarm with the trumpets; and ye shall be remembered before the LORD your God, and ye shall be saved from your enemies. 10. Also in the day of your gladness, and in your appointed seasons, and in your new moons, ye shall blow with the trumpets over your burnt-offerings, and over the sacrifices of your peace-offerings; and they shall be to you for a memorial before your God: I am the LORD your God.' *v.
¶ 11. And it came to pass in the second year, in the second month, on the twentieth day of the month, that the cloud was taken up from over the tabernacle of the testimony. 12. And the children of Israel set forward by their stages out of the wilderness of Sinai; and the cloud abode in the wilderness of Paran.—13. And they took their first journey, according to the commandment of the LORD by the hand of Moses. 14. And in the first place the standard of the camp of the children of Judah set forward according to their hosts; and over his host was Nahshon the son of Amminadab. 15. And over the host of the tribe of the children of Issachar was Nethanel the son of Zuar. 16. And over the host of the tribe of the children of Zebulun was Eliab the son of Helon. 17. And the tabernacle was taken down; and the sons of Gershon and the sons of Merari, who bore the tabernacle, set forward. 18.

9 לְדֹרֹתֵיכֶם׃ וְכִֽי־תָבֹאוּ מִלְחָמָה בְּאַרְצְכֶם עַל־הַצַּר הַצֹּרֵר
אֶתְכֶם וַהֲרֵעֹתֶם בַּחֲצֹצְרֹת וְנִזְכַּרְתֶּם לִפְנֵי יְהוָה אֱלֹהֵיכֶם
י וְנוֹשַׁעְתֶּם מֵאֹיְבֵיכֶם׃ וּבְיוֹם שִׂמְחַתְכֶם וּבְמוֹעֲדֵיכֶם
וּבְרָאשֵׁי חָדְשֵׁכֶם וּתְקַעְתֶּם בַּחֲצֹצְרֹת עַל עֹלֹתֵיכֶם וְעַל
זִבְחֵי שַׁלְמֵיכֶם וְהָיוּ לָכֶם לְזִכָּרוֹן לִפְנֵי אֱלֹהֵיכֶם אֲנִי
יְהוָה אֱלֹהֵיכֶם׃ פ חמישי
11 וַיְהִי בַּשָּׁנָה הַשֵּׁנִית בַּחֹדֶשׁ הַשֵּׁנִי בְּעֶשְׂרִים בַּחֹדֶשׁ נַעֲלָה
12 הֶעָנָן מֵעַל מִשְׁכַּן הָעֵדֻת׃ וַיִּסְעוּ בְנֵי־יִשְׂרָאֵל לְמַסְעֵיהֶם
13 מִמִּדְבַּר סִינָי וַיִּשְׁכֹּן הֶעָנָן בְּמִדְבַּר פָּארָן׃ וַיִּסְעוּ בָּרִאשֹׁנָה
14 עַל־פִּי יְהוָה בְּיַד־מֹשֶׁה׃ וַיִּסַּע דֶּגֶל מַחֲנֵה בְנֵי־יְהוּדָה
טו בָּרִאשֹׁנָה לְצִבְאֹתָם וְעַל־צְבָאוֹ נַחְשׁוֹן בֶּן־עַמִּינָדָב׃ וְעַל־
16 צְבָא מַטֵּה בְּנֵי יִשָּׂשכָר נְתַנְאֵל בֶּן־צוּעָר׃ וְעַל־צְבָא מַטֵּה
17 בְּנֵי זְבוּלֻן אֱלִיאָב בֶּן־חֵלֹן׃ וְהוּרַד הַמִּשְׁכָּן וְנָסְעוּ בְנֵי־
18 גֵרְשׁוֹן וּבְנֵי מְרָרִי נֹשְׂאֵי הַמִּשְׁכָּן׃ וְנָסַע דֶּגֶל מַחֲנֵה רְאוּבֵן

v. 9. צ׳ פתוחה

9. *remembered before the LORD your God.* The music of these clarions, by infusing both courage and cheerfulness in the hearers, will be the means of invoking the Divine aid against the foe; and thus shall Israel in his hour of danger 'be remembered' of God and saved. That the usage of trumpets in war was viewed from this spiritual standpoint is attested by II Chron. XIII, 12–16, as well as I Macc. IV, 40; V, 33.

10. *day of your gladness.* Any public rejoicing, such as after a victory. Tradition here confines the term to Sabbaths.

appointed seasons. Passover, Feast of Weeks, the Day of Memorial, the Day of Atonement, and the Feast of Tabernacles. These were all distinguished by special sacrifices; Lev. XXIII and Num. XXVIII and XXIX.

B. FROM SINAI TO MOAB

(CHAPTERS X, 11–XXI)

X, 11–34. THE DEPARTURE FROM SINAI

Ten months and nineteen days after the arrival at Sinai, the journeying towards Moab and the Holy Land began. Guided by the Cloud they, in due course, encamped in the wilderness of Paran.

12. *their stages.* As in XXXIII, 2. Most Jewish commentators take it to mean the order in which the journeying took place.

abode in the wilderness. As a sign that they were to halt there.

Paran. North of the Sinai Peninsula. Its eastern border is a line drawn from the Dead Sea to the Gulf of Akaba, apparently corresponding to the modern et-Tih. Paran formed an important stage in the wanderings across the wilderness. Before it was reached, there were two halting places at the 'Graves of Lust' (XI, 35) and Hazeroth (XII, 16).

17. *was taken down. i.e.* used to be taken down, and apart, for the journey; the fabric of it, the boards, curtains, and other heavy portions that were packed upon the six wagons provided for the purpose (VII, 5–9).

And the standard of the camp of Reuben set forward according to their hosts; and over his host was Elizur the son of Shedeur. 19. And over the host of the tribe of the children of Simeon was Shelumiel the son of Zurishaddai. 20. And over the host of the tribe of the children of Gad was Eliasaph the son of Deuel. 21. And the Kohathites the bearers of the sanctuary set forward, that the tabernacle might be set up against their coming. 22. And the standard of the camp of the children of Ephraim set forward according to their hosts; and over his host was Elishama the son of Ammihud. 23. And over the host of the tribe of the children of Manasseh was Gamaliel the son of Pedahzur. 24. And over the host of the tribe of the children of Benjamin was Abidan the son of Gideoni. 25. And the standard of the camp of the children of Dan, which was the rearward of all the camps, set forward according to their hosts; and over his host was Ahiezer the son of Ammishaddai. 26. And over the host of the tribe of the children of Asher was Pagiel the son of Ochran. 27. And over the host of the tribe of the children of Naphtali was Ahira the son of Enan. 28. Thus were the journeyings of the children of Israel according to their hosts.—And they set forward. *vi s. ¶29. And Moses said unto Hobab, the son of Reuel the Midianite, Moses' father-in-law: 'We are journeying unto the place of which the LORD said: I will give it you; come thou with us, and we will do thee good; for the LORD hath spoken good concerning Israel.' 30. And he said unto him: 'I will not go; but I will depart to mine own land, and to my kindred.' 31. And he said: 'Leave us not, I pray thee; forasmuch as thou knowest how we are to encamp in the wilderness, and thou shalt

19 לְצִבְאֹתָם וְעַל־צְבָאוֹ אֱלִיצוּר בֶּן־שְׁדֵיאוּר׃ וְעַל־צְבָא מַטֵּה
כ בְּנֵי שִׁמְעוֹן שְׁלֻמִיאֵל בֶּן־צוּרִישַׁדָּי׃ וְעַל־צְבָא מַטֵּה בְנֵי־
21 גָד אֶלְיָסָף בֶּן־דְּעוּאֵל׃ וְנָסְעוּ הַקְּהָתִים נֹשְׂאֵי הַמִּקְדָּשׁ
22 וְהֵקִימוּ אֶת־הַמִּשְׁכָּן עַד־בֹּאָם׃ וְנָסַע דֶּגֶל מַחֲנֵה בְנֵי־
23 אֶפְרַיִם לְצִבְאֹתָם וְעַל־צְבָאוֹ אֱלִישָׁמָע בֶּן־עַמִּיהוּד׃ וְעַל־
24 צְבָא מַטֵּה בְּנֵי מְנַשֶּׁה גַּמְלִיאֵל בֶּן־פְּדָהצוּר׃ וְעַל־צְבָא
כה מַטֵּה בְּנֵי בִנְיָמִן אֲבִידָן בֶּן־גִּדְעוֹנִי׃ וְנָסַע דֶּגֶל מַחֲנֵה בְנֵי־
דָן מְאַסֵּף לְכָל־הַמַּחֲנֹת לְצִבְאֹתָם וְעַל־צְבָאוֹ אֲחִיעֶזֶר
26 בֶּן־עַמִּישַׁדָּי׃ וְעַל־צְבָא מַטֵּה בְּנֵי אָשֵׁר פַּגְעִיאֵל בֶּן־
27 28 עָכְרָן׃ וְעַל־צְבָא מַטֵּה בְּנֵי נַפְתָּלִי אֲחִירַע בֶּן־עֵינָן׃ אֵלֶּה
(ששי לספ') 29 מַסְעֵי בְנֵי־יִשְׂרָאֵל לְצִבְאֹתָם וַיִּסָּעוּ׃ ס וַיֹּאמֶר
מֹשֶׁה לְחֹבָב בֶּן־רְעוּאֵל הַמִּדְיָנִי חֹתֵן מֹשֶׁה נֹסְעִים ׀
אֲנַחְנוּ אֶל־הַמָּקוֹם אֲשֶׁר אָמַר יְהוָה אֹתוֹ אֶתֵּן לָכֶם לְכָה
ל אִתָּנוּ וְהֵטַבְנוּ לָךְ כִּי־יְהוָה דִּבֶּר־טוֹב עַל־יִשְׂרָאֵל׃ וַיֹּאמֶר
אֵלָיו לֹא אֵלֵךְ כִּי אִם־אֶל־אַרְצִי וְאֶל־מוֹלַדְתִּי אֵלֵךְ׃
31 וַיֹּאמֶר אַל־נָא תַּעֲזֹב אֹתָנוּ כִּי ׀ עַל־כֵּן יָדַעְתָּ חֲנֹתֵנוּ בַּמִּדְבָּר
32 וְהָיִתָ לָּנוּ לְעֵינָיִם׃ וְהָיָה כִּי־תֵלֵךְ עִמָּנוּ וְהָיָה ׀ הַטּוֹב

21. *the bearers of the sanctuary.* *i.e.* the holy things of the Sanctuary.

against their coming. *i.e.* before the arrival of the sons of Kohath with the Ark and the other holy vessels. Finding the Tabernacle properly set up, the sons of Kohath would deposit therein the Ark and the other holy vessels.

25. *the rearward.* The work of such a rearguard would consist in collecting stragglers, in taking charge of such as had fainted by the way, and in finding and restoring lost articles.

29–32. HOBAB

Moses requests his father-in-law to remain with them and act as their guide.

29. *Hobab, the son of Reuel.* According to Rabbinic tradition, Hobab is identical with Jethro, the father-in-law of Moses. Reuel was the father of Jethro, or Hobab. Exod. II, 18, where the daughters of Jethro call Reuel their father, presents no difficulty. The Rabbis rightly explain that children oft-times call their grandfather 'father'.

31. *instead of eyes.* As Midian bordered on Sinai and Paran, he was thoroughly familiar with that desert. The Cloud, IX, 15 f, was not a guide; it only indicated the times of breaking up and of resting. Hobab's answer is not given; but it may be inferred from Judges I, 16, IV, 11 that he yielded, and consented to be 'eyes' unto them in the desert.

be to us instead of eyes. 32. And it shall be, if thou go with us, yea, it shall be, that what good soever the LORD shall do unto us, the same will we do unto thee.' ¶ 33. And they set forward from the mount of the LORD three days' journey; and the ark of the covenant of the LORD went before them in the three days' journey, to seek out a resting-place for them. 34. And the cloud of the LORD was over them by day, when they set forward from the camp.*vi a. ¶ 35. And it came to pass, when the ark set forward, that Moses said: 'Rise up, O LORD, and let Thine enemies be scattered; and let them that hate Thee flee before Thee.' 36. And when it rested, he said: 'Return, O LORD, unto the ten thousands of the families of Israel.'

33 הַהוּא אֲשֶׁר יֵיטִיב יְהוָה עִמָּנוּ וְהֵטַבְנוּ לָךְ׃ וַיִּסְעוּ מֵהַר
יְהוָה דֶּרֶךְ שְׁלֹשֶׁת יָמִים וַאֲרוֹן בְּרִית־יְהוָה נֹסֵעַ לִפְנֵיהֶם
34 דֶּרֶךְ שְׁלֹשֶׁת יָמִים לָתוּר לָהֶם מְנוּחָה׃ וַעֲנַן יְהוָה
ששי
לה עֲלֵיהֶם יוֹמָם בְּנָסְעָם מִן־הַמַּחֲנֶה׃* ׆ ס וַיְהִי בִּנְסֹעַ
הָאָרֹן וַיֹּאמֶר מֹשֶׁה קוּמָה ׀ יְהוָה וְיָפֻצוּ אֹיְבֶיךָ וְיָנֻסוּ
36 מְשַׂנְאֶיךָ מִפָּנֶיךָ׃ וּבְנֻחֹה יֹאמַר שׁוּבָה יְהוָה רִבְבוֹת
אַלְפֵי יִשְׂרָאֵל׃ ׆ פ

v. 36. 35. נון הפוכה v. 36. ובנוחו ק'

33–34. ON THE JOURNEY

33. *they set forward.* These words mark the moment of actual departure from Sinai, which has been anticipated in the general statement of *v.* 12.

three days' journey. 'When God commanded Israel to set out from Sinai where they had received many laws and continue their march, the Israelites were glad. Instead of making a day's march from Sinai as God had commanded them, they marched incessantly for three days. They behaved like a boy who runs quickly away after dismissal from school, that his teacher might not call him back' (Midrash).

the ark. On this special occasion only, when they started the journey, did the Ark go in front, in order to inspire them with confidence and courage (Ibn Ezra). Otherwise, the Ark and its appurtenances were carried by the Kohathites in the *middle* of the line of march.

went before them in the three days' journey. This is the rendering of the AV (and Sforno, Luzzatto), and is a departure from the AJ which omits the words 'in the', and thereby attaches an impossible meaning to the text.

34. *was over them by day.* This phrase, taken in conjunction with Psalm CV, 39, 'He spread a cloud for a screen,' would seem to indicate that the Cloud not only served the purpose of a signal but also of a shade, protecting the wanderers from the burning heat of the sun.

35–36. INVOCATION PRAYERS

These verses preserve the invocation prayers in connection with the going forward and the resting of the Ark in the wilderness; and we still feel the thrill of sacred enthusiasm that animated the men of old on hearing them. They are used to this day at the opening and closing of the Ark, whenever the Torah is read in the synagogue. These two verses are enclosed in inverted *Nuns*, to indicate either that they are not here in their original place (Talmud); or that they are taken from another source (possibly from 'the Book of the Wars of the LORD', see XXI, 14) and form a distinct section, scroll, or even 'book' of the Torah. Some of the Rabbis thought of the Book of Numbers as consisting of three parts (I–X, 34; X, 35, 36; XI–XXXVI), and, in consequence, counted *seven* books of the Torah. Thus, according to Rabbi Johanan, 'Wisdom hath hewn out her seven pillars' (Prov. IX, 1) referred to the *Seven* Books of the Torah.

35. *when the ark set forward.* The Ark going forward at the head of Israel's tribes typified God in front of His people protecting and helping them, and leading them on to final victory. 'Through the wilderness Israel went, not knowing from what quarter the sudden raid of a desert people might be made. Swiftly, silently, as if springing out of the very sand, the Arab raiders might bear down upon the travellers. They were assured of the guardianship of Him whose eye never slumbered' (Expositor's Bible).

said. i.e. would say; the tense is the so-called 'frequentative'.

rise up . . . be scattered. 'The impressive war-cry of truth against error, of righteousness against sin' (Abrahams). God's enemies are the enemies of Israel. When God arises against the hosts of Israel, they scatter as the darkness before the sunlight.

36. *unto the ten thousands of the families of Israel.* Heb. רבבות אלפי ישראל. The second 'thousands' is here equivalent to 'families' or 'clans'. Ehrlich takes the whole phrase as a synonym of God—and renders, 'O Thou Who art the ten thousands of the thousands of Israel' —a most appropriate invocation addressed to God as the Ark returned from victory; cf. II Kings II, 12, where Elijah is addressed as 'the chariot of Israel, and the horsemen thereof'; or the Divine title, 'the LORD of Hosts.'

'Long after those desert days, a psalmist laid

11

CHAPTER XI

1. And the people were as murmurers, speaking evil in the ears of the LORD; and when the LORD heard it, His anger was kindled; and the fire of the LORD burnt among them, and devoured in the uttermost part of the camp. 2. And the people cried unto Moses; and Moses prayed unto the LORD, and the fire abated. 3. And the name of that place was called [1]Taberah, because the fire of the LORD burnt among them. ¶ 4. And the mixed multitude that was among them fell a lusting; and the children of Israel also wept on their part, and said: 'Would that we were given flesh to eat! 5. We remember the fish, which we were wont to eat in Egypt for nought; the cucumbers, and the melons, and the leeks, and the onions, and the garlic; 6. but now our soul is dried away; there is nothing at all; we have nought save this manna to look to.'—7. Now the manna was like coriander seed, and the appearance thereof as the appearance of bdellium. 8. The people went about, and gathered it, and

[1] That is, *Burning.*

יא

CAP. XI. יא

א וַיְהִי הָעָם כְּמִתְאֹנְנִים רַע בְּאָזְנֵי יְהוָה וַיִּשְׁמַע יְהוָה וַיִּחַר
אַפּוֹ וַתִּבְעַר־בָּם אֵשׁ יְהוָה וַתֹּאכַל בִּקְצֵה הַמַּחֲנֶה׃
2 וַיִּצְעַק הָעָם אֶל־מֹשֶׁה וַיִּתְפַּלֵּל מֹשֶׁה אֶל־יְהוָה וַתִּשְׁקַע
3 הָאֵשׁ׃ וַיִּקְרָא שֵׁם־הַמָּקוֹם הַהוּא תַּבְעֵרָה כִּי־בָעֲרָה בָם
4 אֵשׁ יְהוָה׃ וְהָאסַפְסֻף אֲשֶׁר בְּקִרְבּוֹ הִתְאַוּוּ תַּאֲוָה וַיָּשֻׁבוּ
ה וַיִּבְכּוּ גַּם בְּנֵי יִשְׂרָאֵל וַיֹּאמְרוּ מִי יַאֲכִלֵנוּ בָּשָׂר׃ זָכַרְנוּ
אֶת־הַדָּגָה אֲשֶׁר־נֹאכַל בְּמִצְרַיִם חִנָּם אֵת הַקִּשֻּׁאִים וְאֵת
הָאֲבַטִּחִים וְאֶת־הֶחָצִיר וְאֶת־הַבְּצָלִים וְאֶת־הַשּׁוּמִים׃
6 7 וְעַתָּה נַפְשֵׁנוּ יְבֵשָׁה אֵין כֹּל בִּלְתִּי אֶל־הַמָּן עֵינֵינוּ׃ וְהַמָּן
8 כִּזְרַע־גַּד הוּא וְעֵינוֹ כְּעֵין הַבְּדֹלַח׃ שָׁטוּ הָעָם וְלָקְטוּ

א׳ נחה v. 4.

hold of the old prayer and offered it, as not antiquated yet by the thousand years that had intervened. "Let God arise, and let His enemies be scattered; let them that hate Him flee before Him" (Psalm LXVIII, 1). We too may take up the immortal though ancient words, and, at the beginnings and endings of all our efforts, offer this old prayer—the prayer which asked for a Divine Presence in the incipiency of our efforts, and the prayer which asked for a Divine Presence on the completion of our work' (Maclaren).

CHAPTER XI
MURMURINGS AND REBELLIONS

This and the following three chapters deal with the successive rebellions of the People after their departure from Sinai that resulted in their being excluded from the Promised Land.

1–3. AT TABERAH

1. *as murmurers.* Rebellious and complaining, instead of bearing their troubles in a spirit of trustful dependence upon God.

the fire of the LORD. The punishment was swift and terrible. It may either have been lightning (Job I, 16), a miraculous outburst of flame (Lev. X, 2), or an ordinary conflagration.

2. *unto Moses; and Moses prayed.* The Midrash says, 'It may be likened unto an earthly king who was angry with his son. What did the son do? He went to his father's friend, saying, Go and seek mercy from my father for me.'

abated. Went out.

3. *Taberah. i.e.* 'Burning.'

4–35. 'THE GRAVES OF LUST'

4. *and the mixed multitude.* The Heb. form is a contemptuous term denoting a number of people gathered together from all quarters, a rabble, or riff-raff. It is identical with the mixed multitude (Exod. XII, 38) of aliens who had attached themselves to the Israelites and accompanied them out of Egypt.

fell a lusting. Began to have a strong craving for flesh food.

the children of Israel also wept. Discontent, like sin, is contagious. 'They were not so much suffering as seeking for some pretext for grumbling' (Sifri).

5. *we remember.* 'The natural dainties of Egypt are set forth in this passage with the fullness and relish which bespeak personal experience' (Speaker's Bible). These words enable us clearly to see into those slave souls who preferred the garlic of Egypt to the bread of freedom.

for nought. Classical writers attest that in Egypt fish was to be had in abundance and was incredibly cheap.

7. *coriander seed.* About the size of a peppercorn; Exod. XVI, 31.

as the appearance of bdellium. See Gen. II, 12. The manna is said to have been white. The comparison probably turns on the *shining* or *sparkling* nature of the bdellium.

8. *as the taste of a cake baked with oil.* lit. 'something juicy made with oil.' In Exod. XVI, 31, it is said to have tasted like wafers made with honey, the 'oily' taste no doubt coming to it after it had been ground and beaten.

ground it in mills, or beat it in mortars, and seethed it in pots, and made cakes of it; and the taste of it was as the taste of a cake baked with oil. 9. And when the dew fell upon the camp in the night, the manna fell upon it.—10. And Moses heard the people weeping, family by family, every man at the door of his tent; and the anger of the LORD was kindled greatly; and Moses was displeased. 11. And Moses said unto the LORD: 'Wherefore hast Thou dealt ill with Thy servant? and wherefore have I not found favour in Thy sight, that Thou layest the burden of all this people upon me? 12. Have I conceived all this people? have I brought them forth, that Thou shouldest say unto me: Carry them in thy bosom, as a nursing-father carrieth the sucking child, unto the land which Thou didst swear unto their fathers? 13. Whence should I have flesh to give unto all this people? for they trouble me with their weeping, saying: Give us flesh, that we may eat. 14. I am not able to bear all this people myself alone, because it is too heavy for me. 15. And if Thou deal thus with me, kill me, I pray Thee, out of hand, if I have found favour in Thy sight; and let me not look upon my wretchedness.' ¶16. And the LORD said unto Moses: 'Gather unto Me seventy men of the elders of Israel, whom thou knowest to be the elders of the people, and officers over them; and bring them unto the tent of meeting, that they may stand there with thee. 17. And I will come down and speak with thee there; and I will take of the spirit which is upon thee, and will put it upon them; and they shall bear the burden of the people with thee, that thou bear it not thyself alone. 18. And say thou unto the people: Sanctify yourselves against to-

וְטָחֲנוּ בָרֵחַיִם אוֹ דָכוּ בַּמְּדֹכָה וּבִשְּׁלוּ בַּפָּרוּר וְעָשׂוּ אֹתוֹ
9 עֻגוֹת וְהָיָה טַעְמוֹ כְּטַעַם לְשַׁד הַשָּׁמֶן׃ וּבְרֶדֶת הַטַּל
י עַל־הַמַּחֲנֶה לָיְלָה יֵרֵד הַמָּן עָלָיו׃ וַיִּשְׁמַע מֹשֶׁה אֶת־
הָעָם בֹּכֶה לְמִשְׁפְּחֹתָיו אִישׁ לְפֶתַח אָהֳלוֹ וַיִּחַר־אַף יְהוָה
11 מְאֹד וּבְעֵינֵי מֹשֶׁה רָע׃ וַיֹּאמֶר מֹשֶׁה אֶל־יְהוָה לָמָה
הֲרֵעֹתָ לְעַבְדֶּךָ וְלָמָּה לֹא־מָצָתִי חֵן בְּעֵינֶיךָ לָשׂוּם אֶת־
12 מַשָּׂא כָּל־הָעָם הַזֶּה עָלָי׃ הֶאָנֹכִי הָרִיתִי אֵת כָּל־הָעָם
הַזֶּה אִם־אָנֹכִי יְלִדְתִּיהוּ כִּי־תֹאמַר אֵלַי שָׂאֵהוּ בְחֵיקֶךָ
כַּאֲשֶׁר יִשָּׂא הָאֹמֵן אֶת־הַיֹּנֵק עַל הָאֲדָמָה אֲשֶׁר נִשְׁבַּעְתָּ
13 לַאֲבֹתָיו׃ מֵאַיִן לִי בָּשָׂר לָתֵת לְכָל־הָעָם הַזֶּה כִּי־יִבְכּוּ
14 עָלַי לֵאמֹר תְּנָה־לָּנוּ בָשָׂר וְנֹאכֵלָה׃ לֹא־אוּכַל אָנֹכִי
טו לְבַדִּי לָשֵׂאת אֶת־כָּל־הָעָם הַזֶּה כִּי כָבֵד מִמֶּנִּי׃ וְאִם־
כָּכָה ׀ אַתְּ־עֹשֶׂה לִּי הָרְגֵנִי נָא הָרֹג אִם־מָצָאתִי חֵן בְּעֵינֶיךָ
וְאַל־אֶרְאֶה בְּרָעָתִי׃ פ
16 וַיֹּאמֶר יְהוָה אֶל־מֹשֶׁה אֶסְפָה־לִּי שִׁבְעִים אִישׁ מִזִּקְנֵי
יִשְׂרָאֵל אֲשֶׁר יָדַעְתָּ כִּי־הֵם זִקְנֵי הָעָם וְשֹׁטְרָיו וְלָקַחְתָּ
17 אֹתָם אֶל־אֹהֶל מוֹעֵד וְהִתְיַצְּבוּ שָׁם עִמָּךְ׃ וְיָרַדְתִּי וְדִבַּרְתִּי
עִמְּךָ שָׁם וְאָצַלְתִּי מִן־הָרוּחַ אֲשֶׁר עָלֶיךָ וְשַׂמְתִּי עֲלֵיהֶם
18 וְנָשְׂאוּ אִתְּךָ בְּמַשָּׂא הָעָם וְלֹא־תִשָּׂא אַתָּה לְבַדֶּךָ׃ וְאֶל־

v. 11. חסר א'

10–15. MOSES' DISCOURAGEMENT AND COMPLAINT

10. *family by family.* The weeping was general and unconcealed.

11. *wherefore have I not found favour in Thy sight.* 'This is the language of despair, not the murmuring of unbelief' (Keil).

15. *my wretchedness.* *i.e.* the failure of his hopes and efforts; cf. the despairing complaint of Elijah in I Kings XIX, 4 and of Jeremiah in Jer. XV, 10. '*My wretchedness:* his failure to fulfil the task which he cannot abandon because God-given—a feeling of woe that arises whenever a spiritual leader toils vainly and wearily with the dull masses, to whom he is tied by feelings of love and duty' (Holzinger).

16–30. THE SEVENTY ELDERS

16. *whom thou knowest to be the elders.* Ripe in years as well as qualified by their wisdom to share the burdens of leadership.

17. *the spirit which is upon thee.* Implying no diminution of the spiritual power of Moses, 'even as a light that kindles other lights is not thereby dimmed' (Sifri).

with thee. Endowed with a portion of Moses' prophetic power, their influence in the camp would silence the murmurings and help towards putting an end to dejection and faithlessness.

18. *sanctify yourselves.* Fit yourselves to receive the promised gift of God.

against to-morrow. In readiness for to-morrow.

morrow, and ye shall eat flesh; for ye have wept in the ears of the LORD, saying: Would that we were given flesh to eat! for it was well with us in Egypt; therefore the LORD will give you flesh and ye shall eat. 19. Ye shall not eat one day, nor two days, nor five days, neither ten days, nor twenty days; 20. but a whole month, until it come out at your nostrils, and it be loathsome unto you; because that ye have rejected the LORD who is among you, and have troubled Him with weeping, saying: 'Why, now, came we forth out of Egypt?' 21. And Moses said: 'The people, among whom I am, are six hundred thousand men on foot; and yet Thou hast said: I will give them flesh, that they may eat a whole month! 22. If flocks and herds be slain for them, will they suffice them? or if all the fish of the sea be gathered together for them, will they suffice them?' 23. And the LORD said unto Moses: 'Is the LORD's hand waxed short? now shalt thou see whether My word shall come to pass unto thee or not.' ¶ 24. And Moses went out, and told the people the words of the LORD; and he gathered seventy men of the elders of the people, and set them round about the Tent. 25. And the LORD came down in the cloud, and spoke unto him, and took of the spirit that was upon him, and put it upon the seventy elders; and it came to pass, that, when the spirit rested upon them, they prophesied, but they did so no more. 26. But there remained two men in the camp, the name of the one was Eldad, and the name of the other Medad; and the spirit rested upon them; and they were of them that were recorded, but had not gone out unto the Tent; and they

הָעָם תֹּאמַר הִתְקַדְּשׁוּ לְמָחָר וַאֲכַלְתֶּם בָּשָׂר כִּי בְּכִיתֶם
בְּאָזְנֵי יְהוָה לֵאמֹר מִי יַאֲכִלֵנוּ בָּשָׂר כִּי־טוֹב לָנוּ בְּמִצְרָיִם
19 וְנָתַן יְהוָה לָכֶם בָּשָׂר וַאֲכַלְתֶּם׃ לֹא יוֹם אֶחָד תֹּאכְלוּן
וְלֹא יוֹמָיִם וְלֹא ׀ חֲמִשָּׁה יָמִים וְלֹא עֲשָׂרָה יָמִים וְלֹא
כ עֶשְׂרִים יוֹם׃ עַד ׀ חֹדֶשׁ יָמִים עַד אֲשֶׁר־יֵצֵא מֵאַפְּכֶם וְהָיָה
לָכֶם לְזָרָא יַעַן כִּי־מְאַסְתֶּם אֶת־יְהוָה אֲשֶׁר בְּקִרְבְּכֶם
21 וַתִּבְכּוּ לְפָנָיו לֵאמֹר לָמָּה זֶּה יָצָאנוּ מִמִּצְרָיִם׃ וַיֹּאמֶר
מֹשֶׁה שֵׁשׁ־מֵאוֹת אֶלֶף רַגְלִי הָעָם אֲשֶׁר אָנֹכִי בְּקִרְבּוֹ
22 וְאַתָּה אָמַרְתָּ בָּשָׂר אֶתֵּן לָהֶם וְאָכְלוּ חֹדֶשׁ יָמִים׃ הֲצֹאן
וּבָקָר יִשָּׁחֵט לָהֶם וּמָצָא לָהֶם אִם אֶת־כָּל־דְּגֵי הַיָּם יֵאָסֵף
לָהֶם וּמָצָא לָהֶם׃ פ
23 וַיֹּאמֶר יְהוָה אֶל־מֹשֶׁה הֲיַד יְהוָה תִּקְצָר עַתָּה תִרְאֶה
24 הֲיִקְרְךָ דְבָרִי אִם־לֹא׃ וַיֵּצֵא מֹשֶׁה וַיְדַבֵּר אֶל־הָעָם אֵת
דִּבְרֵי יְהוָה וַיֶּאֱסֹף שִׁבְעִים אִישׁ מִזִּקְנֵי הָעָם וַיַּעֲמֵד אֹתָם
כה סְבִיבֹת הָאֹהֶל׃ וַיֵּרֶד יְהוָה ׀ בֶּעָנָן וַיְדַבֵּר אֵלָיו וַיָּאצֶל
מִן־הָרוּחַ אֲשֶׁר עָלָיו וַיִּתֵּן עַל־שִׁבְעִים אִישׁ הַזְּקֵנִים וַיְהִי
26 כְּנוֹחַ עֲלֵיהֶם הָרוּחַ וַיִּתְנַבְּאוּ וְלֹא יָסָפוּ׃ וַיִּשָּׁאֲרוּ שְׁנֵי־
אֲנָשִׁים ׀ בַּמַּחֲנֶה שֵׁם הָאֶחָד ׀ אֶלְדָּד וְשֵׁם הַשֵּׁנִי מֵידָד

22. *will they suffice them?* Moses expresses amazement at the Divine promise. His realization of the power of God fails for a moment. Scripture portrays Moses as but human!

23. *is the LORD'S hand waxed short? i.e.* is it too weak or powerless?

25. *in the cloud.* The symbol of His perpetual Presence with them.

they prophesied. A feeling of spiritual ecstasy and exaltation possessed them, causing them to break out into praises of God, and declaring His will and His goodness. By prophecy is here meant, not prediction of the future, but the power of instructing and admonishing the people with an authority that was recognized as having its source in God.

but they did so no more. 'They prophesied that day but never after' (Sifri). They were not intended to be permanent sharers with Moses in his task of leadership. Maimonides compares the recipients of Divine revelations to men whose night is illumined by flashes of lightning. 'To some it is given to behold the lightning flashes in rapid succession; they seem to be in perpetual light, and their night is as clear as day. This was the degree of prophetic excellence obtained by Moses, the greatest of the Prophets. Others perceive the prophetic flash at long intervals; this is the degree of most of the Prophets. By still others a flash of lightning is perceived only once during the whole night. This is the case of those of whom we are told, "They prophesied, but they did so no more."'

26. *Eldad . . . Medad.* Two of the seventy elders had declined the honour and remained in the camp. They were nevertheless seized with the same ecstasy.

of them that were recorded. They belonged to those who were originally registered as being of the seventy elders.

prophesied in the camp. 27. And there ran a young man, and told Moses, and said: 'Eldad and Medad are prophesying in the camp.' 28. And Joshua the son of Nun, the minister of Moses from his youth up, answered and said: 'My lord Moses, shut them in.' 29. And Moses said unto him: 'Art thou jealous for my sake? would that all the LORD's people were prophets, that the LORD would put His spirit upon them!' *vii. 30. And Moses withdrew into the camp, he and the elders of Israel. ¶ 31. And there went forth a wind from the LORD, and brought across quails from the sea, and let them fall by the camp, about a day's journey on this side, and a day's journey on the other side, round about the camp, and about two cubits above the face of the earth. 32. And the people rose up all that day, and all the night, and all the next day, and gathered the quails; he that gathered least gathered ten heaps; and they spread them all abroad for themselves round about the camp. 33. While the flesh was yet between their teeth, ere it was chewed, the anger of the LORD was kindled against the people, and the LORD smote the people with a very great plague. 34. And the name of that place was called [1]Kibroth-hattaavah, because there they buried the people that lusted. 35. From Kibroth-hattaavah the people journeyed unto Hazeroth; and they abode at Hazeroth.

[1] That is, *The graves of lust.*

וַתָּנַח עֲלֵהֶם הָרוּחַ וְהֵמָּה בַּכְּתֻבִים וְלֹא יָצְאוּ הָאֹהֱלָה
27 וַיִּתְנַבְּאוּ בַּמַּחֲנֶה׃ וַיָּרָץ הַנַּעַר וַיַּגֵּד לְמֹשֶׁה וַיֹּאמַר אֶלְדָּד
28 וּמֵידָד מִתְנַבְּאִים בַּמַּחֲנֶה׃ וַיַּעַן יְהוֹשֻׁעַ בִּן־נוּן מְשָׁרֵת
29 מֹשֶׁה מִבְּחֻרָיו וַיֹּאמַר אֲדֹנִי מֹשֶׁה כְּלָאֵם׃ וַיֹּאמֶר לוֹ מֹשֶׁה
הַמְקַנֵּא אַתָּה לִי וּמִי יִתֵּן כָּל־עַם יְהוָה נְבִיאִים כִּי־יִתֵּן יְהוָה
שביעי
ל אֶת־רוּחוֹ עֲלֵיהֶם׃ וַיֵּאָסֵף מֹשֶׁה אֶל־הַמַּחֲנֶה הוּא וְזִקְנֵי
31 יִשְׂרָאֵל׃ וְרוּחַ נָסַע ׀ מֵאֵת יְהוָה וַיָּגָז שַׂלְוִים מִן־הַיָּם וַיִּטֹּשׁ
עַל־הַמַּחֲנֶה כְּדֶרֶךְ יוֹם כֹּה וּכְדֶרֶךְ יוֹם כֹּה סְבִיבוֹת הַמַּחֲנֶה
32 וּכְאַמָּתַיִם עַל־פְּנֵי הָאָרֶץ׃ וַיָּקָם הָעָם כָּל־הַיּוֹם הַהוּא וְכָל־
הַלַּיְלָה וְכֹל ׀ יוֹם הַמָּחֳרָת וַיַּאַסְפוּ אֶת־הַשְּׂלָו הַמַּמְעִיט אָסַף
עֲשָׂרָה חֳמָרִים וַיִּשְׁטְחוּ לָהֶם שָׁטוֹחַ סְבִיבוֹת הַמַּחֲנֶה׃
33 הַבָּשָׂר עוֹדֶנּוּ בֵּין שִׁנֵּיהֶם טֶרֶם יִכָּרֵת וְאַף יְהוָה חָרָה בָעָם
34 וַיַּךְ יְהוָה בָּעָם מַכָּה רַבָּה מְאֹד׃ וַיִּקְרָא אֶת־שֵׁם־הַמָּקוֹם
הַהוּא קִבְרוֹת הַתַּאֲוָה כִּי־שָׁם קָבְרוּ אֶת־הָעָם הַמִּתְאַוִּים׃
לה מִקִּבְרוֹת הַתַּאֲוָה נָסְעוּ הָעָם חֲצֵרוֹת וַיִּהְיוּ בַּחֲצֵרוֹת׃ פ

v. 32. השליו ק'

27. *a young man.* lit. 'the young man'; some one whose name was known but is not given here; possibly some servant of Moses.

28. *shut them in.* Restrain them from continuing their prophetic efforts. He feared that the honour and authority of Moses would be diminished by men prophesying who had not received the spirit from Moses.

29. *would that all the LORD'S people were prophets.* This one saying proves the incomparable greatness of Moses' character. He loves his people more than himself. When a man is really great and good he longs that all should be as he is, and better. So far from being displeased with Eldad and Medad, he yearned for all Israel, elders or not, without the camp or within, to receive the Divine spirit. 'Moses expresses the conviction which is true for all time, that the possession of the spirit is not confined to particular persons or classes' (McNeile).

31–34. FULFILMENT OF THE DIVINE PROMISE

31. *from the sea.* Across the sea; probably the modern Gulf of Akaba.

and let them fall by the camp. The wind lessened, and the quails exhausted by their long flight across the sea fell down from the heights.

two cubits above the face of the earth. Flying at such a low height, they were easily netted.

32. *gathered.* They were arranged in heaps and spread out to be 'cured' in the sun.

33. *very great plague.* Their passionate lust was gratified, but the surfeit killed them; see Psalm LXXVIII, 26–31; CVI, 13–15.

35. *and they abode at Hazeroth.* The site has not been identified.

CHAPTER XII

MIRIAM AND THE VINDICATION OF MOSES

Moses bore with resignation the complaints and murmurings of his People, and—as we shall see—their alternate cowardice and foolhardiness. His foes were also of his own household. This chapter tells how his only brother and only sister offended against him.

12

CHAPTER XII

1. And Miriam and Aaron spoke against Moses because of the Cushite woman whom he had married; for he had married a Cushite woman. 2. And they said: 'Hath the LORD indeed spoken only with Moses? hath He not spoken also with us?' And the LORD heard it.—3. Now the man Moses was very meek, above all the men that were upon the face of the earth.—4. And the LORD spoke suddenly unto Moses, and unto Aaron, and unto Miriam: 'Come out ye three unto the tent of meeting.' And they three came out. 5. And the LORD came down in a pillar of cloud, and stood at the door of the Tent, and called Aaron and Miriam; and they both came forth. 6. And He said: 'Hear now My words: if there be a prophet among you, I the LORD do make Myself known unto him in a vision, I do speak with him in a dream. 7. My servant Moses is

יב

CAP. XII. יב

א וַתְּדַבֵּר מִרְיָם וְאַהֲרֹן בְּמֹשֶׁה עַל־אֹדוֹת הָאִשָּׁה הַכֻּשִׁית
2 אֲשֶׁר לָקָח כִּי־אִשָּׁה כֻשִׁית לָקָח׃ וַיֹּאמְרוּ הֲרַק אַךְ־בְּמֹשֶׁה
3 דִּבֶּר יְהוָה הֲלֹא גַּם־בָּנוּ דִבֵּר וַיִּשְׁמַע יְהוָה׃ וְהָאִישׁ
מֹשֶׁה עָנָו מְאֹד מִכֹּל הָאָדָם אֲשֶׁר עַל־פְּנֵי הָאֲדָמָה׃ ס
4 וַיֹּאמֶר יְהוָה פִּתְאֹם אֶל־מֹשֶׁה וְאֶל־אַהֲרֹן וְאֶל־מִרְיָם
ה צְאוּ שְׁלָשְׁתְּכֶם אֶל־אֹהֶל מוֹעֵד וַיֵּצְאוּ שְׁלָשְׁתָּם׃ וַיֵּרֶד
יְהוָה בְּעַמּוּד עָנָן וַיַּעֲמֹד פֶּתַח הָאֹהֶל וַיִּקְרָא אַהֲרֹן וּמִרְיָם
6 וַיֵּצְאוּ שְׁנֵיהֶם׃ וַיֹּאמֶר שִׁמְעוּ־נָא דְבָרָי אִם־יִהְיֶה נְבִיאֲכֶם
7 יְהוָה בַּמַּרְאָה אֵלָיו אֶתְוַדָּע בַּחֲלוֹם אֲדַבֶּר־בּוֹ׃ לֹא־כֵן

v. 3. עניו ק׳

1. *spoke against Moses.* Miriam seems to have been the instigator of the evil speaking against Moses. The story of Miriam in Scripture is brief, but memorable. She first appears during the Oppression in Egypt, guarding the ark of bulrushes in which Moses was saved from destruction. Then many years later at the crossing of the Red Sea, she led the women's refrain, 'Sing unto the LORD, for He hath triumphed gloriously.' Because of the merit of Miriam—says Jewish legend—a Well accompanied the Israelites on their wanderings till the day of her death. It is a spiritual tragedy that such a prophetic soul should have been guilty of an offence deserving the dire punishment recorded in this chapter.

the Cushite woman. Probably Zipporah, a native of Midian, which is a synonym of Cushan (Hab. III, 7), the home of the North Arabian people called 'Kusi'. Others take the word *Cushite* in the usual sense of 'Ethiopian'. In that case, (the second) marriage of Moses with a South Egyptian woman was the occasion of complaint by Miriam and Aaron. Further details are not given, which fact led legend to step in and fill in the gap, and supply a reason that would serve as the connection between *v.* 1 and 2. (Guedemann traces the growth of that legend in a masterly study in the *Monatsschrift* for 1870).

2. *only with Moses.* Having spoken ill of Moses and thus belittled his importance, they asked, 'Has Moses a monopoly of Divine communications? Can we not claim equality with him?'

and the LORD heard it. God said, Moses is very meek and pays no heed to the injustice meted out to him. I will therefore defend him (Midrash).

3. *now the man Moses was very meek.* These words explain how it was that Moses took no steps to vindicate himself.

'There is about these words, as also about the passages in which Moses no less equivocally records his own faults (XX, 12 f; Exod. IV, 22 f; Deut. I, 37), that simplicity which is witness at once to their genuineness and inspiration. The Heb. word for *meek* (ענו) occurs frequently in the Psalms, and as here is applied by the writers to themselves; cf. Psalm X, 17, and Psalm XXII, 27' (Speaker's Bible).

4. *suddenly.* Reproof and retribution followed without delay.

5. *both came forth.* They were separated from Moses, because a man's whole praise may only be uttered in his absence (Sifri). This praise is given in *v.* 7, 8.

6. *if there be a prophet among you.* Better, *if there be a prophet of the LORD among you.*

I the LORD do make. Better, *I make.*

in a vision . . . dream. 'With some of the higher Prophets, such as Jeremiah, dreams as a source of revelation fell into complete disrepute' (Gray).

7. *trusted in all My house.* Found worthy of God's confidence in everything appertaining to the guidance of the House of Israel. Moses is pre-eminent among the Prophets. While other Prophets chiefly warned their own generation and comforted them with blessings in the remote future, Moses addresses all times, communicating to them everlasting statutes and laws for all generations.

not so; he is trusted in all My house; 8. with him do I speak mouth to mouth, even manifestly, and not in dark speeches; and the similitude of the LORD doth he behold; wherefore then were ye not afraid to speak against My servant, against Moses?' 9. And the anger of the LORD was kindled against them; and He departed. 10. And when the cloud was removed from over the Tent, behold, Miriam was leprous, as white as snow; and Aaron looked upon Miriam; and, behold, she was leprous. 11. And Aaron said unto Moses: 'Oh my lord, lay not, I pray thee, sin upon us, for that we have done foolishly, and for that we have sinned. 12. Let her not, I pray, be as one dead, of whom the flesh is half consumed when he cometh out of his mother's womb.' 13. And Moses cried unto the LORD, saying: 'Heal her now, O God, I beseech Thee.' *m. ¶14. And the LORD said unto Moses: 'If her father had but spit in her face, should she not hide in shame seven days? let her be shut up without the camp seven days, and after that she shall be brought in again.' 15. And Miriam was shut up without the camp seven days; and the people journeyed not till Miriam was brought in again. 16. And afterward the people journeyed from Hazeroth, and pitched in the wilderness of Paran.

8 עַבְדִּי מֹשֶׁה בְּכָל־בֵּיתִי נֶאֱמָן הוּא׃ פֶּה אֶל־פֶּה אֲדַבֶּר־
בּוֹ וּמַרְאֶה וְלֹא בְחִידֹת וּתְמֻנַת יְהוָה יַבִּיט וּמַדּוּעַ לֹא
9 יְרֵאתֶם לְדַבֵּר בְּעַבְדִּי בְמֹשֶׁה׃ וַיִּחַר־אַף יְהוָה בָּם
י וַיֵּלַךְ׃ וְהֶעָנָן סָר מֵעַל הָאֹהֶל וְהִנֵּה מִרְיָם מְצֹרַעַת כַּשָּׁלֶג
11 וַיִּפֶן אַהֲרֹן אֶל־מִרְיָם וְהִנֵּה מְצֹרָעַת׃ וַיֹּאמֶר אַהֲרֹן אֶל־
מֹשֶׁה בִּי אֲדֹנִי אַל־נָא תָשֵׁת עָלֵינוּ חַטָּאת אֲשֶׁר נוֹאַלְנוּ
12 וַאֲשֶׁר חָטָאנוּ׃ אַל־נָא תְהִי כַּמֵּת אֲשֶׁר בְּצֵאתוֹ מֵרֶחֶם
13 אִמּוֹ וַיֵּאָכֵל חֲצִי בְשָׂרוֹ׃ וַיִּצְעַק מֹשֶׁה אֶל־יְהוָה לֵאמֹר אֵל
נָא רְפָא נָא לָהּ׃ * פ מפטיר
14 וַיֹּאמֶר יְהוָה אֶל־מֹשֶׁה וְאָבִיהָ יָרֹק יָרַק בְּפָנֶיהָ הֲלֹא
תִכָּלֵם שִׁבְעַת יָמִים תִּסָּגֵר שִׁבְעַת יָמִים מִחוּץ לַמַּחֲנֶה
טו וְאַחַר תֵּאָסֵף׃ וַתִּסָּגֵר מִרְיָם מִחוּץ לַמַּחֲנֶה שִׁבְעַת יָמִים
16 וְהָעָם לֹא נָסַע עַד־הֵאָסֵף מִרְיָם׃ וְאַחַר נָסְעוּ הָעָם מֵחֲצֵרוֹת
וַיַּחֲנוּ בְּמִדְבַּר פָּארָן׃

8. *mouth to mouth.* The same as 'face to face' (Deut. XXXIV, 10). These phrases denote figuratively 'the clearest, most direct, and most simple communication, the figure being taken from the way in which men communicate to each other things which they desire to be clearly understood and to leave no doubt as to their truth or meaning' (Friedländer).

not in dark speeches. The Talmud expresses this distinction by comparing the vision received by Moses to the reflection given out by a bright mirror (אספקלריא מאירה), whilst the visions of other Prophets were like the blurred images produced by a dim mirror.

the similitude of the LORD. Not the essential nature of God which no man can see, but the similitude in which for the time it pleased Him to veil His glory; as *e.g.* the burning bush.

9. *He departed.* As a judge departs after trying and convicting evil-doers.

10. *Miriam was leprous.* Aaron was exempted from punishment, as he was merely drawn into this attack on his brother. Leprosy was regarded as the Providential punishment for slander (מצורע, מוציא שם רע).

11. *Oh my lord.* Aaron now feels humbled and speaks to Moses as to a superior.

lay not, I pray thee, sin upon us. Do not bring upon us the *consequences* of our sin.

12. *as one dead.* 'Let us not bear the penalty of this wicked folly we have committed. Let her not turn like a corpse, like one born with a body half wasted' (Moffatt).

13. *Moses cried unto the LORD.* Showing fullest forgiveness for both, and sincerest pity for his smitten sister.

heal her, O God, I beseech thee. This prayer is a model of brevity. It says so much in five of the simplest, shortest Hebrew words!

14. *hide in shame seven days.* Would not a father's putting his daughter to shame before all the world entail her retirement for seven days at least? How much more, when her Heavenly Father has seen fit to inflict a public punishment upon Miriam, should she be shut away for at least a similar period!

15. *without the camp.* As was the case with lepers.

till Miriam was brought in again. This was done out of deference to Miriam. 'Miriam waited for her brother Moses one hour, as it is said, "And his sister stood afar off to know what would be done to him" (Exod. II, 4). In return for this sisterly act, the people of Israel waited for Miriam seven days in the desert' (Talmud).

16. *from Hazeroth.* See XI, 35.

wilderness of Paran. See X, 12.

HAFTORAH BEHAALOSECHA הפטרת בהעלתך

ZECHARIAH II, 14–IV, 7

Chapter II

14. 'Sing and rejoice, O daughter of Zion; for, lo, I come, and I will dwell in the midst of thee, saith the LORD. 15. And many nations shall join themselves to the LORD in that day, and shall be My people, and I will dwell in the midst of thee'; and thou shalt know that the LORD of hosts hath sent me unto thee. 16. And the LORD shall inherit Judah as His portion in the holy land, and shall choose Jerusalem again. 17. Be silent, all flesh, before the LORD; for He is aroused out of His holy habitation.

Chapter III

1. And he showed me Joshua the high priest standing before the angel of the LORD, and Satan standing at his right hand to accuse him. 2. And the LORD said unto Satan: 'The LORD rebuke thee, O Satan, yea, the LORD that hath chosen Jerusalem rebuke thee; is not this man a brand plucked out of the fire?' 3. Now Joshua was clothed with filthy garments, and stood before the angel. 4. And he answered and spoke unto those that stood before him, saying: 'Take the

CAP. II. ב

רָנִּי 14
וְשִׂמְחִי בַּת־צִיּוֹן כִּי הִנְנִי־בָא וְשָׁכַנְתִּי בְתוֹכֵךְ נְאֻם־יְהוָה׃
טו וְנִלְווּ גוֹיִם רַבִּים אֶל־יְהוָה בַּיּוֹם הַהוּא וְהָיוּ לִי לְעָם
וְשָׁכַנְתִּי בְתוֹכֵךְ וְיָדַעַתְּ כִּי־יְהוָה צְבָאוֹת שְׁלָחַנִי אֵלָיִךְ׃
16 וְנָחַל יְהוָה אֶת־יְהוּדָה חֶלְקוֹ עַל אַדְמַת הַקֹּדֶשׁ וּבָחַר
17 עוֹד בִּירוּשָׁלִָם׃ הַס כָּל־בָּשָׂר מִפְּנֵי יְהוָה כִּי נֵעוֹר
מִמְּעוֹן קָדְשׁוֹ׃

CAP. III. ג

א וַיַּרְאֵנִי אֶת־יְהוֹשֻׁעַ הַכֹּהֵן הַגָּדוֹל עֹמֵד לִפְנֵי מַלְאַךְ יְהוָה
2 וְהַשָּׂטָן עֹמֵד עַל־יְמִינוֹ לְשִׂטְנוֹ׃ וַיֹּאמֶר יְהוָה אֶל־הַשָּׂטָן
יִגְעַר יְהוָה בְּךָ הַשָּׂטָן וְיִגְעַר יְהוָה בְּךָ הַבֹּחֵר בִּירוּשָׁלִָם
3 הֲלוֹא זֶה אוּד מֻצָּל מֵאֵשׁ׃ וִיהוֹשֻׁעַ הָיָה לָבֻשׁ בְּגָדִים
4 צוֹאִים וְעֹמֵד לִפְנֵי הַמַּלְאָךְ׃ וַיַּעַן וַיֹּאמֶר אֶל־הָעֹמְדִים

Zechariah was one of the exiles who returned from Babylon when Cyrus promulgated his decree of Restoration in the year 537. He began his prophecies about 17 years afterwards. Disastrous seasons and the hostility of neighbours had discouraged the people, and all operations in connection with rebuilding the Temple had long ceased.

At this juncture the Prophets Haggai and Zechariah appeared, roused the people from their despondency and fired them to resume the work which had been suspended.

In our Haftorah, Zechariah assures the people of the Divine assistance in their work of rebuilding the Temple and of national rehabilitation. *Not by might, nor by power, but by My spirit, saith the LORD of Hosts*—these words of Zechariah may be said to proclaim the lesson of all Jewish history; it is certainly the Prophetic teaching of the Maccabean Festival with which his name is linked in the synagogue service.

The Prophet's vision of the 'candlestick all of gold' in chap. IV, with its teaching that God alone is the Source of all light, connects with the Sedrah which opens with the command concerning the Menorah.

14. *I will dwell in the midst of thee.* Through the visible symbol of the restored Temple.

17. *be silent.* All hostile efforts directed against the rebuilding of the Temple, and later any human opposition to God's ultimate purpose, shall fail.

Chapter III

Zechariah's messages are chiefly conveyed by means of visions. The object of the vivid visions, so dramatically described in the remainder of the Haftorah, is to banish the disturbing thoughts and fears which were depressing the people.

1. *Joshua.* The first high priest after the Restoration. He was prominently associated with Zerubbabel, the then Governor of Judah, in the erection of the Second Temple. Zerubbabel was the grandson of Jehoiachin, the last independent king of Judah, who had been carried away captive to Babylon in the year 597.

Satan. One who opposes with false accusations. Satan accuses Joshua and the people of sinfulness, and that they are, therefore, unworthy to rebuild the Temple. Perhaps a similar feeling, arising out of their disappointments, depressed the people. But Satan is rebuked, and the returned exiles are assured that their fears are groundless.

2. *a brand plucked out of the fire.* Something precious (in this case, the Returned Remnant of Israel) snatched from destruction.

3. *filthy garments.* Symbolizing the iniquities of the people that retard the completeness of the Redemption.

filthy garments from off him.' And unto him he said: 'Behold, I cause thine iniquity to pass from thee, and I will clothe thee with robes.' 5. And I said: 'Let them set a fair mitre upon his head.' So they set a fair mitre upon his head, and clothed him with garments; and the angel of the LORD stood by. 6. And the angel of the LORD forewarned Joshua, saying: 7. 'Thus saith the LORD of hosts: If thou wilt walk in My ways, and if thou wilt keep My charge, and wilt also judge My house, and wilt also keep My courts, then I will give thee free access among these that stand by. 8. Hear now, O Joshua the high priest, thou and thy fellows that sit before thee; for they are men that are a sign; for, behold, I will bring forth My servant the Shoot. 9. For behold the stone that I have laid before Joshua; upon one stone are seven facets; behold, I will engrave the graving thereof, saith the LORD of hosts: And I will remove the iniquity of that land in one day. 10. In that day, saith the LORD of hosts, shall ye call every man his neighbour under the vine and under the fig-tree.'

לְפָנָיו לֵאמֹר הָסִירוּ הַבְּגָדִים הַצֹּאִים מֵעָלָיו וַיֹּאמֶר אֵלָיו
ה רְאֵה הֶעֱבַרְתִּי מֵעָלֶיךָ עֲוֺנֶךָ וְהַלְבֵּשׁ אֹתְךָ מַחֲלָצוֹת׃ וָאֹמַר
יָשִׂימוּ צָנִיף טָהוֹר עַל־רֹאשׁוֹ וַיָּשִׂימוּ הַצָּנִיף הַטָּהוֹר עַל־
6 רֹאשׁוֹ וַיַּלְבִּשֻׁהוּ בְּגָדִים וּמַלְאַךְ יְהוָה עֹמֵד׃ וַיָּעַד מַלְאַךְ
7 יְהוָה בִּיהוֹשֻׁעַ לֵאמֹר׃ כֹּה־אָמַר יְהוָה צְבָאוֹת אִם־בִּדְרָכַי
תֵּלֵךְ וְאִם אֶת־מִשְׁמַרְתִּי תִשְׁמֹר וְגַם־אַתָּה תָּדִין אֶת־בֵּיתִי
וְגַם תִּשְׁמֹר אֶת־חֲצֵרָי וְנָתַתִּי לְךָ מַהְלְכִים בֵּין הָעֹמְדִים
8 הָאֵלֶּה׃ שְׁמַע־נָא יְהוֹשֻׁעַ ׀ הַכֹּהֵן הַגָּדוֹל אַתָּה וְרֵעֶיךָ
הַיֹּשְׁבִים לְפָנֶיךָ כִּי־אַנְשֵׁי מוֹפֵת הֵמָּה כִּי־הִנְנִי מֵבִיא אֶת־
9 עַבְדִּי צֶמַח׃ כִּי ׀ הִנֵּה הָאֶבֶן אֲשֶׁר נָתַתִּי לִפְנֵי יְהוֹשֻׁעַ
עַל־אֶבֶן אַחַת שִׁבְעָה עֵינָיִם הִנְנִי מְפַתֵּחַ פִּתֻּחָהּ נְאֻם יְהוָה
י צְבָאוֹת וּמַשְׁתִּי אֶת־עֲוֺן הָאָרֶץ־הַהִיא בְּיוֹם אֶחָד׃ בַּיּוֹם
הַהוּא נְאֻם יְהוָה צְבָאוֹת תִּקְרְאוּ אִישׁ לְרֵעֵהוּ אֶל־תַּחַת
גֶּפֶן וְאֶל־תַּחַת תְּאֵנָה׃

כצ"ל v. 10.

4. *he. i.e.* the angel.

those that stood before him. i.e. attendant angels who are represented as waiting upon him.

take the filthy garments from off him. Symbolizes the removal of the people's sin, forgiveness.

5. *I said.* The idea of a defiled priesthood is intolerable to the Prophet, and he bursts forth with the request that the complete sign of priestly purity and national acceptance be granted.

mitre. Or, 'diadem.' Let Joshua not only be cleansed and clothed, but crowned as well.

6. *forewarned. i.e.* solemnly assured.

7. *if thou wilt walk in My ways.* The first condition of the priesthood is that, not only in the Temple but in his own life, the priest shall observe the Divine requirements of conduct, and always remember to Whose service he is consecrated.

that stand by. Among these attendant angels (*v.* 4). Targum and Kimchi explain 'after death', and take it as an allusion to the immortality of the soul.

8. *thy fellows.* The assistant priests.

men that are a sign. Of God's favour. The restored priesthood is a pledge of the coming of the Messianic Kingdom. Humble and modest as were the beginnings of the Temple, they were portents which contained within them the pledge of the fulfilment of the complete Redemption.

the Shoot. According to Rashi, Zechariah here means Zerubbabel, who as the civic leader will complete, with Joshua as the spiritual leader, the rehabilitated state. A comparison with VI, 12 supports this interpretation.

9. *for behold the stone.* The coping-stone of the Temple (see last verse of the Haftorah, 'head stone') which in this vision is set before Joshua to symbolize the certainty of the rebuilding.

upon one stone are seven facets. i.e. upon every stone in the Temple there shall be 'seven eyes', conveying the idea of the very special watchfulness and care that God will exercise over His house (Kimchi).

The same commentator quotes the interesting opinion of his father that in the number 'seven' we may see a reference to the seven great leaders of the period to whom the Jewish rebirth was due: Joshua, Ezra, Nehemiah, Zerubbabel, Haggai, Zechariah and Malachi.

I will engrave the graving thereof. As the engraving completes and beautifies a work, so God assures the people that the Temple will be completed to every detail (Kimchi).

I will remove the iniquity of that land. Sin, the chief cause of sorrow and suffering, will be removed with the coming of the new Temple.

10. *shall ye call. i.e.* invite. A picture of general felicity and security.

CHAPTER IV

1. And the angel that spoke with me returned, and waked me, as a man that is wakened out of his sleep. 2. And he said unto me: 'What seest thou?' And I said: 'I have seen, and behold a candlestick all of gold, with a bowl upon the top of it, and its seven lamps thereon; there are seven pipes, yea, seven, to the lamps, which are upon the top thereof; 3. and two olive-trees by it, one upon the right side of the bowl, and the other upon the left side thereof.' 4. And I answered and spoke to the angel that spoke with me, saying: 'What are these, my lord?' 5. Then the angel that spoke with me answered and said unto me: 'Knowest thou not what these are?' And I said: 'No, my lord.' 6. Then he answered and spoke unto me, saying: 'This is the word of the LORD unto Zerubbabel, saying: Not by might, nor by power, but by My spirit, saith the LORD of hosts. 7. Who art thou, O great mountain before Zerubbabel? thou shalt become a plain; and he shall bring forth the top stone with shoutings of Grace, grace, unto it.'

CAP. IV. ד

א וַיָּשָׁב הַמַּלְאָךְ הַדֹּבֵר בִּי וַיְעִירֵנִי כְּאִישׁ אֲשֶׁר־יֵעוֹר מִשְּׁנָתוֹ׃
2 וַיֹּאמֶר אֵלַי מָה אַתָּה רֹאֶה וַיֹּאמַר רָאִיתִי וְהִנֵּה מְנוֹרַת
זָהָב כֻּלָּהּ וְגֻלָּהּ עַל־רֹאשָׁהּ וְשִׁבְעָה נֵרֹתֶיהָ עָלֶיהָ שִׁבְעָה
3 וְשִׁבְעָה מוּצָקוֹת לַנֵּרוֹת אֲשֶׁר עַל־רֹאשָׁהּ׃ וּשְׁנַיִם זֵיתִים
4 עָלֶיהָ אֶחָד מִימִין הַגֻּלָּה וְאֶחָד עַל־שְׂמֹאלָהּ׃ וָאַעַן וָאֹמַר
ה אֶל־הַמַּלְאָךְ הַדֹּבֵר בִּי לֵאמֹר מָה אֵלֶּה אֲדֹנִי׃ וַיַּעַן הַמַּלְאָךְ
הַדֹּבֵר בִּי וַיֹּאמֶר אֵלַי הֲלוֹא יָדַעְתָּ מָה־הֵמָּה אֵלֶּה וָאֹמַר
6 לֹא אֲדֹנִי׃ וַיַּעַן וַיֹּאמֶר אֵלַי לֵאמֹר זֶה דְּבַר־יְהוָה אֶל־
זְרֻבָּבֶל לֵאמֹר לֹא בְחַיִל וְלֹא בְכֹחַ כִּי אִם־בְּרוּחִי אָמַר
7 יְהוָה צְבָאוֹת׃ מִי־אַתָּה הַר־הַגָּדוֹל לִפְנֵי זְרֻבָּבֶל לְמִישֹׁר
וְהוֹצִיא אֶת־הָאֶבֶן הָרֹאשָׁה תְּשֻׁאוֹת חֵן ׀ חֵן לָהּ׃

v. 2. ואמר קרי

CHAPTER IV

Another vision. The Prophet's thoughts now turn to Zerubbabel, and the need to encourage him in his work. He would further enforce the lesson that God alone is the source of all Light, as well as power, to rulers and people alike.

2. *candlestick.* Such as stood in the Second Temple.

seven pipes. One to each lamp carrying the supply of oil.

3. *two olive trees.* Representing Joshua and Zerubbabel, who were appointed respectively to the spiritual and civil leadership, and by whom the work in hand would be accomplished (Kimchi); see *v.* 12.

6. *this is the word. i.e.* the message of the LORD to Zerubbabel. As the lights are controlled by an unseen agency, so behind Zerubbabel and his allotted work is the invisible spirit and help of God. All the difficulties in the way will disappear; and, in spite of the hostility and mockings of the people who have hitherto opposed, he will complete the building of the Temple, 'not by might, nor by power, but by My spirit, saith the LORD of hosts.'

7. *who art thou, O great mountain.* Repeating the above idea. Whatever obstacles may arise to hinder him, they will all be overcome.

bring forth the top stone. Amid the joyful acclamations of the people when they see the Temple completed.

Grace, grace, unto it. i.e. may God's grace and favour rest on it!

13

CHAPTER XIII

1. And the LORD spoke unto Moses, saying: 2. 'Send thou men, that they may spy out the land of Canaan, which I give unto the children of Israel; of every tribe of their fathers shall ye send a man, every one a prince among them.' 3. And Moses sent them from the wilderness of Paran according to the commandment of the LORD; all of them men who were heads of the children of Israel. 4. And these were their names: of the tribe of Reuben, Shammua the son of Zaccur. 5. Of the tribe of Simeon, Shaphat the son of Hori. 6. Of the tribe of Judah, Caleb the son of Jephunneh. 7. Of the tribe of Issachar, Igal the son of Joseph. 8. Of the tribe of Ephraim, Hoshea the son of Nun. 9. Of the tribe of Benjamin, Palti the son of Raphu. 10. Of the tribe of Zebulun, Gaddiel the son of Sodi. 11. Of the tribe of Joseph, namely, of the tribe of Manasseh, Gaddi the son of Susi. 12. Of the tribe of Dan, Ammiel the son of Gemalli. 13. Of the tribe of Asher, Sethur the son of Michael. 14. Of the tribe of Naphtali, Nahbi the son of Vophsi. 15. Of the tribe of Gad, Geuel the son of Machi. 16. These are the names of the men that Moses sent to spy out the land. And Moses

CAP. XIII. יג

יג פ פ פ לז 37

א 2 וַיְדַבֵּר יְהוָה אֶל־מֹשֶׁה לֵּאמֹר׃ שְׁלַח־לְךָ אֲנָשִׁים וְיָתֻרוּ
אֶת־אֶרֶץ כְּנַעַן אֲשֶׁר־אֲנִי נֹתֵן לִבְנֵי יִשְׂרָאֵל אִישׁ אֶחָד
3 אִישׁ אֶחָד לְמַטֵּה אֲבֹתָיו תִּשְׁלָחוּ כֹּל נָשִׂיא בָהֶם׃ וַיִּשְׁלַח
אֹתָם מֹשֶׁה מִמִּדְבַּר פָּארָן עַל־פִּי יְהוָה כֻּלָּם אֲנָשִׁים
4 רָאשֵׁי בְנֵי־יִשְׂרָאֵל הֵמָּה׃ וְאֵלֶּה שְׁמוֹתָם לְמַטֵּה רְאוּבֵן
ה 6 שַׁמּוּעַ בֶּן־זַכּוּר׃ לְמַטֵּה שִׁמְעוֹן שָׁפָט בֶּן־חוֹרִי׃ לְמַטֵּה
7 יְהוּדָה כָּלֵב בֶּן־יְפֻנֶּה׃ לְמַטֵּה יִשָּׂשכָר יִגְאָל בֶּן־יוֹסֵף׃
8 9 לְמַטֵּה אֶפְרָיִם הוֹשֵׁעַ בִּן־נוּן׃ לְמַטֵּה בִנְיָמִן פַּלְטִי בֶּן־
י 11 רָפוּא׃ לְמַטֵּה זְבוּלֻן גַּדִּיאֵל בֶּן־סוֹדִי׃ לְמַטֵּה יוֹסֵף
12 לְמַטֵּה מְנַשֶּׁה גַּדִּי בֶּן־סוּסִי׃ לְמַטֵּה דָן עַמִּיאֵל בֶּן־גְּמַלִּי׃
13 14 לְמַטֵּה אָשֵׁר סְתוּר בֶּן־מִיכָאֵל׃ לְמַטֵּה נַפְתָּלִי נַחְבִּי
טו 16 בֶּן־וָפְסִי׃ לְמַטֵּה גָד גְּאוּאֵל בֶּן־מָכִי׃ אֵלֶּה שְׁמוֹת

v. 2. קמץ בז"ק v. 8. קמץ בטרחא

IV. SHELACH LECHA

(CHAPTERS XIII–XV)

THE SPIES AND THEIR REPORT

According to some scholars, the victory of the Israelites over the king of Arad in the extreme south of Canaan, recorded in XXI, 1–3, took place at this stage. The Israelites inflicted an annihilating defeat on the enemy, and called his territory *Hormah*, lit. 'utter destruction'. So striking had been their success, that Moses deemed the moment ripe for undertaking the conquest of the Holy Land from this advanced station of their march. As reported in Deut. I, 22, the Israelites then came to Moses, saying, 'Let us send men before us that they may search the land for us. And they would have succeeded in forcing their way into the heart of Canaan, if they had been animated by the high courage required for such an enterprise. This and the following chapter relate that such was far from being the case. Twelve men are sent to explore the land, and learn its character and that of the inhabitants. After forty days they return. The 'majority report', which is entirely against the possibility of conquest, threatens to demoralize the people by fear.

The incident of the Spies is the turning-point in the lives of all those that had been born in slavery. By the cowardice and murmurings with which they receive the report of the Spies, they show themselves unfit for the tasks of a free nation. They must die in the Wilderness. During thirty-eight years of wandering, a new generation that knew not Egypt was to be reared, in hardship and freedom, for the conquest and possession of the Promised Land.

XIII, 1–24. THE MISSION OF THE SPIES

2. *send thou men.* Heb. *shelach lecha*; lit. 'send for thyself'. The Rabbis stress the word *lecha*, 'for thyself,' and make it imply, 'If thou wishest to send spies, do so.'

of every tribe. In order that the whole people might share in the interest and responsibility of the enterprise.

a prince. Not the same princes that took the leading part in the census (I, 5), but men of importance, capable of grappling with so trying a task.

4. *their names.* Read the note on I, 15 as to the importance of the names in Numbers. In the list before us, several of the names are abbreviated forms; *e.g.* Palti from Paltiel, Gaddi from Gaddiel, and Gemalli from Gamaliel.

הָאֲנָשִׁים אֲשֶׁר־שָׁלַח מֹשֶׁה לָתוּר אֶת־הָאָרֶץ וַיִּקְרָא
17 מֹשֶׁה לְהוֹשֵׁעַ בִּן־נוּן יְהוֹשֻׁעַ׃ וַיִּשְׁלַח אֹתָם מֹשֶׁה לָתוּר
אֶת־אֶרֶץ כְּנָעַן וַיֹּאמֶר אֲלֵהֶם עֲלוּ זֶה בַּנֶּגֶב וַעֲלִיתֶם
18 אֶת־הָהָר׃ וּרְאִיתֶם אֶת־הָאָרֶץ מַה־הִוא וְאֶת־הָעָם הַיֹּשֵׁב
19 עָלֶיהָ הֶחָזָק הוּא הֲרָפֶה הַמְעַט הוּא אִם־רָב׃ וּמָה הָאָרֶץ
אֲשֶׁר־הוּא יֹשֵׁב בָּהּ הֲטוֹבָה הִוא אִם־רָעָה וּמָה הֶעָרִים
כ אֲשֶׁר־הוּא יוֹשֵׁב בָּהֵנָּה הַבְּמַחֲנִים אִם בְּמִבְצָרִים׃ וּמָה
הָאָרֶץ הַשְּׁמֵנָה הִוא אִם־רָזָה הֲיֵשׁ־בָּהּ עֵץ אִם־אַיִן
וְהִתְחַזַּקְתֶּם וּלְקַחְתֶּם מִפְּרִי הָאָרֶץ וְהַיָּמִים יְמֵי בִּכּוּרֵי
שני
21 עֲנָבִים׃ *וַיַּעֲלוּ וַיָּתֻרוּ אֶת־הָאָרֶץ מִמִּדְבַּר־צִן עַד־רְחֹב לְבֹא
22 חֲמָת׃ וַיַּעֲלוּ בַנֶּגֶב וַיָּבֹא עַד־חֶבְרוֹן וְשָׁם אֲחִימַן שֵׁשַׁי
וְתַלְמַי יְלִידֵי הָעֲנָק וְחֶבְרוֹן שֶׁבַע שָׁנִים נִבְנְתָה לִפְנֵי צֹעַן
23 מִצְרָיִם׃ וַיָּבֹאוּ עַד־נַחַל אֶשְׁכֹּל וַיִּכְרְתוּ מִשָּׁם זְמוֹרָה
וְאֶשְׁכּוֹל עֲנָבִים אֶחָד וַיִּשָּׂאֻהוּ בַמּוֹט בִּשְׁנָיִם וּמִן־הָרִמֹּנִים
24 וּמִן־הַתְּאֵנִים׃ לַמָּקוֹם הַהוּא קָרָא נַחַל אֶשְׁכּוֹל עַל אֹדוֹת

v. 22. סבירין ויבאו

called Hoshea the son of Nun Joshua.
17. And Moses sent them to spy out the land of Canaan, and said unto them: 'Get you up here into the South, and go up into the mountains; 18. and see the land, what it is; and the people that dwelleth therein, whether they are strong or weak, whether they are few or many; 19. and what the land is that they dwell in, whether it is good or bad; and what cities they are that they dwell in, whether in camps, or in strongholds; 20. and what the land is, whether it is fat or lean, whether there is wood therein, or not. And be ye of good courage, and bring of the fruit of the land.'—Now the time was the time of the first-ripe grapes. *ii.
—21. So they went up, and spied out the land from the wilderness of Zin unto Rehob, at the entrance to Hamath. 22. And they went up into the South, and came unto Hebron; and Ahiman, Sheshai, and Talmai, the children of Anak, were there.—Now Hebron was built seven years before Zoan in Egypt.—23. And they came unto the valley of Eshcol, and cut down from thence a branch with one cluster of grapes, and they bore it upon a pole between two; they took also of the pomegranates, and of the figs.—24. That place was called the valley of [1]Eshcol, because of the cluster which the children of Israel cut down from thence.—25. And they returned from spying out the

[1] That is, *a cluster*.

16. *Moses called Hoshea . . . Joshua.* Better, *and Moses had called Hoshea the son of Nun Joshua.* The change had already been made at the time of the victory over Amalek, Exod. XVII, 9 f. Hoshea signifies, 'He has helped.' Moses, by prefixing to it a letter of the Divine Name, changed it to Joshua, Heb. *Yehoshua*, *i.e.* 'He will help', at the same time indicating the Source of salvation. According to the Midrash, however, Moses here pronounced over Joshua the prayer, 'May God deliver thee from the counsel of the Spies.'

17. *the South.* Better, *the Negeb*; lit. 'the dry land'; southern Canaan, extending northward from Kadesh to within a few miles of Hebron, and from the Dead Sea westward to the Mediterranean; the steppe region which forms the transition to the true desert.

the mountains. The hill-country in Southern Palestine.

20. *of the fruit.* As a tangible confirmation of their testimony.

the time of the first-ripe grapes. The end of July or beginning of August.

21. *the wilderness of Zin.* N.E. of the wilderness of Paran, and therefore the southern boundary of Canaan.

unto Rehob. In the north of the land, at the base of Mount Hermon, near the sources of the Jordan.

at the entrance to Hamath. The narrow pass between Mount Hermon and the Lebanon, often spoken of in Scripture as the northernmost border of the Holy Land (XXXIV, 8).

22. *Ahiman, Sheshai and Talmai.* Probably the names of clans, since we meet these names in the time of Joshua (Josh. XV, 14).

Anak. lit. 'neck'; the natives of the Negeb seem to have been very tall and lank, a fact that gave rise to the tradition that they were the remnants of a race of giants.

before Zoan. A city of great antiquity, older than 2000 B.C.E., and rebuilt in the beginning of the Nineteenth Egyptian Dynasty.

23. *valley.* Heb. *nachal*, denotes a stream and the gorge through which it flows—a wady.

land at the end of forty days. 26. And they went and came to Moses, and to Aaron, and to all the congregation of the children of Israel, unto the wilderness of Paran, to Kadesh; and brought back word unto them, and unto all the congregation, and showed them the fruit of the land. 27. And they told him, and said: 'We came unto the land whither thou sentest us, and surely it floweth with milk and honey; and this is the fruit of it. 28. Howbeit the people that dwell in the land are fierce, and the cities are fortified, and very great; and moreover we saw the children of Anak there. 29. Amalek dwelleth in the land of the South; and the Hittite, and the Jebusite, and the Amorite, dwell in the mountains; and the Canaanite dwelleth by the sea, and along by the side of the Jordan.' 30. And Caleb stilled the people toward Moses, and said: 'We should go up at once, and possess it; for we are well able to overcome it.' 31. But the men that went up with him said: 'We are not able to go up against the people; for they are stronger than we.' 32. And they spread an evil report of the land which they had spied out unto the children of Israel, saying: 'The land, through which we have passed to spy it out, is a land that eateth up the inhabitants thereof; and all the people that we saw in it are men of great stature. 33. And there we saw the Nephilim, the sons of Anak who come of the Nephilim; and we were in our own sight as grasshoppers, and so we were in their sight.'

כה הָאֶשְׁכּוֹל אֲשֶׁר־כָּרְתוּ מִשָּׁם בְּנֵי יִשְׂרָאֵל׃ וַיָּשֻׁבוּ מִתּוּר
26 הָאָרֶץ מִקֵּץ אַרְבָּעִים יוֹם׃ וַיֵּלְכוּ וַיָּבֹאוּ אֶל־מֹשֶׁה וְאֶל־
אַהֲרֹן וְאֶל־כָּל־עֲדַת בְּנֵי־יִשְׂרָאֵל אֶל־מִדְבַּר פָּארָן קָדֵשָׁה
וַיָּשִׁיבוּ אֹתָם דָּבָר וְאֶת־כָּל־הָעֵדָה וַיַּרְאוּם אֶת־פְּרִי הָאָרֶץ׃
27 וַיְסַפְּרוּ־לוֹ וַיֹּאמְרוּ בָּאנוּ אֶל־הָאָרֶץ אֲשֶׁר שְׁלַחְתָּנוּ וְגַם
28 זָבַת חָלָב וּדְבַשׁ הִוא וְזֶה־פִּרְיָהּ׃ אֶפֶס כִּי־עַז הָעָם הַיֹּשֵׁב
בָּאָרֶץ וְהֶעָרִים בְּצֻרוֹת גְּדֹלֹת מְאֹד וְגַם־יְלִדֵי הָעֲנָק רָאִינוּ
29 שָׁם׃ עֲמָלֵק יוֹשֵׁב בְּאֶרֶץ הַנֶּגֶב וְהַחִתִּי וְהַיְבוּסִי וְהָאֱמֹרִי
ל יוֹשֵׁב בָּהָר וְהַכְּנַעֲנִי יוֹשֵׁב עַל־הַיָּם וְעַל יַד הַיַּרְדֵּן׃ וַיַּהַס
כָּלֵב אֶת־הָעָם אֶל־מֹשֶׁה וַיֹּאמֶר עָלֹה נַעֲלֶה וְיָרַשְׁנוּ אֹתָהּ
31 כִּי־יָכוֹל נוּכַל לָהּ׃ וְהָאֲנָשִׁים אֲשֶׁר־עָלוּ עִמּוֹ אָמְרוּ לֹא
32 נוּכַל לַעֲלוֹת אֶל־הָעָם כִּי־חָזָק הוּא מִמֶּנּוּ׃ וַיֹּצִיאוּ דִּבַּת
הָאָרֶץ אֲשֶׁר תָּרוּ אֹתָהּ אֶל־בְּנֵי יִשְׂרָאֵל לֵאמֹר הָאָרֶץ
אֲשֶׁר עָבַרְנוּ בָהּ לָתוּר אֹתָהּ אֶרֶץ אֹכֶלֶת יוֹשְׁבֶיהָ הִוא
33 וְכָל־הָעָם אֲשֶׁר־רָאִינוּ בְתוֹכָהּ אַנְשֵׁי מִדּוֹת׃ וְשָׁם רָאִינוּ
אֶת־הַנְּפִילִים בְּנֵי עֲנָק מִן־הַנְּפִלִים וַנְּהִי בְעֵינֵינוּ כַּחֲגָבִים
וְכֵן הָיִינוּ בְּעֵינֵיהֶם׃

v. 30. ס׳ רבתי לדעת קצת סופרים

25–33. THE REPORT OF THE SPIES

26. *Kadesh.* Was for many years the seat of encampment for the tribes during the wanderings, and the starting-point for the final march into Canaan. It has been identified with the modern Ain Kadis ('Holy Spring'). 'Out from the barren and desolate stretch of the burning desert-waste we had come with magical suddenness into an oasis of verdure and beauty, unlooked for and hardly conceivable in such a region. Running water gurgled under the waving grass' (Trumbull).

27. *it floweth with milk and honey.* 'Pursuing the tactics of slanderers, they began by extolling the land, so as not to arouse, by too unfavourable a report, the suspicion of the people; and knowing also that no report has a chance of being accepted, unless it contains some truth' (Talmud).

28. *howbeit.* Now comes the announcement of the impossibility of its conquest.

29. *Amalek . . . Hittite.* See note at the end of the chapter.

30. *Caleb stilled the people.* In the next chapter (XIV, 6, 30), Joshua is associated with Caleb in his opposition to the ten faithless men. Being the attendant of Moses, he may have given place to Caleb as the one more likely to be listened to in the then temper of the people.

toward Moses. He restored silence so that Moses might be heard.

we are well able to. lit. 'we shall certainly'.

32. *an evil report of the land.* 'The punishment that God brought upon Miriam was meant as a lesson of the severity with which God punishes slander. Her experience, nevertheless, did not awe the sinful men who, shortly after that incident, made an evil report of the Promised Land, and by their wicked tongues stirred up the whole people in rebellion against God' (Midrash).

that eateth up the inhabitants thereof. That does not produce enough to support them; cf. Ezekiel XXXVI, 8, 11–14, 30 (Gray).

33. *the Nephilim.* The primeval giants mentioned in Gen. VI, 4. The Spies use that name to

14

CHAPTER XIV

1. And all the congregation lifted up their voice, and cried: and the people wept that night. 2. And all the children of Israel murmured against Moses and against Aaron; and the whole congregation said unto them: 'Would that we had died in the land of Egypt! or would we had died in this wilderness! 3. And wherefore doth the LORD bring us unto this land, to fall by the sword? Our wives and our little ones will be a prey; were it not better for us to return into Egypt?' 4. And they said one to another: 'Let us make a captain, and let us return into Egypt.' 5. Then Moses and Aaron fell on their faces before all the assembly of the congregation of the children of Israel. 6. And Joshua the son of Nun and Caleb the son of Jephunneh, who were of them that spied out the land, rent their clothes. 7. And they spoke unto all the congregation of the children of Israel, saying: 'The land, which we passed through to spy it out, is an exceeding good land.*iii. 8. If the LORD delight in us, then He will bring us into this land, and give it

יד

CAP. XIV. יד

א וַתִּשָּׂא כָּל־הָעֵדָה וַיִּתְּנוּ אֶת־קוֹלָם וַיִּבְכּוּ הָעָם בַּלַּיְלָה
2 הַהוּא: וַיִּלֹּנוּ עַל־מֹשֶׁה וְעַל־אַהֲרֹן כֹּל בְּנֵי יִשְׂרָאֵל וַיֹּאמְרוּ
אֲלֵהֶם כָּל־הָעֵדָה לוּ־מַתְנוּ בְּאֶרֶץ מִצְרַיִם אוֹ בַּמִּדְבָּר
3 הַזֶּה לוּ־מָתְנוּ: וְלָמָה יְהוָה מֵבִיא אֹתָנוּ אֶל־הָאָרֶץ הַזֹּאת
לִנְפֹּל בַּחֶרֶב נָשֵׁינוּ וְטַפֵּנוּ יִהְיוּ לָבַז הֲלוֹא טוֹב לָנוּ שׁוּב
4 מִצְרָיְמָה: וַיֹּאמְרוּ אִישׁ אֶל־אָחִיו נִתְּנָה רֹאשׁ וְנָשׁוּבָה
ה מִצְרָיְמָה: וַיִּפֹּל מֹשֶׁה וְאַהֲרֹן עַל־פְּנֵיהֶם לִפְנֵי כָּל־קְהַל
6 עֲדַת בְּנֵי יִשְׂרָאֵל: וִיהוֹשֻׁעַ בִּן־נוּן וְכָלֵב בֶּן־יְפֻנֶּה מִן־
7 הַתָּרִים אֶת־הָאָרֶץ קָרְעוּ בִּגְדֵיהֶם: וַיֹּאמְרוּ אֶל־כָּל־עֲדַת
בְּנֵי־יִשְׂרָאֵל לֵאמֹר הָאָרֶץ אֲשֶׁר עָבַרְנוּ בָהּ לָתוּר אֹתָהּ
8 טוֹבָה הָאָרֶץ מְאֹד מְאֹד: אִם־חָפֵץ בָּנוּ יְהוָה וְהֵבִיא שלישי

heighten the effect of their description of the invincibility of the sons of Anak (W. H. Green).

so we were in their sight. Or, 'so must we have been in their sight.' Those who are in their own eyes as grasshoppers assume, and rightly so, that others have a similar estimate of them.

The Spies traversed the entire land from south to north. The length of the Holy Land is about 180 miles, and its average breadth between the Mediterranean Sea and the River Jordan about 40 miles. The country may be regarded as consisting of three strips running north and south. There is (1) the Maritime Plain—extending inwards from the coast to a distance of from 4 to 15 miles. It is very fertile. It includes the famous Plain of Sharon and the Lowlands of the Philistines. (2) Behind this Maritime Plain, and parallel to it, rises the 'Hill Country', the backbone of the Holy Land. On the east, it falls precipitously down to (3) the Valley of the Jordan and the Dead Sea. Across these lie the Highlands of Gilead and Moab, the modern Transjordania.

In the monumental records, the country is called 'the land of the Canaanites', or the 'land of the Amorites'; from which it may be inferred that these were the tribes originally inhabiting it. At a very early period the Hittites, who formed a powerful kingdom to the north, established themselves in Canaan. At the time of the Israelitish Conquest the land was inhabited by a mixture of tribes. Of these, the principal were the Canaanites (*i.e.* probably 'Lowlanders'), dwelling in the Maritime Plain and the Valley of the Jordan; the Hittites and the Jebusites in the south, in what was afterwards called Judea; the Hivites to the north of these, in what came to be known as Samaria; and, still further north, the Perizzites. The Amorites (*i.e.* probably, the 'Highlanders') were found in the north, and also in the south, to the east of the Jordan. The Philistines had obtained a settlement in the southern part of the Maritime Plain.

CHAPTER XIV

1–10. PANIC, WAILING AND REBELLION

1. *wept that night.* 'When the sound of their weeping reached heaven, God said: "Ye weep now without cause; the time will come when ye shall have good cause to weep on this day." It was then decreed that the Temple be destroyed on this same day, the ninth day of Ab; so that it became forever a day of tears' (Talmud).

4. *let us make a captain.* Heb. **נתנה ראש**; also in Neh. IX, 17. Ehrlich is inclined to see in this phrase an idiomatic expression like נתן קול, and he translates, 'let us *set our mind* to return to Egypt.'

5. *fell on their faces.* Overwhelmed by sorrow and shame.

6. *rent their clothes.* As at the news of some family bereavement or terrible calamity.

8. *if the LORD delight in us.* If they did nothing to alienate God's favour.

unto us—a land which floweth with milk and honey. 9. Only rebel not against the LORD, neither fear ye the people of the land; for they are bread for us; their defence is removed from over them, and the LORD is with us; fear them not.' 10. But all the congregation bade stone them with stones, when the glory of the LORD appeared in the tent of meeting unto all the children of Israel. ¶ 11. And the LORD said unto Moses: 'How long will this people despise Me? and how long will they not believe in Me, for all the signs which I have wrought among them? 12. I will smite them with the pestilence, and destroy them, and will make of thee a nation greater and mightier than they.' 13. And Moses said unto the LORD: 'When the Egyptians shall hear—for Thou broughtest up this people in Thy might from among them—14. they will say to the inhabitants of this land, who have heard that Thou LORD art in the midst of this people; inasmuch as Thou LORD art seen face to face, and Thy cloud standeth over them, and Thou goest before them, in a pillar of cloud by day, and in a pillar of fire by night; 15. now if Thou shalt kill this people as one man, then the nations which have heard the fame of Thee will speak, saying: 16. Because the LORD was not able to bring this people into the land which He swore unto them, therefore He hath slain them in the wilderness. 17. And now, I pray Thee, let the power of the LORD be

אֹתָנוּ אֶל־הָאָרֶץ הַזֹּאת וּנְתָנָהּ לָנוּ אֶרֶץ אֲשֶׁר־הִוא זָבַת חָלָב
9 וּדְבָשׁ׃ אַךְ בַּיהוָה אַל־תִּמְרֹדוּ וְאַתֶּם אַל־תִּירְאוּ אֶת־עַם
הָאָרֶץ כִּי לַחְמֵנוּ הֵם סָר צִלָּם מֵעֲלֵיהֶם וַיהוָה אִתָּנוּ אַל־
י תִּירָאֻם׃ וַיֹּאמְרוּ כָּל־הָעֵדָה לִרְגּוֹם אֹתָם בָּאֲבָנִים וּכְבוֹד
יְהוָה נִרְאָה בְּאֹהֶל מוֹעֵד אֶל־כָּל־בְּנֵי יִשְׂרָאֵל׃ פ
11 וַיֹּאמֶר יְהוָה אֶל־מֹשֶׁה עַד־אָנָה יְנַאֲצֻנִי הָעָם הַזֶּה וְעַד־
אָנָה לֹא־יַאֲמִינוּ בִי בְּכֹל הָאֹתוֹת אֲשֶׁר עָשִׂיתִי בְּקִרְבּוֹ׃
12 אַכֶּנּוּ בַדֶּבֶר וְאוֹרִשֶׁנּוּ וְאֶעֱשֶׂה אֹתְךָ לְגוֹי־גָּדוֹל וְעָצוּם
13 מִמֶּנּוּ׃ וַיֹּאמֶר מֹשֶׁה אֶל־יְהוָה וְשָׁמְעוּ מִצְרַיִם כִּי־הֶעֱלִיתָ
14 בְכֹחֲךָ אֶת־הָעָם הַזֶּה מִקִּרְבּוֹ׃ וְאָמְרוּ אֶל־יוֹשֵׁב הָאָרֶץ
הַזֹּאת שָׁמְעוּ כִּי־אַתָּה יְהוָה בְּקֶרֶב הָעָם הַזֶּה אֲשֶׁר־עַיִן
בְּעַיִן נִרְאָה ׀ אַתָּה יְהוָה וַעֲנָנְךָ עֹמֵד עֲלֵהֶם וּבְעַמֻּד עָנָן
טו אַתָּה הֹלֵךְ לִפְנֵיהֶם יוֹמָם וּבְעַמּוּד אֵשׁ לָיְלָה׃ וְהֵמַתָּה
אֶת־הָעָם הַזֶּה כְּאִישׁ אֶחָד וְאָמְרוּ הַגּוֹיִם אֲשֶׁר־שָׁמְעוּ אֶת־
16 שִׁמְעֲךָ לֵאמֹר׃ מִבִּלְתִּי יְכֹלֶת יְהוָה לְהָבִיא אֶת־הָעָם
17 הַזֶּה אֶל־הָאָרֶץ אֲשֶׁר־נִשְׁבַּע לָהֶם וַיִּשְׁחָטֵם בַּמִּדְבָּר׃ וְעַתָּה

9. *for they are bread for us.* lit. 'they are our bread'; *i.e.* we shall easily destroy them.

their defence. lit. 'their shadow'; a common metaphor of great significance in a hot country (McNeile).

The word לחמנו ('our bread') may refer to the manna, and סר צלם, lit. 'their shadow is removed from over them', to the melting of the manna at noonday (Exod. XVI, 21). The meaning of the passage would then be: 'Fear not the people of the land, for they are like the manna when the shadows pass, *i.e.* when the sun has come out. There is then no manna left. The LORD is with us: our enemies shall melt away—fear them not' (Ephraim Lenczic).

11–25. DIVINE WRATH AND THE INTERCESSION OF MOSES

12. *destroy them.* The Heb. root has this meaning in Exod. XV, 9.

make of thee a nation. Moses would be a second Abraham, and thus the oath sworn to the Patriarchs that their seed should inherit the land would be fulfilled.

13. *Egyptians shall hear.* Moses, the faithful shepherd, leaves an unsurpassed example of self-denial to the children of men. He refuses a glorious future for himself and his descendants, solely because Israel would have no share in it. He begs God to spare His people out of regard for His own Honour. The nations would misunderstand the destruction of Israel, and attribute it to His want of power to lead them into the land He promised them.

17. *let the power of the LORD be great.* Show, in the sight of all the nations, the greatness of Thy power in forbearing with sinners and forgiving sin. 'In God's mercy is also revealed His power. He triumphs by His love and gentleness over the follies and frailties of men, and even in spite of themselves, they must at last fulfil the chosen and holy purposes of God' (Montefiore). Moses then pleads with God to spare His people out of regard for His own self-revealed Thirteen Attributes of Divine Mercy and Forgiveness, enumerated in Exod. XXXIV, 6–7 and reproduced here; see pp. 364–5. In Exod. God is spoken of as רב חסד ואמת, 'abounding in lovingkindness and truth,' to teach mortals that in our dealings with fellow mortals 'lovingkindness' must precede 'truth'. Speak the truth to your fellow men by all means, but be quite sure that you speak it *in love*. Even more instructive is the wording in *v.* 18, רב חסד,

great, according as Thou hast spoken, saying: 18. The LORD is slow to anger, and plenteous in lovingkindness, forgiving iniquity and transgression, and that will by no means clear the guilty; visiting the iniquity of the fathers upon the children, upon the third and upon the fourth generation. 19. Pardon, I pray Thee, the iniquity of this people according unto the greatness of Thy lovingkindness, and according as Thou hast forgiven this people from Egypt even until now.' 20. And the LORD said: 'I have pardoned according to thy word. 21. But in very deed, as I live—and all the earth shall be filled with the glory of the LORD—22. surely all those men that have seen My glory, and My signs, which I wrought in Egypt and in the wilderness, yet have put Me to proof these ten times, and have not hearkened to My voice; 23. surely they shall not see the land which I swore unto their fathers, neither shall any of them that despised Me see it. 24. But My servant Caleb, because he had another spirit with him, and hath followed Me fully, him will I bring into the land whereinto he went; and his seed shall possess it. 25. Now the Amalekite and the Canaanite dwell in the Vale; to-morrow turn ye, and get you into the wilderness by the way to the Red Sea.'*iv. ¶ 26. And the LORD spoke unto Moses and unto Aaron, saying: 27. 'How long shall I bear with this evil congregation,

18 יִגְדַּל־נָא כֹּחַ אֲדֹנָי כַּאֲשֶׁר דִּבַּרְתָּ לֵאמֹר׃ יְהוָה אֶרֶךְ
אַפַּיִם וְרַב־חֶסֶד נֹשֵׂא עָוֺן וָפָשַׁע וְנַקֵּה לֹא יְנַקֶּה פֹּקֵד עֲוֺן
19 אָבוֹת עַל־בָּנִים עַל־שִׁלֵּשִׁים וְעַל־רִבֵּעִים׃ סְלַח־נָא לַעֲוֺן
הָעָם הַזֶּה כְּגֹדֶל חַסְדֶּךָ וְכַאֲשֶׁר נָשָׂאתָה לָעָם הַזֶּה מִמִּצְרַיִם
כ 21 וְעַד־הֵנָּה׃ וַיֹּאמֶר יְהוָה סָלַחְתִּי כִּדְבָרֶךָ׃ וְאוּלָם חַי־אָנִי
22 וְיִמָּלֵא כְבוֹד־יְהוָה אֶת־כָּל־הָאָרֶץ׃ כִּי כָל־הָאֲנָשִׁים
הָרֹאִים אֶת־כְּבֹדִי וְאֶת־אֹתֹתַי אֲשֶׁר־עָשִׂיתִי בְמִצְרַיִם
וּבַמִּדְבָּר וַיְנַסּוּ אֹתִי זֶה עֶשֶׂר פְּעָמִים וְלֹא שָׁמְעוּ בְּקוֹלִי׃
23 אִם־יִרְאוּ אֶת־הָאָרֶץ אֲשֶׁר נִשְׁבַּעְתִּי לַאֲבֹתָם וְכָל־מְנַאֲצַי
24 לֹא יִרְאוּהָ׃ וְעַבְדִּי כָלֵב עֵקֶב הָיְתָה רוּחַ אַחֶרֶת עִמּוֹ
וַיְמַלֵּא אַחֲרָי וַהֲבִיאֹתִיו אֶל־הָאָרֶץ אֲשֶׁר־בָּא שָׁמָּה וְזַרְעוֹ
כה יוֹרִשֶׁנָּה׃ וְהָעֲמָלֵקִי וְהַכְּנַעֲנִי יוֹשֵׁב בָּעֵמֶק מָחָר פְּנוּ וּסְעוּ
לָכֶם הַמִּדְבָּר דֶּרֶךְ יַם־סוּף׃* פ רביעי
26 27 וַיְדַבֵּר יְהוָה אֶל־מֹשֶׁה וְאֶל־אַהֲרֹן לֵאמֹר׃ עַד־מָתַי לָעֵדָה
הָרָעָה הַזֹּאת אֲשֶׁר הֵמָּה מַלִּינִים עָלָי אֶת־תְּלֻנּוֹת בְּנֵי

v. 17. י׳ רבתי

'plenteous in mercy,' lit. 'abounding in lovingkindness'. Here the words 'and truth' are missing altogether, as if to impress upon our minds the teaching that there are occasions when 'lovingkindness' is *all*-important.

19. *according unto the greatness of thy lovingkindness.* And not in accordance with the smallness of their deserts.

from Egypt even until now. The thought that God has always forgiven, gives Moses courage to ask Him still to do so. It is otherwise with our fellowmen. If one has often forgiven us, we are ashamed to ask him again. But with God the gates of prayer, and forgiveness, are never closed.

20. *thy word.* Thy petition.

21. *as I live . . . glory of the LORD.* As truly as I live and as all the peoples of the earth shall know that I am the Omnipotent One, so truly shall I visit with retribution those who distrusted My promises.

22. *these ten times.* A large number of times; cf. Gen. XXXI, 7. They had now filled up the measure of their iniquities, and punishment must inevitably come upon them.

24. *but My servant Caleb.* He alone is mentioned here, because it was he who 'stilled' the agitated people (XIII, 30).

another spirit. Altogether different from that of the other Spies—unfaltering courage and unwavering faith in the Divine promise.

followed Me fully. lit. 'fulfilled to walk behind Me', *i.e.* faithfully confirmed My word that the land was a good land.

possess it. Caleb received Hebron and the neighbouring hill-country; see Josh. XIV, 6–15.

25. *Amalekite and the Canaanite.* Turn away from these formidable nations in another direction, so as not to risk a conflict with them.

vale. Here equivalent to mountain defile, declivity, elevated plain.

into the wilderness. Of the Sinai Peninsula; as distinguished from Palestine on the one hand, and from Egypt on the other.

26–39. THE PUNISHMENT OF THE PEOPLE

27. *how long shall I bear with this evil congregation?* lit. 'how long shall this evil congregation continue to be?' According to Rabbinic tradition the reference here is to the ten Spies.

that keep murmuring against Me? I have heard the murmurings of the children of Israel, which they keep murmuring against Me. 28. Say unto them: As I live, saith the LORD, surely as ye have spoken in Mine ears, so will I do to you: 29. your carcasses shall fall in this wilderness, and all that were numbered of you, according to your whole number, from twenty years old and upward, ye that have murmured against Me; 30. surely ye shall not come into the land, concerning which I lifted up My hand that I would make you dwell therein, save Caleb the son of Jephunneh, and Joshua the son of Nun. 31. But your little ones, that ye said would be a prey, them will I bring in, and they shall know the land which ye have rejected. 32. But as for you, your carcasses shall fall in this wilderness. 33. And your children shall be wanderers in the wilderness forty years, and shall bear your strayings, until your carcasses be consumed in the wilderness. 34. After the number of the days in which ye spied out the land, even forty days, for every day a year, shall ye bear your iniquities, even forty years, and ye shall know My displeasure. 35. I the LORD have spoken, surely this will I do unto all this evil congregation, that are gathered together against Me; in this wilderness they shall be consumed, and there they shall die.' 36. And the men, whom Moses sent to spy out the land, and who, when they returned, made all the congregation to murmur against him, by bringing up an evil report against the land, 37. even those men that did bring up an evil report of the land, died by the plague before the LORD. 38. But Joshua the son of Nun, and Caleb the son of Jephunneh, remained alive of those men that went to spy out the land. 39. And Moses told these words unto all the children of Israel; and the people mourned greatly. 40. And they rose up early in the morning, and got them up to the top of the mountain, saying:

28 יִשְׂרָאֵל אֲשֶׁר הֵמָּה מַלִּינִים עָלַי שָׁמָעְתִּי׃ אֱמֹר אֲלֵהֶם חַי־
אָנִי נְאֻם־יְהוָה אִם־לֹא כַּאֲשֶׁר דִּבַּרְתֶּם בְּאָזְנָי כֵּן אֶעֱשֶׂה
29 לָכֶם׃ בַּמִּדְבָּר הַזֶּה יִפְּלוּ פִגְרֵיכֶם וְכָל־פְּקֻדֵיכֶם לְכָל־
מִסְפַּרְכֶם מִבֶּן עֶשְׂרִים שָׁנָה וָמָעְלָה אֲשֶׁר הֲלִינֹתֶם עָלָי׃
ל אִם־אַתֶּם תָּבֹאוּ אֶל־הָאָרֶץ אֲשֶׁר נָשָׂאתִי אֶת־יָדִי לְשַׁכֵּן
31 אֶתְכֶם בָּהּ כִּי אִם־כָּלֵב בֶּן־יְפֻנֶּה וִיהוֹשֻׁעַ בִּן־נוּן׃ וְטַפְּכֶם
אֲשֶׁר אֲמַרְתֶּם לָבַז יִהְיֶה וְהֵבֵיאתִי אֹתָם וְיָדְעוּ אֶת־הָאָרֶץ
32 אֲשֶׁר מְאַסְתֶּם בָּהּ׃ וּפִגְרֵיכֶם אַתֶּם יִפְּלוּ בַּמִּדְבָּר הַזֶּה׃
33 וּבְנֵיכֶם יִהְיוּ רֹעִים בַּמִּדְבָּר אַרְבָּעִים שָׁנָה וְנָשְׂאוּ אֶת־
34 זְנוּתֵיכֶם עַד־תֹּם פִּגְרֵיכֶם בַּמִּדְבָּר׃ בְּמִסְפַּר הַיָּמִים אֲשֶׁר־
תַּרְתֶּם אֶת־הָאָרֶץ אַרְבָּעִים יוֹם יוֹם לַשָּׁנָה יוֹם לַשָּׁנָה
תִּשְׂאוּ אֶת־עֲוֺנֹתֵיכֶם אַרְבָּעִים שָׁנָה וִידַעְתֶּם אֶת־תְּנוּאָתִי׃
לה אֲנִי יְהוָה דִּבַּרְתִּי אִם־לֹא ׀ זֹאת אֶעֱשֶׂה לְכָל־הָעֵדָה הָרָעָה
הַזֹּאת הַנּוֹעָדִים עָלָי בַּמִּדְבָּר הַזֶּה יִתַּמּוּ וְשָׁם יָמֻתוּ׃
36 וְהָאֲנָשִׁים אֲשֶׁר־שָׁלַח מֹשֶׁה לָתוּר אֶת־הָאָרֶץ וַיָּשֻׁבוּ
וַיַּלִּונוּ עָלָיו אֶת־כָּל־הָעֵדָה לְהוֹצִיא דִבָּה עַל־הָאָרֶץ׃
37 וַיָּמֻתוּ הָאֲנָשִׁים מוֹצִאֵי דִבַּת־הָאָרֶץ רָעָה בַּמַּגֵּפָה לִפְנֵי
38 יְהוָה׃ וִיהוֹשֻׁעַ בִּן־נוּן וְכָלֵב בֶּן־יְפֻנֶּה חָיוּ מִן־הָאֲנָשִׁים הָהֵם
39 הַהֹלְכִים לָתוּר אֶת־הָאָרֶץ׃ וַיְדַבֵּר מֹשֶׁה אֶת־הַדְּבָרִים
מ הָאֵלֶּה אֶל־כָּל־בְּנֵי יִשְׂרָאֵל וַיִּתְאַבְּלוּ הָעָם מְאֹד׃ וַיַּשְׁכִּמוּ
בַבֹּקֶר וַיַּעֲלוּ אֶל־רֹאשׁ־הָהָר לֵאמֹר הִנֶּנּוּ וְעָלִינוּ אֶל־הַמָּקוֹם

v. 31. מלא י׳ v. 36. וילינו ק׳

28. *as ye have spoken.* Your wish expressed in the words, 'Would we had died in this wilderness,' shall be fulfilled.

29. *numbered of you.* In the census detailed in Chap. I.

30. *I lifted up My hand.* 'I have taken an oath.'

33. *bear your strayings.* Although the children were to be spared the fate of their sinning parents, they would not altogether escape the consequences of that falling away from God. 'Strayings' is a departure from the RV which gives the lit. translation of the Heb. **זנות**, the metaphor of marital infidelity used in Scripture to express Israel's disloyalty to God through the worship of strange gods.

34. *My displeasure.* Or, 'the revoking of my promise' (RV Margin).

37. *died by the plague.* By a sudden visitation from God.

40–45. Instead of obeying the Divine injunction to turn southwards (*v.* 25), the people in self-willed defiance make a frantic effort to enter Canaan without delay.

40. *the top of the mountain.* Probably some mountain slope in the Negeb.

'Lo, we are here, and will go up unto the place which the LORD hath promised; for we have sinned.' 41. And Moses said: 'Wherefore now do ye transgress the commandment of the LORD, seeing it shall not prosper? 42. Go not up, for the LORD is not among you; that ye be not smitten down before your enemies. 43. For there the Amalekite and the Canaanite are before you, and ye shall fall by the sword; forasmuch as ye are turned back from following the LORD, and the LORD will not be with you.' 44. But they presumed to go up to the top of the mountain; nevertheless the ark of the covenant of the LORD, and Moses, departed not out of the camp. 45. Then the Amalekite and the Canaanite, who dwelt in that hill-country, came down, and smote them and beat them down, even unto Hormah.

41 אֲשֶׁר־אָמַר יְהוָה כִּי חָטָאנוּ׃ וַיֹּאמֶר מֹשֶׁה לָמָּה זֶּה אַתֶּם
42 עֹבְרִים אֶת־פִּי יְהוָה וְהִוא לֹא תִצְלָח׃ אַל־תַּעֲלוּ כִּי אֵין
43 יְהוָה בְּקִרְבְּכֶם וְלֹא תִּנָּגְפוּ לִפְנֵי אֹיְבֵיכֶם׃ כִּי הָעֲמָלֵקִי
וְהַכְּנַעֲנִי שָׁם לִפְנֵיכֶם וּנְפַלְתֶּם בֶּחָרֶב כִּי־עַל־כֵּן שַׁבְתֶּם
44 מֵאַחֲרֵי יְהוָה וְלֹא־יִהְיֶה יְהוָה עִמָּכֶם׃ וַיַּעְפִּלוּ לַעֲלוֹת אֶל־
רֹאשׁ הָהָר וַאֲרוֹן בְּרִית־יְהוָה וּמֹשֶׁה לֹא־מָשׁוּ מִקֶּרֶב
מה הַמַּחֲנֶה׃ וַיֵּרֶד הָעֲמָלֵקִי וְהַכְּנַעֲנִי הַיֹּשֵׁב בָּהָר הַהוּא וַיַּכּוּם
וַיַּכְּתוּם עַד־הַחָרְמָה׃ פ

15

CHAPTER XV

1. And the LORD spoke unto Moses, saying: 2. Speak unto the children of Israel, and say unto them: ¶ When ye are come into the land of your habitations, which I give unto you, 3. and will make an offering by fire unto the LORD, a burnt-offering, or a sacrifice, in fulfilment of a vow clearly uttered, or as a freewill-offering, or in your appointed seasons, to make a sweet savour unto the LORD, of the herd, or of the flock; 4. then shall he that bringeth his offering present

CAP. XV. טו

טו

א 2 וַיְדַבֵּר יְהוָה אֶל־מֹשֶׁה לֵּאמֹר׃ דַּבֵּר אֶל־בְּנֵי יִשְׂרָאֵל
וְאָמַרְתָּ אֲלֵהֶם כִּי תָבֹאוּ אֶל־אֶרֶץ מוֹשְׁבֹתֵיכֶם אֲשֶׁר אֲנִי
3 נֹתֵן לָכֶם׃ וַעֲשִׂיתֶם אִשֶּׁה לַיהוָה עֹלָה אוֹ־זֶבַח לְפַלֵּא־
נֶדֶר אוֹ בִנְדָבָה אוֹ בְּמֹעֲדֵיכֶם לַעֲשׂוֹת רֵיחַ נִיחֹחַ לַיהוָה

41. *wherefore now do ye transgress.* Your enterprise is contrary to the will of God, nor does the Ark accompany you. The commandment of the LORD in *v.* 42 is given more fully in Deut. I, 42. 'Go not up, neither fight, for I am not among you; lest ye be smitten before your enemies.'

44. *but they presumed.* Their self-confidence rendered futile all the attempts of Moses to induce them to desist.

45. *even unto Hormah.* lit. 'unto *the* Hormah'. They suffer a crushing defeat and are driven back to the Hormah which they had only recently conquered. Their direct march northwards is now definitely barred. Henceforth they can enter Canaan only by passing *through*—and if that is impossible, *around*—the territories situated to the south and east of the Dead Sea, till they have arrived north of the Dead Sea and can cross the Jordan into Western Palestine. It will be some thirty-eight years before a fresh military enterprise is undertaken. 'In estimating the historical value of this story, we must remember that no nation gratuitously invents or accepts accounts of defeats it has never experienced. If Hebrew history tells us that the Israelites on attempting to enter the land they subsequently inhabited met with an overthrow so annihilating as to leave them too weak to do anything but wander helplessly in a wilderness for nearly forty years thereafter, we cannot refuse it credence. The tendency is always to minimize defeats, not to exaggerate them; and a story such as this bears the hallmark of truth' (Wiener).

CHAPTER XV

The priestly and ritual laws mentioned in this chapter seem to be supplementary to the sacrificial code of the Book of Leviticus. They were promulgated during the years of wandering in the desert.

1–16. MEAL OFFERINGS AND LIBATIONS

2. *when ye are come into the land.* These instructions, coming as they did immediately after the doom pronounced upon the generation in the Wilderness, were a welcome intimation that their children should possess the Land of Promise.

3. *offering by fire.* The general term for every sacrifice consumed on the Altar; see Lev. I, 9.
burnt-offering. See Lev. I, 3.
a sacrifice. Termed more fully in Lev. III, 1, 'a sacrifice of peace offerings.'
a vow clearly uttered. See VI, 2.
a sweet savour. See Lev. I, 9.

unto the LORD a meal-offering of a tenth part of an ephah of fine flour mingled with the fourth part of a hin of oil; 5. and wine for the drink-offering, the fourth part of a hin, shalt thou prepare with the burnt-offering or for the sacrifice, for each lamb. 6. Or for a ram, thou shalt prepare for a meal-offering two tenth parts of an ephah of fine flour mingled with the third part of a hin of oil; 7. and for the drink-offering thou shalt present the third part of a hin of wine, of a sweet savour unto the LORD.*v. 8. And when thou preparest a bullock for a burnt-offering, or for a sacrifice, in fulfilment of a vow clearly uttered, or for peace-offerings unto the LORD; 9. then shall there be presented with the bullock a meal-offering of three tenth parts of an ephah of fine flour mingled with half a hin of oil. 10. And thou shalt present for the drink-offering half a hin of wine, for an offering made by fire, of a sweet savour unto the LORD. 11. Thus shall it be done for each bullock, or for each ram, or for each of the he-lambs, or of the kids. 12. According to the number that ye may prepare, so shall ye do for every one according to their number. 13. All that are home-born shall do these things after this manner, in presenting an offering made by fire, of a sweet savour unto the LORD. 14. And if a stranger sojourn with you, or whosoever may be among you, throughout your generations, and will offer an offering made by fire, of a sweet savour unto the LORD; as ye do, so he shall do. 15. As for the congregation, there shall be one statute both for you, and for the stranger that sojourneth with you, a statute for ever throughout your generations; as ye are, so shall the stranger be before the LORD. 16. One law and one ordinance shall be both for you, and for the stranger that sojourneth with you.*vi. ¶ 17. And the LORD spoke unto Moses, saying: 18. Speak unto the children of Israel, and say unto them: ¶ When ye come into the land whither I bring you, 19. then it shall be, that, when ye eat of the bread of the land,

4 מִן־הַבָּקָר אוֹ מִן־הַצֹּאן׃ וְהִקְרִיב הַמַּקְרִיב קָרְבָּנוֹ לַיהוָה
ה מִנְחָה סֹלֶת עִשָּׂרוֹן בָּלוּל בִּרְבִעִית הַהִין שָׁמֶן׃ וְיַיִן
לַנֶּסֶךְ רְבִיעִית הַהִין תַּעֲשֶׂה עַל־הָעֹלָה אוֹ לַזָּבַח לַכֶּבֶשׂ
6 הָאֶחָד׃ אוֹ לָאַיִל תַּעֲשֶׂה מִנְחָה סֹלֶת שְׁנֵי עֶשְׂרֹנִים בְּלוּלָה
7 בַשֶּׁמֶן שְׁלִשִׁית הַהִין׃ וְיַיִן לַנֶּסֶךְ שְׁלִשִׁית הַהִין תַּקְרִיב
חמישי 8 רֵיחַ־נִיחֹחַ לַיהוָה׃ * וְכִי־תַעֲשֶׂה בֶן־בָּקָר עֹלָה אוֹ־זָבַח
9 לְפַלֵּא־נֶדֶר אוֹ־שְׁלָמִים לַיהוָה׃ וְהִקְרִיב עַל־בֶּן־הַבָּקָר
מִנְחָה סֹלֶת שְׁלֹשָׁה עֶשְׂרֹנִים בָּלוּל בַּשֶּׁמֶן חֲצִי הַהִין׃
י וְיַיִן תַּקְרִיב לַנֶּסֶךְ חֲצִי הַהִין אִשֵּׁה רֵיחַ־נִיחֹחַ לַיהוָה׃
11 כָּכָה יֵעָשֶׂה לַשּׁוֹר הָאֶחָד אוֹ לָאַיִל הָאֶחָד אוֹ־לַשֶּׂה
12 בַכְּבָשִׂים אוֹ בָעִזִּים׃ כַּמִּסְפָּר אֲשֶׁר תַּעֲשׂוּ כָּכָה תַּעֲשׂוּ
13 לָאֶחָד כְּמִסְפָּרָם׃ כָּל־הָאֶזְרָח יַעֲשֶׂה־כָּכָה אֶת־אֵלֶּה
14 לְהַקְרִיב אִשֵּׁה רֵיחַ־נִיחֹחַ לַיהוָה׃ וְכִי־יָגוּר אִתְּכֶם גֵּר אוֹ
אֲשֶׁר־בְּתוֹכְכֶם לְדֹרֹתֵיכֶם וְעָשָׂה אִשֵּׁה רֵיחַ־נִיחֹחַ לַיהוָה
טו כַּאֲשֶׁר תַּעֲשׂוּ כֵּן יַעֲשֶׂה׃ הַקָּהָל חֻקָּה אַחַת לָכֶם וְלַגֵּר הַגָּר
16 חֻקַּת עוֹלָם לְדֹרֹתֵיכֶם כָּכֶם כַּגֵּר יִהְיֶה לִפְנֵי יְהוָה׃ תּוֹרָה
ששי אַחַת וּמִשְׁפָּט אֶחָד יִהְיֶה לָכֶם וְלַגֵּר הַגָּר אִתְּכֶם׃ * פ
17 וַיְדַבֵּר יְהוָה אֶל־מֹשֶׁה לֵּאמֹר׃ דַּבֵּר אֶל־בְּנֵי יִשְׂרָאֵל 18
וְאָמַרְתָּ אֲלֵהֶם בְּבֹאֲכֶם אֶל־הָאָרֶץ אֲשֶׁר אֲנִי מֵבִיא אֶתְכֶם
19 שָׁמָּה׃ וְהָיָה בַּאֲכָלְכֶם מִלֶּחֶם הָאָרֶץ תָּרִימוּ תְרוּמָה

4. *then shall he that bringeth his offering.* The following verses prescribe the quantities of flour and oil for the cereal offering, and wine for the drink offering, that must accompany the important sacrifices.

tenth part of an ephah. About seven pints.

fourth part. Rather less than three pints.

6. *for a ram.* The meal and drink offerings were to be increased when the animal sacrificed was of a larger size.

14. *stranger.* See IX, 14.

16. *one law and one ordinance.* Another assertion of the identity, in respect of civil, moral, and religious rights and duties, of the home-born and stranger or proselyte.

17–21. CHALLAH

18. *when ye come into the land.* 'As soon as ye enter upon the soil of the Promised Land, even before ye have subjugated the enemy there, and settled down in comfort' (Sifri).

19. *a portion for a gift.* Or, 'contribution' or 'selected portion'; Heb. *terumah,* see Exod.

כ לַיהוָה׃ רֵאשִׁית עֲרִסֹתֵכֶם חַלָּה תָּרִימוּ תְרוּמָה כִּתְרוּמַת
21 גֹּרֶן כֵּן תָּרִימוּ אֹתָהּ׃ מֵרֵאשִׁית עֲרִסֹתֵיכֶם תִּתְּנוּ לַיהוָה
22 תְּרוּמָה לְדֹרֹתֵיכֶם׃ ס וְכִי תִשְׁגּוּ וְלֹא תַעֲשׂוּ אֵת
23 כָּל־הַמִּצְוֺת הָאֵלֶּה אֲשֶׁר־דִּבֶּר יְהוָה אֶל־מֹשֶׁה׃ אֵת כָּל־
אֲשֶׁר צִוָּה יְהוָה אֲלֵיכֶם בְּיַד־מֹשֶׁה מִן־הַיּוֹם אֲשֶׁר צִוָּה
24 יְהוָה וָהָלְאָה לְדֹרֹתֵיכֶם׃ וְהָיָה אִם מֵעֵינֵי הָעֵדָה נֶעֶשְׂתָה
לִשְׁגָגָה וְעָשׂוּ כָל־הָעֵדָה פַּר בֶּן־בָּקָר אֶחָד לְעֹלָה לְרֵיחַ
נִיחֹחַ לַיהוָה וּמִנְחָתוֹ וְנִסְכּוֹ כַּמִּשְׁפָּט וּשְׂעִיר־עִזִּים אֶחָד
כה לְחַטָּת׃ וְכִפֶּר הַכֹּהֵן עַל־כָּל־עֲדַת בְּנֵי יִשְׂרָאֵל וְנִסְלַח
לָהֶם כִּי־שְׁגָגָה הִוא וְהֵם הֵבִיאוּ אֶת־קָרְבָּנָם אִשֶּׁה לַיהוָה
26 וְחַטָּאתָם לִפְנֵי יְהוָה עַל־שִׁגְגָתָם׃ וְנִסְלַח לְכָל־עֲדַת בְּנֵי
שביעי יִשְׂרָאֵל וְלַגֵּר הַגָּר בְּתוֹכָם כִּי לְכָל־הָעָם בִּשְׁגָגָה׃ ס
27 וְאִם־נֶפֶשׁ אַחַת תֶּחֱטָא בִשְׁגָגָה וְהִקְרִיבָה עֵז בַּת־שְׁנָתָהּ

v. 24. חסר א'

ye shall set apart a portion for a gift unto the LORD. 20. Of the first of your dough ye shall set apart a cake for a gift; as that which is set apart of the threshing-floor, so shall ye set it apart. 21. Of the first of your dough ye shall give unto the LORD a portion for a gift throughout your generations. ¶ 22. And when ye shall err, and not observe all these commandments, which the LORD hath spoken unto Moses, 23. even all that the LORD hath commanded you by the hand of Moses, from the day that the LORD gave commandment, and onward throughout your generations; 24. then it shall be, if it be done in error by the congregation, it being hid from their eyes, that all the congregation shall offer one young bullock for a burnt-offering, for a sweet savour unto the LORD—with the meal-offering thereof, and the drink-offering thereof, according to the ordinance—and one he-goat for a sin-offering. 25. And the priest shall make atonement for all the congregation of the children of Israel, and they shall be forgiven; for it was an error, and they have brought their offering, an offering made by fire unto the LORD, and their sin-offering before the LORD, for their error. 26. And all the congregation of the children of Israel shall be forgiven, and the stranger that sojourneth among them; for in respect

XXV, 2. It is here used in a wide sense to mean a gift in general.

20. *of the first of your dough.* This offering is called חלה *Challah.* The Rabbis, however, laid it down that the dough in order to become subject to the law of Challah must consist of at least one omer of flour (about three quarts). The portion for Challah must be 1/24th of the dough of a private householder, and 1/48th of that of a baker.

as . . . of the threshing floor. This offering of bread from the home is as obligatory as the offering of grain from the threshing-floor at the annual harvest.

21. *unto the LORD. i.e.* unto the priest; 'ye shall also give unto the priest the first of your dough, to cause a blessing to rest on thine house' (Ezek. XLIV, 30).

According to *v.* 18, the law of Challah applied only to Palestine. But in order that this institution should not be forgotten, the Rabbis ordained that it remain in force beyond Palestine and for all time. It is still kept in observant Jewish households where bread is baked. The חלה is, however, thrown into the fire and is not given to the 'priest', because *Kohanim* are to-day precluded from observing the laws of priestly purity, and hence are disqualified from eating anything that is in the nature of a holy sacrifice.

22–28. SIN-OFFERING FOR UNINTENTIONAL SINS

22. *all these commandments.* According to the Talmud, the reference in the present passage is to the sin of idolatry committed unintentionally. That sin, involving as it does apostasy from the fundamental doctrines of Judaism, is equivalent to breaking *all* the commandments of the Torah. Other commentators, like Nachmanides, are inclined to refer these words to any comprehensive breach of the ordinances of the Torah.

24. *in error.* Heb. בשגגה; opposed to sins committed in wilful defiance of God's commandments; see *v.* 40.

shall offer. The whole community is to bring a common sacrifice.

26. *all the congregation shall be forgiven.* This verse is solemnly recited thrice before the opening of the evening service on Kol Nidrè night. And rightly so; because it may be said to be the keynote of the Day of Atonement and its message of forgiveness for *all* sins, and not only of involuntary transgressions. By the sincere repentance which Yom Kippur demands, the sinner shows that his wilful sins also were largely due to ignorance; and hence are treated by God as if they were done 'in error' (בשגגה); see p. 484.

of all the people it was done in error.*vii. ¶ 27. And if one person sin through error, then he shall offer a she-goat of the first year for a sin-offering. 28. And the priest shall make atonement for the soul that erreth, when he sinneth through error, before the LORD, to make atonement for him; and he shall be forgiven, 29. both he that is home-born among the children of Israel, and the stranger that sojourneth among them: ye shall have one law for him that doeth aught in error. 30. But the soul that doeth aught with a high hand, whether he be home-born or a stranger, the same blasphemeth the LORD; and that soul shall be cut off from among his people. 31. Because he hath despised the word of the LORD, and hath broken His commandment; that soul shall utterly be cut off, his iniquity shall be upon him. ¶ 32. And while the children of Israel were in the wilderness, they found a man gathering sticks upon the sabbath day. 33. And they that found him gathering sticks brought him unto Moses and Aaron, and unto all the congregation. 34. And they put him in ward, because it had not been declared what should be done to him. 35. And the LORD said unto Moses: 'The man shall surely be put to death; all the congregation shall stone him with stones without the camp.' 36. And all the congregation brought him without the camp, and stoned him with stones, and he died, as the LORD commanded Moses.*m. ¶ 37. And the LORD spoke unto Moses, saying: 38. 'Speak unto the children of Israel, and bid them that they make them through-

28 לַחַטָּאת׃ וְכִפֶּר הַכֹּהֵן עַל־הַנֶּפֶשׁ הַשֹּׁגֶגֶת בְּחֶטְאָה בִשְׁגָגָה
29 לִפְנֵי יְהוָה לְכַפֵּר עָלָיו וְנִסְלַח לוֹ׃ הָאֶזְרָח בִּבְנֵי יִשְׂרָאֵל
וְלַגֵּר הַגָּר בְּתוֹכָם תּוֹרָה אַחַת יִהְיֶה לָכֶם לָעֹשֶׂה בִּשְׁגָגָה׃
ל וְהַנֶּפֶשׁ אֲשֶׁר־תַּעֲשֶׂה ׀ בְּיָד רָמָה מִן־הָאֶזְרָח וּמִן־הַגֵּר אֶת־
יְהוָה הוּא מְגַדֵּף וְנִכְרְתָה הַנֶּפֶשׁ הַהִוא מִקֶּרֶב עַמָּהּ׃
31 כִּי דְבַר־יְהוָה בָּזָה וְאֶת־מִצְוָתוֹ הֵפַר הִכָּרֵת ׀ תִּכָּרֵת הַנֶּפֶשׁ
הַהִוא עֲוֺנָה בָהּ׃ פ
32 וַיִּהְיוּ בְנֵי־יִשְׂרָאֵל בַּמִּדְבָּר וַיִּמְצְאוּ אִישׁ מְקֹשֵׁשׁ עֵצִים
33 בְּיוֹם הַשַּׁבָּת׃ וַיַּקְרִיבוּ אֹתוֹ הַמֹּצְאִים אֹתוֹ מְקֹשֵׁשׁ עֵצִים
34 אֶל־מֹשֶׁה וְאֶל־אַהֲרֹן וְאֶל כָּל־הָעֵדָה׃ וַיַּנִּיחוּ אֹתוֹ בַּמִּשְׁמָר
לה כִּי לֹא פֹרַשׁ מַה־יֵּעָשֶׂה לוֹ׃ ס וַיֹּאמֶר יְהוָה אֶל־מֹשֶׁה
מוֹת יוּמַת הָאִישׁ רָגוֹם אֹתוֹ בָאֲבָנִים כָּל־הָעֵדָה מִחוּץ
36 לַמַּחֲנֶה׃ וַיֹּצִיאוּ אֹתוֹ כָּל־הָעֵדָה אֶל־מִחוּץ לַמַּחֲנֶה וַיִּרְגְּמוּ
מפטיר אֹתוֹ בָּאֲבָנִים וַיָּמֹת כַּאֲשֶׁר צִוָּה יְהוָה אֶת־מֹשֶׁה׃* פ
37 וַיֹּאמֶר יְהוָה אֶל־מֹשֶׁה לֵּאמֹר׃ 38 דַּבֵּר אֶל־בְּנֵי יִשְׂרָאֵל
וְאָמַרְתָּ אֲלֵהֶם וְעָשׂוּ לָהֶם צִיצִת עַל־כַּנְפֵי בִגְדֵיהֶם לְדֹרֹתָם

v. 28. ה׳ רפה v. 31. פתח באתנח ibid. ה׳ רפה

27. *and if one person sin through error.* According to the Talmud, this too refers to the sin of idolatry.

30. *with an high hand.* lit. 'with a hand raised', as a sign of presumption, as a public defiance of His law.

the same blasphemeth the LORD. No sacrificial atonement is possible for a wilful offence.

from among his people. See note on IX, 13.

31. *his iniquity shall be upon him.* As long as he has not done repentance (Talmud).

32–36. The Sabbath-breaker. A concrete instance of intentional sin.

'In the penal code of Israel, idolatry is regarded as a crime of high treason, as being a subversion of the constitution and a revolt against God. Herein the law exhibits all its rigour, extending to public blasphemy and public violation of the Sabbath' (Joseph Salvador).

33. *and unto all the congregation.* To the Council of Elders who were the congregation by representation; see Exod. XVIII, 25, 26.

34. *should be done to him.* The law against Sabbath-breaking had been made known, but not the method of execution; cf. Lev. XXIV, 12, to which this is a parallel case.

37–41. TZITZIS

38. *fringes.* Heb. **ציצת**. In Ezek. VIII, 3 it denotes a lock of hair. By analogy, it is employed in the present instance to denote a fringe or tassel.

their garments. Only of the men; because of the general rule, that women, whose duties are more absorbing in the home, are free from all

39 וְנָתְנוּ עַל־צִיצִת הַכָּנָף פְּתִיל תְּכֵלֶת׃ וְהָיָה לָכֶם לְצִיצִת
וּרְאִיתֶם אֹתוֹ וּזְכַרְתֶּם אֶת־כָּל־מִצְוֺת יְהוָה וַעֲשִׂיתֶם אֹתָם
וְלֹא־תָתוּרוּ אַחֲרֵי לְבַבְכֶם וְאַחֲרֵי עֵינֵיכֶם אֲשֶׁר־אַתֶּם
מ זֹנִים אַחֲרֵיהֶם׃ לְמַעַן תִּזְכְּרוּ וַעֲשִׂיתֶם אֶת־כָּל־מִצְוֺתָי
41 וִהְיִיתֶם קְדֹשִׁים לֵאלֹהֵיכֶם׃ אֲנִי יְהוָה אֱלֹהֵיכֶם אֲשֶׁר
הוֹצֵאתִי אֶתְכֶם מֵאֶרֶץ מִצְרַיִם לִהְיוֹת לָכֶם לֵאלֹהִים אֲנִי
יְהוָה אֱלֹהֵיכֶם׃

out their generations fringes in the corners of their garments, and that they put with the fringe of each corner a thread of blue. 39. And it shall be unto you for a fringe, that ye may look upon it, and remember all the commandments of the LORD, and do them; and that ye go not about after your own heart and your own eyes, after which ye use to go astray; 40. that ye may remember and do all My commandments, and be holy unto your God. 41. I am the LORD your God, who brought you out of the land of Egypt, to be your God: I am the LORD your God.'

precepts that have to be performed at a specified time (מצות עשה שהזמן גרמא).

a thread of blue. To be intertwined with the 'tassel' itself.

blue. The thread had to be dyed with the blood of a mollusk called חלזון, found in the waters near the coast of Phœnicia. The dye was scarce even in Mishnaic times. Hence the authorities agreed that white wool-threads alone need be inserted.

39. *look upon it.* The Rabbis translated *see it,* which was held to imply that the fringe was reserved for worship during daylight.

and remember. The Tzitzis are to be a constant reminder to the Israelite of all his duties to God, and of the special relationship in which the Israelite stands to God, whose 'colours' he wore. The blue thread in the Tzitzis, say the Rabbis, resembles the sea, the sea resembles the heavens, and the heavens resemble the Throne of Glory. Thus, the outward act of looking upon the Tzitzis was to the Israelite an inward act of spiritual conformity with the precepts of God. It was such fine spiritualization of ceremonial that led to the beautiful verses of Psalm XXXVI ('How precious is Thy lovingkindness, O God, and the children of men take refuge under the shadow of Thy wings. For with Thee is the fountain of life: in Thy light do we see light') being recited by the worshipper on putting on the Tallis.

after your own heart. The heart and the eyes are the agents of Sin—the eye seeth, the heart desireth, and the person executeth (Talmud). The true Israelite, however, arrayed in the sacred covering, reminding him of the Divine Presence, does not stray after the satisfaction of bodily pleasures; but is mindful that he is a member of a 'holy' People, dedicated unto God and holiness; see next *v.*

to go astray. A departure from the RV; see on XIV, 33.

40. *and be holy unto your God.* The aim of this precept is thus distinctly stated to be the furtherance of holiness in the life of the individual and the nation.

In later generations, the law of the fringes was carried out by means of the Arba Kanfos and the Tallis. The former is an undergarment consisting of a rectangular piece of cloth, about three feet long and one foot wide, with an aperture in the centre sufficient to let it pass over the head. To its four corners are fastened the Tzitzis.

The Tallis is a woollen or silken mantle worn over the garments during worship by day (except on the eve of Atonement when it is put on some minutes before nightfall).

'By the thirteenth century it had become unusual for Jews to mark their ordinary outward garments by wearing fringes. But the fringed garment had become too deeply associated with Israel's religious life to be discarded entirely at the dictate of fashion in dress. Pope Innocent III in 1215 compelled the Jew to wear a degrading badge; the fringed garment became all the more an honourable uniform, marking at once God's love for Israel and Israel's determination to "remember to do all God's commandments and be holy unto his God" ' (I. Abrahams).

HAFTORAH SHELACH LECHA

הפטרת שלח לך

JOSHUA II, 1–24

CHAPTER II

1. And Joshua the son of Nun sent out of Shittim two spies secretly, saying: 'Go view the land, and Jericho.' And they went, and came into the house of a harlot whose name was Rahab, and lay there. 2. And it was told the king of Jericho, saying: 'Behold, there came men in hither to-night of the children of Israel to search out the land.' 3. And the king of Jericho sent unto Rahab, saying: 'Bring forth the men that are come to thee, that are entered into thy house; for they are come to search out all the land.' 4. And the woman took the two men, and hid them; and she said: 'Yea, the men came unto me, but I knew not whence they were;

CAP. II. ב

א וַיִּשְׁלַח יְהוֹשֻׁעַ בִּן־נוּן מִן־הַשִּׁטִּים שְׁנַיִם אֲנָשִׁים מְרַגְּלִים
חֶרֶשׁ לֵאמֹר לְכוּ רְאוּ אֶת־הָאָרֶץ וְאֶת־יְרִיחוֹ וַיֵּלְכוּ וַיָּבֹאוּ
2 בֵּית אִשָּׁה זוֹנָה וּשְׁמָהּ רָחָב וַיִּשְׁכְּבוּ־שָׁמָּה׃ וַיֵּאָמַר לְמֶלֶךְ
יְרִיחוֹ לֵאמֹר הִנֵּה אֲנָשִׁים בָּאוּ הֵנָּה הַלַּיְלָה מִבְּנֵי יִשְׂרָאֵל
3 לַחְפֹּר אֶת־הָאָרֶץ׃ וַיִּשְׁלַח מֶלֶךְ יְרִיחוֹ אֶל־רָחָב לֵאמֹר
הוֹצִיאִי הָאֲנָשִׁים הַבָּאִים אֵלַיִךְ אֲשֶׁר־בָּאוּ לְבֵיתֵךְ כִּי
4 לַחְפֹּר אֶת־כָּל־הָאָרֶץ בָּאוּ׃ וַתִּקַּח הָאִשָּׁה אֶת־שְׁנֵי הָאֲנָשִׁים

The Sedrah recounts the story of the twelve Spies sent by Moses to report on Canaan, Joshua himself being one of their number: the Haftorah tells us of the two men sent by Joshua on a similar errand to Jericho. But whereas the report of the former, with its fears and exaggerations, was followed by the tragic consequences of unbelief; the latter, with their inspiring declaration, 'The LORD hath delivered into our hands all the land,' thrilled the people with the assurance of victory that awaited them.

The Book of Joshua records the conquest of Canaan by Israel, the settlement of the Israelite tribes in the land, and the beginning of their consolidation into a nation. Joshua himself is one of the outstanding characters in Scripture; the faithful servant, the victorious soldier, the intrepid general, the wise ruler; and the man of deep faith and humility—his last addresses reviewing the past do not contain a word of his own achievements. The final words of his farewell exhortation to his people to stand firm in their allegiance to God are among the great utterances of history: 'Choose you this day whom you will serve—but as for me and my house, we will serve the LORD' (Joshua XXIV, 15).

1. *Shittim.* lit. 'acacia trees'; the place of the encampment opposite Jericho, on the Eastern side of the Jordan.

secretly. i.e. unbeknown to the children of Israel, as Joshua fears a possible repetition of what took place in the Wilderness. It cannot refer to the inhabitants of Jericho; otherwise there was no need for Scripture to state it (Ehrlich). The Heb. root חרש also denotes earthenware; hence the Midrash paraphrases, 'disguised as potters, or sellers of earthenware.'

and Jericho. i.e. and particularly Jericho.

Jericho. Jericho was at least 1,000 years old when the Israelites prepared to attack this city that barred their route to the whole Western plateau. It was the gateway to the Promised Land, and its capture was of the greatest importance to the Israelites. Garstang's excavations in 1931 on the site of ancient Jericho make an epoch in Biblical studies. Among other results, he has now definitely fixed the date of the capture of Jericho as 1407, and therefore that of the Exodus as 1447 B.C.E.

a harlot. Better, *an innkeeper*, or purveyor of food, from זון 'to provide' (Targum, Rashi, Kimchi). Women were frequently innkeepers in ancient Egypt and Greece.

Rahab. According to Rabbinical tradition, she became a sincere convert to the religion of Israel after the fall of Jericho.

2. *of the children of Israel.* The spies entered the city without at first attracting attention. The inhabitants were evidently accustomed to the passing to and fro of Bedouin and other visitors from beyond the Jordan.

3. *the king of Jericho.* Ever since the finding of the Tel-el Amarna tablets (discovered in Egypt in 1887) we have confirmation of the existence of local 'kings' in Canaanite cities of this period.

4. *and hid them.* lit. 'and hid him'; an idiomatic use of the singular for the plural to indicate that she hid each one separately. She was faithful to the Oriental conception of hospitality which demands protection for the guest at whatever cost.

I knew not. i.e. when they came to me.

5. and it came to pass about the time of the shutting of the gate, when it was dark, that the men went out; whither the men went I know not; pursue after them quickly; for ye shall overtake them.' 6. But she had brought them up to the roof, and hid them with the stalks of flax, which she had spread out upon the roof. 7. And the men pursued after them the way to the Jordan unto the fords; and as soon as they that pursued after them were gone out, the gate was shut. 8. And before they were laid down, she came up unto them upon the roof; 9. and she said unto the men: 'I know that the LORD hath given you the land, and that your terror is fallen upon us, and that all the inhabitants of the land melt away before you. 10. For we have heard how the LORD dried up the water of the Red Sea before you, when ye came out of Egypt; and what ye did unto the two kings of the Amorites, that were beyond the Jordan, unto Sihon and to Og, whom ye utterly destroyed. 11. And as soon as we had heard it, our hearts did melt, neither did there remain any more spirit in any man, because of you; for the LORD your God, He is God in heaven above, and on earth beneath. 12. Now therefore, I pray you, swear unto me by the LORD, since I have dealt kindly with you, that ye also will deal kindly with my father's house—and give me a true token— 13. and save alive my father, and my mother, and my brethren, and my sisters, and all that they have, and deliver our lives from death.' 14. And the men said unto her: 'Our life for yours, if ye tell not this our business; and it shall be, when the LORD giveth us the land, that we will deal kindly and truly with thee.' 15. Then she let them down by a cord through the window; for her house was upon the side of the wall, and she dwelt upon the wall. 16. And she said unto them: 'Get you to the mountain, lest the pursuers

וַתִּצְפְּנוֹ וַתֹּאמֶר כֵּן בָּאוּ אֵלַי הָאֲנָשִׁים וְלֹא יָדַעְתִּי מֵאַיִן
ה הֵמָּה׃ וַיְהִי הַשַּׁעַר לִסְגּוֹר בַּחֹשֶׁךְ וְהָאֲנָשִׁים יָצָאוּ לֹא
יָדַעְתִּי אָנָה הָלְכוּ הָאֲנָשִׁים רִדְפוּ מַהֵר אַחֲרֵיהֶם כִּי
6 תַשִּׂיגוּם׃ וְהִיא הֶעֱלָתַם הַגָּגָה וַתִּטְמְנֵם בְּפִשְׁתֵּי הָעֵץ
7 הָעֲרֻכוֹת לָהּ עַל־הַגָּג׃ וְהָאֲנָשִׁים רָדְפוּ אַחֲרֵיהֶם דֶּרֶךְ
הַיַּרְדֵּן עַל הַמַּעְבְּרוֹת וְהַשַּׁעַר סָגָרוּ אַחֲרֵי כַּאֲשֶׁר יָצְאוּ
8 הָרֹדְפִים אַחֲרֵיהֶם׃ וְהֵמָּה טֶרֶם יִשְׁכָּבוּן וְהִיא עָלְתָה
9 עֲלֵיהֶם עַל־הַגָּג׃ וַתֹּאמֶר אֶל־הָאֲנָשִׁים יָדַעְתִּי כִּי־נָתַן
יְהוָה לָכֶם אֶת־הָאָרֶץ וְכִי־נָפְלָה אֵימַתְכֶם עָלֵינוּ וְכִי
י נָמֹגוּ כָּל־יֹשְׁבֵי הָאָרֶץ מִפְּנֵיכֶם׃ כִּי שָׁמַעְנוּ אֵת אֲשֶׁר־
הוֹבִישׁ יְהוָה אֶת־מֵי יַם־סוּף מִפְּנֵיכֶם בְּצֵאתְכֶם מִמִּצְרָיִם
וַאֲשֶׁר עֲשִׂיתֶם לִשְׁנֵי מַלְכֵי הָאֱמֹרִי אֲשֶׁר בְּעֵבֶר הַיַּרְדֵּן
11 לְסִיחֹן וּלְעוֹג אֲשֶׁר הַחֲרַמְתֶּם אוֹתָם׃ וַנִּשְׁמַע וַיִּמַּס
לְבָבֵנוּ וְלֹא־קָמָה עוֹד רוּחַ בְּאִישׁ מִפְּנֵיכֶם כִּי יְהוָה
אֱלֹהֵיכֶם הוּא אֱלֹהִים בַּשָּׁמַיִם מִמַּעַל וְעַל־הָאָרֶץ מִתָּחַת׃
12 וְעַתָּה הִשָּׁבְעוּ־נָא לִי בַּיהוָה כִּי־עָשִׂיתִי עִמָּכֶם חָסֶד
וַעֲשִׂיתֶם גַּם־אַתֶּם עִם־בֵּית אָבִי חֶסֶד וּנְתַתֶּם לִי אוֹת
13 אֱמֶת׃ וְהַחֲיִתֶם אֶת־אָבִי וְאֶת־אִמִּי וְאֶת־אַחַי וְאֶת־אַחְוֹתַי
14 וְאֵת כָּל־אֲשֶׁר לָהֶם וְהִצַּלְתֶּם אֶת־נַפְשֹׁתֵינוּ מִמָּוֶת׃ וַיֹּאמְרוּ
לָהּ הָאֲנָשִׁים נַפְשֵׁנוּ תַחְתֵּיכֶם לָמוּת אִם לֹא תַגִּידוּ אֶת־
דְּבָרֵנוּ זֶה וְהָיָה בְּתֵת יְהוָה לָנוּ אֶת־הָאָרֶץ וְעָשִׂינוּ עִמָּךְ
טו חֶסֶד וֶאֱמֶת׃ וַתּוֹרִדֵם בַּחֶבֶל בְּעַד הַחַלּוֹן כִּי בֵיתָהּ בְּקִיר

v. 5. קמץ בז״ק v. 7. קמץ בז״ק v. 13. אחיותי ק׳

5. *the gate.* Jericho was strongly fortified, and could effectively be barred and bolted, 'straitly shut up' (VI, 1). This was partly due to the fact that it had only *one* gate.

6. *flax . . . upon the roof.* The flat roofs of Eastern houses were also used for drying flax-stalks.

9. *your terror is fallen upon us.* 'The presence of the host of the Israelites on the opposite bank, and the known tendency of nomads to push into the country when opportunity afforded, must have filled the king and people of Jericho with misgiving and perplexity' (Garstang).

14. *if ye tell not this our business.* The promise of safety given by the spies is conditional on Rahab's secrecy regarding their visit and intentions.

15. *through the window.* Which overlooked the country outside the city.

house upon the side of the wall. 'Pressure upon the limited building-space within the original enclosures seems to have become so great that houses had arisen upon the walls themselves . . . and a number of houses leaned against the inner face of the main city-wall' (Garstang).

16. *get you to the mountain.* The limestone ridges, full of caves, N.W. of Jericho; especially Jebel Kuruntul, a mile from the city, and rising some 1,500 feet above the plain.

16 הַחוֹמָה וּבַחוֹמָה הִיא יוֹשָׁבֶת׃ וַתֹּאמֶר לָהֶם הָהָרָה לֵּכוּ
פֶּן־יִפְגְּעוּ בָכֶם הָרֹדְפִים וְנַחְבֵּתֶם שָׁמָּה שְׁלֹשֶׁת יָמִים
17 עַד שֹׁב הָרֹדְפִים וְאַחַר תֵּלְכוּ לְדַרְכְּכֶם׃ וַיֹּאמְרוּ אֵלֶיהָ
הָאֲנָשִׁים נְקִיִּם אֲנַחְנוּ מִשְּׁבֻעָתֵךְ הַזֶּה אֲשֶׁר הִשְׁבַּעְתָּנוּ׃
18 הִנֵּה אֲנַחְנוּ בָאִים בָּאָרֶץ אֶת־תִּקְוַת חוּט הַשָּׁנִי הַזֶּה
תִּקְשְׁרִי בַּחַלּוֹן אֲשֶׁר הוֹרַדְתֵּנוּ בוֹ וְאֶת־אָבִיךְ וְאֶת־אִמֵּךְ
וְאֶת־אַחַיִךְ וְאֵת כָּל־בֵּית אָבִיךְ תַּאַסְפִי אֵלַיִךְ הַבָּיְתָה׃
19 וְהָיָה כֹּל אֲשֶׁר־יֵצֵא מִדַּלְתֵי בֵיתֵךְ הַחוּצָה דָּמוֹ בְרֹאשׁוֹ
וַאֲנַחְנוּ נְקִיִּם וְכֹל אֲשֶׁר יִהְיֶה אִתָּךְ בַּבַּיִת דָּמוֹ בְרֹאשֵׁנוּ
כ אִם־יָד תִּהְיֶה־בּוֹ׃ וְאִם־תַּגִּידִי אֶת־דְּבָרֵנוּ זֶה וְהָיִינוּ נְקִיִּם
21 מִשְּׁבֻעָתֵךְ אֲשֶׁר הִשְׁבַּעְתָּנוּ׃ וַתֹּאמֶר כְּדִבְרֵיכֶם כֶּן־הוּא
22 וַתְּשַׁלְּחֵם וַיֵּלֵכוּ וַתִּקְשֹׁר אֶת־תִּקְוַת הַשָּׁנִי בַּחַלּוֹן׃ וַיֵּלְכוּ
וַיָּבֹאוּ הָהָרָה וַיֵּשְׁבוּ שָׁם שְׁלֹשֶׁת יָמִים עַד־שָׁבוּ הָרֹדְפִים
23 וַיְבַקְשׁוּ הָרֹדְפִים בְּכָל־הַדֶּרֶךְ וְלֹא מָצָאוּ׃ וַיָּשֻׁבוּ שְׁנֵי
הָאֲנָשִׁים וַיֵּרְדוּ מֵהָהָר וַיַּעַבְרוּ וַיָּבֹאוּ אֶל־יְהוֹשֻׁעַ בִּן־נוּן
24 וַיְסַפְּרוּ־לוֹ אֵת כָּל־הַמֹּצְאוֹת אוֹתָם׃ וַיֹּאמְרוּ אֶל־יְהוֹשֻׁעַ
כִּי־נָתַן יְהוָה בְּיָדֵנוּ אֶת־כָּל־הָאָרֶץ וְגַם־נָמֹגוּ כָּל־יֹשְׁבֵי
הָאָרֶץ מִפָּנֵינוּ׃

v. 18. הת׳ בצרי

light upon you; and hide yourselves there three days, until the pursuers be returned; and afterward may ye go your way.' 17. And the men said unto her: 'We will be guiltless of this thine oath which thou hast made us to swear. 18. Behold, when we come into the land, thou shalt bind this line of scarlet thread in the window which thou didst let us down by; and thou shalt gather unto thee into the house thy father, and thy mother, and thy brethren, and all thy father's household. 19. And it shall be, that whosoever shall go out of the doors of thy house into the street, his blood shall be upon his head, and we will be guiltless; and whosoever shall be with thee in the house, his blood shall be on our head, if any hand be upon him. 20. But if thou utter this our business, then we will be guiltless of thine oath which thou hast made us to swear.' 21. And she said: 'According unto your words, so be it.' And she sent them away, and they departed; and she bound the scarlet line in the window. 22. And they went, and came unto the mountain, and abode there three days, until the pursuers were returned; and the pursuers sought them throughout all the way, but found them not. 23. Then the two men returned, and descended from the mountain, and passed over, and came to Joshua the son of Nun; and they told him all that had befallen them. 24. And they said unto Joshua: 'Truly the LORD hath delivered into our hands all the land; and moreover all the inhabitants of the land do melt away before us.'

hide yourselves there. 'The face of the cliff, weathered by the storm of centuries, presents numerous hiding-places. The spies, once they had gained this mountain under cover of twilight, ran little risk of detection, even though all the roads that converged on Jericho were kept under observation' (Garstang).

17. *guiltless of.* Free from.

19. *his blood shall be upon his head.* They will not be responsible for any members of her family who do not keep within her house when they take the city.

23. *passed over.* The Jordan.

24. *truly.* Heb. כי need not be translated, as it merely introduces the actual words of the speaker.

V. KORACH

(CHAPTERS XVI–XVIII)

THE GREAT MUTINY

In the last Sedrah we had seen the people threatening to appoint a chieftain who was to take them back to Egypt. It was ominous of further serious revolt. When the rebellion broke out, it was widespread though not homogeneous. On the one hand, there were those who were discontented with the leadership of Moses. These were led by Dathan and Abiram, of the tribe of Reuben, the tribe that once possessed but had now lost the 'birthright' in Israel, and was, it seems, chafing for the recovery of that primacy. On the other hand, there were Korah—himself a Levite—and his followers, who were aggrieved with Aaron, to whose family all priestly privileges were now confined. These two groups of malcontents worked separately, and they were in the end cut off by entirely different acts of God (*v.* 32 and 35). Their punishment was signal, since the vindication of Moses and Aaron had to be complete. Otherwise, anarchy would soon have destroyed national unity; and, in its trail, there would have followed the total frustration of whatever Divine Mission was in store for Israel on the arena of history.

The general drift of the story of Korah and his companions is thus quite clear, though we cannot follow all the details. The unprejudiced student finds nothing improbable in the story of such a revolt; and he knows that if it did arise, it could only have taken place in the Desert. During that period alone, the tribes of Reuben and Levi marched side by side, their joint conspiracy growing out of their proximity to one another at that time. 'The two tribes afterwards became entirely parted asunder in their characters and fortunes; the one was incorporated into the innermost circle of the settled civilization of Palestine; the other hovered on the very outskirts of the Holy Land and Chosen People, and dwindled away into a Bedouin tribe. But the story of Korah belongs to a time when Levi was still fresh from the great crisis in Sinai, by which that tribe had been consecrated and divided from the rest; when the recollection of the birthright of Reuben still lingered in the minds of his descendants' (Stanley).

KORAH

The great Mutiny sank deep into the memory of after-generations in Israel. To the Rabbis, this whole movement, of which Korah was the principal spokesman, became typical of all controversies that had their origin in personal motives—'not in the Name of Heaven'—and that could not therefore lead to any beneficient results (Ethics of the Fathers, *v.* 20). In Rabbinic legend, Korah was consumed by jealousy of his kinsman Moses. 'He has passed me by in the appointment of all the high offices'—he is made to exclaim: 'therefore, I will stir up rebellion against him, and overthrow the institutions founded by him.' Korah—they state—began by attempting to make Moses appear ridiculous in the eyes of the people. He had garments made entirely of blue wool for his two hundred and fifty men; and, thus arrayed, he and his company appeared before Moses and asked him whether these garments required fringes. Moses answered, 'Yes.' Korah replied: 'The blue wool of which the entire garment is made, does not make it ritually correct; yet, according to your direction, four threads would!' Again he asked: Does a house filled with books of the Torah require a mezuzah? Moses answered, 'Yes.' Then Korah said: 'The presence of the whole Torah does not fulfil the command, yet thou sayest that the few verses thereof contained in the mezuzah do make the house fit for human habitation!'

Then Korah undertook to show that the laws instituted by Moses were hard beyond endurance. He told the following parable: 'A poor widow had a field. When she came to plough it, Moses forbade her to plough it with an ox and an ass together; when she began to sow, Moses forbade her to sow it with mingled seeds. At the time of the harvest, Moses ordered her to leave unreaped the corners of the field and not to gather up the gleanings, but to leave them for the poor. He furthermore demanded the heave-offering for the priests, and the tithe for the Levites. The woman sold the field and purchased ewes, in the hope that she might live undisturbed. However, when the firstling of the sheep was born, Aaron appeared and demanded it as his due. At shearing-time Aaron reappeared and demanded "the first of the fleece of the sheep", which, according to Moses' Law, was his. He reappeared again and again with new demands, till the long-suffering woman slaughtered the sheep, and in her anger consecrated it to the Sanctuary. Thereupon it all fell to Aaron.' 'Such men,' Korah concluded, 'are Moses and Aaron!'

In brief, Korah was a demagogue, and recoiled from no weapon that would discredit Moses. Perhaps the best judgment on the man and the Cause he sought to destroy is contained in the following curious rabbinic legend. Rabbah bar Bar Chanah—the Munchausen of the Talmud—narrates that, while he was travelling in the desert, an Arab showed him the place where Korah and his companions had been engulfed. There was at the spot a crack in the ground, and on putting his ear to the crack he heard voices cry, 'Moses and his Torah are true, and we are liars.'

16

CHAPTER XVI

1. Now Korah, the son of Izhar, the son of Kohath, the son of Levi, with Dathan and Abiram, the sons of Eliab, and On, the son of Peleth, sons of Reuben, took men; 2. and they rose up in face of Moses, with certain of the children of Israel, two hundred and fifty men; they were princes of the congregation, the elect men of the assembly, men of renown; 3. and they assembled themselves together against Moses and against Aaron, and said unto them: 'Ye take too much upon you, seeing all the congregation are holy, every one of them, and the LORD is among them; wherefore then lift ye up yourselves above the assembly of the LORD?' 4. And when Moses heard it, he fell upon his face. 5. And he spoke unto Korah and unto all his company, saying: 'In the morning the LORD will show who are His, and who is holy, and will cause him to come near unto Him; even him whom He may choose will He cause to come near unto Him. 6. This do:

טז

CAP. XVI. טז

פ פ פ לח 38

א וַיִּקַּח קֹרַח בֶּן־יִצְהָר בֶּן־קְהָת בֶּן־לֵוִי וְדָתָן וַאֲבִירָם בְּנֵי
2 אֱלִיאָב וְאוֹן בֶּן־פֶּלֶת בְּנֵי רְאוּבֵן׃ וַיָּקֻמוּ לִפְנֵי מֹשֶׁה
וַאֲנָשִׁים מִבְּנֵי־יִשְׂרָאֵל חֲמִשִּׁים וּמָאתָיִם נְשִׂיאֵי עֵדָה
3 קְרִאֵי מוֹעֵד אַנְשֵׁי־שֵׁם׃ וַיִּקָּהֲלוּ עַל־מֹשֶׁה וְעַל־אַהֲרֹן
וַיֹּאמְרוּ אֲלֵהֶם רַב־לָכֶם כִּי כָל־הָעֵדָה כֻּלָּם קְדֹשִׁים
4 וּבְתוֹכָם יְהוָה וּמַדּוּעַ תִּתְנַשְּׂאוּ עַל־קְהַל יְהוָה׃ וַיִּשְׁמַע
ה מֹשֶׁה וַיִּפֹּל עַל־פָּנָיו׃ וַיְדַבֵּר אֶל־קֹרַח וְאֶל־כָּל־עֲדָתוֹ
לֵאמֹר בֹּקֶר וְיֹדַע יְהוָה אֶת־אֲשֶׁר־לוֹ וְאֶת־הַקָּדוֹשׁ וְהִקְרִיב
6 אֵלָיו וְאֵת אֲשֶׁר יִבְחַר־בּוֹ יַקְרִיב אֵלָיו׃ זֹאת עֲשׂוּ קְחוּ־

V. KORACH

(CHAPTERS XVI–XVIII)

CHAPTER XVI

1–15. REBELLION OF KORAH, DATHAN, ABIRAM, AND ON

1. *now Korah . . . took men.* In the Heb. Text, *took* is not followed by an object. Most versions follow Ibn Ezra and supply the word 'men'.

sons of Izhar, the son of Kohath. Korah was thus cousin to Moses and Aaron.

with Dathan and Abiram. They were leading men in the tribe of Reuben, who could not forget that theirs was the eldest tribe and from it—they held—should the rulers of Israel be recruited. The men of Levi and Reuben came to join hands —the Rabbis say—because they always marched next each other (II, 16, 17; X, 18, 21), illustrating the old proverb, 'Woe to the wicked, woe to his neighbour.'

On, the son of Peleth. He is not mentioned again either in this chapter or elsewhere. Legend represents him as saved from destruction by his wife. 'When On told his wife that he had joined Korah's rebellion, she said to him, "What benefit shalt *thou* reap from it? Either Moses remains master and thou art his follower, or Korah becomes master and thou art his follower." It was Korah's wife who through her inciting words plunged her husband into destruction, and it was to his wife that On owed his salvation; as it is written in the Book of Proverbs, *every wise woman buildeth her house; but the foolish plucketh it down with her own hands*' (Midrash).

2. *of the congregation.* Hailing not from one tribe only, but from all Israel, summoned for consultation as need arose.

men of renown. Distinguished and influential men.

3. *all the congregation are holy.* With the instinct of the true demagogue, Korah posed as the champion of the People against the alleged dictatorship of Moses and Aaron, the two brothers who usurped all power and authority in Israel.

4. *he fell upon his face.* Either an expression of despair at this sinful rebellion, or of prayer for guidance; *v.* 22.

5. *who are His . . . holy.* God will reveal which tribe He has chosen to be nearest unto Him, and who in that chosen tribe is fitted to be High Priest.

6. *take you censers.* Moses here addresses Korah and those Levites who were envious of the higher privileges of the priesthood. He challenges them to test their claims to equality with Aaron by undergoing a species of ordeal. They are to assume, for once, the functions of priesthood, and God would show whether or not He approved of such assumption.

take you censers, Korah, and all his company; 7. and put fire therein, and put incense upon them before the LORD to-morrow; and it shall be that the man whom the LORD doth choose, he shall be holy; ye take too much upon you, ye sons of Levi.' 8. And Moses said unto Korah: 'Hear now, ye sons of Levi: 9. is it but a small thing unto you, that the God of Israel hath separated you from the congregation of Israel, to bring you near to Himself, to do the service of the tabernacle of the LORD, and to stand before the congregation to minister unto them; 10. and that He hath brought thee near, and all thy brethren the sons of Levi with thee? and will ye seek the priesthood also? 11. Therefore thou and all thy company that are gathered together against the LORD—; and as to Aaron, what is he that ye murmur against him?' 12. And Moses sent to call Dathan and Abiram, the sons of Eliab; and they said: 'We will not come up; 13. is it a small thing that thou hast brought us up out of a land flowing with milk and honey, to kill us in the wilderness, but thou must needs make thyself also a prince over us? *ii. 14. Moreover thou hast not brought us into a land flowing with milk and honey, nor given us inheritance of fields and vineyards; wilt thou put out the eyes of these men? we will not come up.' 15. And Moses was very wroth, and said unto the LORD: 'Respect not Thou their offering; I have

7 לָכֶם מַחְתּוֹת קֹרַח וְכָל־עֲדָתוֹ׃ וּתְנוּ בָהֵן ׀ אֵשׁ וְשִׂימוּ
עֲלֵיהֶן ׀ קְטֹרֶת לִפְנֵי יְהוָה מָחָר וְהָיָה הָאִישׁ אֲשֶׁר־יִבְחַר
8 יְהוָה הוּא הַקָּדוֹשׁ רַב־לָכֶם בְּנֵי לֵוִי׃ וַיֹּאמֶר מֹשֶׁה אֶל־
9 קֹרַח שִׁמְעוּ־נָא בְּנֵי לֵוִי׃ הַמְעַט מִכֶּם כִּי־הִבְדִּיל אֱלֹהֵי
יִשְׂרָאֵל אֶתְכֶם מֵעֲדַת יִשְׂרָאֵל לְהַקְרִיב אֶתְכֶם אֵלָיו לַעֲבֹד
אֶת־עֲבֹדַת מִשְׁכַּן יְהוָה וְלַעֲמֹד לִפְנֵי הָעֵדָה לְשָׁרְתָם׃
י וַיַּקְרֵב אֹתְךָ וְאֶת־כָּל־אַחֶיךָ בְנֵי־לֵוִי אִתָּךְ וּבִקַּשְׁתֶּם גַּם־
11 כְּהֻנָּה׃ לָכֵן אַתָּה וְכָל־עֲדָתְךָ הַנֹּעָדִים עַל־יְהוָה וְאַהֲרֹן
12 מַה־הוּא כִּי תַלּוֹנוּ עָלָיו׃ וַיִּשְׁלַח מֹשֶׁה לִקְרֹא לְדָתָן
13 וְלַאֲבִירָם בְּנֵי אֱלִיאָב וַיֹּאמְרוּ לֹא נַעֲלֶה׃ הַמְעַט כִּי
הֶעֱלִיתָנוּ מֵאֶרֶץ זָבַת חָלָב וּדְבַשׁ לַהֲמִיתֵנוּ בַּמִּדְבָּר כִּי־
שני
14 תִשְׂתָּרֵר עָלֵינוּ גַּם־הִשְׂתָּרֵר׃ אַף לֹא אֶל־אֶרֶץ זָבַת חָלָב
וּדְבַשׁ הֲבִיאֹתָנוּ וַתִּתֶּן־לָנוּ נַחֲלַת שָׂדֶה וָכָרֶם הַעֵינֵי
טו הָאֲנָשִׁים הָהֵם תְּנַקֵּר לֹא נַעֲלֶה׃ וַיִּחַר לְמֹשֶׁה מְאֹד
וַיֹּאמֶר אֶל־יְהוָה אַל־תֵּפֶן אֶל־מִנְחָתָם לֹא חֲמוֹר אֶחָד
16 מֵהֶם נָשָׂאתִי וְלֹא הֲרֵעֹתִי אֶת־אַחַד מֵהֶם׃ וַיֹּאמֶר מֹשֶׁה

v. 11. תלינו ק׳

7. *ye take too much upon you.* Indignantly he retorts upon the rebels in their own words.

8–11. Moses upbraids Korah and the Levites for their discontent with the position already assigned to them.

8. *unto Korah.* While Moses deals with Korah and his group, Dathan and Abiram stand in the background with their grievance; *v.* 12.

11. *that ye murmur against him.* Aaron was not self-appointed. God Himself had called him to his office, and his duties and privileges were duly assigned to him. As a result of this appeal by Moses, some of the Levites—the children of Korah among them—seem to have been detached from the body of rebels. Furthermore, we learn from I Chronicles VI, 22, that in the line of Korah's descendants appeared leaders of sacred song. Several of the Psalms are attributed to the 'Sons of Korah'. See on XXVI, 11.

12–15. Dathan and Abiram contemptuously refuse Moses' summons to attend before him, accuse him of misleading the people, and charge him with playing the prince over the People on the strength of promises he cannot fulfil.

13. *a land flowing with milk and honey.* Insolently—and ironically—they apply to Egypt the very words by which Moses described the Promised Land.

14. *not brought us.* Probably a satiric reference to the disaster that overtook the Israelites when, despite the warning of Moses, they attempted to enter Canaan, recorded in XIV, 45. Wickedly Dathan and Abiram now by insinuation shift the blame for that disaster on Moses! (Wiener).

put out the eyes. Are you trying to blind us to the true facts?

these men. A euphemism for 'us'.

15. *wroth.* Grieved and vexed.

respect not Thou their offering. 'Accept not the offering of incense which they are about to present unto Thee on the morrow' (Rashi).

not taken one ass. 'They accuse me of tyranny. But I have never so far abused my power and position as to accept even the meanest gift from any one of them!' In I Sam. VIII, 11–17, we read what an autocrat of early times had it in his power to do.

not taken one ass from them, neither have I hurt one of them.' 16. And Moses said unto Korah: 'Be thou and all thy congregation before the LORD, thou, and they, and Aaron, to-morrow; 17. and take ye every man his fire-pan, and put incense upon them, and bring ye before the LORD every man his fire-pan, two hundred and fifty fire-pans; thou also, and Aaron, each his fire-pan.' 18. And they took every man his fire-pan, and put fire in them, and laid incense thereon, and stood at the door of the tent of meeting with Moses and Aaron. 19. And Korah assembled all the congregation against them unto the door of the tent of meeting; and the glory of the LORD appeared unto all the congregation. *iii. ¶ 20. And the LORD spoke unto Moses and unto Aaron, saying: 21. 'Separate yourselves from among this congregation, that I may consume them in a moment.' 22. And they fell upon their faces, and said: 'O God, the God of the spirits of all flesh, shall one man sin, and wilt Thou be wroth with all the congregation?' ¶ 23. And the LORD spoke unto Moses, saying: 24. 'Speak unto the congregation, saying: Get you up from about the dwelling of Korah, Dathan, and Abiram.' 25. And Moses rose up and went unto Dathan and Abiram; and the elders of Israel followed him. 26. And he spoke unto the congregation, saying: 'Depart, I pray you, from the tents of these wicked men, and touch nothing of theirs, lest ye be swept away in all their sins.' 27. So they got them up from the dwelling of

אֶל־קֹרַח אַתָּה וְכָל־עֲדָתְךָ הֱיוּ לִפְנֵי יְהוָה אַתָּה וָהֵם
17 וְאַהֲרֹן מָחָר׃ וּקְחוּ ׀ אִישׁ מַחְתָּתוֹ וּנְתַתֶּם עֲלֵיהֶם קְטֹרֶת
וְהִקְרַבְתֶּם לִפְנֵי יְהוָה אִישׁ מַחְתָּתוֹ חֲמִשִּׁים וּמָאתַיִם
18 מַחְתֹּת וְאַתָּה וְאַהֲרֹן אִישׁ מַחְתָּתוֹ׃ וַיִּקְחוּ אִישׁ מַחְתָּתוֹ
וַיִּתְּנוּ עֲלֵיהֶם אֵשׁ וַיָּשִׂימוּ עֲלֵיהֶם קְטֹרֶת וַיַּעַמְדוּ פֶּתַח
19 אֹהֶל מוֹעֵד וּמֹשֶׁה וְאַהֲרֹן׃ וַיַּקְהֵל עֲלֵיהֶם קֹרַח אֶת־כָּל־
הָעֵדָה אֶל־פֶּתַח אֹהֶל מוֹעֵד וַיֵּרָא כְבוֹד־יְהוָה אֶל־כָּל־
שלישי כ הָעֵדָה׃ ס וַיְדַבֵּר יְהוָה אֶל־מֹשֶׁה וְאֶל־אַהֲרֹן לֵאמֹר׃
21 22 הִבָּדְלוּ מִתּוֹךְ הָעֵדָה הַזֹּאת וַאֲכַלֶּה אֹתָם כְּרָגַע׃ וַיִּפְּלוּ
עַל־פְּנֵיהֶם וַיֹּאמְרוּ אֵל אֱלֹהֵי הָרוּחֹת לְכָל־בָּשָׂר הָאִישׁ
23 אֶחָד יֶחֱטָא וְעַל כָּל־הָעֵדָה תִּקְצֹף׃ ס וַיְדַבֵּר יְהוָה
24 אֶל־מֹשֶׁה לֵּאמֹר׃ דַּבֵּר אֶל־הָעֵדָה לֵאמֹר הֵעָלוּ מִסָּבִיב
כה לְמִשְׁכַּן־קֹרַח דָּתָן וַאֲבִירָם׃ וַיָּקָם מֹשֶׁה וַיֵּלֶךְ אֶל־
26 דָּתָן וַאֲבִירָם וַיֵּלְכוּ אַחֲרָיו זִקְנֵי יִשְׂרָאֵל׃ וַיְדַבֵּר אֶל־
הָעֵדָה לֵאמֹר סוּרוּ נָא מֵעַל אָהֳלֵי הָאֲנָשִׁים הָרְשָׁעִים
הָאֵלֶּה וְאַל־תִּגְּעוּ בְּכָל־אֲשֶׁר לָהֶם פֶּן־תִּסָּפוּ בְּכָל־
27 חַטֹּאתָם׃ וַיֵּעָלוּ מֵעַל מִשְׁכַּן־קֹרַח דָּתָן וַאֲבִירָם מִסָּבִיב

16–19. KORAH AND HIS COMPANY ACCEPT MOSES' CHALLENGE

16. *Moses said unto Korah.* To be ready on the morrow and put his claim to the test.

19. *assembled all the congregation.* The rebellion was indeed a serious matter. Korah's demagogy, in addition to his rallying round him the ambitious leaders, had won over to his banner large sections in all the tribes.

20–24. MOSES' INTERCESSION

21. *from among this congregation.* As the whole congregation, favouring Korah, had rendered itself worthy of extermination.

22. *God of the spirits of all flesh.* He who made all hearts can be trusted to distinguish between the guilty and those misled by the guilty.

shall one man sin. Korah, the chief instigator who leads the masses astray; cf. Gen. XVIII, 25 ('That be far from Thee . . . to slay the righteous with the wicked that so the righteous should be as the wicked; that be far from Thee: shall not the Judge of all the earth do right?').

wroth with all the congregation. The dupes of that one man and his misguided confederates.

25–34. DESTRUCTION OF THE REBELS

Nothing could now have prevented the complete disintegration of the People save the destruction of the instigators of the sedition. That destruction, moreover, had to be in so striking a way that it would clearly reveal the Divine purpose.

25. *the elders of Israel.* Ibn Ezra suggests that these were the 70 elders who, according to XI, 16, 17, were to assist Moses in bearing the burden of the people. These remain loyal during the upheaval.

26. *in all their sins.* On account of the great multitude of their sins.

27. *Dathan and Abiram . . . stood at the door.* With a brazen mien, reviling and blaspheming God (Rashi).

Korah, Dathan, and Abiram, on every side; and Dathan and Abiram came out, and stood at the door of their tents, with their wives, and their sons, and their little ones. 28. And Moses said: 'Hereby ye shall know that the LORD hath sent me to do all these works, and that I have not done them of mine own mind. 29. If these men die the common death of all men, and be visited after the visitation of all men, then the LORD hath not sent me. 30. But if the LORD make a new thing, and the ground open her mouth, and swallow them up, with all that appertain unto them, and they go down alive into the pit, then ye shall understand that these men have despised the LORD.' 31. And it came to pass, as he made an end of speaking all these words, that the ground did cleave asunder that was under them. 32. And the earth opened her mouth, and swallowed them up, and their households, and all the men that appertained unto Korah, and all their goods. 33. So they, and all that appertained to them, went down alive into the pit; and the earth closed upon them, and they perished from among the assembly. 34. And all Israel that were round about them fled at the cry of them; for they said: 'Lest the earth swallow us up.' 35. And fire came forth from the LORD, and devoured the two hundred and fifty men that offered the incense.

וְדָתָן וַאֲבִירָם יָצְאוּ נִצָּבִים פֶּתַח אָהֳלֵיהֶם וּנְשֵׁיהֶם
28 וּבְנֵיהֶם וְטַפָּם׃ וַיֹּאמֶר מֹשֶׁה בְּזֹאת תֵּדְעוּן כִּי־יְהוָה שְׁלָחַנִי
29 לַעֲשׂוֹת אֵת כָּל־הַמַּעֲשִׂים הָאֵלֶּה כִּי־לֹא מִלִּבִּי׃ אִם־כְּמוֹת
כָּל־הָאָדָם יְמֻתוּן אֵלֶּה וּפְקֻדַּת כָּל־הָאָדָם יִפָּקֵד עֲלֵיהֶם
ל לֹא יְהוָה שְׁלָחָנִי׃ וְאִם־בְּרִיאָה יִבְרָא יְהוָה וּפָצְתָה
הָאֲדָמָה אֶת־פִּיהָ וּבָלְעָה אֹתָם וְאֶת־כָּל־אֲשֶׁר לָהֶם וְיָרְדוּ
חַיִּים שְׁאֹלָה וִידַעְתֶּם כִּי נִאֲצוּ הָאֲנָשִׁים הָאֵלֶּה אֶת־
31 יְהוָה׃ וַיְהִי כְּכַלֹּתוֹ לְדַבֵּר אֵת כָּל־הַדְּבָרִים הָאֵלֶּה וַתִּבָּקַע
32 הָאֲדָמָה אֲשֶׁר תַּחְתֵּיהֶם׃ וַתִּפְתַּח הָאָרֶץ אֶת־פִּיהָ וַתִּבְלַע
אֹתָם וְאֶת־בָּתֵּיהֶם וְאֵת כָּל־הָאָדָם אֲשֶׁר לְקֹרַח וְאֵת כָּל־
33 הָרְכוּשׁ׃ וַיֵּרְדוּ הֵם וְכָל־אֲשֶׁר לָהֶם חַיִּים שְׁאֹלָה וַתְּכַס
34 עֲלֵיהֶם הָאָרֶץ וַיֹּאבְדוּ מִתּוֹךְ הַקָּהָל׃ וְכָל־יִשְׂרָאֵל אֲשֶׁר
סְבִיבֹתֵיהֶם נָסוּ לְקֹלָם כִּי אָמְרוּ פֶּן־תִּבְלָעֵנוּ הָאָרֶץ׃
לה וְאֵשׁ יָצְאָה מֵאֵת יְהוָה וַתֹּאכַל אֵת הַחֲמִשִּׁים וּמָאתַיִם אִישׁ
מַקְרִיבֵי הַקְּטֹרֶת׃ ס

17

CHAPTER XVII

1. And the LORD spoke unto Moses, saying: 2. 'Speak unto Eleazar the son of Aaron the priest, that he take up the fire-pans

CAP. XVII. יז

א 2 וַיְדַבֵּר יְהוָה אֶל־מֹשֶׁה לֵּאמֹר׃ אֱמֹר אֶל־אֶלְעָזָר בֶּן־אַהֲרֹן

28. *all these works. i.e.* constituting myself the leader, and my brother the High Priest.

not . . . of mine own mind. But at the express Divine command.

29. *these men.* Dathan and Abiram and their followers.

die the common death. A natural death.

visited after the visitation of all men. i.e. suffer no extraordinary or significant fate.

30. *make a new thing.* lit. 'create a creation'; *i.e.* work a miracle which sweeps the rebels out of existence by one stroke; then will their guilt be apparent, and Moses' authority vindicated.

into the pit. lit. 'into Sheol'; regarded as deep down under the earth, and as the place where the wicked go after death.

32. *opened her mouth.* See p. 671.

that appertained unto Korah. All who associated themselves with Korah in his rebellion were suddenly engulfed. See, however, XXVI, 11, 'notwithstanding the sons of Korah died not.'

34. *at the cry of them.* At the mingled sound of the human shrieks and of the earth-convulsions that engulfed the men.

35. *that offered the incense.* The Reubenites who accused Moses of misleading the people were destroyed—like Nadab and Abihu—by fire from the LORD.

CHAPTER XVII

1–5. The brazen censers of the 250 men are to be collected and hammered into plates for the Altar of burnt-offering.

2. *and scatter thou the fire yonder.* Scatter the burning coals in the censers far away from the Altar.

for they are become holy. The censers had previously been private property, but they had, through the fact that incense had been offered in them, acquired sacredness, and must nevermore be used for a secular purpose.

הַכֹּהֵן וְיָרֵם אֶת־הַמַּחְתֹּת מִבֵּין הַשְּׂרֵפָה וְאֶת־הָאֵשׁ זְרֵה־
3 הָלְאָה כִּי קָדֵשׁוּ׃ אֵת מַחְתּוֹת הַחַטָּאִים הָאֵלֶּה בְּנַפְשֹׁתָם
וְעָשׂוּ אֹתָם רִקֻּעֵי פַחִים צִפּוּי לַמִּזְבֵּחַ כִּי־הִקְרִיבֻם לִפְנֵי־
4 יְהוָה וַיִּקְדָּשׁוּ וְיִהְיוּ לְאוֹת לִבְנֵי יִשְׂרָאֵל׃ וַיִּקַּח אֶלְעָזָר
הַכֹּהֵן אֵת מַחְתּוֹת הַנְּחֹשֶׁת אֲשֶׁר הִקְרִיבוּ הַשְּׂרֻפִים
ה וַיְרַקְּעוּם צִפּוּי לַמִּזְבֵּחַ׃ זִכָּרוֹן לִבְנֵי יִשְׂרָאֵל לְמַעַן אֲשֶׁר
לֹא־יִקְרַב אִישׁ זָר אֲשֶׁר לֹא מִזֶּרַע אַהֲרֹן הוּא לְהַקְטִיר
קְטֹרֶת לִפְנֵי יְהוָה וְלֹא־יִהְיֶה כְקֹרַח וְכַעֲדָתוֹ כַּאֲשֶׁר דִּבֶּר
יְהוָה בְּיַד־מֹשֶׁה לוֹ׃ פ
6 וַיִּלֹּנוּ כָּל־עֲדַת בְּנֵי־יִשְׂרָאֵל מִמָּחֳרָת עַל־מֹשֶׁה וְעַל־אַהֲרֹן
7 לֵאמֹר אַתֶּם הֲמִתֶּם אֶת־עַם יְהוָה׃ וַיְהִי בְּהִקָּהֵל הָעֵדָה
עַל־מֹשֶׁה וְעַל־אַהֲרֹן וַיִּפְנוּ אֶל־אֹהֶל מוֹעֵד וְהִנֵּה כִסָּהוּ
8 הֶעָנָן וַיֵּרָא כְּבוֹד יְהוָה׃ וַיָּבֹא מֹשֶׁה וְאַהֲרֹן אֶל־פְּנֵי אֹהֶל רביעי
9 מוֹעֵד׃ ס וַיְדַבֵּר יְהוָה אֶל־מֹשֶׁה לֵּאמֹר׃ הֵרֹמּוּ מִתּוֹךְ
11 הָעֵדָה הַזֹּאת וַאֲכַלֶּה אֹתָם כְּרָגַע וַיִּפְּלוּ עַל־פְּנֵיהֶם׃ וַיֹּאמֶר
מֹשֶׁה אֶל־אַהֲרֹן קַח אֶת־הַמַּחְתָּה וְתֶן־עָלֶיהָ אֵשׁ מֵעַל
הַמִּזְבֵּחַ וְשִׂים קְטֹרֶת וְהוֹלֵךְ מְהֵרָה אֶל־הָעֵדָה וְכַפֵּר
12 עֲלֵיהֶם כִּי־יָצָא הַקֶּצֶף מִלִּפְנֵי יְהוָה הֵחֵל הַנָּגֶף׃ וַיִּקַּח

out of the burning, and scatter thou the fire yonder; for they are become holy; 3. even the fire-pans of these men who have sinned at the cost of their lives, and let them be made beaten plates for a covering of the altar—for they are become holy, because they were offered before the LORD—that they may be a sign unto the children of Israel.' 4. And Eleazar the priest took the brazen fire-pans, which they that were burnt had offered; and they beat them out for a covering of the altar, 5. to be a memorial unto the children of Israel, to the end that no common man, that is not of the seed of Aaron, draw near to burn incense before the LORD; that he fare not as Korah, and as his company; as the LORD spoke unto him by the hand of Moses. ¶ 6. But on the morrow all the congregation of the children of Israel murmured against Moses and against Aaron, saying: 'Ye have killed the people of the LORD.' 7. And it came to pass, when the congregation was assembled against Moses and against Aaron, that they looked toward the tent of meeting; and, behold, the cloud covered it, and the glory of the LORD appeared. 8. And Moses and Aaron came to the front of the tent of meeting.*iv. 9. And the LORD spoke unto Moses, saying: 10. 'Get you up from among this congregation, that I may consume them in a moment.' And they fell upon their faces. 11. And Moses said unto Aaron: 'Take thy fire-pan, and put fire therein from off the altar, and lay incense thereon, and carry it quickly unto the congregation, and make atonement for them; for there is wrath gone out from the LORD: the plague is begun.' 12. And Aaron took as Moses

3. *at the cost of their lives.* Or, 'against their own souls' (RV Text).

covering of the altar. For an *additional* bronze covering of the Altar of burnt-offering; Exod. XXVII, 2.

a sign. A perpetual reminder of the fate that befell the rebels who handled the censers out of which these 'beaten plates' were made.

5. *of the seed of Aaron.* A priest, and not a Levite.

unto him. Better, *regarding him;* Aaron.

6–15. The disaffection had spread so far that many of the people resented the death of Korah and his followers, and held Moses responsible for it. This further shows that the complete suppression of the rebellion was a question of To be or not to be for Israel. The people are visited by an outbreak of plague.

7. *the cloud covered it.* As a symbol of protection to God's loyal servants against the threatening mob.

8. *to the front of the tent.* In response to this Divine manifestation, and to receive the Divine charge for further action.

10. *fell upon their faces.* In prayer and entreaty to God to spare the rebellious people; XVI, 22.

11. *thy fire-pan.* lit. 'the censer'; *i.e.* the censer which belongs to the High Priest and which he used on the Day of Atonement (Lev. XVI, 12) when ministering in the Sanctuary.

make atonement for them. As we see from Lev. XVI, 12, 13, the use of incense played an important part in the Atonement ritual.

wrath gone out from the LORD. Wrath is spoken of as a Divine messenger that is to execute God's punishment upon the guilty. It goes forth to kill, and slays as it proceeds.

spoke, and ran into the midst of the assembly; and, behold, the plague was begun among the people; and he put on the incense, and made atonement for the people. 13. And he stood between the dead and the living; and the plague was stayed. 14. Now they that died by the plague were fourteen thousand and seven hundred, besides them that died about the matter of Korah. 15. And Aaron returned unto Moses unto the door of the tent of meeting, and the plague was stayed.*v. ¶ 16. And the LORD spoke unto Moses, saying: 17. 'Speak unto the children of Israel, and take of them rods, one for each fathers' house, of all their princes according to their fathers' houses, twelve rods; thou shalt write every man's name upon his rod. 18. And thou shalt write Aaron's name upon the rod of Levi, for there shall be one rod for the head of their fathers' houses. 19. And thou shalt lay them up in the tent of meeting before the testimony, where I meet with you. 20. And it shall come to pass, that the man whom I shall choose, his rod shall bud; and I will make to cease from Me the murmurings of the children of Israel, which they murmur against you.' 21. And Moses spoke unto the children of Israel; and all their princes gave him rods, for each prince one, according to their fathers' houses, even twelve rods; and the rod of Aaron was among their rods. 22. And Moses laid up the rods before the LORD in the tent of the testimony. 23. And it came to pass on the morrow, that Moses went into the tent of the testimony; and, behold, the rod of Aaron for the house of Levi was budded, and put forth buds, and bloomed blossoms, and bore ripe almonds. 24. And Moses brought out all the rods from before the LORD unto all the children of Israel; and they looked, and took every man his rod.*vi.

אַהֲרֹן כַּאֲשֶׁר ׀ דִּבֶּר מֹשֶׁה וַיָּרָץ אֶל־תּוֹךְ הַקָּהָל וְהִנֵּה הֵחֵל
13 הַנֶּגֶף בָּעָם וַיִּתֵּן אֶת־הַקְּטֹרֶת וַיְכַפֵּר עַל־הָעָם׃ וַיַּעֲמֹד
14 בֵּין־הַמֵּתִים וּבֵין הַחַיִּים וַתֵּעָצַר הַמַּגֵּפָה׃ וַיִּהְיוּ הַמֵּתִים
בַּמַּגֵּפָה אַרְבָּעָה עָשָׂר אֶלֶף וּשְׁבַע מֵאוֹת מִלְּבַד הַמֵּתִים
טו עַל־דְּבַר־קֹרַח׃ וַיָּשָׁב אַהֲרֹן אֶל־מֹשֶׁה אֶל־פֶּתַח אֹהֶל
מוֹעֵד וְהַמַּגֵּפָה נֶעֱצָרָה׃ • פ חמישי
16 17 וַיְדַבֵּר יְהוָה אֶל־מֹשֶׁה לֵּאמֹר׃ דַּבֵּר ׀ אֶל־בְּנֵי יִשְׂרָאֵל
וְקַח מֵאִתָּם מַטֶּה מַטֶּה לְבֵית אָב מֵאֵת כָּל־נְשִׂיאֵהֶם
לְבֵית אֲבֹתָם שְׁנֵים עָשָׂר מַטּוֹת אִישׁ אֶת־שְׁמוֹ תִּכְתֹּב עַל־
18 מַטֵּהוּ׃ וְאֵת שֵׁם אַהֲרֹן תִּכְתֹּב עַל־מַטֵּה לֵוִי כִּי מַטֶּה אֶחָד
19 לְרֹאשׁ בֵּית אֲבוֹתָם׃ וְהִנַּחְתָּם בְּאֹהֶל מוֹעֵד לִפְנֵי הָעֵדוּת
כ אֲשֶׁר אִוָּעֵד לָכֶם שָׁמָּה׃ • וְהָיָה הָאִישׁ אֲשֶׁר אֶבְחַר־בּוֹ
מַטֵּהוּ יִפְרָח וַהֲשִׁכֹּתִי מֵעָלַי אֶת־תְּלֻנּוֹת בְּנֵי יִשְׂרָאֵל אֲשֶׁר
21 הֵם מַלִּינִם עֲלֵיכֶם׃ וַיְדַבֵּר מֹשֶׁה אֶל־בְּנֵי יִשְׂרָאֵל וַיִּתְּנוּ
אֵלָיו ׀ כָּל־נְשִׂיאֵיהֶם מַטֶּה לְנָשִׂיא אֶחָד מַטֶּה לְנָשִׂיא אֶחָד
לְבֵית אֲבֹתָם שְׁנֵים עָשָׂר מַטּוֹת וּמַטֵּה אַהֲרֹן בְּתוֹךְ מַטּוֹתָם׃
22 23 וַיַּנַּח מֹשֶׁה אֶת־הַמַּטֹּת לִפְנֵי יְהוָה בְּאֹהֶל הָעֵדֻת׃ וַיְהִי
מִמָּחֳרָת וַיָּבֹא מֹשֶׁה אֶל־אֹהֶל הָעֵדוּת וְהִנֵּה פָּרַח מַטֵּה־
24 אַהֲרֹן לְבֵית לֵוִי וַיֹּצֵא פֶרַח וַיָּצֵץ צִיץ וַיִּגְמֹל שְׁקֵדִים׃ וַיֹּצֵא
מֹשֶׁה אֶת־כָּל־הַמַּטֹּת מִלִּפְנֵי יְהוָה אֶל־כָּל־בְּנֵי יִשְׂרָאֵל

v. 20. חצי הספר בפסוקים v. 23. כצ״ל בהעמדה תחת הצ׳

13. *between the dead and the living.* Aaron hastens and takes up a position in front of Wrath. All behind have died: those in front have not been touched; they are living. Thus it is that Aaron stands between the living and the dead, and stays the plague.

16–28. VINDICATION OF AARON

Moses deposits twelve wands for each of the twelve tribes, and an additional rod inscribed with the name of Aaron as head of the tribe of Levi. Ibn Ezra suggests that as the two tribes of the children of Joseph (Ephraim and Manasseh) were reckoned together (Deut. XXVII, 12), the total number of the rods did not exceed twelve. Next morning, Aaron's rod had budded and brought forth fruit, confirming the Divine choice of Levi. Henceforth, Aaron's right to the priesthood is unchallenged.

17. *rods.* Ordinarily carried by the princes as the symbol of tribal authority.
father's house. Tribe.
princes. Those named in chapters II and VII.

18. *Aaron's name.* To indicate that God had appointed Aaron to be the prince of his tribe.

19. *before the testimony. i.e.* in front of the Ark that contained the two Tables of the Testimony.

20. *I shall choose.* For the special duties and privileges of the priesthood.

24. *and they looked.* Here was indeed Divine confirmation of the High Priesthood of Aaron.

¶ 25. And the LORD said unto Moses: 'Put back the rod of Aaron before the testimony, to be kept there, for a token against the rebellious children; that there may be made an end of their murmurings against Me, that they die not.' 26. Thus did Moses; as the LORD commanded him, so did he. ¶ 27. And the children of Israel spoke unto Moses, saying: 'Behold, we perish, we are undone, we are all undone. 28. Every one that cometh near, that cometh near unto the tabernacle of the LORD, is to die; shall we wholly perish?'

18

CHAPTER XVIII

1. And the LORD said unto Aaron: 'Thou and thy sons and thy fathers' house with thee shall bear the iniquity of the sanctuary; and thou and thy sons with thee shall bear the iniquity of your priesthood. 2. And thy brethren also, the tribe of Levi, the tribe of thy father, bring thou near with thee, that they may be joined unto thee, and minister unto thee, thou and thy sons with thee being before the tent of the testimony. 3. And they shall keep thy charge, and the charge of all the Tent; only they shall not come nigh unto the holy furniture and unto the altar, that they die not, neither they, nor ye. 4. And they shall be joined unto thee, and keep the charge of the tent of meeting, whatsoever the service of the Tent may be; but a

וַיִּרְאוּ וַיִּקְחוּ אִישׁ מַטֵּהוּ׃ פ ששי

כה וַיֹּאמֶר יְהוָה אֶל־מֹשֶׁה הָשֵׁב אֶת־מַטֵּה אַהֲרֹן לִפְנֵי הָעֵדוּת

לְמִשְׁמֶרֶת לְאוֹת לִבְנֵי־מֶרִי וּתְכַל תְּלוּנֹּתָם מֵעָלַי וְלֹא

26 יָמֻתוּ׃ וַיַּעַשׂ מֹשֶׁה כַּאֲשֶׁר צִוָּה יְהוָה אֹתוֹ כֵּן עָשָׂה׃ פ

27 וַיֹּאמְרוּ בְּנֵי יִשְׂרָאֵל אֶל־מֹשֶׁה לֵאמֹר הֵן גָּוַעְנוּ אָבַדְנוּ כֻּלָּנוּ

28 אָבָדְנוּ׃ כֹּל הַקָּרֵב ׀ הַקָּרֵב אֶל־מִשְׁכַּן יְהוָה יָמוּת הַאִם

תַּמְנוּ לִגְוֺעַ׃ ס

יח CAP. XVIII. יח

א וַיֹּאמֶר יְהוָה אֶל־אַהֲרֹן אַתָּה וּבָנֶיךָ וּבֵית־אָבִיךָ אִתָּךְ תִּשְׂאוּ

אֶת־עֲוֺן הַמִּקְדָּשׁ וְאַתָּה וּבָנֶיךָ אִתָּךְ תִּשְׂאוּ אֶת־עֲוֺן כְּהֻנַּתְכֶם׃

2 וְגַם אֶת־אַחֶיךָ מַטֵּה לֵוִי שֵׁבֶט אָבִיךָ הַקְרֵב אִתָּךְ וְיִלָּווּ

עָלֶיךָ וִישָׁרְתוּךָ וְאַתָּה וּבָנֶיךָ אִתָּךְ לִפְנֵי אֹהֶל הָעֵדֻת׃

3 וְשָׁמְרוּ מִשְׁמַרְתְּךָ וּמִשְׁמֶרֶת כָּל־הָאֹהֶל אַךְ אֶל־כְּלֵי הַקֹּדֶשׁ

4 וְאֶל־הַמִּזְבֵּחַ לֹא יִקְרָבוּ וְלֹא־יָמֻתוּ גַם־הֵם גַּם־אַתֶּם׃ וְנִלְווּ

עָלֶיךָ וְשָׁמְרוּ אֶת־מִשְׁמֶרֶת אֹהֶל מוֹעֵד לְכֹל עֲבֹדַת הָאֹהֶל

יח׳ v. 3. קמץ בז״ק

25. *token.* A warning to future generations.

27. *behold, we perish.* This and *v.* 28 form a transition to the next chapter in which the Levites guard the Tent, lest any layman should perish by approaching it.

we are undone. A despairing outburst on the part of defeated and disheartened men. Korah, Dathan, and Abiram and their company had perished, and furthermore a plague had swept away several thousands of the people. It looked as if the end had come to all!

28. *shall we wholly perish?* Better, *shall we ever have finished dying?*; 'have we not yet done expiring?' (Benisch). It was in response to this agonizing cry, that Aaron and the Levites were bidden in XVIII to guard the Sanctuary against the approach by any 'stranger'.

CHAPTER XVIII

DUTIES AND EMOLUMENTS OF PRIESTS AND LEVITES

1–7. The rebellion is made the occasion for recalling the Divine choice of the Levites, and for defining the duties and emoluments of the priests and Levites.

1. *bear the iniquity of the sanctuary. i.e.* bear the *consequences* of the iniquity that would be incurred by laymen who, through neglect on the part of the priesthood, performed in the Sanctuary any service assigned to priests or Levites.

of your priesthood. If you allowed any of the ordinary Levites to usurp functions that were the prerogative of Aaron and his sons exclusively.

2. *joined unto thee.* The two other Levitical families, *viz.* the Gershonites and the Merarites, shall assist in the duties of the Sanctuary, but Aaron and his sons shall be the principals.

the tent of the testimony. i.e. in the Inner Sanctuary.

3. *keep thy charge.* See III, 7; perform whatsoever sacred offices they are bidden to do by the priests.

nor ye. The sons of Aaron who would suffer the same fate for having permitted the Levites to transgress.

4. *common man.* A layman.

not draw nigh. To the service in the Sanctuary (Sifri).

ה וְזָר לֹא־יִקְרַב אֲלֵיכֶם׃ וּשְׁמַרְתֶּם אֵת מִשְׁמֶרֶת הַקֹּדֶשׁ
וְאֵת מִשְׁמֶרֶת הַמִּזְבֵּחַ וְלֹא־יִהְיֶה עוֹד קֶצֶף עַל־בְּנֵי יִשְׂרָאֵל׃
6 וַאֲנִי הִנֵּה לָקַחְתִּי אֶת־אֲחֵיכֶם הַלְוִיִּם מִתּוֹךְ בְּנֵי יִשְׂרָאֵל
לָכֶם מַתָּנָה נְתֻנִים לַיהוָה לַעֲבֹד אֶת־עֲבֹדַת אֹהֶל מוֹעֵד׃
7 וְאַתָּה וּבָנֶיךָ אִתְּךָ תִּשְׁמְרוּ אֶת־כְּהֻנַּתְכֶם לְכָל־דְּבַר הַמִּזְבֵּחַ
וּלְמִבֵּית לַפָּרֹכֶת וַעֲבַדְתֶּם עֲבֹדַת מַתָּנָה אֶתֵּן אֶת־כְּהֻנַּתְכֶם
וְהַזָּר הַקָּרֵב יוּמָת׃ פ
8 וַיְדַבֵּר יְהוָה אֶל־אַהֲרֹן וַאֲנִי הִנֵּה נָתַתִּי לְךָ אֶת־מִשְׁמֶרֶת
תְּרוּמֹתָי לְכָל־קָדְשֵׁי בְנֵי־יִשְׂרָאֵל לְךָ נְתַתִּים לְמָשְׁחָה
9 וּלְבָנֶיךָ לְחָק־עוֹלָם׃ זֶה יִהְיֶה לְךָ מִקֹּדֶשׁ הַקֳּדָשִׁים מִן
הָאֵשׁ כָּל־קָרְבָּנָם לְכָל־מִנְחָתָם וּלְכָל־חַטָּאתָם וּלְכָל־
אֲשָׁמָם אֲשֶׁר יָשִׁיבוּ לִי קֹדֶשׁ קָדָשִׁים לְךָ הוּא וּלְבָנֶיךָ׃
י בְּקֹדֶשׁ הַקֳּדָשִׁים תֹּאכְלֶנּוּ כָּל־זָכָר יֹאכַל אֹתוֹ קֹדֶשׁ יִהְיֶה
11 לָּךְ׃ וְזֶה־לְּךָ תְּרוּמַת מַתָּנָם לְכָל־תְּנוּפֹת בְּנֵי יִשְׂרָאֵל לְךָ
נְתַתִּים וּלְבָנֶיךָ וְלִבְנֹתֶיךָ אִתְּךָ לְחָק־עוֹלָם כָּל־טָהוֹר
12 בְּבֵיתְךָ יֹאכַל אֹתוֹ׃ כֹּל חֵלֶב יִצְהָר וְכָל־חֵלֶב תִּירוֹשׁ
13 וְדָגָן רֵאשִׁיתָם אֲשֶׁר־יִתְּנוּ לַיהוָה לְךָ נְתַתִּים׃ בִּכּוּרֵי כָּל־

common man shall not draw nigh unto you.
5. And ye shall keep the charge of the holy things, and the charge of the altar, that there be wrath no more upon the children of Israel.
6. And I, behold, I have taken your brethren the Levites from among the children of Israel; for you they are given as a gift unto the LORD, to do the service of the tent of meeting.
7. And thou and thy sons with thee shall keep your priesthood in everything that pertaineth to the altar, and to that within the veil; and ye shall serve; I give you the priesthood as a service of gift; and the common man that draweth nigh shall be put to death.' ¶
8. And the LORD spoke unto Aaron: 'And I, behold, I have given thee the charge of My heave-offerings; even of all the hallowed things of the children of Israel unto thee have I given them for a consecrated portion, and to thy sons, as a due for ever.
9. This shall be thine of the most holy things, reserved from the fire: every offering of theirs, even every meal-offering of theirs, and every sin-offering of theirs, and every guilt-offering of theirs, which they may render unto Me, shall be most holy for thee and for thy sons.
10. In a most holy place shalt thou eat thereof; every male may eat thereof; it shall be holy unto thee.
11. And this is thine: the heave-offering of their gift, even all the wave-offerings of the children of Israel; I have given them unto thee, and to thy sons and to thy daughters with thee, as a due for ever; every one that is clean in thy house may eat thereof.
12. All the best of the oil, and all the best of the wine, and of the corn, the first part of them which they give unto the LORD, to thee have I given them.
13. The first-ripe fruits of

5. *that there be wrath no more.* As there had been in the case of Korah and his confederates.

6. *given as a gift unto the LORD.* See III, 9; VIII, 16, 19.

7. *that within the veil.* The Holy of Holies, the inmost Sanctuary of the Tabernacle.
as a service of gift. Which must not be regarded as a burden or a misfortune, but as a privilege.

8–20. The dues of the priests from the people —the provisions made for the maintenance of the priests.

8. *I have given . . . for ever.* Or, 'I have given thee that which is reserved (from the Altar) of the contributions made to Me, even all the sacred gifts of the children of Israel, to thee have I given them as a perpetual due' (Kennedy).
heave-offerings. The general term for offerings made to God.

9. *reserved from the fire. i.e.* saved from being totally burnt upon the Altar.
meal-offering. See Lev. II, 2, 3.
guilt-offering. See Lev. VII, 7.

10. To be eaten in a holy place; *viz.* in the 'Court of the Tent of meeting', which in Lev. VI, 19, is designated, 'a holy place.'

11. *and this is thine.* Here begins a second list (*v.* 11–15) of holy gifts that were to be given by the offerers *directly* to the priests, to be eaten at home by all ritually clean members of the priestly families.
heave-offering . . . wave-offering. See Lev. VII, 29–34.

12. *the best.* lit. 'the fat' (in English, 'the cream'), to denote the choicest parts of anything.

13. *first-ripe fruits.* See Deut. XVIII, 4.

all that is in their land, which they bring unto the LORD, shall be thine; every one that is clean in thy house may eat thereof. 14. Every thing devoted in Israel shall be thine. 15. Every thing that openeth the womb, of all flesh which they offer unto the LORD, both of man and beast, shall be thine; howbeit the first-born of man shalt thou surely redeem, and the firstling of unclean beasts shalt thou redeem. 16. And their redemption-money—from a month old shalt thou redeem them—shall be, according to thy valuation, five shekels of silver, after the shekel of the sanctuary—the same is twenty gerahs. 17. But the firstling of an ox, or the firstling of a sheep, or the firstling of a goat, thou shalt not redeem; they are holy: thou shalt dash their blood against the altar, and shalt make their fat smoke for an offering made by fire, for a sweet savour unto the LORD. 18. And the flesh of them shall be thine, as the wave-breast and as the right thigh, it shall be thine. 19. All the heave-offerings of the holy things, which the children of Israel offer unto the LORD, have I given thee, and thy sons and thy daughters with thee, as a due for ever; it is an everlasting covenant of salt before the LORD unto thee and to thy seed with thee.' ¶ 20. And the LORD said unto Aaron: 'Thou shalt have no inheritance in their land, neither shalt thou have any portion among them; I am thy portion and thine inheritance among the children of Israel.*vii. 21. And unto the children of Levi, behold, I have given all the tithe in Israel for an inheritance, in return for their service which they serve, even the service of the tent of meeting. 22. And henceforth the children of Israel shall not come nigh the tent of meeting, lest they bear sin, and die. 23. But the Levites alone shall do the service of the

אֲשֶׁר בְּאַרְצָם אֲשֶׁר־יָבִיאוּ לַיהוָה לְךָ יִהְיֶה כָּל־טָהוֹר
14 טו בְּבֵיתְךָ יֹאכְלֶנּוּ׃ כָּל־חֵרֶם בְּיִשְׂרָאֵל לְךָ יִהְיֶה׃ כָּל־פֶּטֶר
רֶחֶם לְכָל־בָּשָׂר אֲשֶׁר־יַקְרִיבוּ לַיהוָה בָּאָדָם וּבַבְּהֵמָה
יִהְיֶה־לָּךְ אַךְ ׀ פָּדֹה תִפְדֶּה אֵת בְּכוֹר הָאָדָם וְאֵת בְּכוֹר־
16 הַבְּהֵמָה הַטְּמֵאָה תִּפְדֶּה׃ וּפְדוּיָו מִבֶּן־חֹדֶשׁ תִּפְדֶּה
בְּעֶרְכְּךָ כֶּסֶף חֲמֵשֶׁת שְׁקָלִים בְּשֶׁקֶל הַקֹּדֶשׁ עֶשְׂרִים
17 גֵּרָה הוּא׃ אַךְ בְּכוֹר־שׁוֹר אוֹ בְכוֹר כֶּשֶׂב אוֹ־בְכוֹר עֵז
לֹא תִפְדֶּה קֹדֶשׁ הֵם אֶת־דָּמָם תִּזְרֹק עַל־הַמִּזְבֵּחַ וְאֶת־
18 חֶלְבָּם תַּקְטִיר אִשֶּׁה לְרֵיחַ נִיחֹחַ לַיהוָה׃ וּבְשָׂרָם יִהְיֶה־
19 לָּךְ כַּחֲזֵה הַתְּנוּפָה וּכְשׁוֹק הַיָּמִין לְךָ יִהְיֶה׃ כֹּל ׀ תְּרוּמֹת
הַקֳּדָשִׁים אֲשֶׁר יָרִימוּ בְנֵי־יִשְׂרָאֵל לַיהוָה נָתַתִּי לְךָ וּלְבָנֶיךָ
וְלִבְנֹתֶיךָ אִתְּךָ לְחָק־עוֹלָם בְּרִית מֶלַח עוֹלָם הִוא לִפְנֵי
כ יְהוָה לְךָ וּלְזַרְעֲךָ אִתָּךְ׃ וַיֹּאמֶר יְהוָה אֶל־אַהֲרֹן בְּאַרְצָם
לֹא תִנְחָל וְחֵלֶק לֹא־יִהְיֶה לְךָ בְּתוֹכָם אֲנִי חֶלְקְךָ
שביעי 21 וְנַחֲלָתְךָ בְּתוֹךְ בְּנֵי יִשְׂרָאֵל׃ ס וְלִבְנֵי לֵוִי הִנֵּה נָתַתִּי
כָּל־מַעֲשֵׂר בְּיִשְׂרָאֵל לְנַחֲלָה חֵלֶף עֲבֹדָתָם אֲשֶׁר־הֵם
22 עֹבְדִים אֶת־עֲבֹדַת אֹהֶל מוֹעֵד׃ וְלֹא־יִקְרְבוּ עוֹד בְּנֵי
23 יִשְׂרָאֵל אֶל־אֹהֶל מוֹעֵד לָשֵׂאת חֵטְא לָמוּת׃ וְעָבַד הַלֵּוִי

v. 20. קמץ בז"ק

14. *devoted.* See Lev. XXVII, 28. An object wholly given up to God; *i.e.* made over to the Sanctuary. It could not be sold or redeemed.

15–18. DISPOSAL OF FIRSTLINGS

16. *redemption-money.* Of the human first-born.

17. *firstling of an ox . . . goat.* Being available for sacrifice upon the Altar, these were not to be redeemed.

18. *as the wave-breast.* Which in the case of peace-offerings were given unto Aaron and his sons as their due (Lev. VII, 28–34), so shall the flesh of these firstlings also be their perquisite and subject to the same restrictions.

19. *the heave-offerings.* Enumerated in *v.* 8–19.

covenant of salt. i.e. a permanent covenant. As salt preserves food from putrefaction, it became the emblem of permanence.

20. *no inheritance.* They were to have no share in the land of Canaan at the time of its division among the tribes.

I am thy . . . inheritance. Just as the laity were to live upon what was yielded them by the land, so the priests were to live upon what God accorded them; *i.e.* the sacrifices brought to the Altar and the consecrated gifts.

21–24. DUES OF THE LEVITES FROM THE PEOPLE

21. *tithe.* A tenth part.

the tithe in Israel. Was paid on agricultural

הוּא אֶת־עֲבֹדַת אֹהֶל מוֹעֵד וְהֵם יִשְׂאוּ עֲוֹנָם חֻקַּת עוֹלָם
24 לְדֹרֹתֵיכֶם וּבְתוֹךְ בְּנֵי יִשְׂרָאֵל לֹא יִנְחֲלוּ נַחֲלָה׃ כִּי אֶת־
מַעְשַׂר בְּנֵי־יִשְׂרָאֵל אֲשֶׁר יָרִימוּ לַיהוָה תְּרוּמָה נָתַתִּי
לַלְוִיִּם לְנַחֲלָה עַל־כֵּן אָמַרְתִּי לָהֶם בְּתוֹךְ בְּנֵי יִשְׂרָאֵל
לֹא יִנְחֲלוּ נַחֲלָה׃ פ
כה
26 וַיְדַבֵּר יְהוָה אֶל־מֹשֶׁה לֵּאמֹר׃ וְאֶל־הַלְוִיִּם תְּדַבֵּר וְאָמַרְתָּ
אֲלֵהֶם כִּי־תִקְחוּ מֵאֵת בְּנֵי־יִשְׂרָאֵל אֶת־הַמַּעֲשֵׂר אֲשֶׁר
נָתַתִּי לָכֶם מֵאִתָּם בְּנַחֲלַתְכֶם וַהֲרֵמֹתֶם מִמֶּנּוּ תְּרוּמַת
27 יְהוָה מַעֲשֵׂר מִן־הַמַּעֲשֵׂר׃ וְנֶחְשַׁב לָכֶם תְּרוּמַתְכֶם כַּדָּגָן
28 מִן־הַגֹּרֶן וְכַמְלֵאָה מִן־הַיָּקֶב׃ כֵּן תָּרִימוּ גַם־אַתֶּם תְּרוּמַת
יְהוָה מִכֹּל מַעְשְׂרֹתֵיכֶם אֲשֶׁר תִּקְחוּ מֵאֵת בְּנֵי יִשְׂרָאֵל
29 וּנְתַתֶּם מִמֶּנּוּ אֶת־תְּרוּמַת יְהוָה לְאַהֲרֹן הַכֹּהֵן׃ מִכֹּל
מַתְּנֹתֵיכֶם תָּרִימוּ אֵת כָּל־תְּרוּמַת יְהוָה מִכָּל־חֶלְבּוֹ אֶת־
מפטיר ל מִקְדְּשׁוֹ מִמֶּנּוּ׃ וְאָמַרְתָּ אֲלֵהֶם בַּהֲרִימְכֶם אֶת־חֶלְבּוֹ
מִמֶּנּוּ וְנֶחְשַׁב לַלְוִיִּם כִּתְבוּאַת גֹּרֶן וְכִתְבוּאַת יָקֶב׃
31 וַאֲכַלְתֶּם אֹתוֹ בְּכָל־מָקוֹם אַתֶּם וּבֵיתְכֶם כִּי־שָׂכָר הוּא
32 לָכֶם חֵלֶף עֲבֹדַתְכֶם בְּאֹהֶל מוֹעֵד׃ וְלֹא־תִשְׂאוּ עָלָיו
חֵטְא בַּהֲרִימְכֶם אֶת־חֶלְבּוֹ מִמֶּנּוּ וְאֶת־קָדְשֵׁי בְנֵי־יִשְׂרָאֵל
לֹא תְחַלְּלוּ וְלֹא תָמוּתוּ׃

tent of meeting, and they shall bear their iniquity; it shall be a statute for ever throughout your generations, and among the children of Israel they shall have no inheritance. 24. For the tithe of the children of Israel, which they set apart as a gift unto the LORD, I have given to the Levites for an inheritance; therefore I have said unto them: Among the children of Israel they shall have no inheritance.' ¶ 25. And the LORD spoke unto Moses, saying: 26. 'Moreover thou shalt speak unto the Levites, and say unto them: When ye take of the children of Israel the tithe which I have given you from them for your inheritance, then ye shall set apart of it a gift for the LORD, even a tithe of the tithe. 27. And the gift which ye set apart shall be reckoned unto you, as though it were the corn of the threshing-floor, and as the fulness of the winepress. 28. Thus ye also shall set apart a gift unto the LORD of all your tithes, which ye receive of the children of Israel; and thereof ye shall give the gift which is set apart unto the LORD to Aaron the priest. 29. Out of all that is given you ye shall set apart all of that which us due unto the LORD, of all the best thereof, even the hallowed part thereof out of it.*m. 30. Therefore thou shalt say unto them: When ye set apart the best thereof from it, then it shall be counted unto the Levites as the increase of the threshing-floor, and as the increase of the winepress. 31. And ye may eat it in every place, ye and your households; for it is your reward in return for your service in the tent of meeting. 32. And ye shall bear no sin by reason of it, seeing that ye have set apart from it the best thereof; and ye shall not profane the holy things of the children of Israel, that ye die not.'

produce and on cattle to the Levites. It is designated in the Talmud 'first tithe', as distinguished from 'second tithe' and 'the tithe for the poor'; Deut. XIV, 22–29.

24. *no inheritance.* Like the priests, they had no separate territory allotted to them. Their possessions consisted of 48 cities 'with the open land about them'; see XXXV, 7.

25–32. THE DUES OF THE PRIESTS FROM THE LEVITES

The Levites were to contribute to the priests a tithe of that which they had received from the people.

27. *the corn of the threshing-floor.* This tithe by you to the priests shall be regarded as though it were direct from your threshing-floor and winepress.

28. *Aaron the priest.* And his descendants.

29. *the hallowed part.* So called because of its description in *v.* 24 as 'a gift unto the LORD'.

30. *say unto them. i.e.* to the Levites.

counted . . . increase. When the Levites had given as a tithe to the priests the best part from the tithe which they themselves had received from the laity, then the remainder was theirs just as if they had grown it and gathered it themselves.

32. *ye shall bear no sin.* When the tithe of the tithe had been duly contributed in accordance with the preceding instructions, then would the Levites incur no penalty of sin by eating and enjoying the produce of the threshing-floor and winepress as and when they pleased.

I SAMUEL XI, 14–XII, 22

CHAPTER XI

14. Then said Samuel to the people: 'Come and let us go to Gilgal, and renew the kingdom there.' 15. And all the people went to Gilgal; and there they made Saul king before the LORD in Gilgal; and there they sacrificed sacrifices of peace-offerings before the LORD; and there Saul and all the men of Israel rejoiced greatly.

CHAPTER XII

1. And Samuel said unto all Israel: 'Behold, I have hearkened unto your voice in all that ye said unto me, and have made a king over you. 2. And now, behold, the king walketh before you; and I am old and greyheaded; and, behold, my sons are with you; and I have walked before you from my youth unto this day. 3. Here I am; witness against me before the LORD, and before His anointed: whose ox have I taken? or whose ass have I taken? or whom have I defrauded? or whom have I op-

CAP. XI. יא

14 וַיֹּאמֶר שְׁמוּאֵל אֶל־
טו הָעָם לְכוּ וְנֵלְכָה הַגִּלְגָּל וּנְחַדֵּשׁ שָׁם הַמְּלוּכָה׃ וַיֵּלְכוּ כָל־
הָעָם הַגִּלְגָּל וַיַּמְלִכוּ שָׁם אֶת־שָׁאוּל לִפְנֵי יְהוָה בַּגִּלְגָּל
וַיִּזְבְּחוּ־שָׁם זְבָחִים שְׁלָמִים לִפְנֵי יְהוָה וַיִּשְׂמַח שָׁם שָׁאוּל
וְכָל־אַנְשֵׁי יִשְׂרָאֵל עַד־מְאֹד׃

CAP. XII. יב

א וַיֹּאמֶר שְׁמוּאֵל אֶל־כָּל־יִשְׂרָאֵל הִנֵּה שָׁמַעְתִּי בְקֹלְכֶם לְכֹל
2 אֲשֶׁר־אֲמַרְתֶּם לִי וָאַמְלִיךְ עֲלֵיכֶם מֶלֶךְ׃ וְעַתָּה הִנֵּה
הַמֶּלֶךְ ׀ מִתְהַלֵּךְ לִפְנֵיכֶם וַאֲנִי זָקַנְתִּי וָשַׂבְתִּי וּבָנַי הִנָּם
אִתְּכֶם וַאֲנִי הִתְהַלַּכְתִּי לִפְנֵיכֶם מִנְּעֻרַי עַד־הַיּוֹם הַזֶּה׃
3 הִנְנִי עֲנוּ בִי נֶגֶד יְהוָה וְנֶגֶד מְשִׁיחוֹ אֶת־שׁוֹר ׀ מִי לָקַחְתִּי

In the Sedrah, Korah and his associates complained unjustly of the rule of Moses: in the Haftorah, the people displayed ingratitude towards their devoted leader, Samuel, and clamoured for a king to take his place. Both Moses and Samuel protest their utter disinterestedness in the service of the people.

Samuel was the last and greatest of the Judges. The task he was called upon to accomplish was one of extraordinary difficulty. Moses created the nation: it had disintegrated in the wild, anarchic times of the Judges. Samuel had to re-create it, and rebuild it out of ruins. He found a loosely-knit body of tribes and left them a united people. Although himself opposed to monarchy, he made a national monarchy possible. But at the foundation of it, he laid firmly the Biblical conception of the responsibility of the ruler to God. This is one of the main differences between Israel and the other Eastern nations of antiquity. Whereas in Babylon, *e.g.*, a limited monarchy would have been deemed a contradiction in terms, in Israel it is the people that is in possession of sovereign rights, and the king *is under the law*. The Jewish king was bound to respect the liberty, honour, and the property of his subjects, and his powers were strictly limited by the fundamental laws of the Torah (Deut. XVII, 10–20). Prophets, psalmists, and sages all conceived of the king as a shepherd of his people, whose sceptre should be a sceptre of peace, pity, and righteousness.

14–15. RECOGNIZING SAUL AS KING

14. *Gilgal.* Near Jericho. It already had sacred associations. It was the place of Israel's first encampment on crossing into the Holy Land under Joshua. 'Its remoteness from the Philistines made it suitable for an act which was obviously a step towards throwing off their yoke' (Kirkpatrick).

to renew the kingdom there. This sacred place Samuel chose for the solemn consecration of Saul. Saul had proved his worthiness for the kingship, and the people were unanimous in accepting him as their ruler. They solemnly ratified the election by offering public sacrifices to God.

15. *peace-offerings.* Because it was also a national rejoicing over the successful campaign waged by the chosen king; see the first portion of this chapter, *v.* 1–13.

CHAPTER XII. SAMUEL'S FAREWELL ADDRESS

Samuel, though he was still to retain his authority as Prophet, now resigned his office as Judge, and in doing so delivers a Farewell Address. The aged Prophet challenges the assembled people to impeach his official integrity; upbraids them with unbelief and ingratitude in demanding a king; and ends by consoling the people that God will not abandon Israel for His great Name's sake.

2. *I am old and greyheaded.* Having aged prematurely in the service of Israel. He was then only about 50 years old.

my sons are with you. Not *over* you. Samuel had not placed them in positions for which he knew they were not fitted.

from my youth. Samuel's public life commenced from the time when as a child he had ministered to Eli in the Tabernacle; I Sam. I III.

3. *His anointed. i.e.* Saul, His anointed king.
to blind mine eyes. To Justice.

pressed? or of whose hand have I taken a ransom to blind mine eyes therewith? and I will restore it you.' 4. And they said: 'Thou hast not defrauded us, nor oppressed us, neither hast thou taken aught of any man's hand.' 5. And he said unto them: 'The LORD is witness against you, and His anointed is witness this day, that ye have not found aught in my hand.' And they said: 'He is witness.' ¶ 6. And Samuel said unto the people: 'It is the LORD that made Moses and Aaron, and that brought your fathers up out of the land of Egypt. 7. Now therefore stand still, that I may plead with you before the LORD concerning all the righteous acts of the LORD, which He did to you and to your fathers. 8. When Jacob was come into Egypt, then your fathers cried unto the LORD, and the LORD sent Moses and Aaron, who brought forth your fathers out of Egypt, and they were made to dwell in this place. 9. But they forgot the LORD their God, and He gave them over into the hand of Sisera, captain of the host of Hazor, and into the hand of the Philistines, and into the hand of the king of Moab, and they fought against them. 10. And they cried unto the LORD, and said: We have sinned, because we have forsaken the LORD, and have served the Baalim and the Ashtaroth; but now deliver us out of the hand of our enemies, and we will serve Thee. 11. And the LORD sent Jerubbaal, and Bedan, and Jephthah, and Samuel, and delivered you out of the hand of your enemies on every side, and ye dwelt in safety. 12. And when ye saw that Nahash the king of the children of Ammon came against you, ye said unto

וַחֲמוֹר מִי לָקַחְתִּי וְאֶת־מִי עָשַׁקְתִּי אֶת־מִי רַצּוֹתִי וּמִיַּד־
4 מִי לָקַחְתִּי כֹפֶר וְאַעְלִים עֵינַי בּוֹ וְאָשִׁיב לָכֶם׃ וַיֹּאמְרוּ
לֹא עֲשַׁקְתָּנוּ וְלֹא רַצּוֹתָנוּ וְלֹא־לָקַחְתָּ מִיַּד־אִישׁ מְאוּמָה׃
ה וַיֹּאמֶר אֲלֵיהֶם עֵד יְהוָה בָּכֶם וְעֵד מְשִׁיחוֹ הַיּוֹם הַזֶּה
6 כִּי לֹא מְצָאתֶם בְּיָדִי מְאוּמָה וַיֹּאמֶר עֵד׃ וַיֹּאמֶר שְׁמוּאֵל
אֶל־הָעָם יְהוָה אֲשֶׁר עָשָׂה אֶת־מֹשֶׁה וְאֶת־אַהֲרֹן וַאֲשֶׁר
7 הֶעֱלָה אֶת־אֲבוֹתֵיכֶם מֵאֶרֶץ מִצְרָיִם׃ וְעַתָּה הִתְיַצְּבוּ
וְאִשָּׁפְטָה אִתְּכֶם לִפְנֵי יְהוָה אֵת כָּל־צִדְקוֹת יְהוָה אֲשֶׁר־
8 עָשָׂה אִתְּכֶם וְאֶת־אֲבֹתֵיכֶם׃ כַּאֲשֶׁר־בָּא יַעֲקֹב מִצְרָיִם
וַיִּזְעֲקוּ אֲבֹתֵיכֶם אֶל־יְהוָה וַיִּשְׁלַח יְהוָה אֶת־מֹשֶׁה וְאֶת־
אַהֲרֹן וַיּוֹצִיאוּ אֶת־אֲבוֹתֵיכֶם מִמִּצְרַיִם וַיֹּשִׁבוּם בַּמָּקוֹם
9 הַזֶּה׃ וַיִּשְׁכְּחוּ אֶת־יְהוָה אֱלֹהֵיהֶם וַיִּמְכֹּר אֹתָם בְּיַד
סִיסְרָא שַׂר־צְבָא חָצוֹר וּבְיַד־פְּלִשְׁתִּים וּבְיַד מֶלֶךְ מוֹאָב
י וַיִּלָּחֲמוּ בָּם׃ וַיִּזְעֲקוּ אֶל־יְהוָה וַיֹּאמֶר חָטָאנוּ כִּי עָזַבְנוּ
אֶת־יְהוָה וַנַּעֲבֹד אֶת־הַבְּעָלִים וְאֶת־הָעַשְׁתָּרוֹת וְעַתָּה
11 הַצִּילֵנוּ מִיַּד אֹיְבֵינוּ וְנַעַבְדֶךָּ׃ וַיִּשְׁלַח יְהוָה אֶת־יְרֻבַּעַל
וְאֶת־בְּדָן וְאֶת־יִפְתָּח וְאֶת־שְׁמוּאֵל וַיַּצֵּל אֶתְכֶם מִיַּד
12 אֹיְבֵיכֶם מִסָּבִיב וַתֵּשְׁבוּ בֶּטַח׃ וַתִּרְאוּ כִּי נָחָשׁ מֶלֶךְ בְּנֵי־
עַמּוֹן בָּא עֲלֵיכֶם וַתֹּאמְרוּ לִי לֹא כִּי־מֶלֶךְ יִמְלֹךְ עָלֵינוּ

v. 5. ויאמרו סביר v. 10. ויאמרו ק'

5. *and they said.* The Heb. is in the singular, emphasizing the unanimity of the people's endorsement. Hence, the tradition that a Heavenly Voice, *Bath Kol*, uttered these words, 'He, the LORD, is witness to Samuel's purity in regard to all matters hidden from man, even as you are testifying to his purity in regard to known things.'

7–22. SAMUEL RECALLS GOD'S PAST MERCIES AND CHIDES THE PEOPLE

7. *plead with you. i.e.* that I may enter into judgment with you; or, 'rebuke you' (Rashi).

the righteous acts of the LORD. The victories of Israel, as also their reverses, were alike the *righteous acts* of the LORD (Altschul).

8. *your fathers cried.* Because the Egyptians oppressed them. The history is abbreviated.

9–11. Three typical oppressors and four deliverers of Israel during the period of the Judges are here named.

11. *Jerubbaal.* Gideon.

Bedan. Another name for Samson, *i.e. ben Dan*, son of the tribe of Dan (Targum, Rashi).

Jephthah. The mention of Jephthah's name alongside of Samuel's gave rise to the Rabbinic saying that even the meanest person invested with authority must be treated with the respect that would be accorded to the worthiest occupant of that office: יפתח בדורו כשמואל בדורו 'Jephthah in his generation is like Samuel in his generation.'

and Samuel. We would expect, 'and me,' as Samuel himself is speaking. But indirect personal reference is also met elsewhere in me: Nay, but a king shall reign over us; when the LORD your God was your king. 13. Now therefore behold the king whom ye have chosen, and whom ye have asked for; and, behold, the LORD hath set a king over you. 14. If ye will fear the LORD, and serve Him, and hearken unto His voice, and not rebel against the commandment of the LORD, and both ye and also the king that reigneth over you be followers of the LORD your God—; 15. but if ye will not hearken unto the voice of the LORD, but rebel against the commandment of the LORD, then shall the hand of the LORD be against you, and against your fathers. 16. Now therefore stand still and see this great thing, which the LORD will do before your eyes. 17. Is it not wheat harvest to-day? I will call unto the LORD, that He may send thunder and rain; and ye shall know and see that your wickedness is great, which ye have done in the sight of the LORD, in asking you a king.' 18. So Samuel called unto the LORD; and the LORD sent thunder and rain that day; and all the people greatly feared the LORD and Samuel. 19. And all the people said unto Samuel: 'Pray for thy servants unto the LORD thy God, that we die not; for we have added unto all our sins this evil, to ask us a king.' 20. And Samuel said unto the people: 'Fear not; ye have indeed done all this evil; yet turn not aside from following the LORD, but serve the LORD with all your heart; 21. and turn ye not aside; for then should ye go after vain things which cannot profit nor deliver, for they are vain. 22. For the LORD will not forsake His people for His great name's sake; because it hath pleased the LORD to make you a people unto Himself.

13 וַיהוָה אֱלֹהֵיכֶם מַלְכְּכֶם׃ וְעַתָּה הִנֵּה הַמֶּלֶךְ אֲשֶׁר
בְּחַרְתֶּם אֲשֶׁר שְׁאֶלְתֶּם וְהִנֵּה נָתַן יְהוָה עֲלֵיכֶם מֶלֶךְ׃
14 אִם־תִּירְאוּ אֶת־יְהוָה וַעֲבַדְתֶּם אֹתוֹ וּשְׁמַעְתֶּם בְּקֹלוֹ וְלֹא
תַמְרוּ אֶת־פִּי יְהוָה וִהְיִתֶם גַּם־אַתֶּם וְגַם־הַמֶּלֶךְ אֲשֶׁר־
טו מָלַךְ עֲלֵיכֶם אַחַר יְהוָה אֱלֹהֵיכֶם׃ וְאִם־לֹא תִשְׁמְעוּ בְּקוֹל
יְהוָה וּמְרִיתֶם אֶת־פִּי יְהוָה וְהָיְתָה יַד־יְהוָה בָּכֶם
16 וּבַאֲבֹתֵיכֶם׃ גַּם־עַתָּה הִתְיַצְּבוּ וּרְאוּ אֶת־הַדָּבָר הַגָּדוֹל
17 הַזֶּה אֲשֶׁר יְהוָה עֹשֶׂה לְעֵינֵיכֶם׃ הֲלוֹא קְצִיר־חִטִּים
הַיּוֹם אֶקְרָא אֶל־יְהוָה וְיִתֵּן קֹלוֹת וּמָטָר וּדְעוּ וּרְאוּ כִּי־
רָעַתְכֶם רַבָּה אֲשֶׁר עֲשִׂיתֶם בְּעֵינֵי יְהוָה לִשְׁאוֹל לָכֶם
18 מֶלֶךְ׃ וַיִּקְרָא שְׁמוּאֵל אֶל־יְהוָה וַיִּתֵּן יְהוָה קֹלֹת וּמָטָר
בַּיּוֹם הַהוּא וַיִּירָא כָל־הָעָם מְאֹד אֶת־יְהוָה וְאֶת־שְׁמוּאֵל׃
19 וַיֹּאמְרוּ כָל־הָעָם אֶל־שְׁמוּאֵל הִתְפַּלֵּל בְּעַד־עֲבָדֶיךָ אֶל־
יְהוָה אֱלֹהֶיךָ וְאַל־נָמוּת כִּי־יָסַפְנוּ עַל־כָּל־חַטֹּאתֵינוּ רָעָה
כ לִשְׁאֹל לָנוּ מֶלֶךְ׃ וַיֹּאמֶר שְׁמוּאֵל אֶל־הָעָם אַל־תִּירָאוּ
אַתֶּם עֲשִׂיתֶם אֵת כָּל־הָרָעָה הַזֹּאת אַךְ אַל־תָּסוּרוּ מֵאַחֲרֵי
21 יְהוָה וַעֲבַדְתֶּם אֶת־יְהוָה בְּכָל־לְבַבְכֶם׃ וְלֹא תָּסוּרוּ כִּי ׀
אַחֲרֵי הַתֹּהוּ אֲשֶׁר לֹא־יוֹעִילוּ וְלֹא יַצִּילוּ כִּי־תֹהוּ הֵמָּה׃
22 כִּי לֹא־יִטֹּשׁ יְהוָה אֶת־עַמּוֹ בַּעֲבוּר שְׁמוֹ הַגָּדוֹל כִּי הוֹאִיל
יְהוָה לַעֲשׂוֹת אֶתְכֶם לוֹ לְעָם׃

Scripture: cf. Gen. IV, 23 ('Ye wives of Lamech, hear my voice'). Furthermore, his term of office being ended, Samuel is standing as it were outside the era of the Judges and reviews it as a whole.

14. *and also the king.* King and people alike must acknowledge the sovereignty of God and His Law.

15. *and against your fathers.* 'Your leaders, or kings' (Rashi, Kimchi).

17. *is it not wheat harvest.* The time of wheat harvest was May and June. From early spring till late autumn no rain falls in Palestine. During the summer months 'a cloud seldom passes over the sky, and a thunderstorm is a miracle' (G. A. Smith).

20. *done all this evil.* They had sinned because their action reflected the belief that they could trust only in a visible king, whereas their trust should be complete in God. The danger was that now they would put their trust still less in God.

21–22. Yet although you have sinned, sin no more.

21. *vain things.* The idols of the heathens. More generally every 'falling away' or 'turning aside' from God is not merely a negative but a positive submission to אלילים; *i.e.* vain and worthless ideas and pursuits that have neither substance nor worth.

22. *His great name's sake.* That through Israel, God's attributes and nature (expressed in His Name) be understood and His sovereignty acknowledged by all mankind.

19 CHAPTER XIX

1. And the LORD spoke unto Moses and unto Aaron, saying: ¶ 2. This is the statute of the law which the LORD hath commanded, saying: Speak unto the children of Israel, that they bring thee a red heifer, faultless, wherein is no blemish, and upon which never came yoke. 3. And ye shall give her unto Eleazar the priest, and she shall be brought forth without the camp, and

CAP. XIX. יט — יט

פ פ לט 39

א 2 וַיְדַבֵּר יְהוָה אֶל־מֹשֶׁה וְאֶל־אַהֲרֹן לֵאמֹר׃ זֹאת חֻקַּת
הַתּוֹרָה אֲשֶׁר־צִוָּה יְהוָה לֵאמֹר דַּבֵּר ׀ אֶל־בְּנֵי יִשְׂרָאֵל
וְיִקְחוּ אֵלֶיךָ פָרָה אֲדֻמָּה תְּמִימָה אֲשֶׁר אֵין־בָּהּ מוּם

VI. CHUKKAS

(CHAPTERS XIX–XXII, 1)

CHAPTER XIX. THE RED HEIFER

The law set forth in this chapter belongs to the group of commandments dealt with in Lev. XII–XV; see the introductory note, 'Laws of Purification,' p. 459.

It provides for the removal of defilement resulting from contact with the dead. A red heifer, free from blemish and one that had not yet been broken to the yoke, was to be slain outside the camp. It was then to be burned, cedar-wood, hyssop, and scarlet being cast upon the pyre. The gathered ashes, dissolved in fresh water, were to be sprinkled on those who had become contaminated through contact with a dead body.

This ordinance is the most mysterious rite in Scripture, the strange features of which are duly enumerated by the Rabbis. Thus, its aim was to purify the defiled, and yet it defiled all those who were in any way connected with the preparation of the ashes and water of purification. 'It purifies the impure, and at the same time renders impure the pure!' So inscrutable was its nature—they said—that even King Solomon in his wisdom despaired of learning the secret meaning of the Red Heifer regulations. To a high-placed Roman questioner, who expressed his amazement at the procedure in connection with the Red Heifer, Johanan ben Zakkai replied by referring him to a Pagan analogy: 'Just as a person afflicted by melancholy or possessed of an "evil spirit" is freed of his disease by taking certain medicaments or by the burning of certain roots, in the same manner the ashes of the Red Heifer, prepared in the prescribed way and dissolved in water, drive away the "unclean spirit" of defilement resulting from contact with the dead.' The Roman was satisfied with the answer, and went his way. Thereupon the pupils of Johanan said to him: 'That man's attack thou hast warded off with a broken reed, but what answer hast thou for *us*?' 'By your lives,' said the Master, 'the dead man doth not make impure, niether do the ashes dissolved in water make pure: but the law concerning the Red Heifer is a decree of the All-holy, Whose reasons for issuing that decree it behoves not mortals to question.' In brief, the attitude of Judaism as to the meaning of this law is not merely a confession of ignorance, but the realization that we shall never know why such defilement should be removed in that specified manner ('ignorabimus').

Nevertheless there have been many attempts at explanation, at any rate of symbolization, of this law both by Jews and non-Jews. One of them is, The majestic cedar of Lebanon represents pride, and hyssop represents humility; uncleanness and sin and death are all associated ideas: the ceremony, therefore, is a powerful object-lesson, teaching the eternal truth that a holy God can be served only by a holy People.

2. *statute of the law.* Heb. חקת התורה. The word 'statute' is used in connection with all laws and ordinances whose reason is not disclosed to us; see p. 95. 'Because Satan and the heathens taunt Israel with this and similar commandments, Scripture uses in this connection the term חקה "statute", implying, "It is a decree from before Me, and you are not at liberty to cavil at My decrees" ' (Rashi). This law served the generations in Israel as a pure instance of absolute obedience to the decrees of God.

red heifer. Heb. *parah adumah*; a young cow, not a calf or a full-grown cow. The early Jewish conception was that the sacrifice of the red heifer was an expiatory rite to atone for the sin of the Golden Calf תבא פרה ותכפר על מעשה העגל.

faultless. Faultlessly red; two hairs of another colour on its body were sufficient to disqualify it.

no blemish. Such as blindness and others referred to in Lev. XXII, 22–4, as rendering an animal unfit for sacrifice.

upon which never came yoke. A 'virgin' animal in the sense of never having been used for secular purposes.

3. *unto Eleazar.* 'As Aaron had made the Golden Calf, this rite was not to be carried out by him, because the prosecuting counsel cannot become the defending counsel'; *i.e.* Aaron who had caused the sin was not the fitting person

3 אֲשֶׁר לֹא־עָלָה עָלֶיהָ עֹל׃ וּנְתַתֶּם אֹתָהּ אֶל־אֶלְעָזָר הַכֹּהֵן
4 וְהוֹצִיא אֹתָהּ אֶל־מִחוּץ לַמַּחֲנֶה וְשָׁחַט אֹתָהּ לְפָנָיו׃ וְלָקַח
אֶלְעָזָר הַכֹּהֵן מִדָּמָהּ בְּאֶצְבָּעוֹ וְהִזָּה אֶל־נֹכַח פְּנֵי אֹהֶל־
ה מוֹעֵד מִדָּמָהּ שֶׁבַע פְּעָמִים׃ וְשָׂרַף אֶת־הַפָּרָה לְעֵינָיו
6 אֶת־עֹרָהּ וְאֶת־בְּשָׂרָהּ וְאֶת־דָּמָהּ עַל־פִּרְשָׁהּ יִשְׂרֹף׃ וְלָקַח
הַכֹּהֵן עֵץ אֶרֶז וְאֵזוֹב וּשְׁנִי תוֹלָעַת וְהִשְׁלִיךְ אֶל־תּוֹךְ
7 שְׂרֵפַת הַפָּרָה׃ וְכִבֶּס בְּגָדָיו הַכֹּהֵן וְרָחַץ בְּשָׂרוֹ בַּמַּיִם
8 וְאַחַר יָבֹא אֶל־הַמַּחֲנֶה וְטָמֵא הַכֹּהֵן עַד־הָעָרֶב׃ וְהַשֹּׂרֵף
אֹתָהּ יְכַבֵּס בְּגָדָיו בַּמַּיִם וְרָחַץ בְּשָׂרוֹ בַּמָּיִם וְטָמֵא עַד־
9 הָעָרֶב׃ וְאָסַף ׀ אִישׁ טָהוֹר אֵת אֵפֶר הַפָּרָה וְהִנִּיחַ
מִחוּץ לַמַּחֲנֶה בְּמָקוֹם טָהוֹר וְהָיְתָה לַעֲדַת בְּנֵי־יִשְׂרָאֵל
י לְמִשְׁמֶרֶת לְמֵי נִדָּה חַטָּאת הִוא׃ וְכִבֶּס הָאֹסֵף אֶת־אֵפֶר
הַפָּרָה אֶת־בְּגָדָיו וְטָמֵא עַד־הָעָרֶב וְהָיְתָה לִבְנֵי יִשְׂרָאֵל
11 וְלַגֵּר הַגָּר בְּתוֹכָם לְחֻקַּת עוֹלָם׃ הַנֹּגֵעַ בְּמֵת לְכָל־נֶפֶשׁ

she shall be slain before his face. 4. And Eleazar the priest shall take of her blood with his finger, and sprinkle of her blood toward the front of the tent of meeting seven times. 5. And the heifer shall be burnt in his sight; her skin, and her flesh, and her blood, with her dung, shall be burnt. 6. And the priest shall take cedar-wood, and hyssop, and scarlet, and cast it into the midst of the burning of the heifer. 7. Then the priest shall wash his clothes, and he shall bathe his flesh in water, and afterward he may come into the camp, and the priest shall be unclean until the even. 8. And he that burneth her shall wash his clothes in water, and bathe his flesh in water, and shall be unclean until the even. 9. And a man that is clean shall gather up the ashes of the heifer, and lay them up without the camp in a clean place, and it shall be kept for the congregation of the children of Israel for a water of sprinkling; it is a purification from sin. 10. And he that gathereth the ashes of the heifer shall wash his clothes, and be unclean until the even; and it shall be unto the children of Israel, and unto the stranger that sojourneth among them, for a statute for ever. 11. He that toucheth the dead, even any man's dead body, shall be unclean seven days;

to atone for it (Moses Haddarshan, quoted by Rashi). In later times, it was usually—though by no means invariably—the High Priests who officiated on these occasions.

she shall be brought forth. The Heb. is idiomatic, and is equivalent to 'one shall bring her forth'; probably by the person ordered to slaughter her. Such person might be a layman.

4. *toward . . . tent of meeting.* An indication that the blood of the sacrifice was dedicated to the Sanctuary, and thereby acquired its atoning and purifying power.

seven times. As in the case of all sin-offerings; Lev. IV, 6, 17.

6. *cedar wood, and hyssop, and scarlet.* These were also employed in the purgation ritual of the lepers; Lev. XIV, 4. The scarlet may have been symbolic of sin (Isa. I, 18), just as the redness of the heifer.

7. *unclean until the even.* Which implied exclusion from the camp until sunset, and prohibition to partake of the meats of the holy sacrifices.

9. *it shall be kept. i.e.* the ashes.

for a water of sprinkling. Many commentators take its literal meaning to be, 'water for the removal of impurity.' That the ashes were mixed with water is seen from *v.* 17.

purification from sin. Something that removes sin. The ashes of the heifer shall be a medium for the purification from sin; cf. 'water of purification', in VIII, 7.

10. *shall . . . be unclean.* Everyone, priest or layman, who had something to do with the preparation of this water of purification became unclean.

A word must be said on the paradox of the *parah adumah* מטהרת את הטמאים ומטמא את הטהורים, *i.e.* the simultaneous possession of sanctification and defilement. There have been great institutions and movements, in both Jewish and general history, that have sanctified others, and yet have at the same time tended to defile those that created or directed those institutions and movements. The very men who helped others to self-sacrifice and holiness, not infrequently themselves became hard and self-centred, hating and hateful; elevating others, and themselves sinking into inhumanity, impurity, and unholiness. It is a real, if disturbing, fact in the spiritual life of man.

the stranger that sojourneth among them. i.e. the proselyte who assumes the religious duties of Israel.

11–13. The Specific Purpose of the Water for Purification

11. *even any man.* Israelite or non-Israelite.

12 אָדָם וְטָמֵא שִׁבְעַת יָמִים׃ הוּא יִתְחַטָּא־בוֹ בַּיּוֹם הַשְּׁלִישִׁי
וּבַיּוֹם הַשְּׁבִיעִי יִטְהָר וְאִם־לֹא יִתְחַטָּא בַּיּוֹם הַשְּׁלִישִׁי
13 וּבַיּוֹם הַשְּׁבִיעִי לֹא יִטְהָר׃ כָּל־הַנֹּגֵעַ בְּמֵת בְּנֶפֶשׁ הָאָדָם
אֲשֶׁר־יָמוּת וְלֹא יִתְחַטָּא אֶת־מִשְׁכַּן יְהוָה טִמֵּא וְנִכְרְתָה
הַנֶּפֶשׁ הַהִוא מִיִּשְׂרָאֵל כִּי מֵי נִדָּה לֹא־זֹרַק עָלָיו טָמֵא
14 יִהְיֶה עוֹד טֻמְאָתוֹ בוֹ׃ זֹאת הַתּוֹרָה אָדָם כִּי־יָמוּת בְּאֹהֶל
כָּל־הַבָּא אֶל־הָאֹהֶל וְכָל־אֲשֶׁר בָּאֹהֶל יִטְמָא שִׁבְעַת
טו יָמִים׃ וְכֹל כְּלִי פָתוּחַ אֲשֶׁר אֵין־צָמִיד פָּתִיל עָלָיו טָמֵא
16 הוּא׃ וְכֹל אֲשֶׁר־יִגַּע עַל־פְּנֵי הַשָּׂדֶה בַּחֲלַל־חֶרֶב אוֹ בְמֵת
17 אוֹ־בְעֶצֶם אָדָם אוֹ בְקָבֶר יִטְמָא שִׁבְעַת יָמִים׃ וְלָקְחוּ
לַטָּמֵא מֵעֲפַר שְׂרֵפַת הַחַטָּאת וְנָתַן עָלָיו מַיִם חַיִּים אֶל־
שני
18 כֶּלִי׃ וְלָקַח אֵזוֹב וְטָבַל בַּמַּיִם אִישׁ טָהוֹר וְהִזָּה עַל־הָאֹהֶל
וְעַל־כָּל־הַכֵּלִים וְעַל־הַנְּפָשׁוֹת אֲשֶׁר הָיוּ־שָׁם וְעַל־הַנֹּגֵעַ
19 בַּעֶצֶם אוֹ בֶחָלָל אוֹ בַמֵּת אוֹ בַקָּבֶר׃ וְהִזָּה הַטָּהֹר עַל־
הַטָּמֵא בַּיּוֹם הַשְּׁלִישִׁי וּבַיּוֹם הַשְּׁבִיעִי וְחִטְּאוֹ בַּיּוֹם הַשְּׁבִיעִי
כ וְכִבֶּס בְּגָדָיו וְרָחַץ בַּמַּיִם וְטָהֵר בָּעָרֶב׃ וְאִישׁ אֲשֶׁר־יִטְמָא
וְלֹא יִתְחַטָּא וְנִכְרְתָה הַנֶּפֶשׁ הַהִוא מִתּוֹךְ הַקָּהָל כִּי אֶת־

12. the same shall purify himself therewith on the third day and on the seventh day, and he shall be clean; but if he purify not himself the third day and the seventh day, he shall not be clean. 13. Whosoever toucheth the dead, even the body of any man that is dead, and purifieth not himself—he hath defiled the tabernacle of the LORD—that soul shall be cut off from Israel; because the water of sprinkling was not dashed against him, he shall be unclean; his uncleanness is yet upon him. 14. This is the law: when a man dieth in a tent, every one that cometh into the tent, and every thing that is in the tent, shall be unclean seven days. 15. And every open vessel, which hath no covering close-bound upon it, is unclean. 16. And whosoever in the open field toucheth one that is slain with a sword, or one that dieth of himself, or a bone of a man, or a grave, shall be unclean seven days. 17. And for the unclean they shall take of the ashes of the burning of the purification from sin, and running water shall be put thereto in a vessel.*ii. 18. And a clean person shall take hyssop, and dip it in the water, and sprinkle it upon the tent, and upon all the vessels, and upon the persons that were there, and upon him that touched the bone, or the slain, or the dead, or the grave. 19. And the clean person shall sprinkle upon the unclean on the third day, and on the seventh day; and on the seventh day he shall purify him; and he shall wash his clothes, and bathe himself in water, and shall be clean at even. 20. But the man that shall be unclean, and shall not purify himself, that soul shall be cut off from the midst of the assembly, because he hath

12. *shall purify himself.* lit. 'shall remove the sin from himself.'
therewith. With the ashes.

13. *of any man that is dead.* Excluding the dead body of a beast.
the tabernacle. Here used in the larger sense to denote the Camp of Israel; cf. *v.* 3.
cut off. By Divine agency.

14–22. MODE OF PURIFICATION

14. *in a tent.* Here used generally to denote any place wherein people live, because the Israelites at the time dwelt in tents rather than in houses (Ibn Ezra). The same law applies to any dead body that is brought *into* a tent.
everything. Household utensils, wearing apparel, as well as the people who are in the tent at the time.
that cometh into the tent. i.e. whilst the dead body is inside it. Contact with the dead is not required for defilement. Mere presence under the same roof is sufficient.
unclean seven days. Even though these persons or things had no actual contact with the corpse.

15. *no covering.* Not hermetically sealed with a cover.

16. *in the open field.* If one comes up against a dead body or a human bone or grave in the open, that is not under cover, he contracts defilement only after actual contact with any of these.

17. *of the purification from sin.* As in *v.* 9.
running water. lit. 'living water.' According to the Talmud, this water from a running stream had first to be put in a vessel and then the ashes mixed in.

defiled the sanctuary of the LORD; the water of sprinkling hath not been dashed against him: he is unclean. 21. And it shall be a perpetual statute unto them; and he that sprinkleth the water of sprinkling shall wash his clothes; and he that toucheth the water of sprinkling shall be unclean until even. 22. And whatsoever the unclean person toucheth shall be unclean; and the soul that toucheth him shall be unclean until even.

21 מִקְדַּשׁ יְהוָה טִמֵּא מֵי נִדָּה לֹא־זֹרַק עָלָיו טָמֵא הוּא׃ וְהָיְתָה
לָהֶם לְחֻקַּת עוֹלָם וּמַזֵּה מֵי־הַנִּדָּה יְכַבֵּס בְּגָדָיו וְהַנֹּגֵעַ בְּמֵי
22 הַנִּדָּה יִטְמָא עַד־הָעָרֶב׃ וְכֹל אֲשֶׁר־יִגַּע־בּוֹ הַטָּמֵא יִטְמָא
וְהַנֶּפֶשׁ הַנֹּגַעַת תִּטְמָא עַד־הָעָרֶב׃ פ

20 CHAPTER XX

CAP. XX. כ

1. And the children of Israel, even the whole congregation, came into the wilder-

א וַיָּבֹאוּ בְנֵי־יִשְׂרָאֵל כָּל־הָעֵדָה מִדְבַּר־צִן בַּחֹדֶשׁ הָרִאשׁוֹן

כ' v. 1. ב' טעמים

22. *the unclean person.* Who has had contact with a corpse or grave as mentioned in *v.* 18.

that toucheth him. i.e. the person that has any contact with the person mentioned in the foregoing clause. This is a departure from the RV, which has 'that toucheth it'. According to the Rabbis, contact with a corpse is the primary source of ritual impurity (אבי אבות הטומאה). He that has contact with the person thus contaminated becomes a secondary source of impurity (אב הטומאה), which in diminishing intensity is transmitted to food and liquids.

until even. When he becomes 'clean', having bathed his body.

According to the Mishna, the ceremonial of the burning of a Red Heifer was enacted seven times; once by Moses, once by Ezra, and five times after Ezra. It naturally disappeared from Jewish life with the Destruction of the Temple.

Chapter XIX forms the reading for Sabbath Parah, one of the so-called four Extraordinary Sabbaths, on the last Sabbath but one in Adar; or on the last, if the first day of Nisan falls on a Saturday. The reading is to commemorate the purification of the unclean by sprinkling them with the 'water of separation', so that they may be enabled to bring the Passover sacrifice in a state of purity. The Haftorah on Sabbath Parah is Ezek. XXXVI, 16–38, see p. 961.

CHAPTER XX

This chapter is, chronologically, the sequel of XIV, where it is related that the Israelites were condemned to wander forty years, and were foiled in an unauthorized attempt to enter Canaan from the south (XIV, 40–5). The events narrated in the present chapter belong to the last, the fortieth, year of the wanderings. As Ibn Ezra correctly points out, the history of the preceding thirty-eight years is a blank page in the Book of Numbers. And the reason is not far to seek. The men of that generation had been found wanting, and condemned to a dying life in the wilderness. Their story was, therefore, of no further spiritual value to the Israel of the future. And yet, 'the ages of silence in the history of the Hebrews were generally ages of growth. These thirty-eight almost uneventful years are one of those numerous gaps in the nation's history, during which real progress was made. From them Israel emerged transformed from a fugitive body of slaves into a nation; and it is an evidence of the greatness of the character of Moses, that he knew how to wait in silence, till his people were ready to advance to conquest in obedience to God's command' (Foakes-Jackson).

XX, 1. DEATH OF MIRIAM

1. *into the wilderness of Zin.* This, the third and last stage of the journey from Sinai to the Promised Land, started at Kadesh, was continued round the land of Edom (XXI, 4), and ended at the heights of Pisgah in the country of Moab, near the Dead Sea and the fords of the Jordan.

in the first month. Of the fortieth year of wandering.

Kadesh. See on XIII, 26.

Miriam died there. She died towards the end of the desert wanderings, and like her brothers did not reach the Promised Land. She is spoken of as one of the three good leaders of Israel (פרנסים טובים); and to her merit was due the Well, which according to the legend, accompanied the children of Israel as long as she lived.

2–23. STRIKING OF THE ROCK. SIN OF MOSES AND AARON

Over and over again Scripture brings out, on the one hand, the fickleness of the people—their murmurings, mutinies, vehement repentance, and woeful self-assertion; and, on the other ness of Zin in the first month; and the people abode in Kadesh; and Miriam died there, and was buried there. 2. And there was no water for the congregation; and they assembled themselves together against Moses and against Aaron. 3. And the people strove with Moses, and spoke, saying: 'Would that we had perished when our brethren perished before the LORD! 4. And why have ye brought the assembly of the LORD into this wilderness, to die there, we and our cattle? 5. And wherefore have ye made us to come up out of Egypt, to bring us in unto this evil place? it is no place of seed, or of figs, or of vines, or of pomegranates; neither is there any water to drink.' 6. And Moses and Aaron went from the presence of the assembly unto the door of the tent of meeting, and fell upon their faces; and the glory of the LORD appeared unto them.*iii (**ii). 7. And the LORD spoke unto Moses, saying: 8. 'Take the rod, and assemble the congregation, thou, and Aaron thy brother, and speak ye unto the rock before their eyes, that it give forth its water; and thou shalt bring forth to them water out of the rock; so thou shalt give the congregation and their cattle drink.' 9. And Moses took the rod from before the LORD, as He commanded him. 10. And Moses and Aaron gathered the assembly together before the rock, and he said unto them: 'Hear now, ye rebels;

2 וַיֵּשֶׁב הָעָם בְּקָדֵשׁ וַתָּמָת שָׁם מִרְיָם וַתִּקָּבֵר שָׁם׃ וְלֹא־
3 הָיָה מַיִם לָעֵדָה וַיִּקָּהֲלוּ עַל־מֹשֶׁה וְעַל־אַהֲרֹן׃ וַיָּרֶב
הָעָם עִם־מֹשֶׁה וַיֹּאמְרוּ לֵאמֹר וְלוּ גָוַעְנוּ בִּגְוַע אַחֵינוּ לִפְנֵי
4 יְהוָה׃ וְלָמָה הֲבֵאתֶם אֶת־קְהַל יְהוָה אֶל־הַמִּדְבָּר הַזֶּה
ה לָמוּת שָׁם אֲנַחְנוּ וּבְעִירֵנוּ׃ וְלָמָה הֶעֱלִיתֻנוּ מִמִּצְרַיִם
לְהָבִיא אֹתָנוּ אֶל־הַמָּקוֹם הָרָע הַזֶּה לֹא ׀ מְקוֹם זֶרַע וּתְאֵנָה
6 וְגֶפֶן וְרִמּוֹן וּמַיִם אַיִן לִשְׁתּוֹת׃ וַיָּבֹא מֹשֶׁה וְאַהֲרֹן מִפְּנֵי
הַקָּהָל אֶל־פֶּתַח אֹהֶל מוֹעֵד וַיִּפְּלוּ עַל־פְּנֵיהֶם וַיֵּרָא כְבוֹד־
יְהוָה אֲלֵיהֶם׃ * פ שלישי (שני כשהן מחוב')
7 8 וַיְדַבֵּר יְהוָה אֶל־מֹשֶׁה לֵּאמֹר׃ קַח אֶת־הַמַּטֶּה וְהַקְהֵל
אֶת־הָעֵדָה אַתָּה וְאַהֲרֹן אָחִיךָ וְדִבַּרְתֶּם אֶל־הַסֶּלַע
לְעֵינֵיהֶם וְנָתַן מֵימָיו וְהוֹצֵאתָ לָהֶם מַיִם מִן־הַסֶּלַע וְהִשְׁקִיתָ
9 אֶת־הָעֵדָה וְאֶת־בְּעִירָם׃ וַיִּקַּח מֹשֶׁה אֶת־הַמַּטֶּה מִלִּפְנֵי
י יְהוָה כַּאֲשֶׁר צִוָּהוּ׃ וַיַּקְהִלוּ מֹשֶׁה וְאַהֲרֹן אֶת־הַקָּהָל
אֶל־פְּנֵי הַסָּלַע וַיֹּאמֶר לָהֶם שִׁמְעוּ־נָא הַמֹּרִים הֲמִן־הַסֶּלַע

hand, the marvellous constancy of Moses—his humility, faithfulness, generosity, and his sublime patience. Once only was his mighty spirit unable to stand the strain. The meaning of 'ye believed not in Me' (*v.* 12) does not make it quite clear whether the sin was a momentary presumptuousness, or disobedience to a Divine command. It is but a single blot in his career, and in any other man would have been unnoticed. 'Judaism teaches that the greater the man, the stricter the standard by which he is judged and the greater the consequent guilt and punishment, if there is a falling away from that standard' (S. R. Hirsch). For this sin, recorded in this chapter, Moses forfeits his right to enter the Promised Land.

3. *when our brethren perished.* In the revolt of Korah, or at other occasions of 'murmuring'.

4. *and our cattle.* ' "A righteous man regardeth the life of his beast"; and the fact that these people, so near death, still considered the sufferings of their beasts, shows that they were, notwithstanding their attitude towards Moses and Aaron, really pious men. And in truth God did not take amiss their words against Moses and Aaron, for God holds no one responsible for words uttered in distress' (Midrash).

6. *went from the presence of the assembly.* Abarbanel and other commentators understand this in the sense of *fleeing* from before the assembly, and see in this action the lack of faith for which Moses and Aaron were condemned.

8. *take the rod.* With which the miracles had been wrought in Egypt and the rock at Rephidim had been smitten, when likewise the people strove with Moses; Exod. XVII, 4 ('what shall I do unto this people? They be almost ready to stone me').

unto the rock. i.e. the first rock in front of them, and standing in their sight (Nachmanides).

9. *took . . . the LORD.* It had been deposited in the Tabernacle.

10. *ye rebels.* Heb. *morim;* the Midrash connects it with the Greek word for 'fools', and also with the Heb. word for 'teacher', and renders it, 'Hear now, ye who presume to teach your teachers'; *i.e.* ye who imagine yourselves to be wiser than your leaders! 'This impatience with the people was considered reprehensible in Divinely appointed leaders' (Maimonides).

shall we bring you forth. i.e. can we bring forth water out of this rock? In that moment of irritation and gloom, Moses gives expression to doubt in front of the masses as to the fulfilment of God's promise.

11 הַזֶּה נוֹצִיא לָכֶם מָיִם׃ וַיָּרֶם מֹשֶׁה אֶת־יָדוֹ וַיַּךְ אֶת־הַסֶּלַע
בְּמַטֵּהוּ פַּעֲמָיִם וַיֵּצְאוּ מַיִם רַבִּים וַתֵּשְׁתְּ הָעֵדָה וּבְעִירָם׃ ס
12 וַיֹּאמֶר יְהוָה אֶל־מֹשֶׁה וְאֶל־אַהֲרֹן יַעַן לֹא־הֶאֱמַנְתֶּם בִּי
לְהַקְדִּישֵׁנִי לְעֵינֵי בְּנֵי יִשְׂרָאֵל לָכֵן לֹא תָבִיאוּ אֶת־הַקָּהָל
13 הַזֶּה אֶל־הָאָרֶץ אֲשֶׁר־נָתַתִּי לָהֶם׃ הֵמָּה מֵי מְרִיבָה אֲשֶׁר־
רביעי
14 רָבוּ בְנֵי־יִשְׂרָאֵל אֶת־יְהוָה וַיִּקָּדֵשׁ בָּם׃ * ס וַיִּשְׁלַח
מֹשֶׁה מַלְאָכִים מִקָּדֵשׁ אֶל־מֶלֶךְ אֱדוֹם כֹּה אָמַר אָחִיךָ
יִשְׂרָאֵל אַתָּה יָדַעְתָּ אֵת כָּל־הַתְּלָאָה אֲשֶׁר מְצָאָתְנוּ׃
טו וַיֵּרְדוּ אֲבֹתֵינוּ מִצְרַיְמָה וַנֵּשֶׁב בְּמִצְרַיִם יָמִים רַבִּים
16 וַיָּרֵעוּ לָנוּ מִצְרַיִם וְלַאֲבֹתֵינוּ׃ וַנִּצְעַק אֶל־יְהוָה וַיִּשְׁמַע קֹלֵנוּ
וַיִּשְׁלַח מַלְאָךְ וַיֹּצִאֵנוּ מִמִּצְרָיִם וְהִנֵּה אֲנַחְנוּ בְקָדֵשׁ עִיר קְצֵה
17 גְבוּלֶךָ׃ נַעְבְּרָה־נָּא בְאַרְצֶךָ לֹא נַעֲבֹר בְּשָׂדֶה וּבְכֶרֶם וְלֹא
נִשְׁתֶּה מֵי בְאֵר דֶּרֶךְ הַמֶּלֶךְ נֵלֵךְ לֹא נִטֶּה יָמִין וּשְׂמֹאול

v. 17. מלא ו'

are we to bring you forth water out of this rock?' 11. And Moses lifted up his hand, and smote the rock with his rod twice; and water came forth abundantly, and the congregation drank, and their cattle. 12. And the LORD said unto Moses and Aaron: 'Because ye believed not in Me, to sanctify Me in the eyes of the children of Israel, therefore ye shall not bring this assembly into the land which I have given them.' 13. These are the waters of [1]Meribah, where the children of Israel strove with the LORD, and He was sanctified in them.*iv. ¶ 14. And Moses sent messengers from Kadesh unto the king of Edom: 'Thus saith thy brother Israel: Thou knowest all the travail that hath befallen us; 15. how our fathers went down into Egypt, and we dwelt in Egypt a long time; and the Egyptians dealt ill with us, and our fathers; 16. and when we cried unto the LORD, He heard our voice, and sent an angel, and brought us forth out of Egypt; and, behold, we are in Kadesh, a city in the uttermost of thy border. 17. Let us pass, I pray thee, through thy land; we will not pass through field or through vineyard, neither will we drink of the

[1] That is, *Strife*.

11. *smote the rock.* Carried away by anger, Moses still further forgot himself, and instead of speaking to the rock, as he had been commanded, he struck it twice. Had he merely spoken to the rock, the miracle would have been undeniable, and God's Name would then have been sanctified in the eyes of the unbelieving multitude.

12. *because . . . in the eyes of the children of Israel.* In what did the offence really consist for which Moses and Aaron were excluded from the Promised Land? Some commentators hold that Scripture intentionally does not specify the sin of Moses: his sin, like his grave, was to remain unknown to posterity. Such, however, is not the opinion of the Rabbis, who maintain that this sin is sufficiently indicated in *v.* 10 and 11. ' "Thou hast decreed"—said Moses—"that I die in the desert like the generation of the desert that angered Thee. I implore Thee, write in Thy Torah wherefore I have been thus punished, so that future generations may not say I had been like the generation of the desert." God granted his wish, and in several passages, Scripture sets forth the offence for which Moses was not to enter the Promised Land' (Midrash).

13. *waters of Meribah. i.e.* the waters of strife. There is a similar use of the word for a similar occasion in Exod. XVII, 7. To distinguish the two the later occurrence is frequently known as 'Meribath-Kadesh'.

was sanctified in them. God vindicated His Name by His giving water to the people, and by allowing justice to take its course, without respect of persons, in punishing Moses and Aaron (Talmud); cf. Lev. x, 3.

14–21. KING OF EDOM REFUSES PERMISSION TO PASS THROUGH HIS LAND

The Israelites, having failed to enter Canaan from the south, must now seek to enter it by a roundabout way from the east. The refusal of the king of Edom forced the Israelites to take a still more circuitous route round the southern portion of Edom. The journey was a terrible one.

14. *thy brother Israel. i.e.* thy kinsman Israel. The Edomites were descendants of Esau, the twin brother of Jacob; Gen. xxv, 30.

all the travail. lit. 'the weariness.' The sufferings which the Israelites had undergone should have filled the Edomites with brotherly sympathy, and induced them to help their kinsfolk. The unnatural hostility of Edom towards Israel at a later period is the subject of the Book of Obadiah; see p. 137.

16. *an angel.* Here in the literal sense of 'messenger'. The reference is to Moses, the God-sent liberator and guide.

17. *king's highway.* Better, *the king's way.* The public high road made for the king and his armies.

18 עד אשר־נעבר גבלך׃ ויאמר אליו אדום לא תעבר
19 בי פן־בחרב אצא לקראתך׃ ויאמרו אליו בני־ישראל
במסלה נעלה ואם־מימיך נשתה אני ומקני ונתתי מכרם
כ רק אין־דבר ברגלי אעברה׃ ויאמר לא תעבר ויצא
21 אדום לקראתו בעם כבד וביד חזקה׃ וימאן ׀ אדום נתן
חמישי (שלישי כשהן מחוב׳) את־ישראל עבר בגבלו ויט ישראל מעליו׃ פ
22 ויסעו מקדש ויבאו בני־ישראל כל־העדה הר ההר׃
23 ויאמר יהוה אל־משה ואל־אהרן בהר ההר על־גבול
24 ארץ־אדום לאמר׃ יאסף אהרן אל־עמיו כי לא יבא אל־
הארץ אשר נתתי לבני ישראל על אשר־מריתם את־פי
כה למי מריבה׃ קח את־אהרן ואת־אלעזר בנו והעל אתם
26 הר ההר׃ והפשט את־אהרן את־בגדיו והלבשתם את־
27 אלעזר בנו ואהרן יאסף ומת שם׃ ויעש משה כאשר
28 צוה יהוה ויעלו אל־הר ההר לעיני כל־העדה׃ ויפשט
משה את־אהרן את־בגדיו וילבש אתם את־אלעזר בנו
וימת אהרן שם בראש ההר וירד משה ואלעזר מן־ההר׃
29 ויראו כל־העדה כי גוע אהרן ויבכו את־אהרן שלשים
יום כל בית ישראל׃ ס

water of the wells; we will go along the king's highway, we will not turn aside to the right hand nor to the left, until we have passed thy border.' 18. And Edom said unto him: 'Thou shalt not pass through me, lest I come out with the sword against thee.' 19. And the children of Israel said unto him: 'We will go up by the highway; and if we drink of thy water, I and my cattle, then will I give the price thereof; let me only pass through on my feet; there is no hurt.' 20. And he said: 'Thou shalt not pass through.' And Edom came out against him with much people, and with a strong hand. 21. Thus Edom refused to give Israel passage through his border; wherefore Israel turned away from him.*v (**iii). ¶ 22. And they journeyed from Kadesh; and the children of Israel, even the whole congregation, came unto mount Hor. 23. And the LORD spoke unto Moses and Aaron in mount Hor, by the border of the land of Edom, saying: 24. 'Aaron shall be gathered unto his people; for he shall not enter into the land which I have given unto the children of Israel, because ye rebelled against My word at the waters of Meribah. 25. Take Aaron and Eleazar his son, and bring them up unto mount Hor. 26. And strip Aaron of his garments, and put them upon Eleazar his son; and Aaron shall be gathered unto his people, and shall die there.' 27. And Moses did as the LORD commanded; and they went up into mount Hor in the sight of all the congregation. 28. And Moses stripped Aaron of his garments, and put them upon Eleazar his son; and Aaron died there in the top of the mount; and Moses and Eleazar came down from the mount. 29. And when all the congregation saw that Aaron was dead, they wept for Aaron thirty days, even all the house of Israel.

19. *highway.* Heb. *mesillah.* This must be identical with the caravan trade-route that from immemorial times connected Egypt with the lands beyond the Dead Sea and Jordan.

let me only . . . feet. Better, *let me only—there is no hurt—pass through on my feet* (Luzzatto). We ask for nothing that can cause you injury or annoyance.

21. *turned away.* In the direction indicated in *v.* 22.

22–29. DEATH OF AARON

22. *came unto mount Hor.* lit. 'came unto Hor the mountain.' The site is stated to be 'by the border of the land of Edom' (*v.* 23; and 'in the edge' of the land of Edom; XXXIII, 37); probably Jebel Madurah, N.E. of Kadesh and a day's journey from the Dead Sea.

24. *be gathered unto his people.* The Bible phrase for reunion with those who had gone before—an intimation of immortality; see on Gen. XV, 15 and XXV, 8.

ye rebelled. See on *v.* 12. 'The leaders as well as the people with whom they were impatient were "rebels" ' (Dummelow); see *v.* 10.

26. *strip Aaron of his garments. i.e.* the official robes which he wore as High Priest.

upon Eleazar his son. In token that the High Priesthood was transferred to him.

29. *thirty days.* The same number of days as they wept for Moses; Deut. XXXIV, 8.

all the house of Israel. A national mourning for their first High Priest.

In later Jewish thought, Aaron is the ideal peace-maker; and Hillel bids every man to be a

21 CHAPTER XXI

1. And the Canaanite, the king of Arad, who dwelt in the South, heard tell that Israel came by the way of Atharim; and he fought against Israel, and took some of them captive. 2. And Israel vowed a vow unto the LORD, and said: 'If Thou wilt indeed deliver this people into my hand, then I will utterly destroy their cities.' 3. And the LORD hearkened to the voice of Israel, and delivered up the Canaanites; and they utterly destroyed them and their cities; and the name of the place was

CAP. XXI. כא כא

א וַיִּשְׁמַע הַכְּנַעֲנִי מֶלֶךְ־עֲרָד יֹשֵׁב הַנֶּגֶב כִּי בָּא יִשְׂרָאֵל
2 דֶּרֶךְ הָאֲתָרִים וַיִּלָּחֶם בְּיִשְׂרָאֵל וַיִּשְׁבְּ ׀ מִמֶּנּוּ שֶׁבִי׃ וַיִּדַּר
יִשְׂרָאֵל נֶדֶר לַיהוָה וַיֹּאמַר אִם־נָתֹן תִּתֵּן אֶת־הָעָם הַזֶּה
3 בְּיָדִי וְהַחֲרַמְתִּי אֶת־עָרֵיהֶם׃ וַיִּשְׁמַע יְהוָה בְּקוֹל יִשְׂרָאֵל
וַיִּתֵּן אֶת־הַכְּנַעֲנִי וַיַּחֲרֵם אֶתְהֶם וְאֶת־עָרֵיהֶם וַיִּקְרָא שֵׁם־

'disciple of Aaron, loving peace and pursuing peace, loving his fellowmen and bringing them near to the Torah'. According to rabbinic legend, he would go from house to house, and whenever he found one who did not know how to recite the Shema, he taught him to recite it. He did not, however, restrict his activities to 'establishing peace between God and man', but strove to establish peace between man and his fellow. If he discovered that two men had fallen out, he hastened first to the one, then to the other, saying to each: 'If thou didst but know how he with whom thou hast quarrelled regrets his action!' Aaron would thus speak to each separately, until both the former enemies would mutually forgive each other, and as soon as they were again face to face greet each other as friends. This kindness of his led many a sinner to reform, who at the moment when he was about to commit a sin thought to himself, 'How shall I be able to lift up my eyes to Aaron's face, I, to whom Aaron was so kind!' When Aaron died, the angels lamented in the words, 'The law of truth was in his mouth, and unrighteousness was not found in his lips: he walked with Me in peace and uprightness, and did turn many away from iniquity' (Malachi II, 6).

CHAPTER XXI

1–3. BATTLE WITH CANAANITES

1. *Arad.* A royal city of the Canaanites (Josh. XII, 14), situated on a hill now known as Tel' Arad, 17 miles south of Hebron and 50 miles north-east of Kadesh.

the South. Or, 'the Negeb'; lit. 'the dryness,' was the southern district of Canaan that bordered on the desert and was itself largely desert.

of Atharim. Or, 'of the spies' (Targum). As the territory of the king of Arad extended to the desert of Zin, he must have anticipated an invasion and sought to forestall it. Most commentators, however, regard the word as the name of a place.

2. *utterly destroy. i.e.* 'devote,' or place under a ban, dedicate wholly to the Deity.

3. *Hormah.* Heb. חרמה from the same root as חרם a ban, a devoted thing, *i.e.* a thing 'doomed' to destruction. The collective name of all the destroyed cities was Hormah, which was thus a district and not a single town; see on XIV, 45, and introductory note to XIII.

This incident cannot be assigned to the period when the Israelites had begun to compass the land of Edom, for they were nowhere in the neighbourhood of Arad. It therefore must *precede* that event. 'After leaving Sinai, the Israelites proceeded to Kadesh-barnea. From this base, they could march due north and invade Southern Palestine (the Negeb). This they did, and the result is given in the above three verses. It ended in the annihilation of the Canaanite ruler, and his chief city was henceforth called Hormah. Spies were thereupon sent out to explore Canaan proper, as related in Chapter XIII. But their report was unfavourable. On hearing it, the people lost heart, and it became clear that success could not be expected until a new generation had grown up. The order was therefore given to evacuate Kadesh, and proceed towards Edom. But the people suddenly veered round, and refused to obey. In defiance of the Divine command, they embarked on a campaign of conquest. The result was disastrous. They were utterly routed and chased to Hormah (XIV, 45), the scene of their former triumph' (Wiener).

4–9. THE BRAZEN SERPENT

4. *by the way to the Red Sea.* Forbidden to cut through Edom, they had to pass *around* it, by journeying in a southern direction until they reached Ezion-Geber, on the eastern gulf of the Red Sea, the Gulf of Akaba. They then turned eastwards of Mt. Seir; and thereafter northwards towards the steppes of Moab.

to compass. To go round; see on XX, 22–9.

impatient; their endurance gave out because of the unspeakable hardships.

because of the way. The rugged, sandy, and exceptionally dreary plain through which they were passing; and the fact that they were marching, for the time being, away from Canaan and knew not how they were ever to reach it.

הַמָּקוֹם חָרְמָה׃ פ
4 וַיִּסְעוּ מֵהֹר הָהָר דֶּרֶךְ יַם־סוּף לִסְבֹב אֶת־אֶרֶץ אֱדוֹם
ה וַתִּקְצַר נֶפֶשׁ־הָעָם בַּדָּרֶךְ׃ וַיְדַבֵּר הָעָם בֵּאלֹהִים וּבְמֹשֶׁה
לָמָה הֶעֱלִיתֻנוּ מִמִּצְרַיִם לָמוּת בַּמִּדְבָּר כִּי אֵין לֶחֶם
6 וְאֵין מַיִם וְנַפְשֵׁנוּ קָצָה בַּלֶּחֶם הַקְּלֹקֵל׃ וַיְשַׁלַּח יְהוָה
בָּעָם אֵת הַנְּחָשִׁים הַשְּׂרָפִים וַיְנַשְּׁכוּ אֶת־הָעָם וַיָּמָת עַם־
7 רָב מִיִּשְׂרָאֵל׃ וַיָּבֹא הָעָם אֶל־מֹשֶׁה וַיֹּאמְרוּ חָטָאנוּ כִּי־
דִבַּרְנוּ בַיהוָה וָבָךְ הִתְפַּלֵּל אֶל־יְהוָה וְיָסֵר מֵעָלֵינוּ אֶת־
8 הַנָּחָשׁ וַיִּתְפַּלֵּל מֹשֶׁה בְּעַד הָעָם׃ וַיֹּאמֶר יְהוָה אֶל־
מֹשֶׁה עֲשֵׂה לְךָ שָׂרָף וְשִׂים אֹתוֹ עַל־נֵס וְהָיָה כָּל־הַנָּשׁוּךְ
9 וְרָאָה אֹתוֹ וָחָי׃ וַיַּעַשׂ מֹשֶׁה נְחַשׁ נְחֹשֶׁת וַיְשִׂמֵהוּ עַל־
הַנֵּס וְהָיָה אִם־נָשַׁךְ הַנָּחָשׁ אֶת־אִישׁ וְהִבִּיט אֶל־נְחַשׁ
ששי 11 הַנְּחֹשֶׁת וָחָי׃ *וַיִּסְעוּ בְּנֵי יִשְׂרָאֵל וַיַּחֲנוּ בְּאֹבֹת׃ וַיִּסְעוּ
מֵאֹבֹת וַיַּחֲנוּ בְּעִיֵּי הָעֲבָרִים בַּמִּדְבָּר אֲשֶׁר עַל־פְּנֵי מוֹאָב
12 13 מִמִּזְרַח הַשָּׁמֶשׁ׃ מִשָּׁם נָסָעוּ וַיַּחֲנוּ בְּנַחַל זָרֶד׃ מִשָּׁם

v. 6. קמץ בטרחא

called [1]Hormah. ¶ 4. And they journeyed from mount Hor by the way to the Red Sea, to compass the land of Edom; and the soul of the people became impatient because of the way. 5. And the people spoke against God, and against Moses: 'Wherefore have ye brought us up out of Egypt to die in the wilderness? for there is no bread, and there is no water; and our soul loatheth this light bread.' 6. And the LORD sent fiery serpents among the people, and they bit the people; and much people of Israel died. 7. And the people came to Moses, and said: 'We have sinned, because we have spoken against the LORD and against thee; pray unto the LORD, that He take away the serpents from us.' And Moses prayed for the people. 8. And the LORD said unto Moses: 'Make thee a fiery serpent, and set it upon a pole; and it shall come to pass, that every one that is bitten, when he seeth it, shall live.' 9. And Moses made a serpent of brass, and set it upon the pole; and it came to pass, that if a serpent had bitten any man, when he looked unto the serpent of brass, he lived.*vi. 10. And the children of Israel journeyed, and pitched in Oboth. 11. And they journeyed from Oboth, and pitched at Ije-abarim, in the wilderness which is in front of Moab, toward the sunrising. 12. From thence they journeyed, and pitched in the valley of Zered. 13.

[1] That is, *Utter destruction.*

5. *light bread.* Or, 'miserable bread,' the manna, when compared with the appetizing diet of Egypt.

6. *fiery serpents.* lit. 'the serpents, the fiery ones,' whose sting caused violent inflammation.

7. *Moses prayed for the people.* 'Hence we learn,' says the Midrash, 'that when a man is asked to forgive, he must not cruelly refuse to do so. The people had spoken against Moses, but yet in the hour of their extremity Moses readily forgave, and prayed for their deliverance.'

8. *make thee a fiery serpent.* An image of a fiery serpent made out of brass (Ibn Ezra).

9. *when he looked.* 'Did then the brazen serpent possess the power of slaying or of bringing to life? No, but so long as the Israelites looked upwards and subjected their hearts to their Father in Heaven, were they healed. But when they refused, then were they destroyed' (Mishnah). The brazen serpent was 'a token of salvation to put them in remembrance of the commandments of Thy Law, for he that turned toward it was not saved because of that which was beheld but because of Thee, the Saviour of all' (Wisdom of Solomon).

This brazen serpent made by Moses was naturally preserved as an object of veneration by the Israelites. But when in the course of centuries it tended to become, and eventually became, an object of idolatrous worship, it was destroyed by King Hezekiah (II Kings XVIII, 4). He is highly praised by the Rabbis for this act.

10–20. HALTING PLACES

10. *pitched in Oboth.* 'Somewhere on the flinty plateau to the East of Edom' (G. A. Smith).

11. *toward the sunrising.* *i.e.* on the east of Moab.

12. *valley of Zered.* *i.e.* on the wady of Zered, which flows into the Dead Sea at its southern extremity.

13. *on the other side of the Arnon.* *i.e.* north of it.

which is in the wilderness. *i.e.* that part of it which is in the Wilderness.

'The Arnon is an enormous trench across the plateau of Moab. It is about 1,700 feet deep and two miles broad from edge to edge of the cliffs which bound it, but the floor of the Valley over which the stream winds is only forty yards wide. About nineteen miles from the Dead Sea, the trench divides into two branches, each of them again dividing into two. The whole plateau

נָסָעוּ וַיַּחֲנוּ מֵעֵבֶר אַרְנוֹן אֲשֶׁר בַּמִּדְבָּר הַיֹּצֵא מִגְּבֻל
הָאֱמֹרִי כִּי אַרְנוֹן גְּבוּל מוֹאָב בֵּין מוֹאָב וּבֵין הָאֱמֹרִי׃
14 עַל־כֵּן יֵאָמַר בְּסֵפֶר מִלְחֲמֹת יְהוָה אֶת־וָהֵב בְּסוּפָה וְאֶת־
טו הַנְּחָלִים אַרְנוֹן׃ וְאֶשֶׁד הַנְּחָלִים אֲשֶׁר נָטָה לְשֶׁבֶת עָר
16 וְנִשְׁעַן לִגְבוּל מוֹאָב׃ וּמִשָּׁם בְּאֵרָה הִוא הַבְּאֵר אֲשֶׁר
אָמַר יְהוָה לְמֹשֶׁה אֱסֹף אֶת־הָעָם וְאֶתְּנָה לָהֶם מָיִם׃ ס
17 אָז יָשִׁיר יִשְׂרָאֵל אֶת־הַשִּׁירָה הַזֹּאת עֲלִי בְאֵר עֱנוּ־לָהּ׃
18 בְּאֵר חֲפָרוּהָ שָׂרִים כָּרוּהָ נְדִיבֵי הָעָם בִּמְחֹקֵק בְּמִשְׁעֲנֹתָם
19 וּמִמִּדְבָּר מַתָּנָה׃ וּמִמַּתָּנָה נַחֲלִיאֵל וּמִנַּחֲלִיאֵל בָּמוֹת׃
כ וּמִבָּמוֹת הַגַּיְא אֲשֶׁר בִּשְׂדֵה מוֹאָב רֹאשׁ הַפִּסְגָּה וְנִשְׁקָפָה
עַל־פְּנֵי הַיְשִׁימֹן׃ * שביעי פ (רביעי כשהן מחוב׳)

v. 13. קמץ בסגולתא

From thence they journeyed, and pitched on the other side of the Arnon, which is in the wilderness, that cometh out of the border of the Amorites.—For Arnon is the border of Moab, between Moab and the Amorites; 14. wherefore it is said in the book of the Wars of the LORD:

Vaheb in Suphah,
And the valleys of Arnon,
15. And the slope of the valleys
That inclineth toward the seat of Ar,
And leaneth upon the border of Moab.—

16. And from thence to [1]Beer; that is the well whereof the LORD said unto Moses: 'Gather the people together, and I will give them water.' 17. Then sang Israel this song:

Spring up, O well—sing ye unto it—
18. The well, which the princes digged,
Which the nobles of the people delved,
With the sceptre, and with their staves.

And from the wilderness to Mattanah; 19. and from Mattanah to Nahaliel; and from Nahaliel to Bamoth; 20. and from

[1] That is, *A well.*

up to the desert is thus not only cut across, but up and down, by deep ravines, and a very difficult frontier is formed. All the branches probably carried the name Arnon' (G. A. Smith).

14. *the book of the Wars of the LORD.* The lines from that book quoted here support the statement that Arnon was the border of Moab. There is no further mention of this book in the whole of Scripture. Ibn Ezra says, 'It was an independent book in which were written the records of the wars waged by God on behalf of those that fear Him. Many books have been lost and are no longer extant among us; *e.g.* the Words of Nathan and Iddo, and the Chronicles of the Kings of Israel.' Evidently it was a collection of ballads and songs. 'The Book of the Wars of the LORD, like the Sefer Hayashar (Josh. x, 13 and II Sam. I, 18) is a proof that there was no absence of literary activity in the days of Moses. It furthermore proves that the Torah is not the result of such literary activity, otherwise the alleged compiler could have indicated his sources as he has done in this instance' (S. R. Hirsch).

Vaheb. This name of an unidentified town is in the accusative, and requires some verb like, 'we captured,' to be understood before it.

in Suphah. Or, 'in storm.' Perhaps it is the same place as *Suph*, mentioned in Deut. I, 1.

15. *of the valleys.* Not *valley*, for the name Arnon covers a complex of wadies uniting in the long, deep trench that carried their waters to the Dead Sea.

Ar. Ar of Moab, in *v.* 28, which according to Deut. II, 18, lay on the Moabite frontier.

Zunz and Leeser translate *v.* 14 and 15 as follows: 'Therefore mention is made in the Book of the Wars of the LORD of Vaheb in Suphah, and of the brooks of Arnon, and the descent of the brooks, that turneth toward Shebeth-Ar and leaneth upon the border of Moab.' All these names occur in the Book of the Wars of the LORD, and are unknown to us now (Leeser).

16. *Beer. i.e.* 'Well-town'.

17. *then sang Israel this song.* The mention of this town and its well gave occasion for the citation of another short poem, celebrating the way in which the well was opened by the princes and nobles of the people.

sing ye unto it. lit. 'respond unto it', answer as a chorus; cf. Exod. xv, 21. From this arose the legend that it is the well that sang, and that the words of the princes and people were but the chorus to that song *by* the well.

18. *which the princes digged.* The princes took a part in the effort to obtain water for the people.

with the sceptre. Or, 'by order of the lawgiver' (RV Margin).

and from the wilderness . . . Mattanah. Or, 'from the wilderness a gift'—as the last line of the Song of the Well (Budde). The next *v.* would then read: 'And from the gift (*i.e.* the Well) to Nahaliel. . . .'

19. *Nahaliel . . . Bamoth.* These places have not been identified.

20. *Pisgah.* The general name for a series of mountain ranges (called 'mountain of Abarim'

21 וַיִּשְׁלַח יִשְׂרָאֵל מַלְאָכִים אֶל־סִיחֹן מֶלֶךְ־הָאֱמֹרִי לֵאמֹר׃
22 אֶעְבְּרָה בְאַרְצֶךָ לֹא נִטֶּה בְּשָׂדֶה וּבְכֶרֶם לֹא נִשְׁתֶּה מֵי
23 בְאֵר בְּדֶרֶךְ הַמֶּלֶךְ נֵלֵךְ עַד אֲשֶׁר־נַעֲבֹר גְּבֻלֶךָ׃ וְלֹא־נָתַן
סִיחֹן אֶת־יִשְׂרָאֵל עֲבֹר בִּגְבֻלוֹ וַיֶּאֱסֹף סִיחֹן אֶת־כָּל־עַמּוֹ
וַיֵּצֵא לִקְרַאת יִשְׂרָאֵל הַמִּדְבָּרָה וַיָּבֹא יָהְצָה וַיִּלָּחֶם
24 בְּיִשְׂרָאֵל׃ וַיַּכֵּהוּ יִשְׂרָאֵל לְפִי־חָרֶב וַיִּירַשׁ אֶת־אַרְצוֹ
כה מֵאַרְנֹן עַד־יַבֹּק עַד־בְּנֵי עַמּוֹן כִּי עַז גְּבוּל בְּנֵי עַמּוֹן׃ וַיִּקַּח
יִשְׂרָאֵל אֵת כָּל־הֶעָרִים הָאֵלֶּה וַיֵּשֶׁב יִשְׂרָאֵל בְּכָל־עָרֵי
26 הָאֱמֹרִי בְּחֶשְׁבּוֹן וּבְכָל־בְּנֹתֶיהָ׃ כִּי חֶשְׁבּוֹן עִיר סִיחֹן
מֶלֶךְ הָאֱמֹרִי הִוא וְהוּא נִלְחַם בְּמֶלֶךְ מוֹאָב הָרִאשׁוֹן
27 וַיִּקַּח אֶת־כָּל־אַרְצוֹ מִיָּדוֹ עַד־אַרְנֹן׃ עַל־כֵּן יֹאמְרוּ הַמֹּשְׁלִים
28 בֹּאוּ חֶשְׁבּוֹן תִּבָּנֶה וְתִכּוֹנֵן עִיר סִיחוֹן׃ כִּי־אֵשׁ יָצְאָה

Bamoth to the valley that is in the field of Moab, by the top of Pisgah, which looketh down upon the desert.*vii (**iv). ¶ 21. And Israel sent messengers unto Sihon king of the Amorites, saying: 22. 'Let me pass through thy land; we will not turn aside into field, or into vineyard; we will not drink of the water of the wells; we will go by the king's highway, until we have passed thy border.' 23. And Sihon would not suffer Israel to pass through his border; but Sihon gathered all his people together, and went out against Israel into the wilderness, and came to Jahaz; and he fought against Israel. 24. And Israel smote him with the edge of the sword, and possessed his land from the Arnon unto the Jabbok, even unto the children of Ammon; for the border of the children of Ammon was strong. 25. And Israel took all these cities; and Israel dwelt in all the cities of the Amorites, in Heshbon, and in all the towns thereof. 26. For Heshbon was the city of Sihon the king of the Amorites, who had fought against the former king of Moab, and taken all his land out of his hand, even unto the Arnon. 27. Wherefore they that speak in parables say:

in Deut. xxxii, 49) in the plateau of Moab. The highest point was Mount Nebo on which Moses died; Deut. xxxiv, 1.

the desert. Or, 'Jeshimon': the waste desolation north-west of the Dead Sea.

21–32. Conquering the Amorite Kingdoms

In contrast to former pictures of murmuring and mutiny, we now get events which bring out the glad surprise of the new people as their strength is tried against the gigantic Sihon and Og, and the foes are utterly exterminated (Moulton).

21. *Amorites.* Denotes the inhabitants of Syria and Palestine before the time of the Exodus. But from *v.* 26 it would appear that Sihon and his people had but recently wrested from Moab the territory north of the river Arnon.

22. *pass through thy land.* Their objective being the fords of Jordan opposite Jericho.

the king's highway. See on xx, 17.

23. *Jahaz.* On the eastern border of Sihon's land.

24. *the border of the children of Ammon was strong.* Arnon was the southern limit of Sihon's kingdom, and Jabbok was the northern. The Ammonites lay to the east; but as their border fortresses were strong and impregnable, the Amorites had been unable to penetrate into their territory. The reason why the Israelites did not enter the land of the Ammonites is given in Deut. ii, 19.

25. *Heshbon.* The modern Hesban, 2,940 feet above the sea, 18 miles east of Jordan, opposite Jericho.

'The victory over Sihon was of incalculable importance to the Israelites; it strengthened their position and inspired them with self-reliance. They at once took possession of the conquered district and abandoned their nomadic life. The Israelites could now move about freely, being no longer incommoded by the narrow belt of the desert nor by the suspicions of unfriendly tribes' (Graetz).

the towns. lit. 'the daughters'; the villages near and dependent upon the capital, Heshbon. By a similar figure, we speak of 'a mother city'.

26–30. A Historical Note, with Song of Victory

27. *wherefore.* Explains that this song is quoted because of its association with the remark in *v.* 26 concerning the conquest of Moab by Sihon.

they that speak in parables say. Or, 'they that recite ballads say'; Heb. *moshelim*, 'they that speak the *mashal*,' which word might mean either proverb, parable, riddle, song, ode, or ballad. The *moshelim* were bards who expressed in pithy poetic snatches what was uppermost in the popular mind at important occasions in the national life. In the present instance we have a quotation from a popular ballad, referring to

מֵחֶשְׁבּוֹן לֶהָבָה מִקִּרְיַת סִיחֹן אָכְלָה עָר מוֹאָב בַּעֲלֵי
29 בָּמוֹת אַרְנֹן׃ אוֹי־לְךָ מוֹאָב אָבַדְתָּ עַם־כְּמוֹשׁ נָתַן בָּנָיו
ל פְּלֵיטִם וּבְנֹתָיו בַּשְּׁבִית לְמֶלֶךְ אֱמֹרִי סִיחוֹן׃ וַנִּירָם אָבַד
31 חֶשְׁבּוֹן עַד־דִּיבֹן וַנַּשִּׁים עַד־נֹפַח אֲשֶׁר עַד־מֵידְבָא׃ וַיֵּשֶׁב
32 יִשְׂרָאֵל בְּאֶרֶץ הָאֱמֹרִי׃ וַיִּשְׁלַח מֹשֶׁה לְרַגֵּל אֶת־יַעְזֵר
33 וַיִּלְכְּדוּ בְּנֹתֶיהָ וַיּוֹרֶשׁ אֶת־הָאֱמֹרִי אֲשֶׁר־שָׁם׃ וַיִּפְנוּ וַיַּעֲלוּ
דֶּרֶךְ הַבָּשָׁן וַיֵּצֵא עוֹג מֶלֶךְ־הַבָּשָׁן לִקְרָאתָם הוּא וְכָל־
מפטיר 34 עַמּוֹ לַמִּלְחָמָה אֶדְרֶעִי׃* וַיֹּאמֶר יְהוָה אֶל־מֹשֶׁה אַל־תִּירָא
אֹתוֹ כִּי בְיָדְךָ נָתַתִּי אֹתוֹ וְאֶת־כָּל־עַמּוֹ וְאֶת־אַרְצוֹ וְעָשִׂיתָ
לּוֹ כַּאֲשֶׁר עָשִׂיתָ לְסִיחֹן מֶלֶךְ הָאֱמֹרִי אֲשֶׁר יוֹשֵׁב בְּחֶשְׁבּוֹן׃

v. 30. נקוד על ר׳ v. 32. ויורש ק׳

Come ye to Heshbon!
Let the city of Sihon be built and established!
28. For a fire is gone out of Heshbon,
A flame from the city of Sihon;
It hath devoured Ar of Moab,
The lords of the high places of Arnon.
29. Woe to thee, Moab!
Thou art undone, O people of Chemosh;
He hath given his sons as fugitives,
And his daughters into captivity,
Unto Sihon king of the Amorites.
30. We have shot at them—Heshbon is perished—even unto Dibon,
And we have laid waste even unto Nophah,
Which reacheth unto Medeba.

31. Thus Israel dwelt in the land of the Amorites. 32. And Moses sent to spy out Jazer, and they took the towns thereof, and drove out the Amorites that were there. 33. And they turned and went up by the way of Bashan; and Og the king of Bashan went out against them, he and all his people, to battle at Edrei.*m. 34. And the

the jubilation of the Amorites over their conquest of Moab; and another, to the exultation of Israel over the defeat of the Amorites.

come ye to Heshbon. This and the next two verses are the victory song of the Amorites when they in their day had wrested that land from the rulers of Moab. The poet invites the victorious Amorites to lose no time in entering upon and enjoying the greatest trophy in their victory, namely, the captured capital, Heshbon.

the city of Sihon. Let the capital which had fallen into your hands be built up in great splendour, making it worthy to be called City of Sihon (Rashi).

28. *for a fire is gone out of Heshbon.* A figurative way of saying that no sooner had Sihon gained possession of Heshbon than he was able to send forth destruction upon the other towns of Moab.

29. *Chemosh.* The national god of the Moabites.

he hath given . . . into captivity. An expression of half-ironical compassion for the Moabites whom their idol Chemosh was unable to save. The 'sons' and 'daughters' of Chemosh are his votaries who looked to him as to a human father to save them in a time of trouble.

30. *we have shot at them.* This is the second part of the song; *viz.*, the exultation of Israel over the defeat of the Amorites.

even unto Dibon. i.e. the inhabitants of all the places between Heshbon and Dibon have perished. Dibon was afterwards called 'Dibon-Gad' and was situated four miles north of the Arnon. It was at Dibon that the so-called Moabite Stone was discovered in 1868—the most famous of all inscriptions bearing on Bible history. It is a contemporary document of the highest importance, giving the Moabite side of the conflict between Israel and Moab in the ninth pre-Christian century, the days of the Prophet Elijah and King Ahab.

Nophah. Unidentified.

Medeba. The modern Madeba, about four miles S.E. of Heshbon.

32. *Jazer.* In Isaiah XVI, 8, 9 it is mentioned together with Heshbon. According to I Maccabees, V, 8, it was near the Ammonite border.

33–35. Defeat of Og the King of Bashan

33. *went up.* Towards the north.

Bashan. Celebrated for its rich pastures, its healthy herds of cattle, and its oak forests. It extended from the border of Gilead on the south to Mount Hermon on the north.

Og the king of Bashan. In Hebrew folklore, Og is the last of the giants, an antediluvian of superhuman strength who had survived the Flood, and had attained the age of 500 years.

Edrei. The modern Edra'ah, situated on the southern border of Bashan, about 30 miles east of the Sea of Tiberias.

34. *fear him not.* Og was formidable, not only on account of his giant stature (cf. Deut. III, 11) but also on account of the walled cities in his dominions.

LORD said unto Moses: 'Fear him not; for I have delivered him into thy hand, and all his people, and his land; and thou shalt do to him as thou didst unto Sihon king of the Amorites, who dwelt at Heshbon.' 35. So they smote him, and his sons, and all his people, until there was none left him remaining; and they possessed his land.

לה וַיַּכּוּ אֹתוֹ וְאֶת־בָּנָיו וְאֶת־כָּל־עַמּוֹ עַד־בִּלְתִּי הִשְׁאִיר־לוֹ
שָׂרִיד וַיִּירְשׁוּ אֶת־אַרְצוֹ׃

22

CHAPTER XXII

כב

CAP. XXII. כב

1. And the children of Israel journeyed, and pitched in the plains of Moab beyond the Jordan at Jericho.

א וַיִּסְעוּ בְּנֵי יִשְׂרָאֵל וַיַּחֲנוּ בְּעַרְבוֹת מוֹאָב מֵעֵבֶר לְיַרְדֵּן
יְרֵחוֹ׃

CHAPTER XXII

1. *plains of Moab.* Or, 'steppes of Moab'; the open plain immediately to the north of the Dead Sea.

beyond the Jordan. lit. 'on the side of the Jordan'; *i.e.* in this case, the eastern side.

at Jericho. Facing Jericho.

HAFTORAH CHUKKAS הפטרת חקת

JUDGES XI, 1–33

CHAPTER XI

CAP. XI. יא

1. Now Jephthah the Gileadite was a mighty man of valour, and he was the son of a harlot; and Gilead begot Jephthah. 2. And Gilead's wife bore him sons; and when his wife's sons grew up, they drove out Jephthah, and said unto him: 'Thou shalt not inherit in our father's house; for thou art the

א וְיִפְתָּח הַגִּלְעָדִי הָיָה גִּבּוֹר חַיִל וְהוּא בֶּן־אִשָּׁה זוֹנָה וַיּוֹלֶד
2 גִּלְעָד אֶת־יִפְתָּח׃ וַתֵּלֶד אֵשֶׁת־גִּלְעָד לוֹ בָּנִים וַיִּגְדְּלוּ
בְנֵי־הָאִשָּׁה וַיְגָרְשׁוּ אֶת־יִפְתָּח וַיֹּאמְרוּ לוֹ לֹא־תִנְחַל בְּבֵית־

The Haftorah is again from the Book of Judges, which describes the days of lawlessness in Israel; the frequent lapses into the heathenism and immorality of the neighbouring nations; the dire calamities that followed; and the new Judge and Deliverer who would arise and save Israel from bondage and the enemy. For eighteen years Israel had now groaned under the cruel yoke of the Ammonites (1128–1110 B.C.E.). Who and where is the man capable of leading his brethren against the Ammonites? Here the Haftorah opens. It tells the story of Jephthah, the rugged and ruthless warrior but noble patriot and tender-hearted father, whose victory over the enemy was shadowed by a terrible sorrow.

The Sedrah gives the account of Israel's clash with the Amorites. The Northern part of the Amorite kingdom had formerly, it is assumed, belonged to Ammon. This forms the connection between the Sedrah and Haftorah.

1–3. JEPHTHAH'S ANTECEDENTS

1. *a harlot.* Or, 'innkeeper' (Targum Jonathan); or, 'concubine' (Kimchi). In all probability the Heb. word is here used in its usual meaning. The Bible speaks the naked truth; it conceals nothing, whether concerning the individual or the nation. Here it teaches that a man of low, nay infamous, origin, whom his brothers despised, may yet be the destined instrument of deliverance for his people. Jephthah was the first Israelite leader to arise in Transjordania. Two centuries later, another leader, immeasurably the spiritual superior to Jephthah, namely, Elijah the Prophet, also came from the same region.

Gilead. The name of a man living in Gilead; cf. *France* as a family name in France.

2. *Gilead's wife. i.e.* his lawful wife, in contradiction to 'another woman'.

thou shalt not inherit. This unjust act is against the Jewish law of inheritance (Kimchi).

another woman. Heb. אחרת; Ehrlich takes this to be a euphemism, as *Acher* was in later Hebrew.

son of another woman.' 3. Then Jephthah fled from his brethren, and dwelt in the land of Tob; and there were gathered vain fellows to Jephthah, and they went out with him. ¶ 4. And it came to pass after a while, that the children of Ammon made war against Israel. 5. And it was so, that when the children of Ammon made war against Israel, the elders of Gilead went to fetch Jephthah out of the land of Tob. 6. And they said unto Jephthah: 'Come and be our chief, that we may fight with the children of Ammon.' 7. And Jephthah said unto the elders of Gilead: 'Did not ye hate me, and drive me out of my father's house? and why are ye come unto me now when ye are in distress?' 8. And the elders of Gilead said unto Jephthah: 'Therefore are we returned to thee now, that thou mayest go with us, and fight with the children of Ammon, and thou shalt be our head over all the inhabitants of Gilead.' 9. And Jephthah said unto the elders of Gilead: 'If ye bring me back home to fight with the children of Ammon, and the LORD deliver them before me, I will be your head.' 10. And the elders of Gilead said unto Jephthah: 'The LORD shall be witness between us; surely according to thy word so will we do.' 11. Then Jephthah went with the elders of Gilead, and the people made him head and chief over them; and Jephthah spoke all his words before the LORD in Mizpah. ¶ 12. And Jephthah sent messengers unto the king of the children of Ammon, saying: 'What hast thou to do with me, that thou art come unto me to fight against my land?' 13. And the king of the children of Ammon answered unto the messengers of Jephthah: 'Because Israel took away my land, when he

3 אָבִינוּ כִּי בֶּן־אִשָּׁה אַחֶרֶת אָתָּה׃ וַיִּבְרַח יִפְתָּח מִפְּנֵי
אֶחָיו וַיֵּשֶׁב בְּאֶרֶץ טוֹב וַיִּתְלַקְּטוּ אֶל־יִפְתָּח אֲנָשִׁים רֵיקִים
4 וַיֵּצְאוּ עִמּוֹ׃ וַיְהִי מִיָּמִים וַיִּלָּחֲמוּ בְנֵי־עַמּוֹן עִם־יִשְׂרָאֵל׃
ה וַיְהִי כַּאֲשֶׁר־נִלְחֲמוּ בְנֵי־עַמּוֹן עִם־יִשְׂרָאֵל וַיֵּלְכוּ זִקְנֵי גִלְעָד
6 לָקַחַת אֶת־יִפְתָּח מֵאֶרֶץ טוֹב׃ וַיֹּאמְרוּ לְיִפְתָּח לְכָה
7 וְהָיִיתָה לָּנוּ לְקָצִין וְנִלָּחֲמָה בִּבְנֵי עַמּוֹן׃ וַיֹּאמֶר יִפְתָּח
לְזִקְנֵי גִלְעָד הֲלֹא אַתֶּם שְׂנֵאתֶם אוֹתִי וַתְּגָרְשׁוּנִי מִבֵּית
8 אָבִי וּמַדּוּעַ בָּאתֶם אֵלַי עַתָּה כַּאֲשֶׁר צַר לָכֶם׃ וַיֹּאמְרוּ
זִקְנֵי גִלְעָד אֶל־יִפְתָּח לָכֵן עַתָּה שַׁבְנוּ אֵלֶיךָ וְהָלַכְתָּ עִמָּנוּ
וְנִלְחַמְתָּ בִּבְנֵי עַמּוֹן וְהָיִיתָ לָּנוּ לְרֹאשׁ לְכֹל יֹשְׁבֵי גִלְעָד׃
9 וַיֹּאמֶר יִפְתָּח אֶל־זִקְנֵי גִלְעָד אִם־מְשִׁיבִים אַתֶּם אוֹתִי
לְהִלָּחֵם בִּבְנֵי עַמּוֹן וְנָתַן יְהוָה אוֹתָם לְפָנָי אָנֹכִי אֶהְיֶה
י לָכֶם לְרֹאשׁ׃ וַיֹּאמְרוּ זִקְנֵי־גִלְעָד אֶל־יִפְתָּח יְהוָה יִהְיֶה
11 שֹׁמֵעַ בֵּינוֹתֵינוּ אִם־לֹא כִדְבָרְךָ כֵּן נַעֲשֶׂה׃ וַיֵּלֶךְ יִפְתָּח
עִם־זִקְנֵי גִלְעָד וַיָּשִׂימוּ הָעָם אוֹתוֹ עֲלֵיהֶם לְרֹאשׁ וּלְקָצִין
וַיְדַבֵּר יִפְתָּח אֶת־כָּל־דְּבָרָיו לִפְנֵי יְהוָה בַּמִּצְפָּה׃
12 וַיִּשְׁלַח יִפְתָּח מַלְאָכִים אֶל־מֶלֶךְ בְּנֵי־עַמּוֹן לֵאמֹר מַה־לִּי
13 וָלָךְ כִּי־בָאתָ אֵלַי לְהִלָּחֵם בְּאַרְצִי׃ וַיֹּאמֶר מֶלֶךְ בְּנֵי־
עַמּוֹן אֶל־מַלְאֲכֵי יִפְתָּח כִּי־לָקַח יִשְׂרָאֵל אֶת־אַרְצִי בַּעֲלוֹתוֹ

3. *in the land of Tob.* To the north of Gilead.

vain fellows. Or, 'worthless people'; perhaps also men broken by the oppression of the times, such as came to David at the cave of Adullam when he fled from Saul; I Sam. XXII.

they went out with him. On his raiding expeditions. Driven from home, he betook himself to a wild, marauding life on the borders of the tribe. In this way, Jephthah acquired the tactics of warfare, and the art of leading and governing men.

6. *be our chief.* The national emergency needed an intrepid hero, and the thoughts of men turned instinctively to Jephthah whose reputation as a military leader was already established.

9. *I will be your head.* Even after the conflict with Ammon.

11. *the people.* Acclaim the choice of the elders.

spoke all his words before the LORD. i.e. for a solemn confirmation of the terms of the arrangement between the elders and himself.

Mizpah. Not Mizpah in Benjamin, but in Gilead; the scene of a similar solemn compact in the life of the Patriarch Jacob; Gen. XXXI, 49.

12–27. JEPHTHAH'S NEGOTIATIONS

Before taking the field, Jephthah seeks by diplomatic means to arrive at a peaceable settlement.

13. *Arnon . . . Jabbok.* 'The district between the two rivers naturally lay exposed to the incursions of the Ammonites, who lived to the east of it (Num. XXI, 24); but there is no support for the Ammonites' claim to regard it as *my land* at the time of the Israelite invasion when the territory in question was held by the Amorites' (Cooke).

came up out of Egypt, from the Arnon even unto the Jabbok, and unto the Jordan; now therefore restore those cities peaceably.' 14. And Jephthah sent messengers again unto the king of the children of Ammon; 15. and he said unto him: 'Thus saith Jephthah: Israel took not away the land of Moab, nor the land of the children of Ammon. 16. But when they came up from Egypt, and Israel walked through the wilderness unto the Red Sea, and came to Kadesh; 17. then Israel sent messengers unto the king of Edom, saying: Let me, I pray thee, pass through thy land; but the king of Edom hearkened not. And in like manner he sent unto the king of Moab; but he would not; and Israel abode in Kadesh. 18. Then he walked through the wilderness, and compassed the land of Edom, and the land of Moab, and came by the east side of the land of Moab, and they pitched on the other side of the Arnon, but they came not within the border of Moab, for the Arnon was the border of Moab. 19. And Israel sent messengers unto Sihon king of the Amorites, the king of Heshbon; and Israel said unto him: Let us pass, we pray thee, through thy land unto my place. 20. But Sihon trusted not Israel to pass through his border; but Sihon gathered all his people together, and pitched in Jahaz, and fought against Israel. 21. And the LORD, the God of Israel, delivered Sihon and all his people into the hand of Israel, and they smote them; so Israel possessed all the land of the Amorites, the inhabitants of that country. 22. And they possessed all the border of the Amorites, from the Arnon even unto the Jabbok, and from the wilderness even unto the Jordan. 23. So now the LORD, the God of Israel, hath dispossessed the Amorites from before His people Israel, and shouldest thou possess them? 24. Wilt not thou possess that which Chemosh thy god giveth thee to possess? So whomsoever the LORD our God hath dispossessed from before us, them will we possess. 25. And now art thou anything better than Balak the son of Zippor, king of Moab? did he ever strive against Israel, or did he ever fight against them? 26. While Israel dwelt in Heshbon

מִמִּצְרַיִם מֵאַרְנוֹן וְעַד־הַיַּבֹּק וְעַד־הַיַּרְדֵּן וְעַתָּה הָשִׁיבָה
14 אֶתְהֶן בְּשָׁלוֹם׃ וַיּוֹסֶף עוֹד יִפְתָּח וַיִּשְׁלַח מַלְאָכִים אֶל־
טו מֶלֶךְ בְּנֵי עַמּוֹן׃ וַיֹּאמֶר לוֹ כֹּה אָמַר יִפְתָּח לֹא־לָקַח
16 יִשְׂרָאֵל אֶת־אֶרֶץ מוֹאָב וְאֶת־אֶרֶץ בְּנֵי עַמּוֹן׃ כִּי בַּעֲלוֹתָם
מִמִּצְרָיִם וַיֵּלֶךְ יִשְׂרָאֵל בַּמִּדְבָּר עַד־יַם־סוּף וַיָּבֹא קָדֵשָׁה׃
17 וַיִּשְׁלַח יִשְׂרָאֵל מַלְאָכִים ׀ אֶל־מֶלֶךְ אֱדוֹם לֵאמֹר אֶעְבְּרָה־
נָּא בְאַרְצֶךָ וְלֹא שָׁמַע מֶלֶךְ אֱדוֹם וְגַם אֶל־מֶלֶךְ מוֹאָב
18 שָׁלַח וְלֹא אָבָה וַיֵּשֶׁב יִשְׂרָאֵל בְּקָדֵשׁ׃ וַיֵּלֶךְ בַּמִּדְבָּר
וַיָּסָב אֶת־אֶרֶץ אֱדוֹם וְאֶת־אֶרֶץ מוֹאָב וַיָּבֹא מִמִּזְרַח־שֶׁמֶשׁ
לְאֶרֶץ מוֹאָב וַיַּחֲנוּן בְּעֵבֶר אַרְנוֹן וְלֹא־בָאוּ בִּגְבוּל מוֹאָב
19 כִּי אַרְנוֹן גְּבוּל מוֹאָב׃ וַיִּשְׁלַח יִשְׂרָאֵל מַלְאָכִים אֶל־
סִיחוֹן מֶלֶךְ־הָאֱמֹרִי מֶלֶךְ חֶשְׁבּוֹן וַיֹּאמֶר לוֹ יִשְׂרָאֵל
כ נַעְבְּרָה־נָּא בְאַרְצְךָ עַד־מְקוֹמִי׃ וְלֹא־הֶאֱמִין סִיחוֹן אֶת־
יִשְׂרָאֵל עֲבֹר בִּגְבֻלוֹ וַיֶּאֱסֹף סִיחוֹן אֶת־כָּל־עַמּוֹ וַיַּחֲנוּ
21 בְּיָהְצָה וַיִּלָּחֶם עִם־יִשְׂרָאֵל׃ וַיִּתֵּן יְהוָה אֱלֹהֵי־יִשְׂרָאֵל
אֶת־סִיחוֹן וְאֶת־כָּל־עַמּוֹ בְּיַד יִשְׂרָאֵל וַיַּכּוּם וַיִּירַשׁ יִשְׂרָאֵל
22 אֵת כָּל־אֶרֶץ הָאֱמֹרִי יוֹשֵׁב הָאָרֶץ הַהִיא׃ וַיִּירְשׁוּ אֵת
כָּל־גְּבוּל הָאֱמֹרִי מֵאַרְנוֹן וְעַד־הַיַּבֹּק וּמִן־הַמִּדְבָּר וְעַד־
23 הַיַּרְדֵּן׃ וְעַתָּה יְהוָה ׀ אֱלֹהֵי יִשְׂרָאֵל הוֹרִישׁ אֶת־הָאֱמֹרִי
24 מִפְּנֵי עַמּוֹ יִשְׂרָאֵל וְאַתָּה תִּירָשֶׁנּוּ׃ הֲלֹא אֵת אֲשֶׁר יוֹרִישְׁךָ
כְּמוֹשׁ אֱלֹהֶיךָ אוֹתוֹ תִירָשׁ וְאֵת כָּל־אֲשֶׁר הוֹרִישׁ יְהוָה
כה אֱלֹהֵינוּ מִפָּנֵינוּ אוֹתוֹ נִירָשׁ׃ וְעַתָּה הֲטוֹב טוֹב אַתָּה
מִבָּלָק בֶּן־צִפּוֹר מֶלֶךְ מוֹאָב הֲרוֹב רָב עִם־יִשְׂרָאֵל אִם־

15–22. Jephthah proves that the Israelites in the wilderness made a wide detour to avoid the territory of the kinsmen of the Ammonites, the Moabites, who were then in occupation of the land in dispute. When the Israelites took the land, it belonged neither to Moab or Ammon but to their Amorite conquerors; see Num. XX–XXI.

23. *the LORD . . . hath dispossessed the Amorites.* As the children of Israel took the land from the Amorites, his claim was unfounded.

24. *Chemosh.* Was properly the god of the Moabites, with whom, however, the children of Ammon were a kindred people (Gen. XIX, 37–8).

25. *did he ever fight. i.e.* did he ever dare to fight.

and its towns, and in Aroer and its towns, and in all the cities that are along by the side of the Arnon, three hundred years; wherefore did ye not recover them within that time? 27. I therefore have not sinned against thee, but thou doest me wrong to war against me; the LORD, the Judge, be judge this day between the children of Israel and the children of Ammon.' 28. Howbeit the king of the children of Ammon hearkened not unto the words of Jephthah which he sent him. ¶ 29. Then the spirit of the LORD came upon Jephthah, and he passed over Gilead and Manasseh, and passed over Mizpeh of Gilead, and from Mizpeh of Gilead he passed over unto the children of Ammon. 30. And Jephthah vowed a vow unto the LORD, and said: 'If Thou wilt indeed deliver the children of Ammon into my hand, 31. then it shall be, that whatsoever cometh forth of the doors of my house to meet me, when I return in peace from the children of Ammon, it shall be the LORD's, and I will offer it up for a burnt-offering.' 32. So Jephthah passed over unto the children of Ammon to fight against them; and the LORD delivered them into his hand. 33. And he smote them from Aroer until thou come to Minnith, even twenty cities, and unto Abel-cheramim, with a very great slaughter. So the children of Ammon were subdued before the children of Israel.

26 נִלְחַם נִלְחַם בָּם׃ בְּשֶׁבֶת יִשְׂרָאֵל בְּחֶשְׁבּוֹן וּבִבְנוֹתֶיהָ
וּבְעַרְעוֹר וּבִבְנוֹתֶיהָ וּבְכָל־הֶעָרִים אֲשֶׁר עַל־יְדֵי אַרְנוֹן
27 שְׁלֹשׁ מֵאוֹת שָׁנָה וּמַדּוּעַ לֹא־הִצַּלְתֶּם בָּעֵת הַהִיא׃ וְאָנֹכִי
לֹא־חָטָאתִי לָךְ וְאַתָּה עֹשֶׂה אִתִּי רָעָה לְהִלָּחֶם בִּי יִשְׁפֹּט
28 יְהוָה הַשֹּׁפֵט הַיּוֹם בֵּין בְּנֵי יִשְׂרָאֵל וּבֵין בְּנֵי עַמּוֹן׃ וְלֹא
שָׁמַע מֶלֶךְ בְּנֵי עַמּוֹן אֶל־דִּבְרֵי יִפְתָּח אֲשֶׁר שָׁלַח אֵלָיו׃
29 וַתְּהִי עַל־יִפְתָּח רוּחַ יְהוָה וַיַּעֲבֹר אֶת־הַגִּלְעָד וְאֶת־
מְנַשֶּׁה וַיַּעֲבֹר אֶת־מִצְפֵּה גִלְעָד וּמִמִּצְפֵּה גִּלְעָד עָבַר בְּנֵי
ל עַמּוֹן׃ וַיִּדַּר יִפְתָּח נֶדֶר לַיהוָה וַיֹּאמַר אִם־נָתוֹן תִּתֵּן אֶת־
31 בְּנֵי עַמּוֹן בְּיָדִי׃ וְהָיָה הַיּוֹצֵא אֲשֶׁר יֵצֵא מִדַּלְתֵי בֵיתִי
לִקְרָאתִי בְּשׁוּבִי בְשָׁלוֹם מִבְּנֵי עַמּוֹן וְהָיָה לַיהוָה
32 וְהַעֲלִיתִיהוּ עוֹלָה׃ וַיַּעֲבֹר יִפְתָּח אֶל־בְּנֵי עַמּוֹן לְהִלָּחֶם
33 בָּם וַיִּתְּנֵם יְהוָה בְּיָדוֹ׃ וַיַּכֵּם מֵעֲרוֹעֵר וְעַד־בּוֹאֲךָ מִנִּית
עֶשְׂרִים עִיר וְעַד אָבֵל כְּרָמִים מַכָּה גְּדוֹלָה מְאֹד וַיִּכָּנְעוּ
בְּנֵי עַמּוֹן מִפְּנֵי בְּנֵי יִשְׂרָאֵל׃

26. *three hundred years.* The different periods mentioned in the Book of Judges up to the beginning of the Ammonite oppression total 301 years.

30–31. JEPHTHAH'S VOW

31. *and I will offer it up . . . burnt-offering.* Kimchi, Ralbag and Abarbanel maintain that the 'and' before *I will offer it* should be rendered 'or', and the phrase read: 'It shall be the LORD's, *or* I will offer it up as a burnt-offering'; *i.e.* if it be an object permitted for sacrifice I will offer it; otherwise, it shall be dedicated, in some other way, to the LORD. (Support for this rendering is given in the verse, 'Whoso smiteth his father *and* mother,' Exod. XXI, 15, where the obvious meaning is, 'Whoso smiteth his father *or* his mother'). There was thus an implicit reservation in the vow to offer the first living object that met him, namely, 'if it be proper for such purpose.' Jephthah therefore did not offer her up as a burnt-offering, but 'he made a house for her and brought her into it, and she was there separated from mankind and from the ways of the world' (Kimchi).

Whatever interpretation we place upon the tragedy of Jephthah's daughter, his strange unhallowed vow would have been impossible under settled religious conditions, such as preceded and followed the period of the Judges. Legend represents the daughter seeking to prove to her father that the Torah speaks only of animal sacrifice, never of human sacrifices. In vain she cited the example of Jacob, who had vowed to give God a tenth of all his possessions, and yet did not attempt to sacrifice any of his sons. The Rabbis severely blame Jephthah for not having his entirely invalid vow 'annulled' (see Additional Note on Num. XXX). Phinehas the High Priest—whom the Rabbis assume was still living at the time—could have absolved him from his criminal vow; and but for the rivalry between them would have done so. Phinehas said: 'I, the High Priest, should go to that ignoramus! Let him come to *me*.' And Jephthah said: 'I, the Prince of the land, should humiliate myself before one of my subjects!' Both were overtaken by punishment. Jephthah died a horrible death. And as for Phinehas, the Holy Spirit departed from him. The condemnation of Jephthah's vow by the Rabbis has been re-echoed in many tongues and many lands. A thousand years later, Dante wrote:

'Be strong
To keep your vow; yet be not perverse—
As Jephthah once, blindly to execute a rash
resolve.
Better a man should say, I have done wrong,
Than keeping an ill vow, he should do worse.'
(Paradiso).

C. IN MOAB

(Chapters XXII–XXXVI)

VII. BALAK

(Chapters XXII, 2–XXV, 9)

THE BOOK OF BALAAM

The Israelites now enter upon the last stage of their journey to the Promised Land. They are within sight of their goal.

We see an irresistible People about to undertake the conquest of its national home, and a renowned heathen prophet giving solemn testimony to its sublime destiny. Such tribute to Israel's unique character is all the more impressive, as it is that of a stranger, speaking against his intention and interest, under the compulsion of a Higher Power. He proclaims the utter futility of all attempts on the part of man to foil the purposes of God in regard to that People; and in rapturous strains, he foretells the glorious future which awaits Israel. Such is the burden of chapters XXII–XXIV, probably known in ancient times as 'The Book of Balaam' ספר בלעם. (This is the reading found in the Munich Manuscript—the only complete manuscript—of the Talmud, instead of פרשת בלעם as in the printed editions; Baba Bathra, 15*a*.)

CHARACTER OF BALAAM

Balaam's personality is an old enigma which has baffled the skill of commentators. It seems probable that he had from the first learned some elements of pure and true religion in his home in Mesopotamia, the cradle of the ancestors of Israel. He thus belongs, with Melchizedek, Job, and Jethro, to the scattered worshippers of the true God, who are unconnected with Israel. But unlike these, he is represented in Scripture as at the same time heathen sorcerer, true Prophet, and the perverter who suggested a peculiarly abhorrent means of bringing about the ruin of Israel. Because of these fundamental contradictions in character, Bible Critics assume that the Scriptural account of Balaam is a combination of two or three varying traditions belonging to different periods. This is quite unconvincing; it is as if we were to maintain that the current life-story of Francis Bacon, for example, was due to the combination of two or three traditions belonging to different periods of English history, since no one man could at the same time be an illustrious philosopher, a great statesman, and 'the meanest of mankind'. Such a view betrays a slight knowledge of the fearful complexity of the mind and soul of man. It is only in the realm of the Fable that men and women display, as it were in a single flash of light, some *one* aspect of human nature. It is otherwise in real life. 'The heart is deceitful above all things, and desperately wicked: who can know it?' (Jeremiah XVII, 9) is, alas, a far truer summary of human psychology.

In post-Biblical times, most Jewish authorities represent Balaam in an unfavourable, and often in a detestable, light. Although his utterances are a rhapsodic praise of Israel, they pay regard to his intention, which was to curse and not to bless. They therefore speak of him as בלעם הרשע, Balaam the Wicked. An evil eye, a haughty mind, and a proud spirit—they declare—mark his disciples. With Amalek and Haman, he is a permanent type of the enmity of the impious against Israel. All the more noteworthy is the fact that some Jewish opinions are decidedly and emphatically favourable. According to these opinions, he is as a prophet on a level with Moses; and his story is of such importance that it is given in the Law, the Prophets (Micah VI), and the 'Sacred Writings' (Neh. XIII). There was even a suggestion that the utterances of Balaam should find a place in the Shema. Although this was not done, one noted saying of his, מה טבו אהליך יעקב משכנותיך ישראל ('How goodly are thy tents, O Jacob, thy tabernacles, O Israel') forms the opening sentence of every Synagogue service.

In the early Church, the view taken of Balaam is one of unrelieved blackness: he is the embodiment of avarice and unholy ambition. Modern Christian theologians have depicted him as a warning example of self-deception which persuades man in every case that the sin which he commits may be brought within the rules of conscience and revelation; and as the combination of the purest form of religious belief with a standard of conduct immeasurably below it. A violent reaction in his favour set in with Lessing and Herder, long before the rise of the Critical School; and, among these newer estimates, we may mention that of Kalisch who considers Balaam faultless in character and his utterances unsurpassed for poetic beauty in the whole of Scripture: 'firm and inexorable like eternal Fate, he regards himself solely as an instrument of that Omnipotence which guides the destinies of nations by its unerring wisdom. Free from all human passion, he is like a mysterious spirit from a higher and nobler world.' Careful reading of chapters XXII–XXIV, however, shows that those who approve of everything Balaam says or does, are as far from a true estimate of him as those to whom he is a semi-diabolical being.

For the unique incident of the speaking ass, that has for centuries proved a source of merriment to the semi-educated, see introductory note to *v.* 22–34.

22

כב ס ס ס מ 40

2. And Balak the son of Zippor saw all that Israel had done to the Amorites. 3. And Moab was sore afraid of the people, because they were many; and Moab was overcome with dread because of the children of Israel. 4. And Moab said unto the elders of Midian: 'Now will this multitude lick up all that is round about us, as the ox licketh up the grass of the field.'—And Balak the son of Zippor was king of Moab at that time.— 5. And he sent messengers unto Balaam the son of Beor, to Pethor, which is by the River, to the land of the children of his people, to call him, saying: 'Behold, there is a people come out from Egypt; behold, they cover the face of the earth, and they abide over against me. 6. Come now

2 וַיַּרְא בָּלָק בֶּן־צִפּוֹר אֵת כָּל־אֲשֶׁר־עָשָׂה יִשְׂרָאֵל לָאֱמֹרִי׃
3 וַיָּגָר מוֹאָב מִפְּנֵי הָעָם מְאֹד כִּי רַב־הוּא וַיָּקָץ מוֹאָב מִפְּנֵי
4 בְּנֵי יִשְׂרָאֵל׃ וַיֹּאמֶר מוֹאָב אֶל־זִקְנֵי מִדְיָן עַתָּה יְלַחֲכוּ
הַקָּהָל אֶת־כָּל־סְבִיבֹתֵינוּ כִּלְחֹךְ הַשּׁוֹר אֵת יֶרֶק הַשָּׂדֶה
ה וּבָלָק בֶּן־צִפּוֹר מֶלֶךְ לְמוֹאָב בָּעֵת הַהִוא׃ וַיִּשְׁלַח מַלְאָכִים
אֶל־בִּלְעָם בֶּן־בְּעוֹר פְּתוֹרָה אֲשֶׁר עַל־הַנָּהָר אֶרֶץ בְּנֵי־
עַמּוֹ לִקְרֹא־לוֹ לֵאמֹר הִנֵּה עַם יָצָא מִמִּצְרַיִם הִנֵּה כִסָּה
6 אֶת־עֵין הָאָרֶץ וְהוּא יֹשֵׁב מִמֻּלִי׃ וְעַתָּה לְכָה־נָּא אָרָה־

VII. BALAK

(Chapters XXII, 2–XXV, 9)

XXII, 2–4. Balak King of Moab

The Israelites fresh from victory over the Amorite kings were now settled on the border of Moab, and filled both king and people of Moab with dread.

3. *was overcome with dread.* Or, 'loathed'; because they hated the children of Israel, they had a horror of them; cf. Exod. I, 12.

4. *elders of Midian.* Who conducted the general affairs of the desert tribes that had their origin in Midian, east of the Gulf of Akaba. There was no enmity on the part of Israel towards Moab (Deut. II, 29). Neither did Israel in any way cross the path of the Midianites or harbour any ill-will against them. Moses had spent many years in Midian; and Jethro, the Midianite priest, was an honoured guest in Israel's tents. The plot of the Moabites and Midianites against Israel was thus the outcome of 'causeless hatred' (שנאת חנם), the source of the most terrible cruelties in human relations.

5–14. The First Deputation to Balaam

They place their hope in Balaam, far-famed throughout the East as a soothsayer whose curse is irresistible. Balak sends messengers to Balaam inviting him to cast a baneful spell upon this rising People of the desert. In a vision, God forbids Balaam to accompany them.

5. *Balaam.* Heb. 'Bileam', probably a shortened form of בעל העם, 'lord of the people' (Kalisch).

Pethor. Pitru, a town in Mesopotamia, mentioned in Babylonian and Egyptian inscriptions. It was from the land of magic that the great magician was to be brought.

the River. *i.e.* the Euphrates; Deut. I, 7.

land of the children of his people. According to Heb. idiom this means Balaam's native land (Nachmanides). Midrash and Rashi, however, refer it to Balak, and deem him a foreign conqueror of Moab.

6. *come now.* The curse cannot be pronounced at a distance. The diviner must behold those whom he is to blight by his incantations.

curse me this people. The whole ancient world, Greece and Rome no less than the Near Eastern nations, had a firm belief in the real power of blessings and curses. This was especially so in Mesopotamia. Babylonian religion was rooted in demonology. It taught that certain persons had the power of directing or changing the decree of the gods, and could by their spells and incantations secure prosperity or call forth calamity. These masters of magic were employed to discover secrets, to foretell the future, to bless an undertaking, or to bring ruin upon an enemy.

too mighty for me. Cf. Exod. I, 9. Balak's phraseology, as well as his whole attitude, is reminiscent of Pharaoh—both illustrating the fatal madness of those who oppose God's purposes (Gray).

peradventure. 'Hesitancy and assurance, despondency and reckless courage, struggle in his uneasy and foreboding mind' (Kalisch).

whom thou blessest is blessed. An expression of Balak's profound belief in the efficacy of curses; also the language of flattery with the object of securing the expert soothsayer's services before he—Balak—undertakes to fight the Israelites.

לִי אֶת־הָעָם הַזֶּה כִּי־עָצוּם הוּא מִמֶּנִּי אוּלַי אוּכַל נַכֶּה־
בּוֹ וַאֲגָרְשֶׁנּוּ מִן־הָאָרֶץ כִּי יָדַעְתִּי אֵת אֲשֶׁר־תְּבָרֵךְ מְבֹרָךְ
7 וַאֲשֶׁר תָּאֹר יוּאָר׃ וַיֵּלְכוּ זִקְנֵי מוֹאָב וְזִקְנֵי מִדְיָן וּקְסָמִים בְּיָדָם
8 וַיָּבֹאוּ אֶל־בִּלְעָם וַיְדַבְּרוּ אֵלָיו דִּבְרֵי בָלָק׃ וַיֹּאמֶר אֲלֵיהֶם
לִינוּ פֹה הַלַּיְלָה וַהֲשִׁבֹתִי אֶתְכֶם דָּבָר כַּאֲשֶׁר יְדַבֵּר יְהוָה
9 אֵלָי וַיֵּשְׁבוּ שָׂרֵי־מוֹאָב עִם־בִּלְעָם׃ וַיָּבֹא אֱלֹהִים אֶל־
י בִּלְעָם וַיֹּאמֶר מִי הָאֲנָשִׁים הָאֵלֶּה עִמָּךְ׃ וַיֹּאמֶר בִּלְעָם
11 אֶל־הָאֱלֹהִים בָּלָק בֶּן־צִפֹּר מֶלֶךְ מוֹאָב שָׁלַח אֵלָי׃ הִנֵּה
הָעָם הַיֹּצֵא מִמִּצְרַיִם וַיְכַס אֶת־עֵין הָאָרֶץ עַתָּה לְכָה קָבָה־
12 לִּי אֹתוֹ אוּלַי אוּכַל לְהִלָּחֶם בּוֹ וְגֵרַשְׁתִּיו׃ וַיֹּאמֶר אֱלֹהִים
שני (חמישי כשהן מחוב׳) אֶל־בִּלְעָם לֹא תֵלֵךְ עִמָּהֶם לֹא תָאֹר אֶת־הָעָם כִּי בָרוּךְ
13 הוּא׃ וַיָּקָם בִּלְעָם בַּבֹּקֶר וַיֹּאמֶר אֶל־שָׂרֵי בָלָק לְכוּ אֶל־
14 אַרְצְכֶם כִּי מֵאֵן יְהוָה לְתִתִּי לַהֲלֹךְ עִמָּכֶם׃ וַיָּקוּמוּ שָׂרֵי
מוֹאָב וַיָּבֹאוּ אֶל־בָּלָק וַיֹּאמְרוּ מֵאֵן בִּלְעָם הֲלֹךְ עִמָּנוּ׃
טו וַיֹּסֶף עוֹד בָּלָק שְׁלֹחַ שָׂרִים רַבִּים וְנִכְבָּדִים מֵאֵלֶּה׃
16 וַיָּבֹאוּ אֶל־בִּלְעָם וַיֹּאמְרוּ לוֹ כֹּה אָמַר בָּלָק בֶּן־צִפּוֹר אַל־
17 נָא תִמָּנַע מֵהֲלֹךְ אֵלָי׃ כִּי־כַבֵּד אֲכַבֶּדְךָ מְאֹד וְכֹל אֲשֶׁר־
18 תֹּאמַר אֵלַי אֶעֱשֶׂה וּלְכָה־נָּא קָבָה־לִּי אֵת הָעָם הַזֶּה׃ וַיַּעַן
בִּלְעָם וַיֹּאמֶר אֶל־עַבְדֵי בָלָק אִם־יִתֶּן־לִי בָלָק מְלֹא בֵיתוֹ
כֶּסֶף וְזָהָב לֹא אוּכַל לַעֲבֹר אֶת־פִּי יְהוָה אֱלֹהָי לַעֲשׂוֹת

v. 18. קמץ בז״ק

therefore, I pray thee, curse me this people; for they are too mighty for me; peradventure I shall prevail, that we may smite them, and that I may drive them out of the land; for I know that he whom thou blessest is blessed, and he whom thou cursest is cursed.' 7. And the elders of Moab and the elders of Midian departed with the rewards of divination in their hand; and they came unto Balaam, and spoke unto him the words of Balak. 8. And he said unto them: 'Lodge here this night, and I will bring you back word, as the LORD may speak unto me'; and the princes of Moab abode with Balaam. 9. And God came unto Balaam, and said: 'What men are these with thee?' 10. And Balaam said unto God: 'Balak the son of Zippor, king of Moab, hath sent unto me [,saying]: 11. Behold the people that is come out of Egypt, it covereth the face of the earth; now, come curse me them; peradventure I shall be able to fight against them, and shall drive them out.' 12. And God said unto Balaam: 'Thou shalt not go with them; thou shalt not curse the people; for they are blessed.'*ii (**v). 13. And Balaam rose up in the morning, and said unto the princes of Balak: 'Get you into your land; for the LORD refuseth to give me leave to go with you.' 14. And the princes of Moab rose up, and they went unto Balak, and said: 'Balaam refuseth to come with us.' 15. And Balak sent yet again princes, more, and more honourable than they. 16. And they came to Balaam, and said to him: 'Thus saith Balak the son of Zippor: Let nothing, I pray thee, hinder thee from coming unto me; 17. for I will promote thee unto very great honour, and whatsoever thou sayest unto me I will do; come therefore, I pray thee, curse me this people.' 18. And Balaam answered and said unto the servants of Balak: 'If Balak would give me his house full of silver and gold, I can-

7. *the rewards of divination.* lit. 'the instruments of the diviner's art'; here, the reward or pay to be given him (Samuel Hanaggid, the famous Spanish Talmudist, poet and statesman).

8. *lodge here this night.* Balaam is not disinclined to follow the invitation. The name 'Israel' has not even been mentioned. To judge by Balaam's surprise when he caught his first glimpse of the Israelites, his knowledge of them could not have been extensive.

as the LORD may speak unto me. Balaam is a prophet of the true God, in familiar intercourse with Him, and expects to receive some Divine communication in a dream or a vision of the night; cf. Gen. xx, 3. 'This recognition of God's revelation of His purposes concerning Israel to a non-Israelite is striking evidence of the universality of Judaism' (Stanley).

9. *what men are these?* A leading question (Ibn Ezra, Mendelssohn); cf. Gen. III, 9; XVI, 8.

13. *the LORD refuseth.* Balaam suppresses the fact that God had forbidden him to curse Israel.

15–20. A SECOND DEPUTATION

Balak thought that the seer's motive for refusing was to elicit higher reward for his services.

18. *to do anything, small or great; i.e.* to do anything at all against the Divine will.

not go beyond the word of the LORD my
God, to do any thing, small or great.
19. Now therefore, I pray you, tarry ye also
here this night, that I may know what the
LORD will speak unto me more.' 20. And
God came unto Balaam at night, and said
unto him: 'If the men are come to call
thee, rise up, go with them; but only the
word which I speak unto thee, that shalt
thou do.'*iii. 21. And Balaam rose up in the
morning, and saddled his ass, and went

19 קְטַנָּה אוֹ גְדוֹלָה׃ וְעַתָּה שְׁבוּ נָא בָזֶה גַּם־אַתֶּם הַלָּיְלָה
כ וְאֵדְעָה מַה־יֹּסֵף יְהוָה דַּבֵּר עִמִּי׃ וַיָּבֹא אֱלֹהִים ׀ אֶל־
בִּלְעָם לַיְלָה וַיֹּאמֶר לוֹ אִם־לִקְרֹא לְךָ בָּאוּ הָאֲנָשִׁים קוּם
שלישי לֵךְ אִתָּם וְאַךְ אֶת־הַדָּבָר אֲשֶׁר־אֲדַבֵּר אֵלֶיךָ אֹתוֹ תַעֲשֶׂה׃
21 וַיָּקָם בִּלְעָם בַּבֹּקֶר וַיַּחֲבֹשׁ אֶת־אֲתֹנוֹ וַיֵּלֶךְ עִם־שָׂרֵי מוֹאָב׃

19. *tarry ye also here this night.* 'A thorough honest man would without hesitation have repeated his former answer, that he could not be guilty of so infamous a degradation of the sacred character with which he was invested, as to curse those whom he knew to be blessed. But instead of this, he desires the princes of Moab to tarry that night with him also; and for the sake of the reward deliberates whether he might not be able to obtain leave to do that which had been before revealed to him to be contrary to the will of God' (Joseph Butler).

that I may know. After God had distinctly said unto him, 'thou shalt not curse this people,' what need was there for him to say, 'that I may know what the LORD will speak unto me more'? It is evident that he harboured evil thoughts in his heart (Ibn Ezra). 'Balaam said, Perhaps I may persuade Him, and He will agree that I should curse' (Rashi).

20. *rise up, go with them.* 'Audacity may prevail even before God. Balaam's steadfast insistence upon his wish wrested from God His consent to Balaam's journey to Moab. He warned him of its consequences, saying to him, I take no pleasure in the destruction of sinners, but if thou art bound to go to thy destruction, do so' (Talmud).

BALAAM AND THE ASS

We now come to the best-known episode in the story of Balaam; *viz.* the speaking ass. God makes the dumb animal rebuke the blindness and obstinacy of man. Balaam, like many a one before and after him, is saved from dishonour by unforeseen hindrance, and brought to reason through means which human pride despises.

Many expositors, both in ancient and modern times, take the account of the miracle in these verses literally. Nothing is impossible to Omnipotence, they hold; and a speaking ass is no more marvellous than a speaking serpent or any of the other miracles. In the Ethics of the Fathers, the mouth of the earth that swallowed Korah (XVI, 32), the mouth of the well (see note on XXI, 16), and the mouth of Balaam's ass, are classed among those strange and wonderful phenomena that had their origin in the interval between the close of the work of Creation and the commencement of the Sabbath. In this way, the Rabbis gave expression to their conception of the miraculous in the scheme of things. Miracles, they held, were not interruptions of Nature's laws; for *at Creation, God had provided for them in advance, as part of the cosmic plan.* 'The Fathers of the Mishnah, who taught that Balaam's ass was created on the eve of the Sabbath, in the twilight, were not fantastic fools, but subtle philosophers, discovering the reign of universal law through the exceptions, the miracles that had to be created specially and were still a part of the order of the world, bound to appear in due time much as apparently erratic comets are' (Zangwill).

For over a thousand years, however, the literal has largely given place to other interpretations of this incident. One of these explanations —that of Saadyah and Maimonides—considers *v.* 22–34 as enacted in a dream, or vision of the night. This would account for the many incongruous things in these verses. Thus, Balaam appears with but two attendants, and travelling alone without the brilliant accompaniment of princes and 'honourable' ambassadors. Again, he does not show the least astonishment at the startling fact of the ass speaking. In the light of this interpretation, *v.* 22–34 depict the continuance on the subconscious plane of the mental and moral conflict in Balaam's soul; and the dream-apparition of the angel and the speaking ass is but a further warning to Balaam against being misled through avarice to violate God's command. Another explanation holds that the Text nowhere states that the ass gave utterance to human sounds. Its weird behaviour in the presence of the angel, and its wild cries at the cruel beatings, were understood by Balaam to mean the words given in the Text (Luzzatto).

In brief, there is not in Judaism any one authoritative interpretation of the Book of Balaam; and 'in regard to its narrative, readers are free to think what they please' (Josephus). Therefore, those who do not deem any of the above interpretations acceptable, should feel too deeply the *essential veracity* of the story to be troubled overmuch with minute questions about its details. In whatever way we conceive of the narrative, its representation of the strivings of conscience is of permanent human and spiritual value.

with the princes of Moab. 22. And God's anger was kindled because he went; and the angel of the LORD placed himself in the way for an adversary against him.—Now he was riding upon his ass, and his two servants were with him.—23. And the ass saw the angel of the LORD standing in the way, with his sword drawn in his hand; and the ass turned aside out of the way, and went into the field; and Balaam smote the ass, to turn her into the way. 24. Then the angel of the LORD stood in a hollow way between the vineyards, a fence being on this side, and a fence on that side. 25. And the ass saw the angel of the LORD, and she thrust herself unto the wall, and crushed Balaam's foot against the wall; and he smote her again. 26. And the angel of the LORD went further, and stood in a narrow place, where was no way to turn either to the right hand or to the left. 27. And the ass saw the angel of the LORD, and she lay down under Balaam; and Balaam's anger was kindled, and he smote the ass with his staff. 28. And the LORD opened the mouth of the ass, and she said unto Balaam: 'What have I done unto thee, that thou hast smitten me these three times?' 29. And Balaam said unto the ass: 'Because thou hast mocked me; I would there were a sword in my hand, for now I had killed thee.' 30. And the ass said unto Balaam: 'Am not I thine ass, upon which thou hast ridden all thy life long unto this day? was I ever wont to do so unto thee?' And he said: 'Nay.' 31. Then the LORD opened the eyes of Balaam, and he saw the angel of the LORD standing in the way, with his sword drawn in his hand; and he bowed his head, and fell on his

22 וַיִּחַר־אַף אֱלֹהִים כִּי־הוֹלֵךְ הוּא וַיִּתְיַצֵּב מַלְאַךְ יְהוָה בַּדֶּרֶךְ
23 לְשָׂטָן לוֹ וְהוּא רֹכֵב עַל־אֲתֹנוֹ וּשְׁנֵי נְעָרָיו עִמּוֹ׃ וַתֵּרֶא
הָאָתוֹן אֶת־מַלְאַךְ יְהוָה נִצָּב בַּדֶּרֶךְ וְחַרְבּוֹ שְׁלוּפָה בְּיָדוֹ
וַתֵּט הָאָתוֹן מִן־הַדֶּרֶךְ וַתֵּלֶךְ בַּשָּׂדֶה וַיַּךְ בִּלְעָם אֶת־הָאָתוֹן
24 לְהַטֹּתָהּ הַדָּרֶךְ׃ וַיַּעֲמֹד מַלְאַךְ יְהוָה בְּמִשְׁעוֹל הַכְּרָמִים
כה גָּדֵר מִזֶּה וְגָדֵר מִזֶּה׃ וַתֵּרֶא הָאָתוֹן אֶת־מַלְאַךְ יְהוָה
וַתִּלָּחֵץ אֶל־הַקִּיר וַתִּלְחַץ אֶת־רֶגֶל בִּלְעָם אֶל־הַקִּיר וַיֹּסֶף
26 לְהַכֹּתָהּ׃ וַיּוֹסֶף מַלְאַךְ־יְהוָה עֲבוֹר וַיַּעֲמֹד בְּמָקוֹם צָר
27 אֲשֶׁר אֵין־דֶּרֶךְ לִנְטוֹת יָמִין וּשְׂמֹאול׃ וַתֵּרֶא הָאָתוֹן אֶת־
מַלְאַךְ יְהוָה וַתִּרְבַּץ תַּחַת בִּלְעָם וַיִּחַר־אַף בִּלְעָם וַיַּךְ
28 אֶת־הָאָתוֹן בַּמַּקֵּל׃ וַיִּפְתַּח יְהוָה אֶת־פִּי הָאָתוֹן וַתֹּאמֶר
לְבִלְעָם מֶה־עָשִׂיתִי לְךָ כִּי הִכִּיתַנִי זֶה שָׁלֹשׁ רְגָלִים׃
29 וַיֹּאמֶר בִּלְעָם לָאָתוֹן כִּי הִתְעַלַּלְתְּ בִּי לוּ יֶשׁ־חֶרֶב בְּיָדִי
ל כִּי עַתָּה הֲרַגְתִּיךְ׃ וַתֹּאמֶר הָאָתוֹן אֶל־בִּלְעָם הֲלוֹא אָנֹכִי
אֲתֹנְךָ אֲשֶׁר־רָכַבְתָּ עָלַי מֵעוֹדְךָ עַד־הַיּוֹם הַזֶּה הַהַסְכֵּן
31 הִסְכַּנְתִּי לַעֲשׂוֹת לְךָ כֹּה וַיֹּאמֶר לֹא׃ וַיְגַל יְהוָה אֶת־עֵינֵי
בִלְעָם וַיַּרְא אֶת־מַלְאַךְ יְהוָה נִצָּב בַּדֶּרֶךְ וְחַרְבּוֹ שְׁלֻפָה
32 בְּיָדוֹ וַיִּקֹּד וַיִּשְׁתַּחוּ לְאַפָּיו׃ וַיֹּאמֶר אֵלָיו מַלְאַךְ יְהוָה עַל־

v. 26. קמץ בז״ק ibid. מלא ו׳ v. 28. קמץ בז״ק

21–35. THE JOURNEY

22. *God's anger was kindled.* This seems to contradict what is said in *v.* 20, that God gave him permission to go. But that permission was conditional. He might go, but he must speak only what is given him to say. Balaam gladly seized the opportunity of going, for he was hankering after the reward. For the present, he ignored the condition. In his heart he hoped to evade it and satisfy Balak. But God who is the discerner of the thoughts and intents of the heart, sees the double-mindedness of Balaam and gives him to know that there must be no trifling (Dummelow).

angel of the LORD. 'This was an angel of mercy who desired to restrain him from committing a sin and perishing' (Midrash). 'In many unforeseen, singular, and often homely ways, men are checked in the endeavour to carry out the schemes which ambition and avarice prompt. The angel of the LORD who opposes one bent on a bad enterprise often appears in familiar guise. To some men their wives stand in their way, some are challenged by their children' (Expositor's Bible).

an adversary against him. *i.e.* against Balaam's evil self. The angel tried to save Balaam from rushing to his own destruction.

28. *three times.* 'The narrator of this tale had a heart full of pity for the groans of the poor creature' (Holzinger).

29. *I had killed thee.* 'At this, the ass laughed. He is intent on destroying a whole people by word of mouth; and to slay a poor ass he requires a sword' (Midrash).

32. *wherefore hast thou smitten thine ass.* 'I have been commissioned to demand restitution from thee for the injustice thou hast offered to face. 32. And the angel of the LORD said unto him: 'Wherefore hast thou smitten thine ass these three times? behold, I am come forth for an adversary, because thy way is contrary unto me; 33. and the ass saw me, and turned aside before me these three times; unless she had turned aside from me, surely now I had even slain thee, and saved her alive.' 34. And Balaam said unto the angel of the LORD: 'I have sinned; for I knew not that thou stoodest in the way against me; now therefore, if it displease thee, I will get me back.' 35. And the angel of the LORD said unto Balaam: 'Go with the men; but only the word that I shall speak unto thee, that thou shalt speak.' So Balaam went with the princes of Balak. 36. And when Balak heard that Balaam was come, he went out to meet him unto Ir-moab, which is on the border of Arnon, which is in the utmost part of the border. 37. And Balak said unto Balaam: 'Did I not earnestly send unto thee to call thee? wherefore camest thou not *unto me? am I not able indeed to promote thee to honour?' 38. And Balaam said unto Balak: 'Lo, I am come unto thee; have I now any power at all to speak any thing? the word that God putteth in my mouth, that shall I speak.'*iv (**vi). 39. And Balaam went with Balak, and they came unto Kiriath-huzoth. 40. And Balak sacrificed oxen and sheep, and sent to Balaam, and to the princes that were with him. 41. And it came to pass in the morning that Balak took Balaam, and brought him up into Bamoth-baal, and he saw from thence the utmost part of the people.

מַה הִכִּיתָ אֶת־אֲתֹנְךָ זֶה שָׁלוֹשׁ רְגָלִים הִנֵּה אָנֹכִי יָצָאתִי
33 לְשָׂטָן כִּי־יָרַט הַדֶּרֶךְ לְנֶגְדִּי׃ וַתִּרְאַנִי הָאָתוֹן וַתֵּט לְפָנַי
זֶה שָׁלֹשׁ רְגָלִים אוּלַי נָטְתָה מִפָּנַי כִּי עַתָּה גַּם־אֹתְכָה
34 הָרַגְתִּי וְאוֹתָהּ הֶחֱיֵיתִי׃ וַיֹּאמֶר בִּלְעָם אֶל־מַלְאַךְ יְהוָה
חָטָאתִי כִּי לֹא יָדַעְתִּי כִּי אַתָּה נִצָּב לִקְרָאתִי בַּדָּרֶךְ וְעַתָּה
לה אִם־רַע בְּעֵינֶיךָ אָשׁוּבָה לִּי׃ וַיֹּאמֶר מַלְאַךְ יְהוָה אֶל־
בִּלְעָם לֵךְ עִם־הָאֲנָשִׁים וְאֶפֶס אֶת־הַדָּבָר אֲשֶׁר־אֲדַבֵּר
36 אֵלֶיךָ אֹתוֹ תְדַבֵּר וַיֵּלֶךְ בִּלְעָם עִם־שָׂרֵי בָלָק׃ וַיִּשְׁמַע
בָּלָק כִּי־בָא בִלְעָם וַיֵּצֵא לִקְרָאתוֹ אֶל־עִיר מוֹאָב אֲשֶׁר
37 עַל־גְּבוּל אַרְנֹן אֲשֶׁר בִּקְצֵה הַגְּבוּל׃ וַיֹּאמֶר בָּלָק אֶל־
בִּלְעָם הֲלֹא שָׁלֹחַ שָׁלַחְתִּי אֵלֶיךָ לִקְרֹא־לָךְ לָמָּה לֹא־
38 הָלַכְתָּ אֵלָי הַאֻמְנָם לֹא אוּכַל כַּבְּדֶךָ׃ וַיֹּאמֶר בִּלְעָם אֶל־
רביעי (ששי כשהן מחוב') בָּלָק הִנֵּה־בָאתִי אֵלֶיךָ עַתָּה הֲיָכֹל אוּכַל דַּבֵּר מְאוּמָה
39 הַדָּבָר אֲשֶׁר יָשִׂים אֱלֹהִים בְּפִי אֹתוֹ אֲדַבֵּר׃* וַיֵּלֶךְ בִּלְעָם
מ עִם־בָּלָק וַיָּבֹאוּ קִרְיַת חֻצוֹת׃ וַיִּזְבַּח בָּלָק בָּקָר וָצֹאן וַיְשַׁלַּח
41 לְבִלְעָם וְלַשָּׂרִים אֲשֶׁר אִתּוֹ׃ וַיְהִי בַבֹּקֶר וַיִּקַּח בָּלָק אֶת־
בִּלְעָם וַיַּעֲלֵהוּ בָּמוֹת בָּעַל וַיַּרְא מִשָּׁם קְצֵה הָעָם׃

the ass' (Midrash). This *v.* is a classical text for the preaching of humane treatment of animals. 'There is a rule laid down by our Sages, that it is directly prohibited in the Torah to cause pain to an animal, and that rule is based on the words, *Wherefore hast thou smitten thine ass?*' (Maimonides).

contrary. Or, 'headlong'; *i.e.* unto destruction.

34. *I have sinned.* In cruelly beating the animal. 'Balaam knew that Divine punishment could be averted only by penitence, and that the angels have no power to touch a man who, after sinning, says "I have sinned"' (Midrash).

I will get me back. Balaam was now convinced that it was useless hoping to bend God's will to his, and wished to have nothing more to do with Balak. But Balaam must now go as God's messenger and bless Israel.

35. *So Balaam went.* Resolved strictly to adhere to the Divine communications that were to be made to him. Having thus changed his disposition, he received God's revelation and was endowed with the Divine Spirit (Ewald).

36–40. ARRIVAL AND RECEPTION

36. *unto Ir-Moab.* Probably the same as the Ar mentioned in XXI, 15.

37. *to promote thee.* Balak seems surprised that his power to reward the prophet had not secured immediate compliance with his request. He is the type of worldy-minded man who thinks that blessings and curses, nay all things in heaven and on earth, can be bought, if only the buyer will pay a high enough price for them.

39. *Kiriath-huzoth.* Its site is unknown.

40. *and sent to Balaam.* As a sign of hospitality to his honoured guest.

XXII, 41–XXIII, 6. PREPARATIONS FOR THE GREAT INCANTATION

Balaam prepares for his work more after the fashion of a Babylonian soothsayer than in accordance with the spiritual ideas of Hebrew prophecy.

41. *Bamoth-baal.* Either the name of a place

23

CHAPTER XXIII

1. And Balaam said unto Balak: 'Build me here seven altars, and prepare me here seven bullocks and seven rams.' 2. And Balak did as Balaam had spoken; and Balak and Balaam offered on every altar a bullock and a ram. 3. And Balaam said unto Balak: 'Stand by thy burnt-offering, and I will go; peradventure the LORD will come to meet me; and whatsoever He showeth me I will tell thee.' And he went to a bare height. 4. And God met Balaam; and he said unto Him: 'I have prepared the seven altars, and I have offered up a bullock and a ram on every altar.' 5. And the LORD put a word in Balaam's mouth, and said: 'Return unto Balak, and thus thou shalt speak.' 6. And he returned unto him, and, lo, he stood by his burnt-offering, he, and all the princes of Moab. 7. And he took up his parable, and said:

From Aram Balak bringeth me,
The king of Moab from the mountains of the East:
'Come, curse me Jacob,
And come, execrate Israel.'
8. How shall I curse, whom God hath not cursed?
And how shall I execrate, whom the LORD hath not execrated?
9. For from the top of the rocks I see him,

CAP. XXIII. כג

כג

א וַיֹּאמֶר בִּלְעָם אֶל־בָּלָק בְּנֵה־לִי בָזֶה שִׁבְעָה מִזְבְּחֹת וְהָכֵן
2 לִי בָּזֶה שִׁבְעָה פָרִים וְשִׁבְעָה אֵילִים׃ וַיַּעַשׂ בָּלָק כַּאֲשֶׁר
3 דִּבֶּר בִּלְעָם וַיַּעַל בָּלָק וּבִלְעָם פָּר וָאַיִל בַּמִּזְבֵּחַ׃ וַיֹּאמֶר
בִּלְעָם לְבָלָק הִתְיַצֵּב עַל־עֹלָתֶךָ וְאֵלְכָה אוּלַי יִקָּרֵה
יְהוָה לִקְרָאתִי וּדְבַר מַה־יַּרְאֵנִי וְהִגַּדְתִּי לָךְ וַיֵּלֶךְ שֶׁפִי׃
4 וַיִּקָּר אֱלֹהִים אֶל־בִּלְעָם וַיֹּאמֶר אֵלָיו אֶת־שִׁבְעַת הַמִּזְבְּחֹת
ה עָרַכְתִּי וָאַעַל פָּר וָאַיִל בַּמִּזְבֵּחַ׃ וַיָּשֶׂם יְהוָה דָּבָר בְּפִי
6 בִלְעָם וַיֹּאמֶר שׁוּב אֶל־בָּלָק וְכֹה תְדַבֵּר׃ וַיָּשָׁב אֵלָיו
7 וְהִנֵּה נִצָּב עַל־עֹלָתוֹ הוּא וְכָל־שָׂרֵי מוֹאָב׃ וַיִּשָּׂא מְשָׁלוֹ
וַיֹּאמַר מִן־אֲרָם יַנְחֵנִי בָלָק מֶלֶךְ־מוֹאָב מֵהַרְרֵי־קֶדֶם
8 לְכָה אָרָה־לִּי יַעֲקֹב וּלְכָה זֹעֲמָה יִשְׂרָאֵל׃ מָה אֶקֹּב לֹא
9 קַבֹּה אֵל וּמָה אֶזְעֹם לֹא זָעַם יְהוָה׃ כִּי־מֵרֹאשׁ צֻרִים

or, more probably, some local sanctuary of Baal.

the utmost part. The outermost part.

CHAPTER XXIII

1. *build me.* The altar had to be erected by the person for whom the divining was done.

2. *Balak and Balaam. Both* had to be engaged in the sacrifice. This is in accordance with the Babylonian practice of soothsaying (Daiches).

3. *stand by.* Balak had to remain by the burnt-offering, while the diviner did his work.

I will go. To perform the divination ceremonies.

to a bare height. Or, 'alone' (Onkelos). The Heb. שפי has also been taken as an abbreviation of the three words שאול פי י׳, 'to inquire of the mouth of the LORD.'

7–10. BALAAM'S FIRST PROPHECY

When Balaam returns to Balak and his princes, he can but break forth into unstinted blessing of Israel. 'It is a marvellous people, with a unique destiny!'

7. *parable.* Here in the meaning of 'oracular utterance'.

Aram. Usually denotes Syria, here Mesopotamia, and the equivalent of 'Aram-Naharaim'; Gen. XXIV, 10.

mountains of the East. The high ranges of Mesopotamia.

execrate. i.e. provoke against him the anger of God.

9. *from the top of the rocks I see him.* Standing on the mountain peak, and looking not with the eyes of fear or envy, he is overpowered by the view he has of Israel below. Curse he cannot. He feels compelled by an irresistible Divine impulse to break forth into jubilant praise.

that shall dwell alone. Israel has always been a people apart, a people isolated and distinguished from other peoples by its religious and moral laws, by the fact that it has been chosen as the instrument of a Divine purpose.

shall not be reckoned among the nations. The Heb. is in the Hithpael and occurs only here in Scripture; lit. 'does not reckon itself among the nations'. A notable alternative rendering was proposed by Marcus Jastrow. He showed that in Neo-Hebrew the Hithpael of the root חשב signifies 'to conspire' (see his Talmudic Dictionary, I, 508), and believes that this is the meaning intended here. 'Israel is a people that dwelleth alone; *it does not conspire against the nations,*' exclaims Balaam; why then shall he be cursed?

And from the hills I behold him:
Lo, it is a people that shall dwell alone,
And shall not be reckoned among the nations.
10. Who hath counted the dust of Jacob,
Or numbered the stock of Israel?
Let me die the death of the righteous,
And let mine end be like his!

11. And Balak said unto Balaam: 'What hast thou done unto me? I took thee to curse mine enemies, and, behold, thou hast blessed them altogether.' 12. And he answered and said: 'Must I not take heed to speak that which the LORD putteth in my mouth?' *v. 13. And Balak said unto him: 'Come, I pray thee, with me unto another place, from whence thou mayest see them; thou shalt see but the utmost part of them, and shalt not see them all; and curse me them from thence.' 14. And he took him into the field of Zophim, to the top of Pisgah, and built seven altars, and offered up a bullock and a ram on every altar. 15. And he said unto Balak: 'Stand here by thy burnt-offering, while I go toward a meeting yonder.' 16. And the LORD met Balaam, and put a word in his mouth, and said: 'Return unto Balak, and thus shalt thou speak.' 17. And he came to him, and, lo, he stood by his burnt-offering, and

אֶרְאֶנּוּ וּמִגְּבָעוֹת אֲשׁוּרֶנּוּ הֶן־עָם לְבָדָד יִשְׁכֹּן וּבַגּוֹיִם לֹא
י יִתְחַשָּׁב׃ מִי מָנָה עֲפַר יַעֲקֹב וּמִסְפָּר אֶת־רֹבַע יִשְׂרָאֵל
11 תָּמֹת נַפְשִׁי מוֹת יְשָׁרִים וּתְהִי אַחֲרִיתִי כָּמֹהוּ׃ וַיֹּאמֶר
בָּלָק אֶל־בִּלְעָם מֶה עָשִׂיתָ לִי לָקֹב אֹיְבַי לְקַחְתִּיךָ וְהִנֵּה
12 בֵּרַכְתָּ בָרֵךְ׃ וַיַּעַן וַיֹּאמַר הֲלֹא אֵת אֲשֶׁר יָשִׂים יְהוָה
מישי 13 בְּפִי אֹתוֹ אֶשְׁמֹר לְדַבֵּר׃* וַיֹּאמֶר אֵלָיו בָּלָק לְךָ־נָּא אִתִּי
אֶל־מָקוֹם אַחֵר אֲשֶׁר תִּרְאֶנּוּ מִשָּׁם אֶפֶס קָצֵהוּ תִרְאֶה
14 וְכֻלּוֹ לֹא תִרְאֶה וְקָבְנוֹ־לִי מִשָּׁם׃ וַיִּקָּחֵהוּ שְׂדֵה צֹפִים
אֶל־רֹאשׁ הַפִּסְגָּה וַיִּבֶן שִׁבְעָה מִזְבְּחֹת וַיַּעַל פָּר וָאַיִל
טו בַּמִּזְבֵּחַ׃ וַיֹּאמֶר אֶל־בָּלָק הִתְיַצֵּב כֹּה עַל־עֹלָתֶךָ וְאָנֹכִי
16 אִקָּרֶה כֹּה׃ וַיִּקָּר יְהוָה אֶל־בִּלְעָם וַיָּשֶׂם דָּבָר בְּפִיו
17 וַיֹּאמֶר שׁוּב אֶל־בָּלָק וְכֹה תְדַבֵּר׃ וַיָּבֹא אֵלָיו וְהִנּוֹ נִצָּב
עַל־עֹלָתוֹ וְשָׂרֵי מוֹאָב אִתּוֹ וַיֹּאמֶר לוֹ בָּלָק מַה־דִּבֶּר

v. 13. חסר ה'

10. *who hath counted the dust of Jacob.* An expression of amazement at the mighty multitude he sees before him.

the stock. Heb. רבע; lit. 'fourth part'. Balaam's poetic parable is marked by parallelism or 'thought-rhythm' between the two parts of a verse. Now, neither 'stock' nor 'fourth part' *corresponds* to the word 'dust' in the first half of the verse. And yet the parallelism between the two halves of the verse is perfect: forty years ago, a wandering scholar called my attention to the fact that the true meaning of the word רבע is 'ashes', and that therefore the correct rendering of the verse is:—

'Who can count the dust of Jacob,
Or, by number, the ashes of Israel?'

This meaning of רבע is attested by the Samaritan Targum of 'I am but dust and ashes' in Gen. XVIII, 27 (ואנה קטם ורבוע). In 1902, B. Jacob found that also in the Aramaic of the Palestinian Christians, the word רבע is a synonym of 'dust'. Nothing is, of course, more natural than that Balaam, the Aramean, should have made use of an Aramaism in his poetic outburst.

die the death of the righteous. That wish was not to be fulfilled; see XXXI, 8. It would have been better, had he said, 'Let me *live the life* of the righteous.' That is the only way to die their death.

11–17. New Arrangements

What Balaam had seen of the camp of Israel had so impressed him with the numbers, power and unity of Israel that he found it impossible to curse them. The distracted king changes the seer's place of outlook, and to this Balaam consents.

14. *field of Zophim. i.e.* the field of watchers. Probably a plot of high ground used as a post for sentinels.

top of Pisgah. See on XXI, 21.

15. *here.* Better, *thus;* Heb. כה. Balaam shows Balak *how* to stand at the offering of the sacrifice (Daiches).

17. *what hath the LORD spoken?* Balak is impatient, and asks for the result as soon as Balaam returns.

18–24. Balaam's Second Prophecy

The change of place has all been in vain. Balaam, despite himself, must confirm and even transcend his former blessing; God is unchangeable in His purpose to bless His people. There is neither iniquity nor perverseness in Israel, and no magical arts can avail against him. With God as Defender, Israel is certain to be victorious.

18 יְהוָה׃ וַיִּשָּׂא מְשָׁלוֹ וַיֹּאמַר קוּם בָּלָק וּשְׁמָע הַאֲזִינָה
19 עָדַי בְּנוֹ צִפֹּר׃ לֹא אִישׁ אֵל וִיכַזֵּב וּבֶן־אָדָם וְיִתְנֶחָם
כ הַהוּא אָמַר וְלֹא יַעֲשֶׂה וְדִבֶּר וְלֹא יְקִימֶנָּה׃ הִנֵּה בָרֵךְ
21 לָקָחְתִּי וּבֵרֵךְ וְלֹא אֲשִׁיבֶנָּה׃ לֹא־הִבִּיט אָוֶן בְּיַעֲקֹב וְלֹא־
רָאָה עָמָל בְּיִשְׂרָאֵל יְהוָה אֱלֹהָיו עִמּוֹ וּתְרוּעַת מֶלֶךְ בּוֹ׃
22 אֵל מוֹצִיאָם מִמִּצְרָיִם כְּתוֹעֲפֹת רְאֵם לוֹ׃ 23 כִּי לֹא־נַחַשׁ
בְּיַעֲקֹב וְלֹא־קֶסֶם בְּיִשְׂרָאֵל כָּעֵת יֵאָמֵר לְיַעֲקֹב וּלְיִשְׂרָאֵל

the princes of Moab with him. And Balak said unto him: 'What hath the LORD spoken?' 18. And he took up his parable, and said:

Arise, Balak, and hear;
Give ear unto me, thou son of Zippor:

19. God is not a man, that He should lie;
Neither the son of man, that He should repent:
When He hath said, will He not do it?
Or when He hath spoken, will He not make it good?

20. Behold, I am bidden to bless;
And when He hath blessed, I cannot call it back.

21. None hath beheld iniquity in Jacob,
Neither hath one seen perverseness in Israel;
The LORD his God is with him,
And the shouting for the King is among them.

22. God who brought them forth out of Egypt
Is for them like the lofty horns of the wild-ox.

23. For there is no enchantment with Jacob,

v. 18. קמץ בז״ק

18. *arise, Balak.* The soothsayer while giving his answer has to address the person for whom he divines (Daiches).

19. *God is not a man.* With this first utterance, Balaam dashes Balak's hopes to the ground. Man breaks his word: but God is not man.

the son of man. Better, *a son of man; i.e.* a mere mortal.

repent. The Heb. denotes change of mind or purpose.

21. *iniquity in Jacob.* Israel is here, as in *v.* 10, spoken of ideally as a nation without spot or stain. Israel hath not committed any such wrong as would warrant God's withdrawal of His blessing from them, much less His permitting them to suffer destruction.

perverseness. This is the translation of Septuagint and Ibn Ezra; but the Heb. **עמל** means also *calamity*—and the phrase may indicate the absence of disasters in Israel. 'The Israelites are with God—hence there is among them no **און** *iniquity*; and God is with the Israelites—therefore they are free from **עמל**, *calamity*' (Kalisch).

the LORD his God is with him. Israel enjoys the fellowship of God; and hence no weapon hurled against him can prosper.

the shouting for the King. Better, *the trumpet-call of the King; i.e.* they are constantly reminded of the dominion of their God, and summoned to His worship, by the solemn sound (**תרועה**) of the Shofar, which they obey with a joyful readiness, proving the sincerity of their faith and devotion (Kalisch). All holy seasons were announced, and all public sacrifices accompanied, by the 'blast of the trumpet'.

22. *brought them forth.* lit. 'is bringing them forth', representing the Exodus as still in progress, and lasting up to the entrance of Canaan (Gray).

is for them . . . wild-ox. In consequence of God's presence, and of what He does for His people, Israel is as irresistible as the *re'em*—a species of buffalo, now extinct.

23. *with Jacob.* Or, 'in Jacob.' In Israel men do not resort to oracles, enchantments, or magic arts (Rashi). The next half-verse gives the reason. Some translate, 'no enchantment prevails *against* Jacob' (Mendelssohn, Luzzatto, Malbim), implying that the arts of the magician and all the ways of divination are powerless against Israel.

now. Heb. **כעת**; 'at the right time' (Septuagint); 'whenever required' (Rashi). Kalisch translates these two verses as follows:—

'In due time it is told to Jacob
And to Israel what God doeth.'

what God hath wrought. This translation is that of the Septuagint, Rashi, Ibn Ezra, Rashbam. 'The poet reckons it among the advantages of Israel that whenever it is fitting, God causes to be announced what he intends to do' (Kuenen). Another translation is: 'Now one can only say concerning Israel, What hath God wrought!' *i.e.* everything concerning Israel is irrevocably settled by Divine Will, and one can only exclaim in wonder at God's dealings with His people (Dillmann).

Neither is there any divination with Israel;
Now is it said of Jacob and of Israel:
'What hath God wrought!'
24. Behold a people that riseth up as a lioness,
And as a lion doth he lift himself up;
He shall not lie down until he eat of the prey,
And drink the blood of the slain.

25. And Balak said unto Balaam: 'Neither curse them at all, nor bless them at all.' 26. But Balaam answered and said unto Balak: 'Told not I thee, saying: All that the LORD speaketh, that I must do?' *vi (**vii). 27. And Balak said unto Balaam: 'Come now, I will take thee unto another place; peradventure it will please God that thou mayest curse me them from thence.' 28. And Balak took Balaam unto the top of Peor, that looketh down upon the desert. 29. And Balaam said unto Balak: 'Build me here seven altars, and prepare me here seven bullocks and seven rams.' 30. And Balak did as Balaam had said, and offered up a bullock and a ram on every altar.

24 מַה־פָּעַל אֵל׃ הֶן־עָם כְּלָבִיא יָקוּם וְכַאֲרִי יִתְנַשָּׂא לֹא
כה יִשְׁכַּב עַד־יֹאכַל טֶרֶף וְדַם־חֲלָלִים יִשְׁתֶּה׃ וַיֹּאמֶר בָּלָק
26 אֶל־בִּלְעָם גַּם־קֹב לֹא תִקֳּבֶנּוּ גַּם־בָּרֵךְ לֹא תְבָרְכֶנּוּ׃ וַיַּעַן
ששי שביעי (כשהן מחובר׳) בִּלְעָם וַיֹּאמֶר אֶל־בָּלָק הֲלֹא דִּבַּרְתִּי אֵלֶיךָ לֵאמֹר כֹּל
27 אֲשֶׁר־יְדַבֵּר יְהוָה אֹתוֹ אֶעֱשֶׂה׃ * וַיֹּאמֶר בָּלָק אֶל־בִּלְעָם
לְכָה־נָּא אֶקָּחֲךָ אֶל־מָקוֹם אַחֵר אוּלַי יִישַׁר בְּעֵינֵי הָאֱלֹהִים
28 וְקַבֹּתוֹ לִי מִשָּׁם׃ וַיִּקַּח בָּלָק אֶת־בִּלְעָם רֹאשׁ הַפְּעוֹר
29 הַנִּשְׁקָף עַל־פְּנֵי הַיְשִׁימֹן׃ וַיֹּאמֶר בִּלְעָם אֶל־בָּלָק בְּנֵה־
לִי בָזֶה שִׁבְעָה מִזְבְּחֹת וְהָכֵן לִי בָּזֶה שִׁבְעָה פָרִים
ל וְשִׁבְעָה אֵילִם׃ וַיַּעַשׂ בָּלָק כַּאֲשֶׁר אָמַר בִּלְעָם וַיַּעַל פָּר
וָאַיִל בַּמִּזְבֵּחַ׃

24

CHAPTER XXIV

1. And when Balaam saw that it pleased the LORD to bless Israel, he went not, as at the other times, to meet with enchantments, but he set his face toward the wilderness. 2. And Balaam lifted up his eyes, and he saw Israel dwelling tribe by tribe; and the spirit of God came upon him. 3. And he took up his parable, and said:

The saying of Balaam the son of Beor,
And the saying of the man whose eye is opened;

כד CAP. XXIV. כד

א וַיַּרְא בִּלְעָם כִּי טוֹב בְּעֵינֵי יְהוָה לְבָרֵךְ אֶת־יִשְׂרָאֵל וְלֹא־
הָלַךְ כְּפַעַם־בְּפַעַם לִקְרַאת נְחָשִׁים וַיָּשֶׁת אֶל־הַמִּדְבָּר
2 פָּנָיו׃ וַיִּשָּׂא בִלְעָם אֶת־עֵינָיו וַיַּרְא אֶת־יִשְׂרָאֵל שֹׁכֵן
3 לִשְׁבָטָיו וַתְּהִי עָלָיו רוּחַ אֱלֹהִים׃ וַיִּשָּׂא מְשָׁלוֹ וַיֹּאמַר

כג׳ v. 24. קמץ בפשטא

24. *riseth up as a lioness.* Figurative description of an invincible hero (Gen. XLIX, 9), and general prediction of the strength that would mark Israel's progress in coming times.

XXIII, 25–XXIV, 2. REMONSTRANCES AND NEW PREPARATIONS

25. *neither curse them at all.* Balak abandons the hope of a curse, and would be satisfied if the prophet withheld his blessing from Israel. But hoping against hope, he invites Balaam to make a third attempt.

27. *unto another place.* Change of place, thought Balak, might mean a change of fortune!

28. *the top of Peor.* A mountain in the neighbourhood of Pisgah (Deut. III, 27–29).

CHAPTER XXIV

1. *enchantments.* Or, 'omens.' He would no longer, even outwardly, act the sorcerer and retire to a lonely mountain peak for his auguries. He would remain in the presence of Balak, and there and then speak as the Spirit of God moved him. 'He now rose from the character of heathen seer to that of true prophet' (Abarbanel).

his face toward the wilderness. i.e. towards the plain where the Israelites were encamped.

2. *tribe by tribe.* In orderly encampment.

the spirit of God came upon him. His conscience is now stirred to its depth. He no longer addresses Balak as he did when he announced the results of a divination: he speaks to the future, and to all mankind.

3–9. BALAAM'S THIRD PROPHECY

3. *whose eye is opened.* See note on next *v.*

4. The saying of him who heareth the words of God,
Who seeth the vision of the Almighty,
Fallen down, yet with opened eyes:
5. How goodly are thy tents, O Jacob,
Thy dwellings, O Israel!
6. As valleys stretched out,
As gardens by the river-side;
As aloes planted of the LORD,
As cedars beside the waters;
7. Water shall flow from his branches,
And his seed shall be in many waters;
And his king shall be higher than Agag,
And his kingdom shall be exalted.
8. God who brought him forth out of Egypt
Is for him like the lofty horns of the wild-ox;
He shall eat up the nations that are his adversaries,
And shall break their bones in pieces,
And pierce them through with his arrows.
9. He couched, he lay down as a lion,
And as a lioness; who shall rouse him up?
Blessed be every one that blesseth thee,
And cursed be every one that curseth thee.

10. And Balak's anger was kindled against Balaam, and he smote his hands together; and Balak said unto Balaam: 'I called thee to curse mine enemies, and, behold, thou hast altogether blessed them these three

4 נְאֻם בִּלְעָם בְּנוֹ בְעֹר וּנְאֻם הַגֶּבֶר שְׁתֻם הָעָיִן׃ נְאֻם
שֹׁמֵעַ אִמְרֵי־אֵל אֲשֶׁר מַחֲזֵה שַׁדַּי יֶחֱזֶה נֹפֵל וּגְלוּי
ה עֵינָיִם׃ מַה־טֹּבוּ אֹהָלֶיךָ יַעֲקֹב מִשְׁכְּנֹתֶיךָ יִשְׂרָאֵל׃
6 כִּנְחָלִים נִטָּיוּ כְּגַנֹּת עֲלֵי נָהָר כַּאֲהָלִים נָטַע יְהוָה כַּאֲרָזִים
7 עֲלֵי־מָיִם׃ יִזַּל־מַיִם מִדָּלְיָו וְזַרְעוֹ בְּמַיִם רַבִּים וְיָרֹם
8 מֵאֲגַג מַלְכּוֹ וְתִנַּשֵּׂא מַלְכֻתוֹ׃ אֵל מוֹצִיאוֹ מִמִּצְרַיִם
כְּתוֹעֲפֹת רְאֵם לוֹ יֹאכַל גּוֹיִם צָרָיו וְעַצְמֹתֵיהֶם יְגָרֵם
9 וְחִצָּיו יִמְחָץ׃ כָּרַע שָׁכַב כַּאֲרִי וּכְלָבִיא מִי יְקִימֶנּוּ
י מְבָרְכֶיךָ בָרוּךְ וְאֹרְרֶיךָ אָרוּר׃ וַיִּחַר־אַף בָּלָק אֶל־בִּלְעָם
וַיִּסְפֹּק אֶת־כַּפָּיו וַיֹּאמֶר בָּלָק אֶל־בִּלְעָם לָקֹב אֹיְבַי קְרָאתִיךָ
11 וְהִנֵּה בֵּרַכְתָּ בָרֵךְ זֶה שָׁלֹשׁ פְּעָמִים׃ וְעַתָּה בְּרַח־לְךָ
אֶל־מְקוֹמֶךָ אָמַרְתִּי כַּבֵּד אֲכַבֶּדְךָ וְהִנֵּה מְנָעֲךָ יְהוָה
12 מִכָּבוֹד׃ וַיֹּאמֶר בִּלְעָם אֶל־בָּלָק הֲלֹא גַּם אֶל־מַלְאָכֶיךָ
13 אֲשֶׁר־שָׁלַחְתָּ אֵלַי דִּבַּרְתִּי לֵאמֹר׃ אִם־יִתֶּן־לִי בָלָק מְלֹא

v. 5. בראש עמוד סימן בי״ה שמ״ו v. 6. קמץ בז״ק

4. *fallen down, yet with opened eyes.* Overpowered by the inrush of the Divine Spirit which renders the recipient weak and unable to stand on his feet. It is spiritual ecstasy; when the bodily senses become numbed, and only the eyes of the mind are opened to see the Divine vision and to comprehend the Prophetic message.

5. *how goodly are thy tents, O Jacob.* He is swept away in rapt admiration of the Israelite encampments and homes arrayed harmoniously and peacefully, a picture of idyllic happiness and prosperity. According to the Rabbinic interpretation, the 'tents' are the 'tents of Torah', and the 'tabernacles' (lit. 'homes') are the Synagogues. There loomed up before Balaam's mental vision the school-houses and synagogues which have ever been the source and secret of Israel's spiritual strength.

6. *as valleys.* The encampment of Israel is like a series of vast fertile plains, stretching away into the far distance and watered by running streams.

as aloes. A simile of luxuriant prosperity. The aloe-tree furnished one of the most precious of spices.

planted of the LORD. Israel's heritage in Canaan is compared to a Paradise, with wonderful trees of God's own planting.

cedars beside the waters. An image of strength and beauty in combination.

7. *water shall flow from his branches.* He is blessed with an abundant supply of water.

in many waters. In well-watered ground, and thus yield a plentiful harvest.

higher than Agag. 'Agag' was a title common to all Amalekite kings, as 'Pharaoh' was to those of Egypt; probably a metaphor for power and might.

8. *like the lofty horns of the wild-ox.* See on XXIII, 22.

9. *lay down as a lion.* This figure describes the majesty of Israel in time of peace, as XXIII, 24 described his terrific might in war.

blessed be every one that blesseth thee. Far from being affected by blessings and cursings from without, Israel would himself be a source of blessing or cursing to others, according as they treated him. Hence let Balak and all Israel's enemies be warned!

ביתו כסף וזהב לא אוכל לעבר את־פי יהוה לעשות
שביעי טובה או רעה מלבי אשר־ידבר יהוה אתו אדבר׃
14 ועתה הנני הולך לעמי לכה איעצך אשר יעשה העם
טו הזה לעמך באחרית הימים׃ וישא משלו ויאמר נאם
16 בלעם בנו בער ונאם הגבר שתם העין׃ נאם שמע
אמרי־אל וידע דעת עליון מחזה שדי יחזה נפל וגלוי
17 עינים׃ אראנו ולא עתה אשורנו ולא קרוב דרך כוכב
מיעקב וקם שבט מישראל ומחץ פאתי מואב וקרקר
18 כל־בני־שת׃ והיה אדום ירשה והיה ירשה שעיר איביו

times. 11. Therefore now flee thou to thy place; I thought to promote thee unto great honour; but, lo, the LORD hath kept thee back from honour.' 12. And Balaam said unto Balak: 'Spoke I not also to thy messengers that thou didst send unto me, saying: 13. If Balak would give me his house full of silver and gold, I cannot go beyond the word of the LORD, to do either good or bad of mine own mind; what the LORD speaketh, that will I speak?*vii. 14. And now, behold, I go unto my people; come, and I will announce to thee what this people shall do to thy people in the end of days.' 15. And he took up his parable, and said:

The saying of Balaam the son of Beor,
And the saying of the man whose eye is opened;

16. The saying of him who heareth the words of God,
And knoweth the knowledge of the Most High,
Who seeth the vision of the Almighty,
Fallen down, yet with opened eyes:

17. I see him, but not now;
I behold him, but not nigh;
There shall step forth a star out of Jacob,
And a sceptre shall rise out of Israel,
And shall smite through the corners of Moab,
And break down all the sons of Seth.

18. And Edom shall be a possession,
Seir also, even his enemies, shall be a possession;
While Israel doeth valiantly.

v. 17. מלרע

10–14. Balak's Anger

Balaam, having disappointed the king three times, is dismissed by him in anger. In parting, Balaam reveals to him the fate in store for Moab.

14. *announce.* The Heb. is literally 'I will *advise* thee'.

in the end of days. 'The final period of the future so far as it falls within the range of the speaker's perspective' (Driver); Gen. XLIX, 1.

15–17. A vision of Israel's future. Balaam foretells the rise of an illustrious King who will put an end to the independence of Moab.

16. *knoweth the knowledge of the Most High.* To whom God reveals His secret; Amos III, 7.

17. *not now.* But as he will be at some distant date in the future.

a star out of Jacob. The reference is probably to King David, the first monarch to reduce Moab to subjection; II Sam. VIII, 2. In the reign of the Emperor Hadrian, this verse was applied to Bar Cozeba, the leader of the last Jewish War of Independence, whose name was consequently changed to Bar Cocheba, 'the Son of a Star.' His most noted follower was Rabbi Akiba, and the entire Jewish Diaspora seems to have supported the movement. Julius Severus was sent from Britain to quell the Jewish forces. Judea was brought to the lowest ebb; Jerusalem became a heathen city, even its name being changed to Aelia Capitolina; and a Jew was prohibited from entering it on pain of death. Bar Cocheba was slain in 135 A.C.E.

a sceptre. *i.e.* the holder of a sceptre, a ruler of men.

the corners. lit. 'the two temples.' Moab is spoken of under the figure of a human head. He shall smite through its 'two sides'; *i.e.* he shall crush it on either side.

the sons of Sheth. Probably the name of one of the leading tribes of Moab; RV Text translates, 'the sons of tumult.'

18–24. Oracles concerning the Nations

In prophetic ecstasy, Balaam now sees the foes of Israel fall helpless all around, until the vision fades away in the far horizon of history.

18. *shall be a possession.* *i.e.* shall be a conquered state. The reference is probably to David's subjugation of Edom. On this and the succeeding *v.* cf. The Book of Obadiah, p. 137.

19. And out of Jacob shall one have dominion,
And shall destroy the remnant from the city.

¶ 20. And he looked on Amalek, and took up his parable, and said:
Amalek was the first of the nations;
But his end shall come to destruction.

¶ 21. And he looked on the Kenite, and took up his parable, and said:
Though firm be thy dwelling-place,
And though thy nest be set in the rock;
22. Nevertheless Kain shall be wasted;
How long? Asshur shall carry thee away captive.

¶ 23. And he took up his parable, and said:
Alas, who shall live after God hath appointed him?
24. But ships shall come from the coast of Kittim,
And they shall afflict Asshur, and shall afflict Eber,
And he also shall come to destruction.

19 וְיִשְׂרָאֵל עֹשֶׂה חָיִל׃ וְיֵרְדְּ מִיַּעֲקֹב וְהֶאֱבִיד שָׂרִיד מֵעִיר׃
כ וַיַּרְא אֶת־עֲמָלֵק וַיִּשָּׂא מְשָׁלוֹ וַיֹּאמַר רֵאשִׁית גּוֹיִם עֲמָלֵק
21 וְאַחֲרִיתוֹ עֲדֵי אֹבֵד׃ וַיַּרְא אֶת־הַקֵּינִי וַיִּשָּׂא מְשָׁלוֹ וַיֹּאמַר
22 אֵיתָן מוֹשָׁבֶךָ וְשִׂים בַּסֶּלַע קִנֶּךָ׃ כִּי אִם־יִהְיֶה לְבָעֵר קָיִן
23 עַד־מָה אַשּׁוּר תִּשְׁבֶּךָּ׃ וַיִּשָּׂא מְשָׁלוֹ וַיֹּאמַר אוֹי מִי יִחְיֶה
24 מִשֻּׂמוֹ אֵל׃ וְצִים מִיַּד כִּתִּים וְעִנּוּ אַשּׁוּר וְעִנּוּ־עֵבֶר וְגַם־
כה הוּא עֲדֵי אֹבֵד׃ וַיָּקָם בִּלְעָם וַיֵּלֶךְ וַיָּשָׁב לִמְקֹמוֹ וְגַם־
בָּלָק הָלַךְ לְדַרְכּוֹ׃ פ

25. And Balaam rose up, and went and returned to his place; and Balak also went his way.

v. 22. כצ"ל בהעמדה תחת הע'

Seir also. Seir (Gen. XXXII, 3, or Mount Seir, Gen. XXXVI, 8) was an old name of Edom.
his enemies. Stands in opposition to Edom and Seir, both being the enemies of Israel.
doeth valiantly. Is strong and prosperous.

19. *out of Jacob shall one have dominion.* There shall arise in Jacob a powerful ruler.
from the city. Better, *from the cities*, as the Heb. עיר is used collectively. Probably a reference to Joab's action narrated in I Kings XI, 16 (Ibn Ezra).

20. *looked on Amalek.* 'The country of the Amalekites and that of the Kenites (*v.* 21) might just be visible from the Moabite hills, lying far to the south and south-west' (McNeile).
first of the nations. To attack Israel (Onkelos).
come to destruction. In the days of Saul (I Sam. XV, 8); a remnant was subdued by David (II Sam. VIII, 12).

21. *Kenite.* According to Judges I, 16, Jethro, the father-in-law of Moses, belonged to the Kenites, who must originally have formed part of the Midianites.
though firm thy dwelling place. Or, 'ever-enduring is thy habitation' (Gray). A reference to the wellnigh inaccessible rock-dwellings of the Kenites.

22. *Kain.* The poetical name of the tribe.
how long? Before your final doom comes? Assyria will enslave and crush you, and carry you away into captivity. It is, however, possible that (as in Gen. XXV, 18) the reference here is not to Assyria, but to the Ashurim (Gen. XXV, 3).

23. *who shall live. i.e.* who can live.
after God hath appointed him. An obscure verse. Its probable meaning is, Who will be able to survive the terrible catastrophes wrought in Israel by Assyria (Isa. X, 5), appointed by God to be the 'rod' of His anger?

24. *from the coast of Kittim.* Kittim (derived from Kition, a town of Cyprus) was a name also used for Greece. There is here a possible reference to those Mediterranean lands from which later were to come the conquerors of the empires of the East.
afflict. i.e. bring low, subjugate. Divine justice would finally call the Assyrian oppressor himself to account when his allotted work should be done.
Eber. This name is paraphrased by Onkelos as, 'beyond the Euphrates'; *i.e.* all the regions on the other side of the Euphrates. Asshur and Eber would thus denote the World Powers of the East, to whom retribution would be meted out by God.
and he also. 'Asshur and Eber are regarded as a single idea' (Gray).

25. *returned to his place.* As Balaam was slain among the Midianites shortly after (XXXI, 8), he must have set off homewards but tarried at the headquarters of the Midianites, where he met his end.

25

Chapter XXV

1. And Israel abode in Shittim, and the people began to commit harlotry with the daughters of Moab. 2. And they called the people unto the sacrifices of their gods; and the people did eat, and bowed down to their gods. 3. And Israel joined himself unto the Baal of Peor; and the anger of the LORD was kindled against Israel. 4. And the LORD said unto Moses: 'Take all the chiefs of the people, and hang them up unto the LORD in face of the sun, that the fierce anger of the LORD may turn away from Israel.' 5. And Moses said unto the judges of Israel: 'Slay ye every one his men that have joined themselves unto the Baal of Peor.' 6. And, behold, one of the children of Israel came and brought unto his brethren a Midianitish woman in the sight of Moses, and in the sight of all the congregation of the children of Israel, while they were weeping at the door of the tent of meeting.*m. 7. And when Phinehas, the son of Eleazar, the son of Aaron the priest, saw it, he rose up from the midst of the congregation, and took a spear in his hand. 8. And he went after the man of Israel

Cap. XXV. כה

כה

א וַיֵּשֶׁב יִשְׂרָאֵל בַּשִּׁטִּים וַיָּחֶל הָעָם לִזְנוֹת אֶל־בְּנוֹת מוֹאָב׃
2 וַתִּקְרֶאןָ לָעָם לְזִבְחֵי אֱלֹהֵיהֶן וַיֹּאכַל הָעָם וַיִּשְׁתַּחֲווּ
3 לֵאלֹהֵיהֶן׃ וַיִּצָּמֶד יִשְׂרָאֵל לְבַעַל פְּעוֹר וַיִּחַר־אַף־יְהוָה
4 בְּיִשְׂרָאֵל׃ וַיֹּאמֶר יְהוָה אֶל־מֹשֶׁה קַח אֶת־כָּל־רָאשֵׁי הָעָם
וְהוֹקַע אוֹתָם לַיהוָה נֶגֶד הַשָּׁמֶשׁ וְיָשֹׁב חֲרוֹן אַף־יְהוָה
ה מִיִּשְׂרָאֵל׃ וַיֹּאמֶר מֹשֶׁה אֶל־שֹׁפְטֵי יִשְׂרָאֵל הִרְגוּ אִישׁ
6 אֲנָשָׁיו הַנִּצְמָדִים לְבַעַל פְּעוֹר׃ וְהִנֵּה אִישׁ מִבְּנֵי יִשְׂרָאֵל
בָּא וַיַּקְרֵב אֶל־אֶחָיו אֶת־הַמִּדְיָנִית לְעֵינֵי מֹשֶׁה וּלְעֵינֵי כָּל־
מפטיר
7 עֲדַת בְּנֵי־יִשְׂרָאֵל וְהֵמָּה בֹכִים פֶּתַח אֹהֶל מוֹעֵד׃* וַיַּרְא
פִּינְחָס בֶּן־אֶלְעָזָר בֶּן־אַהֲרֹן הַכֹּהֵן וַיָּקָם מִתּוֹךְ הָעֵדָה וַיִּקַּח
8 רֹמַח בְּיָדוֹ׃ וַיָּבֹא אַחַר אִישׁ־יִשְׂרָאֵל אֶל־הַקֻּבָּה וַיִּדְקֹר

XXV, 1–9. The Sin of Baal-Peor

Many Israelites accepted the invitation of the women of Moab and Midian to a sacrificial festival, and then joined them in the worship of Baal-Peor that was associated with, and partly consisted in, the most licentious rites. In xxxi, 16, we are told that it was Balaam who counselled the Midianites to take this evil course, in order to encompass the ruin of the Israelites by their own sins. There is nothing improbable in this heathen prophet, when his enthusiasm for Israel and righteousness had died away, sinking back into the old sorcerer, and telling the Moabites and Midianites that, though he could not curse the Israelites, he knew a way whereby the Israelites would curse themselves.

1. *in Shittim.* The last halting-place of the Israelites before they crossed the Jordan.

3. *joined himself.* lit. 'yoked himself'.

the Baal of Peor. Peor being the name of a mountain (xxiii, 28).

the anger of the LORD was kindled. God sent a plague amongst them.

4. *take all the chiefs of the people.* Assemble them together in council. The words 'with thee' should be added to make it clear that it was the sinners, and not the Israelite chieftains, that were punished.

them. 'Common sense forbids us to refer this pronoun to all the heads of the people' (Paterson). It refers to a certain number of individual malefactors; see next *v.* The Heb. probably denotes some form of impalement.

in face of the sun. In the day-time; see Deut. xxi, 23.

the fierce anger. Manifested in the plague which befell Israel; *v.* 9.

5. *the judges.* The magistrates that had been appointed by Moses to hear and settle all disputes amongst the people (Exod. xviii, 21–26). They are identical with 'the chiefs of the people' in *v.* 4.

his men. The offenders that belonged to his jurisdiction.

6. *one of the children of Israel.* This was Zimri, a prince of one of the Simeonite clans; *v.* 14. He flaunted his immoral association with a Midianitish woman in the sight of Moses and all Israel.

weeping. Over the heinous sin committed and its terrible consequences, and imploring God to end the plague. The moral disintegration of which that shameless action, and at such a time, was a sign—a cynic disregard of law, order and common decency—was part of the plan adopted by the Midianites on the advice of Balaam.

8. *into the chamber.* The inner division of the large vaulted tents that were used as the apartment of the women.

so the plague was stayed. This expression and the incident to which it refers are repeated in Ps. cvi, 30, which also mentions the praiseworthy part played by Phinehas.

into the chamber, and thrust both of them through, the man of Israel, and the woman through her belly. So the plague was stayed from the children of Israel. 9. And those that died by the plague were twenty and four thousand.

אֶת־שְׁנֵיהֶם אֵת אִישׁ יִשְׂרָאֵל וְאֶת־הָאִשָּׁה אֶל־קֳבָתָהּ
9 וַתֵּעָצַר הַמַּגֵּפָה מֵעַל בְּנֵי יִשְׂרָאֵל׃ וַיִּהְיוּ הַמֵּתִים בַּמַּגֵּפָה
אַרְבָּעָה וְעֶשְׂרִים אָלֶף׃

9. *those that died by the plague.* In the census taken immediately after 'the plague' (chap. XXVI), the tribe of Simeon, to whom Zimri belonged, showed the greatest loss in population as compared with the previous census. The Simeonite camp was located in the southern side of the Israelitish encampment, in the vicinity of the Moabites, and hence was more exposed than were the others to the evil Moabitish influences.

HAFTORAH BALAK הפטרת בלק

MICAH V, 6–VI, 8

CHAPTER V

6. And the remnant of Jacob shall be in the midst of many peoples,
As dew from the LORD, as showers upon the grass,
That are not looked for from man,
Nor awaited at the hands of the sons of men.
7. And the remnant of Jacob shall be among the nations, in the midst of many peoples,
As a lion among the beasts of the forest,
As a young lion among the flocks of sheep,
Who, if he go through, treadeth down and teareth in pieces,
And there is none to deliver.

CAP. V. ה

6 וְהָיָה ׀ שְׁאֵרִית יַעֲקֹב בְּקֶרֶב עַמִּים רַבִּים
כְּטַל מֵאֵת יְהוָה כִּרְבִיבִים עֲלֵי־עֵשֶׂב אֲשֶׁר לֹא־יְקַוֶּה לְאִישׁ
7 וְלֹא יְיַחֵל לִבְנֵי אָדָם׃ וְהָיָה שְׁאֵרִית יַעֲקֹב בַּגּוֹיִם בְּקֶרֶב
עַמִּים רַבִּים כְּאַרְיֵה בְּבַהֲמוֹת יַעַר כִּכְפִיר בְּעֶדְרֵי־צֹאן

The Book of Micah from which this Haftorah is taken is one of the so-called Minor Prophets or, more appropriately, the Twelve Prophets (תרי עשר), which at an early date were counted as one book among the twenty-four of Holy Writ. Micah (750–690 B.C.E.) was a contemporary of Isaiah. He was village-born, and spoke as one of the oppressed peasantry, who were ground down by numerous exactions and oppressive treatment on the part of the grandees. He denounced the luxury and degeneracy of city-life, the land-grabbing of the social leaders and the venality of the religious teachers. The chief cities of Judah and Israel that should have been centres of true religion and righteousness, were in his eyes fountains of irreligion and iniquity. Therefore, this Prophet of the poor proclaimed that, even as the Northern Kingdom fell to the Assyrian, Jerusalem would share the same fate. Nevertheless Micah does not doubt Israel's mission to humanity; and, like Isaiah, he foresees the time when the nations shall beat their swords into ploughshares and learn war no more. He has also given the world the noblest definition of true religion: 'What doth the LORD require of thee, but to do justly, and to love mercy, and to walk humbly with thy God.'

The reference in the Haftorah to Balaam who is the outstanding figure of the Sedrah, provides the connection between the two.

7–14. ISRAEL AMONG THE NATIONS

6. *the remnant of Jacob.* The faithful minority in Israel.

as dew. The night-mist in Palestine during the hot months is the only source of life and refreshment for the vegetation, and thus an exquisite image of Divine truth and teaching; Deut. XXXII, 2.

that are not looked for from man, nor awaited at the hands of the sons of men. Israel's message to the world is not from man. Like the dew, it is the gift of heaven.

7. *as a lion.* To those who oppose Israel's message.

8 אֲשֶׁר אִם־עָבַר וְרָמַס וְטָרַף וְאֵין מַצִּיל׃ תָּרֹם יָדְךָ עַל־
9 צָרֶיךָ וְכָל־אֹיְבֶיךָ יִכָּרֵתוּ׃ וְהָיָה בַיּוֹם־הַהוּא נְאֻם־
י יְהוָה וְהִכְרַתִּי סוּסֶיךָ מִקִּרְבֶּךָ וְהַאֲבַדְתִּי מַרְכְּבֹתֶיךָ׃ וְהִכְרַתִּי
11 עָרֵי אַרְצֶךָ וְהָרַסְתִּי כָּל־מִבְצָרֶיךָ׃ וְהִכְרַתִּי כְשָׁפִים מִיָּדֶךָ
12 וּמְעוֹנְנִים לֹא יִהְיוּ־לָךְ׃ וְהִכְרַתִּי פְסִילֶיךָ וּמַצֵּבוֹתֶיךָ מִקִּרְבֶּךָ
13 וְלֹא־תִשְׁתַּחֲוֶה עוֹד לְמַעֲשֵׂה יָדֶיךָ׃ וְנָתַשְׁתִּי אֲשֵׁירֶיךָ מִקִּרְבֶּךָ
14 וְהִשְׁמַדְתִּי עָרֶיךָ׃ וְעָשִׂיתִי בְּאַף וּבְחֵמָה נָקָם אֶת־הַגּוֹיִם
אֲשֶׁר לֹא שָׁמֵעוּ׃

Cap. VI. ו

א שִׁמְעוּ־נָא אֵת אֲשֶׁר־יְהוָה אֹמֵר קוּם רִיב אֶת־הֶהָרִים
2 וְתִשְׁמַעְנָה הַגְּבָעוֹת קוֹלֶךָ׃ שִׁמְעוּ הָרִים אֶת־רִיב יְהוָה
וְהָאֵתָנִים מֹסְדֵי אָרֶץ כִּי רִיב לַיהוָה עִם־עַמּוֹ וְעִם־יִשְׂרָאֵל

8. Let Thy hand be lifted up above Thine adversaries,
And let all Thine enemies be cut off.

9. And it shall come to pass in that day, saith the LORD,
That I will cut off thy horses out of the midst of thee,
And will destroy thy chariots;
10. And I will cut off the cities of thy land,
And will throw down all thy strongholds;
11. And I will cut off witchcrafts out of thy hand;
And thou shalt have no more soothsayers;
12. And I will cut off thy graven images and thy pillars out of the midst of thee;
And thou shalt no more worship the work of thy hands.
13. And I will pluck up thy Asherim out of the midst of thee;
And I will destroy thine enemies.
14. And I will execute vengeance in anger and fury upon the nations,
Because they hearkened not.

Chapter VI

1. Hear ye now what the LORD saith:
Arise, contend thou before the mountains,
And let the hills hear thy voice.
2. Hear, O ye mountains, the LORD's controversy,
And ye enduring rocks, the foundations of the earth;
For the LORD hath a controversy with His people,
And He will plead with Israel.

8. *let Thy hand be lifted up.* A symbol of strength, as contrasted with the hand hanging down in weakness; Exod. XIV, 8.

9. *I will cut off thy horses . . . chariots.* Israel's victory will not depend on the external aids enumerated in this and the following verses, and there will be an end of idolatry.

11. *out of thy hand.* Some divining objects manipulated by the hand.

13. *Asherim.* Groves of sacred trees or poles set up near an altar for idol-worship.

thine enemies. Thus Targum, Rashi, Kimchi.

14. *because they hearkened not.* To those teachings and warnings.

'Amos said that God would punish Israel as well as the nations: Micah says He will punish the nations as well as Israel' (Horton).

Chapter VI

The section following is regarded as dating from the reign of king Manasseh—a period of appalling apostasy, when gruesome heathen rites were followed by prince and people alike. The Prophet enters into an argument with his countrymen, and seeks to wean them from their dreadful delusions as to what constitutes religion and goodness. *v.* 8, *He hath shewed thee, O man, what is good; and what doth the LORD require of thee, but to do justly, and to love mercy, and to walk humbly with thy God*, has been called the most important utterance in the Prophetic literature. It is in fact an epitome of the whole of Scripture. 'In opposition to the most awful mockery of religion is set the purest expression of it, and out of the corruption of the age there shines like a star the purest light of prophecy' (Montefiore).

1–5. God's Great Deeds on Behalf of Israel, and their Neglect of Him

1. *what the LORD saith.* Better, *what the LORD is saying:* The Prophet bids the people listen to the Divine word just at that moment becoming audible to him (Margolis).

arise. This is God's message to the Prophet.

contend thou. State God's case against the erring people.

before the mountains. The everlasting hills that gaze on the generations of human folly and sin are to stand as judges.

2. *hear.* The Prophet forthwith executes the Divine command, and in the ensuing controversy appears on God's behalf as prosecutor.

will plead. Will open an argument with His people.

3 יִתְוַכָּח׃ עַמִּי מֶה־עָשִׂיתִי לְךָ וּמָה הֶלְאֵתִיךָ עֲנֵה בִי׃
4 כִּי הֶעֱלִתִיךָ מֵאֶרֶץ מִצְרַיִם וּמִבֵּית עֲבָדִים פְּדִיתִיךָ וָאֶשְׁלַח
ה לְפָנֶיךָ אֶת־מֹשֶׁה אַהֲרֹן וּמִרְיָם׃ עַמִּי זְכָר־נָא מַה־יָּעַץ
בָּלָק מֶלֶךְ מוֹאָב וּמֶה־עָנָה אֹתוֹ בִּלְעָם בֶּן־בְּעוֹר מִן־הַשִּׁטִּים
6 עַד־הַגִּלְגָּל לְמַעַן דַּעַת צִדְקוֹת יְהוָה׃ בַּמָּה אֲקַדֵּם יְהוָה
אִכַּף לֵאלֹהֵי מָרוֹם הַאֲקַדְּמֶנּוּ בְעוֹלוֹת בַּעֲגָלִים בְּנֵי שָׁנָה׃
7 הֲיִרְצֶה יְהוָה בְּאַלְפֵי אֵילִים בְּרִבְבוֹת נַחֲלֵי־שָׁמֶן הַאֶתֵּן

3. O My people, what have I done unto thee?
And wherein have I wearied thee?
Testify against Me.
4. For I brought thee up out of the land of Egypt,
And redeemed thee out of the house of bondage,
And I sent before thee Moses, Aaron, and Miriam.
5. O My people, remember now what Balak king of Moab devised,
And what Balaam the son of Beor answered him;
From Shittim unto Gilgal,
That ye may know the righteous acts of the LORD.
6. 'Wherewith shall I come before the LORD,
And bow myself before God on high?
Shall I come before Him with burnt-offerings,
With calves of a year old?
7. Will the LORD be pleased with thousands of rams,
With ten thousands of rivers of oil?
Shall I give my first-born for my transgression,
The fruit of my body for the sin of my soul?'

3. *My people.* As a term of affection and endearment. The whole tone of these verses is not that of rebuke but of affectionate appeal. 'God does not mention Israel's sins, but asks only what have been His faults!' (Horton).

what have I done unto thee? What has God done to deserve their neglect—have not His dealings with them been all for their welfare? (Rashi).

4. *Moses, Aaron, and Miriam.* Moses to instruct you in the Divine laws of righteousness and mercy; Aaron to show the way to atonement; Miriam to teach and guide the women (Targum).

5. *devised. i.e.* planned, with Balaam. Not by open attacks, but by insidious and pernicious ways Balak sought Israel's destruction.

and what Balaam answered. With blessings of Israel, instead of curses as Balak demanded. Continuing the retrospect of great Divine mercies, *Shittim* was the last halting-place in the wilderness, *Gilgal* their first station in the Promised Land. At Shittim the people sinned grievously; nevertheless, God's mercy did not weaken, but helped them to cross Jordan and enter Canaan.

6–7. ISRAEL SPEAKS

6. *wherewith shall I come before the LORD.* Impressed by these righteous and merciful acts of God, the people anxiously turn to the Prophet with the question 'What does God really require of us? We are willing to give everything—bullocks without number, oil in vast quantities, yea, our children'. But even in their search for God, the penitent people show their utter lack of understanding as to what is pleasing in God's sight.

7. *thousands of rams . . . rivers of oil.* It is thus not a question of quantity with the deluded people.

the fruit of my body. i.e. my children. 'Can I please God by even sacrificing my children?' Almost a rhetorical question; for human sacrifice was a horrible custom of the Canaanites. Israel's teachers did not rest till the whole people shared their horror of this hideous savage abomination.

8. THE WHOLE DUTY OF MAN

Over against their fantastic and gruesome ways of propitiating God, the Prophet solemnly states the Divine and tender simplicities of God's demands.

8. *it hath been told thee.* It is no *new* revelation which he—the Prophet—is announcing; he is merely echoing and restating the message of Abraham, Moses, Samuel, and Elijah.

O man. Heb. *adam.* The teachings of true religion are of universal appeal, and extend to all the children of men.

Ehrlich points that *adam* means 'man', and not 'O man', as the vocative would have to be *ha-adam.* Consequently, he translates the Prophet's answer to the agonizing cry of the benighted worshipper who asks: 'Shall I offer my child as a sacrifice?' as follows: '*Man* hath told thee that this is good: but what does *the LORD* require of thee? Nothing but to do justly, to love mercy and to walk humbly with thy God.'

to do justly. lit. 'to execute justice'. Justice implies reverence for the personality of every human being as the possessor, by virtue of his humanity, of inalienable rights to life, honour and the fruit of his toil. The whole machinery of the state must be set in motion to protect

8. It hath been told thee, O man, what is good,
And what the LORD doth require of thee:
Only to do justly, and to love mercy, and to walk humbly with thy God.

8 בְּכוֹרִי פִּשְׁעִי פְּרִי בִטְנִי חַטַּאת נַפְשִׁי׃ הִגִּיד לְךָ אָדָם
מַה־טּוֹב וּמָה יְהוָה דּוֹרֵשׁ מִמְּךָ כִּי אִם־עֲשׂוֹת מִשְׁפָּט
וְאַהֲבַת חֶסֶד וְהַצְנֵעַ לֶכֶת עִם־אֱלֹהֶיךָ׃

these inalienable human rights against outrage and injustice. It is heinous sin for any individual by his action to injure the life, honour and possessions of his fellow-man.

to love mercy. Heb. *chesed*, means kindness to the lowly, needy and miserable, as shown in all charitable acts, especially such as go with personal service. And man is 'to *love* mercy'. 'In regard to justice, it is sufficient to carry out its behests; but in regard to mercy, the deed alone is insufficient, even when it is the outcome of a clear sense of duty. *Love* is an essential accompaniment of every deed of mercy' (Hermann Cohen). The Rabbis translate '*to love mercy*' by גמילות חסדים—'the bestowal of lovingkindnesses'; *i.e.* clothing the naked, nursing the sick, comforting those that mourn, burying the dead. When the Temple fell, Johanan ben Zakkai declared: 'We have another means of expiation, equally efficacious, left us; namely, גמילות חסדים, the bestowal of disinterested deeds of lovingkindness upon our fellow-men.' The Rabbis imbued the generations in Israel with a veritable passion for pity; and they denied that anyone who was devoid of pity could be a true descendant of Abraham.

to walk humbly with thy God. In fellowship and communion with God; not ostentatiously, but with inward devotion and noiseless acts of love (Margolis). Rabbi Phinehas ben Yair said, 'Holiness leads to humility; humility leads to the fear of sin; fear of sin leads to saintliness; saintliness leads to the Holy Spirit.' The insistence on humility distinguishes Jewish from Greek ethics. 'Everything heroic in man is insignificant and perishable, and all his wisdom and virtue unable to stand the crucial test, unless they are the fruits of humility. In this there is no exception—neither for any man, any people, or any age' (Hermann Cohen).

In the light of the above interpretation of *v.* 8, the cardinal virtues of human life are Justice, Mercy and Humility. It is questionable, however, whether *to walk humbly* is the correct translation of the Heb. הצנע לכת. A better and higher sense is obtained if we connect it with the later Hebrew צניעות, which denotes modesty, decency, chastity, personal holiness, purity; and translate the third portion of the Prophet's answer *to walk in purity with thy God.* The pillars of Religion are accordingly Justice, Mercy and Purity.

'Micah's ideal is not a minimum of religion, it is a maximum. He provides the great standards by which we may test our acting, our thinking, our religious practice. And this is why Micah's pronouncement has about it an air of finality. The Prophet seems to feel that what he is saying is an eternal truth; we seem to feel it as we read it or we hear it read. Men may come and go, but Micah's ideal must live for ever' (Singer).

25 10. And the LORD spoke unto Moses, saying: 11. 'Phinehas, the son of Eleazar, the son of Aaron the priest, hath turned My wrath away from the children of Israel, in that he was very jealous for My sake among them, so that I consumed not the children of Israel in My jealousy. 12. Wherefore say: Behold, I give unto him My covenant of peace; 13. and it shall be unto him, and to his seed after him, the covenant of an everlasting priesthood; because he was jealous for his God, and made atonement for the children of Israel.' 14. Now the name of the man of Israel that was slain, who was slain with the Midianitish woman, was Zimri, the son of Salu, a prince of a fathers' house among the Simeonites. 15. And the name of the Midianitish woman that was slain was Cozbi, the daughter of Zur; he was head of the people of a fathers' house in Midian. ¶ 16. And the LORD spoke unto Moses, saying: 17. 'Harass the Midianites, and smite them; 18. for they harass you, by their wiles wherewith they have beguiled you in the matter of Peor, and in the matter

כה

פ פ פ מא 41

י 11 וַיְדַבֵּר יְהוָה אֶל־מֹשֶׁה לֵּאמֹר׃ פִּינְחָס בֶּן־אֶלְעָזָר בֶּן
אַהֲרֹן הַכֹּהֵן הֵשִׁיב אֶת־חֲמָתִי מֵעַל בְּנֵי־יִשְׂרָאֵל בְּקַנְאוֹ
אֶת־קִנְאָתִי בְּתוֹכָם וְלֹא־כִלִּיתִי אֶת־בְּנֵי־יִשְׂרָאֵל בְּקִנְאָתִי׃
12 13 לָכֵן אֱמֹר הִנְנִי נֹתֵן לוֹ אֶת־בְּרִיתִי שָׁלוֹם׃ וְהָיְתָה לּוֹ
וּלְזַרְעוֹ אַחֲרָיו בְּרִית כְּהֻנַּת עוֹלָם תַּחַת אֲשֶׁר קִנֵּא לֵאלֹהָיו
14 וַיְכַפֵּר עַל־בְּנֵי יִשְׂרָאֵל׃ וְשֵׁם אִישׁ יִשְׂרָאֵל הַמֻּכֶּה אֲשֶׁר
הֻכָּה אֶת־הַמִּדְיָנִית זִמְרִי בֶּן־סָלוּא נְשִׂיא בֵית־אָב לַשִּׁמְעֹנִי׃
טו וְשֵׁם הָאִשָּׁה הַמֻּכָּה הַמִּדְיָנִית כָּזְבִּי בַת־צוּר רֹאשׁ אֻמּוֹת
בֵּית־אָב בְּמִדְיָן הוּא׃ פ
16 17 וַיְדַבֵּר יְהוָה אֶל־מֹשֶׁה לֵּאמֹר׃ צָרוֹר אֶת־הַמִּדְיָנִים וְהִכִּיתֶם
18 אוֹתָם׃ כִּי צֹרְרִים הֵם לָכֶם בְּנִכְלֵיהֶם אֲשֶׁר־נִכְּלוּ לָכֶם עַל־

v. 12. ו' קטיעה

VIII. PINCHAS

(CHAPTERS XXV, 10–XXX, 1)

XXV, 10–15. PHINEHAS' REWARD

Filled with unsparing hatred of evil and burning indignation against a deed that was a monstrous profanation of God's holy Name, Phinehas executed summary vengeance on Zimri and Cozbi. That action gained Phinehas the reward of hereditary High Priesthood.

11. *very jealous for My sake.* Zimri's conduct within the sacred precincts of the camp was a combination of idolatry and immorality. By his promptness and righteous zeal, Phinehas stayed the moral plague that threatened to destroy the character of Israel. The Rabbis have a saying: 'Phinehas is Elijah'; and in this fearless deed, inspired by motives absolutely pure and holy, he is certainly a counterpart of the Prophet of storm and fire.

12. *My covenant of peace.* lit. 'My covenant, the covenant of peace'; i.e. I assure him of My friendly attitude towards him (Rashi, Gray). Phinehas should be free from any fear of retaliation by the brethren of Zimri, who, being princes, possessed great power (Ibn Ezra). The word 'covenant' is here used, not in the sense of a compact between two persons, but as an unconditional promise on God's part. In addition to the Divine blessing with which Phinehas' action was rewarded, it received the grateful admiration of succeeding ages. In Psalm CVI, we read that his zeal 'was counted unto him for righteousness unto all generations for evermore'.

13. *an everlasting priesthood.* A second promise to Phinehas on God's part—the dignity of the High Priesthood is to be the possession of his descendants. With the exception of a brief interruption in Eli's days, it continued in his family until the fall of the Jewish state.

atonement for the children of Israel. The act of Phinehas was accepted by God as a national atonement; *i.e.* a 'covering' of the nation's sin.

14. *the name of the man.* Just as in the case of good men, so also are the names and families of evil-doers recorded—an immortality of infamy is theirs.

a prince. Of one of the five 'fathers' houses' comprised in the tribe of Simeon (XXVI, 12 f). 'The fact that Zimri was the prince of a great house, was nothing to Phinehas when punishment had to be meted out and the honour of God vindicated' (Rashi).

15. *Zur.* One of the Midianite kings; XXXI, 8.

head of the people of a fathers' house. That the daughter of such a man should have consented to play so immoral a role is an indication of the dangerous lengths to which the Midianites would resort in their efforts to destroy the Israelites through sin (Rashi).

of Cozbi, the daughter of the prince of Midian, their sister, who was slain on the day of the plague in the matter of Peor.' 19. And it came to pass after the plague,

26

Chapter XXVI

1. that the Lord spoke unto Moses and unto Eleazar the son of Aaron the priest, saying: 2. 'Take the sum of all the congregation of the children of Israel, from twenty years old and upward, by their fathers' houses, all that are able to go forth to war in Israel.' 3. And Moses and Eleazar the priest spoke with them in the plains of Moab by the Jordan at Jericho, saying: 4. '[Take the sum of the people,] from twenty years old and upward, as the Lord commanded Moses and the children of Israel, that came forth out of the land of Egypt.'*ii. ¶ 5. Reuben, the first-born of Israel: the sons of Reuben: of Hanoch, the family of the Hanochites; of Pallu, the family of the Palluites; 6. of Hezron, the family of the Hezronites; of Carmi, the family of the Carmites. 7. These are the families of the Reubenites; and they that were numbered of them were forty and three thousand and seven hundred and thirty. 8. And the sons of Pallu: Eliab. 9. And the sons of Eliab: Nemuel, and Dathan, and Abiram. These are that Dathan and Abiram, the elect of the congregation, who strove against Moses and against Aaron in the company of Korah, when they strove against the Lord;

דְּבַר פְּעוֹר וְעַל־דְּבַר כָּזְבִּי בַת־נְשִׂיא מִדְיָן אֲחֹתָם הַמֻּכָּה
19 בְיוֹם־הַמַּגֵּפָה עַל־דְּבַר־פְּעוֹר׃ וַיְהִי אַחֲרֵי הַמַּגֵּפָה׃ ∙ פ

כו Cap. XXVI. כו

א וַיֹּאמֶר יְהוָה אֶל־מֹשֶׁה וְאֶל אֶלְעָזָר בֶּן־אַהֲרֹן הַכֹּהֵן לֵאמֹר׃
2 שְׂאוּ אֶת־רֹאשׁ ׀ כָּל־עֲדַת בְּנֵי־יִשְׂרָאֵל מִבֶּן עֶשְׂרִים שָׁנָה
3 וָמַעְלָה לְבֵית אֲבֹתָם כָּל־יֹצֵא צָבָא בְּיִשְׂרָאֵל׃ וַיְדַבֵּר
מֹשֶׁה וְאֶלְעָזָר הַכֹּהֵן אֹתָם בְּעַרְבֹת מוֹאָב עַל־יַרְדֵּן יְרֵחוֹ
4 לֵאמֹר׃ מִבֶּן עֶשְׂרִים שָׁנָה וָמָעְלָה כַּאֲשֶׁר צִוָּה יְהוָה אֶת־
שני
ה מֹשֶׁה וּבְנֵי יִשְׂרָאֵל הַיֹּצְאִים מֵאֶרֶץ מִצְרָיִם׃* רְאוּבֵן בְּכוֹר
יִשְׂרָאֵל בְּנֵי רְאוּבֵן חֲנוֹךְ מִשְׁפַּחַת הַחֲנֹכִי לְפַלּוּא מִשְׁפַּחַת
6 הַפַּלֻּאִי׃ לְחֶצְרֹן מִשְׁפַּחַת הַחֶצְרוֹנִי לְכַרְמִי מִשְׁפַּחַת
7 הַכַּרְמִי׃ אֵלֶּה מִשְׁפְּחֹת הָרֻאוּבֵנִי וַיִּהְיוּ פְקֻדֵיהֶם שְׁלֹשָׁה
8 וְאַרְבָּעִים אֶלֶף וּשְׁבַע מֵאוֹת וּשְׁלֹשִׁים׃ וּבְנֵי פַלּוּא אֱלִיאָב׃
9 וּבְנֵי אֱלִיאָב נְמוּאֵל וְדָתָן וַאֲבִירָם הוּא־דָתָן וַאֲבִירָם קְרוֹאֵי
הָעֵדָה אֲשֶׁר הִצּוּ עַל־מֹשֶׁה וְעַל־אַהֲרֹן בַּעֲדַת־קֹרַח
י בְּהַצֹּתָם עַל־יְהוָה׃ וַתִּפְתַּח הָאָרֶץ אֶת־פִּיהָ וַתִּבְלַע אֹתָם
וְאֶת־קֹרַח בְּמוֹת הָעֵדָה בַּאֲכֹל הָאֵשׁ אֵת חֲמִשִּׁים וּמָאתַיִם
11 12 אִישׁ וַיִּהְיוּ לְנֵס׃ וּבְנֵי־קֹרַח לֹא־מֵתוּ׃ ס בְּנֵי שִׁמְעוֹן

כה׳ v. 19. פסקא באמצע פסוק   כו׳ v. 7. כצ״ל   v. 9. קריאי ק׳

16–18. War declared against the Midianites

17. *harass the Midianites. i.e.* count them as dangerous enemies and smite them. The Israelites who had been seduced into sin had been severely visited by God. And now, as was just, the Midianites too are to be punished; see xxxi, 1. No punishment is meted out to the Moabites—the Rabbis explain—because these had at least the excuse of fear for their infamous conduct towards the Israelites; whereas the Midianites were actuated by pure hatred.

XXV, 19–XXVI. The Second Census

Nearly forty years had passed since the first numbering of the Israelites, and a new census had become a necessity. The Land was shortly to be divided amongst the tribes for an inheritance; and the exact number of fighting men and families had to be known.

19. *after the plague.* It had seriously diminished the numbers of at least one of the tribes. 'The Divine command to number the Israelites at this juncture may be likened to the case of a shepherd whose flocks have been depleted by an inrush of wolves. When the catastrophe is over, the shepherd lovingly counts his sheep in order to know how many are left alive' (Rashi).

3. *spoke with them. i.e.* with the responsible chiefs of each tribe.

5–51. The census is taken of all the tribes, with the exception of Levi. The families are named for the most part after the descendants of Jacob enumerated in Gen. xlvi, 8–27.

10. *became a sign.* A warning for all time to others.

לְמִשְׁפְּחֹתָם לִנְמוּאֵל מִשְׁפַּחַת הַנְּמוּאֵלִי לְיָמִין מִשְׁפַּחַת
13 הַיָּמִינִי לְיָכִין מִשְׁפַּחַת הַיָּכִינִי׃ לְזֶרַח מִשְׁפַּחַת הַזַּרְחִי
14 לְשָׁאוּל מִשְׁפַּחַת הַשָּׁאוּלִי׃ אֵלֶּה מִשְׁפְּחֹת הַשִּׁמְעֹנִי שְׁנַיִם
טו וְעֶשְׂרִים אֶלֶף וּמָאתָיִם׃ ס בְּנֵי גָד לְמִשְׁפְּחֹתָם לִצְפוֹן
מִשְׁפַּחַת הַצְּפוֹנִי לְחַגִּי מִשְׁפַּחַת הַחַגִּי לְשׁוּנִי מִשְׁפַּחַת
16 הַשּׁוּנִי׃ לְאָזְנִי מִשְׁפַּחַת הָאָזְנִי לְעֵרִי מִשְׁפַּחַת הָעֵרִי׃
17 לַאֲרוֹד מִשְׁפַּחַת הָאֲרוֹדִי לְאַרְאֵלִי מִשְׁפַּחַת הָאַרְאֵלִי׃
18 אֵלֶּה מִשְׁפְּחֹת בְּנֵי־גָד לִפְקֻדֵיהֶם אַרְבָּעִים אֶלֶף וַחֲמֵשׁ
19 מֵאוֹת׃ ס בְּנֵי יְהוּדָה עֵר וְאוֹנָן וַיָּמָת עֵר וְאוֹנָן בְּאֶרֶץ
כ כְּנָעַן׃ וַיִּהְיוּ בְנֵי־יְהוּדָה לְמִשְׁפְּחֹתָם לְשֵׁלָה מִשְׁפַּחַת
הַשֵּׁלָנִי לְפֶרֶץ מִשְׁפַּחַת הַפַּרְצִי לְזֶרַח מִשְׁפַּחַת הַזַּרְחִי׃
21 וַיִּהְיוּ בְנֵי־פֶרֶץ לְחֶצְרֹן מִשְׁפַּחַת הַחֶצְרֹנִי לְחָמוּל מִשְׁפַּחַת
22 הֶחָמוּלִי׃ אֵלֶּה מִשְׁפְּחֹת יְהוּדָה לִפְקֻדֵיהֶם שִׁשָּׁה וְשִׁבְעִים
23 אֶלֶף וַחֲמֵשׁ מֵאוֹת׃ ס בְּנֵי יִשָּׂשכָר לְמִשְׁפְּחֹתָם תּוֹלָע
24 מִשְׁפַּחַת הַתּוֹלָעִי לְפֻוָה מִשְׁפַּחַת הַפּוּנִי׃ לְיָשׁוּב מִשְׁפַּחַת
כה הַיָּשֻׁבִי לְשִׁמְרֹן מִשְׁפַּחַת הַשִּׁמְרֹנִי׃ אֵלֶּה מִשְׁפְּחֹת יִשָּׂשכָר
26 לִפְקֻדֵיהֶם אַרְבָּעָה וְשִׁשִּׁים אֶלֶף וּשְׁלֹשׁ מֵאוֹת׃ ס בְּנֵי
זְבוּלֻן לְמִשְׁפְּחֹתָם לְסֶרֶד מִשְׁפַּחַת הַסַּרְדִּי לְאֵלוֹן מִשְׁפַּחַת
27 הָאֵלֹנִי לְיַחְלְאֵל מִשְׁפַּחַת הַיַּחְלְאֵלִי׃ אֵלֶּה מִשְׁפְּחֹת
28 הַזְּבוּלֹנִי לִפְקֻדֵיהֶם שִׁשִּׁים אֶלֶף וַחֲמֵשׁ מֵאוֹת׃ ס בְּנֵי
29 יוֹסֵף לְמִשְׁפְּחֹתָם מְנַשֶּׁה וְאֶפְרָיִם׃ בְּנֵי מְנַשֶּׁה לְמָכִיר
מִשְׁפַּחַת הַמָּכִירִי וּמָכִיר הוֹלִיד אֶת־גִּלְעָד לְגִלְעָד מִשְׁפַּחַת
ל הַגִּלְעָדִי׃ אֵלֶּה בְּנֵי גִלְעָד אִיעֶזֶר מִשְׁפַּחַת הָאִיעֶזְרִי לְחֵלֶק
31 מִשְׁפַּחַת הַחֶלְקִי׃ וְאַשְׂרִיאֵל מִשְׁפַּחַת הָאַשְׂרִאֵלִי וְשֶׁכֶם

10. and the earth opened her mouth, and swallowed them up together with Korah, when that company died; what time the fire devoured two hundred and fifty men, and they became a sign. 11. Notwithstanding the sons of Korah died not. ¶ 12. The sons of Simeon after their families: of Nemuel, the family of the Nemuelites; of Jamin, the family of the Jaminites; of Jachin, the family of the Jachinites; 13. of Zerah, the family of the Zerahites; of Shaul, the family of the Shaulites. 14. These are the families of the Simeonites, twenty and two thousand and two hundred. ¶ 15. The sons of Gad after their families: of Zephon, the family of the Zephonites; of Haggi, the family of the Haggites; of Shuni, the family of the Shunites; 16. of Ozni, the family of the Oznites; of Eri, the family of the Erites; 17. of Arod, the family of the Arodites; of Areli, the family of the Arelites. 18. These are the families of the sons of Gad according to those that were numbered of them, forty thousand and five hundred. ¶ 19. The sons of Judah: Er and Onan; and Er and Onan died in the land of Canaan. 20. And the sons of Judah after their families were: of Shelah, the family of the Shelanites; of Perez, the family of the Perezites; of Zerah, the family of the Zerahites. 21. And the sons of Perez were: of Hezron, the family of the Hezronites; of Hamul, the family of the Hamulites. 22. These are the families of Judah according to those that were numbered of them, threescore and sixteen thousand and five hundred. ¶ 23. The sons of Issachar after their families: of Tola, the family of the Tolaites; of Puvah, the family of the Punites; 24. of Jashub, the family of the Jashubites; of Shimron, the family of the Shimronites. 25. These are the families of Issachar according to those that were numbered of them, threescore and four thousand and three hundred. ¶ 26. The sons of Zebulun after their families: of Sered, the family of the Seredites; of Elon, the family of the Elonites; of Jahleel, the family of the Jahleelites. 27. These are the families of the Zebulunites according to those that were numbered of them, threescore thousand and five hundred. ¶ 28. The sons of Joseph after their families: Manasseh and Ephraim. 29. The sons of Manasseh: of Machir, the family of the Machirites—and Machir begot Gilead; of Gilead, the family of the Gileadites. 30. These are the sons of Gilead: of Iezer, the family of

11. *the sons of Korah died not.* See on XVI, 11. 'From the earthquake and the consuming flame and the raging plague that put an end to the schemes of those who took counsel together against the chosen of the LORD, the sons of Korah survived—survived to become the founders of a whole family or guild of Psalmists, whose meditations are still with us' (Singer).

32 מִשְׁפַּחַת הַשִּׁכְמִי׃ וּשְׁמִידָע מִשְׁפַּחַת הַשְּׁמִידָעִי וְחֵפֶר
33 מִשְׁפַּחַת הַחֶפְרִי׃ וּצְלָפְחָד בֶּן־חֵפֶר לֹא־הָיוּ לוֹ בָּנִים כִּי
אִם־בָּנוֹת וְשֵׁם בְּנוֹת צְלָפְחָד מַחְלָה וְנֹעָה חָגְלָה מִלְכָּה
34 וְתִרְצָה׃ אֵלֶּה מִשְׁפְּחֹת מְנַשֶּׁה וּפְקֻדֵיהֶם שְׁנַיִם וַחֲמִשִּׁים
לה אֶלֶף וּשְׁבַע מֵאוֹת׃ ס אֵלֶּה בְנֵי־אֶפְרַיִם לְמִשְׁפְּחֹתָם
לְשׁוּתֶלַח מִשְׁפַּחַת הַשֻּׁתַלְחִי לְבֶכֶר מִשְׁפַּחַת הַבַּכְרִי
36 לְתַחַן מִשְׁפַּחַת הַתַּחֲנִי׃ וְאֵלֶּה בְּנֵי שׁוּתָלַח לְעֵרָן מִשְׁפַּחַת
37 הָעֵרָנִי׃ אֵלֶּה מִשְׁפְּחֹת בְּנֵי־אֶפְרַיִם לִפְקֻדֵיהֶם שְׁנַיִם
וּשְׁלֹשִׁים אֶלֶף וַחֲמֵשׁ מֵאוֹת אֵלֶּה בְנֵי־יוֹסֵף לְמִשְׁפְּחֹתָם׃ ס
38 בְּנֵי בִנְיָמִן לְמִשְׁפְּחֹתָם לְבֶלַע מִשְׁפַּחַת הַבַּלְעִי לְאַשְׁבֵּל
39 מִשְׁפַּחַת הָאַשְׁבֵּלִי לַאֲחִירָם מִשְׁפַּחַת הָאֲחִירָמִי׃ לִשְׁפוּפָם
מ מִשְׁפַּחַת הַשּׁוּפָמִי לְחוּפָם מִשְׁפַּחַת הַחוּפָמִי׃ וַיִּהְיוּ בְנֵי־
בֶלַע אַרְדְּ וְנַעֲמָן מִשְׁפַּחַת הָאַרְדִּי לְנַעֲמָן מִשְׁפַּחַת הַנַּעֲמִי׃
41 אֵלֶּה בְנֵי־בִנְיָמִן לְמִשְׁפְּחֹתָם וּפְקֻדֵיהֶם חֲמִשָּׁה וְאַרְבָּעִים
42 אֶלֶף וְשֵׁשׁ מֵאוֹת׃ ס אֵלֶּה בְנֵי־דָן לְמִשְׁפְּחֹתָם לְשׁוּחָם
43 מִשְׁפַּחַת הַשּׁוּחָמִי אֵלֶּה מִשְׁפְּחֹת דָּן לְמִשְׁפְּחֹתָם׃ כָּל־
מִשְׁפְּחֹת הַשּׁוּחָמִי לִפְקֻדֵיהֶם אַרְבָּעָה וְשִׁשִּׁים אֶלֶף וְאַרְבַּע
44 מֵאוֹת׃ ס בְּנֵי אָשֵׁר לְמִשְׁפְּחֹתָם לְיִמְנָה מִשְׁפַּחַת
הַיִּמְנָה לְיִשְׁוִי מִשְׁפַּחַת הַיִּשְׁוִי לִבְרִיעָה מִשְׁפַּחַת הַבְּרִיעִי׃
מה לִבְנֵי בְרִיעָה לְחֶבֶר מִשְׁפַּחַת הַחֶבְרִי לְמַלְכִּיאֵל מִשְׁפַּחַת
46 47 הַמַּלְכִּיאֵלִי׃ וְשֵׁם בַּת־אָשֵׁר שָׂרַח׃ אֵלֶּה מִשְׁפְּחֹת בְּנֵי־
אָשֵׁר לִפְקֻדֵיהֶם שְׁלֹשָׁה וַחֲמִשִּׁים אֶלֶף וְאַרְבַּע מֵאוֹת׃ ס
48 בְּנֵי נַפְתָּלִי לְמִשְׁפְּחֹתָם לְיַחְצְאֵל מִשְׁפַּחַת הַיַּחְצְאֵלִי לְגוּנִי
49 מִשְׁפַּחַת הַגּוּנִי׃ לְיֵצֶר מִשְׁפַּחַת הַיִּצְרִי לְשִׁלֵּם מִשְׁפַּחַת
נ הַשִּׁלֵּמִי׃ אֵלֶּה מִשְׁפְּחֹת נַפְתָּלִי לְמִשְׁפְּחֹתָם וּפְקֻדֵיהֶם

the Iezerites; of Helek, the family of the Helekites; 31. and of Asriel, the family of the Asrielites; and of Shechem, the family of the Shechemites; 32. and of Shemida, the family of the Shemidaites; and of Hepher, the family of the Hepherites. 33. And Zelophehad the son of Hepher had no sons, but daughters; and the names of the daughters of Zelophehad were Mahlah, and Noah, Hoglah, Milcah, and Tirzah. 34. These are the families of Manasseh; and they that were numbered of them were fifty and two thousand and seven hundred. ¶ 35. These are the sons of Ephraim after their families: of Shuthelah, the family of the Shuthelahites; of Becher, the family of the Becherites; of Tahan, the family of the Tahanites. 36. And these are the sons of Shuthelah: of Eran, the family of the Eranites. 37. These are the families of the sons of Ephraim according to those that were numbered of them, thirty and two thousand and five hundred. These are the sons of Joseph after their families. ¶ 38. The sons of Benjamin after their families: of Bela, the family of the Belaites; of Ashbel, the family of the Ashbelites; of Ahiram, the family of the Ahiramites; 39. of Shephupham, the family of the Shuphamites; of Hupham, the family of the Huphamites. 40. And the sons of Bela were Ard and Naaman; [of Ard,] the family of the Ardites; of Naaman, the family of the Naamites. 41. These are the sons of Benjamin after their families; and they that were numbered of them were forty and five thousand and six hundred. ¶ 42. These are the sons of Dan after their families: of Shuham, the family of the Shuhamites. These are the families of Dan after their families. 43. All the families of the Shuhamites, according to those that were numbered of them, were threescore and four thousand and four hundred. ¶ 44. The sons of Asher after their families: of Imnah, the family of the Imnites; of Ishvi, the family of the Ishvites; of Beriah, the family of the Beriites. 45. Of the sons of Beriah: of Heber, the family of the Heberites; of Malchiel, the family of the Malchielites. 46. And the name of the daughter of Asher was Serah. 47. These are the families of the sons of Asher according to those that were numbered of them, fifty and three thousand and four hundred. ¶ 48. The sons of Naphtali after their families: of Jahzeel, the family of the Jahzeelites; of Guni, the family of the Gunites; 49. of Jezer, the family of the Jezerites; of Shillem, the family of the Shillemites. 50.

33. *had no sons, but daughters.* This fact is mentioned here because the question of their inheritance will come up in the next chapter.

These are the families of Naphtali according to their families; and they that were numbered of them were forty and five thousand and four hundred. ¶ 51. These are they that were numbered of the children of Israel, six hundred thousand and a thousand and seven hundred and thirty.*iii. ¶ 52. And the LORD spoke unto Moses, saying: 53. 'Unto these the land shall be divided for an inheritance according to the number of names. 54. To the more thou shalt give the more inheritance, and to the fewer thou shalt give the less inheritance; to each one according to those that were numbered of it shall its inheritance be given. 55. Notwithstanding the land shall be divided by lot; according to the names of the tribes of their fathers they shall inherit. 56. According to the lot shall their inheritance be divided between the more and the fewer.' ¶ 57. And these are they that were numbered of the Levites after their families: of Gershon, the family of the Gershonites; of Kohath, the family of the Kohathites; of Merari, the family of the Merarites. 58. These are the families of Levi: the family of the Libnites, the family of the Hebronites, the family of the Mahlites, the family of the Mushites, the family of the Korahites. And Kohath begot Amram. 59. And the name of Amram's wife was Jochebed, the daughter of Levi, who was born to Levi in Egypt; and she bore unto Amram Aaron and Moses, and Miriam their sister. 60. And unto Aaron were born Nadab and Abihu, Eleazar and Ithamar. 61. And Nadab and Abihu died, when they offered strange

51 חֲמִשָּׁה וְאַרְבָּעִים אֶלֶף וְאַרְבַּע מֵאוֹת׃ אֵלֶּה פְּקוּדֵי בְּנֵי
שלישי יִשְׂרָאֵל שֵׁשׁ־מֵאוֹת אֶלֶף וָאָלֶף שְׁבַע מֵאוֹת וּשְׁלֹשִׁים׃ * פ
52 53 וַיְדַבֵּר יְהוָה אֶל־מֹשֶׁה לֵּאמֹר׃ לָאֵלֶּה תֵּחָלֵק הָאָרֶץ
54 בְּנַחֲלָה בְּמִסְפַּר שֵׁמוֹת׃ לָרַב תַּרְבֶּה נַחֲלָתוֹ וְלַמְעַט
נה תַּמְעִיט נַחֲלָתוֹ אִישׁ לְפִי פְקֻדָיו יֻתַּן נַחֲלָתוֹ׃ אַךְ־בְּגוֹרָל
56 יֵחָלֵק אֶת־הָאָרֶץ לִשְׁמוֹת מַטּוֹת־אֲבֹתָם יִנְחָלוּ׃ עַל־פִּי
57 הַגּוֹרָל תֵּחָלֵק נַחֲלָתוֹ בֵּין רַב לִמְעָט׃ ס וְאֵלֶּה פְקוּדֵי
הַלֵּוִי לְמִשְׁפְּחֹתָם לְגֵרְשׁוֹן מִשְׁפַּחַת הַגֵּרְשֻׁנִּי לִקְהָת
58 מִשְׁפַּחַת הַקְּהָתִי לִמְרָרִי מִשְׁפַּחַת הַמְּרָרִי׃ אֵלֶּה ׀ מִשְׁפְּחֹת
לֵוִי מִשְׁפַּחַת הַלִּבְנִי מִשְׁפַּחַת הַחֶבְרֹנִי מִשְׁפַּחַת הַמַּחְלִי
מִשְׁפַּחַת הַמּוּשִׁי מִשְׁפַּחַת הַקָּרְחִי וּקְהָת הוֹלִד אֶת־עַמְרָם׃
59 וְשֵׁם ׀ אֵשֶׁת עַמְרָם יוֹכֶבֶד בַּת־לֵוִי אֲשֶׁר יָלְדָה אֹתָהּ
לְלֵוִי בְּמִצְרָיִם וַתֵּלֶד לְעַמְרָם אֶת־אַהֲרֹן וְאֶת־מֹשֶׁה וְאֵת
ס מִרְיָם אֲחֹתָם׃ וַיִּוָּלֵד לְאַהֲרֹן אֶת־נָדָב וְאֶת־אֲבִיהוּא אֶת־
61 אֶלְעָזָר וְאֶת־אִיתָמָר׃ וַיָּמָת נָדָב וַאֲבִיהוּא בְּהַקְרִיבָם
62 אֵשׁ־זָרָה לִפְנֵי יְהוָה׃ וַיִּהְיוּ פְקֻדֵיהֶם שְׁלֹשָׁה וְעֶשְׂרִים אֶלֶף

51. *numbered of the children of Israel.* The Levites are excluded from this total of 601,730 which is 1,820 less than the total 38 years before. While the nation as a whole remained nearly stationary, the various tribes show many striking variations. Reuben, Simeon, Gad, Ephraim, and Naphthali decreased in numbers.

52–56. CONCERNING THE DIVISION OF THE LAND

The extent of each territory is to be proportionate to the size of the tribe to whom it is allotted.

55. *divided by lot.* In settling the geographical position of each tribe's inheritance, recourse was had to the 'lot', in order to refer the matter to God unto Whom alone the land belonged. Thus jealousy and strife among the tribes would be prevented. See XXXIII, 54.

57–62. CENSUS OF THE LEVITES

A separate census was necessary, as the Levites were numbered from the age of one month, whilst the other tribes were counted from 20 years of age, as only to such was a parcel of land to be apportioned.

58. *the families of Levi.* The families enumerated in this verse are the issue of the three Levitical families, *viz.* the Gershonites, the Kohathites, and the Merarites, mentioned in the preceding verse. The Libnites were the descendants of the Gershonites (III, 21) ; the Hebronites were Kohathites (III, 19); and the Mahlites and Mushites, Merarites (III, 20, 33). Two other families, *viz.* the Shimeites (III, 21) and Uzzielites (III, 27), as well as a few others, are omitted in the present enumeration, possibly because they had died out.

61. *offered strange fire.* See Lev. x, 1–7.

62. *were twenty and three thousand.* This increase of only 1,000 over the former census (see III, 39) is surprisingly small. It is probable that the Levites suffered a large diminution in numbers on account of their participation in the rebellion of Korah.

fire before the LORD. 62. And they that were numbered of them were twenty and three thousand, every male from a month old and upward; for they were not numbered among the children of Israel, because there was no inheritance given them among the children of Israel. ¶ 63. These are they that were numbered by Moses and Eleazar the priest, who numbered the children of Israel in the plains of Moab by the Jordan at Jericho. 64. But among these there was not a man of them that were numbered by Moses and Aaron the priest, who numbered the children of Israel in the wilderness of Sinai. 65. For the LORD had said of them: 'They shall surely die in the wilderness.' And there was not left a man of them, save Caleb the son of Jephunneh, and Joshua the son of Nun.

כָּל־זָכָר מִבֶּן־חֹדֶשׁ וָמָעְלָה כִּי ׀ לֹא הָתְפָּקְדוּ בְּתוֹךְ בְּנֵי
63 יִשְׂרָאֵל כִּי לֹא־נִתַּן לָהֶם נַחֲלָה בְּתוֹךְ בְּנֵי יִשְׂרָאֵל׃ אֵלֶּה
פְּקוּדֵי מֹשֶׁה וְאֶלְעָזָר הַכֹּהֵן אֲשֶׁר פָּקְדוּ אֶת־בְּנֵי יִשְׂרָאֵל
64 בְּעַרְבֹת מוֹאָב עַל יַרְדֵּן יְרֵחוֹ׃ וּבְאֵלֶּה לֹא־הָיָה אִישׁ
מִפְּקוּדֵי מֹשֶׁה וְאַהֲרֹן הַכֹּהֵן אֲשֶׁר פָּקְדוּ אֶת־בְּנֵי יִשְׂרָאֵל
סה בְּמִדְבַּר סִינָי׃ כִּי־אָמַר יְהוָה לָהֶם מוֹת יָמֻתוּ בַּמִּדְבָּר וְלֹא־
נוֹתַר מֵהֶם אִישׁ כִּי אִם־כָּלֵב בֶּן־יְפֻנֶּה וִיהוֹשֻׁעַ בִּן־נוּן׃ ס

27

CHAPTER XXVII

1. Then drew near the daughters of Zelophehad, the son of Hepher, the son of Gilead, the son of Machir, the son of Manasseh, of the families of Manasseh the son of Joseph; and these are the names of his daughters: Mahlah, Noah, and Hoglah, and Milcah, and Tirzah. 2. And they stood before Moses, and before Eleazar the priest, and before the princes and all the congregation, at the door of the tent of meeting, saying: 3. 'Our father died in the wilderness, and he was not among the company of them that gathered themselves together against the LORD in the company of Korah, but he died in his own sin; and he had no sons. 4. Why should the name of our father be done away from among his family, because he had no son? Give unto us a possession among the brethren of our father.' 5. And Moses brought their cause before the

כז CAP. XXVII. כז

א וַתִּקְרַבְנָה בְּנוֹת צְלָפְחָד בֶּן־חֵפֶר בֶּן־גִּלְעָד בֶּן־מָכִיר בֶּן־
מְנַשֶּׁה לְמִשְׁפְּחֹת מְנַשֶּׁה בֶן־יוֹסֵף וְאֵלֶּה שְׁמוֹת בְּנֹתָיו מַחְלָה
2 נֹעָה וְחָגְלָה וּמִלְכָּה וְתִרְצָה׃ וַתַּעֲמֹדְנָה לִפְנֵי מֹשֶׁה וְלִפְנֵי
אֶלְעָזָר הַכֹּהֵן וְלִפְנֵי הַנְּשִׂיאִם וְכָל־הָעֵדָה פֶּתַח אֹהֶל־מוֹעֵד
3 לֵאמֹר׃ אָבִינוּ מֵת בַּמִּדְבָּר וְהוּא לֹא־הָיָה בְּתוֹךְ הָעֵדָה
הַנּוֹעָדִים עַל־יְהוָה בַּעֲדַת־קֹרַח כִּי־בְחֶטְאוֹ מֵת וּבָנִים לֹא־
4 הָיוּ לוֹ׃ לָמָּה יִגָּרַע שֵׁם־אָבִינוּ מִתּוֹךְ מִשְׁפַּחְתּוֹ כִּי אֵין
ה לוֹ בֵּן תְּנָה־לָּנוּ אֲחֻזָּה בְּתוֹךְ אֲחֵי אָבִינוּ׃ וַיַּקְרֵב מֹשֶׁה אֶת־
מִשְׁפָּטָן לִפְנֵי יְהוָה׃* פ רביעי

כז׳ v. 5. נון רבתי

CHAPTER XXVII. LAWS OF INHERITANCE. JOSHUA THE SUCCESSOR OF MOSES

1–11. THE DAUGHTERS OF ZELOPHEHAD

Landed property was not to be alienated from the family or tribe to which it belonged. However, in the absence of a male heir to an estate, its legal possession by a female heir might on the latter's marriage cause such alienation. Hence the necessity for definite regulation of this question.

3. *our father died in the wilderness.* Prior to the arrival of the Israelites in the Plains of Moab. He died in his own sin. Like the rest of his generation upon whom the general sentence was pronounced that they would die in the wilderness; XIV, 29.

4. *be done away.* Why should our father's rights be done away with because, instead of sons, he left daughters behind him?

among the brethren of our father. Accord unto us the same right of territorial possession as that which applies to the male members of our tribe.

5. *before the LORD.* He submitted their contention to the judgment of God, presumably by going into the 'tent of meeting' and awaiting the revelation of the Divine Will; Exod. XVIII, 19. This is what the daughters of Zelophehad desired. They said: 'God's love is not like the love of a mortal father; the latter prefers his sons to his daughters, but He that created the world extends His love to all His children. His tender mercies are over all His works' (Midrash).

LORD.*iv. 6. And the LORD spoke unto Moses, saying: 7. 'The daughters of Zelophehad speak right: thou shalt surely give them a possession of an inheritance among their father's brethren; and thou shalt cause the inheritance of their father to pass unto them. 8. And thou shalt speak unto the children of Israel, saying: If a man die, and have no son, then ye shall cause his inheritance to pass unto his daughter. 9. And if he have no daughter, then ye shall give his inheritance unto his brethren. 10. And if he have no brethren, then ye shall give his inheritance unto his father's brethren. 11. And if his father have no brethren, then ye shall give his inheritance unto his kinsman that is next to him of his family, and he shall possess it. And it shall be unto the children of Israel a statute of judgment, as the LORD commanded Moses.' ¶ 12. And the LORD said unto Moses: 'Get thee up into this mountain of Abarim, and behold the land which I have given unto the children of Israel. 13. And when thou hast seen it, thou also shalt be gathered unto thy people, as

6 7 וַיֹּ֥אמֶר יְהוָ֖ה אֶל־מֹשֶׁ֥ה לֵּאמֹֽר׃ כֵּ֗ן בְּנ֣וֹת צְלָפְחָד֮ דֹּבְרֹת֒
נָתֹ֨ן תִּתֵּ֤ן לָהֶם֙ אֲחֻזַּ֣ת נַחֲלָ֔ה בְּת֖וֹךְ אֲחֵ֣י אֲבִיהֶ֑ם וְהַֽעֲבַרְתָּ֛
8 אֶת־נַחֲלַ֥ת אֲבִיהֶ֖ן לָהֶֽן׃ וְאֶל־בְּנֵ֥י יִשְׂרָאֵ֖ל תְּדַבֵּ֣ר לֵאמֹ֑ר
אִ֣ישׁ כִּֽי־יָמ֗וּת וּבֵן֙ אֵ֣ין ל֔וֹ וְהַֽעֲבַרְתֶּ֥ם אֶת־נַחֲלָת֖וֹ לְבִתּֽוֹ׃
9 10 וְאִם־אֵ֥ין ל֖וֹ בַּ֑ת וּנְתַתֶּ֥ם אֶת־נַחֲלָת֖וֹ לְאֶחָֽיו׃ וְאִם־אֵ֥ין ל֖וֹ
11 אַחִ֑ים וּנְתַתֶּ֥ם אֶת־נַחֲלָת֖וֹ לַאֲחֵ֥י אָבִֽיו׃ וְאִם־אֵ֣ין אַחִים֮
לְאָבִיו֒ וּנְתַתֶּ֣ם אֶת־נַחֲלָת֗וֹ לִשְׁאֵר֙ הַקָּרֹ֥ב אֵלָ֛יו מִמִּשְׁפַּחְתּ֖וֹ
וְיָרַ֣שׁ אֹתָ֑הּ וְֽהָיְתָה֩ לִבְנֵ֨י יִשְׂרָאֵ֜ל לְחֻקַּ֣ת מִשְׁפָּ֗ט כַּאֲשֶׁ֛ר
צִוָּ֥ה יְהוָ֖ה אֶת־מֹשֶֽׁה׃ פ
12 וַיֹּ֤אמֶר יְהוָה֙ אֶל־מֹשֶׁ֔ה עֲלֵ֛ה אֶל־הַ֥ר הָעֲבָרִ֖ים הַזֶּ֑ה וּרְאֵה֙
13 אֶת־הָאָ֔רֶץ אֲשֶׁ֥ר נָתַ֖תִּי לִבְנֵ֥י יִשְׂרָאֵֽל׃ וְרָאִ֣יתָה אֹתָ֔הּ

7. *the daughters of Zelophehad speak right.* 'Happy is that mortal, whose words are acknowledged to be true by God' (Rashi).

8. *if a man die, and have no son.* A general statement of the law of inheritance is now promulgated. Land was in every case so to pass that the name and fame of the deceased might be, as far as possible, perpetuated.

11. *statute of judgment.* A fixed and authoritative custom; see further XXXVI.

The Order of Inheritance as developed by later Jewish Law is as follows: (1) sons and their descendants; (2) daughters and their descendants; (3) the father; (4) brothers and their descendants; (5) sisters and their descendants; (6) the father's father; (7) the father's brothers and their descendants; (8) the father's sisters and their descendants; (9) the great-grandfather and his collateral descendants; and so on. To this list, the Rabbis added another legal heir, the husband. Each of the sons of the deceased receives an equal share of the estate of his father or of his mother, except the first-born of the father, who receives a double share. In the case of the death of a son during his father's life, his children inherit his portion of the estate. The Rabbis, while denying the daughters a share in the inheritance where there are sons, still make ample provision for their maintenance and support, as long as they remain unmarried. The cost and provision of such maintenance constitute the first charge upon the estate of the deceased. In case the estate was small, the principle was laid down: 'The daughters must be supported, even if the sons are reduced to beggary.'

12–23. JOSHUA APPOINTED SUCCESSOR OF MOSES

Moses is commanded to view the Land of Promise, which he may not enter, and is given an intimation of his approaching death. This command is repeated in Deut. XXXII, and its fulfilment related in XXXIV, the last chapter of the Torah. In the interval, Moses delivered the laws contained in the remaining chapters of Numbers and the addresses that constitute the Book of Deuteronomy—besides the sacred war against Midian. The Midrash accounts for the insertion here of his summons to die in the following way: Moses had just received the Divine instructions concerning the ways in which the Promised Land was to be distributed amongst the tribes, and he said to himself, 'Peradventure, I too may be allotted a share. Peradventure, the Divine decree forbidding me to enter the Promised Land has now been revoked.' But God said unto him, 'My decree stands unchanged.'

12. *mountain of Abarim.* The top of Pisgah, one of the peaks of Mt. Nebo.

and behold the land. Moses had already been told that he should not enter the Promised Land (XX, 12), yet he is allowed the consolation of seeing it with his eyes before his death. Furthermore, Moses was to see how near Israel was now to the Promised Land, and hence his labours had not been in vain.

13. *As Aaron thy brother.* The Rabbis explain this to mean that like Aaron he was to die 'by the mouth of the LORD', *i.e.* his also would be 'death by a Divine kiss'.

Aaron thy brother was gathered; 14. because ye rebelled against My commandment in the wilderness of Zin, in the strife of the congregation, to sanctify Me at the waters before their eyes.'--These are the waters of Meribath-kadesh in the wilderness of Zin.--15. And Moses spoke unto the LORD, saying: 16. 'Let the LORD, the God of the spirits of all flesh, set a man over the congregation, 17. who may go out before them, and who may come in before them, and who may lead them out, and who may bring them in; that the congregation of the LORD be not as sheep which have no shepherd.' 18. And the LORD said unto Moses: 'Take thee Joshua the son of Nun, a man in whom is spirit, and lay thy hand upon him; 19. and set him before Eleazar the priest, and before all the congregation; and give him a charge in their sight. 20. And thou shalt put of thy honour upon him, that all the congregation of the children of Israel may hearken. 21. And he shall stand before Eleazar the priest, who shall inquire for him by the judgment of the Urim before the LORD;

וְנֶאֱסַפְתָּ אֶל־עַמֶּיךָ גַּם־אָתָּה כַּאֲשֶׁר נֶאֱסַף אַהֲרֹן אָחִיךָ׃
14 כַּאֲשֶׁר מְרִיתֶם פִּי בְּמִדְבַּר־צִן בִּמְרִיבַת הָעֵדָה לְהַקְדִּישֵׁנִי
בַמַּיִם לְעֵינֵיהֶם הֵם מֵי־מְרִיבַת קָדֵשׁ מִדְבַּר־צִן׃ ס
טו 16 וַיְדַבֵּר מֹשֶׁה אֶל־יְהוָה לֵאמֹר׃ יִפְקֹד יְהוָה אֱלֹהֵי הָרוּחֹת
17 לְכָל־בָּשָׂר אִישׁ עַל־הָעֵדָה׃ אֲשֶׁר־יֵצֵא לִפְנֵיהֶם וַאֲשֶׁר
יָבֹא לִפְנֵיהֶם וַאֲשֶׁר יוֹצִיאֵם וַאֲשֶׁר יְבִיאֵם וְלֹא תִהְיֶה עֲדַת
18 יְהוָה כַּצֹּאן אֲשֶׁר אֵין־לָהֶם רֹעֶה׃ וַיֹּאמֶר יְהוָה אֶל־מֹשֶׁה
קַח־לְךָ אֶת־יְהוֹשֻׁעַ בִּן־נוּן אִישׁ אֲשֶׁר־רוּחַ בּוֹ וְסָמַכְתָּ אֶת־
19 יָדְךָ עָלָיו׃ וְהַעֲמַדְתָּ אֹתוֹ לִפְנֵי אֶלְעָזָר הַכֹּהֵן וְלִפְנֵי כָּל־
כ הָעֵדָה וְצִוִּיתָה אֹתוֹ לְעֵינֵיהֶם׃ וְנָתַתָּה מֵהוֹדְךָ עָלָיו לְמַעַן
21 יִשְׁמְעוּ כָּל־עֲדַת בְּנֵי יִשְׂרָאֵל׃ וְלִפְנֵי אֶלְעָזָר הַכֹּהֵן יַעֲמֹד

14. *because ye rebelled.* See on XX, 12, 13.

15. *Moses spoke unto the LORD.* Rashi remarks, 'This verse tells us the praise of righteous men who at the hour of their departure from the world abandon all thought of their own wants and think only of the wants of the community.' The solicitude of Moses for the appointment of his successor is singularly and touchingly disinterested.

16. *the God of the spirits of all flesh.* 'God who knows the varying spirits of men, and who therefore knows what type of spirit is required in the man who is to fill the place of Moses' (Ibn Ezra). This same phrase occurs in XVI, 22. According to the Midrash, Moses prayed, 'Sovereign of the universe, Thou knowest the minds of all men, and how the mind of one man differs from that of another. Appoint over them a leader who will be able to bear with the differing minds of every one of Thy children.'

17. *go out . . . come in.* Who combines the capacity of leadership in warfare with the vigorous prosecution of the general duties that devolve upon the head of a nation.

lead . . . bring them in. The image is that of a shepherd and his flock.

which have no shepherd. And are therefore scattered and helpless, exposed to attack on all sides and at all times.

18. *Joshua the son of Nun.* Saying to him, 'Happy art thou inasmuch as thou hast merited to become the leader of the children of God' (Rashi).

in whom is spirit. *i.e.* wisdom, piety, courage, capacity.

lay thine hand upon him. Heb. וסמכת את ידך עליו, a symbolic action to show the transference of his authority to Joshua. From this Heb. word is derived the noun *Semicha*, the act of admission in the Talmudic age to the rights and duties of a Rabbi--ordination. In modern times, when ordination in the olden sense has lapsed, the certificate of admission to the Rabbinate is still called Semicha, as well as by the more general designation *Hattarath Horaah*--'permission to render decisions on ritual questions.'

19. *give him a charge.* *i.e.* instruct him publicly in the duties appertaining to his great and sacred office.

20. *of thy honour upon him.* *i.e.* Moses was to confer honour and dignity upon Joshua publicly; so that, when the people saw the high esteem in which he was held by Moses, they would feel it incumbent upon them to honour him likewise, as well as to obey him. The lit. translation is 'put some of thy majesty upon him', as no man was worthy to receive the whole of Moses' majesty.

21. *stand before Eleazar the priest.* Unlike Moses, he was not to receive Divine communications directly, but indirectly through the medium of Eleazar, the High Priest, after the latter's consultation with God by means of the Urim and Thummim; see Exod. XXVIII, 30.

at his word. Eleazar's.

at his word shall they go out, and at his word they shall come in, both he, and all the children of Israel with him, even all the congregation.' 22. And Moses did as the LORD commanded him; and he took Joshua, and set him before Eleazar the priest, and before all the congregation. 23. And he laid his hands upon him, and gave him a charge, as the LORD spoke by the hand of Moses.*v.

28 CHAPTER XXVIII

1. And the LORD spoke unto Moses, saying: 2. Command the children of Israel, and say unto them: ¶ My food which is presented unto Me for offerings made by fire, of a sweet savour unto Me, shall ye observe to offer unto Me in its due season. 3. And thou shalt say unto them: This is the offering made by fire which ye shall bring unto the LORD: he-lambs of the first year without blemish, two day by day, for a continual burnt-offering. 4. The one lamb shalt thou offer in the morning, and the other lamb shalt thou offer at dusk; 5. and the tenth part of an ephah of fine flour for a meal-offering, mingled with the fourth part of a hin of beaten oil. 6. It is a continual burnt-offering, which was offered in mount Sinai, for a sweet savour, an offering made by fire unto the LORD. 7. And the drink-offering thereof shall be the fourth part of a hin for the one lamb; in the holy place shalt thou pour out a drink-offering of strong drink unto the LORD. 8. And the other lamb shalt thou

וְשָׁאַל לוֹ בְּמִשְׁפַּט הָאוּרִים לִפְנֵי יְהוָה עַל־פִּיו יֵצְאוּ וְעַל־
22 פִּיו יָבֹאוּ הוּא וְכָל־בְּנֵי־יִשְׂרָאֵל אִתּוֹ וְכָל־הָעֵדָה׃ וַיַּעַשׂ מֹשֶׁה
כַּאֲשֶׁר צִוָּה יְהוָה אֹתוֹ וַיִּקַּח אֶת־יְהוֹשֻׁעַ וַיַּעֲמִדֵהוּ לִפְנֵי
23 אֶלְעָזָר הַכֹּהֵן וְלִפְנֵי כָּל־הָעֵדָה׃ וַיִּסְמֹךְ אֶת־יָדָיו עָלָיו וַיְצַוֵּהוּ
כַּאֲשֶׁר דִּבֶּר יְהוָה בְּיַד־מֹשֶׁה׃ * פ חמישי

כח CAP. XXVIII. כח

א 2 וַיְדַבֵּר יְהוָה אֶל־מֹשֶׁה לֵּאמֹר׃ צַו אֶת־בְּנֵי יִשְׂרָאֵל וְאָמַרְתָּ
אֲלֵהֶם אֶת־קָרְבָּנִי לַחְמִי לְאִשַּׁי רֵיחַ נִיחֹחִי תִּשְׁמְרוּ לְהַקְרִיב
3 לִי בְּמוֹעֲדוֹ׃ וְאָמַרְתָּ לָהֶם זֶה הָאִשֶּׁה אֲשֶׁר תַּקְרִיבוּ לַיהוָה
4 כְּבָשִׂים בְּנֵי־שָׁנָה תְמִימִם שְׁנַיִם לַיּוֹם עֹלָה תָמִיד׃ אֶת־
הַכֶּבֶשׂ אֶחָד תַּעֲשֶׂה בַבֹּקֶר וְאֵת הַכֶּבֶשׂ הַשֵּׁנִי תַּעֲשֶׂה
ה בֵּין הָעַרְבָּיִם׃ וַעֲשִׂירִית הָאֵיפָה סֹלֶת לְמִנְחָה בְּלוּלָה
6 בְּשֶׁמֶן כָּתִית רְבִיעִת הַהִין׃ עֹלַת תָּמִיד הָעֲשֻׂיָה בְּהַר סִינַי
7 לְרֵיחַ נִיחֹחַ אִשֶּׁה לַיהוָה׃ וְנִסְכּוֹ רְבִיעִת הַהִין לַכֶּבֶשׂ
8 הָאֶחָד בַּקֹּדֶשׁ הַסֵּךְ נֶסֶךְ שֵׁכָר לַיהוָה׃ וְאֵת הַכֶּבֶשׂ הַשֵּׁנִי

23. *laid his hands.* Moses is Divinely bidden to lay his *hand* upon Joshua (*v.* 18). But Moses goes beyond the Divine command, and lays both his *hands* upon him. So great was his solicitude for the usefulness and success of the man who was to succeed him (Midrash).

CHAPTERS XXVIII AND XXIX
PUBLIC DAILY AND FESTIVAL OFFERINGS

Israel had once more been numbered, and a Leader selected for the conquest of the Land. In this and the following chapter we have a detailed description of the public sacrifices to be brought at the Sanctuary, whether in the daily offering or on each of the Festivals. The sacrifices in these chapters may be regarded as supplementary to Lev. XXIII. The offerings are of four kinds, *viz.* burnt-offerings, meal-offerings, drink-offerings, and sin-offerings.

XXVIII, 2–8. DAILY OFFERINGS

The daily continual (Heb. *tamid*) offering was in later times called 'the Tamid'. Offered throughout the year, it was 'the centre and core of public worship in Judaism' (Kennedy).

2. *food.* See Lev. III, 11 and XXI, 6.
made by fire. See Lev. I, 9.
of a sweet savour. See Lev. I, 9.

3. *without blemish.* A necessary qualification in all holy sacrifices.

4. *at dusk.* Better, *towards even;* see Exod. XII, 6.

5. *tenth part of an ephah.* The 'ephah' was the standard dry measure. The corresponding measure in liquids was the 'hin'. The 'ephah' measured about 70 pints. The 'hin' held nearly 12 pints.

6. *it is a continual burnt-offering.* Resembling the one which was ordained in Exod. XXIX, 38–42, following upon the consecration of Aaron and his sons as priests.

7. *in the holy place.* Or, 'within the sacred court.' According to Rabbinic tradition, over the Altar of sacrifice.
a drink-offering. Of undiluted wine.

present at dusk; as the meal-offering of the morning, and as the drink-offering thereof, thou shalt present it, an offering made by fire, of a sweet savour unto the LORD. ¶ 9. And on the sabbath day two he-lambs of the first year without blemish, and two tenth parts of an ephah of fine flour for a meal-offering, mingled with oil, and the drink-offering thereof. 10. This is the burnt-offering of every sabbath, beside the continual burnt-offering, and the drink-offering thereof. ¶ 11. And in your new moons ye shall present a burnt-offering unto the LORD: two young bullocks, and one ram, seven he-lambs of the first year without blemish; 12. and three tenth parts of an ephah of fine flour for a meal-offering, mingled with oil, for each bullock; and two tenth parts of fine flour for a meal-offering, mingled with oil, for the one ram; 13. and a several tenth part of fine flour mingled with oil for a meal-offering unto every lamb; for a burnt-offering of a sweet savour, an offering made by fire unto the LORD. 14. And their drink-offerings shall be half a hin of wine for a bullock, and the third part of a hin for the ram, and the fourth part of a hin for a lamb. This is the burnt-offering of every new moon throughout the months of the year. 15. And one he-goat for a sin-offering unto the LORD; it shall be offered beside the continual burnt-offering, and the drink-offering thereof.*vi. ¶ 16. And in the first month, on the fourteenth day of the month, is the LORD's passover. 17. And on the fifteenth day of this month shall be a feast; seven days shall unleavened bread be eaten. 18. In the first day shall be a holy convocation; ye shall do no manner of servile work; 19. but ye shall present an offering made by fire, a burnt-offering unto the LORD: two young bullocks, and one ram, and seven he-lambs of the first year; they shall be unto you without blemish; 20. and their meal-offering, fine flour mingled with oil; three tenth parts shall ye offer for a bullock, and two tenth parts for

תַּעֲשֶׂה בֵּין הָעַרְבָּיִם כְּמִנְחַת הַבֹּקֶר וּכְנִסְכּוֹ תַּעֲשֶׂה אִשֵּׁה
רֵיחַ נִיחֹחַ לַיהוָה׃ פ
9 וּבְיוֹם הַשַּׁבָּת שְׁנֵי־כְבָשִׂים בְּנֵי־שָׁנָה תְּמִימִם וּשְׁנֵי עֶשְׂרֹנִים
י סֹלֶת מִנְחָה בְּלוּלָה בַשֶּׁמֶן וְנִסְכּוֹ׃ עֹלַת שַׁבַּת בְּשַׁבַּתּוֹ
עַל־עֹלַת הַתָּמִיד וְנִסְכָּהּ׃ פ
11 וּבְרָאשֵׁי חָדְשֵׁיכֶם תַּקְרִיבוּ עֹלָה לַיהוָה פָּרִים בְּנֵי־בָקָר
שְׁנַיִם וְאַיִל אֶחָד כְּבָשִׂים בְּנֵי־שָׁנָה שִׁבְעָה תְּמִימִם׃
12 וּשְׁלֹשָׁה עֶשְׂרֹנִים סֹלֶת מִנְחָה בְּלוּלָה בַשֶּׁמֶן לַפָּר הָאֶחָד
וּשְׁנֵי עֶשְׂרֹנִים סֹלֶת מִנְחָה בְּלוּלָה בַשֶּׁמֶן לָאַיִל הָאֶחָד׃
13 וְעִשָּׂרֹן עִשָּׂרוֹן סֹלֶת מִנְחָה בְּלוּלָה בַשֶּׁמֶן לַכֶּבֶשׂ הָאֶחָד
14 עֹלָה רֵיחַ נִיחֹחַ אִשֶּׁה לַיהוָה׃ וְנִסְכֵּיהֶם חֲצִי הַהִין יִהְיֶה
לַפָּר וּשְׁלִישִׁת הַהִין לָאַיִל וּרְבִיעִת הַהִין לַכֶּבֶשׂ יָיִן זֹאת
טו עֹלַת חֹדֶשׁ בְּחָדְשׁוֹ לְחָדְשֵׁי הַשָּׁנָה׃ וּשְׂעִיר עִזִּים אֶחָד
ששי לְחַטָּאת לַיהוָה עַל־עֹלַת הַתָּמִיד יֵעָשֶׂה וְנִסְכּוֹ׃ * ס
16 וּבַחֹדֶשׁ הָרִאשׁוֹן בְּאַרְבָּעָה עָשָׂר יוֹם לַחֹדֶשׁ פֶּסַח לַיהוָה׃
17 וּבַחֲמִשָּׁה עָשָׂר יוֹם לַחֹדֶשׁ הַזֶּה חָג שִׁבְעַת יָמִים מַצּוֹת
18 יֵאָכֵל׃ בַּיּוֹם הָרִאשׁוֹן מִקְרָא־קֹדֶשׁ כָּל־מְלֶאכֶת עֲבֹדָה לֹא
19 תַעֲשׂוּ׃ וְהִקְרַבְתֶּם אִשֶּׁה עֹלָה לַיהוָה פָּרִים בְּנֵי־בָקָר
שְׁנַיִם וְאַיִל אֶחָד וְשִׁבְעָה כְבָשִׂים בְּנֵי שָׁנָה תְּמִימִם יִהְיוּ
כ לָכֶם׃ וּמִנְחָתָם סֹלֶת בְּלוּלָה בַשֶּׁמֶן שְׁלֹשָׁה עֶשְׂרֹנִים

v. 10. חב׳ פתוחה

9–10. ADDITIONAL OFFERINGS FOR THE SABBATH

10. *of every sabbath.* It was offered after the daily sacrifice. The same rule applies to all the sacrifices on special occasions.

11–15. NEW MOON OFFERINGS

11. *your new moons.* In pre-Exilic times, the New Moon was celebrated as a minor Festival; see I Sam. XX, 5; II Kings, IV, 23.

15. *a sin-offering.* Offered on all the Feasts (except the Sabbath) as an expiatory sacrifice to atone for any sin of levitical uncleanness committed unwittingly in connection with the Sanctuary or its sacred vessels (Mishnah).

16. *the LORD'S passover.* Better, *a passover unto the LORD.*

16–25. PASSOVER OFFERINGS

18. *an holy convocation.* See Lev. XXIII, 2.
servile work. See on Lev. XXIII, 7.

the ram; 21. a several tenth part shalt thou offer for every lamb of the seven lambs; 22. and one he-goat for a sin-offering, to make atonement for you. 23. Ye shall offer these beside the burnt-offering of the morning, which is for a continual burnt-offering. 24. After this manner ye shall offer daily, for seven days, the food of the offering made by fire, of a sweet savour unto the LORD; it shall be offered beside the continual burnt-offering, and the drink-offering thereof. 25. And on the seventh day ye shall have a holy convocation; ye shall do no manner of servile work. ¶ 26. Also in the day of the first-fruits, when ye bring a new meal-offering unto the LORD in your feast of weeks, ye shall have a holy convocation: ye shall do no manner of servile work; 27. but ye shall present a burnt-offering for a sweet savour unto the LORD: two young bullocks, one ram, seven he-lambs of the first year; 28. and their meal-offering, fine flour mingled with oil, three tenth parts for each bullock, two tenth parts for the one ram, 29. a several tenth part for every lamb of the seven lambs; 30. one he-goat, to make atonement for you. 31. Beside the continual burnt-offering, and the meal-offering thereof, ye shall offer them—they shall be unto you without blemish—and their drink-offerings.

29

CHAPTER XXIX

1. And in the seventh month, on the first day of the month, ye shall have a holy convocation: ye shall do no manner of servile work; it is a day of blowing the horn unto you. 2. And ye shall prepare a burnt-offering for a sweet savour unto the LORD: one young bullock, one ram, seven he-lambs of the first year without blemish; 3. and their meal-offering, fine flour mingled with oil, three tenth parts for the bullock, two tenth parts for the ram, 4. and one tenth part for every lamb of the seven lambs; 5. and one he-goat for a sin-offering, to make atonement for you; 6. beside the burnt-offering of the new moon, and the meal-offering thereof, and the continual burnt-offering and the meal-offering thereof, and their drink-offerings, according unto their ordinance, for a sweet savour, an offering made by fire unto the LORD. ¶ 7. And on the tenth day of this seventh month ye

21 לַפָּר וּשְׁנֵי עֶשְׂרֹנִים לָאַיִל תַּעֲשׂוּ׃ עִשָּׂרוֹן עִשָּׂרוֹן תַּעֲשֶׂה
22 לַכֶּבֶשׂ הָאֶחָד לְשִׁבְעַת הַכְּבָשִׂים׃ וּשְׂעִיר חַטָּאת אֶחָד
23 לְכַפֵּר עֲלֵיכֶם׃ מִלְּבַד עֹלַת הַבֹּקֶר אֲשֶׁר לְעֹלַת הַתָּמִיד
24 תַּעֲשׂוּ אֶת־אֵלֶּה׃ כָּאֵלֶּה תַּעֲשׂוּ לַיּוֹם שִׁבְעַת יָמִים לֶחֶם
אִשֵּׁה רֵיחַ־נִיחֹחַ לַיהוָה עַל־עוֹלַת הַתָּמִיד יֵעָשֶׂה וְנִסְכּוֹ׃
כה וּבַיּוֹם הַשְּׁבִיעִי מִקְרָא־קֹדֶשׁ יִהְיֶה לָכֶם כָּל־מְלֶאכֶת עֲבֹדָה
26 לֹא תַעֲשׂוּ׃ ס וּבְיוֹם הַבִּכּוּרִים בְּהַקְרִיבְכֶם מִנְחָה
חֲדָשָׁה לַיהוָה בְּשָׁבֻעֹתֵיכֶם מִקְרָא־קֹדֶשׁ יִהְיֶה לָכֶם כָּל־
27 מְלֶאכֶת עֲבֹדָה לֹא תַעֲשׂוּ׃ וְהִקְרַבְתֶּם עוֹלָה לְרֵיחַ נִיחֹחַ
לַיהוָה פָּרִים בְּנֵי־בָקָר שְׁנַיִם אַיִל אֶחָד שִׁבְעָה כְבָשִׂים בְּנֵי
28 שָׁנָה׃ וּמִנְחָתָם סֹלֶת בְּלוּלָה בַשָּׁמֶן שְׁלֹשָׁה עֶשְׂרֹנִים לַפָּר
29 הָאֶחָד שְׁנֵי עֶשְׂרֹנִים לָאַיִל הָאֶחָד׃ עִשָּׂרוֹן עִשָּׂרוֹן לַכֶּבֶשׂ
ל הָאֶחָד לְשִׁבְעַת הַכְּבָשִׂים׃ שְׂעִיר עִזִּים אֶחָד לְכַפֵּר עֲלֵיכֶם׃
31 מִלְּבַד עֹלַת הַתָּמִיד וּמִנְחָתוֹ תַּעֲשׂוּ תְּמִימִם יִהְיוּ־לָכֶם
וְנִסְכֵּיהֶם׃ פ

כט CAP. XXIX. כט

א וּבַחֹדֶשׁ הַשְּׁבִיעִי בְּאֶחָד לַחֹדֶשׁ מִקְרָא־קֹדֶשׁ יִהְיֶה לָכֶם
כָּל־מְלֶאכֶת עֲבֹדָה לֹא תַעֲשׂוּ יוֹם תְּרוּעָה יִהְיֶה לָכֶם׃
2 וַעֲשִׂיתֶם עֹלָה לְרֵיחַ נִיחֹחַ לַיהוָה פַּר בֶּן־בָּקָר אֶחָד אַיִל
3 אֶחָד כְּבָשִׂים בְּנֵי־שָׁנָה שִׁבְעָה תְּמִימִם׃ וּמִנְחָתָם סֹלֶת
בְּלוּלָה בַשָּׁמֶן שְׁלֹשָׁה עֶשְׂרֹנִים לַפָּר שְׁנֵי עֶשְׂרֹנִים לָאָיִל׃
4 ה וְעִשָּׂרוֹן אֶחָד לַכֶּבֶשׂ הָאֶחָד לְשִׁבְעַת הַכְּבָשִׂים׃ וּשְׂעִיר־
6 עִזִּים אֶחָד חַטָּאת לְכַפֵּר עֲלֵיכֶם׃ מִלְּבַד עֹלַת הַחֹדֶשׁ
וּמִנְחָתָהּ וְעֹלַת הַתָּמִיד וּמִנְחָתָהּ וְנִסְכֵּיהֶם כְּמִשְׁפָּטָם לְרֵיחַ
7 נִיחֹחַ אִשֶּׁה לַיהוָה׃ ס וּבֶעָשׂוֹר לַחֹדֶשׁ הַשְּׁבִיעִי הַזֶּה

26–31. OFFERINGS FOR THE FEAST OF WEEKS

26. *of the first-fruits.* Of the harvesting of the wheat at Pentecost; Exod. XXXIV, 22.

a new meal-offering. See Lev. XXIII, 16.

XXIX, 1–11. NEW YEAR AND DAY OF ATONEMENT OFFERINGS

7. *ye shall afflict your souls.* A phrase denoting the self-denial and abstention accompanying a fast. Isaiah LVIII, which has always been taken as referring to the Day of Atonement, designates shall have a holy convocation; and ye shall afflict your souls; ye shall do no manner of work; 8. but ye shall present a burnt-offering unto the LORD for a sweet savour: one young bullock, one ram, seven he-lambs of the first year; they shall be unto you without blemish; 9. and their meal-offering, fine flour mingled with oil, three tenth parts for the bullock, two tenth parts for the one ram, 10. a several tenth part for every lamb of the seven lambs; 11. one he-goat for a sin-offering; beside the sin-offering of atonement, and the continual burnt-offering, and the meal-offering thereof, and their drink-offerings.*vii. ¶ 12. And on the fifteenth day of the seventh month ye shall have a holy convocation: ye shall do no manner of servile work, and ye shall keep a feast unto the LORD seven days; 13. and ye shall present a burnt-offering, an offering made by fire, of a sweet savour unto the LORD: thirteen young bullocks, two rams, fourteen he-lambs of the first year; they shall be without blemish; 14. and their meal-offering, fine flour mingled with oil, three tenth parts for every bullock of the thirteen bullocks, two tenth parts for each ram of the two rams, 15. and a several tenth part for every lamb of the fourteen lambs; 16. and one he-goat for a sin-offering; beside the continual burnt-offering, the meal-offering thereof, and the drink-offering thereof. ¶ 17. And on the second day ye shall present twelve young bullocks, two rams, fourteen he-lambs of the first year without blemish; 18. and their meal-offering and their drink-offerings for the bullocks, for the rams, and for the lambs, according to their number, after the ordinance; 19. and one he-goat for a sin-offering; beside the continual burnt-offering, and the meal-offering thereof, and their drink-offerings. ¶ 20. And on the third day eleven bullocks, two rams, fourteen he-lambs of the first year without blemish; 21. and their meal-offering and their drink-offerings for the bullocks, for the rams, and for the lambs, according to their number, after the ordinance; 22. and one he-goat for a sin-offering; beside the continual burnt-offering, and the meal-offering thereof, and the drink-offering thereof. ¶ 23. And on the fourth day ten bullocks, two rams, fourteen he-lambs of the first year without blemish; 24. their meal-offering and their drink-offerings for the bullocks,

מִקְרָא־קֹדֶשׁ יִהְיֶה לָכֶם וְעִנִּיתֶם אֶת־נַפְשֹׁתֵיכֶם כָּל־
8 מְלָאכָה לֹא תַעֲשׂוּ׃ וְהִקְרַבְתֶּם עֹלָה לַיהוָה רֵיחַ נִיחֹחַ
פַּר בֶּן־בָּקָר אֶחָד אַיִל אֶחָד כְּבָשִׂים בְּנֵי־שָׁנָה שִׁבְעָה
9 תְּמִימִם יִהְיוּ לָכֶם׃ וּמִנְחָתָם סֹלֶת בְּלוּלָה בַשָּׁמֶן שְׁלֹשָׁה
י עֶשְׂרֹנִים לַפָּר שְׁנֵי עֶשְׂרֹנִים לָאַיִל הָאֶחָד׃ עִשָּׂרוֹן עִשָּׂרוֹן
11 לַכֶּבֶשׂ הָאֶחָד לְשִׁבְעַת הַכְּבָשִׂים׃ שְׂעִיר־עִזִּים אֶחָד חַטָּאת
שביעי מִלְּבַד חַטַּאת הַכִּפֻּרִים וְעֹלַת הַתָּמִיד וּמִנְחָתָהּ וְנִסְכֵּיהֶם׃
12 ס וּבַחֲמִשָּׁה עָשָׂר יוֹם לַחֹדֶשׁ הַשְּׁבִיעִי מִקְרָא־קֹדֶשׁ
יִהְיֶה לָכֶם כָּל־מְלֶאכֶת עֲבֹדָה לֹא תַעֲשׂוּ וְחַגֹּתֶם חַג לַיהוָה
13 שִׁבְעַת יָמִים׃ וְהִקְרַבְתֶּם עֹלָה אִשֵּׁה רֵיחַ נִיחֹחַ לַיהוָה פָּרִים
בְּנֵי־בָקָר שְׁלֹשָׁה עָשָׂר אֵילִם שְׁנָיִם כְּבָשִׂים בְּנֵי־שָׁנָה
14 אַרְבָּעָה עָשָׂר תְּמִימִם יִהְיוּ׃ וּמִנְחָתָם סֹלֶת בְּלוּלָה בַשָּׁמֶן
שְׁלֹשָׁה עֶשְׂרֹנִים לַפָּר הָאֶחָד לִשְׁלֹשָׁה עָשָׂר פָּרִים שְׁנֵי
טו עֶשְׂרֹנִים לָאַיִל הָאֶחָד לִשְׁנֵי הָאֵילִם׃ וְעִשָּׂרוֹן עִשָּׂרוֹן לַכֶּבֶשׂ
16 הָאֶחָד לְאַרְבָּעָה עָשָׂר כְּבָשִׂים׃ וּשְׂעִיר־עִזִּים אֶחָד חַטָּאת
17 מִלְּבַד עֹלַת הַתָּמִיד מִנְחָתָהּ וְנִסְכָּהּ׃ ס וּבַיּוֹם הַשֵּׁנִי
פָּרִים בְּנֵי־בָקָר שְׁנֵים עָשָׂר אֵילִם שְׁנָיִם כְּבָשִׂים בְּנֵי־
18 שָׁנָה אַרְבָּעָה עָשָׂר תְּמִימִם׃ וּמִנְחָתָם וְנִסְכֵּיהֶם לַפָּרִים
19 לָאֵילִם וְלַכְּבָשִׂים בְּמִסְפָּרָם כַּמִּשְׁפָּט׃ וּשְׂעִיר־עִזִּים אֶחָד
כ חַטָּאת מִלְּבַד עֹלַת הַתָּמִיד וּמִנְחָתָהּ וְנִסְכֵּיהֶם׃ ס וּבַיּוֹם
הַשְּׁלִישִׁי פָּרִים עַשְׁתֵּי־עָשָׂר אֵילִם שְׁנָיִם כְּבָשִׂים בְּנֵי־שָׁנָה
21 אַרְבָּעָה עָשָׂר תְּמִימִם׃ וּמִנְחָתָם וְנִסְכֵּיהֶם לַפָּרִים לָאֵילִם
22 וְלַכְּבָשִׂים בְּמִסְפָּרָם כַּמִּשְׁפָּט׃ וּשְׂעִיר חַטָּאת אֶחָד
23 מִלְּבַד עֹלַת הַתָּמִיד וּמִנְחָתָהּ וְנִסְכָּהּ׃ ס וּבַיּוֹם
הָרְבִיעִי פָּרִים עֲשָׂרָה אֵילִם שְׁנָיִם כְּבָשִׂים בְּנֵי־שָׁנָה
24 אַרְבָּעָה עָשָׂר תְּמִימִם׃ מִנְחָתָם וְנִסְכֵּיהֶם לַפָּרִים לָאֵילִם

v. 15. נקוד על ו' בתרא

it repeatedly as a 'fast', and emphasizes not only its religious but also its social message to the Jewish life. See Lev. XVI, 29, XXIII, 27–9.

no manner of work. See Lev. XXIII, 28.

11. *of atonement*. See Lev. XVI, 15 f.

12–38. OFFERINGS FOR THE FEAST OF TABERNACLES

As it was the Harvest Festival, the joys associated with it found expression in a profusion for the rams, and for the lambs. according to their number, after the ordinance; 25. and one he-goat for a sin-offering; beside the continual burnt-offering, the meal-offering thereof, and the drink-offering thereof. ¶ 26. And on the fifth day nine bullocks, two rams, fourteen he-lambs of the first year without blemish; 27. and their meal-offering and their drink-offerings for the bullocks, for the rams, and for the lambs, according to their number, after the ordinance; 28. and one he-goat for a sin-offering; beside the continual burnt-offering, and the meal-offering thereof, and the drink-offering thereof. ¶ 29. And on the sixth day eight bullocks, two rams, fourteen he-lambs of the first year without blemish; 30. and their meal-offering and their drink-offerings for the bullocks, for the rams, and for the lambs, according to their number, after the ordinance; 31. and one he-goat for a sin-offering; beside the continual burnt-offering, the meal-offering thereof, and the drink-offerings thereof. ¶ 32. And on the seventh day seven bullocks, two rams, fourteen he-lambs of the first year without blemish; 33. and their meal-offering and their drink-offerings for the bullocks, for the rams, and for the lambs, according to their number, after the ordinance; 34. and one he-goat for a sin-offering; beside the continual burnt-offering, the meal-offering thereof, and the drink-offering thereof. *m. ¶ 35. On the eighth day ye shall have a solemn assembly: ye shall do no manner of servile work; 36. but ye shall present a burnt-offering, an offering made by fire, of a sweet savour unto the LORD: one bullock, one ram, seven he-lambs of the first year without blemish; 37. their meal-offering and their drink-offerings for the bullock, for the ram, and for the lambs, shall be according to their number, after the ordinance; 38. and one he-goat for a sin-offering; beside the continual burnt-offering, and the meal-offering thereof, and the drink-offering thereof. ¶ 39. These ye shall offer unto the LORD in your appointed seasons, beside your vows, and your freewill-offerings, whether they be your burnt-offerings, or your meal-offerings, or your drink-offerings, or your peace-offerings.

30

CHAPTER XXX

1. And Moses told the children of Israel according to all that the LORD commanded Moses.

כה וְלַכְּבָשִׂים בְּמִסְפָּרָם כַּמִּשְׁפָּט׃ וּשְׂעִיר־עִזִּים אֶחָד חַטָּאת
26 מִלְּבַד עֹלַת הַתָּמִיד מִנְחָתָהּ וְנִסְכָּהּ׃ ס וּבַיּוֹם הַחֲמִישִׁי
פָּרִים תִּשְׁעָה אֵילִם שְׁנָיִם כְּבָשִׂים בְּנֵי־שָׁנָה אַרְבָּעָה
27 עָשָׂר תְּמִימִם׃ וּמִנְחָתָם וְנִסְכֵּיהֶם לַפָּרִים לָאֵילִם וְלַכְּבָשִׂים
28 בְּמִסְפָּרָם כַּמִּשְׁפָּט׃ וּשְׂעִיר חַטָּאת אֶחָד מִלְּבַד עֹלַת
29 הַתָּמִיד וּמִנְחָתָהּ וְנִסְכָּהּ׃ ס וּבַיּוֹם הַשִּׁשִּׁי פָּרִים שְׁמֹנָה
אֵילִם שְׁנָיִם כְּבָשִׂים בְּנֵי־שָׁנָה אַרְבָּעָה עָשָׂר תְּמִימִם׃
ל וּמִנְחָתָם וְנִסְכֵּיהֶם לַפָּרִים לָאֵילִם וְלַכְּבָשִׂים בְּמִסְפָּרָם
31 כַּמִּשְׁפָּט׃ וּשְׂעִיר חַטָּאת אֶחָד מִלְּבַד עֹלַת הַתָּמִיד
32 מִנְחָתָהּ וּנְסָכֶיהָ׃ ס וּבַיּוֹם הַשְּׁבִיעִי פָּרִים שִׁבְעָה
אֵילִם שְׁנָיִם כְּבָשִׂים בְּנֵי־שָׁנָה אַרְבָּעָה עָשָׂר תְּמִימִם׃
33 וּמִנְחָתָם וְנִסְכֵּהֶם לַפָּרִים לָאֵילִם וְלַכְּבָשִׂים בְּמִסְפָּרָם
34 כְּמִשְׁפָּטָם׃ וּשְׂעִיר חַטָּאת אֶחָד מִלְּבַד עֹלַת הַתָּמִיד
מפטיר
לה מִנְחָתָהּ וְנִסְכָּהּ׃* ס בַּיּוֹם הַשְּׁמִינִי עֲצֶרֶת תִּהְיֶה לָכֶם
36 כָּל־מְלֶאכֶת עֲבֹדָה לֹא תַעֲשׂוּ׃ וְהִקְרַבְתֶּם עֹלָה אִשֵּׁה
רֵיחַ נִיחֹחַ לַיהוָה פַּר אֶחָד אַיִל אֶחָד כְּבָשִׂים בְּנֵי־שָׁנָה
37 שִׁבְעָה תְּמִימִם׃ מִנְחָתָם וְנִסְכֵּיהֶם לַפָּר לָאַיִל וְלַכְּבָשִׂים
38 בְּמִסְפָּרָם כַּמִּשְׁפָּט׃ וּשְׂעִיר חַטָּאת אֶחָד מִלְּבַד עֹלַת
39 הַתָּמִיד וּמִנְחָתָהּ וְנִסְכָּהּ׃ אֵלֶּה תַּעֲשׂוּ לַיהוָה בְּמוֹעֲדֵיכֶם
לְבַד מִנִּדְרֵיכֶם וְנִדְבֹתֵיכֶם לְעֹלֹתֵיכֶם וּלְמִנְחֹתֵיכֶם
וּלְנִסְכֵּיכֶם וּלְשַׁלְמֵיכֶם׃

CAP. XXX. ל

ל

א וַיֹּאמֶר מֹשֶׁה אֶל־בְּנֵי יִשְׂרָאֵל כְּכֹל אֲשֶׁר־צִוָּה יְהוָה אֶת־
מֹשֶׁה׃

כט׳ v. 33. חסר יו״ד

of offerings to God, the bounteous Giver of the harvest.

The numbers of bullocks, totalling seventy altogether, corresponded to the seventy nations of the world, and were intended as an atonement for all mankind.

35. *on the eighth day.* See on Lev. XXIII, 36.

I KINGS XVIII, 46–XIX, 21

CHAPTER XVIII

46. And the hand of the LORD was on Elijah; and he girded up his loins, and ran before Ahab to the entrance of Jezreel.

CHAPTER XIX

1. And Ahab told Jezebel all that Elijah had done, and withal how he had slain all the prophets with the sword. 2. Then Jezebel sent a messenger unto Elijah, saying: 'So let the gods do [to me], and more also, if I make not thy life as the life of one of them by to-morrow about this time.' 3. And when he saw that, he arose, and went for his life, and came to Beer-sheba, which belongeth to Judah, and left his servant there. 4. But he himself went a day's journey into the wilderness, and came and sat down under a broom-tree; and he requested for himself that he might die; and said: 'It is enough; now, O LORD, take away my life; for I am not better than my fathers.' 5. And he lay down and slept under a broom-tree; and, behold, an angel touched him, and said unto him: 'Arise and eat.' 6. And he looked, and, behold, there was at his head a cake baked on the hot stones, and a cruse of water. And he did eat and drink, and laid

CAP. XVIII. יח

46 וְיַד יְהוָה הָיְתָה
אֶל־אֵלִיָּהוּ וַיְשַׁנֵּס מָתְנָיו וַיָּרָץ לִפְנֵי אַחְאָב עַד־בֹּאֲכָה
יִזְרְעֶאלָה׃

CAP. XIX. יט

א וַיַּגֵּד אַחְאָב לְאִיזֶבֶל אֵת כָּל־אֲשֶׁר עָשָׂה אֵלִיָּהוּ וְאֵת כָּל־
2 אֲשֶׁר הָרַג אֶת־כָּל־הַנְּבִיאִים בֶּחָרֶב׃ וַתִּשְׁלַח אִיזֶבֶל
מַלְאָךְ אֶל־אֵלִיָּהוּ לֵאמֹר כֹּה־יַעֲשׂוּן אֱלֹהִים וְכֹה יוֹסִפוּן
3 כִּי־כָעֵת מָחָר אָשִׂים אֶת־נַפְשְׁךָ כְּנֶפֶשׁ אַחַד מֵהֶם׃ וַיַּרְא
וַיָּקָם וַיֵּלֶךְ אֶל־נַפְשׁוֹ וַיָּבֹא בְּאֵר שֶׁבַע אֲשֶׁר לִיהוּדָה וַיַּנַּח
4 אֶת־נַעֲרוֹ שָׁם׃ וְהוּא־הָלַךְ בַּמִּדְבָּר דֶּרֶךְ יוֹם וַיָּבֹא וַיֵּשֶׁב
תַּחַת רֹתֶם אֶחָת וַיִּשְׁאַל אֶת־נַפְשׁוֹ לָמוּת וַיֹּאמֶר ׀ רַב
ה עַתָּה יְהוָה קַח נַפְשִׁי כִּי לֹא־טוֹב אָנֹכִי מֵאֲבֹתָי׃ וַיִּשְׁכַּב
וַיִּישַׁן תַּחַת רֹתֶם אֶחָד וְהִנֵּה־זֶה מַלְאָךְ נֹגֵעַ בּוֹ וַיֹּאמֶר לוֹ

יט׳ v. 3. למדנהאי על v. 4. אחד קרי

The zeal of Phinehas and the zeal of Elijah form the connecting link between the Sedrah and Haftorah.

Under the evil influence of Jezebel, wife of Ahab, the people had been led astray to the worship of Baal. Ahab was a generous ruler, but weak-willed and dominated by his Phoenician wife who had pursued the prophets of God with murderous cruelty. It was high treason to proclaim the God of Israel. Against this dark setting, the figure of Elijah stands out in all its greatness. He meets and confronts the king and queen, and fearlessly pronounces the doom that will follow on their apostasy and outrage of justice. On Mount Carmel, though he is alone and defenceless, his Titanic personality overawes the multitude. He brings the people back to God in an overwhelming act of surrender. Their confession, *Adonay hu ha-elohim*, 'The LORD, He is God,' has become, alongside the declaration of the Unity, Israel's watchword. The events of the Haftorah follow immediately after that historic scene on Mount Carmel.

Elijah's triumph was brief. Jezebel lost no time in informing him that she was neither converted nor dismayed, and that she would take her revenge on Elijah.

46. *the hand of the LORD.* A phrase to denote that the Prophet acted under a Divine impulse.

ran before Ahab. To pay the respect due to Ahab's position as king. An Eastern monarch regularly had runners to escort his chariot.

CHAPTER XIX

1. *all the prophets. i.e.* of Baal.

2. *as the life of one of them. i.e.* of the false prophets whom he had slain.

3. *to Judah.* And therefore outside the jurisdiction of Ahab and Jezebel.

4. *broom-tree.* A kind of flowering broom that grows to the height of about 10 feet and is found in that desert district.

take away my life. Reaction following the great scene on Mount Carmel, and disappointment at its apparent failure, induced a mood of crushing despondency. A sense of the dreariness of a wasted life overspread his soul. 'Like a warrior who has waged all day an unequal strife and at the last received a mortal stroke, he retires from the field to die alone; and when the languor is falling on him, he says, "Now, O LORD, take away my life"' (Davidson).

not better than my fathers. He has made his great effort, and feels he has not been more successful than earlier leaders in Israel in checking apostasy.

6 קוּם אֱכוֹל׃ וַיַּבֵּט וְהִנֵּה מְרַאֲשֹׁתָיו עֻגַת רְצָפִים וְצַפַּחַת
7 מָיִם וַיֹּאכַל וַיֵּשְׁתְּ וַיָּשָׁב וַיִּשְׁכָּב׃ וַיָּשָׁב מַלְאַךְ יְהוָה ׀
שֵׁנִית וַיִּגַּע־בּוֹ וַיֹּאמֶר קוּם אֱכֹל כִּי רַב מִמְּךָ הַדָּרֶךְ׃
8 וַיָּקָם וַיֹּאכַל וַיִּשְׁתֶּה וַיֵּלֶךְ בְּכֹחַ ׀ הָאֲכִילָה הַהִיא אַרְבָּעִים
9 יוֹם וְאַרְבָּעִים לַיְלָה עַד הַר הָאֱלֹהִים חֹרֵב׃ וַיָּבֹא־שָׁם
אֶל־הַמְּעָרָה וַיָּלֶן שָׁם וְהִנֵּה דְבַר־יְהוָה אֵלָיו וַיֹּאמֶר לוֹ
· מַה־לְּךָ פֹה אֵלִיָּהוּ׃ וַיֹּאמֶר קַנֹּא קִנֵּאתִי לַיהוָה ׀ אֱלֹהֵי
צְבָאוֹת כִּי־עָזְבוּ בְרִיתְךָ בְּנֵי יִשְׂרָאֵל אֶת־מִזְבְּחֹתֶיךָ הָרָסוּ
וְאֶת־נְבִיאֶיךָ הָרְגוּ בֶחָרֶב וָאִוָּתֵר אֲנִי לְבַדִּי וַיְבַקְשׁוּ אֶת־
11 נַפְשִׁי לְקַחְתָּהּ׃ וַיֹּאמֶר צֵא וְעָמַדְתָּ בָהָר לִפְנֵי יְהוָה
וְהִנֵּה יְהוָה עֹבֵר וְרוּחַ גְּדוֹלָה וְחָזָק מְפָרֵק הָרִים וּמְשַׁבֵּר
סְלָעִים לִפְנֵי יְהוָה לֹא בָרוּחַ יְהוָה וְאַחַר הָרוּחַ רַעַשׁ לֹא
12 בָרַעַשׁ יְהוָה׃ וְאַחַר הָרַעַשׁ אֵשׁ לֹא בָאֵשׁ יְהוָה וְאַחַר

v. 10. קמץ בז״ק

him down again. 7. And the angel of the LORD came again the second time, and touched him, and said: 'Arise and eat; because the journey is too great for thee.' 8. And he arose, and did eat and drink, and went in the strength of that meal forty days and forty nights unto Horeb the mount of God. ¶ 9. And he came thither unto a cave, and lodged there; and, behold, the word of the LORD came to him, and He said unto him: 'What doest thou here, Elijah?' 10. And he said: 'I have been very jealous for the LORD, the God of hosts; for the children of Israel have forsaken Thy covenant, thrown down Thine altars, and slain Thy prophets with the sword; and I, even I only, am left; and they seek my life, to take it away.' 11. And He said: 'Go forth, and stand upon the mount before the LORD.' And, behold, the LORD passed by, and a great and strong wind rent the mountains, and broke in pieces the rocks before the LORD; but the LORD was not in the wind; and after the wind an earthquake; but the LORD was not in the earthquake; 12. and after the earthquake a fire; but the LORD was not in the fire; and after the fire a still small voice. 13. And it was so, when

7. *too great for thee. i.e.* the journey thou wishest to take (Altschul); suggesting that Mount Horeb was Elijah's goal when he set out on his flight.

9. *unto a cave.* lit. 'into the cave'; *i.e.* the cleft of rock in which Moses was placed when God passed by (Kimchi). The parallel between Moses and Elijah is very real. These two names stand out pre-eminently in Israel's story; both of them endowed above all other men with the power of the Spirit and Titanic force of character.

what doest thou here, Elijah? Thy place is not here in the silent empty wilderness, but among men to fight evil and encourage the faithful.

10. *jealous.* Zealous.

I only, am left. As is more clear below in *v.* 18, Elijah's mood of despondency and despair has led him to exaggerate the darkness of the picture, and to be unjust to the 7,000 men in Israel who had not bent the knee to Baal.

11–14. THE MANIFESTATION OF THE DIVINE PRESENCE

This narrative is one of the profoundest in Scripture. In a magnificent acted parable, Elijah is taught the error of his methods.

12. *a still small voice.* Or, 'a sound of gentle stillness.' The wind, fire and earthquake are often spoken of as heralds of God (Exod. XIX, 18, Psalms XVIII, 7–13); and while they are His agents and subservient to His will, they do not disclose Him so perfectly as the calm which follows the storm. The vision is in the nature of rebuke to the impetuosity of Elijah, and the passion of despair that brought him to this place. He must not imagine that good is vanquished, because evil is mighty, loud, and triumphant. And evil cannot most successfully be overcome by storm and fire. Rather is the Spirit of God manifested, and the purpose of God furthered, in that which is represented by the still small voice; *i.e.* the gentle operation of spiritual forces, the calmness and patience of quiet and indomitable faith, and the persistent work which is the fruit of that patience and faith.

To later generations, Elijah was not the Prophet of storm and fire, but the leader and helper, the reconciler and peace-bringer. 'He shall turn the heart of the fathers to the children, and the heart of the children to their fathers,' said Malachi. 'Elijah will come to bring agreement where there is matter for dispute: to make peace in the world' (Mishnah).

13. *wrapped his face in his mantle.* It is the 'still small voice' that brings home to the Prophet the sense of the Presence of God.

Elijah heard it, that he wrapped his face in his mantle, and went out, and stood in the entrance of the cave. And, behold, there came a voice unto him, and said: 'What doest thou here, Elijah?' 14. And he said: 'I have been very jealous for the LORD, the God of hosts; for the children of Israel have forsaken Thy covenant, thrown down Thine altars, and slain Thy prophets with the sword; and I, even I only, am left; and they seek my life, to take it away.' ¶ 15. And the LORD said unto him: 'Go, return on thy way to the wilderness of Damascus; and when thou comest, thou shalt anoint Hazael to be king over Aram; 16. and Jehu the son of Nimshi shalt thou anoint to be king over Israel; and Elisha the son of Shaphat of Abel-meholah shalt thou anoint to be prophet in thy room. 17. And it shall come to pass, that him that escapeth from the sword of Hazael shall Jehu slay; and him that escapeth from the sword of Jehu shall Elisha slay. 18. Yet will I leave seven thousand in Israel, all the knees which have not bowed unto Baal, and every mouth which hath not kissed him.' ¶ 19. So he departed thence, and found Elisha the son of Shaphat, who was plowing, with twelve yoke of oxen before him, and he with the twelfth; and Elijah passed over unto him, and cast his mantle upon him. 20. And he left the oxen, and ran after Elijah, and said: 'Let me, I pray thee, kiss my father and my mother, and then I will follow thee.' And he said unto him: 'Go back; for what have I done to thee?' 21. And he returned from following him, and took the yoke of oxen, and slew them, and boiled their flesh with the instruments of the oxen, and gave unto the people, and they did eat. Then he arose, and went after Elijah, and ministered unto him.

13 הָאֵשׁ קוֹל דְּמָמָה דַקָּה׃ וַיְהִי ׀ כִּשְׁמֹעַ אֵלִיָּהוּ וַיָּלֶט פָּנָיו
בְּאַדַּרְתּוֹ וַיֵּצֵא וַיַּעֲמֹד פֶּתַח הַמְּעָרָה וְהִנֵּה אֵלָיו קוֹל וַיֹּאמֶר
14 מַה־לְּךָ פֹה אֵלִיָּהוּ׃ וַיֹּאמֶר קַנֹּא קִנֵּאתִי לַיהוָה ׀ אֱלֹהֵי
צְבָאוֹת כִּי־עָזְבוּ בְרִיתְךָ בְּנֵי יִשְׂרָאֵל אֶת־מִזְבְּחֹתֶיךָ
הָרָסוּ וְאֶת־נְבִיאֶיךָ הָרְגוּ בֶחָרֶב וָאִוָּתֵר אֲנִי לְבַדִּי וַיְבַקְשׁוּ
טו אֶת־נַפְשִׁי לְקַחְתָּהּ׃ וַיֹּאמֶר יְהוָה אֵלָיו לֵךְ שׁוּב
לְדַרְכְּךָ מִדְבַּרָה דַמָּשֶׂק וּבָאתָ וּמָשַׁחְתָּ אֶת־חֲזָאֵל לְמֶלֶךְ
16 עַל־אֲרָם׃ וְאֵת יֵהוּא בֶן־נִמְשִׁי תִּמְשַׁח לְמֶלֶךְ עַל־יִשְׂרָאֵל
וְאֶת־אֱלִישָׁע בֶּן־שָׁפָט מֵאָבֵל מְחוֹלָה תִּמְשַׁח לְנָבִיא
17 תַּחְתֶּיךָ׃ וְהָיָה הַנִּמְלָט מֵחֶרֶב חֲזָאֵל יָמִית יֵהוּא וְהַנִּמְלָט
18 מֵחֶרֶב יֵהוּא יָמִית אֱלִישָׁע׃ וְהִשְׁאַרְתִּי בְיִשְׂרָאֵל שִׁבְעַת
אֲלָפִים כָּל־הַבִּרְכַּיִם אֲשֶׁר לֹא־כָרְעוּ לַבַּעַל וְכָל־הַפֶּה
19 אֲשֶׁר לֹא־נָשַׁק לוֹ׃ וַיֵּלֶךְ מִשָּׁם וַיִּמְצָא אֶת־אֱלִישָׁע בֶּן־
שָׁפָט וְהוּא חֹרֵשׁ שְׁנֵים־עָשָׂר צְמָדִים לְפָנָיו וְהוּא בִּשְׁנֵים
כ הֶעָשָׂר וַיַּעֲבֹר אֵלִיָּהוּ אֵלָיו וַיַּשְׁלֵךְ אַדַּרְתּוֹ אֵלָיו׃ וַיַּעֲזֹב
אֶת־הַבָּקָר וַיָּרָץ אַחֲרֵי אֵלִיָּהוּ וַיֹּאמֶר אֶשְּׁקָה־נָּא לְאָבִי
וּלְאִמִּי וְאֵלְכָה אַחֲרֶיךָ וַיֹּאמֶר לוֹ לֵךְ שׁוּב כִּי מֶה עָשִׂיתִי
21 לָךְ׃ וַיָּשָׁב מֵאַחֲרָיו וַיִּקַּח אֶת־צֶמֶד הַבָּקָר וַיִּזְבָּחֵהוּ וּבִכְלִי
הַבָּקָר בִּשְּׁלָם הַבָּשָׂר וַיִּתֵּן לָעָם וַיֹּאכֵלוּ וַיָּקָם וַיֵּלֶךְ אַחֲרֵי
אֵלִיָּהוּ וַיְשָׁרְתֵהוּ׃

v. 14. קמץ בז״ק v. 15. הב׳ בפתח v. 18. מלרע v. 20. הש׳ בח״ק

what doest thou here? Elijah repeats his former reply to this question, and it would appear that his zealous anger for the sins of Israel has prevented him realizing the full import of the vision as above explained (Ralbag).

15–21. ELIJAH'S NEW MISSION

15. *go, return on thy way.* Elijah is shown that there is still work for him to do.

18. *seven thousand.* Elijah had overlooked the 'righteous remnant' in Israel.

19. *cast his mantle upon him.* Elisha understood the meaning of the act.

20. *let me . . . kiss my father.* To ask permission of his parents to accept the call, and in farewell to them. His life was now to take a new direction, as disciple of Elijah, and then as his successor.

go back. And consult your parents.

what have I done to thee? Realize the full significance of the Call.

21. *he returned from following him.* 'He ran back' (Moffatt).

with the instruments of the oxen. That is, with the wooden part of the yoke and plough which he used for fire-wood. His act was to symbolize his break with his former vocation.

and gave unto the people. He made the occasion one of rejoicing to the people who came to take farewell of him and accompany him a distance on his way (Kimchi).

ל 30

פ פ פ מב 42

2. And Moses spoke unto the heads of the tribes of the children of Israel, saying: ¶ This is the thing which the LORD hath commanded. 3. When a man voweth a vow unto the LORD, or sweareth an oath to bind his soul with a bond, he shall not break his word; he shall do according to all that proceedeth out of his mouth. 4. Also when a woman voweth a vow unto the LORD, and bindeth herself by a bond, being in her father's house, in her youth, 5. and her father heareth her vow, or her bond wherewith she hath bound her soul, and her father holdeth his peace at her, then all her vows shall stand, and every bond wherewith she hath bound her soul shall stand. 6. But if her father disallow her in the day that he heareth, none of her vows, or of her bonds wherewith she hath bound her soul, shall stand; and the LORD will forgive her, because her father disallowed her. 7. And if she be married to a husband, while her vows are upon her, or the clear utterance of her lips, wherewith she hath bound her soul; 8. and her husband hear it, whatsoever day

2 וַיְדַבֵּר מֹשֶׁה אֶל־רָאשֵׁי הַמַּטּוֹת לִבְנֵי יִשְׂרָאֵל לֵאמֹר זֶה
3 הַדָּבָר אֲשֶׁר צִוָּה יְהוָה׃ אִישׁ כִּי־יִדֹּר נֶדֶר לַיהוָה אוֹ־
הִשָּׁבַע שְׁבֻעָה לֶאְסֹר אִסָּר עַל־נַפְשׁוֹ לֹא יַחֵל דְּבָרוֹ כְּכָל־
4 הַיֹּצֵא מִפִּיו יַעֲשֶׂה׃ וְאִשָּׁה כִּי־תִדֹּר נֶדֶר לַיהוָה וְאָסְרָה
ה אִסָּר בְּבֵית אָבִיהָ בִּנְעֻרֶיהָ׃ וְשָׁמַע אָבִיהָ אֶת־נִדְרָהּ
וֶאֱסָרָהּ אֲשֶׁר אָסְרָה עַל־נַפְשָׁהּ וְהֶחֱרִישׁ לָהּ אָבִיהָ וְקָמוּ
6 כָּל־נְדָרֶיהָ וְכָל־אִסָּר אֲשֶׁר־אָסְרָה עַל־נַפְשָׁהּ יָקוּם׃ וְאִם־
הֵנִיא אָבִיהָ אֹתָהּ בְּיוֹם שָׁמְעוֹ כָּל־נְדָרֶיהָ וֶאֱסָרֶיהָ אֲשֶׁר־
אָסְרָה עַל־נַפְשָׁהּ לֹא יָקוּם וַיהוָה יִסְלַח־לָהּ כִּי־הֵנִיא אָבִיהָ
7 אֹתָהּ׃ וְאִם־הָיוֹ תִהְיֶה לְאִישׁ וּנְדָרֶיהָ עָלֶיהָ אוֹ מִבְטָא

IX. MATTOS

(CHAPTERS XXX, 2–XXXII)

CHAPTER XXX. CONCERNING VOWS

This chapter emphasizes the solemnity and binding character of religious vows, and in what circumstances vows of women can be annulled by the father or husband.

2–3. SACREDNESS OF VOWS

3. *voweth a vow.* Heb. *neder*; denotes a solemn promise to consecrate something to God, or do something in His service or His honour. A vow was usually made in a time of distress, and its motive was the desire to secure Divine help; cf. Gen. XXVIII, 20–22. Or it might be an expression of gratitude for Divine aid received. 'The manifest emotion with which many a singer in the Psalter records his gratitude to God as he pays his vows, shows that they must often have represented a warm and genuine religious experience' (McFadyen).

a bond. Heb. *issar.* In contrast to *neder*, this may be called a negative vow: a self-imposed pledge to abstain from doing or enjoying something that is perfectly allowable.

break his word. lit. 'profane his word'. The violation of a vow or 'bond' is at once an offence before God, and an act of profanation of man's personality.

according to all that proceedeth out of his mouth. There is a tendency in human nature to forget in health and security the vows that were made in sickness and danger; but the rule remains, Whatever a man has promised unto God, that he must fulfil.

4–6. VOWS OF A YOUNG UNMARRIED WOMAN

After laying down the general principle, Scripture proceeds to qualify it in three special cases of vows made by women under authority; *viz.* (*a*) women before marriage; (*b*) married women; (*c*) women after marriage, *i.e.* widows and divorced women.

4. *in her youth.* A young unmarried woman still under her father's guardianship; *i.e.* till the age of adolescence.

5. *holdeth his peace.* The father's silence amounts to a ratification of the vow.

6. *disallow her.* If the father verbally disapproves of her vow on the day he hears of it, such disapproval amounts to a veto and the vow becomes annulled; see on *v.* 13.

7–9. CASE OF A MARRIED WOMAN WHO MADE THE VOW WHILST SINGLE

7. *while her vows are upon her.* This is the second of the three afore-mentioned cases; *viz.* the vow of a woman who marries whilst under a vow made by her before marriage, whether during the stage of adolescence and with the requisite approval of the father, or when she was a full-grown woman and outside the range of her father's veto.

it be that he heareth it, and hold his peace at her; then her vows shall stand, and her bonds wherewith she hath bound her soul shall stand. 9. But if her husband disallow her in the day that he heareth it, then he shall make void her vow which is upon her, and the clear utterance of her lips, wherewith she hath bound her soul; and the LORD will forgive her. 10. But the vow of a widow, or of her that is divorced, even every thing wherewith she hath bound her soul, shall stand against her. 11. And if a woman vowed in her husband's house, or bound her soul by a bond with an oath, 12. and her husband heard it, and held his peace at her, and disallowed her not, then all her vows shall stand, and every bond wherewith she bound her soul shall stand. 13. But if her husband make them null and void in the day that he heareth them, then whatsoever proceeded out of her lips, whether it were her vows, or the bond of her soul, shall not stand: her husband hath made them void; and the LORD will forgive her. 14. Every vow, and every binding oath to afflict the soul, her husband may let it stand, or her husband may make it void. 15. But if her husband altogether hold his peace at her from day to day, then he causeth all her vows to stand, or all her bonds, which are upon her; he hath let them stand, because he held his peace at her in the day that he heard them. 16. But if he shall make them null and void after that he hath heard them, then he shall bear her iniquity. 17. These are the statutes, which the Lord commanded Moses, between a man and his wife, between a father and his daughter, being in her youth, in her father's house.*ii.

8 שְׂפָתֶיהָ אֲשֶׁר אָסְרָה עַל־נַפְשָׁהּ׃ וְשָׁמַע אִישָׁהּ בְּיוֹם שָׁמְעוֹ
וְהֶחֱרִישׁ לָהּ וְקָמוּ נְדָרֶיהָ וֶאֱסָרֶהָ אֲשֶׁר־אָסְרָה עַל־נַפְשָׁהּ
9 יָקֻמוּ׃ וְאִם בְּיוֹם שְׁמֹעַ אִישָׁהּ יָנִיא אוֹתָהּ וְהֵפֵר אֶת־נִדְרָהּ
אֲשֶׁר עָלֶיהָ וְאֵת מִבְטָא שְׂפָתֶיהָ אֲשֶׁר אָסְרָה עַל־נַפְשָׁהּ
י וַיהוָה יִסְלַח־לָהּ׃ וְנֵדֶר אַלְמָנָה וּגְרוּשָׁה כֹּל אֲשֶׁר־אָסְרָה
11 עַל־נַפְשָׁהּ יָקוּם עָלֶיהָ׃ וְאִם־בֵּית אִישָׁהּ נָדָרָה אוֹ־אָסְרָה
12 אִסָּר עַל־נַפְשָׁהּ בִּשְׁבֻעָה׃ וְשָׁמַע אִישָׁהּ וְהֶחֱרִשׁ לָהּ לֹא
הֵנִיא אֹתָהּ וְקָמוּ כָּל־נְדָרֶיהָ וְכָל־אִסָּר אֲשֶׁר־אָסְרָה עַל־
13 נַפְשָׁהּ יָקוּם׃ וְאִם־הָפֵר יָפֵר אֹתָם ׀ אִישָׁהּ בְּיוֹם שָׁמְעוֹ
כָּל־מוֹצָא שְׂפָתֶיהָ לִנְדָרֶיהָ וּלְאִסַּר נַפְשָׁהּ לֹא יָקוּם אִישָׁהּ
14 הֲפֵרָם וַיהוָה יִסְלַח־לָהּ׃ כָּל־נֵדֶר וְכָל־שְׁבֻעַת אִסָּר לְעַנֹּת
טו נָפֶשׁ אִישָׁהּ יְקִימֶנּוּ וְאִישָׁהּ יְפֵרֶנּוּ׃ וְאִם־הַחֲרֵשׁ יַחֲרִישׁ לָהּ
אִישָׁהּ מִיּוֹם אֶל־יוֹם וְהֵקִים אֶת־כָּל־נְדָרֶיהָ אוֹ אֶת־כָּל־
אֱסָרֶיהָ אֲשֶׁר עָלֶיהָ הֵקִים אֹתָם כִּי־הֶחֱרִשׁ לָהּ בְּיוֹם שָׁמְעוֹ׃
16 17 וְאִם־הָפֵר יָפֵר אֹתָם אַחֲרֵי שָׁמְעוֹ וְנָשָׂא אֶת־עֲוֺנָהּ׃ אֵלֶּה
הַחֻקִּים אֲשֶׁר צִוָּה יְהוָה אֶת־מֹשֶׁה בֵּין אִישׁ לְאִשְׁתּוֹ בֵּין
אָב לְבִתּוֹ בִּנְעֻרֶיהָ בֵּית אָבִיהָ׃* פ שני

31

CHAPTER XXXI

1. And the LORD spoke unto Moses, saying: 2. 'Avenge the children of Israel of the

לא

CAP. XXXI. לא

א 2 וַיְדַבֵּר יְהוָה אֶל־מֹשֶׁה לֵּאמֹר׃ נְקֹם נִקְמַת בְּנֵי יִשְׂרָאֵל

8. *and hold his peace.* As in *v.* 5.

9. *disallow her.* By verbal disapproval, as in *v.* 6.

10–16. VOWS OF A WIDOW AND DIVORCED WOMAN

10. *widow, or . . . divorced.* The vows of such women are fully binding. They fall under the general principle in *v.* 3.

11. *in her husband's house.* In this instance, the husband has the same authority to allow or disallow the vow, as the father had in regard to his young adolescent daughter.

13. *will forgive her.* As it was no fault of hers, if the husband or father cancelled her vow.

14. *to afflict the soul.* By fasting or any kind of abstinence.

16. *he shall bear her iniquity.* If the husband tacitly consented to the vow in the first instance, and afterwards forbade her to fulfil it, then the guilt rests upon him.

CHAPTER XXXI

THE WAR AGAINST THE MIDIANITES

In xxv, 16–18, Moses is bidden to smite the Midianites because they had enticed the Israelites to the licentious and idolatrous worship of Baal-Peor. In the present chapter, he is ordered

Midianites; afterward shalt thou be gathered unto thy people.' 3. And Moses spoke unto the people, saying: 'Arm ye men from among you for the war, that they may go against Midian, to execute the LORD's vengeance on Midian. 4. Of every tribe a thousand, throughout all the tribes of Israel, shall ye send to the war.' 5. So there were delivered, out of the thousands of Israel, a thousand of every tribe, twelve thousand armed for war. 6. And Moses sent them, a thousand of every tribe, to the war, them and Phinehas the son of Eleazar the priest, to the war, with the holy vessels and the trumpets for the alarm in his hand. 7. And they warred against Midian, as the LORD commanded Moses; and they slew every male. 8. And they slew the kings of Midian with the rest of their slain: Evi, and Rekem, and Zur, and Hur, and Reba, the five kings of Midian; Balaam also the son of Beor they slew with the sword. 9. And the children of Israel took captive the women of Midian and their little ones; and all their cattle, and all their flocks, and all their goods, they took for a prey. 10. And all their cities in the places wherein they dwelt, and all their encampments, they burnt with fire. 11. And they took all the spoil, and all the prey, both of man and of beast. 12. And they brought the captives, and the prey, and the spoil, unto Moses, and unto Eleazar the priest, and unto the congregation of the children of Israel, unto the camp, unto the plains of Moab, which are

3 מֵאֵת הַמִּדְיָנִים אַחַר תֵּאָסֵף אֶל־עַמֶּיךָ׃ וַיְדַבֵּר מֹשֶׁה אֶל־
הָעָם לֵאמֹר הֵחָלְצוּ מֵאִתְּכֶם אֲנָשִׁים לַצָּבָא וְיִהְיוּ עַל־
4 מִדְיָן לָתֵת נִקְמַת־יְהוָה בְּמִדְיָן׃ אֶלֶף לַמַּטֶּה אֶלֶף לַמַּטֶּה
ה לְכֹל מַטּוֹת יִשְׂרָאֵל תִּשְׁלְחוּ לַצָּבָא׃ וַיִּמָּסְרוּ מֵאַלְפֵי
6 יִשְׂרָאֵל אֶלֶף לַמַּטֶּה שְׁנֵים־עָשָׂר אֶלֶף חֲלוּצֵי צָבָא׃ וַיִּשְׁלַח
אֹתָם מֹשֶׁה אֶלֶף לַמַּטֶּה לַצָּבָא אֹתָם וְאֶת־פִּינְחָס בֶּן
אֶלְעָזָר הַכֹּהֵן לַצָּבָא וּכְלֵי הַקֹּדֶשׁ וַחֲצֹצְרוֹת הַתְּרוּעָה
7 בְּיָדוֹ׃ וַיִּצְבְּאוּ עַל־מִדְיָן כַּאֲשֶׁר צִוָּה יְהוָה אֶת־מֹשֶׁה
8 וַיַּהַרְגוּ כָּל־זָכָר׃ וְאֶת־מַלְכֵי מִדְיָן הָרְגוּ עַל־חַלְלֵיהֶם אֶת־
אֱוִי וְאֶת־רֶקֶם וְאֶת־צוּר וְאֶת־חוּר וְאֶת־רֶבַע חֲמֵשֶׁת מַלְכֵי
9 מִדְיָן וְאֵת בִּלְעָם בֶּן־בְּעוֹר הָרְגוּ בֶּחָרֶב׃ וַיִּשְׁבּוּ בְנֵי־
יִשְׂרָאֵל אֶת־נְשֵׁי מִדְיָן וְאֶת־טַפָּם וְאֵת כָּל־בְּהֶמְתָּם וְאֶת־
י כָּל־מִקְנֵהֶם וְאֶת־כָּל־חֵילָם בָּזָזוּ׃ וְאֵת כָּל־עָרֵיהֶם
11 בְּמוֹשְׁבֹתָם וְאֵת כָּל־טִירֹתָם שָׂרְפוּ בָּאֵשׁ׃ וַיִּקְחוּ אֶת־כָּל־
12 הַשָּׁלָל וְאֵת כָּל־הַמַּלְקוֹחַ בָּאָדָם וּבַבְּהֵמָה׃ וַיָּבִאוּ אֶל־
מֹשֶׁה וְאֶל־אֶלְעָזָר הַכֹּהֵן וְאֶל־עֲדַת בְּנֵי־יִשְׂרָאֵל אֶת־הַשְּׁבִי

to carry out the command forthwith; and we are given full details of the campaign.

The war against the Midianites presents peculiar difficulties. We are no longer acquainted with the circumstances that justified the ruthlessness with which it was waged, and therefore we cannot satisfactorily meet the various objections that have been raised in that connection. 'Perhaps the recollection of what took place after the Indian Mutiny, when Great Britain was in the same temper, may throw light on this question. The soldiers then, bent on punishing the cruelty and lust of the rebels, partly in patriotism, partly in revenge, set mercy altogether aside' (Expositor's Bible). The Midianites affected were only the clans that lived in the neighbourhood of Moab. This accounts for the persistence of Midianites in later periods of Israelite history.

3. *execute the LORD'S vengeance.* The preceding *v.* refers to Israel's vengeance on Midian; this *v.* speaks of God's vengeance on Midian. Both mean the same thing. The cause of Israel is the cause of God. 'Vengeance' is here used in the broad sense of retributory punishment.

5–18. THE EXPEDITION

5. *delivered. i.e.* placed at the disposal of Moses by the leaders of each tribe.

6. *Phinehas the son of Eleazar the priest.* Phinehas, says Rashi, was especially qualified for this task by the part he played in the Zimri incident (xxv, 14, 15). His role was that of the priest referred to in Deut. xx, 2, whose duty it was to go before the Israelites in battle.

the holy vessels. The Ark and its contents often accompanied the Israelites on their military expeditions; I Sam. IV, 3 f.

in his hand. i.e. at his disposal.

7. *every male.* Every adult male.

8. *Balaam.* On his way to his home in Mesopotamia, he must have remained for some time with the Midianites and been their adviser in the matter of Baal-Peor.

with the sword. The Rabbis say that he was slain after a trial by a Beth Din (Sifri).

11. *prey.* Booty in livestock; *spoil*, in goods.

by the Jordan at Jericho.*iii (**ii). ¶ 13. And Moses, and Eleazar the priest, and all the princes of the congregation, went forth to meet them without the camp. 14. And Moses was wroth with the officers of the host, the captains of thousands and the captains of hundreds, who came from the service of the war. 15. And Moses said unto them: 'Have ye saved all the women alive? 16. Behold, these caused the children of Israel, through the counsel of Balaam, to revolt so as to break faith with the LORD in the matter of Peor, and so the plague was among the congregation of the LORD. 17. Now therefore kill every male among the little ones, and kill every woman that hath known man by lying with him. 18. But all the women children, that have not known man by lying with him, keep alive for yourselves. 19. And encamp ye without the camp seven days; whosoever hath killed any person, and whosoever hath touched any slain, purify yourselves on the third day and on the seventh day, ye and your captives. 20. And as to every garment, and all that is made of skin, and all work of goats' hair, and all things made of wood, ye shall purify.' ¶ 21. And Eleazar the priest said unto the men of war that went to the battle: 'This is the statute of the law which the LORD hath commanded Moses: 22. Howbeit the gold, and the silver, the brass, the iron, the tin, and the lead, 23. every thing that may abide the fire, ye shall make to go through the fire, and it shall be clean; nevertheless it shall be purified with the water of sprinkling; and all that abideth not the fire ye shall make to go through the water. 24. And ye shall wash your clothes on the seventh day, and ye shall be clean, and afterward ye may come into the camp.'*iv. ¶ 25. And the LORD spoke unto Moses, saying: 26. 'Take the sum of the prey that was taken, both of man and of beast,

(שני מחובר) וְאֶת־הַמַּלְקוֹחַ וְאֶת־הַשָּׁלָל אֶל־הַמַּחֲנֶה אֶל־עַרְבֹת מוֹאָב
13 אֲשֶׁר עַל־יַרְדֵּן יְרֵחוֹ׃ ס וַיֵּצְאוּ מֹשֶׁה וְאֶלְעָזָר הַכֹּהֵן
14 וְכָל־נְשִׂיאֵי הָעֵדָה לִקְרָאתָם אֶל־מִחוּץ לַמַּחֲנֶה׃ וַיִּקְצֹף
מֹשֶׁה עַל פְּקוּדֵי הֶחָיִל שָׂרֵי הָאֲלָפִים וְשָׂרֵי הַמֵּאוֹת הַבָּאִים
טו מִצְּבָא הַמִּלְחָמָה׃ וַיֹּאמֶר אֲלֵיהֶם מֹשֶׁה הַחִיִּיתֶם כָּל־
16 נְקֵבָה׃ הֵן הֵנָּה הָיוּ לִבְנֵי יִשְׂרָאֵל בִּדְבַר בִּלְעָם לִמְסָר־
מַעַל בַּיהוָה עַל־דְּבַר־פְּעוֹר וַתְּהִי הַמַּגֵּפָה בַּעֲדַת יְהוָה׃
17 וְעַתָּה הִרְגוּ כָל־זָכָר בַּטָּף וְכָל־אִשָּׁה יֹדַעַת אִישׁ לְמִשְׁכַּב
18 זָכָר הֲרֹגוּ׃ וְכֹל הַטַּף בַּנָּשִׁים אֲשֶׁר לֹא־יָדְעוּ מִשְׁכַּב זָכָר
19 הַחֲיוּ לָכֶם׃ וְאַתֶּם חֲנוּ מִחוּץ לַמַּחֲנֶה שִׁבְעַת יָמִים כֹּל
הֹרֵג נֶפֶשׁ וְכֹל ׀ נֹגֵעַ בֶּחָלָל תִּתְחַטְּאוּ בַּיּוֹם הַשְּׁלִישִׁי וּבַיּוֹם
כ הַשְּׁבִיעִי אַתֶּם וּשְׁבִיכֶם׃ וְכָל־בֶּגֶד וְכָל־כְּלִי־עוֹר וְכָל־
21 מַעֲשֵׂה עִזִּים וְכָל־כְּלִי־עֵץ תִּתְחַטָּאוּ׃ ס וַיֹּאמֶר אֶלְעָזָר
הַכֹּהֵן אֶל־אַנְשֵׁי הַצָּבָא הַבָּאִים לַמִּלְחָמָה זֹאת חֻקַּת הַתּוֹרָה
22 אֲשֶׁר־צִוָּה יְהוָה אֶת־מֹשֶׁה׃ אַךְ אֶת־הַזָּהָב וְאֶת־הַכָּסֶף
23 אֶת־הַנְּחֹשֶׁת אֶת־הַבַּרְזֶל אֶת־הַבְּדִיל וְאֶת־הָעֹפָרֶת׃ כָּל־
דָּבָר אֲשֶׁר־יָבֹא בָאֵשׁ תַּעֲבִירוּ בָאֵשׁ וְטָהֵר אַךְ בְּמֵי נִדָּה
24 יִתְחַטָּא וְכֹל אֲשֶׁר לֹא־יָבֹא בָּאֵשׁ תַּעֲבִירוּ בַמָּיִם׃ וְכִבַּסְתֶּם
רביעי בִּגְדֵיכֶם בַּיּוֹם הַשְּׁבִיעִי וּטְהַרְתֶּם וְאַחַר תָּבֹאוּ אֶל־הַמַּחֲנֶה׃
כה 26 ס וַיֹּאמֶר יְהוָה אֶל־מֹשֶׁה לֵּאמֹר׃ שָׂא אֵת רֹאשׁ מַלְקוֹחַ

18. *for yourselves.* To employ them as domestic servants.

19–24 PURIFICATION OF THE WARRIORS

19. *without the camp seven days.* An enforcement of the law of seven days' defilement and segregation as laid down in XIX, 11.

purify yourselves. A reference to the law in XIX, 12.

and your captives. In order to prevent the spread of their contamination by the Israelites' contact with their garments.

20. *as to every garment.* Everything that had come in contact with a corpse required purifying.

21. *the statute of the law.* Contained in XIX. Eleazar now proceeds to enlarge this 'statute' of the law in order to meet the present circumstances.

23. *everything that may abide the fire.* The Talmud understands these laws to mean that every household utensil which, when employed for preparing food, comes into direct contact with fire, must be cleansed by fire. For others, purification by water is sufficient.

water of sprinkling. See on XIX, 9.

25–34. APPORTIONMENT OF SPOIL

27. *into two parts.* Those who fought and those who remained behind were to receive equal shares; and from each of these shares, a tax was levied for the priests and the Levites.

thou, and Eleazar the priest, and the heads of the fathers' houses of the congregation; 27. and divide the prey into two parts: between the men skilled in war, that went out to battle, and all the congregation; 28. and levy a tribute unto the LORD of the men of war that went out to battle: one soul of five hundred, both of the persons, and of the beeves, and of the asses, and of the flocks; 29. take it of their half, and give it unto Eleazar the priest, as a portion set apart for the LORD. 30. And of the children of Israel's half, thou shalt take one drawn out of every fifty, of the persons, of the beeves, of the asses, and of the flocks, even of all the cattle, and give them unto the Levites, that keep the charge of the tabernacle of the LORD.' 31. And Moses and Eleazar the priest did as the LORD commanded Moses. 32. Now the prey, over and above the booty which the men of war took, was six hundred thousand and seventy thousand and five thousand sheep, 33. and threescore and twelve thousand beeves, 34. and threescore and one thousand asses, 35. and thirty and two thousand persons in all, of the women that had not known man by lying with him. 36. And the half, which was the portion of them that went out to war, was in number three hundred thousand and thirty thousand and seven thousand and five hundred sheep. 37. And the LORD's tribute of the sheep was six hundred and threescore and fifteen. 38. And the beeves were thirty and six thousand, of which the LORD's tribute was threescore and twelve. 39. And the asses were thirty thousand and five hundred, of which the LORD's tribute was threescore and one. 40. And the persons were sixteen thousand, of whom the LORD's tribute was thirty and two persons. 41. And Moses gave the tribute, which was set apart for the LORD, unto Eleazar the priest, as the LORD commanded Moses.*v. 42. And of the children of Israel's half, which Moses divided off from the men that warred—43. now the congregation's half was three hundred thousand and thirty thousand and seven thousand and five hundred sheep, 44. and thirty and six thousand beeves, 45. and thirty thousand and five hundred asses, 46. and sixteen thousand persons—47. even of the children of Israel's half, Moses took one drawn out of every fifty, both of man and of beast, and gave them unto the Levites, that kept the charge of the taber-

הַשְּׁבִי בָּאָדָם וּבַבְּהֵמָה אַתָּה וְאֶלְעָזָר הַכֹּהֵן וְרָאשֵׁי אֲבוֹת
27 הָעֵדָה׃ וְחָצִיתָ אֶת־הַמַּלְקוֹחַ בֵּין תֹּפְשֵׂי הַמִּלְחָמָה
28 הַיֹּצְאִים לַצָּבָא וּבֵין כָּל־הָעֵדָה׃ וַהֲרֵמֹתָ מֶכֶס לַיהוָה
מֵאֵת אַנְשֵׁי הַמִּלְחָמָה הַיֹּצְאִים לַצָּבָא אֶחָד נֶפֶשׁ מֵחֲמֵשׁ
הַמֵּאוֹת מִן־הָאָדָם וּמִן־הַבָּקָר וּמִן־הַחֲמֹרִים וּמִן־הַצֹּאן׃
29 מִמַּחֲצִיתָם תִּקָּחוּ וְנָתַתָּה לְאֶלְעָזָר הַכֹּהֵן תְּרוּמַת יְהוָה׃
ל וּמִמַּחֲצִת בְּנֵי־יִשְׂרָאֵל תִּקַּח ׀ אֶחָד ׀ אָחֻז מִן־הַחֲמִשִּׁים
מִן־הָאָדָם מִן־הַבָּקָר מִן־הַחֲמֹרִים וּמִן־הַצֹּאן מִכָּל־הַבְּהֵמָה
31 וְנָתַתָּה אֹתָם לַלְוִיִּם שֹׁמְרֵי מִשְׁמֶרֶת מִשְׁכַּן יְהוָה׃ וַיַּעַשׂ
32 מֹשֶׁה וְאֶלְעָזָר הַכֹּהֵן כַּאֲשֶׁר צִוָּה יְהוָה אֶת־מֹשֶׁה׃ וַיְהִי
הַמַּלְקוֹחַ יֶתֶר הַבָּז אֲשֶׁר בָּזְזוּ עַם הַצָּבָא צֹאן שֵׁשׁ־מֵאוֹת
33 אֶלֶף וְשִׁבְעִים אֶלֶף וַחֲמֵשֶׁת אֲלָפִים׃ וּבָקָר שְׁנַיִם וְשִׁבְעִים
34 לה אָלֶף׃ וַחֲמֹרִים אֶחָד וְשִׁשִּׁים אָלֶף׃ וְנֶפֶשׁ אָדָם מִן־הַנָּשִׁים
אֲשֶׁר לֹא־יָדְעוּ מִשְׁכַּב זָכָר כָּל־נֶפֶשׁ שְׁנַיִם וּשְׁלֹשִׁים אָלֶף׃
36 וַתְּהִי הַמֶּחֱצָה חֵלֶק הַיֹּצְאִים בַּצָּבָא מִסְפַּר הַצֹּאן שְׁלֹשׁ־
מֵאוֹת אֶלֶף וּשְׁלֹשִׁים אֶלֶף וְשִׁבְעַת אֲלָפִים וַחֲמֵשׁ מֵאוֹת׃
37 וַיְהִי הַמֶּכֶס לַיהוָה מִן־הַצֹּאן שֵׁשׁ מֵאוֹת חָמֵשׁ וְשִׁבְעִים׃
38 וְהַבָּקָר שִׁשָּׁה וּשְׁלֹשִׁים אָלֶף וּמִכְסָם לַיהוָה שְׁנַיִם וְשִׁבְעִים׃
39 וַחֲמֹרִים שְׁלֹשִׁים אֶלֶף וַחֲמֵשׁ מֵאוֹת וּמִכְסָם לַיהוָה אֶחָד
מ וְשִׁשִּׁים׃ וְנֶפֶשׁ אָדָם שִׁשָּׁה עָשָׂר אָלֶף וּמִכְסָם לַיהוָה
41 שְׁנַיִם וּשְׁלֹשִׁים נָפֶשׁ׃ וַיִּתֵּן מֹשֶׁה אֶת־מֶכֶס תְּרוּמַת יְהוָה
חמישי
42 לְאֶלְעָזָר הַכֹּהֵן כַּאֲשֶׁר צִוָּה יְהוָה אֶת־מֹשֶׁה׃ * וּמִמַּחֲצִית
בְּנֵי יִשְׂרָאֵל אֲשֶׁר חָצָה מֹשֶׁה מִן־הָאֲנָשִׁים הַצֹּבְאִים׃
43 וַתְּהִי מֶחֱצַת הָעֵדָה מִן־הַצֹּאן שְׁלֹשׁ־מֵאוֹת אֶלֶף וּשְׁלֹשִׁים
44 אֶלֶף שִׁבְעַת אֲלָפִים וַחֲמֵשׁ מֵאוֹת׃ וּבָקָר שִׁשָּׁה וּשְׁלֹשִׁים
מה 46 אָלֶף׃ וַחֲמֹרִים שְׁלֹשִׁים אֶלֶף וַחֲמֵשׁ מֵאוֹת׃ וְנֶפֶשׁ אָדָם

28. *one soul.* *i.e.* one individual, or, 'head of cattle.' One five-hundredth was to be paid by the soldiers for the benefit of the priests; whilst one-fiftieth of the congregation's share was to go to the support of the Levites.

33. *beeves.* Old English plural of 'beef'; used for live animals.

nacle of the LORD; as the LORD commanded Moses. ¶ 48. And the officers that were over the thousands of the host, the captains of thousands, and the captains of hundreds, came near unto Moses; 49. and they said unto Moses: 'Thy servants have taken the sum of the men of war that are under our charge, and there lacketh not one man of us. 50. And we have brought the LORD's offering, what every man hath gotten, of jewels of gold, armlets, and bracelets, signet-rings, ear-rings, and girdles, to make atonement for our souls before the LORD.' 51. And Moses and Eleazar the priest took the gold of them, even all wrought jewels. 52. And all the gold of the gift that they set apart for the LORD, of the captains of thousands, and of the captains of hundreds, was sixteen thousand seven hundred and fifty shekels.—53. For the men of war had taken booty, every man for himself.—54. And Moses and Eleazar the priest took the gold of the captains of thousands and of hundreds, and brought it into the tent of meeting, for a memorial for the children of Israel before the LORD.*vi (**iii).

32

CHAPTER XXXII

1. Now the children of Reuben and the children of Gad had a very great multitude of cattle; and when they saw the land of Jazer, and the land of Gilead, that, behold, the place was a place for cattle, 2. the children of Gad and the children of Reuben came and spoke unto Moses, and to Eleazar the priest, and unto the princes of the congregation, saying: 3. 'Ataroth, and

47 שִׁשָּׁה עָשָׂר אָלֶף׃ וַיִּקַּח מֹשֶׁה מִמַּחֲצִת בְּנֵי־יִשְׂרָאֵל אֶת־
הָֽאָחֻז אֶחָד מִן־הַחֲמִשִּׁים מִן־הָאָדָם וּמִן־הַבְּהֵמָה וַיִּתֵּן
אֹתָם לַלְוִיִּם שֹׁמְרֵי מִשְׁמֶרֶת מִשְׁכַּן יְהוָה כַּאֲשֶׁר צִוָּה
48 יְהוָה אֶת־מֹשֶׁה׃ וַיִּקְרְבוּ אֶל־מֹשֶׁה הַפְּקֻדִים אֲשֶׁר לְאַלְפֵי
49 הַצָּבָא שָׂרֵי הָאֲלָפִים וְשָׂרֵי הַמֵּאוֹת׃ וַיֹּאמְרוּ אֶל־מֹשֶׁה
עֲבָדֶיךָ נָשְׂאוּ אֶת־רֹאשׁ אַנְשֵׁי הַמִּלְחָמָה אֲשֶׁר בְּיָדֵנוּ וְלֹא־
נ נִפְקַד מִמֶּנּוּ אִישׁ׃ וַנַּקְרֵב אֶת־קָרְבַּן יְהוָה אִישׁ אֲשֶׁר מָצָא
כְלִי־זָהָב אֶצְעָדָה וְצָמִיד טַבַּעַת עָגִיל וְכוּמָז לְכַפֵּר עַל־
51 נַפְשֹׁתֵינוּ לִפְנֵי יְהוָה׃ וַיִּקַּח מֹשֶׁה וְאֶלְעָזָר הַכֹּהֵן אֶת־הַזָּהָב
52 מֵאִתָּם כֹּל כְּלִי מַעֲשֶׂה׃ וַיְהִי ׀ כָּל־זְהַב הַתְּרוּמָה אֲשֶׁר
הֵרִימוּ לַיהוָה שִׁשָּׁה עָשָׂר אֶלֶף שְׁבַע־מֵאוֹת וַחֲמִשִּׁים שָׁקֶל
53 מֵאֵת שָׂרֵי הָאֲלָפִים וּמֵאֵת שָׂרֵי הַמֵּאוֹת׃ אַנְשֵׁי הַצָּבָא
54 בָּזְזוּ אִישׁ לוֹ׃ וַיִּקַּח מֹשֶׁה וְאֶלְעָזָר הַכֹּהֵן אֶת־הַזָּהָב מֵאֵת
שָׂרֵי הָאֲלָפִים וְהַמֵּאוֹת וַיָּבִאוּ אֹתוֹ אֶל־אֹהֶל מוֹעֵד זִכָּרוֹן
לִבְנֵי־יִשְׂרָאֵל לִפְנֵי יְהוָה׃ * פ ששי (שלישי כשהן מחוב')

לב

CAP. XXXII. לב

א וּמִקְנֶה ׀ רַב הָיָה לִבְנֵי רְאוּבֵן וְלִבְנֵי־גָד עָצוּם מְאֹד וַיִּרְאוּ
אֶת־אֶרֶץ יַעְזֵר וְאֶת־אֶרֶץ גִּלְעָד וְהִנֵּה הַמָּקוֹם מְקוֹם מִקְנֶה׃
2 וַיָּבֹאוּ בְנֵי־גָד וּבְנֵי רְאוּבֵן וַיֹּאמְרוּ אֶל־מֹשֶׁה וְאֶל־אֶלְעָזָר

50. *offering.* Of thanksgiving for their victory and safe return home. Ornaments of gold were worn by roving nomads and traders (Gen. XXXVII, 28).

atonement. See Exod. XXX, 15.

54. *into the tent of meeting.* And placed it in the treasury of the Tabernacle; Exod. XXX, 16; Josh. VI, 24.

CHAPTER XXXII

TRIBES REMAINING EAST OF THE JORDAN

The tribes of Reuben, Gad, and the half-tribe of Manasseh desire to settle east of the Jordan. They protest their willingness to accompany the other tribes until Canaan is conquered.

Eastern or Transjordanic Palestine is 150 miles long; its breadth varies from thirty to eighty miles. It is throughout over 2,000 feet above sea-level, with a temperate climate, a land of health and fertility. The middle region—Gilead—bore perfume and medicine for the whole Eastern world. Gilead is covered with forests; and its valleys, by orchards and vineyards. Even more famous was its pasture. 'Flocks and pastures have ever been the wealth, the charm, the temptation of Eastern Palestine—a land of opulence and insecurity' (George Adam Smith).

1. *the land of Jazer.* Referred to in XXI, 32 as having been captured by Moses from the Amorites.

Gilead. Gilead sometimes stands for the whole territory east of the Jordan (*e.g.* in *v.* 29) that was occupied by the Israelites. Sometimes, however, as in *v.* 39 f, it denotes only the land north of the river Jabbok, as far as the river Jarmuk.

3 הַכֹּהֵן וְאֶל־נְשִׂיאֵי הָעֵדָה לֵאמֹר׃ עֲטָרוֹת וְדִיבֹן וְיַעְזֵר
4 וְנִמְרָה וְחֶשְׁבּוֹן וְאֶלְעָלֵה וּשְׂבָם וּנְבוֹ וּבְעֹן׃ הָאָרֶץ אֲשֶׁר
הִכָּה יְהוָה לִפְנֵי עֲדַת יִשְׂרָאֵל אֶרֶץ מִקְנֶה הִוא וְלַעֲבָדֶיךָ
ה מִקְנֶה׃ ס וַיֹּאמְרוּ אִם־מָצָאנוּ חֵן בְּעֵינֶיךָ יֻתַּן אֶת־
הָאָרֶץ הַזֹּאת לַעֲבָדֶיךָ לַאֲחֻזָּה אַל־תַּעֲבִרֵנוּ אֶת־הַיַּרְדֵּן׃
6 וַיֹּאמֶר מֹשֶׁה לִבְנֵי־גָד וְלִבְנֵי רְאוּבֵן הַאַחֵיכֶם יָבֹאוּ לַמִּלְחָמָה
7 וְאַתֶּם תֵּשְׁבוּ פֹה׃ וְלָמָּה תְנִואוּן אֶת־לֵב בְּנֵי יִשְׂרָאֵל
8 מֵעֲבֹר אֶל־הָאָרֶץ אֲשֶׁר־נָתַן לָהֶם יְהוָה׃ כֹּה עָשׂוּ אֲבֹתֵיכֶם
9 בְּשָׁלְחִי אֹתָם מִקָּדֵשׁ בַּרְנֵעַ לִרְאוֹת אֶת־הָאָרֶץ׃ וַיַּעֲלוּ
עַד־נַחַל אֶשְׁכּוֹל וַיִּרְאוּ אֶת־הָאָרֶץ וַיָּנִיאוּ אֶת־לֵב בְּנֵי
יִשְׂרָאֵל לְבִלְתִּי־בֹא אֶל־הָאָרֶץ אֲשֶׁר־נָתַן לָהֶם יְהוָה׃
11 וַיִּחַר־אַף יְהוָה בַּיּוֹם הַהוּא וַיִּשָּׁבַע לֵאמֹר׃ אִם־יִרְאוּ
הָאֲנָשִׁים הָעֹלִים מִמִּצְרַיִם מִבֶּן עֶשְׂרִים שָׁנָה וָמַעְלָה אֵת
הָאֲדָמָה אֲשֶׁר נִשְׁבַּעְתִּי לְאַבְרָהָם לְיִצְחָק וּלְיַעֲקֹב כִּי לֹא־
12 מִלְאוּ אַחֲרָי׃ בִּלְתִּי כָּלֵב בֶּן־יְפֻנֶּה הַקְּנִזִּי וִיהוֹשֻׁעַ בִּן־נוּן
13 כִּי מִלְאוּ אַחֲרֵי יְהוָה׃ וַיִּחַר־אַף יְהוָה בְּיִשְׂרָאֵל וַיְנִעֵם
בַּמִּדְבָּר אַרְבָּעִים שָׁנָה עַד־תֹּם כָּל־הַדּוֹר הָעֹשֶׂה הָרַע
14 בְּעֵינֵי יְהוָה׃ וְהִנֵּה קַמְתֶּם תַּחַת אֲבֹתֵיכֶם תַּרְבּוּת אֲנָשִׁים
טו חַטָּאִים לִסְפּוֹת עוֹד עַל חֲרוֹן אַף־יְהוָה אֶל־יִשְׂרָאֵל׃ כִּי
תְשׁוּבֻן מֵאַחֲרָיו וְיָסַף עוֹד לְהַנִּיחוֹ בַּמִּדְבָּר וְשִׁחַתֶּם לְכָל־
16 הָעָם הַזֶּה׃ ס וַיִּגְּשׁוּ אֵלָיו וַיֹּאמְרוּ גִּדְרֹת צֹאן נִבְנֶה
17 לְמִקְנֵנוּ פֹּה וְעָרִים לְטַפֵּנוּ׃ וַאֲנַחְנוּ נֵחָלֵץ חֻשִׁים לִפְנֵי
בְּנֵי יִשְׂרָאֵל עַד אֲשֶׁר אִם־הֲבִיאֹנֻם אֶל־מְקוֹמָם וְיָשַׁב
18 טַפֵּנוּ בְּעָרֵי הַמִּבְצָר מִפְּנֵי יֹשְׁבֵי הָאָרֶץ׃ לֹא נָשׁוּב אֶל־

v. 7. תניאון קרי

Dibon, and Jazer, and Nimrah, and Heshbon, and Elealeh, and Sebam, and Nebo, and Beon, 4. the land which the LORD smote before the congregation of Israel, is a land for cattle, and thy servants have cattle.' 5. And they said: 'If we have found favour in thy sight, let this land be given unto thy servants for a possession; bring us not over the Jordan.' 6. And Moses said unto the children of Gad and to the children of Reuben: 'Shall your brethren go to the war, and shall ye sit here? 7. And wherefore will ye turn away the heart of the children of Israel from going over into the land which the LORD hath given them? 8. Thus did your fathers, when I sent them from Kadesh-barnea to see the land. 9. For when they went up unto the valley of Eshcol, and saw the land, they turned away the heart of the children of Israel, that they should not go into the land which the LORD had given them. 10. And the LORD's anger was kindled in that day, and He swore, saying: 11. Surely none of the men that came up out of Egypt, from twenty years old and upward, shall see the land which I swore unto Abraham, unto Isaac, and unto Jacob; because they have not wholly followed Me; 12. save Caleb the son of Jephunneh the Kenizzite, and Joshua the son of Nun; because they have wholly followed the LORD. 13. And the LORD's anger was kindled against Israel, and He made them wander to and fro in the wilderness forty years, until all the generation, that had done evil in the sight of the LORD, was consumed. 14. And, behold, ye are risen up in your fathers' stead, a brood of sinful men, to augment yet the fierce anger of the LORD toward Israel. 15. For if ye turn away from after Him, He will yet again leave them in the wilderness; and so ye will destroy all this people.' ¶ 16. And they came near unto him, and said: 'We will build sheepfolds here for our cattle, and cities for our little ones; 17. but we ourselves will be ready armed to go before the children of Israel, until we have brought them unto their place; and our little ones shall dwell in the fortified cities because of the inhabitants of the land. 18. We will not

7. *turn away the heart.* Their request, if granted, would dishearten the other tribes, as it would reduce the fighting strength of Israel.

15. *destroy all this people.* The unworthy desires of these might infect the other tribes, and thus the whole nation would be shut out from entering Canaan and perish.

17. *before the children of Israel.* They will march in the van of the Israelites' army.

fortified cities. To protect them from attack by the neighbouring populations whilst they are away on active service.

return unto our houses, until the children of Israel have inherited every man his inheritance. 19. For we will not inherit with them on the other side of the Jordan, and forward, because our inheritance is fallen to us on this side of the Jordan eastward.'*vii (**iv). ¶ 20. And Moses said unto them: 'If ye will do this thing: if ye will arm yourselves to go before the LORD to the war, 21. and every armed man of you will pass over the Jordan before the LORD, until He hath driven out His enemies from before Him, 22. and the land be subdued before the LORD, and ye return afterward; then ye shall be clear before the LORD, and before Israel, and this land shall be unto you for a possession before the LORD. 23. But if ye will not do so, behold, ye have sinned against the LORD; and know ye your sin which will find you. 24. Build you cities for your little ones, and folds for your sheep; and do that which hath proceeded out of your mouth.' ¶ 25. And the children of Gad and the children of Reuben spoke unto Moses, saying: 'Thy servants will do as my lord commandeth. 26. Our little ones, our wives, our flocks, and all our cattle, shall be there in the cities of Gilead; 27. but thy servants will pass over, every man that is armed for war, before the LORD to battle, as my lord saith.' ¶ 28. So Moses gave charge concerning them to Eleazar the priest, and to Joshua the son of Nun, and to the heads of the fathers' houses of the tribes of the children of Israel. 29. And Moses said unto them: 'If the children of Gad and the children of Reuben will pass with you over the Jordan, every man that is armed to battle, before the LORD, and the land shall be subdued before you, then ye shall give them the land of Gilead for a possession; 30. but if they will not pass over with you armed, they shall have possessions among you in the land of Canaan.' 31. And the children of Gad and the children of Reuben answered, saying: 'As the LORD hath said unto thy servants, so will we do. 32. We will pass over armed before the LORD

19 בָּתֵּינוּ עַד הִתְנַחֵל בְּנֵי יִשְׂרָאֵל אִישׁ נַחֲלָתוֹ׃ כִּי לֹא נִנְחַל
אִתָּם מֵעֵבֶר לַיַּרְדֵּן וָהָלְאָה כִּי בָאָה נַחֲלָתֵנוּ אֵלֵינוּ מֵעֵבֶר
הַיַּרְדֵּן מִזְרָחָה׃ * שביעי פ (רביעי כשהן מחוב')
כ וַיֹּאמֶר אֲלֵיהֶם מֹשֶׁה אִם־תַּעֲשׂוּן אֶת־הַדָּבָר הַזֶּה אִם־
21 תֵּחָלְצוּ לִפְנֵי יְהוָה לַמִּלְחָמָה׃ וְעָבַר לָכֶם כָּל־חָלוּץ אֶת־
22 הַיַּרְדֵּן לִפְנֵי יְהוָה עַד הוֹרִישׁוֹ אֶת־אֹיְבָיו מִפָּנָיו׃ וְנִכְבְּשָׁה
הָאָרֶץ לִפְנֵי יְהוָה וְאַחַר תָּשֻׁבוּ וִהְיִיתֶם נְקִיִּם מֵיְהוָה
וּמִיִּשְׂרָאֵל וְהָיְתָה הָאָרֶץ הַזֹּאת לָכֶם לַאֲחֻזָּה לִפְנֵי יְהוָה׃
23 וְאִם־לֹא תַעֲשׂוּן כֵּן הִנֵּה חֲטָאתֶם לַיהוָה וּדְעוּ חַטַּאתְכֶם
24 אֲשֶׁר תִּמְצָא אֶתְכֶם׃ בְּנוּ־לָכֶם עָרִים לְטַפְּכֶם וּגְדֵרֹת
כה לְצֹנַאֲכֶם וְהַיֹּצֵא מִפִּיכֶם תַּעֲשׂוּ׃ וַיֹּאמֶר בְּנֵי־גָד וּבְנֵי
רְאוּבֵן אֶל־מֹשֶׁה לֵאמֹר עֲבָדֶיךָ יַעֲשׂוּ כַּאֲשֶׁר אֲדֹנִי מְצַוֶּה׃
26 טַפֵּנוּ נָשֵׁינוּ מִקְנֵנוּ וְכָל־בְּהֶמְתֵּנוּ יִהְיוּ־שָׁם בְּעָרֵי הַגִּלְעָד׃
27 וַעֲבָדֶיךָ יַעַבְרוּ כָּל־חֲלוּץ צָבָא לִפְנֵי יְהוָה לַמִּלְחָמָה
28 כַּאֲשֶׁר אֲדֹנִי דֹּבֵר׃ וַיְצַו לָהֶם מֹשֶׁה אֵת אֶלְעָזָר הַכֹּהֵן
וְאֵת יְהוֹשֻׁעַ בִּן־נוּן וְאֶת־רָאשֵׁי אֲבוֹת הַמַּטּוֹת לִבְנֵי יִשְׂרָאֵל׃
29 וַיֹּאמֶר מֹשֶׁה אֲלֵהֶם אִם־יַעַבְרוּ בְנֵי־גָד וּבְנֵי־רְאוּבֵן ׀ אִתְּכֶם
אֶת־הַיַּרְדֵּן כָּל־חָלוּץ לַמִּלְחָמָה לִפְנֵי יְהוָה וְנִכְבְּשָׁה הָאָרֶץ
ל לִפְנֵיכֶם וּנְתַתֶּם לָהֶם אֶת־אֶרֶץ הַגִּלְעָד לַאֲחֻזָּה׃ וְאִם־לֹא
31 יַעַבְרוּ חֲלוּצִים אִתְּכֶם וְנֹאחֲזוּ בְתֹכְכֶם בְּאֶרֶץ כְּנָעַן׃ וַיַּעֲנוּ
בְנֵי־גָד וּבְנֵי רְאוּבֵן לֵאמֹר אֵת אֲשֶׁר דִּבֶּר יְהוָה אֶל־
32 עֲבָדֶיךָ כֵּן נַעֲשֶׂה׃ נַחְנוּ נַעֲבֹר חֲלוּצִים לִפְנֵי יְהוָה אֶרֶץ

v. 25. סבירין ויאמרו

22. *clear before the LORD, and before Israel.* The idea contained in this phrase became a general moral maxim among the Rabbis. 'Man should be clear not only before God but also in the estimation of his fellowmen.' It is not enough that a man's conscience is pure. He must strive to make even his outward actions irreproachable and above suspicion. A man should avoid doing things that *appear* wrong, משום מראית עין.

23. *And know ye your sin*—*i.e.* the punishment for your sin, *which will find you.* The rendering of the RV that has passed into a proverbial expression in the English language, is based upon an ancient notion that sin, like a curse, has, so to speak, an individual existence. The sinner cannot escape its consequence; it will seek and find him out.

30. *among you in the land of Canaan.* They would then be forced to evacuate their possession in Gilead, and fight for territory on the west of Jordan.

into the land of Canaan, and the possession of our inheritance shall remain with us beyond the Jordan.' ¶ 33. And Moses gave unto them, even to the children of Gad, and to the children of Reuben, and unto the half-tribe of Manasseh the son of Joseph, the kingdom of Sihon king of the Amorites, and the kingdom of Og king of Bashan, the land, according to the cities thereof with their borders, even the cities of the land round about. 34. And the children of Gad built Dibon, and Ataroth, and Aroer; 35. and Atroth-shophan, and Jazer, and Jogbehah; 36. and Beth-nimrah, and Beth-haran; fortified cities, and folds for sheep. 37. And the children of Reuben built Heshbon, and Elealeh, and Kiriathaim; 38. and Nebo, and Baal-meon—their names being changed—and Sibmah; and gave their names unto the cities which they builded. 39. And the children of Machir the son of Manasseh went to Gilead, and took it, and dispossessed the Amorites that were therein.*m. 40. And Moses gave Gilead unto Machir the son of Manasseh; and he dwelt therein. 41. And Jair the son of Manasseh went and took the villages thereof, and called them [1]Havvoth-jair. 42. And Nobah went and took Kenath, and the villages thereof, and called it Nobah, after his own name.

33 כְּנָעַן וְאִתָּנוּ אֲחֻזַּת נַחֲלָתֵנוּ מֵעֵבֶר לַיַּרְדֵּן׃ וַיִּתֵּן לָהֶם ׀ מֹשֶׁה
לִבְנֵי־גָד וְלִבְנֵי רְאוּבֵן וְלַחֲצִי ׀ שֵׁבֶט ׀ מְנַשֶּׁה בֶן־יוֹסֵף אֶת־
מַמְלֶכֶת סִיחֹן מֶלֶךְ הָאֱמֹרִי וְאֶת־מַמְלֶכֶת עוֹג מֶלֶךְ הַבָּשָׁן
34 הָאָרֶץ לְעָרֶיהָ בִּגְבֻלֹת עָרֵי הָאָרֶץ סָבִיב׃ וַיִּבְנוּ בְנֵי־גָד
לה אֶת־דִּיבֹן וְאֶת־עֲטָרֹת וְאֵת עֲרֹעֵר׃ וְאֶת־עַטְרֹת שׁוֹפָן וְאֶת־
36 יַעְזֵר וְיָגְבְּהָה׃ וְאֶת־בֵּית נִמְרָה וְאֶת־בֵּית הָרָן עָרֵי מִבְצָר
37 וְגִדְרֹת צֹאן׃ וּבְנֵי רְאוּבֵן בָּנוּ אֶת־חֶשְׁבּוֹן וְאֶת־אֶלְעָלֵא
38 וְאֵת קִרְיָתָיִם׃ וְאֶת־נְבוֹ וְאֶת־בַּעַל מְעוֹן מוּסַבֹּת שֵׁם וְאֶת־
מפטיר שִׂבְמָה וַיִּקְרְאוּ בְשֵׁמֹת אֶת־שְׁמוֹת הֶעָרִים אֲשֶׁר בָּנוּ׃ *
39 וַיֵּלְכוּ בְּנֵי מָכִיר בֶּן־מְנַשֶּׁה גִּלְעָדָה וַיִּלְכְּדֻהָ וַיּוֹרֶשׁ אֶת־
מ הָאֱמֹרִי אֲשֶׁר־בָּהּ׃ וַיִּתֵּן מֹשֶׁה אֶת־הַגִּלְעָד לְמָכִיר בֶּן־
41 מְנַשֶּׁה וַיֵּשֶׁב בָּהּ׃ וְיָאִיר בֶּן־מְנַשֶּׁה הָלַךְ וַיִּלְכֹּד אֶת־חַוֹּתֵיהֶם
42 וַיִּקְרָא אֶתְהֶן חַוֹּת יָאִיר׃ וְנֹבַח הָלַךְ וַיִּלְכֹּד אֶת־קְנָת וְאֶת־
בְּנֹתֶיהָ וַיִּקְרָא לָה נֹבַח בִּשְׁמוֹ׃

[1] That is, *The villages of Jair.*

ה' רפה v. 42.

33. *half-tribe of Manasseh.* The sub-tribes of Manasseh were pure warriors who had taken the most prominent part in the conquest of the Gileadite districts. The word 'half' in the phrase 'half-tribe of Manasseh' is not to be taken in a precise arithmetical sense. It denotes a section. According to XXVI, 29–32 there were eight sub-tribes of Manasseh, six of whom were allotted territory on the west of Jordan.

34. *built Dibon.* *i.e.* rebuilt it; fortified it so as to make it a place of safety for their families; thus also in *v.* 37.

38. *changed.* As they were names of two heathen deities.

40. *unto Machir.* *i.e.* unto the clans of Machir.

41. *Havvoth-jair.* *i.e.* the towns of Jair.

HAFTORAH MATTOS הפטרת מטות

JEREMIAH I–II, 3

CHAPTER I

1. The words of Jeremiah the son of Hilkiah, of the priests that were in Anathoth in the land of Benjamin, 2. to whom the word of the LORD came in the days of Josiah the son of Amon, king of Judah, in

CAP. I. א

א דִּבְרֵי יִרְמְיָהוּ בֶּן־חִלְקִיָּהוּ מִן־הַכֹּהֲנִים אֲשֶׁר בַּעֲנָתוֹת
2 בְּאֶרֶץ בִּנְיָמִן׃ אֲשֶׁר הָיָה דְבַר־יְהוָה אֵלָיו בִּימֵי יֹאשִׁיָּהוּ

This is the first of the three 'Haftorahs of Rebuke' that precede the Ninth of Ab, the anniversary of the Destruction of Jerusalem.

Jeremiah was born of a priestly family about the year 650 B.C.E. His Prophetic call came to him in the reign of Josiah, king of Judah, in the year 626. He witnessed the fall of Nineveh and the annihilation of the Assyrian Empire the thirteenth year of his reign. 3. It came also in the days of Jehoiakim the son of Josiah, king of Judah, unto the end of the eleventh year of Zedekiah the son of Josiah, king of Judah, unto the carrying away of Jerusalem captive in the fifth month. ¶ 4. And the word of the LORD came unto me, saying:

5. Before I formed thee in the belly I knew thee,
And before thou camest forth out of the womb I sanctified thee;
I have appointed thee a prophet unto the nations.

3 בֶּן־אָמוֹן מֶלֶךְ יְהוּדָה בִּשְׁלֹשׁ־עֶשְׂרֵה שָׁנָה לְמָלְכוֹ׃ וַיְהִי
בִּימֵי יְהוֹיָקִים בֶּן־יֹאשִׁיָּהוּ מֶלֶךְ יְהוּדָה עַד־תֹּם עַשְׁתֵּי־
עֶשְׂרֵה שָׁנָה לְצִדְקִיָּהוּ בֶן־יֹאשִׁיָּהוּ מֶלֶךְ יְהוּדָה עַד־גְּלוֹת
4 יְרוּשָׁלַםִ בַּחֹדֶשׁ הַחֲמִישִׁי׃ וַיְהִי דְבַר־יְהוָה אֵלַי
ה לֵאמֹר׃ בְּטֶרֶם אֶצָּוֹרְךָ בַבֶּטֶן יְדַעְתִּיךָ וּבְטֶרֶם תֵּצֵא
6 מֵרֶחֶם הִקְדַּשְׁתִּיךָ נָבִיא לַגּוֹיִם נְתַתִּיךָ׃ וָאֹמַר אֲהָהּ

v. 5. ו' יתירה

in 606; the death of Josiah, Judah's righteous king, in 605; and lived through the two sieges of Jerusalem in 597 and 586, with the attendant destruction of the Jewish state and the consequent transportation of the greater portion of his people to 'the rivers of Babylon'. We last hear of him in Egypt, carried thither by fugitive Judeans; and legend relates that he died a martyr's death at the hands of his brethren. Whatever basis there may be for this legend, it is but too true that Jeremiah the Prophet lived a martyr's life. For the greater part of his career, he was one man against the whole nation. By nature timid and shrinking, he proclaimed the Divine message fearlessly to ruler, noble, priest and people alike.

Jeremiah is the spiritual heir of the great Prophets that preceded him. He combines the tenderness of Hosea, the fearlessness of Amos, and the stern majesty of Isaiah. Like them, he is first of all a preacher of repentance; threatening judgment and, at the same time, holding out the promise of restoration. But even in his darkest moments, when he utterly despairs of the future of the Jewish state, his faith and trust in God do not forsake him. 'Though all be lost,' he seems to say to Israel, 'turn to God in perfect trust, call Him your Father, and His love will regenerate you.' To Jeremiah, Religion is an inward thing, a personal relation between the individual and his Maker, a relation that is untouched by national prosperity and can only be deepened by national ruin. 'The history of Israel begins with the migration of Abraham from the Euphrates to the Jordan; its classical period closes with the compulsory migration of the exiles from the Jordan back to the Euphrates. If Israel had been merely a race like others it would never have survived this fearful catastrophe, and would have disappeared in the Babylonian exile' (Cornill). That it did not so disappear was due to the activity of two men—Jeremiah and his disciple Ezekiel. Jeremiah's message to his despairing brethren in Babylon, 'Seek the welfare of the city wherein ye dwell, and pray unto the LORD for it: for in its welfare shall be your peace,' has been of incalculable influence in the civic life of all Jews throughout the world.

1. *Hilkiah.* Not the priest of that name.

Anathoth. Four miles north-east of Jerusalem. It was the home of Abiathar the High Priest, whom Solomon banished from office. Thus Jeremiah, while of priestly lineage, did not himself act as priest.

land of Benjamin. This hilly territory was 26 miles by 12 miles, about the size of Middlesex.

2. *Josiah.* He reigned from 626–605. He put down the idolatries, abominations and immoralities that had been introduced by Manasseh, and led a great religious revival in Israel. Unfortunately Judah's position between two great empires, Egypt and Babylon, was a most precarious one. Josiah took the side of Babylon, and was slain in the battle of Megiddo by Pharaoh Necho. Jeremiah and the whole people mourned for him 'as one mourneth for an only son'.

3. *Zedekiah.* The youngest son of Josiah, and the last king of Judah. He was well-disposed, but weak and devoid of any true religious zeal. In the eleventh year of his reign, Jerusalem was taken and burned by the Babylonians. He was blinded, taken to Babylon, and died there in prison.

4–10. JEREMIAH'S CALL

5. *knew thee. i.e.* chose thee; cf. Gen. XVIII, 19 ('For I have known him') and Amos III, 2 ('You only have I known of all families of the earth').

sanctified thee. Consecrated thee; *i.e.* set thee apart for My service. 'In the very moment of his call, Jeremiah learnt that he was a child of destiny. His choice for his great work was no haphazard selection. God had planned his life, even before he was born. The riddle and purpose of existence were thus solved for Jeremiah' (Duhm).

unto the nations. As Amos and Isaiah before him, but more so. Israel was now caught in the current of universal politics and its career was inextricably bound up with Assyria, Babylon and Egypt (Peake).

6. Then said I: 'Ah, Lord GOD! behold, I cannot speak; for I am a child.' 7. But the LORD said unto me:

Say not: I am a child;
For to whomsoever I shall send thee thou shalt go,
And whatsoever I shall command thee thou shalt speak.
8. Be not afraid of them;
For I am with thee to deliver thee,
Saith the LORD.

9. Then the LORD put forth His hand, and touched my mouth; and the LORD said unto me:

Behold, I have put My words in thy mouth;
10. See, I have this day set thee over the nations and over the kingdoms,
To root out and to pull down,
And to destroy and to overthrow;
To build, and to plant.

11. Moreover the word of the LORD came unto me, saying: 'Jeremiah, what seest thou?' And I said: 'I see a rod of an [1]almond-tree.' 12. Then said the LORD unto me: 'Thou hast well seen; for I [2]watch over My word to perform it.' ¶ 13. And the word of the LORD came unto me the second time, saying: 'What seest thou?' And I said: 'I see a seething pot; and the face thereof is from the north.' 14. Then the LORD said unto me: 'Out of the north the evil shall break forth upon all the inhabitants of the land. 15. For, lo, I will call all

7 אֲדֹנָי יֱהוִה הִנֵּה לֹא־יָדַעְתִּי דַּבֵּר כִּי־נַעַר אָנֹכִי׃ וַיֹּאמֶר
יְהוָה אֵלַי אַל־תֹּאמַר נַעַר אָנֹכִי כִּי עַל־כָּל־אֲשֶׁר אֶשְׁלָחֲךָ
8 תֵּלֵךְ וְאֵת כָּל־אֲשֶׁר אֲצַוְּךָ תְּדַבֵּר׃ אַל־תִּירָא מִפְּנֵיהֶם
9 כִּי־אִתְּךָ אֲנִי לְהַצִּלֶךָ נְאֻם־יְהוָה׃ וַיִּשְׁלַח יְהוָה אֶת־יָדוֹ
וַיַּגַּע עַל־פִּי וַיֹּאמֶר יְהוָה אֵלַי הִנֵּה נָתַתִּי דְבָרַי בְּפִיךָ׃
י רְאֵה הִפְקַדְתִּיךָ ׀ הַיּוֹם הַזֶּה עַל־הַגּוֹיִם וְעַל־הַמַּמְלָכוֹת
לִנְתוֹשׁ וְלִנְתוֹץ וּלְהַאֲבִיד וְלַהֲרוֹס לִבְנוֹת וְלִנְטוֹעַ׃
11 וַיְהִי דְבַר־יְהוָה אֵלַי לֵאמֹר מָה־אַתָּה רֹאֶה יִרְמְיָהוּ וָאֹמַר
12 מַקֵּל שָׁקֵד אֲנִי רֹאֶה׃ וַיֹּאמֶר יְהוָה אֵלַי הֵיטַבְתָּ לִרְאוֹת
13 כִּי־שֹׁקֵד אֲנִי עַל־דְּבָרִי לַעֲשֹׂתוֹ׃ וַיְהִי דְבַר־יְהוָה ׀
אֵלַי שֵׁנִית לֵאמֹר מָה אַתָּה רֹאֶה וָאֹמַר סִיר נָפוּחַ אֲנִי
14 רֹאֶה וּפָנָיו מִפְּנֵי צָפוֹנָה׃ וַיֹּאמֶר יְהוָה אֵלָי מִצָּפוֹן תִּפָּתַח
טו הָרָעָה עַל כָּל־יֹשְׁבֵי הָאָרֶץ׃ כִּי ׀ הִנְנִי קֹרֵא לְכָל־
מִשְׁפְּחוֹת מַמְלְכוֹת צָפוֹנָה נְאֻם־יְהוָה וּבָאוּ וְנָתְנוּ אִישׁ
כִּסְאוֹ פֶּתַח ׀ שַׁעֲרֵי יְרוּשָׁלַםִ וְעַל כָּל־חוֹמֹתֶיהָ סָבִיב וְעַל

[1] Heb. *shaked*. [2] Heb. *shoked*.

6. *I am a child.* Not necessarily in years. The Heb. word has a wider sense, indicating a child in fitness or experience. These words express the shrinking self-distrust of a sensitive nature, and the humility that characterizes truly great minds; cf. the reply of Moses in the Sedrah, IV, 10.

9. *touched my mouth.* Symbolic of Divine inspiration. The message he would bring would not be *his* message, but the message of God.

10. *set thee.* lit. 'made thee My deputy'.
to root out. Because the Word of God, which the Prophet proclaims, determines the fate of nations and kingdoms.
to plant. Jeremiah's activity would be destructive, but only to prepare the way for the work of restoration.

11, 12. THE SYMBOL OF THE ALMOND-TREE

11. *an almond-tree.* Heb. *shaked*, and the Heb. for 'watching' is *shoked*. There is more than a play on words here. The almond-tree is so named in Hebrew, because, blossoming early in January, it is the first to awake from winter's sleep. On seeing it, the thought flashes across the Prophet's mind that God is awake and watches over His word to fulfil it, without delay. This assurance at the outset of his career, that God would surely execute His purpose, was to steady him, when in the course of his ministry he found himself doomed again and again to disappointment.

13–16. THE SYMBOL OF THE CALDRON

14. *out of the north.* From the North had come the Assyrian invasions, and into the North the Ten Tribes had been led captive. And Babylon, which was to take Judah into exile, also lay to the North.
the evil. Foretold by all the prophets as the result of the nation's sinning.

15. *shall set every one his throne.* The neighbourhood of the city gate was the place where trials were ordinarily held. Here the rulers of the invading army will sit in judgment on the conquered people. This was literally fulfilled; see Jer. XXXIX, 3.

16 כָּל־עָרֵי יְהוּדָה׃ וְדִבַּרְתִּי מִשְׁפָּטַי אוֹתָם עַל כָּל־רָעָתָם
אֲשֶׁר עֲזָבוּנִי וַיְקַטְּרוּ לֵאלֹהִים אֲחֵרִים וַיִּשְׁתַּחֲווּ לְמַעֲשֵׂי
17 יְדֵיהֶם׃ וְאַתָּה תֶּאְזֹר מָתְנֶיךָ וְקַמְתָּ וְדִבַּרְתָּ אֲלֵיהֶם אֵת
כָּל־אֲשֶׁר אָנֹכִי אֲצַוֶּךָּ אַל־תֵּחַת מִפְּנֵיהֶם פֶּן־אֲחִתְּךָ
18 לִפְנֵיהֶם׃ וַאֲנִי הִנֵּה נְתַתִּיךָ הַיּוֹם לְעִיר מִבְצָר וּלְעַמּוּד
בַּרְזֶל וּלְחֹמוֹת נְחֹשֶׁת עַל־כָּל־הָאָרֶץ לְמַלְכֵי יְהוּדָה לְשָׂרֶיהָ
19 לְכֹהֲנֶיהָ וּלְעַם הָאָרֶץ׃ וְנִלְחֲמוּ אֵלֶיךָ וְלֹא־יוּכְלוּ לָךְ כִּי־
אִתְּךָ אֲנִי נְאֻם־יְהוָה לְהַצִּילֶךָ׃

Cap. II. ב

א 2 וַיְהִי דְבַר־יְהוָה אֵלַי לֵאמֹר׃ הָלֹךְ וְקָרָאתָ בְאָזְנֵי יְרוּשָׁלִַם
לֵאמֹר כֹּה אָמַר יְהוָה זָכַרְתִּי לָךְ חֶסֶד נְעוּרַיִךְ אַהֲבַת
3 כְּלוּלֹתָיִךְ לֶכְתֵּךְ אַחֲרַי בַּמִּדְבָּר בְּאֶרֶץ לֹא זְרוּעָה׃ קֹדֶשׁ
יִשְׂרָאֵל לַיהוָה רֵאשִׁית תְּבוּאָתֹה כָּל־אֹכְלָיו יֶאְשָׁמוּ רָעָה
תָּבֹא אֲלֵיהֶם נְאֻם־יְהוָה׃

the families of the kingdoms of the north, saith the LORD; and they shall come, and they shall set every one his throne at the entrance of the gates of Jerusalem, and against all the walls thereof round about, and against all the cities of Judah. 16. And I will utter my judgments against them touching all their wickedness; in that they have forsaken Me, and have offered unto other gods, and worshipped the work of their own hands. 17. Thou therefore gird up thy loins, and arise, and speak unto them all that I command thee; be not dismayed at them, lest I dismay thee before them. 18. For, behold, I have made thee this day a fortified city, and an iron pillar, and brazen walls, against the whole land, against the kings of Judah, against the princes thereof, against the priests thereof, and against the people of the land. 19. And they shall fight against thee; but they shall not prevail against thee; For I am with thee, saith the LORD, to deliver thee.'

Chapter II

1. And the word of the LORD came to me, saying: 2. Go, and cry in the ears of Jerusalem, saying: Thus saith the LORD:

I remember for thee the affection of thy youth,
The love of thine espousals;
How thou wentest after Me in the wilderness,
In a land that was not sown.

3. Israel is the LORD's hallowed portion,
His first-fruits of the increase;
All that devour him shall be held guilty,
Evil shall come upon them,
Saith the LORD.

ב׳ v. 3. קמץ בז״ק

17–19. ENCOURAGEMENT TO JEREMIAH

17. *gird up thy loins.* Prepare thyself for a strenuous task.

lest I dismay thee before them. If thou fearest them, thou wilt fail before them (Kimchi). Jeremiah can only conquer if he does not for one moment lose courage.

18. *the people of the land.* Heb. *am ha-aretz;* probably the National Assembly—'the ancient Hebrew Parliament' (Sulzberger).

19. *shall not prevail. i.e.* shall not finally prevail (Streane). Before the Prophet's death, his warnings would be justified, and his cause vindicated.

Chapter II

1–3. God reminds Israel of her loyalty and affection in the Wilderness. Jeremiah pictures Israel's loyalty to God as that of an affectionate bride, who follows the chosen of her heart even into a wilderness.

2. *affection.* Heb. *chesed.* A very rich and beautiful word, here meaning unquestioned and whole-hearted devotion and total forgetfulness of self, a love more than filial, like that of a youthful, loving bride.

how thou wentest after Me. It was only such love, thought the Prophet, that could account for Israel's willingness to forget the grandeur of Egypt, and brave the terrors of the Wilderness—its hardships, perils and treacherous foes. It was only such love that could cause them gladly to follow the call of God into the Unknown, on a novel quest of the Divine, that was to fill man's earthly existence with new hopes; on an unheard-of adventure in Religion, that was to turn the current of history and humanize mankind.

3. *the LORD'S hallowed portion.* All the nations are the LORD's harvest; but Israel is set apart for Him alone, even as the first-fruits are set apart for the use of the priest. In the Sedrah, IV, 21, Israel is called God's firstborn son.

evil shall come upon them. Woe to anyone who violates that sanctity, and assails Israel.

33

Chapter XXXIII

1. These are the stages of the children of Israel, by which they went forth out of the land of Egypt by their hosts under the hand of Moses and Aaron. 2. And Moses wrote their goings forth, stage by stage, by the commandment of the LORD; and these are their stages at their goings forth. 3. And they journeyed from Rameses in the first month, on the fifteenth day of the first month; on the morrow after the passover the children of Israel went out with a high hand in the sight of all the Egyptians, 4. while the Egyptians were burying them that the LORD had smitten among them, even all their first-born; upon their gods also the LORD executed judgments. 5. And the children of Israel journeyed from Rameses, and pitched in Succoth. 6. And they journeyed from Succoth, and pitched in Etham, which is in the edge of the wilderness. 7. And they journeyed from Etham, and turned back unto Pi-hahiroth, which is before Baal-zephon; and they pitched before Migdol. 8. And they journeyed from Pene-hahiroth, and passed through the midst of the sea into the wilderness; and they went three days' journey in the wilderness of Etham, and pitched in Marah. 9. And they journeyed from Marah, and came unto Elim; and in Elim were twelve springs of water, and threescore and ten palm-trees; and they pitched there. 10. And they journeyed from Elim, and pitched by the Red Sea.*ii. 11. And they journeyed from the Red Sea, and pitched in the wilder-

לג

Cap. XXXIII. לג

פ פ פ מג 43

א אֵלֶּה מַסְעֵי בְנֵי־יִשְׂרָאֵל אֲשֶׁר יָצְאוּ מֵאֶרֶץ מִצְרַיִם לְצִבְאֹתָם
2 בְּיַד־מֹשֶׁה וְאַהֲרֹן׃ וַיִּכְתֹּב מֹשֶׁה אֶת־מוֹצָאֵיהֶם לְמַסְעֵיהֶם
3 עַל־פִּי יְהוָה וְאֵלֶּה מַסְעֵיהֶם לְמוֹצָאֵיהֶם׃ וַיִּסְעוּ מֵרַעְמְסֵס
בַּחֹדֶשׁ הָרִאשׁוֹן בַּחֲמִשָּׁה עָשָׂר יוֹם לַחֹדֶשׁ הָרִאשׁוֹן
מִמָּחֳרַת הַפֶּסַח יָצְאוּ בְנֵי־יִשְׂרָאֵל בְּיָד רָמָה לְעֵינֵי כָּל־
4 מִצְרָיִם׃ וּמִצְרַיִם מְקַבְּרִים אֵת אֲשֶׁר הִכָּה יְהוָה בָּהֶם
ה כָּל־בְּכוֹר וּבֵאלֹהֵיהֶם עָשָׂה יְהוָה שְׁפָטִים׃ וַיִּסְעוּ בְנֵי־
6 יִשְׂרָאֵל מֵרַעְמְסֵס וַיַּחֲנוּ בְּסֻכֹּת׃ וַיִּסְעוּ מִסֻּכֹּת וַיַּחֲנוּ בְאֵתָם
7 אֲשֶׁר בִּקְצֵה הַמִּדְבָּר׃ וַיִּסְעוּ מֵאֵתָם וַיָּשָׁב עַל־פִּי הַחִירֹת
8 אֲשֶׁר עַל־פְּנֵי בַּעַל צְפוֹן וַיַּחֲנוּ לִפְנֵי מִגְדֹּל׃ וַיִּסְעוּ מִפְּנֵי
הַחִירֹת וַיַּעַבְרוּ בְתוֹךְ־הַיָּם הַמִּדְבָּרָה וַיֵּלְכוּ דֶּרֶךְ שְׁלֹשֶׁת
9 יָמִים בְּמִדְבַּר אֵתָם וַיַּחֲנוּ בְּמָרָה׃ וַיִּסְעוּ מִמָּרָה וַיָּבֹאוּ
אֵילִמָה וּבְאֵילִם שְׁתֵּים עֶשְׂרֵה עֵינֹת מַיִם וְשִׁבְעִים תְּמָרִים

v. 8. סבירין מפי

X. MASSEY

(Chapters XXXIII–XXXVI)

XXXIII, 1–49. Itinerary from Egypt to the Jordan

This chapter supplies us with the stages of the journey of the Israelites from Egypt to the Plains of Moab. It was written to serve as a memorial not only of historical interest but of deep religious significance. Every journey and every halting-place had its suggestions for the instruction, admonition, or encouragement of Israel. The Midrash says, 'It may be likened unto a king who had taken his ailing son to a distant place to be cured. On the return journey, the king would lovingly recount to the lad all the experiences they went through at each of their halting-places. "At this spot we slept; at that, we had a cool resting-place from the heat; at the other, you were overcome with pains in the head!" Israel is God's child, upon whom He bestows compassion, even as a father bestows compassion on his son.'

2. *goings forth.* *i.e.* each place from which they went forth to proceed to another place.

3. *with a high hand.* See Exod. XIV, 8.

in the sight of all the Egyptians. The departure was public. There was nothing clandestine or ignominious in the way in which they left the land of their oppressors.

4. *burying.* Israel was joyous and strong, whilst his erstwhile master, Egypt, was bent low and broken.

upon their gods. See Exod. XII, 12 for the meaning of this phrase. The false deities of Egypt were made contemptible in the eyes of their worshippers.

5–15. These verses detail the stages of the journey from Raamses in Egypt to the Wilderness of Sinai. This is related in Exod. XII, 37 and XIX, 2. Two stations, Dophkah and Alush, are not mentioned in Exodus.

ness of Sin. 12. And they journeyed from the wilderness of Sin, and pitched in Dophkah. 13. And they journeyed from Dophkah and pitched in Alush. 14. And they journeyed from Alush, and pitched in Rephidim, where was no water for the people to drink. 15. And they journeyed from Rephidim, and pitched in the wilderness of Sinai. 16. And they journeyed from the wilderness of Sinai, and pitched in Kibroth-hattaavah. 17. And they journeyed from Kibroth-hattaavah, and pitched in Hazeroth. 18. And they journeyed from Hazeroth, and pitched in Rithmah. 19. And they journeyed from Rithmah, and pitched in Rimmon-perez. 20. And they journeyed from Rimmon-perez, and pitched in Libnah. 21. And they journeyed from Libnah, and pitched in Rissah. 22. And they journeyed from Rissah, and pitched in Kehelah. 23. And they journeyed from Kehelah, and pitched in mount Shepher. 24. And they journeyed from mount Shepher, and pitched in Haradah. 25. And they journeyed from Haradah, and pitched in Makheloth. 26. And they journeyed from Makheloth, and pitched in Tahath. 27. And they journeyed from Tahath, and pitched in Terah. 28. And they journeyed from Terah, and pitched in Mithkah. 29. And they journeyed from Mithkah, and pitched in Hashmonah. 30. And they journeyed from Hashmonah, and pitched in Moseroth. 31. And they journeyed from Moseroth, and pitched in Bene-jaakan. 32. And they journeyed from Bene-jaakan, and pitched in Hor-haggidgad. 33. And they journeyed from Hor-haggidgad, and pitched in Jotbah. 34. And they journeyed from Jotbah, and pitched in Abronah. 35. And they journed from Abronah, and pitched in Ezion-geber. 36. And they journeyed from Ezion-geber, and pitched in the wilderness of Zin—the same is Kadesh. 37. And they journeyed from Kadesh, and pitched in mount Hor, in the edge of the land of Edom.—38. And Aaron the priest went up into mount Hor at the commandment of the LORD, and died there, in the fortieth year after the children of Israel were come out of the land of Egypt, in the fifth month, on the first day of the month. 39. And Aaron was a hundred and twenty and three years old when he died in mount Hor. 40. And the Canaanite, the king of

שני י 11 וַיַּחֲנוּ־שָׁם׃ וַיִּסְעוּ מֵאֵילִם וַיַּחֲנוּ עַל־יַם־סוּף׃ *וַיִּסְעוּ מִיַּם־
12 סוּף וַיַּחֲנוּ בְּמִדְבַּר־סִין׃ וַיִּסְעוּ מִמִּדְבַּר־סִין וַיַּחֲנוּ בְּדָפְקָה׃
13 14 וַיִּסְעוּ מִדָּפְקָה וַיַּחֲנוּ בְּאָלוּשׁ׃ וַיִּסְעוּ מֵאָלוּשׁ וַיַּחֲנוּ
טו בִּרְפִידִם וְלֹא־הָיָה שָׁם מַיִם לָעָם לִשְׁתּוֹת׃ וַיִּסְעוּ מֵרְפִידִם
16 וַיַּחֲנוּ בְּמִדְבַּר סִינָי׃ וַיִּסְעוּ מִמִּדְבַּר סִינָי וַיַּחֲנוּ בְּקִבְרֹת
17 18 הַתַּאֲוָה׃ וַיִּסְעוּ מִקִּבְרֹת הַתַּאֲוָה וַיַּחֲנוּ בַּחֲצֵרֹת׃ וַיִּסְעוּ
19 מֵחֲצֵרֹת וַיַּחֲנוּ בְּרִתְמָה׃ וַיִּסְעוּ מֵרִתְמָה וַיַּחֲנוּ בְּרִמֹּן פָּרֶץ׃
כ 21 וַיִּסְעוּ מֵרִמֹּן פָּרֶץ וַיַּחֲנוּ בְּלִבְנָה׃ וַיִּסְעוּ מִלִּבְנָה וַיַּחֲנוּ
22 23 בְּרִסָּה׃ וַיִּסְעוּ מֵרִסָּה וַיַּחֲנוּ בִּקְהֵלָתָה׃ וַיִּסְעוּ מִקְּהֵלָתָה
24 וַיַּחֲנוּ בְּהַר־שָׁפֶר׃ וַיִּסְעוּ מֵהַר־שָׁפֶר וַיַּחֲנוּ בַּחֲרָדָה׃
כה 26 וַיִּסְעוּ מֵחֲרָדָה וַיַּחֲנוּ בְּמַקְהֵלֹת׃ וַיִּסְעוּ מִמַּקְהֵלֹת וַיַּחֲנוּ
27 28 בְּתָחַת׃ וַיִּסְעוּ מִתָּחַת וַיַּחֲנוּ בְּתָרַח׃ וַיִּסְעוּ מִתָּרַח וַיַּחֲנוּ
29 ל בְּמִתְקָה׃ וַיִּסְעוּ מִמִּתְקָה וַיַּחֲנוּ בְּחַשְׁמֹנָה׃ וַיִּסְעוּ מֵחַשְׁמֹנָה
31 וַיַּחֲנוּ בְּמֹסֵרוֹת׃ וַיִּסְעוּ מִמֹּסֵרוֹת וַיַּחֲנוּ בִּבְנֵי יַעֲקָן׃
32 33 וַיִּסְעוּ מִבְּנֵי יַעֲקָן וַיַּחֲנוּ בְּחֹר הַגִּדְגָּד׃ וַיִּסְעוּ מֵחֹר הַגִּדְגָּד
34 וַיַּחֲנוּ בְּיָטְבָתָה׃ וַיִּסְעוּ מִיָּטְבָתָה וַיַּחֲנוּ בְּעַבְרֹנָה׃
לה 36 וַיִּסְעוּ מֵעַבְרֹנָה וַיַּחֲנוּ בְּעֶצְיֹן גָּבֶר׃ וַיִּסְעוּ מֵעֶצְיֹן גָּבֶר
37 וַיַּחֲנוּ בְמִדְבַּר־צִן הִוא קָדֵשׁ׃ וַיִּסְעוּ מִקָּדֵשׁ וַיַּחֲנוּ בְּהֹר
38 הָהָר בִּקְצֵה אֶרֶץ אֱדוֹם׃ וַיַּעַל אַהֲרֹן הַכֹּהֵן אֶל־הֹר
הָהָר עַל־פִּי יְהוָה וַיָּמָת שָׁם בִּשְׁנַת הָאַרְבָּעִים לְצֵאת
בְּנֵי־יִשְׂרָאֵל מֵאֶרֶץ מִצְרַיִם בַּחֹדֶשׁ הַחֲמִישִׁי בְּאֶחָד לַחֹדֶשׁ׃
39 וְאַהֲרֹן בֶּן־שָׁלֹשׁ וְעֶשְׂרִים וּמְאַת שָׁנָה בְּמֹתוֹ בְּהֹר הָהָר׃
מ ס וַיִּשְׁמַע הַכְּנַעֲנִי מֶלֶךְ עֲרָד וְהוּא־יֹשֵׁב בַּנֶּגֶב בְּאֶרֶץ

16–36. At this distance it is exceedingly difficult to identify the exact route of march, more especially as the names were not names of cities or conspicuous landmarks. They have changed with the centuries, and the designation of the temporary landmarks was forgotten (Dummelow).

37–49. This section deals with the march, in the fortieth year, to the borders of Moab and the fords of the Jordan.

Arad, who dwelt in the South in the land of Canaan, heard of the coming of the children of Israel.—41. And they journeyed from mount Hor, and pitched in Zalmonah. 42. And they journeyed from Zalmonah, and pitched in Punon. 43. And they journeyed from Punon, and pitched in Oboth. 44. And they journeyed from Oboth, and pitched in Ije-abarim, in the border of Moab. 45. And they journeyed from Ijim, and pitched in Dibon-gad. 46. And they journeyed from Dibon-gad, and pitched in Almon-diblathaim. 47. And they journeyed from Almon-diblathaim, and pitched in the mountains of Abarim, in front of Nebo. 48. And they journeyed from the mountains of Abarim, and pitched in the plains of Moab by the Jordan at Jericho. 49. And they pitched by the Jordan, from Beth-jeshimoth even unto Abel-shittim in the plains of Moab.*iii (**v). ¶ 50. And the LORD spoke unto Moses in the plains of Moab by the Jordan at Jericho, saying: 51. 'Speak unto the children of Israel, and say unto them: When ye pass over the Jordan into the land of Canaan, 52. then ye shall drive out all the inhabitants of the land from before you, and destroy all their figured stones, and destroy all their molten images, and demolish all their high places. 53. And ye shall drive out the inhabitants of the land, and dwell therein; for unto you have I given the land to possess it. 54. And ye shall inherit the land by lot according to your families—to the more ye shall give the more inheritance, and to the fewer thou shalt give the less inheritance; wheresoever the lot falleth to any man, that shall be his; according to the tribes of your fathers shall ye inherit. 55. But if ye will not drive out the inhabitants of the land from before you, then shall those that ye let remain of them be as thorns in your eyes, and as pricks in your sides, and they shall harass you in the land wherein ye dwell. 56. And it shall come to pass, that as I thought to do unto them, so will I do unto you.'

41 כְּנַעַן בְּבֹא בְּנֵי יִשְׂרָאֵל׃ וַיִּסְעוּ מֵהֹר הָהָר וַיַּחֲנוּ בְּצַלְמֹנָה׃
42 43 וַיִּסְעוּ מִצַּלְמֹנָה וַיַּחֲנוּ בְּפוּנֹן׃ וַיִּסְעוּ מִפּוּנֹן וַיַּחֲנוּ בְּאֹבֹת׃
44 מה וַיִּסְעוּ מֵאֹבֹת וַיַּחֲנוּ בְּעִיֵּי הָעֲבָרִים בִּגְבוּל מוֹאָב׃ וַיִּסְעוּ
46 מֵעִיִּים וַיַּחֲנוּ בְּדִיבֹן גָּד׃ וַיִּסְעוּ מִדִּיבֹן גָּד וַיַּחֲנוּ בְּעַלְמֹן
47 דִּבְלָתָיְמָה׃ וַיִּסְעוּ מֵעַלְמֹן דִּבְלָתָיְמָה וַיַּחֲנוּ בְּהָרֵי הָעֲבָרִים
48 לִפְנֵי נְבוֹ׃ וַיִּסְעוּ מֵהָרֵי הָעֲבָרִים וַיַּחֲנוּ בְּעַרְבֹת מוֹאָב עַל
49 יַרְדֵּן יְרֵחוֹ׃ וַיַּחֲנוּ עַל־הַיַּרְדֵּן מִבֵּית הַיְשִׁמֹת עַד אָבֵל
לישי (חמישי כשהן מחוב')
נ הַשִּׁטִּים בְּעַרְבֹת מוֹאָב׃ * ס וַיְדַבֵּר יְהוָה אֶל־מֹשֶׁה
51 בְּעַרְבֹת מוֹאָב עַל־יַרְדֵּן יְרֵחוֹ לֵאמֹר׃ דַּבֵּר אֶל־בְּנֵי
יִשְׂרָאֵל וְאָמַרְתָּ אֲלֵהֶם כִּי אַתֶּם עֹבְרִים אֶת־הַיַּרְדֵּן אֶל־
52 אֶרֶץ כְּנָעַן׃ וְהוֹרַשְׁתֶּם אֶת־כָּל־יֹשְׁבֵי הָאָרֶץ מִפְּנֵיכֶם
וְאִבַּדְתֶּם אֵת כָּל־מַשְׂכִּיֹּתָם וְאֵת כָּל־צַלְמֵי מַסֵּכֹתָם תְּאַבֵּדוּ
53 וְאֵת כָּל־בָּמוֹתָם תַּשְׁמִידוּ׃ וְהוֹרַשְׁתֶּם אֶת־הָאָרֶץ וִישַׁבְתֶּם־
54 בָּהּ כִּי לָכֶם נָתַתִּי אֶת־הָאָרֶץ לָרֶשֶׁת אֹתָהּ׃ וְהִתְנַחַלְתֶּם
אֶת־הָאָרֶץ בְּגוֹרָל לְמִשְׁפְּחֹתֵיכֶם לָרַב תַּרְבּוּ אֶת־נַחֲלָתוֹ
וְלַמְעַט תַּמְעִיט אֶת־נַחֲלָתוֹ אֶל אֲשֶׁר־יֵצֵא לוֹ שָׁמָּה הַגּוֹרָל
נה לוֹ יִהְיֶה לְמַטּוֹת אֲבֹתֵיכֶם תִּתְנֶחָלוּ׃ וְאִם־לֹא תוֹרִישׁוּ
אֶת־יֹשְׁבֵי הָאָרֶץ מִפְּנֵיכֶם וְהָיָה אֲשֶׁר תּוֹתִירוּ מֵהֶם לְשִׂכִּים
בְּעֵינֵיכֶם וְלִצְנִינִם בְּצִדֵּיכֶם וְצָרְרוּ אֶתְכֶם עַל־הָאָרֶץ אֲשֶׁר
56 אַתֶּם יֹשְׁבִים בָּהּ׃ וְהָיָה כַּאֲשֶׁר דִּמִּיתִי לַעֲשׂוֹת לָהֶם
אֶעֱשֶׂה לָכֶם׃ פ

50–56. COMMANDS WITH REGARD TO THE SETTLEMENT IN CANAAN

52. *drive out. i.e.* dispossess. The reason given for this command is that no inducements to idolatry remain in the Promised Land (see Exod. XXIII, 31–33, XXXIV, 11–17).

their figured stones. See Lev. XXVI, 1.

their high places. The altars and sanctuaries erected on hills and natural mounds, as was the practice of the Canaanites.

Everything that savoured of idolatry was to be swept away, as being offensive to God and religiously perilous to the Israelites.

53. *unto you have I given the land.* The Land is not man's, but God's. 'The earth is the LORD's, and the fulness thereof' (Ps. XXIV, 1). God has a right to do what He will with His own.

54. *by lot.* The system of dividing land by lot persisted down to Roman times. It was in practice in Palestine in the days of R. José, a tanna of the second century (*contra* Kennett, Schweich Lectures 1931, p. 76).

55. *as pricks in your sides.* A source of continual and unabated vexation.

56. *so will I do unto you.* If they left the Canaanites unexpelled, the end would be the expulsion of Israel.

34 CHAPTER XXXIV

1. And the LORD spoke unto Moses, saying: 2. 'Command the children of Israel, and say unto them: When ye come into the land of Canaan, this shall be the land that shall fall unto you for an inheritance, even the land of Canaan according to the borders thereof. 3. Thus your south side shall be from the wilderness of Zin close by the side of Edom, and your south border shall begin at the end of the Salt Sea eastward; 4. and your border shall turn about southward of the ascent of Akrabbim, and pass along to Zin; and the goings out thereof shall be southward of Kadesh-barnea; and it shall go forth to Hazar-addar, and pass along to Azmon; 5. and the border shall turn about from Azmon unto the Brook of Egypt, and the goings out thereof shall be at the Sea. 6. And for the western border, ye shall have the Great Sea for a border; this shall be your west border. 7. And this shall be your north border: from the Great Sea ye shall mark

לד CAP. XXXIV. לד

א 2 וַיְדַבֵּר יְהוָה אֶל־מֹשֶׁה לֵּאמֹר׃ צַו אֶת־בְּנֵי יִשְׂרָאֵל
וְאָמַרְתָּ אֲלֵהֶם כִּי־אַתֶּם בָּאִים אֶל־הָאָרֶץ כְּנָעַן זֹאת הָאָרֶץ
3 אֲשֶׁר תִּפֹּל לָכֶם בְּנַחֲלָה אֶרֶץ כְּנַעַן לִגְבֻלֹתֶיהָ׃ וְהָיָה
לָכֶם פְּאַת־נֶגֶב מִמִּדְבַּר־צִן עַל־יְדֵי אֱדוֹם וְהָיָה לָכֶם
4 גְּבוּל נֶגֶב מִקְצֵה יָם־הַמֶּלַח קֵדְמָה׃ וְנָסַב לָכֶם הַגְּבוּל
מִנֶּגֶב לְמַעֲלֵה עַקְרַבִּים וְעָבַר צִנָה וְהָיָה תּוֹצְאֹתָיו מִנֶּגֶב
ה לְקָדֵשׁ בַּרְנֵעַ וְיָצָא חֲצַר־אַדָּר וְעָבַר עַצְמֹנָה׃ וְנָסַב
הַגְּבוּל מֵעַצְמוֹן נַחְלָה מִצְרָיִם וְהָיוּ תוֹצְאֹתָיו הַיָּמָּה׃
6 וּגְבוּל יָם וְהָיָה לָכֶם הַיָּם הַגָּדוֹל וּגְבוּל זֶה־יִהְיֶה לָכֶם
7 גְּבוּל יָם׃ וְזֶה־יִהְיֶה לָכֶם גְּבוּל צָפוֹן מִן־הַיָּם הַגָּדֹל

v. 4. והיו ק׳

CHAPTER XXXIV

XXXIV, 1–29. THE BOUNDARIES OF THE HOLY LAND

This chapter indicates the *ideal* limits of the Holy Land. 'These, the providential (Gen. xv, 18, Ex. xxiii, 31) and in some sense natural, boundaries of the territory of Israel, were only attained for a brief period during the reigns of David and Solomon' (Dummelow). Great uncertainty exists in regard to many of the geographical terms, especially those connected with the Northern border. S. H. Isaacs, *The True Boundaries of the Holy Land*, Chicago, 1917, is a valuable contribution to the solution of a difficult problem, and has been followed in these comments.

2. *shall fall unto you.* This expression is used because the Land was to be divided by lot.

3–5. THE SOUTHERN BOUNDARY

Starting from the southern extremity of the Dead Sea, it proceeded in a S.W. direction to the region south of Kadesh-barnea; thence to the Brook of Egypt; and then north-westwards to the Mediterranean.

3. *by the side of Edom.* Along the western border of Edom.

south side. i.e. your southern boundary.

the Salt Sea. The Dead Sea.

eastward. On its eastern end.

4. *of Akrabbim.* lit. 'of scorpions'; one of the passes that lead to the northern slope of the Wady-el-Fikreh.

Kadesh-barnea. The modern Ain Quadis. 'Then your frontier shall turn south of the Scorpion Pass and along to Zin, coming out south of Kadesh-barnea, stretching to Hazar-addar, and along to Azmon' (Moffatt).

5. *Brook of Egypt.* The Wady-el-Arish, flowing into the Mediterranean about 20 miles south of Gaza.

and the goings out thereof shall be at the Sea. 'And end at the Mediterranean Sea' (Moffatt).

6. THE WESTERN BORDER

6. *the Great Sea.* The Mediterranean Sea.

shall be your west border. The western border of Palestine is to be the Mediterranean coast. 'The Great Sea—that is the *whole* eastern flank of the Great Sea from its south-eastern to its north-eastern corner—shall be the western boundary of the land. If any point on the coast, between these two corners were meant, the Text would surely have designated that point. As it did not, the whole eastern shore of the Mediterranean must be intended. The western border of the Holy Land, therefore, begins at the south-east corner of the Mediterranean where the "Brook of Egypt" falls into it; thence it runs northward, passing Mount Carmel, Tyre, Zidon, the Lebanons, unto the north-eastern border of the Bay of Alexandretta' (S. H. Isaacs).

7–9. THE NORTHERN BOUNDARY

7. *ye shall mark out your line unto.* 'Ye shall draw your boundary-line' (Kennedy).

mount Hor. This is quite distinct from the mountain of the same name in the Wilderness of Zin, where Aaron died; but no two geographers

8 תְּתָאוּ לָכֶם הֹר הָהָר׃ מֵהֹר הָהָר תְּתָאוּ לְבֹא חֲמָת וְהָיוּ
9 תּוֹצְאֹת הַגְּבֻל צְדָדָה׃ וְיָצָא הַגְּבֻל זִפְרֹנָה וְהָיוּ תוֹצְאֹתָיו
י חֲצַר עֵינָן זֶה־יִהְיֶה לָכֶם גְּבוּל צָפוֹן׃ וְהִתְאַוִּיתֶם לָכֶם
11 לִגְבוּל קֵדְמָה מֵחֲצַר עֵינָן שְׁפָמָה׃ וְיָרַד הַגְּבֻל מִשְּׁפָם
הָרִבְלָה מִקֶּדֶם לָעָיִן וְיָרַד הַגְּבֻל וּמָחָה עַל־כֶּתֶף יָם־
12 כִּנֶּרֶת קֵדְמָה׃ וְיָרַד הַגְּבוּל הַיַּרְדֵּנָה וְהָיוּ תוֹצְאֹתָיו יָם
13 הַמֶּלַח זֹאת תִּהְיֶה לָכֶם הָאָרֶץ לִגְבֻלֹתֶיהָ סָבִיב׃ וַיְצַו
מֹשֶׁה אֶת־בְּנֵי יִשְׂרָאֵל לֵאמֹר זֹאת הָאָרֶץ אֲשֶׁר תִּתְנַחֲלוּ
אֹתָהּ בְּגוֹרָל אֲשֶׁר צִוָּה יְהוָה לָתֵת לְתִשְׁעַת הַמַּטּוֹת
14 וַחֲצִי הַמַּטֶּה׃ כִּי לָקְחוּ מַטֵּה בְנֵי הָרְאוּבֵנִי לְבֵית אֲבֹתָם
וּמַטֵּה בְנֵי־הַגָּדִי לְבֵית אֲבֹתָם וַחֲצִי מַטֵּה מְנַשֶּׁה לָקְחוּ
טו נַחֲלָתָם׃ שְׁנֵי הַמַּטּוֹת וַחֲצִי הַמַּטֶּה לָקְחוּ נַחֲלָתָם מֵעֵבֶר
לְיַרְדֵּן יְרֵחוֹ קֵדְמָה מִזְרָחָה׃ רביעי פ (ששי כשהן מחובר)
16 17 וַיְדַבֵּר יְהוָה אֶל־מֹשֶׁה לֵּאמֹר׃ אֵלֶּה שְׁמוֹת הָאֲנָשִׁים
אֲשֶׁר־יִנְחֲלוּ לָכֶם אֶת־הָאָרֶץ אֶלְעָזָר הַכֹּהֵן וִיהוֹשֻׁעַ בִּן־נוּן׃
18 וְנָשִׂיא אֶחָד נָשִׂיא אֶחָד מִמַּטֶּה תִּקְחוּ לִנְחֹל אֶת־הָאָרֶץ׃

out your line unto mount Hor; 8. from mount Hor ye shall mark out a line unto the entrance to Hamath; and the goings out of the border shall be at Zedad; 9. and the border shall go forth to Ziphron, and the goings out thereof shall be at Hazar-enan; this shall be your north border. 10. And ye shall mark out your line for the east border from Hazar-enan to Shepham; 11. and the border shall go down from Shepham to Riblah, on the east side of Ain; and the border shall go down, and shall strike upon the slope of the sea of Chinnereth eastward; 12. and the border shall go down to the Jordan, and the goings out thereof shall be at the Salt Sea; this shall be your land according to the borders thereof round about.' ¶ 13. And Moses commanded the children of Israel, saying: 'This is the land wherein ye shall receive inheritance by lot, which the LORD hath commanded to give unto the nine tribes, and to the half-tribe; 14. for the tribe of the children of Reuben according to their fathers' houses and the tribe of the children of Gad according to their fathers' houses, have received, and the half-tribe of Manasseh have received, their inheritance; 15. the two tribes and the half-tribe have received their inheritance beyond the Jordan at Jericho eastward, toward the sunrising.'*iv (**vi). ¶ 16. And the LORD spoke unto Moses, saying: 17.'These are the names of the men that shall take possession of the land for you: Eleazar the priest, and Joshua the son of Nun. 18. And ye shall take one prince of every tribe, to take possession of the land. 19. And these are

can be said to agree where it was. Isaacs follows Jewish tradition. He writes: 'If the starting-point of the northern border is the north-eastern corner of the Sea, and the direction of the line is eastward, this line will strike on its way the Mountain of Amanus.'

Targum Jonathan and the Tosefta also identify this Mount Hor with Mount Amanus. Mount Amanus is the modern Giaour Dagh.

8. *the entrance to Hamath.* The Pass across Mount Amanus to the territory of Hamath. Zedad is identified with Baghche Pass.

9. *Ziphron.* Afrin, on the river of the same name.

Hazar-enan. Aintab. This last-named brings us to lands inhabited in ancient times by Hittites. 'Numerous mounds covering the remains of Hittite and other towns attest its former settlement and cultivation' (Sir Chas. Wilson). This accords with Josh. I, 4: 'All the land of the Hittites, and unto the great sea toward the going down of the sun, shall be your border.'

10–12. THE EASTERN BOUNDARY

10. *Shepham.* Apamea, east of the lower valley of the Orontes; now known as Kulat-el-Mudik.

11. *sea of Chinnereth.* Lake of Galilee, or Lake of Tiberias.

16–29. Ten princes are appointed to superintend the allotment of Western Palestine.

19. *and these are the names of the men.* These men were the successors of the 'princes' or heads of the tribes referred to in I, 5–16, also in VII, 12–83. The first three were probably not 'princes', hence they are not given that title.

It was the Divine wish that Caleb though not a 'prince', should be given the honour of being among those who superintend the allotment of Canaan, on account of the distinguished part he had hitherto played in the history of Israel; and the two men mentioned in *v.* 20 and 21 were probably friends of Caleb (Luzzatto).

the names of the men: of the tribe of Judah, Caleb the son of Jephunneh. 20. And of the tribe of the children of Simeon, Shemuel the son of Ammihud. 21. Of the tribe of Benjamin, Elidad the son of Chislon. 22. And of the tribe of the children of Dan a prince, Bukki the son of Jogli. 23. Of the children of Joseph: of the tribe of the children of Manasseh a prince, Hanniel the son of Ephod; 24. and of the tribe of the children of Ephraim a prince, Kemuel the son of Shiphtan. 25. And of the tribe of the children of Zebulun a prince, Elizaphan the son of Parnach. 26. And of the tribe of the children of Issachar a prince, Paltiel the son of Azzan. 27. And of the tribe of the children of Asher a prince, Ahihud the son of Shelomi. 28. And of the tribe of the children of Naphtali a prince, Pedahel the son of Ammihud. 29. These are they whom the Lord commanded to divide the inheritance unto the children of Israel in the land of Canaan.'*v.

19 וְאֵלֶּה שְׁמוֹת הָאֲנָשִׁים לְמַטֵּה יְהוּדָה כָּלֵב בֶּן־יְפֻנֶּה׃
כ 21 וּלְמַטֵּה בְּנֵי שִׁמְעוֹן שְׁמוּאֵל בֶּן־עַמִּיהוּד׃ לְמַטֵּה בִנְיָמִן
22 אֱלִידָד בֶּן־כִּסְלוֹן׃ וּלְמַטֵּה בְנֵי־דָן נָשִׂיא בֻּקִּי בֶּן־יָגְלִי׃
23 לִבְנֵי יוֹסֵף לְמַטֵּה בְנֵי־מְנַשֶּׁה נָשִׂיא חַנִּיאֵל בֶּן־אֵפֹד׃
24 כה וּלְמַטֵּה בְנֵי־אֶפְרַיִם נָשִׂיא קְמוּאֵל בֶּן־שִׁפְטָן׃ וּלְמַטֵּה
26 בְנֵי־זְבוּלֻן נָשִׂיא אֱלִיצָפָן בֶּן־פַּרְנָךְ׃ וּלְמַטֵּה בְנֵי־יִשָּׂשכָר
27 נָשִׂיא פַּלְטִיאֵל בֶּן־עַזָּן׃ וּלְמַטֵּה בְנֵי־אָשֵׁר נָשִׂיא אֲחִיהוּד
28 בֶּן־שְׁלֹמִי׃ וּלְמַטֵּה בְנֵי־נַפְתָּלִי נָשִׂיא פְּדַהְאֵל בֶּן־עַמִּיהוּד׃
29 חמישי אֵלֶּה אֲשֶׁר צִוָּה יְהוָה לְנַחֵל אֶת־בְּנֵי־יִשְׂרָאֵל בְּאֶרֶץ כְּנָעַן׃ פ

35 CHAPTER XXXV

1. And the LORD spoke unto Moses in the plains of Moab by the Jordan at Jericho, saying: 2. 'Command the children of Israel, that they give unto the Levites of the inheritance of their possession cities to dwell in; and open land round about the cities shall ye give unto the Levites. 3. And the cities shall they have to dwell in; and their open land shall be for their cattle, and for their substance, and for all their beasts. 4. And the open land about the cities, which ye shall give unto the Levites, shall be from the wall of the city and outward a thousand cubits round about. 5. And ye shall measure without the city for the east side two thousand cubits, and for the south side two thousand cubits, and for the west side

לה CAP. XXXV. לה

א וַיְדַבֵּר יְהוָה אֶל־מֹשֶׁה בְּעַרְבֹת מוֹאָב עַל־יַרְדֵּן יְרֵחוֹ
2 לֵאמֹר׃ צַו אֶת־בְּנֵי יִשְׂרָאֵל וְנָתְנוּ לַלְוִיִּם מִנַּחֲלַת אֲחֻזָּתָם
עָרִים לָשָׁבֶת וּמִגְרָשׁ לֶעָרִים סְבִיבֹתֵיהֶם תִּתְּנוּ לַלְוִיִּם׃
3 וְהָיוּ הֶעָרִים לָהֶם לָשָׁבֶת וּמִגְרְשֵׁיהֶם יִהְיוּ לִבְהֶמְתָּם
4 וְלִרְכֻשָׁם וּלְכֹל חַיָּתָם׃ וּמִגְרְשֵׁי הֶעָרִים אֲשֶׁר תִּתְּנוּ
ה לַלְוִיִּם מִקִּיר הָעִיר וָחוּצָה אֶלֶף אַמָּה סָבִיב׃ וּמַדֹּתֶם
מִחוּץ לָעִיר אֶת־פְּאַת־קֵדְמָה אַלְפַּיִם בָּאַמָּה וְאֶת־פְּאַת־נֶגֶב

CHAPTER XXXV

LEVITICAL CITIES AND CITIES OF REFUGE. 1–8. LEVITICAL CITIES

Forty-eight cities, with a portion of land attached to each, are to be set aside for the support of the Levites. The carrying into effect of this law is given in Josh. XXI. 'The purpose of this institution seems to be the following. The tribe consecrated to God's service shall, through its equal distribution among the other tribes, be enabled to labour among them for the cause of God; guide those that seek instruction in His Law: and at the same time be saved from utter dispersion by living together in family groups in the Levitical cities. Such distribution among the other tribes was further rendered necessary by the fact that the maintenance of the Levites depended on the tithes, given by the people' (Dillmann). According to Rabbinic tradition, the institution of Levitical cities ceased with the destruction of the first Temple.

2. *cities to dwell in.* The Levites were to have the right to dwell in those cities, but the possession of these cities was vested in the tribe in whose territory the particular city was situated.

open land. Or, 'suburbs.' 'An area consisting of an open space round about the city, serving to beautify it. It was not permitted to build houses there, nor to plant vineyards or to sow a plantation' (Rashi).

5. *two thousand cubits.* From the house of the city ('the city being in the midst'). The first thousand cubits for 'open land'; and the other, for fields and vineyards (Rashi): or, the whole 2,000 cubits for a 'common' (Luzzatto).

two thousand cubits, and for the north side two thousand cubits, the city being in the midst. This shall be to them the open land about the cities. 6. And the cities which ye shall give unto the Levites, they shall be the six cities of refuge, which ye shall give for the manslayer to flee thither; and beside them ye shall give forty and two cities. 7. All the cities which ye shall give to the Levites shall be forty and eight cities: them shall ye give with the open land about them. 8. And concerning the cities which ye shall give of the possession of the children of Israel, from the many ye shall take many, and from the few ye shall take few; each tribe according to its inheritance which it inheriteth shall give of its cities unto the Levites.'*vi (**vii). ¶ 9. And the LORD spoke unto Moses, saying: 10. 'Speak unto the children of Israel, and say unto them: When ye pass over the Jordan into the land of Canaan, 11. then ye shall appoint you cities to be cities of refuge for you, that the manslayer that killeth any person through error may flee thither. 12. And the cities shall be unto you for refuge from the avenger, that the manslayer die not, until he stand before the congregation for judgment. 13. And as to the cities which ye shall give, there shall be for you six cities of refuge. 14. Ye shall give three cities beyond the Jordan, and three cities shall ye give in the land of Canaan; they shall be cities

אַלְפַּיִם בָּאַמָּה וְאֶת־פְּאַת־יָם ׀ אַלְפַּיִם בָּאַמָּה וְאֵת פְּאַת
צָפוֹן אַלְפַּיִם בָּאַמָּה וְהָעִיר בַּתָּוֶךְ זֶה יִהְיֶה לָהֶם מִגְרְשֵׁי
6 הֶעָרִים׃ וְאֵת הֶעָרִים אֲשֶׁר תִּתְּנוּ לַלְוִיִּם אֵת שֵׁשׁ־עָרֵי
הַמִּקְלָט אֲשֶׁר תִּתְּנוּ לָנֻס שָׁמָּה הָרֹצֵחַ וַעֲלֵיהֶם תִּתְּנוּ
7 אַרְבָּעִים וּשְׁתַּיִם עִיר׃ כָּל־הֶעָרִים אֲשֶׁר תִּתְּנוּ לַלְוִיִּם
8 אַרְבָּעִים וּשְׁמֹנֶה עִיר אֶתְהֶן וְאֶת־מִגְרְשֵׁיהֶן׃ וְהֶעָרִים
אֲשֶׁר תִּתְּנוּ מֵאֲחֻזַּת בְּנֵי־יִשְׂרָאֵל מֵאֵת הָרַב תַּרְבּוּ וּמֵאֵת
הַמְעַט תַּמְעִיטוּ אִישׁ כְּפִי נַחֲלָתוֹ אֲשֶׁר יִנְחָלוּ יִתֵּן
מֵעָרָיו לַלְוִיִּם׃ * ששי פ (שביעי כשהן מחוב׳)
9 וַיְדַבֵּר יְהוָה אֶל־מֹשֶׁה לֵּאמֹר׃ דַּבֵּר אֶל־בְּנֵי יִשְׂרָאֵל
וְאָמַרְתָּ אֲלֵהֶם כִּי אַתֶּם עֹבְרִים אֶת־הַיַּרְדֵּן אַרְצָה כְּנָעַן׃
11 וְהִקְרִיתֶם לָכֶם עָרִים עָרֵי מִקְלָט תִּהְיֶינָה לָכֶם וְנָס שָׁמָּה
12 רֹצֵחַ מַכֵּה־נֶפֶשׁ בִּשְׁגָגָה׃ וְהָיוּ לָכֶם הֶעָרִים לְמִקְלָט
מִגֹּאֵל וְלֹא יָמוּת הָרֹצֵחַ עַד־עָמְדוֹ לִפְנֵי הָעֵדָה לַמִּשְׁפָּט׃
13 וְהֶעָרִים אֲשֶׁר תִּתֵּנוּ שֵׁשׁ־עָרֵי מִקְלָט תִּהְיֶינָה לָכֶם׃

v. 5. סבירין לכם v. 8. קמץ בז״ק

6. *cities of refuge.* Places of asylum to shelter the involuntary homicide, see *v.* 9–15. Levitical cities were selected for this purpose; both because they were regarded as having a sacred character, and because they were inhabited by men who could decide in doubtful cases between wilful murder and accidental homicide.

8. *from the many.* The more populous the tribe, the more cities they were to provide for the Levites. East of the Jordan, the Levites had ten such cities, and in Canaan proper 38. The principle of proportionate giving was not literally carried out; the criterion was not the number of the cities given but rather their importance (Nachmanides).

9–15. CITIES OF REFUGE

Six cities of refuge, three on either side of the Jordan, are to be set aside as places of asylum for accidental homicides. Nor did the six Cities of Refuge always need to remain the same. Others might be substituted, provided their situation conformed to the Biblical law with regard to distances and geographical position.

11. *shall appoint you.* lit. 'cause to happen'; *i.e.* make ready, prepare.

may flee thither. Any one guilty of unpremeditated taking of human life could escape to one of these cities and find shelter and protection.

12. *from the avenger.* Heb. *goel*, more usually, *goel haddam*, lit. 'the avenger of blood'; 'redeemer.' It refers to the nearest representative of the family of the slain man, whose duty it was to 'vindicate' the death of the victim. In primitive society, if one member of a family was murdered, an intolerable shame rested upon the family until 'satisfaction' had been inflicted on the manslayer at the hands of the 'redeemer', or avenger of the family honour. It was the sacred aim of the Mosaic legislation to take the decision of the guilt or innocence of the manslayer out of the hands of the 'avenger', and assign it to an impartial tribunal.

before the congregation. The tribunal of elders and judges appointed by the community to which the homicide belongs. In later times, it was understood to refer to a duly constituted Sanhedrin.

14. *cities.* These six cities are specified in Josh. xx, 1–9. Moses in his lifetime set aside three cities for the two and a half tribes on the eastern side of the Jordan, as their land, especially

14 אֵת ׀ שְׁלֹשׁ הֶעָרִים תִּתְּנוּ מֵעֵבֶר לַיַּרְדֵּן וְאֵת שְׁלֹשׁ הֶעָרִים
טו תִּתְּנוּ בְּאֶרֶץ כְּנָעַן עָרֵי מִקְלָט תִּהְיֶינָה׃ לִבְנֵי יִשְׂרָאֵל
וְלַגֵּר וְלַתּוֹשָׁב בְּתוֹכָם תִּהְיֶינָה שֵׁשׁ־הֶעָרִים הָאֵלֶּה לְמִקְלָט
16 לָנוּס שָׁמָּה כָּל־מַכֵּה־נֶפֶשׁ בִּשְׁגָגָה׃ וְאִם־בִּכְלִי בַרְזֶל ׀
17 הִכָּהוּ וַיָּמֹת רֹצֵחַ הוּא מוֹת יוּמַת הָרֹצֵחַ׃ וְאִם בְּאֶבֶן יָד
אֲשֶׁר־יָמוּת בָּהּ הִכָּהוּ וַיָּמֹת רֹצֵחַ הוּא מוֹת יוּמַת הָרֹצֵחַ׃
18 אוֹ בִּכְלִי עֵץ־יָד אֲשֶׁר־יָמוּת בּוֹ הִכָּהוּ וַיָּמֹת רֹצֵחַ הוּא
19 מוֹת יוּמַת הָרֹצֵחַ׃ גֹּאֵל הַדָּם הוּא יָמִית אֶת־הָרֹצֵחַ
כ בְּפִגְעוֹ־בוֹ הוּא יְמִתֶנּוּ׃ וְאִם־בְּשִׂנְאָה יֶהְדֳּפֶנּוּ אוֹ־הִשְׁלִיךְ
21 עָלָיו בִּצְדִיָּה וַיָּמֹת׃ אוֹ בְאֵיבָה הִכָּהוּ בְיָדוֹ וַיָּמֹת מוֹת־
יוּמַת הַמַּכֶּה רֹצֵחַ הוּא גֹּאֵל הַדָּם יָמִית אֶת־הָרֹצֵחַ בְּפִגְעוֹ־
22 בוֹ׃ וְאִם־בְּפֶתַע בְּלֹא־אֵיבָה הֲדָפוֹ אוֹ־הִשְׁלִיךְ עָלָיו כָּל־
23 כְּלִי בְּלֹא צְדִיָּה׃ אוֹ בְכָל־אֶבֶן אֲשֶׁר־יָמוּת בָּהּ בְּלֹא רְאוֹת
וַיַּפֵּל עָלָיו וַיָּמֹת וְהוּא לֹא־אוֹיֵב לוֹ וְלֹא מְבַקֵּשׁ רָעָתוֹ׃

of refuge. 15. For the children of Israel, and for the stranger and for the settler among them, shall these six cities be for refuge, that every one that killeth any person through error may flee thither. 16. But if he smote him with an instrument of iron, so that he died, he is a murderer; the murderer shall surely be put to death. 17. And if he smote him with a stone in the hand, whereby a man may die, and he died, he is a murderer; the murderer shall surely be put to death. 18. Or if he smote him with a weapon of wood in the hand, whereby a man may die, and he died, he is a murderer; the murderer shall surely be put to death. 19. The avenger of blood shall himself put the murderer to death; when he meeteth him, he shall put him to death. 20. And if he thrust him of hatred, or hurled at him any thing, lying in wait, so that he died; 21. or in enmity smote him with his hand, that he died; he that smote him shall surely be put to death: he is a murderer; the avenger of blood shall put the murderer to death when he meeteth him. 22. But if he thrust him suddenly without enmity, or hurled upon him any thing without lying in wait, 23. or with any stone, whereby a man may die, seeing him not, and cast it upon him, so that he died, and he was not

Gilead, was wild border country, and homicide was more frequent there than in Western Palestine. The other three cities were set aside by Joshua.

15. *for the stranger.* Heb. *ger;* the resident alien. The Cities of Refuge were to be for everyone, including both the resident alien and the non-Israelite who was making but a temporary stay in the land of Israel. 'All human life is holy (Exod. XXI, 12), and no innocent blood should be suffered to be shed. Homeborn and stranger alike, therefore, shall have one law in regard to asylum' (Dillmann).

through error. Or, 'unwittingly.' The benefit of asylum is to be limited to unintentional homicides. In ancient Greece and Rome, shrines that gave asylum to murderers were nurseries of criminals. In the time of Tiberius, the swarms of desperadoes at shrines had become so dangerous that the right was limited to a few cities. Conditions were not much better when the Medieval Church began to offer 'sanctuary' to criminals of every description. The Torah alone forbade the granting of protection to the wilful offender. 'If a man come presumptuously upon his neighbour to slay him with guile, thou shalt take him from mine altar that he may die' (Exod. XXI, 14). Even if it was a priest who officiated at the Altar, says the Talmud, he is not to escape punishment, if his act was other than unintentional homicide.

16–23. DISTINCTION BETWEEN MURDER AND MANSLAUGHTER

16. *instrument of iron.* As the fundamental distinction is one of *intention,* everything depends upon the weapon used.

17. *whereby a man may die.* Capable of inflicting a mortal wound.

19. *he shall put him to death.* As he was guilty of deliberate murder, the 'avenger of blood' shall put him to death, even within one of the Cities of Refuge.

20. *if he thrust him of hatred.* Further illustrations of cases of wilful murder. 'Thrust him' means that he pushed him over a cliff, or off the roof of a house.

22. *without enmity.* An explanation of the phrase 'killing a person through error'. The main criterion is the absence of motive. The Rabbis distinguished three grades in unpremeditated homicide: (1) grave carelessness; (2) contributory negligence; (3) complete innocence. Only in case of the second is exile to the Cities of Refuge prescribed. Complete innocence needs no atonement; and for grave carelessness, exile was not deemed a sufficient punishment.

24 וְשָׁפְטוּ הָעֵדָה בֵּין הַמַּכֶּה וּבֵין גֹּאֵל הַדָּם עַל הַמִּשְׁפָּטִים
כה הָאֵלֶּה׃ וְהִצִּילוּ הָעֵדָה אֶת־הָרֹצֵחַ מִיַּד גֹּאֵל הַדָּם וְהֵשִׁיבוּ
אֹתוֹ הָעֵדָה אֶל־עִיר מִקְלָטוֹ אֲשֶׁר־נָס שָׁמָּה וְיָשַׁב בָּהּ עַד־
26 מוֹת הַכֹּהֵן הַגָּדֹל אֲשֶׁר־מָשַׁח אֹתוֹ בְּשֶׁמֶן הַקֹּדֶשׁ׃ וְאִם־
יָצֹא יֵצֵא הָרֹצֵחַ אֶת־גְּבוּל עִיר מִקְלָטוֹ אֲשֶׁר יָנוּס שָׁמָּה׃
27 וּמָצָא אֹתוֹ גֹּאֵל הַדָּם מִחוּץ לִגְבוּל עִיר מִקְלָטוֹ וְרָצַח
28 גֹּאֵל הַדָּם אֶת־הָרֹצֵחַ אֵין לוֹ דָּם׃ כִּי בְעִיר מִקְלָטוֹ יֵשֵׁב
עַד־מוֹת הַכֹּהֵן הַגָּדֹל וְאַחֲרֵי מוֹת הַכֹּהֵן הַגָּדֹל יָשׁוּב הָרֹצֵחַ
29 אֶל־אֶרֶץ אֲחֻזָּתוֹ׃ וְהָיוּ אֵלֶּה לָכֶם לְחֻקַּת מִשְׁפָּט לְדֹרֹתֵיכֶם
ל בְּכֹל מוֹשְׁבֹתֵיכֶם׃ כָּל־מַכֵּה־נֶפֶשׁ לְפִי עֵדִים יִרְצַח אֶת־
31 הָרֹצֵחַ וְעֵד אֶחָד לֹא־יַעֲנֶה בְנֶפֶשׁ לָמוּת׃ וְלֹא־תִקְחוּ כֹפֶר
32 לְנֶפֶשׁ רֹצֵחַ אֲשֶׁר־הוּא רָשָׁע לָמוּת כִּי־מוֹת יוּמָת׃ וְלֹא־

his enemy, neither sought his harm; 24. then the congregation shall judge between the smiter and the avenger of blood according to these ordinances; 25. and the congregation shall deliver the manslayer out of the hand of the avenger of blood, and the congregation shall restore him to his city of refuge, whither he was fled; and he shall dwell therein until the death of the high priest, who was anointed with the holy oil. 26. But if the manslayer shall at any time go beyond the border of his city of refuge, whither he fleeth; 27. and the avenger of blood find him without the border of his city of refuge, and the avenger of blood slay the manslayer; there shall be no bloodguiltiness for him; 28. because he must remain in his city of refuge until the death of the high priest; but after the death of the high priest the manslayer may return into the land of his possession. 29. And these things shall be for a statute of judgment unto you throughout your generations in all your dwellings. 30. Whoso killeth any person, the murderer shall be slain at the mouth of witnesses; but one witness shall not testify against any person that he die. 31. Moreover ye shall take no ransom for

24–29. Legal Procedure in the Case of Accidental Homicide

24. *the congregation.* The tribunal of elders and judges appointed by the congregation.

according to these ordinances. i.e. their decision shall be guided by, and based upon, the regulations and conditions laid down in this chapter.

25. *shall restore him.* They shall send him back under safe escort to the City in which he had taken refuge until the time of the trial. The Asylum, however, is not only a place of protection, but of expiation. 'The condemned must not leave the Asylum under any circumstances, and the consciousness of having taken a human life must never be out of the mind of the homicide' (Talmud).

death of the high priest. Like that of a king, it represented a definite landmark in the national life. And as Asylum was connected with the Altar of the Central Sanctuary and with Cities of the Levites, it was but natural that the death of the High Priest, and not that of the king, should have been selected as the date terminating the exile of the unfortunate manslayer (Dillmann).

Various other explanations have been given as to why the death of the High Priest should be the signal for giving the homicide his freedom. Maimonides thinks that the death of the High Priest was an event that moved the entire people so much that no thoughts of vengeance could arise in the avenger of blood. According to the Talmud, the High Priest should by the power of prayer have made such a calamity as murder an impossibility in Israel. That he had not succeeded in doing so, was a proof that he had failed in his duty. Hence he had to bear the penalty of knowing how welcome his death would be to the man exiled to a City of Refuge!

29. *a statute of judgment.* See on XXVII, 11.

30–34. Concerning Murder

These regulations emphasize the extreme sacredness of human life. 'In ancient custom, loss of life could be compensated for by the death of *any* member of the manslayer's family. Here the Law insists that the murderer only is to forfeit his life' (Gray). Murder, furthermore, is such a heinous crime that it cannot be atoned for by the payment of a money-fine; and not even the man who has unintentionally killed another shall purchase his release from the City of Refuge before the death of the High Priest.

30. *at the mouth of witnesses.* It was stated in *v.* 16–18 that a man guilty of wilful murder should be put to death. The present *v.* and the one following tell us that the tribunal may only carry out the death-sentence if the murder is attested by two witnesses.

31. *no ransom for the life of a murderer.* The wilful murderer cannot have his death-sentence commuted by a money payment. The Rabbis rightly deduced from this wording, that other injuries *could* be thus compounded for; see p. 405.

the life of a murderer, that is guilty of death; but he shall surely be put to death. 32. And ye shall take no ransom for him that is fled to his city of refuge, that he should come again to dwell in the land, until the death of the priest. 33. So ye shall not pollute the land wherein ye are; for blood, it polluteth the land; and no expiation can be made for the land for the blood that is shed therein, but by the blood of him that shed it. 34. And thou shalt not defile the land which ye inhabit, in the midst of which I dwell; for I the LORD dwell in the midst of the children of Israel.'*vii.

36 CHAPTER XXXVI

1. And the heads of the fathers' houses of the family of the children of Gilead, the son of Machir, the son of Manasseh, of the families of the sons of Joseph, came near, and spoke before Moses, and before the princes, the heads of the fathers' houses of the children of Israel; 2. and they said: 'The LORD commanded my lord to give the land for inheritance by lot to the children of Israel; and my lord was commanded by the LORD to give the inheritance of Zelophehad our brother unto his daughters. 3. And if they be married to any of the sons of the other tribes of the children of Israel, then will their inheritance be taken away from the inheritance of our fathers, and will be added to the inheritance of the tribe whereunto they shall belong; so will it be taken away from the lot of our inheritance. 4. And when the jubilee of the children of Israel shall be, then will their

תִקְחוּ כֹפֶר לָנוּס אֶל־עִיר מִקְלָטוֹ לָשׁוּב לָשֶׁבֶת בָּאָרֶץ
33 עַד־מוֹת הַכֹּהֵן׃ וְלֹא־תַחֲנִיפוּ אֶת־הָאָרֶץ אֲשֶׁר אַתֶּם בָּהּ
כִּי הַדָּם הוּא יַחֲנִיף אֶת־הָאָרֶץ וְלָאָרֶץ לֹא־יְכֻפַּר לַדָּם
34 אֲשֶׁר שֻׁפַּךְ־בָּהּ כִּי־אִם בְּדַם שֹׁפְכוֹ׃ וְלֹא תְטַמֵּא אֶת־
הָאָרֶץ אֲשֶׁר אַתֶּם יֹשְׁבִים בָּהּ אֲשֶׁר אֲנִי שֹׁכֵן בְּתוֹכָהּ כִּי
אֲנִי יְהוָה שֹׁכֵן בְּתוֹךְ בְּנֵי יִשְׂרָאֵל׃ * פ שביעי

לו CAP. XXXVI. לו

א וַיִּקְרְבוּ רָאשֵׁי הָאָבוֹת לְמִשְׁפַּחַת בְּנֵי־גִלְעָד בֶּן־מָכִיר בֶּן־
מְנַשֶּׁה מִמִּשְׁפְּחֹת בְּנֵי יוֹסֵף וַיְדַבְּרוּ לִפְנֵי מֹשֶׁה וְלִפְנֵי
2 הַנְּשִׂאִים רָאשֵׁי אָבוֹת לִבְנֵי יִשְׂרָאֵל׃ וַיֹּאמְרוּ אֶת־אֲדֹנִי
צִוָּה יְהוָה לָתֵת אֶת־הָאָרֶץ בְּנַחֲלָה בְּגוֹרָל לִבְנֵי יִשְׂרָאֵל
וַאדֹנִי צֻוָּה בַיהוָה לָתֵת אֶת־נַחֲלַת צְלָפְחָד אָחִינוּ לִבְנֹתָיו׃
3 וְהָיוּ לְאֶחָד מִבְּנֵי שִׁבְטֵי בְנֵי־יִשְׂרָאֵל לְנָשִׁים וְנִגְרְעָה
נַחֲלָתָן מִנַּחֲלַת אֲבֹתֵינוּ וְנוֹסַף עַל נַחֲלַת הַמַּטֶּה אֲשֶׁר
4 תִּהְיֶינָה לָהֶם וּמִגֹּרַל נַחֲלָתֵנוּ יִגָּרֵעַ׃ וְאִם־יִהְיֶה הַיֹּבֵל

32. *fled to his city of refuge.* Neither can the homicide escape exile by a ransom.

33. *ye shall not pollute the land.* The Heb. root חנף means, to act wickedly, to profane, or pollute. If such redemption-money were permitted, human life would be cheapened, and the land would become wholly corrupt.

for blood, it polluteth the land. See Lev. XVIII, 25; Psalm CVI, 38.

34. *for I the LORD dwell in . . . Israel.* Because God dwells in the midst of Israel, therefore Israel and Israel's Land must be undefiled by violence and unholiness. The idea of God's dwelling in the midst of Israel has been epitomized by the Rabbis in the one word *Shechinah; i.e.* God's Indwelling Presence.

CHAPTER XXXVI. LAW OF HEIRESSES

In XXVII, 1–11, the law was laid down that permitted daughters to inherit property in the absence of male issue. But there was a danger that if such heiresses married men belonging to other tribes, their inheritance might pass out of their particular tribe. To guard against this contingency, the ruling in the present chapter is given. The question was raised by the chiefs of the clan of Machir of the half-tribe of Manasseh, whose allotted territory was in Gilead.

1. *fathers' houses.* See on I, 2.

3. *be taken away.* Because their male issue who will be their heirs will be reckoned to the tribe of their father, and thus the property will pass into the possession of another tribe.

4. *the jubilee.* The provisions of the law of Jubilee are given in Lev. XXV. But it was only purchased land that had to be returned to its original owner or his descendant in the Jubilee. Inherited land, such as that belonging to the daughters of Zelophehad, would be outside the provisions of that law; so that, once these women married into another tribe, there was no hope for their property ever returning to their own tribe.

inheritance be added unto the inheritance of the tribe whereunto they shall belong; so will their inheritance be taken away from the inheritance of the tribe of our fathers.' 5. And Moses commanded the children of Israel according to the word of the LORD, saying: 'The tribe of the sons of Joseph speaketh right. 6. This is the thing which the LORD hath commanded concerning the daughters of Zelophehad, saying: Let them be married to whom they think best; only into the family of the tribe of their father shall they be married. 7. So shall no inheritance of the children of Israel remove from tribe to tribe: for the children of Israel shall cleave every one to the inheritance of the tribe of his fathers. 8. And every daughter, that possesseth an inheritance in any tribe of the children of Israel, shall be wife unto one of the family of the tribe of her father, that the children of Israel may possess every man the inheritance of his fathers. 9. So shall no inheritance remove from one tribe to another tribe; for the tribes of the children of Israel shall cleave each one to its own inheritance.'*m. 10. Even as the LORD commanded Moses, so did the daughters of Zelophehad.*m s. 11. For Mahlah, Tirzah, and Hoglah, and Milcah, and Noah, the daughters of Zelophehad, were married unto their father's brothers' sons. 12. They were married into the families of the sons of Manasseh the son of Joseph, and their inheritance remained in the tribe of the family of their father. ¶ 13. These are the commandments and the ordinances, which the LORD commanded by the hand of Moses unto the children of Israel in the plains of Moab by the Jordan at Jericho.

לִבְנֵי יִשְׂרָאֵל וְנוֹסְפָה נַחֲלָתָן עַל נַחֲלַת הַמַּטֶּה אֲשֶׁר
ה תִּהְיֶינָה לָהֶם וּמִנַּחֲלַת מַטֵּה אֲבֹתֵינוּ יִגָּרַע נַחֲלָתָן׃ וַיְצַו
מֹשֶׁה אֶת־בְּנֵי יִשְׂרָאֵל עַל־פִּי יְהוָה לֵאמֹר כֵּן מַטֵּה בְנֵי־
6 יוֹסֵף דֹּבְרִים׃ זֶה הַדָּבָר אֲשֶׁר־צִוָּה יְהוָה לִבְנוֹת צְלָפְחָד
לֵאמֹר לַטּוֹב בְּעֵינֵיהֶם תִּהְיֶינָה לְנָשִׁים אַךְ לְמִשְׁפַּחַת
7 מַטֵּה אֲבִיהֶם תִּהְיֶינָה לְנָשִׁים׃ וְלֹא־תִסֹּב נַחֲלָה לִבְנֵי
יִשְׂרָאֵל מִמַּטֶּה אֶל־מַטֶּה כִּי אִישׁ בְּנַחֲלַת מַטֵּה אֲבֹתָיו
8 יִדְבְּקוּ בְּנֵי יִשְׂרָאֵל׃ וְכָל־בַּת יֹרֶשֶׁת נַחֲלָה מִמַּטּוֹת בְּנֵי
יִשְׂרָאֵל לְאֶחָד מִמִּשְׁפַּחַת מַטֵּה אָבִיהָ תִּהְיֶה לְאִשָּׁה לְמַעַן
9 יִירְשׁוּ בְּנֵי יִשְׂרָאֵל אִישׁ נַחֲלַת אֲבֹתָיו׃ וְלֹא־תִסֹּב נַחֲלָה
מִמַּטֶּה לְמַטֶּה אַחֵר כִּי־אִישׁ בְּנַחֲלָתוֹ יִדְבְּקוּ מַטּוֹת בְּנֵי
מפטיר (מפטיר לספ') י יִשְׂרָאֵל׃ *כַּאֲשֶׁר צִוָּה יְהוָה אֶת־מֹשֶׁה כֵּן עָשׂוּ בְּנוֹת צְלָפְחָד׃ *
11 וַתִּהְיֶינָה מַחְלָה תִרְצָה וְחָגְלָה וּמִלְכָּה וְנֹעָה בְּנוֹת צְלָפְחָד
12 לִבְנֵי דֹדֵיהֶן לְנָשִׁים׃ מִמִּשְׁפְּחֹת בְּנֵי־מְנַשֶּׁה בֶן־יוֹסֵף הָיוּ
13 לְנָשִׁים וַתְּהִי נַחֲלָתָן עַל־מַטֵּה מִשְׁפַּחַת אֲבִיהֶן׃ אֵלֶּה
הַמִּצְוֹת וְהַמִּשְׁפָּטִים אֲשֶׁר צִוָּה יְהוָה בְּיַד־מֹשֶׁה אֶל־בְּנֵי
יִשְׂרָאֵל בְּעַרְבֹת מוֹאָב עַל יַרְדֵּן יְרֵחוֹ׃

חזק

סכום פסוקי דספר במדבר אלף ומאתים ושמנים ושמנה. ארפח
סימן: וחציו והיה האיש אשר אבחר בו מטהו יפרח: ופרשיותיו
עשרה יי' בדד ינחנו סימן: וסדריו שנים ושלשים. לב טהור
ברא לי אלהים סימן: ופרקיו ששה ושלשים. לו חכמו ישכילו
זאת סימן: מניין הפתוחות שתים ותשעים. והסתומות ששים
ושש. הכל מאה וחמשים ושמנה פרשיות. אני חלקך
ונחלתך סימן:

12. *remained in the tribe.* Thus each tribe preserved its own full inheritance.

13. *these are the commandments.* The subscription to the laws in XXII–XXXVI.

The Massoretic Note states the number of verses in the Book of Numbers to be 1,288; its Sedrahs (parshiyoth) 10; its Sedarim, smaller divisions according to the Triennial Cycle, 32; and its Chapters, 36.

HAFTORAH MASSEY הפטרת מסעי

JEREMIAH II, 4–28; III, 4; IV, 1–2

CHAPTER II

4. Hear ye the word of the LORD, O house of Jacob,
And all the families of the house of Israel;
5. Thus saith the LORD:
What unrighteousness have your fathers found in Me,
That they are gone far from Me,
And have walked after things of nought, and are become nought?
6. Neither said they:
'Where is the LORD that brought us up
Out of the land of Egypt;
That led us through the wilderness,
Through a land of deserts and of pits,
Through a land of drought and of the shadow of death,
Through a land that no man passed through,
And where no man dwelt?'
7. And I brought you into a land of fruitful fields,
To eat the fruit thereof and the good thereof;
But when ye entered, ye defiled My land,
And made My heritage an abomination.
8. The priests said not: 'Where is the LORD?'
And they that handle the law knew Me not,

CAP. II. ב

4 שִׁמְעוּ דְבַר־יְהוָה בֵּית
ה יַעֲקֹב וְכָל־מִשְׁפְּחוֹת בֵּית יִשְׂרָאֵל׃ כֹּה ׀ אָמַר יְהוָה מַה־
מָּצְאוּ אֲבוֹתֵיכֶם בִּי עָוֶל כִּי רָחֲקוּ מֵעָלָי וַיֵּלְכוּ אַחֲרֵי
6 הַהֶבֶל וַיֶּהְבָּלוּ׃ וְלֹא אָמְרוּ אַיֵּה יְהוָה הַמַּעֲלֶה אֹתָנוּ מֵאֶרֶץ
מִצְרָיִם הַמּוֹלִיךְ אֹתָנוּ בַּמִּדְבָּר בְּאֶרֶץ עֲרָבָה וְשׁוּחָה
בְּאֶרֶץ צִיָּה וְצַלְמָוֶת בְּאֶרֶץ לֹא־עָבַר בָּהּ אִישׁ וְלֹא־יָשַׁב
7 אָדָם שָׁם׃ וָאָבִיא אֶתְכֶם אֶל־אֶרֶץ הַכַּרְמֶל לֶאֱכֹל פִּרְיָהּ
וְטוּבָהּ וַתָּבֹאוּ וַתְּטַמְּאוּ אֶת־אַרְצִי וְנַחֲלָתִי שַׂמְתֶּם לְתוֹעֵבָה׃
8 הַכֹּהֲנִים לֹא אָמְרוּ אַיֵּה יְהוָה וְתֹפְשֵׂי הַתּוֹרָה לֹא יְדָעוּנִי
וְהָרֹעִים פָּשְׁעוּ בִי וְהַנְּבִיאִים נִבְּאוּ בַבַּעַל וְאַחֲרֵי לֹא־

And the rulers transgressed against Me;
The prophets also prophesied by Baal,
And walked after things that do not profit.

For Jeremiah and his times, as well as the reason for the selection of this chapter for this Sabbath, see the introductory notes on the preceding Haftorah.

II, 4–13. ISRAEL'S INGRATITUDE IN RETURN FOR GOD'S LOVE

4. *hear . . . Jacob . . . Israel.* Jeremiah addresses the nation as a whole.

5. *what unrighteousness.* A rhetorical question. They have found no unrighteousness in Him. Their unfaithfulness to Him has been and is without any reason.

things of nought. Nothingness, folly; denoting the utter futility of idols and idol-worship.

and are become nought. In character and in power. Men's characters become assimilated to the follies which they worship.

6–7. The people's unfaithfulness is rendered more vivid by the reminder in strong colours, of its deliverance from Egyptian bondage, and its preservation from the dangers and terrors of the wilderness.

6. *shadow of death.* Or, 'deep darkness' (RV Margin). 'Just as in the deep darkness men cannot see their way and stray blindly hither and thither, so in the trackless desert they may easily lose themselves, and wander in bewilderment' (Peake).

7. *a land of fruitful fields.* lit. 'a garden land'; a land of fields, vineyards and well-wooded spaces (Kimchi).

ye defiled. By idol-worship.

My heritage. The land I selected for My Divine purpose (Kimchi).

an abomination. By imitating the savage and immoral practices for which the old inhabitants of Canaan were driven out.

8. *the priests said not, Where is the LORD?* They were indifferent to God's will, and thought of nothing less than consulting Him (Streane).

they that handle the law. Those who administer it.

knew Me not. Showed by their conduct they that knew not God's ways.

the rulers. lit. 'the shepherds'; *i.e.* the kings.

the prophets. Members of the Prophetic guilds. Their duty was to urge the people to reform and bring them back to the sense of God, but they had themselves become affected by the prevailing apostasy.

things that do not profit. Idols, that could be no source of help, hope, or comfort in time of distress.

9 יוֹעִלוּ הָלָכוּ׃ לָכֵן עֹד אָרִיב אִתְּכֶם נְאֻם־יְהוָה וְאֶת־בְּנֵי
י בְנֵיכֶם אָרִיב׃ כִּי עִבְרוּ אִיֵּי כִתִּיִּים וּרְאוּ וְקֵדָר שִׁלְחוּ
11 וְהִתְבּוֹנְנוּ מְאֹד וּרְאוּ הֵן הָיְתָה כָּזֹאת׃ הַהֵימִיר גּוֹי אֱלֹהִים
12 וְהֵמָּה לֹא אֱלֹהִים וְעַמִּי הֵמִיר כְּבוֹדוֹ בְּלוֹא יוֹעִיל׃ שֹׁמּוּ
13 שָׁמַיִם עַל־זֹאת וְשַׂעֲרוּ חָרְבוּ מְאֹד נְאֻם־יְהוָה׃ כִּי־שְׁתַּיִם
רָעוֹת עָשָׂה עַמִּי אֹתִי עָזְבוּ מְקוֹר ׀ מַיִם חַיִּים לַחְצֹב
לָהֶם בֹּארוֹת בֹּארֹת נִשְׁבָּרִים אֲשֶׁר לֹא־יָכִלוּ הַמָּיִם׃
14 הַעֶבֶד יִשְׂרָאֵל אִם־יְלִיד בַּיִת הוּא מַדּוּעַ הָיָה לָבַז׃
טו עָלָיו יִשְׁאֲגוּ כְפִרִים נָתְנוּ קוֹלָם וַיָּשִׁיתוּ אַרְצוֹ לְשַׁמָּה עָרָיו
16 נִצְּתָה מִבְּלִי יֹשֵׁב׃ גַּם־בְּנֵי־נֹף וְתַחְפַּנֵס יִרְעוּךְ קָדְקֹד׃

9. Wherefore I will yet plead with you, saith the LORD,
And with your children's children will I plead.

10. For pass over to the isles of the Kittites, and see,
And send unto Kedar, and consider diligently,
And see if there hath been such a thing.

11. Hath a nation changed its gods,
Which yet are no gods?
But My people hath changed its glory
For that which doth not profit.

12. Be astonished, O ye heavens, at this, and be horribly afraid, be ye exceeding amazed,
Saith the LORD.

13. For My people have committed two evils:
They have forsaken Me, the fountain of living waters,
And hewed them out cisterns, broken cisterns,
That can hold no water.

14. Is Israel a servant?
Is he a home-born slave?
Why is he become a prey?

15. The young lions have roared upon him,
And let their voice resound;
And they have made his land desolate,
His cities are laid waste,
Without inhabitant.

16. The children also of Noph and Tahpanhes
Feed upon the crown of thy head.

v. 14. פתח בס״ם v. 15. נצתו קרי v. 16. ותחפנחס קרי

9. *plead.* Argue, contend.

10. *isles of the Kittites.* Cyprus and the neighbouring islands near the coasts of Greece and Italy.

send unto Kedar. An Arabian tribe, but used for Arabia generally. The meaning of the verse is, Send and inquire West and East.

11. *changed its gods.* No other people, is the complaint of the Prophet, has with such thoughtlessness and lack of character changed its ancestral worship. Heathen nations were loyal to their gods, although these were helpless and unreal: Israel has forsaken the true God for that which is false, useless, and a source of degeneration!

12. *O ye heavens.* When God arraigns His people, the whole of Nature is the appropriate audience; and even inanimate Nature must be shocked and appalled at such crass folly.

13. *fountain of living waters.* 'They have ready at hand fresh living water from streams and fountains—pure, cool, perennial and plentiful. But they with great toil and expense hew out cisterns in the rock and *store* their water in them. This water — flat, stagnant, putrid — they prefer to the running water from the fountain. Moreover, these rock-cisterns were very liable to crack, and in the hour of greatest need their water may utterly fail. No comparison could more keenly rebuke the madness of a people who changed their glory for that which doth not profit' (Peake-Thomson).

14–17. ISRAEL'S SIN AND CONSEQUENT CALAMITIES

Not only for her idolatry and ingratitude, but for her faithlessness in relying on Assyria and Egypt, will Judah be punished; see on *v.* 18.

14. *is Israel a servant . . . slave?* Israel is not a slave but a son.

why is he become a prey? How is it then that he has become a slave to neighbouring powers who have despoiled him? The answer is in the next *v.*

15. *the young lions.* Israel's enemies, especially the Assyrians.

16. *the children also of Noph and Tahpanhes.* *i.e.* Egypt, to whom many looked for help.

Noph. Memphis, the capital of Northern Egypt.

17 הֲלוֹא־זֹאת תַּעֲשֶׂה־לָּךְ עָזְבֵךְ אֶת־יְהוָה אֱלֹהַיִךְ בְּעֵת
18 מוֹלִכֵךְ בַּדָּרֶךְ׃ וְעַתָּה מַה־לָּךְ לְדֶרֶךְ מִצְרַיִם לִשְׁתּוֹת
19 מֵי שִׁחוֹר וּמַה־לָּךְ לְדֶרֶךְ אַשּׁוּר לִשְׁתּוֹת מֵי נָהָר׃ תְּיַסְּרֵךְ
רָעָתֵךְ וּמְשֻׁבוֹתַיִךְ תּוֹכִחֻךְ וּדְעִי וּרְאִי כִּי־רַע וָמָר עָזְבֵךְ
אֶת־יְהוָה אֱלֹהָיִךְ וְלֹא פַחְדָּתִי אֵלַיִךְ נְאֻם־אֲדֹנָי יֱהוִה
כ צְבָאוֹת׃ כִּי מֵעוֹלָם שָׁבַרְתִּי עֻלֵּךְ נִתַּקְתִּי מוֹסְרוֹתַיִךְ
וַתֹּאמְרִי לֹא אֶעֱבוֹד כִּי עַל־כָּל־גִּבְעָה גְּבֹהָה וְתַחַת כָּל־
21 עֵץ רַעֲנָן אַתְּ צֹעָה זֹנָה׃ וְאָנֹכִי נְטַעְתִּיךְ שׂוֹרֵק כֻּלֹּה זֶרַע

17. Is it not this that doth cause it unto thee,
That thou hast forsaken the LORD thy God,
When He led thee by the way?

18. And now what hast thou to do in the way to Egypt,
To drink the waters of Shihor?
Or what hast thou to do in the way to Assyria,
To drink the waters of the River?
19. Thine own wickedness shall correct thee,
And thy backslidings shall reprove thee:
Know therefore and see that it is an evil and a bitter thing,
That thou hast forsaken the LORD thy God,
Neither is My fear in thee,
Saith the Lord GOD of hosts.

20. For of old time I have broken thy yoke,
And burst thy bands,
And thou saidst: 'I will not transgress';
Upon every high hill
And under every leafy tree
Thou didst recline, playing the harlot.

21. Yet I had planted thee a noble vine,
Wholly a right seed;
How then art thou turned into the degenerate plant
Of a strange vine unto Me?

v. 19. קמץ בז״ק v. 20. אעבור קרי

Tahpanhes. Daphnae, a fortress of importance on the N.E. frontier, and commanding the road to Palestine. It was to Tahpanhes that Jeremiah was taken by force, after the fall of Jerusalem (Jer. XLIII, 7).

17. The answer to *v.* 14.
when He led thee by the way. i.e. the right way. God showed the Israelites the right path to walk, but they forsook it (Rashi, Kimchi).

18–19. THE FOLLY OF FOREIGN ALLIANCES

18. *what hast thou to do . . . Egypt or . . . Assyria.* Judah's rulers had vacillated between alliances with Egypt and Assyria. Hoshea, the last king of Israel had sought the help of Egypt against Assyria; and Josiah had lost his life in opposing Egypt on behalf of Assyria. What could these alliances profit them, while they were faithless to God?
to drink the waters of. i.e. become the vassal of; equivalent to our phrase, 'to eat the bread of.'
Shihor. The Nile, denoting Egypt.
the River. i.e. the River Euphrates, representing Assyria.

19. *thine own wickedness shall correct thee.* The disasters arising out of the wickedness shall bring about thy betterment.
thy backslidings. The *result* of thy backslidings shall reprove thee.
My fear. The fear of Me in your hearts.

20–25. OBSTINACY IN IDOLATRY

20. *I have broken thy yoke.* In the past God had, beginning from the days of Egypt, delivered Israel from his oppressors (Kimchi).

I will not transgress. This translation is according to the Massoretic correction of the Text. After each deliverance Israel had declared he would never again be unfaithful to God.

upon every high hill. Referring to the immoral practices of the heathen worship for which Israel had forsaken God. These were usually celebrated on hill-tops. 'Such relapse into unholy, primitive cults often accompanies and greatly hastens the disintegration of any society or people. Wherever national life no longer permeates and elevates the masses, these sink into the mire of sensuality, superstition, and animalism' (Duhm).

21–25. The Prophet stresses Israel's backslidings in a variety of figures borrowed from pastoral, agricultural, and home life.

21. *wholly a right seed.* From which good fruit should have come. Israel is sprung from the seed of Abraham, from whom descendants like himself were to be expected (Kimchi).

degenerate plant. How from such a planting and from such careful tending, through instruction and exhortation, could there be such bad fruit? cf. the parable of the vineyard, Isa. v, 2–4.

22. For though thou wash thee with nitre,
And take thee much soap,
Yet thine iniquity is marked before Me,
Saith the Lord GOD.

23. How canst thou say: 'I am not defiled,
I have not gone after the Baalim'?
See thy way in the Valley,
Know what thou hast done;
Thou art a swift young camel traversing her ways;

24. A wild ass used to the wilderness
That snuffeth up the wind in her desire;
Her lust, who can hinder it?
All they that seek her will not weary themselves;
In her month they shall find her.

25. Withhold thy foot from being unshod,
And thy throat from thirst;
But thou saidst: 'There is no hope;
No, for I have loved strangers, and after them will I go.'

26. As the thief is ashamed when he is found,
So is the house of Israel ashamed;
They, their kings, their princes,
And their priests, and their prophets;

27. Who say to a stock: 'Thou art my father,'
And to a stone: 'Thou hast brought us forth,'
For they have turned their back unto Me, and not their face;
But in the time of their trouble they will say:
'Arise, and save us.'

22 אֱמֶת וְאֵיךְ נֶהְפַּכְתְּ לִי סוּרֵי הַגֶּפֶן נׇכְרִיָּה׃ כִּי אִם־תְּכַבְּסִי
בַּנֶּתֶר וְתַרְבִּי־לָךְ בֹּרִית נִכְתָּם עֲוֺנֵךְ לְפָנַי נְאֻם אֲדֹנָי
23 יֱהֹוִה׃ אֵיךְ תֹּאמְרִי לֹא נִטְמֵאתִי אַחֲרֵי הַבְּעָלִים לֹא
הָלַכְתִּי רְאִי דַרְכֵּךְ בַּגַּיְא דְּעִי מֶה עָשִׂית בִּכְרָה קַלָּה
24 מְשָׂרֶכֶת דְּרָכֶיהָ׃ פֶּרֶא ׀ לִמֻּד מִדְבָּר בְּאַוַּת נַפְשׁוֹ שָׁאֲפָה
רוּחַ תַּאֲנָתָהּ מִי יְשִׁיבֶנָּה כׇּל־מְבַקְשֶׁיהָ לֹא יִיעָפוּ בְּחׇדְשָׁהּ
כה יִמְצָאוּנְהָ׃ מִנְעִי רַגְלֵךְ מִיָּחֵף וּגְורֹנֵךְ מִצִּמְאָה וַתֹּאמְרִי
26 נוֹאָשׁ לוֹא כִּי־אָהַבְתִּי זָרִים וְאַחֲרֵיהֶם אֵלֵךְ׃ כְּבֹשֶׁת גַּנָּב
כִּי יִמָּצֵא כֵּן הֹבִישׁוּ בֵּית יִשְׂרָאֵל הֵמָּה מַלְכֵיהֶם שָׂרֵיהֶם
27 וְכֹהֲנֵיהֶם וּנְבִיאֵיהֶם׃ אֹמְרִים לָעֵץ אָבִי אַתָּה וְלָאֶבֶן אַתְּ
יְלִדְתָּנִי כִּי־פָנוּ אֵלַי עֹרֶף וְלֹא פָנִים וּבְעֵת רָעָתָם יֹאמְרוּ
28 קוּמָה וְהוֹשִׁיעֵנוּ׃ וְאַיֵּה אֱלֹהֶיךָ אֲשֶׁר עָשִׂיתָ לָּךְ יָקוּמוּ
אִם־יוֹשִׁיעוּךָ בְּעֵת רָעָתֶךָ כִּי מִסְפַּר עָרֶיךָ הָיוּ אֱלֹהֶיךָ יְהוּדָה׃

28. But where are thy gods that thou hast made thee?
Let them arise, if they can save thee in the time of thy trouble;
For according to the number of thy cities
Are thy gods, O Judah.

v. 24. נפשה קרי   v. 25. וגרונך קרי   v. 27. ילדתנו ק'

22. *take thee much soap.* No outward means of purification will remove her guilt.

23. *not gone after the Baalim.* These words are probably the answer of those who did not agree that participation in 'harmless' local cults was necessarily apostasy. Jeremiah points to the savage cruelties that marked some of these cults.

see thy way in the Valley. Probably a reference to the horrors of Moloch-worship with its child-sacrifices enacted in the Valley of Hinnom.

traversing her ways. Running here and there, backwards and forwards, impelled by her desire. This and the following two verses are figurative of Israel's shameless idolatry in going from the god of one nation to another (Kimchi).

24. *who can hinder it?* From her characteristic habits; equally hard is it to turn Israel from her evil ways (Rashi).

will not weary themselves. Need not weary themselves to find her: she will seek *them.*

25. *withhold thy foot . . . thirst.* Do not wear yourself out in those evil pursuits.

there is no hope. All exhortation is useless. Israel has abandoned herself to her sinful ways.

26–27. FUTILITY OF IDOLS IN TIME OF TROUBLE

26. *as the thief is ashamed. i.e.* the man who is believed to be honourable but is discovered to be a thief (Targum).

they, their kings. All classes will realize the shame of their condition.

their priests, and their prophets. i.e. of Baal.

27. *who say.* This is the reason for their shame.

arise, and save us. In time of great trouble they will realize the helplessness of their gods, and will turn again to Him who is the only Source of help.

CHAPTER III

4\. Didst thou not just now cry unto Me:
'My father,
Thou art the friend of my youth.'

CHAPTER IV

1\. If thou wilt return, O Israel,
Saith the LORD,
Yea, return unto Me;
And if thou wilt put away thy detestable things out of My sight,
And wilt not waver;
2\. And wilt swear: 'As the LORD liveth'
In truth, in justice, and in righteousness;
Then shall the nations bless themselves by Him,
And in Him shall they glory.

CAP. III. ג

4 הֲל֣וֹא מֵעַ֔תָּה קָרָ֥את לִ֖י אָבִ֑י אַלּ֥וּף
נְעֻרַ֖י אָֽתָּה׃

CAP. IV. ד

א אִם־תָּשׁ֨וּב יִשְׂרָאֵ֧ל ׀ נְאֻם־יְהוָ֛ה אֵלַ֖י תָּשׁ֑וּב וְאִם־תָּסִ֧יר
2 שִׁקּוּצֶ֛יךָ מִפָּנַ֖י וְלֹ֥א תָנֽוּד׃ וְנִשְׁבַּ֙עְתָּ֙ חַי־יְהוָ֔ה בֶּאֱמֶ֖ת
בְּמִשְׁפָּ֣ט וּבִצְדָקָ֑ה וְהִתְבָּ֥רְכוּ ב֛וֹ גּוֹיִ֖ם וּב֥וֹ יִתְהַלָּֽלוּ׃

ג׳ v. 4. יתיר י׳

Jewish custom prescribes that the Prophetical Reading shall not end on a note of gloom and despair. Accordingly, verses are added from chapters III and IV, depicting the recognition by Israel of God as Father and Guide (III, 4); and of the better times of Israel's return to God, and of the participation of all humanity in the blessings of that spiritual regeneration (IV, 1, 2).

2\. *in Him.* In God.

ADDITIONAL NOTE TO NUMBERS

VOWS AND VOWING IN THE LIGHT OF JUDAISM

The Rabbis fully endorsed the Biblical demand for man uncompromisingly to honour his word, whether accompanied by a vow or not. Their position on this matter is absolutely clear: 'Let thy yea be yea, and thy nay be nay. He who changes his word commits as heavy a sin as he who worships idols; and he who utters an untruth, is excluded from the Divine Presence.'

A vow to be valid must be uttered aloud; it must be made voluntarily, without any compulsion from without; and the person making it must be fully conscious of its scope and implications. A man may impose a restriction upon himself by vow; he cannot so restrict others. Vows whose fulfilment is rendered impossible by *force majeure* are void.

Scripture discourages vowing. 'If thou shalt forbear to vow, it shall be no sin in thee' (Deut. XXIII, 22): 'Be not rash with thy mouth . . . Better is it that thou shouldest not vow, than that thou shouldest vow and not pay' (Eccl. V, 2, 5). The post-Biblical teachers, whether in Alexandria, Palestine, or Babylon, shared this attitude towards vows. Philo declares, 'The word of the good man should be his oath, firm and unchangeable, founded steadfastly on truth. Therefore vows and oaths should be superfluous. Some men make vows out of wicked hatred of their fellow men; swearing, for example that they will not admit this or that man to sit at the same table with them, or to come under the same roof. Such men should seek to propitiate the mercy of God, so that they may find some cure for the diseases of their souls.' The Rabbis were equally zealous in their attempt to dissuade men from vowing. 'Do not form a habit of making vows,' was an ancient Tannaite teaching; while Samuel, the great teacher in Babylon, roundly declared. 'He who makes a vow, even though he fulfil it, is called a *rosho*, a wicked man.' In the time of the Mishnah, the habit of taking vows was considered a sign of bad breeding, and affected the honour of the vower's parents, just as swearing would nowadays point to a man's low origin. One exception was admitted. The making of vows was tolerated, when it was done in order to rid oneself of bad habits, or in order to encourage oneself to do good; but—says the Shulchan Aruch—even in such cases one should strive for the desired end without the aid of vows. 'Even vows for charitable purposes are not desirable. If one has the money, let him give it straightway without a vow; and if not, let him defer his vow until he have it.'

The fact must, however, be recorded that the mass of the people did not rise to these moral heights, and the popular Oriental passion for vow-making continued unabated. And just because the Rabbis assigned such sacredness to the spoken word, they were faced with a grave problem. For altogether aside from imbecile and rash minds, men in time of danger or under momentary impulse would make vows which they could not fulfil. These self-imposed obligations or abstentions might clash with man's domestic duties, or interfere with his proper relations to his neighbours. In such cases, the Rabbis would consider it their duty to afford a man the facility, under certain definite conditions and restrictions, of *annulling* his thoughtless or impossible vows. Such annulment could never be effected by himself, but only by a Beth Din of three learned men in the Law, after they had carefully investigated the nature and bearing of the vow, and had become convinced that its purpose was not, on the one hand, self-improvement; nor did it, on the other, infringe upon the rights of others. For not all vows or oaths could be absolved. A vow or oath that was made to another person, even be that person a child or a heathen, could not be annulled except in the presence of that person and with his consent; while *an oath which a man had taken in a court of justice, could not be absolved by any other authority in the world.* Far from being animated by a loose regard for morality, the annulment of vows ordained by the Rabbis has an ethical intent, that of saving persons who have made virtually impracticable vows from the guilt of breaking them, and of preventing the hardship and injustice which their fulfilment would entail upon others (Z. Frankel, Schechter).

KOL NIDRÉ

The formula for the annulment of vows that ushers in the Service on the Eve of the Day of Atonement refers to such vows which we had voluntarily promised to the Almighty, and had not kept, or the fulfilment of which might prove to be beyond our ability to carry out. 'But it does not in the least possible degree affect the promises or obligations entered into between man and man, as the latter can only be dissolved by the mutual consent of the parties, nor can it absolve any man from an official oath' (Editor's note, Sephardi Eve of Atonement Prayer Book).

The Kol Nidré has had a curious history. The awe and solemnity with which it is pronounced, the beauty and pathos of the threefold chant, the scattered millions of Israel gathered in every synagogue in the world, are sure signs that the words of the prayer, written like an old inscription, are full of meaning; beneath them lurks the thought that is God-inspired, a conception of the sanctity of Truth' (Editor's note, Ashkenazi Eve of Atonement Prayer Book, in 'The Service of the Synagogue'). And yet its introduction was opposed by some Gaonim over a thousand years ago: it was recast, though not improved, by a noted rabbi in the eleventh century; and has been a welcome weapon in the hands of anti-Semites, who, in defiance of all truth and justice, have used it to prove to their hate-blinded followers that 'the word of a Jew cannot be trusted.' The pioneers of Reform Judaism abolished it a century ago: and every now and then voices are raised in Orthodox communities that, in view of the misunderstandings to which it has given rise, the time has come for its official removal from the Festival Prayer Book. I append the reply I sent to an Overseas Congregation which recently submitted this suggestion to me.

'Proposed alterations in the Liturgy, even of its non-essential portions, call for the greatest care and consideration. The question of altering the Kol Nidré prayer especially bristles with difficulties. Chief among them is this: the prayer as it stands has for centuries been a weapon of malicious attack by enemies of Israel. If, in consequence, the prayer is abolished, we are held as pleading guilty to their charges, and by our action seem to justify these charges. Historic Judaism has, therefore, ever braved these misrepresentations. Conscious of the sacredness and inviolability which attaches to an oath in Jewish Law and life, it indignantly repudiates the construction its maligners place upon this Prayer, and proclaims that the dispensation from vows in it refers only to those in which no other persons or interests are involved; and that no private or public vow, promise or oath which concerns another person, is implied in the Kol Nidré.'

'One further consideration. Recent historical studies have shown the Kol Nidré to be a unique memorial of Jewish suffering and repentance. It arose in Spain, as a result of the Jewish persecutions by the West Goths, in the seventh century. Entire Jewish communities were then doomed to torture and the stake, unless they forswore their Faith, and by most fearful oaths and abjurations bound themselves nevermore to practise any Jewish observances. In this way, even when better times came and the fury of the oppressor abated, the unfortunate members of those communities felt themselves perjured before God and man if they returned to their Holy Faith, or kept even the most sacred of its Festivals. It was to ease the conscience of these crushed and distracted men and women, that the Kol Nidré was formulated. In view of this origin of the prayer—which has only recently become known and which alone explains all its anomalies—various congregations on the Continent that had formerly abolished the Kol Nidré have reintroduced it, realizing that the awakening of historic memories, and the forging of links with the past, are vital factors in Jewish traditional life and worship.'

ספר דברים

THE BOOK OF DEUTERONOMY

ספר דברים

THE BOOK OF DEUTERONOMY

NAME. The name of the Fifth Book of Moses is אלה הדברים, lit. 'these are the words,' from the opening phrase in the Hebrew Text. This title has been shortened in current use to *Devarim*, 'Words.' The oldest name of the Book, however, was משנה תורה, 'the Repetition of the Torah,' a phrase based on XVII, 18. The Greek-speaking Jews translated this name by *Deuteronomion*, *i.e.* 'Second Law'; and this title was taken over by the Latin Bible as *Deuteronomium*, and thence by the English Versions as *Deuteronomy*.

CONTENTS. A full title might be, Moses' Farewell Discourses and Song to Israel. The Lawgiver had brought his People to the borders of the Holy Land. He then recounts in three Discourses the events of the forty years' wanderings; and warns against the temptations awaiting them in Canaan, with promise of Divine judgment for disobedience, and Divine blessing for faithful observance, of God's commandments. Included in the second Discourse is a rehearsal of the principal laws (XII–XXVI), as these were to be observed in the new Land. These laws are given in free reproduction, with hortatory amplification, abbreviation, or even modification to meet new conditions. In his Farewell Song, the dying Leader celebrates God as the Rock of Israel. This is followed by the Farewell Blessing. Standing on the brink of the grave, he gives his parting benediction to the tribes whose religious and political welfare had been the devoted labour of his life. He then ascends the height to the sepulchre which no man knoweth. 'And there hath not arisen a prophet since in Israel like unto Moses.'

NATURE AND INFLUENCE. Deuteronomy is a unique book—distinct from the narrative and historical, the legal, prophetic, and devotional writings of Holy Writ, though it has affinities with each of them. In its literary aspect, it is oratory; and as such it is unsurpassed in its rush of rhythmic sentences, its ebb and flow of exalted passion, its accents of appeal and denunciation: Moses' speech shines as well as his face. And this noble language gives utterance to truths which are always and everywhere sovereign—that God is One, and that man must be wholly His; that God is Righteousness and Faithfulness, Mercy and Love. The central declaration of all this oratory, enshrined by Judaism in its daily devotions, is the Shema—which, as we shall see, teaches the unity of the Creator, the unity of creation, and the unity of mankind.

The God proclaimed by Deuteronomy stands in a relation to Israel and humanity not merely of Judge or Ruler, but of Friend and Father. 'And thou shalt *love* the LORD thy God with all thy heart, with all thy soul, and with all thy might.' This whole-souled love and devotion to God is to be accompanied by a large-hearted benevolence towards man, and indeed towards all sentient beings; by the recognition of the retributive righteousness of God; and by the insistence on the vital importance of family life, and of religious instruction within the home. The influence of this Book of the Farewell Discourses of Moses on both domestic and personal religion in Israel throughout the millennia has never been exceeded by that of any other Book in Scripture.

DIVISIONS. Chapter I, 1–5. Introductory.

I, 6–IV, 40. *First Discourse*—a review of Israel's journeying, with an appeal not to forget the truth promulgated at Horeb.

IV, 44–XXVI. *Second Discourse*—on the religious foundations of the Covenant, together with a *Code of Law*, dealing with worship (XII, 1–XVI, 17), government (XVI, 18–XVIII), criminal law (XIX–XXI, 1–9), domestic life (XXI, 10–XXV), and rituals at the Sanctuary (XXVI).

XXVII–XXX. *Third Discourse*—the enforcement of the Law, and the establishment afresh of the Covenant between Israel and God.

XXXI–XXXIV. *The Last Days of Moses*—the charge to Joshua, the delivery of the Law to the Priests, the Song, the Blessing, and the death of Moses.

1

CHAPTER I

1. These are the words which Moses spoke unto all Israel beyond the Jordan; in the wilderness, in the Arabah, over against Suph, between Paran and Tophel, and Laban, and Hazeroth, and Di-zahab. 2. It is eleven days' journey from Horeb unto Kadesh-barnea by the way of mount Seir. 3. And it came to pass in the fortieth year, in the eleventh month, on the first day of the month, that Moses spoke unto the

CAP. I. א

א

מד 44

א אֵלֶּה הַדְּבָרִים אֲשֶׁר דִּבֶּר מֹשֶׁה אֶל־כָּל־יִשְׂרָאֵל בְּעֵבֶר
הַיַּרְדֵּן בַּמִּדְבָּר בָּעֲרָבָה מוֹל סוּף בֵּין־פָּארָן וּבֵין־תֹּפֶל
2 וְלָבָן וַחֲצֵרֹת וְדִי זָהָב׃ אַחַד עָשָׂר יוֹם מֵחֹרֵב דֶּרֶךְ הַר־
3 שֵׂעִיר עַד קָדֵשׁ בַּרְנֵעַ׃ וַיְהִי בְּאַרְבָּעִים שָׁנָה בְּעַשְׁתֵּי־עָשָׂר

I. DEVARIM

(CHAPTERS I–III, 22)

CHAPTER I, 1–5. INTRODUCTORY

These verses are usually taken to be the general superscription to Deuteronomy. They specify the place and time of the Farewell Discourses of the Lawgiver recorded in this Book.

1. *words. i.e. discourses*, of exhortation and reproof, which form the main contents of Deuteronomy.

unto all Israel. 'These words redound to the praise of Israel. Knowing that they were called together for the purpose of hearing a discourse which would contain strong words of reproof, they nevertheless attended in full number' (Sifri).

beyond the Jordan. Heb. **בעבר הירדן**; 'at the crossing of the Jordan'; or, 'at the banks of the Jordan,' eastern or western. Which one of these is meant in any particular passage can be determined only by the context (Gesenius, Luzzatto, Friedlander); Num. XXXII, 19; Deut. XI, 30. Some commentators see in the words **עבר הירדן** (lit. Transjordania) a *fixed* geographical name of the Moabite side of the Jordan, even for the inhabitants of that land. Along with this went a local usage, determined by the position of the speaker.

in the Arabah. 'The deep valley running North and South of the Dead Sea' (RV Margin). Here the southern portion of this valley is meant, extending to the Gulf of Akabah, which is the north-eastern arm of the Red Sea.

Suph. A shorter form of *yam suph, i.e.* the Red Sea.

Paran. The wilderness of Paran is now called the wilderness of el-Tih, north of the Sinai Peninsula, and west of the Arabah.

Tophel. Some identify this unknown place with el-Tafile, a village about 15 miles south-east of the Dead Sea.

Laban and Hazeroth. Possibly the Libnah and Hazeroth in Num. XXXIII, 17–20.

Di-zahab. The spot has not been identified. The Hebrew implies 'a place productive of gold'.

The five names mentioned above seem to delimit the place where Moses gave one of the discourses to Israel. Their identification is uncertain and full of difficulties. Some of the ancient and medieval teachers have been inclined to treat those names homiletically. By playing on their *meaning*, they associated these places with the murmurings and transgressions of the children of Israel. Thus, Onkelos translates this *v.* as follows: 'These are the words which Moses spake to all Israel beyond Jordan. He reproved them because they had sinned in the Wilderness, and had provoked God to anger in the Plain (*Arabah*) of Moab; over against the Red Sea (*Suph*) they murmured against God; in Paran, they had spoken contemptuously (*tophel*) concerning the manna (*laban*); and in Hazeroth, they angered Him on account of flesh and because they made the Golden Calf (*di-zahab*).'

2. *it is eleven days' journey.* From Horeb, *i.e.* Sinai, the scene of the Giving of the Law, to Kadesh-barnea. The distance is between 160 and 170 miles. In 1838, the traveller Robinson followed the route here specified, and the journey lasted exactly eleven days of ordinary camel-riding.

by the way of mount Seir. Or, 'by the Mount Seir road'—the easternmost track from the Sinai Peninsula to Kadesh.

3. *in the fortieth year.* The date of the discourses. Moses reserved his exhortation for the closing days of his life, in the same way as Jacob (Gen. XLIX), Joshua (Josh. XXIV), Samuel (I Sam. XII), and David (I Kings II). Words spoken at the solemn time of departure from earth have a deep influence upon the hearers.

eleventh. Heb. **עשתי עשר**. In the preceding *v.* the form used for 'eleven' is **אחד עשר**. Koenig rightly points to this fact, among many others, as proof that, unlike the Samaritan and Septuagint Texts, the Heb. Text has from the first been handed down to us with absolute accuracy, and that no attempt was made to 'harmonize' different forms of the same word or phrase.

children of Israel, according unto all that the LORD had given him in commandment unto them; 4. after he had smitten Sihon the king of the Amorites, who dwelt in Heshbon, and Og the king of Bashan, who dwelt in Ashtaroth, at Edrei; 5. beyond the Jordan, in the land of Moab, took Moses upon him to expound this law, saying:

חֹדֶשׁ בְּאֶחָד לַחֹדֶשׁ דִּבֶּר מֹשֶׁה אֶל־בְּנֵי יִשְׂרָאֵל כְּכֹל
4 אֲשֶׁר צִוָּה יְהוָה אֹתוֹ אֲלֵהֶם׃ אַחֲרֵי הַכֹּתוֹ אֵת סִיחֹן מֶלֶךְ
הָאֱמֹרִי אֲשֶׁר יוֹשֵׁב בְּחֶשְׁבּוֹן וְאֵת עוֹג מֶלֶךְ הַבָּשָׁן אֲשֶׁר־
ה יוֹשֵׁב בְּעַשְׁתָּרֹת בְּאֶדְרֶעִי׃ בְּעֵבֶר הַיַּרְדֵּן בְּאֶרֶץ מוֹאָב

4. *Sihon . . . Og.* These signal victories, still fresh in the memory of all, are repeatedly mentioned in Deuteronomy; because the success of Moses' leadership on these occasions heightened his authority and enabled him to address his people on their faults in the past and their duties in the future.

at Edrei. The place where Og was slain (Num. XXI, 35); the modern Dera, 30 miles east of the Lake of Tiberias.

5. *this law.* 'The Heb. word *Torah* does not and never did mean "Law". It means, and always has meant, "Teaching"' (Herford). The word *torah* may refer to moral guidance, or to a single specific teaching, as in Prov. I, 8, 'forsake not the teaching (*torath*) of thy mother.' It is also applied to a body of religious precepts or teachings—such as form the central portion of this Book (Chaps. XII–XXVI). Often it denotes the entire sum of Israel's religious doctrine and life—the *Torah* of Moses.

1–5. Apart from the geographical uncertainties there are many other difficulties in these verses, so long as we regard them as forming the title-page to the whole of Deuteronomy. Thus, *v.* 5 states that 'Moses began to declare this law, saying (לאמר)'. In the light of the current view of these verses, this can only mean that the exposition in question follows *immediately* upon that verse. And yet the succeeding chapters contain no exposition of the Torah; nor, strictly speaking, can the laws in chaps. XII–XXVI be called an 'exposition' of the Torah, seeing that, of the one hundred laws contained in those chapters, seventy are not mentioned in the previous Books of the Pentateuch.

For these and other reasons, many commentators regard *v.* 1–5 as introductory not to the whole Book, but merely to the First Discourse of Moses (I, 6–IV, 40); and, in consequence, their interpretation differs considerably from that given above. One of these commentators is Sforno who paraphrases *v.* 1 and 2 as follows: 'These are the words which Moses repeatedly spoke unto all Israel, beyond Jordan, in the Arabah, over against Suph, between Paran and Tophel and Laban and Hazeroth and Di-zahab; *viz.* "*it is eleven days' journey from Horeb by way of Mount Seir unto Kadesh-barnea.*" And yet it had taken them forty years to accomplish that journey! Such was the veiled admonition that Moses intended to convey to them by these words in each of the places mentioned.' Targum Jonathan, Sifri, and Rashi seem to have understood these verses in the same sense. 'Had Israel been worthy, they could have entered the Land within eleven days; but they were sadly found wanting, and they drew upon themselves the punishment of forty years' wandering' (Sifri). Luzzatto sees this thought continued in *v.* 3–5, which he paraphrases as follows, 'In the fortieth year, after the victories over Sihon and Og, Moses undertook to make clear and expound the veiled meaning embodied in this "teaching". Such declaration and exposition are contained in the First Discourse (I, 6–IV, 40) which he addressed to the People about to undertake the conquest of Canaan.' And in fact, that First Discourse is a historic retrospect of the main incidents from Horeb to Jordan, bringing home to the new generation why it was that the Israelites were doomed to wander forty years in the Wilderness before they could enter the Promised Land, though the direct route was only an eleven days' journey.

A. MOSES' FIRST DISCOURSE

REVIEW OF JOURNEY FROM SINAI TO KADESH WITH EXHORTATION TO OBEDIENCE

(CHAPTERS I, 6–IV, 40)

Moses reviews the experiences of the Israelites in the terrible wilderness through which they passed till they reached Kadesh-barnea. Thence the spies were sent on to Canaan. These brought back word of a good land, but also of cities great and fenced up to heaven, and a population counting giants among them. They so filled the heart of the people with fear, that Israel forgot God and was prepared to return to Egypt. The unfaithful spies and the whole of that generation were therefore to perish in the Wilderness; their children alone were to enter the Promised Land. Moses continues to tell of their presumptuous attempt to defeat that sentence, and the ignominious failure and rout with which it had been visited. Moses himself had been entangled in the rebellious outbreak of the people; and his doom is made known to him, the passage into the Land of Promise to another leadership. But even the eight and thirty years' wandering in the Wilderness lacked not the LORD's watchfulness. Towards the end of the wandering, they passed by Edom, but were forbidden to attack Moab and Ammon. With the crossing of the brook Zered, however, the

¶ 6. The LORD our God spoke unto us in Horeb, saying: 'Ye have dwelt long enough in this mountain; 7. turn you, and take your journey, and go to the hill-country of the Amorites and unto all the places nigh thereunto, in the Arabah, in the hill-country, and in the Lowland, and in the South, and by the sea-shore; the land of the Canaanites, and Lebanon, as far as the great river, the river Euphrates. 8. Behold, I have set the land before you: go in and possess the land which the LORD swore unto your fathers, to Abraham, to Isaac, and to Jacob, to give unto them and to their seed after them.' ¶ 9. And I spoke unto you at that time, saying: 'I am not able to bear you myself alone; 10. the LORD your God hath multiplied you, and, behold, ye are this day as the stars of heaven for multitude.— 11. The LORD, the God of your fathers, make you a thousand times so many more

6 הוֹאִיל מֹשֶׁה בֵּאֵר אֶת־הַתּוֹרָה הַזֹּאת לֵאמֹר׃ יְהוָה
אֱלֹהֵינוּ דִּבֶּר אֵלֵינוּ בְּחֹרֵב לֵאמֹר רַב־לָכֶם שֶׁבֶת בָּהָר
7 הַזֶּה׃ פְּנוּ ׀ וּסְעוּ לָכֶם וּבֹאוּ הַר הָאֱמֹרִי וְאֶל־כָּל־שְׁכֵנָיו
בָּעֲרָבָה בָהָר וּבַשְּׁפֵלָה וּבַנֶּגֶב וּבְחוֹף הַיָּם אֶרֶץ הַכְּנַעֲנִי
8 וְהַלְּבָנוֹן עַד־הַנָּהָר הַגָּדֹל נְהַר פְּרָת׃ רְאֵה נָתַתִּי לִפְנֵיכֶם
אֶת־הָאָרֶץ בֹּאוּ וּרְשׁוּ אֶת־הָאָרֶץ אֲשֶׁר נִשְׁבַּע יְהוָה
לַאֲבֹתֵיכֶם לְאַבְרָהָם לְיִצְחָק וּלְיַעֲקֹב לָתֵת לָהֶם וּלְזַרְעָם
9 אַחֲרֵיהֶם׃ וָאֹמַר אֲלֵכֶם בָּעֵת הַהִוא לֵאמֹר לֹא־אוּכַל
לְבַדִּי שְׂאֵת אֶתְכֶם׃ יְהוָה אֱלֹהֵיכֶם הִרְבָּה אֶתְכֶם וְהִנְּכֶם
11 הַיּוֹם כְּכוֹכְבֵי הַשָּׁמַיִם לָרֹב׃ יְהוָה אֱלֹהֵי אֲבוֹתֵכֶם יֹסֵף

new era began: the dread of Israel fell upon the heathen peoples. In vain Sihon, king of the Amorites, and Og, king of Bashan, resisted: their cities were taken, their people extirpated, their land divided among the tribes of Reuben, Gad and half-Manasseh.

The remainder of Moses' First Discourse will be dealt with in connection with the next Sidrah, p. 755.

6–8. COMMAND TO START FROM HOREB

6. *the LORD our God.* Placed emphatically at the beginning of the sentence as the motive of the whole Discourse. 'The phrase *the LORD our God* has the intimate accent of a common affection. No phrase has been more helpful to piety in all generations' (G. A. Smith).

7. *hill-country.* The central mountain-range of Palestine.

Amorites. The general term for the inhabitants of Canaan prior to the entry of the Israelites; Amos II, 9; see p. 153.

Arabah. Here refers to its northern part, the Jordan Valley, ending in the Dead Sea.

Lowland. Heb. *Shephelah.* The foothills between the Central Range and the Maritime Plain; see Map. It is one of the most fertile tracts in the land.

the South. The *Negeb*; the dry steppe-district south of Judah; see on Num. XIII, 17.

the sea-shore. The Plain extending inwards from the coast of the Mediterranean to a distance of from four to fifteen miles.

Lebanon. The range of mountains to the north of the Holy Land.

the river Euphrates. The ideal limit assigned to the territory of Israel; cf. Gen. XV, 18.

8. *the land, which the LORD sware unto your fathers.* This phrase occurs more than twenty times in Deuteronomy. The Divine love towards the Patriarchs and the Promise to give their children possession of Canaan (see Gen. XII, 7; XXVI, 3 f; and XXVIII, 13 f) led to the selection, and are guarantees for the preservation, of Israel.

9–18. APPOINTMENT OF ASSISTANTS

The first movement forward towards the conquest of the Holy Land revealed the growing numbers of the Israelites. Moses could no longer, unaided, support the burden of so vast a nation. Others had to share responsibility with him. He has in mind not only the appointment of judges on the advice of Jethro (Exod. XVIII), but also the election of seventy elders to help in the administration of the community.

9. *not able to bear.* A reminiscence of Num. XI, 14.

10. *as the stars of heaven.* A simile of wonderful beauty. God had fulfilled His promise to increase the children of the Patriarchs; cf. Gen. XV, 5.

11. *the LORD . . . bless you.* A pious interjection, as in II Sam. XXIV, 3. Moses hastens to bestow his blessing upon Israel in order that his words be not misunderstood as if he lamented the increase of his people (Hoffman). The phrase, 'The LORD, the God of your fathers,' has in substance been taken over into the Prayer Book. It implies the unbroken continuity of the generations in Israel; and, likewise, the unchanging relationship between God and His 'kingdom of priests'.

12. *myself alone bear.* Moses now proceeds to recall how the task of government had grown beyond his powers.

as ye are, and bless you, as He hath promised you!*ii. 12. How can I myself alone bear your cumbrance, and your burden, and your strife? 13. Get you, from each one of your tribes, wise men, and understanding, and full of knowledge, and I will make them heads over you.' 14. And ye answered me, and said: 'The thing which thou hast spoken is good for us to do.' 15. So I took the heads of your tribes, wise men, and full of knowledge, and made them heads over you, captains of thousands, and captains of hundreds, and captains of fifties, and captains of tens, and officers, tribe by tribe. 16. And I charged your judges at that time, saying: 'Hear the causes between your brethren, and judge righteously between a man and his brother, and the stranger that is with him. 17. Ye

עֲלֵיכֶם כָּכֶם אֶלֶף פְּעָמִים וִיבָרֵךְ אֶתְכֶם כַּאֲשֶׁר דִּבֶּר
שני 12 לָכֶם׃ אֵיכָה אֶשָּׂא לְבַדִּי טָרְחֲכֶם וּמַשַּׂאֲכֶם וְרִיבְכֶם׃
13 הָבוּ לָכֶם אֲנָשִׁים חֲכָמִים וּנְבֹנִים וִידֻעִים לְשִׁבְטֵיכֶם
14 וַאֲשִׂימֵם בְּרָאשֵׁיכֶם׃ וַתַּעֲנוּ אֹתִי וַתֹּאמְרוּ טוֹב־הַדָּבָר
טו אֲשֶׁר־דִּבַּרְתָּ לַעֲשׂוֹת׃ וָאֶקַּח אֶת־רָאשֵׁי שִׁבְטֵיכֶם אֲנָשִׁים
חֲכָמִים וִידֻעִים וָאֶתֵּן אוֹתָם רָאשִׁים עֲלֵיכֶם שָׂרֵי אֲלָפִים
וְשָׂרֵי מֵאוֹת וְשָׂרֵי חֲמִשִּׁים וְשָׂרֵי עֲשָׂרֹת וְשֹׁטְרִים לְשִׁבְטֵיכֶם׃
16 וָאֲצַוֶּה אֶת־שֹׁפְטֵיכֶם בָּעֵת הַהִוא לֵאמֹר שָׁמֹעַ בֵּין־אֲחֵיכֶם
17 וּשְׁפַטְתֶּם צֶדֶק בֵּין־אִישׁ וּבֵין־אָחִיו וּבֵין גֵּרוֹ׃ לֹא־תַכִּירוּ

your cumbrance. Your troublesomeness; the people made the leader's task heavier by placing obstacles in his way (Sifri). He did not have their co-operation and assistance.

burden. 'The responsibility of providing the people with food and water, the lack of which caused hostile demonstrations to be made against Moses' (Ibn Ezra).

strife. They were quarrelsome, and at this stage it was essential for him to be relieved of petty judicial functions.

13. *get you.* It is clear from *v.* 15 that Moses, and not the people, made the selection. As the Sifri points out, the Hebrew word denotes taking counsel about a project, not taking action in connection with it.

full of knowledge. Or, 'known.' Because of their outstanding merit.

15. *wise men and full of knowledge.* Compare this with what is stated in *v.* 13, 'wise men, and understanding, and known.' The Rabbis explain that Moses was unable to find men who possessed *all* the desired qualifications.

officers. Officials in the administration of justice and maintenance of civil order, whose duty it was to put in force the instructions of their superiors (Talmud). Some render the Heb. *shoterim* 'recorders', from שטר, 'document.'

16. *hear the causes between.* lit. 'hear between'; *i.e.* not to listen to *ex parte* statements, but to all that is said on both sides (Talmud).

the stranger. In matters involving equity, there must be no difference between an Israelite and the resident alien. 'The care taken by Israelite law to protect strangers finds no parallel in Babylonia' (S. A. Cook). To-day, a great modern state outlaws a section of its own population, and oppresses it far more than it would dare to oppress total aliens.

that is with him. The Rabbis sometimes understand it in the sense of 'inhabiting his house', and, therefore, more in his power. The very life of such a man may depend on *justice* being granted him. The wife of a Chassidic rabbi, having quarrelled with her maid, was setting out to the magistrate to lodge her complaint. Noticing that her husband was about to accompany her, she asked him whither he was bound. 'To the magistrate,' he said. His wife declared that it was beneath his dignity to take any part in a quarrel with a servant. She could deal with the matter herself. The Zaddik replied, 'That may be, but I intend to represent your maid, who, when accused by you, will find no one willing to take her part.' And then, bursting into a passion of tears, he quoted Job XXXI, 13: 'If I did despise the cause of my man-servant or of my maid-servant, when they contended with me, what then shall I do when God riseth up?' A similar story is related of R. Issi in the Midrash.

17. *ye shall not respect . . . . in judgment.* 'You must never show partiality to any person in a case' (Moffatt). The judge must avoid everything that can possibly be construed as a bribe. The Babylonian teacher Samuel was passing over a plank laid across a stream, when a stranger drew nigh and offered his hand to conduct him with safety over the frail bridge. Samuel, on inquiring who he was, learned that he was a suitor who desired him to adjudicate upon his cause. 'Friend, thou hast disqualified me by thy eager courtesy. I am no longer able to judge the case with impartiality'; see also on XVI, 19.

small . . . great alike. i.e. an insignificant person, and a person of importance. There was not to be one law for the rich, and another for the poor. 'Small' and 'great' may also refer to the matters under dispute. A dispute involving a small sum requires the same earnest attention as that involving a large sum (Talmud).

the judgment is God's. The judge should feel that he is God's representative, and that every judicial decision is a religious act; cf. II Chron. XIX, 6 (and the king said to the judges, 'Consider shall not respect persons in judgment; ye shall hear the small and the great alike; ye shall not be afraid of the face of any man; for the judgment is God's; and the cause that is too hard for you ye shall bring unto me, and I will hear it.' 18. And I commanded you at that time all the things which ye should do. ¶ 19. And we journeyed from Horeb, and went through all that great and dreadful wilderness which ye saw, by the way to the hill-country of the Amorites, as the LORD our God commanded us; and we came to Kadesh-barnea. 20. And I said unto you: 'Ye are come unto the hill-country of the Amorites, which the LORD our God giveth unto us. 21. Behold, the LORD thy God hath set the land before thee; go up, take possession, as the LORD, the God of thy fathers, hath spoken unto thee; fear not, neither be dismayed.'*iii. 22. And ye came near unto me every one of you, and said: 'Let us send men before us, that they may search the land for us, and bring us back word of the way by which we must go up, and the cities unto which we shall come.' 23. And the thing pleased me well; and I took twelve men of you, one man for every tribe; 24. and they turned and went up into the mountains, and came unto the valley of Eshcol, and spied it out. 25. And they took of the fruit of the land in their hands, and brought it down unto us, and brought us back word, and said: 'Good is the land which the LORD our God giveth unto us.' 26. Yet ye would not go up, but rebelled against the com-

פָּנִים בַּמִּשְׁפָּט כַּקָּטֹן כַּגָּדֹל תִּשְׁמָעוּן לֹא תָגוּרוּ מִפְּנֵי־אִישׁ
כִּי הַמִּשְׁפָּט לֵאלֹהִים הוּא וְהַדָּבָר אֲשֶׁר יִקְשֶׁה מִכֶּם
18 תַּקְרִבוּן אֵלַי וּשְׁמַעְתִּיו׃ וָאֲצַוֶּה אֶתְכֶם בָּעֵת הַהִוא אֵת
19 כָּל־הַדְּבָרִים אֲשֶׁר תַּעֲשׂוּן׃ וַנִּסַּע מֵחֹרֵב וַנֵּלֶךְ אֵת כָּל־
הַמִּדְבָּר הַגָּדוֹל וְהַנּוֹרָא הַהוּא אֲשֶׁר רְאִיתֶם דֶּרֶךְ הַר
הָאֱמֹרִי כַּאֲשֶׁר צִוָּה יְהוָה אֱלֹהֵינוּ אֹתָנוּ וַנָּבֹא עַד קָדֵשׁ
כ בַּרְנֵעַ׃ וָאֹמַר אֲלֵכֶם בָּאתֶם עַד־הַר הָאֱמֹרִי אֲשֶׁר־יְהוָה
21 אֱלֹהֵינוּ נֹתֵן לָנוּ׃ רְאֵה נָתַן יְהוָה אֱלֹהֶיךָ לְפָנֶיךָ אֶת־
הָאָרֶץ עֲלֵה רֵשׁ כַּאֲשֶׁר דִּבֶּר יְהוָה אֱלֹהֵי אֲבֹתֶיךָ לָךְ
שלישי 22 אַל־תִּירָא וְאַל־תֵּחָת׃ וַתִּקְרְבוּן אֵלַי כֻּלְּכֶם וַתֹּאמְרוּ נִשְׁלְחָה
אֲנָשִׁים לְפָנֵינוּ וְיַחְפְּרוּ־לָנוּ אֶת־הָאָרֶץ וְיָשִׁבוּ אֹתָנוּ דָּבָר
אֶת־הַדֶּרֶךְ אֲשֶׁר נַעֲלֶה־בָּהּ וְאֵת הֶעָרִים אֲשֶׁר נָבֹא אֲלֵיהֶן׃
23 וַיִּיטַב בְּעֵינַי הַדָּבָר וָאֶקַּח מִכֶּם שְׁנֵים עָשָׂר אֲנָשִׁים אִישׁ
24 אֶחָד לַשָּׁבֶט׃ וַיִּפְנוּ וַיַּעֲלוּ הָהָרָה וַיָּבֹאוּ עַד־נַחַל אֶשְׁכֹּל
כה וַיְרַגְּלוּ אֹתָהּ׃ וַיִּקְחוּ בְיָדָם מִפְּרִי הָאָרֶץ וַיּוֹרִדוּ אֵלֵינוּ
וַיָּשִׁבוּ אֹתָנוּ דָבָר וַיֹּאמְרוּ טוֹבָה הָאָרֶץ אֲשֶׁר־יְהוָה אֱלֹהֵינוּ
26 נֹתֵן לָנוּ׃ וְלֹא אֲבִיתֶם לַעֲלֹת וַתַּמְרוּ אֶת־פִּי יְהוָה אֱלֹהֵיכֶם׃

what ye do; for ye judge not for man, but for the LORD; and He is with you in the matter of judgment'). In Jewish teaching all those who administer the law in accordance with right, and thereby maintain the moral foundations—Truth and Justice—upon which human society rests, are performing a Divine task. 'Every judge who renders righteous judgment, Scripture deems him a co-partner of the Holy One, blessed be He, in the work of Creation' (Talmud).

19–46. FROM HOREB TO KADESH-BARNEA

19. *dreadful wilderness.* 'Wherein were fiery serpents and scorpions, and thirsty ground where was no water' (VIII, 15).

22–25. The Mission of the Spies.

22. *ye came near unto me.* By combining what is related here with Num. XIII, we get a full understanding of the incident. The plan originated with the people; it approved itself to Moses; and was sanctioned by God. Moses does not here repeat all the details, because a reminder of all those details is not required for his address of admonition; whereas the historical account in Numbers could well dispense with narrating the circumstance that it was the Israelites who had demanded the sending of the Spies. 'It is evident that a circumstance may be passed over in silence by the historian, which nevertheless the orator selects as lending emphasis to his oration' (Hoffmann). It was important to remind them that the sending of the spies, which led immediately to their rebellion, was their own suggestion (Sifri).

23. *the thing pleased me well.* But it did not please God. It is to be noted that in Num. XIII, 2 the Hebrew is lit. 'send *for thyself* men', and God, as it were, dissociated Himself from the scheme; whereas in the appointment of men to assist Moses, which had God's approval, Scripture relates, 'The LORD said unto Moses, gather *for Me* seventy men' (Num. XI, 16).

24. *into the mountains.* Better, *into the hill-country;* as in *v.* 7.

valley of Eshcol. Near Hebron; Num. XIII, 23.

26–33. The Disaffection of the People.

mandment of the LORD your God; 27. and ye murmured in your tents, and said: 'Because the LORD hated us, He hath brought us forth out of the land of Egypt, to deliver us into the hand of the Amorites, to destroy us. 28. Whither are we going up? our brethren have made our heart to melt, saying: The people is greater and taller than we; the cities are great and fortified up to heaven; and moreover we have seen the sons of the Anakim there.' 29. Then I said unto you: 'Dread not, neither be afraid of them. 30. The LORD your God who goeth before you, He shall fight for you, according to all that He did for you in Egypt before your eyes; 31. and in the wilderness, where thou hast seen how that the LORD thy God bore thee, as a man doth bear his son, in all the way that ye went, until ye came unto this place. 32. Yet in this thing ye do not believe the LORD your God, 33. who went before you in the way, to seek you out a place to pitch your tents in: in fire by night, to show you by what way ye should go, and in the cloud by day.' ¶ 34. And the LORD heard the voice of your words, and was wroth, and swore, saying: 35. 'Surely there shall not one of these men, even this evil generation, see the good land, which I swore to give unto your fathers, 36. save Caleb the son of Jephunneh, he shall see it; and to him will I give the land that he hath trodden upon, and to his children; because he hath wholly followed the LORD.' 37. Also the LORD was angry with me for your sakes, saying: 'Thou also shalt not

27 וַתֵּרָגְנוּ בְאָהֳלֵיכֶם וַתֹּאמְרוּ בְּשִׂנְאַת יְהוָה אֹתָנוּ הוֹצִיאָנוּ
28 מֵאֶרֶץ מִצְרָיִם לָתֵת אֹתָנוּ בְּיַד הָאֱמֹרִי לְהַשְׁמִידֵנוּ׃ אָנָה ׀
אֲנַחְנוּ עֹלִים אַחֵינוּ הֵמַסּוּ אֶת־לְבָבֵנוּ לֵאמֹר עַם גָּדוֹל וָרָם
מִמֶּנּוּ עָרִים גְּדֹלֹת וּבְצוּרֹת בַּשָּׁמָיִם וְגַם־בְּנֵי עֲנָקִים רָאִינוּ
29 שָׁם׃ וָאֹמַר אֲלֵכֶם לֹא־תַעַרְצוּן וְלֹא־תִירְאוּן מֵהֶם׃
ל יְהוָה אֱלֹהֵיכֶם הַהֹלֵךְ לִפְנֵיכֶם הוּא יִלָּחֵם לָכֶם כְּכֹל אֲשֶׁר
31 עָשָׂה אִתְּכֶם בְּמִצְרַיִם לְעֵינֵיכֶם׃ וּבַמִּדְבָּר אֲשֶׁר רָאִיתָ
אֲשֶׁר נְשָׂאֲךָ יְהוָה אֱלֹהֶיךָ כַּאֲשֶׁר יִשָּׂא־אִישׁ אֶת־בְּנוֹ בְּכָל־
32 הַדֶּרֶךְ אֲשֶׁר הֲלַכְתֶּם עַד־בֹּאֲכֶם עַד־הַמָּקוֹם הַזֶּה׃ וּבַדָּבָר
33 הַזֶּה אֵינְכֶם מַאֲמִינִם בַּיהוָה אֱלֹהֵיכֶם׃ הַהֹלֵךְ לִפְנֵיכֶם
בַּדֶּרֶךְ לָתוּר לָכֶם מָקוֹם לַחֲנֹתְכֶם בָּאֵשׁ ׀ לַיְלָה לַרְאֹתְכֶם
34 בַּדֶּרֶךְ אֲשֶׁר תֵּלְכוּ־בָהּ וּבֶעָנָן יוֹמָם׃ וַיִּשְׁמַע יְהוָה אֶת־
לה קוֹל דִּבְרֵיכֶם וַיִּקְצֹף וַיִּשָּׁבַע לֵאמֹר׃ אִם־יִרְאֶה אִישׁ
בָּאֲנָשִׁים הָאֵלֶּה הַדּוֹר הָרָע הַזֶּה אֵת הָאָרֶץ הַטּוֹבָה אֲשֶׁר
36 נִשְׁבַּעְתִּי לָתֵת לַאֲבֹתֵיכֶם׃ זוּלָתִי כָּלֵב בֶּן־יְפֻנֶּה הוּא
יִרְאֶנָּה וְלוֹ־אֶתֵּן אֶת־הָאָרֶץ אֲשֶׁר דָּרַךְ־בָּהּ וּלְבָנָיו יַעַן אֲשֶׁר
37 מִלֵּא אַחֲרֵי יְהוָה׃ גַּם־בִּי הִתְאַנַּף יְהוָה בִּגְלַלְכֶם לֵאמֹר

v. 28. מלרע

27. *in your tents.* Being unwilling to unite for common action. The well-known phrase, *To your tents, O Israel* (I Kings XII, 16) is a formula of dispersion, not a call for military action (H. W. Robinson).

the LORD hated us. To this extreme of unbelief and ingratitude were the people driven by the report of a few among themselves, in spite of their long experience of God's leading. 'The passage is eloquent of the fickleness with which a people will suffer the lessons of its past—facts of Providence it has proved and lived upon—to be overthrown by the opinion of a few "experts" as to a still untried situation' (G. A. Smith).

28. *whither are we going up? i.e.* what unknown dangers are in front of us?

Anakim. Giants; Num. XIII, 22.

30. *He shall fight for you.* The words of encouragement used by Moses at the Red Sea; Exod. XIV, 14.

before your eyes. This phrase occurs ten more times in Deuteronomy. Moses, throughout his address, appeals to the people's experience of God. He is not weaving abstract theories, but drawing on their history.

31. *the LORD thy God bore thee.* Cf. Exod. XIX, 4, 'how I bare you on eagles' wings.'

as a man doth bear his son. The relationship between God and man is here conceived in the tenderest terms, that of a father carrying his infant son when he is too weak or tired to walk; cf. Hosea XI, 1–3. 'It was this usage that prepared the way for the term "Our Father who art in heaven", first used in Pharisaic circles' (Herford).

32. *yet in this thing.* Notwithstanding past experience of the Divine protection and support, ye believed not in the LORD your God.

34–46. God's Anger and Judgments.

36. *Caleb.* See Num. XIV, 24.

37. *for your sakes.* Better, *on your account.* Moses had certainly disobeyed God's command, and thereby incurred His wrath; but this had happened as a consequence of the people's action.

go in thither; 38. Joshua the son of Nun, who standeth before thee, he shall go in thither; encourage thou him, for he shall cause Israel to inherit it.*iv. 39. Moreover your little ones, that ye said should be a prey, and your children, that this day have no knowledge of good or evil, they shall go in thither, and unto them will I give it, and they shall possess it. 40. But as for you, turn you, and take your journey into the wilderness by the way to the Red Sea.' 41. Then he answered and said unto me: 'We have sinned against the LORD, we will go up and fight, according to all that the LORD our God commanded us.' And ye girded on every man his weapons of war, and deemed it a light thing to go up into the hill-country. 42. And the LORD said unto me: 'Say unto them: Go not up, neither fight; for I am not among you; lest ye be smitten before your enemies.' 43. So I spoke unto you, and ye hearkened not; but ye rebelled against the commandment of the LORD, and were presumptuous, and went up into the hill-country. 44. And the Amorites, that dwell in that hill-country, came out against you, and chased you, as bees do, and beat you down in Seir, even unto Hormah. 45. And ye returned and wept before the LORD; but the LORD hearkened not to your voice, nor gave ear unto you. 46. So ye abode in Kadesh many days, according unto the days that ye abode there.

38 גם־אתה לא־תבא שם׃ יהושע בן־נון העמד לפניך הוא
רביעי 39 יבא שמה אתו חזק כי־הוא ינחלנה את־ישראל׃ וטפכם
אשר אמרתם לבז יהיה ובניכם אשר לא־ידעו היום
טוב ורע המה יבאו שמה ולהם אתננה והם יירשוה׃
מ 41 ואתם פנו לכם וסעו המדברה דרך ים־סוף׃ ותענו ׀
ותאמרו אלי חטאנו ליהוה אנחנו נעלה ונלחמנו ככל
אשר־צונו יהוה אלהינו ותחגרו איש את־כלי מלחמתו
42 ותהינו לעלת ההרה׃ ויאמר יהוה אלי אמר להם לא
תעלו ולא־תלחמו כי אינני בקרבכם ולא תנגפו לפני
43 איביכם׃ ואדבר אליכם ולא שמעתם ותמרו את־פי יהוה
44 ותזדו ותעלו ההרה׃ ויצא האמרי הישב בהר ההוא
לקראתכם וירדפו אתכם כאשר תעשינה הדברים ויכתו
מה אתכם בשעיר עד־חרמה׃ ותשבו ותבכו לפני יהוה
46 ולא־שמע יהוה בקלכם ולא האזין אליכם׃ ותשבו בקדש
ימים רבים כימים אשר ישבתם׃

v. 38. מלעיל

'They angered Him also at the waters of Meribah, so that it went ill with Moses for their sakes' (Psalm CVI, 32). The leader must share responsibility for the failings of his flock; see also on III, 26. 'Moses alone realizes all that life in the Promised Land may be; and Moses alone of all the vast assembly is the one who will never see it. *The LORD was angry with me for your sakes*, this is the phrase under which the speaker veils the breakdown of his life-task' (Moulton). Moses refers to the Divine displeasure here, because it leads up to the mention of his successor.

38. *standeth before thee.* The Heb. idiom for 'attend upon', as a servant.

encourage thou him. In its literal sense; *i.e.* make him strong.

39. *ye said should be a prey.* See Num. XIV, 3, 31.

have no knowledge of good or evil. Who are not of an age to incur communal responsibility (cf. pp. 8 and 10); youths under twenty.

40. *by the way to the Red Sea.* See Num. XIV, 25. The explorer, Trumbull, identified this road with the modern pilgrim-track from Suez to Akabah; cf. on *v.* 1 above.

41. *we will go up.* The word 'we' is emphasized in the Hebrew. 'The quick revulsion of popular feeling is true to life. The change was too facile to be real. Mere enthusiasm is no atonement for guilt. Men cannot run away from their moral unworthiness on bursts of feeling' (G. A. Smith).

43. *presumptuous.* See Num. XIV, 41, 44.

44. *the Amorites.* In Num. the opponents are called 'the Amalekite and Canaanite', but, as explained on *v.* 7, 'Amorite' is the general term for the inhabitants of Canaan.

as bees do. The same forcible image for number and ferocity occurs in Isa. VII, 18 and Psalm CXVIII, 12.

Hormah. See on Num. XIV, 45.

45. *wept before the LORD.* 'Tears follow foolhardiness, as foolhardiness does timidity; the psychology of Israel is that of a child' (Bertholet).

hearkened not. Because their weeping was not the outcome of sorrow over sin; but of sorrow over the *consequences* of sin. This feeling the old theologians named 'attrition'; in contrast with the sincere penitence—the sorrow over sin itself—which they called *contrition.* There is all the difference in the world between a man who is contrite and one who is merely 'attrite'.

2

Chapter II

1. Then we turned, and took our journey into the wilderness by the way to the Red Sea, as the LORD spoke unto me; and we compassed mount Seir many days.*v. ¶ 2. And the LORD spoke unto me, saying: 3. 'Ye have compassed this mountain long enough; turn you northward. 4. And command thou the people, saying: Ye are to pass through the border of your brethren the children of Esau, that dwell in Seir; and they will be afraid of you; take ye good heed unto yourselves therefore; 5. contend not with them; for I will not give you of their land, no, not so much as for the sole of the foot to tread on; because I have given mount Seir unto Esau for a possession. 6. Ye shall purchase food of them for money, that ye may eat;

ב

Cap. II. ב

א וַנֵּפֶן וַנִּסַּע הַמִּדְבָּרָה דֶּרֶךְ יַם־סוּף כַּאֲשֶׁר דִּבֶּר יְהוָה
חמישי 2 אֵלָי וַנָּסָב אֶת־הַר־שֵׂעִיר יָמִים רַבִּים׃* ס וַיֹּאמֶר
3 יְהוָה אֵלַי לֵאמֹר׃ רַב־לָכֶם סֹב אֶת־הָהָר הַזֶּה פְּנוּ לָכֶם
4 צָפֹנָה׃ וְאֶת־הָעָם צַו לֵאמֹר אַתֶּם עֹבְרִים בִּגְבוּל אֲחֵיכֶם
בְּנֵי־עֵשָׂו הַיֹּשְׁבִים בְּשֵׂעִיר וְיִירְאוּ מִכֶּם וְנִשְׁמַרְתֶּם מְאֹד׃
ה אַל־תִּתְגָּרוּ בָם כִּי לֹא־אֶתֵּן לָכֶם מֵאַרְצָם עַד מִדְרַךְ כַּף־
6 רָגֶל כִּי־יְרֻשָּׁה לְעֵשָׂו נָתַתִּי אֶת־הַר שֵׂעִיר׃ אֹכֶל תִּשְׁבְּרוּ
מֵאִתָּם בַּכֶּסֶף וַאֲכַלְתֶּם וְגַם־מַיִם תִּכְרוּ מֵאִתָּם בַּכֶּסֶף

46. *Kadesh.* See Num. xx, 1.

many days. An indefinite time. The Traditional explanation states the time to have been 19 years.

according unto the days that ye abode there. Heb. כימים אשר ישבתם. Hoffmann and Driver take this as an example of the Semitic idiom often employed by a writer who is either unable, or has no occasion, to speak explicitly. Rashbam, Mendelssohn, and Luzzatto accordingly render, 'And ye remained in Kadesh the many days that ye abode there'; *i.e.* as is well known to you.

Chapter II

In the first portion of his Discourse, Moses dwelt on the abortive attempt to enter Canaan. He now recalls (II–III, 29) the victories that marked the close of their wanderings, victories that presaged Israel's conquest of the Promised Land. He thus points out that unbelief and rebellion brought shame and punishment; while repentant return to God and obedience to His will were crowned by blessing and triumph.

II, 1–8. Round Mount Seir

After the repulse at Kadesh, the Israelites turned back towards the Red Sea, skirting Mt. Seir, until God commanded them to turn northward, and pass peacefully through Esau's territory.

1. *by the way to the Red Sea. i.e.* in the direction of the north-eastern branch of the Red sea, the Gulf of Akabah.

we compassed mount Seir. Indicates the long and arduous journey in order to go round Edom; see Num. xxi, 4–9.

many days. Thirty-eight years; see *v.* 14 below.

3. *turn you northward.* 'The Israelites must be imagined by this time to have made their way along the south-western and southern border of Edom, as far as the south-east end of the Arabah, so that a turn northwards would at once lead them along the eastern border of Edom in the direction of Moab' (Driver); cf. Judges xi, 18.

4. *ye are to pass through.* This is quite distinct from the earlier attempt to shorten the journey by passing through Edomite territory from Kadesh on the western frontier, permission for which was refused by the king of Edom; Num. xx.

the children of Esau. The eastern portion of Edom was inhabited by free Bedouins, kinsmen of the Israelites. These did not threaten them with war as the Edomites in the western part of the land had done, if they dared pass through their land (Rashbam, Luzzatto).

be afraid of you. The western border of Edom is a series of natural fortresses, making it easy to repel any invading host. Not so the eastern border.

5. *contend not.* lit. 'incite not.' God is the ruler of the whole world. All the nations—not only Israel—were under God's Providential rule, and have had their territories assigned to them. Israel therefore must respect these possessions and not become a mere conquering people, Israel must confine his ambitions to the one Land Divinely assigned to him as the very beginning of his being as a family (S. R. Hirsch).

as for the sole of the foot. They were not permitted even to pass through their land, without their permission.

unto Esau. David fought against the descendants of Esau and made them his 'servants' (II Sam. viii, 14), but he did not dispossess them of their land; and later, in the reign of Jehoram, they again became independent (II Kings viii, 20 f).

7 וּשְׁתִיתֶם׃ כִּי יְהוָה אֱלֹהֶיךָ בֵּרַכְךָ בְּכֹל מַעֲשֵׂה יָדֶךָ יָדַע
לֶכְתְּךָ אֶת־הַמִּדְבָּר הַגָּדֹל הַזֶּה זֶה ׀ אַרְבָּעִים שָׁנָה יְהוָה
8 אֱלֹהֶיךָ עִמָּךְ לֹא חָסַרְתָּ דָּבָר׃ וַנַּעֲבֹר מֵאֵת אַחֵינוּ בְנֵי־
עֵשָׂו הַיֹּשְׁבִים בְּשֵׂעִיר מִדֶּרֶךְ הָעֲרָבָה מֵאֵילַת וּמֵעֶצְיֹן
9 גָּבֶר * ס וַנֵּפֶן וַנַּעֲבֹר דֶּרֶךְ מִדְבַּר מוֹאָב׃ וַיֹּאמֶר
יְהוָה אֵלַי אַל־תָּצַר אֶת־מוֹאָב וְאַל־תִּתְגָּר בָּם מִלְחָמָה
כִּי לֹא־אֶתֵּן לְךָ מֵאַרְצוֹ יְרֻשָּׁה כִּי לִבְנֵי־לוֹט נָתַתִּי אֶת־עָר
10 יְרֻשָּׁה׃ הָאֵמִים לְפָנִים יָשְׁבוּ בָהּ עַם גָּדוֹל וְרַב וָרָם
11 כָּעֲנָקִים׃ רְפָאִים יֵחָשְׁבוּ אַף־הֵם כָּעֲנָקִים וְהַמֹּאָבִים
12 יִקְרְאוּ לָהֶם אֵמִים׃ וּבְשֵׂעִיר יָשְׁבוּ הַחֹרִים לְפָנִים וּבְנֵי
עֵשָׂו יִירָשׁוּם וַיַּשְׁמִידוּם מִפְּנֵיהֶם וַיֵּשְׁבוּ תַּחְתָּם כַּאֲשֶׁר

and ye shall also buy water of them for money, that ye may drink. 7. For the LORD thy God hath blessed thee in all the work of thy hand; He hath known thy walking through this great wilderness; these forty years the LORD thy God hath been with thee; thou hast lacked nothing.' 8. So we passed by from our brethren the children of Esau, that dwell in Seir, from the way of the Arabah, from Elath and from Ezion-geber. ¶ And we turned and passed by the way of the wilderness of Moab. 9. And the LORD said unto me: 'Be not at enmity with Moab, neither contend with them in battle; for I will not give thee of his land for a possession; because I have given Ar unto the children of Lot for a possession.—10. The Emim dwelt therein aforetime, a people great, and many, and tall, as the Anakim; 11. these also are accounted Rephaim, as the Anakim; but the Moabites call them Emim. 12. And in Seir dwelt the Horites aforetime, but the children of Esau succeeded them; and they destroyed them from before them, and dwelt in their stead; as Israel did unto the land of his possession, which the LORD

v. 8. פיסקא באמצע פסוק

7. *hath blessed thee.* Gives the reason for Israel's proud independence of Edom. The Israelites were well able to pay for their necessities.

He hath known. i.e. He hath cared for; the same usage of 'know' is found in Gen. XVIII, 19.

8. *way of the Arabah.* The route from south of the Dead Sea to Hebron.

Elath. The modern Akabah.

Ezion-geber. Also mentioned in I Kings IX, 26 as being 'on the shore of the Red Sea, in the land of Edom'. A fleet which Jehoshaphat had built was wrecked there (I Kings XXII, 48).

The word *Ezion-geber* is followed by a Massoretic note, known as 'a break in the middle of the verse', which indicates that a new paragraph begins with the second half of the verse.

8–12. ON THE BORDER OF MOAB

wilderness. The Heb. מדבר does not always mean 'a desert'. It often denotes 'a place where cattle is driven to pasture', uncultivated land. 'Israel kept so far east, not only to avoid the fertile and settled districts of Edom and Moab but so as not to have to cross the lower stretches of the great canyon between Edom and Moab. These lower stretches are deep, the sides steep, and the roads over them difficult for caravans. The route of Hajj, apparently that of Israel, crosses the much shallower head of this wady on the desert border. Once over it, they were in the wilderness east of Moab' (G. A. Smith).

9. *Ar.* The capital of Moab, situated in the valley of Arnon, on the Moabite frontier; Num. XXI, 15, 28.

the children of Lot. See Gen. XIX, 37.

10–12. These three verses are a parenthetic note on the earlier inhabitants of Moab and Edom, and introduced by Moses probably on writing down his Discourse.

10. *Emim.* 'The dreaded ones'; Gen. XIV, 5.

11. *Rephaim.* See in Gen. XIV, 5; XV, 20.

12. *Horites.* See Gen. XIV, 6 and XXXVI, 20 f; the name has been translated, 'cave-dwellers.' Macalister has discovered at Gezer the remains of a pre-Semitic, cave-dwelling race, using stone implements; and he identifies these with the Horites. A far different view is profounded by J. W. Jack who regards them as being 'one of the most important cultural races of Western Asia during the earlier part of the second millennium. Some time before the Semites arrived on the scene, they occupied the whole of northern Mesopotamia. It was to the Horites or Hurrians that the Hittites directly owed their civilization, including their religion and most of their literature. This ancient race, who were in the country of Seir as early as the time of Abraham, must have exerted a considerable influence on the Hebrews'.

succeeded them. Rashi notes that the verb is unexpectedly in the imperfect tense and gave unto them.—13. Now rise up, and get you over the brook Zered.' And we went over the brook Zered. 14. And the days in which we came from Kadesh-barnea, until we were come over the brook Zered, were thirty and eight years; until all the generation, even the men of war, were consumed from the midst of the camp, as the LORD swore unto them. 15. Moreover the hand of the LORD was against them, to discomfit them from the midst of the camp, until they were consumed. ¶ 16. So it came to pass, when all the men of war were consumed and dead from among the people, 17. that the LORD spoke unto me, saying: 18. 'Thou art this day to pass over the border of Moab, even Ar; 19. and when thou comest nigh over against the children of Ammon, harass them not, nor contend with them; for I will not give thee of the land of the children of Ammon for a possession; because I have given it unto the children of Lot for a possession. —20. That also is accounted a land of Rephaim: Rephaim dwelt therein aforetime; but the Ammonites call them Zamzummim, 21. a people great, and many, and tall, as the Anakim; but the LORD destroyed them before them; and they succeeded them, and dwelt in their stead; 22. as He did for the children of Esau, that dwell in Seir, when He destroyed the Horites from before them; and they succeeded them, and dwelt in their stead even unto this day; 23. and the Avvim, that dwelt in villages as far as Gaza, the Caphtorim, that came forth out of Caphtor, destroyed them, and dwelt in their stead.—

13 עָשָׂה יִשְׂרָאֵל לְאֶרֶץ יְרֻשָּׁתוֹ אֲשֶׁר־נָתַן יְהוָה לָהֶם׃ עַתָּה
קֻמוּ וְעִבְרוּ לָכֶם אֶת־נַחַל זָרֶד וַנַּעֲבֹר אֶת־נַחַל זָרֶד׃
14 וְהַיָּמִים אֲשֶׁר־הָלַכְנוּ ׀ מִקָּדֵשׁ בַּרְנֵעַ עַד אֲשֶׁר־עָבַרְנוּ אֶת־
נַחַל זֶרֶד שְׁלֹשִׁים וּשְׁמֹנֶה שָׁנָה עַד־תֹּם כָּל־הַדּוֹר אַנְשֵׁי
טו הַמִּלְחָמָה מִקֶּרֶב הַמַּחֲנֶה כַּאֲשֶׁר נִשְׁבַּע יְהוָה לָהֶם׃ וְגַם
יַד־יְהוָה הָיְתָה בָּם לְהֻמָּם מִקֶּרֶב הַמַּחֲנֶה עַד תֻּמָּם׃
16 וַיְהִי כַאֲשֶׁר־תַּמּוּ כָּל־אַנְשֵׁי הַמִּלְחָמָה לָמוּת מִקֶּרֶב הָעָם׃
17 18 ס וַיְדַבֵּר יְהוָה אֵלַי לֵאמֹר׃ אַתָּה עֹבֵר הַיּוֹם אֶת־גְּבוּל
19 מוֹאָב אֶת־עָר׃ וְקָרַבְתָּ מוּל בְּנֵי עַמּוֹן אַל־תְּצֻרֵם וְאַל־
תִּתְגָּר בָּם כִּי לֹא־אֶתֵּן מֵאֶרֶץ בְּנֵי־עַמּוֹן לְךָ יְרֻשָּׁה כִּי לִבְנֵי־
כ לוֹט נְתַתִּיהָ יְרֻשָּׁה׃ אֶרֶץ־רְפָאִים תֵּחָשֵׁב אַף־הִוא רְפָאִים
21 יָשְׁבוּ־בָהּ לְפָנִים וְהָעַמֹּנִים יִקְרְאוּ לָהֶם זַמְזֻמִּים׃ עַם גָּדוֹל
וְרַב וָרָם כָּעֲנָקִים וַיַּשְׁמִידֵם יְהוָה מִפְּנֵיהֶם וַיִּירָשֻׁם וַיֵּשְׁבוּ
22 תַחְתָּם׃ כַּאֲשֶׁר עָשָׂה לִבְנֵי עֵשָׂו הַיֹּשְׁבִים בְּשֵׂעִיר אֲשֶׁר
הִשְׁמִיד אֶת־הַחֹרִי מִפְּנֵיהֶם וַיִּירָשֻׁם וַיֵּשְׁבוּ תַחְתָּם עַד הַיּוֹם
23 הַזֶּה׃ וְהָעַוִּים הַיֹּשְׁבִים בַּחֲצֵרִים עַד־עַזָּה כַּפְתֹּרִים הַיֹּצְאִים

implies, 'continued to dispossess them'; *i.e.* gradually dispossessed them.

as Israel did. Refers to the conquest of trans-Jordanic territory (Num. XXXII).

13–15. The Crossing of Zered

This was an important step; hence the mention of the time that had elapsed since Israel left Kadesh, and also that now the doom passed on the men of war because of their murmuring had exhausted itself. Since this doom was no longer resting on their efforts, the people could with every expectation of the Divine help go forward to the conquest of the new country (Welch).

13. *brook.* A torrent-valley — the hollow between hills that is usually dry in summer, but a fast-rushing torrent in the rainy season—a wady.

Zered. See Num. XXI, 12.

14. *the LORD swore unto them.* See Num. XIV, 21 f.

15. *was against them.* The generation of murmurers did not perish entirely from natural causes. God hastened their annihilation, so as to enable their children to pass over the Jordan.

16–25. Ammonites and Amorites

19. *children of Ammon.* Inhabited the district between the Arnon and Jabbok, the tributaries of the Jordan.

20–23. Another archæological note.

20. *Zamzummim.* Nothing is known of them. Their name is held by some to be formed on the analogy of the Greek 'barbaroi', as a people whose speech sounded uncouth (G. A. Smith).

23. *Avvim.* Only mentioned again in Josh. XIII, 3 f, as a Philistine people.

Caphtor. *i.e.* Crete; see Gen. X, 14.

24. Rise ye up, take your journey, and pass over the valley of Arnon; behold, I have given into thy hand Sihon the Amorite, king of Heshbon, and his land; begin to possess it, and contend with him in battle. 25. This day will I begin to put the dread of thee and the fear of thee upon the peoples that are under the whole heaven, who, when they hear the report of thee, shall tremble, and be in anguish because of thee.' ¶ 26. And I sent messengers out of the wilderness of Kedemoth unto Sihon king of Heshbon with words of peace, saying: 27. 'Let me pass through thy land; I will go along by the highway, I will neither turn unto the right hand nor to the left. 28. Thou shalt sell me food for money, that I may eat; and give me water for money, that I may drink; only let me pass through on my feet; 29. as the children of Esau that dwell in Seir, and the Moabites that dwell in Ar, did unto me; until I shall pass over the Jordan into the land which the LORD our God giveth us.' 30. But Sihon king of Heshbon would not let us pass by him; for the LORD thy God hardened his spirit, and made his heart obstinate, that He might deliver him into thy hand, as appeareth this day.*vi. ¶ 31. And the LORD said unto me: 'Behold, I have begun to deliver up Sihon and his land before thee; begin to possess his land.' 32. Then Sihon came out against us, he and all his people, unto battle at Jahaz. 33. And the LORD our God delivered him up before us; and we smote him, and his

24 מִכַּפְתֹּר הִשְׁמִידֻם וַיֵּשְׁבוּ תַחְתָּם׃ קוּמוּ סְּעוּ וְעִבְרוּ אֶת־
נַחַל אַרְנֹן רְאֵה נָתַתִּי בְיָדְךָ אֶת־סִיחֹן מֶלֶךְ־חֶשְׁבּוֹן הָאֱמֹרִי
כה וְאֶת־אַרְצוֹ הָחֵל רָשׁ וְהִתְגָּר בּוֹ מִלְחָמָה׃ הַיּוֹם הַזֶּה אָחֵל
תֵּת פַּחְדְּךָ וְיִרְאָתְךָ עַל־פְּנֵי הָעַמִּים תַּחַת כָּל־הַשָּׁמָיִם
26 אֲשֶׁר יִשְׁמְעוּן שִׁמְעֲךָ וְרָגְזוּ וְחָלוּ מִפָּנֶיךָ׃ וָאֶשְׁלַח מַלְאָכִים
מִמִּדְבַּר קְדֵמוֹת אֶל־סִיחוֹן מֶלֶךְ חֶשְׁבּוֹן דִּבְרֵי שָׁלוֹם
27 לֵאמֹר׃ אֶעְבְּרָה בְאַרְצֶךָ בַּדֶּרֶךְ בַּדֶּרֶךְ אֵלֵךְ לֹא אָסוּר
28 יָמִין וּשְׂמֹאול׃ אֹכֶל בַּכֶּסֶף תַּשְׁבִּרֵנִי וְאָכַלְתִּי וּמַיִם בַּכֶּסֶף
29 תִּתֶּן־לִי וְשָׁתִיתִי רַק אֶעְבְּרָה בְרַגְלָי׃ כַּאֲשֶׁר עָשׂוּ־לִי בְּנֵי
עֵשָׂו הַיֹּשְׁבִים בְּשֵׂעִיר וְהַמּוֹאָבִים הַיֹּשְׁבִים בְּעָר עַד אֲשֶׁר־
אֶעֱבֹר אֶת־הַיַּרְדֵּן אֶל־הָאָרֶץ אֲשֶׁר־יְהוָה אֱלֹהֵינוּ נֹתֵן לָנוּ׃
ל וְלֹא אָבָה סִיחֹן מֶלֶךְ חֶשְׁבּוֹן הַעֲבִרֵנוּ בּוֹ כִּי־הִקְשָׁה יְהוָה
אֱלֹהֶיךָ אֶת־רוּחוֹ וְאִמֵּץ אֶת־לְבָבוֹ לְמַעַן תִּתּוֹ בְיָדְךָ כַּיּוֹם
ששי
31 הַזֶּה׃ * ס וַיֹּאמֶר יְהוָה אֵלַי רְאֵה הַחִלֹּתִי תֵּת לְפָנֶיךָ
32 אֶת־סִיחֹן וְאֶת־אַרְצוֹ הָחֵל רָשׁ לָרֶשֶׁת אֶת־אַרְצוֹ׃ וַיֵּצֵא
33 סִיחֹן לִקְרָאתֵנוּ הוּא וְכָל־עַמּוֹ לַמִּלְחָמָה יָהְצָה׃ וַיִּתְּנֵהוּ
יְהוָה אֱלֹהֵינוּ לְפָנֵינוּ וַנַּךְ אֹתוֹ וְאֶת־בָּנָו וְאֶת־כָּל־עַמּוֹ׃

v. 24. סמך דגושה v. 27. מלא וא"ו v. 33. בניו ק'

24. *rise ye up.* This verse is the continuation of *v.* 19. From Num. XXI, 26 we learn that Heshbon and the surrounding territory had belonged to the Moabites, from whom it had been wrested by Sihon.

25. *this day. i.e.* the day the Israelites cross the Arnon to start on the conquest of Canaan.

under the whole heaven. An oratorical over-statement occurring several times in Scripture.

26–37. VICTORY OVER SIHON

26. *Kedemoth.* The precise site is unknown, but probably somewhere near the upper course of the Arnon. The name occurs later as that of a Levitical city in the territory of Reuben; Josh. XIII, 18.

with words of peace. i.e. messengers with proposals for a peaceful passage through his land, and undertaking to pay for such provisions as would be required; cf. Num. XXI, 21 f.

27. *by the highway.* The Heb. is, 'by the way, by the way'; *i.e.* by the appointed road and nowhere else. In Num. XXI, 22 the phrase is 'by the king's highway'.

29. *as the children of Esua . . . did unto me.* As distinct from the kingdom of Edom; see on *v.* 4.

30. *hardened his spirit.* Similar to the phrase used of Pharaoh; see note on Exod. VII, 3. 'The meaning is, As God rules all, so to Him must be traced all that happens in the world. In some sense all acts, whether good or bad, all agencies, whether beneficent or destructive, have their source and derive their power from Him. But nevertheless men have moral responsibility for their acts, and are fully and justly conscious of ill-desert. It is to be noted that God is never said to harden the heart of a good man. It is always those who are guilty of acts of evil-doing upon whom this works' (Harper).

obstinate. Heb. 'strong.'

as appeareth this day. As experience has now shown.

31. *I have begun.* Sihon's refusal was the beginning of God's move to give Israel his country.

32. *unto battle.* See Num. XXI, 23.

sons, and all his people. 34. And we took all his cities at that time, and utterly destroyed every city, the men, and the women, and the little ones; we left none remaining; 35. only the cattle we took for a prey unto ourselves, with the spoil of the cities which we had taken. 36. From Aroer, which is on the edge of the valley of Arnon, and from the city that is in the valley, even unto Gilead, there was not a city too high for us: the LORD our God delivered up all before us. 37. Only to the land of the children of Ammon thou camest not near; all the side of the river Jabbok, and the cities of the hill-country, and wheresoever the LORD our God forbade us.

3

CHAPTER III

1. Then we turned, and went up the way to Bashan; and Og the king of Bashan came out against us, he and all his people, unto battle at Edrei. 2. And the LORD said unto me: 'Fear him not; for I have delivered him, and all his people, and his land, into thy hand; and thou shalt do unto him as thou didst unto Sihon king of the Amorites, who dwelt at Heshbon.' 3. So the LORD our God delivered into our hand Og also, the king of Bashan, and all his people; and we smote him until none was left to him remaining. 4. And we took all his cities at that time; there was not a city which we took not from them; threescore cities, all the region of Argob, the kingdom of Og in Bashan. 5. All these were fortified

34 וַנִּלְכֹּד אֶת־כָּל־עָרָיו בָּעֵת הַהִוא וַנַּחֲרֵם אֶת־כָּל־עִיר מְתִם
לה וְהַנָּשִׁים וְהַטָּף לֹא הִשְׁאַרְנוּ שָׂרִיד׃ רַק הַבְּהֵמָה בָּזַזְנוּ
36 לָנוּ וּשְׁלַל הֶעָרִים אֲשֶׁר לָכָדְנוּ׃ מֵעֲרֹעֵר אֲשֶׁר עַל־שְׂפַת־
נַחַל אַרְנֹן וְהָעִיר אֲשֶׁר בַּנַּחַל וְעַד־הַגִּלְעָד לֹא הָיְתָה קִרְיָה
אֲשֶׁר שָׂגְבָה מִמֶּנּוּ אֶת־הַכֹּל נָתַן יְהוָה אֱלֹהֵינוּ לְפָנֵינוּ׃
37 רַק אֶל־אֶרֶץ בְּנֵי־עַמּוֹן לֹא קָרָבְתָּ כָּל־יַד נַחַל יַבֹּק וְעָרֵי
הָהָר וְכֹל אֲשֶׁר־צִוָּה יְהוָה אֱלֹהֵינוּ׃

CAP. III. ג — ג

א וַנֵּפֶן וַנַּעַל דֶּרֶךְ הַבָּשָׁן וַיֵּצֵא עוֹג מֶלֶךְ־הַבָּשָׁן לִקְרָאתֵנוּ
2 הוּא וְכָל־עַמּוֹ לַמִּלְחָמָה אֶדְרֶעִי׃ וַיֹּאמֶר יְהוָה אֵלַי אַל־
תִּירָא אֹתוֹ כִּי בְיָדְךָ נָתַתִּי אֹתוֹ וְאֶת־כָּל־עַמּוֹ וְאֶת־אַרְצוֹ
וְעָשִׂיתָ לּוֹ כַּאֲשֶׁר עָשִׂיתָ לְסִיחֹן מֶלֶךְ הָאֱמֹרִי אֲשֶׁר יוֹשֵׁב
3 בְּחֶשְׁבּוֹן׃ וַיִּתֵּן יְהוָה אֱלֹהֵינוּ בְּיָדֵנוּ גַּם אֶת־עוֹג מֶלֶךְ־
הַבָּשָׁן וְאֶת־כָּל־עַמּוֹ וַנַּכֵּהוּ עַד־בִּלְתִּי הִשְׁאִיר־לוֹ שָׂרִיד׃
4 וַנִּלְכֹּד אֶת־כָּל־עָרָיו בָּעֵת הַהִוא לֹא הָיְתָה קִרְיָה אֲשֶׁר
לֹא־לָקַחְנוּ מֵאִתָּם שִׁשִּׁים עִיר כָּל־חֶבֶל אַרְגֹּב מַמְלֶכֶת
ה עוֹג בַּבָּשָׁן׃ כָּל־אֵלֶּה עָרִים בְּצֻרֹת חוֹמָה גְבֹהָה דְּלָתַיִם

34. *utterly destroyed.* Heb. 'treated as *herem*'; *i.e.* placed them under the ban of extermination. Such was the rule of warfare in the days of old, when war was a sacred act. The ruthlessness of those methods is as hideous to us to-day as war itself will—we hope and pray—be to the men and women of the future. And if it is the wholesale nature of the destruction that especially shocks our moral judgment, it is well for us to consider that in the next World War it is especially the defenceless population that will be exposed to annihilation. For the ban in connection with the Canaanites, see on XX, 18.

36. *the city.* The capital, Ar; cf. on *v.* 9.

37. *thou camest not near.* In accordance with the warning in *v.* 19.

forbade us. The Heb. is 'commanded us', and the words 'not to conquer' are understood; as in IV, 23.

CHAPTER III, 1–7. FURTHER VICTORIES

The Israelite hosts, advancing northwards towards Bashan, encounter and defeat Og and conquer his cities.

1. *and went up.* This phrase denotes travelling northward, since there is an almost continuous ascent from South to North (Rashi).

Bashan. The fertile district north of Gilead; see on *v.* 10.

Og. See Num. XXI, 33 f.

2. *fear him not.* Og was a more formidable opponent than Sihon, belonging as he did to the race of giants.

3. *none was left to him.* See on II, 34.

4. *region of Argob.* Probably identical with the modern el-Leja, south of Damascus, and east of Lake Tiberias.

5. *gates.* The Heb. is in the dual, 'double gates,' an indication of the strength of the doors to keep out the enemy.

and bars. The Heb. is in the singular; and there is no reason why it should not be so rendered. Each city had a double gate, with a bar across it when closed.

unwalled towns. Or, 'country towns.'

cities, with high walls, gates, and bars; beside the unwalled towns a great many. 6. And we utterly destroyed them, as we did unto Sihon king of Heshbon, utterly destroying every city, the men, and the women, and the little ones. 7. But all the cattle, and the spoil of the cities, we took for a prey unto ourselves. ¶ 8. And we took the land at that time out of the hand of the two kings of the Amorites that were beyond the Jordan, from the valley of Arnon unto mount Hermon—9. which Hermon the Sidonians call Sirion, and the Amorites call it Senir—10. all the cities of the plain, and all Gilead, and all Bashan, unto Salcah and Edrei, cities of the kingdom of Og in Bashan.—11. For only Og king of Bashan remained of the remnant of the Rephaim; behold, his bedstead was a bedstead of iron; is it not in Rabbah of the children of Ammon? nine cubits was the length thereof, and four cubits the breadth of it, after the cubit of a man.—12. And this land we took in possession at that time; from Aroer, which is by the valley of Arnon, and half the hill-country of Gilead, and the cities thereof, gave I unto the Reubenites and to the Gadites; 13. and the rest of Gilead, and all Bashan, the kingdom of Og, gave I unto the half-tribe of Manasseh; all the region of Argob—all that Bashan is called the land of Rephaim. 14. Jair the son of Manasseh took all the region of Argob, unto the

6 וּבְרִיחַ לְבַד מֵעָרֵי הַפְּרָזִי הַרְבֵּה מְאֹד׃ וַנַּחֲרֵם אוֹתָם
כַּאֲשֶׁר עָשִׂינוּ לְסִיחֹן מֶלֶךְ חֶשְׁבּוֹן הַחֲרֵם כָּל־עִיר מְתִם
7 הַנָּשִׁים וְהַטָּף׃ וְכָל־הַבְּהֵמָה וּשְׁלַל הֶעָרִים בַּזּוֹנוּ לָנוּ׃
8 וַנִּקַּח בָּעֵת הַהִוא אֶת־הָאָרֶץ מִיַּד שְׁנֵי מַלְכֵי הָאֱמֹרִי
9 אֲשֶׁר בְּעֵבֶר הַיַּרְדֵּן מִנַּחַל אַרְנֹן עַד־הַר חֶרְמוֹן׃ צִידֹנִים
· יִקְרְאוּ לְחֶרְמוֹן שִׂרְיֹן וְהָאֱמֹרִי יִקְרְאוּ־לוֹ שְׂנִיר׃ כֹּל ׀ עָרֵי
הַמִּישֹׁר וְכָל־הַגִּלְעָד וְכָל־הַבָּשָׁן עַד־סַלְכָה וְאֶדְרֶעִי עָרֵי
11 מַמְלֶכֶת עוֹג בַּבָּשָׁן׃ כִּי רַק־עוֹג מֶלֶךְ הַבָּשָׁן נִשְׁאַר מִיֶּתֶר
הָרְפָאִים הִנֵּה עַרְשׂוֹ עֶרֶשׂ בַּרְזֶל הֲלֹה הִוא בְּרַבַּת בְּנֵי
עַמּוֹן תֵּשַׁע אַמּוֹת אָרְכָּהּ וְאַרְבַּע אַמּוֹת רָחְבָּהּ בְּאַמַּת־
12 אִישׁ׃ וְאֶת־הָאָרֶץ הַזֹּאת יָרַשְׁנוּ בָּעֵת הַהִוא מֵעֲרֹעֵר
אֲשֶׁר־עַל־נַחַל אַרְנֹן וַחֲצִי הַר־הַגִּלְעָד וְעָרָיו נָתַתִּי לָרֻאוּבֵנִי
13 וְלַגָּדִי׃ וְיֶתֶר הַגִּלְעָד וְכָל־הַבָּשָׁן מַמְלֶכֶת עוֹג נָתַתִּי לַחֲצִי
שֵׁבֶט הַמְנַשֶּׁה כֹּל חֶבֶל הָאַרְגֹּב לְכָל־הַבָּשָׁן הַהוּא יִקָּרֵא
14 אֶרֶץ רְפָאִים׃ יָאִיר בֶּן־מְנַשֶּׁה לָקַח אֶת־כָּל־חֶבֶל אַרְגֹּב
עַד־גְּבוּל הַגְּשׁוּרִי וְהַמַּעֲכָתִי וַיִּקְרָא אֹתָם עַל־שְׁמוֹ אֶת־

v. 11. כתיב בה"א

8–17. Allotment of the Conquered Land

8. *two kings of the Amorites.* Sihon and Og.

9. *Sirion . . . Senir.* An archæological note. 'The several names in the Text, as also that of Sion (Deut. IV, 48), are all descriptive. Rising with its grey snow-capped cone to a height of about 9,500 feet, it is visible from most parts of the Promised Land, and even from the depths of the Jordan Valley and the shores of the Dead Sea. Hence it was *Sion*, the up-raised; or *Hermon*, the lofty peak; or *Senir*, and *Sirion*, the glittering "breastplate" of ice; or above all *Lebanon* the "Mont Blanc" of Palestine, the "White Mountain" of ancient times' (Stanley).

10. *plain.* The Plateau of Moab.

Gilead. The rough and rugged, yet picturesque, hill-country bounded on the west by the Jordan; on the north, by the deep glen of the Yarmuk; on the south, by the valley of Heshbon; and on the east, melting away gradually into the high plateau of Arabia.

Salcah. On the extreme south-east corner of Bashan, situated on very high ground and forming a natural fortress.

11. *for only Og.* This explains why the Israelites were able to enter into possession of the territory. With the death of Og, the formidable race of Rephaim came to an end.

bedstead. This is the meaning which the word has in the Bible. In Aramaic the word signifies 'coffin'; hence there are some who suppose that what is here meant is the king's sarcophagus. Some sites in Eastern Palestine are strewn with stone-coffins. However, the Biblical Hebrew for sarcophagus is always ארון. The bedstead is mentioned in order to indicate the huge size of Og; and it is not improbable that his bed would have been preserved as a curiosity.

Rabbah. Situated 25 miles north-east of the Dead Sea.

the cubit of a man. An ordinary cubit, the length of which was about 18 inches. This does not necessarily mean that the height of Og was nine cubits, as the bed is always longer than the man who occupies it.

12. *this land.* From the valley of Arnon unto Mount Hermon.

Aroer See on II, 36.

13. *the rest of Gilead.* *i.e.* the part north of Jabbok.

border of the Geshurites and the Maacathites, and called them, even Bashan, after his own name, Havvothjair, unto this day.*vii. —15. And I gave Gilead unto Machir. 16. And unto the Reubenites and unto the Gadites I gave from Gilead even unto the valley of Arnon, the middle of the valley for a border; even unto the river Jabbok, which is the border of the children of Ammon; 17. the Arabah also, the Jordan being the border thereof, from Chinnereth even unto the sea of the Arabah, the Salt Sea, under the slopes of Pisgah eastward. ¶ 18. And I commanded you at that time, saying: 'The LORD your God hath given you this land to possess it; ye shall pass over armed before your brethren the children of Israel, all the men of valour. 19. But your wives, and your little ones, and your cattle—I know that ye have much cattle—shall abide in your cities which I have given you;*m. 20. until the LORD give rest unto your brethren, as unto you, and they also possess the land which the LORD your God giveth them beyond the Jordan; then shall ye return every man unto his possession, which I have given you.' 21. And I commanded Joshua at that time, saying: 'Thine eyes have seen all that the LORD your God hath done unto these two kings; so shall the LORD do unto all the kingdoms whither thou goest over. 22. Ye shall not fear them; for the LORD your God, He it is that fighteth for you.'

שביעי טו הַבָּשָׁן חַוֺּת יָאִיר עַד הַיּוֹם הַזֶּה׃ וּלְמָכִיר נָתַתִּי אֶת־הַגִּלְעָד׃
16 וְלָרֽאוּבֵנִי וְלַגָּדִי נָתַתִּי מִן־הַגִּלְעָד וְעַד־נַחַל אַרְנֹן תּוֹךְ
17 הַנַּחַל וּגְבֻל וְעַד יַבֹּק הַנַּחַל גְּבוּל בְּנֵי עַמּוֹן׃ וְהָעֲרָבָה
וְהַיַּרְדֵּן וּגְבֻל מִכִּנֶּרֶת וְעַד יָם הָעֲרָבָה יָם הַמֶּלַח תַּחַת
18 אַשְׁדֹּת הַפִּסְגָּה מִזְרָחָה׃ וָאֲצַו אֶתְכֶם בָּעֵת הַהִוא לֵאמֹר
יְהוָה אֱלֹהֵיכֶם נָתַן לָכֶם אֶת־הָאָרֶץ הַזֹּאת לְרִשְׁתָּהּ חֲלוּצִים
19 תַּעַבְרוּ לִפְנֵי אֲחֵיכֶם בְּנֵי־יִשְׂרָאֵל כָּל־בְּנֵי־חָיִל׃ רַק
נְשֵׁיכֶם וְטַפְּכֶם וּמִקְנֵכֶם יָדַעְתִּי כִּי־מִקְנֶה רַב לָכֶם יֵשְׁבוּ
מפטיר כ בְּעָרֵיכֶם אֲשֶׁר נָתַתִּי לָכֶם׃ עַד אֲשֶׁר־יָנִיחַ יְהוָה ׀ לַאֲחֵיכֶם
כָּכֶם וְיָרְשׁוּ גַם־הֵם אֶת־הָאָרֶץ אֲשֶׁר יְהוָה אֱלֹהֵיכֶם נֹתֵן
לָהֶם בְּעֵבֶר הַיַּרְדֵּן וְשַׁבְתֶּם אִישׁ לִירֻשָּׁתוֹ אֲשֶׁר נָתַתִּי
21 לָכֶם׃ וְאֶת־יְהוֹשׁוּעַ צִוֵּיתִי בָּעֵת הַהִוא לֵאמֹר עֵינֶיךָ
הָרֹאֹת אֵת כָּל־אֲשֶׁר עָשָׂה יְהוָה אֱלֹהֵיכֶם לִשְׁנֵי הַמְּלָכִים
הָאֵלֶּה כֵּן־יַעֲשֶׂה יְהוָה לְכָל־הַמַּמְלָכוֹת אֲשֶׁר אַתָּה
22 עֹבֵר שָׁמָּה׃ לֹא תִּירָאוּם כִּי יְהוָה אֱלֹהֵיכֶם הוּא
הַנִּלְחָם לָכֶם׃

v. 20. סבירין לכם

14. *Jair.* See Num. XXXII, 41.
son. Here used, as frequently in the Bible, in the sense of 'descendant'. In I Chron. II, 21 f, he is said to be the great-grandson of Manasseh's son Machir.
Geshurites and the Maacathites. Two Aramean tribes; cf. Gen. XXII, 24, II Sam. XV, 8.
after his own name. See Num. XXXII, 41.
Havvoth-jair. Tent-villages, each being the homestead of a clan; for the meaning of *havva*, see on Genesis III, 20, p. 12.
unto this day. Until now.

15 *Gilead.* From the context it is clear that the northern half of Gilead is meant.
Machir. See Num. XXXII, 40. The name seems to be used here to denote the half-tribe of Manasseh that had its habitation beyond the Jordan.

16. *unto the Reubenites.* This and the following *v.* are a repetition of *v.* 12 with greater detail of definition.
for a border. i.e. the stream passing through the valley being the boundary.
river Jabbok. The upper part of this river is the western boundary of the territory of the Ammonites.

17. *Arabah.* See on I, 1.
Chinnereth. The city (see Josh. XI, 2) named after the Lake of Kinnereth, known to-day as Lake Tiberias.
the Salt Sea. The Dead Sea; see Gen. XIV, 3.
slopes. Or, 'springs.'
Pisgah. See on XXXIV, 1.

18. *commanded you.* Moses addresses himself to the two and a half tribes.
pass over armed. See Num. XXXII.

20. *beyond the Jordan.* Unlike the same phrase in I, 1, here it denotes the *western* side of the river.

21. *I commanded Joshua.* This is not mentioned in Num. XXXII, as not being relevant to the incident which that chapter relates.

HAFTORAH DEVARIM הפטרת דברים

ISAIAH I, 1–27

Chapter I

1. The vision of Isaiah the son of Amoz, which he saw concerning Judah and Jerusalem, in the days of Uzziah, Jotham, Ahaz, and Hezekiah, kings of Judah.

2. Hear, O heavens, and give ear, O earth,
For the Lord hath spoken:
Children I have reared, and brought up,
And they have rebelled against Me.

Cap. I. א

א חֲזוֹן יְשַׁעְיָהוּ בֶן־אָמוֹץ אֲשֶׁר חָזָה עַל־יְהוּדָה וִירוּשָׁלִָם
2 בִּימֵי עֻזִּיָּהוּ יוֹתָם אָחָז יְחִזְקִיָּהוּ מַלְכֵי יְהוּדָה׃ שִׁמְעוּ שָׁמַיִם
וְהַאֲזִינִי אֶרֶץ כִּי יְהוָה דִּבֵּר בָּנִים גִּדַּלְתִּי וְרוֹמַמְתִּי וְהֵם
3 פָּשְׁעוּ בִי׃ יָדַע שׁוֹר קֹנֵהוּ וַחֲמוֹר אֵבוּס בְּעָלָיו יִשְׂרָאֵל

This Sidrah always precedes the Fast of Av, the anniversary of the Fall of Jerusalem, both at the hands of the Babylonians, and six centuries later at the hands of the Romans, with the consequent dispersion of Israel and the long drawn out suffering, not yet ended, that followed these calamities. The Haftorahs read on the three Sabbaths preceding that Fast are called 'Haftorahs of Rebuke'. For the third Sabbath, Devarim, the opening chapter of Isaiah—the Great Arraignment of Judah—has been selected, in order to warn all generations in Israel of the moral and social transgressions that led to the downfall of the Jewish State.

Isaiah, the son of Amoz, was a native of Jerusalem. His family seems to have been one of rank, and he moved in royal circles. His Prophetic ministry extended for close upon 40 years, from 740–701 B.C.E. These years were the most stirring that the kingdom of Judah had yet passed through; and, throughout that entire period, he was the dominant figure in the land. The momentous event of his time was the rise of Assyria. From being a mere garrison province of Babylon in northern Mesopotamia, Assyria had become a world power. The kingdoms of Syria and Israel fell before the Assyrians in 721; and only as by a miracle was Jerusalem delivered from their grasp in 701.

With the downfall of the kingdom of Israel, Judah became the sole representative and repository of true Religion; and in the fate of that tiny land, the moral destinies of the whole world were involved. In this time of upheaval and spiritual travail, Isaiah brought to King and People the message of the holiness, omnipotence, and sovereignty of God ('Holy, holy, holy, is the Lord of hosts: the whole earth is full of His glory'). With passionate fervour he sought to instil his own vital faith in God and Providence into the heart of his brethren, and interpret for them the crises of history in the light of Divine guidance and righteousness. His efforts brought him into violent conflict with the war party of his day; and throughout his life, he remained an implacable enemy of shallow 'patriots' and opportunist politicians.

Great in thought and great in action, Isaiah united the profoundest religious insight with wide knowledge of men and affairs. The princely personality of the man is reflected in his style. His words are instinct with power, and he is the master of the sublime in universal literature. His moral passion, moreover, marks him as one of the world's greatest orators.

Chapter I. The Great Arraignment

Though Chapter I is not the earliest of Isaiah's prophecies (Rashi), its choice as the opening of the Book is most appropriate. It strikes the fundamental notes of Isaiah's teaching, and at the same time indicates the general line of Prophetic doctrine with a force and clearness unsurpassed in Scripture. The probable date of this prophecy is the time of Sennacherib's campaign in 701 B.C.E., when the Assyrians had overrun the kingdom of Judah, and were now besieging Jerusalem. A less probable date is 734, the year of the Syrian invasion.

1. *vision.* Heb. חזון; what the seer saw with the eye of the spirit; here used collectively for visions, Prophetic revelations. From this opening word, the Sabbath before Tisha-be-Av is called, שבת חזון.

Amoz. A different name from *Amos*, the Prophet.

and Jerusalem. Or, 'and especially Jerusalem.'

This verse is not the heading to the whole Book of Isaiah, but only to the first collection of prophecies (I–XII), none of which is addressed to *foreign* nations.

Uzziah . . . Hezekiah. During the reign of Uzziah, the kingdom enjoyed considerable prosperity; but under his weaker successors, the evils latent in an increase of wealth became pronounced. Isaiah preached repentance and faith, and sternly insisted on the moral aspect of the true religious life.

2–3. The Lord's complaint against His people. He has been a father to Israel, but Israel has proved himself ignorant, disobedient, and ungrateful.

3. The ox knoweth his owner,
And the ass his master's crib;
But Israel doth not know,
My people doth not consider

4. Ah sinful nation,
A people laden with iniquity,
A seed of evil-doers,
Children that deal corruptly;
They have forsaken the LORD,
They have contemned the Holy One of Israel,
They have turned away backward.
5. On what part will ye be yet stricken,
Seeing ye stray away more and more?
The whole head is sick,
And the whole heart faint;
6. From the sole of the foot even unto the head
There is no soundness in it;
But wounds, and bruises, and festering sores:
They have not been pressed, neither bound up,
Neither mollified with oil.

4 לֹא יָדַע עַמִּי לֹא הִתְבּוֹנָן׃ הוֹי ׀ גּוֹי חֹטֵא עַם כֶּבֶד עָוֺן
זֶרַע מְרֵעִים בָּנִים מַשְׁחִיתִים עָזְבוּ אֶת־יְהוָה נִאֲצוּ אֶת־
ה קְדוֹשׁ יִשְׂרָאֵל נָזֹרוּ אָחוֹר׃ עַל־מֶה תֻכּוּ עוֹד תּוֹסִיפוּ סָרָה
6 כָּל־רֹאשׁ לָחֳלִי וְכָל־לֵבָב דַּוָּי׃ מִכַּף־רֶגֶל וְעַד־רֹאשׁ
אֵין־בּוֹ מְתֹם פֶּצַע וְחַבּוּרָה וּמַכָּה טְרִיָּה לֹא־זֹרוּ וְלֹא
7 חֻבָּשׁוּ וְלֹא רֻכְּכָה בַּשָּׁמֶן׃ אַרְצְכֶם שְׁמָמָה עָרֵיכֶם שְׂרֻפוֹת
אֵשׁ אַדְמַתְכֶם לְנֶגְדְּכֶם זָרִים אֹכְלִים אֹתָהּ וּשְׁמָמָה

7. Your country is desolate;
Your cities are burned with fire;
Your land, strangers devour it in your presence,
And it is desolate, as overthrown by floods.

2. *hear, O heavens . . . earth.* Let all creation hear and shudder at Israel's unnatural conduct; see also on Deut. XXX, 19; XXXII, 1; Micah VI, 1. 'In their poetic outbursts, the Prophets not only personify nature, but they *ethicize* nature; *i.e.* they endow it with the capacity of understanding moral distinctions' (Steinthal).

hath spoken. Better, *speaketh* (Ibn Ezra).

rebelled against Me. Faithlessly broken away from Me.

3. *ox . . . ass.* Ingratitude reduces Israel below the level of the dumb animals.

doth not know. Does not wish to know (Rashi). Hosea too finds lack of 'knowledge of the LORD' the source of all moral evil. High and low alike fail to understand the nature and significance of the spiritual gifts God had conferred upon Israel.

doth not consider. i.e. does not try to understand. The Heb. התבונן is the Hithpael and may also mean, 'does not understand *himself*.' *Know thyself* is a moral obligation for nations as well as for individuals. The Jew can only know himself through his Judaism and his past; and the great majority of Jews of to-day are ignorant of the ideals of their Faith, their Scripture, their Sacred Language, and the story of Israel. Such lack of self-knowledge is, at all times, monstrous ingratitude to his Heavenly Father.

4–9. The Prophet speaks. The body politic is diseased to the core. But for the lovingkindness of God, their destruction would have been equal to that of Sodom and Gomorrah.

4. *sinful nation.* Ye who were destined to be a 'holy nation' (Rashi).

a seed of evil-doers. A brood, or generation, consisting of evil-doers.

contemned. Better, *despised*, spurned.

Holy One of Israel. This Divine title is characteristic of Isaiah, occurring 39 times in the Book, and only five times in the rest of Scripture. Holiness is an *essential* attribute of God, signifying His unapproachable exaltation; His abhorrence of all that is untrue, unclean, or sinful; and His eternal righteousness; see p. 302.

turned away . . . backward. Sunk back into idolatry; Ezek. XIV, 3.

5. *on what part.* The whole body being wounded.

6. *pressed.* lit. 'pressed out'; *i.e.* cleansed.

7. *your country.* The figure of speech is now explained by concrete details. The wild Assyrian soldiery wrought indescribable ruin in the land.

your cities. In a boasting inscription, the Assyrians claim to have captured 46 cities of Judah.

strangers. Such as might be expected at the hands of barbarian, enemy strangers. Ibn Ezra translates the Heb. זרים by 'floods'.

in your presence. And you are powerless to prevent it.

8. *daughter of Zion.* The capital remains—but how forlorn. In Hebrew, lands and cities are personified as the mothers of the inhabitants. These too are spoken of collectively as 'the daughter' of the land or city.

8 כְּמַהְפֵּכַת זָרִים׃ וְנוֹתְרָה בַת־צִיּוֹן כְּסֻכָּה בְכָרֶם כִּמְלוּנָה
9 בְּמִקְשָׁה כְּעִיר נְצוּרָה׃ לוּלֵי יְהוָה צְבָאוֹת הוֹתִיר לָנוּ
י שָׂרִיד כִּמְעָט כִּסְדֹם הָיִינוּ לַעֲמֹרָה דָּמִינוּ׃ שִׁמְעוּ
דְבַר־יְהוָה קְצִינֵי סְדֹם הַאֲזִינוּ תּוֹרַת אֱלֹהֵינוּ עַם עֲמֹרָה׃
11 לָמָּה לִּי רֹב־זִבְחֵיכֶם יֹאמַר יְהוָה שָׂבַעְתִּי עֹלוֹת אֵילִים
וְחֵלֶב מְרִיאִים וְדַם פָּרִים וּכְבָשִׂים וְעַתּוּדִים לֹא חָפָצְתִּי׃
12 כִּי תָבֹאוּ לֵרָאוֹת פָּנָי מִי־בִקֵּשׁ זֹאת מִיֶּדְכֶם רְמֹס חֲצֵרָי׃
13 לֹא תוֹסִיפוּ הָבִיא מִנְחַת־שָׁוְא קְטֹרֶת תּוֹעֵבָה הִיא לִי
14 חֹדֶשׁ וְשַׁבָּת קְרֹא מִקְרָא לֹא־אוּכַל אָוֶן וַעֲצָרָה׃ חָדְשֵׁיכֶם
וּמוֹעֲדֵיכֶם שָׂנְאָה נַפְשִׁי הָיוּ עָלַי לָטֹרַח נִלְאֵיתִי נְשֹׂא׃

8. And the daughter of Zion is left
As a booth in a vineyard,
As a lodge in a garden of cucumbers,
As a besieged city.
9. Except the LORD of hosts
Had left unto us a very small remnant,
We should have been as Sodom,
We should have been like unto Gomorrah.

10. Hear the word of the LORD,
Ye rulers of Sodom;
Give ear unto the law of our God,
Ye people of Gomorrah.
11. To what purpose is the multitude of your sacrifices unto Me?
Saith the LORD;
I am full of the burnt-offerings of rams,
And the fat of fed beasts;
And I delight not in the blood
Of bullocks, or of lambs, or of he-goats.
12. When ye come to appear before Me,
Who hath required this at your hand,
To trample My courts?
13. Bring no more vain oblations;
It is an offering of abomination unto Me;
New moon and sabbath, the holding of convocations—
I cannot endure iniquity along with the solemn assembly.
14. Your new moons and your appointed seasons
My soul hateth;
They are a burden unto Me;
I am weary to bear them.

is left. Isolated and helpless, owing to the devastation of the land.

booth . . . lodge. A night-watchman's rough and frail shelter.

9. *the LORD of hosts.* A peculiarly solemn Divine title to denote the all-embracing sovereignty of God, His command of all the forces of nature and all the powers of men.

had left unto us. Of His own grace and mercy, and not for any righteousness of our own (Rashi).

very small. Heb. כמעט. Rashi and most moderns join this to the second half of the verse, and translate it: 'We had all but been as Sodom, and become like unto Gomorrah.' Those cities had perished through lack of such a remnant; see Gen. XVIII, 24 f.

10–17. The true service of God: obedience to the Moral Law as the prerequisite of all worship.

10. *rulers of Sodom . . . people of Gomorrah.* Thus are emphasized both their wickedness and their peril. 'The fate of Sodom had nearly been theirs, the character of Sodom was wholly so' (Davidson). Note that Isaiah, the courtier and aristocrat, blames the *leaders* for the degeneracy of the nation (Marti).

rulers of Sodom. lit. 'judges of Sodom,' who walked in the ways of Sodom.

11. *to what purpose.* None must have known better than the Prophets that acts of worship both kindle and express true religion. But, it is their immortal merit to have proclaimed that the sacrifices of 'judges of Sodom' are an insult to God; cf. Prov. XXI, 27. Throughout this section, it is not the offerings in themselves that are condemned, but the hypocritical character of those who bring the sacrifices. 'The sacrifices were commanded to you that ye call Me to mind and refrain from sin; and, having sinned, that ye confess them at the offering of the sacrifice and repent of your evil ways. If ye do so, the sacrifices are a sweet savour unto Me; but, as it is now, I loathe them' (Kimchi); see pp. 560–2.

12. *to trample My courts.* 'Like the oxen led in to sacrifice; so formal is your attendance' (Cheyne).

13. *vain oblations.* False offerings.

holding of convocations. The sacred convocations, or Festivals; Lev. XXIII, 4.

15. *spread forth your hands.* In prayer. Prayer and festival observance are dear unto God, but not on the part of men whose hands are *full of blood*, through the cruel wrongs perpetrated or tolerated against the innocent and helpless.

טו וּבְפָרִשְׂכֶם כַּפֵּיכֶם אַעְלִים עֵינַי מִכֶּם גַּם כִּי־תַרְבּוּ תְפִלָּה
16 אֵינֶנִּי שֹׁמֵעַ יְדֵיכֶם דָּמִים מָלֵאוּ׃ רַחֲצוּ הִזַּכּוּ הָסִירוּ רֹעַ
17 מַעַלְלֵיכֶם מִנֶּגֶד עֵינָי חִדְלוּ הָרֵעַ׃ לִמְדוּ הֵיטֵב דִּרְשׁוּ
מִשְׁפָּט אַשְּׁרוּ חָמוֹץ שִׁפְטוּ יָתוֹם רִיבוּ אַלְמָנָה׃
18 לְכוּ־נָא וְנִוָּכְחָה יֹאמַר יְהוָה אִם־יִהְיוּ חֲטָאֵיכֶם כַּשָּׁנִים
19 כַּשֶּׁלֶג יַלְבִּינוּ אִם־יַאְדִּימוּ כַתּוֹלָע כַּצֶּמֶר יִהְיוּ׃ אִם־תֹּאבוּ
כ וּשְׁמַעְתֶּם טוּב הָאָרֶץ תֹּאכֵלוּ׃ וְאִם־תְּמָאֲנוּ וּמְרִיתֶם
21 חֶרֶב תְּאֻכְּלוּ כִּי פִּי יְהוָה דִּבֵּר׃ אֵיכָה הָיְתָה
לְזוֹנָה קִרְיָה נֶאֱמָנָה מְלֵאֲתִי מִשְׁפָּט צֶדֶק יָלִין בָּהּ וְעַתָּה
22 מְרַצְּחִים׃ כַּסְפֵּךְ הָיָה לְסִיגִים סָבְאֵךְ מָהוּל בַּמָּיִם׃

15. And when ye spread forth your hands,
I will hide Mine eyes from you;
Yea, when ye make many prayers,
I will not hear;
Your hands are full of blood.

16. Wash you, make you clean,
Put away the evil of your doings
From before Mine eyes,
Cease to do evil;

17. Learn to do well;
Seek justice, relieve the oppressed,
Judge the fatherless, plead for the widow.

18. Come now, and let us reason together,
Saith the LORD;
Though your sins be as scarlet,
They shall be as white as snow;
Though they be red like crimson,
They shall be as wool.

19. If ye be willing and obedient,
Ye shall eat the good of the land;

20. But if ye refuse and rebel,
Ye shall be devoured with the sword;
For the mouth of the LORD hath spoken.

21. How is the faithful city
Become a harlot!
She that was full of justice,
Righteousness lodged in her,
But now murderers.

22. Thy silver is become dross,
Thy wine mixed with water.

W. H. Green rightly reminds us that nothing is further from the truth than to believe that the Prophets preached a kind of Confucianism; *i.e.* civic righteousness, without religion or prayer.

16–17. The vital demand of God—repentance, righteousness, charity.

16. *make you clean.* Cleanse your hearts (Kimchi).

17. *learn to do well.* Well-doing must be *learned* by repeated, habitual action. 'Happy is he that *wisely* considereth the poor,' says the Psalmist. At long last it is recognized that helping others—Philanthropy—is a study, a science! Some connect *learn to do well* with *cease to do evil* of the preceding *v.* Refraining from evil must be supplemented by positive acts of loving-kindness.

justice. Justice—social righteousness that secures for each individual his personal rights.

relieve the oppressed. Or, 'set right the oppressor' by opposition to his course of conduct.

judge. Procure justice for.

plead. Take the part of. Heb. ריבו, lit. 'strive'; *i.e.* do not refrain from strife and struggle in your endeavour to secure justice to the weak and friendless.

18–20. A free offer of pardon to the penitent, but threat of destruction to those who continue in rebellion. The people is given the choice—obedience and prosperity, or disobedience and destruction.

20. *devoured with the sword.* 'A glance at the ravages of the Assyrian soldiery' (Cheyne).

21–26. A dirge (kinah) over the moral decline of Jerusalem.

21. *faithful city.* The once faithful city, faithful of old to her Divine Husband.

harlot. Here in the meaning of 'unfaithful wife'; unfaithful through idolatry and social iniquity to Israel's marriage-bond with God; see p. 581.

justice . . . righteousness. '*Righteousness* (zedek) is the principle of right action in individuals or the community; *judgment* (mishpat) the embodiment of that principle in judicial decisions, use, and wont' (Skinner).

lodged. Permanently dwelt there (Kimchi); see II Chronicles XIX, 5–6.

murderers. Men guilty of miscarriages of justice.

22. *dross . . . mixed.* Aside from the literal meaning, these facts are used figuratively to state that the best of the rulers have become debased.

23 שָׂרַיִךְ סוֹרְרִים וְחַבְרֵי גַּנָּבִים כֻּלּוֹ אֹהֵב שֹׁחַד וְרֹדֵף
שַׁלְמֹנִים יָתוֹם לֹא יִשְׁפֹּטוּ וְרִיב אַלְמָנָה לֹא־יָבוֹא אֲלֵיהֶם׃
24 לָכֵן נְאֻם הָאָדוֹן יְהוָה צְבָאוֹת אֲבִיר יִשְׂרָאֵל הוֹי אֶנָּחֵם
כה מִצָּרַי וְאִנָּקְמָה מֵאוֹיְבָי׃ וְאָשִׁיבָה יָדִי עָלַיִךְ וְאֶצְרֹף כַּבֹּר
26 סִיגָיִךְ וְאָסִירָה כָּל־בְּדִילָיִךְ׃ וְאָשִׁיבָה שֹׁפְטַיִךְ כְּבָרִאשֹׁנָה
וְיֹעֲצַיִךְ כְּבַתְּחִלָּה אַחֲרֵי־כֵן יִקָּרֵא לָךְ עִיר הַצֶּדֶק קִרְיָה
27 נֶאֱמָנָה׃ צִיּוֹן בְּמִשְׁפָּט תִּפָּדֶה וְשָׁבֶיהָ בִּצְדָקָה׃

23. Thy princes are rebellious,
And companions of thieves;
Every one loveth bribes,
And followeth after rewards;
They judge not the fatherless,
Neither doth the cause of the widow come unto them.

24. Therefore said the Lord, the LORD of hosts,
The Mighty One of Israel:
Ah, I will ease Me of Mine adversaries,
And avenge Me of Mine enemies;
25. And I will turn My hand upon thee,
And purge away thy dross as with lye,
And will take away all thine alloy;
26. And I will restore thy judges as at the first,
And thy counsellors as at the beginning;
Afterward thou shalt be called The city of righteousness,
The faithful city.

27. Zion shall be redeemed with justice,
And they that return of her with righteousness.

23. *rebellious.* Law-breakers.

companions of thieves. In partnership with thieves.

bribes. Moffatt renders: 'Your rulers are unruly men, hand in hand with thieves, everyone fond of his bribe, keen upon fees, but careless of the orphan's rights, and of the widow's cause.'

24–27. In the absence of every sign of repentance on the part of the perverse rulers, one means only remains to bring about better conditions—the Judgment. Through punishment of these rulers, God will vindicate His honour, and hasten the Restoration in Zion (Dillmann).

24. *ease Me of.* 'Satisfy myself by bringing retribution upon.'

Mine enemies. God deems such corrupt rulers and oppressors of the poor and helpless, to be His *enemies.*

25–27. The spiritual future of Israel.

25. *My hand upon thee.* With stroke upon stroke, till the transgressors cease and the nation is purified (Rashi, Malbim).

as with lye. Used in purifying metals.

26. *as at the first.* When David was king. Cf. Jer. II, 2, 'I remember for thee the kindness of thy youth'; see p. 713.

27. *with justice.* 'Through justice,' of the people, especially of the new judges.

that return of her. Those in Zion who turn to God (Rashi); or, those who will come back from exile. Both Zion and her children will be redeemed through the justice and righteousness which the regenerate people exhibit.

Isaiah never lost hope that a part of the nation—a Righteous Remnant—would repent. That sanctified minority would survive the Judgment which would befall Israel, and become the seed of a holy, indestructible, eternal People.

3

23. And I besought the LORD at that time, saying: 24. 'O LORD God, Thou hast begun to show Thy servant Thy greatness, and Thy strong hand; for what god is there in heaven or on earth, that can do according to Thy works, and according to Thy mighty acts? 25. Let me go over, I pray Thee, and see the good land that is beyond the Jordan, that goodly hill-country, and Lebanon.' 26. But the LORD was wroth with me for your sakes, and hearkened not unto me; and the LORD said unto me: 'Let it suffice thee; speak no more unto Me of this matter. 27. Get thee up into the top of Pisgah, and lift up thine eyes westward, and northward, and southward, and eastward, and behold with thine eyes; for thou shalt not go over this Jordan. 28. But charge Joshua, and encourage him, and strengthen him; for he shall go over before

ג ס ס ס מה 45

23 וָאֶתְחַנַּן אֶל־יְהוָה בָּעֵת הַהִוא לֵאמֹר׃ אֲדֹנָי יְהוִה אַתָּה
24 הַחִלּוֹתָ לְהַרְאוֹת אֶת־עַבְדְּךָ אֶת־גָּדְלְךָ וְאֶת־יָדְךָ הַחֲזָקָה
אֲשֶׁר מִי־אֵל בַּשָּׁמַיִם וּבָאָרֶץ אֲשֶׁר־יַעֲשֶׂה כְמַעֲשֶׂיךָ
כה וְכִגְבוּרֹתֶךָ׃ אֶעְבְּרָה־נָּא וְאֶרְאֶה אֶת־הָאָרֶץ הַטּוֹבָה אֲשֶׁר
26 בְּעֵבֶר הַיַּרְדֵּן הָהָר הַטּוֹב הַזֶּה וְהַלְּבָנֹן׃ וַיִּתְעַבֵּר יְהוָה בִּי
לְמַעַנְכֶם וְלֹא שָׁמַע אֵלָי וַיֹּאמֶר יְהוָה אֵלַי רַב־לָךְ אַל־
27 תּוֹסֶף דַּבֵּר אֵלַי עוֹד בַּדָּבָר הַזֶּה׃ עֲלֵה ׀ רֹאשׁ הַפִּסְגָּה וְשָׂא
עֵינֶיךָ יָמָּה וְצָפֹנָה וְתֵימָנָה וּמִזְרָחָה וּרְאֵה בְעֵינֶיךָ כִּי־לֹא
28 תַעֲבֹר אֶת־הַיַּרְדֵּן הַזֶּה׃ וְצַו אֶת־יְהוֹשֻׁעַ וְחַזְּקֵהוּ וְאַמְּצֵהוּ

II. VA-ETHCHANAN

(CHAPTERS III, 23–VII, 11)

II, 23–IV, 40. MOSES' FIRST DISCOURSE—CONTINUED

23–29. MOSES' PRAYER AND ITS REJECTION

The signs of God's favour to His people, shown in the victories over the Amorite kings, stirred the personal hope of Moses that he too might see 'the good land that is beyond Jordan'. But it was not to be. He might *view* the land, but he would never cross there. He was to commit the future to Joshua, his successor.

23. *I besought.* He does not base his request on his life of service to Israel, but begs it as an act of grace on the part of God (Rashi).

24. *begun to show.* He yearned to see the *consummation* of the Divine promise.

25. *let me go over.* Not as Leader, but as one in the ranks, to whom the Divine decree might not apply. Hence, 'I besought the LORD *at that time*' (*v.* 23); *i.e.* after he had appointed Joshua as his successor (Malbim).

beyond the Jordan. Here, as in *v.* 20 above, referring to Western Palestine.

that goodly hill-country. i.e. that goodly mountain-land. From where Moses stood the whole of W. Palestine appeared as one compact mountain mass—a thing of surpassing beauty to his mind; cf. XI, 11. The three great landmarks in his life were all connected with mountains. Horeb, where he was called to be the Leader of his people; Sinai, whence issued forth the Divine Proclamation for all time of the Law of conduct; and Nebo, the peak from which he was to behold the Promised Land from afar.

Throughout the Hebrew Scriptures we find a deep love of mountains and mountain scenery. The Rabbis even introduced a special Blessing to be recited on beholding lofty mountains; Authorised Prayer Book, p. 290. All this is something quite exceptional in the Ancient World. No Greek could have written Psalm CXXI, *I will lift up mine eyes unto the hills;* and no Roman could have exclaimed with the Prophet, *Hear, O ye mountains, the LORD'S controversy, and ye enduring foundations of the earth* (Micah VI). 'The Greeks cared nothing for their native ranges; and the Romans were disgustingly practical, and regarded the Alps as an inconvenient barrier to conquest and commerce' (A. Lunn). Ruskin, who is supreme in modern times among the revealers of the glory and mystery of mountain landscape, largely drew his inspiration from the Hebrew Bible, which his mother taught him to read daily.

Lebanon. In the clear air of Palestine, the summit of Lebanon, the most prominent of all the mountains in Syria and Palestine, is visible from the plains of Moab.

26. *for your sakes.* Heb. למענכם; the word is not the same as in I, 37 and is understood by Hirsch to mean *for your good.* 'Had the unbelief of Moses gone unpunished, the people would have been hardened in their own transgression. For their sakes, therefore, it was impossible to overlook it' (Dummelow).

28. *charge.* lit. 'command' him, to do what you may not do! He is to begin the carrying out of the instructions given in Num. XXVII, 19.

he shall go over. The *he* is emphatic.

this people, and he shall cause them to inherit the land which thou shalt see.'
29. So we abode in the valley over against Beth-peor.

4

CHAPTER IV

1. And now, O Israel, hearken unto the statutes and unto the ordinances, which I teach you, to do them; that ye may live, and go in and possess the land which the LORD, the God of your fathers, giveth you.
2. Ye shall not add unto the word which I command you, neither shall ye diminish from it, that ye may keep the command-

כִּי־הוּא יַעֲבֹר לִפְנֵי הָעָם הַזֶּה וְהוּא יַנְחִיל אוֹתָם אֶת־הָאָרֶץ
29 אֲשֶׁר תִּרְאֶה׃ וַנֵּשֶׁב בַּגָּיְא מוּל בֵּית פְּעוֹר׃ פ

ד

CAP. IV. ד

א וְעַתָּה יִשְׂרָאֵל שְׁמַע אֶל־הַחֻקִּים וְאֶל־הַמִּשְׁפָּטִים אֲשֶׁר
אָנֹכִי מְלַמֵּד אֶתְכֶם לַעֲשׂוֹת לְמַעַן תִּחְיוּ וּבָאתֶם וִירִשְׁתֶּם
2 אֶת־הָאָרֶץ אֲשֶׁר יְהוָה אֱלֹהֵי אֲבֹתֵיכֶם נֹתֵן לָכֶם׃ לֹא
תֹסִפוּ עַל־הַדָּבָר אֲשֶׁר אָנֹכִי מְצַוֶּה אֶתְכֶם וְלֹא תִגְרְעוּ

29. *valley.* Glen or ravine.

Beth-peor. This *v.* ends the historical review in the First Discourse that began in I, 6. Accordingly the valley 'over against Beth-peor' must define more closely the location mentioned in I, 5, 'beyond Jordan, in the land of Moab.'

CHAPTER IV, 1–40

The historical review in the preceding three chapters is now followed by an eloquent appeal not to forget what they had seen and heard at Horeb. The Divine Law, if obeyed, shall be their wisdom and understanding in the sight of the peoples. Let them remember the marvellous events at Horeb, and keep far from all idolatry. Idolatry would inevitably be followed by exile. Nevertheless, even in exile, if they sought God in contrition and repentance, they would find Him. Moses concludes with an appeal to their experience of the uniqueness of their God, and pleads for whole-hearted obedience to Him.

1–4. An appeal to their experience that should have taught them the disastrous consequences of disobedience. As to the idea of reward and punishment which pervades this and the succeeding chapters, see on XI, 13.

1. *hearken.* Heb. שמע; understand, take to heart.

statutes. lit. 'engraved decrees'; originally referring to enactments passed by an authoritative body, engraven upon a stone tablet, and exposed in public for the information and guidance of the people. According to the Traditional explanation, *chukkim* are the precepts the reason for the observance of which is withheld from us; such as the prohibition of swine's flesh. One of their main objects is to inculcate discipline and obedience in the heart of every member of the Holy People. 'To obey is better than sacrifice' (I Sam. XV, 22).

ordinances. Judicial decisions arrived at in connection with a matter which had not previously been adjudicated upon, such decisions remaining precedents for the future. The phrase חקים ומשפטים is a standing one in Deuteronomy, but always חקים comes *before* משפטים; in order to indicate the basic importance of unquestioning obedience to the Divine Will.

which I teach. Heb. מלמד. The Jewish people have selected this teaching role of their Lawgiver as the holiest of all his activities, and speak of him not as King Moses, or Moses the Prophet, but as *Mosheh Rabbenu*, 'Moses our Teacher.'

to do them. This is the main purpose of the teaching. 'Not learning, but doing is the principal thing' (Ethics of the Fathers).

that ye may live. 'As a nation! As a matter of fact Israel preserved its identity among the nations, and survived the influences which overwhelmed the religions of its neighbours, by its obedience. The Law was a fence about the people' (G. A. Smith); see on Lev. XVIII, 5.

the God of your fathers. The God who had promised the Patriarchs that the Land would come into the possession of their descendants, was now fulfilling that promise. The same God was imposing His commandments upon them, and would reward their fidelity and punish their disobedience in the years to come.

2. *ye shall not add.* 'A warning against weakening the force of the Divine commandment by additions, omissions, or explanations that would dilute its original meaning, or make it more palatable to human selfishness and desire' (Dillmann). That, however, does not imply that the enactments of the Mosaic code could never be added to or modified as new conditions warranted the change, provided all such modifications were not proclaimed as new revelations from on High (Joseph Karo). 'Israel was not to invent additions to the laws, nor arbitrarily diminish them; *e.g.* using five species, instead of four, in observing the command of the Lulav, or placing five fringes on a Tallis' (Rashi); see on XIII, 1.

ments of the LORD your God which I command you. 3. Your eyes have seen what the LORD did in Baal-peor; for all the men that followed the Baal of Peor, the LORD thy God hath destroyed them from the midst of thee. 4. But ye that did cleave unto the LORD your God are alive every one of you this day.*ii. 5. Behold, I have taught you statutes and ordinances, even as the LORD my God commanded me, that ye should do so in the midst of the land whither ye go in to possess it. 6. Observe therefore and do them; for this is your wisdom and your understanding in the sight of the peoples, that, when they hear all these statutes, shall say: 'Surely this great nation is a wise and understanding people.' 7. For what great nation is there, that hath God so nigh unto them, as the LORD our God is whensoever we call upon Him? 8. And what great nation is there, that hath statutes and ordinances so righteous as all this law,

מִמֶּנּוּ לִשְׁמֹר אֶת־מִצְוֺת יְהוָה אֱלֹהֵיכֶם אֲשֶׁר אָנֹכִי מְצַוֶּה
3 אֶתְכֶם׃ עֵינֵיכֶם הָרֹאוֹת אֵת אֲשֶׁר־עָשָׂה יְהוָה בְּבַעַל
פְּעוֹר כִּי כָל־הָאִישׁ אֲשֶׁר הָלַךְ אַחֲרֵי בַעַל־פְּעוֹר הִשְׁמִידוֹ
4 יְהוָה אֱלֹהֶיךָ מִקִּרְבֶּךָ׃ וְאַתֶּם הַדְּבֵקִים בַּיהוָה אֱלֹהֵיכֶם
שני ה חַיִּים כֻּלְּכֶם הַיּוֹם׃ *רְאֵה ׀ לִמַּדְתִּי אֶתְכֶם חֻקִּים וּמִשְׁפָּטִים
כַּאֲשֶׁר צִוַּנִי יְהוָה אֱלֹהָי לַעֲשׂוֹת כֵּן בְּקֶרֶב הָאָרֶץ אֲשֶׁר
6 אַתֶּם בָּאִים שָׁמָּה לְרִשְׁתָּהּ׃ וּשְׁמַרְתֶּם וַעֲשִׂיתֶם כִּי הִוא
חָכְמַתְכֶם וּבִינַתְכֶם לְעֵינֵי הָעַמִּים אֲשֶׁר יִשְׁמְעוּן אֵת
כָּל־הַחֻקִּים הָאֵלֶּה וְאָמְרוּ רַק עַם־חָכָם וְנָבוֹן הַגּוֹי
7 הַגָּדוֹל הַזֶּה׃ כִּי מִי־גוֹי גָּדוֹל אֲשֶׁר־לוֹ אֱלֹהִים קְרֹבִים
8 אֵלָיו כַּיהוָה אֱלֹהֵינוּ בְּכָל־קָרְאֵנוּ אֵלָיו׃ וּמִי גּוֹי גָּדוֹל

3–4. These verses are to be linked on to *v.* 1, as providing evidence that faithfulness to the Torah spells life, whereas rebellion brings death in its train.

3. *Baal of Peor.* The heathen deity worshipped in Peor (cf. III, 29) with loathsome rites; see Num. XXV, 1 f.

4. *ye that did cleave.* The Heb. דבק is used in connection with whole-souled, disinterested love; *e.g.* to describe Jonathan's loyal affection for David. This *v.* is recited in the synagogue immediately before the Reading of the Law.

5–8. Israel's greatness and wisdom will be manifest in obedience to the Divine Commandment.

5. *I have taught you.* The past tense is somewhat strange after the participle used in *v.* 1. However, this was not the first occasion on which Moses had proclaimed the Divine enactments. He is now merely recapitulating. 'When you reach the goal of your wanderings, remember that I have taught you statutes and judgments for you to observe in the midst of the land' (Nachmanides).

as the LORD my God commanded me. The Jewish teacher is *commanded* to teach the statutes and judgments to young and old in Israel (Hirsch). For many centuries it was held that teaching had to be *free*, without the taint of pecuniary remuneration. Hence the astounding phenomenon that the greatest Doctors of the Talmudic Academies were artisans and handicraftsmen, who eked out their living from these occupations. It was only under the stress of persecution and economic necessity that at last, in the 15th century, some rabbis were compelled to take salaries in compensation for the time which they otherwise might have devoted to find their sustenance.

6. *observe therefore and do them.* Better, *take ye heed to do them* (Koenig).

this. i.e. your faithful observance of the Divine commandments.

in the sight of the peoples. In the estimation of the peoples. After Alexander's conquest of Asia, enlightened Greeks looked upon the Jews as 'philosophers of the East', because of their unique monotheism (G. A. Smith). But the aggrandizement of Israel was not an end in itself: it was to demonstrate to the children of men the Divine in Human History. The sudden rise to power of a horde of slaves, their well-government, prosperity and security, would attract attention. The peoples would ask, What is the secret of Israel's greatness? And, discovering that it rested upon fidelity to the Will of God, they might be induced to pay allegiance to the God of Israel. 'We have here in substance the idea of the missionary purpose of Israel's existence' (Oettli); cf. I Kings X, 1–3; Isa. II, 1–3. This idea was developed, and frequently emphasized in Prophetic and Rabbinic literature.

7. *so nigh unto them.* Israel's religion is unique becuase of the nearness of man to his Maker that it teaches. It proclaims, *No intermediary of any sort is required for the worshipper to approach his God in prayer.* 'The LORD is nigh unto all them that call upon Him, to all that call upon Him in truth,' is the teaching of the Psalmist. The Rabbis only deepened the teaching of Prophets and Psalmists on this head. The charge often brought against Judaism that it knows only a 'distant God' is thus without any foundation.

8. *what great nation is there, that hath statutes and ordinances so righteous?* Israel's religion is likewise unique through the ethical character and which I set before you this day? 9. Only take heed to thyself, and keep thy soul diligently, lest thou forget the things which thine eyes saw, and lest they depart from thy heart all the days of thy life; but make them known unto thy children and thy children's children; 10. the day that thou stoodest before the LORD thy God in Horeb, when the LORD said unto me: 'Assemble Me the people, and I will make them hear My words, that they may learn to fear Me all the days that they live upon the earth, and that they may teach their children.' 11. And ye came near and stood under the mountain; and the mountain burned with fire unto the heart of heaven, with darkness, cloud, and thick darkness. 12. And the LORD spoke unto you out of the midst of the fire; ye heard the voice of words, but ye saw no form; only a voice. 13. And He declared unto you His covenant, which He commanded you to perform, even the ten words; and He wrote them upon two tables of stone. 14. And the LORD commanded

אֲשֶׁר־לוֹ חֻקִּים וּמִשְׁפָּטִים צַדִּיקִם כְּכֹל הַתּוֹרָה הַזֹּאת
9 אֲשֶׁר אָנֹכִי נֹתֵן לִפְנֵיכֶם הַיּוֹם׃ רַק הִשָּׁמֶר לְךָ וּשְׁמֹר
נַפְשְׁךָ מְאֹד פֶּן־תִּשְׁכַּח אֶת־הַדְּבָרִים אֲשֶׁר־רָאוּ עֵינֶיךָ
וּפֶן־יָסוּרוּ מִלְּבָבְךָ כֹּל יְמֵי חַיֶּיךָ וְהוֹדַעְתָּם לְבָנֶיךָ וְלִבְנֵי
י בָנֶיךָ׃ יוֹם אֲשֶׁר עָמַדְתָּ לִפְנֵי יְהוָה אֱלֹהֶיךָ בְּחֹרֵב בֶּאֱמֹר
יְהוָה אֵלַי הַקְהֶל־לִי אֶת־הָעָם וְאַשְׁמִעֵם אֶת־דְּבָרָי אֲשֶׁר
יִלְמְדוּן לְיִרְאָה אֹתִי כָּל־הַיָּמִים אֲשֶׁר הֵם חַיִּים עַל־
11 הָאֲדָמָה וְאֶת־בְּנֵיהֶם יְלַמֵּדוּן׃ וַתִּקְרְבוּן וַתַּעַמְדוּן תַּחַת
הָהָר וְהָהָר בֹּעֵר בָּאֵשׁ עַד־לֵב הַשָּׁמַיִם חֹשֶׁךְ עָנָן וַעֲרָפֶל׃
12 וַיְדַבֵּר יְהוָה אֲלֵיכֶם מִתּוֹךְ הָאֵשׁ קוֹל דְּבָרִים אַתֶּם
13 שֹׁמְעִים וּתְמוּנָה אֵינְכֶם רֹאִים זוּלָתִי קוֹל׃ וַיַּגֵּד לָכֶם
אֶת־בְּרִיתוֹ אֲשֶׁר צִוָּה אֶתְכֶם לַעֲשׂוֹת עֲשֶׂרֶת הַדְּבָרִים

righteousness of its laws for the government of human society. Cardinal Faulhaber, after reviewing the poor-laws, the rights of labour, and the administration of justice found in the Pentateuch, placed the following alternative before the Nazi detractors of the Hebrew Scriptures: either such laws are Divinely inspired, or they are the product of a people endowed above all other peoples with positive *genius* for ethical and social values! 'The cradle of humanity,' he declared, 'is not in Greece; it is in Palestine. Those who do not regard these books as the word of God and as Divine revelation, must admit that Israel is the super-people in the history of the world!' For the tribute to Israel paid a generation before Faulhaber by Leo Tolstoy, see p. 45.

9–24. 'Lest ye forget' that the basic principle of God's Law is the spirituality of God and His abhorrence of all idolatrous representation of Him.

9. *keep thy soul diligently.* lit. 'guard well thy life.' The survival of the nation depends on Israel's memory of and loyalty to the Law of Sinai.

from thy heart. From thy memory; the 'heart' being conceived as the seat of memory.

make them known unto thy children. A second command: These things must also be kept alive in the memory of posterity, so that future generations do not lose their spiritual identity and sink back into heathenism. This transcendent duty towards children and children's children is repeated with the utmost emphasis throughout Deuteronomy. Eventually such insistence on the sacred obligation of religious education led to the first efforts in the world's history to provide elementary instruction to *all* the children of the community: see p. 818. For the content of the religious education that should be accorded to each Jewish child, see p. 926.

10. *the day . . . in Horeb.* When Israel was consecrated as a 'kingdom of priests'. The two-fold obligation is insisted upon: first, they are to learn God's Will and shape their lives in accordance therewith; secondly, to teach their children the Divine Will, so that they too may shape their lives in the light of that Will.

11. *under.* At the foot of (Onkelos, Biur).

with darkness. Better, *amid darkness,* that surrounded the mountain below (Mendelssohn, Driver).

12. *ye saw no form.* Nothing to indicate a material body. He who was *heard* at Horeb was not *seen.*

13. *covenant.* Heb. *berith;* a compact of any kind between man and man (Gen. XII, 32), and between God and man. Here the word is used for the conditions of the Covenant, the terms of the agreement made at Sinai, as binding on Israel; viz. the Ten Commandments.

two tables of stone. See Exod. XXIV, 12; XXXI, 18.

14. *and the LORD commanded me.* lit. 'and me the LORD commanded'; *i.e.* to you He spake the Ten Commandments and these alone; but me He gave during those forty days on the Mount additional instruction for guidance of the Israelite's life throughout all time.

me at that time to teach you statutes and ordinances, that ye might do them in the land whither ye go over to possess it. 15. Take ye therefore good heed unto yourselves—for ye saw no manner of form on the day that the LORD spoke unto you in Horeb out of the midst of the fire—16. lest ye deal corruptly, and make you a graven image, even the form of any figure, the likeness of male or female, 17. the likeness of any beast that is on the earth, the likeness of any winged fowl that flieth in the heaven, 18. the likeness of any thing that creepeth on the ground, the likeness of any fish that is in the water under the earth; 19. and lest thou lift up thine eyes unto heaven, and when thou seest the sun and the moon and the stars, even all the host of

14 וַיִּכְתְּבֵם עַל־שְׁנֵי לֻחוֹת אֲבָנִים׃ וְאֹתִי צִוָּה יְהוָה בָּעֵת
הַהִוא לְלַמֵּד אֶתְכֶם חֻקִּים וּמִשְׁפָּטִים לַעֲשֹׂתְכֶם אֹתָם
טו בָּאָרֶץ אֲשֶׁר אַתֶּם עֹבְרִים שָׁמָּה לְרִשְׁתָּהּ׃ וְנִשְׁמַרְתֶּם
מְאֹד לְנַפְשֹׁתֵיכֶם כִּי לֹא רְאִיתֶם כָּל־תְּמוּנָה בְּיוֹם דִּבֶּר
16 יְהוָה אֲלֵיכֶם בְּחֹרֵב מִתּוֹךְ הָאֵשׁ׃ פֶּן־תַּשְׁחִתוּן וַעֲשִׂיתֶם
17 לָכֶם פֶּסֶל תְּמוּנַת כָּל־סָמֶל תַּבְנִית זָכָר אוֹ נְקֵבָה׃ תַּבְנִית
כָּל־בְּהֵמָה אֲשֶׁר בָּאָרֶץ תַּבְנִית כָּל־צִפּוֹר כָּנָף אֲשֶׁר תָּעוּף
18 בַּשָּׁמָיִם׃ תַּבְנִית כָּל־רֹמֵשׂ בָּאֲדָמָה תַּבְנִית כָּל־דָּגָה אֲשֶׁר־
19 בַּמַּיִם מִתַּחַת לָאָרֶץ׃ וּפֶן־תִּשָּׂא עֵינֶיךָ הַשָּׁמַיְמָה וְרָאִיתָ

15. *for ye saw.* These words till the end of the *v.* are parenthetical. As no form of God was seen at the Revelation on Mt. Sinai, it follows that representing Him under any image is forbidden, as He is a spiritual Being who cannot be pictured under any image.

16. *deal corruptly.* Act perniciously.
figure. The Heb. סמל is found in old Phœnician and Cypriote inscriptions in the sense of 'statue'.
female. How blasphemous and unnatural such a representation is to the Israelite mind can be gathered from the fact that the Heb. language does not even possess a *word* for 'goddess'; cf. I Kings XI, 5, where the Heb. for goddess is 'god'.

17. *likeness of any beast.* 'All the great deities of the Northern Semites had their sacred animals, and were themselves worshipped in animal form, or in association with animal symbols, down to a late date' (W. Robertson Smith).

19. *and lest.* Still the continuation of *take ye therefore good heed* in *v.* 15.
lift up thine eyes unto heaven. The heavenly luminaries exercised a great fascination upon early man. 'Astronomy and adoration entered the world together' (Martineau). The 'host of heaven' was the dominant influence in Babylonian religion. The Egyptians also reverenced the sun, the moon, and the stars as symbols of deities. Associated with this worship was also the superstition that the heavenly bodies influenced the lives of mortals, a superstition which is not yet altogether extinct.
thou be drawn away. lit. 'Thou sufferest thyself to be drawn away,' by their wonderful beauty, their inexplicable movements, and their varied effects upon the world, to worship them.
hath allotted (Onkelos).
unto all the peoples. To be worshipped by them (some Talmud teachers, Rashbam, and Mendelssohn).

RELIGIOUS TOLERANCE

God had *suffered* the heathens to worship the sun, moon, and stars as a stepping-stone to a higher stage of religious belief. That worship of the heathen nations thus forms part of God's guidance of humanity. But as for the Israelites, God had given them first-hand knowledge of Him through the medium of Revelation. It is for this reason that idolatry was *for them* an unpardonable offence; and everything that might seduce them from that Divine Revelation was to be ruthlessly destroyed. Hence the amazing tolerance shown by Judaism of all ages towards the followers of other cults, *so long as these were not steeped in immorality and crime.* Thus the Prophet Malachi declares even the sacrificial offering of heathens to be a glorification of God (see on Mal. I, 11, p. 103). Equally striking is the attitude of the Rabbis toward the heathen world. War had been declared against Canaanites not because of matters of dogma or ritual, but because of the savage cruelty and foul licentiousness of their lives and cult. But the Rabbis never regarded the heathens of their own day as on the same moral level with the Canaanites. Their contemporary heathens in the Roman and Persian Empires obeyed the laws of conduct which the Rabbis deemed vital to the existence of human society, the so-called 'seven commandments given to the children of Noah' (see p. 33, on *v.* 7). They wisely held that in their religious life these heathens merely followed the traditional worship which they had inherited from their fathers before them (מנהג אבותיהן בידיהן), and they could not therefore be held responsible for failure to reach a true notion of the Unity of God, בני נח לא נזהרו על השיתוף. Such followers of other faiths—they taught—were judged by God purely by their moral life. חסידי אומות העולם יש להם חלק לעולם הבא. 'The righteous of all nations have a share in the world to come,' and are heirs of immortality, alongside the righteous in Israel. A later Midrash proclaimed: 'I call heaven and heaven, thou be drawn away and worship them, and serve them, which the LORD thy God hath allotted unto all the peoples under the whole heaven. 20. But you hath the LORD taken and brought forth out of the iron furnace, out of Egypt, to be unto Him a people of inheritance, as ye are this day. 21. Now the LORD was angered with me for your sakes, and swore that I should not go over the Jordan, and that I should not go in unto that good land, which the LORD thy God giveth thee for an inheritance; 22. but I must die in this land, I must not go over the Jordan; but ye are to go over, and possess that good land. 23. Take heed unto yourselves, lest ye forget the covenant of the LORD your God, which He made with you, and make you a graven image, even the likeness of any thing which the LORD thy God hath forbidden thee. 24. For the

אֶת־הַשֶּׁמֶשׁ וְאֶת־הַיָּרֵחַ וְאֶת־הַכּוֹכָבִים כֹּל צְבָא הַשָּׁמַיִם
וְנִדַּחְתָּ וְהִשְׁתַּחֲוִיתָ לָהֶם וַעֲבַדְתָּם אֲשֶׁר חָלַק יְהוָה אֱלֹהֶיךָ
כ אֹתָם לְכֹל הָעַמִּים תַּחַת כָּל־הַשָּׁמָיִם׃ וְאֶתְכֶם לָקַח יְהוָה
וַיּוֹצִא אֶתְכֶם מִכּוּר הַבַּרְזֶל מִמִּצְרָיִם לִהְיוֹת לוֹ לְעַם נַחֲלָה
21 כַּיּוֹם הַזֶּה׃ וַיהוָה הִתְאַנַּף־בִּי עַל־דִּבְרֵיכֶם וַיִּשָּׁבַע לְבִלְתִּי
עָבְרִי אֶת־הַיַּרְדֵּן וּלְבִלְתִּי־בֹא אֶל־הָאָרֶץ הַטּוֹבָה אֲשֶׁר
22 יְהוָה אֱלֹהֶיךָ נֹתֵן לְךָ נַחֲלָה׃ כִּי אָנֹכִי מֵת בָּאָרֶץ הַזֹּאת
אֵינֶנִּי עֹבֵר אֶת־הַיַּרְדֵּן וְאַתֶּם עֹבְרִים וִירִשְׁתֶּם אֶת־הָאָרֶץ
23 הַטּוֹבָה הַזֹּאת׃ הִשָּׁמְרוּ לָכֶם פֶּן־תִּשְׁכְּחוּ אֶת־בְּרִית יְהוָה
אֱלֹהֵיכֶם אֲשֶׁר כָּרַת עִמָּכֶם וַעֲשִׂיתֶם לָכֶם פֶּסֶל תְּמוּנַת

earth to witness that, whether it be Jew or heathen, man or woman, freeman or bondman —only according to their acts doth the Divine spirit rest upon them.' And in the darkest days of the Middle Ages, Solomon ibn Gabirol, the great philosopher and Synagogue hymn-writer, sang

'Thou art the LORD,
And all beings are Thy servants, Thy domain;
And through those who serve idols vain
Thine honour is not detracted from,
For they all aim to Thee to come.'

This is probably the earliest enunciation of religious tolerance in Western Europe.

20. *iron furnace.* One whose fire is fierce enough to melt iron—a symbol of intense suffering and bitter bondage.

a people of inheritance. Involving a relationship that is doubly inalienable. It cannot be renounced by Israel; 'and that which cometh into your mind shall not be at all; in that ye say, We will be as the nations, as the families of the countries, to serve wood and stone. As I live, saith the LORD God, surely with a mighty hand, and with a stretched out arm, and with fury poured out, will I be king over you' (Ezekiel xx, 32–33). Nor will God ever forsake Israel; 'for the LORD will not forsake His people for His great name's sake; because it hath pleased the LORD to make you a people unto Himself' (I Sam. XII, 22).

as ye are this day. The same Heb. phrase as in II, 30.

22. *in this land. He* is not to participate in the inheritance! The words tremble with suppressed emotion, and his soul is full of that thought.

I must not go over Jordan. lit. 'I am not to go over Jordan.' This clause seems unnecessary after, *I must die in this land.* Hence Rashi's comment, Not even my bones will be carried over Jordan to be laid to rest in the sacred soil, as will happen with the bones of Joseph. LORD of the Universe—Moses prayed—the bones of Joseph shall rest in the Holy Land, why then shall I not enter it? The Divine answer was, 'Joseph always acknowledged himself a Hebrew, as it is said, "I was stolen out of the land of the Hebrews." Whereas thou, Moses, didst not always act thus. When the daughters of Jethro told their father, "An Egyptian helped us," thou wast silent and didst not contradict them. Therefore thou shalt not be buried in the Holy Land' (Midrash).

23. *take heed.* This *v.* is not a mere repetition of *v.* 15 f. The fate meted out to Moses should make Israel the more grateful for God's goodness, and at the same time more heedful not to incur God's wrath.

hath forbidden thee. lit. 'hath commanded thee,' not to do (Rashi).

24. *a devouring fire.* Consuming whatever rouses His indignation.

A 'JEALOUS' GOD

a jealous God. The Heb. *el kanna* means, 'a zealous God,' full of zeal for holiness and justice, to Whom man's doings and dealings are not a matter of indifference, but Who renders strict retribution for all idolatry and iniquity. It also means, 'a jealous God.' That may appear a startling description of God. It signifies that God claims the exclusive love of His children, their entire sincerity—and complete self-surrender. He will not allow the veneration and loyalty due to Him alone to be shared with other objects of worship; see on Exod. XX, 5.

LORD thy God is a devouring fire, a jealous God. ¶ 25. When thou shalt beget children, and children's children, and ye shall have been long in the land, and shall deal corruptly, and make a graven image, even the form of any thing, and shall do that which is evil in the sight of the LORD thy God, to provoke Him; 26. I call heaven and earth to witness against you this day, that ye shall soon utterly perish from off the land whereunto ye go over the Jordan to possess it; ye shall not prolong your days upon it, but shall utterly be destroyed. 27. And the LORD shall scatter you among the peoples, and ye shall be left few in number among the nations, whither the LORD shall lead

24 כֹּל אֲשֶׁר צִוְּךָ יְהוָה אֱלֹהֶיךָ׃ כִּי יְהוָה אֱלֹהֶיךָ אֵשׁ אֹכְלָה
הוּא אֵל קַנָּא׃ פ
כה כִּי־תוֹלִיד בָּנִים וּבְנֵי בָנִים וְנוֹשַׁנְתֶּם בָּאָרֶץ וְהִשְׁחַתֶּם
וַעֲשִׂיתֶם פֶּסֶל תְּמוּנַת כֹּל וַעֲשִׂיתֶם הָרַע בְּעֵינֵי יְהוָה־
26 אֱלֹהֶיךָ לְהַכְעִיסוֹ׃ הַעִידֹתִי בָכֶם הַיּוֹם אֶת־הַשָּׁמַיִם וְאֶת־
הָאָרֶץ כִּי־אָבֹד תֹּאבֵדוּן מַהֵר מֵעַל הָאָרֶץ אֲשֶׁר אַתֶּם
עֹבְרִים אֶת־הַיַּרְדֵּן שָׁמָּה לְרִשְׁתָּהּ לֹא־תַאֲרִיכֻן יָמִים
27 עָלֶיהָ כִּי הִשָּׁמֵד תִּשָּׁמֵדוּן׃ וְהֵפִיץ יְהוָה אֶתְכֶם בָּעַמִּים

v. 23. סבירין כאשר

This conception of 'a jealous God' saved Israel from going under in the days of ancient heathendom, as well as in the days of Greece and Rome. 'None of the founders of the great heathen religions had any inkling of this idea of a *jealous* God, a God who would have "none other gods," a God of terrible Truth who would not tolerate any lurking belief in witchcraft, or any sacrificing to the god-king, or any trifling with the stern unity of things' (H. G. Wells).

Our fathers' realization that truth can make no concession to untruth, nor enter into compromise with it, without self-surrender, is responsible for the religious stand they took up in the days of Greece and Rome. 'When Jerusalem fell, Rome was quite prepared to give the God of Israel a place in her Pantheon. Israel absolutely refused such religious annexation: the one, unique and universal God of Israel alone was a living God; Jupiter and his like were things of naught, figments of the imagination. And the same reasons that would not permit the Jews to bend the knee to the gods of pagan Rome, prevented them in later generations from allowing themselves to be absorbed by the two great Religions that issued from Israel's bosom. Here too they found, both in dogma and morality, novelties and concessions that were repugnant to the austere simplicity of their absolute monotheism' (T. Reinach).

And the blessed doctrine of 'a jealous God' is of vital importance for the Jew's attitude towards the neo-paganism of to-day and to-morrow. 'Judaism's mission is just as much to teach the world that there *are* false gods and false ideals, as it is to bring it nearer to the true one. Abraham, the friend of God, began his career, according to the legend, with breaking idols; and it is his particular glory to have been in opposition to the whole world' (Schechter).

25–31. RENEWED WARNING OF IDOLATRY: THREAT OF EXILE, WITH PROMISE OF GRACE ON REPENTANCE

They would be scattered among the peoples, if they fell away from the LORD. But even in those days of tribulation God's mercy would not forsake His people, if they turned to Him in true penitence.

25. *ye shall have been long in the land.* And your long continuance results in a loss of vigour, due to unbroken peace and prosperity. 'Prosperity sometimes acts like a narcotic, and sends the soul to sleep' (Dummelow). The Hebrew word is not וזקנתם 'to grow old and increase in wisdom' (זקן, זה שקנה חכמה), but ונושנתם, lit. 'to grow stale.' They must not imagine that having dwelt for many centuries in Canaan, their tenure was now fixed, and they could neglect the conditions of the Covenant with impunity. (Benjamin Szold makes the opening words כי תוליד, 'when thou shalt beget,' to be equivalent to גם כי תוליד, 'even when thou shalt beget').

do that which is evil. These words are explanatory of what precedes; viz. the making of images. Ibn Ezra explains them as signifying other offences—*e.g.* murder, impurity—which would provoke God.

26. *heaven and earth.* As abiding and outlasting the changes of human life.

ye shall soon utterly perish. Not every individual would be destroyed, but the national life would be brought to an end; see next *v.*

27. *scatter you.* The consequences of idolatry are exile from their native land, dispersion to the four winds of heaven, and diminution in numbers.

28. *wood and stone.* In their own land, they served images as symbols of something higher. But in exile the Israelite would sink to the level of fetish-worshippers and grovel to idols of wood and stone (Hoffmann). Such things cannot, however, permanently satisfy human souls that have known higher things. This very lowering of moral standards called forth a spiritual reaction among the religiously-minded 'remnant' in the Exile.

smell. Or, 'breathe,' as in Isa. XI, 3 (Koenig).

you away. 28. And there ye shall serve gods, the work of men's hands, wood and stone, which neither see, nor hear, nor eat, nor smell. 29. But from thence ye will seek the LORD thy God; and thou shalt find Him, if thou search after Him with all thy heart and with all thy soul. 30. In thy distress, when all these things are come upon thee, in the end of days, thou wilt return to the LORD thy God, and hearken unto His voice; 31. for the LORD thy God is a merciful God; He will not fail thee, neither destroy thee, nor forget the covenant of thy fathers which He swore unto them. 32. For ask now of the days past, which were before thee, since the day that God created man upon the earth, and from the one end of heaven unto the other, whether there hath been any such thing as this great thing is, or hath been heard like it? 33. Did ever a people hear the voice of God speaking out of the midst of the fire, as thou hast heard, and live? 34. Or hath God assayed to go and take Him a nation from the midst of another nation, by trials, by signs, and by wonders, and by war, and by a mighty hand,

וְנִשְׁאַרְתֶּם מְתֵי מִסְפָּר בַּגּוֹיִם אֲשֶׁר יְנַהֵג יְהוָה אֶתְכֶם
28 שָׁמָּה׃ וַעֲבַדְתֶּם־שָׁם אֱלֹהִים מַעֲשֵׂה יְדֵי אָדָם עֵץ וָאֶבֶן
אֲשֶׁר לֹא־יִרְאוּן וְלֹא יִשְׁמְעוּן וְלֹא יֹאכְלוּן וְלֹא יְרִיחֻן׃
29 וּבִקַּשְׁתֶּם מִשָּׁם אֶת־יְהוָה אֱלֹהֶיךָ וּמָצָאתָ כִּי תִדְרְשֶׁנּוּ
ל בְּכָל־לְבָבְךָ וּבְכָל־נַפְשֶׁךָ׃ בַּצַּר לְךָ וּמְצָאוּךָ כֹּל הַדְּבָרִים
הָאֵלֶּה בְּאַחֲרִית הַיָּמִים וְשַׁבְתָּ עַד־יְהוָה אֱלֹהֶיךָ וְשָׁמַעְתָּ
31 בְּקֹלוֹ׃ כִּי אֵל רַחוּם יְהוָה אֱלֹהֶיךָ לֹא יַרְפְּךָ וְלֹא יַשְׁחִיתֶךָ
32 וְלֹא יִשְׁכַּח אֶת־בְּרִית אֲבֹתֶיךָ אֲשֶׁר נִשְׁבַּע לָהֶם׃ כִּי
שְׁאַל־נָא לְיָמִים רִאשֹׁנִים אֲשֶׁר־הָיוּ לְפָנֶיךָ לְמִן־הַיּוֹם אֲשֶׁר
בָּרָא אֱלֹהִים ׀ אָדָם עַל־הָאָרֶץ וּלְמִקְצֵה הַשָּׁמַיִם וְעַד־קְצֵה
הַשָּׁמָיִם הֲנִהְיָה כַּדָּבָר הַגָּדוֹל הַזֶּה אוֹ הֲנִשְׁמַע כָּמֹהוּ׃
33 הֲשָׁמַע עָם קוֹל אֱלֹהִים מְדַבֵּר מִתּוֹךְ־הָאֵשׁ כַּאֲשֶׁר־שָׁמַעְתָּ
34 אַתָּה וַיֶּחִי׃ אוֹ ׀ הֲנִסָּה אֱלֹהִים לָבוֹא לָקַחַת לוֹ גוֹי מִקֶּרֶב

כצ"ל v. 33.

29. *ye will seek the LORD.* This is a great pronouncement of Scripture, proclaiming the omnipotence of תשובה, Repentance. But the sinner must *seek* God; *i.e.* he must feel the 'loss' of God, and take active measures to 'find' Him and regain His favour. And that search must be with the sinner's whole heart and soul. Sincere repentance always and everywhere secures the Divine Mercy. It would be so in the Exile, if they sought God with a radical change of heart, and the devotion of the whole being. And indeed it was in the Exile that repentant Israel found God, rediscovered the Torah, rediscovered itself.

30. *in the end of days.* See on Gen. XLIX, 1; Num. XXIV, 14. Here equivalent to the phrase, 'later on' (Koenig).

31. *a merciful God.* Although He is 'a devouring fire' to those who are perversely wicked, He is merciful and gracious to the sincerely penitent; and His hand is outstretched to receive the sinner returning unto Him.

fail thee. He will not give thee up (Hoffmann); or, He will not withdraw His hand from upholding thee (Rashi).

neither destroy thee. Nor permit thee to go to destruction.

nor forget the covenant. With the Fathers of Israel. This is the basis of Israel's selection and eternal preservation.

32–40. THE UNIQUENESS OF THE GOD OF ISRAEL

Again there is an appeal to history to justify the Divine claims. From the beginning of time, from one end of heaven to the other, no nation had experienced the unparalleled redemption and revelation that were vouchsafed unto Israel. 'He hath not dealt so with any other nation' (Psalm CXLVII, 20).

33. *and live.* The idea often finds expression in Scripture that man cannot have direct communication with God and survive; Exod. XXXIII, 20.

34. *assayed . . . to take Him a nation.* Or, 'adventured' or, 'attempted,' to select a nation for His special service. A bold anthropomorphism that gives striking expression to the profound thought that Israel is, so to speak, 'a Divine experiment in history' (M. Lazarus).

trials. *e.g.* testing the character of Pharaoh by the manifestation of His might; or testing Israel in the iron furnace of suffering, *v.* 20.

signs. Events, either ordinary or extraordinary, having for their purpose the fulfilment of a Divine aim.

wonders. Portents, supernatural phenomena.

war. The overthrow of the Egyptian host.

a mighty hand. The Biblical term to denote any Divine intervention in history (Koenig).

great terrors. *e.g.* the heaping of the waters at the Red Sea. An old Jewish interpretation, found in the Septuagint and the Passover Haggadah, understands this phrase to refer to God's self-manifestation (גילוי שכינה).

and by an outstretched arm, and by great terrors, according to all that the LORD your God did for you in Egypt before thine eyes? 35. Unto thee it was shown, that thou mightest know that the LORD, He is God; there is none else beside Him. 36. Out of heaven He made thee to hear His voice, that He might instruct thee; and upon earth He made thee to see His great fire; and thou didst hear His words out of the midst of the fire. 37. And because He loved thy fathers, and chose their seed after them, and brought thee out with His presence, with His great power, out of Egypt, 38. to drive out nations from before thee greater and mightier than thou, to bring thee in, to give thee their land for an inheritance, as it is this day; 39. know this day, and lay it to thy heart, that the LORD, He is God in heaven above and upon the earth beneath; there is none else. 40. And thou shalt keep His statutes, and His commandments, which I command thee this day, that it may go well with thee, and with thy children after thee, and that thou mayest prolong thy days upon the land, which the LORD thy God giveth thee, for ever.*iii a. ¶ 41. Then Moses separated three cities beyond the Jordan toward the sunrising; 42. that the manslayer might flee thither, that slayeth his neighbour unawares, and hated him not in time past; and that fleeing unto one of

גּוֹי בְּמַסֹּת בְּאֹתֹת וּבְמוֹפְתִים וּבְמִלְחָמָה וּבְיָד חֲזָקָה
וּבִזְרוֹעַ נְטוּיָה וּבְמוֹרָאִים גְּדֹלִים כְּכֹל אֲשֶׁר־עָשָׂה לָכֶם
לה יְהוָה אֱלֹהֵיכֶם בְּמִצְרַיִם לְעֵינֶיךָ׃ אַתָּה הָרְאֵתָ לָדַעַת כִּי
36 יְהוָה הוּא הָאֱלֹהִים אֵין עוֹד מִלְבַדּוֹ׃ מִן־הַשָּׁמַיִם הִשְׁמִיעֲךָ
אֶת־קֹלוֹ לְיַסְּרֶךָּ וְעַל־הָאָרֶץ הֶרְאֲךָ אֶת־אִשּׁוֹ הַגְּדוֹלָה
37 וּדְבָרָיו שָׁמַעְתָּ מִתּוֹךְ הָאֵשׁ׃ וְתַחַת כִּי אָהַב אֶת־אֲבֹתֶיךָ
וַיִּבְחַר בְּזַרְעוֹ אַחֲרָיו וַיּוֹצִאֲךָ בְּפָנָיו בְּכֹחוֹ הַגָּדֹל מִמִּצְרָיִם׃
38 לְהוֹרִישׁ גּוֹיִם גְּדֹלִים וַעֲצֻמִים מִמְּךָ מִפָּנֶיךָ לַהֲבִיאֲךָ לָתֶת־
39 לְךָ אֶת־אַרְצָם נַחֲלָה כַּיּוֹם הַזֶּה׃ וְיָדַעְתָּ הַיּוֹם וַהֲשֵׁבֹתָ
אֶל־לְבָבֶךָ כִּי יְהוָה הוּא הָאֱלֹהִים בַּשָּׁמַיִם מִמַּעַל וְעַל־
מ הָאָרֶץ מִתָּחַת אֵין עוֹד׃ וְשָׁמַרְתָּ אֶת־חֻקָּיו וְאֶת־מִצְוֹתָיו
אֲשֶׁר אָנֹכִי מְצַוְּךָ הַיּוֹם אֲשֶׁר יִיטַב לְךָ וּלְבָנֶיךָ אַחֲרֶיךָ
וּלְמַעַן תַּאֲרִיךְ יָמִים עַל־הָאֲדָמָה אֲשֶׁר יְהוָה אֱלֹהֶיךָ נֹתֵן
לְךָ כָּל־הַיָּמִים׃ * פ שלישי
41 אָז יַבְדִּיל מֹשֶׁה שָׁלֹשׁ עָרִים בְּעֵבֶר הַיַּרְדֵּן מִזְרְחָה שָׁמֶשׁ׃
42 לָנֻס שָׁמָּה רוֹצֵחַ אֲשֶׁר יִרְצַח אֶת־רֵעֵהוּ בִּבְלִי־דַעַת

35. *it was shown.* The experience of God's unique power was first-hand with them, and not derived from speculation or hearsay. Yehudah Hallevi bases on this circumstance the supreme credibility of the Revelation at Sinai: it took place before an entire people.

there is none else beside Him. A clear expression of absolute monotheism; repeated in *v.* 39; VI, 4; VII, 9; X, 17; and XXXII, 39. A Talmudical note on these words is, 'not even magical powers'; *i.e.* the Israelites were to put no faith in witchcraft.

36. *instruct.* Better, *discipline.* What Israel had seen and heard was not merely to impress the mind, but to affect their course of life, and check any tendency to stray after idolatry.

37. *loved thy fathers.* The Patriarchs.

with His presence. In His own person; not through an intermediary.

38. *as it is this day. i.e.* as thou hast already made conquests in the territory east of Jordan, the lands of Sihon and Og.

39. *know this day.* This *v.* and the one following form the peroration of the First Discourse, and summarize the lesson to be learnt from all that has gone before. According to most expositors, this First Discourse gives the historical framework and instruction for the new legislation. The aged Lawgiver exhorts the people to gratitude towards God (I, 6–III, 29), and closes with solemn warnings of the dangers of idolatry that threaten them on entering the Promised Land (IV, 1–40). *v.* 39 has been introduced into the *Oleynoo*, the closing prayer of every Synagogue Service.

41–43. MOSES ASSIGNS THREE CITIES OF REFUGE EAST OF JORDAN

The presence of these verses between the First and Second Discourses of Moses offers considerable difficulty, except on the interpretation of Luzzatto; cf. I, 5. Having finished the exposition of the words, *it is eleven days' journey from Horeb by the way of Mount Seir unto Kadesh-barnea* (I, 2), Moses records that he thereupon set aside the three Cities of Refuge, thus completing the establishment of a portion of Israel on the east of Jordan.

41. *separated.* Set apart.

three cities. There were to be six Cities of Refuge (see Num. XXXV, 9 f), three on each side of the Jordan. The purpose of these cities is expounded in chap. XIX.

42. *unawares.* Better, *unintentionally.*

these cities he might live: 43. Bezer in the wilderness, in the table-land, for the Reubenites; and Ramoth in Gilead, for the Gadites; and Golan in Bashan, for the Manassites. ¶ 44. And this is the law which Moses set before the children of Israel; 45. these are the testimonies, and the statutes, and the ordinances, which Moses spoke unto the children of Israel, when they came forth out of Egypt; 46. beyond the Jordan, in the valley over against Beth-peor, in the land of Sihon king of the Amorites, who dwelt at Heshbon, whom Moses and the children of Israel smote, when they came forth out of Egypt; 47. and they took his land in possession, and the land of Og king of Bashan, the two kings of the Amorites, who were beyond the Jordan toward the sunrising; 48. from Aroer, which is on the edge of the valley of Arnon, even unto mount Sion—the same is Hermon—49. and all the Arabah beyond the Jordan eastward, even unto the sea of the Arabah, under the slopes of Pisgah.*iii s, iv a.

וְהוּא לֹא־שֹׂנֵא לוֹ מִתְּמֹל שִׁלְשֹׁם וְנָס אֶל־אַחַת מִן־הֶעָרִים
43 הָאֵל וָחָי׃ אֶת־בֶּצֶר בַּמִּדְבָּר בְּאֶרֶץ הַמִּישֹׁר לָראוּבֵנִי
44 וְאֶת־רָאמֹת בַּגִּלְעָד לַגָּדִי וְאֶת־גּוֹלָן בַּבָּשָׁן לַמְנַשִּׁי׃ וְזֹאת
מה הַתּוֹרָה אֲשֶׁר־שָׂם מֹשֶׁה לִפְנֵי בְּנֵי יִשְׂרָאֵל׃ אֵלֶּה הָעֵדֹת
וְהַחֻקִּים וְהַמִּשְׁפָּטִים אֲשֶׁר דִּבֶּר מֹשֶׁה אֶל־בְּנֵי יִשְׂרָאֵל
46 בְּצֵאתָם מִמִּצְרָיִם׃ בְּעֵבֶר הַיַּרְדֵּן בַּגַּיְא מוּל בֵּית פְּעוֹר
בְּאֶרֶץ סִיחֹן מֶלֶךְ הָאֱמֹרִי אֲשֶׁר יוֹשֵׁב בְּחֶשְׁבּוֹן אֲשֶׁר
47 הִכָּה מֹשֶׁה וּבְנֵי יִשְׂרָאֵל בְּצֵאתָם מִמִּצְרָיִם׃ וַיִּירְשׁוּ
אֶת־אַרְצוֹ וְאֶת־אֶרֶץ ׀ עוֹג מֶלֶךְ־הַבָּשָׁן שְׁנֵי מַלְכֵי הָאֱמֹרִי
48 אֲשֶׁר בְּעֵבֶר הַיַּרְדֵּן מִזְרַח שָׁמֶשׁ׃ מֵעֲרֹעֵר אֲשֶׁר עַל־
49 שְׂפַת־נַחַל אַרְנֹן וְעַד־הַר שִׂיאֹן הוּא חֶרְמוֹן׃ וְכָל־
הָעֲרָבָה עֵבֶר הַיַּרְדֵּן מִזְרָחָה וְעַד יָם הָעֲרָבָה תַּחַת
אַשְׁדֹּת הַפִּסְגָּה׃ * פ רביעי (שלישי לספ')

v. 42. סבירין האלה v. 43. כצ"ל

43. *Bezer.* Mentioned in Josh. xx, 8.

Ramoth in Gilead. Usually identified with the modern es-Salt; xxi, 36.

Golan. Josephus mentions a district called Gaulanitis east of Lake Tiberias, now named Jaulan, seventeen miles east of the Lake.

B. MOSES' SECOND DISCOURSE

1. Foundations of the Covenant (Chapters IV, 44–XI)

From iv, 44 to the end of xi, the Second Discourse, deals with *the religious foundations* of the Covenant, the spirit in which it is to be kept, and the motives to that right obedience. It defines the relationship between God and Israel, and emphasizes the basic spiritual demands that such relationship imposes upon Israel. Moses solemnly repeats to the new generation that faces him the Ten Commandments given at Sinai; proclaims the Unity of God, together with the Israelite's duty to love Him with all his heart, soul and might; and urges that the same love towards God must be implanted in the hearts of the children. That covenant shall be their distinction among the nations. Moses surveys the forty years of Providential mercies in the Wilderness, and also the succession of murmurings and rebellions. Not for their own righteousness will they conquer, but because of the oath sworn to their Fathers. Let Israel ever keep in mind the lessons of the Wilderness, lest it forget God and perish like the nations whom it is about to dispossess. No truce of any sort is to be made with the peoples of Canaan and their foul and inhuman cults. If Israel faithfully keeps God's commandments, the Land of Promise will enjoy the rain of heaven and be dowered with prosperity. Israel is, in conclusion, solemnly reminded of the alternatives—the Blessing and the Curse—now offered for its acceptance.

Chapter IV, 44–49. Title, Time, and Place of the Discourse

44. *this is the law.* 'Which he is about to set before them in chapters xii–xxvi' (Rashi). This *v.* is recited by the congregation when the Sefer Torah is held up after the Reading. In most rites, the words 'according to the commandment of the Lord by the hand of Moses' are added.

45. *these are the testimonies.* Better, *they are the testimonies.* This *v.* is parenthetical and points out that this Law which Moses is now to set before them is merely a new presentation of the testimonies, statutes, and judgments which He spake unto them when they came out of Egypt (Rashi, Biur).

testimonies. Heb. *edoth*; lit. 'attestations'; solemn declarations of God's will on matters of moral and religious duty.

48. *from Aroer.* Cf. ii, 36.

Mount Sion. Heb. שיאן, see on iii, 9; not to be confused with Mount Zion (Heb. ציון).

5

CHAPTER V

1. And Moses called unto all Israel, and said unto them: ¶ Hear, O Israel, the statutes and the ordinances which I speak in your ears this day, that ye may learn them, and observe to do them. 2. The LORD our God made a covenant with us in Horeb. 3. The LORD made not this covenant with our fathers, but with us, even us, who are all of us here alive this day. 4. The LORD spoke with you face to face in the mount out of the midst of the fire—5. I stood between the LORD and you at that time, to declare unto you the word of the LORD; for ye were afraid because of the fire, and went not up into the mount—saying: ¶ 6. I am the LORD thy God, who brought thee out of the land of Egypt, out of the house of bondage. ¶ 7. Thou shalt have no other gods before Me.

ה

CAP. V. ה

א וַיִּקְרָא מֹשֶׁה אֶל־כָּל־יִשְׂרָאֵל וַיֹּאמֶר אֲלֵהֶם שְׁמַע יִשְׂרָאֵל
אֶת־הַחֻקִּים וְאֶת־הַמִּשְׁפָּטִים אֲשֶׁר אָנֹכִי דֹּבֵר בְּאָזְנֵיכֶם
2 הַיּוֹם וּלְמַדְתֶּם אֹתָם וּשְׁמַרְתֶּם לַעֲשֹׂתָם׃ יְהוָה אֱלֹהֵינוּ
3 כָּרַת עִמָּנוּ בְּרִית בְּחֹרֵב׃ לֹא אֶת־אֲבֹתֵינוּ כָּרַת יְהוָה
אֶת־הַבְּרִית הַזֹּאת כִּי אִתָּנוּ אֲנַחְנוּ אֵלֶּה פֹה הַיּוֹם כֻּלָּנוּ
4 חַיִּים׃ פָּנִים ׀ בְּפָנִים דִּבֶּר יְהוָה עִמָּכֶם בָּהָר מִתּוֹךְ
ה הָאֵשׁ׃ אָנֹכִי עֹמֵד בֵּין־יְהוָה וּבֵינֵיכֶם בָּעֵת הַהִוא לְהַגִּיד
לָכֶם אֶת־דְּבַר יְהוָה כִּי יְרֵאתֶם מִפְּנֵי הָאֵשׁ וְלֹא־עֲלִיתֶם
6 בָּהָר לֵאמֹר׃ ס אָנֹכִי יְהוָה אֱלֹהֶיךָ אֲשֶׁר הוֹצֵאתִיךָ
7 מֵאֶרֶץ מִצְרַיִם מִבֵּית עֲבָדִים׃ לֹא־יִהְיֶה לְךָ אֱלֹהִים

CHAPTER V. ON THE REVELATION AT HOREB. CHAPTER V–VI, 3

The first foundation of the new covenant was the Decalogue—at once the alphabet and summary of the religious life, and the very foundation for all human conduct. The Ten Words formed the basis for the new precepts now to be promulgated (Hoffmann). Moses pronounces the Commandments one by one, as delivered by the Divine Voice amid fire and darkness. He also recalls the impression made on the people by what they had heard—their pledge to do whatever the LORD commanded them, and His approval of their words.

1. *learn them, and observe to do.* Knowledge is an essential pre-requisite to performance.

3. *not . . . with our fathers.* 'The Covenant was entered into only with the coming generation, as the fathers would die in the wilderness' (Abarbanel). Others understand the words to mean, 'not with our fathers alone'; the Covenant survived the men with whom it was made, with binding force upon all future generations.

4. *spoke with you.* *i.e.* revealed Himself to you. Many of those who were listening to Moses had been present as children at Horeb when the Ten Words were spoken.

face to face. *i.e.* a direct revelation, and not a matter of hearsay merely.

5. *I stood between.* As the Israelites did not go near the Mount, they heard the Voice but could not follow the words. Moses was the *meturgeman*, the 'interpreter', who conveyed the Divine message to them (Talmud).

word of the LORD. The collective name for 'The Ten Words'.

ye were afraid. See Exod. xx, 18–21.

saying. The Ten Words now following are almost, but not absolutely, a *verbatim* repetition of the Decalogue as given in Exod. xx. Being part of an exhortation addressed to a new generation, the Lawgiver does not hesitate to expand, or even alter the wording of the Commandments, for the sake of emphasis. In brief, the version in Deuteronomy is more rhetorical, more homiletical, than that in Exod. xx. For the full exposition of the Decalogue see pp. 294 ff. Only additional comments are here given.

6. THE FIRST COMMANDMENT

The Israelites are to recognize that unlike the deities worshipped by the benighted heathens around them—local nature-gods bound to the soil and its products—the God of Israel is the universal ruler of History, the God who redeemed them from Egyptian slavery.

6. *I am the LORD thy God.* Or, 'I, the LORD, am thy God.' The word 'LORD' is the current translation of the Divine Name of four letters (YHWH) as the eternal Power that guides the destinies of men and nations; see p. 6.

thy God. The suffix *thy* refers to 'Israel' collectively, and at the same time to each Israelite individually; as in *v.* 16. The Midrash says: 'Even as thousands may look at a great portrait and each one feel that it looks at *him*, so every Israelite at Horeb felt that the Divine Voice was addressing *him*.'

7–10. SECOND COMMANDMENT

7. *before Me.* Or, 'beside Me.' In addition to Him; see the opening *v.* of the Shema, VI, 4. The monotheism must be absolute. Others translate, 'to my face'; *i.e.* to provoke Him. The provocation is the greater, because these gods are unreal.

8. Thou shalt not make unto thee a graven image, even any manner of likeness, of any thing that is in heaven above, or that is in the earth beneath, or that is in the water under the earth. 9. Thou shalt not bow down unto them, nor serve them; for I the LORD thy God am a jealous God, visiting the iniquity of the fathers upon the children, and upon the third and upon the fourth generation of them that hate Me, 10. and showing mercy unto the thousandth generation of them that love Me and keep My commandments. ¶ 11. Thou shalt not take the name of the LORD thy God in vain; for the LORD will not hold him guiltless that taketh His name in vain. ¶ 12. Observe the sabbath day, to keep it holy, as the LORD thy God commanded thee. 13. Six days shalt thou labour, and do all thy work;

8 אֲחֵרִים עַל־פָּנָיַ׃ לֹא־תַעֲשֶׂה־לְךָ פֶסֶל ׀ כָּל־תְּמוּנָה אֲשֶׁר
בַּשָּׁמַיִם ׀ מִמַּעַל וַאֲשֶׁר בָּאָרֶץ מִתָּחַת וַאֲשֶׁר בַּמַּיִם ׀
9 מִתַּחַת לָאָרֶץ׃ לֹא־תִשְׁתַּחֲוֶה לָהֶם וְלֹא תָעָבְדֵם כִּי אָנֹכִי
יְהוָה אֱלֹהֶיךָ אֵל קַנָּא פֹּקֵד עֲוֺן אָבוֹת עַל־בָּנִים וְעַל־
י שִׁלֵּשִׁים וְעַל־רִבֵּעִים לְשֹׂנְאָי׃ וְעֹשֶׂה חֶסֶד לַאֲלָפִים
11 לְאֹהֲבַי וּלְשֹׁמְרֵי מִצְוֺתָו׃ ס לֹא תִשָּׂא אֶת־שֵׁם־יְהוָה
אֱלֹהֶיךָ לַשָּׁוְא כִּי לֹא יְנַקֶּה יְהוָה אֵת אֲשֶׁר־יִשָּׂא אֶת־שְׁמוֹ
12 לַשָּׁוְא׃ ס שָׁמוֹר אֶת־יוֹם הַשַּׁבָּת לְקַדְּשׁוֹ כַּאֲשֶׁר צִוְּךָ ׀
13 יְהוָה אֱלֹהֶיךָ׃ שֵׁשֶׁת יָמִים תַּעֲבֹד וְעָשִׂיתָ כָּל־מְלַאכְתֶּךָ׃

v. 10. מצותי ק׳

8. *any manner of likeness.* Extends the term 'graven image' to 'the likeness of any form'. *v.* 7 prohibits the worship of other gods; *v.* 8 prohibits the worship of the true God under the form of any image. Hoffmann thinks that the variation in the Heb. text from the form in Exodus was made in view of the sin of the Golden Calf that followed the giving of the Decalogue. The present version makes it clearer that every 'manner of likeness' comes within the category of 'graven image', and therefore of idolatry.

in heaven above. The heavenly bodies worshipped by many nations.

in the earth beneath. Such as the sacred bulls of the Egyptians.

9. *nor serve them.* lit. 'thou shalt not be induced to serve them,' the grammatical form being Hophal (Koenig). Only such sculpture or plastic reproduction as would become objects of idolatrous worship is prohibited here. Hence, the presence of the cherubim in the Tabernacle, and the twelve bronze bullocks under the basin in the Temple. Against art within its own sphere, monotheism wages no war; see p. 375. 'Every picture is an image of a prototype. But does there exist a prototype of the Divine that can be embodied in a picture? Pictures of God must accordingly be pictures of something other than God—of a something other to which the signification of God is given' (Hermann Cohen).

a jealous God. See on IV, 24.

and upon the third. In Exod. 'and' is omitted.

11. THIRD COMMANDMENT

Avoid oaths. For the sacred obligations of sincerity in speech, see VOWS AND VOWING IN THE LIGHT OF JUDAISM, p. 730.

11. *in vain.* Heb. **לשוא**, which may mean either, 'for vanity,' or, 'for falsehood.' The Jerusalem Targum prefaces its translation of this prohibition with the words, 'O my People, my People, House of Israel, swear not by the Name of the LORD thy God for vanity; and swear not by My Name and lie.' Every oath, *even if a true oath*, should be avoided, is the teaching of the Rabbis. It is not generally known that many in Israel have in every age followed the principle of 'Swear not at all', except when a Court of Law exacts an oath in order to ensure the ends of justice. To this day, pious men in Eastern Jewries suffer considerable pecuniary loss rather than enforce their plea by an oath. And it is the practice of a Beth Din to discourage oaths, in the rare instances where one of the litigants insists on the oath being administered.

12–15. FOURTH COMMANDMENT

12. *observe.* Heb. **שמור**; in Exod. **זכור** 'remember'. Tradition explains that the latter refers to the positive precepts in connection with the Sabbath, to its sanctification by wine, prayer and Sabbath joy; whereas 'observe' the Sabbath means, refraining from any desecration through labour by self or dependents. Hence, the addition here concerning the resting of servants and the reminder of the bondage in Egypt (Biur). Tradition also says, 'that both words *observe* and *remember* were communicated by God simultaneously'; *i.e.* the fourth commandment in Deuteronomy, though different in form, does not imply anything that has not been revealed by God on Mount Sinai. Moses uses the stronger word here, because in his exhortation he has a practical object in view; *viz.* the *observance* of God's commands by the people.

as the LORD thy God commanded thee. These words are not in Exodus, being a rhetorical amplification. The reference is to Marah, Exod. XV, 23–27.

14. but the seventh day is a sabbath unto the LORD thy God, in it thou shalt not do any manner of work, thou, nor thy son, nor thy daughter, nor thy man-servant, nor thy maid-servant, nor thine ox, nor thine ass, nor any of thy cattle, nor thy stranger that is within thy gates; that thy man-servant and thy maid-servant may rest as well as thou. 15. And thou shalt remember that thou wast a servant in the land of Egypt, and the LORD thy God brought thee out thence by a mighty hand and by an outstretched arm; therefore the LORD thy God commanded thee to keep the sabbath day. ¶ 16. Honour thy father and thy mother, as the LORD thy God commanded thee; that thy days may be long, and that it may go well with thee, upon the land which the LORD thy God giveth thee. ¶ 17. Thou shalt not murder. Neither shalt thou commit adultery. Neither shalt thou steal. Neither shalt thou bear false witness against thy neighbour. ¶ 18. Neither shalt thou covet thy neighbour's wife; neither shalt thou

14 וְיוֹם הַשְּׁבִיעִי שַׁבָּת ׀ לַיהוָה אֱלֹהֶיךָ לֹא תַעֲשֶׂה כָל־
מְלָאכָה אַתָּה וּבִנְךָ וּבִתֶּךָ וְעַבְדְּךָ וַאֲמָתֶךָ וְשׁוֹרְךָ וַחֲמֹרְךָ
וְכָל־בְּהֶמְתֶּךָ וְגֵרְךָ אֲשֶׁר בִּשְׁעָרֶיךָ לְמַעַן יָנוּחַ עַבְדְּךָ
טו וַאֲמָתְךָ כָּמוֹךָ׃ וְזָכַרְתָּ כִּי־עֶבֶד הָיִיתָ ׀ בְּאֶרֶץ מִצְרַיִם
וַיֹּצִאֲךָ יְהוָה אֱלֹהֶיךָ מִשָּׁם בְּיָד חֲזָקָה וּבִזְרֹעַ נְטוּיָה עַל־
16 כֵּן צִוְּךָ יְהוָה אֱלֹהֶיךָ לַעֲשׂוֹת אֶת־יוֹם הַשַּׁבָּת׃ ס כַּבֵּד אֶת־
אָבִיךָ וְאֶת־אִמֶּךָ כַּאֲשֶׁר צִוְּךָ יְהוָה אֱלֹהֶיךָ לְמַעַן ׀ יַאֲרִיכֻן
יָמֶיךָ וּלְמַעַן יִיטַב לָךְ עַל הָאֲדָמָה אֲשֶׁר־יְהוָה אֱלֹהֶיךָ
17 נֹתֵן לָךְ׃ ס לֹא תִּרְצָח׃ ס וְלֹא תִּנְאָף׃ ס וְלֹא
18 תִּגְנֹב׃ ס וְלֹא־תַעֲנֶה בְרֵעֲךָ עֵד שָׁוְא׃ ס וְלֹא
תַחְמֹד אֵשֶׁת רֵעֶךָ ס וְלֹא תִתְאַוֶּה בֵּית רֵעֶךָ שָׂדֵהוּ

14. *nor thine ox, nor thine ass, nor any of thy cattle.* In place of this detailed enumeration, appropriate to an oration, Exod. has simply, 'nor thy cattle.' Care and kindness to cattle are of such profound importance for the humanizing of man that this duty has its place in the Decalogue. The Rabbis classed cruelty to animals among the most serious of offences; see KINDNESS TO ANIMALS, p. 854.

that thy man-servant . . . thou. This is not in Exod.; but is an explanatory addition.

as well as thou. Heb. כמוך. The slave is to have the same right to his Sabbath-rest as the master. Sabbath-rest thus proclaims the equality of master and man.

15. *thou wast a servant in the land of Egypt.* This is the most important divergence between the two versions. According to Exod. the Sabbath was ordained in commemoration of the six days of creation, 'wherefore the LORD blessed the Sabbath day, and hallowed it.' Man was on that day to set aside the material cares that absorb his attention on the six days of toil. Judaism 'proclaims a truce once in seven days to all personal anxieties and degrading thoughts about the means of subsistence and success in life, and bids us meet together to indulge in larger thoughts. In countries where life is a hard struggle, what more precious, more priceless public benefit can be imagined than this breathing time, this recurring armistice between man and the hostile powers that beset his life, this solemn Sabbatic festival?' (J. R. Seeley). There was, however, another lesson for mankind to learn from the Sabbath institution. The Israelites in Egypt slaved day after day without a rest. By ceasing from toil one day in seven, they would distinguish their work from slavery. And in their new life in the Promised Land they were to avoid imposing upon others what had been so bitter to them.

16. FIFTH COMMANDMENT

16. *commanded thee.* The phrase, 'as the LORD thy God commanded thee,' is new in Deuteronomy, as is also 'and that it may go well with thee'. The latter stresses the truth that a sound national life can only result from a sound family life within the State.

17. SIXTH, SEVENTH, AND EIGHTH COMMANDMENTS

17. *murder . . . neighbour.* These Commandments are here connected by the conjunction 'and'; to indicate that these crimes are to some extent linked together, and that he who breaks one of them is not unlikely to break one of the others as well (Friedländer).

17. NINTH COMMANDMENT

false witness. A different Heb. word is here used for 'false' witness—the same as occurs in *v.* 11 for 'vain'.

18. TENTH COMMANDMENT

18. *covet . . . neighbour's.* The prohibition of coveting a man's wife is here made separate from 'desiring' (a different word, not occurring in Exod.) his possessions—a fundamental distinction of far-reaching moral consequence. There is also new mention of 'his field', an appropriate addition for a people about to enter upon the inheritance of their Land.

חמישי (רביעי לספ׳)
19 וְעַבְדּוֹ וַאֲמָתוֹ שׁוֹרוֹ וַחֲמֹרוֹ וְכֹל אֲשֶׁר לְרֵעֶךָ׃ ס אֶת־
הַדְּבָרִים הָאֵלֶּה דִּבֶּר יְהוָה אֶל־כָּל־קְהַלְכֶם בָּהָר מִתּוֹךְ
הָאֵשׁ הֶעָנָן וְהָעֲרָפֶל קוֹל גָּדוֹל וְלֹא יָסָף וַיִּכְתְּבֵם עַל־
כ שְׁנֵי לֻחֹת אֲבָנִים וַיִּתְּנֵם אֵלָי׃ וַיְהִי כְּשָׁמְעֲכֶם אֶת־הַקּוֹל
מִתּוֹךְ הַחֹשֶׁךְ וְהָהָר בֹּעֵר בָּאֵשׁ וַתִּקְרְבוּן אֵלַי כָּל־רָאשֵׁי
21 שִׁבְטֵיכֶם וְזִקְנֵיכֶם׃ וַתֹּאמְרוּ הֵן הֶרְאָנוּ יְהוָה אֱלֹהֵינוּ
אֶת־כְּבֹדוֹ וְאֶת־גָּדְלוֹ וְאֶת־קֹלוֹ שָׁמַעְנוּ מִתּוֹךְ הָאֵשׁ הַיּוֹם
22 הַזֶּה רָאִינוּ כִּי־יְדַבֵּר אֱלֹהִים אֶת־הָאָדָם וָחָי׃ וְעַתָּה לָמָּה
נָמוּת כִּי תֹאכְלֵנוּ הָאֵשׁ הַגְּדֹלָה הַזֹּאת אִם־יֹסְפִים ׀ אֲנַחְנוּ
23 לִשְׁמֹעַ אֶת־קוֹל יְהוָה אֱלֹהֵינוּ עוֹד וָמָתְנוּ׃ כִּי מִי כָל־
בָּשָׂר אֲשֶׁר שָׁמַע קוֹל אֱלֹהִים חַיִּים מְדַבֵּר מִתּוֹךְ־הָאֵשׁ
24 כָּמֹנוּ וַיֶּחִי׃ קְרַב אַתָּה וּשְׁמָע אֵת כָּל־אֲשֶׁר יֹאמַר יְהוָה
אֱלֹהֵינוּ וְאַתְּ ׀ תְּדַבֵּר אֵלֵינוּ אֵת כָּל־אֲשֶׁר יְדַבֵּר יְהוָה
כה אֱלֹהֵינוּ אֵלֶיךָ וְשָׁמַעְנוּ וְעָשִׂינוּ׃ וַיִּשְׁמַע יְהוָה אֶת־קוֹל
דִּבְרֵיכֶם בְּדַבֶּרְכֶם אֵלָי וַיֹּאמֶר יְהוָה אֵלַי שָׁמַעְתִּי אֶת־
קוֹל דִּבְרֵי הָעָם הַזֶּה אֲשֶׁר דִּבְּרוּ אֵלֶיךָ הֵיטִיבוּ כָּל־אֲשֶׁר
26 דִּבֵּרוּ׃ מִי־יִתֵּן וְהָיָה לְבָבָם זֶה לָהֶם לְיִרְאָה אֹתִי וְלִשְׁמֹר
אֶת־כָּל־מִצְוֺתַי כָּל־הַיָּמִים לְמַעַן יִיטַב לָהֶם וְלִבְנֵיהֶם
27 28 לְעֹלָם׃ לֵךְ אֱמֹר לָהֶם שׁוּבוּ לָכֶם לְאָהֳלֵיכֶם׃ וְאַתָּה פֹּה
עֲמֹד עִמָּדִי וַאֲדַבְּרָה אֵלֶיךָ אֵת כָּל־הַמִּצְוָה וְהַחֻקִּים
וְהַמִּשְׁפָּטִים אֲשֶׁר תְּלַמְּדֵם וְעָשׂוּ בָאָרֶץ אֲשֶׁר אָנֹכִי נֹתֵן
29 לָהֶם לְרִשְׁתָּהּ׃ וּשְׁמַרְתֶּם לַעֲשׂוֹת כַּאֲשֶׁר צִוָּה יְהוָה
ל אֱלֹהֵיכֶם אֶתְכֶם לֹא תָסֻרוּ יָמִין וּשְׂמֹאל׃ בְּכָל־הַדֶּרֶךְ

v. 24. הת׳ בקמץ

desire thy neighbour's house, his field, or his man-servant, or his maid-servant, his ox, or his ass, or any thing that is thy neighbour's.*iv s, v a. ¶ 19. These words the LORD spoke unto all your assembly in the mount out of the midst of the fire, of the cloud, and of the thick darkness, with a great voice, and it went on no more. And He wrote them upon two tables of stone, and gave them unto me. 20. And it came to pass, when ye heard the voice out of the midst of the darkness, while the mountain did burn with fire, that ye came near unto me, even all the heads of your tribes, and your elders; 21. and ye said: 'Behold, the LORD our God hath shown us His glory and His greatness, and we have heard His voice out of the midst of the fire; we have seen this day that God doth speak with man, and he liveth. 22. Now therefore why should we die? for this great fire will consume us; if we hear the voice of the LORD our God any more, then we shall die. 23. For who is there of all flesh, that hath heard the voice of the living God speaking out of the midst of the fire, as we have, and lived? 24. Go thou near, and hear all that the LORD our God may say; and thou shalt speak unto us all that the LORD our God may speak unto thee; and we will hear it, and do it.' 25. And the LORD heard the voice of your words, when ye spoke unto me; and the LORD said unto me: 'I have heard the voice of the words of this people, which they have spoken unto thee; they have well said all that they have spoken. 26. Oh that they had such a heart as this alway, to fear Me, and keep all My commandments, that it might be well with them, and with their children for ever! 27. Go say to them: Return ye to your tents. 28. But as for thee, stand thou here by Me, and I will speak unto thee all the commandment, and the statutes, and the ordinances, which thou shalt teach them, that they may do them in the land which I give them to possess it.' 29. Ye shall observe to do therefore as the LORD your God hath commanded you; ye shall not

19–30. The manner in which the Decalogue was delivered.

19. *no more.* The direct Divine Revelation to the whole people was limited to the Ten Words. The people found it unbearable to listen to the Divine Voice, and the remainder of the Revelation was communicated to them through Moses; *v.* 22–25.

21. *His glory.* Manifested in the fire and smoke; see on Gen. xv, 17.

22. *this great fire will consume us.* Not the Revelation of God, but the physical accompaniments of that Revelation fill them with fear.

26. *Oh that they had such a heart.* 'God too can express a wish of this sort, as freedom of the will has been given to man' (Biur). Alas, that exalted spirit of the Israelites was soon to be followed by a violent reaction—the apostasy of the Golden Calf.

29. *ye shall not turn aside.* This and the following *v.* are the moral exhortation after the historical narrative.

turn aside to the right hand or to the left. 30. Ye shall walk in all the way which the LORD your God hath commanded you, that ye may live, and that it may be well with you, and that ye may prolong your days in the land which ye shall possess.

6 CHAPTER VI

1. Now this is the commandment, the statutes, and the ordinances, which the LORD your God commanded to teach you, that ye might do them in the land whither ye go over to possess it—2. that thou mightest fear the LORD thy God, to keep all His statutes and His commandments, which I command thee, thou, and thy son, and thy son's son, all the days of thy life; and that thy days may be prolonged. 3. Hear therefore, O Israel, and observe to do it; that it may be well with thee, and that ye may increase mightily, as the LORD, the God of thy fathers, hath promised unto thee—a land flowing with milk and honey.*v s, vi a. ¶4. HEAR, O ISRAEL: THE LORD OUR GOD, THE LORD IS ONE. 5. And thou shalt love the LORD

אֲשֶׁר צִוָּה יְהוָה אֱלֹהֵיכֶם אֶתְכֶם תֵּלֵכוּ לְמַעַן תִּחְיוּן וְטוֹב
לָכֶם וְהַאֲרַכְתֶּם יָמִים בָּאָרֶץ אֲשֶׁר תִּירָשׁוּן׃

CAP. VI. ו ו

א וְזֹאת הַמִּצְוָה הַחֻקִּים וְהַמִּשְׁפָּטִים אֲשֶׁר צִוָּה יְהוָה
אֱלֹהֵיכֶם לְלַמֵּד אֶתְכֶם לַעֲשׂוֹת בָּאָרֶץ אֲשֶׁר אַתֶּם עֹבְרִים
2 שָׁמָּה לְרִשְׁתָּהּ׃ לְמַעַן תִּירָא אֶת־יְהוָה אֱלֹהֶיךָ לִשְׁמֹר
אֶת־כָּל־חֻקֹּתָיו וּמִצְוֹתָיו אֲשֶׁר אָנֹכִי מְצַוֶּךָ אַתָּה וּבִנְךָ
3 וּבֶן־בִּנְךָ כֹּל יְמֵי חַיֶּיךָ וּלְמַעַן יַאֲרִכֻן יָמֶיךָ׃ וְשָׁמַעְתָּ
יִשְׂרָאֵל וְשָׁמַרְתָּ לַעֲשׂוֹת אֲשֶׁר יִיטַב לְךָ וַאֲשֶׁר תִּרְבּוּן
מְאֹד כַּאֲשֶׁר דִּבֶּר יְהוָה אֱלֹהֵי אֲבֹתֶיךָ לָךְ אֶרֶץ זָבַת
חָלָב וּדְבָשׁ׃ * פ ששי (חמישי לספ')
4 ה שְׁמַע יִשְׂרָאֵל יְהוָה אֱלֹהֵינוּ יְהוָה ׀ אֶחָד׃ וְאָהַבְתָּ אֵת

ו' v. 4. ע' ד' רבתי

30. *that ye may live.* Cf. IV, 1. The promise is here national not individual; see on IV, 26.

VI, 1–3. These verses conclude that portion of the Second Discourse which deals with the Revelation at Horeb.

1. *now this is.* Better, *and this is.* See *v.* 28 of preceding chapter.

2. *that thou mightest fear.* This sums up the aim and purpose of the general principles of the legislation, as well as of the separate statutes.

THE SHEMA

THE ONENESS OF GOD AND ISRAEL'S UNDIVIDED LOYALTY TO HIM

4–9. After the repetition of the story of the Giving of the Ten Commandments, Moses proceeds to declare the other great foundation of the Torah; *viz.* the oneness of God and Israel's undivided loyalty to Him.

The opening *v.* of this paragraph, called after its first Heb. word *Shema*, sounds the keynote of all Judaism, and has been its watchword and confession of faith throughout the ages. Here the fundamental Truth of the Unity of God is proclaimed. It is followed in *v.* 5–9 by the fundamental Duty founded upon that Truth; *viz.* the devotion to Him of the Israelite's whole being. He is bidden to love God with heart, soul, and might; to remember all the commandments and instruct his children therein; to recite the words of God when retiring or rising; to bind those words on the arm and the head, and to inscribe them on his door-posts and the city gates. 'The later leaders of Jewry showed their spiritual insight when they gave the place they did to this high and winsome message' (Welch). See Additional Note A, THE SHEMA, p. 769.

In the Liturgy, the Shema is said twice daily, and consists of three sections; Deut. VI, 9; XI, 13–21; and Num. XV, 37–41. The second section, Deut. XI, 13–21, contains the promise of reward for the fulfiment of the laws, and of punishment for their transgression. The third section, Num. XV, 37–41, enacts the law concerning the *tzitzith*, as a warning against following the evil inclinations of the heart, and an exhortation to submit to the laws of God in remembrance of the exodus.

4. *Hear, O Israel: the LORD our God, the LORD is One.* Heb. שמע ישראל ד' אלהינו ד' אחד. Or, 'Hear, O Israel: the LORD is our God, the LORD is One' (Sifri, Septuagint, and most Jewish translators and commentators). It sums up the teaching of the First and Second Commandments; The LORD is our God, and He is One. The translation given by AJ, 'Hear, O Israel, the LORD our God, the LORD is One,' is less acceptable; for if the declaration only enunciated the Divine Unity, it would be sufficient to have said, 'Hear, O Israel, the LORD our God is One.' Some moderns follow Rashbam's translation: 'Hear, O Israel, the LORD is our God, the LORD alone.'

In the Heb. the ע of שמע and the ד of אחד are written large. The reason for the ד is evident; it is to distinguish אחד 'one' from אחר 'another god', just as the ר in אחר (Exod. XXXIV, 14) is written large, in order that by error one should thy God with all thy heart, and with all thy soul, and with all thy might. 6. And these

יְהוָה אֱלֹהֶיךָ בְּכָל־לְבָבְךָ וּבְכָל־נַפְשְׁךָ וּבְכָל־מְאֹדֶךָ׃

not utter the blasphemy לא תשתחוה לאל אחד 'thou shalt not bow down to the *one* God'. The reason that induced the Scribes to write the ע in שמע large may possibly be due to the fear of an interchange in their day with שמא, 'perhaps,' and avoid the resulting infidel statement of '*Perhaps*, O Israel, the LORD is our God' (Hirsch). These two large letters form the word עד 'witness'. Every Israelite by pronouncing the Shema becomes one of God's witnesses, testifying to His Unity before the world.

the LORD our God. The Heb. is the Divine Name of Four Letters, the Father and Sustainer of the lives and spirits of all flesh, the everlasting Power Who guides the destinies of men and nations.

the LORD is One. 'In the opening *v.* of the Shema we have a third revelation of God's being. In Gen. XVII, He is made known to us as Almighty; in Exod. VI, as Eternal; and now as the One' (Philippson). He is One, because there is no other God than He; but He is also One, because He is wholly unlike anything else in existence. He is therefore not only One, but the Sole and Unique God.

One. Heb. *echad.* Therefore to Him alone it is right to pray, and not to any being besides Him. The belief that God is made up of several personalities, such as the Christian belief in the Trinity, is a departure from the pure conception of the Unity of God. Israel has throughout the ages rejected everything that marred or obscured the conception of pure monotheism it had given the world, and rather than abandon that pure monotheism, rather than admit any weakening of it, Jews were prepared to wander, to suffer, to die; see p. 920.

5. *and thou shalt love.* This is the first instance in human history that the *love* of God was demanded in any religion. The love of God is the distinctive mark of His true worshippers. The worshipper, as he declares the Unity of God, thereby lovingly and unconditionally surrenders his mind and heart to God's holy will. Such spiritual surrender is called, 'taking upon oneself the yoke of the kingdom of heaven.' קבלת עול מלכות שמים. If the Unity of God is the basis of the Jewish creed, the love of God is to be the basis of the Jewish life. And the noblest spiritual surrender and love of God, the Rabbis held, was so to live and act toward our fellowmen as to make God and His Torah *beloved* in their eyes.

'The meaning of the love of God is that a man should be longing and yearning after the nearness of God, blessed be He, and striving to reach His holiness, in the same manner as he would pursue any object for which he feels a strong passion. He should feel that bliss and delight in mentioning His name, in uttering His praises and in occupying himself with the words of the Torah, which a lover feels towards the wife of his youth, or the father towards his only son. The earlier saints attained to such disinterested love of God; as King David said in Psalm XLII, 2, "As the hart panteth after the water brooks, so panteth my soul after Thee, O God"' (Moses Chayim Luzzatto).

'When the soul sinks in the depths of awe, the spark of the love of God breaks out in flames, and the inward joy increases. Such lovers of God desire only to accomplish His holy will, and lead others unto righteousness' (Eleazar of Worms).

with all thy heart. Because there is one God, we must give Him undivided allegiance. 'The One God demands the whole of man' (Smend). The Rabbis explain *with all thy heart*, to mean 'with all thy desires, including the evil inclination'; *i.e.* make thy earthly passions and ambitions instruments in the service of God.

with all thy soul. We should be prepared to give up our dearest wishes and inclinations for the love of God. The Rabbis take the words *with all thy soul* to mean 'with thy whole life'; *i.e.* love Him with thy heart's last drop of blood, and give up thy life for God, if He requires it. The classical example is that of Rabbi Akiba. He longed for the sublime moment when his daily profession of the love of God might be put to the proof and confirmed by act. That moment came when, after his noble part in the last Jewish War of Independence against Imperial Rome, the Roman executioner was tearing his flesh with combs of iron. 'All my days,' Akiba told his weeping disciples, 'I have longed for this moment when it is given me to love God with my whole life. I loved Him *with all my heart*, and I loved Him *with all my might;* now that I have the opportunity of loving Him *with all my soul*, shall I not rejoice?' It was such understanding of the words of the Shema that gave the Jewish martyrs throughout the ages the comfort and courage to lay down their lives for their Faith. Bachya tells of a medieval Jewish saint who used to pray, 'My God, thou hast given me over to starvation and penury. Into the depth of darkness hast Thou plunged me, and Thy might and strength Thou hast taught me. But even if they burn me with fire, only the more will I love Thee and rejoice in Thee.' Such spiritual surrender, is of course, without any thought of reward or punishment in the Hereafter. As another of the saints boldly expressed it, 'I have no wish for Thy Paradise, nor any desire for the bliss in the world to come. I want Thee and Thee alone.'

On the duty of martyrdom, see p. 489. The supreme sacrifice, however, is demanded only to avoid idolatry, incest, and murder.

words, which I command thee this day, shall be upon thy heart; 7. and thou shalt teach them diligently unto thy children, and shalt talk of them when thou sittest in thy house, and when thou walkest by the way, and when thou liest down, and when thou risest up. 8. And thou shalt bind them for a sign upon thy hand, and they shall be for frontlets between thine eyes. 9. And thou shalt write them upon the door-posts of thy house, and upon thy gates.vi s. ¶ 10. And it shall be, when the LORD thy God shall bring thee into the land which He swore unto thy fathers, to Abraham, to Isaac, and to

6 וְהָיוּ הַדְּבָרִים הָאֵלֶּה אֲשֶׁר אָנֹכִי מְצַוְּךָ הַיּוֹם עַל־לְבָבֶךָ׃
7 וְשִׁנַּנְתָּם לְבָנֶיךָ וְדִבַּרְתָּ בָּם בְּשִׁבְתְּךָ בְּבֵיתֶךָ וּבְלֶכְתְּךָ
שש׳ 8 בַדֶּרֶךְ וּבְשָׁכְבְּךָ וּבְקוּמֶךָ׃ וּקְשַׁרְתָּם לְאוֹת עַל־יָדֶךָ וְהָיוּ
(ספ׳) 9 לְטֹטָפֹת בֵּין עֵינֶיךָ׃ וּכְתַבְתָּם עַל־מְזֻזוֹת בֵּיתֶךָ וּבִשְׁעָרֶיךָ׃
ס וְהָיָה כִּי־יְבִיאֲךָ ׀ יְהוָה אֱלֹהֶיךָ אֶל־הָאָרֶץ אֲשֶׁר נִשְׁבַּע
לַאֲבֹתֶיךָ לְאַבְרָהָם לְיִצְחָק וּלְיַעֲקֹב לָתֶת לָךְ עָרִים

with all thy might. With the full concentration of feeling and power. One Rabbinic explanation is, 'with whatever lot Providence has assigned to thee'; *i.e.* love Him in times of bliss and happiness, and in times of distress and misfortune. Another explanation of *with all thy might* is 'with all thy possessions'; *i.e.* despite whatever material sacrifice thy loyalty to Israel's God and Torah might entail. An eighteenth century moralist understood 'with all thy possessions' to mean, 'even when great wealth is thine' (Panim Yafoth).

6. *these words.* In *v.* 4 and 5; *viz.* the Unity of God and the duty of undivided allegiance to Him, as the epitome of the teaching of the Book.

this day. 'Do not regard the Divine commands as old and stale news; but consider them as something fresh, as a new Royal Proclamation reaching you this very day' (Sifri).

upon thy heart. The heart is conceived as a tablet on which these Divine words shall be inscribed; cf. Jer. xxxi, 32, 33.

7. *teach them diligently.* lit. 'prick them in'; so that the words remain indelibly upon their hearts. 'Let them have a clear, and not a confused or stammering, knowledge of the duties and teachings of their Faith' (Sifri); see p. 925.

and shalt talk of them. They are to be a theme of living interest, early and late, at home and abroad.

when thou sittest in thy house. 'A man should conduct himself with due propriety in his house, so as to set an example to his household; and he should also be gentle with them, and not overawe them' (Zohar).

when thou liest down. The Rabbis based on this the institution of Evening Prayer. It consists of the Shema, preceded by two Benedictions (the one, referring to the Divine ordering of day and night, המעריב ערבים; and the second, eulogizing the love of God shown in the revelation of the Torah, אהבת עולם). The Shema is also followed by two Benedictions (the proclamation of faith, אמת ואמונה; and the prayer for peaceful repose, השכיבנו). The Service continues with the Amidah (the Eighteen Benedictions—three Blessings of Praise; twelve (now thirteen) Petitions; and three Blessings of Thanks) and *Oleynoo.* The Shema is also recited before retiring to rest. To fill one's mind with high and noble thoughts is a wise preparation for the hours of darkness. 'The Shema is a double-edged sword against all the terrors and temptations of the night' (Talmud).

when thou risest up. Hence the institution of the Morning Shema. It is preceded by two Benedictions, and followed by one. These Benedictions are (1) an eulogy of God as the Creator of the light of day, יוצר אור; (2) a eulogy of God as Giver of the Torah, אהבה רבה; and (3) a eulogy of God as the Redeemer of Israel, גואל ישראל. Immediately thereafter come the Eighteen Benedictions. On some days, Tachanun and the Reading of the Torah follow. The Service concludes with *Oleynoo,* Kaddish and some psalms.

8. *bind them.* See p. 261 for the precept of Tephillin. The wording of *v.* 8 and 9 are not to be taken as a figure of speech. 'It seems on the whole to be more probable that the injunction is intended to be carried out literally; and that some material, visible expression of the Israelite's creed is referred to' (Driver).

9. *write them upon the door-posts.* By means of the *mezuzah* affixed to the door-post in Jewish homes. The *mezuzah* is placed in a metal or glass case, and fixed to the right-hand door-post of the outer entrance of every dwelling room in the house. It contains this section of the Shema and xi, 13–20. The word שדי, 'Almighty,' written on the back of the parchment, is rendered visible by means of a small opening in the case. The *mezuzah* is a symbol of God's watchful care over the house and its dwellers. It is a solemn reminder to all who go out and in, that the house is devoted to the ideals of the Shema.

I. Abrahams thus sums up the basic importance of Deut. vi, 4–9: 'It enshrines the fundamental *dogma* (monotheism), the fundamental *duty* (love), the fundamental *discipline* (study of the Law), and the fundamental *method* (union of "letter" and "spirit"), of the Jewish Religion.'

Jacob, to give thee—great and goodly cities, which thou didst not build, 11. and houses full of all good things, which thou didst not fill, and cisterns hewn out, which thou didst not hew, vineyards and olive-trees, which thou didst not plant, and thou shalt eat and be satisfied—12. then beware lest thou forget the LORD, who brought thee forth out of the land of Egypt, out of the house of bondage. 13. Thou shalt fear the LORD thy God; and Him shalt thou serve, and by His name shalt thou swear. 14. Ye shall not go after other gods, of the gods of the peoples that are round about you; 15. for a jealous God, even the LORD thy God, is in the midst of thee; lest the anger of the LORD thy God be kindled against thee, and He destroy thee from off the face of the earth. ¶ 16. Ye shall not try the LORD your God, as ye tried Him in Massah. 17. Ye shall diligently keep the commandments of the LORD your God, and His testimonies, and His statutes, which He hath commanded thee. 18. And thou shalt do that

11 גְּדֹלֹת וְטֹבֹת אֲשֶׁר לֹא־בָנִיתָ׃ וּבָתִּים מְלֵאִים כָּל־טוּב
אֲשֶׁר לֹא־מִלֵּאתָ וּבֹרֹת חֲצוּבִים אֲשֶׁר לֹא־חָצַבְתָּ כְּרָמִים
12 וְזֵיתִים אֲשֶׁר לֹא־נָטָעְתָּ וְאָכַלְתָּ וְשָׂבָעְתָּ׃ הִשָּׁמֶר לְךָ פֶּן
תִּשְׁכַּח אֶת־יְהוָה אֲשֶׁר הוֹצִיאֲךָ מֵאֶרֶץ מִצְרַיִם מִבֵּית
13 עֲבָדִים׃ אֶת־יְהוָה אֱלֹהֶיךָ תִּירָא וְאֹתוֹ תַעֲבֹד וּבִשְׁמוֹ
14 תִּשָּׁבֵעַ׃ לֹא תֵלְכוּן אַחֲרֵי אֱלֹהִים אֲחֵרִים מֵאֱלֹהֵי הָעַמִּים
טו אֲשֶׁר סְבִיבוֹתֵיכֶם׃ כִּי אֵל קַנָּא יְהוָה אֱלֹהֶיךָ בְּקִרְבֶּךָ
פֶּן־יֶחֱרֶה אַף־יְהוָה אֱלֹהֶיךָ בָּךְ וְהִשְׁמִידְךָ מֵעַל פְּנֵי
16 הָאֲדָמָה׃ ס לֹא תְנַסּוּ אֶת־יְהוָה אֱלֹהֵיכֶם כַּאֲשֶׁר
17 נִסִּיתֶם בַּמַּסָּה׃ שָׁמוֹר תִּשְׁמְרוּן אֶת־מִצְוֺת יְהוָה אֱלֹהֵיכֶם
18 וְעֵדֹתָיו וְחֻקָּיו אֲשֶׁר צִוָּךְ׃ וְעָשִׂיתָ הַיָּשָׁר וְהַטּוֹב בְּעֵינֵי

v. 11. ב׳ טעמים

10–19. PERIL OF FORGETTING

The pleasantness of their inheritance in the New Land might breed forgetfulness of their dependence upon the goodness of God, and a disposition to follow the gods of the surrounding nations.

11. *cisterns hewn out.* In the Holy Land water had to be collected during the rainy seasons and stored. For this purpose, cisterns cut out of the rocks are of special value.

13. *thou shalt fear the LORD thy God.* This command is complementary to VI, 5 'thou shalt love the LORD thy God'. Love and fear of God combined constitute the highest reverence. '*The fear of God* acts as a powerful deterrent from evil; the *love of God*, as the highest incentive to living in accordance with the Divine will' (Talmud). 'Indeed יראת ד׳, *the fear of the LORD*, is the nearest equivalent in Hebrew to what we mean when we speak about *religion*' (Welch).

serve. In prayer (Sifri).

by His name shalt thou swear. This is no command to swear; only a bringing out of the religious significance of an oath (Oettli). Primitive man constantly appeals to his gods for the truth and honesty of his transactions; and such appeal to his gods really constituted a profession of his loyalty to those gods. An Israelite is to swear by the Name of God alone, always remembering that it was an unpardonable sin to take God's Name in vain—and that the truly pious refrain from all oaths.

14. *peoples that are round about you.* Not that it was permissible to follow the gods of distant nations, but that the danger of adopting the worship of *neighbouring* peoples was more insidious and real (Rashi).

15. *a jealous God.* See on IV, 24.

destroy thee. As a nation and an independent power.

of the earth. Better, *of the land; i.e.* Palestine.

16. *ye shall not try. i.e.* test, by questioning His power or protection; see on Exod. XVII, 2. Likewise, anyone who obeys the Divine commandments 'on trial', *i.e.* to see if he will be rewarded for doing so, transgresses this prohibition (Mal. III, 10 is an exception).

in Massah. See Exod. XVII, 7.

18. *that which is right and good in the sight of the LORD.* Note the words *and good* in addition to *that which is right.* It is not enough to do *that which is right; i.e.* to act according to the strict letter of the law; as such action often involves hardship and harshness, and the truly pious avoid taking advantage of the letter of strict legality. There is a higher justice, which is equity, and this bids man to be true to something more than the mere letter of his bond. 'Man must act beyond the rule of law' (לפנים משורת הדין), say the Teachers of the Talmud. Jerusalem, they said, was destroyed because its Courts adhered too closely to strict *Din* (justice), and disregarded the principles of *Yosher* (equity). Two examples will make clear what they understood by 'equity'. A Rabbi on being consulted by a poor woman whether a certain coin was good answered her that it was. The next day, she came and told him it had been declared bad. He took it from her, and gave her a good one in exchange. He was not compelled to act so. He was going

יְהוָה לְמַעַן יִיטַב לָךְ וּבָאתָ וְיָרַשְׁתָּ אֶת־הָאָרֶץ הַטֹּבָה
19 אֲשֶׁר־נִשְׁבַּע יְהוָה לַאֲבֹתֶיךָ׃ לַהֲדֹף אֶת־כָּל־אֹיְבֶיךָ מִפָּנֶיךָ
כ כַּאֲשֶׁר דִּבֶּר יְהוָה׃ ס כִּי־יִשְׁאָלְךָ בִנְךָ מָחָר לֵאמֹר
מָה הָעֵדֹת וְהַחֻקִּים וְהַמִּשְׁפָּטִים אֲשֶׁר צִוָּה יְהוָה אֱלֹהֵינוּ
21 אֶתְכֶם׃ וְאָמַרְתָּ לְבִנְךָ עֲבָדִים הָיִינוּ לְפַרְעֹה בְּמִצְרָיִם

which is right and good in the sight of the LORD; that it may be well with thee, and that thou mayest go in and possess the good land which the LORD swore unto thy fathers,
19. to thrust out all thine enemies from before thee, as the LORD hath spoken. ¶ 20.
When thy son asketh thee in time to come, saying: 'What mean the testimonies, and the statutes, and the ordinances, which the LORD our God hath commanded you?'
21. then thou shalt say unto thy son: 'We

beyond the letter of the law, and doing 'that which is right *and good* in the sight of the LORD'.

Rabba, the son of Bar Chana, hired porters to transport some jugs of wine. They, in negligence broke their load; whereupon Rabba seized their garments in compensation. The porters appealed to Rab, who ordered the garments to be returned. When the garments were returned they pleaded, 'We are poor men, we have laboured a full day, exhausted ourselves, and now we have nothing.' Rab decided that their wages be paid. Rabba protested that his action had all along been *legal*. To which Rab replied, 'Indeed it is legal; but Scripture says, "Thou shalt observe the path of the upright," *i.e.* those who act beyond the mere letter of the law.' (If Shakespeare had been aware of this fine Jewish duty, 'to go beyond the letter of the law'—he could not have drawn his Shylock as a Jew.) Rashi understands our *v.* to teach the duty 'of going beyond the rule', and also the concomitant duty of פשרה, 'agreement.' Agreement is reached when each of the litigants forgoes something to which he believes himself entitled by strict law and they become friends. The judgment of the court would have been for the one and against the other; that would be strict law. By agreement, they refrain from insisting on strict law, and friendship is re-established. Thus are fulfilled the words (Zech. VIII, 16), 'execute the judgment of truth *and peace*'; *i.e.* effect peace between the parties by the judgment of truth.

19. *as the LORD hath spoken.* See Exod. XXIII, 27 f.

20–25. THE EXODUS—AN OBJECT-LESSON

The future generation is to be trained to gratitude and reverence towards God by means of the story of the Deliverance from Egypt. The Seder Service is a domestic feast based on the actual usage in the Temple of Jerusalem, and accompanied by a running commentary of prayer and legend and exhortation known as the *Haggadah shel Pesach*. This opens with the questions asked by the youngest child present, who is answered in a recitation of the events of the Exodus of the Midrashic interpretation of Biblical passages (Josh. XXIV, 2–4; Deut. XXVI, 5–8) relating to the Deliverance. Hallel early formed part of the Seder; Nishmath, various hymns, folk-songs, and children's rhymes were added in the course of the centuries.

The Seder in history would require a monograph. In the Middle Ages, the Seder nights were a time of terror to the Jewries of Christian Europe. From the twelfth century onwards, the Satanic charge of using human blood on Passover was responsible for a long series of hideous massacres. Also, it was on the eve of Passover 1190, that the Jews of York resolved to anticipate massacre at the hands of the murderous mob by suicide, and perished almost to a man. 'But the eternal message of hope, revived in the Jewish breast all the more ardently by the Festival of Freedom, saved the martyred people from despair, even in this darkest hour' (Cecil Roth).

20. *in time to come.* lit. 'to-morrow.'
what mean the testimonies . . . ordinances. This whole section is analagous to Exod. XIII, 11 f, where the child asks מה זאת 'What is this?' Evidently the son here is of riper age than in Exod. XIII. The Rabbis describe the latter as תם, 'simple'; and the son in this *v.* as חכם, 'wise.'

21. *we were Pharaoh's bondmen.* These words form the first sentence of the answer to the 'four questions' in the Haggadah. The Seder Service is typical of Jewish education: the ceremonies become object-lessons in religion, national history, and morality. The garnered religious thought and emotion of past generations is made the horizon for the opening mind of the Jewish child. At one point of the Seder, which is largely history raised into religion, it is remarked: 'Every Jew should regard himself as if *he* had personally come out of Egypt.' That spirit dominates the whole of Jewish ceremonial. It all tends to the self-identification of the child with his fathers in the days of old, and to foster in the soul of the Jewish child the resolve to take his part in the Jewish life—whether in the sphere of worship, humanitarian endeavour, or Messianic achievement in and out of the Holy Land.

were Pharaoh's bondmen in Egypt; and the LORD brought us out of Egypt with a mighty hand. 22. And the LORD showed signs and wonders, great and sore, upon Egypt, upon Pharaoh, and upon all his house, before our eyes. 23. And He brought us out from thence, that He might bring us in, to give us the land which He swore unto our fathers. 24. And the LORD commanded us to do all these statutes, to fear the LORD our God, for our good always, that He might preserve us alive, as it is at this day. 25. And it shall be righteousness unto us, if we observe to do all this commandment before the LORD our God, as He hath commanded us.'*vii.

22 וַיּוֹצִיאֵנוּ יְהוָה מִמִּצְרַיִם בְּיָד חֲזָקָה׃ וַיִּתֵּן יְהוָה אוֹתֹת
וּמֹפְתִים גְּדֹלִים וְרָעִים ׀ בְּמִצְרַיִם בְּפַרְעֹה וּבְכָל־בֵּיתוֹ
23 לְעֵינֵינוּ׃ וְאוֹתָנוּ הוֹצִיא מִשָּׁם לְמַעַן הָבִיא אֹתָנוּ לָתֶת
24 לָנוּ אֶת־הָאָרֶץ אֲשֶׁר נִשְׁבַּע לַאֲבֹתֵינוּ׃ וַיְצַוֵּנוּ יְהוָה לַעֲשׂוֹת
אֶת־כָּל־הַחֻקִּים הָאֵלֶּה לְיִרְאָה אֶת־יְהוָה אֱלֹהֵינוּ לְטוֹב
כה לָנוּ כָּל־הַיָּמִים לְחַיֹּתֵנוּ כְּהַיּוֹם הַזֶּה׃ וּצְדָקָה תִּהְיֶה־לָּנוּ כִּי־
נִשְׁמֹר לַעֲשׂוֹת אֶת־כָּל־הַמִּצְוָה הַזֹּאת לִפְנֵי יְהוָה אֱלֹהֵינוּ
כַּאֲשֶׁר צִוָּנוּ׃ * ס שביעי

7

CHAPTER VII

1. When the LORD thy God shall bring thee into the land whither thou goest to possess it, and shall cast out many nations before thee, the Hittite, and the Girgashite, and the Amorite, and the Canaanite, and the Perizzite, and the Hivite, and the Jebusite, seven nations greater and mightier than thou; 2. and when the LORD thy God shall deliver them up before thee, and thou shalt smite them; then thou shalt utterly destroy them; thou shalt make no covenant with them, nor show mercy unto them; 3. neither shalt thou make marriages with them: thy daughter thou shalt not give unto his son, nor his daughter shalt thou

CAP. VII. ז ז

א כִּי יְבִיאֲךָ יְהוָה אֱלֹהֶיךָ אֶל־הָאָרֶץ אֲשֶׁר־אַתָּה בָא־שָׁמָּה
לְרִשְׁתָּהּ וְנָשַׁל גּוֹיִם־רַבִּים ׀ מִפָּנֶיךָ הַחִתִּי וְהַגִּרְגָּשִׁי וְהָאֱמֹרִי
וְהַכְּנַעֲנִי וְהַפְּרִזִּי וְהַחִוִּי וְהַיְבוּסִי שִׁבְעָה גוֹיִם רַבִּים וַעֲצוּמִים
2 מִמֶּךָּ׃ וּנְתָנָם יְהוָה אֱלֹהֶיךָ לְפָנֶיךָ וְהִכִּיתָם הַחֲרֵם
3 תַּחֲרִים אֹתָם לֹא־תִכְרֹת לָהֶם בְּרִית וְלֹא תְחָנֵּם׃ וְלֹא

22. *signs.* See on IV, 34. 'The father's reply points to an Almighty Power that can change the course of Nature for the accomplishment of His Divine purposes' (Koenig).

24. *preserve us alive.* 'God, that He might complete His redemptive work towards Israel, gave it this law, to keep alive in it the spirit of true religion, and to secure in perpetuity its national welfare' (Driver).

25. *and it shall be righteousness unto us.* It will be accounted to us as meritorious, and deserving of God's approval. The phrase is similarly used in Gen. XV, 6, 'and he (Abraham) believed in the LORD: and He counted it to him for righteousness.'

CHAPTER VII

Observance of the Fundamental Laws—the Ten Commandments and the Shema—demands avoidance of intermarriage, and the destruction of all idolatrous worship in the Promised Land.

1. *before thee.* lit. 'from before thee,' *i.e.* to make way for thee. The nations here enumerated are mentioned in Gen. X, 15–18; XV, 19 f; Exod. III, 8, 17; XIII, 5 and elsewhere. The Midrash states that the Girgashites left Canaan before the entry of the Israelites.

2. *utterly destroy.* Heb. החרם תחרים, *i.e.* consider them as a *cherem*, something that must not come near thee. On the 'ban' against the Canaanites, see on XX, 18.

show mercy. Better, *show grace;* or, 'give gifts to' (Talmud). The Rabbis restrict this prohibition, as all others in this connection, to actual idolaters like the ancient Canaanites. It does not apply to ordinary heathens who observe the fundamental laws of human society; see on IV, 19.

3. *marriages.* The evil results of such marriages were perceived by the Patriarchs; Gen. XXIV and XXVIII. Moses had previously warned the people against allying themselves by marriage with their neighbours (Exod. XXXIV, 16), and the warning was repeated by his successor (Josh. XXIII, 12). In our own days, in conditions that are worlds asunder from those in Canaan of old, intermarriage is no less fatal to the continued existence of Israel. 'Every Jew should feel himself bound, even though the duty involves the sacrifice of precious affections, to avoid acts calculated, however remotely, to weaken the stability of the ancestral religion. Every Jew who contemplates marriage outside the pale must regard himself as paving the way to a disruption which would be the final, as it would be the culminating, disaster in the history of his people' (M. Joseph).

take unto thy son. 4. For he will turn away thy son from following Me, that they may serve other gods; so will the anger of the LORD be kindled against you, and He will destroy thee quickly. 5. But thus shall ye deal with them: ye shall break down their altars, and dash in pieces their pillars, and hew down their Asherim, and burn their graven images with fire. 6. For thou art a holy people unto the LORD thy God: the LORD thy God hath chosen thee to be His own treasure, out of all peoples that are upon the face of the earth. 7. The LORD did not set His love upon you, nor choose you, because ye were more in number than any people—for ye were the fewest of all peoples—8. but because the LORD loved you, and because He would keep the oath which He swore unto your fathers, hath the LORD brought you out with a mighty hand, and redeemed you out of the house of bondage, from the hand of Pharaoh king of Egypt.*m. 9. Know therefore that the LORD thy God, He is God; the faithful God, who keepeth covenant and mercy with them that love Him and keep His commandments to a thousand generations; 10. and repayeth them that hate Him to their face, to destroy them; He will not be slack to him that hateth Him, He will repay him to his

תִתְחַתֵּן בָּם בִּתְּךָ לֹא־תִתֵּן לִבְנוֹ וּבִתּוֹ לֹא־תִקַּח לִבְנֶךָ׃
4 כִּי־יָסִיר אֶת־בִּנְךָ מֵאַחֲרַי וְעָבְדוּ אֱלֹהִים אֲחֵרִים וְחָרָה
ה אַף־יְהוָה בָּכֶם וְהִשְׁמִידְךָ מַהֵר׃ כִּי־אִם־כֹּה תַעֲשׂוּ לָהֶם
מִזְבְּחֹתֵיהֶם תִּתֹּצוּ וּמַצֵּבֹתָם תְּשַׁבֵּרוּ וַאֲשֵׁירֵהֶם תְּגַדֵּעוּן
6 וּפְסִילֵיהֶם תִּשְׂרְפוּן בָּאֵשׁ׃ כִּי עַם קָדוֹשׁ אַתָּה לַיהוָה
אֱלֹהֶיךָ בְּךָ בָּחַר ׀ יְהוָה אֱלֹהֶיךָ לִהְיוֹת לוֹ לְעַם סְגֻלָּה
7 מִכֹּל הָעַמִּים אֲשֶׁר עַל־פְּנֵי הָאֲדָמָה׃ לֹא מֵרֻבְּכֶם מִכָּל־
הָעַמִּים חָשַׁק יְהוָה בָּכֶם וַיִּבְחַר בָּכֶם כִּי־אַתֶּם הַמְעַט
8 מִכָּל־הָעַמִּים׃ כִּי מֵאַהֲבַת יְהוָה אֶתְכֶם וּמִשָּׁמְרוֹ אֶת־
הַשְּׁבֻעָה אֲשֶׁר נִשְׁבַּע לַאֲבֹתֵיכֶם הוֹצִיא יְהוָה אֶתְכֶם בְּיָד
מפטיר חֲזָקָה וַיִּפְדְּךָ מִבֵּית עֲבָדִים מִיַּד פַּרְעֹה מֶלֶךְ־מִצְרָיִם׃
9 וְיָדַעְתָּ כִּי־יְהוָה אֱלֹהֶיךָ הוּא הָאֱלֹהִים הָאֵל הַנֶּאֱמָן שֹׁמֵר
הַבְּרִית וְהַחֶסֶד לְאֹהֲבָיו וּלְשֹׁמְרֵי מִצְוֹתָו לְאֶלֶף דּוֹר׃
י וּמְשַׁלֵּם לְשֹׂנְאָיו אֶל־פָּנָיו לְהַאֲבִידוֹ לֹא יְאַחֵר לְשֹׂנְאוֹ אֶל־

v. 9. מצותיו ק׳

4. *he will turn away. i.e.* the heathen who marries thy daughter.

thy son. The Talmud explains this to mean, *thy grandson.* Since the Torah, on this interpretation, calls the child of an Israelite mother and gentile father the 'son' of an Israelite grandfather, it was deduced therefrom that the child is to be regarded as being of the same race and faith *as the mother.* Consequently, the child of a Jewish father and non-Jewish mother follows in Jewish Law the religious status of the mother.

5. *pillars.* Symbols of the sun-god Baal.

Asherim. A tree planted (XVI, 21), or a pole set up (II Kings XVII, 10), as sacred symbols of Astarte, the goddess of fertility.

6–11. REASONS FOR PREVIOUS COMMANDS

6. *thou art a holy people.* See Exod. XIX, 5 f—the classical passage announcing the covenant between God and Israel. Being a holy people, Israel was not to be contaminated by foul and cruel worship. It was to be a People apart from the other nations, and untainted by their heathenish practices.

His own treasure. See on Exod. XIX, 5. 'The character of Israel as the Chosen People does not involve the inferiority of other nations. The universality of Israel's idea of God is sufficient proof against such an assumption. Every nation requires a certain self-consciousness for the carrying out of its mission. Israel's self-consciousness was tempered by the memory of its slavery in Egypt, and the recognition of its being the servant of the LORD. It was the *noblesse oblige* of the God-appointed worker for the entire human race' (Guedemann).

7. *set His love upon you.* The root חשק is used of the 'blind', non-rational love. 'God's love of Israel is like that love (*cheshek*) for which no reason is to be sought, as it is due solely to the desire of the lover' (Albo).

the fewest of all peoples. lit. 'the few out of the totality of peoples'; *i.e.* only a small fragment of the whole of humanity (Herxheimer, Dillmann). Israel is a small nation, but it has been chosen to accomplish world-embracing and eternal things. 'All the great things have been done by the little nations' (Disraeli). 'God has chosen little nations as the vessels by which He carries the choicest wines to the lives of humanity, to rejoice their hearts, to exalt their vision, to stimulate and strengthen their faith' (Lloyd George).

9. *know therefore.* 'This phrase does not mean to know so as to see the fact of, but to know so as to feel *the force* of. It is knowledge that is followed by shame, or by love, or by reverence, or by the sense of a duty' (G. A. Smith).

face. 11. Thou shalt therefore keep the commandment, and the statutes, and the ordinances, which I command thee this day, to do them.

פָּנָיו יְשַׁלֶּם־לוֹ׃ וְשָׁמַרְתָּ אֶת־הַמִּצְוָה וְאֶת־הַחֻקִּים וְאֶת־ 11

הַמִּשְׁפָּטִים אֲשֶׁר אָנֹכִי מְצַוְּךָ הַיּוֹם לַעֲשׂוֹתָם׃

covenant and mercy. Or, 'the merciful covenant,' alluded to in the previous verse; *viz.* the oath which He swore to the Patriarchs.

a thousand generations. A large, indefinite number of generations (Ibn Ezra), 'Those who *love* God form, as it were, centres whence, upon thousands brought within range of their influence, the blessings of His mercy are diffused abroad' (Driver).

10. *to their face.* 'Immediately' (Ehrlich).

HAFTORAH VA-ETHCHANAN — הפטרת ואתחנן

ISAIAH XL, 1–26

CHAPTER XL

1. Comfort ye, comfort ye My people,
Saith your God.
2. Bid Jerusalem take heart,
And proclaim unto her,
That her time of service is accomplished,
That her guilt is paid off;
That she hath received of the LORD's hand
Double for all her sins.

CAP. XL. מ

א 2 נַחֲמוּ נַחֲמוּ עַמִּי יֹאמַר אֱלֹהֵיכֶם׃ דַּבְּרוּ עַל־לֵב יְרוּשָׁלִַם

וְקִרְאוּ אֵלֶיהָ כִּי מָלְאָה צְבָאָהּ כִּי נִרְצָה עֲוֺנָהּ כִּי לָקְחָה

3 מִיַּד יְהוָה כִּפְלַיִם בְּכָל־חַטֹּאתֶיהָ׃ קוֹל קוֹרֵא בַּמִּדְבָּר

4 פַּנּוּ דֶּרֶךְ יְהוָה יַשְּׁרוּ בָּעֲרָבָה מְסִלָּה לֵאלֹהֵינוּ׃ כָּל־גֶּיא

The Prophetic Reading of this Sabbath is the first of the seven 'Haftorahs of Consolation' that follow the Fast of Av. They consist of sublime messages of encouragement that have sustained and fortified Israel during its ordeals of cruelty and persecution throughout the ages.

This chapter opens the Rhapsody of 'Zion Redeemed' that occupies the second half of the Book of Isaiah. For the understanding of the historical situation, it is necessary to recall that the Babylonians had, in the year 586, taken Jerusalem, destroyed the kingdom of Judah, and deported the greater portion of its inhabitants to the banks of the Euphrates. After their exile had lasted 47 years, Babylon itself, the 'mistress of the world', was about to fall at the hands of Cyrus, the founder of the Persian Empire. Great was the commotion among Babylon's subject peoples, not least so among the Jewish exiles. 'Against their enslaver and oppressor, they saw uplifted the irresistible sword of God's instrument, this Persian prince to whose religion the Babylonian idolatry was hateful; a victorious warrior, a wise and just statesman, favourable to Babylon's prisoners and victims, and disposed to restore the exiles of Judah to their own land' (Matthew Arnold); see p. 22.

In this supreme hour is heard the voice of God's Prophet, commanded to comfort Israel, and proclaim the Restoration to Zion.

1–2. The Proclamation of Divine Forgiveness.

1. *comfort ye My people.* This does *not* mean, 'Be comforted, O my people'; but the prophets or all who love Jerusalem, are commanded to comfort Israel. This opening word of this Haftorah, נחמו 'Comfort ye', has given the name to the Sabbath, שבת נחמו.

2. *bid Jerusalem take heart.* Better, *speak to the heart of* (RV), *i.e.* 'speak tenderly.'

Jerusalem. Here the symbol of the whole of Israel.

time of service. Term of punishment.

paid off. Worked off; see Lev. XXVI, 43.

double. More than ample. 'These words of the Prophet are like balm upon a wound, or like a soft breath upon a fevered brow' (Graetz). 'The Hebrew language and genius are seen in the Book of Isaiah at their perfection—this has naturally had its effect on the English translators of the Bible, whose Version nowhere perhaps rises to such beauty as in this Book' (Matthew Arnold).

יִנָּשֵׂא וְכָל־הַר וְגִבְעָה יִשְׁפָּלוּ וְהָיָה הֶעָקֹב לְמִישׁוֹר
ה וְהָרְכָסִים לְבִקְעָה׃ וְנִגְלָה כְּבוֹד יְהוָה וְרָאוּ כָל־בָּשָׂר
6 יַחְדָּו כִּי פִּי יְהוָה דִּבֵּר׃ קוֹל אֹמֵר קְרָא וְאָמַר מָה
7 אֶקְרָא כָּל־הַבָּשָׂר חָצִיר וְכָל־חַסְדּוֹ כְּצִיץ הַשָּׂדֶה׃ יָבֵשׁ
חָצִיר נָבֵל צִיץ כִּי רוּחַ יְהוָה נָשְׁבָה בּוֹ אָכֵן חָצִיר הָעָם׃
8 יָבֵשׁ חָצִיר נָבֵל צִיץ וּדְבַר אֱלֹהֵינוּ יָקוּם לְעוֹלָם׃
9 עַל הַר־גָּבֹהַּ עֲלִי־לָךְ מְבַשֶּׂרֶת צִיּוֹן הָרִימִי בַכֹּחַ קוֹלֵךְ
מְבַשֶּׂרֶת יְרוּשָׁלִָם הָרִימִי אַל־תִּירָאִי אִמְרִי לְעָרֵי יְהוּדָה
י הִנֵּה אֱלֹהֵיכֶם׃ הִנֵּה אֲדֹנָי יֱהוִה בְּחָזָק יָבוֹא וּזְרֹעוֹ מֹשְׁלָה

3. Hark! one calleth:
'Clear ye in the wilderness the way of the LORD,
Make plain in the desert
A highway for our God.
4. Every valley shall be lifted up,
And every mountain and hill shall be made low;
And the rugged shall be made level,
And the rough places a plain;
5. And the glory of the LORD shall be revealed,
And all flesh shall see it together;
For the mouth of the LORD hath spoken it.'

6. Hark! one saith: 'Proclaim!'
And he saith: 'What shall I proclaim?'
'All flesh is grass,
And all the goodliness thereof is as the flower of the field;
7. The grass withereth, the flower fadeth;
Because the breath of the LORD bloweth upon it—
Surely the people is grass.
8. The grass withereth, the flower fadeth;
But the word of our God shall stand for ever.'

9. O thou that tellest good tidings to Zion,
Get thee up into the high mountain;
O thou that tellest good tidings to Jerusalem,
Lift up thy voice with strength;
Lift it up, be not afraid;
Say unto the cities of Judah:
'Behold your God!'
10. Behold, the Lord GOD will come as a Mighty One,
And His arm will rule for Him;
Behold, His reward is with Him,
And His recompense before Him.

3–5. The Prophet hears the sound of Heavenly voices announcing that Israel's Deliverance from exile is at hand. The return from captivity is conceived as a Divine triumphal march.

3. *hark! one calleth.* lit. 'A voice! one is crying.' A Heavenly voice cries to his fellows to make a road through the desert for the return of exiled Israel, with God as the Leader.

clear. Of obstacles.

in the wilderness. The shortest line from Babylon to Judea was nearly all through desert.

4. *every valley . . . plain.* Whatever would obstruct the path of the returning exiles will be smoothed away, in order to make a level and easy road for the returning exiles.

lifted up. Raised.

5. *glory of the LORD.* Israel's redemption will be 'the talk of the world', and lead to a new recognition of the Divine among mankind.

6–8. Second herald: all earthly might is transitory—Israel's oppressors will perish; the word of God alone is eternal.

7. *breath of the LORD.* Probably refers to the sirocco, the scorching wind that often blights the spring vegetation in Palestine.

the people. Here signifying the same as *all flesh*, and, in particular, Israel's enemies who will wither like grass.

8. *the word of our God.* God's immutable purposes as announced to Israel and mankind by Israel's Prophets—'the one permanent factor in human history' (Skinner).

shall stand for ever. The glory of human plans and achievements is as ephemeral as the flower of the field. The word of God alone is forever certain of triumphant fulfilment.

9–11. Third herald: the news announced in Palestine, 'God is coming, bringing His People back to Zion.'

9. *into the high mountain.* So that the glad herald may be heard from afar.

be not afraid. Of being put to shame, through failure of the event announced. Or, fear not the Babylonian authorities, who were still the nominal rulers in Jerusalem (Krauss).

10. *arm.* His power.

reward. Probably the exiles themselves, regarded as spoil recovered from the heathen nations (Skinner).

11 לוֹ הִנֵּה שְׂכָרוֹ אִתּוֹ וּפְעֻלָּתוֹ לְפָנָיו׃ כְּרֹעֶה עֶדְרוֹ יִרְעֶה
12 בִּזְרֹעוֹ יְקַבֵּץ טְלָאִים וּבְחֵיקוֹ יִשָּׂא עָלוֹת יְנַהֵל׃ מִֽי־
מָדַד בְּשָׁעֳלוֹ מַיִם וְשָׁמַיִם בַּזֶּרֶת תִּכֵּן וְכָל בַּשָּׁלִשׁ עֲפַר
13 הָאָרֶץ וְשָׁקַל בַּפֶּלֶס הָרִים וּגְבָעוֹת בְּמֹאזְנָיִם׃ מִֽי־תִכֵּן
14 אֶת־רוּחַ יְהוָה וְאִישׁ עֲצָתוֹ יוֹדִיעֶנּוּ׃ אֶת־מִי נוֹעָץ וַיְבִינֵהוּ
וַֽיְלַמְּדֵהוּ בְּאֹרַח מִשְׁפָּט וַיְלַמְּדֵהוּ דַעַת וְדֶרֶךְ תְּבוּנוֹת
טו יוֹדִיעֶנּוּ׃ הֵן גּוֹיִם כְּמַר מִדְּלִי וּכְשַׁחַק מֹאזְנַיִם נֶחְשָׁבוּ הֵן
16 אִיִּים כַּדַּק יִטּוֹל׃ וּלְבָנוֹן אֵין דֵּי בָּעֵר וְחַיָּתוֹ אֵין דֵּי
17 עוֹלָה׃ כָּל־הַגּוֹיִם כְּאַיִן נֶגְדּוֹ מֵאֶפֶס וָתֹהוּ נֶחְשְׁבוּ־
18 19 לוֹ׃ וְאֶל־מִי תְּדַמְּיוּן אֵל וּמַה־דְּמוּת תַּעַרְכוּ־לוֹ׃ הַפֶּסֶל
נָסַךְ חָרָשׁ וְצֹרֵף בַּזָּהָב יְרַקְּעֶנּוּ וּרְתֻקוֹת כֶּסֶף צוֹרֵף׃

11. Even as a shepherd that feedeth his flock,
That gathereth the lambs in his arm,
And carrieth them in his bosom,
And gently leadeth those that give suck.

12. Who hath measured the waters in the hollow of his hand,
And meted out heaven with the span,
And comprehended the dust of the earth in a measure,
And weighed the mountains in scales,
And the hills in a balance?

13. Who hath meted out the spirit of the LORD?
Or who was His counsellor that he might instruct Him?

14. With whom took He counsel, and who instructed Him,
And taught Him in the path of right,
And taught Him knowledge,
And made Him to know the way of discernment?

15. Behold, the nations are as a drop of a bucket,
And are counted as the small dust of the balance;
Behold, the isles are as a mote in weight.

16. And Lebanon is not sufficient fuel,
Nor the beasts thereof sufficient for burnt-offerings.

17. All the nations are as nothing before Him;
They are accounted by Him as things of nought, and vanity.

18. To whom then will ye liken God?
Or what likeness will ye compare unto Him?

19. The image perchance, which the craftsman hath melted,
And the goldsmith spread over with gold,
The silversmith casting silver chains?

11. *even as a shepherd.* The Almighty God reveals Himself to the returning exiles as a God of infinite tenderness to the weak and the helpless.

12–26. God's Incomparable wisdom and might shown in Creation and the government of the World. And yet there are those, weak in faith, who doubt the possibility of Israel's Deliverance!

12. *measured.* What sort of infinite Being must He be who actually can take all the waters of the universe in the hollow of His hand?
comprehended. Old English for 'held'.
a measure. lit. 'a third,' probably of an ephah.

13. *meted out.* Or, 'estimated,' *i.e.* been able to fathom.
spirit of the LORD. The Divine intelligence. These are rhetorical questions: the answer in this and following verse is, 'No one.'

14. *right.* 'The conception of the orderliness of Creation took almost as firm a hold on the Hebrew mind as the Greek' (Cheyne).

15. *behold.* Having shown God's infinite wisdom and might in Nature, the Prophet proceeds to show it in History.
of a bucket. From a bucket—an illustration of the insignificance of mankind in comparison with the Creator of all things.
small dust. A few grains of dust in the balance, which make no appreciable difference in the weight.
isles. Here, 'the habitable lands.'

16. *fuel.* The forests of Lebanon are not enough wood for a sacrifice commensurate with God's greatness.

17. *vanity.* lit. 'a waste,' emptiness, nothing.

18–20. The absurdity, therefore, of representing God in the form of a man-made idol! The utter folly of such worship.

כ הַמְסֻכָּן תְּרוּמָה עֵץ לֹא־יִרְקַב יִבְחָר חָרָשׁ חָכָם יְבַקֶּשׁ־
21 לוֹ לְהָכִין פֶּסֶל לֹא יִמּוֹט׃ הֲלוֹא תֵדְעוּ הֲלוֹא תִשְׁמָעוּ
הֲלוֹא הֻגַּד מֵרֹאשׁ לָכֶם הֲלוֹא הֲבִינֹתֶם מוֹסְדוֹת הָאָרֶץ׃
22 הַיֹּשֵׁב עַל־חוּג הָאָרֶץ וְיֹשְׁבֶיהָ כַּחֲגָבִים הַנּוֹטֶה כַדֹּק
23 שָׁמַיִם וַיִּמְתָּחֵם כָּאֹהֶל לָשָׁבֶת׃ הַנּוֹתֵן רוֹזְנִים לְאָיִן שֹׁפְטֵי
24 אֶרֶץ כַּתֹּהוּ עָשָׂה׃ אַף בַּל־נִטָּעוּ אַף בַּל־זֹרָעוּ אַף בַּל־
שֹׁרֵשׁ בָּאָרֶץ גִּזְעָם וְגַם נָשַׁף בָּהֶם וַיִּבָשׁוּ וּסְעָרָה כַּקַּשׁ
כה 26 תִּשָּׂאֵם׃ וְאֶל־מִי תְדַמְּיוּנִי וְאֶשְׁוֶה יֹאמַר קָדוֹשׁ׃ שְׂאוּ־
מָרוֹם עֵינֵיכֶם וּרְאוּ מִי־בָרָא אֵלֶּה הַמּוֹצִיא בְמִסְפָּר צְבָאָם
לְכֻלָּם בְּשֵׁם יִקְרָא מֵרֹב אוֹנִים וְאַמִּיץ כֹּחַ אִישׁ לֹא
נֶעְדָּר׃

20. A holm-oak is set apart.
He chooseth a tree that will not rot;
He seeketh unto him a cunning craftsman
To set up an image, that shall not be moved.

21. Know ye not? hear ye not?
Hath it not been told you from the beginning?
Have ye not understood the foundations of the earth?
22. It is He that sitteth above the circle of the earth,
And the inhabitants thereof are as grasshoppers;
That stretcheth out the heavens as a curtain,
And spreadeth them out as a tent to dwell in;
23. That bringeth princes to nothing;
He maketh the judges of the earth as a thing of nought.
24. Scarce are they planted,
Scarce are they sown,
Scarce hath their stock taken root in the earth;
When He bloweth upon them, they wither,
And the whirlwind taketh them away as stubble.
25. To whom then will ye liken Me,
that I should be equal?
Saith the Holy One.
26. Lift up your eyes on high,
And see: who hath created these?
He that bringeth out their host by number,
He calleth them all by name;
By the greatness of His might, and for that He is strong in power,
Not one faileth.

v. 21. קמץ בז״ק

20. *a tree.* See Isa. XLIV, 12–17, for a similar contrast between the costly and the cheap idol, and ridiculing description of the trivial details of idol-manufacture.
not be moved. That will not totter.

21–26. The Creator of Nature is also the Ruler of Mankind.
ye. Mankind as a whole is addressed.
from the beginning. Of Israel's being.
understood the foundations. Which, like the heavens, declare the glory of God.

22. *above the circle of the earth.* The line of the vault of the sky, from horizon to horizon.
curtain. Fine cloth.

23. *princes to nothing.* The Prophet now illustrates God's infinite power and wisdom in the affairs of mankind. The downfall of the King of Media and Crœsus, King of Lydia, before Cyrus must have been fresh in the minds of the exiles (Whitehouse).
judges. Throughout Isaiah, the Heb. word for judges, Shofetim, seems to retain much of its primitive meaning as seen in the Phœnician *suffetes*, 'rulers.'

24. *they wither.* So fleeting and feeble is earthly power and pomp.

26. *lift up your eyes.* 'Regard the heavenly bodies, and consider with understanding that they are merely created things. Their creator is God the Incomparable, who musters them all, and knows the name and nature of each' (Kimchi).
created. Heb. ברא; effortless production, by bare volition. 'No other language possesses a word so exclusively appropriated to the Divine activity' (Skinner).
these. The stars.
calleth. Marshalls them forth.
not one faileth. Each star responds with unswerving obedience to the Divine roll-call.

The verses immediately following (*v.* 27–31) give the application, 'If such be the God of Israel, how can the exiles think that He is indifferent to their fate? The everlasting God is omnipotent, and His understanding is unsearchable. They who trust in Him shall find in Him an inexhaustible source of life and energy.'

ז פ פ פ מו 46

12 וְהָיָה ׀ עֵקֶב תִּשְׁמְעוּן אֵת הַמִּשְׁפָּטִים הָאֵלֶּה וּשְׁמַרְתֶּם
וַעֲשִׂיתֶם אֹתָם וְשָׁמַר יְהוָה אֱלֹהֶיךָ לְךָ אֶת־הַבְּרִית וְאֶת־
13 הַחֶסֶד אֲשֶׁר נִשְׁבַּע לַאֲבֹתֶיךָ׃ וַאֲהֵבְךָ וּבֵרַכְךָ וְהִרְבֶּךָ
וּבֵרַךְ פְּרִי־בִטְנְךָ וּפְרִי־אַדְמָתֶךָ דְּגָנְךָ וְתִירֹשְׁךָ וְיִצְהָרֶךָ
שְׁגַר־אֲלָפֶיךָ וְעַשְׁתְּרֹת צֹאנֶךָ עַל הָאֲדָמָה אֲשֶׁר־נִשְׁבַּע
14 לַאֲבֹתֶיךָ לָתֶת לָךְ׃ בָּרוּךְ תִּהְיֶה מִכָּל־הָעַמִּים לֹא־יִהְיֶה
טו בְךָ עָקָר וַעֲקָרָה וּבִבְהֶמְתֶּךָ׃ וְהֵסִיר יְהוָה מִמְּךָ כָּל־חֹלִי
וְכָל־מַדְוֵי מִצְרַיִם הָרָעִים אֲשֶׁר יָדַעְתָּ לֹא יְשִׂימָם בָּךְ
16 וּנְתָנָם בְּכָל־שֹׂנְאֶיךָ׃ וְאָכַלְתָּ אֶת־כָּל־הָעַמִּים אֲשֶׁר יְהוָה
אֱלֹהֶיךָ נֹתֵן לָךְ לֹא־תָחוֹס עֵינְךָ עֲלֵיהֶם וְלֹא תַעֲבֹד אֶת־
17 אֱלֹהֵיהֶם כִּי־מוֹקֵשׁ הוּא לָךְ׃ ס כִּי תֹאמַר בִּלְבָבְךָ
18 רַבִּים הַגּוֹיִם הָאֵלֶּה מִמֶּנִּי אֵיכָה אוּכַל לְהוֹרִישָׁם׃ לֹא
תִירָא מֵהֶם זָכֹר תִּזְכֹּר אֵת אֲשֶׁר־עָשָׂה יְהוָה אֱלֹהֶיךָ
19 לְפַרְעֹה וּלְכָל־מִצְרָיִם׃ הַמַּסֹּת הַגְּדֹלֹת אֲשֶׁר־רָאוּ עֵינֶיךָ
וְהָאֹתֹת וְהַמֹּפְתִים וְהַיָּד הַחֲזָקָה וְהַזְּרֹעַ הַנְּטוּיָה אֲשֶׁר
הוֹצִאֲךָ יְהוָה אֱלֹהֶיךָ כֵּן־יַעֲשֶׂה יְהוָה אֱלֹהֶיךָ לְכָל־הָעַמִּים
כ אֲשֶׁר־אַתָּה יָרֵא מִפְּנֵיהֶם׃ וְגַם אֶת־הַצִּרְעָה יְשַׁלַּח יְהוָה

7 12. And it shall come to pass, because ye hearken to these ordinances, and keep, and do them, that the LORD thy God shall keep with thee the covenant and the mercy which He swore unto thy fathers, 13. and He will love thee, and bless thee, and multiply thee; He will also bless the fruit of thy body and the fruit of thy land, thy corn and thy wine and thine oil, the increase of thy kine and the young of thy flock, in the land which He swore unto thy fathers to give thee. 14. Thou shalt be blessed above all peoples; there shall not be male or female barren among you, or among your cattle. 15. And the LORD will take away from thee all sickness; and He will put none of the evil diseases of Egypt, which thou knowest, upon thee, but will lay them upon all them that hate thee. 16. And thou shalt consume all the peoples that the LORD thy God shall deliver unto thee; thine eye shall not pity them; neither shalt thou serve their gods; for that will be a snare unto thee. ¶ 17. If thou shalt say in thy heart: 'These nations are more than I; how can I dispossess them?' 18. thou shalt not be afraid of them; thou shalt well remember what the LORD thy God did unto Pharaoh, and unto all Egypt: 19. the great trials which thine eyes saw, and the signs, and the wonders, and the mighty hand, and the outstretched arm, whereby the LORD thy God brought thee out; so shall the LORD thy God do unto all the peoples of whom thou art afraid. 20. Moreover the LORD thy God will send the hornet among them, until they that are left, and they that hide themselves, perish

III. EKEV

(CHAPTERS VII, 12–XI, 25)

VII, 12–16. THE BLESSINGS OF OBEDIENCE

The reward of obedience will be prosperity, vital power, and health.

13. *corn . . . wine . . . oil.* The principal products of Canaan.

15. *diseases of Egypt.* The climate of Egypt is unhealthy, especially at certain seasons of the year. Pliny describes Egypt as 'the mother of worst diseases'; cf. XXVIII, 27, 60.

thou knowest. Thou hast had experience of.

16. *shall not pity them.* See on XX, 17.

17–26. ISRAEL'S STRUGGLE WITH THE CANAANITE NATIONS

God will be his Helper. Let not Israel in the hour of victory come to terms with Idolatry.

17. *are more than I.* 'They are too many for me.'

19. *trials.* See on IV, 34 and XXIX, 3.

20. *hornet.* Cf. Exod. XXIII, 28. A plague of hornets would drive the Canaanites from their hiding-places into the open. Some of the species of hornets found in Palestine have their nests in rock-caves. There is a novel and illuminating explanation of the meaning of the 'hornet'. It was the badge of Thothmes III and his successors, and would thus be a veiled reference to the systematic series of invasions and conquests in Palestine undertaken by that Pharaoh. These invasions had reduced the fighting power and resistance of the Canaanites (Garstang).

from before thee. 21. Thou shalt not be affrighted at them; for the LORD thy God is in the midst of thee, a God great and awful. 22. And the LORD thy God will cast out those nations before thee by little and little; thou mayest not consume them quickly, lest the beasts of the field increase upon thee. 23. But the LORD thy God shall deliver them up before thee, and shall discomfit them with a great discomfiture, until they be destroyed. 24. And He shall deliver their kings into thy hand, and thou shalt make their name to perish from under heaven; there shall no man be able to stand against thee, until thou have destroyed them. 25. The graven images of their gods shall ye burn with fire; thou shalt not covet the silver or the gold that is on them, nor take it unto thee, lest thou be snared therein; for it is an abomination to the LORD thy God. 26. And thou shalt not bring an abomination into thy house, and be accursed like unto it; thou shalt utterly detest it, and thou shalt utterly abhor it; for it is a devoted thing.

8

CHAPTER VIII

1. All the commandment which I command thee this day shall ye observe to do, that ye may live, and multiply, and go in and

21 אֱלֹהֶיךָ בָּם עַד־אֲבֹד הַנִּשְׁאָרִים וְהַנִּסְתָּרִים מִפָּנֶיךָ׃ לֹא
תַעֲרֹץ מִפְּנֵיהֶם כִּי־יְהוָה אֱלֹהֶיךָ בְּקִרְבֶּךָ אֵל גָּדוֹל
22 וְנוֹרָא׃ וְנָשַׁל יְהוָה אֱלֹהֶיךָ אֶת־הַגּוֹיִם הָאֵל מִפָּנֶיךָ מְעַט
מְעָט לֹא תוּכַל כַּלֹּתָם מַהֵר פֶּן־תִּרְבֶּה עָלֶיךָ חַיַּת הַשָּׂדֶה׃
23 וּנְתָנָם יְהוָה אֱלֹהֶיךָ לְפָנֶיךָ וְהָמָם מְהוּמָה גְדֹלָה עַד
24 הִשָּׁמְדָם׃ וְנָתַן מַלְכֵיהֶם בְּיָדֶךָ וְהַאֲבַדְתָּ אֶת־שְׁמָם מִתַּחַת
כה הַשָּׁמָיִם לֹא־יִתְיַצֵּב אִישׁ בְּפָנֶיךָ עַד הִשְׁמִדְךָ אֹתָם׃ פְּסִילֵי
אֱלֹהֵיהֶם תִּשְׂרְפוּן בָּאֵשׁ לֹא־תַחְמֹד כֶּסֶף וְזָהָב עֲלֵיהֶם
וְלָקַחְתָּ לָךְ פֶּן תִּוָּקֵשׁ בּוֹ כִּי תוֹעֲבַת יְהוָה אֱלֹהֶיךָ הוּא׃
26 וְלֹא־תָבִיא תוֹעֵבָה אֶל־בֵּיתֶךָ וְהָיִיתָ חֵרֶם כָּמֹהוּ שַׁקֵּץ ׀
תְּשַׁקְּצֶנּוּ וְתַעֵב ׀ תְּתַעֲבֶנּוּ כִּי־חֵרֶם הוּא׃ פ

ח CAP. VIII. ח

א כָּל־הַמִּצְוָה אֲשֶׁר אָנֹכִי מְצַוְּךָ הַיּוֹם תִּשְׁמְרוּן לַעֲשׂוֹת
לְמַעַן תִּחְיוּן וּרְבִיתֶם וּבָאתֶם וִירִשְׁתֶּם אֶת־הָאָרֶץ אֲשֶׁר־

ז׳ v. 22. סבירין האלה

21. *affrighted at them.* So as to seek safety in flight.

and awful. God alone is to be feared, and the fear of Him would drive out any other.

22. *little and little.* Otherwise, large areas would be left desolate, in which wild beasts would multiply; see II Kings XVII, 24 f, also on Exod. XXIII, 29.

beasts of the field. Wild beasts, as 'field' is here used in the sense of uncultivated territory. The country was at no time in the Biblical age so settled that the jungle lay wholly beyond the range of ordinary experience. 'How constant the war of man against wild animals was in ancient Palestine, may be felt from the promise of their being tamed as one of the elements of the Messianic Age; Isa. XI, 6–8' (G. A. Smith).

23. *discomfit them with a great discomfiture.* 'Rout them in a crushing defeat' (Moffatt).

25. *the silver or the gold that is on them.* The wooden image was usually overlaid with one of the precious metals; see Isa. XL, 19, p. 778.

snared therein. i.e. brought into misfortune, through God's judgment being provoked by the heathenish relic in the Israelite's home.

26. *an abomination.* Heb. תועבה; a contemptuous term for an idolatrous image, unchastity, or dishonest dealing.

be accursed like unto it. Better, *be an accursed thing; i.e.* become a *herem;* cf. p. 549. He who brings an abomination into his house, himself becomes abominable; see the story of Achan, Josh. VII.

CHAPTERS VIII–X, 11. APPEAL TO HISTORY AS A MOTIVE FOR FULFILLING THE FUNDAMENTAL DUTY OF LOVING GOD AND KEEPING HIS COMMANDMENTS

VIII. FATHERLY DISCIPLINE OF GOD—THE LESSONS OF THE WILDERNESS

The long wandering in the Wilderness had been designed to teach Israel humility and a self-distrusting reliance on Him. In those years, when the Israelites were wholly dependent upon God, they had lacked nothing that was essential for their life. Now they were about to take possession of a fertile land; let them take heed not to forget the Divine goodness and guidance.

1. *all the commandment.* Ibn Ezra joins this *v.* to the one following. 'If ye desire to keep all the commandments that ye may live, then remember all the way which the LORD . . . commandments or no.'

live, and multiply. This is said because of the fate of the preceding generation which had been doomed to die in the Wilderness (Ehrlich).

possess the land which the LORD swore unto your fathers. 2. And thou shalt remember all the way which the LORD thy God hath led thee these forty years in the wilderness, that He might afflict thee, to prove thee, to know what was in thy heart, whether thou wouldest keep His commandments, or no. 3. And He afflicted thee, and suffered thee to hunger, and fed thee with manna, which thou knewest not, neither did thy fathers know; that He might make thee know that man doth not live by bread only, but by every thing that proceedeth out of the mouth of the LORD doth man live. 4. Thy raiment waxed not old upon thee, neither did thy foot swell, these forty years. 5. And thou shalt consider in thy heart, that, as a man chasteneth his son, so the LORD thy God chasteneth thee. 6. And thou shalt keep the commandments of the LORD thy God, to walk in His ways, and to fear Him. 7. For the LORD thy God bringeth thee into a good land, a land of brooks of water, of fountains and depths,

2 נִשְׁבַּע יְהוָה לַאֲבֹתֵיכֶם׃ וְזָכַרְתָּ אֶת־כָּל־הַדֶּרֶךְ אֲשֶׁר
הוֹלִיכְךָ יְהוָה אֱלֹהֶיךָ זֶה אַרְבָּעִים שָׁנָה בַּמִּדְבָּר לְמַעַן
עַנֹּתְךָ לְנַסֹּתְךָ לָדַעַת אֶת־אֲשֶׁר בִּלְבָבְךָ הֲתִשְׁמֹר מִצְוֺתָו
3 אִם־לֹא׃ וַיְעַנְּךָ וַיַּרְעִבֶךָ וַיַּאֲכִלְךָ אֶת־הַמָּן אֲשֶׁר לֹא־
יָדַעְתָּ וְלֹא יָדְעוּן אֲבֹתֶיךָ לְמַעַן הוֹדִיעֲךָ כִּי לֹא עַל־הַלֶּחֶם
לְבַדּוֹ יִחְיֶה הָאָדָם כִּי עַל־כָּל־מוֹצָא פִי־יְהוָה יִחְיֶה הָאָדָם׃
4 שִׂמְלָתְךָ לֹא בָלְתָה מֵעָלֶיךָ וְרַגְלְךָ לֹא בָצֵקָה זֶה אַרְבָּעִים
ה שָׁנָה׃ וְיָדַעְתָּ עִם־לְבָבֶךָ כִּי כַּאֲשֶׁר יְיַסֵּר אִישׁ אֶת־בְּנוֹ
6 יְהוָה אֱלֹהֶיךָ מְיַסְּרֶךָּ׃ וְשָׁמַרְתָּ אֶת־מִצְוֺת יְהוָה אֱלֹהֶיךָ
7 לָלֶכֶת בִּדְרָכָיו וּלְיִרְאָה אֹתוֹ׃ כִּי יְהוָה אֱלֹהֶיךָ מְבִיאֲךָ
אֶל־אֶרֶץ טוֹבָה אֶרֶץ נַחֲלֵי מָיִם עֲיָנֹת וּתְהֹמֹת יֹצְאִים

v. 2. מצותיו קרי v. 7. קמץ בז"ק

2. *all the way.* The spiritual purpose of the long journey in the Wilderness is now expounded to the people, presenting a fresh aspect of Divine Providence.

that He might afflict thee. This is defined in *v.* 3, 15–16. God brought privations upon them to teach them how dependent they were upon Him, and how helpless without Him.

to prove thee. i.e. to test thee. It is in adversity that the true nature of a man is seen. When hardships came upon the Israelites, they had stood the test. Although they had murmured and complained, under the restraining influence of Moses they had adhered to God.

3. *and He afflicted thee.* Better, *so He afflicted thee.*

manna. See Exod. XVI.

man doth not live by bread only. Physical food is not the only thing that ensures man's existence. Apart from the normal sustenance, there are Divine forces which sustain man in his progress through life. The words in the Text are of wider application than their reference to the manna. They teach that man has a soul as well as a body, and the needs of the spiritual life should not be neglected. This truth is of especial importance in an age when, in so many countries, men are passionately declaring that man *can* live by bread alone, and that he will.

4. *thy raiment waxed not old.* 'There are some who explain this in the manner of a symbol; *i.e.* the expressions are rhetorical, and not to be understood in their literal sense. They are a vivid metaphor to denote the sustaining Providence of God during the wanderings in the inhospitable desert' (Ibn Ezra).

5. *and thou shalt consider in thine heart.* Better, *and thou shalt know with thine heart; i.e.* with the *conviction* which comes from knowledge—the 'heart' being the seat of intelligence (IV, 29).

chasteneth his son. Better, *disciplineth his son.* Even the hunger and hardship during the wanderings in the desert were part of God's fatherly discipline of His people. Suffering is thus transfigured into what the Rabbis called 'chastisements of love' (יסורין של אהבה). 'God delivereth the afflicted by his affliction' (Job XXXVI, 15). Especially to the Rabbis is the pathway of suffering the necessary road to the beatitudes of the higher life. 'Beloved is suffering; for only through suffering were the good gifts of the Torah, the Holy Land, and Eternal Life given unto Israel. Those who rejoice in their sufferings, they are the *lovers* of God' (Talmud).

7–19. This fatherly discipline of God it is necessary to keep vividly in mind; lest, in the plenty of Palestine, God be forgotten.

7. *a good land . . . hills.* 'An attractive and faithful description of the Palestinian landscape' (Driver); III, 25.

brooks of water. i.e. wadys; see on II, 13.

depths. Heb. *tehomoth;* the underground waters that feed the rivers and fountains; see on IV, 18.

springing forth in valleys and hills; 8. a land of wheat and barley, and vines and fig-trees and pomegranates; a land of olive-trees and honey; 9. a land wherein thou shalt eat bread without scarceness, thou shalt not lack any thing in it; a land whose stones are iron, and out of whose hills thou mayest dig brass. 10. And thou shalt eat and be satisfied, and bless the LORD thy God for the good land which He hath given thee.*ii. 11. Beware lest thou forget the LORD thy God, in not keeping His commandments, and His ordinances, and His statutes, which I command thee this day; 12. lest when thou hast eaten and art satisfied, and hast built goodly houses, and dwelt therein; 13. and when thy herds and thy flocks multiply, and thy silver and thy gold is multiplied, and all that thou hast is multiplied; 14. then thy heart be lifted up, and thou forget the LORD thy God, who brought thee forth out of the land of Egypt, out of the house of bondage; 15. who led thee through the great and dreadful wilderness, wherein were serpents, fiery serpents, and scorpions, and thirsty ground where

8 בַּבִּקְעָה וּבָהָר׃ אֶרֶץ חִטָּה וּשְׂעֹרָה וְגֶפֶן וּתְאֵנָה וְרִמּוֹן
9 אֶרֶץ־זֵית שֶׁמֶן וּדְבָשׁ׃ אֶרֶץ אֲשֶׁר לֹא בְמִסְכֵּנֻת תֹּאכַל־
בָּהּ לֶחֶם לֹא־תֶחְסַר כֹּל בָּהּ אֶרֶץ אֲשֶׁר אֲבָנֶיהָ בַרְזֶל
י וּמֵהֲרָרֶיהָ תַּחְצֹב נְחֹשֶׁת׃ וְאָכַלְתָּ וְשָׂבָעְתָּ וּבֵרַכְתָּ אֶת־
שני
11 יְהוָה אֱלֹהֶיךָ עַל־הָאָרֶץ הַטֹּבָה אֲשֶׁר נָתַן־לָךְ׃* הִשָּׁמֶר
לְךָ פֶּן־תִּשְׁכַּח אֶת־יְהוָה אֱלֹהֶיךָ לְבִלְתִּי שְׁמֹר מִצְוֺתָיו
12 וּמִשְׁפָּטָיו וְחֻקֹּתָיו אֲשֶׁר אָנֹכִי מְצַוְּךָ הַיּוֹם׃ פֶּן־תֹּאכַל וְשָׂבָעְתָּ
13 וּבָתִּים טֹבִים תִּבְנֶה וְיָשָׁבְתָּ׃ וּבְקָרְךָ וְצֹאנְךָ יִרְבְּיֻן וְכֶסֶף
14 וְזָהָב יִרְבֶּה־לָּךְ וְכֹל אֲשֶׁר־לְךָ יִרְבֶּה׃ וְרָם לְבָבֶךָ וְשָׁכַחְתָּ
אֶת־יְהוָה אֱלֹהֶיךָ הַמּוֹצִיאֲךָ מֵאֶרֶץ מִצְרַיִם מִבֵּית עֲבָדִים׃
טו הַמּוֹלִיכְךָ בַּמִּדְבָּר ׀ הַגָּדֹל וְהַנּוֹרָא נָחָשׁ ׀ שָׂרָף וְעַקְרָב
וְצִמָּאוֹן אֲשֶׁר אֵין־מָיִם הַמּוֹצִיא לְךָ מַיִם מִצּוּר הַחַלָּמִישׁ׃

9. *without scarceness.* Among the desert Arabs, 'some tribes taste bread but once a month, others not so often, and it is regarded as a luxury' (Ed. Robinson).

whose stones are iron. i.e. the stones contain, and with treatment yield, iron. What is meant is probably the black basalt, a volcanic product, which contains about one-fifth iron, and is still called iron-stone by the Arabs.

brass. Better, *copper.* Traces of copper works are to be found in the Lebanon and Edom. For an account of ancient mining, see Job. XXVIII, 1–11.

10. *and thou shalt eat.* The good things of the world are provided for man's enjoyment; and, far from doing wrong by finding happiness in them, Judaism desires man to do so.

bless. i.e. thank; thou shalt be moved to praise Him with a grateful heart. The Rabbis understood these words as a command, and based upon them the precept that every meal must be followed by Grace. As 'the earth is the LORD's and the fulness thereof', the Talmud declares, 'Whoever enjoys any worldly pleasure without uttering a benediction of its Divine Giver, commits a theft against God.'

The Grace consists of four parts: thanksgiving for food, for the land of Israel, for the Temple, and general praise and petition. In the light of Judaism, the table is an altar; and every meal is hallowed by prayer, before and after. The ancient Jewish Mystics added a touch of ecstasy to the statutory Grace by singing gleeful table-hymns, Zemiroth. The unique combination in these songs, of adoration of God with genial appreciation of good cheer is a product of the Jewish genius, which interweaves the secular with the sacred, and spreads over the ordinary facts of life the rainbow of the Divine. This saintly custom of table-hymns was soon adopted for the Sabbath by the whole House of Israel. In this way, a Sabbath meal became, literally, a service *of* joy and *with* joy. To those who sing, and teach their little ones to sing, these beautiful hymns and melodies, the Sabbath day is, as it was to their fathers of old, a foretaste of 'that Day which is wholly a Sabbath, and rest in life everlasting'.

14. *thy heart be lifted up . . . forget the LORD.* Wherever there is pride, there is forgetting of God. 'Of a man dominated by pride, the Holy One, blessed be He, says, "I and he cannot dwell in the same universe"' (Talmud). 'Prosperity always tempts man to fretfulness against every idea of restraint. Whenever men forgot God, their whole way of life dropped to a lower level and served baser issues. A reverent and humble recognition of Him and gratitude to Him would prevent their obedience becoming a weariness' (Welch).

15. *fiery serpents.* See Num. XXI, 6.

thirsty ground where was no water. The desert was first of all a place of thirst without shade from the sun, the fierce rays of which cause excessive longing for drink; secondly, the desert was a waterless place.

rock of flint. See Exod. XVII, 6.

was no water; who brought thee forth water out of the rock of flint; 16. who fed thee in the wilderness with manna, which thy fathers knew not; that He might afflict thee, and that He might prove thee, to do thee good at thy latter end; 17. and thou say in thy heart: 'My power and the might of my hand hath gotten me this wealth.' 18. But thou shalt remember the LORD thy God, for it is He that giveth thee power to get wealth; that He may establish His covenant which He swore unto thy fathers, as it is this day. ¶ 19. And it shall be, if thou shalt forget the LORD thy God, and walk after other gods, and serve them, and worship them, I forewarn you this day that ye shall surely perish. 20. As the nations that the LORD maketh to perish before you, so shall ye perish; because ye would not hearken unto the voice of the LORD your God.

16 הַמַּאֲכִלְךָ מָן בַּמִּדְבָּר אֲשֶׁר לֹא־יָדְעוּן אֲבֹתֶיךָ לְמַעַן עַנֹּתְךָ
17 וּלְמַעַן נַסֹּתֶךָ לְהֵיטִבְךָ בְּאַחֲרִיתֶךָ׃ וְאָמַרְתָּ בִּלְבָבֶךָ כֹּחִי
18 וְעֹצֶם יָדִי עָשָׂה לִי אֶת־הַחַיִל הַזֶּה׃ וְזָכַרְתָּ אֶת־יְהוָה
אֱלֹהֶיךָ כִּי הוּא הַנֹּתֵן לְךָ כֹּחַ לַעֲשׂוֹת חָיִל לְמַעַן הָקִים
אֶת־בְּרִיתוֹ אֲשֶׁר־נִשְׁבַּע לַאֲבֹתֶיךָ כַּיּוֹם הַזֶּה׃ פ
19 וְהָיָה אִם־שָׁכֹחַ תִּשְׁכַּח אֶת־יְהוָה אֱלֹהֶיךָ וְהָלַכְתָּ אַחֲרֵי
אֱלֹהִים אֲחֵרִים וַעֲבַדְתָּם וְהִשְׁתַּחֲוִיתָ לָהֶם הַעִדֹתִי בָכֶם
כ הַיּוֹם כִּי אָבֹד תֹּאבֵדוּן׃ כַּגּוֹיִם אֲשֶׁר יְהוָה מַאֲבִיד
מִפְּנֵיכֶם כֵּן תֹּאבֵדוּן עֵקֶב לֹא תִשְׁמְעוּן בְּקוֹל יְהוָה
אֱלֹהֵיכֶם׃ פ

9

CHAPTER IX

1. Hear, O Israel: thou art to pass over the Jordan this day, to go in to dispossess nations greater and mightier than thyself, cities great and fortified up to heaven, 2. a people great and tall, the sons of the Anakim, whom thou knowest, and of whom thou hast heard say: 'Who can stand before the sons of Anak?' 3. Know therefore this day, that the LORD thy God is He who goeth over before thee as a devouring fire; He will destroy them, and He will bring them down before thee; so shalt thou drive them out, and make them to perish quickly, as the LORD hath spoken unto thee.*iii. 4. Speak not thou in thy heart, after that the

CAP. IX. ט

ט

א שְׁמַע יִשְׂרָאֵל אַתָּה עֹבֵר הַיּוֹם אֶת־הַיַּרְדֵּן לָבֹא לָרֶשֶׁת
גּוֹיִם גְּדֹלִים וַעֲצֻמִים מִמֶּךָּ עָרִים גְּדֹלֹת וּבְצֻרֹת בַּשָּׁמָיִם׃
2 עַם־גָּדוֹל וָרָם בְּנֵי עֲנָקִים אֲשֶׁר אַתָּה יָדַעְתָּ וְאַתָּה
3 שָׁמַעְתָּ מִי יִתְיַצֵּב לִפְנֵי בְּנֵי עֲנָק׃ וְיָדַעְתָּ הַיּוֹם כִּי יְהוָה
אֱלֹהֶיךָ הוּא הָעֹבֵר לְפָנֶיךָ אֵשׁ אֹכְלָה הוּא יַשְׁמִידֵם
וְהוּא יַכְנִיעֵם לְפָנֶיךָ וְהוֹרַשְׁתָּם וְהַאֲבַדְתָּם מַהֵר כַּאֲשֶׁר
שלישי
4 דִּבֶּר יְהוָה לָךְ׃ *אַל־תֹּאמַר בִּלְבָבְךָ בַּהֲדֹף יְהוָה אֱלֹהֶיךָ

16. *at thy latter end.* lit. 'in thy later days'; *viz.* when Israel is settled in the Land. The hard experience they had been called upon to endure was part of their training for their independent national existence.

18. *but thou shalt remember.* God would fulfil the promise He made to the Patriarchs; but the continuance of the good fortune of the Israelites would depend upon their own merit. Hence the warning immediately follows, that forgetfulness of God would change national prosperity into adversity.

as it is this day. As the occupation of the Transjordanian lands, and the impending conquest of the Promised Land, are the result of that Covenant.

19. *other gods . . . forewarn.* Local Baals of the Canaanites.

20. *as the nations . . . perish.* Because you will then not be better than those nations.

CHAPTER IX–X, 11. WARNING AGAINST SELF-RIGHTEOUSNESS

Israel's victories over the Canaanites are due not to any exceptional merits of Israel, but to the wickedness of those nations, and because of the Divine promise to the Patriarchs.

1–7. ISRAEL'S VICTORY DUE TO GOD

1. *this day. i.e.* in the immediate future.

fortified up to heaven. Cf. I, 28.

2. *whom thou knowest.* Having come in contact with Og, king of Bashan, who belonged to a race of giants (III, 12).

thou hast heard. From the report of the spies; Num. XIII, 28.

3. *He will.* The *He* is emphatic. The victory is God's, not Israel's.

hath spoken. See Exod. XXIII, 27, 31.

4. *for my righteousness.* 'Because of my deserts.'

whereas for the wickedness. Better, *and for the*

LORD thy God hath thrust them out from before thee, saying: 'For my righteousness the LORD hath brought me in to possess this land'; whereas for the wickedness of these nations the LORD doth drive them out from before thee. 5. Not for thy righteousness, or for the uprightness of thy heart, dost thou go in to possess their land; but for the wickedness of these nations the LORD thy God doth drive them out from before thee, and that He may establish the word which the LORD swore unto thy fathers, to Abraham, to Isaac, and to Jacob. 6. Know therefore that it is not for thy righteousness that the LORD thy God giveth thee this good land to possess it; for thou art a stiffnecked people. ¶ 7. Remember, forget thou not, how thou didst make the LORD thy God wroth in the wilderness; from the day that thou didst go forth out of the land of Egypt, until ye came unto this place, ye have been rebellious against the LORD. 8. Also in Horeb ye made the LORD wroth, and the LORD was angered with you to have destroyed you. 9. When I was gone up into the mount to receive the tables of stone, even the tables of the covenant which the LORD made with you, then I abode in the mount forty days and forty nights; I did neither eat bread nor drink water. 10. And the LORD delivered unto me the two tables of stone written with the finger of God; and on them was written according to all the words, which the LORD spoke with you in the mount out of the midst of the fire in the day of the assembly. 11. And it came to pass at the end of forty days and forty nights, that the LORD gave me the two tables of stone, even the tables of the covenant. 12. And the

אֹתָם ׀ מִלְּפָנֶיךָ לֵאמֹר בְּצִדְקָתִי הֱבִיאַנִי יְהוָה לָרֶשֶׁת
אֶת הָאָרֶץ הַזֹּאת וּבְרִשְׁעַת הַגּוֹיִם הָאֵלֶּה יְהוָה מוֹרִישָׁם
ה מִפָּנֶיךָ׃ לֹא בְצִדְקָתְךָ וּבְיֹשֶׁר לְבָבְךָ אַתָּה בָא לָרֶשֶׁת אֶת־
אַרְצָם כִּי בְּרִשְׁעַת ׀ הַגּוֹיִם הָאֵלֶּה יְהוָה אֱלֹהֶיךָ מוֹרִישָׁם
מִפָּנֶיךָ וּלְמַעַן הָקִים אֶת־הַדָּבָר אֲשֶׁר נִשְׁבַּע יְהוָה לַאֲבֹתֶיךָ
6 לְאַבְרָהָם לְיִצְחָק וּלְיַעֲקֹב׃ וְיָדַעְתָּ כִּי לֹא בְצִדְקָתְךָ יְהוָה
אֱלֹהֶיךָ נֹתֵן לְךָ אֶת־הָאָרֶץ הַטּוֹבָה הַזֹּאת לְרִשְׁתָּהּ כִּי
7 עַם־קְשֵׁה־עֹרֶף אָתָּה׃ זְכֹר אַל־תִּשְׁכַּח אֵת אֲשֶׁר־הִקְצַפְתָּ
אֶת־יְהוָה אֱלֹהֶיךָ בַּמִּדְבָּר לְמִן־הַיּוֹם אֲשֶׁר־יָצָאתָ ׀ מֵאֶרֶץ
מִצְרַיִם עַד־בֹּאֲכֶם עַד־הַמָּקוֹם הַזֶּה מַמְרִים הֱיִיתֶם עִם־
8 יְהוָה׃ וּבְחֹרֵב הִקְצַפְתֶּם אֶת־יְהוָה וַיִּתְאַנַּף יְהוָה בָּכֶם
9 לְהַשְׁמִיד אֶתְכֶם׃ בַּעֲלֹתִי הָהָרָה לָקַחַת לוּחֹת הָאֲבָנִים
לוּחֹת הַבְּרִית אֲשֶׁר־כָּרַת יְהוָה עִמָּכֶם וָאֵשֵׁב בָּהָר אַרְבָּעִים
יוֹם וְאַרְבָּעִים לַיְלָה לֶחֶם לֹא אָכַלְתִּי וּמַיִם לֹא שָׁתִיתִי׃
י וַיִּתֵּן יְהוָה אֵלַי אֶת־שְׁנֵי לוּחֹת הָאֲבָנִים כְּתֻבִים בְּאֶצְבַּע
אֱלֹהִים וַעֲלֵיהֶם כְּכָל־הַדְּבָרִים אֲשֶׁר דִּבֶּר יְהוָה עִמָּכֶם
11 בָּהָר מִתּוֹךְ הָאֵשׁ בְּיוֹם הַקָּהָל׃ וַיְהִי מִקֵּץ אַרְבָּעִים יוֹם
וְאַרְבָּעִים לַיְלָה נָתַן יְהוָה אֵלַי אֶת־שְׁנֵי לֻחֹת הָאֲבָנִים
12 לֻחוֹת הַבְּרִית׃ וַיֹּאמֶר יְהוָה אֵלַי קוּם רֵד מַהֵר מִזֶּה

wickedness. The meaning of this and *v.* 5 is as follows: Do not imagine that there are two reasons for thy possession of the Land; *viz.* thy righteousness, and the wickedness of the inhabitants. True the wickedness of the inhabitants lost them their land; but the reason why the Israelites were taking their place was not their righteousness, but the fulfilment of the Divine promise made to the Fathers (Rashi, Rashbam).

the wickedness of these nations. Recent excavations bear gruesome testimony to the savagery and foul uncleanness of their rites; see on XII, 31.

5. *not for thy righteousness.* This is illustrated in *v.* 8 by the outstanding example of Israel's sin, the Golden Calf.

or for the uprightness of thy heart. This refers to Israel's unbelief and rebellion; see *v.* 20 f.

6. *stiffnecked people.* See on Exod. XXXII, 9.

IX, 8–X, 11. PROOF FROM HISTORY OF ISRAEL'S REBELLION

But for the intercession of Moses, and the gracious forgiveness of God, Israel would have been destroyed for the Golden Calf apostasy.

8. *also in Horeb.* Better, *even in Horeb;* or, *especially in Horeb.* The sin of the Golden Calf is singled out as the most notorious offence committed by the Israelites.

9. *I did neither eat.* While the Revelation imposed upon Moses a long abstinence, they treated it so lightly that they indulged in a heathenish orgy.

10. *written with the finger of God.* See on Exod. XXXI, 18.

the assembly. Heb. *kahal;* any assembly, or its representatives, for organized national action.

LORD said unto me: 'Arise, get thee down quickly from hence; for thy people that thou hast brought forth out of Egypt have dealt corruptly; they are quickly turned aside out of the way which I commanded them; they have made them a molten image.' 13. Furthermore the LORD spoke unto me, saying: 'I have seen this people, and, behold, it is a stiffnecked people; 14. let Me alone, that I may destroy them, and blot out their name from under heaven; and I will make of thee a nation mightier and greater than they.' 15. So I turned and came down from the mount, and the mount burned with fire; and the two tables of the covenant were in my two hands. 16. And I looked, and, behold, ye had sinned against the LORD your God; ye had made you a molten calf; ye had turned aside quickly out of the way which the LORD had commanded you. 17. And I took hold of the two tables, and cast them out of my two hands, and broke them before your eyes. 18. And I fell down before the LORD, as at the first, forty days and forty nights; I did neither eat bread nor drink water; because of all your sin which ye sinned, in doing that which was evil in the sight of the LORD, to provoke Him. 19. For I was in dread of the anger and hot displeasure, wherewith the LORD was wroth against you to destroy you. But the LORD hearkened unto me that time also. 20. Moreover the LORD was very angry with Aaron to have destroyed him; and I prayed for Aaron also the same time. 21. And I took your sin, the calf which ye had made, and burnt it with fire, and beat it in pieces, grinding it very small, until it was as fine as dust; and I cast the dust thereof into the brook that descended out of the mount.—22. And at

כִּי שִׁחֵת עַמְּךָ אֲשֶׁר הוֹצֵאתָ מִמִּצְרָיִם סָרוּ מַהֵר מִן־הַדֶּרֶךְ
13 אֲשֶׁר צִוִּיתִם עָשׂוּ לָהֶם מַסֵּכָה׃ וַיֹּאמֶר יְהוָה אֵלַי לֵאמֹר
14 רָאִיתִי אֶת־הָעָם הַזֶּה וְהִנֵּה עַם־קְשֵׁה־עֹרֶף הוּא׃ הֶרֶף
מִמֶּנִּי וְאַשְׁמִידֵם וְאֶמְחֶה אֶת־שְׁמָם מִתַּחַת הַשָּׁמָיִם
טו וְאֶעֱשֶׂה אוֹתְךָ לְגוֹי־עָצוּם וָרָב מִמֶּנּוּ׃ וָאֵפֶן וָאֵרֵד מִן־
הָהָר וְהָהָר בֹּעֵר בָּאֵשׁ וּשְׁנֵי לוּחֹת הַבְּרִית עַל שְׁתֵּי יָדָי׃
16 וָאֵרֶא וְהִנֵּה חֲטָאתֶם לַיהוָה אֱלֹהֵיכֶם עֲשִׂיתֶם לָכֶם עֵגֶל
מַסֵּכָה סַרְתֶּם מַהֵר מִן־הַדֶּרֶךְ אֲשֶׁר־צִוָּה יְהוָה אֶתְכֶם׃
17 וָאֶתְפֹּשׂ בִּשְׁנֵי הַלֻּחֹת וָאַשְׁלִכֵם מֵעַל שְׁתֵּי יָדָי וָאֲשַׁבְּרֵם
18 לְעֵינֵיכֶם׃ וָאֶתְנַפַּל לִפְנֵי יְהוָה כָּרִאשֹׁנָה אַרְבָּעִים יוֹם
וְאַרְבָּעִים לַיְלָה לֶחֶם לֹא אָכַלְתִּי וּמַיִם לֹא שָׁתִיתִי עַל
כָּל־חַטַּאתְכֶם אֲשֶׁר חֲטָאתֶם לַעֲשׂוֹת הָרַע בְּעֵינֵי יְהוָה
19 לְהַכְעִיסוֹ׃ כִּי יָגֹרְתִּי מִפְּנֵי הָאַף וְהַחֵמָה אֲשֶׁר קָצַף יְהוָה
עֲלֵיכֶם לְהַשְׁמִיד אֶתְכֶם וַיִּשְׁמַע יְהוָה אֵלַי גַּם בַּפַּעַם
כ הַהִוא׃ וּבְאַהֲרֹן הִתְאַנַּף יְהוָה מְאֹד לְהַשְׁמִידוֹ וָאֶתְפַּלֵּל
21 גַּם־בְּעַד אַהֲרֹן בָּעֵת הַהִוא׃ וְאֶת־חַטַּאתְכֶם אֲשֶׁר־עֲשִׂיתֶם
אֶת־הָעֵגֶל לָקַחְתִּי וָאֶשְׂרֹף אֹתוֹ ׀ בָּאֵשׁ וָאֶכֹּת אֹתוֹ טָחוֹן
הֵיטֵב עַד אֲשֶׁר־דַּק לְעָפָר וָאַשְׁלִךְ אֶת־עֲפָרוֹ אֶל־הַנַּחַל
22 הַיֹּרֵד מִן־הָהָר׃ וּבְתַבְעֵרָה וּבְמַסָּה וּבְקִבְרֹת הַתַּאֲוָה

v. 14. קמץ בטרחא

12. *get thee down quickly.* See Exod. XXXII, 7 f.

thy people. God repudiates Israel because of their treachery—'thy (Moses') people,' 'thou (Moses) hast brought forth out of Egypt.'

14. *blot out their name.* See Exod. XXXII, 10, 32.

15. In this historical retrospect, Moses does not follow the strict chronological order as recorded in Exod. XXXII, and the narrative here is much condensed.

17. *broke them before your eyes.* As a sign that God's Covenant with Israel was at an end.

18. *I fell down.* Better, *I cast myself down.*

as at the first. A condensation of the narrative in Exod. XXXII, and a rearrangement of the details, as in *v.* 15.

19. *that time also.* His prayer on their behalf was heard, as on previous occasions; Exod. XIV, 15; XV, 25 (Ibn Ezra).

20. *very angry with Aaron.* Aaron as leader had lacked strength; his, therefore, was much of the responsibility for what had happened.

21. *and I took your sin . . . made.* The destruction of the sin, *i.e.* of the idol that was the occasion of the sin, must precede the removal of the guilt.

I cast the dust thereof. The fact is here omitted that Moses made the people drink of the mingled water and dust, because the point on which he is dwelling is his intercession on their behalf. He is not recapitulating the history of the Golden Calf in detail.

22. *at Taberah.* See Num. XI, 1–3.

Massah. See Exod. XVII, 2 f.

Kibroth-hattaavah. See Num. XI, 4 f.

Taberah, and at Massah, and at Kibroth-hattaavah, ye made the LORD wroth. 23. And when the LORD sent you from Kadesh-barnea, saying: 'Go up and possess the land which I have given you'; then ye rebelled against the commandment of the LORD your God, and ye believed Him not, nor hearkened to His voice. 24. Ye have been rebellious against the LORD from the day that I knew you.—25. So I fell down before the LORD the forty days and forty nights that I fell down; because the LORD had said He would destroy you. 26. And I prayed unto the LORD, and said: 'O Lord GOD, destroy not Thy people and Thine inheritance, that Thou hast redeemed through Thy greatness, that Thou hast brought forth out of Egypt with a mighty hand. 27. Remember Thy servants, Abraham, Isaac, and Jacob; look not unto the stubbornness of this people, nor to their wickedness, nor to their sin; 28. lest the land whence Thou broughtest us out say: Because the LORD was not able to bring them into the land which He promised unto them, and because He hated them, He hath brought them out to slay them in the wilderness. 29. Yet they are Thy people and Thine inheritance, that Thou didst bring out by Thy great power and by Thy outstretched arm.'*iv.

10

CHAPTER X

1. At that time the LORD said unto me: 'Hew thee two tables of stone like unto the first, and come up unto Me into the mount; and make thee an ark of wood. 2. And I will write on the tables the words that were on the first tables which thou didst break, and thou shalt put them in the ark.' 3. So I made an ark of acacia-wood, and hewed two tables of stone like unto the first, and went up into the mount, having the two tables in my hand. 4. And He wrote on the tables, according to the first writing, the ten words, which the LORD spoke unto you in the mount out of the midst of the fire

23 מַקְצִפִים הֱיִיתֶם אֶת־יְהוָה׃ וּבִשְׁלֹחַ יְהוָה אֶתְכֶם מִקָּדֵשׁ
בַּרְנֵעַ לֵאמֹר עֲלוּ וּרְשׁוּ אֶת־הָאָרֶץ אֲשֶׁר נָתַתִּי לָכֶם
וַתַּמְרוּ אֶת־פִּי יְהוָה אֱלֹהֵיכֶם וְלֹא הֶאֱמַנְתֶּם לוֹ וְלֹא
24 שְׁמַעְתֶּם בְּקֹלוֹ׃ מַמְרִים הֱיִיתֶם עִם־יְהוָה מִיּוֹם דַּעְתִּי
כה אֶתְכֶם׃ וָאֶתְנַפַּל לִפְנֵי יְהוָה אֵת אַרְבָּעִים הַיּוֹם וְאֶת־
אַרְבָּעִים הַלַּיְלָה אֲשֶׁר הִתְנַפָּלְתִּי כִּי־אָמַר יְהוָה לְהַשְׁמִיד
26 אֶתְכֶם׃ וָאֶתְפַּלֵּל אֶל־יְהוָה וָאֹמַר אֲדֹנָי יֱהוִה אַל־תַּשְׁחֵת
עַמְּךָ וְנַחֲלָתְךָ אֲשֶׁר פָּדִיתָ בְּגָדְלֶךָ אֲשֶׁר־הוֹצֵאתָ מִמִּצְרַיִם
27 בְּיָד חֲזָקָה׃ זְכֹר לַעֲבָדֶיךָ לְאַבְרָהָם לְיִצְחָק וּלְיַעֲקֹב אַל־
28 תֵּפֶן אֶל־קְשִׁי הָעָם הַזֶּה וְאֶל־רִשְׁעוֹ וְאֶל־חַטָּאתוֹ׃ פֶּן־יֹאמְרוּ
הָאָרֶץ אֲשֶׁר הוֹצֵאתָנוּ מִשָּׁם מִבְּלִי יְכֹלֶת יְהוָה לַהֲבִיאָם
אֶל־הָאָרֶץ אֲשֶׁר־דִּבֶּר לָהֶם וּמִשִּׂנְאָתוֹ אוֹתָם הוֹצִיאָם
29 לַהֲמִתָם בַּמִּדְבָּר׃ וְהֵם עַמְּךָ וְנַחֲלָתֶךָ אֲשֶׁר הוֹצֵאתָ בְּכֹחֲךָ
הַגָּדֹל וּבִזְרֹעֲךָ הַנְּטוּיָה׃ * פ רביעי

CAP. X. י

י
א בָּעֵת הַהִוא אָמַר יְהוָה אֵלַי פְּסָל־לְךָ שְׁנֵי־לוּחֹת אֲבָנִים
2 כָּרִאשֹׁנִים וַעֲלֵה אֵלַי הָהָרָה וְעָשִׂיתָ לְּךָ אֲרוֹן עֵץ׃ וְאֶכְתֹּב
עַל־הַלֻּחֹת אֶת־הַדְּבָרִים אֲשֶׁר הָיוּ עַל־הַלֻּחֹת הָרִאשֹׁנִים
3 אֲשֶׁר שִׁבַּרְתָּ וְשַׂמְתָּם בָּאָרוֹן׃ וָאַעַשׂ אֲרוֹן עֲצֵי שִׁטִּים
וָאֶפְסֹל שְׁנֵי־לֻחֹת אֲבָנִים כָּרִאשֹׁנִים וָאַעַל הָהָרָה וּשְׁנֵי
4 הַלֻּחֹת בְּיָדִי׃ וַיִּכְתֹּב עַל־הַלֻּחֹת כַּמִּכְתָּב הָרִאשׁוֹן אֵת
עֲשֶׂרֶת הַדְּבָרִים אֲשֶׁר דִּבֶּר יְהוָה אֲלֵיכֶם בָּהָר מִתּוֹךְ הָאֵשׁ

ט׳ v. 24. מ׳ קטנה   י׳ v. 2. פתח באתנח

23. *from Kadesh-barnea.* Cf. I, 26, 32.

25. *so I fell down.* See on *v.* 18.

27. *stubbornness.* See on Exod. XXXII, 11–13.

28. *lest the land. i.e.* the inhabitants of the land. In Exod. XXXII, 12, the Egyptians are named.

CHAPTER X, 1–11. RESULTS OF MOSES' INTERCESSION

The grant of the Second Tables; the institution of the priestly and Levitical services; and the permission to march onward and take possession of Canaan.

1. *at that time.* After Moses had succeeded in averting destruction from the people.

3. *so I made an ark.* 'So I had an ark made,' by Bezalel; cf. Exod. XXV, 10 f, 'thou shalt overlay it with pure gold,' *i.e.* have it overlaid.

Some of the Midrashim, followed by Rashi, are of opinion that there were two Arks—a temporary Ark made by Moses on receipt of the Tables, and the permanent one prepared later by Bezalel.

in the day of the assembly; and the LORD gave them unto me. 5. And I turned and came down from the mount, and put the tables in the ark which I had made; and there they are, as the LORD commanded me.—6. And the children of Israel journeyed from Beeroth-benejaakan to Moserah; there Aaron died, and there he was buried; and Eleazar his son ministered in the priest's office in his stead. 7. From thence they journeyed unto Gudgod; and from Gudgod to Jotbah, a land of brooks of water.—8. At that time the LORD separated the tribe of Levi, to bear the ark of the covenant of the LORD, to stand before the LORD to minister unto Him, and to bless in His name, unto this day. 9. Wherefore Levi hath no portion nor inheritance with his brethren; the LORD is his inheritance, according as the LORD thy God spoke unto him.—10. Now I stayed in the mount, as at

ה בְּיוֹם הַקָּהָל וַיִּתְּנֵם יְהוָה אֵלָי׃ וָאֵפֶן וָאֵרֵד מִן־הָהָר וָאָשִׂם
אֶת־הַלֻּחֹת בָּאָרוֹן אֲשֶׁר עָשִׂיתִי וַיִּהְיוּ שָׁם כַּאֲשֶׁר צִוַּנִי
6 יְהוָה׃ וּבְנֵי יִשְׂרָאֵל נָסְעוּ מִבְּאֵרֹת בְּנֵי־יַעֲקָן מוֹסֵרָה שָׁם
7 מֵת אַהֲרֹן וַיִּקָּבֵר שָׁם וַיְכַהֵן אֶלְעָזָר בְּנוֹ תַּחְתָּיו׃ מִשָּׁם
8 נָסְעוּ הַגֻּדְגֹּדָה וּמִן־הַגֻּדְגֹּדָה יָטְבָתָה אֶרֶץ נַחֲלֵי־מָיִם׃ בָּעֵת
הַהִוא הִבְדִּיל יְהוָה אֶת־שֵׁבֶט הַלֵּוִי לָשֵׂאת אֶת־אֲרוֹן
בְּרִית־יְהוָה לַעֲמֹד לִפְנֵי יְהוָה לְשָׁרְתוֹ וּלְבָרֵךְ בִּשְׁמוֹ עַד
9 הַיּוֹם הַזֶּה׃ עַל־כֵּן לֹא־הָיָה לְלֵוִי חֵלֶק וְנַחֲלָה עִם־אֶחָיו
י יְהוָה הוּא נַחֲלָתוֹ כַּאֲשֶׁר דִּבֶּר יְהוָה אֱלֹהֶיךָ לוֹ׃ וְאָנֹכִי
עָמַדְתִּי בָהָר כַּיָּמִים הָרִאשֹׁנִים אַרְבָּעִים יוֹם וְאַרְבָּעִים
לַיְלָה וַיִּשְׁמַע יְהוָה אֵלַי גַּם בַּפַּעַם הַהִוא לֹא־אָבָה יְהוָה

5. *put the tables in the ark.* Cf. I Kings VIII, 9. According to a Rabbinic tradition, Moses also deposited in the Ark the fragments of the First Tables that had been broken. לוחות ושברי לוחות מונחין בארון. 'One should learn from this, to show respect to a scholar who has forgotten his learning through age, sorrow or illness' (Talmud). We must respect the aged, though they be broken by years and trouble.

6–9. The mention of the Ark leads Moses to refer to the appointment of the Levites who were to have it in their charge.

6. *children of Israel journeyed.* This and the succeeding *v.* interrupt the narrative, and may be regarded as a gloss added by Moses when he wrote down the Discourse. In Num. XXXIII, 31 f, we find the stations named in a different order, with the variation in nomenclature that is not infrequent in Scripture. A probable explanation is that the Israelites, after journeying in a southern direction to the land of Edom, had to turn sharply to the north (see on II, 3) and retrace their steps for a short distance.

there Aaron died. By *there* must be understood the last-mentioned place; *viz.* Moserah. As it is unthinkable that, in regard to an important event like the death of Aaron, there should be a divergence in the accounts, Moserah must be thought of as at the foot of Mount Hor mentioned in Num. XX, 22 f, and would indicate the exact spot from which Aaron ascended the mountain.

8. *at that time.* Of the sin of the Golden Calf and its sequel. The tribe of Levi had held aloof from the rest of the people (Exod. XXXII, 26), and, as a reward for their faithfulness, they were appointed to the sacred charge of the Sanctuary.

separated. Better, *set apart.*

to bear the ark. One of the functions of the Levites was to assist the priests in carrying the Ark.

to stand before the LORD. To minister unto Him in offering sacrifice. This duty was reserved for the priests alone; Num. III, 10.

to bless in His name. To pronounce the Priestly Benediction, Num. VI, 23 f.

9. *wherefore.* 'Without any question, the whole tribe of Levi is here set apart for holy, *i.e.* priestly, duties. But it does not at all follow from this, that each single member of the tribe could at will perform each and everyone of these functions, without any gradation or distribution of functions among these servants of God' (Dillmann).

hath no portion. See Num. XVIII, 20. When the Land was divided among the tribes, no part was allotted to the tribe of Levi, both priests and Levites. Their whole time being required for the work of the Sanctuary, they would not be able to attend to the care of the soil.

the LORD is his inheritance. This phrase is like that of the Psalmist (XVI, 5), 'O LORD, the portion of mine inheritance' (Ibn Ezra). The Targum understands it to mean: 'what God will give them; *viz.* the portions of the sacrifices that shall be the inheritance of the tribe of Levi.' See XVIII, 1–8.

spoke unto him. See Num. XVIII, 20. Although the words are there addressed to Aaron and his sons, *i.e.* to the priests, they clearly apply to the tribe of Levi generally.

10. *I stayed in the mount.* This and the succeeding *v.* are a continuation of IX, 18, 19. Moses stayed two periods of forty days on the Mount after the sin of the Golden Calf—the first time, to intercede for the people (alluded to in IX, 18, 25); the second time, for the purpose of receiving the Tables; cf. Exod. XXXIV, 28.

the first time, forty days and forty nights;
and the LORD hearkened unto me that time
also; the LORD would not destroy thee. 11.
And the LORD said unto me: 'Arise, go
before the people, causing them to set
forward, that they may go in and possess
the land, which I swore unto their fathers
to give unto them.'*v. ¶ 12. And now, Israel,
what doth the LORD thy God require of thee,
but to fear the LORD thy God, to walk in all
His ways, and to love Him, and to serve
the LORD thy God with all thy heart and
with all thy soul; 13. to keep for thy good
the commandments of the LORD, and His
statutes, which I command thee this day?
14. Behold, unto the LORD thy God be-
longeth the heaven, and the heaven of
heavens, the earth, with all that therein is.
15. Only the LORD had a delight in thy
fathers to love them, and He chose their
seed after them, even you, above all
peoples, as it is this day. 16. Circumcise
therefore the foreskin of your heart, and be
no more stiffnecked. 17. For the LORD your

11 הַשְׁחִיתֶךָ׃ וַיֹּאמֶר יְהוָה אֵלַי קוּם לֵךְ לְמַסַּע לִפְנֵי
הָעָם וְיָבֹאוּ וְיִירְשׁוּ אֶת־הָאָרֶץ אֲשֶׁר־נִשְׁבַּעְתִּי לַאֲבֹתָם
לָתֵת לָהֶם׃ * פ חמישי
12 וְעַתָּה יִשְׂרָאֵל מָה יְהוָה אֱלֹהֶיךָ שֹׁאֵל מֵעִמָּךְ כִּי אִם־
לְיִרְאָה אֶת־יְהוָה אֱלֹהֶיךָ לָלֶכֶת בְּכָל־דְּרָכָיו וּלְאַהֲבָה
אֹתוֹ וְלַעֲבֹד אֶת־יְהוָה אֱלֹהֶיךָ בְּכָל־לְבָבְךָ וּבְכָל־נַפְשֶׁךָ׃
13 לִשְׁמֹר אֶת־מִצְוֹת יְהוָה וְאֶת־חֻקֹּתָיו אֲשֶׁר אָנֹכִי מְצַוְּךָ הַיּוֹם
14 לְטוֹב לָךְ׃ הֵן לַיהוָה אֱלֹהֶיךָ הַשָּׁמַיִם וּשְׁמֵי הַשָּׁמָיִם
טו הָאָרֶץ וְכָל־אֲשֶׁר־בָּהּ׃ רַק בַּאֲבֹתֶיךָ חָשַׁק יְהוָה לְאַהֲבָה
אוֹתָם וַיִּבְחַר בְּזַרְעָם אַחֲרֵיהֶם בָּכֶם מִכָּל־הָעַמִּים כַּיּוֹם
16 הַזֶּה׃ וּמַלְתֶּם אֵת עָרְלַת לְבַבְכֶם וְעָרְפְּכֶם לֹא תַקְשׁוּ
17 עוֹד׃ כִּי יְהוָה אֱלֹהֵיכֶם הוּא אֱלֹהֵי הָאֱלֹהִים וַאֲדֹנֵי הָאֲדֹנִים

11. *arise.* As Leader of Israel, to bring Israel to Canaan. The forgiveness of Israel's sin is complete.

CHAPTERS X, 12–XI, 32. THE SECOND DISCOURSE OF MOSES: CONCLUDING PORTION

Final review of all the reasons for, and results of, obedience to God.

12. *and now. i.e.* in conclusion. Pride having been shown to be out of place in those who had so often provoked God, and who owed their all to God's forgiveness and the entreaties of Moses, let Israel, in return for God's undeserved mercies, love and fear Him.

what doth the LORD thy God require of thee. Nothing impossible or extraordinary, but what is simple, and within the people's duty—fear, love, service and fulfilment of commandments. The question recalls the great utterance of the prophet Micah (VI, 8), with which it should be compared; see p. 684.

to fear the LORD. 'The fear of the LORD is the beginning of wisdom' (Prov. I, 7); reverence of God is the foundation of religion. The Rabbis, likewise, speak of 'the fear of Heaven' (*i.e.* the religious sense, the feeling for religion) as the key to all Wisdom. 'Whatever man has Learning but no fear of Heaven, to what is he like?' they ask. 'To a keeper of a house, who has the key to the inner chambers, but lacks the key of the outer doors of the house. Of what avail are those others to him?'

and to love Him. See on VI, 5.

13. *for thy good.* Cf. VI, 24. When God asks man to obey His commands, it is not for His benefit, but for man's welfare.

14–15. The *fear* of God should flow from the thought of His infinity and righteousness; the *love* of God from the thought of His love towards the Patriarchs and their posterity.

14. *heaven of heavens.* The highest heaven.

16. *circumcise. i.e.* remove. They are not to allow, as it were, a hard covering to surround their heart, making it impervious to Divine influence. 'Your heart shall be open for recognizing the truth' (Nachmanides).

17. *God of gods.* A Hebraism (like *song of songs*, *heaven of heavens*) for the Supreme Judge; see on III, 24.

the great God. This description of God has been included in the first of the Eighteen Benedictions.

regardeth not persons. 'Is never partial' (Moffatt). Israel must not deliberately sin in the hope of finding mercy through the 'merits of the fathers'. The fact that they were the Chosen People only meant that more was expected of them than of heathens; and, furthermore, that their actions would be judged by higher standards. Cf. Amos III, 2 ('You only have I known of all the families of the earth; *therefore* I will visit upon you all your iniquities'); see p. 153.

nor taketh reward. 'Never to be bribed' (Moffatt). He is no human judge, of whom such might be thought, especially in barbaric society; see on XVI, 19. He is inflexible in His punishment of the iniquitous, and in His protection of the helpless and oppressed.

הָאֵל הַגָּדֹל הַגִּבֹּר וְהַנּוֹרָא אֲשֶׁר לֹא־יִשָּׂא פָנִים וְלֹא יִקַּח
18 שֹׁחַד׃ עֹשֶׂה מִשְׁפַּט יָתוֹם וְאַלְמָנָה וְאֹהֵב גֵּר לָתֶת לוֹ
19 לֶחֶם וְשִׂמְלָה׃ וַאֲהַבְתֶּם אֶת־הַגֵּר כִּי־גֵרִים הֱיִיתֶם בְּאֶרֶץ
כ מִצְרָיִם׃ אֶת־יְהוָה אֱלֹהֶיךָ תִּירָא אֹתוֹ תַעֲבֹד וּבוֹ תִדְבָּק
21 וּבִשְׁמוֹ תִּשָּׁבֵעַ׃ הוּא תְהִלָּתְךָ וְהוּא אֱלֹהֶיךָ אֲשֶׁר־עָשָׂה
אִתְּךָ אֶת־הַגְּדֹלֹת וְאֶת־הַנּוֹרָאֹת הָאֵלֶּה אֲשֶׁר רָאוּ עֵינֶיךָ׃
22 בְּשִׁבְעִים נֶפֶשׁ יָרְדוּ אֲבֹתֶיךָ מִצְרָיְמָה וְעַתָּה שָׂמְךָ יְהוָה
אֱלֹהֶיךָ כְּכוֹכְבֵי הַשָּׁמַיִם לָרֹב׃

CAP. XI. יא — יא

א וְאָהַבְתָּ אֵת יְהוָה אֱלֹהֶיךָ וְשָׁמַרְתָּ מִשְׁמַרְתּוֹ וְחֻקֹּתָיו
2 וּמִשְׁפָּטָיו וּמִצְוֺתָיו כָּל־הַיָּמִים׃ וִידַעְתֶּם הַיּוֹם כִּי ׀ לֹא
אֶת־בְּנֵיכֶם אֲשֶׁר לֹא־יָדְעוּ וַאֲשֶׁר לֹא־רָאוּ אֶת־מוּסַר יְהוָה

י׳ v. 20. קמץ בז״ק

God, He is God of gods, and LORD of lords, the great God, the mighty, and the awful, who regardeth not persons, nor taketh reward.
18. He doth execute justice for the fatherless and widow, and loveth the stranger, in giving him food and raiment.
19. Love ye therefore the stranger; for ye were strangers in the land of Egypt.
20. Thou shalt fear the LORD thy God; Him shalt thou serve; and to Him shalt thou cleave, and by His name shalt thou swear.
21. He is thy glory, and He is thy God, that hath done for thee these great and tremendous things, which thine eyes have seen.
22. Thy fathers went down into Egypt with threescore and ten persons; and now the LORD thy God hath made thee as the stars of heaven for multitude.

11

CHAPTER XI

1. Therefore thou shalt love the LORD thy God, and keep His charge, and His statutes, and His ordinances, and His commandments, alway.
2. And know ye this day; for I speak not with your children that have not known, and that have not seen the

18. *justice for.* The fatherless, the widow, and the stranger, who are too weak to defend themselves against injustice.

19. *love ye therefore the stranger.* This demand to *love* the alien is without parallel in the legislation of any ancient people; see p. 313. In later Hebrew, the word 'stranger' (*ger*) denotes a proselyte, the man or woman who voluntarily joins the ranks of Judaism, and the words of this *v.* are applied to him. 'How great is the duty which the Torah imposes on us with regard to proselytes. Our parents we are commanded to honour and fear; to the prophets we are ordered to hearken. A man may honour and fear and obey without loving. But in the case of "strangers", we are bidden to love them with the whole force of our heart's affection' (Maimonides); see on XXIV, 17–18.

for ye were strangers. From their bitter experience in Egypt, the Israelites were to learn sympathy with the alien in their own land.

20–22. A God of such majesty and justice should command the reverence, devotion and praise of Israel.

20. *thou shalt fear . . . cleave.* The *fear of God* is not a feeling of terror, which repels and causes men to shrink from it. It is that grateful reverence which leads men to cleave and cling to God. The Jewish philosophers coined a special phrase for this feeling: יראה של אהבה, 'loving fear' (Hermann Cohen).

by His name . . . swear. See on VI, 13.

21. *He is thy glory. i.e.* 'to Him alone is thy praise due'; or, 'He is the cause of thy fame,' by the deeds He has done for thee; Exod. XV, 11; Jer. XVII, 14.

22. The crowning evidence of God's claim on the gratitude and obedience of Israel.

CHAPTER XI

1–9. LET PERSONAL EXPERIENCE OF GOD'S WONDROUS DEEDS ON BEHALF OF ISRAEL LEAD TO LOVE AND OBEDIENCE

1. *therefore thou shalt love.* See X, 20, where Israel is exhorted to 'fear' God. The worship of God must be from a motive of love as well as reverential fear.

His charge. The Divine precepts in general.

alway. lit. 'all the days'; see IV, 10.

2. *know ye. i.e.* take note of, pay attention to.

for I speak not. Better, *that I speak not.*

that have not seen. The contrast comes in *v.* 7, 'but your eyes have seen.'

chastisement. Better, *discipline;* see IV, 36. Heb. מוסר denotes *moral education.* The sight of God's wonders 'ought to have exerted upon the Israelites a disciplinary influence, subduing waywardness and pride, and promoting humility and reverence' (Driver). This word מוסר is the word in later Heb. for 'moral exhortation', or 'ethics'.

His greatness. Cf. III, 24; IV, 34.

chastisement of the LORD your God, His greatness, His mighty hand, and His outstretched arm, 3. and His signs, and His works, which He did in the midst of Egypt unto Pharaoh the king of Egypt, and unto all his land; 4. and what He did unto the army of Egypt, unto their horses, and to their chariots; how He made the water of the Red Sea to overflow them as they pursued after you, and how the LORD hath destroyed them unto this day; 5. and what He did unto you in the wilderness, until ye came unto this place; 6. and what He did unto Dathan and Abiram, the sons of Eliab, the son of Reuben; how the earth opened her mouth, and swallowed them up, and their households, and their tents, and every living substance that followed them, in the midst of all Israel; 7. but your eyes have seen all the great work of the LORD which He did. 8. Therefore shall ye keep all the commandment which I command thee this day, that ye may be strong, and go in and possess the land, whither ye go over to possess it; 9. and that ye may prolong your days upon the land, which the LORD swore unto your fathers to give unto them and to their seed, a land flowing with milk and honey.*vi. ¶ 10. For the land, whither thou goest in to possess it, is not as the land of Egypt, from whence ye came out, where thou didst sow thy seed, and didst water it with thy foot, as a garden of herbs; 11. but the land, whither ye go over to possess

3 אֱלֹהֵיכֶם אֶת־גָּדְלוֹ אֶת־יָדוֹ הַחֲזָקָה וּזְרֹעוֹ הַנְּטוּיָה׃ וְאֶת־
אֹתֹתָיו וְאֶת־מַעֲשָׂיו אֲשֶׁר עָשָׂה בְּתוֹךְ מִצְרָיִם לְפַרְעֹה
4 מֶלֶךְ־מִצְרַיִם וּלְכָל־אַרְצוֹ׃ וַאֲשֶׁר עָשָׂה לְחֵיל מִצְרַיִם
לְסוּסָיו וּלְרִכְבּוֹ אֲשֶׁר הֵצִיף אֶת־מֵי יַם־סוּף עַל־פְּנֵיהֶם
ה בְּרָדְפָם אַחֲרֵיכֶם וַיְאַבְּדֵם יְהוָה עַד הַיּוֹם הַזֶּה׃ וַאֲשֶׁר
6 עָשָׂה לָכֶם בַּמִּדְבָּר עַד־בֹּאֲכֶם עַד־הַמָּקוֹם הַזֶּה׃ וַאֲשֶׁר
עָשָׂה לְדָתָן וְלַאֲבִירָם בְּנֵי אֱלִיאָב בֶּן־רְאוּבֵן אֲשֶׁר פָּצְתָה
הָאָרֶץ אֶת־פִּיהָ וַתִּבְלָעֵם וְאֶת־בָּתֵּיהֶם וְאֶת־אָהֳלֵיהֶם
7 וְאֵת כָּל־הַיְקוּם אֲשֶׁר בְּרַגְלֵיהֶם בְּקֶרֶב כָּל־יִשְׂרָאֵל׃ כִּי
עֵינֵיכֶם הָרֹאֹת אֶת כָּל־מַעֲשֵׂה יְהוָה הַגָּדֹל אֲשֶׁר עָשָׂה׃
8 וּשְׁמַרְתֶּם אֶת־כָּל־הַמִּצְוָה אֲשֶׁר אָנֹכִי מְצַוְּךָ הַיּוֹם לְמַעַן
תֶּחֶזְקוּ וּבָאתֶם וִירִשְׁתֶּם אֶת־הָאָרֶץ אֲשֶׁר אַתֶּם עֹבְרִים
9 שָׁמָּה לְרִשְׁתָּהּ׃ וּלְמַעַן תַּאֲרִיכוּ יָמִים עַל־הָאֲדָמָה אֲשֶׁר
נִשְׁבַּע יְהוָה לַאֲבֹתֵיכֶם לָתֵת לָהֶם וּלְזַרְעָם אֶרֶץ זָבַת
ששי י חָלָב וּדְבָשׁ׃ ס כִּי הָאָרֶץ אֲשֶׁר אַתָּה בָא־שָׁמָּה
לְרִשְׁתָּהּ לֹא כְאֶרֶץ מִצְרַיִם הִוא אֲשֶׁר יְצָאתֶם מִשָּׁם
11 אֲשֶׁר תִּזְרַע אֶת־זַרְעֲךָ וְהִשְׁקִיתָ בְרַגְלְךָ כְּגַן הַיָּרָק׃ וְהָאָרֶץ

4. *unto this day.* A mere rhetorical expression, 'since once an enemy is put to death, he is destroyed for ever' (Nachmanides). Some take this phrase here (as in III, 14), in the sense of 'finally, irrevocably'.

6. *Dathan and Abiram.* See Num. XVI. Korah, who was the ringleader of the revolt, is not named here. In the last chapter, X, 8, Moses had spoken of the selection of the Levites, among whom must have been sons of Korah who had not perished (Num. XXVI, 11). It was consequently from consideration of their feelings, that he omitted the name of their father. On similar grounds he is not mentioned in Psalm CVI, 17, since the Psalm was sung by the 'Sons of Korah'.

8. *be strong.* *i.e.* morally, as a consequence of faithfulness to the Torah; and physically, by reason of the Divine aid.

10–17. CANAAN AND EGYPT CONTRASTED

Unlike Egypt, where it never rained and the fields must be watered by human drudgery, Canaan is dependent for its fertility upon the rain of heaven. This would be withheld or granted according to Israel's faithfulness.

10. *from whence ye came out. i.e.* from the part of Egypt whence ye came, *viz.* Goshen (Sifri).

where thou didst sow thy seed. Possibly a portion of the Israelites in Egypt were agriculturists; Egypt 'was so fertile, that it seems even a tribe of shepherds could hardly have refrained from the opportunity which it offered for the richer feeding of their cattle' (G. A. Smith).

with thy foot. i.e. with a wheel—*shaduf*—worked by the foot—a reference to the water-wheel and pump, that are worked by the feet. Illustrations of the *shaduf* appear on the monuments.

as a garden of herbs. Fields in Egypt had to be watered in the same way as a vegetable garden, by arduous labour, artificially, and not by the natural source of rain, the direct boon of Heaven.

11. *a land of hills and valleys.* And, therefore, with a larger rainfall than a flat country.

it, is a land of hills and valleys, and drinketh water as the rain of heaven cometh down; 12. a land which the LORD thy God careth for; the eyes of the LORD thy God are always upon it, from the beginning of the year even unto the end of the year. ¶ 13. And it shall come to pass, if ye shall hearken diligently unto My commandments which I command you this day, to love the LORD your God, and to serve Him with all your heart and with all your soul, 14. that I will give the rain of your land in its season, the former rain and the latter rain, that thou mayest gather in thy corn, and thy wine, and thine oil. 15. And I will give grass in thy fields for thy cattle, and thou shalt eat and be satisfied. 16. Take heed to yourselves, lest your heart be deceived, and ye turn aside, and serve other gods, and worship them; 17. and the anger of the LORD be kindled against you, and He shut up the heaven, so that there shall be no rain, and the ground shall not yield her fruit; and ye perish quickly from off the good land which the LORD giveth you. 18. Therefore shall ye lay up these My words in

אֲשֶׁר אַתֶּם עֹבְרִים שָׁמָּה לְרִשְׁתָּהּ אֶרֶץ הָרִים וּבְקָעֹת
12 לִמְטַר הַשָּׁמַיִם תִּשְׁתֶּה־מָּיִם׃ אֶרֶץ אֲשֶׁר־יְהוָה אֱלֹהֶיךָ
דֹּרֵשׁ אֹתָהּ תָּמִיד עֵינֵי יְהוָה אֱלֹהֶיךָ בָּהּ מֵרֵשִׁית הַשָּׁנָה
13 וְעַד אַחֲרִית שָׁנָה׃ ס וְהָיָה אִם־שָׁמֹעַ תִּשְׁמְעוּ אֶל־
מִצְוֹתַי אֲשֶׁר אָנֹכִי מְצַוֶּה אֶתְכֶם הַיּוֹם לְאַהֲבָה אֶת־יְהוָה
14 אֱלֹהֵיכֶם וּלְעָבְדוֹ בְּכָל־לְבַבְכֶם וּבְכָל־נַפְשְׁכֶם׃ וְנָתַתִּי
מְטַר־אַרְצְכֶם בְּעִתּוֹ יוֹרֶה וּמַלְקוֹשׁ וְאָסַפְתָּ דְגָנֶךָ וְתִירֹשְׁךָ
טו וְיִצְהָרֶךָ׃ וְנָתַתִּי עֵשֶׂב בְּשָׂדְךָ לִבְהֶמְתֶּךָ וְאָכַלְתָּ וְשָׂבָעְתָּ׃
16 הִשָּׁמְרוּ לָכֶם פֶּן־יִפְתֶּה לְבַבְכֶם וְסַרְתֶּם וַעֲבַדְתֶּם אֱלֹהִים
17 אֲחֵרִים וְהִשְׁתַּחֲוִיתֶם לָהֶם׃ וְחָרָה אַף־יְהוָה בָּכֶם וְעָצַר
אֶת־הַשָּׁמַיִם וְלֹא־יִהְיֶה מָטָר וְהָאֲדָמָה לֹא תִתֵּן אֶת־יְבוּלָהּ
וַאֲבַדְתֶּם מְהֵרָה מֵעַל הָאָרֶץ הַטֹּבָה אֲשֶׁר יְהוָה נֹתֵן

v. 12. חסר אל״ף

12. *careth for.* The difference between the fixed climatic conditions of Egypt and those of Canaan can be compared to that between a son in receipt of a fixed annual allowance, and a son in his father's house receiving his portion day by day. Both should be equally filled with gratitude; but, as a fact, the latter would be held more guilty if he were not so (Harper).

13. *to serve Him with all your heart.* 'What is heart-service? Service of the heart is Prayer' (Sifri). The institution of Prayer three times daily goes back to an early period; cf. Daniel VI, 11, 14.

14. *I will give.* Moses speaks in the name of God.

in its season. The agricultural year in Palestine consists of two seasons, the one rainy, and the other dry. The whole of the winter is the rainy season. The heavy rains towards the end of October are the *yoreh*, 'the former rain.' They open the agricultural year. The rainfall increases throughout December, January and February; it begins to abate in March, and is practically over by the end of April. The latter rain, *malkosh*, are the heavy showers of March and April. Coming as they do when the grain is ripening, and being the last before the long summer drought, they are of great importance.

15. *grass.* Better, *herbage*, for human beings as well as for cattle.

in thy fields. A sign of exceptional fertility (Sifri). It will not be necessary to drive the cattle some distance to open pasture-land to enable them to feed. From the fact that Scripture here speaks first of pasture for the cattle and then continues, *thou shalt eat*, the Talmud deduced the regulation that a man must feed his animals before himself partaking of his own meal; see on XXV, 4.

16. *take heed.* Similarly above in VIII, 12, after the words 'eat and be satisfied', the warning note, 'take heed,' is sounded. Satiety easily induces forgetfulness.

your heart be deceived. Into attributing the blessings you enjoy to 'other gods', the local deities worshipped by the heathen inhabitants of old.

17. *shut up the heaven.* Cf. XXVIII, 23 f; Lev. XXVI, 19 f.

and ye perish. When the early rains or the latter rains fail, drought comes occasionally for two years in succession, and that means famine and pestilence.

18. *lay up these My words.* This and the two following *v.* are a repetition, with slight verbal differences, of VI, 6–9. The Sifri joins this on to the words which immediately precede, and your heart and in your soul; and ye shall bind them for a sign upon your hand, and they shall be for frontlets between your eyes. 19. And ye shall teach them your children, talking of them, when thou sittest in thy house, and when thou walkest by the way, and when thou liest down, and when thou risest up. 20. And thou shalt write them upon the door-posts of thy house, and upon thy gates; 21. that your days may be multiplied, and the days of your children, upon the land which the LORD swore unto your fathers to give them, as the days of the heavens above the earth.*vii m. ¶ 22. For if ye shall diligently keep all this commandment which I command you, to do it, to love the LORD your God, to walk in all His ways, and to cleave unto Him, 23. then will the LORD drive out all these nations from before you, and ye shall dispossess nations greater and mightier than yourselves. 24. Every place whereon the sole of your foot shall tread shall be yours: from the wilderness, and Lebanon, from the river, the river Euphrates, even unto the hinder sea shall be your border. 25. There shall no man be able to stand against you: the LORD your God shall lay the fear of you and the dread of you upon all the land that ye shall tread upon, as He hath spoken unto you.

18 לָכֶם׃ וְשַׂמְתֶּם אֶת־דְּבָרַי אֵלֶּה עַל־לְבַבְכֶם וְעַל־נַפְשְׁכֶם
וּקְשַׁרְתֶּם אֹתָם לְאוֹת עַל־יֶדְכֶם וְהָיוּ לְטוֹטָפֹת בֵּין עֵינֵיכֶם׃
19 וְלִמַּדְתֶּם אֹתָם אֶת־בְּנֵיכֶם לְדַבֵּר בָּם בְּשִׁבְתְּךָ בְּבֵיתֶךָ
כ וּבְלֶכְתְּךָ בַדֶּרֶךְ וּבְשָׁכְבְּךָ וּבְקוּמֶךָ׃ וּכְתַבְתָּם עַל־מְזוּזוֹת
21 בֵּיתֶךָ וּבִשְׁעָרֶיךָ׃ לְמַעַן יִרְבּוּ יְמֵיכֶם וִימֵי בְנֵיכֶם עַל
הָאֲדָמָה אֲשֶׁר נִשְׁבַּע יְהוָה לַאֲבֹתֵיכֶם לָתֵת לָהֶם כִּימֵי שביעי מפטיר
22 הַשָּׁמַיִם עַל־הָאָרֶץ׃ * ס כִּי אִם־שָׁמֹר תִּשְׁמְרוּן אֶת־
כָּל־הַמִּצְוָה הַזֹּאת אֲשֶׁר אָנֹכִי מְצַוֶּה אֶתְכֶם לַעֲשֹׂתָהּ
לְאַהֲבָה אֶת־יְהוָה אֱלֹהֵיכֶם לָלֶכֶת בְּכָל־דְּרָכָיו וּלְדָבְקָה־
23 בוֹ׃ וְהוֹרִישׁ יְהוָה אֶת־כָּל־הַגּוֹיִם הָאֵלֶּה מִלִּפְנֵיכֶם וִירִשְׁתֶּם
24 גּוֹיִם גְּדֹלִים וַעֲצֻמִים מִכֶּם׃ כָּל־הַמָּקוֹם אֲשֶׁר תִּדְרֹךְ כַּף־
רַגְלְכֶם בּוֹ לָכֶם יִהְיֶה מִן־הַמִּדְבָּר וְהַלְּבָנוֹן מִן־הַנָּהָר נְהַר־
כה פְּרָת וְעַד הַיָּם הָאַחֲרוֹן יִהְיֶה גְּבֻלְכֶם׃ לֹא־יִתְיַצֵּב אִישׁ
בִּפְנֵיכֶם פַּחְדְּכֶם וּמוֹרַאֲכֶם יִתֵּן ׀ יְהוָה אֱלֹהֵיכֶם עַל־פְּנֵי
כָל־הָאָרֶץ אֲשֶׁר תִּדְרְכוּ־בָהּ כַּאֲשֶׁר דִּבֶּר לָכֶם׃

interprets: In the event of your perishing from the land—*i.e.* of being driven into captivity—even there in the land of exile, you must carry out the ordinances prescribed in VI, 6 f. As these verses are addressed to the nation as a whole, they are in the plural.

19. *teach them your children.* This was taken to mean help them to become *learned* in the Torah, and was therefore understood in the sense of, 'teach them your *sons*.'

21. *as the days of the heavens. i.e.* so long as the visible universe endures; cf. IV, 26.

24. *shall be yours.* With the extent of Israel's dominion as described here, cf. I, 7, Josh. I, 4.

the wilderness. South of the Holy Land.

Lebanon. i.e. the boundary in the north.

Euphrates. Israel's ideal territory is to extend to the Euphrates in the east.

the hinder sea. The Mediterranean. The opposite is the 'front' or 'east' sea (Ezek. XLVII, 18), by which the Dead Sea is designated.

25. *stand.* See on VII, 24. 'It is not force but truth that rules the world; and absolutely no limit can be set to the possibilities which open out to a free, morally robust, and faithful people who have become possessed of higher spiritual ideas than the peoples that surround them' (Harper).

as He hath spoken. See Exod. XXIII, 27.

ISAIAH XLIX, 14–LI, 3

CHAPTER XLIX

14. But Zion said: 'The LORD hath forsaken me,
And the LORD hath forgotten me.'
15. Can a woman forget her sucking child,
That she should not have compassion on the son of her womb?
Yea, these may forget,
Yet will not I forget thee.
16. Behold, I have graven thee upon the palms of My hands;
Thy walls are continually before Me.
17. Thy children make haste;
Thy destroyers and they that made thee waste shall go forth from thee.
18. Lift up thine eyes round about, and behold:
All these gather themselves together, and come to thee.
As I live, saith the LORD,
Thou shalt surely clothe thee with them all as with an ornament,
And gird thyself with them, like a bride.

CAP. XLIX. מט

14 וַתֹּאמֶר צִיּוֹן
טו עֲזָבַנִי יְהוָה וַאדֹנָי שְׁכֵחָנִי׃ הֲתִשְׁכַּח אִשָּׁה עוּלָהּ מֵרַחֵם
16 בֶּן־בִּטְנָהּ גַּם־אֵלֶּה תִשְׁכַּחְנָה וְאָנֹכִי לֹא אֶשְׁכָּחֵךְ׃ הֵן עַל־
17 כַּפַּיִם חַקֹּתִיךְ חוֹמֹתַיִךְ נֶגְדִּי תָּמִיד׃ מִהֲרוּ בָּנָיִךְ מְהָרְסַיִךְ
18 וּמַחֲרִבַיִךְ מִמֵּךְ יֵצֵאוּ׃ שְׂאִי־סָבִיב עֵינַיִךְ וּרְאִי כֻּלָּם
נִקְבְּצוּ בָאוּ־לָךְ חַי־אָנִי נְאֻם־יְהוָה כִּי כֻלָּם כַּעֲדִי תִלְבָּשִׁי

19. For thy waste and thy desolate places
And thy land that hath been destroyed—
Surely now shalt thou be too strait for the inhabitants,
And they that swallowed thee up shall be far away.

v. 18. קמץ בז"ק

This is the second of the Haftorahs of Consolation. These Haftorahs are primarily chosen because of the message of comfort and hope they bring during the weeks that follow the Fast of Av. Yet, in addition, there is a fundamental similarity between the teaching of our Sidrah and Haftorah. The former stresses the vital duty for Israel to maintain its spiritual identity in the face of Canaanite idolatry. This, together with the recognition that man doth not live by bread only, and the proper understanding of the Divine discipline of suffering—would fit Israel for the role of 'the Servant of the LORD', as conceived by the Prophet in this and other portions of his prophecies.

14–21. ZION'S DESPONDENCY AND CONSOLATION

The great body of the Jewish people had lost hope of a national restoration. They thought that Israel's history was definitely closed.

14. *Zion.* Is here pictured as the forsaken wife, mourning for her children. She despairs of her future: 'God hath forgotten me.'
the LORD. RV has here the Divine Name of four letters.

15. *these may forget.* Even a mother's pity for her own helpless infant may fail, but not God's mercy. That is more enduring than the strongest human affection.

16. *have graven thee.* By a bold figure the Prophet poetically represents Zion as being engraved on God's hands, so that it and its ruined walls are continually in His mind.

17–23. THE RETURN OF THE CHILDREN

17. *haste.* From the ends of the earth, to return to Mother Zion.
destroyers . . . waste. Some take these words to refer to the garrison left in Palestine by the Babylonians, and now forced to depart by the Persians after their conquest of Babylon. Kimchi refers them to the wicked in Israel who were the cause of the nation's destruction. The Heb. words, מהרסיך ומחריביך ממך יצאו, have become a popular Jewish saying in the translation, 'Thy destroyers and they that make thee waste *come forth from thee*'; *i.e.* Israel's worst enemies, and those who do most to tarnish Israel's fair name, come from Israel's own camp.

18. *all these . . . come to thee. All* thy children, even 'thy destroyers', *i.e.* the wicked that have gone away from thee (quoted by Ibn Ezra).
with an ornament. Her returning children are likened to the bridal attire that now replaces for Zion the signs of her widowhood.

19–20. 'In place of her present solitude, Zion shall yet look down on a densely-populated city, whose inhabitants are embarrassed for want of room' (Skinner).

19. *too strait.* Too small and too restricted in area, for the multitude of returning exiles.

19 וּתְקַשְּׁרִים כַּכַּלָּה׃ כִּי חָרְבֹתַיִךְ וְשֹׁמְמֹתַיִךְ וְאֶרֶץ הֲרִסֻתֵךְ
כ כִּי עַתָּה תֵּצְרִי מִיּוֹשֵׁב וְרָחֲקוּ מְבַלְּעָיִךְ׃ עוֹד יֹאמְרוּ בְאָזְנַיִךְ
21 בְּנֵי שִׁכֻּלָיִךְ צַר־לִי הַמָּקוֹם גְּשָׁה־לִּי וְאֵשֵׁבָה׃ וְאָמַרְתְּ
בִּלְבָבֵךְ מִי יָלַד־לִי אֶת־אֵלֶּה וַאֲנִי שְׁכוּלָה וְגַלְמוּדָה גֹּלָה
וְסוּרָה וְאֵלֶּה מִי גִדֵּל הֵן אֲנִי נִשְׁאַרְתִּי לְבַדִּי אֵלֶּה אֵיפֹה
22 הֵם׃ כֹּה־אָמַר אֲדֹנָי יֱהוִֹה הִנֵּה אֶשָּׂא אֶל־גּוֹיִם יָדִי
וְאֶל־עַמִּים אָרִים נִסִּי וְהֵבִיאוּ בָנַיִךְ בְּחֹצֶן וּבְנֹתַיִךְ עַל־כָּתֵף
23 תִּנָּשֶׂאנָה׃ וְהָיוּ מְלָכִים אֹמְנַיִךְ וְשָׂרוֹתֵיהֶם מֵינִיקֹתַיִךְ אַפַּיִם
אֶרֶץ יִשְׁתַּחֲווּ־לָךְ וַעֲפַר רַגְלַיִךְ יְלַחֵכוּ וְיָדַעַתְּ כִּי־אֲנִי יְהוָֹה
24 אֲשֶׁר לֹא־יֵבֹשׁוּ קֹוָי׃ הֲיֻקַּח מִגִּבּוֹר מַלְקוֹחַ וְאִם־שְׁבִי
כה צַדִּיק יִמָּלֵט׃ כִּי־כֹה ׀ אָמַר יְהוָֹה גַּם־שְׁבִי גִבּוֹר יֻקָּח
וּמַלְקוֹחַ עָרִיץ יִמָּלֵט וְאֶת־יְרִיבֵךְ אָנֹכִי אָרִיב וְאֶת־בָּנַיִךְ
26 אָנֹכִי אוֹשִׁיעַ׃ וְהַאֲכַלְתִּי אֶת־מוֹנַיִךְ אֶת־בְּשָׂרָם וְכֶעָסִיס
דָּמָם יִשְׁכָּרוּן וְיָדְעוּ כָל־בָּשָׂר כִּי אֲנִי יְהוָֹה מוֹשִׁיעֵךְ וְגֹאֲלֵךְ
אֲבִיר יַעֲקֹב׃

20. The children of thy bereavement
Shall yet say in thine ears:
'The place is too strait for me;
Give place to me that I may dwell.'
21. Then shalt thou say in thy heart:
'Who hath begotten me these,
Seeing I have been bereaved of my children, and am solitary,
An exile, and wandering to and fro?
And who hath brought up these?
Behold, I was left alone;
These, where were they?'

22. Thus saith the Lord GOD:
Behold, I will lift up My hand to the nations,
And set up Mine ensign to the peoples,
And they shall bring thy sons in their bosom,
And thy daughters shall be carried upon their shoulders.
23. And kings shall be thy foster-fathers,
And their queens thy nursing mothers;
They shall bow down to thee with their face to the earth,
And lick the dust of thy feet;
And thou shalt know that I am the LORD,
For they shall not be ashamed that wait for Me.

24. Shall the prey be taken from the mighty,
Or the captives of the victorious be delivered?
25. But thus saith the LORD:
Even the captives of the mighty shall be taken away,
And the prey of the terrible shall be delivered;
And I will contend with him that contendeth with thee,
And I will save thy children.

26. And I will feed them that oppress thee with their own flesh;
And they shall be drunken with their own blood, as with sweet wine;
And all flesh shall know that I the LORD am thy Saviour,
And thy Redeemer, the Mighty One of Jacob.

v. 25. קמץ בז״ק

20. *of thy bereavement.* Of whom thou hast been bereft (Kimchi); *i.e.* thy lost children.

21. *who hath begotten me these?* She cannot believe herself the mother of all these children.

an exile. Applicable only to the former inhabitants, but transferred to Zion, as standing for Israel.

22. *ensign.* Standard, as a signal to mark the spot to which the nations are to assemble the exiles for return to their fatherland.

in their bosom. As little children are carried, carefully and with tenderness.

23. *foster-fathers.* Guardians. The meaning of the metaphor is, Foreign potentates will shield and support thee, and the restoration shall take place under royal sanction (Wiener).

lick the dust. An Oriental metaphor for abject self-humiliation.

24–26. FATE OF THE NATIONS WHO OPPOSE GOD'S WILL

24. *the captives of the victorious* (צדקה also means 'victory'; hence, צדיק, 'victor'). This seems to be in reply to a new utterance of doubt and despondency on the part of the Israelites, 'Shall Israel be really rescued from such a mighty victor as Babylon?' The answer is, 'Yes, I, the LORD, will rescue them.'

26. *feed . . . own flesh.* They will be destroyed by warfare among themselves.

CHAPTER L

1. Thus saith the LORD:
Where is the bill of your mother's divorcement,
Wherewith I have put her away?
Or which of My creditors is it
To whom I have sold you?
Behold, for your iniquities were ye sold,
And for your transgressions was your mother put away.
2. Wherefore, when I came, was there no man?
When I called, was there none to answer?
Is My hand shortened at all, that it cannot redeem?
Or have I no power to deliver?
Behold, at My rebuke I dry up the sea,
I make the rivers a wilderness;
Their fish become foul, because there is no water,
And die for thirst.
3. I clothe the heavens with blackness,
And I make sackcloth their covering.

4. The Lord GOD hath given me
The tongue of them that are taught,
That I should know how to sustain with words him that is weary;
He wakeneth morning by morning,
He wakeneth mine ear
To hear as they that are taught.

CAP. L. נ

א כֹּה ׀ אָמַר יְהוָה אֵי זֶה סֵפֶר כְּרִיתוּת אִמְּכֶם אֲשֶׁר שִׁלַּחְתִּיהָ
אוֹ מִי מִנּוֹשַׁי אֲשֶׁר־מָכַרְתִּי אֶתְכֶם לוֹ הֵן בַּעֲוֺנֹתֵיכֶם
2 נִמְכַּרְתֶּם וּבְפִשְׁעֵיכֶם שֻׁלְּחָה אִמְּכֶם׃ מַדּוּעַ בָּאתִי וְאֵין
אִישׁ קָרָאתִי וְאֵין עוֹנֶה הֲקָצוֹר קָצְרָה יָדִי מִפְּדוּת וְאִם־
אֵין־בִּי כֹחַ לְהַצִּיל הֵן בְּגַעֲרָתִי אַחֲרִיב יָם אָשִׂים נְהָרוֹת
3 מִדְבָּר תִּבְאַשׁ דְּגָתָם מֵאֵין מַיִם וְתָמֹת בַּצָּמָא׃ אַלְבִּישׁ
4 שָׁמַיִם קַדְרוּת וְשַׂק אָשִׂים כְּסוּתָם׃ אֲדֹנָי יֱהֹוִה נָתַן
לִי לְשׁוֹן לִמּוּדִים לָדַעַת לָעוּת אֶת־יָעֵף דָּבָר יָעִיר ׀ בַּבֹּקֶר
ה בַּבֹּקֶר יָעִיר לִי אֹזֶן לִשְׁמֹעַ כַּלִּמּוּדִים׃ אֲדֹנָי יֱהֹוִה פָּתַח־

5. The Lord GOD hath opened mine ear,
And I was not rebellious,
Neither turned away backward.

CHAPTER L

Another cause of despondency to the exiles was the doubt, 'Is the ancient covenant-relation between God and Israel still in existence? Has not God, by exiling Israel, *divorced* Israel?' The answer is, 'Where is your mother's *get*, which alone would make the separation final? It does not exist. Israel, therefore, is still *Israel*, and there is no hindrance to Israel's restoration.'

1. *divorcement.* As there is no such document to prove a formal divorce, the door is open for a reconciliation.

creditors . . . sold you. As poor fathers sold their children in liquidation of debts they owed to pitiless creditors, and thereby forfeited all possession or authority over them.

were ye sold. God surrendered you temporarily to your enemies for a punishment. He now cancels the punishment, and renews the parental relationship.

2. *wherefore, when I came.* The Prophet rebukes the faint-hearted response of the despondent and inert people to the message of Redemption.

is My hand shortened. Not long enough to render assistance? Is there lack of power on the part of God to save and restore?

dry up the sea. As at the exodus from Egypt.

3. *clothe the heavens with blackness.* A reference to God's power in nature as manifested in eclipses (Ibn Ezra).

'THE SERVANT OF THE LORD': THE CONSCIOUSNESS OF HIS MISSION

4–9. This is one of the four passages in the Second Part of Isaiah that either describe the 'Servant of the LORD', or, as here, introduce him as the speaker. These passages are of exceptional beauty and religious depth, but present great difficulties of interpretation. The 'Servant of the LORD' is Ideal Israel, the sanctified minority who are willing to suffer and die for their Faith. They are ready to bear all uncharitableness and persecution at the hands of those of their brethren who may be blind and deaf to the signs of the times, and to the fulfilment of God's purposes in regard to Israel and mankind. See also Isa. XLII, 1–4; XLIX, 1–6; LII, 13–LIII.

4. *them that are taught.* Or, 'the learned.'

to sustain with words. Or, 'to speak a word in season to.'

to hear. He is roused early by his visions, and God makes him receptive of their message and teaching.

5. *neither turned away backward.* 'I did not turn back,' nor hesitate, despite abuse and ill-treatment.

6. I gave my back to the smiters,
And my cheeks to them that plucked off the hair;
I hid not my face from shame and spitting.

7. For the Lord GOD will help me;
Therefore have I not been confounded;
Therefore have I set my face like a flint,
And I know that I shall not be ashamed.

8. He is near that justifieth me;
Who will contend with me? let us stand up together;
Who is mine adversary? let him come near to me.

9. Behold, the Lord GOD will help me;
Who is he that shall condemn me?
Behold, they all shall wax old as a garment,
The moth shall eat them up.

10. Who is among you that feareth the LORD,
That obeyeth the voice of His servant?
Though he walketh in darkness,
And hath no light,
Let him trust in the name of the LORD,
And stay upon his God.

11. Behold, all ye that kindle a fire,
That gird yourselves with firebrands,
Begone in the flame of your fire,
And among the brands that ye have kindled.
This shall ye have of My hand;
Ye shall lie down in sorrow.

6 לִי אֹזֶן וְאָנֹכִי לֹא מָרִיתִי אָחוֹר לֹא נְסוּגֹתִי׃ גֵּוִי נָתַתִּי
לְמַכִּים וּלְחָיַי לְמֹרְטִים פָּנַי לֹא הִסְתַּרְתִּי מִכְּלִמּוֹת וָרֹק׃
7 וַאדֹנָי יֱהֹוִה יַעֲזָר־לִי עַל־כֵּן לֹא נִכְלָמְתִּי עַל־כֵּן שַׂמְתִּי
8 פָנַי כַּחַלָּמִישׁ וָאֵדַע כִּי־לֹא אֵבוֹשׁ׃ קָרוֹב מַצְדִּיקִי מִי־
9 יָרִיב אִתִּי נַעַמְדָה יָּחַד מִי־בַעַל מִשְׁפָּטִי יִגַּשׁ אֵלָי׃ הֵן
אֲדֹנָי יֱהֹוִה יַעֲזָר־לִי מִי־הוּא יַרְשִׁיעֵנִי הֵן כֻּלָּם כַּבֶּגֶד יִבְלוּ
י עָשׁ יֹאכְלֵם׃ מִי בָכֶם יְרֵא יְהוָה שֹׁמֵעַ בְּקוֹל עַבְדּוֹ
אֲשֶׁר ׀ הָלַךְ חֲשֵׁכִים וְאֵין נֹגַהּ לוֹ יִבְטַח בְּשֵׁם יְהוָה וְיִשָּׁעֵן
11 בֵּאלֹהָיו׃ הֵן כֻּלְּכֶם קֹדְחֵי אֵשׁ מְאַזְּרֵי זִיקוֹת לְכוּ ׀
בְּאוּר אֶשְׁכֶם וּבְזִיקוֹת בִּעַרְתֶּם מִיָּדִי הָיְתָה־זֹּאת לָכֶם
לְמַעֲצֵבָה תִּשְׁכָּבוּן׃

6. *gave my back.* The Servant accepts the disgrace to which he was subjected as part of God's discipline.

7. *confounded.* By the tremendous spiritual problem, Why do the righteous suffer? How can a holy, loving, omnipotent God permit His faithful servants to endure such undeserved suffering?

ashamed. This unflinching faith of the Servant has many parallels; *e.g.* Jeremiah (XVII), Job, and the Psalms (XXII).

8. *justifieth me.* 'Showeth me to be in the right, by giving me victory in my cause.' The time-long conflict of Israel with the nations and their idolatries is represented under the figure of a process at law before God's tribunal (Davidson).

stand up together. In litigation or debate.

9. *condemn me.* Prove me in the wrong.

10–11. A message of encouragement and warning based on the Song of the Servant.

10. *among you.* The general body of Israelites, as distinct from the Servant, or Righteous Remnant.

in darkness. In despondency or affliction.

11. *begone in the flame.* 'Fire' and 'firebrands' are images for the designs of the ungodly against Ideal Israel. Their mischievous machinations shall recoil on themselves; Psalm VII, 15.

If *fire* and *firebrands* refer to idolatrous rites, there is here possibly 'an allusion to the strange but apparently authentic fact that in certain forms of heathen worship the devotees, under the stress of excitement, become impervious to the ordinary effects of heat on the human body. If so, the boasted marvels of their fire-walking will not render them immune from the retribution of God' (Elmslie).

CHAPTER LI

1–3. The strain of consolation is resumed. The wonders of God's Providence in the past would once more be repeated. Let not the true believers fear that they are too few to rebuild Zion.

1. *rock . . . pit.* The Patriarchs, the founders of the race.

CHAPTER LI

1. Hearken to Me, ye that follow after righteousness,
Ye that seek the LORD;
Look unto the rock whence ye were hewn,
And to the hole of the pit whence ye were digged.
2. Look unto Abraham your father,
And unto Sarah that bore you;
For when he was but one I called him,
And I blessed him, and made him many.
3. For the LORD hath comforted Zion;
He hath comforted all her waste places,
And hath made her wilderness like Eden,
And her desert like the garden of the LORD;
Joy and gladness shall be found therein,
Thanksgiving, and the voice of melody.

CAP. LI. נא

א שִׁמְעוּ אֵלַי רֹדְפֵי צֶדֶק מְבַקְשֵׁי יְהוָה הַבִּיטוּ אֶל־צוּר
2 חֻצַּבְתֶּם וְאֶל־מַקֶּבֶת בּוֹר נֻקַּרְתֶּם׃ הַבִּיטוּ אֶל־אַבְרָהָם
אֲבִיכֶם וְאֶל־שָׂרָה תְּחוֹלֶלְכֶם כִּי־אֶחָד קְרָאתִיו וַאֲבָרְכֵהוּ
3 וְאַרְבֵּהוּ׃ כִּי־נִחַם יְהוָה צִיּוֹן נִחַם כָּל־חָרְבֹתֶיהָ וַיָּשֶׂם
מִדְבָּרָהּ כְּעֵדֶן וְעַרְבָתָהּ כְּגַן־יְהוָה שָׂשׂוֹן וְשִׂמְחָה יִמָּצֵא
בָהּ תּוֹדָה וְקוֹל זִמְרָה׃

2. *Abraham.* God's Promise to make him a great nation and a blessing to all the families of the earth has been fulfilled; so would the faith of the Righteous Remnant in Zion's restoration be rewarded.

when he was but one. When he had not even a child, God called him to make him a great nation; 'Abraham was one, and he inherited the land,' Ezek. XXXIII, 24.

3. *hath comforted Zion.* The verbs are perfects of certainty (the 'Prophetic future'), and equivalent to *shall surely comfort Zion*, despite the fewness of those who hear the call of Zion.

wilderness. The exiles, no doubt, hesitated to leave the fertile fields of Babylon and argued that Palestine was now a barren wilderness. The Prophet, therefore, assures them that the barren districts in the Holy Land shall be made exceedingly fruitful (Ehrlich). Such marvellous transformations in the fertility of Palestine have been witnessed in our own day.

voice of melody. Even as the *chalutzim* to-day sing at their work.

11 26. Behold, I set before you this day a blessing and a curse: 27. the blessing, if ye shall hearken unto the commandments of the LORD your God, which I command you this day; 28. and the curse, if ye shall not hearken unto the commandments of the LORD your God, but turn aside out of the way which I command you this day, to go after other gods, which ye have not known. ¶ 29. And it shall come to pass, when the LORD thy God shall bring thee into the land whither thou goest to possess it, that thou shalt set the blessing upon mount Gerizim, and the curse upon mount Ebal. 30. Are they not beyond the Jordan, behind the way of the going down of the sun, in the land of the Canaanites that dwell in the Arabah, over against Gilgal, beside the terebinths of Moreh? 31. For ye are to pass over the Jordan to go in to possess the land which the LORD your God giveth you, and ye shall possess it, and dwell therein. 32. And ye shall observe to do all the statutes and the ordinances which I set before you this day.

12

CHAPTER XII

1. These are the statutes and the ordinances, which ye shall observe to do in the land which the LORD, the God of thy fathers, hath given thee to possess it, all the days that

יא ס ס ס מז 47

26 רְאֵה אָנֹכִי נֹתֵן לִפְנֵיכֶם הַיּוֹם בְּרָכָה וּקְלָלָה׃ אֶת־הַבְּרָכָה 27
אֲשֶׁר תִּשְׁמְעוּ אֶל־מִצְוֺת יְהוָה אֱלֹהֵיכֶם אֲשֶׁר אָנֹכִי מְצַוֶּה
28 אֶתְכֶם הַיּוֹם׃ וְהַקְּלָלָה אִם־לֹא תִשְׁמְעוּ אֶל־מִצְוֺת
יְהוָה אֱלֹהֵיכֶם וְסַרְתֶּם מִן־הַדֶּרֶךְ אֲשֶׁר אָנֹכִי מְצַוֶּה
אֶתְכֶם הַיּוֹם לָלֶכֶת אַחֲרֵי אֱלֹהִים אֲחֵרִים אֲשֶׁר לֹא־
29 יְדַעְתֶּם׃ ס וְהָיָה כִּי יְבִיאֲךָ יְהוָה אֱלֹהֶיךָ אֶל־הָאָרֶץ
אֲשֶׁר־אַתָּה בָא־שָׁמָּה לְרִשְׁתָּהּ וְנָתַתָּה אֶת־הַבְּרָכָה
ל עַל־הַר גְּרִזִּים וְאֶת־הַקְּלָלָה עַל־הַר עֵיבָל׃ הֲלֹא־הֵמָּה
בְּעֵבֶר הַיַּרְדֵּן אַחֲרֵי דֶּרֶךְ מְבוֹא הַשֶּׁמֶשׁ בְּאֶרֶץ הַכְּנַעֲנִי
31 הַיֹּשֵׁב בָּעֲרָבָה מוּל הַגִּלְגָּל אֵצֶל אֵלוֹנֵי מֹרֶה׃ כִּי אַתֶּם
עֹבְרִים אֶת־הַיַּרְדֵּן לָבֹא לָרֶשֶׁת אֶת־הָאָרֶץ אֲשֶׁר־יְהוָה
32 אֱלֹהֵיכֶם נֹתֵן לָכֶם וִירִשְׁתֶּם אֹתָהּ וִישַׁבְתֶּם־בָּהּ׃ וּשְׁמַרְתֶּם
לַעֲשׂוֹת אֵת כָּל־הַחֻקִּים וְאֶת־הַמִּשְׁפָּטִים אֲשֶׁר אָנֹכִי נֹתֵן
לִפְנֵיכֶם הַיּוֹם׃

יב CAP. XII. יב

א אֵלֶּה הַחֻקִּים וְהַמִּשְׁפָּטִים אֲשֶׁר תִּשְׁמְרוּן לַעֲשׂוֹת בָּאָרֶץ

IV. RE'EH

(CHAPTERS XI, 26–XVI, 17)

XI, 26–32. THE TWO WAYS

These seven verses form the peroration and summing up of the Second Discourse; and, at the same time, are an introduction to the Code itself, which begins with XII, 1 and ends with XXVI. It is an earnest appeal that a right choice be made between the Two Ways now before Israel. The entire future of the nation depends upon the right choice. This theme is further developed in XXVIII–XXX.

26. *I set before you.* Both as individuals and as a nation they were endowed with free-will, and the choice between the Two Ways rested with themselves. All that Moses could do was clearly to define the alternatives, and point out whither each of them led; cf. XXX, 15.

28. *which ye have not known.* Cf. XXXII, 17, 'new gods that came up of late, whom your fathers dreaded not'; deities that have not shown and, being dead, could not show, the saving power they had experienced at the hand of God.

29. *set the blessing.* To impress the truth of the Two Ways more deeply upon Israel, Moses was to arrange a symbolic representation of the Blessing and Curse; XXVII.

Gerizim . . . Ebal. The two most prominent hills on either side of what is the natural centre of Palestine.

30. *behind the way . . . sun.* What is here described is the main road running from north to south, and passing through the Plain, east of Shechem.

Arabah. See on I, 1.

over against Gilgal. Not the Gilgal of Josh. IV, 19, in the vicinity of Jericho. The word means 'a circle' (of stones), a cairn, and seems to have been used to designate several localities. A Gilgal (Juleijil, the Arabic diminutive for Gilgal) has been discovered near Shechem.

the terebinths of Moreh. See Gen. XII, 6. The association of Moreh with the life of Abraham would have made it a well-known spot to the Israelites.

ye live upon the earth. 2. Ye shall surely destroy all the places, wherein the nations that ye are to dispossess served their gods, upon the high mountains, and upon the hills, and under every leafy tree. 3. And ye shall break down their altars, and dash in pieces their pillars, and burn their Asherim with fire; and ye shall hew down the graven images of their gods; and ye shall destroy their name out of that place. 4. Ye shall

אֲשֶׁר נָתַן יְהוָֹה אֱלֹהֵי אֲבֹתֶיךָ לְךָ לְרִשְׁתָּהּ כָּל־הַיָּמִים
2 אֲשֶׁר־אַתֶּם חַיִּים עַל־הָאֲדָמָה׃ אַבֵּד תְּאַבְּדוּן אֶת־כָּל־
הַמְּקֹמוֹת אֲשֶׁר עָבְדוּ־שָׁם הַגּוֹיִם אֲשֶׁר אַתֶּם יֹרְשִׁים אֹתָם
אֶת־אֱלֹהֵיהֶם עַל־הֶהָרִים הָרָמִים וְעַל־הַגְּבָעוֹת וְתַחַת כָּל־
3 עֵץ רַעֲנָן׃ וְנִתַּצְתֶּם אֶת־מִזְבְּחֹתָם וְשִׁבַּרְתֶּם אֶת־מַצֵּבֹתָם

MOSES' SECOND DISCOURSE (*Continued*)

2. The Rehearsal of the Code

XII–XXVI

At this point we pass to the Code of Laws. All that has gone before may be regarded as the religious and historical prelude to the rehearsal of the statutes and judgments which now follow. So far Moses had been speaking in general terms of the necessity of obedience to the laws of God, reminding them of the Covenant of Horeb, and the fundamental principles of Israel's Religion. He now proceeds to give detailed laws and precepts that were to govern their lives in the Land of Promise.

These laws deal with

(1) Religious institutions and worship (xii, 1–xvi, 17);

(2) Government of the people (xvi, 18–xviii);

(3) Criminal law (xix–xxi, 1–9); and

(4) Domestic life (xxi, 10–xxv).

(5) Conclusion of Code: First-fruits, tithes, and accompanying prayers.

Some commentators detect in all these chapters an elaboration of the basic laws contained in the Decalogue. Thus xii–xiv deal with the worship of God, and are an expansion of the first three of the Ten Commandments. In xv–xvi, 17 we have an enumeration of Holy Festivals analogous to the Sacred Day of the week. Chaps. xvi–xviii deal with civil and religious government, which plays the same part in the national life as the authority of parents plays in the life of the family. The remainder of the section corresponds generally to the second half of the Decalogue, and treats of the relationship of man to his fellow-man.

(1) Religious Institutions and Worship

XII, 1–XVI, 17

This section includes the laws (*a*) concerning the Central Sanctuary; (*b*) distinctiveness in worship; (*c*) against heathen rites and religious seducers; (*d*) of Holiness (concerning clean and unclean, tithes, year of release, firstlings); and (*e*) the Three Feasts.

(*a*) The Law of the Central Sanctuary

XII, 1–28

When Israel is settled in the Land, sacrifices shall be offered only in the spot to be chosen by God.

1. *in the land.* 'Laws that relate to the Land need be observed only in the Land; all other laws must be observed everywhere, in Palestine or out of Palestine' (Sifri).

2. *ye shall surely destroy.* Better, *ye shall utterly destroy.* Their first duty would be the eradication of every trace of heathenism.

hills . . . tree. Worship at these places was accompanied by licentious rites; see *v.* 31 and Hosea iv, 13.

3. *altars . . . pillars.* See on vii, 5.

destroy their name. The very memory of the local Baals is to cease.

out of that place. 'The injunction to destroy idolatrous images applies only to the Holy Land, and not to those places outside it where Jews reside' (Sifri).

4. *not do so.* The Israelites were not, like the Canaanites, to worship God on the 'high mountains, and under every green tree', but were to do so in a Central Sanctuary as stated in the following *v.* Some Rabbis, however, connected this *v.* with the one immediately preceding, and deduced therefrom the prohibition to obliterate in any way the Divine Name in a scroll or book. In later ages, it became customary to bury disused Hebrew books, so as not to dispose of them in any way that would involve destroying something containing a Divine Name. Hence the institution of the *Genizah* in Eastern Jewish Communities, and the periodic burial of disused, tattered, and fragmentary books of Scripture and devotion (שֵׁמוֹת) in Russo-Polish Jewries.

not do so unto the LORD your God. 5. But unto the place which the LORD your God shall choose out of all your tribes to put His name there, even unto His habitation shall ye seek, and thither thou shalt come; 6. and thither ye shall bring your burnt-offerings, and your sacrifices, and your tithes, and the offering of your hand, and your vows, and your freewill-offerings, and the firstlings of your herd and of your flock; 7. and there ye shall eat before the LORD your God, and ye shall rejoice in all that ye put your hand unto, ye and your households, wherein the LORD thy God hath blessed thee. 8. Ye shall not do after all that we do here this day, every man whatsoever is right in his own eyes; 9. for ye are not as yet come to the rest and to the inheritance, which the LORD your God giveth thee. 10. But when ye go over the Jordan, and dwell in the land which the LORD your God causeth you to inherit, and He giveth you rest from all your enemies round about,

וַאֲשֵׁרֵיהֶם תִּשְׂרְפוּן בָּאֵשׁ וּפְסִילֵי אֱלֹהֵיהֶם תְּגַדֵּעוּן וְאִבַּדְתֶּם
4 אֶת־שְׁמָם מִן־הַמָּקוֹם הַהוּא׃ לֹא־תַעֲשׂוּן כֵּן לַיהוָה
ה אֱלֹהֵיכֶם׃ כִּי אִם־אֶל־הַמָּקוֹם אֲשֶׁר־יִבְחַר יְהוָה אֱלֹהֵיכֶם
מִכָּל־שִׁבְטֵיכֶם לָשׂוּם אֶת־שְׁמוֹ שָׁם לְשִׁכְנוֹ תִדְרְשׁוּ
6 וּבָאתָ שָׁמָּה׃ וַהֲבֵאתֶם שָׁמָּה עֹלֹתֵיכֶם וְזִבְחֵיכֶם וְאֵת
מַעְשְׂרֹתֵיכֶם וְאֵת תְּרוּמַת יֶדְכֶם וְנִדְרֵיכֶם וְנִדְבֹתֵיכֶם
7 וּבְכֹרֹת בְּקַרְכֶם וְצֹאנְכֶם׃ וַאֲכַלְתֶּם־שָׁם לִפְנֵי יְהוָה
אֱלֹהֵיכֶם וּשְׂמַחְתֶּם בְּכֹל מִשְׁלַח יֶדְכֶם אַתֶּם וּבָתֵּיכֶם אֲשֶׁר
8 בֵּרַכְךָ יְהוָה אֱלֹהֶיךָ׃ לֹא תַעֲשׂוּן כְּכֹל אֲשֶׁר אֲנַחְנוּ עֹשִׂים
9 פֹּה הַיּוֹם אִישׁ כָּל־הַיָּשָׁר בְּעֵינָיו׃ כִּי לֹא־בָאתֶם עַד־
עָתָּה אֶל־הַמְּנוּחָה וְאֶל־הַנַּחֲלָה אֲשֶׁר־יְהוָה אֱלֹהֶיךָ נֹתֵן
לָךְ׃ וַעֲבַרְתֶּם אֶת־הַיַּרְדֵּן וִישַׁבְתֶּם בָּאָרֶץ אֲשֶׁר־יְהוָה

5. *but unto the place.* This insistence upon the eventual establishment of one Central Sanctuary for all Israel was for the purpose of ensuring unity in national life. The Central Altar was to form a rallying-point to the Israelites wherever they resided, and prove a strong factor in welding the tribes into one compact body. When Jeroboam desired to strengthen the schism in Israel and separate the Ten Tribes from Judah, he set up two new centres of worship.

which the LORD your God. Though Jerusalem was the ultimate place chosen, it is not here in view. God might from time to time designate different places where offerings were to be brought. Thus, in XXVII, 5 f, Israel is commanded to build an altar on Mount Ebal and sacrifice burnt-offerings upon it. Thereafter Shiloh was for centuries the home of God's choice; see Jeremiah VII, 12. Israel was to be guided in this matter by the Prophets. The Prophet Gad tells David to erect an altar in the threshing floor of Araunah in Jerusalem (II Sam. XXIV, 18); and other instances are found in Judges VI, 26; XIII, 16–20; I Kings XVIII, 32. There is no contradiction between the law of the Central Sanctuary and Exod. XX, 21 (XX, 24 in the English Bible). See note, Centralization of Worship, p. 939.

shall choose. Not the place which the worshipper chooses, but the place chosen by God. This is the same truth proclaimed in Exod. XX, 21, which should be translated, '*In whatever place* that *I* cause my name to be mentioned, I will come unto thee and bless thee.'

even unto His habitation. Heb. *leshichno,* which expresses the same thought—the Divine Presence—as the later term, *Shechinah* (Hoffmann).

6. *tithes.* The duty of tithing is expounded in XIV, 22 f.

offering of your hand. Heb. *terumah;* cf. Num. XV, 18 f. The allusion is to the presentation of the first-fruits described in XXVI.

vows . . . freewill-offerings. Voluntary offerings; cf. Lev. XXII, 18 f.

firstlings. The law on the subject is given in XV, 19 f.

7. *there ye shall eat.* The word *ye* refers either to the priests and Levites, or to the persons who bring the sacrifices and their households, according to the character of the offering.

before the LORD. i.e. in the Holy City.

in all that ye put your hand unto. i.e. in all your undertakings. The celebration is thus a thanksgiving for the success of the year's toil.

your households. 'Your wife' (Sifri); *v.* 12 and 18 subsequently enumerating those others who were to participate in the rejoicing.

8–14. PRIVATE ALTARS TO BE PROHIBITED

8. *that we do here this day.* Until the Central Sanctuary had its ultimate fixed abode in Jerusalem, it was permitted to offer sacrifices on private altars. This, in the opinion of many Talmudic teachers, was certainly so in days of unrest, like the time of the Judges. According to other traditions, sacrificing on private altars became again permissible after the Destruction of the Temple. It must have been such a tradition that prompted the Jews in Egypt to erect, after the Fall of the First Temple, a sacrificial sanctuary of their own—the Temple of Onias (Hoffmann).

9. *to the rest . . . inheritance.* The former denotes Shiloh where the Ark first found a resting place; and the latter denotes Jerusalem (Sifri).

that ye dwell in safety;*ii. 11. then it shall come to pass that the place which the LORD your God shall choose to cause His name to dwell there, thither shall ye bring all that I command you: your burnt-offerings, and your sacrifices, your tithes, and the offering of your hand, and all your choice vows which ye vow unto the LORD. 12. And ye shall rejoice before the LORD your God, ye, and your sons, and your daughters, and your men-servants, and your maid-servants, and the Levite that is within your gates, forasmuch as he hath no portion nor inheritance with you. 13. Take heed to thyself that thou offer not thy burnt-offerings in every place that thou seest; 14. but in the place which the LORD shall choose in one of thy tribes, there thou shalt offer thy burnt-offerings, and there thou shalt do all that I command thee. ¶ 15. Notwithstanding thou mayest kill and eat flesh within all thy gates, after all the desire of thy soul, according to the blessing of the LORD thy God which He hath given thee; the unclean and the clean may eat thereof, as of the gazelle, and as of the hart. 16. Only ye shall not eat the blood; thou shalt pour it out upon the earth as water. 17. Thou mayest not eat within thy gates the tithe of thy corn, or of thy wine, or of thine oil, or the firstlings of thy herd or of thy flock, nor any of thy vows which thou vowest, nor thy freewill-offerings, nor the offering of thy hand; 18. but thou shalt eat them before the LORD thy God in the place which the LORD thy God shall choose, thou, and thy son, and thy daughter, and thy man-servant, and thy maid-servant, and the Levite that is within thy gates; and thou

אֱלֹהֵיכֶם מַנְחִיל אֶתְכֶם וְהֵנִיחַ לָכֶם מִכָּל־אֹיְבֵיכֶם מִסָּבִיב
שני 11 וִישַׁבְתֶּם־בֶּטַח׃ וְהָיָה הַמָּקוֹם אֲשֶׁר־יִבְחַר יְהוָה אֱלֹהֵיכֶם
בּוֹ לְשַׁכֵּן שְׁמוֹ שָׁם שָׁמָּה תָבִיאוּ אֵת כָּל־אֲשֶׁר אָנֹכִי
מְצַוֶּה אֶתְכֶם עוֹלֹתֵיכֶם וְזִבְחֵיכֶם מַעְשְׂרֹתֵיכֶם וּתְרֻמַת
12 יֶדְכֶם וְכֹל מִבְחַר נִדְרֵיכֶם אֲשֶׁר תִּדְּרוּ לַיהוָה׃ וּשְׂמַחְתֶּם
לִפְנֵי יְהוָה אֱלֹהֵיכֶם אַתֶּם וּבְנֵיכֶם וּבְנֹתֵיכֶם וְעַבְדֵיכֶם
וְאַמְהֹתֵיכֶם וְהַלֵּוִי אֲשֶׁר בְּשַׁעֲרֵיכֶם כִּי אֵין לוֹ חֵלֶק וְנַחֲלָה
13 אִתְּכֶם׃ הִשָּׁמֶר לְךָ פֶּן־תַּעֲלֶה עֹלֹתֶיךָ בְּכָל־מָקוֹם אֲשֶׁר
14 תִּרְאֶה׃ כִּי אִם־בַּמָּקוֹם אֲשֶׁר־יִבְחַר יְהוָה בְּאַחַד שְׁבָטֶיךָ
שָׁם תַּעֲלֶה עֹלֹתֶיךָ וְשָׁם תַּעֲשֶׂה כֹּל אֲשֶׁר אָנֹכִי מְצַוֶּךָּ׃
טו רַק בְּכָל־אַוַּת נַפְשְׁךָ תִּזְבַּח ׀ וְאָכַלְתָּ בָשָׂר כְּבִרְכַּת יְהוָה
אֱלֹהֶיךָ אֲשֶׁר נָתַן־לְךָ בְּכָל־שְׁעָרֶיךָ הַטָּמֵא וְהַטָּהוֹר יֹאכְלֶנּוּ
16 כַּצְּבִי וְכָאַיָּל׃ רַק הַדָּם לֹא תֹאכֵלוּ עַל־הָאָרֶץ תִּשְׁפְּכֶנּוּ
17 כַּמָּיִם׃ לֹא־תוּכַל לֶאֱכֹל בִּשְׁעָרֶיךָ מַעְשַׂר דְּגָנְךָ וְתִירֹשְׁךָ
וְיִצְהָרֶךָ וּבְכֹרֹת בְּקָרְךָ וְצֹאנֶךָ וְכָל־נְדָרֶיךָ אֲשֶׁר תִּדֹּר
18 וְנִדְבֹתֶיךָ וּתְרוּמַת יָדֶךָ׃ כִּי אִם־לִפְנֵי יְהוָה אֱלֹהֶיךָ תֹּאכְלֶנּוּ
בַּמָּקוֹם אֲשֶׁר יִבְחַר יְהוָה אֱלֹהֶיךָ בּוֹ אַתָּה וּבִנְךָ וּבִתֶּךָ
וְעַבְדְּךָ וַאֲמָתֶךָ וְהַלֵּוִי אֲשֶׁר בִּשְׁעָרֶיךָ וְשָׂמַחְתָּ לִפְנֵי יְהוָה

10. *He giveth you rest.* This did not occur until the reign of David. Hence the statement in II Sam. VII, 1, 'when the king (David) dwelt in his house, and the LORD had given him rest from all his enemies round about,' that the desire to build a Temple arose in his heart. Before that final resting-place in Jerusalem was available, a temporary abode was found in Shiloh; Josh. XVIII, 1.

11. *then it shall come to pass.* In other words, the law of the Central Altar was not meant to come into operation till the time was ripe for building the Temple (I Kings III, 2).

your choice vows. If a man brings an offering, voluntary or otherwise, he must select for that purpose the choicest that he can obtain (Sifri).

12. *within your gates . . . no portion.* See XVIII, 1–8.

13. *thy burnt-offerings.* All the various sacrifices enumerated in *v.* 11.

thou seest. *i.e.* not that *thou* seest as suitable for that purpose, but only as a Prophet sees (*i.e.* selects) for thee, as Elijah did at Mount Carmel (Sifri); see on *v.* 5 above.

15–19. EXTENSION OF PROHIBITION OF PRIVATE SANCTUARY

Even the mere eating of sacrificial foods is forbidden outside the city of the Central Sanctuary.

15. *mayest . . . eat flesh.* See on *v.* 20.

16. *not eat the blood.* See on *v.* 23.

17. *thou mayest not eat.* Mention of burnt-offerings and sacrifices is omitted from the list, because these could only be eaten by the priests within the Temple precincts (Lev. VI, 19, VII, 6); whereas the other sacred foods could be eaten anywhere within the limits of the Holy City.

shalt rejoice before the LORD thy God in all that thou puttest thy hand unto. 19. Take heed to thyself that thou forsake not the Levite as long as thou livest upon thy land. ¶ 20. When the LORD thy God shall enlarge thy border, as He hath promised thee, and thou shalt say: 'I will eat flesh,' because thy soul desireth to eat flesh; thou mayest eat flesh, after all the desire of thy soul. 21. If the place which the LORD thy God shall choose to put His name there be too far from thee, then thou shalt kill of thy herd and of thy flock, which the LORD hath given thee, as I have commanded thee, and thou shalt eat within thy gates, after all the desire of thy soul. 22. Howbeit as the gazelle and as the hart is eaten, so thou shalt eat thereof; the unclean and the clean may eat thereof alike. 23. Only be stedfast in not eating the blood; for the blood is the life; and thou shalt not eat the life with the flesh. 24. Thou shalt not eat it; thou shalt pour it out upon the earth as water. 25. Thou shalt not eat it; that it may go well

19 אֱלֹהֶיךָ בְּכֹל מִשְׁלַח יָדֶךָ׃ הִשָּׁמֶר לְךָ פֶּן־תַּעֲזֹב אֶת־
כ הַלֵּוִי כָּל־יָמֶיךָ עַל־אַדְמָתֶךָ׃ ס כִּי־יַרְחִיב יְהוָה
אֱלֹהֶיךָ אֶת־גְּבֻלְךָ כַּאֲשֶׁר דִּבֶּר־לָךְ וְאָמַרְתָּ אֹכְלָה בָשָׂר
כִּי־תְאַוֶּה נַפְשְׁךָ לֶאֱכֹל בָּשָׂר בְּכָל־אַוַּת נַפְשְׁךָ תֹּאכַל
21 בָּשָׂר׃ כִּי־יִרְחַק מִמְּךָ הַמָּקוֹם אֲשֶׁר יִבְחַר יְהוָה אֱלֹהֶיךָ
לָשׂוּם שְׁמוֹ שָׁם וְזָבַחְתָּ מִבְּקָרְךָ וּמִצֹּאנְךָ אֲשֶׁר נָתַן
יְהוָה לְךָ כַּאֲשֶׁר צִוִּיתִךָ וְאָכַלְתָּ בִּשְׁעָרֶיךָ בְּכֹל אַוַּת
22 נַפְשֶׁךָ׃ אַךְ כַּאֲשֶׁר יֵאָכֵל אֶת־הַצְּבִי וְאֶת־הָאַיָּל כֵּן תֹּאכְלֶנּוּ
23 הַטָּמֵא וְהַטָּהוֹר יַחְדָּו יֹאכְלֶנּוּ׃ רַק חֲזַק לְבִלְתִּי אֲכֹל
הַדָּם כִּי הַדָּם הוּא הַנָּפֶשׁ וְלֹא־תֹאכַל הַנֶּפֶשׁ עִם־הַבָּשָׂר׃
24 כה לֹא תֹּאכְלֶנּוּ עַל־הָאָרֶץ תִּשְׁפְּכֶנּוּ כַּמָּיִם׃ לֹא תֹּאכְלֶנּוּ לְמַעַן

v. 21. חסר יו״ד

19. *as long as thou livest.* lit. 'all thy days.' *upon thy land.* The Levite is to be supported even in the Sabbatical year and the Jubilee, as long as he is resident in the Holy Land. Outside its border, he is to be treated as merely a poor man in need of assistance (Sifri).

20–22. THE SLAUGHTER OF ANIMALS FOR FOOD

In Lev. XVII it is laid down that every animal, even for ordinary consumption, must be slain at the entrance of the Tent of Meeting. This was a temporary precept for the period of the Israelites' sojourn in the Wilderness; see on Lev. XVII, 7. This precept is replaced by another in this chapter of Deuteronomy. Israel was now about to settle in Canaan, and the individual Israelite could not be expected to go to the Central Sanctuary in Shiloh or Jerusalem whenever he wished to partake of meat food.

20. *the desire of thy soul.* In Heb. the 'soul' is conceived as the seat of emotion and appetite.

21. *as I have commanded thee.* This cannot refer to *v.* 15, as in that case the verb would not be in the perfect tense, but the participle would be used (cf. XI, 8, 13, 22, 27, 28; XII, 11, etc.). Tradition connects *as I have commanded thee* with the words, *thou shalt kill.* We have thus an indication that Moses had previously taught the people a method of slaughtering animals. Since this is nowhere mentioned in the Pentateuch, it follows that Shechitah, the Jewish method of slaughter, must have been communicated orally to Israel.

22. *gazelle . . . hart.* These were 'clean' animals, but were not acceptable as offerings on the Altar, not being domestic animals; Lev. I, 2.

may eat thereof alike. A person ritually unclean could not partake of the flesh of a sacrificial animal, but they could join in a non-sacrificial meal.

23–28. WARNING AGAINST BLOOD

This law is mentioned as early as Gen. IX, 4 and repeated Lev. XVII, 11, 14; XIX, 26. The Jewish method of slaughter, and the salting of meat, have as one of their main purposes the draining away of the blood.

23. *the blood is the life.* See on Lev. XVII, 11, 14. *thou shall not eat the life with the flesh.* The Rabbis understood this as meaning that it is forbidden to eat a limb torn from a living animal; see on Gen. IX, 4.

24. *thou shalt not eat it.* The Rabbis understood this and the following apparently superfluous *v.* to signify that even the blood which remains in the animal after the flow of blood has ceased, is prohibited.

pour it out upon the earth. In contrast to the blood of a sacrificial animal (see *v.* 27), or to that of a bird or a hunted animal, which blood is covered over; Lev. XVII, 13.

25. *that it may go well with thee.* Ibn Ezra suggests that the use of blood would have a demoralizing effect upon the moral and physical nature, and pass on a hereditary taint to future generations.

יִיטַב לְךָ וּלְבָנֶיךָ אַחֲרֶיךָ כִּי־תַעֲשֶׂה הַיָּשָׁר בְּעֵינֵי יְהוָה׃
26 רַק קָדָשֶׁיךָ אֲשֶׁר־יִהְיוּ לְךָ וּנְדָרֶיךָ תִּשָּׂא וּבָאתָ אֶל־
27 הַמָּקוֹם אֲשֶׁר־יִבְחַר יְהוָה׃ וְעָשִׂיתָ עֹלֹתֶיךָ הַבָּשָׂר וְהַדָּם
עַל־מִזְבַּח יְהוָה אֱלֹהֶיךָ וְדַם־זְבָחֶיךָ יִשָּׁפֵךְ עַל־מִזְבַּח
28 יְהוָה אֱלֹהֶיךָ וְהַבָּשָׂר תֹּאכֵל׃ שְׁמֹר וְשָׁמַעְתָּ אֵת כָּל־
הַדְּבָרִים הָאֵלֶּה אֲשֶׁר אָנֹכִי מְצַוֶּךָּ לְמַעַן יִיטַב לְךָ וּלְבָנֶיךָ
אַחֲרֶיךָ עַד־עוֹלָם כִּי תַעֲשֶׂה הַטּוֹב וְהַיָּשָׁר בְּעֵינֵי יְהוָה
שלישי 29 אֱלֹהֶיךָ׃ * ס כִּי־יַכְרִית יְהוָה אֱלֹהֶיךָ אֶת־הַגּוֹיִם אֲשֶׁר
אַתָּה בָא־שָׁמָּה לָרֶשֶׁת אוֹתָם מִפָּנֶיךָ וְיָרַשְׁתָּ אֹתָם וְיָשַׁבְתָּ
ל בְּאַרְצָם׃ הִשָּׁמֶר לְךָ פֶּן־תִּנָּקֵשׁ אַחֲרֵיהֶם אַחֲרֵי הִשָּׁמְדָם
מִפָּנֶיךָ וּפֶן־תִּדְרֹשׁ לֵאלֹהֵיהֶם לֵאמֹר אֵיכָה יַעַבְדוּ הַגּוֹיִם
31 הָאֵלֶּה אֶת־אֱלֹהֵיהֶם וְאֶעֱשֶׂה־כֵּן גַּם־אָנִי׃ לֹא־תַעֲשֶׂה
כֵן לַיהוָה אֱלֹהֶיךָ כִּי כָל־תּוֹעֲבַת יְהוָה אֲשֶׁר שָׂנֵא עָשׂוּ
לֵאלֹהֵיהֶם כִּי גַם אֶת־בְּנֵיהֶם וְאֶת־בְּנֹתֵיהֶם יִשְׂרְפוּ בָאֵשׁ
לֵאלֹהֵיהֶם׃

with thee, and with thy children after thee, when thou shalt do that which is right in the eyes of the LORD. 26. Only thy holy things which thou hast, and thy vows, thou shalt take, and go unto the place which the LORD shall choose; 27. and thou shalt offer thy burnt-offerings, the flesh and the blood, upon the altar of the LORD thy God; and the blood of thy sacrifices shall be poured out against the altar of the LORD thy God, and thou shalt eat the flesh. 28. Observe and hear all these words which I command thee, that it may go well with thee, and with thy children after thee for ever, when thou doest that which is good and right in the eyes of the LORD thy God.*iii. ¶ 29. When the LORD thy God shall cut off the nations from before thee, whither thou goest in to dispossess them, and thou dispossessest them, and dwellest in their land; 30. take heed to thyself that thou be not ensnared to follow them, after that they are destroyed from before thee; and that thou inquire not after their gods, saying: 'How used these nations to serve their gods? even so will I do likewise.' 31. Thou shalt not do so unto the LORD thy God; for every abomination to the LORD, which He hateth, have they done unto their gods; for even their sons and their daughters do they burn in the fire to their gods.

26. *which thou hast. i.e.* which are obligatory upon thee.

the place which the LORD shall choose. Notwithstanding the permission granted (*v.* 20–22) in the case of meat for food, solemn offerings of every kind should be brought only at the Central Sanctuary.

(*b*) DISTINCTIVENESS IN WORSHIP

29–31

Not only in regard to the place of sacrifice, but in regard to the mode of Divine Worship, shall the Israelites be distinguished from their heathen neighbours. Israel shall especially beware of the hideous abominations—such as human sacrifice—that accompany their worship. This is one of the many exhortations of this nature that, 'like a chorus, break in upon both the narratives and laws throughout Deuteronomy' (G. A. Smith).

30. *how used these nations to serve.* Better, *used to worship.* The meaning of this warning is strikingly illustrated by the narrative in II Kings XVII, 25 f. Just as these foreign settlers in N. Palestine wished to follow the way of the former inhabitants in regard to worship, so the Israelites might be tempted to inquire after, and follow, the *minhag* of the peoples whose land they would soon inhabit. There would be fatal danger in such a course, even if the imitation confined itself to *forms* of worship. With the alien form, the alien idea would soon find entrance.

31. *every abomination.* It was the immorality and inhumanity of Canaanite religion that rendered it abominable in the eyes of God, and imposed upon the Israelites the duty of exterminating it.

even their sons. To say nothing of ordinary human sacrifices, including the killing of aged parents. R. Akiba cites a particularly loathsome instance of such a murder, which he himself had witnessed.

they burn in the fire to their gods. Human sacrifice was the practice among the primeval Greeks and Romans, Celts, Slavs, and Scandinavians. It was in use among the Germans down to late Roman times; and was widespread among the ancient Semites, especially in times of national danger or disaster. Recent excavations in Palestine, at Gezer, Taanach, and Megiddo, have revealed regular cemeteries round the heathen altars, in which skeletons of scores of infants have been found, showing traces of slaughter and partial consumption by sacrificial fire.

Israel's fight against this hideous aberration of the religious sense began with the story of the sacrifice of Isaac (see p. 201), and was continued throughout the centuries. It is

13

CHAPTER XIII

1. All this word which I command you, that shall ye observe to do; thou shalt not add thereto, nor diminish from it. ¶ 2. If there arise in the midst of thee a prophet, or a dreamer of dreams—and he give thee a sign or a wonder, 3. and the sign or the wonder come to pass, whereof he spoke unto thee—saying: 'Let us go after other gods, which thou has not known, and let us serve them'; 4. thou shalt not hearken unto the words of that prophet, or unto that dreamer of dreams; for the LORD your God putteth you to proof, to know whether

יג

CAP. XIII. יג

א אֵת כָּל־הַדָּבָר אֲשֶׁר אָנֹכִי מְצַוֶּה אֶתְכֶם אֹתוֹ תִשְׁמְרוּ
לַעֲשׂוֹת לֹא־תֹסֵף עָלָיו וְלֹא תִגְרַע מִמֶּנּוּ׃ פ
2 כִּי־יָקוּם בְּקִרְבְּךָ נָבִיא אוֹ חֹלֵם חֲלוֹם וְנָתַן אֵלֶיךָ אוֹת
3 אוֹ מוֹפֵת׃ וּבָא הָאוֹת וְהַמּוֹפֵת אֲשֶׁר־דִּבֶּר אֵלֶיךָ לֵאמֹר
נֵלְכָה אַחֲרֵי אֱלֹהִים אֲחֵרִים אֲשֶׁר לֹא־יְדַעְתָּם וְנָעָבְדֵם׃
4 לֹא תִשְׁמַע אֶל־דִּבְרֵי הַנָּבִיא הַהוּא אוֹ אֶל־חוֹלֵם הַחֲלוֹם
הַהוּא כִּי מְנַסֶּה יְהוָה אֱלֹהֵיכֶם אֶתְכֶם לָדַעַת הֲיִשְׁכֶם

one of the bitter ironies of history, that the one People which for a thousand years fought this horror, and whose religion forbids its followers the eating of any blood in the most rigorous way, should itself have to suffer from the libellous accusation of *ritual* murder and the use of *human* blood for religious purposes. Even in the Twentieth Century, this foul and Satanic lie was officially levelled against Israel in the Beilis trial at Kieff in 1913; and only last year it was broadcast by Nazi leaders in their campaign of ruin against the Jewish population of Germany. In regard to the Nazi resurrection of the fable of ritual murder, it is well to recall that in 1912 no less than 215 non-Jewish leaders in German public life, learning, literature, theology, science, and the arts, issued a protest against this cruel and utterly baseless libel on Judaism. They wrote: 'This unscrupulous fiction, spread among the people, has from the Middle Ages until recent times led to terrible consequences. It has incited the ignorant masses to outrage and massacre, and has driven misguided crowds to pollute themselves with the innocent blood of their Jewish fellow-men. And yet not a shadow of proof has ever been adduced to justify this crazy belief.' See Cecil Roth, *The Ritual Murder Libel and the Jew*, London, 1935; and *A Book of Jewish Thoughts*, Oxford edition, p. 181.

CHAPTER XIII

(c) RELIGIOUS SEDUCERS

Against the danger of religious seduction on the part of false prophets, self-deluded visionaries, and base men.

1. *thou shalt not add thereto.* See on IV, 2. 'Constant changes would tend to disturb the whole system of the Torah, and would lead people to believe that it was not of Divine origin. But permission is at the same time given to the wise men, *i.e.* the Sanhedrin of every generation, to make "fences" round the judgments of the Torah, in order to ensure their keeping. In the same manner, they have the power temporarily to dispense with some religious act prescribed in the Torah, or to allow that which is forbidden, if exceptional circumstances and events require it; but none of the laws can be abrogated permanently' (Maimonides).

This prohibition is of more than theoretic interest in modern Judaism. The various attempts made by revolutionary religious leaders to 'accommodate' Judaism to present-day conditions have all suffered spiritual shipwreck, because they acted in defiance of either *ye shall not add unto the word which I command you*, or of *neither shall ye diminish from it.* On the one hand, some attempted 'to diminish' Judaism by such vital things as the Sabbath, the Hebrew Language, and the Love of Zion. And, on the other hand, there are those who, besides, are prepared 'to add' to the Jewish Heritage things that constitute a serious weakening of the Unity of God, and a radical departure from other fundamental principles of the Jewish Faith.

2–6. A FALSE PROPHET

2. *a prophet.* A false prophet.

a dreamer of dreams. In Scripture, God often communicates with His chosen servants through the medium of dreams (cf. Num. XII, 6); and it would be easy for one who had experienced a dream to regard it as the vehicle of a Divine message.

or a wonder. Better, *or a portent.* Not necessarily a miracle, but a prediction of something that shall happen in the future.

3. *saying.* The sense of the *v.* is, And the sign or the wonder came to pass whereof he spoke unto thee, saying, If what I foretell happens, let us go after other gods.

which thou hast not known. Cf. XI, 28. These are the words of Moses, and are not part of the remarks of the 'prophet'.

4. *thou shalt not hearken.* 'Reason which declares his testimony false is more to be trusted than the eye which sees his signs' (Maimonides).

putteth you to proof. i.e. the fulfilment of the prediction is not evidence of the validity of the

אֹהֲבִים אֶת־יְהוָה אֱלֹהֵיכֶם בְּכָל־לְבַבְכֶם וּבְכָל־נַפְשְׁכֶם׃
ה אַחֲרֵי יְהוָה אֱלֹהֵיכֶם תֵּלֵכוּ וְאֹתוֹ תִירָאוּ וְאֶת־מִצְוֹתָיו
6 תִּשְׁמֹרוּ וּבְקֹלוֹ תִשְׁמָעוּ וְאֹתוֹ תַעֲבֹדוּ וּבוֹ תִדְבָּקוּן׃ וְהַנָּבִיא
הַהוּא אוֹ חֹלֵם הַחֲלוֹם הַהוּא יוּמָת כִּי דִבֶּר־סָרָה עַל־
יְהוָה אֱלֹהֵיכֶם הַמּוֹצִיא אֶתְכֶם ׀ מֵאֶרֶץ מִצְרַיִם וְהַפֹּדְךָ
מִבֵּית עֲבָדִים לְהַדִּיחֲךָ מִן־הַדֶּרֶךְ אֲשֶׁר צִוְּךָ יְהוָה אֱלֹהֶיךָ
7 לָלֶכֶת בָּהּ וּבִעַרְתָּ הָרָע מִקִּרְבֶּךָ׃ ס כִּי יְסִיתְךָ אָחִיךָ
בֶן־אִמֶּךָ אוֹ־בִנְךָ אוֹ־בִתְּךָ אוֹ ׀ אֵשֶׁת חֵיקֶךָ אוֹ רֵעֲךָ אֲשֶׁר
כְּנַפְשְׁךָ בַּסֵּתֶר לֵאמֹר נֵלְכָה וְנַעַבְדָה אֱלֹהִים אֲחֵרִים
8 אֲשֶׁר לֹא יָדַעְתָּ אַתָּה וַאֲבֹתֶיךָ׃ מֵאֱלֹהֵי הָעַמִּים אֲשֶׁר

ye do love the LORD your God with all your heart and with all your soul. 5. After the LORD your God shall ye walk, and Him shall ye fear, and His commandments shall ye keep, and unto His voice shall ye hearken, and Him shall ye serve, and unto Him shall ye cleave. 6. And that prophet, or that dreamer of dreams, shall be put to death; because he hath spoken perversion against the LORD your God, who brought you out of the land of Egypt, and redeemed thee out of the house of bondage, to draw thee aside out of the way which the LORD thy God commanded thee to walk in. So shalt thou put away the evil from the midst of thee. ¶ 7. If thy brother, the son of thy mother, or thy son, or thy daughter, or the wife of thy bosom, or thy friend, that is as thine own soul, entice thee secretly, saying: 'Let us go and serve other gods,' which thou hast not known, thou, nor thy fathers; 8. of the gods of the peoples that are round

v. 5. קמץ בז"ק v. 6. קמץ ברביעי

man's claims, but God is putting you to the test, whether your loyalty to God can withstand the most insidious seductions from His revealed will. This refusal to recognize miracle as necessarily a proof of the truth of a doctrine is typically Jewish. When Sir George Adam Smith writes that it is not in harmony with both the official and the popular mind of ancient Jewry, he does so as a New Testament apologist and in disregard of Rabbinic teaching. The latter can be learned from the story of R. Joshua's unchallenged assertion אין סומכין על הנס, 'Miracles in themselves cannot be invoked as decisive in matters of reason and law.' A thousand years later, Hallevi and Maimonides likewise maintained that miraculous acts can on no account be deemed as an unerring attestation of a Divine mission.

to know whether. These words do not mean that God desires to know whether they loved God, for He already knows it. The expression is an anthropomorphism, Scripture using 'the language of men'. If the Israelites succumbed to the test, it would demonstrate the weakness of their attachment to God; if they came through it successfully, their Faith would be strengthened as a result of the trial.

5. *ye shall walk . . . unto Him.* lit. 'after *the LORD your God* shall ye go, and *Him* shall ye fear, and *His* commandments shall ye keep, and *His* voice shall ye obey, and *Him* shall ye worship, and unto *Him* shall ye cleave.'

6. *brought you out . . . redeemed thee.* He hath spoken rebellion against Him who is your Saviour and Redeemer, Who alone deserves Israel's undivided allegiance and lasting gratitude.

Hoffmann calls attention to the fact that Christian theologians have often explained *v.* 1–6 in relation to the founder of their religion. The rise of Christianity was indeed a test unto Israel; so also were the expansion of Christianity and its triumphant world-dominion an age-long trial of Israel's loyalty to God and His Torah. Israel nobly stood that test and trial. It remained undazzled by the power of the dominant Faith, and undaunted.

'By the torture prolonged from age to age,
By the infamy, Israel's heritage,
By the Ghetto's plague, by the garb's disgrace,
By the badge of shame, by the felon's place,
By the branding tool, by the bloody whip,
And the summons to Christian fellowship'
(Browning).

7–12. SEDUCERS IN ONE'S OWN FAMILY

As against God, even the closest personal ties are not to protect the would-be idolater from unsparing punishment.

7. *the son of thy mother. i.e. even* if he be the son of thy mother. In the days of polygamy, the sons of the same mother were more intimate with one another than with the sons of their father by another wife. 'As so often, the Septuagint and the Samaritan Text misunderstand the Hebrew original, and insert the words, *the son of thy father or* before "the son of thy mother"—which renders it trivial' (Koenig).

or thy daughter. Completing the blood relations. Very significantly and characteristically, father and mother are not mentioned as possible agents of temptation (Bertholet).

8. *nigh . . . or far off.* The gods of Canaan, or those of Babylon, or of any nation under heaven.

about you, nigh unto thee, or far off from
thee, from the one end of the earth even
unto the other end of the earth; 9. thou
shalt not consent unto him, nor hearken
unto him; neither shall thine eye pity him,
neither shalt thou spare, neither shalt thou
conceal him; 10. but thou shalt surely kill
him; thy hand shall be first upon him to
put him to death, and afterwards the hand
of all the people. 11. And thou shalt stone
him with stones, that he die; because he
hath sought to draw thee away from the
LORD thy God, who brought thee out of the
land of Egypt, out of the house of bondage.
12. And all Israel shall hear, and fear, and
shall do no more any such wickedness as
this is in the midst of thee. ¶ 13. If thou
shalt hear tell concerning one of thy cities,
which the LORD thy God giveth thee to
dwell there, saying: 14. 'Certain base
fellows are gone out from the midst of thee,
and have drawn away the inhabitants of
their city, saying: Let us go and serve other
gods, which ye have not known'; 15. then
shalt thou inquire, and make search, and ask
diligently; and, behold, if it be truth, and
the thing certain, that such abomination
is wrought in the midst of thee; 16. thou
shalt surely smite the inhabitants of that
city with the edge of the sword, destroying
it utterly, and all that is therein and the
cattle thereof, with the edge of the sword.
17. And thou shalt gather all the spoil of it
into the midst of the broad place thereof,
and shalt burn with fire the city, and all
the spoil thereof every whit, unto the LORD
thy God; and it shall be a heap for ever;
it shall not be built again. 18. And there

סְבִיבֹתֵיכֶם הַקְּרֹבִים אֵלֶיךָ אוֹ הָרְחֹקִים מִמֶּךָּ מִקְצֵה
9 הָאָרֶץ וְעַד־קְצֵה הָאָרֶץ׃ לֹא־תֹאבֶה לוֹ וְלֹא תִשְׁמַע אֵלָיו
י וְלֹא־תָחוֹס עֵינְךָ עָלָיו וְלֹא־תַחְמֹל וְלֹא־תְכַסֶּה עָלָיו׃ כִּי
הָרֹג תַּהַרְגֶנּוּ יָדְךָ תִּהְיֶה־בּוֹ בָרִאשׁוֹנָה לַהֲמִיתוֹ וְיַד כָּל־
11 הָעָם בָּאַחֲרֹנָה׃ וּסְקַלְתּוֹ בָאֲבָנִים וָמֵת כִּי בִקֵּשׁ לְהַדִּיחֲךָ
מֵעַל יְהוָה אֱלֹהֶיךָ הַמּוֹצִיאֲךָ מֵאֶרֶץ מִצְרַיִם מִבֵּית עֲבָדִים׃
12 וְכָל־יִשְׂרָאֵל יִשְׁמְעוּ וְיִרָאוּן וְלֹא־יוֹסִפוּ לַעֲשׂוֹת כַּדָּבָר
13 הָרָע הַזֶּה בְּקִרְבֶּךָ׃ ס כִּי־תִשְׁמַע בְּאַחַת עָרֶיךָ אֲשֶׁר
14 יְהוָה אֱלֹהֶיךָ נֹתֵן לְךָ לָשֶׁבֶת שָׁם לֵאמֹר׃ יָצְאוּ אֲנָשִׁים
בְּנֵי־בְלִיַּעַל מִקִּרְבֶּךָ וַיַּדִּיחוּ אֶת־יֹשְׁבֵי עִירָם לֵאמֹר נֵלְכָה
טו וְנַעַבְדָה אֱלֹהִים אֲחֵרִים אֲשֶׁר לֹא־יְדַעְתֶּם׃ וְדָרַשְׁתָּ
וְחָקַרְתָּ וְשָׁאַלְתָּ הֵיטֵב וְהִנֵּה אֱמֶת נָכוֹן הַדָּבָר נֶעֶשְׂתָה
16 הַתּוֹעֵבָה הַזֹּאת בְּקִרְבֶּךָ׃ הַכֵּה תַכֶּה אֶת־יֹשְׁבֵי הָעִיר
הַהִוא לְפִי־חָרֶב הַחֲרֵם אֹתָהּ וְאֶת־כָּל־אֲשֶׁר־בָּהּ וְאֶת־
17 בְּהֶמְתָּהּ לְפִי־חָרֶב׃ וְאֶת־כָּל־שְׁלָלָהּ תִּקְבֹּץ אֶל־תּוֹךְ
רְחֹבָהּ וְשָׂרַפְתָּ בָאֵשׁ אֶת־הָעִיר וְאֶת־כָּל־שְׁלָלָהּ כָּלִיל
18 לַיהוָה אֱלֹהֶיךָ וְהָיְתָה תֵּל עוֹלָם לֹא תִבָּנֶה עוֹד׃ וְלֹא־

9. *consent.* 'With the belief of the heart' (Ibn Ezra); *i.e.* thou mayest not let thyself be convinced by what he says, even if thou stop short of doing what he desires.

nor hearken unto him. By actual worship of other gods.

conceal him. By silence.

10. *thou shalt surely kill him.* Not that one is to take the law into his own hand, but that the would-be seducer must stand his trial and be condemned by a court.

thy hand shall be first. In the public infliction of the death penalty, according to XVII, 7. The convicting witness must bear the initial responsibility of the act, cost him what sorrow it may.

Jewish history does not record a single instance of punishment for religious seduction by false prophet or member of one's family.

13–19. A City Tainted with Idolatry

13. *shalt hear.* The news must come to them; they are not to go on a heresy hunt.

14. *if . . . base fellows.* Or, 'If thou shalt hear tell, that, in one of the cities which the LORD thy God giveth thee to dwell there, certain base fellows.'

base fellows. Heb. 'sons of Belial,' *i.e.* 'sons of worthlessness'; the term repeatedly used in Scripture for abandoned criminals, *base* in word, thought, and action.

are gone out. Of set purpose to seduce their brethren.

15. *inquire.* Careful investigation had to be made, because the rumour must be thoroughly tested before action is taken.

the thing certain. The story is substantiated.

16. *destroying it utterly.* See on XX, 17.

17. *broad place.* The market-place.

a heap. Or, 'mound.' Heb. *tel;* cf. Josh. VI, 17, 26.

18. *cleave nought of the devoted thing to thy hand.* The punishment of idolaters must not be made a *profitable* occupation. This prohibition was disregarded by the medieval Church.

shall cleave nought of the devoted thing to thy hand, that the LORD may turn from the fierceness of His anger, and show thee mercy, and have compassion upon thee, and multiply thee, as He hath sworn unto thy fathers; 19. when thou shalt hearken to the voice of the LORD thy God, to keep all His commandments which I command thee this day, to do that which is right in the eyes of the LORD thy God.*iv.

יִדְבַּק בְּיָדְךָ מְאוּמָה מִן־הַחֵרֶם לְמַעַן יָשׁוּב יְהוָה מֵחֲרוֹן
אַפּוֹ וְנָתַן־לְךָ רַחֲמִים וְרִחַמְךָ וְהִרְבֶּךָ כַּאֲשֶׁר נִשְׁבַּע
19 לַאֲבֹתֶיךָ׃ כִּי תִשְׁמַע בְּקוֹל יְהוָה אֱלֹהֶיךָ לִשְׁמֹר אֶת־
כָּל־מִצְוֺתָיו אֲשֶׁר אָנֹכִי מְצַוְּךָ הַיּוֹם לַעֲשׂוֹת הַיָּשָׁר בְּעֵינֵי
יְהוָה אֱלֹהֶיךָ׃ ס רביעי

14 CHAPTER XIV

CAP. XIV. יד

1. Ye are the children of the LORD your God: ye shall not cut yourselves, nor make any baldness between your eyes for the dead. 2. For thou art a holy people unto the LORD thy God, and the LORD hath chosen thee to be His own treasure out of all

א בָּנִים אַתֶּם לַיהוָה אֱלֹהֵיכֶם לֹא תִתְגֹּדְדוּ וְלֹא־תָשִׂימוּ
2 קָרְחָה בֵּין עֵינֵיכֶם לָמֵת׃ כִּי עַם קָדוֹשׁ אַתָּה לַיהוָה
אֱלֹהֶיךָ וּבְךָ בָּחַר יְהוָה לִהְיוֹת לוֹ לְעַם סְגֻלָּה מִכֹּל

Both secular princes and the Inquisition confiscated the possession of heretics. Persecution became more frequent because of the plunder that accompanied it (Guttmann).

Deut. XIII, 13–19 has had a curious history, both in the Synagogue and in the Church. In the Synagogue, it was maintained that this law was not to be carried out, even if only one *mezuzah* were found in the tainted city, as the destruction of the city would involve the cardinal sin of destroying the Name of God inscribed on that *mezuzah*: cf. on XII, 4. Some Rabbis declare, **עיר הנדחת לא היתה ולא עתידה להיות**, 'The case here described, *viz.* the destruction of a city tainted with idolatry, never occurred, nor was likely to occur.' This section, they said in effect, was only added to the Torah for the sake of deepening the understanding of the vital necessity of resisting all temptation to idolatry. This view was not shared by the Church. Deut. XIII, 13–19 was embodied in the Canon Law; and the ghastly records of medieval persecution show that it was not construed as a mere warning against idolatry. In the year 1097, when the Crusaders arrived at Pelagonia in Macedon, and learned that the inhabitants of the town were 'heretics', they paused in their pilgrimage to the Holy Sepulchre, conquered the city, razed it to the ground, and put all its inhabitants to the sword. Again, at the beginning of the thirteenth century, Crusaders annihilated the 20,000 Albigenses, men, women, and children, who had fled to Beziers, in Southern France. Not one was spared. (Lea, *History of the Inquisition in the Middle Ages*, I, pp. 107, 154.)

(*d*) LAWS OF HOLINESS

(CHAPTERS XIV–XV)

The opening words of this chapter are introductory to the regulations following. There being a close kinship between God and Israel, His people were subject to special regulations that would distinguish them from other nations and constantly remind them of the duty of holiness.

XIV, 1–2. AGAINST HEATHEN RITES

1. *ye are the children of the LORD.* Cf. Exod. IV, 22.

'Many ancient nations believed in their descent from gods and demi-gods. But the relation was conceived physically. In the Hebrew Scriptures however, God's fatherhood and Israel's sonship are historical and ethical, and based on God's love, deliverance, and providence' (G. A. Smith). According to the interpretation of Rabbi Judah, the people of Israel were only *children of the LORD* so long as they conformed to the Divine will, and they forfeited the honour when they were disobedient; but Rabbi Meir maintained that, whether their conduct was filial or unfilial, they could never cease being *children of the LORD*.

cut yourselves. As a sign of mourning; see I Kings XVIII, 28. The Israelites were not to gash themselves in their grief: firstly, because any deliberate disfigurement of the body was forbidden; and secondly, because as 'children of God' they were to regard a bereavement as His decree, and, therefore, something to be accepted with resignation. The Sifri gives a homiletic interpretation to the Heb. **לא תתגדדו**; 'Ye shall not cut yourselves up into factions'; *i.e.* a holy people must be a united people (**לא תעשו אגודות אגודות**).

nor make any baldness. This disfigurement was likewise a heathen mourning custom, the hair being sometimes buried with the corpse as an offering to the dead. In Lev. XXI, 5 a similar prohibition had been addressed to the priests; in Deut. the law is given a wider application, in order to embrace the whole of the people who were 'a kingdom of priests'.

between your eyes. i.e. on your forehead, as in VI, 8.

2. *a holy people.* See on VII, 6.

peoples that are upon the face of the earth. ¶ 3. Thou shalt not eat any abominable thing. 4. These are the beasts which ye may eat: the ox, the sheep, and the goat, 5. the hart, and the gazelle, and the roebuck, and the wild goat, and the pygarg, and the antelope, and the mountain-sheep. 6. And every beast that parteth the hoof, and hath the hoof wholly cloven in two, and cheweth the cud, among the beasts, that ye may eat. 7. Nevertheless these ye shall not eat of them that only chew the cud, or of them that only have the hoof cloven: the camel, and the hare, and the rock-badger, because they chew the cud but part not the hoof, they are unclean unto you; 8. and the swine, because he parteth the hoof but cheweth not the cud, he is unclean unto you; of their flesh ye shall not eat, and their carcasses ye shall not touch. ¶ 9. These ye may eat of all that are in the waters: whatsoever hath fins and scales may ye eat; 10. and whatsoever hath not fins and scales ye shall not eat; it is unclean unto you. ¶ 11. Of all clean birds ye may eat. 12. But these are they of which ye shall not eat: the great vulture, and the bearded vulture, and the ospray; 13. and the glede, and the falcon, and the kite after its kinds; 14. and every raven after its kinds; 15. and the ostrich, and the night-hawk, and the sea-mew, and the hawk after its kinds; 16. the little owl, and the great owl, and the horned owl; 17. and the pelican, and the carrion-vulture, and the cormorant; 18. and the stork, and the heron after its kinds,

3 הָעַמִּים אֲשֶׁר עַל־פְּנֵי הָאֲדָמָה׃ ס לֹא תֹאכַל כָּל־
4 תּוֹעֵבָה׃ זֹאת הַבְּהֵמָה אֲשֶׁר תֹּאכֵלוּ שׁוֹר שֵׂה כְשָׂבִים
ה 6 וְשֵׂה עִזִּים׃ אַיָּל וּצְבִי וְיַחְמוּר וְאַקּוֹ וְדִישֹׁן וּתְאוֹ וָזָמֶר׃ וְכָל־
בְּהֵמָה מַפְרֶסֶת פַּרְסָה וְשֹׁסַעַת שֶׁסַע שְׁתֵּי פְרָסוֹת מַעֲלַת
7 גֵּרָה בַּבְּהֵמָה אֹתָהּ תֹּאכֵלוּ׃ אַךְ אֶת־זֶה לֹא תֹאכְלוּ
מִמַּעֲלֵי הַגֵּרָה וּמִמַּפְרִיסֵי הַפַּרְסָה הַשְּׁסוּעָה אֶת־הַגָּמָל
וְאֶת־הָאַרְנֶבֶת וְאֶת־הַשָּׁפָן כִּי־מַעֲלֵה גֵרָה הֵמָּה וּפַרְסָה
8 לֹא הִפְרִיסוּ טְמֵאִים הֵם לָכֶם׃ וְאֶת־הַחֲזִיר כִּי־מַפְרִיס
פַּרְסָה הוּא וְלֹא גֵרָה טָמֵא הוּא לָכֶם מִבְּשָׂרָם לֹא תֹאכֵלוּ
9 וּבְנִבְלָתָם לֹא תִגָּעוּ׃ ס אֶת־זֶה תֹּאכְלוּ מִכֹּל אֲשֶׁר
י בַּמָּיִם כֹּל אֲשֶׁר־לוֹ סְנַפִּיר וְקַשְׂקֶשֶׂת תֹּאכֵלוּ׃ וְכֹל אֲשֶׁר
אֵין־לוֹ סְנַפִּיר וְקַשְׂקֶשֶׂת לֹא תֹאכֵלוּ טָמֵא הוּא לָכֶם׃ ס
11 12 כָּל־צִפּוֹר טְהֹרָה תֹּאכֵלוּ׃ וְזֶה אֲשֶׁר לֹא־תֹאכְלוּ מֵהֶם
13 הַנֶּשֶׁר וְהַפֶּרֶס וְהָעָזְנִיָּה׃ וְהָרָאָה וְאֶת־הָאַיָּה וְהַדַּיָּה לְמִינָהּ׃
14 טו וְאֵת כָּל־עֹרֵב לְמִינוֹ׃ וְאֵת בַּת הַיַּעֲנָה וְאֶת־הַתַּחְמָס וְאֶת־
16 הַשָּׁחַף וְאֶת־הַנֵּץ לְמִינֵהוּ׃ אֶת־הַכּוֹס וְאֶת־הַיַּנְשׁוּף
17 18 וְהַתִּנְשָׁמֶת׃ וְהַקָּאָת וְאֶת־הָרָחָמָה וְאֶת־הַשָּׁלָךְ׃ וְהַחֲסִידָה

3–20. Clean and Unclean Beasts, Fishes and Birds

The twofold purpose of the dietary laws is clearly defined. In the first place, Israel is to be 'holy', *i.e.* distinct, marked off from the other peoples; and these laws powerfully served to maintain the separateness of Israel. In the second place, the creatures which are forbidden are described as 'abominable things'—in themselves loathsome and undesirable as articles of diet; see Introductory Note on Lev. XI, p. 448.

In Deut. we have something more than a mere repetition; there is just the kind of exposition which is appropriate to the circumstances of Moses' farewell to his people.

4. *the ox, the sheep, the goat.* In Lev. XI, we merely have the general classification given in *v.* 6 of this chapter of forbidden animals, with mention of some. Here the animals are named that may be eaten.

5. *the hart . . . mountain-sheep.* Seven varieties of game.

pygarg. Better, *antelope.*

antelope. Better, *wild-ox.*

6. *that parteth . . . cud.* For an explanation of these distinctive features in animals, see on Lev. XI, 3.

7. *these ye shall not eat.* This and the following *v.* correspond to Lev. XI, 4–8.

9. *in the waters.* The law with regard to fishes is slightly abridged here as compared with Lev. XI, 9 f.

11–20. Of birds. Only the unclean are here named. In Lev. XI, these are mentioned in a slightly different order.

13. *glede.* This bird is not mentioned in Lev. XI, 14. According to the Talmud, all the names in this *v.* refer to the same bird, which was known under different designations.

20. *clean winged things.* In Lev. XI, 21 f, a distinction is drawn between 'winged creeping things that go upon all four' and those that do not—the former class being prohibited as food. According to Sifri, the phrase 'clean winged things' corresponds to the permitted 'winged creeping things' in Leviticus; and the unclean species alluded to in the preceding *v.* is the same prohibited kind mentioned in Lev. XI, 23.

and the hoopoe, and the bat. 19. And all winged swarming things are unclean unto you; they shall not be eaten. 20. Of all clean winged things ye may eat. ¶ 21. Ye shall not eat of any thing that dieth of itself; thou mayest give it unto the stranger that is within thy gates, that he may eat it; or thou mayest sell it unto a foreigner; for thou art a holy people unto the LORD thy God. Thou shalt not seethe a kid in its mother's milk.*v. ¶ 22. Thou shalt surely tithe all the increase of thy seed, that which is brought forth in the field year by year. 23. And thou shalt eat before the LORD thy God, in the place which He shall choose to cause His name to dwell there, the tithe of thy corn, of thy wine, and of thine oil, and the firstlings of thy herd and of thy flock; that thou mayest learn to fear the LORD thy God always. 24. And if the way be too long for thee, so that thou art not able to carry it, because the place is too far from thee, which the LORD thy God shall choose to set His name there, when the LORD thy God shall bless thee; 25. then shalt thou turn it into money, and bind up the money in thy hand, and shalt go unto the place which the LORD thy God shall choose. 26. And thou shalt bestow the money for whatsoever thy soul desireth, for oxen, or for sheep, or for wine, or for

19 וְהָאֲנָפָה לְמִינָהּ וְהַדּוּכִיפַת וְהָעֲטַלֵּף׃ וְכֹל שֶׁרֶץ הָעוֹף טָמֵא
כ 21 הוּא לָכֶם לֹא יֵאָכֵלוּ׃ כָּל־עוֹף טָהוֹר תֹּאכֵלוּ׃ לֹא תֹאכְלוּ
כָל־נְבֵלָה לַגֵּר אֲשֶׁר־בִּשְׁעָרֶיךָ תִּתְּנֶנָּה וַאֲכָלָהּ אוֹ מָכֹר
לְנָכְרִי כִּי עַם קָדוֹשׁ אַתָּה לַיהוָה אֱלֹהֶיךָ לֹא־תְבַשֵּׁל גְּדִי
בַּחֲלֵב אִמּוֹ׃ * פ חמישי
22 עַשֵּׂר תְּעַשֵּׂר אֵת כָּל־תְּבוּאַת זַרְעֶךָ הַיֹּצֵא הַשָּׂדֶה שָׁנָה
23 שָׁנָה׃ וְאָכַלְתָּ לִפְנֵי ׀ יְהוָה אֱלֹהֶיךָ בַּמָּקוֹם אֲשֶׁר־יִבְחַר
לְשַׁכֵּן שְׁמוֹ שָׁם מַעְשַׂר דְּגָנְךָ תִּירֹשְׁךָ וְיִצְהָרֶךָ וּבְכֹרֹת
בְּקָרְךָ וְצֹאנֶךָ לְמַעַן תִּלְמַד לְיִרְאָה אֶת־יְהוָה אֱלֹהֶיךָ כָּל־
24 הַיָּמִים׃ וְכִי־יִרְבֶּה מִמְּךָ הַדֶּרֶךְ כִּי לֹא תוּכַל שְׂאֵתוֹ
כִּי־יִרְחַק מִמְּךָ הַמָּקוֹם אֲשֶׁר יִבְחַר יְהוָה אֱלֹהֶיךָ לָשׂוּם
כה שְׁמוֹ שָׁם כִּי יְבָרֶכְךָ יְהוָה אֱלֹהֶיךָ׃ וְנָתַתָּה בַּכָּסֶף וְצַרְתָּ
הַכֶּסֶף בְּיָדְךָ וְהָלַכְתָּ אֶל־הַמָּקוֹם אֲשֶׁר יִבְחַר יְהוָה
26 אֱלֹהֶיךָ בּוֹ׃ וְנָתַתָּה הַכֶּסֶף בְּכֹל אֲשֶׁר־תְּאַוֶּה נַפְשְׁךָ בַּבָּקָר

21. *anything that dieth of itself.* Heb. נבלה; the true meaning of this Heb. term seems to be 'the carcase of an animal which has not been killed according to the method of Shechitah' (Hoffmann). It would thus include not only an animal which died a natural death, but one which has been put to death by shooting.

the stranger. According to Lev. XVII, 15, touching or eating the flesh of a *nevelah* is defiling both to the Israelite and the 'stranger'. In Lev. the 'stranger' meant the non-Israelite who had become a proselyte in the full sense of the word, a *ger tzedek*. Here the 'stranger that is within thy gates' refers to the time when Israel would be settled in their Land and would have in their midst not only proselytes, but also men who while they had abandoned idolatry did not completely take upon themselves the life and religious practices of the Israelite. The Rabbis called this class of resident aliens *ger toshav;* and this *v.* refers to that class, who were neither Israelites by birth or conversion, nor 'foreigners'. See p. 256.

thou shalt not seethe. See on Exod. XXIII, 19.

22–29. TITHES

A tenth of all the yearly produce shall be set aside, taken to the Sanctuary, and eaten there. This tenth is the so-called 'second tithe', as contrasted with the tithe of the produce that was to be given for the maintenance of the Levites; Num. XVIII, 26 f.

22. *all the increase of thy seed.* This is defined in the next *v.* as including corn, wine, and oil.

year by year. The tithe must be computed upon the produce of each year separately.

23. *before the LORD. i.e.* at the Central Sanctuary.

to fear the LORD thy God. The Biblical phrase for being filled with the sense of dependence upon God. And that was the purpose of bidding the Israelite eat this tithe in the Holy City. It would impress upon him the thought that the year's produce was the bounty of God. Furthermore, 'inasmuch as the man and his household would not be likely to consume the whole of the tithe, he would be compelled to give part away in charity' (Maimonides).

24–27. Israelites who dwell too far from the Sanctuary may turn their tithe into money, purchase at the Temple what they desire, and feast before God with their households and Levites.

26. *for strong drink.* Heb. שכר. 'The attempt is sometimes made to argue that the juice of the vine praised or prescribed in Scripture is never an intoxicating liquor. That is clearly contradicted here' (G. A. Smith).

strong drink, or for whatsoever thy soul asketh of thee; and thou shalt eat there before the LORD thy God, and thou shalt rejoice, thou and thy household. 27. And the Levite that is within thy gates, thou shalt not forsake him; for he hath no portion nor inheritance with thee. ¶ 28. At the end of every three years, even in the same year, thou shalt bring forth all the tithe of thine increase, and shalt lay it up within thy gates. 29. And the Levite, because he hath no portion nor inheritance with thee, and the stranger, and the fatherless, and the widow, that are within thy gates, shall come, and shall eat and be satisfied; that the LORD thy God may bless thee in all the work of thy hand which thou doest.*vi.

15

CHAPTER XV

1. At the end of every seven years thou shalt make a release. 2. And this is the manner of the release: every creditor shall release that which he hath lent unto his neighbour; he shall not exact it of his neighbour and

וּבַצֹּאן וּבַיַּיִן וּבַשֵּׁכָר וּבְכֹל אֲשֶׁר תִּשְׁאָלְךָ נַפְשֶׁךָ וְאָכַלְתָּ
27 שָּׁם לִפְנֵי יְהוָה אֱלֹהֶיךָ וְשָׂמַחְתָּ אַתָּה וּבֵיתֶךָ׃ וְהַלֵּוִי
אֲשֶׁר־בִּשְׁעָרֶיךָ לֹא תַעַזְבֶנּוּ כִּי אֵין לוֹ חֵלֶק וְנַחֲלָה עִמָּךְ׃
28 ס מִקְצֵה ׀ שָׁלֹשׁ שָׁנִים תּוֹצִיא אֶת־כָּל־מַעְשַׂר תְּבוּאָתְךָ
29 בַּשָּׁנָה הַהִוא וְהִנַּחְתָּ בִּשְׁעָרֶיךָ׃ וּבָא הַלֵּוִי כִּי אֵין־לוֹ חֵלֶק
וְנַחֲלָה עִמָּךְ וְהַגֵּר וְהַיָּתוֹם וְהָאַלְמָנָה אֲשֶׁר בִּשְׁעָרֶיךָ וְאָכְלוּ
וְשָׂבֵעוּ לְמַעַן יְבָרֶכְךָ יְהוָה אֱלֹהֶיךָ בְּכָל־מַעֲשֵׂה יָדְךָ אֲשֶׁר
תַּעֲשֶׂה׃ * ס ששי

טו

CAP. XV. טו

א 2 מִקֵּץ שֶׁבַע־שָׁנִים תַּעֲשֶׂה שְׁמִטָּה׃ וְזֶה דְּבַר הַשְּׁמִטָּה
שָׁמוֹט כָּל־בַּעַל מַשֵּׁה יָדוֹ אֲשֶׁר יַשֶּׁה בְּרֵעֵהוּ לֹא־יִגֹּשׂ

27. *the Levite.* Cf. XII, 12, 19.

28–29. THE POOR TITHE

This was due in the third and sixth years of the Sabbatical period instead of the second tithe, which, or its equivalent in money, had to be consumed in Jerusalem. In those years, what would have been the Second Tithe is to be retained at home for the poor to consume. The third year is called 'the year of the tithing' in XXVI, 12.

28. *at the end of.* This is not quite the same word as in XV, 1. It rather denotes, 'towards the end of'; *i.e.* after the harvest is gathered in.

all the tithe. Both the first tithe and the second tithe.

shalt lay it up. i.e. place it at the disposal of the Levite and the poor.

29. *and the Levite.* He is to take the first tithe which is due to him; Num. XVIII, 21.

stranger, and the fatherless, and the widow. They are all destitute, and receive the poor tithe.

and be satisfied. On application being made by a destitute person, he must be granted sufficient for his needs.

may bless thee. The purpose of the poor tithe was to teach the salutary doctrine that man's possessions are only truly blessed when he permits others to join with him in their enjoyment. Self-indulgence, without a thought for those in need of assistance, brings no lasting satisfaction; and such a mode of living is without blessing.

CHAPTER XV

THE YEAR OF RELEASE

Every seventh year shall be a year of remission for all debts; this however shall not operate as a motive for refusing loans. Likewise, the seventh year of the individual's service brought freedom to the Hebrew bondman, with liberal parting gifts from his master.

1–11. OF DEBTS

1. *at the end of every seven years.* It is possible that these words signify 'when each seventh year has arrived'; cf. Jer. XXXIV, 14 (see p. 323), where 'at the end of seven years' clearly means, 'in the seventh year.' See, however, comment on next *v.*

a release. Heb. *shemittah.* This 'release' took two forms. (1) The soil was not to be sown; see Exod. XXIII, 10 f, and Lev. XXV, 2 f. (2) The remission of loans.

2. *not exact it of his neighbour.* Or, 'he shall not press his neighbour for payment.' The Jewish traditional view is that the Year of Release in regard to debts does not come into operation until the *end* of the seventh year. This law was intended for an agricultural community, in which each family had its homestead. A debt would only be contracted in case of misfortune. The loan was, therefore, an act of charity, rather than a business transaction. Circumstances had altered altogether when economic life became more complex and people engaged in commerce. Debts contracted in the course of trading belonged to quite a different category, and this law could not fairly be invoked his brother; because the LORD's release hath been proclaimed. 3. Of a foreigner thou mayest exact it; but whatsoever of thine is with thy brother thy hand shall release. 4. Howbeit there shall be no needy among you—for the LORD will surely bless thee in the land which the LORD thy God giveth thee for an inheritance to possess it—5. if only thou diligently hearken unto the voice of the LORD thy God, to observe to do all this commandment which I command thee this day. 6. For the LORD thy God will bless thee, as He promised thee; and thou shalt lend unto many nations, but thou shalt not borrow; and thou shalt rule over many nations, but they shall not rule over thee. ¶ 7. If there be among you a needy man, one of thy brethren, within any of thy gates, in thy land which the LORD thy God giveth thee, thou shalt not harden thy heart, nor shut thy hand from thy needy brother; 8. but thou shalt surely open thy hand unto him, and shalt surely lend him sufficient for his

3 אֶת־רֵעֵהוּ וְאֶת־אָחִיו כִּי־קָרָא שְׁמִטָּה לַיהוָה׃ אֶת־הַנָּכְרִי
4 תִּגֹּשׂ וַאֲשֶׁר יִהְיֶה לְךָ אֶת־אָחִיךָ תַּשְׁמֵט יָדֶךָ׃ אֶפֶס כִּי
לֹא יִהְיֶה־בְּךָ אֶבְיוֹן כִּי־בָרֵךְ יְבָרֶכְךָ יְהוָה בָּאָרֶץ אֲשֶׁר
ה יְהוָה אֱלֹהֶיךָ נֹתֵן־לְךָ נַחֲלָה לְרִשְׁתָּהּ׃ רַק אִם־שָׁמוֹעַ
תִּשְׁמַע בְּקוֹל יְהוָה אֱלֹהֶיךָ לִשְׁמֹר לַעֲשׂוֹת אֶת־כָּל־הַמִּצְוָה
6 הַזֹּאת אֲשֶׁר אָנֹכִי מְצַוְּךָ הַיּוֹם׃ כִּי־יְהוָה אֱלֹהֶיךָ בֵּרַכְךָ
כַּאֲשֶׁר דִּבֶּר־לָךְ וְהַעֲבַטְתָּ גּוֹיִם רַבִּים וְאַתָּה לֹא תַעֲבֹט
7 וּמָשַׁלְתָּ בְּגוֹיִם רַבִּים וּבְךָ לֹא יִמְשֹׁלוּ׃ ס כִּי־יִהְיֶה
בְךָ אֶבְיוֹן מֵאַחַד אַחֶיךָ בְּאַחַד שְׁעָרֶיךָ בְּאַרְצְךָ אֲשֶׁר־
יְהוָה אֱלֹהֶיךָ נֹתֵן לָךְ לֹא תְאַמֵּץ אֶת־לְבָבְךָ וְלֹא תִקְפֹּץ
8 אֶת־יָדְךָ מֵאָחִיךָ הָאֶבְיוֹן׃ כִּי־פָתֹחַ תִּפְתַּח אֶת־יָדְךָ לוֹ

for their cancellation. Consequently in the first century of the present era, Hillel instituted a method whereby the operation of the year of release did not affect debts that had been delivered to the Court before the intervention of the year of release. Without actually handing over the bond or promissory note to the Court, the creditor could secure his debt against forfeiture by appearing before the Beth Din, and making the declaration, 'I announce unto you, judges of this Court, that I shall collect any debt which I may have outstanding with N.N., whenever I desire.' This institution was known as Prosbul.

brother. *i.e.* fellow-Israelite.

the LORD'S release . . . proclaimed. Better, *a release hath been proclaimed unto the LORD; i.e.* in His honour, as the bestower of all wealth and increase (Ibn Ezra).

3. *a foreigner.* Heb. *nochri;* to be distinguished from the *ger* (x, 19). The 'foreigner' merely visits Canaan temporarily, for trade. He is not, like the Israelite (Exod. XXIII, 10 f), under the obligation of surrendering the produce of his land every seventh year; there is, therefore, no reason in his case for any relaxation of his creditor's claims (Driver). It should be noted that the Torah does not declare that the creditor must exact payment; he *may* do so, if he wish.

thy hand shall release. lit. 'let thy hand release.' The Rabbis understood this to mean that payment could not be claimed; but, if the debtor voluntarily offered it, it may be accepted.

4. *needy among you.* This expresses an ideal which would only be realized if the condition of obedience in *v.* 5 were fulfilled. There is thus no contradiction with the statement in *v.* 11, 'the poor shall never cease out of the land.'

6. *as He promised thee.* See VII, 13; Exod. XXIII, 25; Lev. XXVI, 3 f.

thou shalt lend. This is, like *v.* 4 above, a conditional promise that was as unlikely to become actual as the ideal of 'there shall be no poor with thee'. The Israelites began to engage in commerce in the days of King Solomon. Isa. II, 7 and Hos. XII, 8 testify to considerable foreign trade in the long reigns of Uzziah and Jeroboam II. Of later times, the Greek geographer Strabo writes: 'These Jews have penetrated to every city, and it would not be easy to find a single place in the inhabited world which has not received this race, and where it has not become master.' Through no fault of their own, Jews were divorced from agriculture and confined to commerce for over 1,500 years. However, commerce is not their native bent, as is evidenced by the fact that, in recent generations, leadership has almost everywhere been wrested from them by the non-Jewish newcomers in industrial and financial enterprise; see p. 814.

7–11. The Israelite is warned against letting the approach of the Year of Release hinder him from helping his needy brother.

7. *within any of thy gates. i.e.* in one of thy cities (cf. XII, 12); and the Sifri bases therein the rule, 'The poor of thine own city should be helped before those of another city.'

in thy land. The Sifri similarly explains that one must assist the poor in the Holy Land before helping an Israelite who dwelt outside Palestine.

need in that which he wanteth. 9. Beware that there be not a base thought in thy heart, saying: 'The seventh year, the year of release, is at hand'; and thine eye be evil against thy needy brother, and thou give him nought; and he cry unto the LORD against thee, and it be sin in thee. 10. Thou shalt surely give him, and thy heart shall not be grieved when thou givest unto him; because that for this thing the LORD thy God will bless thee in all thy work, and in all that thou puttest thy hand unto. 11. For the poor shall never cease out of the land; therefore I command thee, saying: 'Thou shalt surely open thy hand unto thy poor and needy brother, in thy land.' ¶ 12. If thy brother, a Hebrew man, or a Hebrew woman, be sold unto thee, he shall serve thee six years; and in the seventh year thou shalt let him go free from thee. 13. And when thou lettest him go free from thee, thou shalt not let him go empty; 14. thou shalt furnish him liberally out of thy flock, and out of thy threshing-floor, and out of thy winepress; of that wherewith the LORD thy God hath blessed thee thou shalt give unto him. 15. And thou shalt remember that thou wast a bondman in the land of Egypt, and the LORD thy God redeemed thee; therefore I command thee this thing to-day. 16. And it shall be, if he say unto thee: 'I will not go out from

9 וְהַעֲבֵט תַּעֲבִיטֶנּוּ דֵּי מַחְסֹרוֹ אֲשֶׁר יֶחְסַר לוֹ׃ הִשָּׁמֶר לְךָ
פֶּן־יִהְיֶה דָבָר עִם־לְבָבְךָ בְלִיַּעַל לֵאמֹר קָרְבָה שְׁנַת־
הַשֶּׁבַע שְׁנַת הַשְּׁמִטָּה וְרָעָה עֵינְךָ בְּאָחִיךָ הָאֶבְיוֹן וְלֹא
י תִתֵּן לוֹ וְקָרָא עָלֶיךָ אֶל־יְהוָה וְהָיָה בְךָ חֵטְא׃ נָתוֹן תִּתֵּן
לוֹ וְלֹא־יֵרַע לְבָבְךָ בְּתִתְּךָ לוֹ כִּי בִּגְלַל ׀ הַדָּבָר הַזֶּה
11 יְבָרֶכְךָ יְהוָה אֱלֹהֶיךָ בְּכָל־מַעֲשֶׂךָ וּבְכֹל מִשְׁלַח יָדֶךָ׃ כִּי
לֹא־יֶחְדַּל אֶבְיוֹן מִקֶּרֶב הָאָרֶץ עַל־כֵּן אָנֹכִי מְצַוְּךָ לֵאמֹר
פָּתֹחַ תִּפְתַּח אֶת־יָדְךָ לְאָחִיךָ לַעֲנִיֶּךָ וּלְאֶבְיֹנְךָ בְּאַרְצֶךָ׃ ס
12 כִּי־יִמָּכֵר לְךָ אָחִיךָ הָעִבְרִי אוֹ הָעִבְרִיָּה וַעֲבָדְךָ שֵׁשׁ שָׁנִים
13 וּבַשָּׁנָה הַשְּׁבִיעִת תְּשַׁלְּחֶנּוּ חָפְשִׁי מֵעִמָּךְ׃ וְכִי־תְשַׁלְּחֶנּוּ
14 חָפְשִׁי מֵעִמָּךְ לֹא תְשַׁלְּחֶנּוּ רֵיקָם׃ הַעֲנֵיק תַּעֲנִיק לוֹ
מִצֹּאנְךָ וּמִגָּרְנְךָ וּמִיִּקְבֶךָ אֲשֶׁר בֵּרַכְךָ יְהוָה אֱלֹהֶיךָ תִּתֶּן
טו לוֹ׃ וְזָכַרְתָּ כִּי עֶבֶד הָיִיתָ בְּאֶרֶץ מִצְרַיִם וַיִּפְדְּךָ יְהוָה
16 אֱלֹהֶיךָ עַל־כֵּן אָנֹכִי מְצַוְּךָ אֶת־הַדָּבָר הַזֶּה הַיּוֹם׃ וְהָיָה

9. *thine eye be evil. i.e.* refuse to assist, assuming that the loan will not be refunded.

he cry unto the LORD. God hears the cry of those who are hardly treated; cf. Exod. XXII, 22.

10. *thy heart shall not be grieved. i.e.* the loan must not be made in a grudging spirit; cf. Prov. XIX, 17, 'He that is gracious unto the poor lendeth unto the LORD, and his good deed will He repay unto him.'

11. *for the poor shall never cease.* See on *v.* 4 above.

12–18. THE RELEASE OF SLAVES

A man's misfortune may be so overwhelming that he could not save himself by a loan. To avoid destitution, a Hebrew might sell himself temporarily; *i.e.* become a member of another's household, and earn his food and shelter by his labour. The 'slavery' of the Bible was in no way identical with what was understood by that term in Greece or Rome. The master had many obligations towards the bondman, and the infliction of bodily injury by the master secured the bondman his immediate freedom; see p. 537.

In the seventh year of service the bondman goes free and his master is required at the time of the emancipation liberally to supply the new freedman with an equipment that shall enable him to begin life again with some confidence for the future. This provision is characteristic of the humaneness and philanthropy of the Torah in regard to the bondman.

12. *Hebrew woman.* This is an addition to the law as stated in Exod. XXI, 1–6, and decrees that the same treatment is to be meted out to a man and woman. Exod. XXI, 7 f refers to a different set of circumstances.

be sold. The Heb. could also mean 'sell himself'. According to the Talmud, Scripture here speaks of the case where a person is sold by the court of law because he had committed a burglary and could not repay what he had stolen; Exod. XXII, 2.

14. *liberally.* The compliance with this command must be more than sour obedience of the letter of the law.

out of thy flock . . . winepress. The freed slave is thus to be helped to make a fresh start in life. This principle (הענקה) has become part of Jewish social ethics.

15. *land of Egypt.* Let him remember that he owes his own freedom to the Divine grace; cf. XVI, 12.

16. *I will not go out.* On this and the following verse, see on Exod. XXI, 5 f.

thee'; because he loveth thee and thy house, because he fareth well with thee; 17. then thou shalt take an awl, and thrust it through his ear and into the door, and he shall be thy bondman for ever. And also unto thy bondwoman thou shalt do likewise. 18. It shall not seem hard unto thee, when thou lettest him go free from thee; for to the double of the hire of a hireling hath he served thee six years; and the LORD thy God will bless thee in all that thou doest.*vii. ¶ 19. All the firstling males that are born of thy herd and of thy flock thou shalt sanctify unto the thy LORD God; thou shalt do no work with the firstling of thine ox, nor shear the firstling of thy flock. 20. Thou shalt eat it before the LORD thy God year by year in the place which the LORD shall choose, thou and thy household. 21. And if there be any blemish therein, lameness, or blindness, any ill blemish whatsoever, thou shalt not sacrifice it unto the LORD thy God. 22. Thou shalt eat it within thy gates; the unclean and the clean may eat it alike, as the gazelle, and as the hart. 23. Only thou shalt not eat the blood thereof; thou shalt pour it out upon the ground as water.

כִּֽי־יֹאמַר אֵלֶיךָ לֹא אֵצֵא מֵעִמָּךְ כִּי אֲהֵבְךָ וְאֶת־בֵּיתֶךָ
17 כִּי־טוֹב לוֹ עִמָּךְ׃ וְלָקַחְתָּ אֶת־הַמַּרְצֵעַ וְנָתַתָּה בְאָזְנוֹ
וּבַדֶּלֶת וְהָיָה לְךָ עֶבֶד עוֹלָם וְאַף לַאֲמָתְךָ תַּעֲשֶׂה־כֵּן׃
18 לֹא־יִקְשֶׁה בְעֵינֶךָ בְּשַׁלֵּחֲךָ אֹתוֹ חָפְשִׁי מֵעִמָּךְ כִּי מִשְׁנֶה
שְׂכַר שָׂכִיר עֲבָדְךָ שֵׁשׁ שָׁנִים וּבֵרַכְךָ יְהוָה אֱלֹהֶיךָ בְּכֹל
אֲשֶׁר תַּעֲשֶׂה׃ * פ שביעי
19 כָּל־הַבְּכוֹר אֲשֶׁר יִוָּלֵד בִּבְקָרְךָ וּבְצֹאנְךָ הַזָּכָר תַּקְדִּישׁ
לַיהוָה אֱלֹהֶיךָ לֹא תַעֲבֹד בִּבְכֹר שׁוֹרֶךָ וְלֹא תָגֹז בְּכוֹר
כ צֹאנֶךָ׃ לִפְנֵי יְהוָה אֱלֹהֶיךָ תֹאכְלֶנּוּ שָׁנָה בְשָׁנָה בַּמָּקוֹם
21 אֲשֶׁר־יִבְחַר יְהוָה אַתָּה וּבֵיתֶךָ׃ וְכִי־יִהְיֶה בוֹ מוּם פִּסֵּחַ
22 אוֹ עִוֵּר כֹּל מוּם רָע לֹא תִזְבָּחֶנּוּ לַיהוָה אֱלֹהֶיךָ׃ בִּשְׁעָרֶיךָ
23 תֹּאכְלֶנּוּ הַטָּמֵא וְהַטָּהוֹר יַחְדָּו כַּצְּבִי וְכָאַיָּל׃ רַק אֶת־דָּמוֹ
לֹא תֹאכֵל עַל־הָאָרֶץ תִּשְׁפְּכֶנּוּ כַּמָּיִם׃ פ

17. *also unto thy bondwoman.* The comment of the Sifri is: 'This refers back to the injunction, *thou shalt furnish him liberally* (*v.* 14). Thou mightest say it refers to "thou shalt take an awl, and thrust it through the ear"; therefore the Torah states "and it shall be, if *he* say unto thee"; *he*, not *she*.' Accordingly, the female slave had to leave in the seventh year, and was not subjected to the rule of having the ear bored.

18. *for to the double.* The master gets double value out of a slave of this kind as compared with a hireling, *i.e.* a day-labourer; the slave being a member of the household, the master could get work done by him at night as well as by day.

19–23. OF FIRSTLINGS

This paragraph, dealing with the firstlings of the cattle, should have followed on XIV, 22–29, the law of the tithe. But the last verses which mentioned the 'poor tithe' suggested the subject of the treatment of the poor which occupied this chapter up to this point.

19. *all the firstling males.* For the idea of consecrating the firstborn, see on Exod. XIII, 2.

20. *year by year. i.e.* the offering must not be delayed beyond a year. This is not at variance with what was stated in Exod. XXII, 29 'on the eighth day thou shalt give it Me', for the Mechilta explains that to mean, from the eighth day onwards; cf. Lev. XXII, 27.

21. *be any blemish.* The law of the firstlings is also dealt with in Lev. XXVII, 26, where it is forbidden to sanctify the firstling by using it as an offering for any other purpose. Also in Num. XVIII, 17 f, where the flesh of the firstlings is declared to be the priest's. The words, 'Thou shalt eat it before the LORD,' in this section refer to the person who is entitled to eat it; *i.e.* the priest, as is prescribed in Numbers. As Deut. is a continuation of the preceding Books of the Pentateuch, it was obvious to Moses' hearers who it was that were to eat the firstling, since it had already been ordained and well understood (Hoffmann).

CHAPTER XVI

(*e*) THE THREE PILGRIMAGE FESTIVALS

The law concerning the three annual pilgrimages to the Temple has already been given in Exod. XXIII, 14 f; XXXIV, 18 f; Lev. XXIII, 4 f; and Num. XXVIII, 16 f. What distinguishes the statement of the law in Deut. is the emphasis upon the Central Sanctuary at which all Israel must gather on these Festivals. These Pilgrimage-Feasts had a double signification. They each had reference to a historical event of national importance, but they also marked the three seasons of the agricultural year. 'It is well to keep in view the agricultural aspect of the Three Festivals. It helps us to realize the fact that Israel was once an agricultural people and that its commercial character is not, as is commonly

16

CHAPTER XVI

1. Observe the month of Abib, and keep the passover unto the LORD thy God; for in the month of Abib the LORD thy God brought thee forth out of Egypt by night. 2. And thou shalt sacrifice the passover-offering unto the LORD thy God, of the flock and the herd, in the place which the LORD shall choose to cause His name to dwell there. 3. Thou shalt eat no leavened bread with it; seven days shalt thou eat unleavened bread therewith, even the bread of affliction; for in haste didst thou come forth out of the land of Egypt; that thou mayest remember the day when thou camest forth out of the land of Egypt all the days of thy life. 4. And there shall be no leaven seen with thee in all thy borders seven days; neither shall any of the flesh, which thou sacrificest the first day at even, remain all night until the morning. 5. Thou mayest not sacrifice the passover-offering within any of thy gates, which the LORD thy God giveth thee; 6. but at the place which the LORD thy God shall choose to cause His name to dwell in, there thou shalt sacrifice

טז

CAP. XVI. טז

א שָׁמוֹר אֶת־חֹדֶשׁ הָאָבִיב וְעָשִׂיתָ פֶּסַח לַיהוָה אֱלֹהֶיךָ כִּי
בְּחֹדֶשׁ הָאָבִיב הוֹצִיאֲךָ יְהוָה אֱלֹהֶיךָ מִמִּצְרַיִם לָיְלָה׃
2 וְזָבַחְתָּ פֶּסַח לַיהוָה אֱלֹהֶיךָ צֹאן וּבָקָר בַּמָּקוֹם אֲשֶׁר יִבְחַר
3 יְהוָה לְשַׁכֵּן שְׁמוֹ שָׁם׃ לֹא־תֹאכַל עָלָיו חָמֵץ שִׁבְעַת יָמִים
תֹּאכַל־עָלָיו מַצּוֹת לֶחֶם עֹנִי כִּי בְחִפָּזוֹן יָצָאתָ מֵאֶרֶץ
מִצְרַיִם לְמַעַן תִּזְכֹּר אֶת־יוֹם צֵאתְךָ מֵאֶרֶץ מִצְרַיִם כֹּל
4 יְמֵי חַיֶּיךָ׃ וְלֹא־יֵרָאֶה לְךָ שְׂאֹר בְּכָל־גְּבֻלְךָ שִׁבְעַת יָמִים
וְלֹא־יָלִין מִן־הַבָּשָׂר אֲשֶׁר תִּזְבַּח בָּעֶרֶב בַּיּוֹם הָרִאשׁוֹן
ה לַבֹּקֶר׃ לֹא תוּכַל לִזְבֹּחַ אֶת־הַפָּסַח בְּאַחַד שְׁעָרֶיךָ אֲשֶׁר־
6 יְהוָה אֱלֹהֶיךָ נֹתֵן לָךְ׃ כִּי אִם־אֶל־הַמָּקוֹם אֲשֶׁר־יִבְחַר

thought, inborn, but is the result of the unkindly conditions in later ages. It is good for us and for the world at large to remember that the history of our race has its idyllic side' (M. Joseph).

1–8. THE PASSOVER

1. *the month of Abib.* lit. 'of the green ears of corn'; later known as Nisan.

by night. In Num. XXXIII, 3 it is mentioned, 'on the morrow after the passover, the children of Israel went out.' The deliverance took place during the night (Exod. XII, 31), though the Exodus itself did not begin until the break of the day following the Passover-offering.

2. *and thou shalt sacrifice.* As a token of gratitude for God's mercies.

of the flock and the herd. In Exod. XII, 3 f it is ordained that a lamb was to be used as the Paschal offering; but that restriction was for that special occasion only, not for the perennial observance to be carried out in the Temple. Another explanation is that the lamb was for the Paschal sacrifice, and the ox for the Festival-sacrifice (חגיגה). This is confirmed by what is narrated in II Chron. XXXV, 7 f. In *v.* 13 of that chapter, it is stated that the lambs, which were the Passover-offering, 'they roasted with fire according to the ordinance'; and the oxen, which were 'the holy offerings', were boiled—this being forbidden with the Paschal sacrifice, but allowed with the Festival-sacrifice.

3. *with it. i.e.* with the Paschal offering.

therewith. The whole period of abstinence from leaven is treated as conditioned by the sacrifice of the Passover immediately preceding, and regulated by the same principle established in the first instance for the Passover.

the bread of affliction. So-called because the bread was prepared while the people were in a state of stress and hardship, consequent upon their hasty departure from Egypt (Exod. XII, 34, 39). There is, of course, an obvious association of ideas with servitude in Egypt.

in haste. That alone would make it impossible for the Israelites to think that they had gained their liberty by the might of their hand.

4. *no leaven.* See Exod. XII, 19.

with thee. This is not the traditional Jewish interpretation, which requires the rendering 'of thine'. 'The leaven which belongs to thee thou mayest not see, *i.e.* have in possession; but thou mayest see that which belongs to others' (Sifri).

the first day at even. This means the evening which commences the first day; *i.e.* on the 14th of Nisan. The words 'at even' are not to be understood as signifying that the sacrifice was offered at night, but rather 'towards the evening'.

until the morning. Of the second day of the Festival (the 16th of Nisan), the prohibition to apply also to the Festival-sacrifice (חגיגה).

5. *within any of thy gates.* The law is repeated because the Israelite might think that he should exactly copy the procedure on the fateful night of the release, when each householder had to slay the lamb at the entrance of his house, and stain the door-posts with blood.

the passover-offering at even, at the going down of the sun, at the season that thou camest forth out of Egypt. 7. And thou shalt roast and eat it in the place which the LORD thy God shall choose; and thou shalt turn in the morning, and go unto thy tents. 8. Six days thou shalt eat unleavened bread; and on the seventh day shall be a solemn assembly to the LORD thy God; thou shalt do no work therein. ¶ 9. Seven weeks shalt thou number unto thee; from the time the sickle is first put to the standing corn shalt thou begin to number seven weeks. 10. And thou shalt keep the feast of weeks unto the LORD thy God after the measure of the freewill-offering of thy hand, which thou shalt give, according as the LORD thy God blesseth thee. 11. And thou shalt rejoice before the LORD thy God, thou, and thy son, and thy daughter, and thy man-servant, and thy maid-servant, and the Levite that is within thy gates, and the stranger, and the fatherless, and the widow, that are in the midst of thee, in the place which the LORD thy God shall choose to cause His name to dwell there. 12. And

יְהוָה אֱלֹהֶיךָ לְשַׁכֵּן שְׁמוֹ שָׁם תִּזְבַּח אֶת־הַפֶּסַח בָּעָרֶב
7 כְּבוֹא הַשֶּׁמֶשׁ מוֹעֵד צֵאתְךָ מִמִּצְרָיִם׃ וּבִשַּׁלְתָּ וְאָכַלְתָּ
בַּמָּקוֹם אֲשֶׁר יִבְחַר יְהוָה אֱלֹהֶיךָ בּוֹ וּפָנִיתָ בַבֹּקֶר וְהָלַכְתָּ
8 לְאֹהָלֶיךָ׃ שֵׁשֶׁת יָמִים תֹּאכַל מַצּוֹת וּבַיּוֹם הַשְּׁבִיעִי עֲצֶרֶת
9 לַיהוָה אֱלֹהֶיךָ לֹא תַעֲשֶׂה מְלָאכָה׃ ס שִׁבְעָה שָׁבֻעֹת
תִּסְפָּר־לָךְ מֵהָחֵל חֶרְמֵשׁ בַּקָּמָה תָּחֵל לִסְפֹּר שִׁבְעָה
י שָׁבֻעוֹת׃ וְעָשִׂיתָ חַג שָׁבֻעוֹת לַיהוָה אֱלֹהֶיךָ מִסַּת נִדְבַת
11 יָדְךָ אֲשֶׁר תִּתֵּן כַּאֲשֶׁר יְבָרֶכְךָ יְהוָה אֱלֹהֶיךָ׃ וְשָׂמַחְתָּ
לִפְנֵי ׀ יְהוָה אֱלֹהֶיךָ אַתָּה וּבִנְךָ וּבִתֶּךָ וְעַבְדְּךָ וַאֲמָתֶךָ
וְהַלֵּוִי אֲשֶׁר בִּשְׁעָרֶיךָ וְהַגֵּר וְהַיָּתוֹם וְהָאַלְמָנָה אֲשֶׁר
בְּקִרְבֶּךָ בַּמָּקוֹם אֲשֶׁר יִבְחַר יְהוָה אֱלֹהֶיךָ לְשַׁכֵּן שְׁמוֹ

7. *in the morning.* Of the 16th of Nisan.
go unto thy tents. *i.e.* return home; or, to the temporary dwellings of the pilgrims in Jerusalem (Ehrlich).

8. *six days.* In *v.* 3 and Exod. XIII, 6 f, the command is to eat unleavened bread for seven days. There are several methods of reconciling the two statements. The most obvious is to connect *v.* 8 with what immediately precedes. After leaving the Holy City, unleavened bread is to be eaten for six more days. The Rabbis deduce from the passages that the eating of unleavened bread is obligatory on the first day of the Festival only; on the six other days, the Israelite may not eat that which is leavened, but he is not compelled to eat unleavened bread. He would not contravene the law, if, *e.g.*, he subsisted on fruit.
on the seventh day. Of the Passover Festival.
Passover is the greatest of all the historical festivals, at once the starting-point of Israel's national life and a well-spring of its religious ideas. In the Biblical age, we find the Passover celebrated with especial solemnity at important epochs in the national life; such as the religious revivals which marked the reign of pious kings, like Hezekiah, II Chron. XXX, and Josiah, II Chron. XXXV.

9–12. THE FEAST OF WEEKS

9. *from the time the sickle.* See on Lev. XXIII, 15.

10. *the feast of weeks.* Heb. *Shavuos.* In Exod. XXIII, 16 it is called 'the feast of harvest', and in Num. XXVIII, 26 'the day of the first-fruits', alluding to its agricultural aspect. In the Liturgy it is described as זמן מתן תורתנו 'the Season of the Giving of our Torah', *viz.* the Revelation at Sinai. It is thus both a nature and a historical festival; see pp. 318 and 521.

freewill-offering. *i.e.* with a gift adequate to the ability of the offerer. On Passover, the Israelite's offering was prescribed; but on the Feast of Weeks, each pilgrim offered what he felt disposed to give.

11. *thou shalt rejoice.* Cf. XII, 12, XIV, 29. 'It is a man's duty to be joyful and glad at heart on the festivals, he and his wife and his children and those dependent upon him. Make the children happy by giving them sweets and nuts; and the womenfolk by buying them frocks and jewellery according to your means. It is also a duty to give food to the hungry, to the fatherless, and to the widow, as well as to other poor people' (Shulchan Aruch).

12. *a bondman in Egypt.* 'It was with the view that thou shouldest do these statutes, that I redeemed thee from Egypt' (Rashi).
Unlike Passover and Tabernacles, the Feast of Weeks has no distinctive ceremony. In many rites, the Book of Ruth, presenting a charming picture of agricultural life in ancient Palestine, is

thou shalt remember that thou wast a bondman in Egypt; and thou shalt observe and do these statutes.*m. ¶ 13. Thou shalt keep the feast of tabernacles seven days, after that thou hast gathered in from thy threshing-floor and from thy winepress. 14. And thou shalt rejoice in thy feast, thou, and thy son, and thy daughter, and thy man-servant, and thy maid-servant, and the Levite, and the stranger, and the fatherless, and the widow, that are within thy gates. 15. Seven days shalt thou keep a feast unto the LORD thy God in the place which the LORD shall choose; because the LORD thy God shall bless thee in all thine increase, and in all the work of thy hands, and thou shalt be altogether joyful. 16. Three times in a year shall all thy males appear before the LORD thy God in the place which He shall choose: on the feast of unleavened bread, and on the feast of

12 שָׁם׃ וְזָכַרְתָּ כִּי־עֶבֶד הָיִיתָ בְּמִצְרָיִם וְשָׁמַרְתָּ וְעָשִׂיתָ אֶת־
הַחֻקִּים הָאֵלֶּה׃ * פ מפטיר
13 חַג הַסֻּכֹּת תַּעֲשֶׂה לְךָ שִׁבְעַת יָמִים בְּאָסְפְּךָ מִגָּרְנְךָ
14 וּמִיִּקְבֶךָ׃ וְשָׂמַחְתָּ בְּחַגֶּךָ אַתָּה וּבִנְךָ וּבִתֶּךָ וְעַבְדְּךָ וַאֲמָתֶךָ
טו וְהַלֵּוִי וְהַגֵּר וְהַיָּתוֹם וְהָאַלְמָנָה אֲשֶׁר בִּשְׁעָרֶיךָ׃ שִׁבְעַת
יָמִים תָּחֹג לַיהוָה אֱלֹהֶיךָ בַּמָּקוֹם אֲשֶׁר־יִבְחַר יְהוָה כִּי
יְבָרֶכְךָ יְהוָה אֱלֹהֶיךָ בְּכֹל תְּבוּאָתְךָ וּבְכֹל מַעֲשֵׂה יָדֶיךָ
16 וְהָיִיתָ אַךְ שָׂמֵחַ׃ שָׁלוֹשׁ פְּעָמִים ׀ בַּשָּׁנָה יֵרָאֶה כָל־זְכוּרְךָ
אֶת־פְּנֵי ׀ יְהוָה אֱלֹהֶיךָ בַּמָּקוֹם אֲשֶׁר יִבְחָר בְּחַג הַמַּצּוֹת

v. 16. קמץ בז״ק

read. In many congregations it is also customary to spend the first night of Shavuos in reading selections from the Torah and the Prophets, as well as from Rabbinic literature. The special book of service for this purpose is known as *Tikkun leyl Shavuos*. A more universal custom is to decorate the synagogues with flowers and plants on this Festival; see p. 521. On Shavuos, the Jewish child was first initiated into the study of the Jewish religion and the Hebrew Language.

13–15. FEAST OF TABERNACLES

13. *feast of tabernacles.* The name is explained in Lev. XXIII, 42. It is called 'Feast of Ingathering' in Exod. XXIII, 16, XXXIV, 22.

tabernacle. Is here used in the sense given by Dr. Johnson, 'casual dwelling.'

15. *seven days.* It is noteworthy that the Torah does not add here the observance of Shemini Atzeres, the eighth day of solemn assembly, as in Lev. XXIII, 36. But it is evident that this chapter does not aim at giving a list of all the special days, and that is why there is no mention here of the New Year and Day of Atonement. Its purpose is to describe the three occasions in the year when the Israelite must make a pilgrimage to the Temple (see the summary in the next *v.*). The reason for the omission of Shemini Atzeres is perhaps to be sought in the fact that it was considered 'a separate Festival' שמיני רגל בפני עצמו, and the Israelite was not commanded to make the pilgrimage specially for this eighth day. Being in the Holy City for Tabernacles, he remains there until after Atzeres.

altogether joyful. Since this Festival marked the reaping of the fruits of the year's toil, it was an occasion of great rejoicing. It is sometimes referred to as '*the* Festival', *par excellence.*

'Joyous worship has always been the keynote of the festival of Tabernacles. In Temple days, the priests, with Lulav and Ethrog, went round the Altar in procession to the sound of the Shofar, chanting, 'Save now, I beseech thee, O LORD: O LORD, I beseech thee, send now prosperity' (Ps. CXVIII, 25). The ceremony which appears to have aroused the greatest enthusiasm was the Drawing of water. The Mishnah tells us, 'He that hath not beheld the joy of the Drawing of water hath never seen joy in his life.' There were torch dances by men of piety and renown, and songs and hymns by Levites and people to the accompaniment of flutes, harps, and cymbals.

'The latest feature in the development of the Festival is the festive character given to the last day (*Simchas Torah*), as marking the occasion of the completion and recommencement of the reading of the Law. In the Middle Ages, it became customary to take all the Scrolls from the Ark and to bear them in procession round the Synagogue. Anxious as Jewish parents have always been to stimulate their children's love and interest in their religion, they made it essentially a Children's festival. In some synagogues, children were called to the reading of the Law. Fruits and sweets were distributed amongst them.

'And thus, in ever-changing surroundings, the note of joy in the festival of Tabernacles can be heard through all the centuries; now as the rejoicing over the harvest, now as the joy of Temple-worship, and now again in triumphant homage to the Law, Israel's inalienable birthright, "whence with joy he draws water out of the wells of salvation" ' (H. M. Adler).

16. *three times in a year.* This *v.* occurs substantially in Exod. XXIII, 14–17 and XXXIV, 23.

empty. i.e. without offerings.

weeks, and on the feast of tabernacles; and they shall not appear before the LORD empty; 17. every man shall give as he is able, according to the blessing of the LORD thy God which He hath given thee.

וּבְחַג הַשָּׁבֻעוֹת וּבְחַג הַסֻּכּוֹת וְלֹא יֵרָאֶה אֶת־פְּנֵי יְהוָה
17 רֵיקָם׃ אִישׁ כְּמַתְּנַת יָדוֹ כְּבִרְכַּת יְהוָה אֱלֹהֶיךָ אֲשֶׁר נָתַן־לָךְ׃

HAFTORAH RE'EH הפטרת ראה

ISAIAH LIV, 11–LV, 5

CHAPTER LIV

11. O thou afflicted, tossed with tempest,
And not comforted,
Behold, I will set thy stones in fair colours,
And lay thy foundations with sapphires.

12. And I will make thy pinnacles of rubies,
And thy gates of carbuncles,
And all thy border of precious stones.

13. And all thy children shall be taught of the LORD;
And great shall be the peace of thy children.

14. In righteousness shalt thou be established;
Be thou far from oppression, for thou shalt not fear,
And from ruin, for it shall not come near thee.

15. Behold, they may gather together, but not by Me;
Whosoever shall gather together against thee shall fall because of thee.

CAP. LIV. נד

11 עֲנִיָּה סֹעֲרָה
לֹא נֻחָמָה הִנֵּה אָנֹכִי מַרְבִּיץ בַּפּוּךְ אֲבָנַיִךְ וִיסַדְתִּיךְ
12 בַּסַּפִּירִים׃ וְשַׂמְתִּי כַּדְכֹד שִׁמְשֹׁתַיִךְ וּשְׁעָרַיִךְ לְאַבְנֵי אֶקְדָּח
13 וְכָל־גְּבוּלֵךְ לְאַבְנֵי־חֵפֶץ׃ וְכָל־בָּנַיִךְ לִמּוּדֵי יְהוָה וְרַב
14 שְׁלוֹם בָּנָיִךְ׃ בִּצְדָקָה תִּכּוֹנָנִי רַחֲקִי מֵעֹשֶׁק כִּי־לֹא תִירָאִי
טו וּמִמְּחִתָּה כִּי לֹא־תִקְרַב אֵלָיִךְ׃ הֵן גּוֹר יָגוּר אֶפֶס מֵאוֹתִי
16 מִי־גָר אִתָּךְ עָלַיִךְ יִפּוֹל׃ הִן* אָנֹכִי בָּרָאתִי חָרָשׁ נֹפֵחַ
בְּאֵשׁ פֶּחָם וּמוֹצִיא כְלִי לְמַעֲשֵׂהוּ וְאָנֹכִי בָּרָאתִי מַשְׁחִית

16. Behold, I have created the smith
That bloweth the fire of coals,
And bringeth forth a weapon for his work;
And I have created the waster to destroy.

נד׳ v. 16. הנה ק׳

This is the third of the Haftorahs of Consolation. Its central promise is: 'No weapon that is formed against thee shall prosper; and every tongue that shall rise against thee in judgment thou shalt condemn.' The fulfilment of this promise is dependent on Israel's right choice in regard to the Two Ways, 'Behold I set before you this day a blessing and a curse,' with which the Sidrah opens.

11–17. OUTER AND INNER SPLENDOUR OF ZION

13. *all thy children shall be taught of the LORD.* Or, 'all thy children shall be disciples of the LORD.' Zion's peace will be based not on armed force, but on the God-fearing lives of all its inhabitants. In some ancient manuscripts the second word for 'thy children' (*banayich*) in this verse was read as *bonavich*, 'thy builders.' This proclaims a wonderful truth: the *children* of a nation are the *builders* of its future. And every Jewish child must be reared to become such a builder of his People's better future. This verse ('All thy children shall be taught of the LORD') is an important landmark in the history of civilization. In obedience to it, Israel led the way in universal education. Thus, in his *History of the World*, H. G. Wells records, 'The Jewish religion, because it was a literature-sustained religion, led to the first efforts to provide elementary instruction for all the children of the community.'

14. *be thou far from oppression.* Be steadfast in righteousness, and panic ('terror') shall not touch thee.

15. *not by Me.* All those who now stir up strife with thee shall shatter themselves against thee.

17. No weapon that is formed against thee shall prosper;
And every tongue that shall rise against thee in judgment thou shalt condemn.
This is the heritage of the servants of the LORD,
And their due reward from Me, saith the LORD.

CHAPTER LV

1. Ho, every one that thirsteth, come ye for water,
And he that hath no money;
Come ye, buy, and eat;
Yea, come, buy wine and milk
Without money and without price.
2. Wherefore do ye spend money for that which is not bread?
And your gain for that which satisfieth not?
Hearken diligently unto Me, and eat ye that which is good,
And let your soul delight itself in fatness.
3. Incline your ear, and come unto Me;
Hear, and your soul shall live;
And I will make an everlasting covenant with you,
Even the sure mercies of David.
4. Behold, I have given him for a witness to the peoples,
A prince and commander to the peoples.
5. Behold, thou shalt call a nation that thou knowest not,

17 לְחַבֵּל׃ כָּל־כְּלִי יוּצַר עָלַיִךְ לֹא יִצְלָח וְכָל־לָשׁוֹן תָּקוּם־
אִתָּךְ לַמִּשְׁפָּט תַּרְשִׁיעִי זֹאת נַחֲלַת עַבְדֵי יְהוָה וְצִדְקָתָם
מֵאִתִּי נְאֻם־יְהוָה׃

CAP. LV. נה

א הוֹי כָּל־צָמֵא לְכוּ לַמַּיִם וַאֲשֶׁר אֵין־לוֹ כָּסֶף לְכוּ שִׁבְרוּ
וֶאֱכֹלוּ וּלְכוּ שִׁבְרוּ בְּלוֹא־כֶסֶף וּבְלוֹא מְחִיר יַיִן וְחָלָב׃
2 לָמָּה תִשְׁקְלוּ־כֶסֶף בְּלוֹא־לֶחֶם וִיגִיעֲכֶם בְּלוֹא לְשָׂבְעָה
שִׁמְעוּ שָׁמוֹעַ אֵלַי וְאִכְלוּ־טוֹב וְתִתְעַנַּג בַּדֶּשֶׁן נַפְשְׁכֶם׃
3 הַטּוּ אָזְנְכֶם וּלְכוּ אֵלַי שִׁמְעוּ וּתְחִי נַפְשְׁכֶם וְאֶכְרְתָה
4 לָכֶם בְּרִית עוֹלָם חַסְדֵי דָוִד הַנֶּאֱמָנִים׃ הֵן עֵד לְאוּמִּים
ה נְתַתִּיו נָגִיד וּמְצַוֵּה לְאֻמִּים׃ הֵן גּוֹי לֹא־תֵדַע תִּקְרָא וְגוֹי
לֹא־יְדָעוּךָ אֵלֶיךָ יָרוּצוּ לְמַעַן יְהוָה אֱלֹהַיִךְ וְלִקְדוֹשׁ יִשְׂרָאֵל
כִּי פֵאֲרָךְ׃

And a nation that knew not thee shall run unto thee;
Because of the LORD thy God,
And for the Holy One of Israel, for He hath glorified thee.

נר׳ v. 17. קמץ בז״ק נה׳ v. 4. דגש אחר שורק

17. Israel's vindication in history is assured: neither might nor malice can destroy the Servant of the LORD.

condemn. Overthrow in argument.

this. *i.e.* no weapon forged against Israel shall succeed.

the servants. The worshippers.

their due reward. lit. their righteousness which is of me. צדקה means both 'righteousness' (*i.e.* holiness of life in the individual) and 'victory' (*i.e.* the triumph of right in the world).

CHAPTER LV. THE RETURN TO ZION SHOULD ALSO BE A RETURN TO GOD

1. A call to rich and poor alike to participate in the blessings of the new era, by coming to the Source whence the knowledge of duty springs—the word of God. The cry is like that of the water-carrier in Eastern cities, and blessings are expressed in Oriental imagery, in terms of quickening water, nourishing milk, and gladdening wine. 'One cannot fail to perceive the note of wistfulness in the appeal, suggestive of the dread of an unspeakable disappointment' (Elmslie-Skinner).

2. Why spend time and labour and money on material pursuits that cannot in the end satisfy the soul created for holiness and righteousness?

fatness. Spiritual well-being. Its contrast is 'leanness of soul', Ps. CVI, 15.

3. *the sure mercies of David.* The new covenant shall be the fulfilment of the promise that the Davidic Kingdom would endure; II Sam. VII, 8–16.

4. *I have given him.* David, or the representative of David's family. Zerubbabel, the leader of the returning exiles, was a descendant of David.

5. *thou shalt call.* A return to the description of the unconscious influence which Israel's loyalty to his Divinely-appointed mission is sure to effect.

6 18. Judges and officers shalt thou make thee in all thy gates, which the LORD thy God giveth thee, tribe by tribe; and they shall judge the people with righteous judgment. 19. Thou shalt not wrest judgment; thou shalt not respect persons; neither shalt thou take a gift; for a gift doth blind the eyes of the wise, and pervert the words of the righteous. 20. Justice, justice shalt thou follow, that thou mayest live, and inherit the

טז   ס ס ס מח 48

18 שֹׁפְטִים וְשֹׁטְרִים תִּתֶּן־לְךָ בְּכָל־שְׁעָרֶיךָ אֲשֶׁר יְהוָה אֱלֹהֶיךָ
19 נֹתֵן לְךָ לִשְׁבָטֶיךָ וְשָׁפְטוּ אֶת־הָעָם מִשְׁפַּט־צֶדֶק׃ לֹא־
תַטֶּה מִשְׁפָּט לֹא תַכִּיר פָּנִים וְלֹא־תִקַּח שֹׁחַד כִּי הַשֹּׁחַד
כ יְעַוֵּר עֵינֵי חֲכָמִים וִיסַלֵּף דִּבְרֵי צַדִּיקִם׃ צֶדֶק צֶדֶק

V. SHOFETIM

(CHAPTERS XVI, 18–XXI, 9)

(2) GOVERNMENT OF THE PEOPLE (CHAPTERS XVI, 18–XVIII)

This section defines the status of judges, the king, the priests and prophets—all of them officers of the Hebrew commonwealth.

(*a*) JUDGES AND JUSTICE

18–20. Provision is to be made for an ordered civil government. Justice must be free, accessible, and absolutely impartial; cf. II Chronicles XIX, 5–11.

18. *judges.* Local lay magistrates.

tribe by tribe. i.e. in every town of each tribe.

with righteous judgment. The judges must be both competent and impartial, and are not to be appointed for social or family reasons; see I, 13.

19. *thou.* These commands are in the singular, as though they were an exhortation to each judge individually (Ibn Ezra).

wrest. Pervert; cf. Exod. XXIII, 6.

respect persons. The Heb. idiom for 'showing partiality'; cf. Lev. XIX, 15. Absolute fairness must be shown in the order of the hearing of the cases, whether the case involve a small sum or a large sum, whether the litigant be rich or poor. The Rabbis, however, ruled that an exception be made in the suit of an orphan, whose case must always be heard first; next in order, that of a widow; furthermore, that a woman's cause must be heard before that of a man. The judge is to give everyone a patient and courteous hearing. He is warned against yielding to the subtle temptation of giving an unjust judgment *out of pity to the poor.* 'The judge shall not say, "This man is poor and his opponent is rich, and it is the duty of the latter to help him in his need. I shall therefore decide against the rich man, and thereby cause the poor man to be helped without the taint of almsgiving." Nor shall the judge say, "How can I put this rich man to shame in public, on account of a paltry sum? I shall acquit him now, but shall tell him afterwards to make good the amount" ' (Talmud); see on Exod. XXIII, 3.

a gift. A bribe. The acceptance of any gift by a judge is forbidden; see XXVII, 25. In the East, that judge was regarded as still a just judge who took gifts only from the party in the right. But judicial venality is not unknown in Western lands. The absolutely honest intention to accord justice to all is, even in England, only a recent attainment.

blind the eyes. To the facts of the case and their true bearings; and the judge will find it impossible not to seek to justify the giver of the bribe (Talmud).

words of the righteous. Of men who otherwise would be righteous. Some translate 'cause' instead of *words;* in that case, *righteous* means, 'those who are in the right,' the innocent.

JUSTICE, JUSTICE SHALT THOU FOLLOW

20. *justice, justice.* Or 'that which is altogether just'; or, 'justice, and only justice.' Heb. צדק צדק תרדף. The duplication of the word 'justice', brings out with the greatest possible emphasis the supreme duty of even-handed justice to all. 'Justice, whether to your profit or loss, whether in word or in action, whether to Jew or non-Jew' (Bachya ben Asher). A Chassidic rabbi explained this insistence on 'justice, and only justice' to imply, 'Do not use *unjust* means to secure the victory of justice'—a deep saying. Man is slow to realize that justice is strong enough, Divine enough, to triumph without itself resorting to injustice. In the eyes of the Prophets, justice was a Divine, irresistible force. Isaiah, for example, uses only one word (צדקה) to designate both 'justice' and 'victory' (*i.e.* the triumph of right in the world); see p. 819.

Justice, justice shalt thou follow. These passionate words, may be taken as the keynote of the humane legislation of the Torah, and of the demand for social righteousness by Israel's Prophets, Psalmists and Sages. 'Let justice

תִּרְדֹּף לְמַעַן תִּחְיֶה וְיָרַשְׁתָּ אֶת־הָאָרֶץ אֲשֶׁר־יְהוָה אֱלֹהֶיךָ
21 נֹתֵן לָךְ׃ ס לֹא־תִטַּע לְךָ אֲשֵׁרָה כָּל־עֵץ אֵצֶל מִזְבַּח

land which the LORD thy God giveth thee.
¶ 21. Thou shalt not plant thee an Asherah of any kind of tree beside the altar of the LORD thy God, which thou shalt make thee.

roll down as waters, and righteousness as a mighty stream,' is the cry of Amos. Justice is not the only ethical quality in God or man, nor is it the highest quality; but it is the basis for all the others. 'Righteousness and justice are the foundations of Thy throne,' says the Psalmist: the whole idea of the Divine rests on them.

It must be noted that the idea of justice in Hebrew thought stands for something quite other than in Greek. In Plato's *Republic*, for example, it implies a harmonious arrangement of society, by which every human peg is put into its appropriate hole, so that those who perform humble functions shall be content to perform them in due subservience to their superiors. It stresses the inequalities of human nature; whereas in the Hebrew conception of justice, the equality is stressed. To understand the idea of justice in Israel we must bear in mind the Biblical teaching that man is created in the image of God; that in every human being there is a Divine spark ; and that each human life is sacred, and of infinite worth. In consequence, a human being cannot be treated as a chattel, or a thing, but must be treated as a *personality;* and, as a personality, every human being is the possessor of the right to life, honour, and the fruits of his labour. *Justice is the awe-inspired respect for the personality of others, and their inalienable rights;* even as injustice is the most flagrant manifestation of disrespect for the personality of others (F. Adler). Judaism requires that human personality be respected in every human being—in the female heathen prisoner of war, in the delinquent, even in the criminal condemned to death. The lashes to be inflicted on the evil-doer must be strictly limited, lest 'thy brother seem vile unto thee' (xxv, 3); and, if he be found worthy of death by hanging, his human dignity must still be respected: his body is not to remain hanging over night, but must be buried the same day (xxi, 23).

It is thus seen that whereas in Greek the idea of justice was akin to harmony, in Hebrew it is akin to holiness. Isaiah (v, 16) has for all time declared האל הקדוש נקדש בצדקה, 'The Holy God is sanctified by *justice*.' In brief, where there is no justice, no proper and practical appreciation of the human rights of every human being as sons of the one and only God of righteousness—there we have a negation of religion. The oppressor, the man who tramples on others, and especially on those like the orphan and the stranger who are too weak to defend themselves, is throughout Scripture held forth as *the* enemy of God and man. The final disappearance of injustice and oppression is represented in the New Year Amidah as the goal of human history, and as synonymous with the realization of God's Kingdom on earth, וכל הרשעה כעשן תכלה כי תעביר ממשלת זדון מן הארץ.

However, justice is more than mere abstention from injuring our fellow-men. 'The work of justice is peace; and the effect thereof quietness and confidence forever' (Isa. xxxii, 17). It is a positive conception, and includes charity, philanthropy, and every endeavour to bring out what is highest and best in others. Just as 'truth' is usually preceded in Scripture by 'lovingkindness' (חסד ואמת), to remind us that the truth must be spoken *in love*; even so is 'justice' often accompanied by some synonym of 'lovingkindness' (חסד)—to teach that strict justice must, in its execution, be mitigated by pity and humanity. 'To do justly *and* to love mercy,' is the Prophet's summing up of human duty towards our fellow-men. The world could not exist if it were governed by strict justice alone (מדת הדין)—say the Rabbis; therefore, God judges His human children by justice tempered with mercy (מדת הרחמים). Such being the Jewish understanding of justice (צדקה) it is but natural that in later Hebrew that same word came to denote 'charity' exclusively.

Nor is justice limited to the relation between individuals. It extends to the relation between group and group, and it asserts the claims of the poor upon the rich, of the helpless upon them who possess the means to help. And even as there is *social* justice, prescribing the duties of class to class, so there is *international* justice, which demands respect for the personality of each and every national group, and proclaims that no people can of right be robbed of its national life or territory, its language or spiritual heritage. It is this wider recognition of justice that has called into existence the League of Nations. 'I do not know whether you are aware that the League of Nations was first of all the vision of a great Jew, almost 3,000 years ago —the prophet Isaiah' (J. C. Smuts); see Isa. ii, 1–4.

'The world owes its conception of justice to the Jew,' says an American jurist. 'God gave him to see through the things that are ever changing, the things that never change. Compared with the meaning and majesty of this achievement, every other triumph of every other people sinks into insignificance.'

thou mayest live. The pure administration of justice is thus one of the conditions of Israel's existence as a nation. Our Teachers, from the first of them to the last, brand the perversion of the course of justice, as the most alarming sign of national decay.

22. Neither shalt thou set thee up a pillar, which the LORD thy God hateth.

17 CHAPTER XVII

1. Thou shalt not sacrifice unto the LORD thy God an ox, or a sheep, wherein is a blemish, even any evil thing; for that is an abomination unto the LORD thy God. ¶ 2. If there be found in the midst of thee, within any of thy gates which the LORD thy God giveth thee, man or woman, that doeth that which is evil in the sight of the LORD thy God, in transgressing His covenant, 3. and hath gone and served other gods, and worshipped them, or the sun, or the moon, or any of the host of heaven, which I have commanded not; 4. and it be told thee, and thou hear it, then shalt thou inquire diligently, and, behold, if it be true, and the thing certain, that such abomination is wrought in Israel; 5. then shalt thou bring forth that man or that woman, who have done this evil thing, unto thy gates, even the man or the woman; and thou shalt stone them with stones, that they die. 6. At the mouth of two witnesses, or three witnesses, shall he that is to die be put to death; at the mouth of one witness he shall not be put to death. 7. The hand of the witnesses shall be first upon him to put him to death, and afterward the hand of all the people. So thou shalt put away the evil from the midst of thee. ¶ 8. If there arise a matter too hard for thee in judgment, between blood and blood, between plea and plea,

22 יְהוָה אֱלֹהֶיךָ אֲשֶׁר תַּעֲשֶׂה־לָּךְ׃ וְלֹא־תָקִים לְךָ מַצֵּבָה
אֲשֶׁר שָׂנֵא יְהוָה אֱלֹהֶיךָ׃ ס

יז CAP. XVII. יז

א לֹא־תִזְבַּח לַיהוָה אֱלֹהֶיךָ שׁוֹר וָשֶׂה אֲשֶׁר יִהְיֶה בוֹ מוּם
2 כֹּל דָּבָר רָע כִּי תוֹעֲבַת יְהוָה אֱלֹהֶיךָ הוּא׃ ס כִּי־יִמָּצֵא
בְקִרְבְּךָ בְּאַחַד שְׁעָרֶיךָ אֲשֶׁר־יְהוָה אֱלֹהֶיךָ נֹתֵן לָךְ אִישׁ
אוֹ־אִשָּׁה אֲשֶׁר יַעֲשֶׂה אֶת־הָרַע בְּעֵינֵי יְהוָה־אֱלֹהֶיךָ לַעֲבֹר
3 בְּרִיתוֹ׃ וַיֵּלֶךְ וַיַּעֲבֹד אֱלֹהִים אֲחֵרִים וַיִּשְׁתַּחוּ לָהֶם וְלַשֶּׁמֶשׁ ׀
4 אוֹ לַיָּרֵחַ אוֹ לְכָל־צְבָא הַשָּׁמַיִם אֲשֶׁר לֹא־צִוִּיתִי׃ וְהֻגַּד־
לְךָ וְשָׁמָעְתָּ וְדָרַשְׁתָּ הֵיטֵב וְהִנֵּה אֱמֶת נָכוֹן הַדָּבָר נֶעֶשְׂתָה
ה הַתּוֹעֵבָה הַזֹּאת בְּיִשְׂרָאֵל׃ וְהוֹצֵאתָ אֶת־הָאִישׁ הַהוּא אוֹ
אֶת־הָאִשָּׁה הַהִוא אֲשֶׁר עָשׂוּ אֶת־הַדָּבָר הָרָע הַזֶּה אֶל־
שְׁעָרֶיךָ אֶת־הָאִישׁ אוֹ אֶת־הָאִשָּׁה וּסְקַלְתָּם בָּאֲבָנִים וָמֵתוּ׃
6 עַל־פִּי ׀ שְׁנַיִם עֵדִים אוֹ שְׁלֹשָׁה עֵדִים יוּמַת הַמֵּת לֹא יוּמַת
7 עַל־פִּי עֵד אֶחָד׃ יַד הָעֵדִים תִּהְיֶה־בּוֹ בָרִאשֹׁנָה לַהֲמִיתוֹ
וְיַד כָּל־הָעָם בָּאַחֲרֹנָה וּבִעַרְתָּ הָרָע מִקִּרְבֶּךָ׃ פ

XVI, 21–XVII, 7. AGAINST IDOLATROUS WORSHIP

Idolatry may well be included among laws dealing with government and justice. The Jewish State, as a theocracy, was based on loyalty to God, and idolatry was regarded as high treason. There is a close connection between the commands concerning judges and idolatrous worship: 'He who appoints a judge who is unfit for his office, is as if he were to build an Asherah, a centre of heathen worship' (Talmud).

21. *Asherah.* See on VII, 5.

22. *pillar.* See on VII, 5 and Exod. XXIII, 24. *which the LORD thy God hateth.* These additional words distinguish the heathen pillars from the innocent pillars mentioned in Gen. XXVIII, 18; XXXV, 14 (Ibn Ezra, Dillmann).

CHAPTER XVII

1. The sacrificing of blemished or injured animals (XV, 21; Lev. XXII, 20–22) is a profanation of the service of God; Malachi I, 8, see p. 103.

2–7. DETECTING AND PUNISHMENT OF IDOLATRY

3. *which I have commanded not. i.e.* which I have not permitted you to worship.

4. *it be told thee . . . the thing certain.* The judges were not to act on mere report, but must institute a process of searching inquiry; see XIII, 15.

6. *two . . . witnesses.* Whose validity as witnesses is unimpeachable, and who must agree in their testimony, if the sentence is to be carried out. There was no torture of the accused to compel confession, or to exact the testimony *desired* by the Court, such as there was in Greece and in the trials of the Inquisition. A leading principle of Jewish law is, No man can by his own testimony incriminate himself in a capital charge (אין אדם משים עצמו רשע).

7. *shall be first.* On the convicting witnesses rests the duty of being first to inflict the extreme penalty with their own hands; so they would feel more seriously the responsibility of their testimony.

8–13. THE SUPREME COURT

Not a Court of Appeal, but a High Court at the Central Sanctuary for cases too hard for the local courts. Such a Court is mentioned in and between stroke and stroke, even matters of controversy within thy gates; then shalt thou arise, and get thee up unto the place which the LORD thy God shall choose. 9. And thou shalt come unto the priests the Levites, and unto the judge that shall be in those days; and thou shalt inquire; and they shall declare unto thee the sentence of judgment. 10. And thou shalt do according to the tenor of the sentence, which they shall declare unto thee from that place which the LORD shall choose; and thou shalt observe to do according to all that they shall teach thee. 11. According to the law which they shall teach thee, and according to the judgment which they shall tell thee, thou shalt do; thou shalt not turn aside from the sentence which they shall declare unto thee, to the right hand, nor to the left. 12. And the man that doeth presumptuously, in not hearkening unto the priest that standeth to minister there before the LORD thy God, or unto the judge, even that man shall die; and thou shalt exterminate the evil from Israel. 13. And all the people shall hear, and fear, and do no more presumptuously.*ii. ¶ 14. When thou art come unto the land which the LORD thy God giveth thee, and shalt possess it, and shalt dwell therein; and shalt say: 'I will set a king over me, like all the nations that are round about me';

8 כִּי יִפָּלֵא מִמְּךָ דָבָר לַמִּשְׁפָּט בֵּין־דָּם ׀ לְדָם בֵּין־דִּין לְדִין
וּבֵין נֶגַע לָנֶגַע דִּבְרֵי רִיבֹת בִּשְׁעָרֶיךָ וְקַמְתָּ וְעָלִיתָ אֶל־
9 הַמָּקוֹם אֲשֶׁר יִבְחַר יְהוָה אֱלֹהֶיךָ בּוֹ׃ וּבָאתָ אֶל־הַכֹּהֲנִים
הַלְוִיִּם וְאֶל־הַשֹּׁפֵט אֲשֶׁר יִהְיֶה בַּיָּמִים הָהֵם וְדָרַשְׁתָּ
י וְהִגִּידוּ לְךָ אֵת דְּבַר הַמִּשְׁפָּט׃ * וְעָשִׂיתָ עַל־פִּי הַדָּבָר
אֲשֶׁר יַגִּידוּ לְךָ מִן־הַמָּקוֹם הַהוּא אֲשֶׁר יִבְחַר יְהוָה וְשָׁמַרְתָּ
11 לַעֲשׂוֹת כְּכֹל אֲשֶׁר יוֹרוּךָ׃ עַל־פִּי הַתּוֹרָה אֲשֶׁר יוֹרוּךָ
וְעַל־הַמִּשְׁפָּט אֲשֶׁר־יֹאמְרוּ לְךָ תַּעֲשֶׂה לֹא תָסוּר מִן־הַדָּבָר
12 אֲשֶׁר־יַגִּידוּ לְךָ יָמִין וּשְׂמֹאל׃ וְהָאִישׁ אֲשֶׁר־יַעֲשֶׂה בְזָדוֹן
לְבִלְתִּי שְׁמֹעַ אֶל־הַכֹּהֵן הָעֹמֵד לְשָׁרֶת שָׁם אֶת־יְהוָה
אֱלֹהֶיךָ אוֹ אֶל־הַשֹּׁפֵט וּמֵת הָאִישׁ הַהוּא וּבִעַרְתָּ הָרָע
13 14 מִיִּשְׂרָאֵל׃ וְכָל־הָעָם יִשְׁמְעוּ וְיִרָאוּ וְלֹא יְזִידוּן עוֹד׃ * ס כִּי־ שני
תָבֹא אֶל־הָאָרֶץ אֲשֶׁר יְהוָה אֱלֹהֶיךָ נֹתֵן לָךְ וִירִשְׁתָּהּ
וְיָשַׁבְתָּה בָּהּ וְאָמַרְתָּ אָשִׂימָה עָלַי מֶלֶךְ כְּכָל־הַגּוֹיִם אֲשֶׁר

* v. 10. חצי הספר בפסוקים

II Chronicles XIX, 8 f. Jewish Tradition—both Talmud and Josephus—attests to the continued existence of such a Court from the days of Moses to the destruction of the Jewish State, and beyond. In the first century of the present era, the Sanhedrin in Jerusalem made the laws and acted as Court of Appeal. It consisted of 70 members in addition to the presiding officer, who was generally the High Priest. In the Provincial towns, there were smaller Sanhedrins of twenty-three members.

8. *hard.* Or, 'extraordinary.'

between blood and blood. Whether the act of killing was intentional or accidental (Biur).

plea and plea. Cases of disputed rights and claims regarding property.

stroke and stroke. Cases where bodily injury has been inflicted, and it is hard to assess the damages fairly.

matters of controversy within thy gates. i.e. the local judges are of divided opinion (Rashi).

the place. See on XII, 5.

9. *the priests the Levites. i.e.* the priests, who were of the tribe of Levi.

the judge. Heb. שפט; the head of the Court of the Central Sanctuary.

in those days. 'Even though he be inferior to the judges who preceded him, you are in duty bound to accept his decision. Only the judge of your own day must be your judge' (Rashi); see on XIX, 17.

declare. lit. 'announce'.

11. *not turn aside.* 'Even if in your eyes they seem to tell you that right is left, and left is right, hearken unto them' (Sifri).

12. *the man that doeth presumptuously.* The decisions of this Court must be strictly obeyed. Refusal to do so would, in a theocracy, be tantamount to revolt against the Constitution, and involve capital punishment for the offender. Tradition explains this *v.* to refer to a judge (זקן ממרה) who defies the ruling of the Supreme Court.

the priest. The ecclesiastical president of the tribunal.

(*b*) THE KING

14–20. These verses define the selection, the qualifications, and the duties of the king. It is legitimate to have a king, but he must be a native Israelite and be a constitutional monarch who governs in accordance with the Torah. He was to have no standing cavalry to keep his people in subjection, nor establish a harem; and he was himself to study and obey the laws of the realm.

15. thou shalt in any wise set him king over thee, whom the LORD thy God shall choose; one from among thy brethren shalt thou set king over thee; thou mayest not put a foreigner over thee, who is not thy brother. 16. Only he shall not multiply horses to himself, nor cause the people to return to Egypt, to the end that he should multiply horses; forasmuch as the LORD hath said unto you: 'Ye shall henceforth return no more that way.' 17. Neither shall he multiply wives to himself, that his heart turn not away; neither shall he greatly multiply to himself silver and gold. 18. And it shall be, when he sitteth upon the throne of his kingdom, that he shall write him a copy of this law in a book, out of that which

טו סְבִיבֹתָי׃ שׂוֹם תָּשִׂים עָלֶיךָ מֶלֶךְ אֲשֶׁר יִבְחַר יְהוָה אֱלֹהֶיךָ
בּוֹ מִקֶּרֶב אַחֶיךָ תָּשִׂים עָלֶיךָ מֶלֶךְ לֹא תוּכַל לָתֵת עָלֶיךָ
16 אִישׁ נָכְרִי אֲשֶׁר לֹא־אָחִיךָ הוּא׃ רַק לֹא־יַרְבֶּה־לּוֹ סוּסִים
וְלֹא־יָשִׁיב אֶת־הָעָם מִצְרַיְמָה לְמַעַן הַרְבּוֹת סוּס וַיהוָה
17 אָמַר לָכֶם לֹא תֹסִפוּן לָשׁוּב בַּדֶּרֶךְ הַזֶּה עוֹד׃ וְלֹא יַרְבֶּה־
לּוֹ נָשִׁים וְלֹא יָסוּר לְבָבוֹ וְכֶסֶף וְזָהָב לֹא יַרְבֶּה־לּוֹ מְאֹד׃
18 וְהָיָה כְשִׁבְתּוֹ עַל כִּסֵּא מַמְלַכְתּוֹ וְכָתַב לוֹ אֶת־מִשְׁנֵה
19 הַתּוֹרָה הַזֹּאת עַל־סֵפֶר מִלִּפְנֵי הַכֹּהֲנִים הַלְוִיִּם׃ וְהָיְתָה

15. *thou shalt in any wise set.* lit. 'thou mayest certainly set.' Monarchy is not commanded, like the appointment of judges, but *permitted.* This explains the possibility of the opposition to the setting up of a king in I Samuel VIII.

shall choose. The king must be God's choice; cf. I Sam. x, 24, 'See ye him whom the LORD hath chosen.' God's choice was expressed through the Prophet of that particular generation.

foreigner. In the latter days of the Second Temple, the Romans made Herod and his kinsmen—who were of Edomite descent—kings of Judea. When one of these Herodian kings, Agrippa I, read this *v.* in the Court of the Temple at the close of a Year of Release, 'he burst into tears, deeming himself unworthy of kinghood on account of his alien ancestry; whereupon the people reassured him with the words, "Thou art our brother, thou art our brother" ' (Talmud).

16. *not multiply horses.* For war. He was not to cherish military ambitions. 'The early kings possessed horses in direct proportion to the strength of their military establishments; and the mark of their strength was the number of their horses' (Radin).

the people. This cannot mean 'the whole people'; otherwise, it would mean self-annihilation for him (Dillmann). Scripture warns against a body of Israelites being devoted by the king for the purchase of horses in Egypt.

return to Egypt. Cf. Exod. XIII, 17; XIV, 13; and Num. XIV, 3; see on XXVIII, 68.

to the end . . . horses. 'Several of the Hebrew kings,' said a German Professor some years ago, 'seem to have plied a considerable trade in horses'—a remark that was greeted with ironic applause by his students. The Professor continued, however, 'This trade, though not very honourable for kings, is not quite as dishonourable as the trade in human beings that was carried on by German princes during the eighteenth century, in the sale of their subjects as mercenaries in foreign wars.' See also I Kings x, 28.

17. *turn not away.* To idolatry, as did Solomon's (I Kings XI, 4 f). The evils and intrigues of harem-rule are commonplaces in the history of every Eastern court.

silver and gold. This warning is necessary in order to protect the people against exploitation by a despotic monarch.

18. *a copy of this law.* Heb. משנה התורה הזאת; lit. 'a repetition of this law,' wrongly understood by the Septuagint to refer to the whole of the Fifth Book of Moses, and therefore they called it Deuteronomy, 'the Second Law.' According to the Talmud, the king possessed two copies of the Torah; one in his private treasure, and one which he carried about with him. At the crowning of a British monarch, the Bible is delivered to him with the words, 'We present you with this Book, the most valuable thing the world affords. Here is wisdom; this is the royal law; these are the lively (*i.e.* living) oracles of God'; cf. II Chron. XXIII, 11.

the priests the Levites. The custodians of the Law which was kept by the side of 'the ark of the Covenant'; see Deut. XXXI, 26. The king's copy had to be transcribed from their codex.

19. *all the days of his life.* It was to be his *vade mecum*, the object of his continual meditation and the guide of his daily life; Josh. I, 8; Psalm I, 2.

and these statutes. Or, 'and especially these statutes' (Koenig). Whenever a king in Israel threw off the yoke of the Torah and disregarded its precepts of righteousness, then the evils of despotic Oriental rule made their appearance unchecked. Cruelty, callous indifference to the welfare of the weaker and poorer classes, avarice, corruption, and disorder in all public affairs were rampant; and these are precisely the sins which the true prophets of Israel were continually denouncing (Harper).

is before the priests the Levites. 19. And it shall be with him, and he shall read therein all the days of his life; that he may learn to fear the LORD his God, to keep all the words of this law and these statutes, to do them; 20. that his heart be not lifted up above his brethren, and that he turn not aside from the commandment, to the right hand, or to the left; to the end that he may prolong his days in his kingdom, he and his children, in the midst of Israel.*iii.

18 CHAPTER XVIII

1. The priests the Levites, even all the tribe of Levi, shall have no portion nor inheritance with Israel; they shall eat the offerings of the LORD made by fire, and His inheritance. 2. And they shall have no inheritance among their brethren; the LORD is their inheritance, as He hath spoken unto them. ¶ 3. And this shall be the priests' due from the people, from them that offer a sacrifice, whether it be ox or sheep, that they shall give unto the priest the shoulder, and the two cheeks, and the maw. 4. The first-fruits of thy corn, of thy wine, and of thine oil, and the first of the fleece of thy sheep, shalt thou give him. 5. For the LORD thy God hath chosen him out of all thy tribes, to stand to minister in the name of the LORD, him and his sons for ever.*iv. ¶ 6. And if a Levite come from any of thy gates out of all Israel, where he sojourneth, and come with all the desire of his soul unto the

עִמּוֹ וְקָרָא בוֹ כָּל־יְמֵי חַיָּיו לְמַעַן יִלְמַד לְיִרְאָה אֶת־יְהוָה
אֱלֹהָיו לִשְׁמֹר אֶת־כָּל־דִּבְרֵי הַתּוֹרָה הַזֹּאת וְאֶת־הַחֻקִּים
כ הָאֵלֶּה לַעֲשֹׂתָם׃ לְבִלְתִּי רוּם־לְבָבוֹ מֵאֶחָיו וּלְבִלְתִּי סוּר
מִן־הַמִּצְוָה יָמִין וּשְׂמֹאול לְמַעַן יַאֲרִיךְ יָמִים עַל־מַמְלַכְתּוֹ
הוּא וּבָנָיו בְּקֶרֶב יִשְׂרָאֵל׃ * ס שלישי

יח CAP. XVIII. יח

א לֹא־יִהְיֶה לַכֹּהֲנִים הַלְוִיִּם כָּל־שֵׁבֶט לֵוִי חֵלֶק וְנַחֲלָה עִם־
2 יִשְׂרָאֵל אִשֵּׁי יְהוָה וְנַחֲלָתוֹ יֹאכֵלוּן׃ וְנַחֲלָה לֹא־יִהְיֶה־לּוֹ
3 בְּקֶרֶב אֶחָיו יְהוָה הוּא נַחֲלָתוֹ כַּאֲשֶׁר דִּבֶּר־לוֹ׃ ס וְזֶה
יִהְיֶה מִשְׁפַּט הַכֹּהֲנִים מֵאֵת הָעָם מֵאֵת זֹבְחֵי הַזֶּבַח אִם־
4 שׁוֹר אִם־שֶׂה וְנָתַן לַכֹּהֵן הַזְּרֹעַ וְהַלְּחָיַיִם וְהַקֵּבָה׃ רֵאשִׁית
ה דְּגָנְךָ תִּירֹשְׁךָ וְיִצְהָרֶךָ וְרֵאשִׁית גֵּז צֹאנְךָ תִּתֶּן־לוֹ׃ כִּי בוֹ
בָּחַר יְהוָה אֱלֹהֶיךָ מִכָּל־שְׁבָטֶיךָ לַעֲמֹד לְשָׁרֵת בְּשֵׁם־ רביעי
6 יְהוָה הוּא וּבָנָיו כָּל־הַיָּמִים׃ * ס וְכִי־יָבֹא הַלֵּוִי מֵאַחַד
שְׁעָרֶיךָ מִכָּל־יִשְׂרָאֵל אֲשֶׁר־הוּא גָּר שָׁם וּבָא בְּכָל־אַוַּת

יז' v. 19. סבירין בה v. 20. מלא ו'

20. *his heart be not lifted up.* 'If pride is to be shunned by a king, how much the more is it to be shunned as a besetting sin in an ordinary mortal' (Nachmanides).

above his brethren. To the Israelite king his subjects were to be his 'brethren'; see p. 927.

the commandment. This commandment concerning the king and his duties.

may prolong his days. The king's loyalty to the Torah and its regulations concerning the monarchy, would establish his throne in the affections of his people and secure it to his children after him.

CHAPTER XVIII

(c) PRIESTS AND LEVITES

1–8. The priests and Levites were not to possess any allotments of land. The history of the European peoples would have been a happier one than it has been, if the priesthood had been debarred from ownership of land.

1. *the priests the Levites.* See on x, 9.

the offerings of the LORD. These were (*a*) the burnt-offering; (*b*) the meal-offering; (*c*) the thank-offering; and (*d*) the trespass-offering. Certain specific parts in all of these sacrifices belonged to the priests.

His inheritance. God's inheritance; *i.e.* what was appropriated to Him, and from Him to the tribe of Levi; such as, heave-offerings, tithes and first-fruits.

2. *as He hath spoken unto them.* See Numbers XVIII, 20.

3. *priests' due.* The reference is here to further 'dues' not previously mentioned in Numbers; viz., those which accrued from the animals slaughtered for ordinary consumption, as distinguished from those brought as sacrifices.

6. *if a Levite come.* Only a portion of the tribe of Levites would live in Jerusalem. Most of them would be scattered among the tribes. Unlike the non-Levites living on the land in their own clan, these Levites had necessarily no fixed abode; cf. Judges XVII, 7–9, XIX; I Sam. II, 36. The officiating priests would tend to close their ranks against the wandering priests. It is here enacted that should any of these latter come to the Central Sanctuary, he should be allowed to minister and share in the priestly emoluments.

place which the LORD shall choose; 7. then he shall minister in the name of the LORD his God, as all his brethren the Levites do, who stand there before the LORD. 8. They shall have like portions to eat, beside that which is his due according to the fathers' houses. ¶ 9. When thou art come into the land which the LORD thy God giveth thee, thou shalt not learn to do after the abominations of those nations. 10. There shall not be found among you any one that maketh his son or his daughter to pass through the fire, one that useth divination, a soothsayer, or an enchanter,

7 נַפְשׁ֑וֹ אֶל־הַמָּק֖וֹם אֲשֶׁר־יִבְחַ֥ר יְהוָֽה׃ וְשֵׁרֵ֕ת בְּשֵׁ֖ם יְהוָ֣ה
8 אֱלֹהָ֑יו כְּכָל־אֶחָיו֙ הַלְוִיִּ֔ם הָעֹמְדִ֥ים שָׁ֖ם לִפְנֵ֥י יְהוָֽה׃ חֵ֥לֶק
9 כְּחֵ֖לֶק יֹאכֵ֑לוּ לְבַ֥ד מִמְכָּרָ֖יו עַל־הָאָבֽוֹת׃ ס כִּ֤י אַתָּה֙ בָּ֣א
אֶל־הָאָ֔רֶץ אֲשֶׁר־יְהוָ֥ה אֱלֹהֶ֖יךָ נֹתֵ֣ן לָ֑ךְ לֹֽא־תִלְמַ֣ד לַעֲשׂ֔וֹת
י כְּתוֹעֲבֹ֖ת הַגּוֹיִ֥ם הָהֵֽם׃ לֹֽא־יִמָּצֵ֣א בְךָ֔ מַעֲבִ֥יר בְּנֽוֹ־וּבִתּ֖וֹ בָּאֵ֑שׁ
11 קֹסֵ֣ם קְסָמִ֔ים מְעוֹנֵ֥ן וּמְנַחֵ֖שׁ וּמְכַשֵּֽׁף׃ וְחֹבֵ֖ר חָ֑בֶר וְשֹׁאֵ֥ל

8. *like portions to eat.* lit. 'they shall eat portion as portion'; *i.e.* share and share alike.

beside . . . fathers' houses. lit. 'besides his sellings according to the fathers'. This refers to the proceeds of the sale of his local possessions which a Levite inherited from his ancestors (Lev. xxv, 33) or of private dues accruing to him. If a Levite had such extra income, his brother-Levites were not permitted to say to him, 'You have enough, you must not expect or accept any priestly emoluments!' He still has his right to share alike with the others.

Modern writers seldom do justice to the priesthood. They exalt the prophet, and almost invariably depreciate the priest. It is true that 'the centre of gravity in religion lies for the priest elsewhere than for the prophet; it lies in man's attitude, not toward his fellow men, but toward God; not in his social, but in his personal life' (Kuenen). To the priest, man is more than a social being; he has also an individual life of his own, his joys and sorrows, his historical claims, his traditions of the past, and his hopes for the future; and all these are brought by the priest under the influence of religion, to become sanctified through their relation with God. All the details of human life are with the priest so many opportunities for the worship of God (Schechter).

The priest's indispensable function was to conserve the spiritual discoveries of the past by means of religious institutions. He gave the daily bread of religion to the people, treasured up whatever had been gained, and kept the people nurtured on it and admonished by it. To picture the priest as exalting external observance at the expense of moral values, is a controversial fiction. Though Malachi had much to complain of the priests of his day, his estimate of what Levi had been in the past is no exaggeration. 'The law of truth was in his mouth, and unrighteousness was not found in his lips; he walked with Me in peace and uprightness, and did turn many away from iniquity.' See further the note at the end of the chapter.

(*d*) PROPHETS

9–22. The description of the place of the prophet in Israel is preceded by a stern and detailed denunciation of any dealings with soothsayers and wizards—a restatement of the injunction in Lev. XIX, 26, 31. The people may naturally desire to know the future or to learn the Divine mind; and they will be living among nations who hold that the will of the gods was best learned through augury and sorcery. But Israel does not need such means of obtaining Divine guidance. 'Alone in the antique world, Israel has the high honour of having broken with this entire system of approaching the Divine' (Welch). *Its* communion with the spiritual world was through a spiritual channel—that of the prophet. As it is said in Num. XXIII, 23, 'There is no enchantment in Jacob, neither is there any divination in Israel: at the right time it is said to him what God doeth.'

The problem of sorcery confronts every administrator of primitive races. 'Attempts to advance them to a higher life in our own day are being rendered futile by the sorcerer; at his instigation the darkest crimes are committed. To what depths of wickedness his practices can bring men is seen in the horrors of the secret cult of the negroes of Haiti' (Harper).

10. *pass through the fire.* Human sacrifice was an essential part of Moloch worship.

divination. This is the most general term for the magical practices that follow. A Gold Coast official recently complained that the numbing effect of omen-taking and consultation with soothsayers had not hitherto received the attention it deserved.

one that useth divination. lit. 'cloud-gazer'; an observer of clouds or omens, a soothsayer.

enchanter. Or, 'augur.'

sorcerer. One who uses magical appliances in the shape of drugs or herbs for curing, or for inflicting, diseases.

or a sorcerer, 11. or a charmer, or one that consulteth a ghost or a familiar spirit, or a necromancer. 12. For whosoever doeth these things is an abomination unto the LORD; and because of these abominations the LORD thy God is driving them out from before thee. 13. Thou shalt be whole-hearted with the LORD thy God.*v. 14. For these nations, that thou art to dispossess, hearken unto soothsayers, and unto diviners; but as for thee, the LORD thy God hath not suffered thee so to do. 15. A prophet will the LORD thy God raise up unto thee, from the midst of thee, of thy brethren, like unto me; unto him ye shall hearken; 16. according to all that thou didst desire of the LORD thy God in Horeb in the day of the assembly, saying: 'Let me not hear again the voice of the LORD my God, neither let me see this great fire any more, that I die not.' 17. And the LORD said unto me: 'They have well said that which they have spoken. 18. I will raise them up a prophet from among their brethren, like unto thee; and I will put My words in his mouth, and he shall speak unto them all that I shall command him. 19. And it shall come to pass, that whosoever will not hearken unto My words

12 אוֹב וְיִדְּעֹנִי וְדֹרֵשׁ אֶל־הַמֵּתִים׃ כִּי־תוֹעֲבַת יְהוָה כָּל־עֹשֵׂה
אֵלֶּה וּבִגְלַל הַתּוֹעֵבֹת הָאֵלֶּה יְהוָה אֱלֹהֶיךָ מוֹרִישׁ אוֹתָם
ישי 13 14 מִפָּנֶיךָ׃ תָּמִים תִּהְיֶה עִם יְהוָה אֱלֹהֶיךָ׃* כִּי ׀ הַגּוֹיִם הָאֵלֶּה
אֲשֶׁר אַתָּה יוֹרֵשׁ אוֹתָם אֶל־מְעֹנְנִים וְאֶל־קֹסְמִים יִשְׁמָעוּ
טו וְאַתָּה לֹא כֵן נָתַן לְךָ יְהוָה אֱלֹהֶיךָ׃ נָבִיא מִקִּרְבְּךָ מֵאַחֶיךָ
16 כָּמֹנִי יָקִים לְךָ יְהוָה אֱלֹהֶיךָ אֵלָיו תִּשְׁמָעוּן׃ כְּכֹל אֲשֶׁר־
שָׁאַלְתָּ מֵעִם יְהוָה אֱלֹהֶיךָ בְּחֹרֵב בְּיוֹם הַקָּהָל לֵאמֹר
לֹא אֹסֵף לִשְׁמֹעַ אֶת־קוֹל יְהוָה אֱלֹהָי וְאֶת־הָאֵשׁ הַגְּדֹלָה
17 הַזֹּאת לֹא־אֶרְאֶה עוֹד וְלֹא אָמוּת׃ וַיֹּאמֶר יְהוָה אֵלָי
18 הֵיטִיבוּ אֲשֶׁר דִּבֵּרוּ׃ נָבִיא אָקִים לָהֶם מִקֶּרֶב אֲחֵיהֶם
כָּמוֹךָ וְנָתַתִּי דְבָרַי בְּפִיו וְדִבֶּר אֲלֵיהֶם אֵת כָּל־אֲשֶׁר
19 אֲצַוֶּנּוּ׃ וְהָיָה הָאִישׁ אֲשֶׁר לֹא־יִשְׁמַע אֶל־דְּבָרַי אֲשֶׁר

v. 13. בקצת ספרים הת׳ רבתי v. 16. קמץ בז״ק

11. *charmer.* As of serpents; a dealer in spells.

a ghost. Heb. *ob.* Saul, desirous of speaking to Samuel on the night before the fateful battle of Gilboa (I Sam. XXVIII, 7), said unto his servants, 'Seek me a woman that hath a familiar spirit' (*i.e.* that divineth by a ghost). From Isaiah VIII, 19 it would seem that the *ob* was a kind of ventriloquist who impersonated the dead by speaking in a faint voice from the ground.

or a familiar spirit. Heb. ידעני. Coming from the root ידע ('know') it would seem to correspond to the English word *wizard*, which originally meant 'wise or knowing one', without any hint of sorcery or evil.

necromancer. An inquirer of the dead. 'In the Hebrew religion the spiritual part of man was conceived not as ghostly, but under the attribute of holy. It is a significant fact that stories of ghosts or apparitions are almost absent from the Old Testament; and necromancy, which attempts to come into communication with the dead, that is, to deal with ghosts, was especially abhorrent' (F. Adler).

13. *thou shalt be whole-hearted.* And not given over in part to demoniac powers, or other evil superstitions of the heathen. 'Walk with Him whole-heartedly and hope in Him. Pry not into the veiled future, but accept whatever lot befalls you. Then will you be His people and His portion' (Rashi).

Whole-heartedness is one of the great requirements of Religion; hence תמים is written with a large initial letter.

14. *hath not suffered thee so to do.* To turn to soothsayers, because God would raise up a Prophet from amongst the Israelites themselves, and thus reveal to them whatever they desired to know from God.

15. *a prophet.* In each generation.

like unto me. Not of the same rank as Moses (XXXIV, 10), but of the line of Prophets of which Moses is the 'father'.

16. *in Horeb.* Israel had refused the high honour of hearing directly the voice of God. As Moses was the intermediary at Horeb, so the Prophets shall be the intermediaries in their generation.

18. *command him.* The office of the Prophet is thus conceived not so much as a foreteller, but in spiritual succession to Moses as the teacher and religious guide of his age, though the gift of predicting the future where this serves a moral purpose, cannot be denied him.

19. *require.* I will seek out his disobedience, and judge him for it. 'The rigorous punishment would deter anyone from coming forward as a prophet, who had not an absolute conviction of his Divine call' (Dillmann).

which he shall speak in My name, I will require it of him. 20. But the prophet, that shall speak a word presumptuously in My name, which I have not commanded him to speak, or that shall speak in the name of other gods, that same prophet shall die.' 21. And if thou say in thy heart: 'How shall we know the word which the LORD hath not spoken?' 22. When a prophet speaketh in the name of the LORD, if the thing follow not, nor come to pass, that is the thing which the LORD hath not spoken; the prophet hath spoken it presumptuously, thou shalt not be afraid of him.

כ יְדַבֵּר בִּשְׁמִי אָנֹכִי אֶדְרֹשׁ מֵעִמּוֹ׃ אַךְ הַנָּבִיא אֲשֶׁר יָזִיד
לְדַבֵּר דָּבָר בִּשְׁמִי אֵת אֲשֶׁר לֹא־צִוִּיתִיו לְדַבֵּר וַאֲשֶׁר
21 יְדַבֵּר בְּשֵׁם אֱלֹהִים אֲחֵרִים וּמֵת הַנָּבִיא הַהוּא׃ וְכִי
תֹאמַר בִּלְבָבֶךָ אֵיכָה נֵדַע אֶת־הַדָּבָר אֲשֶׁר לֹא־דִבְּרוֹ
22 יְהוָה׃ אֲשֶׁר יְדַבֵּר הַנָּבִיא בְּשֵׁם יְהוָה וְלֹא־יִהְיֶה הַדָּבָר
וְלֹא יָבֹא הוּא הַדָּבָר אֲשֶׁר לֹא־דִבְּרוֹ יְהוָה בְּזָדוֹן דִּבְּרוֹ
הַנָּבִיא לֹא תָגוּר מִמֶּנּוּ׃ ס

19

CHAPTER XIX

1. When the LORD thy God shall cut off the nations, whose land the LORD thy God giveth thee, and thou dost succeed them, and dwell in their cities, and in their houses; 2. thou shalt separate three cities for thee in the midst of thy land, which the LORD thy God giveth thee to possess it. 3. Thou

יט CAP. XIX. יט

א כִּי־יַכְרִית יְהוָה אֱלֹהֶיךָ אֶת־הַגּוֹיִם אֲשֶׁר יְהוָה אֱלֹהֶיךָ
נֹתֵן לְךָ אֶת־אַרְצָם וִירִשְׁתָּם וְיָשַׁבְתָּ בְעָרֵיהֶם וּבְבָתֵּיהֶם׃
2 שָׁלוֹשׁ עָרִים תַּבְדִּיל לָךְ בְּתוֹךְ אַרְצְךָ אֲשֶׁר יְהוָה אֱלֹהֶיךָ

22. *follow not.* The test of the false prophet was the non-fulfilment of the specific prediction that he announced as the credentials of his Divine call, though signs and miracles performed by a 'prophet', are not necessarily a proof of his truth (XIII, 2, 6). 'The ultimate criterion of the true prophet is the moral character of his utterance' (Dummelow).

Even as the kingship ensured stability to national and social life, and the priesthood gave stability in religion, so the Prophetic order secured spiritual progress and averted stagnation. The Prophets are the inspired declarers of the Divine will. 'The mere foretelling of future events is the lowest stage of prophecy, and in the eyes of the great Prophets of Israel it was of quite secondary importance. Their aim was to fathom the secrets of holiness; and their striving, by means of admonition and moral suasion, to guide the peoples in the paths which lead mankind to spiritual and political well-being' (Shemtob ibn Shemtob).

The competence of the Prophet, however, is not unlimited. He too is bound by the Torah, to which he may neither add nor subtract, except as a temporary measure of extreme urgency (*horaath shaah*). Nor may he venture, solely in virtue of the prophetic gifts with which he is endowed, to give a ruling in matters of Law. In this respect he must yield place to the Judge, the sage in whom alone is vested the authority to interpret and to apply the sanctions of the Law according to the accepted norms of Biblical interpretation.

'There is no quarrel between prophet and priest; nor was there ever one. As guardians of the Law of God, they both cherish common ideals. The prophets never preached the abrogation of the Law. What they did stress—and it is what the most resolute formalist can endorse word for word—was that only the heart which is right with God can find fit and proper expression in the well-ordered Temple-worship, and be brought nearer to the Eternal by ritual and ceremony. Nor did the good and genuine priest—for there were false priests as there were false prophets—ever hold that one could shelter himself behind sacrifices from the judgment of Heaven upon his moral turpitude and waywardness of conduct' (I. Epstein).

(3) CRIMINAL LAW AND WARFARE

(CHAPTERS XIX–XXI, 1–9)

(a) LAWS RELATING TO CRIME

XIX, 1–13. CITIES OF REFUGE

Three cities shall be set aside in the future territory to serve as 'sanctuary' to the manslayer; see Num. XXXV, 9–34 and Deut. IV, 41–3. In this way the immemorial custom of blood-revenge that to this day rests like a curse upon many Bedouin tribes is curbed; and the heathen conception of 'sanctuary' for the wilful murderer is abolished.

1. *dost succeed.* Or, 'shalt dispossess.'

3. *prepare thee the way.* Affording every facility to the fugitive to reach the place of refuge. According to the Talmud, a sign-post bearing the inscription, 'To the City of Refuge,' was at every cross-road, pointing out the direction in which the City of Refuge lay.

flee thither. The three Cities of Refuge should be equidistant from one another.

borders. Territory.

shalt prepare thee the way, and divide the borders of thy land, which the LORD thy God causeth thee to inherit, into three parts, that every manslayer may flee thither. 4. And this is the case of the manslayer, that shall flee thither and live: whoso killeth his neighbour unawares, and hated him not in time past; 5. as when a man goeth into the forest with his neighbour to hew wood, and his hand fetcheth a stroke with the axe to cut down the tree, and the head slippeth from the helve, and lighteth upon his neighbour, that he die; he shall flee unto one of these cities and live; 6. lest the avenger of blood pursue the manslayer, while his heart is hot, and overtake him, because the way is long, and smite him mortally; whereas he was not deserving of death, inasmuch as he hated him not in time past. 7. Wherefore I command thee, saying: 'Thou shalt separate three cities for thee.' 8. And if the LORD thy God enlarge thy border, as He hath sworn unto thy fathers, and give thee all the land which He promised to give unto thy fathers—9. if thou shalt keep all this commandment to do it, which I command thee this day, to love the LORD thy God, and to walk ever in His ways—then shalt thou add three cities more for thee, beside these three; 10. that innocent blood be not shed in the midst of thy land, which the LORD thy God giveth thee for an inheritance, and so blood be upon thee. ¶ 11. But if any man hate his neighbour, and lie in wait for him, and rise up against him, and smite him mortally that he die; and he flee into one of these cities; 12. then the elders of his city shall send and fetch him thence, and deliver him into the hand of the avenger of blood, that he may die. 13. Thine eye shall not pity him, but thou shalt put away the blood of the innocent from Israel, that it may go well with thee.*vi. ¶ 14. Thou shalt not remove thy neighbour's landmark, which they of old time have set, in thine inheritance which thou shalt inherit, in the

3 נֹתֵן לְךָ לְרִשְׁתָּהּ׃ תָּכִין לְךָ הַדֶּרֶךְ וְשִׁלַּשְׁתָּ אֶת־גְּבוּל
אַרְצְךָ אֲשֶׁר יַנְחִילְךָ יְהוָה אֱלֹהֶיךָ וְהָיָה לָנוּס שָׁמָּה כָּל־
4 רֹצֵחַ׃ וְזֶה דְּבַר הָרֹצֵחַ אֲשֶׁר־יָנוּס שָׁמָּה וָחָי אֲשֶׁר יַכֶּה
אֶת־רֵעֵהוּ בִּבְלִי־דַעַת וְהוּא לֹא־שֹׂנֵא לוֹ מִתְּמֹל שִׁלְשֹׁם׃
ה וַאֲשֶׁר יָבֹא אֶת־רֵעֵהוּ בַיַּעַר לַחְטֹב עֵצִים וְנִדְּחָה יָדוֹ
בַגַּרְזֶן לִכְרֹת הָעֵץ וְנָשַׁל הַבַּרְזֶל מִן־הָעֵץ וּמָצָא אֶת־
6 רֵעֵהוּ וָמֵת הוּא יָנוּס אֶל־אַחַת הֶעָרִים־הָאֵלֶּה וָחָי׃ פֶּן־
יִרְדֹּף גֹּאֵל הַדָּם אַחֲרֵי הָרֹצֵחַ כִּי יֵחַם לְבָבוֹ וְהִשִּׂיגוֹ
כִּי־יִרְבֶּה הַדֶּרֶךְ וְהִכָּהוּ נָפֶשׁ וְלוֹ אֵין מִשְׁפַּט־מָוֶת כִּי
7 לֹא שֹׂנֵא הוּא לוֹ מִתְּמוֹל שִׁלְשׁוֹם׃ עַל־כֵּן אָנֹכִי מְצַוְּךָ
8 לֵאמֹר שָׁלֹשׁ עָרִים תַּבְדִּיל לָךְ׃ וְאִם־יַרְחִיב יְהוָה
אֱלֹהֶיךָ אֶת־גְּבֻלְךָ כַּאֲשֶׁר נִשְׁבַּע לַאֲבֹתֶיךָ וְנָתַן לְךָ אֶת־
9 כָּל־הָאָרֶץ אֲשֶׁר דִּבֶּר לָתֵת לַאֲבֹתֶיךָ׃ כִּי־תִשְׁמֹר אֶת־
כָּל־הַמִּצְוָה הַזֹּאת לַעֲשֹׂתָהּ אֲשֶׁר אָנֹכִי מְצַוְּךָ הַיּוֹם לְאַהֲבָה
אֶת־יְהוָה אֱלֹהֶיךָ וְלָלֶכֶת בִּדְרָכָיו כָּל־הַיָּמִים וְיָסַפְתָּ לְךָ
י עוֹד שָׁלֹשׁ עָרִים עַל הַשָּׁלֹשׁ הָאֵלֶּה׃ וְלֹא יִשָּׁפֵךְ דָּם נָקִי
בְּקֶרֶב אַרְצְךָ אֲשֶׁר יְהוָה אֱלֹהֶיךָ נֹתֵן לְךָ נַחֲלָה וְהָיָה
עָלֶיךָ דָּמִים׃ פ
11 וְכִי־יִהְיֶה אִישׁ שֹׂנֵא לְרֵעֵהוּ וְאָרַב לוֹ וְקָם עָלָיו וְהִכָּהוּ
12 נֶפֶשׁ וָמֵת וְנָס אֶל־אַחַת הֶעָרִים הָאֵל׃ וְשָׁלְחוּ זִקְנֵי עִירוֹ
13 וְלָקְחוּ אֹתוֹ מִשָּׁם וְנָתְנוּ אֹתוֹ בְּיַד גֹּאֵל הַדָּם וָמֵת׃ לֹא־
ששי תָחוֹס עֵינְךָ עָלָיו וּבִעַרְתָּ דַם־הַנָּקִי מִיִּשְׂרָאֵל וְטוֹב לָךְ׃
14 ס לֹא תַסִּיג גְּבוּל רֵעֲךָ אֲשֶׁר גָּבְלוּ רִאשֹׁנִים בְּנַחֲלָתְךָ

v. 11. סבירין האלה

5. *fetcheth a stroke.* 'As his hand lets drive with the axe' (Moffatt), the iron slips off the handle, and, instead of hitting the tree, strikes a man.

6. *the avenger of blood.* The nearest kinsman of the dead man; Num. XXXV, 12.

because the way is long. To the Central Sanctuary, if these three equidistant Cities of Refuge are not provided.

8. *enlarge thy border.* If Israel comes to possess all the territory that was promised to Abraham (Gen. XV, 18), then three more Cities of Refuge should be added.

10. *blood be upon thee. i.e.* blood-guiltiness be upon thee. If no provision of such Cities of Refuge were made, the guilt of bloodshed would rest upon the land; see on XXI, 1–9.

11. *lie in wait for him.* This and the succeeding two verses provide a safeguard against the abuse of the right of sanctuary. A fair trial and acquittal is secured to the innocent slayer; but the wilful murderer cannot, as among Arab tribes, compound for his crime by payment to the kinsmen of the victim. He must die.

land that the LORD thy God giveth thee to possess it. ¶ 15. One witness shall not rise up against a man for any iniquity, or for any sin, in any sin that he sinneth; at the mouth of two witnesses, or at the mouth of three witnesses, shall a matter be established. 16. If an unrighteous witness rise up against any man to bear perverted witness against him; 17. then both the men, between whom the controversy is, shall stand before the LORD, before the priests and the judges that shall be in those days. 18. And the judges shall inquire diligently; and, behold, if the witness be a false witness, and hath testified falsely against his brother; 19. then shall ye do unto him, as he had purposed to do unto his brother; so shalt thou put away the evil from the midst of thee. 20. And those that remain shall hear, and fear, and shall henceforth commit no more any such evil in the midst of thee. 21. And thine eye shall not pity: life for life, eye for eye, tooth for tooth, hand for hand, foot for foot.

אֲשֶׁר תִּנְחַל בָּאָרֶץ אֲשֶׁר יְהוָה אֱלֹהֶיךָ נֹתֵן לְךָ לְרִשְׁתָּהּ׃
טו ס לֹא־יָקוּם עֵד אֶחָד בְּאִישׁ לְכָל־עָוֺן וּלְכָל־חַטָּאת
בְּכָל־חֵטְא אֲשֶׁר יֶחֱטָא עַל־פִּי ׀ שְׁנֵי עֵדִים אוֹ עַל־פִּי
16 שְׁלֹשָׁה־עֵדִים יָקוּם דָּבָר׃ כִּי־יָקוּם עֵד־חָמָס בְּאִישׁ לַעֲנוֹת
17 בּוֹ סָרָה׃ וְעָמְדוּ שְׁנֵי־הָאֲנָשִׁים אֲשֶׁר־לָהֶם הָרִיב לִפְנֵי
יְהוָה לִפְנֵי הַכֹּהֲנִים וְהַשֹּׁפְטִים אֲשֶׁר יִהְיוּ בַּיָּמִים הָהֵם׃
18 וְדָרְשׁוּ הַשֹּׁפְטִים הֵיטֵב וְהִנֵּה עֵד־שֶׁקֶר הָעֵד שֶׁקֶר עָנָה
19 בְאָחִיו׃ וַעֲשִׂיתֶם לוֹ כַּאֲשֶׁר זָמַם לַעֲשׂוֹת לְאָחִיו וּבִעַרְתָּ
כ הָרָע מִקִּרְבֶּךָ׃ וְהַנִּשְׁאָרִים יִשְׁמְעוּ וְיִרָאוּ וְלֹא־יֹסִפוּ לַעֲשׂוֹת
21 עוֹד כַּדָּבָר הָרָע הַזֶּה בְּקִרְבֶּךָ׃ וְלֹא תָחוֹס עֵינֶךָ נֶפֶשׁ
בְּנֶפֶשׁ עַיִן בְּעַיִן שֵׁן בְּשֵׁן יָד בְּיָד רֶגֶל בְּרָגֶל׃ ס

ע׳ 19. הטעם נסוג אחור

14. REMOVING A LANDMARK

14. *landmark.* The line of stone defining the boundary of a man's field. In Deut. XXVII, 17 it is said, 'Cursed be he that removeth his neighbour's landmark,' in order thereby to enlarge his own estate. Such removal was equivalent to theft. Before the introduction of land-measurement, removing landmarks was a crime more difficult to combat than to-day.

In later times, this prohibition of removing a neighbour's landmark (*hassagath gevul*) received an ethical extension. Thereby any unfair encroachment upon another man's honour or livelihood, any 'poaching on another man's preserves' or sphere of activity, is strictly prohibited.

they of old time. Those of a former age. Moses is here addressing future generations. Num. XXXIV gives the precise divisions of the land under the superintendence of Eleazar, Joshua and one prince out of every tribe.

15–21. PLOTTING WITNESSES

Before guilt can be established, whether in a case of manslaughter, murder, the removal of a landmark, or any other injury to life or property, it is here enacted that the testimony must come from the mouth of at least two witnesses.

Whereas, in Jewish Law, *intention* to commit a crime was no punishable offence, it is otherwise with plotting witnesses (**עדים זוממים**). In their case, intention is of the very essence of their crime, and they are to receive the punishment they had intended for the innocent victim. The Schools differed as to their punishment, if they had succeeded in their criminal intention.

16. *unrighteous witness.* lit. 'a witness of violence', *i.e.* a witness who purposes to do harm.

perverted witness. lit. 'a turning aside', *i.e.* rebellion against the Law of God. In XIII, 6 the same word is used in reference to the sin of idolatry.

17. *both the men.* Both parties must be present at the hearing of the case; see on I, 16.

before the LORD. *i.e.* before the priests and judges who are God's representatives in judgment.

in those days. Whoever the judge of your day may be, due regard must be paid him. 'Jephthah in his generation was the equal of Samuel in his'; see on XVII, 9.

19. *as he had purposed.* The false witness shall suffer the penalty he had sought to bring on another, in accordance with the *lex talionis*, *v.* 21.

20. *shall hear.* According to the Talmud, it was customary for the court to issue the public proclamation, 'Such and such a person has been punished for being a false witness.'

21. *shall not pity.* Wilful murder must be punished by death; see on Exod. XXI, 12 and 14.

life for life. See pp. 309 and 403.

20

CHAPTER XX

1. When thou goest forth to battle against thine enemies, and seest horses, and chariots, and a people more than thou, thou shalt not be afraid of them; for the LORD thy God is with thee, who brought thee up out of the land of Egypt. 2. And it shall be, when ye draw nigh unto the battle, that the priest shall approach and speak unto the people, 3. and shall say unto them: 'Hear, O Israel, ye draw nigh this day unto battle against your enemies; let not your heart faint; fear not, nor be alarmed, neither be ye affrighted at them; 4. for the LORD your God is He that goeth with you, to fight for you against your enemies, to save you.' 5. And the officers shall speak unto the people, saying: 'What man is there that hath built a new house, and hath not dedicated it? let him go and return to his house, lest he die in the battle, and another man dedicate it. 6. And what man is there that hath planted a vineyard, and hath not used the fruit thereof? let him go and return unto his house, lest he die in the battle, and another man use the fruit thereof. 7. And what man is there that hath betrothed a wife, and hath not taken her? let him go and return unto his house, lest he die in the battle, and another man take her.' 8. And the officers shall speak further unto the people, and they

כ

CAP. XX. כ

א כִּֽי־תֵצֵא לַמִּלְחָמָה עַל־אֹיְבֶךָ וְרָאִיתָ סוּס וָרֶכֶב עַם רַב
מִמְּךָ לֹא תִירָא מֵהֶם כִּֽי־יְהוָה אֱלֹהֶיךָ עִמָּךְ הַמַּעַלְךָ
2 מֵאֶרֶץ מִצְרָיִם׃ וְהָיָה כְּקָרָבְכֶם אֶל־הַמִּלְחָמָה וְנִגַּשׁ
3 הַכֹּהֵן וְדִבֶּר אֶל־הָעָם׃ וְאָמַר אֲלֵהֶם שְׁמַע יִשְׂרָאֵל אַתֶּם
קְרֵבִים הַיּוֹם לַמִּלְחָמָה עַל־אֹיְבֵיכֶם אַל־יֵרַךְ לְבַבְכֶם
4 אַל־תִּירְאוּ וְאַל־תַּחְפְּזוּ וְאַל־תַּעַרְצוּ מִפְּנֵיהֶם׃ כִּי יְהוָה
אֱלֹהֵיכֶם הַהֹלֵךְ עִמָּכֶם לְהִלָּחֵם לָכֶם עִם־אֹיְבֵיכֶם לְהוֹשִׁיעַ
ה אֶתְכֶם׃ וְדִבְּרוּ הַשֹּׁטְרִים אֶל־הָעָם לֵאמֹר מִֽי־הָאִישׁ אֲשֶׁר
בָּנָה בַיִת־חָדָשׁ וְלֹא חֲנָכוֹ יֵלֵךְ וְיָשֹׁב לְבֵיתוֹ פֶּן־יָמוּת
6 בַּמִּלְחָמָה וְאִישׁ אַחֵר יַחְנְכֶנּוּ׃ וּמִֽי־הָאִישׁ אֲשֶׁר נָטַע
כֶּרֶם וְלֹא חִלְּלוֹ יֵלֵךְ וְיָשֹׁב לְבֵיתוֹ פֶּן־יָמוּת בַּמִּלְחָמָה
7 וְאִישׁ אַחֵר יְחַלְּלֶנּוּ׃ וּמִֽי־הָאִישׁ אֲשֶׁר אֵרַשׂ אִשָּׁה וְלֹא
לְקָחָהּ יֵלֵךְ וְיָשֹׁב לְבֵיתוֹ פֶּן־יָמוּת בַּמִּלְחָמָה וְאִישׁ אַחֵר
8 יִקָּחֶנָּה׃ וְיָסְפוּ הַשֹּׁטְרִים לְדַבֵּר אֶל־הָעָם וְאָמְרוּ מִֽי־

CHAPTER XX

(*b*) LAWS OF WARFARE

Israel is bidden to display human kindness even in wartime: thus, the betrothed is to be exempt from service; offers of peace are to be made to every city attacked; and fruit-trees are not to be destroyed during a siege. The conduct of war is to be guided by reason and mercy. Israelite kings were famed for their humanity (I Kings XX, 31); while contemporary Assyrian monarchs delighted in inhuman savagery, and made it a rule to devastate forests and cultivated fields; Isa. XIV, 8.

1–9. EXEMPTION FROM SERVICE

1. *horses.* The Heb. is in the singular, used in a collective sense. 'In Mine eyes their multitude of horses are as one horse; hence, fear not' (Rashi).
more than thou. lit. 'a people too great for thee.'
who brought thee out. The recollection of God's work for Israel in the past, is a pledge of what He will do for them in the future.

2. *the priest.* Specially appointed for the purpose, and designated in Rabbinical literature as, 'the priest anointed for the war.'

3. *fear not.* In your hearts.
neither be ye affrighted. In action.

5. *dedicated it.* Rashi renders, 'and hath not begun to live in it.' His heart will be set upon his house, and not upon the battle. Hence, he may flee from battle and cause his companions to do likewise.

6. *not used the fruit thereof.* lit. 'hath not made it profane', by common use. According to Lev. XIX, 23–25, the produce of any fruit-tree was not to be used during its first three years. In the fourth year, the fruit was to be dedicated to God. In the fifth year, the fruit became 'profane'; *i.e.* it was permitted to be eaten. Hence the words, 'he hath not made it profane' mean no more than, 'he hath not used the fruit thereof.'

8. *faint-hearted.* Fear is infectious, and the presence of such persons in the host would be a source of weakness and danger.

In these verses, 1–8, we have 'a shrewd psychological understanding of the dangerous contagion of cowardice, as well as of its probable self-conquest, if given freedom of choice. The contagion of courage would then probably act upon the trembler, and the fear of confessing himself faint-hearted might nerve him to bravery.

shall say: 'What man is there that is fearful and faint-hearted? let him go and return unto his house, lest his brethren's heart melt as his heart.' 9. And it shall be, when the officers have made an end of speaking unto the people, that captains of hosts shall be appointed at the head of the people.*vii. ¶ 10. When thou drawest nigh unto a city to fight against it, then proclaim peace unto it. 11. And it shall be, if it make thee answer of peace, and open unto thee, then it shall be, that all the people that are found therein shall become tributary unto thee, and shall serve thee. 12. And if it will make no peace with thee, but will make war against thee, then thou shalt besiege it. 13. And when the LORD thy God delivereth it into thy hand, thou shalt smite every male thereof with the edge of the sword; 14. but the women, and the little ones, and the cattle, and all that is in the city, even all the spoil thereof, shalt thou take for a prey unto thyself; and thou shalt eat the spoil of thine enemies, which the LORD thy God hath given thee. 15. Thus shalt thou do unto all the cities which are very far off from thee, which are not of the cities of these nations. 16. Howbeit of the cities of these peoples, that the LORD thy God giveth thee for an inheritance, thou shalt save alive nothing that breatheth, 17. but thou shalt utterly destroy them: the Hittite, and the Amorite, the Canaanite, and the

הָאִישׁ הַיָּרֵא וְרַךְ הַלֵּבָב יֵלֵךְ וְיָשֹׁב לְבֵיתוֹ וְלֹא יִמַּס אֶת־
9 לְבַב אֶחָיו כִּלְבָבוֹ׃ וְהָיָה כְּכַלֹּת הַשֹּׁטְרִים לְדַבֵּר אֶל־
שביעי
י הָעָם וּפָקְדוּ שָׂרֵי צְבָאוֹת בְּרֹאשׁ הָעָם׃* ס כִּי־תִקְרַב
11 אֶל־עִיר לְהִלָּחֵם עָלֶיהָ וְקָרָאתָ אֵלֶיהָ לְשָׁלוֹם׃ וְהָיָה
אִם־שָׁלוֹם תַּעַנְךָ וּפָתְחָה לָךְ וְהָיָה כָּל־הָעָם הַנִּמְצָא־בָהּ
12 יִהְיוּ לְךָ לָמַס וַעֲבָדוּךָ׃ וְאִם־לֹא תַשְׁלִים עִמָּךְ וְעָשְׂתָה
13 עִמְּךָ מִלְחָמָה וְצַרְתָּ עָלֶיהָ׃ וּנְתָנָהּ יְהוָה אֱלֹהֶיךָ בְּיָדֶךָ
14 וְהִכִּיתָ אֶת־כָּל־זְכוּרָהּ לְפִי־חָרֶב׃ רַק הַנָּשִׁים וְהַטַּף
וְהַבְּהֵמָה וְכֹל אֲשֶׁר יִהְיֶה בָעִיר כָּל־שְׁלָלָהּ תָּבֹז לָךְ
טו וְאָכַלְתָּ אֶת־שְׁלַל אֹיְבֶיךָ אֲשֶׁר נָתַן יְהוָה אֱלֹהֶיךָ לָךְ׃ כֵּן
תַּעֲשֶׂה לְכָל־הֶעָרִים הָרְחֹקֹת מִמְּךָ מְאֹד אֲשֶׁר לֹא־מֵעָרֵי
16 הַגּוֹיִם־הָאֵלֶּה הֵנָּה׃ רַק מֵעָרֵי הָעַמִּים הָאֵלֶּה אֲשֶׁר יְהוָה
17 אֱלֹהֶיךָ נֹתֵן לְךָ נַחֲלָה לֹא תְחַיֶּה כָּל־נְשָׁמָה׃ כִּי־הַחֲרֵם
תַּחֲרִימֵם הַחִתִּי וְהָאֱמֹרִי הַכְּנַעֲנִי וְהַפְּרִזִּי הַחִוִּי וְהַיְבוּסִי

Compare this genial wisdom with the grim "Shot at dawn" of contemporary military law; with that stark brutality of the ritual of Moloch which has sent shell-shocked conscripts in their teens to a dishonoured grave. The Jewish law, at once more merciful and more intelligent, is the combination of universal service with freedom: making militarism its slave, and not its master' (Zangwill).

9. *captains of hosts.* The army was to be divided into detachments, with a captain for each.

10–18. CAPTURE OF HEATHEN CITIES

10. *proclaim peace unto it.* War is to be regarded as the last resort. First of all there must be offers of peace. If these are accepted, no one is to be harmed in person or in possession; the city becomes tributary to Israel. All Traditional commentaries agree that these offers of peace had to be made to *all* enemy cities, to those of the Canaanites as well. The latter were, in addition, to abandon idolatry and adhere to the Seven Commandments given to the descendants of Noah (*i.e.* the establishment of courts of justice, and the prohibition of blasphemy, idolatry, incest, murder, robbery and unnatural cruelty); see p. 33.

15. *very far off.* Which do not belong to the nations mentioned in *v.* 17 (and also in VII, 1–3).

16. *nothing that breatheth.* If they refuse the offers of peace, and are unwilling to give up idolatry and observe the precepts of Natural Religion; see on *v.* 10.

17. *Hittite . . . Jebusite.* Only six nations are mentioned here, whereas in VII, 1–3 seven nations are named. Ibn Ezra accounts for the omission of 'Girgashite' here because it was the smallest of the seven nations, and negligible. The Jerusalem Talmud states: 'A three-fold message Joshua sent to the Promised Land before the Israelites entered it. It was to the following effect: "Whosoever wishes to leave the country, let him do so; whosoever desires to make peace, his desire will be granted; and whosoever is determined on war, battle will be joined with him." The Girgashites left Canaan, and migrated to North Africa; the Gibeonites made peace; and the thirty-one kings of the cities of Canaan chose to make war, and fell.' It is clear from Joshua XI, 19 that peace-offers were made in every case. The stratagem of the Gibeonites may have been due to a desire to obtain some extra privileges.

18 כַּאֲשֶׁר צִוְּךָ יְהוָה אֱלֹהֶיךָ׃ לְמַעַן אֲשֶׁר לֹא־יְלַמְּדוּ אֶתְכֶם
לַעֲשׂוֹת כְּכֹל תּוֹעֲבֹתָם אֲשֶׁר עָשׂוּ לֵאלֹהֵיהֶם וַחֲטָאתֶם
19 לַיהוָה אֱלֹהֵיכֶם׃ ס כִּי־תָצוּר אֶל־עִיר יָמִים רַבִּים
לְהִלָּחֵם עָלֶיהָ לְתָפְשָׂהּ לֹא־תַשְׁחִית אֶת־עֵצָהּ לִנְדֹּחַ עָלָיו
גַּרְזֶן כִּי מִמֶּנּוּ תֹאכֵל וְאֹתוֹ לֹא תִכְרֹת כִּי הָאָדָם עֵץ הַשָּׂדֶה
כ לָבֹא מִפָּנֶיךָ בַּמָּצוֹר׃ רַק עֵץ אֲשֶׁר־תֵּדַע כִּי לֹא־עֵץ

Perizzite, the Hivite, and the Jebusite; as the LORD thy God hath commanded thee; 18. that they teach you not to do after all their abominations, which they have done unto their gods, and so ye sin against the LORD your God. ¶ 19. When thou shalt besiege a city a long time, in making war against it to take it, thou shalt not destroy the trees thereof by wielding an axe against them; for thou mayest eat of them, but thou shalt not cut them down; for is the tree of the field man, that it should be besieged of thee? 20. Only the trees

18. *that they teach you not.* 'This plainly indicates that, if they are willing to give up their idolatrous abominations, they are to be spared' (Sifri).

BANNING THE CANAANITES

The moral difficulty in *v.* 10–18 has been variously met by Jewish and non-Jewish authorities. The traditional Jewish view is sufficiently indicated in the comments above. Non-Jewish exegetes of the older school point out that the ban was a pre-Mosaic institution, not confined to the Semitic world. It is found in peoples as far apart as the Romans and the Mexicans: among them all it was but an exhibition of cruelty for cruelty's sake. In Israel alone was it moralized—turned into a potent and terrible weapon for the safe-guarding of the Sacred Cause entrusted to Israel's keeping. Israel's preservation from depravity and decay was the main anxiety of the Lawgiver. Just as in modern days the preservation of the State is reckoned in every country the supreme law which overrides every other consideration, so was in Israel the preservation of Israel's religious character. And rightly so, for the whole moral and spiritual future of mankind was involved in that preservation.

Furthermore, the search for a new homeland, and the conquest of such homeland, are not isolated phenomena in World History. The fact is that *the population of nearly every European country to-day had conquered its present homeland and largely destroyed the original inhabitants.* Thus, the Saxons all but exterminated the Romanized Celts; and, in turn, the Saxons were 'harried' by the Normans on their conquest of England. Even more dreadful was the enslavement or extermination of the native races by both Catholic and Protestant settlers in their Overseas possessions. Now, no nation has ever been called upon to justify the taking of such lands, or its conduct towards the natives who thus passed under its control. The peoples exhaust the vocabulary of praise for those of their national heroes who secured that homeland or colonial possessions for them. Israel alone has such an ethical justification for the conquest of Canaan and the banning of its inhabitants. In Lev. XVIII, dealing with the bestialities and moral depravities of the Canaanites, we read: *v.* 26–28, 'Ye shall not do any of these abominations . . . (for all these abominations have the men of the land done, which were before you, and the land is defiled); that the land vomit not you out also, when ye defile it, as it vomited out the nation that was before you.'

It is thus seen that the Canaanites were put under the ban, not for false belief but for vile action; because of the human sacrifices and foul immorality of their gruesome cults. The judicial extirpation of the Canaanites is but another instance of the fact that the interests of man's moral progress occasionally demand the employment of stern and relentless methods. 'Here is no partiality of a merely national God befriending His worshippers at the expense of others, without regard to justice; here rather is a Power making for righteousness and against iniquity; yea, a Power acting with a beneficent regard to the good of humanity, burying a putrefying carcase out of sight, lest it should taint the air. In the execution of His righteous purposes, Almighty God is guided by one supreme aim, namely, the elevation of human character. It is to be observed, that *Israel itself is threatened with a similar judgment, in the event of its yielding to the depraved rites and practices of heathendom*' (Bruce).

19–20. DESTRUCTION OF TREES

A precautionary warning to Israel—in view of such practices by nomadic warriors—not to devastate the land they are setting out to conquer.

19. *is the tree . . . man?* The trees of a besieged city must not be cut down, because they are vital to man (Ibn Ezra). The Rabbis deduce from this *v.* a prohibition of the wanton destruction of anything useful to man (**בל תשחית**).

20. *not trees for food.* Should the trees, however, not be fruit-bearing, and hence not vital to man, then by all means let them be cut down, if military necessity demands it.

מַאֲכָל הוּא אֹתוֹ תַשְׁחִית וְכָרָתָּ וּבָנִיתָ מָצוֹר עַל־הָעִיר
אֲשֶׁר־הִוא עֹשָׂה עִמְּךָ מִלְחָמָה עַד רִדְתָּהּ׃ פ

of which thou knowest that they are not trees for food, them thou mayest destroy and cut down, that thou mayest build bulwarks against the city that maketh war with thee, until it fall.

CAP. XXI. כא

כא

א כִּי־יִמָּצֵא חָלָל בָּאֲדָמָה אֲשֶׁר יְהוָה אֱלֹהֶיךָ נֹתֵן לְךָ
2 לְרִשְׁתָּהּ נֹפֵל בַּשָּׂדֶה לֹא נוֹדַע מִי הִכָּהוּ׃ וְיָצְאוּ זְקֵנֶיךָ
3 וְשֹׁפְטֶיךָ וּמָדְדוּ אֶל־הֶעָרִים אֲשֶׁר סְבִיבֹת הֶחָלָל׃ וְהָיָה
הָעִיר הַקְּרֹבָה אֶל־הֶחָלָל וְלָקְחוּ זִקְנֵי הָעִיר הַהִוא עֶגְלַת
4 בָּקָר אֲשֶׁר לֹא־עֻבַּד בָּהּ אֲשֶׁר לֹא־מָשְׁכָה בְּעֹל׃ וְהוֹרִדוּ
זִקְנֵי הָעִיר הַהִוא אֶת־הָעֶגְלָה אֶל־נַחַל אֵיתָן אֲשֶׁר לֹא־
ה יֵעָבֵד בּוֹ וְלֹא יִזָּרֵעַ וְעָרְפוּ־שָׁם אֶת־הָעֶגְלָה בַּנָּחַל׃ וְנִגְּשׁוּ
הַכֹּהֲנִים בְּנֵי לֵוִי כִּי בָם בָּחַר יְהוָה אֱלֹהֶיךָ לְשָׁרְתוֹ וּלְבָרֵךְ
6 בְּשֵׁם יְהוָה וְעַל־פִּיהֶם יִהְיֶה כָּל־רִיב וְכָל־נָגַע׃ וְכֹל זִקְנֵי

21

Chapter XXI

1. If one be found slain in the land which the LORD thy God giveth thee to possess it, lying in the field, and it be not known who hath smitten him; 2. then thy elders and thy judges shall come forth, and they shall measure unto the cities which are round about him that is slain. 3. And it shall be, that the city which is nearest unto the slain man, even the elders of that city shall take a heifer of the herd, which hath not been wrought with, and which hath not drawn in the yoke. 4. And the elders of that city shall bring down the heifer unto a rough valley, which may neither be plowed nor sown, and shall break the heifer's neck there in the valley. 5. And the priests the sons of Levi shall come near—for them the LORD thy God hath chosen to minister unto Him, and to bless in the name of the LORD; and according to their word shall every controversy and

Chapter XXI

This chapter contains various laws concerning the sacredness of human life, and regard for the rights and dignity of human nature.

1–9. On the Expiation of an Untraced Murder

If a slain man be found in the open country, the murderer being unknown, the elders of the nearest town shall slay a young heifer in an uncultivated valley with a stream, and testify that they neither shed this blood nor saw it shed, and pray for forgiveness. In Israel, murder is not only a crime committed against a fellow-man, but also a sin against God in whose image man was made; hence, no money-compensation was permitted in the case of the wilful murderer (Num. xxxv, 33), 'for the soul is not the possession of the nearest of kin, but of the Holy One, blessed be He' (Maimonides). 'According to the oldest Hellenic idea, the murderer violated only the family sphere. Mosaism, however, by virtue of its conception of the human being as of Divine image, recognized in murder above all a sin against the Holy God, the Creator and Master of human life, Gen. IX, 5–6, which sin has to be atoned for by the extermination of the guilty murderer from the Holy Land defiled by blood-guilt' (Oehler). When the murderer is not known, the whole community is held responsible for the crime perpetrated on one of its members; see on *v.* 7.

1. *in the field.* The open country.

2. *thy elders.* Of the towns in the vicinity.

thy judges. Each village would naturally desire to get rid of the responsibility of providing a heifer, and its elders would be apt to exaggerate the distance between their home and the body. Hence, the presence of the judges was required, as arbiters and overseers, that all matters connected with the measurement and resultant responsibility are equitably settled (Welch).

3. *not been wrought with. i.e.* not been used for ploughing or subjected to any forced labour; and, therefore, unprofaned by common use.

4. *a rough valley.* lit. 'a strong valley'; *i.e.* a rough, uncultivated, unfrequented territory, with a perennial brook. Its running water would carry away the blood of the heifer, and thus symbolize the removal of the defilement from the land.

The Rabbis' explanation of these ceremonies is, 'Let the heifer which has never produced fruit (*i.e.* which has never been set to do any work) be killed in a spot which has never produced fruit (*i.e.* a rough, uncultivated ground), to atone for the death of a man who was debarred (through being prematurely made to die) from producing fruit.' According to Maimonides, the object of this rite was to assist in the discovery of the murderer by the publicity attending the performance thereof.

5. *the priests.* Their presence is to impart a religious character to the ceremony.

controversy . . . stroke. See on XVII, 8.

every stroke be. 6. And all the elders of that city, who are nearest unto the slain man, shall wash their hands over the heifer whose neck was broken in the valley.*m. 7. And they shall speak and say: 'Our hands have not shed this blood, neither have our eyes seen it. 8. Forgive, O LORD, Thy people Israel, whom Thou hast redeemed, and suffer not innocent blood to remain in the midst of Thy people Israel.' And the blood shall be forgiven them. 9. So shalt thou put away the innocent blood from the midst of thee, when thou shalt do that which is right in the eyes of the LORD.

הָעִיר הַהִוא הַקְּרֹבִים אֶל־הֶחָלָל יִרְחֲצוּ אֶת־יְדֵיהֶם עַל־
*פטיר 7 הָעֶגְלָה הָעֲרוּפָה בַנָּחַל׃ * וְעָנוּ וְאָמְרוּ יָדֵינוּ לֹא שָׁפְכָה
8 אֶת־הַדָּם הַזֶּה וְעֵינֵינוּ לֹא רָאוּ׃ כַּפֵּר לְעַמְּךָ יִשְׂרָאֵל
אֲשֶׁר־פָּדִיתָ יְהוָה וְאַל־תִּתֵּן דָּם נָקִי בְּקֶרֶב עַמְּךָ יִשְׂרָאֵל
9 וְנִכַּפֵּר לָהֶם הַדָּם׃ וְאַתָּה תְּבַעֵר הַדָּם הַנָּקִי מִקִּרְבֶּךָ
כִּי־תַעֲשֶׂה הַיָּשָׁר בְּעֵינֵי יְהוָה׃

v. 7. שפכו ק׳

6. *wash their hands.* Innocent blood shed by violence sticks to the hands of the murderer, and all the seas cannot wash away its stain. It is otherwise with those who—the actual murderer being unknown—are held to be only morally responsible for the crime. In their case, the washing of the hands is a symbolic act to disown the community's guilt; Ps. XXVI, 6. No trace of this symbolic action is found in Greek or Roman life (*contra* Matth. XXVII, 24).

7. *speak.* Respond liturgically.
our hands . . . eyes. 'Could it possibly occur to anyone to suspect the elders of murder? No! By this avowal the elders of the town declare, He did not come to us hungry, and we failed to feed him; he did not come to us friendless, and we failed to befriend him' (Sifri). Thus did the Rabbis bring home to the people the great principle of mutual responsibility and moral interdependence of men and classes.

8. *forgive.* This is spoken by the priests. They ask forgiveness because the people of the vicinity had sinned in failing adequately to safeguard the roads against danger (Ibn Ezra).

9. *so shalt thou put away.* If the murderer is discovered after the ceremony had been performed, he must be put to death. 'Then shalt thou be doing that which is right in the eyes of the LORD.'
innocent blood. Which cries to God for vengeance against the murderer; Gen. IV, 10; Job XVI, 18.

HAFTORAH SHOFETIM הפטרת שפטים

ISAIAH LI, 12–LII, 12

CHAPTER LI

12. I, even I, am He that comforteth you;
Who art thou, that thou art afraid of man that shall die,
And of the son of man that shall be made as grass;

CAP. LI. נא

12 אָנֹכִי אָנֹכִי הוּא מְנַחֶמְכֶם מִי־אַתְּ וַתִּירְאִי
1 מֵאֱנוֹשׁ יָמוּת וּמִבֶּן־אָדָם חָצִיר יִנָּתֵן׃ וַתִּשְׁכַּח יְהוָה עֹשֶׂךָ

This is the fourth of the Haftorahs of Consolation: Israel shall be redeemed from exile, and be the means of extending God's salvation to all mankind. The Haftorah brings a programme of religion—to plant heaven and establish the earth for the children of men. The Sidrah, in one of its luminous commands—'justice, justice, shalt thou follow'—gives the fundamental prerequisite for all human living on earth.

12–16. THE ALMIGHTY GOD IS ZION'S COMFORTER

12. *afraid of man.* Such as the King of Babylon.
son of man. i.e. a member of the human race, of frail humanity.
made as grass. Given up to destruction.

13. And hast forgotten the LORD thy Maker,
That stretched forth the heavens,
And laid the foundations of the earth;
And fearest continually all the day
Because of the fury of the oppressor,
As he maketh ready to destroy?
And where is the fury of the oppressor?
14. He that is bent down shall speedily be loosed;
And he shall not go down dying into the pit,
Neither shall his bread fail.
15. For I am the LORD thy God,
Who stirreth up the sea, that the waves thereof roar;
The LORD of hosts is His name.
16. And I have put My words in thy mouth,
And have covered thee in the shadow of My hand,
That I may plant the heavens,
And lay the foundations of the earth,
And say unto Zion: 'Thou art My people.'

נֹטֶה שָׁמַיִם וְיֹסֵד אָרֶץ וַתְּפַחֵד תָּמִיד כָּל־הַיּוֹם מִפְּנֵי חֲמַת
14 הַמֵּצִיק כַּאֲשֶׁר כּוֹנֵן לְהַשְׁחִית וְאַיֵּה חֲמַת הַמֵּצִיק׃ מִהַר
טו צֹעֶה לְהִפָּתֵחַ וְלֹא־יָמוּת לַשַּׁחַת וְלֹא יֶחְסַר לַחְמוֹ׃ וְאָנֹכִי
יְהוָה אֱלֹהֶיךָ רֹגַע הַיָּם וַיֶּהֱמוּ גַּלָּיו יְהוָה צְבָאוֹת שְׁמוֹ׃
16 וָאָשִׂם דְּבָרַי בְּפִיךָ וּבְצֵל יָדִי כִּסִּיתִיךָ לִנְטֹעַ שָׁמַיִם וְלִיסֹד
17 אָרֶץ וְלֵאמֹר לְצִיּוֹן עַמִּי־אָתָּה׃ הִתְעוֹרְרִי הִתְעוֹרְרִי
קוּמִי יְרוּשָׁלַםִ אֲשֶׁר שָׁתִית מִיַּד יְהוָה אֶת־כּוֹס חֲמָתוֹ

17. Awake, awake,
Stand up, O Jerusalem,
That hast drunk at the hand of the LORD
The cup of His fury;
Thou hast drunken the beaker, even the cup of staggering,
And drained it.

v. 13. קמץ בסגולתא v. 16. קמץ בז״ק

13. *oppressor.* The Babylonian rulers. Ehrlich refers this to Cyrus, the great conqueror, who then filled the hearts of men, and also of the overwhelming number of the Jewish exiles, with alarm.

as he maketh ready to destroy. 'As if he intended to destroy you' (Ehrlich).

where is the fury of the oppressor? Cyrus has no intention to destroy you. On the contrary.

14. *pit.* Grave.

15. *stirreth up the sea.* Restrains its fury, so that its waves beat in vain against the shore. 'By the roar and crash of the ocean on the beach, the Hebrew prophet sought to render the futile rage of the world, as it dashed on the steadfast will of God' (G. A. Smith).

16. *I have put.* He Who had in the beginning created the heavens and the earth would now, through the Righteous Remnant, the sanctified minority in Israel, create a new heaven and a new earth. This *v.* is of wonderful depth, and is in fact a summary of Israel's place and function in the spiritual life of humanity.

put My words in thy mouth. God's message to man was through Israel. 'As long as the world lasts, all who want to make progress in righteousness will come to Israel for inspiration, as the people who have the sense for righteousness most glowing and strongest' (Matthew Arnold).

covered thee. Wonderful as had been the Election of Israel, equally so has been Israel's preservation through all the fires and floods of history. Both such Divine Election and miraculous Preservation were for purposes that embrace all mankind. The Prophet now enumerates three of these purposes.

that I may plant the heavens. The new heavens and the new earth; see LXV, 17. With the break-up of the heathen kingdoms and the restoration of Israel begins a new epoch for humanity. Heb. לנטע שמים, lit. 'to plant Heaven.' Heaven is here compared to a *seed* that will grow into a tree, and yield fruit and shelter to the children of men. And Heaven may be planted! Whenever we teach a child by word or example a noble thought, deed, or way of life, we plant Heaven. In the same way, Heaven can be planted in the soul of a people, or peoples. Israel was chosen and Providentially preserved, in order that through Israel God might plant Heaven—*i.e.* righteousness and mercy—in the soul of humanity.

lay the foundations of the earth. i.e. to teach mankind what are the true foundations of human society: not 'blood and iron', but Truth, Justice, Peace—ideals which the Servant of the Lord was to teach the children of men.

thou art My people. Israel to remain throughout history a witness of God among the nations.

17–23. THE END OF ZION'S TRIBULATION

17. *awake, awake.* From thy despair! Since her fall, Jerusalem is in a stupor, having drained the staggering cup of misfortune and ruin to its very dregs.

18. There is none to guide her
Among all the sons whom she hath brought forth;
Neither is there any that taketh her by the hand
Of all the sons that she hath brought up.
19. These two things are befallen thee;
Who shall bemoan thee?
Desolation and destruction, and the famine and the sword;
How shall I comfort thee?
20. Thy sons have fainted, they lie at the head of all the streets,
As an antelope in a net;
They are full of the fury of the LORD,
The rebuke of thy God.
21. Therefore hear now this, thou afflicted,
And drunken, but not with wine;
22. Thus saith thy Lord the LORD,
And thy God that pleadeth the cause of His people:
Behold, I have taken out of thy hand
The cup of staggering;
The beaker, even the cup of My fury,
Thou shalt no more drink it again;
23. And I will put it into the hand of them that afflict thee;
That have said to thy soul:
'Bow down, that we may go over';
And thou hast laid thy back as the ground,
And as the street, to them that go over.

18 אֶת־קֻבַּעַת כּוֹס הַתַּרְעֵלָה שָׁתִית מָצִית׃ אֵין מְנַהֵל לָהּ
מִכָּל־בָּנִים יָלָדָה וְאֵין מַחֲזִיק בְּיָדָהּ מִכָּל־בָּנִים גִּדֵּלָה׃
19 שְׁתַּיִם הֵנָּה קֹרְאֹתַיִךְ מִי יָנוּד לָךְ הַשֹּׁד וְהַשֶּׁבֶר וְהָרָעָב
כ וְהַחֶרֶב מִי אֲנַחֲמֵךְ׃ בָּנַיִךְ עֻלְּפוּ שָׁכְבוּ בְּרֹאשׁ כָּל־חוּצוֹת
21 כְּתוֹא מִכְמָר הַמְלֵאִים חֲמַת־יְהוָה גַּעֲרַת אֱלֹהָיִךְ׃ לָכֵן
22 שִׁמְעִי־נָא זֹאת עֲנִיָּה וּשְׁכֻרַת וְלֹא מִיָּיִן׃ כֹּה־אָמַר אֲדֹנַיִךְ
יְהוָה וֵאלֹהַיִךְ יָרִיב עַמּוֹ הִנֵּה לָקַחְתִּי מִיָּדֵךְ אֶת־כּוֹס
הַתַּרְעֵלָה אֶת־קֻבַּעַת כּוֹס חֲמָתִי לֹא־תוֹסִיפִי לִשְׁתּוֹתָהּ
23 עוֹד׃ וְשַׂמְתִּיהָ בְּיַד מוֹגַיִךְ אֲשֶׁר־אָמְרוּ לְנַפְשֵׁךְ שְׁחִי וְנַעֲבֹרָה
וַתָּשִׂימִי כָאָרֶץ גֵּוֵךְ וְכַחוּץ לַעֹבְרִים׃

CAP. LII. נב

א עוּרִי עוּרִי לִבְשִׁי עֻזֵּךְ צִיּוֹן לִבְשִׁי ׀ בִּגְדֵי תִפְאַרְתֵּךְ יְרוּשָׁלִַם

CHAPTER LII

1. Awake, awake,
Put on thy strength, O Zion;
Put on thy beautiful garments,
O Jerusalem, the holy city;
For henceforth there shall no more come into thee
The uncircumcised and the unclean.

נב׳ v. 1. מלרע

18. *none to guide her.* A drunken person needs someone to guide him.

19. *two things.* In this verse and the two following, the Prophet pictures the misery wrought by the siege and destruction of Jerusalem; ruin (desolation and destruction), and the death of her citizens (famine and the sword).

how shall I comfort thee? Or, 'by whom shall I comfort thee?' *i.e.* by citing which other nation whose sufferings have been as overwhelming as thine (Rashi, Ibn Ezra).

20. *at the head of.* At the corners of.

as an antelope in a net. 'Israel, the mountain-people, is likened to a gazelle, which all its swiftness and grace have not saved from the hunter's snare' (Cheyne).

full of the fury. The despondency that has come upon them through God's wrath.

21. *not with wine.* But with affliction from God.

23. *said to thy soul.* Those who afflicted Israel have at all times demanded of Israel that it give up its *soul* for them to go over. This Israel has ever refused to do; only its *back* would it give for the oppressor to go over. Therefore it survived. When others are thus fallen, they rise not again; המה כרעו ונפלו (Psalm xx, 9).

that we may go over. Eastern conquerors would walk, or even ride, over the backs of captive foes.

CHAPTER LII

Jerusalem will rise again from its present degradation. Let her array herself as a queen, surrounded by her restored children. The mountains and waste places of Judea shall rejoice at the Lord's triumphal return to Zion.

1–6. THE TRIUMPH OF ZION

1. *unclean.* No alien garrison is to remain within her.

2 עִיר הַקֹּדֶשׁ כִּי לֹא יוֹסִיף יָבֹא־בָךְ עוֹד עָרֵל וְטָמֵא׃ הִתְנַעֲרִי
מֵעָפָר קוּמִי שְּׁבִי יְרוּשָׁלָםִ הִתְפַּתְּחוּ מוֹסְרֵי צַוָּארֵךְ שְׁבִיָּה
3 בַּת־צִיּוֹן׃ כִּי־כֹה אָמַר יְהוָה חִנָּם נִמְכַּרְתֶּם וְלֹא
4 בְכֶסֶף תִּגָּאֵלוּ׃ כִּי כֹה אָמַר אֲדֹנָי יֱהֹוִה מִצְרַיִם יָרַד־
ה עַמִּי בָרִאשֹׁנָה לָגוּר שָׁם וְאַשּׁוּר בְּאֶפֶס עֲשָׁקוֹ׃ וְעַתָּה מַה־
לִּי־פֹה נְאֻם־יְהוָה כִּי־לֻקַּח עַמִּי חִנָּם מֹשְׁלָו יְהֵילִילוּ נְאֻם־
6 יְהוָה וְתָמִיד כָּל־הַיּוֹם שְׁמִי מִנֹּאָץ׃ לָכֵן יֵדַע עַמִּי שְׁמִי לָכֵן
7 בַּיּוֹם הַהוּא כִּי־אֲנִי־הוּא הַמְדַבֵּר הִנֵּנִי׃ מַה־נָּאווּ עַל־
הֶהָרִים רַגְלֵי מְבַשֵּׂר מַשְׁמִיעַ שָׁלוֹם מְבַשֵּׂר טוֹב מַשְׁמִיעַ
8 יְשׁוּעָה אֹמֵר לְצִיּוֹן מָלַךְ אֱלֹהָיִךְ׃ קוֹל צֹפַיִךְ נָשְׂאוּ קוֹל
9 יַחְדָּו יְרַנֵּנוּ כִּי עַיִן בְּעַיִן יִרְאוּ בְּשׁוּב יְהוָה צִיּוֹן׃ פִּצְחוּ רַנְּנוּ
יַחְדָּו חָרְבוֹת יְרוּשָׁלָםִ כִּי־נִחַם יְהוָה עַמּוֹ גָּאַל יְרוּשָׁלָםִ׃

2. Shake thyself from the dust;
Arise, and sit down, O Jerusalem;
Loose thyself from the bands of thy neck,
O captive daughter of Zion.

3. For thus saith the LORD:
Ye were sold for nought;
And ye shall be redeemed without money.

4. For thus saith the LORD God:
My people went down aforetime into Egypt to sojourn there;
And the Assyrian oppressed them without cause.

5. Now therefore, what do I here, saith the LORD,
Seeing that My people is taken away for nought?
They that rule over them do howl, saith the LORD,
And My name continually all the day is blasphemed.

6. Therefore My people shall know My name;
Therefore they shall know in that day
That I, even He that spoke, behold, here I am.

7. How beautiful upon the mountains
Are the feet of the messenger of good tidings,
That announceth peace, the harbinger of good tidings,
That announceth salvation;
That saith unto Zion:
'Thy God reigneth!'

8. Hark, thy watchmen! they lift up the voice,
Together do they sing;
For they shall see, eye to eye,
The LORD returning to Zion.

9. Break forth into joy, sing together,
Ye waste places of Jerusalem;
For the LORD hath comforted His people,
He hath redeemed Jerusalem.

v. 2. התפתחי קרי v. 5. משליו ק'

2. *sit down.* On thy throne (Rashi).
loose thyself from the bands. Better, *loosen for thyself the bonds of thy captivity.*

3. *sold for nought.* Her captors paid no price and, therefore, have no claim upon her.
redeemed without money. 'Egypt and Assyria never became Israel's purchasers and legal owners; so it is now with Babylon. Babylon has no permanent property in Israel whom it so heavily oppresses; therefore the Lord, who punished Israel by giving him over for a time to his enemies, will now restore him' (M. Arnold).

4. *without cause.* Without having acquired any right over Israel by services rendered to God.

5. *what do I here.* Why do I linger and cause My sons to linger here? (Rashi). The situation is unendurable, and inconsistent with the honour of God! If Egyptian and Assyrian tyranny have passed away, why should not Babylonian?
howl. Exult over Israel's defeat, which they take to be the defeat of Israel's God; see Ezek. XXXVI, 20.

6. *know My name.* 'Know the significance of My name and learn My power.'
behold, here I am. This phrase simply repeats the sense of the preceding clause.

7–12. The joy of the inhabitants of Jerusalem at the exiles' return. The coming of the tidings, that the exiles are coming back to Zion, is described by the Prophet as though he saw from a hill the arrival of the exultant Israelites preceded by those bearing the holy vessels that shared their captivity; see on v. 11.

7. *upon the mountains.* The herald is seen hastening over the hills with his message of joy and salvation.
thy God reigneth. He hath established His everlasting kingdom in Zion.

8. *eye to eye. i.e.* face to face; as one looks into the eyes of a friend.

10. The LORD hath made bare His holy arm
In the eyes of all the nations;
And all the ends of the earth shall see
The salvation of our God.

11. Depart ye, depart ye, go ye out from thence,
Touch no unclean thing;
Go ye out of the midst of her; be ye clean,
Ye that bear the vessels of the LORD.

12. For ye shall not go out in haste,
Neither shall ye go by flight;
For the LORD will go before you,
And the God of Israel will be your rearward.

י חָשַׂף יְהוָה אֶת־זְרוֹעַ קָדְשׁוֹ לְעֵינֵי כָּל־הַגּוֹיִם וְרָאוּ כָּל־
11 אַפְסֵי־אָרֶץ אֵת יְשׁוּעַת אֱלֹהֵינוּ׃ סוּרוּ סוּרוּ צְאוּ מִשָּׁם
12 טָמֵא אַל־תִּגָּעוּ צְאוּ מִתּוֹכָהּ הִבָּרוּ נֹשְׂאֵי כְּלֵי יְהוָה׃ כִּי לֹא
בְחִפָּזוֹן תֵּצֵאוּ וּבִמְנוּסָה לֹא תֵלֵכוּן כִּי־הֹלֵךְ לִפְנֵיכֶם יְהוָה
וּמְאַסִּפְכֶם אֱלֹהֵי יִשְׂרָאֵל׃

v. 10. קמץ בז״ק

9. *hath comforted.* The 'perfect of certainty', viewing a future action as if it had already taken place.

10. *hath made bare.* In readiness for action.

11. *go ye out from thence.* This is spoken to the fellow-Israelites in exile.
of her. Of Babylon.
be ye clean. Purify yourselves.
that bear the vessels. The holy vessels taken to Babylon at the destruction of the Temple; see Ezra I, 7 f.

12. *not in haste.* Or, 'not in flight,' as was the departure from Egypt (Exod. XII, 33). The exodus from Babylon shall be public and triumphant.
your rearward. Your rearguard. God would both lead them, collect the stragglers, and also protect them from any foe who dared to pursue (Rashi).

21

כא ס ס ס מט 49

10. When thou goest forth to battle against thine enemies, and the LORD thy God delivereth them into thy hands, and thou carriest them away captive, 11. and seest among the captives a woman of goodly form, and thou hast a desire unto her, and wouldest take her to thee to wife; 12. then thou shalt bring her home to thy house; and she shall shave her head, and pare her nails; 13. and she shall put the raiment of her captivity from off her, and shall remain in thy house, and bewail her father and her mother a full month; and after that thou mayest go in unto her, and be her husband, and she shall be thy wife. 14. And it shall be, if thou have no delight in her, then thou shalt let her go whither she will; but thou shalt not sell her at all for money,

י כִּֽי־תֵצֵא לַמִּלְחָמָה עַל־אֹיְבֶיךָ וּנְתָנוֹ יְהוָה אֱלֹהֶיךָ בְּיָדֶךָ
11 וְשָׁבִיתָ שִׁבְיוֹ׃ וְרָאִיתָ בַּשִּׁבְיָה אֵשֶׁת יְפַת־תֹּאַר וְחָשַׁקְתָּ
12 בָהּ וְלָקַחְתָּ לְךָ לְאִשָּׁה׃ וַהֲבֵאתָהּ אֶל־תּוֹךְ בֵּיתֶךָ וְגִלְּחָה
13 אֶת־רֹאשָׁהּ וְעָשְׂתָה אֶת־צִפָּרְנֶיהָ׃ וְהֵסִירָה אֶת־שִׂמְלַת
שִׁבְיָהּ מֵעָלֶיהָ וְיָשְׁבָה בְּבֵיתֶךָ וּבָכְתָה אֶת־אָבִיהָ וְאֶת־
אִמָּהּ יֶרַח יָמִים וְאַחַר כֵּן תָּבוֹא אֵלֶיהָ וּבְעַלְתָּהּ וְהָיְתָה
14 לְךָ לְאִשָּׁה׃ וְהָיָה אִם־לֹא חָפַצְתָּ בָּהּ וְשִׁלַּחְתָּהּ לְנַפְשָׁהּ

VI. KI THETZE

(CHAPTERS XXI, 10–XXV)

(4) LAWS OF DOMESTIC LIFE AND HUMAN KINDNESS

(*a*) XXI, 10–21. FAMILY LAWS

10–14. MARRIAGE WITH A CAPTIVE OF WAR

A female war-captive was not to be made a concubine till after an interval of a month. The bitter moments of the captive's first grief had to be respected. She must not subsequently be sold or treated as a slave.

10. *goest forth to battle.* Outside Palestine.

12. *bring her home.* This law inculcates thoughtfulness and forbearance under circumstances in which the warrior, elated by victory, might deem himself at liberty to act as he pleased (Driver). 'After the countless rapes of conquered women with which recent history has made us so painfully familiar, it is like hearing soft music to read of the warrior's duty to the enemy woman, of the necessary marriage with its set ritual and its due delay. And the Legislator proceeds to trace the course of the husband's duty in the event of the conquered alien woman failing to bring him the expected delight. "Then thou shalt let her go whither she will; but thou shalt not sell her at all for money, thou shalt not deal with her as a slave, because thou hast humbled her" ' (Zangwill).

shave . . . nails. Rites of purification and renunciation of her former heathendom, so as to render herself fit and worthy of acceptance in the fold of Israel; Lev. XIV, 9. Onkelos translates, 'she shall suffer her nails to grow'; and the Rabbis explain the whole procedure as designed to render her unattractive to the captor, and deter him from marrying her; see on *v.* 14.

13. *raiment of her captivity.* The clothes worn when she was taken captive were to be laid aside by reason of their heathen impurity.

a full month. For her grief to spend itself and to accustom herself to her new condition of life.

she shall be thy wife. And enjoy the full rights and duties of a Jewish wife; Exod. XXI, 10.

14. *no delight in her. i.e.* no longer any delight in her. The Rabbis deemed such a marriage a concession to human weakness, as a preventive against worse manifestations of the unbridled passions of man. Even though permissible, such an alliance should be discouraged. 'Holy Writ,' they say, 'here clearly indicates that a wife taken in this fashion will probably end by becoming an object of aversion to her husband.'

let her go. Divorce her; and, if she should be ill, he must not do so before her complete recovery (Sifri).

whither she will. As she will. She has complete freedom.

not sell her. Nor by any other method dispose of her (Ibn Ezra); see on Exod. XXI, 8.

deal with her as a slave. 'Make merchandise of her' (AV). He must not reduce her in the home to the level of a bondwoman (Sifri).

humbled her. Dishonoured her.

thou shalt not deal with her as a slave,
because thou hast humbled her. ¶ 15. If a
man have two wives, the one beloved, and
the other hated, and they have borne him
children, both the beloved and the hated;
and if the first-born son be hers that was
hated; 16. then it shall be, in the day that
he causeth his sons to inherit that which
he hath, that he may not make the son
of the beloved the first-born before the
son of the hated, who is the first-born;
17. but he shall acknowledge the first-born,
the son of the hated, by giving him a double
portion of all that he hath; for he is the
first-fruits of his strength; the right of the
first-born is his. ¶ 18. If a man have a
stubborn and rebellious son, that will not
hearken to the voice of his father, or the
voice of his mother, and though they
chasten him, will not hearken unto them;
19. then shall his father and his mother lay
hold on him, and bring him out unto the
elders of his city, and unto the gate of his
place; 20. and they shall say unto the
elders of his city: 'This our son is stubborn
and rebellious, he doth not hearken to our
voice; he is a glutton, and a drunkard.'
21. And all the men of his city shall stone

וּמָכֹר לֹא־תִמְכְּרֶנָּה בַּכָּסֶף לֹא־תִתְעַמֵּר בָּהּ תַּחַת אֲשֶׁר
טו עִנִּיתָהּ׃ ס כִּי־תִהְיֶיןָ לְאִישׁ שְׁתֵּי נָשִׁים הָאַחַת
אֲהוּבָה וְהָאַחַת שְׂנוּאָה וְיָלְדוּ־לוֹ בָנִים הָאֲהוּבָה וְהַשְּׂנוּאָה
16 וְהָיָה הַבֵּן הַבְּכֹר לַשְּׂנִיאָה׃ וְהָיָה בְּיוֹם הַנְחִילוֹ אֶת־בָּנָיו
אֵת אֲשֶׁר־יִהְיֶה לוֹ לֹא יוּכַל לְבַכֵּר אֶת־בֶּן־הָאֲהוּבָה עַל־
17 פְּנֵי בֶן־הַשְּׂנוּאָה הַבְּכֹר׃ כִּי אֶת־הַבְּכֹר בֶּן־הַשְּׂנוּאָה יַכִּיר
לָתֶת לוֹ פִּי שְׁנַיִם בְּכֹל אֲשֶׁר־יִמָּצֵא לוֹ כִּי־הוּא רֵאשִׁית
18 אֹנוֹ לוֹ מִשְׁפַּט הַבְּכֹרָה׃ ס כִּי־יִהְיֶה לְאִישׁ בֵּן סוֹרֵר
וּמוֹרֶה אֵינֶנּוּ שֹׁמֵעַ בְּקוֹל אָבִיו וּבְקוֹל אִמּוֹ וְיִסְּרוּ אֹתוֹ וְלֹא
19 יִשְׁמַע אֲלֵיהֶם׃ וְתָפְשׂוּ בוֹ אָבִיו וְאִמּוֹ וְהוֹצִיאוּ אֹתוֹ אֶל־
כ זִקְנֵי עִירוֹ וְאֶל־שַׁעַר מְקֹמוֹ׃ וְאָמְרוּ אֶל־זִקְנֵי עִירוֹ בְּנֵנוּ
21 זֶה סוֹרֵר וּמֹרֶה אֵינֶנּוּ שֹׁמֵעַ בְּקֹלֵנוּ זוֹלֵל וְסֹבֵא׃ וּרְגָמֻהוּ

15–17. The Right of the First-born

Succession to property is a source of discord in a family, as is the favouritism of parents. But the double portion due to the first-born son is inalienable, though his mother be the less loved wife.

15. *beloved . . . hated.* Relative terms only, denoting that one is preferred to the other, as Leah and Rachel (it is in this sense that Mal. I, 2, 3, p. 102, is to be understood). Rabbi Ishmael said, 'Human experience shows that, in every bigamous marriage, one wife is always more loved than the other.'

16. *in the day.* Not necessarily at the approach of death, but at any time when he announces what the division of his property is to be *at his death.* The Rabbis forbid a man to distribute his possessions, Lear-like, in his life-time; and they also warn a man against any discrimination between his children, aside from the privileges of the first-born.

he may not make. He is legally incapable of making.

before. In preference to.

17. *acknowledge.* lit. 'recognize'.

double portion. Twice as much as any of the other sons.

of all that he hath. The Talmud deduces from this that the first-born is not entitled to claim a double portion from the estate that will accrue *after* the father's death.

first-fruits of his strength. Cf. Gen. XLIX, 3.

18–21. A Disobedient Son

Israelite parents were particularly affectionate, and even indulgent. However, an incorrigible son whom milder measures failed to reclaim, might be tried by the elders at the gate, and was liable to death by stoning.

18. *stubborn and rebellious.* A son who throws off the authority of his parents as well as of God.

father . . . mother. Mark the equality of the parents, as in the Fifth Commandment.

chasten. See on VIII, 5.

19. *unto the gate.* The gateway; the Oriental forum.

20. *glutton.* Includes not only gluttony, but is a term for a general debauchee, 'riotous liver' (RV).

21. *all the men . . . stone him.* The Hebrew parent did not possess the power of life and death over his child. In Greece, weak children were *exposed, i.e.* left on a lonely mountain to perish; and in Rome, a father could at will put even a grown-up son to death. In Israel, however, even when vice and insubordination in an adolescent son had become intolerable, the parents must appeal to the decision of an impartial tribunal. The death-penalty could only be inflicted by the community, with the sanction of the elders of the city.

him with stones, that he die; so shalt thou put away the evil from the midst of thee; and all Israel shall hear, and fear.*ii. ¶ 22. And if a man have committed a sin worthy of death, and he be put to death, and thou hang him on a tree; 23. his body shall not remain all night upon the tree, but thou shalt surely bury him the same day; for he that is hanged is a reproach unto God; that thou defile not thy land which the LORD thy God giveth thee for an inheritance.

22

CHAPTER XXII

1. Thou shalt not see thy brother's ox or his sheep driven away, and hide thyself from them; thou shalt surely bring them back unto thy brother. 2. And if thy brother be not nigh unto thee, and thou know him not, then thou shalt bring it home to thy house, and it shall be with thee until thy brother require it, and thou shalt restore it to him. 3. And so shalt thou do with his ass; and so shalt thou do with his garment; and so shalt thou do with every lost thing of thy brother's,

כָּל־אַנְשֵׁי עִירוֹ בָאֲבָנִים וָמֵת וּבִעַרְתָּ הָרָע מִקִּרְבֶּךָ וְכָל־
שני
22 יִשְׂרָאֵל יִשְׁמְעוּ וְיִרָאוּ׃ * ס וְכִי־יִהְיֶה בְאִישׁ חֵטְא
23 מִשְׁפַּט־מָוֶת וְהוּמָת וְתָלִיתָ אֹתוֹ עַל־עֵץ׃ לֹא־תָלִין
נִבְלָתוֹ עַל־הָעֵץ כִּי־קָבוֹר תִּקְבְּרֶנּוּ בַּיּוֹם הַהוּא כִּי־קִלְלַת
אֱלֹהִים תָּלוּי וְלֹא תְטַמֵּא אֶת־אַדְמָתְךָ אֲשֶׁר יְהוָה אֱלֹהֶיךָ
נֹתֵן לְךָ נַחֲלָה׃ ס

CAP. XXII. כב

כב

א לֹא־תִרְאֶה אֶת־שׁוֹר אָחִיךָ אוֹ אֶת־שֵׂיוֹ נִדָּחִים וְהִתְעַלַּמְתָּ
2 מֵהֶם הָשֵׁב תְּשִׁיבֵם לְאָחִיךָ׃ וְאִם־לֹא קָרוֹב אָחִיךָ אֵלֶיךָ
וְלֹא יְדַעְתּוֹ וַאֲסַפְתּוֹ אֶל־תּוֹךְ בֵּיתֶךָ וְהָיָה עִמְּךָ עַד דְּרֹשׁ
3 אָחִיךָ אֹתוֹ וַהֲשֵׁבֹתוֹ לוֹ׃ וְכֵן תַּעֲשֶׂה לַחֲמֹרוֹ וְכֵן תַּעֲשֶׂה
לְשִׂמְלָתוֹ וְכֵן תַּעֲשֶׂה לְכָל־אֲבֵדַת אָחִיךָ אֲשֶׁר־תֹּאבַד

The Rabbis tell us that this law was never once carried out; and, by the regulations with which the infliction of the death-penalty was in this case surrounded, it could not be carried out (see also on XXII, 22). Its presence in the Torah was merely to serve as a warning, and bring out with the strongest possible emphasis the heinous crime of disobedience to parents.

(*b*) XXI, 22–XXII, 4. LAWS OF KINDNESS

22–23. THE EXPOSED CORPSE OF A CRIMINAL

22. *a sin worthy of death.* lit. 'a sin of judgment of death'; if a man lies under sentence of death.

and thou hang him. After he had been put to death; the fiendish punishment of crucifying men alive, nailing them to the cross and prolonging their death-agonies for days, was a Roman invention. There were four methods of execution in ancient Israel—stoning, burning, the sword, and strangulation. Hanging was sometimes added after death, in token of infamy, or as a further deterrent; Josh. X, 26.

23. *bury him.* Burial, and not cremation, is the Jewish method of disposal of the dead; see p. 80.

a reproach unto God. Or, 'involves the cursing of the judges' (Rashbam), by his relations. The former explanation is the more probable. 'It is a slight to the King, because man is made in the Divine image' (Rashi); and the dignity of humanity must be respected even in a criminal. Death, Judaism teaches, atones his sin; therefore, his body shall, at the earliest moment, receive the same reverent treatment that is due to any other deceased. The hanging was delayed till near sunset, so that the body might without delay be taken down for burial.

defile not thy land. A corpse is the primary source of ritual impurity (אבי אבות הטומאה); and, if the corpse were permitted to remain on the tree till it decomposes and falls apart, or it becomes food to the birds, such impurity would spread far and wide (Luzzatto).

CHAPTER XXII

1–3. RESTORING LOST PROPERTY

We have in these three verses a repetition of the law in Exod. XXIII, 4, 5, regarding our duty of restoring the strayed ox or ass, and of the lifting up of the fallen beast of burden. The law is here widened to include other lost articles that require restoration to their owners. Exodus speaks of the things belonging to 'thine enemy'; here the wider term, 'thy brother,' is used. Whether thy neighbour be thy brother or enemy, his property must be protected and restored.

1. *ox . . . sheep.* These names are typical, and the law applies to all domestic animals alike.

hide thyself from them. Fail to notice them or trouble about them, saying, 'It is no concern of mine.'

2. *restore it.* Failure to do so is accounted theft, and punished with a fine one-fifth over and above the value, if denied on oath; Lev. V, 20–24 (Chap. VI, 1–7 in English Bible).

which he hath lost, and thou hast found; thou mayest not hide thyself. ¶ 4. Thou shalt not see thy brother's ass or his ox fallen down by the way, and hide thyself from them; thou shalt surely help him to lift them up again. ¶ 5. A woman shall not wear that which pertaineth unto a man, neither shall a man put on a woman's garment; for whosoever doeth these things is an abomination unto the LORD thy God. ¶ 6. If a bird's nest chance to be before thee in the way, in any tree or on the ground, with young ones or eggs, and the dam sitting upon the young, or upon the eggs, thou shalt not take the dam with the young; 7. thou shalt in any wise let the dam go, but the young thou mayest take unto thyself; that it may be well with thee, and that thou mayest prolong thy days.*iii. ¶ 8. When thou buildest a new house, then thou shalt make a parapet for thy roof, that thou bring not blood upon thy house, if any man fall from thence. ¶ 9. Thou shalt not sow

4 מִמֶּנּוּ וּמְצָאתָהּ לֹא תוּכַל לְהִתְעַלֵּם׃ ס לֹא־תִרְאֶה
אֶת־חֲמוֹר אָחִיךָ אוֹ שׁוֹרוֹ נֹפְלִים בַּדֶּרֶךְ וְהִתְעַלַּמְתָּ מֵהֶם
ה הָקֵם תָּקִים עִמּוֹ׃ ס לֹא־יִהְיֶה כְלִי־גֶבֶר עַל־אִשָּׁה
וְלֹא־יִלְבַּשׁ גֶּבֶר שִׂמְלַת אִשָּׁה כִּי תוֹעֲבַת יְהוָה אֱלֹהֶיךָ
כָּל־עֹשֵׂה אֵלֶּה׃ פ
6 כִּי יִקָּרֵא קַן־צִפּוֹר ׀ לְפָנֶיךָ בַּדֶּרֶךְ בְּכָל־עֵץ ׀ אוֹ עַל־
הָאָרֶץ אֶפְרֹחִים אוֹ בֵיצִים וְהָאֵם רֹבֶצֶת עַל־הָאֶפְרֹחִים
7 אוֹ עַל־הַבֵּיצִים לֹא־תִקַּח הָאֵם עַל־הַבָּנִים׃ שַׁלֵּחַ תְּשַׁלַּח
אֶת־הָאֵם וְאֶת־הַבָּנִים תִּקַּח־לָךְ לְמַעַן יִיטַב לָךְ וְהַאֲרַכְתָּ
שלישי 8 יָמִים׃ * ס כִּי תִבְנֶה בַּיִת חָדָשׁ וְעָשִׂיתָ מַעֲקֶה לְגַגֶּךָ
9 וְלֹא־תָשִׂים דָּמִים בְּבֵיתֶךָ כִּי־יִפֹּל הַנֹּפֵל מִמֶּנּוּ׃ לֹא־

4. ASSISTING TO LIFT FALLEN BEASTS

4. *help him.* lit. 'help with him'; *i.e.* in company with the owner. The owner must not stand by idle and leave the work to others. A Chassidic Rabbi lamented that this law was little observed. and he devoted himself to its fulfilment. He was continually to be seen in the streets, helping one man to load his wagon, another to drag his cart out of the mire.

(*c*) XXII, 5–12. MISCELLANEOUS LAWS—FIRST GROUP

5. DISTINCTION OF SEX IN APPAREL

5. An interchange of attire between man and woman would promote immodesty and, in consequence, immorality. This law is probably directed against rites in Syrian heathenism, which included exchange of garments by the sexes and led to gross impurities.

6–7. SPARING THE MOTHER-BIRD

The ground of sympathy here is the sacredness of the parental relationship. The mother-bird is sacred as a mother; and length of days is promised to those who regard the sanctity of motherhood in this sphere, as it is promised to those who observe the Fifth Commandment. 'When the mother is sent away, she does not see the taking of her young ones, and does not feel any pain. The eggs over which the bird sits, and the brood that are in need of the mother, are generally unfit for food. Consequently, this commandment will cause man to leave the whole nest untouched. The Torah provides that such grief should not be caused to cattle (Lev. XXII, 28) or birds; how much more careful must we be that we should not cause grief to our fellow men' (Maimonides); see XXV, 4 f.

7. *prolong thy days.* Rabbi Akiba, referring to this promise of long life, supposes the case of a man who climbs a tower and takes the young from the nest, sparing the mother-bird in accordance with this commandment. But on his way down, he falls and dies. To this question, 'Where is the well-being and prolonging of days in this case?' Akiba answers, 'In the Life to Come where all goes well, and all is abiding.'

8. PARAPETS TO HOUSE-ROOFS

As the houses in all Eastern countries possessed flat roofs which were used for walking, sleeping, and other domestic purposes, it was necessary to erect a parapet to prevent accidental falling off. According to the Rabbis, the parapet was to be at least two cubits high.

8. *blood.* Blood-guiltiness; failure to protect human life exposes the builder, owner, or resident of the house to blood-guiltiness in the eyes of God. The Rabbis extended this prohibition to cover all cases where danger to life exists through our negligence; such as keeping a dangerous dog, or placing a broken ladder against a wall.

9. AGAINST MIXING SEEDS

This law—as well as the two laws following it against ploughing with an ox and an ass together, and the wearing of a garment composed of a mixture of wool and linen—is based on the idea that God has made distinctions in the natural world which it is wrong for a man to obliterate by processes of intermixing; see on Lev. XIX, 19.

thy vineyard with two kinds of seed; lest the fulness of the seed which thou hast sown be forfeited together with the increase of the vineyard. ¶ 10. Thou shalt not plow with an ox and an ass together. 11. Thou shalt not wear a mingled stuff, wool and linen together. ¶ 12. Thou shalt make thee twisted cords upon the four corners of thy covering, wherewith thou coverest thyself. ¶ 13. If any man take a wife, and go in unto her, and hate her, 14. and lay wanton charges against her, and bring up an evil name upon her, and say: 'I took this woman, and when I came nigh to her, I found not in her the tokens of virginity'; 15. then shall the father of the damsel, and her mother, take and bring forth the tokens of the damsel's virginity unto the elders of the city in the gate. 16. And the damsel's father shall say unto the elders: 'I gave my daughter unto this man to wife, and he hateth her; 17. and, lo, he hath laid wanton charges, saying: I found not in thy daughter the tokens of virginity;

תִּזְרַע כַּרְמְךָ כִּלְאָיִם פֶּן־תִּקְדַּשׁ הַמְלֵאָה הַזֶּרַע אֲשֶׁר תִּזְרָע
י וּתְבוּאַת הַכָּרֶם׃ ס לֹא־תַחֲרֹשׁ בְּשׁוֹר־וּבַחֲמֹר יַחְדָּו׃
11 12 לֹא תִלְבַּשׁ שַׁעַטְנֵז צֶמֶר וּפִשְׁתִּים יַחְדָּו׃ ס גְּדִלִים
תַּעֲשֶׂה־לָּךְ עַל־אַרְבַּע כַּנְפוֹת כְּסוּתְךָ אֲשֶׁר תְּכַסֶּה־בָּהּ׃
13 14 ס כִּי־יִקַּח אִישׁ אִשָּׁה וּבָא אֵלֶיהָ וּשְׂנֵאָהּ׃ וְשָׂם לָהּ
עֲלִילֹת דְּבָרִים וְהוֹצִא עָלֶיהָ שֵׁם רָע וְאָמַר אֶת־הָאִשָּׁה
הַזֹּאת לָקַחְתִּי וָאֶקְרַב אֵלֶיהָ וְלֹא־מָצָאתִי לָהּ בְּתוּלִים׃
טו וְלָקַח אֲבִי הַנַּעֲרָ וְאִמָּהּ וְהוֹצִיאוּ אֶת־בְּתוּלֵי הַנַּעֲרָ אֶל־
16 זִקְנֵי הָעִיר הַשָּׁעְרָה׃ וְאָמַר אֲבִי הַנַּעֲרָ אֶל־הַזְּקֵנִים אֶת־
17 בִּתִּי נָתַתִּי לָאִישׁ הַזֶּה לְאִשָּׁה וַיִּשְׂנָאֶהָ׃ וְהִנֵּה־הוּא
שָׂם עֲלִילֹת דְּבָרִים לֵאמֹר לֹא־מָצָאתִי לְבִתְּךָ בְּתוּלִים

v. 9. קמץ בז"ק v. 15. רה קרי ibid. רה קרי v. 16. רה קרי

9. *two kinds.* Heb. *kilayim,* mutually exclusive kinds.

forfeited. lit. 'to become consecrated'; the resultant crop would have to be consigned to the flames. The man would lose both his grapes and his other crop, as a penalty for his irreligious act.

10. Yoking an Ox and an Ass

10. *ox and an ass.* They differ greatly in their nature, in size, and strength; it is, therefore, cruel to the weaker animal to yoke them together.

11. Shaatnes

11. *mingled stuff.* The etymology and meaning of this word are both uncertain. Some derive it from the Egyptian. The reason underlying the prohibition may possibly be the same as that against mixing seeds, *v.* 9. The Rabbis class it with the prohibition of swine's flesh and other *chekkim,* which provoke the ridicule of scoffers, Jewish and non-Jewish, but which the loyal Israelite nevertheless willingly obeys, because they are the commands of his Father Who is in Heaven.

12. Tzitzis

12. *twisted cords.* Heb. *gedilim;* lit. 'twisted threads,' identified by the Rabbis with the *tzitzis* in Num. xv, 37–41. Among all peoples, knots have been used as reminders and symbols. The *tzitzis* are a constant reminder of the special relationship in which the Israelite stands to God, and the consequent duty of withstanding temptation to sin. There is a well-known Talmudic story of a reprobate and riotous liver who was recalled to his better self by the *tzitzis* he wore, so as to break completely with his wicked past.

(*d*) XXII, 13–XXIII, 9. HOLINESS OF MARRIAGE

13–21. Charges against a Bride

He who falsely accuses his wife of unchastity during betrothal shall be rebuked, fined, and he loses the right ever to divorce her. However, if such charge be true, it is a case of capital punishment. Betrothal in Bible times united the bridal couple as husband and wife for all purposes, save living together; and any infidelity on the part of the wife was considered adultery; see on *v.* 23. 'In considering these plain-spoken laws (*v.* 13–21), it is just to remember that they represent an upward stage in the struggle against the animal passions of men. That we do not need some of them to-day is due to the fact that their enforcement under religious sanction was needed at the time of their origin. It is only ignorance or ingratitude which can cavil at their spirit or their form' (G. A. Smith).

13. *and hate her.* The man had entered on marriage merely for the satisfaction of his passions, and then turned against his wife by a revulsion of feeling frequent in such characters (Bertholet); see on XXI, 14, and cf. II Sam. XIII, 15.

15. *the tokens.* Such evidence was regarded as essential by many ancient races, though the absence of those tokens is by no means conclusive of guilt. Some of the Rabbis, therefore, took the phrase concerning the tokens as a metaphorical expression (בורריו את הדבר כשמלה חדשה) for clearly establishing the falsity of his charge by witnesses and expert evidence.

and yet these are the tokens of my daughter's virginity.' And they shall spread the garment before the elders of the city. 18. And the elders of that city shall take the man and chastise him. 19. And they shall fine him a hundred shekels of silver, and give them unto the father of the damsel, because he hath brought up an evil name upon a virgin of Israel; and she shall be his wife; he may not put her away all his days. ¶ 20. But if this thing be true, that the tokens of virginity were not found in the damsel; 21. then they shall bring out the damsel to the door of her father's house, and the men of her city shall stone her with stones that she die; because she hath wrought a wanton deed in Israel, to play the harlot in her father's house; so shalt thou put away the evil from the midst of thee. ¶ 22. If a man be found lying with a woman married to a husband, then they shall both of them die, the man that lay with the woman, and the woman; so shalt thou put away the evil from Israel. ¶ 23. If there be a damsel that is a virgin betrothed unto a man, and a man find her in the city, and lie with her; 24. then ye shall bring them both out unto the gate of that city, and ye shall stone them with stones that they die: the damsel, because she cried not, being in the city; and the man, because he hath humbled his neighbour's wife; so thou shalt put away the evil from the midst of thee. ¶ 25. But if the man find the damsel that is betrothed in the field, and the man take hold of her, and lie with her; then the man only that

וְאֵלֶּה בְּתוּלֵי בִתִּי וּפָרְשׂוּ הַשִּׂמְלָה לִפְנֵי זִקְנֵי הָעִיר׃
18 וְלָקְחוּ זִקְנֵי הָעִיר־הַהִוא אֶת־הָאִישׁ וְיִסְּרוּ אֹתוֹ׃ וְעָנְשׁוּ 19
אֹתוֹ מֵאָה כֶסֶף וְנָתְנוּ לַאֲבִי הַנַּעֲרָה כִּי הוֹצִיא שֵׁם רָע
עַל בְּתוּלַת יִשְׂרָאֵל וְלוֹ־תִהְיֶה לְאִשָּׁה לֹא־יוּכַל לְשַׁלְּחָהּ
כ כָּל־יָמָיו׃ ס וְאִם־אֱמֶת הָיָה הַדָּבָר הַזֶּה לֹא־נִמְצְאוּ
21 בְתוּלִים לַנַּעֲרָ׃ וְהוֹצִיאוּ אֶת־הַנַּעֲרָ אֶל־פֶּתַח בֵּית־אָבִיהָ
וּסְקָלוּהָ אַנְשֵׁי עִירָהּ בָּאֲבָנִים וָמֵתָה כִּי־עָשְׂתָה נְבָלָה
בְּיִשְׂרָאֵל לִזְנוֹת בֵּית אָבִיהָ וּבִעַרְתָּ הָרָע מִקִּרְבֶּךָ׃ ס
22 כִּי־יִמָּצֵא אִישׁ שֹׁכֵב ׀ עִם־אִשָּׁה בְעֻלַת־בַּעַל וּמֵתוּ גַּם־
שְׁנֵיהֶם הָאִישׁ הַשֹּׁכֵב עִם־הָאִשָּׁה וְהָאִשָּׁה וּבִעַרְתָּ הָרָע
23 מִיִּשְׂרָאֵל׃ ס כִּי יִהְיֶה נַעֲרָ בְתוּלָה מְאֹרָשָׂה לְאִישׁ
24 וּמְצָאָהּ אִישׁ בָּעִיר וְשָׁכַב עִמָּהּ׃ וְהוֹצֵאתֶם אֶת־שְׁנֵיהֶם
אֶל־שַׁעַר ׀ הָעִיר הַהִוא וּסְקַלְתֶּם אֹתָם בָּאֲבָנִים וָמֵתוּ אֶת־
הַנַּעֲרָ עַל־דְּבַר אֲשֶׁר לֹא־צָעֲקָה בָעִיר וְאֶת־הָאִישׁ עַל־
דְּבַר אֲשֶׁר־עִנָּה אֶת־אֵשֶׁת רֵעֵהוּ וּבִעַרְתָּ הָרָע מִקִּרְבֶּךָ׃
כה ס וְאִם־בַּשָּׂדֶה יִמְצָא הָאִישׁ אֶת־הַנַּעֲרָ הַמְאֹרָשָׂה
וְהֶחֱזִיק־בָּהּ הָאִישׁ וְשָׁכַב עִמָּהּ וּמֵת הָאִישׁ אֲשֶׁר־שָׁכַב

נערה ק' v. 20. 21. 23. 24. 25.

18. *chastise him.* Inflict the corporal punishment, 'thirty-nine stripes,' upon him (Talmud).

19. *an hundred shekels.* Nominally £13 15*s.*; then the equivalent of a far greater sum.

unto the father. Whose family name had been defamed. 'If the damsel is an orphan the fine goes to her' (Talmud).

put her away. Divorce her.

20. *this thing.* The charge, see on *v.* 15.

be true. And—add the Rabbis—if at the time she had been warned by witnesses of the serious consequences of her conduct.

21. *to the door of her father's house.* Not at the city gate, because it was her father's house which she had dishonoured.

wanton deed. Or, 'folly' (AV). Heb. *nevalah.* 'The Heb. word does not indicate weakness of reason, but a rooted incapacity to discern moral and religious relations, leading to an intolerant repudiation in practice of the claims which they impose' (Driver).

wanton deed in Israel. Or, 'folly.' Her action is an offence against the national standard, a crime against the national conscience. 'She did not merely degrade herself, but every virgin in Israel' (Sifri).

22. Adultery

22. *both of them die.* The man as well as the woman; cf. Lev. xx, 10. There is to be no double standard of conjugal morality in Israel.

As in the case of all capital offences, the Rabbis required that the guilty parties be warned of the seriousness of their proposed action. Without such warning (*hathraah*), the death penalty could not be carried out. Furthermore, the law of evidence in capital offences and the proof of premeditation were made so severe that a death verdict was almost impossible. R. Tarphon and R. Akiba said, 'If we would have been in the Sanhedrin, a man would never have been executed by it.' A few lines before it is stated, 'A Sanhedrin that executes a person once in seven years is called destructive.' R. Eleazar ben Azaryah says, 'Once in seventy years.'

lay with her shall die. 26. But unto the damsel thou shalt do nothing; there is in the damsel no sin worthy of death; for as when a man riseth against his neighbour, and slayeth him, even so is this matter. 27. For he found her in the field; the betrothed damsel cried, and there was none to save her. ¶ 28. If a man find a damsel that is a virgin, that is not betrothed, and lay hold on her, and lie with her, and they be found; 29. then the man that lay with her shall give unto the damsel's father fifty shekels of silver, and she shall be his wife, because he hath humbled her; he may not put her away all his days.

23

Chapter XXIII

1. A man shall not take his father's wife, and shall not uncover his father's skirt. ¶ 2. He that is crushed or maimed in his privy parts shall not enter into the assembly of the Lord. ¶ 3. A bastard shall not enter into the assembly of the Lord; even to the tenth generation shall none of his enter into the assembly of the Lord. ¶ 4. An Ammonite or a Moabite shall not enter into the assembly of the Lord; even to the tenth generation shall none of them enter into the assembly of the Lord for ever; 5.

26 עִמָּהּ לְבַדּוֹ׃ וְלַנַּעֲרָ לֹא־תַעֲשֶׂה דָבָר אֵין לַנַּעֲרָ חֵטְא מָוֶת
כִּי כַּאֲשֶׁר יָקוּם אִישׁ עַל־רֵעֵהוּ וּרְצָחוֹ נֶפֶשׁ כֵּן הַדָּבָר
27 הַזֶּה׃ כִּי בַשָּׂדֶה מְצָאָהּ צָעֲקָה הַנַּעֲרָ הַמְאֹרָשָׂה וְאֵין
28 מוֹשִׁיעַ לָהּ׃ ס כִּי־יִמְצָא אִישׁ נַעֲרָ בְתוּלָה אֲשֶׁר לֹא־
29 אֹרָשָׂה וּתְפָשָׂהּ וְשָׁכַב עִמָּהּ וְנִמְצָאוּ׃ וְנָתַן הָאִישׁ הַשֹּׁכֵב
עִמָּהּ לַאֲבִי הַנַּעֲרָ חֲמִשִּׁים כָּסֶף וְלוֹ־תִהְיֶה לְאִשָּׁה תַּחַת
אֲשֶׁר עִנָּהּ לֹא־יוּכַל שַׁלְּחָהּ כָּל־יָמָיו׃ ס

Cap. XXIII. כג

כג

א לֹא־יִקַּח אִישׁ אֶת־אֵשֶׁת אָבִיו וְלֹא יְגַלֶּה כְּנַף אָבִיו׃ ס
2 לֹא־יָבֹא פְצוּעַ־דַּכָּה וּכְרוּת שָׁפְכָה בִּקְהַל יְהוָה׃ ס
3 לֹא־יָבֹא מַמְזֵר בִּקְהַל יְהוָה גַּם דּוֹר עֲשִׂירִי לֹא־יָבֹא לוֹ
4 בִּקְהַל יְהוָה׃ ס לֹא־יָבֹא עַמּוֹנִי וּמוֹאָבִי בִּקְהַל
יְהוָה גַּם דּוֹר עֲשִׂירִי לֹא־יָבֹא לָהֶם בִּקְהַל יְהוָה עַד־

כב׳ v. 26. 27. 28. 29. רה ק׳

23–27. A Betrothed Virgin

26. *no sin.* Where there is compulsion, *force majeure*, there is no sin, or any of the legal consequences of sin.

27. *cried.* The woman is given the benefit of the doubt (Rashbam, Sforno). A similar provision, with similar phrasing, is found in the newly-discovered Hittite Law, going back to the year 1350 B.C.E. It seems, therefore, that in the laws concerning rape we have the Common Law of the more advanced Semitic nations, just as we have seen in the Code of Hammurabi parallels to the Civil Legislation in Exodus; see p. 403.

28–29. A Virgin not Betrothed

The man must pay the 'bride-price' and marry her, without right of divorce.

Chapter XXIII

1. Prohibition of Marriage with Stepmother

This law was aimed at the ancient heathen custom of inheriting women in the same way as other possessions of the deceased.

1. *his father's skirt.* Or, 'his father's bed-cover'; a euphemism for marital relation; see Ruth III, 9.

2–9. Classes Excluded from Congregation

2. *enter into the assembly of the LORD.* Be counted as belonging to the community. He shall not therefore be permitted to marry an Israelite woman. The first to be excluded are the self-mutilated or unsexed in the service of some heathen cult. Isa. LVI, 3 f speaks of men whose mutilation was not voluntary.

3. *bastard.* Heb. ממזר. This does *not* mean a child born out of wedlock, but the child of an adulterous or an incestuous marriage (*i.e.* one with the forbidden degrees of kinship as laid down in Lev. XVIII and XX).

tenth generation. i.e. never. The numeral 'ten' here denotes an indefinitely large number; cf. Gen. XXXI, 7.

4. *Ammonite or a Moabite.* From the use of the masculine and not the feminine, the Talmud deduces that it is only the male Ammonite and the male Moabite that are excluded. But the females could, after proselytization, marry male Israelites; *e.g.* Ruth, who was a Moabitess, entered the Jewish fold and became the ancestress of King David.

According to the Rabbis this prohibition in regard to the admission of Ammon, Moab, Edom, and Egypt into the community ceased with Assyrian conquest, which drove the inhabitants from their original homes and led to a commingling of tribes and races.

because they met you not with bread and with water in the way, when ye came forth out of Egypt; and because they hired against thee Balaam the son of Beor from Pethor of Aramnaharaim, to curse thee. 6. Nevertheless the LORD thy God would not hearken unto Balaam; but the LORD thy God turned the curse into a blessing unto thee, because the LORD thy God loved thee. 7. Thou shalt not seek their peace nor their prosperity all thy days for ever. *iv. ¶ 8. Thou shalt not abhor an Edomite, for he is thy brother; thou shalt not abhor an Egyptian, because thou wast a stranger in his land. 9. The children of the third generation that are born unto them may enter into the assembly of the LORD. ¶ 10. When thou goest forth in camp against thine enemies, then thou shalt keep thee from every evil thing. 11. If there be among you any man, that is not clean by reason of that which chanceth him by night, then shall he go abroad out of the camp, he shall not come within the camp. 12. But it shall be, when evening cometh on, he shall bathe himself in water; and when the sun is down, he may come within the camp. 13. Thou shalt have a place also without the camp, whither thou shalt go forth abroad. 14. And thou shalt have a paddle among thy weapons; and it shall be, when thou sittest down abroad, thou shalt dig therewith, and shalt turn back and cover that which cometh from thee. 15. For the LORD thy God walketh in the midst of thy camp,

ה עוֹלָם׃ עַל־דְּבַר אֲשֶׁר לֹא־קִדְּמוּ אֶתְכֶם בַּלֶּחֶם וּבַמַּיִם
בַּדֶּרֶךְ בְּצֵאתְכֶם מִמִּצְרָיִם וַאֲשֶׁר שָׂכַר עָלֶיךָ אֶת־בִּלְעָם
6 בֶּן־בְּעוֹר מִפְּתוֹר אֲרַם נַהֲרַיִם לְקַלְלֶךָּ׃ וְלֹא־אָבָה יְהוָה
אֱלֹהֶיךָ לִשְׁמֹעַ אֶל־בִּלְעָם וַיַּהֲפֹךְ יְהוָה אֱלֹהֶיךָ לְּךָ אֶת־
7 הַקְּלָלָה לִבְרָכָה כִּי אֲהֵבְךָ יְהוָה אֱלֹהֶיךָ׃ לֹא־תִדְרֹשׁ
רביעי 8 שְׁלֹמָם וְטֹבָתָם כָּל־יָמֶיךָ לְעוֹלָם׃ * ס לֹא־תְתַעֵב
אֲדֹמִי כִּי אָחִיךָ הוּא לֹא־תְתַעֵב מִצְרִי כִּי־גֵר הָיִיתָ
9 בְאַרְצוֹ׃ בָּנִים אֲשֶׁר־יִוָּלְדוּ לָהֶם דּוֹר שְׁלִישִׁי יָבֹא לָהֶם
י בִּקְהַל יְהוָה׃ ס כִּי־תֵצֵא מַחֲנֶה עַל־אֹיְבֶיךָ וְנִשְׁמַרְתָּ
11 מִכֹּל דָּבָר רָע׃ כִּי־יִהְיֶה בְךָ אִישׁ אֲשֶׁר לֹא־יִהְיֶה
טָהוֹר מִקְּרֵה־לָיְלָה וְיָצָא אֶל־מִחוּץ לַמַּחֲנֶה לֹא יָבֹא
12 אֶל־תּוֹךְ הַמַּחֲנֶה׃ וְהָיָה לִפְנוֹת־עֶרֶב יִרְחַץ בַּמָּיִם
13 וּכְבֹא הַשֶּׁמֶשׁ יָבֹא אֶל־תּוֹךְ הַמַּחֲנֶה׃ וְיָד תִּהְיֶה לְךָ
14 מִחוּץ לַמַּחֲנֶה וְיָצָאתָ שָּׁמָּה חוּץ׃ וְיָתֵד תִּהְיֶה לְךָ עַל־
אֲזֵנֶךָ וְהָיָה בְּשִׁבְתְּךָ חוּץ וְחָפַרְתָּה בָהּ וְשַׁבְתָּ וְכִסִּיתָ
טו אֶת־צֵאָתֶךָ׃ כִּי יְהוָה אֱלֹהֶיךָ מִתְהַלֵּךְ ׀ בְּקֶרֶב מַחֲנֶךָ

5. *with bread.* In Deut. II, 29, the Moabites *sold* the bread and water to the Israelites. As for the Ammonites, there is no record of their willingness to do even as much for them.

they hired. In the Heb. the singular is used, because Moab alone hired Balaam against Israel; Num. XXII, 5.

6. *turned the curse.* See Num. XXIII, 11, 25, and XXIV, 10.

7. *not seek their peace. i.e.* thou shall not invite them to be on terms of amity with thee, as a punishment for their inhuman treatment of Israel. 'Not hatred, but indifference, is commanded here' (Oettli).

8. *thy brother.* Thy blood-brother, therefore, must not be placed under a ban of exclusion.

an Egyptian. The oppression of the Egyptians was the act of the Pharaohs rather than the will of the people. Israel had found a home in Egypt, and the Israelites were 'guests' (גרים) in that land. For this the Egyptians must be remembered with gratitude. National gratitude is as rare as national self-criticism: Israel is the classical example of both.

stranger. Heb. גר; here in the meaning of 'guest'.

(*e*) XXIII, 10–25. MISCELLANEOUS LAWS
A SECOND GROUP

10–15. HOLINESS OF THE CAMP

10. *every evil thing.* This refers to both personal and moral pollution. The camp was hallowed by the Divine Presence, and must therefore be a place of purity. Uncleanliness leads to ungodliness. Morals, religion, and even the elementary rules of sanitation, were absent in ancient camps. It was to be otherwise in Israel.

11. *chanceth him by night.* See Lev. XV, 16.

13. *a place.* 'A prepared place' (Targum). Sanitation is of vital importance in a camp. In this respect also, the Mosaic Law is thousands of years in advance of its age.

15. *unseemly thing.* lit. 'nakedness of anything'; *i.e.* anything that one would be ashamed of.

turn away from thee. The camp must be 'holy', otherwise there is no place in it for God.

to deliver thee, and to give up thine enemies before thee; therefore shall thy camp be holy; that He see no unseemly thing in thee, and turn away from thee. ¶ 16. Thou shalt not deliver unto his master a bondman that is escaped from his master unto thee; 17. he shall dwell with thee, in the midst of thee, in the place which he shall choose within one of thy gates, where it liketh him best; thou shalt not wrong him. ¶ 18. There shall be no harlot of the daughters of Israel, neither shall there be a sodomite of the sons of Israel. 19. Thou shalt not bring the hire of a harlot, or the price of a dog, into the house of the LORD thy God for any vow; for even both these are an abomination unto the LORD thy God. ¶ 20. Thou shalt not lend upon interest to thy

לְהַצִּֽילְךָ֙ וְלָתֵ֤ת אֹיְבֶ֙יךָ֙ לְפָנֶ֔יךָ וְהָיָ֥ה מַחֲנֶ֖יךָ קָד֑וֹשׁ וְלֹֽא־
16 יִרְאֶ֤ה בְךָ֙ עֶרְוַ֣ת דָּבָ֔ר וְשָׁ֖ב מֵאַחֲרֶֽיךָ׃ ס לֹא־
תַסְגִּ֥יר עֶ֖בֶד אֶל־אֲדֹנָ֑יו אֲשֶׁר־יִנָּצֵ֥ל אֵלֶ֖יךָ מֵעִ֥ם אֲדֹנָֽיו׃
17 עִמְּךָ֞ יֵשֵׁ֣ב בְּקִרְבְּךָ֗ בַּמָּק֧וֹם אֲשֶׁר־יִבְחַ֛ר בְּאַחַ֥ד שְׁעָרֶ֖יךָ
18 בַּטּ֣וֹב ל֑וֹ לֹ֖א תּוֹנֶֽנּוּ׃ ס לֹא־תִהְיֶ֥ה קְדֵשָׁ֖ה מִבְּנ֣וֹת
19 יִשְׂרָאֵ֑ל וְלֹֽא־יִהְיֶ֥ה קָדֵ֖שׁ מִבְּנֵ֥י יִשְׂרָאֵֽל׃ לֹא־תָבִיא֩ אֶתְנַ֨ן
זוֹנָ֜ה וּמְחִ֣יר כֶּ֗לֶב בֵּ֛ית יְהוָ֥ה אֱלֹהֶ֖יךָ לְכָל־נֶ֑דֶר כִּ֧י תוֹעֲבַ֛ת
כ יְהוָ֥ה אֱלֹהֶ֖יךָ גַּם־שְׁנֵיהֶֽם׃ ס לֹא־תַשִּׁ֣יךְ לְאָחִ֔יךָ

16–17. FUGITIVE SLAVES

The number of slaves was comparatively small in Israel; and the slave-trade could not have been extensive, since no slave-markets are mentioned in Scripture. Slaves had human rights in Jewish law, and were generally well-treated. In all Jewish history, there is no record of a servile insurrection, nor of runaway slaves. In the latter case, he was not to be restored to his master. 'What an honourable contrast to the law of Hammurabi, which condemned to death anyone who sheltered a runaway slave!' (McFadyen). Among the Greeks and Romans the runaway bondman was, on recapture, branded with a red-hot iron. Readers of *Uncle Tom's Cabin* will remember that, as late as the middle of the last century, fugitive slaves were tracked and pursued by blood-hounds. In this Mosaic law, however, we have the same legislation which is the peculiar boast of England to have introduced into the modern world:

'Slaves cannot breathe in England . . .
They touch our country, and their shackles fall' (Cowper).

On the position of the slave in Greece and Rome, see p. 537. Among the Greeks, slave-hunting was a not unfamiliar sport among them. As to Rome, Seneca records that the most gruesome punishments — torture, crucifixion, being thrown to the wild beasts in the arena—were inflicted on the slave for slight misdoings. Even the Stoics debated whether in a shipwreck one should sacrifice a valuable horse to save a slave. The Romans could not understand the humane treatment which the Judeans extended to their slaves. During the Hadrianic persecutions, one of the grave counts against Rabbi Eleazar ben Perata was that he had set free his slaves.

16. *a bondman.* A fleeing non-Israelitish slave, seeking refuge in Palestine from the harsh treatment of an unjust master, Jew or non-Jew, outside Palestine.

17. *with thee.* He was not only free, but was to be protected and helped to earn his livelihood and lead a useful life.

within one of thy gates. In any city of Israel, in any part of the land.

not wrong him. Better, *not vex him*, by words; this forbids wounding his feelings by speaking mockingly of his past or his race; see on Lev. XIX, 33.

18–19. IMMORALITY

18. *harlot.* In Canaanite cults, there were males and females who committed acts of immorality as part of the idolatrous worship.

19. *hire of a harlot.* A departure from the RV. The profits, either in money or kind, earned in an infamous way must not be brought to the Sanctuary in fulfilment of a vow or for any other religious purpose.

a dog. The Semitic term for a male person who practised immoral conduct as a religious rite. The Rabbis, however, took the phrase in its literal sense, as anything obtained in exchange of a dog.

abomination. We dishonour God with gifts secured by unrighteous and impure means.

20–21. INTEREST

Israel is a brotherhood whose sons are linked together by kindly feeling. Hence, an Israelite must lend money to a necessitous brother without expectation of any profit whatsoever. It is otherwise in the case of the alien merchant, who requires money not to relieve his poverty but as a business investment; see on Exod. XXII, 24, and Lev. XXV, 36, 37.

20. *not lend upon interest.* lit. 'not exact interest,' moderate or excessive. In Old English *usury* means 'interest'.

'One of the great duties of charity is here prescribed—to assist persons in reduced circumstances with timely loans, so that they may be brother: interest of money, interest of victuals, interest of any thing that is lent upon interest. 21. Unto a foreigner thou mayest lend upon interest; but unto thy brother thou shalt not lend upon interest; that the LORD thy God may bless thee in all that thou puttest thy hand unto, in the land whither thou goest in to possess it. ¶ 22. When thou shalt vow a vow unto the LORD thy God, thou shalt not be slack to pay it; for the LORD thy God will surely require it of thee; and it will be sin in thee. 23. But if thou shalt forbear to vow, it shall be no sin in thee. 24. That which is gone out of thy lips thou shalt observe and do;

21 נֶ֣שֶׁךְ כֶּ֔סֶף נֶ֖שֶׁךְ אֹ֑כֶל נֶ֕שֶׁךְ כָּל־דָּבָ֖ר אֲשֶׁ֥ר יִשָּֽׁךְ׃ לַנָּכְרִ֣י
תַשִּׁ֔יךְ וּלְאָחִ֖יךָ לֹ֣א תַשִּׁ֑יךְ לְמַ֨עַן יְבָרֶכְךָ֜ יְהוָ֣ה אֱלֹהֶ֗יךָ בְּכֹל֙
מִשְׁלַ֣ח יָדֶ֔ךָ עַל־הָאָ֕רֶץ אֲשֶׁר־אַתָּ֥ה בָא־שָׁ֖מָּה לְרִשְׁתָּֽהּ׃
22 ס כִּֽי־תִדֹּ֥ר נֶ֙דֶר֙ לַיהוָ֣ה אֱלֹהֶ֔יךָ לֹ֥א תְאַחֵ֖ר לְשַׁלְּמ֑וֹ כִּֽי־
23 דָרֹ֨שׁ יִדְרְשֶׁ֜נּוּ יְהוָ֤ה אֱלֹהֶ֙יךָ֙ מֵעִמָּ֔ךְ וְהָיָ֥ה בְךָ֖ חֵֽטְא׃ וְכִ֥י
24 תֶחְדַּ֖ל לִנְדֹּ֑ר לֹא־יִהְיֶ֥ה בְךָ֖ חֵֽטְא׃ מוֹצָ֥א שְׂפָתֶ֖יךָ תִּשְׁמֹ֣ר
וְעָשִׂ֑יתָ כַּאֲשֶׁ֨ר נָדַ֜רְתָּ לַיהוָ֤ה אֱלֹהֶ֙יךָ֙ נְדָבָ֔ה אֲשֶׁ֥ר דִּבַּ֖רְתָּ

enabled to maintain themselves by their own industry, without resorting to the degrading necessity of accepting alms. If the poor man was to derive any real assistance from the loan granted him, it was absolutely indispensable that no more was to be required of him than the actual amount that had been lent' (H. Adler).

21. *unto a foreigner thou mayest lend upon interest.* In contrast to the גר, the *resident* alien, the נכרי, 'foreigner,' is only temporarily in the land of Israel. He was usually a merchant in transit through Palestine. 'The caravan trade was very extensive, and the foreign trader enjoyed ample protection in the customs and laws of the land. The uninterrupted course of trade and absence of complaints relative to acts of violence against caravans speak plainly in favour of this fact. Some differentiation between the Israelite and foreigner was inevitable. The foreigner could not very well be expected, in a year which the Israelites celebrated as a Release Year, to remit the debt of his Israelitish debtor. Nor could he be expected to lend money to his Israelitish customer without taking interest. If an equal basis for trading between Israelites and foreigners was to be established, it could be attained only in this way; that the restrictions of the Release Year and the law of interest that were not binding on the foreigner *a priori* were also void for the Israelite, in so far as trade with foreigners was concerned' (Guttmann).

This permission to exact interest from a foreigner applied only to sums borrowed for mercantile purposes. When the Gentile needed the money for his subsistence, there was no longer any difference between Israelite and foreigner. 'And if thy brother be waxen poor, and his hand fail with thee, then thou shalt uphold him; yea, *though he be a stranger or a sojourner;* that he may live with thee. Take thou no usury of him or increase; but fear thy God' (Lev. XXV, 35, 36). The Talmud maintains the interest prohibition throughout, even in regard to foreigners; and nowhere do we find stronger condemnation of the usurer than in Rabbinical literature. The Rabbis teach that the testimony of a usurer must not be accepted in a court of justice. He is classed in the same category with thieves and professional gamblers. These noble sentiments in regard to usury only deepen the moral tragedy of the Jew in the Middle Ages. Debarred from normal means of livelihood, money dealings were forced upon him throughout Christian Europe. 'If we prohibit the Jews from following trades and other civil occupations, we compel them to become usurers,' said Martin Luther. When on the eve of the French Revolution, the National Assembly hesitated in emancipating the Jews because of the charge of usury, a noted delegate, the Abbé Gregoire, pleaded: 'O nations, if you record the past faults of the Jews, let it be to deplore your own work.' However, if much may be brought forward in extenuation of the past, nothing can be said in defence of contemporary Jewish money-lenders. 'No amount of money given in charity, nothing but the abandonment of this hateful trade, can atone for this great sin against God, Israel, and Humanity' (H. Adler).

not lend. Rabbinic law forbids the Jewish lender to demand interest from Jew and non-Jew alike, and forbids the Jewish borrower from a Jew to pay it.

22–24. Vows

22. *not be slack to pay it.* The sacred and binding character of the vow is given in Num. XXX, 3.

No one is under any obligation to make a vow. It is a purely voluntary act; but once made, it must be faithfully fulfilled. Ecclesiastes (*v.* 4) says, 'Better is it that thou shouldest not vow, than that thou shouldest vow and not pay.' See VOWS AND VOWING IN THE LIGHT OF JUDAISM, p. 730.

24. *that which is gone out of thy lips thou shalt observe.* 'You must be careful to perform any promise you have made' (Moffatt). A much-needed warning as to the sacred duty of keeping one's word; see p. 499.

חמישי
כה בְּפִיךָ׃ ס כִּי תָבֹא בְּכֶרֶם רֵעֶךָ וְאָכַלְתָּ עֲנָבִים
26 כְּנַפְשְׁךָ שָׂבְעֶךָ וְאֶל־כֶּלְיְךָ לֹא תִתֵּן׃ ס כִּי תָבֹא
בְּקָמַת רֵעֶךָ וְקָטַפְתָּ מְלִילֹת בְּיָדֶךָ וְחֶרְמֵשׁ לֹא תָנִיף
עַל קָמַת רֵעֶךָ׃ ס

according as thou hast vowed freely unto the LORD thy God, even that which thou hast promised with thy mouth.*v. ¶ 25. When thou comest into thy neighbour's vineyard, then thou mayest eat grapes until thou have enough at thine own pleasure; but thou shalt not put any in thy vessel. ¶ 26. When thou comest into thy neighbour's standing corn, then thou mayest pluck ears with thy hand; but thou shalt not move a sickle unto thy neighbour's standing corn.

כד CAP. XXIV. כד

א כִּי־יִקַּח אִישׁ אִשָּׁה וּבְעָלָהּ וְהָיָה אִם־לֹא תִמְצָא־חֵן
בְּעֵינָיו כִּי־מָצָא בָהּ עֶרְוַת דָּבָר וְכָתַב לָהּ סֵפֶר כְּרִיתֻת
2 וְנָתַן בְּיָדָהּ וְשִׁלְּחָהּ מִבֵּיתוֹ׃ וְיָצְאָה מִבֵּיתוֹ וְהָלְכָה וְהָיְתָה
3 לְאִישׁ־אַחֵר׃ וּשְׂנֵאָהּ הָאִישׁ הָאַחֲרוֹן וְכָתַב לָהּ סֵפֶר כְּרִיתֻת
וְנָתַן בְּיָדָהּ וְשִׁלְּחָהּ מִבֵּיתוֹ אוֹ כִי יָמוּת הָאִישׁ הָאַחֲרוֹן אֲשֶׁר־
4 לְקָחָהּ לוֹ לְאִשָּׁה׃ לֹא־יוּכַל בַּעְלָהּ הָרִאשׁוֹן אֲשֶׁר־שִׁלְּחָהּ
לָשׁוּב לְקַחְתָּהּ לִהְיוֹת לוֹ לְאִשָּׁה אַחֲרֵי אֲשֶׁר הֻטַּמָּאָה
כִּי־תוֹעֵבָה הִוא לִפְנֵי יְהוָה וְלֹא תַחֲטִיא אֶת־הָאָרֶץ אֲשֶׁר
ששי
ה יְהוָה אֱלֹהֶיךָ נֹתֵן לְךָ נַחֲלָה׃ ס כִּי־יִקַּח אִישׁ אִשָּׁה

4

CHAPTER XXIV

1. When a man taketh a wife, and marrieth her, then it cometh to pass, if she find no favour in his eyes, because he hath found some unseemly thing in her, that he writeth her a bill of divorcement, and giveth it in her hand, and sendeth her out of his house, 2. and she departeth out of his house, and goeth and becometh another man's wife, 3. and the latter husband hateth her, and writeth her a bill of divorcement, and giveth it in her hand, and sendeth her out of his house; or if the latter husband die, who took her to be his wife; 4. her former husband, who sent her away, may not take her again to be his wife, after that she is defiled; for that is abomination before the LORD; and thou shalt not cause the land to sin, which the LORD thy God giveth thee for an inheritance.*vi. ¶ 5. When a man taketh a new wife, he shall not go

25–26. IN A NEIGHBOUR'S FIELD AND VINEYARD

25. *at thine own pleasure.* The passer-by may pick and eat as much as his appetite demands, but no more. The Rabbis limit this privilege to the labourer who is engaged in gathering in the grapes.

vessel. The bag or wallet into which field or garden produce was put. Hunger, not greed, may be satisfied. Kindness must not be abused.

CHAPTER XXIV

(*f*) 1–4. DIVORCE

What we have here is no law instituting or commanding divorce. This institution is taken for granted, as in Lev. XXI, 7, and Num. XXX, 10. We are merely given one regulation in regard to it; *viz.*, that a man who has divorced his wife may not remarry her, if her second husband divorced her or died. See Additional Note, MARRIAGE AND DIVORCE IN JUDAISM, p. 930.

1. *some unseemly thing.* Heb. **ערות דבר**. The School of Shammai translated these words by 'a thing of *indecency*', and maintained that divorce could only be allowed if the wife was guilty of unchastity; whereas the School of Hillel rendered them by, 'indecency *in anything*,' implying that a wife may be divorced also for reasons other than unchastity.

bill of divorcement. lit. 'a writing of cutting off,' a certificate of total separation from her with whom he had hitherto lived 'as one flesh' (Gen. II, 24). The later name for the document was גט. Divorce was no longer to be at the arbitrary will and pleasure of the husband and by mere word of mouth, but upon reason given and by means of a formal document which demanded the intervention of a public authority. The marriage bond is holy; but whilst it is inviolable, it is not indissoluble.

4. *defiled.* To her former husband only, by her marriage with another man. The strong expression *defiled* is used in order to condemn the easy passage of a woman between one man and another, which must always entail some degradation of the wifely ideal, and might lead to virtual adultery though the *formality* of the law would be observed (Nachmanides, Sforno). 'Woman is a moral personality and not a *thing*, that a man may hand over to another, and then take back again at pleasure' (Koenig). David remarried Michal (II Sam. III, 14), but she was taken from him, and not divorced by him.

cause the land to sin. Immorality defiles the land.

out in the host, neither shall he be charged with any business; he shall be free for his house one year, and shall cheer his wife whom he hath taken. ¶ 6. No man shall take the mill or the upper millstone to pledge; for he taketh a man's life to pledge. ¶ 7. If a man be found stealing any of his brethren of the children of Israel, and he deal with him as a slave, and sell him; then that thief shall die; so shalt thou put away the evil from the midst of thee. ¶ 8. Take heed in the plague of leprosy, that thou observe diligently, and do according to all that the priests the Levites shall teach you, as I commanded them, so ye shall observe to do. 9. Remember what the LORD thy God did unto Miriam, by the way as ye came forth out of Egypt. ¶ 10. When thou dost lend thy neighbour any manner of loan, thou shalt not go into his house to fetch his pledge. 11. Thou shalt stand without, and the man to whom thou dost

חֲדָשָׁה לֹא יֵצֵא בַּצָּבָא וְלֹא־יַעֲבֹר עָלָיו לְכָל־דָּבָר נָקִי
יִהְיֶה לְבֵיתוֹ שָׁנָה אֶחָת וְשִׂמַּח אֶת־אִשְׁתּוֹ אֲשֶׁר־לָקָח׃
לֹא־יַחֲבֹל רֵחַיִם וָרָכֶב כִּי־נֶפֶשׁ הוּא חֹבֵל׃ ס כִּי־ 6 7
יִמָּצֵא אִישׁ גֹּנֵב נֶפֶשׁ מֵאֶחָיו מִבְּנֵי יִשְׂרָאֵל וְהִתְעַמֶּר־בּוֹ
וּמְכָרוֹ וּמֵת הַגַּנָּב הַהוּא וּבִעַרְתָּ הָרָע מִקִּרְבֶּךָ׃ ס הִשָּׁמֶר 8
בְּנֶגַע־הַצָּרַעַת לִשְׁמֹר מְאֹד וְלַעֲשׂוֹת כְּכֹל אֲשֶׁר־יוֹרוּ אֶתְכֶם
הַכֹּהֲנִים הַלְוִיִּם כַּאֲשֶׁר צִוִּיתִם תִּשְׁמְרוּ לַעֲשׂוֹת׃ זָכוֹר אֵת 9
אֲשֶׁר־עָשָׂה יְהוָה אֱלֹהֶיךָ לְמִרְיָם בַּדֶּרֶךְ בְּצֵאתְכֶם
מִמִּצְרָיִם׃ ס כִּי־תַשֶּׁה בְרֵעֲךָ מַשַּׁאת מְאוּמָה לֹא־תָבֹא י
אֶל־בֵּיתוֹ לַעֲבֹט עֲבֹטוֹ׃ בַּחוּץ תַּעֲמֹד וְהָאִישׁ אֲשֶׁר אַתָּה 11

(*g*) XXIV, 5–XXV, 4. LAWS OF EQUITY AND HUMANITY

5. Exemption from War

Another instance of the universality of these laws of mercy—their penetrative sympathy, and their superhuman impartiality, courtesy, and consideration (Welch).

5. *charged with any business*. There shall not be laid upon him any public duties and responsibilities.

cheer. lit. 'make to rejoice.'

6. Millstone not to be taken in Pledge

The mill consisted of two circular stones, one above the other. The removal of one would make the other useless, and would deprive the family of its daily supply of bread.

6. *a man's life*. To deprive a man of any tools indispensable for his livelihood is equivalent to depriving him of his life. This was also forbidden among the Greeks and Romans, and in the ancient Common Law of England.

7. Man-stealing

A repetition, with expansion, of the law in Exod. XXI, 16; see p. 308.

7. *deal with him as a slave*. Or, 'as a chattel'; the same phrase is used in XXI, 14.

shall die. The Code of Hammurabi decrees death for stealing a slave, the interest being not in human but in property rights.

8–9. Leprosy

8. *take heed*. The laws of leprosy are to be rigorously followed. These are laid down in Lev. XIII and XIV. 'Even though the leper be a king like Uzziah, they must not honour him (by exempting him from the prescribed restrictions), but must shut him out from the camp in isolation' (Rashbam).

9. *Miriam*. Prophetess and sister of Moses though she was, when smitten with leprosy, she was yet separated from the camp seven days; Num. XII, 14 f.

10–13. Taking and Restoring a Pledge

As usury was forbidden in Israel, and there were elaborate precautions against excessive indebtedness, there were fewer possibilities of oppression in connection with debt than elsewhere. It was permitted to give pledges, but in the taking of these, the creditor must spare the debtor's feelings. He may not insolently invade the debtor's house, and select as a pledge any article that he deems fit. The dignity, as well as the need, of the poor man must be respected. 'Even finer than the humanitarianism of these laws is their noble respect for human personality. Deuteronomy strikes the note of what is finest in Hebrew ethics and one of its great contributions to the world. Perhaps it is seen most finely, because most simply, in the direction, *When thou dost lend thy neighbour any manner of loan, thou shalt not go into his house to fetch the pledge*. For every Israelite, however poor, has the right to invite into or to exclude from the four walls of the cabin he calls his home' (Welch).

11. *thou shalt stand without*. Unless he invites thee to enter. Just because he requires our help, we are to remember how it deteriorates the poor to be dealt with in an unceremonious, tactless way, even by the benevolent (Harper).

12 נֹשֶׁה בוֹ יוֹצִיא אֵלֶיךָ אֶת־הַעֲבוֹט הַחוּצָה׃ וְאִם־אִישׁ עָנִי
13 הוּא לֹא תִשְׁכַּב בַּעֲבֹטוֹ׃ הָשֵׁב תָּשִׁיב לוֹ אֶת־הַעֲבוֹט
כְּבוֹא הַשֶּׁמֶשׁ וְשָׁכַב בְּשַׂלְמָתוֹ וּבֵרֲכֶךָּ וּלְךָ תִּהְיֶה צְדָקָה
שביעי 14 לִפְנֵי יְהוָה אֱלֹהֶיךָ׃ ס לֹא־תַעֲשֹׁק שָׂכִיר עָנִי וְאֶבְיֹן
טו מֵאַחֶיךָ אוֹ מִגֵּרְךָ אֲשֶׁר בְּאַרְצְךָ בִּשְׁעָרֶיךָ׃ בְּיוֹמוֹ תִתֵּן
שְׂכָרוֹ וְלֹא־תָבוֹא עָלָיו הַשֶּׁמֶשׁ כִּי עָנִי הוּא וְאֵלָיו הוּא נֹשֵׂא
אֶת־נַפְשׁוֹ וְלֹא־יִקְרָא עָלֶיךָ אֶל־יְהוָה וְהָיָה בְךָ חֵטְא׃ ס
16 לֹא־יוּמְתוּ אָבוֹת עַל־בָּנִים וּבָנִים לֹא־יוּמְתוּ עַל־אָבוֹת אִישׁ

lend shall bring forth the pledge without unto thee. 12. And if he be a poor man, thou shalt not sleep with his pledge; 13. thou shalt surely restore to him the pledge when the sun goeth down, that he may sleep in his garment, and bless thee; and it shall be righteousness unto thee before the LORD thy God.*vii. ¶ 14. Thou shalt not oppress a hired servant that is poor and needy, whether he be of thy brethren, or of thy strangers that are in thy land within thy gates. 15. In the same day thou shalt give him his hire, neither shall the sun go down upon it; for he is poor, and setteth his heart upon it; lest he cry against thee unto the LORD, and it be sin in thee. ¶ 16. The fathers shall not be put to death for the children, neither shall the children be put to death for the fathers; every man shall be put

13. *sleep in his garment.* If the debtor be a poor man he would probably give as security some necessary article of clothing, such as the *simlah,* worn for protection against wind and rain, and used as a covering during sleep. In Palestine the nights are mostly cold, and the poor man has no covering save his clothes. Hence the command that the creditor return such garment at nightfall, and not heartlessly deprive him of what is an essential of everyday life. Such heartlessness was peculiarly offensive to Israelite feeling; Amos II, 8, p. 152.

and bless thee. A generous treatment of the poor will call forth their blessing.

it shall be righteousness. An act of kindness such as this, is an act of צדקה in its double sense of 'charity' and 'righteous living'.

The spirit of the above law is in absolute contrast to the Greek and Roman attitudes towards the poor; see p. 929.

14–15. TREATMENT OF WORKMEN

The workman is not to be wronged by being kept waiting for his wage. It must be punctually paid him the day he earns it; Lev. XIX, 13.

14. *or of thy strangers.* One and the same law must protect the Israelite and the non-Israelite worker.

15. *in the same day.* He must receive the wages *on the same* day; *i.e.* as soon as his day's work is over; Lev. XIX, 13, 'the wages of a hired servant shall not abide with thee all night until the morning.'

upon it. The sun must not go down whilst the wages are still unpaid.

setteth his heart upon it. Because he needs it to buy food for his family in the evening. Rashi translates the Heb. words, 'for it he risks his life' in his work.

lest he cry. Cf. the end of *v.* 13.

16. INDIVIDUAL RESPONSIBILITY

In ancient times the family of a criminal often suffered supreme punishment with him.

Though the family is a moral unity, and the ethical solidarity of the nation is never to be lost sight of, no judge or tribunal must assume the power of putting the parents to death for a sin committed by the children, nor of putting the children to death for a sin committed by the parents. Ezekiel strikingly emphasized this fundamental teaching: 'The soul that sinneth, *it* shall die; the son shall not bear the iniquity of the father with him, neither shall the father bear the iniquity of the son with him' (XVIII, 4, 20).

16. *for the fathers.* Or, 'in addition to the fathers' (Koenig). In II Kings XIV, 6, Amaziah king of Judah slays 'his servants who had slain the king his father. But the children of the murderers he put not to death', in obedience to this law of Deuteronomy. Some explain the prohibition to mean the fathers shall not be permitted to die *instead* of the children, nor shall the children be permitted to die *instead* of the fathers. This was actually the case in Babylonian Law. If, through faulty construction, a house collapsed and a child was killed, then it was not the jerry-builder, but the *child* of the jerry-builder, that was put to death; see 'Son for son, and daughter for daughter, in Code Hammurabi', p. 403.

17–18. INJUSTICE TO THE STRANGER, ORPHAN, AND WIDOW

'It is astonishing to find how many of the laws—especially in the great-hearted Book of Deuteronomy—are expressly designed to protect the interests of the impoverished and defenceless members of society' (McFadyen). 'No other system of jurisprudence in any country at any to death for his own sin. ¶ 17. Thou shalt not pervert the justice due to the stranger, or to the fatherless; nor take the widow's raiment to pledge. 18. But thou shalt remember that thou wast a bondman in Egypt, and the LORD thy God redeemed thee thence; therefore I command thee to do this thing. ¶ 19. When thou reapest thy harvest in thy field, and hast forgot a sheaf in the field, thou shalt not go back to fetch it; it shall be for the stranger, for the fatherless, and for the widow; that the LORD thy God may bless thee in all the work of thy hands. ¶ 20. When thou beatest thine olive-tree, thou shalt not go over the boughs again; it shall be for the stranger, for the fatherless, and for the widow. 21. When thou gatherest the grapes of thy vineyard, thou shalt not glean it after thee; it shall be for the stranger, for the fatherless, and for the widow. 22. And thou shalt remember that thou wast a bondman in the land of Egypt; therefore I command thee to do this thing.

17 בְּחֶטְאוֹ יוּמָתוּ׃ ס לֹא תַטֶּה מִשְׁפַּט גֵּר יָתוֹם וְלֹא תַחֲבֹל
18 בֶּגֶד אַלְמָנָה׃ וְזָכַרְתָּ כִּי עֶבֶד הָיִיתָ בְּמִצְרַיִם וַיִּפְדְּךָ יְהוָֹה
אֱלֹהֶיךָ מִשָּׁם עַל־כֵּן אָנֹכִי מְצַוְּךָ לַעֲשׂוֹת אֶת־הַדָּבָר הַזֶּה׃
19 ס כִּי תִקְצֹר קְצִירְךָ בְשָׂדֶךָ וְשָׁכַחְתָּ עֹמֶר בַּשָּׂדֶה לֹא־
תָשׁוּב לְקַחְתּוֹ לַגֵּר לַיָּתוֹם וְלָאַלְמָנָה יִהְיֶה לְמַעַן יְבָרֶכְךָ
כ יְהוָֹה אֱלֹהֶיךָ בְּכֹל מַעֲשֵׂה יָדֶיךָ׃ ס כִּי תַחְבֹּט זֵיתְךָ לֹא
21 תְפַאֵר אַחֲרֶיךָ לַגֵּר לַיָּתוֹם וְלָאַלְמָנָה יִהְיֶה׃ כִּי תִבְצֹר
כַּרְמְךָ לֹא תְעוֹלֵל אַחֲרֶיךָ לַגֵּר לַיָּתוֹם וְלָאַלְמָנָה יִהְיֶה׃
22 וְזָכַרְתָּ כִּי־עֶבֶד הָיִיתָ בְּאֶרֶץ מִצְרָיִם עַל־כֵּן אָנֹכִי מְצַוְּךָ
לַעֲשׂוֹת אֶת־הַדָּבָר הַזֶּה׃ ס

25

CHAPTER XXV

1. If there be a controversy between men, and they come unto judgment, and the judges judge them, by justifying the righteous, and condemning the wicked, 2. then it shall be, if the wicked man deserve to be beaten, that the judge shall

כה

CAP. XXV. כה

א כִּי־יִהְיֶה רִיב בֵּין אֲנָשִׁים וְנִגְּשׁוּ אֶל־הַמִּשְׁפָּט וּשְׁפָטוּם
2 וְהִצְדִּיקוּ אֶת־הַצַּדִּיק וְהִרְשִׁיעוּ אֶת־הָרָשָׁע׃ וְהָיָה אִם־

period is marked by such humanity in respect to the unfortunate' (Houghton). The stranger, fatherless, and widow should be treated with a generous perception of the peculiar difficulties of their lot. Care for them is characteristic of Jewish civilization generally, whether in ancient, medieval, or modern times.

19–23. GENEROSITY TO THE LANDLESS

19. *forgot a sheaf.* As this commandment could not be *consciously* observed, Rabbi Zadok grieved over the fact that he had never carried out this mitzvah. When at last he forgot some sheaves on his fields, he rejoiced, and made a festival for himself and his household.

20. *olive-tree.* The Rabbis declared that the law of leaving the corner of the field unreaped (Lev. XIX, 9) so that the poor might come and take it, applied also to trees. 'In gathering olives, the fruit is brought to the ground either by shaking the boughs or beating them with a long palm branch. At the present time, the trees are beaten on a certain day announced by a crier, after which the poor are allowed to glean what is left. Gleaning is a beautiful and kindly custom still surviving to some extent in Palestine, but fast disappearing before the introduction of modern methods of harvesting' (Dummelow).

CHAPTER XXV

1–3. AGAINST EXCESSIVE PUNISHMENT

In ancient societies, that had no system of imprisonment for lighter crimes, corporal punishment was of necessity much more frequent than in modern times. There was, therefore, great need for regulating it, if its possible barbarities were to be prevented.

1. *controversy.* Litigation.
justifying the righteous. Acquit the innocent.

2. *to be beaten.* No stripes were to be inflicted before or during the investigation; and the application of torture to extort confession from a criminal (or evidence from witnesses) was unknown in Israel. Only *after* he was found guilty was the punishment to take place.

judge . . . before his face. In his presence, as a precaution against indiscriminate or unlimited flogging.

by number. The literal meaning is the number is to be proportionate to his wickedness (Ibn Ezra, Mendelssohn, and all moderns). The Traditional explanation combines the last Heb. word of *v.* 2 with the first word of *v.* 3, and deduces therefrom that the 39 stripes are to be carefully counted, cause him to lie down, and to be beaten before his face, according to the measure of his wickedness, by number. 3. Forty stripes he may give him, he shall not exceed; lest, if he should exceed, and beat him above these with many stripes, then thy brother should be dishonoured before thine

בֵּן הַכּוֹת הָרָשָׁע וְהִפִּילוֹ הַשֹּׁפֵט וְהִכָּהוּ לְפָנָיו כְּדֵי רִשְׁעָתוֹ
3 בְּמִסְפָּר׃ אַרְבָּעִים יַכֶּנּוּ לֹא יֹסִיף פֶּן־יֹסִיף לְהַכֹּתוֹ עַל־
4 אֵלֶּה מַכָּה רַבָּה וְנִקְלָה אָחִיךָ לְעֵינֶיךָ׃ לֹא־תַחְסֹם שׁוֹר

and the number inflicted to be in accordance with the physical strength of the offender.

3. *stripes.* By means of a leathern belt, and not by rods or any instrument that might prove fatal.

he shall not exceed. The Rabbis fixed the maximum at 39, for fear of exceeding the legal number by miscount.

be dishonoured. Or, 'seem vile.' Become an object of contempt, by destroying his human dignity which must be respected even in a criminal. The Rabbis point out that 'previous to receiving his punishment the wrong-doer is termed the *wicked man*, but that after being punished he is designated *thy brother*. Once a man has expiated his offence, let his past be entirely forgotten; and let him be received once again into the brotherhood of Israel!' That punishment must have a decidedly moral aim; *viz.* the improvement of the criminal. 'It may in some cases be a man's duty to punish, and in other cases to pardon, but it is in all cases a man's duty to be merciful to a criminal' (Seeley). The wonderful spirit of humanity of this Biblical law is quite absent from the codes of ancient and even relatively modern times. In nearly all those codes, the intention seems to be both to humiliate the offender and to inflict torment.

4. Kindness to Animals

The love of God regards not only the poor and the slave, but takes account also of the lower animals.

4. *not muzzle the ox.* This prohibition applies to all animals employed in labour, and not to the ox alone. 'A righteous man regardeth the life of his beast' (Prov. xii, 10)—he has consideration for its feelings and needs. It is a refinement of cruelty to excite the animal's desire for food and to prevent its satisfaction. Prof. Cornill writes:—

'What a truly humanitarian sentiment finds expression in the law, *Thou shalt not muzzle the ox when he treadeth out the corn.* The brute should not perform hard labour, and at the same time have food before its eyes without the possibility of eating therefrom. I remember some time ago to have read that one of the richest Italian real-estate owners, at the grape-harvest, fastened iron muzzles to his miserable, fever-stricken workmen, so that it might not occur to these poor peasants, working for starvation wages under the glowing sun of Southern Italy, to satiate their burning thirst and their gnawing hunger with a few of the millions of grapes of the owner.' Jewish legislation extended the prohibition of muzzling the ox to workmen employed on production of articles of food; they must not be prevented from eating them; see p. 850.

The claims of the lower animals on human pity and consideration are characteristic of the *Hebrew* Scriptures. 'In Psalm xxxvi, 7, there is an implication that, morally speaking, there is no complete break of continuity in the scale of sentient life; and (Gen. viii, 1; Jer. xxi, 6) the domesticated animals are, in fact, regarded as part of the human community. In the Decalogue, the animals that labour with and for man have their share of Sabbath rest, and the produce of the fields during the Sabbatical year (Exod. xxiii, 11) is to be for them as for the poor' (Harper).

The duties to our dumb friends have been strangely overlooked in most ethical systems, not excluding Christianity. Paul dismisses as an idle sentimentalism the notion of man's duty to animals. 'Is it for oxen that God careth?' he asks mockingly. And this remained the attitude of the Church till recent times. 'In the range and circle of duties,' says the historian Lecky, 'inculcated by the early Fathers, those to animals had no place.' In the Talmud, however, kindness to animals (צער בעלי חיים) becomes the basis of a whole code of laws. A great Rabbi is said to have been punished with long and continued physical pain because, when a calf which was about to be killed ran to him bleating for protection, he repulsed the animal, exclaiming, 'Go, that is thy destiny.' In a beautiful legend which the poet Coleridge has paraphrased, the Rabbis tell how Moses, while he is still Jethro's shepherd, seeks out a stray lamb and tenderly carries the tired creature in his arms back to the fold, and how a voice from Heaven cries, 'Thou art worthy to be My people's pastor.' 'This sympathy for the dumb animals is all the more remarkable because the terrible scenes in the Roman arena are only too clear an indication of the inhumanity which prevailed in the civilized world during the Talmudic period' (M. Joseph).

It is only in our day that legislation at long last forbade cruelty to animals. Until the middle of the nineteenth century, it was nowhere illegal—except in Jewish Law. It is, therefore, but another of the 'conventional lies of our civilization', eyes. ¶ 4. Thou shalt not muzzle the ox when he treadeth out the corn. ¶ 5. If brethren dwell together, and one of them die, and have no child, the wife of the dead shall not be married abroad unto one not of his kin; her husband's brother shall go in unto her, and take her to him to wife, and perform the duty of a husband's brother unto her. 6. And it shall be, that the first-born that she beareth shall succeed in the name of his brother that is dead, that his name be not blotted out of Israel. 7. And if the man like not to take his brother's wife, then his brother's wife shall go up to the gate unto the elders, and say: 'My husband's brother refuseth to raise up unto his brother a name in Israel; he will not perform the duty of a husband's brother unto me.' 8. Then the elders of his city shall call him, and speak unto him; and if he stand, and say: 'I like not to take her'; 9. then shall his brother's wife draw

ה בְּדִישׁוֹ׃ ס כִּי־יֵשְׁבוּ אַחִים יַחְדָּו וּמֵת אַחַד מֵהֶם וּבֵן
אֵין־לוֹ לֹא־תִהְיֶה אֵשֶׁת־הַמֵּת הַחוּצָה לְאִישׁ זָר יְבָמָהּ יָבֹא
6 עָלֶיהָ וּלְקָחָהּ לוֹ לְאִשָּׁה וְיִבְּמָהּ׃ וְהָיָה הַבְּכוֹר אֲשֶׁר תֵּלֵד
7 יָקוּם עַל־שֵׁם אָחִיו הַמֵּת וְלֹא־יִמָּחֶה שְׁמוֹ מִיִּשְׂרָאֵל׃ וְאִם־
לֹא יַחְפֹּץ הָאִישׁ לָקַחַת אֶת־יְבִמְתּוֹ וְעָלְתָה יְבִמְתּוֹ הַשַּׁעְרָה
אֶל־הַזְּקֵנִים וְאָמְרָה מֵאֵן יְבָמִי לְהָקִים לְאָחִיו שֵׁם בְּיִשְׂרָאֵל
8 לֹא אָבָה יַבְּמִי׃ וְקָרְאוּ־לוֹ זִקְנֵי־עִירוֹ וְדִבְּרוּ אֵלָיו וְעָמַד
9 וְאָמַר לֹא חָפַצְתִּי לְקַחְתָּהּ׃ וְנִגְּשָׁה יְבִמְתּוֹ אֵלָיו לְעֵינֵי
הַזְּקֵנִים וְחָלְצָה נַעֲלוֹ מֵעַל רַגְלוֹ וְיָרְקָה בְּפָנָיו וְעָנְתָה

if the duty of preventing cruelty to animals is invoked against one of the major requirements of Jewish life—Shechitah.

As is well known, the Rabbinical regulations concerning Shechitah, the Jewish mode of slaughtering animals intended for food, are in part due to a desire to prevent the slightest unnecessary suffering to the animal. 'Since the need of procuring food necessitates the slaying of animals, the Law enjoins that the death of the animal should be the easiest. It is not allowed to torment the animal by cutting the throat in a clumsy manner, by pole-axing, or by cutting off a limb while the animal is still alive' (Maimonides). The Jewish method of slaughter is one continuous cut with the sharpest of knives, applied by a skilled operator. Such cut severs all the great blood-vessels of the neck, and produces *instantaneous* insensibility in the animal. A leading physiologist declares: 'I should be happy to think that my own end were likely to be as swift and painless as the end of these cattle killed in this way undoubtedly is' (Prof. C. Lovatt Evans). Similar opinions in regard to Shechitah have been given some years ago by no less than 446 non-Jewish Professors of physiology and veterinary surgeons in the principal European countries. If, nevertheless, Shechitah is prohibited in enlightened lands like Switzerland and Norway, this is due to the ignorance on the part of the electorate as to what the Jewish method of slaughter actually is. In Nazi Germany such prohibition was enacted not so much out of sympathy with the beast, as out of a desire to inflict pain on human beings: 'they sacrifice men, and kiss calves' (Hosea XIII, 2).

(*h*) 5–10. LEVIRATE MARRIAGE

Levirate marriage (in Latin, *levir* is a husband's brother) is the technical name for the marriage with the widow of a childless brother (יבום). To avert the calamity of the family line becoming extinct, of a man's name perishing and his property going to others, the surviving brother of such a childless man was required to marry the widow, so as to raise up an heir to that man's name. This custom occurs in various forms among many ancient peoples. It existed in Israel in Patriarchal times (Gen. XXXVIII), but is here modified in important particulars.

5. *dwell together.* Not necessarily in the same community, but at the same time (Talmud).

no child. Heb. *ben*, in the sense of child, whether male or female. The Rabbis extended its meaning in this instance to grandchild, from this or any other wife.

married abroad. One who is outside the family.

the duty of the husband's brother. He shall take the place of the dead brother; *i.e.* he shall 'build up the house' which the deceased had begun, and perpetuate his name.

8. *speak unto him.* 'The elders counsel him as to what is the best course for him to follow' (Sifri). There are cases in which the levirate marriage was inadvisable, and they counselled that the rite of Chalitzah take its place. The latter course has been almost universally followed in later centuries, especially after the formal excommunication of all polygamists by Rabbenu Gershom in the year 1000.

9. *loose his shoe.* Or, 'strip his sandal.' The loosening of one's shoe by another was emblematic of the transfer of property. It betokened the giving up to that other of some property or right; Ruth IV, 7.

spit in his face. This is a departure from the rendering of AJ, as of RV, as their rendering is contrary both to fact and Heb. idiom. Spitting nigh unto him in the presence of the elders, and loose his shoe from off his foot, and spit in his face; and she shall answer and say: 'So shall it be done unto the man that doth not build up his brother's house.' 10. And his name shall be called in Israel The house of him that had his shoe loosed. ¶ 11. When men strive together one with another, and the wife of the one draweth near to deliver her husband out of the hand of him that smiteth him, and putteth forth her hand, and taketh him by the secrets; 12. then thou shalt cut off her hand, thine eye shall have no pity. ¶ 13. Thou shalt not have in thy bag diverse weights, a great and a small. 14. Thou shalt not have in thy house diverse measures, a great and a small. 15. A perfect and just weight shalt thou have; a perfect and just measure shalt thou have; that thy days may be long upon the land which the LORD thy God giveth thee. 16. For all that do such things, even all that do unrighteously, are an abomination unto the LORD thy God. *m. ¶ 17. Remember what Amalek did unto thee by the way as ye came forth out of Egypt; 18. how he met thee by the way, and smote the hindmost of thee, all that were enfeebled in thy rear, when thou wast faint and weary; and he feared not God. 19. There-

וְאָמְרָה כָּכָה יֵעָשֶׂה לָאִישׁ אֲשֶׁר לֹא־יִבְנֶה אֶת־בֵּית אָחִיו׃
11 וְנִקְרָא שְׁמוֹ בְּיִשְׂרָאֵל בֵּית חֲלוּץ הַנָּעַל׃ ס כִּי־יִנָּצוּ
אֲנָשִׁים יַחְדָּו אִישׁ וְאָחִיו וְקָרְבָה אֵשֶׁת הָאֶחָד לְהַצִּיל אֶת־
12 אִישָׁהּ מִיַּד מַכֵּהוּ וְשָׁלְחָה יָדָהּ וְהֶחֱזִיקָה בִּמְבֻשָׁיו׃ וְקַצֹּתָה
13 אֶת־כַּפָּהּ לֹא תָחוֹס עֵינֶךָ׃ ס לֹא־יִהְיֶה לְךָ בְּכִיסְךָ אֶבֶן
14 וָאָבֶן גְּדוֹלָה וּקְטַנָּה׃ לֹא־יִהְיֶה לְךָ בְּבֵיתְךָ אֵיפָה וְאֵיפָה
טו גְּדוֹלָה וּקְטַנָּה׃ אֶבֶן שְׁלֵמָה וָצֶדֶק יִהְיֶה־לָּךְ אֵיפָה שְׁלֵמָה
וָצֶדֶק יִהְיֶה־לָּךְ לְמַעַן יַאֲרִיכוּ יָמֶיךָ עַל הָאֲדָמָה אֲשֶׁר־
16 יְהוָה אֱלֹהֶיךָ נֹתֵן לָךְ׃ כִּי תוֹעֲבַת יְהוָה אֱלֹהֶיךָ כָּל־עֹשֵׂה
אֵלֶּה כֹּל עֹשֵׂה עָוֶל׃ * פ מפטיר
17 זָכוֹר אֵת אֲשֶׁר־עָשָׂה לְךָ עֲמָלֵק בַּדֶּרֶךְ בְּצֵאתְכֶם מִמִּצְרָיִם׃
18 אֲשֶׁר קָרְךָ בַּדֶּרֶךְ וַיְזַנֵּב בְּךָ כָּל־הַנֶּחֱשָׁלִים אַחֲרֶיךָ וְאַתָּה
19 עָיֵף וְיָגֵעַ וְלֹא יָרֵא אֱלֹהִים׃ וְהָיָה בְּהָנִיחַ יְהוָה אֱלֹהֶיךָ ׀

before him 'on the ground' (Talmud, Rashi) was to symbolize the contempt for the man who brings disgrace upon himself and his family by refusing the privilege to raise up unto his brother a name in Israel.
answer. Solemnly assert.

10. *had his shoe loosed.* Or, 'whose sandal was stripped off.' After that, he could nevermore marry her, nor could any of his brothers. She was free to marry 'a stranger'.

11–12. FLAGRANT IMMODESTY

Even in extenuating circumstances, flagrant immodesty is to be dealt with without pity.

11. *strive together.* lit. 'are wrestling together.'
taketh. Seizes with violence.

12. *cut off.* The Rabbis commuted this severe penalty into a money-fine, varying 'in accordance with the status of the culprit and the victim'. There is no other case of mutilation in the Torah.

13–16. HONEST WEIGHTS AND MEASURES

13. *diverse weights.* A large one for buying, and a small one for selling.

15. *thy days may be long.* Fair dealing, integrity in trade, must necessarily promote social happiness and prolong the life of a nation. 'It is a known fact that every kingdom based on justice will stand. Justice is like a building. Injustice is like the cracks in that building, which cause it to fall without a moment's warning' (Ibn Ezra). 'A false balance is an abomination unto the LORD: but a just weight is His delight' (Prov. XI, 1).

16. *all that do unrighteously.* A comprehensive summing-up. 'All that do unrighteously either by mouth or deed, in secret or in open' (Ibn Ezra).

17–19. REMEMBERING AMALEK

Whilst Israel was to make justice and brotherly love its guiding rule, it was not to forget that Amalek had perpetuated a cowardly and unprovoked attack on the feeble and hindmost, when the Israelites were marching from Egypt; Exod. XVII, 8–16.

18. *met thee.* Better, *fell on thee.*
smote the hindmost. He attacked the rear of the Israelites, the faint and weary stragglers enfeebled by the march.
he feared not God. He was devoid of pity and fundamental humanity; see p. 208.

19. *blot out.* A people so devoid of natural religion as to kill non-combatants had forfeited all claim to mercy.

לְךָ מִכָּל־אֹיְבֶיךָ מִסָּבִיב בָּאָרֶץ אֲשֶׁר יְהוָה־אֱלֹהֶיךָ נֹתֵן
לְךָ נַחֲלָה לְרִשְׁתָּהּ תִּמְחֶה אֶת־זֵכֶר עֲמָלֵק מִתַּחַת הַשָּׁמָיִם
לֹא תִּשְׁכָּח׃

fore it shall be, when the LORD thy God hath given thee rest from all thine enemies round about, in the land which the LORD thy God giveth thee for an inheritance to possess it, that thou shalt blot out the remembrance of Amalek from under heaven; thou shalt not forget.

HAFTORAH KI THETZE הפטרת כי תצא

ISAIAH LIV, 1–10

CAP. LIV. נד

א רָנִּי עֲקָרָה לֹא יָלָדָה פִּצְחִי רִנָּה וְצַהֲלִי לֹא־חָלָה כִּי־
2 רַבִּים בְּנֵי־שׁוֹמֵמָה מִבְּנֵי בְעוּלָה אָמַר יְהוָה׃ הַרְחִיבִי ׀
מְקוֹם אָהֳלֵךְ וִירִיעוֹת מִשְׁכְּנוֹתַיִךְ יַטּוּ אַל־תַּחְשֹׂכִי הַאֲרִיכִי
3 מֵיתָרַיִךְ וִיתֵדֹתַיִךְ חַזֵּקִי׃ כִּי־יָמִין וּשְׂמֹאול תִּפְרֹצִי וְזַרְעֵךְ
4 גּוֹיִם יִירָשׁ וְעָרִים נְשַׁמּוֹת יוֹשִׁיבוּ׃ אַל־תִּירְאִי כִּי־לֹא
תֵבוֹשִׁי וְאַל־תִּכָּלְמִי כִּי־לֹא תַחְפִּירִי כִּי בֹשֶׁת עֲלוּמַיִךְ
ה תִּשְׁכָּחִי וְחֶרְפַּת אַלְמְנוּתַיִךְ לֹא תִזְכְּרִי־עוֹד׃ כִּי בֹעֲלַיִךְ
עֹשַׂיִךְ יְהוָה צְבָאוֹת שְׁמוֹ וְגֹאֲלֵךְ קְדוֹשׁ יִשְׂרָאֵל אֱלֹהֵי כָל־

CHAPTER LIV

1. Sing, O barren, thou that didst not bear,
Break forth into singing, and cry aloud, thou that didst not travail;
For more are the children of the desolate
Than the children of the married wife, saith the LORD.

2. Enlarge the place of thy tent,
And let them stretch forth the curtains of thy habitations, spare not;
Lengthen thy cords, and strengthen thy stakes.

3. For thou shalt spread abroad on the right hand and on the left;
And thy seed shall possess the nations,
And make the desolate cities to be inhabited.

4. Fear not, for thou shalt not be ashamed.
Neither be thou confounded, for thou shalt not be put to shame;
For thou shalt forget the shame of thy youth,
And the reproach of thy widowhood shalt thou remember no more.

5. For thy Maker is thy husband,
The LORD of hosts is His name:
And the Holy One of Israel is thy Redeemer,
The God of the whole earth shall He be called.

v. 3. מלא ו׳ ibid. קמץ בז״ק v. 4. קמץ בז״ק

The fifth Haftorah of Consolation. Its message is the everlasting mercy of God. 'For the mountains shall depart, and the hills be removed; but My kindness shall not depart from thee.' This entails for the Israelites the sacred duty of imitating God's ways of lovingkindness, by loyal observance of the precepts of humanity and pity proclaimed in the Sidrah.

JERUSALEM REBUILT

1. *more are the children.* Zion's cities shall be repopulated; Jerusalem desolate was like a woman forsaken. Now with her exiles returned, she is like the wife re-united with husband and children.

2. *enlarge.* Because of the increase of Zion's population.

tent. i.e. Jerusalem.

thy habitations. The other cities of Israel. All of Zion's children who have become estranged from her, wherever they may be dispersed, shall renew their allegiance and return to her leading.

3. *possess. i.e.* dispossess those of alien race who have occupied the desolate Jewish cities during the Exile.

4. *the shame of thy youth.* The defeats and humiliations in Israel's earlier history.

thy widowhood. i.e. the Exile, when God, 'Zion's husband,' seemed to have withdrawn from her. 'Widowhood' has a wider significance than in colloquial English, being used to denote a woman abandoned by her husband.

6. For the LORD hath called thee
As a wife forsaken and grieved in spirit;
And a wife of youth, can she be rejected?
Saith thy God.

7. For a small moment have I forsaken thee;
But with great compassion will I gather thee.

8. In a little wrath I hid My face from thee for a moment;
But with everlasting kindness will I have compassion on thee,
Saith the LORD thy Redeemer.

9. For this is as the waters of Noah unto Me;
For as I have sworn that the waters of Noah
Should no more go over the earth,
So have I sworn that I would not be wroth with thee,
Nor rebuke thee.

10. For the mountains may depart,
And the hills be removed;
But My kindness shall not depart from thee,
Neither shall My covenant of peace be removed,
Saith the LORD that hath compassion on thee.

6 הָאָרֶץ יִקְרָא׃ כִּֽי־כְאִשָּׁה עֲזוּבָה וַעֲצוּבַת רוּחַ קְרָאָךְ
7 יְהוָה וְאֵשֶׁת נְעוּרִים כִּי תִמָּאֵס אָמַר אֱלֹהָיִךְ׃ בְּרֶגַע קָטֹן
8 עֲזַבְתִּיךְ וּבְרַחֲמִים גְּדוֹלִים אֲקַבְּצֵךְ׃ בְּשֶׁצֶף קֶצֶף הִסְתַּרְתִּי
פָנַי רֶגַע מִמֵּךְ וּבְחֶסֶד עוֹלָם רִחַמְתִּיךְ אָמַר גֹּאֲלֵךְ יְהוָה׃
9 כִּי־מֵי נֹחַ זֹאת לִי אֲשֶׁר נִשְׁבַּעְתִּי מֵעֲבֹר מֵי־נֹחַ עוֹד
10 עַל־הָאָרֶץ כֵּן נִשְׁבַּעְתִּי מִקְּצֹף עָלַיִךְ וּמִגְּעָר־בָּךְ׃ כִּי הֶהָרִים
יָמוּשׁוּ וְהַגְּבָעוֹת תְּמוּטֶנָה וְחַסְדִּי מֵאִתֵּךְ לֹא־יָמוּשׁ וּבְרִית
שְׁלוֹמִי לֹא תָמוּט אָמַר מְרַחֲמֵךְ יְהוָה׃

v. 9. נ"א כימי

7–8. God's anger is but momentary; cf. Psalm xxx, 6. Although the years of the Exile seemed interminably long, they will prove but a brief space in the vast sweep of Israel's history.

9–10. Yet another utterance of comfort.

9. *for this. i.e.* the Exile and the comfort. The Exile is compared to the Flood; and the comfort, to the Divine promise that the Flood should never recur.

26 CHAPTER XXVI

1. And it shall be, when thou art come in unto the land which the LORD thy God giveth thee for an inheritance, and dost possess it, and dwell therein; 2. that thou shalt take of the first of all the fruit of the ground, which thou shalt bring in from thy land that the LORD thy God giveth thee; and thou shalt put it in a basket, and shalt go unto the place which the LORD thy God shall choose to cause His name to dwell there. 3. And thou shalt come unto the priest that shall be in those days, and say unto him: 'I profess this day unto the LORD thy God, that I am come unto the land which the LORD swore unto our fathers to give us.' 4. And the priest shall take the basket out of thy hand, and set it down before the altar of the LORD thy God. 5. And thou shalt speak and say before the LORD thy God: 'A wandering Aramean was my father, and he went down into Egypt, and sojourned there, few in number; and he became there a nation, great, mighty, and populous. 6. And the Egyptians dealt ill with us, and afflicted us, and laid upon us hard bondage. 7. And we cried unto the LORD, the God of our fathers, and the

CAP. XXVI. כו

כו

פ פ פ נ 50

א וְהָיָה כִּי־תָבוֹא אֶל־הָאָרֶץ אֲשֶׁר יְהוָה אֱלֹהֶיךָ נֹתֵן לְךָ
2 נַחֲלָה וִירִשְׁתָּהּ וְיָשַׁבְתָּ בָּהּ׃ וְלָקַחְתָּ מֵרֵאשִׁית ׀ כָּל־פְּרִי
הָאֲדָמָה אֲשֶׁר תָּבִיא מֵאַרְצְךָ אֲשֶׁר יְהוָה אֱלֹהֶיךָ נֹתֵן לָךְ
וְשַׂמְתָּ בַטֶּנֶא וְהָלַכְתָּ אֶל־הַמָּקוֹם אֲשֶׁר יִבְחַר יְהוָה אֱלֹהֶיךָ
3 לְשַׁכֵּן שְׁמוֹ שָׁם׃ וּבָאתָ אֶל־הַכֹּהֵן אֲשֶׁר יִהְיֶה בַּיָּמִים הָהֵם
וְאָמַרְתָּ אֵלָיו הִגַּדְתִּי הַיּוֹם לַיהוָה אֱלֹהֶיךָ כִּי־בָאתִי אֶל־
4 הָאָרֶץ אֲשֶׁר נִשְׁבַּע יְהוָה לַאֲבֹתֵינוּ לָתֶת לָנוּ׃ וְלָקַח
הַכֹּהֵן הַטֶּנֶא מִיָּדֶךָ וְהִנִּיחוֹ לִפְנֵי מִזְבַּח יְהוָה אֱלֹהֶיךָ׃
ה וְעָנִיתָ וְאָמַרְתָּ לִפְנֵי ׀ יְהוָה אֱלֹהֶיךָ אֲרַמִּי אֹבֵד אָבִי וַיֵּרֶד
מִצְרַיְמָה וַיָּגָר שָׁם בִּמְתֵי מְעָט וַיְהִי־שָׁם לְגוֹי גָּדוֹל עָצוּם
6 וָרָב׃ וַיָּרֵעוּ אֹתָנוּ הַמִּצְרִים וַיְעַנּוּנוּ וַיִּתְּנוּ עָלֵינוּ עֲבֹדָה
7 קָשָׁה׃ וַנִּצְעַק אֶל־יְהוָה אֱלֹהֵי אֲבֹתֵינוּ וַיִּשְׁמַע יְהוָה אֶת־

VII. KI THAVO

(CHAPTERS XXVI–XXIX, 8)

(5) CONCLUSION OF CODE

(a) XXVI, 1–11. FIRST-FRUITS AND ACKNOWLEDGMENT OF DIVINE PROVIDENCE

The present chapter prescribes the rituals that were to accompany the presentation of the first-fruits and the tithe at the Sanctuary. It was to be an occasion of thanksgiving to God, by whose favour the Israelites had been rescued from the hardships of the past, and raised to become a great nation that dwelt in comfort in a rich and fertile land. This beautiful prayer leads us to believe that other sacrifices at the Sanctuary were likewise not offered in silence; cf. Joel II, 17, p. 894.

2. *of the first of all the fruit.* Not the first of every kind of fruit, but only of the seven kinds mentioned in Deut. VIII, 8 as typical of the fruitfulness of the Land. These are:—wheat, barley, vines, figs, pomegranates, olives, and date-honey.

3. *I profess.* Heb. הגדתי, 'I solemnly proclaim.' Verses 5–10 are a brief epitome of early Jewish history, and constitute the 'profession'. The Rabbis made the exposition of these verses an important part of the Passover Haggadah.

thy God. Thy is used because the priest is here conceived as standing in a special relationship to God; cf. 'The God of Abraham,' in the Liturgy.

I am come. The thank-offering would be the visible proof that the land was now in the possession of the Israelites, and that the Divine Promise had been faithfully fulfilled.

5. *speak.* Testify. This prayer (*v.* 5–10) had to be recited in the Hebrew language. Those who could not do so, repeated it after the priest. To avoid putting anyone to shame, it was eventually ruled that all must repeat the words after the priest.

a wandering Aramean. Or, 'a nomad Aramean.' Ibn Ezra, Rashbam, and Sforno refer this to Jacob, because of his straying and unsettled life; cf. Jacob 'fled into the country of Aram' (Hosea XII, 13). The Heb. for *wandering* often means 'astray', 'ready to perish'; cf. Psalm CXIX end. The Passover Haggadah renders it, 'An Aramean (*i.e.* Laban) sought to destroy my father.'

few in number. Seventy souls in all.

7. *our affliction.* See Exod. I, 11.

LORD heard our voice, and saw our affliction, and our toil, and our oppression. 8. And the LORD brought us forth out of Egypt with a mighty hand, and with an outstretched arm, and with great terribleness, and with signs, and with wonders. 9. And He hath brought us into this place, and hath given us this land, a land flowing with milk and honey. 10. And now, behold, I have brought the first of the fruit of the land, which Thou, O LORD, hast given me.' And thou shalt set it down before the LORD thy God, and worship before the LORD thy God. 11. And thou shalt rejoice in all the good which the LORD thy God hath given unto thee, and unto thy house, thou, and the Levite, and the stranger that is in the midst of thee. *ii. ¶ 12. When thou hast made

8 קֹלֵנוּ וַיַּרְא אֶת־עָנְיֵנוּ וְאֶת־עֲמָלֵנוּ וְאֶת־לַחֲצֵנוּ׃ וַיּוֹצִאֵנוּ
יְהוָה מִמִּצְרַיִם בְּיָד חֲזָקָה וּבִזְרֹעַ נְטוּיָה וּבְמֹרָא גָּדֹל
9 וּבְאֹתוֹת וּבְמֹפְתִים׃ וַיְבִאֵנוּ אֶל־הַמָּקוֹם הַזֶּה וַיִּתֶּן־לָנוּ
10 אֶת־הָאָרֶץ הַזֹּאת אֶרֶץ זָבַת חָלָב וּדְבָשׁ׃ וְעַתָּה הִנֵּה
הֵבֵאתִי אֶת־רֵאשִׁית פְּרִי הָאֲדָמָה אֲשֶׁר־נָתַתָּה לִּי יְהוָה
וְהִנַּחְתּוֹ לִפְנֵי יְהוָה אֱלֹהֶיךָ וְהִשְׁתַּחֲוִיתָ לִפְנֵי יְהוָה אֱלֹהֶיךָ׃
11 וְשָׂמַחְתָּ בְכָל־הַטּוֹב אֲשֶׁר נָתַן־לְךָ יְהוָה אֱלֹהֶיךָ וּלְבֵיתֶךָ
שני 12 אַתָּה וְהַלֵּוִי וְהַגֵּר אֲשֶׁר בְּקִרְבֶּךָ׃ ס כִּי תְכַלֶּה לַעְשֵׂר

9. *milk and honey.* This further brings out the contrast with the state of nomads.

10. *which Thou, O LORD, hast given me.* Refers to the Land and not to the fruits. The above prayer contains two features that are characteristic of all Jewish prayer: (1) recognition of Israel's historic relationship to God; (2) recognition of God as the Source of all blessings.

thou shalt set it down. The bringer of the first-fruits would resume hold of the basket whilst making the declaration contained in *v.* 5–10, and would now, once again, solemnly deposit it before the Altar.

11. *thou shalt rejoice.* The yearly dedication of the first-fruits must be made a family festivity in which, as in the case of the fixed annual Feasts mentioned in XVI, 9–17, the Levite, who had no portion in the land, as well as the 'stranger', were to participate.

The following description of the Procession of the first-fruits to the Temple is given in the Mishnah:—

'How do they set apart the first-fruits? When a man goes down to his field and sees for the first time a ripe fig or a ripe cluster of grapes or a ripe pomegranate, he binds it round with reed-grass and says, "Lo, these are first-fruits."

'How do they take up the first-fruits to Jerusalem? The men of all smaller towns that belonged to the Maamad (*i.e.* the local delegation to the Temple, see p. 429) gathered together in the town of the Maamad, and spent the night in the open place of the town. Early in the morning the officer of the Maamad said, "Arise ye, and let us go up to Zion, unto the LORD our God."

'They that were near to Jerusalem brought fresh figs and grapes and they that were far off brought dried figs and raisins. Before them went the ox, having its horns overlaid with gold and a wreath of olive-leaves on its head. The flute was played before them until they drew nigh to Jerusalem. When they had drawn nigh to Jerusalem, they sent messengers before them and bedecked their first-fruits. The rulers and the prefects and the treasurers of the Temple went forth to meet them. According to the honour due to them that came in, used they to go forth. And all the craftsmen in Jerusalem used to rise up before them and greet them, saying, "Brethren, men of such-and-such a place, ye are welcome."

'The flute was played before them until they reached the Temple Mount. When they reached the Temple Mount, even Agrippa the king would take his basket on his shoulder and enter in as far as the Temple Court. When they reached the Temple Court, the Levites sang the song, "*I will exalt thee, O LORD, for thou hast raised me up, and not made mine enemies to triumph over me.*"

'While the basket was yet on his shoulder, a man would recite the passage from *I profess this day unto the LORD thy God,* until he reached the end of the passage. R. Judah says, Until he reached the words *A wandering Aramean was my father.* When he reached the word *Aramean,* he took down the basket from his shoulder and held it by the rim. And the priests put his hand beneath it and waved it; and the man then recited the words from *A wandering Aramean* until he finished the passage. Then he left the basket by the side of the Altar, and bowed himself down and went his way.

'The rich brought their first-fruits in baskets overlaid with silver and gold, while the poor brought them in wicker baskets of peeled willow-branches: and baskets and first-fruits were given to the priests' (Bikkurim, Chapter III).

(*b*) 12–15. TRIENNIAL DISTRIBUTION OF TITHES, AND PRAYER

There were three tithes. The first tithe was applied to the maintenance of the landless Levites; Num. XVIII, 21–32. The second tithe was taken by the owner to Jerusalem where he an end of tithing all the tithe of thine increase in the third year, which is the year of tithing, and hast given it unto the Levite, to the stranger, to the fatherless, and to the widow, that they may eat within thy gates, and be satisfied, 13. then thou shalt say before the LORD thy God: 'I have put away the hallowed things out of my house, and also have given them unto the Levite, and unto the stranger, to the fatherless, and to the widow, according to all Thy commandment which Thou hast commanded me; I have not transgressed any of Thy commandments, neither have I forgotten them. 14. I have not eaten thereof in my mourning, neither have I put away thereof, being unclean, nor given thereof for the dead; I have hearkened to the voice of the LORD my God, I have done according to all that Thou hast commanded me. 15. Look forth from Thy holy habitation, from heaven, and bless Thy people Israel, and the land which Thou hast given us, as Thou didst swear unto our fathers, a land flowing with milk and honey.'*iii. ¶16. This day the LORD thy God commandeth thee to do these statutes and ordinances; thou shalt therefore observe and do them with all thy heart, and with all thy soul. 17. Thou hast avouched the LORD this day to be thy God, and that thou wouldest

אֶת־כָּל־מַעְשַׂר תְּבוּאָתְךָ בַּשָּׁנָה הַשְּׁלִישִׁת שְׁנַת הַמַּעֲשֵׂר
וְנָתַתָּה לַלֵּוִי לַגֵּר לַיָּתוֹם וְלָאַלְמָנָה וְאָכְלוּ בִשְׁעָרֶיךָ
13 וְשָׂבֵעוּ׃ וְאָמַרְתָּ לִפְנֵי יְהוָה אֱלֹהֶיךָ בִּעַרְתִּי הַקֹּדֶשׁ מִן
הַבַּיִת וְגַם נְתַתִּיו לַלֵּוִי וְלַגֵּר לַיָּתוֹם וְלָאַלְמָנָה כְּכָל־
מִצְוָתְךָ אֲשֶׁר צִוִּיתָנִי לֹא־עָבַרְתִּי מִמִּצְוֺתֶיךָ וְלֹא שָׁכָחְתִּי׃
14 לֹא־אָכַלְתִּי בְאֹנִי מִמֶּנּוּ וְלֹא־בִעַרְתִּי מִמֶּנּוּ בְּטָמֵא וְלֹא־
נָתַתִּי מִמֶּנּוּ לְמֵת שָׁמַעְתִּי בְּקוֹל יְהוָה אֱלֹהָי עָשִׂיתִי כְּכֹל
טו אֲשֶׁר צִוִּיתָנִי׃ הַשְׁקִיפָה מִמְּעוֹן קָדְשְׁךָ מִן־הַשָּׁמַיִם וּבָרֵךְ
אֶת־עַמְּךָ אֶת־יִשְׂרָאֵל וְאֵת הָאֲדָמָה אֲשֶׁר נָתַתָּה לָנוּ כַּאֲשֶׁר
שלישי 16 נִשְׁבַּעְתָּ לַאֲבֹתֵינוּ אֶרֶץ זָבַת חָלָב וּדְבָשׁ׃* ס הַיּוֹם הַזֶּה
יְהוָה אֱלֹהֶיךָ מְצַוְּךָ לַעֲשׂוֹת אֶת־הַחֻקִּים הָאֵלֶּה וְאֶת־
הַמִּשְׁפָּטִים וְשָׁמַרְתָּ וְעָשִׂיתָ אוֹתָם בְּכָל־לְבָבְךָ וּבְכָל־
17 נַפְשֶׁךָ׃ אֶת־יְהוָה הֶאֱמַרְתָּ הַיּוֹם לִהְיוֹת לְךָ לֵאלֹהִים
וְלָלֶכֶת בִּדְרָכָיו וְלִשְׁמֹר חֻקָּיו וּמִצְוֺתָיו וּמִשְׁפָּטָיו וְלִשְׁמֹעַ

v. 14. קמץ בז״ק

and the members of his family consumed it, or else redeemed it for money; Deut. XIV, 22 f. In the third year, this second tithe was devoted entirely to the poor and dependent classes (XIV, 29), whose sufferings so often excite the compassion or indignation of the Prophets and Psalmists. It was later called מעשר עני, 'the tithe of the poor.' The third year was also known as 'the year of removal'. In it the landowner had to remove all his tithes out of the house; that is, pay all his arrears. This 'removal' was accompanied by a solemn declaration, and a prayer for Divine blessing on Israel.

12. *the year of tithing.* Of the poor-tithe.

13. *put away the hallowed things.* 'I have removed the tithe out of my house. I have not secretly kept it back for personal use, but have given it away to those to whom the Torah charges me to give it.'

the hallowed things. Heb. *kodesh; i.e.* the tithe, as holy to God.

14. *in my mourning.* lit. 'as a mourner'. The second tithe, like all sacrificial meats, had to be eaten in a spirit of joy.

being unclean. In that state it was unlawful to eat anything that was hallowed.

nor given thereof for the dead. Not used any part of the tithe to provide a coffin or grave-clothes for a dead person (Sifri), or towards a meal in the house of mourning. Some commentators refer these words to the Egyptian custom of placing articles of food inside the tomb. According to others, the allusion is to actual sacrifices offered to the dead in order to render them propitious to the survivors. However, the cult of the dead is opposed to both the letter and spirit of the Torah; see XVIII, 11 and Psalm CVI, 28.

15. *look forth.* 'Even as we have fulfilled our obligations unto Thee, O God, so do Thou fulfil Thy promise unto us, by blessing us and making the land Thou hast given us a land flowing with milk and honey.'

(*c*) 16–19. FORMULATION OF THE COVENANT BETWEEN GOD AND ISRAEL

17. *avouched.* Avowed, acknowledged; lit. 'thou hast caused the LORD to say' (Herxheimer); probably a technical, legal term by which either of the two parties to a covenant made the other utter a declaration of his obligation under it. Israel, by pledging himself to obedience to all that God hath enjoined, has given occasion to Him to declare Himself to be Israel's God.

walk in His ways, and keep His statutes, and His commandments, and His ordinances, and hearken unto His voice. 18. And the LORD hath avouched thee this day to be His own treasure, as He hath promised thee, and that thou shouldest keep all His commandments; 19. and to make thee high above all nations that He hath made, in praise, and in name, and in glory; and that thou mayest be a holy people unto the LORD thy God, as He hath spoken.*iv.

27 CHAPTER XXVII

1. And Moses and the elders of Israel commanded the people, saying: 'Keep all the commandment which I command you this day. 2. And it shall be on the day when ye shall pass over the Jordan unto the land which the LORD thy God giveth thee, that thou shalt set thee up great stones, and plaster them with plaster. 3. And thou shalt write upon them all the words of this law, when thou art passed over; that thou mayest go in unto the land which the LORD thy God giveth thee, a land flowing with

18 בְּקֹלוֹ׃ וַיהוָה הֶאֱמִירְךָ הַיּוֹם לִהְיוֹת לוֹ לְעַם סְגֻלָּה כַּאֲשֶׁר
19 דִּבֶּר־לָךְ וְלִשְׁמֹר כָּל־מִצְוֺתָיו׃ וּלְתִתְּךָ עֶלְיוֹן עַל כָּל־הַגּוֹיִם
אֲשֶׁר עָשָׂה לִתְהִלָּה וּלְשֵׁם וּלְתִפְאָרֶת וְלִהְיֹתְךָ עַם־קָדֹשׁ
לַיהוָה אֱלֹהֶיךָ כַּאֲשֶׁר דִּבֵּר׃ * רביעי

כז CAP. XXVII. כז

א וַיְצַו מֹשֶׁה וְזִקְנֵי יִשְׂרָאֵל אֶת־הָעָם לֵאמֹר שָׁמֹר אֶת־כָּל־
2 הַמִּצְוָה אֲשֶׁר אָנֹכִי מְצַוֶּה אֶתְכֶם הַיּוֹם׃ וְהָיָה בַּיּוֹם אֲשֶׁר
תַּעַבְרוּ אֶת־הַיַּרְדֵּן אֶל־הָאָרֶץ אֲשֶׁר־יְהוָה אֱלֹהֶיךָ נֹתֵן לָךְ
3 וַהֲקֵמֹתָ לְךָ אֲבָנִים גְּדֹלוֹת וְשַׂדְתָּ אֹתָם בַּשִּׂיד׃ וְכָתַבְתָּ
עֲלֵיהֶן אֶת־כָּל־דִּבְרֵי הַתּוֹרָה הַזֹּאת בְּעָבְרֶךָ לְמַעַן אֲשֶׁר
תָּבֹא אֶל־הָאָרֶץ אֲשֶׁר־יְהוָה אֱלֹהֶיךָ ׀ נֹתֵן לְךָ אֶרֶץ זָבַת

18. *the LORD hath avouched thee.* In the same way, God hath given occasion to the Israelites to say that they were His treasured People, in accordance with Exodus XIX, 5, 6.

19. *make thee high above all nations.* Such is the glorious distinction in store for an Israel that is obedient and loyal. The idea is elaborated in XXVIII, 10, 'And all the peoples of the earth shall see that thou art called by the name of the LORD.'

as He hath spoken. See Exodus XIX, 6, 'And ye shall be unto me a kingdom of priests and an holy nation.'

D. MOSES' THIRD DISCOURSE
ENFORCEMENT OF THE LAW
(XXVII–XXX)

CHAPTER XXVII. PROCEDURE ON CROSSING JORDAN

The nation, upon entering the land, was to declare the terms of its tenure by expressive ceremonies. These are four in number. The Law was to be written on twelve stones at Mt. Ebal; an Altar was to be erected there; the Covenant was to be ratified on Ebal and Gerizim; and twelve dooms on various malefactors were to be pronounced; see Josh. VIII, 30–35.

1–4. Erection of Stones for the inscription of the Law—a symbolic act, declaring that the Israelites took possession of the land by virtue of their covenant with God, and on condition of their own faithfulness thereto.

1. *the elders.* They are here associated with Moses, because upon them would soon devolve the responsibility of securing the fulfilment of the Law.

commanded the people. 'It thus becomes the duty of each individual Israelite to guard and defend the precepts of the Torah and to secure their observance' (Hirsch).

2. *on the day.* At the time; *i.e. after* the crossing of the Jordan. Many commentators see in this a reference to the twelve stones taken out of Jordan by Joshua (IV, 3).

great stones. As they were to contain 'all the words of this law'. Some commentators have held that only a brief summary of the Law could have been inscribed on the stones. However, since the discovery of the Hammurabi Code, consisting of 232 paragraphs, with a lengthy introduction and conclusion, in all about 8,000 words, engraved on one block of diorite, it is seen that the laws of Deuteronomy, or even the whole Torah, could have been written on twelve stones. The Behistun inscription of Darius is, in its triple form, twice as long as the Code (XII–XXVI), and is carved on the solid rock. There is, therefore, no reasonable doubt that, as Saadyah and Ibn Ezra hold, the 613 Precepts of the Torah were inscribed on those great stones.

with plaster. A coating of lime or chalk as a background for the writing in black or another colour. This was quite usual in Egypt. Such writing would not long survive the winter rainstorms of Palestine; but the purpose was not so much permanency, as that the Law be before the eyes of the Israelites at the time when they heard the Blessings and the Curses.

4 חָלָב וּדְבַשׁ כַּאֲשֶׁר דִּבֶּר יְהוָֹה אֱלֹהֵי־אֲבֹתֶיךָ לָךְ׃ וְהָיָה
בְּעָבְרְכֶם אֶת־הַיַּרְדֵּן תָּקִימוּ אֶת־הָאֲבָנִים הָאֵלֶּה אֲשֶׁר
אָנֹכִי מְצַוֶּה אֶתְכֶם הַיּוֹם בְּהַר עֵיבָל וְשַׂדְתָּ אוֹתָם בַּשִּׂיד׃
ה וּבָנִיתָ שָּׁם מִזְבֵּחַ לַיהוָֹה אֱלֹהֶיךָ מִזְבַּח אֲבָנִים לֹא־תָנִיף
6 עֲלֵיהֶם בַּרְזֶל׃ אֲבָנִים שְׁלֵמוֹת תִּבְנֶה אֶת־מִזְבַּח יְהוָֹה
7 אֱלֹהֶיךָ וְהַעֲלִיתָ עָלָיו עוֹלֹת לַיהוָֹה אֱלֹהֶיךָ׃ וְזָבַחְתָּ שְׁלָמִים
8 וְאָכַלְתָּ שָּׁם וְשָׂמַחְתָּ לִפְנֵי יְהוָֹה אֱלֹהֶיךָ׃ וְכָתַבְתָּ עַל־
הָאֲבָנִים אֶת־כָּל־דִּבְרֵי הַתּוֹרָה הַזֹּאת בַּאֵר הֵיטֵב׃ ס
9 וַיְדַבֵּר מֹשֶׁה וְהַכֹּהֲנִים הַלְוִיִּם אֶל־כָּל־יִשְׂרָאֵל לֵאמֹר
הַסְכֵּת ׀ וּשְׁמַע יִשְׂרָאֵל הַיּוֹם הַזֶּה נִהְיֵיתָ לְעָם לַיהוָֹה אֱלֹהֶיךָ׃
י וְשָׁמַעְתָּ בְּקוֹל יְהוָֹה אֱלֹהֶיךָ וְעָשִׂיתָ אֶת־מִצְוֺתָו וְאֶת־חֻקָּיו

v. 8. ב׳ פתוחה v. 9. קמץ בז״ק v. 10. מצותיו קרי

milk and honey, as the LORD, the God of thy fathers, hath promised thee. 4. And it shall be when ye are passed over the Jordan, that ye shall set up these stones, which I command you this day, in mount Ebal, and thou shalt plaster them with plaster. 5. And there shalt thou build an altar unto the LORD thy God, an altar of stones; thou shalt lift up no iron tool upon them. 6. Thou shalt build the altar of the LORD thy God of unhewn stones; and thou shalt offer burnt-offerings thereon unto the LORD thy God. 7. And thou shalt sacrifice peace-offerings, and shalt eat there; and thou shalt rejoice before the LORD thy God. 8. And thou shalt write upon the stones all the words of this law very plainly.' ¶ 9. And Moses and the priests the Levites spoke unto all Israel, saying: 'Keep silence, and hear, O Israel; this day thou art become a people unto the LORD thy God. 10. Thou shalt therefore hearken to the voice of the LORD thy God, and do His commandments and His statutes, which

4. *mount Ebal.* See XI, 29.

5–8. Building an Altar

This command is not contrary to chap. XII that an Altar be erected only in the Central Sanctuary, as the latter law came into force only after the conquest of the Holy Land.

It is noteworthy that the building of an Altar, *i.e.* the institution of Public Worship, was to be the first duty of the Israelites on their entering into Canaan. Throughout the ages, provision for public worship and the religious instruction of the children was ever the first care of the loyal Jew on coming into a new land.

5. *no iron tool.* See Exod. XX, 22. 'The purpose of the Altar is to promote peace between Israel and his Father in Heaven. Let it not, therefore, be polluted by the touch of an iron tool, the symbol of division and destruction' (Talmud).

6. *unhewn stones.* lit. 'whole,' or, 'peaceful stones,' the adjective שלמות being of the same root as שלום, 'peace.' The Altar, whose purpose is the expiation of sin, can only fulfil its mission when peace and brotherhood reign in Israel.

7. *peace-offerings.* An emblem of Israel's peaceful association with God.

shall eat there. The sacrificial meal was to form part of the ceremony of ratification; Exod. XXIV, 11.

8. *upon the stones.* Not on the stones of the Altar, which were rough and unhewn, but upon those of *v.* 4.

very plainly. Heb. באר היטב, so that the words of the Law could be easily read and understood. 'In 70 languages,' is the deep comment of the Rabbis, as its message was for all the children of men. They welcomed any serious attempt to make the Scriptures known and understood by those unable to read the Hebrew Original. 'The words, *baer hetev*, demanding that the words on the stones of the Altar be lucidly explained gave rise to the School of Sopherim, the Scribes, whose office it was to read the Book of the Law of God, distinctly, giving the sense, and causing the people to understand the reading (Nehemiah VIII, 8). In time, this activity resulted in the various Targumim, the versions in the Aramaic vernacular of Onkelos and Jonathan ben Uzziel, and in the Greek of Aquila, the pupil of Akiba. In the course of the ages, the Scribe of old became the Rabbi of to-day. He expounds the Law at the solemn convocations in the synagogue, applies it to the every-day needs and problems besetting the lives of the worshipper, and perpetuates it by teaching it diligently to the children of the community under his guidance' (Schechter).

The fulfilment of the command concerning the stones and Altar is given in Josh. VIII, 30–32.

9–10. 'Noblesse Oblige'

9. *this day.* The erection of the Altar and the initiation of the sacrificial rites connected therewith, that were to take effect on the Israelites' entry into Canaan, made them become God's people, charged with the obligation of fulfilling His commandments and statutes. The consequences of obedience and disobedience are given in the next chapter.

I command thee this day.'*v. ¶ 11. And Moses charged the people the same day, saying: 12. 'These shall stand upon mount Gerizim to bless the people, when ye are passed over the Jordan: Simeon, and Levi, and Judah, and Issachar, and Joseph, and Benjamin; 13. and these shall stand upon mount Ebal for the curse: Reuben, Gad, and Asher, and Zebulun, Dan, and Naphtali. 14. And the Levites shall speak, and say unto all the men of Israel with a loud voice: ¶ 15. Cursed be the man that maketh a graven or molten image, an abomination unto the LORD, the work of the hands of the craftsman, and setteth it up in secret. And all the people shall answer and say: Amen. ¶ 16. Cursed be he that dishonoureth his father or his mother. And all the people shall say: Amen. ¶ 17. Cursed be he that removeth his neighbour's landmark. And all the people shall say: Amen. ¶ 18. Cursed be he that maketh the blind to go astray in the way. And all the people shall say: Amen. ¶ 19. Cursed be he that perverteth the justice due to the stranger, fatherless, and widow. And all the people shall say: Amen. ¶ 20. Cursed be he that lieth with his father's wife; because he hath uncovered his father's

חמישי
11 אֲשֶׁר אָנֹכִי מְצַוְּךָ הַיּוֹם׃ * ס וַיְצַו מֹשֶׁה אֶת־הָעָם בַּיּוֹם
12 הַהוּא לֵאמֹר׃ אֵלֶּה יַעַמְדוּ לְבָרֵךְ אֶת־הָעָם עַל־הַר גְּרִזִּים
בְּעָבְרְכֶם אֶת־הַיַּרְדֵּן שִׁמְעוֹן וְלֵוִי וִיהוּדָה וְיִשָּׂשכָר וְיוֹסֵף
13 וּבִנְיָמִן׃ וְאֵלֶּה יַעַמְדוּ עַל־הַקְּלָלָה בְּהַר עֵיבָל רְאוּבֵן גָּד
14 וְאָשֵׁר וּזְבוּלֻן דָּן וְנַפְתָּלִי׃ וְעָנוּ הַלְוִיִּם וְאָמְרוּ אֶל־כָּל־אִישׁ
טו יִשְׂרָאֵל קוֹל רָם׃ ס אָרוּר הָאִישׁ אֲשֶׁר יַעֲשֶׂה פֶסֶל
וּמַסֵּכָה תּוֹעֲבַת יְהוָה מַעֲשֵׂה יְדֵי חָרָשׁ וְשָׂם בַּסָּתֶר וְעָנוּ
16 כָל־הָעָם וְאָמְרוּ אָמֵן׃ ס אָרוּר מַקְלֶה אָבִיו וְאִמּוֹ
17 וְאָמַר כָּל־הָעָם אָמֵן׃ ס אָרוּר מַסִּיג גְּבוּל רֵעֵהוּ וְאָמַר
18 כָּל־הָעָם אָמֵן׃ ס אָרוּר מַשְׁגֶּה עִוֵּר בַּדָּרֶךְ וְאָמַר
19 כָּל־הָעָם אָמֵן׃ ס אָרוּר מַטֶּה מִשְׁפַּט גֵּר־יָתוֹם
כ וְאַלְמָנָה וְאָמַר כָּל־הָעָם אָמֵן׃ אָרוּר שֹׁכֵב עִם־אֵשֶׁת אָבִיו
21 כִּי גִלָּה כְּנַף אָבִיו וְאָמַר כָּל־הָעָם אָמֵן׃ ס אָרוּר שֹׁכֵב

11–14. MANNER OF THE SOLEMN BLESSING AND DOOM

The ceremony was antiphonal in character, the Levites speaking, and the people responding with an Amen. According to Tradition, the Levites stood round the Ark in some spot in the valley, midway between Gerizim and Ebal. They would first turn towards Gerizim and pronounce the Blessing, and the whole multitude on the slopes answered *Amen.* Turning then to Ebal, they would pronounce the Doom, followed by the same response. 'Never did human imagination conceive a scene so imposing, so solemn, so likely to impress the whole people with deep and enduring awe, as the final ratification of their polity commanded by the dying Lawgiver' (Milman).

12. *to bless.* The Blessings, however, are not mentioned. According to the Talmud, a Blessing and a Doom were pronounced alternately, the Blessing being in each case the negative form of the Doom. Thus the first Blessing would be, 'Blessed is the man who maketh not a graven or molten image,' and so on.

14. *the Levites.* The Levitical priests.
speak. Solemnly pronounce.

15–26. THE SOLEMN DOOMS

In their clarity and succinctness, these denunciations recall the Decalogue. They relate to extreme cases of irreligion and immorality: (1) idolatry; (2) dishonour of parents; (3) removal of landmarks; (4) want of humanity to the blind; (5) injustice to the helpless; (6–9) incest and immorality; (10) murder; (11) bribery; and (12) general disobedience of the Law. The offences selected are such as could not readily be brought to justice before a human tribunal.

15. *cursed be.* Or, 'cursed is.' The words announce the inevitable result in God's righteous government of a certain line of conduct.
Amen. 'So be it'; see p. 591. On the prohibition, cf. IV, 16.

16. *dishonoureth.* The Heb. is the exact opposite of 'honour thy father and thy mother'; cf. Exod. XXI, 17; Lev. XX, 9.

17. *his neighbour's landmark.* See Deut. XIX, 14.

18. *the blind.* This includes the inexperienced and morally weak, who by disingenuous advice can be led to commit irretrievable, or even fatal, mistakes (Rashi); see p. 500.

19. *that perverteth the justice.* See Deut. XXIV, 17. Moffatt renders, 'A curse on the man who tampers with the rights of an alien, an orphan, or a widow.'

20. *his father's skirt.* See on Deut. XXIII, 1; Lev. XVIII, 8.

skirt. And all the people shall say: Amen. ¶ 21. Cursed be he that lieth with any manner of beast. And all the people shall say: Amen. ¶ 22. Cursed be he that lieth with his sister, the daughter of his father, or the daughter of his mother. And all the people shall say: Amen. ¶ 23. Cursed be he that lieth with his mother-in-law. And all the people shall say: Amen. ¶ 24. Cursed be he that smiteth his neighbour in secret. And all the people shall say: Amen. ¶ 25. Cursed be he that taketh a bribe to slay an innocent person. And all the people shall say: Amen. ¶ 26. Cursed be he that confirmeth not the words of this law to do them. And all the people shall say: Amen.'

22 עִם־כָּל־בְּהֵמָה וְאָמַר כָּל־הָעָם אָמֵן׃ ס אָרוּר שֹׁכֵב
עִם־אֲחֹתוֹ בַּת־אָבִיו אוֹ בַת־אִמּוֹ וְאָמַר כָּל־הָעָם אָמֵן׃ ס
23 24 אָרוּר שֹׁכֵב עִם־חֹתַנְתּוֹ וְאָמַר כָּל־הָעָם אָמֵן׃ ס אָרוּר
כה מַכֵּה רֵעֵהוּ בַּסָּתֶר וְאָמַר כָּל־הָעָם אָמֵן׃ ס אָרוּר
לֹקֵחַ שֹׁחַד לְהַכּוֹת נֶפֶשׁ דַּם נָקִי וְאָמַר כָּל־הָעָם אָמֵן׃ ס
26 אָרוּר אֲשֶׁר לֹא־יָקִים אֶת־דִּבְרֵי הַתּוֹרָה־הַזֹּאת לַעֲשׂוֹת
אוֹתָם וְאָמַר כָּל־הָעָם אָמֵן׃ פ

28

Chapter XXVIII

1. And it shall come to pass, if thou shalt hearken diligently unto the voice of the Lord thy God, to observe to do all His commandments which I command thee this day, that the Lord thy God will set thee high above all the nations of the earth. 2. And all these blessings shall come upon thee, and overtake thee, if thou shalt hearken unto the voice of the Lord thy God. 3. Blessed shalt thou be in the city, and blessed shalt thou be in the field. 4. Blessed shall be the fruit of thy body, and the fruit of thy land, and the fruit of thy cattle, the increase of thy

Cap. XXVIII. כח

כח

א וְהָיָה אִם־שָׁמוֹעַ תִּשְׁמַע בְּקוֹל יְהוָה אֱלֹהֶיךָ לִשְׁמֹר
לַעֲשׂוֹת אֶת־כָּל־מִצְוֹתָיו אֲשֶׁר אָנֹכִי מְצַוְּךָ הַיּוֹם וּנְתָנְךָ
2 יְהוָה אֱלֹהֶיךָ עֶלְיוֹן עַל כָּל־גּוֹיֵי הָאָרֶץ׃ וּבָאוּ עָלֶיךָ כָּל־
הַבְּרָכוֹת הָאֵלֶּה וְהִשִּׂיגֻךָ כִּי תִשְׁמַע בְּקוֹל יְהוָה אֱלֹהֶיךָ׃
3 4 בָּרוּךְ אַתָּה בָּעִיר וּבָרוּךְ אַתָּה בַּשָּׂדֶה׃ בָּרוּךְ פְּרִי־בִטְנְךָ
וּפְרִי אַדְמָתְךָ וּפְרִי בְהֶמְתֶּךָ שְׁגַר אֲלָפֶיךָ וְעַשְׁתְּרוֹת צֹאנֶךָ׃

21. *any manner of beast.* See Lev. xviii, 23.

22. *with his sister.* By either parent; cf. Lev. xviii, 9, 17. As such marriages were often contracted before the Giving of the Torah, it was necessary to emphasize their heinousness.

23. *mother-in-law.* 'The Persians married their nearest blood-relatives; thus, Cambyses had two of his sisters in his harem. Similar abominations had to be fought in the early Church' (Koenig).

24. *smiteth his neighbour.* 'By calumny' (Rashi), which smites the honour, peace, and happiness of one's neighbour; cf. Exod. xxi, 12.

25. *bribe.* Cf. Exod. xxiii, 8; Deut. xvi, 19.

26. *that confirmeth not.* 'A comprehensive summing up of the foregoing in general terms, making the Torah, as a whole, binding on every individual Israelite, as contrasted with Israel' (Wiener).

Chapter XXVIII

The Blessings and the Warnings

After the solemn rehearsal of the Dooms, there follows a description of their effect and import. 'The Prophet has taught the higher law; he has rooted all human duty, both to God and man, in love of God; and now he tries to enlist man's natural fear and hope as allies of his highest principle' (Harper). The Warning (תוכחה), as this chapter is called in Hebrew, is far more detailed than the parallel Warning in Lev. xxvi. On the significance of these Warnings, see p. 542; and p. 555, on their similarity with Code Hammurabi. 'The language rises in this chapter to its sublimest strains: and the prophecies respecting the dispersion and sufferings of the Jewish people in latter days are among the most remarkable in Scripture' (Speaker's Bible).

1–14. The Blessings

2. *overtake thee.* The blessings (and curses *v.* 15) are personified as actual beings overtaking their objects.

3–6. Six forms of blessing, covering Israel's life in town and field, in offspring, crops, cattle, harvest, and daily bread.

5. *thy basket . . . kneading-trough.* Metaphors for the annual harvest of fruit and daily bread.

kine, and the young of thy flock. 5. Blessed shall be thy basket and thy kneading-trough. 6. Blessed shalt thou be when thou comest in, and blessed shalt thou be when thou goest out.*vi. 7. The LORD will cause thine enemies that rise up against thee to be smitten before thee; they shall come out against thee one way, and shall flee before thee seven ways. 8. The LORD will command the blessing with thee in thy barns, and in all that thou puttest thy hand unto; and He will bless thee in the land which the LORD thy God giveth thee. 9. The LORD will establish thee for a holy people unto Himself, as He hath sworn unto thee; if thou shalt keep the commandments of the LORD thy God, and walk in His ways. 10. And all the peoples of the earth shall see that the name of the LORD is called upon thee; and they shall be afraid of thee. 11. And the LORD will make thee over-abundant for good, in the fruit of thy body, and in the fruit of thy cattle, and in the fruit of thy land, in the land which the LORD swore unto thy fathers to give thee. 12. The LORD will open unto thee His good treasure the heaven to give the rain of thy land in its season, and to bless all the work of thy hand; and thou shalt lend unto many nations, but thou shalt not borrow. 13. And the LORD will make thee the head, and not the tail; and thou shalt be above only, and thou shalt not be beneath; if thou shalt hearken unto the commandments of the LORD thy God, which I command thee this day, to observe and to do them; 14. and shalt not turn aside from any of the words which I command you this day, to the right hand, or to the left, to go after other gods to serve them. ¶ 15. But it shall come to pass, if thou wilt not hearken unto the voice of the LORD thy God, to observe to do all His commandments and His

ה 6 בָּרוּךְ טַנְאֲךָ וּמִשְׁאַרְתֶּךָ׃ בָּרוּךְ אַתָּה בְּבֹאֶךָ וּבָרוּךְ אַתָּה
ששי 7 בְּצֵאתֶךָ׃ * יִתֵּן יְהוָה אֶת־אֹיְבֶיךָ הַקָּמִים עָלֶיךָ נִגָּפִים
לְפָנֶיךָ בְּדֶרֶךְ אֶחָד יֵצְאוּ אֵלֶיךָ וּבְשִׁבְעָה דְרָכִים יָנוּסוּ
8 לְפָנֶיךָ׃ יְצַו יְהוָה אִתְּךָ אֶת־הַבְּרָכָה בַּאֲסָמֶיךָ וּבְכֹל מִשְׁלַח
9 יָדֶךָ וּבֵרַכְךָ בָּאָרֶץ אֲשֶׁר־יְהוָה אֱלֹהֶיךָ נֹתֵן לָךְ׃ יְקִימְךָ
יְהוָה לוֹ לְעַם קָדוֹשׁ כַּאֲשֶׁר נִשְׁבַּע־לָךְ כִּי תִשְׁמֹר אֶת־
י מִצְוֺת יְהוָה אֱלֹהֶיךָ וְהָלַכְתָּ בִּדְרָכָיו׃ וְרָאוּ כָּל־עַמֵּי הָאָרֶץ
11 כִּי שֵׁם יְהוָה נִקְרָא עָלֶיךָ וְיָרְאוּ מִמֶּךָּ׃ וְהוֹתִרְךָ יְהוָה
לְטוֹבָה בִּפְרִי בִטְנְךָ וּבִפְרִי בְהֶמְתְּךָ וּבִפְרִי אַדְמָתֶךָ עַל
12 הָאֲדָמָה אֲשֶׁר נִשְׁבַּע יְהוָה לַאֲבֹתֶיךָ לָתֶת לָךְ׃ יִפְתַּח
יְהוָה ׀ לְךָ אֶת־אוֹצָרוֹ הַטּוֹב אֶת־הַשָּׁמַיִם לָתֵת מְטַר־אַרְצְךָ
בְּעִתּוֹ וּלְבָרֵךְ אֵת כָּל־מַעֲשֵׂה יָדֶךָ וְהִלְוִיתָ גּוֹיִם רַבִּים
13 וְאַתָּה לֹא תִלְוֶה׃ וּנְתָנְךָ יְהוָה לְרֹאשׁ וְלֹא לְזָנָב וְהָיִיתָ רַק
לְמַעְלָה וְלֹא תִהְיֶה לְמָטָּה כִּי־תִשְׁמַע אֶל־מִצְוֺת ׀ יְהוָה
14 אֱלֹהֶיךָ אֲשֶׁר אָנֹכִי מְצַוְּךָ הַיּוֹם לִשְׁמֹר וְלַעֲשׂוֹת׃ וְלֹא תָסוּר
מִכָּל־הַדְּבָרִים אֲשֶׁר אָנֹכִי מְצַוֶּה אֶתְכֶם הַיּוֹם יָמִין וּשְׂמֹאול
לָלֶכֶת אַחֲרֵי אֱלֹהִים אֲחֵרִים לְעָבְדָם׃ פ
טו וְהָיָה אִם־לֹא תִשְׁמַע בְּקוֹל יְהוָה אֱלֹהֶיךָ לִשְׁמֹר לַעֲשׂוֹת

v. 14. יתיר ו׳

6. *comest in . . . goest out.* The blessing of safety in all the manifold activities of ordinary life.

7–13. The Divine blessing will rest also on their larger enterprises whether in peace or war. Theirs will be a victory over enemies; material success in all forms of labour, accompanied by religious and cultural supremacy among the nations.

7. *seven ways.* A round number, indicating a great quantity. The compact array of the advancing foe is contrasted with his dispersion, in manifold directions, after defeat.

9. *a holy people.* Set apart for Himself, and therefore inviolable.

10. *called upon thee.* *i.e.* that He is thy Owner, and, as such, surrounds thee with His protection.

12. *good treasure.* The celestial reservoirs, in which the rain was conceived to be stored; cf. Job. XXXVIII, 22.

shalt lend. A sign of wealth, as well as of power and independence.

13. *only.* Here in the meaning of 'nothing but'; ever rising in reputation.

15–68. THE WARNINGS

In the remainder of this chapter, the Lawgiver sets forth in words of awful power the fact that God's laws have a reverse, as well as an obverse, side; that the Divine Covenant was indeed a hope

את־כל־מצותיו וחקתיו אשר אנכי מצוך היום ובאו
16 עליך כל־הקללות האלה והשיגוך: ארור אתה בעיר
17 18 וארור אתה בשדה: ארור טנאך ומשארתך: ארור פרי־
19 בטנך ופרי אדמתך שגר אלפיך ועשתרת צאנך: ארור
כ אתה בבאך וארור אתה בצאתך: ישלח יהוה בך את־
המארה את־המהומה ואת־המגערת בכל־משלח ידך
אשר תעשה עד השמדך ועד־אבדך מהר מפני רע
21 מעלליך אשר עזבתני: ידבק יהוה בך את־הדבר עד
כלתו אתך מעל האדמה אשר־אתה בא־שמה לרשתה:
22 יככה יהוה בשחפת ובקדחת ובדלקת ובחרחר ובחרב
23 ובשדפון ובירקון ורדפוך עד אבדך: והיו שמיך אשר על־
24 ראשך נחשת והארץ אשר־תחתיך ברזל: יתן יהוה את־

statutes which I command thee this day; that all these curses shall come upon thee, and overtake thee. 16. Cursed shalt thou be in the city, and cursed shalt thou be in the field. 17. Cursed shall be thy basket and thy kneading-trough. 18. Cursed shall be the fruit of thy body, and the fruit of thy land, the increase of thy kine, and the young of thy flock. 19. Cursed shalt thou be when thou comest in, and cursed shalt thou be when thou goest out. 20. The LORD will send upon thee cursing, discomfiture, and rebuke, in all that thou puttest thy hand unto to do, until thou be destroyed, and until thou perish quickly; because of the evil of thy doings, whereby thou hast forsaken Me. 21. The LORD will make the pestilence cleave unto thee, until He have consumed thee from off the land, whither thou goest in to possess it. 22. The LORD will smite thee with consumption, and with fever, and with inflammation, and with fiery heat, and with drought, and with blasting, and with mildew; and they shall pursue thee until thou perish. 23. And thy heaven that is over thy head shall be brass, and the earth that is under thee shall be iron. 24. The LORD will make the rain of thy land powder and dust; from heaven

and an encouragement, but also a responsibility and a warning. 'The sublimity of the denunciations surpasses anything in the oratory or the poetry of the whole world. Nothing, except the real horrors of Jewish history, can approach the tremendous maledictions which warned Israel against the violation of the Law' (Milman). 'Three times does the wave of holy passion rise and fall. At first the exuberance of the woes enumerated overpowers our attention; the musically parallel sentences, which in other speeches make perorations, here come for intervals of relief. Another stream of denunciation brings the serving the LORD with joyfulness, and with gladness of heart by reason of the abundance of all things, into contrast with the serving of the enemy in hunger, and in thirst, and in nakedness, and in want of all things; and the siege laid by the enemy is extended in picture to the last horrors the mind can conceive. Yet another flood of speech begins with the "glorious and fearful" Name; and there passes before us the fading of the life of promise into plagues and exile; in exile, the trembling heart, and failing of eyes, and pining of soul; until for a final climax the original salvation of Israel is reversed in a voluntary returning to the land of bondage, the people selling themselves to their enemies for bondmen and bondwomen, a climax yet more final than this, for "no man shall buy you" ' (Moulton).

The curses are national and not individual. They are all of them conditional, declaring what God would bring on Israel in the event of its complete apostasy. Israel's survival of the Divine Judgment is due to the fact that Israel always possessed a 'righteous remnant'.

16–19. These curses take the same verbal form as the blessings, *v.* 1–6, and express failure in every department of national life.

20–26. Disastrous years, fevers, droughts, and ruinous defeat in battle.

20. *cursing.* The general term, particulars of which follow.

discomfiture. Inability to complete a task undertaken (Ibn Ezra).

rebuke. Failure to enjoy the fruit of one's labours through constant anxiety and vexation.

21. *pestilence.* Any dangerous epidemic.

22. *will smite thee.* With seven plagues; five on men, and two on crops. The identification of the names of the plagues is by Macalister.

consumption. A wasting fever of the Mediterranean type.

fever. Malaria.

inflammation. Typhoid fever.

fiery heat. lit. 'irritation', erysipelas.

24. *powder and dust.* An allusion to the sirocco, with its fogs of sand and dust.

shall it come down upon thee, until thou be destroyed. 25. The LORD will cause thee to be smitten before thine enemies; thou shalt go out one way against them, and shalt flee seven ways before them; and thou shalt be a horror unto all the kingdoms of the earth. 26. And thy carcasses shall be food unto all fowls of the air, and unto the beasts of the earth, and there shall be none to frighten them away. ¶ 27. The LORD will smite thee with the boil of Egypt, and with the emerods, and with the scab, and with the itch, whereof thou canst not be healed. 28. The LORD will smite thee with madness, and with blindness, and with astonishment of heart. 29. And thou shalt grope at noondays, as the blind gropeth in darkness, and thou shalt not make thy ways prosperous; and thou shalt be only oppressed and robbed alway, and there shall be none to save thee. 30. Thou shalt betroth a wife, and another man shall lie with her; thou shalt build a house, and thou shalt not dwell therein; thou shalt plant a vineyard, and shalt not use the fruit thereof. 31. Thine ox shall be slain before thine eyes, and thou shalt not eat thereof; thine ass shall be violently taken away from before thy face, and shall not be restored to thee; thy sheep shall be given unto thine enemies; and thou shalt have none to save thee. 32. Thy sons and thy daughters shall be given unto another people, and thine eyes shall look, and fail with longing for them all the day; and there shall be nought in the power of thy hand. 33. The fruit of thy land, and all thy labours, shall a nation which thou knowest not eat up;

מְטַר אַרְצְךָ אָבָק וְעָפָר מִן־הַשָּׁמַיִם יֵרֵד עָלֶיךָ עַד הִשָּׁמְדָךְ׃
כה יִתֶּנְךָ יְהוָה ׀ נִגָּף לִפְנֵי אֹיְבֶיךָ בְּדֶרֶךְ אֶחָד תֵּצֵא אֵלָיו
וּבְשִׁבְעָה דְרָכִים תָּנוּס לְפָנָיו וְהָיִיתָ לְזַעֲוָה לְכֹל מַמְלְכוֹת
26 הָאָרֶץ׃ וְהָיְתָה נִבְלָתְךָ לְמַאֲכָל לְכָל־עוֹף הַשָּׁמַיִם וּלְבֶהֱמַת
27 הָאָרֶץ וְאֵין מַחֲרִיד׃ יַכְּכָה יְהוָה בִּשְׁחִין מִצְרַיִם וּבַעְפֹלִים
28 וּבַגָּרָב וּבֶחָרֶס אֲשֶׁר לֹא־תוּכַל לְהֵרָפֵא׃ יַכְּכָה יְהוָה
29 בְּשִׁגָּעוֹן וּבְעִוָּרוֹן וּבְתִמְהוֹן לֵבָב׃ וְהָיִיתָ מְמַשֵּׁשׁ בַּצָּהֳרַיִם
כַּאֲשֶׁר יְמַשֵּׁשׁ הָעִוֵּר בָּאֲפֵלָה וְלֹא תַצְלִיחַ אֶת־דְּרָכֶיךָ
ל וְהָיִיתָ אַךְ עָשׁוּק וְגָזוּל כָּל־הַיָּמִים וְאֵין מוֹשִׁיעַ׃ אִשָּׁה תְאָרֵשׂ
וְאִישׁ אַחֵר יִשְׁגָּלֶנָּה בַּיִת תִּבְנֶה וְלֹא־תֵשֵׁב בּוֹ כֶּרֶם תִּטַּע
31 וְלֹא תְחַלְּלֶנּוּ׃ שׁוֹרְךָ טָבוּחַ לְעֵינֶיךָ וְלֹא תֹאכַל מִמֶּנּוּ חֲמֹרְךָ
גָּזוּל מִלְּפָנֶיךָ וְלֹא יָשׁוּב לָךְ צֹאנְךָ נְתֻנוֹת לְאֹיְבֶיךָ וְאֵין לְךָ
32 מוֹשִׁיעַ׃ בָּנֶיךָ וּבְנֹתֶיךָ נְתֻנִים לְעַם אַחֵר וְעֵינֶיךָ רֹאוֹת
33 וְכָלוֹת אֲלֵיהֶם כָּל־הַיּוֹם וְאֵין לְאֵל יָדֶךָ׃ פְּרִי אַדְמָתְךָ וְכָל־
יְגִיעֲךָ יֹאכַל עַם אֲשֶׁר לֹא־יָדָעְתָּ וְהָיִיתָ רַק עָשׁוּק וְרָצוּץ
34 כָּל־הַיָּמִים׃ וְהָיִיתָ מְשֻׁגָּע מִמַּרְאֵה עֵינֶיךָ אֲשֶׁר תִּרְאֶה׃

v. 27. ובטחורים ק׳ v. 30. ישכבנה ק׳

25. *a horror unto.* Or, 'a shuddering unto'; an awe-inspiring spectacle.

26. *frighten.* As Rizpah's mother-love did, II Sam. XXI, 10. So complete would be the rout, that the dead would lie unburied.

27–37. Incurable diseases, mental blindness, a prey to cruel invaders, and ignominious exile.

27. *the boil of Egypt.* Cf. Deut. VII, 15.

28. *astonishment of heart.* Dismay; confusion of mind.

29. *grope.* Reduced to blind helplessness.

as the blind gropeth in darkness. 'Rabbi José said, All my days I grieved at my not being able to explain this verse; for, what difference can it be to the blind man, whether he gropeth in the light or in the dark? Until one night I was walking in the road, and met a blind man with a lighted torch in his hand. "Son," said I, "why dost thou carry that torch? thou canst not see its light." "Friend," replied the blind man, "true it is I cannot see, but as long as I carry this torch in my hand, the sons of men see me, take pity on me, and save me from pitfalls, from thorns and briers"' (Talmud). Thus, the apparently superfluous phrase *in darkness* was to emphasize the greatness of the calamity that would befall Israel. Even at noonday they were to grope as the blind do in the darkness, without a ray of light to exhibit their distress to the compassion of men.

30. *not use the fruit thereof.* See XX, 6. The helpless inhabitants would be at the mercy of insatiable conquerors, so that they could call nothing they possessed—not even their wives and children—their own.

31. *before thine eyes.* Whilst thou art looking on, unable to raise a hand to prevent it.

32. *thy sons and thy daughters.* History records several large deportations of Israelites to distant lands beyond the Euphrates.

and thou shalt be only oppressed and crushed alway; 34. so that thou shalt be mad for the sight of thine eyes which thou shalt see. 35. The LORD will smite thee in the knees, and in the legs, with a sore boil, whereof thou canst not be healed, from the sole of thy foot unto the crown of thy head. 36. The LORD will bring thee, and thy king whom thou shalt set over thee, unto a nation that thou hast not known, thou nor thy fathers; and there shalt thou serve other gods, wood and stone. 37. And thou shalt become an astonishment, a proverb, and a byword, among all the peoples whither the LORD shall lead thee away. ¶ 38. Thou shalt carry much seed out into the field, and shalt gather little in; for the locust shall consume it. 39. Thou shalt plant vineyards and dress them, but thou shalt neither drink of the wine, nor gather the grapes; for the worm shall eat them. 40. Thou shalt have olive-trees throughout all thy borders, but thou shalt not anoint thyself with the oil; for thine olives shall drop off. 41. Thou shalt beget sons and daughters, but they shall not be thine; for they shall go into captivity. 42. All thy trees and the fruit of thy land shall the locust possess. ¶ 43. The stranger that is in the midst of thee shall mount up above thee higher and higher; and thou shalt come down lower and lower. 44. He shall lend to thee, and thou shalt not lend to him; he shall be the head, and thou shalt be the tail. 45. And all these curses shall come upon thee, and shall pursue thee, and

לה יַכְּכָה יְהוָֹה בִּשְׁחִין רָע עַל־הַבִּרְכַּיִם וְעַל־הַשֹּׁקַיִם אֲשֶׁר
36 לֹא־תוּכַל לְהֵרָפֵא מִכַּף רַגְלְךָ וְעַד קָדְקֳדֶךָ׃ יוֹלֵךְ יְהוָֹה
אֹתְךָ וְאֶת־מַלְכְּךָ אֲשֶׁר תָּקִים עָלֶיךָ אֶל־גּוֹי אֲשֶׁר לֹא־
יָדַעְתָּ אַתָּה וַאֲבֹתֶיךָ וְעָבַדְתָּ שָּׁם אֱלֹהִים אֲחֵרִים עֵץ וָאָבֶן׃
37 וְהָיִיתָ לְשַׁמָּה לְמָשָׁל וְלִשְׁנִינָה בְּכֹל הָעַמִּים אֲשֶׁר־יְנַהֶגְךָ
38 יְהוָֹה שָׁמָּה׃ זֶרַע רַב תּוֹצִיא הַשָּׂדֶה וּמְעַט תֶּאֱסֹף כִּי יַחְסְלֶנּוּ
39 הָאַרְבֶּה׃ כְּרָמִים תִּטַּע וְעָבָדְתָּ וְיַיִן לֹא־תִשְׁתֶּה וְלֹא
מ תֶאֱגֹר כִּי תֹאכְלֶנּוּ הַתֹּלָעַת׃ זֵיתִים יִהְיוּ לְךָ בְּכָל־גְּבוּלֶךָ
41 וְשֶׁמֶן לֹא תָסוּךְ כִּי יִשַּׁל זֵיתֶךָ׃ בָּנִים וּבָנוֹת תּוֹלִיד וְלֹא־
42 יִהְיוּ לָךְ כִּי יֵלְכוּ בַּשֶּׁבִי׃ כָּל־עֵצְךָ וּפְרִי אַדְמָתֶךָ יְיָרֵשׁ
43 הַצְּלָצַל׃ הַגֵּר אֲשֶׁר בְּקִרְבְּךָ יַעֲלֶה עָלֶיךָ מַעְלָה מָּעְלָה
44 וְאַתָּה תֵרֵד מַטָּה מָּטָּה׃ הוּא יַלְוְךָ וְאַתָּה לֹא תַלְוֶנּוּ
מה הוּא יִהְיֶה לְרֹאשׁ וְאַתָּה תִּהְיֶה לְזָנָב׃ וּבָאוּ עָלֶיךָ כָּל־
הַקְּלָלוֹת הָאֵלֶּה וּרְדָפוּךָ וְהִשִּׂיגוּךָ עַד הִשָּׁמְדָךְ כִּי־לֹא
שָׁמַעְתָּ בְּקוֹל יְהוָֹה אֱלֹהֶיךָ לִשְׁמֹר מִצְוֹתָיו וְחֻקֹּתָיו אֲשֶׁר

v. 42. פתח בס״פ

34. *be mad.* *i.e.* be driven mad.

36. *thy king.* II Kings XXIV reports that Jehoiakim was carried captive to Babylon with 10,000 of his subjects.
serve other gods, wood and stone. 'Transportation to a heathen land would mean absorption into the religion, as well as into the life, of heathenism' (Welch).

37. *a proverb.* A taunt.
byword. lit. 'the object of biting remarks.'

38–44. Impoverished Israel reduced to dependence on the resident foreigner.

41. *shall not be thine.* With transportation to a foreign land, estrangement from their fathers, Faith and People must inevitably follow. Such estrangement is deemed a curse in Mal. III, 24; see p. 970. Byalik calls attention to a similar estrangement of the children from their Faith and People in the present age, and considers it the supreme tragedy of the Spiritual Golus of the emancipation era.

43. *the stranger.* He who had received the charity of the Israelites, to him would they now have to look for commiseration. They must learn to live as servants where they had once been masters.

45–48. The reason for these terrible calamities.

45. *because.* A return to the keynote of this whole chapter, *v.* 15.

46. *for a sign and for a wonder.* The calamities shall testify to the truth of the Divine interposition in history. As soon as they were prepared to acknowledge that what they suffered was not unmerited, there was still soundness in them, and they would receive mercy at the hands of God.
upon thy seed for ever. *i.e.* as long as they maintained their disobedience and rebelliousness. But, as stated in Deut. XXX, 2, 3, should they

overtake thee, till thou be destroyed; because thou didst not hearken unto the voice of the LORD thy God, to keep His commandments and His statutes which He commanded thee. 46. And they shall be upon thee for a sign and for a wonder, and upon thy seed for ever; 47. because thou didst not serve the LORD thy God with joyfulness, and with gladness of heart, by reason of the abundance of all things; 48. therefore shalt thou serve thine enemy whom the LORD shall send against thee, in hunger, and in thirst, and in nakedness, and in want of all things; and he shall put a yoke of iron upon thy neck, until he have destroyed thee. ¶ 49. The LORD will bring a nation against thee from far, from the end of the earth, as the vulture swoopeth down; a nation whose tongue thou shalt not understand; 50. a nation of fierce countenance, that shall not regard the person of the old, nor show favour to the young. 51. And he shall eat the fruit of thy cattle, and the fruit of thy ground, until thou be destroyed; that also shall not leave thee corn, wine, or oil, the increase of thy kine, or the young of thy flock, until he have caused thee to perish. 52. And he shall besiege thee in all thy gates, until thy high and fortified walls come down, wherein thou didst trust, throughout all thy land; and he shall besiege thee in all thy gates throughout all thy land, which the LORD thy God hath given thee. 53. And thou shalt eat the fruit of thine own body, the flesh of thy sons and of thy daughters whom the LORD thy God hath given thee; in the siege and in the straitness, wherewith thine enemies shall straiten thee. 54. The man that is tender among you, and very delicate, his eye shall be evil against his brother, and against the wife of his bosom, and against the remnant of his children whom he hath remaining; 55. so that he will not give to any of them of the flesh of his children whom he shall eat, because he hath nothing left him; in the siege and in the straitness, wherewith thine enemy shall straiten thee in all thy gates. 56. The tender and delicate woman among you, who would not adventure to set the sole of her foot upon the ground for delicateness and tenderness, her eye shall be evil against the husband of her bosom, and

46 47 צִוָּֽךְ׃ וְהָיוּ בְךָ לְאוֹת וּלְמוֹפֵת וּבְזַרְעֲךָ עַד־עוֹלָם׃ תַּחַת
אֲשֶׁר לֹא־עָבַדְתָּ אֶת־יְהוָה אֱלֹהֶיךָ בְּשִׂמְחָה וּבְטוּב לֵבָב
48 מֵרֹב כֹּל׃ וְעָבַדְתָּ אֶת־אֹיְבֶיךָ אֲשֶׁר יְשַׁלְּחֶנּוּ יְהוָה בָּךְ
בְּרָעָב וּבְצָמָא וּבְעֵירֹם וּבְחֹסֶר כֹּל וְנָתַן עֹל בַּרְזֶל עַל־
49 צַוָּארֶךָ עַד הִשְׁמִידוֹ אֹתָךְ׃ יִשָּׂא יְהוָה עָלֶיךָ גּוֹי מֵרָחֹק
מִקְצֵה הָאָרֶץ כַּאֲשֶׁר יִדְאֶה הַנָּשֶׁר גּוֹי אֲשֶׁר לֹא־תִשְׁמַע
נ לְשֹׁנוֹ׃ גּוֹי עַז פָּנִים אֲשֶׁר לֹא־יִשָּׂא פָנִים לְזָקֵן וְנַעַר לֹא
51 יָחֹן׃ וְאָכַל פְּרִי בְהֶמְתְּךָ וּפְרִי־אַדְמָתְךָ עַד הִשָּׁמְדָךְ אֲשֶׁר
לֹא־יַשְׁאִיר לְךָ דָּגָן תִּירוֹשׁ וְיִצְהָר שְׁגַר אֲלָפֶיךָ וְעַשְׁתְּרֹת
52 צֹאנֶךָ עַד הַאֲבִידוֹ אֹתָךְ׃ וְהֵצַר לְךָ בְּכָל־שְׁעָרֶיךָ עַד רֶדֶת
חֹמֹתֶיךָ הַגְּבֹהֹת וְהַבְּצֻרוֹת אֲשֶׁר אַתָּה בֹּטֵחַ בָּהֵן בְּכָל־
אַרְצֶךָ וְהֵצַר לְךָ בְּכָל־שְׁעָרֶיךָ בְּכָל־אַרְצְךָ אֲשֶׁר נָתַן יְהוָה
53 אֱלֹהֶיךָ לָךְ׃ וְאָכַלְתָּ פְרִי־בִטְנְךָ בְּשַׂר בָּנֶיךָ וּבְנֹתֶיךָ אֲשֶׁר
נָתַן־לְךָ יְהוָה אֱלֹהֶיךָ בְּמָצוֹר וּבְמָצוֹק אֲשֶׁר־יָצִיק לְךָ
54 אֹיְבֶךָ׃ הָאִישׁ הָרַךְ בְּךָ וְהֶעָנֹג מְאֹד תֵּרַע עֵינוֹ בְאָחִיו
נה וּבְאֵשֶׁת חֵיקוֹ וּבְיֶתֶר בָּנָיו אֲשֶׁר יוֹתִיר׃ מִתֵּת ׀ לְאַחַד
מֵהֶם מִבְּשַׂר בָּנָיו אֲשֶׁר יֹאכֵל מִבְּלִי הִשְׁאִיר־לוֹ כֹּל
בְּמָצוֹר וּבְמָצוֹק אֲשֶׁר יָצִיק לְךָ אֹיִבְךָ בְּכָל־שְׁעָרֶיךָ׃
56 הָרַכָּה בְךָ וְהָעֲנֻגָּה אֲשֶׁר לֹא־נִסְּתָה כַף־רַגְלָהּ הַצֵּג עַל־
הָאָרֶץ מֵהִתְעַנֵּג וּמֵרֹךְ תֵּרַע עֵינָהּ בְּאִישׁ חֵיקָהּ וּבִבְנָהּ
57 וּבְבִתָּהּ׃ וּבְשִׁלְיָתָהּ הַיּוֹצֵת ׀ מִבֵּין רַגְלֶיהָ וּבְבָנֶיהָ אֲשֶׁר
תֵּלֵד כִּי־תֹאכְלֵם בְּחֹסֶר־כֹּל בַּסֵּתֶר בְּמָצוֹר וּבְמָצוֹק אֲשֶׁר

v. 57. חסר אל״ף

'bethink themselves' and 'return', then would they reap the blessings of restoration and prosperity.

49–55. Measure for measure. Invasion by a far-off nation. The horrors of siege.

49. *bring a nation against thee.* The Assyrians and Babylonians.

50. *fierce countenance.* Unyielding to considerations of humanity or pity.

53. *eat the fruit of thine own body.* Hunger would so brutalize them; see II Kings VI, 25–29.
straiten thee. 'Press you hard' (Moffatt).

54. *shall be evil.* He would grudge even this ghastly food to those nearest to him.

against her son, and against her daughter; 57. and against her afterbirth that cometh out from between her feet, and against her children whom she shall bear; for she shall eat them for want of all things secretly; in the siege and in the straitness, wherewith thine enemy shall straiten thee in thy gates. ¶ 58. If thou wilt not observe to do all the words of this law that are written in this book, that thou mayest fear this glorious and awful Name, the LORD thy God; 59. then the LORD will make thy plagues wonderful, and the plagues of thy seed, even great plagues, and of long continuance, and sore sicknesses, and of long continuance. 60. And He will bring back upon thee all the diseases of Egypt, which thou wast in dread of; and they shall cleave unto thee. 61. Also every sickness, and every plague, which is not written in the book of this law, them will the LORD bring upon thee, until thou be destroyed. 62. And ye shall be left few in number, whereas ye were as the stars of heaven for multitude; because thou didst not hearken unto the voice of the LORD thy God. 63. And it shall come to pass, that as the LORD rejoiced over you to do you good, and to multiply you; so the LORD will rejoice over you to cause you to perish, and to destroy you; and ye shall be plucked from off the land whither thou goest in to possess it. 64. And the LORD shall scatter thee among all peoples, from the one end of the earth even unto the other end of the earth; and there thou shalt serve other gods, which thou hast not known, thou nor thy fathers, even wood and stone. 65. And among these nations shalt thou have no repose, and there shall be no rest for the sole of thy foot; but the LORD shall give thee there a trembling heart, and failing of eyes, and languishing of soul. 66. And thy life shall hang in doubt before thee; and thou shalt fear night and day, and shalt have no assurance of thy life. 67. In the morning thou shalt say: 'Would

58 יָצִיק לְךָ אֹיִבְךָ בִּשְׁעָרֶיךָ׃ אִם־לֹא תִשְׁמֹר לַעֲשׂוֹת אֶת־
כָּל־דִּבְרֵי הַתּוֹרָה הַזֹּאת הַכְּתֻבִים בַּסֵּפֶר הַזֶּה לְיִרְאָה
59 אֶת־הַשֵּׁם הַנִּכְבָּד וְהַנּוֹרָא הַזֶּה אֵת יְהוָה אֱלֹהֶיךָ׃ וְהִפְלָא
יְהוָה אֶת־מַכֹּתְךָ וְאֵת מַכּוֹת זַרְעֶךָ מַכּוֹת גְּדֹלֹת וְנֶאֱמָנוֹת
ס וָחֳלָיִם רָעִים וְנֶאֱמָנִים׃ וְהֵשִׁיב בְּךָ אֵת כָּל־מַדְוֵה מִצְרַיִם
61 אֲשֶׁר יָגֹרְתָּ מִפְּנֵיהֶם וְדָבְקוּ בָּךְ׃ גַּם כָּל־חֳלִי וְכָל־מַכָּה
אֲשֶׁר לֹא כָתוּב בְּסֵפֶר הַתּוֹרָה הַזֹּאת יַעְלֵם יְהוָה עָלֶיךָ
62 עַד הִשָּׁמְדָךְ׃ וְנִשְׁאַרְתֶּם בִּמְתֵי מְעָט תַּחַת אֲשֶׁר הֱיִיתֶם
כְּכוֹכְבֵי הַשָּׁמַיִם לָרֹב כִּי־לֹא שָׁמַעְתָּ בְּקוֹל יְהוָה אֱלֹהֶיךָ׃
63 וְהָיָה כַּאֲשֶׁר־שָׂשׂ יְהוָה עֲלֵיכֶם לְהֵיטִיב אֶתְכֶם וּלְהַרְבּוֹת
אֶתְכֶם כֵּן יָשִׂישׂ יְהוָה עֲלֵיכֶם לְהַאֲבִיד אֶתְכֶם וּלְהַשְׁמִיד
אֶתְכֶם וְנִסַּחְתֶּם מֵעַל הָאֲדָמָה אֲשֶׁר־אַתָּה בָא־שָׁמָּה
64 לְרִשְׁתָּהּ׃ וֶהֱפִיצְךָ יְהוָה בְּכָל־הָעַמִּים מִקְצֵה הָאָרֶץ וְעַד־
קְצֵה הָאָרֶץ וְעָבַדְתָּ שָּׁם אֱלֹהִים אֲחֵרִים אֲשֶׁר לֹא־יָדַעְתָּ
סה אַתָּה וַאֲבֹתֶיךָ עֵץ וָאָבֶן׃ וּבַגּוֹיִם הָהֵם לֹא תַרְגִּיעַ וְלֹא־
יִהְיֶה מָנוֹחַ לְכַף־רַגְלֶךָ וְנָתַן יְהוָה לְךָ שָׁם לֵב רַגָּז וְכִלְיוֹן
66 עֵינַיִם וְדַאֲבוֹן נָפֶשׁ׃ וְהָיוּ חַיֶּיךָ תְּלֻאִים לְךָ מִנֶּגֶד וּפָחַדְתָּ
67 לַיְלָה וְיוֹמָם וְלֹא תַאֲמִין בְּחַיֶּיךָ׃ בַּבֹּקֶר תֹּאמַר מִי־יִתֵּן
עֶרֶב וּבָעֶרֶב תֹּאמַר מִי־יִתֵּן בֹּקֶר מִפַּחַד לְבָבְךָ אֲשֶׁר

v. 62. קמץ בז"ק

56–68. CONCLUDING WARNING

58. *fear this glorious and awful Name.* The adjective 'glorious' has reference to the majesty of God to Whom fear (*i.e.* reverence) is due; 'awful' denotes God's awe-inspiring nature. *Name* is occasionally used as a synonym for Deity, or as denoting the Divine Presence; cf. Lev. XXIV, 11.

59. *wonderful.* Extraordinary, exceptional.

63. *the LORD rejoiced over you.* When a son walks in the right way, it is the father's joy to help him and to show him kindness. Should, however, the son fall into evil ways, then it is equally the father's 'joy' to find some means—even painful ones—to bring him back to the right path. In like manner, God 'rejoices' to bring upon sinful Israel the trials and sufferings of exile, in order thereby to purify and elevate him, and thus restore him to His favour.

64. *shall scatter thee . . . and stone.* See on *v.* 36.

65. *among these nations.* Israel is to have no rest—never-ceasing anxiety, life in perpetual jeopardy, an unendurable present, and a future of undefined terrors.

failing of eyes. Usually taken to mean the

68 תִּפְחַד וּמִמַּרְאֵה עֵינֶיךָ אֲשֶׁר תִּרְאֶה׃ וֶהֱשִׁיבְךָ יְהוָה מִצְרַיִם
בָּאֳנִיּוֹת בַּדֶּרֶךְ אֲשֶׁר אָמַרְתִּי לְךָ לֹא־תֹסִיף עוֹד לִרְאֹתָהּ
וְהִתְמַכַּרְתֶּם שָׁם לְאֹיְבֶיךָ לַעֲבָדִים וְלִשְׁפָחוֹת וְאֵין קֹנֶה׃
69 ס אֵלֶּה דִבְרֵי הַבְּרִית אֲשֶׁר־צִוָּה יְהוָה אֶת־מֹשֶׁה לִכְרֹת
אֶת־בְּנֵי יִשְׂרָאֵל בְּאֶרֶץ מוֹאָב מִלְּבַד הַבְּרִית אֲשֶׁר־כָּרַת
אִתָּם בְּחֹרֵב׃ * פ שביעי

כט

CAP. XXIX. כט

א וַיִּקְרָא מֹשֶׁה אֶל־כָּל־יִשְׂרָאֵל וַיֹּאמֶר אֲלֵהֶם אַתֶּם רְאִיתֶם
אֵת כָּל־אֲשֶׁר עָשָׂה יְהוָה לְעֵינֵיכֶם בְּאֶרֶץ מִצְרַיִם לְפַרְעֹה
2 וּלְכָל־עֲבָדָיו וּלְכָל־אַרְצוֹ׃ הַמַּסּוֹת הַגְּדֹלֹת אֲשֶׁר רָאוּ

כח' v. 67. קמץ בז"ק

it were even!' and at even thou shalt say: 'Would it were morning!' for the fear of thy heart which thou shalt fear, and for the sight of thine eyes which thou shalt see. 68. And the LORD shall bring thee back into Egypt in ships, by the way whereof I said unto thee: 'Thou shalt see it no more again'; and there ye shall sell yourselves unto your enemies for bondmen and for bondwomen, and no man shall buy you. ¶ 69. These are the words of the covenant which the LORD commanded Moses to make with the children of Israel in the land of Moab, beside the covenant which He made with them in Horeb.*vii.

29

CHAPTER XXIX

1. And Moses called unto all Israel, and said unto them: ¶ Ye have seen all that the LORD did before your eyes in the land of Egypt unto Pharaoh, and unto all his

gradual extinction of all hope; or, the eyes refuse their office, because they see only horror.

languishing of soul. A mind tortured and restless.

66. *life shall hang in doubt before thee.* Like an object suspended by a tender thread and held in front of one's eyes—about to fall down and break at any moment; but see next comment.

no assurance of thy life. 'Thou shalt expect every moment to be thy last' (Driver). Better, *thou shalt not believe in thy life; i.e.* thou canst not believe that these happenings are happening to *thee*, that they are real; deluding thyself with the vain hope that it is all an evil dream (Steinthal).

67. *in the morning thou shalt say.* Even as he that suffers acute pain yearns for the hours to pass. This *v.* graphically depicts the agonized uncertainty, protracted by day and by night.

68. *bring thee back into Egypt.* A culminating calamity. God repeals the prohibition mentioned in XVII, 16, and they would be returned to Egypt, to the degradation of their erstwhile Egyptian serfdom. At the destruction of Jerusalem by the Romans, both Titus and Hadrian consigned multitudes of Jews into slavery; and Egypt received a large proportion of those slaves.

in ships. They came forth from Egypt '600,000 men on foot', a disciplined host of free warriors, but would be carried thither cooped up in slave-ships. The Romans had a fleet in the Mediterranean, and this was an easier and safer way of transporting prisoners than by land across the desert.

sell yourselves. Better, *offer yourselves for sale;* ye will in vain seek and yearn to be bought as man-servants and maid-servants (Rashi).

no man shall buy you. Josephus records that when, at the Destruction of Jerusalem, the Roman troops grew weary of slaughter, 97,000 of the younger prisoners were spared. Those over seventeen years were sent to the mines, or to the arenas to fight as gladiators or against wild beasts; those under seventeen were sold as slaves; but the market was so glutted that, though offered at nominal prices, none would buy them! Those who remained unpurchased were sent into confinement, where they perished by hundreds and thousands from hunger.

69. SUPERSCRIPTION

'If, in Hellas, the beautiful was conceived to be the fruit of joyful play; if, in Rome, serious will was held to lead to power and right; in Jerusalem, everything high and holy was deemed to be the vintage of suffering and sorrow' (Steinthal).

69. *these are the words of the covenant.* A summary description of the contents of the whole chapter.

beside the covenant . . . in Horeb. A reference to the parallel section of the Warning in Lev. XXVI.

CHAPTER XXIX

In this and the succeeding chapters, Moses sums up the argument in the previous discourses. He reviews the journey of Israel from Egypt to Moab. Israel now stands ready to enter God's Covenant; let none dream to escape the curse of disobedience. God's wrath will be manifest to all in Israel's Exile. Yet even then, Repentance

servants, and unto all his land; 2. the great
trials which thine eyes saw, the signs and
those great wonders; 3. but the LORD hath
not given you a heart to know, and eyes
to see, and ears to hear, unto this day.
4. And I have led you forty years in the
wilderness; your clothes are not waxen
old upon you, and thy shoe is not waxen
old upon thy foot. 5. Ye have not eaten
bread, neither have ye drunk wine or strong
drink; that ye might know that I am the
LORD your God.*m. 6. And when ye came
unto this place, Sihon the king of Heshbon,
and Og the king of Bashan, came out against
us unto battle, and we smote them. 7.
And we took their land, and gave it for an
inheritance unto the Reubenites, and to the
Gadites, and to the half-tribe of the
Manassites. 8. Observe therefore the
words of this covenant, and do them, that
ye may make all that ye do to prosper.

3 עֵינֶיךָ הָאֹתֹת וְהַמֹּפְתִים הַגְּדֹלִים הָהֵם׃ וְלֹא־נָתַן יְהוָה
לָכֶם לֵב לָדַעַת וְעֵינַיִם לִרְאוֹת וְאָזְנַיִם לִשְׁמֹעַ עַד הַיּוֹם
4 הַזֶּה׃ וָאוֹלֵךְ אֶתְכֶם אַרְבָּעִים שָׁנָה בַּמִּדְבָּר לֹא־בָלוּ
ה שַׂלְמֹתֵיכֶם מֵעֲלֵיכֶם וְנַעַלְךָ לֹא־בָלְתָה מֵעַל רַגְלֶךָ׃ לֶחֶם
לֹא אֲכַלְתֶּם וְיַיִן וְשֵׁכָר לֹא שְׁתִיתֶם לְמַעַן תֵּדְעוּ כִּי אֲנִי
מפטיר 6 יְהוָה אֱלֹהֵיכֶם׃ וַתָּבֹאוּ אֶל־הַמָּקוֹם הַזֶּה וַיֵּצֵא סִיחֹן מֶלֶךְ־
7 חֶשְׁבּוֹן וְעוֹג מֶלֶךְ־הַבָּשָׁן לִקְרָאתֵנוּ לַמִּלְחָמָה וַנַּכֵּם׃ וַנִּקַּח
אֶת־אַרְצָם וַנִּתְּנָהּ לְנַחֲלָה לָרְאוּבֵנִי וְלַגָּדִי וְלַחֲצִי שֵׁבֶט
8 הַמְנַשִּׁי׃ וּשְׁמַרְתֶּם אֶת־דִּבְרֵי הַבְּרִית הַזֹּאת וַעֲשִׂיתֶם אֹתָם
לְמַעַן תַּשְׂכִּילוּ אֵת כָּל־אֲשֶׁר תַּעֲשׂוּן׃

will bring return from Exile. Let Israel note the simplicity of the Divine Commandment, and the issues of life and death dependent on obedience or disobedience of it.

1. *seen all that the LORD did.* They had been witnesses of God's special watchfulness over them, in guiding them safely through the wilderness, and in aiding them to crush their enemies.

2. *great trials. i.e.* provings, trials; see on IV, 34.

3. *a heart to know.* The constant succession of God's mercies had no proper effect on them, as the spiritual power was not theirs to appreciate the full meaning of Israel's history; cf. on Isaiah VI, 9 and 10, and also p. 303.

4. *led you forty years.* The narrative here suddenly changes to the first person singular, with God as the speaker.

your clothes are not waxen old. You had no need to trouble yourselves with material cares.

5. *that ye . . . LORD.* To teach you dependence on God's guidance and sustaining care.

8. *observe therefore the words of this covenant.* Now that you have succeeded, be humble even in the midst of your triumphs; observe all the words of the Covenant, and do them.

ISAIAH LX

CHAPTER LX

1. Arise, shine, for thy light is come,
And the glory of the LORD is risen upon thee.
2. For, behold, darkness shall cover the earth,
And gross darkness the peoples;
But upon thee the LORD will arise,
And His glory shall be seen upon thee.
3. And nations shall walk at thy light,
And kings at the brightness of thy rising.

4. Lift up thine eyes round about, and see:
They all are gathered together, and come to thee;
Thy sons come from far,
And thy daughters are borne on the side.
5. Then thou shalt see and be radiant,
And thy heart shall throb and be enlarged;
Because the abundance of the sea shall be turned unto thee,
The wealth of the nations shall come unto thee.

CAP. LX. ס

א 2 קוּמִי אוֹרִי כִּי־בָא אוֹרֵךְ וּכְבוֹד יְהוָה עָלַיִךְ זָרָח׃ כִּי־
הִנֵּה הַחֹשֶׁךְ יְכַסֶּה־אֶרֶץ וַעֲרָפֶל לְאֻמִּים וְעָלַיִךְ יִזְרַח יְהוָה
3 וּכְבוֹדוֹ עָלַיִךְ יֵרָאֶה׃ וְהָלְכוּ גוֹיִם לְאוֹרֵךְ וּמְלָכִים לְנֹגַהּ
4 זַרְחֵךְ׃ שְׂאִי סָבִיב עֵינַיִךְ וּרְאִי כֻּלָּם נִקְבְּצוּ בָאוּ־לָךְ
ה בָּנַיִךְ מֵרָחוֹק יָבֹאוּ וּבְנֹתַיִךְ עַל־צַד תֵּאָמַנָה׃ אָז תִּרְאִי
וְנָהַרְתְּ וּפָחַד וְרָחַב לְבָבֵךְ כִּי־יֵהָפֵךְ עָלַיִךְ הֲמוֹן יָם חֵיל

6. The caravan of camels shall cover thee,
And of the young camels of Midian and Ephah,
All coming from Sheba;
They shall bring gold and frankincense,
And shall proclaim the praises of the LORD.

v. 4. המ׳ בפתח

The Sidrah brings the close of the Second Discourse of the Lawgiver with the Divine promise to make Israel, 'high above all nations.' The Haftorah of the sixth Sabbath of Consolation gives the highest spiritual interpretation of that promise ('The LORD shall arise upon thee, and His glory shall be seen upon thee. And nations shall come to thy light'). It proclaims in ecstatic terms the glories which Jerusalem will enjoy in the era of Divine favour. The light of Deliverance, so long waited for, is about to shine. 'Thick darkness enfolds the earth, the darkness which typifies alienation from God. But God has begun to reveal Himself anew—not as yet to the whole earth, but to its central people, Israel. As "the children of Israel had light in their dwellings" when there was "thick darkness in all the land of Egypt", so now there are beaming over Israel the first rays of a newly risen sun' (Cheyne).

1. *arise.* Zion is addressed: arise out of the night of despair and oppression.
thy light is come. Thy salvation is at hand (Kimchi).

2. *shall cover.* Better, *doth cover.* The Prophet sees the kingdoms of the earth breaking up amid gloom and misery; with Israel alone is light and joy in the LORD (M. Arnold).

3. *at thy light.* Or, 'towards thy light'; from the outer darkness, to share the Divine light with Israel.

4. *thy sons.* The longing of her heart can only be satisfied by the restoration of her banished children.
borne on the side. lit. 'supported on the side'; *i.e.* on the hip, the arm of the mother supporting the child's back—the Eastern manner of carrying children.

5–9. Zion is enriched with wealth which the nations bring as offerings wherewith to restore the Temple service and rebuild Jerusalem.

5. *throb.* Throb with happy excitement, 'as a man trembles at an unexpected deliverance' (Ibn Ezra).
enlarged. *i.e.* have a sense of freedom and happiness; Ps. CXVIII, 5.
abundance of the sea. The rich cargoes from the distant lands.

6. *cover thee.* From the lands of the East and the South long trains of camels, together with caravans carrying gold and incense, are seen wending their way to Zion.
Midian, Ephah. Tribes of Northern Arabia.
Sheba. Ancient Sabæa; modern Yemen.
praises. *i.e.* the praiseworthy deeds.

6 גּוֹיִם יָבֹאוּ לָךְ׃ שִׁפְעַת גְּמַלִּים תְּכַסֵּךְ בִּכְרֵי מִדְיָן וְעֵיפָה
כֻּלָּם מִשְּׁבָא יָבֹאוּ זָהָב וּלְבוֹנָה יִשָּׂאוּ וּתְהִלּוֹת יְהוָה
7 יְבַשֵּׂרוּ׃ כָּל־צֹאן קֵדָר יִקָּבְצוּ לָךְ אֵילֵי נְבָיוֹת יְשָׁרְתוּנֶךְ
8 יַעֲלוּ עַל־רָצוֹן מִזְבְּחִי וּבֵית תִּפְאַרְתִּי אֲפָאֵר׃ מִי־אֵלֶּה
9 כָּעָב תְּעוּפֶינָה וְכַיּוֹנִים אֶל־אֲרֻבֹּתֵיהֶם׃ כִּי־לִי ׀ אִיִּים יְקַוּוּ
וָאֳנִיּוֹת תַּרְשִׁישׁ בָּרִאשֹׁנָה לְהָבִיא בָנַיִךְ מֵרָחוֹק כַּסְפָּם
וּזְהָבָם אִתָּם לְשֵׁם יְהוָה אֱלֹהַיִךְ וְלִקְדוֹשׁ יִשְׂרָאֵל כִּי
י פֵאֲרָךְ׃ וּבָנוּ בְנֵי־נֵכָר חֹמֹתַיִךְ וּמַלְכֵיהֶם יְשָׁרְתוּנֶךְ כִּי
11 בְקִצְפִּי הִכִּיתִיךְ וּבִרְצוֹנִי רִחַמְתִּיךְ׃ וּפִתְּחוּ שְׁעָרַיִךְ תָּמִיד
יוֹמָם וָלַיְלָה לֹא יִסָּגֵרוּ לְהָבִיא אֵלַיִךְ חֵיל גּוֹיִם וּמַלְכֵיהֶם
12 נְהוּגִים׃ כִּי־הַגּוֹי וְהַמַּמְלָכָה אֲשֶׁר לֹא־יַעַבְדוּךְ יֹאבֵדוּ

7. All the flocks of Kedar shall be gathered together unto thee,
The rams of Nebaioth shall minister unto thee;
They shall come up with acceptance on Mine altar,
And I will glorify My glorious house.

8. Who are these that fly as a cloud,
And as the doves to their cotes?

9. Surely the isles shall wait for Me,
And the ships of Tarshish first,
To bring thy sons from far,
Their silver and their gold with them,
For the name of the LORD thy God,
And for the Holy One of Israel, because He hath glorified thee.

10. And aliens shall build up thy walls,
And their kings shall minister unto thee;
For in My wrath I smote thee,
But in My favour have I had compassion on thee.

11. Thy gates also shall be open continually,
Day and night, they shall not be shut;
That men may bring unto thee the wealth of the nations,
And their kings in procession.

12. For that nation and kingdom that will not serve thee shall perish;
Yea, those nations shall be utterly wasted.

7. *Kedar . . . Nebaioth.* Pastoral tribes in North Arabia.
minister. By providing animals for sacrifices.
glorify. Beautify.

8. *doves to their cotes.* Having looked landward and watched the coming of the caravans, the Prophet now looks seaward and sees the white-sailed ships speeding across the Mediterranean to Palestinian harbours, as if they were a flight of doves returning to their nests. The emphasis is also on the swiftness of their flight, for 'they fly more swiftly on their return to their nests with food for their young than when they departed' (Kimchi).

9. *isles.* The distant coast-lands; *i.e.* their inhabitants.
wait. In believing expectation of the blessings in which they would participate.
Tarshish. A Phœnician settlement outside Gibraltar. In the days of the Prophet, therefore, the Jewish Dispersion had already spread to the westernmost end of the Mediterranean and beyond.
their silver and their gold. Of the Israelites (Luzzatto, Malbim). They will 'pull up all their stakes' in the Diaspora, and will return with all that they have to the land of their fathers. It is quite needless to make '*their* silver and *their* gold' refer to the nations. This only gives some non-Jewish commentators an opportunity to denounce the imaginary exploitation contemplated by the author of these chapters whom they call Trito-Isaiah, and his alleged appeal to covetousness and pride of race.

10–14. The nations will gladly and humbly build Jerusalem.

10. *aliens.* The heathen nations who destroyed will also rebuild the city. This will be a signal proof of Divine favour.
thy walls. An essential to a city in antiquity.

11. *in procession.* Or, 'led with them' (RV). 'Accompanied by a large retinue' (Kimchi); or, 'one after another' (Luzzatto). Realizing that their prosperity depends on their relations with Israel (see next *v.*), the kings of the distant lands come in procession, one after the other, to Zion, accompanied by their retinue and followers.

12. *that nation.* Every nation shall fail unless it serves the LORD, the righteous God of Israel, through Whom alone is salvation. 'It was to be a voluntary submission before the evidence of Jerusalem's spiritual superiority' (G. A. Smith).

13 וְהַגּוֹיִם חָרֹב יֶחֱרָבוּ׃ כְּבוֹד הַלְּבָנוֹן אֵלַיִךְ יָבוֹא בְּרוֹשׁ
תִּדְהָר וּתְאַשּׁוּר יַחְדָּו לְפָאֵר מְקוֹם מִקְדָּשִׁי וּמְקוֹם רַגְלַי
14 אֲכַבֵּד׃ וְהָלְכוּ אֵלַיִךְ שְׁחוֹחַ בְּנֵי מְעַנַּיִךְ וְהִשְׁתַּחֲווּ עַל־
כַּפּוֹת רַגְלַיִךְ כָּל־מְנַאֲצָיִךְ וְקָרְאוּ לָךְ עִיר יְהוָה צִיּוֹן קְדוֹשׁ
טו יִשְׂרָאֵל׃ תַּחַת הֱיוֹתֵךְ עֲזוּבָה וּשְׂנוּאָה וְאֵין עוֹבֵר וְשַׂמְתִּיךְ
16 לִגְאוֹן עוֹלָם מְשׂוֹשׂ דּוֹר וָדוֹר׃ וְיָנַקְתְּ חֲלֵב גּוֹיִם וְשֹׁד
מְלָכִים תִּינָקִי וְיָדַעַתְּ כִּי־אֲנִי יְהוָה מוֹשִׁיעֵךְ וְגֹאֲלֵךְ אֲבִיר
17 יַעֲקֹב׃ תַּחַת הַנְּחֹשֶׁת אָבִיא זָהָב וְתַחַת הַבַּרְזֶל אָבִיא
כֶסֶף וְתַחַת הָעֵצִים נְחֹשֶׁת וְתַחַת הָאֲבָנִים בַּרְזֶל וְשַׂמְתִּי
18 פְקֻדָּתֵךְ שָׁלוֹם וְנֹגְשַׂיִךְ צְדָקָה׃ לֹא־יִשָּׁמַע עוֹד חָמָס
בְּאַרְצֵךְ שֹׁד וָשֶׁבֶר בִּגְבוּלָיִךְ וְקָרָאת יְשׁוּעָה חוֹמֹתַיִךְ
19 וּשְׁעָרַיִךְ תְּהִלָּה׃ לֹא־יִהְיֶה־לָּךְ עוֹד הַשֶּׁמֶשׁ לְאוֹר יוֹמָם
וּלְנֹגַהּ הַיָּרֵחַ לֹא־יָאִיר לָךְ וְהָיָה־לָךְ יְהוָה לְאוֹר עוֹלָם

13. The glory of Lebanon shall come unto thee,
The cypress, the plane-tree, and the larch together;
To beautify the place of My sanctuary,
And I will make the place of My feet glorious.

14. And the sons of them that afflicted thee
Shall come bending unto thee,
And all they that despised thee shall bow down
At the soles of thy feet;
And they shall call thee The city of the LORD,
The Zion of the Holy One of Israel.

15. Whereas thou hast been forsaken and hated,
So that no man passed through thee,
I will make thee an eternal excellency,
A joy of many generations.

16. Thou shalt also suck the milk of the nations,
And shalt suck the spoil of kings;
And thou shalt know that I the LORD am thy Saviour,
And I, the Mighty One of Jacob, thy Redeemer.

17. For brass I will bring gold,
And for iron I will bring silver,
And for wood brass,
And for stones iron;
I will also make thy officers peace,
And righteousness thy magistrates.

18. Violence shall no more be heard in thy land,
Desolation nor destruction within thy borders;
But thou shalt call thy walls Salvation,
And thy gates Praise.

19. The sun shall be no more thy light by day,
Neither for brightness shall the moon give light unto thee;
But the LORD shall be unto thee an everlasting light,
And thy God thy glory.

13. *glory of Lebanon. i.e.* the trees for which Lebanon was famous will be brought to beautify the *place, i.e.* the surroundings of the Temple. Afforestation will be one of the first undertakings of the new Judea.

place of My feet. The Temple; Ezek. XLIII, 7.

15–18. THE TRANSFORMATION OF ZION

15. *whereas thou hast been.* Instead of thy being.

eternal excellency. A thing of beauty and a joy to all the generations in the world's story.

16. *suck.* Cf. Deuteronomy XXXIII, 19.

the spoil of kings. Heb. שד מלכים (cf. 'ye shall suck the glory of the nations,' Isa. LXVI, 12). The meaning is, The kings, like their peoples, will contribute to the strength of the new Zion. This translation is a departure from AJ.

17. *for brass.* For the less valuable that has been lost, there will be the more valuable in the new Zion; I Kings X, 21 f.

thy magistrates. Translate: 'I will make Peace thy government, and Righteousness thy magistrates,' to take the place of the tyranny of the foreign governors and alien garrison (Cheyne).

18. *Salvation.* Because affording perfect security.

Praise. Or, 'renown.'

19. *the sun.* Thou shalt no longer have need for the sun to shine (Rashi), as the continual

20. Thy sun shall no more go down,
Neither shall thy moon withdraw itself;
For the LORD shall be thine everlasting light,
And the days of thy mourning shall be ended.

21. Thy people also shall be all righteous,
They shall inherit the land for ever;
The branch of My planting, the work of My hands,
Wherein I glory.

22. The smallest shall become a thousand,
And the least a mighty nation;
I the LORD will hasten it in its time.

כ וֵאלֹהַיִךְ לְתִפְאַרְתֵּךְ׃ לֹא־יָבוֹא עוֹד שִׁמְשֵׁךְ וִירֵחֵךְ לֹא
יֵאָסֵף כִּי יְהוָה יִהְיֶה־לָּךְ לְאוֹר עוֹלָם וְשָׁלְמוּ יְמֵי אֶבְלֵךְ׃
21 וְעַמֵּךְ כֻּלָּם צַדִּיקִים לְעוֹלָם יִירְשׁוּ אָרֶץ נֵצֶר מַטָּעוֹ* מַעֲשֵׂה
22 יָדַי לְהִתְפָּאֵר׃ הַקָּטֹן יִהְיֶה לָאֶלֶף וְהַצָּעִיר לְגוֹי עָצוּם אֲנִי
יְהוָה בְּעִתָּהּ אֲחִישֶׁנָּה׃

v. 21. מטעי קרי

presence of God Himself shall cause Zion to dwell in eternal light. Of course we are here in the region of pure ecstasy and mystic symbolism.

20. *go down.* Set.

everlasting. Continuous. Not that the sun and moon shall cease to exist, but that the New Jerusalem shall not be dependent on these natural luminaries (Ehrlich, Davidson). The light of the Shechinah makes the light of the material sun and moon unnecessary.

21. *all righteous.* They have been purified by God and lead godly lives. The Rabbis built on this verse their teaching, 'All Israel have a share in the world to come,' all are heirs of immortality.

for ever. There will never again be need for the stern discipline of exile (Kimchi).

22. *the smallest shall become a thousand, and the least.* Or, 'the least shall become a clan, and the smallest.' Though the returning exiles are but a fraction of the former population of Judah, the new Zion would increase wonderfully in strength and number.

in its time. When the hour of salvation arrives.

29 9. Ye are standing this day all of you before the LORD your God: your heads, your tribes, your elders, and your officers, even all the men of Israel, 10. your little ones, your wives, and thy stranger that is in the midst of thy camp, from the hewer of thy wood unto the drawer of thy water; 11. that thou shouldest enter into the covenant of the LORD thy God—and into His oath—which the LORD thy God maketh with thee this day;*ii. 12. that He may establish thee this day unto Himself for a people, and that He may be unto thee a God, as He spoke unto thee, and as He swore unto thy fathers, to Abraham, to Isaac, and to Jacob. 13. Neither with you only do I make this covenant and this oath; 14. but with him that standeth here with us this day before the LORD our God, and also with him that is not here with us this day—*iii. 15. for ye know how we dwelt in the land of Egypt; and how we came through the midst of the nations through which ye passed; 16. and ye have seen their detestable things, and their idols, wood and stone, silver and gold, which were with

כט

51 נא פ פ פ

9 אַתֶּם נִצָּבִים הַיּוֹם כֻּלְּכֶם לִפְנֵי יְהוָה אֱלֹהֵיכֶם רָאשֵׁיכֶם
י שִׁבְטֵיכֶם זִקְנֵיכֶם וְשֹׁטְרֵיכֶם כֹּל אִישׁ יִשְׂרָאֵל׃ טַפְּכֶם
נְשֵׁיכֶם וְגֵרְךָ אֲשֶׁר בְּקֶרֶב מַחֲנֶיךָ מֵחֹטֵב עֵצֶיךָ עַד שֹׁאֵב
11 מֵימֶיךָ׃ לְעָבְרְךָ בִּבְרִית יְהוָה אֱלֹהֶיךָ וּבְאָלָתוֹ אֲשֶׁר יְהוָה
שני 12 אֱלֹהֶיךָ כֹּרֵת עִמְּךָ הַיּוֹם׃* לְמַעַן הָקִים־אֹתְךָ הַיּוֹם לוֹ
לְעָם וְהוּא יִהְיֶה־לְּךָ לֵאלֹהִים כַּאֲשֶׁר דִּבֶּר־לָךְ וְכַאֲשֶׁר
13 נִשְׁבַּע לַאֲבֹתֶיךָ לְאַבְרָהָם לְיִצְחָק וּלְיַעֲקֹב׃ וְלֹא אִתְּכֶם
לְבַדְּכֶם אָנֹכִי כֹּרֵת אֶת־הַבְּרִית הַזֹּאת וְאֶת־הָאָלָה הַזֹּאת׃
14 כִּי אֶת־אֲשֶׁר יֶשְׁנוֹ פֹּה עִמָּנוּ עֹמֵד הַיּוֹם לִפְנֵי יְהוָה אֱלֹהֵינוּ
שלישי טו וְאֵת אֲשֶׁר אֵינֶנּוּ פֹּה עִמָּנוּ הַיּוֹם׃* כִּי־אַתֶּם יְדַעְתֶּם אֵת אֲשֶׁר־
יָשַׁבְנוּ בְּאֶרֶץ מִצְרָיִם וְאֵת אֲשֶׁר־עָבַרְנוּ בְּקֶרֶב הַגּוֹיִם אֲשֶׁר
16 עֲבַרְתֶּם׃ וַתִּרְאוּ אֶת־שִׁקּוּצֵיהֶם וְאֵת גִּלֻּלֵיהֶם עֵץ וָאֶבֶן

VIII. NITZAVIM

(CHAPTERS XXIX, 9–XXX)

XXIX, 9–28. MOSES' THIRD DISCOURSE CONTINUED

Moses reviews the different orders of people before him, all assembled to enter into a Covenant with God: heads of tribes, elders, officers, all the men of Israel, the little ones, the wives, the strangers; he thinks of others who shall hereafter take part in such solemn acts. He warns every man or woman, every family or tribe, against nourishing evil in their hearts, and trusting to escape in the general righteousness. He proclaims how the sinful individual shall be separated for doom, the land of a sinful tribe overthrown in a curse. But he adds words of mercy; and he makes solemn appeals to choose life and not death (Moulton).

9. *standing this day all of you.* Moses spake these words to the multitudes of Israel whom he had assembled to stand before God on the day of his death (Rashi).
your heads, your tribes. i.e. the heads of your tribes (Rashi, Ibn Ezra).

10. *thy stranger.* The non-Israelite element that accompanied them out of Egypt; Exod. XII, 38; Num. XI, 4.
hewer of thy wood . . . water. The strangers performing menial duties for the individual Israelites. Thus, all classes of the population are to be included in the Covenant.

11. *and into His oath.* A covenant sealed by an oath; Gen. XXVI, 28.

13–28. ISRAEL, PRESENT AND FUTURE, IS A UNITY

The Covenant is one which must be held to bind not only the living who were present that day, but their distant posterity as well.

15. *for ye know.* 'For ye have experience of the idolatry rife both in Egypt and among the other nations bordering on Canaan; and can judge consequently of the necessity of including future generations in the terms of the obligation' (Driver).
came through the midst of the nations. The trying experiences they endured in their contact with Edom and Ammon, Moab and Midian.

16. *detestable things.* A contemptuous designation for idols, with an implied reference to the immoral rites that went hand in hand with idol-worship.
their idols. lit. 'inanimate blocks', fetishes.
silver and gold. The costly ornaments with which their worshippers beautified them (Talmud).

them—17. lest there should be among you man, or woman, or family, or tribe, whose heart turneth away this day from the LORD our God, to go to serve the gods of those nations; lest there should be among you a root that beareth gall and wormwood; 18. and it come to pass, when he heareth the words of this curse, that he bless himself in his heart, saying: 'I shall have peace, though I walk in the stubbornness of my heart—that the watered be swept away with the dry'; 19. the LORD will not be willing to pardon him, but then the anger of the LORD and His jealousy shall be kindled against that man, and all the curse that is written in this book shall lie upon him, and the LORD shall blot out his name from under heaven; 20. and the LORD shall separate him unto evil out of all the tribes of Israel, according to all the curses of the covenant that is written in this book of the law. 21. And the generation to come, your children that shall rise up after you, and the foreigner that shall come from a far land, shall say, when they see the plagues of that land, and the sicknesses wherewith the LORD hath made it sick; 22. and that the whole land thereof is brimstone, and salt, and a burning, that it is not sown, nor beareth, nor any grass groweth therein, like the overthrow of Sodom and Gomorrah, Admah and Zeboiim, which the LORD overthrew in His anger, and in His wrath; 23. even all the nations shall

17 כֶּסֶף וְזָהָב אֲשֶׁר עִמָּהֶם׃ פֶּן־יֵשׁ בָּכֶם אִישׁ אוֹ־אִשָּׁה אוֹ
מִשְׁפָּחָה אוֹ־שֵׁבֶט אֲשֶׁר לְבָבוֹ פֹנֶה הַיּוֹם מֵעִם יְהוָה
אֱלֹהֵינוּ לָלֶכֶת לַעֲבֹד אֶת־אֱלֹהֵי הַגּוֹיִם הָהֵם פֶּן־יֵשׁ בָּכֶם
18 שֹׁרֶשׁ פֹּרֶה רֹאשׁ וְלַעֲנָה׃ וְהָיָה בְּשָׁמְעוֹ אֶת־דִּבְרֵי הָאָלָה
הַזֹּאת וְהִתְבָּרֵךְ בִּלְבָבוֹ לֵאמֹר שָׁלוֹם יִהְיֶה־לִּי כִּי
בִּשְׁרִרוּת לִבִּי אֵלֵךְ לְמַעַן סְפוֹת הָרָוָה אֶת־הַצְּמֵאָה׃
19 לֹא־יֹאבֶה יְהוָה סְלֹחַ לוֹ כִּי אָז יֶעְשַׁן אַף־יְהוָה וְקִנְאָתוֹ
בָּאִישׁ הַהוּא וְרָבְצָה בּוֹ כָּל־הָאָלָה הַכְּתוּבָה בַּסֵּפֶר הַזֶּה
כ וּמָחָה יְהוָה אֶת־שְׁמוֹ מִתַּחַת הַשָּׁמָיִם׃ וְהִבְדִּילוֹ יְהוָה
לְרָעָה מִכֹּל שִׁבְטֵי יִשְׂרָאֵל כְּכֹל אָלוֹת הַבְּרִית הַכְּתוּבָה
21 בְּסֵפֶר הַתּוֹרָה הַזֶּה׃ וְאָמַר הַדּוֹר הָאַחֲרוֹן בְּנֵיכֶם אֲשֶׁר
יָקוּמוּ מֵאַחֲרֵיכֶם וְהַנָּכְרִי אֲשֶׁר יָבֹא מֵאֶרֶץ רְחוֹקָה וְרָאוּ
אֶת־מַכּוֹת הָאָרֶץ הַהִוא וְאֶת־תַּחֲלֻאֶיהָ אֲשֶׁר־חִלָּה יְהוָה
22 בָּהּ׃ גָּפְרִית וָמֶלַח שְׂרֵפָה כָל־אַרְצָהּ לֹא תִזָּרַע וְלֹא
תַצְמִחַ וְלֹא־יַעֲלֶה בָהּ כָּל־עֵשֶׂב כְּמַהְפֵּכַת סְדֹם וַעֲמֹרָה
23 אַדְמָה וּצְבֹיִים אֲשֶׁר הָפַךְ יְהוָה בְּאַפּוֹ וּבַחֲמָתוֹ׃ וְאָמְרוּ
כָּל־הַגּוֹיִם עַל־מֶה עָשָׂה יְהוָה כָּכָה לָאָרֶץ הַזֹּאת מֶה חֳרִי

v. 22. וצבוים ק'

17. *lest there should be among you.* An elliptical phrase. The full sense is: 'I adjure you to enter into this oath and covenant, for fear lest there should be among you. . . .'

gall. Heb. *rosh*, a poisonous herb.

gall and wormwood. Poison and bitterness—the consequences of idolatry. The sinner is here pictured as a bitter root bearing deadly fruit, destroying the life of a nation.

18. *bless himself in his heart.* Congratulate or delude himself. Because of God's oath to Israel, this man flatters himself that he is secure, no matter how recklessly he indulges in evil.

in the stubbornness of my heart. 'Though I persist in the strong wayward impulses of my heart'; cf. Jer. XXIII, 17.

that the watered be swept away with the dry. Or, 'to sweep away the well-watered soil with the dry'; a proverbial phrase, denoting a hurricane of destruction that would annihilate the community through the sinfulness of individual members here and there. As often in Scripture, the consequences of the idolater's self-congratulation are here represented ironically as his purpose. Others translate: 'to add drunkenness to thirst'; *i.e.* to increase desire by indulgence; as indulgence increases desire, and desire in turn hastens to satisfy itself by indulgence (Maimonides, M. Lazarus).

19. *shall be kindled. i.e.* shall break forth in a destructive fire; cf. Psalm XVIII, 9.

shall lie upon him. The Heb. root of this word is used to denote the crouching of a wild beast at the moment of pouncing upon its prey. So here, retribution will pounce upon the evil-doer unawares.

20. *shall separate him.* 'If the sinners be a whole tribe, then shall it be sundered from the other tribes, and its members carried away into exile' (Ibn Ezra)—a fate which later befell the Ten Tribes (II Kings XVII, 6).

21–28. The whole land and people will suffer for apostasy, and future generations and the most distant nations will learn with horror God's judgment upon the depopulated land.

22. *brimstone . . . wrath.* The imagery is drawn from the desolate surroundings of the Dead Sea; Gen. XIX, 24–29.

Admah and Zeboiim. See Gen. XIV, 2.

say: 'Wherefore hath the LORD done thus unto this land? what meaneth the heat of this great anger?' 24. then men shall say: 'Because they forsook the covenant of the LORD, the God of their fathers, which He made with them when He brought them forth out of the land of Egypt; 25. and went and served other gods, and worshipped them, gods that they knew not, and that He had not allotted unto them; 26. therefore the anger of the LORD was kindled against this land, to bring upon it all the curse that is written in this book; 27. and the LORD rooted them out of their land in anger, and in wrath, and in great indignation, and cast them into another land, as it is this day.'—28. The secret things belong unto the LORD our God; but the things that are revealed belong unto us and to our children for ever, that we may do all the words of this law.*iv (**ii).

CHAPTER XXX

1. And it shall come to pass, when all these things are come upon thee, the blessing and the curse, which I have set before thee, and thou shalt bethink thyself among all the nations, whither the LORD thy God hath driven thee, 2. and shalt return unto the LORD thy God, and hearken to His voice according to all that I command thee this day, thou and thy children, with all thy heart, and with all thy soul; 3. that then

24 הָאַף הַגָּדוֹל הַזֶּה׃ וְאָמְרוּ עַל אֲשֶׁר עָזְבוּ אֶת־בְּרִית יְהוָה
אֱלֹהֵי אֲבֹתָם אֲשֶׁר כָּרַת עִמָּם בְּהוֹצִיאוֹ אֹתָם מֵאֶרֶץ
כה מִצְרָיִם׃ וַיֵּלְכוּ וַיַּעַבְדוּ אֱלֹהִים אֲחֵרִים וַיִּשְׁתַּחֲווּ לָהֶם
26 אֱלֹהִים אֲשֶׁר לֹא־יְדָעוּם וְלֹא חָלַק לָהֶם׃ וַיִּחַר־אַף יְהוָה
בָּאָרֶץ הַהִוא לְהָבִיא עָלֶיהָ אֶת־כָּל־הַקְּלָלָה הַכְּתוּבָה
27 בַּסֵּפֶר הַזֶּה׃ וַיִּתְּשֵׁם יְהוָה מֵעַל אַדְמָתָם בְּאַף וּבְחֵמָה
28 וּבְקֶצֶף גָּדוֹל וַיַּשְׁלִכֵם אֶל־אֶרֶץ אַחֶרֶת כַּיּוֹם הַזֶּה׃ הַנִּסְתָּרֹת
לַיהוָה אֱלֹהֵינוּ וְהַנִּגְלֹת לָנוּ וּלְבָנֵינוּ עַד־עוֹלָם לַעֲשׂוֹת
אֶת־כָּל־דִּבְרֵי הַתּוֹרָה הַזֹּאת׃* רביעי (שני ס כשהן מחוב׳)

CAP. XXX. ל

ל

א וְהָיָה כִי־יָבֹאוּ עָלֶיךָ כָּל־הַדְּבָרִים הָאֵלֶּה הַבְּרָכָה וְהַקְּלָלָה
אֲשֶׁר נָתַתִּי לְפָנֶיךָ וַהֲשֵׁבֹתָ אֶל־לְבָבֶךָ בְּכָל־הַגּוֹיִם אֲשֶׁר
2 הִדִּיחֲךָ יְהוָה אֱלֹהֶיךָ שָׁמָּה׃ וְשַׁבְתָּ עַד־יְהוָה אֱלֹהֶיךָ
וְשָׁמַעְתָּ בְקֹלוֹ כְּכֹל אֲשֶׁר־אָנֹכִי מְצַוְּךָ הַיּוֹם אַתָּה וּבָנֶיךָ
3 בְּכָל־לְבָבְךָ וּבְכָל־נַפְשֶׁךָ׃ וְשָׁב יְהוָה אֱלֹהֶיךָ אֶת־שְׁבוּתְךָ

כט׳ v. 27. ל׳ רבתי v. 28. י״א נקודות

25. *not allotted unto them.* See on IV, 19.

27. *as it is this day.* As we see it to be the case now; cf. II, 30.

28. *the secret things . . . that we may do.* 'The secret things (of the sin) are for God to discover but the judgment when revealed is before us for ever as a warning' (Moulton). In Jewish thought, this *v.* has been made into a great law of life. There are limits to what mortal beings can know. Certain things are in the hands of God alone, and must be left with Him. But there are other things which are 'revealed'—the words and ordinances of the Torah—and to these we and all successive generations must render willing obedience. Benjamin Szold pointed out that the accentuation likewise emphasizes this truth. If we follow the accents (גרשיים), this *v.* reads: 'The secret things belong to the LORD our God *and* the revealed things; for us and our children it is to carry out all the words of this Law.'

This *v.* is one of the fifteen passages of the Bible in which words (לנו ולבנינו ע) are dotted. The most probable explanation of these dots is, that they were intended to call attention to important homiletical teachings in connection with the words thus dotted.

CHAPTER XXX

MOSES' THIRD DISCOURSE: CONCLUDED

1–10. OMNIPOTENCE OF REPENTANCE: RETURN FROM EXILE

A fuller restatement of the vital lesson taught in IV, 29–31. Punishment is not God's last word unto Israel. If Israel seeks God, Israel will find mercy at the hands of the LORD, and be brought back to the Land of his fathers.

1. *and thou shalt bethink thyself.* A consoling prediction that Israel's woes would lead to Israel's betterment (תשובה).

2. *shalt return.* Israel would take to heart the hard lessons taught him by his exile.

3. *God will turn thy captivity.* He will change thy fortune, restore thee to thy former happy state (Luzzatto, Ewald). The Talmud renders it, 'And the LORD thy God will return with thy captivity.' When Israel was in exile, God was, so to speak, in exile along with him. The Divine Cause which it is Israel's mission to champion was in eclipse; see p. 886.

the LORD thy God will turn thy captivity, and have compassion upon thee, and will return and gather thee from all the peoples, whither the LORD thy God hath scattered thee. 4. If any of thine that are dispersed be in the uttermost parts of heaven, from thence will the LORD thy God gather thee, and from thence will He fetch thee. 5. And the LORD thy God will bring thee into the land which thy fathers possessed, and thou shalt possess it; and He will do thee good, and multiply thee above thy fathers. 6. And the LORD thy God will open thy heart, and the heart of thy seed, to love the LORD thy God with all thy heart, and with all thy soul, that thou mayest live.*v (**iii). 7. And the LORD thy God will put all these curses upon thine enemies, and on them that hate thee, that persecuted thee. 8. And thou shalt return and hearken to the voice of the LORD, and do all His commandments which I command thee this day. 9. And the LORD thy God will make thee over-abundant in all the work of thy hand, in the fruit of thy body, and in the fruit of thy cattle, and in the fruit of thy land, for good; for the LORD will again rejoice over thee for good, as He rejoiced over thy fathers; 10. if thou shalt hearken to the voice of the LORD thy God, to keep His commandments and His statutes which are written in this book of the law; if thou turn unto the LORD thy God with all thy heart, and with all thy soul.*vi. ¶ 11. For this commandment which I command thee this day, it is not too hard for thee, neither is it far off. 12. It is not in heaven, that thou shouldest say: 'Who shall go up for us to heaven, and bring it unto us, and make us to hear it, that we may do it?' 13. Neither is it beyond the sea, that thou shouldest say: 'Who shall go over the sea for us,

וְרִחֲמֶךָ וְשָׁב וְקִבֶּצְךָ מִכָּל־הָעַמִּים אֲשֶׁר הֱפִיצְךָ יְהוָה
4 אֱלֹהֶיךָ שָׁמָּה׃ אִם־יִהְיֶה נִדַּחֲךָ בִּקְצֵה הַשָּׁמָיִם מִשָּׁם
ה יְקַבֶּצְךָ יְהוָה אֱלֹהֶיךָ וּמִשָּׁם יִקָּחֶךָ׃ וֶהֱבִיאֲךָ יְהוָה אֱלֹהֶיךָ
אֶל־הָאָרֶץ אֲשֶׁר־יָרְשׁוּ אֲבֹתֶיךָ וִירִשְׁתָּהּ וְהֵיטִבְךָ וְהִרְבְּךָ
6 מֵאֲבֹתֶיךָ׃ וּמָל יְהוָה אֱלֹהֶיךָ אֶת־לְבָבְךָ וְאֶת־לְבַב זַרְעֶךָ
חמישי שלישי (כשהן מחוברין) לְאַהֲבָה אֶת־יְהוָה אֱלֹהֶיךָ בְּכָל־לְבָבְךָ וּבְכָל־נַפְשְׁךָ לְמַעַן
7 חַיֶּיךָ׃* וְנָתַן יְהוָה אֱלֹהֶיךָ אֵת כָּל־הָאָלוֹת הָאֵלֶּה עַל־
8 אֹיְבֶיךָ וְעַל־שֹׂנְאֶיךָ אֲשֶׁר רְדָפוּךָ׃ וְאַתָּה תָשׁוּב וְשָׁמַעְתָּ
בְּקוֹל יְהוָה וְעָשִׂיתָ אֶת־כָּל־מִצְוֺתָיו אֲשֶׁר אָנֹכִי מְצַוְּךָ
9 הַיּוֹם׃ וְהוֹתִירְךָ יְהוָה אֱלֹהֶיךָ בְּכֹל ׀ מַעֲשֵׂה יָדֶךָ בִּפְרִי
בִטְנְךָ וּבִפְרִי בְהֶמְתְּךָ וּבִפְרִי אַדְמָתְךָ לְטֹבָה כִּי ׀ יָשׁוּב
י יְהוָה לָשׂוּשׂ עָלֶיךָ לְטוֹב כַּאֲשֶׁר־שָׂשׂ עַל־אֲבֹתֶיךָ׃ כִּי
תִשְׁמַע בְּקוֹל יְהוָה אֱלֹהֶיךָ לִשְׁמֹר מִצְוֺתָיו וְחֻקֹּתָיו הַכְּתוּבָה
בְּסֵפֶר הַתּוֹרָה הַזֶּה כִּי תָשׁוּב אֶל־יְהוָה אֱלֹהֶיךָ בְּכָל־
ששי 11 לְבָבְךָ וּבְכָל־נַפְשֶׁךָ׃* ס כִּי הַמִּצְוָה הַזֹּאת אֲשֶׁר
אָנֹכִי מְצַוְּךָ הַיּוֹם לֹא־נִפְלֵאת הִוא מִמְּךָ וְלֹא־רְחֹקָה הִוא׃
12 לֹא בַשָּׁמַיִם הִוא לֵאמֹר מִי יַעֲלֶה־לָּנוּ הַשָּׁמַיְמָה וְיִקָּחֶהָ
13 לָּנוּ וְיַשְׁמִעֵנוּ אֹתָהּ וְנַעֲשֶׂנָּה׃ וְלֹא־מֵעֵבֶר לַיָּם הִוא לֵאמֹר
מִי יַעֲבָר־לָנוּ אֶל־עֵבֶר הַיָּם וְיִקָּחֶהָ לָּנוּ וְיַשְׁמִעֵנוּ אֹתָהּ

4–6. Though the Israelites be scattered to the four winds of heaven, yet will God reunite them in the Land of the Fathers, and work in Israel a change of heart.

6. *open thy heart.* So that it be no longer closed up, impenetrable, and unreceptive of spiritual teaching. God would help Israel to fulfil his ideal of duty. The words of Jer. XXXI. 32, 'I will put my law in their inward parts, and in their hearts will I write it,' are taken by Nachmanides to express this particular teaching of Deuteronomy.

7-10. Israel will again enjoy the blessings of obedience on his own land.

11–14. THE NATURE OF GOD'S COMMANDMENT

God's commandment is not too hard nor distant; but nigh, clear, and practicable. Sheer life and death, good and evil, are set before Israel. Obedience means blessing; disobedience, destruction.

11. *this commandment.* In the collective sense, meaning all the laws in Deuteronomy.

too hard. Or, 'too wonderful,' to understand and beyond one's power to do; nothing abstruse or esoteric, like the heathen mysteries (Hirsch).

neither is it far off. Out of reach, out of ken, far removed from the sphere of ordinary life.

12. *it is not in heaven.* It is not something inaccessible or supernatural, making it necessary for a man to scale the heights of heaven to find it, and bring it down to earth!

13. *beyond the sea.* In some distant land, among strange peoples.

and bring it unto us, and make us to hear it, that we may do it?' 14. But the word is very nigh unto thee, in thy mouth, and in thy heart, that thou mayest do it.*vii (**iv). ¶ 15. See, I have set before thee this day life and good, and death and evil, 16. in that I command thee this day to love the LORD thy God, to walk in His ways, and to keep His commandments and His statutes and His ordinances; then thou shalt live and multiply, and the LORD thy God shall bless thee in the land whither thou goest in to possess it. 17. But if thy heart turn away, and thou wilt not hear, but shalt be drawn away, and worship other gods, and serve them;*m. 18. I declare unto you this day, that ye shall surely perish; ye shall not prolong your days upon the land, whither thou passest over the Jordan to go in to possess it. 19. I call heaven and earth to witness against you this day, that I have set before thee life and death, the blessing and the

14 וְנַעֲשֶׂנָּה׃ כִּי־קָרוֹב אֵלֶיךָ הַדָּבָר מְאֹד בְּפִיךָ וּבִלְבָבְךָ שביעי (רביעי כשהן מחוב')
טו לַעֲשֹׂתוֹ׃ * ס רְאֵה נָתַתִּי לְפָנֶיךָ הַיּוֹם אֶת־הַחַיִּים
16 וְאֶת־הַטּוֹב וְאֶת־הַמָּוֶת וְאֶת־הָרָע׃ אֲשֶׁר אָנֹכִי מְצַוְּךָ
הַיּוֹם לְאַהֲבָה אֶת־יְהוָה אֱלֹהֶיךָ לָלֶכֶת בִּדְרָכָיו וְלִשְׁמֹר
מִצְוֺתָיו וְחֻקֹּתָיו וּמִשְׁפָּטָיו וְחָיִיתָ וְרָבִיתָ וּבֵרַכְךָ יְהוָה
17 אֱלֹהֶיךָ בָּאָרֶץ אֲשֶׁר־אַתָּה בָא־שָׁמָּה לְרִשְׁתָּהּ׃ וְאִם־
יִפְנֶה לְבָבְךָ וְלֹא תִשְׁמָע וְנִדַּחְתָּ וְהִשְׁתַּחֲוִיתָ לֵאלֹהִים
מפטיר
18 אֲחֵרִים וַעֲבַדְתָּם׃ * הִגַּדְתִּי לָכֶם הַיּוֹם כִּי אָבֹד תֹּאבֵדוּן
לֹא־תַאֲרִיכֻן יָמִים עַל־הָאֲדָמָה אֲשֶׁר אַתָּה עֹבֵר אֶת־
19 הַיַּרְדֵּן לָבוֹא שָׁמָּה לְרִשְׁתָּהּ׃ הַעִידֹתִי בָכֶם הַיּוֹם אֶת־
הַשָּׁמַיִם וְאֶת־הָאָרֶץ הַחַיִּים וְהַמָּוֶת נָתַתִּי לְפָנֶיךָ הַבְּרָכָה

14. *the word is very nigh.* The word of God is on the lips of fathers and children, teachers and taught. Man can carry the Torah, unlike the Sanctuary, everywhere with him. 'When thou walkest, it shall lead thee; when thou liest down, it shall watch over thee; and when thou awakest, it shall talk with thee' (Prov. VI, 22). R. Jose the son of Kisma applied those words to the Torah, thus: *when thou walkest, it shall lead thee*—in this world; *when thou liest down, it shall watch over thee*—in the grave; *and when thou wakest, it shall talk with thee*—in the world to come.

that thou mayest do it. Moses does not say it is *easy*, 'but more justly and finely, that it carries with it the conscience and provocation to its fulfilment by man' (G. A. Smith).

15–20. PERORATION TO THE DISCOURSES OF DEUTERONOMY

A final reminder, as in XI, 26, that two ways lie before them, one leading to life and good, the other to death and evil. The choice lies in their own hands. Only if they choose wisely will they enjoy long life and prosperity upon the land which they were about to inherit.

19. *I call heaven and earth to witness.* Heaven and earth are chosen as witnesses because they abide for ever, outlasting all the changes of human life; IV, 26, Micah VI, 1.

FREE-WILL IN JUDAISM

therefore choose life. Jewish ethics is rooted in the doctrine of human responsibility, that is, *freedom of the will.* 'All is in the hands of God, except the fear of God,' is an undisputed maxim of the Rabbis. And 'to subject our will to the will of our Father in Heaven' is the great purpose of man's life on earth. Josephus states that the doctrine of Free-will was maintained by the Pharisees both against the Sadducees who attributed everything to chance, and the Essenes who ascribed all the actions of man to predestination and Divine Providence. 'Free-will is granted to every man. If he desires to incline towards the good way, and be righteous, he has the power to do so; and if he desires to incline towards the unrighteous way, and be a wicked man, he has also the power to do so. Since this power of doing good or evil is in our own hands, and since all the wicked deeds which we have committed have been committed with our full consciousness, it befits us to turn in penitence and forsake our evil deeds; the power of doing so being still in our hands. Now this matter is a very important principle; nay, it is the pillar of the Law and of the commandments' (Maimonides).

We are free agents in so far as our choice between good and evil is concerned. This is an undeniable fact of human nature; but it is an equally undeniable fact that the sphere in which that choice is exercised is limited for us by heredity and environment. As the earth follows the sun in its vast sweep through heavenly space, and yet at the same time daily revolves on its axis, even so man, in the midst of the larger national and cultural whole of which he is a part, ever revolves in his own orbit. His sphere of individual conduct is largely of man's own making. It depends upon him alone whether his life be a cosmos—order, law, unity ruling in it; or whether it be chaos—desolate and void, and darkness for evermore hovering over it. Thus, in the moral universe man ever remains his own master. Though man cannot always even half control his destiny, God has given the reins of man's conduct altogether into his hands. See Exod. XX, 11, p. 298.

curse; therefore choose life, that thou mayest live, thou and thy seed; 20. to love the LORD thy God, to hearken to His voice, and to cleave unto Him; for that is thy life, and the length of thy days; that thou mayest dwell in the land which the LORD swore unto thy fathers, to Abraham, to Isaac, and to Jacob, to give them.

כ וְהַקְּלָלָה וּבָחַרְתָּ בַּחַיִּים לְמַעַן תִּחְיֶה אַתָּה וְזַרְעֶךָ׃ לְאַהֲבָה
אֶת־יְהוָה אֱלֹהֶיךָ לִשְׁמֹעַ בְּקֹלוֹ וּלְדָבְקָה־בוֹ כִּי הוּא חַיֶּיךָ
וְאֹרֶךְ יָמֶיךָ לָשֶׁבֶת עַל־הָאֲדָמָה אֲשֶׁר נִשְׁבַּע יְהוָה לַאֲבֹתֶיךָ
לְאַבְרָהָם לְיִצְחָק וּלְיַעֲקֹב לָתֵת לָהֶם׃

20. *to love the LORD thy God.* Note the three ascending stages in the godly life: *viz.* (1) to love God; (2) to obey God; (3) and to cleave unto God.

for that is thy life. To love God, to obey Him, to cleave to Him, is to have life and length of days. Ibn Ezra translates, with RV Text, 'for he is thy life,' and interprets the phrase in a mystical sense as, 'God is our life.'

HAFTORAH NITZAVIM הפטרת נצבים

ISAIAH LXI, 10–LXIII, 9

CHAPTER LXI

10. I will greatly rejoice in the LORD,
My soul shall be joyful in my God;
For He hath clothed me with the garments of salvation,
He hath covered me with the robe of victory,
As a bridegroom putteth on a priestly diadem,
And as a bride adorneth herself with her jewels.

11. For as the earth bringeth forth her growth,
And as the garden causeth the things that are sown in it to spring forth;
So the Lord GOD will cause victory and glory
To spring forth before all the nations.

CAP. LXI. סא

שׂוֹשׂ אָשִׂישׂ בַּיהוָה תָּגֵל נַפְשִׁי
בֵּאלֹהַי כִּי הִלְבִּישַׁנִי בִּגְדֵי־יֶשַׁע מְעִיל צְדָקָה יְעָטָנִי כֶּחָתָן
11 יְכַהֵן פְּאֵר וְכַכַּלָּה תַּעְדֶּה כֵלֶיהָ׃ כִּי כָאָרֶץ תּוֹצִיא צִמְחָהּ
וּכְגַנָּה זֵרוּעֶיהָ תַצְמִיחַ כֵּן ׀ אֲדֹנָי יְהוִה יַצְמִיחַ צְדָקָה וּתְהִלָּה
נֶגֶד כָּל־הַגּוֹיִם׃

This is the last of the Haftorahs of Consolation. It is invariably read on the Sabbath before Rosh Hashanah. The opening words of the Haftorah reflect the spiritual exaltation which at that season possesses the soul of the loyal and God-fearing Israelite.

10–11. Zion's Hymn of Gladness.

10. *I will greatly rejoice.* The speaker is Jerusalem (Targum).

salvation. Deliverance.

putteth on a priestly diadem. Or, 'decketh himself with a garland.' Song of Solomon III, 11. This ancient Jewish custom ceased after the Roman wars, when, as a sign of passionate grief over the ruin of the nation, even brides were not permitted to wear such crowns.

11. *as the earth . . . growth.* 'The Prophet compares the salvation of Israel from Exile to the sprouting of the seed from the earth. The seed decays in the earth, and yet it quickens with life; it then renews itself to something better and fresher than it formerly was, and in ever so much greater quantities than before. In the same way, Israel was many years in Exile, disintegrating and despairing; and yet when the hour of Redemption struck he sprouted, renewed his youth, and increased in number, dignity, and greatness beyond his earlier state. And all the nations shall witness and acknowledge this wonderful event' (Kimchi).

Cap. LXII. סב

א לְמַ֣עַן צִיּ֗וֹן לֹ֤א אֶחֱשֶׁה֙ וּלְמַ֥עַן יְרוּשָׁלִַ֖ם לֹ֣א אֶשְׁק֑וֹט עַד־
2 יֵצֵ֤א כַנֹּ֙גַהּ֙ צִדְקָ֔הּ וִישׁוּעָתָ֖הּ כְּלַפִּ֥יד יִבְעָֽר׃ וְרָא֤וּ גוֹיִם֙
צִדְקֵ֔ךְ וְכָל־מְלָכִ֖ים כְּבוֹדֵ֑ךְ וְקֹ֤רָא לָךְ֙ שֵׁ֣ם חָדָ֔שׁ אֲשֶׁ֛ר פִּ֥י
3 יְהוָ֖ה יִקֳּבֶֽנּוּ׃ וְהָיִ֛ית עֲטֶ֥רֶת תִּפְאֶ֖רֶת בְּיַד־יְהוָ֑ה וּצְנ֥וֹף
4 מְלוּכָ֖ה בְּכַף־אֱלֹהָֽיִךְ׃ לֹא־יֵאָמֵ֨ר לָ֜ךְ ע֣וֹד עֲזוּבָ֗ה וּֽלְאַרְצֵךְ֙
לֹא־יֵאָמֵ֥ר עוֹד֙ שְׁמָמָ֔ה כִּ֥י לָ֛ךְ יִקָּרֵא֙ חֶפְצִי־בָ֔הּ וּלְאַרְצֵ֖ךְ
ה בְּעוּלָ֑ה כִּֽי־חָפֵ֤ץ יְהוָה֙ בָּ֔ךְ וְאַרְצֵ֖ךְ תִּבָּעֵֽל׃ כִּֽי־יִבְעַ֤ל בָּחוּר֙
בְּתוּלָ֔ה יִבְעָל֖וּךְ בָּנָ֑יִךְ וּמְשׂ֤וֹשׂ חָתָן֙ עַל־כַּלָּ֔ה יָשִׂ֥ישׂ עָלַ֖יִךְ
6 אֱלֹהָֽיִךְ׃ עַל־חוֹמֹתַ֣יִךְ יְרוּשָׁלִַ֗ם הִפְקַ֙דְתִּי֙ שֹֽׁמְרִ֔ים כָּל־הַיּ֤וֹם
וְכָל־הַלַּ֙יְלָה֙ תָּמִ֖יד לֹ֣א יֶחֱשׁ֑וּ הַמַּזְכִּירִים֙ אֶת־יְהוָ֔ה אַל־דֳּמִ֖י
7 לָכֶֽם׃ וְאַל־תִּתְּנ֥וּ דֳמִ֖י ל֑וֹ עַד־יְכוֹנֵ֞ן וְעַד־יָשִׂ֧ים אֶת־יְרוּשָׁלִַ֛ם

Chapter LXII

1. For Zion's sake will I not hold My peace,
And for Jerusalem's sake I will not rest,
Until her triumph go forth as brightness,
And her salvation as a torch that burneth.

2. And the nations shall see thy triumph,
And all kings thy glory;
And thou shalt be called by a new name,
Which the mouth of the Lord shall mark out.

3. Thou shalt also be a crown of beauty in the hand of the Lord,
And a royal diadem in the open hand of thy God.

4. Thou shalt no more be termed Forsaken,
Neither shall thy land any more be termed Desolate;
But thou shalt be called, My delight is in her,
And thy land, Espoused;
For the Lord delighteth in thee,
And thy land shall be espoused.

5. For as a young man espouseth a virgin,
So shall thy sons espouse thee;
And as the bridegroom rejoiceth over the bride;
So shall thy God rejoice over thee.

6. I have set watchmen
Upon thy walls, O Jerusalem,
They shall never hold their peace
Day or night:
'Ye that are the Lord's remembrancers,
Take ye no rest,

7. And give Him no rest,
Till He establish,
And till He make Jerusalem
A praise in the earth.'

---

v. 3. וצניף קרי

Chapter LXII

A soliloquy of the Prophet regarding his purpose to labour unremittingly on behalf of Zion.

1. *I will not.* Cease to proclaim my message concerning Zion.
her triumph. Her vindication.

2. *a new name.* Of dignity and honour. The name is given in *v.* 4 (Kimchi, Luzzatto).

3. *in the hand.* So held out of affection (Luzzatto); or, for the admiration of the world (Cheyne).

4. *delight in her.* Heb. *Hephzi-bah;* II Kings XXI, 1.
espoused. Heb. *Beulah;* a land forsaken of its owners is said to be 'widowed'.

5. *thy sons.* The land is the bride, and the people is regarded as her 'lord', which is the lit. meaning of the Heb. *baal,* 'husband.'

6–9. A delay in the expected Deliverance.

6. *I have set watchmen.* God is the speaker. He hath set angelic beings (Targum, Rashi, Ewald, Cheyne) as an invisible bodyguard of the city. Some understand by *watchmen,* Prophets, or, 'mourners of Zion,' who constantly pray for the rehabilitation and welfare of Jerusalem.
day nor night. Unlike other watchmen who wake at night and sleep by day.
ye . . . remembrancers. The Prophet now adjures these celestial watchmen continually to remind God of Zion, until He restore it. A remembrancer is the keeper of the King's conscience. A king of Persia had a slave who was daily to call to him, 'Remember the Athenians!' Cf. Ezek. XXIX, 16.

8 תְהִלָּה בָּאָרֶץ׃ נִשְׁבַּע יְהוָה בִּימִינוֹ וּבִזְרוֹעַ עֻזּוֹ אִם־אֶתֵּן
אֶת־דְּגָנֵךְ עוֹד מַאֲכָל לְאֹיְבַיִךְ וְאִם־יִשְׁתּוּ בְנֵי־נֵכָר תִּירוֹשֵׁךְ
9 אֲשֶׁר יָגַעַתְּ בּוֹ׃ כִּי מְאַסְפָיו יֹאכְלֻהוּ וְהִלְלוּ אֶת־יְהוָה
י וּמְקַבְּצָיו יִשְׁתֻּהוּ בְּחַצְרוֹת קָדְשִׁי׃ עִבְרוּ עִבְרוּ בַּשְּׁעָרִים
פַּנּוּ דֶּרֶךְ הָעָם סֹלּוּ סֹלּוּ הַמְסִלָּה סַקְּלוּ מֵאֶבֶן הָרִימוּ נֵס
11 עַל־הָעַמִּים׃ הִנֵּה יְהוָה הִשְׁמִיעַ אֶל־קְצֵה הָאָרֶץ אִמְרוּ
לְבַת־צִיּוֹן הִנֵּה יִשְׁעֵךְ בָּא הִנֵּה שְׂכָרוֹ אִתּוֹ וּפְעֻלָּתוֹ לְפָנָיו׃
12 וְקָרְאוּ לָהֶם עַם־הַקֹּדֶשׁ גְּאוּלֵי יְהוָה וְלָךְ יִקָּרֵא דְרוּשָׁה
עִיר לֹא נֶעֱזָבָה׃

CAP. LXIII. סג

א מִי־זֶה ׀ בָּא מֵאֱדוֹם חֲמוּץ בְּגָדִים מִבָּצְרָה זֶה הָדוּר
בִּלְבוּשׁוֹ צֹעֶה בְּרֹב כֹּחוֹ אֲנִי מְדַבֵּר בִּצְדָקָה רַב לְהוֹשִׁיעַ׃

8. The LORD hath sworn by His right hand,
And by the arm of His strength:
Surely I will no more give thy corn
To be food for thine enemies;
And strangers shall not drink thy wine,
For which thou hast laboured;
9. But they that have garnered it shall eat it,
And praise the LORD,
And they that have gathered it shall drink it
In the courts of My sanctuary.

10. Go through, go through the gates,
Clear ye the way of the people;
Cast up, cast up the highway,
Gather out the stones;
Lift up an ensign over the peoples.
11. Behold, the LORD hath proclaimed
Unto the end of the earth:
Say ye to the daughter of Zion:
'Behold, thy salvation cometh;
Behold, His reward is with Him,
And His recompense before Him.'
12. And they shall call them The holy people,
The redeemed of the LORD;
And thou shalt be called Sought out,
A city not forsaken.

CHAPTER LXIII

1. 'Who is this that cometh from Edom,
With crimsoned garments from Bozrah?
This that is glorious in his apparel,
Stately in the greatness of his strength?'—
'I that speak in victory, mighty to save.'—

8. *by His right hand.* 'By His might.'
food for thine enemies. The foe will no more rob them of their harvests.

9. *praise.* See on Lev. XIX, 24.

10–12. Prepare for the Return!

10. *go through.* Pass through the cities and proclaim, Prepare ye, etc. (Ibn Ezra).
cast up. A road for the return of the exiles.
lift up an ensign. That the nations shall come to thy light, and kings to the brightness of thy rising.

12. *The holy people.* The priesthood of humanity; cf. Exod. XIX, 6.
Sought out. *i.e.* much sought after.

CHAPTER LXIII. THE WARRIOR FROM EDOM

1–6. The time for the restoration of Israel has come, that the world might be saved through Israel. So sure are God's purposes of fulfilment, that even if mortal instruments fail, God Himself will intervene for His people. In a short drama of wonderful forcefulness of phrase and pictorial power, a startled watchman perceives the majestic figure of a Divine Being approaching Zion. He asks the meaning of the blood-stained garments; and is told that it is God Himself returning from single combat, executing vengeance upon Edom, as the type of enemies who knew neither righteousness nor pity in their dealings with Israel. 'The image presented is one of the most impressive and awe-inspiring in Scripture, and it is difficult to say which is most to be admired, the dramatic vividness of the vision, or the reticence which conceals the actual work of slaughter, and concentrates the attention on the Divine Hero as He emerges victoriously from the conflict' (Skinner). Rashi draws special attention to the marked anthropomorphism of this passage, representing God under the image of a fierce, human warrior.

1. *Bozrah.* A city in Edom.
speak in victory. The Divine figure does not give His name, only announces one of His unique qualities—great in act as in word, fulfilling His promise that He would come to the aid of His People.

2 3 מַדּוּעַ אָדֹם לִלְבוּשֶׁךָ וּבְגָדֶיךָ כְּדֹרֵךְ בְּגַת׃ פּוּרָה ׀ דָּרַכְתִּי
לְבַדִּי וּמֵעַמִּים אֵין־אִישׁ אִתִּי וְאֶדְרְכֵם בְּאַפִּי וְאֶרְמְסֵם
4 בַּחֲמָתִי וְיֵז נִצְחָם עַל־בְּגָדַי וְכָל־מַלְבּוּשַׁי אֶגְאָלְתִּי׃ כִּי
ה יוֹם נָקָם בְּלִבִּי וּשְׁנַת גְּאוּלַי בָּאָה׃ וְאַבִּיט וְאֵין עֹזֵר
וְאֶשְׁתּוֹמֵם וְאֵין סוֹמֵךְ וַתּוֹשַׁע לִי זְרֹעִי וַחֲמָתִי הִיא
6 סְמָכָתְנִי׃ וְאָבוּס עַמִּים בְּאַפִּי וַאֲשַׁכְּרֵם בַּחֲמָתִי וְאוֹרִיד
7 לָאָרֶץ נִצְחָם׃ חַסְדֵי יְהוָה ׀ אַזְכִּיר תְּהִלּוֹת יְהוָה
כְּעַל כֹּל אֲשֶׁר־גְּמָלָנוּ יְהוָה וְרַב־טוּב לְבֵית יִשְׂרָאֵל אֲשֶׁר־
8 גְּמָלָם כְּרַחֲמָיו וּכְרֹב חֲסָדָיו׃ וַיֹּאמֶר אַךְ־עַמִּי הֵמָּה
9 בָּנִים לֹא יְשַׁקֵּרוּ וַיְהִי לָהֶם לְמוֹשִׁיעַ׃ בְּכָל־צָרָתָם ׀ לֹא
צָר וּמַלְאַךְ פָּנָיו הוֹשִׁיעָם בְּאַהֲבָתוֹ וּבְחֶמְלָתוֹ הוּא גְאָלָם
וַיְנַטְּלֵם וַיְנַשְּׂאֵם כָּל־יְמֵי עוֹלָם׃

2. 'Wherefore is Thine apparel red,
And Thy garments like his that treadeth in the winevat?'—

3. 'I have trodden the winepress alone,
And of the peoples there was no man with Me:
Yea, I trod them in Mine anger,
And trampled them in My fury;
And their lifeblood is dashed against My garments,
And I have stained all My raiment.

4. For the day of vengeance that was in My heart,
And My year of redemption are come.

5. And I looked, and there was none to help.
And I beheld in astonishment, and there was none to uphold;
Therefore Mine own arm brought salvation unto Me,
And My fury, it upheld Me.

6. And I trod down the peoples in Mine anger,
And made them drunk with My fury,
And I poured out their lifeblood on the earth.'

7. I will make mention of the mercies of the LORD,
And the praises of the LORD,
According to all that the LORD hath bestowed on us;
And the great goodness toward the house of Israel,
Which He hath bestowed on them according to His compassions,
And according to the multitude of His mercies.

8. For He said: 'Surely, they are My people,
Children that will not deal falsely';
So He was their Saviour.

9. In all their affliction He was afflicted,
And the angel of His presence saved them;
In His love and in His pity He redeemed them;
And He bore them, and carried them all the days of old.

v. 2. פתח בס״פ v. 9. לו קרי

2. *winevat.* Winepress—a standing figure of vengeance and carnage in battle.

3. *of the peoples.* They are united in a common fear and hatred of Judah, and are cursed because they came not to the help of the LORD; cf. Judges v, 23.

4. *day . . . year.* The day of vengeance is the necessary preliminary to the year of redemption. God's mercy belongs to a year, His vengeance to a day (Luzzatto).

6. *drunk.* A figure for stupefying disaster.

7–9. Israel's Prayer. Grateful remembrance of God's tender sympathy in the past, and importunate prayer for its renewal.

7. *make mention.* Commemorate.
praises. Praiseworthy acts; deeds of renown.

8. *My people.* Cf. Hosea XI, 1.
so He was their saviour. Better, *so He became their saviour.*

9. *in all their affliction He was afflicted.* This is the ancient Jewish interpretation, following the Traditional Reading (Keri) and not the Text (Kethib); it is defended by Ibn Ezra and Luzzatto, and is now adopted by most moderns. For the meaning, cf. Judges X, 16 ('The LORD's soul was grieved because of the misery of Israel'); and Psalm XCI, 15 ('I will be with him in trouble,' עמו אנכי בצרה). God Himself suffers—the whole cause of the Divine is in temporary eclipse whenever Tyranny becomes mighty on earth and vents its barbarism in afflicting Israel.
angel of His presence. Cf. Exod. XXXIII, 2; a Divine Manifestation that can be perceived. The מלאך הפנים ('Angel of the Presence') plays an important part in later Jewish mysticism.
carried them. As on eagle's wings; Exod. XIX, 4.

31

Chapter XXXI

1. And Moses went and spoke these words unto all Israel. 2. And he said unto them: 'I am a hundred and twenty years old this day; I can no more go out and come in; and the Lord hath said unto me: Thou shalt not go over this Jordan. 3. The Lord thy God, He will go over before thee; He will destroy these nations from before thee, and thou shalt dispossess them; and Joshua, he shall go over before thee, as the Lord hath spoken.*ii. 4. And the Lord will do unto them as He did to Sihon and to Og, the kings of the Amorites, and unto their land; whom He destroyed. 5. And the Lord will deliver them up before you, and ye shall do unto them according unto all the commandment which I have commanded you. 6. Be strong and of good courage, fear not, nor be affrighted at them; for the Lord thy God, He it is that doth go

Cap. XXXI. לא

לא

פ פ פ נב 52

א וַיֵּלֶךְ מֹשֶׁה וַיְדַבֵּר אֶת־הַדְּבָרִים הָאֵלֶּה אֶל־כָּל־יִשְׂרָאֵל׃
2 וַיֹּאמֶר אֲלֵהֶם בֶּן־מֵאָה וְעֶשְׂרִים שָׁנָה אָנֹכִי הַיּוֹם לֹא־
אוּכַל עוֹד לָצֵאת וְלָבוֹא וַיהוָה אָמַר אֵלַי לֹא תַעֲבֹר אֶת־
3 הַיַּרְדֵּן הַזֶּה׃ יְהוָה אֱלֹהֶיךָ הוּא ׀ עֹבֵר לְפָנֶיךָ הוּא־יַשְׁמִיד
אֶת־הַגּוֹיִם הָאֵלֶּה מִלְּפָנֶיךָ וִירִשְׁתָּם יְהוֹשֻׁעַ הוּא עֹבֵר
שני 4 לְפָנֶיךָ כַּאֲשֶׁר דִּבֶּר יְהוָה׃* וְעָשָׂה יְהוָה לָהֶם כַּאֲשֶׁר עָשָׂה
לְסִיחוֹן וּלְעוֹג מַלְכֵי הָאֱמֹרִי וּלְאַרְצָם אֲשֶׁר הִשְׁמִיד אֹתָם׃
ה וּנְתָנָם יְהוָה לִפְנֵיכֶם וַעֲשִׂיתֶם לָהֶם כְּכָל־הַמִּצְוָה אֲשֶׁר
6 צִוִּיתִי אֶתְכֶם׃ חִזְקוּ וְאִמְצוּ אַל־תִּירְאוּ וְאַל־תַּעַרְצוּ מִפְּנֵיהֶם

IX. VAYYELECH

(Chapter XXXI)

E. THE LAST DAYS OF MOSES (Chapters XXXI–XXXIV)

The remainder of the Book deals with the close of Moses' life, and incorporates his Farewell Song and Blessing which recapitulate and enshrine in poetry his message unto Israel. One other Song of Moses, Psalm xc, 'the Prayer of Moses the Man of God,' may likewise have been the product of the latest period of the Lawgiver's life. It is a meditation on the lot of humanity, and contrasts the fleeting generations of man with the mountains at whose feet the Israelites wandered, and with the eternity of Him who existed before ever those mountains were brought forth. Stanley speaks of it as 'the funeral hymn of the world'; and in Watts' noble version it has become a cherished spiritual possession of the English-speaking race:—

'O God, our help in ages past,
Our hope for years to come,
Our shelter from the stormy blast,
And our eternal home.

Before the hills in order stood,
Or earth received her frame,
From everlasting Thou art God,
To endless years the same.

A thousand ages in Thy sight
Are like an evening gone;
Short as the watch that ends the night
Before the rising sun.'

Chapter XXXI

(1) COMMITTAL OF THE LAW TO THE KEEPING OF THE PRIESTS

1–8. Appointment of Joshua

Moses announces the approaching close of his leadership and the appointment of his successor.

2. *go out and come in.* Though, when he died, his eye had not become dim nor had his natural strength abated, he could no longer attend to the activities of public life.

and the LORD hath said unto me. See on iii, 27. This is referred to five times by Moses, and comes again and again as a pathetic break in the majesty of his periods. It forms a most important thread of connection through the different parts of the book (Moulton).

thou shalt not go over this Jordan. Even though I were yet capable to 'go out and come in', I must bow to the Divine decree (Biur).

3. *He will go over.* You need have no fear that my impending death will weaken you. Joshua will lead you in warfare under Divine guidance.

5. *do unto them.* See vii, 1 f; xx, 16 f.

6. *not fail thee.* See on iv, 31.

with thee; He will not fail thee, nor forsake thee.'*iii (**v). ¶ 7. And Moses called unto Joshua, and said unto him in the sight of all Israel: 'Be strong and of good courage; for thou shalt go with this people into the land which the LORD hath sworn unto their fathers to give them; and thou shalt cause them to inherit it. 8. And the LORD, He it is that doth go before thee; He will be with thee, He will not fail thee, neither forsake thee; fear not, neither be dismayed.' ¶ 9. And Moses wrote this law, and delivered it unto the priests the sons of Levi, that bore the ark of the covenant of the LORD, and unto all the elders of Israel.*iv. 10. And Moses commanded them, saying: 'At the end of every seven years, in the set time of the year of release, in the feast of tabernacles, 11. when all Israel is come to appear before the LORD thy God in the place which He shall choose, thou shalt read this law before all Israel in their hearing. 12. Assemble the people, the men and the women and the little ones, and thy stranger that is within thy gates, that they may hear, and that they may learn, and fear the LORD

שלישי (חמישי כשהן מחוב׳) כִּי ׀ יְהוָה אֱלֹהֶיךָ הוּא הַהֹלֵךְ עִמָּךְ לֹא יַרְפְּךָ וְלֹא יַעַזְבֶךָּ׃
7 ס וַיִּקְרָא מֹשֶׁה לִיהוֹשֻׁעַ וַיֹּאמֶר אֵלָיו לְעֵינֵי כָל־יִשְׂרָאֵל
חֲזַק וֶאֱמָץ כִּי אַתָּה תָּבוֹא אֶת־הָעָם הַזֶּה אֶל־הָאָרֶץ אֲשֶׁר
נִשְׁבַּע יְהוָה לַאֲבֹתָם לָתֵת לָהֶם וְאַתָּה תַּנְחִילֶנָּה אוֹתָם׃
8 וַיהוָה הוּא ׀ הַהֹלֵךְ לְפָנֶיךָ הוּא יִהְיֶה עִמָּךְ לֹא יַרְפְּךָ וְלֹא
9 יַעַזְבֶךָּ לֹא תִירָא וְלֹא תֵחָת׃ וַיִּכְתֹּב מֹשֶׁה אֶת־הַתּוֹרָה
רביעי הַזֹּאת וַיִּתְּנָהּ אֶל־הַכֹּהֲנִים בְּנֵי לֵוִי הַנֹּשְׂאִים אֶת־אֲרוֹן
י בְּרִית יְהוָה וְאֶל־כָּל־זִקְנֵי יִשְׂרָאֵל׃ וַיְצַו מֹשֶׁה אוֹתָם
לֵאמֹר מִקֵּץ ׀ שֶׁבַע שָׁנִים בְּמֹעֵד שְׁנַת הַשְּׁמִטָּה בְּחַג
11 הַסֻּכּוֹת׃ בְּבוֹא כָל־יִשְׂרָאֵל לֵרָאוֹת אֶת־פְּנֵי יְהוָה
אֱלֹהֶיךָ בַּמָּקוֹם אֲשֶׁר יִבְחָר תִּקְרָא אֶת־הַתּוֹרָה הַזֹּאת
12 נֶגֶד כָּל־יִשְׂרָאֵל בְּאָזְנֵיהֶם׃ הַקְהֵל אֶת־הָעָם הָאֲנָשִׁים
וְהַנָּשִׁים וְהַטַּף וְגֵרְךָ אֲשֶׁר בִּשְׁעָרֶיךָ לְמַעַן יִשְׁמְעוּ וּלְמַעַן

v. 7 קמץ בסגולתא

7. *in the sight of all Israel.* So that Joshua's authority might not henceforth be questioned. Moses now repeats before all Israel the words he had formerly spoken to Joshua alone; III, 28.

9–13. PUBLIC READING OF THE TORAH

Moses having committed the Torah to writing, delivers it into the hands of the priests and elders—the religious and secular heads of the nation—and enjoins upon them to have it read periodically to the assembled people. Religion in Judaism was not to be the concern of the priests only, who are to share in its truths with a small esoteric circle of political leaders. The priests are merely its guardians and teachers, and the whole body of religious truth is intended to be the everlasting possession of the entire people. This commandment strikes the keynote of the spiritual democracy established by Moses. The Torah is the heritage of the *congregation* of Jacob; XXXIII, 4.

10. *in the set time of the year of release.* According to Tradition, the reference here is to the 'Sabbatical year', called in XV, 1 'the year of release'. The Feast of Tabernacles referred to is that immediately following the conclusion of the Sabbatical year. And there seems to be a special reason why that period was chosen for this public reading of the Law. It was in order to testify that, although there had been neither sowing nor reaping during that year, the Israelites were nevertheless sustained by the mercies of God, to Whose word they were resolved ever to remain loyal, whether in prosperity or adversity (Hoffmann).

11. *thou shalt read.* This is addressed to the nation who delegates the performance of this duty to its representatives (Hirsch). In the days of Josephus, it was done by the High Priest. An early Mishnah declares it to be the function of the King.

this law. Rabbinic Tradition reports that the King read from the beginning of Deuteronomy to the end of the first section of the Shema (I–VI, 9), the second section of the Shema (XI, 13–21), and concluded with XIV, 22 to the end of XXVIII.

12. *men and the women and the little ones.* 'The men were assembled,' says Rashi, quoting the Talmud, 'to learn'; the women, 'to hear'; the little ones, 'to cause recompense to those who bring them.' 'Let neither woman nor child be excluded from this audience, nay, nor yet the slaves. For it is good that these laws should be so graven on their hearts and stored in the memory that they can never be effaced. Let your children also begin by learning the laws, most beautiful of lessons and a source of felicity' (Josephus). None realized more clearly than the Rabbis the spiritual power that comes from the mouth of babes and sucklings (Psalm VIII, 3). 'The moral universe rests upon the breath of school children,' is one of their deep sayings.

hear . . . learn . . . observe. Merely 'to hear' the Torah read once every seven years in a public assembly would not be sufficient. It was to be 'learnt'; *i.e.* made an object of study. Further the Torah must be made the rule of life, and its teachings 'observed'.

your God, and observe to do all the words of this law; 13. and that their children, who have not known, may hear, and learn to fear the LORD your God, as long as ye live in the land whither ye go over the Jordan to possess it.'*v (**vi). ¶ 14. And the LORD said unto Moses: 'Behold, thy days approach that thou must die; call Joshua, and present yourselves in the tent of meeting, that I may give him a charge.' And Moses and Joshua went, and presented themselves in the tent of meeting. 15. And the LORD appeared in the Tent in a pillar of cloud; and the pillar of cloud stood over the door of the Tent. 16. And the LORD said unto Moses: 'Behold, thou art about to sleep with thy fathers; and this people will rise up, and go astray after the foreign gods of the land, whither they go to be among them, and will forsake Me, and break My covenant which I have made with them. 17. Then My anger shall be kindled against them in that day, and I will forsake them, and I will hide My face from them, and they shall be devoured, and many evils and troubles shall come upon them; so that they will say in that day: Are not these evils come upon us because our God is not among us? 18. And I will surely hide My face in that day for all the evil which they shall have wrought, in that they are turned unto other gods. 19. Now therefore write ye this song for you, and teach thou it the children of

יִלְמְדוּ וְיָרְאוּ אֶת־יְהוָה אֱלֹהֵיכֶם וְשָׁמְרוּ לַעֲשׂוֹת אֶת־
13 כָּל־דִּבְרֵי הַתּוֹרָה הַזֹּאת׃ וּבְנֵיהֶם אֲשֶׁר לֹא־יָדְעוּ יִשְׁמְעוּ
וְלָמְדוּ לְיִרְאָה אֶת־יְהוָה אֱלֹהֵיכֶם כָּל־הַיָּמִים אֲשֶׁר אַתֶּם
חַיִּים עַל־הָאֲדָמָה אֲשֶׁר אַתֶּם עֹבְרִים אֶת־הַיַּרְדֵּן שָׁמָּה
לְרִשְׁתָּהּ׃ * חמישי פ (ששי כשהן מחוב׳)
14 וַיֹּאמֶר יְהוָה אֶל־מֹשֶׁה הֵן קָרְבוּ יָמֶיךָ לָמוּת קְרָא אֶת־
יְהוֹשֻׁעַ וְהִתְיַצְּבוּ בְּאֹהֶל מוֹעֵד וַאֲצַוֶּנּוּ וַיֵּלֶךְ מֹשֶׁה וִיהוֹשֻׁעַ
טו וַיִּתְיַצְּבוּ בְּאֹהֶל מוֹעֵד׃ וַיֵּרָא יְהוָה בָּאֹהֶל בְּעַמּוּד עָנָן
16 וַיַּעֲמֹד עַמּוּד הֶעָנָן עַל־פֶּתַח הָאֹהֶל׃ וַיֹּאמֶר יְהוָה אֶל־
מֹשֶׁה הִנְּךָ שֹׁכֵב עִם־אֲבֹתֶיךָ וְקָם הָעָם הַזֶּה וְזָנָה ׀ אַחֲרֵי ׀
אֱלֹהֵי נֵכַר־הָאָרֶץ אֲשֶׁר הוּא בָא־שָׁמָּה בְּקִרְבּוֹ וַעֲזָבַנִי
17 וְהֵפֵר אֶת־בְּרִיתִי אֲשֶׁר כָּרַתִּי אִתּוֹ׃ וְחָרָה אַפִּי בוֹ בַיּוֹם־
הַהוּא וַעֲזַבְתִּים וְהִסְתַּרְתִּי פָנַי מֵהֶם וְהָיָה לֶאֱכֹל וּמְצָאֻהוּ
רָעוֹת רַבּוֹת וְצָרוֹת וְאָמַר בַּיּוֹם הַהוּא הֲלֹא עַל כִּי־
18 אֵין אֱלֹהַי בְּקִרְבִּי מְצָאוּנִי הָרָעוֹת הָאֵלֶּה׃ וְאָנֹכִי הַסְתֵּר
אַסְתִּיר פָּנַי בַּיּוֹם הַהוּא עַל כָּל־הָרָעָה אֲשֶׁר עָשָׂה
19 כִּי פָנָה אֶל־אֱלֹהִים אֲחֵרִים׃ וְעַתָּה כִּתְבוּ לָכֶם אֶת־

13. *and that their children . . . may hear, and learn.* The 'children' are identical with 'the little ones' in the preceding verse. Their presence in such an assembly would mean their initiation into the knowledge of the Torah, and of the duties which it prescribes. Here we have another instance of the vital importance of religious education, so characteristic of the Book of the Farewell Orations of the Lawgiver. The Rabbis worked in the spirit of the Lawgiver when they determined to make the Torah the Book of the People by translating it into the vernacular, and expounding it for the masses. They went far beyond the requirement of reading to the people a portion of Deuteronomy every seven years. They divided the Torah in 156 portions, and had a portion read on each Sabbath in the Synagogue, so as to cover the whole Torah in three years. In the large and influential Jewry of Babylon, the custom prevailed of completing the whole of the Torah in the course of one year; and this eventually became the rule throughout the Diaspora. An appropriate selection from the Prophets—the Haftorah—early accompanied the Pentateuchal lesson on Sabbaths, Festivals, and Fasts.

14–23. INTRODUCTION TO THE SONG OF MOSES

The purpose of the Song, and the circumstances in which Moses received the command to compose and teach it.

14. *give him a charge.* lit. 'command him,' appoint him to the office of Leader.

16. *sleep with thy fathers.* See on Gen. XLVII, 30.

go astray. The lit. meaning of the verb indicates the immorality of heathen worship.

whither they go to be among them. The land amidst whose people the Israelites go to dwell.

17. *because our God is not among us?* An acknowledgment of their guilt and of the justice of their punishment.

19. *write ye this song for you.* The Song in the following chapter. Moses and Joshua were both to write it. According to Ibn Ezra, this command is addressed to each Israelite. The Rabbis deduced from this the commendation to each Israelite that he write for himself a copy of the Torah. In recent centuries, the custom has grown up for the sopher (scribe) who completes the writing of a Scroll to trace the final sentences of the Torah in outline merely. At the festive celebration called the Siyyum,

Israel; put it in their mouths, that this song may be a witness for Me against the children of Israel.*vi (**vii). 20. For when I shall have brought them into the land which I swore unto their fathers, flowing with milk and honey; and they shall have eaten their fill, and waxen fat; and turned unto other gods, and served them, and despised Me, and broken My covenant; 21. then it shall come to pass, when many evils and troubles are come upon them, that this song shall testify before them as a witness; for it shall not be forgotten out of the mouths of their seed; for I know their imagination how they do even now, before I have brought them into the land which I swore.' 22. So Moses wrote this song the same day, and taught it the children of Israel. 23. And he gave Joshua the son of Nun a charge, and said: 'Be strong and of good courage; for thou shalt bring the children of Israel into the land which I swore unto them; and I will be with thee.' ¶ 24. And it came to pass, when Moses had made an end of writing the words of this law in a book, until they were finished,*vii. 25. that Moses commanded the Levites, that bore the ark of the covenant of the LORD, saying: 26. 'Take this book of the Law, and put it by the side of the ark of the covenant of the LORD your God, that it may be there for a witness against thee. 27. For I know thy rebellion, and thy stiff neck; behold, while I am yet alive with you this day, ye have been rebellious against the LORD; and how much more after my death?*m.

י (שביעי הן מחוב') הַשִּׁירָה הַזֹּאת וְלַמְּדָהּ אֶת־בְּנֵי־יִשְׂרָאֵל שִׂימָהּ בְּפִיהֶם
כ לְמַעַן תִּהְיֶה־לִּי הַשִּׁירָה הַזֹּאת לְעֵד בִּבְנֵי יִשְׂרָאֵל׃* כִּי־
אֲבִיאֶנּוּ אֶל־הָאֲדָמָה ׀ אֲשֶׁר־נִשְׁבַּעְתִּי לַאֲבֹתָיו זָבַת חָלָב
וּדְבַשׁ וְאָכַל וְשָׂבַע וְדָשֵׁן וּפָנָה אֶל־אֱלֹהִים אֲחֵרִים
21 וַעֲבָדוּם וְנִאֲצוּנִי וְהֵפֵר אֶת־בְּרִיתִי׃ וְהָיָה כִּי־תִמְצֶאןָ
אֹתוֹ רָעוֹת רַבּוֹת וְצָרוֹת וְעָנְתָה הַשִּׁירָה הַזֹּאת לְפָנָיו לְעֵד
כִּי לֹא תִשָּׁכַח מִפִּי זַרְעוֹ כִּי יָדַעְתִּי אֶת־יִצְרוֹ אֲשֶׁר
הוּא עֹשֶׂה הַיּוֹם בְּטֶרֶם אֲבִיאֶנּוּ אֶל־הָאָרֶץ אֲשֶׁר נִשְׁבָּעְתִּי׃
22 וַיִּכְתֹּב מֹשֶׁה אֶת־הַשִּׁירָה הַזֹּאת בַּיּוֹם הַהוּא וַיְלַמְּדָהּ
23 אֶת־בְּנֵי יִשְׂרָאֵל׃ וַיְצַו אֶת־יְהוֹשֻׁעַ בִּן־נוּן וַיֹּאמֶר חֲזַק
וֶאֱמָץ כִּי אַתָּה תָּבִיא אֶת־בְּנֵי יִשְׂרָאֵל אֶל־הָאָרֶץ אֲשֶׁר־
24 נִשְׁבַּעְתִּי לָהֶם וְאָנֹכִי אֶהְיֶה עִמָּךְ׃ וַיְהִי ׀ כְּכַלּוֹת מֹשֶׁה
שביעי כה לִכְתֹּב אֶת־דִּבְרֵי הַתּוֹרָה־הַזֹּאת עַל־סֵפֶר עַד תֻּמָּם׃* וַיְצַו
26 מֹשֶׁה אֶת־הַלְוִיִּם נֹשְׂאֵי אֲרוֹן בְּרִית־יְהוָה לֵאמֹר׃ לָקֹחַ
אֵת סֵפֶר הַתּוֹרָה הַזֶּה וְשַׂמְתֶּם אֹתוֹ מִצַּד אֲרוֹן בְּרִית־
27 יְהוָה אֱלֹהֵיכֶם וְהָיָה־שָׁם בְּךָ לְעֵד׃ כִּי אָנֹכִי יָדַעְתִּי אֶת־
מֶרְיְךָ וְאֶת־עָרְפְּךָ הַקָּשֶׁה הֵן בְּעוֹדֶנִּי חַי עִמָּכֶם הַיּוֹם מַמְרִים
מפטיר 28 הֱיִתֶם עִם־יְהוָה וְאַף כִּי־אַחֲרֵי מוֹתִי׃* הַקְהִילוּ אֵלַי אֶת־

v. 21. פתח בס"פ   v. 23. קמץ בסגולתא

each letter in those sentences is filled in by a different man, who thereby symbolically takes part in the writing of a Sacred Scroll.

put it in their mouths. Let them know it by heart.

20. *into the land . . . and waxen fat.* The comfort and luxury of such a land would probably demoralize them, and cause them to go astray.

and despised Me. Or, 'and provoke Me to anger' (Targum, Rashi).

21. *as a witness.* For God. Whenever the people will murmur and ask, 'Why has all this evil befallen us?' it will vindicate the retributive justice of God.

for it shall not be forgotten. A Divine assurance that, be Israel's misfortunes what they may, Israel will never altogether forget its destiny, and cease to be 'the people of the Book'.

their imagination. Their imaginings—in an undesirable sense; their evil passions and tendencies.

23. *and he gave.* Better, *and He gave.* This continues *v.* 15. The subject is God (Rashi).

24–30. MOSES HANDS THE LAW TO THE LEVITES TO BE DEPOSITED IN THE ARK

26. *by the side of the ark. In* the Ark were the Ten Words, the ten foundation principles of the Sinaitic Covenant. The entire Book of the Law, which contained both the laws of the Sinai Covenant and those of the Covenant in the Plains of Moab (XXVIII, 69), was placed *by the side* of the Ark (Koenig).

The Traditional explanation is that the Sefer was placed on a ledge projecting from the Ark; others hold that it was placed within the ark, by the side of the Tables of Testimony.

for a witness. When in the days of Josiah (II Kings XXII, 8–17) this Book of the Law was found in the Temple, it was indeed a witness for

28. Assemble unto me all the elders of your tribes, and your officers, that I may speak these words in their ears, and call heaven and earth to witness against them. 29. For I know that after my death ye will in any wise deal corruptly, and turn aside from the way which I have commanded you ; and evil will befall you in the end of days; because ye will do that which is evil in the sight of the LORD, to provoke Him through the work of your hands.' 30. And Moses spoke in the ears of all the assembly of Israel the words of this song, until they were finished:

כָּל־זִקְנֵי שִׁבְטֵיכֶם וְשֹׁטְרֵיכֶם וַאֲדַבְּרָה בְאָזְנֵיהֶם אֵת
הַדְּבָרִים הָאֵלֶּה וְאָעִידָה בָּם אֶת־הַשָּׁמַיִם וְאֶת־הָאָרֶץ׃
29 כִּי יָדַעְתִּי אַחֲרֵי מוֹתִי כִּי־הַשְׁחֵת תַּשְׁחִתוּן וְסַרְתֶּם מִן
הַדֶּרֶךְ אֲשֶׁר צִוִּיתִי אֶתְכֶם וְקָרָאת אֶתְכֶם הָרָעָה בְּאַחֲרִית
הַיָּמִים כִּי־תַעֲשׂוּ אֶת־הָרַע בְּעֵינֵי יְהוָה לְהַכְעִיסוֹ בְּמַעֲשֵׂה
ל יְדֵיכֶם׃ וַיְדַבֵּר מֹשֶׁה בְּאָזְנֵי כָּל־קְהַל יִשְׂרָאֵל אֶת־דִּבְרֵי
הַשִּׁירָה הַזֹּאת עַד תֻּמָּם׃

v. 28. בראש עמוד סימן בי״ה שמ״ו

God in Israel, and instrumental in bringing Israel back to his Father Who is in Heaven.

28. *and call heaven and earth to witness.* A reference to the opening words of the Song in the next chapter.

29. *in the end of days.* A phrase indicating some distant future; Gen. XLIX, 1. The apostasy here predicted became widespread in the days of some of the Judges; cf. Judges II, 11–16; III, 7.

through the work of your hands. This does not mean 'your actions'; but by analogy of IV, 28, it refers to the idols, the product of their hands.

30. *all the assembly of Israel.* Gathered for the purpose. This *v.* forms the transition to the Song.

HAFTORAH SABBATH SHUVAH הפטרת שבת שובה

HOSEA XIV, 2–10; MICAH VII, 18–20; JOEL II, 15–27

CHAPTER XIV

CAP. XIV. יד

2. Return, O Israel, unto the LORD thy God;
For thou hast stumbled in thine iniquity.

3. Take with you words,
And return unto the LORD;
Say unto him: 'Forgive all iniquity,
And accept that which is good;
So will we render for bullocks the offering of our lips.

2 שׁוּבָה יִשְׂרָאֵל עַד יְהוָה
3 אֱלֹהֶיךָ כִּי כָשַׁלְתָּ בַּעֲוֺנֶךָ׃ קְחוּ עִמָּכֶם דְּבָרִים וְשׁוּבוּ אֶל־
יְהוָה אִמְרוּ אֵלָיו כָּל־תִּשָּׂא עָוֺן וְקַח־טוֹב וּנְשַׁלְּמָה פָרִים

Hosea is the Prophet of the Decline and Fall of Northern Israel. He is a deeply affectionate nature, whose message is the unwearying love of God to Israel. 'Let Israel come back to God, and call upon Him in its anguish. Let Israel seek the LORD, it is still time'—such is the burden of his prophecy. The passion of his soul reaches its fullest expression in the concluding chapter of his Book. This is appropriately enough the Haftorah for the Sabbath of Repentance, שבת שובה lit. 'The Sabbath of *Return, O Israel, unto the LORD*.' The very term, *Teshuvah*, *i.e.* 'a turning away from sin and a turning towards God,' is taken from the word שובה in its opening verse. The doctrine of Repentance which is derived from it, is of fundamental importance in Judaism; see p. 195.

A CALL TO REPENTANCE

2. *return . . . unto the LORD.* God's love and mercy are unending. Even after the pronouncement of doom, there is hope and forgiveness for repentant Israel.

3. *take with you words.* God does not require gifts or sacrifices, but sincere confession and penitent words expressing the resolve to amend (Midrash).

4 שְׂפָתֵינוּ׃ אַשּׁוּר ׀ לֹא יוֹשִׁיעֵנוּ עַל־סוּס לֹא נִרְכָּב וְלֹא־
נֹאמַר עוֹד אֱלֹהֵינוּ לְמַעֲשֵׂה יָדֵינוּ אֲשֶׁר־בְּךָ יְרֻחַם יָתוֹם׃
ה 6 אֶרְפָּא מְשׁוּבָתָם אֹהֲבֵם נְדָבָה כִּי שָׁב אַפִּי מִמֶּנּוּ׃ אֶהְיֶה
7 כַטַּל לְיִשְׂרָאֵל יִפְרַח כַּשּׁוֹשַׁנָּה וְיַךְ שָׁרָשָׁיו כַּלְּבָנוֹן׃ יֵלְכוּ
8 יֹנְקוֹתָיו וִיהִי כַזַּיִת הוֹדוֹ וְרֵיחַ לוֹ כַּלְּבָנוֹן׃ יָשֻׁבוּ יֹשְׁבֵי
9 בְצִלּוֹ יְחַיּוּ דָגָן וְיִפְרְחוּ כַגָּפֶן זִכְרוֹ כְּיֵין לְבָנוֹן׃ אֶפְרַיִם
מַה־לִּי עוֹד לָעֲצַבִּים אֲנִי עָנִיתִי וַאֲשׁוּרֶנּוּ אֲנִי כִּבְרוֹשׁ רַעֲנָן
י מִמֶּנִּי פֶּרְיְךָ נִמְצָא׃ מִי חָכָם וְיָבֵן אֵלֶּה נָבוֹן וְיֵדָעֵם כִּי־
יְשָׁרִים דַּרְכֵי יְהוָה וְצַדִּקִים יֵלְכוּ בָם וּפֹשְׁעִים יִכָּשְׁלוּ בָם׃

מיכה ז

18 מִי־אֵל כָּמוֹךָ נֹשֵׂא עָוֹן וְעֹבֵר עַל־פֶּשַׁע לִשְׁאֵרִית נַחֲלָתוֹ

4. Asshur shall not save us;
We will not ride upon horses;
Neither will we call any more the work of our hands our gods;
For in Thee the fatherless findeth mercy.'
5. I will heal their backsliding,
I will love them freely;
For Mine anger is turned away from him.
6. I will be as the dew unto Israel;
He shall blossom as the lily,
And cast forth his roots as Lebanon.
7. His branches shall spread,
And his beauty shall be as the olive tree,
And his fragrance as Lebanon.
8. They that dwell under his shadow shall again
Make corn to grow,
And shall blossom as the vine;
The scent thereof shall be as the wine of Lebanon.
9. Ephraim [shall say]:
'What have I to do any more with idols?'
As for Me, I respond and look on him;
I am like a leafy cypress-tree;
From Me is thy fruit found.

10. Whoso is wise, let him understand these things,
Whoso is prudent, let him know them.
For the ways of the LORD are right,
And the just do walk in them;
But transgressors do stumble therein.

MICAH VII

18. Who is a God like unto Thee, that pardoneth the iniquity,
And passeth by the transgression of the remnant of His heritage?
He retaineth not His anger for ever,
Because he delighteth in mercy.

יד׳ v. 4. קמץ בז״ק v. 10. כצ״ל

4. *Asshur shall not save us.* Israel will no longer put their trust in alliances with foreign, idol-worshipping nations—Assyria or Egypt.

will not ride upon horses. A reference to the help looked for from Egypt; see I Kings x, 28.

5–7. God's gracious and loving reply to those words of repentance and faith.

6. *as the lily.* A symbol of beauty and fruitfulness; but his roots shall be unmovable as Lebanon.

7. *his fragrance as Lebanon.* On the lower slopes of Lebanon are aromatic shrubs, lavender, and myrtle; Song of Songs IV, 8.

9. *is thy fruit found.* 'Thy good cometh.'

10. *stumble therein.* They stumble as if the ways were actually crooked, because their wrong thoughts and desires pervert the meaning of the Divine commands. Thus they do wrong and stumble, even when they would claim to be walking in the ways of the LORD.

MICAH VII

For the life of Micah, see p. 682. He was a contemporary of Isaiah, and like him dreamt of the time when the nations would learn war no more. Micah was the Prophet of the poor, and fearlessly denounced luxury, irreligion, and degeneracy. In these concluding verses of his Book, he revels in the thought of the Divine Forgiveness. These verses are also read, after the Book of Jonah, at Minchah on the Day of Atonement.

18. *like unto Thee.* 'The Prophet does not mean that other gods have a real existence, but speaks from the point of view of the other nations who believe that they do really exist' (Cheyne); Exod. XV, 11.

that pardoneth the iniquity. This and other phrases are a reminiscence of the supreme revelation of the Divine Attributes accorded to Moses on Sinai—'merciful and gracious, slow to anger and abounding in lovingkindness and truth; keeping mercy unto thousands, forgiving iniquity, transgression, and sin.' These

19. He will again have compassion upon us;
He will subdue our iniquities;
And Thou wilt cast all their sins into the depths of the sea.
20. Thou wilt show faithfulness to Jacob, mercy to Abraham,
As Thou hast sworn unto our fathers from the days of old.

19 לֹא־הֶחֱזִיק לָעַד אַפּוֹ כִּי־חָפֵץ חֶסֶד הוּא׃ יָשׁוּב יְרַחֲמֵנוּ
יִכְבֹּשׁ עֲוֹנֹתֵינוּ וְתַשְׁלִיךְ בִּמְצֻלוֹת יָם כָּל־חַטֹּאותָם׃
כ תִּתֵּן אֱמֶת לְיַעֲקֹב חֶסֶד לְאַבְרָהָם אֲשֶׁר־נִשְׁבַּעְתָּ לַאֲבֹתֵינוּ
מִימֵי קֶדֶם׃

Joel II

15. Blow the horn in Zion,
Sanctify a fast, call a solemn assembly;
16. Gather the people,
Sanctify the congregation,
Assemble the elders,
Gather the children,
And those that suck the breasts;
Let the bridegroom go forth from his chamber,
And the bride out of her pavilion.

יואל ב

טו תִּקְעוּ שׁוֹפָר בְּצִיּוֹן
16 קַדְּשׁוּ־צוֹם קִרְאוּ עֲצָרָה׃ אִסְפוּ־עָם קַדְּשׁוּ קָהָל קִבְצוּ
זְקֵנִים אִסְפוּ עוֹלָלִים וְיֹנְקֵי שָׁדָיִם יֵצֵא חָתָן מֵחֶדְרוֹ וְכַלָּה

Thirteen Divine Attributes have always had a wonderful fascination for the Jew, and are the recurrent refrain of the prayers on the Day of Atonement; see on Exod. xxxiv, 6 f.

remnant of His heritage. The Prophets hold fast to the belief in a purified minority in Israel, a righteous nucleus that is indestructible. And historic Israel that has suffered all things, endured all things, and survived all things for its Faith, may well speak of itself as that Remnant, and daily pray: 'O Guardian of Israel, guard the remnant of Israel, and suffer not Israel to perish, who say, Hear O Israel. O Guardian of an only nation, guard the remnant of an only nation, and suffer not an only nation to perish, who proclaim the unity of thy name, saying, The LORD our God, the LORD is One. O Guardian of a holy nation, guard the remnant of a holy nation, and suffer not a holy nation to perish, who thrice repeat the three-fold sanctification unto the Holy One' (Authorised Prayer Book, p. 64).

delighteth in mercy. In the Neilah Amidah, we pray: 'Thou delightest not in the destruction of the world, but thou art a God ready to forgive: Thou delightest in the repentance of the wicked, and hast no pleasure in their death' (Authorised Prayer Book, p. 268).

19. *subdue.* Or, 'suppress' (Kimchi). Sins in Scripture are personified as enemies; or as wild animals which man has it in his power to master; Gen. IV, 7.

20. *faithfulness.* lit. 'truth.'

Jacob . . . Abraham. In God's sight Jacob and Abraham are alive (Cheyne). The Rabbis declared, 'Jacob our father is not dead; even as his children are alive, so is he alive.' *Jacob* and *Abraham* are therefore equivalent to, 'the seed of Jacob and Abraham.'

The above three verses, with a slight interpolation between verses 19 and 20, are recited during the Tashlich ceremony (Authorised Prayer Book, p. 254), on the afternoon of the First Day of New Year; or, on the Second Day, if the First fall on Sabbath.

Joel II

Joel, a Prophet of Repentance, of unknown date, depicts Divine Judgment under the form of a terrible locust plague, which threatens the land with destruction. The people fast and pray unto God, 'and the LORD hath pity on His people'—an appropriate selection for the Sabbath before the Day of Atonement. Joel foresees the day when the LORD will pour out His spirit upon all flesh, 'when your old men shall dream dreams, your young men shall see visions'—when youth shall have the knowledge of age, and age the enthusiasm of youth. Is not such rejuvenation of the soul and renewal of the spirit, the main purpose of the Day of Atonement?

15–17. All are to take part in public humiliation and fast.

15. *horn.* The ram's horn, the *shofar*, summoning the people to a religious gathering.

16. *sanctify the congregation.* *i.e.* hold a sacred religious meeting.

pavilion. Nuptial tent.

17 מֵחֻפָּתָהּ׃ בֵּין הָאוּלָם וְלַמִּזְבֵּחַ יִבְכּוּ הַכֹּהֲנִים מְשָׁרְתֵי
יְהוָה וְיֹאמְרוּ חוּסָה יְהוָה עַל־עַמֶּךָ וְאַל־תִּתֵּן נַחֲלָתְךָ
לְחֶרְפָּה לִמְשָׁל־בָּם גּוֹיִם לָמָּה יֹאמְרוּ בָעַמִּים אַיֵּה
18 19 אֱלֹהֵיהֶם׃ וַיְקַנֵּא יְהוָה לְאַרְצוֹ וַיַּחְמֹל עַל־עַמּוֹ׃ וַיַּעַן יְהוָה
וַיֹּאמֶר לְעַמּוֹ הִנְנִי שֹׁלֵחַ לָכֶם אֶת־הַדָּגָן וְהַתִּירוֹשׁ וְהַיִּצְהָר
כ וּשְׂבַעְתֶּם אֹתוֹ וְלֹא־אֶתֵּן אֶתְכֶם עוֹד חֶרְפָּה בַּגּוֹיִם׃ וְאֶת־
הַצְּפוֹנִי אַרְחִיק מֵעֲלֵיכֶם וְהִדַּחְתִּיו אֶל־אֶרֶץ צִיָּה וּשְׁמָמָה
אֶת־פָּנָיו אֶל־הַיָּם הַקַּדְמֹנִי וְסֹפוֹ אֶל־הַיָּם הָאַחֲרוֹן וְעָלָה
21 בָאְשׁוֹ וְתַעַל צַחֲנָתוֹ כִּי הִגְדִּיל לַעֲשׂוֹת׃ אַל־תִּירְאִי אֲדָמָה
22 גִּילִי וּשְׂמָחִי כִּי־הִגְדִּיל יְהוָה לַעֲשׂוֹת׃ אַל־תִּירְאוּ בַּהֲמוֹת
שָׂדַי כִּי דָשְׁאוּ נְאוֹת מִדְבָּר כִּי־עֵץ נָשָׂא פִרְיוֹ תְּאֵנָה וָגֶפֶן

17. Let the priests, the ministers of the LORD,
Weep between the porch and the altar,
And let them say: 'Spare Thy people, O LORD,
And give not Thy heritage to reproach,
That the nations should make them a byword:
Wherefore should they say among the peoples:
Where is their God?'
18. Then was the LORD jealous for His land,
And had pity on His people.
19. And the LORD answered and said unto His people:
'Behold, I will send you corn, and wine, and oil,
And ye shall be satisfied therewith;
And I will no more make you a reproach among the nations;
20. But I will remove far off from you the northern one,
And will drive him into a land barren and desolate,
With his face toward the eastern sea,
And his hinder part toward the western sea;
That his foulness may come up, and his ill savour may come up,
Because he hath done great things.'

21. Fear not, O land, be glad and rejoice;
For the LORD hath done great things.

22. Be not afraid, ye beasts of the field;
For the pastures of the wilderness do spring,
For the tree beareth its fruit,
The fig-tree and the vine do yield their strength.

17. *between the porch and the altar.* The inner part of the Court of the priests.
make them a byword. For wretchedness.
where is their God? Such would be the taunt of the heathen.

18–20. God's answer to the Prayer of Penitence.

18. *was the LORD jealous.* Because the heathen argued that He was unable to relieve His people.

19. *satisfied.* Will have it in abundance.

20. *the northern one.* The army of locusts. The 'army' that had devastated the land came from the Syrian desert in the north of Palestine. A swarm of locusts is appalling in its power of collective devastation. In quantity it is a thing incredible: it literally darkens the sky. Locusts are the incarnation of hunger, and a swarm clears the land of all vegetation as with a razor. The locusts are then driven by the wind into the desert or the Sea; and their dead bodies are often cast up in heaps, putrefying the atmosphere; see p. 248.
his face. The van of the swarm was near the Eastern (*i.e.* the Dead) Sea, and its rear extended to the Western (*i.e.* Mediterranean) Sea.
hath done great things. In destruction (Rashi, Kimchi). The locust army was the instrument of God, in that it had turned the people to repentance (Horton). The Prophets *ethicize* nature, and poetically invest lower animals, and even inanimate objects, with rational powers; cf. on Isa. I, 3.

21–27. JOY IN DELIVERANCE

21. *the LORD hath done great things.* In good, for Israel, 'to compensate for the evil wrought by the plague' (Ibn Ezra).

22. *ye beasts of the field.* They too are bidden to rejoice. In Chap. I, 18 and 20, the Prophet laments, 'How do the beasts groan (lit. "sob")! yea, the beasts of the field pant unto Thee'; see p. 854.

23. *the former rain in just measure.* The Heb. המורה לצדקה may also mean 'the instructor in Righteousness', in which sense it has been

23. Be glad then, ye children of Zion, and rejoice
In the LORD your God;
For he giveth you the former rain in just measure,
And He causeth to come down for you the rain,
The former rain and the latter rain, at the first.

24. And the floors shall be full of corn,
And the vats shall overflow with wine and oil.

25. And I will restore to you the years that the locust hath eaten,
The canker-worm, and the caterpillar, and the palmer-worm,
My great army which I sent among you.

26. And ye shall eat in plenty and be satisfied,
And shall praise the name of the LORD your God,
That hath dealt wondrously with you;
And My people shall never be ashamed.

27. And ye shall know that I am in the midst of Israel,
And that I am the LORD your God, and there is none else;
And My people shall never be ashamed.

23 נָתְנוּ חֵילָם׃ וּבְנֵי צִיּוֹן גִּילוּ וְשִׂמְחוּ בַּיהוָה אֱלֹהֵיכֶם כִּי־
נָתַן לָכֶם אֶת־הַמּוֹרֶה לִצְדָקָה וַיּוֹרֶד לָכֶם גֶּשֶׁם מוֹרֶה
24 וּמַלְקוֹשׁ בָּרִאשׁוֹן׃ וּמָלְאוּ הַגֳּרָנוֹת בָּר וְהֵשִׁיקוּ הַיְקָבִים
כה תִּירוֹשׁ וְיִצְהָר׃ וְשִׁלַּמְתִּי לָכֶם אֶת־הַשָּׁנִים אֲשֶׁר אָכַל
הָאַרְבֶּה הַיֶּלֶק וְהֶחָסִיל וְהַגָּזָם חֵילִי הַגָּדוֹל אֲשֶׁר שִׁלַּחְתִּי
26 בָּכֶם׃ וַאֲכַלְתֶּם אָכוֹל וְשָׂבוֹעַ וְהִלַּלְתֶּם אֶת־שֵׁם יְהוָה
אֱלֹהֵיכֶם אֲשֶׁר־עָשָׂה עִמָּכֶם לְהַפְלִיא וְלֹא־יֵבֹשׁוּ עַמִּי
27 לְעוֹלָם׃ וִידַעְתֶּם כִּי בְקֶרֶב יִשְׂרָאֵל אָנִי וַאֲנִי יְהוָה
אֱלֹהֵיכֶם וְאֵין עוֹד וְלֹא־יֵבֹשׁוּ עַמִּי לְעוֹלָם׃

taken by some Jewish and non-Jewish expositors; cf. Deut. XVIII, 15; Mal. III, 1, 23 (IV, 5 in English Bibles).

24. *floors.* Threshing-floors.

25. *canker-worm.* Three kinds of locusts had come in successive years.

26. *ashamed.* Disappointed.

27. *in the midst of Israel.* His Helper and Saviour.

none else. An assertion of absolute monotheism.

Chapter XXXII

1. Give ear, ye heavens, and I will speak;
And let the earth hear the words of my mouth.
2. My doctrine shall drop as the rain,
My speech shall distil as the dew;
As the small rain upon the tender grass,
And as the showers upon the herb.
3. For I will proclaim the name of the Lord;
Ascribe ye greatness unto our God.

4. The Rock, His work is perfect;
For all His ways are justice;
A God of faithfulness and without iniquity,
Just and right is He.

Cap. XXXII. לב

לב פ פ פ נג 53

א הַאֲזִינוּ הַשָּׁמַיִם וַאֲדַבֵּרָה וְתִשְׁמַע הָאָרֶץ אִמְרֵי־פִי׃
2 יַעֲרֹף כַּמָּטָר לִקְחִי תִּזַּל כַּטַּל אִמְרָתִי
כִּשְׂעִירִם עֲלֵי־דֶשֶׁא וְכִרְבִיבִים עֲלֵי־עֵשֶׂב׃
3 כִּי שֵׁם יְהוָה אֶקְרָא הָבוּ גֹדֶל לֵאלֹהֵינוּ׃
4 הַצּוּר תָּמִים פָּעֳלוֹ כִּי כָל־דְּרָכָיו מִשְׁפָּט
אֵל אֱמוּנָה וְאֵין עָוֶל צַדִּיק וְיָשָׁר הוּא׃
ה שִׁחֵת לוֹ לֹא בָּנָיו מוּמָם דּוֹר עִקֵּשׁ וּפְתַלְתֹּל׃

X. HAAZINU

(Chapter XXXII)

(2) The Song of Moses

XXXII, 1–44

Moses began his ministry at the Red Sea with a song of praise and triumph, and he ends his life of service to God and Israel with another hymn of joy on the banks of Jordan, and in view of the Promised possession. Both songs are an anticipation of the glorious future beyond the wilderness-life. The majestic Farewell Song, distinguished by fire, force, and the sweep of its rhetoric, is a didactic ode. Moses takes his stand in the spirit at a point of time long subsequent to his own death: he makes a retrospective survey of Israel's history, and develops the lessons deducible from it. The result is a vindication of the ways of God in His relations to Israel. The Divine lovingkindness and unchanging faithfulness are contrasted with Israel's faithlessness and ingratitude. God is the loving father, whereas Israel is the wayward, disobedient child. The successive disasters which would befall Israel are a just retribution for his senseless and ungrateful conduct. But let not the heathen exult and say that Israel lies helpless and crushed. God would in the end intervene for Israel, and the Lawgiver calls upon the nations to rejoice in the salvation of the People of God.

1–3. Appeal to Universe for Attention

1. *give ear, ye heavens, and I will speak.* He appeals to heaven and earth as eternal witnesses of the Divine truths he is about to declare; see xxx, 19; Isa. i, 2.

2. *doctrine.* Better, *teaching*, message or instruction; cf. Prov. iv, 2. The message conveyed by the Song shall, like rain and dew falling on plants, penetrate to the hearts of the Israelites; refresh, stimulate, and give birth to a new spiritual life. The Song, therefore, is not only one of warning, but of comfort also, to awaken new hope in a suffering Israel.

distil as the dew. God's word is as the dew which, though it falls gently and unheard, yet has a wonderful reviving power; cf. Micah v, 6.

small rain. The tender grass needs the small drops for its revival. Even so is the Divine teaching tempered to meet the wants of the weak and the young.

showers upon the herb. The grown-up grass needs the strong forceful showers.

3. *the name of the LORD.* This *v.* states the reason of the invoking of heaven and earth in *v.* 1, and the wish expressed in *v.* 2. He will proclaim the Name of the Lord; *i.e.* His character as revealed in His dealings with Israel.

4–6. God's Faithfulness and Israel's Folly

A contrast between the unchangeable rectitude of God and the fickle behaviour of His people.

4. 'This *v.* gives a concise and forcible declaration of the ethical perfection of God, maintained by Him uniformly in His moral government of the world' (Driver).

the Rock. 'Nine times in the course of this single hymn is repeated this most expressive figure, taken from the granite crags of Sinai, and carried thence through psalms and hymns of all nations, like one of the huge fragments which it represents, to regions as remote in

5. Is corruption His? No; His children's is the blemish;
A generation crooked and perverse.
6. Do ye thus requite the LORD,
O foolish people and unwise?
Is not He thy father that hath gotten thee?
Hath He not made thee, and established thee?*ii.

7. Remember the days of old,
Consider the years of many generations;
Ask thy father, and he will declare unto thee,
Thine elders, and they will tell thee.
8. When the Most High gave to the nations their inheritance,
When he separated the children of men,
He set the borders of the peoples
According to the number of the children of Israel.
9. For the portion of the LORD is His people,
Jacob the lot of His inheritance.
10. He found him in a desert land,
And in the waste, a howling wilderness;
He compassed him about, He cared for him,
He kept him as the apple of His eye.

6 הַ לַיהוָה תִּגְמְלוּ־זֹאת עַם נָבָל וְלֹא חָכָם
שני הֲלוֹא־הוּא אָבִיךָ קָּנֶךָ הוּא עָשְׂךָ וַיְכֹנְנֶךָ׃*
7 זְכֹר יְמוֹת עוֹלָם בִּינוּ שְׁנוֹת דֹּר־וָדֹר
שְׁאַל אָבִיךָ וְיַגֵּדְךָ זְקֵנֶיךָ וְיֹאמְרוּ־לָךְ׃
8 בְּהַנְחֵל עֶלְיוֹן גּוֹיִם בְּהַפְרִידוֹ בְּנֵי אָדָם
יַצֵּב גְּבֻלֹת עַמִּים לְמִסְפַּר בְּנֵי יִשְׂרָאֵל׃
9 כִּי חֵלֶק יְהוָה עַמּוֹ יַעֲקֹב חֶבֶל נַחֲלָתוֹ׃
י יִמְצָאֵהוּ בְּאֶרֶץ מִדְבָּר וּבְתֹהוּ יְלֵל יְשִׁמֹן
יְסֹבְבֶנְהוּ יְבוֹנְנֵהוּ יִצְּרֶנְהוּ כְּאִישׁוֹן עֵינוֹ׃

v. 6. ה׳ רבתי והיא תיבה בפני עצמה

aspect as in distance from its original birth-place' (Stanley). It denotes the Divine unchangeableness and its refuge for men. Ages pass away, but the rock remains a place of safety in time of storm and flood.

perfect. Irreproachable.

a God of faithfulness. 'Faithful to give the righteous his due reward in the life after death. Even though to our seeming this reward be unduly delayed in its coming, God will certainly keep faith in bringing it to pass' (Rashi).

iniquity. Better, *injustice*. Maimonides makes the recognition of the justice of God one of the fundamental principles of the Jewish Faith, even as the Rabbis make it one of the fundamental duties of the Jew (צידוק הדין).

5. *His children's is the blemish.* The Heb. Text is very difficult, and the Ancient Versions render little help. M. Friedländer took מומם as a parallel form to חנם, ריקם, with the meaning of 'fault-laden': 'Is corruption His? No, O ye His fault-laden children, ye perverse and crooked generation.'

The sinning of Israel is not a blemish upon the goodness of God. He gave them a Law which would render them happy, but they choose sin and its subsequent sorrows (Leeser).

6. *requite.* Will ye thus treat your Father and Benefactor?

gotten thee. lit. 'acquired thee,' by delivering them out of Egypt.

hath He not made thee? Constituted thee a nation (Rashi).

and established thee. Set thee upon a firm basis so as to play a great and lasting part in world-history.

7–14. THE LESSON OF HISTORY

7. *the days of old.* The story of Israel's birth as a nation.

many generations. Or, 'each generation.'

father . . . elders. The depositaries of religious tradition.

8–14. THE ANSWER OF THE FATHERS AND ELDERS

When God first allotted the nations a place and a heritage, as described in Gen. X and XI, He had respect to the special necessities of the Israelites.

9. *for the portion of the LORD is His people.* Israel belonged to God in a more intimate sense than any other ethnic group.

10. *He found him in a desert land.* This v. and those immediately following depict God's fatherly care of Israel. Israel is represented as an abandoned, starving child left to die in a wilderness (cf. Ezekiel XVI, 3–6). God finds and rescues him. Israel's history begins with the forty years' march through the desert—where he must have perished, had not God supplied the food and the necessary protection.

howling wilderness. Where wild beasts howl.

compassed him about. By a pillar of cloud by day, and a pillar of fire by night.

cared for him. Or, 'gave him understanding'

11. As an eagle that stirreth up her nest,
Hovereth over her young,
Spreadeth abroad her wings, taketh them,
Beareth them on her pinions—
12. The LORD alone did lead him,
And there was no strange god with Him.*iii.

13. He made him ride on the high places of the earth,
And he did eat the fruitage of the field;
And He made him to suck honey out of the crag,
And oil out of the flinty rock;
14. Curd of kine, and milk of sheep,
With fat of lambs,
And rams of the breed of Bashan, and he-goats,
With the kidney-fat of wheat;
And of the blood of the grape thou drankest foaming wine.
15. But Jeshurun waxed fat, and kicked—
Thou didst wax fat, thou didst grow thick, thou didst become gross—

11 כְּנֶשֶׁר יָעִיר קִנּוֹ עַל־גּוֹזָלָיו יְרַחֵף
יִפְרֹשׂ כְּנָפָיו יִקָּחֵהוּ יִשָּׂאֵהוּ עַל־אֶבְרָתוֹ׃
שלישי 12 יְהוָה בָּדָד יַנְחֶנּוּ וְאֵין עִמּוֹ אֵל נֵכָר׃
13 יַרְכִּבֵהוּ עַל־בָּמֳתֵי אָרֶץ וַיֹּאכַל תְּנוּבֹת שָׂדָי
וַיֵּנִקֵהוּ דְבַשׁ מִסֶּלַע וְשֶׁמֶן מֵחַלְמִישׁ צוּר׃
14 חֶמְאַת בָּקָר וַחֲלֵב צֹאן עִם־חֵלֶב כָּרִים
וְאֵילִים בְּנֵי־בָשָׁן וְעַתּוּדִים עִם־חֵלֶב כִּלְיוֹת חִטָּה

And he forsook God who made him,
And contemned the Rock of his salvation.

v. 13. ו' יתירה ibid. קמץ בז"ק

(Onkelos, Rashi); Israel's spiritual wants were cared for, inasmuch as he received the Law in that desert.

the apple of His eye. The pupil of his eye; the Heb. phrase is equivalent to the English, 'as his very life.'

11. *as an eagle.* God's loving care for Israel is likened to the tender affection that is shown by the eagle towards its young when it teaches them to fly.

stirreth up her nest. When the time comes for the young to leave the nest, the mother-bird does not rouse them suddenly, but strikes her wings against the surrounding branches. Having thus gently awakened them, she 'stirs up' the nest, and allures them to imitate her fluttering in flight.

hovereth over her young. She hovers over them in loving solicitude, and has her wings in readiness to catch them, should they become exhausted.

spreadeth abroad her wings, taketh them. If the young are too weak or too timid to fly, the eagle takes them upon her outspread wings and carries them—a picture of the fostering care, the discipline and training to independence, that Israel received at the Divine hands.

13–14. Israel would enjoy all the luxuries of a pastoral people in abundance.

13. *ride on the high places.* A figure of speech denoting the triumphant and undisputed possession of the land, even of its high mountain fastnesses, which the Prophet-poet foresees as an accomplished fact.

of the earth. Better, *of the land.*

honey . . . rock. Even from the rocks He had given them honey, and the flinty soul produced the olive tree. Palestine is by its flora (it has 3,000 species of flowers), and by its innumerable caves and fissures of the dry limestone rocks, well suited to honey-culture.

suck. Enjoy with relish.

14. *curd of kine . . . wine.* The very products for which the Trans-Jordanic lands they had just conquered were famous.

Bashan. Famous for its cattle.

the kidney-fat of wheat. The best and the most nutritious wheat, even as the fat of the kidneys is the choicest of fat.

15–18. ISRAEL'S INGRATITUDE

15. *Jeshurun.* This title of honour for *Israel* is formed from the root ישר, 'to be righteous,' and designates Israel under its ideal character as 'the Upright One'. It is used here ironically, as a rebuke to Israel's ingratitude and perfidy.

waxed fat, and kicked. Like an ox grown intractible through good feeding, and refusing to bear the yoke of the master.

become gross. Or, 'wast gorged with food' (Driver).

God. Heb. אלוה is used only in poetry; it is a singular obtained from אלהים.

contemned. lit. 'and treated as a נבל,' a senseless person who only deserves contempt. 'How often in their superstition do men act as if God could be tricked; and in their immorality, as if He were senseless' (G. A. Smith).

טו וְדַם־עֵנָב תִּשְׁתֶּה־חָמֶר׃ וַיִּשְׁמַן יְשֻׁרוּן וַיִּבְעָט
שָׁמַנְתָּ עָבִיתָ כָּשִׂיתָ וַיִּטֹּשׁ אֱלוֹהַּ עָשָׂהוּ
16 וַיְנַבֵּל צוּר יְשֻׁעָתוֹ׃ יַקְנִאֻהוּ בְּזָרִים
17 בְּתוֹעֵבֹת יַכְעִיסֻהוּ׃ יִזְבְּחוּ לַשֵּׁדִים לֹא אֱלֹהַּ
אֱלֹהִים לֹא יְדָעוּם חֲדָשִׁים מִקָּרֹב בָּאוּ
18 לֹא שְׂעָרוּם אֲבֹתֵיכֶם׃ צוּר יְלָדְךָ תֶּשִׁי
ביעי
19 וַתִּשְׁכַּח אֵל מְחֹלְלֶךָ׃* וַיַּרְא יְהוָה וַיִּנְאָץ
כ מִכַּעַס בָּנָיו וּבְנֹתָיו׃ וַיֹּאמֶר אַסְתִּירָה פָנַי מֵהֶם
אֶרְאֶה מָה אַחֲרִיתָם כִּי דוֹר תַּהְפֻּכֹת הֵמָּה
21 בָּנִים לֹא־אֵמֻן בָּם׃ הֵם קִנְאוּנִי בְלֹא־אֵל
כִּעֲסוּנִי בְּהַבְלֵיהֶם וַאֲנִי אַקְנִיאֵם בְּלֹא־עָם
22 בְּגוֹי נָבָל אַכְעִיסֵם׃ כִּי־אֵשׁ קָדְחָה בְאַפִּי
וַתִּיקַד עַד־שְׁאוֹל תַּחְתִּית וַתֹּאכַל אֶרֶץ וִיבֻלָהּ
23 וַתְּלַהֵט מוֹסְדֵי הָרִים׃ אַסְפֶּה עָלֵימוֹ רָעוֹת

16. They roused Him to jealousy with strange gods,
With abominations did they provoke Him.
17. They sacrificed unto demons, no-gods,
Gods that they knew not,
New gods that came up of late,
Which your fathers dreaded not.
18. Of the Rock that begot thee thou wast unmindful,
And didst forget God that bore thee.*iv.

19. And the LORD saw, and spurned,
Because of the provoking of His sons and His daughters.
20. And He said: 'I will hide My face from them,
I will see what their end shall be;
For they are a very froward generation,
Children in whom is no faithfulness.
21. They have roused Me to jealousy with a no-god;
They have provoked Me with their vanities;
And I will rouse them to jealousy with a no-people;
I will provoke them with a vile nation.
22. For a fire is kindled in My nostril,
And burneth unto the depths of the nether-world,
And devoureth the earth with her produce,
And setteth ablaze the foundations of the mountains.
23. I will heap evils upon them;
I will spend Mine arrows upon them;

v. 15. קמץ בז"ק v. 17. חול v. 18. י' זעירא v. 21. חול ibid. קמץ בז"ק

16. *roused Him to jealousy.* See on IV, 24.
strange gods. False gods, served with 'abominations', *i.e.* wicked and idolatrous practices.

17. *demons.* Heb. שדים. In Assyrian, *shidu* are the demi-gods usually represented by the bull-colossi in front of palaces.
new gods. Upstart deities recently invented or imported.
dreaded not. The Heb. verb is from the root שער, 'hair'; gods in whose presence your fathers 'shuddered' not, and the hair of their head did not stand on end (Sifri, Rashi).

18. *of the Rock that begot thee . . . bore thee.* A figure as bold as it is beautiful. God is represented as a Father, to whom Israel owed its existence as a people; and, at the same time, as a Mother, travailing with her infant, and forever watching over it with tender affection.

19–25. THE MERITED PUNISHMENT

19. *provoking.* Vexation, disappointment at the unmerited dishonour.

20. *hide My face.* Leave them to themselves.
a froward generation. lit. 'a generation given to perverseness,' *i.e.* evasions of truth and right; a falsehood-loving race (Driver).
no faithfulness. No loyalty to a tender Parent.

21. *vanities.* lit. 'breaths'—something insubstantial, vaporous, unreal; hence false gods.
no-people. Measure for measure. Just as they had angered God by adopting a no-god, so would God anger them by bringing against them a no-people; *i.e.* a horde of barbarians.
a vile nation. Or, 'foolish nation' (RV). Ignorant and, hence, barbarous and inhuman in its habits and methods (Ibn Ezra). And this people will win successes over Israel!

22. *setteth ablaze . . . mountains.* Possibly a reference to volcanic activity, conceived as an expression of Divine anger.

23. *spend Mine arrows.* Exhaust the whole quiverful of evils upon them. 'The evils, like arrows, fall *suddenly* upon their unprotected victims' (Ibn Ezra).

24. The wasting of hunger, and the devouring of the fiery bolt,
And bitter destruction;
And the teeth of beasts will I send upon them,
With the venom of crawling things of the dust.
25. Without shall the sword bereave,
And in the chambers terror;
Slaying both young man and virgin,
The suckling with the man of gray hairs.

26. I thought I would make an end of them,
I would make their memory cease from among men;
27. Were it not that I dreaded the enemy's provocation,
Lest their adversaries should misdeem,
Lest they should say: Our hand is exalted,
And not the LORD hath wrought all this.'

28. For they are a nation void of counsel,
And there is no understanding in them.*v.
29. If they were wise, they would understand this,
They would discern their latter end.
30. How should one chase a thousand,
And two put ten thousand to flight,
Except their Rock had given them over,
And the LORD had delivered them up?

24 חִצַּי אֲכַלֶּה־בָּם׃ מְזֵי רָעָב וּלְחֻמֵי רֶשֶׁף
וְקֶטֶב מְרִירִי וְשֶׁן־בְּהֵמֹת אֲשַׁלַּח־בָּם
כה עִם־חֲמַת זֹחֲלֵי עָפָר׃ מִחוּץ תְּשַׁכֶּל־חֶרֶב
וּמֵחֲדָרִים אֵימָה גַּם־בָּחוּר גַּם־בְּתוּלָה
26 יוֹנֵק עִם־אִישׁ שֵׂיבָה׃ אָמַרְתִּי אַפְאֵיהֶם
27 אַשְׁבִּיתָה מֵאֱנוֹשׁ זִכְרָם׃ לוּלֵי כַּעַס אוֹיֵב אָגוּר
פֶּן־יְנַכְּרוּ צָרֵימוֹ פֶּן־יֹאמְרוּ יָדֵנוּ רָמָה
28 וְלֹא יְהוָה פָּעַל כָּל־זֹאת׃ כִּי־גוֹי אֹבַד עֵצוֹת הֵמָּה
חמישי
29 וְאֵין בָּהֶם תְּבוּנָה׃* לוּ חָכְמוּ יַשְׂכִּילוּ זֹאת
ל יָבִינוּ לְאַחֲרִיתָם׃ אֵיכָה יִרְדֹּף אֶחָד אֶלֶף
וּשְׁנַיִם יָנִיסוּ רְבָבָה אִם־לֹא כִּי־צוּרָם מְכָרָם

31. For their rock is not as our Rock,
Even our enemies themselves being judges.
32. For their vine is of the vine of Sodom,
And of the fields of Gomorrah;
Their grapes are grapes of gall,
Their clusters are bitter;

24. *fiery bolt.* Of fever. Others understand by רשף, fiery darts that produce pestilence; Hab. III, 5.
bitter destruction. Deadly pestilence and malignant plague.

25. *without . . . terror.* War, the climax to these natural horrors. Death will stalk through the streets and invade the homes. Neither age nor sex is spared.

26–33. THE STAY OF GOD'S VENGEANCE

God's resolve on Israel's annihilation was stayed by the consideration of the adversaries' taunts. Nothing could save Israel, but God's respect for His own Name.

26. *I thought.* Better, *I would have said.*
make an end. Or, 'cleave them in pieces.'

27. *enemy's provocation.* The taunts of Israel's foes. They would fail to see God's retributive justice in it all.
misdeem. Misapprehend.

29. *If they were wise.* If those enemies were wise, they would look at things in the right light, past their temporary triumph over Israel. They would see their own inevitable undoing, as soon as Israel returned to God.

30. *how should one chase a thousand.* Their victory over Israel is not their work. How should Israel be so completely crushed, unless it were that God had abandoned His people?

31. *for their rock is not as our Rock.* 'All this the heathens have understood; viz. that God had delivered Israel into their hands and that, therefore, the victory belonged neither to them nor to their gods' (Rashi).
themselves being judges. They must admit that such deeds as were performed by Israel's God stand unrivalled; cf. Exod. XIV, 25.

32. *the vine of Sodom.* Neither is the victory over Israel due to God's approval of the deeds and spirit of the heathens. They are corrupt in root and fruit. The nations are compared to a vine whose stock is derived from Sodom and Gomorrah; hence, tainted by the corruption of which these cities are a type. Ancient writers (Strabo, Pliny, and Tacitus) speak of *apples of Sodom* that 'have a colour as if they were fit to be eaten; but, if you pluck them with your hands, they dissolve into smoke and ashes' (Josephus).
gall. Poison; XXIX, 17. The grapes on a vine of Sodom are a mockery—fair outside, but ashes within.

31 וַיהוָה הִסְגִּירָם׃ כִּי לֹא כְצוּרֵנוּ צוּרָם
32 וְאֹיְבֵינוּ פְּלִילִים׃ כִּי־מִגֶּפֶן סְדֹם גַּפְנָם
וּמִשַּׁדְמֹת עֲמֹרָה עֲנָבֵמוֹ עִנְּבֵי־רוֹשׁ
33 אַשְׁכְּלֹת מְרֹרֹת לָמוֹ׃ חֲמַת תַּנִּינִם יֵינָם
34 וְרֹאשׁ פְּתָנִים אַכְזָר׃ הֲלֹא הוּא כָּמֻס עִמָּדִי
לה חָתוּם בְּאוֹצְרֹתָי׃ לִי נָקָם וְשִׁלֵּם
לְעֵת תָּמוּט רַגְלָם כִּי קָרוֹב יוֹם אֵידָם
36 וְחָשׁ עֲתִדֹת לָמוֹ׃ כִּי־יָדִין יְהוָה עַמּוֹ
וְעַל־עֲבָדָיו יִתְנֶחָם כִּי יִרְאֶה כִּי־אָזְלַת יָד
37 וְאֶפֶס עָצוּר וְעָזוּב׃ וְאָמַר אֵי אֱלֹהֵימוֹ
38 צוּר חָסָיוּ בוֹ׃ אֲשֶׁר חֵלֶב זְבָחֵימוֹ יֹאכֵלוּ
יִשְׁתּוּ יֵין נְסִיכָם יָקוּמוּ וְיַעְזְרֻכֶם
39 יְהִי עֲלֵיכֶם סִתְרָה׃ רְאוּ ׀ עַתָּה כִּי אֲנִי אֲנִי הוּא
וְאֵין אֱלֹהִים עִמָּדִי אֲנִי אָמִית וַאֲחַיֶּה
ששי מָחַצְתִּי וַאֲנִי אֶרְפָּא וְאֵין מִיָּדִי מַצִּיל׃
מ כִּי־אֶשָּׂא אֶל־שָׁמַיִם יָדִי וְאָמַרְתִּי חַי אָנֹכִי לְעֹלָם׃

33. Their wine is the venom of serpents,
And the cruel poison of asps.

34. 'Is not this laid up in store with Me,
Sealed up in My treasuries?

35. Vengeance is Mine, and recompense,
Against the time when their foot shall slip;
For the day of their calamity is at hand,
And the things that are to come upon them shall make haste.*vi.

36. For the LORD will judge His people,
And repent Himself for His servants;
When He seeth that their stay is gone,
And there is none remaining, shut up or left at large.

37. And it is said: Where are their gods,
The rock in whom they trusted;

38. Who did eat the fat of their sacrifices,
And drank the wine of their drink-offering?
Let him rise up and help you,
Let him be your protection.

39. See now that I, even I, am He,
And there is no god with Me;
I kill, and I make alive;
I have wounded, and I heal;
And there is none that can deliver out of My hand.*vi.

40. For I lift up My hand to heaven,
And say: As I live for ever,

v. 39. חול

33. *asps.* Cobras, poisonous snakes.

34–43. The Lot of Israel's Enemies

34. *is not this laid up in store with Me.* Such corruption and moral poison as is the life and example of the heathens could not remain forever unpunished. God would, therefore, interpose on His people's behalf. The punishment to be meted out to Israel's enemies has been duly written down and sealed in the Divine archives.

35. *vengeance.* Is here used in the general sense of punishment. God's long-suffering towards the heathen doers of evil must not be taken for forgetfulness on His part. Retribution would assuredly come.
against the time when. As soon as.
the day of their calamity. The occasion of their sudden and irreparable disaster.

36–42. Hitherto Moses spoke to the Israelites words of warning, so that the Song might testify against them in the day of their calamity. In the remainder of this Song, he utters words of consolation—what would befall them, if they turned from their evil ways in consequence of the calamities that befell them (Rashi).

36. *for the LORD will judge His people.* The very extremity of Israel's need will move Him to vindicate Israel against foes and detractors.
and repent Himself for His servants. Or, 'have compassion on his servants,' in their desolate and downtrodden state.
none remaining . . . large. 'Nothing is left, except the things imprisoned or abandoned' (Luzzatto).
shut up or left at large. Or, 'bond or free' (Gesenius).

37–39. God would speak to them through the extremity of their need, bring them to own, by the logic of facts, that the gods in whom they trusted were unworthy of their regard, and so making it possible for Himself to interpose on their behalf (Driver). Moses endeavours to strengthen 'their faith in a moral government of the world. In spite of the conditions which might well make men despair, the world was one in a Divine purpose. And Israel, to whom this Divine purpose had been revealed, could endure through this dark night of the world. It alone had hope, and men who can hope can endure' (Welch).

39. *see now that I, even I, am He.* Let Israel now see from the calamities it has suffered and

41. If I whet My glittering sword,
And My hand take hold on judgment;
I will render vengeance to Mine adversaries,
And will recompense them that hate Me.
42. I will make Mine arrows drunk with blood,
And My sword shall devour flesh;
With the blood of the slain and the captives,
From the long-haired heads of the enemy.'

43. Sing aloud, O ye nations, of His people;
For He doth avenge the blood of His servants,
And doth render vengeance to His adversaries,
And doth make expiation for the land of His people.*vii.

¶ 44. And Moses came and spoke all the words of this song in the ears of the people, he, and Hoshea, the son of Nun. 45. And when Moses made an end of speaking all these words to all Israel, 46. he said unto them: 'Set your heart unto all the words wherewith I testify against you this day; that ye may charge your children therewith to observe to do all the words of this law. 47. For it is no vain thing for you; because

41 אִם־שַׁנּוֹתִי בְּרַק חַרְבִּי   וְתֹאחֵז בְּמִשְׁפָּט יָדִי
אָשִׁיב נָקָם לְצָרָי   וְלִמְשַׂנְאַי אֲשַׁלֵּם׃
42 אַשְׁכִּיר חִצַּי מִדָּם   וְחַרְבִּי תֹּאכַל בָּשָׂר
מִדַּם חָלָל וְשִׁבְיָה   מֵרֹאשׁ פַּרְעוֹת אוֹיֵב׃
43 הַרְנִינוּ גוֹיִם עַמּוֹ   כִּי דַם־עֲבָדָיו יִקּוֹם
שביעי וְנָקָם יָשִׁיב לְצָרָיו   וְכִפֶּר אַדְמָתוֹ עַמּוֹ׃ *

פ

44 וַיָּבֹא מֹשֶׁה וַיְדַבֵּר אֶת־כָּל־דִּבְרֵי הַשִּׁירָה־הַזֹּאת בְּאָזְנֵי הָעָם
מה הוּא וְהוֹשֵׁעַ בִּן־נוּן׃ וַיְכַל מֹשֶׁה לְדַבֵּר אֶת־כָּל־הַדְּבָרִים
46 הָאֵלֶּה אֶל־כָּל־יִשְׂרָאֵל׃ וַיֹּאמֶר אֲלֵהֶם שִׂימוּ לְבַבְכֶם
לְכָל־הַדְּבָרִים אֲשֶׁר אָנֹכִי מֵעִיד בָּכֶם הַיּוֹם אֲשֶׁר תְּצַוֻּם
אֶת־בְּנֵיכֶם לִשְׁמֹר לַעֲשׂוֹת אֶת־כָּל־דִּבְרֵי הַתּוֹרָה הַזֹּאת׃
47 כִּי לֹא־דָבָר רֵק הוּא מִכֶּם כִּי־הוּא חַיֵּיכֶם וּבַדָּבָר הַזֶּה
תַּאֲרִיכוּ יָמִים עַל־הָאֲדָמָה אֲשֶׁר אַתֶּם עֹבְרִים אֶת־הַיַּרְדֵּן

v. 41. קמץ בז״ק

from what it has learnt of the utter helplessness of the idols and their worshippers, that the God of Israel is the only true God; and that with Him alone is the power of life and death.

40–42. Divine Retribution on Israel's Foes

40. *I lift up My hand to heaven.* Equivalent to, 'I swear.'

as I live for ever. An emphatic variation of the usual phrasing of an oath, As I live.

41. *if.* When.

take hold on judgment. The figure is that of God marching forth as a warrior with justice ('judgment') as his invincible weapon. The 'judgment' over the foes would be remorseless and complete.

that hate Me. Israel's enemies are God's enemies.

43. Conclusion of the Song

43. *sing aloud, O ye nations, of His people.* The Poet calls upon the nations to join Israel in its song of deliverance. That deliverance has been so great that even the heathen, seeing it, must rejoice at it and celebrate it in song. 'They will see His justice and His faithfulness and will gain new confidence in the stability and moral character of the forces which rule the world' (Harper).

his adversaries. They alone who had brought Israel to the brink of destruction are threatened with vengeance, and not the heathen in general who are invited to rejoice with Israel.

and doth make expiation for the land of His people. The expiation is for the massacred innocent Israelites whose blood was in the land of Israel, and for other defilements wrought either by enemies or earlier by backsliding Israelites on the soil of the Promised Land.

44. *Hoshea the son of Nun.* Hoshea, the original name of Joshua, before he came into prominence as Moses' lieutenant and future successor (Num. xiii, 16), was still the name by which he was popularly known. 'Why is Joshua here called Hoshea? It is to show up his modesty. Although he was now about to become the Divinely-appointed Leader of Israel, he still felt himself the same humble youth that he was in the days of his obscurity' (Sifri).

45–47. The Law is Israel's Life

46. *that ye may charge.* One more reference to the duty of impressing the coming generation with the necessity of observing the Torah.

47. *no vain thing.* Or, 'no empty thing'; the Torah is no mere book of empty words, without meaning or message.

it is your life, and through this thing ye shall prolong your days upon the land, whither ye go over the Jordan to possess it.'*m. ¶ 48. And the LORD spoke unto Moses that selfsame day, saying: 49. 'Get thee up into this mountain of Abarim, unto mount Nebo, which is in the land of Moab, that is over against Jericho; and behold the land of Canaan, which I give unto the children of Israel for a possession; 50. and die in the mount whither thou goest up, and be gathered unto thy people; as Aaron thy brother died in mount Hor, and was gathered unto his people. 51. Because ye trespassed against Me in the midst of the children of Israel at the waters of Meribath-kadesh, in the wilderness of Zin; because ye sanctified Me not in the midst of the children of Israel. 52. For thou shalt see the land afar off; but thou shalt not go thither into the land which I give the children of Israel.'

שָׁמָּה לְרִשְׁתָּהּ׃ • פ מפטיר
48 49 וַיְדַבֵּר יְהוָה אֶל־מֹשֶׁה בְּעֶצֶם הַיּוֹם הַזֶּה לֵאמֹר׃ עֲלֵה
אֶל־הַר הָעֲבָרִים הַזֶּה הַר־נְבוֹ אֲשֶׁר בְּאֶרֶץ מוֹאָב אֲשֶׁר
עַל־פְּנֵי יְרֵחוֹ וּרְאֵה אֶת־אֶרֶץ כְּנַעַן אֲשֶׁר אֲנִי נֹתֵן לִבְנֵי
נ יִשְׂרָאֵל לַאֲחֻזָּה׃ וּמֻת בָּהָר אֲשֶׁר אַתָּה עֹלֶה שָׁמָּה וְהֵאָסֵף
אֶל־עַמֶּיךָ כַּאֲשֶׁר־מֵת אַהֲרֹן אָחִיךָ בְּהֹר הָהָר וַיֵּאָסֶף אֶל־
51 עַמָּיו׃ עַל אֲשֶׁר מְעַלְתֶּם בִּי בְּתוֹךְ בְּנֵי יִשְׂרָאֵל בְּמֵי־מְרִיבַת
קָדֵשׁ מִדְבַּר־צִן עַל אֲשֶׁר לֹא־קִדַּשְׁתֶּם אוֹתִי בְּתוֹךְ בְּנֵי
52 יִשְׂרָאֵל׃ כִּי מִנֶּגֶד תִּרְאֶה אֶת־הָאָרֶץ וְשָׁמָּה לֹא תָבוֹא אֶל־
הָאָרֶץ אֲשֶׁר־אֲנִי נֹתֵן לִבְנֵי יִשְׂרָאֵל׃

ye shall prolong your days. Obedience to the Torah tends to length of life, in that it restrains from sin, which shortens it. A life led in harmony with the demands of the Torah is a life of health and cheerfulness and holiness. 'The fear of the LORD prolongeth days, but the years of the wicked shall be shortened' (Prov. x, 27).

48–52. MOSES ORDERED TO ASCEND MOUNT NEBO

48. *that selfsame day.* The day on which Moses rehearsed the Song in the hearing of the people.

49. *into this mountain of Abarim.* The mountain range in the north-west of Moab, overlooking the north end of the Dead Sea.

unto mount Nebo. The summit of the afore-mentioned range of mountains.

50. *and be gathered unto thy people.* Be joined in soul to the souls of thy people who have preceded thee. A similar expression is used of the death of Abraham (Gen. xxv, 8) and of Jacob (Gen. XLIX, 33).

as Aaron thy brother died. Moses had witnessed the passing of Aaron on Mount Hor.

51. *ye trespassed against Me.* lit. 'ye brake faith with Me'; see on Numbers xx, 12.

in the midst of the children of Israel. It seems that these words are intended to be emphatic. Moses had made Pharaoh acknowledge the greatness of God; the princes of Edom and mighty men of Moab trembled at this achievement (Exod. xv)—but all this was among those outside Israel. In Israel itself, both princes and masses remained unimpressed. Moses' work, therefore, was in this sense not a success—'ye sanctified me not *in the midst of the children of Israel*'; see on Lev. XXII, 32.

52. *afar off.* From a distance.

II SAMUEL XXII

Chapter XXII

1. And David spoke unto the Lord the words of this song in the day that the Lord delivered him out of the hand of all his enemies, and out of the hand of Saul; 2. and he said:

The Lord is my rock, and my fortress,
 and my deliverer;

3. The God who is my rock, in Him
 I take refuge;
My shield, and my horn of salvation,
 my high tower, and my refuge;
My saviour, Thou savest me from
 violence.

4. Praised, I cry, is the Lord,
And I am saved from mine enemies.

5. For the waves of Death compassed
 me,
The floods of [1]Belial assailed me.

6. The cords of [1]Sheol surrounded me;
The snares of Death confronted me.

7. In my distress I called upon the
 Lord,
Yea, I called unto my God;
And out of His temple He heard my
 voice,
And my cry did enter into His ears.

8. Then the earth did shake and quake,
The foundations of heaven did tremble;
They were shaken, because He was wroth.

[1] That is, the nether-world.

Cap. XXII. כב

א וַיְדַבֵּר דָּוִד לַיהוָה אֶת־דִּבְרֵי הַשִּׁירָה הַזֹּאת בְּיוֹם הִצִּיל
יְהוָה אֹתוֹ מִכַּף כָּל־אֹיְבָיו וּמִכַּף שָׁאוּל׃
2 3 וַיֹּאמַר יְהוָה סַלְעִי וּמְצֻדָתִי וּמְפַלְטִי־לִי׃ אֱלֹהֵי
צוּרִי אֶחֱסֶה־בּוֹ מָגִנִּי וְקֶרֶן יִשְׁעִי מִשְׂגַּבִּי
4 וּמְנוּסִי מֹשִׁעִי מֵחָמָס תֹּשִׁעֵנִי׃ מְהֻלָּל
ה אֶקְרָא יְהוָה וּמֵאֹיְבַי אִוָּשֵׁעַ׃ כִּי אֲפָפֻנִי מִשְׁבְּרֵי־
6 מָוֶת נַחֲלֵי בְלִיַּעַל יְבַעֲתֻנִי׃ חֶבְלֵי
שְׁאוֹל סַבֻּנִי קִדְּמֻנִי מֹקְשֵׁי־
7 מָוֶת׃ בַּצַּר־לִי אֶקְרָא יְהוָה וְאֶל־
אֱלֹהַי אֶקְרָא וַיִּשְׁמַע מֵהֵיכָלוֹ
8 קוֹלִי וְשַׁוְעָתִי בְּאָזְנָיו׃ וַיִּתְגָּעַשׁ
וַתִּרְעַשׁ הָאָרֶץ מוֹסְדוֹת הַשָּׁמַיִם

v. 8. ויתגעש קרי

This magnificent Song of Thanksgiving, which is almost identical with Psalm xviii, forms an appropriate parallel to the Farewell Song of Moses read on this Sabbath. David traces Divine Providence in his own marvellous escapes from persecution and peril, and renders thanks to God Almighty for his deliverance and victories. Such also was the last lesson that Moses endeavoured to impress upon Israel in his Song—trust in Providence, loyalty to God, and gratitude for His infinite mercies. On the character of David, see p. 458.

Chapter XXII

1. Title

1. *in the day that.* At the time when.

out of the hand. And especially out of the hand of Saul, the most implacable of his enemies.

2–4. Invocation

2. *my rock.* David's early warfare had been mostly waged from mountain strongholds and hiding places, and he draws his figures of speech from those early experiences.

my horn of salvation. i.e. the Power that saves and delivers me. 'The horn is symbol of victorious strength, and is borrowed from animals who push with their horns' (Rashi).

5–7. Prayer in Peril

5. *waves of Death.* Dire adversity threatened to engulf him.

Belial. 'Ungodliness'; here in the meaning of destruction, mortal peril.

6. *Sheol.* The nether-world, the grave. Sheol and Death are like hunters lying in wait for their prey with nets and snares.

7. *His temple.* In heaven (Kimchi).

8–20. His Prayer is Answered

'The manifestation of God's power to deliver is poetically described as the physical appearance of God Himself, accompanied by earthquake and thunderstorm. He is conceived as dwelling in the heart of the thunderstorm, surrounded by fires which break forth as lightning through the cloud' (Dummelow).

8. *then.* Forthwith earthquake, lightning and storm show God's power against His and Israel's enemies.

9. Smoke arose up in His nostrils,
And fire out of His mouth did devour;
Coals flamed forth from Him.
10. He bowed the heavens also, and came down;
And thick darkness was under His feet.
11. And He rode upon a cherub, and did fly;
Yea, He was seen upon the wings of the wind.
12. And He made darkness pavilions round about Him,
Gathering of waters, thick clouds of the skies.
13. At the brightness before Him
Coals of fire flamed forth.
14. The LORD thundered from heaven,
And the Most High gave forth His voice.
15. And he sent out arrows, and scattered them;
Lightning, and discomforted them.
16. And the channels of the sea appeared,
The foundations of the world were laid bare,
By the rebuke of the LORD,
At the blast of the breath of His nostrils.

17. He sent from on high, He took me;
He drew me out of many waters;
18. He delivered me from mine enemy most strong,
From them that hated me, for they were too mighty for me.
19. They confronted me in the day of my calamity;
But the LORD was a stay unto me.
20. He brought me forth also into a large place;
He delivered me, because He delighted in me.

9 יִרְגְּזוּ וַיִּתְגָּעֲשׁוּ כִּי־חָרָה לוֹ׃ עָלָה
עָשָׁן בְּאַפּוֹ וְאֵשׁ מִפִּיו
י תֹּאכֵל גֶּחָלִים בָּעֲרוּ מִמֶּנּוּ׃ וַיֵּט
שָׁמַיִם וַיֵּרַד וַעֲרָפֶל תַּחַת
11 רַגְלָיו׃ וַיִּרְכַּב עַל־כְּרוּב וַיָּעֹף וַיֵּרָא
12 עַל־כַּנְפֵי־רוּחַ׃ וַיָּשֶׁת חֹשֶׁךְ סְבִיבֹתָיו
13 סֻכּוֹת חַשְׁרַת־מַיִם עָבֵי שְׁחָקִים׃ מִנֹּגַהּ
14 נֶגְדּוֹ בָּעֲרוּ גַּחֲלֵי־אֵשׁ׃ יַרְעֵם מִן־שָׁמַיִם
טו יְהוָה וְעֶלְיוֹן יִתֵּן קוֹלוֹ׃ וַיִּשְׁלַח
16 חִצִּים וַיְפִיצֵם בָּרָק וַיָּהֹמֹם׃ וַיֵּרָאוּ אֲפִקֵי
יָם יִגָּלוּ מֹסְדוֹת תֵּבֵל בְּגַעֲרַת
17 יְהוָה מִנִּשְׁמַת רוּחַ אַפּוֹ׃ יִשְׁלַח מִמָּרוֹם
18 יִקָּחֵנִי יַמְשֵׁנִי מִמַּיִם רַבִּים׃ יַצִּילֵנִי
מֵאֹיְבִי עָז מִשֹּׂנְאַי כִּי אָמְצוּ
19 מִמֶּנִּי׃ יְקַדְּמֻנִי בְּיוֹם אֵידִי וַיְהִי
כ יְהוָה מִשְׁעָן לִי׃ וַיֹּצֵא לַמֶּרְחָב
21 אֹתִי יְחַלְּצֵנִי כִּי־חָפֵץ בִּי׃ יִגְמְלֵנִי
יְהוָה כְּצִדְקָתִי כְּבֹר יָדַי יָשִׁיב

21. The LORD rewarded me according to my righteousness;
According to the cleanness of my hands hath He recompensed me.

v. 15. ויהם קרי

foundations of heaven. The mountains, which seem like pillars supporting the sky.

9. 'The startling boldness of the language will be intelligible if the distinctive character of Hebrew symbolism is borne in mind. It is no "gross anthropomorphism", for the Psalmist did not intend that the mind's eye should shape his figures into a concrete form. His aim is vividly to express the manifestation of the wrath of God, and he does so in figures which are intended to remain as purely mental conceptions, not to be realized as though God appeared in any visible shape' (Kirkpatrick).

11. *upon a cherub.* A winged angelic being; here the personification of the storm-cloud.

He was seen. Heb. **וירא**. In Ps. XVIII, it is **וידא**, 'yea, He flew swiftly.'

12. *pavilions.* Better, *his pavilion*—a tent which shrouds God's Majesty.

13. *at the brightness.* Ps. XVIII, 13, reads: 'At the brightness before Him, there passed through His thick clouds hail-stones and coals of fire.'

14. *Most High.* Heb. *Elyon.* Abraham Geiger confidently asserted this Divine title to be of late origin, not earlier than Maccabean times. Its occurrence in the recently discovered Ras-Shamra Tablets proves it to be pre-Mosaic.

gave forth His voice. Thundered; Ps. XXIX, 3 f.

16. *foundations . . . bare.* Nature is convulsed to its lowest depths. The drying up of the Red Sea is woven into the imagery of the storm.

17. *drew me.* The same word as is used of drawing Moses out of the Nile.

22 לִי׃ כִּי שָׁמַרְתִּי דַּרְכֵי יְהוָה וְלֹא
23 רָשַׁעְתִּי מֵאֱלֹהָי׃ כִּי כָל־מִשְׁפָּטָו
24 לְנֶגְדִּי וְחֻקֹּתָיו לֹא־אָסוּר מִמֶּנָּה׃ וָאֶהְיֶה
כה תָמִים לוֹ וָאֶשְׁתַּמְּרָה מֵעֲוֺנִי׃ וַיָּשֶׁב יְהוָה לִי
26 כְּצִדְקָתִי כְּבֹרִי לְנֶגֶד עֵינָיו׃ עִם־
חָסִיד תִּתְחַסָּד עִם־גִּבּוֹר תָּמִים
27 תִּתַּמָּם׃ עִם־נָבָר תִּתָּבָר וְעִם־
28 עִקֵּשׁ תִּתַּפָּל׃ וְאֶת־עַם עָנִי
29 תּוֹשִׁיעַ וְעֵינֶיךָ עַל־רָמִים תַּשְׁפִּיל׃ כִּי־
אַתָּה נֵירִי יְהוָה וַיהוָה יַגִּיהַּ
ל חָשְׁכִּי׃ כִּי בְכָה אָרוּץ גְּדוּד בֵּאלֹהַי
31 אֲדַלֶּג־שׁוּר׃ הָאֵל תָּמִים
דַּרְכּוֹ אִמְרַת יְהוָה צְרוּפָה מָגֵן
32 הוּא לְכֹל הַחֹסִים בּוֹ׃ כִּי מִי־אֵל מִבַּלְעֲדֵי
33 יְהוָה וּמִי צוּר מִבַּלְעֲדֵי אֱלֹהֵינוּ׃ הָאֵל
מָעוּזִּי חָיִל וַיַּתֵּר תָּמִים

22. For I have kept the ways of the LORD,
And have not wickedly departed from my God.
23. For all His ordinances were before me;
And as for His statutes, I did not depart from them.
24. And I was single-hearted toward Him,
And I kept myself from mine iniquity.
25. Therefore hath the LORD recompensed me according to my righteousness,
According to my cleanness in His eyes.

26. With the merciful Thou dost show Thyself merciful,
With the upright man Thou dost show Thyself upright;
27. With the pure Thou dost show Thyself pure;
And with the crooked Thou dost show Thyself subtle.
28. And the afflicted people Thou dost save;
But Thine eyes are upon the haughty, that Thou mayest humble them.

29. For Thou art my lamp, O Lord;
And the LORD doth lighten my darkness.
30. For by Thee I run upon a troop;
By my God do I scale a wall.
31. As for God, His way is perfect;
The word of the LORD is tried;
He is a shield unto all them that take refuge in Him.

32. For who is God, save the LORD?
And who is a Rock, save our God?
33. The God who is my strong fortress,
And who letteth my way go forth straight;
34. Who maketh my feet like hinds',
And setteth me upon my high places;

v. 23. משפטיו קרי

20. *large place.* The opposite phrase for 'straits' and distress.

21–31. GOD'S DELIGHT IN GOODNESS AND MERCY

21. *righteousness.* David does not lay claim to perfect righteousness but to single-hearted devotion to God.

cleanness of my hands. Obviously this Song must have been written before David's great sin.

24. *single-hearted.* And with undivided devotion; see Deut. XVIII, 13.

mine iniquity. My besetting sin.

26. *merciful.* David had been merciful to Saul and his house, and God had been merciful to him.

27. *subtle.* God shows His perfection to those who walk in His ways, but opposes those who oppose Him. The *crooked* man is given over by God to follow his own crooked way, till it brings him to ruin; for example, Pharaoh (Rashi). The Rabbis, who made the Imitation of God a great ethical ideal, laid it down that such imitation must be confined to His qualities of lovingkindness and righteousness, and must not embrace His attributes of severity and rigid justice, jealousy (Deut. VI, 15) or the quality indicated in the words 'with the crooked Thou wilt show Thyself subtle'. These qualities are not for mortals to imitate (Schechter).

29. *darkness.* Night of woe or danger.

30. *by Thee.* By trust in Thee (Rashi).

upon a troop. See I Sam. XXX.

a wall. The capture of Zion; II Sam. V, 6–8.

31. *His way is perfect.* 'Rendering unto each man according to his deserts' (Kimchi).

35. Who traineth my hands for war,
So that mine arms do bend a bow of brass.
36. Thou hast also given me Thy shield of salvation;
And Thy condescension hath made me great.
37. Thou hast enlarged my steps under me,
And my feet have not slipped.

38. I have pursued mine enemies, and destroyed them;
Neither did I turn back till they were consumed.
39. And I have consumed them, and smitten them through, that they cannot arise;
Yea, they are fallen under my feet.
40. For Thou hast girded me with strength unto the battle;
Thou hast subdued under me those that rose up against me.
41. Thou hast also made mine enemies turn their backs unto me;
Yea, them that hate me, that I might cut them off.
42. They looked, but there was none to save;
Even unto the LORD, but He answered them not.
43. Then did I beat them small as the dust of the earth,
I did stamp them as the mire of the streets, and did tread them down.
44. Thou also hast delivered me from the contentions of my people;
Thou hast kept me to be the head of the nations;
A people whom I have not known serve me.
45. The sons of the stranger dwindle away before me;
As soon as they hear of me, they obey me.
46. The sons of the stranger fade away,
And come halting out of their close places.
47. The LORD liveth, and blessed be my Rock;
And exalted be the God, my Rock of salvation;

34 דַּרְכּוֹ׃ מְשַׁוֶּה רַגְלַיו כָּאַיָּלוֹת וְעַל־
לה בָּמוֹתַי יַעֲמִדֵנִי׃ מְלַמֵּד יָדַי
36 לַמִּלְחָמָה וְנִחַת קֶשֶׁת־נְחוּשָׁה זְרֹעֹתָי׃ וַתִּתֶּן־
37 לִי מָגֵן יִשְׁעֶךָ וַעֲנֹתְךָ תַּרְבֵּנִי׃ תַּרְחִיב צַעֲדִי
38 תַּחְתֵּנִי וְלֹא מָעֲדוּ קַרְסֻלָּי׃ אֶרְדְּפָה
אֹיְבַי וָאַשְׁמִידֵם וְלֹא אָשׁוּב עַד־
39 כַּלּוֹתָם׃ וָאֲכַלֵּם וָאֶמְחָצֵם וְלֹא יְקוּמוּן וַיִּפְּלוּ
מ תַּחַת רַגְלָי׃ וַתַּזְרֵנִי חַיִל
41 לַמִּלְחָמָה תַּכְרִיעַ קָמַי תַּחְתֵּנִי׃ וְאֹיְבַי
42 תַּתָּה לִּי עֹרֶף מְשַׂנְאַי וָאַצְמִיתֵם׃ יִשְׁעוּ וְאֵין
43 מֹשִׁיעַ אֶל־יְהוָה וְלֹא עָנָם׃ וְאֶשְׁחָקֵם
כַּעֲפַר־אָרֶץ כְּטִיט־חוּצוֹת אֲדִקֵּם
44 אֶרְקָעֵם׃ וַתְּפַלְּטֵנִי מֵרִיבֵי עַמִּי תִּשְׁמְרֵנִי
לְרֹאשׁ גּוֹיִם עַם לֹא־יָדַעְתִּי
מה יַעַבְדֻנִי׃ בְּנֵי נֵכָר יִתְכַּחֲשׁוּ־לִי לִשְׁמוֹעַ
46 אֹזֶן יִשָּׁמְעוּ לִי׃ בְּנֵי נֵכָר יִבֹּלוּ וְיַחְגְּרוּ
47 מִמִּסְגְּרוֹתָם׃ חַי־יְהוָה וּבָרוּךְ צוּרִי וְיָרֻם

v. 33. דרכי קרי .v. 34. רגלי קרי .v. 40. חסר א'

tried. Refined, like pure gold.

32–43. Victory belongs to God.

34. *feet like hinds'.* Agile, swift and sure. They are so constructed that they can stand on the narrowest and most slippery crags. Hence, the phrase means sure-footedness—an indispensable qualification in mountain-warfare, as David's largely was.

my high places. His mountain strongholds.

35. *bow of brass.* His is the ability to bend a *metal* bow; cf. Odyssey XXI, 409.

36. *condescension.* Mendelssohn renders the word, 'chastisement': God's punishment of David's failings has contributed to his greatness!

37. *enlarged.* Given me free space for my foothold.

40. *strength.* He recognizes that all his personal advantages are gifts of God.

42. *looked.* For help.

43. *tread them down.* Or, 'spread them abroad.' *i.e.* fling them away as worthless refuse.

48 אֱלֹהֵי צוּר יִשְׁעִי׃ הָאֵל הַנֹּתֵן נְקָמֹת
49 לִי וּמֹרִיד עַמִּים תַּחְתֵּנִי׃ וּמוֹצִיאִי
מֵאֹיְבָי וּמִקָּמַי תְּרוֹמְמֵנִי מֵאִישׁ חֲמָסִים
נ 51 תַּצִּילֵנִי׃ עַל־כֵּן אוֹדְךָ יְהוָה בַּגּוֹיִם וּלְשִׁמְךָ אֲזַמֵּר׃ מִגְדִּיל
יְשׁוּעוֹת מַלְכּוֹ וְעֹשֶׂה־חֶסֶד
לִמְשִׁיחוֹ לְדָוִד וּלְזַרְעוֹ עַד־עוֹלָם׃

48. Even the God that executeth vengeance for me,
And bringeth down peoples under me,

49. And that bringeth me forth from mine enemies;
Yea, Thou liftest me up above them that rise up against me;
Thou deliverest me from the violent man.

50. Therefore I will give thanks unto Thee, O LORD, among the nations,
And will sing praises unto Thy name.

51. A tower of salvation is He to His king;
And showeth mercy to His anointed,
To David and to his seed, for evermore.

v. 51. מגדול קרי

44–46. Establishment of David's dominion.

44. *contentions.* Dissensions, civil war with Ishbosheth. Israel was now a united people.

hast kept me. In Ps. XVIII, 'hast made me.'

head of the nations. Ruling over the heathen peoples around.

46. *out of their close places.* Terrified into surrendering.

47–51. Concluding Thanksgiving. 'Vengeance is God's vindication of the righteousness and integrity of His servants. Such a thanksgiving as this does not show a spirit of vindictiveness in David, but is a recognition that God had pleaded his cause and maintained his right' (Kirkpatrick).

49. *violent man.* Saul, in his relation to David.

50. *the nations.* The new peoples under his dominion.

51. *a tower of salvation is He.* In Ps. XVIII the reading is, 'great salvation giveth He.' The former is used in the Grace on Sabbaths and Festivals; the latter in the ordinary Grace after Meals; see Authorised Prayer Book, p. 285.

33

CHAPTER XXXIII

1\. And this is the blessing, wherewith Moses the man of God blessed the children of Israel before his death. 2. And he said:

The LORD came from Sinai,
And rose from Seir unto them;
He shined forth from mount Paran,
And He came from the myriads holy,
At His right hand was a fiery law unto them.

CAP. XXXIII. לג

לג פ פ פ נד 54

א וְזֹאת הַבְּרָכָה אֲשֶׁר בֵּרַךְ מֹשֶׁה אִישׁ הָאֱלֹהִים אֶת־בְּנֵי
2 יִשְׂרָאֵל לִפְנֵי מוֹתוֹ׃ וַיֹּאמַר יְהֹוָה מִסִּינַי בָּא וְזָרַח מִשֵּׂעִיר
לָמוֹ הוֹפִיעַ מֵהַר פָּארָן וְאָתָה מֵרִבְבֹת קֹדֶשׁ מִימִינוֹ אֵשְׁדָּת

v. 2. תרין מילין קרי

XI. VEZOTH HA-BERACHAH

(CHAPTERS XXXIII–XXXIV)

(3) THE BLESSING OF MOSES

CHAPTER XXXIII

The Song opens the final day of Deuteronomy, and in the course of that day the long-expected summons comes. 'The whole people understand the mysterious doom, and line the route by which Moses sets out on the journey from which there will be no return. Like a father laying his hands from a death-bed on the heads of his children, the departing Leader blesses the several tribes, as he passes along; then turning to behold the whole multitude for the last time, Moses lifts his hands in general blessing:

"There is none like unto God, O Jeshurun,
Who rideth upon the heaven as thy help,
And in His excellency on the skies.
The eternal God is a dwelling place,
And underneath are the everlasting arms."

Simple, bare prose tells the rest: the solitary ascent into the mount, the long gaze over the Land of Promise, the death. But no wealth of poetic imagination could have made a close for Deuteronomy more harmonious with the body of the book. The life of the lonely Leader has passed out into solitude: and "no man knoweth of his sepulchre unto this day"' (Moulton).

1. *and this is the blessing.* This Blessing is a complement as well as a counterpart to the Song in the preceding chapter. Whereas the Song is an admonition, depicting the calamities that were to befall a wayward and disloyal Israel, here is all-blessing, foreshadowing a bright and happy destiny. As to form and contents, it is modelled on the Blessing of Jacob; Gen. XLIX.

the man of God. Moses is given this title in Josh. XIV, 6, and in the heading of Psalm XC, 'A Prayer of Moses the Man of God.' The title is sometimes applied to the Prophets; *e.g.* I Sam. IX, 6.

before his death. Just prior to his death, probably the very day on which he died; cf. Gen. XXVII, 7.

2–5. INTRODUCTION

God, revealing Himself majestically unto His people in the desert, gave them a Law through Moses, and united the tribes with God as their king. A similar opening is found in Judges V, Habakkuk III, and Psalm LXVIII.

The happiness and felicity of the tribes of Israel is all traced back to the Divine Revelation which God bestowed upon His people, as He came with them through the wilderness.

2. *the LORD came from Sinai.* The mountain of Revelation, to make His abode in Israel's midst. Sinai was the starting-point in the manifestation of the Divine glory to Israel.

and rose. A metaphor of sunrise. God had 'dawned' on them; had 'risen' for them, and had shed forth the light of His Law upon Israel, so that henceforth they walked in His light.

from Seir. The hill-country of Edom, to the east of Sinai.

mount Paran. Perhaps the mountain-range forming the southern boundary of Canaan. The Divine Presence journeyed, as it were, with Israel from Sinai, through Seir, through Paran, and then finally through the desert; aiding and guarding them, even until they became established in the good inheritance Divinely promised to the Fathers.

holy. Better, *of holy ones.* As in Psalm LXVIII, 18, God is here poetically depicted as coming forth from the angelic hosts that surround His throne.

a fiery law. A Law given out of the midst of the fire (Deut. V, 19–23, Targum); 'a Law of fire' (Mendelssohn, Hirsch). This translation takes the Heb. אש דת, with the Massoretes, as two words. The second of these words, דת 'Law', however, occurs only in the latest books of Scripture. Many translators, therefore, follow the *Kethib* and translate the phrase, 'at His right hand were streams for them.'

3. Yea, He loveth the peoples,
All His holy ones—they are in Thy hand;
And they sit down at Thy feet,
Receiving of Thy words.

4. Moses commanded us a law,
An inheritance of the congregation of Jacob.

5. And there was a king in Jeshurun,
When the heads of the people were gathered,
All the tribes of Israel together.

6. Let Reuben live, and not die
In that his men become few.

7. And this for Judah, and he said:
Hear, LORD, the voice of Judah,
And bring him in unto his people;
His hands shall contend for him,
And Thou shalt be a help against his adversaries.*ii.

3 לָמוֹ׃ אַף חֹבֵב עַמִּים כָּל־קְדֹשָׁיו בְּיָדֶךָ וְהֵם תֻּכּוּ לְרַגְלֶךָ
4 יִשָּׂא מִדַּבְּרֹתֶיךָ׃ תּוֹרָה צִוָּה־לָנוּ מֹשֶׁה מוֹרָשָׁה קְהִלַּת
ה יַעֲקֹב׃ וַיְהִי בִישֻׁרוּן מֶלֶךְ בְּהִתְאַסֵּף רָאשֵׁי עָם יַחַד שִׁבְטֵי
6 7 יִשְׂרָאֵל׃ יְחִי רְאוּבֵן וְאַל־יָמֹת וִיהִי מְתָיו מִסְפָּר׃ ס וְזֹאת
לִיהוּדָה וַיֹּאמַר שְׁמַע יְהוָה קוֹל יְהוּדָה וְאֶל־עַמּוֹ תְּבִיאֶנּוּ
יָדָיו רָב לוֹ וְעֵזֶר מִצָּרָיו תִּהְיֶה׃* פ שני

v. 5. קמץ בז״ק v. 7. הר׳ בקמץ

3. *He loveth the peoples.* *i.e.* the tribes of Israel; cf. Gen. XXVIII, 3. If the word 'peoples' is taken literally, the meaning is that, although the Divine Law was given to Israel alone, God's love embraces all peoples. 'The LORD is good to all; and his tender mercies are over all His works' (Ps. CXLV, 9).

His holy ones. Either of the 'tribes', or of the peoples. If the latter, then the good and pious of all nations are meant, as well as of Israel. RV has 'his saints'; *i.e.* Israel's Saints.

are in Thy hand. Under Thy protection and guardianship.

they sit down at Thy feet. Like pupils in the presence of the master, ready to receive instruction.

receiving of Thy words. The next *v.* defines 'thy words', *i.e.* 'the Law which Moses commanded us, as an inheritance of the congregation of Jacob.'

4. *inheritance.* Better, *heritage;* Heb. מורשה, not ירושה, 'inheritance.' The latter may be spent by the heir at his discretion. A מורשה, however, is an entailed estate, inalienable, and must remain in the family to be handed on from father to son undiminished. Such is the Torah unto Israel. It is transmitted from age to age and generation to generation, so that it is never forgotten.

the congregation of Jacob. The words of this verse have deservedly become a national motto in Israel. They form part of the little child's Morning Prayer; see Authorised Prayer Book, p. 328.

5. *and there was a king in Jeshurun.* Thus began God's Kingdom over Israel.

all the tribes of Israel together. In the presence of the whole People gathered together to enter into the covenant at Sinai.

The above section, especially *v.* 1–3, is among the most difficult passages in Scripture. The different translations are, therefore, both numerous and uncertain. In a popular commentary it is not possible to take note of them all.

6–25. THE BLESSINGS OF THE TRIBES

6. REUBEN

6. *let Reuben live.* The Heb. idiom is equivalent to 'long live Reuben', or, 'God save Reuben' (as in I Kings I, 25).

and not die. Living in Transjordania, he was exposed to constant attacks from numerous enemies.

in that his men become few. Let not the death of Reuben take place through a diminution in his numbers. At the first census taken in the time of Moses, the number of Reubenites capable of bearing arms was 46,500 men (Num. I, 21). At the second, it had dwindled to 43,730 men (Num. XXVI, 7). In David's time much of their territory was conquered by the Moabites. Mesha, in the ninth century B.C.E., when describing his victories against the Eastern tribes, does not even mention the tribe of Reuben.

7. JUDAH

7. *hear, LORD, the voice of Judah.* 'Hear, O LORD, the prayer of Judah when he goeth forth to battle; and bring him back to his people in peace' (Onkelos). Judah was the first to undertake the conquest of the unconquered portion of Palestine; and for some time, his possessions were an *enclave*, surrounded by the Canaanites. Hence this prayer that he be united to the other tribes.

his hands shall contend for him. He needs and deserves Divine help, as he will be fighting the fight of all Israel.

8 וּלְלֵוִי אָמַר תֻּמֶּיךָ וְאוּרֶיךָ לְאִישׁ חֲסִידֶךָ אֲשֶׁר נִסִּיתוֹ
9 בְּמַסָּה תְּרִיבֵהוּ עַל־מֵי מְרִיבָה׃ הָאֹמֵר לְאָבִיו וּלְאִמּוֹ
לֹא רְאִיתִיו וְאֶת־אֶחָיו לֹא הִכִּיר וְאֶת־בָּנָו לֹא יָדָע כִּי שָׁמְרוּ
י אִמְרָתֶךָ וּבְרִיתְךָ יִנְצֹרוּ׃ יוֹרוּ מִשְׁפָּטֶיךָ לְיַעֲקֹב וְתוֹרָתְךָ
11 לְיִשְׂרָאֵל יָשִׂימוּ קְטוֹרָה בְּאַפֶּךָ וְכָלִיל עַל־מִזְבְּחֶךָ׃ בָּרֵךְ
יְהוָה חֵילוֹ וּפֹעַל יָדָיו תִּרְצֶה מְחַץ מָתְנַיִם קָמָיו וּמְשַׂנְאָיו
12 מִן־יְקוּמוּן׃ ס לְבִנְיָמִן אָמַר יְדִיד יְהוָה יִשְׁכֹּן לָבֶטַח

8. And of Levi he said:
Thy Thummim and Thy Urim be with Thy holy one,
Whom Thou didst prove at Massah,
With whom Thou didst strive at the waters of Meribah;
9. Who said of his father, and of his mother: 'I have not seen him';
Neither did he acknowledge his brethren,
Nor knew he his own children;
For they have observed Thy word,
And keep Thy covenant.
10. They shall teach Jacob Thine ordinances,
And Israel Thy law;
They shall put incense before Thee,
And whole burnt-offering upon Thine altar.
11. Bless, LORD, his substance,
And accept the work of his hands;
Smite through the loins of them that rise up against him,
And of them that hate him, that they rise not again.

12. Of Benjamin he said:
The beloved of the LORD shall dwell in safety by Him;
He covereth him all the day,
And He dwelleth between his shoulders.*iii.

v. 9. בניו קרי

8–11. LEVI

We note the omission of Simeon, who is joined with Levi in Jacob's Blessing, Gen. XLIX, 5. The probable explanation is that Jacob had foretold that both Simeon and Levi should have their territories divided up among the other tribes. As Simeon's possessions consisted of only 19 unconnected cities within the territory of Judah (Josh. XIX, 2–9), the tribe of Simeon was regarded as included in Judah.

In blessing Levi, Moses prays that the privilege of guarding the Urim and the Thummim may remain with Levi, who had proved his fidelity to the Divine cause in the Wilderness.

8. *thy Thummim and thy Urim.* Objects connected with the breast-plate of the High Priest.

holy one. i.e. the tribe of Levi, personified as an individual.

didst prove. At Massah (Exod. XVII, 1–7) and at Meribah (Num. XX, 1–13), when the piety of Moses and Aaron, the two great sons of Levi, was put to a severe test.

9. *who said of his father . . . children.* This describes in emphatic language the disinterested spirit in which the tribe of Levi discharges its office: the disregard of even the closest family ties, when they interfere with the performance of religious duties. Thus, the Levites slew every man his companion and every man his neighbour, as a punishment for their worship of the Golden Calf; Exod. XXXII, 27.

and keep Thy covenant. See Mal. II, 5–7 ('My covenant was with him of life and peace. The law of truth was in his mouth, and unrighteousness was not found in his lips; he walked with me in peace and uprightness, and did turn away many from iniquity. For the priest's lips should keep knowledge, and they should seek the law at his mouth').

10. *Thine ordinances.* Such being the Levites' record, they are worthy of having the prerogative of teaching Israel the precepts of God as laid down in the Torah, and designed for the maintenance of justice between man and man. The God of Israel 'is distinguished from the gods of Israel's neighbours, and towers above them as the God in Whose name justice was administered, and of Whom it could be said that He was not known where the laws of honour and good faith were violated. The priest, His interpreter, is the bearer and appointed upholder of right' (Kuenen).

they shall put . . . upon Thine altar. In addition to being the guardians and teachers of right in Israel, theirs is the charge of the Altar.

11. *his substance.* Better, *his might* (Driver); *i.e.* his ability for the efficient performance of his duties.

the loins. The seat of bodily strength.

them that hate him. Those who are opposed to the priestly prerogatives, like Korah (Num. XVI).

12. BENJAMIN

12. *the beloved of the LORD.* Even as Benjamin was the favourite of Jacob, Moses sees in that parental love for Benjamin a reflection of God's love for that tribe.

shall dwell in safety by Him. God shall ever be at the side of Benjamin to aid and shield

שלישי
13 עָלָיו חֹפֵף עָלָיו כָּל־הַיּוֹם וּבֵין כְּתֵפָיו שָׁכֵן׃ * ס וּלְיוֹסֵף
אָמַר מְבֹרֶכֶת יְהוָה אַרְצוֹ מִמֶּגֶד שָׁמַיִם מִטָּל וּמִתְּהוֹם רֹבֶצֶת
14 טו תָּחַת׃ וּמִמֶּגֶד תְּבוּאֹת שָׁמֶשׁ וּמִמֶּגֶד גֶּרֶשׁ יְרָחִים׃ וּמֵרֹאשׁ
16 הַרְרֵי־קֶדֶם וּמִמֶּגֶד גִּבְעוֹת עוֹלָם׃ וּמִמֶּגֶד אֶרֶץ וּמְלֹאָהּ
וּרְצוֹן שֹׁכְנִי סְנֶה תָּבוֹאתָה לְרֹאשׁ יוֹסֵף וּלְקָדְקֹד נְזִיר
17 אֶחָיו׃ בְּכוֹר שׁוֹרוֹ הָדָר לוֹ וְקַרְנֵי רְאֵם קַרְנָיו בָּהֶם עַמִּים
יְנַגַּח יַחְדָּו אַפְסֵי־אָרֶץ וְהֵם רִבְבוֹת אֶפְרַיִם וְהֵם אַלְפֵי

13. And of Joseph he said:
Blessed of the LORD be his land;
For the precious things of heaven, for the dew,
And for the deep that coucheth beneath,
14. And for the precious things of the fruits of the sun,
And for the precious things of the yield of the moons,
15. And for the tops of the ancient mountains,
And for the precious things of the everlasting hills,
16. And for the precious things of the earth and the fulness thereof,
And the good will of Him that dwelt in the bush;
Let the blessing come upon the head of Joseph,
And upon the crown of the head of him that is prince among his brethren.
17. His firstling bullock, majesty is his;
And his horns are the horns of the wild-ox;
With them he shall gore the peoples all of them, even the ends of the earth;
And they are the ten thousands of Ephraim,
And they are the thousands of Manasseh.*iv.

18. And of Zebulun he said:
Rejoice, Zebulun, in thy going out,
And, Issachar, in thy tents.

v. 13. קמץ בז״ק

him. Rashi explains this 'nearness' of Benjamin to God to mean that the Temple would be situated in his territory. The Temple itself was just within the rocky border of Benjamin, whilst its courts were in Judah.

He covereth him. As with a canopy.

all the day. For ever. Once Jerusalem—which was in Benjamin's territory—had been chosen as the spot for the Sanctuary, the Shechinah never left it for another spot.

between his shoulders. Josh. xv, 8, uses the same Hebrew word for 'shoulder' to denote the side of the hill on which Jerusalem and the Temple were to stand.

13–17. JOSEPH

The twin tribe, Ephraim and Manasseh, receives the temporal blessings of fertility of soil and military prowess, accompanied by uninterrupted enjoyment of the Divine favour.

13. *the precious things of heaven.* The gifts of nature—rain, sunshine, warmth—that are indispensable for fertility.

for the dew. Cf. Isaac's blessing of Jacob (Gen. XXVII, 28), 'God give thee of the dew of heaven.'

for the deep. The fountains and floods which spring up from the depths of the earth.

coucheth. Old English for 'croucheth'.

14. *fruits of the sun.* Every form of yearly produce matured by the light and warmth of the sun.

yield of the moons. 'The produce of the months'; *i.e.* the fruit and vegetation of successive seasons.

15. *tops of the ancient mountains.* The vegetation which so luxuriantly adorns the peaks and slopes of the mountain-ranges of Palestine.

16. *precious things of the earth.* After speaking of the fertility of the hills and mountains, the Seer turns to the precious products of the plains and valleys.

that dwelt in the bush. See Exod. III, 2–10, when God, after making Himself known to Moses 'in a flame of fire out of the midst of the bush', promises to become the Redeemer of Israel.

prince among his brethren. Eminent among his brethren; the last two lines (in the English) are a quotation from Gen. XLIX, 26.

17. *firstling bullock.* *i.e.* Ephraim, to whom Jacob had given the precedence over the elder brother Manasseh; Gen. XLVIII, 19.

and his horns. The figure of the bull is here employed as the emblem of strength.

wild-ox. See on Num. XXIII, 22.

he shall gore. Ephraim shall extend his conquests over remote peoples.

and they are. Better, *and these be; i.e.* the reference is to the myriads of the men of Ephraim, and the thousands of the men of Manasseh.

18*a*. ZEBULUN

18. *going out.* *i.e.* general activity; here probably a reference to the maritime enterprises of the tribe. The territory of Zebulun stretched

19. They shall call peoples unto the mountain;
There shall they offer sacrifices of righteousness;
For they shall suck the abundance of the seas,
And the hidden treasures of the sand.

20. And of Gad he said:
Blessed be He that enlargeth Gad;
He dwelleth as a lioness,
And teareth the arm, yea, the crown of the head.
21. And he chose a first part for himself,
For there a portion of a ruler was reserved;
And there came the heads of the people,
He executed the righteousness of the LORD
And His ordinances with Israel.*v.

רביעי
18 מְנַשֶּׁה׃ * ס וְלִזְבוּלֻן אָמַר שְׂמַח זְבוּלֻן בְּצֵאתֶךָ וְיִשָּׂשכָר
19 בְּאֹהָלֶיךָ׃ עַמִּים הַר־יִקְרָאוּ שָׁם יִזְבְּחוּ זִבְחֵי־צֶדֶק כִּי שֶׁפַע
כ יַמִּים יִינָקוּ וּשְׂפֻנֵי טְמוּנֵי חוֹל׃ ס וּלְגָד אָמַר בָּרוּךְ
21 מַרְחִיב גָּד כְּלָבִיא שָׁכֵן וְטָרַף זְרוֹעַ אַף־קָדְקֹד׃ וַיַּרְא
רֵאשִׁית לוֹ כִּי־שָׁם חֶלְקַת מְחֹקֵק סָפוּן וַיֵּתֵא רָאשֵׁי עָם
חמישי
22 צִדְקַת יְהוָה עָשָׂה וּמִשְׁפָּטָיו עִם־יִשְׂרָאֵל׃ * ס וּלְדָן אָמַר

22. And of Dan he said:
Dan is a lion's whelp,
That leapeth forth from Bashan.

v. 19. קמץ בז״ק v. 21. קמץ בז״ק

from what is now known as Lake Tiberias to the Mediterranean, which fact gave it an active share in the sea-traffic. Jacob's blessing is, 'Zebulun shall dwell at the beach of the sea, and he shall be for an haven of ships.'

18*b*–19. ISSACHAR

in thy tents. In the enjoyment of rest; in the quiet pursuit of a peaceful life, possibly an agricultural one. While Zebulun chose adventure and enterprise, Issachar preferred 'a stay-at-home' existence. The Talmud interprets 'tents' as homes for the study of the Law. In I Chron. XII, 32, the men of Issachar are said to have been the religious teachers in Israel. Scripture here links Zebulun, the merchant and man of action, with Issachar, the student, the man of spirit; as if to show how necessary it is that these two types should always work in co-operation.

19. *call peoples.* They shall invite the tribes to join them in thanksgiving to God.

the mountain. Zion, the place which God shall choose as His sanctuary. This is nowhere expressly named in Deuteronomy, and is here likewise left undefined.

sacrifices of righteousness. Due, fitting, legal sacrifices; Ps. IV, 6.

for. Gives the reason why the two tribes invite 'the peoples' to worship: it is because of the rich blessings which Zebulun and Issachar enjoy.

suck . . . the seas. A reference to Zebulun's fishing and sea-carrying trade.

hidden treasures of the sand. Probably a reference to Issachar's manufacture of glass, which, according to Josephus, Targum Jonathan and Talmud, took place on the sands of Acre.

20–21. GAD

20. *that enlargeth Gad.* Gad's territory was east of Jordan—the territory of Sihon, king of the Amorites, and was larger than the territory of any of the Western tribes. Gad's 'enlarger' is God.

as a lioness. Gad was famed for courage and success in war; I Chron. XII, 8 f.

arm . . . crown. The hosts of his enemies . . . and their leaders.

21. *and he chose a first part.* Gad is praised for his foresight in being the first of all the tribes to choose his territory; Num. XXXII, 1 f.

portion of a ruler. Or, 'commander's portion,' a district worthy of a martial leader. The meaning of this and the following line is very uncertain.

there came the heads. He took his part in the conquest of Western Palestine.

he executed the righteousness of the LORD. He (Gad) fulfilled that which he had promised; *viz.* to cross the Jordan and assist the other tribes to dispossess their enemies (Num. XXXII, 31 f). This is probably a case of the Perfect of certainty—the future action being viewed as past. In this way he did his duty in carrying out the righteous will and ordinances of God who had decreed that Israel should inherit the land of Canaan.

22. DAN

22. *lion's whelp.* In the Blessing of Jacob (Gen. XLIX, 17), Dan is compared to a serpent for mischievous subtlety. Here he is spoken of as a lion for agility, as a young lion leaping forth from the crevices and caves of the rocks of Bashan, a land celebrated for the size and strength of its cattle (Deut. XXXII, 14). Both similes refer to the nimbleness and adventurous spirit for which the tribe of Dan was celebrated. Samson was a Danite.

23. And of Naphtali he said:
O Naphtali, satisfied with favour,
And full with the blessing of the LORD:
Possess thou the sea and the south.

24. And of Asher he said:
Blessed be Asher above sons;
Let him be the favoured of his brethren,
And let him dip his foot in oil.
25. Iron and brass shall be thy bars;
And as thy days, so shall thy strength be.

26. There is none like unto God, O Jeshurun,
Who rideth upon the heaven as thy help,
And in His excellency on the skies.*vi.
27. The eternal God is a dwelling-place,
And underneath are the everlasting arms;
And He thrust out the enemy from before thee,
And said: 'Destroy.'

23 דָּן גּוּר אַרְיֵה יְזַנֵּק מִן־הַבָּשָׁן׃ וּלְנַפְתָּלִי אָמַר נַפְתָּלִי שְׂבַע
24 רָצוֹן וּמָלֵא בִּרְכַּת יְהוָה יָם וְדָרוֹם יְרָשָׁה׃ ס וּלְאָשֵׁר
אָמַר בָּרוּךְ מִבָּנִים אָשֵׁר יְהִי רְצוּי אֶחָיו וְטֹבֵל בַּשֶּׁמֶן רַגְלוֹ׃
כה 26 בַּרְזֶל וּנְחֹשֶׁת מִנְעָלֶךָ וּכְיָמֶיךָ דָּבְאֶךָ׃ אֵין כָּאֵל יְשֻׁרוּן
ששי 27 רֹכֵב שָׁמַיִם בְּעֶזְרֶךָ וּבְגַאֲוָתוֹ שְׁחָקִים׃* מְעֹנָה אֱלֹהֵי קֶדֶם
וּמִתַּחַת זְרֹעֹת עוֹלָם וַיְגָרֶשׁ מִפָּנֶיךָ אוֹיֵב וַיֹּאמֶר הַשְׁמֵד׃

28. And Israel dwelleth in safety,
The fountain of Jacob alone,
In a land of corn and wine;
Yea, his heavens drop down dew.

23. NAPHTALI

23. *satisfied with favour.* Satiated with good will. 'Ancient and modern writers vie with one another in praising the soil and climate of the territory owned by Naphtali' (Driver).

possess thou the sea. The sea of Kinnereth; *i.e.* Lake Tiberias.

the south. On the west side of the sea of Kinnereth, Naphtali's territory was 'so styled in contrast to the main possessions of the tribe which were further north' (Driver). Its soil was specially fruitful in the region of Huleh and on the shore of the sea. The 'fruits of Kinnereth' are celebrated in the Talmud.

24–25. ASHER

24. *blessed be Asher above sons.* An exposition of the meaning of the name Asher ('happy'). He was to be blessed 'above sons'; *i.e.* to enjoy exceptional prosperity.

the favoured. Favoured of his brethren, so that they delight in his good fortune,

dip his foot in oil. A metaphor for great abundance. The olive tree was specially fruitful in the territory of Asher.

25. *iron and brass shall be thy bars.* Asher's dwelling shall be impregnable. His territory being in the far north and also on the sea-coast, it needed to be strongly fortified.

as thy days, so shall thy strength be. 'May your strength last like your days' (Moffatt); or, 'as thy younger days, so shall thy old age be' (Leeser).

26–29. EPILOGUE: GOD, THE ABIDING SOURCE OF ISRAEL'S SECURITY, PROSPERITY AND VICTORY

Like the introductory section, *v.* 2–6, the epilogue celebrates the felicity, material and spiritual, of the nation as a whole, through the goodness and protecting care of God.

26. *there is none like unto God, O Jeshurun.* 'There is no God, but the God of Israel' (Onkelos).

rideth upon the heaven as thy help. The Seer compares God to a king in his chariot, and he sees God ride upon the heavens to bring victory to Israel.

in His excellency. In His loftiness and surpassing grandeur.

27. *the eternal God is a dwelling-place.* He is Israel's home and refuge; even, as Moses himself declares, 'O Lord, Thou hast been our dwelling place in all generations' (Ps. XC, 1).

the everlasting arms. i.e. arms whose strength shall never be exhausted. He who is enthroned in heaven above is also the God who is with His people below. 'When thou passest through the waters, I will be with thee; and through the rivers, they shall not overflow thee; when thou walkest through the fire, thou shalt not be burned; neither shall the flame kindle upon thee' (Isa. XLIII, 2). Not only is God a dwelling-place for His people, He is their unfailing support. His everlasting arms, which do not grow weary, are ever bearing them up and sustaining them.

He thrust out the enemy from before thee. God proved that He is His people's everlasting Friend and Helper by the fact that He dislodged their enemies.

28. *dwelleth in safety . . . alone.* 'Every individual Israelite would dwell in isolated security, each one singly under his vine and under his fig-tree. There would be no need to mass themselves together for self-protection against any external enemy' (Rashi).

the fountain of Jacob. 'The succession of generations in Israel figured as a stream ever welling forth freshly from its source' (Driver).

29. Happy art thou, O Israel, who is like unto thee?
A people saved by the LORD,
The shield of thy help,
And that is the sword of thy excellency!
And thine enemies shall dwindle away before thee;
And thou shalt tread upon their high places.vii.

28 וַיִּשְׁכֹּן יִשְׂרָאֵל בֶּטַח בָּדָד עֵין יַעֲקֹב אֶל־אֶרֶץ דָּגָן וְתִירוֹשׁ
29 אַף־שָׁמָיו יַעַרְפוּ־טָל׃ אַשְׁרֶיךָ יִשְׂרָאֵל מִי כָמוֹךָ עַם נוֹשַׁע
בַּיהוָה מָגֵן עֶזְרֶךָ וַאֲשֶׁר־חֶרֶב גַּאֲוָתֶךָ וְיִכָּחֲשׁוּ אֹיְבֶיךָ לָךְ
וְאַתָּה עַל־בָּמוֹתֵימוֹ תִדְרֹךְ׃* ס שביעי

34

CHAPTER XXXIV

1. And Moses went up from the plains of Moab unto mount Nebo, to the top of Pisgah, that is over against Jericho. And the LORD showed him all the land, even Gilead as far as Dan; 2. and all Naphtali, and the land of Ephraim and Manasseh, and all the land of Judah as far as the hinder sea; 3. and the South, and the Plain, even the valley of Jericho the city of

לד

CAP. XXXIV. לד

א וַיַּעַל מֹשֶׁה מֵעַרְבֹת מוֹאָב אֶל־הַר נְבוֹ רֹאשׁ הַפִּסְגָּה אֲשֶׁר
עַל־פְּנֵי יְרֵחוֹ וַיַּרְאֵהוּ יְהוָה אֶת־כָּל־הָאָרֶץ אֶת־הַגִּלְעָד עַד־
2 דָּן׃ וְאֵת כָּל־נַפְתָּלִי וְאֶת־אֶרֶץ אֶפְרַיִם וּמְנַשֶּׁה וְאֵת כָּל־
3 אֶרֶץ יְהוּדָה עַד הַיָּם הָאַחֲרוֹן׃ וְאֶת־הַנֶּגֶב וְאֶת־הַכִּכָּר

29. *who is like unto thee?* What nation on earth is like unto Israel! A unique people, in the care of a unique God.

saved. Victorious, and not by the weapons of war, but by the protecting love of God.

that is the sword of thy excellency. God's protection of Israel is Israel's excellent and triumphant sword.

shall dwindle away. Or, 'shall yield feigned obedience' (RV); the insincere homage rendered by the vanquished to the conqueror.

tread upon their high places. See on XXXII, 13.

'With such golden words Moses takes leave of his people. Israel should have been a brave mountaineer people, if Moses' will had been fulfilled. The land lies apart, surrounded by mountains, seas and deserts—a Divinely blessed corner of the earth that, with industrious cultivation and the security that comes from unity, could have flourished wonderfully. To the north and south of Judea were the trade routes of the ancient world. By its very position alone, it could have become the happiest people of the world, if it had made use of its position and remained faithful to the spirit of its Laws' (Herder).

4. THE DEATH OF MOSES

CHAPTER XXXIV

Before his eyes close for ever, Moses beholds from afar the Promised Land from the top of Pisgah, and dies there according to God's decree. His incomparable rank as a prophet and unique place in the history of Israel.

1. *went up . . . Nebo.* From that height he came down no more.

'Amidst the tears of the people, the women beating their breasts and the children giving way to uncontrolled wailing, he withdrew. At a certain point in his ascent he made a sign to the weeping multitude to advance no further, taking with him only the elders, the high priest Eleazar and the general Joshua. At the top of the mountain, he dismissed the elders, and then, as he was embracing Eleazar and Joshua, and still speaking to them, a cloud suddenly stood over him, and he vanished in a deep valley' (Josephus).

unto mount Nebo, to the top of Pisgah. 'Pisgah' was the specific name for a series of mountain-ranges in the high plateau of Moab. In Deut. XXXII, 49, as well as in Num. XXVII, 12, these ranges are designated by the more general name of הר העברים, *i.e.* 'the mountain of the regions beyond'. Nebo was the special name of one of these mountain-ranges (cf. Num. XXI, 20).

even Gilead as far as Dan. Better, *all the land—Gilead unto Dan* (G. A. Smith).

In the clear air of Palestine, he saw the Land lying before him. From the top of Pisgah all Western Palestine is in sight—the undulating forests of Southern Gilead, the snow-clad top of Hermon, mounts Tabor and Gilboa, Ebal and Gerizim, the heights of Benjamin and Judah, the Mount of Olives, and Zion, Bethlehem and Hebron and Beersheba. Sifri states that Moses was given something more than a mere physical glimpse of the Holy Land. He was shown all the land of Israel as it then was in its prosperity, and as it would be in the days of its adversity. He was given a prophetic vision of the main episodes in the future history of Israel; so that he saw Samson and Gideon, Deborah and David, taking up his unfinished task of leadership and was vouchsafed a vision of all that would happen unto Israel till the Judgment Day.

3. *the South.* The Negeb; southern Judea.

valley of Jericho. The Plain through which Jordan flows into the Dead Sea.

palm-trees, as far as Zoar. 4. And the LORD said unto him: 'This is the land which I swore unto Abraham, unto Isaac, and unto Jacob, saying: I will give it unto thy seed; I have caused thee to see it with thine eyes, but thou shalt not go over thither.' 5. So Moses the servant of the LORD died there in the land of Moab, according to the word of the LORD. 6. And he was buried in the valley of the land of Moab over against Bethpeor; and no man knoweth of his sepulchre unto this day. 7. And Moses was a hundred and twenty years old when he died; his eye was not dim, nor his natural force abated. 8. And the children of Israel wept for Moses in the plains of Moab thirty days; so the days of weeping in the mourning for Moses were ended. 9. And Joshua the son of Nun was full of the spirit of wisdom; for Moses had laid his hands upon him; and the children of Israel hearkened unto him, and did as the

4 בִּקְעַ֛ת יְרֵח֥וֹ עִ֣יר הַתְּמָרִ֖ים עַד־צֹֽעַר׃ וַיֹּ֨אמֶר יְהוָ֜ה אֵלָ֗יו
זֹ֤את הָאָ֙רֶץ֙ אֲשֶׁ֨ר נִשְׁבַּ֜עְתִּי לְאַבְרָהָ֨ם לְיִצְחָ֤ק וּֽלְיַעֲקֹב֙
לֵאמֹ֔ר לְזַרְעֲךָ֖ אֶתְּנֶ֑נָּה הֶרְאִיתִ֣יךָ בְעֵינֶ֔יךָ וְשָׁ֖מָּה לֹ֥א תַעֲבֹֽר׃
ה וַיָּ֨מָת שָׁ֜ם מֹשֶׁ֧ה עֶֽבֶד־יְהוָ֛ה בְּאֶ֥רֶץ מוֹאָ֖ב עַל־פִּ֥י יְהוָֽה׃
6 וַיִּקְבֹּ֨ר אֹת֤וֹ בַגַּי֙ בְּאֶ֣רֶץ מוֹאָ֔ב מ֖וּל בֵּ֣ית פְּע֑וֹר וְלֹא־יָדַ֥ע
7 אִישׁ֙ אֶת־קְבֻ֣רָת֔וֹ עַ֖ד הַיּ֥וֹם הַזֶּֽה׃ וּמֹשֶׁ֗ה בֶּן־מֵאָ֧ה וְעֶשְׂרִ֛ים
8 שָׁנָ֖ה בְּמֹת֑וֹ לֹא־כָהֲתָ֥ה עֵינ֖וֹ וְלֹא־נָ֥ס לֵחֹֽה׃ וַיִּבְכּוּ֩ בְנֵ֨י
יִשְׂרָאֵ֧ל אֶת־מֹשֶׁ֛ה בְּעַרְבֹ֥ת מוֹאָ֖ב שְׁלֹשִׁ֣ים י֑וֹם וַיִּתְּמ֕וּ יְמֵ֥י
9 בְכִ֖י אֵ֥בֶל מֹשֶֽׁה׃ וִיהוֹשֻׁ֣עַ בִּן־נ֗וּן מָלֵא֙ ר֣וּחַ חָכְמָ֔ה כִּֽי־סָמַ֥ךְ
מֹשֶׁ֛ה אֶת־יָדָ֖יו עָלָ֑יו וַיִּשְׁמְע֨וּ אֵלָ֤יו בְּנֵֽי־יִשְׂרָאֵל֙ וַֽיַּעֲשׂ֔וּ

4. *thou shalt not go over thither.* 'To labour and not to see the end of our labours; to sow and not to reap; to be removed from this earthly scene before our work has been appreciated, and when it will be carried on not by ourselves but by others—is a law so common in the highest characters of history, that none can be said to be altogether exempt from its operation' (Stanley).

5. *so Moses the servant of the LORD.* Ibn Ezra remarks that even in the act of dying Moses was still the servant of God, obeying the command of the Master.

died there. Scripture thus stresses the fact that Moses was human in regard to death, even as he was as to birth; see on Exod. II, 1.

according to the word of the LORD. lit. 'at the mouth of the LORD'. God, say the Rabbis, spares the righteous the bitterness of death, and takes away their souls with a kiss.

6. *he was buried in the valley.* In some depression on the Pisgah range. According to Rabbinic legend, God buried Moses in a grave that had been prepared for him at Creation (Ethics of the Fathers, v, 6).

no man knoweth of his sepulchre. It has been hidden from human ken, say the Rabbis, so that it might not become a place of pilgrimage for those who deify national heroes. He lies in an unknown sepulchre and unvisited tomb. It is the seal of his self-effacement.

unto this day. These words, as the whole of the latter portion of this chapter, were added by Joshua. This is the opinion of Rabbi Judah. Poetic and touchingly beautiful are the words of Rabbi Meir: 'These verses, the Holy One, blessed be He, dictated, and Moses wrote them down in tears.' Such also was the view of Philo:—'The Divine Spirit fell upon him, and he prophesied with discernment while still alive the story of his own death; told, ere the end, how the end came; told how he was buried with none present, surely by no mortal hands but by immortal powers; how all the nation wept and mourned for him a whole month and made open display, private and public, of their sorrow, in memory of his vast benevolence and watchful care for each one of them and for all.'

7. *nor his natural force abated.* lit. 'neither had his freshness fled'. He suffered none of the infirmities of age, and the natural freshness of his body had not become dried up.

8. *the mourning for Moses were ended.* The days of mourning even for the best men must have an end. It is wrong unduly to prolong them. The workman passes, but the work must be continued. 'No sooner did the sun of Moses set, than the sun of Joshua rose' (Talmud).

9. *spirit of wisdom.* But another name for the Spirit of God (Ibn Ezra).

Moses had laid his hands upon him. Thus endowing him with a portion of his spirit, and imparting the necessary qualification to be his successor; Num. XXVII, 18.

10. *and there hath not arisen . . . like unto Moses.* The pre-eminence of Moses is one of the Articles of Maimonides' Creed. 'To lead into freedom a people long crushed by tyranny; to discipline and order such a mighty host; to harden them into fighting men, before whom warlike tribes quailed and walled cities went down; to repress discontent and jealousy and mutiny require some towering character—a character blending in highest expression the

LORD commanded Moses. 10. And there hath not arisen a prophet since in Israel like unto Moses, whom the LORD knew face to face; 11. in all the signs and the wonders, which the LORD sent him to do in the land of Egypt, to Pharaoh, and to all his servants, and to all his land; 12. and in all the mighty hand, and in all the great terror, which Moses wrought in the sight of all Israel.

י כַּאֲשֶׁר צִוָּה יְהֹוָה אֶת־מֹשֶׁה׃ וְלֹא־קָם נָבִיא עוֹד בְּיִשְׂרָאֵל
11 כְּמֹשֶׁה אֲשֶׁר יְדָעוֹ יְהֹוָה פָּנִים אֶל־פָּנִים׃ לְכָל־הָאֹתֹת
וְהַמּוֹפְתִים אֲשֶׁר שְׁלָחוֹ יְהֹוָה לַעֲשׂוֹת בְּאֶרֶץ מִצְרָיִם
12 לְפַרְעֹה וּלְכָל־עֲבָדָיו וּלְכָל־אַרְצוֹ׃ וּלְכֹל הַיָּד הַחֲזָקָה
וּלְכֹל הַמּוֹרָא הַגָּדוֹל אֲשֶׁר עָשָׂה מֹשֶׁה לְעֵינֵי כָּל־יִשְׂרָאֵל׃

חזק

נשלמו חמשה חומשי תורה. תהלה לאל גדול ונורא:

סכום פסוקי דספר דברים תשע מאות וחמשים וחמשה הנ״ה סימן: וחציו. ועשית על פי הדבר אשר יגידו לך: ופרשיותיו אחד עשר אסרו חג בעבותים סימן: וסדריו עשרים ושבעה יפיח אמונה יגיד צדק סימן: ופרקיו שלשים וארבעה אודה י״י בכל לבב סימן: מניין הפתוחות שלשים וארבעה והסתומות מאה ועשרים וארבעה הכל מאה וחמשים ושמנה פרשיות וכסא כבוד ינחילם סימן:

סכום הפסוקים של כל התורה חמשת אלפים ושמנה מאות וארבעים וחמשה ואור החמה יהיה שבעתים סימן: וחציו. וישם עליו את החשן ויתן אל החשן את האורים ואת התמים: מניין פתוחות של כל התורה מאתים ותשעים יבא דודי לגנו ויאכל פרי מגדיו סימן: והסתומות שלש מאות ושבעים ותשעה או אסרה אסר על נפשה בשבעה סימן: נמצאו מניין כל הפרשיות פתוחות וסתומות שש מאות וששים ותשעה לא תחסר כל בה סימן:

qualities of politician, patriot, philosopher, and statesman—the union of the wisdom of the Egyptian with the unselfish devotion of the meekest of men. . . . To dispute about the inspiration of such a man were to dispute about words. From the depths of the Unseen such characters must draw their strength; from fountains that flow only to the pure in heart must come their wisdom. Of something more real than matter; of something higher than the stars; of a light that will endure when suns are dead and dark; of a purpose of which the physical universe is but a passing phase, such lives tell' (Henry George).

face to face. See on Num. XII, 8.

12. *In the sight of all Israel.* 'Such was the end of the Hebrew Lawgiver—a man who, considered merely in an historical light, without any reference to his Divine inspiration, has exercised a more extensive and permanent influence over the destinies of his own nation and mankind at large than any other individual recorded in the annals of the world' (Milman).

According to Jewish custom, the completion of any of the Five Books of the Torah is marked in the Synagogue by the congregation exclaiming, חזק חזק ונתחזק, 'Be strong, be strong, and let us strengthen one another.' *Be strong. i.e.* to carry out the teaching contained in the Book just completed.

The Massoretic Notes state the number of verses in the Book of Deuteronomy to be 955; its Sedrahs (parshiyoth) 11; its chapters 34; and the number of verses in the whole Torah to be 5,845.

Chapters XXXIII *and* XXXIV *form the Reading for Rejoicing of the Law. When the last verses of* XXXIV *have been read, the Torah is immediately begun again by the reading of Gen.* I–II, 3.

JOSHUA I

Chapter I

1. Now it came to pass after the death of Moses the servant of the Lord, that the Lord spoke unto Joshua the son of Nun, Moses' minister, saying: 2. 'Moses My servant is dead; now therefore arise, go over this Jordan, thou, and all this people, unto the land which I do give to them, even to the children of Israel. 3. Every place that the sole of your foot shall tread upon, to you have I given it, as I spoke unto Moses. 4. From the wilderness, and this Lebanon, even unto the great river, the river Euphrates, all the land of the Hittites, and unto the Great Sea toward the going down of the sun, shall be your border. 5. There shall not any man be able to stand before thee all the days of thy life; as I was with Moses, so I will be with thee; I will not fail thee, nor forsake thee. 6. Be strong and of good courage; for thou shalt cause this people to inherit the land which I swore unto their fathers to give them. 7. Only be strong and very courageous, to observe to do according to all the law, which Moses My servant commanded thee; turn not from it to the right hand or to the left, that thou mayest have good success whithersoever thou goest. 8. This book of the law shall not depart out of thy mouth, but thou shalt meditate therein day and night, that thou mayest observe to do according to all that is written therein; for then thou shalt make thy ways prosperous, and

א וַיְהִי אַחֲרֵי מוֹת מֹשֶׁה עֶבֶד יְהוָה וַיֹּאמֶר יְהוָה אֶל־יְהוֹשֻׁעַ
2 בִּן־נוּן מְשָׁרֵת מֹשֶׁה לֵאמֹר׃ מֹשֶׁה עַבְדִּי מֵת וְעַתָּה קוּם
עֲבֹר אֶת־הַיַּרְדֵּן הַזֶּה אַתָּה וְכָל־הָעָם הַזֶּה אֶל־הָאָרֶץ אֲשֶׁר
3 אָנֹכִי נֹתֵן לָהֶם לִבְנֵי יִשְׂרָאֵל׃ כָּל־מָקוֹם אֲשֶׁר תִּדְרֹךְ
כַּף־רַגְלְכֶם בּוֹ לָכֶם נְתַתִּיו כַּאֲשֶׁר דִּבַּרְתִּי אֶל־מֹשֶׁה׃
4 מֵהַמִּדְבָּר וְהַלְּבָנוֹן הַזֶּה וְעַד־הַנָּהָר הַגָּדוֹל נְהַר־פְּרָת כֹּל
אֶרֶץ הַחִתִּים וְעַד־הַיָּם הַגָּדוֹל מְבוֹא הַשָּׁמֶשׁ יִהְיֶה גְּבוּלְכֶם׃
ה לֹא־יִתְיַצֵּב אִישׁ לְפָנֶיךָ כֹּל יְמֵי חַיֶּיךָ כַּאֲשֶׁר הָיִיתִי עִם־
6 מֹשֶׁה אֶהְיֶה עִמָּךְ לֹא אַרְפְּךָ וְלֹא אֶעֶזְבֶךָּ׃ חֲזַק וֶאֱמָץ
כִּי אַתָּה תַּנְחִיל אֶת־הָעָם הַזֶּה אֶת־הָאָרֶץ אֲשֶׁר־נִשְׁבַּעְתִּי
7 לַאֲבוֹתָם לָתֵת לָהֶם׃ רַק חֲזַק וֶאֱמַץ מְאֹד לִשְׁמֹר לַעֲשׂוֹת
כְּכָל־הַתּוֹרָה אֲשֶׁר צִוְּךָ מֹשֶׁה עַבְדִּי אַל־תָּסוּר מִמֶּנּוּ יָמִין
8 וּשְׂמֹאול לְמַעַן תַּשְׂכִּיל בְּכֹל אֲשֶׁר תֵּלֵךְ׃ לֹא־יָמוּשׁ סֵפֶר
הַתּוֹרָה הַזֶּה מִפִּיךָ וְהָגִיתָ בּוֹ יוֹמָם וָלַיְלָה לְמַעַן תִּשְׁמֹר
לַעֲשׂוֹת כְּכָל־הַכָּתוּב בּוֹ כִּי־אָז תַּצְלִיחַ אֶת־דְּרָכֶךָ וְאָז

v. 6. פתח באתנח v. 7. סבירין ממנה ibid. מלא ו'

Israel's story did not close with the death of Moses. This is one of the lessons which the choice of this chapter as the Prophetical Reading for the last Sidrah of the Pentateuch is to teach. The reading of the first chapter of Joshua, which opens the section of Scripture known as 'The Prophets', is to remind us that though Moses is dead, his work and message are eternal, and remain the undying task of all future generations in Israel to fulfil.

The Book of Joshua records the conquest of the Promised Land (I–XII); the Division of the Land (XIII–XXI — Israel's 'Domesday Book') and Joshua's Farewell Addresses (XXII–XXIV).

Moses' Successor

1. *the LORD spoke.* This characteristic phrase of Scripture is one of the most obvious indications of what we call 'inspiration'. We are not in a position to define the exact mode in which the Divine message was communicated. Was it an inner conviction borne in upon the soul, voiceless but clear and definite? We cannot tell. '*How* God reveals Himself to His chosen messengers will scarcely ever be understood. It is the greatest of mysteries; although *that* he reveals Himself is the greatest of certainties' (Marti).

Moses' minister. This designation, which is otherwise quite unnecessary, gives the reason why Joshua was worthy of such revelation: he had ministered unto Moses (Elijah Wilna).

2. *Moses My servant.* Not everyone who calls himself 'servant of the Lord' does God Himself so designate (Sifri).

4. *the land of the Hittites.* The Hittite Empire shall be the northern boundary of the Holy Land.

Great Sea. The Mediterranean Sea.

your border. This was attained during the reigns of David and Solomon; see p. 717.

8. *this book of the law.* The copy written by Moses and delivered to the Levites and elders; Deut. XXXI, 9.

meditate therein. As it was the duty of Israel's ruler to do; see Deut. XVII, 19.

then thou shalt have good success. 9. Have not I commanded thee? Be strong and of good courage; be not affrighted, neither be thou dismayed; for the LORD thy God is with thee whithersoever thou goest.'[1] ¶ 10. Then Joshua commanded the officers of the people, saying: 11. 'Pass through the midst of the camp, and command the people, saying: Prepare you victuals; for within three days ye are to pass over this Jordan, to go in to possess the land, which the LORD your God giveth you to possess it.' ¶ 12. And to the Reubenites, and to the Gadites, and to the half-tribe of Manasseh, spoke Joshua, saying: 13. 'Remember the word which Moses the servant of the LORD commanded you, saying: The LORD your God giveth you rest, and will give you this land. 14. Your wives, your little ones, and your cattle, shall abide in the land which Moses gave you beyond the Jordan; but ye shall pass over before your brethren armed, all the mighty men of valour, and shall help them; 15. until the LORD have given your brethren rest, as unto you, and they also have possessed the land which the LORD your God giveth them; then ye shall return unto the land of your possession, and possess it, which Moses the servant of the LORD gave you beyond the Jordan toward the sunrising.' ¶ 16. And they answered Joshua, saying: 'All that thou hast commanded us we will do, and whithersoever thou sendest us we will go. 17. According as we hearkened unto Moses in all things, so will we hearken unto thee; only the LORD thy God be with thee, as He was with Moses. 18. Whosoever he be that shall rebel against thy commandment, and shall not hearken unto thy words in all that thou commandest him, he shall be put to death; only be strong and of good courage.'

[1] Sephardim conclude here.

9 תַּשְׂכִּיל׃ הֲלוֹא צִוִּיתִיךָ חֲזַק וֶאֱמָץ אַל־תַּעֲרֹץ וְאַל־תֵּחָת כִּי
י עִמְּךָ יְהוָה אֱלֹהֶיךָ בְּכֹל אֲשֶׁר תֵּלֵךְ׃ * וַיְצַו יְהוֹשֻׁעַ אֶת־
11 שֹׁטְרֵי הָעָם לֵאמֹר׃ עִבְרוּ ׀ בְּקֶרֶב הַמַּחֲנֶה וְצַוּוּ אֶת־הָעָם
לֵאמֹר הָכִינוּ לָכֶם צֵידָה כִּי בְּעוֹד ׀ שְׁלֹשֶׁת יָמִים אַתֶּם עֹבְרִים
אֶת־הַיַּרְדֵּן הַזֶּה לָבוֹא לָרֶשֶׁת אֶת־הָאָרֶץ אֲשֶׁר יְהוָה
12 אֱלֹהֵיכֶם נֹתֵן לָכֶם לְרִשְׁתָּהּ׃ וְלָרְאוּבֵנִי וְלַגָּדִי וְלַחֲצִי
13 שֵׁבֶט הַמְנַשֶּׁה אָמַר יְהוֹשֻׁעַ לֵאמֹר׃ זָכוֹר אֶת־הַדָּבָר אֲשֶׁר
צִוָּה אֶתְכֶם מֹשֶׁה עֶבֶד־יְהוָה לֵאמֹר יְהוָה אֱלֹהֵיכֶם מֵנִיחַ
14 לָכֶם וְנָתַן לָכֶם אֶת־הָאָרֶץ הַזֹּאת׃ נְשֵׁיכֶם טַפְּכֶם וּמִקְנֵיכֶם
יֵשְׁבוּ בָּאָרֶץ אֲשֶׁר נָתַן לָכֶם מֹשֶׁה בְּעֵבֶר הַיַּרְדֵּן וְאַתֶּם
תַּעַבְרוּ חֲמֻשִׁים לִפְנֵי אֲחֵיכֶם כֹּל גִּבּוֹרֵי הַחַיִל וַעֲזַרְתֶּם
טו אוֹתָם׃ עַד אֲשֶׁר־יָנִיחַ יְהוָה ׀ לַאֲחֵיכֶם כָּכֶם וְיָרְשׁוּ גַם־
הֵמָּה אֶת־הָאָרֶץ אֲשֶׁר־יְהוָה אֱלֹהֵיכֶם נֹתֵן לָהֶם וְשַׁבְתֶּם
לְאֶרֶץ יְרֻשַּׁתְכֶם וִירִשְׁתֶּם אוֹתָהּ אֲשֶׁר ׀ נָתַן לָכֶם מֹשֶׁה
16 עֶבֶד יְהוָה בְּעֵבֶר הַיַּרְדֵּן מִזְרַח הַשָּׁמֶשׁ׃ וַיַּעֲנוּ אֶת־יְהוֹשֻׁעַ
לֵאמֹר כֹּל אֲשֶׁר־צִוִּיתָנוּ נַעֲשֶׂה וְאֶל־כָּל־אֲשֶׁר תִּשְׁלָחֵנוּ
17 נֵלֵךְ׃ כְּכֹל אֲשֶׁר־שָׁמַעְנוּ אֶל־מֹשֶׁה כֵּן נִשְׁמַע אֵלֶיךָ רַק
18 יִהְיֶה יְהוָה אֱלֹהֶיךָ עִמָּךְ כַּאֲשֶׁר הָיָה עִם־מֹשֶׁה׃ כָּל־אִישׁ
אֲשֶׁר־יַמְרֶה אֶת־פִּיךָ וְלֹא־יִשְׁמַע אֶת־דְּבָרֶיךָ לְכֹל אֲשֶׁר־
תְּצַוֶּנּוּ יוּמָת רַק חֲזַק וֶאֱמָץ׃

v. 9. קמץ בז״ק *כאן מסיימין הספרדים v. 18. נ״א אל

9. *have not I commanded thee.* See Deut. XXXI, 7.

11. *prepare you victuals.* Commissariat is of primary importance in campaigning, especially in a hostile country.

12. *Reubenites.* He reminds them of the promise they gave Moses to cross Jordan and assist their brethren in the conquest of Canaan; Num. XXXII, 20–32.

13. *rest.* Cf. Deut. XII, 9.

17. *only the LORD thy God be with thee. i.e.* that thou walk in the ways of Moses, so that the LORD be with thee (Kimchi).

18. *rebel.* They desire strict military discipline. *only be strong and of good courage.* The Rabbis understood this call for courage to apply with especial force in the realm of the spirit: 'There are four directions in which a man needs constantly to strengthen himself; namely, in Torah (*i.e.* in his grasp of religious fundamentals) and Good Deeds (beneficence is the result of habitual action), in Prayer (daily worship not only expresses, but kindles the flame of devotion in the soul), and in *Derech Eretz* (*i.e.* harmonious relationship with his fellow-men).'

ADDITIONAL NOTES TO DEUTERONOMY

THE SHEMA

ITS MEANING AND HISTORY

A

THE MEANING OF THE SHEMA

'Hear, O Israel, the LORD is our God, the LORD is One.' These words enshrine Judaism's greatest contribution to the religious thought of mankind. They constitute the primal confession of Faith in the religion of the Synagogue, declaring that the Holy God worshipped and proclaimed by Israel is One; and that He alone is God, Who was, is, and ever will be. That opening sentence of the Shema rightly occupies the central place in Jewish religious thought; for every other Jewish belief turns upon it: all goes back to it; all flows from it. The following are some of its far-reaching implications, negative and positive, that have been of vital importance in the spiritual history of man.

ITS NEGATIONS

Polytheism. This sublime pronouncement of absolute monotheism was a declaration of war against all *polytheism*, the worship of many deities, and *paganism*, the deification of any finite thing or being or natural force. It scornfully rejected the star-cults and demon worship of Babylonia, the animal worship of Egypt, the nature worship of Greece, the Emperor worship of Rome, as well as the stone, tree, and serpent idolatries of other heathen religions, with their human sacrifices, lustful rites, their barbarism and inhumanity. Polytheism breaks the moral unity of man, and involves a variety of moral standards; that is to say, no standard at all. The study of Comparative Religion clearly shows that, in polytheism, 'side by side with a High God of Justice and Truth, the cults of a goddess of sensual love, a god of intoxicating drink, or of thieves and liars, might be maintained' (Farnell). It certainly is not the soil on which a high and consistent ethical system grows. This is true of even its highest forms, such as the heathenism of the Greeks. 'The Olympian divinities merely copied and even exaggerated the pleasures and pains, the perfections and imperfections, the loftiness and baseness of life on earth. Man could not receive any moral guidance from them. The Greeks possessed nothing even remotely resembling a Decalogue to restrain and bind them' (Kastein). Despite the love of beauty that characterized the Greeks, and despite their iridescent minds, they remained barbarians religiously and morally; and their race was held up by their pupils, the Romans of Imperial days, as the prototype of everything that was mendacious, cruel, grasping and unjust. The fruit of Greek heathen teaching is, in fact, best seen in the horrors of the arena, the wholesale crucifixions, and the unspeakable bestialities of these same pupils, the Romans of Imperial days.

Quite other were the works of Hebrew Monotheism. Its preaching of the One, Omnipotent God liberated man from slavery to nature; from fear of demons and goblins and ghosts; from all creatures of man's infantile or diseased imagination. And that One God is One who 'is sanctified by righteousness', who is of purer eyes than to endure the sight of evil, or to tolerate wrong. This has been named *ethical monotheism*. There may have been independent recognition of the unity of the Divine nature among some peoples; *e.g.* the unitary sun-cult of Ikhnaton in Egypt, or some faint glimpses of it in ancient Babylon. But in neither of these systems of worship was it essentially ethical, completely transfused with the Moral Law, and holding moral conduct to be the beginning and end of the religious life. Likewise, moral thinking and moral practices had indeed existed from immemorial times everywhere; but the sublime idea that morality is something Divine, spiritual in its inmost essence —this is the distinctive teaching of the Hebrew Scriptures. In Hebrew monotheism, ethical values are not only the highest of human values, but exclusively the only values of eternal worth. 'There is none upon earth that I desire beside Thee,' exclaims the Hebrew Psalmist. These words are but a poetic translation of the Shema in terms of religious experience.

Dualism. The Shema excludes *dualism*, any assumption of two rival powers of Light and Darkness, of the universe being regarded as the arena of a perpetual conflict between the principles of Good and Evil. This was the religion of Zoroaster, the seer of ancient Persia. His teaching was far in advance of all other heathen religions. Yet it was in utter contradiction to the belief in One, Supreme Ruler of the World, shaping the light, and at the same time controlling the darkness (Isa. XLV, 7). In the Jewish view, the universe with all its conflicting forces, is marvellously harmonized in its totality; and, in the sum, evil is overruled and made a new source of strength for the victory of the good. 'He maketh peace in His high places.' Zoroastrianism is alleged by some to be responsible for many folklore elements in Jewish theology, especially for its angelology. But though later generations in Judaism did speak of Satan and a whole hierarchy of angels, these were invariably thought of as absolutely the *creatures* of God. To attribute Divine powers to any of these beings, and deem them independent of God, or in any way on a par with the Supreme Being, would at all times have been deemed in Jewry to be wild blasphemy. It is noteworthy that the Jewish Mystics placed man—

because he is endowed with free will—higher in the scale of spiritual existence than any mere 'messenger', which is the literal translation of the word *angel*, as well as of its Hebrew original, מלאך.

Pantheism. And the Shema excludes *pantheism*, which considers the totality of things to be the Divine. The inevitable result of believing that all things are divine, and all equally divine, is that the distinction between right and wrong, between holy and unholy, loses it meaning. Pantheism, in addition, robs the Divine Being of conscious personality. In Judaism, on the contrary, though God pervades the universe, He transcends it. 'The heavens are the work of Thy hands. They shall perish but Thou shalt endure; yea, all of them shall wax old like a garment; as a vesture Thou shalt change them, and they shall be changed. But Thou art the same, and Thy years shall have no end' (Psalm CII, 26–8). The Rabbis expressed the same thought when they said: 'The Holy One, blessed be He, encompasses the universe, but the universe does not encompass Him.' And so far from submerging the Creator in His created universe, they would have fully endorsed the lines,

'Though earth and man were gone,
And suns and universes ceased to be,
And Thou wert left alone,
Every existence would exist in Thee'
(Emily Brontë).

Belief in the Trinity. In the same way, the Shema excludes *the trinity* of the Christian creed as a violation of the Unity of God. Trinitarianism has at times been indistinguishable from tritheism; *i.e.* the belief in three separate gods. To this were added later cults of the Virgin and the saints, all of them quite incompatible with pure monotheism. Judaism recognizes no intermediary between God and man; and declares that prayer is to be directed to God alone, and to no other being in the heavens above or on earth beneath.

Its Positive Implications

Brotherhood of Man. The belief in the unity of the Human Race is the natural corollary of the Unity of God, since the One God must be the God of the whole of humanity. It was impossible for polytheism to reach the conception of One Humanity. It could no more have written the tenth chapter of Genesis, which traces the descent of all the races of man to a common ancestry, than it could have written the first chapter of Genesis, which proclaims the One God as the Creator of the universe and all that is therein. Through Hebrew monotheism alone was it possible to teach the Brotherhood of Man; and it was Hebrew monotheism which first declared, 'Thou shalt love thy neighbour as thyself. And the stranger that sojourneth with you shall be unto you as the homeborn among you, and thou shalt love him as thyself' (Lev. XIX, 18, 34).

Unity of the Universe. The conception of monotheism has been the basis of modern science, and of the modern world-view. Belief in the Unity of God opened the eyes of man to the unity of nature; 'that there is a unity and harmony in the *structure* of things, because of the unity of their *Source*' (L. Roth). A noted scientist wrote: —'The One, Sole God—conceived as the Supreme and Absolute Being who is the Source of all the moral aspirations of man—that conception of the Deity accustomed the human spirit to the idea of Reason underlying all things, and kindled in man the desire to learn that Reason' (Dubois-Reymond). Likewise, A. N. Whitehead declares that the conception of absolute cosmic regularity is monotheistic in origin. And 'every fresh discovery confirms the fact that in all Nature's infinite variety there is one single Principle at work; that there is one controlling Power which—in the words of our Adon Olam hymn—is of no beginning and no end, existing before all things were formed, and remaining when all are gone' (Haffkine).

Unity of History. And this One God—Judaism teaches—is the righteous and omnipotent Ruler of the universe. In polytheism, it was practically impossible to arrive at 'the conception of a single Providence ruling the world by fixed laws; the multitude of divinities suggests the possibility of discord in the divine cosmos; and instils a sense of the capricious and incalculable in the unseen world' (Farnell). Not so Judaism, with its passionate belief in a Judge of all the earth, who can and will do right. As early as the days of the Second Temple, the idea of the Sovereignty of God was linked with the Shema. The Rabbis ordained that the words, 'Hear, O Israel, the LORD is our God, the LORD is One,' should be immediately followed by ברוך שם כבוד מלכותו לעולם ועד, 'Blessed be His name, Whose glorious kingdom is for ever and ever'—the proclamation of the ultimate triumph of justice on earth. Jewish monotheism thus stresses the supremacy of the will of God for righteousness over the course of history: '*One* will rules all to *one* end—the world as it ought to be' (Moore).

The Messianic Kingdom. The cardinal Jewish teaching of a living God who rules history, has changed the heart and the whole outlook of humanity. Not only the hallowing of human life, but the hallowing of history flows from this doctrine of a Holy God, who is hallowed by righteousness. It is only the Jew, and those who have adopted Israel's Scriptures as their own, who see all events in nature and history as parts of one all-embracing plan; who behold God's world as a magnificent unity; and who look forward to that sure triumph of justice in humanity on earth which men call the Kingdom of God. And it is only the Jew, and those who have gone to school to the Jew, who can pray, וימליך מלכותיה, 'May His kingdom come.'

Highest among the implications of the Shema is the passionate conviction of the Jew that the day must dawn when all mankind will call upon the One God, when all the peoples will recognize that they are the children of One Father. Nine hundred years ago, Rashi commented as follows on the six words of the Shema: 'He Who now is our God and is not yet recognized by the nations as their God, will yet be the *one* God of the whole world. As it is written in Zephaniah III, 9, *I will restore to the peoples a pure language, that they may call upon the name of the LORD to serve Him with one consent;* and it is said in Zechariah XIV, 9, *And the LORD shall be king over all the earth; in that day shall the LORD be One, and His Name One.*'

A word must be added in regard to the two proof-texts cited by Rashi. The first, 'I will restore to the peoples a pure language, that they may call upon the name of the LORD,' must be reckoned among the most remarkable utterances of the Prophets. It foretells a wonderful transformation of spirit that will come over the peoples of the earth. They are now only groping dimly after the true God, and stammering His praise. But the time will come when they shall adore Him with a full knowledge of Him; and *with one consent* (lit. 'shoulder to shoulder', *i.e.* without any superiority of one over the other), they will form a universal chorus to chant His praise. 'The amazing thing about this prophecy is that it foresees the time when the curse of Babel will be removed from the children of men, and the confusion of tongues will end: one *world-language*, based on man's moral and religious needs, will be the speech in the Kingdom of the Spirit on earth' (Sellin).

As to the words, 'And the LORD shall be king over all the earth; in that day shall the LORD be One, and His Name One,' they are combined with the Shema Yisroel in the Musaph Prayer of the New Year—one of the most solemn portions of the Jewish Liturgy. They also form the last sentence of the Oleynoo prayer, and thus end every statutory Jewish service—morning, afternoon, and evening. There could be no more fitting conclusion for the Jew's daily devotions than this universalist hope of God's Kingdom.

THE HISTORY OF THE SHEMA

The work of the Rabbis. Who unveiled to the masses of the Jewish people the spiritual wonders enshrined in the Shema? It is the immortal merit of the Rabbis in the centuries immediately before and after the common era, that these religious treasures did not remain the possession of the few, but became the heritage of the whole House of Israel. Thanks to the Rabbis, the fulness of that sacred truth gradually saturated the souls of the lowliest, as of the highest, in Israel. The recitation of the Shema was part of the regular daily worship in the Temple. They took it over to the Synagogue, and gave it central place in the morning and evening prayers of every Jew. We may judge the important part it played in the rabbinic consciousness from the fact that the whole Mishnah opens with the question, 'From what hour is the evening Shema to be read?' It is the Rabbis who raised the six words שמע ישראל ד׳אלהינו ד׳אחד to a confession of Faith; who ordained that they be repeated by the entire body of worshippers when the Torah is taken out on Sabbaths and Festivals; in the Sanctification (*Kedusha*) on these sacred occasions; after the Neilah service, as the culmination of the great Day of Atonement; and in man's last hour, when he is setting out to meet his Heavenly Father face to face. In this way, the Shema became the soul-stirring, collective self-expression of Israel's spiritual being. But even in the private prayer of the individual Jew, the Rabbis spared no effort to enhance the solemnity of its utterance. It is to be said audibly, they ordained, the ear hearing what the lips utter; and its last word *echod* ('One') was to be pronounced with special emphasis. All thoughts other than God's Unity must be shut out. It must be spoken with entire collection and concentration of heart and mind (כוונה); the reading of the Shema may not be interrupted even to respond to the salutation of a king. If the words of the Shema are uttered devoutly and reverently—the Rabbis taught—they thrill the very soul of the worshipper and bring him a realization of communion with the Most High. 'When men in prayer declare the Unity of the Holy Name in love and reverence, the walls of earth's darkness are cleft in twain, and the face of the Heavenly King is revealed, lighting up the universe' (Zohar).

The Shema of martyrdom. The unwearied national pedagogy of the Rabbis bore blessed fruit. The Shema became the first prayer of innocent childhood, and the last utterance of the dying. It was the rallying-cry by which a hundred generations in Israel were welded together into one Brotherhood to do the will of their Father in heaven; it was the watchword of the myriads of martyrs who agonized and died for the Unity, 'as the *ultima ratio* of their religion' (Herford). During every persecution and massacre, from the time of the Crusades to the wholesale slaughter of the Jewish population in the Ukraine in the years 1919 to 1921, *Shema Yisroel* has been the last sound on the lips of the victims. All the Jewish martyrologies are written round the Shema. The Jewish Teachers in medieval Germany introduced a regular Benediction for the recital of the Shema at the hour of 'sanctification of the Name'; *i.e.* when a man is facing martyrdom. It is as follows: 'Blessed art Thou, O LORD our God, King of the Universe, who hast sanctified us by Thy commandments and bade us love Thee with all our heart and all our soul, and to sanctify Thy glorious and awful Name in public. Blessed art Thou, O LORD, Who sanctifiest Thy Name amongst the many.' Numberless were the dire occasions when this Benediction was spoken. One instance will suffice. When the hordes of the Crusaders reached Xanten, near the Rhine (June 27, 1096), the Jews of that place were partaking of their Sabbath-eve meal together. The arrival of the Crusaders meant, of course, certain death to them, and the meal was discontinued. But they did not leave the hall until the saintly R. Moses ha-Cohen first said Grace, enlarging the regular text with prayers appropriate to the awful moment. The Grace was concluded with the Shema. Thereupon they went to the synagogue where they all met with martyrdom. It is such happenings, which decimated the Jewish communities in the Rhine region by massacre, and self-immolation to escape baptism, that caused the contemporary Synagogue poet, Kalonymos ben Yehudah, to sing:

'Yea, they slay us and they smite,
Vex our souls with sore affright;
All the closer cleave we, LORD,
To thine everlasting word.
Not a line of all their Mass
Shall our lips in homage pass;
Though they curse, and bind, and kill,
The living God is with us still.
We still are Thine, though limbs are torn;
Better death than life forsworn.
From dying lips the accents swell,
"Thy God is One, O Israel";
And bridegroom answers unto bride,
"The LORD is God, and none beside,"
And, knit with bonds of holiest faith,
They pass to endless life through death.'

The reading of the Shema indeed fulfilled the promise of the Rabbis that it clothes man with invincible lion-strength. It endowed the Jew with the double-edged sword of the spirit against the unutterable terrors of his long night of suffering and exile.

Defence of the Unity. The Rabbis not only trained Israel to the understanding of the vital significance of the Divine Unity; they also defended the Jewish God-idea whenever its purity was threatened by enemies from without or within. They permitted no toying with polytheism, be its disguises ever so ethereal; they brooked no departure, even by a hair's breadth, from the most rigorous monotheism; and rejected absolutely everything that might weaken or obscure it. The fight against idolatry and paganism begun by the Prophets was continued by the Pharisees. Abraham, the father of the Hebrew people, they taught, started on his career as an idol-wrecker. In legends, parables, and discourses, they showed forth the folly and futility of idol-worship, and pointed to the infamy and moral degradation evidenced by the Roman deification of the reigning Emperor. Josephus records that, when Caligula ordered the symbols of his divinity to be erected in the Temple at Jerusalem, tens of thousands of Jews declared their readiness to be trampled to death under the heels of the Roman cavalry, rather than suffer the Jewish belief in the Unity of God to be outraged. 'In the world-wide Roman Empire, it was the Jews alone who refused the erection of statues and the paying of divine homage to Caligula. They thereby saved the honour of the human race, when all the other peoples slavishly obeyed the decree of the Imperial madman' (Fuerst). The Rabbis defended the Unity of God against the Jewish Gnostics, those ancient heretics who blasphemed the God of Israel, ridiculed the Scriptures, and asserted a duality of Divine Powers. And they defended it against the Jewish Christians, who darkened the sky of Israel's monotheism by teaching a novel doctrine of God's 'sonship'; by identifying a man, born of woman, with God; and by advocating the doctrine of a Trinity. Said a Palestinian Rabbi of the fourth century: 'Strange are those men who believe that God has a son and suffered him to die. The God who could not bear to see Abraham about to sacrifice his son, but exclaimed, "Lay not thine hand upon the lad," would He have looked on calmly while His son was being slain, and not have reduced the whole world to chaos!'

In the Middle Ages. Throughout the Middle Ages, the Jewish Teachers continued the religious education of the people begun in earlier centuries. They upheld the cause of pure Monotheism at the Religious Disputations in which they were compelled to participate by the triumphant and all-powerful Church. That portion of their defence of Judaism which found expression in literary form, like the 'Book of Victory' (Sefer Nizzachon), is of lasting value. Such likewise is the book of Isaac Troki, a Polish Karaite of the sixteenth century, 'the Defence of the Faith,' which evoked the warm praise of Voltaire. Of especial importance is the work of the Jewish philosophers, whose effort represents a distinct enrichment of the world's religious thinking. Saadyah, Gabirol, Bachya, Hallevi, Maimonides purge the concept of God of all anthropomorphism, and vindicate the unity and uniqueness of Israel's God-conception. Solomon Ibn Gabirol, renowned alike as philosopher and Synagogue poet, begins his *Royal Crown*, with the words, 'Thou art One, the first great Cause of all: Thou art One, and none can penetrate—not even the wisest in heart—the unfathomable mystery of Thy Unity. Thou art One; Thy Unity can neither be lessened nor increased, for neither plurality nor change nor any attribute can be applied to Thee. Thou art One, but the imagination fails in any attempt to define or limit Thee. Therefore I said, "I will take heed to my ways, that I sin not with my tongue." '

In the present day. The long and arduous warfare begun by the Prophets and continued by the Rabbis is not yet ended. The Unity of God has its antagonists in the present day, as in former ages. Even advanced non-Jewish writers on religion are, as a rule, but hesitating witnesses to the Unity of God; and liberal Christian theologians wax quite eloquent in depicting the amenities of life under polytheism. They plead that it helped to interfuse the whole life with 'religion'; to intensify the 'joy of life' and delight in the world of nature; and that it made for religious tolerance.

On closer examination, these partisan claims

collapse entirely. As for tolerance, even enlightened Greek polytheism permitted three of the greatest thinkers of the Periclean age—Socrates, Protagoras, and Anaxagoras—to be put to death on religious grounds. The Jews came into contact with Greek polytheism in its later stages. But neither Antiochus Epiphanes who attempted to drown Judaism in the blood of its faithful children, nor Apion, the frenzied spokesman of the anti-Semites in Alexandria, displayed particular tolerance.

Again, the alleged interfusion of the whole of life with 'religion' under polytheism did not save the votaries of Greek polytheism from moral laxity, licentiousness and *inhuman* behaviour both in war and in peace. As to intensifying the 'joy of life'—that 'joy of life', even among the Greeks, seems to have been the prerogative of the few. Thus, Greek society was broad-based on unrighteousness, *i.e.* on human slavery; and in Greece, 'the animated tool,' as Aristotle defined the slave, was denied all human rights. It is, furthermore, difficult to see wherein the 'joy of life' consisted for the human sacrifices regularly offered by the heathen Semites and Slavs, Germans and Greeks. In regard to the last-named, it is not generally remembered that we find traces of human sacrifice throughout the Hellenic world, in the cult of almost every god, and in all periods of the independent Greek states. In the Roman Empire, this hideous accompaniment of polytheism continued till the fourth century of our present era; while in India the burning of widows was abolished only in the year 1840!

The other claims on behalf of polytheism are seen to be equally untenable. Delight in the world of nature was not confined to the polytheists. It could not have been alien to the people that produced the Song of Songs, and is therefore not the possession of heathenism alone. No less a scientist and thinker than Alexander von Humboldt has shown that the æsthetic contemplation of nature only began when the landscape was freed from its gods, and men could rejoice in nature's own greatness and beauty.

Various secular writers on religion go far beyond modernist theologians in their depreciation of monotheism. Unlike those theologians, they do not halt between two opinions, and they know no hesitancies. Ernest Renan ascribed the rise of belief in One God to the desert surroundings of the early Hebrews. 'The desert is monotheistic,' he announced. He omitted, however, to explain why, if so, the other Semitic desert-dwellers had remained polytheists; or why the primeval inhabitants of the Sahara, Gobi and Kalahari deserts were not monotheists. Anti-Semites go further still. In order to belittle Israel's infinite glory as the Prophet of Monotheism, they decry the Unity of God as 'a bare, barren, arithmetical idea'; as merely 'the minimum of religion'. (It is strange that the alleged 'minimum of religion' should have given the Decalogue to the world; should have produced the Psalms, the book of devotion of civilized humanity; should have succeeded in shattering all idols, turning the course of history, and freeing the children of men from the stone heart of heathen antiquity.) Some of these anti-Semites contrast the bountiful abundance displayed by Greece in its hundreds of gods and goddesses, by India in its thousands of fantastic deities, with the one God of Israel. '*Only* one God—how mean, how meagre!' —they exclaim. It would serve no purpose to repeat further strictures on monotheism on the part of men who deem that, in attacking Jews, one need be neither logical nor fair; and that one may say anything of Jews and Judaism so long as it covers them with ridicule. But Truth is on the march; and the number of those thinkers is growing who recognize that 'the Shema is the basis of all higher, ethical, spiritual religion; an imperishable pronouncement, reverberating to this day in every idealistic conception of the universe' (Gunkel).

Conclusion. 'It was undeniably a stroke of true religious genius—a veritable prompting by the Holy Spirit, רוח הקודש,—to select, as Prof. Steinthal reminds us, out of the 4,875 verses of the Pentateuch this one verse (Deut. VI, 4) as the inscription for Israel's banner of victory. Throughout the entire realm of literature, secular or sacred, there is probably no utterance to be found that can be compared in its intrinsic intellectual and spiritual force, or in the influence it exerted upon the whole thinking and feeling of civilized mankind, with the six words which have become the battle-cry of the Jewish people for more than twenty-five centuries' (Kohler).

B

REWARD AND PUNISHMENT IN JUDAISM

Chapter x, 13–21, which forms the middle portion of the Shema, proclaims the doctrine of the Retributive Righteousness of God. Both rewards and punishments are here agricultural, and in particular refer to the rainfall, which is a matter of life and death in a land like Palestine.

Judaism teaches that obedience to the will of God is rewarded, and disobedience punished. This doctrine is bound up with the fundamental belief of Judaism in a God of Justice. Because God is just, He will not treat the righteous and the wicked in the same manner. In some way, it must be better with the former than with the latter, through the justice of God. But such reward—whether conceived as material blessing or, as in later ages, when it became more and more spiritualized—is not made the *motive* for virtue. That must be love of God and His commandments, a free enthusiasm for doing His will.

Throughout his Farewell Discourses, Moses demands obedience to the Divine will out of pure and disinterested love of God. His words in Deuteronomy breathe an ardent love and spiritual awe of the invisible God, a heart-religion such as we meet in the greatest of the Psalms and the highest portions of Prophecy. Throughout these same Discourses, however, we find, as in no other Biblical book, the appeal to material reward for obedience, and material punishment for disobedience, repeatedly and urgently pressed. 'This is due,' it has been explained, 'to the personal position of Moses. In himself he is a lofty, spiritual nature, yearning with a parent's love to a people incapable of rising to his spiritual plane; a people yet in the childhood of what we call real life, to be enticed with promises and frightened with threats. And alternately he pours his spiritual fervour into their dull ears, and then falls back helplessly on to the material considerations which alone will move them' (Moulton). He boldly makes use of every motive that actually influences men—gratitude to God, feeling of dependence on Him, and fear of God—in order to win them to the higher life. 'He does not ask men to serve God because it will be profitable to them, but because they love God; and he endeavours to make them love God by reciting all His love and friendliness and patience to His people, and by pointing out the evil which His love is seeking to ward off. Having before his mind the results of evil conduct, he does urge men to escape from the wrath that may rest upon them. But the only means so to escape is to yield to the love of God' (Harper).

How far there is correspondence in actual life between righteousness and happiness, and between misery and sin, is a recurrent problem both in Biblical and post-Biblical Judaism. Deuteronomy and Ezekiel declare that men get in this world exactly what they deserve. Job, Jeremiah, Habakkuk, the Psalms, and Ecclesiastes courageously face the bitter facts of life, and point out how often it goes well with the wicked and ill with the righteous. This world-riddle becomes less distracting under the influence of the belief in the immortality of the soul.

Since the time of the Maccabees, the belief in immortality had become wellnigh universal among the masses of the Jewish people. R. Jannai could thus remain quite unperturbed by his recognition, that 'it is not in our power to explain either the prosperity of the wicked, or the affliction of the righteous'. 'Faithful is thy Employer,' says R. Tarphon, 'to pay thee the reward of thy labour, and know that the grant of the reward of the righteous will be in the future life.' New spiritual conceptions became prominent; such as the great saying of the illustrious Babylonian teacher Rab, 'In the world to come there is neither eating nor drinking . . . but the righteous enjoy the radiance of the Shechinah.'

In connection with this world-riddle, the Rabbis never lost sight of two things. One, that suffering is not an absolute evil: it educates, it purifies, it can be an instrument of Divine love; see on VIII, 5. Through it, Israel came into possession of the best gifts—the Torah, the Holy Land, and Eternal Life. Rab declared, 'He who suffers no affliction and persecution, does not belong to Israel'; *i.e.* has not known the highest spiritual experience of God's chosen ones. And the second thing is, that in the deepest sense, righteousness is its own reward. Ben Azzai taught that even as one sin begets another, so the reward of a good deed is that it leads to another good deed! שכר מצוה מצוה. The Rabbis would have rejected the thought that in this world righteousness should permanently produce misery, and wickedness invariably lead to happiness, as both irrational and blasphemous. Nevertheless, they taught men to disregard the thought of reward altogether; and to do their duty לשמה, *lishmoh*, for its own sake. Rabbi Eleazar explained the opening verse of Psalm CXII, 'Blessed is the man that delighteth greatly in His commandments,' to mean, 'he delights greatly in His commandments, but not in the reward connected with them.' This is in line with the teaching of one of the earliest Sages, Antigonos of Socoh, 'Be not like servants that minister to their master for the sake of receiving a reward; but be like servants who minister to their master without the condition of receiving a reward; and let the fear of Heaven be upon you' (Ethics of the Fathers).

'It is true that the ordinary man may be incapable of such pure devotion; and, in his case, promises of reward and punishment are necessary. But such promises are merely a means to an end, the end being the attainment of such spiritual exaltation in which the love of good will be the sole stimulus to good. Let men serve God at first for reward; they will end by serving Him without any such motive. He who desires to serve God from love must not serve to win the future world, but he does the right and eschews the wrong, because he is a man, and owes it to his manhood to perfect himself' (Maimonides).

C

JEWISH EDUCATION

Its Scope

Though it was never intended that women become learned in the Torah, a clear understanding of the fundamentals of Jewish faith and duty was required of the Jewish woman. In ancient times, the Mishnah (Ned. IV) speaks of the Scripture instruction of sons and daughters as the normal practice. In the Middle Ages, Judah the Pious writes: 'Girls too should receive instruction in the Holy Law. It is true that the Rabbis taught that girls need not be instructed in the Talmud. This only means that it is not necessary for them to pursue Talmudic learning, but girls must share in religious and moral instruction. Everyone should know the Divine laws and commandments; youths should learn them in the Hebrew language, women and girls may learn them in their mother tongue. The instruction of girls must be given in a gentle and pleasant manner.'

It is but too true that in past centuries the standard of education for Jewish girls was immeasurably lower than it was in the case of boys. This did not then much matter, as in the sheltered life of the olden ghetto the morale of Jewish women remained unharmed by this narrow educational ideal. 'The Jewish woman vied with her husband in an admiration for a religious culture which she was not permitted to share; her greatest pride was to have sons learned in the Torah. She was, above everything, modest and chaste, and she could immolate herself as a martyr when the need arose' (M. Joseph). Yet even in those ages, a whole devotional literature arose, *e.g.* the Techinnoth, in the Judeo-German vernacular, which was exclusively intended for the use of girls and women, to acquaint them with Scripture, and enable them to understand the teachings of Jewish ritual and ethics.

Earlier than among any other people, Jewish law and custom ordained the provision of elementary instruction to all the children of the community, rich and poor alike. 'Be ye heedful of the children of the poor, for from them does the Torah go forth,' was the warning of the Rabbis. And the Jewish knowledge which is to endow every Jewish boy or girl with the Jewish outlook and Jewish loyalty cannot be acquired in the few hundred hours of instruction they receive in the current Religion Classes. It must extend over years, and not end with adolescence. 'Nicht Religionsstunden, sondern Religionsjahre,' said the illustrious Leopold Zunz, the founder of the new Jewish learning. The continuation teaching of the Jewish youth and the Jewish adult need not necessarily be carried on in formal classes. But a deep yearning, and constant striving, for acquaintance with Jewish thought, and the classical sources of Jewish inspiration, are indispensable for real, conscious, and not merely accidental, membership in the House of Israel.

Its Content

As the aim of Jewish education is the consecration of the Jewish child to Judaism and his preparation for a life of beneficence for Israel and humanity, it must consist of the following four elements.

(1) *Jewish Religion.—i.e.* the Jewish beliefs concerning God, the Torah and Israel; the teachings and practices, the symbols and institutions which have come down to the House of Israel through the ages. Such knowledge does not come of itself, and cannot be satisfactorily picked up from other Jewish studies. The growing boy and girl will in the future be often called upon to state and defend their religious position. They should be helped to a formulation of Jewish belief by means of systematic instruction.

(2) *The Hebrew Language.* Hebrew is Israel's historic language, and the key to all Israel's treasures; and, being the key and receptacle of Israel's message to mankind, no other language, whether living or dead, has had such a vast and eternal span of influence. It is the most important of human tongues, the language of languages, the Sacred Tongue. Every Jewish child is entitled to the possession of an intimate, even if not extensive, knowledge of the Sacred Tongue, which shall give that child a lot and portion in the synagogue, the heart of Jewish communal life. A Hebrew-less Jewry has no future, because it cannot fairly be said to have a present.

(3) *The Sacred Scriptures.* The beginnings of Israel's history as related in the Pentateuch should early form part of the child's soul-life, But we must go beyond the Pentateuch, and teach the whole Bible story. The main stress must be laid on the living truths underlying the narration of the facts. It is these truths, enshrined not only in Bible history, but in prophecy, psalm, proverb and moral discourse, that are of transcendent worth to the spiritual development of the child. Through these truths, the Bible is a Tree of Life to them that grasp it.

(4) *Jewish History.* Jewish History is a continuous revelation, with a divine lesson for each generation. Nobody can understand the Jew—the Jew cannot understand himself—if he knows nothing of Jewish history beyond the *Chumesh,* or the Bible or even Josephus. Every Jew should know the outstanding events and personalities of every age in Jewish history, with appropriate selections from our imperishable literary monuments. Only he who has wept over the tragedy of Israel and has been inspired by the story of our martyrs, who knows something of the wealth of our literature and of our contributions to the humanization of man, can have the proud Jewish consciousness that he is a member of a holy and indomitable People, or understand the meaning of the Unity of Israel, with its great ethical corollaries, the warning against the profanation of the Jewish Name *(Chillul Hashem)* and the sublime duty of hallowing the Name of God *(Kiddush Hashem).*

D

MONARCHY AND FREEDOM IN ISRAEL

I

The Biblical theory of government is among the greatest contributions ever made to the political life of man. Such, however, is far from being the general opinion. This looks upon the two ancient

Jewish kingdoms as petty Oriental despotisms, whose State life was never of any importance to the larger world.

Both Jewish and non-Jewish writers are responsible for this ignorance and radical misconception of Israel's remarkable achievements as a political entity.

On the one hand, many Jewish writers have been under the influence of the German-American Reform Movement in Judaism, which minimizes and attempts to eliminate the national element from the consciousness of the Jew of to-day. These writers, approaching the question with a theological bias, dismiss the political history of ancient Israel as, on the whole, 'a gloomy record of bad government, tyranny and oppression.' We shall see how recklessly this die-hard partisan view runs counter to the facts of history, as marshalled by a whole series of scholars, from John Michaelis and Joseph Salvador to Justice Sulzberger and Prof. T. H. Robinson.

On the other hand, non-Jewish writers often look upon Israel's national existence as a mere 'preparation' for Christianity; or, they share the late Sir Henry Maine's superstition that 'nothing, except the blind forces of Nature, moves in the world to-day, that is not Greek in origin'. They, therefore, bid us turn to Greece, if we would learn the origins of free government.

Now, as to Greece, the 158 petty, quarrelling, fratricidal States that are comprised under that geographical term have left behind little indeed that is worthy of emulation in political life. Thus, the Athenians chose their judges by lot, and their generals by mass meeting. 'The Greeks had no political unity. Every small city-state was an independent, sovereign community. This raised the hatred between city and city, still more the hatred between class and class in each city, to a dangerous pitch. At Athens, some of the men of the old ruling families formed an association, every member of which had to take an oath, "I will be an enemy to the popular party and will try to do it every harm that I can"' (Edwyn Bevan). The Greeks displayed to the full that fatal vice of factiousness which imbues politics with fanaticism, and proscribes opponents by massacre or exile. 'The various forms of government that the Greeks established were all experiments, which, owing to the fact that they were carried to their extreme logical conclusion, culminated in absurdity. Whether they tried an aristocracy, a tyranny, a democracy or a Spartan system of military communism, there was always some section of the people who were fettered and oppressed. Nietzsche rightly calls them, "the political fools of ancient history"' (Kastein).

In absolute contrast to this, there existed in Israel *one* form of State, constructed on a definite principle, and a political constitution that was truly representative of the spirit and aspirations of the community. The normal form of government was the monarchy; and the conception of kinghood it embodied was unique throughout antiquity. 'Down to modern times,' says T. H. Huxley, 'no State had a constitution in which the interests of the people are so largely taken into account, in which the *duties* so much more than the privileges of rulers are insisted upon, as that drawn up for Israel in Deuteronomy and Leviticus.'

II

The King

Among all other Oriental peoples, the word 'king' connotes an irresponsible despot, vested with unchallenged authority. All law is the expression of his will; and, while it binds every other member of the community, the monarch himself is free to disregard or to supersede it. He owes no formal duties to his subjects, and is answerable to none for his actions. To the Eastern mind, a 'limited monarchy' was a contradiction in terms.

It was otherwise in Israel. There it is God who is the real King and the sole supreme authority; and the monarch is but the agent of the Divine King, entrusted with an indicated commission for which he is responsible to God who chose him. No Jewish ruler would ever have dared to claim Divine honours, and, like the Egyptian and Roman emperors, order sacrifices to be offered to him. In Israel, the monarch is under the Law, and is bound to respect the life, honour, and possessions of his subjects. We must keep these things in mind if we are to realize Israel's unique and original attitude to the monarchy. And then let us turn to the twenty-first chapter of the First Book of Kings. Naboth's vineyard was hard by king Ahab's palace at Jezreel. Ahab was anxious either to buy it, or to give Naboth a better vineyard in exchange. However, as Jezreel was a walled city, the law of Jubilee did not apply to it, and the inheritance of his fathers if sold by Naboth, would not eventually revert to the seller, but would be for ever lost to the family. He, therefore, received the king's proposal with horror, and refused. Ahab showed his annoyance. When Jezebel, his foreign queen, hears the story, she is quite unable to comprehend her husband's difficulties. A king is nothing, who is not prepared to take what he wants, is her view of the situation. 'I will give thee the vineyard of Naboth the Jezreelite,' she says. The law which could not be changed by force, she evades by fraud. With Ahab's acquiescence she assumes royal powers for the purpose. It may be that Naboth in his indignation at the king's proposal had uttered some hasty words, though quite insufficient to warrant the course adopted by Jezebel. She has Naboth accused of blasphemy and treason; he is duly tried in the local courts; and, having been found guilty on perjured testimony, is made to pay the supreme penalty for his alleged crimes. When Ahab is about to take possession of the vineyard, he is confronted by Elijah. The Prophet of Truth and Justice denounces him as a murderer and robber, and foretells the vengeance of Heaven that would descend upon his entire House. It is interesting to compare this incident in Scripture with the conduct of the later Roman Emperor Diocletian. It was his habit to charge with treason any of his subjects whose estates he desired; to have the owner executed; and then confiscate those estates. Of course, there was no Elijah to raise his voice against the Imperial procedure. The Diocletian incident is typical of Roman rule in the Provinces of the Empire. It was unbelievably merciless. The hideous misgovernment of Palestine by the Roman Procurators as recorded by Josephus is not exceptional. 'Roman administration sucked the life-blood out of its Eastern subjects, and diminished their will to live' (W. R. Inge). In the matter of humane government, Rome has as little to teach us as has Greece.

Normally—*i.e.* outside Israel—the subject's life, honour, and property were throughout antiquity at the absolute disposal of the sovereign. And this was so not only in regard to individuals. In Egypt, the lives of vast multitudes of men were sacrificed in connection with the frenzied building schemes of the Pharaohs. Herodotus tells us that in the time of Necho II (609–588 B.C.E.), no less than 120,000 labourers were worked to death in the construction of a canal connecting the Nile and the Red Sea. The contemporary Jewish ruler, king Jehoiakim, tried to emulate the example of Necho II, and he built himself palaces by means of *forced labour*. In other countries, such a thing was taken to be the unquestioned prerogative of the king. But absolute power in a ruler was incomprehensible to the Jewish mind; and that enterprise was deemed an outrage against law and reason, against immemorial custom and all human decency. Like Elijah before him, Jeremiah the Prophet arose, and came to the door of Jehoiakim's palace, crying: 'Woe unto him that buildeth his house by unrighteousness, and his chambers by injustice; that useth his neighbour's service without wages, and giveth him not his hire. He shall be buried with the burial of an ass, drawn and cast forth beyond the gates of Jerusalem' (Jer. XXII, 13, 19).

The king in Israel recognized his responsibility not only to God and the Divine Law, but to the human community that had enthroned him as its leader as well. It is not the king but the people who is in possession of sovereign rights, and the people was free to impose fresh conditions on each new monarch at his accession. A refusal to accept these new conditions cost Solomon's son, Rehoboam, the greater part of his kingdom (I Kings XII, 16). And, as a rule, the kings did not dare to break the covenant entered into with their subjects at their accession. The exceptions to this rule are, Ahab, who was dominated by his Tyrian wife; and Jehoiakim, who was imposed on Judah by a foreign conqueror. Thus it comes that even the great Prophets, who certainly never shrank from denouncing social iniquity wherever it was found, say little of *royal* malpractices in either realm. And the Psalmists could bid their royal ruler 'ride on prosperously in behalf of truth, and meekness, and righteousness' (Ps. XLV, 5); and could pray, 'Give the king thy judgments, O God. In his days shall the righteous flourish, and the souls of the needy shall he save. He shall redeem their soul from oppression and violence, and precious shall their blood be in his sight' (Ps. LXXII, 1, 7, 13, 14). They all cherish the Messianic dream that days are coming when the king shall be shepherd to his people, when the king's sceptre shall be a sceptre of peace, and upon him shall rest the spirit of wisdom and counsel and the fear of the LORD (Isa. XI, 2).

This truly democratic relation between the governor and the governed in Israel is indicated in the Scriptural words, 'And it shall be, when he sitteth upon the throne of his kingdom, that he shall write him a copy of this law in a book . . . and he shall read therein all the days of his life . . . that his heart be not lifted up above his brethren.' On this a recent Schweich lecturer has the following admirable comment: 'In Israel, the king exists for the sake of his people. He has power and authority; but they are not given him for his own pleasure, but for the safety and well-being of the nation over whom he rules. He does not stand on a higher level than others, except in so far as his duties give him a loftier place. He is *primus inter pares*, and though he must of necessity have special authority, yet he belongs to the same order as his people: he is one of them. While to every other ancient monarch the subject was a slave, to the Israelite king he was *a brother*' (T. H. Robinson).

III

Ethical Foundations

The conception of a constitutional and law-abiding king, to whom the meanest of his subjects was a 'brother', is not the only unique characteristic of the Mosaic Commonwealth. It is well to enumerate a few others of the ethical foundations of the Mosaic Polity.

(1) The Supremacy of Justice in the State

It is noteworthy that the Biblical regulations concerning justice *precede* those of the appointment of the king (XVII, 14–20): justice is to be above the monarchy. This is certainly without a parallel in ancient times. Only in the modern world do we find similar instances of national reverence for justice. England's advance on the road of freedom, is largely due to the fact that, at an early date in her history, the administration of justice became independent of the king. To-day, however, there are at least two leading European states who openly and deliberately destroy the independence of their Courts of Law, and turn them into instruments of State policy.

'Justice must be guided solely by State interests,' says a Nazi ruler. 'Every judge must remember that his decisions are intended to promote nothing but the prevailing policy of the State,' is the pronouncement of the Soviet commissar for justice. As far as these two governments are concerned, the Divine demand of 'Justice, and only justice, shalt thou pursue', was made in vain. Civilization is once again witnessing travesties of, and outrages on, justice that recall the darkest days of the Middle Ages.

(2) Dignity of Labour

The recognition of the dignity of labour could not be looked for in Athens and Rome. In these societies, labour was relegated to the slave, who was merely 'an animated tool' without any human claims or rights. In every such society, work itself—even that of a physician or schoolmaster—becomes dishonourable; and, as in Sparta, is forbidden to the free citizen.

In sharpest contrast to the above, the Jewish Sages are unanimous in their insistence that work ennobles and sanctifies, and that idleness is the door to temptation and sin. They were themselves toilers, earning their daily bread by following some handicraft as masons, tailors, sandal-makers, carpenters. The most renowned of all the Rabbis, Hillel the Elder, was a wood-cutter.

In Israel, man remained master of labour; labour did not mean the bondage of man. The Sabbath gave the labourer every week a day of freedom and leisure. This was quite incomprehensible to the Greeks and Romans. Their writers—Tacitus, Juvenal, Plutarch—make merry over the idea of presenting one day in every seven to the worker! The far-reaching humanitarian significance of the Sabbath was, of course, undreamt of by them; and even 'our modern spirit with all its barren theories of civic and political rights, and its strivings towards freedom and equality, has not thought out and called into existence a single institution that, in its beneficent effects upon the labouring classes, can in the slightest degree be compared to the Weekly Day of Rest promulgated in the Sinaitic wilderness' (Proudhon). It was many ages before its man-redeeming implications began to be seen. The Mosaic restrictions as to the *days of weekly* work that might be demanded of the labourer, laid down a principle of immeasurable importance for the social legislation of the future. At long last, after three thousand years, humanity has taken the next step; *viz.* that of regulating the *hours of daily* labour. This slowness in recognizing the needs of labour is no doubt due to the fact that, till quite recent times, classical literature monopolized the education of the governing classes of the European peoples. As with the Greeks and Romans, idleness became the mark of nobility; and it was deemed to be beneath the man of gentle birth to worry over the condition of serfs or toilers (Bloch).

(3) Property and Poverty

Among the Romans, the idea of property took precedence over the idea of humanity. Thus, if the debtor was unable to repay the sum advanced to him, the Roman creditor could imprison him in a private dungeon, chain him to a block, sell him into slavery, or slay him. With such a deification of property, it is small wonder that poverty was in itself considered dishonouring; and that pity for the poor was looked upon as a sickly sentimentality, unworthy of the free man. Virgil praises one of his heroes because he never felt any sympathy with sufferers through want; Seneca thinks it natural to recoil in horror from a poor man; and Plautus declares feeding the hungry to be cruelty, because it merely prolongs a life of misery.

In Israel, property was never a *noli me tangere;* neither was the possession of the individual over it deemed to be absolute, as is shown by the Sabbatical and tithe laws. 'He who says, What is mine is mine and what is thine is thine, that man speaks like a citizen of Sodom' (Ethics of the Fathers, v, 13).

Such subordination of the rights of property to those of humanity explains the place and claims of the poor in the Jewish Commonwealth. It was a new conception in the history of the world—a conception that could as little have been derived from Egypt, as from Greece and Rome then unborn. 'The Hebrew commonwealth was a commonwealth whose ideal it was that every man should sit under his own vine and fig-tree, with none to vex him or make him afraid; in which, for even the bond slave there should be hope; in which, for even the beast of burden there should be rest. With the blast of the jubilee trumpets the slave goes free, and a re-division of the land secures again to the poorest his fair share in the bounty of the common Creator. The reaper must leave something for the gleaner; even the ox cannot be muzzled as he treadeth out the corn' (Henry George).

IV

Democratic Institutions

Foremost among these are the Prophets. The vigilance of the Prophets, throughout Jewish history, against every abuse perpetrated by the brute force of the oppressor—whoever he be—was ceaseless. Samuel warns the tribes of Israel against the ways of the Eastern despot; and, long before Elijah, Nathan the Prophet hurls his 'Thou art the man!' at the royal sinner. In view of the unique role the Prophets played in the moral evolution of the Jewish people, even a secularist like John Stuart Mill perceived the overwhelming influence of the Prophets in upholding ideals of true democracy. He saw in them the living equivalent of the modern freedom of speech and liberty of the press. Such likewise is the verdict of all modern scholars:

'It was part of the spirit of Prophecy to be dumbfounded at human ferocity as at something against nature and reason. In the presence of the iniquities of the world, the heart of the Prophets bled as though from a wound of the Divine Spirit, and their cry of indignation re-echoed the wrath of the Deity. Greece and Rome had their rich and poor, just as Israel had in the days of Jeroboam II, and the various classes continued to slaughter one another for centuries; but no voice of justice and pity arose from the fierce tumult. Therefore the words of the Prophets have more vitality at the present time, and answer better to the needs of modern souls, than all the classic masterpieces of antiquity' (James Darmesteter).

Next in importance in the moulding and administration of the Jewish state was the National Council. The researches of the late Justice Mayer Sulzberger in the domain of Israelite politics have thrown much light on the nature of the legislative body in ancient Israel. The general impression, he says, left on the mind by reading the Pentateuch and the Book of Joshua is that Israel was governed by a Chief (Prince, Judge, King) who was at the head of the military and civil authorities; and that, alongside of him, was a High Priest who controlled the ecclesiastical establishment; that the Chief had a Council, probably bi-cameral, to determine national policies; that the smaller chamber was composed of twelve princes (Nesiim), and the larger of seventy elders (Zekenim), and that the two constituted the Edah (Congregation or Parliament) of the nation. The Edah did not disappear with the Mosaic age. Throughout the succeeding centuries, we find the same democratic institution in the state, exercising executive, political, and high judicial powers. This National Council became fully developed in the early days of the kingdom, under the name of Am ha-aretz (see pages 80-81 and 955). It made and unmade kings (*e.g.* II Kings XXI, 24, XXIII, 30); and, as the trial of Jeremiah for 'blasphemy' amply proves (Jer. XXVI), it exercised the highest judicial powers in the State. Eventually it re-emerged after the Exile as the Gerusia, the Great Synagogue, and the Sanhedrin.

The above is witness to *a wonderful capacity for self-government on the part of our ancestors.* We may disregard the kingdom of the Ten Tribes who had lapsed into idolatry, and confine our attention to the kingdom of Judah. That kingdom existed as an independent state from 933 to 586 B.C.E.; and during the entire period of these 347 years, we do not detect the faintest trace of a single civil war, nor of an attempt at a change of dynasty (I. Friedlander). The only exception, that of Athaliah, the daughter of Ahab, confirms the rule. For she was not a Judean, but a princess of the Northern Kingdom, a daughter of Jezebel. She had usurped the throne of Judah, and was overthrown by the faithful Judeans after an illegitimate reign of six years. Of how many other peoples, ancient or modern, can this be said, that they persisted for a period of 347 years without a change of dynasty or civil war? And it was not a vegetative existence which that little kingdom led during that long period. The greater portion of the Prophetic literature was produced within that time; social justice and freedom of speech were maintained; and national independence was preserved, in spite of Judah's position as the little buffer-state between the Great Powers of that age, as the small bit of iron between the hammer of Assyria and the anvil of Egypt.

In view of all this, more and more students of the political facts of Bible history will endorse the following judgment:

'There is no historical record of any other nation which, as early as a millennium before the present era, had overcome the forces both of despotism and of unbridled democracy. The Jewish people at large had as keen an outlook and as wide a vision in political as in religious affairs; and while the modern monotheistic conception of the universe is largely the product of their genius, so the modern conception of a rational, democratic, representative government owes its origin to the same ancestry. The remarkable phenomenon that the English people and their American descendants, the only nations that have really comprehended and utilized the principles of parliamentary government, took the Jewish Bible as their text-book in times of stress and storm, will thus be explained' (Sulzberger).

To conclude with the weighty words of a Master of Balliol: 'It is not without significance that the great struggle for political freedom in this country was led by men who drew much of their inspiration from the Old Testament, the sacred fountain of the spirit of nationality and national religion. This free religious spirit is one of the main causes why England outstripped all other European countries in its political development, and becomes their teacher in the methods of free government' (Edward Caird).

E

ON MARRIAGE, DIVORCE, AND THE POSITION OF WOMAN, IN JUDAISM

Marriage

Its Meaning. Marriage is that relationship between man and woman under whose shadow alone there can be true reverence for the mystery, dignity and sacredness of life. Scripture represents marriage not merely as a Mosaic ordinance, but as part of the scheme of Creation, intended for all humanity. Its sacredness thus goes back to the very birth of man.

They do less than justice to this Divine institution who view it in no other light than a civil contract. There is a vital difference between a marriage and a contract. In a contract the mutual rights and obligations are the result of an agreement, and their selection and formulation may flow from the momentary whim of the parties. In the marriage relation, however, such rights and obligations are high above the arbitrary will of both husband and wife: they are determined and imposed by Religion as well as the Civil Law. The failure of the contract view to bring out this higher sphere of duty and conscience which is of the very essence of marriage, led a philosopher like Hegel to denounce that view as a 'Schaendlichkeit'.

Its purpose. The purpose of marriage is twofold—(*a*) posterity, and (*b*) companionship.

(*a*) The duty of building a home and of rearing a family (Gen. I, 28, 'Be fruitful and multiply') figures in the Rabbinic codes as the first of the 613 Mitzvoth of the Torah. To this commandment is due the sacredness and centrality of the child in Judaism—something which even the enlightened nations of antiquity could not understand. Tacitus deemed it a contemptible prejudice of the Jews that 'it is a crime among them to kill any child'. What a lurid flashlight these words throw on Græco-Roman society! It is in such a society that Judaism proclaimed the Biblical view that the child was the highest of human treasures. 'O Lord God, what wilt Thou give me, seeing that I go childless?' was Abraham's agonizing cry. Of what value were earthly possessions to him, if he was denied a child who would continue his work after him. This attitude of the Father of the Hebrew people has remained that of his descendants throughout the ages. A childless marriage was deemed to have failed of its main purpose; and, in ancient times, was admitted as ground for divorce after ten years. In little children—it was taught—God gives humanity a chance to make good its mistakes. They are 'the Messiahs of mankind'—the perennial regenerative force in humanity. No wonder that Jewish infant mortality is everywhere lower than the non-Jewish—often only one-half of that among the general population.

(*b*) Companionship is the other primary end of the marriage institution. Woman is to be the helpmate of man, עזר כנגדו. A wife is a man's other self, all that man's nature demands for its completion physically, socially, and spiritually. In marriage alone can man's need for physical and social companionship be directed to holy ends. It is this idea which is expressed by the term *kiddushin* ('hallowing') applied to Jewish marriage—the hallowing of two human beings to life's holiest purposes. In married life, man finds his truest and most lasting happiness; and only through married life does human personality reach its highest fulfilment. 'A man shall leave his father and mother and cleave to his wife,' says Scripture. Note that it is man who is to cleave to his wife, and not the woman, physically the weaker, who is to cleave to her husband; because in the higher sphere of the soul's life, woman is the ethical and spiritual superior of man. 'Even as the wife is'—say the Rabbis, 'so the husband is.' The celibate life is the unblessed life: Judaism requires its saints to show their sanctity *in* the world, and amid the ties and obligations of family life. 'He who has no wife abides without good, help, joy, blessing or atonement. He who has no wife cannot be considered a whole man' (Talmud). The satisfaction of the needs of physical and social companionship outside the sacred estate of matrimony, unhallowed by religion and unrestrained by its commandments, Judaism considers an abomination. And such extra-marital relations are prohibited just as sternly with non-Jewish women as with Jewish. Thus, Joseph resists the advances of the *heathen* temptress with the words: 'How can I do this great wickedness, and sin against God?' (Gen. XXXIX, 9); and the Book of Proverbs is clear on the attitude of Judaism to the 'strange woman'—married or unmarried (see Chapters II, V–VII). No less emphatically than in Scripture is purity demanded by the Rabbis. The New Testament accepted the Jewish view on the subject in its entirety. The whole of Gospel teaching on this subject, even Matthew V, 28, is to be found in the Talmud.

The Marriage Ceremony. The Marriage Service consists of the blessings of Betrothal, the formula of Marriage, the reading of the Kethubah, and the seven blessings of Sanctification. In later times was added the breaking of the glass. Originally a considerable time intervened between the Betrothal (אירוסין), by which the bridal couple became bound for all purposes save living together, and the Nuptials proper (נישואין). Since the sixteenth century, however, Betrothal is always combined with the Nuptials. The solemnization of both the Betrothal and Nuptials opens with the benediction over a cup of wine. Wine is a symbol of joy, joyousness at a wedding being a religious duty; and in the Wedding Grace, 'we bless our God in Whose abode is joy.' The couple drink from both cups of wine—an indication of their resolve henceforth to share whatever destiny Providence may allot to them. The Betrothal blessing reads:—

> 'Blessed art thou, O Lord our God, King of the Universe, who hast sanctified us by thy commandments, and hast given us command concerning forbidden marriages; who hast disallowed unto us those that are betrothed, but hast sanctioned unto us such as are wedded to us by the rite of the canopy and the sacred covenant of wedlock. Blessed art thou, O Lord, who sanctifiest thy people Israel by the rite of the canopy and the sacred covenant of wedlock.'

The commands concerning forbidden marriages are given in Leviticus XVIII and XX; see the Table of Prohibited Marriages in force among Jews to-day, p. 559. The 'rite of the canopy' is the chuppah, under which the bride and bridegroom stand during the Service, and is a symbol of the hometaking of the bride by the bridegroom. After this benediction there follows the bridegroom's Declaration, which constitutes the essence of the ceremony. He places a ring upon the forefinger of the right hand of the bride, and says: 'Behold, thou art consecrated unto me by this ring according to the Law of Moses and of Israel.' The general use of the ring is post-Talmudic; its place was formerly taken by any object of value. The formula is at least 2,000 years old, and expresses the resolve to lead their common life according to the rule and manner of Judaism. After this, the Kethubah is read. The Kethubah was introduced by Simeon ben Shetach in the first pre-Christian century as a protection to the wife in the event of her becoming widowed or divorced. This document testifies that on such and such a date, the bridegroom said to his bride: 'Be thou my wife according to the Law of Moses and of Israel. I will work for thee; I will honour thee; I will support and maintain thee in accordance with the custom of Jewish husbands who work for their wives, and honour, support, and maintain them in truth.' The husband further undertakes the obligation of a certain fixed sum for her prior claim on his estate. 'All my property even the mantle on my shoulders, shall be mortgaged for the security of this contract and that sum.' Then begins the solemnization of the Nuptials proper in seven Blessings. The fourth and seventh of these read:

> 'Blessed art thou, O Lord our God, King of the Universe, who hast made man in thine image, after thy likeness, and hast prepared unto him, out of his very self, a perpetual fabric. Blessed art thou, O Lord, Creator of man.
>
> 'Blessed art thou, O Lord our God, King of the Universe, who hast created joy and gladness, bridegroom and bride, mirth and exultation, pleasure and delight, love, brotherhood, peace and fellowship. Soon may there be heard in the cities of Judah and in the streets of Jerusalem the voice of joy and gladness, the voice of the bridegroom and the voice of the bride, the jubilant voice of bridegrooms from their canopies, and of youths from their feasts of song. Blessed art thou, O Lord, who makest the bridegroom to rejoice with the bride.'

It is seen that the Blessings 'cover the whole of Israel's history. Each new home is thus brought into relation with the story of Creation and with Israel's Messianic Hope' (Abrahams). At the conclusion of the Blessings, a glass is broken by the bridegroom—a reminder of the Destruction of Jerusalem (זכר לחורבן). Another symbolization may also be mentioned: just as one step shatters the glass, so can one act of unfaithfulness for ever destroy the holiness and happiness of the Home. The Service concludes nowadays with the pronouncement of the priestly benediction.

Monogamy. The Biblical ideal of human marriage is the monogamous one. The Creation story and all the ethical portions of Scripture speak of the union of a man with *one* wife. Whenever a Prophet alludes to marriage, he is thinking of such a union—lifelong, faithful, holy. Polygamy seems to have wellnigh disappeared in Israel after the Babylonian Exile. Early Rabbinic literature presupposes a practically monogamic society; and out of 2,800 Teachers mentioned in the Talmudim, one only is stated to have had two wives. In the fourth century Aramaic paraphrase (Targum) of the Book of Ruth, the kinsman (IV, 6) refuses to 'redeem' Ruth, saying, 'I cannot marry her, because I am already married; I have no right to take an additional wife, lest it lead to strife in my home.' Such paraphrase would be meaningless if it did not reflect the general feeling of the people on this question.

Monogamy in Israel was thus not the result of European contact. As a matter of fact, monogamy was firmly established in Jewish life long before the rise of Christianity. The New Testament does not prohibit polygamy, but only demands that a bishop or presbyter shall have but one wife (I Tim. III, 2). As late as Luther's day, bigamy was not unknown in Western Europe; and in the thirteenth century, for example, monogamy was but a name, at any rate in the upper classes of society. The Church, too, found it difficult to enforce strict monogamy among Eastern Christians.

Divorce

In the first pre-Christian century, there was a fundamental cleavage in the religious schools of Palestine in regard to Divorce. The dispute turned over the interpretation of Deut. XXIV, 1; but, as so often in theological controversy, the words of the Sacred Text were merely the pegs upon which to hang conflicting theories of life on the part of the disputants. The School of Shammai maintained that a marriage could be dissolved only by unchastity on the part of the wife, because adultery alone sapped the foundation of marriage and made its continuance impossible. The School of Hillel argued that divorce should be permitted for any reason which entailed a rupture of domestic harmony resulting in a daily violation of one of the main purposes of marriage—companionship. The Jewish sectaries (the Essenes, the 'Zadokites' of Damascus, the Samaritans and Jewish Christians) opposed, in addition, the marrying a second wife, as long as the divorced wife was alive. Official Judaism, throughout the ages, followed the principle of the School of Hillel; and, of course, the unnatural prohibition for the parties to marry again is quite unknown to it. We shall see that in recent generations the civilized nations are more and more coming to adopt the Jewish attitude on this basic and vital question.

Not that Judaism ever lost sight of the fact that divorce was a calamitous necessity. 'I hate divorce,' is the Divine message by the Prophet Malachi (II, 16). 'The very altar weeps for one who divorces the wife of his youth,' says the Talmud. Later legislation made the writing and the delivery of the *Get* difficult and protracted, in order to facilitate attempts at reconciliation. The rabbi was bidden to exhaust every possible expedient to dissuade husband and wife from proceeding to divorce. 'If there is a doubt as to the originator of the quarrel, the husband is not believed when he asserts that the wife has commenced the dispute, as all women are presumed to be lovers of domestic peace' (Schulchan Aruch).

Characteristics of Jewish Divorce. (*a*) In theory, the power of divorce is in the hands of the husband. However, in the case of the wife's adultery, he is compelled to divorce her; connivance and condonation are not tolerated in Jewish Law. 'Adultery is not merely infidelity towards the conjugal partner, but a violation of a Divine order, a crime which cannot be condoned by the offended party' (Z. Frankel, L. Löw). Divorce is also compulsory where a man has married within one of the prohibited degrees. (Incestuous 'marriages' require no divorce, as these are null and void *ab initio*. On the distinction between incestuous marriages and those within the prohibited degrees, see p. 489.) There are also a few cases in which the Torah deprives the husband of the right to divorce his wife (Deut. XXII, 19 and 29). Furthermore, the wife might sue for a divorce in the Jewish Courts, which could for certain causes—*e.g.*, loathsome occupation or disease—compel him to free her. The uniform aim of the Rabbis throughout the succeeding centuries was to develop the law in the direction of greater equality between the man and the woman. At last, in the year 1000, Rabbenu Gershom decreed that the wife, unless she was unfaithful, could not be divorced *except of her free will.* Maimonides went even further: 'If a woman says, "My husband is repulsive to me, and I cannot live with him," the husband is compelled to divorce her, because she is not like a captive woman that she should be forced to consort with a man whom she hates.'

Such restriction of the husband's power to divorce was practicable only as long as the Jewish Rabbinic Courts had legal power to enforce their decisions. With the disappearance of that power, hardships have arisen in connection with divorce and *chalitzah*, difficulties which perhaps only a Central Sanhedrin in Jerusalem will in time be able to remove. The most serious of these is that of the Agunah, the woman whose husband has merely vanished. In favour of such a deserted wife, the laws of evidence as to the reported death of her husband have from the first been relaxed, and no effort is spared to free her from her uncertain state. While learned rabbis are to-day seeking a radical solution of this urgent question, it is a pity that the Agunah problem has become a tool in the hands of men whose purpose is the overthrow of Traditional Judaism, and some of whom recoil from no exaggeration in pursuit of that purpose. Jewish forsaken wives are relatively a very small minority when compared with the vast number of those in other faiths and legal systems who are deserted, are denied divorce or are granted it only on condition that they commit adultery, and those who are divorced without right to remarry.

(*b*) Jewish divorce can take place by mutual consent, even as marriage is itself a matter of mutual consent. In English law, it is difficult to obtain divorce where both parties want it. If both desire to be free, it savours of 'collusion', and may involve the intervention of the King's Proctor and the denial or revocation of divorce, even though one spouse is innocent of matrimonial offence and the other guilty. Divorce as a result of mutual consent continued to be in force in Europe, including Saxon England, till the eighth century. It is to-day granted in various countries—*e.g.*, Belgium, Switzerland and some of the United States of America.

It must be added that despite the ease with which, in theory, the marriage-tie may be dissolved in Jewish Law, divorce is less frequent among Jews than among the other populations of the various countries; see *Jewish Encyclopedia*, VIII, 340. Thus in the year 1933, there were in England, 2,549 marriages according to Jewish Law, but only 40 decrees *nisi*. In 1934, there were 2,600 marriages, and 46 such decrees. The strikingly small number of Jewish divorces is largely due to the fact that, 'among Jews, there is an absence of drunkenness, always a fruitful source of domestic strife and misconduct' (H. Adler).

(*c*) Perhaps the most characteristic feature of the Jewish Law of Divorce is its absolute prohibition of the adulterer to marry the adulteress. Even in cases where such a marriage had, through suppression of the true facts, been entered into, *it must be dissolved.* A leader of the Anglican Church regrets that the sacred institution of marriage is so often used to whitewash an adulterous pair. 'I should be glad to see the marriage of an adulterer with his or her paramour absolutely forbidden' (W. R. Inge).

New Testament Divorce. It is impossible to evade reference to the New Testament position of the question of divorce. According to Matt. XIX, 3, divorce was to be permitted, albeit for the one and sole reason of adultery. But it is now generally recognized that the Founder of Christianity desired the prohibition of divorce to be *absolute*, and taught that a divorced man or woman who married again was guilty of adultery (Mark X, 2–12). The Roman Catholic Church accordingly refuses in any way to recognize divorce, though in very rare cases it grants decrees of nullity. Outside that Church, however, the conscience of mankind has long been struggling with the problem of divorce as inherited from the Gospels. Nearly all Protestant States, and some Catholic ones, legislate to-day with due regard to the imperfections of human nature. They not only recognize adultery as a ground for divorce, but realize that there are other causes as well (*e.g.*, drunkenness, disease, felony) that destroy the moral foundations of the family, interfere with the upbringing of the children, embitter the lives of two human beings, and often lead them to degradation and crime.

Divorce in England. English law until the other day demanded, in the case of the wife's petition, the committing of adultery, *in addition to desertion, cruelty or some other enormity*, as the indispensable condition for divorce. It was a definite incentive to perjury and immorality, and gave rise to an infamous class of professional helpers to procure a divorce. The evidence given before the Royal Commission of 1909 confirmed the fact that the Jewish outlook, which recognizes the dissolution of a marriage when the happiness of the home is impossible, was in general harmony with progressive thought, while the Christian outlook was in direct conflict with it. In regard to the Jewish population, prior to the passing of the Divorce Act of 1857, the Jewish Ecclesiastical Authorities granted divorces on grounds established by Jewish Law, and continued to do so till 1866. Since that date, no Jewish divorce as between parties domiciled in England is given by the London Beth Din, or any responsible Rabbi, unless a divorce, previously decreed by a Court, had been made absolute.

It is well known that not all Jews to-day follow Rabbinical law in the matter of marriage and divorce. Thus, in 1909, C. G. Montefiore proclaimed that the extreme New Testament utterances on divorce showed 'unerring ethical instinct', whereas it was 'to the eternal dishonour' of Hillel that he favoured divorce on other grounds besides adultery. This impelled Achad Ha-am to produce one of his most brilliant essays (על שתי הסעפים, 'Judaism and the Gospels'), and subject Mr. Montefiore's views to an annihilating criticism. Neither the moderate nor the radical wing of Reform Judaism endorses Mr. Montefiore's position in this matter. Moderate reformers respect, in regard to marriage, the laws of the prohibited degrees, retain the essentials of the Traditional marriage service, and hold that 'it is logical that the Synagogue which insists upon marriage between Jews being performed in accordance with Jewish rites, should also insist upon the divorce being performed in accordance with the same rites' (L. M. Simmons). Radical Reformers in Europe and America have ever looked upon both marriage and divorce as purely civil acts, and hold that the civil law alone in regard to these matters possesses for Jews absolute validity. And as each one of the American States has its own divorce law, there are thus forty-eight different laws of marriage and divorce for the Liberal Jews in America! Some of these State laws are notoriously and even ludicrously lax; but no serious objection has been voiced against them by Liberal rabbis, except against the law of the State of Rhode Island. And this for a curious reason. That State—founded by the apostle of religious freedom, Roger Williams, the friend of Milton and Cromwell—rules that Jews, as all other religious bodies, be governed by their own regulations as to marriage and divorce.

Over against the secularist view in some sections of contemporary Jewry, the following words of the late Dr. Friedländer clearly define the attitude of Traditional Jews to the modern State on this vital question: 'We acknowledge the principle laid down in the Talmud, "The law of the Country is binding upon us" (דינא דמלכותא דינא), but only in so far as our civil relations are concerned. With regard to religious questions, our own religious Code must be obeyed. Marriage laws include two elements—civil relations and religious duties. As regards the former, we abide by the decisions of the civil Courts of the country. We must, therefore, not solemnize a marriage which the law of the Country would not recognize; we must not religiously dissolve a marriage by גט, unless the civil Courts of law have already decreed the divorce. On the other hand, we must not content ourselves with civil marriage or civil divorce; religiously, neither civil marriage nor civil divorce can be recognized, unless supplemented by marriage or divorce according to religious forms. Furthermore, marriages allowed by the civil law, but prohibited by our religious law, cannot be recognized before the tribunal of our Religion.'

The Position of Woman in Judaism

It is astonishing to note the amount of hostile misrepresentation that exists in regard to woman's position in Bible times. 'The relation of the wife to the husband was, to all intents and purposes, that of a slave to her master,' are the words of a writer in the *Encyclopædia of Religion and Ethics.* That this judgment is radically false may be proved from hundreds of instances throughout Scripture. God created man and woman in His image (Gen. I, 27)—both man and woman are in their spiritual nature akin to God; and both are invested with the same authority to subdue the earth and have dominion over it. The wives of the Patriarchs are almost the equals of their husbands; later generations regard them as quite alike. Miriam, alongside her brothers, is reckoned as one of the three emancipators from Egypt (Micah VI, 4); Deborah is 'Judge' in Israel, and leader in war of independence; and to Hannah her husband speaks: 'Why weepest thou? Am not I better to thee than ten sons?' In later centuries, we find woman among the Prophets (Huldah); and in the days of the Second Temple, on the throne (Queen Salome Alexandra). Nothing can well be nobler praise of woman than Prov. XXXI; and as regards the reverence due to her from her children, the mother was always placed on a par with the father (Exod. XX, 12; Lev. XIX, 3). A Jewish child would not have spoken to his grief-stricken mother as did Telemachus, the hero's son in the Odyssey: 'Go to the chamber, and mind thine own housewiferies. Speech shall be for man, for all, but for me in chief; for mine is the lordship in the house.'

The property rights of woman became clearly defined in the Talmudic period. Her legal status under Jewish law 'compares to its advantage with that of contemporary civilizations' (G. F. Moore). 'In respect to possessing independent estate, the Jewish wife was in a position far superior to that of English wives before the enactment of recent legislation' (Abrahams). An infinitely more important proof of her dominating place in Jewish life is the undeniable fact, that the hallowing of the Jewish home was her work; and that the laws of chastity were observed in that home, both by men and women, with a scrupulousness that has hardly ever been equalled. The Jewish Sages duly recognized her wonderful spiritual influence, and nothing could surpass the delicacy with which respect for her is inculcated: 'Love your wife as yourself, and honour her more than yourself. Be careful not to cause woman to weep, for God counts her tears. Israel was redeemed from Egypt on account of the virtue of its women. He who weds a good woman, it is as if he had fulfilled all the precepts of the Torah' (Talmud).

The respect and reverence which womanhood enjoyed in Judaism are not limited to noble and beautiful *sayings*. That respect and reverence were translated into life. True, neither minnesingers nor troubadours sang for Jewish women; and the immemorial chastity of the Jewess could not well go with courts of love and chivalric tournaments. And yet, one test alone is sufficient to show the abyss, in actual life, between Jewish and non-Jewish chivalry down to modern times. That test is wife-beating. On the one hand, both Rabbenu Tam, the renowned grandson of Rashi, and Rabbi Meir of Rothenburg, the illustrious jurist, poet, martyr and leader of thirteenth-century Judaism, could declare: 'This is a thing not done in Israel'; and the Shulchan Aruch prescribe it as the Beth Din's duty to punish a wife-beater, to excommunicate him, and—if this be of no avail—to compel him to divorce his wife with full Kethubah (Eben Ha-ezer, CLIV, 3). Among non-Jews, on the other hand, no less an authority on the Middle Ages than G. C. Coulton writes: 'To chastise one's wife was not only customary, not only expressly permitted by the statutes of some towns, but even formally granted by the Canon Law.' Even in our own country, as late as the fifteenth century, 'wife-beating was a recognized right of man, and was practised without shame by high as well as low' (G. M. Trevelyan). In the reign of Charles II, this recognized right of man began to be doubted; 'yet the lower ranks of the people who were always fond of the Common Law still claim and exert their ancient privilege' (Blackstone). Even more strange was the public sale of wives that was not unknown among the very poor. Thomas Hardy wrote his powerful novel, *The Mayor of Casterbridge*, on such a sale. Some years ago, *The Times* (January 4, 8, 11, 17, 1924) traced a number of these sales throughout the nineteenth century; and Prof. A. R. Wright has shown that folk-custom to have survived in various parts of England into the twentieth century.

In modern times, friend and foe of the Jew alike speak with admiration of his home, and echo the praise of the heathen seer: 'How beautiful are thy tents, O Jacob, thy dwelling-places, O Israel.' The following description may well be quoted here of the Sabbath eve of a humble toiler in the London Ghetto a half-century ago:—

'The roaring Sambatyon of life was at rest in the Ghetto; on thousands of squalid homes the light of Sinai shone.

'The Ghetto welcomed the Sabbath Bride with proud song and humble feast, and sped her parting with optimistic symbolisms of fire and wine, of spice and light and shadow. All around, their neighbours sought distraction in the blazing public-houses, and their tipsy bellowings resounded through the streets and mingled with the Hebrew hymns. Here and there the voice of a beaten woman rose on the air. But no Son of the Covenant was among the revellers or the wife-beaters; the Jews remained a chosen race, a peculiar people, faulty enough, but redeemed at least from the grosser vices—a little human islet won from the waters of animalism by the genius of ancient engineers' (I. Zangwill).

F

THE HALLOWING OF HISTORY

I

Israel is the author of the idea of History. The Egyptians and Babylonians left behind them annals of events, chronicles of dynasties, and boastful inscriptions of victories; but nothing that can be dignified by the name of historical writing. It is only in Israel that the whole human scene on earth was conceived as a unity, from its very beginning to the end of time. Thus Scripture does not begin with the Exodus, or even with the Call of Abraham, but with the Creation of the world and the birth of man. We are, of course, dogmatically told that 'the writing of history begins, like so many other things, with the Greeks'. But this is part of the Hellenic myth dominant in academic quarters. The Greeks could not rise to the concept of universal History without the belief in the *unity of mankind;* a conception they only learned centuries later through the Septuagint Version of the Hebrew Scriptures. Furthermore, the universe to the Greeks was not the creation of one supreme Mind but the confused inter-play of blind natural forces going on forever in a vain, endless recurrence, leading nowhither. Hence, they could not see any higher meaning in the story of man. Such also has ever been the opinion of those who share the Greek view of God and the universe, as did the free-thinkers of the eighteenth century. To them, 'history is little more than a register of the crimes, follies and misfortunes of mankind' (Gibbon). Not so the Teachers in Israel. They conceived of God as a Moral Power, and saw Him at work in the world. They traced the line of Divine action in the lives of men and nations. They saw in history a continuous revelation of Divine thought and purpose across the abyss of time. In clarion tones they proclaimed that Right was irresistible; and *that what ought to be must be, and will be.* They taught men to see the vision of 'the kingdom of God'—human society based on righteousness—as the Messianic goal of history. Schiller's profound utterance, *Die Weltgeschichte ist das Weltgericht* ('History is one long Day of Judgment'), which would have been unintelligible to a Greek or Roman, is but a striking epitome of Hebrew thought. And no view of the course of history is worth anything that is *not* essentially one with the Biblical position. Froude has eloquently restated it in the noble words: 'History is a voice for ever sounding across the centuries the laws of right and wrong. Opinions alter, manners change, creeds rise and fall, but the moral law is written on the tablets of eternity. For every false word or unrighteous deed, for cruelty and oppression, for lust or vanity, the price has to be paid at last; not always by the chief offenders, but paid by someone. Justice and truth alone endure and live.'

II

Israel, moreover, was the first to conceive of *history as a guide to the generations of men*, as is done throughout Deuteronomy, and to grasp its vital importance in the education of the individual as of the human group. A recent historian of British civilization has well put it: 'The past does not die; so long as spiritual continuity is maintained, the present life of a community is its whole accumulated past; and only by understanding that past can it understand itself or determine its future. A people, unconscious of its history, is like a man smitten with loss of memory, who wanders aimlessly, till he comes to grief' (Wingfield-Stratford). It is history that preserves men and nations from loss of memory, from loss of spiritual identity. 'Man is made man by history. The Jew is what he is by the history of his fathers, and he would be losing his better self were he to lose hold of his past history' (J. Jacobs).

The field of Jewish history is immeasurably vast; the Jew is met with everywhere, and his story opens very near the beginning of human civilization. And that story has, as no other, left its mark on the souls of men. 'The first part of Jewish history, the Biblical part, is a source from which, for many centuries, millions of human beings have derived instruction, solace, and inspiration. Its heroes have long ago become types, incarnations, of great ideals. The events it relates serve as living ethical formulæ. But a time will come—perhaps it is not very far off—when the second half of Jewish history, that people's life after the Biblical period, will be accorded the same treatment. The thousand years' martyrdom of the Jewish People, its unbroken pilgrimage, its tragic fate, its teachers of religion, its martyrs, philosophers, champions—this whole epic will, in days to come, sink deep into the memory of men. It will speak to the heart and conscience of men, and secure respect for the silvery hair of the Jewish People' (Dubnow).

III

Even a brief history of Jewish history, *i.e.* a critical estimate of Jewish historians, ancient, medieval and modern—cannot here be attempted. A few words might, however, be added on the *task of the Jewish historian* at the present day.

His primary aim should be neither to lament the past, nor to denounce, or to idealize it; but *to understand it.* He is, therefore, no longer to confine himself to the martyrdoms of the Jewish People, as the medieval chroniclers did; or even exclusively to the strivings of the Jewish spirit in the world of thought—which so largely claimed the attention of Graetz. Both the story of the martyrdoms and the spiritual strivings are, of course, basic. But, in addition, the historian to-day must seek to explain the position of the Jews in the national history of the countries where they dwelt. This calls, on the one hand, for a detailed study of Jewish communities—their institutions, cultural values, and religious endeavour; and, on the other hand, for a knowledge of the Jew's social, economic, and political relations to the general population. In this way alone can we in time hope to understand the 'cross-fertilization' of Jewish and non-Jewish ideas and influences in literature, folklore and life. The truth will then dawn upon the student that Judaism, in addition to being a body of doctrine and faith, a way of life and salvation, is also a *civilization*, a civilization that has made distinct contributions in every sphere of human life, human thought, and human achievement.

IV

'The history of Israel is *the great living proof of the working of Divine Providence* in the affairs of the world. Alone among the nations, Israel has shared in all great movements since mankind became conscious of their destinies. If there is no Divine purpose in the long travail of Israel, it is vain to seek for any such purpose in man's life. In the reflected light of that purpose, each Jew should lead his life with an added dignity' (J. Jacobs).

G

DEUTERONOMY: ITS ANTIQUITY AND MOSAIC AUTHORSHIP

1. Deuteronomy and the Religious Revival under King Josiah (621 b.c.e.)

King Josiah was the grandson of idolatrous King Manasseh, whose reign of fifty-five years was the longest in the annals of the Jewish People, and the darkest. Manasseh was swayed by a fanatical hatred for the Faith of his fathers. He nearly succeeded in uprooting True Religion in Israel, and flooded the land with obscene and gruesome idolatries. The Temple itself did not escape profanation: the sacred Altar was desecrated; the Ark itself was removed from out of the Holy of Holies; and new altars were erected for various weird cults. His years were one long Reign of Terror to the loyal minority who attempted to withstand the tide of religious barbarism. 'Manasseh shed innocent blood very much, till he had filled Jerusalem from one end to another,' says the author of the Book of Kings; and, according to a tradition preserved by Josephus, day by day a fresh batch of the Prophetic Order was led to execution. The aged Isaiah, it is said, met a martyr's death by being sawn asunder in a forest-tree in which he hid himself when attempting to escape from the fury of the tyrant.

No wonder that, when two years after the death of Manasseh, Josiah, a child of eight, came to the throne, the sacred books and teachings of Israel's Faith had been all but forgotten. However, in the group of influential persons responsible for the education and policy of the young King, there was a strong revulsion of feeling from the apostasy of the previous two generations, and a sincere yearning for a return to the historical Jewish national worship. It was, no doubt, due to the fact of having grown to manhood under such influences, that Josiah decided in the eighteenth year of his reign to repair the Temple, which had been permitted under his predecessors to fall into a shameful state of neglect. In the course of this restoration of the Temple, a discovery was made that was to prove of far-reaching importance for the spiritual revival of Israel. Under the accumulated rubbish and ruins of the decayed Temple-walls, Hilkiah the High Priest came upon a scroll which he handed to the King's scribe with the words, 'I have found the book of the law in the house of the Lord.' Shaphan the scribe brought the scroll to King Josiah, saying:

> 'Hilkiah, the priest, hath delivered me a book. And Shaphan read it before the king. And it came to pass when the king had heard the words of the book of the law, that he rent his clothes. And the king commanded Hilkiah the priest . . . and Shaphan, the scribe, . . . saying, Go ye, inquire of the Lord for me, and for the people, and for all Judah, concerning the words of this book that is found; for great is the wrath of the Lord that is kindled against us, because our fathers have not hearkened unto the words of this book to do according unto all that which is written concerning us' (ii Kings xxii, 3–14).

The following questions arise in connection with this narrative:

(*a*) What is here meant by 'the book of the law?'

Jewish and non-Jewish tradition and opinion hold that the scroll brought to the King was the Book of Deuteronomy. Some interpret Hilkiah's words ('I have found *the* book of the law!') to mean that he had found the autograph copy of Deuteronomy (ביד משה in the account given in i Chron. xxxiv, 14, being taken to mean, 'written by the hand of Moses himself'). Hence the extraordinary interest of all concerned in the discovery of this Book of the Law, and the effect of such discovery on the conscience of the King.

Neither is it accidental that the rediscovery of Deuteronomy in Josiah's day coincided with the rebuilding of the Jerusalem Sanctuary. Throughout the Ancient East, books of religious law and sacred documents were deposited in Temples at their erection, and were often found when the buildings were repaired. Naville, the renowned Egyptologist, instances from the Egyptian 'Book of the Dead' an exact parallel to the Hilkiah incident. He further adduces evidence that this custom was known and observed in Palestine at the time of Solomon. In that case, the copy of the Book of Deuteronomy in question would at least date from that reign. It had been immured in a foundation wall when the Temple was first built. In the time of Josiah, the breaches in the Temple-walls had become so considerable that great sums were required for 'the carpenters, the builders and the masons; and for buying timber and hewn stone to repair the House' (ii Kings xxii, 6). In the process of demolition, either the workmen must have come upon a foundation deposit, or the Book must have fallen out from a crevice; and the High Priest picked it up among the rubbish. In view of this general Eastern custom, and especially of the Egyptian parallel, 'there is no longer any justification for seeing any mystery or mystification in the incident of the finding of the Book of the Law by Hilkiah, the High Priest' (Jirku).

(*b*) How are we to explain the behaviour of the King?

The behaviour of the King—he is stirred to the depths of his being by the message of the Book, and yet that message is new to him—is easy of explanation. Though during the half-century and longer of the royal apostasy the public reading of the Torah had been interrupted, and though the Book itself had disappeared or had been destroyed by idolatrous priests, men still knew of the existence of such a Book, and had sufficient idea of its contents to be able to recognize it when the old Temple copy was suddenly brought to light. But so little were its contents *common knowledge* that, on its first reading, the King was struck with terror at its solemn prediction of the evils which would overtake a sinful Israel. 'The ignorance of the King, brought up by the priesthood, may well be accounted for by supposing him to have been vaguely taught the general precepts of the Law, but to have seen or heard for the first time this special Book' (Milman).

Ancient and medieval history records several instances of codes of law or sacred documents disappearing, and of their rediscovery generations, and even centuries, later. Such, for example, was the fate that overtook the code of Charlemagne in the ninth century. 'Before the close of the century in which he died, the whole body of his laws had fallen into utter disuse throughout the whole extent of his dominions. The charters, laws and chronicles of the later Carlovingian princes indicate either an absolute ignorance or an entire forgetfulness of the legislation of Charlemagne' (Sir James Stephen). The general neglect of the Scriptures in the age before the Reformation furnishes a partial illustration of the disappearance of Deuteronomy; even as the recovery, at the time of the Renaissance, of the original Hebrew Text of the Bible for the Western peoples is a parallel to its re-emergence under Josiah. In our own day, wherever the extirpation of religion is part of the State policy, as in Soviet Russia, we can quite imagine men and women who may have a superficial knowledge of the observances and beliefs of Judaism, but who had never read, or heard of, Deuteronomy, or any other Scripture.

2. Doubts in Regard to the Discovery of Deuteronomy

Nothing could be simpler than the above explanation of the finding of the scroll of Deuteronomy during the repair of the Temple. Bible Critics think otherwise. For over 150 years, they have declared that Deuteronomy, the Book of the Farewell Orations of Moses, was not the work of the Lawgiver, but was a spurious production written *during the generation of Josiah*. Some of them maintain further that this spurious work was hidden in the Temple with the intention that it should be brought to light, reach the King, and influence him in a definite way.

Not a word of all this appears in II Kings XXII, which describes the finding of the Book of the Law in the Temple; and there is nothing in that account that can justifiably serve as a basis for so strange a hypothesis. Hilkiah speaks of '*the* book of the law', ספר התורה, *i.e.* the well-known Torah. He could not have used such a phrase—it would not have been understood—if it were not known that such a book had been in existence before. It is clear that the finding of the book was regarded as the discovery of an old lost Scripture, a book of the Law of Moses. It was this fact alone which gave it authority. The King, when the book had been read to him, rent his garments, and sent to inquire of the LORD what it portended for him and his people; for 'great is the wrath of the LORD that is kindled against us because our fathers have not hearkened unto the words of this book'. The King was thus convinced of the Divine character of the Book, and also of its existence in the time of his forefathers. And it was this conviction alone that led to the religious revolution associated with his name—a revolution which succeeded despite all the machinery of heathenism that would recoil from nothing to thwart it. Not a whisper of doubt as to the Mosaic origin of the book is heard on any side, not from priests whose revenues it seriously interefered with, nor from prophets on many of whom it bore hardly less severely. 'It is plainly inconceivable that the whole nation should have at once adopted, without objection or criticism, a book of the existence of which no one knew anything before that time, a book which demanded radical modification of worship as well as of the whole religious life' (B. Jacob).

Though many of the Critics do not hesitate to bring the grave moral charge of forgery in connection with the Book, they are themselves not at all agreed on the question whether the author belonged to the prophetic circle or to the priestly class; whether the Book was the work of one man, or of a 'school'; whether it was produced in the time of Josiah, Manasseh, Hezekiah or even earlier; whether it originally was the same as we now have it, or it consisted of merely the code of laws—the historical orations having been added later; whether that code of laws came from one hand, or represented the gradual growth of centuries; whether some portion of the Book was Mosaic, or none of it; and whether it even *claimed* to be a work of Moses, or it made no such claim.

It was the English deists of the sixteenth century who first set afloat the theory that Deuteronomy was an essential forgery of the subtle priest, Hilkiah. That theory will not bear serious examination. This priest, whose ministrations in the Zion Sanctuary are not marked by any particular devotion or zeal, would not be the man to undertake to make it the one and only Place of Worship in Israel; neither was he the man to write those exhortations to godliness and humanity that have made Deuteronomy a pure stream of righteousness to the children of men. And surely this crafty ecclesiastic would not have invented laws (Deuteronomy XVIII, 6) which seriously infringed the vested privileges of the Jerusalem priesthood—unless we are to attribute to him a height of folly that would be psychologically inexplicable. In our generation, W. R. Smith, Dillmann, Kittel, Driver and many others have repudiated this absurd theory.

Even less convincing, but far more shocking to the moral sense, is the attempt to find the forger among the Prophets. A pioneer of nineteenth century Bible criticism in England, Bishop Colenso, thinks it likely that Jeremiah was the falsifier. 'What the inner voice ordered him to do,' Colenso has the shamelessness to write, 'he would do without hesitation, as by direct command of God, and all considerations of morality or immorality would not be entertained.' Verily, there are some things that do not deserve to be refuted: they should be exorcized.

It is refreshing to turn to the words of Rudolf Kittel written in 1925: 'There is no real evidence to prove that a pious or impious deceit was practised on Josiah. The assumption of forgery may be one of those hypotheses which, once set up, is so often repeated that finally every one believes it has been proven. Then one seems ultra-conservative and unscientific not to believe it. Who, nowadays, would take upon himself the odium of being behind the times?'

3. Internal Evidence as to the Antiquity of Deuteronomy

The internal evidence *against* the late composition of Deuteronomy, and *for* its Mosaic authorship, is overwhelming. From whatever side the question is examined, we find that the Book and the history of Josiah's times do not fit each other. To take a few examples. In the reign of Josiah, or in that of his immediate predecessors, the injunction to exterminate the Canaanites (xx, 16–18) and the Amalekites (xxv, 17–19), who had long since disappeared, would have been as utterly out of date as a royal proclamation in Great Britain at the present day ordering the expulsion of the Danes (W. H. Green). And how can a Code belong to the time of Josiah which, while it provides for the possible selection of a king in the future, nowhere implies an actual monarchical government? It finds it necessary to ordain that the king must be a native and not a foreigner (XVIII, 15), when the undisputed line of succession had for ages been fixed in the family of David. It furthermore regulates that the king must not 'cause the people to return to Egypt', as they seemed ready to do on every grievance in the days of Moses (Num. XIV, 4), but which no one ever dreamed of doing after they were fairly established in Canaan. In brief, regarding this whole law of monarchy, H. M. Wiener rightly says, 'As part of the work of Moses, all is clear; place it in a later age, all is confusion.'

This same judgment must be pronounced in regard to dozens of other matters in Deuteronomy. Thus, Israel is treated in its unbroken unity as a nation: *one* Israel is spoken of. There is not the slightest hint of the great secession of the Ten Tribes which had rent Israel in twain. Furthermore, in Deuteronomy the hope and the promise is that Israel is to be, 'high above all nations'; and the Law actually contemplates foreign wars (xx,10–15). This is quite understandable of the Mosaic generation, just about to embark on the conquest of Canaan. In the days of Josiah, however, it was a question whether Judah could even maintain its own existence. It had been brought to the edge of ruin by the Assyrian world-power, and within two decades of Josiah's day, its inhabitants were to be exiled to the banks of the Euphrates. Again, Edom is mentioned as the people to be most favoured by Israel; whereas from the time of David onwards, Edom was Judah's bitterest enemy, and is unsparingly denounced by Jeremiah, as by Isaiah before him. Lastly, in a book assumed to be specially produced to effect reformation in *worship*, how are we to explain the presence of such laws as regulate birds' nests or parapets upon a roof? Or, for that matter, what relevancy is there, for such a purpose, in Moses' historical retrospect? 'As part of the work of Moses, all is clear; place it in a later age, all is confusion.'

4. Centralization of Worship

The above considerations, and scores more of the same force and moment, have long been urged against the hypothesis of the late production of Deuteronomy. How is it that they have made so little impression upon the mass of the Critics?

The reason is as follows: the assumption that Deuteronomy is a product of Josiah's age is the basis of the theory on which the Critics have built their whole reconstruction of Bible history and religion. That theory—*viz., the Centralization of Worship in ancient Israel*—they have raised to a *dogma*, which it is in their opinion sheer heresy to question. Till the time of Josiah, they tell us, the ancient Israelite could sacrifice at any place he desired; numberless local shrines, 'high places,' dotted the land; and, though there was a good deal of pagan revelry, natural piety was a living thing among the people. But with the appearance of Deuteronomy the local cults were uprooted, religion was separated from 'life', and worship was centred in Jerusalem. There arose the idea of a Church; religion was now contained in a book; and it became an object of study, a theology. All these things, we are told, flowed from the centralization of worship; and such centralization was the result exclusively of the finding of Deuteronomy in the days of Josiah.

What is the truth in regard to centralization of worship, and these claims of the Wellhausen school of Bible Critics?

Briefly, not a single one of the Critical claims in connection with their dogma of centralization is in agreement with the historical facts. Centralization of worship did not originate in the age of Josiah; it was not the dominant motive of his reformation; neither was there any freedom of indiscriminate sacrifice before his day.

(*a*) *Centralization of worship did not originate in the age of Josiah.* It was present from the beginnings of Israel as a nation (Baxter). One need not be a great Bible scholar to know that, four hundred years before Josiah, the splendid *Temple of Solomon* was built on Mount Zion. That Temple was built by 'a levy out of all Israel' (I Kings v, 13); and for its dedication, Solomon assembles 'the elders of Israel and all the heads of the tribes' (VIII, 1). It is the central shrine of the whole House of Israel. (Wellhausen says, 'this view of Solomon's Temple is unhistorical,' because no king after Solomon is left uncensured for having tolerated the continuance of 'the high places'. It is the old familiar argument—see page 556—that the Law could not have existed because it can be shown that it was broken! According to such logic, there could never have been any Prohibition law in America.)

And for centuries before Solomon, there was the Central Sanctuary *at Shiloh.* Elkanah, the father of Samuel, 'went out of his city from year to year to worship and to sacrifice unto the LORD of hosts in Shiloh' (I Samuel I, 3). We are told of 'all the Israelites coming hither' (II, 15); and that the presiding priest represented 'all the tribes of Israel'.

But even centuries before Shiloh, we have the *Sanctuary at Sinai.* Nothing in Scripture is more minutely or more solemnly described than the building of the Mosaic tabernacle. Hypercritics have, in obedience to their programme, denied its existence. However, the study of comparative religions and their sacred structures has rendered their position absurd. Kittel's considered opinion is: 'It is part of the knowledge which has been confirmed in recent times, that in Moses' day and during the Desert wanderings there was a sacred tent (Tent of Meeting), which was the religious centre of the congregation in the Desert.'

(*b*) *Centralization of worship was not the dominant motive in Josiah's reformation.* Josiah's reformation from beginning to end was a crusade against the idolatry which had flooded the land, the Jerusalem sanctuary included; and the 'high places' were put down as part of this stern suppression of all idolatrous practices. Of a movement for centralization of worship as such, the narrative gives not a single hint. The whole condition of Jerusalem and Judah, as described in II Kings XXIII, was in flagrant violation of far more fundamental statutes than that of the central Sanctuary in Deuteronomy. And it cannot be repeated with sufficient emphasis that there *are* far more fundamental laws in Deuteronomy than this law concerning the Sanctuary. It has its place in chap XII, and recurs in the regulations for feasts, tithing, and priestly duty; but it is quite incorrect to say that this is the one grand idea which inspires the Book.

(*c*) *There was no freedom of indiscriminate altar-building in early Israel.* The alleged legitimacy, before the reformation of Josiah, of sacrificing wherever one desired, is based upon a wrong interpretation of Exodus XX, 21 (in English Bibles, XX, 24). 'An altar of earth thou shalt make unto Me, and shalt sacrifice thereon thy burnt offerings and thy peace offerings, thy sheep, and thine oxen; in every place where I cause My name to be remembered I will come unto thee and I will bless thee' (the last clause should be translated, 'in *whatever place I record My name*, I will come unto thee, and will bless thee'). This law does *not* authorize worship 'at the altars of earth and unhewn stones in all corners of the land', as claimed by W. Robertson Smith and those of his school. The law does not speak of 'altars', but only of 'an altar'; and that altar was to be erected 'in whatever place I record My name': *i.e.*, in any place sanctified by a special revelation of God. There is here nothing that conflicts with the command concerning centralization of worship in Deut. XII. There we have the general rule of worship at the Central Sanctuary; but that general rule does not forbid that, under proper Divine authority, exceptional sacrifices might be offered elsewhere. The clearest proof of this is that *Deuteronomy itself* orders the building of an Altar on Mount Ebal, precisely in the manner of Exodus XX, 21. Critics unanimously assign Exod. XX, 21, to what they call 'the Book of the Covenant', which they deem to be many centuries older than Josiah. But the 'Book of the Covenant' has the same ideal of centralization as Deuteronomy! It takes for granted a Central Shrine, and prescribes that three times in the year all males shall present themselves there before the Lord (Exod. XXIII, 17).

In view of all the above, one need not be surprised to learn that the alleged evil effects which followed the eventual enforcement of this ancient law of centralization of worship are purely imaginary. 'Centralization is the necessary consequence of monotheism and of the actual or ideal unity of Israel. The regulation of life according to Divine Law, the rise of a canon and a theology, are incidental to the development of every religion that has ever controlled and modified the life of a people' (B. Jacob).

Not all Scholars have remained blind to the true facts regarding the alleged lateness of the law of Centralization summarized above. From the very first, the hollowness of the Critical hypothesis was recognized by Sayce (Oxford), Hoffmann (Berlin), Naville (Geneva), Robertson (Glasgow), and W. H. Green (Princeton). Their protests were disregarded, but new recruits were found in Hommel, Dahse, Wiener, Moeller, Orr, Jacob and many others. In recent years, several outstanding Critics—Max Löhr, Th. Oesterreicher, W. Staerk—have come to realize that especially this fundamental pillar of the Bible Critical view has proved a delusion and a snare. In 1924, W. Staerk wrote:—'For over 100 years Old Testament studies have been under the spell of this hypothesis (*i.e.*, centralization of worship), which in its results has been fatal to the proper understanding of Israel's religion.'

5. The Unity and Mosaicity of Deuteronomy

No Book of the Bible bears on its face a stronger impress of unity—unity of thought, language, style and spirit—than Deuteronomy. And there is no reason to doubt that the various Discourses proceed from one hand, and that the same hand was responsible for the Code of laws. The alleged discrepancies between some of its statements and those in the other books of the Pentateuch, are largely the result of what Delitzsch called 'hunting for contradictions'. These alleged differences between the historical accounts in the earlier books and the rhetorical presentation of the same matter in the Farewell Addresses of the dying Lawgiver, are all of them capable of a natural explanation.

In recent decades, attention has been called to the fact that in some portions of Deuteronomy Israel is addressed in the singular (collectively), and in other portions in the plural; and it is urged that this is evidence of dual authorship. Anyone who is familiar with the Prophetic writings knows that the singular and the plural constantly interchange. This feature is found likewise in other literatures, English included. H. M. Wiener adduces the following from Sir Walter Scott's ' St. Ronan's Well ' (the italics are Wiener's):

> 'Why, *thou* suspicious monitor, have I not repeated a hundred times . . . And what need *you* come upon me, with *your* long lesson. *Thou* art, indeed, a curious animal. No man like you for stealing other men's inventions, and cooking them up in *your* own way. However, Harry, bating a little self-conceit and assumption, *thou* art as honest a fellow as ever man put faith in—clever, too, in *your* own style, though not quite the genius *you* would fain pass for. Come on *thine* own terms, and come as speedily as *thou* canst.'

As to the Mosaic authorship, the discoveries, since the beginning of this century, of the ancient Semitic codes confirm the antiquity of Deuteronomy. Thus, when King Amaziah punished his father's murderers, he refrained from having their families killed with them (II Kings XIV, 6), because the Law of Moses (Deut. XXIV, 16) forbade such procedure. To-day we know that the old Hittite law of the fifteenth pre-Christian century—contemporaneous with Moses—contains this same principle. Furthermore, the law concerning the rape of a betrothed or married woman in Deuteronomy has striking similarities to the law on the subject in the Hammurabi, the Hittite, and the Assyrian Codes. What reason, therefore, is there to assume that these laws of Deuteronomy are later than the Mosaic period? Paul Volz, who—together with Benno Jacob and Umberto Cassuto—has recently dealt a staggering blow to the Documentary Theory by demolishing all proof for the so-called Elohist source, has once again recorded his conviction that, on the strictly scientific evidence now available, Moses must have been a genius of the first order, a supreme Lawgiver who shaped an inchoate human mass into a great spiritual nation. *Can* we deny such a genius the ability to deliver his Farewell Discourses? 'When we carefully examine the arguments that have been collected in the work of more than a century of criticism, we find that not a shadow of a case can be made against the authenticity of the Mosaic speeches' (Wiener). The same holds true in reference to the Code of laws. Max Löhr and W. Staerk see no valid reason why the Deuteronomic legislation should not be Mosaic. And they are not the only scholars who have come to see the force of Dean Milman's words: 'If there are difficulties in connection with the Mosaic date of Deuteronomy, endeavour to assign Deuteronomy to any other period in the Jewish annals, and judge whether difficulties do not accumulate twenty-fold.'

Die-hard adherents of the Wellhausen school of Pentateuch criticism may derive what comfort they may from the following two concluding selections. The first is: 'Speaking for all branches of science, we may say that a hypothesis which has stood for half a century has done its duty. Measured by this standard, Wellhausen's theory is as good as the best. However, there is increasing evidence that it has had its day; and that those scholars who, from the first, expressed serious doubts of it are right' (Kittel).

The other selection cuts at the root of the whole method of deciding historical questions merely by so-called literary tests. It reads as follows: 'Must there not be something essentially illusory in a method which never gives or can give any independent proofs of its conclusions; and which too leads each new set of inquirers to reject what their next predecessors had been thought to have most clearly established?' (Speaker's Commentary).

H

THE AUTHORSHIP OF THE SECOND PART OF ISAIAH

Chapters XL–LXVI

These chapters differ considerably from those in the first half of Isaiah (chapters I–XXXIX). There the Prophet is speaking to the citizens of the independent state of Judah; here the Jewish exiles in Babylon are addressed—whose Temple has been destroyed, whose city Jerusalem is desolate and forsaken, and the people themselves suffering the physical and moral miseries of captivity. Thus there is a span of some 150 years between the political and social conditions reflected in the two parts of the Book. Furthermore, the predominant note in the prophecies of the first part of Isaiah is *warning*, lest Israel suffer destruction through rebellion against God; the note of the second part is *comfort*—Israel having suffered more than due for its sins.

Are both parts of the Book the work of one hand, Isaiah, the statesman-prophet of Jerusalem? Or, Is the second part the work of an unknown prophet in Babylon, whose anonymous writings were later appended to the Prophecies of Isaiah?

This question can be considered dispassionately. It touches no dogma, or any religious principle in Judaism; and, moreover, does not materially affect the understanding of the prophecies, or of the human conditions of the Jewish people that they have in view.

Until the beginning of the nineteenth century, it was almost the universal belief that the whole Book of Isaiah is by one hand. As early as 200 B.C.E. (Ecclesiasticus XLVIII, 23–25), chapters XL–LXVI were looked upon as the prediction of national disaster by Isaiah, and the consolation which the Prophet bequeathed to his brethren who were doomed in later times to the fate of exile. In these chapters it was held, the Prophet, is by the Spirit carried forward out of his own age; so that, in spirit, he is living amidst the exiles one hundred and fifty years after his day. Prediction, though not by any means the whole of prophecy, is yet of its very essence. This is particularly true of the prophecies of Isaiah. Thus, he *foretold* the fall of the Northern Kingdom; and we read that he prepared a written record of his teaching in another connection and deposited it as a sealed document for future days. 'Bind up the testimony, seal the instruction among my disciples. And I will wait for the LORD, that hideth His face from the house of Jacob, and I will hope in Him' (Isa. VIII, 16, 17). Why then could not his Prophetic gaze penetrate the future that awaited his people across the generations, and send his exiled brethren a message of comfort and hope? There is thus nothing inherently improbable in the traditional belief; and, though it finds few modern supporters, it has had able defenders among scholars, Jewish and non-Jewish; to name only Luzzatto in the nineteenth century, and Kaminka in the twentieth.

However, nearly all scholars to-day assume that the author of the later chapters was not identical with the author of chapters I–XXXIX. Ibn Ezra was the first who maintained that they are the work of a contemporary of the events which they presuppose. And it has often been pointed out that neither the appearance of Cyrus nor the captivity of Israel is ever *predicted* in them; they are everywhere assumed as facts known to the readers. The name 'Isaiah', it is argued, does not occur in the second part, nor any personal reference that could connect the author with the older Prophet. It is also held to be significant that, in the Synagogue, the order in which the Great Prophets were originally arranged was Jeremiah, Ezekiel, Isaiah—suggesting that those responsible for this ancient arrangement were conscious that elements were contained in the Book of Isaiah which were of a later date than the Prophet Ezekiel. For these reasons, among others, modern scholars refer to the author of chapters XL–LXVI as the Second Isaiah, or some equivalent term like Deutero-Isaiah, or Isaiah of Babylon.

None of the arguments for the dual authorship of Isaiah explain how the name of that Prophet whose outpouring brought about a resurrection of Jewish life in the Holy Land should have been clean forgotten; and forgotten by the very people who cherished the name of the earlier seer for prophecies which were of no direct concern to them (Kaminka). Neither is the newer view strengthened by those who would restrict the work of the Second Isaiah to chapters XL–LV, and confer the authorship of the remaining eleven chapters to 'Trito-Isaiah', or divide them among a third *and fourth* Prophet of that later age. The arguments on which such further subdivision is based are extremely precarious. And even from the literary angle, that procedure disregards the 'Law of parsimony' in Nature. The prophecies in chapters XL–LV reveal one of the world's greatest masters of literature; and no less so do the portions assigned by the Critics to 'Trito-Isaiah'. In grandeur, spiritual insight, and religious power, these chapters reach a level that is not surpassed by Isaiah of Jerusalem. It is no small strain on credulity to believe in two or three contemporary literary and spiritual geniuses of the first order (Wiener).

It may be added that the Critics are hopelessly at variance as to the place where those prophecies have been written. Some favour Babylon; others, Palestine, Egypt, or Phœnicia.

ZECHARIAH II, 14–IV, 7

CHAPTER II

14. 'Sing and rejoice, O daughter of Zion; for, lo, I come, and I will dwell in the midst of thee, saith the LORD. 15. And many nations shall join themselves to the LORD in that day, and shall be My people, and I will dwell in the midst of thee'; and thou shalt know that the LORD of hosts hath sent me unto thee. 16. And the LORD shall inherit Judah as His portion in the holy land, and shall choose Jerusalem again. 17. Be silent, all flesh, before the LORD: for He is aroused out of His holy habitation.

CAP. II. ב

14 רָנִּי
וְשִׂמְחִי בַּת־צִיּוֹן כִּי הִנְנִי־בָא וְשָׁכַנְתִּי בְתוֹכֵךְ נְאֻם־יְהוָה׃
טו וְנִלְווּ גוֹיִם רַבִּים אֶל־יְהוָה בַּיּוֹם הַהוּא וְהָיוּ לִי לְעָם
וְשָׁכַנְתִּי בְתוֹכֵךְ וְיָדַעַתְּ כִּי־יְהוָה צְבָאוֹת שְׁלָחַנִי אֵלָיִךְ׃
16 וְנָחַל יְהוָה אֶת־יְהוּדָה חֶלְקוֹ עַל אַדְמַת הַקֹּדֶשׁ וּבָחַר
17 עוֹד בִּירוּשָׁלִָם׃ הַס כָּל־בָּשָׂר מִפְּנֵי יְהוָה כִּי נֵעוֹר
מִמְּעוֹן קָדְשׁוֹ׃

CHAPTER III

1. And he showed me Joshua the high priest standing before the angel of the LORD, and Satan standing at his right hand to accuse him. 2. And the LORD said unto Satan: 'The LORD rebuke thee, O Satan, yea, the LORD that hath chosen Jerusalem rebuke thee; is not this man a brand plucked out of the fire?' 3. Now Joshua was clothed with filthy garments, and stood before the angel. 4. And he answered and spoke unto those

CAP. III. ג

א וַיַּרְאֵנִי אֶת־יְהוֹשֻׁעַ הַכֹּהֵן הַגָּדוֹל עֹמֵד לִפְנֵי מַלְאַךְ יְהוָה
2 וְהַשָּׂטָן עֹמֵד עַל־יְמִינוֹ לְשִׂטְנוֹ׃ וַיֹּאמֶר יְהוָה אֶל־הַשָּׂטָן
יִגְעַר יְהוָה בְּךָ הַשָּׂטָן וְיִגְעַר יְהוָה בְּךָ הַבֹּחֵר בִּירוּשָׁלִָם
3 הֲלוֹא זֶה אוּד מֻצָּל מֵאֵשׁ׃ וִיהוֹשֻׁעַ הָיָה לָבֻשׁ בְּגָדִים
4 צוֹאִים וְעֹמֵד לִפְנֵי הַמַּלְאָךְ׃ וַיַּעַן וַיֹּאמֶר אֶל־הָעֹמְדִים

Zechariah was one of the exiles who returned from Babylon when Cyrus promulgated his decree of Restoration in the year 537. He began his prophecies about 17 years afterwards. Disastrous seasons and the hostility of neighbours had discouraged the people, and all operations in connection with rebuilding the Temple had long ceased.

At this juncture the Prophet Zechariah appears, rouses the people from their despondency and assures them of the Divine assistance in their work of rebuilding the Temple and of national rehabilitation. '*Not by might, nor by power, but by My spirit, saith the LORD of Hosts*' is his message. These words of Zechariah may be said to proclaim the lesson of all Jewish history; it is certainly the Prophetic teaching of the Maccabean Festival with which his name is linked in the synagogue service. Even a brief résumé of Maccabean events (such as is given at the end of the second Haftorah for Chanukah, p. 947) will show the appropriateness of these chapters for the anniversary of the re-dedication of the Temple after its defilement by the Syrians.

14. *I will dwell in the midst of thee.* Through the visible symbol of the restored Temple.

17. *be silent.* All hostile efforts—now on the part of the Samaritans and other opponents, and later any human opposition to God's ultimate purpose—shall fail.

CHAPTER III

Zechariah's messages are chiefly conveyed by means of visions. The object of these visions, so dramatically described in the remainder of the Haftorah, is to banish the disturbing fears which were depressing the people.

1. *Joshua.* The first high priest after the Restoration. He was prominently associated with Zerubbabel, the then Governor of Judah, in the erection of the Second Temple. Zerubbabel was the grandson of Jehoiachin, the last independent king of Judah.

Satan. One who opposes with false accusations. Satan accuses Joshua and the people of sinfulness, and that they are, therefore, unworthy to rebuild the Temple. Perhaps a similar feeling, arising out of their disappointments, depressed the people. But Satan is rebuked; and the returned exiles assured that their fears are groundless.

2. *a brand plucked out of the fire.* Something precious (in this case, the Returned Remnant of Israel) snatched from destruction.

3. *filthy garments.* Symbolizing the iniquities of the people that retard the completeness of the Redemption.

that stood before him, saying: 'Take the filthy garments from off him.' And unto him he said: 'Behold, I cause thine iniquity to pass from thee, and I will clothe thee with robes.' 5. And I said: 'Let them set a fair mitre upon his head.' So they set a fair mitre upon his head, and clothed him with garments; and the angel of the LORD stood by. 6. And the angel of the LORD forewarned Joshua, saying: 7. 'Thus saith the LORD of hosts: If thou wilt walk in My ways, and if thou wilt keep My charge, and wilt also judge My house, and wilt also keep My courts, then I will give thee free access among these that stand by. 8. Hear now, O Joshua the high priest, thou and thy fellows that sit before thee; for they are men that are a sign; for, behold, I will bring forth My servant the Shoot. 9. For behold the stone that I have laid before Joshua; upon one stone are seven facets; behold, I will engrave the graving thereof, saith the LORD of hosts: And I will remove the iniquity of that land in one day. 10. In that day, saith the LORD of hosts, shall ye call every man his neighbour under the vine and under the fig-tree.'

לְפָנָיו לֵאמֹר הָסִירוּ הַבְּגָדִים הַצֹּאִים מֵעָלָיו וַיֹּאמֶר אֵלָיו
ה רְאֵה הֶעֱבַרְתִּי מֵעָלֶיךָ עֲוֺנֶךָ וְהַלְבֵּשׁ אֹתְךָ מַחֲלָצוֹת׃ וָאֹמַר
יָשִׂימוּ צָנִיף טָהוֹר עַל־רֹאשׁוֹ וַיָּשִׂימוּ הַצָּנִיף הַטָּהוֹר עַל־
6 רֹאשׁוֹ וַיַּלְבִּשֻׁהוּ בְּגָדִים וּמַלְאַךְ יְהוָה עֹמֵד׃ וַיָּעַד מַלְאַךְ
7 יְהוָה בִּיהוֹשֻׁעַ לֵאמֹר׃ כֹּה־אָמַר יְהוָה צְבָאוֹת אִם־בִּדְרָכַי
תֵּלֵךְ וְאִם אֶת־מִשְׁמַרְתִּי תִשְׁמֹר וְגַם־אַתָּה תָּדִין אֶת־בֵּיתִי
וְגַם תִּשְׁמֹר אֶת־חֲצֵרָי וְנָתַתִּי לְךָ מַהְלְכִים בֵּין הָעֹמְדִים
8 הָאֵלֶּה׃ שְׁמַע־נָא יְהוֹשֻׁעַ ׀ הַכֹּהֵן הַגָּדוֹל אַתָּה וְרֵעֶיךָ
הַיֹּשְׁבִים לְפָנֶיךָ כִּי־אַנְשֵׁי מוֹפֵת הֵמָּה כִּי־הִנְנִי מֵבִיא אֶת־
9 עַבְדִּי צֶמַח׃ כִּי ׀ הִנֵּה הָאֶבֶן אֲשֶׁר נָתַתִּי לִפְנֵי יְהוֹשֻׁעַ
עַל־אֶבֶן אַחַת שִׁבְעָה עֵינָיִם הִנְנִי מְפַתֵּחַ פִּתֻּחָהּ נְאֻם יְהוָה
י צְבָאוֹת וּמַשְׁתִּי אֶת־עֲוֺן הָאָרֶץ־הַהִיא בְּיוֹם אֶחָד׃ בַּיּוֹם
הַהוּא נְאֻם יְהוָה צְבָאוֹת תִּקְרְאוּ אִישׁ לְרֵעֵהוּ אֶל־תַּחַת
גֶּפֶן וְאֶל־תַּחַת תְּאֵנָה׃

v. 10. כצ"ל

4. *he. i.e.* the angel.

those that stood before him. i.e. attendant angels who are represented as waiting upon him.

take the filthy garments from off him. Symbolizes the removal of the people's sin, forgiveness.

5. *I said.* The idea of a defiled priesthood is intolerable to the Prophet, and he bursts forth with the request that the complete sign of priestly purity and national acceptance be granted.

mitre. Or, 'diadem.' Let Joshua not only be cleansed and clothed, but crowned as well.

6. *forewarned. i.e.* solemnly assured.

7. *if thou wilt walk in My ways.* The first condition of the priesthood is that, not only in the Temple but in his own life, the priest shall observe the Divine requirements of conduct, and always remember to Whose service he is consecrated.

that stand by. Among these attendant angels (v. 4). Targum and Kimchi explain 'after death', and take it as an allusion to the immortality of the soul.

8. *thy fellows.* The assistant priests.

men that are a sign. Of God's favour. The restored priesthood is a pledge of the coming of the Messianic Kingdom. Humble and modest as were the beginnings of the Temple, they were portents which contained within them the pledge of the fulfilment of the complete Redemption.

the Shoot. According to Rashi, Zechariah here means Zerubbabel, who as the civic leader will complete, with Joshua as the spiritual leader, the rehabilitated state. A comparison with VI, 12, supports this interpretation.

9. *for behold the stone.* The head or coping stone of the Temple (see last verse of the Haftorah, 'head stone') which in this vision is set before Joshua to symbolize the certainty of the rebuilding.

upon one stone are seven facets. i.e. upon every stone in the Temple there shall be 'seven eyes', conveying the idea of the very special watchfulness and care that God will exercise over His house (Kimchi).

The same commentator quotes the interesting opinion of his father that in the number 'seven' we may see a reference to the seven great leaders of the period to whom the Jewish rebirth was due: Joshua, Ezra, Nehemiah, Zerubbabel, Haggai, Zechariah and Malachi.

I will engrave the graving thereof. As the engraving completes and beautifies a work, so God assures the people that the Temple will be completed to every detail (Kimchi).

I will remove the iniquity of that land. Sin, the chief cause of sorrow and suffering, will be removed with the coming of the new Temple.

10. *shall ye call. i.e.* invite. A picture of general felicity and security.

Chapter IV

1. And the angel that spoke with me returned, and waked me, as a man that is wakened out of his sleep. 2. And he said unto me: 'What seest thou?' And I said: 'I have seen, and behold a candlestick all of gold, with a bowl upon the top of it, and its seven lamps thereon; there are seven pipes, yea, seven, to the lamps, which are upon the top thereof; 3. and two olive-trees by it, one upon the right side of the bowl, and the other upon the left side thereof.' 4. And I answered and spoke to the angel that spoke with me, saying: 'What are these, my lord?' 5. Then the angel that spoke with me answered and said unto me: 'Knowest thou not what these are?' And I said: 'No, my lord.' 6. Then he answered and spoke unto me, saying: 'This is the word of the LORD unto Zerubbabel, saying: Not by might, nor by power, but by My spirit, saith the LORD of hosts. 7. Who art thou, O great mountain before Zerubbabel? thou shalt become a plain; and he shall bring forth the top stone with shoutings of Grace, grace unto it.'

CAP. IV. ד

א וַיָּשָׁב הַמַּלְאָךְ הַדֹּבֵר בִּי וַיְעִירֵנִי כְּאִישׁ אֲשֶׁר־יֵעוֹר מִשְּׁנָתוֹ׃
2 וַיֹּאמַר אֵלַי מָה אַתָּה רֹאֶה וָאֹמַר רָאִיתִי וְהִנֵּה מְנוֹרַת
זָהָב כֻּלָּהּ וְגֻלָּהּ עַל־רֹאשָׁהּ וְשִׁבְעָה נֵרֹתֶיהָ עָלֶיהָ שִׁבְעָה
3 וְשִׁבְעָה מוּצָקוֹת לַנֵּרוֹת אֲשֶׁר עַל־רֹאשָׁהּ׃ וּשְׁנַיִם זֵיתִים
4 עָלֶיהָ אֶחָד מִימִין הַגֻּלָּה וְאֶחָד עַל־שְׂמֹאלָהּ׃ וָאַעַן וָאֹמַר
ה אֶל־הַמַּלְאָךְ הַדֹּבֵר בִּי לֵאמֹר מָה אֵלֶּה אֲדֹנִי׃ וַיַּעַן הַמַּלְאָךְ
הַדֹּבֵר בִּי וַיֹּאמֶר אֵלַי הֲלוֹא יָדַעְתָּ מָה־הֵמָּה אֵלֶּה וָאֹמַר
6 לֹא אֲדֹנִי׃ וַיַּעַן וַיֹּאמֶר אֵלַי לֵאמֹר זֶה דְּבַר־יְהוָה אֶל־
זְרֻבָּבֶל לֵאמֹר לֹא בְחַיִל וְלֹא בְכֹחַ כִּי אִם־בְּרוּחִי אָמַר
7 יְהוָה צְבָאוֹת׃ מִי־אַתָּה הַר־הַגָּדוֹל לִפְנֵי זְרֻבָּבֶל לְמִישֹׁר
וְהוֹצִיא אֶת־הָאֶבֶן הָרֹאשָׁה תְּשֻׁאוֹת חֵן ׀ חֵן לָהּ׃

v. 2. ואמר קרי

Chapter IV

Another vision. The Prophet's thoughts now turn to Zerubbabel, and the need to encourage him in his work. He would further enforce the lesson that God alone is the source of all Light, as well as power, to rulers and people alike.

2. *candlestick.* Such as stood in the Second Temple.

seven pipes. One to each lamp carrying the supply of oil.

3. *two olive-trees.* Representing Joshua and Zerubbabel, who were appointed respectively to the spiritual and civil leadership, and by whom the work in hand would be accomplished; see *v.* 12 (Kimchi).

6. *this is the word. i.e.* the message of the LORD to Zerubabbel. As the lights are controlled by an unseen agency, so behind Zerubbabel and his allotted work is the invisible spirit and help of God. All the difficulties in the way will disappear; and, in spite of the hostility and mockings of the people who have hitherto opposed, he will complete the building of the Temple, 'not by might, nor by power, but by My spirit, saith the LORD of hosts.'

7. *who art thou, O great mountain?* Repeating the above idea. Whatever obstacles may arise to hinder him, will all be overcome.

bring forth the top stone. Amid the joyful acclamations of the people when they see the Temple completed.

Grace, grace unto it. i.e. may God's grace and favour rest on it!

I KINGS VII, 40–50

CHAPTER VII

40. And [1]Hiram made the pots, and the shovels, and the basins. ¶So Hiram made an end of doing all the work that he wrought for king Solomon in the house of the LORD: 41. the two pillars, and the two bowls of the capitals that were on the top of the pillars; and the two networks to cover the two bowls of the capitals that were on the top of the pillars; 42. and the four hundred pomegranates for the two networks, two rows of pomegranates for each network, to cover the two bowls of the capitals that were upon the top of the pillars; 43. and the ten bases, and the ten lavers on the bases; 44. and the one sea, and the twelve oxen under the sea; 45. and the pots, and the shovels, and the basins; even all these vessels, which Hiram made for king Solomon, in the house of the LORD, were of burnished brass. 46. In the plain of the Jordan did the king cast them, in the clay ground between Succoth and Zarethan. 47. And Solomon left all the vessels unweighed, because they were exceeding many; the weight of the brass could not be found out. 48. And Solomon made all the vessels that were in the house of the LORD: the golden altar, and the table whereupon the showbread was, of gold; 49. and the candlesticks, five on the right side, and five on the left, before the

[1] Heb. *Hirom.*

CAP. VII. ז

מ וַיַּעַשׂ חִירוֹם אֶת־הַכִּיֹּרוֹת
וְאֶת־הַיָּעִים וְאֶת־הַמִּזְרָקוֹת וַיְכַל חִירָם לַעֲשׂוֹת אֶת־כָּל־
41 הַמְּלָאכָה אֲשֶׁר עָשָׂה לַמֶּלֶךְ שְׁלֹמֹה בֵּית יְהוָה׃ עַמֻּדִים
שְׁנַיִם וְגֻלֹּת הַכֹּתָרֹת אֲשֶׁר־עַל־רֹאשׁ הָעַמֻּדִים שְׁתָּיִם
וְהַשְּׂבָכוֹת שְׁתַּיִם לְכַסּוֹת אֶת־שְׁתֵּי גֻּלּוֹת הַכֹּתָרֹת אֲשֶׁר
42 עַל־רֹאשׁ הָעַמּוּדִים׃ וְאֶת־הָרִמֹּנִים אַרְבַּע מֵאוֹת לִשְׁתֵּי
הַשְּׂבָכוֹת שְׁנֵי־טוּרִים רִמֹּנִים לַשְּׂבָכָה הָאֶחָת לְכַסּוֹת אֶת־
43 שְׁתֵּי גֻּלֹּת הַכֹּתָרֹת אֲשֶׁר עַל־פְּנֵי הָעַמּוּדִים׃ וְאֶת־הַמְּכֹנוֹת
44 עֶשֶׂר וְאֶת־הַכִּיֹּרֹת עֲשָׂרָה עַל־הַמְּכֹנוֹת׃ וְאֶת־הַיָּם הָאֶחָד
מה וְאֶת־הַבָּקָר שְׁנֵים־עָשָׂר תַּחַת הַיָּם׃ וְאֶת־הַסִּירוֹת וְאֶת־
הַיָּעִים וְאֶת־הַמִּזְרָקוֹת וְאֵת כָּל־הַכֵּלִים הָאֹהֶל אֲשֶׁר עָשָׂה
46 חִירָם לַמֶּלֶךְ שְׁלֹמֹה בֵּית יְהוָה נְחֹשֶׁת מְמֹרָט׃ בְּכִכַּר
הַיַּרְדֵּן יְצָקָם הַמֶּלֶךְ בְּמַעֲבֵה הָאֲדָמָה בֵּין סֻכּוֹת וּבֵין
47 צָרְתָן׃ וַיַּנַּח שְׁלֹמֹה אֶת־כָּל־הַכֵּלִים מֵרֹב מְאֹד מְאֹד לֹא
48 נֶחְקַר מִשְׁקַל הַנְּחֹשֶׁת׃ וַיַּעַשׂ שְׁלֹמֹה אֵת כָּל־הַכֵּלִים
אֲשֶׁר בֵּית יְהוָה אֵת מִזְבַּח הַזָּהָב וְאֶת־הַשֻּׁלְחָן אֲשֶׁר עָלָיו
49 לֶחֶם הַפָּנִים זָהָב׃ וְאֶת־הַמְּנֹרוֹת חָמֵשׁ מִיָּמִין וְחָמֵשׁ מִשְּׂמֹאל

v. 45. האלה קרי

Appropriately to Chanukah, the Festival of the Re-dedication of the Second Temple, this section contains a description of the appurtenances for the First Temple; also (v. 48–50) of the golden utensils for the interior of the House made under Solomon's supervision, and the consecrated gifts bequeathed by his father David (v. 50).

40. *Hiram.* A famous brass worker, the son of a Tyrian father, who was also a skilled artist, and an Israelitish mother.

44. *and the one sea.* An enormous circular vessel ten cubits (about 18 feet) in diameter and five cubits (about 9 feet) in depth. It was richly decorated, and was supported on the backs of twelve brazen oxen, three looking towards each of the cardinal points of the compass. See *v.* 23–26 of this chapter.

46. *in the plains of the Jordan.* Hiram set up his foundry in the valley of Jordan at the spot where he found suitable soil ('clay ground') for his moulds.

between Succoth and Zarethan. Succoth was on the other, the east side of the river, in Gad. Zarethan was on the west side of Jordan, about 24 miles north of the Dead Sea.

47. The amount of brass used was so great that no attempt was made to keep an account of it.

48. *the golden altar.* The altar of incense.

49. *the flowers.* The flower-like ornaments of the candlesticks.

To appreciate the significance of the Temple in the life of ancient Israel, we must continue reading the next chapter of the First Book of

Sanctuary, of pure gold; and the flowers, and the lamps, and the tongs, of gold; 50. and the cups, and the snuffers, and the basins, and the pans, and the fire-pans, of pure gold; and the hinges, both for the doors of the inner house, the most holy place, and for the doors of the house, that is, of the temple, of gold.

לִפְנֵי הַדְּבִיר זָהָב סָגוּר וְהַפֶּרַח וְהַנֵּרֹת וְהַמֶּלְקָחַיִם זָהָב׃
נ וְהַסִּפּוֹת וְהַמְזַמְּרוֹת וְהַמִּזְרָקוֹת וְהַכַּפּוֹת וְהַמַּחְתּוֹת זָהָב
סָגוּר וְהַפֹּתוֹת לְדַלְתוֹת הַבַּיִת הַפְּנִימִי לְקֹדֶשׁ הַקֳּדָשִׁים
לְדַלְתֵי הַבַּיִת לַהֵיכָל זָהָב׃

Kings, Solomon's Prayer of Dedication (set aside as the Haftorah for the first and eighth days of Tabernacles); or, better still, during Chanukah, the story of the Re-dedication of the Temple as told in the First Book of Maccabees. There is nothing finer in the whole history of heroism, or more soul-stirring in the annals of religion, than the account of this handful of Jewish warriors who were 'prepared to live or die nobly' in order that the light of revealed truth and righteousness be not extinguished in a heathen world. The following is a selection from the first four chapters of I Maccabees:—

'And King Antiochus wrote to his whole kingdom, that all should be one people, and that each should forsake his own laws. And he sent letters unto Jerusalem and the cities of Judah that they should profane the Sabbaths and feasts, pollute the sanctuary, and build altars and temples and shrines for idols; and whosoever shall not do according to the word of the King, he shall die. And he appointed overseers over all the people, and he commanded the cities of Judah to sacrifice, city by city. And they did evil things in the land; and they made Israel to hide themselves in every place of refuge which they had. And they rent in pieces the Books of the Law which they found, and set them on fire. And whosoever was found with any Book of the Covenant, and if any consented to the Law, the king's sentence delivered him to death.

'And in those days rose up Mattathias, a priest from Jerusalem; and he dwelt at Modin. And he had five sons, John, Simon, Judah (who was called Maccabæus), Eleazar, Jonathan. And he saw the blasphemies that were committed in Judah and in Jerusalem, and Mattathias and his sons rent their clothes, and put on sackcloth, and mourned exceedingly.

'And the king's officers, that were enforcing the apostasy, came into the city Modin. And many of Israel came unto them, and Mattathias and his sons were gathered together. And the king's officers spake to Mattathias, saying, "Thou art a ruler and an honourable and great man in this city, and strengthened with sons and brethren; now therefore come thou first and do the commandment of the king, as all nations have done, and the men of Judah, and they that remain in Jerusalem; so shalt thou and thy house be in the number of the king's friends, and thou and thy children shall be honoured with silver and gold, and many rewards." And Mattathias answered and said with a loud voice, "*Though all the nations that are under the king's dominion obey him, and fall away every one from the religion of their fathers, yet will I and my sons and my brethren walk in the covenant of our fathers.*" And Mattathias cried out in the city with a loud voice, saying, "Whosoever is zealous for the Law, and maintaineth the Covenant, let him follow me."

'Then were gathered together unto them every one that offered himself willingly for the Law. And all they that fled from the evils were added to them, and became a stay unto them. And they mustered a host, and pulled down the altars; and they pursued after the sons of pride, neither suffered they the sinner to triumph.'

'And the days of Mattathias drew near that he should die, and his son Judah rose up in his stead. And all his brethren helped him, and they fought with gladness the battle of Israel. King Antiochus sent forty thousand footmen, and seven thousand horse to go into the land of Judaea, and to destroy it. And Judah, who was called Maccabaeus, said, "Victory in battle standeth not in the multitude of a host, but strength is from Heaven. They come unto us in fulness of insolence and lawlessness, to destroy us and our wives and children: but we fight for our lives and our Law. It is better for us to die in battle, than to look upon the evils of our nation and the Sanctuary. Nevertheless, as may be the will in Heaven, so shall He do." And they that were with Judah joined battle, and the heathens were discomfited when they saw the boldness of them that were with Judah, and how they were ready either to live or die nobly. And Judah and his brethren said, "Behold, our enemies are discomfited, let us go up to cleanse the Sanctuary, and to dedicate it afresh." And they built a new altar after the fashion of the former; and they built the Sanctuary and the inner parts of the House. And they made the holy vessels new, and they brought the candlestick, and the altar, and the table, into the Temple. On the five and twentieth day of the ninth month, which is the month Kislev, at what time and on what day the heathens had profaned it, even on that day was it dedicated afresh. And all the people fell upon their faces, and worshipped and gave praise unto Heaven.'

ADDITIONAL READING: NUMBERS XXVIII, 9–15

ISAIAH LXVI

CHAPTER LXVI

1. Thus saith the LORD:
The heaven is My throne,
And the earth is My footstool;
Where is the house that ye may build unto Me?
And where is the place that may be My resting-place?
2. For all these things hath My hand made,
And so all these things came to be,
Saith the LORD;
But on this man will I look,
Even on him that is poor and of a contrite spirit,
And trembleth at My word.
3. He that killeth an ox is as if he slew a man;
He that sacrificeth a lamb, as if he broke a dog's neck.
He that offereth a meal-offering, as if he offered swine's blood;
He that maketh a memorial-offering of frankincense, as if he blessed an idol;
According as they have chosen their own ways,
And their soul delighteth in their abominations;

CAP. LXVI. סו

א כֹּה אָמַר יְהוָה הַשָּׁמַיִם כִּסְאִי וְהָאָרֶץ הֲדֹם רַגְלָי אֵי־זֶה
2 בַיִת אֲשֶׁר תִּבְנוּ־לִי וְאֵי־זֶה מָקוֹם מְנוּחָתִי׃ וְאֶת־כָּל־אֵלֶּה
יָדִי עָשָׂתָה וַיִּהְיוּ כָל־אֵלֶּה נְאֻם־יְהוָה וְאֶל־זֶה אַבִּיט אֶל־
3 עָנִי וּנְכֵה־רוּחַ וְחָרֵד עַל־דְּבָרִי׃ שׁוֹחֵט הַשּׁוֹר מַכֵּה־אִישׁ
זוֹבֵחַ הַשֶּׂה עֹרֵף כֶּלֶב מַעֲלֵה מִנְחָה דַּם־חֲזִיר מַזְכִּיר
לְבֹנָה מְבָרֵךְ אָוֶן גַּם־הֵמָּה בָּחֲרוּ בְּדַרְכֵיהֶם וּבְשִׁקּוּצֵיהֶם

v. 2. קמץ בז"ק ibid. למדנחאי אֶל־ v. 3. כצ"ל

The Second Temple is nearing completion, and the Prophet corrects false ideas concerning the Temple building and the worship therein. He contrasts the faithful Israelites with the apostates, given to idolatrous practices, and doomed to extinction. The chapter concludes with the renewed assurance of the triumph of the Faithful Remnant, and the universal worship of the one God. Verse 23 that enshrines this hope in the phrase, 'From one New Moon to another, and from one Sabbath to another,' makes the section an appropriate Haftorah for this Sabbath.

1. *Where is the house?* God's presence cannot be limited to one spot. ('Behold heaven and the heaven of heavens cannot contain Thee; how much less this house that I have builded!' I Kings VIII, 27). The purpose of the Temple was to lead men to reverence and uprightness, and the sacrifices were to help the worshipper expel evil thoughts and desires from his heart, and burn them as burnt offerings on the altar (Kimchi). If these conditions did not exist, the Temple was not a house fit for God's glory.

2. *all these things. i.e.* heaven and earth came into existence at the word of God (Abarbanel). *will I look.* Not to external splendours of the building or to the elaborate ceremonial within does God look, but to the existence of a humble and sincere piety among the worshippers who make their will subservient to God ('that trembleth at My word').

3. The lit. translation of the first part of this verse is: 'The slaughterer of an ox, a slayer of a man, etc.' This is often explained to mean that he who offers the statutory sacrifices but is not animated by a sincere spirit is no better than he who takes a leading part in some horrible and unholy cult involving human sacrifices. No Prophet, however, would be guilty of such an exaggeration. More probably the Prophet has in mind those who combined outward observance of Jewish ceremonial with the detestable rites of some debased fetish-worship which existed among those left in Israel after the Assyrian conquest (II Kings XVII, 33 f). There is no reason, however, to assume that these heathen worshippers indulged, or were permitted by the Persian authorities to indulge, in human sacrifices. The words מכה איש only mean 'striketh a man' (Ibn Ezra), and not 'slayeth a man'. The Heb. root of מכה is used for 'inflicting stripes', and may therefore here refer to sacred flagellations or scourgings which, as is well known, formed part of many pagan secret cults. He that sacrificeth an ox at God's Temple, complains our Prophet, is at the same time acting as flagellator or sacred scourger at heathen mystery worship!

4 נַפְשָׁם חָפֵצָה׃ גַּם־אֲנִי אֶבְחַר בְּתַעֲלֻלֵיהֶם וּמְגוּרֹתָם אָבִיא
לָהֶם יַעַן קָרָאתִי וְאֵין עוֹנֶה דִּבַּרְתִּי וְלֹא שָׁמֵעוּ וַיַּעֲשׂוּ הָרַע
ה בְּעֵינַי וּבַאֲשֶׁר לֹא־חָפַצְתִּי בָּחָרוּ׃ שִׁמְעוּ דְּבַר־יְהוָה
הַחֲרֵדִים אֶל־דְּבָרוֹ אָמְרוּ אֲחֵיכֶם שֹׂנְאֵיכֶם מְנַדֵּיכֶם לְמַעַן
6 שְׁמִי יִכְבַּד יְהוָה וְנִרְאֶה בְשִׂמְחַתְכֶם וְהֵם יֵבֹשׁוּ׃ קוֹל
שָׁאוֹן מֵעִיר קוֹל מֵהֵיכָל קוֹל יְהוָה מְשַׁלֵּם גְּמוּל לְאֹיְבָיו׃
7 בְּטֶרֶם תָּחִיל יָלָדָה בְּטֶרֶם יָבוֹא חֵבֶל לָהּ וְהִמְלִיטָה
8 זָכָר׃ מִי־שָׁמַע כָּזֹאת מִי רָאָה כָּאֵלֶּה הֲיוּחַל אֶרֶץ בְּיוֹם
אֶחָד אִם־יִוָּלֵד גּוֹי פַּעַם אֶחָת כִּי־חָלָה גַּם־יָלְדָה צִיּוֹן אֶת־
9 בָּנֶיהָ׃ הַאֲנִי אַשְׁבִּיר וְלֹא אוֹלִיד יֹאמַר יְהוָה אִם־אֲנִי
י הַמּוֹלִיד וְעָצַרְתִּי אָמַר אֱלֹהָיִךְ׃ שִׂמְחוּ אֶת־יְרוּשָׁלִַם
וְגִילוּ בָהּ כָּל־אֹהֲבֶיהָ שִׂישׂוּ אִתָּהּ מָשׂוֹשׂ כָּל־הַמִּתְאַבְּלִים
11 עָלֶיהָ׃ לְמַעַן תִּינְקוּ וּשְׂבַעְתֶּם מִשֹּׁד תַּנְחֻמֶיהָ לְמַעַן תָּמֹצּוּ

4. Even so I will choose their mockings,
And will bring their fears upon them;
Because when I called, none did answer;
When I spoke, they did not hear,
But they did that which was evil in Mine eyes,
And chose that in which I delighted not.

5. Hear the word of the LORD,
Ye that tremble at His word:
Your brethren that hate you, that cast you out for My name's sake, have said:
'Let the LORD be glorified,
That we may gaze upon your joy,'
But they shall be ashamed.
6. Hark! an uproar from the city,
Hark! it cometh from the temple,
Hark! the Lord rendereth recompense to His enemies.
7. Before she travailed, she brought forth;
Before her pain came,
She was delivered of a man-child.
8. Who hath heard such a thing?
Who hath seen such things?
Is a land born in one day?
Is a nation brought forth at once?
For as soon as Zion travailed,
She brought forth her children.
9. Shall I bring to the birth, and not cause to bring forth?
Saith the LORD;
Shall I that cause to bring forth shut the womb?
Saith thy God.

10. Rejoice ye with Jerusalem,
And be glad with her, all ye that love her;
Rejoice for joy with her,
All ye that mourn for her;

11. That ye may suck, and be satisfied
With the breast of her consolations;
That ye may drink deeply with delight
Of the abundance of her glory.

כצ״ל v. 8.

4. *their mockings.* Because they—the apostate and obstinate transgressors—have *chosen* to do that which mocks Me (*v.* 3), I will *choose* for them suffering that will mock their hopes.
their fears. i.e. the very things they fear, I will bring upon them.

5–6. Addressed to the faithful whose hopes are ridiculed by their adversaries.

5. *your brethren. i.e.* the semi-idolatrous schismatics.
cast you out. That refuse to associate with you (Cheyne).
let the LORD be glorified . . . joy. These are the taunting words of the insolent opponents.

6. *an uproar.* The Prophet already seems to hear the sound of the coming judgment against the mockers.

7–14. The Prophet again breaks off with words of comfort to the faithful community. Though ridiculed by their adversaries, increase of population (*v.* 7), peace and prosperity (*v.* 12) shall be theirs.

7. Zion is the mother, and the verse describes the swift increase in her population through the re-inforcement of faithful children from all parts.

8. *is a land born in one day?* Emphasizes the rapidity of this remarkable increase.

9. The work of Restoration and salvation shall be complete. God will not leave it unfinished.

10. A call to the children restored, and those still in Exile, to rejoice with Jerusalem.
all ye that mourn for her. All those in Exile, and those who since the Return have been depressed at the slow realization of their hopes in Zion.

11. The figure of Zion as Mother is retained.

12 וְהִתְעַנַּגְתֶּם מִזִּיז כְּבוֹדָהּ׃ כִּי־כֹה ׀ אָמַר יְהוָה הִנְנִי
נֹטֶה־אֵלֶיהָ כְּנָהָר שָׁלוֹם וּכְנַחַל שׁוֹטֵף כְּבוֹד גּוֹיִם וִינַקְתֶּם
13 עַל־צַד תִּנָּשֵׂאוּ וְעַל־בִּרְכַּיִם תְּשָׁעֳשָׁעוּ׃ כְּאִישׁ אֲשֶׁר אִמּוֹ
14 תְּנַחֲמֶנּוּ כֵּן אָנֹכִי אֲנַחֶמְכֶם וּבִירוּשָׁלִַם תְּנֻחָמוּ׃ וּרְאִיתֶם
וְשָׂשׂ לִבְּכֶם וְעַצְמוֹתֵיכֶם כַּדֶּשֶׁא תִפְרַחְנָה וְנוֹדְעָה יַד־יְהוָה
טו אֶת־עֲבָדָיו וְזָעַם אֶת־אֹיְבָיו׃ כִּי־הִנֵּה יְהוָה בָּאֵשׁ יָבוֹא
וְכַסּוּפָה מַרְכְּבֹתָיו לְהָשִׁיב בְּחֵמָה אַפּוֹ וְגַעֲרָתוֹ בְּלַהֲבֵי־
16 אֵשׁ׃ כִּי בָאֵשׁ יְהוָה נִשְׁפָּט וּבְחַרְבּוֹ אֶת־כָּל־בָּשָׂר וְרַבּוּ
17 חַלְלֵי יְהוָה׃ הַמִּתְקַדְּשִׁים וְהַמִּטַּהֲרִים אֶל־הַגַּנּוֹת אַחַר
אַחַד בַּתָּוֶךְ אֹכְלֵי בְּשַׂר הַחֲזִיר וְהַשֶּׁקֶץ וְהָעַכְבָּר יַחְדָּו
18 יָסֻפוּ נְאֻם־יְהוָה׃ וְאָנֹכִי מַעֲשֵׂיהֶם וּמַחְשְׁבֹתֵיהֶם בָּאָה

v. 17. אחת קרי

12. For thus saith the LORD:
Behold, I will extend peace to her like a river,
And the wealth of the nations like an overflowing stream,
And ye shall suck thereof;
Ye shall be borne upon the side,
And shall be dandled upon the knees.
13. As one whom his mother comforteth,
So will I comfort you;
And ye shall be comforted in Jerusalem.
14. And when ye see this, your heart shall rejoice,
And your bones shall flourish like young grass;
And the hand of the LORD shall be known toward His servants,
And He will have indignation against His enemies.

15. For, behold, the LORD will come in fire,
And His chariots shall be like the whirlwind;
To render His anger with fury,
And His rebuke with flames of fire.
16. For by fire will the LORD contend,
And by His sword with all flesh;
And the slain of the Lord shall be many.
17. They that sanctify themselves and purify themselves
To go unto the gardens,
Behind one in the midst,
Eating swine's flesh, and the detestable thing, and the mouse,
Shall be consumed together, saith the LORD.

18. For I [know] their works and their thoughts; [the time] cometh, that I will gather all nations and tongues; and they shall come, and shall see My glory. 19. And I will work a sign among them, and I will send such as escape of them unto the nations, to Tarshish, Pul and Lud, that draw the bow, to Tubal and Javan, to the isles afar off, that have not heard My fame, neither have seen My glory; and they shall declare My glory among the nations.

12. Peace and prosperity shall stream into Zion, like a river that overflows its banks.

shall be borne upon the side. Continues the figure of the nursling in the preceding verse. The nations become their foster-mothers.

13. *as one whom his mother comforteth.* 'As the grown man, coming back with wounds and weariness upon him to be comforted of his mother' (G. A. Smith), finds there the comfort he seeks, so will God comfort the men of Zion. God is our Mother.

14. *your bones shall flourish.* Your bodily frames shall be filled with renewed vigour.

15–16. The Prophet returns to the coming judgment of God against His enemies.

17. Once more a reference to the idolatries of the apostates.

they that sanctify themselves. Words used satirically of the preparation by these people for their heathenish rites (Kimchi).

unto the gardens. i.e. to join in the abominable cults often practised there (Isa. LXV, 3).

behind one in the midst. The Massoretes read the feminine form אחת for 'one'. The reference therefore is to an *asherah*, a grove of sacred trees or poles set up near an altar for idol-worship in the garden. If the word is read *as written*, אחד, the reference would be to a priest who led the company of worshippers.

the mouse. Its flesh was, with that of the other 'detestable things', eaten as part of the mystic rites of this heathen cult.

19. *I will work a sign among them. i.e.* the nations, by a mighty act of judgment and retribution. Those of the peoples that survive are represented as going to far-off lands to tell of God, His greatness and glory.

Tarshish. The town of Tartessus in Spain.
Pul and Lud. Probably districts in N. Africa.
Javan. Greece.

לְקַבֵּץ אֶת־כָּל־הַגּוֹיִם וְהַלְּשֹׁנוֹת וּבָאוּ וְרָאוּ אֶת־כְּבוֹדִי׃
19 וְשַׂמְתִּי בָהֶם אוֹת וְשִׁלַּחְתִּי מֵהֶם ׀ פְּלֵיטִים אֶל־הַגּוֹיִם
תַּרְשִׁישׁ פּוּל וְלוּד מֹשְׁכֵי קֶשֶׁת תֻּבַל וְיָוָן הָאִיִּים הָרְחֹקִים
אֲשֶׁר לֹא־שָׁמְעוּ אֶת־שִׁמְעִי וְלֹא־רָאוּ אֶת־כְּבוֹדִי וְהִגִּידוּ
כ אֶת־כְּבוֹדִי בַּגּוֹיִם׃ וְהֵבִיאוּ אֶת־כָּל־אֲחֵיכֶם ׀ מִכָּל־הַגּוֹיִם ׀
מִנְחָה ׀ לַיהוָה בַּסּוּסִים וּבָרֶכֶב וּבַצַּבִּים וּבַפְּרָדִים
וּבַכִּרְכָּרוֹת עַל הַר קָדְשִׁי יְרוּשָׁלִַם אָמַר יְהוָה כַּאֲשֶׁר יָבִיאוּ
21 בְנֵי יִשְׂרָאֵל אֶת־הַמִּנְחָה בִּכְלִי טָהוֹר בֵּית יְהוָה׃ וְגַם־
22 מֵהֶם אֶקַּח לַכֹּהֲנִים לַלְוִיִּם אָמַר יְהוָה׃ כִּי כַאֲשֶׁר הַשָּׁמַיִם
הַחֲדָשִׁים וְהָאָרֶץ הַחֲדָשָׁה אֲשֶׁר אֲנִי עֹשֶׂה עֹמְדִים לְפָנַי
23 נְאֻם־יְהוָה כֵּן יַעֲמֹד זַרְעֲכֶם וְשִׁמְכֶם׃ וְהָיָה מִדֵּי־חֹדֶשׁ בְּחָדְשׁוֹ
וּמִדֵּי שַׁבָּת בְּשַׁבַּתּוֹ יָבוֹא כָל־בָּשָׂר לְהִשְׁתַּחֲוֺת לְפָנַי אָמַר
24 יְהוָה׃ וְיָצְאוּ וְרָאוּ בְּפִגְרֵי הָאֲנָשִׁים הַפֹּשְׁעִים בִּי כִּי תוֹלַעְתָּם
לֹא תָמוּת וְאִשָּׁם לֹא תִכְבֶּה וְהָיוּ דֵרָאוֹן לְכָל־בָּשָׂר׃
וְהָיָה מִדֵּי־חֹדֶשׁ בְּחָדְשׁוֹ וּמִדֵּי שַׁבָּת בְּשַׁבַּתּוֹ יָבוֹא
כָל־בָּשָׂר לְהִשְׁתַּחֲוֺת לְפָנַי אָמַר יְהוָה׃

v. 23. סבירין יבואו

20. And they shall bring all your brethren out of all the nations for an offering unto the LORD, upon horses, and in chariots, and in litters, and upon mules, and upon swift beasts, to My holy mountain Jerusalem, saith the LORD, as the children of Israel bring their offering in a clean vessel into the house of the LORD. 21. And of them also will I take for the priests and for the Levites, saith the LORD. 22. For as the new heavens and the new earth, which I will make, shall remain before Me, saith the LORD, so shall your seed and your name remain.

23. And it shall come to pass,
That from one new moon to another,
And from one sabbath to another,
Shall all flesh come to worship before Me,
Saith the LORD.

24. And they shall go forth, and look
Upon the carcasses of the men that have rebelled against Me;
For their worm shall not die,
Neither shall their fire be quenched;
And they shall be an abhorring unto all flesh.

And it shall come to pass,
That from one new moon to another,
And from one sabbath to another,
Shall all flesh come to worship before Me,
Saith the Lord.

20. Impressed by what they thus hear, these far-off nations shall bring to Jerusalem all the Israelites dwelling among them, and in a manner appropriate to the greatness of the occasion.

21. *and of them also will I take for priests and Levites.* Of the converted Gentiles who bring, and from the Jews who are brought back, I will take to assist the priests and Levites in their service (Kimchi). This thought is quite in accordance with the universalist spirit in Isaiah.

22 and 23. In this new (and better) order of things, the race and influence of Israel will continue for ever, leading to the fulfilment of Israel's mission, *i.e.* the universal worship of the One God, with Jerusalem as the devotional capital of mankind.

23. *from one new moon to another.* lit. 'as often as there is a new moon on its new moon, etc.', *i.e.* on every New Moon and Sabbath; New Moon by New Moon and Sabbath by Sabbath.

24. A survey again of the conflict against evil, and its final defeat, through which the above great goal is reached. Delitzsch points out that, in effect, the thought is the same as in the concluding sentence of other sections of the second half of Isaiah—'there is no peace unto the wicked' (XLVIII, 22, and LVII, 21). Under the figure of the worm that dieth not, and the fire that is not quenched, we have here a symbolical representation of the lasting remorse that, on the realization of their wickedness, troubles the souls of evil-doers. The knowledge of this, which will be clear to all ('And they shall go forth and look'), will become a restraining moral influence. It will be a factor in the attainment of the great consummation (the universal worship of the one true God) described in the previous verse.

they shall go forth. The worshippers.

According to ancient Jewish custom, *v.* 23 is read a second time after *v.* 24, so as to conclude the book (of which this is the last chapter) with words of comfort and encouragement. There is a similar direction in regard to concluding Malachi, Lamentations and Ecclesiastes. In each case, the last verse but one is reprinted in the Heb. text, and repeated during the reading in the Synagogue.

HAFTORAH MACHAR CHODESH הפטרת מחר חדש

(Eve of New Moon)

I SAMUEL XX, 18–42

Chapter XX

18. And Jonathan said unto him: 'To-morrow is the new moon; and thou wilt be missed, because thy seat will be empty. 19. And in the third day thou shalt hide thyself well, and come to the place where thou didst hide thyself in the day of work, and shalt remain by the stone Ezel. 20. And I will shoot three arrows to the side-ward, as though I shot at a mark. 21. And, behold, I will send the lad: Go, find the arrows. If I say unto the lad: Behold, the arrows are on this side of thee; take them, and come; for there is peace to thee and no hurt, as the LORD liveth. 22. But if I say thus unto the boy: Behold, the arrows are beyond thee; go thy way; for the LORD hath sent thee away. 23. And as touching the matter which I and thou have spoken of, behold, the LORD is between me and thee for ever.' ¶ 24. So David hid himself in the field; and when the new moon was come, the king sat him down to the meal to eat. 25. And the king sat upon his seat, as at other times, even upon the seat by the wall; and Jonathan stood up, and Abner sat by Saul's side; but David's place was empty. 26. Nevertheless Saul spoke not any thing that day; for he thought: 'Something hath befallen him, he is unclean; surely he is not clean.' 27. And it came to pass on the morrow after the new moon, which was the

Cap. XX. כ

18 וַיֹּֽאמֶר־ל֥וֹ יְהוֹנָתָ֖ן מָחָ֣ר חֹ֑דֶשׁ וְנִפְקַ֕דְתָּ כִּ֥י יִפָּקֵ֖ד
19 מוֹשָׁבֶֽךָ׃ וְשִׁלַּשְׁתָּ֙ תֵּרֵ֣ד מְאֹ֔ד וּבָאתָ֙ אֶל־הַמָּק֔וֹם אֲשֶׁר־
נִסְתַּ֥רְתָּ שָּׁ֖ם בְּי֣וֹם הַֽמַּעֲשֶׂ֑ה וְיָ֣שַׁבְתָּ֔ אֵ֖צֶל הָאֶ֥בֶן הָאָֽזֶל׃
כ וַאֲנִ֕י שְׁלֹ֥שֶׁת הַחִצִּ֖ים צִדָּ֣ה אוֹרֶ֑ה לְשַֽׁלַּֽח־לִ֖י לְמַטָּרָֽה׃
21 וְהִנֵּה֙ אֶשְׁלַ֣ח אֶת־הַנַּ֔עַר לֵ֖ךְ מְצָ֣א אֶת־הַחִצִּ֑ים אִם־אָמֹ֨ר
אֹמַ֜ר לַנַּ֗עַר הִנֵּ֧ה הַחִצִּ֣ים ׀ מִמְּךָ֣ וָהֵ֗נָּה קָחֶ֧נּוּ וָבֹ֛אָה כִּֽי־שָׁל֥וֹם
22 לְךָ֛ וְאֵ֥ין דָּבָ֖ר חַי־יְהוָֽה׃ וְאִם־כֹּ֤ה אֹמַר֙ לָעֶ֔לֶם הִנֵּ֥ה הַחִצִּ֖ים
23 מִמְּךָ֣ וָהָ֑לְאָה לֵ֕ךְ כִּ֥י שִֽׁלַּחֲךָ֖ יְהוָֽה׃ וְהַ֨דָּבָ֔ר אֲשֶׁ֥ר דִּבַּ֖רְנוּ
24 אֲנִ֣י וָאָ֑תָּה הִנֵּ֧ה יְהוָ֛ה בֵּינִ֥י וּבֵינְךָ֖ עַד־עוֹלָֽם׃ וַיִּסָּתֵ֥ר
דָּוִ֖ד בַּשָּׂדֶ֑ה וַיְהִ֣י הַחֹ֔דֶשׁ וַיֵּ֧שֶׁב הַמֶּ֛לֶךְ עַֽל־הַלֶּ֖חֶם לֶאֱכֽוֹל׃
כה וַיֵּ֣שֶׁב הַ֠מֶּלֶךְ עַל־מ֨וֹשָׁב֜וֹ כְּפַ֣עַם ׀ בְּפַ֗עַם אֶל־מוֹשַׁב֙ הַקִּ֔יר
וַיָּ֙קָם֙ יְה֣וֹנָתָ֔ן וַיֵּ֥שֶׁב אַבְנֵ֖ר מִצַּ֣ד שָׁא֑וּל וַיִּפָּקֵ֖ד מְק֥וֹם דָּוִֽד׃
26 וְלֹֽא־דִבֶּ֥ר שָׁא֛וּל מְא֖וּמָה בַּיּ֣וֹם הַה֑וּא כִּ֤י אָמַר֙ מִקְרֶ֣ה
27 ה֔וּא בִּלְתִּ֥י טָה֛וֹר ה֖וּא כִּי־לֹ֥א טָהֽוֹר׃ וַיְהִ֗י מִֽמָּחֳרַ֤ת

v. 20. ה׳ רפה v. 24. אל קרי

There is hardly a more beautiful figure in history than Jonathan. Truly he was 'a very perfect knight', the very essence of chivalry. To the Rabbis, he stands for all time as the type of disinterested, self-denying friendship (Ethics of the Fathers, v, 17). His greatness was manifested in the very clash of duty between his loyalty to his father and his love of David. Jonathan's was a task of rare difficulty, to combine duty to his father with devotion to his friend. Yet he fails in neither. To Saul he was an affectionate son and faithful officer; and 'no cloud of envy intercepted his admiration of the great warrior, the sweet singer of Israel, who hereafter was to supersede him' (Jowett). It is fortunate that the opening incident of the chapter, occurring on a *Machar Chodesh*—the eve of the New Moon, enables the story of Jonathan's friendship and self-abnegation to be included among the Lessons from the Prophets.

Saul, half-crazed by jealousy of David's popularity and growing hold on the people, seeks to destroy him. David places himself in the power of Jonathan, who at first is quite unwilling to believe evil of his father. He decides to sound his father and warn David.

18. *new moon.* The New Moon was in ancient times celebrated as an important festive occasion.

19. *in the day of work.* lit. 'on the day of the deed'. Probably a reference to the occasion when Jonathan interceded with Saul for David's life (XIX, 2–4).

stone Ezel. A cairn called Ezel.

20. *arrows.* This shows that archery was a familiar sport in ancient Israel.

23. *the LORD is between me and thee.* There is a sworn covenant between us.

26. *not clean.* The peace-offering sacrifice could not be eaten by anyone who was not ceremoniously clean (Lev. VII, 20 f).

second day, that David's place was empty; and Saul said unto Jonathan his son: 'Wherefore cometh not the son of Jesse to the meal, neither yesterday, nor to-day?' 28. And Jonathan answered Saul: 'David earnestly asked leave of me to go to Beth-lehem; 29. and he said: Let me go, I pray thee; for our family hath a sacrifice in the city; and my brother, he hath commanded me; and now, if I have found favour in thine eyes, let me get away, I pray thee, and see my brethren. Therefore he is not come unto the king's table.' ¶ 30. Then Saul's anger was kindled against Jonathan, and he said unto him: 'Thou son of perverse rebellion, do not I know that thou hast chosen the son of Jesse to thine own shame, and unto the shame of thy mother's nakedness? 31. For as long as the son of Jesse liveth upon the earth, thou shalt not be established, nor thy kingdom. Wherefore now send and fetch him unto me, for he deserveth to die.' 32. And Jonathan answered Saul his father, and said unto him: 'Wherefore should he be put to death? what hath he done?' 33. And Saul cast his spear at him to smite him; whereby Jonathan knew that it was determined of his father to put David to death. 34. So Jonathan arose from the table in fierce anger and did eat no food the second day of the month; for he was grieved for David, and because his father had put him to shame. ¶ 35. And it came to pass in the morning, that Jonathan went out into the field at the time appointed with David, and a little lad with him. 36. And he said unto his lad: 'Run, find now the arrows which I shoot.' And as the lad ran, he shot an arrow beyond him. 37. And when the lad was come to the place of the arrow which Jonathan had shot, Jonathan cried after the lad, and said: 'Is not the arrow beyond thee?' 38. And Jonathan cried after the lad: 'Make speed, hasten, stay not.' And Jonathan's lad gathered up the arrows, and came to his master. 39. But the lad knew not any thing; only Jonathan and David knew the matter. 40. And Jonathan gave his weapons unto his lad, and said unto him: 'Go, carry them to the city.' 41. And as soon as the lad was gone, David arose out of a place toward the South, and fell on his face to the ground, and bowed down three times; and they kissed one another, and wept one with

הַחֹדֶשׁ הַשֵּׁנִי וַיִּפָּקֵד מְקוֹם דָּוִד וַיֹּאמֶר שָׁאוּל אֶל־יְהוֹנָתָן
בְּנוֹ מַדּוּעַ לֹא־בָא בֶן־יִשַׁי גַּם־תְּמוֹל גַּם־הַיּוֹם אֶל־הַלָּחֶם׃
28 וַיַּעַן יְהוֹנָתָן אֶת־שָׁאוּל נִשְׁאֹל נִשְׁאַל דָּוִד מֵעִמָּדִי עַד־בֵּית
29 לָחֶם׃ וַיֹּאמֶר שַׁלְּחֵנִי נָא כִּי זֶבַח מִשְׁפָּחָה לָנוּ בָּעִיר וְהוּא
צִוָּה־לִי אָחִי וְעַתָּה אִם־מָצָאתִי חֵן בְּעֵינֶיךָ אִמָּלְטָה נָּא
וְאֶרְאֶה אֶת־אֶחָי עַל־כֵּן לֹא־בָא אֶל־שֻׁלְחַן הַמֶּלֶךְ׃
ל וַיִּחַר־אַף שָׁאוּל בִּיהוֹנָתָן וַיֹּאמֶר לוֹ בֶּן־נַעֲוַת הַמַּרְדּוּת
הֲלוֹא יָדַעְתִּי כִּי־בֹחֵר אַתָּה לְבֶן־יִשַׁי לְבָשְׁתְּךָ וּלְבֹשֶׁת
31 עֶרְוַת אִמֶּךָ׃ כִּי כָל־הַיָּמִים אֲשֶׁר בֶּן־יִשַׁי חַי עַל־הָאֲדָמָה
לֹא תִכּוֹן אַתָּה וּמַלְכוּתֶךָ וְעַתָּה שְׁלַח וְקַח אֹתוֹ אֵלַי כִּי
32 בֶן־מָוֶת הוּא׃ וַיַּעַן יְהוֹנָתָן אֶת־שָׁאוּל אָבִיו וַיֹּאמֶר אֵלָיו
33 לָמָּה יוּמַת מֶה עָשָׂה׃ וַיָּטֶל שָׁאוּל אֶת־הַחֲנִית עָלָיו
לְהַכֹּתוֹ וַיֵּדַע יְהוֹנָתָן כִּי־כָלָה הִיא מֵעִם אָבִיו לְהָמִית אֶת־
34 דָּוִד׃ וַיָּקָם יְהוֹנָתָן מֵעִם הַשֻּׁלְחָן בָּחֳרִי־אָף וְלֹא־אָכַל
בְּיוֹם־הַחֹדֶשׁ הַשֵּׁנִי לֶחֶם כִּי נֶעְצַב אֶל־דָּוִד כִּי הִכְלִמוֹ
לה אָבִיו׃ וַיְהִי בַבֹּקֶר וַיֵּצֵא יְהוֹנָתָן הַשָּׂדֶה לְמוֹעֵד דָּוִד
36 וְנַעַר קָטֹן עִמּוֹ׃ וַיֹּאמֶר לְנַעֲרוֹ רֻץ מְצָא־נָא אֶת־הַחִצִּים
אֲשֶׁר אָנֹכִי מוֹרֶה הַנַּעַר רָץ וְהוּא־יָרָה הַחֵצִי לְהַעֲבִרוֹ׃
37 וַיָּבֹא הַנַּעַר עַד־מְקוֹם הַחֵצִי אֲשֶׁר יָרָה יְהוֹנָתָן וַיִּקְרָא
יְהוֹנָתָן אַחֲרֵי הַנַּעַר וַיֹּאמֶר הֲלוֹא הַחֵצִי מִמְּךָ וָהָלְאָה׃
38 וַיִּקְרָא יְהוֹנָתָן אַחֲרֵי הַנַּעַר מְהֵרָה חוּשָׁה אַל־תַּעֲמֹד וַיְלַקֵּט
39 נַעַר יְהוֹנָתָן אֶת־הַחִצִּי וַיָּבֹא אֶל־אֲדֹנָיו׃ וְהַנַּעַר לֹא־יָדַע
מ מְאוּמָה אַךְ יְהוֹנָתָן וְדָוִד יָדְעוּ אֶת־הַדָּבָר׃ וַיִּתֵּן יְהוֹנָתָן
אֶת־כֵּלָיו אֶל־הַנַּעַר אֲשֶׁר־לוֹ וַיֹּאמֶר לוֹ לֵךְ הָבֵיא הָעִיר׃
41 הַנַּעַר בָּא וְדָוִד קָם מֵאֵצֶל הַנֶּגֶב וַיִּפֹּל לְאַפָּיו אַרְצָה וַיִּשְׁתַּחוּ
שָׁלֹשׁ פְּעָמִים וַיִּשְׁקוּ ׀ אִישׁ אֶת־רֵעֵהוּ וַיִּבְכּוּ אִישׁ אֶת־רֵעֵהוּ

v. 38. החצים קרי

34. *grieved for David.* He grieves not for the insult to himself, but for the shame done to his friend before the whole court.

41. *until David exceeded. i.e.* in weeping. The thought of separation from his friend overwhelmed him.

42. *go in peace.* Jonathan comforts David with the reassurance of his undying love and devotion. Saul's violence soon assumes a another, until David exceeded. 42. And Jonathan said to David: 'Go in peace, forasmuch as we have sworn both of us in the name of the LORD, saying: The LORD shall be between me and thee, and between my seed and thy seed, for ever.'

42 עַד־דָּוִד הִגְדִּיל׃ וַיֹּאמֶר יְהוֹנָתָן לְדָוִד לֵךְ לְשָׁלוֹם אֲשֶׁר
נִשְׁבַּעְנוּ שְׁנֵינוּ אֲנַחְנוּ בְּשֵׁם יְהוָה לֵאמֹר יְהוָה יִהְיֶה ׀ בֵּינִי
וּבֵינֶךָ וּבֵין זַרְעִי וּבֵין זַרְעֲךָ עַד־עוֹלָם׃

murderous fury—85 priests are slain for having given bread to the hungry fugitive David. If Jonathan had, at the moment of farewell, only thought of providing his friend with a few loaves of bread, that massacre might have been averted (Talmud). When the tragic end came, and both Saul and Jonathan died for their people, David lamented them in the most beautiful elegy in literature:

Thy glory, O Israel, is slain upon thy high places!
How are the mighty fallen! . . .
Saul and Jonathan were lovely and pleasant in their lives,
And in their death they were not divided;
They were swifter than eagles,
They were stronger than lions.
Ye daughters of Israel, weep over Saul,
Who clothed you in scarlet delicately,
Who put ornaments of gold upon your apparel.
How are the mighty fallen in the midst of the battle!
O, Jonathan, slain upon thy high places,
I am distressed for thee, my brother Jonathan;
Very pleasant hast thou been unto me:
Thy love to me was wonderful,
Passing the love of women.
How are the mighty fallen,
And the weapons of war perished!

When, to the example of David and Jonathan, we add the deep friendship of two women, Ruth and Naomi: ('Whither thou goest I will go; and where thou lodgest, I will lodge: thy people shall be my people, and thy God my God; where thou diest, will I die, and there will I be buried: the LORD do so to me and more also, if aught but death part thee and me,') we realize that the Bible is also the supreme Book of Friendship.

HAFTORAH SHEKALIM הפטרת שקלים

ADDITIONAL READING: EXODUS XXX, 11–16

II KINGS XI, 17–XII, 17

CHAPTER XI — CAP. XI. יא

17.[1] And Jehoiada made a covenant between the LORD and the king and the people, that they should be the LORD's people; between the king also and the people.

17 *וַיִּכְרֹת יְהוֹיָדָע אֶת־הַבְּרִית בֵּין יְהוָה
וּבֵין הַמֶּלֶךְ וּבֵין הָעָם לִהְיוֹת לְעָם לַיהוָה וּבֵין הַמֶּלֶךְ וּבֵין

[1] Sephardim begin here.

* כאן מתחילין הספרדים

The historical background of the Haftorah is of deep interest. In its opening sentences, it gives us the concluding scenes of the only revolution in the history of the Kingdom of Judah during the 347 years of its existence. And that revolution was directed against a foreign princess who had attempted to exterminate the native dynasty of the House of David.

Athaliah, daughter of Ahab, king of Israel, had married Jehoram, king of Judah, and had used her influence to foster the worship of Baal in Judah. On the death of her husband, she was the queen-mother—a position which carried great power with it. But when her son died at the hands of Jehu, she would have had to yield her position to her son's widow; and, therefore, this true daughter of Jezebel, proceeded to murder all her grandchildren, and to ascend the throne of Judah herself. Only one little grandson was saved, the infant Jehoash, or Joash, who was concealed by an aunt, married to Jehoiada the High Priest. For six years Athaliah, that inhuman woman, usurped the throne in Jerusalem. In the seventh year, the High Priest Jehoiada brought forward young Joash from his hiding place, and the royal bodyguard and the representatives of the nation greeted the legitimate ruler with wild enthusiasm. He was crowned in the Temple, and Athaliah met the retribution she deserved.

17. *and Jehoiada made a covenant.* This joyous renewal of the covenant was a fitting sequel to the end of the unholy reign of Athaliah, and her Phœnician idolatry.

Jehoiada. True type of High Priest and

18. And all the people of the land went to the house of Baal, and broke it down; his altars and his images broke they in pieces thoroughly, and slew Mattan the priest of Baal before the altars. And the priest appointed officers over the house of the LORD. 19. And he took the captains over hundreds, and the Carites, and the guard, and all the people of the land; and they brought down the king from the house of the LORD, and came by the way of the gate of the guard unto the king's house. And he sat on the throne of the kings. 20. So all the people of the land rejoiced, and the city was quiet; and they slew Athaliah with the sword at the king's house.

18 הָעָם׃ וַיָּבֹאוּ כָל־עַם הָאָרֶץ בֵּית־הַבַּעַל וַיִּתְּצֻהוּ אֶת־
מִזְבְּחֹתָו וְאֶת־צְלָמָיו שִׁבְּרוּ הֵיטֵב וְאֵת מַתָּן כֹּהֵן הַבַּעַל
הָרְגוּ לִפְנֵי הַמִּזְבְּחוֹת וַיָּשֶׂם הַכֹּהֵן פְּקֻדֹּת עַל־בֵּית יְהוָה׃
19 וַיִּקַּח אֶת־שָׂרֵי הַמֵּאוֹת וְאֶת־הַכָּרִי וְאֶת־הָרָצִים וְאֵת ׀ כָּל־
עַם הָאָרֶץ וַיֹּרִידוּ אֶת־הַמֶּלֶךְ מִבֵּית יְהוָה וַיָּבוֹאוּ דֶּרֶךְ־
כ שַׁעַר הָרָצִים בֵּית הַמֶּלֶךְ וַיֵּשֶׁב עַל־כִּסֵּא הַמְּלָכִים׃ וַיִּשְׂמַח
כָּל־עַם־הָאָרֶץ וְהָעִיר שָׁקָטָה וְאֶת־עֲתַלְיָהוּ הֵמִיתוּ בַחֶרֶב
בֵּית ׳מֶלֶךְ׃

CHAPTER XII[1]

[2]1. Jehoash was seven years old when he began to reign. 2. In the seventh year of Jehu began Jehoash to reign; and he reigned forty years in Jerusalem; and his mother's name was Zibiah of Beer-sheba. 3. And Jehoash did that which was right in the eyes of the LORD all his days wherein Jehoiada the priest instructed him. 4. Howbeit the high places were not taken away; the people still sacrificed and offered in the high places.

CAP. XII. יב

א 2 *בֶּן־שֶׁבַע שָׁנִים יְהוֹאָשׁ בְּמָלְכוֹ׃ בִּשְׁנַת־שֶׁבַע לְיֵהוּא מָלַךְ
יְהוֹאָשׁ וְאַרְבָּעִים שָׁנָה מָלַךְ בִּירוּשָׁלִָם וְשֵׁם אִמּוֹ צִבְיָה
3 מִבְּאֵר שָׁבַע׃ וַיַּעַשׂ יְהוֹאָשׁ הַיָּשָׁר בְּעֵינֵי יְהוָה כָּל־יָמָיו
4 אֲשֶׁר הוֹרָהוּ יְהוֹיָדָע הַכֹּהֵן׃ רַק הַבָּמוֹת לֹא־סָרוּ עוֹד

[1] Ashkenazim begin here.
[2] In English Bibles the chapter begins with *v.* 2.

יא׳ v. 18. מזבחותיו קרי v. 20. המלך קרי יב׳ *כאן מתחילין האשכנזים

religious leader, whose advice and guidance during his life-time were followed by king Jehoash with blessed results to the nation.

18. *all the people of the land.* This cannot mean a mob of country-folk; for how could such a mob have become entrenched within the Temple citadel, without the knowledge of a vigorous ruler like Athaliah. Neither can it mean the city rabble; otherwise *v.* 20 ('and the city was quiet') would be meaningless. Besides, the city rabble would be spoken of as *anshey ha-ir.* All difficulties disappear if we follow Justice Sulzberger's explanation (see p. 80), of *am ha-aretz* as the National Council. Jehoiada had won over the members of that body, as well as the military chiefs, before he attempted the overthrow of Athaliah. The Am ha-aretz made and unmade kings; see II Kings XXI, 23; XXIII, 30. In the light of the above, the beginning of the verse should read, *And the whole National Council went to the house of Baal, etc.*

19. *the Carites.* A foreign body-guard of the king.

people of the land. As in the preceding verse; Jehoiada and the National Council, accompanied by the soldiery, brought the King to the Palace and there enthroned him.

20. *the city was quiet.* The National Council rejoiced over the success of their revolution, and, when the proceedings became known, the bulk of the population remained quiet. Evidently Athaliah, the foreign murderess, was not beloved in Jerusalem.

CHAPTER XII

2. *his mother's name.* The queen mother's power being only second to that of the king, her name is almost invariably given.

3. *all his days wherein Jehoiada instructed. i.e.* not all the days of his life, but only as long as he was under the guiding influence of Jehoiada.

4. *the high places.* Idol-worship at the high places was suppressed by Hezekiah; was renewed by King Manasseh and finally uprooted by his grandson Josiah.

5–17. REPAIR OF THE TEMPLE

The Additional Portion for Sabbath Shekalim, Exod. XXX, 11–16, is a reminder of the half-shekel given by each individual to the services of the Tabernacle. Similarly, in the Haftorah the people bring their offerings in money to repair the breaches in the Temple. Although the Temple is no more, this special Sabbath continues to stress the thought that each member of the community is under the obligation to give his measure of support to the stability of the Tabernacle and the perpetuation of his Religion.

¶ 5. And Jehoash said to the priests: 'All the money of the hallowed things that is brought into the house of the LORD, in current money, the money of the persons for whom each man is rated, all the money that it cometh into any man's heart to bring into the house of the LORD, 6. let the priests take it to them, every man from him that bestoweth it upon him; and they shall repair the breaches of the house, whereso-ever any breach shall be found.' 7. But it was so, that in the three and twentieth year of king Jehoash the priests had not repaired the breaches of the house. 8. Then king Jehoash called for Jehoiada the priest, and for the other priests, and said unto them: 'Why repair ye not the breaches of the house? now therefore take no longer money from them that bestow it upon you, but deliver it for the breaches of the house.' 9. And the priests consented that they should take no longer money from the people, neither repair the breaches of the house. ¶ 10. And Jehoiada the priest took a chest, and bored a hole in the lid of it, and set it beside the altar, on the right side as one cometh into the house of the LORD; and the priests that kept the threshold put therein all the money that was brought into the house of the LORD. 11. And it was so, when they saw that there was much money in the chest, that the king's scribe and the high priest came up, and they put up in bags and counted the money that was found in the house of the LORD. 12. And they gave the money that was weighed out into the hands of them that did the work, that had the oversight of the house of the LORD; and they paid it out to the carpenters and the builders, that wrought upon the house of the LORD, 13. and to the masons and the hewers of stone, and for buying timber and hewn stone to repair the breaches of the house of the LORD, and for all that was laid out for

ה הָעָם מְזַבְּחִים וּמְקַטְּרִים בַּבָּמוֹת׃ וַיֹּאמֶר יְהוֹאָשׁ אֶל־
הַכֹּהֲנִים כֹּל כֶּסֶף הַקֳּדָשִׁים אֲשֶׁר יוּבָא בֵית־יְהוָה כֶּסֶף
עוֹבֵר אִישׁ כֶּסֶף נַפְשׁוֹת עֶרְכּוֹ כָּל־כֶּסֶף אֲשֶׁר יַעֲלֶה עַל
6 לֶב־אִישׁ לְהָבִיא בֵּית יְהוָה׃ יִקְחוּ לָהֶם הַכֹּהֲנִים אִישׁ
מֵאֵת מַכָּרוֹ וְהֵם יְחַזְּקוּ אֶת־בֶּדֶק הַבַּיִת לְכֹל אֲשֶׁר־יִמָּצֵא
7 שָׁם בָּדֶק׃ וַיְהִי בִּשְׁנַת עֶשְׂרִים וְשָׁלֹשׁ שָׁנָה לַמֶּלֶךְ
8 יְהוֹאָשׁ לֹא־חִזְּקוּ הַכֹּהֲנִים אֶת־בֶּדֶק הַבָּיִת׃ וַיִּקְרָא הַמֶּלֶךְ
יְהוֹאָשׁ לִיהוֹיָדָע הַכֹּהֵן וְלַכֹּהֲנִים וַיֹּאמֶר אֲלֵהֶם מַדּוּעַ
אֵינְכֶם מְחַזְּקִים אֶת־בֶּדֶק הַבָּיִת וְעַתָּה אַל־תִּקְחוּ־כֶסֶף
9 מֵאֵת מַכָּרֵיכֶם כִּי־לְבֶדֶק הַבַּיִת תִּתְּנֻהוּ׃ וַיֵּאֹתוּ הַכֹּהֲנִים
לְבִלְתִּי קְחַת־כֶּסֶף מֵאֵת הָעָם וּלְבִלְתִּי חַזֵּק אֶת־בֶּדֶק
י הַבָּיִת׃ וַיִּקַּח יְהוֹיָדָע הַכֹּהֵן אֲרוֹן אֶחָד וַיִּקֹּב חֹר בְּדַלְתּוֹ
וַיִּתֵּן אֹתוֹ אֵצֶל הַמִּזְבֵּחַ בַּיָּמִין בְּבוֹא־אִישׁ בֵּית יְהוָה
וְנָתְנוּ־שָׁמָּה הַכֹּהֲנִים שֹׁמְרֵי הַסַּף אֶת־כָּל־הַכֶּסֶף הַמּוּבָא
11 בֵית־יְהוָה׃ וַיְהִי כִּרְאוֹתָם כִּי־רַב הַכֶּסֶף בָּאָרוֹן וַיַּעַל
סֹפֵר הַמֶּלֶךְ וְהַכֹּהֵן הַגָּדוֹל וַיָּצֻרוּ וַיִּמְנוּ אֶת־הַכֶּסֶף הַנִּמְצָא
12 בֵית־יְהוָה׃ וְנָתְנוּ אֶת־הַכֶּסֶף הַמְתֻכָּן עַל־יַד עֹשֵׂי הַמְּלָאכָה
הַפְּקֻדִים בֵּית יְהוָה וַיּוֹצִיאֻהוּ לְחָרָשֵׁי הָעֵץ וְלַבֹּנִים
13 הָעֹשִׂים בֵּית יְהוָה׃ וְלַגֹּדְרִים וּלְחֹצְבֵי הָאֶבֶן וְלִקְנוֹת
עֵצִים וְאַבְנֵי מַחְצֵב לְחַזֵּק אֶת־בֶּדֶק בֵּית־יְהוָה וּלְכֹל

v. 10. מימין קרי   v. 12. ידי קרי   ibid. המפקדים קרי

5. *all the money of the hallowed things.* Includes all the payments that came into the treasury; which are here specified (Biur).

the money of the persons for whom each man is rated. For the redemption of vows; or of persons dedicated to the LORD; Lev. XXVII, 2–8.

money that it cometh . . . of the LORD. Free-will offerings.

7–9. The arrangement did not work well. Not unnaturally. The priests were deflected from their rightful work, and sent out as tax-collectors to gather in the money; see II Chron. XXIV, 5: 'And he gathered together the priests and the Levites, and said to them, Go out unto the cities of Judah, and gather of all Israel money to repair the house of your God from year to year, and see that ye hasten the matter.'

8. *why repair ye not.* The priests were waiting until a sufficient sum had accumulated to take the repairs in hand. The King had unworthy suspicions of them, and introduced a new system (Kimchi).

9. *the priests consented.* They were pleased to be relieved of a responsibility which should not have been imposed on them (Ralbag).

12. *that did the work.* The headmen or the master workmen, responsible for the work.

the house to repair it. 14. But there were not made for the house of the LORD cups of silver, snuffers, basins, trumpets, any vessels of gold, or vessels of silver, of the money that was brought into the house of the LORD; 15. for they gave that to them that did the work, and repaired therewith the house of the LORD. 16. Moreover they reckoned not with the men, into whose hand they delivered the money to give to them that did the work; for they dealt faithfully. 17. The forfeit money, and the sin money, was not brought into the house of the LORD; it was the priests'.

14 אֲשֶׁר־יֵצֵא עַל־הַבַּיִת לְחַזְּקָה׃ אַךְ לֹא יֵעָשֶׂה בֵּית יְהוָה
סִפּוֹת כֶּסֶף מְזַמְּרוֹת מִזְרָקוֹת חֲצֹצְרוֹת כָּל־כְּלִי זָהָב וּכְלִי־
טו כָסֶף מִן־הַכֶּסֶף הַמּוּבָא בֵית־יְהוָה׃ כִּי־לְעֹשֵׂי הַמְּלָאכָה
16 יִתְּנֻהוּ וְחִזְּקוּ־בוֹ אֶת־בֵּית יְהוָה׃ וְלֹא יְחַשְּׁבוּ אֶת־
הָאֲנָשִׁים אֲשֶׁר יִתְּנוּ אֶת־הַכֶּסֶף עַל־יָדָם לָתֵת לְעֹשֵׂי
17 הַמְּלָאכָה כִּי בֶאֱמֻנָה הֵם עֹשִׂים׃ כֶּסֶף אָשָׁם וְכֶסֶף חַטָּאוֹת
לֹא יוּבָא בֵּית יְהוָה לַכֹּהֲנִים יִהְיוּ׃

14. *but there were not made . . . cups of silver.* At the time when the repairs were in hand, and when it did not seem that there would be sufficient money for the renewal of the sacred vessels. Subsequently when the repairs were finished there was found to be a surplus, which, according to II Chron. XXIV, 12, was used for supplying new vessels for the Temple service (Kimchi).

16. *they dealt faithfully.* All the overseers were men of integrity.

17. *the money for the guilt offerings.* *i.e.* the money left over after the purchase of the animal, from the amount dedicated to these offerings. This money was not used for the repairs.

HAFTORAH ZACHOR הפטרת זכור

ADDITIONAL READING: DEUTERONOMY XXV, 17–19

I SAMUEL XV, 1–34

CHAPTER XV

CAP. XV. טו

1. And Samuel said unto Saul: 'The LORD sent me to anoint thee to be king over His people, over Israel; now therefore hearken thou unto the voice of the words of the

א וַיֹּאמֶר שְׁמוּאֵל אֶל־שָׁאוּל אֹתִי שָׁלַח יְהוָה לִמְשָׁחֳךָ לְמֶלֶךְ
עַל־עַמּוֹ עַל־יִשְׂרָאֵל וְעַתָּה שְׁמַע לְקוֹל דִּבְרֵי יְהוָה׃

The Additional Reading recalls how Amalek ruthlessly attacked the defenceless and the weak of the Israelites in the wilderness, 'and he feared not God.' The Amalekites showed their implacable enmity not only at Rephidim, but also opposed Israel's entrance into the Holy Land. It was an hereditary hatred; they were the allies of the Midianites when these harried the Israelites in the days of the Judges. The feud between the tribes of Israel and this untamable race of savages was thus of long duration. The command for exterminating them with which the Haftorah opens, may have been given in consequence of their raids having become more numerous and sanguinary under their present king; *v.* 33. It was clear to Samuel that the struggle with these ancient and ever-hostile opponents was a matter of life and death to Israel.

The moral difficulty in connection with this command is very real. It seems to be in violent contrast to the Divine law which forbids vengeance, private vengeance. However, the truest mercy sometimes lies in the dispensation of sternest justice, and Israel here was the instrument of Divine Retribution.

Sabbath Zachor precedes the Festival of Purim, the story of which is recorded in the Book of Esther. Haman, the arch-enemy of the Jews, was deemed to be a descendant of the Amalekite king in the Haftorah. Sabbath Zachor reminds us of their inhumanity. Its charge to the generations in Israel is to blot out from the human heart the cruel Amalek spirit.

1. *to be king over His people.* Not *thy* (Saul's) people. God's people, to be ruled according to the Divine word and will.

LORD. [1]2. Thus saith the LORD of hosts: I remember that which Amalek did to Israel, how he set himself against him in the way, when he came up out of Egypt. 3. Now go and smite Amalek, and utterly destroy all that they have, and spare them not; but slay both man and woman, infant and suckling, ox and sheep, camel and ass.' ¶ 4. And Saul summoned the people, and numbered them in Telaim, two hundred thousand footmen, and ten thousand men of Judah. 5. And Saul came to the city of Amalek, and lay in wait in the valley. 6. And Saul said unto the Kenites: 'Go, depart, get you down from among the Amalekites, lest I destroy you with them; for ye showed kindness to all the children of Israel, when they came up out of Egypt.' So the Kenites departed from among the Amalekites. 7. And Saul smote the Amalekites, from Havilah as thou goest to Shur, that is in front of Egypt. 8. And he took Agag the king of the Amalekites alive, and utterly destroyed all the people with the edge of the sword. 9. But Saul and the people spared Agag, and the best of the sheep, and of the oxen, even the young of the second birth, and the lambs, and all that was good, and would not utterly destroy them; but everything that was of no account and feeble, that they destroyed utterly. ¶ 10. Then came the word of the LORD unto Samuel, saying: 11. 'It repenteth Me that I have set up Saul to be king; for he is turned back from following Me, and hath not performed My commandments.' And it grieved Samuel; and he cried unto the LORD all night. 12. And Samuel rose early

[1] Ashkenazim begin here.

2 כֹּה* אָמַר יְהוָה צְבָאוֹת פָּקַדְתִּי אֵת אֲשֶׁר־עָשָׂה עֲמָלֵק
3 לְיִשְׂרָאֵל אֲשֶׁר־שָׂם לוֹ בַּדֶּרֶךְ בַּעֲלֹתוֹ מִמִּצְרָיִם׃ עַתָּה
לֵךְ וְהִכִּיתָה אֶת־עֲמָלֵק וְהַחֲרַמְתֶּם אֶת־כָּל־אֲשֶׁר־לוֹ וְלֹא
תַחְמֹל עָלָיו וְהֵמַתָּה מֵאִישׁ עַד־אִשָּׁה מֵעֹלֵל וְעַד־יוֹנֵק
4 מִשּׁוֹר וְעַד־שֶׂה מִגָּמָל וְעַד־חֲמוֹר׃ וַיְשַׁמַּע שָׁאוּל
אֶת־הָעָם וַיִּפְקְדֵם בַּטְּלָאִים מָאתַיִם אֶלֶף רַגְלִי וַעֲשֶׂרֶת
ה אֲלָפִים אֶת־אִישׁ יְהוּדָה׃ וַיָּבֹא שָׁאוּל עַד־עִיר עֲמָלֵק וַיָּרֶב
6 בַּנָּחַל׃ וַיֹּאמֶר שָׁאוּל אֶל־הַקֵּינִי לְכוּ סֻּרוּ רְדוּ מִתּוֹךְ
עֲמָלֵקִי פֶּן־אֹסִפְךָ עִמּוֹ וְאַתָּה עָשִׂיתָה חֶסֶד עִם־כָּל־בְּנֵי
7 יִשְׂרָאֵל בַּעֲלוֹתָם מִמִּצְרָיִם וַיָּסַר קֵינִי מִתּוֹךְ עֲמָלֵק׃ וַיַּךְ
שָׁאוּל אֶת־עֲמָלֵק מֵחֲוִילָה בּוֹאֲךָ שׁוּר אֲשֶׁר עַל־פְּנֵי
8 מִצְרָיִם׃ וַיִּתְפֹּשׂ אֶת־אֲגַג מֶלֶךְ־עֲמָלֵק חָי וְאֶת־כָּל־הָעָם
9 הֶחֱרִים לְפִי־חָרֶב׃ וַיַּחְמֹל שָׁאוּל וְהָעָם עַל־אֲגָג וְעַל־
מֵיטַב הַצֹּאן וְהַבָּקָר וְהַמִּשְׁנִים וְעַל־הַכָּרִים וְעַל־כָּל־הַטּוֹב
וְלֹא אָבוּ הַחֲרִימָם וְכָל־הַמְּלָאכָה נְמִבְזָה וְנָמֵס אֹתָהּ
י הֶחֱרִימוּ׃ וַיְהִי דְּבַר־יְהוָה אֶל־שְׁמוּאֵל לֵאמֹר׃ נִחַמְתִּי
11 כִּי־הִמְלַכְתִּי אֶת־שָׁאוּל לְמֶלֶךְ כִּי־שָׁב מֵאַחֲרַי וְאֶת־דְּבָרַי
לֹא הֵקִים וַיִּחַר לִשְׁמוּאֵל וַיִּזְעַק אֶל־יְהוָה כָּל־הַלָּיְלָה׃
12 וַיַּשְׁכֵּם שְׁמוּאֵל לִקְרַאת שָׁאוּל בַּבֹּקֶר וַיֻּגַּד לִשְׁמוּאֵל

* כאן מתחילין האשכנזים

3. *utterly destroy.* lit. 'ban' or 'devote'. They were not to be taken as spoil. The Israelites were to derive no material profit from this punitive war.

4. *in Telaim.* Probably Telem (Josh. xv, 24), a place in southern Judah.

6. *the Kenites.* A tribe to which Jethro, the father-in-law of Moses, belonged. Some of them dwelt among the Amalekites, South of Judah.

7. *Havilah.* The eastern boundary of the district in northen Arabia inhabited by the Amalekites.
Shur. The western part of the desert, bordering on Egypt.

8. *all the people. i.e.* all that fell into his hands. Some bands survived and carried on guerilla warfare against the Israelites; but from this time they ceased to be formidable.

9. *spared Agag.* Saul did so, perhaps from a fellow-feeling with a king; cf. I Kings xx, 32.
the best of the sheep. Apparently to derive material profit from a campaign that was to be undertaken only to serve higher ends.

11. *it repenteth Me.* An expression signifying an apparent change in the Divine attitude towards people, brought about by a change in their character and conduct.
it grieved Samuel. For Saul, concerning whom he had held such high hopes.
cried. Interceded for Saul.

12. *Carmel.* In Judah, about 7 miles S. of Hebron.
setting him up a monument. To commemorate his victory.
Gilgal. In the Jordan valley. Perhaps to sacrifice there of the spoil in thanksgiving for the victory (Ralbag); see *v.* 15 and 21.

to meet Saul in the morning; and it was told
Samuel, saying: 'Saul came to Carmel, and,
behold, he is setting him up a monument,
and is gone about, and passed on, and gone
down to Gilgal.' 13. And Samuel came to
Saul; and Saul said unto him: 'Blessed be
thou of the LORD; I have performed the
commandment of the LORD.' 14. And
Samuel said: 'What meaneth then this
bleating of the sheep in mine ears, and the
lowing of the oxen which I hear?' 15. And
Saul said: 'They have brought them from
the Amalekites; for the people spared the
best of the sheep and of the oxen, to sacrifice
unto the LORD thy God; and the rest we
have utterly destroyed.' 16. Then Samuel
said unto Saul: 'Stay, and I will tell thee
what the LORD hath said to me this night.'
And he said unto him: 'Say on.' ¶ 17.
And Samuel said: 'Though thou be little
in thine own sight, art thou not head of the
tribes of Israel? And the LORD anointed
thee king over Israel; 18. and the LORD sent
thee on a journey, and said: Go and utterly
destroy the sinners the Amalekites, and
fight against them until they be consumed.
19. Wherefore then didst thou not hearken
to the voice of the LORD, but didst fly upon
the spoil, and didst that which was evil in
the sight of the LORD?' 20. And Saul said
unto Samuel: 'Yea, I have hearkened to the
voice of the LORD, and have gone the way
which the LORD sent me, and have brought
Agag the king of Amalek, and have utterly
destroyed the Amalekites. 21. But the
people took of the spoil, sheep and oxen,
the chief of the devoted things, to sacrifice
unto the LORD thy God in Gilgal.' 22.
And Samuel said:

'Hath the LORD as great delight in burnt-offerings and sacrifices,
As in hearkening to the voice of the LORD?
Behold, to obey is better than sacrifice,
And to hearken than the fat of rams.
23. For rebellion is as the sin of witchcraft,
And stubbornness is as idolatry and teraphim.

Because thou hast rejected the word of the
LORD, He hath also rejected thee from being

לֵאמֹר בָּא־שָׁאוּל הַכַּרְמֶלָה וְהִנֵּה מַצִּיב לוֹ יָד וַיִּסֹּב וַיַּעֲבֹר
13 וַיֵּרֶד הַגִּלְגָּל׃ וַיָּבֹא שְׁמוּאֵל אֶל־שָׁאוּל וַיֹּאמֶר לוֹ שָׁאוּל
14 בָּרוּךְ אַתָּה לַיהוָה הֲקִימֹתִי אֶת־דְּבַר יְהוָה׃ וַיֹּאמֶר שְׁמוּאֵל
וּמֶה קוֹל־הַצֹּאן הַזֶּה בְּאָזְנָי וְקוֹל הַבָּקָר אֲשֶׁר אָנֹכִי שֹׁמֵעַ׃
טו וַיֹּאמֶר שָׁאוּל מֵעֲמָלֵקִי הֱבִיאוּם אֲשֶׁר חָמַל הָעָם עַל־
מֵיטַב הַצֹּאן וְהַבָּקָר לְמַעַן זְבֹחַ לַיהוָה אֱלֹהֶיךָ וְאֶת־הַיּוֹתֵר
16 הֶחֱרַמְנוּ׃ וַיֹּאמֶר שְׁמוּאֵל אֶל־שָׁאוּל הֶרֶף וְאַגִּידָה לְּךָ
אֵת אֲשֶׁר דִּבֶּר יְהוָה אֵלַי הַלָּיְלָה וַיֹּאמְרוּ לוֹ דַּבֵּר׃
17 וַיֹּאמֶר שְׁמוּאֵל הֲלוֹא אִם־קָטֹן אַתָּה בְּעֵינֶיךָ רֹאשׁ שִׁבְטֵי
18 יִשְׂרָאֵל אָתָּה וַיִּמְשָׁחֲךָ יְהוָה לְמֶלֶךְ עַל־יִשְׂרָאֵל׃ וַיִּשְׁלָחֲךָ
יְהוָה בְּדָרֶךְ וַיֹּאמֶר לֵךְ וְהַחֲרַמְתָּה אֶת־הַחַטָּאִים אֶת־
19 עֲמָלֵק וְנִלְחַמְתָּ בוֹ עַד־כַּלּוֹתָם אֹתָם׃ וְלָמָּה לֹא־שָׁמַעְתָּ
בְּקוֹל יְהוָה וַתַּעַט אֶל־הַשָּׁלָל וַתַּעַשׂ הָרַע בְּעֵינֵי יְהוָה׃
כ וַיֹּאמֶר שָׁאוּל אֶל־שְׁמוּאֵל אֲשֶׁר שָׁמַעְתִּי בְּקוֹל
יְהוָה וָאֵלֵךְ בַּדֶּרֶךְ אֲשֶׁר־שְׁלָחַנִי יְהוָה וָאָבִיא אֶת־אֲגַג
21 מֶלֶךְ עֲמָלֵק וְאֶת־עֲמָלֵק הֶחֱרַמְתִּי׃ וַיִּקַּח הָעָם מֵהַשָּׁלָל
צֹאן וּבָקָר רֵאשִׁית הַחֵרֶם לִזְבֹּחַ לַיהוָה אֱלֹהֶיךָ בַּגִּלְגָּל׃
22 וַיֹּאמֶר שְׁמוּאֵל הַחֵפֶץ לַיהוָה בְּעֹלוֹת וּזְבָחִים
כִּשְׁמֹעַ בְּקוֹל יְהוָה הִנֵּה שְׁמֹעַ מִזֶּבַח טוֹב לְהַקְשִׁיב
23 מֵחֵלֶב אֵילִים׃ כִּי חַטַּאת־קֶסֶם מֶרִי וְאָוֶן וּתְרָפִים
הַפְצַר יַעַן מָאַסְתָּ אֶת־דְּבַר יְהוָה וַיִּמְאָסְךָ מִמֶּלֶךְ׃

v. 15. פתח בס״פ v. 16. ויאמר קרי v. 20. פתח בס״פ

15. *they have brought them from the Amalekites.* Saul appears to lay the blame upon the people. *to sacrifice unto the LORD thy God.* Saul thought that this would justify his action.

17. *though thou be little in thine own sight.* If he heeded the voice of his army in an act of disobedience, he was not fit to lead.

20. *I have hearkened . . . and have brought Agag.* He had destroyed the Amalekites; and the people had brought the spoil not for themselves, but for sacrifice.

22. *delight in burnt offerings.* Samuel's reply is couched in the rhythmical form of parallelism, the characteristic of Heb. poetry. In a few immortal words he summarizes the ethical teaching of the Hebrew prophets and asserts in clearest terms the superiority of moral to ritual worship.

23. *teraphim.* Idolatrous images. Deliberate disobedience towards God is compared to witchcraft, because both bow to an authority other than Divine; in the one case, to the individual will or passion; and in the other, to the idol. The comparison is especially appropriate here, as Saul has been zealous in abolishing witchcraft in Israel. Samuel accuses him of being as guilty as those he had himself condemned.

king.' 24. And Saul said unto Samuel: 'I have sinned; for I have transgressed the commandments of the LORD, and thy words; because I feared the people, and hearkened to their voice. 25. Now therefore, I pray thee, pardon my sin, and return with me, that I may worship the LORD.' 26. And Samuel said unto Saul: 'I will not return with thee; for thou hast rejected the word of the LORD, and the LORD hath rejected thee from being king over Israel.' 27. And as Samuel turned about to go away, he laid hold upon the skirt of his robe, and it rent. 28. And Samuel said unto him: 'The LORD hath rent the kingdom of Israel from thee this day, and hath given it to a neighbour of thine, that is better than thou. 29. And also the Glory of Israel will not lie nor repent; for He is not a man, that He should repent.' 30. Then he said: 'I have sinned; yet honour me now, I pray thee, before the elders of my people, and before Israel, and return with me, that I may worship the LORD thy God.' 31. So Samuel returned after Saul; and Saul worshipped the LORD. ¶ 32. Then said Samuel: 'Bring ye hither to me Agag the king of the Amalekites.' And Agag came unto him in chains. And Agag said: 'Surely the bitterness of death is at hand.' 33. And Samuel said:

As thy sword hath made women childless,
So shall thy mother be childless among
women.

And Samuel hewed Agag in pieces before the LORD in Gilgal. ¶ 34. Then Samuel went to Ramah; and Saul went up to his house to Gibeath-shaul.

24 וַיֹּאמֶר שָׁאוּל אֶל־שְׁמוּאֵל חָטָאתִי כִּי־עָבַרְתִּי אֶת־פִּי־
יְהוָה וְאֶת־דְּבָרֶיךָ כִּי יָרֵאתִי אֶת־הָעָם וָאֶשְׁמַע בְּקוֹלָם׃
כה וְעַתָּה שָׂא נָא אֶת־חַטָּאתִי וְשׁוּב עִמִּי וְאֶשְׁתַּחֲוֶה לַיהוָה׃
26 וַיֹּאמֶר שְׁמוּאֵל אֶל־שָׁאוּל לֹא אָשׁוּב עִמָּךְ כִּי
מָאַסְתָּה אֶת־דְּבַר יְהוָה וַיִּמְאָסְךָ יְהוָה מִהְיוֹת מֶלֶךְ עַל־
27 יִשְׂרָאֵל׃ וַיִּסֹּב שְׁמוּאֵל לָלֶכֶת וַיַּחֲזֵק בִּכְנַף־מְעִילוֹ וַיִּקָּרַע׃
28 וַיֹּאמֶר אֵלָיו שְׁמוּאֵל קָרַע יְהוָה אֶת־מַמְלְכוּת
29 יִשְׂרָאֵל מֵעָלֶיךָ הַיּוֹם וּנְתָנָהּ לְרֵעֲךָ הַטּוֹב מִמֶּךָּ׃ וְגַם
נֵצַח יִשְׂרָאֵל לֹא יְשַׁקֵּר וְלֹא יִנָּחֵם כִּי לֹא אָדָם הוּא לְהִנָּחֵם׃
ל וַיֹּאמֶר חָטָאתִי עַתָּה כַּבְּדֵנִי נָא נֶגֶד־זִקְנֵי עַמִּי וְנֶגֶד יִשְׂרָאֵל
31 וְשׁוּב עִמִּי וְהִשְׁתַּחֲוֵיתִי לַיהוָה אֱלֹהֶיךָ׃ וַיָּשָׁב שְׁמוּאֵל
32 אַחֲרֵי שָׁאוּל וַיִּשְׁתַּחוּ שָׁאוּל לַיהוָה׃ וַיֹּאמֶר שְׁמוּאֵל
הַגִּישׁוּ אֵלַי אֶת־אֲגַג מֶלֶךְ עֲמָלֵק וַיֵּלֶךְ אֵלָיו אֲגַג מַעֲדַנֹּת
33 וַיֹּאמֶר אֲגָג אָכֵן סָר מַר־הַמָּוֶת׃ וַיֹּאמֶר שְׁמוּאֵל
כַּאֲשֶׁר שִׁכְּלָה נָשִׁים חַרְבֶּךָ כֵּן־תִּשְׁכַּל מִנָּשִׁים אִמֶּךָ
34 וַיְשַׁסֵּף שְׁמוּאֵל אֶת־אֲגָג לִפְנֵי יְהוָה בַּגִּלְגָּל׃ וַיֵּלֶךְ
שְׁמוּאֵל הָרָמָתָה וְשָׁאוּל עָלָה אֶל־בֵּיתוֹ גִּבְעַת שָׁאוּל׃

24. *feared the people.* Saul now admits the true reason of his lapse. He did not lead, though king, but was led.

29. *the Glory of Israel.* He who is the Source of their strength and confidence.

He is not a man, that He should repent. He is not changeable like man, but permanent in His purpose. He desires the good of Israel, and it is for their good that Saul should be deprived of sovereignty. There is no contradiction here to the expression in *v.* 10. It is because God is unchangeable in His purposes that 'change of attitude in men from good to evil, seems to develop a corresponding change of attitude towards them in God' (Sime).

30. *honour me now.* A touching and natural request. Saul had been sufficiently humiliated; and, as he was still king, it was necessary that his authority should be upheld before the people.

31. *so Samuel returned after Saul.* He had vindicated himself as representative of God's will, and now allowed Saul to precede him.

32. *in chains.* Some translate 'tremblingly', others, 'cheerfully.'

the bitterness of death is at hand. He had lost kingdom and liberty, and death held no further bitterness for him.

33. *childless.* He had practised the old Amalekite method of murdering the weak and defenceless, on the borders of Judah. Samuel, who in more than one way was the last of the Judges, seized a sword and with his own hand struck the murderer dead. It was national vengeance, not vengeance taken by Samuel in his own cause.

34. *then Samuel went to Ramah.* He saw Saul no more. He loved and grieved for Saul, and mourned for the failure of a career that had seemed so promising. 'He had begun his reign as a knightly hero in the splendour of manly strength, good fortune and victory; he died, harassed, embittered, deranged, giving himself the death blow, avoided and forsaken by every one—by his trusted seer and counsellor, by his greatest warrior, and, finally, by the last of his faithful followers' (Kittel).

HAFTORAH PARAH הפטרת פרה

ADDITIONAL READING: NUMBERS XIX, 1–22

EZEKIEL XXXVI, 16–38

CHAPTER XXXVI

16. Moreover the word of the LORD came unto me, saying: 17. 'Son of man, when the house of Israel dwelt in their own land, they defiled it by their way and by their doings; their way before Me was as the uncleanness of a woman in her impurity. 18. Wherefore I poured out My fury upon them for the blood which they had shed upon the land, and because they had defiled it with their idols; 19. and I scattered them among the nations, and they were dispersed through the countries; according to their way and according to their doings I judged them. 20. And when they came unto the nations, whither they came, they profaned My holy name; in that men said of them: These are the people of the LORD, and are gone forth out of His land. 21. But I had pity for My holy name, which the house of Israel had profaned among the nations, whither they came. 22. Therefore say unto the house of Israel: Thus saith the Lord GOD: I do not this for your sake, O house of Israel, but for My holy name, which ye have profaned among the nations, whither

CAP. XXXVI. לו

16 וַיְהִי דְבַר־יְהוָה אֵלַי לֵאמֹר׃ בֶּן־אָדָם בֵּית יִשְׂרָאֵל
17 יֹשְׁבִים עַל־אַדְמָתָם וַיְטַמְּאוּ אוֹתָהּ בְּדַרְכָּם וּבַעֲלִילוֹתָם
18 כְּטֻמְאַת הַנִּדָּה הָיְתָה דַרְכָּם לְפָנָי׃ וָאֶשְׁפֹּךְ חֲמָתִי עֲלֵיהֶם
עַל־הַדָּם אֲשֶׁר־שָׁפְכוּ עַל־הָאָרֶץ וּבְגִלּוּלֵיהֶם טִמְּאוּהָ׃
19 וָאָפִיץ אֹתָם בַּגּוֹיִם וַיִּזָּרוּ בָּאֲרָצוֹת כְּדַרְכָּם וְכַעֲלִילוֹתָם
כ שְׁפַטְתִּים׃ וַיָּבוֹא אֶל־הַגּוֹיִם אֲשֶׁר־בָּאוּ שָׁם וַיְחַלְּלוּ אֶת־
שֵׁם קָדְשִׁי בֶּאֱמֹר לָהֶם עַם־יְהוָה אֵלֶּה וּמֵאַרְצוֹ יָצָאוּ׃
21 וָאֶחְמֹל עַל־שֵׁם קָדְשִׁי אֲשֶׁר חִלְּלֻהוּ בֵּית יִשְׂרָאֵל בַּגּוֹיִם
22 אֲשֶׁר־בָּאוּ שָׁמָּה׃ לָכֵן אֱמֹר לְבֵית־יִשְׂרָאֵל כֹּה
אָמַר אֲדֹנָי יֱהוִה לֹא לְמַעַנְכֶם אֲנִי עֹשֶׂה בֵּית יִשְׂרָאֵל כִּי
אִם־לְשֵׁם־קָדְשִׁי אֲשֶׁר חִלַּלְתֶּם בַּגּוֹיִם אֲשֶׁר־בָּאתֶם שָׁם׃

v. 20. סבירין ויבואו

The Additional Reading lays down the regulations for bodily purification. The object of these laws, our Sages say, was to impress on the Israelites the need of moral purification after the apostasy in connection with the Golden Calf.

Moral purification is likewise the theme of the Haftorah taken from the Book of Ezekiel. How Israel is to emerge from the grave of the Exile, renew its life on its own soil, and open an era of undefiled service of God—such is the teaching of the Haftorah. God had justly sent Israel into captivity, says the Prophet; its disasters were inevitable, seeing that God is a God of Holiness and Right. But the heathens had misunderstood this punishment, taking it as a sign of God's inability to save His people (Rashi, Kimchi). In this way, Israel had occasioned the profanation of God's Name. To vindicate His own honour, God will restore them; not because Israel deserved restoration, but because God's Glory demanded it. This Restoration will, however, be accompanied by moral renewal; on the one hand, God will implant 'a new heart and a new spirit' in the nation; and, on the other hand, Israel's soul will be swept by sincere Repentance that will cause it to be ashamed of its evil past. When the sinful nation has thus been purified, and the desolate land re-peopled, then the heathen will know that the whole is God's doing.

16–18. The uncleanness, religious and moral, of their ways was the real cause of the suffering of the people and their banishment.

17. *their doings.* Their idolatry.

18. *blood which they had shed.* The Prophet probably has in mind the abominable rite of child-sacrifice which they copied from the heathens surrounding them.

20. *profaned My holy name.* Doubly so; by their own wrong-doing and by forcing God to punish them.

are gone forth out of His land. 'He was not able to protect His people!' was the taunt of the heathen, which constituted a monstrous *chillul hashem*, a profanation and degradation of the idea of God.

22–24. To vindicate His own honour, God will restore them, 'for so only can His sole Godhead, which the ruin of His people had caused to be questioned, be generally acknowledged in the world; He *can* restore Israel, for of His own free grace He forgives their sins and transforms their hard heart.'

22. *I do not this for your sake. Because* Israel was His own people, He must strictly punish Israel for its sins; cf. Amos III, 2 (p. 153). His Name was inseparably connected with Israel. To that fact the nation owed its preservation.

23 וְקִדַּשְׁתִּי אֶת־שְׁמִי הַגָּדוֹל הַמְחֻלָּל בַּגּוֹיִם אֲשֶׁר חִלַּלְתֶּם
בְּתוֹכָם וְיָדְעוּ הַגּוֹיִם כִּי־אֲנִי יְהוָה נְאֻם אֲדֹנָי יְהוִה בְּהִקָּדְשִׁי
24 בָכֶם לְעֵינֵיהֶם׃ וְלָקַחְתִּי אֶתְכֶם מִן־הַגּוֹיִם וְקִבַּצְתִּי אֶתְכֶם
כה מִכָּל־הָאֲרָצוֹת וְהֵבֵאתִי אֶתְכֶם אֶל־אַדְמַתְכֶם׃ וְזָרַקְתִּי
עֲלֵיכֶם מַיִם טְהוֹרִים וּטְהַרְתֶּם מִכֹּל טֻמְאוֹתֵיכֶם וּמִכָּל־
26 גִּלּוּלֵיכֶם אֲטַהֵר אֶתְכֶם׃ וְנָתַתִּי לָכֶם לֵב חָדָשׁ וְרוּחַ
חֲדָשָׁה אֶתֵּן בְּקִרְבְּכֶם וַהֲסִרֹתִי אֶת־לֵב הָאֶבֶן מִבְּשַׂרְכֶם
27 וְנָתַתִּי לָכֶם לֵב בָּשָׂר׃ וְאֶת־רוּחִי אֶתֵּן בְּקִרְבְּכֶם וְעָשִׂיתִי
28 אֵת אֲשֶׁר־בְּחֻקַּי תֵּלֵכוּ וּמִשְׁפָּטַי תִּשְׁמְרוּ וַעֲשִׂיתֶם׃ וִישַׁבְתֶּם
בָּאָרֶץ אֲשֶׁר נָתַתִּי לַאֲבֹתֵיכֶם וִהְיִיתֶם לִי לְעָם וְאָנֹכִי
29 אֶהְיֶה לָכֶם לֵאלֹהִים׃ וְהוֹשַׁעְתִּי אֶתְכֶם מִכֹּל טֻמְאוֹתֵיכֶם
וְקָרָאתִי אֶל־הַדָּגָן וְהִרְבֵּיתִי אֹתוֹ וְלֹא־אֶתֵּן עֲלֵיכֶם רָעָב׃
ל וְהִרְבֵּיתִי אֶת־פְּרִי הָעֵץ וּתְנוּבַת הַשָּׂדֶה לְמַעַן אֲשֶׁר לֹא־
31 תִקְחוּ עוֹד חֶרְפַּת רָעָב בַּגּוֹיִם׃ וּזְכַרְתֶּם אֶת־דַּרְכֵיכֶם
הָרָעִים וּמַעַלְלֵיכֶם אֲשֶׁר לֹא־טוֹבִים וּנְקֹטֹתֶם בִּפְנֵיכֶם עַל
32 עֲוֺנֹתֵיכֶם וְעַל תּוֹעֲבוֹתֵיכֶם׃ לֹא לְמַעַנְכֶם אֲנִי־עֹשֶׂה נְאֻם
אֲדֹנָי יְהוִה יִוָּדַע לָכֶם בּוֹשׁוּ וְהִכָּלְמוּ מִדַּרְכֵיכֶם בֵּית
33 יִשְׂרָאֵל׃ כֹּה אָמַר אֲדֹנָי יְהוִה בְּיוֹם טַהֲרִי אֶתְכֶם מִכֹּל
34 עֲוֺנוֹתֵיכֶם וְהוֹשַׁבְתִּי אֶת־הֶעָרִים וְנִבְנוּ הֶחֳרָבוֹת׃ וְהָאָרֶץ

כצ"ל v. 23. 25.

ye came. 23. And I will sanctify My great name, which hath been profaned among the nations, which ye have profaned in the midst of them; and the nations shall know that I am the LORD, saith the Lord GOD, when I shall be sanctified in you before their eyes. 24. For I will take you from among the nations, and gather you out of all the countries, and will bring you into your own land. 25. And I will sprinkle clean water upon you, and ye shall be clean; from all your uncleannesses, and from all your idols, will I cleanse you. 26. A new heart also will I give you, and a new spirit will I put within you; and I will take away the stony heart out of your flesh, and I will give you a heart of flesh. 27. And I will put My spirit within you, and cause you to walk in My statutes, and ye shall keep Mine ordinances, and do them. 28. And ye shall dwell in the land that I gave to your fathers; and ye shall be My people, and I will be your God. 29. And I will save you from all your uncleannesses; and I will call for the corn, and will increase it, and lay no famine upon you. 30. And I will multiply the fruit of the tree, and the increase of the field, that ye may receive no more the reproach of famine among the nations. 31. Then shall ye remember your evil ways, and your doings that were not good; and ye shall loathe yourselves in your own sight for your iniquities and for your abominations. 32. Not for your sake do I this, saith the Lord GOD, be it known unto you; be ashamed and confounded for your ways, O house of Israel. 33. Thus saith the Lord GOD: In the day that I cleanse you from all your iniquities, I will cause the cities to be inhabited, and the waste places shall be

23. *when I shall be sanctified in you.* Or, 'when I show myself holy in you.' Israel is the subject *through* which God will show Himself to be the Omnipotent and Holy God to the nations. 'The great act of reinstatement would make the heathen honour God's majesty, as the sufferings of Israel made them despise it' (Lofthouse).

25. *I will sprinkle clean water.* Figurative for moral purification and inward spiritual renewal.
uncleannesses. Of idolatry, whose worship involved both ritual and moral uncleanness.

26. *a new heart.* Obedient, submissive, and desiring the good. 'Heart' is the Heb. term for the whole inward being.
a new spirit. Steadfast, and predisposed to revere God.
the stony heart. Hard and rebellious.
heart of flesh. Tender, sensitive to Divine admonition and influence, and capable of being moulded thereby.

27. *to walk in My statutes.* The spirit of God will appear both as an inward impulse to fulfil God's will, and as a power to do it.

31. *then shall ye remember your evil ways.* The Divine mercies described in the previous verses will 'heap coals of fire on their head'. They will bring vividly to their memory the former national sins, and the consequent justice of their exile. A deep and sincere repentance will be the result.

32. *not for your sake.* 'It is doubtless meant as consolation to the people when the Prophet declares that their deliverance does not depend on their deserts' (Toy).
be ashamed. Self-loathing for its past misdeeds would be a sign of possessing the 'new heart and new spirit'.

33–35. The land will enjoy prosperity, the

builded. 34. And the land that was desolate shall be tilled, whereas it was a desolation in the sight of all that passed by. 35. And they shall say: This land that was desolate is become like the garden of Eden; and the waste and desolate and ruined cities are fortified and inhabited. 36. Then the nations that are left round about you shall know that I the LORD have builded the ruined places, and planted that which was desolate; I the LORD have spoken it, and I will do it.[1] ¶ 37. Thus saith the Lord GOD: I will yet for this be inquired of by the house of Israel, to do it for them; I will increase them with men like a flock. 38. As the flock for sacrifice, as the flock of Jerusalem in her appointed seasons, so shall the waste cities be filled with flocks of men; and they shall know that I am the LORD.'

[1] Sephardim end here.

הַנְּשַׁמָּה תֵּעָבֵד תַּחַת אֲשֶׁר הָיְתָה שְׁמָמָה לְעֵינֵי כָּל־עוֹבֵר׃
לה וְאָמְרוּ הָאָרֶץ הַלֵּזוּ הַנְּשַׁמָּה הָיְתָה כְּגַן־עֵדֶן וְהֶעָרִים הֶחֳרֵבוֹת
36 וְהַנְּשַׁמּוֹת וְהַנֶּהֱרָסוֹת בְּצוּרוֹת יָשָׁבוּ׃ וְיָדְעוּ הַגּוֹיִם אֲשֶׁר
יִשָּׁאֲרוּ סְבִיבוֹתֵיכֶם כִּי ׀ אֲנִי יְהוָה בָּנִיתִי הַנֶּהֱרָסוֹת
37 נָטַעְתִּי הַנְּשַׁמָּה אֲנִי יְהוָה דִּבַּרְתִּי וְעָשִׂיתִי׃* כֹּה
אָמַר אֲדֹנָי יֱהוִה עוֹד זֹאת אִדָּרֵשׁ לְבֵית־יִשְׂרָאֵל לַעֲשׂוֹת
38 לָהֶם אַרְבֶּה אֹתָם כַּצֹּאן אָדָם׃ כְּצֹאן קָדָשִׁים כְּצֹאן
יְרוּשָׁלִַם בְּמוֹעֲדֶיהָ כֵּן תִּהְיֶינָה הֶעָרִים הֶחֳרֵבוֹת מְלֵאוֹת
צֹאן אָדָם וְיָדְעוּ כִּי־אֲנִי יְהוָה׃

* כאן מסיימין הספרדים v. 35, 38. הר׳ בצירי

towns will be rebuilt, and filled with a teeming population.

36. *I the LORD have builded.* This redemption and restoration shall be manifest to the nations as the work of God and not of man.

37. *I will be inquired of. i.e.* I will be accessible to their prayers.

38. *as the flock.* As numerous as the sheep with which the Temple courts and streets of Jerusalem were crowded at the Festival Season.

HAFTORAH HACHODESH — הפטרת החדש

ADDITIONAL READING: EXODUS XII, 1–20

EZEKIEL XLV, 16–XLVI, 18

CHAPTER XLV

16. All the people of the land shall give this offering for the prince in Israel. 17. And it shall be the prince's part to give the burnt-offerings, and the meal-offerings, and the drink-offerings, in the feasts, and in the new moons, and in the sabbaths, in all the appointed seasons of the house of Israel; he shall prepare the sin-offering, and the meal-offering, and the burnt-offering, and the peace-offerings, to make atonement for the house of Israel.

CAP. XLV. מה

16 כֹּל הָעָם
17 הָאָרֶץ יִהְיוּ אֶל־הַתְּרוּמָה הַזֹּאת לַנָּשִׂיא בְּיִשְׂרָאֵל׃ וְעַל־
הַנָּשִׂיא יִהְיֶה הָעוֹלוֹת וְהַמִּנְחָה וְהַנֶּסֶךְ בַּחַגִּים וּבֶחֳדָשִׁים
וּבַשַּׁבָּתוֹת בְּכָל־מוֹעֲדֵי בֵּית יִשְׂרָאֵל הוּא־יַעֲשֶׂה אֶת־
הַחַטָּאת וְאֶת־הַמִּנְחָה וְאֶת־הָעוֹלָה וְאֶת־הַשְּׁלָמִים לְכַפֵּר

For the life and message of Ezekiel see p. 178, and the Introductory Note to the Haftorahs of Tetzaveh and Parah, pp. 350 and 961.

The Additional Reading describes the paschal sacrifice on the first Passover in Egypt, as well as the rules and preparation of the perennial celebration of that Festival. The Haftorah, likewise, touches upon the Passover sacrifices in the course of the Prophet's description of the Restored Temple.

The last portion of the Book of Ezekiel (chaps. XL–XLVIII) is a description of the New Jerusalem that is to arise when the Exile is over. 'The Prophet, transported in thought to the Jerusalem to come, reconstructs the Temple, describes its proportions and forms, organizes the future priesthood, the new cult, lays out the geographical plan of the reorganized kingdom, and divides it among the tribes that have come back from the four corners of exile. This plan of the constitution of the

[1] ¶ 18. Thus saith the Lord GOD: In the first month, in the first day of the month, thou shalt take a young bullock without blemish; and thou shalt purify the sanctuary. 19. And the priest shall take of the blood of the sin-offering, and put it upon the door-posts ot the house, and upon the four corners of the settle of the altar, and upon the posts of the gate of the inner court. 20. And so thou shalt do on the seventh day of the month for every one that erreth, and for him that is simple; so shall ye make atonement for the house. 21. In the first month, in the fourteenth day of the month, ye shall have the pass-over; a feast of seven days; unleavened bread shall be eaten. 22. And upon that day shall the prince prepare for himself and for all the people of the land a bullock for a sin-offering. 23. And the seven days of the feast he shall prepare a burnt-offering to the LORD, seven bullocks and seven rams without blemish daily the seven days; and a he-goat daily for a sin-offering. 24. And he shall prepare a meal-offering,

[1] Sephardim begin here.

18 בְּעַד בֵּית־יִשְׂרָאֵל׃ * כֹּה־אָמַר אֲדֹנָי יֱהֹוִה בָּרִאשׁוֹן
בְּאֶחָד לַחֹדֶשׁ תִּקַּח פַּר־בֶּן־בָּקָר תָּמִים וְחִטֵּאתָ אֶת־
19 הַמִּקְדָּשׁ׃ וְלָקַח הַכֹּהֵן מִדַּם הַחַטָּאת וְנָתַן אֶל־מְזוּזַת
הַבַּיִת וְאֶל־אַרְבַּע פִּנּוֹת הָעֲזָרָה לַמִּזְבֵּחַ וְעַל־מְזוּזַת שַׁעַר
כ הֶחָצֵר הַפְּנִימִית׃ וְכֵן תַּעֲשֶׂה בְּשִׁבְעָה בַחֹדֶשׁ מֵאִישׁ
21 שֹׁגֶה וּמִפֶּתִי וְכִפַּרְתֶּם אֶת־הַבָּיִת׃ בָּרִאשׁוֹן בְּאַרְבָּעָה
עָשָׂר יוֹם לַחֹדֶשׁ יִהְיֶה לָכֶם הַפָּסַח חָג שְׁבֻעוֹת יָמִים
22 מַצּוֹת יֵאָכֵל׃ וְעָשָׂה הַנָּשִׂיא בַּיּוֹם הַהוּא בַּעֲדוֹ וּבְעַד כָּל־
23 עַם הָאָרֶץ פַּר חַטָּאת׃ וְשִׁבְעַת יְמֵי־הֶחָג יַעֲשֶׂה עוֹלָה
לַיהוָה שִׁבְעַת פָּרִים וְשִׁבְעַת אֵילִים תְּמִימִם לַיּוֹם שִׁבְעַת

* כאן מתחילין הספרדים

future is half-ideal, half-allegorical' (Darmesteter). In the New Jerusalem, the Temple becomes both spiritually and materially the centre of the whole nation and its life; and the name of the City is for the future to be, *The LORD is there.* 'Ezekiel realized that great things on earth are only produced by union. He, therefore, regarded it as the aim and task of his prophetic and pastoral mission to educate individuals, not only to be religious, but to be members of a community' (Cornill). That such a community be a holy community and serve ideal ends was, however, dependent on the people being prevented from again lapsing into their former sins. Hence, the new constitution for the nation in chaps. XL–XLVIII. Thereby the new Temple would be saved from the repetition of its profanations, and Israel rendered worthy of the God Who would make His dwelling in their midst. In this earliest of literary Utopias, the king's power is strictly limited. As wars are no more, his is no longer any military leadership; and the Prince of the nation is little else than its representative in the Temple. A rich reservation of land is assigned to him, which he tills like every other Israelite. The priests and Levites receive a definite portion of land as the material foundation of their existence.

16. *offering.* *i.e.* the dues that were to be given to the Temple; see *v.* 13–15. The National Council, on behalf of the people, were to hand the dues to the Prince; he would thus possess a common stock from which the priests could draw.

17. *to give the burnt-offerings.* From the contributions specified in the preceding verses, the Prince, as the head of the nation, would be held responsible for the supply of sacrifices at the appointed seasons.

he shall prepare the sin-offering. *i.e.* provide the offering.

18–20. To ensure the purity of the Sanctuary, which may have been endangered by error or ignorance, Passover and Tabernacles were, according to Ezekiel's vision, to be preceded on the first of the month by a day of expiation or atonement. The ritual therewith is so novel that, on the one hand, some Rabbis held that it could only refer to the Third Temple, in the days to come; and, on the other hand, there were attempts to exclude the Book of Ezekiel from the Canon of Scripture.

20. *so thou shalt do on the seventh day.* According to XLIII, 25 (Haftorah Tetzaveh), the consecration of the altar was to last seven days. When that was completed, atonement could be made for the unintentional errors committed during the services of consecration (Kimchi).

erreth. Unwittingly.

him that is simple. One who has trespassed in ignorance of the law.

21–25. The Festival sacrifices. These differ in many particulars from those in Leviticus. One Rabbi declares that this Chapter will only properly be explained 'when Elijah appears'.

22. *shall the prince prepare for himself.* Shall provide it from his own resources.

24. *ephah.* About $1\frac{1}{10}$ bushels.

hin. About $1\frac{1}{2}$ gallons.

an ephah for a bullock, and an ephah for a ram, and a hin of oil to an ephah. 25. In the seventh month, in the fifteenth day of the month, in the feast, shall he do the like the seven days; to the sin-offering as well as the burnt-offering, and the meal-offering as well as the oil.

Chapter XLVI

1. Thus saith the Lord God: The gate of the inner court that looketh toward the east shall be shut the six working days; but on the sabbath day it shall be opened, and in the day of the new moon it shall be opened. 2. And the prince shall enter by the way of the porch of the gate without, and shall stand by the post of the gate, and the priests shall prepare his burnt-offering and his peace-offerings, and he shall worship at the threshold of the gate; then he shall go forth; but the gate shall not be shut until the evening. 3. Likewise the people of the land shall worship at the door of that gate before the Lord in the sabbaths and in the new moons. 4. And the burnt-offering that the prince shall offer unto the Lord shall be in the sabbath day six lambs without blemish and a ram without blemish; 5. and the meal-offering shall be an ephah for the ram, and the meal-offering for the lambs as he is able to give, and a hin of oil to an ephah. 6. And in the day of the new moon it shall be a young bullock without blemish; and six lambs, and a ram; they shall be without blemish; 7. and he shall prepare a meal-offering, an ephah for the bullock, and an ephah for the ram, and for the lambs according as his means suffice, and a hin of oil to an ephah. 8. And when the prince shall enter, he shall go in by the way of the porch of the gate, and he shall go forth by the way thereof. 9. But when the people of the land shall come before the Lord in the appointed seasons, he that entereth by the way of the north

24 הַיָּמִים וְחַטָּאת שְׂעִיר עִזִּים לַיּוֹם׃ וּמִנְחָה אֵיפָה לַפָּר
וְאֵיפָה לָאַיִל יַעֲשֶׂה וְשֶׁמֶן הִין לָאֵיפָה׃ בַּשְּׁבִיעִי בַּחֲמִשָּׁה
כה עָשָׂר יוֹם לַחֹדֶשׁ בֶּחָג יַעֲשֶׂה כָאֵלֶּה שִׁבְעַת הַיָּמִים כַּחַטָּאת
כָּעֹלָה וְכַמִּנְחָה וְכַשָּׁמֶן׃

Cap. XLVI. מו

א כֹּה־אָמַר אֲדֹנָי יֱהֹוִה שַׁעַר הֶחָצֵר הַפְּנִימִית הַפֹּנֶה קָדִים
יִהְיֶה סָגוּר שֵׁשֶׁת יְמֵי הַמַּעֲשֶׂה וּבְיוֹם הַשַּׁבָּת יִפָּתֵחַ וּבְיוֹם
2 הַחֹדֶשׁ יִפָּתֵחַ׃ וּבָא הַנָּשִׂיא דֶּרֶךְ אוּלָם הַשַּׁעַר מִחוּץ וְעָמַד
עַל־מְזוּזַת הַשַּׁעַר וְעָשׂוּ הַכֹּהֲנִים אֶת־עוֹלָתוֹ וְאֶת־שְׁלָמָיו
וְהִשְׁתַּחֲוָה עַל־מִפְתַּן הַשַּׁעַר וְיָצָא וְהַשַּׁעַר לֹא־יִסָּגֵר עַד־
3 הָעָרֶב׃ וְהִשְׁתַּחֲווּ עַם־הָאָרֶץ פֶּתַח הַשַּׁעַר הַהוּא בַּשַּׁבָּתוֹת
4 וּבֶחֳדָשִׁים לִפְנֵי יְהוָה׃ וְהָעֹלָה אֲשֶׁר־יַקְרִב הַנָּשִׂיא לַיהוָה
ה בְּיוֹם הַשַּׁבָּת שִׁשָּׁה כְבָשִׂים תְּמִימִם וְאַיִל תָּמִים׃ וּמִנְחָה
אֵיפָה לָאַיִל וְלַכְּבָשִׂים מִנְחָה מַתַּת יָדוֹ וְשֶׁמֶן הִין לָאֵיפָה׃
6 וּבְיוֹם הַחֹדֶשׁ פַּר בֶּן־בָּקָר תְּמִימִם וְשֵׁשֶׁת כְּבָשִׂים וָאַיִל
7 תְּמִימִם יִהְיוּ׃ וְאֵיפָה לַפָּר וְאֵיפָה לָאַיִל יַעֲשֶׂה מִנְחָה
8 וְלַכְּבָשִׂים כַּאֲשֶׁר תַּשִּׂיג יָדוֹ וְשֶׁמֶן הִין לָאֵיפָה׃ וּבְבוֹא
9 הַנָּשִׂיא דֶּרֶךְ אוּלָם הַשַּׁעַר יָבוֹא וּבְדַרְכּוֹ יֵצֵא׃ וּבְבוֹא עַם

25. *in the feast.* The Feast of Tabernacles, the harvest festival.

Chapter XLVI

1–15. The rights of the Prince in the Sanctuary are strictly prescribed.

2. *shall stand by the post of the gate.* The Prince had no right of entry within it. He stood at the threshold of the eastern gate, opposite the altar, watching his sacrifice.

3. *people of the land.* Heb. *am ha-aretz*, the National Council. They have almost the same privilege as the Prince. They worship at the door of the same gate.

8. *shall go forth.* The Prince is to leave the inner gate as he entered it; he is not to pass through the Inner Court. The procedure of the Prince is thus minutely ordered that it may be understood that, though certain privileges are accorded his rank, he has no authority within the sacred precincts.

9. *in the appointed feasts.* The three Pilgrim Festivals of the year (Passover, Pentecost, and Tabernacles) when all were to appear at the Temple in Jerusalem. Ezekiel lays down the regulations to prevent overcrowding. The members of the National Council, like every worshipper, were to pass reverently as near the Holy of Holies as was allowed, but pass on. Public worship was not to degenerate into a public spectacle.

gate to worship shall go forth by the way of the south gate; and he that entereth by the way of the south gate shall go forth by the way of the north gate; he shall not return by the way of the gate whereby he came in, but shall go forth straight before him. 10. And the prince, when they go in, shall go in the midst of them; and when they go forth, they shall go forth together. 11. And in the feasts and in the appointed seasons the meal-offering shall be an ephah for a bullock, and an ephah for a ram, and for the lambs as he is able to give, and a hin of oil to an ephah. ¶ 12. And when the prince shall prepare a freewill-offering, a burnt-offering or peace-offerings as a freewill-offering unto the LORD, one shall open for him the gate that looketh toward the east, and he shall prepare his burnt-offering and his peace-offerings, as he doth on the sabbath day; then he shall go forth; and after his going forth one shall shut the gate. ¶ 13. And thou shalt prepare a lamb of the first year without blemish for a burnt-offering unto the LORD daily; morning by morning shalt thou prepare it. 14. And thou shalt prepare a meal-offering with it morning by morning, the sixth part of an ephah, and the third part of a hin of oil, to moisten the fine flour; a meal-offering unto the LORD continually by a perpetual ordinance. 15. Thus shall they prepare the lamb, and the meal-offering, and the oil, morning by morning, for a continual burnt-offering.[1] ¶ 16. Thus saith the Lord GOD: If the prince give a gift unto any of his sons, it is his inheritance, it shall belong to his sons; it is their possession by inheritance. 17. But if he give of his inheritance a gift to one of his servants, it shall be his to the year of liberty; then it shall return to the prince; but as for his inheritance, it shall be for his sons. 18. Moreover the prince shall not take of the people's inheritance, to thrust them wrongfully out of their possession; he shall give inheritance to his sons out of his own possession; that My people be not scattered every man from his possession.'

הארץ לפני יהוה במועדים הבא דרך שער צפון
להשתחות יצא דרך־שער נגב והבא דרך־שער נגב יצא
דרך־שער צפונה לא ישוב דרך השער אשר־בא בו כי
י נכחו יצאו׃ והנשיא בתוכם בבואם יבוא ובצאתם יצאו׃
11 ובחגים ובמועדים תהיה המנחה איפה לפר ואיפה לאיל
12 ולכבשים מתת ידו ושמן הין לאיפה׃ וכי־יעשה הנשיא
נדבה עולה או־שלמים נדבה ליהוה ופתח לו את־השער
הפנה קדים ועשה את־עלתו ואת־שלמיו כאשר יעשה
13 ביום השבת ויצא וסגר את־השער אחרי צאתו׃ וכבש
בן־שנתו תמים תעשה עולה ליום ליהוה בבקר בבקר
14 תעשה אתו׃ ומנחה תעשה עליו בבקר בבקר ששית
האיפה ושמן שלישית ההין לרס את־הסלת מנחה ליהוה
טו חקות עולם תמיד׃ ויעשו את־הכבש ואת־המנחה ואת־
16 השמן בבקר בבקר עולת תמיד׃* כה־אמר אדני
יהוה כי־יתן הנשיא מתנה לאיש מבניו נחלתו היא לבניו
17 תהיה אחזתם היא בנחלה׃ וכי־יתן מתנה מנחלתו לאחד
מעבדיו והיתה לו עד־שנת הדרור ושבת לנשיא אך
18 נחלתו בניו להם תהיה׃ ולא־יקח הנשיא מנחלת העם
להונתם מאחזתם מאחזתו ינחל את־בניו למען אשר לא־
יפצו עמי איש מאחזתו׃

[1] Sephardim end here.

v. 9 יצא קרי   v. 15 יעשו ק'   * כאן מסיימין הספרדים

10. *the prince . . . shall go in the midst of them.* Of the *am ha-aretz*, the National Council. Those who take the words 'people of the land' literally, explain that on the Festival days, when the people would be there in great numbers, the Prince was to mingle freely with them. In no other way does a ruler do himself greater honour (Altschul).

16–18. THE PRINCE'S ESTATE

16. *give a gift.* The Prince was at liberty to give part of his estate inalienably to his own sons.

17. *of his servants.* If he presented any gifts to them, this gift reverted to the princely estate in the year of Release.

18. *shall not take of the people's inheritance.* The Prince is to be subject to property-laws, like any other citizen. He is prohibited from appropriating, under any pretext whatsoever, land of the common people. The story of Naboth's vineyard was never again to be enacted in Israel. The Prophet thus ends his Book with the double ideal of Holiness in Worship, and Justice to Fellow-man.

HAFTORAH SABBATH HAGADOL הפטרת שבת הגדול

MALACHI III, 4–24

CHAPTER III

4. Then shall the offering of Judah and Jerusalem
Be pleasant unto the LORD,
As in the days of old,
And as in ancient years.

5. And I will come near to you to judgment;
And I will be a swift witness
Against the sorcerers, and against the adulterers,
And against false swearers;
And against those that oppress the hireling in his wages,
The widow, and the fatherless,
And that turn aside the stranger from his right,
And fear not Me,
Saith the LORD of hosts.
6. For I the LORD change not;
And ye, O sons of Jacob, are not consumed.
7. From the days of your fathers ye have turned aside
From Mine ordinances, and have not kept them.
Return unto Me, and I will return unto you,
Saith the LORD of hosts.
But ye say: 'Wherein shall we return?'

CAP. III. ג

4 וְעָֽרְבָה֙ לַֽיהוָ֔ה מִנְחַ֥ת יְהוּדָ֖ה וִירוּשָׁלִָ֑ם כִּימֵ֣י
ה עוֹלָ֔ם וּכְשָׁנִ֖ים קַדְמֹנִיֹּֽת׃ וְקָרַבְתִּ֣י אֲלֵיכֶם֮ לַמִּשְׁפָּט֒ וְהָיִ֣יתִי ׀
עֵ֣ד מְמַהֵ֗ר בַּֽמְכַשְּׁפִים֙ וּבַמְנָ֣אֲפִ֔ים וּבַנִּשְׁבָּעִ֖ים לַשָּׁ֑קֶר
וּבְעֹשְׁקֵ֣י שְׂכַר־שָׂ֠כִיר אַלְמָנָ֨ה וְיָת֤וֹם וּמַטֵּי־גֵר֙ וְלֹ֣א יְרֵא֔וּנִי
6 אָמַ֖ר יְהוָ֥ה צְבָאֽוֹת׃ כִּ֛י אֲנִ֥י יְהוָ֖ה לֹ֣א שָׁנִ֑יתִי וְאַתֶּ֥ם בְּנֵֽי־
7 יַעֲקֹ֖ב לֹ֥א כְלִיתֶֽם׃ לְמִימֵ֨י אֲבֹתֵיכֶ֜ם סַרְתֶּ֤ם מֵֽחֻקַּי֙ וְלֹ֣א

For a characterization of the times and message of Malachi see p. 102.

The Haftorah ends with the announcement of the reappearance of Elijah the Prophet. Passover, as the Festival of Redemption in the past, was always associated with the Redemption of the Future (פסח לעתיד), when mankind would be delivered from all oppression, physical and spiritual. Elijah was traditionally regarded as the advance messenger who would appear at Passover-time and announce the dawn of that Messianic era.

Malachi preaches to a despondent generation, when spiritual lassitude possessed both high and low, and doubt paralyzed the souls of men. Sordidness, callousness and moral disintegration met him at every turn: and at the same time men asked, Where is God? Malachi answers the challenge by announcing the speedy advent of a great Judgment Day.

4. *be pleasant unto the LORD.* When, as stated in the previous verse, they will be offered 'in righteousness'.

ancient years. Parallel to the phrase, 'days of old,' and probably referring to the age of David and Solomon.

5. *to judgment.* An answer to the doubters who, perplexed by the social wrongs about them and the prosperity of evil doers, asked 'Where is the God of Judgment?' (II, 17).

swift witness. 'Judgment will not wait till witnesses are produced, for I, knowing all secrets, am witness as well as judge' (Altschul).

oppress the hireling. Defraud the hired day labourer of his hard-earned pay.

widow and the fatherless. Exploitation of the weak (widow, fatherless, stranger) who cannot defend their rights, is accounted an unpardonable sin in Scripture.

fear not Me. Being God-less, they are devoid of natural piety; and their dealings with the weak and helpless show a lack of fundamental humanity.

6. *I the LORD change not . . . are not consumed.* I change not in My nature, being ever the same both in loving good and hating evil as in the purpose for which you are selected as My people. Therefore, My judgment is but to purify you for the fulfilment of your destiny (Kimchi).

7–12. The neglect of tithes and the punishment therefor.

7. *return. i.e.* turn away from sin and turn

8. Will a man rob God?
Yet ye rob Me.
But ye say: 'Wherein have we robbed Thee?'
In tithes and heave-offerings.

9. Ye are cursed with the curse,
Yet ye rob Me,
Even this whole nation.

10. Bring ye the whole tithe into the store-house,
That there may be food in My house,
And try Me now herewith,
Saith the LORD of hosts,
If I will not open you the windows of heaven,
And pour you out a blessing,
That there shall be more than sufficiency.

11. And I will rebuke the devourer for your good,
And he shall not destroy the fruits of your land;
Neither shall your vine cast its fruit before the time in the field,
Saith the LORD of hosts.

12. And all nations shall call you happy;
For ye shall be a delightsome land,
Saith the LORD of hosts.

13. Your words have been all too strong against Me,
Saith the LORD.
Yet ye say: 'Wherein have we spoken against Thee?'

14. Ye have said: 'It is vain to serve God;
And what profit is it that we have kept His charge,
And that we have walked mournfully
Because of the LORD of hosts?

שְׁמַרְתֶּם שׁוּבוּ אֵלַי וְאָשׁוּבָה אֲלֵיכֶם אָמַר יְהוָה צְבָאוֹת
8 וַאֲמַרְתֶּם בַּמֶּה נָשׁוּב׃ הֲיִקְבַּע אָדָם אֱלֹהִים כִּי אַתֶּם
קֹבְעִים אֹתִי וַאֲמַרְתֶּם בַּמֶּה קְבַעֲנוּךָ הַמַּעֲשֵׂר וְהַתְּרוּמָה׃
9 בַּמְּאֵרָה אַתֶּם נֵאָרִים וְאֹתִי אַתֶּם קֹבְעִים הַגּוֹי כֻּלּוֹ׃ הָבִיאוּ
אֶת־כָּל־הַמַּעֲשֵׂר אֶל־בֵּית הָאוֹצָר וִיהִי טֶרֶף בְּבֵיתִי וּבְחָנוּנִי
נָא בָּזֹאת אָמַר יְהוָה צְבָאוֹת אִם־לֹא אֶפְתַּח לָכֶם אֵת
11 אֲרֻבּוֹת הַשָּׁמַיִם וַהֲרִיקֹתִי לָכֶם בְּרָכָה עַד־בְּלִי־דָי׃ וְגָעַרְתִּי
לָכֶם בָּאֹכֵל וְלֹא־יַשְׁחִת לָכֶם אֶת־פְּרִי הָאֲדָמָה וְלֹא־
12 תְשַׁכֵּל לָכֶם הַגֶּפֶן בַּשָּׂדֶה אָמַר יְהוָה צְבָאוֹת׃ וְאִשְּׁרוּ
אֶתְכֶם כָּל־הַגּוֹיִם כִּי־תִהְיוּ אַתֶּם אֶרֶץ חֵפֶץ אָמַר יְהוָה
13 צְבָאוֹת׃ חָזְקוּ עָלַי דִּבְרֵיכֶם אָמַר יְהוָה וַאֲמַרְתֶּם
14 מַה־נִּדְבַּרְנוּ עָלֶיךָ׃ אֲמַרְתֶּם שָׁוְא עֲבֹד אֱלֹהִים וּמַה־
בֶּצַע כִּי שָׁמַרְנוּ מִשְׁמַרְתּוֹ וְכִי הָלַכְנוּ קְדֹרַנִּית מִפְּנֵי יְהוָה
טו צְבָאוֹת׃ וְעַתָּה אֲנַחְנוּ מְאַשְּׁרִים זֵדִים גַּם־נִבְנוּ עֹשֵׂי

15. And now we call the proud happy;
Yea, they that work wickedness are built up;
Yea, they try God, and are delivered.'

toward God. The Heb. word for Repentance, תשובה, is derived from this root.

wherein shall we return. Pretending not to know where in their conduct there was any need for repentance.

8. *in tithes and heave-offerings.* They have neglected or refused to pay the sacred dues for the maintenance of the Temple Service. 'Israel's preservation as the people of God could only be effectively secured by a strict observance of the ceremonial obligations laid upon it, and by its holding firmly aloof from the disintegrating influence to which unrestricted intercourse with its neighbours would inevitably expose it' (Driver).

9. *with the curse.* Locusts and failure of crops.

10. *meat in My house.* Sustenance for those ministering in the Temple.

11. *the devourer.* The locust; a dire plague of Palestine.

cast. Fail to ripen.

13–24. Encouragement to the impatient.

13. *strong.* Hard, in censure. This is addressed to those who murmured at God's apparent indifference to their troubles and His tolerance of the prosperity of the wicked; see *v.* 14 and 15. They say: There is neither a judge nor justice in the universe (Kimchi).

14. *His charge.* All religious duties.

walked mournfully. Humbling themselves, and mourning at the signs of God's anger in their disasters.

15. *and now . . . happy.* Since their own religious observances bring them no profit.

proud. The lax and worldly, who looked down

16. Then they that feared the LORD
Spoke one with another;
And the LORD hearkened, and heard,
And a book of remembrance was written before Him,
For them that feared the LORD, and that thought upon His name.
17. And they shall be Mine, saith the LORD of hosts,
In the day that I do make, even Mine own treasure;
And I will spare them, as a man spareth
His own son that serveth him.
18. Then shall ye again discern between the righteous and the wicked,
Between him that serveth God
And him that serveth Him not.
19. For, behold, the day cometh,
It burneth as a furnace;
And all the proud, and all that work wickedness, shall be stubble;
And the day that cometh shall set them ablaze,
Saith the Lord of hosts,
That it shall leave them neither root nor branch.
20. But unto you that fear My Name
Shall the sun of righteousness arise with healing in its wings;
And ye shall go forth, and gambol
As calves of the stall.
21. And ye shall tread down the wicked;
For they shall be ashes under the soles of your feet
In the day that I do make,
Saith the LORD of hosts.

22. Remember ye the law of Moses My servant,
Which I commanded unto him in Horeb for all Israel,
Even statutes and ordinances.

23. Behold, I will send you
Elijah the prophet
Before the coming
Of the great and terrible day of the LORD.

16 רִשְׁעָה גַּם בָּחֲנוּ אֱלֹהִים וַיִּמָּלֵטוּ׃ אָז נִדְבְּרוּ יִרְאֵי יְהוָה
אִישׁ אֶל־רֵעֵהוּ וַיַּקְשֵׁב יְהוָה וַיִּשְׁמָע וַיִּכָּתֵב סֵפֶר זִכָּרוֹן
17 לְפָנָיו לְיִרְאֵי יְהוָה וּלְחֹשְׁבֵי שְׁמוֹ׃ וְהָיוּ לִי אָמַר יְהוָה
צְבָאוֹת לַיּוֹם אֲשֶׁר אֲנִי עֹשֶׂה סְגֻלָּה וְחָמַלְתִּי עֲלֵיהֶם
18 כַּאֲשֶׁר יַחְמֹל אִישׁ עַל־בְּנוֹ הָעֹבֵד אֹתוֹ׃ וְשַׁבְתֶּם וּרְאִיתֶם
19 בֵּין צַדִּיק לְרָשָׁע בֵּין עֹבֵד אֱלֹהִים לַאֲשֶׁר לֹא עֲבָדוֹ׃ כִּי
הִנֵּה הַיּוֹם בָּא בֹּעֵר כַּתַּנּוּר וְהָיוּ כָל־זֵדִים וְכָל־עֹשֵׂה
רִשְׁעָה קַשׁ וְלִהַט אֹתָם הַיּוֹם הַבָּא אָמַר יְהוָה צְבָאוֹת
כ אֲשֶׁר לֹא־יַעֲזֹב לָהֶם שֹׁרֶשׁ וְעָנָף׃ וְזָרְחָה לָכֶם יִרְאֵי שְׁמִי
שֶׁמֶשׁ צְדָקָה וּמַרְפֵּא בִּכְנָפֶיהָ וִיצָאתֶם וּפִשְׁתֶּם כְּעֶגְלֵי
21 מַרְבֵּק׃ וְעַסּוֹתֶם רְשָׁעִים כִּי־יִהְיוּ אֵפֶר תַּחַת כַּפּוֹת
22 רַגְלֵיכֶם בַּיּוֹם אֲשֶׁר אֲנִי עֹשֶׂה אָמַר יְהוָה צְבָאוֹת׃ זִכְרוּ
תּוֹרַת מֹשֶׁה עַבְדִּי אֲשֶׁר צִוִּיתִי אוֹתוֹ בְחֹרֵב עַל־כָּל־יִשְׂרָאֵל
23 חֻקִּים וּמִשְׁפָּטִים׃ הִנֵּה אָנֹכִי שֹׁלֵחַ לָכֶם אֵת אֵלִיָּה הַנָּבִיא

v. 16. קמץ בז״ק v. 22. ז׳ רבתי

with cold and haughty indifference upon their poorer brethren (Driver).

are built up. Prosperous.

try God. They deliberately defy God, and yet escape His judgment which they challenge by their lives.

16. *that feared the LORD.* In face of all this, the truly pious spoke words of trust and faith, reassuring one another that God is 'a God of faithfulness and there is no iniquity in Him'.

book of remembrance. The figure is derived from the custom of Persian monarchs to have the names of public benefactors inscribed in a book; see Esther VI, 1.

thought upon His name. Those who reflected upon the ways and attributes of the Lord as revealed in His Name (Kimchi, Ibn Ezra).

17. *in the day that I do make.* The Day of Judgment. The faithful minority will be safe.

own treasure. They will be God's own possession and treasure, סגלה—the privileged term once applied to all Israel.

20. *the sun of righteousness arise.* The rightness of the cause of those 'that fear My name' will become patent to all. Their deliverance will be a vindication of their loyalty and faith.

with healing in his wings. 'Wings' figuratively for 'rays'. As the rays of the physical sun spread healing and life around, so shall your signal deliverance, shining out like the sun, banish the troubles now afflicting you, and endow you with health and happiness.

gambol. 'Break into life and energy, like young calves leaping forth from the dark pen into the early sunshine' (G. A. Smith).

24 לִפְנֵי בּוֹא יוֹם יְהוָה הַגָּדוֹל וְהַנּוֹרָא׃ וְהֵשִׁיב לֵב־אָבוֹת
עַל־בָּנִים וְלֵב בָּנִים עַל־אֲבוֹתָם פֶּן־אָבוֹא וְהִכֵּיתִי אֶת־
הָאָרֶץ חֵרֶם׃ הִנֵּה אָנֹכִי שֹׁלֵחַ לָכֶם אֵת אֵלִיָּה הַנָּבִיא
לִפְנֵי בּוֹא יוֹם יְהוָה הַגָּדוֹל וְהַנּוֹרָא׃

24. And he shall turn the heart of the fathers to the children,
And the heart of the children to their fathers;
Lest I come and smite the land with utter destruction.

Behold, I will send you
Elijah the prophet
Before the coming
Of the great and terrible day of the LORD.

21. *ashes.* A grim metaphorical representation of the complete victory of right over wrong.

22–24. Final exhortation.

22. *remember ye the law of Moses.* This epilogue to Malachi is an excellent summary of the teaching of the Prophets.

23. *Elijah.* Far more than the prophet of zeal and fire of the Biblical narrative, he is to later generations the helper and healer, the reconciler and peace-bringer, the herald of the days of the Messiah.

the great and terrible day. Of Judgment announced in the preceding chapter. 'Terrible' in the sense of 'awesome'.

24. *he shall turn the heart.* The heart was considered the seat of thought as well as emotion. 'Elijah' will therefore effect a reconciliation between the old and the new, not merely by awakening sympathy of one for the other, but by endowing them with a full understanding of the religious and moral obligations unitedly held by both sections.

of the children to their fathers. It is the home divided against itself, the estrangement of the youth from the elders, that especially fills the Prophet with pain and horror as something unnatural—a curse which, if unremoved, must blight the land. First reconciling parents and children, Elijah will turn the hearts of both to God.

23. *he shall turn.* *v.* 23 is repeated, as it is against Jewish custom to conclude a Reading from the Scriptures with words of threat or doom.

BLESSINGS BEFORE AND AFTER THE HAFTORAH

ברכות ההפטרה

Before reading the Lesson from the Prophets, the following is said by the Maftir :—

Blessed art thou, O Lord our God, King of the universe, who hast chosen good prophets, and hast found pleasure in their words which were spoken in truth.

Blessed art thou, O Lord, who hast chosen the Law, and Moses thy servant, and Israel thy people, and prophets of truth and righteousness.

בָּרוּךְ אַתָּה יְיָ אֱלֹהֵינוּ מֶלֶךְ הָעוֹלָם · אֲשֶׁר בָּחַר בִּנְבִיאִים טוֹבִים וְרָצָה בְדִבְרֵיהֶם הַנֶּאֱמָרִים בֶּאֱמֶת
בָּרוּךְ אַתָּה יְיָ · הַבּוֹחֵר בַּתּוֹרָה וּבְמשֶׁה עַבְדּוֹ וּבְיִשְׂרָאֵל עַמּוֹ וּבִנְבִיאֵי הָאֱמֶת וָצֶדֶק :

[*Sephardim conclude each Haftorah with the words :—*

Our Redeemer! The Lord of Hosts is his name, the Holy One of Israel.]

[גֹּאֲלֵנוּ יְיָ צְבָאוֹת שְׁמוֹ קְדוֹשׁ יִשְׂרָאֵל :

After the Lesson from the Prophets, the Maftir says the following :—

Blessed art thou, O Lord our God, King of the universe, Rock of all worlds, righteous through all generations, O faithful God, who sayest and doest, who speakest and fulfillest, all whose words are truth and righteousness. Faithful art thou, O Lord our God, and faithful are thy words, and not one of thy words shall return void, for thou art a faithful and merciful God and King. Blessed art thou, O Lord, God, who art faithful in all thy words.

בָּרוּךְ אַתָּה יְיָ אֱלֹהֵינוּ מֶלֶךְ הָעוֹלָם · צוּר כָּל־הָעוֹלָמִים צַדִּיק בְּכָל־הַדּוֹרוֹת הָאֵל הַנֶּאֱמָן הָאוֹמֵר וְעוֹשֶׂה הַמְדַבֵּר וּמְקַיֵּם שֶׁכָּל־דְּבָרָיו אֱמֶת וָצֶדֶק : נֶאֱמָן אַתָּה הוּא יְיָ אֱלֹהֵינוּ וְנֶאֱמָנִים דְּבָרֶיךָ וְדָבָר אֶחָד מִדְּבָרֶיךָ אָחוֹר לֹא־יָשׁוּב רֵיקָם · כִּי אֵל מֶלֶךְ נֶאֱמָן וְרַחֲמָן אָתָּה · בָּרוּךְ אַתָּה יְיָ · הָאֵל הַנֶּאֱמָן בְּכָל־דְּבָרָיו :

Have mercy upon Zion, for it is the home of our life, and save her that is grieved in spirit speedily, even in our days. Blessed art thou, O Lord, who makest Zion joyful through her children.

רַחֵם עַל־צִיּוֹן כִּי הִיא בֵּית חַיֵּינוּ וְלַעֲלוּבַת נֶפֶשׁ תּוֹשִׁיעַ בִּמְהֵרָה בְיָמֵינוּ : בָּרוּךְ אַתָּה יְיָ · מְשַׂמֵּחַ צִיּוֹן בְּבָנֶיהָ :

Gladden us, O Lord our God, with Elijah the prophet, thy servant, and with the kingdom of the house of David, thine anointed. Soon may he come and rejoice our hearts. Suffer not a stranger to sit upon his throne, nor let others any longer inherit his glory; for by thy holy name thou didst swear unto him, that his light should not be quenched for ever. Blessed art thou, O Lord, the Shield of David.

שַׂמְּחֵנוּ יְיָ אֱלֹהֵינוּ בְּאֵלִיָּהוּ הַנָּבִיא עַבְדֶּךָ וּבְמַלְכוּת בֵּית דָּוִד מְשִׁיחֶךָ · בִּמְהֵרָה יָבֹא וְיָגֵל לִבֵּנוּ · עַל־כִּסְאוֹ לֹא־יֵשֶׁב זָר וְלֹא יִנְחֲלוּ עוֹד אֲחֵרִים אֶת־כְּבוֹדוֹ · כִּי בְשֵׁם קָדְשְׁךָ נִשְׁבַּעְתָּ לּוֹ שֶׁלֹּא יִכְבֶּה נֵרוֹ לְעוֹלָם וָעֶד · בָּרוּךְ אַתָּה יְיָ · מָגֵן דָּוִד :

For the Law, for the divine service, for the prophets, and for this Sabbath day, which thou, O Lord our God, hast given us for holiness and for rest, for honour and for glory,—for all these we thank and bless thee, O Lord our God, blessed be thy name by the mouth of every living being continually and for ever. Blessed art thou, O Lord, who sanctifiest the Sabbath.

עַל־הַתּוֹרָה וְעַל־הָעֲבוֹדָה וְעַל־הַנְּבִיאִים וְעַל־יוֹם הַשַּׁבָּת הַזֶּה שֶׁנָּתַתָּ־לָּנוּ יְיָ אֱלֹהֵינוּ לִקְדֻשָּׁה וְלִמְנוּחָה לְכָבוֹד וּלְתִפְאָרֶת · עַל־הַכֹּל יְיָ אֱלֹהֵינוּ אֲנַחְנוּ מוֹדִים לָךְ וּמְבָרְכִים אוֹתָךְ · יִתְבָּרַךְ שִׁמְךָ בְּפִי כָל־חַי תָּמִיד לְעוֹלָם וָעֶד · בָּרוּךְ אַתָּה יְיָ · מְקַדֵּשׁ הַשַּׁבָּת :

נְגִינוֹת לִקְרִיאַת הַתּוֹרָה

CANTILLATION OF THE TORAH

Arranged by the Revs.
H. MAYEROWITSCH AND G. PRINCE

[1] *in middle of verse* [2] *at end of verse* [3] *at end of section*

אַזְלָא־גֵּרֵשׁ
קַדְמָא־וְאַזְלָא
תְּלִישָׁא־גְדוֹלָה
Te - li - sho ge - do - lo Kad - mo ve - az - lo Az - lo - Ge-resh
תְּבִיר
מֵרְכָא
תְּבִיר
דַּרְגָּא
גֵּרְשַׁיִם
Geir - sha yim Dar - go Te - vir Mer - cho Te - vir
קַרְנֵי פָרָה
שַׁלְשֶׁלֶת
Shal - she les Kar - nei pho-ro
מֵרְכָא־כְפוּלָא
יֶרַח־בֶּן־יוֹמוֹ
Ye - rach ben yo - mo Mer - cho che - fu - loh
מוּנַּח
preceding
Mu - nach
מוּנַּח
preceding
Mu - nach
פַּשְׁטָא קָטֹן
When on one word.
Pash - to ko - ton

נְגִינוֹת לְהַפְטָרָה

CANTILLATION OF THE PROPHETS

[1] *in middle of verse*

[2] *at end of verse*

[3] *at the end of Haftorah*

קַדְמָא־וְאַזְלָא
אַזְלָא־גֵּרֵשׁ
גֵּרְשַׁיִם
Kad - mo — ve - az - lo —— Az - lo Ge - resh Geir - sha —— yim
דַּרְגָּא
תְּבִיר
תְּבִיר מֵרְכָא
Dar - go —— Te - vir —— Mer - cho Te - vir ——
מוּנַּח
Mu - nach
preceding
מוּנַּח
Mu - nach ——
preceding

VERSIONS AND COMMENTATORS CONSULTED

A. ANCIENT VERSIONS AND AUTHORITIES

Jerusalem Targum, see *Targum*.

Jonathan Targum, see *Targum*.

Josephus, Flavius (37–95 A.C.E.) Jewish historian and apologist. 'Antiquities of the Jews.'

Massorah. lit. 'The Tradition'. The original Bible text was unvowelled. The *Massoretes* fixed the Traditional reading of the Sacred Text and its exact pronunciation, largely by means of vowel-points. Their activity began after the Talmudic period, and extended to the tenth century.

Mechilta. Oldest Rabbinic Commentary on Exodus.

Midrash. The ancient homiletical expositions of the Torah, the Five Scrolls (*i.e.* Song of Songs, Ruth, Lamentations, Ecclesiastes, and Esther), and other portions of Scripture.

Onkelos, see *Targum*.

Philo Judaeus (20 B.C.E.–40 A.C.E.). Renowned Jewish philosopher in Alexandria. Author of allegorical commentaries on the Pentateuch.

Rabbis, the. The religious authorities in the Talmudim and Midrashim.

Samaritan Pentateuch. The Samaritan adaptation of the Hebrew Text; see also *Targum*.

Septuagint. The Greek translation of the Bible made by the Jews in Egypt in the third century B.C.E. The word *Septuagint* means seventy, because it was believed to be the work of seventy-two scholars selected for that purpose by one of the Ptolemy rulers.

Sifra. Oldest Rabbinic Commentary on Leviticus.

Sifri. Or, *Sifré*. Oldest Rabbinic Commentary on Numbers and Deuteronomy.

Symmachus. A literal Greek version of the Pentateuch by a Hellenistic Jew of the second century.

Targum. Ancient translations or paraphrases of the Bible into the Aramaic vernacular then spoken by the Jews. The most important of these is the translation of the Pentateuch that is ascribed to *Onkelos*, the Proselyte, a Mishnah teacher of the first century. *The Jonathan Targum* is a freer paraphrase of the Bible, ascribed to Jonathan ben Uzziel, a pupil of Hillel. An earlier and fragmentary version of this paraphrase is known as the *Jerusalem Targum*. The *Samaritans* also have an Aramaic *Targum*, embodying their traditional interpretation of the Torah.

Talmud. Body of Jewish law and legend comprising the *Mishnah* and the *Gemara*, and containing the authoritative explanation of the Torah by the Rabbis of Palestine and Babylon, from the years 100 B.C.E. to 500 A.C.E.

B. MEDIEVAL JEWISH AUTHORITIES AND COMMENTATORS

Abarbanel (or, Abrabanel), Don Isaac (1437–1509). Spanish exegete and statesman.

Bechor Shor, Joseph. French exegete of the twelfth century.

Chizkuni. Thirteenth century French commentator.

Gersonides, see *Ralbag*.

Hallevi, Yehudah (1085–1140). Religious philosopher and greatest medieval Hebrew poet. 'The Cuzari.'

Ibn Ezra, Abraham (1092–1167). Famous Spanish-Jewish grammarian, Bible exegete, philosopher, traveller, and poet.

Kimchi, David (1160–1235). Franco-Spanish exegete and grammarian. His commentary profoundly influenced the Authorized Version of 1611.

Maimonides, Moses (1135–1204). Foremost medieval Jewish philosopher. In his 'Guide of the Perplexed', he deals with difficult Bible terms and conceptions.

Nachmanides, Moses (1194–1268). Great Spanish Talmudist, Bible commentator and mystic.

Ralbag. *i.e.* Rabbi Levi ben Gerson (1288–1344). French exegete, philosopher, and scientist.

Rashbam. *i.e.* Rabbi Samuel ben Meir (1085–1174). Rashi's grandson. Stresses the 'plain, natural sense' in his commentaries.

Rashi. *i.e.* Rabbi Solomon ben Isaac of Troyes (1040–1105). French Bible exegete and greatest commentator of the Talmud. No other commentary on the Pentateuch has had a more enduring popularity or exerted an equal influence in Jewry.

Saadyah, Gaon (882–942), born in Egypt. Religious philosopher and exegete. Translator of Bible into Arabic.

Sforno, Obadiah (1475–1550). Italian physician and exegete. Teacher of Reuchlin.

Shulchan Aruch. Authoritative code of Rabbinic Judaism compiled by Joseph Karo, 1564, and enlarged by Moses Isserles, 1578.

Zohar. Mystical commentary on the Pentateuch. Probably thirteenth century.

C. MODERN VERSIONS IN ENGLISH

Authorized Version. Also known as the King James's Version, 1611—Of unsurpassed literary beauty.

Benisch, Abraham (1811–1878). 'Jewish School and Family Bible,' 4 vols. London, 1851–1861.

Leeser, Isaac (1806–1868). The Twenty-four Books of the Holy Scriptures, Philadelphia, 1853—This work and that of Benisch were the first Jewish versions in English of the entire Bible.

Revised Version, 1884. Preserves the beauties of the Authorized Version, but corrects its mistakes in the light of modern scholarship.

M. Friedlander. A Jewish Appendix to the Revised Version, 1896.

American Jewish Version. 'With the aid of previous versions and with constant consultation of Jewish Authorities.' Jewish Publication Society of America, Philadelphia, 1917.

Moffatt, James. A New Translation of the Bible, 1925—in colloquial English.

D. MODERN COMMENTATORS, TRANSLATORS, AND WRITERS ON BIBLE SUBJECTS—JEWISH

Only the principal names referred to are given, and only works consulted in the preparation of this Volume

Abrahams, Israel (1858–1925). Anglo-Jewish scholar.

Adler, Hermann (1839–1911). Chief Rabbi.

Altschul, David. Seventeenth century. 'Metzudath David' and 'Metzudath Tziyon', popular commentaries on the Prophetical books.

Blau, Ludwig (1861–1936). Hungarian Bible scholar. 'Zur Einleitung in die Heilige Schrift.' 'Masoretische Studien.'

Bloch, J. S. (1850–1923). Austrian-Jewish apologist.

Büchler, A. (1867–1939). Principal of Jews' College, London. 'Studies in Sin and Atonement.'

Cassuto, Umberto (1883–). Italian Jewish scholar.

Cohen, Hermann (1842–1918). Kantian philosopher of religion. 'Juedische Schriften.' 'Religion der Vernunft aus den Quellen des Judentums.'

Daiches, Samuel (1878–). Anglo-Jewish scholar.

Darmesteter, James (1849–1894). French Orientalist. 'The Prophets of Israel.'

Ehrlich, A. B. (1848–1920). Russian-American exegete. 'Mikra ki-Pheschuto.' 'Randglossen.'

Frankel, Z. (1801–1875). First Principal of Breslau Seminary. 'Mosaisch-talmudisches Eherecht.'

Friedländer, Michael (1833–1910). English scholar and commentator. 'The Jewish Religion.'

Geiger, Abraham (1810–1874). German religious leader and Bible critic.

Guttmann, Michael (1872–). Rector of Rabbinical Seminary, Budapest. 'Das Judentum und die Umwelt.'

Herxheimer, S. (1801–1884). Author of complete commentary on the Holy Scriptures.

Hirsch, Samson R. (1808–1888). German religious leader and commentator.

Hoffmann, David (1843–1921). Bible and Talmud scholar. 'Leviticus.' 'Deuteronomium.'

Jacob, Benno (1862–). German Bible exegete.

Jacobs, Joseph (1854–1916). Anglo-Jewish scholar. 'Jewish Ideals.'

Jampel, S. (1874–1934). German exegete and popular writer on Bible archæology. 'Die Hagada aus Aegypten.'

Jastrow, Marcus (1829–1903). American Bible scholar and Talmudist.

Joseph, Morris (1848–1930). Anglo-Jewish Minister. 'Judaism as Life and Creed.'

Kalisch, M. M. (1828–1885). English Bible commentator.

Kohler, Kaufmann (1843–1926). German-American scholar. 'Jewish Theology.'

Krauss, Samuel (1866–). Bible and Talmud scholar.

Leeser, Isaac (1806–1868). American Bible translator and author of exegetical glosses.

Lencziz, Ephraim. Early seventeenth century. Polish-Bohemian preacher and commentator.

Löw, Leopold (1811–1875). Theologian and Talmudist. 'Eherechtliche Studien.'

Luzzatto, S. D. (1800–1865). Great Italian Hebraist and commentator.

Mahler, Eduard (1857–). Hungarian Orientalist and authority on Jewish chronology.

Malbim, M. L. (1809–1879). Russian Rabbi and exegete.

Margolis, Max L. (1866–1932). American scholar and Bible translator. 'The Book of Micah.'

Mendelssohn, Moses (1729–1786). German philosopher, Bible translator and commentator (*Biur*).

Montefiore, C. G. (1858–**1938**). Hibbert Lecturer, 1892. 'The Synoptic Gospels.'

Mueller, D. H. (1846–1912). Austrian Assyriologist.

Philippson, Ludwig (1811–1889). German preacher and commentator.

Reggio, Isaac Samuel (1784–1855). Austro-Italian scholar.

Schechter, S. (1847–1915). Theologian, Talmudist, and Essayist. 'Aspects of Rabbinic Theology.'

Steinthal, H. (1823–1899). German philosopher. 'Zu Bibel u. Religionsphilosophie.'

Sulzberger, Mayer (1843–1923). American jurist.

Szold, Benjamin (1829–1902). American Bible scholar.

Wesseley, N. H. (1725–1805). Hebraist. 'Leviticus' in Mendelssohn's edition of the Pentateuch.

Wiener, H. M. (1874–1929). English Bible scholar. 'Essays in Pentateuchal Criticism.'

Wogue, Lazare (1817–1897). French scholar and exegete.

Yahuda, A. S. (1878–). English Egyptologist. 'The Language of the Pentateuch.'

Zangwill, Israel (1864–1926). English man of letters. 'The Voice of Jerusalem,' 'Children of the Ghetto.'

Zunz, Leopold (1794–1886). Founder of the New Jewish Learning. Edited the Bible translation that is most in use among German-speaking Jews.

E. MODERN COMMENTATORS, TRANSLATORS, AND WRITERS ON BIBLE SUBJECTS—NON-JEWISH

Only the principal names referred to are given, and only works consulted in the preparation of this Volume

Baxter, W. L. (1841–1937). Scottish Bible scholar. 'Sanctuary and Sacrifice.'

Cheyne, T. K. (1841–1915). English Bible critic. 'Isaiah,' 'Hosea,' 'Micah.'

Cornill, C. H. (1854–1920). German exegete. 'Jeremias.' 'The Prophets of Israel.'

Delitzsch, Franz (1813–1890). Rabbinic scholar and commentator. 'Genesis.' 'Jesaia.'

Dillmann, A. (1823–1894). German philologist and exegete. 'Pentateuch.' 'Jesaia.'

Driver, S. R. (1846–1914). English Bible commentator.

Ewald, Heinrich (1803–1875). German historian and exegete.

Garstang, John (1876–). British Archæologist. 'The Foundations of Bible History: Joshua, Judges.'

Green, W. H. (1825–1900). American Hebraist.

Hall, R. H. (1873–1930). British archæologist.

Herford, R. Travers (1868–). Rabbinic scholar. 'The Pharisees.'

Hommel, Fritz (1854–1937). German Orientalist. 'Ancient Hebrew Tradition.'

Kittel, Gerhard (1888–). German Rabbinic scholar. 'Die Probleme des pal. Spätjudentums.'

Kittel, Rudolf (1853–1933). Bible historian.

Koenig, Eduard (1846–1936). German Hebraist. 'Genesis.' 'Das Deuteronomium.'

Milman, Dean (1791–1868). English historian. 'The History of the Jews.'

Moore, G. F. (1851–1931). American Bible scholar.

Naville, Edouard (1844–1930). Swiss Egyptologist.

Orr, James. Scottish Bible scholar. 'The Problem of the Old Testament.'

Otto, Rudolf (1869–1937). German philosopher of religion. 'The Idea of the Holy.'

Petrie, Flinders (1853–). English Egyptologist.

Robinson, T. H. (1881–). English Bible scholar.

Sayce, A. H. (1845–1933). British Orientalist.

Smith, G. A. (1856–). Scottish Bible scholar.

Stanley, Dean (1815–1881). English Divine. 'History of the Jewish Church.'

Welch, Adam C. (1864–). Scottish Hebraist. 'The Code of Deuteronomy.'

In addition to the works of the Jewish and non-Jewish authors mentioned above, the standard commentaries on the books of the Pentateuch and on the *Prophets* were consulted; also various volumes in the Cambridge Bible for Schools, the Temple, the Century, the Modern Reader's, and Expositor's Bible, as well as the One Volume (Dummelow), New (Guillaume), Pulpit, and Speaker's Commentaries.

CHRONOLOGICAL TABLE

IN CONNECTION WITH THE SEDRAS AND THEIR HAFTORAHS

	B.C.E.
Abraham	*circa* 1900
Isaac	„ 1800
Jacob	„ 1750
Joseph	„ 1700
Joseph in Egypt	„ 1650
Expulsion of Hyksos	„ 1587
Joshua—entrance into Canaan	1407
Rameses II	1300–1234
(*According to Mahler* :)	1347–1280
Menremptah	1234–1214
Date of Exodus	1230
(*For Mahler's view, see p.* 251 ; *for Garstang's, see p.* 635)	
Deborah	*circa* 1150
Jephthah	„ 1110
Samson	„ 1100
Saul	1028–1013
David	1013–973
Solomon	973–933
Jeroboam I and the Division of the Kingdom	933
Ahab	876–853

	B.C.E.
Elijah	*circa* 870
Elisha	„ 850
Joash	837–798
Jeroboam II	790–749
Amos and Hosea, Prophetic activity of	760–734
Isaiah, call of	740
Micah	740
Fall of the Northern Kingdom	722
Jeremiah, call of	626
Josiah	638–609
Capture of Jerusalem by the Babylonians	597
Ezekiel, call of	592
First Destruction of the Temple	586
Obadiah	*circa* 585
Cyrus takes Babylon	538
First Return of Babylonian Exiles	537
Zechariah and the Rebuilding of the Temple	520
Ezra and the Second Return from Babylon	458
Maccabean Rising	167
Second Destruction of Jerusalem	A.C.E. 70

ABBREVIATIONS

A.C.E.	After the Christian Era.
AJ	American Jewish Version—adopted as the Translation in this edition.
AV	Authorized Version, 1611.
B.C.E.	Before the Christian Era.
Better	Indicates a rendering which is preferable to that given in the Translation of AJ.
cf.	Compare; see.
chap.	Chapter. Whenever the reference is to a chapter in the same book of the Pentateuch, the Roman numeral alone is given.
f.	After the number of a verse, indicates that the reference extends to the verse or verses following.
fig.	Figuratively speaking.
Heb.	Hebrew; the original Hebrew word or Text; in the original Hebrew.
i.e.	That is.
lit.	Literally; the *literal* meaning of the Hebrew word or phrase translated.
RV	Revised Version, 1884.
v.	Verse or verses.
°	indicates where the division of the chapters, and consequent numbering of the verses, differ in English Bibles from the Hebrew Text.
*	followed by a Roman numeral, indicates each of the seven divisions (parshiyoth) into which the Weekly Portion (Sidrah) is divided. Whenever the Ashkenazi and Sephardi usages differ, the small letter *a* or *s* follows the Roman numerals.
**	followed by a Roman numeral, indicates each of the seven divisions when two Weekly Portions are combined.

The Books of the Bible are abbreviated as follows: Gen., Exod., Lev., Num., Deut., Josh., Judg., I Sam., II Sam., Isa., Jer., Ezek., Zech., Mal., Ps., Prov., Lam., Eccl., Dan., I Chron., II Chron.

All Scripture references are according to the chapter-division and verse-numbering of the Hebrew Text.

In the transliteration of Hebrew words into English (*Shema*, *tzedakah*, and *haftorah*, and not Shᵉmaʻ or Shemang, sᵉdaqah and haphṭarah), the aim is not to bewilder the ordinary lay reader, for whom this work is primarily intended.

GENERAL INDEX OF NAMES AND SUBJECTS IN THE COMMENTARY

This Index is not intended as a concordance to the Biblical Text. No references are given to standard expositors of the Text (Rashi, Ibn Ezra, Dillmann, etc.).

Special Comments are indicated by small capitals; Introductory or Additional Notes, by large capitals. An asterisk (*) marks the more important references.

C

O

P

R

S

T